# TOOL AND MANUFACTURING ENGINEERS HANDBOOK

## VOLUME II
## FORMING

# SOCIETY OF MANUFACTURING ENGINEERS

## OFFICERS AND DIRECTORS, 1983-1984

# TOOL AND MANUFACTURING ENGINEERS HANDBOOK

**Fourth Edition**

## VOLUME II
## FORMING

*A reference book for manufacturing engineers, managers, and technicians*


**Charles Wick,** CMfgE
Editor-in-Chief

**John T. Benedict**
Senior Staff Editor

**Raymond F. Veilleux**
Associate Editor


Revised under the supervision of the SME Publications Committee in cooperation with the SME Technical Divisions

Society of Manufacturing Engineers
One SME Drive
Dearborn, Michigan

**TMEH**™

ISBN No. 0-87263-135-4

Library of Congress Catalog No. 82-60312

Society of Manufacturing Engineers (SME)



First edition published 1949 by McGraw-Hill Book Co. in cooperation with SME under earlier Society name, American Society of Tool Engineers (ASTE), and under title: *Tool Engineers Handbook*. Second edition published 1959 by McGraw-Hill Book Co. in cooperation with SME under earlier Society name, American Society of Tool and Manufacturing Engineers (ASTME), and under title: *Tool Engineers Handbook*. Third edition published 1976 by McGraw-Hill Book Co. in cooperation with SME under current Society name, and under title: *Tool and Manufacturing Engineers Handbook*.

Printed in the United States of America

# PREFACE

The first edition, published as the *Tool Engineers Handbook* in 1949, established a useful and authoritative editorial format that was successfully expanded and improved upon in the publication of highly acclaimed subsequent editions, published in 1959 and 1976 respectively. Now, with continuing dramatic advances in manufacturing technology, increasing competitive pressure both in the United States and abroad, and a significant diversification of informational needs of the modern manufacturing engineer, comes the need for further expansion of the Handbook. As succinctly stated by Editor Frank W. Wilson in the preface to the second edition: "...no 'Bible' of the industry can indefinitely survive the impact of new and changed technology."

Although greatly expanded and updated to reflect the latest in manufacturing technology, the nature of coverage in this edition is deeply rooted in the heritage of previous editions, constituting a unique compilation of practical data detailing the specification and use of modern manufacturing equipment and processes. Yet, the publication of this edition marks an important break with tradition in that this volume, dedicated solely to forming technology, is the second of five volumes to be published in the coming years, to comprise the fourth edition. Volume I, *Machining*, was published in March 1983. Other volumes of this edition will include: *Materials, Finishing and Coating*; *Quality Control and Assembly*; and *Management*.

The scope of this edition is multifaceted, offering a ready reference source of authoritative manufacturing information for daily use by engineers, managers, and technicians, yet providing significant coverage of the fundamentals of manufacturing processes, equipment, and tooling for study by the novice engineer or student. Uniquely, this blend of coverage has characterized the proven usefulness and reputation of SME Handbooks in previous editions and continues in this edition to provide the basis for acceptance across all segments of manufacturing.

The scope of this volume encompasses both conventional and special forming methods, covering in detail the fundamentals, capabilities and limitations, and applications of all processes. Included are discussions of presses and machines used, dies and other tooling, operating parameters, troubleshooting guidelines, and safety considerations. Individual chapters are devoted to sheet metal formability, die and mold materials, lubricants, die design, powder metallurgy, and plastics forming.

Every aspect of forming technology is provided in-depth coverage in this volume, presented in a completely new, easy-to-read format. An exhaustive index that cross references processes, equipment, tools, and workpiece materials enhances readability and facilitates the quick access of information. Liberal presentation of illustrations, graphs, and tables speeds information gathering and problem solving.

The reference material contained in this volume is the product of incalculable hours of unselfish contribution by hundreds of individuals and organizations, as listed at the beginning of each chapter. No written words of appreciation can sufficiently express the special thanks due these many forward-thinking professionals. Their work is deeply appreciated by the Society; but more important, their contributions will undoubtedly serve to advance the understanding of forming technology throughout industry and will certainly help spur major productivity gains in the years ahead. Industry as a whole will be the beneficiary of their dedication.

Further recognition is due the members of the SME Publications Committee for their expert guidance and support as well as the many members of the SME Technical Activities Board, particularly the members of the Material Forming Council.

The Editors

SME staff who participated in the editorial development and production of this volume include:

**EDITORIAL**

**Thomas J. Drozda**
Division Manager, Editorial

**Charles Wick**
Manager, Reference Publications

**John T. Benedict**
Senior Staff Editor

**Raymond F. Veilleux**
Associate Editor

**Gerri J. Andrews**
Technical Copy Editor

**Shirley A. Barrick**
Editorial Secretary

**Judy A. Justice**
Word Processor Operator

**TYPESETTING**

**Susan J. Leinart**
Assistant Supervisor

**Shari L. Rogers**
Typesetter Operator

**GRAPHICS**

**Johanne D. Kanney**
Assistant Manager

**Michael McRae**
Keyliner

**Christine Marie**
Keyliner

# SME

The Society of Manufacturing Engineers is a professional engineering society dedicated to advancing manufacturing technology through the continuing education of manufacturing engineers, managers, and technicians. The specific goal of the Society is "to advance scientific knowledge in the field of manufacturing engineering and to apply its resources to research, writing, publishing, and disseminating information."

The Society was founded in 1932 as the American Society of Tool Engineers (ASTE). From 1960 to 1969, it was known as the American Society of Tool and Manufacturing Engineers (ASTME), and in January 1970 it became the Society of Manufacturing Engineers.

The changes in name reflect the evolution of the manufacturing engineering profession, and the growth and increasing sophistication of a technical society that has gained an international reputation for being the most knowledgeable and progressive voice in the field. The Society has some 70,000 members in 65 countries, most of whom are affiliated with SME's 270-plus senior chapters. The Society also sponsors more than 110 student chapters at universities and colleges.

As a member of the World Federation of Engineering Organizations, SME is the universally acknowledged technical society serving the manufacturing industries.

# CONTENTS

## VOLUME II—FORMING

# SYMBOLS AND ABBREVIATIONS

The following is a list of symbols and abbreviations in general use throughout this volume. Supplementary and/or derived units, symbols, and abbreviations which are peculiar to specific subject matter are listed within chapters.

## A

| | |
|---|---|
| A | Ampere |
| ABS | Acrylonitrile butadiene styrene or Adjustable-bed stationary press |
| a-c | Alternating current |
| ADC | Allyl diglycol carbonate |
| AISI | American Iron and Steel Institute |
| AK | Aluminum killed |
| Al | Aluminum |
| Alnico | Nickel-iron-aluminum-cobalt magnetic alloys |
| amp | Ampere |
| AMSA | American Metal Stamping Association |
| ANSI | American National Standards Institute |
| AOD | Argon-oxygen decarburization |
| AS | As sintered |
| ASME | American Society of Mechanical Engineers |
| ASP | Antisegregation process |
| ASTM | American Society for Testing and Materials |

## B-C

| | |
|---|---|
| BDC | Bottom dead center |
| BET | Brunauer-Emmett-Teller |
| Bhn | Brinell hardness number |
| BLS | Federal Bureau of Labor Statistics |
| BMC | Bulk molding compound |
| BOD | Biological oxygen demand |
| BOF | Basic-oxygen furnace |
| BSA | Benzene sulfonic acid |
| BSI | British Standards Institute |
| Btu | British thermal unit |
| C | Celsius, Coulomb, Carbon or Constant |
| CAD/CAM | Computer-aided design/computer-aided manufacturing |
| CAOHC | Council for Accreditation in Occupational Hearing Conservation |
| $CCl_4$ | Carbon tetrachloride |
| $CH_4$ | Methane |
| CIP | Cold isostatic pressing |
| CL | Centerline |
| CNC | Computer numerical control |
| Co | Cobalt |
| $CO_2$ | Carbon dioxide |
| COD | Chemical oxygen demand |
| CPM | Crucible Particle Metallurgy |
| cps | Cycles per second |
| Cr | Chromium |
| Cr-Ni | Chrome-nickel |
| CRS | Cold-rolled steel |
| CRT | Cathode ray tube |
| Cu | Copper |
| $Cu_2O$ | Copper oxide |
| CVD | Chemical vapor deposition |

## D-E

| | |
|---|---|
| DAP | Diallyl phthalate |
| dB | Decibel |
| d-c | Direct current |
| deg or ° | Degree |
| deg/ft | Degree per foot |
| deg/m | Degree per meter |
| diam | Diameter |
| DIN | Deutscher Normenausschuss (German standards organization) |
| DR | Draw ratio |
| EDM | Electrical discharge machining |
| EDPT | Examination, diagnosis, prescription and treatment |
| EHF | Electrohydraulic forming |
| EP | Epoxy or Extreme pressure |
| Eq. | Equation |
| ESR | Electroslag remelting |
| ETFE | Ethylene tetrafluoroethylene copolymer |

## F-G

| | |
|---|---|
| F | Fahrenheit |
| FA | Furfuryl alcohol |
| FDA | Food and Drug Administration |
| Fe | Iron |
| $Fe_3O_4$ | Iron oxide |
| FEP | Fluorinated ethylene propylene |
| Fig. | Figure |
| FLD | Forming limit diagram |
| fpm | Foot per minute |
| fps | Foot per second |
| ft | Foot |
| $ft^3$ | Cubic foot |
| ft-lb | Foot-pound |
| g | Gram or Gravity value |
| GCA | Grid-circle analyzer |

| | |
|---|---|
| g/cc | Gram per cubic centimeter |
| g/cm$^3$ | Gram per cubic centimeter |
| g/m$^3$ | Gram per cubic meter |
| GPa | Giga pascal |

## H-I

| | |
|---|---|
| $H_2$ | Hydrogen gas |
| HAZ | Heat-affected zone |
| HERF | High-energy-rate forming |
| Hg | Mercury |
| HIP | Hot isostatic pressing |
| $H_2O$ | Water |
| hp | Horsepower |
| HRS | Hot-rolled steel |
| HSLA | High strength, low alloy |
| HVF | High-velocity forming |
| Hz | Cycles per second |
| IACS | International Annealed Copper Standard (Electrical Conductivity) |
| ID | Inside diameter |
| in. or ″ | Inch |
| in.$^2$ | Square inch |
| in./ft | Inch per foot |
| in./in. | Inch per inch |
| in./in./s | Inch per inch per second |
| in./s | Inch per second |
| ipm | Inch per minute |
| ips | Inch per second |

## J-K-L

| | |
|---|---|
| J | Joule |
| JIC | Joint Industry Conference |
| kA | Kiloampere |
| KE | Kinetic energy |
| kg | Kilogram |
| kg/m$^2$ | Kilogram per square meter |
| kg/s | Kilogram per second |
| kJ | Kilojoule |
| kN | Kilonewton |
| kN/m | Kilonewton per meter |
| kPa | Kilopascal |
| ksi | 1000 pounds per square inch |
| kV | Kilovolt |
| kW | Kilowatt |
| lb | Pound |
| lbf | Pound force |
| lb/s | Pound per second |
| LDR | Limiting draw ratio |
| LED | Light-emitting diode |
| LIM | Liquid injection molding |
| LP | Liquid petroleum |

## M

| | |
|---|---|
| m | Meter or Mass |
| m$^2$ | Square meter |
| max | Maximum |
| MDI | Manual data input |
| MF | Freon MF, Freon-11, $CCl_3F$, trichlorofluoromethane |
| Mg | Magnesium |
| MHz | Megahertz |
| MIG | Metallic inert gas |
| mil | 0.001 in. |
| min | Minute or Minimum |
| MJ | Megajoule |
| mm | Millimeter |
| mm$^2$ | Square millimeter |
| m/min | Meter per minute |
| mm/m | Millimeter per meter |
| mm/min | Millimeter per minute |
| mm/mm | Millimeter per millimeter |
| mm/mm/s | Millimeter per millimeter per second |
| mm/s | Millimeter per second |
| MN | Meganewton |
| Mn | Manganese |
| Mo | Molybdenum |
| $MoS_2$ | Molybdenum disulfide |
| MPa | Megapascal |
| MPIF | Metal Powder Industries Federation |
| m/s | meter per second |

## N-O

| | |
|---|---|
| N | Newton |
| $N_2$ | Nitrogen |
| NaOH | Sodium hydroxide |
| NASA | National Aeronautics and Space Administration |
| NbC | Niobium carbide |
| NC | Numerical control |
| NEMA | National Electrical Manufacturers Association |
| NFPA | National Fire Protection Association |
| Ni | Nickel |
| Ni-Mo | Nickel-molybdenum |
| NiO | Nickel oxide |
| NIOSH | National Institute for Occupational Safety and Health |
| N/mm$^2$ | Newton per square millimeter |
| No. | Number |
| $O_2$ | Oxygen |
| OBI | Open-back inclinable press |
| OBS | Open-back stationary press |
| OD | Outside diameter |
| OSHA | Occupational Safety and Health Administration |
| oz | Ounce |

## P

| | |
|---|---|
| P | Phosphorus, Poise or Crossover point |
| Pa | Pascal |
| PC | Programmable controller |
| PCTFE | Polychlorotrifluoroethylene |
| PET | Polyethylene terephthalate |
| PETN | Pentaerythritol tetranitrate |
| PM | Powder metallurgy |
| PP | Polypropylene |
| ppm | Parts per million |
| PPO | Polyphenylene oxide |
| PS | Polystyrene |
| psi | Pounds per square inch |
| psia | Pounds per square inch, absolute |
| psig | Pounds per square inch, gage |
| PTFE | Polytetrafluoroethylene |
| PUR | Polyurethane |
| PVC | Polyvinyl chloride |
| PVD | Physical vapor deposition |

## R-S

| | |
|---|---|
| R or r | Radius |
| $R_{A, B, C \text{ or } H}$ | Rockwell hardness—A, B, C or H scales |
| rad | Radius |
| RDX | Cyclotrimethylene trinitramine |
| RIM | Reaction injection molding |
| rms | Root mean square |
| rpm | Revolution per minute |
| s | Second |
| S | Sulfur |
| SA | Shape analysis |
| SAE | Society of Automotive Engineers |
| SAN | Styrene acrylonitrile |
| sec | Second |
| sfm | Surface feet per minute |
| Si | Silicon |
| SI | International System of Units |
| SMC | Sheet molding compound |
| Sn | Tin |
| $SO_2$ | Sulfur dioxide |
| spm | Strokes per minute |

## T

| | |
|---|---|
| Ta | Tantalum |
| TAN-E | Total acid number—electrometric |
| TBN-E | Total base number—electrometric |
| TDC | Top dead center |
| TF | Freon TF, Freon-113, $CClF_2$-$CClF_2$, dichloro-tetrafluoroethane |
| TFE | Teflon, tetrafluoroethylene |
| Ti | Titanium |
| TiC | Titanium carbide |
| $TiCl_4$ | Titanium tetrachloride |
| TIG | Tungsten inert gas |
| TIR | Total indicator reading |
| TL | Trim line |
| TMC | Thick molding compound |
| TMEH | Tool and Manufacturing Engineers Handbook |
| TNT | Trinitrotoluene |
| tons/in.$^2$ | Tons per square inch |
| TSA | Talene sulfonic acid |

## U-V-W

| | |
|---|---|
| UNS | Unified numbering system |
| USP | United States Pharmacopoeia |
| V | Vanadium, Volt or Velocity |
| VAD | Vacuum-arc degassing |
| VAR | Vacuum-arc remelting |
| V-Process | A licensed vacuum molding method |
| W | Watt or Tungsten |
| WC-Co | Tungsten carbide with cobalt binder |
| $WS_2$ | Tungsten sulfide |

## X-Y-Z

| | |
|---|---|
| XSA | Exlene sulfonic acid |
| $Y_2O_3$ | Yttrium oxide |
| YPE | Yield point elongation |
| Zn | Zinc |
| Zr | Zirconium |

| | |
|---|---|
| $\delta$ | Delta |
| $\rho$ | Rho |
| ° | Degree |
| $ | Dollar |
| $\mu$F | Capacitance |
| $\mu$in. | Microinch |
| $\mu$m | Micrometer |
| $\mu$s | Microsecond |
| % | Percent |
| $\pi$ | Pi (3.14159...) |
| $\pm$ | Plus or minus |

CHAPTER

# 1

# Sheet Metal Formability

# SHEET METAL FORMABILITY

From a manufacturing viewpoint, the main requirement for most applications of sheet metal is good formability. Formability is generally understood to mean the capability of being extensively deformed into intricate shapes without fracture or defects in the finished part. The manufacturing operation by which this is done is called press forming, deep drawing, or stamping. Figure 1-1 is a generalized representation of forming operations performed in producing a sheet metal stamping.

Press forming is the most common sheet metal forming method. In this process, a flat blank is formed into a finished shape between a pair of matched dies. Other forming methods exist, but in all of them two principal kinds of deformation, drawing and stretching, are involved.

The properties of the sheet metal required for good drawability are not the same as those required for good stretchability. The relative severity of a process in terms of drawing and stretching depends on the shape of the part being formed. It also depends on mechanical factors of the forming operation, such as die design, lubrication, and press speed. As a consequence, the formability of a sheet metal cannot be expressed by a single property; instead, it is a combination of several properties and formability differs from one part or operation to the next. Table 1-1 lists some important variables and their effects on the forming process.[1] Analysis of the mechanics of forming operations highlights the properties of the sheet that are of major importance to drawability and stretchability.

CHAPTER CONTENTS:



## DEFINITIONS OF SELECTED TERMS

**bending stress** A stress involving both tensile and compressive forces, which are not uniformly distributed. Its maximum value depends on the amount of flexure that a given application can accommodate. Resistance to bending may be called "stiffness." It is a function of the modulus of elasticity and, for any metal, is not affected by alloying or heat treatment.

**circle grid** A regular pattern of circles, typically 0.1″ (2.5 mm) diam, marked on a sheet metal blank.

**circle-grid analysis** The analysis of deformed circles to determine the severity with which a sheet metal blank has been stretched.

**compressive ultimate strength** The maximum stress that a brittle material can withstand without fracturing when subjected to compression.

**compressive yield strength** The maximum stress that a metal subjected to compression can withstand without a predefined amount of deformation.

**creep** The flow or plastic deformation of metals that are held for long periods of time at stresses lower than the yield strength. Creep effect is particularly important when the temperature of stressing approaches the metal's recrystallization temperature.

**deep drawing** Characterized by production of a parallel-wall cup from a flat blank. The blank may be circular, rectangular, or of a more complex shape. The blank is drawn into the die cavity by action of a punch. Deformation is restricted to the flange areas of the blank. No deformation occurs under the bottom of the punch—the area of the blank that was originally within the die opening. As the punch forms the cup, the amount of material in the flange decreases. Also called cup drawing or radial drawing.

**deformation limit** In drawing, the limit of deformation is reached when the load required to deform the flange becomes greater than the load-carrying capacity of the cup wall. The deformation limit (limiting drawing ratio, LDR) is defined as the ratio of the maximum blank diameter that can be drawn into a cup without failure, to the diameter of the punch.

**drawing** In general terms, drawing describes the operations used to produce cups, cones, boxes, and shell-like parts. The sheet metal being worked wraps around the punch as it descends into the die cavity. Essentially, the metal is drawn or pulled from the edges into the cavity. Shallow drawing applies when the depth of the part is less than one-half the part radius. Deep-drawn parts are deeper than one-half the part radius.

**ductility** The property that permits permanent deformation before fracture by stress in tension.

**elastic limit** The maximum stress a metal can withstand without exhibiting a permanent deformation upon complete release of the stress. Since the elastic limit may be determined only by successively loading and unloading a test specimen, it is more practical to determine the stress at which Hooke's law (deformation is

*Contributors of sections of this chapter are: John L. Duncan, Professor, Mechanical Engineering Department, McMaster University; C. Howard Hamilton, Director-Materials Synthesis and Processing Department, Science Center, Rockwell International; Stuart P. Keeler, Manager-Research and Development, Great Lakes Steel Division, National Steel Corp.; Harmon D. Nine, Staff Research Scientist, Physics Department, Research Laboratories, General Motors Corp.; Philip A. Stine, Program Manager, Applied Science and Technology Laboratory, General Electric Co.; William L. Weeks, Materials Engineer and Sheet Metal Forming Consultant;*

# CHAPTER 1

## DEFINITIONS OF SELECTED TERMS

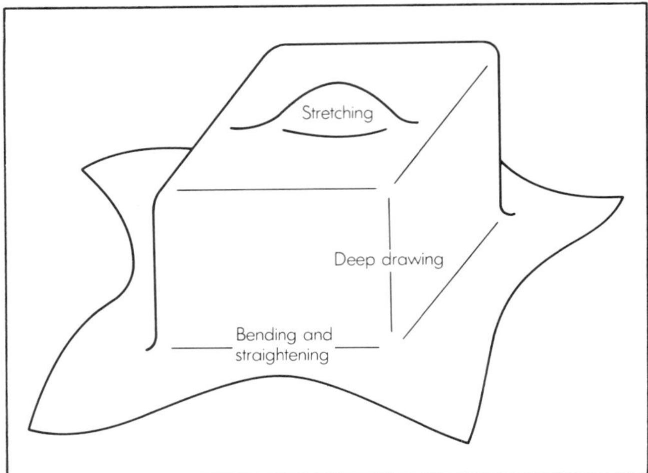


**Fig. 1-1 A complex stamping embodies several modes of forming.**

proportional to stress) no longer holds. It must be remembered that repeated loads which produce any degree of permanent deformation also produce strain-hardening effects in most metals, which in turn, increase the elastic range for load applications after the initial one. The point above which the ratio of stress to strain is no longer constant (straight line) is called the "proportional limit," and it is customary to accept the value of this point as the equivalent of the so-called "elastic limit."

**elongation** The amount of permanent extension in the vicinity of the fracture in the tension test; usually expressed as a percentage of the original gage length, such as 25% in 2" (50 mm).

**endurance limit** The maximum stress that a metal can withstand without failure during a specified large number of cycles of stress. If the term is employed without qualification, the cycles of stress are usually such that they produce complete reversal of flexural stress.

**engineering stress** The load per unit area necessary to elongate a specimen. Computation based on original cross-sectional area.

**FLD** *See* Forming Limit Diagram.

**formability parameters**

*n value* Work-hardening (strain-hardening) exponent; relates to stretching.

*r value* Anisotropy coefficient; relates to drawing.

*m value* Strain rate sensitivity factor; strain rate hardening exponent; relates to change of mechanical properties with rate of force application.

**forming** In the context of this "Sheet Metal Formability" chapter, the term forming covers all operations required to form a flat sheet into a part. These operations include deep drawing, stretching, bending, buckling, etc.

**Forming limit diagram (FLD)** A diagram describing the limits that sheet metal can be stretched under different conditions.

**TABLE 1-1**
**Variables in the Press Forming Process**

MAJOR VARIABLES:

Sheet material
- *n*-value (ability to strain harden, a measure of stretchability of material)
- *r*-value (resistance to thinning, a measure of deep drawability of material)
- anisotropy in the plane of the sheet ($r_0$, $r_{45}$, $r_{90}$ values, a measured tendency to earing)
- uniformity of thickness

Lubricant
- pressure sensitivity
- temperature sensitivity
- stability
- thickness and position of application

Blank
- size
- shape

Tooling
- stiffness of die and blankholder plates (use of shims to flex blankholder plate)
- surface roughness
- die radius (may sometimes be alterable)

MINOR VARIABLES:

Sheet material
- strain rate sensitivity of yield stress
- surface roughness (affects lubrication)

Blank
- edge condition (burred, heavily worked)
- location on die plate

Press
- ram speed
- method of blankholding
- stiffness of frame, accuracy of movement in guides

**hardness** Defined in terms of the method of measurement: (1) usually the resistance to indentation, (2) stiffness or temper of wrought products, (3) machinability characteristics.

**internal friction** Ability of a metal to transform vibratory energy into heat. Internal friction generally refers to low stress levels of vibration; damping has a broader connotation, since it may refer to stresses approaching or exceeding the yield strength.

**major stretch (strain)** The largest amount that a given circle is stretched (strained).

**minor stretch (strain)** The smallest amount that a given circle is stretched (strained). This occurs at a perpendicular direction to the major stretch (strain).

**modulus of elasticity** The ratio of stress to strain; corresponds

***Contributors, cont.:*** *Michael L. Wenner, Senior Staff Research Engineer, Mathematics Department, Research Laboratories, General Motors Corp.*

***Reviewers of sections of this chapter are:*** *A. K. Ghosh, Manager-Metals Processing and C. Howard Hamilton, Director-Materials Synthesis and Processing Department, Science Center, Rockwell International; Howard A. Kuhn, Professor-Mechanical Engineering, Director of Freshman Engineering Programs, School of Engineering, University of Pittsburgh; David J. Meuleman, Applications Research Engineer, Great Lakes Steel Division, National Steel Corp.; Harmon D. Nine, Staff Research Scientist, Physics Department, Research Laboratories, General Motors Corp.;*

# DEFINITIONS OF SELECTED TERMS

to slope of elastic portion of stress-strain curve in mechanical testing. The stress is divided by the unit elongation. The tensile or compressive elastic modulus is called "Young's modulus"; the torsional elastic modulus is known as the "shear modulus" or "modulus of rigidity."

**necking failure** The failure of a formed part by thinning abruptly in a narrow localized area. An extreme case of necking failure is splitting.

**permanent set** Inelastic deformation.

**plastic anisotropy** Directional difference in mechanical properties relative to rolling direction applied in producing the sheet metal.

**Poisson's ratio** The ratio of the lateral expansion to the longitudinal contraction under a compressive load, or the ratio of the lateral contraction to the longitudinal expansion under a tensile load, provided the elastic limit is not exceeded.

**reduction in area** The difference between the original cross-sectional area and the smallest area at the point of rupture, usually stated as a percentage of the original area.

**resilience** The amount of energy stored in a unit volume of metal as a result of applied loads.

**shear strength** The maximum stress that a metal can withstand before fracturing when the load is applied parallel to the plane of stress; contrasted with tensile or compressive force, which is applied perpendicular to the plane of stress. Under shear stress, adjacent planes of a metal tend to slide over each other.

**springback** The elastic characteristic of metal evidenced when a cup is removed from a draw die and springs open, making its inside diameter larger at the flange end. The cylindrical wall is slightly tapered.

**stamping** In its broadest interpretation, the term stamping encompasses all pressworking operations on sheet metal. In its narrowest sense, stamping is the production of shallow indentations in sheet metal.

**strain** A measure of the change in size or shape of a body, due to force, in reference to its original size or shape. Tensile or compressive strain is the change, due to force, per unit of length in an original linear dimension, in the direction of the force.

**strain hardening** Mechanical deformation of metal at temperatures less than one-half the melting point. Macroscopic regions of compression and tension, and microscopic disorientations of atoms from equilibrium or unstressed positions, may persist at the deformation temperature. Also called cold working.

**stress** The intensity of force within a body which resists a change in shape. It is measured in pounds per square inch or pascals. Stress is normally calculated on the basis of the original cross-sectional dimensions. The three kinds of stresses are tensile, compressive, and shearing.

**stretching** Stretching is defined as an extension of the surface of the sheet in all directions. In stretching, the flange of the flat blank is securely clamped. Deformation is restricted to the area initially within the die. The stretching limit is the onset of metal failure.

**tensile strength** The maximum tensile stress that a material is capable of withstanding without breaking under a gradually and uniformly applied load. Its value is obtained by dividing the maximum load observed during tensile straining by the specimen cross-sectional area before straining. Other terms that are commonly used are ultimate tensile strength, and less accurately, breaking strength.

**torsional strength** The maximum stress that a metal can withstand before fracture when subjected to a torque or twisting force. Stress in torsion involves shearing stress, which is not uniformly distributed.

**toughness** As determined by static tests, toughness is considered to be the work per unit volume required to fracture a metal. It is equal to the total area under the stress-strain curve, represents the total energy-absorbing capacity, and includes both elastic and plastic deformation. Toughness in practice is more often considered to be resistance to shock or impact, which is a dynamic property.

**ultimate strength** *See* tensile strength.

**unit stress** The amount of stress per unit area on a section of a loaded body.

**yield point** In mild or medium-carbon steel, the stress at which a marked increase in deformation occurs without an increase in load; also called proportional limit. In other steels and in nonferrous metals this phenomenon is not observed. Refer also to yield strength.

**yield strength** The stress at which a material exhibits a specified permanent plastic yielding or set; a limiting deviation from proportionality of stress to strain. An offset of 0.2% is used for many metals, such as aluminum-based and magnesium-based alloys, while 0.5% total elongation under load is frequently used for copper alloys. Also called proof stress.

## DRAWING

In an idealized forming operation in which drawing is the only deformation process that occurs, the clamping force of the hold-down dies is just sufficient to permit the material to flow radially into the die cavity without wrinkling. Deformation of the sheet takes place in the flange and over the lip of the die; no deformation occurs over the nose of the punch. Analysis indicates that the flange is compressed circumferentially and pulled radially in the plane of the sheet into the side wall of the part. This is analogous to wire drawing in that a large cross section is drawn into a smaller cross section of greater length; and for this reason, this kind of forming process is called drawing to distinguish it from stretching. The capability of the metal to withstand drawing depends on two factors. One is the ability of the material in the flange region to flow easily in the plane of the sheet under a condition of pure shear. This means it is desirable to have low flow strength in all directions of the plane of the sheet.

The other drawability factor is the ability of the material in the side wall to resist deformation in the thickness direction.

***Reviewers, cont.***: *William H. Pearson, Project Manager, Atlas Alloys Division, Rio Algom Ltd.; Richard I. Phillips, Assistant Professor, Department of Industrial Education and Technology, Southwest Missouri State University; Philip A. Stine, Program Manager, Applied Science and Technology Laboratory, General Electric Co.; Ronald J. Traficante, Senior Materials Development Engineer, Engineering Office, Chrysler Corp.; William L. Weeks, Materials Engineer Consultant; Michael L. Wenner, Senior Staff Research Engineer, Mathematics Department, Research Laboratories, General Motors Corp.*

# CHAPTER 1

## DRAWING

The punch prevents side-wall material from changing dimension in the circumferential direction; the only way it can flow is by elongating and becoming thinner. Thus, the ability of the material in the side wall to withstand the load imposed by drawing down the flange is determined by its resistance to thinning. Hence, high flow strength in the thickness direction of the sheet is desirable.

Taking both factors into account, in drawing operations it is desirable to maximize the ability of material to flow in the plane of the sheet and also maximize the resistance of the material to flow in a direction perpendicular to the sheet. Low flow strength in the plane of the sheet is of little use if the material also has low flow strength in the thickness direction.

It is difficult to measure the flow strength of sheet metal in the thickness direction. However, the ratio of strengths in the plane and thickness directions can be obtained by determining the ratio of true strains in the width and thickness directions in a simple tension test. For a given steel strained in a particular direction, this ratio is a constant called the plastic strain ratio and is expressed as:

$$r = \frac{\bar{\epsilon}_w}{\bar{\epsilon}_t} \tag{1}$$

where:

$r$ = plastic strain ratio
$\bar{\epsilon}_w$ = true strain in width direction
$\bar{\epsilon}_t$ = true strain in thickness direction

The properties in the plane of the sheet usually are different in different directions. Therefore, it is necessary to use the average of the strain ratios measured parallel to, transverse to, and 45° to the rolling direction. The average strain ratio is expressed as:

$$\bar{r} = \frac{r_L + 2r_{45} + r_T}{4} \tag{2}$$

where:

$\bar{r}$ = average strain ratio
$r_L$ = strain ratio in longitudinal direction
$r_T$ = strain ratio in transverse direction
$r_{45}$ = strain ratio measured at 45° to rolling direction

An average strain ratio of unity is indicative of equal flow strengths in the plane and thickness directions of the sheet. If the strength in the thickness direction is greater than the average strength in different directions in the plane of the sheet, the average strain ratio is greater than unity. In this case, the material is resistant to uniform thinning. In general, the average strain ratio, $\bar{r}$ ($r_m$ is also used), is directly related to depth of draw; and the higher the $\bar{r}$ value, the deeper the draw that is feasible. This relationship is illustrated in Fig. 1-2.[2]

The average strain ratio is a partial measurement of the plastic anisotropy of the sheet. Since it gives the ratio of an average flow strength in the plane of the sheet to the flow strength normal to the plane of the sheet, it is called "normal"

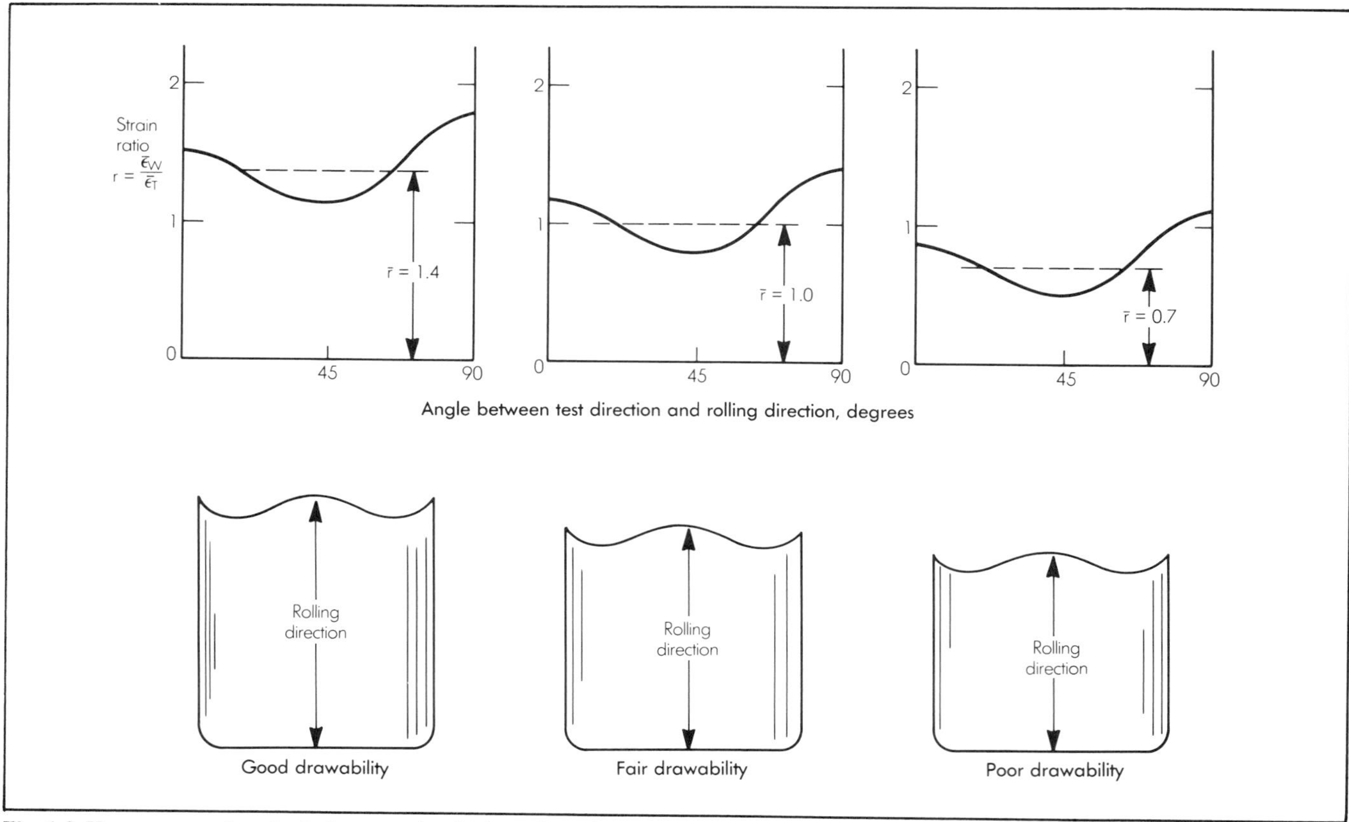


**Fig. 1-2 Upper curves show typical manner in which strain ratio, *r*, varies with test direction in low-carbon steel. The average strain ratio, $\bar{r}$, is a measure of normal anisotropy. The relationship of this parameter to drawability is indicated by relative size of cups below each curve. Each cup represents the deepest cup that could be drawn from material with the average strain ratio indicated.**

anisotropy to distinguish it from the variations in the flow strength in the plane of the sheet. On the other hand, the variation of the strain ratio in different directions in the plane of the sheet, $\Delta r$, is a measurement of the "planar" anisotropy, where $\Delta r$ is expressed as:

$$\Delta r = \frac{r_L + r_T - 2r_{45}}{2} \quad (3)$$

where:

$\Delta r$ = strain ratio variation

A completely isotropic material has a strain ratio of unity in all directions; i.e., $\bar{r} = 1$ and $\Delta r = 0$. The two parameters $\bar{r}$ and $\Delta r$ are convenient measures of plastic anisotropy of a sheet material. Figure 1-3 illustrates the relationship between normal anisotropy and planar anisotropy.

In deep-drawn parts, the defect known as earing is related to planar anisotropy. When sheet metal is rolled at the mill, a fiber structure is formed in the direction of rolling. The fibers actually are rolled-out impurities. The sheet metal is, therefore, stronger and has a greater elongation capability in the direction of rolling. This nonuniform strength causes four ears or lobes to occur, even though a circular blank is used. Earing becomes more severe when the sheet metal is cold worked to quarter-hard or harder tempers. In practice, enough extra metal is left on the stamped cup so that trimming removes the wavy edge ("ears").

## STRETCHING

In an idealized stretch forming operation, a blank of sheet metal is clamped firmly around the periphery or flange to prevent the material in the flange from moving into the die cavity as the punch descends. In this case, hold-down dies prevent radial flow of the flange. All deformation occurs over the punch, at which time the sheet deforms by elongating and thinning. As in tension testing, if the deformation exceeds the ability of the material to undergo uniform straining, it is localized and fracture is imminent. This stage is similar to the elongation at maximum load in a tension test, which is called uniform elongation, $e_u$.

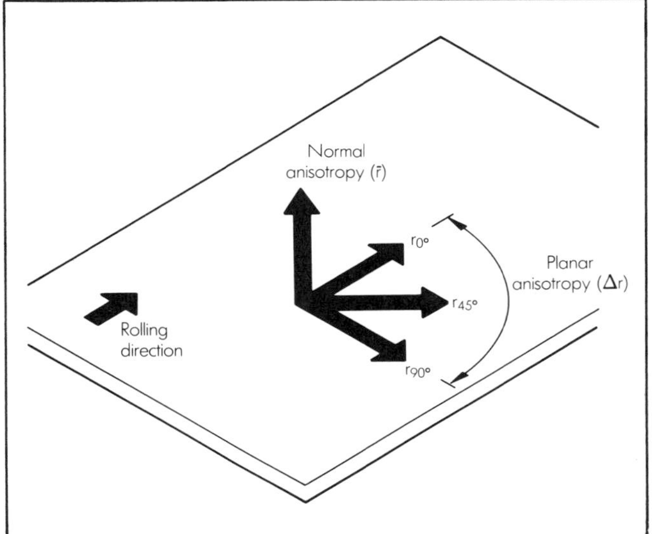


**Fig. 1-3 Planar anisotropy accounts for strain ratio variations in different directions in the plane of the sheet.**

For some metals, including low-carbon sheet steel, the shape of the plastic portion of the tension stress-strain curve, expressed in terms of true stress and true strain, may be closely described by the parabolic equation:

$$\sigma = K\epsilon^n \quad (4)$$

where:

$\sigma$ = true stress
$\epsilon$ = true strain
$n$ = strain-hardening exponent
$K$ = strength coefficient

In this equation, it is $n$, the strain-hardening exponent, that is the measure of the metal's ability to resist localized straining and thus withstand complex nonuniform deformation. In fact, if $e_u$, the uniform elongation, is expressed as true strain, it is numerically equal to $n$.

A metal with a low value for $n$ sustains localized straining early in the stretching process and fails before much uniform strain occurs. On the other hand, a metal that has a high $n$ value tends to strain uniformly even under nonuniform stress conditions. Thus, for good stretchability, a high strain-hardening exponent, $n$, is desirable.

In reality, the stress system in stretching is biaxial and not uniaxial. Under biaxial conditions, plastic instability appears as diffuse necking rather than localized necking. Thus, biaxial conditions increase the likelihood of nonuniform straining. Nevertheless, the conclusions drawn from the simple uniaxial tensile case have been proven valid: namely, that a high strain-hardening exponent, $n$, acts to distribute plastic strain and thereby increases the total stretchability of the material.

## COMPLEX FORMING OPERATIONS

In practical press forming operations, the stretching-drawing interaction is usually complex. Critical regions may occur in small areas anywhere on the part. It has, however, been established that the parameters $n$ (strain-hardening exponent) and $\bar{r}$ (average strain ratio), in some combination, are important measurements of the formability of the sheet. Many metals, including steel, have common tensile properties that change with the speed of deformation. Strain rate hardening, quantified by the strain rate hardening exponent, $m$, relates the yield (flow) strength of metals to the speed of testing. The positive $m$ values of most steels contribute to dentability, impact strength, and formability.

### Strain Rate Hardening

Another important parameter, therefore, is the strain rate hardening exponent, $m$, which is a measurement of the change in flow stress with an incremental change in strain rate. An equation parallel to the strain-hardening equation (Eq. 4), can be written for strain rate hardening as follows:

$$\sigma = K\dot{\epsilon}^m \quad (5)$$

where:

$\sigma$ = true stress
$\dot{\epsilon}$ = strain rate
$K$ = strength coefficient
$m$ = strain rate hardening exponent

The $m$ value influences the distribution of strain in a manner similar to the $n$ value. A positive $m$ value reduces the localization of strain in the presence of a stress gradient. During neck formation, a positive strain rate hardening opposes the rapid localization of the neck and causes the neck to be more diffused. In a reverse manner, a negative $m$ value promotes the localization of the strain and generates a more severe strain gradient. Therefore, both the sign and the magnitude of the $m$ value are important.

Example:

For low-carbon, AK steel: $n = 0.210$, $m = +0.01$, $h = 1.2''$ (30 mm)

For 2036-T4 aluminum: $n = 0.245$, $m = 0.006$, $h = 0.9''$ (23 mm)

In spite of the lower $n$ value for AK steel in the example, the value for the stretched dome height, $h$, is one-third greater than the value for $h$ for 2036-T4 aluminum. This suggests that strain rate hardening, though small, could be playing an important role in strain uniformity. The $m$ factor has a significant effect on post-uniform deformation during which work hardening is balanced by geometrical softening.

Both the impact strength and dent resistance of automotive body panels depend upon dynamic yield strength. Unlike the yield strength of most automotive aluminum alloys, the yield strength of steel increases with forming speed. For SAE 945 steel, the yield strength increases approximately 20 ksi (138 MPa) for a $10^4$ increase in strain rate. The high post-uniform deformation of steel is related to the positive $m$ value of steel. This post-uniform deformation provides an additional increment of useful deformation after maximum load, and increases the total elongation of the steel.

### Other Factors

Although strain ratio and strain hardening are the principal property parameters that determine success in stamping a part without resulting in fracture, other properties are also important to the acceptability of a formed part. For instance, if the sheet has a large yield point elongation, areas of a stamping that are only slightly deformed plastically often show surface markings. These are variously called Lüders' lines, stretcher strains, or Piobert lines; they disfigure the surface and may cause rejection of the stamping. Also, high yield strength in a sheet makes it necessary to increase hold-down pressures on the blank. This can change the drawing-stretching actions, can lead to buckling, and may cause fracture.

# PHYSICAL PROPERTIES

In metalforming operations, work is performed within established limits—above the yield strength and below the fracture strength—using forces that may be tensile, compressive, shearing, or some combination. For a given workpiece material, it is necessary to have information on these strength properties along with data on strain-hardening and strain rate sensitivity.

The relationship between the mechanical properties of sheet metal and forming performance has been studied extensively in many investigations. As noted previously, it is generally agreed that the performance of sheet steels in a drawing-type operation is related to the plastic strain ratio, $r$, while the performance in a stretch-type operation is related to the strain-hardening exponent, $n$.

## DUCTILITY

To take form, a metal must be ductile; a ductile metal can be defined as any metal that can be drawn out or hammered thin. A relationship that is utilized in forming sheet metal is one in which the metal can be drawn or elongated in one dimension while it becomes thin in other dimensions. It can be hammered thin or stretched biaxially under balanced conditions. By hammering (drawing), it is possible to elongate commercial sheet metals 100% or more.

Metal is weakest in shear. When shearing of metal is performed in a controlled manner, the process is called "cutting." (See "Shearing," Chapter 11.) When a similar shear force is applied in an uncontrolled manner, or in an area in which it is not desired, it is described as tearing. The shear strength of metal is approximately one-half of its ultimate strength under tension forces.

Sheet metal formability depends on ductility and on the plastic deformation which starts after stretching the metal enough to exceed its elastic limit (yield point) and which ends when local neck-down, prior to fracture, occurs. Metal is ductile and, when properly worked, can assume almost any shape. What causes metal to fail? One cause is that the producer introduces potential failure sites, such as voids or a nonmetallic inclusion in the metal. Also, by improper alloy additions, adjacent areas of extreme strength differences can develop, causing a "minishear" action to tear the metal during forming operations. Why does failure occur repeatedly at a particular location? The chances of a void or hard and soft adjacent particles being at the same place on numerous metal blanks is not likely. Such failures are more likely to be caused by attempts to form the part in a manner that is limited by the metal's inherent weakness in shear.

## PLANAR SHEAR

Commonly accepted definitions of shear include an action or stress resulting from applied forces, which causes two contiguous parts of a body to slide relative to each other in a direction parallel to their plane of contact. When the shearing stress is acting in the plane of the sheet, it is called "planar shear," to distinguish it from shearing due to a cutting action obtained by applying stress perpendicular to the sheet surface, as with cutting shear knives.

What happens when one area of a sheet of metal is securely clamped while adjacent areas are forced to move? If the process is carried too far beyond the yield point, the metal tears by planar shear.

## TENSION TESTING

As a source of data relevant to formability, one of the most useful tests is the tension test. In this test, a standard-shaped specimen is used and the pulling force is uniaxially applied. The tension test can quickly and reproducibly determine a number of physical properties that are related to formability.

The primary output from the tension test is a measurement of the load required to elongate the specimen for each increment of specimen elongation. Although this information can be presented in many ways, the most common is to plot engineering stress against engineering strain, as shown in Fig. 1-4.

Engineering stress, $\sigma_E$, is the load, $P$, to elongate the sample normalized by the cross-sectional area, $A_o$, of the initial specimen. More specifically,

$$\sigma_E = \frac{P}{A_o} \tag{6}$$

where:

$\sigma_E$ = engineering stress
$P$ = load
$A_o$ = original cross-sectional area

Engineering stress allows direct comparison of specimens with different cross-sectional areas.

Engineering strain, $\epsilon$, is the increase in length of line or gage length, $\Delta l$, divided by the original length, $l_o$, times 100:

$$\epsilon = \frac{\Delta l}{l_o} \times 100 = \frac{l_f - l_o}{l_o} \times 100 \tag{7}$$

where:

$\epsilon$ = engineering strain
$\Delta l$ = increase in length
$l_o$ = original length
$l_f$ = final length

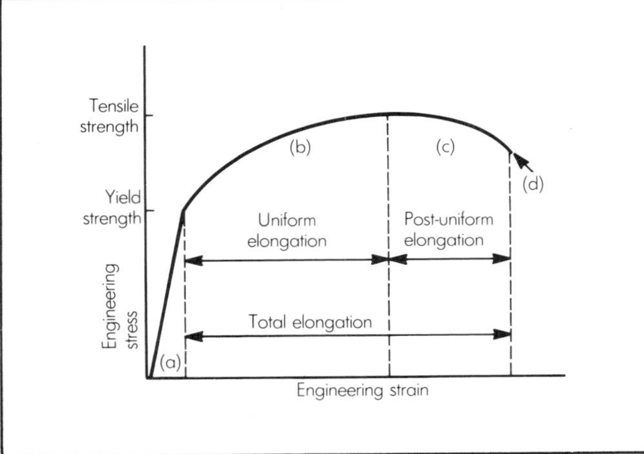


**Fig. 1-4 Classic engineering stress-strain curve shows various stages of elongation deformation.**

## Stages of Deformation[3]

Metal undergoes several stages of deformation during the tensile test. Referring to Fig. 1-4, the metal first deforms in an elastic manner (zone *a*). Loading and unloading to any point on the curved line does not cause permanent or plastic deformation of the metal. The slope of the line is the Young's modulus of the metal. The Young's modulus value is used in many calculations of deflection, stiffness, and springback. Typical values are 30 x $10^6$ psi (207 GPa) for steel and 10 x $10^6$ psi (69 GPa) for aluminum.

At some stress value, called the yield strength, the metal reaches its proportional limit and starts to deform plastically. This means that when the specimen is stressed beyond the yield strength and unloaded (thereby removing the elastic component), a permanent elongation remains. This elongation or deformation is uniformly distributed along the gage section. Thus, the deformation is labeled "uniform elongation."

During the uniform elongation portion of the tensile test, two variables have been changing. The metal has been work hardening with each increment of deformation. This means an increase in load is required to deform the specimen an additional increment of length.

Each additional increment of length increase also causes the cross-sectional area of the specimen to decrease (specimen volume must remain constant). The reduction in cross-sectional area causes the applied load to be more effective in deforming the metal. This effect is called "geometrical softening."

As the tensile specimen is elongated, the amount of work hardening decreases and the amount of geometrical softening increases. When the two amounts balance each other, a load maximum is reached (tensile strength) and deformation can continue under decreasing load.

Assuming that one slice through the specimen is slightly weaker than the others, the next increment of deformation causes a reduction in load necessary to sustain deformation in that slice. The other elements of the specimen stop deforming because they do not quite reach the balance point between work hardening and geometrical softening. Thus, all additional elongation is restricted to a localized zone.

As the specimen elongates, a reduction in width occurs, resulting in a "diffuse neck." The onset of diffuse necking terminates uniform elongation because additional increments of deformation are not uniformly distributed throughout the entire length of the specimen.

Continuing deformation causes another type of neck to form. This neck is a highly localized band across the specimen. The phenomenon is called "localized necking."

Finally, the specimen fractures (zone *d*, Fig. 1-4) and separates into two pieces. This final separation terminates all deformation and signifies the end of total elongation.

Examination of Fig. 1-4 reveals that the total elongation can be divided into two components—uniform elongation (zone *b*) plus post-uniform elongation (zone *c*). Each is controlled by a different characteristic of the metal.

## Yield Point

Yield point or proportional limit is the point in the tension test at which elastic deformation ends and plastic deformation begins. It is significant because the yield point must be exceeded if a permanent change in shape is to occur—and the yield point, along with ultimate strength, determines the amount of plastic deformation that is attainable. Yield point also is a factor in determining the amount of springback that occurs when the part is removed from the press; springback, in turn, is related to the tendency of some formed parts to warp out of shape.

Discontinuous yielding, associated with nitrogen or carbon segregation in low-carbon steels, causes the surface strains (Lüders' lines) in formed parts, which were discussed previously. In a tension test of such a material, there may be an initial higher load followed by a drop in load and subsequent discontinuous load elongation phenomena. The upper yield point is dependent on specimen preparation, alignment, test speed, and uncontrollable variables. It is, therefore, not reported; and instead, the lower yield strength, or minimum load during discontinuous yielding, is used to establish the yield strength of metals exhibiting yield point elongation.

# CHAPTER 1

## PHYSICAL PROPERTIES

### Yield Point Elongation

The amount of discontinuous yielding is measured up to the elongation at which the load starts to rise continuously and is reported as the yield point elongation (YPE). It has been found that if the YPE is less than 1.5%, no adverse effects due to surface strain lines should occur in formed sheet metal parts. More than 1.5% YPE requires temper rolling or flex leveling to eliminate the strain hazard during forming.

### Yield Strength

As there is no apparent yield point in the load vs. elongation curve for fresh rimmed steel or stabilized steels such as aluminum killed or interstitial free steels, an offset in the curve or fixed amount of deformation is used during the tension test to determine the yielding of such metals. For low-magnification (10x) plots, a 0.5% extension is used. For high-magnification (250x) plots, a 0.2% offset from the modulus slope line is used. Normally, the 0.5% extension is preferred for low-carbon steels. The yield strength of low-carbon steels used for forming ranges from 20.3-34.8 ksi (140-240 MPa). When the strength is lower than 20.3 ksi (140 MPa), problems due to denting and weakness of the steel affect the final part. When the strength is higher than 33 ksi (225 MPa), springback and warpage of formed parts can become critical. This is especially troublesome in shallow box-shaped parts. For high-strength, low-alloy steels, a typical yield strength is 50.8 ksi (350 MPa).

### Plastic Strain Ratio

When sheet metal is elongated beyond the yield point, it thins in two dimensions—through the thickness and across the width. The relative amount of thinning is important in sheet metal forming, and it can be derived from data obtained during the tension test. As noted previously, the $r$ value changes with respect to test direction and relative to the sheet rolling direction; hence, it must be obtained at various angles to give an average $\bar{r}$ (or $r_m$) value. Typical $\bar{r}$ values for low-carbon steels used in forming sheet metal parts are listed in Table 1-2.

Special processed steels and interstitial free steels which maintain extremely low carbon and nitrogen levels have a different distribution of $r$ in the sheet with average values to $\bar{r}$ = 2.4. Why is the $r$ value important in formed parts? If the sheet metal has a high $\bar{r}$ value, it resists thinning during forming. In deep-drawn applications, this provides more metal to support the load used when forming the metal.

For most industrial stampings, an $\bar{r}$ of 1.8 to 2.0 is adequate when deep drawing is involved, and materials with lesser values can be used for the majority of stampings.

**TABLE 1-2**
**Typical Values of Plastic Strain Ratio**

| Type of Steel | Plastic Strain Ratio, $r_0$ | $r_{45}$ | $r_{90}$ | $\bar{r}$ |
|---|---|---|---|---|
| Rimmed—Normalized | 0.9 | 1.1 | 0.9 | 1.0 |
| Rimmed—Annealed | 1.3 | 1.0 | 1.4 | 1.2 |
| Aluminum Killed (CR 40%) | 1.4 | 1.2 | 1.6 | 1.4 |
| Aluminum Killed (CR 70%) | 1.6 | 1.4 | 1.9 | 1.6 |

### Strain Hardening Capacity

After the yield strength has been exceeded, plastic deformation results in a hardening and strengthening process which continues until the ultimate load is reached. A measure of strain hardening is the yield-tensile ratio. As noted previously, another measure is the uniform elongation, $e_u$, which is the elongation at maximum load.

It has been observed that for many metals and especially for low-carbon steel, a plot of the logarithm of the true stress, $\sigma$, versus the logarithm of true strain, $\epsilon$, follows a straight line. The slope of this line is the strain-hardening exponent, $n$, defined by the relationship expressed in Eq. (4), where $K$ = strength coefficient, determined as the true stress when $\epsilon$ = 1.0.

The $n$ value is related to $e_u$ by the equation:

$$n = ln(1 + e_u) \qquad (8)$$

where:

$n$ = strain-hardening exponent
$e_u$ = uniform elongation

In low-carbon steels the $n$ value is highest when the material is normalized. It is lowered by cold working. A typical low-carbon steel has an $n$ value of 0.20-0.22. A value of 0.24-0.25 is considered high for these steels, while those with an $n$ below 0.18 are considered to have low ductility and strain-hardening capacity.

### Tensile Strength

The ultimate load in the tension test is used to calculate the tensile strength based on the original cross-section area of the specimen. Although the tensile strength is the most frequently referenced value to describe a metal's strength, it is a convenience measure only and does not give the true tension strength, which must be calculated from the instantaneous cross-section area at ultimate load. It is difficult to determine the latter value, so the former tensile strength is used to indicate how much load a material can stand before necking down and breaking.

The tensile strength of most low-carbon steels used for forming ranges between 40.6 and 50.8 ksi (280 and 350 MPa). Rimmed steels generally have lower strengths than aluminum killed steels, while interstitial free steels have strengths around 45 ksi (310 MPa).

### Elongation

Total elongation is, as the name implies, the total increase in length of the tensile specimen between the start of permanent deformation and fracture. The broken ends of the specimen are fitted together, and a total elongation is measured over some gage length. In normal practice, this gage length is 2" (51 mm) and elongations of between 30 and 50% are usual for forming materials. The value does not relate to actual formability limits because if a shorter gage length were used, higher values could be obtained for the same material. The total elongation over 2" is a convenient measure of ductility and is frequently used to compare materials.

**Evolution.** Originally, total elongation was the most popular of the two elongations as a measure of the formability of steel. The total elongation or total strain was related to the ductility of the steel. This was related, in turn, to the ductility of the steel required to produce a given stamping without fracture.

In the late 1960's and early 1970's the importance of forming limit diagrams and strain distributions was studied in great detail. These two formability parameters were found to be related directly to the work-hardening capacity of the steel and therefore to the work-hardening exponent, $n$. The $n$ value and uniform elongation are related for most low-carbon steels. Therefore, uniform elongation became a popular measurement.

**Current practice.** Currently, total elongation again has become an important measure of formability. Instead of only low-carbon, low-strength steel, a wide variety of metals are being used for stampings, including higher strength steel, dual-phase steel, stainless steel, aluminum, copper, brass, zinc, and magnesium. When comparing this wide spectrum of metals, one obtains radically different amounts of post-uniform elongation.

In stretching a sheet of metal over a rigid punch, the post-uniform deformation is useful deformation that makes a significant contribution toward producing an unbroken stamping. Total formability, therefore, includes both uniform elongation and post-uniform elongation, which is measured by the total elongation.

Total elongation is dependent on the amount of post-uniform elongation (Fig. 1-4). The amount of post-uniform elongation is a summation of two factors. One is the strain rate hardening exponent, $m$. The other is the influence of inclusions and other particles which lead to early fracture. Post-uniform elongation thus is dependent on steel cleanliness and test direction.

Total elongation is an important measurement of the formability of the new dual-phase steels. In addition, certain forming operations, such as bending, hole expansion, and elongation of a blanked edge, appear to correlate directly to total elongation. Thus, total elongation has regained its importance.

### Tension Test Significance

It is apparent from the foregoing discussion that the tension test, or modifications of it, tell a great deal about how much formability a given sheet metal contains. Among other things, it provides a convenient basis for comparisons between materials. It can also be used to evaluate a new material based on a general knowledge of formable sheet metals.

In practice, however, the test should not be the master. The final decision on formability rests in actual forming of the part in question. The consensus of expert opinion is that not one test, but a battery of tests is required to fully define the general formability of a metal. Correlation between a single test and sheet metal formability may exist for one given stamping; however, this correlation seldom is transferable to other stampings.

# SHEET METAL FORMING

Sheet metal formability is undergoing a transition from an art to a science. Formability—within each forming mode—can be related to specific metal formability parameters. These parameters may or may not decrease as the yield strength of a high-strength steel increases. The important point to bear in mind is that they change gradually and predictably as the yield strength of the steel increases. No discontinuous drop in formability is experienced. In fact, certain formability modes are insensitive to yield strength. Therefore, knowing the change in formability parameters expected, compensation can be made in part design, tool design, lubricant selection, and press parameters.

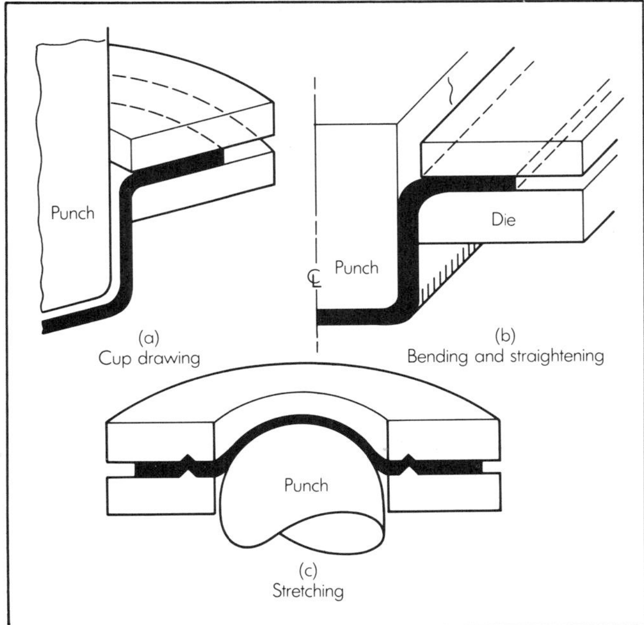


**Fig. 1-5 Primary forming modes in a complex stamping. Each mode is dependent on a different metal property.**

A complex forming operation is usually composed of several primary forming modes, each of which is dependent on a different mechanical property. Therefore, the suitability of a sheet steel for an operation has to be decided on the basis of its formability in each of these several modes.[4]

## FORMING MODES

The three most common primary forming modes are cup drawing, bending and straightening, and stretching, illustrated in Fig. 1-5. Blanking, punching, flanging, and trimming are considered secondary forming operations.

### Cup Drawing Mode

In cup drawing, also referred to as radial drawing, a circular blank is usually drawn into a circular die by a flat-bottom, cylindrical punch (see Fig. 1-5, view *a*). As the flange is pulled toward the die opening, the decrease in blank circumference causes a circumferential compression of the metal. Unless controlled by blankholder pressure, this circumferential compression can easily generate radial buckles in the flange.

### Bending and Straightening Mode

The bending and straightening mode is often confused with the cup drawing mode. In both cases, metal is pulled from a flange, bent over a die radius, and then restraightened. However, in bending and straightening (see Fig. 1-5, view *b*), the die line is straight, the flange length does not change, and no circumferential compression or buckles are generated.

During deformation, the outer fiber (convex side of the

bend) is first elongated as it bends over the die radius. It is then compressed as the sheet is straightened. The inner fiber (concave side) undergoes the reverse sequence of compression followed by tension. Thus, no radial elongation or sheet thinning is observed in a pure bending and straightening operation.

### Stretching Mode

In stretching (see Fig. 1-5, view *c*), a blank is clamped at the die ring by hold-down pressure or lock beads. A domed punch is pushed into the blank, causing tensile elongation of the metal in all directions of the dome. The thickness of the sheet must therefore decrease. This deformation is called biaxial stretch forming.

If the punch is long compared to its width (for a rectangular die opening), tensile elongation of the clamped blank occurs only in one direction—across the small punch radius. This tensile elongation is offset by a reduction in sheet thickness. This very common type of deformation is called plane strain stretching.

One important problem which develops when a formed edge is elongated or stretched is that any damage in the blanking or shearing operation, as evidenced by a burr or rounding of the edge, reduces the formability of the edge.

### Complex Stampings

The complex stamping shown in Fig. 1-6 should help to place the individual forming modes in perspective. The flange can be divided into four corners connected by four straight segments.

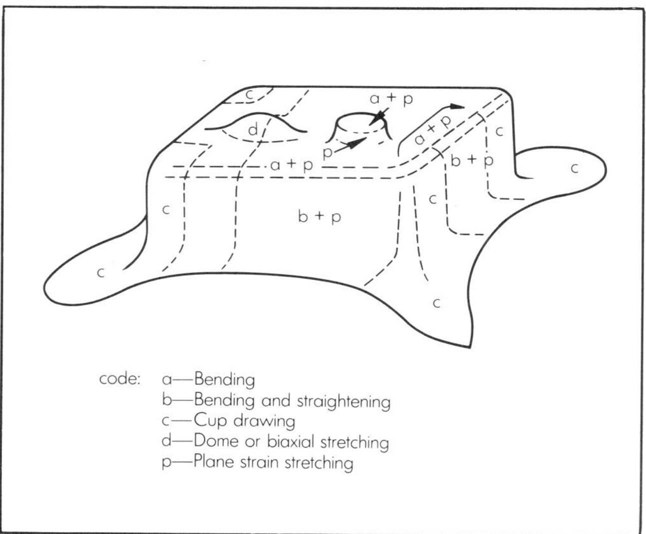


**Fig. 1-6 Breakdown of a stamping into its component forming modes. Dotted line shows typical length of line generated to fulfill design requirement.**

The four corners are created by cup drawing, and each represents one-quarter of a cylindrical cup. The straight line segments joining the corners are created by bending and straightening. However, if hold-down pressure or draw beads create a high radial tensile stress over the die radius, plane strain stretching is added to the bending and straightening action. The bottom radii are a combination of bending (one-half of the bending and straightening operation) plus plane strain stretching. The dome on the bottom of the pan is formed by biaxial stretching, while the embossment and character line are formed by plane strain stretching and bending.

## FORMING LIMITS

For a particular stamping, the limiting factors can be grouped according to the specific forming mode—cup drawing, bending and straightening, or stretching—and the applicable process parameters and metal physical properties.

### Cup Drawing Limits

In cup drawing, the punch button is pushed against the cup bottom to pull the flange into the cup wall. The cup wall must be able to carry the load required to deform the flange and overcome friction. If the cup wall can carry a larger force without necking down, a larger blank can then be drawn into a deeper cup. One method of characterizing this resistance of the cup wall to necking down is by the normal anisotropy of the metal, or the $\bar{r}$. The higher the $\bar{r}$, the greater the deep drawability of the metal.

Typical $\bar{r}$ values for steel are indicated in the following table:

| Type of Steel | $\bar{r}$ Value |
|---|---|
| Hot-rolled 1008 | 0.8-1.0 |
| Cold-rolled 1008, rimmed | 1.0-1.4 |
| Cold-rolled 1008, aluminum killed (AK) | 1.3-1.9 |
| Hot-rolled, high-strength, low-alloy (HSLA) | 0.8-1.0 |
| Cold-rolled HSLA | 1.0-1.4 |

Based on the $\bar{r}$ values, hot-rolled HSLA steels, whether 50 or 80 ksi (345 or 552 MPa) yield strength, can be drawn to a cup depth equivalent to hot-rolled 1008 steels. Cold-rolled HSLA steels have cup drawability equivalent to cold-rolled 1008 rimmed steels. A more direct measure of cup drawability is the limiting drawing ratio, *LDR*, which equals $D_b/D_p$ where $D_b$ is the maximum blank diameter that can be successfully drawn with a punch of diameter, $D_p$. A comparison between an 80 ksi (552 MPa) yield strength, cold-rolled HSLA steel with a low $\bar{r}$ of 1.0, and a 27 ksi (186 MPa) yield, cold-rolled AK steel with a high $\bar{r}$ of 1.8 shows only a 25% reduction in the *LDR*, but a 300% increase in yield strength. Dramatic increases in yield strength can be achieved with only small reductions in cup drawability.

### Bending and Straightening Limits

The limiting factor in the bending and straightening mode is the ability of the inner fiber of the metal to withstand the tensile strain in straightening after being cold worked in compression during bending. In the case of bending only, the outer fiber element must withstand the required tensile strain. In both cases, the ability of the metal to withstand the bending and straightening deformation mode can be correlated to the total elongation of the metal as measured by a tensile test. The higher the total elongation, the sharper the bend radius that can be formed. Typical percentages of total elongation in a 2" (51 mm) gage length are indicated in the following table:

| Yield Strength | Percentage of Longitudinal Elongation | Percentage of Transverse Elongation |
|---|---|---|
| 30 ksi (207 MPa) | 48 | 46 |
| 50 ksi (345 MPa) | 35 | 30 |
| 80 ksi (552 MPa) | 20 | 20 |

These measurements are important in three ways. First, the gain in yield strength is accompanied by a loss in total elongation. Thus, an increase in yield strength requires an increase in bend radius for equal thickness. As a result, formability in this mode is inversely proportional to yield strength.

Second, the longitudinal total elongation of the 50 ksi (345 MPa) yield strength steel is greater than the transverse total elongation. Thus, the preferred bending and straightening axis is across the rolling direction of the fiber. Blank orientation can significantly improve formability in this mode.

Third, inclusion shape control of the 80 ksi (552 MPa) yield strength steel is important in elevating the level of the transverse total elongation to that of the longitudinal direction. Inclusion shape control can improve the transverse bending and straightening capacity of HSLA steels.

## Stretching Limits

Stretching capacity of a metal is related to its ability to delay or resist the onset of a tensile instability or necking. One measure of this resistance to necking is the work-hardening exponent, or $n$ value (from $\sigma = K\epsilon^n$). The higher the $n$ value, the larger the uniform elongation, the greater the resistance to necking.

This relationship between yield strength of steel and the $n$ value is shown in Fig. 1-7. The $n$ value influences stretchability in two ways. First, a higher $n$ value improves ability of the metal to resist localization of strain in the presence of a stress gradient. This generates a more uniform distribution of strain and permits more effective utilization of available metal.

Second, the biaxial stretching portion of the forming limit diagram (FLD) is dependent on the $n$ value. (See "Analytical Methods," later in this chapter.) The FLD (see Fig. 1-8) specifies the maximum strain that sheet metal can withstand without necking for a wide combination of strain states. The level of this standard shaped curve for low-carbon steel is fixed by the intercept of the $e_2 = 0$ axis; this point is labeled the $FLD_0$. The dependence of the $FLD_0$ on the $n$ value for different thicknesses is shown in Fig. 1-9.

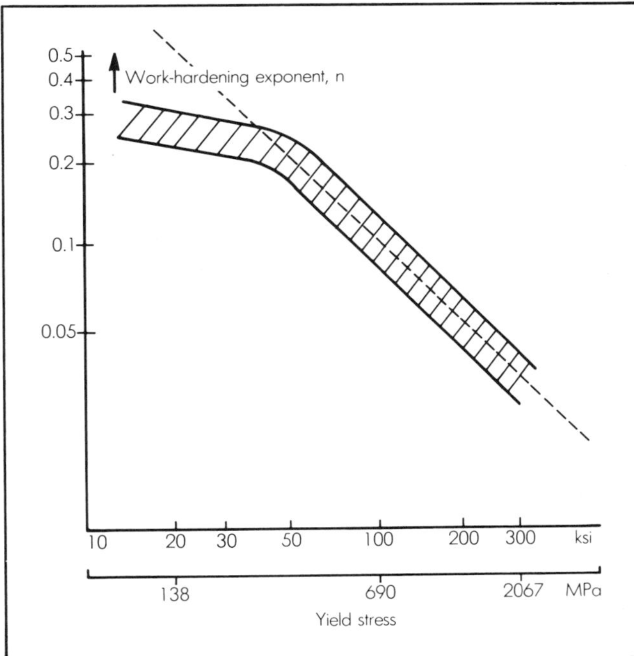


**Fig. 1-7 Relationship of work-hardening exponent, *n*, to yield strength.**

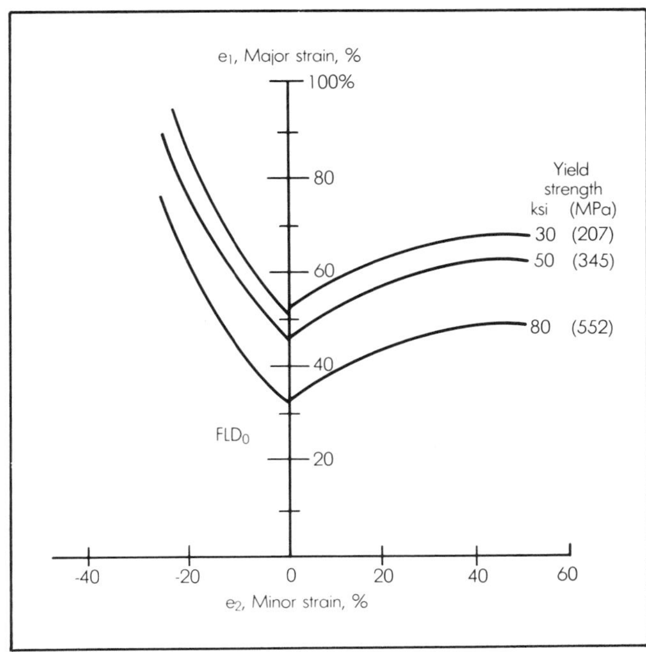


**Fig. 1-8 Forming limit diagram for three 0.08" (2 mm) thick low-carbon steels.**

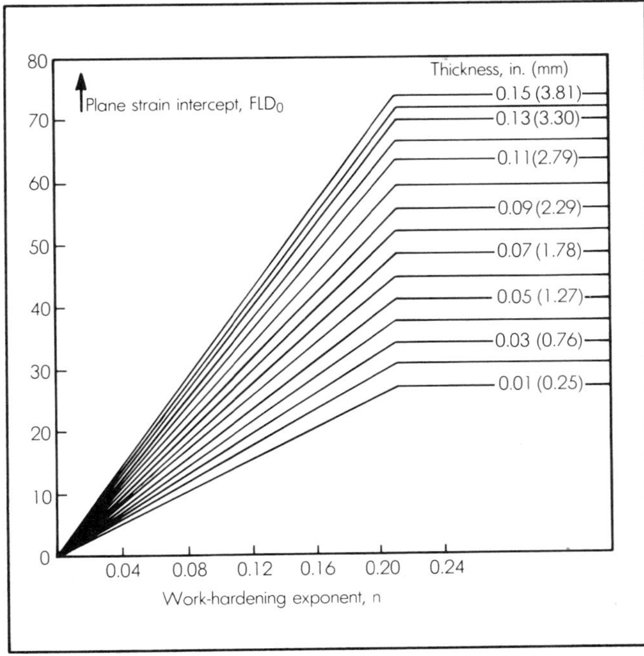


**Fig. 1-9 Graphic relationship among work-hardening exponent, *n*; sheet thickness; and the plane strain intercept of the forming limit diagram, $FLD_o$.**

It can be noted in Fig. 1-7 that the $n$ values of a 30 ksi (207 MPa) and a 50 ksi (345 MPa) yield strength steel are approximately equal (within the scatter band). In addition, the FLD's for these two steels are quite close (see Fig. 1-8). Forming experience has confirmed that stretchability of 30 and 50 ksi (207 and 345 MPa) yield strength steels is approximately equal.

# SHEET METAL FORMING

A reduction in stretchability is observed for an 80 ksi (552 MPa) yield strength steel because of the lower $n$ value.

## Influencing Factors

In the previous section the formability of high-strength steels is compared with ordinary 1008 steels, assuming the influence of design, tooling, lubricant, and press adjustments does not change. However, all variables in the forming system are closely interrelated, and a change in one variable (steel properties, for example) requires modifications in the other variables. A number of these interactions can be illustrated with the aid of the schematic drawing in Fig. 1-6.

**Part design**. The part design requires that a specific length of line be generated, whether it originates by stretching or by bending and straightening. The stretchability of an 80 ksi (552 MPa) yield strength steel is reduced in comparison to that of an ordinary 1008 steel. However, if die radii, hold-down pressure, draw bead radii, etc., are carefully selected, the required length of line can be generated by replacing the stretch forming component by pulling metal from the flange. Thus, proper tool design can optimize the forming modes for which high-strength steels are most suited.

In one study, 50 and 80 ksi (345 and 552 MPa) yield strength steels were directly substituted for a 30 ksi (207 MPa) yield strength 1008 steel. Without any tooling, lubricant, or press adjustments, the 80 ksi (552 MPa) yield strength steel resisted stretching over the punch (because of the high yield strength) but compensated for this resistance by pulling more metal into the die from the flange. Modifications by the part designer or toolmaker which can provide this replacement of stretch forming by bending and straightening deformation of flange metal are desirable.

The four flange corners are more susceptible to wrinkling or buckling if the yield strength of the metal is increased or if the sheet thickness is reduced. This greater tendency of a high-strength steel to wrinkle can be compensated for by increased hold-down pressures. However, increased hold-down pressures result in increased binder (flange) forces unless the lubricant coefficient of friction is reduced to offset the increased pressures.

**Deformation parameter**. The increased forces required to deform the higher strength steels generate higher interface pressures. Lubricants may have to be upgraded to withstand these increased interface pressures without lubricant breakdown. Furthermore, careful lubricant selection is required to avoid increased tool wear.

The reduced work-hardening exponent, $n$, of the high-strength steel indicates a reduced ability to resist localization of strain in the presence of a stress gradient. Therefore, part and tool designs should compensate by reducing stress gradients. Included in a long list of possible modifications are increasing punch and die radii, selecting lubricants to encourage uniform distribution of deformation, avoiding plane strain stretching, reducing flange loads, reducing depths of embossments, bringing in more metal from the flange, etc. Proper part and die design changes can help compensate for reduced stretchability of the new higher strength-to-weight ratio metals.

Other deformation parameters are less well defined. One example is springback. In bending, springback increases with increased yield strength. This can be corrected by appropriate overbending, overcrowning, or subsequent restriking. In stretch forming, however, the interaction of deformation with metal properties is very complex and predictions of springback are difficult. Additional information on springback is given in Chapter 4, "Sheet Metal Blanking and Forming."

Some other considerations which must also be taken into account in the secondary forming operations include increased press loads to blank, punch, and shear; blanking clearances; and edge cracking during flanging.

## THE ROLE OF LUBRICATION

Friction and lubrication are of vital importance in most metalforming operations. Effective lubrication systems result in low friction levels which reduce the loads imposed on tooling and workpieces. This can eliminate problems with tooling or workpiece failures or permit a reduction in the number of steps required to form a part. Lower force levels also reduce tooling deflection and can improve the dimensional accuracy of the product.

Lubrication is an important process variable in sheet metal forming since it controls the friction between the die and the sheet. Lubricants are chosen to minimize metallic transfer (galling) and wear, to regulate surface finish, and to control the force that draws the sheet into the die cavity. Even though friction is a relatively small part of the force required to form sheet metal, it directly influences formability by affecting the ratio of draw to stretch and the strain distribution in various regions in a stamping. The friction component may often be critical in the stamping of materials with reduced formability due to cost or weight restraints.

### Metal Flow

A primary function of lubrication in sheet metal forming is to permit metal flow in a controlled manner. Metal flow requirements vary from point to point on a particular stamping and also vary from one stamping to another. A given lubricant can cause a different response in each set of dies. Each individual application should be considered in terms of its specific conditions and requirements.

In current practice, lubricant requirements and effectiveness are considered in conjunction with drawbeads, which control the flow of sheet metal into the die cavity to prevent either splitting or wrinkling. A drawbead consists of a semicylindrical, raised rod on one binder surface and a matching groove on the opposing binder surface.

### Surface Roughness

Sheet metal surface roughness and material properties interact with lubricant viscosity in a complex way to change friction. Effects similar to those of lubrication are obtained by varying the surface roughness of the blank. Like poor lubrication, rough surfaces may retard metal being drawn in from the flange and thereby force higher strains in the punch stretching region. Conversely, rough surfaces can also entrap and carry more lubrication into the deformation zone, thereby reducing the friction and nonuniformity of the strain distribution. At the other extreme, a blank that is too smooth may "run in" too fast, resulting in either a lack of material for trimming or buckles which lock the metal. Each apparent lubrication problem, therefore, must be investigated separately.

### Lubrication Regimes

The type of lubrication regime that occurs in a metalforming operation has a strong influence on frictional conditions, as well as on important factors such as product surface finish and tooling wear rates. Four main lubrication regimes occur in sheet metal forming with liquid or solid lubricants: the thick-film regime; the thin-film regime; the mixed regime; and the boundary regime. Additional information is provided in Chapter 3, "Lubricants." The characteristics of lubrication and friction are different in each regime, and it is vital to recognize these differences in sheet metal forming processes.

The majority of metalforming operations are characterized by high pressures and low speeds. Under such conditions, the metal surfaces are separated by an extremely thin lubricant film of molecular thickness. Analysis on lubrication of sheet metal forming operations indicates that the lubricant's mechanical properties and boundary lubricity, as well as workpiece surface roughness and deformation speed, have important influences on lubrication. Thus, it seems likely that while thick-film or boundary lubrication may occur under unusual circumstances, significant regions in most processes operate in a thin-film or mixed regime. It is, therefore, desirable to be able to estimate the lubricant film thickness in different parts of the interface between workpiece and tooling. This permits selection of important lubrication parameters on a logical basis and estimation of resultant frictional conditions.

The term *sheet metal forming* covers a wide variety of operations. Some of these operations, such as bending, are usually unlubricated, while others, such as shallow drawing, do not place stringent requirements on the lubricant. On the other hand, operations such as deep drawing and ironing (see Chapter 4, "Sheet Metal Blanking and Forming") require careful attention to lubrication to ensure success.

## SHEET STEEL MATERIALS

In recent years, sheet steel and other sheet metals with higher strength and better formability have become available. Formable and weldable high-strength steels in the 50-80 ksi (345-552 MPa) yield strength range are being specified in product design. For a broad comparison, steels can be arranged in a general formability classification system according to their yield strength and tensile characteristics, as shown in Table 1-3.

**TABLE 1-3**
**Formability Classification of Steels**

| Material | Tensile Strength, ksi | Tensile Strength, MPa | Yield Strength, ksi | Yield Strength, MPa | Formability Factor |
|---|---|---|---|---|---|
| Mild steel | 55 | 379 | 35 | 241 | 1 |
| | 65 | 448 | 45 | 310 | |
| High-tensile, low-yield steel | 80 | 552 | 30 | 207 | 1.2 |
| | 90 | 621 | 40 | 276 | |
| Medium-tensile, medium-yield steel | 60 | 414 | 45 | 310 | 1.7 |
| | 75 | 517 | 55 | 379 | |
| High-tensile, high-yield steel | 105 | 724 | 90 | 621 | 3.1 |
| | 135 | 931 | 100 | 690 | |

### Low-Carbon Sheet Steel

Regular low-carbon sheet steel, a type commonly used in the automotive industry, has a typical yield strength in the 25-35 ksi range (172-241 MPa). These materials are easily formed and welded with high-volume, mass-production techniques. Their combination of strength, modulus, and fabricability means that the design of even low-cost components can meet all the performance requirements.

Structurally, low-carbon sheet steel is excellent. It is expected to continue to be widely used. Typical low-carbon sheet steels and their properties are summarized in Table 1-4.

**Availability**. Low-carbon sheet steels are available in products cold rolled to as thin as 0.014" (0.36 mm) and hot rolled to as thick as 0.50" (12.7 mm) and thicker. Specific availability of hot and cold-rolled products as well as maximum widths at various thicknesses vary. In selecting these products, it is best to consult the producers.

**SAE 1006 and 1008**. Both SAE 1006 and 1008 steel are soft steels that are highly ductile and easily formed and shaped. These grades are commonly selected when maximum formability is required and strength is secondary. They are usually produced as rimmed steels or fully aluminum-killed products when optimum formability is required.

**SAE 1010 and 1012**. These steels are slightly stronger than SAE 1006 and 1008. They are also less ductile and less formable. They are often selected for applications in which forming requirements are not excessively severe and part strength is of some concern.

### High-Strength Sheet Steels

Low-carbon sheet steels provide an effective balance of strength and modulus for many components. However, many components can be designed more effectively by using higher strength steels at reduced thicknesses.

A range of high-strength steels is available in strength levels from 35-80 ksi (241-552 MPa). These steels offer many of the same advantages as the low-carbon steels. Because of this, they are compatible with existing manufacturing equipment. They can be formed, joined, and painted at high production rates.

The wide range of qualities of high-strength steels permits optimization of selection in terms of cost, formability, and weldability. At the same time, these steels meet part performance requirements of strength, fatigue, and toughness. Table 1-5 lists the various qualities and strength levels to which high-strength steels are produced. In this table, formability increases from left to right.

In its consideration of high-strength steels, one steel company

**TABLE 1-4**
**Typical Properties of Low-Carbon Steel**

| Designation | Chemistry C | Chemistry Mn | Yield Point | Tensile Strength | Percentage of Elongation in 2" (51 mm), Typical |
|---|---|---|---|---|---|
| SAE 1006 | 0.08 max | 0.45 max | 25-32 ksi | 40-53 ksi | 35-45% |
| SAE 1008 | 0.10 max | 0.50 max | 174-221 MPa | 276-365 MPa | |
| SAE 1010 | 0.08-0.13 | 0.30-0.60 | 30-35 ksi | 45-55 ksi | 30-40% |
| SAE 1012 | 0.10-0.15 | 0.30-0.60 | 207-241 MPa | 310-379 MPa | |

**TABLE 1-5**
**High-Strength Steel, Yield Strength and Mill-Applied Qualities**

| Minimum Yield ksi | Minimum Yield MPa | Structural Quality | Semikilled, Capped, Rimmed | High-Strength Low-Alloy Fully Killed | High-Strength Low-Alloy Killed, Inclusion Shape Control |
|---|---|---|---|---|---|
| 35 | 241 | • | | • | • |
| 40 | 276 | • | | • | • |
| 45 | 310 | • | • | • | • |
| 50 | 345 | • | • | • | • |
| 60 | 414 | | • | • | • |
| 70 | 483 | | • | • | • |
| 80 | 552 | | | • | • |

has these rules of thumb regarding formability: (1) In stretching operations, allowances should be made for a 20-60% sacrifice in the formability of high-strength sheet steel; and (2) in edge stretching operations, allowances for 20-50% sacrifice should be made.

On the other hand, formability loss in drawing and bending is only 10-30%. The conclusion is that the part and the dies should be designed if possible for drawing and bending in preference to stretching and edge stretching. In general, as the yield strength increases, the formability decreases in a gradual, predictable manner. This relationship is illustrated in Fig. 1-10.

Generally, the higher the strength level, the more restricted the limits of sheet product dimensions when compared to low-carbon sheet products. The 35 ksi (241 MPa) steels are available in cold-rolled products as thin as approximately 0.020" (0.51 mm) and in hot-rolled products similar to low-carbon steels as thick as 0.50" (12.7 mm) and thicker. The 50 ksi (345 MPa) steels are available in cold-rolled products as thin as approximately 0.025" (0.64 mm), and 80 ksi (552 MPa) steels as thin as approximately 0.035" (0.89 mm). Both of these strength levels are available in plate products as thick as 0.50" (12.7 mm) and thicker. A description of the various qualities and their properties is provided in Table 1-6.

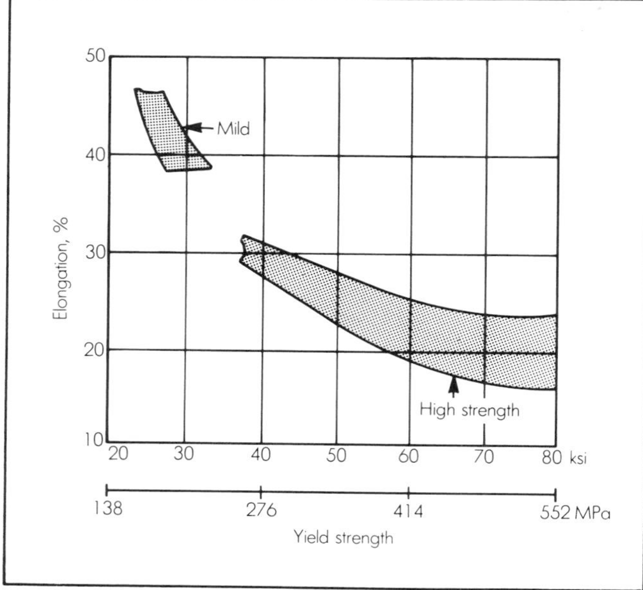


**Fig. 1-10 For the families of mild steel and high-strength steel, formability (elongation) decreases in a gradual, predictable manner, as an inverse function of yield strength.** *(Bethlehem Steel Corp.)*

Structural quality steels are produced through three different chemistry approaches: the addition of carbon-manganese, the addition of nitrogen, and the addition of phosphorus. All of these steels are normally produced by semikilled, capped, or rimmed deoxidation practices. When compared with the high-strength, low-alloy steels, they may be less homogeneous, formable, weldable, and tough.

**Carbon-manganese steel.** Although carbon and manganese are added to increase the strength of steel, they impair its ductility and weldability.

**Nitrogenized steel.** In addition to carbon and manganese, nitrogen is added to these steels to increase strength and hardness. The addition of nitrogen enables the producer to use slightly lower carbon and/or manganese levels than are used in the carbon-manganese grades, thus improving formability.

Nitrogenized steels are also characterized by accelerated strain aging properties. This characteristic enables the steel to attain yield strength increases of as much as 25% in the finished part over the as-received condition. The increase in yield strength is accompanied by a loss of ductility and toughness.

**Phosphorized steel.** Like nitrogenized steels, the phosphorized steels are characterized by the addition of a strengthening element—phosphorus. The carbon and/or manganese content of the metal may be reduced slightly from the carbon-manganese grades. Stretchability, weldability, and toughness are comparable to that of carbon-manganese and nitrogenized steels, and drawability is somewhat better than that of nitrogenized and carbon-manganese steels.

**TABLE 1-6**
**Structural Quality Steel Properties**

| Yield Point, ksi | Yield Point, MPa | Tensile Strength, ksi | Tensile Strength, MPa | Percentage of Elongation in 2" (51 mm) |
|---|---|---|---|---|
| 35 | 241 | 47-52 | 324-359 | 28 |
| 40 | 276 | 52-57 | 359-393 | 27 |
| 45 | 310 | 57-62 | 393-427 | 25 |
| 50 | 345 | 62-67 | 427-462 | 22 |

## High-Strength, Low-Alloy Steel

The HSLA steels are strengthened by the addition of microalloying elements such as columbium, vanadium, titanium, and zirconium, or by having low levels of alloying elements such as silicon, chromium, molybdenum, copper, and nickel. The use of these elements enables producers to significantly reduce the carbon and/or manganese levels to improve formability, toughness, and weldability when compared to structural quality steels. Figure 1-11 shows elongation vs. yield strength for plain carbon steels and HSLA steels.

The principal differences between these types of steel, and among the grades within them, are the deoxidation practices and the spread between yield point and tensile strength.

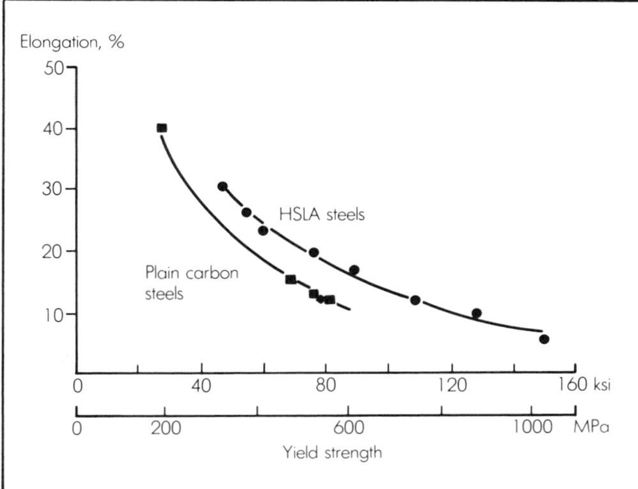


**Fig. 1-11 Elongation (formability) versus yield strength for plain carbon steels and high-strength, low-alloy steels.**

The major element affecting tensile strength is carbon. High-strength steels with higher carbon levels generally have a greater yield strength to tensile strength spread (20 ksi; 138 MPa). Thus, for steel specified to a minimum yield strength, a higher tensile strength and improved fatigue characteristics are attainable with the higher carbon levels. The greater yield strength to tensile strength spread also coincides with better formability. Lower carbon steels with other alloying elements for strength properties do, however, merit consideration for applications in which weldability and other fabricating and performance factors are primary considerations in material selection.

Deoxidation practices can significantly affect the quality of steel. Semikilled steels, like capped and rimmed steels, are less homogeneous than killed steels. As a result, they are not as formable nor are they as tough. Killed steels are more homogeneous with improved toughness and formability.

Sulfide inclusion control can be obtained in killed steels through the addition of small amounts of zirconium, titanium, or rare earth elements. This results in a steel with optimum formability in both the longitudinal and transverse directions. The deoxidation practices increase the cost of producing the steel.

The formability properties of HSLA steels can be summarized as follows:

- Their performance is comparable to mild steels in simple bending areas as well as in straight line areas of draw dies.
- In stretching, performance is similar to mild steels except for reduced elongation to the point of fracture and poor strain distribution. Stretched shapes must, therefore, be less demanding for the high-strength steels.
- Regarding drawing, areas of radial cup shaped deep draws are borderline. Abnormal tonnages are required to avoid wrinkles, and the tendency is toward fractures and laminations.
- With regard to springback, although HSLA steels generally have a greater degree of springback than mild steels, problems are manageable within normal part design and die practices.

## Ultrahigh-Strength Steels

These steels should be considered when part strength is critical. They are characterized by good weldability and formability that, while limited, is adequate for roll-forming or press-brake operations.

At the lower yield range, specially processed low-carbon steels can be produced in a cold-rolled condition to minimum yield points of 85 ksi (586 MPa).

Titanium, vanadium, or columbium-bearing, low-carbon steels can be produced in a cold-rolled, annealed condition at yield point minimums of 100 ksi (689 MPa), 120 ksi (827 MPa), and 140 ksi (965 MPa). Low-carbon martensitic steels are available in strengths up to 200 ksi (1379 MPa) yield strength.

## Strength in Finished Part

All steels are characterized by an ability to work harden and strengthen from strain induced during part forming. In addition, many steels age harden at ambient temperatures or at elevated temperatures such as those incurred during painting-baking cycles. These two properties are important in imparting additional strength to the finished part and should be taken into consideration when steel is being compared to other materials. Strength increases in the finished part due to straining and aging of 20-30 ksi (138-207 MPa) are not uncommon. Most steels have individual strain aging characteristics, and the purchaser should consult with the steel producer for specifics.

A new family of dual-phase steels is characterized by very rapid work-hardening characteristics. Increases of 20,000 psi (138 MPa) in yield point can be obtained in areas of a part which have less than 3% strain. This characteristic enables relatively low strength steel to be used in producing high-strength parts that require complex forming.

## Strain Rate Sensitivity

One of the characteristics of some metals is that common tensile test properties change with the speed of testing. This important property is called strain rate sensitivity. A common and simple measure of strain rate sensitivity is the change of yield strength as the speed of deformation is changed.[5]

**Equations.** While there are a number of equations which can describe this behavior, the following are most widely used:

$$\sigma_T = K\dot{\epsilon}^m \tag{9}$$

where:

$\sigma_T$ = true stress
$K$ = constant defined as the stress at a strain rate of $\dot{\epsilon} = 1$
$\dot{\epsilon}$ = true strain rate
$m$ = strain rate hardening exponent

and:

$$\sigma_T = K\epsilon^n \qquad (10)$$

where:

$\epsilon$ = true strain
$n$ = strain-hardening (work-hardening) exponent

The strain-hardening and strain rate hardening effects usually are combined into one equation:

$$\sigma_T = K\epsilon^n\dot{\epsilon}^m \qquad (11)$$

**Energy absorption**. Of increasing importance to the design engineer are the effects of impact loading, controlled crush, and energy absorption on vehicle components. A knowledge of the change in mechanical properties of a material with changes in strain rate (strain rate sensitivity) is paramount in understanding and designing for vehicle crash protection. Studies show that for both low-carbon steels and high-strength, low-alloy steels, yield and tensile strengths increase with increasing strain rate. The total elongations remain constant.

Absorbed energy tends to increase with increasing strain rate. Figure 1-12 shows examples of relative increases in yield strength with strain rate for a number of steels and for an aluminum alloy. In a practical sense, ferrous alloys are stronger at high loading rates than expected from ordinary mechanical property measurements. This provides dent resistance, impact loading resistance, and energy absorption.

## NONFERROUS SHEET METAL FORMABILITY

The formability parameters and methods of analysis for nonferrous sheet metal are similar to those used for steel. The correlation of physical and mechanical properties to formability, however, differs from one material to another. Expert knowledge and careful treatment of data are required to achieve valid formability comparisons among different groups of materials.

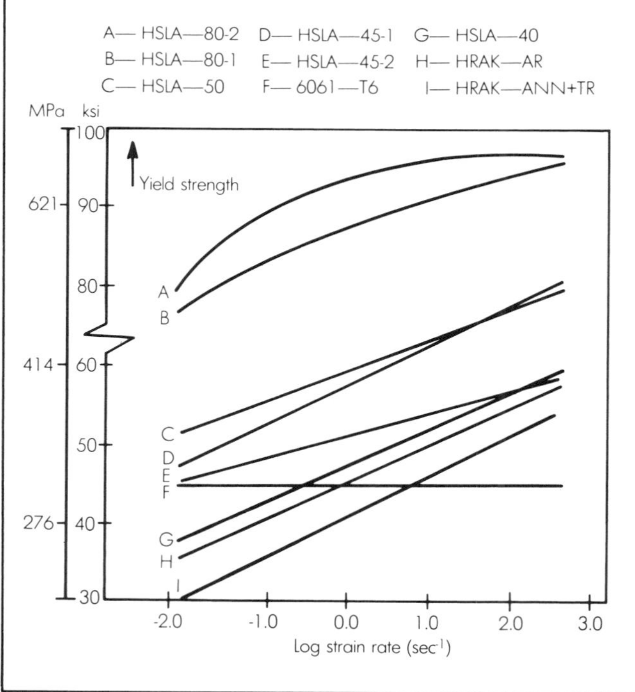


**Fig. 1-12 Effect of strain rate on yield strength.**

### Sheet Aluminum Alloy Formability

Aluminum and its alloys are among the most readily formable of the commonly fabricated metals. Aluminum alloys for sheet metal forming applications are available in various combinations of strength and formability. There are, of course, differences between aluminum alloys and other metals in the deformation that is attainable, as well as differences in some aspects of tool design and in operation procedural details. These differences are caused primarily by the lower tensile and yield strengths of aluminum alloys and by their comparatively low rate of work hardening and low strain rate sensitivity. The compositions and tempers also affect aluminum alloy formability.

The strain-hardening alloys of the 5xxx series have excellent formability in the annealed temper. However, in the conventional "0" temper, they are susceptible to formation of Luder lines during deformation. Use of such materials generally is restricted to interior or nonvisible panels. This limitation does not apply to the Lüders' line resistant variations of the "0" temper. The heat-treatable alloys have good to excellent formability, with formability generally varying inversely in relation to strength of the alloy. Table 1-7 lists typical formability characteristics of automobile body aluminum sheet alloys.[6]

**High-Volume Production.** Aluminum sheet has recently begun to be specified in applications that require high-volume forming techniques, such as mechanical stamping with hard tooling. High strength-to-weight ratio and excellent corrosion resistance are the primary engineering advantages of aluminum over low-carbon steel in such applications.[7]

In evaluating the ease with which a particular stamping can be formed from aluminum sheet, three basic forming parameters—the shape of the part, the specific alloy and the tooling (or process)—should be considered.

**Aluminum forming characteristics.** Aluminum stampings often are considered replacements for stampings of low-carbon steel. Choosing between an aluminum alloy and a low-carbon steel for a particular application requires detailed analysis and should take into consideration the following general comments:

- Formability of medium-strength aluminum alloys in deep draw and biaxial stretch cup type forming operations is about two-thirds that of low-carbon steel.
- Minimum bend radii are approximately three times those for steel. The lower bendability is related to aluminum's characteristically low reduction in area. Aluminum cannot be severely strained in local areas that have sharp formations.
- Aluminum's high notch sensitivity requires that blanking tools—particularly those with sharp edges—be designed for close tolerances. Tools must be sharp and precise to minimize formation of burrs and reduce edge-splitting tendencies in subsequent bending or flange-stretching operations. Lancing of blanks to improve interior metal flow should be avoided.
- Yield strengths of steels generally increase with increasing strain rate, while yield strengths of typical aluminum alloys are relatively unaffected by strain rate.
- In mechanical presses, the highest speed in the stroke

**TABLE 1-7**
**Typical Formability Characteristics—Aluminum Sheet Alloys**

| Alloy | Thickness, in. (mm) | Olsen Values[1] in. (mm) | $n$ Value[2] | $r$ Value[3] | Relative Formability Rating[4] |
|---|---|---|---|---|---|
| 2036-T4 | 0.031-0.051 (0.80-1.30) | 0.36 (9.14) | 0.23 | 0.75 | B |
| 2037-T4 | 0.031-0.051 (0.80-1.30) | 0.37 (9.40) | 0.24 | 0.70 | B |
| 5182-0 | 0.031-0.051 (0.80-1.30) | 0.39 (9.91) | 0.33 | 0.80 | A |
| 5182 | 0.031-0.051 (0.80-1.30) | 0.40 (10.16) | 0.31 | 0.67 | A |
| 6009-T4 | 0.031-0.051 (0.80-1.30) | 0.38 (9.65) | 0.23 | 0.70 | A |
| 6010-T4 | 0.031-0.051 (0.80-1.30) | 0.36 (9.14) | 0.22 | 0.70 | B |

[1] Using 1″ (25.4 mm) diam top die and approximately 2.2 ksi (15 MPa) hold-down pressure and polyethylene film as lubricants, testing at approximately 0.05 in./s (1.3 mm/s).
[2] The $n$ value is known as the strain-hardening coefficient and is obtained by laboratory measurement. It indicates the ability of an alloy to stretch by providing uniform elongation. The more formable aluminum alloys have values of 0.20-0.25. Intermediate tempers normally have values from 0.12-0.15.
[3] The $r$ value is derived from a tensile test and is the ratio of the change in width of a specimen to the change in thickness. It is a measure of drawability.
[4] The ratings of A, B, and C are relative ratings in decreasing order of merit.

cycle occurs during workpiece contact. The low strain rate sensitivity of aluminum creates high stresses in the metal during initial metal movement, especially during deep drawing. It is compensated for by lower blank hold-down pressure, by increased draw-ring and punch-nose radii, and by use of lubricants formulated for aluminum. Aluminum is sensitive to lubrication as a result of its oxide layer.

- Because the elastic modulus of aluminum is lower than that of steel, formed aluminum panels have more elastic recovery, or springback, than formed steel panels. This must be compensated for by increasing overcrown in the draw die and/or incorporating locking beads in the binder, to ensure that all material has been "set" by plastic deformation.

**Forming limit diagrams (FLD's).** The FLD is a useful representation of aluminum sheet formability. Basically, it depicts the biaxial combinations of strain that can occur without failure. A variety of FLD shapes are found for aluminum alloys. However, a number of aluminum alloys have FLD's with shapes similar to that of low-carbon steel. This similarity is illustrated in Fig. 1-13. Additional information on Forming Limit Diagrams is given under "Analytical Methods," in this chapter.

## Wrought Zinc Alloy Formability

The material properties used to characterize the formability of steel do not correlate with the properties that characterize the formability of the various zinc alloy series. When drawing is being considered, the plastic strain ratio at 0° to the rolling direction is a better indicator of the alloy's performance than the normal anisotropy coefficient used with other materials. In assessing the stretch forming characteristics of zinc alloys, the strain-hardening exponent, $n_{90}$, does not accurately predict behavior. Because of the high strain rate sensitivity of zinc alloys, the $m$ value, as well as the total elongation, should be considered. More work is needed in this area to develop a reliable correlation. Therefore, caution should be used in attempting to compare the formability of zinc alloys to different types of materials based strictly on mechanical property test data. The absolute data may not correlate directly with the ability of the material to withstand certain forming operations,

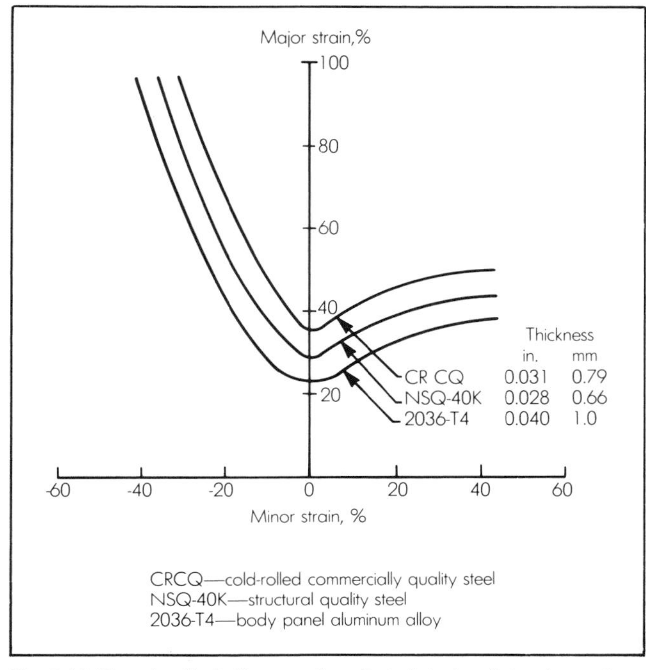


**Fig. 1-13 Forming limit diagrams for selected steel and aluminum sheet materials.**

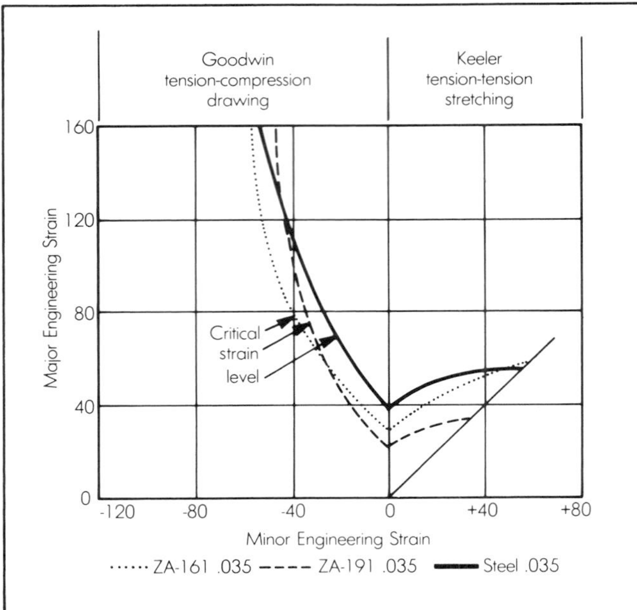


**Fig. 1-14 Forming limit diagrams for representative steel and zinc alloys.**

and/or it may not fully describe the material's capability. The latter is especially true for zinc alloys.

The forming limit diagrams for the various zinc alloy series can be used to evaluate any forming process in conjunction with circular grid strain analyses in the same way that the FLD for steel is used. Forming limit diagrams for representative steel and zinc alloys are shown in Fig. 1-14.[8]

## Nonferrous Formability Data

Punch stretching accompanied by flange draw-in is called "combined stretching." The combined stretching depends on the pure stretchability and deep drawability, that is, mainly on the $n$ and $\bar{r}$ values. Figure 1-15 illustrates some typical relationships between the forming limit (as measured by stretching depth, $h_{max}$) and $n$ or $r$ value for shells of different geometry.[9] The relationship between $h_{max}$ and $r$ in sheet steels is strong, although it exhibits effects varying from forming geometry. In nonferrous materials that have virtually the same $r$ value, the forming limit, $h_{max}$, is closely related to the $n$ value for all the different geometries of forming (in this particular set of tests). The stress-strain relationship characterized by the $n$ value is very important and also quite complex. As shown in Fig. 1-16, the stress-strain curves for different materials and deformation modes differ significantly from each other; hence, it is unlikely that a single $n$ value would express the work-hardening property for the entire measured strain range.[10]

## SIMULATIVE FORMABILITY TESTS

When complex stampings are broken down into their component operations, each operation can be simulated and studied in the laboratory. Tests that subject sheet metal to the same types of deformation found in stamping are used to evaluate formability. These simulative tests enable the effects of surface textures of materials, lubrication, anisotropy, and large surface areas to be evaluated. Figure 1-17 shows, schematically, the interrelationship between forming operations, material properties, and simulative tests. In addition to the tests discussed here, the simulative tests also include a number of other cup/dome, bend, and hole-expansion tests.

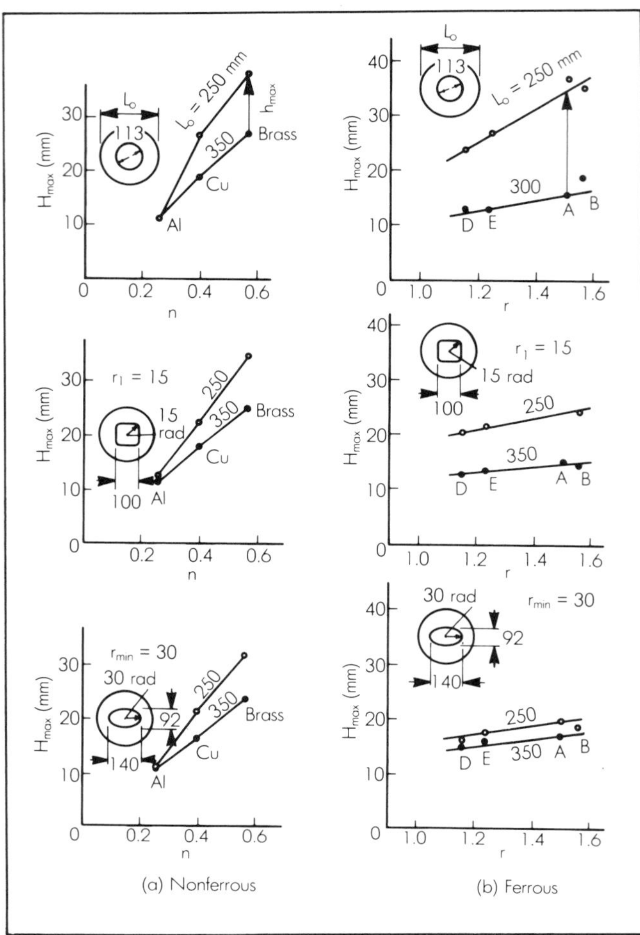


**Fig. 1-15 Relationship between stretching depth and *n* or *r* value for different forming geometry. (Dimensions are in mm.)**

## Olsen and Erichsen Tests

The Erichsen (Europe) and Olsen (North America) tests are similar in that they are both ball-punch deformation tests that simulate stretch forming. The principal difference is in the size of the ball, 0.875″ (22.23 mm) for the Olsen and approximately 0.8″ (20 mm) for the Erichsen tests. In both tests, a ball-punch penetrator is pressed into a metal sheet clamped over a cup. The end point of the test is indicated by a drop in load, indicating necking in the specimen. Maximum cup height is measured when necking occurs. The cup-test value is reported as the ratio of cup height to cup diameter. A typical cupping test is shown in Fig. 1-18. The procedures for conducting Olsen and Erichsen tests are described in ASTM Specification E643.78.

The Swift test is commonly used to simulate deep drawing. The test consists of drawing a circular blank specimen into a cylindrical cup. It has not been entirely standardized because results are affected by many factors: die opening, die approach radius, surface finish, thickness, blank lubrication, hold-down pressure, and material properties. The Swift index or limiting draw ratio, *LDR*, is obtained with a 2″ (51 mm) diam flat-bottom punch and draw die appropriate for thickness of the specimen. A circular blank is cut to a diameter smaller than the expected draw limit. The blank is drawn to maximum punch load, which occurs before the cup is fully formed. Successively larger blanks are drawn until one fractures before being drawn completely through the die. The diameter of the largest blank that can be drawn without fracturing, divided by cup diameter, determines the limiting draw ratio, *LDR*.

## Correlation of Results

Results of simulative forming tests correlate well with results of tension tests. Specifically, results of cup ductility tests, such

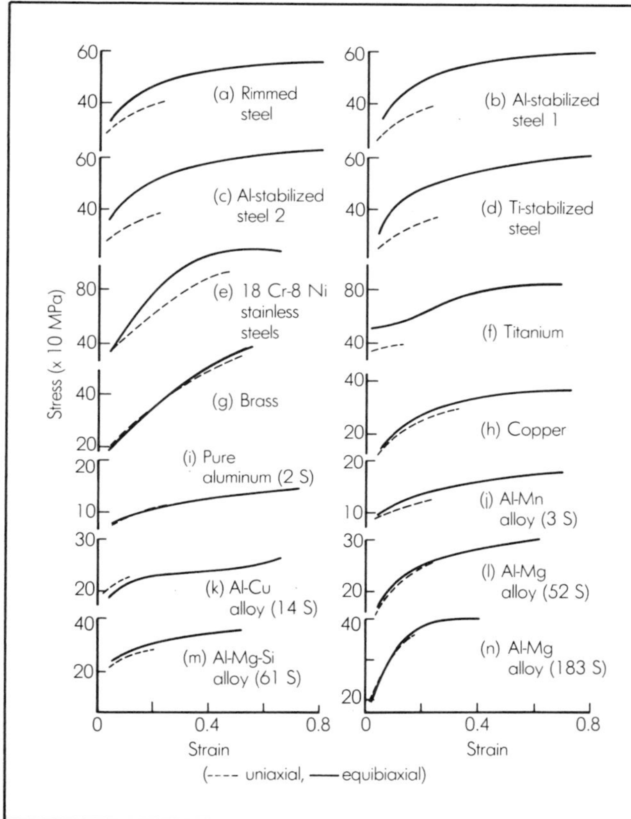


**Fig. 1-16 Stress-strain curves for various materials, assuming isotropy.**

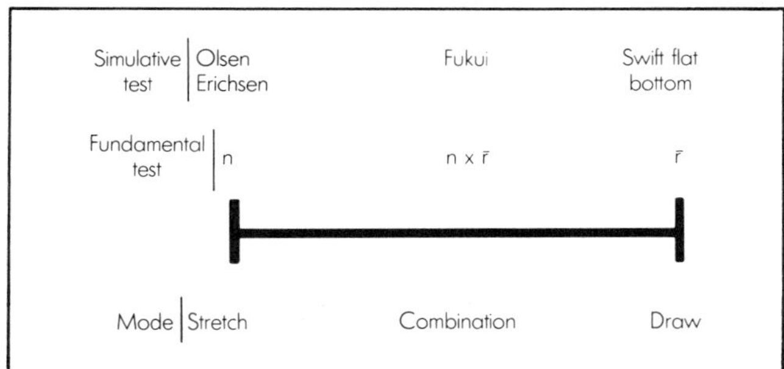


**Fig. 1-17 Forming classification. Certain material properties and simulative tests can be correlated between the two extremes (stretching and drawing).**

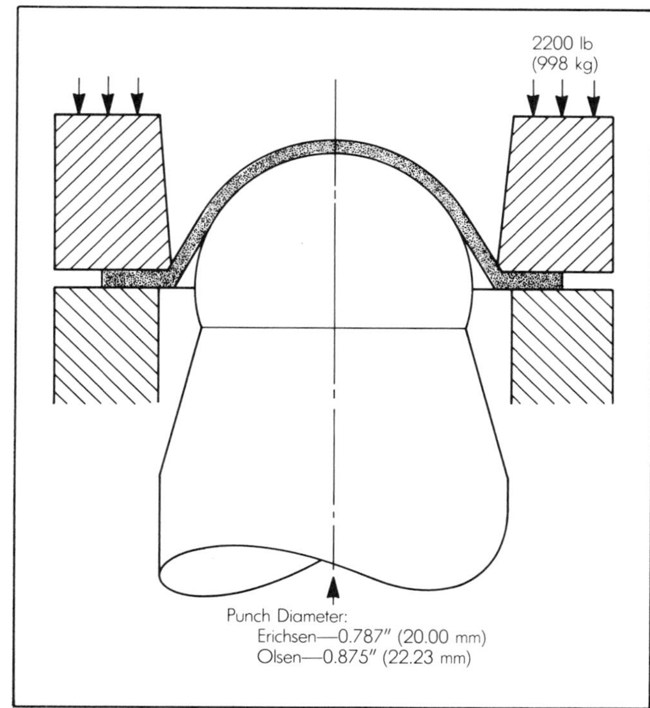


**Fig. 1-18 Erichsen or Olsen Cup test.**

as the Olsen and Swift tests, show good correlation with values of tensile elongation, the strain-hardening exponent, and the plastic strain ratio. In production forming, the material properties that apply to flange stretching are tensile elongation and plastic strain ratio. Ease of forming ribs and troughs in parts is related to the plastic strain ratio and can best be predicted from tests that produce conditions of plane strain. The formability test must be matched to a particular stamping for valid correlation with press performance data.

## Fukui Test

Combined stretching and drawing are simulated in the Fukui Conical Cup test (see Fig. 1-19). Since a majority of stampings are complex combinations of many separate operations, including stretching, drawing, bending, etc., the Fukui test often is more meaningful than the Olsen test.

The Fukui Conical Cup test is based on forcing a disc of sheet steel into a cone with a hemispherical punch. A 60° conical die is used so that no clamping force is required to hold the blank. The apparatus and procedure are derived from the need for a test that combines biaxial stretching over a punch and drawing-in over a radius as occurs in most press forming operations.

## Hemispherical Punch Test

Limitations inherent in the Olsen Cup test led to efforts to develop an improved dome stretching test for evaluation of pure stretch forming operations. Important features of the test (see Fig. 1-20) include a common punch diameter of 4″ (102 mm) and a locking bead to insure pure metal stretch.

## Usefulness of Test Results

Simulative tests, such as mechanical property tests, are limited in value for the evaluation of sheet metal formability.

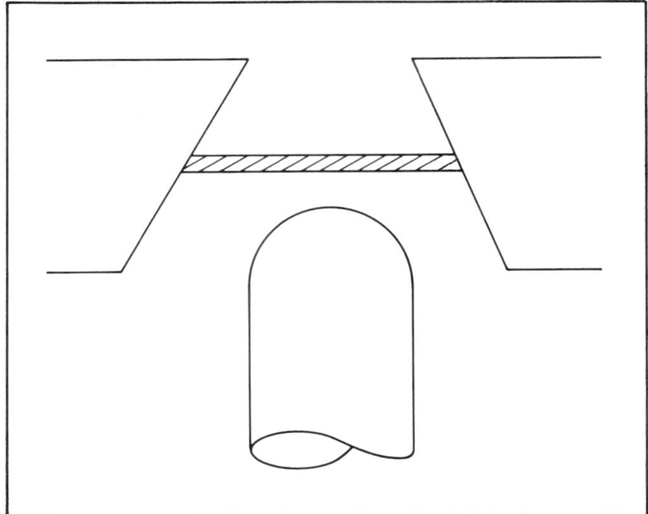
Fig. 1-19 Fukui Conical Cup test.

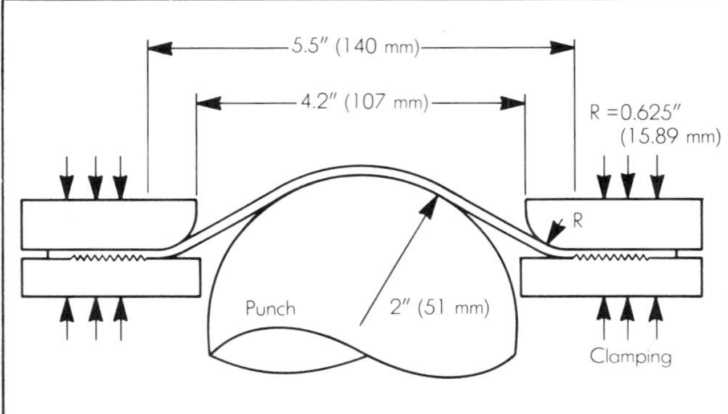

Fig. 1-20 Hemispherical punch test.

This is because the exact placement of a stamping on the classification spectrum varies or is unknown. Several combinations of forming operations may be found in various locations of the part. The relative amounts of stretching and drawing vary with material properties, lubrication, die conditions, time, and the depth of the stamping. The fundamental and simulative tests are limited to comparing various materials.

## SUPERPLASTIC METALFORMING

In metalforming, one of the significant emerging technologies is based on superplasticity—the property that permits the forming of metal as if it were a polymer or glass. The basic definition of a superplastic metal is that it can develop extremely high tensile elongations at elevated temperatures and under controlled rates of deformation.[11] As shown in Fig. 1-21, a conventional metal or alloy would develop perhaps 10-30% tensile elongation in an ordinary tensile test. This ductility is normally unchanged even though the temperatures may be increased. However, a superplastic material develops extremely high tensile elongations characteristically exceeding 300% elongation and not infrequently achieving as high as 2000-3000% tensile elongation. This is achieved at elevated temperatures and controlled strain rates. The other characteristic

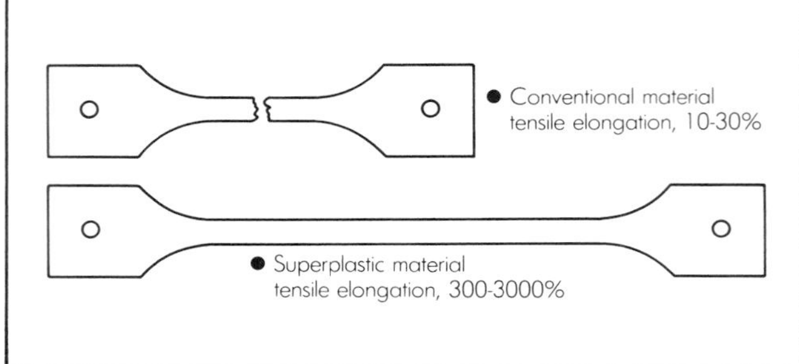

Fig. 1-21 Specimens illustrating superplasticity, which is the capability of certain alloys to develop extremely high tensile elongations at elevated temperatures and controlled strain rates.

normally observed concurrently with the high tensile deformation is a substantial reduction in the flow stress of the material. That is, the forces and stresses required to cause this deformation can be as little as 1/2 to 1/20th that of the conventional alloy under the same conditions. It is these two factors (high tensile elongation and low flow stress) that provide the exceptional potential available through superplastic forming.

A characteristic of a superplastic alloy is the strong sensitivity of flow stress to strain rate. This characteristic is quantified by the following relationship:

$$\sigma = K\epsilon^m \qquad (12)$$

where:

$\sigma$ = flow stress
$K$ = material constant
$\epsilon$ = strain rate
$m$ = strain rate sensitivity exponent

The value of $m$ for a superplastic material is not a constant function of strain rate. It normally follows a bell curve.

### Superplasticity Requirements

The most fundamental requirements for superplasticity are (1) grain size must be fine and stable and normally less than about 10 microns, although the grain size requirement may vary with material and other conditions; (2) the temperature at which the deformation proceeds is usually in excess of one-half the absolute melting point; and (3) the rate of straining must be controlled since superplasticity is observed only within a specified strain rate range. As the strain rate increases beyond the superplastic region, the ductility drops dramatically; and if the strain rate is decreased below the superplastic strain rate, the ductility likewise drops dramatically.

### Materials

While most ferrous and nonferrous metal and alloy systems have the potential for being superplastically formed, titanium alloys and high-strength aluminum alloys are regarded as having outstanding potential for application of this technology. Several alloy systems, such as zinc-aluminum (Zn-Al) and aluminum-copper-zinc (Al-Cu-Zn), have been developed specifically for their superplastic properties, and most titanium-based alloys exhibit superplasticity as conventionally produced sheet material. The superplastic characteristics of various alloys are shown in Table 1-8.

**TABLE 1-8**
**Superplastic Characteristics of Various Alloys**

| Alloy | Superplastic Temperature | | Elongation Tests | | | Flow Stress | |
|---|---|---|---|---|---|---|---|
| | °F | °C | Elongation, % | at Strain Rate $s^{(-1)}$ at | m* | (MPa) | (psi) |
| Titanium: Ti-6Al-4V | 1701 | 927 | 1000-2000 | $2 \times 10^{-4}$ | 0.8 | 10 | 1450 |
| Aluminum: | | | | | | | |
| Supral 100 | 842 | 450 | 600-1000 | $10^{-3}$ | 0.38 | 9 | 1305 |
| 08050 | 1049 | 565 | 500 | $10^{-3}$ | 0.3 | 2.8 | 406 |
| 7475 (Fine Grain) | 961 | 516 | 1200 | $2 \times 10^{-4}$ | 0.75 | 2 | 290 |
| Zinc: Zn-22Al | 392 | 200 | 2000 | $10^{-2}$ | 0.5 | 10 | 1450 |
| Iron: | | | | | | | |
| Fe-1.6C (+1.5Cr) | 1202 | 650 | 1200 | $10^{-4}$ | 0.46 | 45 | 6526 |
| Fe-26Cr-6.5Ni (IN 744) | 1652 | 900 | 1000 | $5 \times 10^{-4}$ | --- | 28 | 4061 |
| Nickel: IN 199 (PM) | 1850 | 1010 | 1000 | --- | 0.5 | 35 | 5076 |

*Strain rate sensitivity exponent.

### Advantages

Superplastic forming offers a number of advantages. First, because of the very high tensile elongation and resistance of superplastic material to localized necking and rupture, complex parts are readily formed. Since the forming typically is caused by gas pressure, it is necessary to use only a single configurational tool; that is, a tool designed to provide the shape of the part required. This results in both low cost of die fabrication and reduced lead time, since it is not necessary to fabricate a mating die and impose the costly hand-work operations necessary to cause the dies to mate accurately. The gas pressures normally used for superplastic forming are quite low, typically less than 300 psi (2 MPa). This permits the use of inexpensive die materials and can permit the forming of large complex parts with low press load capacity.

Perhaps the most important benefit of the superplastic forming process is related to the design of structural components. Because it is capable of forming complex parts, superplastic forming greatly increases the design flexibility. This can result in reduced part and fastener counts, thereby resulting in more efficient structural designs and systems that are lighter in weight.

The other area of keen importance is that of fabrication costs. The fabrication labor costs are greatly reduced since there are fewer parts; consequently, less time is expended in fabrication assembly. Both of these factors result in lower costs for the component. It is noted that the greatest benefits of this technology depends on a coupling of the design and manufacturing functions to result in the most efficient structure with the lowest cost.

### Limitations

Superplastic materials do not offer advantages in conventional deep drawing processes under isothermal conditions. The reason is that to draw in the flange, the material in contact with the punch nose as well as the cup walls must first work harden. At temperatures necessary for superplastic forming, no significant work hardening occurs; thus, if the friction between punch and blank is high, the punch typically pierces the blank or fails in the cup walls. The most significant disadvantage of superplastic forming is its inherently low forming rate (particularly for sheet structural parts), which is measured in terms of several inches per minute or less. This limitation disqualifies the superplastic alloys for high-production parts.

### Process Selection

In general, superplastic forming merits consideration when the part design requires complex, relatively deep shapes with compound curves or when redesigning of built-up, multiple-piece structures can reduce the part and fastener count and simplify assembly operations. The process would not be specified for easy-to-fabricate parts that require little tooling. Additional information on the superplastic forming process and its applications is provided in Chapter 4, "Sheet Metal Blanking and Forming."

## ANALYTICAL METHODS

Sheet metal forming is an experience-oriented technology. Throughout the years, a great deal of know-how and experience have been accumulated in this field, largely by trial-and-error methods. The complex physical phenomena describing a metalforming process are difficult to express mathematically. The metal flow, the friction at the tool-workpiece interface, the heat generation and transfer during plastic deformation, and the behavior and properties of the material are difficult to predict and analyze.

The development of analytical methods to study and describe mechanisms in metalforming has been active since 1940. Although considerable progress has been made, the techniques currently available are limited in their quantitative applicability. They have, however, become useful as qualitative guides.

Grid strain analysis involves etching a pattern of fine circles onto the sheet steel before pressing. During pressing, the circles are deformed into ellipses which can be measured to determine major and minor strains produced in the component. An estimate of how close the metal is to failure can be obtained by reference to the forming limit diagram (FLD), which is a plot of the major and minor strains at fracture over a wide range of conditions, from deep drawing (tension-compression) to stretch forming (tension-tension). A knowledge of how close the metal is to failure enables an estimate to be made of the criticality of the press forming operation. The strain values and the ratio of major to minor strain give information on the type of deformation in various areas of the press-formed part; for example, whether the metal has been drawn or stretched. This information provides insight into the press forming operation that can be used to solve problems in die development work and part design.

## CIRCULAR GRID SYSTEM

The circular grid system is widely used to evaluate sheet metal formability. It permits immediate and direct measurement of the maximum elongation of the sheet at any location. The grid consists of a pattern of small circles, typically 0.1″ (2.5 mm) diam, electrochemically etched into the surface of the blank prior to forming. Analysis of the deformed circles after forming (see Fig. 1-22) indicates the level of mechanical properties required in the sheet to form the part without breakage. Alternatively, it suggests the type and amount of rework to be performed on dies so that the part may be formed from a given grade of sheet metal.

### Imprinting the Pattern

Electrochemical marking is commonly used to etch the circular grid pattern onto the test metal sheet. This process eliminates the problems encountered with techniques such as scribing, printing, and photoprinting.

In this process, an "electrical stencil" is placed on the cleaned blank. A felt pad, soaked with electrolyte, is then placed on top of the blank, and an electrode—which may be either flat or "rocking"—is placed above the felt pad. The type of electrolyte used depends on the material to be gridded. Leads from a 14-volt power source are attached to the electrode and the blank. Current varies from 15-200 A, depending on stencil size and line density.

Application time ranges from 15 seconds for a flat electrode to under one minute for a rocker or roller type of electrode. The depth of the etched mark is 0.0005″ (0.013 mm) or less and is controlled by the application time. After etching, the solution on the blank is neutralized and a polarized oil is applied to prevent rusting.

Several hundred grids can be obtained from each stencil. For large areas, the stencil is stepped along the sheet until the desired area is covered; however, this is usually not necessary since only one or two potentially critical areas need be gridded on each panel. Once the pattern is etched into the sheet, the grid is not removed by rubbing the part over the die nor is it removed by applications of oil or chemicals.

The marked sheet is placed in a tryout press and formed, approaching as nearly as possible the conditions under which the part is to be formed in production. This is important because such variables as the type of lubricant used, the rate at which deformation occurs, and the force exerted on the hold-down ring have a substantial effect on the distribution of stresses in the blank and on the resulting deformation or strain.

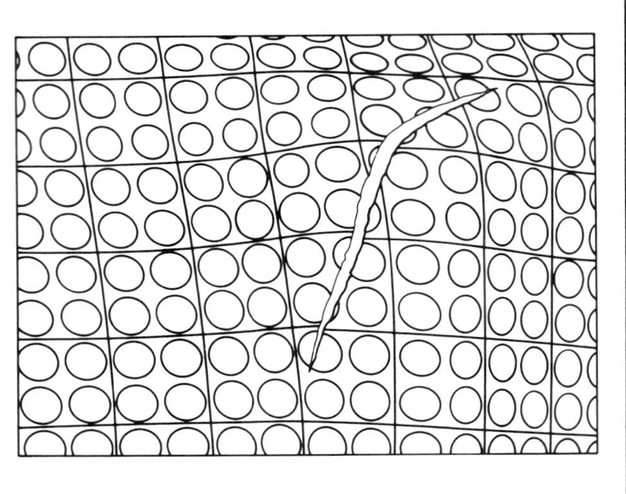

**Fig. 1-22 Strain patterns in a formed sheet metal part are made visible by deformation of circles. Analysis enables failure cause to be identified and eliminated.**

### Measuring Strain

Strain is a measurement of linear deformation; that is, the amount by which a unit length of metal is stretched. Each type of material has an allowable strain also called the critical strain level. If the critical strain level is exceeded, the metal fails, usually by tearing. To evaluate how well the metal responds to a given set of forming conditions, the actual strain must be measured at each potential failure location. Strain is identified with the standard symbol $\epsilon$ and is measured in percentages:

$$\epsilon = \frac{l_f - l_o \times 100}{l_o} = \frac{\Delta l \times 100}{l_o} \qquad (13)$$

where:

$l_o$ = original length
$l_f$ = final length
$\Delta l$ = difference between final and original length

Depending on the accuracy desired, a selection can be made from several grid measuring techniques. For relatively small volume, routine measuring (±5% accuracy is sufficient), simple flexible rulers or calibrated strips are satisfactory. For high-volume operations, measurement of the outcome of circle-grid testing is done most effectively either by use of stereo binoculars fitted with a calibrated reticle or by use of a specially marked mylar tape on which diverging lines are marked to allow a direct reading of the strain (elongation of circles in one or both axes). A computerized measuring system is also gaining acceptance.

When the material is strained, a circle becomes an ellipse (see Fig. 1-23). The largest surface strain is along the major axis of the ellipse. The formula for calculating strain is:

$$\epsilon = \frac{l_a - d_o \times 100}{d_o} \qquad (14)$$

where:

$\epsilon$ = strain
$l_a$ = length, major axis
$d_o$ = diameter of original circle

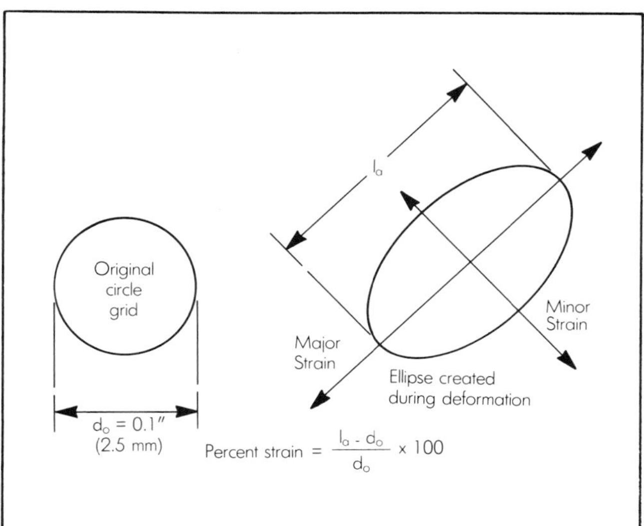


**Fig. 1-23 Circles stretch into ellipses as a result of strain. Maximum strain is along major axis.**

A similar calculation is made to determine the cross strain or the strain along the minor axis of the ellipse.

The grid spacing must be small enough to detect point-to-point variations in the strain distribution. For this reason, the circle diameters range from 0.1-0.2″ (2.5-5 mm). In research experiments, diameters 0.05″ (1.3 mm) and smaller may be used.

One important safety factor to be kept in mind is that when a stamping tears during forming, the tear is a visible indication that the metal has been worked beyond its formability limit. A more formable material, different lubricants, or reworked tools are needed. Modification of the tools is often more economical than paying the increased cost of premium materials or lubricants during the life of a product model.

Many stampings are close to failure, but yet not to the point at which they tear. These are called "critical" stampings. During die tryout, conditions may permit critical stampings to be formed successfully. The conditions include the use of slow speeds, careful blanking, spot lubrication, carefully adjusted tools, and selected blanks. In production, conditions less than optimum may prevail and breakage may result. Breakage during production runs is costly. Modifications then are time consuming when time is at a premium. The ability to predict failure—to identify critical stampings—is very desirable, and the circular grid system provides at least a partial solution to this problem.

The goal in measuring strain is to find the safety factor for each combination of material, lubricant, die set, and press. This safety factor indicates how close to failure a particular area of the finished part is. It is defined as the percent strain difference between the critical strain and the peak strain found in the stamping.

## FORMING LIMIT DIAGRAM

The forming limit diagram (FLD) is sometimes referred to as a "formability map." The FLD shows, for different strain rates, the maximum strain that a sheet metal can sustain before onset of localized thinning. For steel, the FLD is dependent upon sheet gage and the strain-hardening exponent, $n$.

### Formability Map

In the forming limit diagram (see Fig. 1-24) the bands indicating the critical strain level separate failure and nonfailure conditions for annealed and lightly rolled low-carbon sheet steel. The portion of the graph on the right represents tension-tension strains. These most commonly occur over the head of the punch or under conditions of stretching in which the blank is clamped and the punch is pushed into the sheet. The major and minor axes of the ellipse are both larger than the diameter of the original grid circle.

The portion of the graph on the left is for conditions encountered in deep drawing, or the tension-compression strain states. Here the major axis of the ellipse is greater than the original diameter of the circle, while the minor axis is shortened or compressed to less than the circle diameter. The curve apparently continues as a straight line to very high strain levels (such as 225% tension and 85% compression). These very high strains are possible because compressing the metal from the sides contributes to material elongation in the other direction.

The critical strain level drops to lower values as the material is cold worked. It is relatively insensitive to variations in cleanliness, gage, direction in the sheet, and other properties.

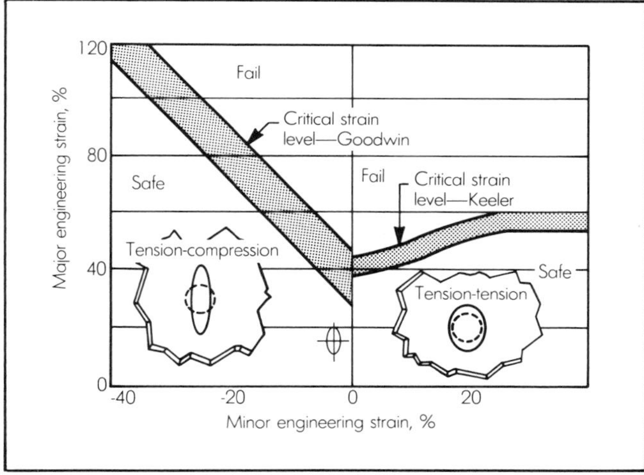


**Fig. 1-24 Basic forming limit diagram. Critical strain band separates failure from nonfailure conditions. Vertical axis is for maximum strain (major axis of ellipse). Horizontal axis is for strain along minor axis of ellipse.**

### Strain Distribution

The requirement for a satisfactory stamping is to obtain as uniform a strain distribution as possible, under the critical level (see Fig. 1-25). The more uniformly the strain is distributed, the lower the peak strain is and the higher the safety factor is for equal depths of the stamping.

The important criterion is how uniformly a particular steel distributes the strain in the presence of a stress gradient. It must be emphasized, however, that material properties—and corresponding grades of steel—are not the only variables that influence strain distribution. Small changes in other factors—lubrication, die design, etc.—can overshadow large variations in material properties.

## COMPUTER SYSTEM

The sequence of operations for General Motors Corporation's grid-circle analyzer (GCA), a computerized system for

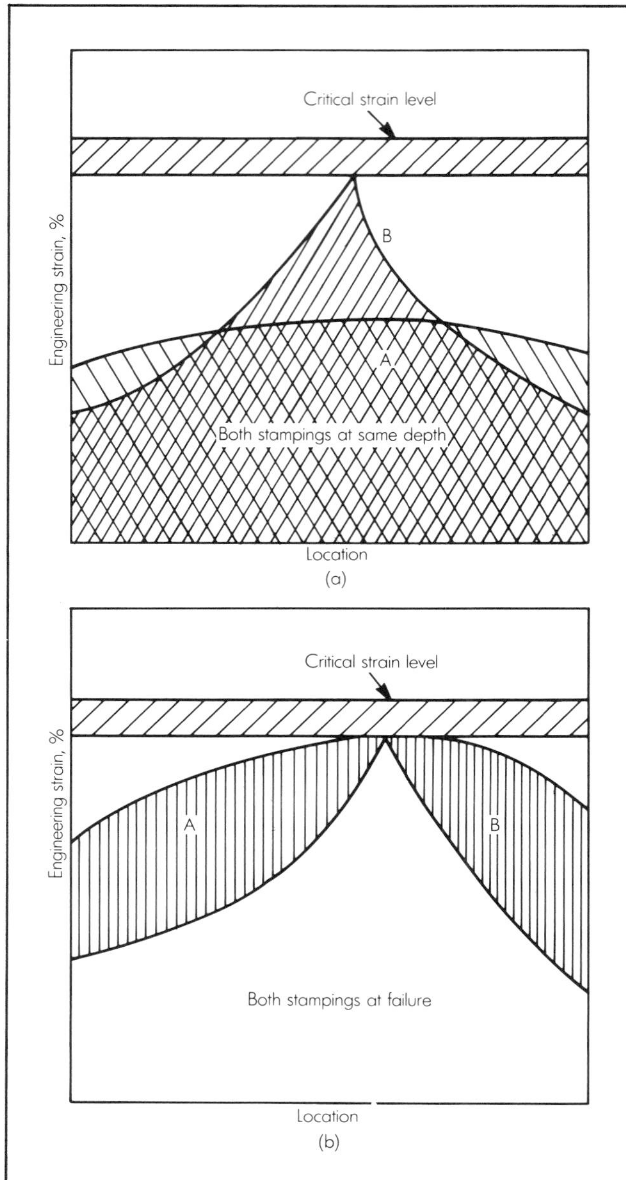


**Fig. 1-25 Schematic strain distribution of two materials formed over the same punch. Because it distributes the same total strain more uniformly, (a) material A does not fail, while material B does and (b) material A absorbs much more strain before it fails.**

optically transforming the results of a grid-circle experiment into an FLD is shown in Fig. 1-26. The system uses a solid-state camera and computer to convert formed metal distortions directly into major and minor strains, which can be plotted as an FLD. Time to measure one ellipse by GCA is 15 seconds.

## SHAPE ANALYSIS

Shape analysis is a method for determining the forming severity of a stamped part. Forming severity indicates, through a numerical value, how near the part is to fracture failure. Shape analysis is based on stretching and deep drawing actions in sheet metal forming. These actions occur when a blank is stretched over a punch nose and drawn into a die cavity. They influence each other and react with the tooling to affect the onset and character of failure. The shape analysis concept is extendable to any sheet metal undergoing similar kinds of strain. Determining the forming severity permits reduction in strain and improvement in material economy and process efficiency by changes in material, forming process, or part shape. The method can also be applied to parts of various designs, parts made of different materials and with different tooling, and parts on which different drawing lubricants are used.

### Shape Analysis Method Summary

In shape analysis, the critical forming area of a part is selected for analysis. A line representing the profile of half a cup shape is marked on the part through the critical area. The cup center, the outer edge of the cup, and the boundary between stretch and draw types of strains are marked. Measurements of line lengthening due to forming action are made. Proportions of the stretch and draw cups are calculated. Laboratory cups made with the same material give forming parameters that are compared to the measurements, and the forming severity is calculated. From the forming severity and other parameters, the need for changes in shape, process, or material can be determined. Analysis may be made of other areas and compared for severity.

### Basic Procedure for Shape Analysis

Areas, lines, and points used in shape analysis are shown in Fig. 1-27. Symbols are identified in Table 1-9. The basic shape analysis procedure consists of part selection, line analysis, measuring, and calculating.

**Part selection**. A portion of the part featuring a section of a cup shape should be selected. This can be the corner of a rectangular pan or the end of an elliptical or trough shape. Among these areas, the deepest and steepest formation is usually the most critical. Localized necking or incipient fracturing may be present. When such critical strains are elsewhere on a part, they may be traceable to efforts by press operators to compensate for the deeper formation.

The selected portion of the part is divided into two areas. The bottom area resembles a dome shape over the punch nose where the metal undergoes biaxial strain. This contour resembles various laboratory cups, such as the Olsen, Erichsen, and Dome Height Stretch cups. The principal factor affecting formability of these cups is the strain-hardening exponent, $n$. In the wall or cylindrical area, strain relates to such draw cups as the Swift, Engelhardt, and Single Blank Limiting Draw Ratio cups. The principle factor affecting formability of these draw cups is average anisotropy, $\bar{r}$.

These two groups of cups establish forming parameter limits of the material which appear in the calculations. Small shop presses can make these tests. A test part for analysis is formed with the blank gridded by circle strain patterns. The marked pattern should extend from the center of the part bottom outward to the corner or edge of the part.

**Line analysis**. The analysis line, $AL$, represents the profile cross section of the cup-shaped area, a half cup from bottom center to its outer limit. The location and ends of this line are important in obtaining useful measurements. The line is marked on the part as if a vertical cut were being made from the dome center out to the edge. It passes through the failure area. The center of the cup dome, the inner terminal, $IT$, is marked. This is not the part center but the projected center of the cup

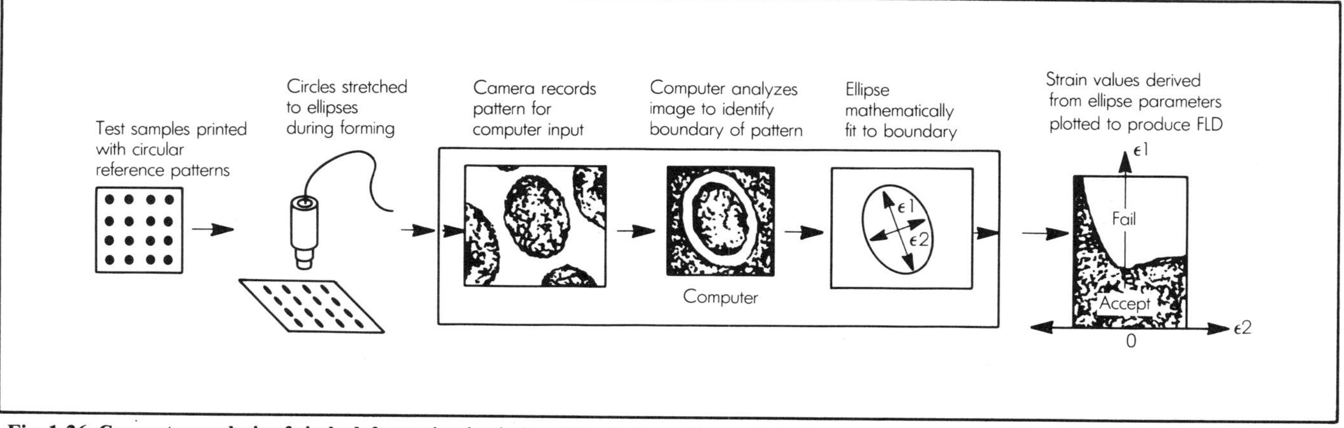


**Fig. 1-26 Computer analysis of circle deformation in circle-grid technique. Computerized measurements use solid-state camera focused on a formed dome. Cathode ray tube in foreground shows two of the ellipses magnified for measurements.**

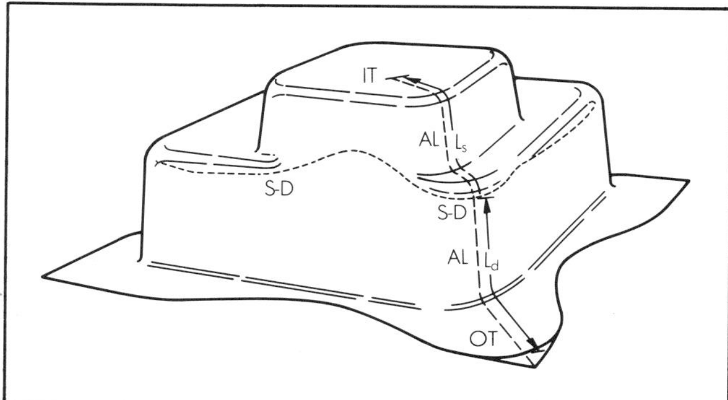


**Fig. 1-27 Deep-drawn pan illustrating analysis line locations for measurements using shape analysis technique.**

bottom at which the cup dome midpoint would be located.

As the analysis line passes down from the biaxially strained dome to the draw formed cylindrical portion, it passes through the stretch-draw boundary, *S-D*. Often the fracture failures are found near it. Identification is by the die impact mark made on the workpiece by the die ring as the sheet began to move into the die cavity. This mark in the metal is easily seen when the die ring has a tight radius edge. Circle-grid strain markings show a transition from biaxial stretch to elongation in draw in this area. Other identifying marks in the metal may be the beginning of scratches and sliding marks resulting from its movement over the die ring.

The outer terminal, *OT*, is marked at the outer limit in which material has effectively contributed to the cup formation. Although the outer terminal is frequently at the outer edge, the metal in the corner flanges does not draw into the die and is not strained by the forming action. This unstrained area can be observed by unaltered circle-grid marks. A draw bead can also prevent metal movement toward the cup.

**Measuring.** Two groups of measurements are taken. From the first group, the added length of the analysis line from blank to final shape for each kind of forming is measured. To do this, the circle-grid pattern is required. The distance, $L_s$, along the part surface from the inner terminal, *IT*, to the stretch-draw boundary, *S-D*, is measured. For stretching, the original distance, $L_{os}$, of this line is obtained by counting grid circles and

**TABLE 1-9**
**Identification of Symbols for Shape Analysis**

| Symbol | Identification |
|---|---|
| *AL* | Analysis line |
| *IT* | Inner terminal of analysis line |
| *OT* | Outer terminal of analysis line |
| *S-D* | Stretch-draw boundary between biaxial stretch and deep draw forming |
| $L_s$ | Final length biaxial stretch portion of analysis line |
| $L_d$ | Final length deep draw portion of analysis line |
| $L_{os}$ | Original length biaxial stretch portion of analysis line |
| $L_{od}$ | Original length deep draw portion of analysis line |
| $L_{ds}$ | Final total analysis line length |
| $L_o$ | Original total analysis line length |
| $C_{hs}$ | Part stretch cup height |
| $C_{hd}$ | Part draw cup height |
| $C_{ws}$ | Biaxial stretch cup width at stretch-draw boundary |
| $C_{wd}$ | Draw cup width at die ring |
| $E_{bw}$ | Effective blank width derived from $L_o$ (2 x $L_o$) |
| *STR* | Amount of forming contributed to analysis line by biaxial stretch |
| *DRAW* | Amount of forming contributed to analysis line by deep draw |
| $R_s$ | Stretch cup height to width ratio of the part |
| $R_d$ | Draw cup blank to cup width ratio of the part |
| *$O_d$ | Biaxial stretch material cup forming parameter |
| ***LDR* | Deep draw material cup forming parameter |
| *SEV* | Forming severity value obtained from shape analysis calculations |

* $O_d$ is the value of a 1″ (25.4 mm) Olsen laboratory cup height in inches (millimeters) formed using oiled polyethylene lubrication on the punch. Dome height test cup ratio, h/w, is equally valid when using oiled polyethylene on punch.

** Limited Draw Ratio, *LDR*, the value of critical blank size/cup size from a Swift Cup Test or from a Single Blank Draw Cup Test, polyethylene and oil.

multiplying the number obtained by the unit fraction. Then the distance, $L_d$, from the stretch-draw boundary, *S-D*, to the outer terminal, *OT*, is measured along the part surface. Similarly, for drawing, the original distance, $L_{od}$, is determined by grid circle counting.

The second group of measurements (see Fig. 1-28) is used to determine the stretch cup and draw cup dimensions of the part. Toolmaker measuring devices are helpful in taking these measurements. Vertical height, $C_{hs}$, from the level of the inner terminal down to the stretch-draw boundary is measured. The horizontal distance from inner terminal to stretch-draw boundary is measured. This is equal to half the stretch cup width, $C_{ws}$. These measurements describe the stretch cup portion of the analysis line. For the draw cup portion, the vertical height, $C_{hd}$, from stretch-draw boundary to the outer terminal is measured. The horizontal distance from the inner terminal to the base of the draw cup is measured. This is equal to half the draw cup width, $C_{wd}$. The base of the draw cup is at the bend from cup wall to the outer flange which has not been drawn into the cup.

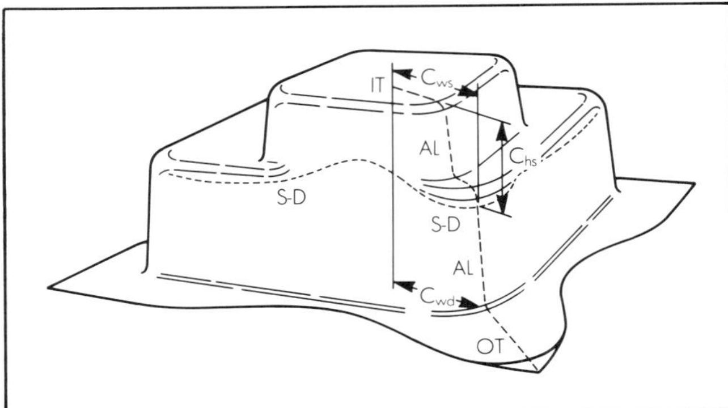


**Fig. 1-28 Deep-drawn pan illustrating measurements taken for shape analysis.**

**TABLE 1-10**
**Equations for Shape Analysis Calculations**

Analysis Line Lengthening:

$$STR = \frac{L_s - L_{os}}{L_{ds} - L_o} \quad \text{where } L_{ds} = L_d + L_s \qquad (15)$$

$$DRAW = \frac{L_d - L_{od}}{L_{dx} - L_o} \quad \text{where } L_o = L_{od} + L_{os} \qquad (16)$$

Cup Forming Ratios:

$$R_s = \frac{C_{hs}}{C_{ws}}$$

NOTE

$C_{ws}$ should approximate 2 x $L_{os}$, since the analysis line profile accounts for half cup. (17)

$$R_d = \frac{E_{bw}}{C_{wd}} \quad \text{where } E_{bw} = 2 \times L_o \qquad (18)$$

Forming Severity:

$$SEV = \frac{(R_s \times STR) + (R_d \times DRAW) - DRAW}{DRAW(LDR - O_d) + O_d - DRAW} \qquad (19)$$

NOTE

Substitution of *LDR* and $O_d$ values in the Forming Severity equation with *LDR* and $O_d$ values for other materials gives *SEV* values for those materials under identical forming conditions.

**Calculating**. The ratio of analysis line lengthening due to stretching can be obtained by calculating Eq. (15) in Table 1-10. The ratio of line lengthening due to draw can be found by calculating Eq. (16). When compared, these ratio values show the relative amount of stretching and drawing used to obtain the shape. This information is used in applying analysis results to indicate process changes or material specifications. Stretch and draw cup proportions can be obtained by calculating Eq. (17) and Eq. (18). For Eq. (4), effective blank width, $E_{bw}$, is 2 x $L_o$, twice the original analysis line length.

The final equation, Eq. (19), compares cup shape ratios and line lengthening ratios to the theoretical material forming parameters from the cup tests, a three-way comparison. This gives the forming severity, *SEV*, which shows how close the part is to the theoretical forming limit value of 1.0 which would be achieved by full utilization of the analysis line.

An example of forming shape analysis data is given in Table 1-11 for a terne coated drawing quality steel used in a typical deep-drawn pan used in automotive applications. The value obtained for *SEV* is 0.78.

## Interpretation and Application

When interpreting and applying shape analysis data, a *SEV* value of 0.78, obtained from the data of Table 1-11, indicates a tolerable level of strain from forming. As a working basis for estimations, an *SEV* value of 1.0 indicates failure, and visible evidence of this should appear on the part as fractures. An *SEV* value of 0.9 is unacceptably close to failure; an *SEV* value of 0.8 indicates the upper limit of acceptable strain; and an *SEV* value of 0.6 or below indicates economies may be effected within the triad relationship of material, shape, and process.

An *SEV* value of 0.78 indicates a considerable use of available shape and process, which indicates a considerable use of available formability of the material. If it were significantly lower, a smaller amount of material might be used by reducing blank size. This would require increased resistance to draw-in by friction, such as that caused by higher binder pressure or a less-slippery drawing lubricant. Deterioration of tooling causing scoring, for instance, also increases friction. At an *SEV* value of 0.78, this scoring would quickly increase severity into an unacceptable range.

Substitution of less-formable material, such as commercial-quality steel for drawing-quality steel or aluminum for steel, is not indicated. Aluminum alloy 5182-0, which has material forming parameters of $O_d$ = 0.34 and *LDR* = 2.09, is calculated to have an *SEV* value of 0.91, assuming identical forming conditions.

From values calculated for *STR* and *DRAW* (see Table 1-9), estimates may be made as to whether to increase the proportion of stretching to drawing or to increase the proportion of drawing to stretching to change the *SEV* value. In the example given in Table 1-11, the *STR* value of 0.355 indicates a good proportion of stretching in view of the step in the profile of the cup. If the profile were a smooth curve, more material would be available for stretching and increased binder pressure could be used, risking possible higher scrap rates as the tools become worn.

**TABLE 1-11**
**Shape Analysis Values for Steel Deep-Drawn Cup**

| Symbol | Value in. | Value mm |
|---|---|---|
| $L_s$ | 9.7 | 246 |
| $L_d$ | 11.5 | 292 |
| $L_{os}$ | 8.6 | 218 |
| $L_{od}$ | 9.5 | 241 |
| $L_{ds}$ | 21.2 | 538 |
| $L_o$ | 18.1 | 460 |
| $C_{hs}$ | 3.6 | 91 |
| $C_{ws}$ | 15.5 | 393 |
| $C_{wd}$ | 17.8 | 452 |
| $E_{bw}$ | 36.2 | 919 |
| $O_d$ | 0.38 | --- |
| $LDR$ | 2.28 | --- |
| Calculated Ratio Values | | |
| $STR$ | 0.355 | |
| $DRAW$ | 0.645 | |
| $R_s$ | 0.232 | |
| $R_d$ | 2.034 | |
| $SEV$ | 0.78 | |

## COMPUTER-AIDED MODELING

Research activity is aimed at enabling the computer to have a significant role in evaluating alternatives and optimizing the designing and manufacturing of sheet metal parts. In approaching an understanding of the application of mathematical modeling and computers to sheet metal forming analysis and prediction, one begins by recognizing that the familiar formability parameters and relationships are the main ingredients for constructing a numerical model.

The sheet metal is described by its $n$, $r$, and $m$ values; its yield and tensile strengths; and the forming limit diagram. The lubricant affects the punch-sheet interaction, and draw beads determine the conditions on the binder surface. To these factors are added a geometrical description of the punch and die and the equations of sheet metal plasticity. The output is the strain in the finished part and a prediction of any failure mode (necking, fracturing, wrinkling, etc.). Computer modeling of draw dies is in its infancy, and the general mathematical problem has not yet been solved. Hence, it is important to note that the computer models are presently used (1) as research tools and (2) for analysis of certain critical areas of stampings.

It is expected that, eventually, the computer will aid in making forming decisions on a broad basis. It will select material based not only on mechanical properties but also on overall part cost. Die dimensions will be worked out; dies will be constructed; and parts will be finished and delivered to final inspection—all with the aid of a computer.

The objective is to eliminate the "cut-and-try" aspect of sheet metal designing and fabrication, a fine-tuning process that can take as long as two years from initial die design to startup on the production line.

### Predicting Part Formability

In predicting the success or failure of an automobile body stamping for a given die design, the computer is playing a significant role. In the technique represented by the graph shown in Fig. 1-29, experimental data and computer calculations combine to determine the feasibility of forming the part from a particular sheet metal material.

The data is presented as a forming limit diagram (FLD). Above a maximum combination of major and minor strain, the sheet metal will fail. The FLD is determined experimentally for each material.

A model based on the mathematical theory of plasticity is then used to calculate the strains that would occur in the metal during the stamping of a particular shape. Using parameters such as forces generated by the tool, material properties, and panel geometry, the computer calculates strain paths such as the one shown in Fig. 1-29 for various locations on the sheet. The most critical strain path is then isolated.

To determine this critical path, calculated strains at various punch depths are compared with the maximum allowable strain on the FLD. In this example of an automobile body stamping, the maximum attainable punch depth is reached when the maximum calculated strain intercepts the FLD. Since this depth is less than the design depth, the part would develop a split and would fail.

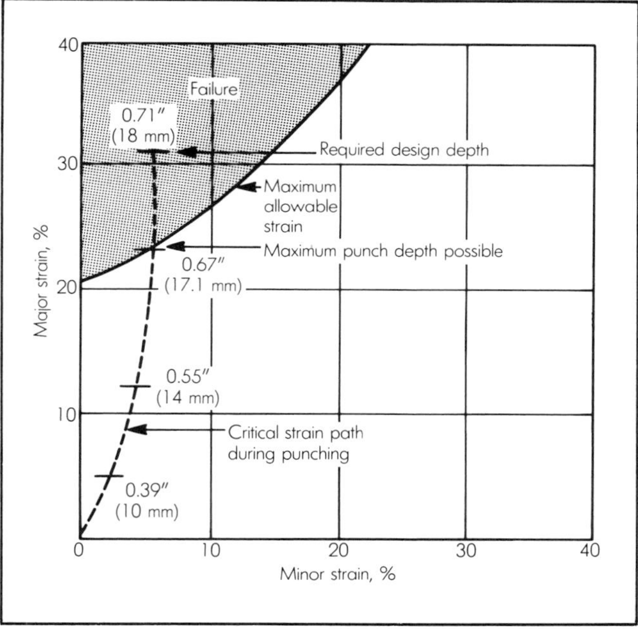


**Fig. 1-29 Graph developed for predicting part formability. Experimental data and computer calculations are combined to assess feasibility of forming the part from a particular sheet metal material. This forming limit diagram delineates the failure zone, above a maximum feasible combination of major and minor strain.**

### Model for Stretch Flanging

When a flange bend occurs along a convex curve, the flange edge becomes stretched. The maximum amount of stretching permissible must not be exceeded during the stamping operation if metal tearing is to be avoided. With computerized mathematical modeling, formability limits can be determined accurately and approached closely in production without part failure.

The flanging mathematical model not only reduces the lead time required to bring a new part into production but also provides wider design latitude in some cases. As the graphs in

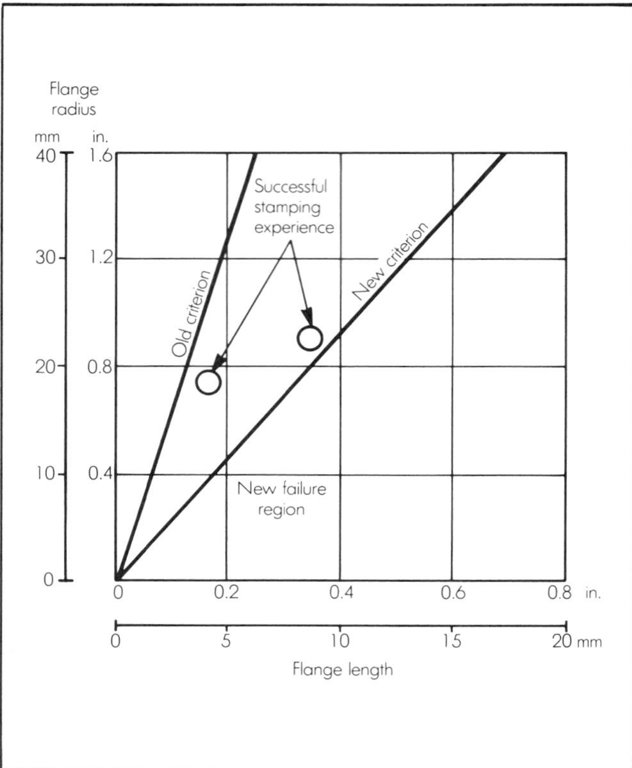


**Fig. 1-30 This graph shows, for typical production part, the former stretch flange criterion and the new criterion that was developed with the aid of computer math model.**

Fig. 1-30 illustrate for a typical production part, the former design criterion for flange length-to-radius design was much more restrictive than the new mathematical model.

### Computer Research Underway

Development of useful predictive capabilities is based on the philosophy that calculations to evaluate the consequences of metalforming operations must be tailored to specific applications. This is in contrast to an all-inclusive approach in which various types of forming operations and part shapes might be analyzed by a single, general-purpose, computer program.

The latter approach—although attractive at first glance—is impractical. Forming operations are so complex that computing requirements for such an all-inclusive calculation are much too large to be practical. In addition, an all-purpose program may not even be necessary, since the success of a forming operation often depends only on the formability of a few isolated critical areas.

Each critical area can be effectively treated in a specially designed computer program to suit specific geometric features and forming processes. To date at one company, two such forming processes, stretch flanging and stretch forming of channels and pockets, have been programmed successfully. Experience from these programs is leading the way toward similar programs for bending and drawing.

At another research laboratory, computer-aided modeling and simulating of the sheet metal forming processes is intended to provide information for production planning, for selecting equipment and tooling, and for predicting failure during forming. Mathematical models and computer programs have been developed and validated to analyze and simulate such widely used sheet metal forming processes as brake bending, rubber forming, and punch stretch forming.

# FORMABILITY PREDICTION AND EVALUATION

It is recognized that fractures which occur during forming can be due to part design, tooling irregularities, steel quality, lubrication, or various press or shop conditions. Steel quality has been measured for many years by standard tests for determining yield strength, uniform elongation, total elongation, tensile strength, and resistance to thinning (plastic strain ratio). Lubricants have been characterized using various tests to obtain the coefficient of friction.

Until recently, the weak link in the analysis system has been the inability to quantitatively determine whether failures are attributable to a difficult design or to tooling irregularities. Now, however, by using both the forming limit diagram and shape analysis concepts in the analysis of parts from prototype through production, this weak link can be eliminated. At the General Electric Co. an ongoing forming analysis procedure exemplifies this approach in a sophisticated application that combines the circle grid, forming limit diagram, and shape analysis systems.

The use of accepted analysis techniques to separate a design problem from a tooling problem is desirable because it permits quick identification of the true cause of a problem, which allows rapid implementation of corrective action. It also permits any improvement achieved by corrective action to be quantitatively measured.

## SURFACE PATTERN FOR ANALYSES

Electrochemical etching is used to apply the circular-grid pattern on sheet metals that will be formed on prototype or production dies. A recommended pattern consists of four 0.1″ (2.5 mm) diam circles within any number of 0.25″ (6.4 mm) squares (see Fig. 1-31, view *a*). The circles and squares are distorted during the forming process. Measurement of this distortion allows both the forming limit diagram and shape analysis techniques to be carried out. Electrochemical etching equipment is available from various manufacturers.

## FORMING LIMIT DIAGRAM (FLD) CONCEPT

The FLD, originally developed by G. M. Goodwin and S. P. Keeler, allows forming severity to be obtained from the strains that occur during sheet metal forming. Measurement of the critical strains on many production and laboratory parts formed from 0.035″ (0.89 mm) cold-rolled steel resulted in the compilation of the original Keeler-Goodwin diagram (see Fig. 1-32).

Critical strains are those strains measured after local thinning has started. The critical strain level for a given material is obtained by measuring the final major and minor ellipse diameters (see Fig. 1-31, view *b*) in the severely deformed region of the part and converting them into engineering strain. This major-minor strain combination defines one point on the critical strain level curve of the FLD.

## FLD's for Various Materials

Forming limit diagrams have been developed for many materials and material thicknesses since the original FLD was published. These FLD's are available in the literature or from steel and aluminum suppliers. By using them, part evaluation can be simplified, because it is only necessary to measure the critical part strains and then plot them on an FLD that is readily available.

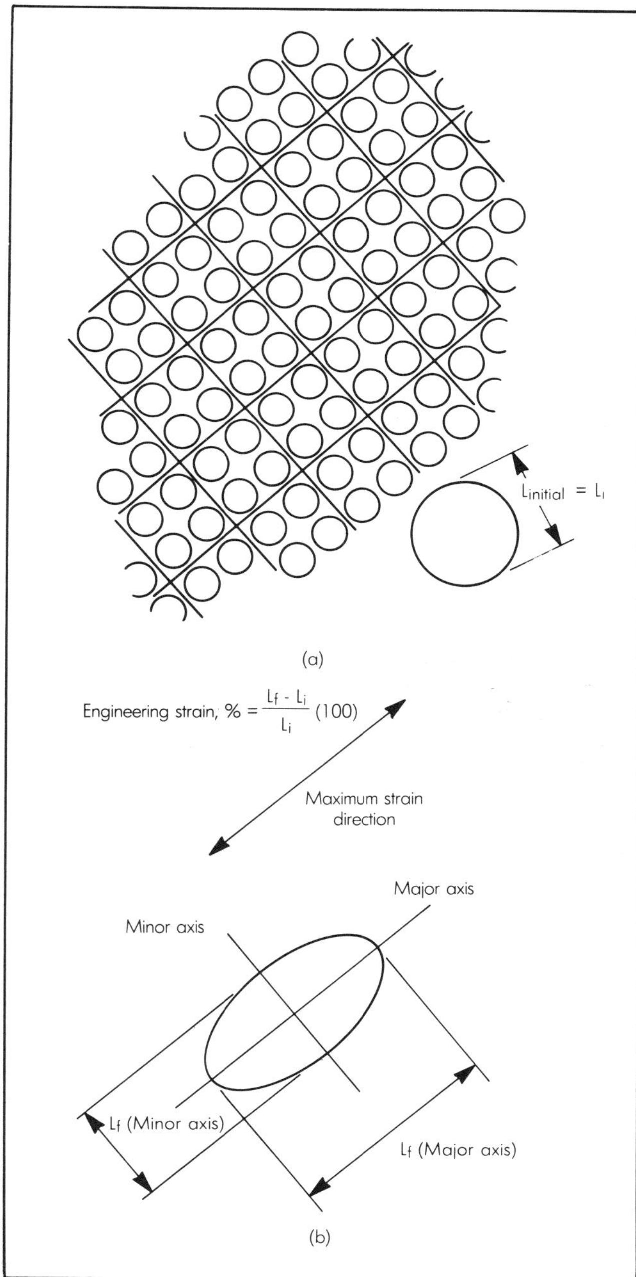


**Fig. 1-31 Typical grid pattern: (a) undeformed and (b) deformed; and elongation equation.**

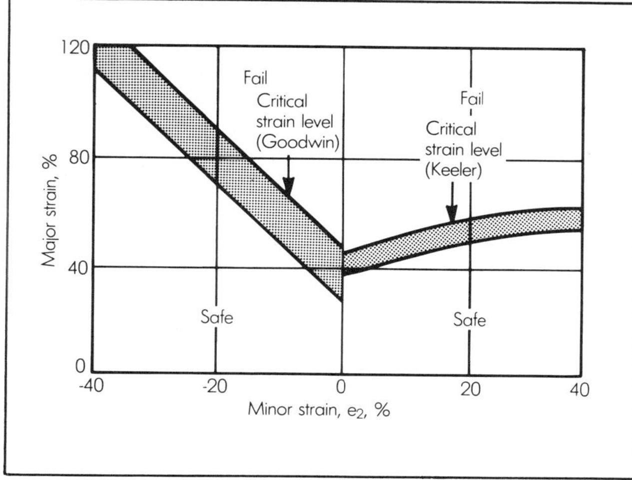


**Fig. 1-32 Forming limit diagram illustrates tension-compression strain rate (left) and tension-tension strain (right).**

## FLD Modified For Shop Applications

Two definitions of the critical strain level exist in industry. Personnel working in production shops consider visible localized thinning (necking) or splits unacceptable. Persons working in laboratories consider the initial onset of local thinning critical. Experience has shown that placing bands representing both definitions of the critical strain level on the FLD is beneficial from a practical viewpoint, because it accurately describes what is observed in the shop. Normal variations in press shop conditions cause fractures when the most severe strains are at the onset of necking. An FLD that contains both severity levels is shown in Fig. 1-33.

The limitations of the material from which a part is to be formed must be included in any part analysis. The forming limit of this material is determined by its thickness and properties. This means that the critical strain bands must be positioned properly on the FLD for the specified material.

Low-carbon steels are used for a large percentage of sheet metal parts. The following procedures show how the FLD can be optimized for analysis of a given low carbon steel part. The FLD can be corrected only for thickness if part analysis is required before material properties can be determined, or it can be corrected for both material thickness and material properties. It is very important to use the correct FLD for the material, material thickness, and material properties.

- To correct the FLD for thickness only:

1. Place a point indicating the measured thickness at the proper location within the vertical thickness range on the right side of Fig. 1-34.
2. Draw a horizontal line until it intercepts the major strain axis on the left side of this figure.
3. Record this major strain value for use later with the information in Fig. 1-33.
4. Figure 1-33, *a*, indicates the major-minor strain axes while Fig. 1-33, *b*, shows the critical strain bands and the major strain index point. Place the information in Fig. 1-33, *a*, on white paper and that in Fig. 1-33, *b*, on clear plastic.
5. Draw a horizontal line in Fig. 1-33, *a*, beginning at the major strain value (obtained for material thickness

from Fig. 1-34), until it intersects the vertical line at 0% minor strain.

6. Place the clear plastic sheet (Fig. 1-33, *b*) over Fig. 1-33, *a*, and locate the (major strain) index point at the intersection of the major strain value and zero minor strain.

- To correct the FLD for both thickness and material properties (uniform elongation, $e_u$):

1. Beginning at the proper thickness on the right side of Fig. 1-34, follow the two segmented lines that represent this material thickness (horizontal for $e_u$ greater than 23.5% and sloping to the origin for $e_u$ less than 23.5%) until the measured value for the material's uniform elongation is reached.

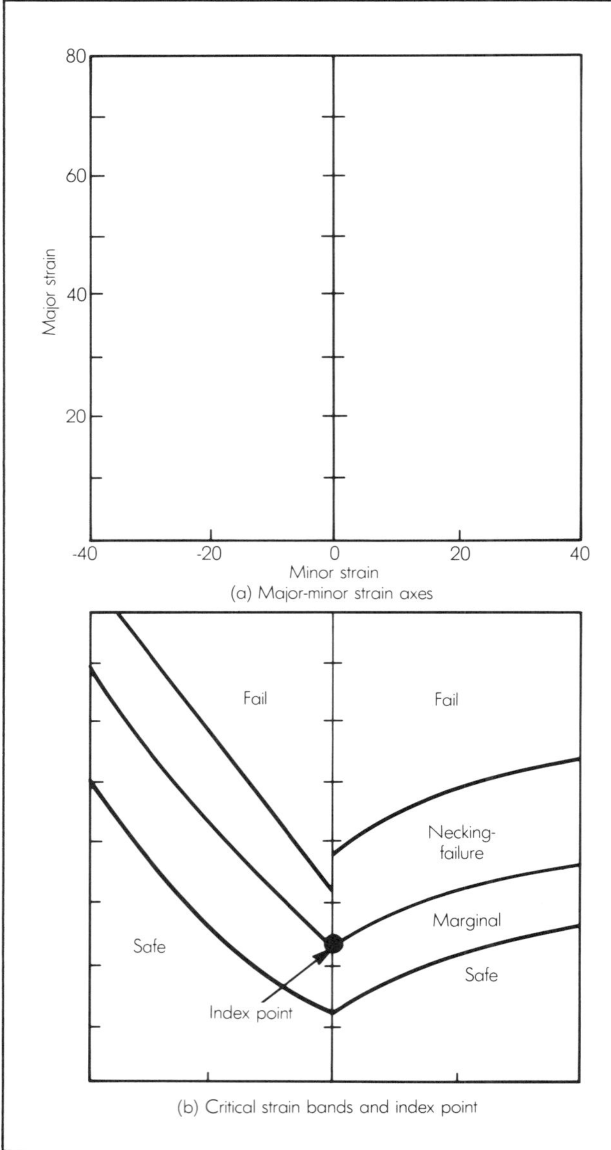


**Fig. 1-33 Modified forming limit diagram: (a) major-minor strain axes and (b) critical strain bands and index point.**

2. Draw a horizontal line until it intercepts the major strain axis on the left side of Fig. 1-34.
3. Proceed as instructed in Steps 3 through 6 for correcting FLD for material thickness only.

Normally it is necessary to measure the major/minor engineering strains of approximately six ellipses in each critical region and to plot them on an FLD to determine which is the most severely deformed ellipse. Once these measurements are completed, only the data point for the most severely deformed ellipse is retained on the FLD.

The FLD analysis is therefore a point analysis that allows areas of localized high strain or tooling irregularities to be identified. Sophisticated equipment is available to precisely measure the major-minor ellipse diameter on the formed part. Normally, however, for part analyses, a flexible ruler or dividers are adequate to measure ellipse diameters after forming.

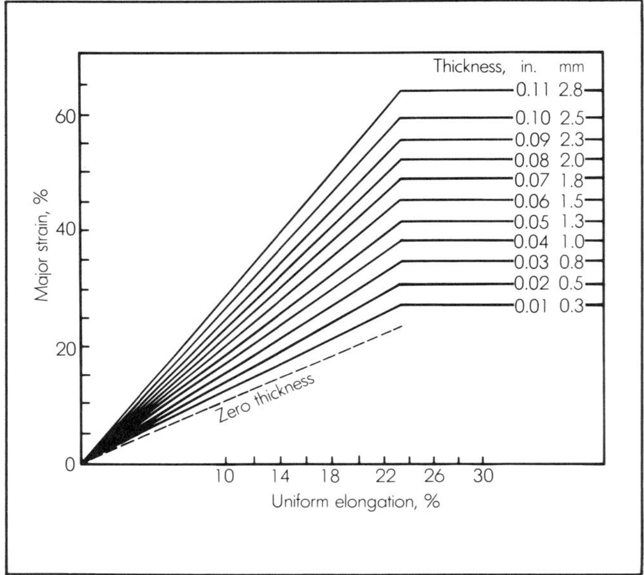


**Fig. 1-34 Graph used for positioning of forming limit diagram strain bands.**

## SHAPE ANALYSIS (SA)

Shape analysis was initially conceived by A. S. Kasper. It is a line analysis technique that breaks the critical portion of the part as identified by the FLD into stretch and draw. This technique, since it is a line analysis, extends beyond the localized strains and therefore determines the average design severity.

A brief description of Kasper's SA is given earlier in this chapter. The basic diagram of the technique (the stretch-draw chart) contains three key parameters (see Fig. 1-35).

### Material Capability

In using the stretch-draw chart, the first parameter, the forming line, determines the material's capabilities. The end points of the forming line are most easily obtained from the material properties (total elongation and plastic anisotropy) and the equation shown in Fig. 1-35. These material properties are obtainable from a standard tensile test. It has been proven that these end points can be joined by a straight line.

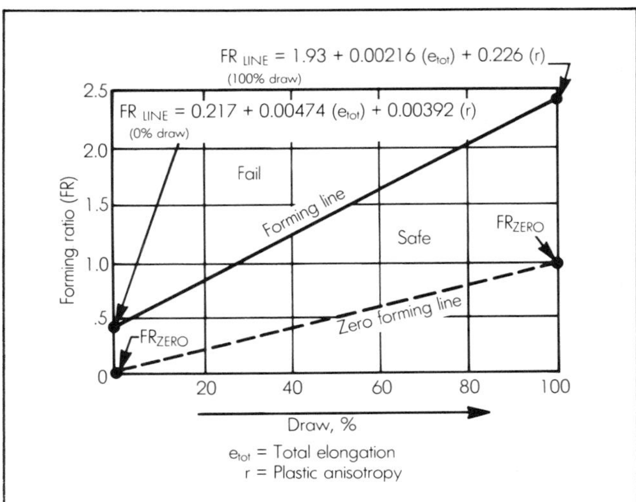


**Fig. 1-35 Shape analysis stretch-draw chart.**

## Percent Draw

The second parameter of the stretch-draw chart, the percent draw, is obtained from the circle grid on the formed part. The portion of the material deformed to produce the critical region of the part must be identified and split into stretch and draw areas before the calculations can be performed.

**Stretch/draw separation.** To separate into stretch and draw areas, an analysis line is drawn on the part (see Fig. 1-36). The die impact line that is visible on the part is identified as the boundary between stretch and draw areas. It is now necessary to determine the portion of material formed by drawing. This determination is done on a part with the recommended electroetched grid pattern of four 0.1″ (2.5 mm) diam circles within a 0.25″ (6.4 mm) square by setting dividers at 0.1″ (2.5 mm), and traversing down the sidewall and into the flange along the analysis line, until the dividers match the major diameter of the grid pattern. This location identifies the outer draw boundary. The inner stretch boundary is obtained in the same fashion, except in this case one traverses up the sidewall and toward the blank center along the analysis line until the material is no longer affected by the critically formed region.

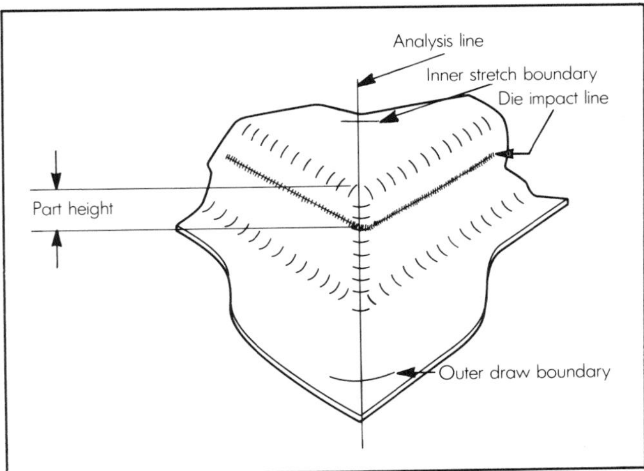


**Fig. 1-36 Boundary identification used to calculate percent draw.**

**Percent draw calculations.** After all three boundaries have been determined, it is possible to measure or calculate the formed lengths required to obtain the percent draw. The final stretch length, $S_F$, is the distance between the die impact line and the inner stretch boundary. The final draw length, $D_F$, is the distance between the outer draw boundary and the die impact line. These lengths can be conveniently measured with a flexible scale. The original stretch, $S_I$, and draw, $D_I$, lengths can be obtained by counting the number of squares between the die impact and the appropriate boundary. To obtain the initial lengths, the number of squares is multiplied by 0.25 if the analysis line runs parallel to the sides of the squares and by 0.3535 if the analysis line runs parallel to the square diagonals. The percent draw is then calculated:

$$\%\ draw = \left[\frac{(D_F - D_I)}{(F - I)}\right]100 \quad (20)$$

where:

$D_F$ = distance between outer draw boundary and die impact line
$D_I$ = initial or original draw length
$S_I$ = initial stretch length
$F = S_F + D_F$
$I = S_I + D_I$

## Forming Ratio

The forming ratio is the third parameter on the stretch-draw chart. Prior to calculating this ratio, the part height, $P_h$, must be measured from the die impact line to the closed end of the gridded part (see Fig. 1-36). The part width stretch, $PW_s$, is twice the distance from the inner stretch boundary to the inner surface of the part. The final required length is the part width draw, $PW_D$. The $PW_D$ is equal to twice the distance from the inner stretch boundary to the outer surface of the part. It is known that the percent stretch equals 100 minus percent draw and that the effective blank width, $BW$, equals 2I. It is now possible to calculate the stretch forming ratio and draw forming ratio as follows:

$$(FR_S) = \left(\frac{P_h}{PW_s}\right) \times \left(\frac{percent\ stretch}{100}\right) \quad (21)$$

where:

$FR_S$ = stretch forming ratio
$P_h$ = part height
$PW_s$ = part width stretch

and:

$$(FR_D) = \left(\frac{BW}{PW_D}\right) \times \left(\frac{percent\ draw}{100}\right) \quad (22)$$

where:

$FR_D$ = draw forming ratio
$BW$ = blank width
$PW_D$ = part width draw

The total forming ratio, $FR$, that is plotted in Fig. 1-35 is obtained by adding the $FR_S$ and $FR_D$. This describes shape analysis.

### Application Technique

The shape analysis technique has been further refined to allow a direct comparison between it and the combined FLD. This refinement was achieved using Kasper's definition for severity, *SEV*:

$$SEV = \frac{(FR_{calc} - FR_{zero})}{(FR_{line} - FR_{zero})} \tag{23}$$

where:

$SEV$ = 0.8 at bottom of FLD marginal regions and 1.3 at top of necking failure region
$FR_{calc}$ = the "unknown," the forming ratio that is calculated by solving the severity equation
$FR_{zero}$ = 1 at 100% draw
$FR_{line}$ = quantity defined in Fig. 1-35

Information in the literature defines the severity as 0.8 at the bottom of the combined FLD marginal region and as 1.3 at the top of the necking failure region. Solving the severity equation for $FR_{calc}$ at 0% and 100% draw for these severity values defines the marginal and necking failure regions on the stretch-draw chart. All forming ratios, *FR*, except $FR_{calc}$ are defined in Fig. 1-35.

The result is a modified stretch-draw chart that allows a direct comparison between the FLD and SA results (see Fig. 1-37).

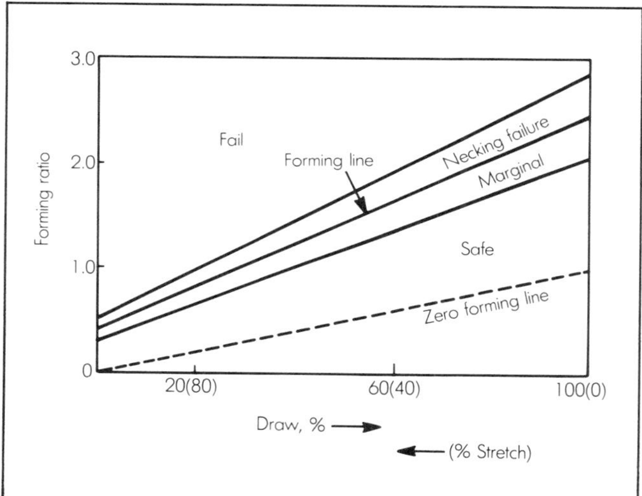


**Fig. 1-37 Modified stretch-draw chart: shape analysis diagram for determining severity of design. Percent draw is read from left to right; percent stretch (in brackets) is read from right to left.**

## COMPARING FLD AND SA RESULTS

The use of forming limit diagram and shape analysis techniques together proves to be a powerful tool, because it allows one to determine if fractures are caused by the design or by tooling irregularities. This separation of design and tooling problems is very important, because once the real cause of metal splitting is determined, everyone can work together to implement the necessary corrective action. Thus, accepted techniques (not opinion) can be used to determine the true cause of the problem.

A severe design is the cause of fractures when equivalent high severities are observed on both the FLD and SA charts; and tooling irregularities are the cause of the problem when SA indicates a "safe" design yet very high strains are observed on the FLD. These techniques allow the benefit of corrective action to be quantitatively measured and compared with previous forming conditions.

## APPLICATION OF TECHNIQUES

The following example shows how the FLD and SA techniques eliminated an unacceptable fracture rate and allowed a gage reduction on a part that had been a problem for many years.

Fractures were encountered in the sidewall of a drawn corner formed from an unclipped blank (see Fig. 1-38, *a*). The FLD and SA results (see Fig. 1-39) both revealed "necking failure" severity. Equivalent high severity from both techniques has proven that a severe design was the cause of the problem. It was necessary to drastically change the part geometry and/or material flow to eliminate a design problem. The FLD and SA showed during a preliminary investigation that a substantial increase in material flow lowered the design difficulty to between "safe" and "marginal" when the blank corners were clipped before forming (see Fig. 1-38, *b*). The ability of these techniques to quantitatively measure the benefit of this change resulted in rapid implementation of the clipped corner design.

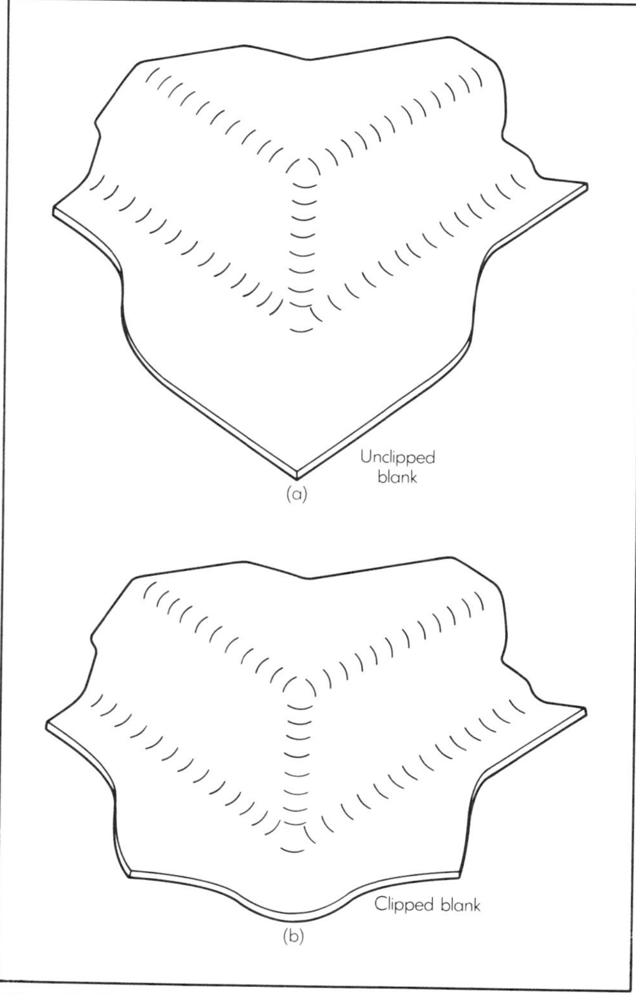


**Fig. 1-38 Unclipped blank and clipped blank (for improved formability).**

# BIBLIOGRAPHY

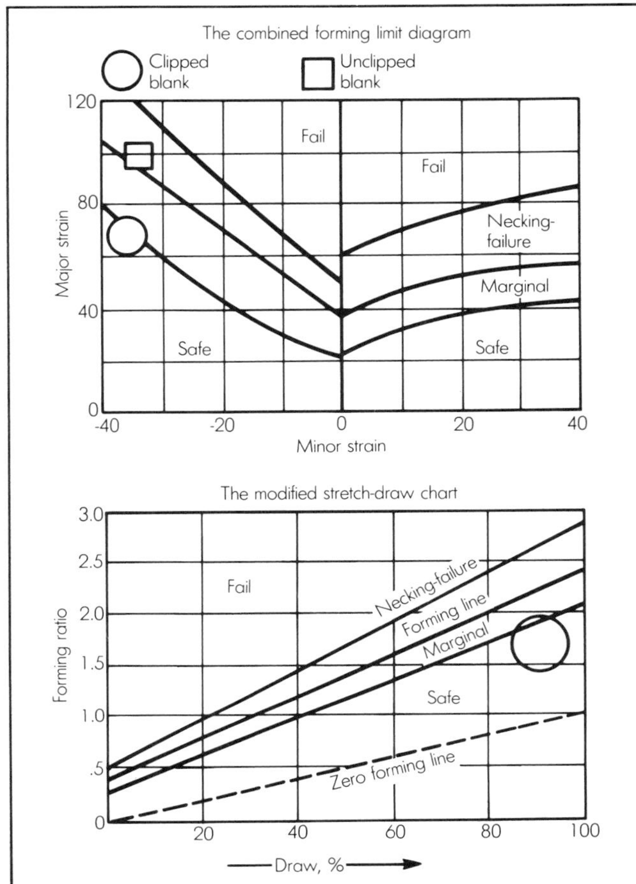


**Fig. 1-39 Graphic plots used for application of forming limit diagram and shape analysis to a shop problem.**

### References


1. R. M. Hobbs, *Source Book on Forming of Steel Sheet*, Metals Park, OH: American Society for Metals, 1976.
2. Stuart P. Keeler, "Understanding Sheet Metal Formability," *Machinery* (February-July 1968). Six articles.
3. National Steel Corporation, *Tensile Elongations—Uniform and Total*, Automotive Technical Bulletin GI-4G9.
4. American Iron and Steel Institute, "Modern Sheet Steels—What They Are and How They're Worked," *Manufacturing Engineering* (October 1977), p. 22.
5. National Steel Corporation, *The Importance of Strain Rate Hardening*, Automotive Technical Bulletin GI-3D9.
6. The Aluminum Association Inc., *Data on Aluminum Alloy Properties and Characteristics for Automotive Applications*, Publication T9, I979.
7. "Properties and Selection: Nonferrous Alloys and Pure Metals," *Metals Handbook*, 9th ed., Vol. 2, Metals Park, OH: American Society for Metals, 1979.
8. D. L. Dollar, *Formability of Wrought Zinc Alloys*, SME Technical Paper MF77-588, 1977.
9. Donald P. Koistinen and Neng-Ming Wang, *Mechanics of Sheet Forming*, NY: Plenum Press, 1978.
10. *Ibid.*
11. C. H. Hamilton, "Superplastic Forming of Aluminum," Paper presented at Toulouse International Show of Technologies and Energies of the Future, Toulouse, France, 1981.


### Bibliography


Adams, D. G.; Kasper, A. S.; Kurajian, G. M. *The Effects of Mechanical Properties on Elastic Recovery of Biaxially Stretched Panels*. SME Technical Paper MFR75, 1975.

Battelle Columbus Laboratories. *Superplastic Forming of Magnesium-Base Alloys*, Illus. No. 92, Current Awareness Bulletin, October 24, 1980.

Dinda, S.; James, K. F.; Keeler, S. P. *How to Use Circle Grid Analysis For Die Tryout*, Metals Park, OH: American Society for Metals, 1980.

Dreger, Donald R. "More Metals Go Superplastic." *Machine Design* (September 25, 1980), pp. 95-102.

Duncan, J. L. "Aspects of Draw Die Forming of Sheet Metal." Paper presented at Australian Conference on Manufacturing Engineering, 1977.

Duncan, J. L., and Altan, T. *New Directions in Sheet Metal Forming Research*. Annals of the CIRP, Vol. 29/1/1980, pp. 153-156.

Duncan, J. L., and Embury, J. D. *Fundamentals of Dual-Phase Steels*, Proceedings of symposium sponsored by the Metallurgical Society of AIME, 1981.

Duncan, J. L.; Shabel, B. S.; Filho, J. G. *A Tensile Strip Test for Evaluating Friction in Sheet Metal Forming*. SAE Technical Paper 780391, 1978.

Eary, Donald F. "New Tools for Measuring Sheet Metal Formability." *Metal Stamping* (September 1976), pp. 7-10.

Embury, J. D., and Duncan, J. L. "Formability Maps." *Annual Review Material Science*, Vol. 11 (1981), pp. 505-521.

Goodwin, Gorton M. *Formability Index*. SME Technical Paper MF71-165, 1971.

Granzow, Wayne G. *The Effect of Mechanical Properties on Formability of Low Carbon Steel Sheets*. SME Technical Paper EM75-371, 1975.

Hamilton, C. H. "Formability Analysis, Modeling, and Experimentation." *Forming of Superplastic Metals*. Proceedings of symposium sponsored by the Metallurgical Society of AIME, 1977.

Hecker, S. S., and Ghosh, A. K. "The Forming of Sheet Metal." *Scientific American* (November 1976), pp. 100-108.

Hobbs, Robert M. *The Use of Grid Strain Analysis for Die Development and Process Control in Australian Press Shops*. SME Technical Paper MFR77-15, 1977.

Irving, Robert R. "Why Automotive is Putting Its Faith in High Strength Steels." *Iron Age* (January 14, 1981), pp. 47-52.

Keeler, Stuart P. "Circular Grids Help Solve Stamping Problems." *The Tool and Manufacturing Engineer* (May 1969), pp. 14-17.

___________. "Forming Limit Criteria—Sheets." Paper presented at Sagamore Conference, ASM, 1974.

___________. "Sheet Metal Forming in the 80s." *Metal Progress*, (July 1980), pp. 25-29.

Lahoti, G. D., and Altan, T. *Input/Output Relationships in Metal Forming*. SME Technical Paper EM75-375, 1975.

McLaughlan, B. D. "Evaluating Formability—A Supplier's Procedure." Paper presented at SME conference: Sheet Metal Forming for the 80s, 1981.

Newby, J. R. "Formability Fundamentals." *Sheet Metal Industries* (November 1978), pp. 1185-1193.

Nine, Harmon D. "Testing Lubricants for Sheet Metal Forming." Paper presented to the AIME, 1982.

Post, Charles T. "Grain Structure Holds Key to Superplastic Aluminum." *Iron Age* (November 3, 1980), pp. 88-91.

Schneider, E. J. "High Strength Steel for the 80s." Paper presented at SME conference: Sheet Metal Forming for the 80s, 1981.

Stine, P. A. "Sheet Forming Analyses Significantly Increase Productivity." ASM-IDDRG Seminar, 1975.

Swenson, W. E.; Traficante, R. J.; Vadhavkar, A. V.; Fecek, M. G.; Shah, V. C. *The Effects of Material Properties on Aluminum Body Panel Design and Formability*. SME Technical Paper MF81-987, 1981.

Van Minh, H.; Sowerby, R.; Duncan, J. L. "Variability of Forming Limit Curves." *International Journal of Mechanical Science*, vol. 16 (1974), pp. 31-44.

Wang, Neng-Ming. *A Mathematical Model of Drawbead Forces in Sheet Metal Forming*. GM Research Technical Publication GMR-3644, 1981.

Wenner, Michael L. *On Work Hardening and Springback in Plane Strain Draw Forming*. GM Research Technical Publication GMR-3645, 1981.

CHAPTER

2

# Die and Mold Materials

# DIE AND MOLD MATERIALS

Essential requirements for any die or mold, with respect to optimum performance and economy, include the following:

1. Proper design, discussed in other chapters of this volume, including Chapter 6, "Die Design for Sheet Metal Forming."
2. Proper materials, discussed in this chapter.
3. Accurate manufacture. Machining and grinding practices are discussed in Volume I of this Handbook series.
4. Correct heat treatment, discussed in this chapter and Volume III.
5. Proper setup, use, and maintenance, discussed in other chapters of this volume.

**CHAPTER CONTENTS:**



## MATERIAL SELECTION

A wide variety of materials are used for dies and molds, and many dies and molds contain several materials. Most of the more common materials used are discussed in this chapter. (Diamonds for wire drawing dies are described in Chapter 13, "Wire Drawing, Extruding and Heading.") No single material is best for all forming applications because of the extensive range of conditions and requirements encountered in various operations. Selecting the proper material for a specific application can improve workpiece quality, increase productivity, and reduce costs.

Factors affecting the selection of a proper die or mold material for a specific application include:

1. The operations to be performed, including their severity, forces applied, temperatures encountered, and lubricants used.
2. The workpiece material, including its hardness, thickness, and condition, as well as the size of the workpiece.
3. The production rate and quantity, accuracy, and finish requirements.
4. The press or machine to be used, including its type and condition.
5. The design of the die or mold.
6. The accuracy and rigidity of the setup.
7. The cost per part produced, based upon the material, manufacturing, heat treatment, and maintenance costs, as well as the life of the die or mold.
8. The current availability of the die or mold material.
9. The properties of the material, including resistance to wear, heat, and deformation, and the ease with which it can be machined, heat treated, and ground.

Different applications require specific characteristics and properties for the material to be used, as discussed later in this chapter. For many materials, the chemical analyses and heat treatments can be adjusted to change the properties. The relative evaluation of properties for various materials, however, is of necessity qualitative, and the proper choice for a specific application cannot always be made with assurance. Consultation with the material supplier, die or mold producer, and heat treater is recommended, to advise them of the specifics of the application.

In many instances, the choice is not limited to a single material that can be used for an application. It is desirable, however, to select the one material that provides the most economical overall performance, based on the factors just discussed. A continuing evaluation of the materials used is important, employing accumulated performance data.

## CARBON AND LOW-ALLOY STEELS

Wrought plain-carbon and low-alloy steels, in the form of plates, rounds, and shapes, are often used in the fabrication of auxiliary die components, as well as some die parts. Applications for dies are mainly those in which strength and weldability, rather than wear resistance, are the primary requirements.

Some of the more common plain-carbon and low-alloy steels used for die components are listed in Table 2-1. Advantages of using these materials include economy, availability, easy machinability in their annealed conditions, and their capability of being heat treated to provide a high surface hardness and fairly tough core. The alloy steels can be heat treated to higher strength levels with optimum impact properties. These grades are often carried in stock in the heat-treated condition for the convenience of users, and resulfurized

***Contributors of sections of this chapter are:*** *Lewis F. Bogart, President, Tool Chemical Co., Inc.; Peter B. Hopper, Product Metallurgist, Crucible Specialty Metals Div., Colt Industries; Herbert S. Kalish, Vice President, Technical and International Director, Adamas Carbide Corp.; Russell M. Melvin, Die Design Supervisor, The Budd Co.; Raymond J. Severson, Vice President, Ampco Metals Div., Ampco-Pittsburgh Corp.;*

# CHAPTER 2

## CARBON AND LOW-ALLOY STEELS

**TABLE 2-1**
**Wrought Plain-Carbon and Low-Alloy Steels Commonly Used for Die Components**

| AISI/SAE No. | UNS No. | Composition, %* | | | | | |
|---|---|---|---|---|---|---|---|
| | | C | Mn | Ni | Cr | Mo | Si |
| 1010 | G10100 | 0.08/0.13 | 0.30/0.60 | | | | 0.10/0.20 |
| 1012 | G10120 | 0.10/0.15 | 0.30/0.60 | | | | 0.10/0.20 |
| 1015 | G10150 | 0.13/0.18 | 0.30/0.60 | | | | 0.10/0.20 |
| 1017 | G10170 | 0.15/0.20 | 0.30/0.60 | | | | 0.10/0.20 |
| 1020 | G10200 | 0.18/0.23 | 0.30/0.60 | | | | 0.10/0.20 |
| 1040 | G10400 | 0.37/0.44 | 0.60/0.90 | | | | 0.15/0.30 |
| 1060 | G10600 | 0.55/0.65 | 0.60/0.90 | | | | 0.15/0.30 |
| 1080 | G10800 | 0.75/0.88 | 0.60/0.90 | | | | 0.15/0.30 |
| 4140 | G41400 | 0.38/0.43 | 0.75/1.00 | | 0.80/1.10 | 0.15/0.25 | 0.15/0.30 |
| 4150 | G41500 | 0.48/0.53 | 0.75/1.00 | | 0.80/1.10 | 0.15/0.25 | 0.15/0.30 |
| 4340 | G43400 | 0.38/0.43 | 0.60/0.80 | 1.65/2.00 | 0.70/0.90 | 0.20/0.30 | 0.15/0.30 |
| 4615 | G46150 | 0.13/0.18 | 0.45/0.65 | 1.65/2.00 | | 0.20/0.30 | 0.15/0.30 |
| 6150** | G61500 | 0.48/0.53 | 0.70/0.90 | | 0.80/1.10 | | |
| 8620 | G86200 | 0.18/0.23 | 0.70/0.90 | 0.40/0.70 | 0.40/0.60 | 0.15/0.25 | 0.15/0.30 |
| 8640 | G86400 | 0.38/0.43 | 0.75/1.00 | 0.40/0.70 | 0.40/0.60 | 0.15/0.25 | 0.15/0.30 |

* Plain carbon steels: Maximum P 0.040%, maximum S 0.050%.
** Contains 0.15% minimum V.

grades are available for improved machinability in the hardened condition.

A limitation to the use of plain-carbon and low-alloy steels is their poor hot hardness. Their hardness decreases with increasing temperatures encountered in forming operations, and care is required when grinding components made from these materials. Care is also required in heat treatment to maintain dimensional stability and to prevent cracking. The plain-carbon steels generally require straightening after heat treatment, but alloy steels, requiring a less severe quench to achieve hardness, suffer less distortion.

For severe forming operations, steel die components are sometimes hard chrome plated to prevent galling; however, the plate may spall off, especially if the die components have small radii. Nitriding of alloy steels that contain chromium and molybdenum generally minimizes or prevents galling, but the nitrided surfaces can spall off in some severe applications, especially with die components having small radii and/or complex contours.

Forming dies subjected to high stresses are sometimes made from forged and heat-treated carbon and alloy steels. One large manufacturing concern has replaced a water-hardening tool steel with AISI/SAE 1060 steel, hardened to $R_C$ 58-60, for blanking and trimming steel to 0.090" (2.29 mm) thick. Advantages include lower cost, increased toughness, and the capability of performing more regrinds because of the deeper hardened case attained.

### HOT-ROLLED STEELS

Hot-rolled low-carbon steels are relatively inexpensive and are used extensively for die components for which machining and/or welding are required. These materials can be purchased in standard-size bars and plates from stock. Large plates may be cut to required sizes and contours with torches and templates, thus substantially reducing machining costs during die construction. These materials can be case hardened to provide limited hardness and toughness for short-run dies.

Hot-rolled steels hold their shape well when machined and welded. This is because of the minimal surface stresses caused by hot rolling at the steel mill. A limitation of hot-rolled steels is their poor wear resistance. When used for die components, these materials gall and cause scoring of the workpiece surfaces in applications subjecting the dies to wear.

Because of their low cost, good machinability and weldability, and minimum distortion during machining or welding, hot-rolled steels are often preferred for many die components. Applications include welded die bases and holders, support members, blankholder plates, die-shoe plates, mounting plates for trim steels, and parallels for use under or over dies. Other uses include fabricated strippers and stripper stops, punch fastening plates, fabricated slide drivers, guide blocks for pads, strippers and stripper stops, fabricated ejectors, nitrogen and oil reservoir manifolds, and shape gages for locating blanks or stampings in dies.

### COLD-ROLLED STEELS

Cold-rolled low-carbon steels have smoother surface finishes, closer dimensional tolerances, and higher strengths than hot-rolled low-carbon steels because of their cold-roll processing at the steel mill. They are generally used for die components for which hardening is not required, but wear surfaces are often cyanided.

*__Contributors, cont.__: J. F. Thompson, Technical Service Engineer, Universal-Cyclops Specialty Steel Div., Cyclops Corp.; David C. Vale, Product Manager, Specialty Products Group, Kennametal Inc.; William H. Wills, Tool Steel Product Metallurgist, AL Tech Specialty Steel Corp.; Zinc Institute Inc., Fraser Industrial Mall.*

*__Reviewers of sections of this chapter are__: A. M. Bayer, Technical Director, Teledyne Vasco; Lewis F. Bogart, President, Tool Chemical Co., Inc.; Arthur E. Chambers, President, Carbidex Corp.; Carl W. Dralle, Vice President, Market and Product Development, Ampco Metal, An Ampco-Pittsburgh Co.; Edward S. Hilty, President, Carbidie; Peter B. Hopper, Product Metallurgist, Specialty Metals Div., Crucible Inc., Colt Industries;*

The major advantage of cold-rolled steels is that they can often be used without machining, thus reducing costs. Such cost reductions frequently exceed the initial high price of the materials—about 50% more than hot-rolled steels. Cold-rolled steels, however, have internal stresses which are relieved by machining or welding. This can cause sufficient bowing, warping, or twisting to require additional costly operations, which often negates the use of cold-rolled steels for die components needing machining or welding.

Applications of cold-rolled steels for die components include keepers, stock guides, knockout bars and rods, and keys that withstand the thrust of trim and flange steels. Other uses for these materials include pad stop plates, air-line header blocks, and studs for spring locations and springs to return slides.

# CAST IRONS AND STEELS

Wrought irons are used only occasionally for dies, one example being bases for welded composite tool-steel cutting sections for trim dies. Castings of iron or steel, however, are used extensively for large dies to form, draw, or trim sheet metal. While such dies are sometimes made in one piece, they are often of composite construction. Composite dies have inserts made from carbon, alloy, or tool steel or other materials, or liners placed at sections most subject to wear or breakage.

In recent years, the advent of styrofoam patterns has decreased casting costs considerably. Patterns are now easy to cut and assemble and they are light in weight, thus reducing handling costs. They are incinerated by the cast molten metal, thus eliminating the need for pattern storage. These cost reductions have decreased the need for fabricated, hot-rolled steel weldments. Castings are normally less expensive, require less machining, and are structurally strong. Most cast irons and all cast steels can be hardened conventionally or by induction or flame hardening.

Composite dies and castings with inserts increase flexibility. The inserts can generally be changed to accommodate alterations in workpiece design or to produce different parts. Dies with inserts, however, are more costly; and because the inserts wear less than the softer casting, the uneven joint lines between inserts and castings can cause marking of the workpieces, thus necessitating reworking of the dies.

A possible limitation to the use of castings is the time required between starting to make the patterns and receiving castings from the foundry. Production scheduling may not allow time for this delay; and weldments are often substituted for castings.

## CAST IRONS FOR DIES

Irons are comparatively low in cost and are easily cast and machined. For uniform properties and improved machinability, they should be free of excessively large flake graphite, large primary carbides, and excessive phosphates. Another advantage of irons is their ability to resist galling. These materials, however, have relatively poor weldability. Irons used for casting dies include unalloyed, alloyed, and ductile irons (see Table 2-2).

### Unalloyed Cast Irons

Advantages of unalloyed cast irons, such as the one listed in Table 2-2, include their low cost (the least expensive of all irons), their ready availability, their capability of being flame hardened with a water quench, and their very good machinability. A major limitation is that their structural strengths are only fair. As a result, they are generally used on simple applications. The weldability of unalloyed cast irons is very poor, making any necessary repairs difficult. Most castings are also fairly porous, which can create problems.

Castings of unalloyed irons are used for many die applications in which no actual operations are performed on the irons themselves. These applications include upper and lower die shoes, upper die holding pads, slides, slide adapters, and slide drivers (with tool steel inserts).

### Alloyed Cast Irons

Alloyed cast irons, such as the one listed in Table 2-2, are used extensively for heavy-duty dies to form, flange, or restrike sheet metal on the irons themselves. Castings are also used to hold tool steel inserts for trimming, forming, or combined piercing and forming operations. Wear resistance of these materials is excellent, and metals can be moved over their surfaces with a minimum of scratching or galling. Machinability is good, flame hardening is common, and the castings can be repaired by welding with proper care.

A major limitation of alloyed cast irons, like unalloyed cast irons, is their lack of structural strength. The brittle nature of these materials requires careful consideration when designing die sections that must have high strength. For some applications, stronger materials, such as ductile irons or cast steels (discussed later in this chapter), or Meehanite, must be used. High-strength, wear-resistant iron castings produced by the Meehanite licensed process have only limited use for dies.

Applications of alloyed cast irons include form punches, upper and lower blankholders for double-action draw dies, upper and lower stretch forming dies, upper pads for use where metal movement exists or forming is done, and master and holding surfaces of redraw dies. Other applications include the master surfaces of flanging dies and collapsible slides for forming dies.

### Ductile Cast Irons

Ductile irons, sometimes called nodular irons, have most of the desirable properties of unalloyed and alloyed cast irons,

*__Reviewers, cont.__: Herbert S. Kalish, Vice President, Technical and International Director, Adamas Carbide Corp.; Russell M. Melvin, Die Design Supervisor, Stamping & Frame Products Group, The Budd Co.; Mike Molitor, REN Plastics; James Moore, Wayne Foundry & Stamping Co.; J. F. Thompson, Technical Service Engineer, Universal-Cyclops Specialty Steel Div., Cyclops Corp.; David C. Vale, Product Manager, Specialty Products Group, Kennametal Inc.; Harry R. Warren, Executive Assistant to the Vice President and General Manager, Central Hardboard Div., Masonite Corp.; William H. Wills, Tool Steel Product Metallurgist, AL Tech Specialty Steel Corp.; Ed Wojtowicz, Manager-Engineering & Tooling, Alloy Technology International, Inc.; Zinc Institute Inc., Fraser Industrial Mall.*

**TABLE 2-2**
**Compositions and Properties of Cast Irons Commonly Used for Dies**

| | Type of Cast Iron | | |
|---|---|---|---|
| | Unalloyed Cast Iron | Alloyed Cast Iron | Ductile Cast Iron* |
| Composition, % | | | |
| C | 3.0-3.6 | 3.0-3.6 | 3.0-3.6 |
| Combined C | 0.60 min | 0.60 min | |
| Mn | 0.50-1.0 | 0.50-1.0 | 0.20-0.60 |
| Mo | | 0.35-0.50 | |
| Cr | | 0.35-0.50 | |
| Ni | | | 0-1.0 |
| P | 0.20 max, 0.15 desired | 0.20 max, 0.15 desired | 0.10 max |
| S | 0.15 max | 0.15 max | |
| Si | 2.0** | 1.25-2.25 | 2.0-3.0 |
| Brinell hardness: | | | |
| Working areas | 174-223 | 183-241 | 150-225 |
| All other areas requiring machining | 223 max | 241 max | 225 max |
| Unalloyed | | | 150-200 |
| Alloyed | | | 175-225 |
| After flame hardening | 400 (water quench) | 450 (air cool) | Unalloyed: poor<br>Alloyed: to 450 |
| Comparative characteristics: | | | |
| Cost | Low | About 15% more than unalloyed cast iron | About 30% more than unalloyed cast iron |
| Machinability | Very good | Good | Unalloyed: very good<br>Alloyed: good |
| Wear resistance | Very good | Best | Unalloyed: fairly good<br>Alloyed: good |
| Toughness | Fair | Fair | Unalloyed: excellent<br>Alloyed: very good |
| Strength | Fair | Fair | Unalloyed: very good to 80,000 psi (552 MPa)<br>Alloyed: excellent, to 90,000 psi (621 MPa) |
| Weldability | Very poor | Fair | Poor |

* The compositions of ductile cast irons can be modified by the addition of a higher percentage of manganese, or the addition of chromium, molybdenum, or magnesium, to provide the desired microstructure and hardness.

** The percentage of silicon and other elements in unalloyed cast irons is sometimes adjusted to obtain the desired microstructure and hardness.

with the added features of higher structural strength and toughness levels approaching those of steel because of their spheroidal free graphite. These materials are available in two grades: unalloyed and alloyed.

Unalloyed ductile irons are used where added strength—to 80,000 psi (552 MPa)—is required. Applications include die shoes having thin sections, slides, and slide adapters.

Alloyed ductile irons are used where even higher strength—to 90,000 psi (621 MPa)—and more wear resistance are needed. Applications include punches, thin-section die pads, cams for dies, blankholder rings, and lower die posts for collapsible cam dies. Flame hardened, alloyed ductile iron dies have replaced more expensive cast iron dies with steel inserts.

A limitation of the use of ductile iron castings is that they must be stress relieved, which increases their cost. Castings of these materials also cost about 30% more than unalloyed iron castings, and weldability is poor. Steel castings should be considered for high strength requirements if repair welds are anticipated.

## STEEL CASTINGS FOR DIES

Steel castings used for dies include medium-carbon, high-carbon, and alloy steels. Some of the more commonly used steels are listed in Table 2-3.

### Medium-Carbon Steels

Steel castings having a medium carbon content, such as the medium-carbon mild steel casting in Table 2-3, are used for die

**TABLE 2-3**
**Composition and Properties of Steel Castings Commonly Used for Dies**

| | Type of Steel Castings | | | |
|---|---|---|---|---|
| | Medium-Carbon Mild Steel | High-Carbon Mild Steel | Alloy Steel | High-Carbon, High-Chromium Steel |
| Composition, % | | | | |
| C | 0.25-0.40 | 0.65-0.80 | 0.40-0.60 | 1.5-1.8 |
| Mn | 0.50-0.85 | 0.50-0.80 | 0.90-1.20 | 0.5-0.8 |
| Cr | | | 0.90-1.25 | 11.5-14.0 |
| Mo | | | 0.35-0.50 | 0.5-1.0 |
| V | | | Optional | 0.2-1.0 |
| Cu | | | Optional | |
| Co | | | | Optional |
| Ni | | | Optional | Optional |
| P | 0.05 max | 0.05 max | 0.045 max | 0.025 max |
| S | 0.06 max | 0.06 max | 0.05 max | 0.025 max |
| Si | | | | 0.4-0.6 |
| Brinell hardness before machining | 120-180 | 185-250 | 185-250 | 269 max |
| Heat treatment | Full anneal or normalize and temper, not less than 900 °F (482°C), to required hardness. | Full anneal or normalize and temper to required hardness. Flame harden to $R_C$58-60. | Flame harden and air cool to $R_C$50-56. | $R_C$59-61 after machining or die tryout. |
| Comparative characteristics: | | | | |
| Cost | Lowest, but twice that of unalloyed cast iron. | About 225% of unalloyed cast iron. | About 225% of unalloyed cast iron. | About 650% of unalloyed cast iron. |
| Machinability | Best | Good | Good | Poor |
| Wear resistance | Fair | Good | Good | Excellent |
| Toughness | Very good | Fair | Very good | Poor |
| Flame hardening properties | Poor | Very good | Excellent | Very poor |
| Strength | Good | Good | Very good | Fair |

components that require higher structural strengths and toughness than can be obtained with cast irons. They have the lowest cost and best machinability of the various steel castings used for dies, but their cost is about twice that of unalloyed cast irons. Flame hardening properties of medium-carbon steels are poor, but these materials can be welded readily, similar to hot-rolled steels. Their uses include general purpose applications, such as die shoes, pads, keepers, and other components in which wear is at a minimum and no need exists for flame hardening.

Limitations of these materials are that they cannot be used when forming is done on the castings themselves, and the castings must be annealed or normalized and tempered to attain the required hardness. Availability is limited to foundries in which steel is poured, and in these foundries, styrofoam cannot be used as a disappearing pattern; the styrofoam pattern must be removed from the sand before the molten steel is poured.

### High-Carbon Steels

Castings made from high-carbon steels are used for punches, inserts, and other die components in which savings in material and machining costs are realized in comparison to the use of tool steels. They are usually flame hardened in localized areas, but are sometimes hardened by annealing or normalizing and tempering. Such castings are not recommended for applications in which there is a tendency toward galling, seizing, or metal pickup, and they should not be used for delicate dies which might break or distort during heat treatment.

### Alloy Steel Castings

Castings made from alloy steels, such as the one in Table 2-3, have good machinability and wear resistance, very good toughness, high strength, and excellent flame hardening properties. These characteristics, together with good weldability for repairs, makes them versatile die materials.

Applications for alloy steel castings include punches, die inserts, collapsible slides, and 45° clinching dies requiring the toughness of steels which can be flame hardened in critical areas. Flame hardening only the critical working areas provides tougher, unhardened material in the more fragile, thin sections of the die components. These materials can be fully flame hardened with air cooling.

Such castings are also applied for low and medium production requirements in forming and cutting operations, often with savings in material and machining costs. Another application is the flanging of thin, long surfaces where the joint surfaces of adjacent tool steel inserts can cause marks on the workpieces. By making long inserts of flame hardened, alloy steel castings, fewer joint surfaces exist and possible damage to the workpieces is minimized.

### High-Alloy Steel Castings

High-alloy steel castings, such as the high-carbon, high-chromium type in Table 2-3, are also used for die components. Excellent wear resistance is the primary advantage of these materials, resulting in little or no maintenance under high-production conditions.

Uses for high-alloy steel castings include inserts for blanking, trimming, forming, and drawing dies in high-production applications in which galling or wear are problems. A possible limitation is high initial cost of the materials. The need for heat treatment before and after machining and the need for rework after hardening to remove scale and any distortion add to the cost.

# STAINLESS AND MARAGING STEELS

Martensitic stainless steels and maraging steels are being used for some dies and molds, especially those of intricate design and requiring long life. While these materials have a high initial cost, the cost per part formed or molded in long production runs is often lower than with dies or molds made from other materials.

## STAINLESS STEELS

Stainless steels of martensitic, hardenable metallurgical structure are used for dies and molds. These materials have a ferritic structure in the annealed conditions; but when they are cooled quickly from above the critical temperature range, which is about 1600° F (870° C), they develop a martensitic structure.

The martensitic stainless steels that are most commonly used for dies and molds, in order of increasing chromium contents, strengths, and abrasion resistance, are AISI Types 410 (UNS S41000), 410 (UNS S42000), and 440C (UNS S44004). Type 410 stainless steel, which contains 11.50-13.50% chromium, can be hardened to about $R_C41$, with a tensile strength of 195 ksi (1344 MPa). Type 440C, which contains 16.00-18.00% chromium and a maximum of 0.75% molybdenum, can be hardened to about $R_C57$, with a tensile strength of 285 ksi (1965 MPa).

## MARAGING STEELS

Maraging steels, generally containing 18% nickel, are used for aluminum die-casting dies and core pins, intricate plastic molds, hot-forging and extrusion dies, punches, and blanking and cold-forming dies. Applications to plastic molds are most common for compression molds requiring high pressures. A major advantage of maraging steels, especially for intricate dies and molds with close tolerance requirements, is the simple precipitation-hardening (aging) treatment. Steels supplied in the solution-annealed condition are relatively soft ($R_C$ 30-35) and readily machinable. Depending upon the specific type of steel, hardnesses to $R_C60$ can be produced after machining.

Full hardening of maraging steels is attained by means of a simple aging treatment, generally about three hours at 900° F (482° C) and requiring no protective atmosphere. Since quenching is not required, cracking or distortion from thermal stresses is eliminated. Shrinkage during heat treatment is uniform and predictable. All these factors reduce the cost of manufacturing dies and molds. The steels can be nitrided to increase both surface hardness and wear resistance.

The original maraging steels contain 7-12% cobalt as their strengthening agent. More recently, maraging steels containing no cobalt have been introduced, with titanium as the primary strengthening agent. Mechanical properties and processing of both types of maraging steels are essentially the same.

# TOOL STEELS

Tool steels are special grades of carbon, alloy, or high-speed steels capable of being hardened and tempered, and are the most widely used materials for dies and molds. They are usually melted in electric furnaces and produced under high-quality, tool steel practice to meet special requirements. Tool steels are produced in the form of hot and cold-finished bars, special shapes, forgings, hollow bar, hot extrusions, wire, drill rod, plate, sheets, strip, tool bits, powdered metal products, and castings. They are made in small quantities compared to the high-volume production of carbon and alloy steels.

Tool steels are used for a wide variety of applications, including those in many nontooling areas, in which strength, toughness, resistance to wear, and other properties are selected for optimum performance. A comprehensive discussion of high-speed steels used for cutting tools is presented in Volume I, *Machining*, of this Handbook series. This section is confined to tool steels used in the construction of dies and molds.

## CLASSIFICATION OF TOOL STEELS

A method of identification and type classification of tool steels has been developed by the American Iron and Steel Institute (AISI) to follow the most commonly used and generally accepted terminology. The present commonly used tool steels have been grouped into eight major classifications, with the tool steels under each classification assigned a prefix letter, as indicated in Table 2-4. The chemical compositions of tool steels most commonly used for metal forming dies and molds are presented in Table 2-5.

## ALLOYING ELEMENTS

The type of alloying elements added to tool steels and the amount added affect the properties of the various tool steels. Some elements are added to enhance specific properties for certain applications.

**TABLE 2-4**
**Tool Steel Groups and Prefix Letters**

| Tool Steel Headings | Identifying Prefix |
|---|---|
| Standard high-speed tool steels: | |
| Molybdenum types (except M50-M59) | M |
| Tungsten types | T |
| Intermediate high-speed tool steels: | |
| Molybdenum types | M50-M59 |
| Hot-work tool steels: | |
| Chromium types | H1-H19 |
| Tungsten types | H20-H39 |
| Molybdenum types | H40-H59 |
| Cold-work tool steels: | |
| High-carbon, high-chromium types | D |
| Medium-alloy, air-hardening types | A |
| Oil-hardening types | O |
| Shock-resisting tool steels | S |
| Mold steels | P |
| Special-purpose tool steels, low-alloy types | L |
| Water-hardening tool steels | W |

## Carbon Content

The most important alloying element affecting the properties of tool steels is carbon. It is carbon which enables a tool steel to harden through austenitic transformation. This transformation occurs by heating the steel above its critical temperature, followed by martensite formation upon cooling with sufficient speed through the martensite temperature range to about 150° F (66° C). In general, increased carbon contents provide higher hardnesses after heat treatment and improved wear resistance in service, accompanied by some sacrifice in toughness.

## Manganese Additions

The addition of manganese increases the hardenability of tool steels. Even small amounts have significant effects on depth of hardening in carbon tool steels. The addition of 2.00% manganese in Type A6 tool steel enables this cold-work die material to be air hardened strongly at a relatively low austenitizing temperature.

## The Use of Silicon

Silicon improves the toughness of low-alloy tool steels of the shock resisting group. When added to hot-work tool steels, silicon raises the critical points and reduces scaling tendencies. Silicon also increases hardenability and resistance to tempering. This element is added to the graphitic free-machining steels to promote the formation of free carbon.

**TABLE 2-5**
**Chemical Compositions of Tool Steels Commonly Used for Dies and Molds**

| AISI/SAE Type | UNS No. | Chemical Content, % | | | | | | | | |
|---|---|---|---|---|---|---|---|---|---|---|
| | | C | Mn | Si | W | Mo | Cr | V | Co | Ni |
| Medium-alloy, air-hardening, cold-work tool steels: | | | | | | | | | | |
| A2 | T30102 | 1.00 | | | | 1.00 | 5.00 | | | |
| A6 | T30106 | 0.70 | 2.00 | | | 1.25 | 1.00 | | | |
| A8 | T30108 | 0.55 | | | 1.25 | 1.25 | 5.00 | | | |
| A11 | | 2.45 | 0.50 | 0.90 | | 1.30 | 5.25 | 9.75 | | |
| High-carbon, high-chromium, cold-work tool steels: | | | | | | | | | | |
| D2 | T30402 | 1.50 | | | | 1.00 | 12.00 | 1.00 | | |
| D3 | T30403 | 2.25 | | | | | 12.00 | | | |
| D4 | T30404 | 2.25 | | | | 1.00 | 12.00 | | | |
| D5 | T30405 | 1.50 | | | | 1.00 | 12.00 | 3.00 | | |
| D7 | T30407 | 2.35 | | | | 1.00 | 12.00 | 4.00 | | |
| Chromium-type, hot-work tool steels: | | | | | | | | | | |
| H11 | T20811 | 0.35 | | | | 1.50 | 5.00 | 0.40 | | |
| H12 | T20812 | 0.35 | | | 1.50 | 1.50 | 5.00 | 0.40 | | |
| H13 | T20813 | 0.35 | | | | 1.50 | 5.00 | 1.00 | | |
| H19 | T20819 | 0.40 | | | 4.25 | | 4.25 | 2.00 | 4.25 | |

(*continued*)

**TABLE 2-5—*Continued***

| AISI/SAE Type | UNS No. | Chemical Content, % | | | | | | | | |
|---|---|---|---|---|---|---|---|---|---|---|
| | | C | Mn | Si | W | Mo | Cr | V | Co | Ni |
| Tungsten-type, hot-work tool steel: | | | | | | | | | | |
| H21 | T20821 | 0.35 | | | 9.00 | | 3.50 | | | |
| Low-alloy, oil-hardening tool steels: | | | | | | | | | | |
| 01 | T31501 | 0.90 | 1.00 | | 0.50 | | 0.50 | | | |
| 06 | T31506 | 1.45 | 0.80 | 1.00 | | 0.25 | | | | |
| Shock-resisting tool steels: | | | | | | | | | | |
| S1 | T41901 | 0.50 | | | 2.50 | | 1.50 | | | |
| S5 | T41905 | 0.55 | 0.80 | 2.00 | | 0.40 | | | | |
| S7 | T41907 | 0.50 | | | | 1.40 | 3.25 | | | |
| Water-hardening tool steels: | | | | | | | | | | |
| W1 | T72301 | 0.60-1.40 | | | | | | | | |
| W2 | T72302 | 0.60-1.40 | | | | | | 0.25 | | |
| Special-purpose tool steel: | | | | | | | | | | |
| L6 | T61206 | 0.70 | | | | 0.25* | 0.75 | | | 1.50 |
| Tungsten-type, high-speed tool steels: | | | | | | | | | | |
| T1 | T12001 | 0.75 | | | 18.00 | | 4.00 | 1.00 | | |
| T15 | T12015 | 1.50 | | | 12.00 | | 4.00 | 5.00 | 5.00 | |
| Molybdenum-type, high-speed tool steels: | | | | | | | | | | |
| M2 | T11302 | 0.85; 1.00 | | | 6.00 | 5.00 | 4.00 | 2.00 | | |
| M4 | T11304 | 1.30 | | | 5.50 | 4.50 | 4.00 | 4.00 | | |
| M42 | T11342 | 1.10 | | 0.30; 0.55 | 1.50 | 9.50 | 3.75 | 1.15 | 8.00 | |
| Mold steel: | | | | | | | | | | |
| P20 | T51620 | 0.35 | | | | 0.40 | 1.70 | | | |

* Optional

## Tungsten and Molybdenum

Both tungsten and molybdenum are crucial alloying elements for hot-work and high-speed steels. This is because they provide hot hardness (the ability to maintain hardness at elevated temperatures), increased resistance to tempering, and wear-resistant carbides that are harder than chromium carbides. Molybdenum has about double the potency of tungsten in its effect on hot hardness. Relatively small amounts of molybdenum are frequently added to low-alloy tool steels for improved hardenability.

## Chromium Content

Chromium, a moderately strong carbide former, contributes to wear resistance in the cold-work die steels. This is especially true for the high-carbon, high-chromium types, the D group. Chromium also promotes resistance to tempering and hot hardness in hot-work and high-speed tool steels. Additions of chromium also improve the hardenability of tool steels.

### Vanadium Additions

Vanadium, a very strong carbide former, is added to hot-work and high-speed tool steels for increased wear resistance. This alloying element also improves hot hardness and tempering resistance, particularly in high-speed steels, and promotes grain refinement.

### The Use of Cobalt

Cobalt is added to improve hot hardness and resistance to tempering in both high-speed and hot-work tool steels. This alloying element remains entirely in solid solution in the steels and does not form carbides.

### Functions of Nickel

Like cobalt, nickel goes into solid solution and does not form carbides. Improved toughness and lower critical points normally result from the additions of nickel. In general, high nickel contents (above about 2%) are not desirable in tool steels because of the element's strong tendency to stabilize the austenite, thus increasing difficulty in annealing.

## PRODUCTION VARIABLES

There are many variables in the production of tool steels that influence the properties of the materials. These variables include melting practice, hot reduction, annealing, straightening, and the use of powder metallurgy (PM) processes.

### Melting Practice

Optimum performance from forming dies and molds depends upon superior cleanliness, good chemistry control, freedom from harmful gases (particularly oxygen and hydrogen), and minimum porosity and segregation in the tooling material used. This is particularly true when unblemished, highly polished surfaces are required for applications such as forming rolls and plastic molds, or when high operational stresses are involved, particularly in the transverse direction of larger die or mold sections.

The advent of argon-oxygen decarburization (AOD) and vacuum-arc degassing (VAD) melting has resulted in improved cleanliness and reduced gas content, as well as closer composition control, in the production of tool steels. Special melting techniques, such as consumable-electrode, vacuum-arc remelting (VAR) and electroslag remelting (ESR), are used where further improvement in cleanliness and quality is required. These methods also ensure greater internal soundness (minimum porosity and center segregation).

The VAR and ESR practices are particularly applicable to the production of larger die and mold sections, in which the retention of internal quality becomes more difficult with conventional air melting practice. Internal quality refinement attained in larger bars or plates results in improved toughness in the transverse direction. This is highly beneficial when critically stressed working surfaces must be close to the center areas of the tooling.

### Hot Reduction

Hot working in the production of tool steels is usually accomplished by pressing, hammering, or rolling or by a combination of these operations. Normally, either pressing or hammering is used for the initial ingot breakdown of the higher alloyed tool steels, such as the high-speed and high-carbon, high-chromium types. These processes more effectively break up segregated structures through their kneading action.

Sufficient hot reduction (from original ingot to finished shape) is essential to provide normal grain size, minimize internal porosity, and effectively refine carbide size and distribution. This is especially critical in higher alloyed tool steels. Internal quality is necessary to maintain adequate strength, toughness, and working surface integrity in dies and molds. In general, optimum internal quality and grain refinement in tool steels is accomplished with as few reheatings as practical during hot reduction to finished size.

### Annealing

Proper annealing of tool steels is essential to provide optimum machinability and/or formability during production of the dies or molds. Normally, low annealed hardnesses and uniformly spheroidized microstructures are desirable for best machinability, formability, and size stability during heat treatment (discussed later in this chapter).

### Straightening

Care must be exercised in the final straightening of tool steel bars and plates to avoid excessive cold-working stresses that could lead to abnormal distortion during subsequent heat treatment. Stress relieving, within the temperature range of 1000-1300° F (538-704° C), should be employed on any bar or plate suspected of having been overly cold worked during straightening.

### Powder Metallurgy Processing

Some tool steels are produced by powder metallurgy (PM) processes. These processes are discussed in detail in Chapter 17, "Powder Metallurgy." The use of PM processing is generally applied to highly alloyed grades, for which the benefits imparted by the process may be needed the most. The AISI Type A11 is an air-hardening, cold-work tool steel produced using PM techniques. This grade would be almost impossible to manufacture using normal methods.

The production of PM tool steels consists essentially of atomizing prealloyed molten steel into powdered particles. The powder is consolidated into compacts or preforms by hot isostatic compaction, pressing, forging, or other means, followed by a sintering operation. These compacts or preforms may then be subsequently hot worked to the desired finish form or used in the preform condition without further hot working.

Tool steel products made by PM are characterized by minimum segregation and fine-grain, uniform microstructures usually containing small carbide particles. Major advantages of these products, discussed comprehensively in Volume I, *Machining*, of this Handbook series, include better size stability during heat treatment and improved grindability, which can reduce the costs of producing dies and molds.

## SELECTING TOOL STEELS

Selecting the proper tool steel for a specific application requires careful consideration of many factors. One approach is to use a material that has proved successful in the past for a certain die or mold and operation. It is essential, however, to have an understanding of the reasoning behind using different tool steels for various applications, thus permitting some judgment in the selection process.

## Desirable Properties

Many different properties are desirable for tool steels used to make dies and molds for various operations. These properties can be separated into the following two groups:

1. Primary or surface properties. These are inherent performance characteristics which pertain directly to the properties the steel possesses to perform the required operation.
2. Secondary or fabricating properties. These are material characteristics which affect the manufacture of the die or mold.

**Primary properties.** These include wear resistance, toughness, and heat resistance. An additional primary property required for hot-work tool steel applications is resistance to heat checking or thermal fatigue cracking. Heat checking is characterized by a network of fine cracks that appear on the working surfaces of tooling as a result of stresses associated with alternate rapid heating and cooling during service.

Although hardness is a property developed in heat treatment, rather than an inherent property, it is still very important. Without adequate hardness, the steel would not be able to withstand the loads imposed upon the die or mold. There is a direct relationship between resistance to deformation and hardness of the steel, as illustrated in Fig. 2-1. Variations in the steel grade and heat-treated condition, however, cause variations in this relationship, so design values should not be scaled from this graph.

**Secondary properties.** These include the many characteristics that influence the ability to make a die or mold, as well as the cost of manufacturing. Some of these are machinability, grindability, polishability, hardenability, and distortion and safety in heat treatment. Availability and cost of the tool steels are also important considerations.

Some desirable primary and secondary properties for tool steels to be used in different operations are presented in Table 2-6. This table is intended only as a preliminary guide in tool steel selection and is too general to be applied universally.

## Property Compromises

In examining the properties of tool steels it becomes apparent that some compromising is required. As the alloy content of a tool steel is changed to provide greater wear and heat resistance, the toughness usually decreases. If the alloy content is adjusted to provide increased toughness, the wear and heat resistance may decrease. In addition, the secondary properties change, possibly resulting in higher alloy steels that may be more difficult to machine and grind. The challenge of selecting tool steels is to get an optimum blend of both primary and secondary properties, matching these properties to the requirements of the job.

If a punch is being manufactured to have an intended life of only 100 holes, it would be wasteful to make it from a tool steel having properties to produce 10,000 holes. The added alloy in such a steel would cause more difficulty than necessary to manufacture the punch.

To properly match the various tool steels to the operations to be performed, it is important to know how one tool steel compares to others with respect to primary and secondary properties. This information is presented in Table 2-7.

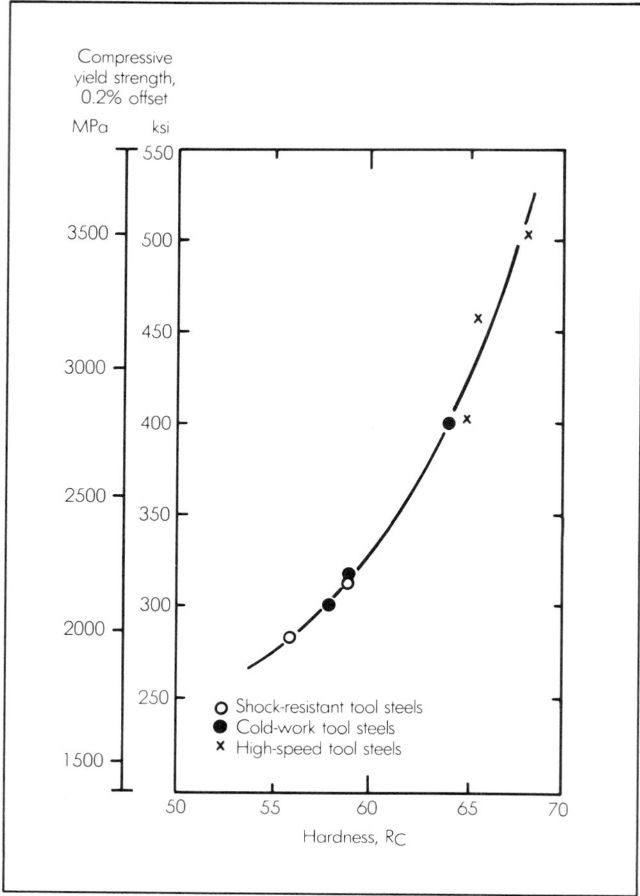


**Fig. 2-1 Relationship between resistance to deformation (compressive strength) and hardness of tool steels.**

## Recommended Applications

A list of metalforming and cutting operations for dies, molds, and die components, and the tool steel grades generally recommended for each application, are presented in Table 2-8. The tool steel grades recommended are intended as starting points only. Compromises often have to be made with respect to both grade selection and hardness, depending upon careful consideration of anticipated problems for the specific application. Close cooperation with the tool steel supplier, the builder of the die or mold, and the heat treater is also essential.

## HEAT TREATMENT OF TOOL STEELS

Development of the optimum properties in any tool steel is dependent on adherence to correct heat-treating procedures. Proper heat-treating methods take into account metallurgical considerations as well as practical factors affecting such aspects as distortion and tool finish.

The important metallurgical factors in the heat-treating procedure include preheating, heating to the proper hardening temperature (also termed austenitizing temperature), adequate holding time, proper quenching, and tempering. Details of these aspects are summarized by tool steel grade in Table 2-9.

**TABLE 2-6**
**Desirable Properties of Tool Steels for Various Operations**

| Operation | Desirable Properties | |
|---|---|---|
| | Primary | Secondary |
| Shearing and blanking: | | |
| Cold: | | |
| light duty | Wear resistance | Low distortion |
| heavy duty | Wear resistance and toughness | Safety in heat treating |
| Hot: | | |
| light duty | Wear and heat resistance | Safety in heat treating |
| heavy duty | Heat resistance and toughness; resistance to heat checking | Safety in heat treating |
| Forming (including press operations, forging, plastic molding, and die casting): | | |
| Cold | Wear resistance and toughness | Machinability and polishability |
| Hot | Heat resistance and toughness; resistance to heat checking | Machinability |
| Drawing | Wear resistance | Polishability and low distortion |
| Extruding and heading: | | |
| Cold | Wear resistance | Low distortion |
| Hot | Heat resistance and toughness; resistance to heat checking | Low distortion |
| Rolling and roll forming: | | |
| Cold | Wear resistance | Polishability |
| Hot | Heat resistance and toughness; resistance to heat checking | |

## Preheating the Steels

Preheating prior to hardening is recommended for most tool steels. The primary purpose of preheating is to reduce thermal shock when the tool enters the high heat employed in hardening and to reduce the soaking time required at the high-heat temperature. Reduced thermal shock minimizes cracking propensity and distortion effects. Lowered soaking times at high heat, resulting from preheating, reduce decarburization and scaling in air.

## Hardening Temperatures

Choice of the proper hardening temperature depends primarily upon the service requirements of the die or mold. The most desirable balance of strength and toughness is a prerequisite for optimum tool life. Hardening temperatures at the high ends of the recommended ranges favor development of maximum hardness with reduced toughness. Hardening temperatures at the lower ends of the ranges favor better toughness with slightly lowered attainable hardness.

The extremities of the recommended hardening ranges are fixed by two metallurgical considerations. The minimum hardening temperature must exceed the critical temperatures of the individual tool steel type in order to transform the internal structure. This transformation brings about the condition resulting in hardening during subsequent cooling. The maximum recommended hardening temperature is established as the temperature above which adverse grain growth and incipient melting occur.

The hardening temperature ranges shown in Table 2-9 represent the safe austenitizing ranges for tool steels of standard composition. Choice of the specific hardening temperature within the recommended range is best established on the basis of actual tool life results. When no prior tool life data is available, a hardening temperature is recommended at the midpoint of the range. Proper soaking times at the hardening temperature are fixed by the tool steel type, the size of the die or mold, and the heating medium. Tool steels hardened below 2000° F (1093° C) require 20-30 minutes soaking time per inch (0.8-1.2 min/mm) of thickness, whereas those tool steels hardened above 2000° F require but 2-5 minutes per inch (0.1-0.2 min/mm) soak time.

## Cooling the Steels

The method of cooling following hardening is an important part of the heat-treating process. Tool steels with low alloy content require quenching in oil or brine, whereas more highly alloyed tool steels can be cooled in air. The recommended quenching method (Table 2-9) produces full hardness for the grades shown. When a choice of quenching method is indicated, it is better to use the method having a slower cooling rate for reasons of reduced distortion and lower risk of cracking. The tool must be cooled to less than 150° F (66° C) before tempering, but preferably not below room temperature.

## Tempering Treatment

Tempering is a necessary part of the heat-treating process. Tempering is performed to relieve the locked-in stresses resulting from the volumetric changes of hardening. Without tempering, the die or mold would be brittle and would fail prematurely in service. Tempering relieves the stresses of hardening and imparts added toughness and shock resistance to the tool.

**TABLE 2-7**
**Comparative Properties of Tool Steels Commonly Used for Dies and Molds**

| AISI/SAE Type | Typical Hardness, $R_C$ | Primary Properties, relative deg. | Secondary Properties* | | | | | | |
|---|---|---|---|---|---|---|---|---|---|
| | | | Machin-ability | Grind-ability | Polish-ability | Depth of Hardening | Distortion | Avail-ability | Initial Cost |
| A2 | 61 | Wear resistance<br>Hot hardness<br>Toughness | 5 | 7 | 8 | 9 | 10 | 10 | 8 |
| A6 | | Wear resistance<br>Hot hardness<br>Toughness | | | | | | | |
| A8 | 58 | Wear resistance<br>Hot hardness<br>Toughness | 6 | 8 | 8 | 9 | 10 | 3 | 8 |
| A11 | 61 | Wear resistance<br>Hot hardness<br>Toughness | 4 | 3.5 | 7 | 10 | 10 | 5 | 3 |
| D2 | 61 | Wear resistance<br>Hot hardness<br>Toughness | 3.5 | 3.5 | 6 | 10 | 10 | 10 | 8 |
| D4 | 61 | Wear resistance<br>Hot hardness<br>Toughness | 3 | 3 | 5.5 | 10 | 9 | 3 | 7 |
| D7 | 62 | Wear resistance<br>Hot hardness<br>Toughness | 2 | 1 | 5 | 10 | 8 | 2 | 6 |
| H11 | 47 | Wear resistance<br>Hot hardness<br>Toughness | 7 | 9 | 10 | 10 | 9 | 7 | 9 |
| H12 | 47 | Wear resistance<br>Hot hardness<br>Toughness | 7 | 9 | 10 | 10 | 9 | 6 | 9 |
| H13 | 47 | Wear resistance<br>Hot hardness<br>Toughness | 7 | 8.5 | 10 | 10 | 9 | 10 | 8 |
| H19 | 47 | Wear resistance<br>Hot hardness<br>Toughness | 6 | 6.5 | 8 | 8 | 8 | 2 | 5 |
| H21 | 47 | Wear resistance<br>Hot hardness<br>Toughness | 5.5 | 7 | 8 | 8 | 8 | 7 | 6 |
| 01 | 61 | Wear resistance<br>Hot hardness<br>Toughness | 7 | 9 | 9 | 6 | 7 | 10 | 9 |

TABLE 2-7—*Continued*

| AISI/SAE Type | Typical Hardness, $R_C$ | Primary Properties, relative deg. | Secondary Properties* Machinability | Grindability | Polishability | Depth of Hardening | Distortion | Availability | Initial Cost |
|---|---|---|---|---|---|---|---|---|---|
| 06 | 61 | Wear resistance<br>Hot hardness<br>Toughness | 8 | 10 | 6 | 6 | 7 | 5 | 9 |
| S1 | 55 | Wear resistance<br>Hot hardness<br>Toughness | 6.5 | 8 | 8 | 6 | 6 | 4 | 8 |
| S5 | 55 | Wear resistance<br>Hot hardness<br>Toughness | 7 | 9 | 9 | 5 | 6 | 10 | 9 |
| S7 | 55 | Wear resistance<br>Hot hardness<br>Toughness | 7.5 | 8 | 10 | 7 | 6 | 8 | 9 |
| W1 | 63 | Wear resistance<br>Hot hardness<br>Toughness | 10 | 10 | 9 | 1 | 1 | 8 | 9 |
| W2 | 63 | Wear resistance<br>Hot hardness<br>Toughness | 10 | 10 | 9 | 1 | 1 | 5 | 9 |
| L6 | 59 | Wear resistance<br>Hot hardness<br>Toughness | 6.5 | 9 | 9 | 6 | 6 | 7 | 9 |
| T1 | 65 | Wear resistance<br>Hot hardness<br>Toughness | 4 | 3 | 5 | 9 | 8 | 3 | 3 |
| T15 | 66 | Wear resistance<br>Hot hardness<br>Toughness | 2 | 0.5 | 3 | 9 | 8 | 5 | 1 |
| M2 | 65 | Wear resistance<br>Hot hardness<br>Toughness | 4 | 4 | 6 | 9 | 8 | 10 | 6 |
| M4 | 65 | Wear resistance<br>Hot hardness<br>Toughness | 3.5 | 1 | 4 | 9 | 8 | 5 | 5 |
| M42 | 67 | Wear resistance<br>Hot hardness<br>Toughness | 3.5 | 2 | 3 | 9 | 8 | 8 | 3 |
| P20 | 31 | Wear resistance<br>Hot hardness<br>Toughness | 8.5 | 10 | 10 | 6 | 7 | 10 | 9 |

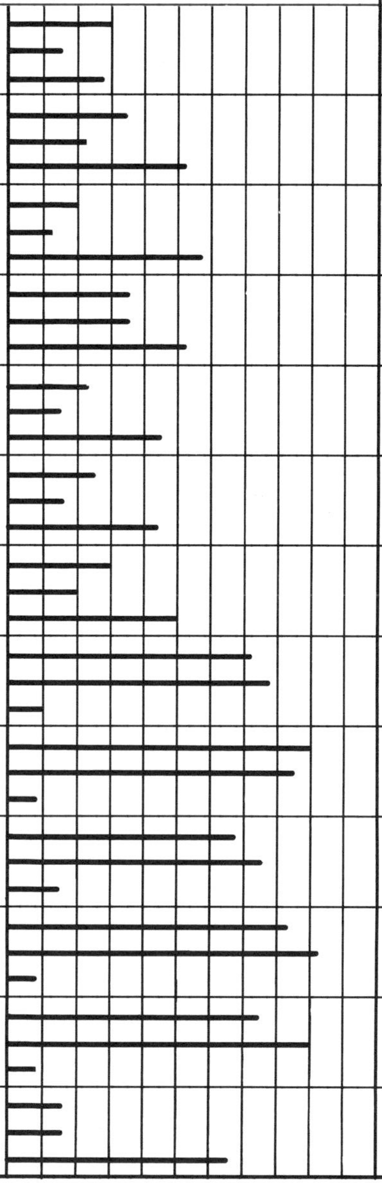

* The higher the number, the better the property; lowest numbers indicate the poorest properties.

**TABLE 2-8**
**Recommended Tool Steels for Various Forming Applications**

| Operation and Tools | Recommended Grade, AISI/SAE Type | Alternate Grades | Hardness, $R_C$ |
|---|---|---|---|
| Bending dies | A11 | A2,02 | 58-64 |
| Blanking dies | A11 | A2,D2,S7,01 | 58-64 |
| Coining dies | A11 | A2,D2 | 58-62 |
| Cold heading | | | |
| heading dies | W1 | --- | 58-62 |
| heading die inserts | M4 | D2 | 60-64 |
| shearing dies | M2 | D2,M4 | 58-63 |
| upsetting dies | M2 | A2,D2 | 58-64 |
| trimming dies | M2 | T1 | 60-64 |
| chamfering cutters | M4 | M42 | 62-65 |
| heading punches | W1 | M2,M4 | 58-60 |
| indenting punches | M2 | M4 | 60-64 |
| blanking punches | D2 | A2,S5 | 58-62 |
| piercing punches | M2 | D2,A2 | 58-62 |
| upsetting punches | M2 | A2,S5 | 58-64 |
| die-insert holders | H11 | H13 | 45-50 |
| cutoff blades | M2 | W1,01 | 60-64 |
| quills and knockout pins | A2 | W1,M2 | 59-63 |
| Deep drawing dies for: | | | |
| steel | A11 | A2,M4,D2 | 62-65 |
| aluminum | A11 | A2,D2 | 62-64 |
| brass | A11 | M4,D2 | 62-65 |
| Die casting of | | | |
| aluminum and magnesium: | | | |
| dies | H13 | H11 | 42-52 |
| inserts and cores | H13 | H11 | 46-52 |
| dieholders | 4140 | P20 | 28-32 |
| ejector pins | H13 | --- | 42-46 |
| plungers | H13 | H11 | 46-50 |
| slides | H13 | H11 | 46-52 |
| shot sleeves | H13 | H11 | 44-48 |
| nozzles | H13 | H11 | 32-42 |
| brass: | | | |
| dies | H19 | H21,H13 | 40-44 |
| inserts and cores | H19 | H21,H13 | 40-44 |
| dieholders | 4140 | P20 | 28-32 |
| ejector pins | H13 | M2 | 42-46 |
| plungers | H13 | H21 | 40-44 |
| zinc alloys: | | | |
| dies and inserts | P20 | H13,S7 | 28-48 |
| plungers | H13 | H11 | 42-48 |
| ejector pins | H13 | H11 | 39-44 |
| cores and slides | H13 | H11,P20 | 39-44 |
| Drawing punches | A11 | D2,M2,A2 | 62-65 |
| Extrusion of cold | | | |
| steel dies and punches | M2 | M4,02 | 60-66 |
| aluminum dies and punches | A11 | A2,D2 | 56-62 |
| Extrusion of hot | | | |
| aluminum and magnesium: | | | |
| dies | H11 | H12,H13 | 48-50 |
| dummy and backer blocks | H11 | H12,H13 | 44-48 |
| liners | H11 | H12,H13 | 42-46 |
| rams | H11 | H12,H13 | 40-42 |
| mandrels | H11 | H12,H13 | 48-52 |

TABLE 2-8—*Continued*

| Operation and Tools | Recommended Grade, AISI/SAE Type | Alternate Grades | Hardness, $R_C$ |
|---|---|---|---|
| brass: | | | |
| dies for tubes and round shapes | H21 | H19 | 39-42 |
| dies for other shapes | H21 | H19 | 31-37 |
| dummy and backer blocks | H11 | H21 | 40-45 |
| liners | H12 | H11 | 40-44 |
| rams | H12 | H11 | 40-44 |
| mandrels | H12 | H11,H19 | 40-46 |
| steel: | | | |
| dies | H21 | H11 | 43-47 |
| dummy blocks | H21 | H19 | 40-44 |
| mandrels | H11 | H13 | 42-46 |
| billet shears | H21 | H12,H11 | 46-52 |
| trimmer dies | A2 | H13 | 56-58 |
| Forging of | | | |
| aluminum: | | | |
| punches and dies | H11 | H12,H13 | 44-48 |
| die inserts | H11 | H12,H13 | 46-50 |
| brass punches, dies and inserts | H21 | H11,H13 | 48-52 |
| steel: | | | |
| punches, dies, and inserts | H13 | H12,H19 | 44-48 |
| trim dies | D2 | A2 | 58-60 |
| Lamination dies | A11 | T15,D2 | 62-64 |
| Plastic molds | | | |
| dies | A2 | H13,S7 | 50-60 |
| dieholders | 4140 | P20 | 28-32 |
| ejector pins | H13 | | |
| PM compacting dies | M4 | A11,D2 | 56-64 |
| Punches | | | |
| cold | | | |
| light duty | S5 | A11,D2 | 58-62 |
| heavy duty | S5 | M2,S7 | 58-62 |
| hot | H13 | --- | 48-58 |
| Rolls, beading, forming, and seaming | D2 | A11,D2 | 58-64 |
| Shear blades | | | |
| cold | | | |
| light duty | D2 | A2,01 | 56-68 |
| heavy duty | S5 | S7 | 55-60 |
| hot | | | |
| light duty | S5 | H13,S7 | 55-60 |
| heavy duty | H21 | H13,H12 | 45-50 |
| Spinning | | | |
| mandrels | A2 | H11,P20 | 50-58 |
| rollers | M2 | M4 | 58-62 |
| Stamping dies | A2 | D2 | 58-64 |
| Swaging dies | | | |
| cold | S5,S7 | A2,D2 | 56-60 |
| hot | H13 | H12,H11 | 48-52 |

(*Crucible Specialty Metals Div., Colt Industries*)

**TABLE 2-9**
**Heat Treatment of Tool Steels Commonly Used for Dies and Molds**

| AISI/ SAE Type | Preheating Range, °F (°C) | Hardening Range, °F (°C)* | Quench Medium | Tempering Range, °F (°C) | Typical Hardness Range, $R_C$ |
|---|---|---|---|---|---|
| A2 | 1400-1450 (760-788) | 1700-1800 (927-982) | Air | 350-1000 (177-538) | 57-62 |
| A6 | 1200-1250 (649-677) | 1525-1600 (829-871) | Air | 300-800 (149-427) | 54-60 |
| A8 | 1400-1450 (760-788) | 1800-1850 (982-1010) | Air | 350-1100 (177-593) | 50-60 |
| A11 | 1450-1550 (788-843) | 1950-2150 (1066-1177) | Air, salt, or oil | 1000-1050 (538-566)** | 55-65 |
| D2 | 1450-1500 (788-816) | 1800-1875 (982-1024) | Air | 400-1000 (204-538) | 54-61 |
| D4 | 1450-1500 (788-816) | 1775-1850 (968-1010) | Air | 400-1000 (204-538) | 54-61 |
| D7 | 1450-1500 (788-816) | 1850-1950 (1010-1066) | Air | 300-1000 (149-538) | 58-65 |
| H11 | 1450-1500 (788-816) | 1825-1875 (996-1024) | Air | 1000-1200 (538-649)† | 38-55 |
| H12 | 1450-1500 (788-816) | 1825-1875 (996-1024) | Air | 1000-1200 (538-649)† | 38-55 |
| H13 | 1450-1500 (788-816) | 1825-1875 (996-1024) | Air | 1000-1200 (538-649)† | 38-55 |
| H19 | 1450-1500 (788-816) | 2000-2200 (1093-1204) | Air or oil | 1000-1300 (538-704)† | 40-59 |
| H21 | 1500-1550 (816-843) | 2000-2200 (1093-1204) | Air or oil | 1100-1250 (593-677)† | 36-54 |
| 01 | 1100-1200 (593-649) | 1450-1500 (788-816) | Oil | 300-500 (149-260) | 57-62 |
| 06 | 1100-1200 (593-649) | 1450-1500 (788-816) | Oil | 350-600 (177-316) | 58-63 |
| S1 | 1200-1250 (649-677) | 1650-1800 (899-982) | Oil | 400-1200 (204-649) | 40-58 |
| S5 | 1200-1250 (649-677) | 1600-1700 (871-927) | Oil | 350-800 (177-427) | 50-60 |
| S7 | 1200-1300 (649-704) | 1700-1750 (927-954) | Air or oil | 400-1150 (204-621) | 45-57 |
| W1 | 1100-1200 (593-649) | 1400-1550 (760-843) | Brine or water | 350-650 (177-343) | 50-64 |
| W2 | 1100-1200 (593-649) | 1400-1550 (760-843) | Brine or water | 350-650 (177-343) | 50-64 |
| L6 | 1100-1200 (593-649) | 1450-1550 (788-843) | Oil | 300-1100 (149-593) | 45-62 |
| T1 | 1500-1600 (816-871) | 2300-2375 (1260-1302) | Air, salt, or oil | 1000-1100 (538-593)† | 60-66 |
| T15 | 1500-1600 (816-871) | 2200-2300 (1204-1260) | Air, salt, or oil | 1000-1100 (538-593)† | 63-68 |

TABLE 2-9—*Continued*

| AISI/ SAE Type | Preheating Range, °F (°C) | Hardening Range, °F (°C)* | Quench Medium | Tempering Range, °F (°C) | Typical Hardness Range, $R_C$ |
|---|---|---|---|---|---|
| M2 | 1350-1550 (732-843) | 2175-2250 (1191-1232) | Air, salt, or oil | 1000-1100 (538-593)† | 60-65 |
| M4 | 1350-1550 (732-843) | 2200-2250 (1204-1232) | Air, salt, or oil | 1000-1100 (538-593)† | 61-66 |
| M42 | 1350-1550 (732-843) | 2175-2210 (1163-1191) | Air, salt, or oil | 950-1100 (510-593)** | 65-70 |
| P20‡ | | | | | |

* Hardening temperature ranges are 25° F (14° C) lower than those shown when salt bath heating is used.
** Triple tempering is recommended with two hours for each temper.
† Double tempering is recommended with two hours for each temper.
‡ Normally supplied in the prehardened condition, $R_C$ 30-32.

Tempering is accomplished by heating to the desired temperature for an appropriate length of time (generally two to three hours) and then air cooling to room temperature. Tool steel compositions such as high-speed and hot-work grades require two or even three separate tempers because of the greater amount of retained austenite in the microstructure.

## Designing for Heat Treating

Design considerations for the die or mold are important in reducing the risk of cracking in heat treatment. These considerations include:

1. Use generous radii to eliminate sharp corners.
2. Avoid abrupt section changes.
3. Avoid deep stamp marks.
4. Remove decarburization resulting from processing at the steel mill.

Sharp corners, drastic section changes, and deep stamp marks are the most common design factors contributing to cracking in heat treatment. These factors have the common characteristic of acting as stress raisers in the heat-treated tool. The intensified stresses can exceed the tensile strength of the tool, causing it to rupture. A detailed discussion of design factors is presented in Chapter 6, "Die Design for Sheet Metal Forming."

Tool steel mill bar purchased in the hot-rolled and annealed condition contains a layer of decarburization which must be removed before heat treatment. The presence of decarburization on the finished tool surface results in a soft surface having excessively high tensile stresses that promote cracking. Information pertaining to the required amount of surface removal from a hot-rolled and annealed mill bar can be obtained from the producer or from the *Tool Steel Products Manual.*[1]

## Heat-Treating Equipment

An extensive range of heat-treating equipment is available to toolmakers. Most heat-treating furnaces used for dies or molds are either salt-bath, vacuum, controlled-atmosphere, or muffle type.

**Salt-bath furnaces.** These furnaces offer the advantage of protecting the tool from the harmful effects of the atmosphere during heat treating. Dies or molds immersed in molten salt do not develop an oxide skin or harmful decarburization. In addition, heating is accomplished quickly and uniformly from all sides due to the intimate contact of the tool and heating medium. The molten salt mixture is contained in a brick-lined receptacle. Heating is usually accomplished by two submerged electrodes, or the furnace may be gas fired. Electrical resistance of the salt generates heat as voltage is applied to the electrodes.

Composition of the salt mixture determines the useful heating range of the salt. High temperatures, above 2000° F (1093° C), are achieved in salt mixtures rich in barium chloride. Midrange temperatures of 1000-2000° F (538-1093° C) employ chloride salt mixtures of sodium, barium, and calcium. Nitrate salts are required for temperatures below 1000° F (538° C).

**Vacuum furnaces.** Use of vacuum furnaces for heat treating tool steels has gained wide acceptance. Reasons accounting for the success of vacuum procedures include versatility, efficient utilization of energy, improved tool quality, and improved environmental factors. In the process of vacuum heat treating, the die or mold is heated in a vacuum and the tool surface is completely protected from the harmful effects of the atmosphere.

A variety of vacuum furnace equipment is available. The simplest type consists of a single chamber used for both heating and cooling. The single-chamber furnace may be sufficient for most air-hardening tool steels, but it is inadequate for those tools requiring rapid cooling. A three-chamber vacuum furnace represents maximum flexibility in respect to heating and cooling cycles. A three-chamber furnace is constructed with movable doors between each compartment and doors at both ends of the furnace. The arrangement facilitates a steady flow of work from one compartment to another, thus promoting efficiency.

In the operation of a vacuum furnace, vacuum levels of 0.050 mm of mercury (0.067 Pa) pressure or lower are normally used. Dies or molds heat treated at vacuum levels below this level are clean, bright, and free of decarburization. Vacuum furnaces are designed to include a gas or oil quench. In gas quenching, the furnace is back-filled with nitrogen. The gas quenching method has been successfully used for air hardening dies or molds of nominal size. Oil quenching is required for tools for which rapid cooling to 1100° F (593° C) is necessary to prevent grain boundary precipitation.

**Furnaces with controlled atmospheres.** Controlled atmospheres are often used in the heat treating of tool steels in sealed furnaces. Protective gases used for heat treating dies or molds are in the form of a generated atmosphere, dissociated ammonia, or bottled inert gas. Generated atmospheres are made by the partial combustion of a hydrocarbon gas such as methane. The resultant gas is primarily nitrogen with controlled amounts of carbon monoxide for carbon potential control. Carbon dioxide and water vapor must be removed in a generated gas because of their high decarburizing potential.

An atmosphere of 75% hydrogen and 25% nitrogen is produced when ammonia is passed over a heated catalyst. The gas mixture is used for bright annealing many types of steels and has been successfully used for the bright hardening of tool steels.

**Muffle-type furnaces.** The long-used method of heat treating in muffle furnaces is still employed when some minor amount of decarburization or scaling can be tolerated in the heat-treated dies or molds. A retort is sometimes used to protect the tool from direct exposure to the heating medium, whether gas or electric. In this method, sufficient grinding stock is required to be left on the die or mold to allow for decarburization removal after heat treatment. A more comprehensive discussion of heat treatment is presented in Volume III of this Handbook series.

## SURFACE TREATMENTS FOR DIES AND MOLDS

Various surface treatments of tool steels have been used to improve the performance of dies and molds, principally with respect to wear resistance. The most popular surface treatments used in industry for tool steels have been nitriding, oxidizing, and chromium plating. Carburizing is also a popular surface-hardening method, used primarily for steels with low to medium carbon contents. Because of their high carbon content, most tool steels are not normally carburized.

### Nitriding of Tool Steels

The nitriding process imparts a hard surface to the die or mold by the penetration of nitrogen atoms into the material and the formation of hard nitrides. Nitriding can prevent or minimize galling, but the nitrided surface can spall from small radii.

A nitrided case has a hardness of $R_C$ 70-74. Depth of the nitride case varies considerably, depending upon the nitriding process and the time/temperature parameters employed. Case depth must be adjusted to avoid brittleness. Nitriding is accomplished either in a molten salt bath, in gaseous ammonia, or by the glow discharge method (ion implantation).

**Salt-bath nitriding.** Molten salt baths composed of cyanide salts impart nitrogen to the steel at temperatures in the range of 950-1200° F (510-649° C). Case depths produced by the molten salt method are typically in the range of 0.0001-0.001″ (0.003-0.03 mm).

**Gaseous ammonia nitriding.** In the ammonia gas process, nascent reactive nitrogen is released when the gas comes in contact with hot steel. The nitrogen diffuses inward developing a hard case. The process is conducted typically at 980-1000° F (527-538° C) for times of 10-80 hours. The gaseous method accomplishes deeper nitrogen penetration than the molten salt method can accomplish and is therefore especially useful where heavy case depths are required.

**Nitriding by ion implantation.** In glow discharge nitriding, the workpiece is made into the negative electrode in a vacuum furnace. A glow discharge is formed around the workpiece at a potential of 300V in a vacuum of 0.001-0.010 mm of mercury (0.0013-0.013 Pa) pressure. Nitrogen is introduced in controlled amounts, and nitrogen ions are implanted in the workpiece by virtue of their kinetic energy. Principal advantage of the glow discharge nitriding process is the control of nitrogen concentration and case depth.

### Oxidizing Treatment

Some dies and molds are produced with a black oxide film which extends tool life. The oxide film reduces direct metal-to-metal contact between tool and workpiece and retains cutting lubricant, thus promoting improved tool life. The oxide film can be developed by a steam treatment or by immersion in a molten oxidizing salt.

**Steam oxidizing.** In using the steam oxidizing method, a sealed retort furnace is employed which incorporates the addition of steam in controlled amounts. The steam treatment is normally performed simultaneously with the tempering operation, typically in the 1000-1050° F (538-566° C) temperature range.

**Salt oxidizing.** The technique of oxidizing dies or molds in a molten salt bath employs a mixture of sodium nitrite and sodium hydroxide. Tools develop a tenacious oxide film when immersed in the oxidizing salt mixture at 300° F (149° C) for approximately 15 minutes. Most oxide films applied to tools are typically 0.0001-0.0002″ (0.003-0.005 mm) deep.

### Chromium Plating

Chromium plating is employed to advantage for some dies or molds on which friction is a critical factor in tool life. A chromium-plated surface has a reduced coefficient of friction as compared to a machined steel surface. It is also useful in minimizing or preventing galling for some severe applications, but the plating may spall from small radii. This method can also be used to build up worn areas of a die or mold. A typical chrome plate thickness used for antifriction purposes is 0.001-0.005″ (0.03-0.13 mm) and has a hardness of $R_C$ 65-75.

In chromium plating, the workpiece is made into the cathode in an electrolytic cell and chromium metal is plated on the surface from an anodic source. Hydrogen is also released at the cathode, which makes the die or mold sensitive to hydrogen embrittlement. A post stress-relief treatment must be performed on chromium-plated tools to insure the removal of hydrogen. Exposure to temperatures of 400-500° F (204-260° C) is employed for periods of 3-4 hours to accomplish hydrogen removal. More details on chromium plating are presented in Volume III, *Materials, Finishing and Coating*, of this Handbook series.

### Vapor Deposition Coatings

Among the most promising of new coating methods are those based on vapor deposition (refer to Volume III). Extensive testing of tools coated with titanium nitride shows promising results for metalforming tools such as punches, dies, and rolls. Increased tool life is attributed to the lubricous hard qualities of titanium nitride which resists galling and metal pickup.

**Physical vapor deposition.** In the process termed physical vapor deposition (PVD), the finished die or mold is placed in a chamber where it is bombarded with titanium ions in the presence of nitrogen, producing a thin layer of titanium nitride. The PVD process is conducted at temperatures below the tempering temperature.

**Chemical vapor deposition.** The chemical vapor deposition (CVD) process requires a high temperature and therefore necessitates subsequent vacuum reheat treating after coating. In CVD, the die or mold is heated to approximately 1900° F

(1038° C) in the presence of titanium tetrachloride gas and methane or nitrogen. Two separate layers of first titanium carbide and then titanium nitride are deposited on the tool.

**Coating thickness and materials.** A deposited layer thickness of 0.0002-0.0003" (0.005-0.008 mm) is typical for the vapor deposition processes. Both the PVD and CVD processes can be adapted to a variety of coating materials, such as hafnium nitride, aluminum oxide, tungsten carbide, and nickel borides.

# STEEL-BONDED CARBIDES

Steel-bonded carbides belong to the family of cemented carbides and are produced by the powder metallurgy (PM) process discussed in Chapter 17, "Powder Metallurgy." These materials differ, however, from conventional cemented carbides, discussed next in this chapter, in that they have variable physical properties (particularly hardness) obtained by heat treatment of their matrices.

## GRADES AVAILABLE

These sintered ferrous alloys, sold under the trade name of Ferro-Tic (a registered trademark of Alloy Technology International, Inc.), are made in several grades. Different grades contain from 20-70% (by volume) titanium carbide, tungsten carbide, titanium-tungsten double carbides, or other refractory carbides as their hard phase. The balance of the content, the heat-treatable matrix or binder, is a carbon or alloy steel containing at least 60% iron. By controlling the composition, the material grade can be tailored to specific property requirements.

The grade used most commonly for dies and molds contains neither tungsten nor cobalt. Main constituents of this grade are about 45% titanium carbide and approximately 55% alloy tool steel. The tool steel contains 3% molybdenum, 10% chromium, and 0.80% carbon. This grade has a compressive strength in excess of 450,000 psi (3100 MPa) and a transverse rupture strength of about 200,000 psi (1380 MPa).

## ADVANTAGES

Advantages of steel-bonded carbides for dies and molds include machinability in the annealed condition, hardenability, good wear resistance, minimum friction, and the ability to withstand heavy compressive loads at high temperatures. Annealing of these materials to hardness levels of $R_C$ 43-46 permits machining (discussed later in this section) with conventional steel-cutting tools.

The wear resistance of steel-bonded carbides is much better than that of most tool steels and approaches that of some cemented tungsten carbides with cobalt binder. This is the result of the titanium carbide particles, about 0.0002-0.0003" (0.005-0.008 mm) diam and having a Vickers hardness of 3300, embedded in the hardened matrix. These materials are less brittle than cemented tungsten carbides, thus reducing the possibility of chipping.

For many applications, dies and molds made from steel-bonded carbides are providing higher quality parts with less scrap, increased productivity as a result of less downtime, and reduced costs. In comparison to production runs in which dies made from high-carbon, high-chromium tool steels were used, production runs between regrinds of 10 times as long and increases in die life of 50 or more times have been reported. While steel-bonded carbides cost about 20% more than the more expensive tool steels, they are less costly than sintered tungsten carbides.

## APPLICATIONS

Steel-bonded carbides are being used primarily for single-station and progressive dies employed in severe stamping operations, such as forming, drawing, notching, and blanking, including the production of laminations. Rigid presses with good parallelism between moving and stationary members are essential for the use of these die materials. Excessive deflection reduces the productivity and life of the dies. The applications of steel-bonded carbides for plastic molds include gate and mold inserts, and nozzles.

## DIE DESIGN AND CONSTRUCTION

Sectional construction is generally preferable for dies made from steel-bonded carbides because it permits easier manufacture of complex sections and facilitates the replacement of worn components. For high-production dies, it is most economical to provide die sections with tapped holes in their bottom surfaces. This allows the sections to be clamped to die shoes from below and permits the maximum number of regrinds.

Draw-die inserts or rings require suitable steel retainer rings that are precompressed to absorb and counteract the stresses exerted radially on the bore of the die. This can be accomplished by providing an interference shrink fit or by means of a taper fit (see Fig. 2-2), drawing the rings together onto a support plate with bolts. If shrink fitting is performed, care is required to minimize or prevent the absorption of heat from the expanded ring, which could reduce the hardness of the steel-bonded carbide.

When die sets are used, they should be of four-post design for increased rigidity. Hardened, precision-ground bushings and pins are preferable for accurate parallelism. Strippers and knockouts must also be sturdy and well guided, and pressure pads should be spring loaded instead of the positive type. Safety devices to detect misfeeds, buckling of the stock, and other malfunctions are essential for die protection.

Optimum rigidity is also important for punches made from steel-bonded carbides. Punches of straight design with nested bases are preferable to L or T-shaped designs because less material is required and they are easier to grind. Brazing or welding is not generally recommended, and punches are usually attached to the punch plates with screws.

Clearances between the punches and dies is generally slightly larger than when tool steels are used. A clearance of 7-8% of the stock thickness per cutting side is recommended for blanking or piercing carbon or alloy steels, as well as nonferrous materials. For stainless steel or prehardened spring steel, the clearance is generally 9-10% of stock thickness per cutting side.

When sharp outside corners are required on stampings, the die sections should be split at the corners. Corners on the punches, however, must be rounded with radii of 0.003-0.004" (0.08-0.10 mm) to avoid chipping or rapid wear.

## MACHINING AND GRINDING PROCEDURES

With only a few variations, the machining and grinding of

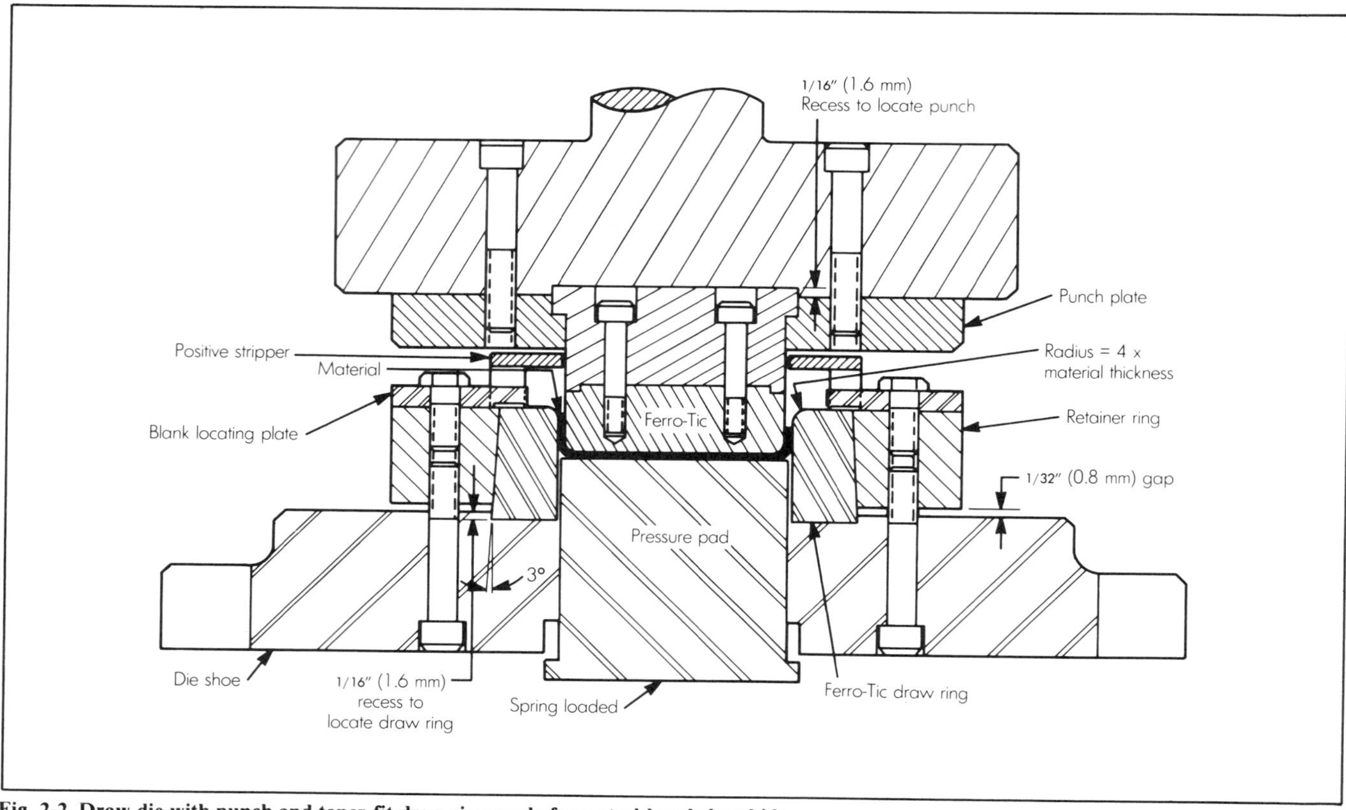


**Fig. 2-2 Draw die with punch and taper-fit draw ring made from steel-bonded carbide.**

steel-bonded carbides is essentially the same as for other materials. In fact, it is possible to remove about 50% more stock per minute than is removed in machining high-carbon, high-chromium tool steels, such as AISI Type D2.

## Machining Practice

When steel-bonded carbides are being machined, low cutting speeds are essential to preserve the cutting edges of the tools and to avoid overheating, which can cause premature hardening of the metals. A maximum cutting speed of 30 sfm (9.1 m/min) is recommended for turning, milling, and sawing. For drilling, the cutting speed can vary from 125-250 sfm (38-76 m/min). Tapping should be done by hand or with a slow machine.

**Cut depths.** Relatively heavy cuts are also important to avoid glazing and undesirable work hardening. Depths of cut should never be less than 0.003" (0.08 mm) but can be as heavy as 1/4" (6.4 mm) or more on rigid machines. Feed rates for turning vary from 0.003-0.012 ipr (0.08-0.30 mm/rev) and for milling, 0.003-0.010" (0.08-0.25 mm) per tooth. Down (climb) milling should be used whenever possible in preference to up (conventional) milling.

**Cutting tools.** Tungsten carbide tools, classification numbers C-1 and C-2, are used extensively for turning operations. The tools or inserts generally have a 0-5° negative rake, 5° side rake, and nose radius of 0.030" (0.76 mm). High-speed steel tools are common for milling, drilling, and tapping. Carbon steel blades having 8 or 10 teeth per inch are satisfactory for sawing. Good results have been obtained in cutting threads with five-flute, high-speed steel taps having a negative rake angle, shallow flutes, and narrow lands.

**Cutting fluids.** Cutting fluids should not be used in machining steel-bonded carbides. This is because the fluids have a tendency to combine with the carbide grains in the chips and form an undesirable lapping compound that can quickly destroy the cutting edges of tools.

**Electrical discharge machining (EDM).** This process is used extensively, especially for finishing die components that have been premachined by sawing, milling, drilling, and other conventional processes. Best results are generally obtained with graphite-based, copper-impregnated electrodes. The wire EDM process is preferable because less heat is generated with the smaller contact area.

## Grinding Practice

Relatively soft, open-structure, vitrified-bond, aluminum oxide wheels of 80-120 grain size are recommended for grinding steel-bonded carbides. Nickel-coated, resin-bonded, synthetic diamond wheels of 150-180 grain size are only used occasionally for precision finishing operations.

Grinding should be done into the edges of the die components, not away from them, to prevent breakout of carbide particles. To avoid overheating, stock removal per pass should be minimal and table movement rapid. Care should be exercised to ensure that any decarburized metal is removed in the grinding operation.

When surface grinding is performed, the table speed should be 50-60 fpm (15.2-18.3 m/min)—about twice that normally used for surface grinding most tool steels. A table crossfeed of 0.010-0.030" (0.25-0.76 mm) per stroke and wheel downfeed of 0.0002-0.001" (0.005-0.03 mm) per stroke are common. For cylindrical grinding, the slowest available rotary speed should be used for the workpiece, with a wheel traverse rate of 8 fpm (2.4 m/min) and infeed rates of 0.002" (0.05 mm) per pass for roughing and 0.0002-0.0005" (0.005-0.013 mm) per pass for finishing.

Lapping and polishing, if done, should be in the direction that the metal flows in the drawing operation to be performed. All sharp edges should be stoned to a small radius.

### HEAT TREATMENT

The heat treatment of steel-bonded carbides is conventional. However, only the steel matrix is hardened, with the titanium carbide particles being unaffected. The cycle consists of heating to 1975° F (1079° C), preferably in a vacuum furnace, quenching with nitrogen or another inert gas, tempering by heating to 950° F (510° C) for one hour, air cooling to room temperature, retempering at 950° F, and again air cooling. This treatment produces a hardness of $R_C$ 66-70.

The need for decarburization-free heat treatment is essential. If a vacuum furnace is not available, the metals can be heated in an atmosphere-controlled furnace and quenched in oil. If an atmosphere-controlled furnace is not available, the die components can be wrapped in airtight bags of stainless steel foil for heating. Quenching should be done with the components still in the bags.

Rough-machined, annealed components are often stress relieved prior to finish machining and hardening. This is accomplished by heating the components to 1200° F (649° C) for one hour and cooling in air. By finish machining the material in the annealed and stress-relieved condition, the need for grinding after hardening becomes minimal.

Like tool steels, steel-bonded carbides undergo a slight growth during hardening in the conversion of the matrix from austenite to martensite. Stability, however, is good, with minimal distortion. An expansion of 0.00025 in./in. (mm/mm) is common.

## CEMENTED TUNGSTEN CARBIDE

Tungsten carbides cemented with cobalt have replaced steels for many tools used in metalforming operations, primarily because of their high abrasion (wear) resistance and compressive strengths. These materials are normally used for long production runs in which their higher initial cost can be economically justified as the result of longer tool life, reduced downtime, and decreased cost per part produced. Some stamping operations, such as the production of small holes in hard and tough materials, can only be done with tungsten carbide punches. Precise tolerances are maintained for long periods, thus improving product quality and reducing rejects.

The high elastic modulus (stiffness under bending loads) of cemented tungsten carbides permits their use for punches with length-to-diameter ratios exceeding 4:1. These materials also reduce the severity of galling, which is a problem common with punches and dies made from tool steels.

A possible limitation to the use of tungsten carbides, in addition to their higher initial cost, is the greater difficulty in grinding them (discussed later in this section), with resultant problems in finishing difficult shapes. Tungsten carbides are more brittle (nonductile) and have some physical properties lower than tool steels. Depending upon manufacturing techniques, their cobalt content, and the design of the punches and dies, however, it is feasible to make complex-shaped, high-strength, cemented carbide tooling for forming and blanking operations.

### APPLICATIONS

Cemented tungsten carbide dies are being used extensively for drawing wire, bars, and tubes; extruding steels and nonferrous alloys; cold and hot heading dies; swaging hammers and mandrels; and powder compacting punches and dies. Tungsten carbide is also used to make dies to draw sheet metal parts. Other important applications include punching, coining, sizing, and ironing tools for beverage and food cans and the production of a variety of laminations and other stamped metal parts.

Typical products produced by tungsten-carbide forming tools include automotive parts such as piston pins, bearing cups for universal joints, spark plug shells, bearing races for front-wheel drives, air pump rotors, transmission gear blanks, and valves. In the construction and farm equipment industries, tungsten carbide is used to form hitch pins, track link bushings, hydraulic hose fittings, diesel piston pins, and a variety of gear blanks. Tungsten carbide is also used in manufacturing fasteners, drawn and ironed beverage cans, cartridge cases, wrench sockets, bicycle drive cups, motor laminations, electronic terminals, and many other stamped parts.

### PRODUCTION OF CEMENTED CARBIDES

Tungsten carbides are produced by a powder metallurgy (PM) process. Details of blending and carburizing the powders, adding the binder, compacting, and sintering are presented in Chapter 3, "Cutting Tool Materials," of Volume I, *Machining*, of this Handbook series. Properties of the cemented tungsten carbides are determined by the compositions of the materials, the size of the particles used, the production techniques, and the metallurgical structure of the materials.

Although sintering of cemented carbides results in a density of virtually 100%, porosity can occur from several different causes. One cause is excessive carbon content. Such a defect cannot be cured in the finished part. Another source of difficulty can be carbon deficiency, which results in a brittle condition known as eta phase. These conditions must be avoided because neither can be tolerated in the finished parts.

Porosity can also be caused by improper techniques employed in processing the powders and by the introduction of impurities during the production of the cemented carbides. Most porosity caused by impurities or reasons other than improper carbon balance can be eliminated by the employment of better manufacturing techniques. If porosity or voids are not at the surfaces, hot isostatic pressing (HIP) after sintering will close the voids. This process also improves the average transverse rupture strength as well as the surface integrity after grinding. Tools made from carbides pressed isostatically are particularly desirable for applications in which pits cannot be tolerated on the tool surfaces, such as high-stress applications

# CEMENTED TUNGSTEN CARBIDE

and those in which thin materials are formed.

The HIP technique, being used extensively as a standard production operation, especially for forming dies, is generally done with an inert gas (such as argon) in a pressure chamber at 5000-20,000 psi (34.5-138 MPa), with temperatures ranging from 2200-2550° F (1200-1400° C). Additional details of the HIP process are presented in Chapter 17, "Powder Metallurgy."

## CEMENTED CARBIDE PROPERTIES

The cemented carbide materials used most extensively for forming operations are the so-called straight tungsten carbides with cobalt binder, a family of two-phase WC-Co compositions. Occasionally, tantalum carbide is added for lubricity, for increased hot strength, or for inhibited grain growth, but other additives are normally avoided for die materials.

Tungsten carbide grains in these materials range from less than 1 micron (0.00004") to 10 microns (0.0004"), and cobalt contents vary from 3-25%. The effect of binder content on some physical properties is shown in Fig. 2-3.

Desirable properties of the straight tungsten carbides used for forming-die applications include high hardness at room and elevated temperatures, high abrasion or wear resistance, high modulus of elasticity, high compressive strength (much higher than its tensile strength), and low rate of thermal expansion. Some of the major properties of tungsten carbides compared to tool steels are presented in Table 2-10.

### Hardness

The hardness of a straight tungsten carbide, depends primarily upon the percentage of cobalt binder that it contains. In general, the more binder, the lower the hardness (see Fig. 2-4). This graph also illustrates that fine-grain tungsten carbides have a higher hardness than coarse-grain materials. There is a linear relationship in the increase in hardness from $R_A$ 84 ($R_C$ 65) for a material with 25% cobalt to $R_A$ 94.3 ($R_C$ 83.5) for one with less than 1.5% cobalt. Fine-grain compositions with the same cobalt content have a higher hardness of between 1-2 points on the Rockwell A scale than materials with coarse grains. The coarse-grain carbides are generally stronger.

At elevated temperatures, tungsten carbides retain their hardness much better than steels and most other tool materials. Above 1000° F (538° C), however, the cobalt binder can melt out (oxidize). The success of hot-forming applications with tungsten carbide tooling depends upon the workpiece material and temperature, the contact time, and the type and application method of the coolant/lubricant.

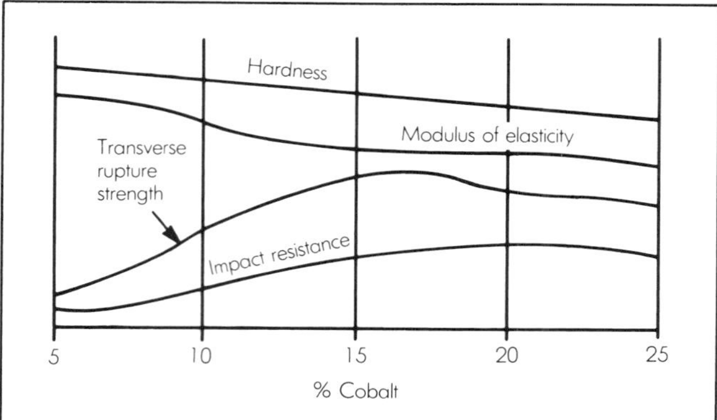


**Fig. 2-3 Relative properties of straight tungsten carbides with various percentages of cobalt binder.** (*Kennametal Inc.*)

**TABLE 2-10**
**Comparison of Approximate Properties of Straight Tungsten Carbides and Tool Steels**

| Material Property | Tungsten Carbides | Tool Steels |
|---|---|---|
| Hardness, | | |
| $R_C$ | 65-83.5 | 66 |
| $R_A$ | 84-94.3 | |
| Abrasion resistance | to 825 | 14 |
| Tensile strength, ksi (MPa) | to 200 (1379) | to 290 (2000) |
| Compressive strength, ksi (MPa) | to 900 (6205) | to 290 (2000) |
| Modulus of elasticity, ksi x $10^3$ (GPa) | to 94 (0.65) | 30 (0.21) |
| Specific gravity | to 15.0 | 7.7-8.7 |
| Impact resistance | poor to good | good |
| Hot hardness at 1200° F (649° C), $R_C$ | 45-77.9 | 33-38 |
| $R_A$ | 73-90.8 | |
| Corrosion resistance | good | fair |

(*Kennametal Inc.*)

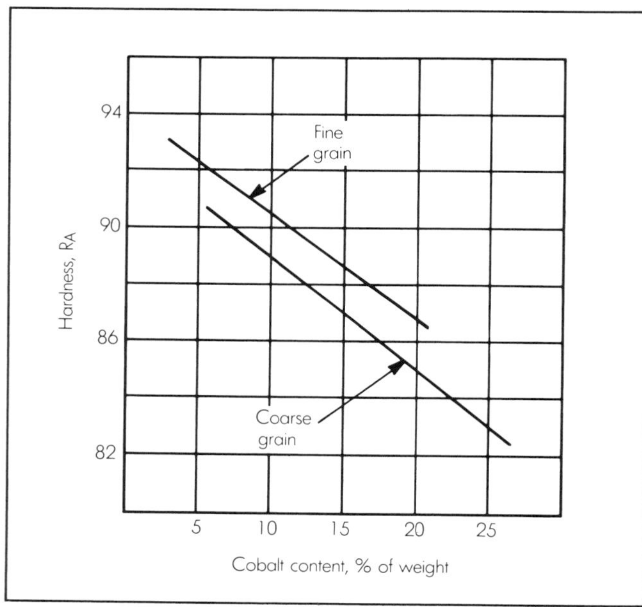


**Fig. 2-4 Effect of cobalt content and grain size on the hardness of straight tungsten carbides.** (*Adamas Carbide Corp.*)

### Wear Resistance

The wear or abrasion resistance of straight tungsten carbides also depends primarily upon the percentages of cobalt binder they contain. In general, the lower the binder content, the higher the wear resistance, and the finer the grain size, the better the wear resistance (see Fig. 2-5). Maximum wear or abrasion resistance is obtained with materials having fine grains and a cobalt content in the range of 3-6%.

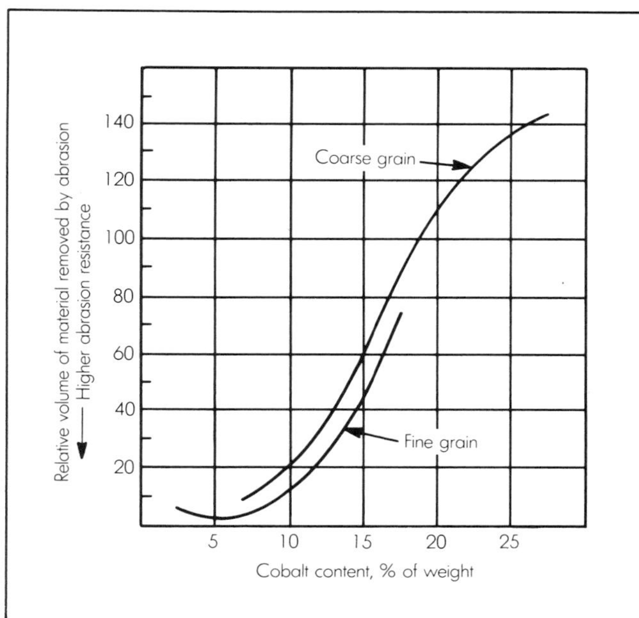


**Fig. 2-5 Effect of cobalt content and grain size on the abrasion resistance of straight tungsten carbides.** (*Adamas Carbide Corp.*)

Cobalt content and grain size, however, also affect the material strength. The higher the cobalt content, the higher the strength; and for some compositions, the coarser the grain size, the higher the strength. For most forming operations, high strengths are needed and materials with low cobalt contents can only be used for fine-wire drawing and low-impact applications. Also, coarse grains are not generally used for materials with a cobalt content less than 6%, but are often employed for carbides with higher cobalt contents, particularly in the 20-25% range.

The addition of tantalum carbide improves the abrasion resistance of these materials slightly because it inhibits grain growth and maintains controlled grain sizes. In general, the small quantities of tantalum carbide (as little as 0.2%) sometimes added to materials are added to control grain size, and larger quantities (usually a maximum of 5%) are added to increase lubricity or to increase the resistance of the carbide to deformation in hot forming operations.

The abrasion or wear resistance of tungsten carbides are measured with dry sand, wet sand, or metal-to-metal tests. In the metal-to-metal test, a carbide ring is run against a test block. The area of the groove worn in the block is used to determine the volume of material removed by abrasion.

## Transverse Rupture Strength

Since standard tensile tests give erratic results with tungsten carbides because of the notch sensitivity of the materials, the carbide industry has chosen the transverse rupture test as a standard for determining relative strengths. The test measures the strength of the material by determining the maximum stress at the extreme fiber when using a three-point loading on a standard test specimen (see Fig. 2-6). The tensile strengths of tungsten carbides have been determined to be 45-50% of their transverse rupture strengths, and these values can be used in stress analysis calculations.

The effect of cobalt content and grain size on transverse rupture strengths is illustrated in Fig. 2-7. As the cobalt content increases, the strengths increase. With respect to fracture toughness and resistance to chipping, however, coarse-grain materials are far superior to fine-grain materials with the same cobalt contents. As a result, generally most materials with cobalt contents above 9-10% are made with coarse-grain tungsten carbide when high strength is needed.

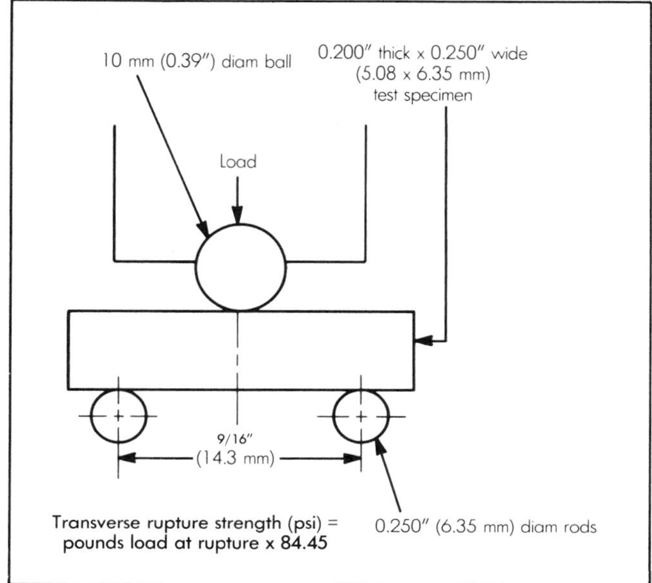


**Fig. 2-6 Test method for determining the transverse rupture strengths of tungsten carbides.** (*Kennametal Inc.*)

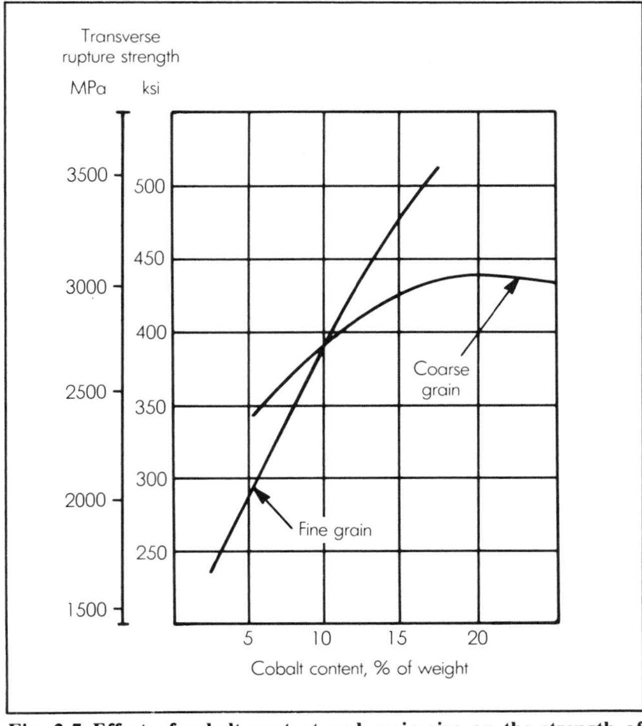


**Fig. 2-7 Effect of cobalt content and grain size on the strength of straight tungsten carbides.** (*Adamas Carbide Corp.*)

# CEMENTED TUNGSTEN CARBIDE

Certain compositions exist which are exceptions to this general rule, but the majority of cemented tungsten carbides produced for forming-die operations are made from mixed, medium, or coarse grains. The use of coarse grains increases as the cobalt content rises from about 12% to the maximum of 25%.

### Fracture Toughness

Currently under evaluation are two methods of determining the fracture toughness of tungsten carbides—the Palmquist method and the Terra-Tek method. The Palmquist method measures fracture toughness (the resistance of a material to crack propagation) by means of a Vickers hardness indentation and measurement of the resulting crack lengths. The Terra-Tek method measures fracture toughness by applying hydraulic pressure to a chevron slot in a cylindrical specimen. Both of these new methods are still under evaluation to determine their usefulness as indicators for production applications.

### Elastic Modulus

The elastic modulus of tungsten carbide is two to three times that of steel. If the same load were applied to a tungsten carbide punch and a steel punch (having the same geometry), the tungsten carbide punch would deflect only 1/3 to 1/2 as much as the steel punch.

### Corrosion Resistance

Since carbides themselves are virtually inert, the corrosion resistance of tungsten carbide is largely determined by the corrosion resistance of the binder metal. In a corrosive environment, such as that created by some grinding and metalforming lubricants or coolants, cobalt binder can be leached from the tungsten carbide. What remains is a skeletal surface structure of tungsten carbide particles. Since there is little cobalt binder left to hold the particles together, the particles can abrade away more easily. This can lead to edge chipping, accelerated wear, galling, and even breakage in some cases. Lubricant/coolant suppliers should be asked if their products are compatible with tungsten carbide. Lubricants containing active sulfur usually attack the cobalt binder. Normally, corrosion of metalforming punches and dies, such as those used for extrusion tooling, is not a serious problem. However, it is a problem with punches and dies used in the manufacturing of drawn and ironed beverage cans and some other stampings.

## GRADE CLASSIFICATIONS

The classification of cemented carbides is a controversial subject because the materials are available in a wide variety of compositions with different properties from many suppliers. The unofficial C-classification system commonly used in the United States for cutting tools, as discussed in Chapter 3, "Cutting Tool Materials," of Volume I, *Machining*, of this Handbook series, is not recommended for carbide forming dies because of the considerable overlapping of the classes.

In the *World Directory and Handbook of Hardmetals*,[2] the carbide grades produced by various manufacturers are listed and classified with respect to relative cobalt content, grain structure, and wear and impact resistance.

The most recent general classification of cemented carbides for forming operations is presented in Table 2-11. This data is published in *General Aspects of Tool Design and Tool Materials for Cold and Warm Forging*, Document No. 4/82, prepared by the International Cold Forging Group.[3] The appendix of this document lists the different grades of various carbide producers classified into Groups A through F (see Table 2-11).

The carbide cold-forming tools in examples discussed in this document have a life ranging from 200,000 to more than 1,000,000 parts, compared to a typical life of 10,000 to 300,000 parts for tools made from tool steels. Actual life, however, varies with the application and its severity, the complexity of the part being formed, the hardness and/or abrasiveness of the workpiece material, and the precision required.

## GRADE SELECTION

Past experience in using tungsten carbides is most helpful in selecting the proper grade or composition for a specific application. Good production records should be maintained so that the experience can be used as a guide for new applications, as well as to improve current applications. Such records should include the exact grade of carbide used; the workpiece material and condition; the type of lubricant and/or coolant used and method of application; the press speed and forces and press condition; the details of any tool failures and suspected causes; and the number of pieces produced.

For new applications, the supplier of the material should be contacted for technical help. When either cemented carbide or a tool steel are being considered, selection must be based upon the number of parts to be produced and the relevant need for wear resistance vs. strength. Consideration must also be given to the difference in cost between carbide and steel. The initial cost of carbide is significantly higher, and subsequent finishing can add substantially to the cost. Each application must be evaluated individually, comparing total cost of the tool with its expected life and overall maintenance costs. The number of parts produced per dressing (sharpening and/or polishing) should always be considered.

For impact applications, or when high strengths are required, tungsten carbide grades containing 11-25% cobalt are generally recommended, with materials having the higher cobalt content used for more severe impact operations. Applications requiring little or no impact are usually performed with carbides having a low cobalt content (6-10%). The more severe the wear application, the lower the cobalt content required. A compromise always has to be made, however, between wear resistance and strength because as the value of one property increases, the value of the other decreases.

Cemented tungsten carbides provide more gall resistance (resistance of metal pickup onto the tool) than tool steels. When galling occurs with carbide tools, special compositions containing tantalum and/or titanium carbide should be tried. For corrosive applications, carbide grades with a nickel binder can be used to reduce corrosive effects; and for some special low-impact applications, titanium-carbide-base, nickel-binder materials are useful.

Hot metalforming applications are generally performed with carbide grades having coarse grain structures and high cobalt contents, often with 3-5% tantalum carbide added, providing excellent impact strength and good resistance to thermal shock. One major producer of carbides generally supplies hot-forming punches made from tungsten carbide containing 12% cobalt and having a hardness of $R_A$88, although hot forming dies are usually made from a carbide containing 20% cobalt, with a hardness of $R_A$84.7. Such punches and dies have been applied successfully with workpiece temperatures to 1500° F (816° C) on a short exposure basis.

For backward-extrusion punches, a tungsten carbide grade

**TABLE 2-11**
**Compositions and Properties of Cemented Carbides for Forming**[3]

| Group | A | B | C | D | E | F |
|---|---|---|---|---|---|---|
| Composition, %: | | | | | | |
| Co | 5-7 | 8-10 | 11-13 | 14-17 | 18-22 | 23-30 |
| Ta or NbC | 0-2.5 | 0-2.5 | 0-2.5 | 0-2.5 | 0-2.5 | 0-2.5 |
| TiC, max | 1 | 1 | 1 | 1 | 1 | 1 |
| WC | Balance | Balance | Balance | Balance | Balance | Balance |
| Average WC grain size, $\mu$m ($\mu$in.) | 1-5 (0.00004-0.0002) | 1-5 (0.00004-0.0002) | 1-5 (0.00004-0.0002) | 1-5 (0.00004-0.0002) | 1-5 (0.00004-0.0002) | 1-5 (0.00004-0.0002) |
| Density, g/cm$^3$ (lb/in.$^3$) | 14.7-15.1 (0.53-0.55) | 14.4-14.7 (0.52-0.53) | 14.1-14.4 (0.51-0.52) | 13.8-14.2 (0.50-0.51) | 13.3-13.8 (0.48-0.50) | 12.6-13 (0.46-0.47) |
| Hardness: | | | | | | |
| room temperature: | | | | | | |
| Vickers | 1450-1550 | 1300-1400 | 1200-1250 | 1100-1150 | 950-1000 | 800-850 |
| $R_A$ | 90.5-91.0 | 89.0-90.0 | 88.0-88.5 | 87.0-87.5 | 85.5-86.0 | 83.5-84.0 |
| at 300° C (572° F): | | | | | | |
| Vickers | 1200 | 1050 | 1000 | 900 | 750 | 600 |
| Transverse rupture strength, N/mm$^2$ (ksi): | | | | | | |
| room temperature | >1800 (261) | >2000 (290) | >2200 (319) | >2500 (363) | >2500 (363) | >2300 (334) |
| 300° C (572° F) | >1600 (232) | >1800 (261) | >2000 (290) | >2300 (334) | >2200 (319) | >1900 (276) |
| Compressive strength, N/mm$^2$ (ksi) | | | | | | |
| room temperature | >4100 (595) | >3800 (551) | >3600 (522) | >3300 (479) | >3100 (450) | >2700 (392) |
| 300° F (572° F) | >3100 (450) | >2900 (421) | >2800 (406) | >2700 (392) | >2500 (363) | >2300 (334) |
| Young's modulus, N/mm$^2$ (ksi) | 630 000 (91,400) | 610 000 (88,500) | 570 000 (82,700) | 540 000 (78,300) | 500 000 (72,500) | 450 000 (65,300) |
| Thermal expansion coefficient, room temperature to 400° C (752° F): | | | | | | |
| per °C | $4.9 \times 10^{-6}$ | $5.0 \times 10^{-6}$ | $5.4 \times 10^{-6}$ | $5.6 \times 10^{-6}$ | $6.3 \times 10^{-6}$ | $7.0 \times 10^{-6}$ |
| per °F | $8.8 \times 10^{-6}$ | $9.0 \times 10^{-6}$ | $9.7 \times 10^{-6}$ | $10.1 \times 10^{-6}$ | $11.3 \times 10^{-6}$ | $12.6 \times 10^{-6}$ |

Note: N/mm$^2$ is equivalent in value to MPa.

containing 12% cobalt, with a hardness of $R_A$88, an average transverse rupture strength of 430,000 psi (2965 MPa), and a compressive strength of 635,000 psi (4378 MPa), is commonly used. When compressive loads on the front of the punches start to exceed 300,000 psi (2068 MPa), a grade with a lower cobalt content (11%), a higher hardness ($R_A$89.3), a higher compressive strength of 705,000 psi (4861 MPa), and the same transverse rupture strength is often employed.

For backward or forward-extrusion dies with medium impact requirements, a tungsten carbide containing 15.5% cobalt, with a hardness of $R_A$88.5, a transverse rupture strength of 475,000 psi (3275 MPa), and a compressive strength of 670,000 psi (4619 MPa), is widely used. For more severe impact requirements, a carbide with a higher cobalt content (19.5%) and a lower hardness ($R_A$86.8) can be employed. Lower cobalt grades, with increased wear resistance, are generally satisfactory for applications with less-severe impact requirements.

Heading dies are frequently made of coarse-grain tungsten carbides containing 20% or more cobalt. Powder-compacting dies are often made of a tungsten carbide containing as little as 5.5% cobalt, but punches, rams, and core pins for the PM process generally require carbides with about 11% cobalt.

## DESIGN CONSIDERATIONS

Special design techniques are required for the successful application of tungsten carbide materials. Sharp edges, notches, or abrupt changes in cross section are stress risers and should be avoided. Dies should be designed to keep the carbides in compression because the compressive strengths of these materials are much higher than their tensile strengths. Draw radii or approach angles, punch and die clearances, and reliefs are similar to those for steel dies. Bearing heights for carbide draw dies, however, may be lower (see Table 2-12), and back relief is required for best performance.

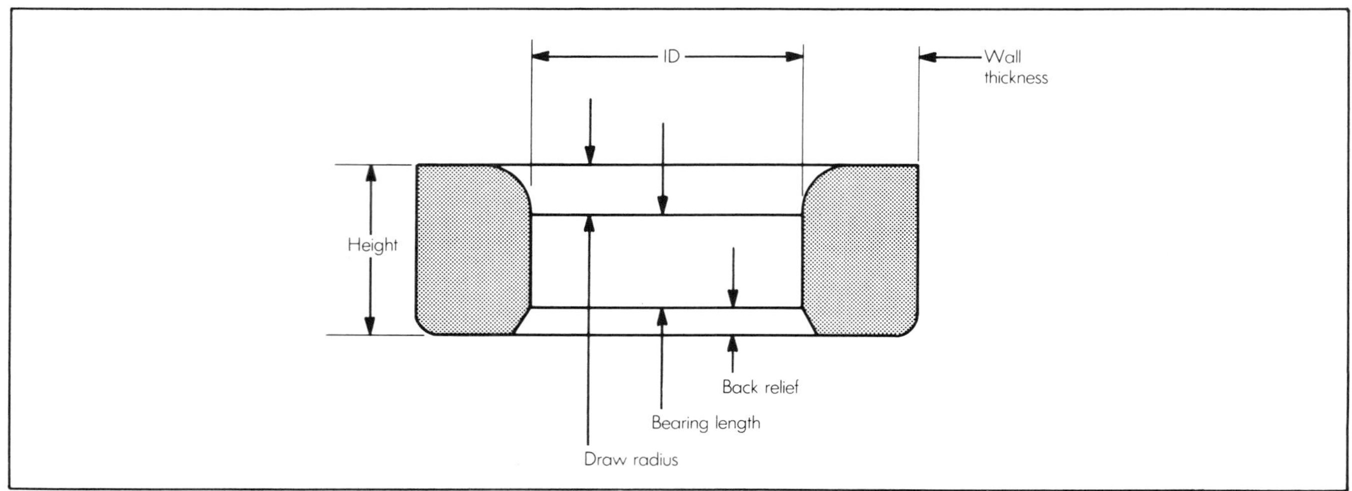


**TABLE 2-12**
**Typical Dimensions for Carbide Draw Dies**

| Inside Diameter, in. (mm) | Wall Thickness, in. (mm) | Bearing Length, in. (mm) | Back Relief Length, in. (mm) |
|---|---|---|---|
| to 1/2 (12.7) | 5/16 (7.9) | 1/8 (3.2) | 1/16 (1.6) |
| 1/2 to 1 (12.7 to 25.4) | 3/8 (9.5) | 3/16 (4.8) | 3/32 (2.4) |
| 1 to 1 1/2 (25.4 to 38.1) | 1/2 (12.7) | 1/4 (6.4) | 1/8 (3.2) |
| 1 1/2 to 2 1/2 (38.1 to 63.5) | 9/16 (14.3) | 5/16 (7.9) | 1/8 (3.2) |
| 2 1/2 to 5 (63.5 to 127) | 5/8 (15.9) | 3/8 (9.5) | 5/32 (4.0) |
| 5-10 (127 to 254) | 3/4 (19.1) | 7/16 (11.1) | 3/16 (4.8) |
| 10-15 (254 to 381) | 7/8 (22.2) | 1/2 (12.7) | 1/4 (6.4) |

When a carbide die insert is subjected to high-impact loads and internal bursting pressures, it must be adequately supported externally by pressing or shrinking the carbide ring into a hardened steel case. Suitable steels for die cases include SAE 4140, 4340, and 6145, as well as AISI Type H13 tool steel, hardened to $R_C$ 38-48. The outside diameter of the steel case should be two to three times the outside diameter of the carbide ring when high internal pressures are involved. While carbide can be shrunk into steel successfully, steel cannot generally be shrunk into carbide. With the thermal expansion of steel being about three times that of carbide, the steel can break the carbide with only a moderate increase in temperature.

Shrink allowances listed in Table 2-13 are only general guidelines. Actual calculations with the formulas given in Fig. 2-8 are preferred. Calculations should be performed for any new or unusual designs, such as dies for forming parts to complex geometry, for drawing or ironing thin-walled cylinders, for operations at elevated temperatures, and for applications that exert high internal pressures on the dies.

A die for blanking discs (see Fig. 2-9) incorporates a punch which is a carbide ring shrunk into a hardened steel case. When the carbide ring does not require a case or holder, it can be

**TABLE 2-13**
**Approximate Shrink Allowances for Carbide Cylinders Mounted Inside Steel Rings**

| Outside Diameter of Carbide Cylinder, in. (mm) | Medium Diametral Interference, in. (mm) | Heavy Diametral Interference, in. (mm) |
|---|---|---|
| 1/2 to 3/4 (12.7 to 19) | 0.0020 (0.051) | 0.0025 (0.064) |
| 3/4 to 1 (19 to 25.4) | 0.0025 (0.064) | 0.0038 (0.097) |
| 1 to 1 1/4 (25.4 to 31.7) | 0.0035 (0.089) | 0.0050 (0.127) |
| 1 1/4 to 1 1/2 (31.7 to 38.1) | 0.0040 (0.102) | 0.0063 (0.160) |
| 1 1/2 to 2 (38.1 to 50.8) | 0.0050 (0.127) | 0.0075 (0.190) |
| 2 to 2 1/2 (50.8 to 63.5) | 0.0070 (0.178) | 0.0100 (0.254) |
| 2 1/2 to 3 (63.5 to 76.2) | 0.0080 (0.203) | 0.0125 (0.318) |
| 3 to 3 1/2 (76.2 to 88.9) | 0.0100 (0.254) | 0.0150 (0.381) |
| 3 1/2 to 4 (88.9 to 101.6) | 0.0110 (0.279) | 0.0175 (0.444) |
| 4 to 5 (101.6 to 127) | 0.0140 (0.356) | 0.0200 (0.508) |
| 5 to 6 (127 to 152.4) | 0.0165 (0.419) | 0.0250 (0.635) |
| 6 to 7 (152.4 to 177.8) | 0.0200 (0.508) | 0.0300 (0.762) |

(*Kennametal Inc.*)

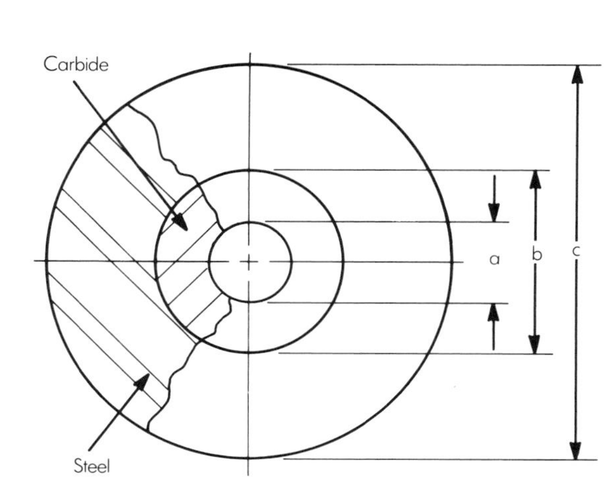


$\delta$ — Diametral interference
P — Pressure between cylinders
$E_s$ — Modulus of elasticity of steel
$E_c$ — Modulus of elasticity of carbide
$\mu_s$ — Poisson's ratio of steel
$\mu_c$ — Poisson's ratio of carbide

$$\delta = \frac{bP}{E_s}\left(\frac{b^2 + c^2}{c^2 - b^2} + \mu_s\right) + \frac{bP}{E_c}\left(\frac{a^2 + b^2}{b^2 - a^2} + \mu_c\right)$$

If a steel ring is to be shrunk on a solid carbide cylinder, the diametral interference can be calculated by considering "a" to equal zero in the above formula. In the design shown, the tangential stress at the inner surface of the steel due to shrink is:

$$\sigma_t = \frac{P\,(b^2 + c^2)}{c^2 - b^2}$$

The maximum compressive prestress at the inner surface of carbide due to shrink is:

$$\sigma_t = \frac{-\,2\,Pb^2}{b^2 - a^2}$$

**Fig. 2-8 Methods of determining diametral interference and compressive prestress when shrinking carbide rings into steel cases. (*Kennametal Inc.*)**

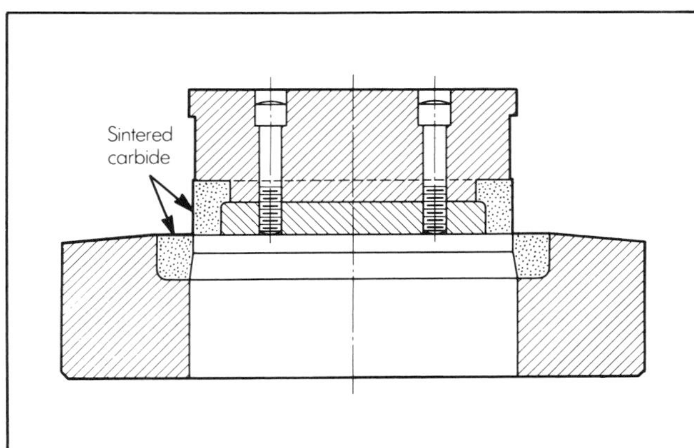


**Fig. 2-9 Punch and die with tungsten carbide inserts for blanking discs.**

bolted or clamped directly in place (see Fig. 2-10).

For blanking dies, carbide inserts may incorporate soft nickel-iron or steel plugs (usually brazed in place), which are drilled and tapped for hold-down screws and dowels (see Fig. 2-11). A high-nickel (35-40%), low-expansion alloy is recommended for plugs or tapping inserts. Another method of retention sometimes employed is to tap holes directly in the carbide by electrical discharge machining (EDM). This method is only employed when space does not allow the use of plugs or tapping inserts, because EDM often results in chipping of the carbide unless extreme care is exercised.

Draw dies, such as the one shown in Fig. 2-12, have a solid carbide punch and a carbide die ring shrunk into its case. In designs with sleeved carbide draw punches, retention is generally accomplished with an inner steel shank mechanically holding the carbide in place (see Fig. 2-13). The carbide dies are shrunk into steel cases.

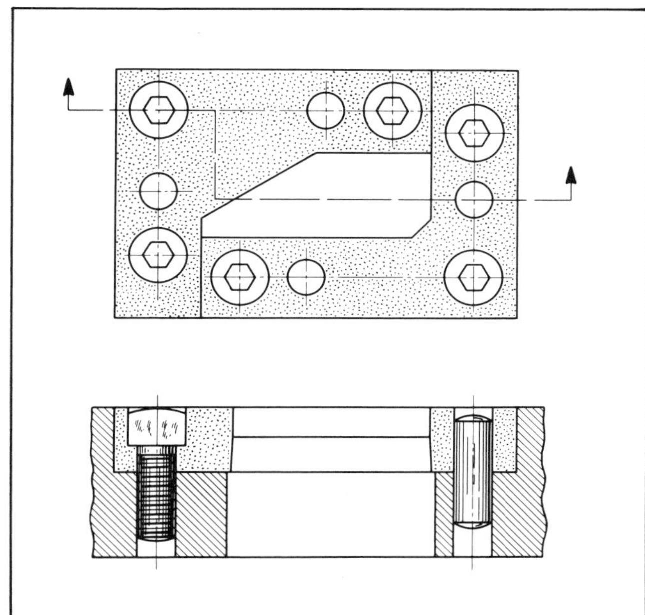

**Fig. 2-10 Carbide die held with screws and dowels.**

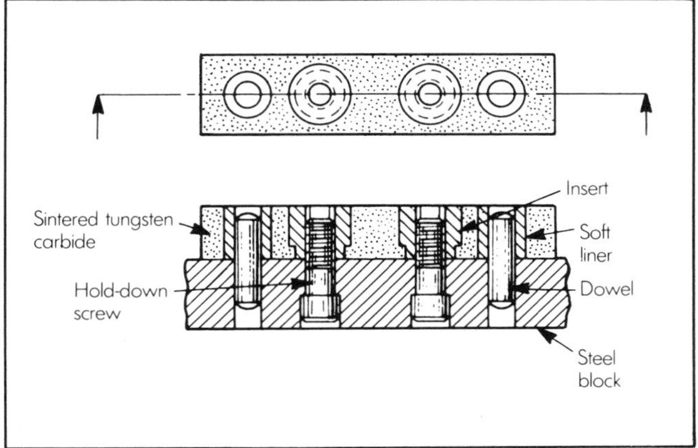


**Fig. 2-11 Carbide blanking die having soft steel plugs for screws and dowels.**

# CEMENTED TUNGSTEN CARBIDE

Dies using carbide inserts or segments (see Fig. 2-14) are similar in design to sectional steel dies. Such dies are generally used for applications in which irregular shapes are to be blanked or punched, or in which maintaining close relationships between holes in the die segments is necessary.

## FINISHING OF CARBIDES

Unsintered, compacted carbide parts can be formed to the required shape by conventional machining. These parts are dewaxed and generally presintered at a low temperature, 350-850° C (662-1562° F). However, because precise tolerances cannot be maintained during sintering, because shrinkage encountered is variable, and because the as-sintered surface finish is generally between 50-100 $\mu$in. (1.27 and 2.54 $\mu$m), subsequent finishing is normally required for metalforming punches and dies. Finishing can be done by diamond-wheel grinding or carefully applied EDM.

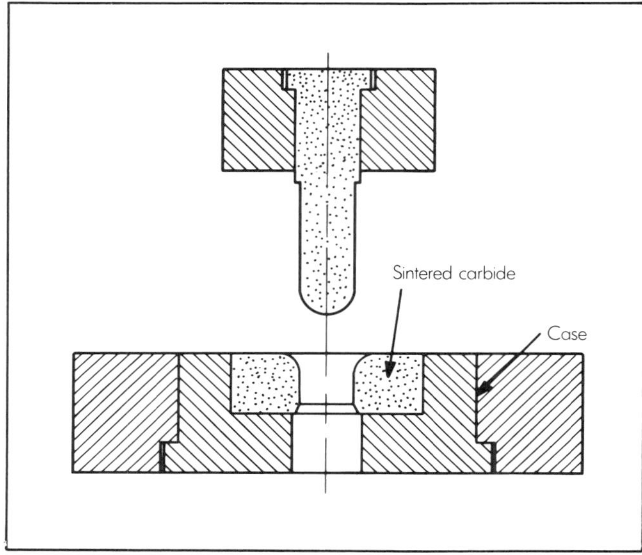


**Fig. 2-12 Draw die with solid carbide punch and carbide die shrunk into its case.**

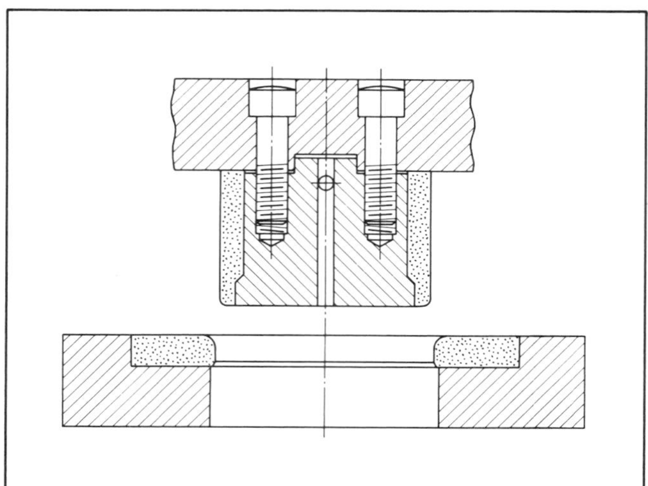

**Fig. 2-13 Method of retaining a sleeved carbide punch.**

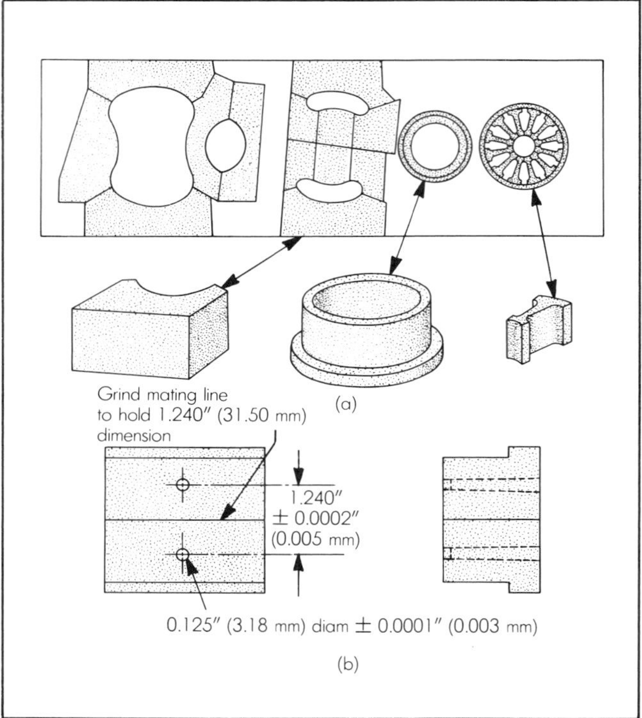


**Fig. 2-14 Dies with carbide segments: (a) segments held in position with bolts and dowels (not shown); (b) mating surfaces of segments are precision ground for required dimension between holes.**

### Grinding Practice

Good grinding equipment and techniques are essential for finishing tungsten carbides and can mean the difference between success or failure of the tools. Extreme care must be exercised, particularly with materials having low cobalt contents and high hardnesses. If grinding is done incorrectly (with excessive pressure or a loaded wheel) or too rapidly, small surface cracks (crazing) occur, which may or may not be detected after the grinding operation. If undetected, the cracks may cause premature failure of the tools because carbide is very notch sensitive.

Cemented tungsten carbides having high cobalt contents (20-25%) can sometimes be machined by turning with single-point diamond tools, or with high-hardness, cemented carbide cutting tools, and small stock removals. It is also possible to use silicon carbide grinding wheels for shaping cemented carbide parts containing 15% or more cobalt. It is always recommended, however, that diamond wheel grinding be used, particularly for finishing die components.

**Grinding wheels.** Diamond wheels permit fast stock removal. Wheels having 100-150 grit size are recommended for roughing; and 180-220 grit size or finer, for finishing. A reinforced Bakelite core adds to wheel stability, and metal cores should be avoided. Metal-coated diamond abrasives often provide increased grinding ratios (the volume of carbide removed per unit volume of wheel wear). Soft grade wheels are preferable because of the hardness of the carbides. When the wheels have been mounted, the mounts should stay on the wheels during the full life of the wheels.

Grinding pressure helps to keep the wheel free cutting, but periodic dressing of the diamond wheels with a soft silicon carbide stick is recommended to keep the wheel face open. Brake-controlled dressing attachments placed on the grinding machine table and fitted with silicon carbide wheels are often used for trueing the diamond wheels.

**Grinding fluid.** A generous, continuous flow of grinding fluid should be directed at the contact area between wheel and workpiece because intermittent cooling can produce thermal cracks. The use of a proper fluid, compatible with the carbide being ground, and subsequent monitoring and maintenance of the fluid are essential to avoid leaching of the cobalt binder. The ground or partially ground die components should be wiped dry immediately after grinding. If necessary, the components can be cleaned with isopropyl alcohol.

A thin solution of good, sulfur-free, soluble oil and water (80 parts water to 1 part oil) has been found satisfactory as a grinding fluid. The pH of the fluid should have a nominal value of 8.5, and the alkalinity should be low, about 2000 ppm. The fluid should be kept clean and inspected regularly for pH level, alkalinity, and suspended solids.

**Grinding machines.** The machines employed to grind cemented tungsten carbides must be rigid and in good condition, with sufficient capacity to hold the weight of the punch or die components.

Wheel speeds should be about 5000 sfm (25.4 m/s). Table speeds should be approximately 85 sfm (26 m/min) for rough grinding, and faster for finishing. Cross feeds of 1/3 to 1/2 the wheel width are generally best for roughing; and cross feeds of about 1/32" (0.8 mm) are usually best for final finishing passes. Down feeds should be small, in increments of 0.0001" (0.003 mm).

## Polishing Die Components

In most instances, especially for drawing and extrusion dies as well as many forming, shaping, and PM compacting dies, a polished finish is needed on the carbide components. Polishing is generally done with diamond paste or diamond polishing compounds. For flat surfaces, diamond lapping operations are most suitable. For contoured surfaces, special tools and fine-diamond polishing compounds are used. Surfaces of the die components should be free of nicks, grinding grooves, and cracks. Surface finishes of 1-2 μin. (0.025-0.051 μm) are sometimes specified.

## Electrical Discharge Machining

Sintered carbide materials can be formed by electrical discharge machining (EDM), either with the solid-electrode or traveling-wire technique. With either of these methods, however, there is always some surface damage to the carbide. This is the result of extremely high temperatures (at the vaporization point of the material) in a concentrated area, which causes thermal cracks in the carbide surface.

The severity of cracking depends primarily upon the current (amperage) used in the EDM process. Depths of cracks can range from 0.0001-0.020" (0.003-0.51 mm), but are generally less than 0.001" (0.03 mm). Such cracks should be removed by a light EDM finishing pass, followed by grinding, polishing, and/or honing. Good results have been obtained in removing cracks by the abrasive-flow finishing process, using semisolid or liquid abrasive carriers.

## TROUBLESHOOTING

Fracture failures occur with cemented tungsten carbide dies because the materials do not yield significantly before the initiation of cracks. Accurate failure analysis is necessary to improve die performance. As discussed previously in this section, detailed production records should be maintained so that the most common failure patterns are evident.

## Backward Extrusion Punches

A transverse break (at right angles to the axis of the punch) is a result of punch bending. This is often caused by press misalignment and should be corrected immediately. Improved tool life may also be obtained by using a tungsten carbide composition with higher strength. Caution is necessary, however, because a tungsten carbide composition that is too soft will upset (shorten in length with a corresponding increase in diameter).

Another type of failure occurs when the punch tip (usually a disc-shaped piece) pulls off and away from the working end at, or just behind, the punch land. This is a result of tensile stresses that develop as the workpiece is stripped from the punch during withdrawal. It may be caused by improper or insufficient lubricant. The land area should be checked for galling. The punch entry may be too deep, causing excessive friction on withdrawal. Regular repolishing of the working surfaces also reduces the frequency of punch tip pull-off. Lubricating the top and bottom surfaces of the workpiece material is also helpful.

The clothespin fracture is the most common mode of failure for a backward-extrusion punch. It often starts due to compressive yield of the tool material, which results in surface tension around the periphery of the punch at the working end. This leads to the development of tensile cracks at right angles to the tensile stress (along the axis of the punch at the working end). With further use, a crack progresses toward the center of the punch to the opposite side, eventually resulting in a split punch. These types of cracks may go straight across the face of the punch or may form a pie-shaped segment.

Small surface scratches at the waterfall radius or on the working land of the punch may develop as a result of use; for example, a hard particle forced between the punch and the workpiece could cause small surface scratches. Grinding or EDM grooves or cracks may also be present in this critical working area. Regardless of the source, these scratches do represent stress risers and may lead to premature failure. To improve tool life, the forces on the punch may be reduced by a change in geometry or a change in properties of the material being worked.

## Forward and Backward-Extrusion Dies

Axial fractures are generally the result of insufficient interference between the carbide die and the steel support ring. Stress calculations should be rechecked to assure that the carbide die stays in compression during the maximum working load. Dies with hexagonal shapes usually fracture along the fillet. The largest possible radius should be used to reduce this stress concentration.

It is difficult to determine the cause of most circumferential fractures. A change in the cross-sectional area of the die or the die case produces an uneven stress. If this stress difference is great enough, fracture may occur during use of the die. Discontinuous stresses (highly stressed areas next to low or zero stress areas) are often set up by die or workpiece geometry, and may result in circumferential fracture. Sharp corners, notches, or grinding grooves set up stress concentrations which can cause both circumferential and axial fractures, depending upon the direction of the stress concentration and the loads involved.

Galling (buildup of workpiece material on the tool) may also lead to premature fracture, because it can increase the load applied to the die. Regular maintenance (punch or die polishing) minimizes this problem. Improper selection of the tungsten carbide grade is also a cause for failure. It may be necessary to conduct a complete metallurgical analysis of the tungsten carbide to determine the cause of failure.

As previously mentioned, any tungsten carbide grade used for hot forming oxidizes if the tool reaches and maintains a temperature of 1000° F (538° C) or more. The severity of oxidation depends upon time and temperature. The oxide layer that develops leads to rapid wear. If attempting thermal stress relief is desirable, a temperature of 800° C (1472° F) in an inert atmosphere for 2-3 hours should be used initially. Some modification of time and temperature may be necessary.

### Can Tooling

Can-body punches employed in ironing operations normally wear out by a corrosive-wear mechanism. This is inevitable, but tool life can be prolonged by using a noncorrosive coolant which is cleaned regularly and maintained at the alkalinity and pH previously discussed. The use of a corrosion-resistant grade of carbide may also increase tool life significantly. Carbides having a corrosion-resistant binder, however, are not generally as strong as carbides having a cobalt binder.

Can ironing dies are worn by the same mechanism as described for can-body punches. They may also crack axially if insufficient interference exists between the carbide die and the steel case, or if the bore of the case has a rough surface finish. Cupping, cut-edge, and draw dies are also susceptible to corrosion wear. Cut-edge dies may chip due to misalignment, which must be corrected. Heavy stock or hard workpiece material may also cause chipping. The use of a stronger grade carbide, one with more cobalt, may help, but there is no substitute for accurate alignment, precise and rigid die construction, and proper maintenance practices.

# NONFERROUS METALS

Several nonferrous metals, including aluminum bronzes, beryllium coppers, zinc-based alloys, antimonial lead, and bismuth alloys, are used for dies and molds, generally for specific applications.

## ALUMINUM BRONZES

Proprietary aluminum bronzes (see Table 2-14) are used primarily for dies and molds to form materials when scratching, scoring, or galling cannot be tolerated. These materials are available as sand castings, centrifugal castings, and extruded shapes. They are also available in the form of electrodes for weld overlay on the working surfaces of steel or cast-iron dies, or for the weld repair of dies. Different alloys of these so-called hard bronzes have Brinell hardnesses ranging from 207 to 375. The harder alloys are more difficult to machine, but the cast shapes require only minimum machining. Heat treatment is not required, thus minimizing finishing requirements.

### Advantages

The major advantage of aluminum bronzes is their excellent resistance to scratching, scoring, and galling of the workpiece materials. They also have good resistance to impact and deformation because of their high compressive strengths, which results in long life. A low coefficient of friction, about 0.08 compared to 0.11 for many tool steels, allows easier, smoother metal flow. Easy repair is another important advantage.

### Applications

Aluminum bronze dies and molds are usually employed in applications in which smooth surface finishes are required on the workpieces. They are also employed in applications in which materials must be formed that are difficult to produce with steel dies. Aluminum bronzes are not recommended for blanking or forging dies. Materials formed include low-carbon and stainless steels; aluminum, magnesium, and titanium alloys; and prefinished materials. The aluminum bronzes are sometimes used as inserts for cast-iron and cast-steel dies employed for high production requirements. The higher cost of these materials is generally offset by savings in finishing the workpieces. For large cast-iron or steel dies, for which aluminum bronze would be uneconomical, the radii of the dies are often overlaid using aluminum bronze welding rods.

One common application is deep-drawing dies, especially when forming the tougher grades of stainless steels. In addition to the improved quality of parts produced, smaller blanks can be used because draw beads are not necessary. Higher pressure-pad pressures, however, are necessary. In one application for deep drawing stainless-steel cooking utensils, die life was doubled, maintenance was reduced 45%, and workpiece finishing costs were lowered 25%. Aluminum bronzes are not recommended for drawing copper, brass, bronze, or unpickled steels.

Draw rings, pressure pads, and noses of steel punches are sometimes made of aluminum bronzes, especially when they are to be used in forming tough stainless steels. Galling and scratching of the workpiece surfaces are eliminated because there is no metal pickup, and long life results due to the low friction between the dissimilar metals.

Forming rolls for the production of stainless steel tubing and other shapes are often made from aluminum bronzes. In addition to improving workpiece finish and wear resistance, such rolls resist adhesion of welding spatter. Straightening dies for roll-formed aluminum house siding are also made from aluminum bronzes.

Other applications for aluminum bronzes include bending dies for press brakes, wing dies for vertical tube benders, dies for rotary swaging of stainless steel and aluminum alloy tubing, and gang arbors (snakes) for bending tubing.

### Die Design

The design of dies made from aluminum bronzes varies with the operation to be performed, workpiece material (thickness and condition), type of press or machine used, ram and hold-down pressures, surface finish desired, lubricant employed, and quantity of workpieces required.

When used for drawing, the die must be solidly supported and well seated in a cavity of a steel or iron member. A shrink-type interference fit of 0.001 in./in. (mm/mm) of diameter is

**TABLE 2-14**
**Compositions, Properties, and Applications of Aluminum Bronzes for Dies**

| Ampco Alloy | Chemical Composition, % Al | Fe | Others | Cu | Ultimate Compressive Strength, ksi (MPa) | Brinell Hardness, 3000 kg Load | Rockwell Hardness | Applications |
|---|---|---|---|---|---|---|---|---|
| 20: | | | | | | | | |
| sand cast | 11.0-12.0 | 3.2-4.5 | 0.50 | Balance | 150 (1034) | 212 | B96 | For short-run production and medium-duty requirements |
| centrifugally cast | | | | | 155 (1069) | 223 | B97 | |
| extruded | | | | | 155 (1069) | 207 | B95 | |
| 21: | | | | | | | | |
| sand cast | 12.5-13.5 | 3.7-5.2 | 0.50 | Balance | 175 (1207) | 286 | C29 | |
| centrifugally cast | | | | | 190 (1310) | 286 | C29 | |
| extruded | | | | | 190 (1310) | 286 | C29 | |
| 22: | | | | | | | | |
| sand cast | 13.6-14.6 | 4.2-5.7 | 0.50 | Balance | 200 (1379) | 332 | C35 | For long-run production and severe-duty requirements |
| centrifugally cast | | | | | 210 (1448) | 332 | C35 | |
| extruded | | | | | 210 (1448) | 332 | C35 | |
| 25: | | | | | | | | |
| sand cast | 14.5-16.0 | 4.0-7.0 | 3.8-8.0 | Balance | 220 (1517) | 364 | C38 | |
| centrifugally cast | | | | | 225 (1551) | 375 | C39 | |
| extruded | | | | | 225 (1551) | 375 | C39 | |

(*Ampco Metal Div., Ampco-Pittsburgh Corp.*)

suggested. The usual procedure is to shrink the aluminum bronze die by packing it in dry ice, rather than to expand the backup member.

The radii on draw dies and punches must be generous. For draw dies, the radii should be about four times the thickness of the metal to be drawn; for punches, the radii should be about eight times the metal thickness. Clearance between the punch and die should be proportional to the metal thickness plus an allowance (generally 7-20% of the metal thickness) to minimize wall friction.

Composite or segmental dies consist of rings or narrow strips of aluminum bronze placed in retainers at wear areas on cast-iron or steel dies. For long production runs, full rings or blocks of aluminum bronze are sometimes used. Larger radii are required and higher pressures must be exerted on the pressure pads when composite dies are employed. Solid dies permit smaller radii, lower pressures on the pressure pads, and the use of smaller blanks. With solid dies, draws can be made closer to the edges of the blanks, thus reducing material losses when trimming.

## Machining and Finishing Dies

Aluminum bronzes have the inherent ability to develop very smooth surface finishes when machined properly. Turning, boring, facing, and similar operations are generally performed with conventional carbide cutting tools. For roughing operations, cutting speeds to 350 sfm (107 m/min) are employed, with a feed rate of 0.005-0.020 ipr (0.13-0.51 mm/rev). For finishing, cutting speeds to 800 sfm (244 m/min) and feed rates of 0.002-0.005 ipr (0.05-0.13 mm/rev) are recommended. A soluble-oil cutting fluid is generally used.

Drilling and tapping of aluminum bronzes are difficult and should be avoided if other methods of assembling the die components can be used. If drilling is required, carbide-tipped, straight-flute drills should be employed, with a cutting speed of 70-150 sfm (21.3-45.7 m/min) and a feed rate of 0.002-0.007 ipr (0.05-0.18 mm/rev). Holes should be chamfered before tapping is performed to prevent edge breakout. Fair results have been obtained by using taps having a 0° rake angle, a 10-15° chamfer for a length of two to three threads, and a spiral point extending beyond the first full thread.

Grinding of aluminum bronzes is generally done with vitrified-bond, silicon-carbide or aluminum-oxide wheels, with wheel speeds of 5000-6000 sfm (25.4-30.5 m/s) and work speeds of 25-150 rpm. Polishing can be done with silicon-carbide abrasive cloth having a grain size of 240 or 320. Crocus cloth is sometimes used for final finishing.

## Die Operation

For optimum performance, the first 35 or so workpieces produced with a new die made of aluminum bronze should be formed using a strained, thick slurry of water and unslacked lime as a buffing compound. Alternatively, this run-in can be done using a silicon-Teflon dry lubricant. After the run-in period, conventional sulfur-free lubricants can be used, with a dry lubricant added if desired. For drawing stainless steels, the lubricant should have a higher film strength than that used for drawing carbon steels. It is essential that smooth blanks, without burrs or turned edges, be used with aluminum bronze dies.

## BERYLLIUM COPPERS

Cast alloys of beryllium, cobalt, and copper have characteristics comparable to those of the proprietary aluminum bronzes just discussed. These alloys are sometimes used for molds to form plastics, plunger tips for die-casting dies, and other components. Ample exhaust ventilation is essential in making such components to minimize concentrations of beryllium in the air, which can cause a health hazard.

## ZINC-BASED ALLOYS

Zinc alloys are used extensively for punches, dies, and molds to form, draw, blank, and trim steel and aluminum alloys, plastics, and other materials. Applications are predominant in the automotive and aircraft industries for producing prototypes and limited quantities of large parts. Frequently, one member of a two-piece die set is made of zinc alloy and the other (usually, the punch) is made of a softer material, such as antimonial lead, especially for drop hammer operations on soft sheet metals. Zinc alloy construction is generally required for both die members when steel sheets are being formed, when sharp definition is needed, when production runs are long, or when binder rings are necessary.

Tools made from these alloys are often capable of forming 10,000 or more parts before they have to be replaced or repaired. When abraded and worn areas are repaired by welding, 25,000 or more parts can be produced. There may be some creep of the material under extreme-pressure conditions, and close tolerances cannot be maintained in blanking operations.

### Advantages

Zinc alloys provide a low cost and fast method of making punches, dies, and molds having a dense, smooth working surface. These materials are easy to melt, cast, machine, grind, polish, weld, remelt, and recast. Casting provides sharp definition of contours because of the fluidity of the alloys, and accuracy of the castings minimizes the need for costly finishing.

Other important advantages of these alloys include no scratching of the workpiece material, good abrasion resistance, inherent self-lubricating properties, and high impact and compressive strengths. Their low melting temperatures reduce energy costs, and the tools can be remelted and recast a number of times without loss of mechanical properties. Care must be taken, however, to ensure that contaminants, such as iron or lead, are minimized and that excessive casting temperatures, which might cause de-alloying and immoderate grain growth, are avoided.

### Alloys Available

Various proprietary zinc alloys, some called Kirksite alloys, are available. Many contain about 3 1/2 to 4 1/2% aluminum, 2 1/2 to 3 1/2% copper, and 0.02 to 0.10% magnesium. Some contain additional magnesium or copper, or minor amounts of nickel or titanium. As with zinc die-casting alloys, practically pure zinc (a minimum of 99.99%) is used in these alloys to keep the impurities of lead, tin, iron, and cadmium low.

Mechanical properties vary with the specific alloy. Typical property values include tensile strengths of 30-40 ksi (207-276 MPa), compressive strengths of about 65 ksi (448 MPa), and Brinell hardnesses to approximately 105.

### Casting Practice

Most zinc alloys melt at 717-745° F (381-396° C) and are cast at 800-850° F (427-454° C). During solidification to room temperature, shrinkage is about 0.13"/ft (10.8 mm/m) and the castings weigh approximately 0.25 lb/in.$^3$ (6.9 g/cm$^3$).

Zinc alloys are generally sand cast in plaster (sometimes wood) patterns or in preformed plaster, but rarely in steel molds. For superior results, shrink patterns are made for all die members (allowing for the thickness of the workpiece material), which are cast in sand. Mounting surfaces are machined, critical die surfaces may be checked against model surfaces, and hand grinding is performed for final accuracy and/or clearances. In some cases, only one die member is cast and it is used as a mold for casting the opposite die member, usually of lead. A separating layer of insulating material must be used in such cases. Urethane, cast in place, is also used for some applications. Details of casting procedures are presented in Chapter 16, "Casting."

### Machining the Castings

With accurate patterns or molds and correct casting techniques, little machining or finishing of zinc alloy castings is required. Machining of the castings, however, presents no problems. It should be done at high cutting speeds with light cuts, using polished tools having generous rake and clearance angles. Drills used should have large spiral flutes, thin webs, an included point angle of 100°, and a lip clearance angle of at least 10°. When made from high-speed steels, the drills should operate at a cutting speed of 300 sfm (91 m/min) or more.

For turning and boring the castings, high-speed steel or cast alloy tools are generally used. A top rake angle of 10°, an end clearance angle of 15°, and a side clearance angle of 50° are recommended for the tools. If carbide tools are used, the end clearance should be under, not over, 8°. A cutting speed of 300 sfm (91 m/min) is suggested for roughing operations, and 600 sfm (183 m/min) for finishing.

Cutters with staggered, coarse teeth, 10° clearance angles, and 10° rake angles are used for milling at high speeds. Coarse-tooth blades (6 teeth per inch) are suggested for sawing, with a blade speed of 150 fpm (45.7 m/min) or more. Feed pressure exerted during sawing should be sufficient to remove about 9 in.$^2$/min (58 cm$^2$/min) of stock.

Zinc alloy castings can be plated with any common metal coating, including hard chromium.

## ANTIMONIAL LEAD

Punches made of antimonial lead are sometimes used with dies made of zinc alloy, especially for drop hammer operations on soft metals. Lead-antimony alloys are available with various percentages of antimony to suit specific requirements. The balance of the contents of these alloys is lead, but from 0.25-0.75% tin is often added to improve the casting properties. The alloys generally best suited for forming operations contain 6-7% antimony, which provides the best combination of mechanical properties, including adequate ductility, hardness, and tensile strength. These alloys have a melting range of 539-552° F (282-289° C), a Brinell hardness of about 12, a tensile strength of approximately 7000 psi (48.3 MPa), and a density of 0.39 lb/in.$^3$ (10.8 g/cm$^3$).

Antimonial-lead punches are made by casting into the cavity of zinc alloy dies. The antimonial lead is sufficiently ductile to accurately assume the dimensions of the zinc alloy die under impact. These alloys, like zinc alloys, can be remelted and recast.

## BISMUTH ALLOYS

The alloys of bismuth, often called low-melting-point alloys, are used chiefly as matrix material for securing punch and die parts in small die sets, and as-cast punches and dies for short-run forming and drawing operations. The compositions and properties of several bismuth alloys are presented in Table 2-15.

**TABLE 2-15**
**Compositions and Properties of Some Bismuth Alloys**

| | | | | | | | | |
|---|---|---|---|---|---|---|---|---|
| | Composition, % | | | | | | | |
| Bismuth | 44.7 | 49.0 | 50.0 | 42.5 | 48.0 | 55.5 | 58.0 | 40.0 |
| Lead | 22.6 | 18.0 | 26.7 | 37.7 | 28.5 | 44.5 | --- | --- |
| Tin | 8.3 | 12.0 | 13.3 | 11.3 | 14.5 | --- | 42.0 | 60.0 |
| Cadmium | 5.3 | --- | 10.0 | 8.5 | --- | --- | --- | --- |
| Other | 19.1 | 21.0 | --- | --- | 9.0 | --- | --- | --- |
| | Properties | | | | | | | |
| Melting temperature, °F (°C) | 117 (47) | 136 (58) | 158 (70) | 159-194 (70-90) | 217-440 (103-227) | 255 (124) | 281 (138) | 281-388 (138-198) |
| Tensile strength, ksi (MPa) | 5.4 (37.2) | 6.3 (43.4) | 5.99 (41.3) | 5.4 (37.2) | 13 (89.6) | 6.4 (44.1) | 8 (55.2) | 8 (55.2) |
| Bhn | 12 | 14 | 9.2 | 9 | 19 | 10.2 | 22 | 2 |

# PLASTICS FOR DIES AND MOLDS

Many dies and molds, as well as jigs, fixtures, and models, are made from plastics, discussed in Chapter 18, "Plastics Forming." Die and mold applications are primarily for prototypes and limited-volume production runs.

## ADVANTAGES OF USING PLASTICS

A major advantage of using plastics for dies and molds is the short lead time needed with them. If patterns, prototype parts, or models are available for casting or for layup of the resins, plastics can be molded to complex contours quickly, in a fraction of the time required to produce metal dies or molds. Other advantages include their low initial cost, minimum finishing requirements, light weight, and toughness and flexibility.

The small amount of machining sometimes required can be done readily, as discussed in Chapter 18; and the tools can be repaired and reworked easily. The light weight of the tools facilitates moving them to other presses or machines. Resiliency of the plastics ensures smooth finishes on the workpieces.

## LIMITATIONS OF PLASTICS

The strengths, 10-40 ksi (69-276 MPa), and hardnesses of plastics are lower than those of metallic die materials. As a result, the requirements of the application must be considered and the die or mold carefully designed. Low edge strength, reduced wear resistance, and limited resistance to elevated temperatures must be given careful consideration.

The normal life of dies and molds made of plastics is the production of about 20,000 parts. Surface coating or casting, however, can generally restore the tools to their initial conditions. The use of metallic inserts at areas of highest stress extends the life of such tools.

Smooth workpiece blanks are essential for the successful use of dies made from plastics. The low tensile strengths and soft surfaces of plastics do not withstand the shearing action of burrs or rough edges.

## TYPICAL APPLICATIONS

Plastics are used extensively for dies, primarily for forming aluminum alloys and other light metals, but also for forming low-carbon and stainless steels. For blanking and trimming operations, the dies are generally provided with metal inserts. Ironing of wall sections is not recommended since a sufficient compressive force cannot be obtained to perform the required sizing. Spanking or bottoming in dies made of plastics is of little value for the removal of wrinkles formed in metal stampings.

Many molds for forming parts are now being made from plastics. Other applications include stretch forming dies (form blocks), snakes for bending, and dies for stretch forming operations.

## PLASTICS USED

The plastics originally used for dies and molds were predominantly polyesters and phenolics. Instability of these materials, however, caused dimensional changes that required frequent checking and modification of the tools. Now, the harder epoxies and improved polyurethane resins available are being used practically exclusively for dies and molds. Graphite fibers and fabrics are being employed to produce heat-resistant molds of plastics for forming parts made from composite materials.

### Polyesters

Polyesters are used with glass reinforcements, containing up to 50% glass in the form of cloth, strands, or chopped fibers. Applications are for molds to produce polyester workpieces on which dimensional tolerances are not important.

Advantages of polyesters include low cost (when considering resin cost alone) and good mechanical properties, such as durability, strength, and heat resistance (when formulated with special resins). Polyesters are nonreactive with other materials and are essentially noncorrosive. Limitations include low dimensional stability and shrink rates that vary between 2 and 7% when the polyesters are used as laminates.

# CHAPTER 2

## PLASTICS FOR DIES AND MOLDS

### Phenolics

Phenolics were used for stretch forming blocks and some molds and models; however, they are seldom used now.

### Epoxies

Epoxies, together with polyurethanes (discussed next), have virtually preempted the field of plastics for dies and molds. Advantages of epoxies include high dimensional stability, low shrinkage, nonreactivity with other materials, and excellent chemical resistance. Room-temperature curing simplifies toolmaking, and excellent adhesion to most materials facilitates the fabrication of dies and molds. Good wettability aids the impregnation of fiberglass cloth when used for laminated construction.

Epoxies for tooling applications are available as casting and laminating resins in a wide range of viscosities and are compounded with a variety of additives to suit specific requirements. Most epoxies are rigid and have low impact strength, which can cause failure in some applications. Good hygiene practices and proper protective measures are recommended.

### POLYURETHANES

Polyurethanes are a versatile family of plastics that combine the flexibility of rubber with the hardness of structural plastics. The many available polyurethanes, commonly called urethanes, are made by chemically combining a variety of alcohols with specific isocyanates to provide desired properties for specific applications. Recently developed hybrid urethanes have good impact resistance and toughness and are not moisture sensitive, permitting them to be laminated with fiberglass.

A major application for urethanes is low-cost die pads for forming, drawing, and bending. The pads generally have no shape, but require containment on their bottoms and sides. The urethane reacts to the displacement of a punch in much the same way as a liquid reacts; the volume remains constant while the shape changes. (Refer to Chapter 10, "Bending and Straightening.")

Vertical force of the press ram is changed to uniform, multidirectional force on the workpiece, and the urethane returns to its original shape when the ram rises. Advantages include minimum stretching and thinning of the workpiece material and compensation for variations in thickness of the starting blanks and for misalignment of the press or die components. Since the urethane is nonmarking, prepainted and prepolished materials can be formed. The same die can often be used to form several workpieces.

Urethanes are now being used more extensively than rubber for diaphragms employed in flexible-die forming processes (discussed in Chapter 4, "Sheet Metal Blanking and Forming," and Chapter 5, "Presses for Sheet Metal Forming"). Other applications for urethanes include punches (the urethanes usually being bonded to steel plates), wiping edges for forming and flanging dies, internal supports (snakes) for tube bending, and pressure pads and strippers.

### DIE AND MOLD CONSTRUCTION

Dies and molds made from plastics are generally constructed by casting, facing, laminating, or a combination of these methods.

### Casting Dies and Molds

Casting of plastics (see Fig. 2-15) is similar to normal casting procedures discussed in Chapter 16, "Casting." A prototype workpiece, wood or plaster model, or pattern can be used as the mold, with suitable framework. To reduce the weight and cost of large castings, lightweight cores are often constructed. Stones, gravel, sand, sawdust, and walnut-shell aggregates are used as core filler materials.

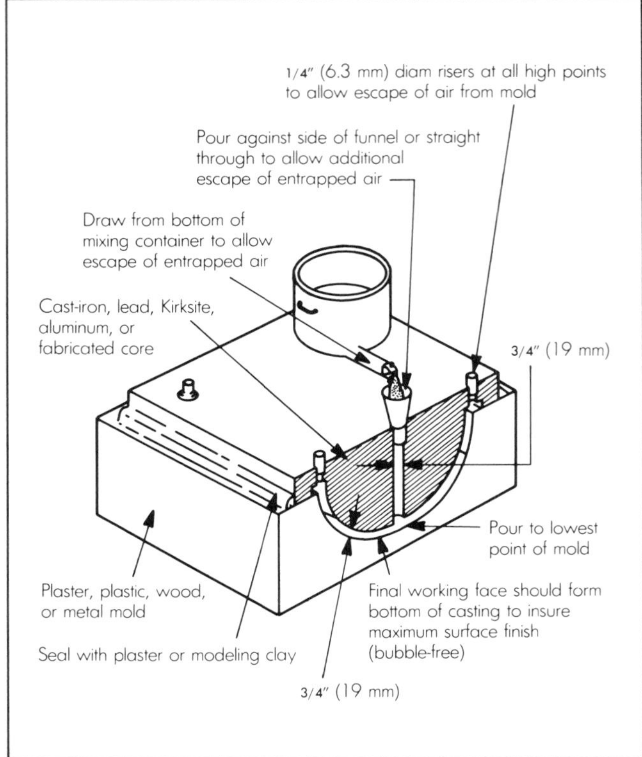

1/4" (6.3 mm) diam risers at all high points to allow escape of air from mold
Pour against side of funnel or straight through to allow additional escape of entrapped air
Draw from bottom of mixing container to allow escape of entrapped air
Cast-iron, lead, Kirksite, aluminum, or fabricated core
3/4" (19 mm)
Pour to lowest point of mold
Plaster, plastic, wood, or metal mold
Final working face should form bottom of casting to insure maximum surface finish (bubble-free)
Seal with plaster or modeling clay
3/4" (19 mm)

**Fig. 2-15 Casting an epoxy tool. (*Rezolin, Inc.*)**

### Facings of Plastics

Facings or coatings of plastics are often provided on the wear surfaces of dies and molds. The facings are sometimes cast or brushed on the mold and backed with a laminate or casting. A typical draw die with an epoxy face cast on the epoxy core of the die and punch ring, as well as the backup ring and knockout made from cast iron or zinc-based alloy, is shown in Fig. 2-16. Figure 2-17 illustrates a flanging die with epoxy surfaces cast on a plastic core, a steel punch, and a cast-iron ring. Chips, pellets, or cut shot of aluminum are often used in the mass-cast cores of epoxy.

### Laminated Construction

Laminating is the process of bonding together layers of resin-soaked reinforcement (such as fiberglass cloth) into a single structure of the desired thickness. It can be done by hand contact or spray layup (refer to Chapter 18, "Plastics Forming"). The mold or surface on which the laminate is to be made must be smooth and waxed. A parting agent is applied to the mold surface, followed by the first resin surface coat. After this coat becomes tacky, a layer of reinforcement, prewetted with resin, is applied, followed by successive layers of laminating resin and reinforcement until the desired thickness is attained.

The laminating method is generally used to make large dies

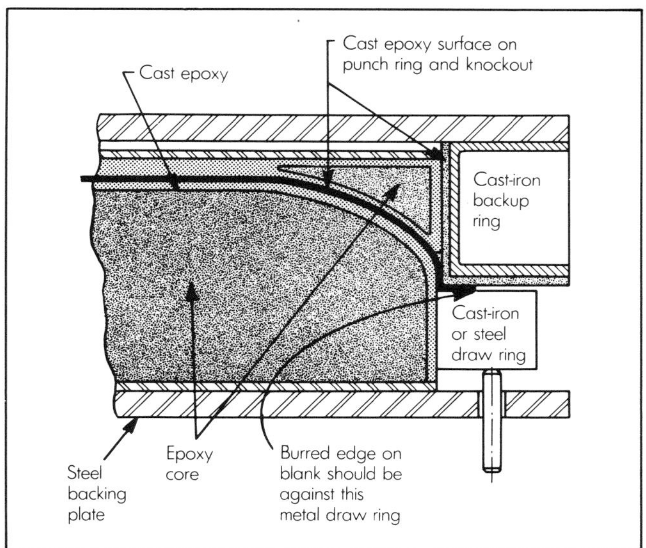


**Fig. 2-16 Draw die with epoxy cast on epoxy cores and cast-iron rings.**

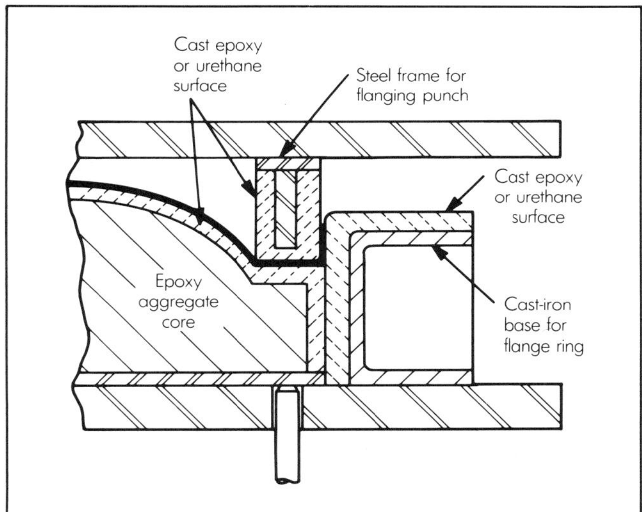


**Fig. 2-17 Flange die with epoxy surfaces cast on die, punch, and ring members.**

and molds that require good surface control and accuracy. The tools are usually reinforced with a backup structure made of egg-crate-like construction. Angle supports, fiberglass or metal tubing, or other materials are used. Molds made from heat-resistant laminates are sometimes provided with copper cooling coils embedded behind the laminations to conduct heat away from them.

### Combined Construction

Dies and molds can be made with a combination of casting, facing, or laminating methods. Surface coats of plastics are often brushed on the form, followed by a cast on a laminated backup. For some molds, a thin layer of metal is applied to the surface before the backup is applied. A flanging die used to form sheet metal by hand is illustrated in Fig. 2-18. This tool employs a combination of materials for minimum cost and good service.

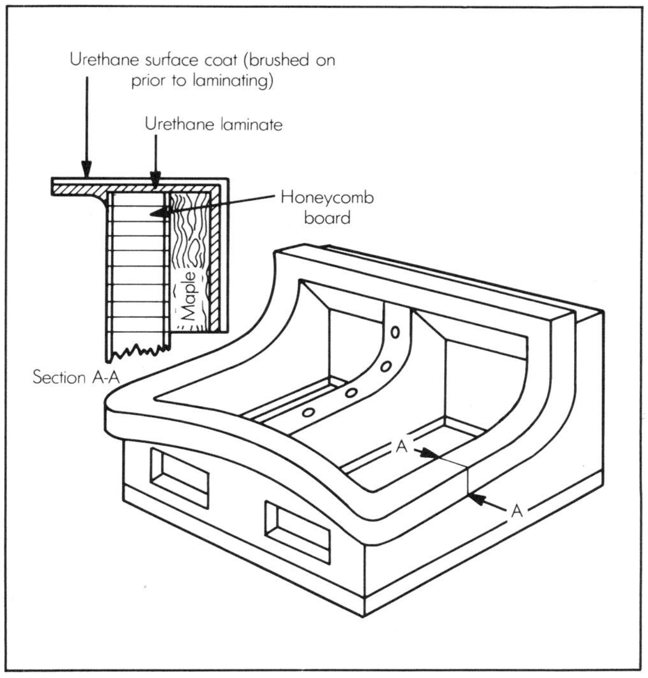


**Fig. 2-18 Flanging die used to form sheet metal by hand is made from a combination of materials.**

# OTHER NONMETALLIC DIE MATERIALS

In addition to plastics, just discussed, several other nonmetallic materials are used for forming dies, chucks, mandrels, and other components. Their applications, however, are generally limited to forming prototype or experimental parts from aluminum alloys and other light metals, or for short production runs.

## HARDWOODS

Dies are sometimes made of hardwoods, such as maple or beech, for blanking, forming, or shallow drawing of light metals, but applications are limited. Such woods are hard, dense, and close grained, and do not have a tendency to splinter. The woods used, however, must be carefully selected, cured, and kiln dried. For more severe operations, wood dies are faced with metal or plastic, or provided with steel inserts at areas of highest stress.

Mandrels for low-production spinning are often made of wood. The wooden blocks used sometimes consist of strips or layers of wood that are cross laminated and glued together prior to turning to the required shape. Other applications include forming shoes for expanding operations and dies (form blocks) for stretch forming, discussed in Chapter 7, "Expanding, Shrinking and Stretch Forming."

# BIBLIOGRAPHY

## HARDBOARDS

Hardboards are high-density panels of compressed wood fiber and lignin (a natural binder). These materials are used for forming and drawing dies, plastic molds, spinning mandrels, and stretch forming dies, as well as jigs, fixtures, templates, and patterns. Advantages of hardboards include good dimensional stability, light weight, smooth surfaces, uniform density, and abrasion resistance.

One common hardboard, produced by Masonite Corp., is available in thicknesses of 1/8 to 3/8" (3.2 to 9.5 mm). The boards can be readily laminated with adhesives to produce any thickness required. For blanking and piercing dies, steel cutting plates are usually inserted in the boards. For longer production runs, forming dies, molds, and mandrels can be faced with metal or plastic, or provided with steel inserts.

## DENSIFIED WOOD

Various woods are impregnated with a phenolic resin, after which the laminated assembly is compressed to about 50% of the original thicknesses of the wood layers. One proprietary material, Benelex, made by Masonite Corp., is a dense, lignin-resin cellulose laminate consisting of hardboards laminated under high pressure and heat. A small amount of phenol resin is added to the fiber to increase the hardness of the material.

Densified wood is used for punches and dies to form and draw aluminum alloys and other light metals. In drawing operations, scoring of the workpieces is minimized because of the low coefficient of friction of densified wood when properly finished. Dies made from these materials can be used for short to moderate production runs, depending upon the operation and its severity. Service life is often extended by the use of metal inserts.

## RUBBER

Molded rubber dies and rubber covered punches are used for some difficult forming operations, such as deep fluting and bulging. Rubber pads or diaphragms are also used for flexible-die forming processes (discussed in Chapter 4, "Sheet Metal Blanking and Forming," and Chapter 5, "Presses for Sheet Metal Forming"), but polyurethane diaphragms are now being employed extensively for these methods. Synthetic rubbers, such as neoprene, are used for certain pressworking operations like hot-forming of magnesium.

## CORK

Soft, medium, and hard cork layers, compressed into sheet form, are sometimes used with, or in place of, rubber pads. Cork deforms only slightly in any direction other than that of the applied load, while rubber flows in all directions.

### References


1. American Iron and Steel Institute, *Steel Products Manual—Tool Steels*, (Washington, DC, September 1981).
2. Brooks, J. A. *World Directory and Handbook of Hardmetals*. 3rd ed., (London, England: Engineers' Digest Ltd., 1982).
3. *General Aspects of Tool Design and Tool Materials for Cold and Warm Forging*, Document No. 4/82, International Cold Forging Group. (Surrey, England: Portcullis Press Ltd., 1982).


### Bibliography


Bogart, L. Frank. *Laminates of Non-Moisture Sensitive Urethanes Open Up Production Tooling to Plastic*. SME Technical Paper EM80-294, 1980.

Knott, Tom. *Tooling for Plastic Forming*. SME Technical Paper EM80-295, 1980.

Lamoureux, Paul. *Carbon Fiber Fabric Reinforced Plastic Tools*. SME Technical Paper TE80-337, 1980.

McCleary, Gail P. "Stamping Dies—Tool Steel or Tungsten Carbide?" *Manufacturing Engineering* (February 1978), pp. 56-58.

Palmer, Frank R.; Luerssen, George V.; and Pendleton, Jr., Joseph S. *Tool Steel Simplified*, 4th ed. Radnor, PA: Chilton Co., 1978.

Payson, P. *The Metallurgy of Tool Steels*. New York: John Wiley & Sons, 1962.

Roberts, George A., and Cary, Robert A. *Tool Steels*, 4th ed. Metals Park, OH: American Society for Metals, 1980.

Vale, David C. "Tooling with Carbide—Metalforming Applications." *Manufacturing Engineering* (September 1980) pp.98-99.

Vecchi, John C. *Carbide Die Maintenance and Service*. SME Technical Paper MR81-957, 1981.

Weber, John S. *Stamping Laminations with Steel-Bonded Titanium Carbide Dies*. SME Technical Paper MR82-900, 1982.

Wilson, R. *Metallurgy and Heat Treatment of Tool Steels*. New York: McGraw-Hill, 1975.

Younkin, Charles N. *Cold Work Die Steels*. SME Technical Paper TE76-918, 1976.

CHAPTER

# 3

# Lubricants

# LUBRICANTS

This chapter presents general information on metalforming lubricants, including their types, selection, and application. Additional, more detailed, process-oriented information and reference data are given in the various other chapters of this volume. Also, in Volume I, *Machining*, an extensive general coverage of the subject is provided in Chapter 4, "Cutting Fluids and Industrial Lubricants."

Lubrication is vitally important in metalforming operations. Effective lubrication results in controlled friction, with consequential reductions in force and power requirements and in tooling stresses and deflections. Tooling wear can be reduced by proper lubrication, and product quality can be improved by elimination of surface damage and harmful residual stresses.

A lubricant's main function is to minimize surface contact between the tooling and workpiece. If too much surface contact occurs, metal pickup on the tooling can damage the product and cause high maintenance costs from excessive tool wear. If friction is too high, temperature can exceed material limits and reduce production speeds. Workpiece surface quality is directly related to the properties and behavior of lubricants, whether surface contact occurs or not. In general, the lubrication function influences workpiece quality, process productivity, and cost.

**CHAPTER CONTENTS:**



## PRINCIPLES OF LUBRICATION

In discussing lubrication for metalforming processes, it is useful to distinguish between the different modes or "regimes" that can occur. The principal variable to be considered is the thickness of the lubricant film interposed between the surfaces. The four regimes of lubrication are illustrated in Fig. 3-1.[1]

### FILM THEORY

For most practical metalforming processes, determining and identifying the lubrication regime is difficult. It is also difficult to assess accurate values of friction for most processes; the use of a constant coefficient of friction is not appropriate. In most processes, lubrication is a combination of all the possible regimes, and thus friction varies during deformation. Lubricant properties must be matched as closely as possible with the properties of the workpiece and with process conditions to direct or to control the lubrication regime that is most likely to produce the desired results.

#### Thick-Film Lubrication

In thick-film lubrication (Fig. 3-1, *a*), the film minimum thickness is large compared with either the molecular size of the lubricant or the surface roughness of the tooling or workpiece. Thus, the lubricant may be regarded as a continuum (liquid or solid) between smooth surfaces.

The tool and workpiece surfaces are completely separated by the lubricant film. Friction is a function of the viscosity of the lubricant undergoing shear in the contact region. For conventional drawing and extrusion, thick-film lubrication has potential advantages because 30-40% of the total drawing force is expended in overcoming friction. For some applications, possible drawbacks are the matte finish that results and the prospect of producing metallurgical properties that are not desired in the workpiece.

The analyses of thick-film lubrication in metalforming have been facilitated by the discovery that the lubricant film can be divided up into a series of zones. In each zone it is possible to make some simplifying assumptions about the lubrication system. For example, in considering the lubricant film between the ironing ring and the workpiece in the ironing operation shown in Fig. 3-2, the film can be divided into three zones: an inlet zone, a work zone, and an outlet zone.

The amount of lubricant entrained in the inlet zone and the film shape are determined by the tooling. In the work zone, the pressure in the lubricant film is controlled by workpiece plasticity. This means that the pressure gradients in the work zone are small compared with those in the inlet zone.

In the outlet zone, the conditions resemble those in the inlet zone. The pressure is largely controlled by lubricant hydrodynamics, but the

*__Contributors of sections of this chapter are:__ Joseph Ivaska, Jr., Director of Engineering, Tower Oil & Technology Co.; Paul J. Kenney, Product Manager, Metalworking Lubricants, Acheson Colloids Co.; Nick L. Matthews, Lubricant Division, Russell Products; Ronald J. Newhouse, Manager, Marketing Services, Franklin Oil Corp.*

*__Reviewers of sections of this chapter are:__ William B. Burr, Sales Manager, Pillsbury Chemical & Oil, Inc.; Thomas A. Fairman, Director of Research, The H. A. Montgomery Co.; Angelo M. Fucinari, Service Engineer, The H. A. Montgomery Co.; Joseph Ivaska, Jr., Director of Engineering, Tower Oil & Technology Co.; Robert K. Rauth, President, Pillsbury Chemical & Oil, Inc.; B. M. Robin, Vice President—Technical, E. F. Houghton & Co.; Robert R. Rogers, Product Manager, Chemical Products, DoALL Co.; Harris R. Vahle, Vice President—Operations, Pillsbury Chemical & Oil, Inc.; C. K. Venkateswaran, Production Engineering, AC Spark Plug Div., General Motors Corp.; William L. Weeks, Materials Engineer Consultant; J. George Wills, Chief Technical Editor, Mobile Oil Corp.*

elasticity of the tooling and workpiece also may be important. The outlet zone has a minor role in the lubrication process. Its main function is to allow the lubricant pressure to fall back to ambient. This means that the film thickness in the outlet zone is slightly less than that at the outlet boundary of the work zone.

In practice, an analysis must take into account the variation of lubricant viscosity with pressure and temperature. The viscosity of a typical mineral oil lubricant doubles with each increase in pressure of 5000 psi (35 MPa) and is halved with each increase in temperature of 59° F (15° C).[2]

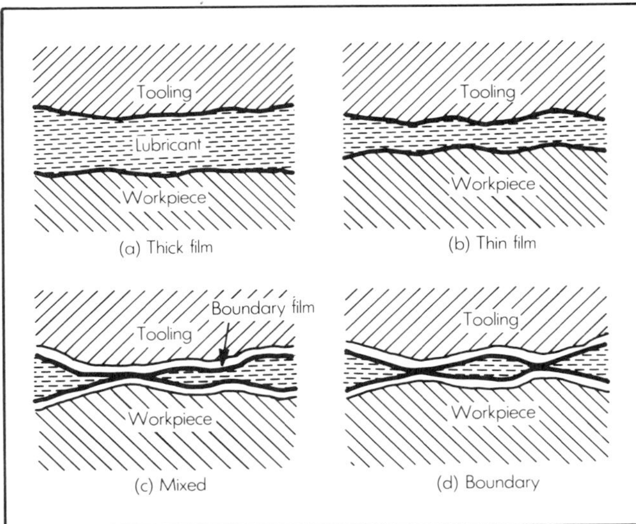


**Fig. 3-1 Regimes of lubrication.**

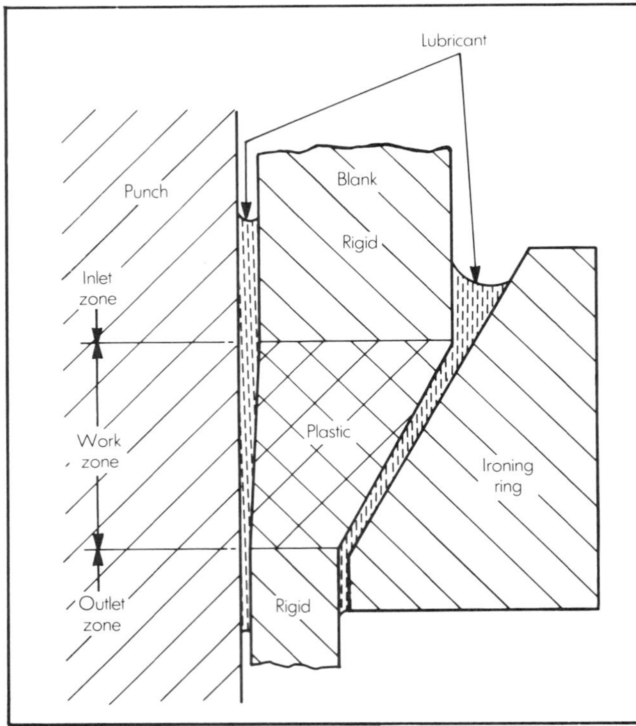


**Fig. 3-2 Lubrication in ironing operation.**

## Thin-Film Lubrication

If the minimum thickness of lubricant film is reduced or if surface roughness is increased, the system may enter the thin-film lubrication regime (see Fig. 3-1, *b*). In this mode, the minimum film thickness is of the same order as the surface roughness, but it is still much larger than the molecular size of the lubricant. Under these circumstances, the lubricant may be treated as a continuum, but roughness of the surfaces must be considered in the analysis.

The properties of the lubricant—its flow behavior under conditions of pressure, temperature, and shear—are equally important. Lubricant effectiveness is directly dependent on the pressure coefficient of viscosity. Because of their high speed requirements, cold rolling and high-speed wire drawing are among the relatively few metalworking processes for which sustained thin-film lubrication is practicable.

## Mixed-Film Lubrication

Further reduction in the minimum film thickness results in potential contact between roughness peaks (asperities). The lubricant, however, contains materials that react chemically with the surfaces, forming tightly adhering boundary films with a thickness on the order of the lubricant molecular size. These films prevent direct metal-to-metal contact between asperities. Part of the load between the surfaces is carried by the thick film in the roughness valleys, and part is carried by the thin boundary films over the peaks. This results in the mixed-film lubrication regime illustrated in Fig. 3-1, *c*.

## Boundary-Film Lubrication

The final lubrication regime of importance in metalforming is shown in Fig. 3-1, *d*. This is purely a boundary-film lubrication regime in which all of the load between the surfaces is carried on thin boundary films on the asperity peaks. The coefficient of friction is usually in the range of 0.1-0.3.

## Solid-Film Lubrication

Thick-film lubrication can be produced with lubricating solids as well as with liquids. Solid lubricants vary a great deal in chemical character and in physical properties. In the broadest sense, the products resulting from the interaction of liquid lubricants or semisolid organic boundary lubricants could be described as "solid lubricants," because it is in the solid phase that they become effective. More specifically, however, the term "solid lubrication" describes the reduction of friction and wear through the use of inorganic solids having low shear strengths. Organic materials such as Teflon, powder, and low-shear lamellar pigments also are used. The desired mechanism involves complete separation of surfaces by the solid lubricant (which, in some instances, is soap, wax, or polymer-based, dry film). However, in metal-deformation processes, in which plastic flow of the substrate causes film stretching, solid-film lubrication is often a boundary lubrication process.

An important criterion for effective solid-film lubrication is the lubricant's adherence to the surfaces. Good adherence to the metal surfaces ensures that shear occurs in the lubricant films; thus, with films of low-shear solids which are relatively thick, friction is low. As with boundary lubricants, an important consideration in the selection of a solid lubricant is its ability to interact (physically adsorb or chemisorb) or react with metallic substrates at the sliding interface. Should this ability be lacking, mechanical interlocking promoted by an optimum surface roughness often enhances solid lubrication. Otherwise, an adhesive or binder can be used to bond a solid-lubricant pigment to the substrates. Other criteria for selection of solid lubricants are their volatility, thermal stability, hardness, crystal structure, and insulation value and the mobility of the molecules permitting adsorption.

### Film Performance

In performing its friction reduction and control functions, the lubricant uses different mechanisms in each of the regimes. In the thick-film regime, the lubricant completely separates the tool and workpiece, and the bulk properties of the fluid are paramount. As the film gets thinner, the influence of the bulk properties lessens and the surface-lubricant interaction begins to become important. In mixed boundary film, although areas of thin-film lubrication exist, the asperites come into close proximity and a portion of the lubricant's additive package is attracted to the metal surface, where it forms an adhering boundary film. Finally, in the boundary-film regime, it is the reactivity of the lubricant's additives, along with its ability to form a chemically bound film, that provides a low friction layer. These are the mechanisms by which the lubricant functions to minimize contact between the tool and workpiece and, thereby, to control wear.

The boundary regime offers a classic illustration showing how this occurs. The extreme-pressure (EP) agent forms a surface chemical film that has a lower shear strength than that of the base metal; hence, controlled wear occurs in this layer, thus preventing a more catastrophic metal-to-metal contact.

The thick and thin-film lubrication regimes (sometimes called, collectively, "full-film" lubrication) are most effective in reducing friction and wear. With these regimes, the coefficient of friction often is less than 0.03 and virtually no wear of the dies or surface damage to the product occurs. Solid particles behave as films. Full-film operation is impracticable during at least part of many metalforming operations. For example, it is impossible to provide full-film lubrication during the starting and stopping phases of rolling and drawing operations. For this reason, the chemical properties of lubricants (which affect boundary lubrication) are just as important as the physical properties (which affect thick-film lubrication).

Most metal deformation processes are performed predominantly with boundary or mixed-film lubrication. Friction is a function of the bulk physical properties of the lubricant as they chemically interact with the properties of the surfaces. The film is extremely thin and usually is discontinuous. Heavy loads that are characteristic of boundary lubrication cause contact between a large number of asperities. Lubricants that are effective in boundary lubrication act to prevent or reduce the junction growth of asperities and result in interfacial slip. They also delay the plastic flow of asperites and impede contact, galling, and friction.

## OPERATING PARAMETERS

The lubrication regime that occurs in a given metalforming process is dependent on several factors of the process:

- Contact macrogeometry (varies with process and die design).
- Load (contact force, tool to workpiece).
- Speed (surface speed, tool to workpiece).
- Environment (air, moisture, drawing compound, etc.).
- Lubricant properties.
- Contact microgeometry (microtopography or surface finish).

For thick-film lubrication with liquid lubricants, relatively high speed and low load, a critical contact geometry, and a relatively viscous lubricant are required. In addition, more subtle influences on the lubrication mechanism should be considered, such as the possible role of surface microgeometry in the generation of thick-film lubrication in high-speed sliding applications in the presence of very low-viscosity liquids. Typical features connected with other metal-deformation processes control the lubrication mechanism in other ways. For example, slow speeds and high loads dictate that lubrication must be the boundary type.

The lubrication mechanism is also critically influenced by temperature at the sliding interface. Increases in temperature affect the physical and chemical properties—viscosity, reactivity, stability, and volatility—of the lubricant. The effect of pressure is also important, but less significant than that of temperature. As long as the temperature is not high enough to cause deterioration or loss of liquid lubricants, pressure counteracts the effects of temperature on viscosity to some extent.

Most of these effects on lubricants prevent the establishment of, or cause the loss of, thick-film lubrication in metalforming processes. On the other hand, the conditions that force lubrication to become the boundary type are high ambient temperature, high loads, and slow speeds. These conditions ultimately produce the frictional heat and surface activation required before boundary lubricants can chemically alter the interface. Thus, distress to the surfaces is necessary to enable the surfaces to survive under boundary lubrication conditions.

## MATERIAL SURFACE PROPERTIES

There is a direct relationship between surface properties of the material worked and the lubricant that is applied to a particular surface. Some materials are more difficult to lubricate than others. Certain surface treatments and coatings require special care. Fabricating problems, such as white rust, staining of nonferrous metals, and peeling and blistering of painted or coated stock, can occur when improper lubricants are used. To facilitate understanding of the interrelationships that are involved, material surfaces can be grouped into four categories: normal, active, inactive, and coated.

### Normal Surfaces

Most normal surfaces are material surfaces that have a natural affinity enabling them to retain lubricants readily; they generally do not require special wetting or polarity agents to obtain sufficient lubrication. The material is relatively clean and free of such contaminants as heavy-oxide films and extraneous gases (nitrogen, oxygen, carbon dioxide). Cold-rolled steel, hot-rolled steel, and aluminum-killed steel have surfaces of this type. They tend to hold lubricant that is applied to them.

### Active Surfaces

An active material surface is one in which the bond strength between the lubricant additive and metal atom is great. The attractive energy of the metallic surface is high. This tends to encourage desirable chemical reactions. As a result, chemically active additives and wetting agents such as oleic acid, lard oil, and some emulsifiers (such as soaps) are effective in lubricating such materials and coatings as brass, copper, aluminum, terneplate, zincrometal, and tinplate.

### Inactive Surfaces

An inactive surface is one in which the strength of the bond

**TABLE 3-1**
**Composite Lubrication Guide for Metal Forming**

| Forming Operation | Straight* Mineral Oils | EP-Type Mineral Oils | Water-* Soluble Oils | EP Heavy-Duty Soluble Oils | Synthetic Solubles | Semi-Synthetic Solubles | Solvent Type Lubes | Inorganic Soaps | Pigment | Organic Soaps and Waxes | Dry Films | Dispersions | Glasses |
|---|---|---|---|---|---|---|---|---|---|---|---|---|---|
| Cold forging | | | | | | | | • | | | • | • | |
| Cold heading | | • | | | | | | • | | | • | | |
| Warm and hot forming | | • | | | | | | | | | | • | • |
| Extrusions | | • | | | | | | | | • | • | • | • |
| Hot forging | | | | | • | | | | | • | • | • | • |
| Roll forming | • | • | • | • | • | • | • | | | | | | |
| Roll bending | • | | | | | | | | | • | | | |
| Rod and wire | | • | | • | • | | | • | • | | • | | |
| Spinning | | • | | | • | | | | | • | | | |
| Swaging | | • | | | | | | | | • | | | |
| Tube bending | | • | • | • | | | | | • | • | • | | |
| Blanking and forming | • | • | • | • | • | • | • | | • | • | | | |
| Drawing | • | • | • | • | • | • | | | • | • | • | | |
| Fine blanking | | • | | | | | • | | | • | | | |
| Four slide | • | • | | • | • | • | • | | | | | | |
| Laminations | | | | | • | • | • | | | | | | |
| Punching and perforating | | • | • | • | • | • | • | | | • | • | | |
| Transfer die systems | | • | • | • | • | • | | | | • | | | |
| Transfer presses | | • | • | • | • | • | | | | • | | | |
| Stretch forming | • | • | • | • | | | | | • | • | | | |

Note: Information on expanded lubrication properties, application techniques, and specific forming operations is included in the respective forming chapters.

* Under certain nonrigorous conditions, these lubricants are applicable to the indicated processes. Their effectiveness, however, is limited; and, usually, they are not the "preferred" lubricant.

**TABLE 3-2**
**High-Pressure Lubricant Applications**

| Forming Operation | Composition | Dispersing Media | Remarks |
|---|---|---|---|
| Forging: Aluminum, brass, carbon steels, high strength and super-alloys, stainless steels | Graphite, $MoS_2$, or other pigment | Water, oil, solvent | Provides strong thin film, excellent die wetting, promotes metal flow, provides high temperature stability. |
| Forging, extrusion, wire and tube drawing | Graphite, $MoS_2$, zinc phosphate and soap, metallic coatings, oxylates, and other pigments | Water, oil, solvent | Strong thin film, in some cases reacted with metal surface, promotes metal flow, prevents metal-to-metal contact. |
| Diecasting | Release agents, graphite or other pigments | Water, solvent | Promotes metal flow, prevents metal-to-metal contact. |
| Cold heading, extrusion hot-metal forming | Graphite, $MoS_2$, zinc phosphate and soap, metallic coatings | Water, oil, solvent | Strong thin film, firmly bonded to metal surface, eases metal flow. |
| Severe deep drawing, punching, piercing: ferrous and nonferrous | Extreme-pressure agents, lubricity agents: sulfurized chlorinated, sulfochlorinated, phosphates, film-strength improvers, pigments, fatty acids, and others | Water, oil | Selection based on total needs, i.e., cleanability, corrosion protection, staining, tool life and composition, operational severity. |
| Stamping and drawing: ferrous and nonferrous metals | Extreme-pressure agents, lubricity agents: sulfurized chlorinated, sulfochlorinated, organic phosphate esters, polymers, fatty acids, and others | Water, oil, solvent | Selection based on total needs, operational severity, tooling, corrosive protection, staining considerations, cleanability. |

**TABLE 3-3**
**Lubricant Selection Factors**

| Operation | Tooling | Material | Application Method | Subsequent Operations | Special Considerations |
|---|---|---|---|---|---|
| Drawing | Tool steel | Steel | Drip | Cleaning | Pollution |
| Forming | High speed | Commercial | Roller | Alkaline | Odor |
| Perforating | Urethane | Hot roll | Air spray | Vapor | Nonmisting |
| Blanking | Carbide | Drawing | Airless spray | No degreasing | Food |
| Coining | Chrome treated | Stainless | Flooding | Weld | Procurement |
| Shaving | Hastelloy | Silicon | Precoat | Braze | Cost |
| Extruding | Nitrite | Spring | | Paint | Toxicity |
| Progressive | | High carbon | | Anneal | Disposal |
| Transfer | | High strength, low alloy | | Plate | Safety |
| Cold heading | | Nonferrous | | Rust prevention | Personnel |
| Upsetting | | Brass | | Heat treating | Dermatitis |
| | | Aluminum | | | Storage |
| | | Copper | | | |
| | | Treated Surfaces | | | |
| | | Galvanized | | | |
| | | Terne | | | |
| | | Aluminized | | | |
| | | Coated | | | |
| | | Vinyl and paint | | | |
| | | Paper | | | |
| | | Lacquer | | | |
| | | Epoxy | | | |

between the lubricant additive and the metal atom is low. The attractive energy of the metallic surface also is low. This lessens the tendency for chemical reactions with lubricant chemical additives. When working with inactive surfaces such as stainless steel, titanium, and nickel, the lubricant should have a high film strength. Suitable lubricants contain hydrocarbons, polymers, polar and wetting agents, and extreme-pressure agents. Aluminum metal is a "special case"; since its active surface usually is coated with an inactive oxide film, it needs a high-film strength lubricant.

### Coated Surfaces

Nonmetallic surface treatments and coatings include vinyl, paint, lacquer, paper, plastic, and other organic coatings. Lubricants used on these coatings must be compatible and clean and must not cause the surface coating to peel, blister, blush, or stain. Lubricants that work well on coated surfaces are synthetic and chemical solubles and certain natural emulsions.

If the coated surface is electroplated or is a bimetal, it should be treated as an "active surface," for purposes of specifying the lubricant.

## LUBRICANT SELECTION

A metalworking lubricant performs a number of functions. Primarily, of course, it keeps the tool and workpiece separated, preventing direct metal-to-metal contact. This is done with extreme pressure agents and other additives. Through its lubricity agents and wetting agents, the lubricant provides "slip." It cools the work surface and prevents rust. In addition, bacterial growth is inhibited by the germicides and bactericides contained in the lubricant. General information on lubricant selection is given in Table 3-1. Usage and applications of high-temperature, high-pressure lubricants are summarized in Table 3-2.

To make a proper selection of lubricant, consideration must be given to such factors as the type of operations being performed, tooling design and materials, kind of metal being formed, speed of presses, lubricant application methods, subsequent operations, and a number of other factors. Table 3-3 lists the kinds of interrelated items that should be taken into account when a lubricant is being selected.

# TYPES OF LUBRICANTS

The many varied conventional liquid lubricant materials used for lubricating punches and dies can usually be divided into two broad categories: oil based and water dilutable. Both types may use similar additives—sulfurized fats or oils; chlorine, usually in the form of chlorinated paraffin wax ("honey oil"); and phosphorus. Fats are added to improve wetting of the stock with lubricant and also to increase slipperiness or oiliness. In addition, water-dilutable lubricants may contain amine soaps, metallic soaps, and/or other emulsifiers. With the proper amounts of the various additives, as well as the use of inhibitors, they can be used in drawing and stamping compounds.

The new "synthetics" are another broad group of lubricants. They generally contain no mineral oil. Semisynthetics may contain some mineral oil; the remaining ingredients are water-soluble compounds and wetting agents, along with extreme-pressure (EP) additives, corrosion deterrents, and antifoam inhibitors.[3]

Another group of lubricants includes solid films, solid particles (pigments), and eutectic salts. These are covered later in this chapter under "Lubricant Formulations."

## LUBRICANT PROPERTIES

The difference between success or failure in many metalforming operations can be attributed to properties of lubricants that can be formulated to suit a particular operation. Table 3-4 lists properties that characterize metalforming lubricants. As shown, the various physical and chemical properties are broken down into five categories: barrier films, wetting agents, additives, special properties, and dry-film lubricants.

A compound usually can be formulated to provide the properties that are most important for lubricating a specific operation. To formulate and compound a lubricant and tailor it to the requirements, it is necessary to know the material surfaces that are being worked; metal gauge; application

**TABLE 3-4**
**Drawing Compound Properties**

| Barrier Films | Wetting Agents | Additives | Special Properties | Dry Films |
|---|---|---|---|---|
| Oil | Animal fat | EP Type | Cleaning inducers | Phosphates |
| Soap | Vegetable | Sulfur | Weld-through | Graphite |
| Wax | derivatives | Chlorine | Annealing | Oxides |
| Pigment | Polymers | Phosphorous | Brazing | Teflon |
| Polymer | Lardates | Friction modifiers | No degreasing | Electrofilm |
| | (Synthetic) | Rust preventive | Easy painting | Molydisulfide |
| | Water | | Oil base | Ceramic |
| | Solvent | | Water base | Polymer |
| | Stearates | | Adhesives | |
| | Emulsifiers | | Paper clad | |
| | | | Biodegradability | |
| | | | Long-term storage | |
| | | | Outdoor storage | |

techniques; cleaning and removal methods; subsequent operations; and any special considerations that are peculiar to the process, plant, or setup. For example, by looking at Table 3-4, it is evident that, if desired, lubricants can be made for easy cleaning, good rust protection, compatibility with welding and heat treating, biodegradability, and no degreasing.

## INGREDIENTS

There are three basic ingredients in the makeup of a typical metalforming lubricant. Theoretically, a lubricant cross-section may be one layer, two layers, or three layers—consisting of a carrier (vehicle); a polarity or wetting agent; and, in some instances, an extreme-pressure agent or parting agent.

General information on various types of straight oil and water extendible lubricants for stamping and drawing is summarized in Tables 3-5 and 3-6.[4]

The main component of most drawing compounds is their vehicle, which may be oil, solvent, water, or a combination of several vehicles. The second ingredient is a wetting or polarity agent. Some of the commonly used agents are animal fats, fatty acids, long chain polymers, and emulsifiers. The third basic ingredient added to many stamping lubricants is an EP agent such as chlorine, sulfur, or phosphorus. Physical barriers such as calcium carbonate, talc, mica, or graphite also may be added.

Numerous combinations of carriers, additives, and EP agents can be used in formulating lubricants for metal stamping operations. The objective is effective matching of the lubricant with the manufacturing operation and the piece part.

### Oil-Based Lubricants

Petroleum-based lubricants are especially useful when high load characteristics are present. The diverse combinations that can be created with the use of different blending oils and additives can successfully perform punching, heavy forming, drawing, extruding, coining, blanking, and embossing. The stamping operations are performed on various types of machines, such as transfer presses, draw presses, punch presses, fine blanking presses, and four slide equipment.

### Water-Based Lubricants

In recent years, there has been substantial growth in the use of water-soluble lubricant emulsions. They may or may not contain oil; they are relatively easy to clean; and they facilitate disposal and pollution control. Some of the heavy-duty water-soluble lubricants are comparable to petroleum-based lubricants in their performance. They are well-suited for use in recirculating systems of transfer presses; and, when properly applied, they work well with progressive tooling. The water-soluble lubricants are applicable to drawing operations and can perform some unusually complex, severe metal stamping operations.

### Synthetic, Soluble Lubricants

This new class of lubricants has been undergoing rapid development and its usage is growing. Some synthetic lubricants perform well at extreme pressures; hence, they are useful for

**TABLE 3-5**
**Stamping and Drawing Lubricants—Straight Oils**
**Applications Summary**

| Type | Uses | Advantages | Disadvantages |
|---|---|---|---|
| Mineral oil (physical film) | Limited use; light forming; not for punching, blanking, or trimming operations. | Inexpensive. Readily available. Easy to apply. | No EP quality. Moderate rust protection. |
| Mineral fatty oil (physical film, lard oil) | Nonferrous material; stamping, piercing, forming. | Inexpensive. Readily available. Easy to apply. No reaction. Removable with solvent. | Minimal EP. Moderate rust protection. Becomes rancid. |
| Mineral fatty chlorinated oil (physical, chemical film) | Carbon steel and stainless steel; stamping and drawing. | Minimal stain. Adequate EP. Good lubricity. Job tailored. | Corrosive unless inhibited. Solvent cleaning. Carry-off (viscosity). Cost. |
| Mineral fatty sulfur oil | Extruding, blanking, punching, heavy-gauge piercing. | High EP. Handles severe jobs. | Attacks carbide tooling. Stains nonferrous. Flattens alkali cleaner. Odor. |
| Mineral fatty sulfur chlorinated oil | Combination jobs, piercing and drawing, extruding. | Good EP. | Similar, but more extreme than mineral fatty sulfur oil. |
| Chlorinated bases | Severe heavy-gauge drawing; medium to heavy-gauge stainless steel; stamping, piercing, drawing. | High EP. Versatile (cut with oil). | Difficult cleaning. High cost. |
| Metallic soaps | Augmenting other EP additives. | High EP. | May deplete phosphate system. Contaminates cleaners. |
| Phosphate esters | With chlorine and/or sulfur. | Add EP. Increase effectiveness. | Cost. |

many metal stamping operations. These lubricants are exceptionally cleanable. They perform well on coated, painted paper-clad, and vinyl-clad surfaces, as well as on terneplate and aluminum. Secondary operations such as welding and painting often can be performed without prior degreasing or cleaning. Many of the synthetics are biodegradable and readily disposable.

Synthetic lubricants are solutions of chemicals in water. They are different from petroleum-based lubricants. Their characteristics must be understood, and the lubricants must be used properly to perform a particular metalforming operation satisfactorily. Suitable procedures and controls should be established to obtain effective performance and to maintain the chemical balance of synthetic lubricants at their optimum levels. The areas to be reviewed for overall compatibility include tooling, material, system contamination control, application method, startup procedure lubricant control, and subsequent operations.

### Solvent-Based Lubricants

The solvent-based lubricants give good results when used with many different coatings, such as paint, vinyl, paper, and lacquer. These applications have expanded the need for clean stamping lubricants, which in some processes, require no cleaning or degreasing. Secondary operations such as welding, painting, and the addition of sealants, gaskets, and packings can be performed after degreasing. Solvent-based lubricants are used to stamp appliance and TV components and electrical hardware, including laminations. Care must be taken to avoid solvent reaction or stripping of the organic film.

### Specialty Stamping Lubricants

Appropriate types of lubricants for various special processing operations and suggested dilution ratios (if the lubricants are water soluble) are shown in Table 3-7.

## LUBRICANT FORMULATIONS

Lubricant formulations for metalforming differ widely in physical form and chemical composition. The components of the formulations are divided into liquids, solids, and additives and formulation aids.

**TABLE 3-6**
**Stamping and Drawing Lubricants—Water Extendibles**
**Applications Summary**

| Type | Uses | Advantages | Disadvantages |
|---|---|---|---|
| Mineral soluble oils | Nonferrous material; light forming. | No reaction or staining. Inexpensive. | No EP. Becomes rancid. Minimal rust protection. |
| Fatty soluble oils | Nonferrous material; drawing, piercing, and forming. | No reaction or staining. Good tool life. Minimum water spotting. Good wetting. | Fairly high cost. |
| Fatty chlorinated soluble oils | Majority of drawing and stamping jobs. | Most versatile compound. Rust protection. Forms stable emulsion. Easily cleaned. Minimal carry-off. Low cost (total usage). | Reapplication needed on multiple draw operations. High initial cost. |
| Fatty sulfur soluble oils | Ferrous material; limited use. | No distinctive features. | Reacts with nonferrous material. Attacks carbide. Depletes alkaline cleaners. |
| Fatty chlorinated sulfur soluble oils | Medium to heavy-gauge ferrous material; punching, piercing, extruding. | High level of activity. | Reacts with nonferrous material. Attacks carbide. Depletes alkaline cleaners. |
| Liquid soaps | Carbon steel; light to medium forming. Nonferrous material; medium drawing. | Self-cleaning. Excellent wetting and lubricity. | No EP. Can stain nonferrous material. Can etch carbide. Can cause white rust on zinc. |
| Soap fat paste compounds | Nonpigmented material, same as for liquid soaps. Pigmented material; severe drawing and good stainless steel drawing compound. | Will carry through on subsequent operations. | Messy. Pigment is hard to clean. Cannot be vapor degreased. Not well suited to punch and pierce processes. |
| Synthetics | Good for stretching and forming. | Retains lubricity at high mix rations. Self-cleaning. Can be used as specialty lubricant. | Limited EP. Cannot be vapor degreased. Can build up on tools at low mix ratios. |

Note: Rust protection depends on formulation. Biocide additives deter rancidity.

**TABLE 3-7**
**Specialty Stamping Lubricants**

- Lamination compounds
  - Solvent cutbacks. Fast evaporation. Clean burn-off.
  - Water-soluble fatty oils. Lower cost. Better die life in lower dilution ratios, cleaner burn-off. Less odor and fewer safety hazards. Use ratios 9:1 to 20:1.
  - Light viscosity chlorinated fatty oil. Must be degreased.
- Paintable films and bondable films (Watch mill oil condition)
  - Fatty soluble oil at 10 to 1, paint or bond.
  - Synthetics at 10 to 1, paint only.
  - Solvent-type vanishing film (paint or bond).
- Aerospace, nuclear and contamination free surface
  - No halogen bearing compounds—sulfur chlorine.
  - Water-soluble fatty oils or selected synthetics.
- Prepaint vinyl clad vanishing film, etc.
  - Water-soluble fatty oil at dilution ratios of 10 to 1 and higher.
  - Synthetics at 10 to 1 and higher.
  - Solvent cutbacks check for paint softening, high priced, will only do very mild operations.
- F.D.A. approved
  - U.S.P. white oil, very expensive. Ratios: 20:1 to 40:1.
  - Fatty soluble oil with special emulsifiers. Use ratios 10:1 to 30:1, with water.
- Tinplate, terneplate and galvanized
  - Mineral fatty oils.
  - Fatty soluble oils. Ratios: 10:1 to 20:1 (pH 7 to 8.5)
  - Synthetic. Use ratios 10:1 to 20:1 (pH 7 to 8.5)
  - Solvent vanishing films.

## Liquids

Liquid components include:

- Mineral oils.
- Natural oils (fatty oils).
- Synthetic oils.
- Compounded oils.
- Extreme-pressure oils.
- Emulsions (soluble oils).
- Solutions (mixtures of water with other fluids or additives).
- Eutectic salts (liquids under process conditions).
- Glasses (liquids under process conditions).

**Mineral oils**. The viscosities of mineral oils used in metalworking range from that of kerosene (and even lower when the mineral oil fraction is used as a solvent or as a vehicle) to that of very heavy oils such as asphaltic residues, which are apparent solids. Straight mineral oils are useful when the process can take advantage of the physical properties of the oil (mainly viscosity) to promote fluid-film lubrication. Otherwise, the low-viscosity representatives of this type are satisfactory as coolants and heat-transfer media, but function poorly as boundary lubricants. However, because many deformation processes are carried out under mild boundary-lubrication conditions, and because mineral oils are inexpensive, the more viscous fractions are used extensively. The high-viscosity mineral oils contain significant concentrations of polar compounds and nonhydrocarbon constituents; thus, they show appreciable boundary-lubrication ability. For many applications, mineral oils are compounded with polar and reactive additives to further increase their boundary-lubrication properties.

Technical advantages of mineral oil as a base stock for metalforming lubricants include availability in a number of viscosity ranges, controlled compressibility, and stability to molecular shear under high stress. Within certain viscosity ranges, a choice of chemical type can be made. Boundary-lubrication value is dependent on chemical type. The ability of the base stock to be improved in value by additives is also influenced by its chemical type.

**Natural oils**. Palm oil, rapeseed oil, lard oil, and other natural oils are used in metalforming, either neat, in combination with mineral oils, or at times admixed with water. Usually they are used to produce better boundary lubrication than can be achieved with straight mineral oils. They are more effective in the boundary regime than are mineral oils, because they contain free fatty acids which can form boundary films. When added to mineral oils, fatty oils are known as "oiliness" agents. In addition, fatty oils have a relatively low pressure coefficient of viscosity, which contributes to their good performance in metal rolling processes as thin-film hydrodynamic lubricants.

**Synthetic oils**. Synthetic oils are usually pure chemical species. For metalforming processes, synthetic oils are used because they are more resistant to degradation at high temperatures than are mineral oils. Synthetic oils usually show better viscosity-temperature characteristics, lower volatility and flammability, and better oxidative and thermal stability than mineral oils. For operations at extreme temperature, during which evaporation or decomposition occur, synthetic fluids that may leave very little carbonaceous residue are available.

For boundary lubrication, certain synthetic fluids are more effective than straight mineral oils of equivalent viscosity.

**Compounded oils**. Compounded or "formulated" oils represent mixtures of mineral or synthetic oils containing "oiliness" agents (fatty oils or fatty acids) and other additives to reduce friction in boundary lubrication. Compounded oils may be comprised of as much as 30% fatty oils by weight and 5% fatty acids. Although used extensively in metalforming, compounded oils have two disadvantages: (1) they tend to stain metals if not completely removed before annealing or further processing and (2) they have a fairly low critical temperature. Above this temperature they lose effectiveness as boundary lubricants and develop poor antiweld properties.

**Extreme-pressure oils**. For operations requiring good antiweld properties, extreme-pressure (EP) oils are used. EP oils are mineral oils or synthetic fluids containing highly active chemical compounds in additive concentrations. Some EP oils are quite crude; for example, elemental sulfur may be dissolved in a mineral oil or a fatty oil, and although they are effective as lubricants, such oils containing free or only loosely bonded sulfur might produce undesirable staining. On the other hand, tightly bound sulfur is not very effective as an EP agent.

Other chemicals in EP oils are chlorine, phosphorus, and sulfur. These elements are usually added to the base stock (as are some sulfur-bearing materials) in the form of organic

# TYPES OF LUBRICANTS

compounds—for example, chlorinated hydrocarbons in the case of chlorine. Some of these compounds are quite complex in structure, and they often contribute other properties to the base oil.

**Emulsions**. All the previously described oils can be used in oil-water combinations as lubricant-coolants. These "soluble oils," usually are a compounded oil or an EP oil containing an emulsifier that requires little energy to disperse in water to form a stable emulsion.

The effectiveness of emulsions in metalforming is largely a function of their cooling capacity. However, to take advantage of the lubricating power of the combinations, emulsions should be "loose" enough to break in the interfaces of contacts requiring lubrication. On the other hand, they should be stable under all other conditions of use, including recirculation. Rich emulsions containing 10% and sometimes as much as 20% oil are the choice for most metalforming processes in which soluble oils are used.

**Solutions**. Water solutions are used in metal-deformation processes. They are usually concentrated aqueous solutions of inorganic salts (rust inhibitors such as sodium nitrite or sodium borate), water-soluble detergents, and amines. Often, the lubricating agent is a hydrophilic polyglycol synthetic fluid. Although water solutions are fire-resistant and attractive in appearance, they have limited lubricating ability and they tend to build up inorganic deposits on the tooling and workpiece.

**Eutectic salts**. Salt melts containing magnesium chloride or fusions of zinc chloride with zinc sulfate, and melts based on lead chloride have been studied as lubricants for the hot working of both ferrous and nonferrous metals. Eutectic salts that form high-viscosity liquids at high temperatures act similarly to conventional mineral oils at lower temperatures; that is, boundary effects are minimal and lubrication is predominantly a physical process that depends on the melt viscosity of the salt. Other eutectics are believed to deposit a low-melting-point metal in liquid form at the contact interface. This film, which acts as a boundary lubricant, is protected from oxidation by the surrounding molten salt. Corrosion does not appear to be a problem with nonhygroscopic salts (or for those of low hygroscopicity) if the workpiece is kept hot and the salts are removed immediately after working. Salts are easily removable with water.

**Glasses**. Glasses can be formulated which melt to highly viscous liquids that wet metals. They have been used in hot-deformation processes for working metals and alloys with high melting points. Before deformation, the billet is heated to a high temperature and the tool is heated to some lower temperature. The sharp temperature gradient through the glass film (glass is molten on the billet and solid near the tool) produces a viscosity gradient that is important to lubrication. However, this indirect control over film viscosity limits the processing speed because of time-temperature effects. Better control over tool and workpiece temperature would extend the utility of glasses as lubricants. One of the main disadvantages of glasses is the difficulty of removing the glass and the tenacious products resulting from its reaction with the workpiece.

## Dry-Film Lubricant

Prelubricated stock is suitable for some high-volume jobs in which drawing, blanking, or forming can be performed satisfactorily with a single application of a lubricant. Dry-film lubricants fall into three categories: soaps, waxes, and polymers.

Dry soap films and polymer coatings are applied to sheet or coil stock from an aqueous solution and subsequently allowed to dry before stacking or recoiling of metal.

Use of preheated solution and/or heated oven facilitates drying the film. Wax films are applied from a hot melt using suitable roll coating equipment to deposit a thin film of lubricant.

Soap films are frequently modified by addition of alkali salts. The best known combination is soap borax, which is inexpensive and effective in severe deformation of heavy gauge hot-rolled steel.

High humidity seriously impairs lubricity and corrosion protection of soap films. Polymer coatings and wax films, though more expensive, are not affected by high humidity and therefore are more reliable.

In recent years, developments from investigations into polymer chemistry have resulted in availability of polymer-based, hot-melt, dry-film lubricants, which are 100% concentrated (no water, oil, etc.) into solid form. Melted to a liquid [105-125° F (41-52° C)] and spray-applied by a fog chamber over the mill oil, these lubricants dry quickly—thus eliminating the cost of precleaning and drying. The polymer-based, hot-melt, dry-film drawing lubricants are applicable to both ferrous and nonferrous metals, in production processes on hot-rolled steel, cold-rolled steel, stainless steel, galvanized steel, and aluminum, in various metal thicknesses. They require a special fog chamber applicator facility.

## Solids

A variety of solids are used as lubricants for metal-deformation processes:

- Dry powdered soaps.
- Lamellar inorganic solids.
- Nonlamellar inorganic solids.
- Organic solids.
- Metallic films.

The term "solid lubricants" covers a wide variety of physical forms and chemical compounds. Physically, the solid lubricant can take the form of a bulk solid, a thin film, or a dispersion in liquid or grease. Chemically, it can be organic or inorganic, reactive or inert.

**Soaps**. Metallic stearates and palmitates have been used for years in mild cold-working operations. These soaps have good "oiliness," but poor antiweld properties. They lubricate well in boundary contacts only at temperatures below their melting points. Above their melting points, soaps have little lubricating value. Melting points of some soaps are given in Table 3-8. Soaps formed by the alkali metals are soluble in water, whereas soaps of other metals are not.

**Lamellar inorganic solids**. The most widely used solid in metalforming is graphite. Graphite is typical of inorganic solids that are resistant to high temperatures and that have low shear strengths as a result of their layer-lattice structures. Although graphite is effective in both cold and hot-deformation processes, it does not satisfy one of the important requirements of a good boundary lubricant—that of interaction with the metals of the surfaces to be lubricated. Because graphite is only mechanically interlocked, or at most physically adsorbed, other lamellar solids are more effective for some processes. The performance of graphite is also very sensitive to the environment in which it must function; it begins to oxidize at about 850° F (454° C), and removal of adsorbed vapors from its surfaces destroys its effectiveness.

**TABLE 3-8**
**Melting Points of Fatty-Acid Soaps**

| | Melting Point of Salt, °C (°F) | | | | | | | |
|---|---|---|---|---|---|---|---|---|
| Cation | Enanthate ($C_7$) | Caprylate ($C_8$) | Pelargonate ($C_9$) | Laurate ($C_{12}$) | Myristate ($C_{14}$) | Palmitate ($C_{16}$) | Stearate ($C_{18}$) | Oleate ($C_{18}$) |
| Ammonium (neutral) | 112 (234) | 114 (237) | 115 (239) | 75 (167) | 75 (167)* | --- | --- | --- |
| Ammonium (acid) | 45 (113) | 54 (129) | --- | 77 (171) | 84 (183) | 89 (192) | 93 (199) | 78 (172) |
| Potassium (acid) | --- | 80 (176)* | --- | 80 (176)* | 95 (203)* | 100 (212)* | 100 (212)* | 95 (203) |
| Lithium | --- | --- | --- | 229 (444) | 224 (435) | 224 (435) | 221 (430) | --- |
| Barium | 238 (460) | --- | --- | 260 (500) | --- | --- | --- | 100 (212) |
| Calcium | --- | --- | 216 (421) | 182 (360) | --- | 155 (311) | 150 (302)* | 83 (181) |
| Magnesium | --- | --- | --- | 150 (302) | 132 (270) | 121 (250) | 132 (270) | --- |
| Lead | 85 (185) | 100 (212) | 98 (208) | 104 (219) | 109 (228) | 112 (234) | 116 (241) | 50 (122) |
| Silver | --- | --- | --- | 212 (414) | 211 (412) | 209 (408) | 205 (401) | --- |
| Zinc | 131 (268) | 135 (275) | 131 (268) | 128 (262) | --- | 129 (264) | 130 (266) | 70 (158) |
| Copper (ic) | --- | 265 (509) | 260 (500) | 112 (234) | --- | 115 (239)* | 125 (257) | 100 (212) |
| Nickel (ic) | --- | --- | --- | 44 (111) | --- | 80 (176) | 80 (176)* | 19 (66) |
| Cobalt (ic) | --- | --- | --- | --- | --- | 70 (158)* | 72 (162)* | --- |

* Melting point varies, depending upon purity of compound. These values are at low end of the range.

Other lamellar solids which are used extensively in metalworking include molybdenum disulfide, mica, and talc. Selection among these solids is not based solely upon their relative abilities to lubricate. Other considerations, such as cost or the difficulty of removing a dark-colored lubricating pigment from the workpiece, are decisive.

**Nonlamellar inorganic solids**. Many nonlamellar solids have been overlooked as lubricating pigments, although certain nonlamellar inorganic solids (lime and phosphate coatings) have been used for years as coatings by themselves and as surface treatments prior to the use of soaps and other lubricants. Lime is applied in slurry form and dried to leave a film which aids soap lubricants in drawing operations. Zinc and manganese phosphate conversion coatings are used (sometimes alone but usually as pretreatments) to enhance the effectiveness of soaps, lamellar solids, and/or liquid lubricants. In such cases, lubricant entrapment by the "chemically etched" or roughened surfaces is the essential feature of enhancement. In recent years conversion coatings consisting of a fluoride-phosphate application and an anodizing treatment have shown considerable promise as pretreatments in the deformation of titanium alloys. For extreme temperatures [2000° F (1100° C) and higher], a number of metal chlorides, oxides, and fluorides have been studied. Most of these materials act as solid lubricants below their melting points, and some have shown good lubricating properties in the molten state.

**Organic solids**. Organic pigments, polymers, and waxes have been used as solid lubricants in both cold and hot deformation. Polytetrafluoroethylene (PTFE) is the polymer which is known best for its utility. Its stability [to above 600° F (316° C)], chemical inertness, and low-friction properties are outstanding among organic compounds. Chemical relatives of PTFE (fluorocarbon telomers) also have shown excellent performance in cold-deformation processes. The main disadvantages of fluorocarbon polymers are their high cost and the difficulty in applying them to ensure optimum performance. Other less expensive and less stable organic polymers have some merit; for example, sheet polyethylene has been used for high-contact-pressure forming.

Even for hot extrusion, some of the unstable thermoplastic resins, such as acrylics, and thermosetting resins, such as phenol-formaldehyde polymers, have been identified as promising lubricants. In most of these cases, however, it is not clear whether the carbon-containing decomposition products contribute to the solid lubrication or whether the viscous effects of softening are responsible. Other resins which have shown promise for high-temperature processes are epoxies and polyamides. As with glass, plastic solid lubricants may be used either as collars located at the tool entry or as films.

**Metallic films**. Metallic films and diffusion-bonded coatings have been developed for forming difficult-to-work alloys such as titanium and tantalum. Electroplated films of chromium, cobalt, copper, gold, iron, nickel, platinum, and silver have been studied as coatings for titanium. Subsequently, induced diffusion of such dissimilar metals showed that friction was lowest for nickel, silver, and chromium. Copper and lead are commonly used in the United States as coatings for drawing stainless steels.

## Additives and Formulation Aids

It is difficult to identify which components in metalworking lubricants should be classified as additives. The lubricants are usually multicomponent formulations, and the functions of some components are often complex and interacting. An additive is a chemical component that favorably influences either the chemical or physical properties of a lubricant. Its concentration usually represents a few percent or less of a solid (usually soluble) or a liquid in an oil-based stock. However, in metalworking lubricants, the additive may be present in up to 50% concentration; in some cases, the liquid major component might be only a vehicle or adjunct-function fluid which does not qualify as a lubricant at all. Therefore, the term *additive* is used

**TABLE 3-9**
**Principal Additives Used in Metalworking Lubricants**

| Additive | Chemical Type | Function |
|---|---|---|
| Antioxidants | Organic amines, phenols, sulfides, hydroxysulfides, often of barium and zinc | Prevent oxidative deterioration causing viscosity change and formation of acids, gums, varnish, and insoluble carbon deposits |
| Corrosion inhibitors | Organic amines and metal salts of organic sulfonates, phosphites, and phosphates, certain unsaturated fatty acids | Prevent corrosion of bearing surfaces, containers for lubricants, and metals of lubrication system and workpieces |
| Oiliness, antiwear, and extreme-pressure agents | Fatty acids, organic phosphates, and phosphites; chlorinated paraffins and other organic compounds containing chlorine, sulfur, and phosphorus; metal salts of organic thiophosphates and thiocarbamates; lead soaps | Reduce friction and prevent wear, galling, scoring, and seizure of metal surfaces in sliding |
| Metal deactivators or passivators | Organic diamines, heterocyclic sulfur-nitrogen compounds | Passify the catalytic effect of metals (especially copper) on oxidation of lubricants |
| Detergent dispersants | Nitrogen and polyethylene glycol-substituted methacrylate polymers, organic sulfonates containing calcium, barium, and magnesium | Prevent collection of deposits on metal surfaces; to prevent agglomeration of insoluble deposits |
| Viscosity-index improvers | Isobutylene and methacrylate polymers | Reduce magnitude of temperature-induced viscosity changes in lubricant |
| Pour-point depressants | High-molecular-weight alkyl aromatic, acrylate, and methacrylate polymers | Prevent solidification of lubricants at low temperatures |
| Antifoam agents | Polyorganosiloxanes | Prevent formation of stable foam |
| Emulsifiers | Organic sulfonates, esters of fatty acids, polyoxyethylene acids, and alcohols | Homogenize oil-water lubricants |
| Antimicrobial agents | Tar acids, chlorine-containing compounds, certain alcohols | Prevent growth of bacteria and fungi which results in insoluble matter; to prevent frothing, discoloration, odor formation, corrosion, and demulsification. |
| Thickeners and tackifiers | Carbon black, silica, bentone clays, polybutenes, polyisobutylenes | Body or thicken lubricant; to make lubricant tack and adherent |
| Solid lubricants | Usually inorganic, lamellar solids—graphite, $MoS_2$ | Increase boundary-lubrication capability; lubricants for high temperatures |
| Odor-masking agents and dyes | Essential oils and perfumes, oil-soluble dyes, and pigments | Mask undesirable odor or color; to yield characteristic odor or color |
| Vehicles, solvents and adjunct-function components | Water, low and high-boiling organic solvents | Enhance cooling properties; to aid lubricant application |
| | Diglycol stearate | Couple thickeners and additives to base oil; to prevent bleeding of greases |
| | Low-surface-energy fluorocarbons | Prevent migration of oils to undesired locations |

to cover liquids employed as vehicles, solvents, and other application aids, as well as the materials that are considered conventional additives.

Examples of the types of additives used to influence chemical properties of the lubricant are:

- Antioxidants.
- Corrosion inhibitors.
- Oiliness, antiwear, and extreme-pressure agents.
- Metal deactivators or passivators.
- Detergent dispersants.

Additives used to improve physical properties of lubricants are:

- Viscosity-index improvers.
- Pour-point depressants.
- Antifoam agents.
- Emulsifiers.
- Antimicrobial agents.
- Thickeners and tackifiers.
- Solid lubricants.
- Odor-masking agents and dyes.
- Vehicles, solvents, and essentially nonlubricative components.

Of the physical additives, the last seven types listed are most frequently included in metalworking lubricants. The functions and mechanisms of action of the 14 types of additives are presented in Table 3-9.

# LUBRICANT APPLICATION METHODS

The method of application is an important factor in determining effectiveness of metalforming lubrication. This is apparent when considering how it relates to the way the lubricant performs. Use too little and performance is impaired; use too much and costs go up; misdirect the lubricant and it is not applied at the critical locations. Cleaning, disposal, and housekeeping costs are influenced by application of lubricant.[5]

Some stamping plants use considerably more lubricant than the job requires. The objective in applying a drawing compound or lubricant is to apply the correct compound or lubricant where needed, at the right time, and in the proper amount. In general, lubricant is needed at the punch for punch and pierce operations and form and stretch-form operations; for drawing operations, it is needed at the die radii.

## BENEFITS

The job requirement is the main factor in selecting the type of lubricant; and the lubricant, in turn, is a key determinant for the application method. Other important considerations include the type of press and the press feed, and the type of die, whether single or multistation. The following are benefits attainable from correct lubricant application:

- Reduced lubricant usage.
- Increased press speed.
- Longer die life.
- Cleaner operations.
- Reduced shop maintenance (cleanup).
- Reduced scrap.
- Reduced lubricant carryoff.
- Simplified waste disposal.

## BASIC METHODS

Five basic methods exist for applying die lubricants, whether they be heavy drawing lubricants or light mineral oils for fast blanking. Selection should be made after considering the advantages and disadvantages of each method, with emphasis on compatibility with the overall manufacturing operations. In some forming operations, a combination of methods is required to obtain effective lubrication. As illustrated in Fig. 3-3, the commonly used application methods are manual, drip, roller, spraying, and flooding.

### Manual Application

The most basic way to apply lubricant is by hand, with a brush, sponge, swab, or roller or by dipping. All of these manual methods require very little equipment; and, initially, seem to be economical. However, any manual method can be expensive. The two principal cost factors are wasted lubricant and high labor cost caused by excessive time to perform the operation.

**Advantages**. The various brushes, swabs, etc., are readily available, inexpensive, and require no maintenance. Manual application is useful in short-run work for applying lubricant at a selected place on the workpiece, for reapplication to formed parts, and on second operations.

**Disadvantages**. The disadvantages of manual application are significant. This method is usually wasteful. It may require the operator to reach into the die area, which may be dangerous and (in some instances) would violate OSHA regulations. If the operator is careless and applies lubricant insufficiently or erratically, die wear will increase. Manual application necessitates an open container, which can lead to contamination and other problems.

### Drip Application

The first rudimentary drip applicators probably were made by punching a hole in the bottom of a can and allowing lubricant to drip continuously on the strip stock. Progress has brought carefully designed, sophisticated systems with various accessories such as felt wiper pads and rollers. A typical drip applicator is mounted after the stock or roll feed. Drip application of lubricant can be used for small parts that are being blanked and formed, and where light-bodied, easy-flowing lubricants are used. When heavy, viscous lubricants are applied by dripping, it may be necessary to spread the lubricant with rollers.

**Advantages**. Well-engineered drip systems are relatively inexpensive and are readily available. A petcock or regulating valve enables adjustment to assure that the correct flow of lubricant is applied consistently. Usually, the applicator can be mounted to apply the lubricant where it is most needed—for instance, at a critical station of a die or behind (rather than before) a roll feed, to reduce slippage.

**Disadvantages**. These systems typically lack provision for

# LUBRICANT APPLICATION METHODS

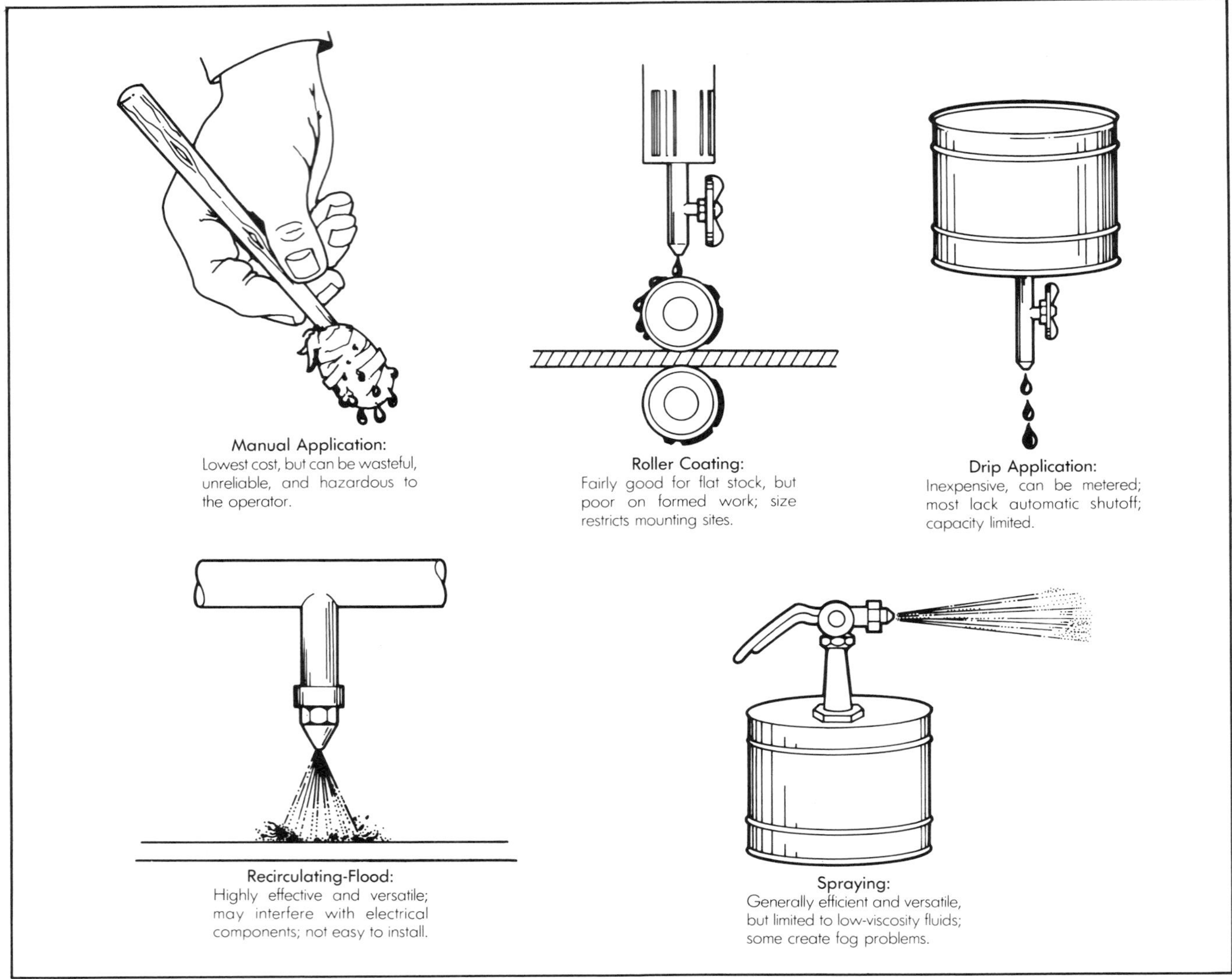

Manual Application:
Lowest cost, but can be wasteful, unreliable, and hazardous to the operator.
Roller Coating:
Fairly good for flat stock, but poor on formed work; size restricts mounting sites.
Drip Application:
Inexpensive, can be metered; most lack automatic shutoff; capacity limited.
Recirculating-Flood:
Highly effective and versatile; may interfere with electrical components; not easy to install.
Spraying:
Generally efficient and versatile, but limited to low-viscosity fluids; some create fog problems.


**Fig. 3-3 Methods of applying die lubricants.**

agitation. This requires use of a stable compound that does not separate into its constituents. Also, this application method does not provide automatic shutoff when the equipment stops. Without an automatic shutoff valve, the operator must close the metering valve when the press is stopped. Unless this is done promptly, lubricant is wasted and parts become oily and messy. When a large stock area is to be lubricated, a drip applicator is not suitable because of relatively small reservoir capacity. Usually, the reservoir requires frequent filling, which, in itself, can be wasteful. An empty reservoir can lead to quality problems, productivity loss, and accelerated die wear.

## Roller Coating

The roller coater method of application is widely used for applying lubricant. There are three types of roller coaters: unpowered, plain; unpowered with recirculating system; and powered. Certain features common to all three types should be kept in mind when determining design aspects of the system that is to be installed. First, the location of the roller coater is important. The preferred position is between the fabricating equipment and the feeding mechanism. Placing the coater before the coil feed can allow lubricant to be mechanically wiped off the metal surface and can cause slippage in the coil feeding mechanism. Another important point is positive control of the lubricant that is being applied. An effective method is to link lubricant flow to the equipment feeding mechanism by a flow valve on the roller coater or a pressure switch on the machine.

**System design considerations.** The viscosity of the lubricant being applied by a roller coater influences selection of pump components. When light oils or water-based fluids are used, a centrifugal pump is suitable for lubricant recirculation. For heavy oils, a gear type pump is needed. Roller coater material is another important point. Rolls can be made from steel, neoprene, felt, urethane, or polyurethane. The roller surface can be altered to retain lubricant. Special grooves or surface texturizing can be added, to make the roller more adaptable for the specific lubricant that is being used. Care is needed to avoid lubricant "pooling" between movements of stock feed into the presses. When working nonferrous materials or specially coated stock, a soft roller made of either felt, neoprene, or polyurethane should be used to avoid scratching or marring the surface.

**Unpowered, plain roller**. The unpowered roller coater is used extensively. In operation, the coil feeding mechanism pushes the stock through the rollers and lubricant drips on or between the rollers. The stock is coated with lubricant as it passes through the applicator rollers. Either or both sides of the material can be lubricated, as shown in Fig. 3-4.[6]

*Advantages*. This system is inexpensive and readily available. It is easy to maintain and provides some degree of control over the amount of lubricant and the uniformity of lubricant film.

*Disadvantages*. The plain, unpowered roller is adequate for some short-run jobs involving sheet and strip, but it shares many disadvantages with the drip applicators. It requires a stable lubricant compound. It usually requires that the operator shut the lubricant off when the press is stopped. Reservoir capacity often is quite limited. Many models do not provide for roll tension, which means that lubricant film control is uncertain. Because of space restrictions, roller coaters typically must be mounted ahead of the stock feed. This does not cause problems with a hitch or gripper feed, but it can cause slippage when used with roller feeds.

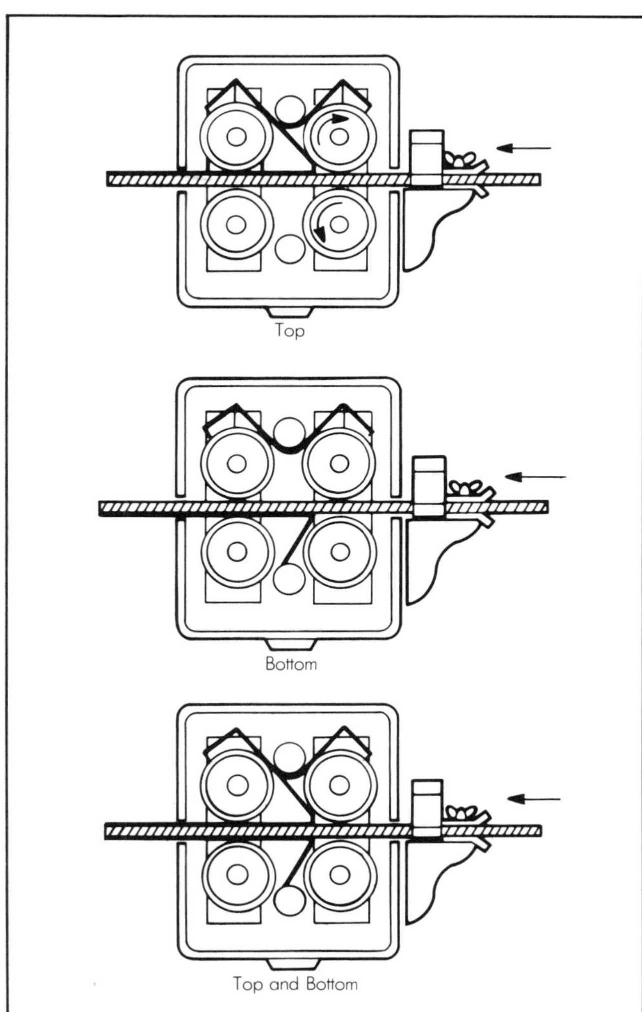


**Fig. 3-4 Three methods of lubricant application by roller coater.**

**Unpowered roller with recirculation**. These systems give continuous lubrication and reduce lubricant consumption. The roller should be located after the feed stock, eliminating slippage problems. The rollers also act as stock guides.

*Advantages*. Unpowered roller coaters used with recirculating systems are more effective than the roller-drip combination. The excess lubricant is squeezed off by the wiper rollers; then, it is returned to the reservoir, where it is filtered and available for reapplication. These systems are readily available. The recirculation gives continuous lubrication and at the same time decreases total consumption, since spillage is reduced and unused lubricant is recovered. Some designs can be mounted after the stock feed, thereby eliminating the slippage problem. Adjustable roller tension provides control in applying the lubricant film.

*Disadvantages*. The principal disadvantage is comparatively high cost for initial purchase, installation, and setup.

**Powered roller with recirculation**. For large blanks and wide sheets, powered roller coaters integrated with recirculating lubrication systems have been developed, with initial applications in the automotive and appliance industries.

*Advantages*. Powered rollers share the advantages of unpowered roller coater systems, including the ability to coat wide widths evenly. With either roller system, the lubricating function is performed efficiently and the pressworking operation is relatively clean, both at the press and the adjacent area.

*Disadvantages*. A common disadvantage of roller coaters is that they cannot be used to lubricate formed or partially formed work—as in operations involving progressive dies—or to lubricate work prior to secondary operations. Similarly, in a transfer or eyelet machine, the lubricant film may not be durable enough to last through the first few stations; a secondary means of applying additional lubricant must be developed. Sometimes this is accomplished merely by supplementing the roller coater with a drip-type unit within the die area. Often, however, this is not feasible and another approach must be taken.

## Spraying

Lubricant spray application is the most versatile system. The most commonly used type is the air spray system. A newer type is the airless spray system, which is gaining in usage. A third type, the electrostatic spray, has limited application.

**Air spray system**. Special nozzles and related accessories have been developed to make air spraying compatible with die lubrication. Currently available spray guns are compact in size and can be provided with offset fittings to enable mounting in small areas. Most of the units have adjustable nozzles for control of lubricant volume.

*Advantages*. Air spray systems are readily available and relatively inexpensive, although cost varies with complexity of the requirements. This system can be integrated with press operations and can be used for single or multistation equipment. Lubricant usage can be controlled precisely, and special nozzles are available for pattern spray. The air spray systems are well-suited to automation or semiautomation. They can be connected into the press control circuit to operate only when and where needed. They can be used in transfer and progressive and secondary operations. Such requirements are met by installing a number of spray nozzles at the proper locations.

*Disadvantages*. Air spray systems create a fog or mist. They need a continuous air supply, and they cannot be used with high-viscosity drawing compounds and lubricants. In many installations, a mist collector must be used.

**Airless spray system**. These systems usually are activated by the press ram. They use a mechanical method of producing high pressure on the lubricant. Pressure is applied by means of an intensifier and is conveyed through a pressure-resistant hose to an orifice in the nozzle, from which the lubricant is expelled as a fine spray. Figure 3-5 illustrates an airless spray system.

*Advantages*. This system does not use air. There is no atomizing effect; no mist or fog. The unit can be adjusted to deliver a heavy intermittent drip or a light film, and it can handle high-viscosity compounds. There is no bounce or overspray; the lubricant can be directed at a particular area in the die and can be timed to operate off the equipment cycle. Heavy films can be applied to formed work, and this system is readily adapted to automated pressworking.

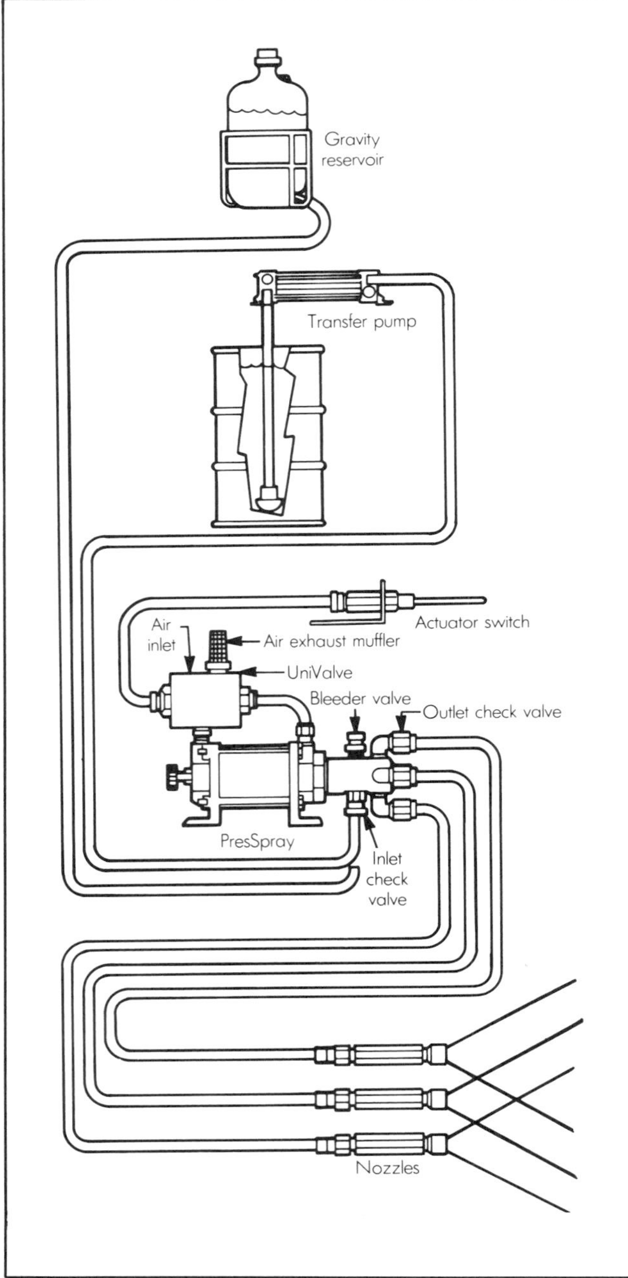


**Fig. 3-5 Airless spray lubricant systems.**

*Disadvantages*. Initial cost is relatively high. Also, this system is complex; hence, it requires careful installation and more maintenance than the air spray system.

**Electrostatic spray**. In principle, this system resembles an electrostatic paint spraying system; the lubricant is attracted to the work and "wraps around" it, with virtually no overspray or bounce. When it is feasible to use such a system, and when the application offers cost justification, this system can be very effective. Applications, however, are quite limited, due to various considerations, including restrictions on the type of lubricant that can be used.

## Flooding

The flood lubrication system consists of a pump, a sump, filters, and as many lubricant supply points as the job requires. The flooding provides a cooling effect, as well as effective lubrication. In addition, since lubricant is returned continuously to the sump, is filtered, and then is recirculated, a heavy flow volume can be used when necessary, without wasting the lubricant. The only significant lubricant loss occurs through carryoff, which can be reduced by using dilute solutions with low viscosity.

**Advantages**. Since the lubricant is flooded, a highly diluted water-soluble compound can be used. Regardless of the number of stations in a progressive die or transfer press, positive lubrication at all stations is simply a matter of providing enough supply points. This is done by attaching small diameter tubing. Die life may be increased substantially in some applications. This is attributable to the beneficial cooling action, plus delivery of an abundant supply of lubricant to the critical points. The cooling effect also enables use of increased press speeds. Avoidance of slug pickup is a side benefit attributed to the water-soluble lubricants that are used with the flood systems.

**Disadvantages**. Standard presses often do not have built-in recirculating systems, which are needed for flooding. To use this system in an existing press, it may be necessary to perform the design and installation as an in-plant project. The press's lubrication system must be shielded. Die cushions can be a source of difficulty. Sensing systems must be waterproofed. Dies should be vented. Electrical systems may need to be rerouted. Initial cost for design and installation of a flood system is higher than for other systems. One such unit is shown in Fig. 3-6.

## Current Practice

Of the five die lubricant application methods available—hand, drip, roller, spray, and flood—the last three are most commonly used in modern metalforming operations. Typically, recirculating roller coating is used for single-point application; and spraying or flooding is used for multipoint application. For best results, the lubricant and application method should be established during the job planning stage, in the early phase of tooling and production engineering. Furthermore, it must be recognized that overall responsibility includes the provision of adequate means for disposal of lubricants after they have performed their function.

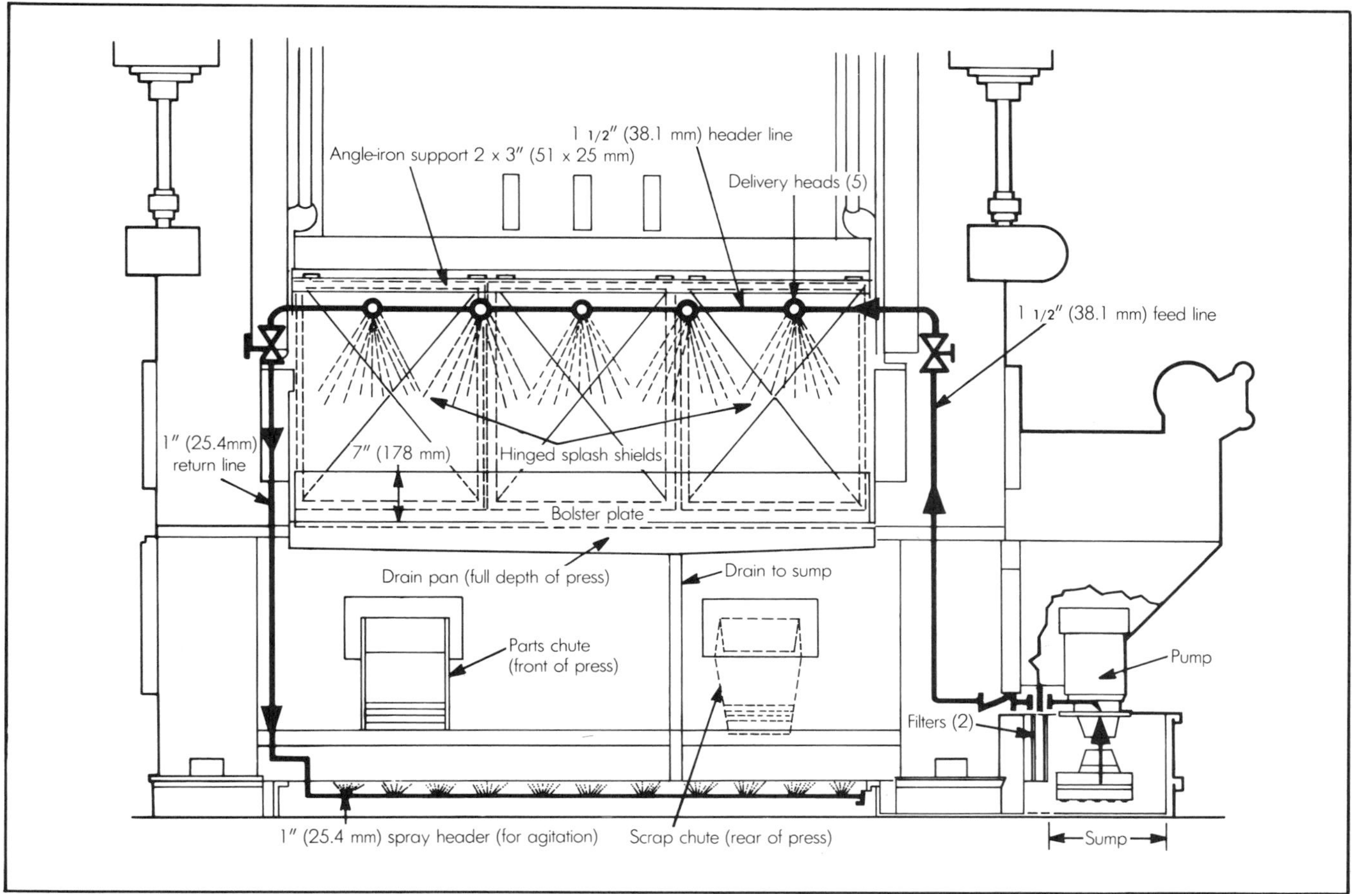


**Fig. 3-6 Recirculating flood die-lubricant system on a straight-side press.**

# WASTE TREATMENT AND DISPOSAL

Lubricant disposal is discussed fully in Chapter 4, Volume I, *Machining,* of this Handbook series. The following, therefore, deals briefly with waste treatment and disposal of synthetic lubricants.

Some synthetic lubricants can cause difficulties in treatment systems. Because of this, it is important to identify the lubricant involved and establish an evaluation procedure that considers waste treatment compatibility.

## WASTE TREATMENT

The most common mistake in waste treatment lies in trying to treat the synthetic effluent as if it were a petroleum oil-type product. Since synthetics contain no petroleum and form chemically true solutions, there is no emulsion to split. Therefore, the use of emulsion-splitting chemicals may induce extra problems in the treatment process while accelerating cost.

Also of concern is that many water-based synthetics contain wetting additives that can cause a tight emulsion to form in conjunction with tramp oil contaminants. Such an emulsion may be more resistant to standard treatment techniques than petroleum-based oil. A chemically true synthetic resists tramp oil pickup. Since the tramp oil contaminants merely float on the surface, skimmers remove the oil phase without the need for treatment with chemicals.

The question to ask is: How can it be determined if a given synthetic will pose problems in a treatment process? A sample of the test lubricant should be mixed with the hydraulic oil that is currently being used in-house; about 5% by volume should be added and shaken vigorously. The oil should float to the surface within approximately 15 minutes. Many synthetics pass this test within 60-90 seconds. The faster the oil rejection time, the more compatible the synthetic will be with the waste treatment procedure, thus improving the efficiency of surface skimmers.

## BIODEGRADABILITY

One accepted definition of the term biodegradable uses Biological Oxygen Demand (BOD) and Chemical Oxygen Demand (COD) as the determining parameters. BOD measures the ability of bacteria to oxidize readily available organic matter in the effluent, while COD measures the oxygen requirements to achieve this degradation.

With petroleum oils, BOD values are generally low, while

COD is high. This indicates that it is difficult for bacteria to break down organic matter that is present in the material. Synthetics generally show a high BOD which can be equal to 50-70% of the COD. Such a profile indicates an active bacterial action to achieve degradation of organics, thus placing an oxygen demand on the effluent. Generally, this indicates that the synthetic is biodegradable.

Furthermore, biodegradability is defined in terms of compatibility with most municipal waste treatment systems. Properly formulated synthetics should reduce treatment costs for the user and should still be compatible with municipal systems. The crucial challenge presented to the compounder of lubricants is how to achieve microbial inhibition to prevent rancidity in the lubricant on the job without also inhibiting the growth of microbial degradation organisms in treatment systems upon disposal.

Responsibility for this information is often assigned to the lubricant supplier to demonstrate compatibility. It is desirable that a microbiological study be made using a living culture mix of bacteria, yeasts and mold that are acclimated to decompose synthetic lubricants. Studies should be made to determine the concentration at which a synthetic material can be treated without inhibiting biological activity. Disposal recommendations would then include dilution ratios for disposal of the lubricant to minimize the chance of incompatibility with the waste treatment system.

Those who use lubricants must realize that aqueous-based synthetics are chemically different from soluble oil. Once the previously mentioned screening tests have been performed successfully, chemical treatment requirements can generally be reduced. Neutralization of the effluent is nearly always recommended.

If the natural untreated waste stream efficiently rejects tramp oil, air flotation and skimming systems operate more efficiently. The use of polyelectrolytes can further provide for removal of suspended solids and organics. Addition of high levels of acid, caustics, alum, ferric chloride, etc., can be greatly reduced or eliminated. Of course, if the waste stream receives high levels of contamination from various sources in the production process, all factors must be considered in the screening process. It is important that the effluent sample be representative of the primary in-house sources of pollution.

# CLEANING

Residues of drawing and stamping compounds must be removed from metal surfaces to prepare the parts for in-process storage or subsequent operations. Usually, these surfaces must be cleaned prior to other operations, such as plating, painting, enameling, rustproofing, welding, or adhesive bonding of some other material to the surface of the parts.

Because a stamped part is not completed until all of the subsequent operations have been performed, it is important to understand the role and influence of the lubricant upon the cost and effectiveness of cleaning and upon the ensuing secondary operations.

## TYPES OF CLEANERS

The types of cleaners generally used for removing drawing compounds fall in the broad categories of solvent cleaners and alkaline cleaners. Acid cleaners sometimes are used for special applications that require removal of tarnish from metals.

### Solvent Cleaners

Certain drawing compounds containing oils, fats, and waxes can be removed by organic solvents, such as:

- Petroleum solvents—kerosene, naptha, or stoddard solvent applied by wiping or immersion.
- Nonflammable solvents—trichlorethylene or perchlorethylene, used in vapor degreasers.
- Special formulated solvents—emulsion cleaners, emulsifiable solvents, or diphase cleaners.

Care should be taken because some solvents are flammable and also because some of the organic vapors are toxic.

### Alkaline Cleaners

Alkaline cleaners are widely used for removal of drawing compounds in soak cleaning and spray cleaning operations. They are also used for barrel cleaning, electrocleaning, and ultrasonic cleaning. Alkaline cleaners generally are used to remove soils for in-process cleaning and to prepare metals for operations such as painting or plating.

Alkaline cleaners are formulated with alkaline builders, chelating agents, and surfactants. They are formulated to clean by a combination of mechanisms, including saponification, emulsification, dispersion, chelation, wetting, and solvency. Solvents and corrosion inhibitors also are included in formulations for some applications. Specific cleaners are prepared for ferrous and nonferrous metals to avoid undue etch or tarnish.

## CLEANER SELECTION FACTORS

In addition to the type and composition of the lubricant that is to be removed, selection of a cleaner should be based upon consideration of the following factors:

- Dirt and soil to be removed.
- Surface to be cleaned.
- Degree of cleanliness needed.
- Water supply.
- Safety considerations.
- Disposal of spent solutions.
- Method of application.

## GENERAL GUIDELINES

In terms of overall "system" planning, it is desirable to predetermine and match the lubricant properties with the cleaning operation. For effective operations, it is important to specify and maintain adequate wash temperatures and to avoid overuse and excessive dilution of cleaners. Alkaline cleaners used at high temperatures generally can remove and clean most petroleum-based lubricants and water-soluble compounds. Vapor degreasers, on the other hand, are not effective in cleaning water-soluble compounds and should not be used for pigmented or paste lubricants or compounds.

Low-temperature cleaning, which includes acid cleaning, is growing in usage, because of the savings in both energy and cleaning costs. Heavy residual oils, fats, and other insolubles contaminate these types of cleaners more readily—since they clean by lifting off the foreign particles and lubricants that are present on the metal surface. The resulting buildup of contaminants then must be removed from the cleaner, or the cleaner must be replaced. If low-temperature cleaning operations are part of the production system, it is, therefore, important to select compatible lubricants.

In terms of complexity and cost of the so-called "subsequent" operations, the greatest potential for savings can be gained when it is feasible to use the recently developed "extra clean" synthetic or the chemical solubles for the lubricant specification.

# LUBRICANT QUALITY CONTROL

Numerous quality-control techniques are available to the lubricant user for checking incoming shipments and maintaining in-process control. Tests on incoming materials ensure that the material meets specifications, and in-process checks lead to accurate compensation for the lubricant that is consumed, evaporated, or carried away in the deformation process. In-process checks also protect against spoilage or contamination by foreign materials. Electron microscopy is an effective means of detecting and identifying particles; electron and X-ray beam techniques are also used to identify materials.

## STANDARDS

All quality-control test procedures are not described here. The American Society for Testing and Materials (ASTM) has adequately described standard tests in their entirety. The following physical tests for oil lubricants have been standardized by ASTM and are used to determine various properties:

- Viscosity (ASTM D88).
- Flash point (ASTM D92).
- Fire point (ASTM D92).
- Gravity (ASTM D287).
- Percent sulfur (ASTM D129).
- Percent chlorine (ASTM D808).
- Saponifiable matter (ASTM D855).
- Free fatty acid (ASTM D128).
- Soap and emulsifier (ASTM D855).
- Foaming (ASTM D3519 and D3601).
- Sheet metal forming lubricant evaluation (ASTM D4173).

Additional standards to determine properties of emulsified lubricants include:

- Moisture (ASTM D95).
- Ash (ASTM D482).
- Sulfated residue (ASTM D128).

## TESTING

Inorganic solid lubricants are often used in the most severe and high-temperature deformation processes. These solids are almost always dispersed in a fluid medium. The fluid medium may contribute significantly to the total lubricant effectiveness, or it may serve strictly as a carrier fluid which allows efficient application of the solid lubricant.

Some of the common tests used to check and control solid lubricants dispersed in fluid carriers can determine solids content, particle size, suspension properties, consistency, and ash content.

### Solids Content

After accurately weighing the lubricant sample, the carrier fluid is removed by heating (to remove the volatile solvents and water) and filtration (to remove the oil). Oven temperatures of 230° F (110° C) are commonly employed, with drying time being about 3 hr. Devices are also available which automatically dry and weigh the samples, employing higher temperatures (350° F or 175° C) and shorter cycle times.

### Particle Size

A diluted sample of lubricant is placed on a glass slide and viewed through a transmitted-light microscope. A calibrated eyepiece allows the viewer to measure minimum and maximum particle sizes and to determine a rough particle-size distribution. Electronic counting devices are also available which measure the particles as they pass through an orifice and automatically plot a size-distribution curve.

### Suspension

The suspension properties or, conversely, the settling tendencies can be determined by:

- Centrifuging.
- Colorimetric tests—transmitted light.
- Gravimetric settling.

### Consistency

A Zahn cup, Saybolt apparatus, or Brookfield viscometer is commonly employed to measure viscosities of fluid dispersions, with various cone-penetration tests being used on heavy grease or paste materials. Applicable standards include:

- Zahn cup (ASTM D3794).
- Saybolt (ASTM D88).
- Kinematic (ASTM D445).
- Brookfield (ASTM D2393, D2849).
- Cone-penetration (ASTM D217, D937, D1321).

### Ash

Water carriers are first removed by drying. Volatile carriers such as alcohol are removed by drying and are exposed to an open flame to flash off any remaining fluid. Less volatile petroleum carriers are usually burned off. The residues are then weighed, subjected to a temperature of 1510° F (820° C) for 2 1/2 to 3 hr, and reweighed. This test is not employed with $MoS_2$ or $WS_2$ products, since they form oxides that vaporize and recrystallize on the furnace interior. Talc, mica, etc., do not significantly decompose at this temperature and are included in the total ash content of the product.

### General Considerations

It is important that all dispersions be thoroughly agitated

before samples are taken for quality-control purposes. It is also recommended that lubricants containing solids be continually agitated during use to assure uniform results. This is not necessary with very thick materials in which the solids are physically unable to settle.

Initial examination of soap-type lubricants can be performed through color and density comparisons with agreed-upon standards. Soaps can also be characterized by solubility limits in water at a certain temperature. Foaming tendency can be measured with a simple food blender test. Most soaps are a complex mixture of many compounds, and a simple melting point is not easily obtained. Liquid soaps or soaps added to water can be checked for viscosity by using the Zahn cup, Ford cup, or Brookfield viscometer.

Organic solids can be checked similarly; in a dispersion, the solids content can be checked by gravimetric means or a centrifuge test. The diluent can be removed by drying and weighing the solid residue as mentioned previously.

Tests such as saponification number, total acid number—electrometric (TAN-E), total base number—electrometric (TBN-E), or color indicator are usually used in checking compounded oils. They are also useful for soaps and organic solids.

Since soaps may be used as solids or as liquid solutions, the inspection methods for incoming materials can also be applied to the materials during use. The temperature, viscosity, and solids content of liquid solutions should be controlled.

Metallic film specifications can be controlled through chemical analysis of the plating solutions. Brass and bronze solutions are usually checked for free cyanide, carbonates, metallic copper, and zinc; lead solutions are normally checked only for metallic lead; and tin solutions are checked for sodium stannate and metallic tin.

The exact methods of carrying out quality-control tests and the more specific tests for determining particular properties of a specific compound can usually be obtained from the supplier of the lubricant.

Standards and laboratory tests are useful aids to lubricant selection and quality control. Acceptability of metal-deformation lubricants is, however, contingent on performance. Specialized test procedures can be performed for processing problems. These tests are generally conducted in the plant under existing operating conditions. A variety of test procedures are used with adaptations to suit individual problems. Data from these tests must be critically evaluated to assure that an acceptable correlation exists between laboratory and production performance.

### STORAGE

Year-round indoor storage is best for practically all metalworking lubricants and coolants. Ideal indoor storage provides for moderate heating in winter [50-70° F (10-21° C)] and ventilation in summer [70-90° F (21-32° C)]. Many oil and aqueous metalworking fluids contain organic fatty compounds, soaps, and oils which are sensitive to prolonged heat and to freezing. Hence, extremes of temperature in storage should be avoided. If indoor storage cannot be arranged, sheltered outdoor storage in summer, with air ventilation around drum stock, is the next best choice. In winter, aqueous fluids, emulsions, complex soap/fat dispersions, and sulfurized oils must be stored indoors for adequate protection. Otherwise, the aqueous fluids may freeze, the organic dispersions may be degraded, and crystalline sulfur suspensions may be precipitated. Stocks of emulsions, aqueous suspensions, and fatty-compound lubricants should normally not be stored more than 6 months under any conditions. More stable metalworking oil products can be held for about 12 months or longer under ideal conditions.

If drums are stored outdoors, they should be laid on their sides on raised wooden runners, or if they must be stacked upright, they should be tilted with the bungs in the three o'clock or nine o'clock positions to avoid leakage of accumulated rainwater.

When bulk tank storage is required, localized temperature extremes must be avoided. In winter, if the fluid is heated by immersion heaters and no sensitive heater control is provided, oil circulation past heater surfaces must be a minimum of 5 fps (1.5 m/s), with higher circulation rates preferable.

### RECOVERY

Metalworking fluid recovery is usually practiced only with oil fluids. Although aqueous fluids may be maintained during service by means of settling tanks, bulk replenishment, filters, and centrifuges, they are usually disposed of after a reasonable period. This service period varies considerably with the type of fluid or emulsion and the class of service required. Typical use periods may range from as little as 3 to 4 months up to a year. Oil fluid recovery with heaters, centrifuges, filters, etc., is common practice.

## TROUBLESHOOTING

As covered previously, pressworking lubricants are used to reduce and control friction and to provide tool protection, rust inhibition, cooling, acceptably finished pieces, and minimum scrap. The general guidelines in Table 3-10 are provided as a starting point for investigation of problems and determination of corrective actions. Key aspects for consideration in troubleshooting include viscosity, mixture, lubricity and EP agents, and complex compounds.[7]

### VISCOSITY

For pressworking lubricants, viscosity—a measure of resistance to flow at a specific temperature—is the key physical property that must be monitored. Low viscosity lubricants are used for light-duty, high-speed work. Higher viscosity lubricants are used for heavier duty, slower speed operations, and the forming of thick metals.

### MIXTURE

This property of lubricants refers to both the compounding of additives and the dilution of a concentrate with water, kerosene, or light oils.

Water-soluble concentrates usually are designed for dilution with water in ratios varying from 1:1 to 1:60 or more. The more water used, the lower the lubricant cost per part formed and the greater the cooling effect that is provided. However, increasing the percentage of water changes the lubricity, die protection, and rust prevention, and may result in die galling.

Dilutions of concentrate in water are generally in the range

**TABLE 3-10**
**Pressworking Problem-Solving Guide**

| Variable | Scoring | Wrinkling* | Breakage | Poor Concentricity |
|---|---|---|---|---|
| | Problems, Causes and Possible Solutions | | | |
| Press | Ram off center or traveling too fast. | Hold-down pressure uneven or too low. | Ram off center or traveling too fast. Hold-down pressure too high. | Ram misaligned. Excessive wear of vertical ways or post. |
| Material | Too hard. Impurities or foreign substances. Laminated stock. | Too thin or soft. | Too hard or brittle. Foreign inclusions. Wrong blank size. Laminated stock. | Blank wrong size or shape. |
| Dies | Misalignment of punch and die. Too soft. Too little clearance. Not properly polished. Die ring land too long. | Radius on die too large. Too much clearance. | Misalignment of punch and die. Radius on punch and/or die ring too small. | Misalignment of punch and die. |
| Lubricant | Improper product application. Additive percentage too low. Need cushioning agents. Need better wetting. Mix thicker. Increase film strength. | Improper product application. Too much slip. Wrong viscosity. Thin the mixture. | Improper product application. Mixture too thin. Product too heavy. Increase film strength. | Improper product application. Mixture too thick. |

* Draw beads are used to control wrinkling.

of 1:1 to 1:20, to provide the best combination of desirable characteristics. Such mixtures have sufficient oil concentrate and chemical additives to protect the dies and workpieces in most pressworking applications.

These recommended dilution ratios also apply to kerosene and light oil. Kerosene, however, reduces lubricity and can cause premature die wear and excessive scrap. Mineral oil is slightly higher in viscosity than kerosene and is a better lubricant. Also, since it is not as good a solvent as kerosene, it is milder to exposed skin.

## LUBRICITY AND EP AGENTS

The chemistry of a lubricant includes the additions of various lubricity and extreme-pressure (EP) agents that make the fluid slipperier and more wear and weld-resistant. These agents include fat, phosphorus, chlorine, and sulfur. Percentages of the agents used for any given application are dictated by the ductility of the metal, configuration of the part, temperatures generated, press cycle time, and other factors.

The content of viscosity and lubricity agents (which control slipperiness) can cause pressworking problems, if improperly specified. Lubricity agents function under all temperature conditions, but are least effective below 50° F (10° C) and above 1200° F (649° C). Fat is a good lubricity additive, since it is attracted to most metal surfaces and does not stain metal.

Extreme-pressure additives form a chemical/mechanical film that minimizes metal-to-metal contact, thus providing antiwear and antiweld properties. The film is temperature/pressure activated, and the additive types and percentages vary with severity of the operation. Phosphorus is the least active EP additive, and is generally limited to less severe pressworking operations that generate temperatures up to about 400° F (204° C). For heavier operations, with temperatures up to about 572° F (300° C), chlorine can be added. Sulfur is often used as an EP additive for the most severe operations, with temperatures up to about 1380° F (750° C), but it is limited to the forming of ferrous metals.

## COMPLEX COMPOUNDS

Most pressworking operations can be handled satisfactorily with lubricants having the proper viscosity, mixture, and additives discussed. However, when washability, sharp corner radii, poor metal, die finish peculiarities, or other problems occur, it may be necessary to work with a lubricant supplier in developing a more complex compound.

In addition to the ingredients previously discussed, these compounds may contain such solid separating or cushioning agents as soap, talc, mica, graphite, molybdenum disulfide, pigments, fibers, or Teflon. These ingredients alter film strength, die protection properties, and the effective viscosity and lubricity. Their mechanism is not so much chemical as physical. They physically keep the punch, die, and workpiece from contacting each other.

While these more complex compounds may solve some pressworking problems, they can also cause problems in subsequent washing, welding, painting, or plating and in maintaining plant cleanliness. However, when needed they can materially reduce scrap and increase productivity. Tight control of their storage, application, and removal is necessary for efficient production.

# CHAPTER 3

## BIBLIOGRAPHY


### References

1. W. R. D. Wilson, *A Review of Recent Research on the Mechanics of Metal Forming Lubrication*, SME Technical Paper MS77-341, 1977.
2. Donald P. Koistinen and Neng-Ming Wang, *Mechanics of Sheet Metal Forming*, NY: Plenum Press, 1978.
3. Joseph Ivaska, Jr., "Synthetic Lubricants in Pressworking," *Proceedings of FabTech International*, Society of Manufacturing Engineers and Fabricating Manufacturers Association, Inc., 1981.
4. Ronald J. Newhouse, "Modern Metal-Forming Lubrication," *Tooling & Production* (October 1981).
5. R. I. Hamilton, *Picking the Right Method for Applying Die Lubricants*, SME Technical Paper MF76-988, 1976.
6. Joseph Ivaska, Jr., *Lubrication Requirements for Transfer Presses, Transfer Die Systems and Progressive Dies*, SME Technical Paper MFR79-03, 1979.
7. Donald Hixson, "Pressworking Lubricants," *Manufacturing Engineering* (February 1979), p. 56.

### Bibliography

American Society of Metals. *Metals Handbook, Forming.* vol. 4, Metals Park, OH, 1969.

Bastian, E. L. "Modern Developments in Fluids & Metal Forming Operations." *Lubrication Engineering* (July 1969), pp. 278-84.

Hamilton, R. I. *Modern Advances in Blanking, Piercing, and Stamping Lubricants.* SME Technical Paper MF74-625, 1974.

Ivaska, Joseph, Jr. "Analysis of Lubrication Problems in Roll Forming." *Proceedings of FabTech International*, Society of Manufacturing Engineers and Fabricating Manufacturers Association Inc., 1981.

Jentgen, R. L. *The Key Role of Lubrication in Metal Deformation Processes.* SME Technical Paper MFR72-01, 1972.

__________. "Lubrication in Metal Deformation Processes," Monograph, Battelle Memorial Institute.

Lloyd, D. H. "Lubrication for Press Forming." *Sheet Metal Industries* (March, April, May, July 1966).

*Lubricants—A Productive Tool in the Metal Stamping Process.* SME Technical Paper TE77-499, 1977.

"Metal Deformation Processing," DMIC Report 226, Vol. II, Battelle Memorial Institute, Defense Information Center, 1966.

Nachtman, Elliot S. *A Review of Surface-Lubricant Interactions During Metal Forming.* SME Technical Paper MS77-338, 1977.

Otrhalek, J. V. *Selection of Cleaning Process to Remove Stamping and Drawing Compounds from Metal Surfaces.* SME Technical Paper MR77-951, 1977.

*Overview of Lubricant Properties for Four-Slide Metal Forming.* SME Technical Paper MFR79-02, 1979.

Plevy, T. A. "A Review of Sheet and Strip Lubricants and Their Application Prior to Forming Operations." *Sheet Metal Industries* (February 1980), pp. 137-147.

Schey, J. A. *Metal Deformation Processes; Friction and Lubrication.* NY: Marcel Dekker, Inc., 1970.

Schey, J. A., Ratnagar, H. S., and Cheng, H. S. "Surface Deformation of Aluminum Compressed with Viscous Lubricants." *Journal of Lubrication Technology*, vol. 96 (1974), pp. 591-594.

Spallina, Elroy M. *Systems Approach to the Selection of Lubrication for Metal Stamping and Drawing.* SME Technical Paper, MF75-180, 1975.

*Standard Handbook of Lubrication Engineering.* NY: McGraw Hill Book Co., 1968.

Swindell, K. C., and Wainwright, P. "Lubrication in Metal-Forming Processes." *Sheet Metal Industries* (April 1981), pp. 290-295.

Tsao, Y. H., and Sargent, L. B. *Friction and Slip in the Cold Rolling of Metals.* ASLE Technical Paper, 76-LC-5A-1, 1976.

Wilson, W. R. D. "Workpiece Surface Roughening in a Hydrodynamically Lubricated Metal Forming Process." *Journal of Lubrication Technology*, vol. 99 (1977), pp. 10-14.

Wilson, W. R. D. and Cazeault, P. "Measurement of Frictional Conditions in Lubricated Strip Drawing." *Proceedings NAMRC IV*, Battelle Memorial Institute, 1976, pp. 165-170.

Wojtowicz, W. J. *Lubricating Characteristics of Drawing Compounds.* SME Technical Paper MF70-502, 1970.

Zintak, Dennis, ed. *Improving Production with Coolants and Lubricants.* Dearborn, MI: Society of Manufacturing Engineers, 1982.

CHAPTER

# 4

# Sheet Metal Blanking and Forming

# SHEET METAL BLANKING AND FORMING

Metal stampings are an indispensable, pervasive part of the contemporary industrialized society. An examination of most machines and products would disclose metal stampings in the assembly. Currently, stampings are widely used in machines, tools, vehicles of all kinds, household appliances, hardware, office equipment, electrical and electronic equipment, containers, buildings, clothing, and most manufactured products. Applications of metal stampings in various fields are listed in Table 4-1.[1]

This chapter provides basic information on the various processes for blanking and forming sheet metal. Chapter 1 lays the formability groundwork in fundamentals such as theory and analytical methods. Subsequent chapters cover tooling, equipment and operations for each of the major sheet metal and bulk forming processes.

CHAPTER CONTENTS:



## STAMPING PRESS OPERATIONS

In this chapter, stamping is used as a general term to cover all pressworking operations on sheet metal; it is not confined to forming and drawing processes. The stamping of parts from sheet metal is a straightforward operation in which the metal is shaped or cut through deformation by shearing, punching, drawing, stretching, bending, coining, etc. Production rates are high and secondary machining is generally not required to produce finished parts within tolerances.

A stamped part may be produced by one or a combination of three fundamental press operations applied to a given material. These include:

1. Cutting (blanking, punching, perforating, or lancing) to a predetermined configuration by exceeding the shear strength of the material.
2. Drawing (bending or forming) whereby the desired part shape is achieved by overcoming the tensile resistance of the material.
3. Coining (compression, squeezing, or forging) which accomplishes surface displacement by overcoming the compressive strength of the material.

Whether applied to blanking or forming, the underlying principles of the stamping process may be described as the use of force and pressure to cut or form a piece of sheet metal into the desired shape. Part shape is produced by the punch and die, which are positioned in the stamping press as shown schematically in Fig. 4-1. In most production operations, the sheet metal is placed over the die and the descending punch is forced into the workpiece by the press.

Inherent characteristics of the stamping process make it versatile and foster wide usage. Costs tend to be low, since complex parts can be made in a few operations at high production rates. Sheet metal has a high strength-to-weight factor, enabling production of parts that are lightweight and strong. Part interchangeability is assured because virtually identical parts are produced by the dies. Stamped parts can be made from a large number of different metals and alloys.

### MATERIALS USED FOR STAMPINGS

Most metal stampings are made from steel in sheet form. The following are the principal characteristics and requirements needed in raw materials to be used for stampings in press work:

- Comparatively low cost.
- High strength.
- Good surface finish.
- Uniform crystalline metal structure.
- Uniformity of dimensions.
- Workability.

A variety of raw materials can be used for metal stamping production. In most applications, the strength of the material is an important consideration. However, other characteristics such as formability, appearance, and predictable performance often are contributing factors in the selection of materials and production methods. In general,

***Contributors of sections of this chapter are:*** *Sokka M. Doraivelu, Visiting Scientist, AFWAL/MLLM, Wright-Patterson Air Force Base; Lowell W. Foster, President, Lowell W. Foster Associates, Inc.; Harold L. Gegel, Senior Scientist, AFWAL/MLLM, Wright-Patterson Air Force Base; Jay S. Gunasekera, Visiting Scientist, AFWAL/MLLM, Wright-Patterson Air Force Base; C. Howard Hamilton, Director—Materials Synthesis & Processing, Science Center, Rockwell International; Kenneth F. James, Staff Development Engineers, Manufacturing Engineering and Development, Technical Center, General Motors Corp.; Cor Langewis, P.E., Langewis Consulting & Engineering, Inc.; Alvin G. Neumann, Technical Consultants International; Richard I. Phillips, Assistant Professor, Department of Industrial Education and Technology, Southwest Missouri State University.*

***Reviewers of sections of this chapter are:*** *Sokka M. Doraivelu, Senior Scientist, Manufacturing Dept., Universal Energy Systems; Lowell W. Foster, President, Lowell W. Foster Associates, Inc.;*

# STAMPING PRESS OPERATIONS

**TABLE 4-1**
**Principal Fields of Application for Metal Stampings**

| Field | Applications |
|---|---|
| Machines and Tools | Machine elements, machine tool components, tools, tool components, sewing machines, automatic machines, agricultural implements, material handling equipment, lawn mowers, fans, control instruments, pulleys, turbine blades, textile machinery. |
| Household Appliances | Furniture, washing machines, burners, stoves, ranges, furnaces, radiators, heaters, refrigerators, kitchenware, cooking utensils, saucepans, kettles, egg poachers, can openers, cutlery, tea pots, waffle irons, toasters, vacuum cleaners, wash tubs, bath tubs, sinks, radio, TV sets, record players, tape recorders, hair dryers, lamps, lanterns, bells, gongs, baby carriages, mail boxes, cigarette boxes and cases, trays, ash trays, safety razor blades, electric razors. |
| Clothing | Buttons, eyelets, buckles. |
| Vehicles | Airplanes, automobiles, motor cars, bicycles, railway coaches, tanks, tractors, wheels for vehicles. |
| Hardware | Building hardware, door knobs, locks, pipe couplings, hinges, bathroom and kitchen fixtures, light metal sash, garbage cans. |
| Buildings | Houses, roofing, bridges, cement reinforcements. |
| Office | Computers, calculators, word processors, typewriters, copiers, office machines, advertising novelties, calendars, tags, envelope clasps. |
| Shops | Cash registers, cash boxes, menu holders, toys, jewelry, cameras. |
| Electricity | Motors, generators, transformers, wiring devices (switches, receptacles, lampholders), meters and measuring instruments, telephone, telegraph, electronics, electrical conduit, stripping devices, lighting fixtures. |
| Containers | Cans, tin boxes, drums, drum lids, caps, buckets, canisters; containers for food, medicines, and chemical materials. |
| Miscellaneous | Guns, cartridges, coins, medals, insignia, bird cages, caskets, coffins, watches, collapsible tubes, dental instruments, metal signs, musical instruments, shovels, thimbles, art, metal trades, capsules. |

all materials that are available in the form of sheets or strips and that do not shatter under impact can be worked with press tools. Materials used for stampings can be grouped in three categories: ferrous metals, nonferrous metals, and nonmetallic materials.

## Ferrous Metals

This group contains alloys in which the principal element is iron. If a special functional requirement does not dictate material selection, the first choice for stamping usually is low-carbon (0.05-0.20%), cold-rolled or hot-rolled steel. Cold-rolled steel (CRS) is available in gages up to 1/16" (1.6 mm) in the United States and up to 3/16" (4.76 mm) in Canada, while hot-rolled steel (HRS) is supplied in heavier gages. Low-carbon steels are the predominant material used for stampings, although there is a trend toward increasing use of high-strength, low-alloy (HSLA) steels.

In some applications, special specifications or considerations must be fulfilled to increase the material's strength and resistance to unusually rigorous adverse conditions (oxidation, corrosion, temperature, etc.). In these instances, alloy steels such as high-carbon steels, silicon steels, stainless steels, and heat-resistant steels often are used in stampings. These alloys, however, typically are more difficult to work in dies and presses, especially during forming operations.

## Nonferrous Metals

Aluminum in a range of alloys and tempers is used extensively for stampings. Copper and its alloys of brass, beryllium copper, phosphor bronze, cupronickel, and nickel silver also are used. Alloys based on magnesium, zinc, titanium, and nickel also are widely used for stampings. Alloys of other nonferrous metals, including zirconium, tantalum, niobium, tungsten, molybdenum, and vanadium, and precious metals, including gold, silver, platinum, and palladium, are used for special applications.

## Nonmetallic Materials

Some nonmetallic materials have sufficient hardness and consistency to permit stamping with standard dies. The so-called dinking, hollow, or steel rule dies (similar to cookie cutters) are used for softer materials. Natural nonmetallic materials, such as paper, cardboard, leather, rubber, cork, mica, asbestos, felt, and wood, and other nonmetallic materials, such as celluloid, vulcanized sheet fiber, and linoleum, are outside the scope of this handbook. Plastics, however, are covered in Chapter 18, "Plastics Forming."

***Reviewers, cont.**: Harold L. Gegel, Senior Scientist, AFWAL/MLLM, Wright-Patterson Air Force Base; A.K. Ghosh, Manager—Metals Processing, Science Center, Rockwell International; Jay S. Gunasekera, Senior Lecturer (Production), Mechanical Engineering Department, Monash University (Australia); C. Howard Hamilton, Director—Materials Synthesis & Processing, Science Center, Rockwell International; Kenneth F. James, Staff Development Engineer, Manufacturing Engineering and Development, Technical Center, General Motors Corp.; Hugh Juchler, Engineering Manager, Burkland Inc.; Howard A. Kuhn, Professor—Mechanical Engineering, University of Pittsburgh;*

# STAMPING PRESS OPERATIONS

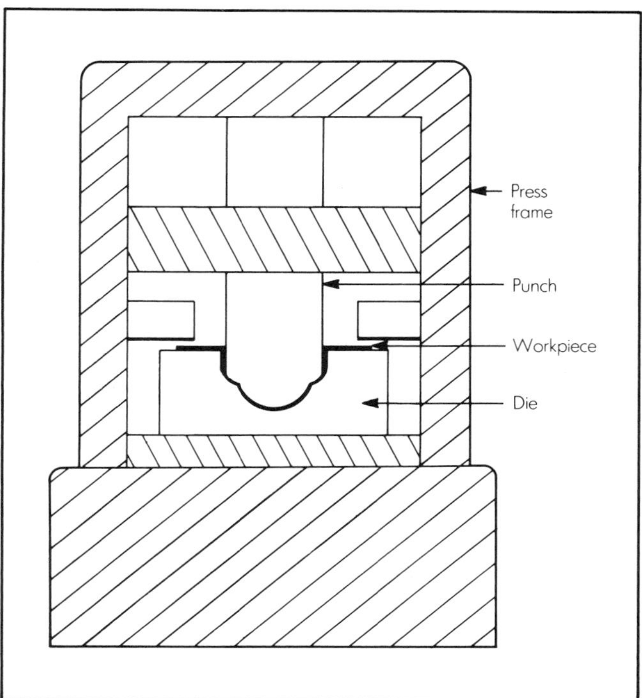


**Fig. 4-1 Basic production setup for stamping operation. Pressure is applied by the press. The sheet metal is formed into the shape determined by the punch and die.**

## Thickness

The thickness of sheet metal used for stampings varies widely from that of foil as thin as 0.003" (0.08 mm) to that of metal as thick as 1/2" (12.7 mm) or more. The majority of stampings, however, are made from metal having a thickness in the range of 0.020-0.080" (0.51-2.03 mm). No rigid standard exists for defining the expressions *light*, *medium*, and *heavy* which are used in describing the gages of sheet metal. In general, sheets up to 0.031" (0.79 mm) are considered light gage; sheets from 0.031-0.109" (2.77 mm) are considered medium gage; and those above 0.109" are considered heavy gage. The term *plate* (rather than sheet) is usually applied to metals having a thickness greater than 1/4" (6.3 mm).

## BLANKING AND FORMING OVERVIEW

Blanking (cutting) and forming operations are the primary stamping or pressworking operations. Manufacturing of sheet metal components involves a combination of these two operations, which are carried out for mass production using power shears, slitters and presses.

Cutting operations are classified by either the purpose of the cutting action or the shape it produces. Shearing, cutoff, parting, and blanking operations are employed to produce blanks; punching, slotting, and perforating operations are employed to cut holes; notching, seminotching, lancing, parting, and cutoff are used for progressive working; and trimming, slitting, and shaving are used for size control. Fine blanking, high-speed blanking, and roll blanking are nonconventional cutting operations developed to meet special requirements.

Forming operations include bending, drawing, spinning, embossing, and miscellaneous operations such as coining, ironing, bulging, crimping, dimpling, necking, and swaging. Bending and drawing operations are futher classified and identified in industry based on the functions performed and appearance of the formed product. Most of these pressworking operations are listed, illustrated, and briefly described in Table 4-2. Basic theory of the primary operations and their characteristic metal flow are described in fundamental terms in this chapter.

**TABLE 4-2**
**Pressworking Operations**

SHEARING (See Chapter 11):

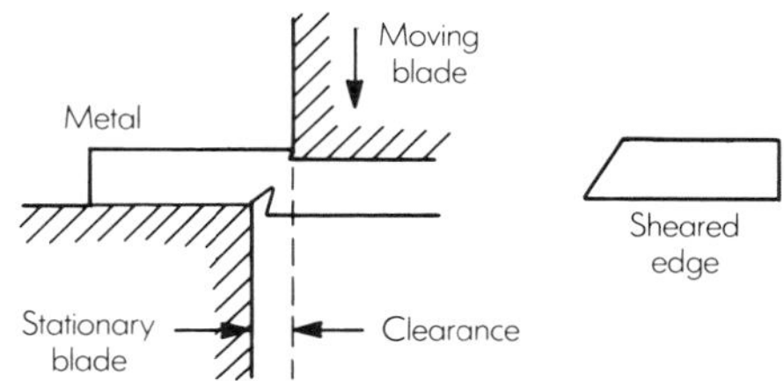


Shearing is the cutting action along a straight line to separate metal by two moving blades. Machines used for shearing are called squaring shears. In shearing, a narrow strip of metal is plastically deformed to the point where it fractures at the surfaces in contact with the blades. The fracture then propagates inward to provide complete separation. It is used for producing blanks.

CUTOFF:

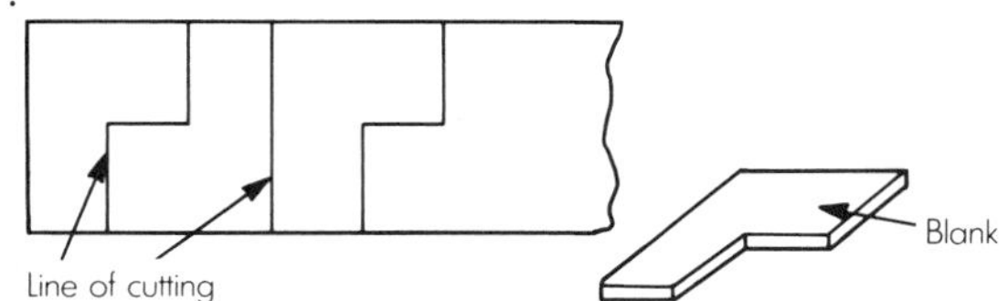


Cutoff is the cutting action along a line. It may involve one or more cuts where the line of cutting is straight, angular, jogged, or curved. It is performed in a die operated by a press, similar to blades in shears. The use of cutoff operations is limited to blank shapes that nest readily. However, it is more versatile because it is not limited to straight-line cuts, as is shearing. A small amount of scrap or waste sheet metal may be produced at the start or finish of the strip or coil of sheet metal.

***Reviewers, cont.***: *Cor Langewis, P.E., Langewis Consulting & Engineering, Inc.; David J. Meuleman, Applications Research Engineer, National Steel Corp.; Alvin G. Neumann, Technical Consultants International; William H. Pearson, Project Specialist, Atlas Alloys; Richard I. Phillips, Assistant Professor, Department of Industrial Education and Technology, Southwest Missouri State University; Edward A. Reed, Manufacturing Consultant; Ronald J. Traficante, Senior Materials Development Engineer, Engineering Office, Chrysler Corp.; Felix Wahrenberger, Vice President—Sales, Schmid Corporation of America; William L. Weeks, Metallurgical Engineer.*

**TABLE 4-2—*Continued***

PARTING:

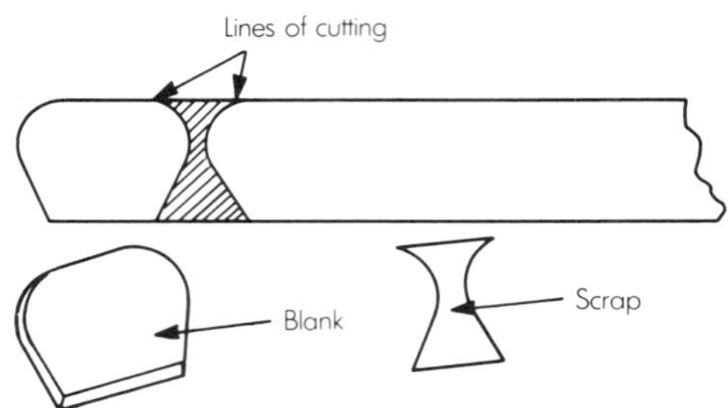


Parting is an operation that involves two cutoff operations to produce blanks from the strip as shown in the figure. During parting, some scrap is produced. Therefore, parting is the next best method (after cutoff) for cutting blanks. It is used when the blanks do not nest perfectly. Parting is carried out in presses using a die.

BLANKING:

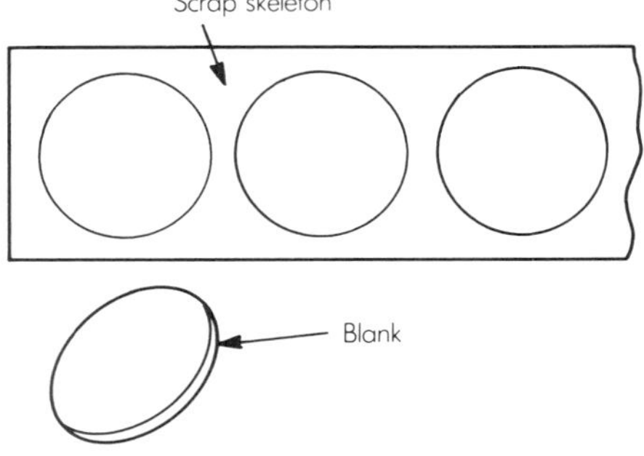


Blanking involves shearing a piece out of stock (strip of sheet metal) to a predetermined contour. It results in excessive waste of metal compared to cutoff and parting. However, the blank shape makes the use of blanking a necessity in most cases. It is performed in a die operated by a press.

PUNCHING (PIERCING):

Punching involves the cutting of clean holes with resulting scrap slugs. This operation is often called piercing, although piercing is properly used to identify the operation for producing holes by tearing action, which is not typical of cutting operations. In general, the term *punching* is widely used to describe die-cut holes regardless of size and shape. Punching is performed in a press with a die.

SLOTTING:

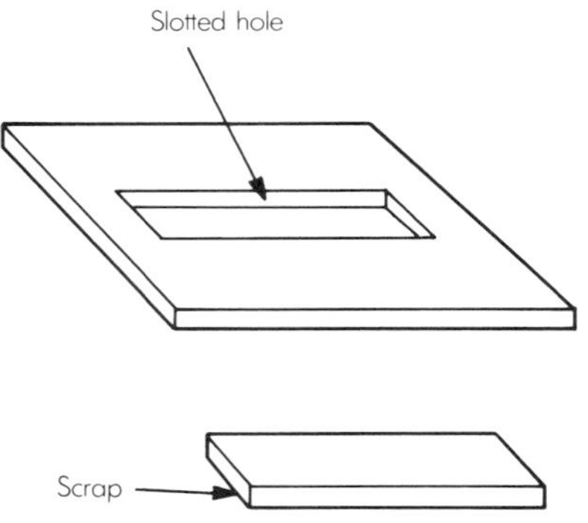


Slotting is a punching operation in which elongated and rectangular holes are cut.

PERFORATING:

Perforating is also a punching operation. It is used to punch many holes in a product with a specific pattern for decorative purposes or to permit the passage of light, gas, or liquid.

NOTCHING AND SEMINOTCHING:

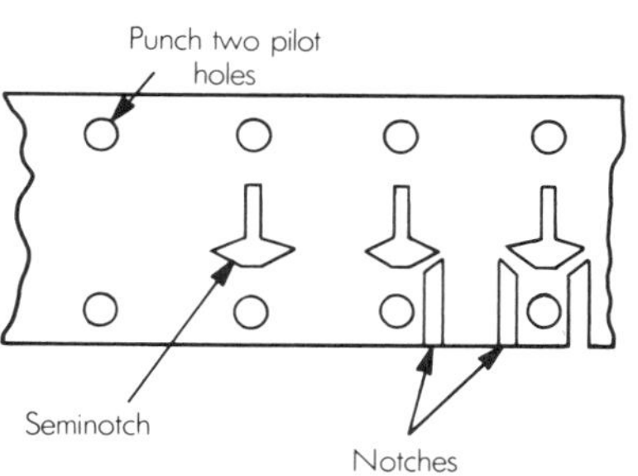

**TABLE 4-2—*Continued***

Notching is a cutting operation used for removing a piece of metal from the edge of a strip to a required blank. By making several notches, notching gradually produces a blank contour before the blank is detached. In some cases notching is done on the product itself. Generally, progressive dies are used for notching. The term *seminotching* represents the same cutting operation if it is done at the central portion of the strip.

LANCING:

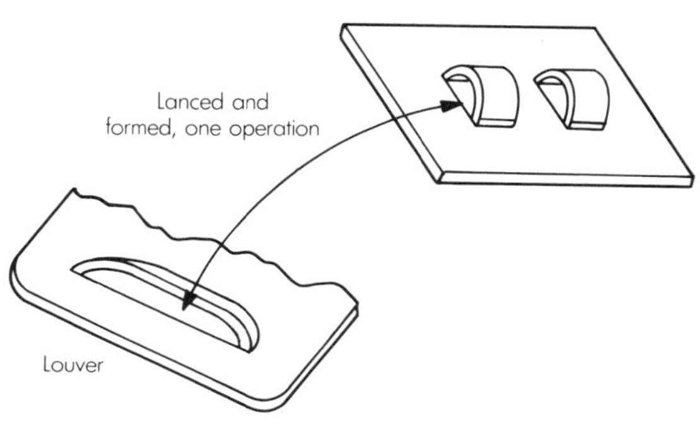


Lancing is cutting along a line in the product without freeing the scrap from the product. It is performed using a progressive die operated on a press. Lancing cuts are necessary to create louvers, which are formed in sheet metal for venting functions.

TRIMMING:

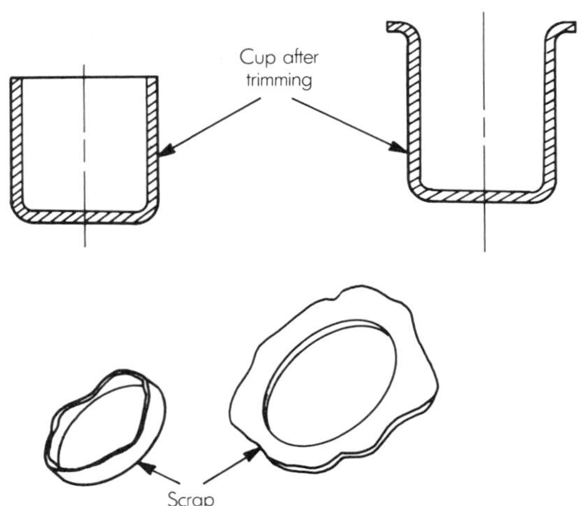


Trimming is the operation of cutting scrap off a fully or partially formed product to an established trim line. It is comparatively easier to trim the flanges of a drawn cup than the wall of the cup. For some irregular panels, trimming is done in a series of dies with notchlike cutting. The edge of a cup is sometimes trimmed by pinching or pushing the flange or lip of the cup over the cutting edge of a stationary punch.

SHAVING:

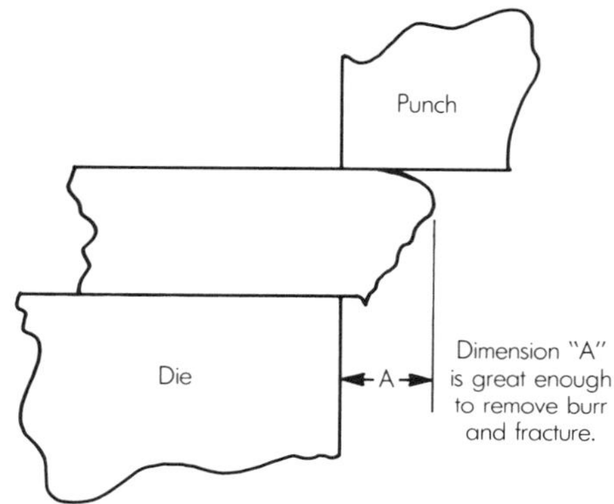


Shaving involves cutting off metal in a chip fashion to obtain accurate dimensions and also to remove the rough fractured edge of the sheet metal. Shaving is performed using dies with a very small clearance, as shown in the figure. It is considered to be a secondary shearing operation.

SLITTING:

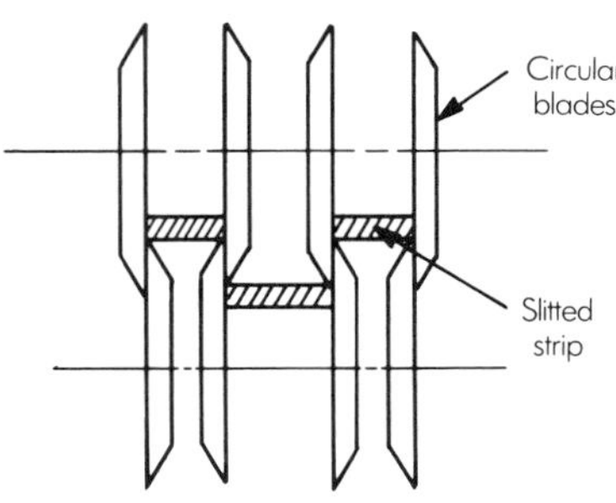


Slitting is cutting along single lines. A gang of circular blades cuts strips from a sheet. This operation is also used to cut along lines of given length or contour in a sheet or in products.

**TABLE 4-2—*Continued***

BENDING:

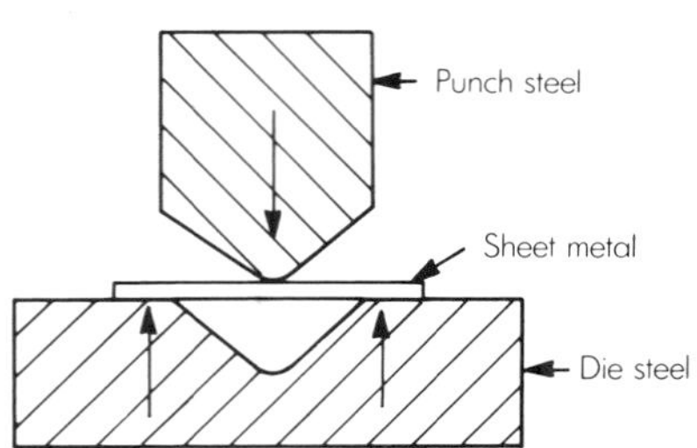


Bending is a process by which a straight length of sheet metal is plastically deformed to a required curved length, as illustrated in the figure. It is common forming operation for changing sheet and plate into channel, drums, tanks, etc. In addition, it is part of the deformation in many other forming operations.

STRAIGHT FLANGING:

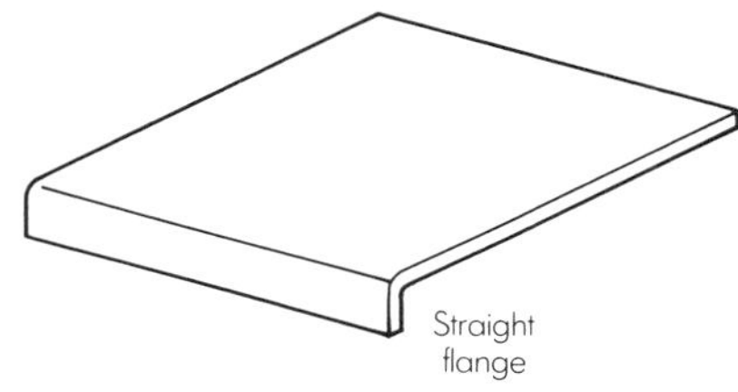


Straight flanging is a bending operation in which the line of bending is straight. It is the easiest operation to perform, and there are few restrictions on the flange width.

STRETCH FLANGING:

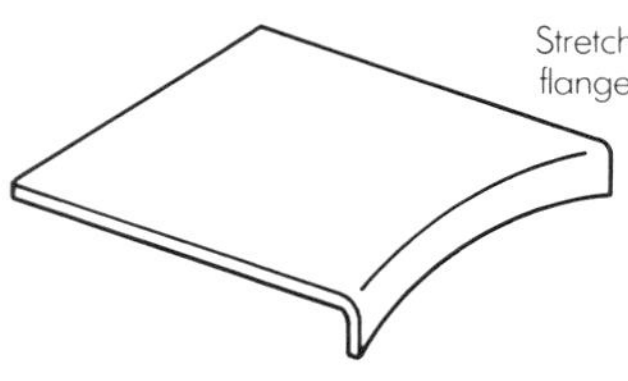


Stretch flanging is also a bending operation, but the line of bending is not straight. It is a concave curvature, as shown in the figure. The flange is known as a stretch flange and the process is called stretch flanging because the material undergoes tension when the flange is being formed. Tearing or breaking of the edge is common. To reduce the possibility of tensile tears, the width of stretch flanges must be limited.

SHRINK FLANGING:

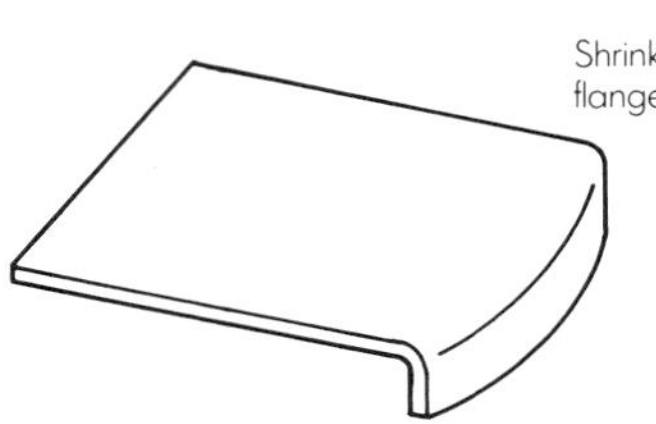


During shrink flanging, the line of bending is a convex curve and the metal is under severe compressive stress, so wrinkles are likely to occur. Therefore, the flange width must be limited. An alternative is the design of preplanned offsets in the flange to take up excess metal.

JOGGLING:

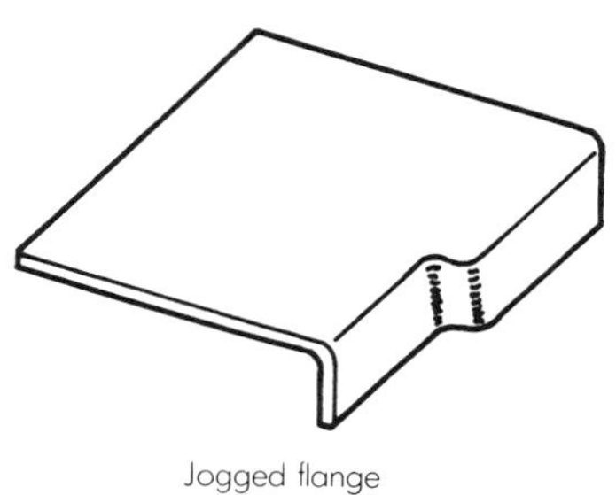


Joggling is a flanging operation by which an offset is produced at a desired place in the flange, as shown in the figure. A joggle consists of two adjacent, continuous or nearly continuous, short radius bends of opposite curvature.

REVERSE FLANGING:

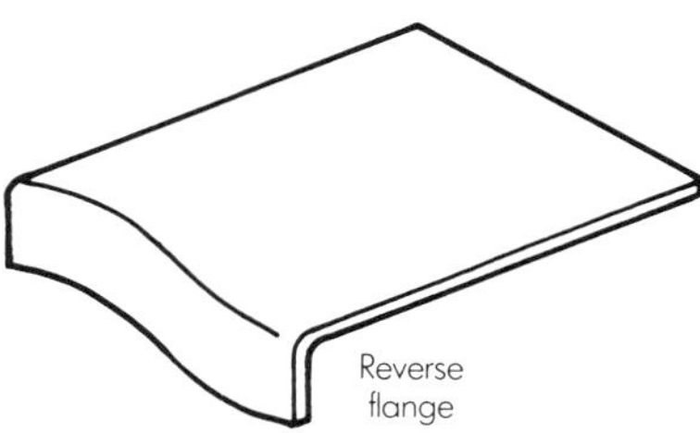


Reverse flanging is similar to joggling. In this case the product has at least one shrink flange and one stretch flange which are connected by a joggle.

TABLE 4-2—*Continued*

HOLE FLANGING:

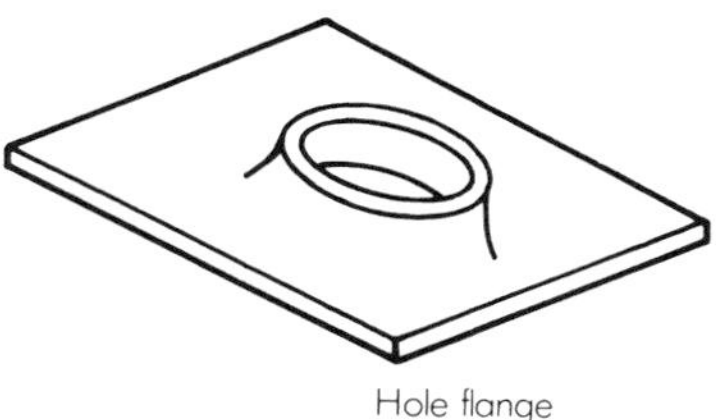
Hole flange

Hole flanging involves stretch flanging of a hole in the product. Higher hole flanges require a smaller punched hole diameter to provide the additional metal.

STRETCH FORMING (See Chapter 7):

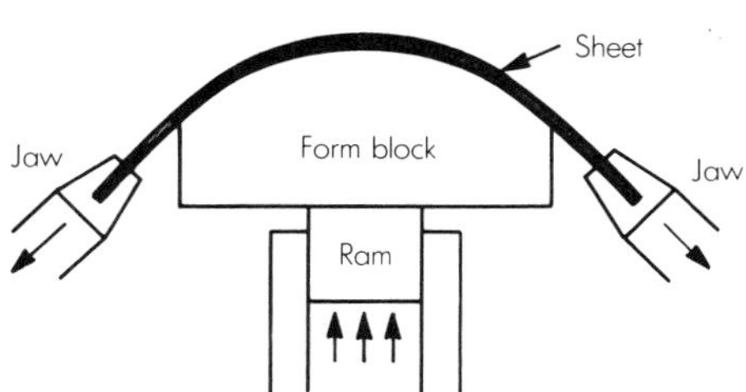


Stretch forming is the process of forming by the application of primarily tensile forces to stretch the sheet metal over a tool or formblock as shown in the figure. The process is an outgrowth of the stretcher leveling of rolled sheet. This operation is used most extensively in the aircraft industry to produce parts of large radius of curvature, frequently with double curvature.

SHALLOW AND DEEP DRAWING:

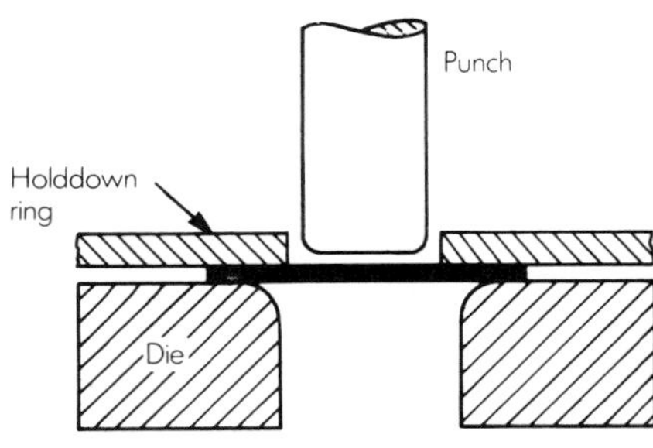


Drawing is used for shaping flat sheets into cup-shaped workpieces. If the depth of the cup formed is equal to or more than the radius of the cup, the process is known as deep drawing. Otherwise, it is considered shallow drawing. Drawing is performed by placing a blank of appropriate size over a shaped die and pressing the metal into the die with a punch. It requires blankholder pressure to press the blank against the die to prevent wrinkling.

IRONING:

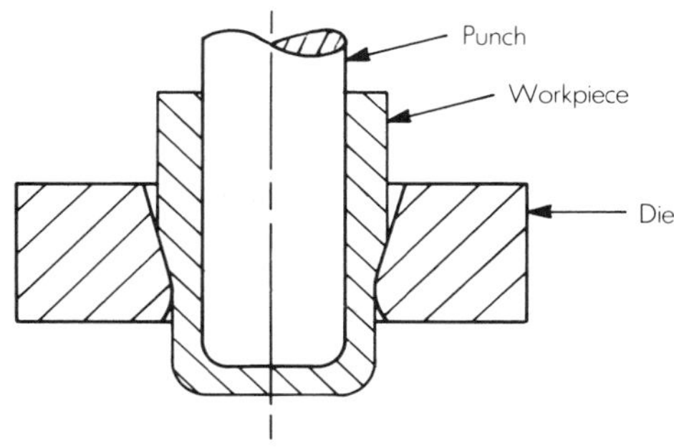


Ironing is the process of smoothing and thinning the wall of a shell or cup by forcing the shell or cup through a die with a punch, as shown in the figure. The working of the metal is severe, and annealing of parts is often necessary between ironing processes.

EMBOSSING:

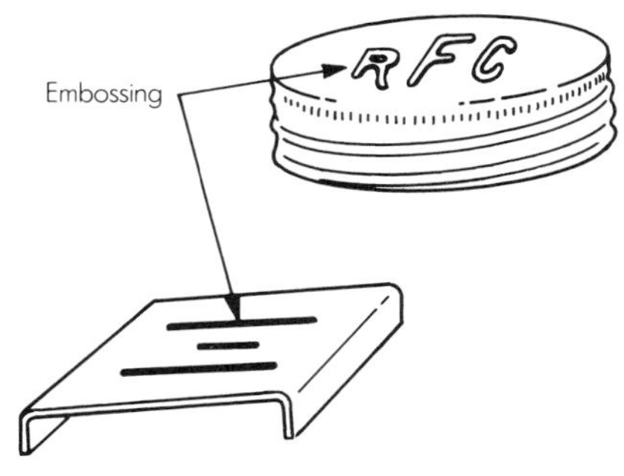


Embossing is the process that produces relatively shallow indentation or raised designs with theoretically no change in metal thickness. This group of operations is used to deform sheet metal away from the blank or product edge or in the central region. The common characteristic of all embossments is well-defined localized stretching of sheet metal into crisp contours. Forming of beads, ribs, and letters on sheet metal is done with embossing operations.

**TABLE 4-2—*Continued***

COINING:

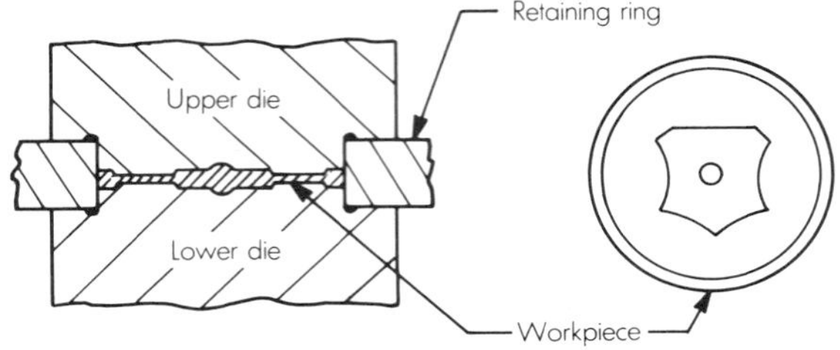


Coining is used for sheet metal working as well as for bulk forming. During this operation, metal is intentionally thinned or thickened to achieve the required indentations or raised designs. Coining is widely used for lettering on sheet metal or components such as coins. It is done in a closed die in which all surfaces of the sheet metal are confined or restricted, resulting in a well-defined imprint of the die on the workpiece.

SPINNING (See Chapter 9):

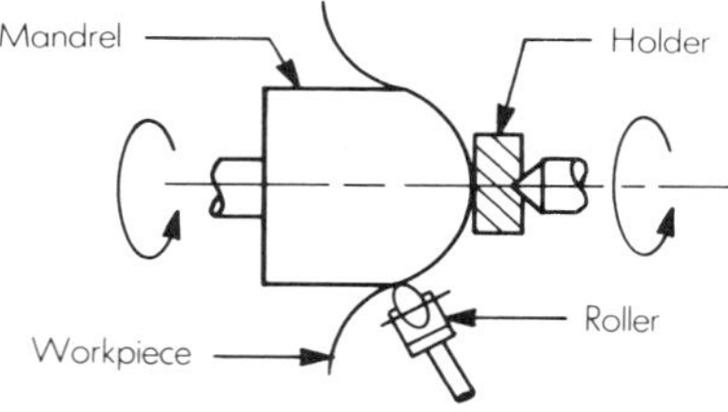


Spinning is a method of forming sheet metal or tubing into seamless hollow cylinders, cones, hemispheres, or other circular shapes by the combined forces of rotation and pressure. It does not result in any change in thickness. The operation is usually done in a lathe by pressing a tool against a circular metal blank that is rotated by a headstock.

SHEAR FORMING (See Chapter 9):

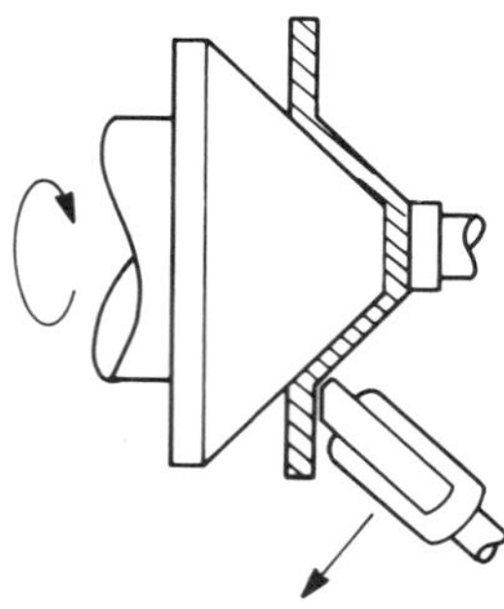

Shear forming, also known as flow turning, is similar to spinning, but during flow turning the metal is intentionally thinned by shear forces. This is also known as power spinning. It is sometimes done at hot-working condition because the metal undergoes severe shear deformation which demands high ductility. This process is done in a lathe.

BULGING:

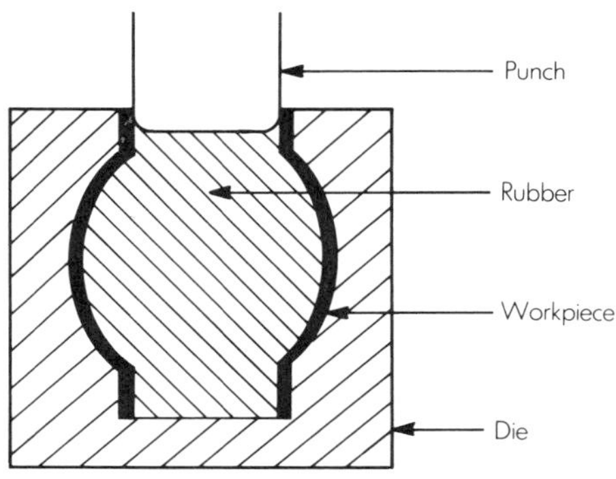


In bulging, an internal pressure is applied to form a tube to the desired shape. The internal pressure can be delivered by expanding a segmented punch through a fluid, or by using an elastomer, as illustrated.

NECKING AND SWAGING:

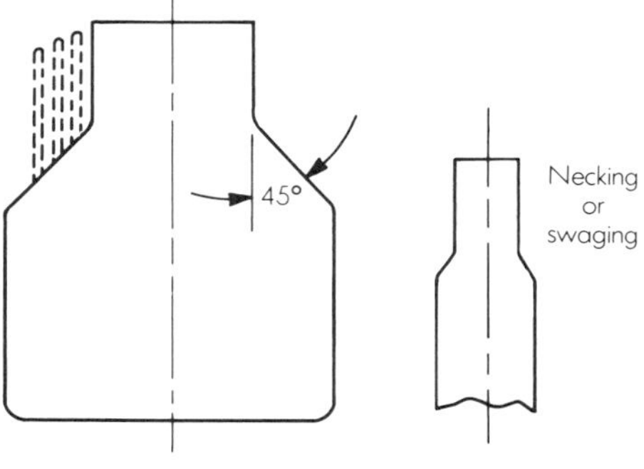


Necking and swaging reduce the diameter on the tube or drawn cup. Necking is accomplished between dies in a manner similar to other drawing operations. It can also be performed by spinning and swaging. Swaging is primarily used to reduce diameter, and it represents the squeezing operation in which part of the metal under compression plastically flows into contours of the die; the remaining metal is unconfined and flows generally at an angle to the direction of applied pressure.

**TABLE 4-2—*Continued***

CORRUGATING:

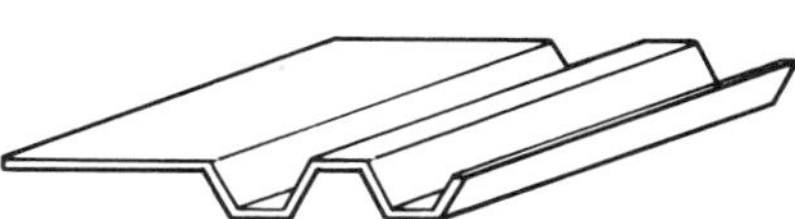

Corrugating involves making parallel bends across either the length or width of the sheet to increase the section modules of the sheet. The bends may be "U", "V" or any desired shape. Corrugating is performed with a punch and die in brake press.

CURLING AND WIRING:

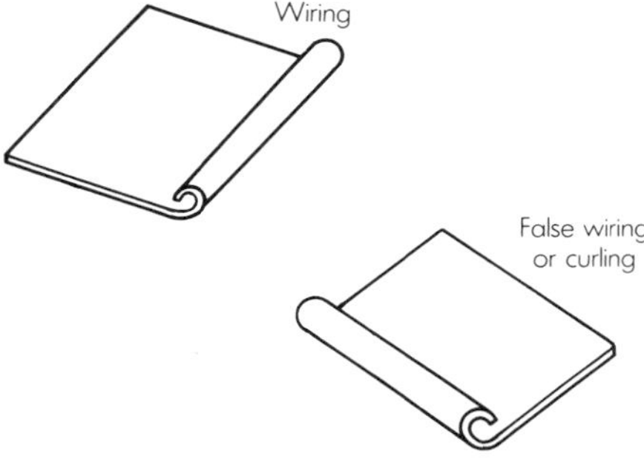


During wiring, the metal is curled up and over a length of wire to strengthen the edge of sheet metal. When the wire is not used, the operation is known as curling. Curling and wiring are used on flat parts or on round parts such as cams or drums. On round parts, curling is done in a lathe (like spinning) and also is done using a die operated on a press. Generally, it is combined with flanging operations in press working.

HEMMING AND SEAMING:

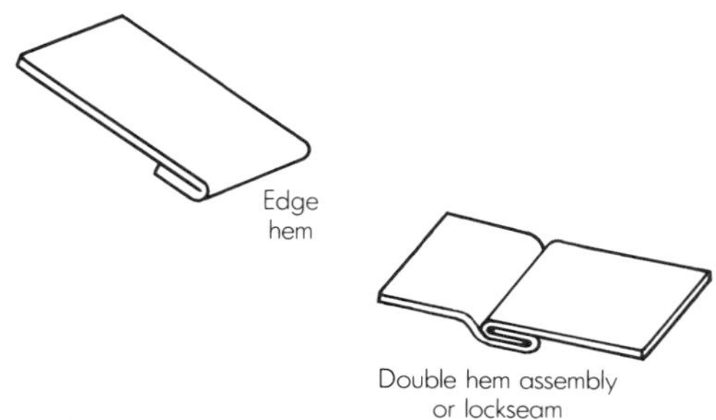


Hemming and seaming are the processes of joining two edges of sheet metal by multiple bending, as shown in the figure. A hem is folded at the edge of the sheet metal to remove the burred edge and improve the appearance of the edge. As used in the clothing industry, the term *seam* applies to an area in which two edges have been joined.

DIMPLING:

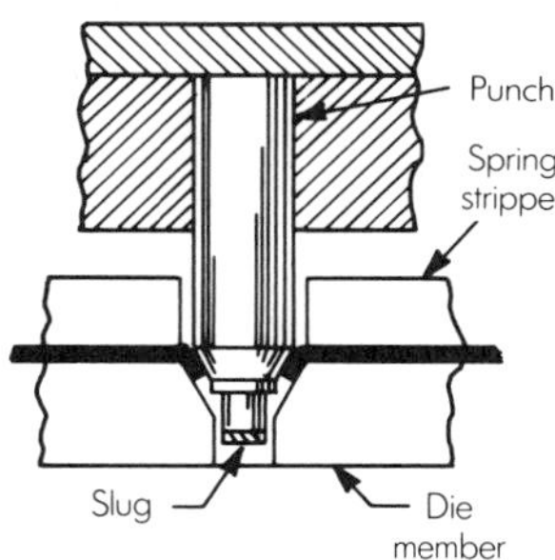


Dimpling is a process for producing a small conical flange around a hole in sheet metal parts that are to be assembled with flush or flat-headed rivets. Dimpling is commonly applied to sheets that are too thin for countersinking.

## NOMENCLATURE

The following glossary consists of terms commonly used in sheet metal blanking and forming operations. It was compiled from various sources. The two principal references are *Bliss Power Press Handbook*[2] and *Die Design Handbook*.[3]

**annealing** Softening or strain relieving of material by application of heat above the critical temperature for the correct time interval and then cooling slowly enough to avoid hardening.

**bead** A narrow ridge in a sheet metal workpiece or part, commonly formed for reinforcement.

**blank** The piece of sheet material, usually flat, produced in cutting dies and usually subjected to further press operations.

**blank, developed** *See* developed blank.

**blank development** (1) The technique of determining the size and shape of a blank; (2) the resultant flat pattern.

**blankholder** The part of a drawing or forming die that holds the workpiece against the draw ring to control metal flow.

**blanking** The operation of cutting or shearing a piece out of stock to a predetermined contour.

**blanking die** A die used for shearing or cutting blanks usually from flat sheets or strips. The single blanking die used for producing one blank at each stroke of the press is the simplest of all dies, consisting essentially of punch, die block, and stripper.

# STAMPING PRESS OPERATIONS

**buckling** A bulge, bend, kink, or other wavy condition of the workpiece caused by compressive stresses.

**bulging** The process of increasing the diameter of a cylindrical shell (usually to a spherical shape) or of expanding the outer walls of any shell or box shape whose walls were previously straight.

**bulldozer** Slow-acting horizontal mechanical press with large bed used for bending, straightening, etc. The work, which is done between dies, may be performed either hot or cold. The machine is closely allied to a forging machine.

**camber** A slight convexity or rounding of sheet, strip, or plate as might appear along the edge.

**canning (oil canning)** Distortion of a flat or nearly flat metal surface which can be deflected by finger pressure, but which will return to its original position when the pressure is removed. The process of forming such areas is referred to as canning.

**carbon steel** A steel that owes its specific properties chiefly to the presence of carbon, without substantial amounts of other alloying elements; also termed "ordinary steel," "straight carbon steel," or "plain carbon steel."

**coining** A closed-die squeezing operation in which all surfaces of the work are confined or restrained.

**crimping** A forming operation used to set down, or close in, a seam.

**cup** (1) A sheet metal part, the product of the first drawing operation. (2) Any cylindrical part or shell closed at one end.

**cupping** Usually the first operation in deep drawing.

**curling** The act of forming an edge of circular cross section along a sheet or workpiece or at the end of a shell or tube.

**deep drawing** The drawing of deeply recessed parts from sheet material through plastic flow of the material when the depth of the recess equals or exceeds the minimum part width.

**developed blank** Blank which yields a finished part without trimming or with the least amount of trimming.

**die stamping** The general term for a sheet metal part that is formed, shaped, or cut by a die in a press in one or more operations.

**dimpling** Localized indent forming of sheet metal to permit the head of a rivet or a bolt to fasten flush with the surface of the sheet.

**directionality in sheet metal** A property resulting from the rolling process in sheet metal fabrication at the mill so that the sheet metal's tensile strength and other properties are different in the rolling direction as compared to the transverse direction.

**dishing** The act of forming a large-radiused concave surface in a part.

**disk (disc)** A circular blank.

**distortion** Any deviation from a desired contour or shape.

**double seaming** The process of joining two edges of metal, each edge being flanged, curled, and crimped within the other.

**draw radius** The radius at the edge of a die or punch over which the material is drawn.

**draw ring** A ring-shaped die part (either the die ring itself or a separate ring) over which the inner edge of the metal is drawn by the punch.

**drawability** (1) A quantitative measure of the maximum possible reduction in a drawing process. (2) Reduction in diameter from the blank to a deep-drawn shell of maximum depth.

**drawing** (1) A variety of forming operations, such as deep drawing a sheet blank, redrawing a tubular part, and drawing rod, wire, and tube. The usual drawing process in reference to the working of sheet metal in a press is a method for producing a cuplike form from a sheet metal disc by holding it firmly between blankholding surfaces to prevent formation of wrinkles while the punch travel produces the required shape. (2) *See* Tempering.

**ductility** The property of a material that permits plastic working in tension and compression, as in drawing or stretching, and permanent deformation without rupture.

**earing** The formation of ears or scalloped edges around the top of a drawn shell, resulting from directional differences in the plastic-working properties of rolled metal with, across, and at angles to the direction of rolling.

**embossing** A process for producing raised or sunken designs in sheet material by means of male and female dies, theoretically with no change in metal thickness. Common examples are letters, ornamental pictures, and ribs for stiffening. The heaviest embossing is usually done in knuckle-joint presses. Heavy embossing and coining are similar operations.

**eyelet method** The fundamental eyelet method appears to have been the cut-and-carry method of feeding with the double roll feed. An adaptation of this method is the transfer feed process.

**fin** *See* flash.

**flange** A projecting rim or edge of a part, usually narrow and of approximately constant width for stiffening or fastening.

**flash (fin)** The excess metal which is squeezed or forced out from between the upper and lower dies in drop forging and in some squeezing operations in presswork.

**flattening** Removing irregularities of a metal surface by a variety of methods, such as stretching, rolling, and/or roller leveling of sheet and strip.

**forming** Making any change in the shape of a metal piece which does not intentionally reduce the metal thickness and which produces a useful shape.

**galling** The friction-induced roughness of two metal surfaces in direct sliding contact.

**Guerin process** A rubber pad forming process. *See* rubber pad forming.

**hole flanging** Turning up or drawing out a flange or rim around a hole (usually round) in the bottom or side of a shell or in a flat plate. It is essentially the reverse of necking.

**hot working (pressing)** Forming or other pressworking at temperatures sufficiently high to prevent strain hardening.

**inside-out redrawing** *See* reverse redrawing.

**ironing** The press operation of reducing the thickness of a shell wall while retaining the original thickness of the bottom, and reducing the inside diameter by only a small amount. This is the opposite of a true drawing operation in which reducing the diameter is the primary consideration and wall thickness may be increased slightly.

**joggle** (1) An offset (usually with parallel surfaces) in the surface of a sheet or part. (2) The process or act of offsetting the surface of a sheet or part.

**lancing** Slitting and forming a pocket-shaped opening in a part.

**lightening hole** A hole punched in a part to save weight.

**mild steel** Usually SAE 1010 to 1029 steel.

**minimum bend radius** Smallest bend radius used commercially for a given material.

**normalizing** Normalizing of steel is the process of heating the steel above the critical temperature and cooling it freely in air. It is a special case of annealing. Normalizing does leave the metal in a uniform, unstressed condition, but may not leave it machinable. *See* annealing.

**nosing** The act of forming a curved portion, with reduced diameters, at the end of a tubular part.

**notching** The cutting out of various shapes from the edge of a strip, blank, or part.

**overbending** Bending metal a greater amount than specified for the finished piece, to compensate for springback.

**perforating** The punching of many holes, usually identical and arranged in regular pattern, in a sheet, workpiece blank or previously formed part. The holes are usually round, but may be any shape. The operation is also called multiple punching. *See* piercing.

**piercing** The general term for cutting (shearing or punching) openings, such as holes and slots in sheet material, plate, or parts. This operation is similar to blanking; the difference being that the slug or piece produced by piercing is scrap, whereas the blank produced by blanking is the useful part.

**plastic flow** The phenomenon that takes place when metals or other substances are stretched or compressed permanently without rupture.

**plastic working** The processing of metals or other substances by causing permanent change in shape without rupture.

**plasticity** That property or characteristic which permits substances to undergo permanent change in shape without rupturing. Practically, it is the property possessed by useful materials that permits stretching or compressing them into useful shapes.

**power press** A term used loosely to designate any mechanical press (usually as distinct from a hydraulic press).

**preformed part** A partially formed part which will be subjected to one or more subsequent forming operations.

**press** A machine tool having a stationary bed and a slide or ram that has reciprocating motion at right angles to the bed surface, the slide being guided in the frame of the machine.

**press brake** *See* bending brake.

**press forming** Any forming operation performed with tooling by means of a mechanical or hydraulic press.

**puckering** Wavy condition of a deep-drawn part around the walls, in contrast to wrinkling, which occurs at the edges.

**punch** (1) The male part of a die, as distinguished from the female part which is called the die. The punch is usually the upper member of the complete die assembly and is mounted on the slide or in a die set for alignment (except in the inverted die). (2) In double-action draw dies, the punch is the inner portion of the upper die, which is mounted on the plunger (inner slide) and does the drawing. (3) The act of piercing or punching a hole. Also referred to as punching.

**punching** Die shearing of a closed contour in which the sheared out part is scrap.

**rabbit ear** Recess in die corner to allow for wrinkling or folding of the blank.

**redrawing** The second and successive deep drawing operations in which the cuplike shells are deepened and reduced in cross-sectional dimensions (sometimes in wall thickness, by ironing). Redrawing is done in both single-action dies and in double-action dies.

**restriking** A sizing or light coining operation in which compressive strains are introduced in the stamping to counteract or offset tensile strains set up in previous operations. For example, restriking is used to counteract springback in a bending operation.

**reverse redrawing** The second and subsequent drawing operations which are performed in the opposite direction of the original drawing; that is, the punch pushes against the outside of the shell at the bottom of the part. It is often referred to as inside-out redrawing and is used to avoid wrinkling.

**rough blank** Blank for a forming or drawing operation, usually of irregular outline, with necessary stock allowance for process metal which is trimmed after forming or drawing to the desired size.

**rubber pad forming** A forming operation for shallow parts in which a confined, pliable, rubber pad attached to the press slide is forced by hydraulic pressure to become a mating die for a punch or group of punches that have been placed on the press bed or baseplate. A process developed in the aircraft industry for limited production of a large number of diversified parts. This is the Guerin process. Although this process was used originally on aluminum and magnesium alloys, it is now used on light gages of mild and stainless steel.

**seam** (1) The fold or ridge formed at the juncture of two pieces of sheet material. (2) An extended, narrow defect on the metal surface, resulting from a blow hole or inclusion which has been stretched during processing.

**seaming** The process of joining two edges of sheet material to produce a seam. Machines that do this work are referred to as seaming machines or seamers.

**seizing** Welding of metal from the workpiece to a die member under the combined action of pressure and sliding friction.

**shear** (1) A machine or tool for cutting metal and other material by the closing motion of two sharp, closely adjoining edges; for example, squaring shear and circular shear. (2) An inclination between two cutting edges, such as between two straight knife blades or between punch cutting edge and the die cutting edge, so that a reduced area will be cut each time. This reduces the necessary force, but increases the required length of working stroke. This method is referred to as angular shear. (3) The act of cutting by shearing dies or blades, as in a squaring shear.

**sheet** Any material or piece of uniform thickness and of considerable length and breadth as compared to its thickness is called a sheet or plate. In reference to metal, such pieces under 1/4″ thick are called sheets and those 1/4″ thick and over are called plates. Occasionally, the limiting thickness for steel to be designated as "sheet steel" is number ten Manufacturer's Standard Gage for sheet steel, which is 0.1345″ (3.42 mm) thick.

**sizing** A secondary pressworking operation to obtain dimensional accuracy by metal flow.

**slitting** Cutting or shearing along single lines either to cut strips from a sheet or to cut along lines of a given length or contour in a sheet or workpiece.

**slug** Small pieces of material (usually scrap) which are produced in punching holes in sheet material.

**springback** (1) The elastic recovery of metal after stressing. (2) The extent to which metal tends to return to its original shape or contour after undergoing a forming operation. This is compensated for by over-bending or by a secondary operation of restriking (squeezing).

**stamp** (1) The act of impressing by pressure (sink in) lettering or designs in the surface of sheet material or parts. (2) The act of forming or drawing by pressworking. (3) The general term used to denote all pressworking.

**stamping** (1) A general term covering press operations. (2) Forming and drawing press operations.

**strain** The deformation, or change in size or shape, produced by stress in a body. Unit strain is the amount of deformation per unit length.

**strain hardening** The increase in hardness and strength in a metal caused by plastic deformation at temperatures below the recrystallization range.

**stress** The internal force set up within a body by outside applied forces or loads. Unit stress is the amount of load per unit area.

**stretch forming** The shaping or forming of a sheet by stretching it over a formed shape. Used largely in aircraft work.

**tempering** The heat-treating process for reducing brittleness and removing internal stresses and strains in hardened steel. The process, sometimes called "drawing," consists of heating the hardened parts to the required temperature in a bath of oil, molten lead, or other liquid, and then removing them from the bath and quenching them.

**trimming** A secondary cutting or shearing operation on previously formed, drawn, or forged parts in which the surplus metal or irregular outline or edge is sheared off to form the desired shape and size.

**trimming allowance** Excess material beyond or outside the finished part, which is necessary because of variations or irregularities in material and processing. This excess is removed in a secondary or finishing operation.

**wiper forming (wiping)** Method of curving sections and tubing over a form block or die in which this form block is rotated relative to a wiper block or slide block.

**wrinkling** The wavy condition that appears on some formed, comparatively thin walled, metal parts due to buckling caused by unbalanced compressive stresses in the drawing or forming operation. This condition often takes place in the flange of a deep-drawn part.

# BLANKING

Preparing a sheet metal blank or workpiece from coils, strips, or sheets by a cutting operation is the first step in the production of most sheet metal parts. When the piece of sheet metal cut from stock is to become the manufactured part, the piece is called the blank or workpiece (see Fig. 4-2) and the process is known as blanking. The blank sometimes is the finished product and requires no further working; in most cases, however, it is formed or drawn to make the desired product. Additional cutting operations often are performed on the blank to complete the product. Blanks that are to be formed or drawn are usually referred to as developed blanks. Blanks may be simple round discs, squares, rectangles, or cylinders, or they may be more complex shapes.

High-volume production cutting of sheet metal using slitters, power shears, and dies in presses can be classified by shape or purpose of the cutting action into operations for producing blanks, for cutting holes, for progressive working, or for size control.[4] Operations for producing blanks are subdivided into shearing, cutoff, parting, and blanking (see Table 4-2).

## TERMINOLOGY

The terminology dealing with the processes of sheet metal cutting or separation can sometimes be confusing. Several words may be used to describe one process; or, conversely, one word may have several different meanings. For example, the term *shear* can refer to a specific process by which straight cuts are made on metal or it can refer to a machine. Some people refer to the overall process of cutting as shearing. Metal has shear strength and resists shear force. (These terms are explained later in this chapter.) Finally, shear refers to the relief angle or shear angle on a punch or die or shear blade to provide efficient cutting.

Because of this ambiguity, some common terms relating to sheet metal separation processes are closely examined in this section. One unusual aspect of these processes is that most of them do not produce chips, although trimming is an exception to this statement.

### Shearing

Shearing is a cutting process performed between two cutting edges; it does not form a chip. It may be a straight cut on a machine called a squaring shear (refer to Chapter 11), or it may be done between a punch and die.

### Blanking

Any part cut from a sheet of metal that is not scrap is called a blank. Blanking, however, is a specific operation of cutting by which a part is cut from a sheet or strip of metal by a punch and die with the cut touching no edge of the sheet or strip. The part (blank) that has been cut out is used, and the remaining portion of the original sheet or strip of metal becomes scrap. The blank may be used as is, subjected to notching or punching, or transferred to the forming area for possible press-brake bending or deep drawing.

### Punching

As shown in Fig. 4-2, the opposite of blanking is punching. Although the punching process is identical to that of blanking, the difference between the two operations lies in which part is used and which part is scrapped. In blanking, the part cut from the original metal is saved; in punching, the part that is cut out (called a slug) is scrapped and the original metal is saved. Holes of any shape—usually round, square, or triangular—can be punched. For additional information on punching, Chapter 12 should be referenced.

### Piercing

Piercing is a process that is often confused with punching. It consists of cutting (or tearing) a hole in metal; however, it does not generate a slug. Instead, the metal is pushed back to form a jagged flange on the back side of the hole. A pierced hole looks somewhat like a bullet hole in a sheet of metal.

### Extruding

A process similar to piercing is extruding. Extruding is another word with several meanings in the metals area. Pertaining to metal separation, it refers not only to punching a slug from a piece of metal (as in punching), but also to forming a flange on the backside of the hole (as in piercing). Forming of parts by cold, warm, and hot extruding is discussed in Chapter 13.

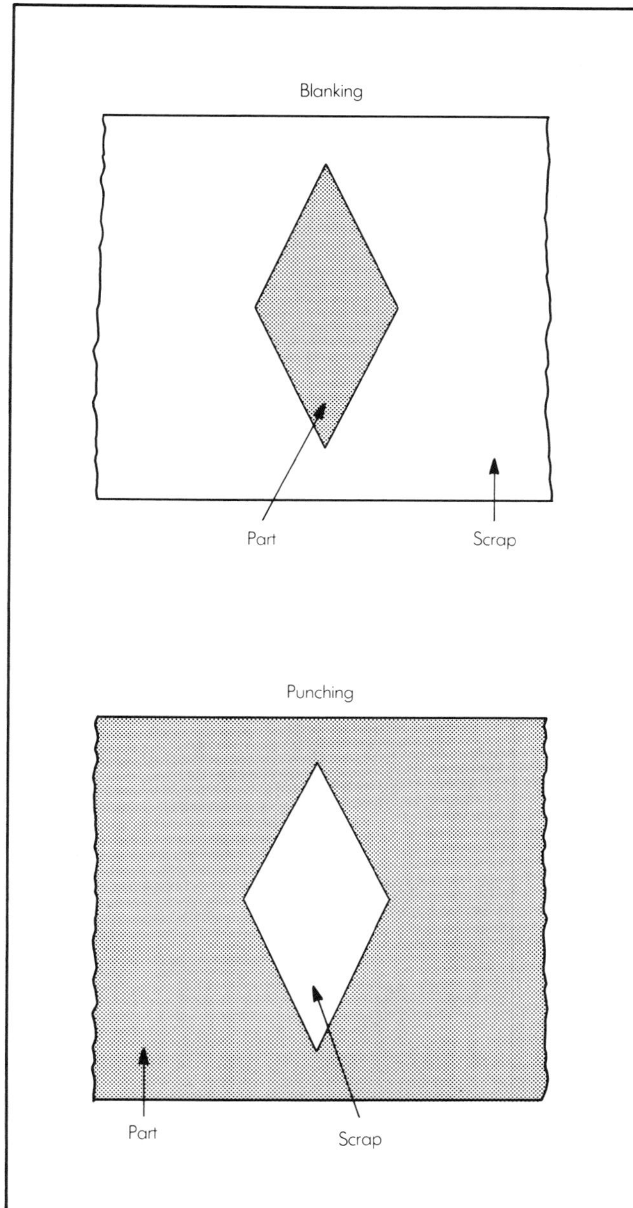


**Fig. 4-2 Comparison of basic stamping operations. In punching, the metal inside the part is removed; in blanking, the metal around the part is removed. In other operations (not shown), metal from the edge is removed in notching, slitting makes an incomplete cut in the metal, and lancing bends cut metal to form a louver or tab.**

### Notching

Notching is another process by which a slug is removed from a blank. The cutting line of the slug must touch one edge of the blank or strip (as opposed to punching). A notch can be made in any shape and is generally cut to release metal for bending or fitting up. For additional information, Chapter 12 should be referenced.

### Parting

Parting is a process similar to notching, except that the cut-out part is kept and the original strip is scrapped. The cut must touch the edge of the metal and may extend over part or all of the metal surface. Some scrap is always generated in this process.

### Cutoff

Shearing is both a generic term and one used to describe a cutting process by which a straight cut is made across metal using a squaring shear. When a similar cut is made using a punch and die, the process is called cutoff. The cut produced by this process may be either a straight or curved cut. The process differs from shearing in that a punch and die are used; it differs from parting in that no scrap is generated (except at the beginning or end of the strip).

### Nibbling

Nibbling is a variation of notching, with overlapping notches being cut into the metal. This process may be used to cut almost any desired shape; it is also effective for cutting flanges, collars, etc., from heavier thicknesses of metal. For further information, Chapter 12 should be referenced.

### Perforating

Perforating is the process of punching a number of uniformly spaced holes in a piece of metal. The holes may be any shape, and they usually cover the entire sheet of metal. During the punching operation, care must be taken to avoid warping the perforated workpiece.

## THE BLANKING/PUNCHING PROCESS

The blanking/punching process is a complex operation. The shear cutting, blanking, or punching action results from material being placed between two sharp, closely adjoined edges that have a closing motion. The material is stressed in shear to the point of fracture while going through three phases: elastic deformation (impact), penetration, and fracture (see Fig. 4-3). For purposes of analysis and discussion, it is useful to divide the process into the operational sequence and the cause and effect of generated forces.

### Operational Sequence

Punching a hole or producing a blank requires the same sequence of events: impact, penetration, and fracture. Contrary to appearances, the entire sequence is not a smoothly integrated series of events.[5]

**Impact**. The initial contact between the punch and the stock involves impact and deformation. As the stock begins to resist the penetration of the punch, sufficient force is developed to overcome the weight of the slide ram system and the punch stops moving. When the clearances in the ram, the pitman connection, the crank bearing, and the main bearings are taken up, the punch again impacts the stock. As the cutting edges close on the material, deformation occurs on both sides, near the cutting edge.

**Penetration**. The punch continues to penetrate the stock until sufficient resistance is developed to cause the press frame to stretch. As the frame elongates vertically, the punch velocity must be reduced, resulting in a slight hesitation. When the frame deflection is such that the stored energy can overcome the resistance, the punch resumes its penetration until fracture is imminent. The cutting edges then cut or penetrate the material, causing fracture lines.

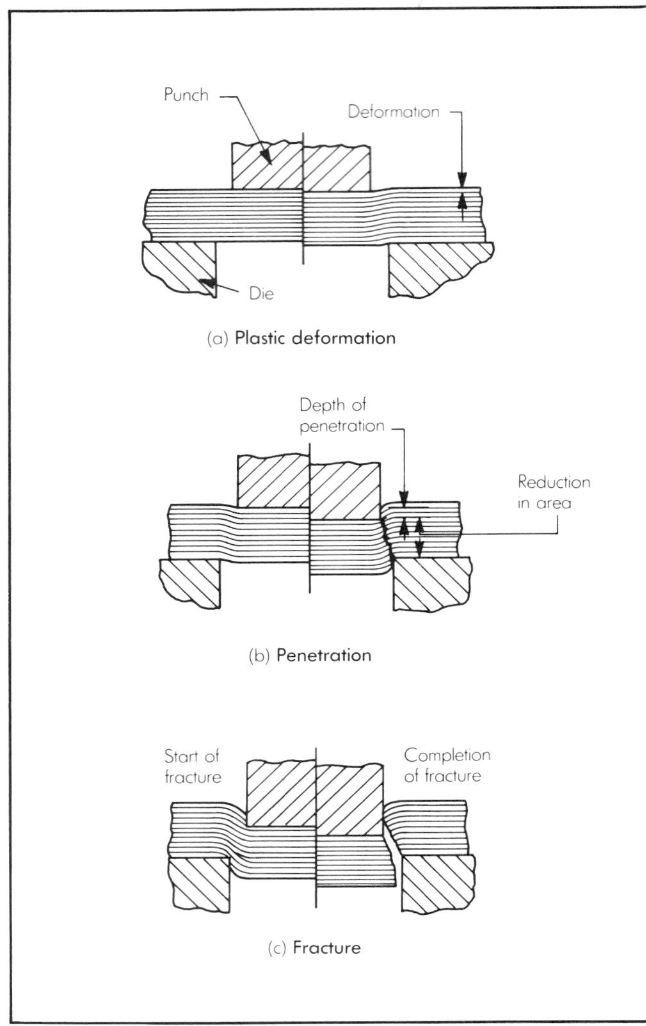


**Fig. 4-3 Three phases of shear cutting, as performed in blanking and punching.**

**Fracture**. The phenomenon of fracture is accomplished in three distinct stages—crack initiation, slow crack extension, and rapid crack extension. The sketches shown in Fig. 4-4 illustrate the progressive nature of fracture, from initiation to completion.

*Crack initiation*. Because the punching load is generally distributed over a relatively sharp cutting edge, the stress is very high. Both the punch and the stock are subjected to the same stress, but the stock is not as resistant to the stress and a crack is initiated. As long as the crack remains closed, external force must be applied to extend it. This effect is encountered because as an elastic solid is deformed during loading, the work done in overcoming its resistance to deformation is stored in the deformed part and can be regained during unloading. The stress pattern for the closed crack indicates that energy is stored at the front of the crack and along both sides.

*Slow crack extension*. As the punch continues its penetration, an external force is applied to the crack and the crack is gradually extended. As the crack begins to open, the rate of extension is increased.

*Rapid crack extension*. The opening crack is self-propagating and requires no external force. All of the stored energy is released into the opening crack, and extension is rapid until complete separation occurs. It is interesting to note that the rapid extension reaches a terminal velocity that varies with the material type. The released energy is usually greater than that required to reach terminal velocity, and the excess energy causes the initiation and extension of other cracks. In essence, the excess energy causes the original crack to fork.

Fracture usually begins on both sides of the stock. The punch initiates fracture from the top side, and the die cavity starts a crack from the underside. As the cracks approach each other, the stress concentrations at their ends veer, causing a rupture across the intermediate area, and the rupture is spread downward by the punch. This phenomenon is more readily apparent in thick materials.

The self-propagating nature of fracture makes it necessary for the punch to penetrate only half the stock thickness to make a hole and produce a blank or slug. Fracture is complete when the upper and lower fracture lines meet. At this point the work is done, but the punch must continue to move through the material to clear the slug or blank.

## Cause and Effect of Generated Forces

Impact has a pronounced effect on the punch and on the material being punched. Because solids are theoretically not compressible, material displacement must occur when a solid is subjected to opposing forces. When the punch slams into the material initially, the sudden resistance stops the face of the punch while the opposite end continues to move downward. Since the loaded punch is shortened and the volume remains the same, lateral displacement or bulging must occur.

**Bulging**. Bulging of the punch point causes a lateral thrust on the material being punched. The direction of least resistance to displacement is vertical, and a bulge develops around the periphery of the punch point.

**Reaction**. The reaction force of the material is generated by the die cavity. Consequently, the reaction is concentrated at a locus of points near the edge periphery of the punch. This permits the center of the punch face to project beyond the edges. As the press clearances are taken up, the time element permits the loads to be equalized. Suddenly, the press delivers another blow and the original displacement is intensified.

As punch penetration continues, frame elongation provides another time period during which the punch attempts to equalize the load distribution. Again the power builds up, the punch is confined between two extremely heavy loads, and further displacement occurs. During this total time period, shock waves travel upward along the length of the punch. The shock waves are attenuated as they travel through the punched material, and a major dissipation occurs when the waves are absorbed by the mass of the punch retainer. As each hesitation occurs, however, another series of waves starts to travel upward.

**Fracture**. When ultimate fracture takes place, a violent reaction is generated within the punch. The load at the face of the punch is abruptly removed, and the punch immediately tries to regain its original dimensional stability. The stored energy drives the punch face downward and generates a series of alternations during which the punch is either too long or too short. Gradually, the amplitude of the oscillations is reduced to zero and the punch is in equilibrium.

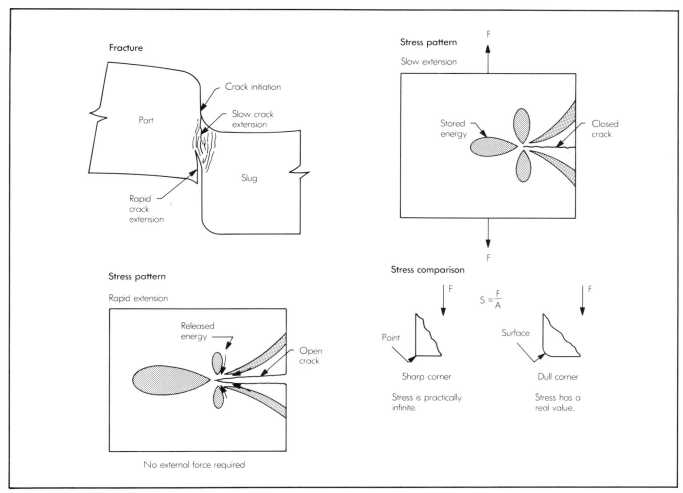

**Fig. 4-4 Illustration of fracture, from initiation to completion.** (*Danly Machine Co.*)

Meanwhile, the direction of shock wave travel through the punch is reversed. Instead of encountering increasing diameters, the shock waves now meet decreasing diameters. Head breakage or breakage at the blend-radius tangent points often results from this type of stress concentration. On rare occasions, the shock wave moving downward joins an upward-traveling wave; both waves then move in phase and snap the shank within its retainer.

As the punch load is removed abruptly, the sudden extension of the point reduces its cross-sectional dimensions. The residual energy stored in the stock strip and the suddenly acquired space between the punch and the hole cause a fluttering action that tends to polish or burnish the land. A similar combination of stored energy and space for movement causes the slug to undergo rather violent gyrations.

## ZONES OF A SHEARED PART

A part edge which has been cut usually has four major zones (see Fig. 4-5). Perhaps the most obvious portion is the burr. With proper punch or die clearance adjustment the burr should be small enough so that in most cases it will not require removal. If clearance between the punch and die is too great, the burr may be sufficiently large to cause problems. If the clearance is

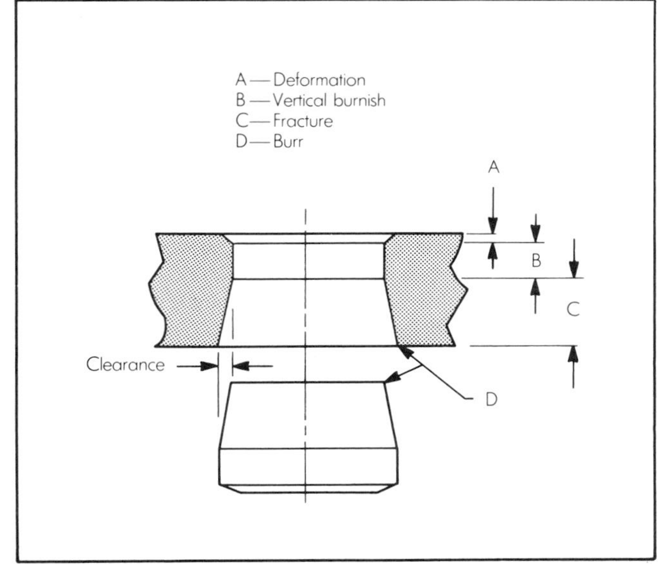


**Fig. 4-5 Four zones of a shear cut.**

too small, a phenomenon called secondary shear takes place. This is caused by the fracture lines' missing each other and actually producing two fracture areas.

As the upper blade or punch descends and makes contact with the workpiece, the metal becomes elastically deformed. If the force is removed during this stage, no deformation or cutting takes place. Of course, the blade or punch usually continues to descend and plastic deformation begins to take place at the lower die. This is the second zone—the zone of plastic deformation, which is the flattened area along the bottom of the cut. This deformation is localized because of the small amount of clearance between the shear blades or between the punch and die.

As the force continues, the descending blade or punch penetrates the metal. This depth of penetration is the shiny area seen on the edge of the cut part. After shearing occurs, the blade slides over this area and burnishes it; hence, it is called the burnish or the burnished zone.

When a sheared part is viewed, the burnished zone stands out in shiny contrast to the rough area adjoining it. This rough area is called the fracture zone and is the result of sudden failure as the penetration increases from 15 to 60% of the metal thickness. This percentage varies depending upon the metal's strength, ductility, and thickness. As the shear forces exceed the shear strength, the metal fails and fracture is completed. This fracture creates the rough area (burr zone) on the edge of the cut part.

## Shear Zone Factors

The extent of each of the four characteristic shear zones (deformation, burnish, fracture, and burr) and their interrelationships depends upon:[6]

1. Thickness of material.
2. Kind and hardness of material.
3. Amount of clearance between cutting edges.
4. Condition of cutting edges.
5. Support or firmness of material on both sides of cut.
6. Diameter of hole or blank in relation to material thickness.

If all the preceding conditions are met and the edge condition is not acceptable, other pressworking methods may be employed. One of the common finishing methods is shaving, which removes a small amount of material to smooth the fracture angle. Another is the fine blanking process, which uses a special press and die set to compress the material in the shear plain during the cutting cycle and eliminates the fracture angle. Information on fine blanking is presented later in this chapter.

## Deformation

Deformation adjacent to the cut plane is an inherent condition of sheared edges. Its amount depends upon the six factors listed previously. Soft, thick materials deform the most.

The angular fracture and the quality of cut, punched hole, or blank is dependent upon the amount of clearance between the two opposing cutting edges.

Increasing the clearance between the cutting edges increases the deformation due to the moment arm ($A$ in Fig. 4-6). Material adjacent to the cutting edge is put in tension and stretched excessively. Figure 4-6 also illustrates the problem of nibbling due to the moment arm, $A$, and the unsupported material that is free to bend as it is compressed by the punch. The combined unbalanced forces in nibbling or notching cause the punch to deflect; and if not properly guided, the punch will shear into the die and damage the cutting edges. To overcome this problem, a hold-down should be used to support the material and preferably at least a 20% overall die clearance should be used with a concaved-face punch. Additional information on clearances is provided in Chapter 6.

## Penetration

Penetration is the sum distance of the deformation and vertical burnish height as seen in Fig. 4-7. It is expressed as a percentage of the material thickness and is defined as the distance the punch must travel before the metal fractures. The percentage of penetration varies with the type and hardness of the material. As the material becomes harder, the percentage of penetration decreases. It increases where holes are less than 1.5 times the material thickness, due to the high compressive stress in the material cut zone.

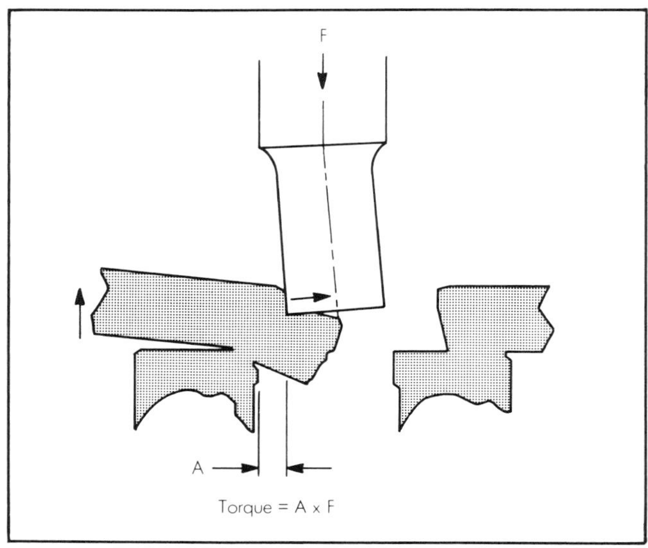


**Fig. 4-6 Nibbling, when performed with incorrect tooling, results in deformation.**

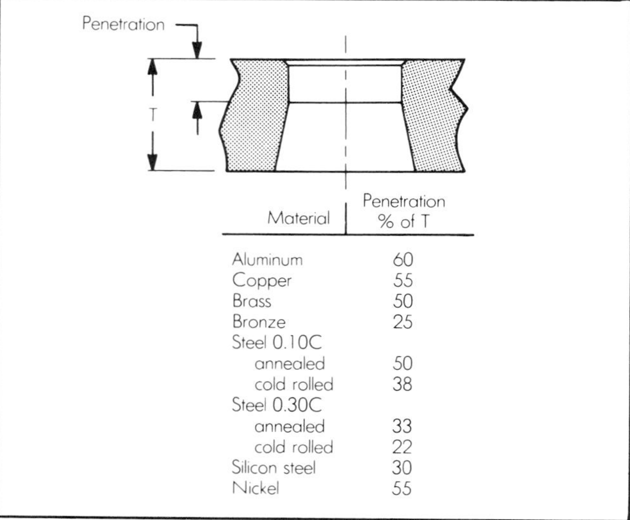


| Material | Penetration % of T |
|---|---|
| Aluminum | 60 |
| Copper | 55 |
| Brass | 50 |
| Bronze | 25 |
| Steel 0.10C | |
| annealed | 50 |
| cold rolled | 38 |
| Steel 0.30C | |
| annealed | 33 |
| cold rolled | 22 |
| Silicon steel | 30 |
| Nickel | 55 |

**Fig. 4-7 Penetration expressed as a percent of stock thickness.**

## FORCE CALCULATIONS

Blanking and punching are the basic die-cutting operations. As noted previously in this chapter, blanking is the cutting of stock around the complete perimeter of a shape to form a workpiece blank. Punching is the cutting of a slug from stock to produce a hole. The major factors in successful blanking and punching generally can be applied to other die-cutting processes. These factors are punch/die clearance (see Chapter 6) and punching force or load.

### Theory of Cutting

When sheet metal is being cut by blanking and punching, the force applied to the metal is basically a shear force. The total force is comprised of equal and opposite forces spaced a small distance (clearance) apart on the metal. The ability of a material to resist this force is called shear strength. The shear strength of a material is directly proportional to its tensile strength and hardness. The shear strength increases as the tensile strength and hardness of a material increase.

Two types of shear strength that must be considered are true shear strength and die shear strength. The strength of a metal being cut on a squaring shear is referred to as the true shear strength. True shear strength is generally estimated to be equal to a metal's tensile strength.

Cutting with a punch and die is more efficient, in terms of energy, than cutting with a shear. For this reason, a punch and die needs less shear force to make a given cut than squaring shears. This lower amount of shear strength required is referred to as the die shear strength and can be estimated to be about 0.75 times the true shear strength for most carbon steels and aluminum alloys (see Chapter 11, "Shearing"). For example, for a 1020 steel with a tensile strength of 60,000 psi (414 MPa), the true shear strength is 60,000 psi and the die shear strength is 0.75 x 60,000, or 45,000 psi (310 MPa).

There are occasions when it is necessary to calculate cutting force. Some of these occasions may be when specifications are being prepared for ordering a new press; when equipment for a stamping operation is being selected from existing equipment; or when it is necessary to determine whether a particular thickness or type of metal can be cut on a given machine.

### Blanking or Punching Force

The cutting force formula is derived from the basic relationship that force equals area times shearing stress. Blanking or punching force for various metals and gages can be calculated with the aid of Table 4-3 and Table 4-4.

**Equations**. Assuming no shear on the punch or die, the formula for calculating the force required to blank or punch a given material for any shape is:

$$F = SLT \tag{1}$$

for round holes:

$$F = S\pi DT \tag{2}$$

where:

$F$ = blanking or punching force, lbf
$S$ = shear strength of material, psi
$L$ = sheared length, in.
$D$ = diameter, in.
$T$ = material thickness, in.
$\pi$ = 3.1416

**TABLE 4-3**
**Shear and Tensile Strengths**

| Material | Shear Strength psi | Shear Strength MPa | Tensile Strength psi | Tensile Strength MPa |
|---|---|---|---|---|
| Aluminum 1100-H14 | 11,000 | 75.8 | 18,000 | 124.1 |
| Aluminum 20224-T4 | 41,000 | 282.7 | 68,000 | 468.9 |
| SAE 3240 | 150,000 | 1034.2 | 105,000 | 723.9 |
| SAE 4130 | 55,000 | 379.2 | 90,000 | 620.5 |
| SAE 4130 | 65,000 | 448.2 | 100,000 | 689.5 |
| SAE 4130 | 75,000 | 517.1 | 125,000 | 861.8 |
| SAE 4130 | 90,000 | 620.5 | 150,000 | 1034.2 |
| SAE 4130 | 105,000 | 723.9 | 180,000 | 1241.1 |
| Stainless (18-8) | 70,000 | 482.6 | 95,000 | 655.0 |
| Steel (0.1 C) | 45,000 | 310.3 | 60,000 | 413.7 |
| Steel (0.25 C) | 50,000 | 344.7 | 70,000 | 482.6 |
| Copper-hard | 35,000 | 241.3 | 50,000 | 344.8 |
| Brass-hard | 50,000 | 344.7 | 78,000 | 537.8 |
| Tin | 6,000 | 41.4 | 5,000 | 34.5 |
| Zinc | 20,000 | 137.9 | 24,000 | 165.5 |

**TABLE 4-4**
**Inch and Metric Equivalents of U.S. Gage Numbers**

| U.S. Gage No. | Inch | mm | U.S. Gage No. | Inch | mm |
|---|---|---|---|---|---|
| 0000000 | 0.5 | 12.7 | 16 | 0.063 | 1.59 |
| 000000 | 0.4689 | 11.91 | 17 | 0.0564 | 1.43 |
| 00000 | 0.4378 | 11.11 | 18 | 0.05 | 1.27 |
| 0000 | 0.406 | 10.32 | 19 | 0.04 | 1.11 |
| 000 | 0.375 | 9.53 | 20 | 0.038 | 0.95 |
| 00 | 0.344 | 8.73 | | | |
| 0 | 0.313 | 7.94 | 21 | 0.0344 | 0.87 |
| | | | 22 | 0.031 | 0.79 |
| 1 | 0.281 | 7.14 | 23 | 0.028 | 0.71 |
| 2 | 0.266 | 6.75 | 24 | 0.025 | 0.64 |
| 3 | 0.25 | 6.35 | 25 | 0.022 | 0.56 |
| 4 | 0.234 | 5.95 | | | |
| 5 | 0.219 | 5.56 | 26 | 0.019 | 0.48 |
| | | | 27 | 0.017 | 0.44 |
| 6 | 0.203 | 5.16 | 28 | 0.016 | 0.40 |
| 7 | 0.188 | 4.76 | 29 | 0.014 | 0.38 |
| 8 | 0.172 | 4.37 | 30 | 0.013 | 0.32 |
| 9 | 0.156 | 3.97 | | | |
| 10 | 0.141 | 3.57 | 31 | 0.011 | 0.28 |
| | | | 32 | 0.010 | 0.26 |
| 11 | 0.125 | 3.18 | 33 | 0.009 | 0.24 |
| 12 | 0.109 | 2.78 | 34 | 0.009 | 0.22 |
| 13 | 0.094 | 2.38 | 35 | 0.008 | 0.20 |
| 14 | 0.078 | 1.98 | | | |
| 15 | 0.070 | 1.79 | 36 | 0.007 | 0.18 |
| | | | 37 | 0.007 | 0.17 |
| | | | 38 | 0.006 | 0.16 |

**TABLE 4-5**
**Force Required to Punch Mild Steel**

| Metal Gage | Metal Thickness, in. (mm) | Hole Diameter, in. (mm) | | | | | | | | | | | | | | |
|---|---|---|---|---|---|---|---|---|---|---|---|---|---|---|---|---|
| | | 1/8 (3.2) | 3/16 (4.8) | 1/4 (6.4) | 5/16 (7.9) | 3/8 (9.5) | 7/16 (11.1) | 1/2 (12.7) | 9/16 (14.3) | 5/8 (15.9) | 11/16 (17.5) | 3/4 (19.1) | 13/16 (20.6) | 7/8 (22.2) | 15/16 (23.8) | 1 (25.4) |
| | | Force Required, tons (kN) | | | | | | | | | | | | | | |
| 20 | 0.036 (0.91) | 0.35 (3.1) | 0.53 (4.7) | 0.71 (6.3) | 0.88 (7.8) | 1.1 (9.8) | 1.2 (10.7) | 1.4 (12.5) | 1.6 (14.2) | 1.8 (16) | 1.9 (17) | 2.1 (18.7) | 2.3 (20.5) | 2.5 (22.2) | 2.7 (24) | 2.8 (25) |
| 18 | 0.048 (1.22) | 0.47 (4.2) | 0.71 (6.3) | 0.94 (8.4) | 1.2 (10.7) | 1.4 (12.5) | 1.7 (15) | 1.9 (17) | 2.1 (18.7) | 2.4 (21.3) | 2.6 (23) | 2.8 (25) | 3.1 (27.6) | 3.3 (29.4) | 3.5 (31) | 3.8 (33.8) |
| 1/16 or 16 | 0.060 (1.52) | 0.59 (5.2) | 0.89 (7.9) | 1.2 (10.7) | 1.5 (13.3) | 1.8 (16) | 2.1 (18.7) | 2.4 (21.3) | 2.7 (24) | 2.9 (25.8) | 3.2 (28.5) | 3.5 (31) | 3.8 (33.8) | 4.1 (36.5) | 4.4 (39) | 4.7 (41.8) |
| 14 | 0.075 (1.90) | 0.74 (6.6) | 1.1 (9.8) | 1.5 (13.3) | 1.9 (17) | 2.2 (19.6) | 2.6 (23) | 2.9 (25.8) | 3.3 (29.4) | 3.7 (33) | 4.1 (36.5) | 4.4 (39) | 4.8 (42.7) | 5.2 (46.3) | 5.5 (49) | 5.9 (52.5) |
| 12 | 0.105 (2.67) | 1.0 (8.9) | 1.6 (14.2) | 2.1 (18.7) | 2.6 (23) | 3.1 (27.6) | 3.6 (32) | 4.1 (36.5) | 4.7 (41.8) | 5.2 (46.3) | 5.7 (50.7) | 6.2 (55.2) | 6.7 (59.6) | 7.2 (64) | 7.7 (68.5) | 9.3 (82.7) |
| 1/8 or 11 | 0.120 (3.05) | 1.2 (10.7) | 1.8 (16) | 2.4 (21.3) | 3.0 (26.7) | 3.5 (31) | 4.1 (36.5) | 4.7 (41.8) | 5.3 (47) | 5.9 (52.5) | 6.5 (57.8) | 7.1 (63.2) | 7.7 (68.5) | 8.3 (73.8) | 8.8 (78.3) | 9.4 (83.6) |
| 10 | 0.135 (3.43) | | 2.0 (17.8) | 2.7 (24) | 3.3 (29.4) | 4.0 (35.6) | 4.6 (41) | 5.3 (47) | 6.0 (53.4) | 6.6 (58.7) | 7.3 (65) | 8.0 (71) | 8.6 (76.5) | 9.3 (82.7) | 10.0 (89) | 10.6 (94.3) |
| 3/16 | 0.187 (4.75) | | 2.8 (25) | 3.7 (33) | 4.6 (41) | 5.5 (49) | 6.5 (57.8) | 7.4 (65.8) | 8.3 (73.8) | 9.2 (81.8) | 10.2 (90.7) | 11.1 (98.7) | 12.0 (106.8) | 12.9 (114.8) | 13.8 (122.8) | 14.8 (131.7) |
| 1/4 | 0.250 (6.35) | | | 4.9 (43.6) | 6.2 (55.2) | 7.4 (65.8) | 8.6 (76.5) | 9.8 (87.2) | 11.0 (98) | 12.3 (109.4) | 13.5 (120) | 14.8 (131.7) | 16.0 (142.3) | 17.2 (153) | 18.5 (164.6) | 19.7 (175.3) |
| 5/16 | 0.312 (7.92) | | | | 7.8 (69.4) | 9.2 (81.8) | 10.8 (96) | 12.3 (109.4) | 13.8 (122.8) | 15.4 (137) | 16.9 (150.3) | 18.4 (163.7) | 20.0 (178) | 21.5 (191.3) | 23.0 (204.6) | 24.6 (218.8) |
| 3/8 | 0.375 (9.52) | | | | | 11.1 (98.7) | 13.0 (115.6) | 14.8 (131.7) | 16.6 (147.7) | 18.5 (164.6) | 20.3 (180.6) | 22.1 (196.6) | 24.0 (213.5) | 25.8 (229.5) | 27.7 (246.4) | 29.5 (262.4) |
| 1/2 | 0.500 (12.70) | | | | | | 17.2 (153) | 19.7 (175.3) | 22.1 (196.6) | 24.6 (218.8) | 27.1 (241) | 29.5 (262.4) | 32.0 (284.7) | 34.4 (306) | 36.9 (328.3) | 39.4 (350.5) |
| 5/8 | 0.625 (15.87) | | | | | | | | | 30.8 (274) | 33.8 (300.7) | 36.9 (328.3) | 40.0 (355.8) | 43.0 (382.5) | 46.1 (410) | 49.2 (437.7) |
| 3/4 | 0.750 (19.05) | | | | | | | | | | 40.6 (361.2) | 44.3 (394) | 48.0 (427) | 51.9 (461.7) | 55.4 (492.8) | 59.0 (525) |
| 7/8 | 0.875 (22.22) | | | | | | | | | | | 51.6 (459) | 56.0 (498) | 60.2 (535.5) | 64.6 (574.7) | 69.0 (613.8) |
| 1 | 1.00 (25.40) | | | | | | | | | | | | 64.0 (569.3) | 68.8 (612) | 73.8 (656.4) | 78.8 (701) |

Note: Force requirements are based on mild steel having a shear strength of 50,000 psi (345 MPa). For punching materials having a different shear strength, use a multiplier (see Table 4-6). For example, to punch a 15/16" (23.8 mm) diam hole through 1" (25.4 mm) thick, ASTM A36 steel having a shear strength of 60,000 psi (414 MPa), the value from this table, 73.8 tons (656.5 kN), would be multiplied by 1.2 (from Table 4-7) to obtain 88.6 tons (788 kN) as the force required.

Example:

Calculate the force required to punch a 0.50″ (12.7 mm) diam hole in 20 gage aluminum 2024-T4. From Table 4-3, the shear strength of the material is 41,000 psi (282.7 MPa). From Table 4-4, the thickness of 20 gage is 0.038″ (0.95 mm). Using these values, the force required is calculated:

$$F = 41{,}000 \times 3.14 \times 0.50 \times 0.038$$
$$= 2{,}446.1 \text{ lb} = 1.2 \text{ tons}$$

To express the result in metric terms, use the conversion factor (one pound force equals 4.4448 newton):

$$F = 2{,}446.1 \times 4.448 = 10\,880.3 \text{ N} = 10.88 \text{ kN}$$

For convenience, the tonnage required to punch or blank round holes in various metal thicknesses has been calculated and charted in Table 4-5. For example, a 1/2″ diam hole punched through 1/4″ thick mild steel requires 9.8 tons (87.2 kN). The chart also can be used for materials other than mild steel by multiplying the chart figure by a "chart multiplier" obtained from Table 4-6. For example, the chart multiplier for 6061-T6 aluminum is 0.58 which means that its shear strength is 58% of the value for mild steel. Therefore, a 1/2″ diam hole punched through 1/4″ thick 6061-T6 aluminum would require 9.8 x 0.58 or 5.68 tons (50.5 kN). Force requirements for holes above 1″ diam can be obtained by adding the forces for two diameters that total the desired diameter.[7]

When shear strength is unknown, but tensile strength is given, the shear strength can be estimated by taking a percentage of the tensile strength. The percentage varies with the material type and thickness. Figure 4-8 gives the percentages obtained from sampling three types of material.[8]

**Nomograph.** Punching force for various materials can also be determined with customary inch-pound units from the nomograph in Fig. 4-9. For example, if a 3″ diam hole is to be punched in a 0.051″ 2024-T4 aluminum part, the punching force can be found using the following information and guidelines:

1. Using 9.42″ ($\pi D$) as the length of sheared edge, find 0.051″ on Scale 1 (at Point 1) and 9.42″ on Scale 4 (at Point 2).
2. Connect Points 1 and 2.
3. Note that the line connecting Points 1 and 2 intersects Scale 2 at 0.480″, or Point 3.
4. From Table 4-3, determine the shear strength for the material. In this case, the shear strength for 2024-T4 aluminum is 41,000 psi.
5. From Point 4 on Scale 5 (representing 41,000 psi), draw a line to Point 3 on Scale 2.
6. Note that the line connecting Points 3 and 4 intersects Scale 3 at Point 5, giving a reading of 9.8 tons.

**Metric nomograph.**[9] If, in the preceding example, all quantities are expressed in SI metric terms, the metric version of the nomograph (Fig. 4-10) can be used as follows to determine punching force:

1. Find the total length of the cut (3.14 x 76 mm = 0.24 m) on Scale 2, or Point 1.
2. Find the metal thickness (1.29 mm) on Scale 4, or Point 2.
3. Connect these two points with a straight edge to find the area in shear on Scale 3, or Point 3.

**TABLE 4-6**
**Multiplying Factor for Shear Strength of Various Metals Compared to Mild Steel**

| Material | Chart Multiplier |
|---|---|
| Aluminum | |
| 1100-0 | 0.19 |
| 1100-H14 | 0.22 |
| 3003-H14 | 0.28 |
| 2024-T4 | 0.82 |
| 5005-H18 | 0.32 |
| 6063-T5 | 0.36 |
| 6061-T4 | 0.48 |
| 6061-T6 | 0.58 |
| 7075-T6 | 0.98 |
| Brass, Rolled Sheet | |
| Soft | 0.64 |
| 1/2 Hard | 0.88 |
| Hard | 1.00 |
| Copper | |
| 1/4 Hard | 0.50 |
| Hard | 0.70 |
| Steel | |
| Mild A-7 Structural | 1.00 |
| Boiler Plate | 1.10 |
| Structural A-36 | 1.20 |
| Structural Cor-Ten (ASTM-A242) | 1.28 |
| Cold-rolled C-1018 | 1.20 |
| Hot-rolled C-1050 | 1.40 |
| Hot-rolled C-1095 | 2.20 |
| Hot-rolled C-1095, Annealed | 1.64 |
| Stainless 302, Annealed | 1.40 |
| Stainless 304, Cold-rolled | 1.40 |
| Stainless 316, Cold-rolled | 1.40 |

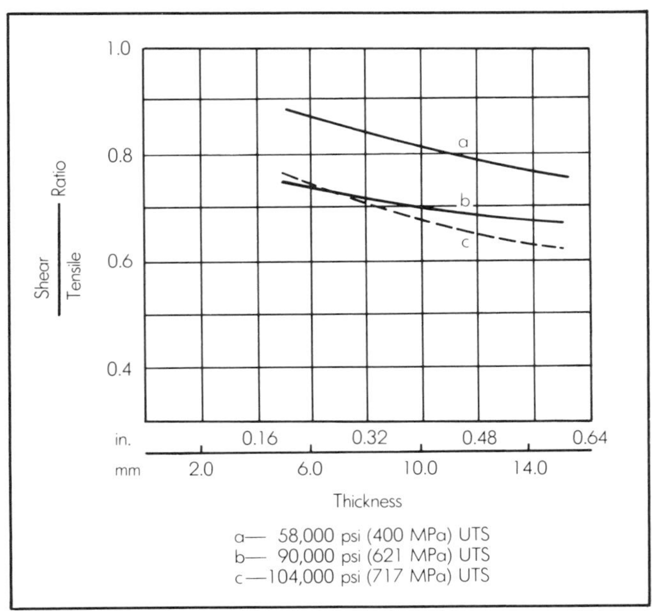


**Fig. 4-8 Relationship of shear strength to tensile strength.**

4. From this point on Scale 3, draw a line to the metal shear strength (282.7 MPa) on Scale 1, or Point 4.
5. Extending this line, read the force requirement in kilonewtons (87) on Scale 5, or Point 5.
6. To check the answer for agreement with the result obtained when using the original nomograph in Fig. 4-9, divide the result (87 kN) by the conversion factor (8.9). The result should be 9.8 tons.

## Stripping Force

The punching process requires two actions, punching and stripping (extracting the punch). A stripping force develops due to the resiliency or springback of the punched material that grips the punch. Additional friction is created by cold welding and galling that occurs on the punch surface if tooling is not maintained properly.

Stripping force is generally expressed as a percentage of the

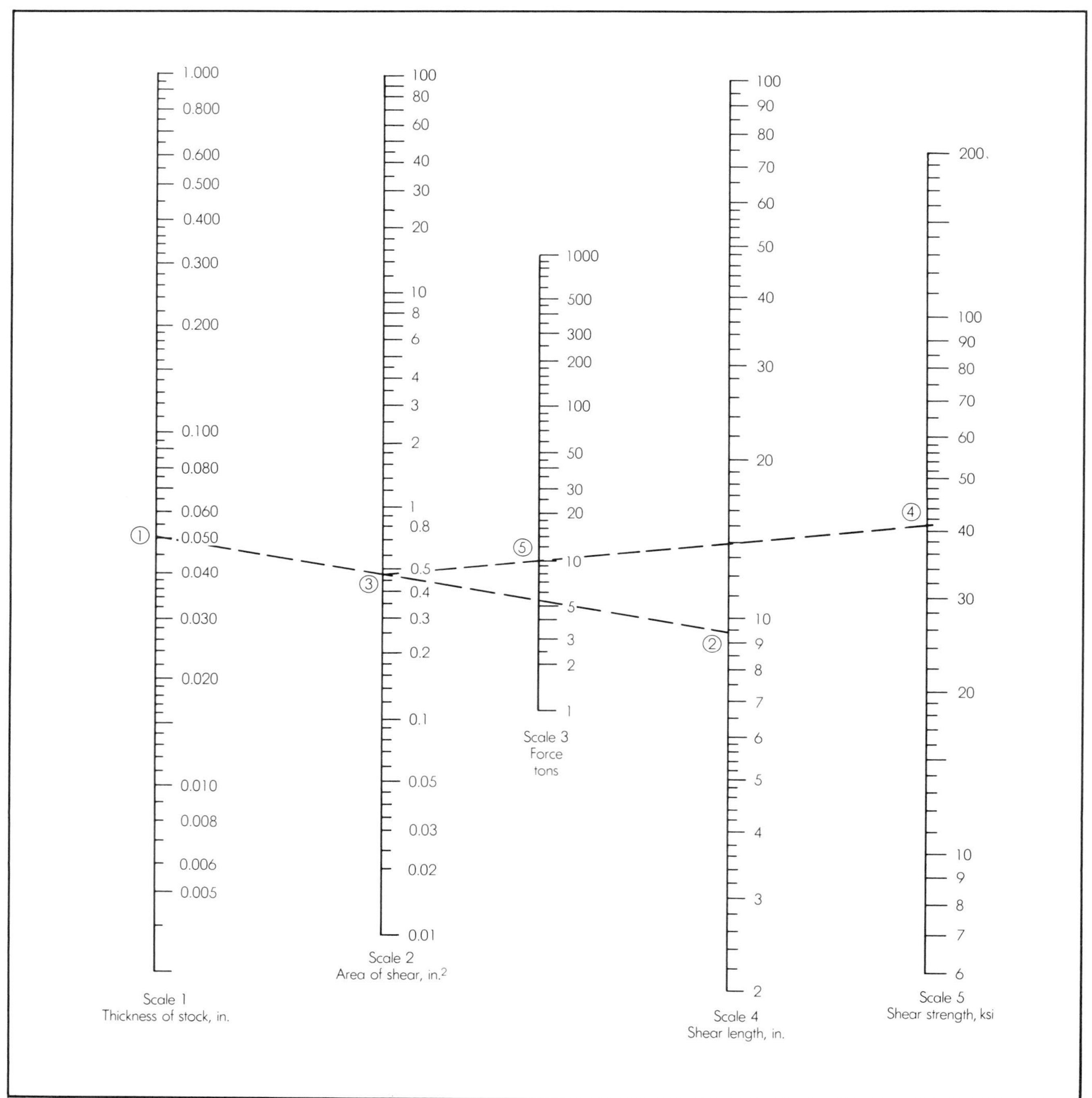


**Fig. 4-9 Nomograph for determining punching force in tons.**

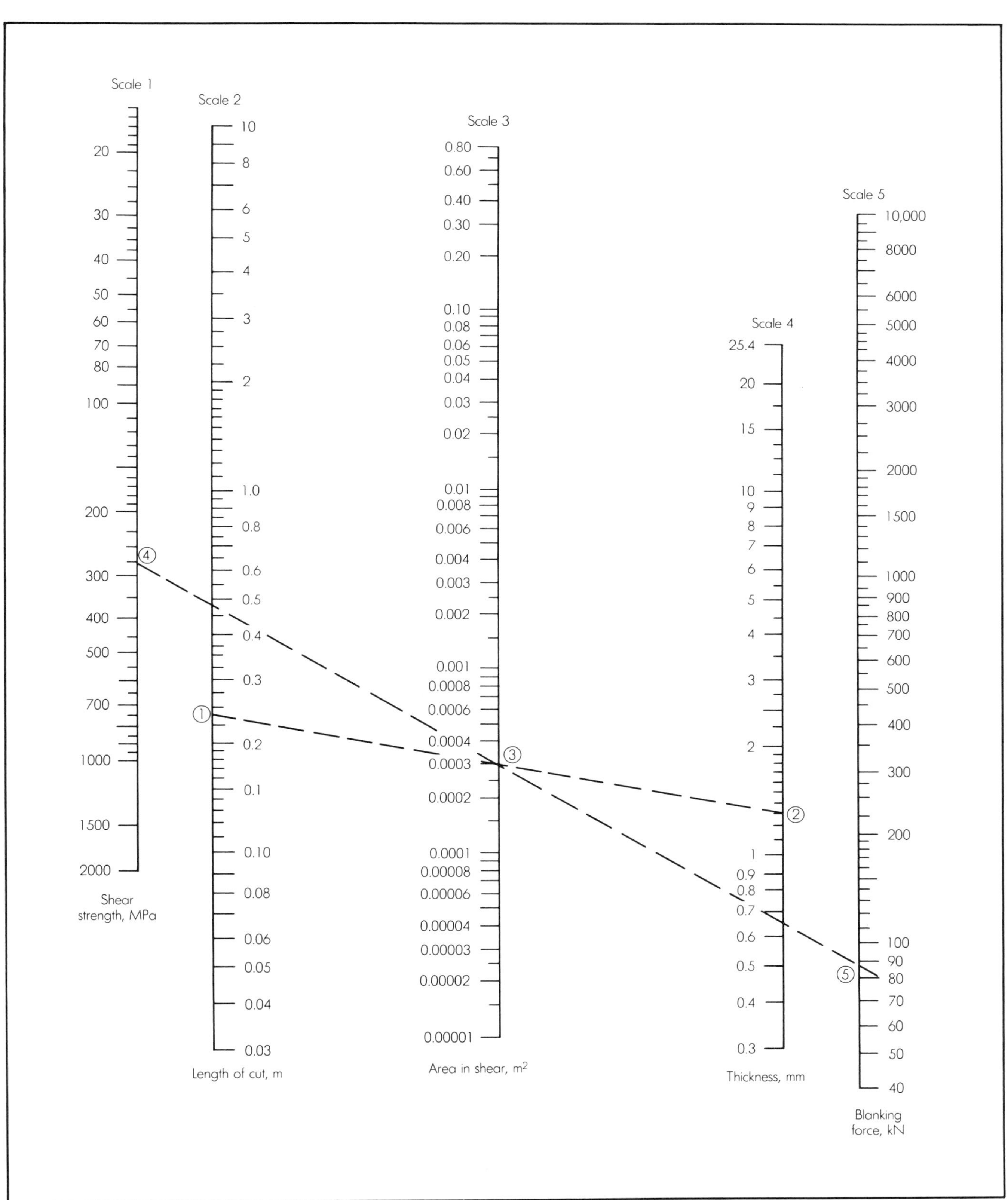


**Fig. 4-10 Nomograph for determining punching force in kilonewtons.**

force required to punch the hole. This percentage greatly changes with the type of material being punched and the amount of clearance between the cutting edges. Figure 4-11 is a graph showing the effect of these two conditions.

The surface finish of the punch changes with the number of holes being punched; and if a lubricant is not used, the effect can be very severe. A good grade of die cutting lubricant substantially reduces the stripping force.

**Stripping force equation**. The force required to strip a punch is difficult to determine, since it is influenced by the type of metal pierced, the area of metal in contact with the punch, the punch/die clearance, punch sharpness, spring positioning with respect to the punch, and other factors. The following empirical equation is used for rough approximations:

$$F = L \times T \times 1.5 \quad (3)$$

where:

$F$ = stripping force, ton
$L$ = length of cut, in.
$T$ = material thickness, in.

When using metric units, the equation is:

$$F = L \cdot T \cdot 20\,600 \quad (4)$$

where:

$F$ = stripping force, kN
$L$ = length of cut, m
$T$ = material thickness, m

**Stripping methods**. As shown in Fig. 4-12, stripping can be accomplished with a spring (urethane or die rubber) loaded plate that holds the material firmly against the die or a positive stripper plate set a short distance above the material. With a positive stripper, the material is lifted with the ascending punch until the material contacts the stripper and is freed of the punch.

## Reducing Shear Forces

A progressive shearing action is commonly used to reduce the required force. This is accomplished by stepping or staggering punches when more than one punch is used so that they do not cut at the same time, or it is accomplished by grinding a shear angle on the punch and die edges. In either method, the work is being done over a greater distance with less force, but the total work performed is the same as if no stepping or shear existed on the punches.

Special high-capacity tooling (refer to Chapter 6) is another method that can be used to reduce the shear force requirement in short-run production. For example, in punching large (2"; 51 mm) holes in thick metal, use of a hydraulic press with a special (high-capacity shear) punch enables a 15 ton (12.5 MPa) capacity press to produce holes that normally require 40 tons (36 MPa) with a mechanical press.

With minimal penetration of the punch and resultant breakthrough shock, the silicon steels, alloy and high-carbon steels, and some of the stainless steels (based on their hardness) could require equipment with as much as 50% greater capacity than calculated forces. The reversal of stresses in equipment when blanking these materials is so sudden and severe that improperly selected equipment can be seriously damaged.

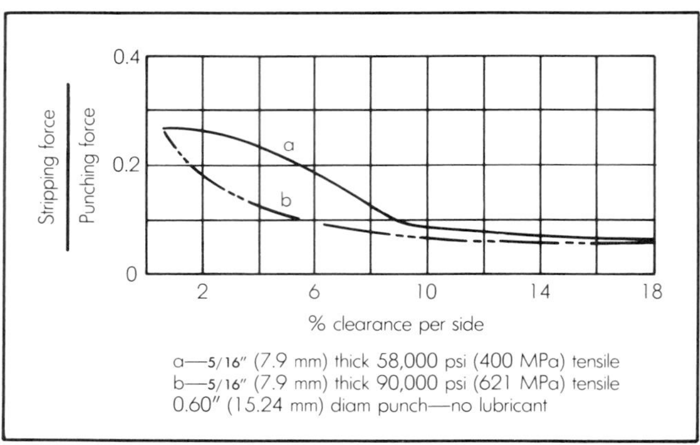


**Fig. 4-11 Stripping force varies with clearance.**

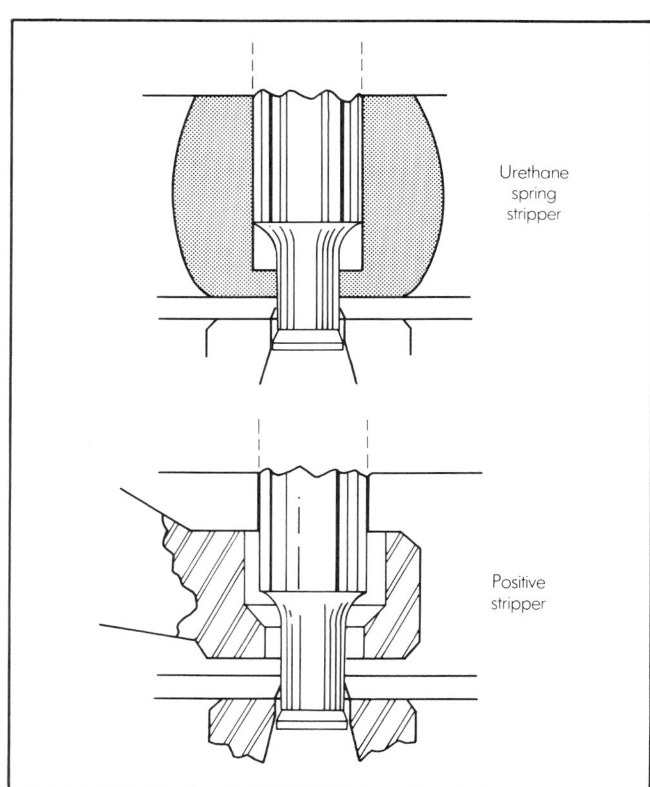


**Fig. 4-12 Spring and positive type stripping.**

## Stock Requirement

To determine the amount of stock required in pressworking operations to produce a particular part, per Fig. 4-13, the equation is:

$$W = C \times S \times P \times 7.3 \quad (5)$$

where:

$W$ = weight of stock for 1000 parts, lb
$C$ = dimension between blanks, in.
$S$ = width of the stock, in.
$P$ = weight of stock, lb/ft$^2$

Using metric units, the equation is:

$$W = C \cdot S \cdot P \cdot 1050 \quad (6)$$

where:

$W$ = stock weight for 1000 parts, kg
$C$ = dimension between blanks, m
$S$ = stock width, m
$P$ = stock weight, kg/m$^2$

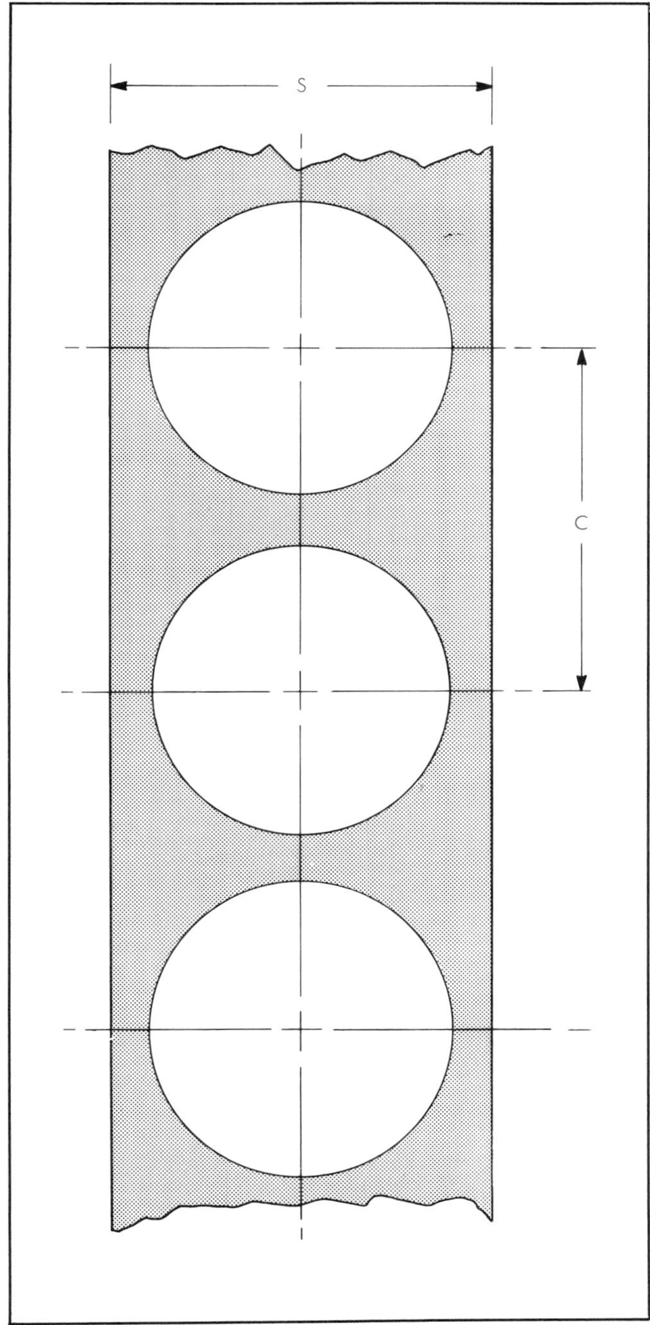


**Fig. 4-13 Simple blank layout for determining stock requirement.**

## BLANK DESIGN

Blanks can be cut from either flat or preformed stock. The flat blank usually requires subsequent operations. The development of the shape of the blank is determined by the end product. For example, circular blanks are used for round products such as drum heads and drawn cylindrical shells. Rectangular and irregularly shaped blanks are used to provide material for further working such as bending, flanging, or bulging. In addition to the material required for a finished part, the blank normally contains additional stock to permit holding during working and final trimming. Typical blanked semifinished parts are laminations for motors, transformers, and padlock cases made from stacked stampings.

Blanks, theoretically, are limited in size only to the width that can be produced by a rolling mill and to the cubic size of the ingot being rolled. The largest practical blanks from sheet or coil are used in the automotive industry for floors and roofs of cars. Other large-sized blanks may be found in the home appliance industry. The precious-metal industry generally has the smallest blanks, such as the gold foil used for electrical contact tips, these blanks being almost microscopic in size.

Blanks that are run in power presses with feed equipment vary in thickness from a few thousandths of an inch up to 1/4″ (0.08-6.4 mm). Blanks that are greater in thickness are generally low-production items blanked from strip. Production requirements also control the type of operation used.

The inherent advantage of parts blanked in a die on a punch press or similar equipment is that they can be duplicated constantly within given tolerances. The tolerances vary with type of material, thickness, and in some cases, the end product. For example, a blank for a motor lamination requires extreme accuracy with minimum burr, and a can end must be held to closer specifications than a drum head.

Economy of operation is relevant only to the particular operation. It can be maximum utilization of the stock or production with minimum scrap, but essentially it is the lowest unit cost for that specific operation. Economy of operation must be a combination of proper tooling for material and production requirements, total number of parts to be produced, number of parts per run or parts required in a unit of time, accuracy requirements, physical size and weight of the part, and material from which the part is to be blanked.

The amount of scrap generated in a blanking operation should be held to a minimum based on the blank sheet. When blanking is performed in multiples, stock layouts (see Fig. 4-14) should be checked for maximum stock utilization and the direction of burrs, assuming this is an important factor. Scrap allowances vary with the metal used; for example, in blanking aluminum approximately 0.050″ (1.27 mm) thick, a scrap allowance of 3/16″ (5 mm) is generally permissible on the side of the sheet, with approximately 3/32″ (2 mm) between the blanks. With specially shaped blanks, the requirement may increase. Usual practice allows a burr up to 10% of material thickness on light-gage stock and up to 0.001″ (0.03 mm) on stock less than 0.010″ (0.3 mm) thick, or 5% of material thickness.

## FINE BLANKING

Fine blanking and piercing is a process developed in Switzerland for producing blanks and holes with smoother edges and closer tolerances than are possible with conventional stamping practice. This is done in a single-station die with one stroke on a triple-action press (see Chapter 5). This process is

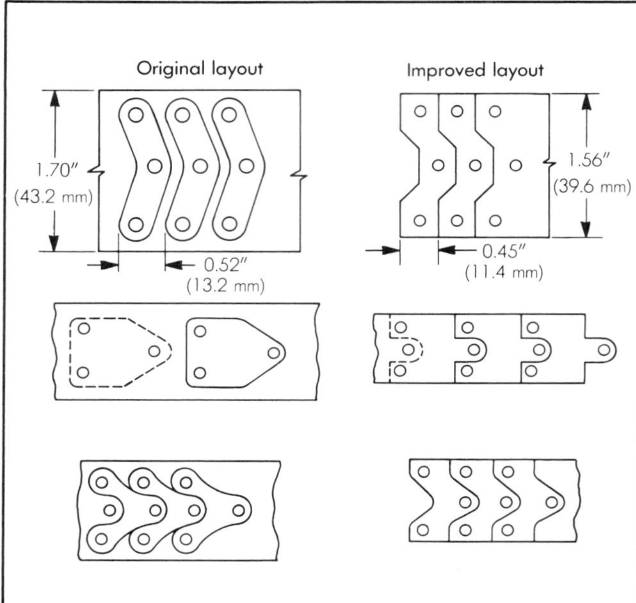


**Fig. 4-14 Example of stock layout improvement for economical blanking with minimum scrap.**

used extensively in Europe and is being applied increasingly in the United States.

## Advantages

Conventional blanking or stamping operations produce parts with sheared surfaces that are only partially—generally one third—cleanly sheared, the remaining two thirds showing a rough break as illustrated in Fig. 4-15. When functional demands are made on these sheared/break surfaces concerning tolerances or quality of surface finish, the piece parts must be reworked by such methods as shaving, milling, reaming, broaching or grinding. For the production of precision devices, it is often necessary that at least two, but generally more, secondary operations be performed per piece-part.[10]

Using fine blanking, precise finished components with inner and outer forms cleanly sheared over the whole material thickness are produced in one operation (see Fig. 4-15), thereby effecting significant production cost savings. To achieve these benefits, a triple action press and a specially constructed tool are required. The sequence of operations during one press stroke is shown in Fig. 4-16.

Savings in cost and time are important advantages of the fine blanking process for many applications. As stated previously, smooth edges and close dimensional accuracies of the parts produced eliminate or minimize subsequent operations required for functional surfaces. Fine blanking produces completely sheared edges without die breakage.

Accuracy attained in fine blanking depends on the thickness and tensile strength of the material being fine blanked and the configuration of the part being produced. Tolerances of ±0.001" (0.03 mm) can be consistently held on thin parts made from low-carbon steel, and ±0.003" (0.08 mm) on thicker parts. The smooth sheared edges can be held perpendicular to the material surface within 0.001 in./in. (0.03 mm/mm) and surface finishes of 32 $\mu$ in. (0.81 $\mu$ m) or less are possible. Flatness maintained is the same as that of the material fed into the die.

Another major advantage of fine blanking is that hole diameters, slot widths, and wall thicknesses can be made smaller than with conventional stampings—as small as 50% of material thickness in low-carbon steels. Also, other operations such as bending, embossing, and coining can be combined in the same operation, and the press can be used for conventional stamping dies when not required for fine blanking.

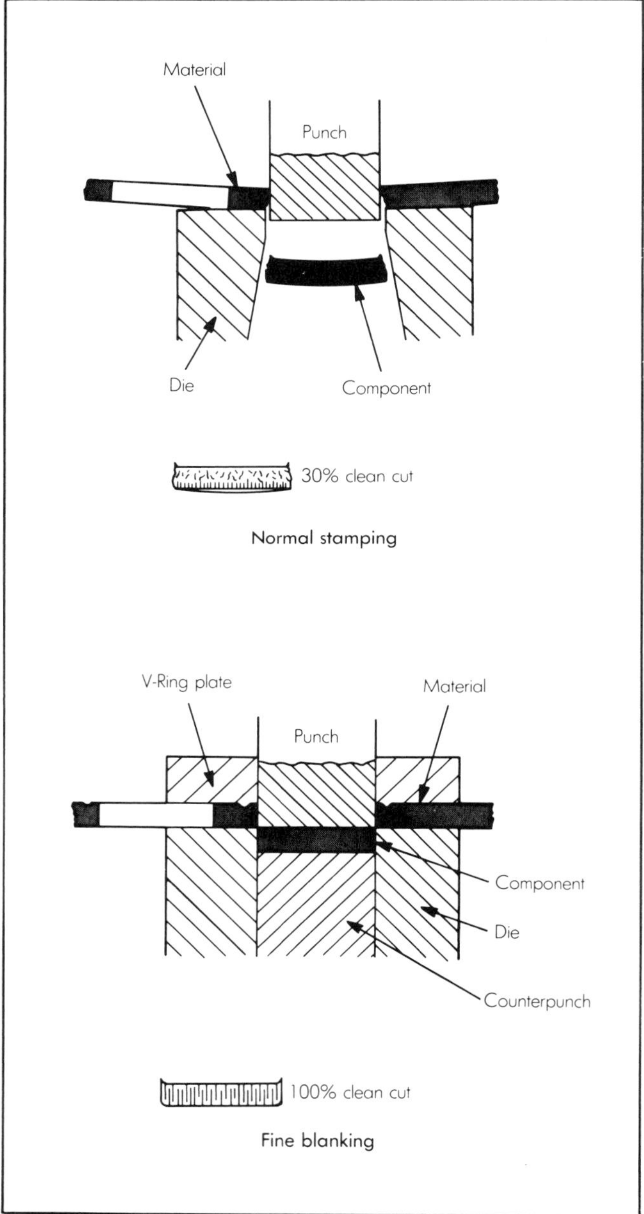


**Fig. 4-15 Elements of conventional stamping compared with fine blanking. Before the material is fine blanked, it is firmly clamped so that it can flow only in the cutting direction. On the outside of the component's cutting line, the material is sandwiched by the die and the V-ring plate (stinger); inside of the cutting line, the punch and the counter-punch locate and control the material. The clearance between punch and die measures only a few 100ths of a millimeter (1/1000 of an inch) and the cutting speed is relatively slow. (*Schmid Corp. of America*)**

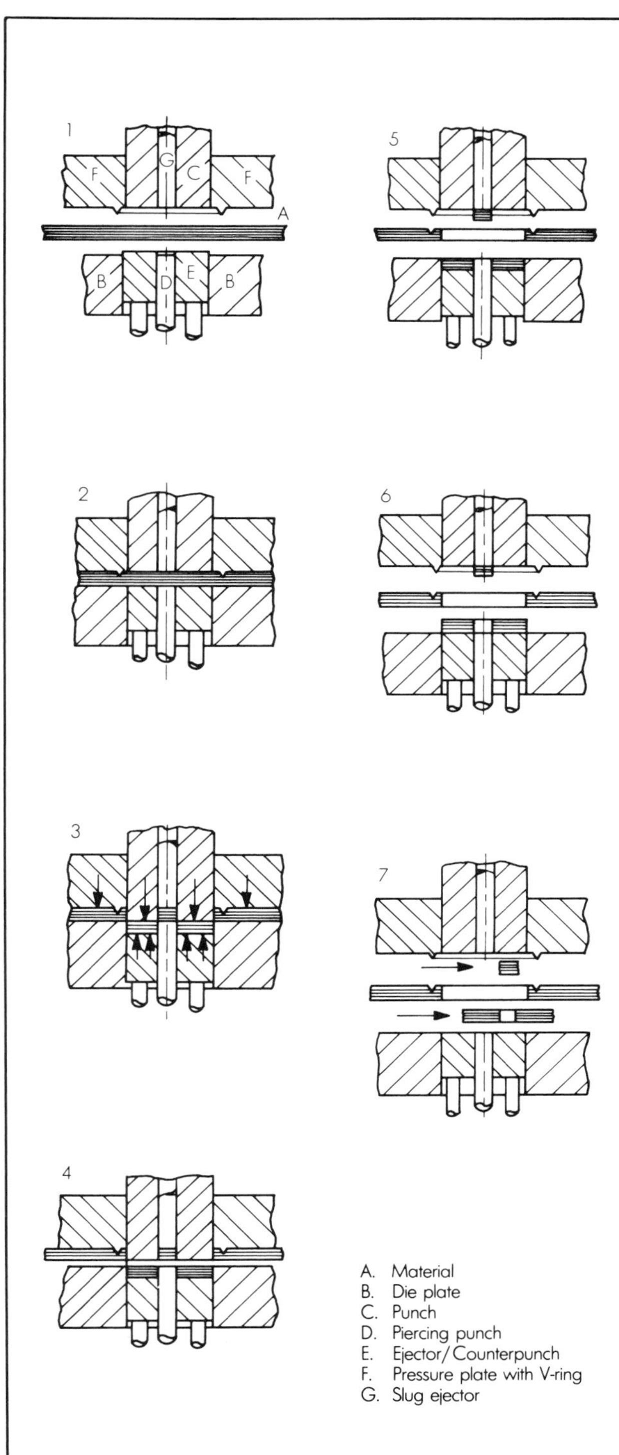


**Fig. 4-16 Fine blanking cycle: (1) Material is fed into the die; (2) Die closes and V-ring is embedded in the material; (3) Part is blanked—V-ring pressure is maintained, blanking pressure is exerted, and counterpressure is exerted against the part; (4) Die begins to open; (5) Slugs are ejected from top down; (6) Part is ejected from bottom up by reversing the counterpressure (7) Parts and slugs are removed from the die area—cycle is ready to repeat. (*Wagner Fineblanking*)**

## Materials Handled

Many different materials are being fine blanked. These include ferrous materials such as low and medium-carbon steels and some alloy and stainless steels, as well as nonferrous materials such as brass, copper, and aluminum alloys. In fact, any material suitable for cold forming can be fine blanked.

The best nonalloyed steels for fine blanking are those with low carbon content, generally with a maximum allowable of about 0.70% C. However, thin parts have been fine blanked from plain steels containing up to 0.95% C. Alloy steels should have a low yield strength and high elasticity—the more brittle the material, the poorer the results. For economical production and long die life, the tensile strength of the material should not exceed 85 ksi (586 MPa), except for thin sheets up to about 0.12″ (3 mm) thick, where materials with tensile strengths up to 114 ksi (786 MPa) have been fine blanked successfully.

**Limitations.** Fine blanking is best for applications in which manufacturing costs can be reduced by minimizing or eliminating secondary operations in producing smooth, accurate functional edges, or for improving product edge quality. When the edges produced in conventional stamping are satisfactory for a specific application, fine blanking can seldom be justified economically.

A fine blanking press can cost about twice that of a conventional press with equal capacity, and tooling costs may be up to 70% more than a standard compound die. Also, the fine blanking process is slower than conventional stamping. Despite these disadvantages, substantial savings are gained in many applications.

With respect to the design of the fine blanked part, the size of the part and material thickness are limited only by the die area and force available on the press. The process is generally limited to materials with a minimum thickness of about 0.03″ (0.8 mm) and a maximum of about 5/8″ (15.9 mm). Parts made from materials up to about 5/32″ (4 mm) thick are most common, but applications for precision blanking of thicker materials, which often make the process competitive with machining, are increasing.

Sharp corners cannot be produced with fine blanking, since it could cause tearing of the material and chipping of the tooling. The process does produce edge rollover, usually from 10 to 25% of the material thickness. Also, small burrs, generally having a maximum height of about 0.010″ (0.25 mm), are formed, but these can be easily removed by tumbling or by a light grinding operation.

## Applications

Most early applications of fine blanking involved the production of instrument, watch, and office machine components such as levers, fingers, tooth segments, gear wheels, cams, and similar parts. Now, the process is also being increasingly applied to a wider variety of materials and thicker stock in many industries, including the automotive, textile machinery, farm equipment, ordnance, machine tool, printing machine, and household appliance industries. Tooth forms (gears, racks, sprockets, ratchets, and splines) are easily produced and are common applications.

Fine blanking is an accepted process in many fields of production. The potential cost savings depend on the number and complexity of secondary operations that can be eliminated. The use of progressive tools is expanding the range of new applications of fine blanked parts involving forming operations.

Figure 4-17 shows various forming operations that are feasible for fine blanking.

### The Fine Blanking Process

The fine blanking and piercing process is more of a cold extruding operation than a cutting operation. It is comparable to conventional blanking with a compound die, but with several important differences. First, one or two raised vee-shaped rings or wedges (sometimes called stingers), which are located adjacent to and outside the cutting line, restrict the flow of material away from the cutting edge and press the material to be cut against the punch.

Another important difference is the independent adjustment and accurate control of the three hydraulic pressures (clamping, counterpressure, and blanking) on the triple-action press. A further difference is that only a small clearance is provided between the punch and die—generally about ½ to 1% of the stock thickness, plus corresponding closer tolerances on the punch and die. Also, the punch enters the die only a slight amount—equal to the radius on the die, which is generally about 5% of the material thickness. These features combine to prevent fracture cracking of the material, resulting in parts with smooth edges and holes fully sheared throughout the thickness of the material.

Information on fine blanking equipment and tooling is contained in Chapter 5, "Presses for Sheet Metal Forming," and Chapter 6, "Die Design for Sheet Metal Forming."

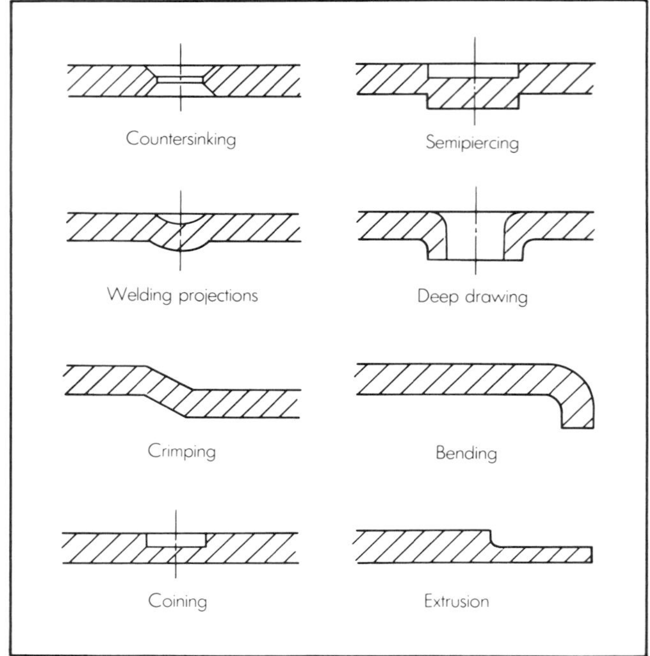


**Fig. 4-17 Various forming operations are feasible with fine blanking.**

# FORMING

Forming is a broad term for the metalworking processes in which the shape of a punch and die is reproduced directly in the metal. Bending, drawing, ironing, bulging, and various compression processes are included here as general subclasses under forming.

Chapter 9 covers spinning; and Chapter 19, "Special Forming Methods," includes information on explosive forming and other high-energy-rate forming processes.

## BENDING AND FLANGING

Bending and flanging are methods of forming shapes by stressing metal beyond its yield strength but below the ultimate strength. Flanging is similar to the bending of sheet metal, except that during flanging, the bent down metal is short compared to overall part size. There is no well-defined bent-over length that distinguishes bending from flanging. As explained later in this chapter, however, flanges and bends have distinctly different functions.

### Bending

Bends are made in sheet metal to gain rigidity and to produce a part of desired shape to perform a particular function. Bending is commonly used to produce structural stampings such as braces, brackets, supports, hinges, angles, and channels. Bending in several directions can produce parts that otherwise would require a drawing operation. Bending is usually done to a 90° angle, but other angles are sometimes produced.

The simplest form of bending, air bending, is illustrated by a beam supported at two points, with a load applied to the midpoint, as shown in Fig. 4-18. The load produces compressive stresses in the inner layers of the bend and tensile stresses in the outer layers. If the stress exceeds the material yield strength, the beam takes a permanent set or bend. All of the material in the bend zone is not stressed equally. The material in the inner and outer surfaces is stressed the most, and the stress gradually diminishes toward a neutral axis between the two surfaces. At that point, the stress is zero, and there is no length change. Additional information on sheet metal bending with press brakes and on tube bending is contained in Chapter 10, "Bending and Straightening."

### Flanging

Flanging is a forming operation in which a narrow strip at the edge of a sheet is bent down along a straight or curved line. Flanges can be open, at 90°, or at an acute angle—all of which are shown in Fig. 4-19. A flange is used for appearance, rigidity, edge strengthening, and removal of a sheared edge, as well as for an accurately positioned fastening surface.

**Types of flanges**. The three major types of flanges are the straight, stretch, and shrink flanges, shown in Fig. 4-20. The joggled flange in Fig. 4-20, view *f*, is a combination of all three major types. The reverse flange, Fig. 4-20, view *g*, is a combination of the stretch and shrink flanges; and the hole flange, Fig. 4-20, view *h*, is a special case of the stretch flange.

*Straight flange*. The straight flange is a simple bend with no longitudinal stresses imposed on the material except at the bend radius (see Fig. 4-21); therefore, within reason, a flange of any desired width can be made.

*Stretch flange*. The stretch flange is unique in that the flange has been stretched in the length direction during the flanging operation. The greatest longitudinal stretch occurs at the edge of the flange and diminishes to zero at the bend radius. A stretch flange forms with a concave outline, as shown in Fig. 4-20, view *b*; a concave surface contour, as shown in Fig. 4-20, view *c*; or a combination of the two conditions.

*Shrink flange*. The shrink flange is the opposite of the stretch flange, having shrunk in the length direction during the flanging operation. The greatest compressive stress occurs at the edge of the flange and diminishes to zero at the bend radius. A shrink flange forms with a convex outline, as shown in Fig. 4-20, view *d*; a convex surface contour, as shown in Fig. 4-20, view *e*; or a combination of the two conditions.

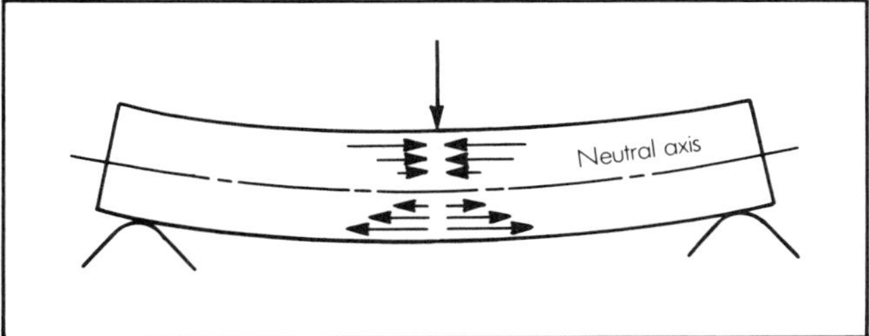


**Fig. 4-18 Simple beam deflection within elastic limits.**

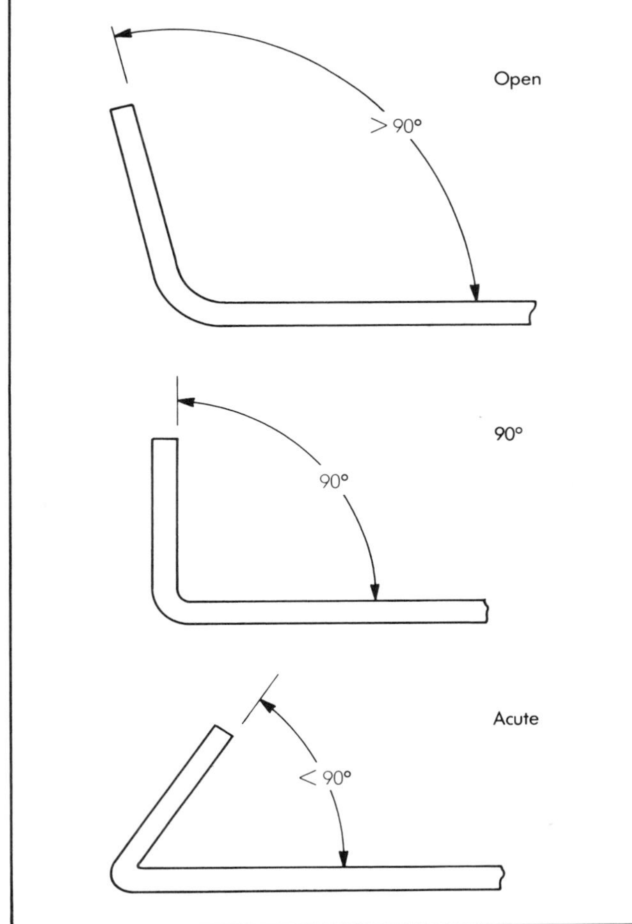


**Fig. 4-19 Flange angles of bend.**

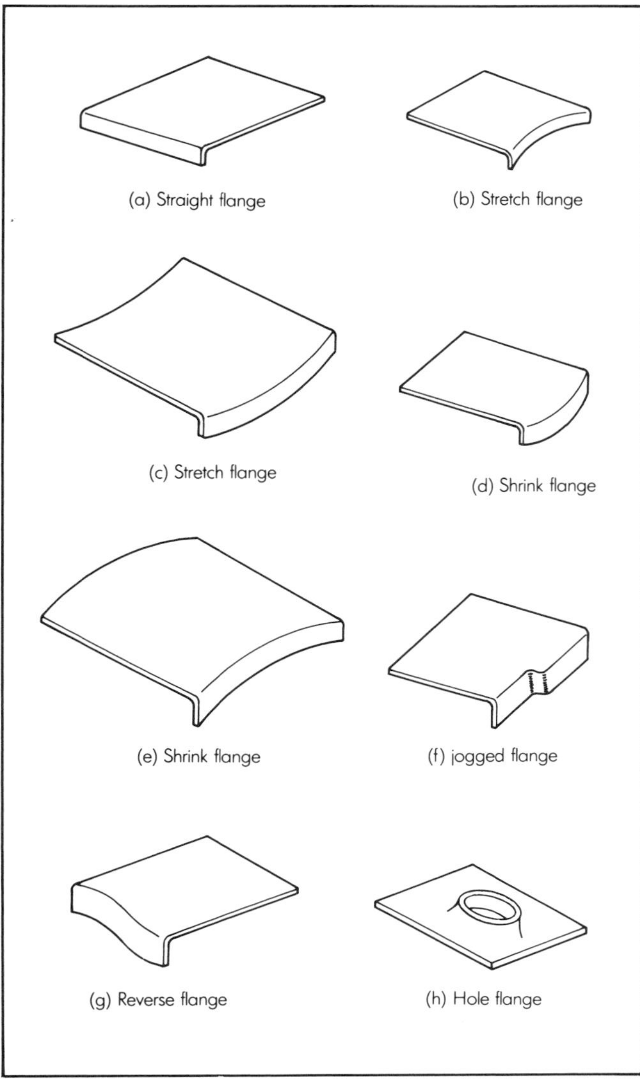


**Fig. 4-20 The major types of flanges are straight, stretch, and shrink.**

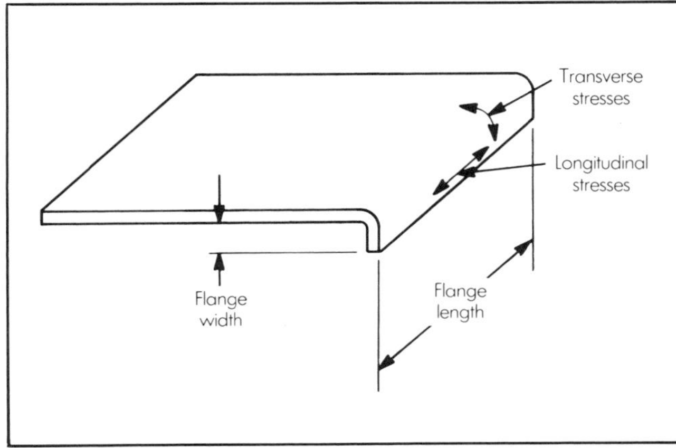


**Fig. 4-21 Straight flange.**

**Tooling to make flanges**. Typical flange tooling is shown in Fig.4-22. Normally, a part is formed before flanging. After the formed part is placed on the male punch and positioned by appropriate locators, the pad descends to clamp the part. The wiper steel then descends wiping the edges down over the male steels.

The wiping operation of the wiper steel against the outside flange surface is severe, since the wiper steel is susceptible to galling. An 06 graphitic oil hardening tool steel is a good material for this application.

The male steels should be sufficiently hard to maintain the proper flange radius, but should also be tough enough to resist corner chipping. The radius of flanges that are subsequently hemmed by conventional methods is kept fairly sharp; therefore, such flanges are susceptible to chipping. An S7 tool steel is a good material for this application. The force required to bend or flange a sheet is calculated as shown in Fig. 4-23.

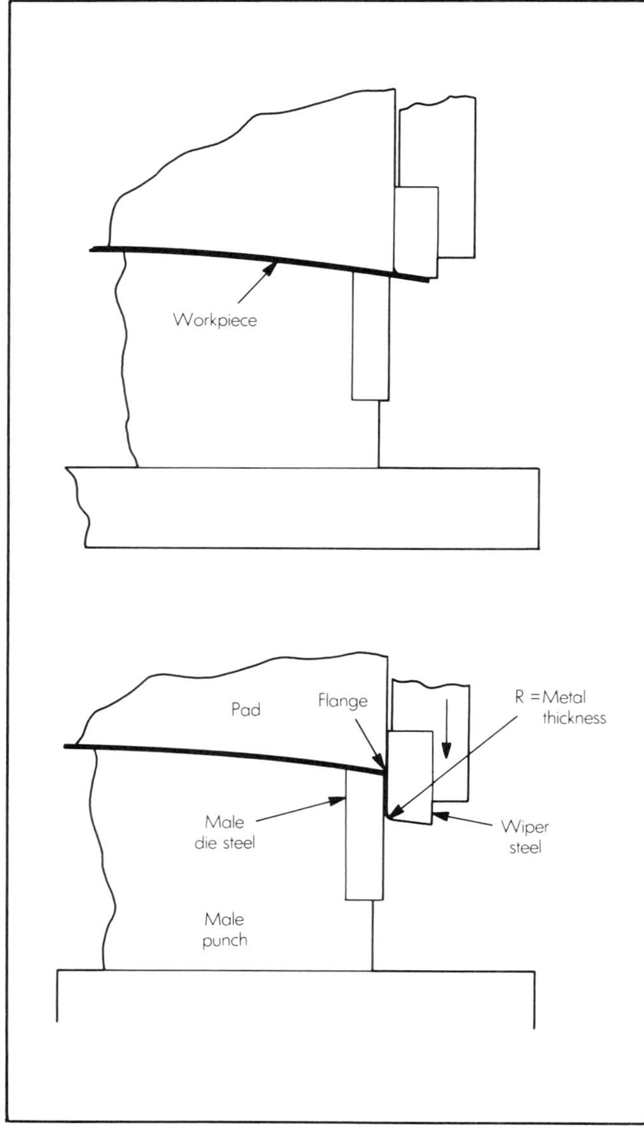

Fig. 4-22 Typical flange tooling.

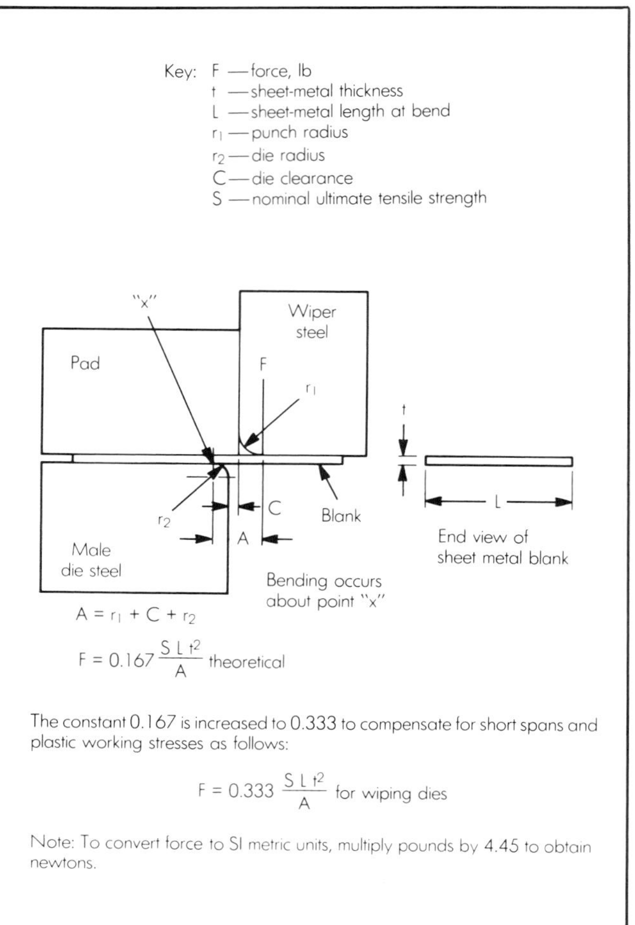

Fig. 4-23 Flange force calculation.

**Quality of flanges**. As noted earlier, both stretch and shrink flanges are strained nonuniformly during the flanging operation. Some portion of the resulting stress is elastic. This stress can sometimes result in substantial distortion of the previously formed part. Two ways of compensating for this effect are:

1. Change the contour of the formed part prior to flanging.
2. Change the contour of the male punch and pad of the flanging die. This is usually the easiest solution.

Recoil is shown in Fig. 4-24. This is a particular problem when appearance is of great concern, such as in the case of automotive outer panels. Recoil is caused by insufficient pad pressure or by a pad that gives insufficient part coverage. Figure 4-25 shows two designs for recoil control. A rule of thumb for determining sufficient pad force is as follows:

$$Pad\ force = \frac{SLt}{3} \tag{7}$$

where:

$F$ = force, lb
$S$ = ultimate strength of the material, psi
$L$ = flange length, in.
$t$ = material thickness, in.

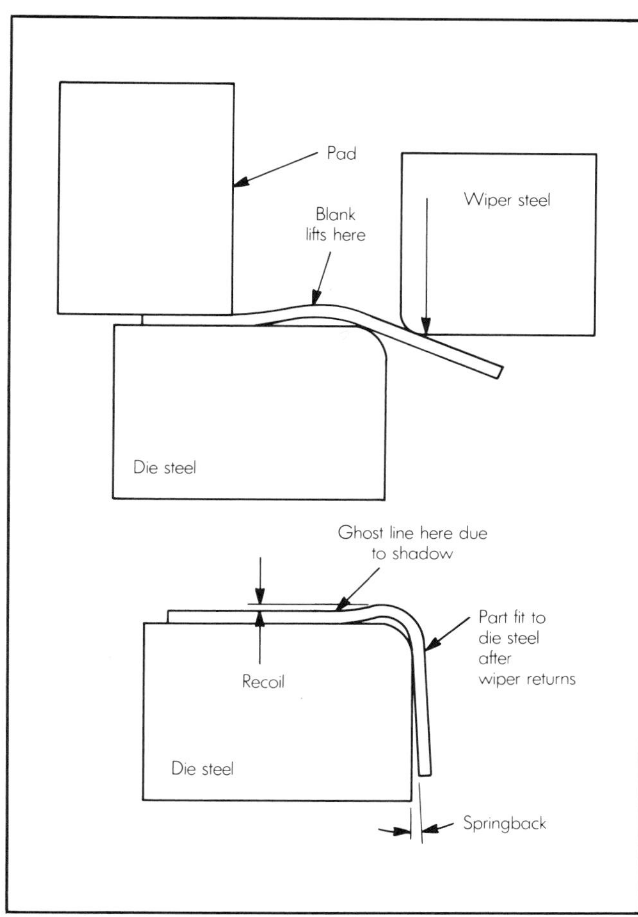


Fig. 4-24 Metal recoil or springback during bending.

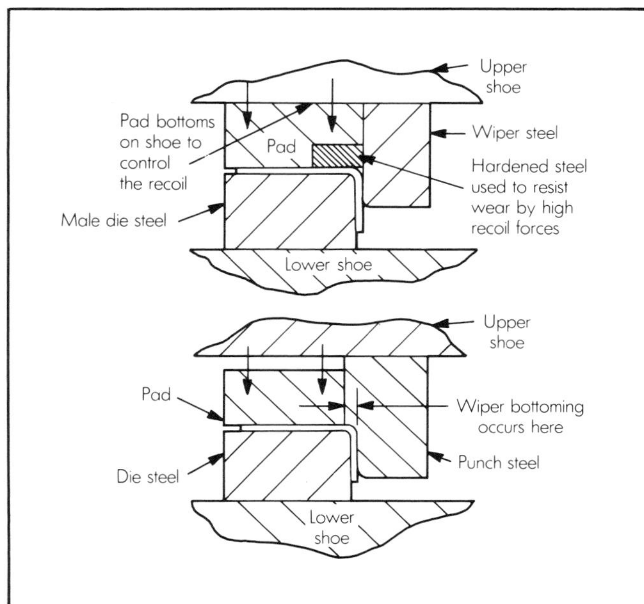


Fig. 4-25 Two designs for recoil control.

To express force in SI metric units, lbf should be multiplied by 4.448, to obtain newtons.

*Wrinkling*. A common problem of shrink flanges is wrinkling. This is a buckling phenomenon and is a function of the ability of the flange to resist the compressive stresses during the forming operation while the material is not confined. The condition can be improved by limiting flange width, increasing material thickness, providing offsets in the flange to take up excess metal, and reducing clearance between the wiper steel and the male die steel to iron out wrinkles that occur. The ironing solution may result in galling conditions on the wiper steel, creating appearance problems.

*Splitting*. Edge splitting is a common occurrence with stretch flanges. The susceptibility to splitting is a function of the tensile stress at the edge, the material properties, and the edge condition resulting from the trimming operation. Tensile stress can be reduced by reducing the flange width or by providing notches or scallops as shown in Fig. 4-26. Aluminum-killed steel with a high strain ratio ($r$ value) withstands a higher edge stretch than rimmed steel or other steels with lower strain ratios. An effective means of reducing susceptibility to splitting is to use correct tool conditions during blanking, to reduce work hardening of the cut edge. Sharp, unchipped cutting edges with a tool clearance that is 15%, ± 5% of material thickness, should be used.

The onset of edge splitting can be determined from geometry, and the limits of formability can be determined. A simple general equation expresses the strain at the edge of the stretch flange, where most failures begin.

$$e_x = \frac{R_2}{R_1} - 1 \qquad (8)$$

where:

$e_x$ = strain at flange edge
$R_1$ = flange edge radius before forming
$R_2$ = flange edge radius after forming

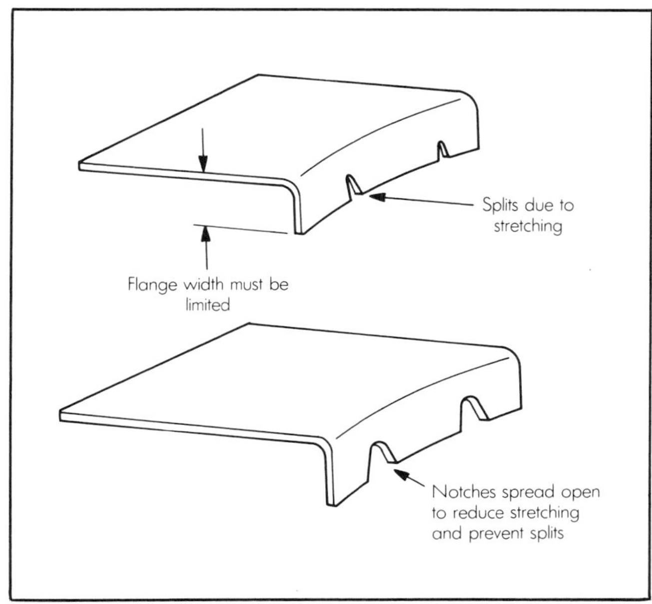


Fig. 4-26 Notches or scallops prevent splitting of a stretch flange.

# BENDING AND FLANGING

This is seen in Fig. 4-27 for a flat surface. It also applies to flanges expanded from a cylindrical surface as seen in Fig. 4-28. In this case, $R_1$ is the cylinder radius and $R_2$ is the outer rim radius.

The difference between original and final radii is not identical to final flange width, which narrows during forming. Counting etched circles applied before forming gives a correct value when either $R_1$ or $R_2$ cannot be measured directly. Flange forming limits depend on material properties, worked metal at the edge, and burrs at the edge. Table 4-7 gives strain limits for materials with burr-free edges. These limits relate to tensile properties. Materials may be tested by expanding a drilled, deburred hole with a lubricated conical punch. Limit is taken as initiation of a crack or localized neck at the flange edge.

Figure 4-29 shows remaining formability or strain limits in the table if burrs are present. Burr height/thickness is the ratio of burr height above the edge to material thickness. Burrs and thinning of metal indicate the presence of cold working, which also reduces formability. Increase in hardness at the edge is proportional to reduction in forming limit. Edge condition improvement raises the forming limit by removing burrs and, where necessary, annealing the edge before forming.

Tabs and notches at the edge of a flange localize strains and often reduce the forming limit severely. Tabs reduce formability. The larger the tab, the worse the reduction. The smaller the tab root radius, the worse it is, as indicated in Fig. 4-30.

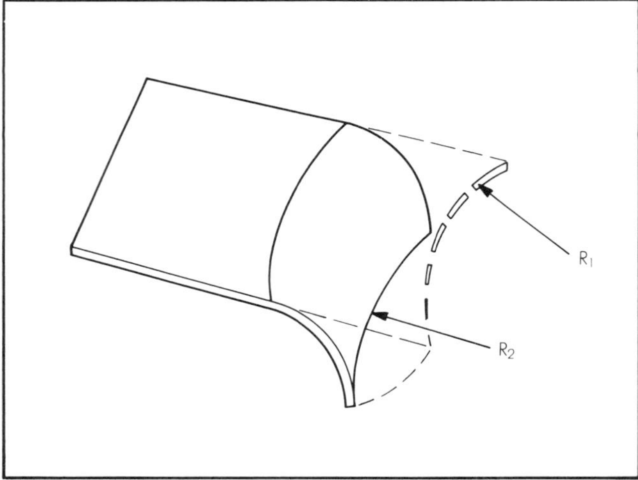


**Fig. 4-27 Stretched flange—flat sheet.**

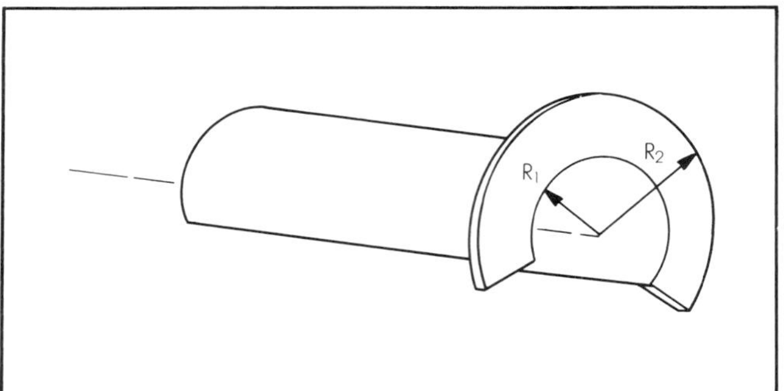


**Fig. 4-28 Stretched flange—curved sheet.**

**TABLE 4-7**
**Flange Edge Maximum Strain Limit**

| Material | Strain Limit (no burrs) |
|---|---|
| Low-carbon steel, hot-rolled drawing-quality, special-killed | 0.65 |
| Low-carbon steel, cold-rolled | 0.40 |
| Low-carbon rimmed steel, cold-rolled drawing-quality, special-killed | 0.50 |
| Renitrogenized/rephosphorized, hot-rolled steel | 0.50 |
| Renitrogenized/rephosphorized, cold-rolled steel | 0.40 |
| High-strength, low-alloy steel YS50 ksi | 0.40 |
| Aluminum 5182-0, body stock | 0.20 |

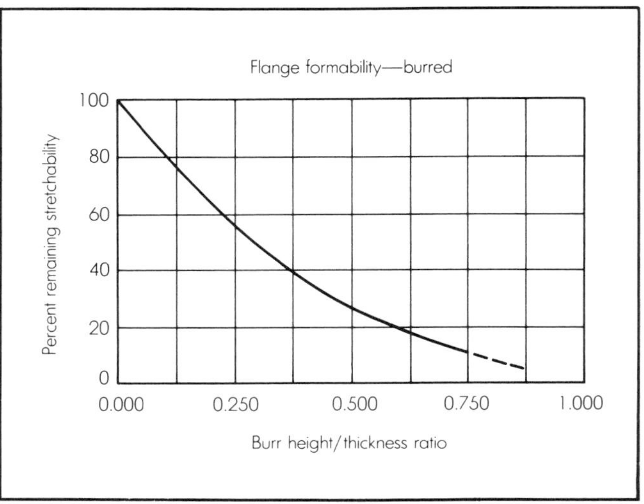


**Fig. 4-29 Flange formability in relation to burring.** (*Chrysler Corporation*)

Notches that are cut deeply and broadly at the base can relieve edge splitting at the expense of the flange strength function. Smaller notches reduce forming limits in much the same way as tabs. The larger radius at the notch bottom eases its bad effect on forming limit. Wider notches also reduce the detrimental stress localization effect on forming limit.

*Springback*. Depending on the application, springback can be an important consideration. It is difficult to predict because it is affected by many variables. Some factors that increase springback are:

- Higher material strength.
- Thinner material.
- Lower Young's modulus.
- Larger die radius.
- Greater wiper steel clearance.
- Greater number of degrees of bend.
- Less irregularity in part outline.
- Flatter part surface contour.

If a flanged part has sufficient irregularity with respect to either the outline or surface contour, the springback will be very slight. An approximation of the springback of a straight bend for low-carbon, low-strength steel and a zero wiping-steel clearance is shown in Fig. 4-31. The springback for large wiping-steel clearances can be as much as five times the amount shown on the graph.

The springback for other materials is reasonably proportional to the difference between strength and Young's modulus.

Hole flange depths for 6010-T4 and 2036-T4 aluminum can be greatly increased by the use of a backup pressure pad as shown in Fig. 4-32.

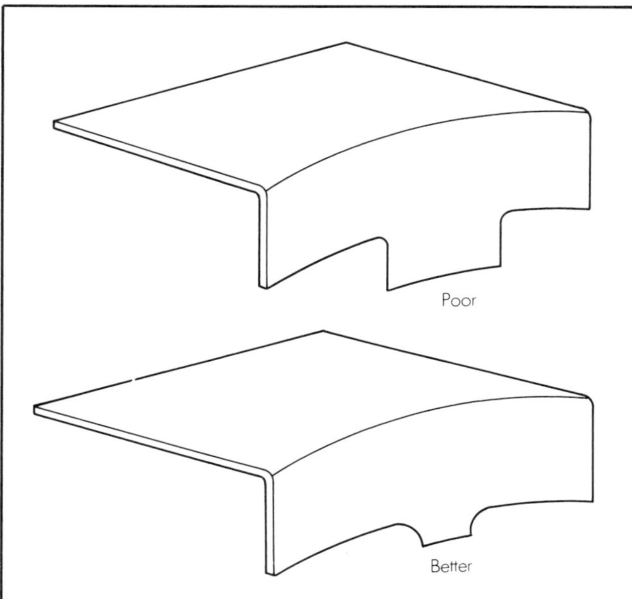


**Fig. 4-30 Tabs on stretch flanges.**

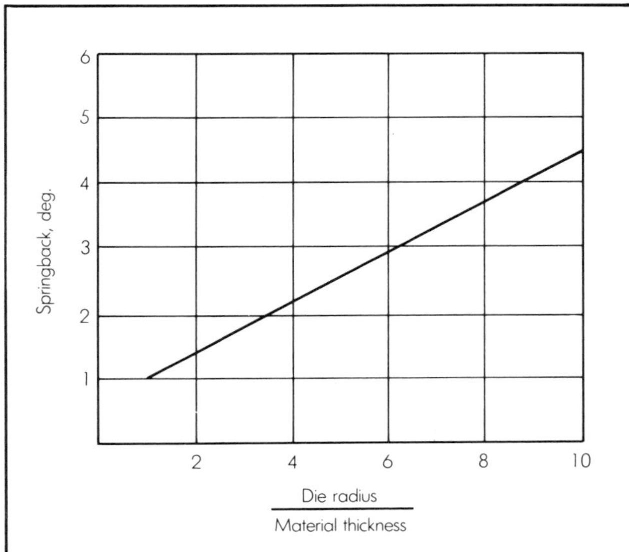


**Fig. 4-31 Springback for a straight 90° bend of low-carbon, aluminum-killed steel with zero wiping steel clearance.**

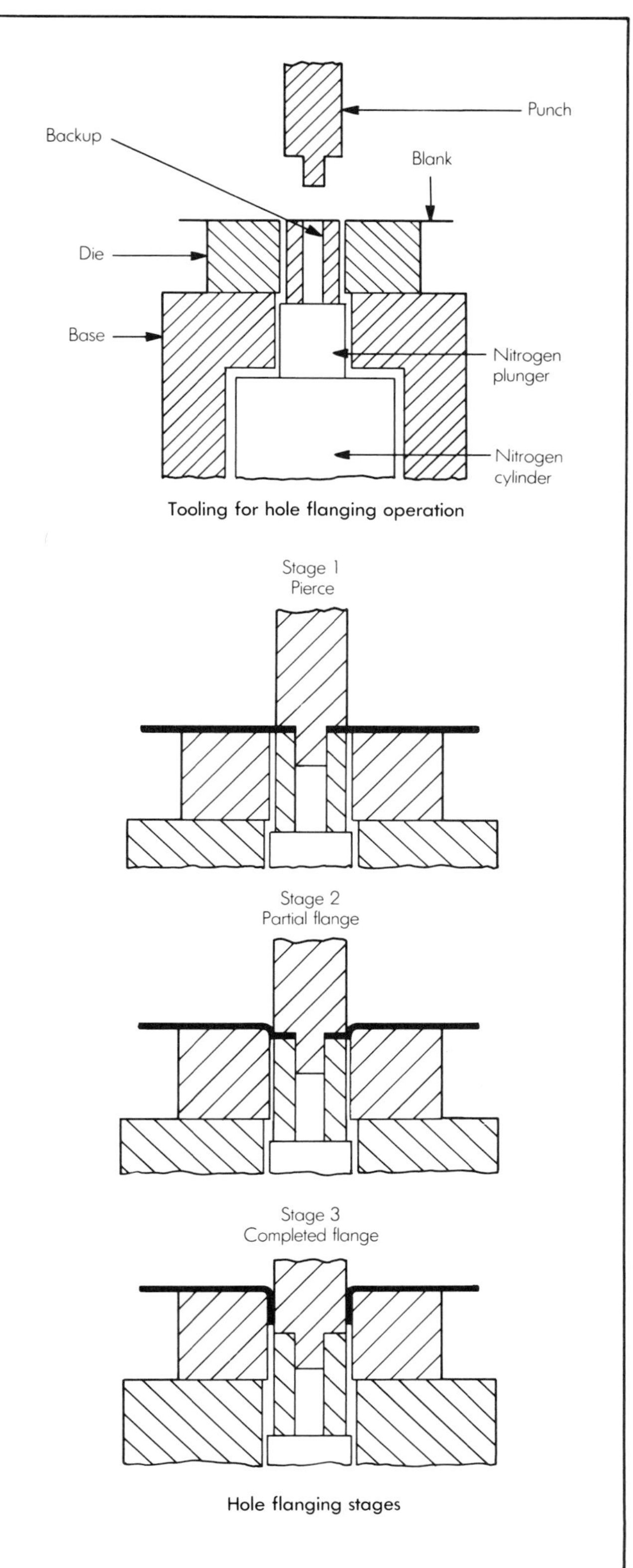


**Fig. 4-32 A backup pressure pad enables production of increased hole flange depths. (*Aluminum Company of America*)**

## Hemming

A hem is a flange that has been bent more than 180°. Hems are primarily used for appearance and for the attachment of one sheet metal part to another. They are not as rigid or accurate as a flange; but they very effectively remove a dangerous sheared edge. They are used extensively in automobiles to join inner and outer door and trunk lid stampings.

**Types of hems**. Four different types of hems are shown in Fig. 4-33. The tear drop hem is used for materials that do not have the ductility required to form the flattened hem. The open hem and rope hem are used for attachment to other sheet metal parts. The rope hem is used for materials with insufficient ductility to form the open hem.

**Tooling for hems**. Although flanges and hems can be made in one operation, as shown in Fig. 4-34, generally, hemming is performed on a part that has been flanged in a previous operation.

A typical hemming operation is shown in Fig. 4-35. The flanged part is accurately positioned on the adapter. The pre-hem steel descends, bending the 90° flange to a 45° flange. Then the hem steel continues to descend, completing the operation.

The tooling for a rope hem used for 6010-T4 and 2036-T4 aluminum is shown in Fig. 4-36.

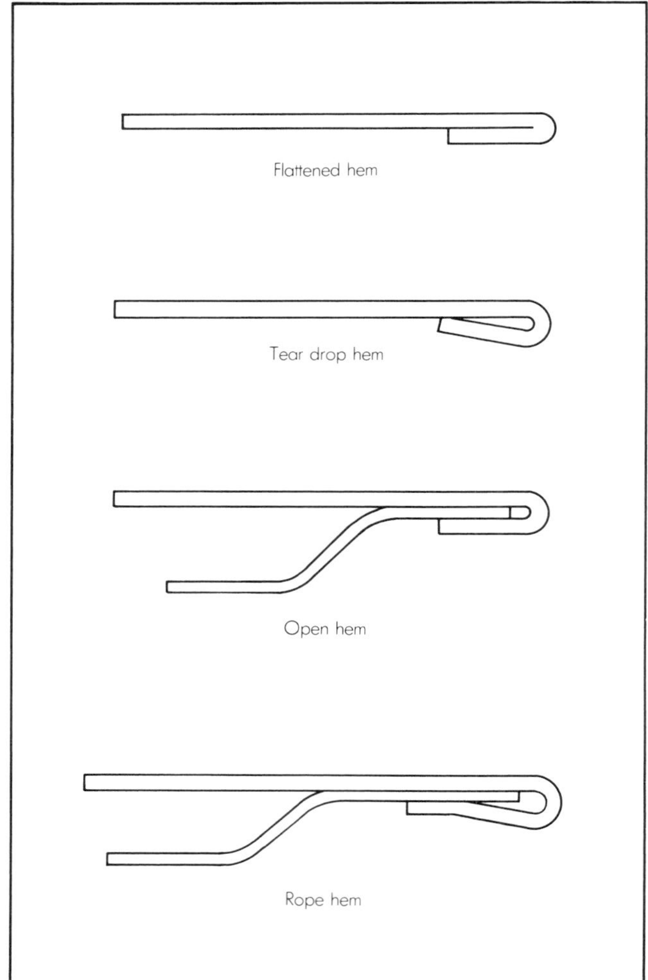


**Fig. 4-33 Four types of hems.**

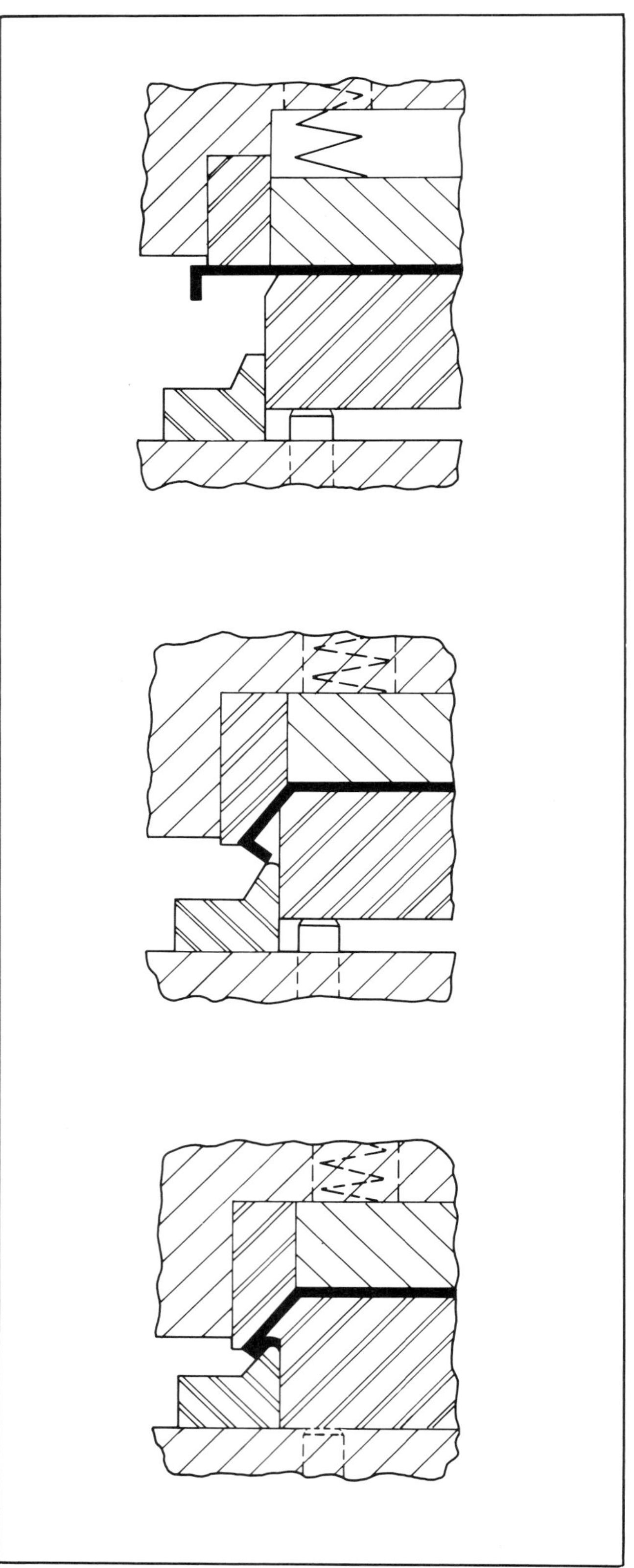

**Fig. 4-34 A flanging and hemming die.**

**Quality of hems.** Some hem quality problems, such as edge splitting, wrinkling, and part distortion, are the same as those for flanging, and the solutions are similar. However, unlike flanging, a major difficulty with hemming is maintaining an accurate part outline. The reason is "roll-in" or "roll-out." Roll-in is shown in Fig. 4-35. The amount of roll-in or roll-out is difficult to predict because it is affected by all of the following factors:

- Material thickness.
- Material strength.
- Flange die radius.
- Outline curvature—direction and degree.
- Surface contour curvature—direction and degree.
- Flange length.

Because of the unpredictability of the location of the hemmed outline, the solution to maintaining an accurate part outline is a trial-and-error changing of the position of the flange outline and length. The experience of the die tryout operator is invaluable in reducing the time involved in this tedious job.

A well-timed hemming operation, in which the pre-hem steel hits most of the flanged edge at the same time, is essential to a good part. Mistiming can result in recoil and shifting of the part on the adapter.

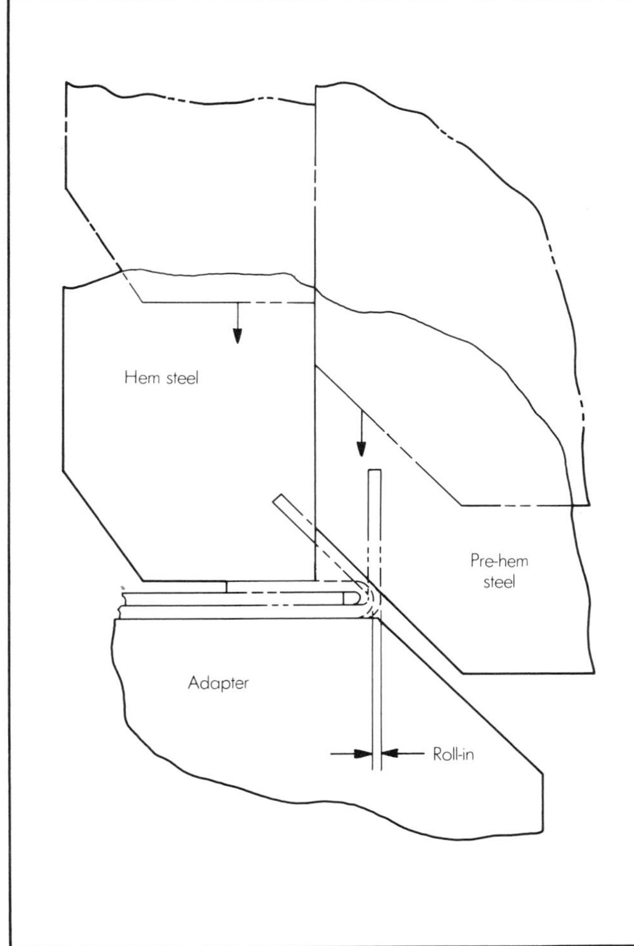


**Fig. 4-35 Typical hemming die operation.**

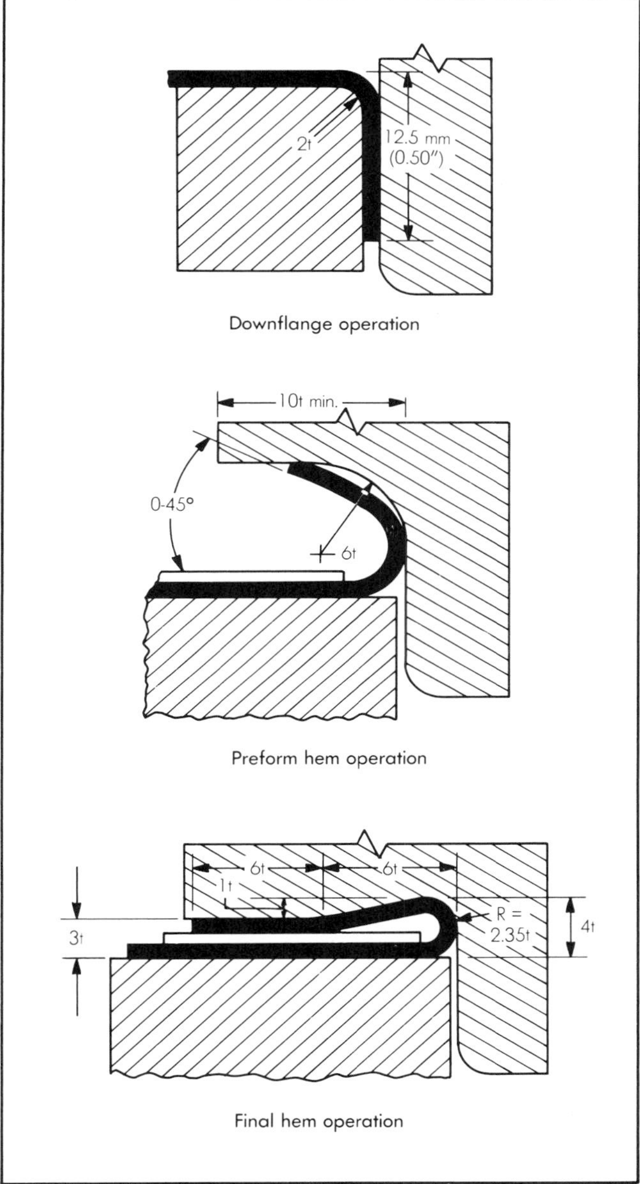


**Fig. 4-36 Rope hem tooling for aluminum alloys.** (*Aluminum Company of America*)

## DRAWING

Drawing is a process of cold forming a flat precut metal blank into a hollow vessel without excessive wrinkling, thinning, or fracturing. The various forms produced may be cylindrical or box shaped, with straight or tapered sides or a combination of straight, tapered, and curved sides. The parts may vary from 1/4" (6 mm) diam parts or smaller to aircraft or automotive parts large enough to require mechanical handling equipment.

The process of drawing basically involves forcing the flat sheet of metal into a die cavity with a punch. The force exerted by the punch must be sufficient to draw the metal over the edge of the die opening and into the die. The metal flow is similar to that of a viscous fluid.

# DRAWING

The metal being drawn must have a combination of strength and ductility, to avoid rupture in the critical area where the metal blends from the punch face to the vertical portion of the punch. This area is subjected to the stress that occurs when the metal is pulled from the flat blank into the die. The blank must have sufficient ductility to permit metal flow toward the die opening by the combination of compressive and tensile forces that are applied.

## Blankholder Force

The compressive forces on the metal in the area beyond the edge of the die cause the metal to buckle. If buckled or wrinkled metal were pulled into the die, the buckled metal would increase the strain in the nose area to the point where the metal would rupture soon after the draw began. To prevent this buckling reaction, blankholder force pressure is applied to the blank. The amount of blankholder pressure is generally one-third of that required for drawing. For simple shapes, metal thickness must also be considered. The thinner the metal, the more blankholder force required.

It should be noted that blankholder force is a widely debated, controversial subject and that, in a practical sense, most values are found empirically. The amount of blankholder force should be just sufficient to prevent wrinkling. It depends on the draw reduction, the stock thickness, the stock properties, the die lubrication, and other factors; and for a particular application, it can be best determined experimentally by trial-and-error.

Three primary reactions of the metal to an application of drawing force (pressure) and blankholding force (pressure) are:

1. Metal in the periphery of the blank area thickens slightly.
2. Metal in the periphery of the blank area moves toward the die under combined compressive and tensile forces that result from punch pressure.
3. Metal in the area adjacent to the punch nose becomes thinner because of the stress imposed upon it by resistance that the metal in the flange area encounters in overcoming compression and friction forces.

## Redrawing

The term *redrawing* is used for a variety of operations in which a part is reduced in its lateral dimensions by means of single or double-action dies without reducing the wall thickness. Regular redrawing is done by positioning the part under the punch, which forces the cup into the die, reducing the bottom dimensions, and increasing the side-wall height. Reverse or inside-out redrawing is done by positioning the cup over a die ring; the punch contacts the outside of the bottom, turning the part inside-out into the die opening.

**Number of operations**. When the height of the cup drawn from the blank is larger than the diameter of the required part, the cup must be redrawn, according to recommended percentages, until the required diameter is obtained. Knowing the blank diameter, the number of operations needed to reduce the blank diameter to the required part diameter can be determined. General practice is to make a 40-45% reduction of blank diameter for the first draw. For the second draw, the reduction is 30%; and for the third draw, the reduction is 16%. These percentages are given only as a general guide.

Percent reduction refers to the figure obtained by the following equation:

$$R = 100\,\frac{D - d}{d} \qquad (9)$$

where:

$R$ = percent reduction
$D$ = diameter being reduced
$d$ = diameter to which the blank or shell is being reduced

The number of draws required for a rectangular shell depends upon the ratio of the corner radius to the height of the draw. The heights that may reasonably be expected from one draw are listed in Table 4-8.

**TABLE 4-8**
**Cup Draw Lengths for Various Corner Radii**

| Corner Radii | | Length of Draw | |
|---|---|---|---|
| in. | mm | in. | mm |
| 3/32 to 3/16 | 2.4 to 4.8 | 1 | 25 |
| 3/16 to 3/8 | 4.8 to 9.5 | 1 1/2 | 38 |
| 3/8 to 1/2 | 9.5 to 12.7 | 2 | 51 |
| 1/2 to 3/4 | 12.7 to 19.1 | 3 | 76 |

The amount that a rectangular part can be reduced in one draw depends upon the corner radius and diminishes as the corner radius becomes smaller. For example, a box with a 1/8″ (3.2 mm) radius could not be reduced as much as one with corners of 3/8″ (9.5 mm) radius. Theoretically, the corner radius should be as large as possible, but the size is limited by practical considerations. The larger the radius, the sooner the blank is released from under the blankholder or pressure pad, allowing the metal to wrinkle and encouraging the possibility of a fracture at the corner.

Successful operation of the dies depends to a considerable extent upon the corner clearance, as the big difficulty in rectangular drawing is thickening at the corners. In a one-operation die, the corner clearance should be somewhat more than the thickness of the stock.

Corner clearances for single, double, and multiple draws cannot be determined solely by analysis. The usual practice is to make the finishing die; then draw the part by hand; and by a method of cut and try, determine both the size of the blank for the first operation and the number of draws necessary to finish the part.

**Reductions in drawing**. One important factor in the success or failure of a drawing operation is the thickness-diameter ratio, or the relationship of the metal thickness to the blank or previous shell diameter; this ratio is expressed as $t/d$. As this ratio decreases, the tendency to wrinkle increases and necessitates more blankholding pressure to control the flow properly and prevent wrinkles from starting.

The ratio $t/d$ is used in Fig. 4-37 as a tentative means of determining maximum reductions permissible under single and double-action draws. The top limit of about 48% seems to be substantiated by practice and theory concerning the strains set up in the draw. The 30% limit for double-action redraws is dictated by practice and is modified by corner radii, friction, and the angle of the blankholding faces with respect to the shell wall. Because of strain-hardening stresses set up in the metal,

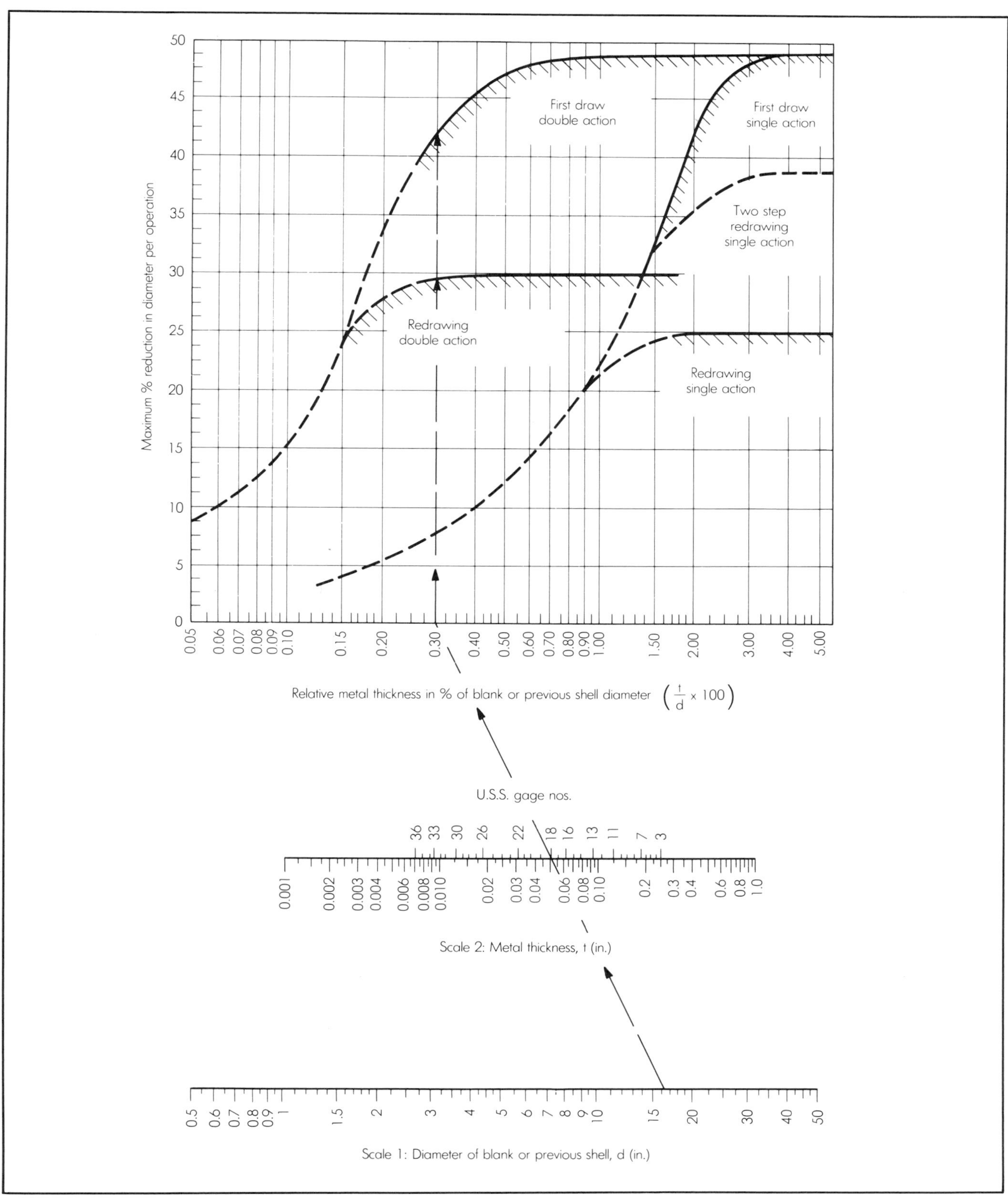


**Fig. 4-37 Chart for determining tentative maximum reductions in diameter by various methods.**

## DRAWING

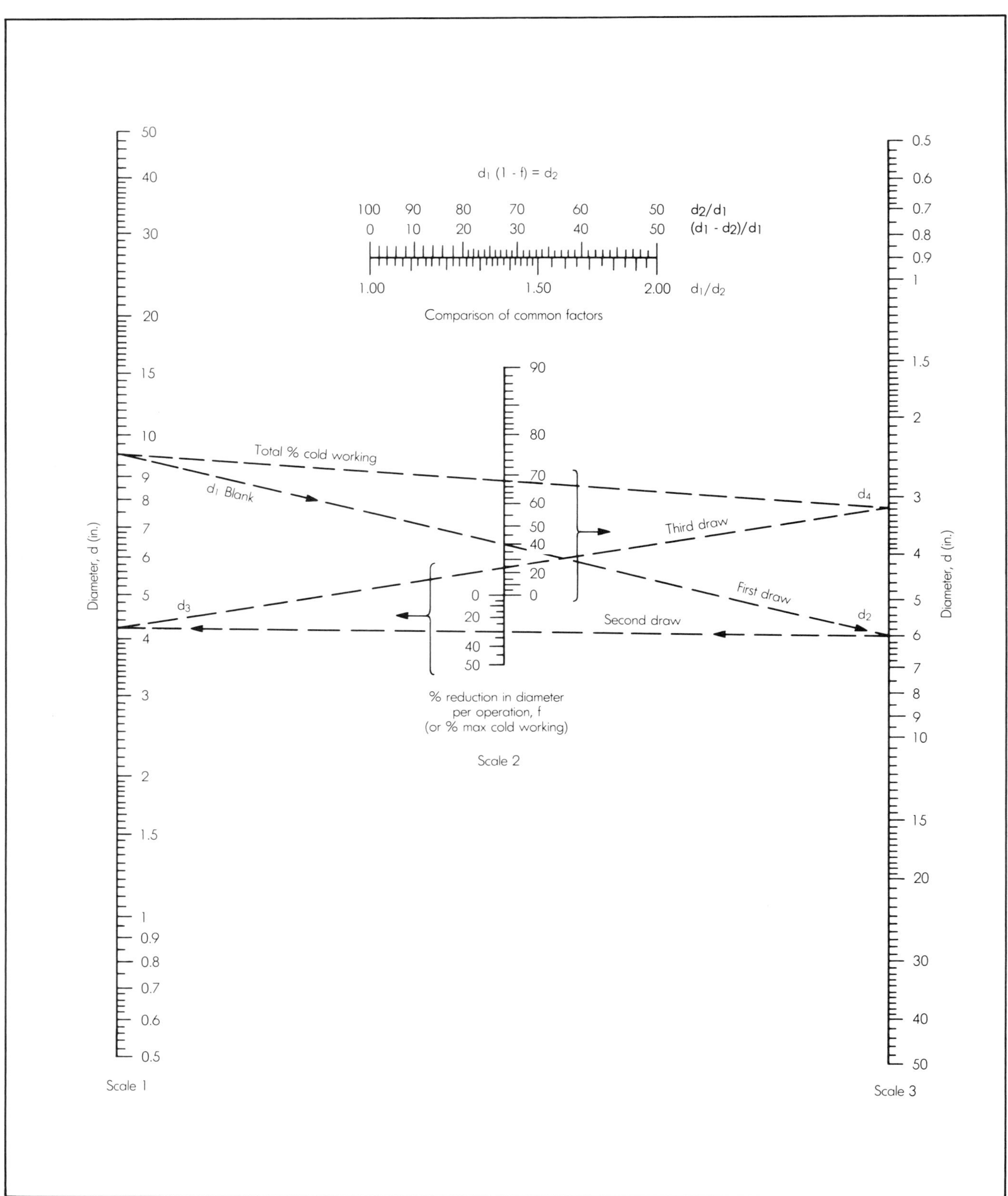


Fig. 4-38 Nomograph for determining shell diameters from percentage reductions.

the third and subsequent draws would not exceed 20% reduction without an annealing operation. The reduction percentages obtained from Fig. 4-37 should be considered tentative, since they may be exceeded under certain conditions and under other circumstances they may be reduced.

To determine drawing reductions for a blank with an approximate diameter of 16.6″ and a thickness of 0.050″, the nomograph in Fig. 4-37 would be used as follows:

1. Connect point 16.6 on Scale 1 and point 0.050 on Scale 2 with a line.
2. The projection of this line intersects the graph at 0.30 (0.3 of 1%).
3. The vertical projection of this point on the "first draw, double-action" curve at 42 establishes an approximate limit of 42% reduction for the first draw using a double-action die. Similarly, intersections as shown establish reduction limits of approximately 28 and 7 1/2%, respectively, for double-action and single-action redrawing.

When the maximum ratio of height divided by the diameter exceeds 5:8 or a possible 3:4, more than one reduction is required. Table 4-9 enumerates the probable number of reductions using this ratio.

Figure 4-38 is a nomograph for determining tentative diameters from percentage reductions. The dotted lines show the use of the chart for the reduction of a 10″ diam blank to a 3 3/16″ diam shell. A line drawn from the 10″ diam on Scale 1 through the 40% point on Scale 2 shows a first-draw diameter of 6″ on Scale 3. For the second draw, going from the 6″ point on Scale 3 through the 30% point on Scale 2 shows a second-draw diameter (on Scale 1) of 4.2″. A line from the 4.2″ point to a 3.18″ diameter on Scale 3 crosses the middle line (Scale 2) at 25%, which is acceptable.

As the metal is cold worked, it work hardens. In single-operation processing in which parts may be stored between operations, an annealing operation is required. On transfer presses, when heat is retained in the part, work hardening is not a limiting factor.

The total reduction is also indicated in Fig. 4-38 by a point at which a line drawn from the initial diameter on Scale 1 to the final diameter on Scale 3 crosses the center line (Scale 2). In this example, the line crosses at 68%. If the part requires any further reduction, it should be annealed.

Figure 4-39 shows, graphically, the formability of deep draw quality, low-carbon steel and aluminum sheets for various wall thicknesses and percentage reductions. The data is applicable to the general range of part shapes that are shown alongside the graph.

## Press Speed

One of the many factors that determine whether the wall of a drawn part will rupture is the speed of deformation that the metal can sustain, particularly at the moment when drawing begins.

Usual drawing speed for shapes other than cylinders in low-carbon steel is 55 fpm in single-action presses. In double-action presses, the speed is from 30-55 fpm. These rates can be increased to about 70 fpm under ideal conditions, such as when drawing cylindrical shapes with draw-quality steel, effective lubricants, blankholders at optimum pressure, slides accurately aligned, and optimum radii on punches and dies. Typical drawing speeds for various materials are listed in Table 4-10.

Since the velocity of the slide of a mechanical press varies from zero at the top and bottom of the stroke to maximum at midstroke, it is necessary to determine velocity of the press slide at the time that drawing begins in order to know whether or not a mechanical press is suitable for a particular drawing job.

## Metal Flow

**Deep-drawing cylindrical cup.** When the punch of a drawing press forces a portion of a metal blank through the bore of the draw ring, a number of different forces interact (see Fig. 4-40) to cause plastic flow of the material. Volume and thickness of the

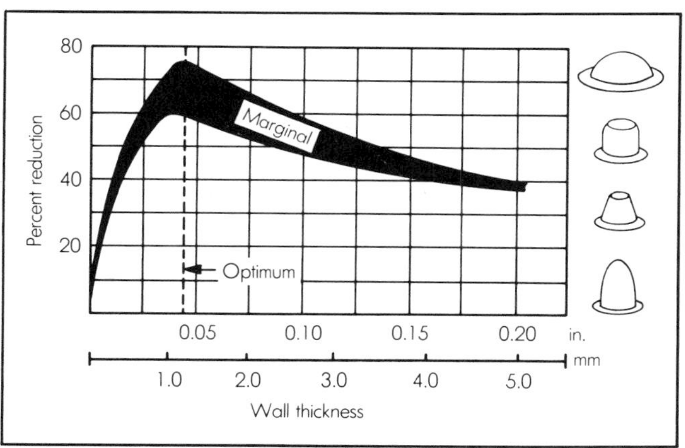


**Fig. 4-39 Graphic representation showing formability of deep draw quality, low-carbon steel and aluminum sheets, applicable to circular configurations such as hemispheres, cones, cups, and bullet-shaped parts.** (*Verson Allsteel Press Co.*)

**TABLE 4-9**
**Probable Number of Reductions for Height-Diameter Ratios**

| Ratio, height to diam.* | Probable Number of Reductions |
|---|---|
| Up to 0.7 | 1 |
| 0.7-1.5 | 2 |
| 1.5-3 | 3 |
| 3-4.7 | 4 |

* To compute the height-diameter ratio, divide inside shell height by mean shell diameter.

**TABLE 4-10**
**Typical Drawing Speeds for Various Materials**

| Material | Drawing Speed, fpm | m/min |
|---|---|---|
| Aluminum | 150-175 | 45.7-53.3 |
| Brass | 175-200 | 53.3-61 |
| Copper | 125-150 | 38.1-45.7 |
| Steel | 18-50 | 5.5-15.2 |
| Steel, stainless | 30-40 | 9.1-12.2 |
| Zinc | 125-150 | 38.1-45.7 |

metal remain essentially constant, and the final shape of the cup is similar to the contour of the punch.

The progressive stages of cupping are shown schematically in Fig. 4-41. After a small stroke of the punch (cupping stage A), the metal volume element (2) of the blank is bent and wrapped around the punch nose. Simultaneously and subsequently, the outer portions of the blank (depicted by 3, 4, and 5) move radially toward the center of the blank, as shown in cupping stages B and C. The various volume elements decrease in circumferential length (not shown) and correspondingly increase in radial length until they reach the bore of the draw ring. They then bend over, conforming to the edge of the die. After becoming part of the shell wall, the elements are straight. During drawing, Area 1 (for the specific example illustrated) is unchanged in the bottom of the cup. The areas that become the side wall of the shell (2, 3, and 4) change in shape from angular segments to longer parallel-sided shapes as they are drawn over the inner edge of the draw ring; from this point on, no further metal flow takes place.

In general, metal flow by cupping may be summarized as follows:

1. Little or no metal deformation takes place in the blank area that forms the bottom of the cup. This is indicated by unchanged distances between marking lines and radial boundaries of annular quandrants remaining radial in the base of the shell.
2. The metal flow during forming of the cup wall uniformly increases with cup height. This is indicated by the marking lines, which remain concentric but also show increasing distances between lines. Radial boundaries of the blank segments become parallel when they are drawn over the inner edge of the draw ring, where they assume their final dimensions in the cup wall.
3. The metal flow of the volume elements at the periphery of the blank is extensive and involves an increase in metal thickness caused by severe circumferential compression (see Fig. 4-40). This increase in wall thickness at the open end of the cup wall, although observable in practice, is not shown in the figures. The increase is usually slight because it is restricted by the clearance between the punch and the bore wall of the die ring.

**Metal flow in rectangular shells.** The drawing of a rectangular shell involves varying degrees of flow severity. Some parts of the shell may require severe cold working; and others, simple bending. In contrast to circular shells in which pressure is uniform on all diameters, some areas of rectangular and irregular shells may require more pressure than others. True drawing occurs at the corners only; at the sides and ends, metal movement is more closely allied to bending. The stresses at the corner of the shell are compressive on the metal moving toward the die radius and are tensile on the metal that has already moved over the radius. The metal between the corners is in tension only on the side wall and in the flange areas.

The variation in flow in different parts of the rectangular shell divides the blank into stretch and draw areas, as described in Chapter 1, "Sheet Metal Formability."

**Wrinkling and puckering.** The shaping of a shell necessitates severe cold working and involves plastic flow of the metal; therefore, any condition retarding the flow must be avoided to minimize the stress to which the metal is subjected.

The metal may buckle rather than shrink in any location of the blank, if it is very thin and if a sufficiently wide area is free to move away from the tools. The buckles produced by this buckling are called "wrinkles" when they occur at the edge of the blank and "puckers" when they appear in any other part of the blank. The formation of wrinkles in the flange area is to be expected, since the stress direction is circumferential. This wrinkling must be controlled because it may adversely affect the normal metal flow.

Since relatively thin metals have a high wrinkling tendency, blankholding pressures required for such draws are higher than for draws with relatively thick metals. When the thickness-diameter ratio of the blank is low, high blankholding pressure is required; when this ratio is high, little or no blankholding pressure is required. Also, in general, as the thickness-diameter ratio of the blank decreases, the amount of drawing that is feasible decreases correspondingly, and the tools for these draws must be finished with greater care.

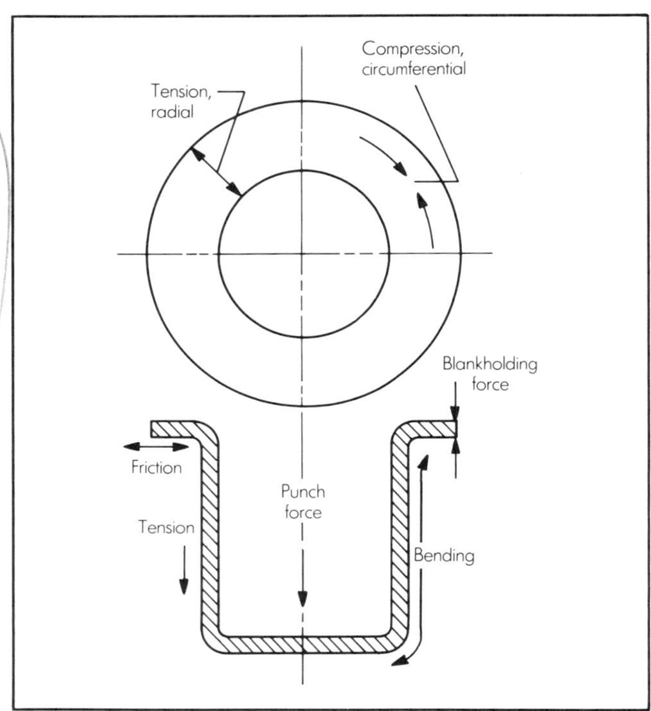


**Fig. 4-40 Forces involved in metal flow during cupping.**

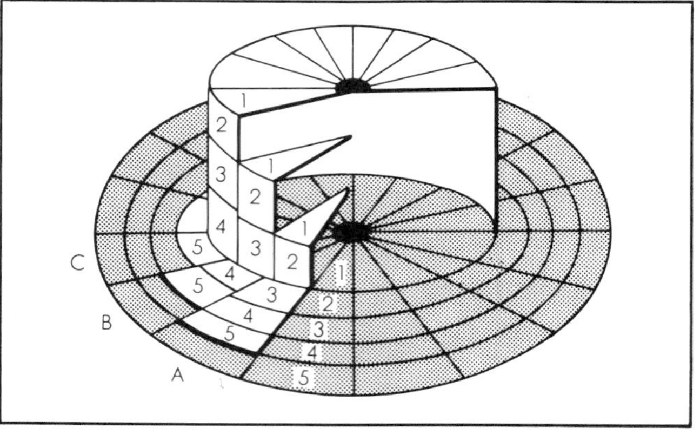


**Fig. 4-41 Sequential flow of metal shows progressive stages of cupping.**

The shape of the shell section governs, to some extent, whether wrinkles or puckers will be more prevalent under conditions of poor control. Straight-sided shells are typical shapes in which wrinkles often occur; whereas puckers are most likely to appear in domed or tapered shells. If the die radius and/or the punch radius is too large, even though the sides are straight, the conditions approach those of domed shapes and both wrinkles and puckers tend to occur.

**Controlling metal flow.** The two draw dies shown in Fig. 4-42 illustrate good control of flow (view *a*) and poor control of flow (view *b*). In view *a*, the tool faces are in close contact with the blank at all points, but insufficient blankholder pressure may encourage wrinkles to occur in the shell. In view *b*, there is poor control of the metal flow because only the tip of the punch is in contact with the blank, leaving much of the center area of the blank free to pucker. Depending upon the material, increased blankholder pressure may or may not produce a good shell. Other causes of poor control of metal flow include uneven blankholder pressure and suspended metal in the wall (where draw-in is uneven, due to faulty design contour).

Draw beads are sometimes included in the blankholder faces to provide more resistance to metal flow, thus aiding control of metal movement into the die bore. The beads need not be continuous around the die, and more than one is sometimes placed in areas requiring great retarding of metal flow. Figure 4-43 shows two common types of draw beads. Draw beads may be provided in a die in several different ways.[11]

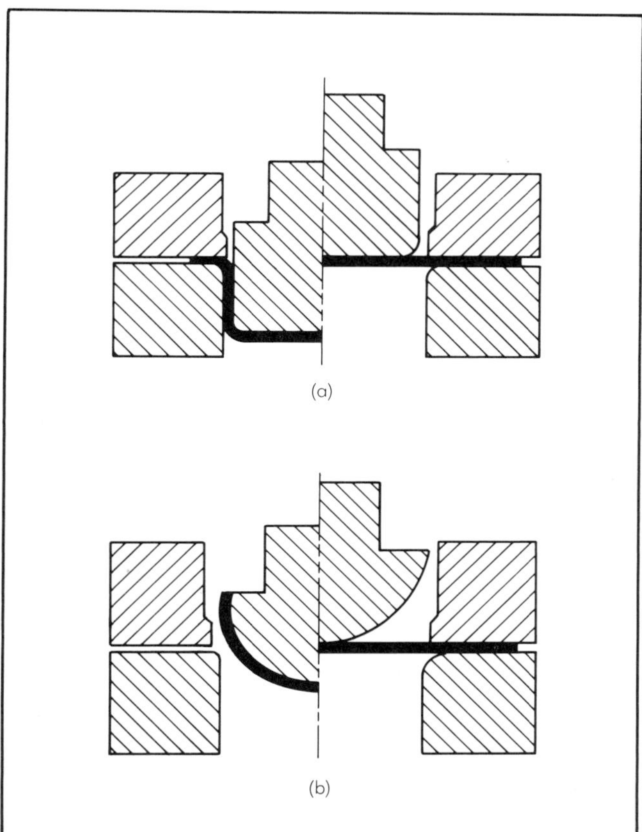


**Fig. 4-42 Two draw dies illustrate (a) good and (b) poor control of metal flow in cupping. The contour of the punch determines initial contact with the blank.**

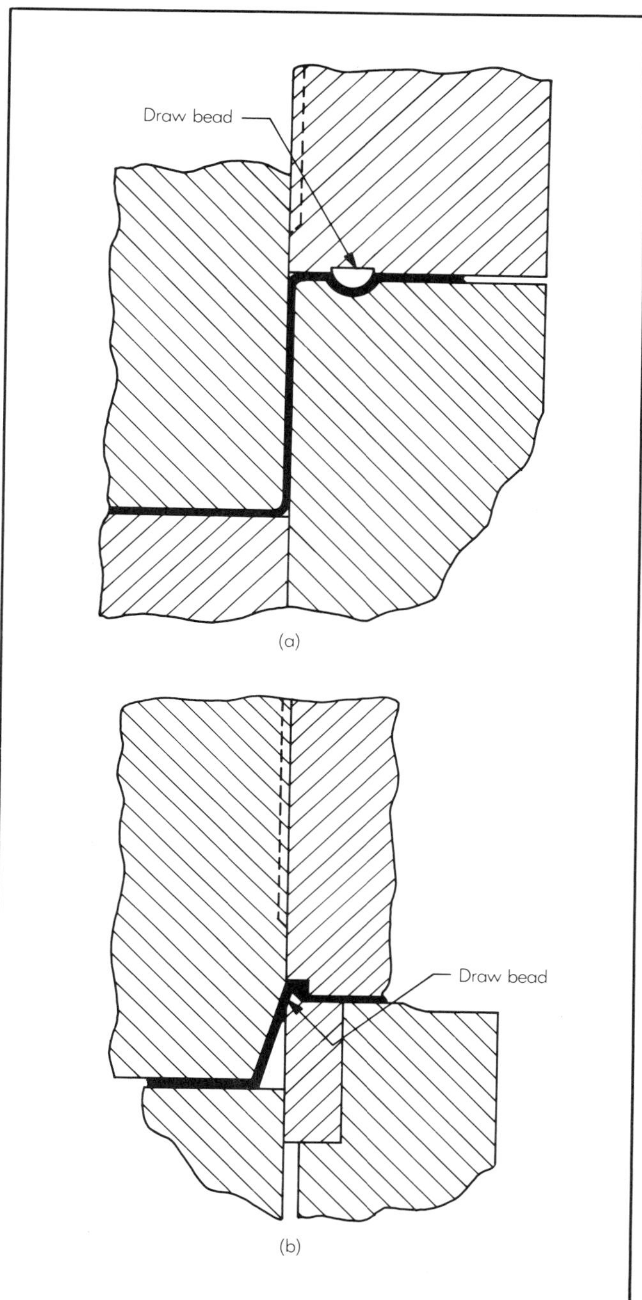


**Fig. 4-43 Two examples of draw beads to control metal flow during deep drawing: (a) molding type, offset in blankholder; (b) lock type, inserted in the draw ring.**

## Blanking

As covered previously in this chapter, the first step in the drawing of a round cup is the punching out of a circular blank. Depending on the required production rate, tool design, available metal widths, etc., one or more blanks can be punched out with each stroke of the press. Material may be in coil or sheet form. A typical layout for a five-out operation for coil feed is shown in Fig. 4-44. Five blanks, shown cross-hatched, are punched-out simultaneously.

Coil width, $W$, can be calculated as follows:

$$W = \sin 60° (N - 1)(CE + X) + CE + 2Y \quad (10)$$

where:

$W$ = width, in. or mm
$N$ = number of blanks per stroke of the press
$CE$ = blank diameter, in. or mm
$X$ = skeleton width, in. or mm
$Y$ = edge clearance, in. or mm

The coil stock must be advanced a distance of $CE + X$ for each press stroke.

The number of blanks produced per stroke has a significant effect on the overall metal economics, as shown in Fig. 4-45. Suitable coil widths should be selected with production needs, equipment limitations and metal availability taken into account. Certain coil widths that have an extra slitting or waste premium cost should be avoided.

For sheet-fed presses, scroll-sheared sheets are used as shown in Fig. 4-46, with metal economics close to the cost level for coil-fed operations.

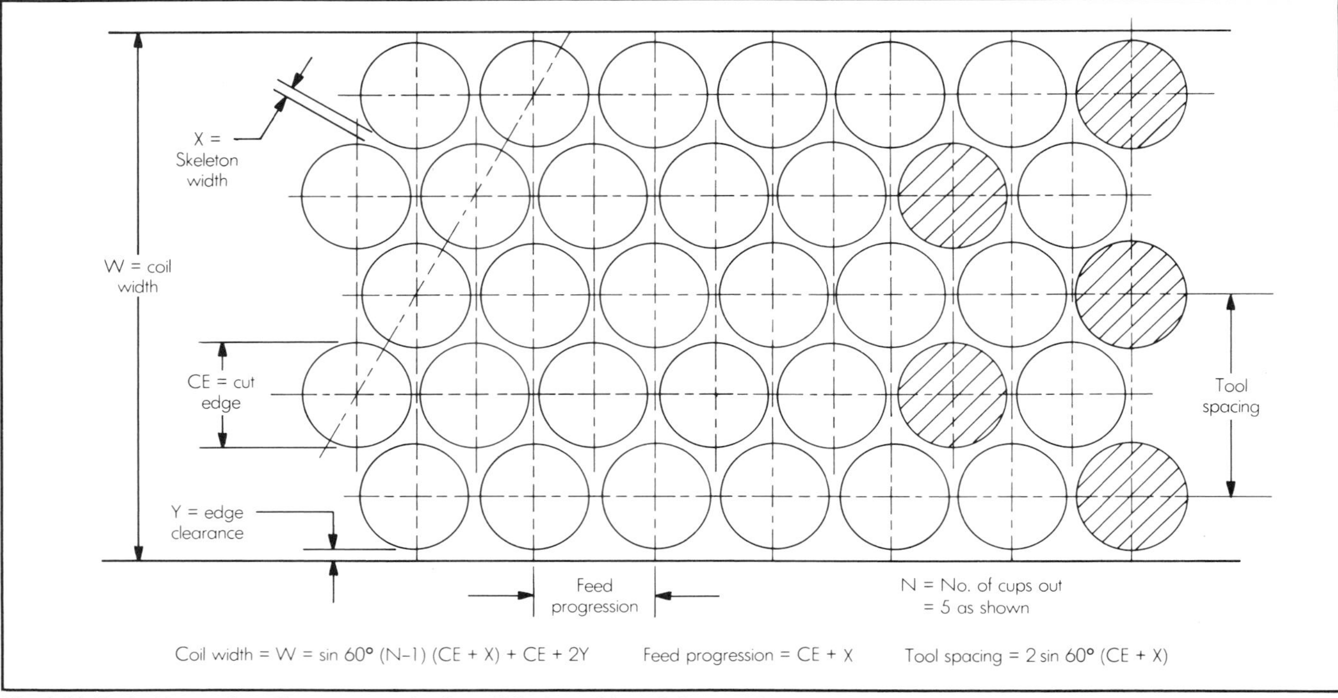


**Fig. 4-44 Typical layout for a five-out operation for coil feed punching of circular blanks.**

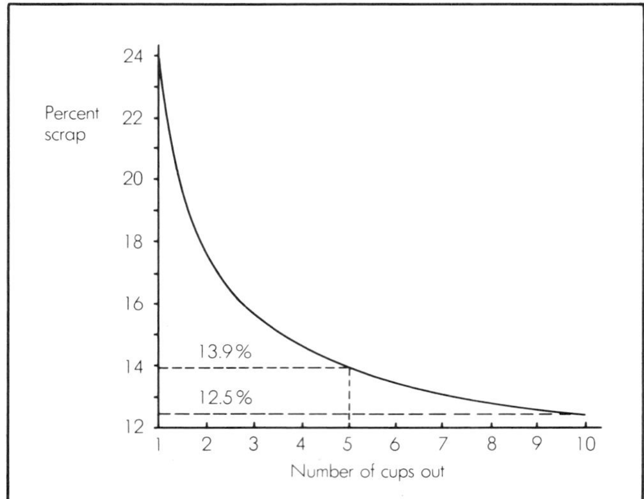


**Fig. 4-45 Relationship of coil skeleton scrap and number of cups produced per stroke.**

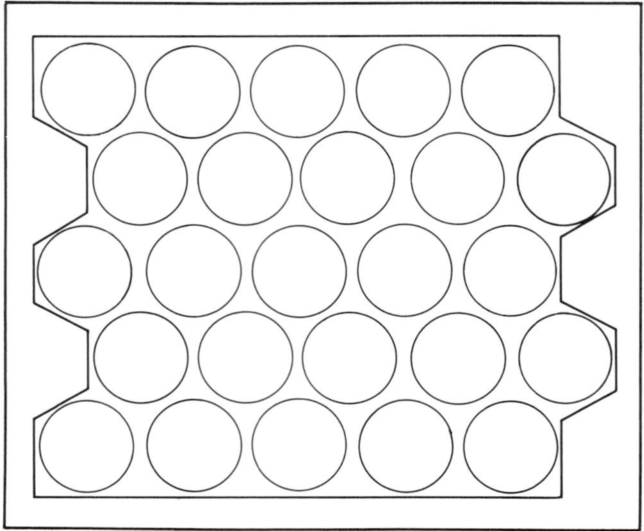

**Fig. 4-46 Scroll-sheared sheets.**

## Drawing Limits

The drawing of a circular cup is accomplished by clamping the blank between two disc-shaped dies, the blankholder and draw pad (see Fig. 4-47); an advancing punch forces the blank through the dies and draws it into a cup-shaped container.

The work that can be done in a single pass is limited and depends on metal conditions, die design, lubrication, blank diameter to blank thickness ratio, etc.

The work done can be expressed as the drawing reduction, which is the reduction in diameter from blank to inside cup.

*Percentage reduction*

$$= \frac{\text{Blank diam} - \text{inside cup diam}}{\text{Inside cup diam}} \times 100\% \qquad (11)$$

The limiting draw ratio, *LDR*, is used to show the maximum drawing reduction possible:

$$LDR = \frac{\text{Max blank diam}}{\text{Cup inside diam}} \qquad (12)$$

The maximum draw reduction with ordinary tooling is about 48% for aluminum; but with steel or tin plate, 52-56% reductions are possible.

It can be seen that a 50% reduction means an *LDR* of 2 and, therefore, the *LDR* for aluminum should be less than 2 (1.92 for 48%) and the *LDR* for tin plate should be higher than 2 (for example, 2.17 for 54% reduction). The greater the blank diameter/stock thickness ratio, the smaller the possible reduction or *LDR*. Limiting draw ratio is related mathematically to material properties, and the strain ratio, $r$, and work-hardening exponent, $n$, are primary determinants of *LDR* (see Chapter 1).

## Multiple Draws

If required cup diameter is smaller than can be obtained with a maximum reduction in one pass, multiple draws are needed. These can be done with a straight redraw (see Fig. 4-48) or with a reverse redraw (see Fig. 4-49) whereby the cup is actually turned inside-out.

With a straight redraw, the metal is severely worked as it is bent 90° in two different directions during the redraw. In general, stresses are less severe with a reverse redraw where the metal is formed in one direction only. A compromise is shown in Fig. 4-50, where the bottom of the cup of the first draw has a taper and the metal is not required to make two 90° bends during redraw. This method, however, puts a limitation on the amount of reduction in the first draw. At the beginning of the draw, the metal around the tapered nose of the punch is not supported and also the draw reduction at the beginning of the draw is much larger than the final amount. The unsupported metal can easily wrinkle, and the amount of reduction and the angle of the punch nose are very critical—especially when the blank diameter/metal thickness ratio is large.

Blanking, first draw, and redraw can be performed either with one stroke of a double-action press with air cushions providing the third action, or with triple-action presses. A cross-section of a draw and reverse redraw die is shown in Fig. 4-51. Here, the finished cup is pushed through the die. Multiple draws can also be performed by separate redraw dies located in the same die set or in a separate press, with the first drawn cups being moved from die to die by a transfer mechanism.

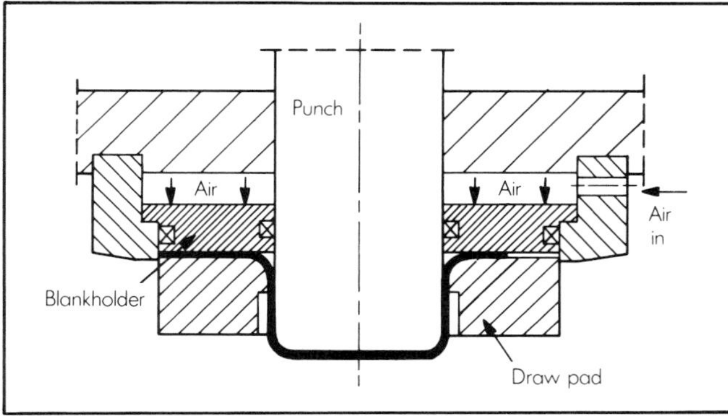


**Fig. 4-47 A blank and draw operation.**

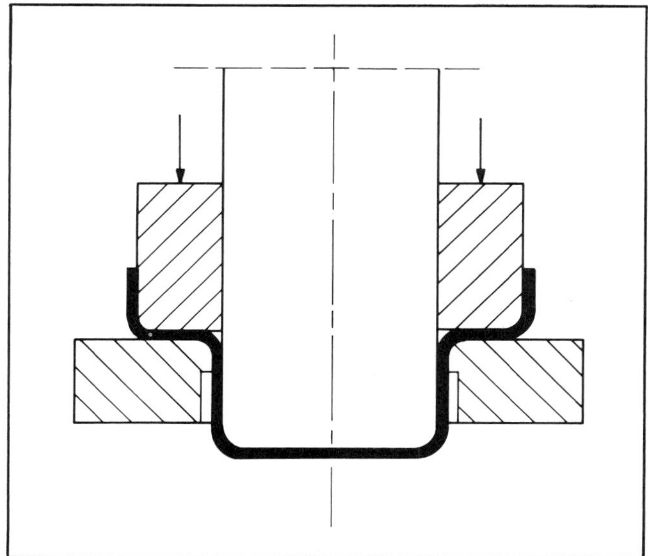

**Fig. 4-48 Straight redraw operation.**

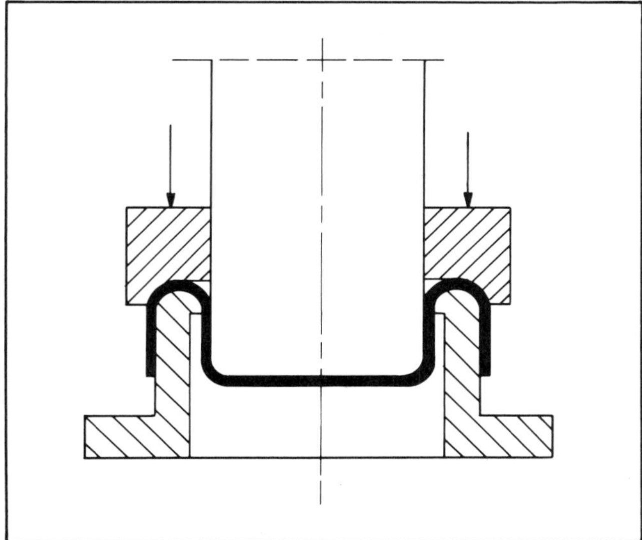

**Fig. 4-49 Reverse redraw operation.**

## Drawing Force Calculation

For drawing cylindrical shells having circular cross sections, the maximum drawing force may be calculated from the following equation:

$$P = n\pi d t \sigma_B \tag{13}$$

where:

$P$ = drawing force, lb or kN
$\sigma_B$ = tensile strength of the blank material, psi or MPa
$d$ = punch diameter, in. or mm
$t$ = sheet thickness, in. or mm

$$n = \frac{\sigma_D}{\sigma_B} = \frac{\text{Drawing stress}}{\text{Tensile strength}}$$

For material having good drawing qualities, the factor $n$ can be ascertained from the following equation:

$$n = 1.2\frac{DR - 1}{LDR - 1} \tag{14}$$

where:

$n$ = drawing force factor
$DR$ = draw ratio
$LDR$ = limiting draw ratio

**Round shells**. Drawing forces required for round shells depend upon a number of variables. As a guide, Fig. 4-52 may be used for computing the maximum drawing force. The nomograph is based upon a free draw with sufficient clearance so that there is no ironing and upon a maximum reduction of

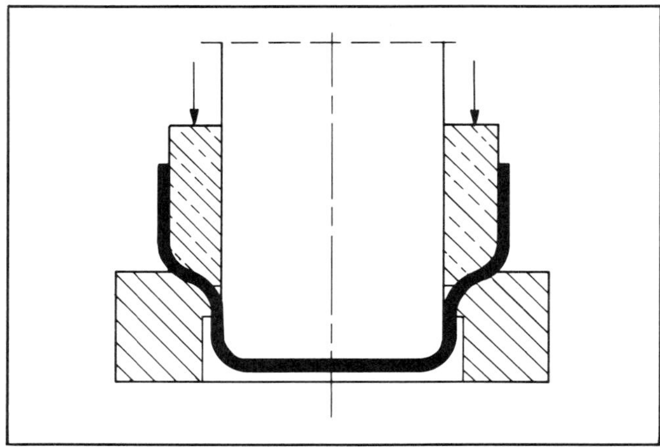

**Fig. 4-50 Direct redraw using inclined plane for first draw.**

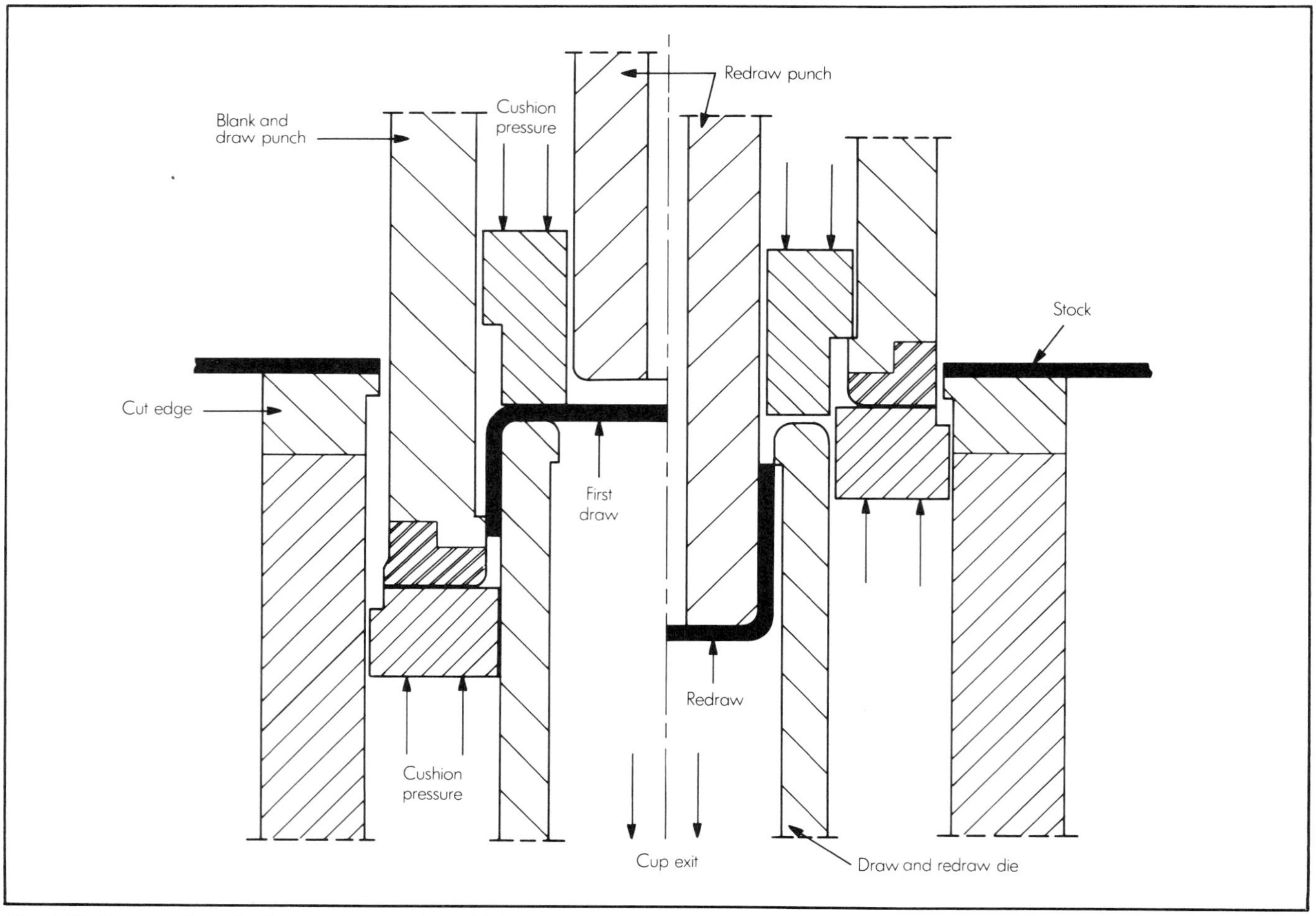

**Fig. 4-51 Cross-section of a draw and reverse draw die for a double-action press.**

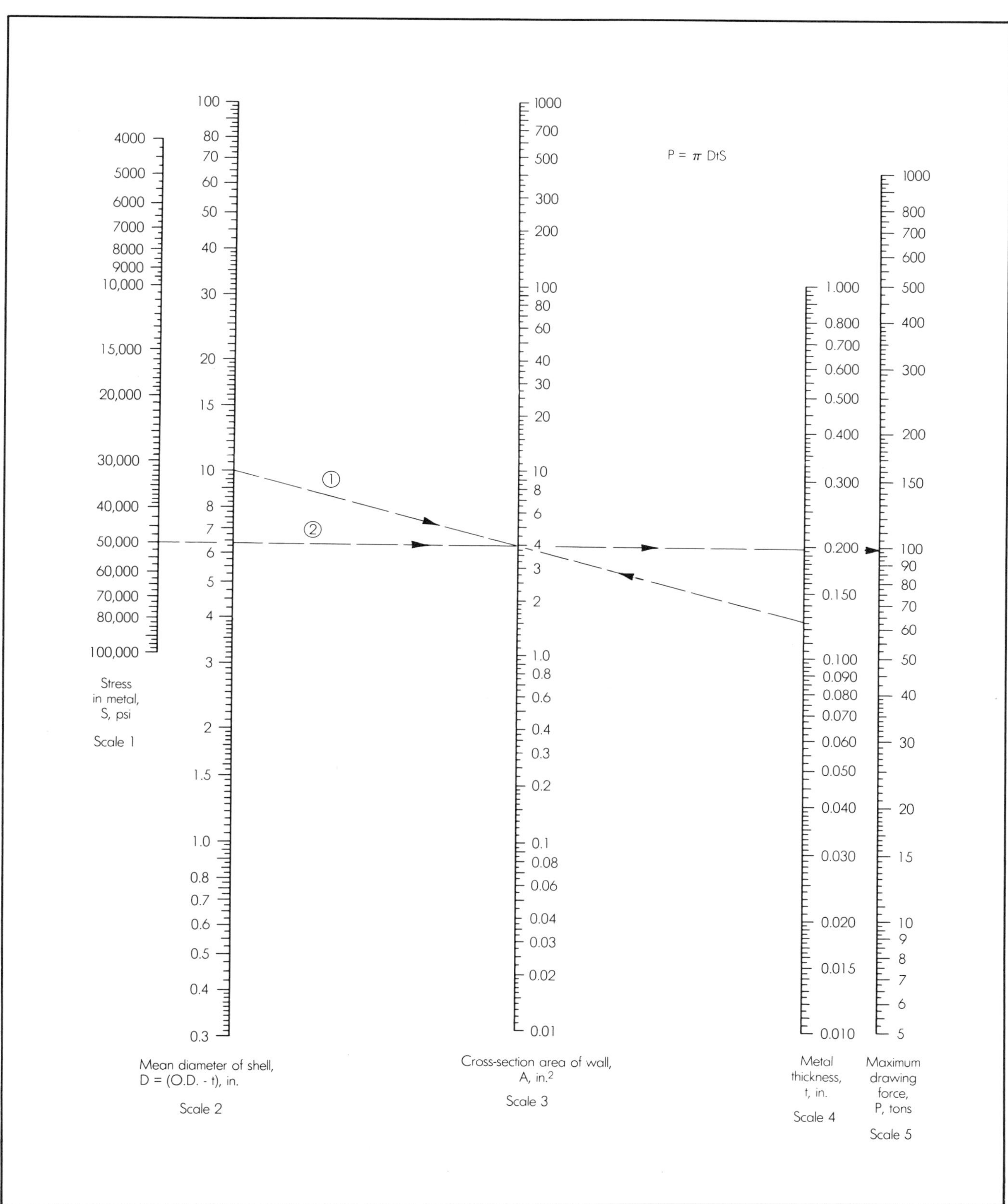


**Fig. 4-52 Drawing force nomograph, inch-pound units.**

# DRAWING

about 50%. The nomograph actually gives the load to fracture the shell or the tensile strength near the bottom of the shell. A typical example of its use is in determining the force required for deep drawing steel stock, 1/8″ thick and with a tensile strength of 50,000 psi, into a shell 10″ diam. The following steps would be taken:

1. Connect Point 10 on Scale 2 with Line 1 to Point 0.125 on Scale 4.
2. The intersection of Line 1 with Scale 3 is at 4.0, which is the approximate area.
3. Connect this point with Line 2 to Point 50,000 on Scale 1.
4. Project the line to the right to intersect Scale 5 at 98 tons, the drawing force required.

The force applied to the punch to draw a shell is equal to the product of the cross-sectional area and the yield strength, *S*, of the metal. Taking into consideration the relationship between the blank and shell diameters and a constant, *C*, of 0.6-0.7 to cover friction and bending, the force, *P*, for a cylindrical shell may be expressed by the empirical equation:

$$P = \pi d t S\left(\frac{D}{d} - C\right) \qquad (15)$$

where:

$P$ = drawing force, lb
$D$ = blank diameter, in.
$d$ = shell diameter, in.
$t$ = metal thickness, in.
$S$ = tensile strength, psi
$C$ = constant

**Rectangular shells**. Drawing force for producing rectangular drawn shells may be calculated from the equation:

$$P = tS(2\pi r C_1 + L C_2) \qquad (16)$$

where:

$P$ = drawing punch force, lb
$t$ = metal thickness, in.
$S$ = nominal tensile strength, psi
$r$ = corner radius of rectangular shell, in.
$L$ = total length of straight sides of rectangular shell, in.
$C_1$ = 0.5 for a very low shell, up to about 2 for a shell having a depth of five or six times the corner radius, $r$
$C_2$ = 0.2 for easy draw radius, ample clearance, and no holding pressure; or about 0.3 for similar free flow and a normal blankholding force of about $P/3$; or a maximum of 1 for a metal clamped too tightly to flow.

Values for $C_1$ and $C_2$ are approximate.

**Metric nomograph**. Drawing force required is a significant factor in press selection. This section presents data and a nomograph for determining drawing force when working in SI metric measurement units.

*Draw force nomograph*. Shown in Fig. 4-53, the drawing force nomograph requires knowledge of the following:

- Stress in the metal.
- Mean diameter of the shell.
- Cross sectional area of the wall.
- Metal thickness.

To use this information in calculating the maximum drawing force, proceed as follows:

1. Starting with Scale 2, the mean diameter of the shell, which equals the outside diameter of the shell minus metal thickness, find the appropriate value on Scale 2 in millimeters.
2. Find metal thickness, also in millimeters, on Scale 4.
3. Connect the appropriate points on Scales 2 and 4.
4. Determine the cross-sectional area by the point of intersection on Scale 3. The operation of finding this point is denoted by the encircled Numeral 1 on the nomograph.

Next, it is necessary to find the stress in the metal due to drawing. Just how the value of stress in metal (Scale 1) is found will be dealt with shortly. For the moment, assuming that the value is known, proceed as follows:

1. Connect the appropriate point on Scale 1 with the line of intersection on Scale 3.
2. By drawing a line through the point of intersection on Scale 3 until it connects with Scale 5, find the maximum drawing force in kilonewtons.

If a sequence of drawing operations is performed in a single die—as in a progressive die—or if a sequence of draw dies is set up in a single press, a separate calculation must be made for each operation or each die. The total of the individual calculations is then matched against press capabilities.

*Determining the stress*. Use of the nomograph depends on a reasonably accurate determination of the stress in the metal. The stress developed in most metals employed in drawing applications can be found in the graphs in Fig. 4-54.

To use these graphs, it is first necessary to determine the percent reduction between the blank and the drawn shell. This means the first draw—not the last draw—if a sequence of draw operations is involved. If a sequence of draws is performed, the percent reduction is determined sequentially for each of the successive draws. The implication here is that the drawing pressure must be calculated for the individual draws, since the actual unit stress is a variable and is not accumulative.

It will be noted that actual unit stress increases linearly with percent reduction. Each line representing a metal has both a light and dark portion. The dark portion starts with the yield point of the metal and terminates with the fracture point. In other words, the dark (or heavy) section of the line represents the working portion of the metal. The extension of each line all the way to the right—to the theoretical 100% reduction—provides the metal's modulus of strain hardening.

It should also be noted that different terminal values are given for the aluminums shown in Fig. 4-54. These values depend on the hardness of the aluminum, a condition that should be noted before actual unit stress is determined. The reason, of course, is that calculations based on unit stresses that exceed those indicated by the actual working portion of the curve will cause the workpiece to fracture in the drawing operation.[12]

## Cup Height

When blank diameter and cup diameter are known and the punch nose radius is taken into account, calculation of cup height can be quite complex. Nevertheless, the calculated cup height is only an approximation, since the metal stretches and becomes thin close to the bottom area of the cup and thickens at

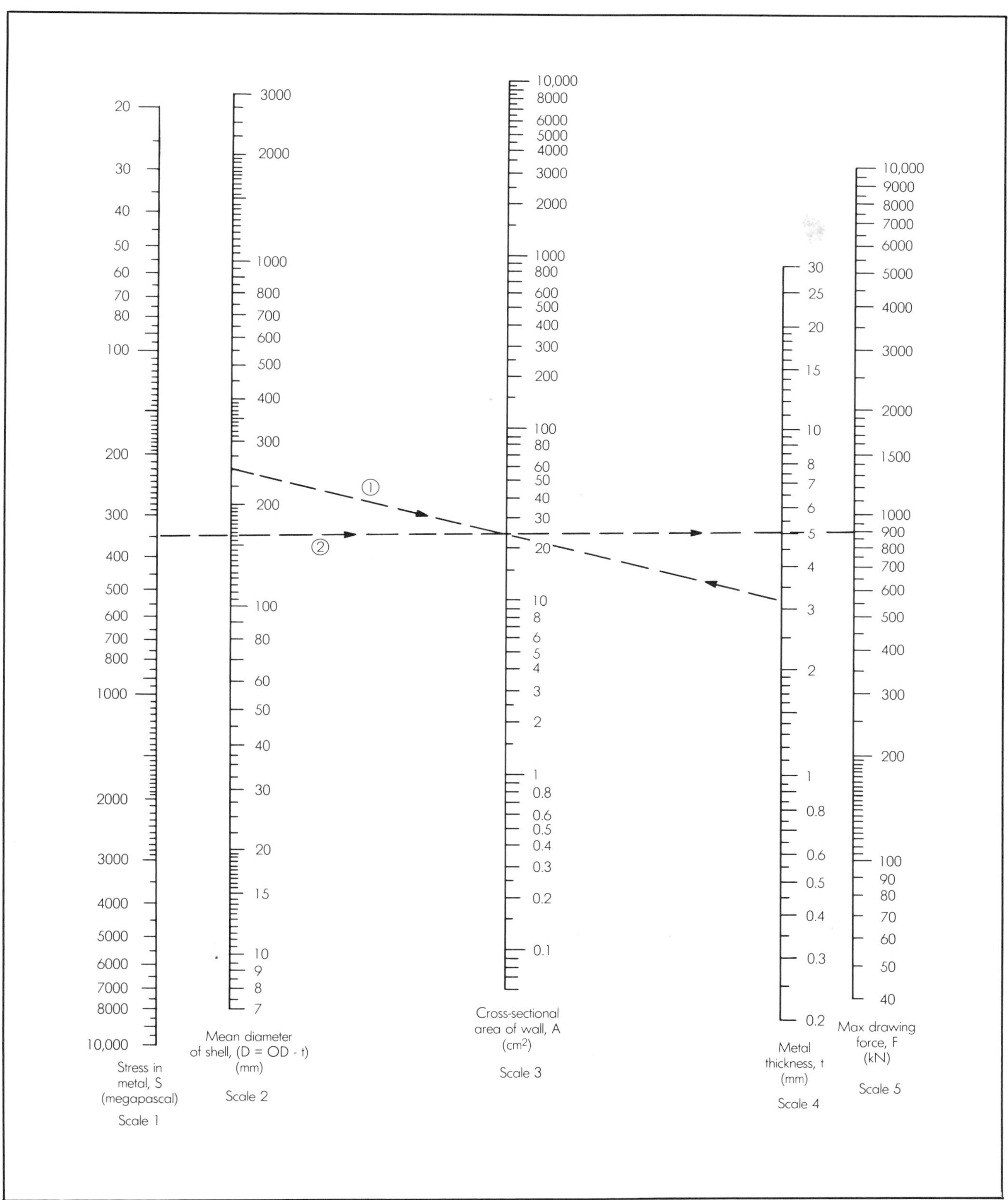


**Fig. 4-53 Drawing force nomograph, SI metric units.**

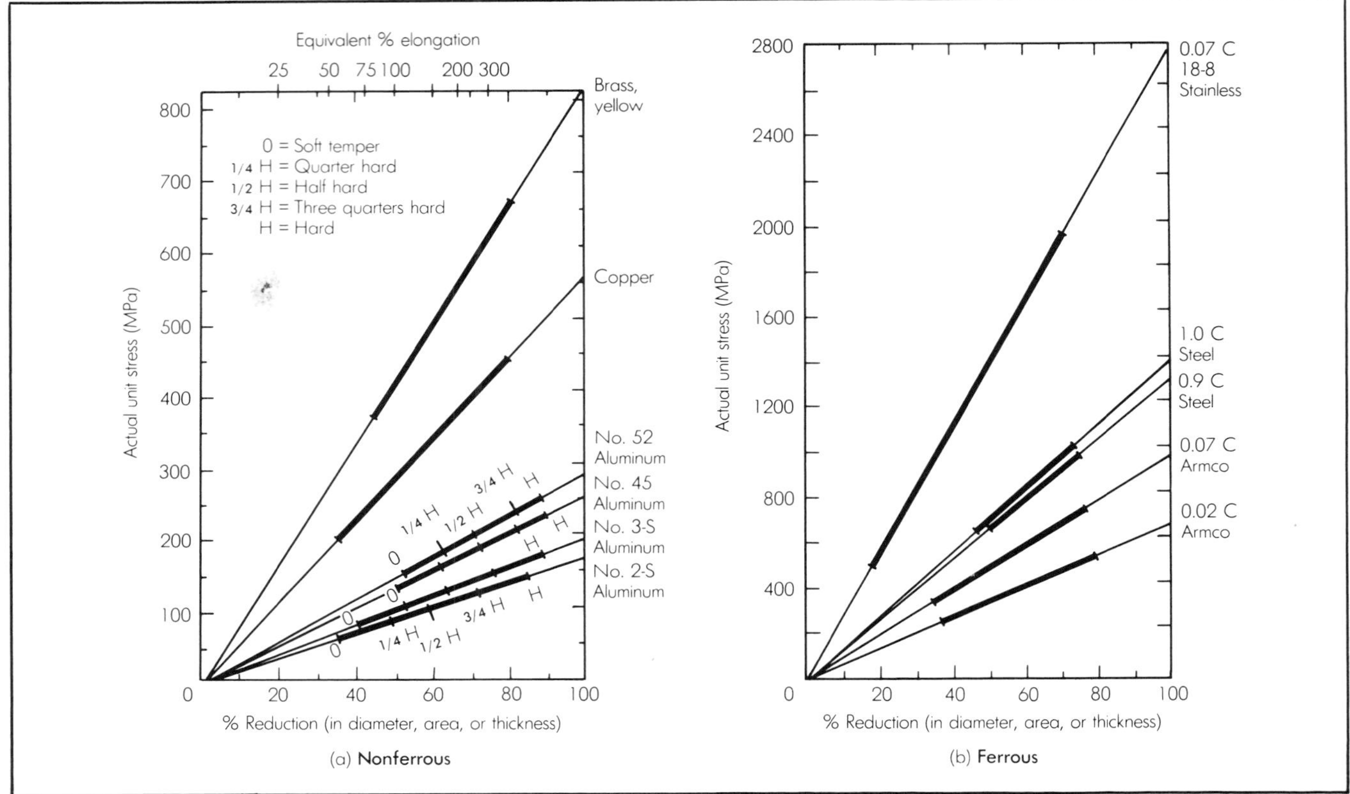


**Fig. 4-54 Graphs showing (a) unit stress for nonferrous metals and (b) unit stress for ferrous metals.**

the top of the cup. These actions affect cup height, especially if the draw reductions are high. Therefore, for simplicity, the bottom radius is usually ignored and the following equation is used in conjunction with Fig. 4-55 to give a usable approximation of the expected cup height for the first draw:

$$H_1 = \frac{D_1^2 - D_2^2}{4(D_2 + T)} \qquad (17)$$

where:

$H_1$ = cup height, first draw, in. or mm
$D_1$ = blank diameter, in. or mm
$D_2$ = inside cup diameter of the first draw, in. or mm
$T$ = metal thickness, in. or mm

For thin metals, the metal thickness is sometimes omitted and the equation becomes:

$$H_1 = \frac{D_1^2 - D_2^2}{4D_2} \qquad (18)$$

The cup height of the second draw is calculated in the same way:

$$H_2 = \frac{D_1^2 - D_3^2}{4(D_3 + T)} \qquad (19)$$

where:

$H_2$ = Cup height, second draw, in. or mm
$D_3$ = Cup diameter, second draw, in. or mm

Example:

By using these equations, it can be seen that for a maximum reduction of 48% of aluminum, the maximum cup height will be 0.35 times the blank diameter or 0.675 times the cup diameter. At 48% reduction, if cup diameter of the first draw is 0.52 $D_1$, or 0.52 = 1 - 0.48, then:

$$H_1 = \frac{D_1^2 - (0.52D_1)^2}{4 \times 0.52D_1}$$

or:

$$H_1 = \frac{D_1 - 0.2704D_1}{2.08}$$

or:

$$H_1 = 0.35D_1$$

To find the relation of cup height/cup diameter, if cup diameter is 0.52 $D_1$, or $D_1$ = $D_2$ divided by 0.52 = 1.923 $D_2$, then:

$$H_1 = \frac{(1.923D_2)^2 - D_2^2}{4 \times D_2} = \frac{3.698D_2 - D_2}{4} = 0.675D_2$$

This means that if the desired height of the cup exceeds 35% of the blank diameter or 67.5% of the inside cup diameter, more than one draw is required. For steel, these percentages are somewhat higher.

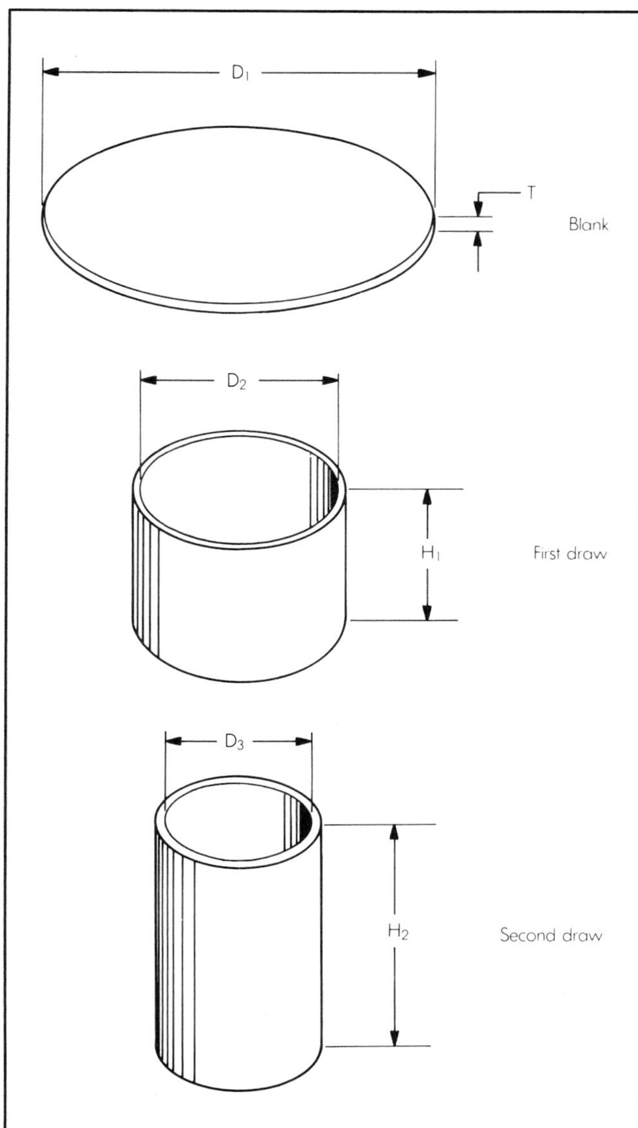


Fig. 4-55 Illustration of the sequence used to calculate cup height.

Final reduction for double-drawn cups can be calculated from the following:

$$R_f = R_1 + R_2 - R_1 R_2 \quad (20)$$

where:

$R_f$ = final reduction
$R_1$ = first reduction
$R_2$ = second reduction

Example:

For a double draw with a 40% reduction in the first draw and 30% reduction in the second draw, the final reduction from blank size would be determined as follows:

$$R_f = 0.4 + 0.3 - (0.4 \times 0.3) = 0.58, \text{ or } 58\%.$$

Calculating as in Eq.(17) and Eq. (18), the cup height for these reductions is 1.67 times the inside cup diameter. This means that if a cup is required of a height greater than 1.67 times the inside diameter, either more than two draws are needed or larger reductions should be used.

## Earing

The earing characteristic (illustrated in Fig. 4-56) is frequently noted on drawn cups with and without flanges. For a brief description of earing, refer to the section "Drawing" in Chapter 1.

As a circular blank is drawn into a cup, the metal between draw pad and blankholder (see Figs. 4-47 and 4-57) is subjected to radial tensile stress as well as compressive hoop stress. Unfortunately, stock used in making cans and other sheet steels is not strictly isotropic; its strength is not the same in all directions. Due to the method of fabrication (rolling), sheet metals have properties that are not the same in different directions; this characteristic is called anisotropy.

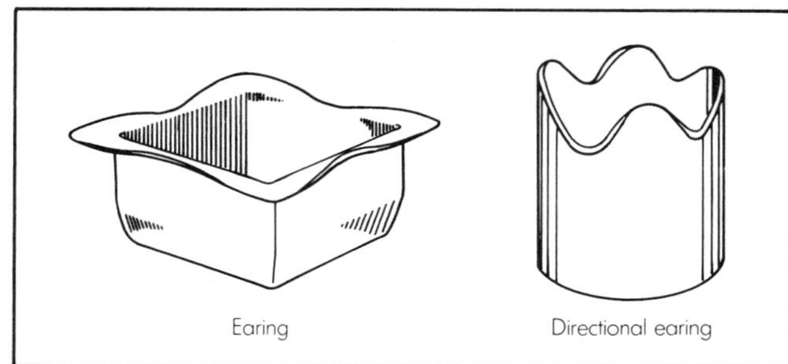


**Fig. 4-56 Typical earing.**

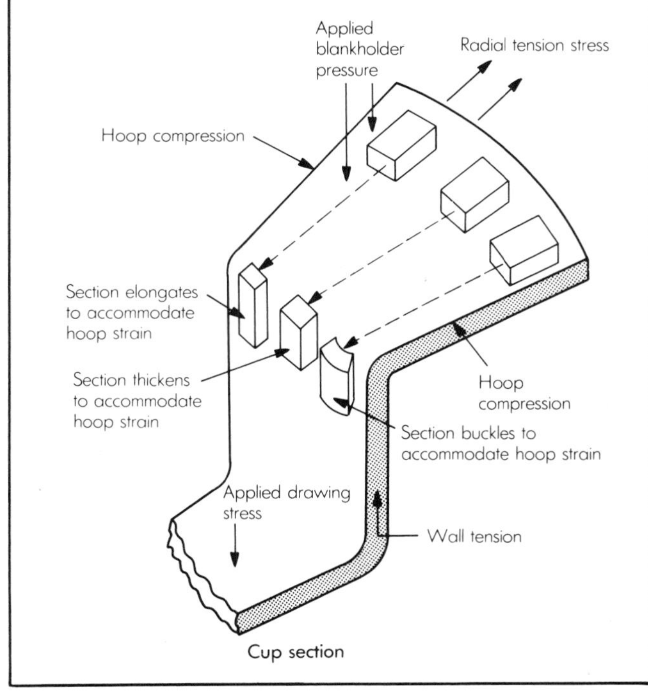


**Fig. 4-57 Schematic drawing of a cup section shows stresses and types of deformation that occur during the drawing process.**

# CHAPTER 4

# DRAWING

As described in Chapter 1, "Sheet Metal Formability," there are two kinds of anisotropy to consider:

1. Planar Anisotropy. Here the properties vary in the plane of the sheet. The tensile strength in the rolling direction differs from the tensile strength perpendicular to the rolling direction.
2. Normal Anisotropy. Under these conditions, the strength of the material across the thickness direction differs from the properties in the plane of the sheet.

During the drawing process, material in the flange of the cup between draw pad and blankholder must move from a large diameter (blank size) to a much smaller size, that is, the cup diameter. As shown in Fig. 4-57, the metal is subjected to a compressive hoop stress as well as a radial tensile stress and can deform by buckling, elongating, or thickening. Buckling is avoided by proper tool design, sufficient blankholder pressure, and the correct draw reduction.

A test sample in a tensile tester elongates under load, and the specimen becomes narrower or thinner. One way to assess drawing material is the plastic strain ratio or so-called *r* value, which is the ratio of the width strain to the thickness strain. A high *r* value means that the material of the test strip gets narrower rather than thinner. A good drawing material has a high *r* value (greater than 1), which means that it flows easily in the plane of the sheet, but not in the thickness direction.

A material that flows easily in the thickness direction (*r* less than 1) has an undesirable tendency to thin under the influence of wall tension during drawing—and thinning of the cup wall could lead to metal failure.

Typical *r* values range from 1.0 to 2.0 for various steels and are usually below 1.0 for aluminum.

The planar anisotropy and variations in the normal anisotropy cause undesirable earing of the material during drawing. Earing usually accompanies local wrinkling of the cup wall. Between the ears of the cup are valleys in which the material has thickened under the compressive hoop stress instead of elongating under the radial tensile stress. This thicker metal forces the die open against the blankholder pressure and allows the metal in the thinner areas around the ears to wrinkle. The die design, die radii, draw reduction, and lubricant are factors that affect earing.

For aluminum, grooving of the blankholder reduces earing and wrinkling. The use of a lower grade or more-diluted lubricant often reduces wrinkling and earing. Ironing the top of the cup in the draw pad also reduces thickness of the valleys between the ears. Earing can be expressed as a percentage and calculated as follows:

$$\frac{Avg.\ ht.\ of\ ears - Avg.\ ht.\ of\ valleys}{Avg.\ ht.\ of\ valleys} \times 100\%. \qquad (21)$$

A good drawing material should exhibit less than 4% earing. Earing is very undesirable. It can lead to pinching or clipping in the draw dies because at the end of the draw, the full blankholder load is concentrated on the tips of the ears. These ear tips can be pinched off due to the high unit load, and an accumulation of the clippings in the dies can be a serious problem.

Various means can be used to prevent ear pinching. On some presses the dies can be designed in such a way that the blankholder lifts off the blank at the precise end of the draw. This requires precise setting and shimming of the dies after regrinding to maintain the original die height.

In double-action presses with a cam-actuated blanking ram, the dies can be designed so that the blankholder always stays away from the draw pad by about 80% of the stock thickness and cannot snap shut at the end of the draw.

## Drawing Parameters

The most common failure of a drawing operation is rupturing of metal in a critical area because of insufficient strength to withstand the force required to draw the metal from the blank area into the die. Many factors determine whether this area has sufficient strength: (1) the relationship of the diameter of the blank to the diameter of the cup, (2) the contour of the punch edge and the contour of the die edge, (3) the type of lubricant being used to minimize friction between the metal being drawn and the surfaces of the blankholder and the die, (4) the ductility of the metal being drawn, and (5) the speed of the press.

## Blank Development

It is usually advisable, when laying out the blank, to plan for a form that produces corners somewhat higher than the sides and ends. Wear on the die occurs at the corners; and when it does, the metal thickens, resulting in a drawn part that is low at the corners if allowance for this wear has not been made on the blank.

The maximum inside diameter of a cup that can be drawn from a blank without excessively straining the bottom of the cup ranges from 40-45% of the blank diameter. Typically, the cup height (for steel) is approximately one-half the blank diameter.

One of the first steps in establishing the process of operations for drawing a cylindrical part is to determine the blank diameter. Then, by comparing this with the diameter of the part, the number of operations necessary to reduce the diameter of the blank to that of the part can be determined on the basis of recommended percentages that do not subject the critical area of the drawn part to excessive stresses. Generally, the second draw, or redraw, should have a reduction of 30% when additional reductions are required. Annealing may be necessary if parts are stockpiled between operations, especially for severe drawing operations.

**Cup**. Blank diameters that are calculated should be considered approximate. Because of variations in wall thickness of the drawn part and the ductility of the metal being drawn, the blank size cannot be calculated accurately. The calculated blank diameters are used for material-requirement estimates and for cutting blanks to be tried out in the drawing die. The tryout of these blanks indicates revisions that must be made to the theoretical blank diameter.

Three methods are used to determine the blank diameter: computation, layout, and direct formula.

*Computation*. For parts that have a complex cross-section, the blank diameter is determined one of two ways:

1. The contour of the part is divided into basic geometric segments for which area formulas are given in reference books. These areas are then added together, and the diameter of the blank is found by using this value and performing a calculation with the following formula:

$$\text{Blank diam} = 1.128\sqrt{\text{sum of areas}} \qquad (22)$$

2. According to the second theorem of Pappus, the area swept by a line of any contour, as it revolves about a center axis, is equal to the length of the line multiplied by

the circumference swept by the center of gravity of that line. The area of the contour of a part may be determined by this rule as shown in Fig. 4-58.

After the length of each section and the horizontal location of the center of gravity of each section is determined, the horizontal location of the center of gravity of the entire contour—Line $X$ for Point $P$—is determined by the following equation:

$$X = \frac{L_1 D + L_2 Z + L_3 E + L_4 F}{L_1 + L_2 + L_3 + L_4} \quad (23)$$

The area swept by this section is then obtained by:

$$A = (L_1 + L_2 + L_3 + L_4)2\pi X \quad (24)$$

and the blank diameter is obtained by:

$$D = \sqrt{8X(L_1 + L_2 + L_3 + L_4)} \quad (25)$$

*Layout.* For parts having a complex cross section, as illustrated in Fig. 4-59, the following steps would be taken to determine the blank diameter:

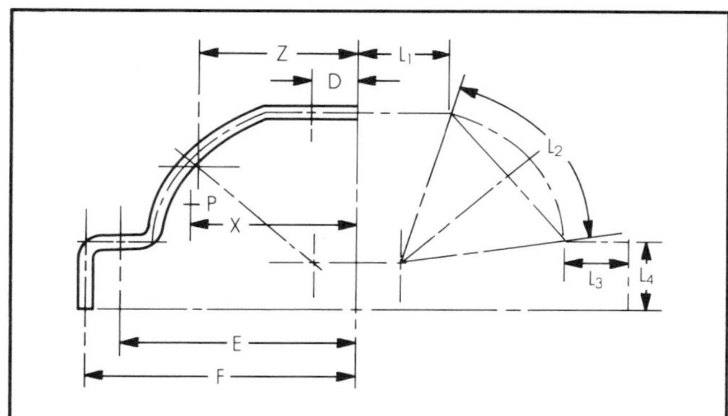


**Fig. 4-58 Determination of blank diameter for a symmetrical shell.**

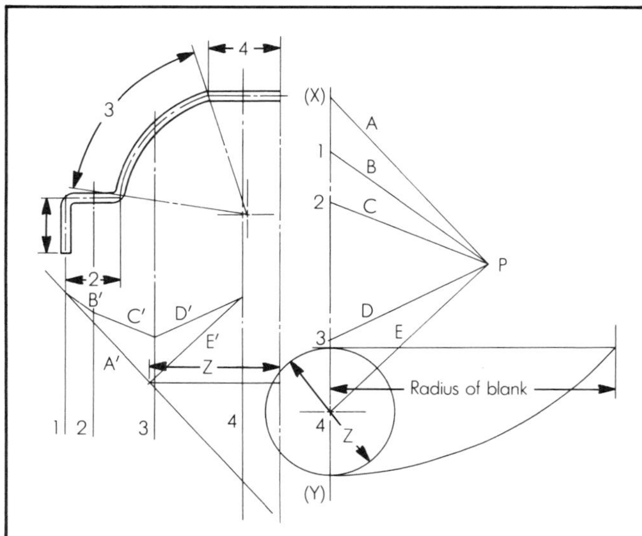


**Fig. 4-59 Graphic determination of blank diameter for a symmetrical shell.**

1. Make an accurate layout of the part, including a line through the center of the stock.
2. Number each dissimilar geometric section starting at the extreme edge of the part.
3. Draw a vertical line, $XY$, and mark off the length of each section accurately, starting with Section 1 at the top of the line. Number each section to correspond to the same portion of the shell.
4. Through the center of gravity of each section, draw a line downward, parallel to Line $XY$. The center of gravity of an arc lies on a line which is perpendicular to and bisects the chord and is two-thirds the distance from the chord to the arc.
5. From Point $X$, draw Line $A$ at 45° to Point $P$, which is about midway between $X$ and $Y$. Draw Line $A'$ intersecting the lines drawn in Step 4.
6. Connect $P$ to the ends of the sections on Line $XY$, obtaining Lines $B$, $C$, $D$, and $E$. Draw parallel Lines $B'$, $C'$, $D'$, and $E'$. Note that $B'$ begins where Line $A'$ intersects the first center-of-gravity line (Line 1), $C'$ begins where $B'$ intersects Line 2, and $D'$ begins where $C'$ intersects Line 3 and continues until the point where it intersects the last center-of-gravity line (Line 4). From that point, $E'$ is drawn, parallel to $E$, to intersect $A'$.
7. Through the intersection of $A'$ and $E'$, draw a horizontal line, $Z$, to the centerline of the shell. Construct a circle on Line $XY$, using Point 4 as the center and $Z$ as the diameter. Using Point $X$ as the center, scribe an arc tangent to the small circle.
8. Draw a horizontal line tangent to the top of the small circle until it intersects the large arc. The distance from this to Line $XY$ is the radius of the required blank.

*Direct formula.* For parts to be drawn in a plain cylinder with a flange, the following formula would be used:

$$D = \sqrt{d^2 + 4dh} \quad (26)$$

where:

$D$ = blank diameter, in. or mm
$d$ = diameter of shell, in. or mm
$h$ = height of shell, in. or mm

Variations of this equation are shown in Fig. 4-60 for various similar flanged and unflanged shells.

**Shapes for rectangular drawing.** It is common practice to cut out a trial blank having a width equal to the required width at the bottom of the drawn part plus the heights of each side, and a length approximately equal to the length of the drawn part plus the heights at each end (see Fig. 4-61). The resulting rectangular blank is beveled and rounded at the corners until, by repeated trial draws, the correct shape is developed. A simpler method, although it does not provide correct measurements for final dimensions of the blanking punch, enables the diemaker to quickly determine approximate shape for the blank, and it is sufficiently accurate to eliminate many trial drawings. Using this method, the following steps would be taken:

1. Draw a plan view of the finished shell or lines representing the shape of the work at the bottom, giving the corners the required radius (Fig. 4-61).
2. Next draw the sides and ends, making the length, $L$, and the width, $W$, equal to the length and width, respectively,

of the drawn part and deducting in each case twice the radius, *R*, at the corners.

3. Transfer the shape of the blank to another piece of the same stock and then draw the blank. The outline made prior to the drawing operation will serve as a record and show changes that should be made in the outline to obtain a more even edge along the top of the drawn rectangular part. When a blank of the correct shape is obtained, it is used in laying out the blanking die.

If the part must be drawn quite deeply, it is not feasible to produce an even edge along the top, and the usual practice is to finish this edge with trimming shears or a separate trimming die.

As stated previously, when laying out a blank, it usually is advisable to anticipate and provide an allowance for the wear that normally occurs at the corners of the die.

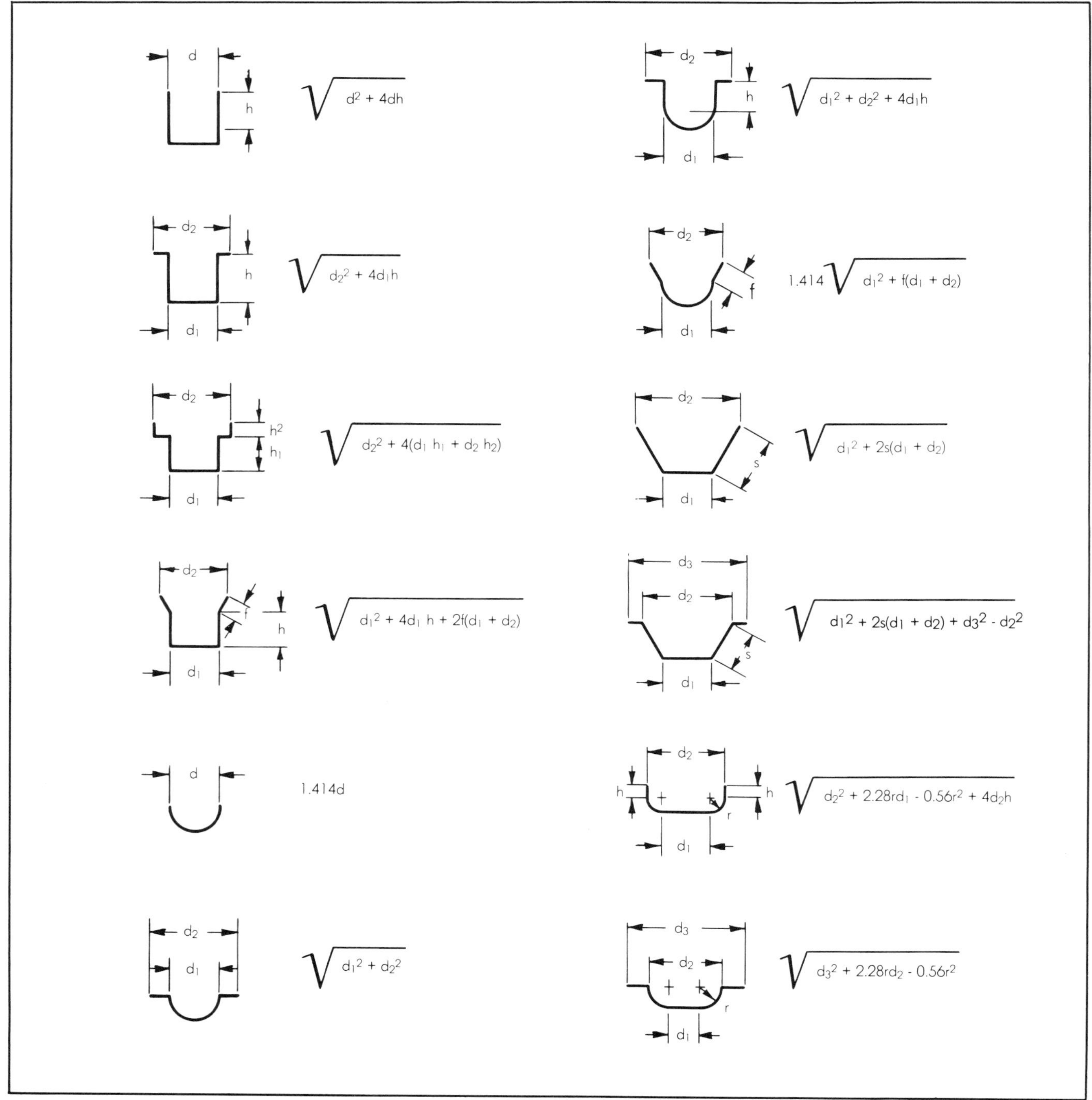


**Fig. 4-60 Equations for blank-diameter determination for symmetrical shells.**

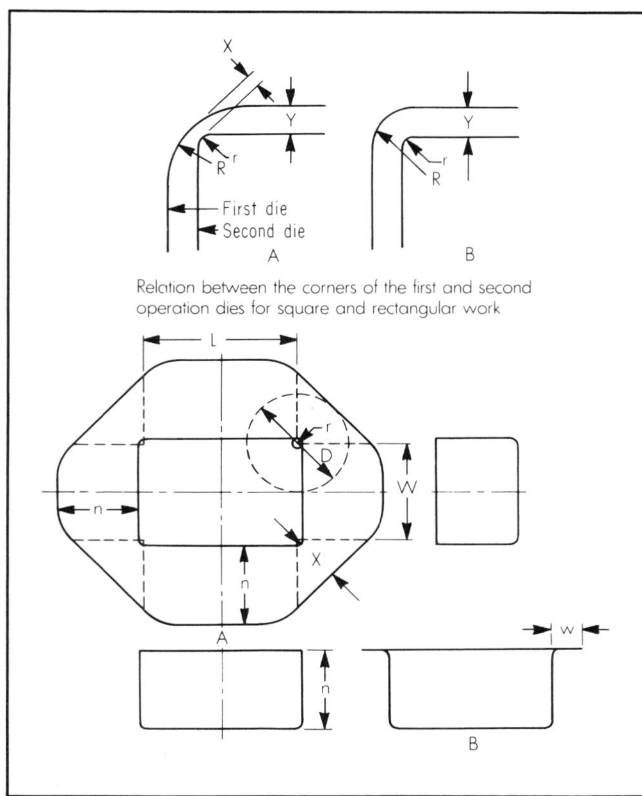


**Fig. 4-61 Method for determining approximate shape of blanks for drawing rectangular parts.**

## IRONING

In blanking, metal is fractured in shear; in drawing, it is worked primarily by application of a tensile load on the side walls. Ironing is distinguished from blanking and drawing by the fact that the primary working stress is compressive. (Other compression processes, such as coining and swaging, are described later in this chapter.)

Ironing of a container wall can be described as an operation whereby the wall thickness of the shell is reduced and its surface is smoothed.

The idea of making a container taller by thinning of the wall (ironing) is not new. An Italian, Luigi Stampacchia, obtained a U.S. patent in 1898 on the process of double-drawing and consequently ironing of cans. It was not widely used, because the process of ironing was not well understood and the necessary die materials such as carbide and high-alloy tool steels were not available.

Originally, ironing was mainly used for shell casings and similar items. Walls were fairly thick, reductions in thickness relatively small, and the ironing was rather easy. Patents on the ironing of cans appeared in the late 1930's and 1940's, describing the mechanics of ironing and die construction in detail. Soon, drawn and ironed beverage cans replaced the conventional cans which had a soldered side and separate bottom.

### The Ironing Process

Ironing, which (as stated previously) is the reduction in thickness of drawn shell walls by pulling them through tight dies, is related to both shell drawing and wire drawing. It is done to obtain a wall that is thin compared with the shell bottom; to obtain a uniform wall; to obtain a tapered wall, such as those in cartridge cases; or merely to correct the natural wall thickening toward the top edge of a drawn shell.

The theoretical maximum reduction in wall thickness per operation due to ironing is approximately 50%. In such a case, the cross-section area of the (unstrained) metal before ironing is about double the cross-section area after ironing.

### Typical Tooling

Basically, in the ironing process, a drawn cup is placed on a punch or ram and is pushed through a die that has a smaller in side diameter than the outside diameter of the cup (see Fig. 4-62, view *a*). The wall thickness is thereby reduced, and the wall elongated and given a smooth, uniform surface. This is done by providing clearance space between the punch and the die wall. When the walls of the shell must be thinner at the top than toward the bottom, the punch is given a taper corresponding to the desired variation in wall thickness. Unless the material being worked is especially ductile, reductions should be limited to 10-12% of the thickness of the shell wall in one operation. The bottom of the shell is unaffected by ironing operations and retains the original metal thickness. Two-step ironing dies (see Fig. 4-62, view *b*) permit a second reduction of up to 75% of the first, depending upon the spacing of the dies.

In ironing, the cup is not simply pulled through the die by the push of the punch against the bottom of the cup. The ironed portion of the cup wall between cup bottom and ironing die is too thin to transmit the force required for ironing. Usually, the cup body is pulled through the die by a combination of forces:

1. The wall tension of the cup, created by the push of the punch against the cup bottom.
2. A friction force created by the ironing action and the friction between the cup wall and the surface of the punch.

### Computation Aids[13]

To minimize complexity and enable straightforward presentation, customary inch-pound measurement units are used throughout this section on computation aids for ironing wall thickness and force calculations. When working in SI metric units, direct use may be made of conversion factors for inches to millimeters; tons force to kilonewtons; and pounds per square inch to megapascals.

**Without ironing.** Figure 4-63 shows the natural change (without ironing) in thickness accompanying a change in diameter. The results which it gives apply to the upper edge of

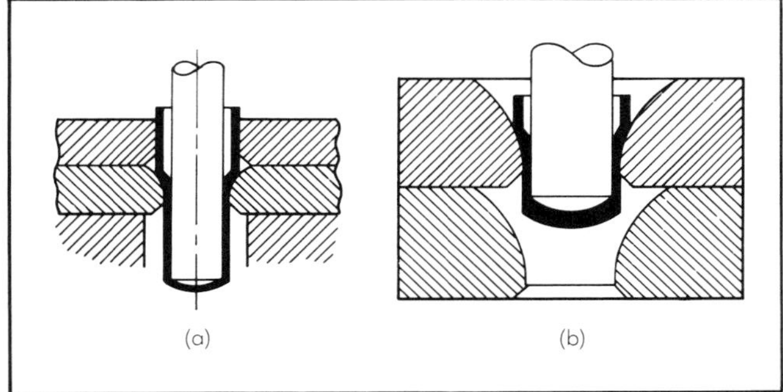


**Fig. 4-62 Basic principle of ironing: (a) operation partially completed; (b) two-step die. Ironing often is the final operation in a series of draws.**

# IRONING

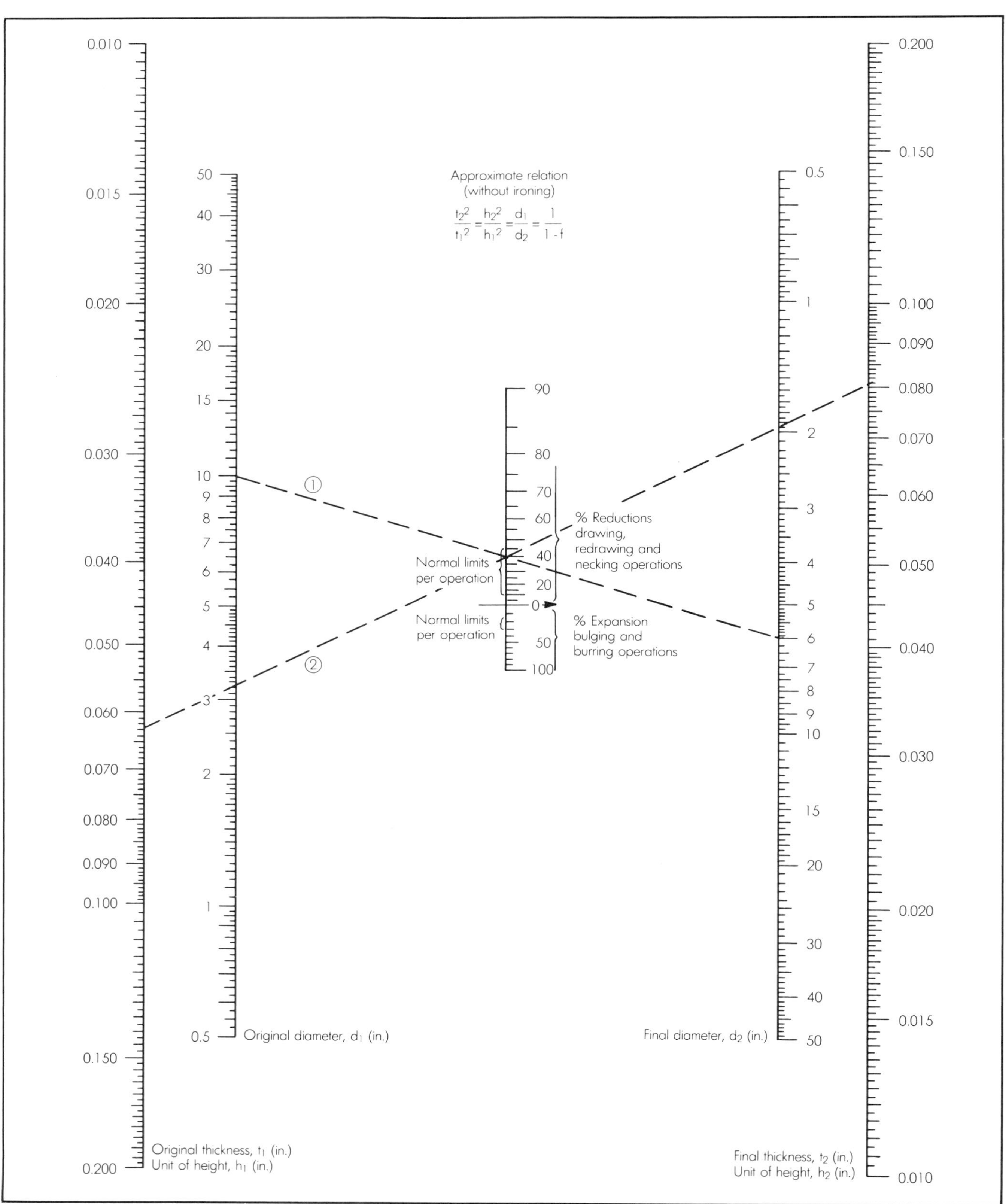


**Fig. 4-63 Nomograph for wall thickness (reduction) and blank diameter relationship for drawing without ironing.** (*E. W. Bliss Co.*)

drawn shells, since the wall thickness tapers from a maximum at that point to a minimum at the bottom corner, where it may be as much as 10 or 15% less than the original metal thickness. Even at the top edge, the metal thickness is likely to be a little less than the theoretical thickness given by the chart, because of the thinning effect of bending over the drawing edge. A sharper radius or a deeper draw increases this thinning effect.

Figure 4-63 is always read from left to right, drawing a line between the original diameter (of blank or shell) and the final diameter (of shell), on the two inner scales, to obtain the maximum percent reduction or expansion on the center scale. A second line drawn through this point, starting from the original metal thickness on the left-hand scale, indicates the approximate maximum wall thickness at the upper edge of the final shell. An example is indicated by the dotted lines. It is noted on Fig. 4-63 that this is based upon a draw with sufficient clearance between the punch and die so that no ironing will occur.

**With ironing**. If the clearance between punch and die is made equal to the metal thickness (0.0625″, in the example) there is an ironing load added to the drawing load (sufficient to remove 0.0805 - 0.0625 = 0.018″). For a parallel wall, it is necessary to iron the wall down to the thickness of the thinnest section (which is appreciably less than the original metal thickness).

Figure 4-64 offers a convenient means of approximating the force required in ironing. Referring to the example shown in dotted lines, it can be noted that the two inner scales are used first, to establish the pivot point on the center scale. Thus, a shell ironed to a finished diameter of 4″, with a displacement of 0.010″ of the total metal thickness, requires an ironing force of about 3.8 tons, assuming that the metal is spheroidized steel

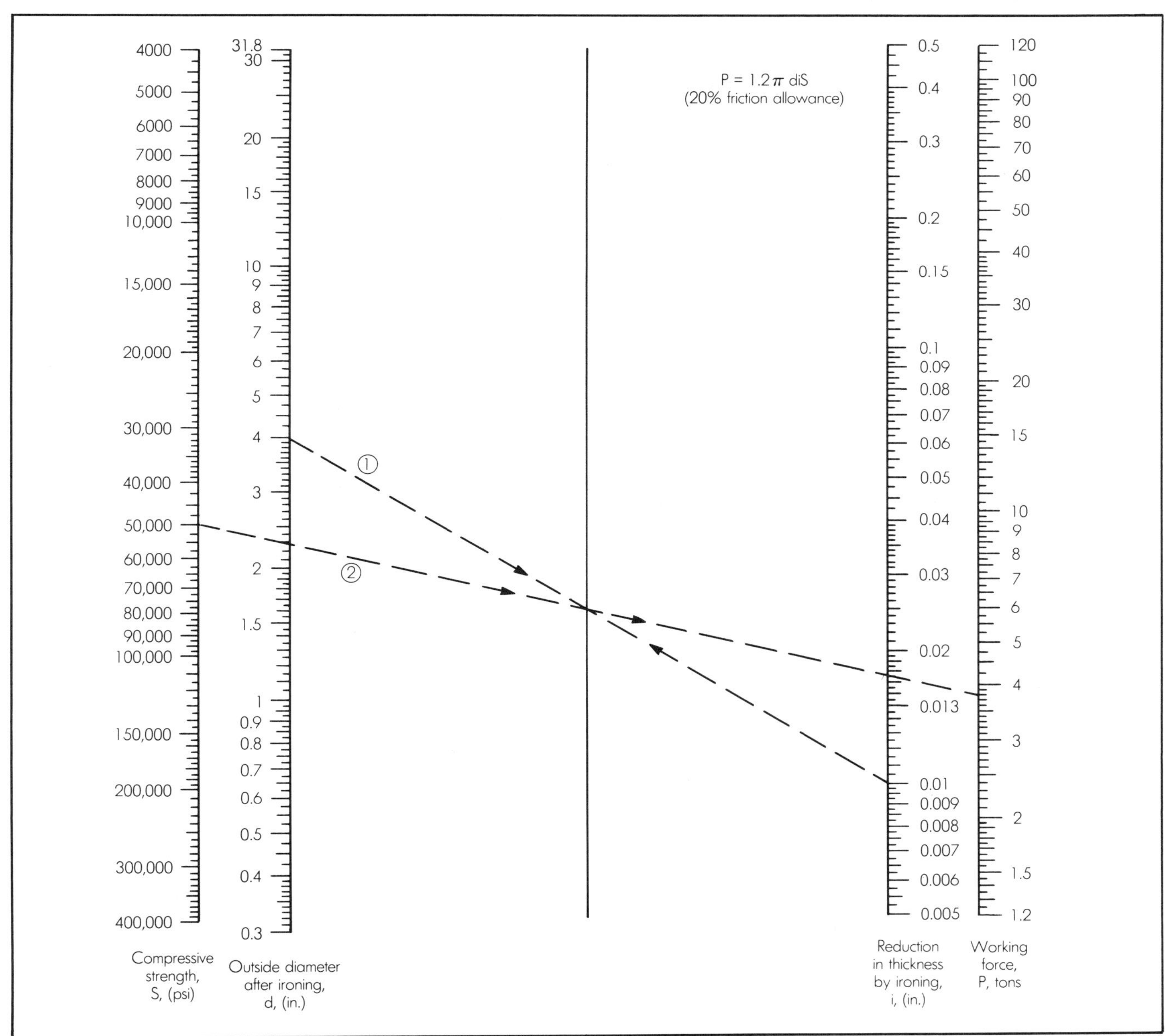


**Fig. 4-64 Nomograph for approximate determination of force required for ironing.** (*E. W. Bliss Co.*)

moderately strain hardened and therefore offering a compressive resistance of about 90,000 psi. This ironing force must be added to the drawing or redrawing load figured separately. The formula is:

$$P = 1.2\pi diS \quad (27)$$

where:

$P$ = maximum force required, ton (approx.)
$d$ = outside diameter, after ironing, in.
$i$ = wall thickness reduction, in.
$S$ = compressive resistance of the metal, under strain-hardening conditions, psi

The foregoing empirical formula includes a 20% allowance for surface friction, in addition to work expended in the metal forming. This is an arbitrary figure, suitable for well-polished dies and effective lubrication. Lack of lubricant, tool mark rings, picking-up on the surface, and other factors can cause the friction load to increase significantly.

If the wall of a shell is ironed thinner by the same amount for the entire length of the shell, the work done is approximately the product of the length of the shell or of the ironed surface and the force required for ironing (see Fig. 4-64).

In this case, the formula is:

$$W = PL \quad (28)$$

where:

$W$ = work, in.-ton
$P$ = force, ton
$L$ = length, in.

When a reducing operation accompanies the ironing, the drawing force should be added to the ironing force.

If the ironing operation is performed mainly to correct the natural changes in wall thickness due to drawing and reduces the thickest portion near the top of the shell to equal the thinnest portion near the bottom, the average ironing force equals about half the maximum, as calculated in Eq. (28).

## BULGING

Bulging is a metalforming process used to expand a tubular or cylindrical blank or part. The forming may be limited to a portion of a part, as in the expanding of pipe ends and the forming of rolling or stiffening beads in steel drums or washer tubs (see Fig. 4-65), or the entire part may be formed, as in the production of missile venturi sections. The two principal methods of bulge forming are mechanical bulging and hydrostatic bulging.

Bulging or expanding can be performed on parts made of materials with any practical ductility, and the process controls the accuracy of both the size and shape of parts formed. Tolerances of ±0.1% of diameter are readily achieved. Many applications have reduced size variations to 0.05% of diameter when uniform material physical properties permit.

Bulge forming often offers significant economy over alternative manufacturing methods for some parts. In addition to the relative economy of tooling and equipment for bulging or expanding, other cost savings result from enhanced strength and improved dimensional stability and consistency of shape obtained in parts formed by this process. Conical sheet metal parts are formed from cylindrical blanks with considerable reduction of tooling and labor and elimination of scrap loss inherent in developed blanks for such parts. Bulging has been applied to a wide size range of materials.

### Mechanical Bulging

Relatively symmetrical shapes may be produced by segmented bulging dies in which the various segments, held together by springs, are pushed apart by the punch to expand a superimposed shell. The main disadvantage of this method is that the resulting surface is marred by slight flats; however, if this slight marring is not objectionable, segmented dies are easily operated and maintained.

Bulging by mechanical methods that utilize a segmented, radially expanding mandrel or die set has been used successfully for parts as small as 2" (51 mm) diam when conditions of length, wall thickness, physical properties, and amount of bulging required are favorable. There is no inherent limitation to the maximum diameter bulged by mechanical expanding. Several special expanding machines have been built with maximum diametral capacity in the range of 120-150" (3-3.8 m). For mechanical expanding, part-length limitations are related to wall thickness, part diameter, die-set radial travel required, and material physical properties. When the part length to be expanded exceeds three diameters, the wall thickness is limited to approximately 1-2% of the part diameter. Refer to Chapter 7, "Expanding, Shrinking, and Stretch Forming," for details on cone-type expanding.

Another method of mechanical bulging involves inserting steel balls and grease, to make up a volume equal to that of the cubic content of the finished piece, into the shell that has been placed in a split die, and subsequently using the punch to compress the filler to form or bend the shell.

It is advisable to use annealed shells for bulging. If the expansion must be considerable, the work may best be accomplished in two, three, or even more steps. It may be necessary to anneal between operations. The more ductile metals such as aluminum, copper, soft brass, silver, and low-carbon steel may be enlarged about 30% of the blank diameter in one operation.

The comparative advantages of mechanical bulging include:

1. Sealing or containing hydrostatic pressure inside the workpiece is not a problem.
2. Elongation of the workpiece perimeter is evenly distributed, since die friction prevents localized elongation of weak spots.
3. Outer restraining tooling and structures are required only in certain cases to produce radii or localized bosses.
4. Equipment is readily adaptable to automated, high-speed production.

### Hydrostatic Bulging

The hydrostatic method of bulge forming uses a fluid or rubber, usually polyurethane, to apply internal pressure to the inside of the workpiece as the die is closed.

The comparative advantages of hydrostatic bulging include:

1. There is no inherent limitation of the minimum diameter or length of a part that may be formed.
2. There is no marking of the workpiece by the internal pressure medium.
3. The reduction of workpiece wall thickness is minimized by freedom of the workpiece to shorten during the bulging operation.

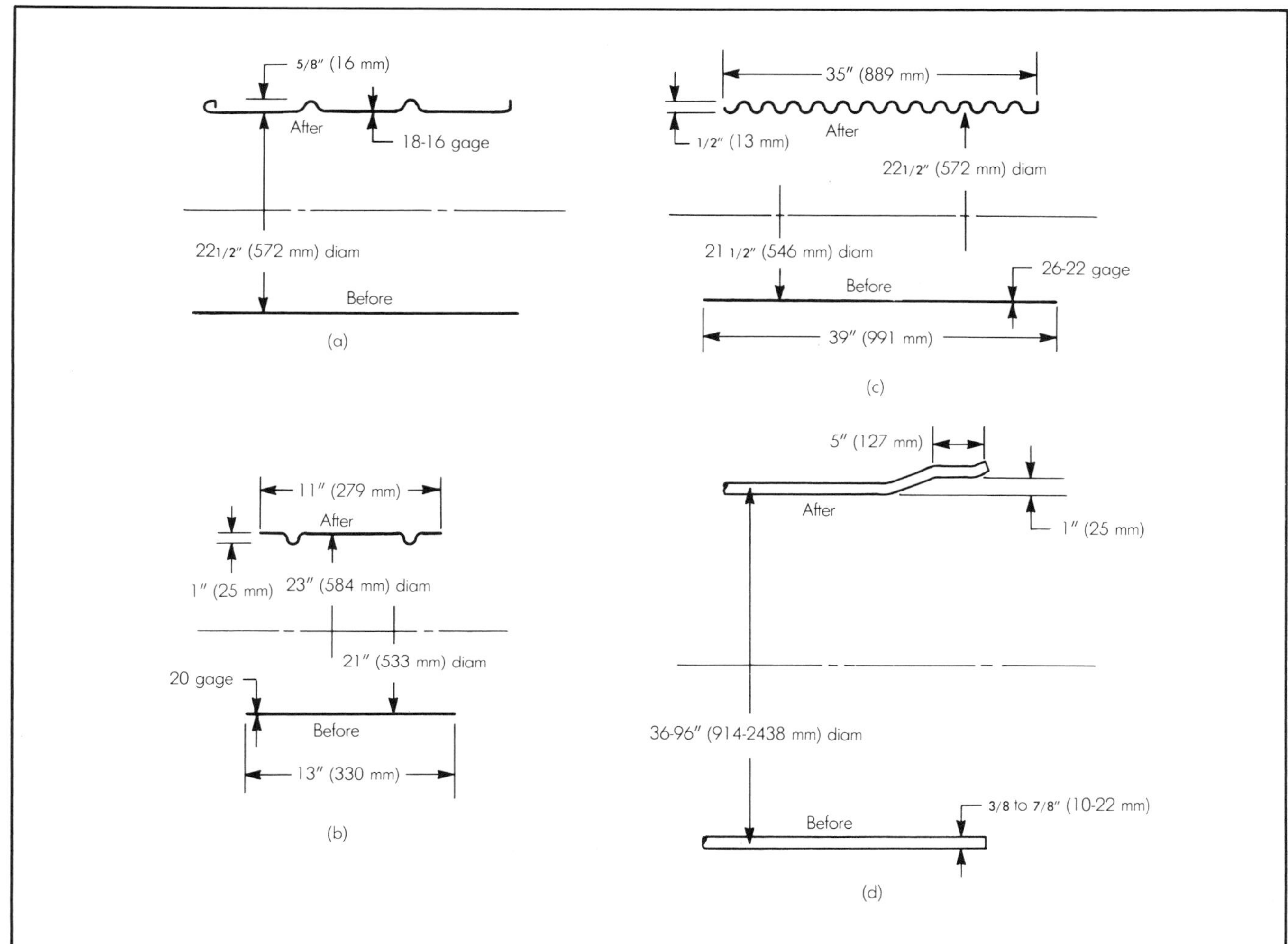


**Fig. 4-65 Typical bulge-formed parts before and after bulging: (a) standard 55 gallon (208 L) drum body; (b) drier drum; (c) lightweight 55 gallon drum body; and (d) large-bore pipe.**

Urethane bulging dies usually have either vertical or horizontal split cavities made of steel; the punch used with them is usually made of polyurethane. The die cavities must be machined smooth to avoid surface marring of the outside of the workpiece. The force required to deform the polyurethane and move the metal is transmitted to the punch by the ram of either a mechanical or hydraulic press or a special bulging or expanding machine. The punch may be mounted either on the press bed or on the slide. A positive means of holding the die sections tightly together, such as a locking ring, screw, toggle clamp, blankholding slide, or other device, must be used during the actual stroke.

In operation, urethane acts as a solid when deflected; that is, its volume remains constant while its shape changes. In bulging, the urethane changes the vertical force of the ram to uniform, multidirectional pressure on the blank. At the same time, the urethane deflects, forcing the blank metal outward into the die spaces provided. When the force is removed on the upstroke of the ram, the urethane returns to its original shape, permitting easy withdrawal of the punch. The amount a part is bulged is determined by the degree of deflection of the urethane punch.

For many bulging applications, polyurethane is the most practical and economical material to use as the punch, because it is highly wear and abrasion-resistant and is unaffected by oils and ozone. Also, the polyurethane will not mar the inside of the workpiece, and there are no fluid leakage problems. However, care should be taken to avoid cutting the polyurethane.

## COMPRESSION OPERATIONS

Coining, swaging, and sizing are metal-compression processes employed to impart a pattern, configuration, or decoration to parts produced from flat-rolled material. Figure 4-66 illustrates the differences between coining, beading, and embossing operations. Sizing and swaging are closely related to coining.

### Coining

Coining is the most severe of the metal-squeezing operations in the amount of pressure applied to each square inch of material. In this process, the metal thickness is changed, as is the internal structure of the workpiece. Because a closed die is generally used to confine the metal, the workpiece becomes an accurate reproduction of the die cavity.

# CHAPTER 4

## COMPRESSION OPERATIONS

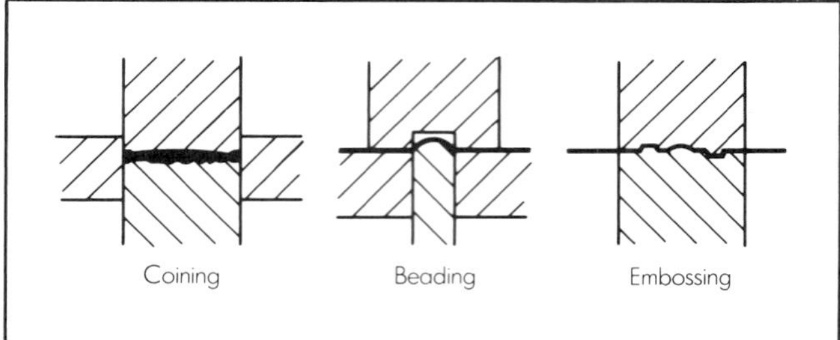


**Fig. 4-66 Comparison of coining, beading, and embossing operations.**

Theoretically metals are not compressible, but many metals are viscous and therefore flow under pressure. The highest pressure in a squeezing operation is required to set the part at the very bottom of the press stroke. As movement progresses, the fluidity of the metal decreases and the pressure to sustain the movement must be increased. Both lateral and vertical movements can be achieved, and many parts that require nonuniform metal thickness can be successfully and economically manufactured only by coining.

The coining process is used to manufacture medallions, jewelry, metal buttons, and coins of all types. The process is the most practical for producing smooth surfaces that also include a design.

**Coining pressure**. Accurate determination of the force and pressure requirements for a coining operation requires careful analysis. The factors determining pressure are (1) area to be squeezed, (2) resistance created within the metal (compressive strength), (3) freedom of flow, and (4) work hardenability of the metal.

Unit pressures on materials during coining range from three to five times the compressive strength of the material. If the required pressure must be determined exactly, laboratory tests should be conducted using either a hydraulic press or a mechanical press equipped with a strain gage. A mechanical press of the knuckle-joint type is preferred for both testing and manufacturing coined objects. (Refer to Chapter 5, "Presses for Sheet Metal Forming.") The knuckle-joint press provides a slow squeeze and dwell at the bottom of its stroke. It is recommended that the pressure obtained during tests in a hydraulic press be increased a minimum of 100% when a mechanical press is to be used for production of the part that was tested previously.

**Materials**. Materials that can be successfully coined are gold, silver, mild steels of the low-carbon type, brass, bronze, and copper. High-carbon steels, as well as those of the sulfur type, commonly fracture during coining.

**Advantages and limitations**. The advantages of parts produced by coining include dimensional accuracy, polished surfaces, increased strength, and economy both in material and manufacturing. The limitations of coining processes are that die steels must be used that can withstand the high unit pressures generated and that metal movement of die components must be held to a minimum.

### Sizing

Sizing operations are closely related to coining in that sizing, like coining, changes the metal thickness and configuration by squeezing and working metal beyond the yield point.

Most sizing operations are performed in open dies; therefore, the entire workpiece is not confined in the die and the only contact between the workpiece and the die occurs in the section in which the sizing takes place. There is usually no restriction to metal flow. Sizing is used to sharpen corners on stampings, flatten areas around pierced holes, etc. Some malleable-iron castings and drop forgings are sized in this manner.

Pressures required for sizing are usually considerably lower than those required to produce a complete part by coining. The pressure determination is, however, a factor of the (1) area to be sized, (2) type of material, and (3) amount of change in metal thickness. When the area is to be determined, it is important that the contact area between the die and the workpiece be kept to a minimum to minimize the total load.

Sizing operations by pressing are usually performed on semifinished parts for which accuracy is required or on which the surface must be prepared for an additional operation or assembly.

Both mechanical and hydraulic presses can be used for sizing, but stop blocks must be used on hydraulic presses and are sometimes used on mechanical presses when close tolerances are to be held. The stop blocks are usually a part of the die. When a sizing press is selected for this operation, it is advisable to allow a liberal safety factor (as much as 2:1) over the theoretically calculated load.

### Swaging

Swaging is also closely related to coining in the family of compression operations. In swaging, which is somewhat more severe than sizing, the shape of the blank or slug is considerably altered as part of it flows into the contours of the die. The swaging process differs from coining, however, in that the remaining metal is unconfined and generally flows at an angle to the direction of applied force. Compared with sizing, there is greater restriction to metal flow, although more metal is moved. Swaging is applied to the production of parts such as small gears or cams or other small parts of irregular contour. Rotary swaging is discussed in Chapter 14, "Swaging," and rotary forging in Chapter 15, "Hot Forging."

### Embossing

In the manufacturing of metal parts with a die set and press, embossing is the process used to create shallow designs theoretically without changing the metal thickness.

Embossing differs from coining in that with embossing the same design is created on both sides of the workpiece, one side being depressed and the other raised, whereas with coining a different design is created on each side. During embossing, therefore, the metal is bent along the lines of the design. Some stretching and compressing takes place along the design lines, the amount depending on the extent to which the design height is changed.

The press to be used for embossing depends upon the area to be squeezed and the type of material. To determine the area, it is necessary to consider only the area in contact with the die. Therefore, in designing the die, it is important to provide die relief for all surfaces that are not to be embossed. The size of the press can be greatly reduced by proper die design, since it is not necessary for the die to make contact over the entire surface of the workpiece.

Pressures required for embossing are those necessary to overcome the elastic limit of the material along the design lines. If the ultimate strength of the material is used in the calculations, an adequate safety factor is provided during press selection.

Steel dies with matching upper and lower die configurations are generally used for embossing. If the workpiece is of relatively thin material and does not require sharp impressions, however, a urethane pad may be substituted for either the upper or the lower metal punch, thereby reducing the die cost.

The advantage of embossing is that complicated designs can be economically and accurately reproduced in metallic parts at a high rate of speed. Single or progressive dies can be used. Limitations on embossing include difficulty in maintaining uniform thickness of the part and difficulty in creating sharp impressions.

Embossing operations are generally used in manufacturing tableware, jewelry, number or nameplates, and localized patterns (usually shallow).

### Beading

Beading is a process used to form shallow, round troughs of uniform width (either recessed or raised) in a straight, curved, or circular form. Pressures required to form strengthening or ornamental beads in sheet metal parts are approximately the same as those required for embossing operations and are considerably less than those required for coining. Beads increase overall rigidity without increasing material thickness. They can be produced in either single or progressive operations.

Beading is applied to round can or container bodies in a rolling operation between male and female roll forms. Both semiautomatic and automatic machines are available for this operation, and occasionally trimming and flanging are combined with beading.

The metal in the area of the bead is subjected to stretching, bending, and drawing. Actual squeezing of the metal in the head is uncommon, since a nonbottoming die set is generally used. The greatest amount of force required is that due to stretching of the metal in the bead. The total force required to form a bead is a product of the yield strength of the metal, the length of the bead, and the metal thickness. The force should be sufficient to cause movement of the metal, thus exceeding the yield strength but not reaching the ultimate strength. When calculating the total force for press selection, an adequate safety factor should be provided if the ultimate strength of the metal is used instead of the yield strength.

The size of a bead is limited by the amount of metal that can be moved without fracture. Table 4-11 provides data for beads in sheet aluminum.

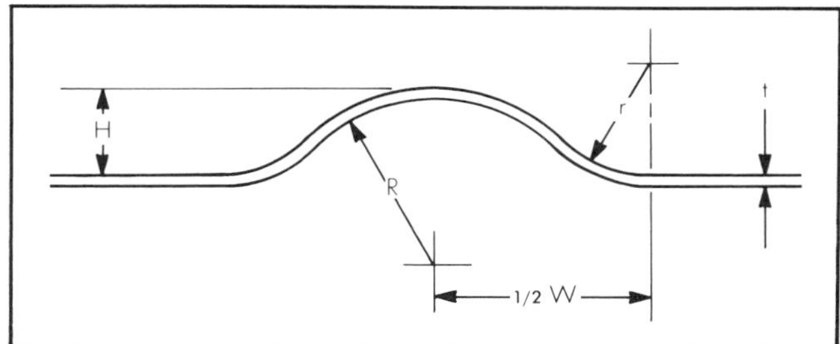


**TABLE 4-11**
**Allowable Dimensions for Locked-In Aluminum Beads, in. (mm)**

| Bead No. | H | 1/2 W | R | r | Suitable Gages |
|---|---|---|---|---|---|
| 1 | 0.050 (1.27) | 1/8 (3.2) | 7/64 (2.8) | 0.070 (1.78) | 0.020 (0.51) |
| 2 | 0.100 (2.54) | 1/4 (6.4) | 7/32 (5.6) | 0.140 (3.56) | 0.020-0.025 (0.51-0.63) |
| 3 | 0.150 (3.81) | 3/8 (9.5) | 21/64 (8.3) | 0.210 (5.33) | 0.020-0.032 (0.51-0.81) |
| 4 | 0.200 (5.08) | 1/2 (12.7) | 7/16 (11.1) | 0.280 (7.11) | 0.020-0.040 (0.51-1.02) |
| 5 | 0.250 (6.35) | 5/8 (15.9) | 35/64 (13.9) | 0.350 (8.89) | 0.020-0.051 (0.51-1.30) |
| 6 | 0.300 (7.62) | 3/4 (19.1) | 21/32 (16.7) | 0.420 (10.67) | 0.020-0.064 (0.51-1.63) |
| 7 | 0.350 (8.89) | 7/8 (22.2) | 49/64 (19.4) | 0.490 (12.45) | 0.020-0.064 (0.51-1.63) |
| 8 | 0.400 (10.16) | 1 (25.4) | 7/8 (22.2) | 0.560 (14.22) | 0.020-0.064 (0.51-1.63) |

## CREEP FORMING

Creep forming is the deformation of metal at a stress level below its yield point and the application of heat to the metal for a time sufficient to permit metallurgical creep to cause relaxation of the induced elastic stresses to such a level that plastic deformation to the desired shape is achieved.

This process is used almost exclusively by the aerospace industry. Applications range from jet engine parts to large, comparatively thin, and relatively shallow-contour components for which one-piece construction and the resultant product life-cycle costs or payload benefits offset the unit costs of creep forming. The materals that are predominately creep formed are aluminum and titanium alloys for skins in missiles and airplanes. One of the production applications is the forming of airplane wing skins.

Typically, most creep forming is conducted with the material in a highly heat-treated condition. This eliminates the need for postforming heat treatment and the associated furnaces and fixtures. The highly heat-treated condition also limits the maximum temperature that can be used, because adverse metallurgical effects occur at higher temperatures. This condition limits the rate at which creep can occur and results in a forming time per part of between four and eight hours.

The principal economic advantage of creep forming is the low capital investment (equipment and tooling) required as compared with other processes capable of forming comparable sections. The need for heat-cycle time and the effect of heat-cycle time on reactive alloys, combined with tooling sensitivity to design changes, constitute the principal economic limitations.

The methods and equipment used for creep forming are normally developed by the user for specific applications. Equipment typically consists of a die, a clamping fixture, and a furnace sufficiently large enough to accommodate both the tooling and the part.

Creep forming does not lend itself readily to automation because of the large size of parts processed and the characteristics of the process itself. In addition, the process finds its greatest usefulness in relatively small production quantities in which its low initial investment is attractive.

## RUBBER PAD FORMING

The principle of rubber pad forming is that when the underlying rubber is placed in a cylinder and pressure is brought to bear upon it by applying a force to a ram of a press, the force causes a resultant reaction on every surface with which the rubber comes in contact. This resultant reaction is used for forming sheet metals to a required shape using form blocks or punches and dies.

## Guerin Process

The Guerin process employs a rubber pad on the ram of the press and a form block that is placed on the lower platen mounted on the press bed. This process is the oldest and most widely used, but it is limited to the forming of relatively shallow parts of light materials, normally not exceeding 1.2-1.5" (30-38 mm) deep.

**Drawing**. Parts with straight flanges, stretch flanges, and beaded parts formed from developed blanks are most suitable for this process. Figure 4-67 is a schematic section through the equipment and tooling utilized in the process. This illustrates the container loaded with rubber fixed on the ram of the press bed supporting a single form block. The inability of the Guerin process to shrink metal is caused by wrinkling. The pressures are not sufficiently high to compact the rubber enough to prevent wrinkles. A mere increase in pressure would not solve this problem, since wrinkles can begin to form before any pressure is built up on the rubber to prevent their formation. Once a wrinkle occurs, the rubber pressure tends to maintain it rather than iron it out flat. As a result, this process is not suited for forming shrink flanges.

**Blanking and piercing**. In the Guerin process, rubber pads can be used for blanking and punching as well as for forming. The use of rubber pads results in better edges on the blanked workpiece than are possible with bandsawing, and in edges that are as good as those obtained by routing. An edge radius up to the thickness of the metal can be produced on some heavy gage metals. The form block is provided with a sharp cutting edge where the blank is to be sheared. In a hard metal block, this edge can be cut into the form block. The shearing edge should be undercut from 3 to 6°. The trim metal beyond the line of shear must be clamped firmly so that the work metal breaks over the sharp edge instead of forming around it. This clamping is done by means of a lock ring or a raised extension of the form block.

For punching circular or square holes on a circular sheet, a die ring with sharp edges to cut the blank is used. Undercut is given to allow the scrap to fill down and to facilitate smooth cutting. A sheet is placed over the die, and the ram is brought down. The sheet is clamped against the die, and the portion to be pierced is pushed inside. Since the edges are sharp, the blank is pierced.

## Marforming Process

This method was developed to form shrink flanges and deep draw shells. Figure 4-68 shows that the process uses a deep rubber pad on the ram of the press with a stationary punch fixed on the press bed. A steel pressure plate cut to fit the container and to slip freely over the punch provides the bottom support for the rubber pad in the container. As the ram is lowered, the blank is clamped between the rubber pad and the blankholder before forming begins. As the ram continues to descend, the blank is drawn over the punch. The pressure in the pneumatic cushion must be controlled. Such constant control of pressure on the blankholder provides smooth forming and eliminates wrinkling. The variable draw radii in a rubber pad permit the material to draw more easily than the fixed radius of a steel die. It is also possible to draw square and rectangular boxes and hemispherical and tapered stampings with this process.

## Rubber-Die Process

This process is used to draw shallow-recessed parts. In this process, a die is used instead of a punch. The die is mounted on the press bed and fits in the container exactly. A sheet is placed on the die, and the ram is brought down. As it descends, the rubber pad in the container pushes the sheet into the cavity. Initially, the rubber pressure acts uniformly over the entire surface, but when the rubber pushes the sheet into the die cavity, the pressure is increased in that region because the rubber is squeezed into a smaller area. Therefore, due to difference in pressures on the flange and the die cavity, the sheet is drawn. The blankholder plate is not necessary for this process.

## Dieless Process

In this process, a draw ring is used instead of a die with the external contour of the component. The material is pushed inside a circular hole in an annular ring. Since the rubber flows in hemispherical form when it is pushed against a hole, hemispherical components can be produced without difficulty.

## Fluid Cell Process

The fluid cell process was developed from the Guerin process. It uses higher pressure and is designed primarily for forming slightly deeper parts, using a rubber pad as either the die or punch. A flexible hydraulic fluid cell forces an auxiliary

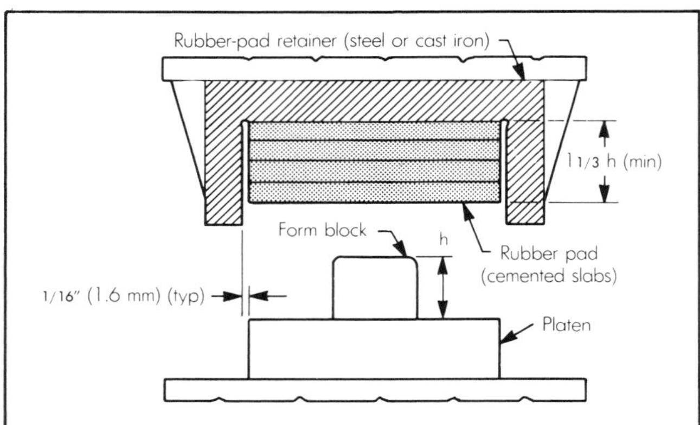


**Fig. 4-67 Tooling and setup for rubber-pad forming by the Guerin process.**

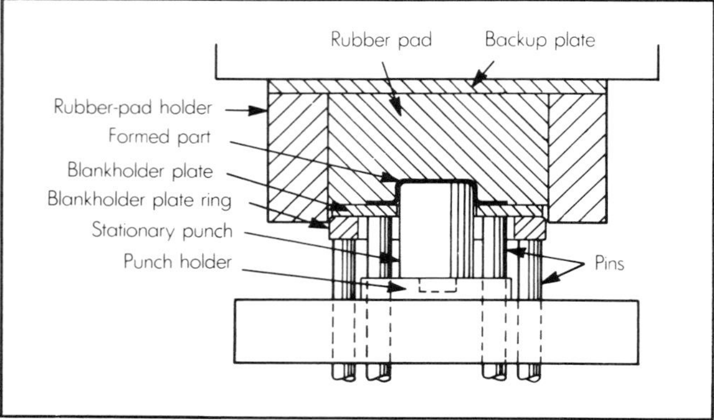


**Fig. 4-68 Tooling and setup for rubber-pad forming by the Marform process.**

rubber pad to follow the contour of the form block and exert a nearly uniform pressure at all points.

The distribution of pressure on the sides of the form block permits forming of wider flanges than are possible with the Guerin process. Also, shrink flanges, joggles, and beads and ribs in flanges and web surfaces can be formed in one operation to sharp detail in aluminum, low-carbon steel, stainless steel, heat-resisting alloys, and titanium. Special processes for fluid cell forming are discussed in Chapter 5.

### Fluid Forming

This process differs from those previously described in that the die cavity is not completely filled with rubber, but with hydraulic fluid retained by a cup-shaped rubber diaphragm. This cavity is called the pressure dome. A replaceable wear sheet is cemented to the lower surface of the diaphragm.

More severe draws can be made with this process than with processes using conventional draw dies, because oil pressure against the diaphragm causes the metal to be held tightly against the sides as well as against the tip of the punch.

Reductions in blank diameter of 60-70% are common for a first draw. When redrawing is necessary, reductions can reach 40%. Low-carbon steel, stainless steel, and aluminum in thicknesses from 0.010-0.065″ (0.25-1.65 mm) are commonly formed. Parts made of heat-resisting alloys and copper alloys are also formed by the process. Special presses are used for this process, as discussed in Chapter 5, "Presses for Sheet Metal Forming."

### Demarest Process

Cylindrical and conical parts can also be formed by a modified rubber bulging punch. The punch, equipped with a hydraulic cell, is placed inside the workpiece, which in turn is placed inside the die. Hydraulic pressure expands the punch. Figure 4-69 shows a fuel tank section made by the Demarest process.

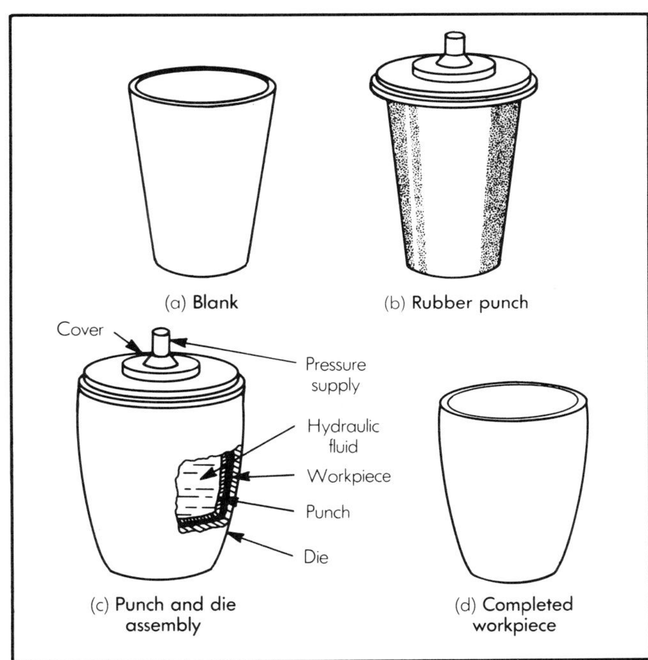


**Fig. 4-69 Forming a fuel tank section by the Demarest process.**

## SUPERPLASTIC FORMING

As discussed in Chapter 1, "Sheet Metal Formability," materials that can be stretched to unusually large strains (approaching 500%) without localized necking are said to be superplastic. In general, superplastic materials can be formed into more complex shapes using lower loads and can attain higher strains without fracturing than materials with conventional stress-strain characteristics.

### Key Factors

A key factor in superplasticity is the capability of certain metal alloys to develop extremely high tensile elongations at elevated temperatures and under controlled deformation rates. The other characteristic that is normally observed is a substantial reduction in the flow stress of the material. This means that the forces and stresses required to cause deformation can be as much or as little as 1/2 to 1/20th that of the conventional alloy under the same conditions. It is these two factors (high tensile elongation and low flow stress) that provide the exceptional potential that is anticipated for superplastic forming.

While the requirements for superplasticity are well understood, the first of these, that is, the fine stable grain size, is perhaps the most difficult to achieve in metals and alloys. It is for this reason that superplasticity has been demonstrated only for a limited number of materials.

In most metals and alloys, the temperature range is not a problem to achieve nor is the rate of straining. However, the requirement for the fine stable grain size is difficult to achieve and retain because of the elevated temperature. Unless the grain growth is inhibited by some microstructural feature, this grain size would normally increase beyond the limits of superplasticity once the temperature achieves more than one half the melting point. As a result, relatively few alloys demonstrate superplasticity, and those that do normally require special processing and/or alloying compositions to achieve the fine stable grain size.

### Typical Process

The typical process that utilizes this unique characteristic of superplasticity is called superplastic forming and is illustrated in Fig. 4-70. In this process, the superplastic blank is inserted between two die elements or tools, one of which is configured to the part required. In this case the lower die is the configuration die. The upper die piece is utilized to provide application of the gas pressure which is introduced to cause forming.

The tooling and the superplastic blank are then placed between heated elements, as shown, and heated to a temperature suitable for superplastic forming. A clamping pressure is applied to this sandwich of heated platens and tooling to contain the gas pressure, and the gas pressure is then imposed over the top of the sheet causing it to blow form or stretch form into the die cavity. The rate of pressure application must be controlled, since it translates directly into the strain rate imposed on the material—a critical factor in achieving superplasticity and superplastic forming. Once the forming has been achieved, the die assembly is opened, the formed part is removed, and then trimming and subsequent processing operations are performed similarly to those of parts formed by conventional forming.

A cross section of this forming operation is shown in Fig. 4-71. In this example, the superplastic sheet is formed into a rectangular die cavity; and as illustrated, as the gas pressure is imposed over the top of the sheet, a bubble is formed into the lower die cavity and stretches plastically in a creeplike deformation mode into the die cavity until it fully mates with the configuration of the die, at which time the forming is completed. The gas pressures required for superplastic forming vary from 15-100 psi (0.1-0.7 MPa), although normal forming operations utilize less than 300 psi (2 MPa) gas pressure. Forming times vary from 2 minutes to about 2 hours, depending on the material and the extent of deformation required. The temperature for forming superplastic aluminum materials is normally in the range of 842-968° F (450-520° C), depending on the specific alloy.

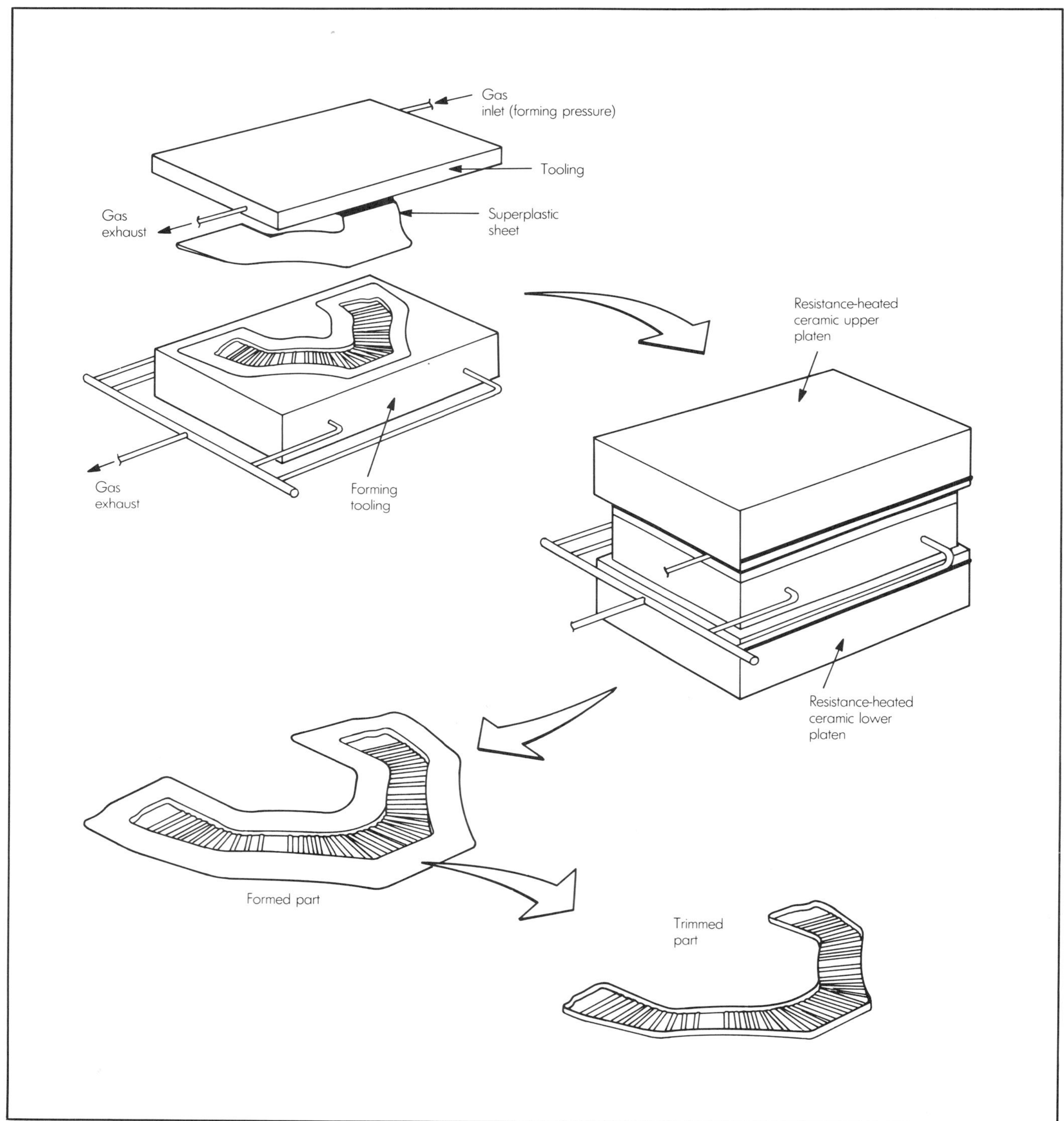


**Fig. 4-70 Superplastic forming process, schematic view of sequence.**

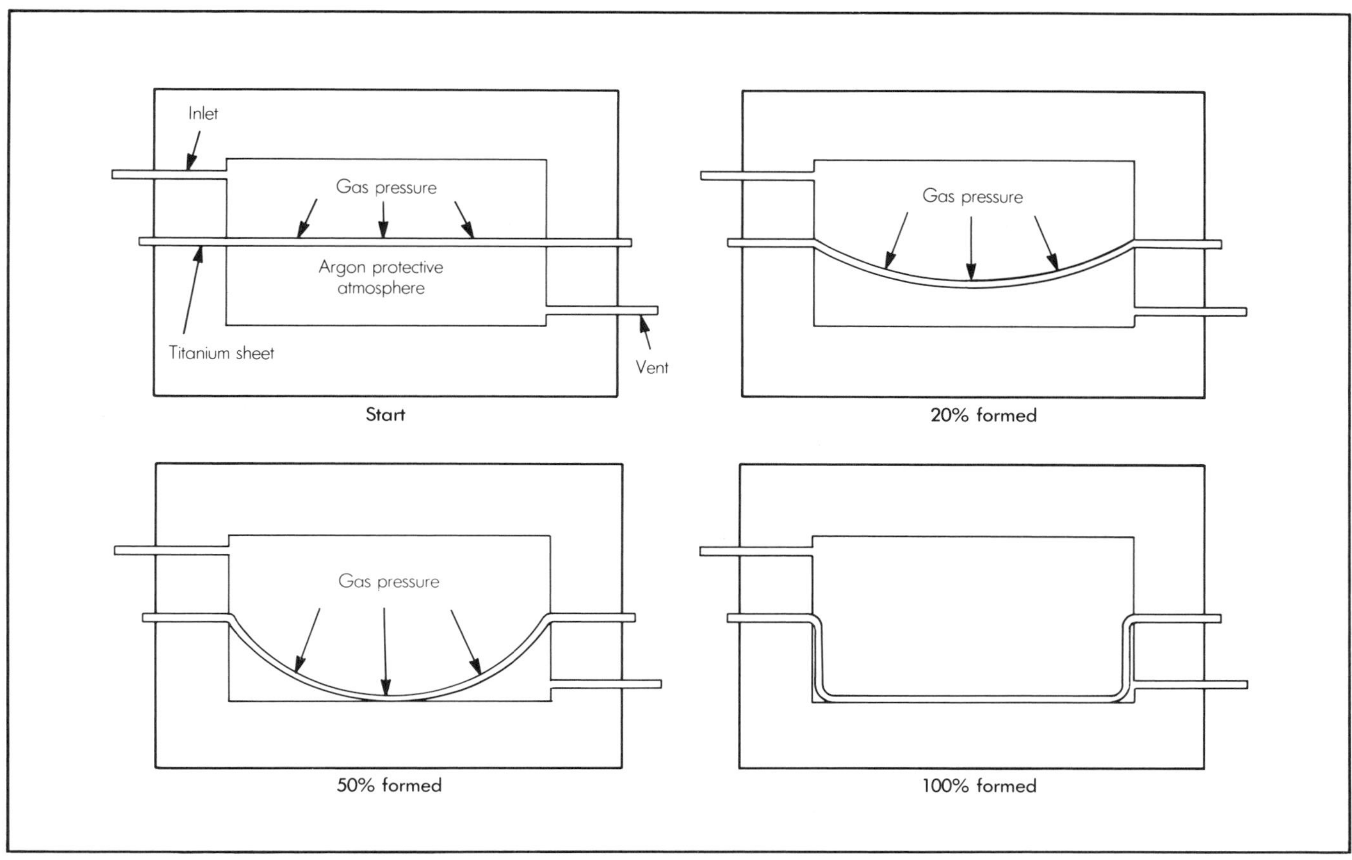


**Fig. 4-71 Cross-sectional view of superplastic forming during various stages of the process.**

# TOLERANCES FOR STAMPINGS

The approach to specifying tolerances for stampings should not be the same as for machined parts. Machined parts allow closer tolerances than stampings. Correct dimensioning and determination of tolerances for stampings should be realistic and conform to the true functional requirements.[14]

The best rationale consists in using empirical, practical data taken from actual products that are functionally similar to the new product that is to be produced. In the absence of previous experience, the following simple procedure may be taken as a guide for determining tolerances. Minimal clearance between operating components is the space that barely permits their assembly and correct operation under service conditions. Maximum clearance is the distance that still allows proper functioning of the assembly. In this way, the two tolerance limits can be established to a good approximation.

## PRACTICAL DATA

Some data on tolerances in metal stampings is presented here as a guide. This data has been collected in actual practice in the field. It consists simply of recommendations; deviations from it are frequent. It refers to short run jobs in which tools of the lowest cost are anticipated. Closer tolerances are possible; however, they require more sophisticated tooling and manufacturing processes which, of course, increase production costs. Additional information on tolerances is provided in Chapter 6, "Die Design for Sheet Metal Forming," in this volume; and in Chapter 2, "Tolerance Control," in Volume I *Machining* of this Handbook series.

## FLAT STAMPINGS

In stampings, the die-cut surfaces are not precisely straight or perpendicular to the general surface of the stamping. They are composed of a land that is smooth and parallel and a break that is uneven, rough, and tapered. The land is usually smaller than the break in a hole or on a blank. When tolerances are being checked, the land portion should be measured.

### Flatness

Parts should be designed so that straight edges can be maintained on the flat blanks of formed parts wherever possible. This results in economy and ease of production, since the blank can be sheared from flat blanks with relatively inexpensive dies.

The chief factors governing flatness are material temper and tool design. Under ordinary circumstances, a flatness of 0.005-0.010 in./in. (0.13-0.25 mm/mm) can be maintained. If closer tolerances are required, some corrective operation such as coining, straightening, or grinding is needed. Such corrective operations increase costs. Care should be taken to avoid the mistake of confusing flatness with parallelism.

## Squareness and Eccentricity

To obtain squareness of sheared parts, a tolerance of ±0.003" (0.08 mm) is allowable for part dimensions given in decimals, and ±0.010" (0.25 mm) on fractional dimensions for each inch of the surface length. When metric units are used, the corresponding tolerance is expressed in millimeters. This tolerance is for squareness only and is not to be added to the linear tolerance.

The radius tolerance for eccentricity between the hole and outside diameter of washers punched with stock dies is 0.004" (0.10 mm) on 1" (25.4 mm) outside diameters or less, and 0.008" (0.20 mm) on outside diameters greater than 1".

## Punched Holes

When specifying stampings with punched holes, it should be recognized that only about one-third the thickness of the metal is sheared cleanly to the size of the punch. The remainder fails in shear by the pressure on the sheared slug, producing a rough hole that tapers outward from the diameter of the punch to the diameter of the die. This face is especially important when the periphery of the hole is intended to act as a bearing surface. Table 4-12 presents general guides for blank dimensions and punched-hole diameters, including center-to-center distances and the distance from the edge of blanked part. Tolerances for punched holes are given in Table 4-13.

Tolerances for punched holes and outer contours for blanks vary with stock quality, thickness, and hardness; with the size and shape of the part; with the condition, design, and accuracy of the tool; with the number of stations in progressive dies; and with other factors.

The tolerance values in Fig. 4-72 refer to light-gage stock (up to 0.031"; 0.78 mm). For medium-gage stock (up to 0.062"; 1.57 mm), tolerances should be increased by 25-50%; for heavy-gage stock (over 0.062"; 1.57 mm) they should be increased by 100-200%.

Tolerances for center distances between holes located in the same plane depend chiefly upon the production method employed:

1. When punched simultaneously with the same die: ±0.003" (0.08 mm).
2. When punched with separate, single operation dies: ±0.005" (0.13 mm).
3. When punched in progressive dies, made in separate stations, according to quantity of stations between operations and type of progression gage: ±0.005 to ±0.015" (0.13 to 0.38 mm).

Tolerances for hole location from the edge of a stamping or from a bend are:

1. For light and medium stock up to 0.062" (1.57 mm): ±0.008 to ±0.010" (0.20 to 10.25 mm).
2. For heavy stock from 0.062-0.125" (1.57-3.18 mm): ±0.015 to ±0.020" (0.38 to 0.51 mm).
3. For very heavy stock over 0.125" (3.18 mm): ±0.030 to ±0.035" (0.76 to 0.89 mm).

Holes in bent legs must be located from the inside. In this way, variations of sheet metal thickness do not influence the location tolerances. When functional gaging is being used, the hole size also is a key factor in establishing the allowable tolerance for hole positioning.

## Blanking and Piercing

Table 4-14 gives blanking and piercing (punching) tolerances that can generally be maintained on steel, brass, copper, or aluminum parts. Greater tolerances are usually required on fiber, rubber, and softer materials.

If closer tolerances are required than those given in the preceding paragraphs, the holes must be punched after forming. This means lower production rates, higher tooling cost, and higher workpiece cost.

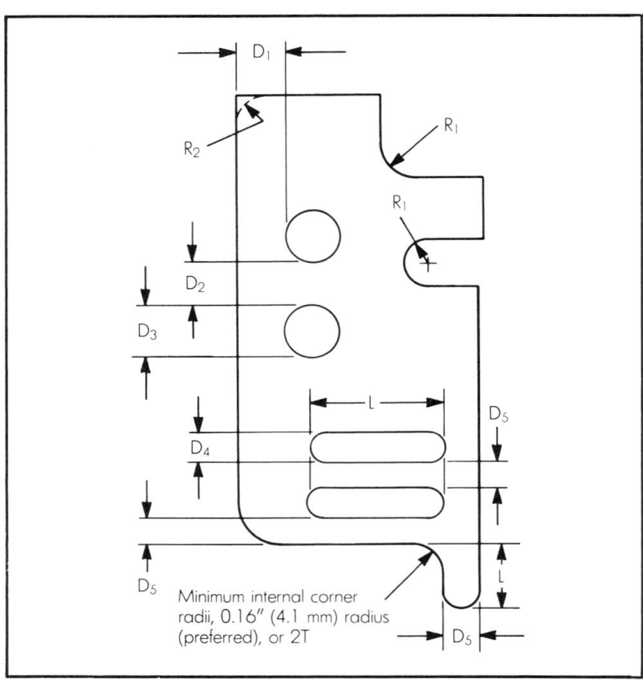


**TABLE 4-12**
**Minimum Practical Punching and Blanking Dimensions**

| | Punch Press | | |
|---|---|---|---|
| $R_1$ | 0.16" (4.1 mm) preferred or 2T | | |
| $R_2$ | 2T min | | |
| | T | Nonferrous | Ferrous |
| $D_1$ or $D_2$ | Through 0.062" (1.57 mm) | 0.12" (3.1 mm) | 0.12" (3.1 mm) |
| | 0.063-0.38" (1.60-0.97 mm) | 0.12" or 1.5T whichever is greater | 2T |
| $D_3$ | 1.0T or 0.098" (2.49 mm) min except 0.120" (3.05 mm) min for alloy steels | | |
| | T | | Width |
| $D_4$ or $D_5$ | Through 0.032" (0.81 mm) | | 0.06" (1.5 mm) |
| | 0.033-0.125" (0.84-3.18 mm) | | 2T |
| | 0.126-0.38" (3.20-9.65 mm) | | 2.5T |

**TABLE 4-13**
**Maximum Punched-Hole Tolerances for Aluminum and Steel Sheet**

| Nominal Punched-Hole Diameter, incl., in. (mm) | Equivalent Drill Size, in. (mm) | Sheet Thickness, in. (mm) 0.025-0.042 (0.63-1.07) | 0.050-0.072 (1.27-1.83) | 0.078-0.093 (1.98-2.36) | 0.102-0.156 (2.59-3.96) | 0.187-0.250 (4.75-6.35) |
|---|---|---|---|---|---|---|
| | | Maximum Punched-Hole Tolerance, in. (mm) | | | | |
| 0.125-0.141 (3.17-3.58) | 1/8 to 9/64 (3.2 to 3.6) | +0.002 (0.05) | | | | |
| 0.144-0.228 (3.66-5.79) | No. 27 to No. 1 (3.6 to 5.8) | +0.003 (0.08) | +0.006 (0.15) | +0.008 (0.20) | +0.011 (0.28) | |
| | | | -0.001 (0.03) | -0.002 (0.05) | -0.003 (0.08) | |
| 0.234-0.413 (5.94-10.49) | 15/64 to Z (6.0 to 10.5) | +0.004 (0.10) | | | | +0.021 (0.53) -0.003 (0.08) |
| 0.422-0.688 (10.72-17.48) | 27/64 to 11/16 (10.7 to 17.5) | +0.006 (0.15) | | | | |
| 0.703-0.984 (17.86-24.99) | 45/64 to 63/64 (17.9 to 25.0) | +0.009 (0.23) | +0.009 (0.23) | | | |
| 1.000 and up (25.40) | 1 and up (25.4) | +0.010 (0.25) | +0.010 (0.25) | +0.010 (0.25) | | |

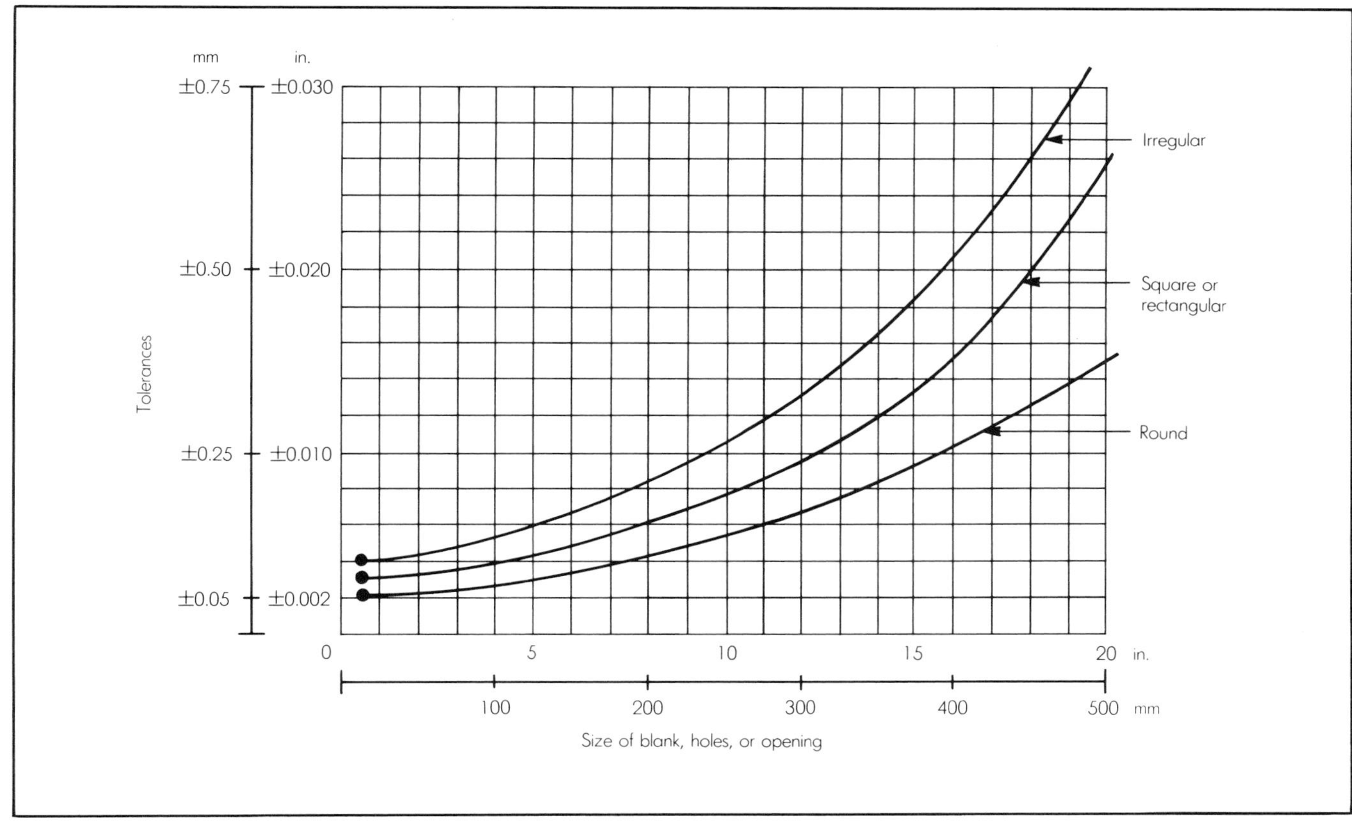


**Fig. 4-72 Tolerances for various types and sizes of blanks.**

# TOLERANCES FOR STAMPING

**TABLE 4-14**
**Blanking and Piercing Tolerances**

| Material Thickness, in. (mm) | Size of Blanked or Pierced Opening: Up to 3″ (76 mm) wide | Over 3″, up to 8″ (203 mm) wide | Over 8″, up to 24″ (610) mm wide |
|---|---|---|---|
| | Tolerance*, in. (mm) | | |
| 0.025 (0.63) | 0.003 (0.08) | 0.005 (0.13) | 0.008 (0.20) |
| 0.030 (0.76) | 0.003 (0.08) | 0.006 (0.15) | 0.010 (0.25) |
| 0.060 (1.52) | 0.004 (0.10) | 0.008 (0.20) | 0.012 (0.30) |
| 0.084 (2.13) | 0.005 (0.13) | 0.009 (0.23) | 0.014 (0.36) |
| 0.125 (3.17) | 0.006 (0.15) | 0.010 (0.25) | 0.016 (0.41) |
| 0.187 (4.75) | 0.010 (0.25) | 0.016 (0.41) | 0.025 (0.63) |
| 0.250 (6.35) | 0.015 (0.38) | 0.020 (0.51) | 0.035 (0.89) |

* All tolerances are plus for blanking and minus for piercing.

## Incomplete Blanks

In the case of incomplete blanks, the tolerances must be increased as follows because of the inherent lower accuracy of production techniques:

1. For parting short lengths up to 6″ (152 mm): ±0.005 to ±0.008″ (0.13 to 0.20 mm).
2. For parting long stampings: ±0.010 to ±0.015″ (0.25 to 0.38 mm).
3. For cutting off light-gage, short lengths: ±0.015″ (0.38 mm).
4. For cutting off light-gage, long parts: ±0.030″ (0.76 mm).
5. For cutting off heavy-gage, short lengths: ±0.025″ (0.64 mm).
6. For cutting off heavy-gage, long parts: ±0.040″ (1.02 mm).

Width tolerances for both parting and cutting-off correspond to commercial tolerances for slitting strips and coils. Concentricity is the relationship of one dimension to another. Tolerances on concentricity should be specified only if necessary for correct functioning. Commercial radius concentricity tolerances are ±0.010 to ±0.020″ (0.25 to 0.51 mm).

## Burr Height

Burr height limits should be specified only if the function of the part demands it. Removal of burrs or removal of sharp edges should be avoided because of the additional expense.

## FORMED STAMPINGS

Tolerances are restrictive specifications and should be made only as close as necessary in the functioning of the stamped part. Unnecessarily close tolerances increase tool and production costs, lower the die life, and may make up to 100% inspection mandatory.

### Press Brake Formed

The average dimensional tolerances in workpieces formed in press brakes are:

1. For regular small parts: ±0.030″ (0.76 mm).
2. For large and complicated shapes: ±0.060″ (1.52 mm) or more.

### Die Formed

The average dimensional tolerances in workpieces formed in dies are:

1. For small workpieces or for portions of work: ±0.010″ (0.25 mm).
2. For off-sets (see Fig. 4-73): ±0.010″ (0.25 mm).
3. For channel forming (see Fig. 4-74): tolerances on dimensions *A* and *B* can be held within 0.020″ (0.25 mm).
4. For angles, specify tolerances in degrees, not in straight dimensions. Usual tolerance limits are ±1°, except when one leg is shorter than 1″ (25 mm); then the tolerances are ±2°.
5. For internal bending radii, specify liberal tolerances: ±0.010″ (0.25 mm) for R < 0.060″ (1.52 mm) and ±0.020″ (0.51 mm) for R > 0.060″ (1.52 mm).

### Drawn Shells

No standard, customary tolerance values are available for drawn shells. Every plant has its own standards. In establishing such tolerances for drawn shells, the following points should be considered:

1. Wall thickness of drawn shells deviates from bottom thickness; some portions are thinner and some portions are thicker.
2. Do not specify both outside diameter and inside diameter with close tolerances—only one of them can be reasonably held.

### Stock Thickness

The standard thickness tolerances given by sheet metal manufacturers range from about 10-20%. These allowed thickness variations prohibit close tolerance limits on form and shapes. Figure 4-75 illustrates how thickness variations influence accuracy of formed stamping shapes.

In channel forming (see Fig. 4-75), the clearance between the punch and the female die cavity, $\alpha$, must be accurately estimated for the highest thickness value. Consequently, the bending angle will be different depending on whether the stock is at the high or low limit of commercial tolerance. These guidelines should be kept in mind when specifying tolerance limits for formed parts.

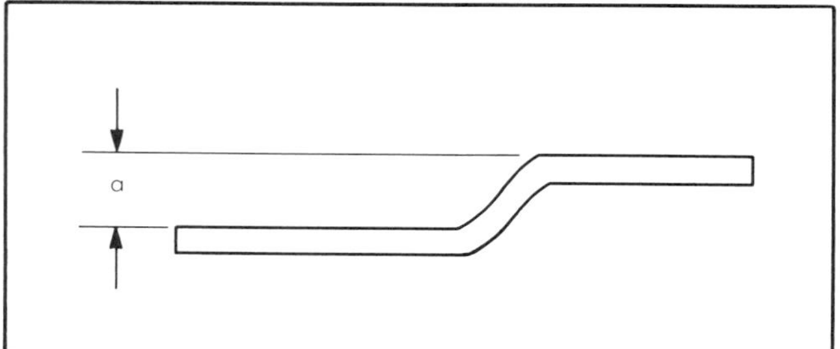


**Fig. 4-73 For a die-formed offset, the dimensional tolerance is ±0.010″ (0.25 mm).**

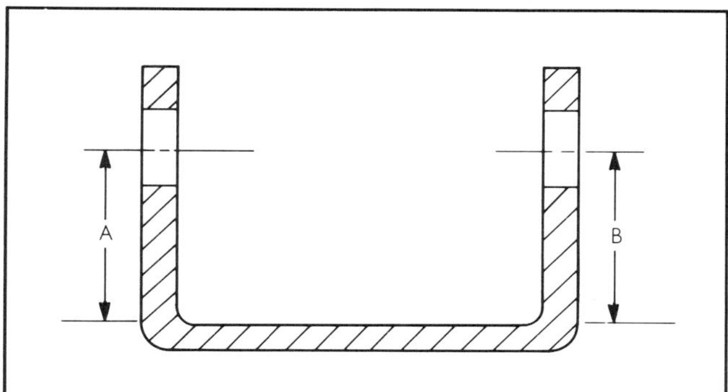


**Fig. 4-74 For die-formed channels, tolerances on dimension *A* can be held within 0.020″ (0.25 mm).**

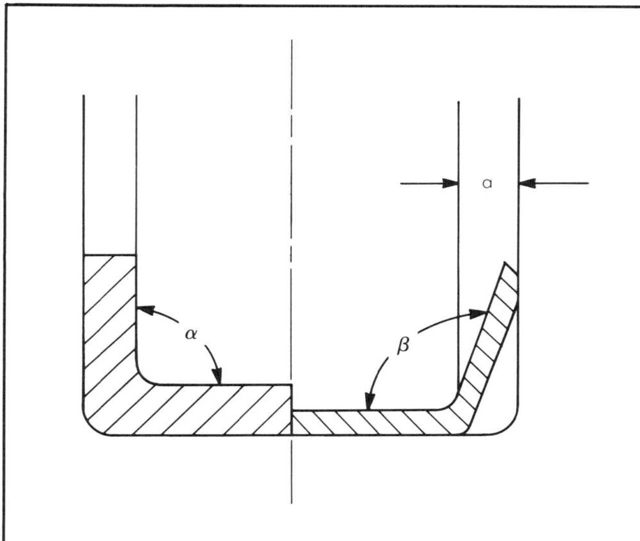


**Fig. 4-75 Sheet metal thickness variations influence the accuracy of formed stamping shapes.**

## HIGH-VOLUME PRODUCTION

The piece-part design function is not normally based upon the method of manufacturing. The designed part is usually concerned with interchangeability in mass production, and with a fit relationship with mating parts.

The part design does not predetermine how the part is to be produced; the drawing shows the end product and all information needed to manufacture it. The die design, in turn, derives tooling tolerances from the part design. Standard tooling tolerances are based on company or industry standards, and are supported by a background of manufacturing experience. In general terms, tolerances are concerned with physical size or features on a part, or with geometric characteristics of the features.

### Geometric Tolerancing

A sophisticated system that provides complete coverage of standard practices for dimensioning of sizes and geometric characteristics is given in the American National Standard ANSI Y14.5-1982, "Geometric Dimensioning and Tolerancing" (which includes metrication).

While most widely used for design, tooling, and production of machined parts, Standard Y14.5 is applicable to all manufacturing processes, including stamping. Currently, there is increasing recognition and growing application of geometric dimensioning and tolerancing principles and practices to high-volume production of sheet metal stampings ranging in size and complexity from small brackets to large panels for automobile bodies.

### Typical Applications

**Hole patterns**. The choice of manufacturing methods, and the decision as to whether to produce a part as a stamping or a casting, or to machine it from raw stock, depends upon the design, materials, quantity to be produced, and other factors. Regardless of the production method, tolerances related to function, interchangeability, and mating between adjacent parts are important. Hole patterns in parts typify the criticality of tolerances.

*Datum*. On engineering drawings using geometric dimensioning and tolerancing practices, datums are points, lines, planes, cylinders, and other shapes that are assumed to be exact for purposes of computation. The precise location and geometric relationship (form) of various part features are established by direct reference to the datums. Geometric tolerancing using positional tolerancing and datum references may be needed to assure the kinds of stamped parts the manufacturing engineer is required to produce at acceptable levels of quality and cost.

Figure 4-76 shows a simple part that can be used for illustrative purposes. The die design derives tolerance specifications from the part drawing. The making of the die, blank layout, etc., are assisted by geometric dimensioning and tolerancing methods because of the specific "part function" information conveyed by these engineering drafting practices. In addition, these practices are compatible with normal toolmaking standards, where punches are sized toward the high hole size limit for wear, sharpening, and shear action with the taper on the punches.

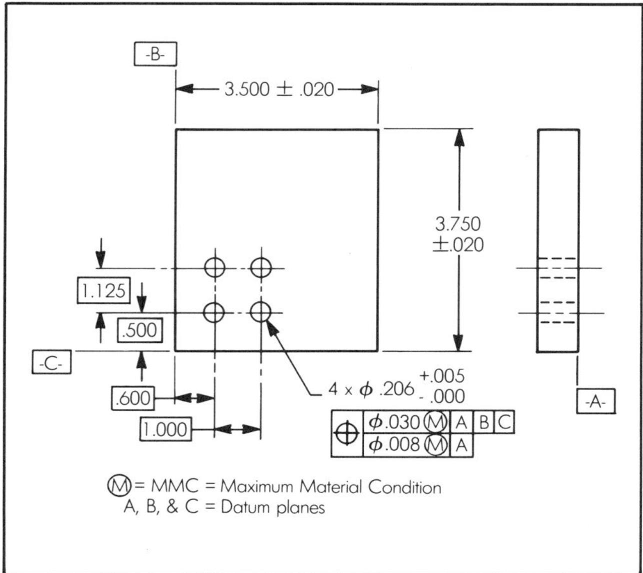


**Fig. 4-76 This simple part drawing with drilled holes illustrates the application of geometric dimensioning, position tolerancing, and datum references.**

# TOLERANCES FOR STAMPING

*Positional tolerance*. This procedure utilizes the "maximum material condition" that is shown on the drawing in Fig. 4-76. The finished parts gain positional tolerance, since any departure from the maximum material size (low size limit) of the hole is a one-on-one increase in hole location (positional) tolerance. Verification of such parts is aided by the specific requirements, and functional gaging may be used. In such application, using geometric tolerancing methods, the toolmaking is facilitated and greater tool life is attained due to increased piece-part working tolerances.

**Contours**. Another application in which geometric tolerancing is useful in producing sheet metal or stamped parts is profile tolerancing for defining odd shapes or contours. For example, if the part shown in Fig. 4-77 were defined with conventional plus or minus tolerancing, layout of all allowable variations would show that the contour allowed by the tolerance

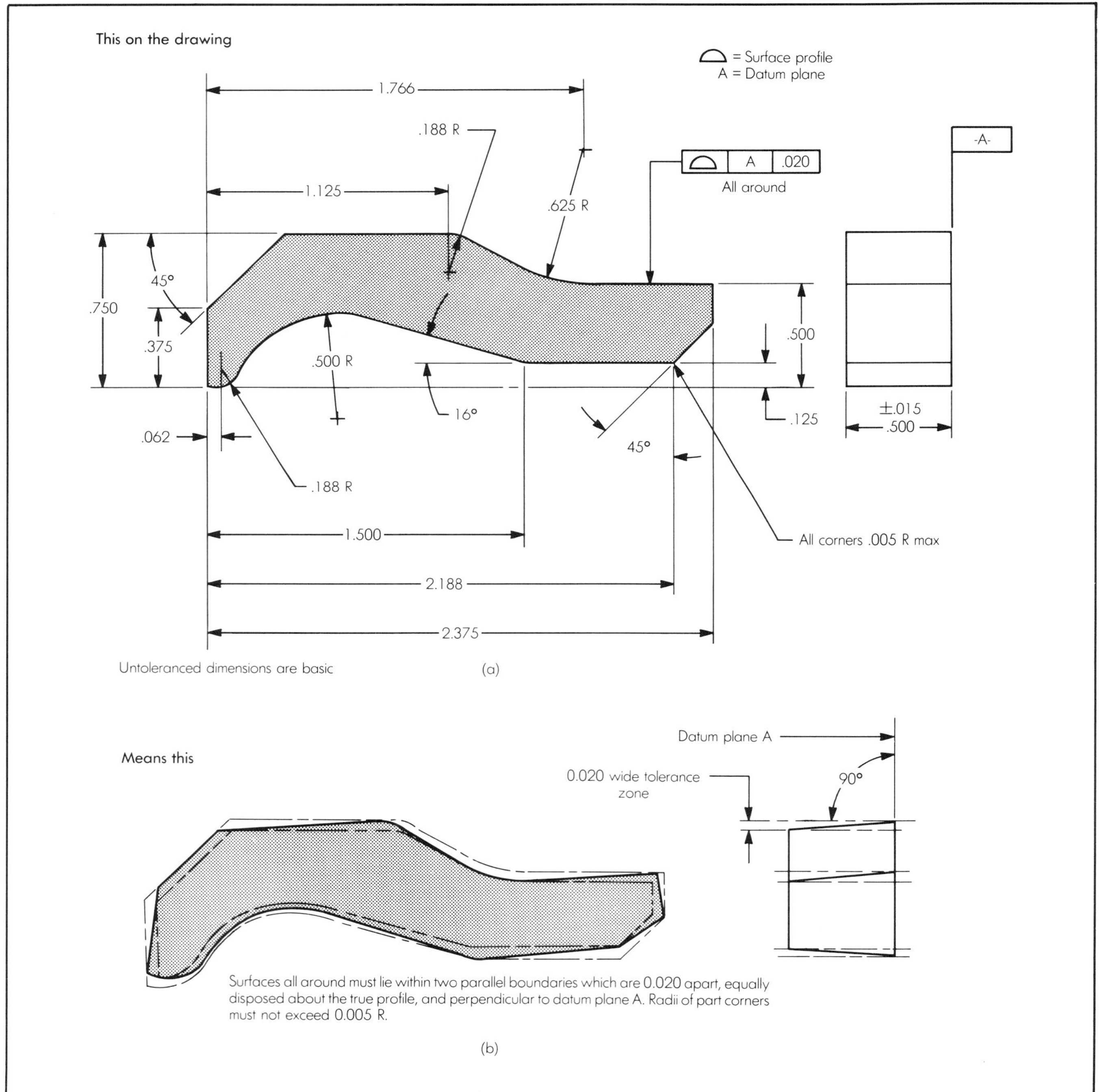


**Fig. 4-77 Illustration of profile tolerancing, to specify the profile of a complete surface. View *a* shows application of a feature control symbol to the part surface; view *b* depicts the intended interpretation of the profile tolerance control specification.**

would not deviate uniformly. In some areas the tolerance would allow the part to vary substantially; and in other areas, the part would have little tolerance. In some parts, it may be desirable to allow this condition. However, in most cases, the part must deviate from an exact shape in a uniform manner.

*Profile tolerance.* If this is a requirement, a profile tolerance may be applied. First, this would require the part to be defined in basic or exact dimensions. This definition or designation may be accomplished by placing a box around dimensions that must be exact, or by adding a suitable note. A feature control symbol with the profile tolerance may then be applied to the surface as shown in Fig. 4-77, view *a*. This would require all elements of the surface to fall within the specified tolerance zone as indicated in the feature control symbol. In Fig. 4-77, the interpretation of the application in view *a* is shown in view *b*.

*Tolerance location.* Profile tolerancing may be applied in a bilateral or unilateral manner. If the tolerance zone is to be equally disposed about the basic lines, the arrow is pointed directly at the surface as shown in Fig. 4-78, view *a*. If the tolerance zone is to be either to the inside or to the outside of the basic line, the direction of the tolerance zone should be indicated with a phantom line as shown in views *b* and *c*.

In some cases, it may be desirable to have the tolerance vary on different parts of the contour. This may be accomplished by identifying points and using feature control symbols with different tolerances between the different points. Profile tolerancing may be applied to the entire surface or to the elements of a surface. Datums are also often used in conjunction with profile tolerancing to ensure function and interchangeability.[15]

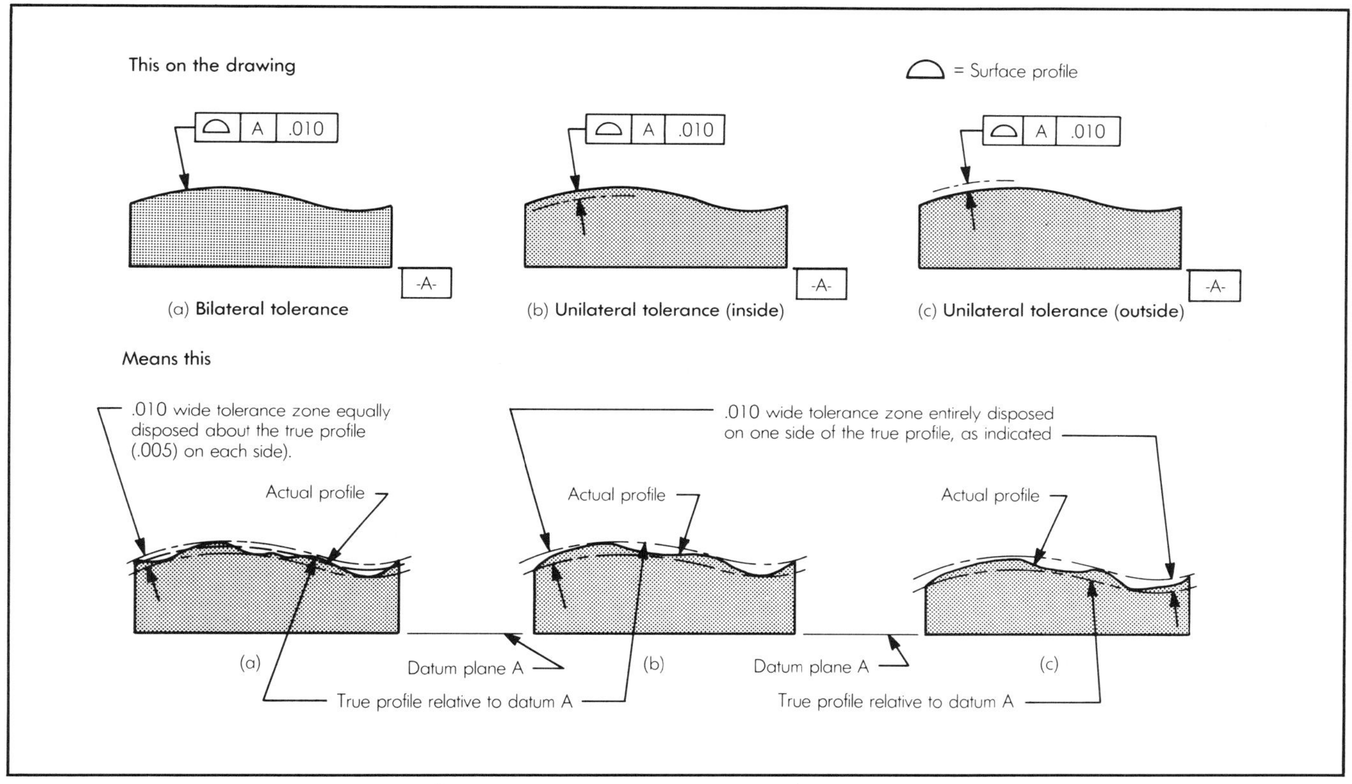


**Fig. 4-78 Application of a "profile of a surface" tolerance to a basic contour. Views *a*, *b*, and *c* represent bilateral and unilateral profile tolerancing.**

### References

1. Frederico Strasser, *Functional Design of Metal Stampings*, Dearborn, MI: Society of Manufacturing Engineers, 1971.
2. *Bliss Power Press Handbook*, Toledo: E. W. Bliss Co., 1950.
3. Frank W. Wilson, *Die Design Handbook*, 2nd ed., New York: McGraw-Hill Book Co. and Society of Manufacturing Engineers, 1965.
4. Donald F. Eary and Edward A. Reed, *Techniques of Pressworking Sheet Metal*, 2nd ed., Englewood Cliffs, NJ: Prentice-Hall Inc., 1974.
5. Harding R. Hugo, *How to Improve Stamping Die Performance*, Cleveland: Society of Manufacturing Engineers, 1979.
6. Ted F. Brolund, *Punching and Shearing Science*, Paper No. 100C, W. A. Whitney Corp. Training Center, Rockford, IL.
7. *Ibid.*
8. Brolund, *op. cit.*
9. Daniel B. Dallas, "Metricating the Pressworking Equations," *Manufacturing Engineering* (February 1976).
10. *Fine-Blanking Practical Handbook*, Hallwag AG, Bern, Switzerland: Feintool AG, Lyss.
11. Wilson, *op. cit.*
12. Daniel B. Dallas, "Metricating the Pressworking Equations," *Manufacturing Engineering* (March 1976).
13. "Computations for Metal Working in Presses," Catalog 960, E. W. Bliss Div., Gulf and Western Manufacturing Co., Salem, OH, 1977.
14. Karl A. Keyes, Editor, *Pressworking: Stampings and Dies*, Dearborn, MI: Society of Manufacturing Engineers, 1980.
15. American National Standard Institute, *Dimensioning and Tolerancing*, ANSI Y14.5-1982, American Society of Mechanical Engineers, New York, 1983.

# BIBLIOGRAPHY

## Bibliography


Adams, D. G.; Kasper, A. S.; Kurajian, G. M. *The Effects of Mechanical Properties on the Elastic Recovery of Biaxially Stretched Panels*. SME Technical Report MFR75-07, 1975.

Curry, David T. "Taking Sheet Metal to the Limit." *Machine Design* (February 22, 1979), pp. 170-174.

Dallas, Daniel B. *Pressworking Aids (metric and inch) for Designers and Diemakers*. Dearborn, MI: Society of Manufacturing Engineers, 1978.

Industrial Perforators Association. *Designers, Specifiers, and Buyers Handbook for Perforated Metals*. Milwaukee, 1981.

*Fineblanking: Principles, Design, Advantages*. E. R. Wagner Manufacturing Co., Milwaukee.

Ford, Martin G. *Fine Blanking Tools and Die Design*. SME Technical Paper MF72-105, 1972.

"Fundamentals of Fineblanking." *American Machinist*, Special Report 713, "Metalforming." (July 1979), pp. 103-122.

"Fundamentals of Stamping." *Precision Metal* (May 1982), pp. 31-36.

Gettelman, Ken. "Where is High-Speed Stamping Today?" *Modern Machine Shop* (January 1982), pp. 58-64.

Granzow, Wayne G. *The Effect of Mechanical Properties on the Formability of Low Carbon Steel Sheets*. SME Technical Paper EM75-371, 1975.

*How to Design Metal Stampings*. Dayton Rogers Mfg. Co., Minneapolis, 1980.

Juchler, Hugo. "Fineblanking Gets Down to the Wire." *Tooling and Production* (April 1982), pp. 80-84.

Lundy, Wilson T. *The Efficient Production of Part Blanks via Computer-Aided Manufacturing*. Paper presented at FabTech International, Society of Manufacturing Engineers and the Fabricating Manufacturers Association, 1981.

Machover, Carl, and Blauth, Robert E. *The CAD/CAM Handbook*. Computervision Corp., Bedford, MA, 1980.

*Metal and Ceramics*. CAB Current Awareness Bulletin. Battelle Columbus Laboratories, Columbus, OH, May 22, 1981.

Newby, J. R. "Formability Fundamentals," *Sheet Metal Industries* (November 1978), pp. 1182-1191.

"Notched Laminations by CNC." *American Machinist* (August 1982), pp. 125-127.

Paslay, Paul R. *Mechanisms Involved in Metal Forming*. SME Technical Paper EM75-372, 1975.

National Association of Punch Manufacturers. *Perforating Technology: The Hole Story*. Pivot Punch Corp. Lockport, NY.

Rizzo, Russ J. "How to Stamp Chalky Metals." *Modern Machine Shop* (September 1981), pp. 96-99.

Wenner, Michael L. *On Work Hardening and Springback in Plane Strain Draw Forming*. Research Publication GMR-3645. General Motors Research Laboratories, Warren, MI, 1981.

Wick, Charles. "Deep Drawing the HSLA Steels." *Manufacturing Engineering* (January 1975), pp. 30-31.

__________. "Fine Blanking ½ inch Coil Stock." *Manufacturing Engineering* (May 1978), pp. 50-53.

__________. "Heavy Metal Stamping." *Manufacturing Engineering* (August 1977), pp. 50-52.

CHAPTER

# 5

# Presses for Sheet Metal Forming

# PRESSES FOR SHEET METAL FORMING

Presses are powered machines having stationary beds and slides (rams) which have controlled reciprocating motions toward and away from the beds, guided by their frames. They supply energy to press-mounted dies that form and cut materials.

Presses discussed in this chapter are used to form and cut (blank, trim, punch, etc.) sheet metal, and in some cases, thicker materials such as plates. Presses used for different processes are described in other chapters of this volume.

CHAPTER CONTENTS:



## PRESS NOMENCLATURE

The following glossary of terms commonly used in the press, die, and stamping industries to describe presses and their parts and characteristics is adapted from ANSI Standard B5.49[1], the *Bliss Power Press Handbook*[2], and the *Die Design Handbook*[3]:

**accumulator, hydraulic** A device for storing fluid under pressure as a source of energy.

**adjustable bed** The bed or table of a gap-frame press, such as a horn press, which is bolted to the vertical front surface of the press. It is supported and adjusted (up and down) by means of a screw or screws usually operated by hand. This term also refers to the bed of a large straight-side press mounted and guided in the press frame and provided with a suitable mechanism, usually power operated, for varying the die space shutheight. Adjustable-bed presses are also referred to as knee-type presses.

**adjustable stroke** The capability of varying length of stroke on a press.

**adjustment, slide** The distance that a press slide position can be altered to change the shutheight of the die space. The adjustment may be by hand or by power mechanism.

**automatic press stop** A machine-generated signal for stopping the action of a press, usually after a complete cycle, by disengaging the clutch mechanism and engaging the brake mechanism.

**bed, press** The stationary part of the press serving as a table to which is affixed the bolster, or sometimes, the lower die directly.

**blankholder slide** The outer slide of a multiple-action press. It is usually operated by toggles or cams.

**bolster plate** A plate attached to the top of the press bed for locating and suppporting the die assembly. It usually has holes or T-slots for attaching the lower die or die shoe. Moving bolster plates are self powered for transferring dies in and out of the press for die setting. Also called rolling bolsters, they may be integral with or mounted to a carriage. They are not to be confused with sliding bolsters, the purpose of which is moving the lower die in and out of the press for workpiece feeding.

**capacity, press** The rated force that a press is designed to exert at a predetermined distance above the bottom of the stroke of the slide.

**closed height** *See* shutheight.

**clutch** A coupling mechanism used on a mechanical press to couple the flywheel to the crankshaft, either directly or through a gear train. (Note: Types of clutches are discussed subsequently in this chapter.)

**connection** A connecting member to convey motion and force from an orbiting member to a slide or lever. Also called the pitman, connecting link, or eccentric strap.

**crown** The upper part (head) of a press frame. On hydraulic presses, the crown usually contains the cylinder; on mechanical presses, the crown contains the drive mechanism.

**cushion, die** An accessory for a press which provides a resistive force with motion required for some operations, such as blankholding, drawing or redrawing, maintaining uniform pressure on a workpiece, and knocking out or stripping. Also called pads or jacks. Although usually mounted in or under the press bed, they are also used in or on the slide. (Note: Types of cushions are discussed subsequently in this chapter.)

**daylight** *See* shutheight.

**deflection** The amount of the deviation from a straight line or plane when a force is applied to

***Contributors of sections of this chapter are:*** *James W. Bowman, Director of Marketing, Pacific Press & Shear Co.; M. F. Einecker, Staff Electrical Engineer, Danly Machine Corp.; Jerome B. Pfeffer, Manager—Quintus Department, ASEA Pressure Systems Inc.; Robert Soman, P.E., Consulting Engineer.*

***Reviewers of sections of this chapter are:*** *Rune Adolfsson, Technical Department, Metallurgical Industries Div., ASEA; John Augustyniak, Director of Engineering, Pneu Power Press Corp.; Roland J. Bergman, Vice President—Marketing, Tranemo Corp.; James W. Bowman, Director of Marketing, Pacific Press & Shear Co.; Fred R. Brown, Sales Manager, F. J. Littell Machine Co.; Romeo Couture, Engineering, Greenerd Press & Machine Co.; A. Cristofano, Manager of Hydraulic Engineering, Verson Allsteel Press Co.; Reeve W. Dean, Assistant to the President, Niagara Machine & Tool Works; Kurt Diekmann, Product Sales Manager, Metal Forming Div., Waterbury Farrel Div., Textron Inc.; Edward Dunbar, General Sales Manager, U.S. Baird Corp.;*

# CHAPTER 5

## PRESS NOMENCLATURE

a press member. Generally used to specify allowable bending of bed, slide, or frame at rated capacity with load of predetermined distribution.

**die space** The maximum space (volume) or any part of the maximum space within a press for mounting a die.

**drag-link motion** *See* quick-return motion.

**dwell** A portion of the press cycle during which the movement of a member is zero or at least insignificant. Usually refers to the interval when the blankholder in a drawing operation is holding the blank while the punch is making the draw.

**eccentric gear** A main press-drive gear with an eccentric(s) as an integral part. The unit rotates about a common shaft with the eccentric transmitting the rotary motion of the gear into vertical motion of the slide through a connection.

**eccentric shaft** A crank with a crankpin of such size that it contains or surrounds the shaft. The eccentric, with its connection, is used in the eccentric press and is also used for driving auxiliary attachments, such as liftouts and feeds.

**effective draw** The maximum limits of forming depth which can be accomplished with multiple-action presses. As shown on a motion diagram for a typical double action or the upper action of a triple-action press, effective draw is the distance the inner slide is from the bottom of its stroke at the point at which the outer slide begins its dwell. For the lower action of a triple-action press, it is the distance the lower slide is from the top of its stroke when the inner slide begins its dwell—sometimes called maximum draw or maximum depth of draw.

**energy curve** A graphical representation to show available flywheel energy as a function of stroke rate on a variable-speed press.

**ejector** *See* knockout.

**feeds** Various devices that move stock or workpieces to, in, or from a die. (Note: Types of feeds are discussed subsequently in this chapter.)

**flywheel** A heavy, rotating wheel, attached to a shaft, whose principal purpose is to store kinetic energy during the nonworking portion of the press cycle and to release energy during the working portion of the press cycle.

**frame** The main structure of a press.

**gibs** Guides or shoes which ensure the proper parallelism, squareness, and sliding fit between press components such as the slide and frame. They are usually adjustable to compensate for wear and to establish operating clearance.

**Guerin process** A rubber-pad forming process discussed subsequently in this chapter.

**inner slide** The slide of any double or triple-action press upon which the punch is mounted.

**JIC** Joint Industry Conference.

**knee** *See* adjustable bed.

**knockout** A mechanism for releasing workpieces from a die; also called ejector, kickout, or liftout. Crossbars, cams, springs, or air cushions are commonly used to actuate slide knockouts.

**liftout** *See* knockout.

**load, press** Amount of force exerted in a given operation.

**lower slide** The third slide on a triple-action press; also called the third action.

**motion diagram** A graph or curve which shows the motion of a slide relative to the motion of the driving member, such as the rotation of a crank. It may also show slide velocity and/or acceleration. For a multiple-action press, the motion diagram shows the relative motion and position between the slides.

**overload relief device** A mechanism designed to relieve overloads to structural members of the press and/or tooling. The devices can be mechanical, hydropneumatic, or hydraulic and can be located in the slide, connections, bed, or tie rods. These devices have limited strokes, often less than 1" (25.4 mm) of travel.

**pitman** *See* connection.

**platen** The sliding member, slide, or ram of a hydraulic press.

**plunger** *See* inner slide.

**pneumatic toggle links** Special main links of a toggle press which are equipped with pneumatic cushions and a linkage to give air pressure controlled flexibility. These links compensate for variations in material thickness under the blankholder and also can be adjusted to exert different pressures at different corners of the blankholder.

**prefill valve** A pressure-actuated valve required for controlling the prefilling (or exhausting) of oil during the fast traverse operation of the hydraulic press ram cylinder.

**press** A machine having a stationary bed and a slide (ram) which has a controlled reciprocating motion toward and away from the bed surface and at a right angle to it, the slide being guided in the frame of the machine to give a definite path of motion.

*arbor* A manual or power-operated press used to force arbors or mandrels into or out of holes and for similar assembly or disassembly operations.

*arch* A small crank press having its columns or uprights curved or arched outward to permit a wider bed and wider slide flange, left to right between the columns, or to permit a longer stroke length.

*automatic* A press in which the work, either separate parts or strip or sheet stock, is fed through the press in synchronism with the press operating cycle and by means other than manual.

*bench* Any small press of a size to be mounted on a bench or table. These presses are almost always gap frame and may be fixed or inclinable.

*bottom drive* Any press with the drive mechanism located

---

*__Reviewers, cont.__: M. F. Einecker, Staff Electrical Engineer, Danly Machine Corp.; Erik R. Enberg, Marketing Manager, Perfecto Industries, Inc.; Engineering Dept., E. W. Bliss Div., Gulf & Western Manufacturing Co.; Engineering Dept., The Minster Machine Co.; Edward Freeland, Manager—Product Liability, E. W. Bliss Div., Gulf & Western Manufacturing Co.; Robert W. Gardner, Chief Engineer, Hydraulic Presses, Schuler Inc.; Gordon A. Gettum, Vice President Engineering, Niagara Machine & Tool Works; Hans Grill, Manager Engineering & Development, Schuler Inc.; Walter C. Johnson, Vice President/Marketing, Verson Allsteel Press Co.; Robert H. Kemp, P. E., Chief Engineer, L & J Press Corp.; Floyd Kunce, Oak Products, Inc.; Werner K. Lehmann, President, SESCO, Inc.; D. K. Jim Loukidis, Vice President—Engineering Sales, Famco Machine Div., Belco Industries, Inc.; Robert G. Lown, Vice President, Greenerd Press & Machine Co.; Robert P. Mallia, General Sales Manager, Cooper—Weymouth, Peterson, Div. of Reed National Corp.; V. J. Mankowsky, Vice President—Sales Engineering, Clearing, A Div. of U.S. Industries, Inc.; T. E. Marquardt, General Manager, Industrial Machinery Div., Komatsu America Corp.; Ronald G. Mason, Manager—Coil Processing Equipment, Niagara Machine & Tool Works; Roger T. Miller, National Sales Manager, Lauffer Presses Inc.; R. B. Omo, Chief Design Engineer, Cleveland Punch & Shear, Sales Div. of Bath Iron Works Corp.;*

within or under the bed. Connections of the drive to slide or slides are within or alongside the uprights.
*bulldozer* A slow-acting horizontal press with a large bed used for bending, straightening, and other operations.
*C frame* A press having uprights or housing resembling the form of the letter C.
*cam* A mechanical press in which one or more of the slides are cam actuated.
*center drive* A geared press with the crankshaft driven from the center.
*crank* A press, the slide of which is actuated by a crankshaft or an eccentric shaft.
*dieing* A high-speed vertical press, the slide of which is actuated by pull rods extending to the drive mechanism below the bed.
*double action* A press having two independent, parallel movements by means of two slides, one slide moving within the other.
*double crank* A crank press in which the slide is driven by two connections attached to two cranks.
*eccentric* A mechanical press in which an eccentric is used to move the slide instead of a crankshaft.
*enclosed* A press having most of its operating parts enclosed within the frame, guards, and plates.
*endwheel* A gap-frame mechanical press with the flywheel at the back and the crankshaft or eccentric shaft located front to back.
*eyelet* A multiple-slide press usually employing a cut-and-carry or transfer feed for sequential operations in successive stations.
*fine blanking* A special triple-action press designed specifically for fine-blanking operations.
*flywheel* A mechanical press which has the flywheel mounted directly on the main crankshaft or eccentric shaft without gearing. Also called a plain or nongeared press.
*foot* A small press powered by foot pressure.
*four-point* A press whose slide is actuated by four connections.
*four-slide* A press (also called a multislide machine) equipped with a progressive die for automatically producing small, intricately shaped parts.
*front-to-back shaft* A mechanical press in which the main shaft and other driveshafts are positioned in a front-to-back direction.
*gap frame See* C frame.
*geared* A press whose main crank or eccentric is connected to the driving source by one or more sets of gears.
*high production* A specialized version of a mechanical press designed for high stroke rates. The frame is extra rigid; the drive may be nongeared or single geared and is almost always variable speed.
*horizontal* A press in which the slide moves horizontally.
*horn (horning)* A gap-frame press that has a straight front and is equipped with or arranged for a horn (a cantilever block or post which acts as the die or to which the die is fastened).
*hydraulic* A press having its slide (ram) actuated by a hydraulic cylinder and piston.
*inclinable* A press whose main frame may be tilted backward, usually 20-30°, to facilitate ejection of workpieces by gravity through an open back.
*inclined* A press having the frame built in a fixed, inclined position.
*knuckle joint* A press in which the slide is directly actuated by a single toggle (or knuckle) joint which is closed and opened by means of a connection and crank. It is generally a powerful, short-stroke press which has a slight dwell of the slide at the bottom of its stroke and is used for embossing, coining, sizing, heading, swaging, and extruding.
*left-to-right shaft* A press in which the main shaft and other driveshafts are positioned in a left-to-right direction.
*link drive (drag link)* A press in which the slide is driven by a linkage mechanism to optimize the time-motion characteristics.
*mechanical* A press having a slide or slides actuated by mechanical means.
*multiple slide (plunger)* (a) A press having individual slides (plungers) built into the main slide or (b) a press having more than one slide in which each slide has its own connections to the main shaft.
*notching* A press used for notching internal and external circumferences and also for notching along a straight line. These presses are generally equipped with automatic feeds or indexing mechanisms because only one notch is made per stroke. Loading and unloading of the workpieces can be done manually or automatically.
*OBI See* open-back inclinable.
*OBS See* open-back stationary.
*one-piece frame* A press having a frame that combines the bed, uprights, and crown into a single structure.
*one-point See* single-point.
*open-back* A gap press designed to facilitate feeding from front to back and ejecting from the back.
*open-back inclinable (OBI)* A gap-frame press that has an opening at the back between the two side members of the frame and is arranged to be inclinable to facilitate part feeding and removal by gravity.
*open-back stationary (OBS)* A gap-frame press that has an opening at the back between the two side members of the frame and is arranged to be upright or permanently inclined.

***Reviewers, cont.**: Stuart P. Opel, Marketing Assistant, Sick Optik—Elektronik, Inc.; Jerome B. Pfeffer, Manager Quintus Dept., ASEA Pressure Systems Inc.; Lloyd C. Pillsbury, Vice President, Wintriss Controls Group, Data Instruments Inc.; Edward A. Reed, Consultant, Chevrolet-Flint Manufacturing, General Motors Corp. (retired); John Reeves, President, Pneu Power Press Corp.; Charles G. Rezack, Marketing Manager, Hydraulic Press Equipment, Verson Allsteel Press Co.; James M. Rice, Allen-Bradley Co.; Heinz Roth, Vice President, Schmid Corporation of America; K. W. Salisbury, Engineering Manager, Air-Hydraulics, Inc.; Robert Soman, P.E., Consulting Engineer; L. W. Springer, Marketing Manager, Multipress Inc.; Ugo Tonon, District Sales Manager, Machine Div., Torin Corp.; Eugene J. Verret, Manager—Corporate Product Safety, Allen-Bradley Co.; Felix Wahrenberger, Vice President, Schmid Corporation of America; Courtney A. Warner, P.E., President, Metform International Ltd.; Bernard Wels, Division Manager—Safety and Automation Systems, Weldotron Corp.; Robert G. Whitesides, Vice President—Sales, Dake Division, JSJ Corp.; D. V. Wiberg, Supervisor—Plant & Equipment Engineering, A. O. Smith Corp.; Christopher Zeilenga, P.E., General Manager Product Reliability, Verson Allsteel Press Co.*

# PRESS NOMENCLATURE

*open-rod* A hydraulic press with vertical rods instead of uprights to guide the slide.
*oscillating-die* A small, high-speed press in which punch and die have reciprocating motion which coincides with the strip or coil motion during the working stroke. When the punch is clear of the work and stripper, the die and punch then move back to their original positions to begin the next stroke. The strip or coil has continuous motion.
*overhanging* A gap press in which the frame overhangs the bed.
*overhead drive See* top drive.
*perforating* A high-speed, straight-side, crank press usually furnished with a narrow slide, a slide stripper plate, and a special roll feed for progressively feeding sheet, strip, or coil stock to be perforated.
*power* A term used loosely to designate any press using electrical power as compared to manual power.
*punch (punching)* (a) A term used loosely to designate an OBI mechanical press or (b) an endwheel gap press of the fixed-bed type used commonly for piercing (punching) operations.
*reducing* A long-stroke, single-action, single-crank press for redrawing (reducing) and other operations on deep workpieces. Drive parts are of increased torque and energy capacity to provide for increased loading above the bottom of the stroke.
*rubber pad* A single-action hydraulic press having its slide equipped with a rubber pad for rubber-pad forming. (See Guerin process.)
*screw* A press whose slide or platen is operated by a screw instead of by a crank or other means. Screw presses may be either manually or power driven.
*single action* A press with a single slide.
*single-end drive* A press with the crankshaft or eccentric shaft driven from one end.
*single-piece frame See* one-piece frame.
*single point* A press with force applied to the slide through one connection. Usually refers to a single-crankshaft or single-eccentric-shaft press.
*solid frame See* one-piece frame.
*spotting (die spotter or tryout)* A press, usually of low capacity in relation to die area or die rating, employed for final finishing of dies to indicate (spot) inaccuracies and also to test mating and functioning of parts.
*straight side* A mechanical press with uprights or housings which have plain, flat sides (usually vertical) that bound or enclose the left and right sides of the die space. A straight-side hydraulic press is called a housing press.
*tie-rod frame* A straight-side press having a frame made up of bed, crown, and uprights held together by prestressed tie rods.
*toggle* (a) A mechanical press in which a slide or slides are actuated by one or more toggle joints; (b) a term applied to double and triple-action presses.
*toggle drawing* A press in which the outer or blankholder slide is actuated by a series of toggle joints and the inner slide is actuated by the crankshaft or eccentric shaft.
*top drive* A press with the drive mechanism above the slide.
*transfer* A press having an integral mechanism for transfer and control of the workpiece.
*trimming* A special-purpose press for shearing and trimming operations.
*triple action* A press having three independent, parallel movements by means of three slides, two from above and one from below the die space.
*twin-end drive* A geared press with the crankshaft or eccentric shaft driven from both ends.
*two-point* A press with force applied to the slide through two connections.
*underdrive See* bottom drive.
*watch (watchmaker's)* A small, endwheel gap press having a comparatively high die space to allow the use of sub-presses for accurate work.

**pressure attachment** *See* cushion.
**pressure curve** A graphical representation to show allowable press as a function of slide displacement during the working portion of the stroke.
**quick-return (drag-link) motion** A motion used on some types of mechanical presses to provide fast, upward travel of the slide, thus allowing faster stroking rates while maintaining slower downward motion for drawing and other operations.
**ram** *See* slide.
**riser block** Plates or pieces inserted between the top of a press bed and bolster or on the bolster to decrease the height of the die space. A one-piece riser with openings to register with the bed openings is called a ring riser or sub-bolster.
**shutheight** The distance from the top of the bed to the bottom of the slide of a vertical press, with stroke down and adjustment up. On moving bolster presses, the shutheight is measured from the top of the bolster (when the bolster is integral with the carriage) or the top of the carriage (when the bolster is separate).
**slide** The main reciprocating member of a press, guided in the press frame, to which the punch or upper die is fastened. Sometimes called the ram. The inner slide of a double-action press is called the plunger or punch-holder slide; the outer slide of a double-action press is called the blankholder slide; the third slide of a triple-action press is called the lower slide; and the slide of a hydraulic press is often called the platen.
**slide separation** The distance between the face of die-mounting surface of the inner slide and the outer slide of multiple-action presses at open position.
**stroke** The distance between the terminal points of the reciprocating motion of a press slide.
**strokes per minute (spm)** The specified continuous running speed of a press. It is not the number of permissible single trippings of a press and consequently does not measure the possible production per minute, except when a press is run continuously. The number of single trippings per minute varies with different types and makes of clutches as well as with the dexterity of the operator.
**table** *See* adjustable bed.
**throat (gap) depth** The distance from the slide centerline to the frame of a gap-frame press.
**throw** The distance from the centerline of the crankshaft or main shaft to the centerline of the crankpin or eccentric in crank or eccentric presses. Equal to one-half of the stroke.
**tie rods** Steel rods, threaded at both ends for nuts, used to prestress straight-side press frames. They are also used to reduce deflection in gap-frame presses, but require careful installation, as discussed later in this chapter.
**toggle joint** A connecting mechanism consisting of two links freely pinned together at one end and connected by free pins to other press parts at their other or outer ends.
**tonnage** *See* capacity, press.
**top stop** A machine-generated signal for stopping a press at the

top of a stroke (after each cycle).

**tripping mechanism** Any auxiliary mechanism, manually, mechanically, or automatically operated, which engages and disengages the clutch for starting and stopping the press.

**uniform stroke motion** A type of motion obtainable with a drag-link mechanism in which a fairly uniform slide speed is obtained during a large portion of the working stroke.

# TYPES OF PRESSES

Presses are classified by one or a combination of characteristics which include the source of power and the number of slides. Other classification methods, discussed in subsequent sections of this chapter, are the types of frames and construction, types of drive, and intended applications.

## SOURCE OF POWER

The source of power for press operation can be manual, mechanical, hydraulic, pneumatic, or pneumatic/hydraulic.

### Manual Presses

Manual presses are either hand or foot powered through levers, screws, or gears. The most common press of this type is the arbor press used for various assembly operations. These presses are often converted to power operation by the addition of air or hydraulic cylinders.

### Mechanical Presses

Mechanical presses utilize flywheel energy which is transferred to the workpiece by gears, cranks, eccentrics, or levers. As discussed in detail in a subsequent section of this chapter, mechanical presses can be nongeared or geared, with single or multiple-reduction gear drives, depending upon the press size and force requirements.

### Hydraulic Presses

Hydraulic presses provide working force through the application of fluid pressure on a piston by means of pumps, valves, intensifiers, and accumulators. While mechanical presses are still the predominant type in use, hydraulic presses are being increasingly applied because of their improved performance and reliability. The types of hydraulic presses, their construction and operation, and their advantages are discussed later in this chapter.

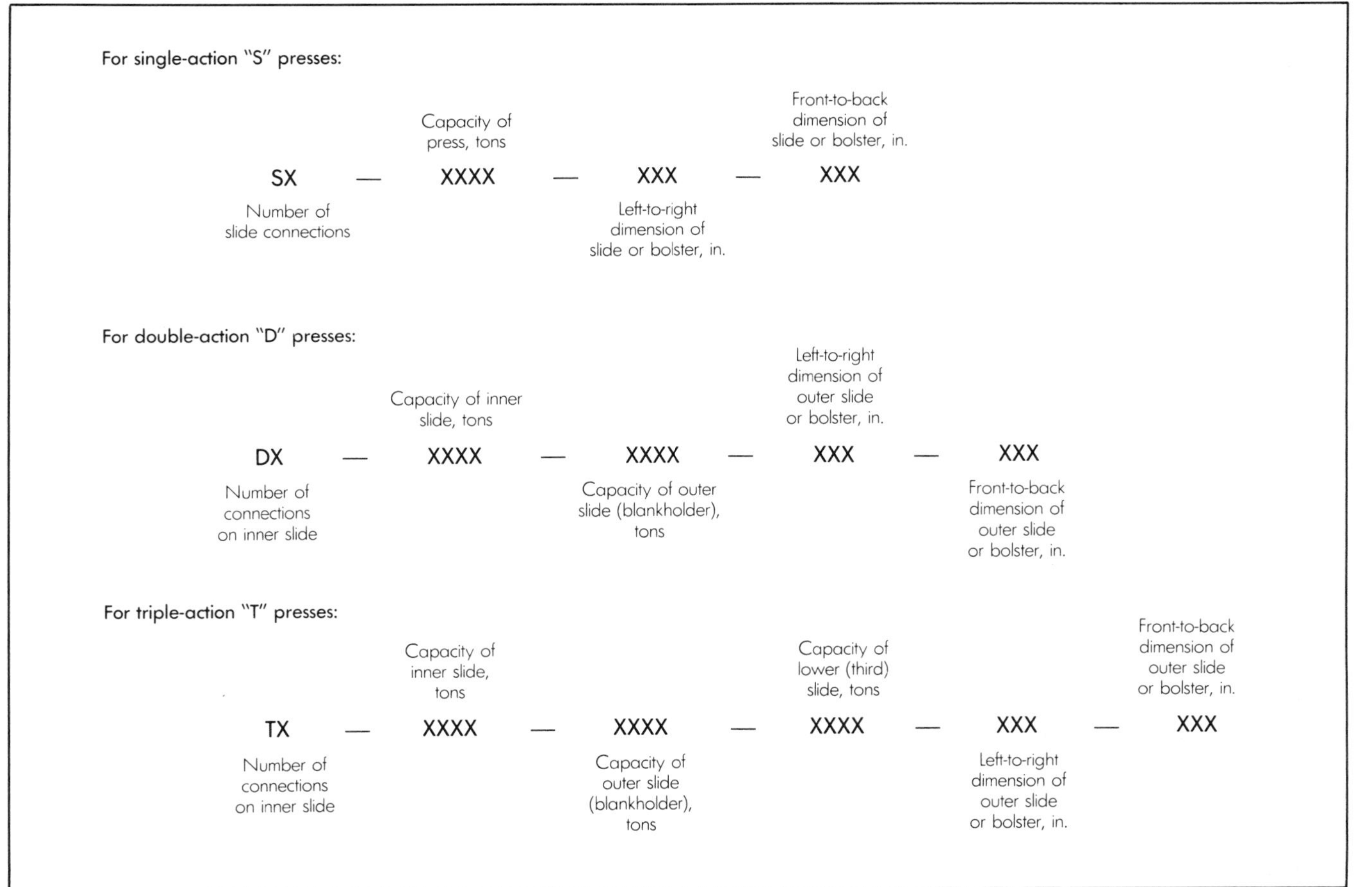


**Fig. 5-1 Designations used for press identification under JIC classification system.**

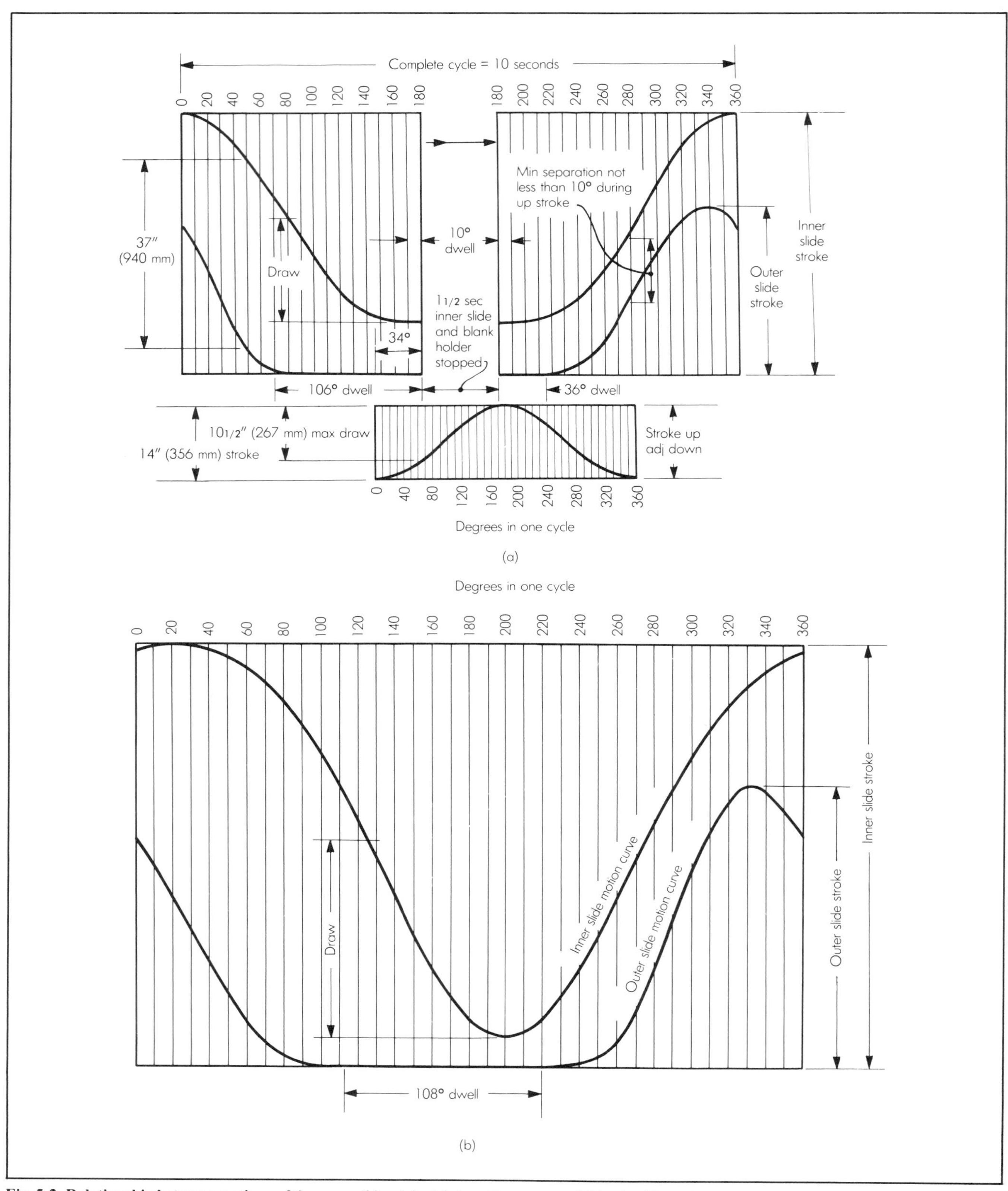


**Fig. 5-2 Relationship between motions of the press slides: (a) a triple-action press and (b) a double-action press.** (*Clearing, A Div. of U.S. Industries, Inc.*)

### Pneumatic Presses

Using air cylinders to exert the required force, pneumatic presses are usually smaller in size and capacity than mechanical or hydraulic presses. They are generally employed for lighter duty operations. Advantages include low cost, high speed, and minimum maintenance.

## NUMBER OF SLIDES

With respect to function, presses may be classified by the number of slides incorporated and are referred to as single, double, and triple-action presses. On multislide machines, each slide may use a common energy source or each may have a separate, independent power source.

The Joint Industry Conference (JIC), a committee of press builders and large-press users formed some years ago, set guidelines for uniformity with respect to nomenclature, bed and ram sizes, force ranges, and symbols for presses. Although JIC is not in existence today, most press builders adhere to the standards either completely or in part. Under the JIC press classification system with respect to the number of slides, the first letter in the designation is *S* for single-action, *D* for double-action, and *T* for triple-action presses. Other designations used for visible identification of presses suggested under the JIC classification system are given in Fig. 5-1. Most press builders place these markings at a prominent position on the fronts of the presses.

### Single-Action Presses

A single-action press has one reciprocating slide (tool carrier) acting against a fixed bed. Presses of this type, which are the most widely used, can be employed for many different metal stamping operations, including blanking, embossing, coining, and drawing. Depending upon the depth of draw, single-action presses often require the use of a die cushion for blankholding. In such applications, a blankholder ring is depressed by the slide (through pins) against the die cushion, usually mounted in the bed of the press. Die cushions are discussed later in this chapter.

### Double-Action Presses

A double-action press has two slides moving in the same direction against a fixed bed. These slides are generally referred to as the outer blankholder slide and the inner draw slide. The blankholder slide is a hollow rectangle, while the inner slide is a solid rectangle that reciprocates within the blankholder.

Double-action presses are more suitable for drawing operations, especially deep drawing, than single-action presses. In single-action presses, force is required to depress the cushion. In double-action presses, the blankholder slide has a shorter stroke and dwells at the bottom of its stroke, before the punch mounted on the inner slide contacts the work. As a result, practically the entire capacity of the press is available for drawing. Another advantage is that the four corners of the blankholder are individually adjustable so that nonuniform forces can be exerted on the work when required. A double-action press equipped with a die having an open bottom permits pushing the stamping through the die to perform other operations, such as ironing, after drawing.

Deep-draw operations and irregular-shaped stampings generally require the use of a double-action press. Most operations performed on double-action presses require a cushion either for liftout or reverse drawing of the stamping.

### Triple-Action Presses

A triple-action press has three moving slides, two slides moving in the same direction as in a double-action press and a third or lower slide moving upward through the fixed bed in a direction opposite to the blankholder and inner slides. This action permits reverse-drawing, forming, or beading operations against the inner slide while both upper actions are dwelling.

Cycle time for a triple-action press is necessarily longer than for a double-action press because of the time required for the third action. Since most drawn stampings require subsequent restriking and/or trimming operations, which are done in faster, single-action presses, most stamping manufacturers consider the triple-action press too slow.

### Relative Slide Motions

The relationship between the motions of the three slides of a triple-action press is shown in Fig. 5-2, view *a*. The relative motion of the slides on a double-action press (view *b*) is similar to the two curves in view *a* except that little or no dwelling occurs with the inner slide. The motion of the slide of a single-action press is similar to that of the inner slide of a double-action press.

# PRESS SELECTION

Proper selection of a press is essential for successful and economical operation. The purchase of a press represents a substantial capital investment, and return on investment depends upon how well the press performs the job required. No general-purpose press exists that can provide maximum productivity and economy for all applications. Compromises usually have to be made to permit a press to be employed for more than one job. Careful consideration should be given to both present and future production requirements.

Important factors influencing the selection of a press include size, force, energy, and speed requirements. The press must be capable of exerting force in the amount, location, and direction, as well as for the length of time, needed to perform the specified operation(s). Other considerations must include the size and geometry of the workpieces, operation(s) to be performed, number of workpieces to be produced, production rate needed, accuracy and finish requirements, equipment costs, and other factors.

## SIZE REQUIREMENTS

Bed and slide areas of the press must be large enough to accommodate the dies to be used and to provide space for die changing and maintenance. Space is required around the dies for accessories such as keepers, pads, cam return springs, and gages; it is also needed for attaching the dies to the press. Shutheight of the press, with adjustment, must also be suitable for the dies.

# PRESS SELECTION

Presses with as short a stroke as possible should be selected because they permit higher speed operation, thus increasing productivity. Stroke requirements, however, depend upon the height of the parts to be produced. Blanking can be done with short strokes, but some forming and drawing operations require long strokes, especially for ejection of the parts.

Size and type of press to be selected also depends upon the method and direction of feeding; the size of sheet, coil stock, blank, or workpiece to be formed; the type of operation; and the material being formed and its strength. Material or workpiece handling and die accessibility generally determine whether the press should be of gap-frame or straight-side construction (discussed later in this chapter) and whether it should be inclined or inclinable.

Physical size of a press can be misleading with respect to its capacity. Presses having the same force rating can vary considerably in size depending upon differences in length of stroke, pressing speed, and number of strokes per minute.

Force required to perform blanking and forming operations, as discussed in Chapter 4 of this volume, "Sheet Metal Blanking and Forming," determines the press capacity, expressed in tons or kilonewtons (kN). The position on the stroke at which the force is required and the length of stroke must be considered.

Mechanical presses are generally rated near the bottom of the stroke, as discussed later in this chapter. It is customary to provide the torque necessary to exert the rated press force at some given point above the bottom of the stroke, and capacity decreases above this point. Operations requiring force application higher in the stroke should be performed on presses with greater torque in their drives and more flywheel energy.

Energy or work (force times distance), expressed in inch-tons or joules (J), varies with the operation. Blanking and punching require the force to be exerted over only a short distance; drawing, forming, and other operations, over a longer distance. The major source of energy in mechanical presses is the flywheel, the energy varying with the size and speed of the flywheel. Energy available increases with the square of the flywheel speed.

Possible problems are minimized by selecting a press having the proper frame capacity, drive-motor rating, flywheel energy, and clutch torque capacity.

## PRESS SPEEDS

Press speed is a relative term that varies with the point of reference. Fast speeds are generally desirable, but they are limited by the operations performed, the distances above stroke bottoms where the forces must be applied, and the stroke lengths. High speed, however, is not necessarily the most efficient or productive. Size and configuration of the workpiece, the material from which it is made, die life, maintenance costs, and other factors must be considered to determine the highest production rate at the lowest cost per workpiece. A lower speed may be more economical because of possible longer production runs with less downtime.

### Speed Ranges

Simple blanking and shallow forming operations can be performed at high speeds. Mechanical presses have been built that operate to 2000 spm with 1" (25.4 mm) stroke, but applications at this maximum speed are rare. Speeds of 600-1400 spm are more common for blanking operations, and thick materials are often blanked at much slower speeds. For drawing operations, contact velocities are critical with respect to the workpiece material and presses are generally operated at slide speeds from 10-300 spm, with the slower speeds for longer stroke drawing operations.

### Requirements for High-Speed Operation

High-production presses that operate to about 200 spm generally do not require special dynamic balancing. Those operating from 200-600 spm, with force ratings of 25-400 tons (222-3558 kN), usually have crankshaft counterweighting to minimize vibration. Presses that operate at speeds over 600 spm, with force ratings generally less than 200 tons (1779 kN), are available with adjustable or fixed stroke lengths. Adjustable types have a maximum speed for each stroke length; fixed-stroke presses are dynamically balanced for the maximum speed. Many of these presses have equipoise balancing consisting of a counterreciprocating device to offset the main drive, compensating for both rotating and reciprocating unbalance.

All high-speed presses require rigid frames and beds to minimize deflection and increase shock-absorbing capabilities. Alignment of the slide to the bed of the press is critical and requires minimum-clearance gibbing or antifriction bearings. The presses are usually furnished with automatic recirculation systems to provide lubricant to all wear surfaces, with the systems interlocked with the press drives to stop the presses if the oil pressure falls below a safe limit.

Automatic, high-speed, accurate means for feeding and unloading the presses and fast, reliable safety systems are essential. Most high-speed presses are equipped with variable-speed motor drives. It is recommended that high-speed presses be mounted on inertia blocks or isolation mounts to isolate them from the plant foundation.

Mechanical presses that have been built to operate to speeds of 2000 spm, with force ratings to 50 tons (445 kN), have special drives, hydrostatic bearing systems, and a hydraulic bed lock to eliminate all clearances in shutheight adjustments. These presses are generally operating in the speed range of 1000-1400 spm for improved die performance and life, more consistent quality of the workpieces produced, easier material handling, and reduced power consumption.

### Limitations of High-Speed Operation

Press speeds above about 700 spm increase the amount of noise generated and may require the use of sound enclosures. High-speed operation also increases the amount of heat generated and decreases the shutheight because of stretching of the drive connections, but this can generally be controlled. Other possible limitations include decreased accuracy, repeatability, and die life.

## MECHANICAL VS. HYDRAULIC PRESSES

Mechanical presses are the most predominant type used for blanking, forming, and drawing of sheet metal, but hydraulic presses are being increasingly applied. There are applications for which hydraulic presses offer certain advantages, and in some cases, are the only machines that can be employed. For example, very high force requirements can only be met with hydraulic presses. A comparison of characteristics and preferred uses for both mechanical and hydraulic presses is presented in Table 5-1.

## PRESS SYSTEMS

Presses integrated with material-handling equipment, feeding and unloading devices, and other manufacturing equipment

**TABLE 5-1**
**Comparative Characteristics of Mechanical and Hydraulic Presses**

| Characteristic | Mechanical Presses | Hydraulic Presses |
|---|---|---|
| Force | Variable (depends upon slide position). | Relatively constant (does not depend upon slide position). |
| Stroke length | Limited. | Capable of long strokes (100" [2540 mm] or more). |
| Slide speed | Higher speed capability. Highest at mid-stroke. Can be variable. | Slower pressing speeds with rapid advance and retraction. Variable speeds uniform throughout stroke. |
| Capacity | About 6000 tons (53 MN) maximum practical. | 50,000 tons (445 MN) or more. |
| Control | Full stroke generally required before reversal. | Adjustable, can reverse slide at any position. |
| Preferred uses | Operations requiring maximum pressure near bottom of stroke. Cutting operations (blanking, shearing, piercing). Forming and drawing to depths of about 4" (100 mm). High-production applications. Progressive and transfer die operations. | Operations requiring steady pressure through-out stroke. Deep drawing. Die tryout. Flexible-die forming. Drawing irregular shaped parts. Straightening. Hubbing of mold and die cavities. Operations requiring high and variable forces. Operations requiring variable or partial strokes. |

for automated, synchronized operation are being used more extensively. The reasons include improved quality, increased productivity, lower costs, and reduced inventories. Press systems are not limited to high-production applications; the development of means for making quick die changes has increased their flexibility and made short runs economical. Improved controls, feeds, transfer devices, and unloaders, which are critical to the efficiency of press systems, are discussed later in this chapter.

### FASTER DIE CHANGING

Many methods have been developed to permit faster die changes. One method is to equip the press with a powered slide adjustment. Hydraulic or air cylinders can be mounted in the press bolster to serve as jacks for lifting dies free of the bolster; then a forklift truck can be used to change the dies rapidly. Bolsters can also be drilled and connected to a supply of compressed air so that air jets can be used to lift and support the dies. Bolsters of this design are sometimes referred to as floating bolsters.

Fast die-changing systems are available that employ universal mounting fixtures and quick-acting or automatic clamps. One system uses standard upper and lower plates for holding the dies and press-mounted fixtures which can also be used to produce the dies on diemaking machines. Each plate has integral stops on its front corners and four bushed holes for positioning over dowels in the fixtures. With dies mounted on the plates, the plates are slipped into slots in the standard fixtures bolted to the ram and bolster plate of the press. Double-acting air cylinders on the fixtures accurately locate and securely clamp the dieholding plates, and shutheight is set with a power slide adjustment. With this system, a press operator can quickly change dies.

Moving bolsters and automatic die clamps are common accessories for large, long-bed presses. Dies for the next production run are set up on a spare bolster alongside the press while dies on the other bolster are in use. Wheels on the bolsters are driven by air motors and roll on rails which extend from front to back through the press. Hydraulic lifts facilitate positioning the bolsters in the press, and pins are provided for accurate location with respect to the centerline of the press. Air-powered, swing-type clamps can be provided for the upper tools, and hydraulic clamps for securing the moving bolster to the press bed. Some press builders provide air-over-oil hydraulic clamps for both upper and lower tools.

# MECHANICAL PRESSES

Mechanical presses are machines having a slide or slides actuated by mechanical means. They are sometimes referred to as power presses to differentiate them from hydraulic presses. All mechanical presses employ flywheel energy which is transferred to the workpiece by gears, cranks, eccentrics, or levers. They are available in many different types and sizes and with various drives.

### TYPES OF FRAMES AND CONSTRUCTION

Basic functions of a press frame are to contain the loads imposed with a minimum of deflection, which requires ample rigidity. The two major types of press frames are gap frame and straight side. Straight-side presses are sometimes constructed with column-type frames. Important criteria for selecting the type of frame to be used include accessibility and operating characteristics, convenience of feeding and unloading, stiffness, and profile.

#### Press Construction

Press frames are made of cast iron, cast steel, or welded or bolted-steel construction. Some frames are made from machined posts or pillars. Many press builders are now using computers for frame design to optimize material utilization and ensure maximum stiffness, strength, and performance. The five most common types of construction are as follows:

1. One-piece frame of cast iron, cast steel, or steel weldments.
2. Four-piece, steel, tie-rod frame. This construction consists of the bed, two uprights, and the crown held together by steel tie rods (usually four) which are preshrunk in excess of the rated force. The tie rods can be heated to obtain the proper expanded length, the nuts are tightened, and the rods are allowed to cool to produce the required tension, with the frame parts in compression. Pretensioning of tie rods by heating is becoming obsolete with the availability of hydraulically actuated tie-rod nuts and hydraulic tensioning devices. As load is applied to the press, the tension stresses in the tie rods increase while the compressive prestresses in the frame parts decrease in direct proportion to the load. This type of construction is employed on most large, straight-side presses.
3. Bolted frame. This construction consists of the bed, two side members, and the crown keyed and held together by bolts. This type of construction is used frequently for single and double-crank, gap-frame presses.
4. Modified tie-rod frame. This construction combines the tie-rod and bolted types of frames.
5. Solid frame with tie rods. With this type of construction, steel tie rods are shrunk into the solid frame.

Hardness of the material from which the press frame is made affects frame strength, but has a negligible effect on the press rigidity. Softer materials used for press frames deflect to about the same degree as harder materials. Rigidity, however, can generally be increased by adding material at selected locations. Press beds are usually covered by thick steel or cast-iron bolster plates having tapped holes or T-slots for die bolts or other fastening devices.

Except for the values given in ANSI Standard B5.52M, "General Purpose Single-Point, Gap-Type (Metric), Mechanical Power Presses," which are discussed later in this chapter, no industry standards exist for bed or slide deflection. A new ANSI standard for straight-side, single-action presses is to be published soon. Press builders and some users have their own standards, generally expressed as the maximum deflection in inches per foot or millimeters per meter of span under rated load. Specifications for maximum bending deflections of beds and slides generally vary from 0.0005-0.002 in./ft (0.042-0.17 mm/m) between tie rods or column centers. Press frames can be built with less deflection, but to reduce the deflection about 50% would require an increase in material mass of approximately 100%.

## Gap-Frame Presses

The housings of a gap-frame (also called C-frame) press are cut back below the gibs to form the shape of a letter C. Presses of this type are the most versatile and common in use and are lower in cost than straight-side presses. They provide unobstructed access to the dies from three sides, and their backs are usually open for the ejection of stampings and/or scrap. Press feeding, discussed later in this chapter, can be done conveniently from the side or front (on open-back presses). Gap-frame presses generally have a lower overall height than straight-side presses of the same capacity, which is important when overhead clearance is limited.

**Types available.** Gap-frame presses are available in several different designs, some of which are shown in Fig. 5-3. The types include permanently upright presses, such as the adjustable-bed stationary (ABS) and open-back stationary (OBS) presses illustrated; permanently inclined presses; and open-back inclinable (OBI) presses, which are the most common. The inclined presses often facilitate feeding and permit finished stampings to fall out by gravity or to be blown out by air at the rear of the press.

Gap-frame presses are made with either one or two points of suspension (discussed later in this chapter). Large gap-frame presses are generally equipped for mounting cushions for workpiece liftout or for shallow-draw operations. Powered slide-adjustment systems are available for faster die changing.

These presses are commonly arranged with their crankshafts extending from right to left of the die space. They are also available with the crankshaft extending from front to back, with the flywheel or gear at the rear of the press. For some

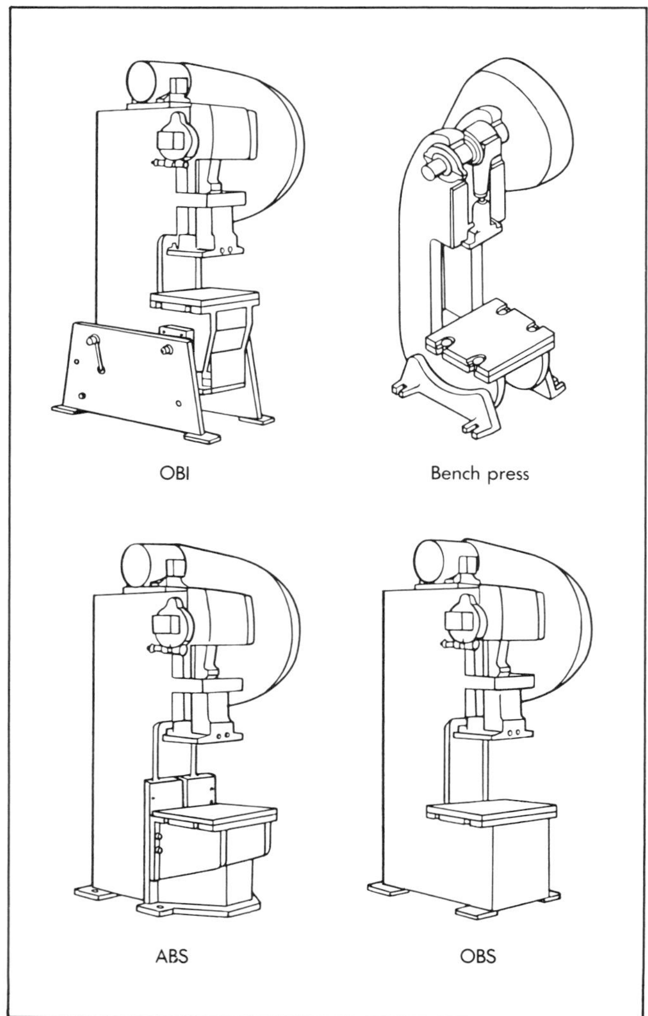


**Fig. 5-3 Several types of gap-frame presses: OBI—open-back inclinable, ABS—adjustable-bed stationary, OBS—open-back stationary; and bench press.**[4]

applications, these so-called endwheel presses (with front-to-back crankshaft configurations) eliminate the inconvenience of a flywheel or gear in proximity with the operator or feed unit and permit handling workpieces such as large rings without interference.

A special type of gap-frame press known as an adjustable-bed, knee, or horning press is also available. This type of press differs from the conventional design in that the lower jaw which supports the bolster is eliminated, which sacrifices some rigidity, and is replaced by a screw-adjustable table for varying the shutheight. The table can be custom designed for special applications. Sometimes, means are provided for swinging the table from under the slide (see Fig. 5-4). This provides access to a horizontal hole in the press frame for mounting a horn or post to perform operations on hollow, cylindrical workpieces. With the table under the slide, this type of press can be used for punching, piercing, blanking, riveting, stamping, wiring, and assembling. With the table swung aside and a horn or special attachment installed, bending, flanging, forming, seaming, and other operations can be performed.

**Press capacities.** Gap-frame presses are available from small bench types of 1 ton (8.9 kN) force capacity to OBI's of 300 ton (2669 kN) capacity. Such presses with two-point suspension are made with capacities to 300 tons (2669 kN) or more. Table 5-2 gives the capacities of JIC standard, geared and nongeared, gap-frame presses, rated at different distances above the bottoms of their strokes. A discussion of geared and nongeared presses is presented later in this chapter. The capacities of metric-size, gap-frame presses, specified in ANSI Standard B5.52M, are presented in Table 5-3.

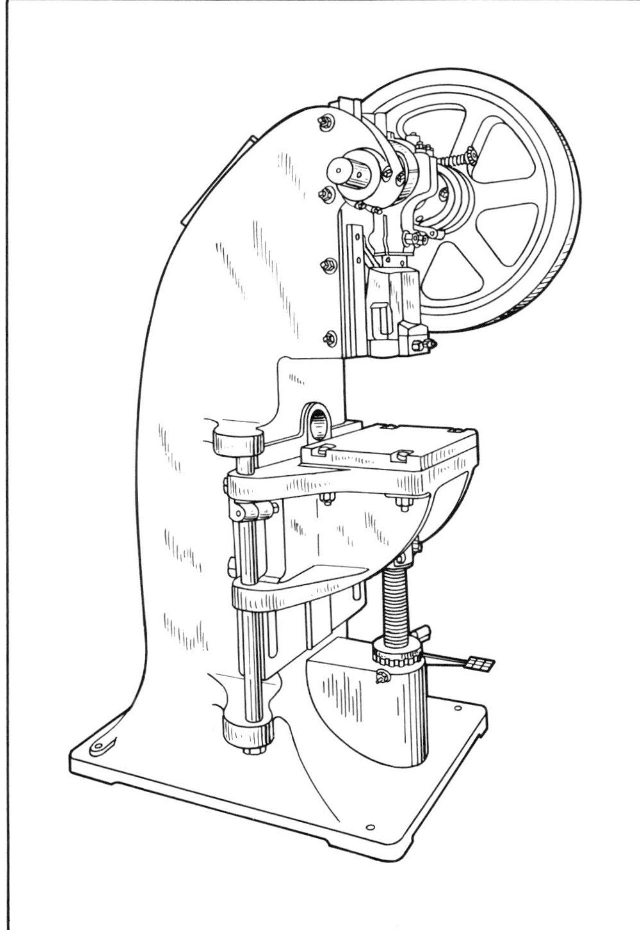

**Fig. 5-4 Horn press with adjustable swinging table.** (*The V & O Press Co.*)

**Press stiffness.** While gap-frame presses have many desirable features, they have the disadvantage of more deflection under load than straight-side presses of the same capacity. Also, due to the geometry of the gap construction, the deflection results in an out-of-parallel condition between the top surface of the press bolster and the bottom surface of the slide. Proper location of the dies, especially progressive dies, is critical because single-point, gap-frame presses are not generally designed for off-center loading unless plunger guides are used. Excessive deflection can damage the dies or press and can result in the production of unacceptable parts. The degree of misalignment is proportional to the force required. If punch and die alignment are critical, either from the standpoint of workpiece accuracy or excessive die wear, gap-frame presses should not be used.

**TABLE 5-2**
**Strokes and Rated Capacities of JIC Standard Gap-Frame Presses**

| Press Capacity, tons (kN) | Rating Distance Above Bottom of Slide Stroke, in. (mm) | | Stroke, in. (mm) | |
|---|---|---|---|---|
| | Nongeared | Geared | Standard | Max |
| 22 (195.7) | 1/32 (0.8) | 1/8 (3.2) | 2 1/2 (63.5) | 4 (101.6) |
| 32 (284.7) | 1/32 (0.8) | 1/8 (3.2) | 3 (76.2) | 5 (127) |
| 45 (400.3) | 1/16 (1.6) | 1/4 (6.4) | 3 (76.2) | 6 (152.4) |
| 60 (533.8) | 1/16 (1.6) | 1/4 (6.4) | 3 1/2 (88.9) | 7 (177.8) |
| 75 (667.2) | 1/16 (1.6) | 1/4 (6.4) | 4 (101.6) | 8 (203.2) |
| 110 (978.6) | 1/16 (1.6) | 1/4 (6.4) | 5 (127) | 10 (254) |
| 150 (1334.4) | --- | 1/4 (6.4) | 6 (152.4) | 12 (304.8) |
| 200 (1779.2) | --- | 1/4 (6.4) | 8 (203.2) | 12 (304.8) |

**TABLE 5-3**
**Rated Capacities of ANSI Standard Single-Point, Gap-Type, Mechanical Power Presses (Metric)[4]**

| Press Capacity, kN (tons) | Rating Distance Above Bottom of Slide Stroke, mm (in.) | |
|---|---|---|
| | Nongeared | Geared |
| 20 (2.25) | 0.5 (0.02) | --- |
| 50-100 (5.6-11.2) | 1.0 (0.04) | 1.6 (0.06) |
| 140-300 (15.7-33.7) | 1.0 (0.04) | 3.0 (0.12) |
| 400-1000 (45-112) | 1.6 (0.06) | 6.0 (0.24) |
| 1400-2240 (157-252) | --- | 6.0 (0.24) |

A standard that is common to many press builders specifies a maximum deflection of 0.0015 in./in. (mm/mm) of throat depth, measured from the back of the throat to the centerline of the crankshaft. Total deflection of the gap area, however, is made up of both vertical and angular deflection and is a function of the gap height and depth. Angular deflection is the most critical because it can produce misalignment between the punch and die. ANSI Standard B5.52M for metric-size, gap-type presses specifies both linear and angular deflections that are allowable (see Fig. 5-5).

For some applications, the deflection of gap-frame presses is not tolerable. If it is impractical or uneconomical to transfer such operations to straight-side presses, the deflection of the gap-frame presses can be reduced by the use of tie rods across their open fronts. Adding tie rods, however, sacrifices some of the benefits of die accessibility on gap-frame presses. Most press builders recommend using a gap-frame press of increased capacity, rather than adding tie rods to a smaller capacity press.

Tie rods can be installed using lugs available from press builders. When the rods are properly prestressed, a significant reduction in deflection results. A more effective method of using tie rods is to install the tie rods with proper-proportioned tubular spacers, which ensure accurate spacing between the press crown and bolster. Without spacers, the tie rods can be overstressed and can cause die misalignment. The use of tubular spacers, however, requires accurate machining of the tie-rod lugs and the spacers to length. Proper prestressing of the rods and spacers can reduce deflection more than using tie rods alone.

Comparison of results obtained in reducing deflection by using tie rods only or tie rods and spacers on a 200 ton (1779 kN) gap-frame press are presented in Table 5-4. Without tie rods, this press has a deflection under rated load of 0.026" (0.66 mm). Using tie rods alone or tie rods and spacers, without any preload, the deflection is reduced to 0.0178" (0.452 mm). By prestressing the tie rods alone or tie rods and spacers, the deflection is further reduced, as shown in the table. With the combination of tie rods and spacers prestressed by a one-fourth turn of the nuts, total deflection in this test was reduced to 0.0134" (0.340 mm).

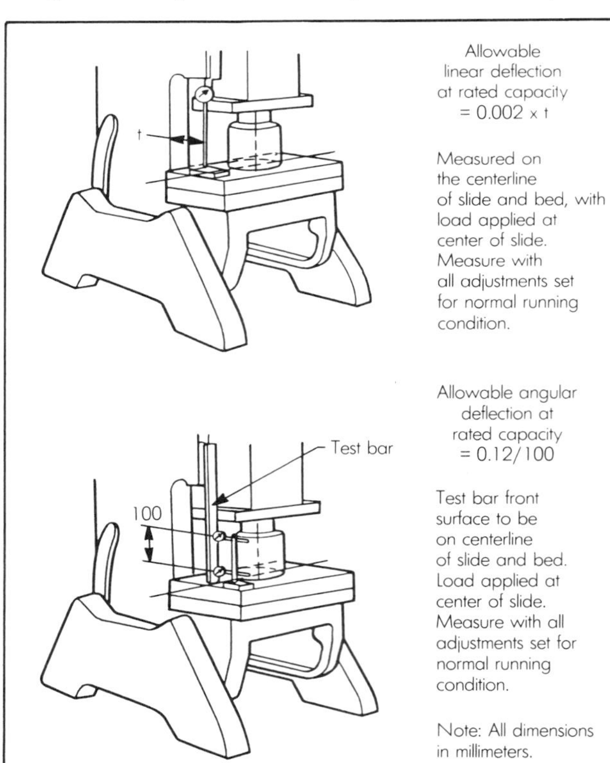
Allowable
linear deflection
at rated capacity
= 0.002 x t
t
Measured on
the centerline
of slide and bed, with
load applied at
center of slide.
Measure with
all adjustments set
for normal running
condition.
Allowable angular
deflection at
rated capacity
= 0.12/100
Test bar
100
Test bar front
surface to be
on centerline
of slide and bed.
Load applied at
center of slide.
Measure with all
adjustments set for
normal running
condition.
Note: All dimensions
in millimeters.

**Fig. 5-5. Allowable linear and angular deflection for metric-size, gap-type presses.**[5]

For the purpose of comparison, a straight-side press of tie-rod-frame construction, having a similar shutheight, might have a total deflection under load of 0.010" (0.25 mm). This deflection, however, is symmetrical and does not result in any angular misalignment, as results with gap-frame presses.

## Straight-Side Presses

Presses with straight-side frames consist of a crown, two uprights, a bed which supports the bolster, and a slide which reciprocates between the two straight sides or housings. The crown and bed are connected with the uprights by tie rods or by bolting and keying together, or all members can be cast or welded into one piece. Fabricated construction of members made by one press builder is illustrated in Fig. 5-6. Continuous, welded, box-type construction is commonly used to minimize twisting, especially when the press is to be subjected to off-center loading. Each construction method has certain advantages and limitations. Solid-frame, straight-side presses are generally less expensive than tie-rod presses, but their size is limited because they must be transported from builder to user in one piece.

Tie-rod construction provides several advantages. If the press slide becomes stuck at the bottom of its stroke, it is possible to remove the stress applied to the rods by heating them, thereby enabling the cause of the problem to be corrected. To facilitate this procedure, hydraulically operated tie-rod nuts are available, generally as original equipment.

Another advantage of tie-rod construction is that tie rods provide some overload protection. Figure 5-7 shows an example of deflection curves for solid frames and for tie-rod frames with cast iron and steel uprights. With a tie-rod frame, the crown separates from the uprights at about 200% of press capacity and the stiffness of the frame under additional load is determined by the rods alone. Rate of deflection changes from about 0.010" (0.25 mm) to 0.036" (0.91 mm) per 100% of press capacity, and the frame is only 28% as stiff after crown separation. As a result, load buildup because of accidental interference increases at a slower rate, thus decreasing the possibility of a catastrophic accident. Use of a hydraulic overload device, however, provides more positive protection for short displacements.

**Press capacities.** Straight-side presses are available for single or multiple-action operation and in a number of sizes from small-capacity, special-purpose machines to those having capacities of 2000 tons (17 792 kN) or more. Some large, straight-side presses are capable of exerting forces to 6000 tons (53 376 kN). High-speed, straight-side presses are discussed previously in this chapter, and transfer presses are described in a subsequent section.

The JIC standard for single-point, straight-side presses specifies 16 capacity ratings ranging from 50-2000 tons (445-17 792 kN), with a single die-space pattern for each rating. For multiple-point presses, this standard covers 16 capacity ratings ranging from 50-2000 tons (449-17 792 kN), with a variety of die-space patterns for each rating.

# MECHANICAL PRESS FRAMES AND CONSTRUCTION

**TABLE 5-4**
**Effect of Tie Rods on Deflection of a Gap-Frame Press**

| Elongation, Stress, and Deflection | Tie Rods Only | Tie Rods and Spacers | Tie Rods Only | Tie Rods and Spacers | Tie Rods Only | Tie Rods and Spacers |
|---|---|---|---|---|---|---|
| | Prestress | | | | | |
| | 1/4 Turn of Nuts | | 1/8 Turn of Nuts | | Zero | |
| Tie rod elongation from prestress, in. (mm) | 0.0353 (0.897) | 0.0472 (1.199) | 0.0176 (0.447) | 0.0232 (0.589) | 0 | 0 |
| Tie rod elongation from load, in. (mm) | 0.0212 (0.538) | 0.0122 (0.310) | 0.0212 (0.538) | 0.0212 (0.538) | 0.0212 (0.538) | 0.0212 (0.538) |
| Total tie rod elongation, in. (mm) | 0.0565 (1.435) | 0.0594 (1.509) | 0.0388 (0.986) | 0.0444 (1.128) | 0.0212 (0.538) | 0.0212 (0.538) |
| Tie rod prestress, psi (kPa) | 10,300 (71 018) | 13,600 (93 772) | 5172 (35 661) | 6800 (46 886) | 0 | 0 |
| Final tie rod stress, psi (kPa) | 16,600 (114 457) | 17,300 (119 283) | 11,400 (78 603) | 11,400 (78 603) | 6200 (42 749) | 6200 (42 749) |
| Press deflection from prestress, in. (mm) | -0.0137 (0.348) | -0.0081 (0.206) | -0.0069 (0.175) | -0.0041 (0.104) | 0 | 0 |
| Press deflection from load, in. (mm) | +0.0040 (0.102) | +0.0053 (0.135) | +0.0109 (0.277) | +0.0109 (0.277) | +0.0178 (0.452) | +0.0178 (0.452) |
| Total press deflection, in. (mm) | 0.0177 (0.450) | 0.0134 (0.340) | 0.0178 (0.452) | 0.0150 (0.381) | 0.0178 (0.452) | 0.0178 (0.452) |

Notes:

1. Results obtained on a 200 ton (1779 kN) gap-frame press having a deflection under rated load without tie rods of 0.026″ (0.66 mm).
2. Tie rods used are 3″ (76 mm) diam x 102″ (2590 mm) long, with 4 nut threads per in.; spacer area is 10.5 in.$^2$ (6774 mm$^2$).
3. When the nuts are not tightened or are tightened only 1/8 turn, separation occurs between the spacer and the tie-rod lugs. As a result, the full effect of the spacers is not obtained.

The maximum ratings for the JIC standard are for 1/4″ (6.3 mm) above bottom of stroke on straight-side presses with single-end, geared drives and are 1/2″ (12.7 mm) above bottom of stroke on presses with eccentric gear or twin-end geared drives. A tentative ANSI standard rates capacities of metric-size presses at 1.6 mm (0.06″) above bottom of stroke for nongeared drives; 6.0 mm (0.24″) above for single-end, geared drives; and 13 mm (0.5″) above for eccentric and twin-end geared drives. Press drives are discussed later in this chapter.

**Die accessibility.** Dies mounted in straight-side presses are accessible primarily from the front and rear. Openings are generally provided in the uprights, giving some limited access to the right and left ends of the die space, and are used for automatic feeding and unloading. Hand feeding and unloading are limited to the front and back of the press and necessitate safety provisions discussed later in this chapter. The wide range of bed sizes available with these presses allows selecting the narrowest front-to-back dimension commensurate with the dies to be used. Moving bolsters are often used on large, straight-side presses to facilitate die changing.

**Press stiffness.** Straight-side presses are stiffer than gap-frame presses. They have no angular deflection, and vertical deflection of their uprights under load is practically symmetrical when they are symmetrically loaded. As a result, usually no problems are created with respect to punch and die alignment.

Vertical stiffness of a press frame depends upon the cross-sectional area of the uprights on solid or bolted-and-keyed frames. With tie-rod frames, stiffness depends upon the cross-sectional areas of the uprights and tie rods, and the proportion of one to the other. Adequate stiffness is necessary for the die to function properly and to prevent excessive snap-through during blanking or severe punching operations. Too much stiffness, however, can cause a proportionately greater load on all press members, including the drive, in cases of excessive stock thickness or double headers (two blanks or stampings in the die simultaneously).

In addition to the deflection (or elongation) of the upright members, the bed, bolster, and slide of a straight-side press also deflect under load. No JIC standards are available for maximum allowable deflection of these members. The standards of press builders for bed deflection vary from 0.002 in./ft (0.17 mm/m) of span for general-purpose presses to 0.0005-0.001 in./ft (0.042-0.08 mm/m) for high-speed presses and presses in which progressive dies are employed, with the load evenly distributed over two-thirds of the nominal left-to-right dimension.

Although the slide and bolster are not strictly members of the press frame, their deflections must be carefully considered. Press builder's standards for slide deflection are the same as those for the bed. Bolster thicknesses specified in JIC and ANSI standards are usually adequate unless the bolster contains large

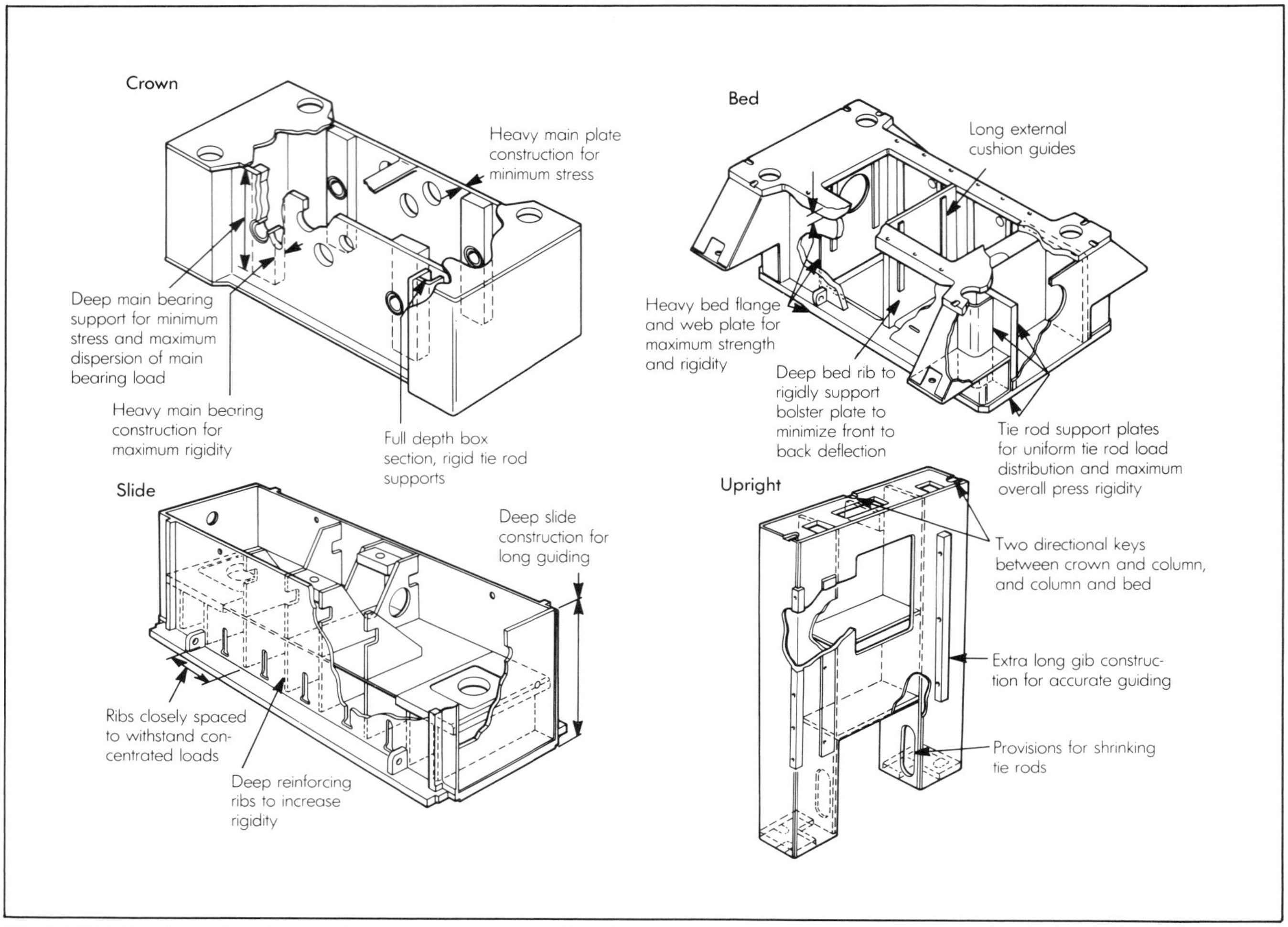

Fig. 5-6 **Fabricated members for a straight-side press.** (*Verson Allsteel Press Co.*)

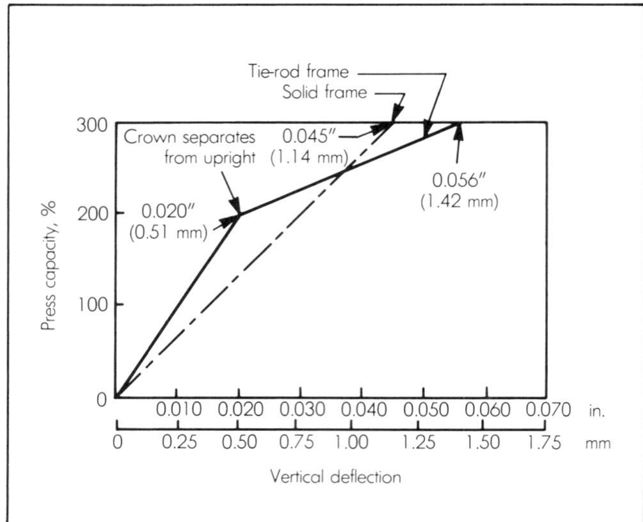


**Fig. 5-7 Typical deflection curves for straight-side presses with solid frames and with tie-rod frames.**

holes for scrap shedding or unless highly concentrated loads are applied at the center of the bolster. Cast-iron bolsters are not as stiff as steel bolsters of the same thickness. In some cases, this requires an increase in bolster thickness if cast iron is used.

## Round-Column Presses

Column-type presses are similar to straight-side presses, but they have round columns, pillars, or posts instead of the side uprights. Most column-type presses have four columns, but some have two or three columns. Bushings of the bronze-sleeve or ball-type surround the columns for good guidance. Column presses are available for horizontal operation, permitting gravity ejection of stampings and/or scrap.

## Press Slide Connections

Mechanical straight-side presses are generally arranged so that the rotary motion of their drives (discussed later in this chapter) are transmitted to their reciprocating slides through one, two, or four connections (pitmans). Depending upon the number of connections, the presses are referred to as being of single-point, two-point, or four-point suspension. Although uncommon, some long-bed presses have been made with three in-line connections. On double-action presses, the number of connections refers only to the main slide. Blankholder slides are generally of four-point suspension.

The number of points of slide suspension is determined by the left-to-right and front-to-back dimensions of the slide face. Location of the applied press loads in relation to the number of slide connections influences the performance of the press and the quality of the parts produced.

**Single-point suspension.** Presses with small, nearly square slide-face areas, usually 42 in.$^2$ (27 097 mm$^2$) or less, are generally of single-point suspension. The parts of the one connection are sized to carry the rated press capacity.

When a single-point slide is loaded at any position other than directly under the connection, the slide tilts. The amount of tilt depends upon the clearance between the slide guides and the gibs (discussed next in this section) and upon the amount of load. Reducing the clearance, increasing the length of contact between guides and gibs, and decreasing the load or moving it closer in line with the connection help keep the slide level. Single-point presses are not recommended, however, when significant off-center loading is to be applied.

Presses with single-point suspension are also not generally recommended for precision, long-run operations because die wear can be excessive. Care in locating the dies with respect to the center of the slide, however, can reduce die wear. When progressive dies are used, the loading at the various stations should be balanced.

**Two-point suspension.** Presses with two-point suspension generally have rectangular slides with a front-to-back dimension not exceeding about 54″ (1372 mm). Each connection is designed for a maximum of 50-60% of the rated press load, depending upon the press manufacturer. The maximum load should ideally be placed at the midpoint between the connections to avoid overloading. Also, it should be remembered that the slide tilts in the front-to-back direction if the resultant load on the slide is not in the same plane as the connections. Workpiece quality and die life are both improved if the dies are set in line with the connections.

**Four-point suspension.** Presses with four-point suspension generally provide the highest accuracy and longest die life. The rating for each connection is usually either one-fourth or one-third of the press capacity, depending upon the press builder.

The four pitmans on these presses are better able to reduce tilting in either direction when off-center loading occurs. Press builders, however, recommend that the loads be centered as much as possible or that, if off-center loading is necessary, the loads be distributed as evenly as possible, making sure that the load on any connection is within its capacity.

## Slide Adjustment

An adjusting-screw arrangement is generally provided between the lower ends of the connections (pitmans) and the slide to permit varying the shutheight between specified limits to accommodate different dies. On smaller OBI and single-point, gap-frame presses, the shutheight is usually adjusted by hand, with a special wrench employed for the adjusting screw nut. Wedge adjustment is common for short adjustments. On some large, single-point presses, hand adjustment is accomplished through a set of gears. Such hand adjustments are slow, but if adjustments are required only infrequently, they are generally satisfactory.

Large, single-point presses and most modern, multiple-point presses have air or electric motor drives for adjusting the shutheight. Speed of adjustment generally depends upon the size of the press and the length of adjustment and varies between 2-4 ipm (51-102 mm/min). Motorized units are available with dial or pushbutton settings and digital readouts for faster setting and improved accuracy. Integral or separate brakes are generally provided to maintain precision control.

## Slide Guiding

Guiding of press slides is required to keep the lower faces of the slides parallel to the upper faces of the bed or bolsters during the portion of the stroke when operations are being performed. This is accomplished with gibs, or gibbing, attached to the uprights or press frame to guide the slide. The degree of accuracy of slide adjustment that is maintained depends upon the type of gibs and the fit or clearance between the gibs and the wear surfaces on the slide.

Required accuracy varies widely depending upon the operation. For example, when thin metal 0.010″ (0.25 mm) thick or less is blanked or punched, the parallelism must be held within 0.001″ (0.03 mm). Since the clearances between the punches and dies for such operations are of similar magnitude, the press guides (sometimes supplemented by heel blocks in the case of lateral loads) must maintain the required tolerance if any offset or lateral loads are imposed, because the guide posts in the dies cannot be expected to do so.

Contrasted to this requirement for close-tolerance guiding for blanking or punching operations, accurate guiding of the punch-holding slide in a double-action press can sometimes cause trouble when unsymmetrical deep draws are being made. In such cases, it may be advantageous to have some float to allow the punches to seek registry in the die cavities, thus preventing possible ironing or tearing of the workpiece material.

**Parallelism.** In a single-point press, the slide guides basically determine parallelism of the slide face with respect to the bed or bolster, both in the front-to-back and right-to-left directions. In a two-point press, slide guides determine parallelism only in the front-to-back direction. Out-of-parallel conditions in the right-to-left direction because of faulty adjusting-screw timing, variations in throw between the cranks or eccentrics, or bicycling (periodic tilting of the slide in opposite directions) due to timing errors in the drive cannot be corrected by adjusting the slide guides.

In a four-point press, parallelism is determined strictly by the press-drive and adjusting-screw accuracy and timing. Out-of-parallel conditions at midstroke, however, can be caused by improper centering of the slide guide adjustment.

No JIC standards exist for parallelism of slide to bed, but the standards of most press builders specify about 0.001 in./ft (0.08 mm/m) of die space at bottom of stroke and 0.003 in./ft (0.25 mm/m) of die space at midstroke.

**Runout.** This is the amount that the path of any point on the slide face varies from the vertical during the stroke of the press. The effect of slide guide accuracy on runout for single-point, two-point, and four-point presses is the same as its effect on parallelism.

No JIC standards are available for runout, and manufacturer's standards vary. A proposed ANSI standard for metric-size presses specifies a maximum of 0.1 mm (0.004″) for the first 100 mm (3.94″) of stroke and 0.01 mm (0.0004″) for each additional increment of 100 mm, the readings being taken on the lower one-third of the downward stroke of the press. Measurements are made by reading an indicator clamped to the slide face and contacting a square mounted on the press bolster.

**Clearance.** Clearances between press slide guides and gibs are required to compensate for inaccuracies in machining and in the throw and timing of two and four-point presses, and to allow for expansion and contraction of the guides and gibs. With the bronze-to-cast-iron or cast-iron-to-cast-iron gibbing normally used, some slight clearance must also exist for the oil or grease lubricant.

If sufficient clearance is not provided, excessive pressure on the guides occurs at some point during the stroke, resulting in galling of the mating surfaces. The amount of clearance also affects the repetitive registry of punch with die. If the clearance between punch and die is less than the clearance between the press guides, the punch can mount the die, thereby causing premature wear. Clearance between the press guides also depends upon the length of the gibs. A reasonable allowance can be 0.003-0.006" (0.08-0.15 mm), the exact amount varying with gib length. For high-speed presses, the clearance between a gib-type guide and the press slide at normal operating temperature is generally no more than 0.0015" (0.038 mm).

Clearances between the mating surfaces of press guides can be reduced by using self-lubricating, reinforced-phenolic liners. The modulus of elasticity of this material is about 1/50 that of steel. As a result, deformation of the liners due to the inaccuracies discussed does not raise compressive stresses in the liners excessively, providing the liners are of sufficient thickness.

Near-zero clearances can be achieved by using preloaded, rolling-contact (ball or roller) bearing guides. When offset or lateral loads are encountered, however, tending to cause the press slide to tilt, only a few rolling-contact members at the top and bottom of the guides take the loads. As a result, stresses exerted on the balls or rollers can be very high.

**Guide lengths.** Length of guide for the purpose of this discussion refers to the length of slide gib that is contained within the slide guides during the working portion of the stroke. The out-of-parallel conditions resulting from a short guide as compared to a long guide are illustrated in Fig. 5-8, view *a*. View *b* shows the effects on parallelism with variations in the amount that the slide face extends below the guides at bottom of stroke.

With the same clearances and guide lengths, parallelism is not affected, but the resultant misalignment is significantly greater. The closer the guides extend toward the stock pass line, the more effective they are in controlling alignment.

Differences of opinion exist as to whether it is more effective to have pairs of gibs far apart (wide gibs) or close together (narrow gibs), but the affect of the distance between gibs on parallelism and alignment is generally nil. Offset loads on wide gibs, however, cause greater gib loading, so the gib area should be larger to compensate for this.

**Offset loading.** In a single-point press, offset loads are considered to be any loads that are not on the centerline of the press. In a two-point press, any loads that are not on the centerline of the suspension points or that are beyond the suspension points are considered to be offset loads. In a four-point press, offset loads are any loads that are outside the four points of suspension.

The ability of a press slide to resist offset loads depends upon the following factors:

1. The geometry and bearing area of the gibbing.
2. The type of lower connection (ball, saddle, or pin type).
3. The orientation of the lower connection (wristpin front-to-back or right-to-left).

Press gibs are intended primarily to maintain correct

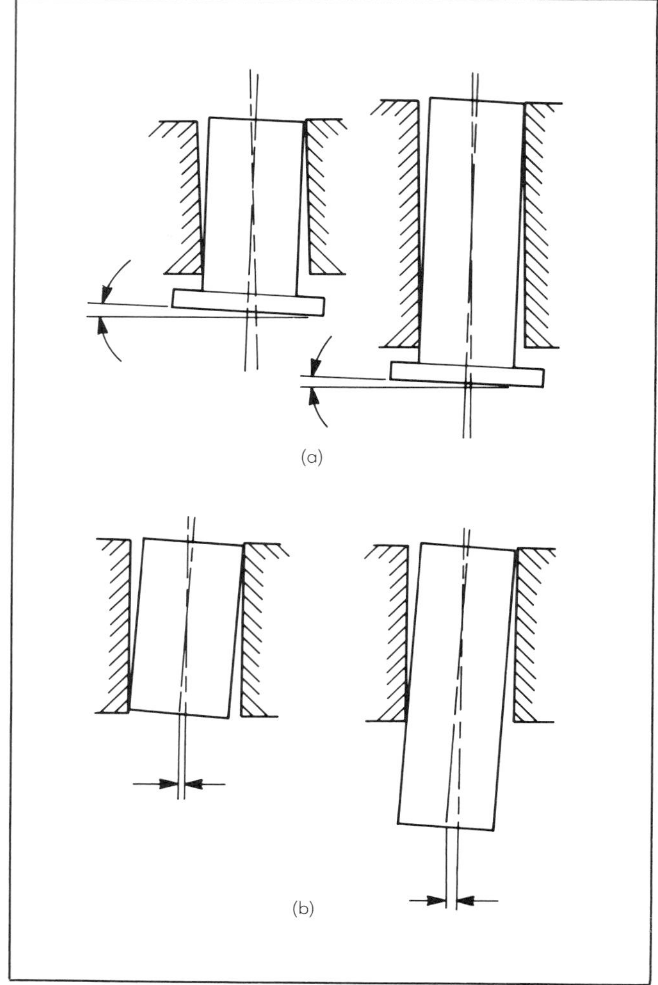


**Fig. 5-8 Effects of guide lengths on: (a) out-of-parallel condition and (b) parallelism.**

alignment of the slide; they have only limited capacity for resisting the forces of significant offset loads. Saddle and pin-type connections, however, can support significant offset loads, but the direction of the offset load must be in line with the wristpins of the connections. Also, the magnitude of the load and the amount of offset is limited by the proportions of the lower connections. The best practice is to design and locate dies in the press so as to minimize offset loading.

**Lateral loading.** Lateral loads are considered to be those horizontal loads that are not completely contained within the dies. One example is a shearing load in which the shear blade or punch is not backed up in the die.

As is the case with offset loads, press guides are not intended to withstand high lateral loads. It is always good practice, when substantial lateral loads are encountered, to build backup means into the dies. This can be accomplished by using heel blocks, by heeling the punch into the die before shearing takes place, or by using other methods (refer to Chapter 6, "Die Design for Sheet Metal Forming").

**Types of slide guides.** Two types of guiding used extensively in small, single-point, gap-frame presses are shown in Fig. 5-9.

# MECHANICAL PRESS FRAMES AND CONSTRUCTION

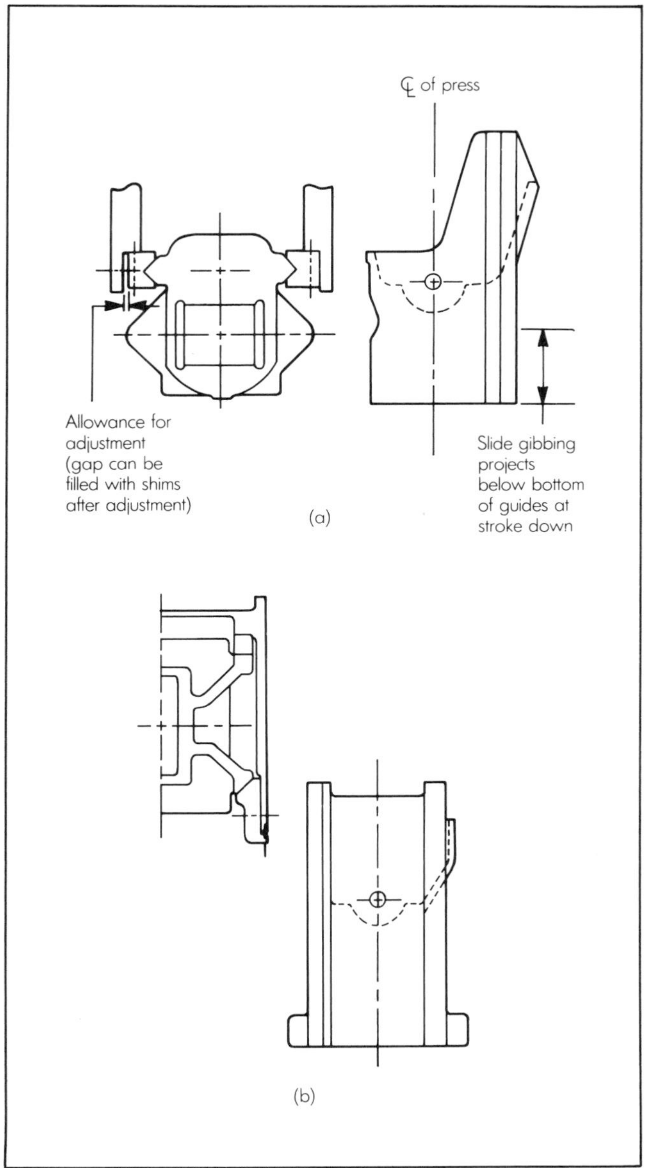


**Fig. 5-9 Two types of guiding used extensively in small, single-point, gap-frame presses: (a) V-gibs and (b) basic box-type guiding.**

View *a* illustrates V-gibs; view *b*, basic box-type guiding. With V-gibs, one gib is fixed and the other is adjustable, using jackscrews and studs in a push-pull arrangement. Location of the slide guides, whether or not they are symmetrical with the centerline of the press, bears no relation to the effectiveness of the guiding system.

Various configurations of gibbing used with the box-type guiding system are illustrated in Fig. 5-10. View *a* shows a flat rear gib which presents a maximum area to forces created by the horizontal component of the pressing force. (This force is to the rear in the case of a press with a crankshaft in the right-to-left direction.) The front gib is mounted at an angle of 45° to the press centerline so that adjustment in one direction changes the clearance in both the front-to-back and right-to-left directions.

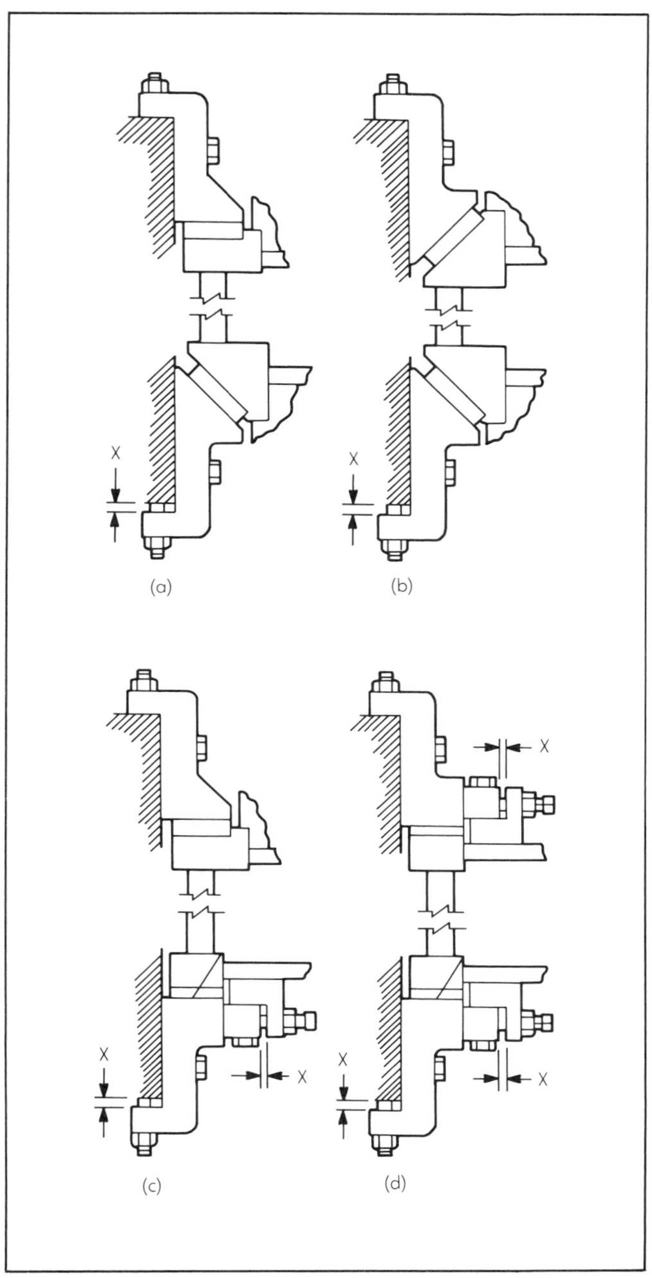


**Fig. 5-10 Various configurations of gibbing used with the box-type guiding system: (a) flat rear gib and 45° front gib, (b) front and rear 45° gibs, (c) and (d) square gibbing. Allowance for adjustment is indicated by X.**

View *b* of Fig. 5-10 shows both front and rear gibs mounted at an angle of 45° to the press centerline. This arrangement has two deficiencies. First, the press slide has a tendency to rotate in the horizontal plane, especially if the slide is approximately square. Secondly, it is more difficult to set up gibs of this type because there are no square surfaces to use as references.

Two configurations known as square gibbing are shown in views *c* and *d* of Fig. 5-10. An inherent advantage of this type of guiding system is its ability to accurately set gib clearance. With square gibbing, a movement of 0.001″ (0.03 mm) of the gib affects the clearance by 0.001″. With a 45° gib, a movement of 0.001″ of the gib changes the clearance by only 0.0007″ (0.018 mm). Thus, with square gibbing, it is possible to get a more direct feel for the amount to be moved, and a more accurate setting generally results. Another advantage of square gibbing over 45° gibbing is that front-to-back adjustment of square gibbing does not affect the right-to-left setting, and vice versa.

Six and eight-point, square-type gibs (see Fig. 5-11) are employed extensively on large-bed, high-force, straight-side presses. The six-point, square-type gibs (view *a*) are more common on solid-frame presses. Eight-point, square-type gibs (view *b*), which are adjustable right-to-left and front-to-back, are used frequently on tie-rod presses. The eight-point design is also generally preferred for progressive-die operations because it tends to resist any rotating movement of the slide caused by off-center loading.

## Counterbalances

Counterbalances on presses perform several functions, including the following:

1. Counterbalance the moving weight of the press slide and the driving components attached to it, as well as the die members attached to the slide. A properly counterbalanced press may stop somewhat more quickly with less load on the brake.
2. Take up backlash from clearances in bearings, in adjusting-screw threads, and between gear teeth, thus ensuring accurate bottom-of-stroke and shutheight positions. By reducing shock loads, wear of the press members is reduced.
3. Assist in making slide adjustments by minimizing the weight that has to be moved. If adjustment is done manually, less force is required. If the adjustment is motorized, life of the unit can be increased and/or a smaller motor used.
4. Improve safety by preventing the press slide from falling inadvertently due to failure of the brake, connection, or other members.
5. Reduce noise levels caused by drive gears on the press.
6. Permit high-speed operation by reducing vibration.

There are two basic types of counterbalances: spring and air cylinder.

**Spring counterbalances.** The use of springs for counterbalances on presses is limited, generally being restricted to presses with very short strokes, and in many cases, relatively high speeds. For such applications, the load curve of a spring counterbalance can be designed to minimize vibrational forces set up by the slide motion.

A disadvantage of spring counterbalances is that they are designed for a specific application and cannot be readily changed with respect to load capacity. The springs also have a limited life and are subject to fatigue breakage. When spring counterbalance systems are used, safety requirements specify that they have the capability of holding the slide and its attachments at midstroke without the brake applied and that they have means to retain system parts in the event of breakage.

**Air counterbalances.** The use of one to four or more air cylinders provides an effective and economical means for counterbalancing, and such systems are common for all types of presses. The systems furnish a practically constant force, and the amount of counterbalancing is easily changed by means of a pressure control valve to accommodate various die weights. Presses can be equipped with automatic counterbalance systems that automatically adjust the air pressure to conform with the actual die weight. Ample-size surge tanks are necessary to prevent excessive build-up of pressure resulting from the press stroke or when the slide is adjusted. For some presses having short strokes, self-contained cylinders without surge tanks are often used. Check valves prevent air from surging back into the main air line.

*Cylinder mounting.* Counterbalance cylinders are generally mounted to a stationary member of the press frame (the crown or the uprights), with the cylinder rod connected to the slide. Pull-type cylinders, the most commonly used on mechanical presses, are mounted to the crown with the cylinder rod creating an upward lifting force on the slide. Push-type cylinders are mounted to the press upright or frame with the rod pushing the slide.

With both pull and push-type cylinders, a floating connection must be provided at both ends of the cylinders to allow for any movement necessary in the slide as it is adjusted in the press gibs. To eliminate undue strain and possible breakage, a flexible joint is often provided in the piping that connects the cylinder to the surge tank.

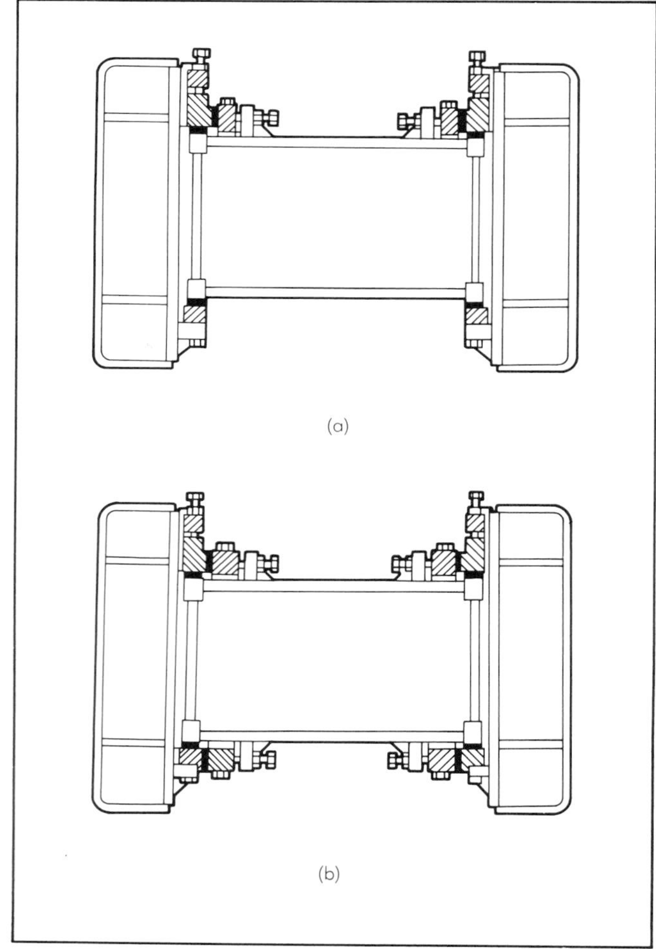


**Fig. 5-11 Square-type gibs: (a) six point and (b) eight point.** (*Verson Allsteel Press Co.*)

*Safety requirements.* When air counterbalances are used, safety requirements specify the following:

1. The cylinder must incorporate means to retain the piston and rod in case of breakage or loosening.
2. The system must have adequate capability to hold the slide and its attachments at any point in the stroke, without the brake being applied. A chart of attachment weights and proper counterbalance pressures to achieve the requirements should be attached near the counterbalance regulating controls.
3. The cylinder must incorporate means to prevent failure of capability (sudden loss of pressure) in the event of air supply failure.
4. Air-controlling equipment must be protected against foreign material and water entering the pneumatic system. A means of air lubrication must be provided when needed.

## Die Cushions

Die cushions, often and more accurately referred to as pressure pads, are used to apply pressure to flat blanks for drawing operations. They also serve as liftout or knockout devices to remove stampings from the dies. Dies are sometimes built with integral blankholders (refer to Chapter 6, "Die Design for Sheet Metal Forming"), using compression springs or pieces of rubber or urethane to supply the holding pressure; but this method of supplying holding pressure can cause problems with respect to force requirements and uniformity of force, especially in deep-drawing operations. Other limitations to the use of springs are that adjustments generally require changing the springs and their working travel is limited (about 25% of their free lengths at zero loads). Nitrogen die cylinders, discussed in Chapter 6, are being used extensively in place of springs.

Double and triple-action presses feature integral blankholders and do not require cushions for drawing operations. Cushions are sometimes employed on double-action presses, however, for liftout or triple-action draws or to keep the bottoms of the stampings flat, hold their shapes, or prevent slippage while drawing. For such applications, the cushions must be equipped with locking devices to hold the cushions at the bottom of stroke for a predetermined length of the return stroke of the press slide.

Single-action presses do not have an integral means for blankholding and require the use of cushions or other means of applying uniform pressure to the blanks for drawing operations, except for shallow draws in thick stock. The most common types of pressure-control means for drawing operations on single-action presses are pneumatic and hydropneumatic die cushions.

Most die cushions are located in the press beds, but there are applications that require installation within or on the press slides. In either case, the functions are similar and the operations are the same. The recommended capacity of a die cushion (the amount of force it is capable of exerting) is generally about 15-20% of the rated press force. Strokes of the cushions are usually one-half the strokes of the press slides, but should not exceed the bolster thickness less 1/2" (12.7 mm).

Cushions with different strokes and with higher capacities are available, but the size of the press-bed opening limits the size, type, and capacity of the cushions. Consideration must be given to the press capacity at the point at which the draw is to begin, because the force and energy required to depress the cushion is added to that required to draw the stamping. As a result, the force and energy needed for a high-capacity cushion may not leave enough for the operation to be performed.

**Pneumatic cushions.** In cushions of this type, the maximum pressure is controlled by the diameter and number of cylinders and the available air pressure. Shop line pressure is generally used, but it is possible to use a booster or intensifier to increase the air pressure. Most cushions are normally rated at a pressure of 100 psi (689.5 kPa), and it is generally recommended that the pressure not exceed 200 psi (1379 kPa). Surge tanks, if required, must conform to local codes and are generally approved for a maximum pressure of 125 psi (862 kPa).

A pneumatic die cushion for a single-point press normally uses one cylinder and one piston. Two or more cushions may be placed on top of one another, however, when a high-capacity unit is required in a limited-bed area in which vertical space is available. For multiple-point presses, when the pressure pad area requirement is too large for one cushion, multiple cushions can be arranged alongside one another. The cushions may be individually adjustable or tied together. A multiple-die cushion is often preferable to a hydropneumatic die cushion because of the speed restrictions of the latter. Presses to be used with progressive dies can be equipped with a cushion whose position may be changed from right to left in the press bed.

A commonly used pneumatic cushion (see Fig. 5-12) has a single cylinder with internal guiding only. Downward movement of the blankholder, through pressure pins, forces the cylinder against a cushion of air inside the cylinder and moves the air back into the surge tank. On the upstroke of the press slide, air in the surge tank returns the cylinder. Self-contained designs that function without the need for surge tanks are available when space in or below the press bed permits their use.

Guiding of the cushions is critical to maintain their top surfaces parallel to the bottom face of the press slide. Parallelism of the top of the cushion to the top of the press bed is generally maintained within 0.004 in./ft (0.33 mm/m). Cushions are available with cylinders having both external and internal guides, which are especially desirable for off-center loads. Post-type cushions, using posts to resist off-center forces, have the guides spread the maximum distance possible for increased rigidity.

Any significant offset loading on a cushion creates high pressures on the guide liners. Cushions with long guides, such as

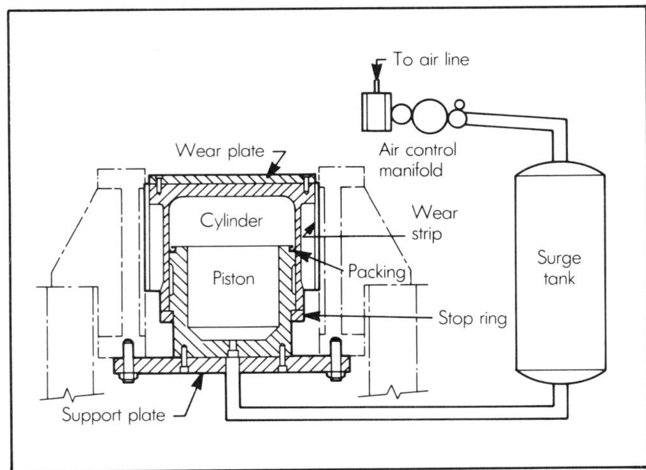


**Fig. 5-12 Schematic diagram of a pneumatic die cushion.**

post-guided cushions, are better than other designs; but eventually, offset loads cause excessive wear of the guides. The use of balancing-type pressure pins to compensate for offset loading is recommended.

Locking devices are usually double-acting hydraulic cylinders tied to the pneumatic cushions to control and delay the stripping action of the cushions. Valving in the lock withdraws the cushion to relieve all pressure from the stamping, and the cushion is held in this position until the lock is released, permitting the cushion to move upward. The return stroke of the cushion is adjustable by means of a speed-control valve which allows the oil to flow back at a controlled rate, thereby controlling the speed of the cushion on the upstroke, preventing the blankholder from overtaking the die, and minimizing any shock at the completion of its return stroke.

**Hydropneumatic cushions.** These die cushions are used when higher forces are required or when space does not permit the use of double or triple-stage cushions. Hydropneumatic cushions are slower acting than the pneumatic cushions; therefore, they are usually used on large presses and on slow presses. They can be adjusted to hold a large, light blank for deep drawing or shallow forming or to grip heavy-gage material as tightly as required for curved-surface or flat-bottom forming.

A typical hydropneumatic cushion is connected to a surge tank as shown in Fig. 5-13. Two individually controlled air lines are required, one connected to the operating valve of the cushion and the other connected to the top of the surge tank. The air pressure supplied to the operating valve determines the capacity of the cushion on the downstroke. The pressure of the air in the surge tank determines the stripping force available on the upstroke. The surge tank may be separate from or integral with the cushion, depending upon the space available beneath the press bed.

The pressure of the air in the surge tank is transmitted to the hydraulic fluid, which is free to pass upward through the check valve and force the cushion piston upward. Pressure is also exerted against the face of the operating valve stem, but it is not sufficient to overcome the opposing air pressure working on the operating air piston.

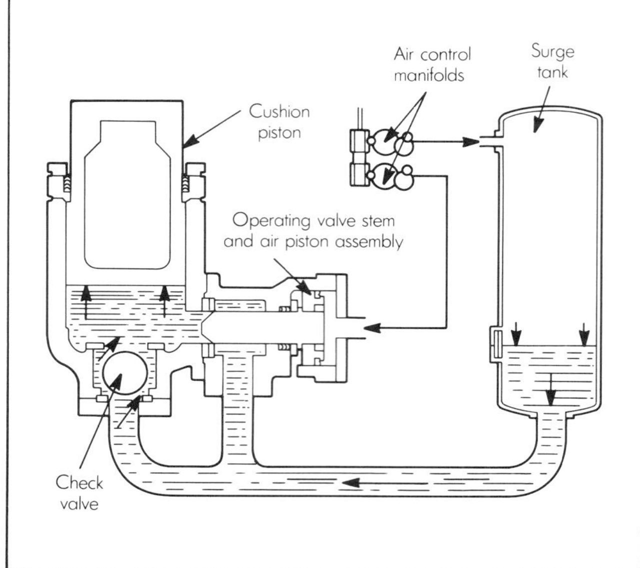


**Fig. 5-13 Schematic diagram of a hydropneumatic die cushion.**

When a downward force is applied to the cushion, the check valve is immediately closed and the pressure of the fluid that is trapped beneath the piston begins to rise. When the pressure against the small face of the operating valve stem reaches a predetermined point, it exceeds the magnitude of the air pressure on the larger area of the air piston and opens the operating valve. As long as the cushion piston continues its downward movement, the fluid beneath it is maintained under constant pressure by the throttling action of the operating valve; the additional fluid replaced by the piston is forced through the valve to the surge tank. Oil pressures are generally limited to about 1000 psi (6.9 MPa).

When the stroke has been completed and the downward force on the cushion piston is removed, the pressure of the fluid beneath the piston is immediately lessened, reducing the air pressure on the air piston and thereby closing the operating valve. Fluid from the surge tank under pressure from the air behind it passes upward through the check valve and raises the cushion piston to top stroke.

The use of hydropneumatic cushions is limited to slow operating speeds—about 50 fpm (15 m/min). When long cushion strokes are required, slow operating speeds must be used. Conversely, faster operating speeds can be used only with very short strokes. If the cushion is operated at high speed, the operating valve is forced open too rapidly, causing the air piston to strike the end of its travel. The piston bounces back and oscillates rapidly with a series of extremely hard hammer blows. This results in unsatisfactory operation and damage to the operating valve. The stripping force of a hydropneumatic cushion is much less than its blankholding force.

**Air pressure requirements.** The following equations may be used for determining the amount of air pressure required to obtain a certain cushion capacity. These equations do not take into consideration friction or loss of air pressure due to the length of piping.

For pneumatic cushions and stripping pressure on hydropneumatic cushions:

$$p = \frac{P}{A_1} \tag{1}$$

For hydropneumatic cushions:

$$p = \frac{PA_3}{A_1 A_2} \tag{2}$$

where:

$p$ = air pressure, psi
$P$ = cushion capacity, lb
$A_1$ = area, cushion piston, in.$^2$
$A_2$ = area, operating air piston, in.$^2$
$A_3$ = area, operating valve stem face, in.$^2$

For metric usage, the air pressure in psi should be multiplied by 6.895 to obtain the air pressure in kilopascals (kPa).

## Reducing Reversal Loads

Reversal or snap-through loads are a major cause of noise and press breakdown, especially in blanking amd severe punching operations. The breakthrough in workpiece material after the punch has penetrated 20-30% of the material thickness (refer to Chapter 4, "Sheet Metal Blanking and Forming") suddenly releases high energy that propels the press slide downward at speeds to 100 fps (30.5 m/s). At the bottom of the slide travel, press members are subjected to high reverse loads.

Several methods have been developed to minimize the effect of reverse loads and damage to the press, including the use of properly designed shock mounts and the use of counterpressures built into the dies. One press builder offers a snap-through arrestor (see Fig. 5-14) for mechanical presses. This unit, employing two hydraulic cylinders in the press bolster, senses an increase in fluid velocity when breakthrough starts. A fast-acting valve shifts the system from a low-pressure to a high-pressure mode. All the fluid in the cylinders is retained to provide maximum restraining force.

Acceleration of the press slide at breakthrough immediately closes the velocity-sensitive valve, and rapid counterloading is produced to absorb the energy released from the slide. A high-pressure accumulator cushions the system in this mode. Reduction in the released energy due to breakthrough is about 70%.

## MECHANICAL PRESS DRIVES

The structural characteristics of a press that are required to resist the forces produced during the working portion of its cycle are described in the preceding section of this chapter. In addition to these characteristics, a press must have a drive capable of furnishing the necessary torque to exert the pressing forces when required and must also have sufficient energy to sustain the forces through the distances required.

Mechanical presses are available with various types of drives. Selection of a particular type depends primarily upon the application for which the press is intended, as well as the stroke and speed requirements.

### Nongeared and Geared Drives

Three major types of drives for mechanical presses are:

1. Nongeared, or flywheel, drive.
2. Single-reduction gear drive.
3. Multiple-reduction gear drive.

With all three types of drives, a flywheel is used to store energy. The source of power is an electric motor which returns the flywheel to operating speed between press strokes. Permissible slowdown of the flywheel during the operation depends upon the characteristics of the drive motor and is generally about 7-10% in nongeared presses and 10-20% in geared presses.

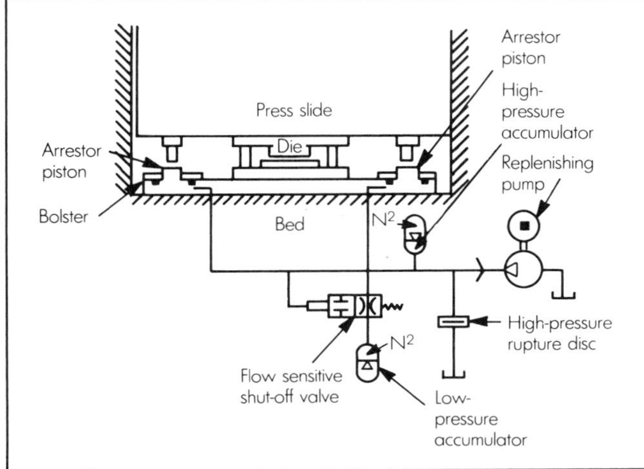


**Fig. 5-14 Snap-through arrestor with high and low-pressure hydraulic circuits for absorbing the shock from reversal loads.** (*E. W. Bliss Div., Gulf & Western Manufacturing Co.*)

**Nongeared drive.** The flywheel-type drive transmits the energy of the flywheel directly to the main shaft of the press without intermediate gearing (see Fig. 5-15, *a*). The main shaft may be mounted right-to-left (parallel to the front of the press) with the flywheel on either side, or the shaft may be mounted front-to-back (with the flywheel at the back of the press).

Presses with this simple drive are generally used for light blanking; punching; shallow forming; small operations requiring high-speed progressive dies; or other light, high-speed operations for which energy requirements are small. Limited flywheel energy requires that work be performed near the bottom of the stroke. Nongeared presses operate at higher speeds than geared types.

**Single-reduction gear drive.** This type of drive (see Fig. 5-15, *b* and *c*) transmits the energy of the flywheel to the main shaft through one gear reduction. Such drives generally operate presses at speeds of about 30-150 spm and are recommended for heavier blanking operations, shallow drawing, and similar operations requiring more energy than available with nongeared drives.

**Multiple-reduction gear drive.** This type of drive (see Fig. 5-15, *d*) transmits flywheel energy to the main shaft through two or more gear reductions. The gears reduce the strokes per minute of the press slide (generally 10-30 spm) without reducing the nominal flywheel speed. Presses with this type of drive are used for deep-drawing operations in which considerable energy is needed due to the long stroke that is required. They are also used for deep-drawing operations in which the maximum drawing speed of the workpiece material limits the slide speed.

Large presses with heavy slides use a multiple-gear drive because it is impractical to accelerate and decelerate large masses at high speeds. Dependent upon the force capacity of the press and the length of stroke, speeds generally range from 8-30 spm.

### Single and Twin-Drive Presses

Whether a mechanical press has a single or multiple-reduction gear drive, energy can be transmitted to the main shaft from one or two gears on each shaft. With one pair of gears (see Fig. 5-15, *b*), the press is referred to as having single-end drive; with two pairs of gears (view *c*), the press is called a twin-end-drive press.

Twin-end-drive arrangements are used on presses having long, left-to-right dimensions to reduce the torsional strain on the shafts. This results from applying force to both sides of the point of resistance. Crank presses of low force capacities, short stroke, and narrow span from bearing to bearing are generally single-end drive. The shafts on these presses are not subjected to as high a torsional (angular) deflection as the shafts on presses having a wider span between bearings. A twin-end drive is generally used for all long-stroke presses, whether they have a narrow or wide span between bearings.

For large-bed presses, a quadruple drive is often used. Such presses have two long crankshafts, with each crankshaft having a twin-end drive.

### Drive Location

Most presses are the top-drive (overdrive) type in which the driving mechanism is located in the press crown and pushes the slide down to perform the operation.

Underdrive presses (see Fig. 5-16) have the mechanism

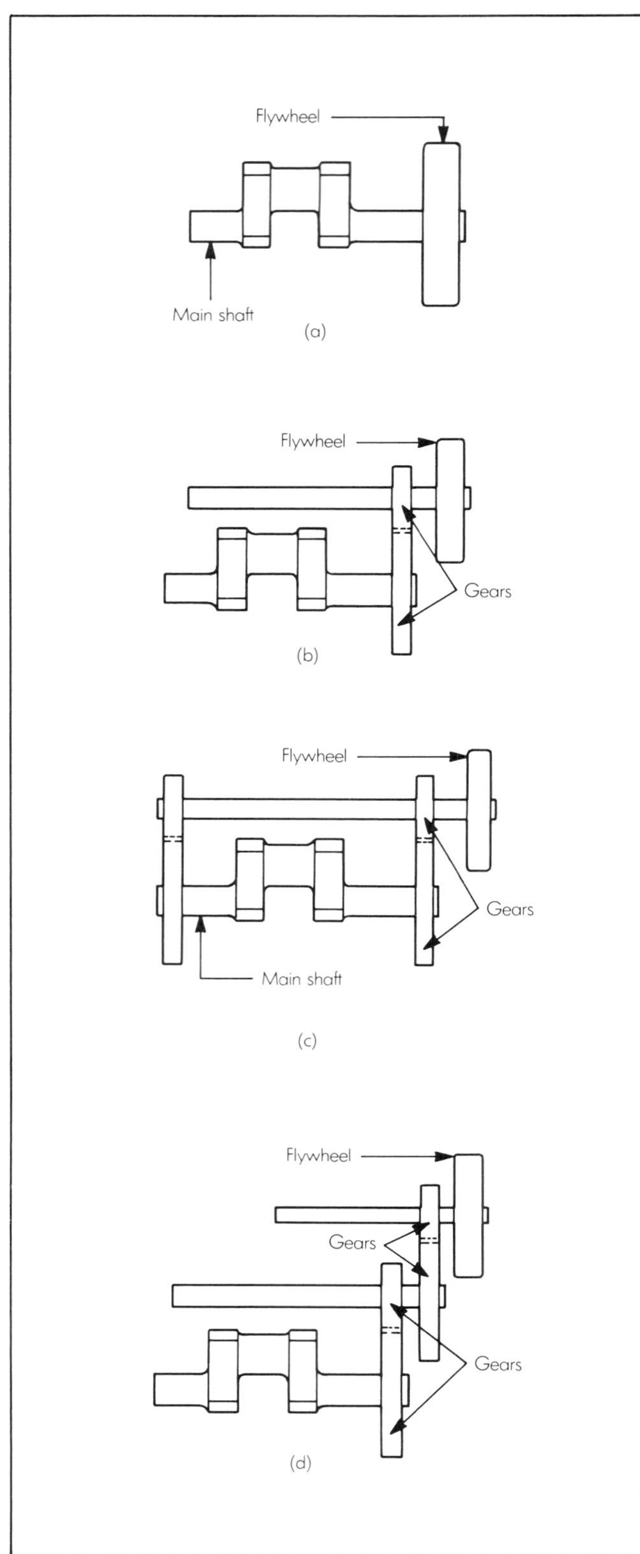


**Fig. 5-15 Mechanical press drives: (a) nongeared (flywheel) type; (b) single-reduction, single-end, gear type; (c) single-reduction, twin-end, gear type; and (d) multiple-reduction, gear type.**

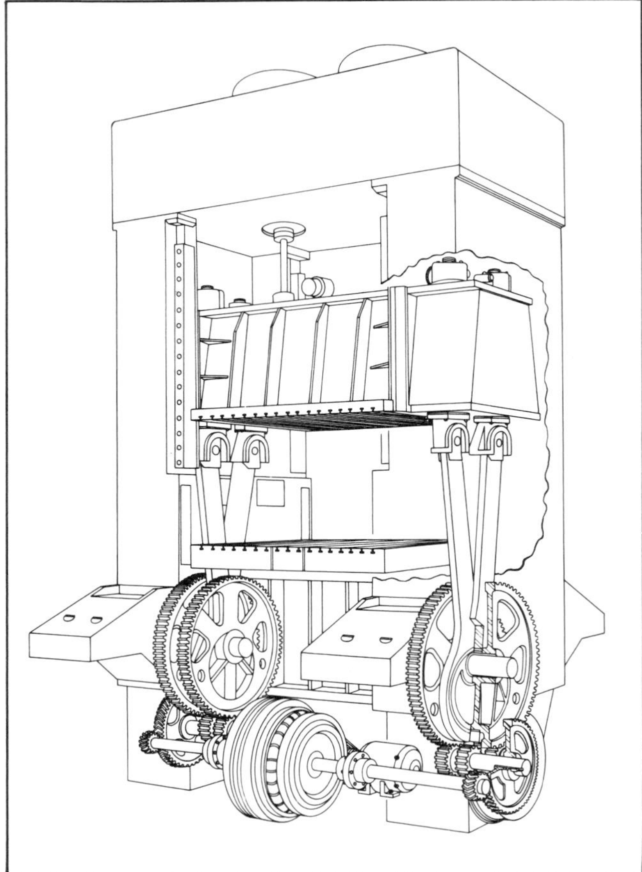

**Fig. 5-16 Underdrive, straight-side press.** (*Clearing, A Div. of U.S. Industries, Inc.*)

under the bed with connecting linkage in the uprights to pull the slide downward. The mechanisms of large underdrive presses are below floor level, thus requiring only a minimum ceiling height; but either a basement or trench-type pit is required for servicing. Machine repair does not result in obstruction of the production floor.

## Method of Slide Actuation

In all power presses the work is performed by the slide or slides through reciprocating motion to and from the press bed or bolster. In mechanical presses (see Fig. 5-17), slide motion originates from the following:

1. Crankshafts incorporating crankpins or eccentrics.
2. Eccentrics cast or welded integrally with or bolted to rotating main gears.
3. A pair of knuckles folded and straightened by a pitman-crankpin mechanism.
4. Oscillating rocker shafts and toggles.
5. Cams.
6. Drag links.

**Crankshafts.** Main shafts in single-action presses of the nongeared type are of conventional crank, semieccentric, or full-eccentric design. The number of throws (offsets) or eccentrics on the shaft is determined by the number of points of suspension of the slide.

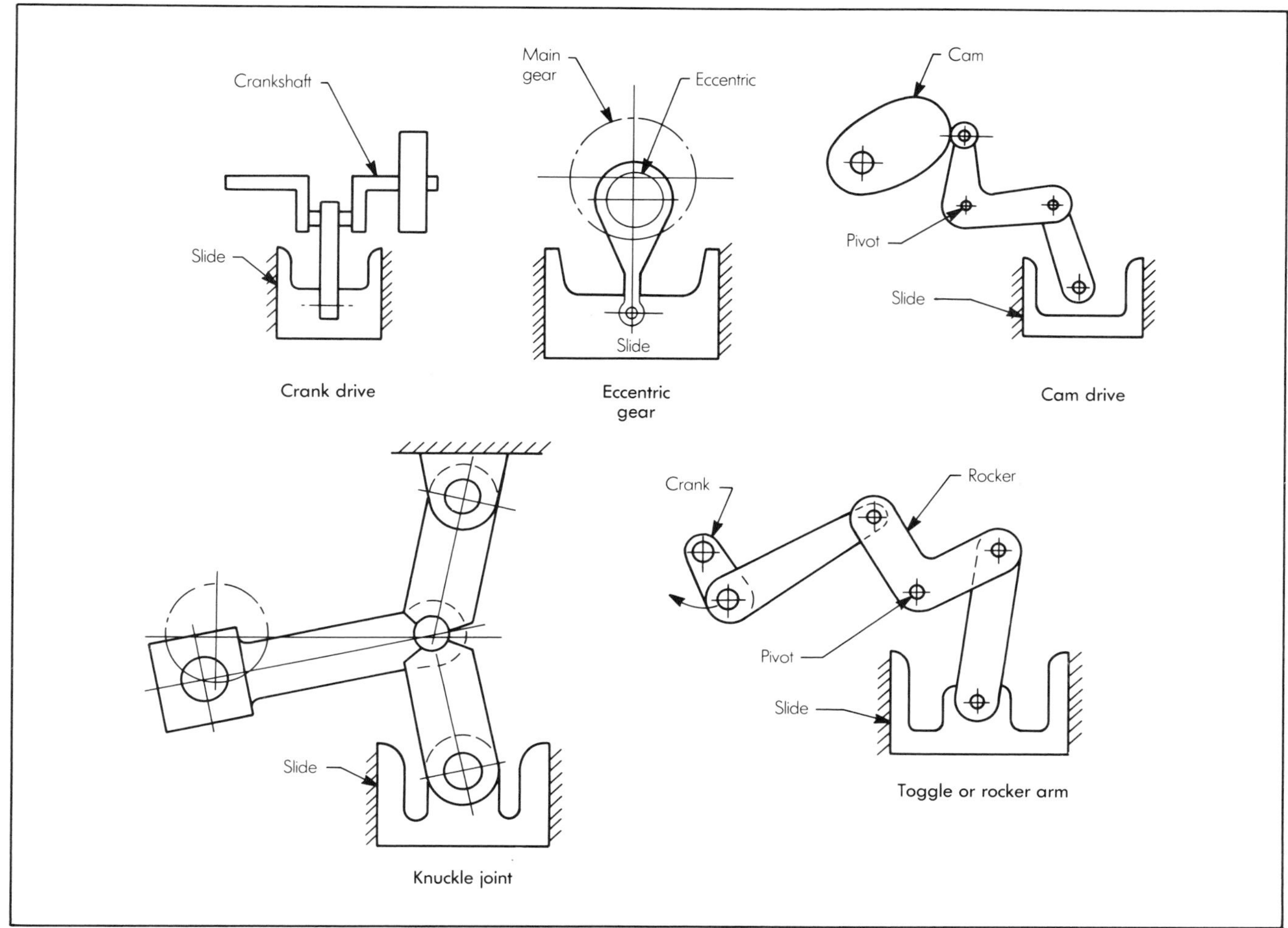


**Fig. 5-17 Schematic representation of methods of slide actuation in mechanical presses.** (*Danly Machine Corp.*)

The crankshaft is the most common means used for actuating slides for presses up to about 600 tons (5338 kN). For comparatively short strokes, the throw is obtained by means of a full eccentric machined on the shaft. Conventional crankshafts are used for longer strokes. Double cranks are used for wide presses, and some presses are built with more than two cranks.

Conventional crank construction can be used for press strokes up to three times the shaft diameter. The full-eccentric design, which is the stiffest, can be used for strokes to approximately 1 1/2 times the shaft diameter.

**Eccentric gear.** Eccentric-gear presses incorporate a slide actuated by an eccentric cast or welded integrally with, or keyed and bolted to, the main gears (see Fig. 5-18). The gear eccentric is mounted on either a rotating or nonrotating shaft which is sometimes used as a power take-off for auxiliary equipment. Torsional stresses are not present in shafts of eccentrically driven presses as they are in those of crankshaft-driven presses.

**Knuckle joint.** Presses employing knuckle joints (see Fig. 5-19) develop tremendous pressures near the bottom of the stroke. They are often used for compression operations, such as coining, requiring high pressures during a short portion of the stroke. The force is applied through a crank or eccentric to the joint connecting two levers of equal lengths. The levers are actuated through a nonadjustable connection from the shaft in the back of the press frame. The slide motion is achieved through straightening the two hinged levers that suspends the slide from the crown.

**Toggles.** A crank or eccentric actuates a series of levers, linked in tandem in a sequence of movements through two or more dead-center positions or dissipation points. These are spaced at closely related intervals to accomplish an effective dwell of the holding member. In the toggle or rocker arm mechanism the force is always exerted against one end of a series of levers, but should not be confused with the knuckle-joint motion.

Toggle action is widely used in double-action presses to obtain the proper stroking characteristics for the blankholder. Figure 5-20 shows that the reciprocating action of the toggle-driven slide is faster than and dwells longer than the crank-driven and knuckle-joint slides. The use of toggles to operate the outer (blankholding) slide on double-action presses relieves the crankshaft of blankholding strain, which is carried directly to the press frame.

Pneumatic toggle links are available for light-duty, single and double-crank presses. Placing cushions on the links makes adjustments more convenient, increases the range of work that

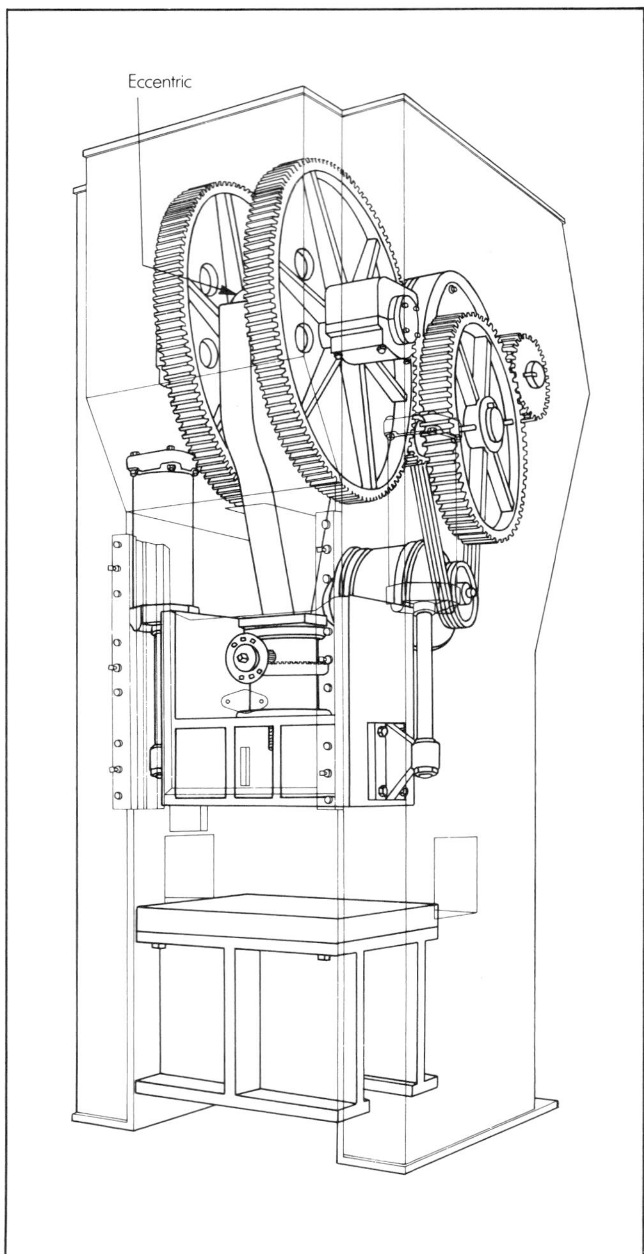


**Fig. 5-18 Single-action, straight-side, eccentric-type, mechanical press.** (*Verson Allsteel Press Co.*)

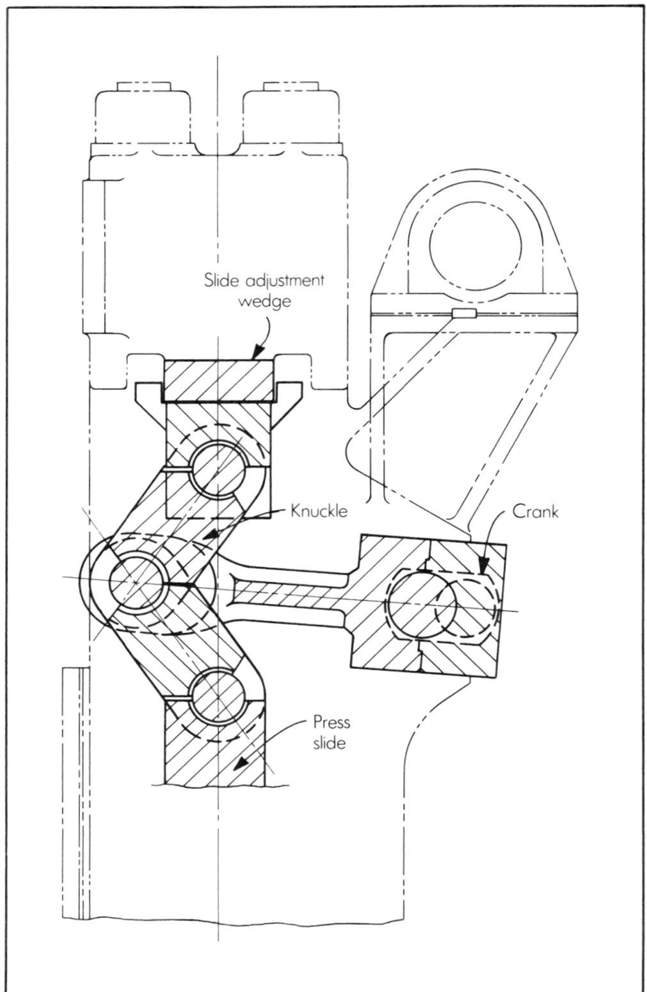


**Fig. 5-19 Knuckle-joint press.**

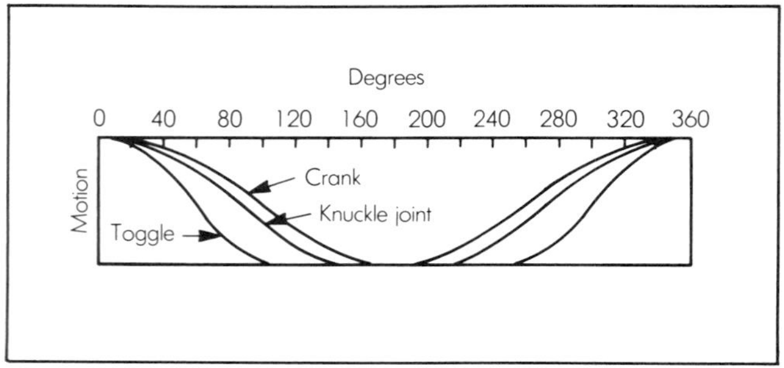


**Fig. 5-20 Relative motions and degrees of dwell obtained with crank, knuckle-joint, and toggle actions.**

can be performed, and automatically compensates for changes in thickness of the workpiece material. Provisions can be made for disconnecting the toggle mechanism and attaching the outer slide to the inner slide for single-action operation.

**Cams.** Cams are utilized to produce motions at angles and in planes not obtainable from simple crankshaft mechanisms. The motions of cams, cranks, and eccentrics are frequently combined, as on single and multiple-action presses on which one or more dwells or certain hold-down or stripping motions are required. The double-action cam press essentially embodies the same motions as the double-action toggle press, but can generally be operated at higher speeds. They are usually limited to small-capacity presses of relatively narrow widths and are primarily used for blanking and cupping operations.

**Drag link.** A drag-link mechanism consists of a power-driven crank, two intermediate links, and a fourth link connecting the drive to the slide of the press. By changing the relative lengths and geometric arrangement of the links, a wide variety of motions can be provided. For example, the full force capacity of the press can be exerted high above the bottom of the stroke and the force can be maintained nearly constant throughout the stroke. Proper design of the link drive can also reduce the impact velocity (required because of the metallurgical limits of some workpiece materials), with a fast approach and return of the slide, thus compensating for the slowdown and maintaining the same production rate.

## FORCE, ENERGY AND TORQUE CONSIDERATIONS

The force rating of a mechanical press, expressed in tons or kilonewtons (kN), is often the major consideration in the selection and application of the press. Torque and energy (work) capacities, however, are also critical, especially for deep-drawing operations, and should be given careful attention.

### Force Capacity

The force capacity of a mechanical press is the maximum force that should be exerted by the slide or slide-mounted dies against a workpiece at a specified distance above bottom of stroke, as discussed previously in this chapter (refer to Tables 5-2 and 5-3). It is a relative measure of the torque capacity of the press drive and an actual measure of the structural capacity (size and physical strength) of the press components to withstand the applied load and resist deflection within the specified tolerances.

It has been customary to associate the force ratings of mechanical presses with the shaft diameters at the main bearings. The maximum strokes for single-end-drive presses of various force ratings and of different shaft diameters are presented in Table 5-5. Methods of determining the forces required to blank, form, and draw workpieces are discussed in Chapter 4 of this volume, "Sheet Metal Blanking and Forming." For drawing operations, the force required to offset the pressure of die cushions must be added to determine total force requirements.

It is advisable to maintain a wide margin of safety between the calculated force required for any job and the force capacity of the press, because of the tendency of certain materials to work-harden and also because of conditions inherent in most dies. Force requirements for cutting, (blanking, punching, etc.) are customarily figured on the basis of sharp dies with correct clearances. As the dies wear or become dull, the forces may be double the original requirements. This is particularly true when materials 0.020" (0.51 mm) thick or less are worked. Drawing and forming operations are greatly affected by die clearances, and worn or mismatched dies may make a noticeable difference in force requirements. Press failure or breakage, resulting in unsafe operating conditions, is frequently the result of using dull dies.

### Distance Above Bottom of Stroke

Proper selection of a press for a specific application depends upon where in the stroke the maximum force is to be applied. Only forces less than the capacity of the press should be applied further up on the stroke than the distance specified in the press rating.

The reduced force capacities of straight-side presses [rated at full capacity 1/2" (12.7 mm) above bottom of stroke] for force applications at various distances above bottom of stroke are shown in Fig. 5-21. For example, if a stroke of 6" (152 mm) is required, with maximum force applied 2" (50.8 mm) above bottom of stroke, only 60% of the rated force capacity of the press should be applied. Since many presses are rated at different distances from the bottom of the stroke, a chart such as the one shown should be obtained from the builder for each press. Table 5-6 gives data for approximate force capacities at bottom of stroke and at midstroke for various sizes and types of presses with different strokes.

**TABLE 5-5**
**Maximum Strokes for Mechanical Presses with Single-End Drives**

| Press Capacity, tons (kN) | Shaft Diameter at Main Bearing,* in. (mm) | Shaft Diameter at Crankpin,* in. (mm) | Maximum Stroke,** in. (mm) |
|---|---|---|---|
| 60 (534) | 4 (102) | 5 1/2 (140) | 6 (152) |
| 75 (667) | 4 1/2 (114) | 6 1/2 (165) | 8 (203) |
| 110 (979) | 5 1/2 (140) | 8 (203) | 10 (254) |
| 150 (1334) | 6 1/2 (165) | 9 (229) | 12 (305) |
| 200 (1779) | 7 1/2 (190) | 10 1/2 (267) | 14 (356) |

* Diameters are approximate and vary slightly with different press manufacturers.
** Based on a maximum torsional stress of about 12,000 psi (82.7 MPa).

### Torque Capacity

The drives of mechanical presses provide a constant torque, but due to the mechanical advantage of the linkage, the forces transmitted through their clutches to rotating members and reciprocating slides vary from a minimum at midstroke to infinity at the bottom of the stroke. The torque value equals the force times the perpendicular distance from the force to the axis about which the force is applied.

Torque limitations of a press are determined by the size of the drive components (shaft, clutch, gears) that transmit flywheel energy in the form of torque to the slide, by the stroke length, and by the distance above bottom where the force is applied. Presses rated higher in the stroke (above bottom dead center) require greater torque capacity in the drive components and more flywheel energy. Exerting too high a torque causes press members to fail.

### Energy Requirements

In addition to knowing that a press and its drive can provide adequate force at a certain distance above stroke bottom, it is equally important to determine whether the press has sufficient work (energy) capacity. This is the ability to deliver enough force through the distance required to make a particular part. The product of force times distance (working stroke) is the energy load on the press, usually expressed in inch-tons or joules (J)—1 in.-ton equals 226J.

As energy is expended in forming a part in the die, the flywheel slows down. If the amount of energy used is within the design limitations of the press drive, the motor returns the energy used to the flywheel, bringing it back to its starting speed before the press ram reaches the top of its stroke, and starts the next stroke. For intermittent press operation, 20% is considered the maximum the flywheel may be slowed down in removing

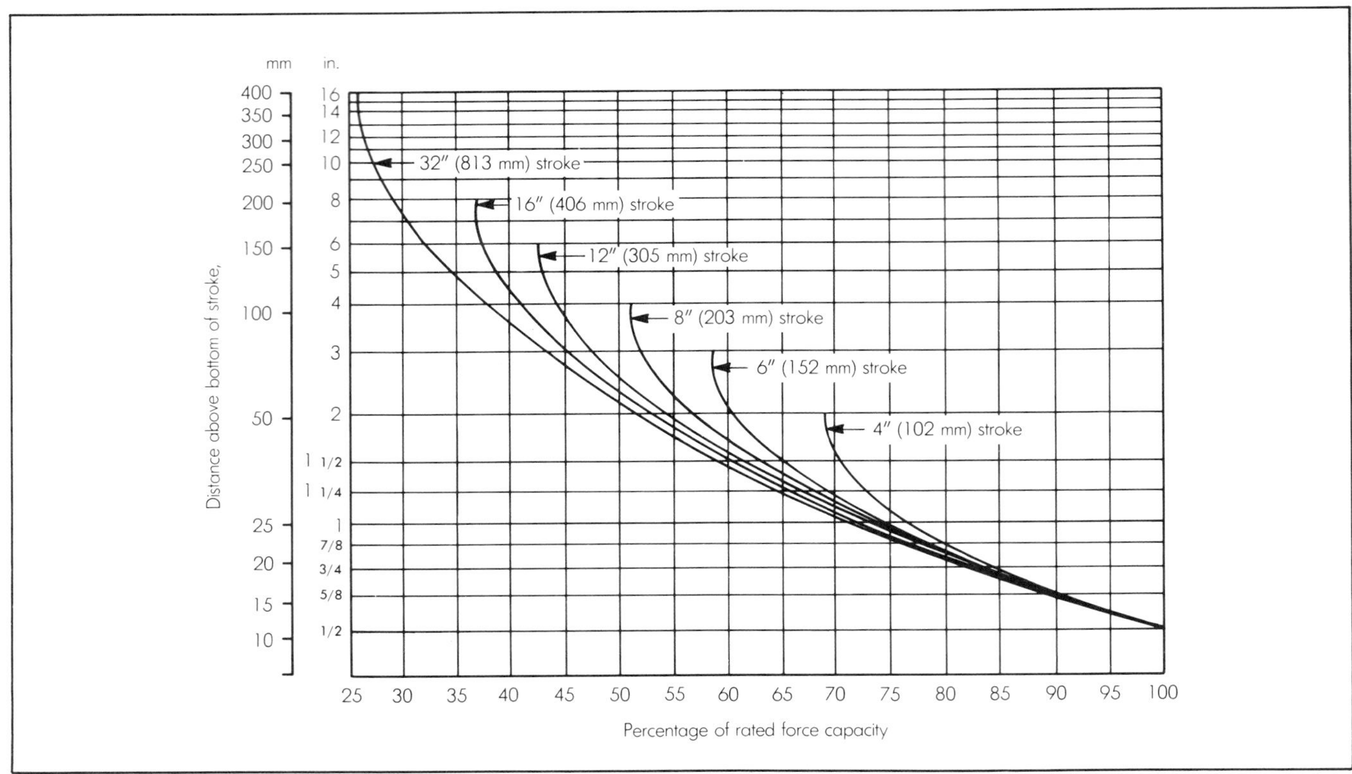


**Fig. 5-21 Percentage of rated force capacity for straight-side presses at various distances above bottom of stroke.** (*Danly Machine Corp.*)

**TABLE 5-6**
**Approximate Force Capacities of Presses**

| Shaft Diam, in. (mm) | Type of Drive | | Stroke of Press, in. (mm) | | | | | | | | | | | |
|---|---|---|---|---|---|---|---|---|---|---|---|---|---|---|
| | | | 3 (76) | 4 (102) | 5 (127) | 6 (152) | 8 (203) | 10 (254) | 12 (305) | 14 (356) | 16 (406) | 18 (457) | 20 (508) | 22 (559) |
| | | Approximate Force Capacity, tons (kN) | | | | | | | | | | | | |
| | | at Bottom | at Midstroke | | | | | | | | | | | |
| Straight-Side, Single-Crank Presses | | | | | | | | | | | | | | |
| 1 | Single | 3 | --- | --- | --- | --- | --- | --- | --- | --- | --- | --- | --- | --- |
| (25.4) | | (26.7) | --- | --- | --- | --- | --- | --- | --- | --- | --- | --- | --- | --- |
| 1 1/2 | Single | 6 3/4 | 3 | 2 1/4 | --- | --- | --- | --- | --- | --- | --- | --- | --- | --- |
| (38) | | (60) | (26.7) | (20) | --- | --- | --- | --- | --- | --- | --- | --- | --- | --- |
| 2 | Single | 12 | 7 1/2 | 5 1/2 | 4 1/4 | --- | --- | --- | --- | --- | --- | --- | --- | --- |
| (51) | | (107) | (66.7) | (49) | (37.8) | --- | --- | --- | --- | --- | --- | --- | --- | --- |
| 2 1/2 | Single | 19 | 14 | 11 | 8 1/2 | 7 | --- | --- | --- | --- | --- | --- | --- | --- |
| (63.5) | | (169) | (124.5) | (98) | (75.6) | (62.3) | --- | --- | --- | --- | --- | --- | --- | --- |
| 3 | Single | 32 | 20 | 15 | 12 | 9 | 8 | --- | --- | --- | --- | --- | --- | --- |
| (76) | | (285) | (178) | (133.4) | (107) | (80) | (71) | --- | --- | --- | --- | --- | --- | --- |
| 3 1/2 | Single | 44 | 31 1/2 | 23 1/2 | 19 | 16 | 14 | 11 1/2 | --- | --- | --- | --- | --- | --- |
| (89) | | (391) | (280) | (209) | (169) | (142) | (124.5) | (102.3) | --- | --- | --- | --- | --- | --- |
| 4 | Single | 58 | 44 | 36 | 30 | 24 | 18 | 13 | 9 | --- | --- | --- | --- | --- |
| (102) | | (516) | (391) | (320) | (267) | (213.5) | (160) | (115.6) | (80) | --- | --- | --- | --- | --- |
| 4 1/2 | Single | 74 | 60 | 50 | 40 | 35 | 26 | 19 | 12 | --- | --- | --- | --- | --- |
| (114) | | (658) | (534) | (445) | (356) | (311) | (231) | (169) | (107) | | | | | |

**TABLE 5-6—*Continued***

| Shaft Diam, in. (mm) | Type of Drive | Stroke of Press, in. (mm) / Approximate Force Capacity, tons (kN) at Bottom | 3 (76) | 4 (102) | 5 (127) | 6 (152) | 8 (203) | 10 (254) | 12 (305) | 14 (356) | 16 (406) | 18 (457) | 20 (508) | 22 (559) |
|---|---|---|---|---|---|---|---|---|---|---|---|---|---|---|
| | | | at Midstroke | | | | | | | | | | | |
| **Straight-Side, Single-Crank Presses** | | | | | | | | | | | | | | |
| 5 (127) | Single | 93 (827) | 73 (649) | 64 (569) | 56 (498) | 47 (418) | 35 (311) | 28 (249) | 22 (196) | 18 (160) | 14 (124.5) | --- | --- | --- |
| 6 (152) | Single | 135 (1201) | --- | 108 (961) | 94 (836) | 80 (712) | 60 (534) | 48 (427) | 39 (347) | 35 (311) | 32 (285) | 30 (267) | 27 (240) | --- |
| 7 (178) | Single | 190 (1690) | --- | --- | 135 (1201) | 122 (1085) | 98 (872) | 78 (694) | 69 (614) | 62 (552) | 46 (409) | 36 (320) | 31 (276) | --- |
| 8 (203) | Single | 255 (2268) | --- | --- | --- | 174 (1548) | 147 (1308) | 117 (1041) | 93 (827) | 82 (729) | 70 (623) | 55 (489) | 45 (400) | 37 (329) |
| 8 (203) | Twin | 255 (2268) | --- | --- | --- | --- | 225 (2002) | 196 (1744) | 162 (1441) | 142 (1263) | 121 (1076) | 110 (979) | 95 (845) | 85 (756) |
| 9 (229) | Single | 345 (3069) | --- | --- | 265 (2357) | 245 (2180) | 205 (1824) | 163 (1450) | 135 (1201) | 125 (1112) | 115 (1023) | 91 (810) | 75 (667) | 63 (560) |
| 9 (229) | Twin | 345 (3069) | --- | --- | --- | --- | --- | 274 (2438) | 227 (2019) | 193 (1717) | 169 (1503) | 152 (1352) | 135 (1201) | 120 (1068) |
| 10 (254) | Single | 440 (3914) | --- | --- | --- | 340 (3025) | 282 (2509) | 227 (2019) | 185 (1646) | 150 (1334) | 123 (1094) | 117 (1041) | 111 (987) | 105 (934) |
| 10 (254) | Twin | 440 (3914) | --- | --- | --- | --- | --- | 354 (3149) | 310 (2758) | 267 (2375) | 233 (2073) | 206 (1833) | 185 (1646) | 166 (1477) |
| 11 (279) | Single | 545 (4848) | --- | --- | --- | 450 (4003) | 376 (3345) | 300 (2669) | 252 (2242) | 210 (1868) | 180 (1601) | 170 (1512) | 159 (1414) | 145 (1290) |
| 11 (279) | Twin | 545 (4848) | --- | --- | --- | --- | --- | 450 (4003) | 410 (3647) | 362 (3220) | 332 (2953) | 278 (2473) | 250 (2224) | 225 (2002) |
| 12 (305) | Single | 665 (5916) | --- | --- | --- | --- | 485 (4315) | 390 (3469) | 320 (2847) | 280 (2491) | 240 (2135) | 210 (1868) | 190 (1690) | 170 (1512) |
| 12 (305) | Twin | 665 (5916) | --- | --- | --- | --- | --- | 550 (4893) | 510 (4537) | 460 (4092) | 405 (3603) | 360 (3203) | 325 (2891) | 285 (2535) |
| 13 (330) | Single | 790 (7028) | --- | --- | --- | --- | 595 (5293) | 500 (4448) | 415 (3692) | 350 (3114) | 300 (2669) | 250 (2224) | 220 (1957) | 195 (1735) |
| 13 (330) | Twin | 790 (7028) | --- | --- | --- | --- | --- | --- | 605 (5382) | 570 (5071) | 515 (4581) | 461 (4101) | 427 (3799) | 376 (3345) |
| 14 (356) | Single | 920 (8184) | --- | --- | --- | --- | 707 (6289) | 615 (5471) | 510 (4537) | 460 (4092) | 380 (3380) | 310 (2758) | 280 (2491) | 250 (2224) |
| 14 (356) | Twin | 920 (8184) | --- | --- | --- | --- | --- | --- | 737 (6556) | 700 (6227) | 630 (5604) | 565 (5026) | 510 (4537) | 465 (4137) |
| **Straight-Side, Double-Crank Presses** | | | | | | | | | | | | | | |
| 2 1/2 (63.5) | Single | 19 (169) | 16 (142) | 12 (107) | 8 (71) | --- | --- | --- | --- | --- | --- | --- | --- | --- |
| 3 (76) | Single | 32 (285) | 20 (178) | 15 (133.4) | 13 (115.6) | 10 (89) | 5 (44.5) | --- | --- | --- | --- | --- | --- | --- |
| 3 1/2 (89) | Single | 44 (391) | 31 (276) | 23 (205) | 19 (169) | 16 (142) | 9 (80) | --- | --- | --- | --- | --- | --- | --- |

**TABLE 5-6—*Continued***

| Shaft Diam, in. (mm) | Type of Drive | Stroke of Press, in. (mm) | | | | | | | | | | | |
|---|---|---|---|---|---|---|---|---|---|---|---|---|---|
| | | | 3 (76) | 4 (102) | 5 (127) | 6 (152) | 8 (203) | 10 (254) | 12 (305) | 14 (356) | 16 (406) | 18 (457) | 20 (508) | 22 (559) |
| | | Approximate Force Capacity, tons (kN) | | | | | | | | | | | |
| | | at Bottom | at Midstroke | | | | | | | | | | |
| Straight-Side, Double-Crank Presses | | | | | | | | | | | | | |
| 4<br>(102) | Single | 58<br>(516) | 41<br>(365) | 33<br>(294) | 29<br>(258) | 22<br>(196) | 19<br>(169) | 12<br>(107) | --- | --- | --- | --- | --- | --- |
| 4 1/2<br>(114) | Single | 74<br>(658) | 59<br>(525) | 51<br>(454) | 40<br>(356) | 34<br>(302) | 25<br>(222) | 19<br>(169) | --- | --- | --- | --- | --- | --- |
| 5<br>(127) | Single | 93<br>(827) | 73<br>(649) | 64<br>(569) | 56<br>(498) | 47<br>(418) | 36<br>(320) | 28<br>(249) | 21<br>(187) | --- | --- | --- | --- | --- |
| 6<br>(152) | Single | 135<br>(1201) | --- | 101<br>(898) | 91<br>(810) | 82<br>(729) | 60<br>(534) | 48<br>(427) | 39<br>(347) | --- | --- | --- | --- | --- |
| 7<br>(178) | Single | 200<br>(1779) | --- | --- | 135<br>(1201) | 122<br>(1085) | 102<br>(907) | 76<br>(676) | 66<br>(587) | 54<br>(480) | --- | --- | --- | --- |
| 8<br>(203) | Single | 290<br>(2580) | --- | --- | --- | 180<br>(1601) | 145<br>(1290) | 117<br>(1041) | 99<br>(881) | 72<br>(641) | 68<br>(605) | --- | --- | --- |
| 8<br>(203) | Twin | 290<br>(2580) | --- | --- | --- | 260<br>(2313) | 230<br>(2046) | 196<br>(1744) | 160<br>(1423) | 140<br>(1245) | 120<br>(1068) | 108<br>(961) | 96<br>(854) | --- |
| 9<br>(229) | Single | 400<br>(3558) | --- | --- | --- | 250<br>(2224) | 205<br>(1824) | 165<br>(1468) | 137<br>(1219) | 110<br>(979) | 98<br>(872) | 90<br>(801) | 85<br>(756) | --- |
| 9<br>(229) | Twin | 400<br>(3558) | --- | --- | --- | 333<br>(2962) | 310<br>(2758) | 273<br>(2429) | 227<br>(2019) | 195<br>(1735) | 170<br>(1512) | 150<br>(1334) | 133<br>(1183) | --- |
| 10<br>(254) | Single | 525<br>(4670) | --- | --- | --- | 340<br>(3025) | 285<br>(2535) | 227<br>(2019) | 187<br>(1664) | 155<br>(1379) | 144<br>(1281) | 128<br>(1139) | 112<br>(996) | --- |
| 10<br>(254) | Twin | 525<br>(4670) | --- | --- | --- | --- | --- | 375<br>(3336) | 315<br>(2802) | 265<br>(2357) | 233<br>(2073) | 205<br>(1824) | 185<br>(1646) | 170<br>(1512) |
| 11<br>(279) | Single | 700<br>(6227) | --- | --- | --- | 450<br>(4003) | 375<br>(3336) | 305<br>(2713) | 250<br>(2224) | 200<br>(1779) | 190<br>(1690) | 175<br>(1557) | 152<br>(1352) | 135<br>(1201) |
| 11<br>(279) | Twin | 700<br>(6227) | --- | --- | --- | --- | --- | 470<br>(4181) | 420<br>(3736) | 365<br>(3247) | 315<br>(2802) | 275<br>(2446) | 250<br>(2224) | 225<br>(2002) |
| 12<br>(305) | Single | 900<br>(8006) | --- | --- | --- | 580<br>5160 | 485<br>(4315) | 390<br>(3469) | 325<br>(2891) | 270<br>(2402) | 240<br>(2135) | 223<br>(1984) | 192<br>(1708) | 185<br>(1646) |
| 12<br>(305) | Twin | 900<br>(8006) | --- | --- | --- | --- | --- | 610<br>(5427) | 540<br>(4804) | 470<br>(4181) | 410<br>(3647) | 360<br>(3203) | 320<br>(2847) | 290<br>(2580) |
| 13<br>(330) | Single | 1150<br>(10 230) | --- | --- | --- | 740<br>(6583) | 621<br>(5524) | 498<br>(4430) | 415<br>(3692) | 355<br>(3158) | 315<br>(2802) | 285<br>(2535) | 250<br>(2224) | 235<br>(2091) |
| 13<br>(330) | Twin | 1150<br>(10 230) | --- | --- | --- | --- | --- | 800<br>(7117) | 700<br>(6227) | 630<br>(5604) | 520<br>(4626) | 470<br>(4181) | 430<br>(3825) | 385<br>(3425) |
| 14<br>(356) | Single | 1400<br>(12 454) | --- | --- | --- | 900<br>(8006) | 770<br>(6850) | 610<br>(5427) | 510<br>(4537) | 425<br>(3781) | 380<br>(3380) | 350<br>(3114 | 310<br>(2758) | 275<br>(2446) |
| 14<br>(356) | Twin | 1400<br>(12 454) | --- | --- | --- | --- | --- | 958<br>(8522) | 850<br>(7562) | 730<br>(6494) | 640<br>(5693) | 565<br>(5026) | 510<br>(4537) | 455<br>(4048) |

(*E.W. Bliss Div., Gulf & Western Manufacturing Co.*)

Note: Force capacities given are entirely independent of work or energy ratings. A long-stroke press, if loaded to maximum force capacity through its maximum working stroke, will undoubtedly require additional flywheel and motor capacity.

energy from it. The motor must be of sufficient size to restore the energy in time for the next stroke. Increasing the number of production strokes requires a larger motor, assuming the same energy is lost per stroke.

If not enough energy is available to form a specific part on the press, slowdown of the flywheel during the working portion of the press stroke becomes excessive. The results could be loss of press speed on each successive stroke, belt slippage and wear, and/or overloading of the main drive motor. If flywheel slowdown is severe enough due to the use of most or all the energy available during a stroke, motor overheating can cause thermal overloads in the motor starter to break the circuit and stop the press. Even more critical is the possibility of the press sticking at the bottom of the stroke. If this happens, considerable work is required to get the jam released.

A general rule-of-thumb is that a standard press should have at least work capacity equal to its force rating times the distance from the bottom of stroke at which it is rated. For example, a 100 ton (890 kN) press rated at 1/4″ (6.3 mm) from stroke bottom would usually be capable of providing only 25 in.-tons (5650 J) of energy to do work on a continuous basis. For presses using multistation dies, the energy requirements at all stations must be added.

Kinetic energy stored in the rotating flywheel of the press is the major source of energy to perform work. The amount available is determined by the size and weight of the flywheel and the speed at which it rotates. Useful energy available in a flywheel can be calculated from the following equation:

$$E = \frac{N^2 \times D^2 \times W}{5.25 \times 10^9} \qquad (3)$$

where:

$E$ = available flywheel energy, in.-tons
$N$ = rotary speed of flywheel, rpm
$D$ = diameter of flywheel, in.
$W$ = weight of flywheel, lb

The value of $E$ presupposes a slowdown of about 10%, the maximum allowable for continuous press operation. For single-stroke operations, the value of $E$ can usually be doubled to correspond to a slowdown of about 20%. This equation is based upon a radius of gyration of approximately $0.375D$. Approximate energies from other sizes of flywheels are presented in Table 5-7.

The metric version of this formula is:

$$E = \frac{N^2 \cdot D^2 \cdot W}{6.8 \times 10^6} \qquad (4)$$

where:

$E$ = available flywheel energy, kJ
$N$ = rotary speed of flywheel, rpm
$D$ = diameter of flywheel, m
$W$ = weight of flywheel, kg

Since the flywheel energy increases as the square of its speed, fast rotation is desirable when large amounts of energy are required. Geared presses allow the flywheel to be rotated faster, while the slide speed is reduced. Gearing does not increase the force or energy capacity. The gear ratio is primarily a means for obtaining an efficient flywheel speed. Flywheel rim speed is limited to about 6000 sfm (1829 m/min) for cast iron and to about 9000 sfm (2743 m/min) for steel flywheels.

Energy curves vary with each different press, their shapes and values depending on flywheel weight and speed, type of drive, percentage of slowdown allowable, press speed and stroke, and other factors. However, characteristic energy and tonnage curves are shown in Fig. 5-22 for a geared OBI press operating at 30 spm and having a 20% allowable slowdown. Coordinates for this graph are given in percentages to divorce it from any specific press.

Assuming the press is rated at 100 tons (890 kN) and has a 10″ (254 mm) stroke, force is the controlling factor when the work is done between 0.35″ (8.9 mm) above the bottom of the stroke (Point $A$, Fig. 5-22) and stroke bottom. However, when the work is engaged more than 0.35″ (8.9 mm) above stroke bottom, energy becomes the limiting factor to prevent flywheel slowdown from exceeding the 20% allowable. Also, if the work is engaged 1″ (25.4 mm) above the bottom of the stroke, the force requirement should not exceed 36.5 tons (325 kN) (Point $B$) to prevent excessive slowdown, even though the power train would, in fact, be capable of delivering 55 tons (489 kN) (Point $C$).

Since blanking and similar cutting operations only require the application of force over a short distance, less energy is usually needed. Frequency of load application, however, is an important consideration, since higher press speeds reduce the time allowed for the flywheel to recover its speed. If the press drive supplies power for automatic feeding as well as stamping, the energy drain may be high enough to keep the flywheel from recovering. In cases such as these, the press drive motor must be large enough to supply all the energy demands of the total system during the working portion of the stroke.

## Motor Selection

The primary function of the main drive motor on most mechanical presses is to restore energy to the flywheel. During flywheel slowdown, most of the energy is derived from the flywheel, with some contribution by the motor. Following the working stroke, the motor must restore the energy expended by the flywheel while returning the wheel to speed. If the energy capacity of the press is not adequate to satisfy the operation, slowdown of the flywheel during the working portion of the stroke becomes excessive, resulting in overloading of the motor. Stopping of the press can occur if insufficient time exists between production strokes to permit recovery of flywheel speed.

When slowdown is rapid and the working stroke is long, it is desirable to use a high starting torque with relatively low starting current, good heat-dissipation capacity, and sufficient slip (slowdown). The slip designation of a motor is the amount the motor slows down at rated full-load torque. Under conditions of moderate slowdown and short working strokes, general-purpose motors can be used satisfactorily.

Many presses employ alternating-current (a-c) induction motors having slip ratings of 3-5%, 5-8%, or 8-13%, the choice depending upon flywheel design, press speed, and other parameters. For short-stroke presses operating at speeds above 40 spm, general-purpose motors with a slip rating of 3-5% are often satisfactory. Motors with a slip rating of 5-8% are often used for press speeds of 20-40 spm. For long-stroke presses operating at speeds less than 20 spm, high-slip (8-13%) motors are usually required. Figure 5-23 shows how the torque varies with slowdown for these three most common classes of press drive motors.

Totally enclosed, fan-cooled motors are sometimes used to reduce maintenance costs by keeping contaminants out, but open-design motors with sealed insulation systems are more

**TABLE 5-7**
**Approximate Energies from Cast Iron Flywheels Rotating at 300 rpm***

| Size of Flywheel, | | | | Energy per Inch Width of Flywheel Face | | | |
|---|---|---|---|---|---|---|---|
| Outside Diameter | | Inside Diameter | | Total Energy at 300 rpm, | | Energy Expended with 15% Speed Decrease from 30 rpm, | |
| in. | mm | in. | mm | in.-tons | kJ | in.-tons | kJ |
| 32 | 813 | 24 | 610 | 11.6 | 2.6 | 3.3 | 0.7 |
| 34 | 864 | 24 | 610 | 13.8 | 3.1 | 3.9 | 0.9 |
| 36 | 914 | 26 | 660 | 19.7 | 4.5 | 5.5 | 1.2 |
| 38 | 965 | 26 | 660 | 26.6 | 6.0 | 7.4 | 1.7 |
| 40 | 1016 | 26 | 660 | 34.2 | 7.7 | 9.5 | 2.1 |
| 42 | 1067 | 26 | 660 | 43.3 | 9.8 | 12.3 | 2.8 |
| 44 | 1118 | 28 | 711 | 51.0 | 11.5 | 14.2 | 3.2 |
| 46 | 1168 | 30 | 762 | 59.8 | 13.5 | 16.9 | 3.8 |
| 48 | 1219 | 32 | 813 | 70.5 | 15.9 | 19.8 | 4.5 |
| 50 | 1270 | 32 | 813 | 84.5 | 19.1 | 23.9 | 5.4 |
| 52 | 1321 | 34 | 864 | 97.5 | 22.0 | 27.5 | 6.2 |
| 54 | 1372 | 34 | 864 | 116.3 | 26.3 | 32.8 | 7.4 |
| 56 | 1422 | 34 | 864 | 138.5 | 31.3 | 39.2 | 8.9 |
| 58 | 1473 | 34 | 864 | 162.0 | 36.6 | 45.9 | 10.4 |
| 60 | 1524 | 38 | 965 | 176.5 | 39.9 | 49.9 | 11.3 |
| 64 | 1626 | 40 | 1016 | 231.0 | 52.2 | 64.7 | 14.6 |
| 68 | 1727 | 40 | 1016 | 305.0 | 68.9 | 85.5 | 19.3 |
| 72 | 1829 | 40 | 1016 | 396.0 | 89.5 | 111.1 | 25.1 |

**TABLE 5-7—*Continued***

Maximum Safe Speeds for Various Size Flywheels Made from Cast Iron, Based on a Maximum Rim Speed of 6000 sfm (1829 m/min)

| Flywheel OD, In. (mm) | 32 (813) | 34 (864) | 36 (914) | 38 (965) | 40 (1016) | 42 (1067) | 44 (1118) | 46 (1168) | 48 (1219) | 50 (1270) | 52 (1321) | 54 (1372) | 56 (1422) | 58 (1473) | 60 (1524) | 64 (1626) | 68 (1727) | 72 (1829) |
|---|---|---|---|---|---|---|---|---|---|---|---|---|---|---|---|---|---|---|
| Max. speed, rpm | 716 | 677 | 620 | 600 | 572 | 545 | 520 | 495 | 477 | 458 | 446 | 425 | 414 | 395 | 381 | 358 | 337 | 318 |

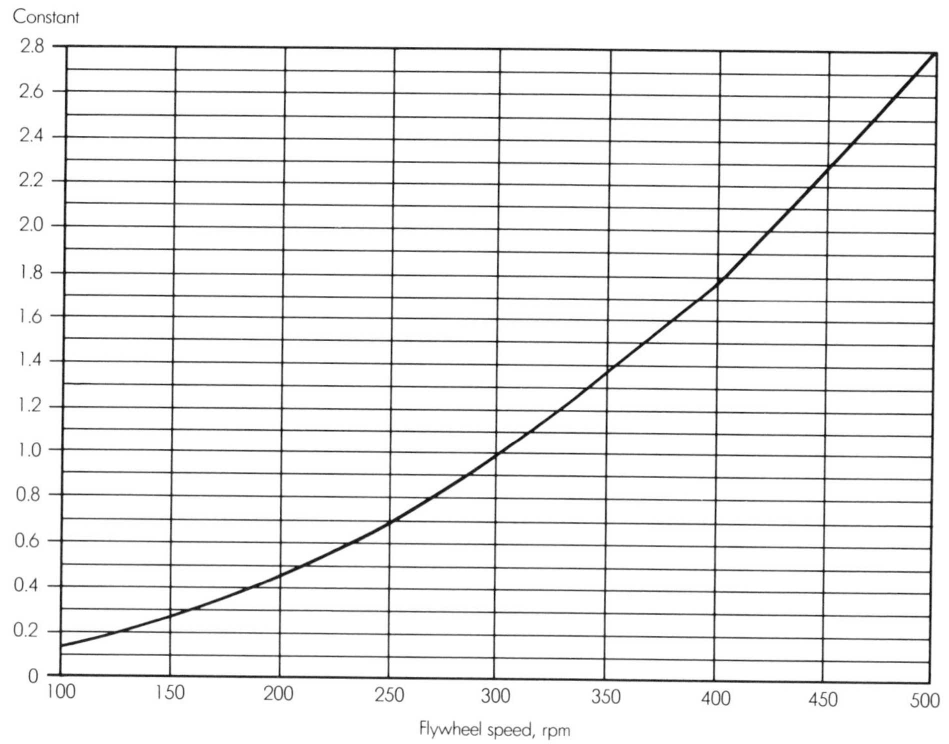

* For speeds other than 300 rpm, multiply the energies given in the table by the constant found on the curve.
Example: For a flywheel with an OD of 40″ (1016 mm) and ID of 26″ (660 mm), operating at 450 rpm, the total energy would be 34.2 x 2.3 = 78.7 in.-tons (17.8 kJ). The energy expended with a 15% decrease in speed would be 9.5 x 2.3 = 21.8 in.-tons (4.9 kJ).

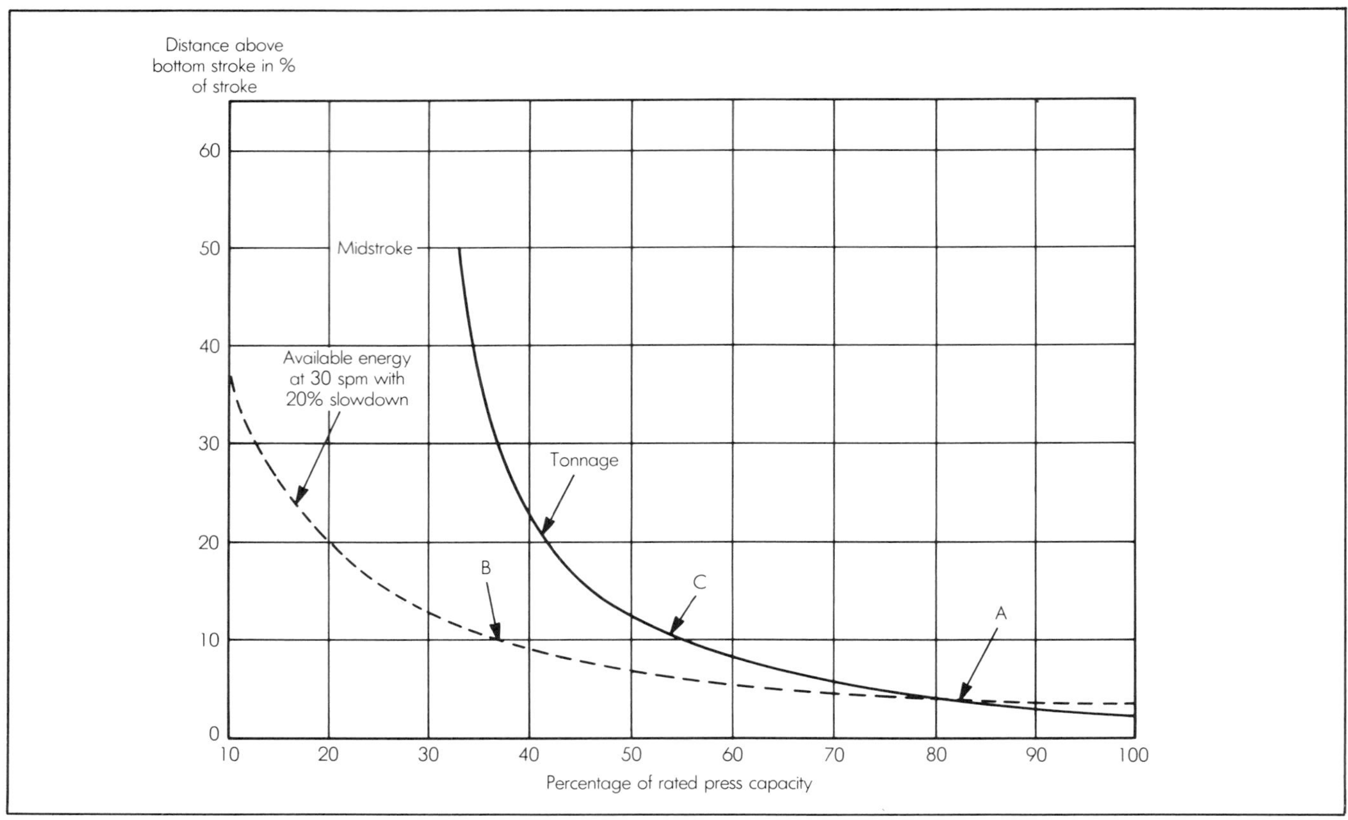


**Fig. 5-22 Characteristic energy and force curves for a geared OBI press operating at 30 spm.**

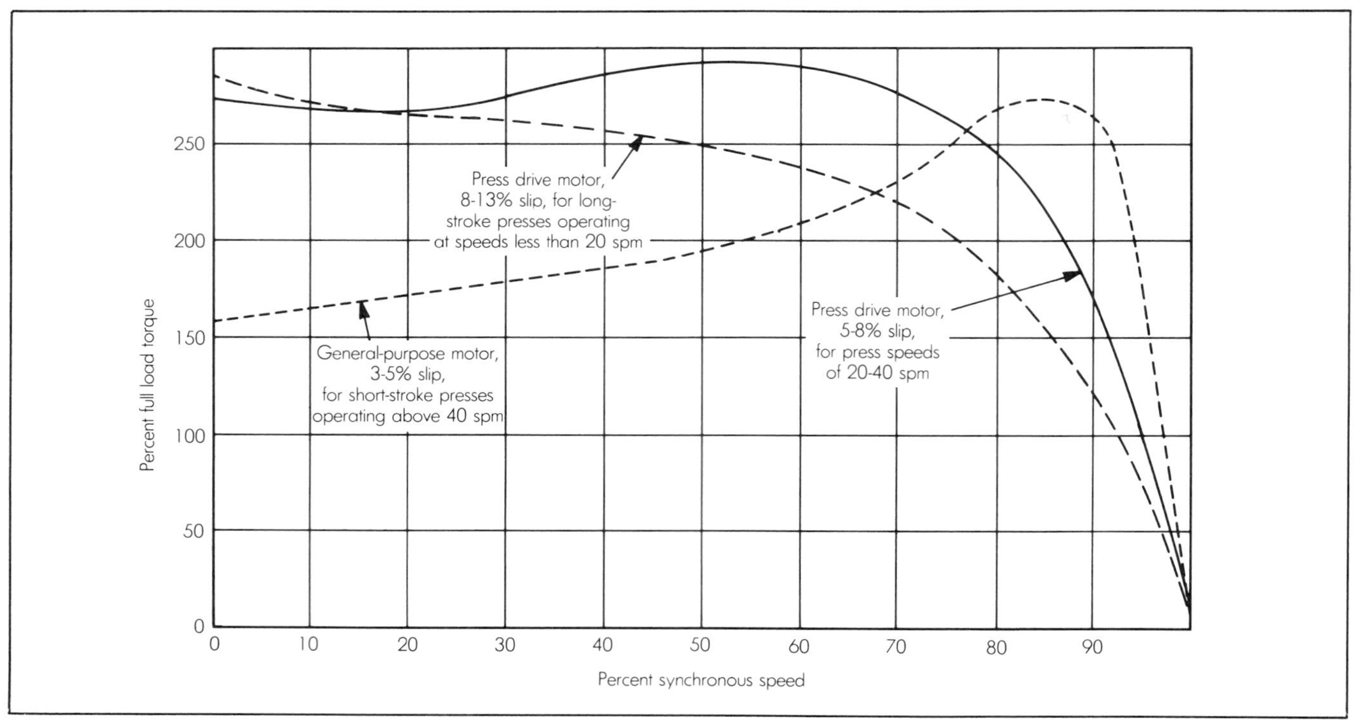


**Fig. 5-23 Variations in available torque for three common classes of press drive motors.**

common. Speeds of the main drive motors for mechanical presses are often 900 rpm for nongeared designs and 1200 or 1800 rpm for geared presses. Lower motor speeds decrease the noise level.

Determining the proper motor power for a specific application requires careful consideration of energy requirements, stroking mode and rate, and press inertia. Empirical methods based on data that has given satisfactory results for similar applications are sometimes used to select motor power, flywheel energy, and other design criteria. Analytical methods require solving exponential equations involving many independent variables. More recently, the use of computer programs for determining duty cycles has facilitated the process, with less chance for errors.

**Constant-speed drives.** On many mechanical presses, the flywheels are belt driven by single-speed, a-c induction motors. Constant-speed drives are generally satisfactory when work requirements are not expected to vary substantially.

**Adjustable-speed drives.** Drives of this type permit adjusting the speed to the optimum for different work requirements, thus lengthening die life, reducing scrap, and permitting higher production rates with lower unit costs. Press speeds can also be varied to suit workpiece material requirements, automatic feeding and unloading equipment, and press systems—series of presses connected by automatic material-handling units. The capability of using low speeds for setup reduces press downtime. Operating ranges, however, are generally limited to a maximum speed ratio of 3:1 due to the loss of flywheel energy in the lower speed range.

*Adjustable-speed motor drives.* Adjustable-speed, direct-current (d-c) motor drives operate from a-c power, employing motor-generator sets or solid-state units such as silicon-controlled rectifiers (SCR's) to convert a-c to d-c.

*Mechanical, adjustable-speed drives.* These drives use a single-speed, a-c motor with a belt and movable-sheave arrangement that changes the speed of the output shaft. They are normally supplied with speed ratios of 2:1, 3:1, and in some cases, 4:1 and are often used on small, high-speed presses.

*Eddy-current drives.* These drives employ a single-speed, a-c induction motor with an eddy-current coupling that changes the speed of the output shaft. While the speed ratios of these constant-torque drives are theoretically infinite, the most efficient ratio is generally from 2:1 to 3:1.

*Constant-energy drives.* These compact drives eliminate the need for a conventional flywheel and friction clutch unit (discussed later in this chapter), but a small pneumatic friction brake is required. The drive is transmitted from the press motor to an air-cooled inertia wheel which runs at nearly constant speed. Clutch coils are mounted within the rim of this wheel, and field excitation of these coils produces torque and engages a clutch to drive the output shaft. Brake coils are mounted on a stationary frame, and the brake rotor is keyed to the output shaft.

The inertia wheel of a constant-energy drive always runs at the same speed except for a slight slowdown during each working cycle. Speed of press operation is changed by varying the slip rate between the inertia wheel and the clutch rotor. This is accomplished with closed-loop control systems which change the magnitude of the current supplied to the electromagnetic coils. These drives permit rapid advancement of the press slide, a reduced speed for drawing operations (when required by the workpiece material), and rapid return, thus maintaining required production rates.

## Overload Protection

As discussed later in this chapter under the subject of safety requirements, presses should be operated within the force and attachment weight ratings specified by the builders of the presses. In addition to being unsafe, overloading of presses can be a costly practice because of potential damage to the press and dies.

Most presses, especially large ones, are designed with a factor of safety that can compensate for some overloading. Constant overloading, however, can increase maintenance requirements and possibly cause damage or breakage.

**Causes of overloading.** Overloading of presses occurs, generally unintentionally, because of one or more of the following reasons:

1. Inaccurate calculation of force and energy requirements for the workpiece to be produced. Any estimates made should be conservative, especially for complex dies. It is recommended that calculations be confirmed before starting production by checking actual press loading after the dies are installed. This can be done by using strain gage instrumentation or other deformation measuring techniques such as deflection or crown lift indicators. Once established, the force and stroke requirements should be stamped on each die for reference in future applications.
2. Applying maximum force higher in the stroke than the distance above bottom of stroke specified in the press rating.
3. Setting the slide adjustment too low, especially if closed dies are used.
4. Cycling the press with two or more workpieces in the die simultaneously (called double heading or die doubling). The use of malfunction detectors, such as photoelectric cells, sonic detectors, sensor probes, and switches, used in conjunction with sequential electronic controls to stop the press in the event of a workpiece not being properly discharged, can help eliminate the possibility of this problem.
5. Variations in material thickness during a production run. Inspection of incoming material can minimize this problem.
6. Variations in hardness or toughness of the workpiece material. Again, material inspection can reduce the possibility of this trouble.
7. High reversal or snap-through loads, encountered especially in blanking operations, as discussed previously in this chapter. Methods such as the snap-through arrestor described can reduce the effects of these loads. Redesigning the dies can sometimes minimize this problem.
8. Leaving stampings, tools, or other objects on the press bolster or in the die area. Proper press care is the only solution to this problem.
9. Using dull or worn dies. Proper die maintenance minimizes this problem.
10. Improper die design or setup. For example, installing a small, narrow die in the center of a wide press can cause overloading. The die should be of such a size that the resultant load is uniformly distributed over the center two-thirds of the right-to-left dimension of the press bolster. On two-point presses, however, a separate, smaller die can be installed under each connection.

11. Improper or infrequent press maintenance. A good maintenance program consistently performed is the solution.

**Protection units.** Some protection from overloading is provided on most presses. For example, clutches can sometimes be adjusted to slip when an excessive torque requirement is encountered, but this is not effective for bottom-of-stroke work. Drive-motor cutouts are provided to protect the motor against overheating. In addition, some means to protect the press and dies from destructive force overloading is sometimes desirable. Such a means, however, provides only short-stroke protection.

Both replaceable and permanent overload protection units are sometimes used on mechanical presses. Replaceable units are of either the stretch-link or shear-washer type. Stretch-link units are used only on under-drive presses and are more of an overload indicator than a protective mechanism. Shear washers, or collars, mounted on the slide adjustment, break when overloaded and provide limited displacement on the adjustment nut to relieve overloading. Also, if sized properly for maximum permissible load, they tend to fail inadvertently in fatigue.

So-called "electrical shear pins" in couplings have been used for protection from overload. Press circuitry is electrically interlocked with the pin, and any overload condition that causes the pin to shear results in stopping the press. A disadvantage is the downtime required to replace the broken pin.

The permanent overload protection unit shown in Fig. 5-24 consists of an accumulator, air/oil pump, filters, control valves and pressure switches, and hydraulic overload cylinder for each slide connection. The short-stroke, high-pressure cylinder is hydraulically charged and prestressed to a preselected trip-out setting. When the setting is exceeded, the unit collapses to its minimum height. Dumping of the hydraulic system is directly related to exerted force and system precharge pressure.

A limit switch detects collapsing of the overload unit and de-energizes the clutch and brake control circuit to stop the press. No matter where the overload may fall within the die area of the press with one, two, or four-point slide connection, the system protects against damage because of a single valve within the closed hydraulic system. Force setting of the overload is directly proportional to the air pressure applied.

Another permanent mechanism uses air cylinders and linkage to (or hydraulic jacks on) the press tie rods that allow the press crown to lift if the preset pressure is exceeded. Friction clutches (discussed next in this section) can sometimes be used for drive overload protection by regulating the air pressure. With automatic reduction of the pressure near the bottom of the stroke, some structural protection is also provided. With electric clutches, current can be adjusted. Slip couplings can be used with either full or part revolution clutches on crankshaft presses.

A hydropneumatic overload-relief bed (see Fig. 5-25) can be built into a press so that if an unusual stress arises which would overtax the capacity of the press, the relief bed will yield to compensate for this condition. The bed can be adjusted to a little more than the pressure required to perform the operation;

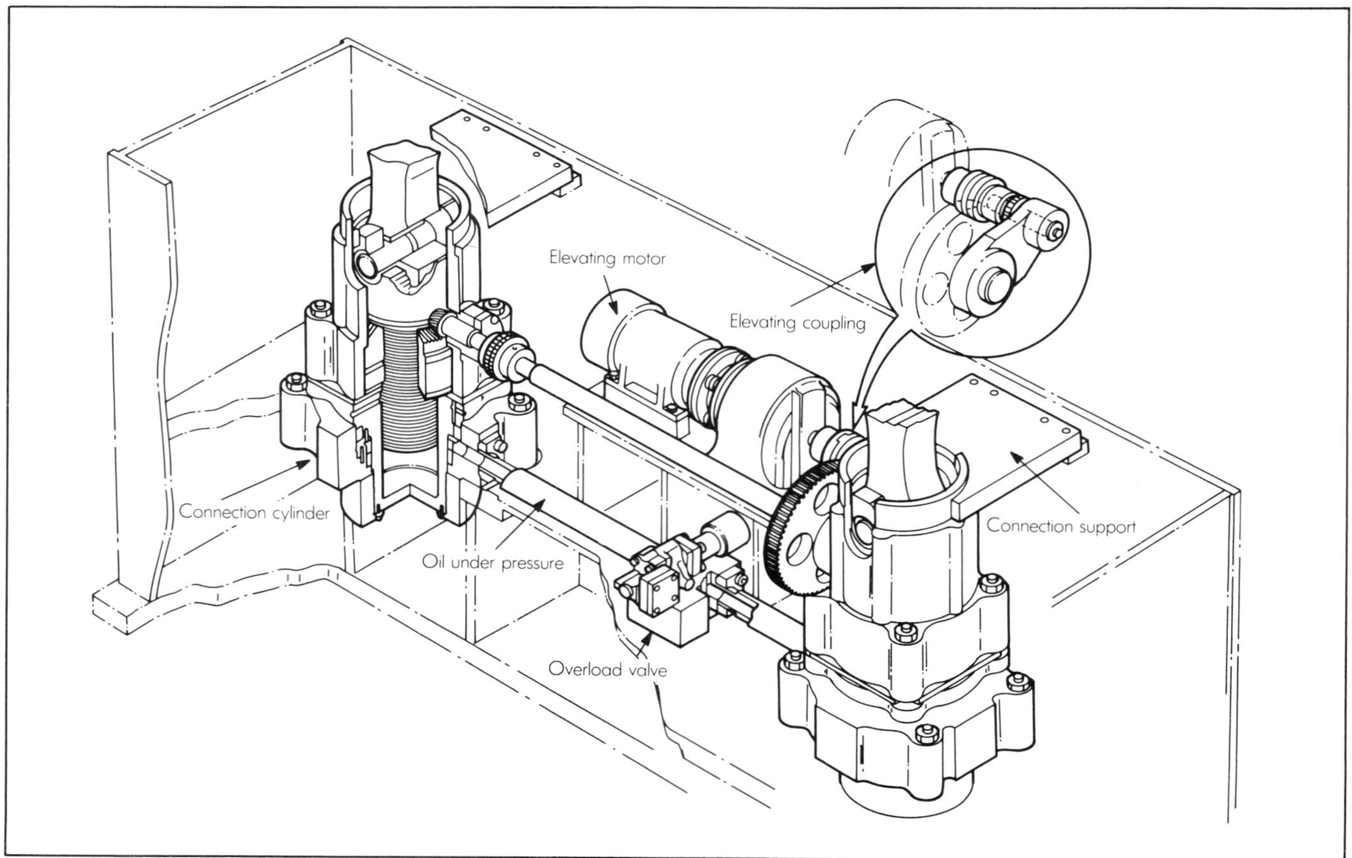


**Fig. 5-24 Permanent overload protection unit has a prestressed hydraulic cylinder.** (*Verson Allsteel Press Co.*)

and in case of an overload, the relief valve is forced open and some fluid moves out to the surge tank. On the upstroke of the press, this fluid is returned to the hydraulic cylinder, raising the press bed to normal working position. Working pressures to 2000 psi (13.8 MPa) can be obtained by adjusting the pressure in the air cylinder that actuates the combination relief and check valve in the hydraulic cylinder. The pressure in the bed builds up to the working load only during a brief period near the bottom of the press stroke.

Instruments are available for measuring loads, controlling the press, preventing the repetition of overloads, calibrating dies to ensure proper application, and monitoring die wear. Portable meters measure force, monitors measure the load and can stop the press after the rated load is exceeded, and analyzers provide a CRT readout of both direct and reverse loads. The instruments plug into a receptacle on any press that has been equipped with small, electronic, strain-sensing pickups bonded to the frame. Each press has its own calibration characteristic that is recorded on the receptacle. When this so-called "press factor" is dialed into the instrument being used, the system is calibrated for the particular press and is able to measure the load as a percentage of full press capacity.

Another portable press tonnage indicator consists of a solid-state, direct-reading instrument with either two or four sensor units. Sensors are bolted permanently to the press frame, and the portable plug-in amplifier unit contains the controls and meter. The load sensors are full-bridge force transducers, steel encapsulated and factory sealed. A similar system has strain gage sensors for up to four channels and a dial indicating instrument with outputs that can be used for recording or monitoring.

Strain gage overload protection units can also be used to stop the press when the force limit has been exceeded. The strain gages measure stretching or compressing of press members (usually the frame or connection). Any change in electrical resistance of the gage wire grid is proportional to the applied load. Amplified signals from the gages are used for readout and can be used to stop press operation.

Systems are available using piezoelectric crystal sensors mounted on the press frames. Deflection of the frame under load squeezes the sensors, creating a small electric current proportional to the load on the press. This current is constantly monitored, converted to force loads, and continuously displayed. If the load exceeds the preset limit, a control circuit

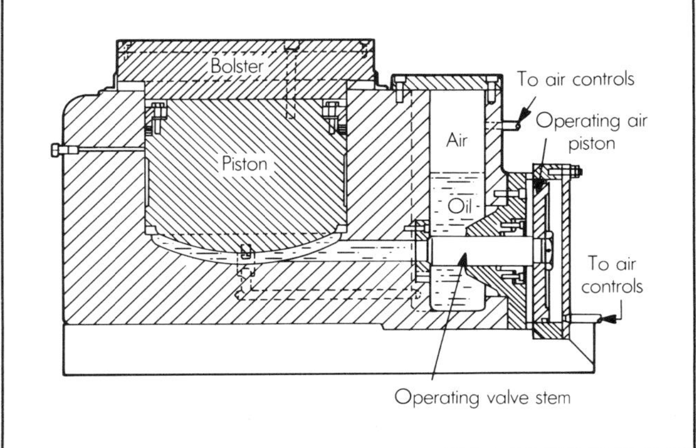


**Fig. 5-25 Hydropneumatic overload-relief bed can be built into press.** *(E. W. Bliss Div., Gulf & Western Manufacturing Co.)*

immediately stops the press. Options for such systems include workpiece counters, strip-chart recorders, bearing temperature monitors, and microprocessor interfaces.

Load measuring elements are sometimes made integral parts of the dies for certain applications. This arrangement is particularly useful for multistation dies for which the forces vary for different stations. Devices are available that monitor loads by measuring the current used by the drive motor; devices are also available for monitoring the sound generated by the dies during operation.

## PRESS CLUTCHES AND BRAKES

Clutches and brakes are essential components required for the proper operation of mechanical presses. A clutch is a mechanism for coupling the flywheel to the shaft, either directly or through a gear train, to provide timing and control of the intermittent, reciprocating movement of the press slide. A brake is a mechanism for stopping the slide and other press components after the clutch has been disengaged.

### Types of Clutches

Clutches for mechanical presses are either the full-revolution or part-revolution type. No clutch is required on a press with a direct drive. Clutches are mounted on the main shafts, intermediate shafts, or driveshafts of presses; the highest speed shafts are the most efficient for torque transmission, but those mounted on the slowest speed shafts generate less heat.

**Full-revolution clutch.** This type of clutch, once engaged, cannot be disengaged until the crankshaft has completed a full revolution and the press slide a full stroke. Positive clutches (discussed later in this section) are almost always the full-revolution type. Usually, a tripping device releases spring pressure to move engaging members, which by nature require a full revolution before they can be disengaged. Disengagement is generally accomplished by a throwout cam arrangement which is part of the clutch mechanism.

The use of full-revolution clutches for single-stroke operations is not recommended unless the ANSI and OSHA safety requirements discussed later in this chapter are met. Conversion packages are available from most press builders and other manufacturers to update presses to conform to OSHA requirements. Full-revolution clutches that do conform are still desirable for certain operations, using the single-stroke mode. They are also used with automatic feeds, resulting in fewer clutch engagements, with resultant longer clutch life.

**Part-revolution clutch.** This type of clutch can be disengaged at any point before the crankshaft has completed a full revolution and the press slide a full stroke. These clutches are usually air engaged and generally have friction mechanisms. Some types of positive engagement clutches, however, are also air engaged and capable of being disengaged within the stroke of the slide. Other clutches, such as eddy-current or hydraulically operated types, are sometimes used for part-revolution operation.

### Types of Brakes

Brakes for mechanical presses may be the constant-drag type (typical for presses with full-revolution clutches) or a type that is disengaged while the clutch is engaged (most typical for presses with part-revolution clutches). The brakes may be separate units, or they may be incorporated with the clutches.

# CHAPTER 5

# PRESS CLUTCHES AND BRAKES

## Clutch and Brake Selection

Selection of a proper clutch (see Table 5-8) for a specific press depends primarily upon the torque required to deliver adequate force to the slide and upon the acceleration needed to start components with each stroke of the press. Heat generated by acceleration is not a factor with positive clutches, but may have to be considered when friction clutches are being used.

Brake selection is dependent upon the deceleration of moving components that have to be stopped with each stroke of the press. The brake capacity must be sufficient to stop the motion of the slide quickly and to hold the slide and its attachments at any point in its travel. Satisfactory stopping time is an important safety consideration.

Safety requirements for clutches and brakes, including single-stroke mechanisms, control systems, brake system monitoring, and guards and devices, are discussed in a subsequent section of this chapter.

## Positive Clutches

With positive clutches—still used on small presses, especially gap-frame types—the driven and driving members of the clutches are interlocked when engaged. These clutches can be either mechanically actuated (see Fig. 5-26) or air operated. Keys, pins, or multiple jaws are used for engagement; and throwout cams, springs, or other means, for disengagement. In the case of air-operated clutches, air valves are used. An auxiliary cam is often provided for single-stroke operation.

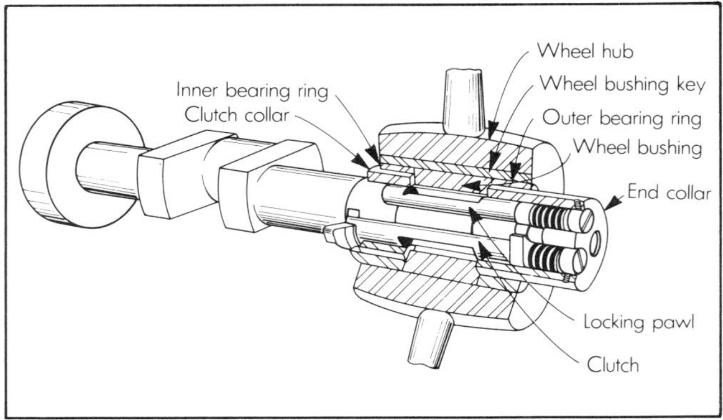


**Fig. 5-26 Mechanically-actuated positive clutch mounted on press crankshaft.** (*E. W. Bliss Div., Gulf & Western Manufacturing Co.*)

Positive clutches are mounted on the crankshaft or eccentric of the press. Brakes for presses equipped with positive clutches are placed on the outer end of the shaft, opposite the drivewheel end. The brakes are generally the continuous-acting (drag-friction) type, with yoke, band, or double-shoe construction.

Advantages of positive clutches include low cost, compactness, simple operation, rapid acceleration, and low inertia. Drag-type friction brakes are commonly used with positive clutches, but releasing brakes are necessary if the presses are used with automatic feeds.

The slide of a press having a positive clutch is usually stopped at its upper position. Lowering (inching) or backing up (lifting) of the slide during the die setting must be done by turning the flywheel or main gear by hand, chain block, or a hand bar passed through the crankshaft. Many flywheel-type presses (nongeared) have bar holes provided in the rim of the flywheel into which a turnover bar may be placed. When such bars are used, they should be the spring-loaded type to ensure ejection, thus preventing the bars from remaining in the holes and being forgotten.

## Friction Clutches and Brakes

Presses with friction clutches allow the slides to be stopped or started at any point in the stroke. This feature is convenient for setting and adjusting dies, especially in large presses. With a well-designed, air-friction clutch, sudden power failure causes the press to stop immediately. Friction clutches using high-pressure oil or magnetic attraction have been employed to some degree.

Most friction clutches are air engaged and spring released. Brakes are spring engaged and air released. Some clutches are combined with integral brakes; others are constructed as individual units for separate mounting. The brakes for presses equipped with friction clutches are drum type or single or multiple-disc type and are operated in unison with the clutches. A piston-type integral clutch and brake is shown in Fig. 5-27. Some designs use diaphragms or air tubes for actuation instead of pistons with packings.

**TABLE 5-8**
**Comparison of Various Types of Friction Clutches and Brakes**

| Type of Friction Clutch and Brake | Advantages | Disadvantages |
|---|---|---|
| Backshaft mounted, combined clutch and brake* (Fig. 5-27) | Simple construction. Ease of maintenance. No overlap between clutch and brake. | Comparatively high inertia, resulting in heat buildup when single stroking at high rates. |
| Crankshaft mounted, clutch and brake (combined or separate) | Simple construction. Ease of maintenance. Low inertia (due to slow speed, thus permitting high single-stroking rates). | Uneconomical on larger presses, over 200 tons (1779 kN). |
| Low-inertia clutch and brake (Fig. 5-28, clutch only) | Applicable to larger presses. Low heat buildup, making higher single-stroking rates possible. | Higher cost. Special consideration necessary to prevent overlap of clutch and brake. |
| Wet clutch and brake combination | Unlimited single-stroking rates (heat exchanger prevents heat buildup) | Higher cost. Required addition of circulating, oil cooling system. Requires special training and tools for maintenance. |

* Combined clutch and brake is sometimes mounted on the intermediate shaft to reduce inertia.

# PRESS CLUTCHES AND BRAKES

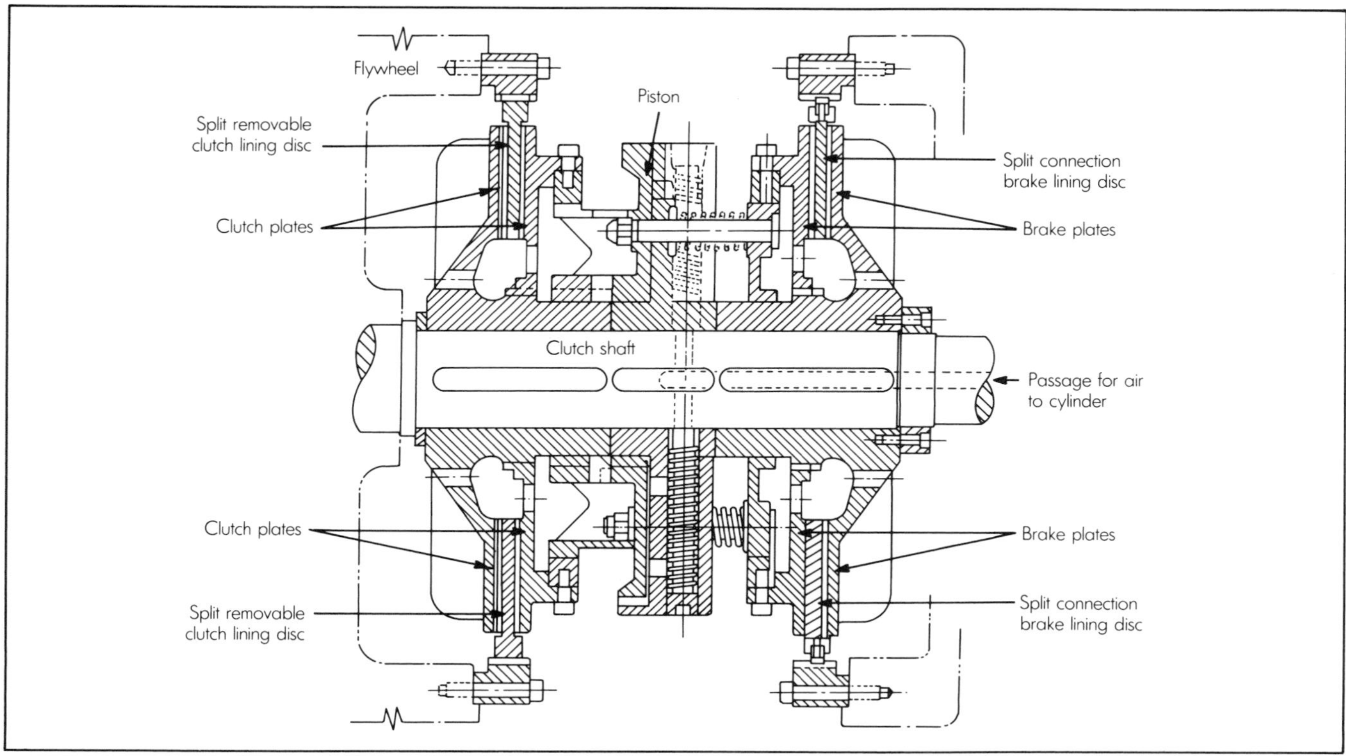


**Fig. 5-27 Piston-type integral clutch and brake.** (*Verson Allsteel Press Co.*)

**Wet clutch.** So-called wet clutch and brake units have the clutch and brake operating in a sealed housing filled with oil. A film of oil between the friction discs and intermediate contact plates absorbs most of the heat. Wet clutch and brake units made by one manufacturer employ planetary gear sets.

**Two-speed clutch.** This unit (see Fig. 5-28) has two air-operated, friction clutches mounted axially on the flywheel and arranged to drive the press through two concentric shafts. One clutch pickup member is attached directly to the driveshaft, and the other is connected to a pair of reduction gears. The high-speed clutch operates during the approach and return portions of the cycle, and the low-speed clutch operates during the working part of the stroke. Completely automatic control is accomplished with a four-way, solenoid air valve, energized by an adjustable, rotary-cam limit switch. A selector switch permits the press to be operated at two speeds or continuously at low or high speed.

**Eddy-current clutches and brakes.** These units are generally a part of the eddy-current drive described previously in this chapter under the subject of adjustable-speed drives. The clutches can be started, stopped, and reversed with variable torque and are often used for large presses. Advantages include (1) the capability for rapid cycling and operation under various degrees of slip for different slide speeds and (2) reduced maintenance because there are no frictional surfaces or mechanical connections between driver and driven members. Units consist of a variable-speed, clutch and brake rotor assembly directly connected to the press driveshaft, and a stationary brake field assembly. Driving torque is transmitted by electromagnetic attraction between the flywheel and the clutch rotor; braking torque is developed similarly between the brake field assembly and the brake rotor.

Control of both clutching and braking actions is accomplished by varying the current supplied to the coils. Eddy-current brakes are not suitable for use as holding brakes, and a mechanical brake is generally provided to hold the press slide between cycles.

**Constant-energy drives.** With this type of drive, also described previously under the subject of adjustable-speed drives, a conventional flywheel and friction clutch unit are not required. A small, pneumatic friction brake, however, is needed.

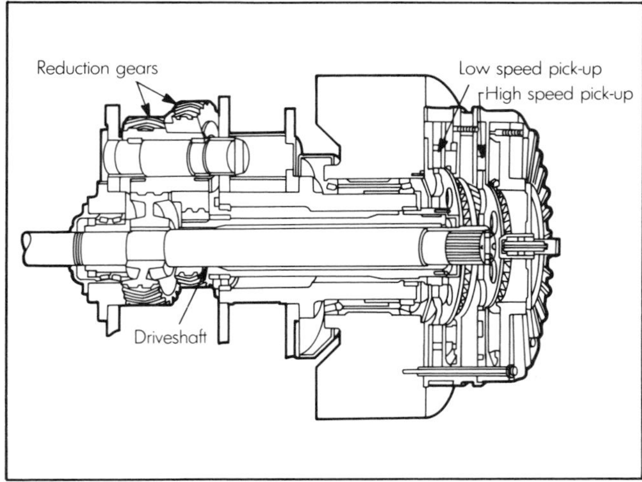


**Fig. 5-28 Two-speed clutch has two air-operated friction clutches.** (*Danly Machine Corp.*)

# CHAPTER 5

# PRESS CONTROLS

## PRESS CONTROLS

The subject of press controls deals with the electrical, electromechanical, pneumatic, hydraulic, electronic, and associated equipment used to control the operation of power presses. The complexity of these controls ranges from a simple, single-motor, starter and disconnect switch to a sophisticated, multimotor, multifunction control incorporating a variety of sensors, control systems, and devices. Regardless of the type of control system used, the resulting operation must yield consistent, predictably high, production rates without jeopardizing the safety of either operating personnel, press, or dies. Proper design, application, and installation are critical factors, whereas easy accessibility, efficient operation, minimum downtime, and limited maintenance are desirable features for press controls. Self-checking and diagnostic capabilities are becoming increasingly important.

Safety requirements from OSHA and in ANSI B11.1 and other safety requirements for the critical clutch and brake controls, including control reliability and brake system monitoring, are discussed in the next section of this chapter under the subject of press safety.

### Control Systems

Systems used for the control of mechanical power presses are predominantly either electromechanical or solid state, or a combination of the two. More recently, programmable controllers (PC's) and computer numerical control (CNC) systems are also being used, particularly in conjunction with more complex automated systems. All press controls should be applied in accordance with NFPA Standard No. 79 (replaces JIC starting in 1984) and should be installed in accordance with the National Electrical Code (ANSI Standard C1 and NFPA Standard No. 70), applicable local codes, and recognized industry standards.

**Electromechanical systems.** Various designs utilizing relays, pneumatic timers, and rotary-cam limit switches have controlled power presses for years. During the past 15 years these systems have grown more complex as redundancy and self-checking techniques developed and additional accessory equipment was added.

**Solid-state control systems.** Solid-state press control systems have been available for more than 20 years from various press builders and control manufacturers. These systems use solid-state electronic gating devices in conjunction with a rotary-cam limit switch and often also use a press position-sensing device driven by the main crank of the press. The position sensor or encoder converts mechanical positions to electrical signals for control purposes. Advantages of these systems over relays include longer life, less maintenance, self-checking diagnostic capabilities, and often, reduced space requirements. Unfortunately, these systems can be difficult to troubleshoot, if for no other reason than less maintenance means less experience.

**Programmable controllers (PC's).** These are versatile, modular-constructed, microprocessor-based, solid-state devices which are capable of examining all sensing devices and input control signals many times per second; applying preprogrammed, easily-revised logic, including mathematics, to these signals; making decisions; and energizing corresponding output devices to properly operate, self-diagnose, and/or completely shut down the machine as required. (Refer also to Chapter 5, "Machine Controls," in Volume I of this Handbook series).

These PC devices are being used especially for multipress and multifunction automated lines in which features such as automatic die changing are often provided. In addition to their self-diagnostic capability, PC's can be programmed to provide accurate, up-to-date management information, such as production, maintenance, and downtime records. A possible limitation to the use of solid-state controls, including PC's, is their unique characteristics as compared to those of electromechanical controls. For example, careful consideration must be given to their different performance characteristics and failure modes, as well as their response to various environmental conditions.

**CNC systems.** Computerized numerical controls are starting to be used more extensively because of their capability for fast and reliable monitoring of operations, as well as their self-checking and diagnostic features. So far as press controls are concerned, however, the gap between PC and CNC capability is rapidly closing. Examples of CNC use include operations in which blanking, notching, perforating, and piercing have been controlled using CNC to activate various punches as required for the specific application, thus minimizing setup and changeover times. On some automated blanking presses, CNC's are used to automatically establish optimum speeds, stock feed rates, and feed-roll acceleration and deceleration rates.

### Electrical Control Equipment

Many components (see Fig. 5-29) are required for press controls, some of the more common of which are discussed in this section. All electrical devices should meet NEMA requirements and should be UL approved. Press wiring, color coded and marked for easy circuit identification, should be carried in oiltight protective conduits.

**Power disconnect.** A fused main disconnect switch or circuit breaker must be provided with every press control system to isolate the machine from the source of power. The switch or breaker must be sized for heavy-duty starting of the press flywheel and must also be capable of being locked in the Off position. Operating handles should be on the exterior of the control enclosures, not more than 78" (1980 mm) from the floor, and must have provisions for interlocking with the enclosure doors to prevent unauthorized entry.

Sometimes, an auxiliary disconnect switch is also provided. This permits cutting off power to the drive and adjustment motors, clutch and brake controls, and mechanical device controls, while retaining power for lubrication and for hydraulic overload motors and controls, as well as for power receptacles and lighting circuits. For multimotor control systems, branch circuit fuses are required for the smaller motors.

**Motor starters.** All press controls must incorporate a type of drive motor starter with three-phase overloads and three-wire control that disconnects the motor from the power source in the event of control-voltage or power-source failure; they must also require operation of the Start button to restart the motor after power is restored. The Start button of the main drive motor must be guarded to protect against accidental operation.

When a reversing starter is supplied for the main drive motor, a zero-speed detector should be included to prevent starting the motor in the opposite direction before it is stopped. Such a detector is often used to control a "Flywheel Stopped" light on the master control panel. Press stroking should be prevented unless the main drive motor is powered in the forward direction. When a flywheel brake is supplied, it should be interlocked with the starter for the main drive motor to remove driving power when the brake is applied.

Reduced-voltage starters must be used for main drive motors when required because of limited power sources. Full-

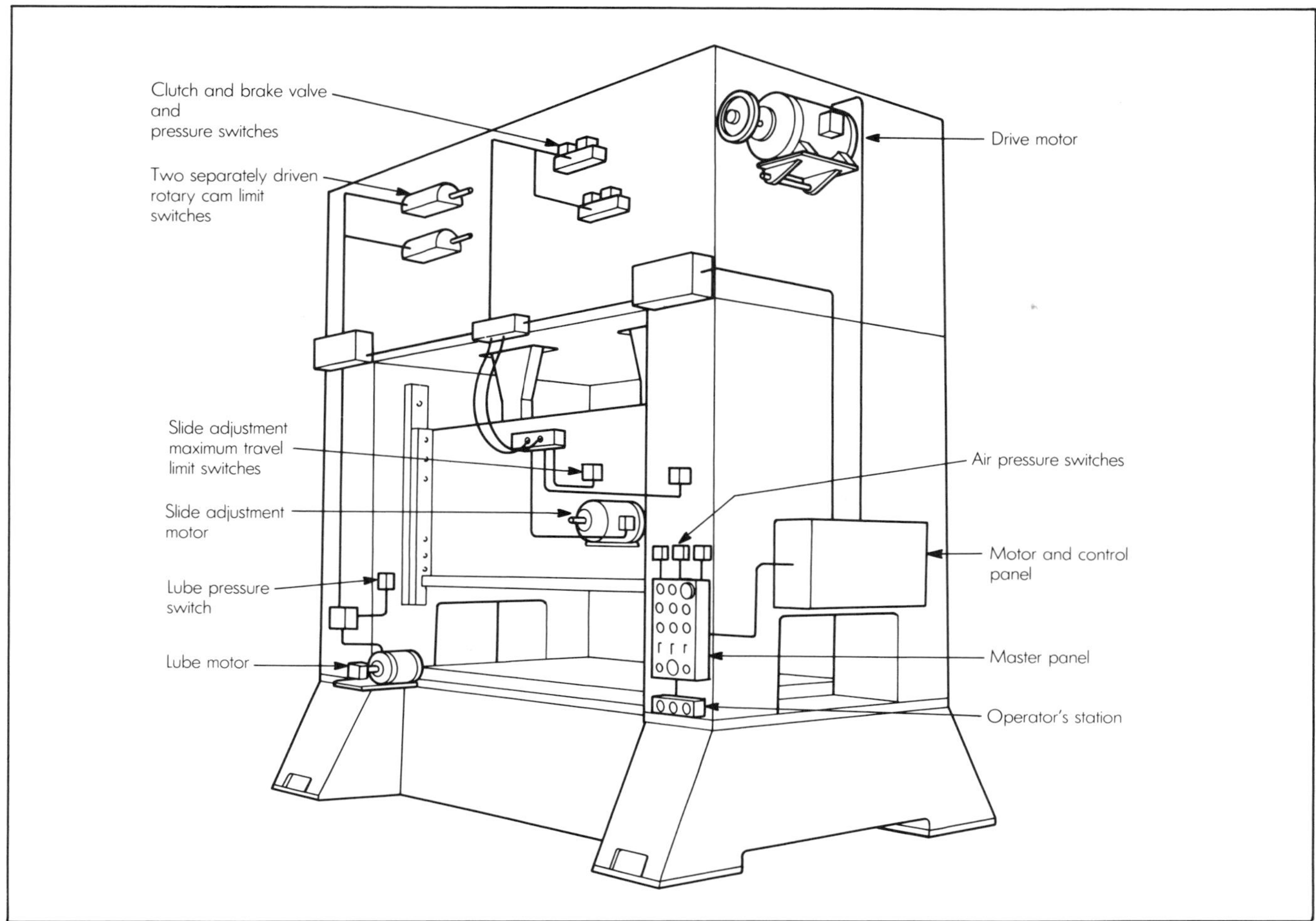


**Fig. 5-29 Typical control components on a straight-side press.** (*Verson Allsteel Press Co.*)

voltage starters, however, should be supplied for all slide-adjustment and slow-inching drive motors. This is necessary because these intermittent-duty motors are generally sized, based on the 275% starting/stalled torque rating of an NEMA Design D motor. Their starters usually include a redundant contactor that closes under no-load conditions and is controlled so that whenever the motor is stopped, it locks out in the event that a starter contact has welded in the closed position. An over-temperature switch is often included in the windings of these motors as a better means of protection and for sensing the motor current.

**Transformers.** All a-c control circuits and solenoid-valve coils are normally powered by a nominal 120V alternating current. Since most presses are supplied from 230 or 460V power sources, one or more step-down transformers with isolated secondary windings are required to supply the 120V alternating current.

Whenever higher voltage is necessary for operation of any part of the press, it must be isolated from any control device handled by the operator. However, motor starters with integral Start/Stop buttons are permitted to use 230 or 460V line voltage control. Control circuits operated with direct current should be powered by not more than 240V, isolated from any higher voltages.

**Grounding.** Electrical circuits for all press controls must be protected against the possibility of an accidental ground in the control circuits, causing false operation of the press. Unless control circuitry is duplicated in both power lines, it is required that one line be permanently grounded and the connection be indicated by a light on the master panel. Motor controls should be single-sided and grounded. Isolated, double-sided circuitry, either ungrounded or with a center-tap ground having provision for removal of the intentional ground, is recommended for the clutch/brake control. Ground-fault indicating lights should be provided on the master panel.

All electrical enclosures, device housings, motor frames, run-button stands, and similar components should be grounded to and through the press frames. Grounding surfaces should be clean and not painted until after assembly. A grounding conductor should be included in cables or flexible conduits that are connected to movable electrical devices. To further protect against shock hazard and fire, the installation of presses should conform to NFPA Code No. 70.

**Relays.** When electromechanical relays are used, they should be selected to provide long, reliable service. They should be designed so that if a contact should weld, further operation of the remaining contacts is prevented. Inclusion of redundancy and self-checking features is highly recommended in all portions of the control circuit affecting machine and/or personnel safety.

**Control panels.** All operator control devices used for motor control, setup, stroke selection, fault indication, and other functions should be located on a common NEMA 12 master control panel, usually located at the right front of the press. The Start button on this panel for the main drive motor must be guarded. A large, red, mushroom-head, Stop Control button (sometimes called "Emergency Stop") to halt press motion is sometimes located on this panel. Release of this button must not, by that action alone, cause press motion to restart.

Requirements for inch control, stroking selection, two-hand trip and two-hand control, single-stroke mechanism, and other components associated with clutch and brake controls are discussed in the next section of this chapter under the subject of press safety.

**Rotary-cam limit switch(es).** Mechanical or electrical failure of these switches may result in the press's failing to stop when required, such as at the end of each "single" stroke, or when a Run button is released during the "holding" time. Loss of the antirepeat feature may also result. The switch driving mechanism, including all couplings, gears, sprockets, and associated parts, should be securely assembled and of rugged design. A positive keyed connection is preferable to setscrews, which have a tendency to vibrate and loosen. The use of two separately driven switches or a motion detector is recommended.

## Air-Control Equipment

Air-control equipment (see Fig. 5-30) must be protected against foreign material and water entering the system. A means of air lubrication must be provided when needed.

All magnetic air valves used for clutch actuation should be the three-way, normally closed, poppet-type design. Spool valves should never be used for this purpose because they have pistons sliding in close-fitting sleeves and may stick due to dirt, corrosion, or improper lubrication.

A self-checking assembly of two three-way valves is usually best for reliable control. A schematic cross section of one such self-checking, series-flow, dual air valve is shown in Fig. 5-31. Each of the three-way valve units is raised for operation by means of a diaphragm. Failure of either magnet or pilot, or too slow an exhaust from the operating unit, closes the safety unit. This shuts off line air and exhausts any trapped air through the safety exhaust port.

Air pressure for clutches and brakes may be monitored at the surge tank to ensure that adequate pressure is available where it is needed. Air pressure for counterbalances and auxiliary equipment, such as cushions and knockouts, may be sensed at a surge line or tank in preference to the line from the supply regulator.

Manifolds, which simplify piping and maintenance and include pressure regulators, check valves, and blow down valves, are desirable. Means should be provided to shut off,

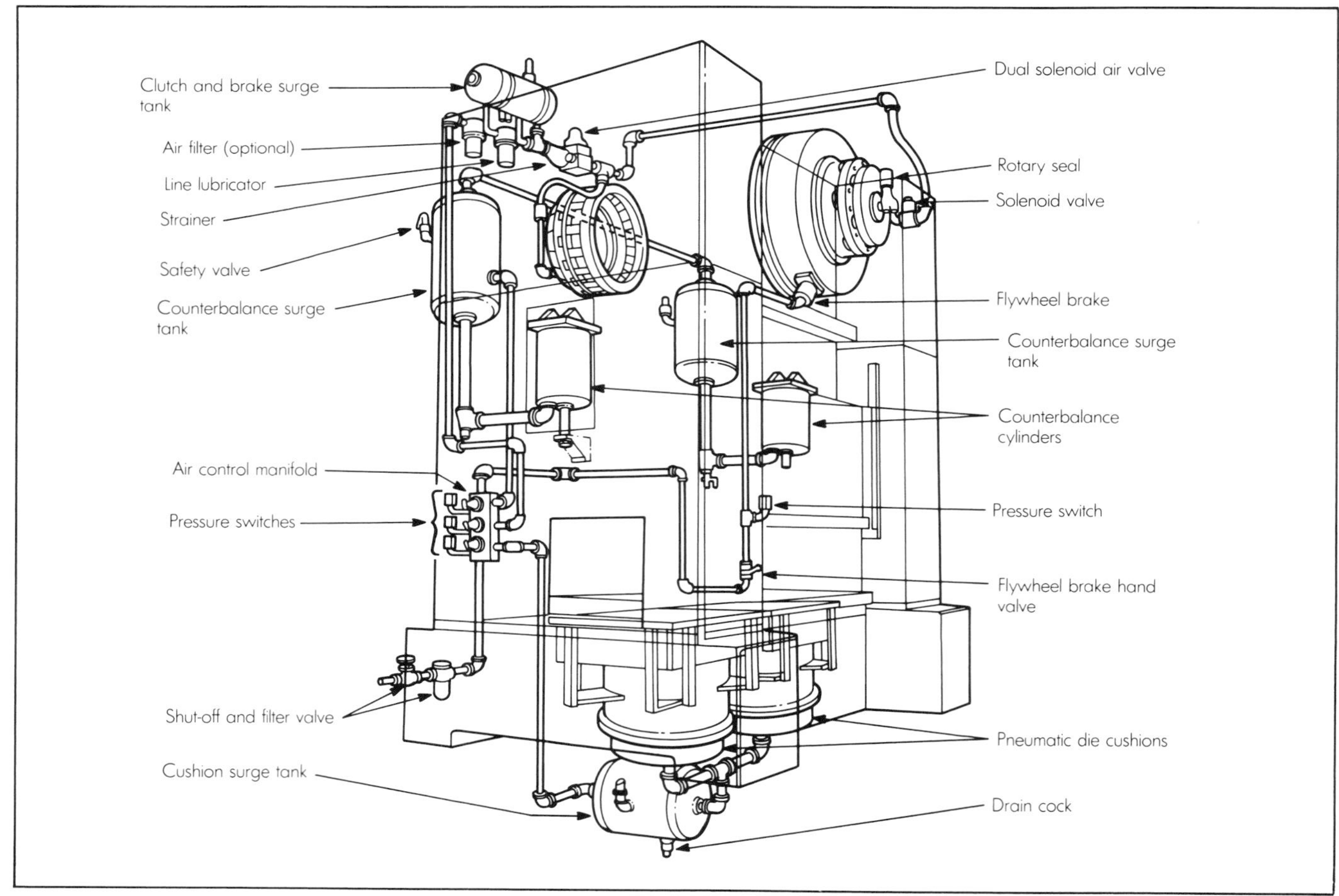


**Fig. 5-30 Pneumatic piping, tanks, and controls for a press.** (*Verson Allsteel Press Co.*)

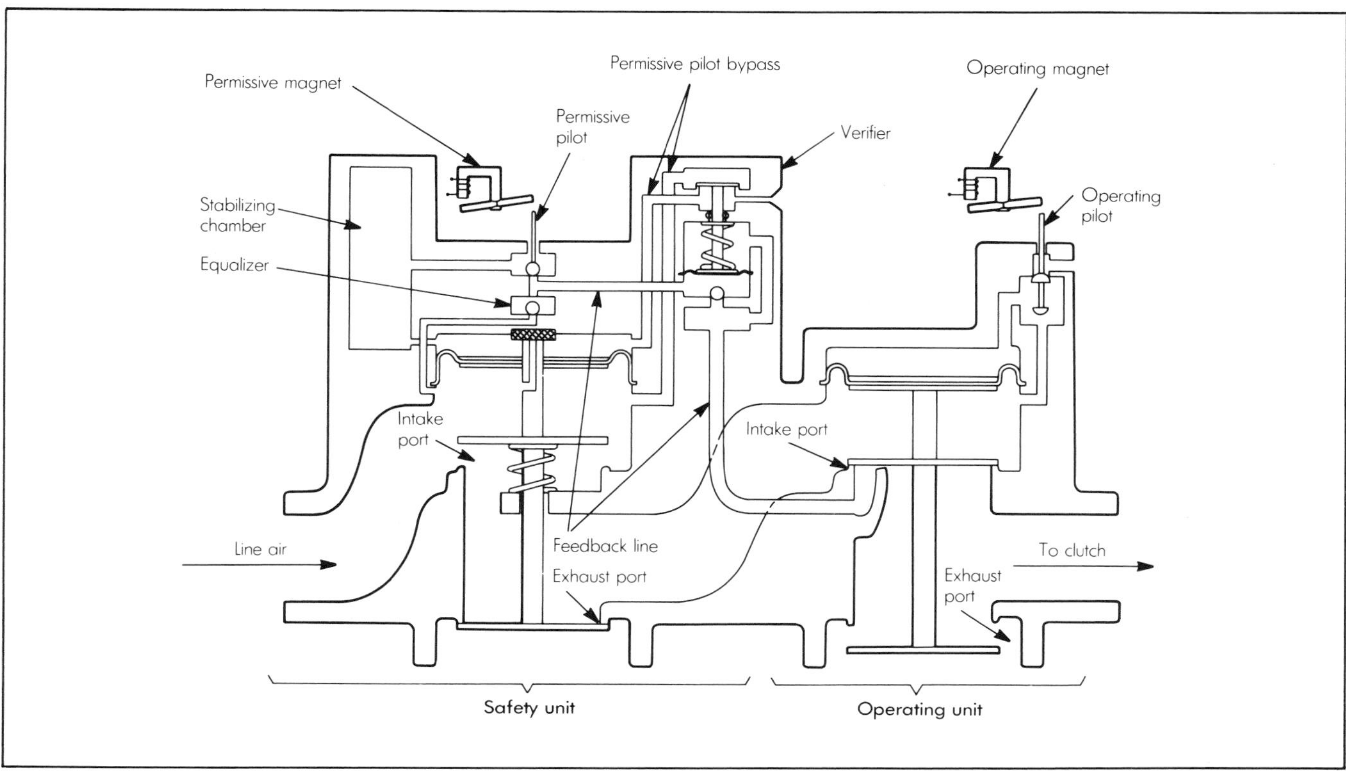


**Fig. 5-31 Schematic cross section of self-checking, series-flow magnetic air valve. Failure of either magnet or pilot, or too slow an exhaust, shuts off line air.**

blow down, and lock off the air supply to the press. All air pressure vessels must conform to the latest edition of the ANSI/ASME Boiler and Pressure Vessel Code; they should also be supplied with relief valves, fusible plugs, and drain cocks.

### Hydraulic Equipment

The maximum anticipated working pressures in any hydraulic system used on a mechanical press must not exceed the safe working pressure rating of the lowest rated component in that system. Mechanisms operated by hydraulic or air cylinders should have provisions for shutting off the bleeding pressure from all components that might cause unexpected operation or motion.

## MECHANICAL PRESS SAFETY

Press safety depends upon the proper design, manufacture, installation, setup, operation, and maintenance of the presses, dies, and related equipment. Safeguarding is complicated by the wide variety of operations and conditions encountered due to variations in size, speed, and type of press used; the size, thickness, and kind of workpiece to be produced; the design and construction of the dies; the required accuracy of the workpieces; the skill of the operators; the number of workpieces needed; and the method of feeding, including scrap and workpiece removal methods.

Safety precautions that minimize risk associated with human exposure are essential. A good safety program (refer to Chapter 20, "Safety in Forming," in this volume) can minimize accidents, human injuries, and damage to presses, dies, and other equipment.

### Safety Nomenclature

Information pertaining to safety requirements as they relate to mechanical presses is available in ANSI Standard B11.1, "Safety Requirements for the Construction, Care, and Use of Mechanical Presses." Most of the provisions of this standard are included in Section 1910.217 of the Occupational Safety and Health Act (OSHA), Public Law 91-596. Some of the more important definitions (not previously discussed) included in the ANSI B11.1 and OSHA standards, with explanations for clarification, are:

**antirepeat** The part of the clutch/brake electrical control system designed to limit the press to a single stroke if the tripping means is held in its operating position. Antirepeat also requires release of all tripping mechanisms before another stroke can be initiated. Antirepeat is also called single-stroke reset or reset circuit. (Explanation: The function of antirepeat is to prevent the successive strokes which could occur if the antirepeat control did not exist. Antirepeat is the electrical control equivalent of a mechanical single-stroke mechanism, associated with full-revolution clutches. Both systems incorporate the feature requiring release of all tripping mechanisms prior to enabling a new stroke.)

**brake monitor** A sensor designed, constructed, and arranged to monitor any decrease in the performance of the press braking system.

**concurrent** Acting in conjunction; used to describe a situation wherein two or more controls exist in an operated condition at the same time. (Explanation: Specifically, as applied to the operation of run buttons or inch controls, the use of the word *concurrent* means that the clutch will be activated after each hand of the operator is holding a control in the operated position. The use of the word *concurrent* is intended to exclude any inference that a simultaneous moment of actuation must exist between the operations of the individual two-hand controls.)

**continuous** Uninterrupted, multiple strokes of the slide without intervening stops (or other clutch-control action) at the end of individual strokes.

**device** Part of the press control or an attachment that (1) restrains the operator from inadvertently reaching into the point of operation; (2) prevents normal press operation if the operator's hands are inadvertently within the point of operation; or (3) automatically withdraws the operator's hands if the operator's hands are inadvertently within the point of operation as the dies close.

*presence-sensing device* A device designed, constructed, and arranged to create a sensing field or area and to deactivate the clutch control of the press when an operator's hand or any other part of the operator's body is within such field or area.

*movable-barrier device* A movable barrier arranged to enclose the point of operation before the press stroke can be started. (Explanation: A movable-barrier device differs from an interlocked press barrier guard in that the device is controlled by the press-tripping controls; that is, operating the press, or slide, control first closes the movable barrier, which when closed, in conjunction with the press control causes slide operation. The movable barrier opens automatically when the slide is in or is approaching a stopped condition. Movable-barrier devices are self-powered. The interlocking method used with a movable-barrier device is normally more complicated than that used with an interlocked press barrier guard.)

*Type A movable barrier device* A self-powered movable barrier, which in normal single-stroke operation is designed to (1) close off access to the point of operation in response to operation of the press-tripping control; (2) prevent engagement of the clutch prior to closing of the barrier; (3) hold itself in the closed position; and (4) remain in the closed position until the slide has completed its stroke and has stopped at top of stroke. The device must not itself pose a source of injury; it must close softly.

*Type B movable barrier device* A self-powered movable barrier, which in normal single-stroke operation is designed to (1) close off access to the point of operation in response to operation of the press-tripping control; (2) prevent engagement of the clutch prior to closing of the barrier; and (3) hold itself in the closed position during the hazardous portion of the stroke of the slide. (Explanation: Stated another way, this requirement implies that the barrier is permitted to open automatically during the upstroke of the slide. The device must not in itself pose a source of injury.)

*holdout or restraint device* A mechanism, including attachments to the operator's hands, that when anchored and properly adjusted, prevents the operator's hands from entering the point of operation.

*pullback (out) device* A mechanism attached to the operator's hands and connected to the upper die or slide of the press that is intended, when properly adjusted, to withdraw the operator's hands as the dies close, if the operator's hands are inadvertently within the point of operation.

*two-hand trip* A clutch-actuating means requiring concurrent use of both hands of the operator to trip presses with full-revolution clutches.

*two-hand control device* A two-hand trip that further requires concurrent pressure from both hands of the operator during a substantial part of the die-closing portion of the stroke of the press. (Explanation: Two-hand trip and two-hand control devices are listed together to better explain the difference in safeguarding capabilities. A two-hand trip requires only a momentary concurrent application to push buttons, or other operating mechanisms, to set the slide ultimately into motion. Instantaneous removal of the hands cannot recall the action or stop the motion. A two-hand control device requires holding the buttons depressed for a portion of the downward stroke of the slide. Premature removal of hands results in a stopping action. A two-hand trip is applicable to full-revolution clutch equipment, and a two-hand control device is used with part-revolution clutch equipment only.)

**guard** A barrier that physically prevents entry of the operator's hands or fingers into the point of operation. (Explanation: In ANSI Standard B11.1 and the OSHA requirements, the use of the word *guard* is reserved exclusively for referring to physical barriers or enclosures designed for safeguarding at the point of operation. In contrast, a *device* may be electronic in nature or of a restraining type.

*die-enclosure guard* An enclosure attached to the die shoe or stripper, or both, in a fixed position.

*fixed-barrier guard* A die space barrier attached to the press frame.

*interlocked press barrier guard* A barrier interlocked so that the press stroke cannot be started normally unless the guard itself, or its hinged or movable sections, encloses the point of operation. (Explanation: The interlocked press barrier guard has a hinged or movable section [or the complete barrier is movable on tracks, for example] utilizing a simple interlock switch which is closed when the guard is in its protecting position. The hinged or movable section normally is manually powered, although some large guards may use a pneumatic cylinder, which in turn is manually controlled, with a selector switch, for example. Even though the guard should be in its protecting position before the press can be tripped [and opening the guard while the press slide is in motion results in deactivating the clutch-control circuit], nevertheless, stroking of the slide is independent of the movable section; that is, providing the movable section is closed, the slide may be single-stroked in an automatic mode or operated on a continuous basis with the press controls.)

*adjustable-barrier guard* A barrier requiring adjustment for each job or die setup.

**inch** An intermittent motion imparted to the slide (on machines using part-revolution clutches) by momentary operation of the inch-operating means. Operation of the inch-operating means engages the driving clutch so that a small portion of one stroke or indefinite stroking can occur, depending upon the length of time the inch-operating means is held in its operating position. Inch is a function used by the die setter for setup of dies and tooling, but is not intended for use during production operations by the operator. (Explanation:

Occasionally, a timing mechanism is used within the inch control circuit to give a predetermined maximum time interval to each inch actuation. This is usually called timed inch. Under any circumstances, it should be noted that the increment of slide travel obtained at each actuation is dependent upon time, speed of press, and position of slide within stroke and that inch, as used in the standard, has no relationship to the common unit of lineal measure. Inch is sometimes accomplished through a separate motor driving the press directly at slow speed. Inch is sometimes called jog, but the term *jog* has a different meaning for the purposes of the standard.)

**jog** An intermittent motion imparted to the slide by momentary operation of the drive motor, after the clutch is engaged with the flywheel at rest. (Explanation: It should be noted that in the heating effects on both motor and starter, jog places much more severe conditions on the drive motor and drive starter than normal operational conditions.)

**pinch point** Any point, other than the point of operation, at which it is possible for a part of the human body to be caught between the moving parts of a press or auxiliary equipment, between moving and stationary parts of a press or auxiliary equipment, or between the material and moving part or parts of the press or auxiliary equipment. (Explanation: The expression *pinch point*, as used in the standard, refers only to parts of the machine or parts associated with it that create a hazard. The expression is not used to describe hazards caused by the tooling at the point of operation, since these hazards are a different problem and require different treatment.)

**point of operation** The area of the press in which material is actually positioned and work is being performed during any process, such as shearing, punching, forming, or drawing.

**repeat** An unintended or unexpected successive stroke of the press resulting from a malfunction.

**single stroke** One complete stroke of the slide, usually initiated from a full open (or up) position, followed by closing (or down), and then a return to the full open position.

**single-stroke mechanism** A mechanical arrangement used on a full-revolution clutch to limit the travel of the slide to one complete stroke at each engagement of the clutch.

**stop control** An operator control designed to immediately deactivate the clutch control and activate the brake to stop slide motion. (Explanation: The term *Emergency Stop* is sometimes used to refer to this control, even though its use is most commonly not on an emergency basis. Sometimes, the control causes motor shutdown, in addition to clutch disengagement. Also, quite commonly, a top stop control is used to stop continuous stroking at top of stroke or at another predetermined point in stroke. A top stop control action is delayed, after actuation of the operating means, to cause stopping at the predetermined point in stroke.)

**stroking selector** The part of the clutch/brake control that determines the type of stroking when the operating means is actuated. The stroking selector generally includes positions for Off (clutch control), Inch, Single Stroke, Continuous (when Continuous is furnished) modes, and sometimes, Automatic mode. Supervisory control is required.

**trip (or tripping)** Activation of the clutch to run the press.

**turnover bar** A bar used in die setting to manually turn the crankshaft of the press. (Explanation: Two methods of ensuring the removal of the turnover bar from the barring hole have been found acceptable. They are: (1) use of spring action on the end of the bar and (2) use of storage pockets for the bar, incorporating an interlock switch.)

## Press Construction and Modification

Responsibility for the construction, reconstruction, and modification of mechanical power presses is presented in Section 3 of ANSI Standard B11.1. Hazards to personnel from moving parts (other than point-of-operation hazards) are to be eliminated by design, when possible, or by providing protection against the hazards in accordance with ANSI Safety Standard for Mechanical Power Transmission Apparatus, B15.1. Most of this code is contained in Section 1910.219 of the OSHA Standards. In cases in which hazards cannot be eliminated, the manufacturer must warn against them.

Press components must also be designed, secured, or covered to minimize hazards caused by breakage, loosening, and falling or by release of mechanical energy (as might be the case with broken springs). One basis for the design of brackets (if used) is their ability to support twice the static weight of components to be contained.

**Brake and clutch requirements.** Depending on design, a wide variety of brake types may exist, as discussed previously in this chapter. The brake may be a separate unit, or it may be combined with the clutch. Friction brakes provided for stopping or holding the slide must be set with compression springs. The brake capacity must be sufficient to stop the motion of the slide quickly and to hold the slide and its attachments at any point in its travel.

*Presses with full-revolution clutches.* When these presses are used for single-stroke operations, a mechanical single-stroke mechanism is required. If the single-stroke mechanism is dependent upon spring action, the spring(s) must be the compression type, operating on a rod or guided within a hole or tube, and designed to prevent interleaving of the spring coils in the event of breakage.

Construction standards for foot pedals (treadles), hand levers, and two-hand trips for operating presses with full-revolution clutches are also included in ANSI Standard B11.1. Limitations on the use of two-hand tripping devices on such presses as point-of-operation safety devices are discussed later in this section on press safety.

*Presses with part-revolution clutches.* These clutches must release and the brake must be applied when the external clutch-engaging means is removed, deactivated, or de-energized. A red-colored stop control must be provided with the clutch/brake control system. Momentary operation of the stop control must immediately deactivate the clutch and apply the brake. The stop control has to override any other control, and reactuation of the clutch must require use of the operating control that has been selected.

A stop control should be available to each operator. A top stop control (yellow) is recommended as an additional control for continuous-operating machines in which the speed or type of operation makes stopping at the top of stroke (or other predetermined point) a desirable feature.

A means of selecting the mode of operation must be supplied with the clutch/brake control to select the type of operation of the press. Fixing of selection must be by means capable of supervision by the employer. The recommended arrangement is Off, Inch, Single Stroke, and Continuous, as the control is turned clockwise. However, if design of the press component and its controls does not incorporate an Inch, a Single Stroke, or a Continuous mode, then the mode(s) so excluded would likewise be excluded on the stroking selector. There is no absolute intention to require a key-locking arrangement for the stroking selector switch, but it is desirable. When used in some production systems, a lockable selector switch such as this may not be practical.

The inch-operating means must be designed to prevent the worker's hands from entering the point of operation by requiring one of the following:

1. The clutch be actuated by the concurrent use of both hands.
2. The inch-operating means be a single control protected against accidental actuation and so located that the worker cannot reach into the point of operation while operating the single control.

Two-hand controls for single-stroke operation, when furnished, must conform to the following requirements:

1. Each hand control must be protected against unintended operation and must be arranged by design, construction, and/or separation so that the concurrent use of both hands is required to actuate the press. The use of rings around the palm-operated buttons protects them from unintentional operation. Precautions in design or installation are needed to prevent operation of two buttons by the use of one hand and the elbow of the same arm and to inhibit other circumvention of the two-hand requirement.
2. The control system must be designed to permit an adjustment which requires concurrent pressure from both hands during the die-closing portion of the stroke. A control adjustment is needed to establish a point in the die-closing portion of the stroke, prior to which slide motion is halted if either mechanism is released, but after which slide motion automatically continues if either mechanism is released.
3. The control system must incorporate an electrical anti-repeat feature.
4. The control system must be designed to require all of the operator hand controls to be released before an interrupted stroke can be resumed. This requirement pertains only to two-hand controls for single-stroke operation that were manufactured and installed after February 17, 1971.

Controls for more than one operating station must be designed to be activated and deactivated in complete sets of two-hand controls per operating station (excluding the stop control), by means capable of being supervised by the employer. The clutch/brake control system must be designed and constructed to prevent actuation of the clutch if all operating stations are bypassed.

A clutch/brake control system which contains both single-stroke and continuous functions must be designed so that the completion of the continuous circuit can be supervised by the employer. The initiation of Continuous mode must require a prior action or decision by the operator in addition to the selection of Continuous mode on the stroking selector, before actuation of the operating means results in continuous stroking.

One arrangement capable of meeting the intention of this standard is shown in Fig. 5-32. The following sequence is necessary to obtain continuous stroking: the supervisory Off/On selector switch must be turned on with a key; the stroking selector must be turned to Continuous mode; the setup button must be momentarily depressed; and then within a predetermined period of time, the operating means must be actuated.

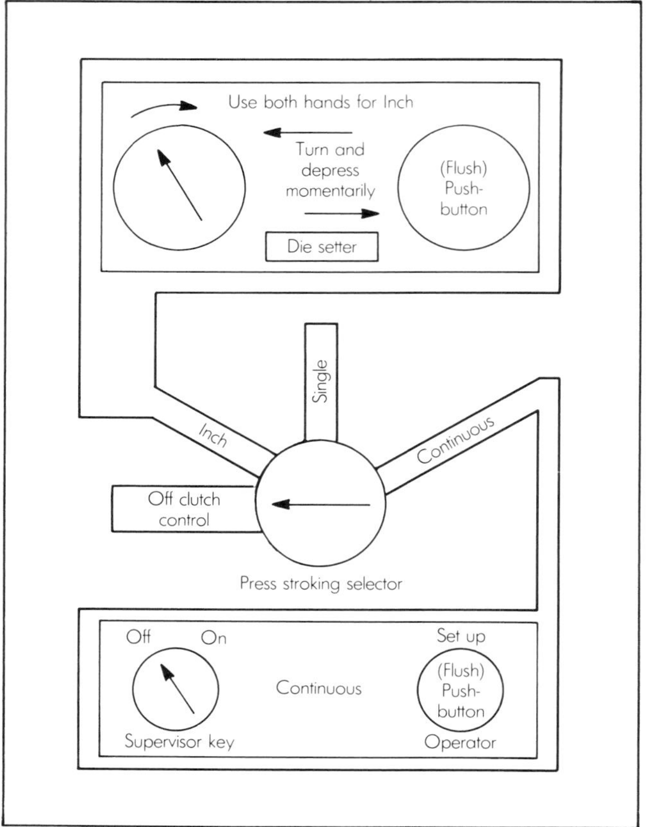


**Fig. 5-32 One arrangement for meeting standard requirements for continuous press operation. Two other arrangements are described in ANSI Standard B11.1.**

Two other arrangements for governing continuous press action are described in ANSI Standard B11.1. Another arrangement used in some controls requires the setup button to be depressed after the cycle has been initiated in the same manner as for Single Stroke mode.

If foot control is provided, the selection method between hand and foot control must be separate from the stroking selector and designed so that the selection can be supervised by the employer. Use of a foot control or pedal requires the use of a properly applied point-of-operation device or guarding. While several methods of ensuring supervisory control exist, one method is to use key locks and another is to use a removable foot control, which is held in supervised storage when not required for use, in conjunction with a dummy plug arrangement.

Foot-operated controls, if used, must be protected to prevent unintended operation by falling or moving objects or by accidental stepping onto the foot control directly from above. Such controls take the form of a foot-operated electrical switch to operate a solenoid or solenoid-operated air valve, or they may take the form of a foot-operated air valve.

The control of air-clutch machines must be designed to prevent a significant increase in the normal stopping time due to a failure within the operating-valve mechanism, and to inhibit further operation if such failure does occur. Inspection to determine mechanical condition is difficult, and the results to be obtained from such inspections are not positive. A so-called tandem or dual air-valve arrangement is commonly used to satisfy this requirement. Two exceptions to this requirement are:

1. It does not apply to presses intended only for continuous, automatic-feeding applications. (The application of such arrangements may actually be detrimental to normal operation.)
2. The requirement pertains only to those clutch/brake air-valve controls manufactured and installed after February 17, 1971.

The clutch/brake control must incorporate an automatic means to prevent initiation or continued activation of the single-stroke or continuous functions unless the press-drive motor is energized in the forward direction. A control-circuit interlock contact on the drive-motor starter (forward direction contactor), to permit run functions only when the contactor is energized, is one method of meeting this requirement.

The clutch/brake control must automatically deactivate in the event of failure of the power or pressure supply for the clutch-engaging means. Reactivation of the clutch must require restoration of normal air supply, energization of the main drive motor, and use of the tripping mechanism(s). This requirement may be satisfied on air-friction clutch machines by use of an air-pressure switch on the incoming air supply. Sensing the air pressure at the clutch/brake solenoid air valve, or better still at a surge tank, if used, is more effective.

The clutch/brake control must automatically deactivate in the event of failure of the air supply of the counterbalance(s). Reactivation of the clutch must require restoration of a normal air supply, energization of the main drive motor, and use of the tripping mechanism(s). An air-pressure switch in the counterbalance air system, downstream from pressure regulators, is an effective method of meeting this requirement.

Selection of turnover bar operation must be by a means capable of being supervised by the employer. A separate pushbutton, in a circuit activated only if the drive motor is de-energized, must be employed to activate the clutch.

*Control component failure.* Electrical clutch/brake control circuits must incorporate features to minimize the possibility of an unintended stroke if a control component, including relays, limit switches, and static output circuits, fails to function properly. Acceptable methods of controlling normal stopping of the slide include interruption of the clutch (and brake, if separate) valve current through the cycle-control rotary limit switch, or a series of contacts of two or more independent relays or static circuits. Adjustable stopping controls, using counters or timers, may be used with suitable limit switch backup.

**Control reliability and brake-system monitoring.** Operating with hands out of the die operation is recommended. However, when an operator is required to feed or remove parts by placing one or both hands in the point of operation, and a two-hand-control, presence-sensing device or Type B movable barrier (on a press equipped with a part-revolution clutch) is used for safeguarding, a reliable control system and brake monitor (discussed next) must be used. The exception that the requirement for interrupted stroke pertains only to two-hand controls for single-stroke operations manufactured and installed after February 17, 1971 (discussed previously) is not applicable. The control of air-clutch machines must be designed to prevent a significant increase in the normal stopping time due to a failure within the operating valve or other parts of the press braking system. It must also be designed to inhibit further operation if such failure occurs when a part-revolution clutch is employed.

An increase in stopping time with a press braking system (not necessarily just the operating valve mechanism) can be influenced by any one or a combination of the following factors:

1. Brake deterioration (wear).
2. Change in clutch/brake air pressure.
3. Change in counterbalance air pressure.
4. Dirt in the air exhaust system (especially the muffler).
5. Change in the slide/die weight.
6. Change in press speed.
7. Need for clutch/brake spring adjustment.
8. Failure of the clutch valve.

*Control reliability.* The control system must be constructed so that a failure within the system does not prevent the normal stopping action from being applied to the press when required, but does prevent initiation of a successive stroke until the failure is corrected. The failure must be detectable by a simple test, or it must be indicated by the control system. This requirement does not apply to those elements of the control system that have no effect on the protection against point-of-operation injuries.

*Brake-system monitoring.* Brake monitoring is not required on mechanical power presses with full-revolution clutches. It is also not required on presses with part-revolution clutches whenever hands-out-of-the-die feeding (including hand tools) is used or when one of the following types of safeguards is used: fixed-barrier guards, interlocked-barrier guards, Type A movable barrier device, or pullback (out) device. When required, the brake monitor must be so constructed as to automatically prevent the activation of a successive stroke if the stopping time or braking distance deteriorates to the point that the safety distance does not meet the following requirements:

1. For presence-sensing, point-of-operation devices or two-hand control devices, the safety distance from the sensing field or the two-hand station to the point of operation must be greater than the distance determined by the following formula:

$$D_s = C_H \times T_s \quad (5)$$

where:

$D_s$ = minimum safety distance, in. (mm)
$C_H$ = hand-speed constant, 63 ips (1600 mm/s)
$T_s$ = stopping time of press measured at about 90° position of crankshaft rotation, s

The hand-speed constant of 63 ips (1600 mm/s) is derived from OSHA (1974) regulations. Under certain circumstances, a higher hand-speed constant may be necessary. Small parts in conjunction with fast operator speed should be viewed with particular concern, and many safety experts feel that the constant should be closer to 98 ips (2489 mm/s).

2. For a two-hand trip used as a device, the safety distance between the two-hand trip and the point of operation must be greater than the distance determined by the following formula:

$$D_m = C_H \times T_m \quad (6)$$

where:

$D_m$ = minimum safety distance, in. (mm)
$C_H$ = hand-speed constant, 63 ips (1600 mm/s)
$T_m$ = maximum time the press takes for die closure after it has been tripped, s

# MECHANICAL PRESS SAFETY

For full-revolution clutch presses with only one engaging point, $T_m$ is equal to the time necessary for 1 1/2 revolutions of the crankshaft. For full-revolution clutch presses with more than one engaging point, $T_m$ is calculated from the following formula:

$$T_m = \left(\frac{1}{2} + \frac{1}{N}\right) T_r \quad (7)$$

where:

$N$ = number of engaging points per revolution
$T_r$ = time necessary to complete one revolution of the crankshaft, s

A brake monitor used with a Type B movable barrier device must be installed in a manner to detect slide top-stop overrun beyond the normal limit reasonably established by the employer. The brake monitor must be installed on a press so that it indicates when the performance of the braking system has deteriorated to the extent specified. The brake monitor must also be constructed and installed to monitor brake-system performance on each stroke in single-stroke operations.

Brake monitors may be a permanent part of the presses, or press controls, being tied into the press controls for continuous monitoring of each stroke. Many types, including pneumatic, electromechanical, electro-optical, and electronic types, are commercially available with various features and degrees of sophistication.

Top-position-type brake monitors check braking distance, not the time it takes to stop from the initiation of a signal. Advantages of top-position monitors are that they are simple and relatively inexpensive and they satisfy OSHA requirements when the press control system meets OSHA reliability specifications.

Full-cycle or stop-time types of brake monitors check the stopping time rather than the distance. These monitors are higher in cost and more complex than top-position types and should be kept locked to prevent unauthorized resetting. Their timers can usually be set so that stopping time can be checked at any point in the cycle.

Stopping time of a press, used to calculate safety distance, can be measured with some types of full-cycle monitors having readout capabilities, with brake stop-time monitors, or with some other means. Portable devices are available for mounting externally on various presses.

## Press Operation

In addition to a properly equipped press with a point-of-operation safeguard to suit the operation, properly trained operators, correct procedures, adequate supervision, ample work area, and avoidance of overloading are essential for safe and efficient press operation. A checklist of some important items for press operator safety is presented in Table 5-9.

**Instruction to operators.** The employer must train and instruct the operator in the safe method of working before work is started on any operation. The employer must ensure by adequate supervision that correct operating procedures are being followed and that proper point-of-operation safeguards are being used. The relative maturity of young or inexperienced workers should be evaluated before assigning them to press operations, and appropriate training procedures should be undertaken.

**Work area.** The employer must provide clearance between machines so that movement of one operator does not interfere with the work of another. Ample room for cleaning machines and handling material, workpieces, and scrap must also be provided. All surrounding floors must be kept in good condition and free from obstructions, grease, oil, and water.

**Overloading.** Employers must operate their presses within the force and attachment weight ratings specified by the manufacturer. Standard press force ratings are specified at a given point above bottom of stroke, as discussed previously in this chapter. In the practical circumstance, many operations encounter their maximum loads higher in the stroke than this specified point. This can overload the press motor. Another point not always understood is that reverse (or tension) loading is imposed by "snap through" during severe blanking operations. Depending on die design, adjustment, speed, and material, this reverse load may be a severe overload of the equipment, leading to fatigue failures because of improper application of press equipment. The reverse (tension) loading capability of most presses is generally 15-20% of the forward (compressive) capability. Load monitoring systems are available to monitor total load to protect the press frame and to monitor load vs. stroke position to detect energy problems, as well as reverse loads.

## Noise Control

Employers are responsible for providing and ensuring permissible noise levels. Permissible noise exposure varies from a maximum noise level of 90 dBA for a duration of 8 hours per day to 115 dBA for 1/4 hour or less. Many press manufacturers have done considerable work in reducing noise by improving the design and manufacture of gears and by using new construction techniques. Tooling, however, is a major contributor to noise. The use of stepped punches, increased shear on the tools, urethane strippers, and other die designs can reduce noise.

Noise can be reduced in press rooms and press areas by providing baffles of sound-absorptive material over the presses and on walls or ceilings. One method consists of placing partial (operative where required) enclosures of lead or other materials over openings on the machines. Sheet lead, lead-impregnated vinyl, sheet lead sandwiched between layers of polyurethane foam, lead-loaded epoxy, and sheet lead laminated to a variety of substrates provide good sound isolation. Total enclosures are being used successfully, especially for high-speed laminating presses. Mufflers, barriers, and damping materials applied to thin-metal panels (such as those used for control cabinets and for material-handling chutes and bins) are also being used effectively to control noise. Mufflers can substantially reduce air exhaust noises without affecting operation when properly applied.

Noise amplification and transmission by the foundation and floor can be eliminated by mounting presses on vibration isolators. One type of isolator has ductile iron fingers and a bearing plate supported on a neoprene cushion to isolate vibration in all directions.

Ear protection in the form of plugs or muffs for employees must be provided and used when noise levels cannot be adequately controlled by changes in the machines or environment. It is advisable to modify the design or surroundings of machines now in use, provide adequate maintenance, and institute a noise detection and reduction program.

**TABLE 5-9**
**Checklist of Some Important Items for Press Operator Safety**

BEFORE STARTING THE PRESS:

WARNING
Be sure the power to the press is off and the flywheel is at rest.

1. Clean the press and the area around the press.
2. Inspect the press visually. Check the dies and any feeding and ejecting mechanism. Check tooling, clamps, bolts, and locknuts holding the dies and bolster plate in position. Check all operating air and lubrication gages for proper pressure.
3. Check the point of operation safeguarding and equipment for proper location and condition.
4. Report any defects discovered by inspection.

WARNING
Repair defects immediately. Never operate press in defective condition.

5. If tooling requires lubrication, do not reach into the die area. Always use long-handled brushes, swabs, rollers, or remote lubrication equipment.
6. Be sure that stock is of proper thickness and type and that tubs and skids are properly located.

STARTING THE PRESS:

1. When satisfied that the press and the work area around the press are in proper condition for operation, turn power on.
2. Check remaining air and lubrication gages for proper pressure.
3. If the clutch and brake are functioning properly, start main motor and bring the flywheel up to speed. (This is not recommended for presses with full revolution clutches.)
4. Press the main motor stop button.
5. Inch the slide through one complete stroke with flywheel coasting.

CAUTION
Be alert for any binding or jamming of moving parts.

6. If press performs satisfactorily, start the main motor, bring the flywheel up to speed, and check for correct slide stroking sequence in response to each stroke selector switch setting on the control panel. If the equipment does not function properly, have a maintenance person check the electrical and air circuits.

OPERATING THE PRESS:

WARNING
Never place any part of the body in the point of operation or other pinch, shear, or crushing hazard points.
Never eliminate or bypass any of the point of operation safety devices or guards installed on the press.
Never attempt to circumvent the safety function of an operator's two-hand control in any way.
Never operate a foot-controlled press unless a properly applied point of operation guard is provided to keep the operator's hands out of the die space area.

1. Use hand feeding tools when required and make sure they are in good condition.
2. Do not talk when operating the press. If it is necessary to talk, stop the press.
3. Report any malfunction or unusual operations of the press immediately.

WARNING
Never continue operating a malfunctioning press—get it fixed!

4. When feeding the press, never sit or stand on anything that could cause a fall, slip, or stumble into the point of operation or other hazardous area.

INTERRUPTION OF OPERATION:

WARNING
Never leave a running press unattended.

1. When the operation of the press is interrupted for any reason, no matter how short the time, press the main motor stop button and, with the flywheel coasting, inch the slide to the bottom of stroke. Always leave the slide at the bottom of stroke.

WARNING
Never leave the press unattended until the flywheel has come to rest.

2. If a foot switch is being used, unplug and remove from the press if possible.
3. When restarting the press, follow the procedures listed under STARTING THE PRESS.

MAINTAINING AND SERVICING THE PRESS:

This may involve major mechanical, pneumatic, hydraulic, or electrical repairs; procedures involving the lubrication system; cleaning; removal of a stuck or jammed part in a die; or other procedures.

1. Always be sure the electrical power to the press is off by installing a padlock on the main power disconnect, external operating handle mechanism after the handle has been placed in the "off" position. A warning tag should also be temporarily installed on the main power disconnect operating handle advising others that the press in out of service. An appropriate tag marked "do not close main power switch" should be utilized.
2. Check to ensure that main power is off by attempting to start the main (flywheel) drive motor. It should not operate.
3. If the slide cannot be placed into the die's maximum closed position due to the nature of the work to be performed and if the slide must be positioned in the die's maximum open position, a die safety block should be put into place between the stationary bolster and the movable (slide) bolster in the die area of the press. The die safety block must be provided with an electrical interlock plug which additionally causes a disconnect of the press 120V control circuit to assure nonelectrical operation of the press electrical control system when the die safety block is removed from its storage facility on the press frame.

(*Danly Machine Corp.*)

# MECHANICAL PRESS SAFETY

## Safeguarding the Point of Operation

Employers are responsible for providing and ensuring the usage of either a point-of-operation guard or a properly applied and adjusted point-of-operation device on every operation performed on a press production system. This requirement does not apply when the point-of-operation opening is 1/4″ (6.3 mm) or less.

**Point-of-operation guards.** Every point-of-operation guard must meet the following design, construction, application, and adjustment requirements:

1. It must prevent entry of hands or fingers into the point of operation by reaching through, over, under, or around the guard. Suggested permissible openings shown in Fig. 5-33 are usually reasonable, but circumstances may exist in which they do not apply.
2. It must not, in itself, create a pinch point between the guard and moving machine parts. It is recommended that at least 1″ (25 mm) be provided to avoid the possibility of pinch points.
3. It must utilize fasteners not readily removable by the operator, to minimize the possibility of misuse or removal of essential parts.
4. It must facilitate its inspection.
5. It must offer maximum visibility of the point of operation consistent with the other requirements.

*Die-enclosure guards.* When individual die guards, called die-enclosure guards in the Standards, are used they must be attached to the die shoes or strippers in fixed positions. This single-purpose type of guard provides positive operator protection because the die is completely enclosed and the guard is a permanent part of it. Since each guard is designed for a specific die, no adjustments are necessary. Modifications are necessary only when dies are modified and/or the product is changed.

Transparent plastics may be used for die-enclosure guards (see Fig. 5-34) since they provide visibility. The plastic should be of a type that does not shatter, and the guard design should permit authorized removal of the plastic for cleaning or replacement. Such guards may also be made from slotted material, rods or bars (with openings having their long dimension in the direction of movement), expanded or perforated metal, or woven wire.

Two-piece telescoping guards are sometimes used, particularly for longer stroke operations. One shield is made stationary on the fixed part of the die, and the other is attached to the punch holder or press slide. Moving tubes which telescope over stationary rods are also used for this purpose.

*Fixed-barrier guards.* When fixed-barrier guards are used, they must be attached securely to the frame of the press or to the bolster plate (see Fig. 5-35). These guards provide maximum possible protection, can be used with presses having part or full-revolution clutches, and are the least expensive positive

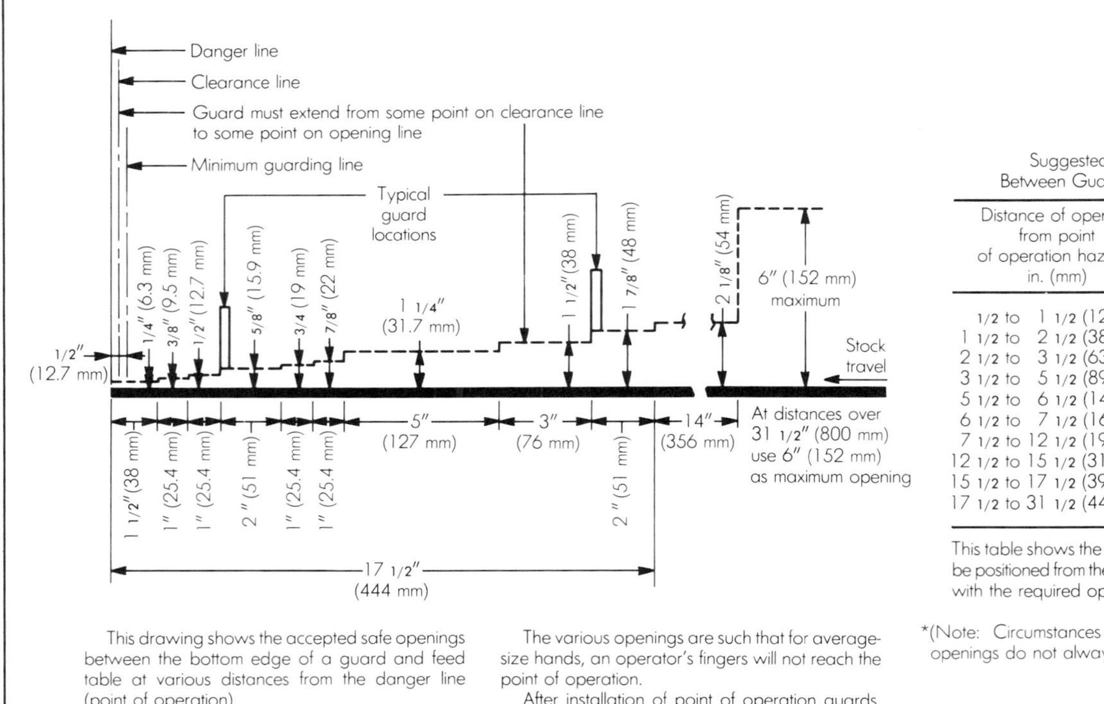


Suggested Safe Openings Between Guard and Feed Table*

| Distance of opening from point of operation hazard, in. (mm) | Maximum width of opening, in. (mm) |
|---|---|
| 1/2 to 1 1/2 (12.7-38) | 1/4 (6.3) |
| 1 1/2 to 2 1/2 (38-63.5) | 3/8 (9.5) |
| 2 1/2 to 3 1/2 (63.5-89) | 1/2 (12.7) |
| 3 1/2 to 5 1/2 (89-140) | 5/8 (15.9) |
| 5 1/2 to 6 1/2 (140-165) | 3/4 (19) |
| 6 1/2 to 7 1/2 (165-190) | 7/8 (22) |
| 7 1/2 to 12 1/2 (190-317) | 1 1/4 (32) |
| 12 1/2 to 15 1/2 (317-394) | 1 1/2 (38) |
| 15 1/2 to 17 1/2 (394-444) | 1 7/8 (48) |
| 17 1/2 to 31 1/2 (444-800) | 2 1/8 (54) |

This table shows the distances that guards shall be positioned from the danger line in accordance with the required openings.

*(Note: Circumstances may exist where these openings do not always apply.)

**Fig. 5-33 Suggested permissible openings between bottom edges of guards and top surface of feed table at various distances from danger line (point of operation).**

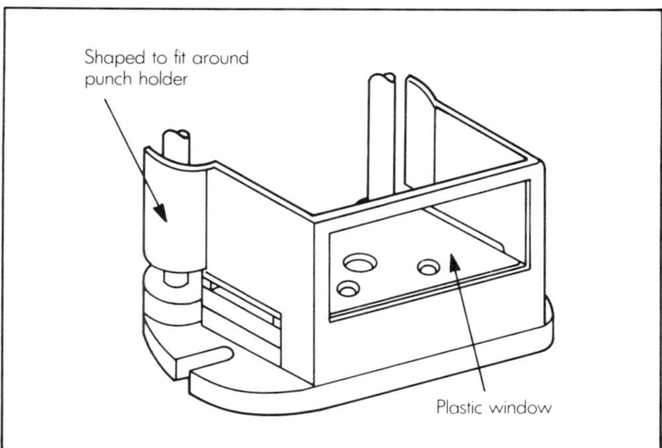


**Fig. 5-34 Die-enclosure guard completely encloses and is a permanent part of die for positive protection. Transparent plastic window provides visibility.**

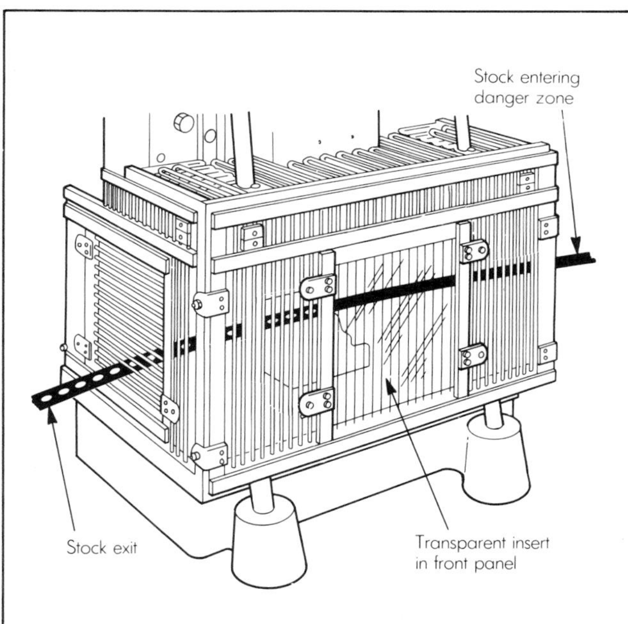


**Fig. 5-35 Fixed-barrier guards on a power press.**

guarding method. They are limited, however, to specific operations in which operator involvement in the danger zone is not required. Another limitation is that press adjustment and repair, as well as die changes, generally require removal of the guard, thus increasing downtime.

*Interlocked press barrier guards.* These guards contain a hinged or movable section designed for die changing (when the die size is small enough to so permit) or for removing a jammed part or material or scrap. The guards must be electrically interlocked with the press-clutch control so that the clutch cannot be activated unless the guard itself, or the hinged or movable sections of the guard, is in the protecting position.

The hinged or movable sections of an interlocked press barrier guard must not be used for manual feeding. Through interlocking, the guard must prevent opening of the interlocked section and reaching into the point of operation prior to die closure or prior to the cessation of slide motion.

*Adjustable-barrier guards.* When an adjustable-barrier guard (see Fig. 5-36) is used, it must be securely attached to the press bed or frame, bolster plate, or die shoe. Adjustable front and side panels of slotted metal or rods are fastened to a framework so that they can conveniently accommodate different sizes of dies and still provide the necessary protection to prevent hand entry. The brackets can be fastened permanently to the press. Connecting links are used to adjust the barrier to proper location. A front support bar is used to carry two front sections. Side sections, fastened to the front sections, can be set at any angle so that the operator can control the stock at a safe location from the point of operation.

These guards must be adjusted and operated in conformity with Fig. 5-33 and the five requirements for point-of-operation guards stated previously. If the adjustment and operation of an adjustable-barrier guard is not closely supervised, inadequate guarding may result.

Adjustable-barrier guards can provide maximum protection when properly adjusted and are relatively inexpensive. Disadvantages are that they often require adjustment and maintenance and they can easily be tampered with by the operator. Also, press adjustment and repair often require removal of the guard.

*Inadequate enclosures.* Any enclosure which does not meet the five requirements for point-of-operation guards (given earlier), as well as Fig. 5-33, must be used only in conjunction with a point-of-operation device.

**Point-of-operation devices.** A point-of-operation device must protect the operator by one or more of the following:

1. Preventing or stopping normal stroking of the press, or both, if the operator's hands are inadvertently placed in the point of operation.
2. Preventing the operator from inadvertently reaching into the point of operation, or withdrawing the operator's hands if they are inadvertently located in the point of operation as the dies close.

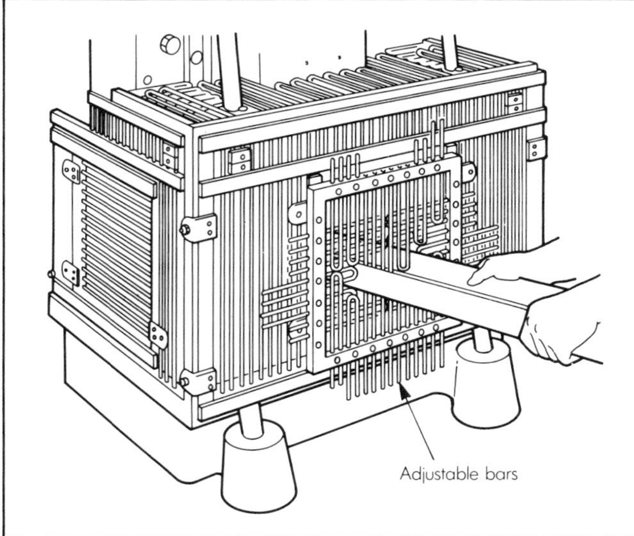


**Fig. 5-36 Adjustable-barrier guard must be attached to press bed, bolster plate, or die shoe. Adjustment must conform with dimensional requirements of Fig. 5-33.**

3. Preventing the operator from inadvertently reaching into the point of operation at all times.
4. Requiring application of both of the operator's hands to machine operating controls and locating such controls a safe distance from the point of operation so that the slide completes its downward travel or stops before the operator can reach into the point of operation.
5. Enclosing the point of operation before a press stroke can be initiated and maintaining this closed condition until the motion of the slide has ceased.
6. Enclosing the point of operation before a press stroke can be initiated, to prevent an operator from reaching into the point of operation prior to die closure or prior to cessation of slide motion during the downward stroke.

*Movable-barrier devices.* Type A and Type B movable barrier devices are discussed previously in this section under the subject of "Safety Definitions." A Type A device must protect the operator in the manner specified in Requirement 5 of point-of-operation devices; and Type B, in the manner specified in Requirement 6.

When used with a power press having a full-revolution clutch, a movable-barrier device must be operated only with a single-stroke mechanism. It must also be applied in such a way that it makes impossible any attempt, after tripping the clutch, to open the device and reach into the point of operation prior to die closure.

When used with presses having part-revolution clutches, a movable-barrier device must be interlocked into the clutch/brake control system to prevent or stop activation of the clutch unless the device is in its closed (protecting) position.

*Presence-sensing devices.* When a presence-sensing device (see Fig. 5-37) is used, it must protect the operator as provided in Requirement 1 for point-of-operation devices. The device must be interlocked into the control circuit to prevent or stop slide motion if the operator's hand or another part of the operator's body is within the sensing field of the device during the downstroke of the press slide. These devices must not be used on presses having full-revolution clutches and must not be used as a tripping means to initiate slide motion.

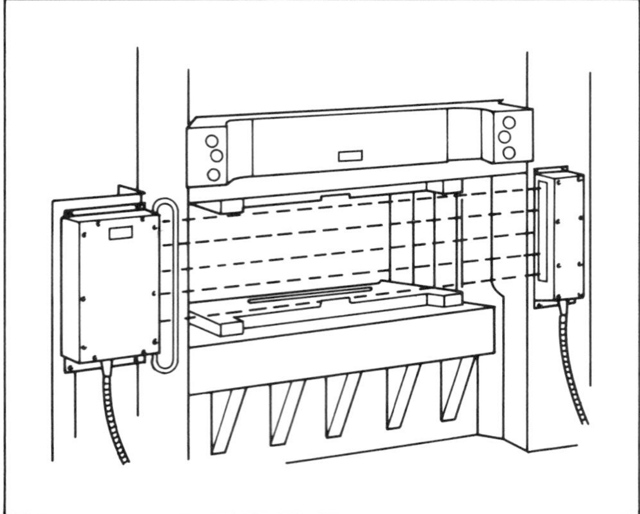

**Fig. 5-37 Electronic device does not obstruct operator visibility or movements. Press clutch/brake must be able to stop slide anywhere in its stroke.**

Although the use of a presence-sensing device to trip the press may increase productivity and is employed in Europe, it is not permitted on mechanical presses in the United States without a variance from OSHA. One firm in the United States has been using this system for several years, under an experimental variance, with a reported gain in productivity.

Presence-sensing devices must be constructed so that a failure within a system does not prevent the normal stopping action from being applied to the press when required, but does prevent the initiation of a successive stroke until the failure is corrected. The failure must be indicated by the system.

Muting (bypassing of the protective function) of these devices, during the upstroke of the press slide, is permitted for parts ejection, circuit checking, and feeding. Muting can be accomplished by interface or auxiliary control, but must be accomplished so that a failure within the muting system does not allow undetected and unprotected operation. A simple limit switch wired in parallel with the presence-sensing device is unsafe. Failure of the light source or power supply, excessive ambient light, temperature variations, or other environmental factors should not adversely affect the protection offered to the operator.

The safety distance from the sensing field to the point of operation must be greater than the distance determined by Eq. (6), presented previously under the subject of brake-system monitoring. Guards must be used to protect all areas of entry to the point of operation that are not protected by the presence-sensing device.

Ultrasonic, capacitance, and optical electronic (photoelectric) types of presence-sensing devices are available. The ultrasonic devices create a screen of inaudible, high-frequency sound; a sensing medium detects any intrusion. With capacitance devices, the die area is protected by an antenna energized to create a capacitance field of radio-frequency waves. Intrusions of the field are sensed by a change of capacitance, which stops the press.

Presence-sensing devices of the optical-electronic (photoelectric) type are made using visible light or infrared light. With devices using visible light, one or more beams from light sources are transmitted across the area of die entry to receiving photocells. Intrusions interrupt the beam(s) and transmit a signal to stop the press.

Presence-sensing devices using infrared light are generally either of the scanning-beam or diode-array type. A scanning-beam device utilizes light from a single, solid-state, light-emitting diode (LED) source. The light beam travels across the area to be protected many times per second, forming a continuous curtain of light. The scanning beam is returned by a retroreflector to a photocell, located in the same housing as the source. Such light curtains can be bent around corners to provide two or three-sided protection. With other infrared devices, coded pulses are applied sequentially to a linear array of LED's to form a grid across the area to be protected.

*Pullback (out) devices.* When a pullback (out) device is used, it must protect the operator as specified in Requirement 2 for point-of-operation devices. These devices must include attachments for each of the operator's hands. The attachments must be connected to and operated only by the press slide or the upper die. Attachments must be adjusted to prevent the operator from reaching into the point of operation or to withdraw the operator's hands from the point of operation before the dies close.

A separate pullback (out) device must be provided for each

operator if more than one operator runs a press. Each device in use must be visually inspected and checked for proper adjustment at the start of each operator shift, following a new die setup, and when operators are changed. Necessary maintenance or repair, or both, shall be performed and completed before the press is operated, and records of inspections and maintenance must be kept.

*Holdout or restraint devices.* A holdout or restraint device, when used, must protect the operator as specified in Requirement 3 for point-of-operation devices. The devices must include attachments for each of the operator's hands. Such attachments must be securely anchored and adjusted in such a way that the operator is restrained from reaching into the point of operation. A separate set of restraints must be provided for each operator if more than one operator is required on a press.

Disadvantages of pullback and holdout devices are that they limit the movement of the operator and may cause discomfort; require frequent inspection, adjustments, and maintenance; and do not prevent others (such as foremen) from placing their hands in the point of operation.

*Two-hand control devices.* When a two-hand control is used as a device, it must protect the operator as specified in Requirement 4 for point-of-operation devices. Two-hand control devices can only be used when the press has a part-revolution clutch or direct drive capable of being stopped during the stroke. During single stroking of the press, two-hand control devices require that the hands be on the control during the closing portion of the strokes; they are only one type of safety device used on presses for production applications. A disadvantage of them is that they do not protect against machine failures that prevent normal stopping action.

When press operations require more than one operator, separate two-hand control stations must be provided for each operator and must be designed to require concurrent application of all operators' controls to activate the slide. Removal of a hand from any control button must cause the slide to stop. There must be concurrent use of both hands of all operators to start the stroke and to continue the die-closing portion of the stroke when single stroking the press.

Each two-hand control must meet the construction requirements described previously in this section under the subject of presses with part-revolution clutches. The safety distance between each two-hand control device and the point of operation must be greater than the distance determined by Eq. (6) presented previously under the subject of brake-system monitoring. Two-hand controls may be permanently mounted. When they cannot be permanently mounted because of the type of operation, administrative procedures to ensure awareness of the proper safety distance—including an explanation to the operator(s)—are acceptable.

*Two-hand trip used as a device.* This generally applies to the use of concurrently operated two-hand tripping means on presses with full-revolution clutches. There is no control of the stroke, because when a full-revolution clutch is engaged, it cannot be disengaged until the end of the stroke. Consequently, no holding time is possible during the die-closing portion of the stroke.

The two-hand trip, when used, shall protect the operator as specified in Requirement 4 for point-of-operation devices. When used in press operations requiring more than one operator, separate two-hand trips must be provided for each operator and must be designed to require concurrent application of all operators to activate the slide.

Some clutches have multiple engaging points which decrease the time lag after tripping. Some older full-revolution clutches require proper maintenance to maintain their reliability. A significant possibility exists with many arrangements that the clutch can be mechanically tripped with the flywheel either at rest or in motion. For this reason, no part of the body or hand tools should be in the point of operation when a press drive motor is first started.

Each two-hand trip must meet the construction requirements described previously in this section under the subject of presses with part-revolution clutches. The safety distance between the two-hand trip and the point of operation must be greater than the distance determined by Eq. (7) and Eq. (8) presented previously under the subject of brake-system monitoring. Ideally, two-hand trips should be mounted a safe distance from the point of operation. When this is not possible because of the type of operation, administrative procedures to ensure awareness of the proper safety distance—including an explanation to the operator(s)—are acceptable.

### Other Safety Considerations

The methods used to feed stock, blanks, or stampings to presses, as well as the means for unloading (discussed in detail in a preceding section of this chapter) are important considerations in establishing safe operating procedures. Proper die design, fastening, handling, and setting (discussed in Chapter 6 of this volume, "Die Design for Sheet Metal Forming") are also critical factors in press safety.

Metal signs warning of possible hazards and giving basic safety fundamentals and procedures should be permanently attached to all presses, attachments, and controls. The signs should be located at strategic positions for easy viewing and most effective use. If damaged, the signs should be replaced immediately.

## PRESS LUBRICATION AND MAINTENANCE

Proper lubrication and maintenance are essential to safety, efficient production, minimum costs, and long press life.

### Lubrication of Presses

Lubrication requirements vary with the size and complexity of the press, as well as the specific operation and press speed. Recommendations of the press builders with respect to the type of lubricant to be used, the amount that is necessary, and the frequency of application should be followed carefully.

Either oil or grease is used for press lubrication, with application by manual, centralized, or recirculating oil systems. A detailed discussion of lubricants is presented in Chapter 3, "Lubricants," and Chapter 4, "Cutting Fluids and Industrial Lubricants," in Volume I of this Handbook series.

**Manual lubricating systems.** Point-to-point lubrication, with a fitting provided for each bearing and wear surface, is the simplest lubricating method and requires the lowest capital investment. Instead of bearings and surfaces having to be individually lubricated with a hand pump or gun, some systems provide centralized headers with lubricant lines to several bearings and surfaces.

Major disadvantages of manual lubricating are the time required for the process, the danger of human error (missing one or more lubrication points), and possible contamination from dirty containers or other sources. Such systems, however, are often adequate for smaller presses having only a few points requiring lubrication.

**Centralized systems.** Several types of systems are available for supplying the proper amount of oil or grease to required points from a central source. The major advantage of such systems is that the possibility of human error is eliminated, thus minimizing the chance of lubrication failures.

With one centralized system, a number of measuring valves are mounted on a tube which is alternately pressurized and is vented from a central pump. When pressurized, the piston in each valve displaces a metered amount of lubricant. When pressure is removed, springs in the valves return the pistons to their starting positions. Check valves prevent lubricant from returning from the bearings.

Other systems use pressurized valve blocks to distribute metered amounts of lubricant, and some have individual pumps to supply each bearing. Central sources of pressure are hand guns, hand-operated pumps, or motorized pumps with automatic timers.

**Recirculating oil systems.** These systems are becoming increasingly popular, especially for larger, more complex mechanical presses. An important advantage over centralized systems is that the oil is recovered for reuse.

An automatic, recirculating oil system for a straight-side mechanical press is shown in Fig. 5-38. The system employs a motor-driven pump; a coarse, mechanical filter on the intake side of the pump; a fine, micronic filter on the discharge side; and an oil reservoir in the bed of the press. In addition to lubricating all points of wear, the large volume of oil circulated also cleans surfaces by flushing away foreign particles and controls expansion by cooling. Piston-type distribution blocks (feeders) ensure proper metering of the oil. Pressure switches or cycle monitors stop the press in the event of oil stoppage.

## Press Maintenance

Regulations by OSHA as well as regulations contained in ANSI Standard B11.1 require that the employer be responsible for establishing and following a program of periodic and regular inspection of production systems using presses to ensure that all their parts, auxiliary equipment, and point-of-operation

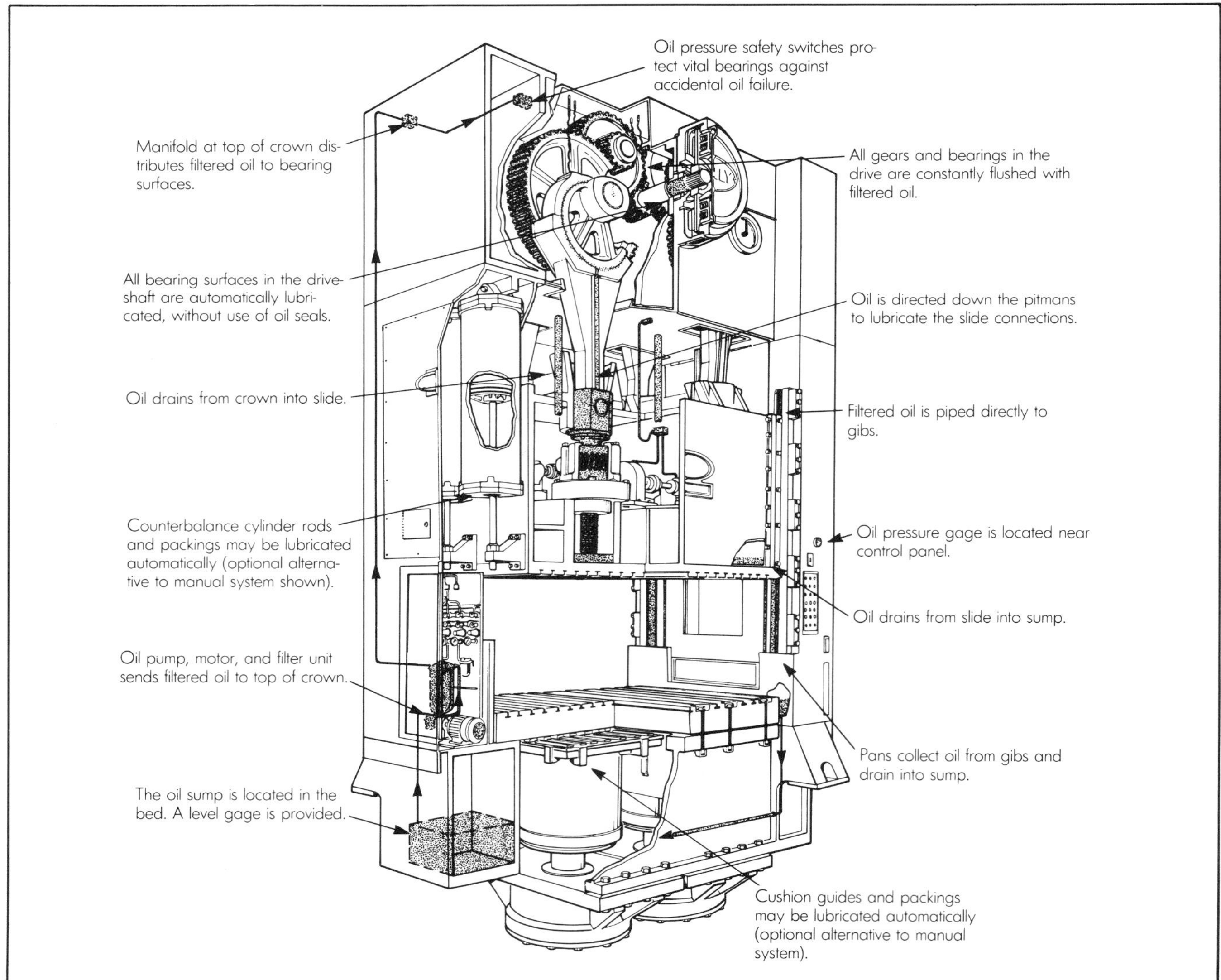
Oil pressure safety switches protect vital bearings against accidental oil failure.
Manifold at top of crown distributes filtered oil to bearing surfaces.
All gears and bearings in the drive are constantly flushed with filtered oil.
All bearing surfaces in the driveshaft are automatically lubricated, without use of oil seals.
Oil is directed down the pitmans to lubricate the slide connections.
Oil drains from crown into slide.
Filtered oil is piped directly to gibs.
Counterbalance cylinder rods and packings may be lubricated automatically (optional alternative to manual system shown).
Oil pressure gage is located near control panel.
Oil drains from slide into sump.
Oil pump, motor, and filter unit sends filtered oil to top of crown.
Pans collect oil from gibs and drain into sump.
The oil sump is located in the bed. A level gage is provided.
Cushion guides and packings may be lubricated automatically (optional alternative to manual system).

**Fig. 5-38 Automatic recirculating oil system for a mechanical press.** (*Danly Machine Corp.*)

safeguarding are in safe operating condition and adjustment. The employer must also be able to demonstrate that the inspections are made, and records of safety-related maintenance work must be kept.

To meet these requirements, it is recommended that a visual inspection of operations, safeguards, and auxiliary equipment be made at least once per shift. At weekly, or perhaps monthly, intervals, each press should be examined and so indicated on individual press record forms. Some press features may require less frequent attention.

An itemized check list and report form (see Fig. 5-39) should be developed for each press. Items on the form illustrated are

PRESS INSPECTION RECORD

(refer to manufacturer's recommendation)

Machine no. ______________ Date ______________

Manufacturer's serial no. ______________

| Satisfactory | Unsatisfactory | Operation | Unsatisfactory condition | Date of correction |
|---|---|---|---|---|
| ____ | ____ | All parts and screws (for looseness) | ____ | ____ |
| ____ | ____ | Lubrication | ____ | ____ |
| ____ | ____ | Bearing clearances | ____ | ____ |
| ____ | ____ | Slide gib clearances | ____ | ____ |
| ____ | ____ | Drive gears and keys (for looseness) | ____ | ____ |
| ____ | ____ | Clutch adjustment | ____ | ____ |
| ____ | ____ | Brake adjustment | ____ | ____ |
| ____ | ____ | Main-drive V-belt adjustment | ____ | ____ |
| ____ | ____ | Air gage (for accuracy) | ____ | ____ |
| ____ | ____ | Air connections (for leaks) | ____ | ____ |
| ____ | ____ | Proper pressure settings | ____ | ____ |
| ____ | ____ | Air valve and solenoid | ____ | ____ |
| ____ | ____ | Limit-switch setting | ____ | ____ |
| ____ | ____ | Limit-switch condition | ____ | ____ |
| ____ | ____ | Limit-switch drive | ____ | ____ |
| ____ | ____ | Control panel (for loose connections) | ____ | ____ |
| ____ | ____ | Pushbuttons and wiring | ____ | ____ |
| ____ | ____ | Counterbalance cylinders | ____ | ____ |
| ____ | ____ | Pneumatic die cushions | ____ | ____ |
| ____ | ____ | Point-of-operation guards or devices | ____ | ____ |
| ____ | ____ | ____ | ____ | ____ |
| ____ | ____ | ____ | ____ | ____ |
| ____ | ____ | ____ | ____ | ____ |

Corrective measures: ______________

____ Press approved for operation

____ Press NOT approved for operation

Inspected by: ______________ Date ______________

Corrections made by: ______________ Date ______________

Press approved for production by: ______________ Date ______________

**Fig. 5-39 Suggested inspection form for mechanical presses.** (*Clearing, A Div. of U.S. Industries, Inc.*)

not all inclusive and vary for different presses. Immediate action must be taken to correct all items found unsatisfactory in the report.

**Maintenance program.** A complete maintenance program can be organized to coordinate several levels of activity, such as routine inspections, preventive maintenance, replacement or repair of parts as required, and complete reinspection after repair. A maintenance file should be kept for each press, and all maintenance reports and service records should be kept for future reference.

*Routine inspections.* The first level of inspection should be performed when each work shift changes, when operators change, and whenever the dies are changed. More frequent inspections may be dictated by the particular conditions of the job being run. This inspection can be carried out by trained press operators, diesetters, or shop supervisory personnel as part of their normal duties. This inspection should include items such as lubricant levels, oil leaks, loose fasteners, unusual noises, loose belts, unusual vibrations, and erratic speeds, as well as the operation of electrical controls and of safeguarding equipment.

The clutch solenoid valve should always be included in this inspection. The solenoid valve action must be immediate and positive. A sluggish or improperly operating clutch solenoid valve is not safe and must be replaced immediately. A worn valve should be replaced only with a new valve; an attempt should never be made to repair an old or worn-out valve. Replacement clutch valves should always be the double, self-checking type. The valve lubrication supply from the air line lubricator should be checked, and the valve air supply must be clean and moisture free.

The next level of inspection must be performed by maintenance personnel on a weekly basis, at a minimum, and more frequently if required by operating conditions. At this inspection, the entire press, its auxiliary equipment, and the surrounding area should be cleaned. The press should be inspected for such items as leaks in pneumatic components, damaged oil lines, and the condition of air and oil filters. At these inspections, excess moisture should be drained from the clutch system, counterbalance cylinders, die cushion cylinders, and surge tank. All of the electrical controls should be cycled through their normal functions and should be inspected for proper operation. Fault-detection circuits should be similarly checked. Relays should be inspected for defective contact points; freedom of armature motion; and consistent, immediate response. Foot controls should be inspected to make certain that connecting wires are not broken or pulled loose.

Another level of inspection should be performed by maintenance personnel at monthly intervals. Items that were not checked at previous inspections should be included in the monthly inspection and may include the following: lubricator fault switches, solenoid air valves, electrical controls, and V-belts.

An inspection should be performed to establish the general condition of the press and auxiliary equipment on either an annual or semiannual basis, depending on the total operating time. This inspection should include the following: bearing clearances, slide parallelism, gib clearance, electrical components and connectors, connection screws, air components, and the press floor mounting. In presses equipped with recirculating oil systems, the oil should be drained and replaced. Critical machine parts should be inspected for cracks and broken sections. A thorough inspection at this level can give management a basis for budgeting realistic machine replacement costs and scheduling major repairs and overhauls.

It should be noted that the power press and components which are discussed in each of the previously mentioned levels of inspection are only a few of those which must be inspected. The examples are only illustrative of the parts to be inspected and are not to be construed as a comprehensive listing. A complete inspection can only be obtained by consulting the maintenance publications for the specific press and auxiliary equipment.

*Preventive maintenance.* Some of the inspection steps that have been discussed include preventive maintenance measures. There are items, however, which can be covered by pure preventive maintenance procedures. Regularly applied preventive maintenance minimizes shutdowns and eliminates the cause of many operating hazards. Procedures and precautions for diesetting are discussed in Chapter 6, "Die Design for Sheet Metal Forming." The following is a brief list of some of the basic items to be considered in a preventive maintenance program:

1. The press and its associated equipment must be lubricated regularly. This is best accomplished by a trained and well-equipped maintenance crew. Oil and/or grease levels should be inspected and refilled as necessary.
2. The brake, and compensating springs if utilized on the press, may require adjustment at frequent intervals.
3. The counterbalance should be adjusted to accommodate different die weights.
4. The cutting dies should be kept well sharpened, and forming dies should be kept dressed. This reduces the loading on the press and keeps bearing wear to a minimum.
5. All press jams and tooling wrecks should be reported to the responsible maintenance or plant engineering departments. Serious press damage, with the possibility of resultant injuries, can be prevented if damaged components are detected and replaced immediately.
6. Recurring troubles, even those of a minor nature, should be reported to the responsible department. Minor changes in design, heat treating, or surface hardening of a machine component part can often significantly increase the life of that part.

*Preventing accidents during maintenance.* Electrical power supplies should be disconnected and locked in the Off position during maintenance and repair operations. Air and hydraulic supplies should be shut off, and pressures discharged by bleeding to prevent unexpected operations or movements. Spring pressures should also be relieved.

An inspection should be made to ensure that the flywheel has completely stopped. The press slide should be at the bottom dead center of its stroke, especially if the clutch and the brake units are to be disassembled or removed. It is also advisable to remove the die and related accessories.

The press and work and surrounding areas should be kept clean. Handling equipment such as cranes or trucks should be used for heavy components, making sure that the capacity of the equipment is not exceeded. Solid work platforms, scaffolding, or portable elevators with good footing and adequate space should also be employed, avoiding the use of ladders or climbing on the press. Other safety precautions are discussed in Chapter 20 of this volume, "Safety in Forming."

*Checking repairs.* After all repairs and maintenance procedures have been completed, the work should be inspected by the mechanic, and all tools, rigging, and handling equipment should be removed. The press should be rotated completely through a cycle, being checked for interference at that time, before it is operated under power. Power should be restored to the equipment only after all personnel concerned with the project have reported clear of the area. The mechanic should then start the press and run it for an adequate length of time to determine that all parts, especially the lubrication system and clutch controls, are functioning properly. Before the press is released for production operation, all power transmission guards, cover plates, inspection covers, and point-of-operation guards must be replaced, adjusted as necessary, and checked.

**Repair or replace.** Inspection procedures indicate when one or more of the components can be repaired. In other cases, the inspection shows that some parts have deteriorated to the point at which productive and safe operation is no longer obtainable. In such instances, the components should be replaced immediately.

Old presses that are still in fairly good condition can generally be rebuilt to provide safe and efficient service. Worn-out presses, however, are usually unsafe and inefficient, and can shorten die life and produce unsatisfactory stampings. An objective approach must be developed for evaluating the condition of a press and associated equipment. Then, careful judgment must be made to either update or replace the press. Brazing or welding of cracks in press frames can be a satisfactory repair method if properly done, but the cause of the cracking should be determined and eliminated prior to repairing.

## PRESS FEEDING AND UNLOADING

A wide variety of equipment is available to transfer blanks, stampings, or material to, from, and between presses. Such equipment includes feed units for blanks, workpieces, or strip or coil stock; coil processing lines; and unloading, conveying, and transfer units. Equipment selection depends upon many factors, including the size and shape of the material or workpiece, type of press, die design, safety considerations, production volume and accuracy requirements, cost, and scrap collection and removal.

### Blank and Stamping Feeds

Feeding of blanks or previously formed stampings to presses is accomplished in several ways. Selection of a specific method depends upon many factors including safety considerations, production requirements, and cost.

**Manual feeding.** Feeding of blanks or stampings by hand is still a common practice, but this method is generally limited to low-production requirements which do not warrant the cost of semiautomatic or automatic feeds. Manual feeding, however, requires the use of a guard or, if a guard is impossible, hand feeding tools and a point-of-operation safety device. The use of tools and a safety device eliminates the need for the operator to place hands or fingers within the point of operation and safeguards the operator who inadvertently reaches into the point of operation, as discussed previously in this chapter under the subject of mechanical press safety.

A variety of hand-held feeding tools are available for loading and unloading dies. These include special pliers, tongs, tweezers, vacuum lifters, magnetic pickups, hooks, and other tools in a variety of sizes and types. Most are made from aluminum or other light, ductile material. Some are spring loaded and provided with finger-guarding loops.

**Chute feeds.** Simple, low-cost chutes are often used for feeding small parts, with the blanks or stampings generally sliding by gravity along skid rails in the bottoms of the chutes. Side members guide the workpieces, and rollers are sometimes added to facilitate sliding of the parts. A typical gravity chute feed for loading press dies is illustrated in Fig. 5-40. Production rates to 1800 parts per hour are not uncommon with such feeds.

Slide chutes are designed for a specific die and blank or stamping and are generally attached permanently to the die, thus reducing setup time. To provide a proper slide angle, usually 20-30°, the dies are often operated in OBI presses. With the die set at an angle in the press, unloading is facilitated.

Chute feeds require barrier guard enclosures for operator protection, with just enough of an opening in the enclosures for the blanks or stampings to slide through to the dies. The guarding is made of open-type or transparent material so that the operator can view the die area. It is designed to swing open or to be easily removed for setup or die repair. Electrical interlocks of the guard to the press ensure that the guard is in place before the press cycles.

Blanks or stampings are generally placed in the inclined chutes manually, but the setup can be automated by using hoppers, prestacked magazines, or other means to supply the chutes. "Windows" are provided at the point at which the workpieces enter the chutes when proper orientation is required.

**Push feeds.** These feeds (see Fig. 5-41) are used when blanks must be oriented in specific relation to the die, or when irregularly shaped parts are fed that do not slide down a chute and orient themselves properly in the die nest. Workpieces can be manually placed in a nest in a slide, one at a time, and the slide pushed until the piece falls into the die nest. An interlock is generally provided so that the press cannot be operated until the slide has correctly located the part in the die. Slide length should be sufficient to allow placement of workpieces in the pusher slide nest outside a barrier guard enclosure. Strippers, knockouts, or air can be used to eject finished parts from the die. In some cases, holes can be provided in the bottom plates of the slides through which finished pieces fall on the return stroke of the pusher.

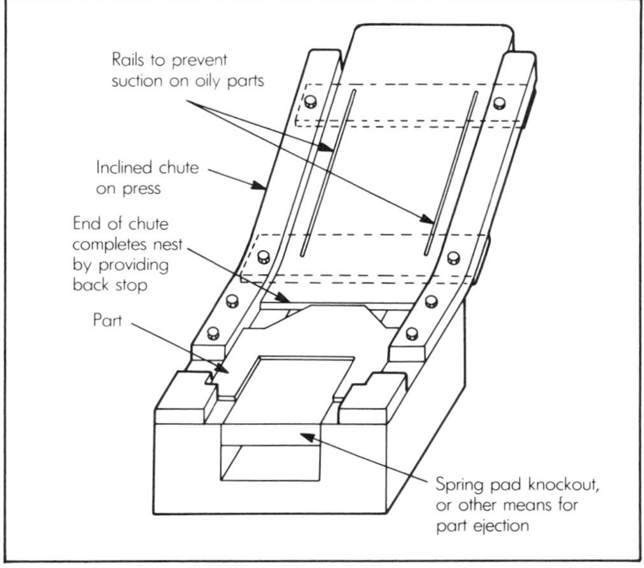


**Fig. 5-40 Gravity chute feed for loading press dies.**

# PRESS FEEDING AND UNLOADING

Another type of push feed, called a follow feed (see Fig. 5-42), is used when the shape of the blanks or stampings permits pushing similar workpieces and precise orientation by nesting is not required. Such feeds generally consist of a flat plate, on which parts are pushed one behind the other, and of side plates, which serve as guides. One or more parts may be pushed into the die area simultaneously, depending on the operation and workpieces. In some applications, completed parts can be pushed from the back of the die by incoming parts. In other cases, air or other ejection means may be required.

Both push and follow feeds can be used with magazines to increase production rates and minimize manual handling of blanks or parts. The slide pushes the bottom part from the stack in the magazine into the die.

Many such feeds are operated with manually reciprocated slides, but they can be automated by actuating the feed slide through mechanical attachment to the press slide or crankshaft.

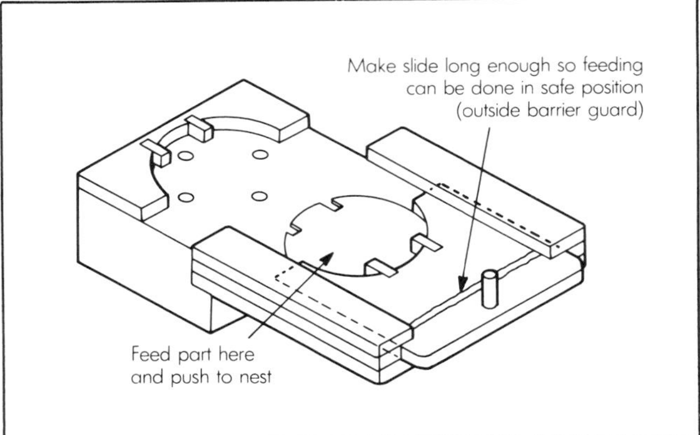


**Fig. 5-41 Push feed is used when blanks must be oriented in relation to the die.**

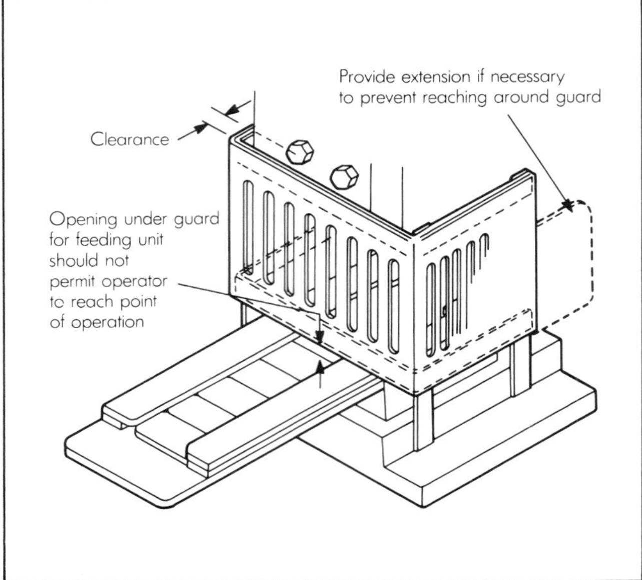


**Fig. 5-42 Follow feed is often used when shape of blanks or stampings permits pushing similar workpieces and orientation is not required.** (*Liberty Mutual*)

Slide feeds can also be operated hydraulically, pneumatically, or with electric drives, in synchronization with the press slide. In some applications parts are pushed onto a conveyor, shuttle carriage, or other mechanism for transfer to the die instead of being pushed directly into the die.

**Sliding dies.** Partially formed parts that cannot be fed to secondary operations by means of gravity chute or push or follow feeds can be fed automatically or semiautomatically by other means. One semiautomatic method uses sliding dies or bolsters, in which the lower die slides forward from under the punch and outside the danger zone during each feeding operation and then returns to operating position for the downward ram stroke. The die can be reciprocated by hand, by foot treadle, or by automatic means in synchronization with the press slide. Operator protection must also be assured by the use of safety guards or devices. Die or bolster slides are incorporated as original equipment on some presses.

**Lift-and-transfer devices.** In some automated installations, blanks are lifted one at a time from stacks by vacuum or suction cups and moved to the die by transfer units. Separation of the top blank from a stack is usually done magnetically, pneumatically, or mechanically. The top level of a stack can be controlled by a height-detection system that regulates a stack elevating cylinder. Two or more stacks can be arranged to be automatically moved into the elevating station when the previous stack has been used. Blank feeds for transfer presses are discussed later in this chapter under the subject of transfer presses.

**Dial feeds.** Another method of feeding secondary operations that is being increasingly applied because of greater safety and increased productivity is the dial feed. Such feeds consist of rotary indexing tables having nests or fixtures for holding workpieces as they are carried to the press tooling. Parts can be placed in the nests or fixtures at the loading station (away from the point of operation) manually or by the use of hoppers, chutes, magazines, vibratory feeders, robots, or other means. Dial feeds can be built into or added to presses.

Dial feeds can be actuated several ways. Ratchet drives, which are generally used for low-speed operations, have a reciprocating index slide and pawl for driving and are positioned by a cam-operated, positive-locking pawl. Friction drives use a reciprocating band to move the dial and index ring into position on the forward stroke. Then a spring-loaded stop pawl engages the index ring and holds it stationary while the band returns to its starting position. Geneva-wheel drives are also used to provide positive intermittent motion from a continuous rotary drive. Roller gear drives, which are generally smoother acting and more versatile than Geneva drives, use a worm having a dwell provided in its lead. Air or hydraulic drives, independent of the press operation, are also used for dial feeds.

One type of dial feed consists of a turntable mounted in front of the press instead of directly under the tooling. It has a mechanical transfer arm which lifts each workpiece from the turntable and positions it accurately on the die, then swings back out of the way and trips the press. Finished parts are automatically ejected from the die by air. Because this feeder is not an integral part of the press, it can be mounted on any press without requiring special tooling or machine modifications, as required with most dial feeds. Also, it can be removed and installed easily, permitting use of the press without the feeder if required.

Motion of the turntable, transfer arm, and pickup hand is controlled by a separate electric motor and variable-speed drive. Mechanical, vacuum, or magnetic pickup methods can be provided on the end of the transfer arm to handle parts of various size and configuration. Interchangeable nest plates can be mounted on the turntable to handle different parts.

**Robots.** Industrial robots are being used extensively for press loading (see Fig. 5-43) and other industrial applications. These mechanical arms, manipulators, or universal transfer and positioning units are descendants of the iron hands or swinging arms (discussed next in this section) long used for press loading and unloading. The big difference between them and true robots is that true robots can be programmed to perform different operations. Various types of tooling can be attached to the arms to handle different sizes and shapes of workpieces. Not only do such units increase safety, but they also boost production rates substantially.

Robots are particularly suitable for low-volume production requirements and for operations in which large differences exist in size and geometry of the workpieces to be handled. Two basic types available are servo and nonservo robots. Servo robots have good accuracy and programmability, but are more costly. Nonservo robots, with fixed stops, have good positional accuracy and are less costly, but programming is limited and slower.

## Press Feeds for Coil Stock

A broad selection of press feeds is available because of the wide variety of applications and the extensive range of material widths and thicknesses now sold in coil form. A careful analysis is required to match the feed to the press and dies to be used for maximum productivity with minimum costs. Major requirements for any feed unit include ample capacity, fast operation, proper synchronization with the press operation, accurate feed lengths, minimum material waste, reliability, and safety.

Two major classifications of automatic press feeds for coil stock are slide (or gripper) and roll feeds. Both of these can be further subdivided into press or independently driven types.

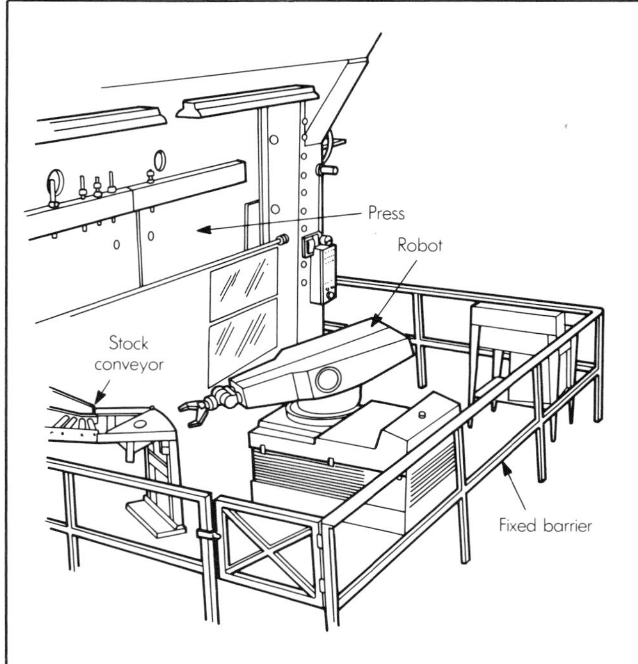


**Fig. 5-43 Industrial robot used for press loading.**

**Mechanical slide feeds.** Press-driven slide feeds (see Fig. 5-44) have a gripper arrangement which clamps and feeds the stock during its forward movement and releases it on the return stroke. Material is prevented from backing up during the return stroke of the gripper by a drag unit (frictional brake) or roller checks (rolls with a one-way clutch that allows stock to move in one direction only).

Grippers reciprocate on rods or slides between adjustable positive stops to ensure accuracy. Some feeds have sufficient power to pull stock through a nonpowered straightener when required, thus reducing the cost of the installation. Marring of material supplied by slide feeds can be minimized by using special gripping fingers or inserts or by gripping the stock on its scrap portions.

Gripper devices on most mechanical slide feeds are shoes, blocks, or cylinders. Some use a feed block with a holder having an adjustable blade, usually carbide tipped. Others have a pair of eccentric gripping cylinders. Stock supports are often necessary for feeding thin stock to prevent buckling. Many slide feeds are mounted on the press bolsters, and some smaller units are mounted permanently on the dies, thus reducing setup times.

Press-driven slide feeds are powered by the press crankshaft, usually through an adjustable connecting rod. An adjustable, eccentric-type driving plate on the crankshaft permits changing the length of stock fed.

Mechanical slide feeds are available in a variety of designs, sizes, and capacities. They are generally best for narrow coil stock and short feed lengths. Excessive inertia can be a problem with wide and thick material, long feed lengths, and fast press speeds. Arrangements other than conventional left-to-right feeding may also be difficult, depending upon the location of the press crankshaft extension and the arrangement of the die. Special linkage may be required.

**Hitch-type feed.** These units, sometimes called Dickerman feed units because of the originator, differ from press-driven, mechanical slide feeds in that actuation is by a simple, flat cam

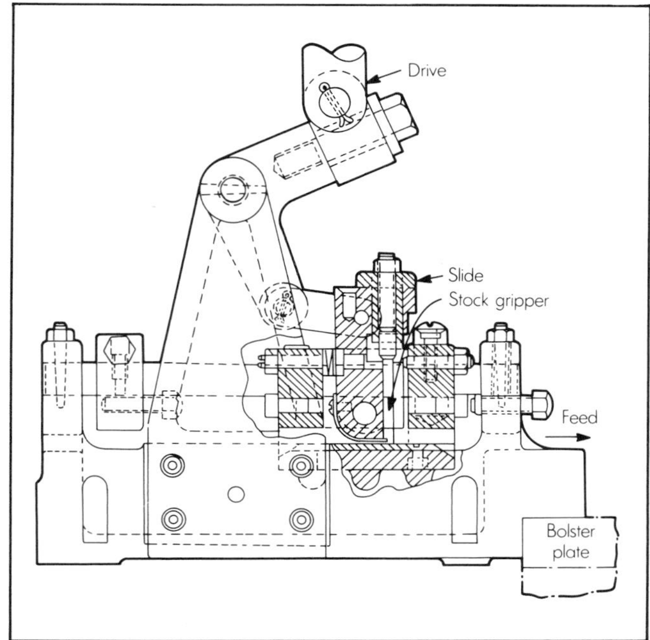


**Fig. 5-44 Press-driven slide feed.** (*U.S. Baird Co.*)

## PRESS FEEDING AND UNLOADING

attached to the ram or punch holder (see Fig. 5-45), instead of by the press crankshaft. On the downstroke of the press, one or more springs are compressed by the cam action; then on the upstroke, the springs provide the force to feed stock into the die. Different models are made with gripper plates, blades, or cylinders to move the stock. On the cylinder grip types, overriding clutches permit the cylinders to rotate in only one direction for stock feeding. This type permits feeding polished material without marring.

Hitch feeds are one of the oldest and least expensive feeding devices still in wide use. Because of their low cost, they are often left permanently attached to the dies, thus reducing setup time. They can be mounted to feed stock in any direction and can be used on air or hydraulic presses, as well as on mechanical presses without accessible crankshaft extensions. Feed length changes are accomplished by changing the low-cost, flat cams.

These feeds are best suited for coil stock up to medium thickness and for relatively short feed progressions. Long feed lengths are generally not feasible because of practical limits with respect to cam size and press stroke, but some feeds have a rack slide provided in the feed body to permit longer feed increments. Also, some units have open-side gripping cylinders that grip just the material edge, thus permitting wide coil stock to be fed.

**Air slide feeds.** These feeds are providing a rapidly growing method of feeding coil stock, particularly for short-run job shops, because of their low initial cost and versatility. Like mechanical slide feeds, most have grippers or clamps that reciprocate on guide rails or slides between adjustable positive stops to push and/or pull stock into a die.

They differ in that they are powered by an air cylinder instead of the press crankshaft or cams and springs, with actuation and timing of valves by cam-operated limit switches or by an adjustable rod or screw on the press ram or punch.

Coil stock is controlled throughout the cycle by two clamps—one gripping the material during feeding and the other holding it while the feed head returns for the next cycle. The clamps can be air actuated or mechanical. If mechanical holding clamps, such as one-way clutches or cam checks, are used, the material is free to be moved forward by pilots in the die during the backstroke of the feed. With an air-operated holding clamp, a stock release device must be employed with dies having pilots.

Some compact air feeds can be mounted on the dies, or on the press bolsters close to the dies, thereby reducing or eliminating buckling problems with thin stock. Coil stock can be fed in any direction or at any angle to the die. Since there is no mechanical linkage to the press crankshaft, feeding cycles can be varied to start whenever desired. They can be used on air or hydraulic presses, as well as on mechanical presses without accessible crankshafts. Material can be pushed or pulled, any remaining skeleton stock can be pulled, and two or more coils can be fed simultaneously by the same feeder. Setup and feed length adjustment is simple and rapid, generally by means of stop block adjusting screws or a hand crank. Some units can be quickly moved from press to press or can be left permanently mounted on dies.

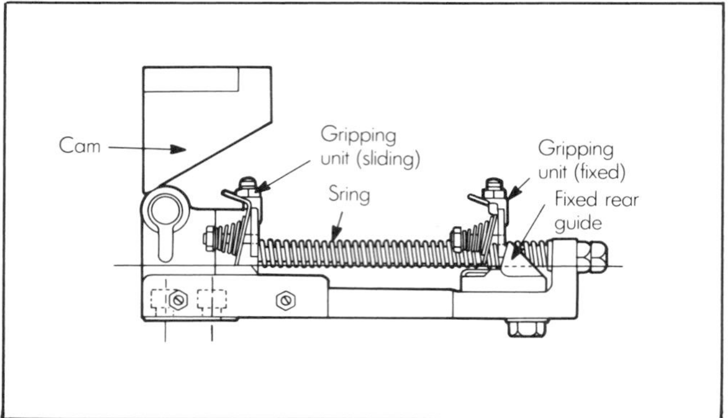


**Fig. 5-45 Hitch feed is actuated by a cam attached to press ram or punch holder.** (*Dickerman Div., Reed National Corp.*)

While the maximum single-stroke feed length on most standard units is 36" (914 mm), units with a length capability of 60" (1524 mm) have been produced. Longer lengths can be fed at reduced production rates by using a sequence counting or repeater device which recycles the feed the required number of times before cycling the press. Depending on press speed and desired feed length, the press can control the feed cycle, or the feed unit can signal the press that the feed cycle is completed.

Some users have modified their air feeds to be used for different length progressions, either alternately or in a fixed sequence, by the properly timed, automatic insertion of a block between the stop and the feed head. Air slide feeds are also good for thin and compressible materials, but antibuckling supports may sometimes be required. Flexible inserts can be mounted in the clamps to minimize marring the materials.

Coil stock widths are also limited to a maximum of 36" (914 mm) on air slide units. Wider and thicker stock can be fed, however, with double air units which grip the material along each edge.

Possible disadvantages of air slide feeds include speed limitations; cost of providing a reliable supply of clean and dry, but slightly oiled, air; and for some applications, inadequate pulling power. Some air feeds are capable of speeds to 300 spm and 400 ipm (10 160 mm/min) with short progressions, but roll feeds (discussed later in this section) are generally required for high-speed operation. Air consumption and maintenance costs have been reduced substantially by improvements in the design of modern air slide feeds.

**Hydraulic slide feeds.** These feeds are usually made to special order only. They cost more than air feeds, but can handle thicker stock. They operate similarly to air slide feeds, with gripper heads reciprocating between positive stops, but they are powered by a hydraulic cylinder instead of air. Gripping pressure can be adjusted to suit the material being fed. Valve actuation can be from the press crankshaft or ram.

**Motor-driven slide feeds.** Slide feeds with independent motor drives are sometimes employed when the feed units are to be used on different presses. Feed lengths are adjustable, timing can be varied for different portions of the press cycle, and independent units can be mounted to feed in any direction. Eccentric feed-block motion and feed-blade gripping are generally used on small models, and air grippers are provided on some large models.

**Roll feeds.** These feeds advance coil stock by pressure exerted between intermittently driven, opposed rolls which allow the stock to dwell during the working part of the press stroke. They are available in several types and in a wide variety of sizes suitable for almost any width and thickness of stock. While their design and construction often entail a higher cost than slide feeds, they are often more economical to operate, depending on the application.

Increased durability, minimum maintenance and material marking, and long life are important advantages accounting for the extensive use of roll feeds. They can feed narrow or wide, thin or thick material in short or long lengths, with high speeds for short increments.

Intermittent rotation or indexing of the feed rolls, with the rolls rotating in only one direction, is accomplished in several ways. On conventional press-driven types, the rolls are indexed through a one-way clutch by a rack-and-pinion or bellcrank mechanism that is actuated by an adjustable eccentric on the press crankshaft extension. Cam-indexed roll feeds are also powered from the press crankshaft, usually by a timing belt drive. These feeds generally provide the highest accuracy attainable for short feed lengths. Independent roll feeds have self-contained electric motor, air, or hydraulic power drives. An increasingly popular type is servo electric, digitally controlled.

A difference of opinion exists among some feed manufacturers as to whether one or both rolls should be driven. On some feeds, only one feed roll is driven and the other is free wheeling. It is claimed that improved accuracy and performance can sometimes be attained with an idling grip roll when thinner stock is being fed. More commonly, however, the upper and lower rolls are geared together to provide a dual drive. Both designs are often satisfactory, but dual drive is generally preferred when progressive tooling is used and piloting is necessary or when thicker material is employed and heavier loops are required. The dual drive is said to minimize the possibility that one roll will coast when the feed cycle is complete or that the stock will move when the rolls are closing for the next cycle. Also, when higher speeds or velocities are used, some feed manufacturers claim there is less chance of the roll's skidding against the stock at the start of the feed cycle with dual drive.

*Single-roll feeds.* These feeds generally consist of one pair of opposed pinch rolls (see Fig. 5-46), but four rolls (two pairs in tandem on the entry side of the die area) are sometimes used for heavier stock. This type of feed is used when no scrap skeleton is left by the die, when the stock is rigid enough to be pushed into or pulled from the die, or when parts are left in the coil stock and rewound in preparation for subsequent operations.

*Double-roll feeds.* Two sets of pinch rolls are used by double-roll feeds, one on either side of the die area. They are powered by the press crankshaft and synchronized by a cross driveshaft to push and pull the stock. These feeds are used when a scrap skeleton is produced by compound or progressive dies.

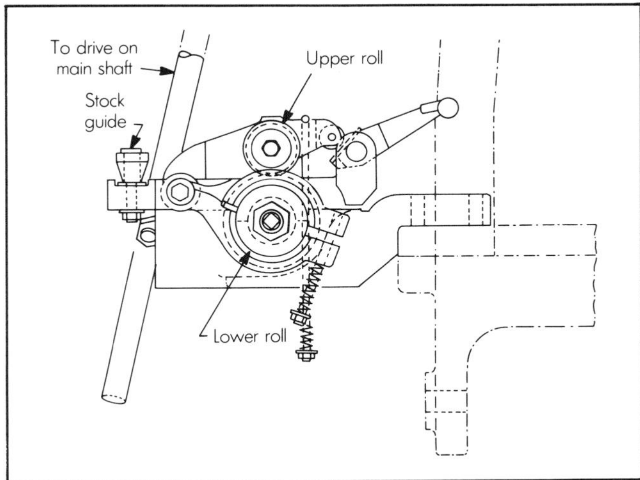


**Fig. 5-46 Single-roll feed.** (*E. W. Bliss Div., Gulf & Western Manufacturing Co.*)

They are also used for thin stock which might otherwise sag or buckle and for deep draw applications. In addition to assisting in removing the skeleton from the die, the outgoing rolls are frequently used to direct the skeleton to an optional press-driven scrap cutter.

*Feed rolls.* The rolls exert squeezing pressure on the stock by various means, including springs, cams, screwdown devices, and air or hydraulic cylinders. Means are provided to raise and lower the upper rolls when a new coil is being threaded into the press. Automatic roll lifters are incorporated for use with piloted dies. This is generally accomplished with press-actuated cams, eccentrics, or an air or hydraulic cylinder and linkage that is electrically timed through a rotary cam switch. Antibackup rolls can be supplied to prevent stock from slipping backward when the feed rolls are automatically lifted.

Rolls used on these feeds—normally hardened and ground steel—are mounted in antifriction bearings. Typically, rolls are hollow and/or of lightweight construction to reduce inertia and to respond quickly to braking.

While a smooth ground finish on the rolls is satisfactory for most applications, a variety of other finishes and coatings are available. Hob-knurled or grooved rolls, which increase the pulling power, are recommended for thicker materials with rough, scaly surfaces. At the opposite extreme, hard, chromium-plated rolls are widely used for feeding aluminum, silicon and stainless steels, and other materials with smooth surfaces which must be protected from marking or scoring. Rubber, neoprene, and polyurethane-coated rolls are also available for feeding material such as printed, painted, plastic, composite, vinyl, or anodized stock without marring.

*Press-driven roll feeds.* These feeds are powered by either a rack-and-pinion or a bellcrank mechanism from the press crankshaft. The rack-and-pinion feed is more common for heavy stamping and drawing operations, as well as for long feed lengths on larger OBI and straight-side presses. It provides a smooth, harmonic drive, free of jerking action.

Economical bellcrank drives are used extensively for high-speed operation, narrow coil stock, or short feed lengths on small OBI presses. These drives apply a uniform pull throughout the stroke. They also minimize wear when short lengths are being fed. With the bellcrank design, the clutch housing of the feed unit oscillates through a short arc by a balljoint-and-rod connection from the driving disc on the press crankshaft extension. Feed lengths can be increased by using compound gearing.

The drive for rack-and-pinion roll feeds is from an eccentric crank disc, usually adjustable, mounted on a hub attached to the press crankshaft extension (see Fig. 5-47). On adjustable types, feed length is changed by moving a slider block either manually or by means of a motor. This block is connected to the roll feed by a connecting rod having a rack on its lower end. On the upstroke of the rod, the rack rotates gearing and a driveshaft—through an overrunning or one-way clutch on the feed unit—to index the rolls and advance the stock. On the downstroke, the clutch is disengaged and the feed rolls are stationary. Brakes are provided in or on the rolls to apply drag, to reduce gear backlash, and to control roll inertia. The condition of the brake and its setting controls feed accuracy.

While the feed cycle on these units is generally limited to 180° of press crankshaft rotation, several manufacturers offer a rotary drag-link, shaper-motion drive to increase or decrease the amplitude of the feed cycle. Shorter feed cycles, sometimes in as little as 90° of crankshaft rotation, can be offered for draw

# PRESS FEEDING AND UNLOADING

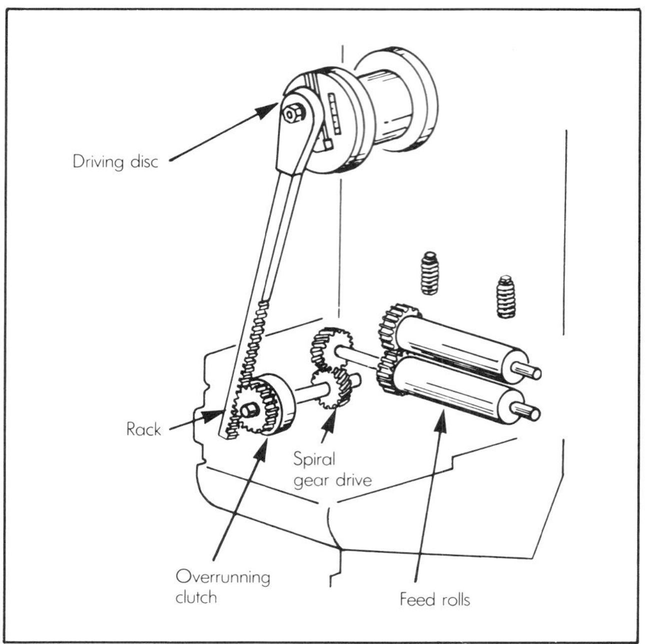


**Fig. 5-47 Rack-and-pinion roll feed has adjustable driving disc attached to press crankshaft.** (*F. J. Littell Machine Co.*)

operations, for use with special dies, or for meeting die-protection requirements. Feeding during a longer portion of the press cycle, up to 270°, allows faster press operation while keeping the material velocity within acceptable limits.

*Clutches for roll feeds.* Clutches are a critical component of roll feeds. They are essentially dividing heads and must be accurate for precise feeding without slippage. Some feeds are equipped with clutches consisting of an inner and outer race. The annular space between the races is filled with special-shaped roller cams that lock to the supporting shaft when rotated in one direction and release in the other direction. Other manufacturers offer multipawl and ratchet-style clutches on their roll feeds for closer indexing. These clutches consist of ratchet wheels having hundreds of teeth that are engaged by double or quadruple rows of pawls. This combination permits the potential engagement of any one of the pawls with many ratchet teeth for possible indexing stations in the thousands.

*Roll-feed options.* Many options are available with press-driven roll feeds, including automatic roll lifters, antibackup rolls, and power run-in. Power run-in consists of separate, motor-driven rolls for positioning material in the die without cycling the press. Another popular option includes a manually operated, microadjusting feature to permit fine tuning of the preset feed length from floor level while the press is running. Still another option is a motorized, floor-level-operated, full-feed-length adjustment, usually furnished with visual length indicators or readouts. These feeds can be permanently mounted on extensions to the press bolster or on separate frame-mounted brackets with adjustment to vary the feed-line height. With appropriate linkage, the feeds can be arranged to feed in any direction.

Obtaining maximum feed length for conventional press-driven roll feeds is primarily a function of the roll diameters and gearing. For practical reasons, feed length is generally limited to a 20-36" (508-914 mm) range, with a maximum limit of about 48" (1219 mm). Feed lengths of this order can be accomplished with step-up gearing and/or upper and lower feed rolls of different diameters. With shorter feed lengths, speeds up to 550 spm or material velocities of 1200 ipm (30 480 mm/min) are possible on some rack-and-pinion or bellcrank-type units.

Roll feeds made by one manufacturer differ from conventional press-driven roll feeds in that they do not use a clutch, nor do they require brakes on the rolls. A special roll-lifting arrangement allows the rolls to be parted from the stock at the instant the material has been delivered, while the rolls are backing up. The reversing action of the roll, combined with stock drags, checks stock inertia. Without the additional clutch linkage and roll brakes, some models are capable of operating at precise accuracies with speeds to 1200 spm or material velocities of 2400 ipm (60 960 mm/min).

*Cam roll feeds.* Single or double-type cam roll feeds are capable of the highest accuracies and speeds attainable with any press feeding device for coil stock. However, they cost more than conventional press-driven roll feeds. While these feeds are also driven from the press crankshaft, the reciprocating feed motion is produced by a rotary indexing cam. Other major advantages of cam roll feeds are:

1. Setup, adjustments, and operation do not require skilled operators.
2. No brakes or clutches are needed.
3. Maintenance is minimal.

It is generally preferable to mount these feeds on new or rebuilt presses with tight fits to take full advantage of their potential for high-speed operation and for maintaining close tolerances.

Two major classifications of cam roll feeds exist: the fixed-index type and the change-gear type. With the fixed-index type, the feed range cannot be changed. Adjusting the feed length within the established range requires replacing one or both feed rolls with rolls of a different diameter. As a result, they are generally restricted to high-speed, long-run applications such as laminations and can tops.

The newer change-gear type allows faster changing and a wider range of feed lengths, while retaining the speeds and accuracies of cam roll feeds. This makes them economically feasible for short-run operations, as well as for operations employing the increasingly popular high-speed presses and for job-shop applications with long runs. Both types can provide feed lengths up to a maximum of about 36" (914 mm), depending on the feed-roll diameter and number of cam stops. It has been estimated that about 90% of the existing press-working applications are for lengths 12" (305 mm) or less.

A more recent development is adjustable cam feeds using reciprocating feed rolls that are adjustable by linkage to give the desired feed length. Adjustments may be manual or motorized. A readout is provided to show the feed-length setting.

Feeding cycles, as well as acceleration and deceleration characteristics, are controlled by the cam. The cams can be computer designed for specific applications in which it is necessary to minimize shock loading, backlash, material inertia, vibration, and wear. No trial-and-error adjustments are necessary with properly designed cams. Feeding can start sooner in the press cycle, as little as 90° on short-stroke presses; or it can finish later, as much as 220° or more, depending on requirements. Increasing the length of the feed cycle, where stroke length permits, lowers the strain on the feed unit and permits faster operation.

On cam roll feeds produced by most manufacturers, driving is accomplished via the press crankshaft by a timing belt with its teeth meshing with pulley grooves (see Fig. 5-48). These feed units contain parallel, flat cams and follower plates with from one to eight stops for indexing the feed rolls. Feed length is equal to the feed-roll circumference divided by the number of stops on the follower plates.

*Independent roll feeds.* Independently driven roll feeds provide the only practical method of feeding wide coils of material in long lengths. Essentially no limit exists with respect to lengths that can be fed with independent roll feeds, and these feeds are extremely versatile; progressions can be changed simply and rapidly, generally while the press is operating. Operation is feasible from any side of the press. Speed capabilities often exceed those of the large, slow presses with which they are generally used.

These feeds are available in various types having different self-contained drives to power the feed rolls either directly or through gearing. Automatic operation with the press is usually accomplished electrically with rotary-type limit switches. Versatile rack-and-pinion types are generally less expensive and good for short runs and varied operations, but they are slower.

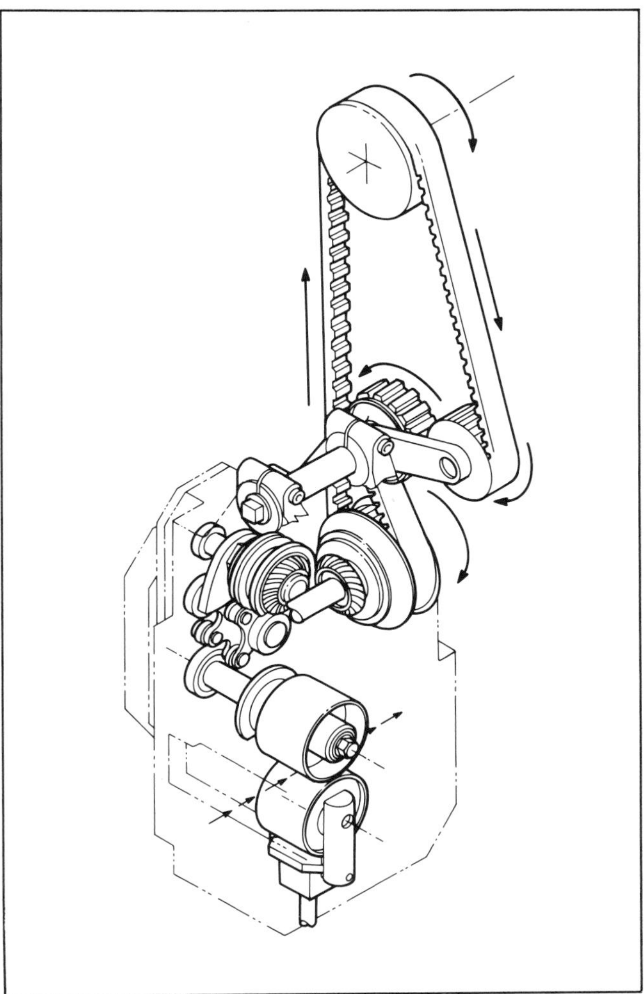

**Fig. 5-48 Timing belt is used for high-speed operation of fixed-index, cam roll feed.** (*F. J. Littell Machine Co.*)

Electronic, digitally controlled, independent roll feeds, while sophisticated and expensive, are becoming increasingly popular, especially with large stamping firms. This is because of their fast, simple feed-length and speed adjustments and their capability of feeding practically any length and width of coil stock at high speeds. Also, they provide smooth, controlled acceleration and deceleration and their high-speed capabilities often permit continuous operation of coil-fed stamping lines, even with long feed lengths.

Digitally controlled, closed-loop, servo drive systems made by one firm use a digital crystal clock as a command unit, and a pulse generator for feedback. The pulse generator, coupled to the d-c motor that drives the feed rolls (or a measuring wheel in contact with the material), supplies signals indicating position and velocity of the feed rolls. Digital command signals, preset with length and speed dials or thumbwheel switches on the control console, are compared by a digital controller with the feedback signals from the pulse generator. A d-c voltage proportional to the error is generated and used to control the motor speed and direction to achieve the desired position by reducing the error signal to zero.

More sophisticated controls with microprocessors and solid-state, plug-in modules are also available to suit various requirements. A card or tape reader can be added for further automation. Some controls are being used to control double-roll feeds, with separate motors on each side, having no connecting driveshaft between the ingoing and outgoing rolls. This permits controlling the outgoing feed rolls without affecting the ingoing rolls, thus permitting compensation for any stretching or shrinking of the material. Others are being used to control all functions of completely integrated production lines, including uncoilers, levelers, loops, feeders, and stackers.

*Joggle feeding.* Joggle, zig-zag, oscillating, or shuttle feeding is being used increasingly on servo-electric and other independent feeds, because it often permits better material utilization—more blanks per coil—using more economical, wider coils and simpler single-station dies. Press-mounted, mechanically driven zig-zag feeds are also used. They are driven from the press crankshaft extensions and usually operate at higher speeds than the independent feeds. Units used for this method simultaneously advance the material and shuttle it from side to side so that two or more staggered or nested blanks are produced, one per press stroke, across the coil width. Using a wider coil to produce interspersed blanks results in a reduction in scrap compared to use of a narrower coil that would produce a single blank with higher unit material cost. A schematic drawing of a zig-zag feed is shown in Fig. 5-49. The feed unit shuttles horizontally on stationary guide rods and slide bearings.

Feeding coil stock to transfer presses, rather than blanks, has usually been recommended only when the blanks produced in the presses are square or rectangular and scrap loss is minimal. Now, however, joggle feeding sometimes makes coil stock economically attractive for round or irregular-shaped blanks. In some applications, scrap has been reduced more than 30%, with material savings as high as 12%.

## Coil Lines

Coil stock is being increasingly used to supply material to presses. A major advantage is reduced cost compared to strip stock cut from coils and processed by the mill or a service center. Safety is improved, and inventory costs and floor-space requirements are generally less with coil stock. Another important advantage of using coil stock is more efficient production because of faster setup, less press downtime, and increased speed with continuous operations.

Use of coil stock, however, requires investment in a coil processing line (see Fig. 5-50), which can vary in complexity and cost depending upon the application. The basic functions of most lines include uncoiling, straightening or leveling, measuring, and feeding. Coil lines for shearing or slitting are discussed in Chapter 11, "Shearing." This section is confined to a description of coil lines for pressworking. Coil lines for processes such as pickling, annealing, galvanizing, and coating, generally used by mills, service centers, or specialty shops, are not discussed in this volume.

**Uncoiling.** Handling equipment for loading coils onto reel spindles or into cradles at the beginning of a line can include turnstiles, rotators, fork trucks, coil cars, ramps, chain hoists, or overhead cranes. Coils range in weight from about 100-100,000 lb (45-45 360 kg), with widths of 1/4 to 96" (6 to 2438 mm) and outside diameters to 84" (2134 mm).

*Reels.* These units, which hold the coils on their inside diameters, are used extensively for uncoiling (payoff). They are generally best for applications requiring protection of the stock surface from damage, or for thinner materials. Plates or arms are provided to contain stock in the payoff reels, and systems for automatic self-centering of the stock are available.

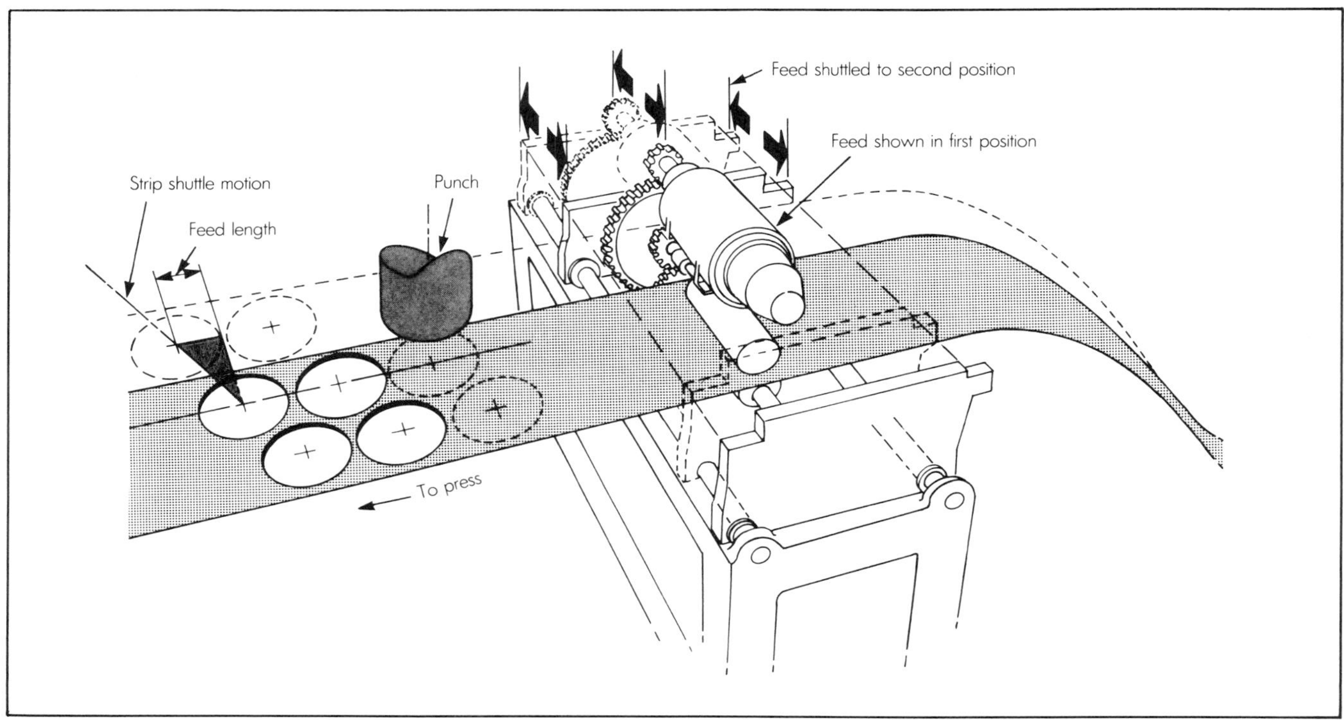


**Fig. 5-49 Zig-zag feed simultaneously advances and shuttles material to get more blanks per coil.** (*F. J. Littell Machine Co.*)

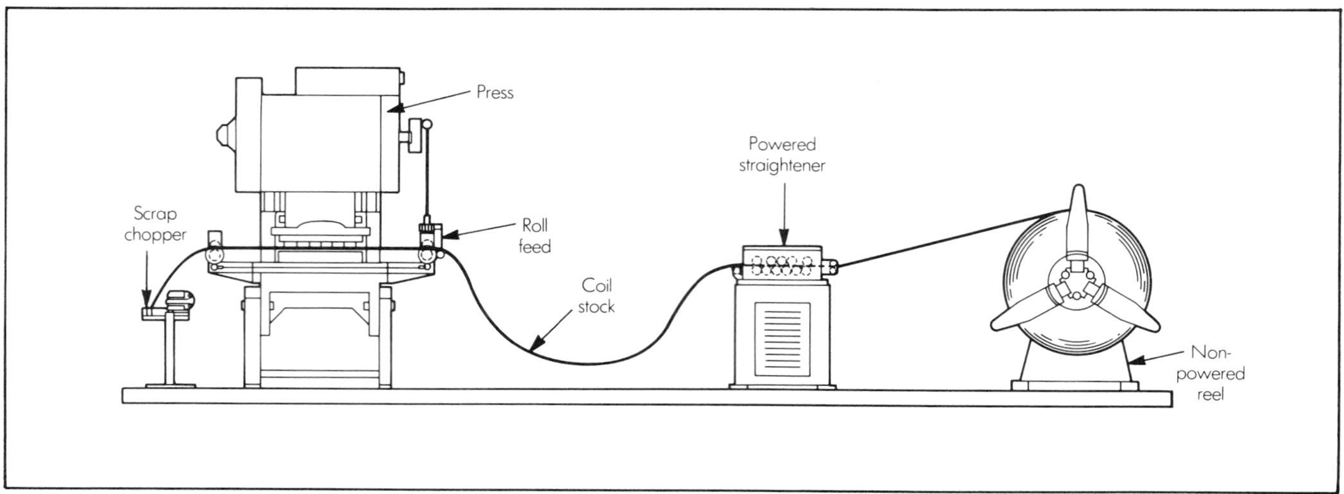


**Fig. 5-50 Coil line containing nonpowered reel, straightener, feed, press, and scrap chopper.** (*Cooper-Weymouth, Peterson*)

Powered and nonpowered reels are available. Spindle or mandrel-type reels for heavier coils are generally equipped with powered, automatic expansion devices. Double-cone or double-expanding-mandrel reels, which provide support at both sides, are often used for heavy, wide coils. Double-end reel swivel units having two reels on the same base are sometimes employed for high-production requirements, one reel being set up while the other is being used.

Double-expanding and double-cone reels provide support of the coils at both sides and are often used for heavy, wide coils. Double-cone reels have a tendency to deform the inner wraps of a coil more than expanding mandrels. Desired back tension and effective stopping of coils on double-cone reels may cause problems due to the smaller area of surface contact on the inside diameters of the coils compared to expanding mandrels.

Powered clamping or hold-down rolls that ride on the outside diameter of the coil are common on reels for highly tempered, thick, or springy material or for wide stock. Stock-surge or payout-control systems are often provided with powered-reel uncoiling equipment. Such systems form a slack loop or hump of controlled-length stock that must be stopped momentarily and periodically for the blanking operation.

Pinch rolls and peelers may be required to pull stock from a reel uncoiler or to advance the stock into a leveler. Other options include variable-speed and reversing drives, automatic threading units, and brakes and clutches. Uncoiling reels are sometimes combined on the same base with a straightener to reduce floor space requirements. When rewinding of the coil is necessary, the power required may exceed the power needed for unwinding.

*Cradles.* These units, also used for uncoiling, support the coils on their outside diameters with rolls. Cradles are best suited for coils of thicker stock and applications in which protection of the stock surface is not critical. Advantages of cradles include formation of the slack loop in the natural direction of coil curvature, the ability to form a slack loop in a 180° arc (thereby conserving space), and simpler control as the coil depletes.

Powered and nonpowered cradles are available, but powered types are predominant. Adjustable vertical plates, some with edge rolls, keep the stock centered. The powered cradles can be provided with stock-surge systems to form slack loops, with the loop lengths controlled by sensors.

Air or hydraulic-cushioned support rolls are available for cradles to handle heavy coils. For painted, coated, or smoothly finished stock, the rolls can be covered with polyurethane or other material. Options for uncoiling cradles include pinch rolls, peelers, motorized hold-downs, automatic threading units, and support rolls of various diameter and arrangements. As with reels, cradles are sometimes combined with straighteners to conserve space.

**Straightening/leveling.** Uncoiled stock is flattened, removing the set created in coiling, by flexing the material between adjustable rollers positioned above and below the pass line. Levelers resemble flatteners (straighteners), but they have more rolls, which are smaller in diameter, mounted closer together, and supported by adjustable backup rolls.

**Length controls.** Controls for the lengths of coil stock to be blanked or formed are generally incorporated in the coil feed units on the presses, discussed next in this chapter. Various control methods are used by different equipment manufacturers. Some employ digital measurement systems, with required lengths preset by thumbwheels or pushbuttons. Positive-stop systems and computer-controlled units for continuous monitoring are also available. Accuracy of the control varies primarily with the material, line speed, and length and generally ranges from ±0.005 to 1/8" (0.13 to 3.2 mm).

**Scrap cutters.** Scrap cutters or choppers (see Fig. 5-51) are used in conjunction with a double-roll feed and are employed to cut the scrap skeleton that is produced in some stamping operations. Most scrap cutters are press actuated, powered from an eccentric mounted on the end of the press crank. They are in effect a shear, using upper and lower blades to cut the material. The bracket on which the scrap cutter and roll feed are mounted is generally adjustable vertically to accommodate different die heights. The connection of the scrap cutter to the press crank is also made adjustable. Some scrap cutters are actuated from the press ram, and others are free-standing, with independent power. Scrap cutters usually have an adjustment feature that permits them to be positioned in the direction of stock flow so that shearing occurs at the thinnest cross section of the scrap web, which is important when handling thick material.

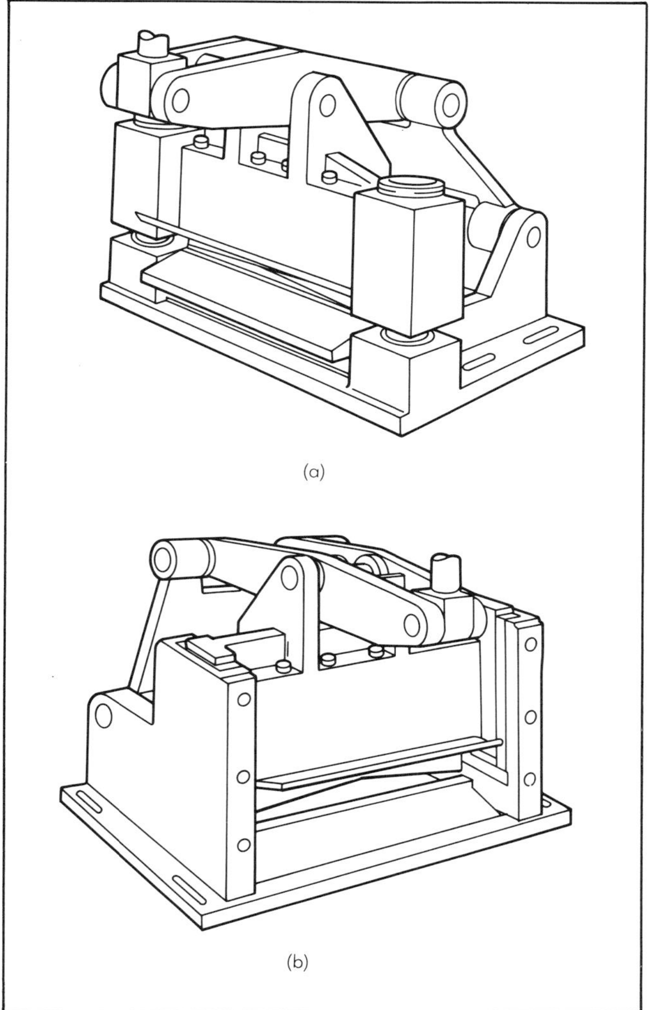


**Fig. 5-51 Scrap cutters: (a) post-type with blade-carrying upper guided on posts and (b) gib-type, for heavier capacity, with slide and blade guided in square gibbing within the frame.** (*Sesco, Inc.*)

# PRESS FEEDING AND UNLOADING

**Stackers.** Stacking units are generally used at the ends of blanking lines. Some are arranged for gravity drop of the blanks into piles, and others have powered lowering tables for the stacks. A means can be provided to separate acceptable and reject blanks.

## Press Unloading

Methods employed to unload stampings from presses vary depending upon workpiece size, weight, and geometry; production requirements; material from which the stamping is made; press and die design; surface-quality requirements; and safety considerations.

**Gravity and air ejection.** Gravity is the simplest and least expensive method of unloading presses, but it is not applicable for many operations. In some cases, dies can be designed so that the stampings fall through a hole in the press bed. The use of OBI presses facilitates unloading by means of gravity when there are no holes in the beds; stampings fall out the open backs of the presses. When press inclination is not practical, chutes are sometimes provided to carry the stampings away. Air ejection is still common for lightweight parts, but this method is expensive and noisy.

**Kickers, lifters, and shuttle extractors.** Kickers consist of pivoted levers, generally air actuated, that are mounted in the dies and throw stampings out of the dies when the dies open. Lifters are similar, but simply move vertically and require other means for stamping ejection. Pan shuttle-type extractors (see Fig. 5-52) swing to and from the die area, catching stampings as they are stripped from the punches or upper dies and dropping them outside the presses. Actuation of the pans can be from either the press rams or the independent drives.

**Mechanical hands.** Mechanical hands, often called iron hands, are air or electrically actuated mechanisms commonly used to remove stampings from presses. Gripping fingers or jaws are mounted on arms which swing (see Fig. 5-53) or reciprocate into the die area to lift the stampings and place them on a mechanism for transfer to the next press or operation. Standard units are available as swing-arm or straight-path types.

Interchangeable jaws or fingers are designed to grip the flanges of stampings. Vacuum cups or electromagnetic elements are used in place of jaws or fingers for curved surfaces and fragile or easily damaged workpieces. Figure 5-54, view *a*, illustrates a reciprocating unloader equipped with a vacuum cup to pick up stampings. A jaw for gripping a vertical flange is shown in view *b*; a jaw for an easily accessible, horizontal flange is shown in view *c*; and a jaw for restricted areas, in view *d*.

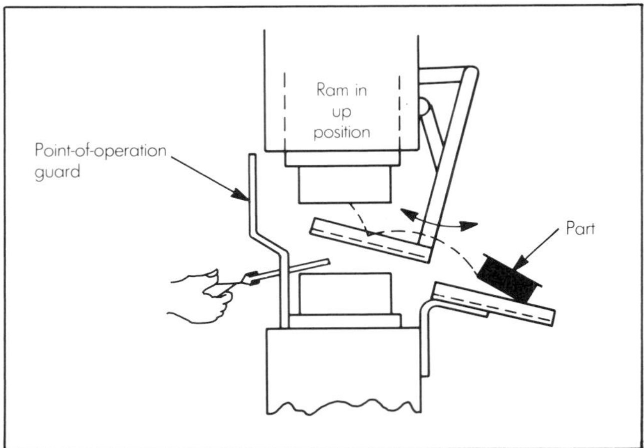


**Fig. 5-52 Pan, shuttle-type extractor swings to and from the die area.**

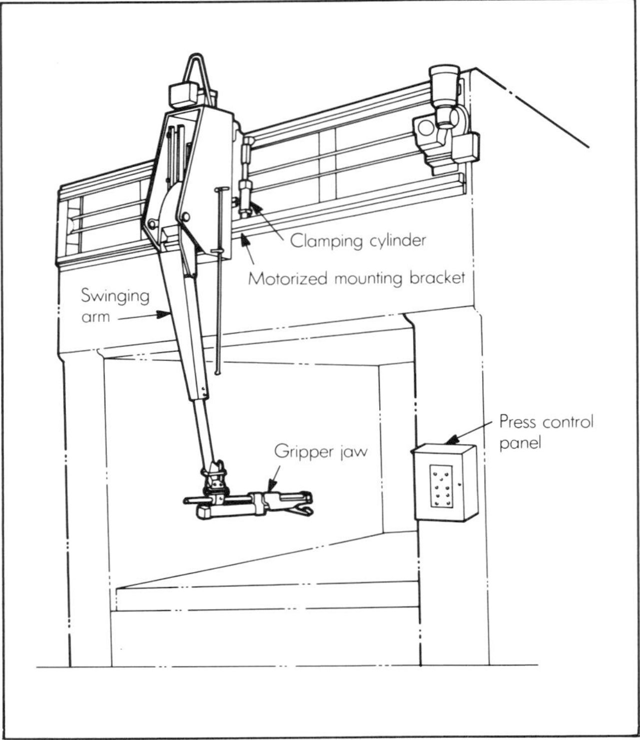


**Fig. 5-53 Gripping jaw is mounted on swinging arm of mechanical hand.**

**Robots.** Industrial robots, discussed previously in this section, are also used for press unloading. An important advantage of robots is their programmability to suit various workpieces and requirements.

**Strip recoiling.** Some workpieces, such as small terminals, produced from coil stock, are left in the strip which is recoiled for subsequent separation of the parts at assembly.

## Work Transfer Between Presses

Several methods are used to automatically transfer stampings from press to press for high-production requirements. When applicable, the use of chutes, on which the stampings slide, provide the lowest cost method. Power-driven, slat or belt conveyors are commonly employed. Adjustable-speed drives for the conveyors are often desirable to suit various cycle times.

**Shuttle-type transfer devices.** These units are used extensively. With some units, the stampings are pushed by reciprocating fingers that extend and retract as required; others use the lift-and-carry (walking-beam) method. Shuttle units are driven by hydraulic, pneumatic, or electric power, or they are driven mechanically from the press. Adjustable side rails are often provided to accommodate workpieces having different widths.

**Lift-and-carry devices.** One lift-and-carry device, which employs a parallelogram motion, is illustrated in Fig. 5-55. Two rails move into slots milled in a die, rise vertically to lift a stamping from the die, retract and lower to deposit the stamping on a set of idle rails, and return to pick up the next stamping. Each time the presses cycle, the stampings are

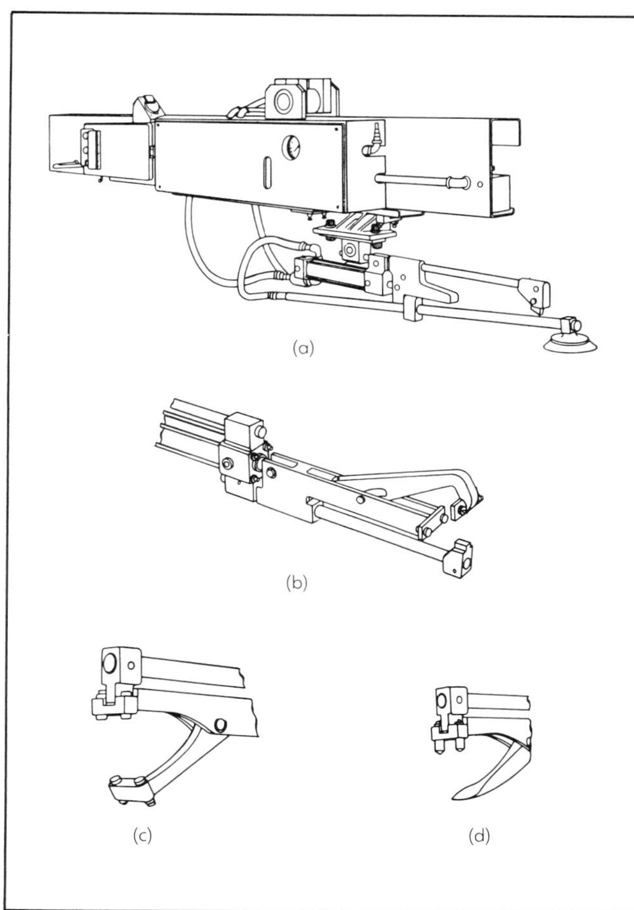

Fig. 5-54 Air-operated press unloading devices. (*Press Automation Systems, Inc.*)

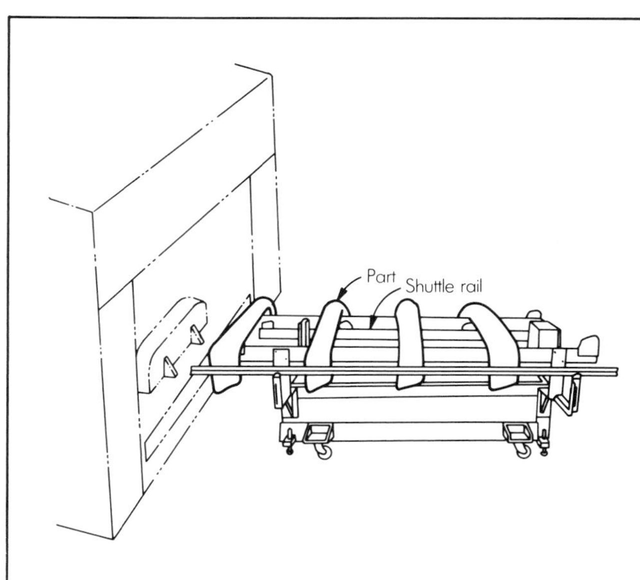

Fig. 5-55 Lift-and-carry transfer device for stampings. (*Press Automation Systems, Inc.*)

progressively moved from one press to the next. This type of transfer unit maintains full control of the stampings from unloading them from one die through loading them into the next die.

**Turnover and/or turnaround devices.** These devices are sometimes added to transfer systems to change the positions of the stampings as they pass from one press to another. Turnaround devices generally consist of turntables that lift the stampings, rotate them the required amount, and lower them onto the transfer system. Turnover devices often have one arm and use one or more vacuum cups (see Fig. 5-56). In operation, the stamping is transferred above the arm, the arm is raised, the cup or cups engage the stamping, vacuum pulls the stamping against the cups, and the arm rotates about 180°. At the end of the arm movement, the vacuum is released and the arm returns to its horizontal position. Some devices are of the ferris-wheel type.

**Robots.** Industrial robots, electrically interlocked to two or more presses, are also being used for the automatic unloading, transferring, and loading of stampings. Advantages include increased flexibility, with programmability permitting different stampings to be produced over the same press line.

**Transfer with CNC.** Transfer systems controlled by programmable CNC units are available for automating press lines. Such systems are independent of the presses, can be adapted to stampings of all sizes, and are easily reset. As shown in Fig. 5-57, the transfer slides are arranged on overhead gantry frames. Differences in the distances between presses are compensated for by shortening or lengthening the girders. The transfer slides have integral drives, transfer level is programmable in three coordinates, and transfer rates can be varied along certain sections. Grippers or suction cups are used to handle the stampings.

Modular construction of the CNC transfer units permits use with conveyor belts, buffer storage devices, and turnover or turnaround units. Manual data input (MDI) is employed to enter information directly into the control memory, or cassettes can be used to enter programs. Pushbuttons are provided to call up stored programs.

**Stackers/loaders.** Stackers or conveyor loaders are often provided at the ends of the lines to stack or remove finished stampings that are unloaded from the last press. Low-profile, under-the-die conveyors are used for some applications.

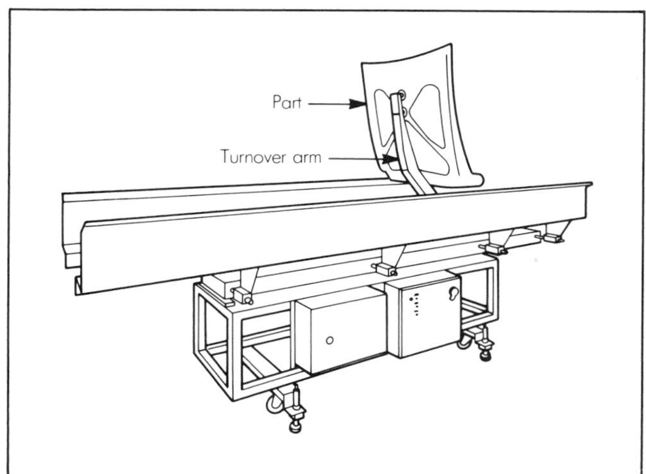

Fig. 5-56 Panel turnover device using vacuum cups to grip workpiece. (*Press Automation Systems, Inc.*)

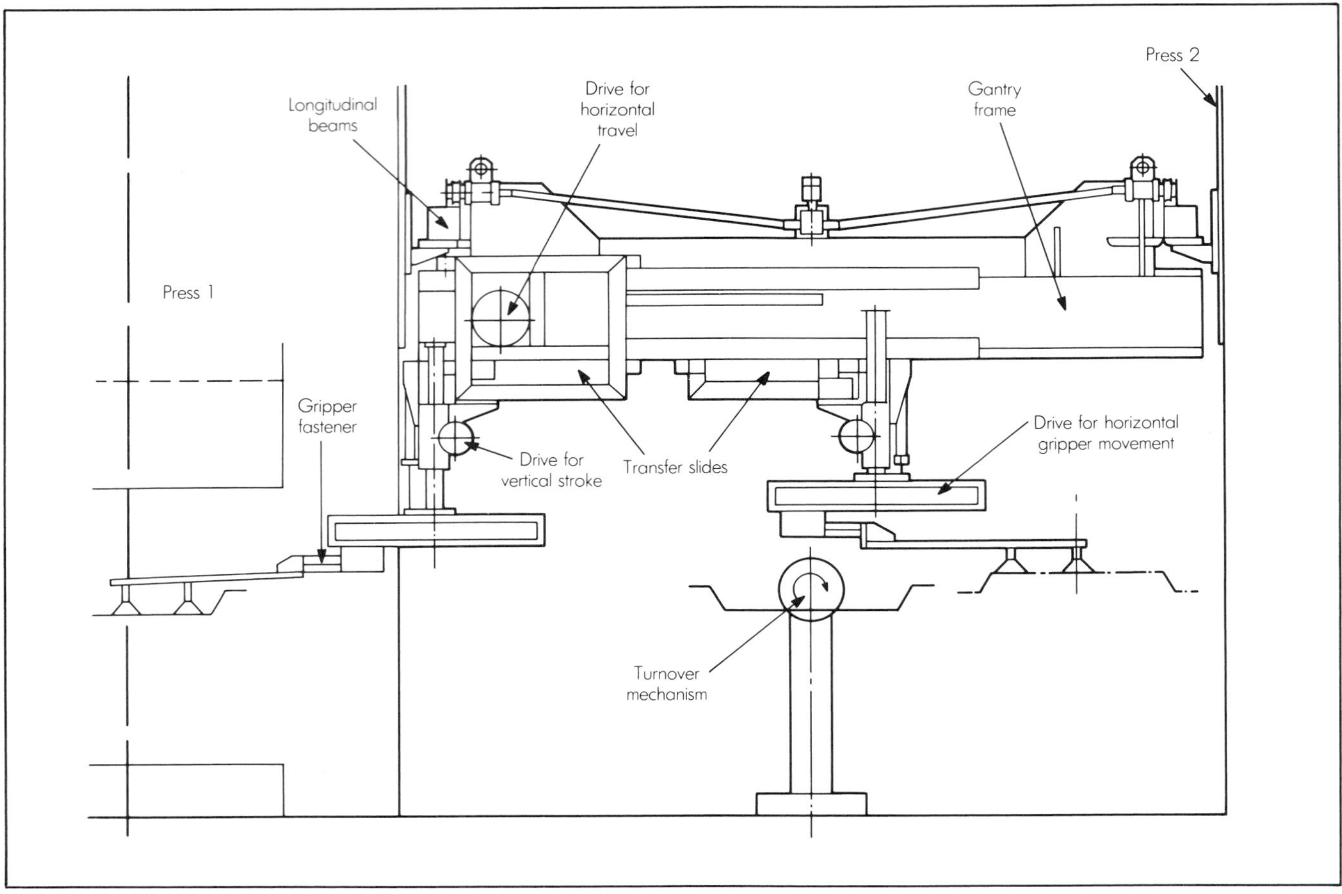


**Fig. 5-57 Transfer system controlled by programmable CNC unit.** (*Schuler Inc.*)

# HYDRAULIC PRESSES

Hydraulic presses are machines that use one or more cylinders and pressurized fluid to provide the required motion and force to form or blank workpieces. While mechanical presses are still the predominant type, hydraulic presses are being increasingly applied. About one out of every four presses in U.S. industry today is hydraulic, and the use of hydraulic presses is even more extensive in Europe.

Major reasons for the increased use of hydraulic presses in recent years are their improved performance and reliability. Improved hydraulic circuits and new valves with higher flow capacities and faster response times are major factors.

Specific applications exist in which hydraulic presses offer definite advantages and, in some cases, are the only machines that can be employed. For example, very high force requirements can only be met economically with hydraulic presses. In some applications, the capability of a hydraulic press to dwell on the workpiece can produce more accurate and stable parts. For coining, embossing, and assembling operations, control of the pressure, rather than distance, can overcome problems associated with variations in stock thickness. A comparison of characteristics and preferred uses for both mechanical and hydraulic presses is presented in Table 5-1.

## ADVANTAGES OF HYDRAULIC PRESSES

The greatest advantage of a hydraulic press is its adjustability, which increases the versatility of the machine. With a nonfixed cycle and full force availability at any point in the stroke, a hydraulic press is compatible with various dies and operations. Hydraulic presses have been built with stroke lengths of 100″ (2540 mm) and more. To obtain the long-stroke capabilities of hydraulic presses, mechanical presses require taller and more massive frames.

### Variable Force

The force exerted by a hydraulic press is infinitely adjustable from about 20% of its maximum rated capacity by simply varying the pressure relief valve setting. This is important in protecting dies designed for limited capacities and for various operations on different workpiece materials. The preset force is relatively constant throughout the stroke. It is practically impossible to overload a hydraulic press because the press only operates to the preset force, regardless of variations in stock thickness, inaccurate dies, doubleheaders, or other factors.

Full force capacities of hydraulic presses can be applied at any point in their strokes, regardless of stroke lengths, thus permitting their use for both short and long-stroke applications. This capability allows the use of a hydraulic press with a lower force rating than that needed for a mechanical press on which the operation requires the application of force high above bottom of stroke. For example, on a 500 ton (4.4 MN) mechanical press, only 175 tons (1.6 MN) are available for an operation requiring the application of force 5" (127 mm) up on the stroke. A mechanical press comparable to a 500 ton hydraulic press for this operation would require a 1350 ton (12 MN) force capacity (see Fig. 5-58).

### Variable Stroke and Speed

Compared to the fixed stroke of a mechanical press, the stroke of a hydraulic press can be easily adjusted to stop and reverse the slide at any position in the stroke. The speed of hydraulic presses is also variable; slide speed can be slowed from rapid advance to pressing speed just prior to contacting the workpiece. This can lengthen die life by reducing shock loads. Variable speed also permits selecting the optimum speed for each operation and workpiece material, thus ensuring high-quality parts and reducing setup time.

### Other Advantages

Variable capacity is another feature of hydraulic presses. Bed size, stroke length, press speed, and force capacity are not necessarily interdependent. Hydraulic presses are available with large beds and low force ratings, small beds and high force ratings, and a wide variety of stroke lengths. While standard-size hydraulic presses are available, many are purchased especially designed to suit user requirements. Hydraulic presses are more compact than mechanical presses of comparable capacity.

Since hydraulic presses have fewer moving parts than mechanical presses, there is generally less downtime and maintenance required. Hydraulic presses are essentially self-lubricating; the only additional lubrication required is that needed for the slide gibbing or column bearings. With properly designed and mounted hydraulic systems, the presses provide quiet operation.

## PRESS LIMITATIONS

Hydraulic presses still have slower speeds than mechanical presses. The speed, however, depends upon stroke length, and many applications exist in which hydraulic presses can outperform mechanical presses. There are small, automatic-cycling hydraulic presses operating at 900 spm for short-stroke applications. Pressing speeds range to about 600 ipm (15 240 mm/min), with approach and return speeds as high as 2000 ipm (50 800 mm/min).

Even with slower speeds, hydraulic presses are ideally suited for many applications, particularly hand-fed operations and small lot sizes. Automatic feeds require the use of an external or auxiliary power unit, integrated with the press control system.

Shock loads resulting from the sudden acceleration of press slides at the bottom of their strokes when metal has been sheared in blanking and piercing operations are particularly critical. Most builders of hydraulic presses have developed systems to relieve the downward force on the slide at the moment of die breakthrough, and some of these systems are described later in this section.

## FRAME CONSTRUCTION

Hydraulic presses are available in a number of frame configurations, including straight-side, column-type, C-frame, open-back stationary (OBS), and special-purpose designs. They are made in horizontal and vertical-acting models, with the vertical type being predominant.

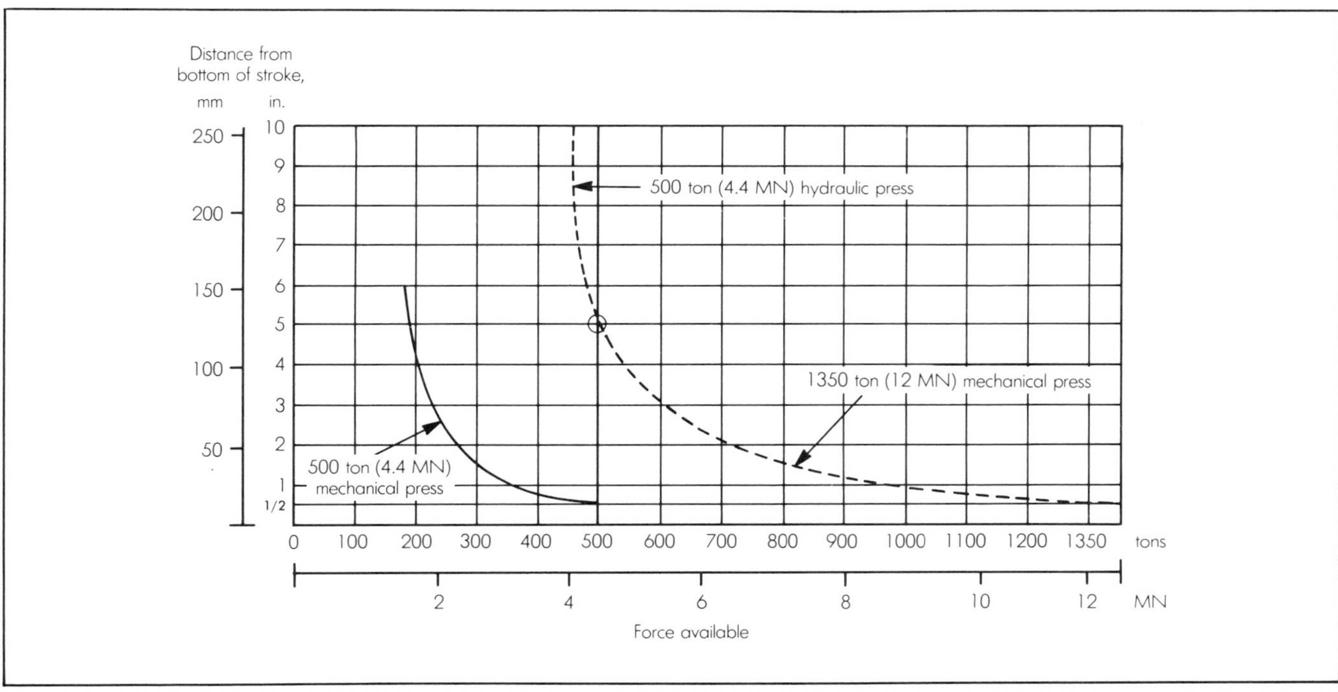


**Fig. 5-58 Comparative requirements for mechanical and hydraulic presses to exert 500 tons (4.4 MN) of force 5" (127 mm) up on stroke.** (*Clearing, A Div. of U.S. Industries, Inc.*)

# CHAPTER 5

## HYDRAULIC PRESSES

### Straight-Side Presses

Straight-side hydraulic presses (see Fig. 5-59) are available with single or two-point (connection) suspensions, having one or two cylinders, and may be single, double, or triple acting. Force capacities generally range from 50-5000 tons (0.4-44.5 MN) for conventional metalforming and blanking operations to 85,000 tons (756.5 MN) for hot forging (refer to Chapter 15 of this volume, "Hot Forging").

**Press components.** Major components of a straight-side hydraulic press consist of the bed, side housings (uprights), crown, and slide (platen). Side housings often have openings to permit feeding strip or coil stock from the side. The bed often has a removable bolster and sometimes contains one or more die cushions for deep-drawing operations.

Housings are either solid welded members or fabricated steel uprights; or the whole structure is joined together with steel tie rods, as with the construction of mechanical straight-side presses discussed previously in this chapter. Band-type, loop frames are sometimes used for short-stroke, high-force applications such as coining and hubbing (sometimes called hobbing).

The crown is an integral member of the press structure, usually containing the power unit, hydraulic cylinder(s), and oil reservoir. Depending upon the press design, the power unit (motor-driven pump) is sometimes mounted independent of the press, together with intensifiers and/or accumulators.

The slide (platen) and upper bolster travel vertically between the side members. Various types of gibbing arrangements, similar to those used on mechanical presses, are employed to guide the slide and maintain accurate alignment. Adjustable, eight-point, square-type gibbing is used on many hydraulic presses.

**Applications.** Straight-side hydraulic presses are used extensively for production applications for which good slide and bed alignment is essential for accuracy. Their rigid construction permits off-center loading.

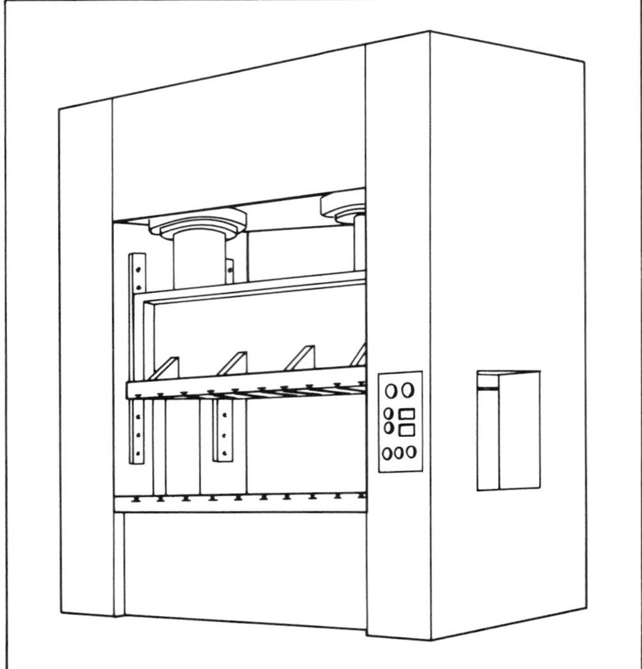

**Fig. 5-59 Straight-side hydraulic press with dual cylinders.** (*Pacific Press & Shear Co.*)

Operations in which these presses are used encompass the full range of metalforming and blanking operations. Presses with large bolster and slide areas permit producing large parts which may require blanking, punching, forming, and often, deep drawing of the same part. Controlled and adjustable speed, stroke length, and force facilitate the use of progressive dies for producing complex parts.

Accuracy and controllability of some modern, straight-side hydraulic presses equipped with double-acting cylinders make them ideal for steel-rule blanking applications. In many cases, the low-cost, steel-rule dies (discussed in chapter 6 of this volume, "Die Design for Sheet Metal Forming") can be designed to blank, pierce, form, and trim in a single stroke.

**Die cushions.** One or more die cushions (discussed previously in this chapter under the subject of mechanical presses) are often installed in the beds of straight-side hydraulic presses for deep-drawing applications. Hydraulic cushions can be operated from the main power unit and require less space than air cushions. Adjustability of the presses simplifies setup and enables selection of the optimum speed for the material to be drawn. When the main motor and pump are used to operate hydraulic cushions, however, press performance with respect to force and speed can be affected.

Each die-cushion cylinder is connected to individual control valves and to an air/oil accumulator tank which provides the return force for the cushions. The cushions maintain constant force on the metal blanks during drawing to control metal flow and minimize wrinkling. Force exerted on the blankholder can be varied and can be controlled by adjusting valve settings.

**Other accessories.** The versatility of straight-side hydraulic presses can be further increased by the addition of heated platens for forming materials such as titanium and magnesium. Electrically heated, water-cooled platens are used for laminating operations and compression molding of rubber and thermosetting plastics.

Special holding circuits can be provided for applications requiring dwell time under a specified load. Extruding and compacting devices can also be employed to take advantage of the long, steady, full-power stroke, and the presses can be readily adapted to completely automated production systems.

### Round-Column Presses

Column-type hydraulic presses are similar to straight-side presses, but they have round columns, rods, or posts instead of the side frames. Presses with four columns are the most common, but some presses have two or three columns. These presses are of simpler construction and generally cost less than straight-side presses.

Column presses are popular when a variety of applications are required, when production runs are short, and when initial cost is a factor. An important advantage is good accessibility to the dies from all sides. These presses are generally not recommended, however, when high production rates are needed and extremely accurate guiding of the slide is required.

### C-Frame Presses

Hydraulic presses with C frames (see Fig. 5-60), also called gap-frame presses, are a more recent development. The two solid steel housings on each press are cut back below the gibs to form the shape of a letter C, similar to the gap-frame mechanical presses discussed earlier in this chapter. The ample throat and open sides of these presses provide easy access to the die area from three sides and permit loading/unloading wide or irregular-shaped workpieces.

Most C-frame hydraulic presses have a single cylinder, but some special-purpose machines have been built with two cylinders (one horizontal and one vertical, each with a different force capacity). An electric motor rotates a pump to draw oil from the reservoir and supply it to the cylinder. A valving and electrical system responds to control demands to advance and retract the slide or ram and to apply the desired amount of force. The force ratings of C-frame hydraulic presses generally range from 1-1000 tons (8.9-8896 kN).

C-frame hydraulic presses are designed to perform a wide variety of operations that require high force concentration in a relatively small area. They are commonly used for punching, blanking, forming, sizing, straightening, riveting, and assembly operations. When equipped with a single die cushion, they are also employed for deep-drawing work. Other applications include trimming of diecastings, cut-off, and broaching.

### OBI and OBS Presses

Hydraulic presses with C frames are also available in open-back inclinable (OBI) and open-back stationary (OBS) designs. A typical OBS press is illustrated in Fig. 5-61. These presses are designed to have stroking speeds comparable to mechanical presses of similar design. Force ratings generally range from 6-250 tons (53-2224 kN). Advantages include the ability to feed from front to back of the press, as well as from either side, and the ability to eject workpieces from the rear of the press.

These single-cylinder presses have compact frames; integral, box-type slides; and full-length gibbing. A self-contained, high-speed power unit is mounted within the upper area of the frame. The presses can be equipped with removable bolsters, a die cushion in the bed for deep-drawing operations, and automatic feeding or material-handling systems for high-speed production applications.

### Other Designs

Hydraulic presses are available in a wide variety of other designs to suit specific applications. Some of these, discussed later in this chapter under the subject of special-purpose presses, are die setting or spotting presses, flexible-die forming presses, fine blanking presses, and portal presses.

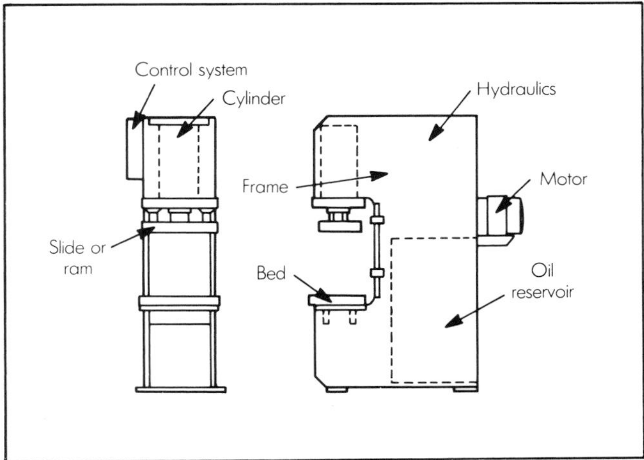


**Fig. 5-60 Hydraulic press with C (gap) frame.** (*Greenerd Press & Machine Co.*)

Additional hydraulic presses and machines are described in other chapters of this volume, as follows:

| Chapter | Title |
|---|---|
| 7 | Expanding, Shrinking and Stretch Forming |
| 9 | Spinning |
| 10 | Bending and Straightening |
| 11 | Shearing |
| 12 | Punching |
| 13 | Wire Drawing, Extruding and Heading |
| 15 | Hot Forging |
| 16 | Casting |
| 17 | Powder Metallurgy |
| 18 | Plastic Forming |
| 19 | Special Forming Methods |

## SELF-CONTAINED WORKHEADS

Self-contained hydraulic workheads (cylinders), movable along channels, are available with or without press frames. They are equipped with roller mounting, a pressure gage, and a

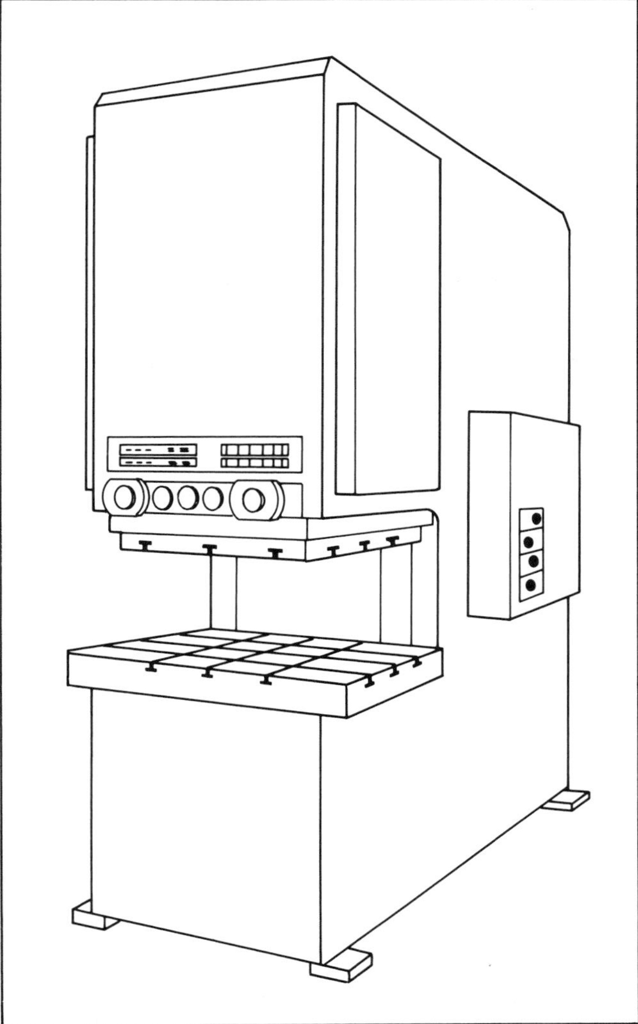

**Fig. 5-61 Typical C-frame hydraulic press of open-back stationary (OBS) design.** (*Pacific Press & Shear Co.*)

# HYDRAULIC PRESSES

flat ram nose for pressing. A release valve automatically returns the ram to its starting position. Tables that are movable front to back between the press frames can be provided.

The workheads, with force ratings of 1-200 tons (0.01-1.78 MN), are made for hand, air, or electric operation. Hand-operated models are equipped with screw-type rams that can be advanced rapidly to the workpiece with a handwheel. Air-operated units require no hand pumping and are available with foot control valves. Electric models are made with single or double-acting cylinders. They provide automatic, rapid ram approach, and variable ram speed with fingertip control. Units with double-acting cylinders can be used for lifting as well as pressing.

## TOOL-CASTING PRESSES

Hydraulic presses are available that cast their own tools for prototype forming of sheet metal parts. The cast tools are then used in the same presses to produce the required number of parts. When the job is completed, the tooling is melted in the press and collected in a reservoir for reuse.

These machines are basically double-acting hydraulic presses, 50-125 tons (0.4-1.1 MN) force capacity, having reservoirs for a bismuth-type alloy that melts at about 160° F (71° C). Melting is accomplished with a built-in electric heater. Tooling is cast with the fluid metal surrounding a sample workpiece, which is then solidified by applying cold water.

## AUTOMATIC TOOL CLAMPING

Some builders of hydraulic presses offer automatic tool clamping systems. One system consists of four clamping units in the press ram and four in the press bed. The units are clamped by mechanically actuated spring washers and unclamped hydraulically.

The next tool to be used in the press is placed on a twin-station turret located behind the press. The tool to be changed is unclamped and moved onto the turret manually. Then the turret is rotated 180° and the new tool is moved into position and clamped. Advantages include reduced toolchanging time (requiring about 1 minute), increased space on the press bed (by eliminating clamping brackets), and safer operations.

## LIMITING DOWNSTROKE

On many hydraulic presses, downstroke is limited by provisions in the tooling, such as kiss blocks. Some press builders offer adjustable positive stops that permit stroke limiting to act independently of the ram force. Distance reversal limit switches, pressure limit switches, and digital electronic controls are also employed to automatically return the ram after the desired stroke. Mechanical press stops, predominant on hydraulic presses of European design, are adjustable and provide good repeat accuracy.

## REDUCING SHOCK LOADS

Builders of hydraulic presses offer several different systems to relieve the downward force on and acceleration of the slide at the moment of die breakthrough in blanking and piercing operations, thus minimizing shock loads. Some use automatic decompression of oil in the cylinder by supplying pressurized oil under the piston to absorb and dissipate shock. Another builder offers an optional cushioning cylinder to arrest and dissipate shock and reduce noise.

With a system offered by another press builder, two catching cylinders are provided to serve as shock absorbers. These single-acting cylinders, built into the bed of the press, stop the ram automatically and almost instantly at the moment the punch breaks through the material. This is accomplished by rapidly diverting pressure from the main cylinder to the catching cylinders. The catching cylinders also raise the upper platen to the top of its stroke. A shock dissipator is provided to damp decompression waves (sonic hydraulic vibrations) and prevent damage to the piping and hydraulic components.

When blanking is performed on hydraulic presses equipped with mechanical stops, the stops can be combined with secondary cushioning cylinders built within the main cylinder housings to dissipate snap-through shock and lessen noise levels. With this design, blanking can be done at 100% of rated press capacity without damage to the cylinder or hydraulic components.

## PRESSURE SYSTEMS

Major components of the pressure systems used on hydraulic presses include the pressure medium, motor-driven pumps, cylinders and pistons, valves, and piping. Control of the valves determines the direction of flow and the volume of the medium that is directed into the cylinder(s) to actuate movements of the press slide.

### Pressure Medium

Most hydraulic presses employ oil as the pressure medium, but some, especially hot forging presses, use water, steam, or fire-resistant fluids (refer to Chapter 15 of this volume, "Hot Forging"). The medium is usually under a pressure of 2500 psi (17.24 MPa) for most hydraulic presses, but pressures to 10,000 psi (69 MPa) are not uncommon.

### Pressure Supply

Most hydraulic presses are self-contained, with their own motor-driven pumps and hydraulic systems. Radial or axial-piston pumps or radial-vane pumps are used. Since there are no provisions for storing energy with self-contained systems, the motor and pump must be large enough to meet the load requirements. Some designs employ two pumps, one for low pressure and the other for high pressure, resulting in less noise generation. Press-mounted oil reservoirs are generally equipped with a strainer and/or filter, air breather, oil-level gage, and in some cases, an immersion heater and cooler.

Semiaccumulator and accumulator pressure supply systems are generally used for large hydraulic presses with higher force ratings. The systems are capable of supplying large volumes of hydraulic fluid at a relatively constant pressure in a short time. The systems generally use pumps of smaller volume capacity than self-contained systems use because the pumps can recharge the accumulators during the idle portions of the press cycles.

### Hydraulic Cylinders

Single-acting cylinders are used extensively on hydraulic presses, but it is necessary to provide separate, auxiliary cylinders to return the upper platen (slide) to its top position. Double-acting cylinders are often preferred when the mass to be moved is not too heavy and when a high return speed is desirable.

One builder offers presses having a double-acting hydraulic cylinder that moves with the slide throughout the stroke. The cylinder is inverted and mounted within the press slide, with the piston rod attached to a flange at the top of the press. Hydraulic knockouts can be incorporated at the lower end of the cylinders. The knockout system can be preadjusted or bypassed.

Force capacity of a hydraulic press is dependent upon the cross-sectional area of the piston(s) and the pressure developed by the pump(s). When the required force is known, the desired operating pressure determines the size of the cylinder(s). Higher pressures and smaller cylinder bore diameters are used for fast press speeds; lower pressures and larger diameters, for slow speeds. The amount of work that a hydraulic press can deliver equals the force exerted on the piston(s) multiplied by the stroke. Some hydraulic presses are designed with various diameters within one cylinder.

### Valves and Piping

Good, fast-response, heavy-duty valves are essential for optimum performance and minimum maintenance. With some designs, the valves are of modular construction and stacked together to reduce the need for interconnecting piping. Plug-in type valves with cartridge elements are used by some press builders. The cartridge elements are seat valves that can be combined to meet different functions, such as directional control or pressure regulating. The piping for hydraulic presses is generally seamless steel tubing with forged steel fittings.

### Hydraulic Circuits

Hydraulic circuits used with self-contained pressure supply systems on modern metalworking presses can be categorized into two basic types: single cylinder and parallel circuit. The type of circuit used for any press is governed essentially by the number of cylinders on the press, the type of work to be performed, and the operating characteristics of the hydraulic circuit. Each circuit has its advantages and limitations. While the circuits become more complex with the addition of auxiliary equipment and features, the following discussion pertains to simple, basic hydraulic circuits.

**Single-cylinder circuit.** The single-cylinder circuit (see Fig. 5-62) is the basic circuit used for all single-point hydraulic presses. The system is capable of high-speed performance and consists of a motor-driven pump and a single valve-manifold system.

**Parallel circuit.** The parallel circuit (see Fig. 5-63) is a heavy-duty circuit used on large two-cylinder presses requiring precision accuracy and high forces over long stroke lengths. It consists essentially of two synchronized, single-cylinder circuits connected to the same motor. Each cylinder has its own pump and valve system, but also has electrical and hydraulic connections that permit the parallel systems to operate as one integral unit.

**Other circuits.** Many other circuits are used for hydraulic presses. One common design uses a single-acting main cylinder and two side cylinders for pullback, with the cylinders and system counterbalanced. Another circuit employs a double-acting cylinder with counterbalance.

## PRESS CONTROLS

Properly designed and applied controls are essential for the maximum protection of personnel, presses, and dies and to ensure optimum production rates with a minimum of downtime. Reliability of the controls is critical, and self-checking and diagnostic capabilities are important advantages.

The controls used for hydraulic presses are similar to those employed for mechanical presses (discussed previously in this chapter), with the addition of pressure gages and controls for

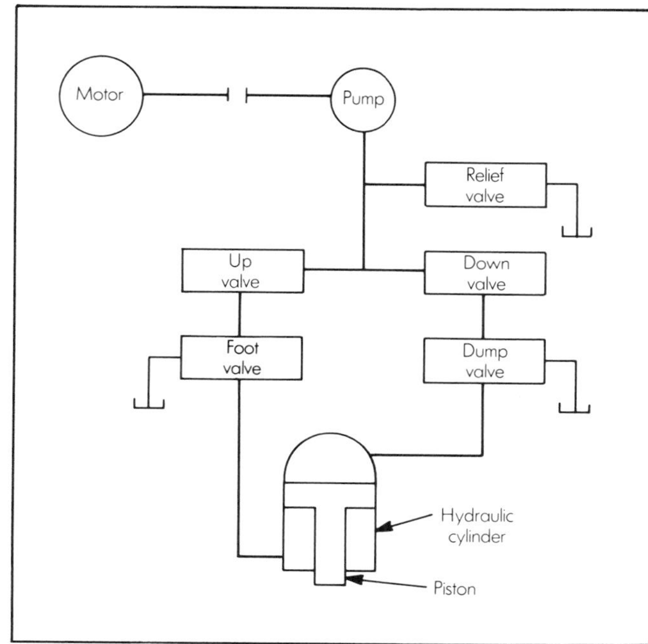


**Fig. 5-62 Single-cylinder circuit used for single-point hydraulic presses.** (*Pacific Press & Shear Co.*)

varying the force applied, stroke length, and ram speed.

Control systems employed include electromechanical systems, programmable controllers (PC's), solid-state controls, and microprocessors. Some electronic control systems provide for digital setting of all pressures and movements. The PC's permit fast setting of forming or blanking pressure, stroke length, dwell time, pull-out pressure, and other functions, as well as the sequence of functions for different applications.

Some microprocessor controls provide a data entry keyboard for simplified programming of slide stroke positions, forces applied, and auxiliary functions. Data can be stored in the control memory for future use on the same job. The controls are available with a visual display of data for setup, operation, and production counts; fault indications; and diagnostic information.

The maximum anticipated working pressures in any hydraulic system must not exceed the safe working pressure rating of the lowest rated component in that system. Mechanisms operated by hydraulic cylinders should have provisions for shutting off and bleeding pressure from all components that might cause unexpected operation or motion.

## HYDRAULIC PRESS SAFETY

Detailed information on hydraulic press safety is available in ANSI Standard B11.2, "Safety Requirements for the Construction, Care, and Use of Hydraulic Presses." Objectives of this standard are the same as for ANSI Standard B11.1 on mechanical presses (discussed previously in this chapter)—to establish performance standards that eliminate hazards to personnel by establishing requirements for the construction, care, and use of the presses.

Many of the definitions and requirements in the hydraulic press standard are the same or similar to those in the mechanical press standard, including safeguarding the point of operation (discussed previously).

# CHAPTER 5

## HYDRAULIC PRESSES

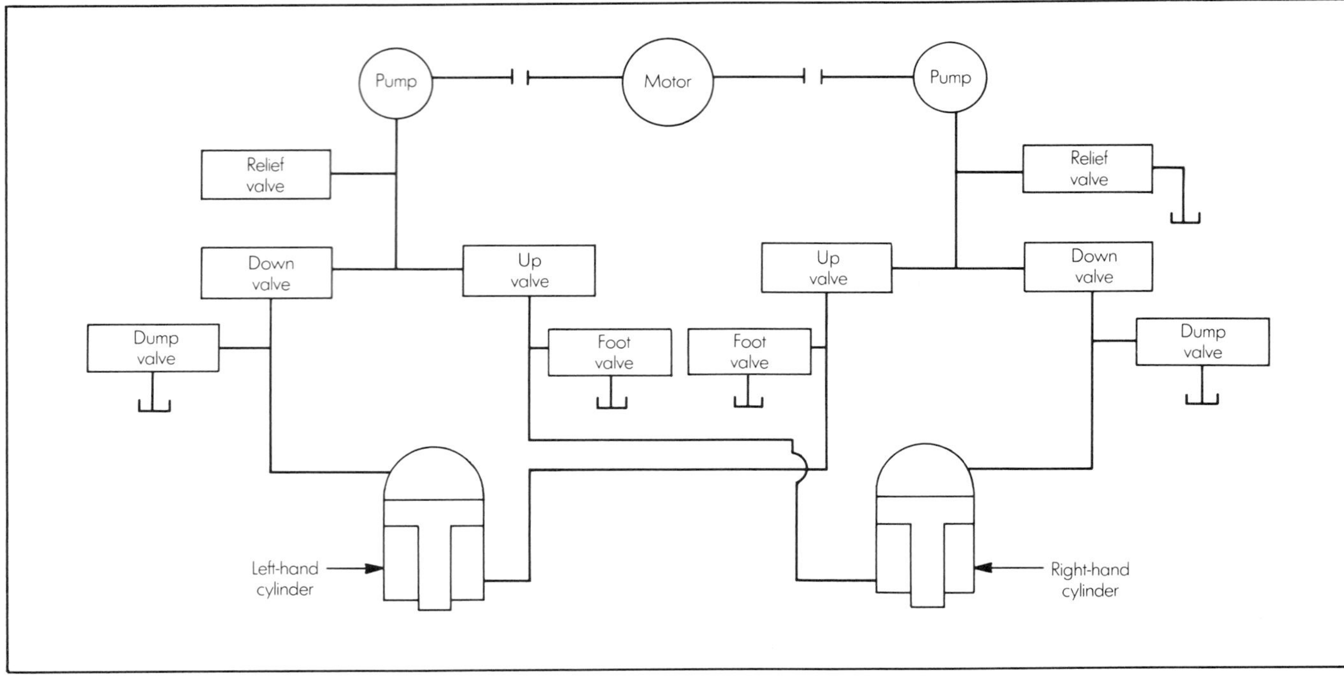


**Fig. 5-63 Parallel circuit used on large, two-cylinder, hydraulic presses.** (*Pacific Press & Shear Co.*)

Requirements of the B11.2 standard pertaining to construction apply to all new hydraulic presses, as well as used presses before being put into operation or installed at a new location, after the approval date (April 30, 1982) of the standard. It is recommended that required modifications to all existing hydraulic presses be accomplished within five years after the approval date. Point-of-operation guarding, devices, etc., should be installed as soon as possible.

### General Electrical and Pneumatic Requirements

The hydraulic press control shall incorporate means to prevent motion unless at least one pump motor is running or adequate control and/or pilot pressure is available. A control circuit interlock contact on at least one pump-motor starter to allow press operation only when the contactor is energized is one method of meeting this requirement.

The press control must be designed so that in the event of power failure, restoration of power does not result in any unintended motion of the slide(s). Requirements for power disconnecting means, motor start buttons, voltage supply, and grounding of electrical circuits are the same as for mechanical presses (previously discussed in this chapter).

Pneumatic controls must be protected against foreign material and water entering the pneumatic system of the press if this creates a safety hazard. A means of air lubrication must be provided when needed.

### Counterbalance System

A counterbalance system shall be provided when necessary for protection of the operator and shall have sufficient capacity to stop the motion of the slide(s) and its attachments quickly at any point in travel. Drifting of the slide(s) shall be limited to a speed that does not present a hazard to the operator. The counterbalance requirement may not be necessary where gravity motion is not possible.

Depending upon design, a wide variety of counterbalancing systems may exist. Spring and air counterbalances are discussed earlier in this chapter under the subject of mechanical press construction. The system should be designed so that loss of power effectively stops and controls the slide(s) and its attachments. Where multiple-return cylinders are used, consideration should be given to using a separate counterbalance valve on each cylinder. Where a single-return cylinder is used, redundancy of valves should be considered to ensure reliability. The counterbalance valve should be mounted as close to the cylinder as possible, with emphasis on the reliability of the connection.

### Hydraulic Press Components and Circuits

**Components.** The press shall show the maximum force as determined by pressure settings in accordance with press design. Where applicable, counterbalance pressure settings for die weights shall be affixed to the press. Hydraulic equipment, including valves, accumulators, surge tanks, fluid, etc., shall be used within their design capacity. Over-pressure protection shall be consistent with the design rating of the press. Some methods of accomplishing this include using:

1. A preset, locked (sealed) pressure-control valve.
2. A hydraulic fuse.
3. A self-limiting pump or pressure source.

**Circuits.** Where severe shock would result, the hydraulic circuit shall incorporate a means of decompression before reversing the directional control. Design provisions shall be made to prevent intensification of system pressure where it would create a hazard. Intensification is particularly a problem with accumulator systems, cylinder ratios, and breakthrough shock (that is, blanking operations). Design and circuit application shall minimize the possibility of unintended slide closing in case of valve failure.

Hydraulic piping, including pipe, tubing, hose, and associated fittings, shall be selected to provide adequate service factors, based upon rated operating parameters, to minimize the possibility of unintended motion in the event of failure. Hydraulic circuit designs shall incorporate means to minimize hydraulic shock as a factor in piping failure. Hydraulic piping runs shall be designed and constructed to minimize structurally borne or self-generated vibration.

**Accumulators.** An accumulator is a source of stored energy and remains under pressure even when the pump motor is off unless other precautions are taken. Auxiliary equipment that does not present a hazard, such as cushion accumulators, is excluded from requirements of the standard.

Accumulator applications shall include the following:

1. Shut-off. Whenever possible, circuits shall be designed to vent or isolate accumulator fluid pressure when the power is shut off.
2. Charge. Accumulators operating above 200 psi (1380 kPa) pressure shall be charged with nitrogen unless the fluid media used will not support combustion, in which case air is permissible.
3. Safety. Accumulators shall incorporate means to prevent the gas charge from entering the press hydraulic system.

**Cylinder(s).** A means shall be provided to prevent pistons from causing a hazard by stroking beyond their design limits. One hazard is that a single-acting piston could leave its cylinder if stroked beyond its design limits. Items that may be used to meet this requirement include a cam-operated valve or a full-force positive stop.

**Fluid media conditioning.** Fluid media conditioning is required to minimize hazards due to system malfunctions caused by failure of components such as pumps, valves, and actuators. A means shall be provided to meet the manufacturer's recommended level of fluid quality. Some common means of accomplishing this are:

1. Pressure or return-line filtration.
2. Recirculating filtration.
3. External conditioning.
4. Micronic air breathers.

Where necessary, a means shall be provided for heating and/or cooling to maintain the fluid temperature level within the manufacturer's recommended operating limits.

**Slide-lock mechanism.** When provided, the slide lock shall prevent the slide(s) from closing in an unintended manner. With slide-lock mechanisms designed to hold less than full press force, a means shall be provided to prevent the forces from exceeding the design capabilities of the slide-lock mechanism.

## Hydraulic Press Operation

A properly equipped press with a suitable point-of-operation safeguard, properly trained operators, correct procedures, adequate supervision, ample work area, and avoidance of overloading are essential for safe and efficient operation.

**Overloading.** Hydraulic presses must be operated within their design limitations such as force capacity, eccentric loading, concentrated loading, attachment weight ratings, and shock loading due to breakthrough.

**Lubrication.** The fluid medium used, often hydraulic oil, not only serves as the pressure means, but also internally lubricates all the pumps and valves. Conditioning of the fluid by filtration or other means is required, however, to maintain its quality; and it may be necessary to heat and/or cool the fluid, as previously described, to maintain the recommended temperature level.

The lubrication of wear surfaces such as the press gibbing is accomplished with manual, centralized, or recirculating systems, as described earlier in this chapter for mechanical presses.

**Maintenance.** Since hydraulic presses have fewer moving parts than mechanical presses, maintenance is generally less of a problem. Skilled personnel and consistently regular maintenance procedures are required however to prevent leaks, especially with operations involving higher pressures and speeds. Leakage problems with hydraulic presses have been minimized by improved designs of pumps, valves, and circuits. A complete maintenance program coordinating routine inspections, preventive maintenance, replacement or repair of parts as required, and a checkout after repair is discussed under the preceding section on mechanical presses.

**Inspection.** Firms using hydraulic presses are responsible for establishing and following a program of periodic inspection of the presses to ensure that all their parts, auxiliary equipment, and safeguards are in safe operating condition and adjustment. It is recommended that a visual inspection of operations, safeguards, and auxiliary equipment be made at least once per shift. At annual intervals, or at the specific schedule recommended by the press manufacturer, each machine should be examined.

**Feeds and dies.** The methods used to feed stock, blanks, or stampings to hydraulic presses, as well as means for unloading, are similar to those for mechanical presses, discussed in detail in a preceding section of this chapter. Proper die design, fastening, handling, and setting, discussed in Chapter 6 of this volume, "Die Design for Sheet Metal Forming," are also critical factors in press safety.

## Responsibility of Press User

Just as the hydraulic power press itself is not functional until the user installs a die unique to the product being made, a complete, functional, safeguarded machine does not exist until the user installs a point-of-operation guard or device made necessary by that operation, and then further assures its use. Even if a form of point-of-operation safeguarding exists prior to installation of the die, adjustment (for instance, of an adjustable barrier guard or pullback device) is usually necessary for the particular operation. Even a two-hand control may require, for example, adjustment of the distance of separation from the point of operation or of the "holding time" before it is an effective means of safeguarding.

One or more of the following methods shall be used for safeguarding the point of operation:

1. Ensure that the operator is physically prevented from entering or is removed from the point of operation as the slide(s) closes.
2. Prevent or stop slide(s) motion if the operator is within the point of operation.
3. In applications which preclude the use of any of the above, such as certain straightening or maintenance operations, implement and document such methods of operations to protect the operator to the fullest extent possible.

# PNEUMATIC PRESSES

Pneumatic presses use pressurized air to exert the required force. They are smaller in size and capacity than most mechanical and hydraulic presses and are generally employed for light-duty operations. Some pneumatic presses, however, are used for heavy-duty cutting, punching, and notching operations.

## ADVANTAGES OF PNEUMATIC PRESSES

Important advantages of pneumatic presses include low cost, minimum maintenance, and high ram velocities. These presses eliminate the need for crankshafts, motors, clutches, brakes, and other components required on mechanical presses. As a result, there is less downtime for adjustments, repairs, and replacements. Installation of pneumatic presses is simple, requiring only connection to an adequate air supply; and the presses are fast cycling, with quick response.

Another major advantage of pneumatic presses is their adjustability with respect to force, speed, stroke, and shutheight. The preset pressure is essentially constant throughout the stroke, with a slight reduction for the compression of return springs on presses of single-acting design. Pneumatic presses are of compact design, generally being rectangular assemblies having low profiles. They can be mounted for operation in any position.

## POSSIBLE LIMITATIONS

Limited capacities and short strokes of pneumatic presses may present problems, depending upon the application. The impact forces of these presses are most effective when the energies of the rapidly moving rams can be absorbed with short tool penetrations. As a result, the presses are generally best suited for coining, shallow embossing, blanking of thin materials, and similar operations. Pneumatic presses of high capacity require a considerable volume of air, which should be an economic consideration in press selection.

## APPLICATIONS OF PNEUMATIC PRESSES

Pneumatic presses are being used extensively on roll forming lines (discussed in Chapter 8, "Roll Forming") for both preforming and postforming operations such as punching, notching, lancing, and cutoff of formed parts to required lengths. Other applications include production stamping operations such as blanking, piercing, cutting, trimming, forming, embossing, and coining, as well as assembly operations. The presses are especially well suited for use with steel-rule dies and unitized tooling.

## TYPES OF PNEUMATIC PRESSES

Pneumatic presses are available in several types, with a wide range of die areas. Some are actually air-operated, precision die sets consisting of upper and lower shoes on which punches and dies are mounted and having guide or leader pins and bushings for proper alignment.

### Press Construction

Pneumatic presses are made with one, two, four, or more posts or columns, or they are of gap-frame design. They have single or multiple air-actuated cylinders and are arranged for bench or floor mounting. On most presses, except those of larger size, the rams are returned to their upper positions by springs. Presses are available, however, with double-acting cylinders to provide power on their return strokes for lifting, positive stripping, and other functions.

Standard equipment generally includes air and electric controls, pressure regulators, and air filters and lubricators. Controls and safety guards are similar to those used for mechanical and hydraulic presses. Some pneumatic presses have air logic controls, eliminating the need for electrical connections, but response time is generally slower. Control equipment using air, however, must be protected against foreign material and water entering the system, as discussed previously under the section on controls for mechanical presses. Many optional items are available, including index tables, air reserve tanks, and mufflers for exhaust parts.

### Air Consumption

The amount of air required varies considerably for different pneumatic presses. Factors affecting air consumption include the pressure of the supply air, length of stroke, press speed (strokes per minute), the number of cylinders used on the press, and the air volume required per inch of stroke per cylinder.

Air consumption can be calculated from the following formula:

$$A = FLN \tag{8}$$

where:

$A$ = free air consumption, cfm
$F$ = air volume factor from Table 5-10
$L$ = length of ram stroke, in.
$N$ = press speed, spm

For metric usage, cfm should be multiplied by 0.028 to obtain $m^3/min$.

Example:

Air consumption for a pneumatic press having one double-acting cylinder with an area of 28 in.$^2$ (0.018 $m^2$), operating with a supply pressure of 110 psi (758 kPa), a ram stroke of 2" (51 mm), and speed of 30 spm, is:

$$A = 0.28 \times 2 \times 30 = 16.8 \text{ cfm } (0.47 \text{ m}^3/\text{min})$$

Care is required in the selection of an air compressor and the installation of adequate supply lines and reservoirs to maintain consistent press performance and production. Power requirements, based on the use of a single-stage compressor with an adiabatic compression cycle, can be calculated from the following formula:

$$P = FLN \tag{9}$$

where:

$P$ = compressor power requirement, hp
$F$ = power factor from Table 5-11
$L$ = length of ram stroke, in.
$N$ = press speed, spm

**TABLE 5-10**
**Air Volume Factor for Determining Air Consumption with Eq. (8)**

| Cylinder Area, in.$^2$ (m$^2$) | Air Supply Pressure, psi (kPa) | | | | | | | |
|---|---|---|---|---|---|---|---|---|
| | 80 (552) | 90 (621) | 100 (689) | 110 (758) | 120 (827) | 130 (896) | 140 (965) | 150 (1034) |
| | Air Volume Factor | | | | | | | |
| Single-acting: | | | | | | | | |
| 12 (0.008) | 0.045 | 0.049 | 0.054 | 0.059 | 0.064 | 0.069 | 0.073 | 0.078 |
| 24 (0.015) | 0.089 | 0.097 | 0.108 | 0.117 | 0.127 | 0.137 | 0.146 | 0.156 |
| 36 (0.023) | 0.134 | 0.148 | 0.162 | 0.176 | 0.190 | 0.205 | 0.219 | 0.233 |
| 50 (0.032) | 0.187 | 0.203 | 0.226 | 0.245 | 0.265 | 0.285 | 0.304 | 0.324 |
| Double-acting: | | | | | | | | |
| 12 (0.008) | 0.09 | 0.10 | 0.11 | 0.12 | 0.13 | 0.14 | 0.15 | 0.16 |
| 28 (0.018) | 0.21 | 0.23 | 0.25 | 0.28 | 0.30 | 0.32 | 0.34 | 0.37 |
| 50 (0.032) | 0.38 | 0.42 | 0.46 | 0.50 | 0.54 | 0.58 | 0.62 | 0.66 |
| 78 (0.050) | 0.58 | 0.64 | 0.70 | 0.77 | 0.83 | 0.89 | 0.95 | 1.01 |

(*Famco Machine Div., Belco Industries, Inc.*)

**TABLE 5-11**
**Power Factor for Determining Compressor Power Required with Eq. (9)**

| Cylinder Area, in.$^2$ (m$^2$) | Air Supply Pressure, psi (kPa) | | | | | | | |
|---|---|---|---|---|---|---|---|---|
| | 80 (552) | 90 (621) | 100 (689) | 110 (758) | 120 (827) | 130 (896) | 140 (965) | 150 (1034) |
| | Power Factor | | | | | | | |
| Single-acting: | | | | | | | | |
| 12 (0.008) | 0.007 | 0.008 | 0.010 | 0.011 | 0.012 | 0.014 | 0.016 | 0.017 |
| 24 (0.015) | 0.014 | 0.016 | 0.019 | 0.022 | 0.025 | 0.028 | 0.031 | 0.034 |
| 36 (0.023) | 0.022 | 0.025 | 0.029 | 0.033 | 0.037 | 0.043 | 0.047 | 0.051 |
| 50 (0.032) | 0.030 | 0.035 | 0.041 | 0.047 | 0.052 | 0.059 | 0.066 | 0.071 |
| Double-acting: | | | | | | | | |
| 12 (0.008) | 0.014 | 0.017 | 0.020 | 0.023 | 0.026 | 0.029 | 0.032 | 0.036 |
| 28 (0.018) | 0.033 | 0.039 | 0.045 | 0.053 | 0.060 | 0.067 | 0.073 | 0.083 |
| 50 (0.032) | 0.060 | 0.071 | 0.083 | 0.095 | 0.108 | 0.121 | 0.134 | 0.148 |
| 78 (0.050) | 0.092 | 0.102 | 0.126 | 0.146 | 0.165 | 0.185 | 0.205 | 0.226 |

(*Famco Machine Div., Belco Industries, Inc.*)

For metric usage, hp should be multiplied by 0.746 to obtain kW.

Example:

For the same press described in the preceding example, and operating with the same supply pressure, ram stroke, and press speed, the power required is:

$P = 0.053 \times 2 \times 30 = 3.2$ hp (2.4 kW)

There are several methods of reducing air consumption, including the use of toggle-type presses and the use of hydraulics in combination with air.

**Toggle-type.** One builder offers pneumatic presses of toggle design that multiply supply air pressure many times.

**Air-hydraulic.** Presses are available that use air cylinders in combination with hydraulic booster cylinders for reduced air requirements and smoother operation. Such presses are capable of delivering ram pressures from 50-100 or more times the pressure of the supply air. Press speed is controlled by a hydraulic valve.

### Force Ratings

Pneumatic presses are generally rated for both impact pressure and holding (stall) pressure. The impact pressure is usually 2 to 2 1/2 times the holding pressure. Presses are available with impact force ratings of 1/4 to 300 tons (2.2 to 2669 kN).

# SPECIAL-PURPOSE PRESSES

There are a number of special types of presses available to suit specific application requirements. Some of the more common of these special-purpose presses are discussed in this section.

## DIE-SETTING PRESSES

Presses used for final finishing of dies to indicate inaccuracies, and also to test mating and functioning of parts, are called die-setting, spotting, die-development, or tryout presses. They are often used in toolrooms for die construction, with hand grinders being employed to remove cutter marks. Then, punches are spotted to dies (and vice versa), using red lead or blueing, and necessary corrections are made.

The presses are also used to determine the size and shape of blanks, lengths of bends, shape and depth of draws, and other development work which must be done before a die or a set of dies can be completed.

In addition to saving time and money in design evaluation and in the testing, correcting, and finishing of dies, these presses permit sample workpieces to be made before the dies are delivered. In some cases, the presses are used for short production runs.

Die-setting presses are usually of low capacity in relation to die area or die rating and are generally of single-stroking design, with slow speeds. Hydraulic presses are most common for these operations, but mechanical and pneumatic presses are sometimes used. Advantages of hydraulic presses for these applications include their smaller size and lower cost compared to mechanical presses with the same bed area and force capacity; their capability for slide inching and precise adjustment; their slow slide speed; and their ability to exert full force capacity at any point in the slide stroke and to stop the slide at any position. Accurate guiding for precise alignment of the dies is essential. The presses are available with a wide range of bed and slide sizes to suit the dies to be finished and tested.

Hydraulic tryout presses have been built with swing-down upper bolsters (hydraulically released from the press slides) to hold the top halves of dies and with shuttle-type lower bolsters for the bottom halves (see Fig. 5-64), thus increasing safety and productivity in handling large, heavy dies. Hydraulically actuated, tapered pins automatically locate both bolsters for precise alignment after the bolsters return to the spotting position. For barbering and grinding operations, actuation of the moving bolsters transfers the die halves to convenient work stations which are not beneath the press slide. Press controls permit slowing down, inching, stopping, or reversing the slide at any position in the stroke. Full force capacity of the press is available at any point in the press stroke.

## DIEING MACHINES

Dieing machines, sometimes called die presses, are used for high-speed precision stamping operation on small workpieces, often with progressive dies and coil feeds. These machines are actually inverted mechanical presses with their drive mechanisms located under the beds (see Fig. 5-65). Advantages include accurate die alignment and a low center of gravity. No floor pits are required, and the machines can be installed in rooms with low ceilings.

Four guide rods (pillars), extending from a lower crosshead, pass upward through long, adjustable bushings in the bed. The rods are fastened to an upper crosshead (platen) to which a punch or upper die is attached. The lower crosshead is reciprocated by a flywheel-driven crankshaft, through connecting rods, thus pulling the punch or upper die down on the die mounted on the bed. Chain-driven adjusting nuts are provided above the upper crosshead for adjusting shutheight. The machines are available with capacity ratings ranging from 25-200 tons (222-1779 kN), speeds of 100-600 spm, and stroke lengths of 1-2" (25-51 mm).

## LAMINATION PRESSES

So-called "lamination presses" are high-speed, automatic, mechanical presses frequently used for stamping laminations, but also employed for shallow-drawing operations, progressive-die operations, and other operations. The short-stroke presses are generally of straight-side, tie-rod construction, but C-frame types are also used. Variable speed drives are standard. Coil-stock reels, straighteners, and feeders are offered as optional equipment.

One builder of lamination presses features two actions: a mechanical drive for high-speed stroking and a hydraulic lift action for slide withdrawal. The hydraulic lift provides accessibility for visual inspection and maintenance of the die without having to remove the die from the press. The presses are available with rated capacities of 30-300 tons (267-2669 kN), strokes of 1-3" (25.4-76.2 mm), and speeds of 133-1500 spm.

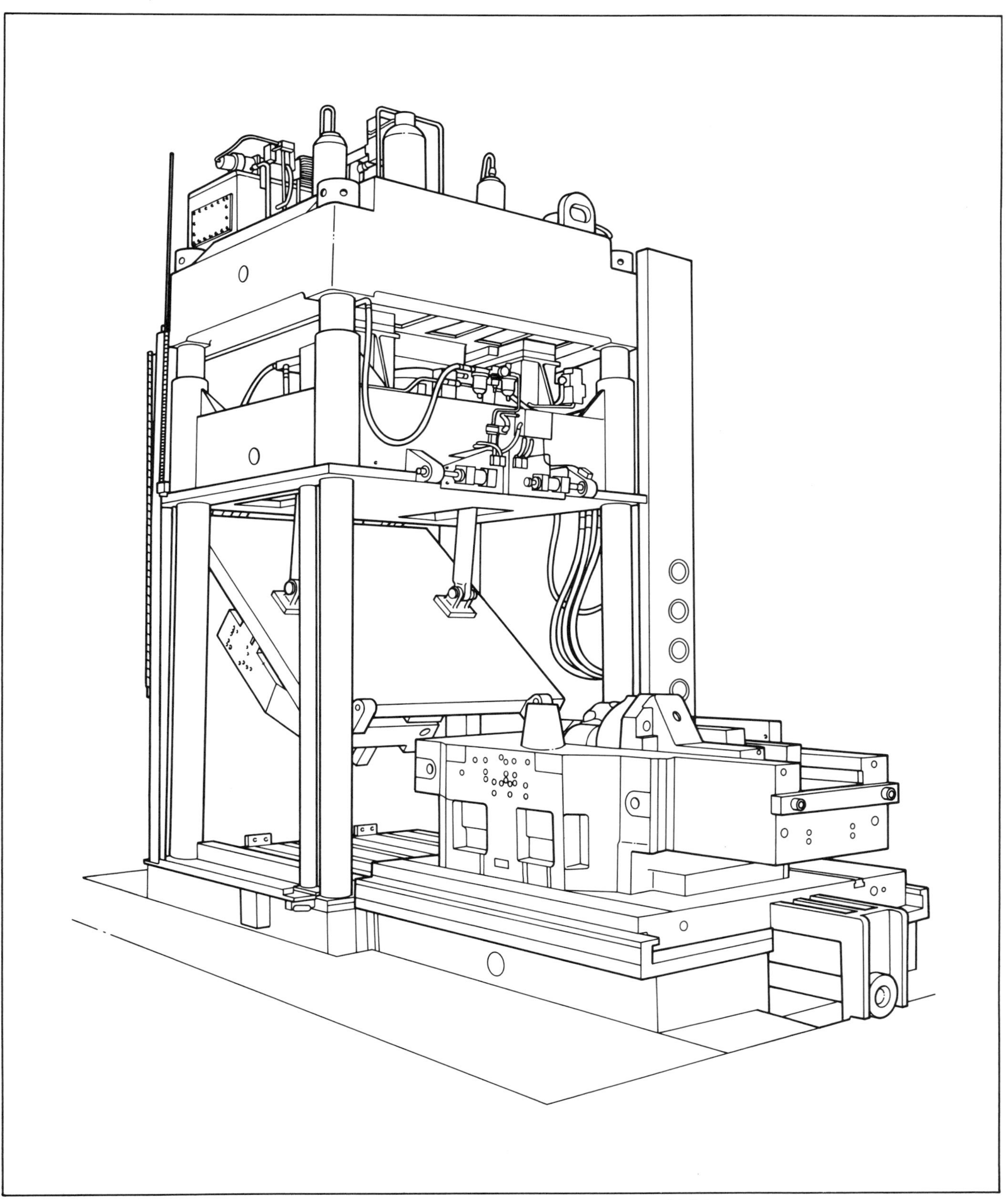

**Fig. 5-64 Hydraulic tryout press with swing-down upper bolster and shuttle-type lower bolster.** (*Dake*)

# CHAPTER 5

## SPECIAL-PURPOSE PRESSES

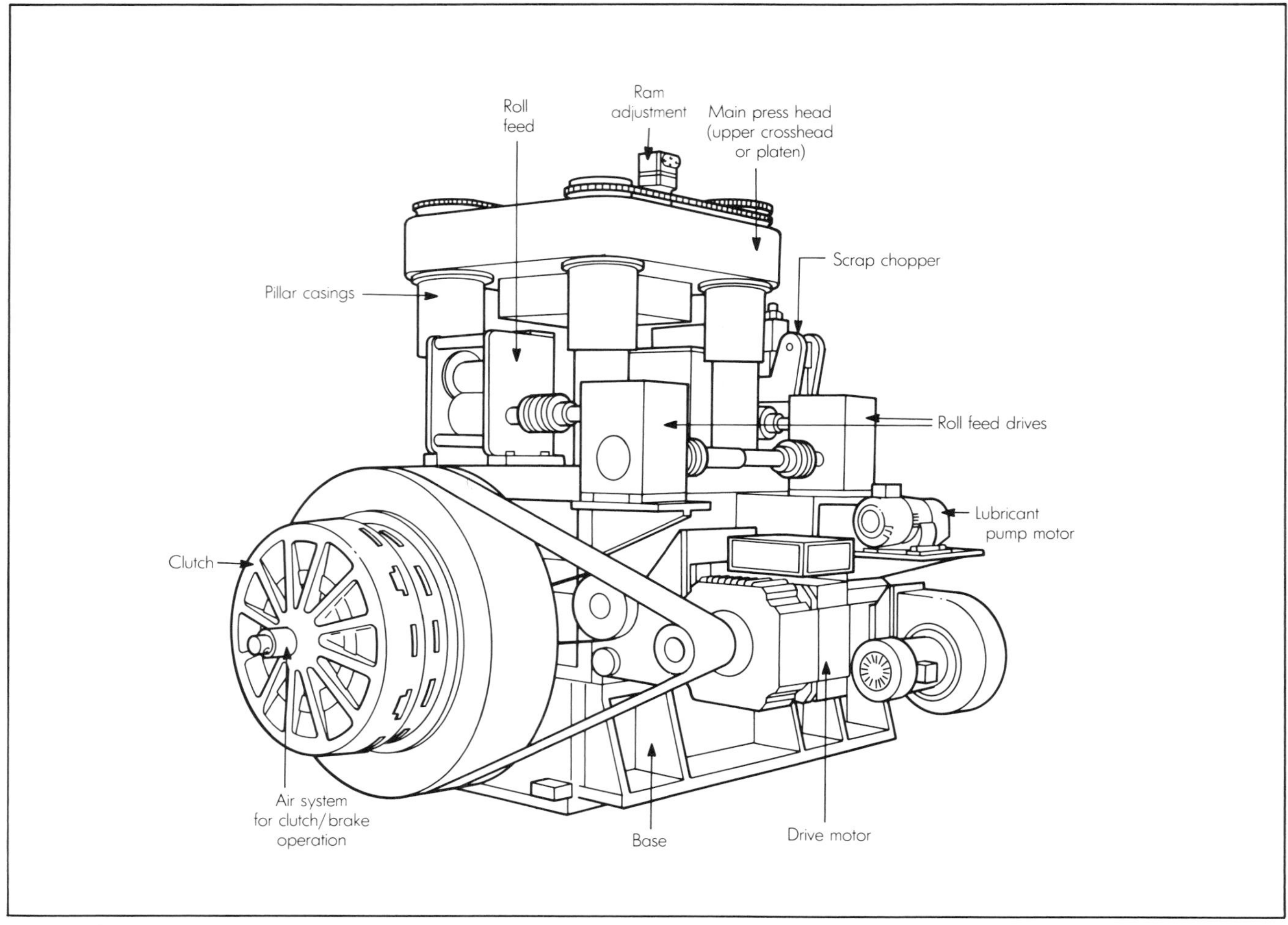


**Fig. 5-65 Dieing machine provides accurate alignment and low center of gravity.** (*Metform International Ltd.*)

Presses built by this manufacturer also feature four solid posts fitted with hardened and ground steel inserts that serve as bearing surfaces for a roller bearing slide. This provides zero-clearance motion throughout the stroke and prevents lateral movement of the slide when it is subjected to uneven loading. Crankshaft assemblies for these presses are of scotch yoke design, instead of the conventional pitman, to provide a strong connection with fewer moving parts, thus contributing to improved accuracy. Other features include micrometer adjustment of shutheight and overload protection.

### FLEXIBLE-DIE FORMING PRESSES

Forming and sometimes blanking with flexible dies (rubber pads or diaphragms backed by high-pressure oil), discussed in Chapter 4, "Sheet Metal Blanking and Forming," is an economical method because it requires only half a die and materials of different thicknesses can be formed with the same tool. Also, one pad or diaphragm can be used to produce different workpieces, thus reducing tooling costs. No scratch marks are produced on the side of the blank facing the flexible die.

Another advantage of flexible-die forming is that localized stress concentrations are avoided because of the uniformly distributed pressure achieved with a rubber pad or diaphragm, and the gradual wrapping of the blank around the tool. A limitation is that the process is slower than forming with mating die halves, thus generally restricting applications to low-volume requirements. However, depending upon workpiece complexity and size, the method may be competitive for production runs to 20,000 of a particular part.

Flexible-die forming is used extensively by the aircraft and aerospace industries, as well as other manufacturers with low-volume requirements. The three major types of flexible-die forming are rubber pad, fluid cell, and fluid forming, which are performed on either standard or special hydraulic presses.

#### Presses for Rubber-Pad Forming

Rubber-pad forming is done with the Guerin or Marform processes (refer to Chapter 4). In the Guerin process, a solid or laminated rubber pad is confined in a retainer on the ram of a press and a form block or punch is mounted on the lower platen. This process is generally limited to forming shallow workpieces of simple shape, with maximum form-block heights of about 4" (100 mm). Cycle times average approximately 1 minute or less. The Marform process is similar except that a die cushion and blankholder are provided to control the pressure and prevent wrinkling during forming, thus permitting deeper draws.

# SPECIAL-PURPOSE PRESSES

Conventional hydraulic presses and hydraulic presses specifically designed for the process are both used for rubber-pad forming. For Marforming, single-action presses are equipped with die cushions and blankholders. Force capacities and die areas of the presses must be sufficient for the operations to be performed.

One builder offers hydraulic, rubber-pad presses employing wire-wound frames (see Fig. 5-66), and separate guiding columns, generally designed with force ratings of 5600-56,000 tons (49.8-498 MN). The wire is stressed to place the press frame under high compression prior to loading. When the press is loaded, the frame remains in slight compression and the major structural members never operate in the tensile mode.

These presses are equipped with a forged-steel retainer for the rubber. The retainer can be provided with a replaceable insert to allow forming with higher pressures. For example, a press can be used at twice the maximum forming pressure over the normal table working area by cutting the work area in half. In such cases, however, the maximum tool heights must be reduced when using high-pressure inserts.

Rubber pad forming presses adapt readily to different degrees of automation with various material-handling systems or the use of pallets for feeding, thus increasing productivity. The presses are also used for forming at elevated temperatures. Hot forming is often used for hard or brittle materials that are difficult to form, and to produce more complex shapes. Blanks and form blocks are heated outside the press by conduction, infrared heaters, or other means.

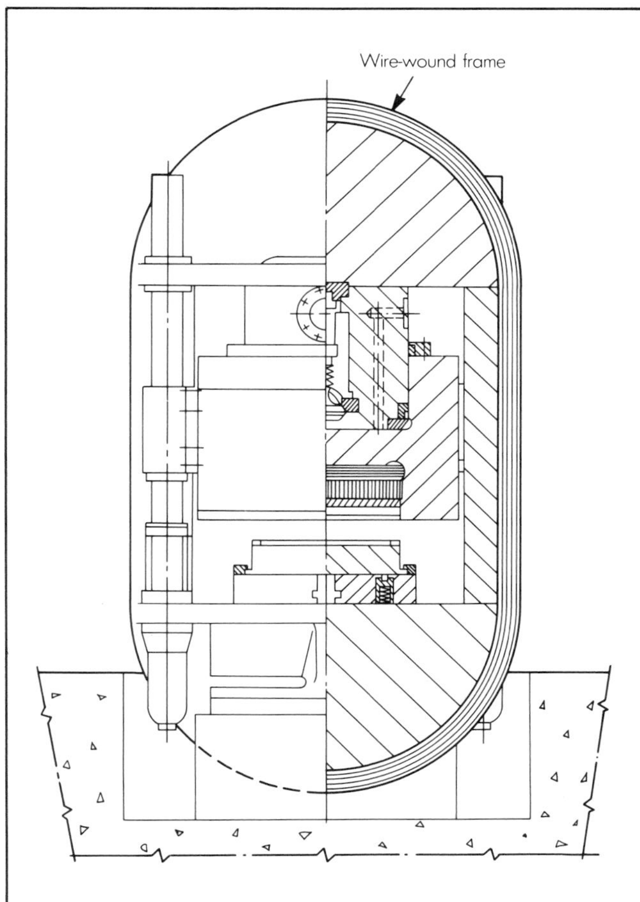


**Fig. 5-66 Rubber-pad hydraulic press with wire-wound frame.** (*ASEA Pressure Systems Inc.*)

## Fluid-Cell Presses

In the fluid-cell process (refer to Chapter 4), high-pressure oil is supplied to a fluid cell (a flexible bladder) in a pressure chamber to form blanks over form blocks or into dies. Improved radial pressure distribution resulting from the oil-filled cell permits this process to form slightly deeper recessed parts, as well as more complex parts with reentrant features, than are possible with the rubber-pad method just described. The fluid-cell method is also capable of forming difficult joggles, beads and ribs in flanges and webs, and all types of wide flanges, including C-shaped and shrink flanges. Tooling height can be as much as 10″ (254 mm).

A number of different parts, including different-shaped workpieces, can be formed in each cycle, the number depending upon press size and capacity, and workpiece size. Cycle time for forming generally varies from 1-3 minutes. Floor-to-floor time depends upon the time required for loading and unloading. Productivity can be increased by using pallet-handling systems.

Special hydraulic presses, without conventional slides or pistons, are used for fluid-cell forming. Two types are the Verson-Wheelon and the ASEA Quintus presses.

**Verson-Wheelon presses.** These consist of horizontal, cylindrical press housings made from laminated, prestressed steel and serving as pressure chambers. Side rails are equipped with built-in counteracting hydraulic cylinders to assist in resisting the tendency of the press housing to go out of round under loads. A fluid cell is provided in the roof of the housing bore, and the bottom of the chamber accommodates a rolling tray holding the tooling and workpieces. Blanks are placed over punches or dies on trays that are power driven into the chamber by a fluid motor with a rack-and-pinion arrangement. High-pressure hydraulic fluid is pumped into the cell, causing the bladder to expand, thus forcing a flexible pad to form the blanks over punches or into dies (see Fig. 5-67). The press is then depressurized, and the tray is removed for unloading and reloading.

These presses are available with operating pressures of 5000-20,000 psi (34.5-138 MPa), having rated force capacities of 2500-82,000 tons (22.2-730 MN). Work areas exceeding 50 x 164″ (1270 x 4166 mm) can be provided. Bladders for the fluid cells are made from neoprene or polyurethane. An automatic, vacuum-pad, hold-up system eliminates bladder sag, thus permitting the use of higher tooling. The presses are furnished with duplex trays, allowing one tray to be unloaded and reloaded while the other tray is in the pressure chamber. The trays can be provided with platens that can be heated to 600° F (316° C) for hot forming.

**ASEA Quintus presses.** These consist of cylindrical frames (pressure vessels) lying on their sides. The frames are circumferentially wound with prestressed high-strength wire to place them in compression, thus preventing tensile stresses when the presses are operated. The upper half of each frame houses the fluid cell into which oil is pumped to create high forming pressure against a flexible diaphragm made from specially cured polyurethane. A polyurethane wear pad that protects the diaphragm is anchored within the pressure chamber, just below the diaphragm (see Fig. 5-68). A vacuum system ensures that the diaphragm and the wear pad return to their original positions after each cycle.

# SPECIAL-PURPOSE PRESSES

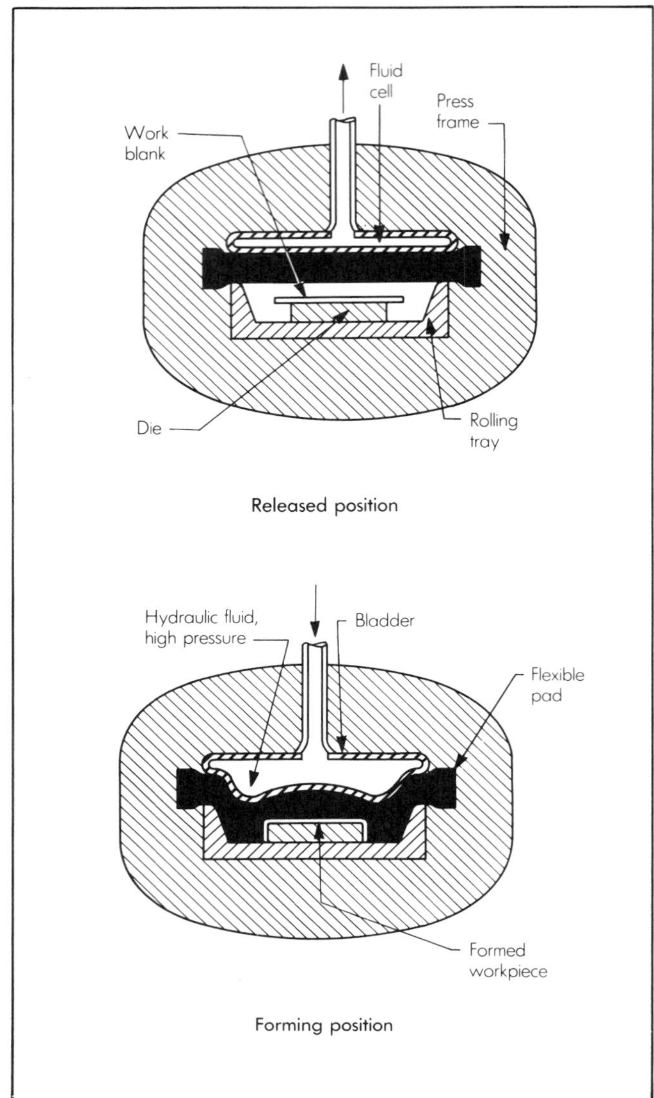


**Fig. 5-67 Cycling of a fluid-cell press.** (*Verson Allsteel Press Co.*)

Trays, onto which the blanks and form blocks or dies are loaded, are rolled into the lower half of the press frame through end openings in the chamber. The press can be equipped with one or more roller-guided trays at each end for alternate unloading and reloading of the pressure chamber. Automatic multipallet systems with computer control are also available.

These presses use direct pumping of hydraulic oil for pressures to 14,500 psi (100 MPa). Pressure intensifiers are used for higher pressures, 20,000 psi (138 MPa) or more. The self-contained hydraulic systems consist of multiple pumps, an oil reservoir tank, a heat exchanger, and filters. Rated force capacities of the presses range from 700-18,000 tons (62-160 MN). Interchangeable domes allow one press to handle large-diameter blanks at low pressures, 4600 psi (31.7 MPa), and small-diameter blanks at high pressures, to 29,000 psi (200 MPa). Tooling heights to 28″ (711 mm) and blanks to 75″ (1905 mm) diam can be accommodated. Cycle times generally vary between 15 and 30 seconds per workpiece.

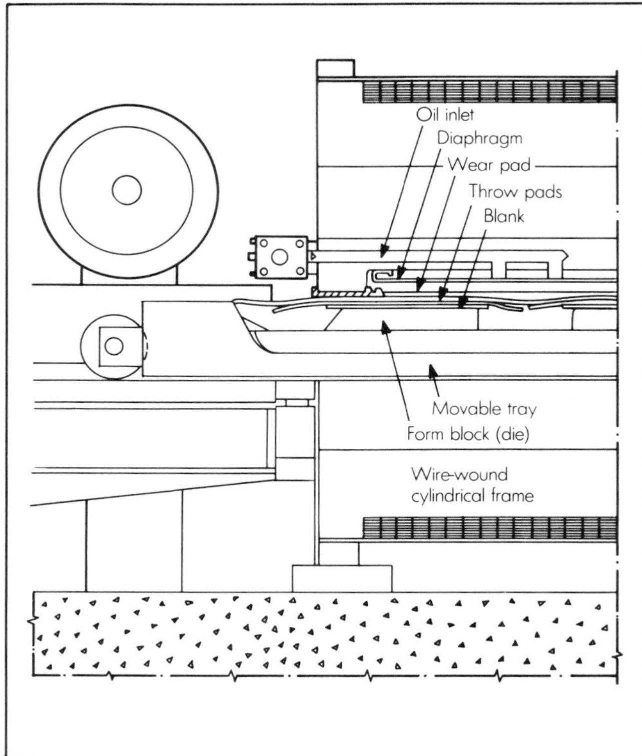


**Fig. 5-68 Loading the pressure chamber of a fluid-cell press.** (*ASEA Pressure Systems Inc.*)

## Presses for Fluid Forming

Special hydraulic presses used for fluid forming have a forming chamber (pressure dome) attached to their slides. The cavities are filled with hydraulic fluid, which is retained by a flexible diaphragm made from rubber. The diaphragm serves both as a blankholder and as a universal die for producing various-shaped parts. A single tool (generally a punch, but in some cases, a cavity die) is mounted on the ram of a hydraulic cylinder in the press bed, and a pressure pad surrounds the tool. The operating sequence is illustrated schematically in Fig. 5-69.

Adjustability and precise control of the pressure in fluid forming permits deeper draws than with conventional dies, the handling of materials that cannot be formed by deep drawing, and the production of a wide range of complex shaped parts in one operation (refer to Chapter 4). Controlled metal flow minimizes localized stress concentrations and buckling of workpiece sidewalls, and the wrapping action of the process results in less thinning of the material. Parts produced are as accurate as the single punch or die used.

Two types of special hydraulic presses used for fluid forming are the Verson Hydroform and the ASEA Quintus presses.

**ASEA Quintus presses.** These presses, having wire-wound frames (as previously discussed under rubber pad and fluid cell presses) are available with force ratings ranging from 700-17,000 tons (6.2-151.2 MN). Interchangeable domes allow one press to handle large-diameter blanks to 75″ (1900 mm) diam at low pressures, 4600 psi (31.7 MPa), and small-diameter blanks at high pressures, to 29,000 psi (200 MPa). Tooling heights to 28″ (711 mm) can be accommodated, and cycle time varies between 15 and 30 seconds per workpiece.

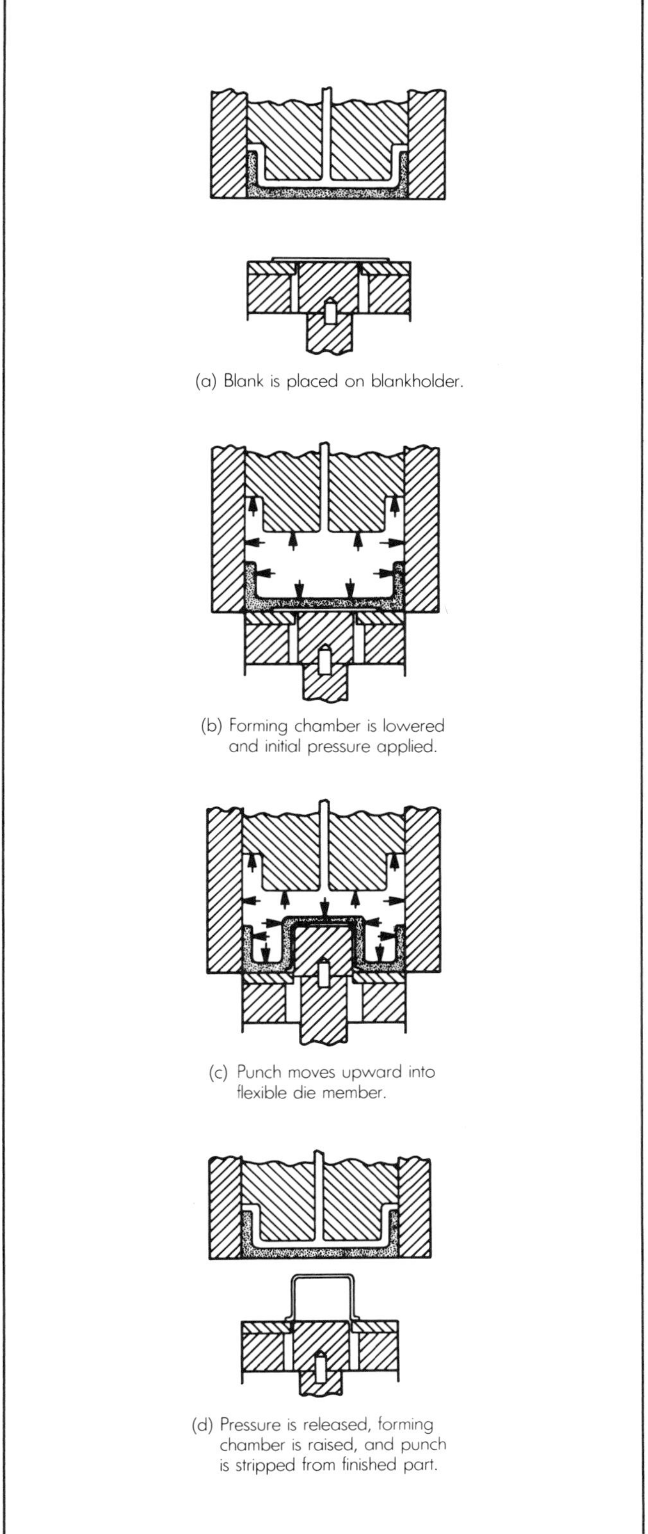

(a) Blank is placed on blankholder.
(b) Forming chamber is lowered and initial pressure applied.
(c) Punch moves upward into flexible die member.
(d) Pressure is released, forming chamber is raised, and punch is stripped from finished part.


**Fig. 5-69 Operational sequence for the fluid forming process.** (*Verson Allsteel Press Co.*)

The presses have a telescoping ram system (see Fig. 5-70) for pressure control and punch movement. An outer ram controls the dome pressure, and an inner ram moves the punch. Dome pressure is varied and controlled by the movement of the outer portion of the dome, which changes the confined volume of oil in the dome.

A preprogrammed paper cam (cut with scissors) controls the dome pressure in relation to the draw depth. The cam is moved by the punch, and the curve produced by the cam covers or uncovers 96 photocells which govern an electrohydraulic control valve. This valve controls oil pressure to the outer cylinder, the pressure being directly proportional to, but much lower than, the dome pressure.

**Verson Hydroform presses.** These presses (see Fig. 5-71) are designed so that all loading is transmitted through solid parent metal with no loading on weldments. They are available with maximum forming pressures of 6000-15,000 psi (41.4-103.4 MPa) and force ratings of 700-4473 tons (4.8-30.8 MN). Maximum blank diameters are 12-40″ (305-1016 mm); punch diameters, 10-34″ (254-864 mm); and draw depths, 7-12″ 178-305 mm).

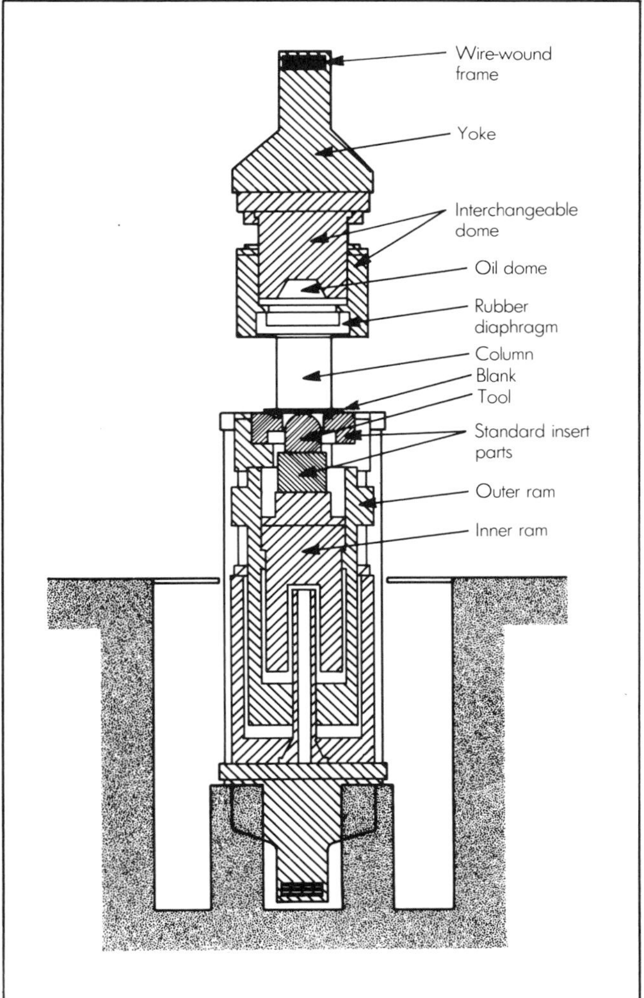


**Fig. 5-70 Hydraulic press with wire-wound frame for fluid forming.** (*ASEA Pressure Systems Inc.*)

# SPECIAL-PURPOSE PRESSES

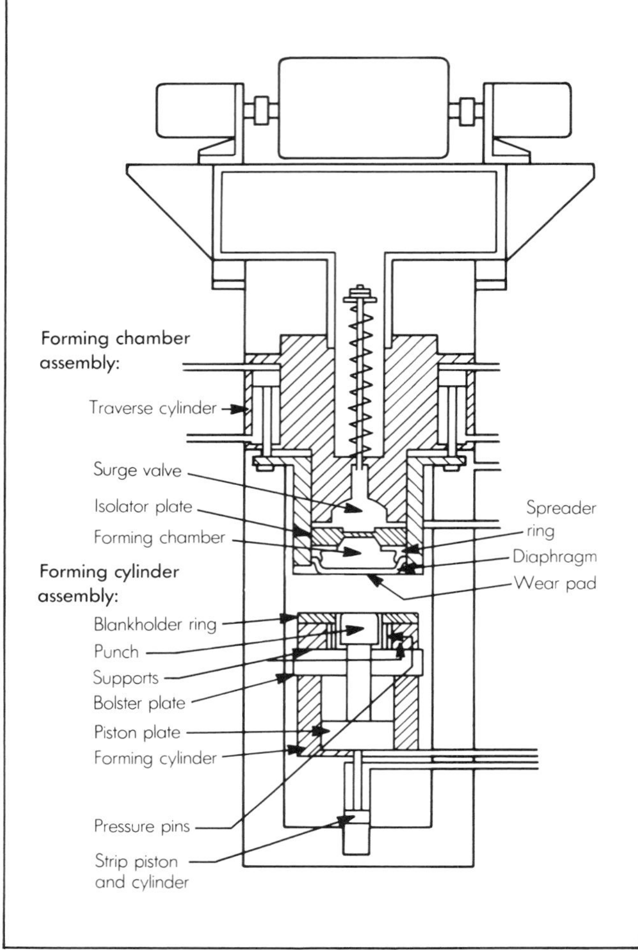


**Fig. 5-71 Details of fluid forming press.** (*Verson Allsteel Press Co.*)

One gage on each press monitors the actual forming pressure during the cycle; a second gage monitors the programmed pressures for the cycle. An easily set, programmable controller ensures automatic cycling. Programmable limit switches monitor movement of the lower punch or die.

A sliding, semiautomatic, hydraulic toolchanger is furnished on these presses to facilitate die changing. When required, the presses can be used as conventional single-action hydraulic presses with standard tooling. Automatic blank loaders and workpiece ejectors are available as optional equipment.

## FINE-BLANKING PRESSES

The fine-blanking process, discussed in Chapter 4 of this volume, "Sheet Metal Blanking and Forming," is generally performed in special triple-action presses designed specifically for the purpose. The presses are available in a range of sizes varying in capacity from 25-2500 tons (222-22 240 kN) or more.

Basic components of most fine-blanking presses are the frame, upper and lower tables for supporting the tooling, a power system, a stock feeder and lubricator, a control system, and a tool safety device. The frames are generally of welded plate construction, with four-column or double-frame web design, but some smaller presses have single-casting frames. Most presses are designed for vertical operation of the ram, but horizontal presses are available. On vertical presses, ram movement for shearing is usually upward, but some presses have downward movement.

### Press Requirements

Essential requirements for fine-blanking presses include the following:

- Means for applying the three necessary forces—clamping, shearing, and opposing (counter)—all independently and infinitely adjustable.
- Rapid advance and return of the ram, but with reduced and adjustable ram speed during shearing, and adjustable stroke.
- A precise point of ram reversal after shearing to prevent the punch from entering the die because of small clearance.
- A heavy-duty frame, more rigid than typical stamping presses, and precise ram guidance to withstand high forces, absorb vibration, and ensure accurate alignment.
- Adequate controls, accessories, and safety devices.

### Source of Power

Fine-blanking presses are available with either a combination of mechanical and hydraulic power or all hydraulic power. Small presses, with capacities to about 350 tons (3114 kN), are usually mechanical/hydraulic, and large-capacity presses are usually all hydraulic.

On mechanical/hydraulic presses, a double toggle performs the shearing and related operations. A separate hydraulic system, preset for the required pressures, provides the clamping force and counterforce.

On all-hydraulic presses, the three forces required are applied hydraulically and are independently and infinitely adjustable. The ram speed is fast for advance and return, but slow and constant during shearing. Ram speed during shearing, however, is adjustable, being made slower for thicker materials and those having higher tensile strengths. An all-hydraulic press rated at 700 tons (6227 kN) is shown in Fig. 5-72.

### Press Controls

Controls generally provided on fine-blanking presses include the following:

- A selector switch for inching, single-stroke, or automatic operation.
- Controls for setting all three forces, ram speed, and feed increments. Various systems make use of cams, electric or electronic sequencers, or programmable controllers.
- A tool-safety device that stops the press automatically if a workpiece or slug remains in the tooling.
- Guards connected to the control system to keep the operator from the die area when the press is in operation.

### Press Accessories

Automated installations of fine-blanking presses include a stock loader. This can be either a strip feeder or a decoiler, usually with a roll-type stock straightener. Some operations require only a pull-through feeder, while others need a push-and-pull feeder. Grippers for the feed units are sometimes operated pneumatically for light-duty operations, and generally hydraulically for heavy-duty requirements.

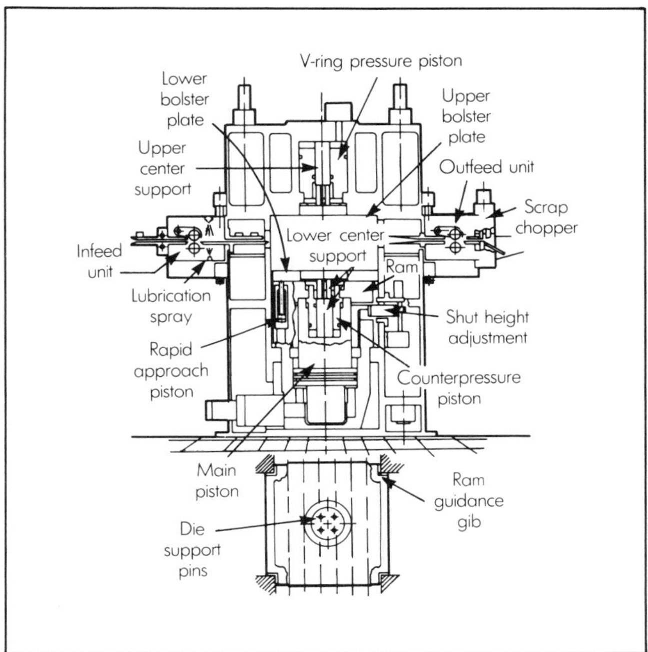


**Fig. 5-72 Triple-action, fine-blanking hydraulic press rated at 700 tons (6227 kN).** (*Feintool Equipment Corp., Schuler Inc.*)

A lubricating unit is essential to apply lubricant to both the top and bottom surfaces of the stock. This is sometimes a mist-free spray system automatically synchronized with the stock feed unit. Lubricant is also often applied with felt-covered or brush-type rollers.

Scrap choppers are usually the guillotine type, with the blades operated pneumatically or hydraulically. Light workpieces and slugs can be blown clear of the die by air jets, but heavy parts require mechanical extraction. Means are available for separating the workpieces and slugs; and in some cases, the workpieces are automatically oriented, burr-side up, for transfer to an abrasive belt grinder. The die areas of fine-blanking presses are often enclosed to ensure safety and reduce noise.

## FOUR-SLIDE MACHINES

Four-slide or multislide machines are versatile presses equipped with progressive dies for automatically producing small, intricately shaped parts to close tolerances. Originally developed to form wire, these machines are now also used to progressively form sheet-metal parts. The machines straighten the metal as it is taken from a coil, feed it in exact lengths, form and cut off the parts, and form them further if required, thus minimizing or eliminating the need for secondary operations. Substantial material savings are generally obtained compared to other pressworking methods.

Parts formed on four-slide machines are comparable to those formed in progressive dies on presses, but more difficult operations can be accomplished without the expense of providing slides in the dies. Slides that can be timed independently are a standard part of four-slide machines, and they can be tooled inexpensively. Forms can be completed within the dies or over a block at the forming end of the machine. The form tools can dwell at closure while other operations are performed by auxiliary slides. If the part cannot be completed in one cycle, it can be transferred further out on the mandrel and completed in succeeding cycles (called multistage forming). Four-slide presses are generally eccentric operated, but toggle presses are available for heavy coining operations.

Four-slide machines are available in a range of sizes and for operation in the horizontal or vertical plane. The layout of a typical horizontal machine is presented in Fig. 5-73. All working components are mounted on the machine table. Camshafts, driven by a variable-speed motor through a flywheel and gears, actuate the press section and slides in synchronized movements.

Cams control the motion of all forming tools. One or more die heads in the press area are equipped with progressive dies and can be adjusted along the longitudinal axis of the machine. The machine slides are fitted with the tooling necessary for forming parts around the mandrels or arbors, usually referred to as the kingposts. Machine accessories include multiple-roll straighteners for wire or flat stock, adjustable-stroke feed units, auxiliary slides, tapping units, welders, roll feeds, and units for point, winding, threading, and assembling.

Stock entering the press section goes through a progressive sequence in the die(s). Parts are then cut from the coil; and if additional forming is required, they are held for forming at the kingpost. Forming action at the kingpost is accomplished with two, three, four, or more of the machine slides. If springback is encountered with the formed parts, corrections can be made by adjusting the tooling. The design of dies for four-slide machines is discussed in Chapter 6 of this volume, "Die Design for Sheet Metal Forming."

Workpiece size is limited on four-slide machines. The maximum stock width is generally about 3" (76 mm), but some machines accept material to 8" (203 mm) wide. Another possible limitation is the long setup time required, usually 2-4 hours. This may make them uneconomical for short production runs. Another possible limitation is that less force can be applied than for most presses.

## TRANSFER PRESSES

Transfer techniques in metalforming, in which multiple operations are performed in succession on a single press, are accomplished with progressive or transfer dies (refer to Chapter 6 in this volume, "Die Design for Sheet Metal Forming") in conventional presses or on special transfer presses having integral transfer mechanisms. Selection of a specific method depends upon many factors including workpiece design and material, production requirements, die and press costs, and press availability. This section is confined to a discussion of automatic, high-production transfer presses, which are single presses equipped with multiple die stations.

### Advantages

Performing multiple operations on a single press can increase productivity and decrease costs. Transfer presses eliminate the need for secondary operations; annealing requirements between operations; and in-process inspection, storage, and handling of workpieces.

The use of transfer presses reduces labor, floor space, energy, and maintenance requirements, compared to using several presses to perform the operations. Other advantages include safer and quieter operation, more efficient utilization of raw material, and improved quality and uniformity of the stampings produced.

# CHAPTER 5

## SPECIAL-PURPOSE PRESSES

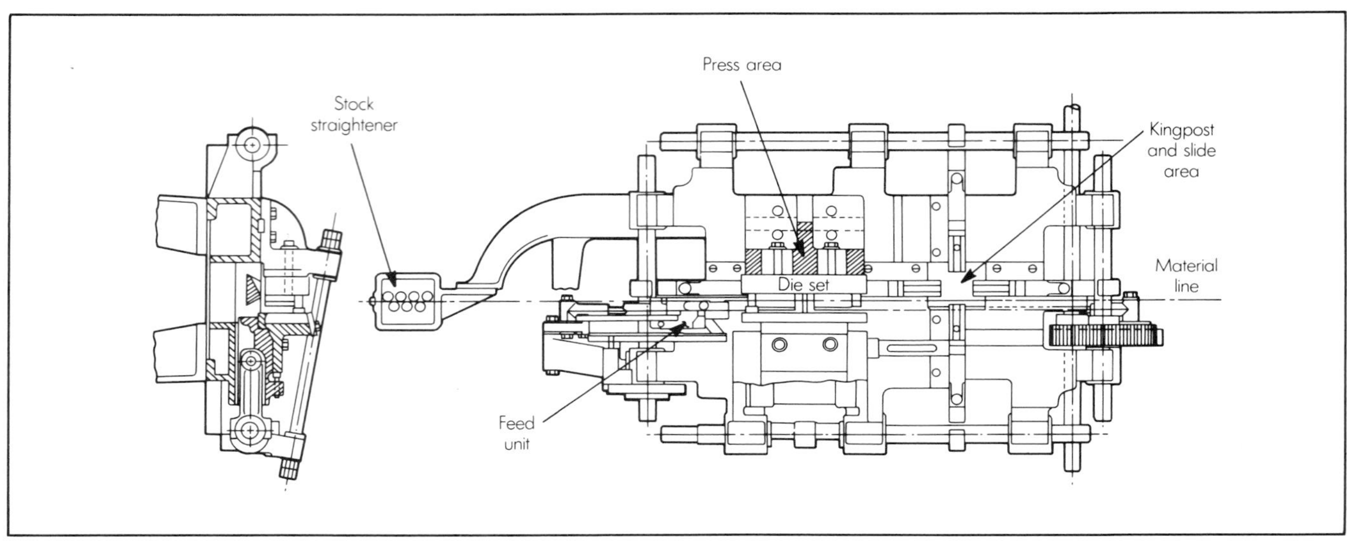


**Fig. 5-73 Four-slide machine. Stock passes through press section, then on to kingpost for final forming.** (*A. H. Nilson Machine Co.*)

### Applications

Transfer presses should be considered whenever 4000 or more identical stampings requiring three or more operations are needed daily. A total production run of 30,000-50,000 identical parts is generally economical between tooling changes. Most transfer presses are designed to make more than one part, and they are often used for families of parts that are similar in size, shape, and thickness. One press is being used to produce 22 different parts.

Stampings are being produced in a wide range of sizes and shapes. Any configuration that can be grasped by mechanical fingers is suitable, and the parts do not have to be concentric. Practically any operation that can be done in any other press can be performed on transfer presses. Typical operations include blanking, piercing, forming, trimming, drawing, flanging, embossing, and coining.

Major users of transfer presses are the automotive and appliance industries. Automotive parts produced on these presses include wheel covers, tail-light assemblies, control and suspension arms, transmission parts, catalytic converters, and timing-gear case covers. Appliance components include refrigerator, freezer, washer, and dryer parts.

Transfer presses have been built with capacities to 6000 tons (53.4 MN) for automatically producing stampings from coil stock or blanks to 3/8" (9.5 mm) thick. These presses have from 3-18 stations, with an 8-48" (203-1219 mm) center distance between stations and a 6-38" (152-965 mm) slide stroke; they operate at 4-40 spm.

### Press Selection

Selection of a specific transfer press requires careful analysis of the design of the workpiece or family of parts to be produced, the materials from which they are made, and the number and types of operations to be performed. Such analyses determine the bed size, shutheight, stroke, and speed requirements. Die space must be sufficient to accommodate all the dies, the feed and transfer units, and means for loading and unloading. Limiting factors with respect to press speed include the depth of the workpieces and capabilities of the die and transfer unit.

Ample rigidity is essential to withstand off-center loading, and precise parallelism is needed to produce accurate parts. Sufficient press capacity (force and energy) is necessary to prevent overloading. The capacity needed must be based on the total requirements for all stations plus die cushion and stripping force requirements, as well as the distribution of loading.

Straight-side mechanical presses of tie-rod construction, with two-point suspension for each slide, are generally employed. Twin-end drives of the crankshaft or eccentric-gear types are most common. Cam drives are sometimes used to provide more uniform stroke speed and force, as well as dwells during the stroke. Toggle drives are employed to provide greater force with shorter strokes.

It is rare that the force requirements of the individual dies are distributed evenly over the total die area. As a result, it is generally necessary to use a press of increased capacity to accommodate off-center loading. When force requirements vary widely between operations or when the number of operations requires excessive press width, multiple-column construction is used with two or three slides. Such presses have a single bed and crown, but individual slides between columns with independent or a common drive. Each slide can have different dimensions and exert a different force, but all slides are synchronized to function as one.

A 4600 ton (40.9 MN), four-column, three-slide transfer press, 54 ft (16.5 m) long, is shown in Fig. 5-74. The right-hand and center slides are each rated at 2000 tons (17.8 MN); the left-hand slide, 600 tons (5.3 MN). Heavy coining is done with the single die mounted in the center-slide position. This press operates at 18 spm to produce brake backing plates and other automotive parts.

### Coil Stock or Blanks

Transfer presses are supplied with coil feeds or blank destackers. For some cold extruding operations (refer to Chapter 13 of this volume, "Wire Drawing, Extruding and Heading"), slugs are supplied from a hopper. The choice between coil stock and blanks is influenced by the shape of the workpieces, the most efficient use of the raw materials, availability of separate blanking presses, and the effect and frequency of coil loading on the production rate.

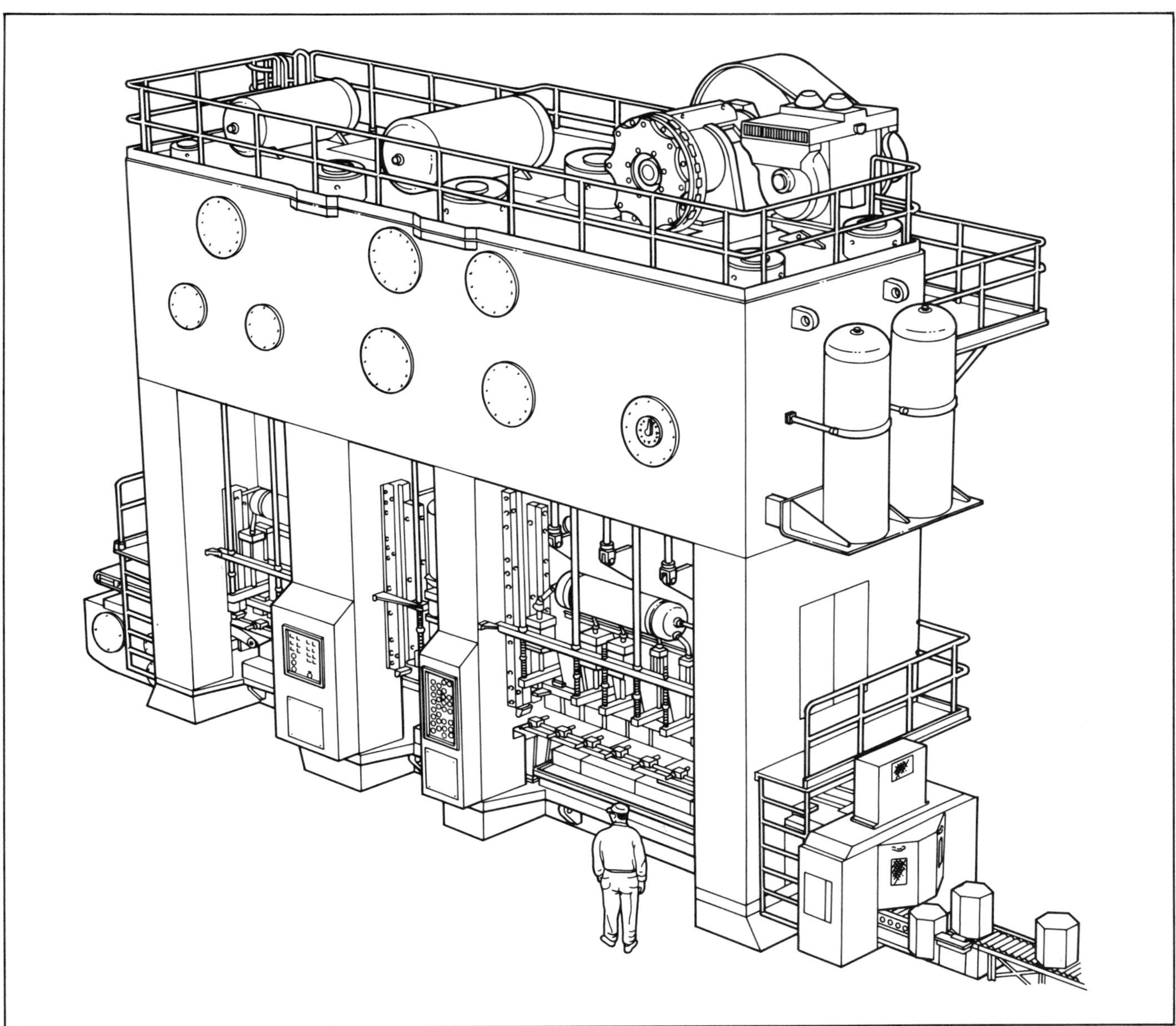

**Fig. 5-74 A four-column, three-slide transfer press with a rated force capacity of 4600 tons (40.9MN).** (*Verson Allsteel Press Co.*)

Coil feeding, with blanking done in the transfer press, is often preferable when the blank is square or rectangular and scrap loss is minimal. If the blanks are round or irregular shaped, a joggle or zig-zag-type coil feed (discussed previously in this chapter) should be considered. Such feeds can provide material savings to 12%, permit using more economical double-width coils, and reduce downtime for coil changing. With coil feeding, scrap is generally removed from front to back in the press, over the blanking station.

Precut blanks are supplied to transfer presses by magazine or stack feeds. Stacks of blanks are moved into position automatically either in-line on a shuttle-type roller conveyor (see Fig. 5-75, view *a*) or by a dial indexing table (view *b*). Shuttle-type stack feeds with in-line conveyors lend themselves to automatic blanking with the blanking presses linked to the transfer presses and delivering blanks on demand. Dial-type stack feeds automatically reposition a new stack of blanks when required without stopping production.

Each stack of blanks is automatically and continuously elevated to the feeding position by a cylinder. The blanks are picked up, one at a time, from the top of the stack by either suction cups or magnets. Feed fingers on the transfer unit carry each blank to the first die station.

## Transfer Units

Several types of transfer units are offered by different builders of transfer presses. Most use a combination cam and gear feed powered directly from the main press drive. They are available for single-axis (in-line) or three-axis, lift-and-carry movements.

# SPECIAL-PURPOSE PRESSES

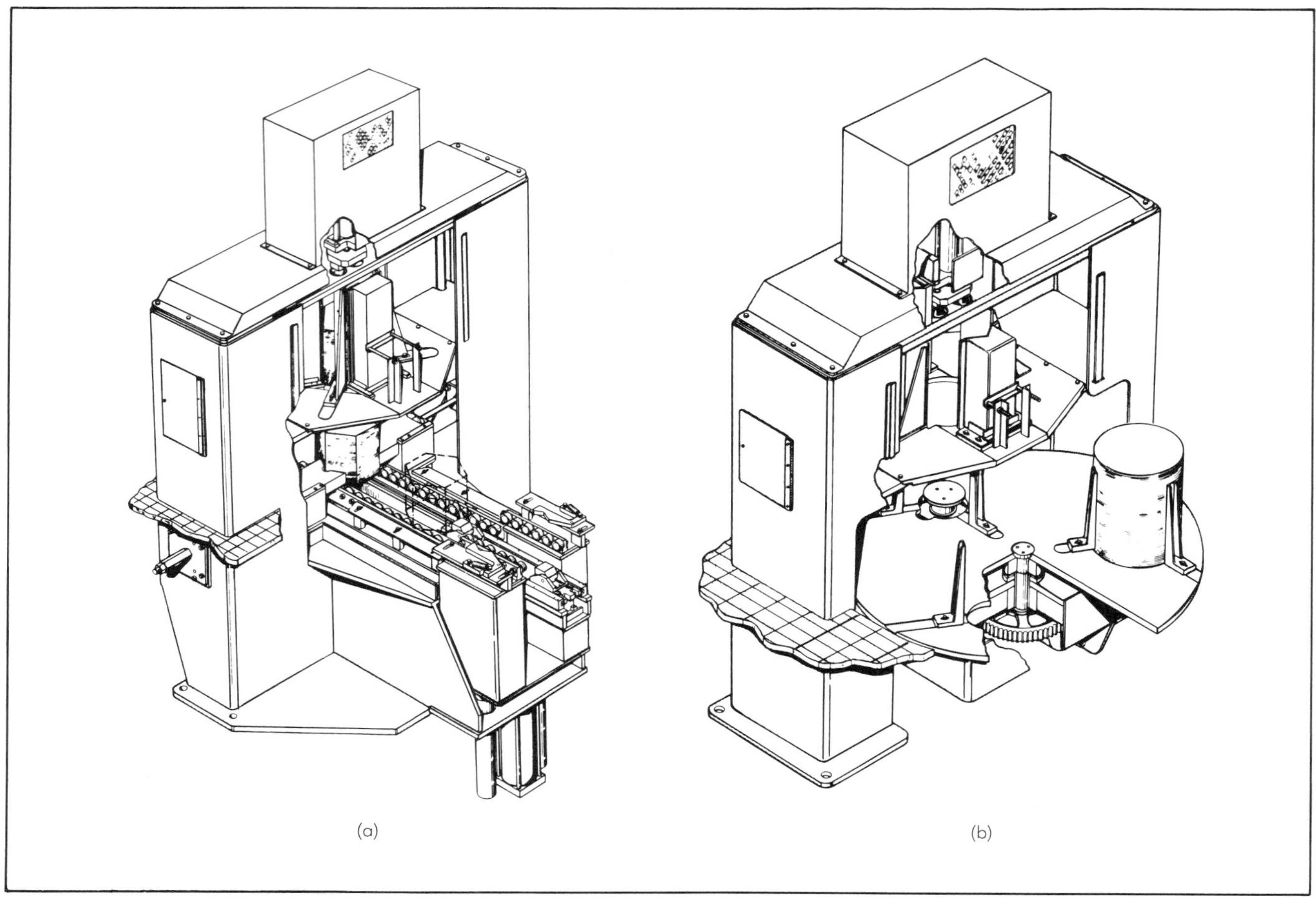


**Fig. 5-75 Stacks of precut blanks are supplied to transfer presses by: (a) roller conveyor or (b) dial indexing table.** (*Verson Allsteel Press Co.*)

**Single-axis transfers.** These units are used whenever the stampings can be moved over relatively flat die surfaces. One design consists of two feed bars, one along the front and the other along the rear of the dies, which can be any length to extend the full length of the tooling area. The bars move with a horizontal reciprocating motion, the stroke corresponding to the center distance between stations. Bar movements are protected against overloads or misfeeds by safety slip clutches on the power takeoff shaft and the bar racks.

A pair of feed fingers for each die station is mounted on the bars. Rack-and-pinion drives on the feed bars cause the fingers to automatically extend towards and retract away from the stampings during each cycle. Air or electric sensors are provided on the fingers to signal proper sequencing or the loss of stampings.

As the press ram rises, the feed fingers advance to grasp the stampings, which are lifted from the dies by cushions. The feed bars move horizontally to transfer each stamping to the next die station. The fingers then retract and the bars return to their starting positions, ready for the next cycle. Gripping the opposed sides of each stamping ensures positive control throughout the transfer cycle.

**Lift-and-carry transfer.** These units lift the stampings above the lower dies, move them to the next stations, and lower them into the dies (see Fig. 5-76), generally over pilots for precise positioning. The lifting action of these units eliminates the need for cushions in the press bed for this purpose.

The feed bars of lift-and-carry units are similar to those for single-axis transfers except that a lower rack-and-pinion mechanism is provided to raise and lower the bars. Finger motion is also similar, but gripping jaws are added. The jaws automatically open and close to clamp the stampings during transfer and to release them at the subsequent stations. Positive gripping with jaws permits faster transfer. Workpiece turnover capabilities can be provided with these transfer units.

## Press Controls

Extensive electronic controls are necessary for automatic, continuous monitoring of all essential functions and sequencing of transfer presses. Many systems include a graphic display board or diagnostic fault panel that indicates the reasons for press stoppages and shows the specific locations of troubles.

Functions generally monitored include the load and temperature of the main drive motor, the temperatures of critical bearings, performance of the feed unit and lubrication system, workpiece locations at each station, overloads, and air and hydraulic pressures. Various safety devices for automatically stopping the press include sensing units on the fingers and overload clutches on the transfer unit, overload connections in the main slide(s), and the lubrication system.

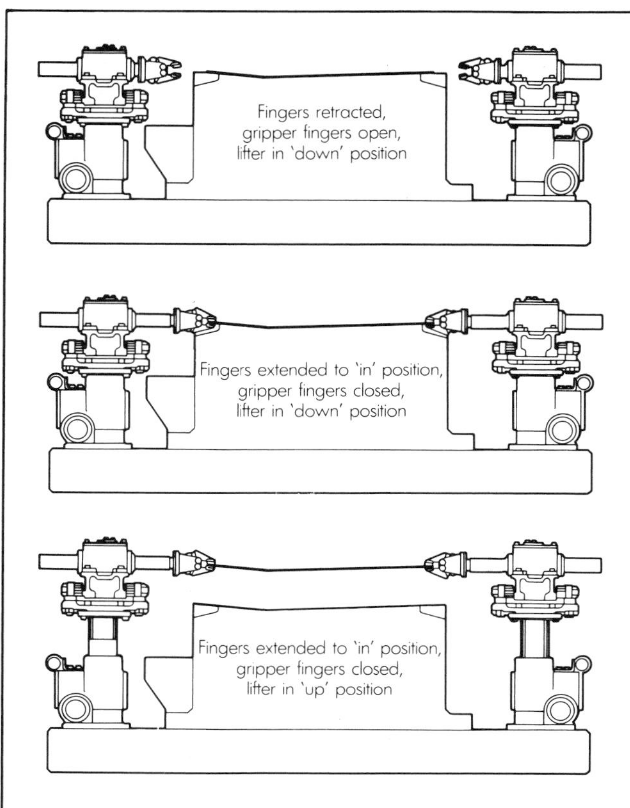


**Fig. 5-76 Operation of lift-and-carry transfer unit.** (*Verson Allsteel Press Co.*)

Sensing of workpiece presence is sometimes accomplished by passing low-voltage current from one transfer finger through the stamping to the finger on the opposite side of the workpiece at each station. If either finger at any station is not contacting the workpiece adequately, the current is interrupted and the press stopped. Safety detectors are provided at the entry end to protect the press and tooling against running double or triple blanks. Some of these detectors weigh the incoming blanks and automatically dump them if more than a single blank is present.

Transfer presses are available with means for digital inputs to reduce setup time. Selector and thumbwheel switches are used to preset production quantity, die height, transfer distance, distance between feed bars, and blank thickness. Manual operations still required include (1) changing the dies and feed bars on a moving bolster outside the press and (2) adjusting air pressures for the knockouts and die cushions.

### Accessories for Transfer Presses

Accessories often required for the most efficient use of transfer presses include an inching drive to facilitate setup, an automatic oil and grease lubrication system, knockouts in the slide(s) over each die station for stripping workpieces, and die cushions at required stations for drawing or stripping purposes.

Moving bolsters and automatic die clamping, discussed previously in this chapter, are desirable for rapid toolchanging. Individual dies on the slide(s) and bolster can also be changed independently.

Adjustable-speed motor drives (discussed previously in this chapter) are frequently used to permit changing the press speed for different applications. To reduce the speed for some drawing operations, while maintaining required production rates, constant-energy, adjustable-speed drives are employed. Such drives permit rapid advance, a reduced speed for drawing, and rapid return.

Speed of the press is changed by varying the slip rate between the inertia wheel and the clutch rotor. This is accomplished with a closed-loop control system which changes the magnitude of the current supplied to the electromagnetic coils.

## DIE-SET TRANSFER PRESSES

These presses (see Fig. 5-77) have cam-driven slides with built-in transfer mechanisms that provide positive workpiece control. They are available with force capacities of 15-250 tons (133-2224 kN), with speeds ranging from 25-300 spm, depending upon the force rating. This type of transfer press is used to produce smaller workpieces than the transfer presses discussed in the preceding section of this chapter. Maximum blank diameters that can be handled range from 1-7" (25-178 mm), and maximum punch penetrations into the dies vary from 5/8 to 4 3/4" (16-121 mm), depending upon the force capacity rating of the press.

Simple die sets can be used with these presses, and center distances can be adjusted to provide up to 14 stations. The press beds are machined to accept movable, cam-operated, pers are aas modules for the number of stations to be used.

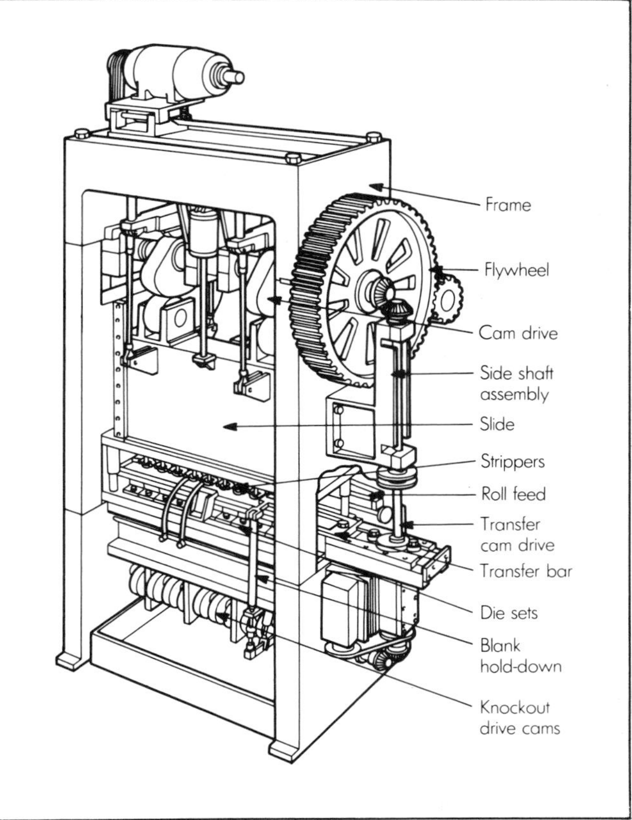


**Fig. 5-77 Die-set transfer press with cam-driven slide and integrated transfer mechanism.** (*Waterbury Farrel Div., Textron Inc.*)

To prevent material wrinkling in the first forming station, a cam-driven blank hold-down is available. Holding sleeves may be applied at subsequent stations to eliminate the use of cushions. For changing the number of stations, transfer drive packages are available. These consist of a transfer cam for the correct center distance and a transfer slide and gripping fingers for the specified number of stations.

The integral transfer mechanism is driven by a cam through a side shaft assembly, which in turn, is driven from the main camshaft through bevel gears. Adjustable fingers transfer the workpieces from station to station. The cam-driven slide requires less operating stroke to produce the same depth of draw as a crank-actuated slide. This shorter stroke permits lower press heights for comparable depths of draw, higher speeds, and lower forming velocities.

Material supplied to the die-set transfer presses can be in the form of strip or coil stock, blanks, cups, or preforms, and various feed units (discussed previously in this chapter) can be used. Scrap shears can be integrated with any of the feed units.

## MULTISTATION-PLUNGER TRANSFER PRESS

This type of transfer press, often referred to as an eyelet machine, has the tooling in each separate station actuated by individual cam-actuated plungers. Each machine consists of as many as 12 single-plunger presses mounted in a single frame. The name eyelet persists from the original machines used to produce eyelets and similar parts. Modern multistation transfer machines, however, are being used to produce a wide variety of deep-drawn parts, as well as to perform many other operations, including blanking and piercing, ironing, bulging, curling, necking, flanging, threading, knurling, and trimming.

### Advantages

The motion of each plunger and its punch is individually adjustable to the action of a fixed-time transfer mechanism. By adjusting the motion of each plunger to the transfer, as well as to the work performed, every workpiece reaches the top of the die, ready for transfer, at the same time.

All plungers pause simultaneously, each with its punch still fully inserted in the work, until the transfer fingers have firmly grasped the part. As a result, the parts are always under complete control of either the punches or the transfer fingers.

A portion of each cycle can be used for operations such as side piercing and thread rolling. Force can be applied high up on the stroke, often allowing the use of a smaller capacity press for drawing operations. Presses can be mounted in tandem to permit additional operations on workpieces requiring them.

### Stock Requirements

Strip or coil stock, blanks, cups, or preforms can be fed to the press. With strip or coil stock, a blanking punch is mounted on the press slide or a plunger, and blanking is performed at the first station. A stagger-feed system can be used to automatically shift the stock from side to side, thus providing double-row blanking in one pass. A scrap shear can be integrated with the feed unit, eliminating the need for a take-up reel and simplifying scrap handling.

### Plunger Actions

Each press station has its own individual set of lifter and plunger cams mounted on a common shaft (see Fig. 5-78). The plunger cam drives the plunger down by means of the roller follower. The lifter cam raises the plunger by acting on the lifter arm. Both cam followers are rigidly connected through the lifter rod. Upstroke motion is adjusted by moving the lifter arm up or down on the lifter rod. Depth of draw into the die on the downstroke determines length of the punch.

### Transfer Mechanism

The integrated, universal transfer mechanism, also cam driven, advances and returns once for each work cycle. As it completes its return stroke, the spring-loaded transfer fingers slip around and grip the work which waits at the top of the die. At transfer engagement, all punches are stationary and fully in

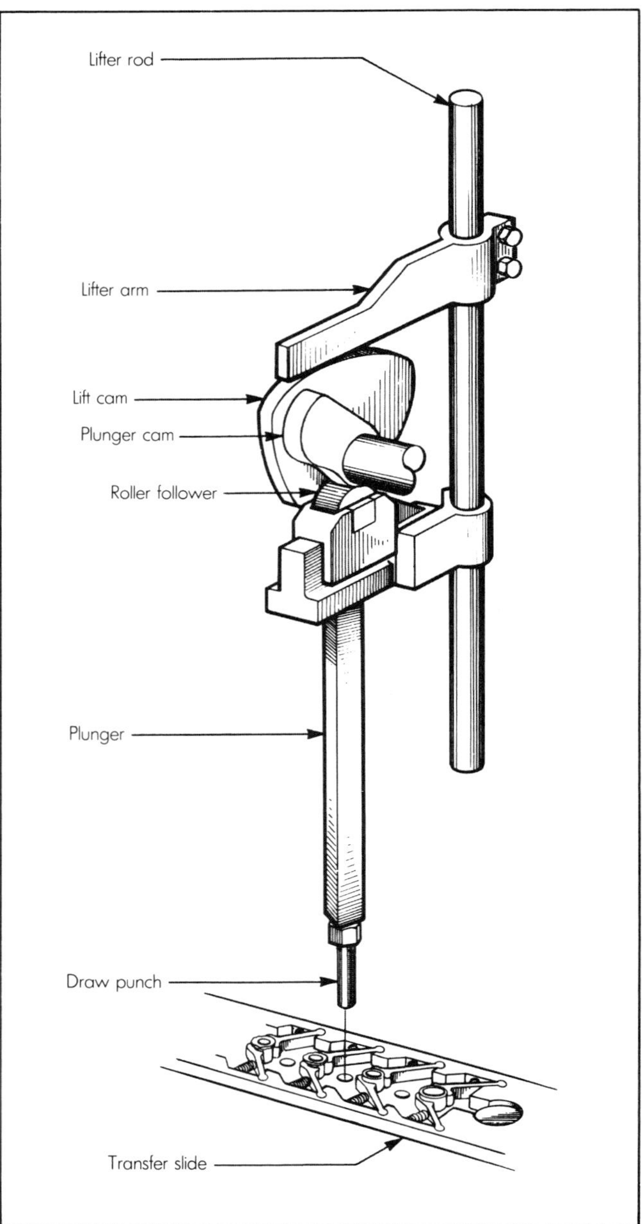


**Fig. 5-78 Independent, cam-operated plunger for multistation transfer press. (*Waterbury Farrel Div., Textron Inc.*)**

the work. As the punches withdraw, strippers keep the work in place between stationary transfer fingers. When all punches clear, the transfer advances the work to the next station. The fingers hold the work until the punch carries it into the die. Then the cycle repeats.

## PORTAL PRESSES

Portal presses are hydraulic machines for forming large plates to 10" (254 mm) thick. Plates can be formed with single and double curvatures by means of conventional tools. The presses are used extensively in making ship hulls, long pipes, pressure vessels, tank ends, domes, and other components.

### Press Construction

The portal press has an upper beam and two side frames which form a vertically movable portal (see Fig. 5-79). Each frame consists of two rectangular columns and an upper and lower semicircular yoke. The open side frames are wrapped with prestressed high-strength steel wire to obtain even load distribution and eliminate stress concentrations. The frames are guided in a fixed lower beam which rests on the press foundation.

Two or four double-acting hydraulic cylinders, located below floor level in the lower beam, raise and lower the upper beam. Servo-controlled, variable-delivery, axial-piston pumps provide variable speed. Pressure sensing units for each cylinder stop the press when the maximum preset force is reached.

Tables, on which punches and dies are mounted, are provided on the upper and lower beams, and they can be arranged to be moved along the beams. Beams and tables can be extended through the side frames for gap-press forming operations and to facilitate toolchanging. An optional moving bolster can be used to load/unload tools and workpieces to the front or back of the press.

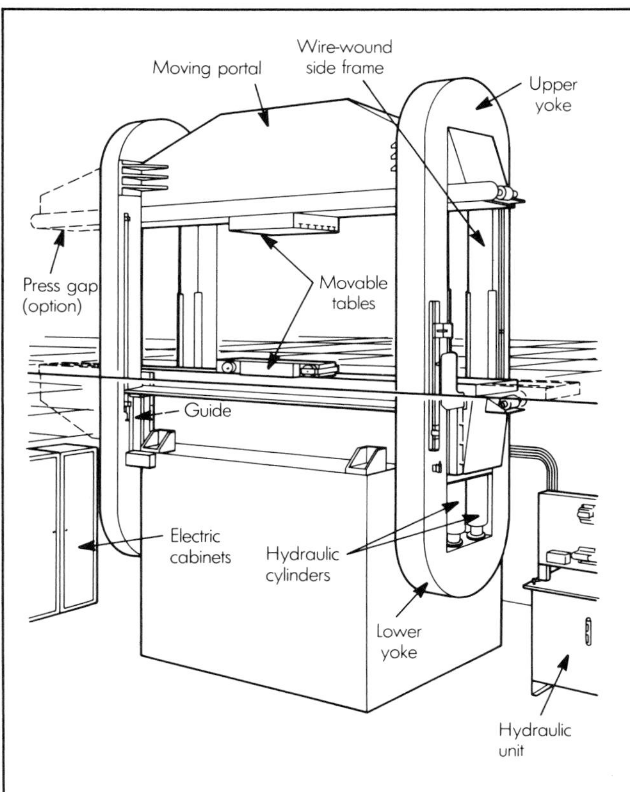


**Fig. 5-79 Hydraulic portal press for forming large, thick plates.** (*ASEA Pressure Systems Inc.*)

Portal presses are available with force ratings of 1000-10,000 tons (8.9-89 MN). Left-to-right spans of 4-6 m (13-20 ft) are standard; spans to 12 m (40 ft) can be provided for special purposes. Stroke lengths available are 1000-2200 mm (39-87"), with daylight openings of 2000-3800 mm (78-150"). Pressing speeds are from 7-12 mm/s (0.28-0.47 in./s), with rates of 100 mm/s (3.94 in./s) advance and retraction.

### Press Controls

In addition to standard press controls, plate deformation values can be preset and read on a digital display for accurate and fully controlled forming. Sensors are available for mounting in the centers of the lower tools for measuring pressing depth when cylindrical or spherical forming is performed. The sensors are connected to the hydraulic pumps for controlling press strokes. Just before a preset value is reached, the press slows to a creep speed and stops within 0.2 mm (0.008") of the preset value. This system can be arranged to compensate for springback.

To use computerized control systems, the presses and material-handling equipment must be provided with measuring systems. Thumbwheel switches are employed to preset the advance stroke, press stroke, and return stroke, based on previous experience or calculations. For repetitive work, all operation data for forming the first plate is recorded by the computer and repeated for forming additional plates. Programming can be improved each time the system is used. The computerized control systems measure plate deformation during the forming cycle and can be used to compensate for springback of workpieces.

### Material and Tool Handling

Portal presses are available with various degrees of automation. Integrated material and tool-handling systems are provided by lateral travel of the upper and lower tool tables, and plate manipulator carriages. Hydraulically operated, movable carriages with gripping and lifting devices permit handling large plates for stepwise pressing to single or double-curvature forms.

#### References

1. "Glossary of Mechanical Press Terms," ANSI Standard B5.49, American Society of Mechanical Engineers, New York.
2. E. W. Bliss Div., Gulf & Western Manufacturing Co., *Bliss Power Press Handbook*, Southfield, MI, 1950.
3. Frank W. Wilson, Philip D. Harvey, and Charles B. Gump, *Die Design Handbook*, Society of Manufacturing Engineers, Dearborn, MI, 1965.
4. "Mechanical Power Presses, General Purpose Single Point, Gap Type (Metric)," ANSI Standard B5.52M, American Society of Mechanical Engineers, New York.
5. *Ibid.*

# BIBLIOGRAPHY

## Bibliography


Bell, Lewis H. *Guidelines to Power Press Noise Reduction*. SME Technical Paper TE80-338, 1980.

"Brake Monitoring." *Manufacturing Engineering* (February 1976), pp. 24-30.

__________. "Four-slides, Part 1—The Press with a Difference." *Manufacturing Engineering* (February 1978), pp. 34-40.

Dallas, Daniel B. "Metricating the Pressworking Equations—Part 1." *Manufacturing Engineering* (February 1976), pp. 36-41.

Daniels, Harold R. *Mechanical Press Handbook*, 3rd. ed. Boston: Cahners Publishing Co., Inc., 1969.

Fisher, Nicholas. *Principles of Mechanical Power Presses*. SME Technical Paper MF76-285,1976.

Hufford, Donald L. *Blank Feeding Equipment*. SME Technical Paper MF77-596, 1977.

Janitz, John A. "Pressworking: Toward Higher Speeds, Greater Efficiencies." *Manufacturing Engineering* (August 1982), pp. 91-92.

Johnson, Walter C. *Total System, Heavy Tonnage, High Production Transfer Presses*. SME Technical Paper MS79-958,1979.

Lown, Robert G. *Hydraulic Presses in the 80's*. SME Technical Paper MF82-918, 1982.

Mankowsky, Vincent J. *The Selection of Conventional Metal Forming Presses*. SME Technical Paper MF69-522, 1969.

"Mechanical Power Press Safety Engineering Guide." PB80-195340, National Technical Information Service, Springfield, VA, (September 1976).

*Power Press Safety Manual*, 3rd ed. National Safety Council, Chicago, 1979.

Wick, Charles. "Advances in Press Feeds for Coil Stock, Part 1: Slide Feeds, Part 2: Roll Feeds, Part 3: Independent Roll Feeds." *Manufacturing Engineering* (February 1980), pp. 68-71; (March 1980), pp. 84-88; and (April 1980), pp. 112-114.

__________. "Don't Overlook Energy in Press Selection." *Manufacturing Engineering* (July 1975), pp. 26-27.

__________. "Power Press Safety." *Manufacturing Engineering* (February 1972), pp. 19-25; (March 1972), pp. 16-21; (April 1972), pp. 26-29; and (May 1972), pp. 22-26.

CHAPTER

# 6

# Die Design for Sheet Metal Forming

# DIE DESIGN FOR SHEET METAL FORMING

Die design is a specialized profession that combines the elements of craft, art, and science. The objective is to prepare drawings that can be translated into stamping dies by skilled craftsmen known as diemakers. The stamping dies, in turn, are mounted in presses in which they blank, bend, form, draw, extrude, trim, pierce, and coin sheet metal into finished parts or into components which may be assembled with other parts (which may or may not be stampings) to form finished products.

The presses used to produce stamped parts are treated in detail in Chapter 5, "Presses for Sheet Metal Forming." The sheet metal stampings produced with this technology are treated in Chapter 4, "Sheet Metal Blanking and Forming."

This chapter deals with the design and engineering of the dies themselves. Additional information on dies for specific forming and cutting operations, as well as materials used in making the dies, are discussed in the following chapters in this volume:

| Chapter | Title |
|---|---|
| 2 | Die and Mold Materials |
| 4 | Sheet Metal Blanking and Forming |
| 7 | Expanding, Shrinking and Stretch Forming |
| 8 | Roll Forming |
| 9 | Spinning |
| 10 | Bending and Straightening |
| 11 | Shearing |
| 12 | Punching |
| 19 | Special Forming Methods |

## CHAPTER CONTENTS:



## DIE NOMENCLATURE

A glossary of terms commonly used in the press, die, and stamping industries to describe presses and their parts and characteristics, as well as the feeding and safeguarding of the point of operation, is presented in Chapter 5, "Presses for Sheet Metal Forming." The following is a glossary of terms commonly used in die design:

**blank** The flat stamping produced in a blanking die. Use of the word *blank* to describe a stamping usually implies the need for subsequent operations of cutting, forming, or drawing.

**blankholder** As a double-action forming or drawing operation takes place, the blankholder restrains the metal in its movement. Force exerted on the metal by the blankholder provides this restraining action. During drawing operations, if the force is insufficient, the metal wrinkles; if it is excessive, the metal tears.

**bolster plate** A plate attached to the top of the bed of the press, on which the die is mounted. The bolster plate contains numerous drilled holes and/or T-slots for attaching the lower die or die shoe. Bolsters in larger presses also contain holes for insertion of pressure pins, which are actuated by die cushions.

**die** Generic term used to denote the entire press tooling used to cut or form material. This word is also used to denote just the female half of the press tool. The female die steel works in opposition to the punch steel.

**die pad** A movable plate or pad in a female die, usually for part ejection by mechanical means, springs, or fluid cushions.

**die set** The assembly of the upper and lower die shoes (punch and dieholders), which usually includes the guide pins, guide pin bushings, and heel blocks. This assembly, which takes many forms, shapes, and sizes, is frequently purchased as a commercially available unit.

**diesetter** An individual who places dies in or removes dies from presses, and who makes the necessary adjustments to cause the tooling to function properly and safely.

**die shoes** The upper and lower plates or castings which make up a die set (punch and dieholder). Also a plate or block upon which a dieholder is mounted, functioning primarily as a base for the complete die assembly. It is bolted or clamped to the bolster plate or the face of the press slide.

**die space** The maximum space (volume), or any part of the maximum space, within a press for mounting a die.

**die springs** Heavy wire springs used to exert force on a stripper plate, pressure plate, or cam slides. These springs are purchased items. Careful

***Contributors of sections of this chapter are:*** *Daniel B. Dallas, Consultant; Harding R. Hugo, Consultant; Karl A. Keyes, Consultant; George Tann, President, Congress Tool & Die, Div. of Tann Co.*

***Reviewers of sections of this chapter are:*** *Douglas E. Booth, Vice President, Livernois Automation; Anto Lindberg, Vice President—Engineering, Moore Special Tool Co., Inc.; Ben Rapien, Chief Die Engineer, Cincinnati Incorporated; Edward A. Reed, Consultant.*

# DIE NOMENCLATURE

calculations are normally required to determine the number and size of the die springs required, and to minimize travel for maximum life.

**draft** The taper given to a die to allow the part to fall through the die or to be removed.

**draw bead** An insert or riblike projection on the draw ring or hold-down surfaces that aids in controlling the rate of metal flow during draw operations. Draw beads are especially useful in controlling the rate of metal flow in irregular-shaped stampings. (*See* also blankholder.)

**ejector** A mechanism for removing work or material from between the dies.

**guide pin bushings** Bushings, pressed into a die shoe, which allow the guide pins to enter in order to maintain punch-die alignment. Entry must be effected prior to engagement of punch and die. (*See* also guide pins.)

**guide pins** Hardened, ground, round pins or posts which maintain alignment between punch and die during die fabrication, setup, operation, and storage. If the press slide is out of alignment, the guide pins cannot make the necessary correction unless heel plates are engaged before the pins enter the bushings.

**heel block** A block or plate usually mounted on or attached to a lower die, and serving to prevent or minimize deflection of punches or cams.

**hold-down plate (pressure pad)** Pressurized plate designed to hold the workpiece down during a press operation. In practice, this plate often serves as a stripper and is also called a stripper plate.

**keeper** Block used to retain the stripper plate for the designed range of travel. Keepers are used as an alternative to shoulder screws and are considered an improved design.

**knockout** The knockout, also called a shedder, clears the press tool of a stamped part at the end of the press cycle. In so doing, it serves as an internal stripper plate; that is, it fits within the die member, whereas the stripper fits around the punch.

**liftout** The mechanism also known as knockout.

**line dies** A sequence of stamping dies, all of which perform operations on a part with manual attendance. As an example, a part blanked out of coil stock may advance through a forming die, a piercing die, a trim die, and/or other dies.

**nitrogen die cylinders** Commercially available, gas-charged cylinders manufactured specifically for die applications. These cylinders are used in place of springs or die cushions in applications in which high initial pressure is required, usually in draw, form, and cam dies. Uniformity of pressure is attained by linking cylinders to an accumulator.

**pad** The general term used for that part of a die which delivers holding pressure to the metal being worked.

**pilot** Bullet-nosed component used in dies to maintain correct position of advancing strip. As the strip advances through a sequence of operations, the pilot entry into prepunched holes ensures precise registration of the part at each station of the strip.

**pin plate** A replaceable wear plate which fastens to the working surface of the cushion or lower slide and accepts the force from the pressure pins.

**pressure pins** Pins that extend downward from moving components in the die to bear on the pressure plate. (*See* pressure plate.)

**pressure plate** A plate located beneath the bolster which acts against the resistance of a group of cylinders mounted to the pressure plate to provide uniform pressure throughout the press stroke when the press is symmetrically loaded.

**progression** The constant dimension between adjacent stations in a progressive die. As such, it is the precise distance the strip must advance between successive cycles of the press. Accuracy of the progression is guaranteed by piloting and by the feed unit.

**progressive die** A die with two or more stations arranged in line for performing two or more operations on a part, one operation usually being performed at each station.

**punch** Male member of the punch-die combination.

**shedder** *See* knockout.

**shedder pin** Small, spring-actuated pin generally inserted in a punch member, but sometimes in a die section. The purpose of this pin is to act as an oil-seal breaker and to "kick off" a stamped part or scrap slug which tends to adhere to the tooling.

**slug** The piece of scrap metal produced by punching a hole.

**spring cans** Sheet metal cylinders open at one end and closed at the other. These commercially available items are used to retain the various segments of a spring in the event that it breaks. Without spring cans, various parts of broken springs could enter and jam openings between various die members, and could be a hazard to the press operator.

**stamping** The end product of a press operation, or a series of operations, wherein the workpiece is generated by processing flat (or preformed) strip or sheet stock between the opposing members of a die.

**steel rule die** A metalcutting die employing a thin strip of steel (printer's rule) formed to the outline of a part and a thin steel punch mounted to a suitable die set.

**stop** A device for positioning stock or parts in a die.

**stripper** A plate designed to surround the piercing punch steels or the piercing punches. Its purpose, quite literally, is to strip the sheet metal stock from the punching members during the withdrawal cycle. Strippers are also employed for the purpose of guiding small precision punches in close tolerance dies, to guide scrap away from dies, and to assist in the cutting action. Strippers are made in two types: fixed and movable.

**stripper bolt** Precision screws. Uniformity of the length of the shoulders on shoulder screws or caps on cap screws keeps the strippers (and other components on which these screws are used) parallel with the die shoes and also limits and defines the stroke of the stripper.

**turnover bar** A bar used in diesetting to manually turn the crankshaft of the press.

**unitized tooling** A type of die in which the upper and lower members are incorporated into a self-contained unit, which is arranged in such a way that it holds the die members in alignment. This type of tooling includes continental, sub-press, pushthrough, pancake, or short-run dies.

**vent** A small hole in a punch or die for admitting air to avoid suction holding or for relieving pockets of trapped air that would prevent proper die closure or action.

# DIE COMPONENTS

Sheet metal stamping dies are unique in their design; no two are alike. There are, however, numerous die components that are identical or similar in design. Because many of these components are commercially available, the designer need not include all their dimensions in the die drawings and the diemaker need not take the time to make the components. They can be purchased more economically as standard items.

## DIE SETS

Typical die sets (see Fig. 6-1) range in size from extremely small sets, such as those used to produce watch parts, to extremely large sets, such as those used to produce automotive stampings. Standard die sets are specified in ANSI Standards B5.25 and B5.25M (metric). Steel, cast iron, and cast steel are typical materials used in die sets. Large, special-design die sets are cast to order from custom-made patterns.

Alignment between the upper and lower members of a die set is maintained by pins with matched or ball bushings. Large sets also use heel blocks on two or more sides or corners as aids in maintaining alignment of the die shoes before the pins and bushings are engaged. Purchased die sets can be obtained in three grades: commercial, precision, and superprecision. Superprecision die sets are not standard and specifications must be negotiated between the customer and the die set manufacturer.

Types of die set pins and bushings available are shown in Figs. 6-2 and 6-3. A hole-punching unit that requires a separate

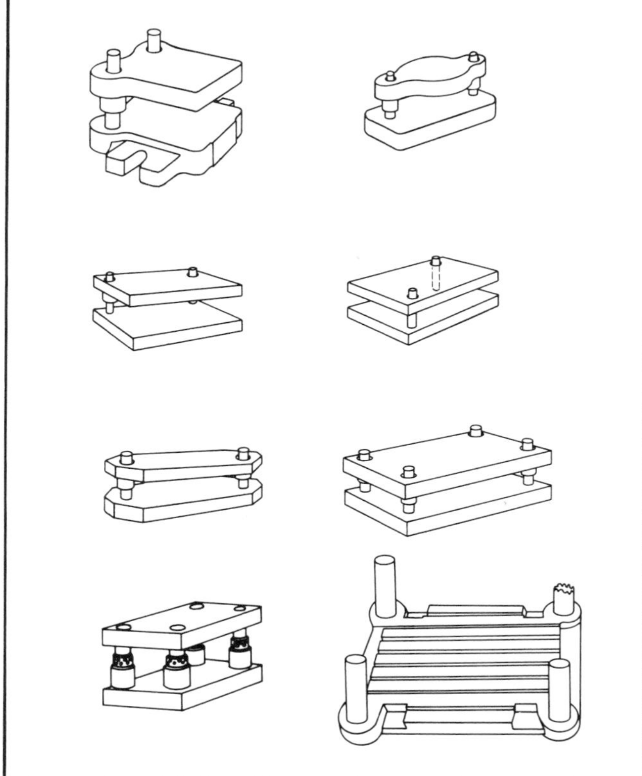

Fig. 6-1 Typical commercially available die sets.

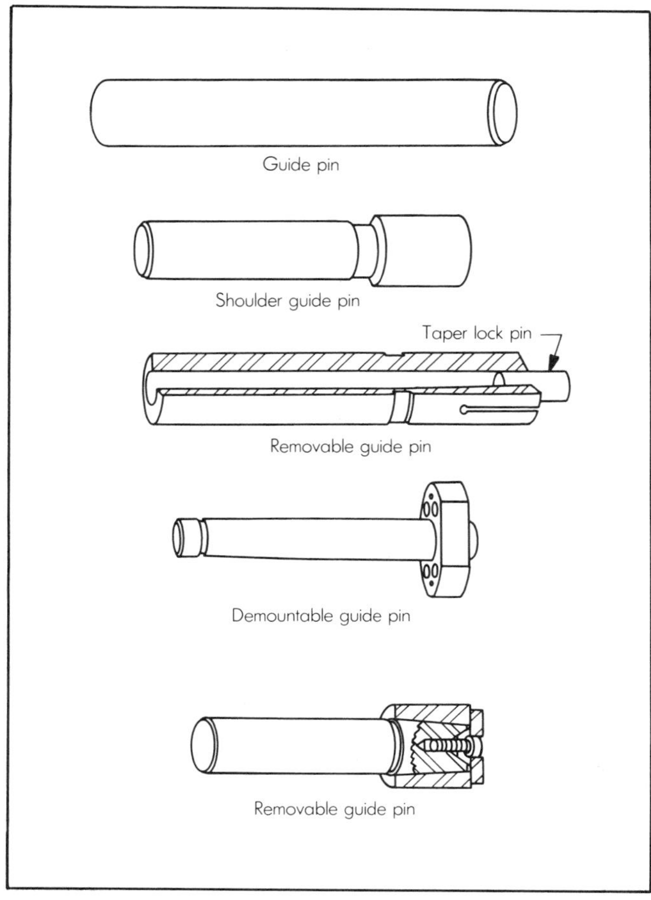


Fig. 6-2 Commercial standard guide pins.

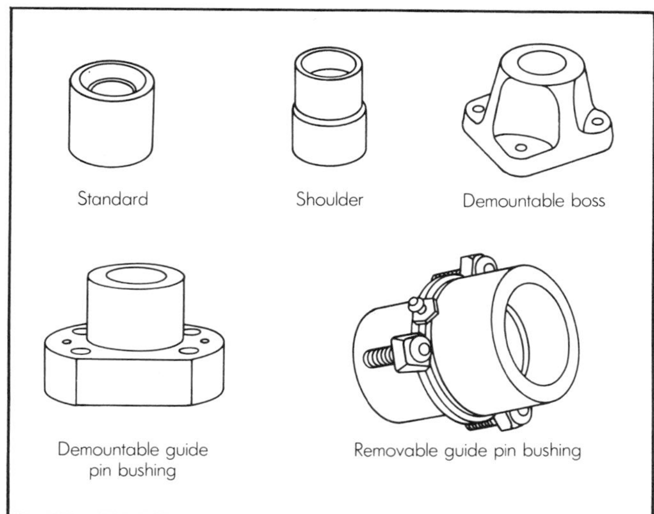


Fig. 6-3 Commercial standard guide-pin bushings.

die set or other means for alignment is shown in Fig. 6-4, view *a*, while view *b* depicts a self-enclosing hole-punching unit requiring no die set because of its self-contained alignment.

## STRIPPERS

Two types of strippers are generally used—the fixed type and the movable type (with pressure from air, nitrogen, or springs). Fixed strippers are permanently attached to the die and may also guide the stock. Stock clearances are critical. Movable types strip the stock from tools, but may also apply hold-down pressure to prevent distortion of part or web while force is being applied to the material.

Methods for retaining strippers are shown in Fig. 6-5. Practical designs allow the removal of strippers from large dies while they are in the press and from the working side of small dies to facilitate repairs without complete disassembly of the dies. Pressure strippers may guide punches or do some forming. For such applications, the strippers must be well guided for accurate alignment and positioning. The lower edge of a draw-die ring may be undercut to catch the edge of a drawn shell and to strip it from the draw punch (see Fig. 6-6).

## KNOCKOUTS

Knockouts usually push or lift parts from die cavities. A commonly used positive knockout for stripping parts from an inverted compound die is illustrated in Fig. 6-7. A knockout rod forces the knockout plate to strip the part from the die. The part is prevented from adhering to the plate by an oil-seal breaker pin.

Blanked parts may be shed just before the top of the stroke in an inclined press so that they drop away from the working area of the die. Cam-actuated knockouts may shed heavy blanks, 2 lb (0.9 kg) or heavier, in a straight-sided press at a preset position below the top of the stroke to prevent damage to die surfaces or injury to the operator.

## STOPS

One or more stops (gages) are required for most dies. A solid registering stop or a temporary stop is used only for starting stock through a progressive die. Typical stops are shown in Figs. 6-8 through 6-11. Hand-operated, lever-type starting stops (see Fig. 6-9, view *a*) locate the ends of strip stock or large holes and notches in the material, and are suited for hand-feed operations or power-feed setups. A similar type allows the stop to move under the stock when the die closes. Push stops (view *b*) are used to locate the starting ends of strips in progressive dies.

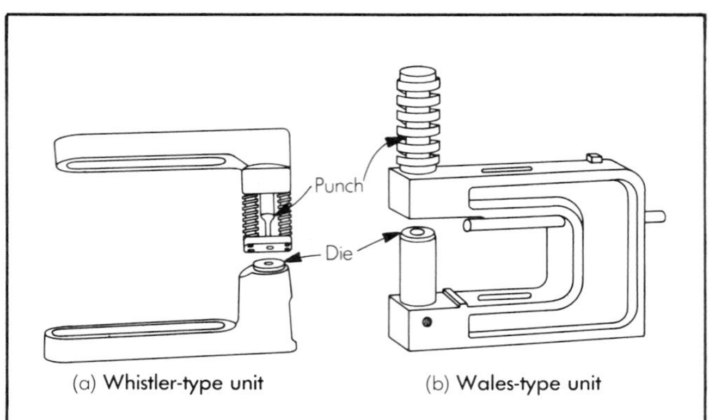


**Fig. 6-4 Hole-punching units.**

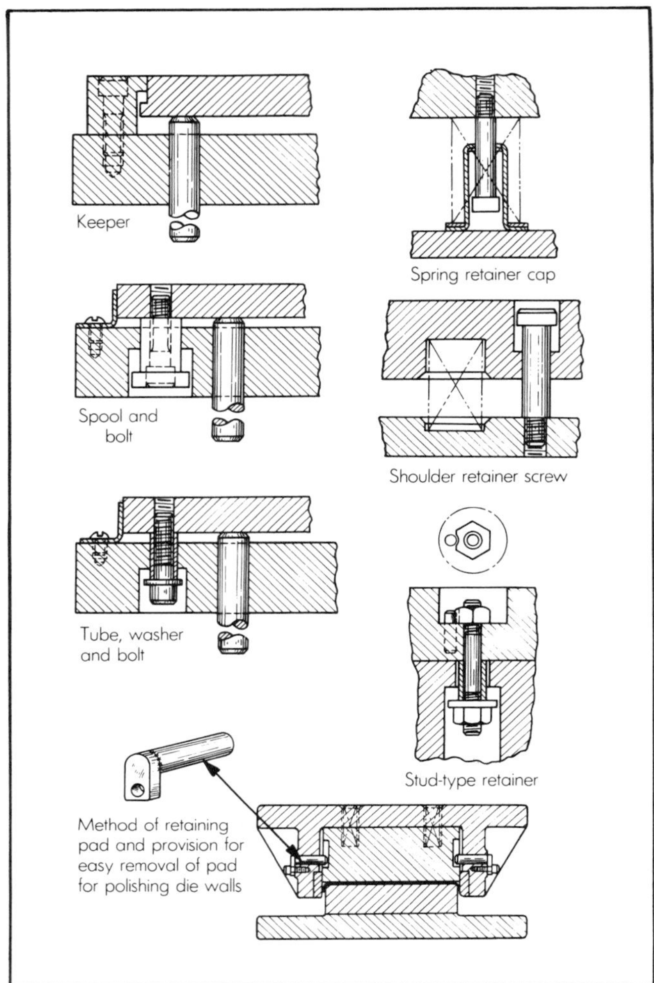


**Fig. 6-5 Methods for retaining stripper plates.**

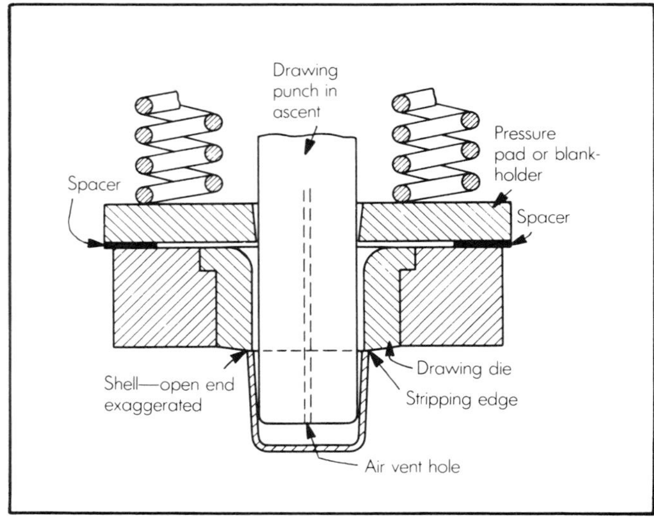


**Fig. 6-6 Lower edge of a draw ring performing the function of a stripper.**

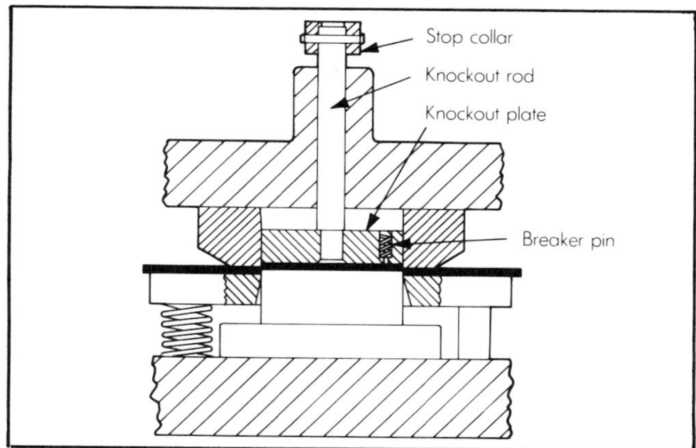

**Fig. 6-7 Positive knockout for stripping parts from an inverted compound die.**

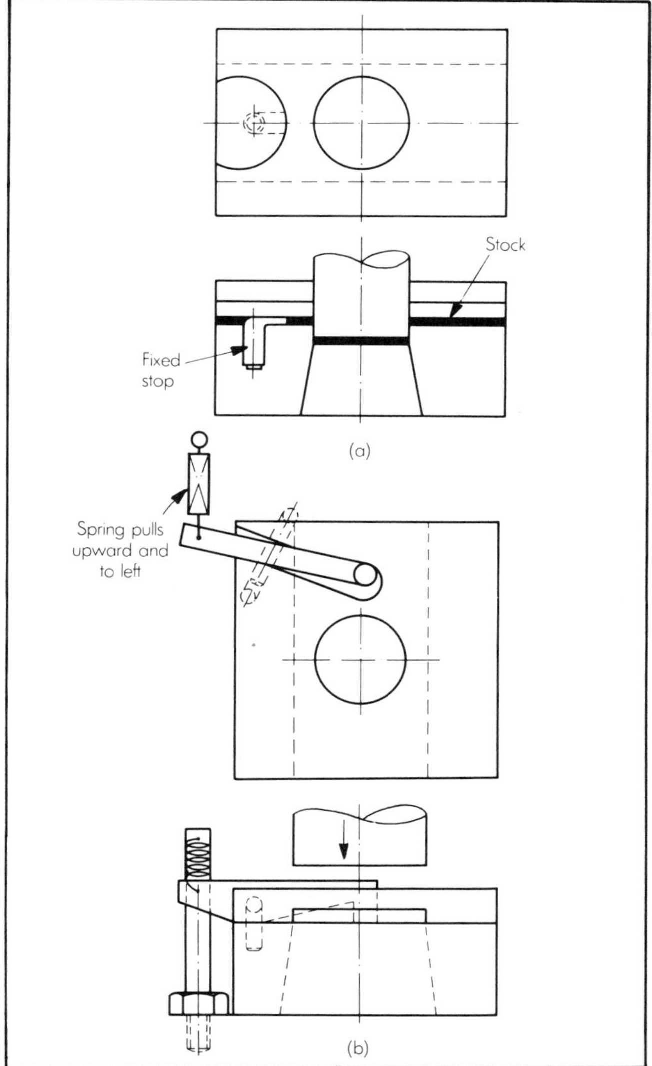

**Fig. 6-8 Commonly used stops: (a) fixed stop is manually operated (stock must be lifted over the stop before progressing); and (b) movable stop (when die closes, stop is raised above stock).**

Pull stops (view *c*) are moved out of the way after locating the stock and then act like stock pushers to hold material against back rails.

Disappearing stops shown in Fig. 6-10 include: round type (view *a*), air ejector type (view *b*), and flat type (view *c*). With the adjustable stop illustrated in view *d*, release of the setscrew allows the stop to be rotated to the proper location. A first stop and a running gage for progressive dies are shown in Fig. 6-11. In addition to stops for progressive dies, pilots are incorporated for accurate positioning by either pulling or pushing the stock slightly.

## KICKER (SHEDDER) PINS

Kicker pins are spring-actuated pins extending from dies to prevent the stamped part from adhering to a working surface, generally because of an oil-film seal. They are usually built into strippers, knockouts, blank punches, formed tool surfaces, and the like.

## STOCK PUSHERS

Stock pushers are used to ensure proper registration of part or strip to gaging surface or surfaces. Typical stock pushers are shown in Fig. 6-12.

## GUIDES

Stock guides direct stock material along suitable slots or grooves. In some progressive dies in which deep draws are produced, a combination stock guide and lifter is used (see Fig. 6-13).

## HEEL AND WEAR PLATES

Heels are incorporated in dies to hold punches, dies, and the blankholder in alignment and to prevent damage to dies if the press ram has too much play. A typical large-die, heel-block installation is shown in Fig. 6-14, view *a*. Notching punches or punches that cut along the edge of stock (french cuts) may have a heel which enters the die opening before any cutting action starts (view *b*). This tends to minimize punch breakage due to side loads and also ensures maintaining proper clearance between the cutting steels. Wear plates protect die parts receiving greatest wear. They are made of hardened tool steel or aluminum bronze. In some high-production dies, carbide wear strips are used.

## STOP BLOCKS

Stop blocks are blocks or posts mounted to die shoes to assist the diesetter in the proper positioning of mating punches and dies or the entering of punches into die cavities to the proper depth. Stop blocks, with suitable spacers, also prevent damage to dies in storage from punch and die members hitting together.

## PERFORATORS (PUNCHES)

Typical perforators (punches) and methods for mounting and securing them are shown in Fig. 6-15. Standards for these tooling components are listed in Table 6-1. Specifications for variable, press-fit, punch-guide bushings are presented in ANSI Standard B94.23. Perforators are made of a good grade of tool steel properly hardened and ground. After grinding, vertical lapping of the cutting portion of the punch is recommended, particularly for operations in which thin stock is cut, shaving operations, or operations in which die clearances are less than

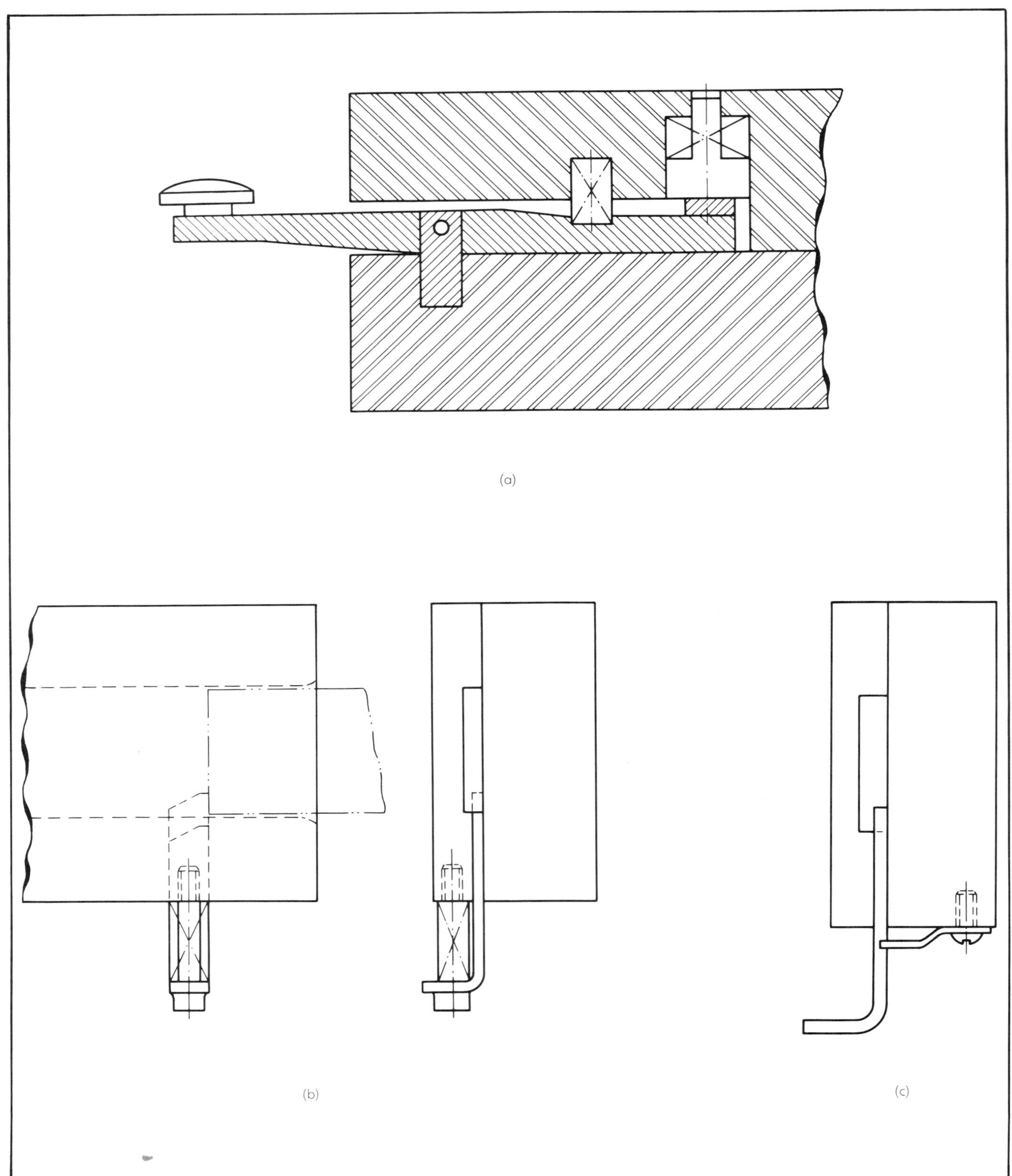


Fig. 6-9 Starting stops: (a) lever type, (b) push type, and (c) pull type.

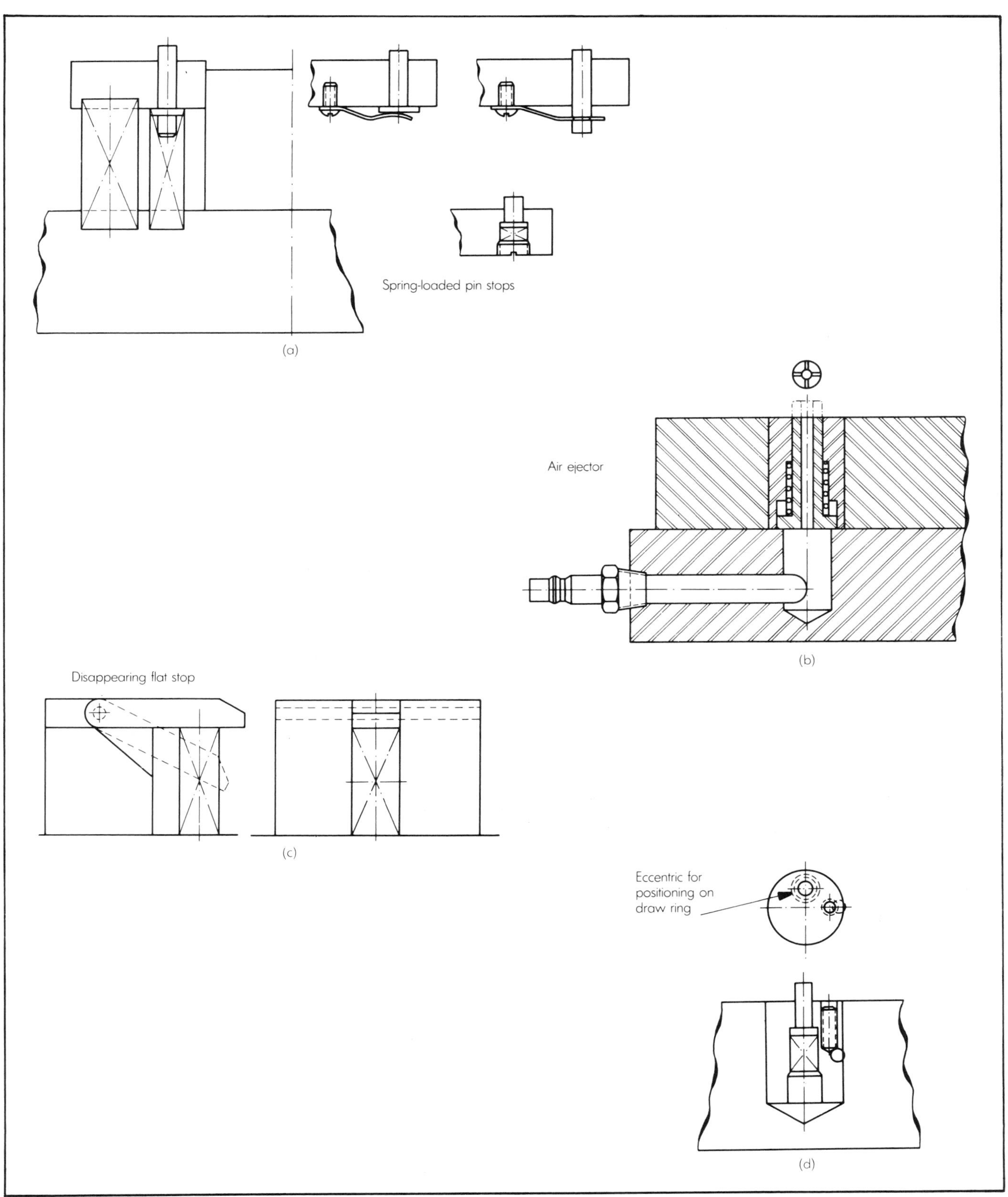


**Fig. 6-10 Disappearing stops.**

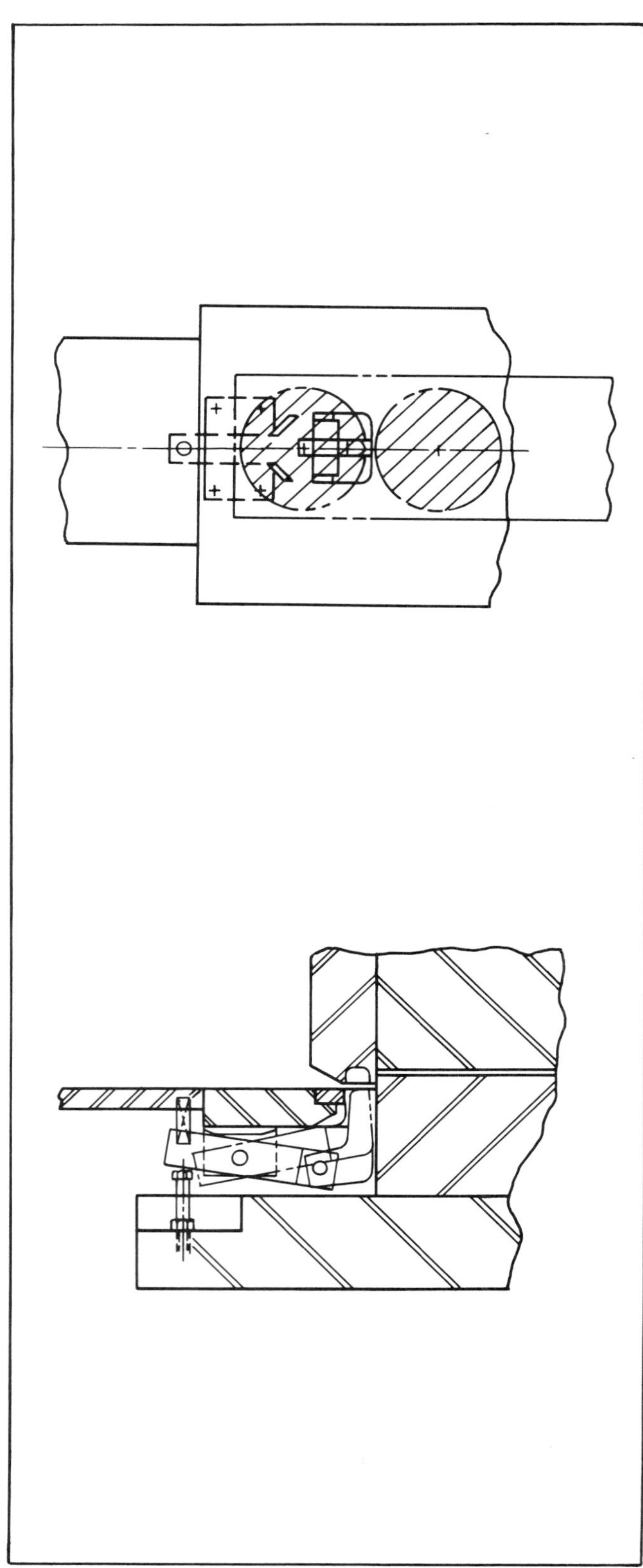

**Fig. 6-11 First stop and running gage for progressive dies.** (*Livernois Automation Co.*)

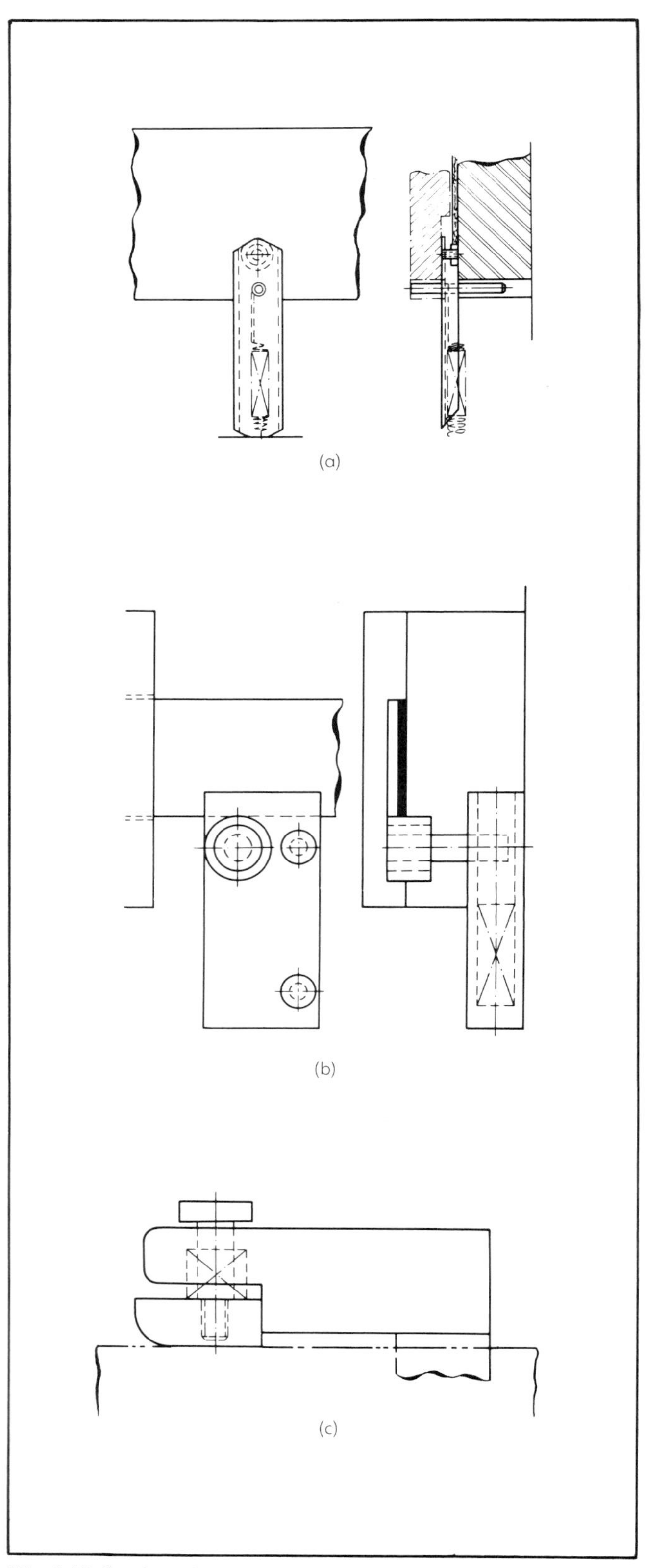


**Fig. 6-12 Stock pushers: (a) roller-stock pusher, (b) stock guide and pusher, and (c) stock-gaging pusher.**

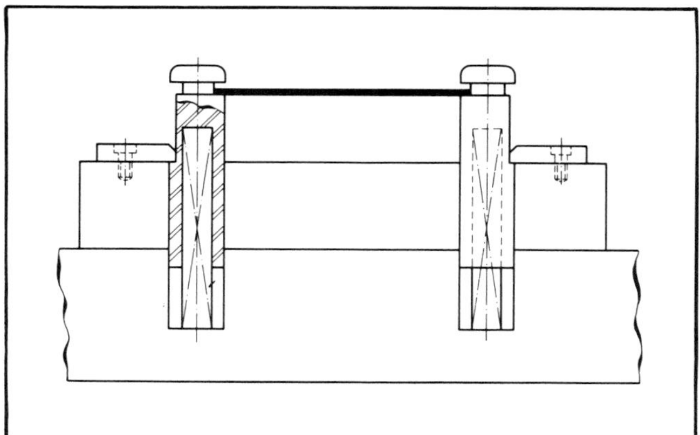

Fig. 6-13 Stock lifters. They also guide the stock in its advancement through the die.

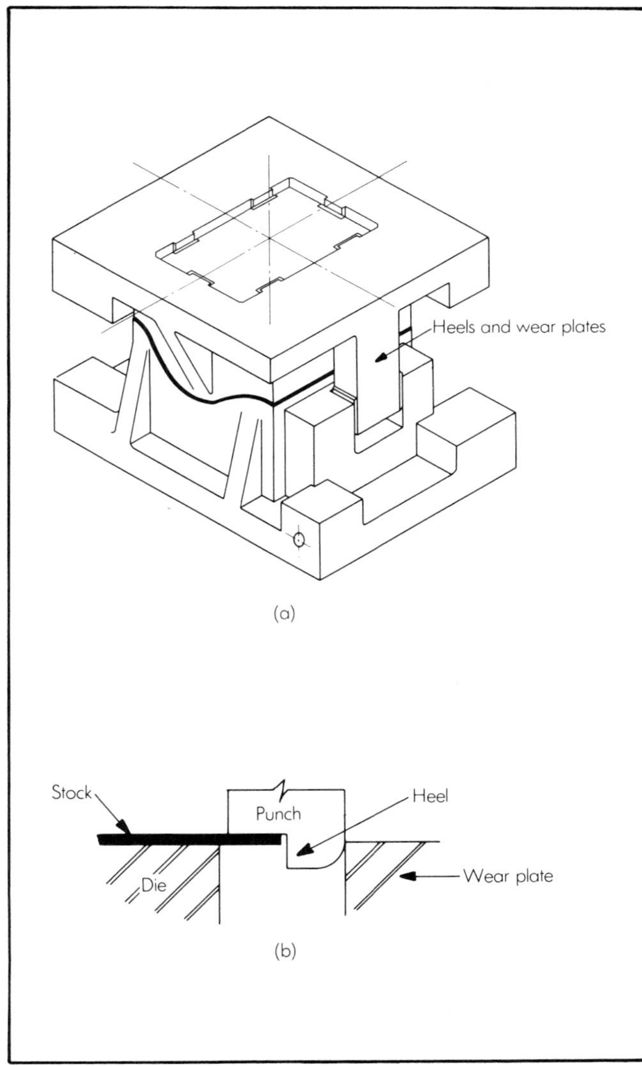


Fig. 6-14 Heel and wear plates: (a) on a large die and (b) heel that enters die opening before cutting starts.

normal. The breakage of punches is generally the result of severe shock and/or misalignment during penetration. Breakage can be minimized by maintaining perpendicularity between the stock and the punches.

## PILOTS

Pilots accurately register stock in progressive dies. To be effective, a pilot must be strong enough to align the stock without bending. For this reason, a pilot with the largest possible diameter is preferred. Typical pilots are shown in Fig. 6-16. Pilots should be made of a good grade of tool steel, heat treated to maximum toughness and a hardness of $R_C$ 56-60. Pilot holes should extend through the dieholder to clear slugs produced during misfeeds.

## PILOT HOLDERS

A pilot holder is usually a block of steel which can be fastened to the punch shoe. Some commercial holders, such as the ball-lock type of holder (see Fig. 6-16), can be used. Holders for press fit of the pilots are also used.

## MISFEED DETECTORS

Misfeed detectors are devices to stop the presses in case of misfeeds (see Fig. 6-17). Detectors should ensure that the stock is in proper position for the pilots to enter. They generally incorporate a spring-loaded detector to actuate a limit switch and are commonly employed in progressive dies. Designed like a perforator, the point is smaller in diameter than the pilot hole by the amount of over or under-feeding allowed. A spring-loaded pilot linked to a limit switch through a lever (see Fig. 6-18) prevents press operation if the workpiece is improperly located. This type of design, however, is subject to failure of both the rod or lever actuating device and the limit switch. The design shown in Fig. 6-19 is more reliable, although it still depends on a mechanically operated limit switch because it is operated directly by the detector. The best design (see Fig. 6-20) is a reliable proximity-type magnetic sensor which does not require physical contact with the sliding parts.

The buckling of stock, the incorrect positioning of blanks or parts, slug pileup, and various misfeeds in dies can be detected by mechanical probes, fingers, feelers, etc. Movements actuate limit switches or sensors which directly or indirectly control press operations and, if desired, also operate various lights, buzzers, etc., to warn the press operator.

## DIE BUTTONS

Small die steels called die buttons are available in the same shapes and general size range as perforators and punches. Standards for these tooling components are listed in Table 6-2. The button opening is always larger than the punch point size, generally by a percentage of the thickness of the material being pierced. As seen in Fig. 6-21, buttons can be retained by press fitting as well as by the use of ball locks or shoulders. Press fitting is satisfactory when the need to replace the button is infrequent. Stripping forces act only on the punch and do not affect the button.

## RETAINERS

Punch and die button retainers are provided in several shapes, depending on the die space or mounting method used (see Fig. 6-22). Specifications for basic ball-lock, punch and

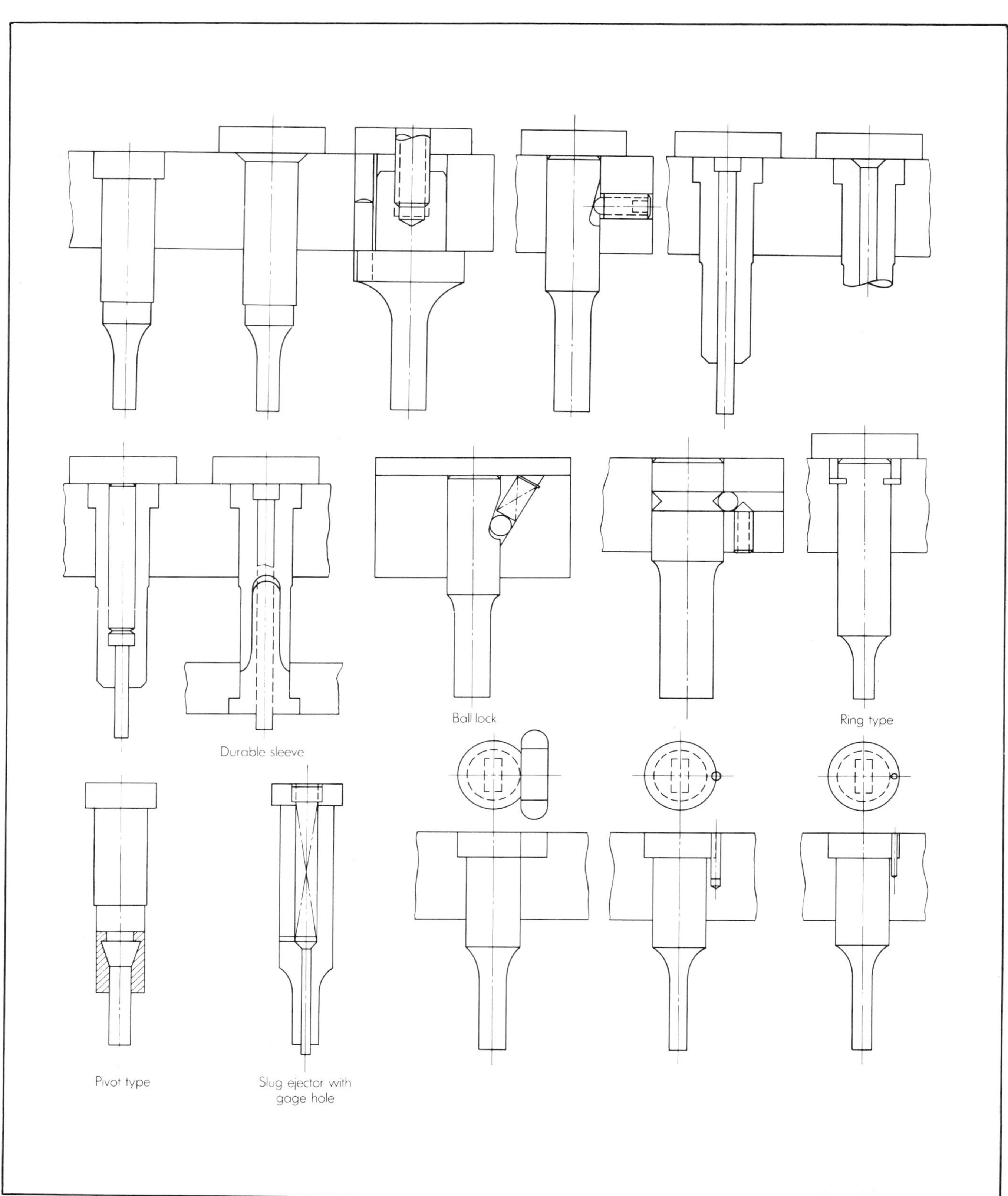


**Fig. 6-15 Typical perforating punches and mounting methods.**

**TABLE 6-1**
**ANSI Standards for Various Types of Punches**

| Standard | Title |
|---|---|
| B94.14 | Punches, Basic Head Type |
| B94.14.1 | Punches, Basic Head Type (Metric) |
| B94.18 | Punches, Basic Ball-Lock, Light and Heavy Duty |
| B94.18.1 | Punches, Basic Ball-Lock, Light and Heavy Duty (Metric) |
| B94.22 | Punches, Variable, Head Type |
| B94.22.1 | Punches, Variable, Head Type (Metric) |
| B94.38 | Punches, Variable, Angle-Head Type, and Related Quill Bushings |
| B94.39 | Punches, Basic, Combination Angle-Head Type, and Related Quill Bushings |
| B94.40 | Punches, Wire Type |
| B94.41 | Punches, Basic, Angle-Head Type, and Related Quill Bushings |
| B94.44 | Punches, Basic, Cylindrical-Head Type, and Related Quill Bushings |

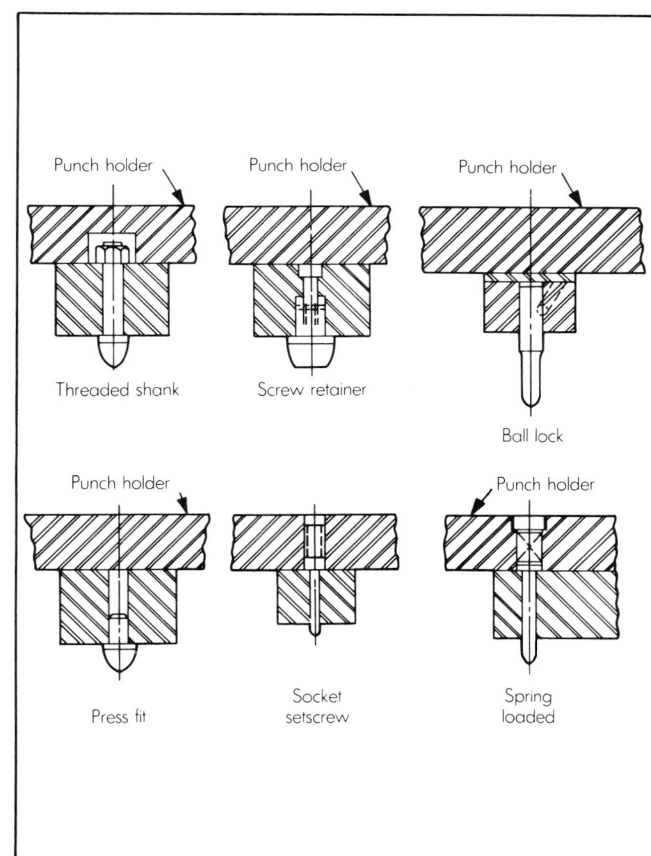


**Fig. 6-16 Various pilots and methods of retaining them.**

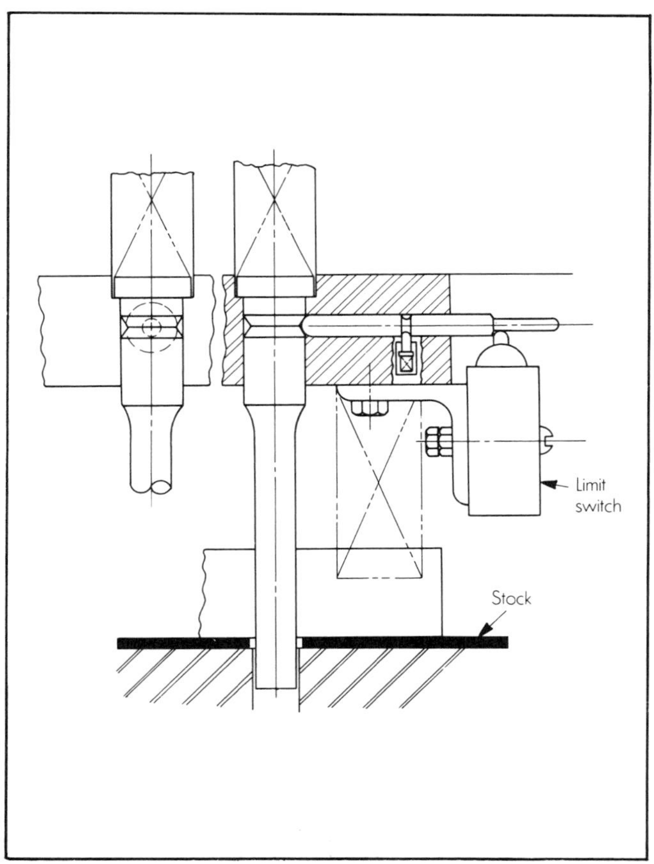


**Fig. 6-17 Automatic limit-switch press stop for misfeeds.**

# DIE COMPONENTS

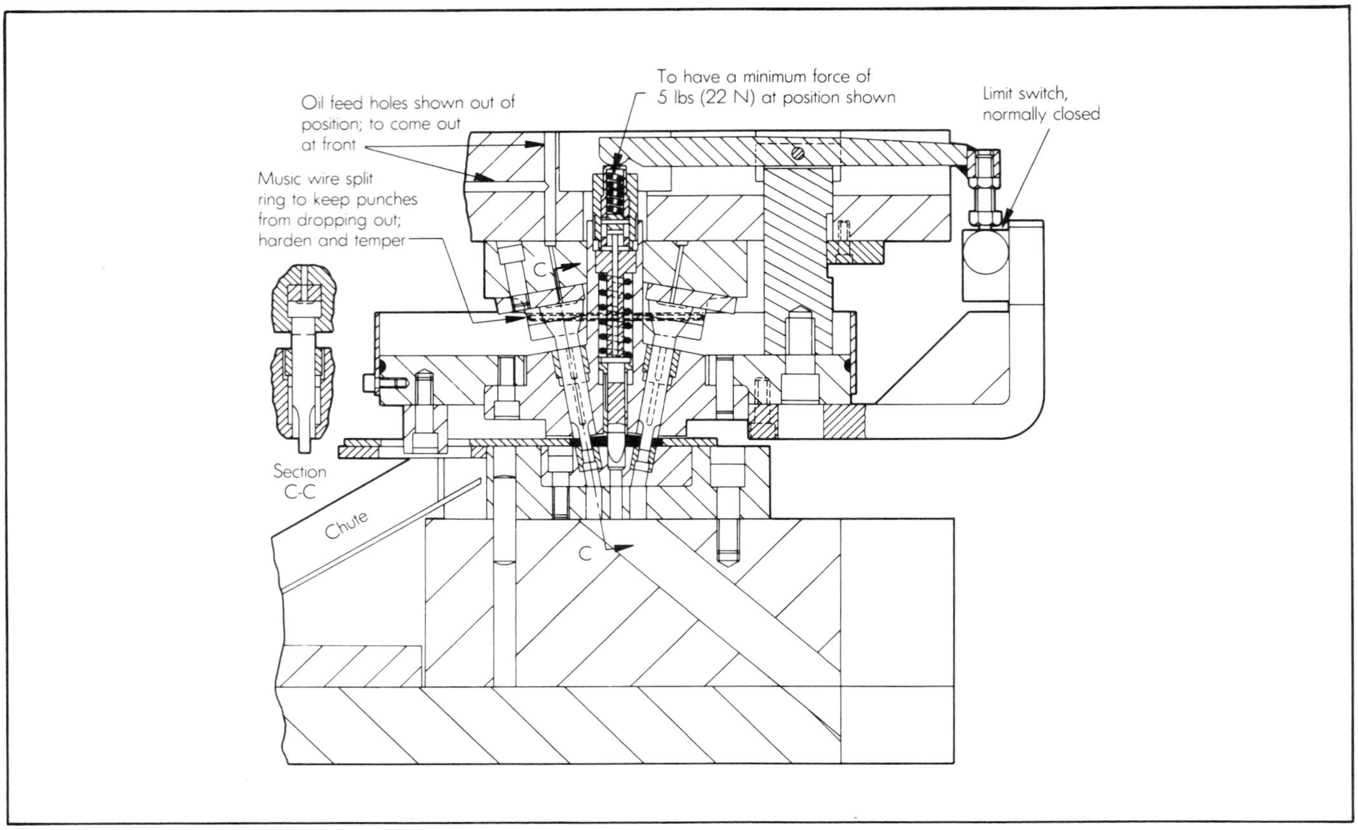

**Fig. 6-18 Shaving die protected by lever-actuated limit switch.**

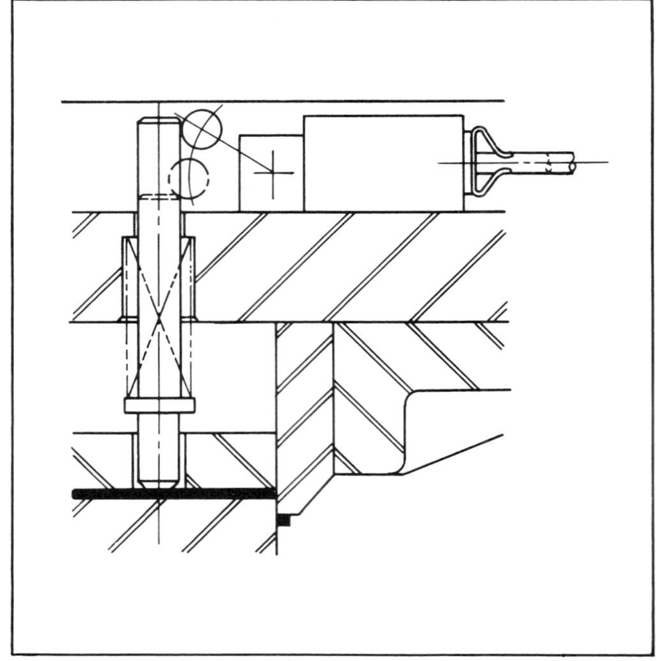

**Fig. 6-19 Automatic limit-switch press stop operated directly by contact with pilot.** (*Livernois Automation Co.*)

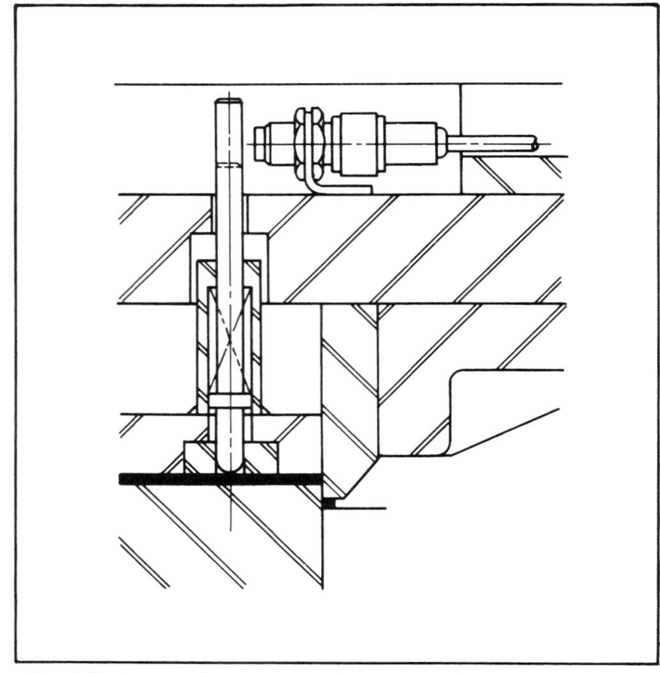

**Fig. 6-20 Automatic press stop by means of a magnetic sensor.** (*Livernois Automation Co.*)

**TABLE 6-2**
**ANSI Standards for Various Types of Die Buttons**

| Standard | Title |
|---|---|
| B94.27 | Die Buttons, Basic Taper Relief, Press Fit |
| B94.28 | Die Buttons, Basic Straight Relief, Press Fit |
| B94.29 | Die Buttons, Basic Ball Lock |
| B94.29.1 | Die Buttons, Basic Ball Lock (Metric) |
| B94.30 | Die Buttons, Variable, Press Fit |
| B94.43 | Die Buttons, Variable, Press Fit, Headless and Head Types, Step Relief |

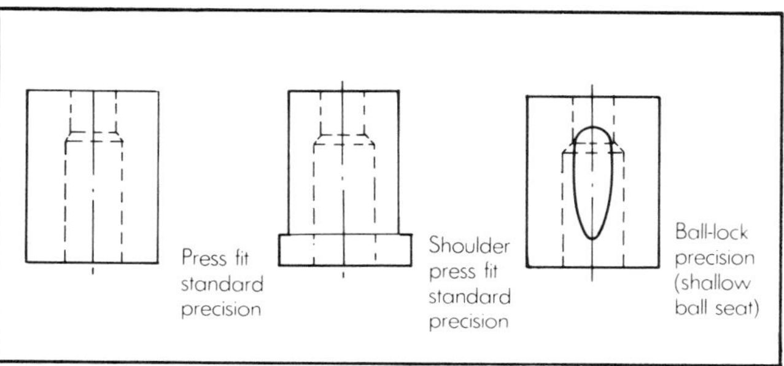


**Fig. 6-21 Basic die buttons.**

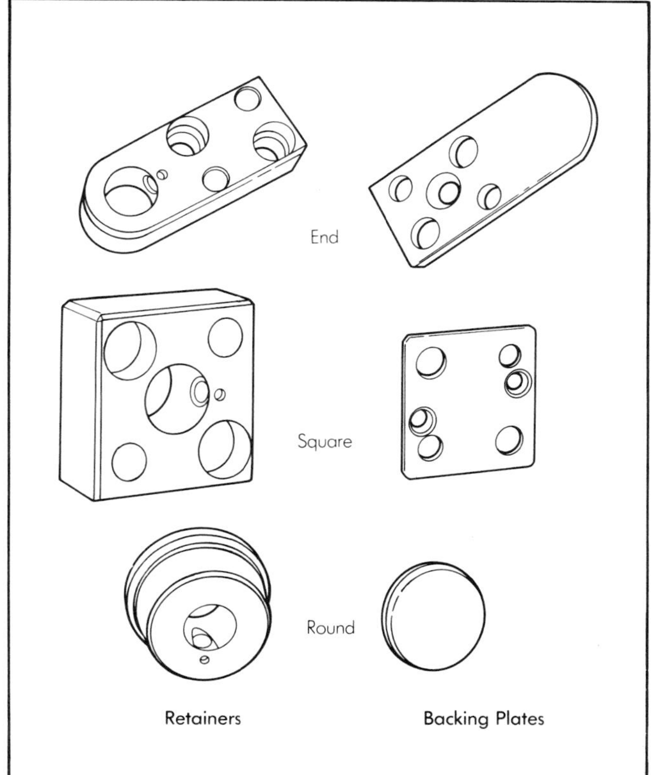


**Fig. 6-22 Retainers and backing plates.** (*Richard Brothers Punch Co.*)

die-button retainers, both light and heavy duty, are presented in ANSI Standards B94.16 and B94.16.1 (metric). When close spacing of two or three punches is required, end retainers are useful although they are generally used only for pilots. For very close spacing of many punches, special one-piece retainers can be made or obtained commercially. Hardened backing plates may be required to back up the punches, but improved design retainers now available require no backup plate.

## SPRING RETAINERS

Spring retainers are used to permit stripper plates or pads to be removed without loose springs dropping out. Two types of commercial spring retainers are shown in Fig. 6-23.

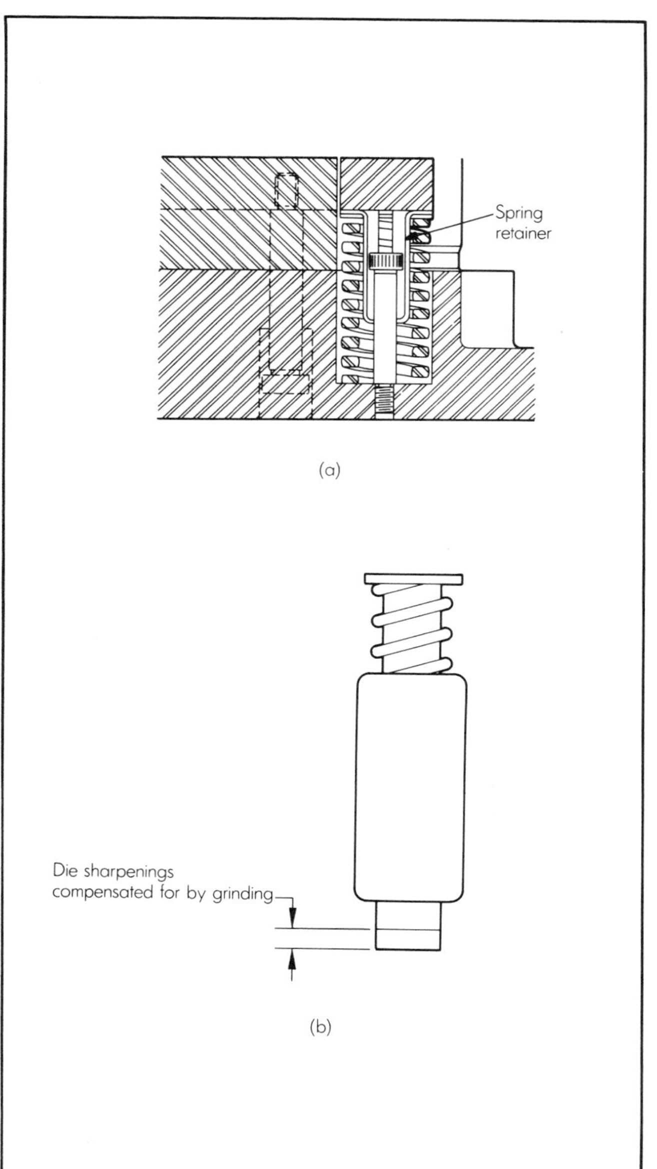


**Fig. 6-23 Spring retainers: (a) with external spring and (b) with self-contained, preloaded spring.**

# LOCATION OF STAMPINGS IN DIES

Qualified areas for locating stampings in dies are those areas which fulfill the requirements of the following three main types of tests:

1. Arithmetical test. The selected surface of registry must not cause a limit stack with respect to allowable tolerances. If the surfaces cannot be selected, they must be qualified; that is, they must be produced to tolerances closer than those required and specified by the product engineer.
2. Mechanical test. The size, shape, and finish of the selected surfaces of registry must withstand the operating forces exerted and also the necessary holding forces.
3. Geometrical test. This test pertains to the distribution of the surfaces of registry so that the workpiece is positionally stable. If surfaces of registry are not thus qualified, the process planner must consider suitable redesign with the product engineer.

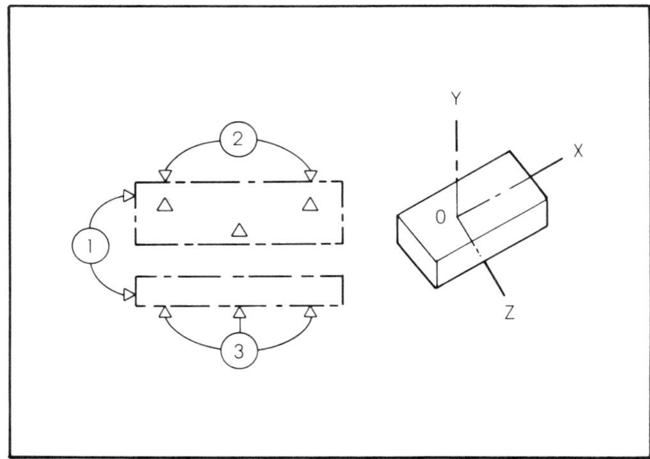

**Fig. 6-24 The 3-2-1 locating system.**

In the 3-2-1 locating system (see Fig. 6-24), six points are the minimum number required to fix a square or rectangular shape in space. Three points establish a plane; two points define a straight line; and one point designates a point in space. Combined, they total six points. A small pyramid symbol is used to designate a locating point. In Fig. 6-25, this symbol is used to illustrate a locating system for a rectangular solid. Variations of the illustrated system can be used to fix location of a cylinder, cone, disc, or other geometric shapes.

The surface of the device used by the die designer to establish the locating points specified by the process planner is known as a seat of registry. The corresponding area on the workpiece is known as a surface of registry.

Process planning symbols can be used to avoid lengthy writing in the preliminary stages of planning the utilization of critical areas for primary and secondary manufacturing operations. Figure 6-25 illustrates use of such symbols.

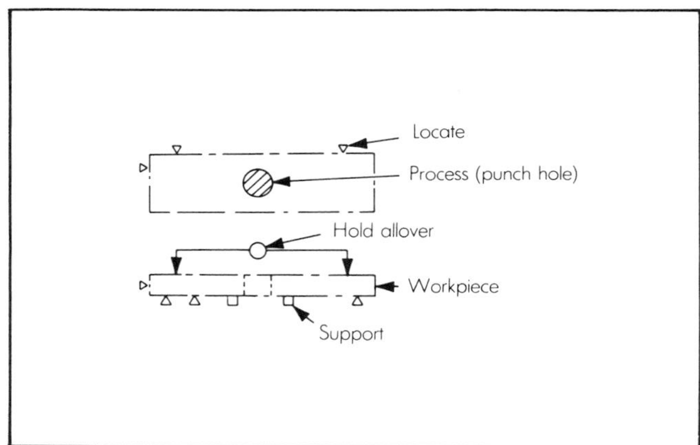

**Fig. 6-25 Application of process symbols.**

# DESIGN CHECKLIST

Reference to a list of check questions can aid the designer during the preliminary and final stages of die design. Checklists are generally created to maintain company standards. Such lists serve as a reminder in planning both overall design and the details of design, rather than a series of set rules rigidly applying to all die designs. Specific lists are often developed for each type of die.

The following checklist is largely based on the more common mistakes in the design of various types of dies. While not complete, the list may suggest to the designer other problems and difficulties of design associated with those listed. The list can be referred to after sketches of tentative or alternate designs have been made, or after the exact function of each element and detail of various designs have been reviewed.

1. Does thickness or shear strength of the stock indicate the need for heavy die construction, with guided and/or heeled punches?
2. Does hardness or abrasiveness of the stock require alloy or carbide punches and dies?
3. Is stock thin enough to require punches with shedder pins?
4. Will guided, quilled, or sleeved punches be necessary for small holes?
5. Do large holes require sectional die construction or shear on the punches?
6. Do tabbed or elongated holes or notches necessitate heeled or guided punches or shear on the punches?
7. Will ductility or resilience of stock modify bending, forming, or drawing punch design?

8. Will the press accommodate the die set specified?
9. Are minimum clearances specified to allow the slug or blanked part to drop through the die?
10. After analyzing the part design, which is more practical: inserted sectional or solid punch and die construction?
11. Can standard die buttons and punches be used?
12. Should punches and pilots be removable, adjustable, or equipped with spacer plates for resetting after grinding?
13. Will a cam-actuated punch (for angular cutting) require a special guide, a sleeve, or a special cam design?
14. Can removable or gagged punch design allow versatility in punching various hole patterns?
15. Should interchangeable punch and die design (with suitable holders, plates, etc.) be considered to facilitate production of various hole patterns?
16. Have different lengths of stepped punches been considered for multihole production to distribute the punching pressure?
17. Has the slot in a solid stripper been checked for stock clearance?
18. Do spring strippers have pockets and sufficient space for the springs?
19. Should guide pins and bushings for punches and pilots be incorporated in a spring-loaded stripper?
20. Is the stripper designed to also clamp and guide the stock or workpiece?
21. Will the part be removed from the die cavity by a knockout, lifter, or shedder; manually; by air; or by a robot?
22. Have pushers or spring-loaded, cammed, or pin-type stock guides been considered?
23. For a given die, is an adjustable solid stop allowing various stop lengths to be cut off preferable to the other types?
24. What devices are necessary for operator, die, and press safety?
25. Has venting for trapped air been considered?
26. Will the die allow automatic feeds to be used with little or no change in design?
27. Will scrap cutters be incorporated?
28. How will scrap be removed from the die?

# PLANNING DIE PROCESSING

The basic procedures and principles of process planning for sheet metal parts are in general the same for all classifications of parts. However, the techniques used for the preliminary steps of processing large panels are considerably different from those applied to the processing of symmetrical geometric shapes. In both cases, the part material is subjected to the same stresses, tensile and compressive, and the material strain characteristics vary with the severity of the configuration.

However, the source of information and specifications for planning production of an irregularly shaped appearance panel is basically different from that for planning production of a solely functional part. Although the appearance panels of a sheet metal assembly have structural value, one of the more important design considerations is styling for sales appeal. In contrast, some functional components of the same product are formed from sheet metal for reasons of economy.

The modern automobile offers the best example of the application of both types of sheet metal components. The front fenders of a passenger car become an integral part of the stylist's design, which is worked out as an artist's rendering in chalkboard drawings, in clay models, and finally in styling drawings.

The process engineer, in order to meet process engineering responsibilities within the allotted lead time for the product, must get preliminary information on the size and shape of the fender directly from the clay model. The clay model at this stage is also an aid to the process engineer and others in the evaluation of product producibility. Many minor changes are agreed upon by the stylist, the design engineers, and the process engineer to keep the product within the known range of material and sheet metalworking techniques. When the clay model is approved, templates and critical measurement are made to develop styling drawings. The styling drawings are used to develop the master surface plates as well as advance information for dies and experimental evaluation of drawn shapes.

The master surface plate, which is the source of size and shape specifications for the mylar drawing, the master model, checking fixtures, and prototype tooling, is actually the starting point for the responsibility for part specifications in manufacturing. Up to this point, the stylist is responsible, as can be seen in the flow chart illustrated in Fig. 6-26. Actually, to conserve lead time, the master model is built while the engineering drawings are being developed.

Electronic and optical recording systems are gradually changing this processing. In some cases, computer-made tapes are eliminating the need for costly models, which are subject to variations due to changes in ambient conditions. The use of computer-aided design and computer-aided manufacturing (CAD/CAM) is discussed later in this section.

It is important for the die engineer to have advance information from the clay model in the form of a female plaster and design lines. This information permits work to be started on draw-die developments and die positions, and also on patterns for the major die castings for major body panels, well in advance of completion of the master model. When the master model is completed with all significant engineering changes (including those recommended by the process engineer upon viewing the clay model), female plasters for making male machining and spotting aids for finishing castings for the draw, trim, or flange punches are made. The same or similar procedures used for dies may be used for checking fixtures and prototype work.

As mentioned earlier, a female plaster is made from the original clay model in the testing procedure. Then, a male model, as shown in Fig. 6-27, is made from this female plaster. The accuracy of these models is adequate for the preliminary transferring of size and shape specifications.

The procedure used in the development of a draw die for an irregularly shaped panel, such as a fender, requires several steps to establish die position, draw-die wrap to establish the draw ring, and the necessary allowances of shapes required for

## PLANNING DIE PROCESSING

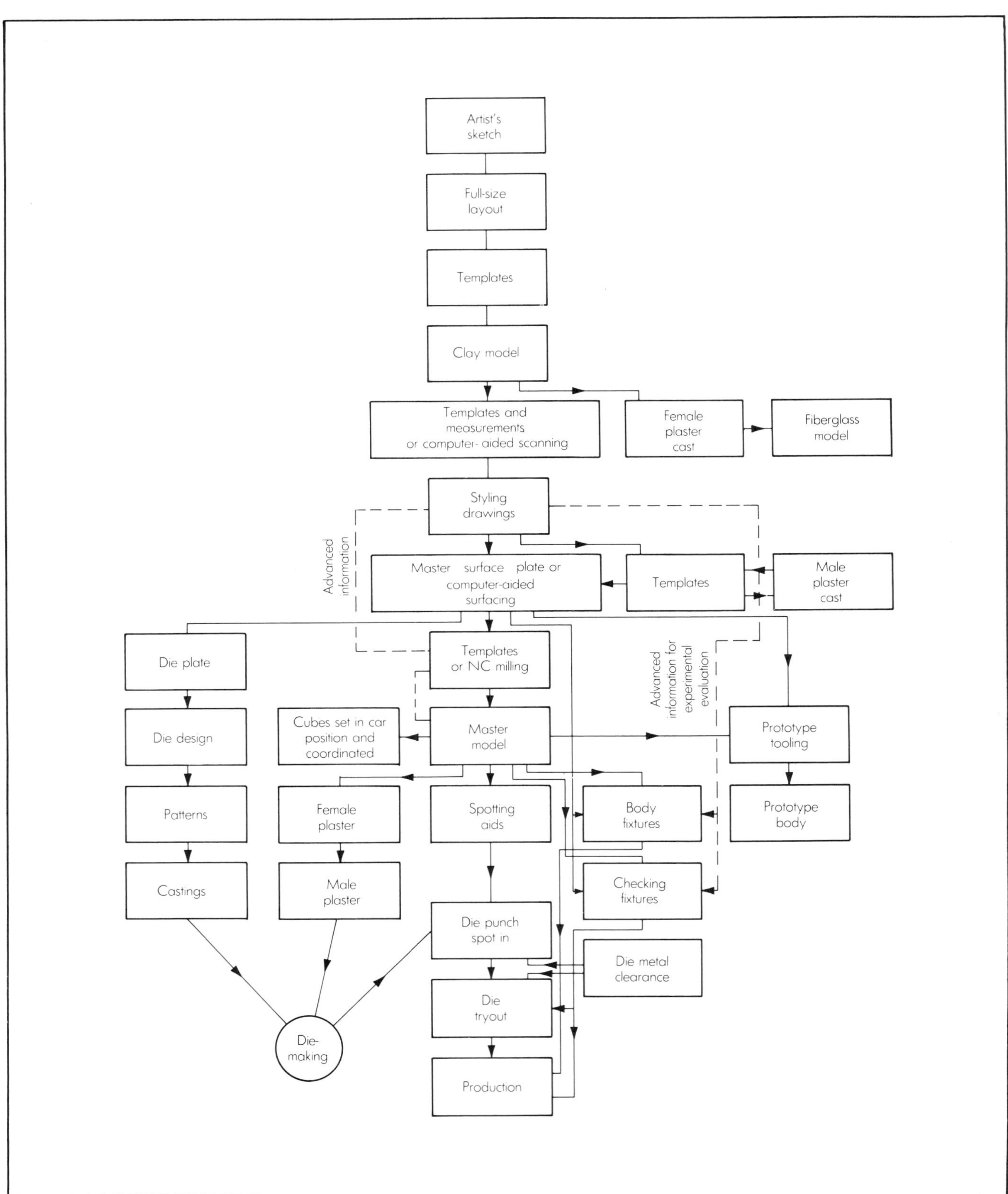


**Fig. 6-26 Flow chart of information from styling to die engineering. Many of these operations have now been eliminated by the use of CAD/CAM.**

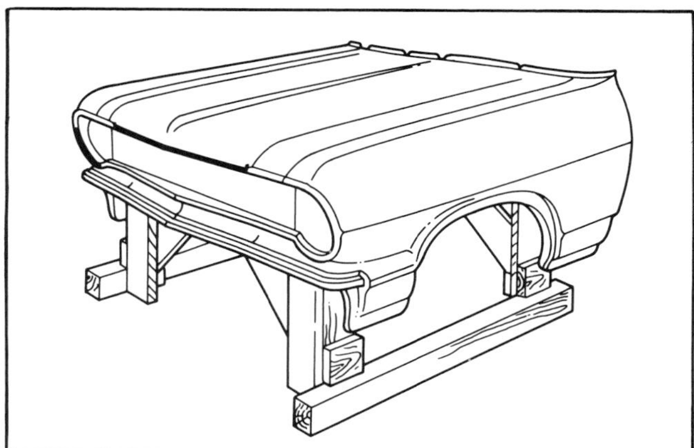

Fig. 6-27 Male model of an automobile hood and fenders.

subsequent trim and flange die conditions. The procedure is also reviewed to determine minimum size of blank for material savings with nested blanks. Sometimes, the change of a minor punch opening can reduce costs.

The plaster models taken from this preliminary model of the hood and fenders, for example, are used to develop draw-die position and wrap, as well as the flange and trim lines. The draw setup shown in Fig. 6-28 shows the male plaster removed from the female plaster. The method of developing the flange and trim lines is shown in section. The flange line development is important to panel appearance, and the trim line development in the draw is important to secondary operations.

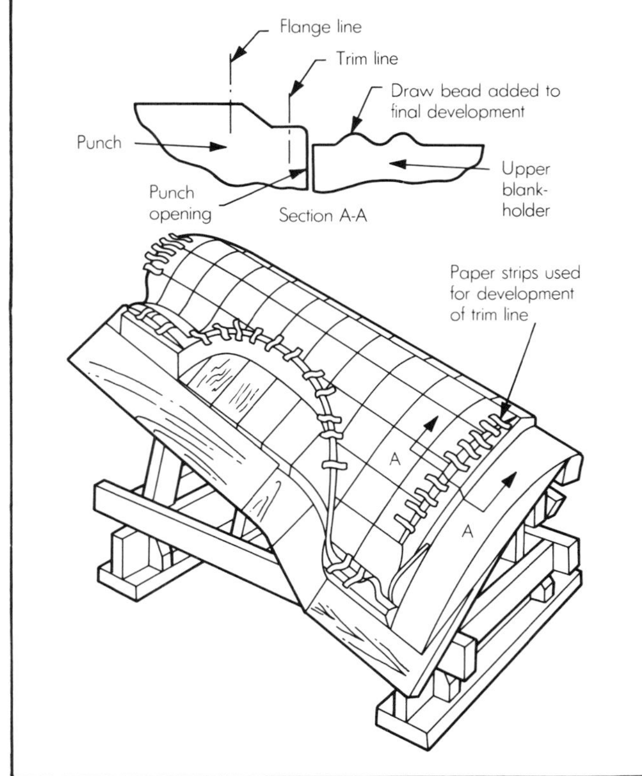


Fig. 6-28 Preliminary draw plaster.

A female plaster (see Fig. 6-29) is taken from the male. The draw ring and punch entry angle are planned to give a controlled flow of metal. The flow of metal in this configuration of die is not readily computed as in the cup shape and, therefore, must be studied and determined as outlined. Much of this development work, including draw-ring developments, trim lines, and girth developments, is being accomplished by the use of computers. For complicated designs, experimental dies, usually made of Kirksite, are built, preferably to full size, to develop optimum metal flow conditions and in some cases to establish sheet stock requirements for the panel.

Concurrent with this development, steps are taken to finalize the master surface plate and the master model (see Fig. 6-26). The wood and plastic model shown in Fig. 6-30 is the master for a fender "cubed" in car positions. This final model is used to prepare the final spotting aids and machining models used to build the dies. In many cases, to remain within the lead time, the patterns for the die, particularly the draw die, are built from preliminary specifications and then finished to the final specifications of the master model or numerical control (NC) tapes.

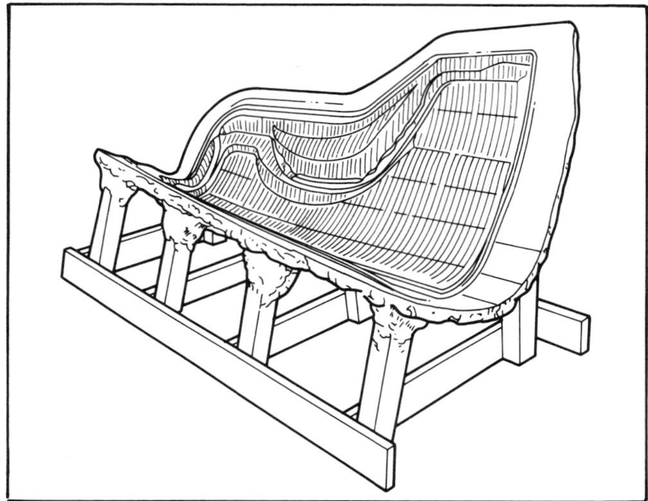

Fig. 6-29 Female plaster with preliminary wrap developed to give a wrinkle-free condition and made from a male development.

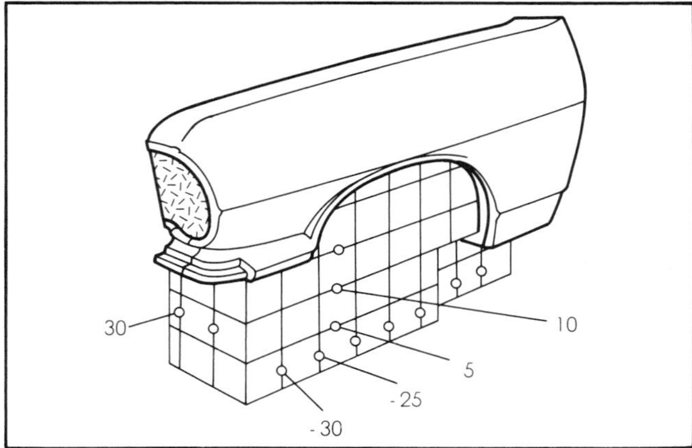


Fig. 6-30 Final wood and plastic model. In many instances, negative values have been eliminated by establishing a zero line at the front of the car.

## USE OF CAD/CAM

Substantial cost savings, improved quality, and much shorter lead times are being realized by the use of computer-aided design and computer-aided manufacturing (CAD/CAM) for designing and engineering components, as well as for producing dies. A data base created with CAD is used with CAM to program NC or CNC machines for producing models and dies.

After approval of a full-sized clay model of an automobile in the design studio, a computerized, three-dimensional digitizer is used to automatically extract coordinate data (dimensions and design geometry) from the model by scanning. This eliminates the time-consuming tasks of manually measuring points on the surfaces, fitting templates to the model, and making drawings. The digitizer transforms the physical form of the model into digital form by means of a computer-driven coordinate measuring machine. Scanning is accomplished with a mechanical probe or with noncontact video cameras or lasers.

With specially developed software programs, the raw digital data defining the surface is smoothed and refined. Using computer graphics, the product designers engineer various openings, joints, and flanges and design and analyze structural components. A cathode-ray tube (CRT) display screen, function keyboard, and light pen or two-dimensional digitizer are used for this design process. A plotter (NC drafting machine) is used to produce drawings to design specifications and to produce parts lists. The drawings are as accurate as master surface plates or mylars.

In die processing, display of the panel to be produced on the CRT eliminates the need for studying part drawings and making models. With three-dimensional viewing on the CRT, the process engineer can evaluate various tip positions, design the draw-die binder surface and punch, determine required blank size, and specify operations to be performed and presses to be used. Tapes can then be made for use on NC or CNC machines to produce models and/or dies.

A limitation of CAD/CAM is that sophisticated systems, such as those used by automotive producers, are very costly and generally not economically feasible or readily adaptable for the large number of jobbing shops that produce dies and molds. Such jobbing shops, however, can use NC graphic systems (without the need for in-house computers and programming procedures) integrated with their customer's data base. This makes it possible to complete die or mold designs from the customer's design data. In some cases, jobbing shops have NC tape-preparation devices for machining the sculptured surfaces of dies from design data supplied by the customer. In other cases, large producers supply tapes for use on NC machines in jobbing shops. Limitations to the use of CAD/CAM by automotive producers has been greatly reduced with the advent of turnkey CAD/CAM computer systems.

## RULES FOR DESIGN

The process planning engineer is confronted with producibility problems which result from the intricacy of the product design or from specific capabilities and conditions of the die; in most cases these problems are interrelated, but a good die condition does not always permit attractive styling. From experience, however, the following rules have been developed which should be considered when potential problems are recognized in the analysis of a proposed panel or in the design of the dies:

1. Avoid localized contact of punch with metal. The part should be positioned so that the punch contact area is distributed for the best utilization of the strain range of the material.
2. Draw parts to final shape in a minimum number of operations. The tipping of a part to completely form the right-hand side while the left-hand side requires additional operations is illustrated in Fig. 6-31, view *a*. Had the designer tipped the part to partially form the left-hand side, additional operations would have been required on the right-hand side, resulting in possible marking of the appearance surfaces.
3. Favor critical characteristics. Figure 6-31, view *b*, illustrates how the more critical line is favored in the

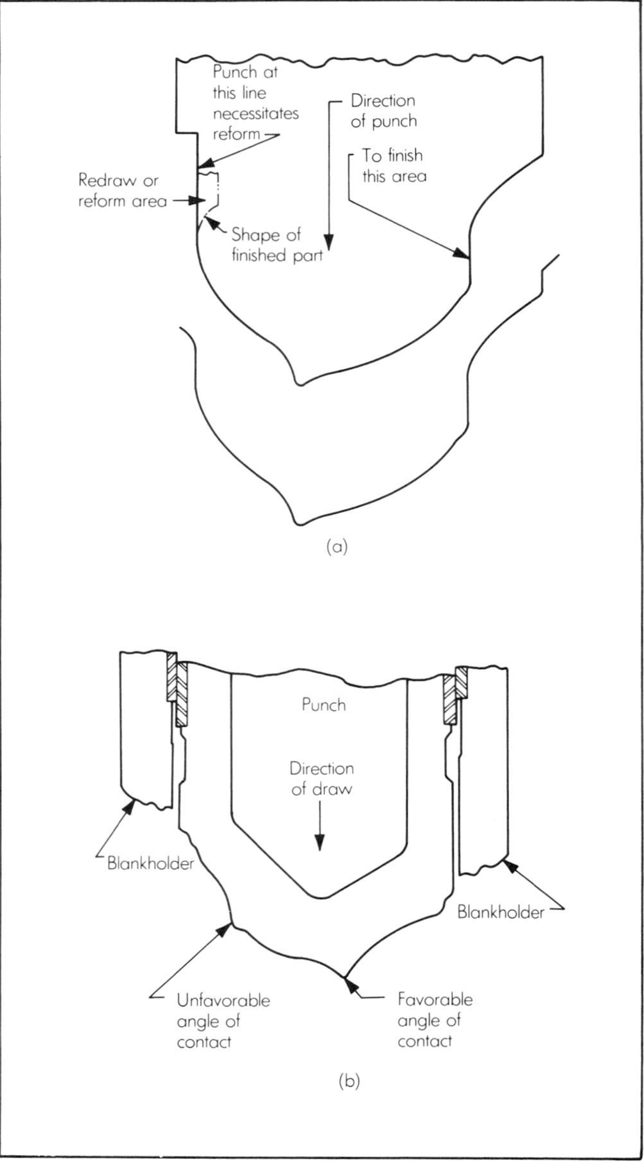


**Fig. 6-31 Punch tipping (a) to equalize punch control area and (b) to favor character lines and angle of forming.**

positioning of a part in a draw die. The more rounded surface of the protrusion on the left-hand side will cause less noticeable draw lines than the lower and sharper surface.

4. Overcrown to compensate for springback. Large areas having plane surfaces with nonsupporting characteristics often require special treatment. Springback and a weak supporting structure may be compensated for by additional crown on the punch. Development of this crown depends on experience with the type of panel and on whether the surface configuration offers any supporting strength.
5. Avoid an excess or shortage of metal from blankholder action. The wrap and the draw-die blankholder relation must not cause metal excess or shortage in appearance surfaces because such strains cannot be removed by drawing action.
6. Work the metal to establish shallow shapes. The length of the draw ring or binder line should be less than the punch part length to ensure that stretch occurs, thus elongating the metal to the permanent fabricated shape. A perfect wrap should be avoided on the face of the punch before the drawing action starts in order to stretch the surface so that it has a permanent set.
7. Minimize the effect of the length of adjacent contours. Drastic differences in lengths of lines in adjacent contours might require stretching the metal excessively through line *X* (Fig. 6-32) to prevent wrinkles along line *Y*. The problem is partially solved by more generous radii to provide metal in the deficient areas.
8. Avoid sharp radii for flow of appearance surfaces. In the case illustrated in Fig. 6-33, the initial contact of the punch at *Y* locally stresses the metal; and as the punch carries the metal into the die, the metal is further elongated by the restraining action of the blankholder and continues to move over point *Y*. The effect is usually noticeable on the appearance side of the panel.
9. Allow for subsequent flanging and trimming operations. In Fig. 6-34, note that material has been provided for the flange which has been partially formed. The trim line is accessible for trimming in a conventional trim die operation instead of by cam or indirect trimming.
10. Control location of contact marks. Figure 6-35 shows the contact mark on a panel, made in an incorrectly designed die, carried into the exposed flange. With the correct die design, the mark can be produced outside the specified 0.62″ (15.7 mm) exposed width.
11. Control metal flow close to critical shapes. When difficult shapes, such as the pyramidal shapes in Fig. 6-36, are formed, the draw ring should be kept as close as possible to the shape, and then the metal flow should be controlled by balancing the restraining action by the use of beads and blankholding pressure.

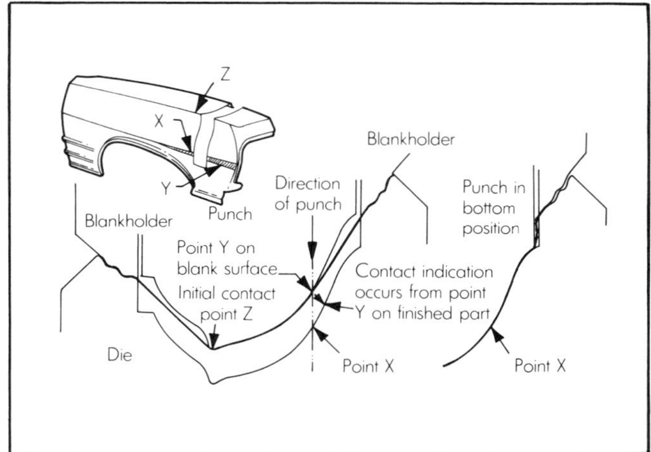


**Fig. 6-33 Punch contact and wear points.**

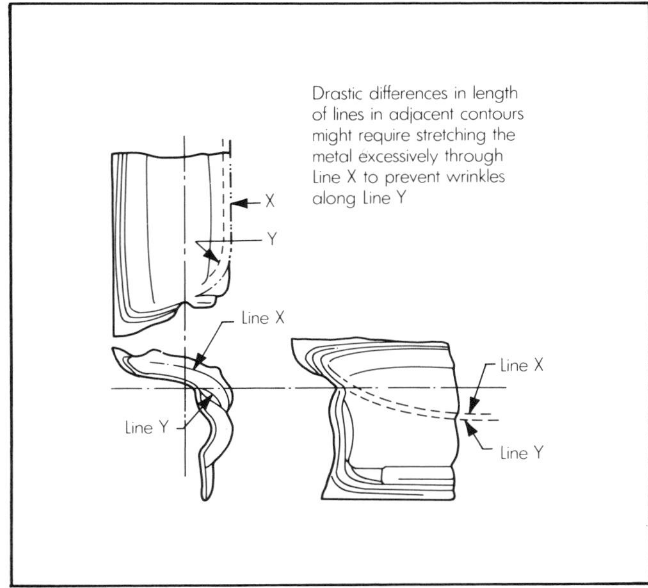


**Fig. 6-32 Adjacent contour effect.**

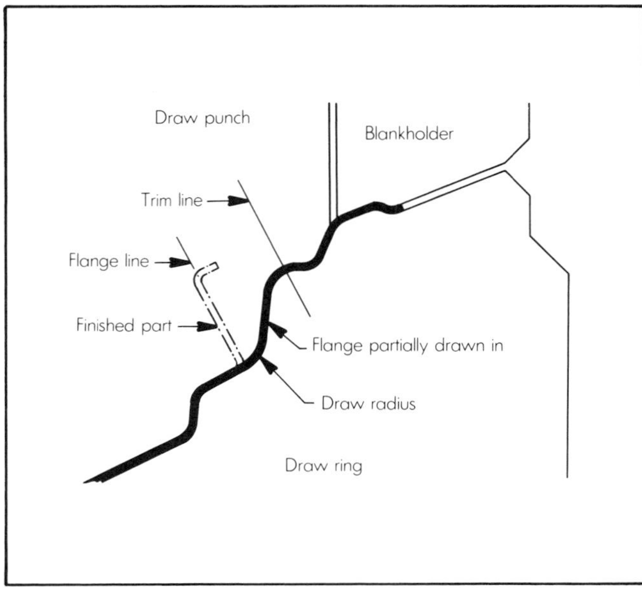


**Fig. 6-34 Development of trim and flange lines.**

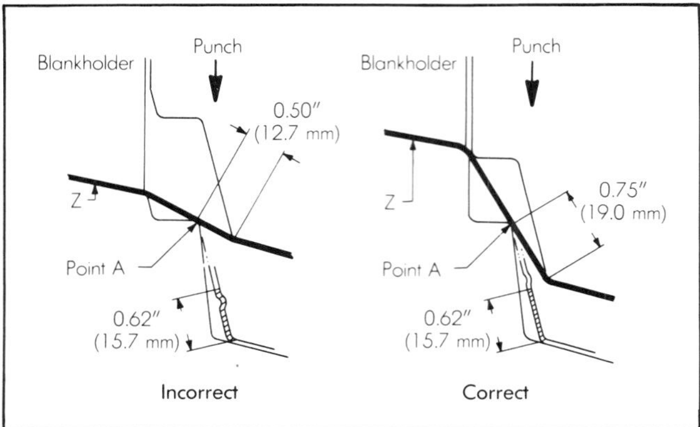


**Fig. 6-35 Trim-edge and draw-ring development.**

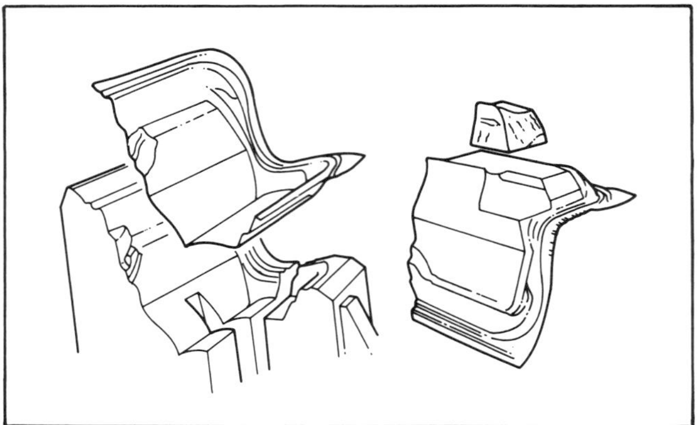

**Fig. 6-36 Control of metal flow close to critical shapes.**

# CUTTING DIES

Die cutting is the application of shear forces to coil or sheet material with a tool consisting of a mating punch and die mounted in a press, as discussed in Chapter 4, "Sheet Metal Blanking and Forming." The stock is stressed between the cutting edges of the punch and the die; and as the punch penetrates the material, compressive and tensile stresses build up and fracture occurs along the lines of stress (see Fig. 6-37). Separation of the die-cut stock generally occurs with mild steel when approximately one third of the thickness of the stock has been penetrated. However, when harder materials are die cut, penetration by the punch may be somewhat less than one-third the material thickness, and softer materials may require almost full penetration.

The various types of die cutting that may be performed include (1) blanking, (2) punching, (3) perforating, (4) slotting, (5) notching and seminotching, (6) lancing, (7) trimming, (8) slugging, (9) piercing, and (10) parting or cutoff.

## BLANKING AND PUNCHING

Blanking and punching are the basic die-cutting operations. Blanking is the cutting of stock around the complete perimeter of a shape to form a workpiece blank. Punching is the cutting of a slug from stock to produce a hole. The major factors in successful blanking and punching can generally be applied to the other die-cutting operations. These factors are punch/die clearance and punching force.

## CLEARANCE

Die cutting requires a certain amount of clearance between the punch and the die. Figure 6-38 shows a cross section of a punch and die illustrating the characteristics of blanks or slugs formed by normal and abnormal clearances. As a punch begins to penetrate the stock, the edges of the punch and the die first deform and then cut into the material. As the stock is stressed further by the punch, a fracture begins to form in the material. Proper clearance between the cutting edges enables the fracture to form a clean edge. Proper clearance is a function of the kind, thickness, and temper of the work material, as well as the size of the hole or blank being produced. A small ratio of hole or blank size to stock thickness requires greater clearance than a larger ratio.

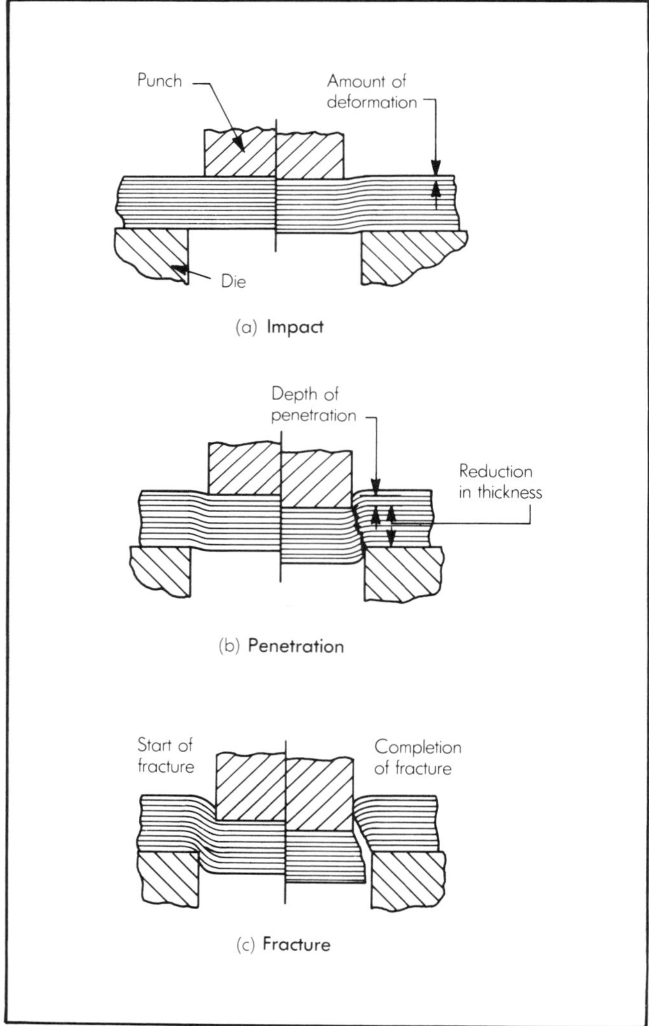


**Fig. 6-37 Steps in shearing metal. Clearances shown are exaggerated.**

Characteristics of the cut edges on both the stock and the blank are shown in Fig. 6-38. The upper corner, *A*, of the cut edge of the stock and the lower corner, *A'*, of the blank will have rounded corners where the punch and die edges, respectively, make contact with the material. This rounded edge is due to the plastic deformation that first takes place and is more pronounced when soft metals are being cut. Excessive clearance will also cause a large radius at these corners, as well as a burr on opposite corners (view *a*).

In an ideal die-cutting operation, the punch penetrates the material to a depth equal to about one third of material thickness before fracture occurs, and it forces an equal part of the material into the die opening. The portion of the material penetrated will be highly burnished, appearing as a bright cut band around the entire contour of the cut adjacent to the edge radius, as indicated at *B* and *B'1* in Fig. 6-38. When clearance is not sufficient, additional banks of metal must be cut before complete separation is accomplished, as shown in view *b*. With correct clearance, the angle of fracture permits a clean break below the cut bank because the upper and lower fractures extend toward one another. Excessive clearance results in a tapered cut edge, since for any cutting operation the opposite side of the material that the punch enters will, after cutting, be the same size as the die opening.

The width of the cut band is an indication of the hardness of the material. Provided that the die clearance and material thickness are constant, the wider the cut band, the softer the material. The harder metals permit less penetration by the punch than do ductile metals; dull tools create the effect of too small a clearance as well as a burr on the die side of the stock. Clearances are universally expressed as a percentage of stock thickness and, for clarity, should apply to one side only; that is, the clearance for a round hole is one-half the difference between punch and die diameters.

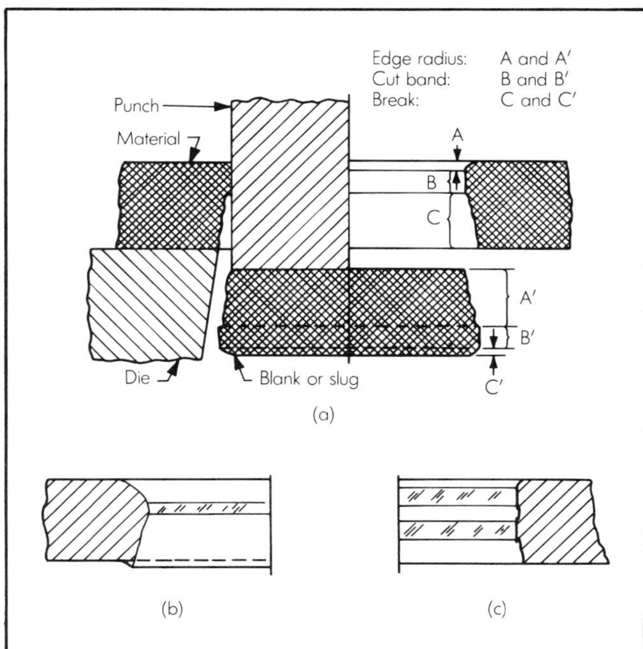


**Fig. 6-38 Die-cut edge characteristics: (a) normal clearance, (b) excessive clearance, and (c) insufficient clearance.**

Types of die-cut edges that are representative of the types that can be obtained and used by varying punch/die clearances (see Fig. 6-39) include the following:

1. Type I edges—These edges are obtained at the upper limits of clearance for usable die cutting. This type of hole or blank has a large edge radius, a large angle on the side, and a large tensile burr. Type I edge clearances are generally used on structural metalworking machines to punch a wide range of thicknesses; they are also generally used when the main purpose of the operation is to produce holes. If blanks are to be produced, Type I edges may be used if the large edge radius and burr are not important.
2. Type II edges—These have a large edge radius, a normal tensile burr, and a medium edge angle. Such edge clearances enable maximum die life to be obtained, as well as a hole or blank that is acceptable for general purposes.
3. Type III edges—Generally suitable for most purposes, these edges have a normal edge radius and show only a shallow edge angle. They are desirable for work-hardenable material that is to undergo severe forming. These clean, stress-free edges reduce the possibility of edge forming to a minimum.
4. Type IV edges—These edges are desirable for parts that require edge finishing, such as polishing. Type IV edges have a minimum edge radius, are nearly perpendicular to the face of the stock, and have heavy compressive and

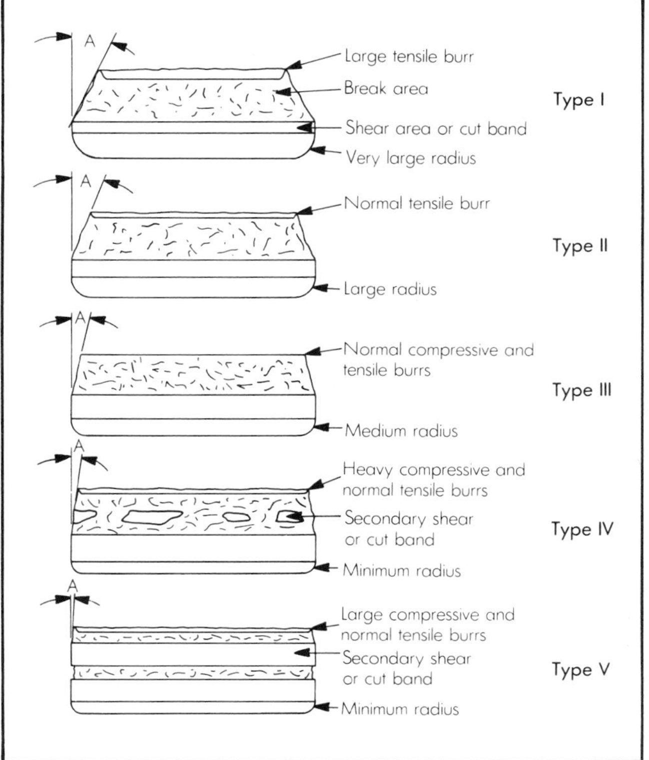


**Fig. 6-39 Five basic types of die-cut edges as variations of punch-to-die clearance.**

normal tensile burrs. Such an edge may be easily recognized by the spotty secondary shear areas on its break.

5. Type V edges—These have a minimum edge radius, are perpendicular to the stock face, and show complete secondary shear. Clearances for such edges may cause poor die life for cutting hard material, but may be useful on softer materials such as brass, lead, soft copper, and aluminum.

As a rule, clearances per side are less for soft materials than for hard materials (see Table 6-3). Clearances for punching electrical-steel laminations are listed in Table 6-4, arranged in the order of decreasing silicon content. The data indicates that the greater the silicon content is, the greater the die clearance required will be. A softer stock will require smaller die clearance, but greater angular clearance to prevent scoring of die walls. Angular clearances, per side in 1 1/2″ (38 mm) length and ground after hardening, are 0.001-0.002″ (0.03-0.05 mm) for hard stock and 0.002-0.003″ (0.05-0.08 mm) for soft stock.

A rule of thumb that is used extensively is to provide a total punch-to-die clearance of 10% of material thickness for mild steel and 6% for brass and other soft metals. Such clearances, however, represent a compromise to reduce the risk of slug pulling and result in a reduced number of parts that can be produced before the tooling requires regrinding. For many applications, larger clearances (in some cases, from 22-30% of material thickness) are being used, resulting in reduced force requirements and permitting die cutting many more parts before tool regrinding is necessary because of reduced punch and die wear. The use of large clearances, however, requires rigid presses, dies, and setups; precise alignments; smooth finishes on the tools; and good lubricants. Other factors that should be considered in determining clearances include the effect of the ratio of hole size to stock thickness, the proximity of adjacent holes or part edges, and the intended function of the workpiece.

Location of the proper clearance determines either hole or blank size; the punch controls hole size; and the die controls blank size. A hole punched to size results when the die is made to size plus double the die clearance. A blank is sheared to size when the punch is made to size less twice the die clearance. Clearances for shaving dies can be as low as 1 1/2 to 2 1/2% of stock thickness, depending upon the hardness of the workpiece material and whether removal is done in a single operation or in two successive operations.

## BLANKING OR PUNCHING FORCES

Formulas, tables, and a nomograph for determining cutting forces required to blank or punch various materials are presented in Chapter 4, "Sheet Metal Blanking and Forming."

The formulas, while providing force required for punching, are not in themselves the only factor used in the selection of proper press equipment. Providing either the punch or the die with shear equal to metal thickness (see Fig. 6-40, view *a*) could reduce the force requirements by one third to one half. By stepping the punches, as shown in view *b*, a reduction in force requirements may be obtained when more than one hole is punched. When punches or dies are reground, care must be taken to retain the stepping or the shear built into the tools. Stepping height should be slightly greater than the punch-penetration depth. When in doubt, stepping the punches one half of the stock thickness is considered a safe practice.

Alloy steels, high-carbon steels, and some stainless steels (based on their hardness), with minimal penetration of the

**TABLE 6-3**
**Side Clearances for Different Die-Cut Edge Types in Various Materials**

| | Die-Cut Edge Type | | | | |
|---|---|---|---|---|---|
| | Type I | Type II | Type III | Type IV | Type V |
| Blank Material | Clearance, percentage of blank thickness | | | | |
| High-carbon and alloy steel | 26 | 18 | 15 | 12 | |
| Mild steel (1020) | 21 | 12 | 9 | 6.5 | 2 |
| Stainless steel (304) | 23 | 13 | 10 | 4 | 1.5 |
| Copper: | | | | | |
| Hard | 25 | 11 | 8 | 3.5 | 1.25 |
| Soft | 26 | 8 | 6 | 3 | 0.75 |
| Phosphor bronze | 25 | 13 | 11 | 4.5 | 2.5 |
| Brass: | | | | | |
| Hard | 24 | 10 | 7 | 4 | 0.80 |
| Soft | 21 | 9 | 6 | 2.5 | 1 |
| Aluminum: | | | | | |
| Hard | 20 | 15 | 10 | 6 | 1 |
| Soft (250) | 17 | 9 | 7 | 3 | 1 |
| Magnesium | 16 | 6 | 4 | 2 | 0.75 |
| Lead | 22 | 9 | 7 | 5 | 2.5 |

**TABLE 6-4**
**Clearances per Side for Lamination Dies**

| Grade of Steel | Material Thickness, gage, in., (mm) | | |
|---|---|---|---|
| | 29 gage, 0.0155″ (0.394) | 26 gage, 0.0186″ (0.472) | 24 gage, 0.0249″ (0.632) |
| | Clearance per Side, in. (mm) | | |
| Transformer grades | 0.0007 (0.018) | 0.00085 (0.0216) | 0.001 (0.03) |
| Dynamo special | 0.0007 (0.018) | 0.00085 (0.0216) | 0.001 (0.03) |
| Dynamo | 0.0006 (0.015) | 0.00075 (0.0190) | 0.0009 (0.023) |
| Electrical | 0.0006 (0.015) | 0.00075 (0.0190) | 0.0009 (0.023) |
| Armature | 0.0005 (0.013) | 0.00065 (0.0165) | 0.0008 (0.020) |
| Export armature | 0.0005 (0.013) | 0.00065 (0.0165) | 0.0008 (0.020) |

punch and resultant breakthrough shock, could require equipment with as much as 50% greater capacity than calculated forces. The reversal of stresses, often referred to as snap-through, in equipment when blanking these materials is so sudden and severe that improperly selected equipment can be seriously damaged.

Figure 6-41 shows an oscilloscope trace of punch penetration through 201 stainless steel. In a press cycle, the first load

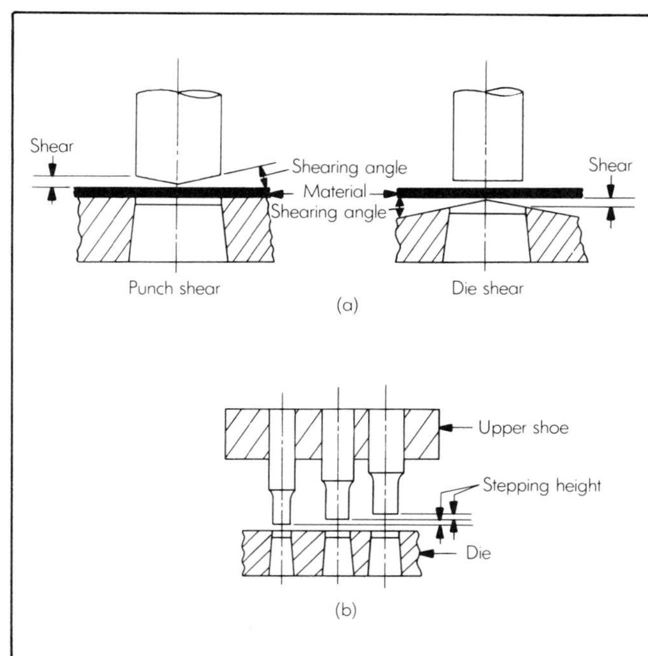


**Fig. 6-40 Shear (a) and stepping (b) added to punches to reduce press force requirements.**

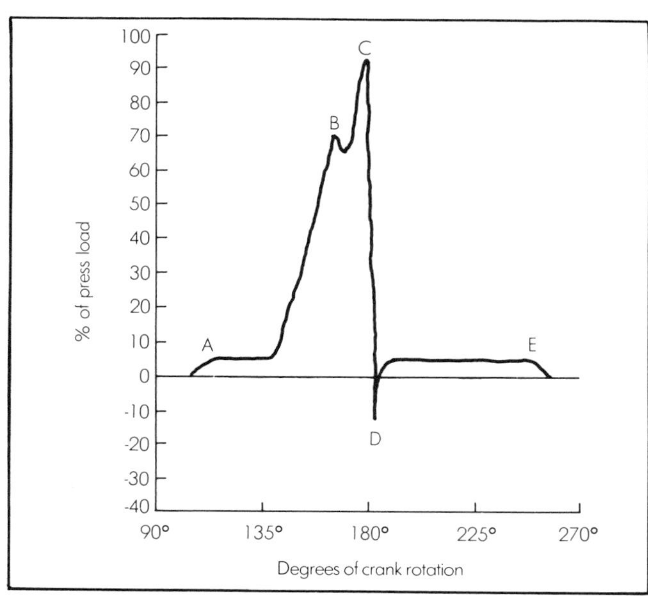


**Fig. 6-41 Oscilloscope trace of press loads during punching.**

imposed is at Point *A*, which represents hold-down and stripper forces. The curve increases sharply to Point *B*, then takes a slight dip and a rise to Point *C*. The sharp decline following Point *C* is a negative force, and Point *D* indicates the severe reversal of stresses. Point *E* is the removal of hold-down or stripper forces. The severity of the reversal stresses should be limited based on the press being used. The industry generally limits the Point *D* load to 8-10% of press capacity on single-point, C-frame presses and 12-15% of press capacity on straight-side presses. If breakthrough loads are greater than 15%, special equipment is required.

## DIE DESIGN

A blanking die is generally cheaper to make and faster in operation than a trim die. Depending upon the tolerances of a part, it may be better to blank before forming than to trim all around the edges after forming. A single blanking die can produce either a right-hand or a left-hand part, while two trim dies (right and left-handed) are needed for trimming around the edges of the two parts.

A flat blank sheared by a blank-through type of blanking die (see Fig. 6-42) drops through the die block (lower shoe) and

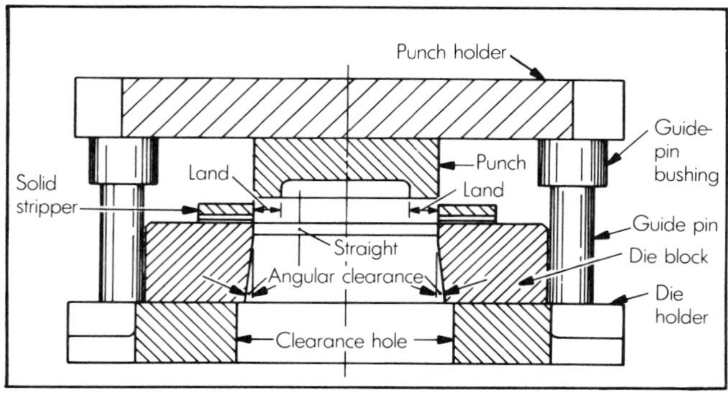


**Fig. 6-42 Drop-through blanking die showing straight, land, and angular clearance.**

onto the bolster plate, often provided with an unloading chute, or drops through a hole in both die block and bolster plate. In a return-blank die (see Fig. 6-43), the blank is pushed up into the die cavity, after which it is ejected by a spring-loaded knockout. Different spring pressures are important for various applications. The stripper removes the stock from the punch as the press slide rises and the die opens. Return-blank die designs frequently incorporate positive knockouts actuated through linkages in the press ram instead of through spring pressure. A return-blank die is slower in operation due to the need for blank removal and costs more to build than a drop-through die because of the additional die sections required.

The perforating die shown in Fig. 6-44 is a typical single-station design for producing holes in flat stock that is manually or mechanically fed and is kept on a straight path through the die by the stock guides. The amount of stock travel is controlled by the method of feeding, by stops of various designs, or by direct or indirect piloting. The spring-loaded stripper clamps and helps position the stock during the punching of the three holes.

Spring-loaded knockout
Upper shoe
Die
Stock
Outside (punch) stripper
Punch
Lower shoe
Stripper spring
Open die
Knockout bolt
Stripper bolt
Stripper travel
Start of blanking
Knockout travel
Scrap
Punch mounting and spacer block
Closed die

**Fig. 6-43 Return-blank blanking die.**

The die shown in Fig. 6-45 vertically punches a central hole in the bottom of a copper bowl and, by cam action, a hole in the side of the bowl. The stripper plate guides the vertical punch and prevents distortion in the flat bottom of the bowl as the punch is withdrawn. It also positions and holds the bottom while the open end fits around the locator. The side punch sleeve allows punch removal. Slugs from both holes drop through a clearance hole in the lower shoe. Deep parts of this type must be handled manually, and tongs are generally used to meet safety requirements for loading and unloading. It should be noted that the side punch is returned by spring action as the cam withdraws with the slide. A more positive punch-return mechanism is shown in Fig. 6-46. In this mechanism, the punch is positively advanced and returned by a punch shoulder which slides freely in a T-slot in the cam.

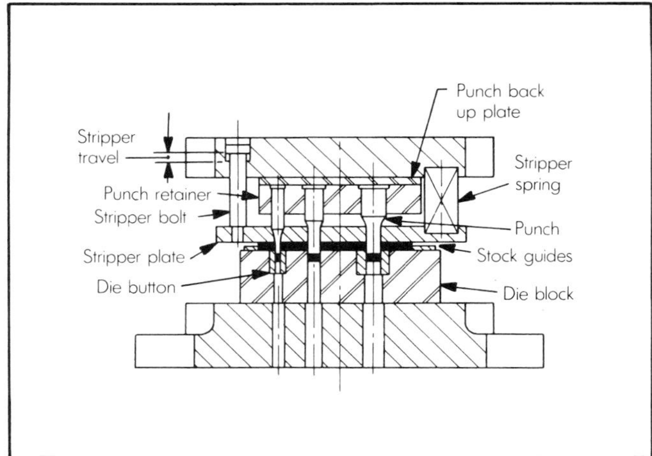


**Fig. 6-44 Perforating die.**

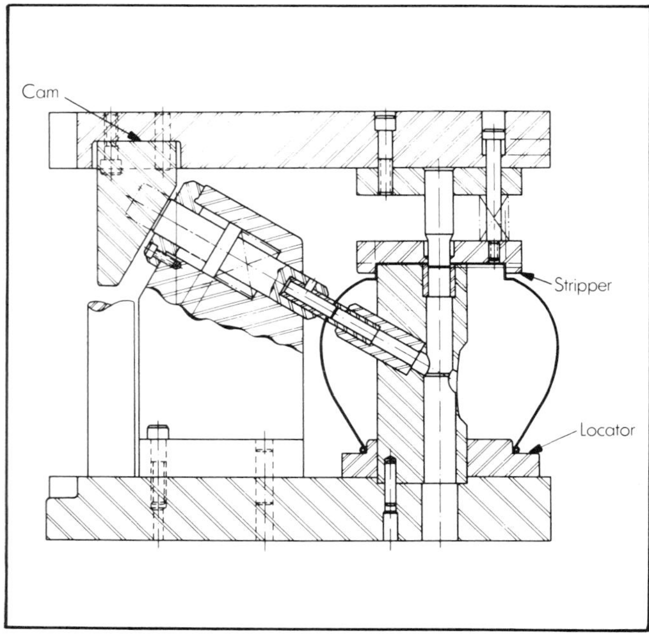


**Fig. 6-45 Vertical and angular punching.** (*Knapp-Monarch Co.*)

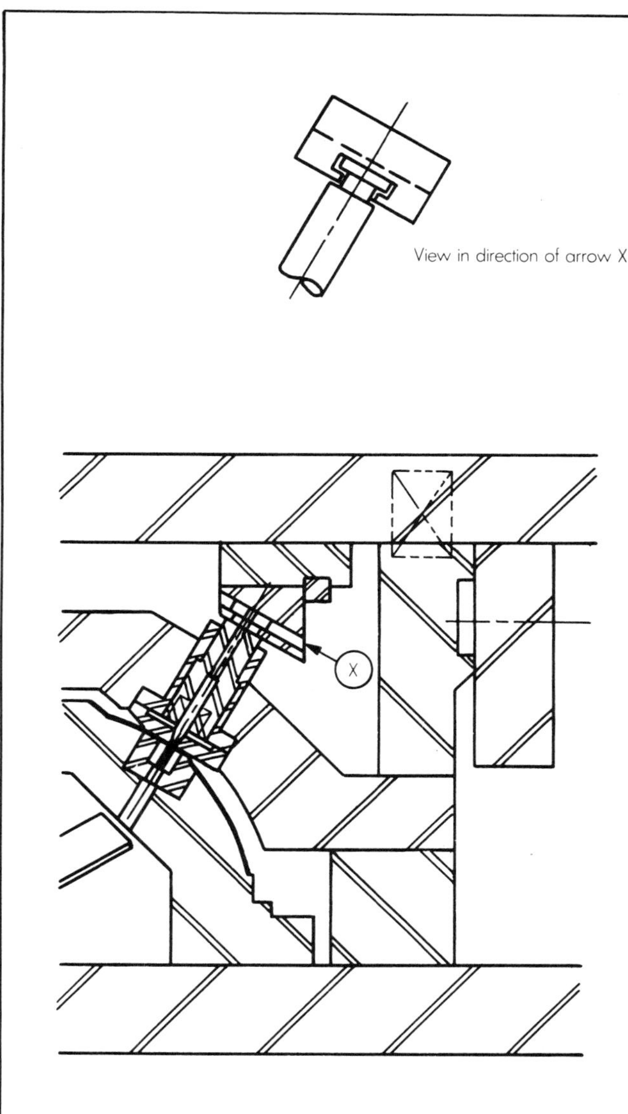


Fig. 6-46 Angular punching with positive aerial cam punch advance and return. (*Livernois Automation Co.*)

## Punches

Standard punches are available for a wide variety of round, oblong, and square holes. The manufacturers furnish these punches in the general proportions listed in Table 6-5 and illustrated in Fig. 6-47 as well as in any design to special order. Also available are die buttons corresponding to a punch size. Commercial punching units, having interchangeable punches and die buttons, may be quickly set up in presses or press brakes to accommodate hole-pattern changes. Classified common shapes, such as flatted round, hexagonal, keyhole, hourglass, and triangular, are offered by most punch manufacturers. Specifications for these classified-shape punches only require the use of a minimum number of dimensions. Recommended dimensions for heavy and normal-duty shouldered punches are given in Table 6-6 and illustrated in Fig. 6-48.

**TABLE 6-5**
**Dimensions of Commercially Available, Standard Basic Punches Shown in Fig. 6-47**

| | | | D | | |
|---|---|---|---|---|---|
| A* | B | C | Shoulder Type** | Ball-Lock Type† | E |
| 0.062-0.186 | 0.43 | 0.1875 | 1.50-2.50 | --- | 0.31 |
| 0.062-0.249‡ | 0.50 | 0.2500 | 1.50-2.50 | --- | 0.37 |
| 0.093-0.311 | 0.56 | 0.3125 | 1.50-3.00 | --- | 0.43 |
| 0.125-0.374 | 0.62 | 0.3750 | 1.75-3.00 | 2.50-4.00 | 0.50 |
| 0.187-0.499 | 0.81 | 0.5000 | 2.00-3.50 | 2.50-4.00 | 0.62 |
| 0.375-0.624 | 0.93 | 0.6250 | 2.00-3.50 | 2.50-4.00 | 0.75 |
| 0.500-0.749 | 1.06 | 0.7500 | 2.25-4.00 | 2.50-4.00 | 0.87 |
| 0.687-0.999 | 1.25 | 1.0000 | 2.50-4.00 | 3.00-4.00 | 1.12 |

Note: All dimensions in inches.

* In 0.0005″ increments.
** In 0.25″ increments.
† In 0.50″ increments.
‡ Size and length range for wire-type punches.

## Steel Rule Dies

Many types of steel rule dies (also called cookie-cutter or low-cost dies) are used regularly for a wide range of applications. All such dies make use of low-cost materials, and all are constructed in a fraction of the time needed to make conventional dies for the same operations. Two distinctly different operating principles separate the various types into the classifications of (1) single-element dies and (2) two-element dies.

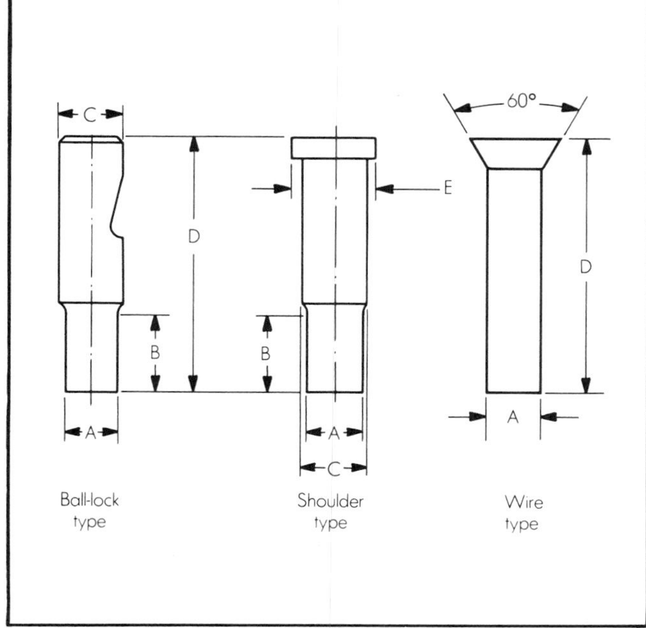


**Fig. 6-47 Standard dimensions of commercial punches (see Table 6-5).**

**TABLE 6-6**
**Punch Dimensions Shown in Fig. 6-48**

| P +0.0005,-0.0000 | D +0.0002,+0.0005 | H +0.000,-0.010 | T +0.010,-0.000 | B +0.06,-0.00 |
|---|---|---|---|---|
| Normal-duty punches for mild steel, 0.022-0.093″ thick | | | | |
| 0.062-0.188 | 0.2500 | 0.37 | 0.12 | 0.50-0.75 |
| 0.093-0.218 | 0.3125 | 0.43 | 0.12 | 0.56-1.00 |
| 0.125-0.250 | 0.3750 | 0.50 | 0.19 | 0.62-1.00 |
| 0.187-0.375 | 0.5000 | 0.62 | 0.19 | 0.81-1.00 |
| 0.375-0.500 | 0.6250 | 0.75 | 0.25 | 0.93-1.25 |
| 0.500-0.687 | 0.7500 | 0.87 | 0.25 | 1.06-1.25 |
| 0.687-0.937 | 1.0000 | 1.12 | 0.25 | 1.25 |
| Heavy-duty punches* for mild steel, over 0.093″ thick | | | | |
| 0.093-0.188 | 0.3125 | 0.43 | 0.12 | 0.56-0.75 |
| 0.125-0.218 | 0.3750 | 0.50 | 0.19 | 0.62-0.75 |
| 0.187-0.250 | 0.5000 | 0.62 | 0.19 | 0.81 |
| 0.250-0.375 | 0.6250 | 0.75 | 0.25 | 0.93 |
| 0.375-0.625 | 0.7500 | 0.87 | 0.25 | 1.06 |
| 0.625-0.875 | 1.0000 | 1.12 | 0.25 | 1.25 |

Note: All dimensions in inches.

R = 0.010-0.020″
F = 0.625″ min. for normal-duty punches, and 1.000″ min. for heavy-duty punches.

*Points must be altered below standard.

**Single-element dies.** All of the older, better known types of rule die tooling fall into this category, which includes dinkers, clickers, one-piece forms, block dies, and cutting and creasing dies. For the most part, these are single-element tools consisting of a die section only and having no opposing punch. They employ printer's rule or similar strip steel, with a sharp edge, bent or formed to the outline shape of the part desired. Suitably mounted, the shaped knives are operated against a flat metal platen or a hard wood block to produce a desired blank by cutting or cleaving action.

Dies of this type are widely used for the cutting of paper, cardboard, fiber, rubber, felt, leather, and similar soft materials, and occasionally for the blanking of thin, soft metals. The printer's or die-cutter's rule is suitably held within a kerf sawed from a die board 5/8 or 3/4″ (16 or 19 mm) thick and consisting of five to seven plies of gum or maple wood (see Fig. 6-49).

Cutting rule heights are standard, from 0.918 to 0.923″ and 0.937″ (23.32 to 23.44 mm and 23.80 mm). The kerf is often cut intermittently with gaps tying in the framework. When gaps are used in the die board, in one-piece forms, the rule is notched or bridged so that the upper cutting surface is continuous. Pieces of rule may also be used and are inserted in the kerf with a mallet. In clicker dies, the ends of the rule are brazed to preserve continuity and to strengthen the cutting form.

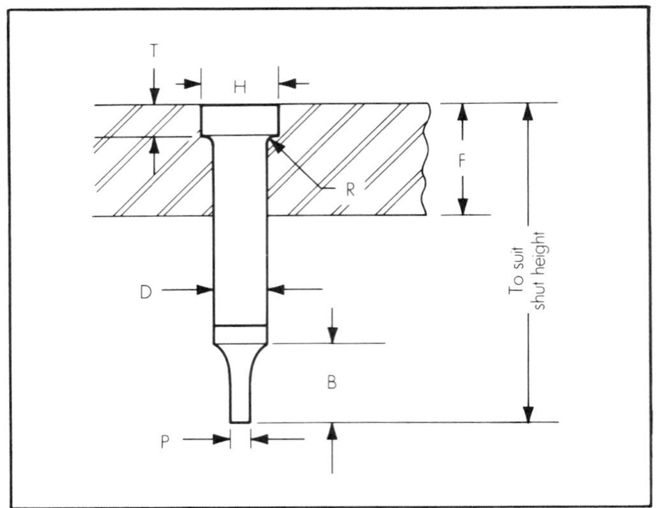


**Fig. 6-48 Recommended dimensions for normal and heavy-duty shouldered punches (see Table 6-6).**

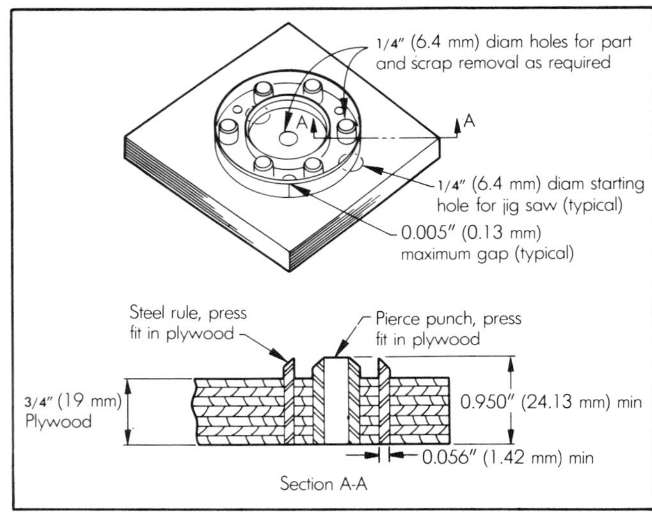


**Fig. 6-49 Steel rule die for cutting paper, fiber, rubber, felt, leather, and other soft materials.**

The steel rule should be inserted or attached at 90° ±1/4° to the surface of the die board. Generally, they are hardened to $R_C$ 52-55, although this hardness may not be necessary for some materials. These dinking rules are purchased in soft to hard condition. They are readily worked in the $R_C$ 40-50 hardness range and are generally cut to size in all prehardened conditions.

Stripper material is usually 5/16 to 3/8" (8 to 9.5 mm) thick, extending somewhat over the height of the cutting rules. It is usually made of neoprene, cork sheet, or rubber. These single-element tools may be mounted in almost any form of press. In some instances they are operated in printing presses. Although useful and economical within their area of application, the operating principle limits their application in the metalworking industries.

**Two-element dies.** The two-element steel rule die does not produce parts by cutting action. Instead, it employs a rule to exert force to produce a fracture in shear to the outline desired. Although not precisely the same, the action is similar to that of the conventional punch and die. Construction methods and specifications vary for these two-element dies, and developments have resulted in the granting of various patents on dies and associated equipment.

Steel rule and wood, or a similar substance, may be used for the upper die section, but somewhat more attention must be given to construction detail, and better grades of materials must be employed. The punch-like section is made from relatively thin steel plate, usually of a hardenable steel, which is mounted on a subplate. Because of the need to contain the stresses involved in shearing steel sheet and plate, considerable know-how is required to construct and operate this type of tool properly. Neoprene, springs, or other suitable ejectors are used to remove the blank and strip the waste. Punches may be installed to pierce while blanking the workpiece.

Metalworking rule dies are best operated in specially designed master die sets (see Fig. 6-50), which permit interchangeability and corrective adjustment for stability and alignment. While commonly utilized as compound blank and pierce or notching tools, the metalworking rule die has been extended to areas permitting combined operations in dies which blank, form, trim, and pierce in a single hit (see Fig. 6-51).

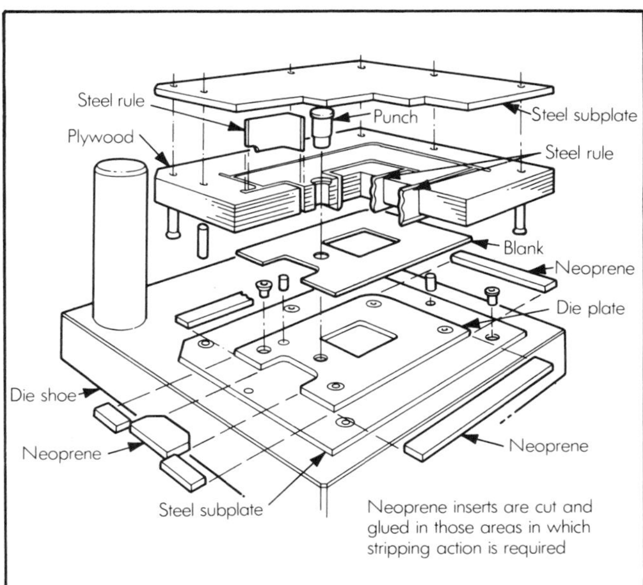


**Fig. 6-50 Exploded assembly view of a steel rule die.**

Various other designs of metalworking rule tooling, such as progressive and trimming dies, have been used with some success. In general, this tooling is not recommended for small parts. However, on larger parts, tool economies show an increased saving proportionate to size.

One steel rule die user recommends the steel rule thicknesses listed in Table 6-7. A land is ground on the steel rule, as shown in Fig. 6-52, with a minimum bevel length of 0.015" (0.38 mm). Standard methods of applying shear to the die may be used if the press force capacity is exceeded. Conventional punch and die clearances are used for the material being blanked. The shear plate shown in Fig. 6-51 may be made of high carbon steel such as SAE 1080 or 1095, or alloy steel such as SAE 4130 or 8630 and heat treated to $R_C$ 39-44. Large sections may be flame hardened.

## Other Cutting Dies

Other designs of cutting dies commonly used include:

1. Pinch-trimming dies—The trimming operation in which pinch-trimming dies are employed is usually combined with drawing, forming, sizing, or flanging and produces a uniform trimmed edge of doubtful quality. The edge is usually feathered. The type of die shown in Fig 6-53, *a*, is simple to maintain.
2. Brehm trimming (shimmy) dies—The design and action of this die (see Fig. 6-53, *b*) make it possible to trim shells, boxes, cups, and the like and to include tabs, notches, and angles. The stamping to be trimmed is dropped into a recess in the die, flange up. A floating arbor or locating pad is mounted in the punch and contacts the stamping first. The die is floating but positively controlled by cams on the downstroke, causing it to move from left to right and front to back, thus trimming in all directions.

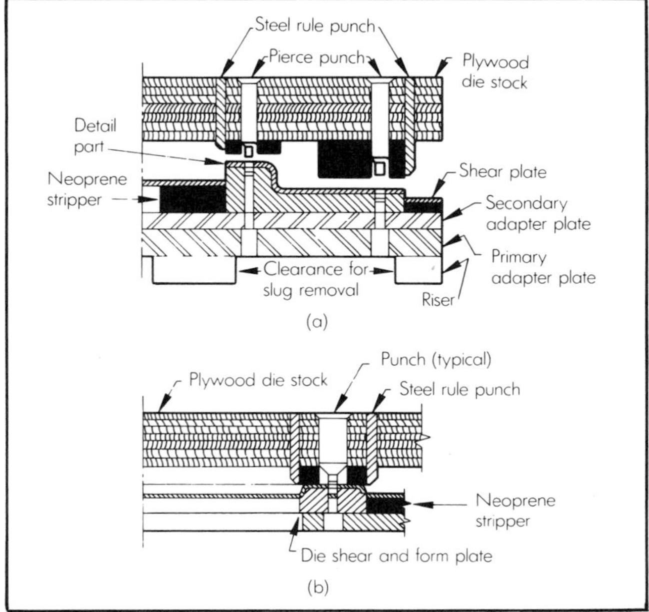


**Fig. 6-51 Steel rule dies: (a) for piercing and trimming a preformed workpiece and (b) for forming, piercing, and blanking a workpiece.** (*Template Industries, Inc.*)

**TABLE 6-7**
**Recommended Steel Rule Thicknesses for Various Materials**

| Material Thickness, in. (mm) | Material: Steel, Mild | Steel, 4130 | Steel, Stainless, 302 | Aluminum, Soft | Aluminum, 2024-T | Aluminum, 7075-T | Brass, 1/2 Hard |
|---|---|---|---|---|---|---|---|
| | Steel Rule Thickness, in. (mm) | | | | | | |
| 0.010 (0.25) | 0.056 (1.42) | 0.056 (1.42) | 0.056 (1.42) | 0.042 (1.07) | 0.056 (1.42) | 0.056 (1.42) | 0.056 (1.42) |
| 0.031 (0.79) | 0.056 (1.42) | 0.056 (1.42) | 0.056 (1.42) | 0.056 (1.42) | 0.056 (1.42) | 0.056 (1.42) | 0.056 (1.42) |
| 0.062 (1.57) | 0.056 (1.42) | 0.056 (1.42) | 0.084 (2.13) | 0.056 (1.42) | 0.056 (1.42) | 0.056 (1.42) | 0.056 (1.42) |
| 0.078 (1.98) | 0.056 (1.42) | 0.084 (2.13) | 0.084 (2.13) | 0.056 (1.42) | 0.056 (1.42) | 0.056 (1.42) | 0.056 (1.42) |
| 0.093 (2.36) | 0.084 (2.13) | 0.084 (2.13) | 0.084 (2.13) | 0.056 (1.42) | 0.084 (2.13) | 0.084 (2.13) | 0.056 (1.42) |
| 0.125 (3.18) | 0.084 (2.13) | 0.112 (2.84) | 0.112 (2.84) | 0.084 (2.13) | 0.084 (2.13) | 0.084 (2.13) | 0.084 (2.13) |
| 0.150 (3.81) | 0.112 (2.84) | 0.112 (2.84) | --- | 0.084 (2.13) | 0.112 (2.84) | 0.112 (2.84) | 0.084 (2.13) |

3. Shaving dies—Shaving dies are used to obtain finished edges or surfaces and sizes on light and heavy stampings, forgings, tubing, etc., for low or high production. If precision is required, rough and finish shaving operations are used, with the finish operation removing from 0.001-0.002" (0.03-0.05 mm). Holes can be shaved in complicated blanks with concentricity equivalent to that of a precision-boring operation. This type of die is used extensively in the manufacture of timepieces, typewriters, adding machines, automobiles, etc.; its action is similar to that of broaching.

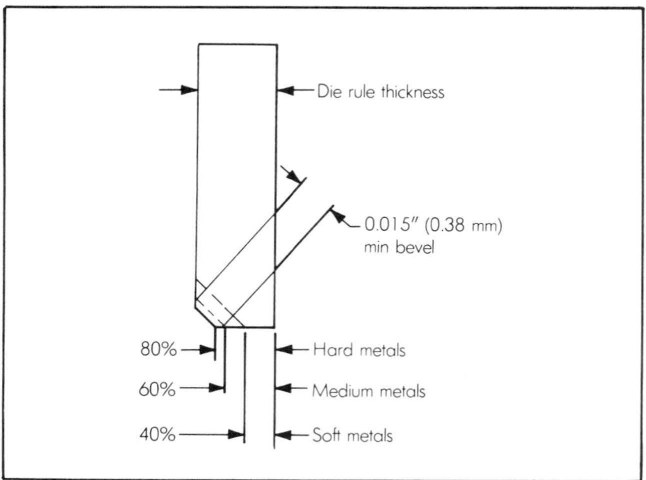


**Fig. 6-52 Grinding specifications for steel rule dies.** (*Template Industries, Inc.*)

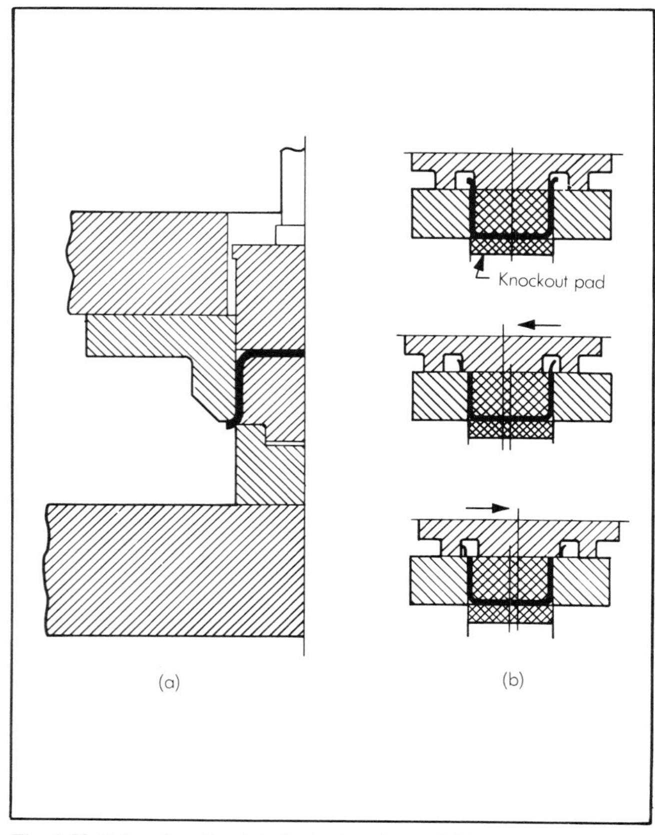


**Fig. 6-53 Trimming dies: (a) pinch trimming and (b) shimmy trimming.**

# FORMING DIES

Dies are used for many sheet metal forming operations. The more common forming operations accomplished with press-mounted dies include bending and flanging, embossing, beading, drawing, ironing, bulging, and compression operations.

## BENDING AND FLANGING

The forming processes of bending and flanging are discussed in Chapter 4, "Sheet Metal Blanking and Forming." Details with respect to bend allowances, force requirements, types of bending, and press brake dies are presented in Chapter 10, "Bending and Straightening."

The forming die shown in Fig. 6-54, used in a conventional press, was designed to form a part to close limits (see Fig. 6-55). All punches and the heel blocks incorporate carbide inserts. The vertical form punch limits the height of the bent ear to 0.185" (4.70 mm) ±0.005" (0.13 mm). A flattening punch holds the

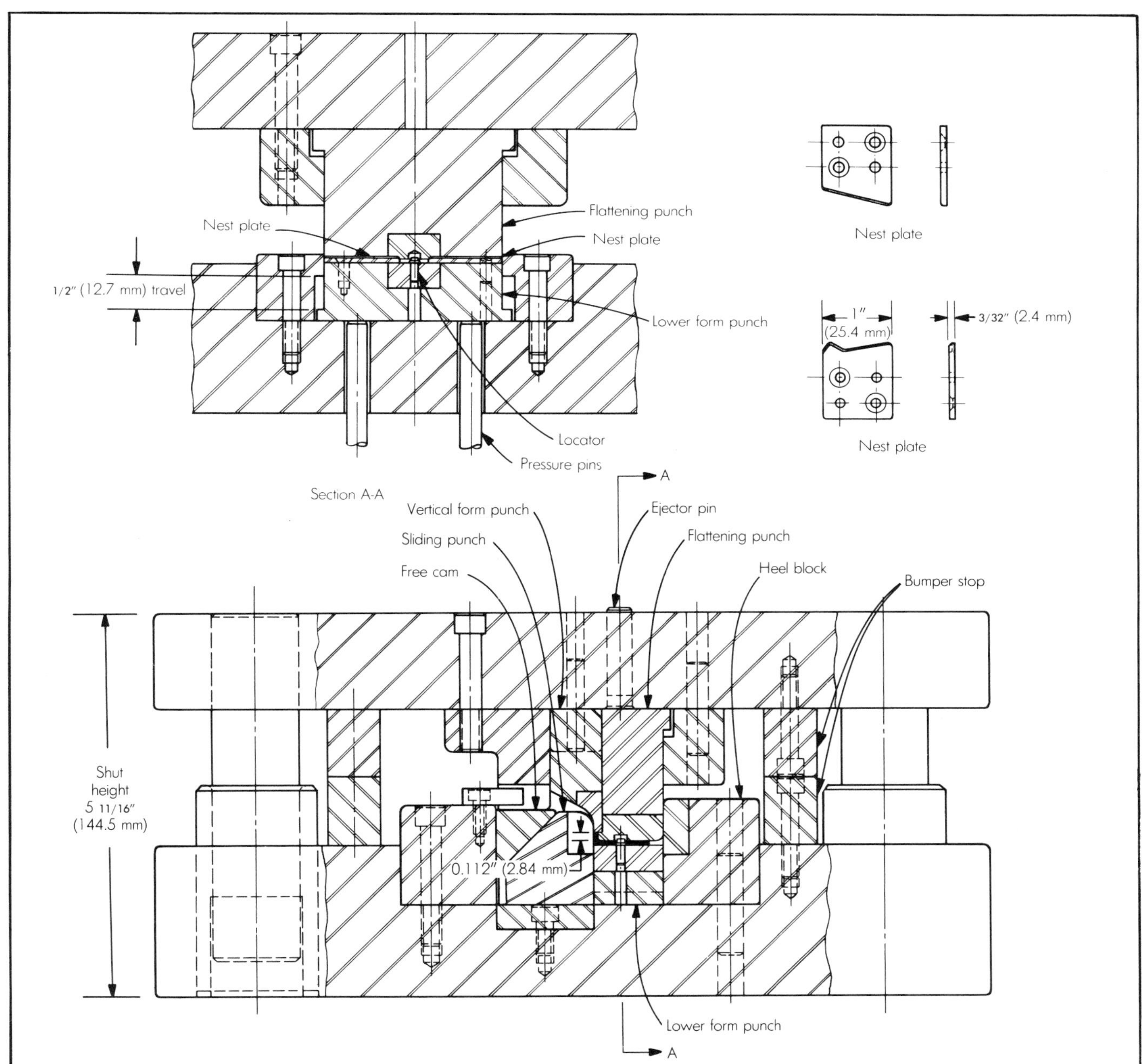


**Fig. 6-54 Forming die with carbide inserts.** (*National Cash Register Co.*)

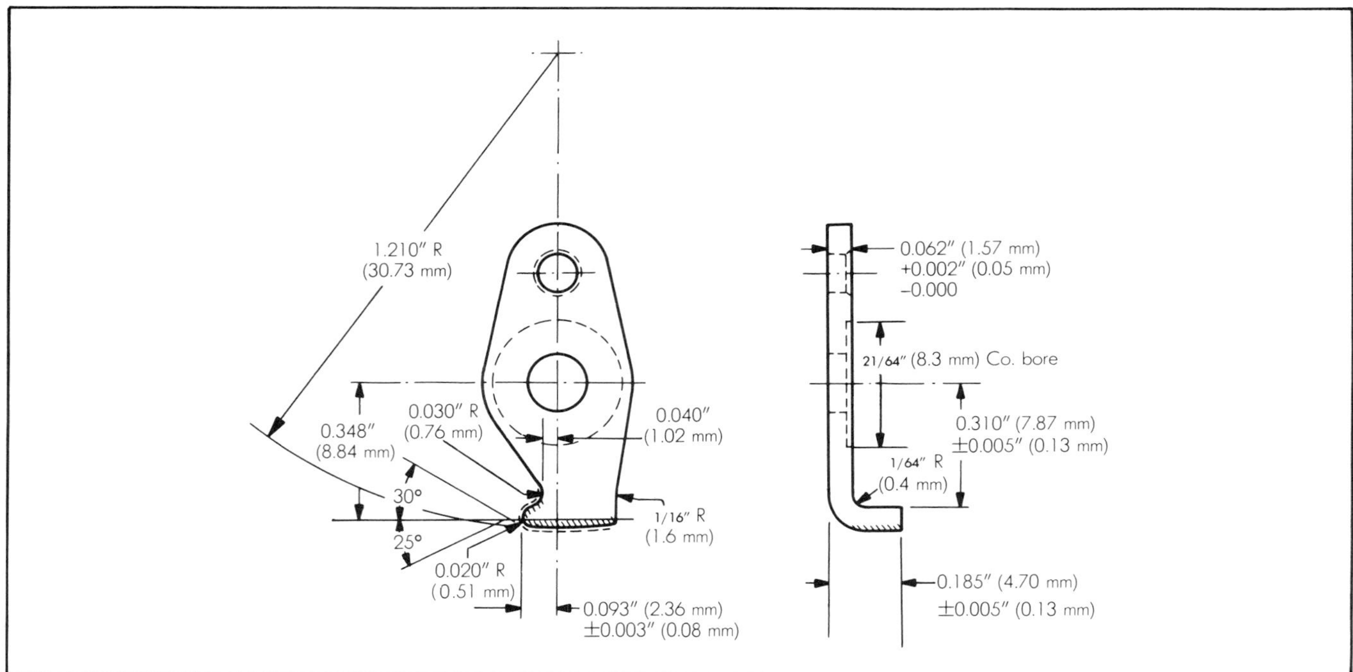


**Fig. 6-55 Part formed in die illustrated in Fig. 6-54.**

radius of the bend to 1/64″ (0.4 mm) and is backed up by the heel block. The sliding punch swages a 1.210″ (30.73 mm) radius on the bent ear through the action of the free cam. A locating pin is provided on the lower form punch. The contour of the part is machined in the face of the flattening punch. The 90° bend is formed between the sliding punch and the flattening punch. This is a triple-action die, with one action accomplished through pressure pins which force the lower form punch 1/2″ (12.7 mm) upward.

The size of the part formed in the die shown in Fig. 6-56 requires an air-operated lifter to push it up and out of the die. The back edge of the part is flanged vertically, while its front

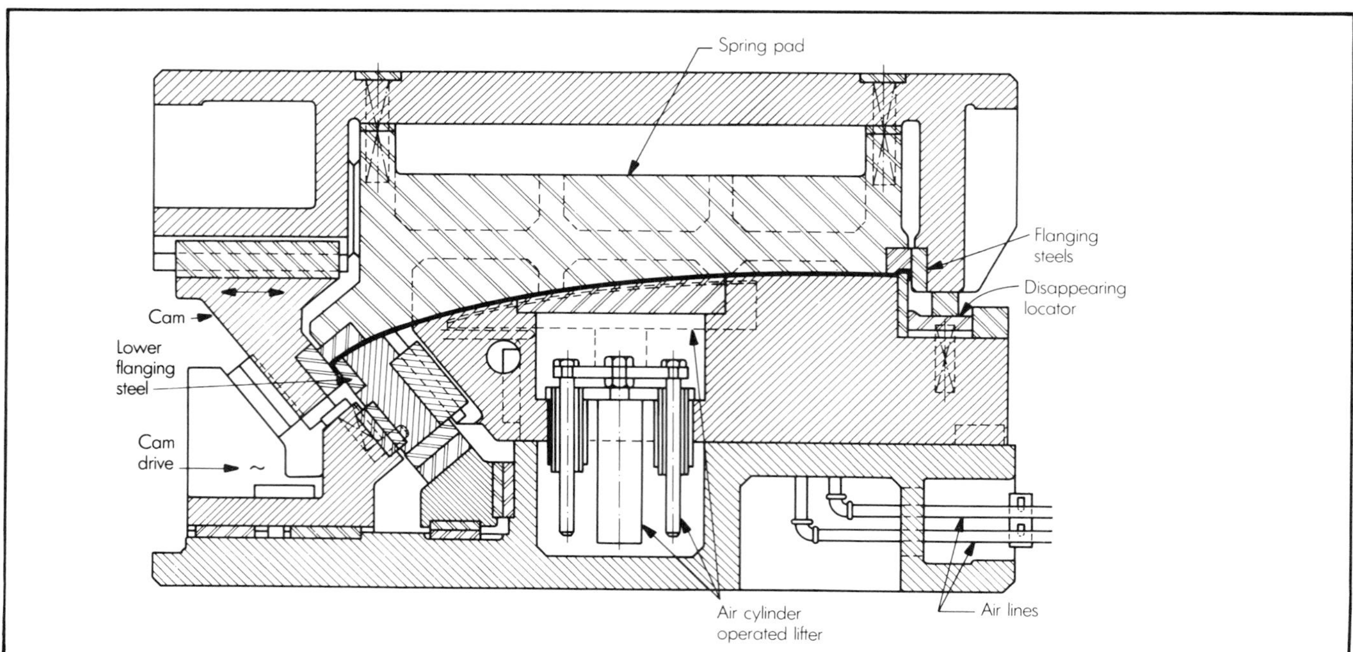


**Fig. 6-56 Automobile-hood flange and cam flange die (section from front to back).**

edge is flanged at any angle by the descending cammed punch forced inward by the cam driver. The spring-loaded pad clamps the hood to prevent it from moving during the two flanging operations. Disappearing locators, spaced around the edge of the blank, locate and position it before the pressure pad, with its clamping action, descends. On the upstroke of the press, the lower flanging steel is retracted by another cam mechanism (not shown) to allow the stamping to be raised by the lifter.

While various cam designs are often incorporated in dies for cutting operations, they are also frequently used in forming at an angle to the press ram. The dogleg cam driver (see Fig. 6-57) reciprocates through a slot in the cam slide and ensures positive cam-slide travel in both directions. The heel block resists the return and forming thrusts of the vertical portion of the driver. More commonly used are spring-returned designs such as that shown in Fig. 6-58, having a protective housing around the projecting members of the assembly. Spring returns are the most inexpensive cam-return methods; but if the spring fails, the dies and the parts may be damaged. A positive return method to replace the spring return is shown in Fig. 6-59. In this positive method, the cam slide is driven and returned by a tabbed gib which slides freely in slots in both the cam slide and the driver.

Cams, slides, and other driving and driven surfaces of die parts are frequently made with wear plates having surfaces at angles that enable maximum efficiency to be obtained (see Fig. 6-60). Drawings should show their forward and return positions for necessary travel, clearance, and pickup.

Straight brass pipe is formed into a sickle curve in the die shown in Fig. 6-61. Two pilots are pushed into the ends of the pipe, which is forced through the curved die cavity. Circular outside beads, under compression of the excess metal, are then formed on both ends of the pipe, which must be cut to exact length to obtain the required bead dimensions. On the upstroke, the operating lever is pulled back to open the split die, and the ejector lever is pushed in to loosen the workpiece, which falls through the die. The die-closing cam keeps the split die blocks tightly together during the downstroke. Production is 300 parts per hour in a 7 1/2" (190 mm) stroke, 40 ton (356 kN) press.

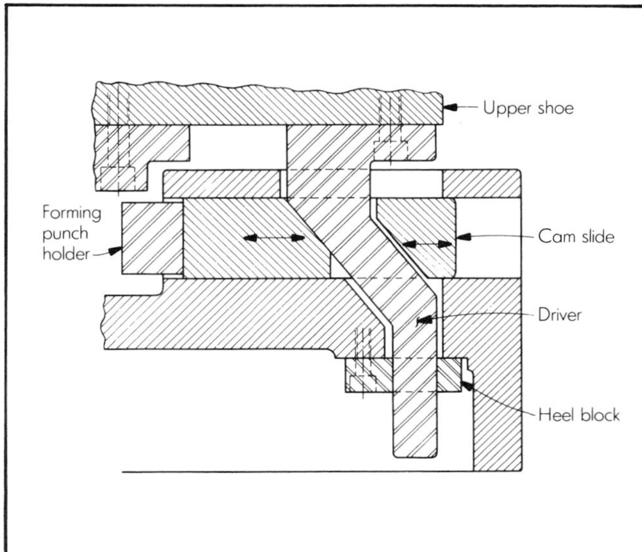


**Fig. 6-57 Forming die with positive dogleg cam drive and return.**

## EMBOSSING AND BEADING

These forming processes for creating shallow designs and round troughs are discussed in Chapter 4, "Sheet Metal Blanking and Forming."

## DRAWING

The drawing process of forming metal blanks into hollow vessels is also described in Chapter 4, "Sheet Metal Blanking and Forming." The discussion includes comprehensive data (including formulas, tables, and nomographs) on metal flow, force requirements, redrawing (percentage reduction), and blankholder forces.

### Punch and Die Contours

One of the most significant factors in obtaining the reduction of the blank diameter is the contour of the area at which the face of the punch is radiused into the side of the punch and the contour of the area at which the wall of the die is radiused into

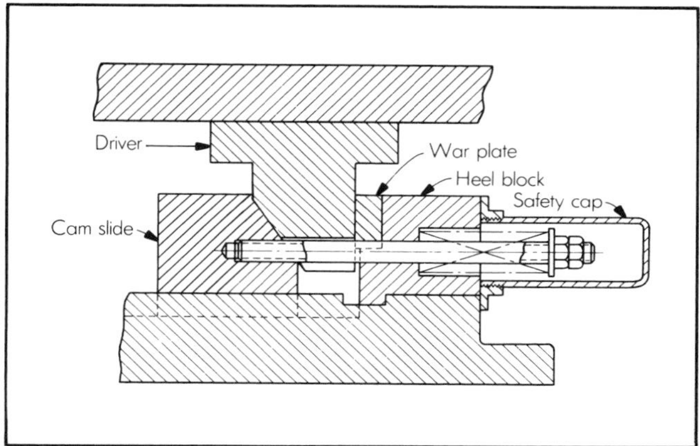


**Fig. 6-58 Forming die with spring-returned cam slide.**

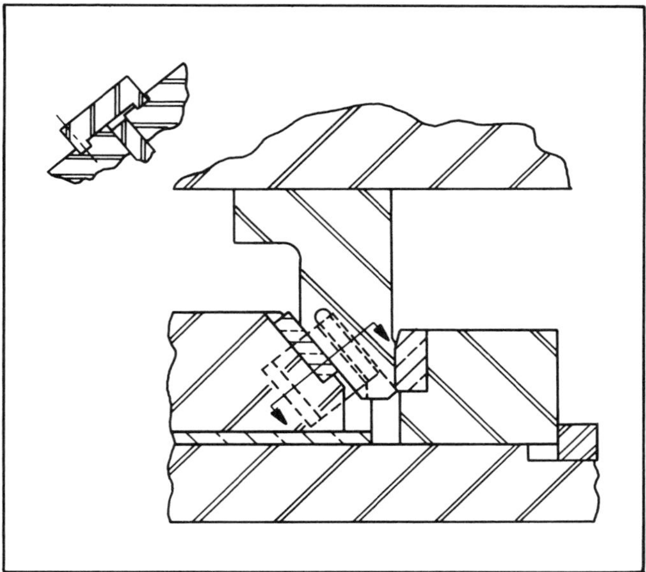

**Fig. 6-59 Forming die cam slide with positive tabbed-gib drive and return.** (*Livernois Automation Co.*)

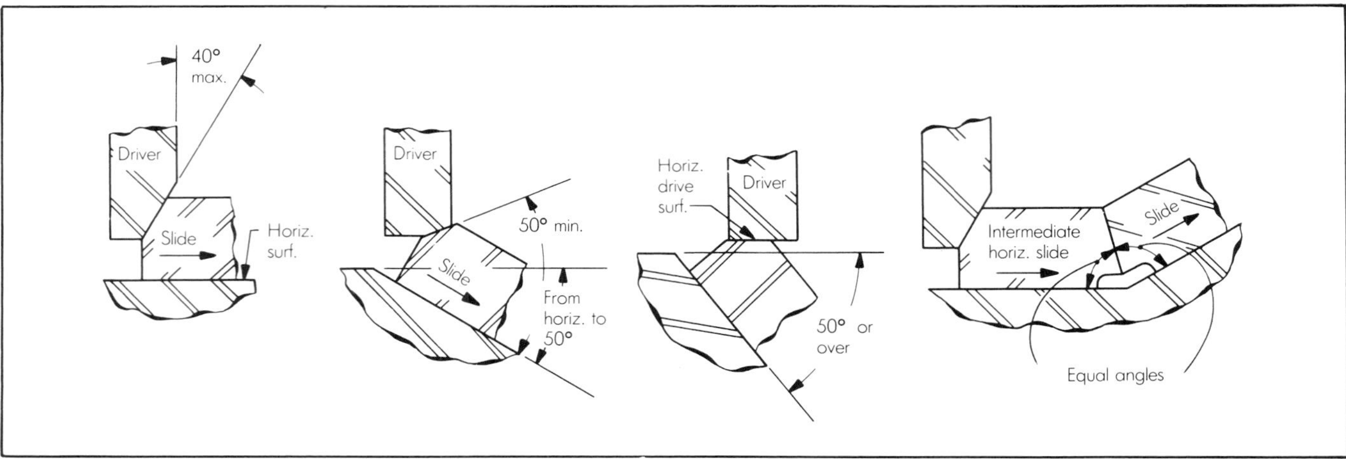


**Fig. 6-60 Standard cam slide and driver angles.**

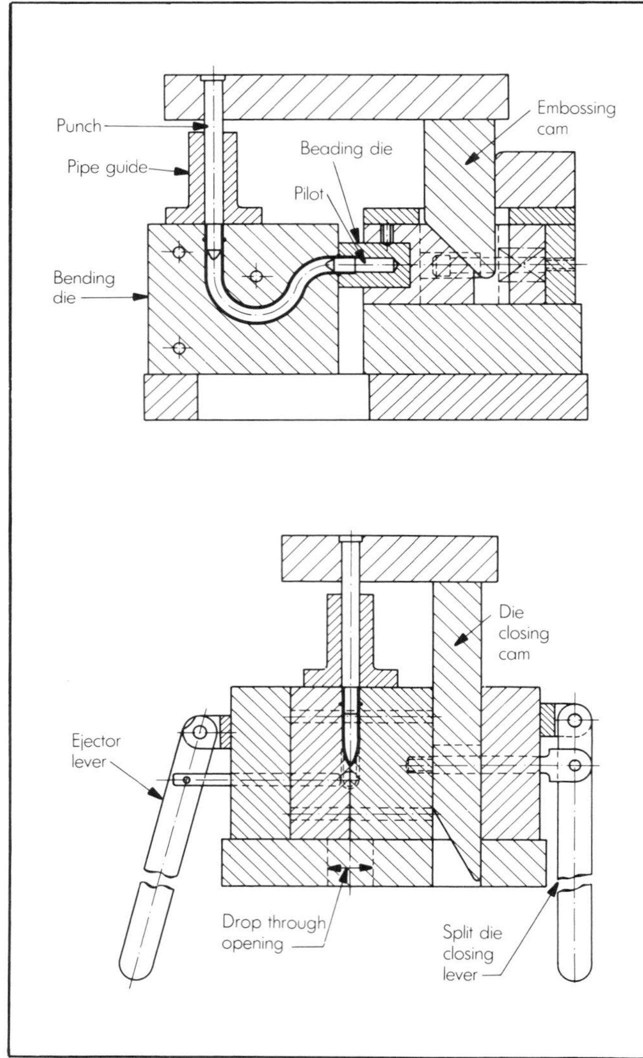


**Fig. 6-61 Tube forming and beading die.**

the face of the die. If these transition contours are too abrupt, the critical area in the bottom of the cup will be so severely stressed that the strength left to overcome the flow resistance of the metal on the die face will be insufficient and the bottom of the part will tear. If these contours are too sweeping, a puckering will occur in the length of unsupported metal at the point at which, in the beginning of the draw, the metal is tangent to the transition contour of the die.

Usual practice is to specify a punch edge radius of approximately five times the metal thickness. The punch radius, however, is often determined by part design and often varies from four to ten times the metal thickness. The surface of the radius and the sides of the punch should also be polished in the direction of metal flow to minimize friction. Because the die edge is subjected to high sliding pressures, it is particularly important that this area be polished to provide a smooth surface on the drawn part and to provide maximum die life.

The curved working surface of a draw die or draw ring, for best practice, should have a radius of four times the stock thickness for stock 1/64 to 1/8" (0.4 to 3.2 mm) thick, although a radius of six to eight times stock thickness is required for drawing heavy-gage metals without a blankholder.

The die space usually allowed for drawing any metal should be proportional to the metal thickness plus clearance to reduce wall friction. This allowance ranges from 7-20% of the metal thickness depending on the type of material and the operation. As the shearing strength of the stock decreases, the allowance must be increased. Table 6-8 provides factors for determining typical die-clearance dimensions.

## Draw Dies

The die shown in Fig. 6-62 is designed to be used in a single-action press with an air cushion that supplies the blankholding pressure. This type of setup can be used for shallow draws, deep draws such as those used in making washer and drier tubs, and draws used to make shapes such as engine oil pans. When cushion size is a limiting factor, hydropneumatic cushions can be used on mechanical presses or hydraulic presses.

A typical double-action die (see Fig. 6-63) incorporates a blankholder, attached to the outer press slide, that clamps the blank before the punch (fastened to the inner slide) descends and draws the part. While pushing the part into the die, the

**TABLE 6-8**
**Draw-Die Clearances**

| Blank Thickness T, in. (mm) | Draw-Die Clearance First Draws | Redraws | Sizing Draws* |
|---|---|---|---|
| To 0.015 (0.38) | 1.07-1.09T | 1.08-1.1T | 1.04-1.05T |
| 0.016-0.050 (0.41-1.27) | 1.08-1.1T | 1.09-1.12T | 1.05-1.06T |
| 0.051-0.125 (1.30-3.18) | 1.1-1.12T | 1.12-1.14T | 1.07-1.09T |
| 0.126 or more (3.20) | 1.12-1.14T | 1.15-1.2T | 1.08-1.1T |

* Used for straight-sided shells when diameter or wall thickness is important or when it is necessary to improve the surface finish.

punch assembly also forces down the air cushion, which lifts the part out of the die after the slide retracts. On the return stroke of the press, the blankholder prevents the drawn part from being carried up by the punch and it dwells in its down position until the blankholding slide starts on its upstroke. If a controlled delay of the air cushion is necessary to avoid the opposing forces of the blankholder and the air cushion, which could buckle the part, timing pins or other devices must be provided.

**Direct redrawing.** Figure 6-64 illustrates the type of double-action die used for direct redrawing. On the downstroke of the press, the sleeve enters the part to be redrawn. As the sleeve presses on the part, the punch continues down, pulling the wall from around the sleeve into the smaller diameter. The purpose of the sleeve is to prevent the wall from distorting while it is being pulled into the smaller diameter. In direct redrawing, the metal makes two 90° bends. In making the first bend, the inside of the metal is compressed and the outside is stretched. In making the second bend, the inside is stretched and the outside is compressed.

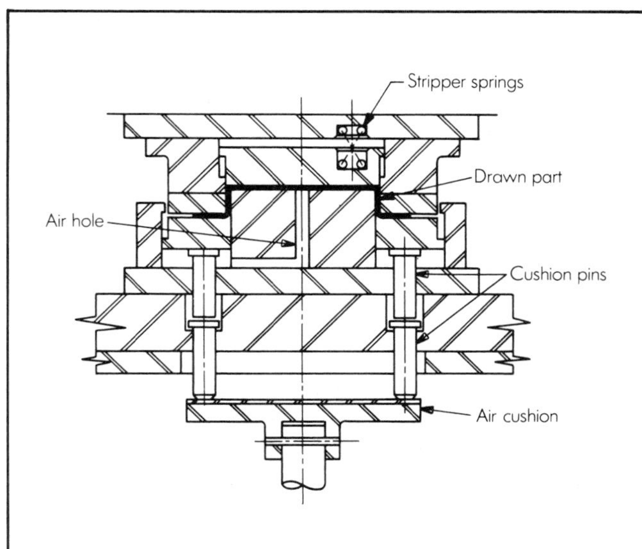


Fig. 6-62 Drawing die with air-cushion blankholding.

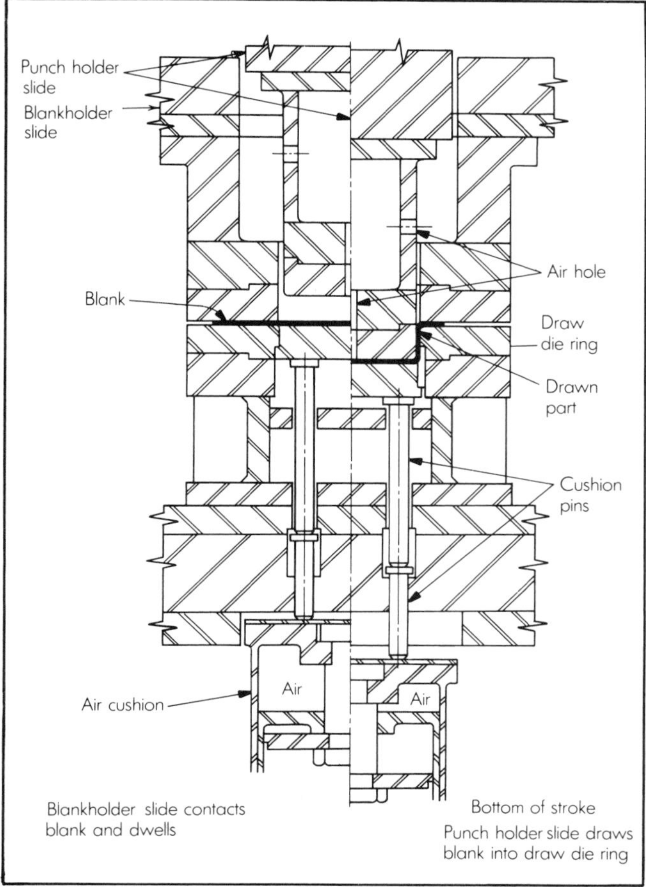


Fig. 6-63 Typical double-action cylindrical drawing die.

The inverted redraw die of Fig. 6-65 reduces the diameter of a copper shell from 7.856″ (199.54 mm) to 6.517″ (165.53 mm) as the shell flows between the surfaces of the blankholder and the draw ring. On the upstroke, the knockout plate pushes the redrawn shell down and out of the cast-iron die.

When deep cups are being drawn, there is no hard-and-fast rule as to the punch-nose radius that is desirable for each successive die, except that each radius should be smaller in proportion to that of the preceding shell. When the radius is too sharp on the first draws, thinning occurs on the sidewalls of subsequently drawn parts and extends upward on them with each succeeding draw.

**Reverse redrawing.** Figure 6-66 shows a die for reverse redrawing, in which the part to be redrawn is turned inside out. The bottom of the part is pushed down into the inside diameter of the sleeve. It is still necessary for the metal to make two 90° bends; but because it is not subjected to stresses first in one direction and then in the other, greater percentages of reduction may be obtained in each operation. This avoidance of stresses might also result in the elimination of one or more annealing operations.

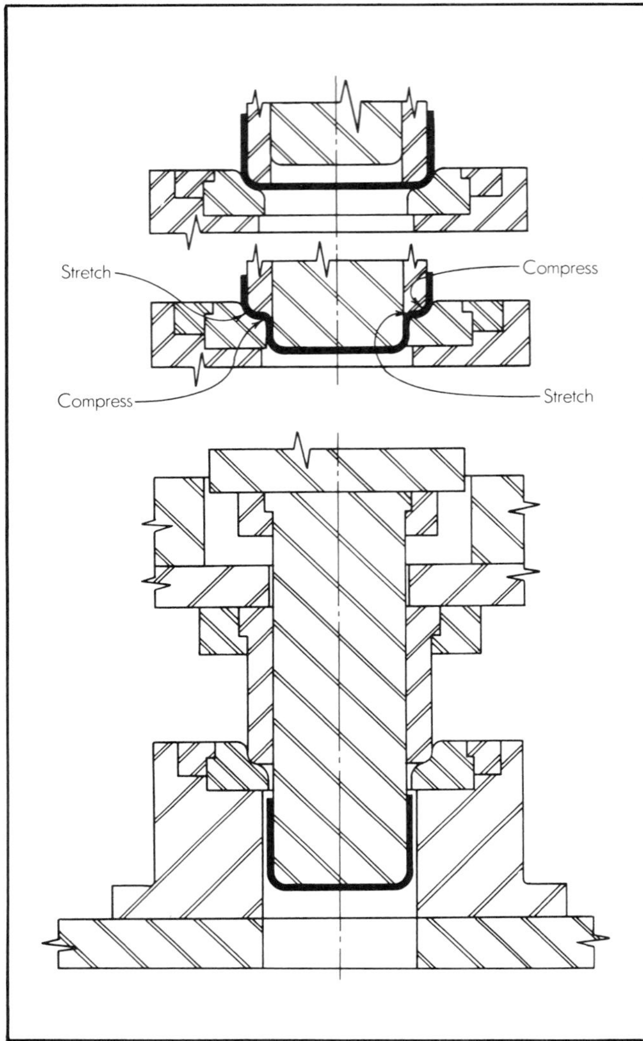


Fig. 6-64 Direct redrawing die in a double-action press.

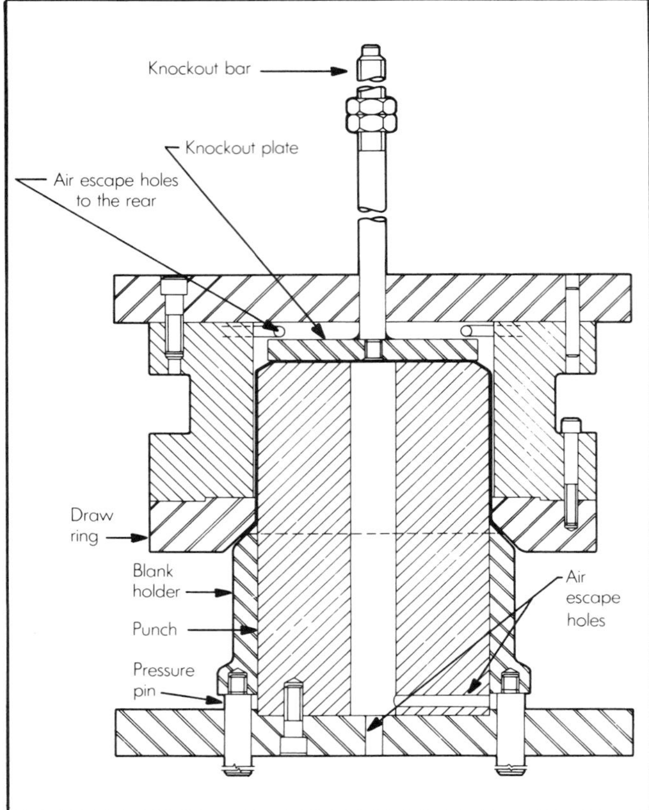


Fig. 6-65 Inverted redrawing die using an air cushion.

A reverse redrawing die usually requires a longer press stroke and closer inspection of the blanks to see that they are free of nicks and scratches, especially at the edges. The radius of the sleeve should be as large as practical—ten times the thickness of the work material, if possible.

**Rectangular dies.** A typical die for drawing rectangular parts is shown in Fig. 6-67. The blankholder incorporates four pressure strips, or pressure restrictors, ground to a thickness that allows uniform distribution of pressure on the blank throughout the drawing operation.

**Large draw dies.** Dies for large, deep draws, such as for automobile front fenders, body quarter panels, roof panels, bathtubs, refrigerator cabinets, and washing machine tubs, are more complicated than those previously discussed, because the metal movement is gained by a combination of stretching and compression. This necessitates very accurate control of metal flow by a blankholder and enough draw beads to retard the flow of metal when necessary while at the same time allowing the punch to move the stock into the die.

Hot or cold-rolled steel stock, pickled in oil, of approximately $R_B45$ hardness is recommended. In many applications of drawing, it is possible to make a rather broad adjustment between die construction and stock characteristics; however, in large, deep draws, the mechanical difficulties encountered make it imperative that the physical characteristics of the stock be held within close limits. From the standpoint of the most economical operation, a stock stretch not exceeding 20% is generally an optimum condition.

The usual practice of establishing draw lines for irregular shapes has been to construct a master wood model of the article; however, computers are now being used extensively for this purpose (refer to the previous discussion "Use of CAD/CAM" in this chapter). Measurements of a model, if used, are to the inside of the stock, and usually all flanges and pierced holes in the finished part are incorporated. Good practice is to mount the master model on a positioning fixture, although other methods of supporting it in position are sometimes used.

The basic movement of the punch holder in the press is at a 90° angle to the plane of the bolster or bed to which the die is attached. An irregularly shaped, large part is very frequently positioned for drawing in such a manner that its major axis (design or datum line) is at an angle to the horizontal to permit the best results to be obtained. The angle of tip should establish the shallowest draw possible for the particular part and should be such that contact of the punch with the stock is as uniform as possible, permitting a consistent pull of stock from the draw ring.

With the tip angle established, it is customary to intersect the

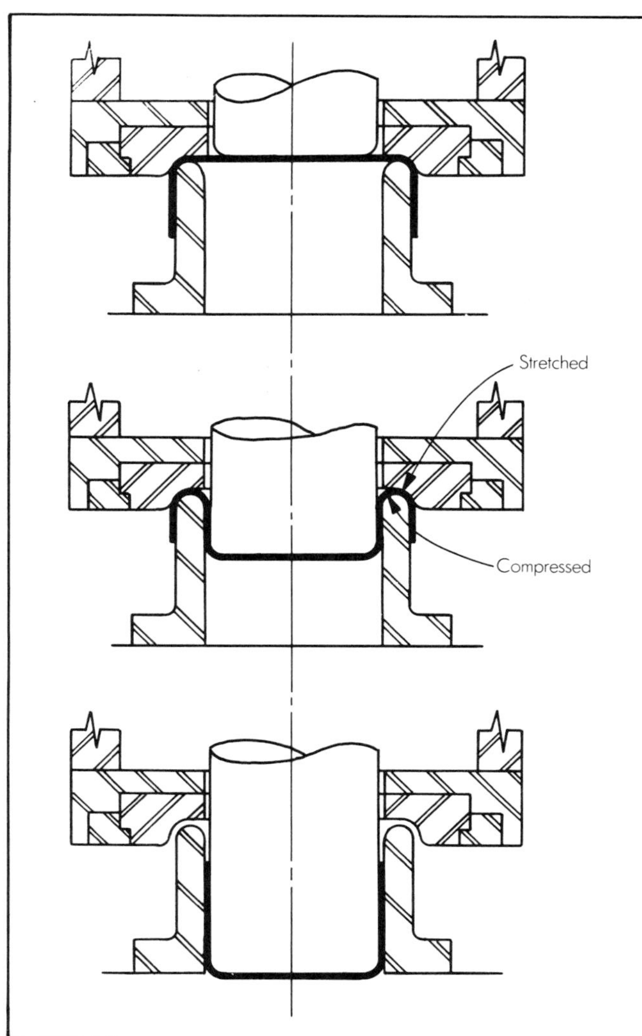


Fig. 6-66 Reverse redrawing in a double-action press.

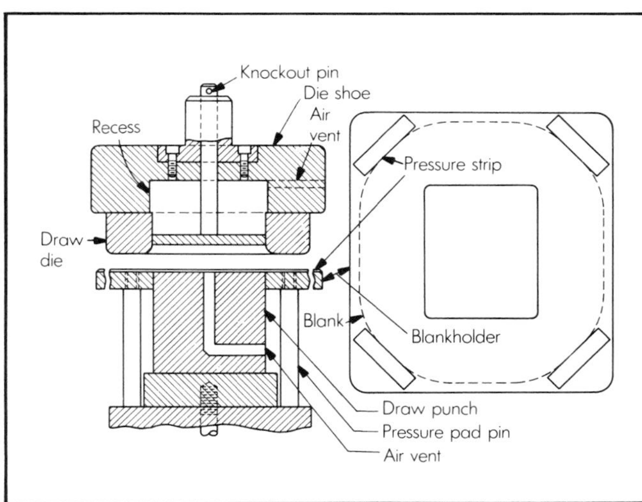


Fig. 6-67 Die for drawing rectangular parts.

model surface by imaginary horizontal planes spaced at frequent intervals, projecting the lines of intersection upon a metal template or upon paper layout sheets. The lines so projected are utilized to develop the surfaces of the punch and die. Much of this metalcutting was formerly done by hand. Under industrial practices, the points of the tip and the draw-line contours are projected from the model to a steel template or to paper layout sheets and later utilized to rectify the profiling and contouring done by an automatic profiling machine or other means. Presently, considerable success is being experienced in using computers for complete draw-die ring, punch, and trim development with many automotive stamped parts, particularly for body parts which do not change drastically from model to model or year to year.

Good practice endeavors to get all the panel contours and flange break lines established in the draw, allowing from 1/32 to 1/8" (0.8 to 3.2 mm) of overdraw depending upon the radius at that point, to facilitate reflanging and establishing a satisfactory vertical trim condition that eliminates costly cam-trim dies. Satisfactory establishment of contours and break lines is shown in Fig. 6-68. Dies for drawing metal parts similar to the parts shown in Fig. 6-68 are shown in Fig. 6-69.

When a uniform pull of stock from the blankholder cannot be attained, the usual practice is to install draw beads in the draw-die face to control stock movement at areas where the stock runs in excessively or, if surplus has to run in to prevent breakage, to put a step in the draw line to pull excessive stock out and keep draw marks from getting into the finished panel.

Draw beads, providing more resistance to metal flow than that provided by the blankholder, can control metal flow and, where stretching is desirable, can help stretch metal areas. Draw beads momentarily heat the metal and to some extent improve its drawing characteristics. Draw beads may be installed in several ways, the manner of installation being chosen by the diemaker. When the draw beads are installed and matching channels are spotted in the draw ring, with metal clearance provided in the channels, the die is ready to be tested.

After the die is tried out, the area of the blank will probably need to be modified to a certain extent. The blank for the tryout is normally a square blank sheared to approximate size. After the metal flow has been observed, the diemaker may find that more metal has been allowed in the blank than is necessary, and the blank size will then be reduced. In many cases, irregular shapes are developed, which have to be blanked, using nesting layout methods to utilize the least amount of material per stamping.

If the draw approaches a U shape, a wrapping fixture is sometimes used to prebend the blank into a shape that will lie on the binder with contact all around the blank. This prebending aids in securing uniform drawing of the metal and helps in preventing wrinkles and cracks.

## IRONING

Frequently, the final operation in a series of draws consists of ironing the shell walls to reduce the thickness of the metal and ensure a smooth, uniform surface throughout. This process, typical tooling, and methods of determining force requirements are discussed in Chapter 4, "Sheet Metal Blanking and Forming."

## BULGING

Bulging is a metalforming process for expanding tubular or cylindrical blanks or parts. Both mechanical and hydrostatic bulging are discussed in Chapter 4.

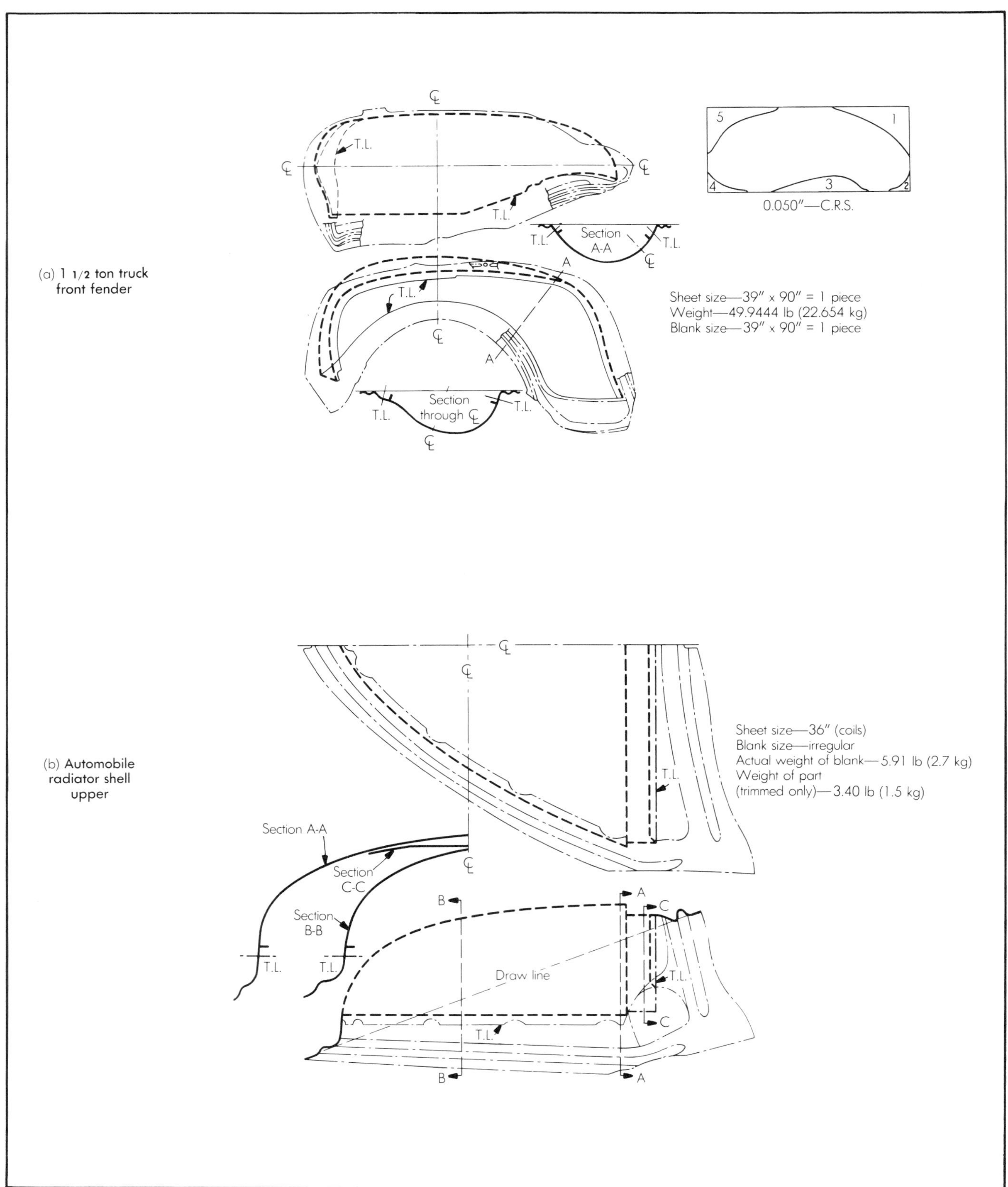


**Fig. 6-68 Draw-line contours and flange break lines established for large drawing operations.**

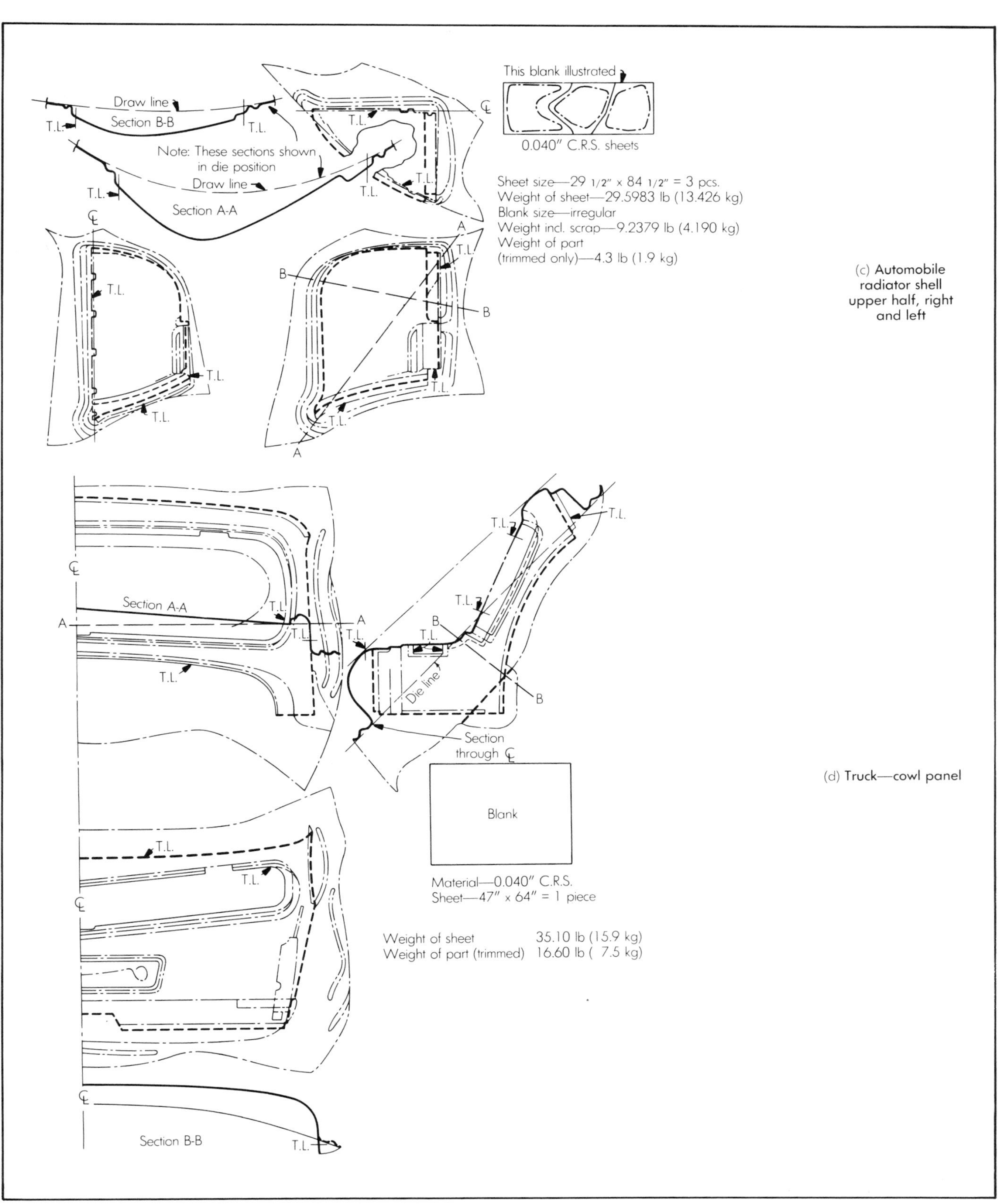


(c) Automobile radiator shell upper half, right and left

(d) Truck—cowl panel

**Fig. 6-68—*Continued***

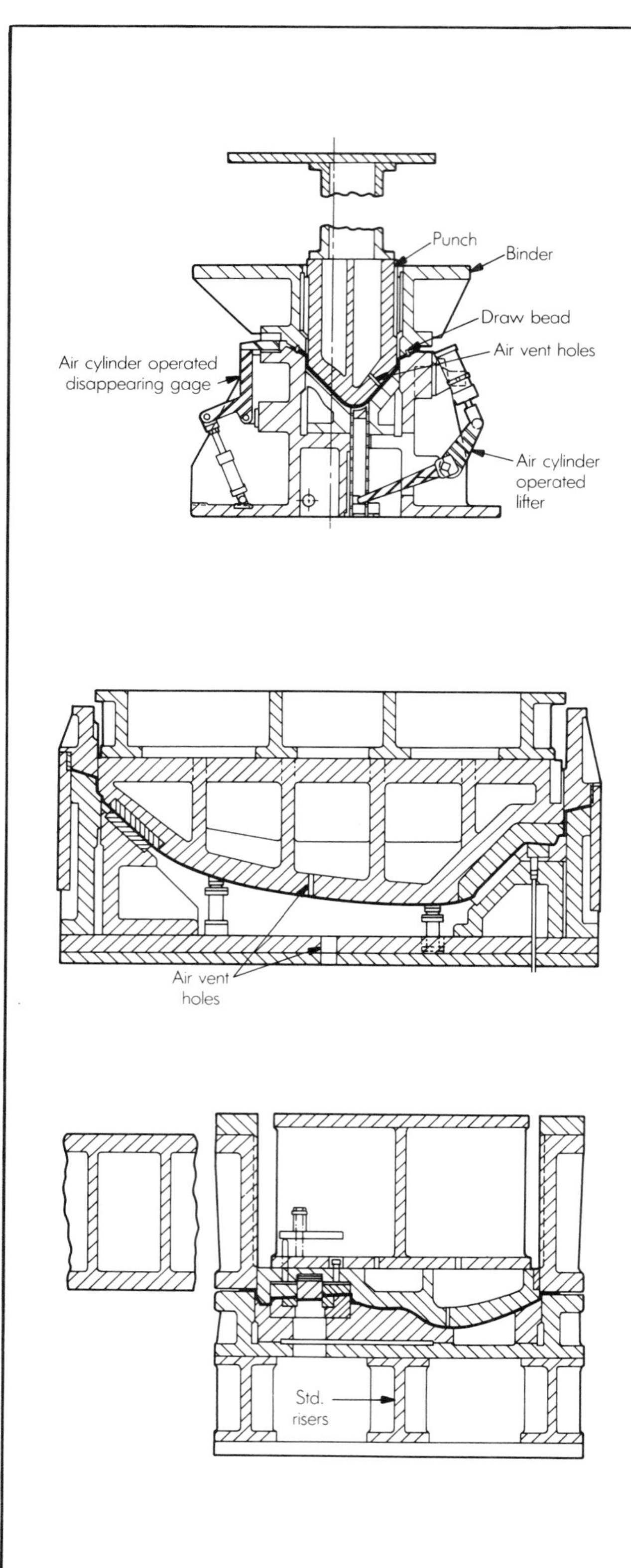


Fig. 6-69 Dies for drawing metal parts similar to those shown in Fig. 6-68.

## COMPRESSION OPERATIONS

The metal compression processes of coining, swaging, and sizing, used to impart a pattern, configuration, or decoration on parts produced from flat-rolled material, are discussed in Chapter 4. A die used to coin an indentation in the bottom of a cup is shown in Fig. 6-70. The cup is placed on the post and the coined area is confined by the die ring while the coining punch indents the bottom of the cup. The coining punch is designed to slide up and down inside the die ring and is actuated by a positive knockout bar to eject the part from the die. A locator properly positions the cup in a previously cut notch. Components of this die are mounted on a standard two-post die set.

A die for swaging the bevel and two welding projections on a type segment is shown in Fig. 6-71. First, the preblanked segment is placed in the die. Then, as the slide descends, the bevel and welding projections are swaged into the part. For ease of manufacture, the die is sectionalized. The impression is machined into the insert, which is set into the main die block. This block is stepped to serve as a part locator. End stops are also fastened to the main die block. The hand-operated ejection lever lifts a pin to eject the segment from the die cavity.

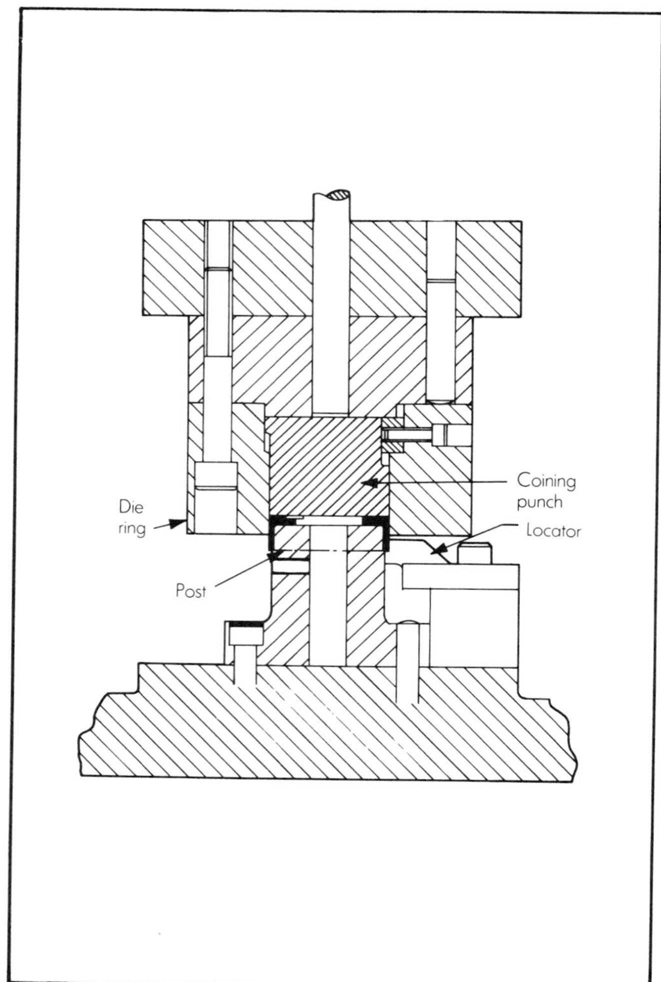


Fig. 6-70 Die to coin an indentation in the bottom of a cup. (*Coinex, Inc.*)

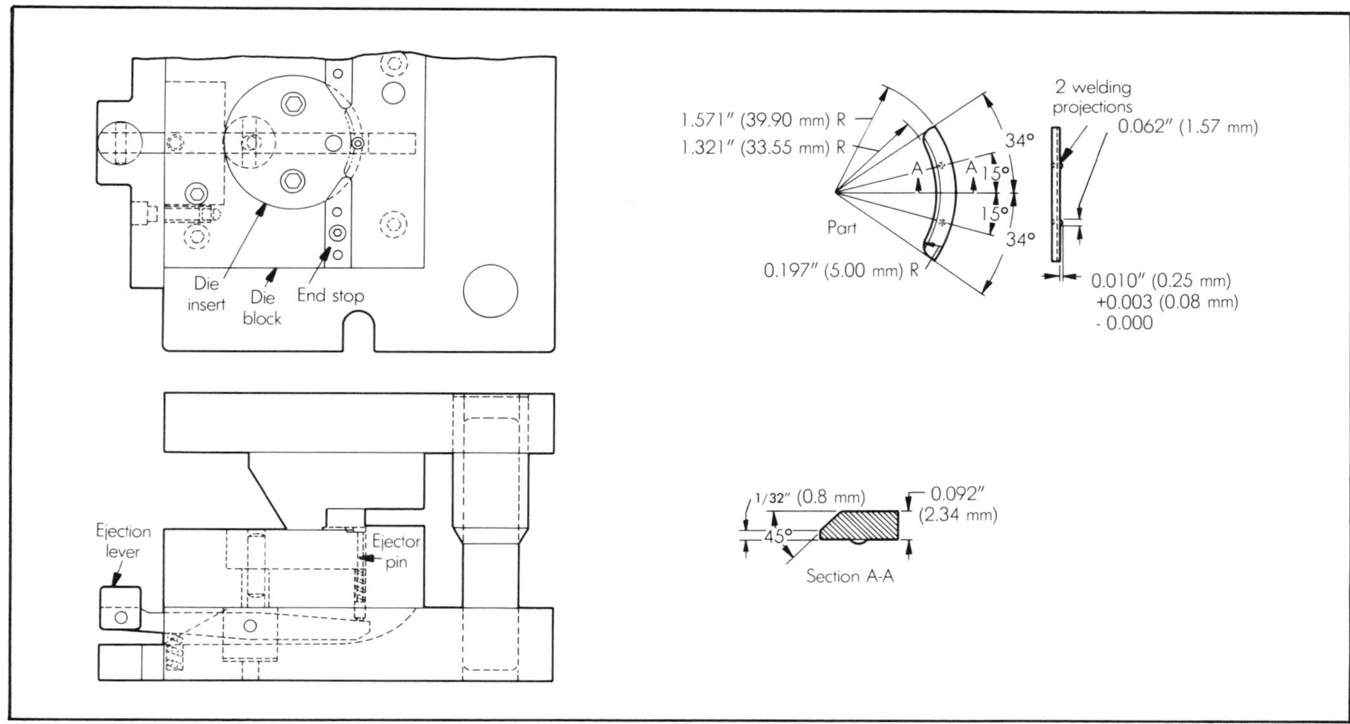


**Fig. 6-71 Die to swage the bevel and welding projections on a type segment.** (*National Cash Register Co.*)

# MULTIPLE-OPERATION PROCESSES

Multiple operations may be carried out on sheet metal stock either at a single die station or at multiple stations with a single stroke of the press. Such operations are commonly classified by the characteristics of the die if a single-station die is used or by the characteristics of the part-progression method if a multiple-station die is used.

## SINGLE-STATION OPERATIONS

The terms compound and combination have frequently been used interchangeably to define any one-station die, of which the elements are designed around a common centerline (usually vertical) and in which two or more operations are completed during a single press stroke. The dies are classified as follows:

1. Compound dies—Press tools in which only cutting operations are done, usually blanking and punching.
2. Combination dies—Press tools in which a cutting operation (usually blanking) is combined with a shaping or deforming operation (bending, forming, drawing, coining, etc.).

### Compound Dies

The compound blank-and-punch die shown in Fig. 6-72 is a blanking die with two punches added. A knockout pin, actuated by the press ram, pushes the punched blank down and out of the blanking-die cavity. The stock is supported by the stripper, which keeps the stock in contact with the blanking die. On the upstroke of the press, this stripper removes the stock from the blanking punch. The finished part is ejected from the blanking die by a knockout pin when the press ram (carrying the upper die) reaches top dead center.

When accurate hole location with respect to the shaved portion of a blank must be maintained, a compound shave-and-punch die effects both of these operations in a single press stroke. As such, it is similar to a compound blank-and-punch die except that its design provides for nesting and rigid clamping of the previously blanked parts, as well as accurate removal of thin shavings.

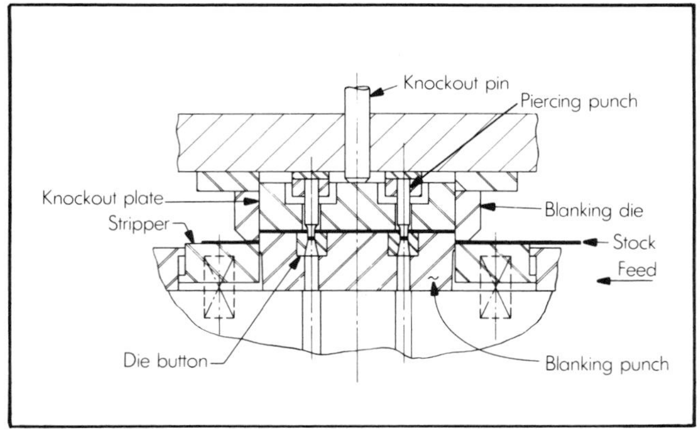


**Fig. 6-72 Compound blank-and-punch die.**

# MULTIPLE-OPERATION PROCESSES

Another compound type, used when the width or length of the part equals the stock width, is the punch-and-cutoff die (see Fig. 6-73). The holemaking punch is mounted in the crescent-shaped cutoff punch. The perforated and cutoff part held down by the spring-loaded stripper falls off the back of the die when the slide of the inclined press ascends. The stock is guided by the tunnel stripper and positioned by the end stop.

## Combination Dies

In the combination die shown in Fig. 6-74, the dome of a preformed part is drawn downward against a rubber cushion.

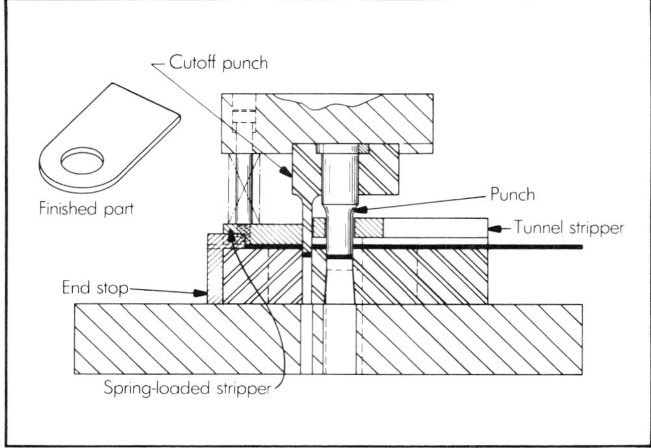


**Fig. 6-73 Punch-and-cutoff die.** (*Toledo Pressed Steel Co.*)

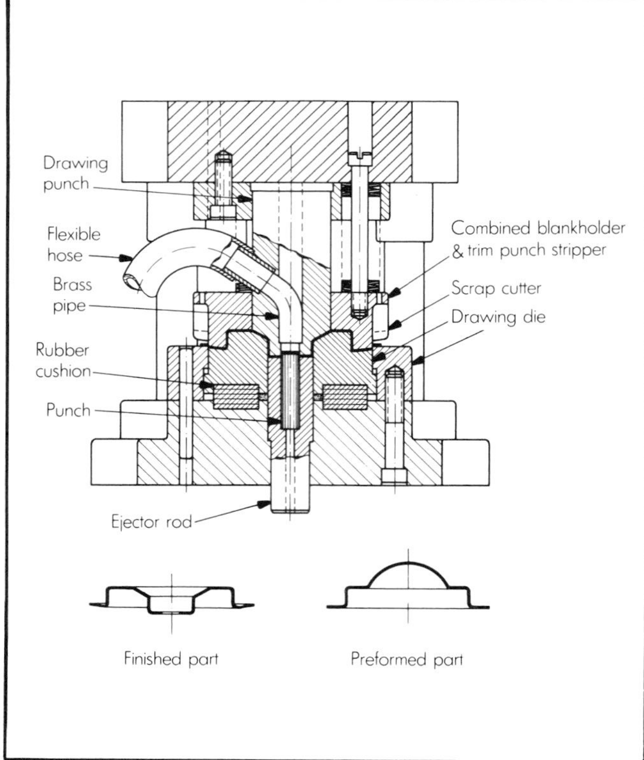


**Fig. 6-74 Combination draw-punch-trim die.**

The trimmed ring is split in half by two scrap cutters. The punched slugs are evacuated by vacuum from the punching die (centrally located in the draw punch) through the brass pipe and rubber hose. The finished part is pushed upward by the ejector rod and out of the trim die by the draw die (actuated by the rubber cushion). It is stripped from the draw punch by the spring-loaded combination stripper and blankholder. This die represents an interesting application; however, cutting with the moving die member is generally not considered to be good die practice.

In the first operation of the combination die shown in Fig. 6-75, the circular blank and the cup are produced by the combined blanking, punch, and draw die. This punch forces the pressure plate down until its groove is in front of the groove in the pressure ring containing the balls. The balls travel downward with the pressure plate, allowing the downward travel of the pressure ring. The blank-and-draw punch continues to descend to draw the cup to a 1″ (25 mm) diameter and to pinch-trim the top of the inverted cup. At the end of the stroke, the central hole is punched and the finished cup is pushed down and out of the die cavity by the knockout ring and pins.

## MULTIPLE-STATION OPERATIONS

Progressive and transfer operations are multiple operations performed by means of a die having several stations, each of which performs a different operation as the stock passes through the die. The design may include components or devices to position, locate, or guide the stock. Idle stations, at which no work is performed, are used to spread out closely spaced operations or to better distribute the forces required to perform the work.

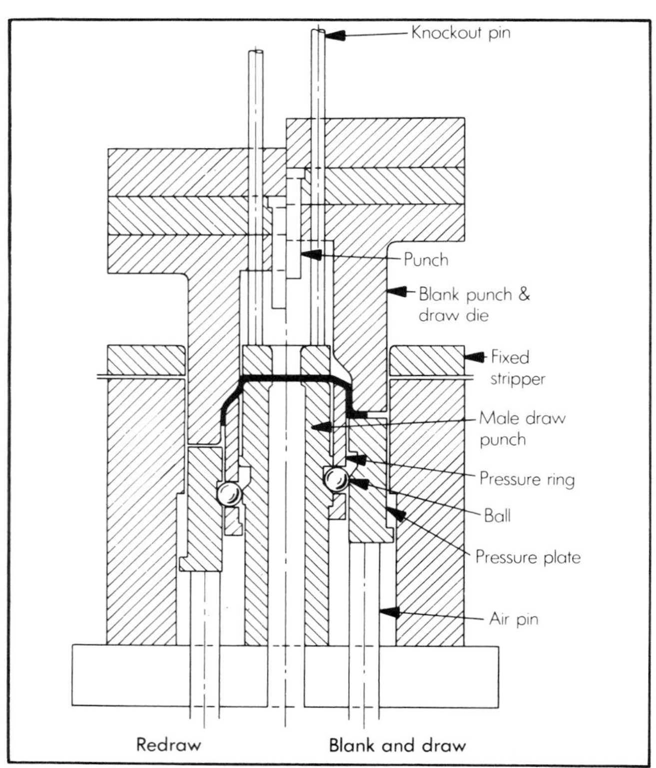


**Fig. 6-75 Combination blank, draw, redraw, punch, and pinch-trim die.**

In progressive operations, parts, usually made from continuous coil stock, are connected by a carrier strip until the final parting or cutoff operation. In transfer operations, the parts are blanked before or at the beginning of the operations and mechanical transfer devices move the workpieces from station to station. Progressive and transfer operations both have advantages and disadvantages, and each has its own special applications. The choice between the two types of operations depends entirely upon relative economics, part and die design, production requirements, and equipment available.

Progressive operations can usually be run at higher speeds and with shorter press strokes than comparable transfer operations. Parts that are designed for minimum scrap loss by nesting, thereby eliminating the carrier strip, as illustrated in Fig. 6-76, may provide highly economical production when run through progressive dies.

However, the carrier strip required for other part designs may give rise to certain problems in progressive operations. Transfer operations should be considered if the connecting strip interferes with metal flow during forming, the parts must be formed at different angles from the plane of the carrier strip, scrap can be reduced, or the camber of the sheet or coil strip affects the progression. The transfer system generally allows drawing or other operations around the entire perimeter of a part without carrier-strip interference, and a part may be tilted from the horizontal plane, or even inverted.

The elimination of a great deal of scrap loss, as shown in Fig. 6-77, is a major advantage of transfer operations. Not only can the carrier strip be eliminated, but blanks can be cut from the sheet stock in nested positions to reduce scrap between blanks. Another important advantage of transfer dies is elimination of the need for costly, manual secondary operations sometimes required with progressive dies. Transfer blanks can also be cut to take advantage of the grain direction of the metal stock or can be salvaged from scrap material.

On the other hand, transfer dies generally have a higher initial cost than progressive dies. Additionally, they are difficult to modify from one progression to another. Therefore, the cost advantages of progressive operations and transfer operations should be closely compared, especially when shorter production runs are required.

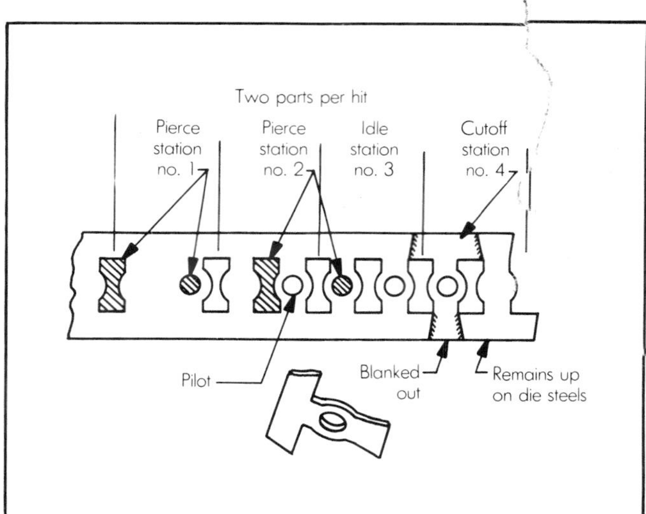


**Fig. 6-76 Typical progressive-die part layout for minimum scrap loss.**

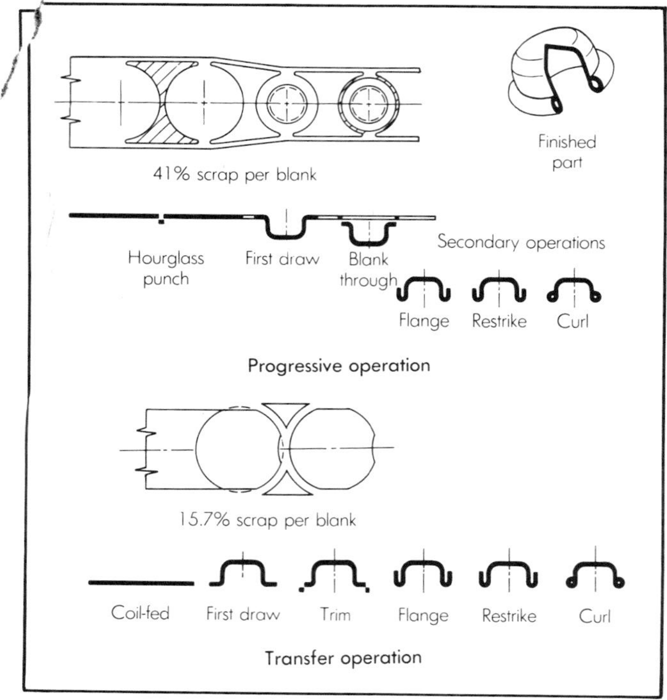


**Fig. 6-77 Material scrap loss of a progressive operation compared with a transfer operation for the same part.**

## Design Parameters

Progressive and transfer pressworking operations have several basic design parameters in common. These parameters are:

1. Dwell, the portion of the press stroke necessary to completely clear the die and punch from the part so that the part may be advanced.
2. Pitch (also called progression), the distance between the centerlines of two adjacent work stations in the die. This dimension must be constant between successive stations throughout the die.
3. Press stroke.
4. Operational speed, including drawing speed for the material to be fabricated, press speed, and ram speed.

**Dwell.** Correct dwell is a common requirement for both progressive and transfer operations. Dwell is the part of the upward stroke of the press ram that clears the part and has to be a minimum of twice the height of the part. The dwell period cannot be used to move the strip in progressive operations or to index the part in transfer operations.

**Pitch.** Pitch must be the shortest practical distance between working stations which will not sacrifice the strength of the die steels between die cavities. In progressive operations, the shorter the pitch, the less scrap material is created. To reduce scrap, the pitch is shortened to the minimum necessary to prevent excessively weak dies. Pitch must be increased in proportion to increases in material thickness. In transfer operations, pitch is determined by creating the optimum die condition that can be obtained without sacrificing workpiece material. Excessive transfer pitch may be reduced by incorporating an idle station between work stations. As pitch is

reduced, the operation can be run at higher speed and the press stroke can be shortened, part height and metal thickness allowing.

**Press stroke.** The stroke of the press in both progressive and transfer operations must be longer than that actually required to form the part. The excess portion of the stroke is necessary to provide time for the automatic shuttling of parts to subsequent stations. The press strokes in both transfer and progressive operations are diagrammed in Fig. 6-78. Although a progressive press stroke is equal to approximately three to four times part height, a transfer press stroke with ram drive is about five to six times part height because of the time necessary to move the transfer fingers in and out of the die area. A cam-driven transfer mechanism requires a press stroke of three to four times part height, which is comparable to requirements for progressive dies.

**Operation speed.** No operation, whether single or multiple, can be affected at a press speed greater than the drawing speed of the metal being worked. Inertia, however, becomes a factor in operating speed for multiple operations. The movement of a workpiece or series of workpieces through a die is subject to inertia laws. In a progressive operation, the inertia of the parts is controlled by the strip or strips connecting them. In transfer operations, however, the parts must either be locked in the die or held firmly by the transfer mechanism at all times. This locking or holding of parts is referred to as part control. Separate parts moving too fast through the press may move out of alignment with their stations after release by the transfer fingers; such loss of part control can result in damage to parts, dies, and presses.

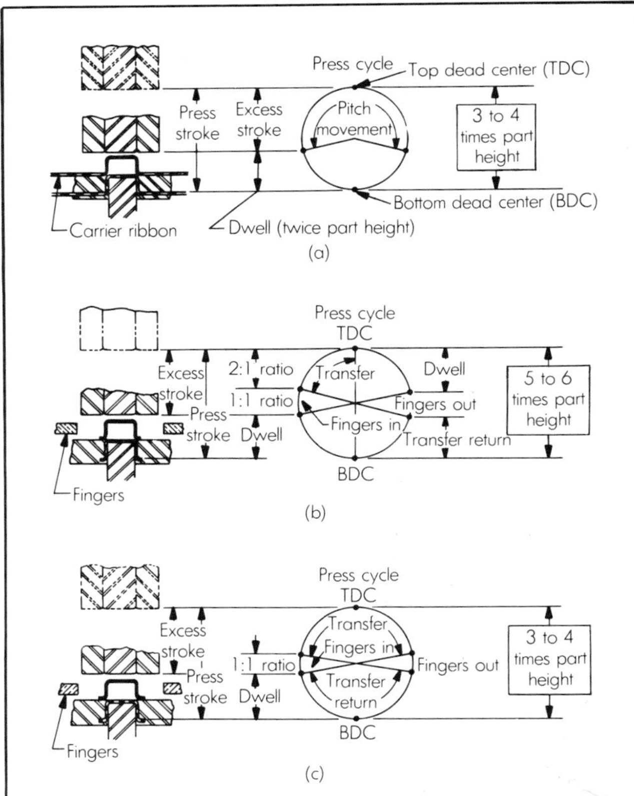


**Fig. 6-78 Press-stroke diagrams for progressive and transfer operations: (a) progressive, (b) ram-operated transfer, and (c) cam-operated transfer.** (*Livernois Automation Co.*)

## Progressive Dies

Individual operations performed in a progressive die are often relatively simple; but when they are combined in several stations, the most practical and economical strip design for optimum operations of the die often becomes difficult to devise.

The sequence of operations on a strip and the details of each operation must be carefully developed to assist in the design of a die to produce good parts. A tentative sequence of operations, called an operational strip, should be established and the following items considered as the final sequence of operations is developed:

1. Pilot holes and/or notches should be punched in the first station. Other holes may have to be punched that will not be affected by subsequent noncutting operations.
2. The blank for drawing or forming operations should be developed to permit free movement of metal.
3. It is good design practice to distribute punched areas over several stations if the punched areas are close together or are close to the edge of the die opening. This practice can lengthen die life.
4. The shape of the blank should be analyzed to determine if it can be divided into simple shapes so that punches of simple contours may cut out some areas at one station and remaining areas at later stations. This suggests the use of commercially available punch shapes wherever they are practical.
5. Idle stations should be used to strengthen die blocks, stripper plates, and punch retainers and to facilitate strip movement.
6. A determination should be made as to whether strip grain direction will adversely affect or facilitate an operation.
7. Forming or drawing operations should be planned to take place in either an upward or downward direction, and the direction that ensures the best die design and strip movement should be selected.
8. The shape of the finished part may dictate that the cutoff operation should precede the last noncutting operation. Care must be taken to properly control the workpiece after cutoff has occurred.
9. Adequate carrier strips or tabs should be designed.
10. Strip layout should be checked for minimum scrap; a multiple layout should be used if feasible.
11. Cutting and forming areas should be located to provide uniform loading of the press slide.
12. The strip should be designed so that scrap and part can be ejected without interference.

The layout approaches to drawing similar cups, in which metal movement from the strip into the cup must be provided for, are shown in Fig. 6-79 and 6-80. The lancing of the strip in the first station of Fig. 6-79 provides suspension and allows little or no distortion of the edges of the strip during drawing and restriking. An idle station between the lance station and the draw station allows minimum strip distortion during the lancing operation. Stock lifters allow all operations to be done without interference between the die members and the cups. Pressure pads are located at the draw and restrike stations.

An I-shaped relief cutout is notched in the first station in the layout illustrated in Fig. 6-80. During all the drawing stages, metal is pulled in from the cutout edges as well as from the edges of the strip,thus narrowing its width. This type of relief cutout

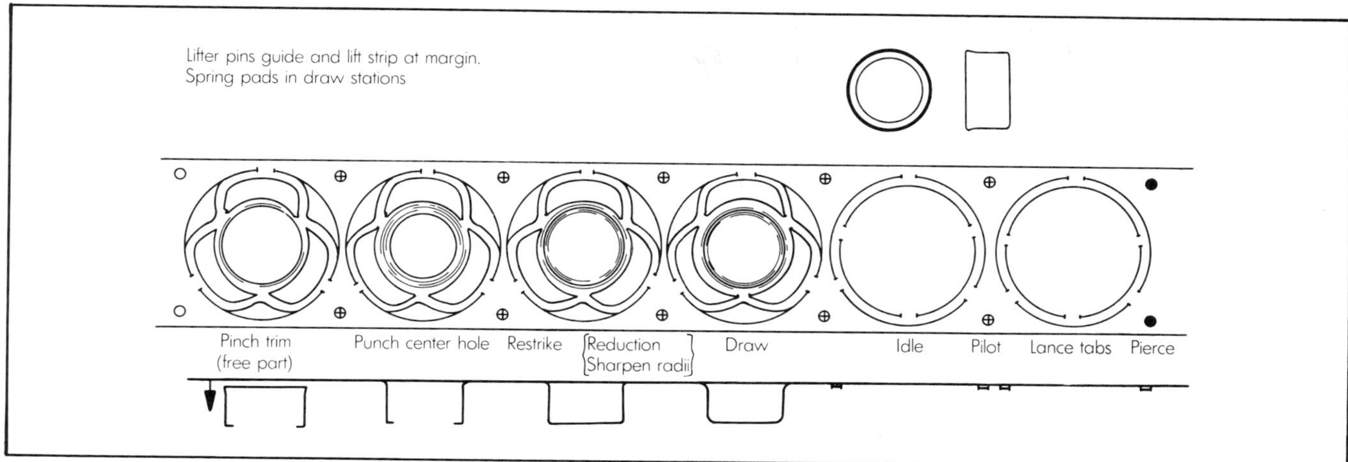


**Fig. 6-79 Progressive strip layout for undistorted strip edges.**

can be used when a series of shallow draws are to be made without wrinkling the strip skeleton. The 0.064″ (1.63 mm) strip stock in the layout illustrated in Fig. 6-77 requires three draws to avoid fractures. Both layouts follow the common practice of punching all holes and severing the completed cup from the strip after all drawing and restriking operations are completed.

The strip layout shown in Fig. 6-81 is typical for a lamination die using carbide punches and die sections. Since carbide die construction is relatively complex and expensive, limit switches are commonly incorporated to detect misfeeds, through linkage to pilots, and then instantaneously to stop the press.

The die shown in Fig. 6-82 produces a simple bracket from

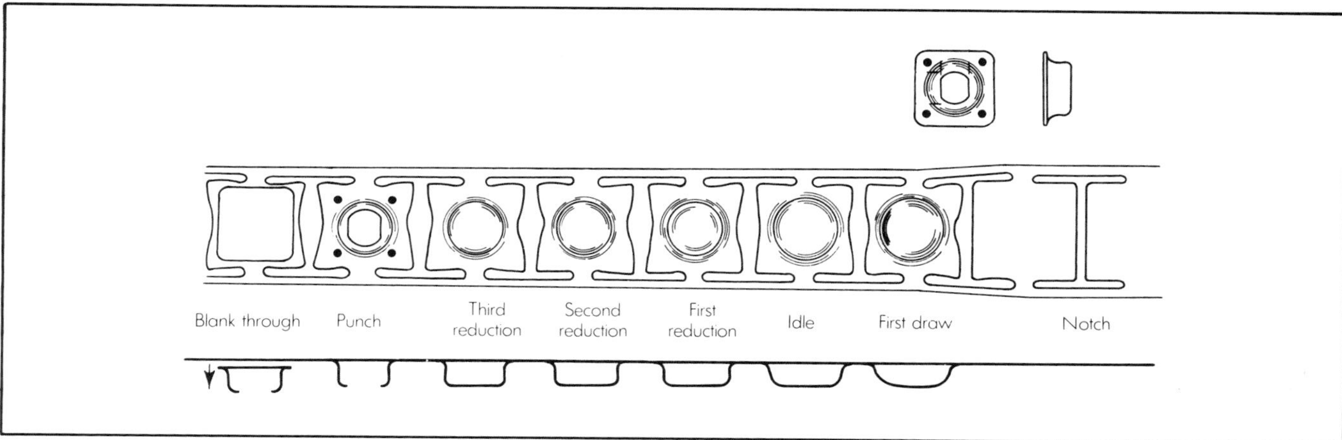


**Fig. 6-80 Progressive strip layout with narrow strip.**

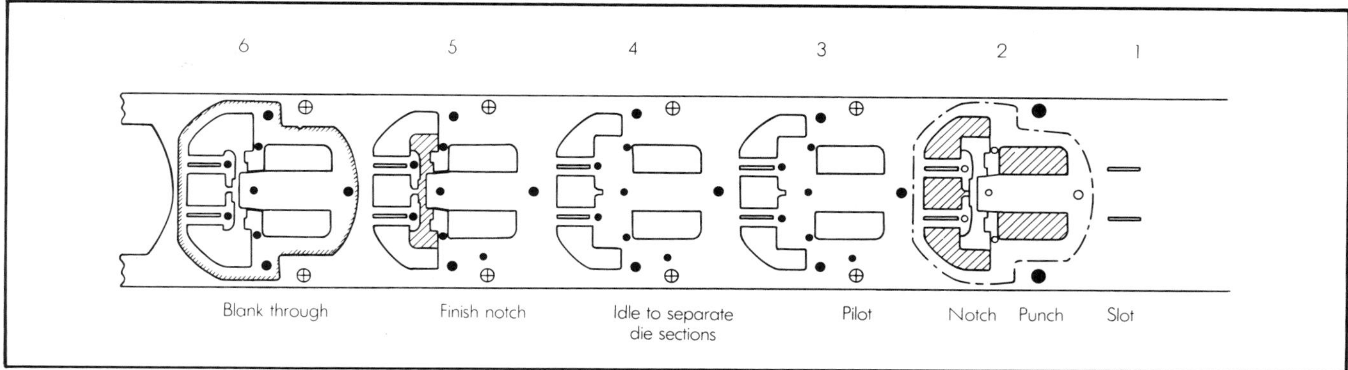


**Fig. 6-81 Strip layout for progressive punching, slotting, notching, and blanking in a carbide lamination die.**

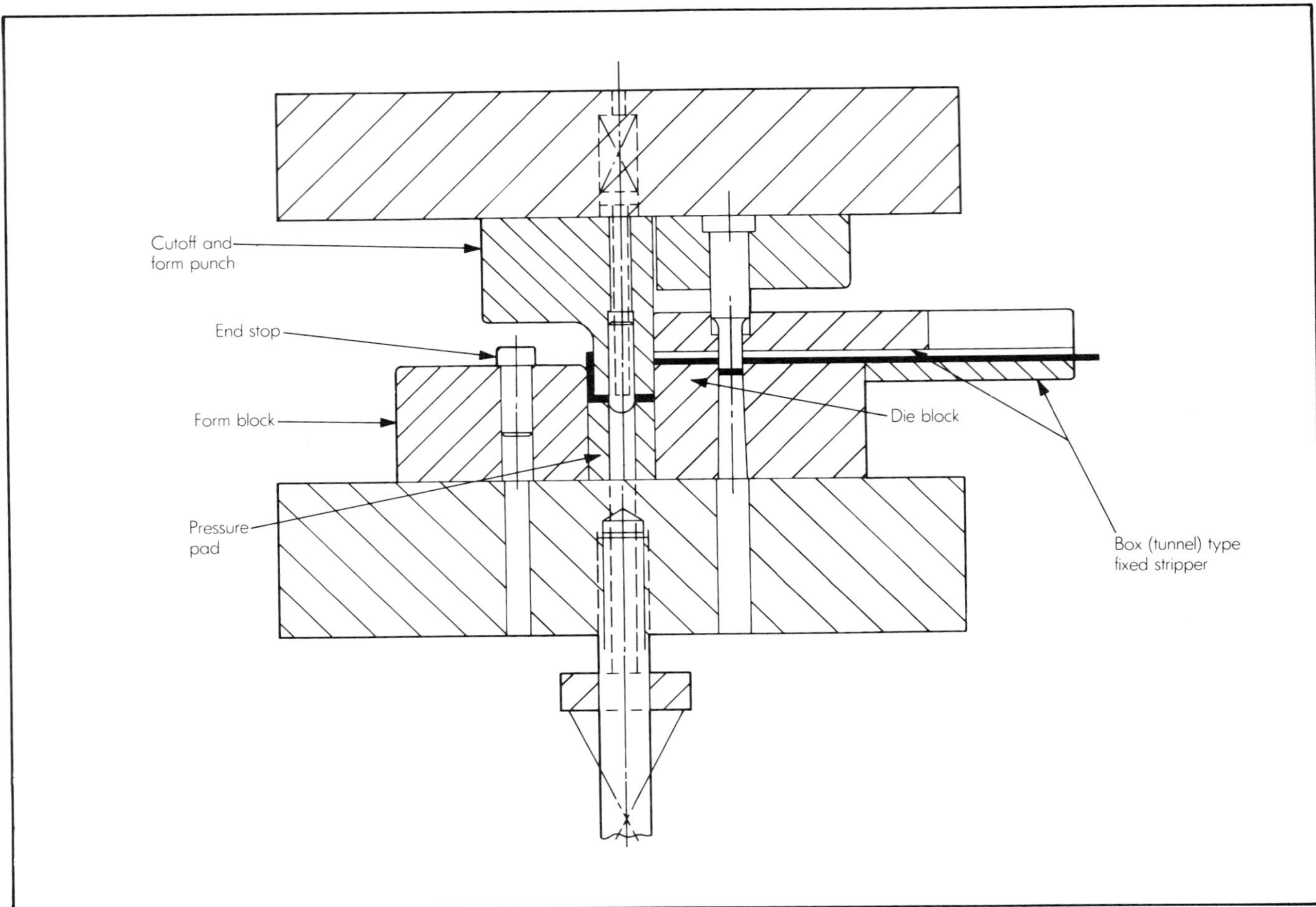


**Fig. 6-82 Progressive punch, cutoff, and form die.**

steel coil stock. The final (second) station incorporates a combination cutoff and forming punch. A pressure pad actuated by a spring-loaded pressure plate and two pins (not shown) holds the workpiece during the cutoff and form (bending) operation. A positive end stop is inserted in the form block. A box or tunnel-type fixed stripper is mounted on the punching die block. This is a scrapless die, since the bracket is of the same width as the coil stock.

A thermostat pointer is produced by the die shown in Fig. 6-83. The punch and the first pilot are guided by bushings in the stripper plate. The second pilot provides accuracy in matching the sides of the pointer as it holds the strip during the first notching, and a third pilot (not shown) holds the strip during the second notching. One of the heeled notching punches, provided with kicker pins (not shown), cuts one side of the pointer, and the other notching punch (not shown) cuts the other side. The punch holder is hardened and jig-ground for close alignment of pilots and punches. The cutoff punch parts the finished pointer from the strip. A bridged, spring-loaded pressure pad holds the workpiece as it is formed downward by a forming punch. A cam-actuated feed, which is set to feed the stock less than the pitch, allows the pilots to pull the strip into the correct position and prevents overfeeding and buckling.

## Transfer Dies

Transfer dies are used extensively because of their ability to reduce material and labor requirements. Multistation transfer dies often perform a series of comparatively simple operations. Blanks are generally loaded manually into a magazine shuttle, from which they are picked up by the first set of transfer arms and deposited in the first station of the die. After being automatically transferred through successive stations, the parts are ejected at the end of the die, thus reducing labor costs by eliminating material handling.

Transfer dies are usually designed with individual stations that can be easily dismantled for use in separate presses for the production of replacement parts. The dies at individual stations are of various design to suit the operations to be performed. Magnets are sometimes embedded in the die sections and support plates to stabilize the workpieces at each station.

Punching of opposed holes in a part is accomplished conventionally with cam-driven punches. To eliminate the danger of punched slugs remaining in the die, a cammed knockout device shown in Fig. 6-84 was developed. This device is normally at rest in a forward position, directly in the path of the advancing punches. During die closure, the device is cammed back out of position to permit slug entry. As the

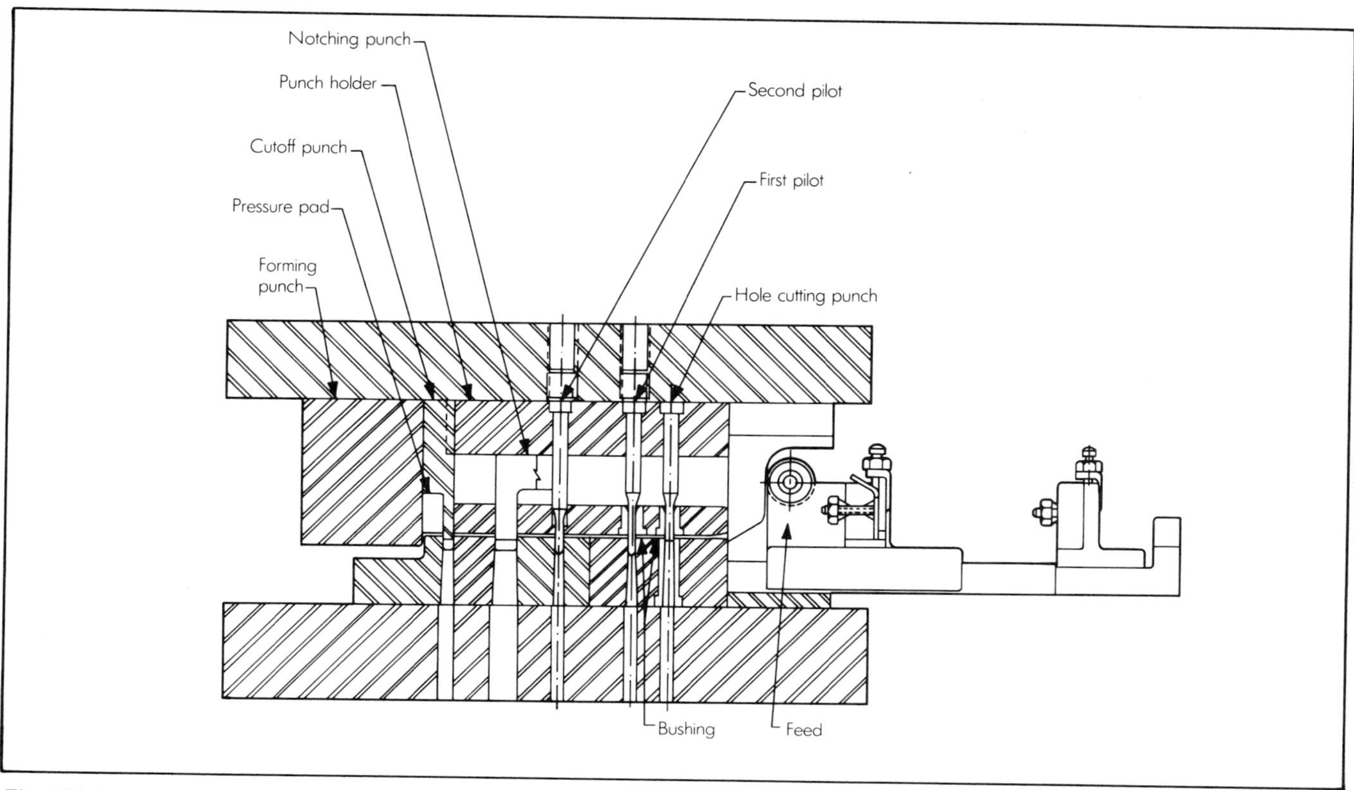


**Fig. 6-83 Progressive punch, notch, cutoff, and form die.**

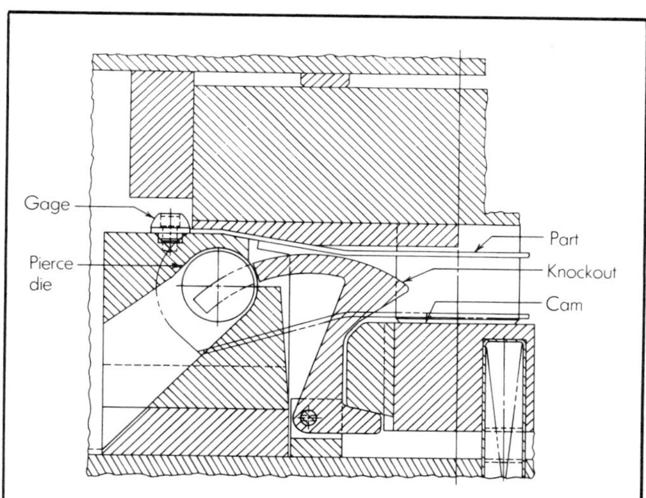


**Fig. 6-84 Cammed knockout device for removing slugs from punching station in a transfer die.** (*Livernois Automation Co.*)

punching operation is completed, the cam moves the knockout forward, thus stripping the slugs from the die and into an escape chute.

Extrusion of hole flanges can be performed by a cam station that resembles a shimmy die used in trimming the edges of drawn shells (see Fig. 6-85). The heart of this station is a floating punch nested in a locating die. The punch performs the extruding operation on in-line holes by moving first to the right, then to the left. The operation is initiated when the workpiece contacts a spring pad located in the upper die. This pad forces the part downward and into position on the locating die. Descending cams then bring two form blocks into contact with the part, cam timing being such that both blocks arrive in position simultaneously and dwell for the remainder of the operation. As the cams continue their descent, an insert in the left-hand cam picks up a plunger in its form block, forcing the plunger to advance against the floating punch in the locating die. At the same time, a similar plunger in the right-hand block is also brought into contact with the punch. The cams are designed so that the plungers and floating punch maintain a coordinated movement, first to the right, then to the left.

In this design, the forming operations might be performed in a progressive die, but a progressive operation would require extra metal for the carrier strips and the areas between blanks. Metal is saved by multiple blanking of flat pieces in staggered patterns. Also in the transfer design, idling parts remain at transfer level, while those in the punching and extruding stations are lowered into the working area. These movements are not possible in a progressive die because of the carrier strip.

A brass part produced and the tools used in an eyelet machine (a transfer-type press) are shown in Fig. 6-86. The operations include blanking, drawing, pinch trimming, flanging, coining, and punching. The first operation blanks a 1.223″ (31.06 mm) diam blank from a brass strip 0.020″ (0.51 mm) thick and 1 9/32″ (32.5 mm) wide. The blanking punch places the blank into the carrier pad to be transferred to the second station, where it is cupped. The hold-down in the second station

# FOUR-SLIDE OPERATIONS

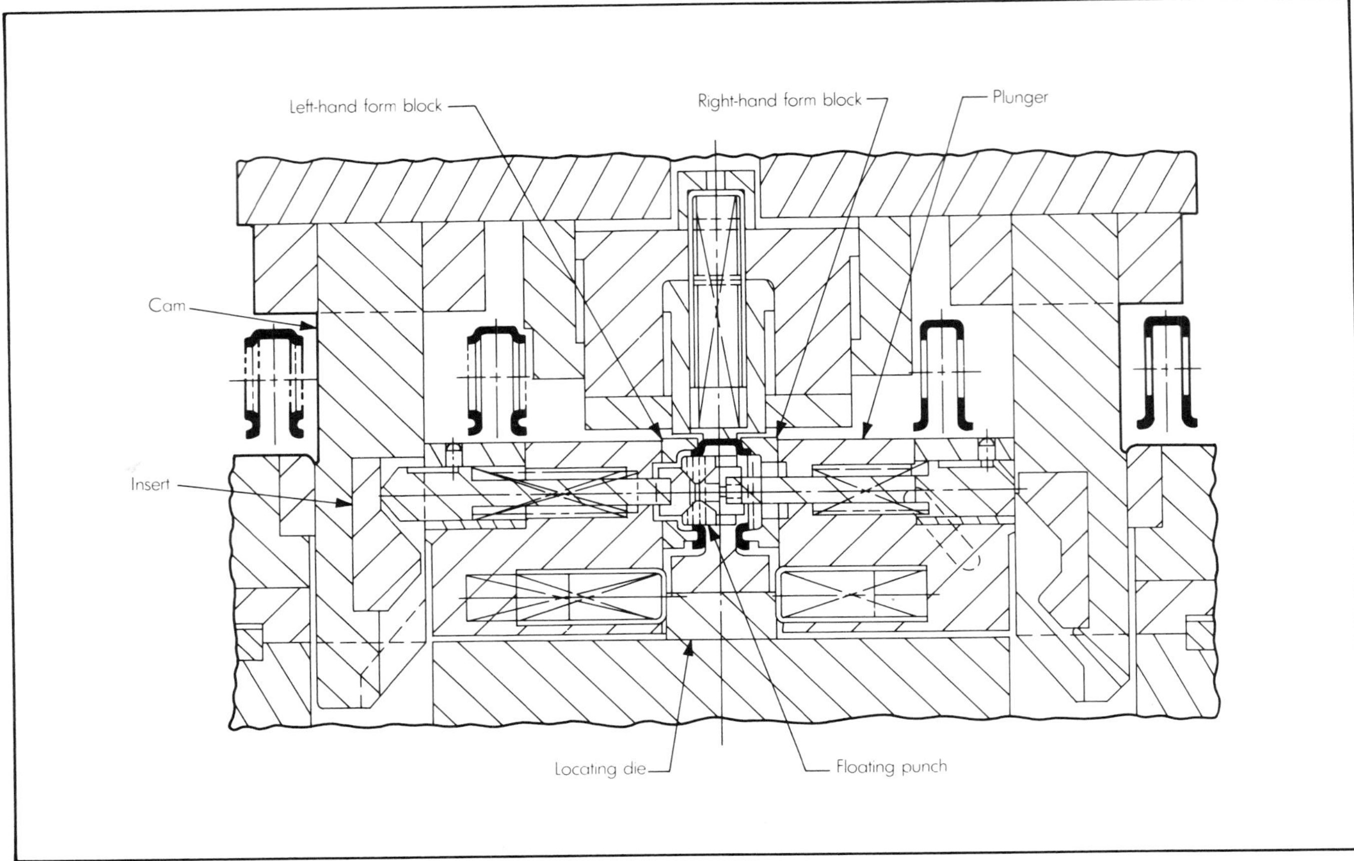


**Fig. 6-85 Cam system for an extruding station in a transfer die.** (*Livernois Automation Co.*)

grips the blank while it is drawn by the punch into the carbide die. Station 3 squares the top edge in preparation for pinch trimming in Station 4. The pinch-trim punch has a replaceable, hardened-steel tip held in place by the pilot. The die at this station has a carbide insert. Stations 2, 3, and 4 each have an ejector to lift the part to the level of the transfer fingers so that it can be moved to the next station. The operations in Stations 5 and 6 are performed at the level of transfer and do not require ejectors.

At Station 5, the part is held in the forming die while the sleeve, actuated by the sleeve retainer, forms the flange. The punch guides the inside of the part and holds the bottom flat. The part is sized in Station 6, and an area in the bottom is coined 0.0055″ (0.140 mm) deep and 0.175″ (4.44 mm) diam in Station 7. The hole is punched in the bottom of the cup at Station 8.

## FOUR-SLIDE OPERATIONS

Four-slide or multislide machines are discussed in Chapter 5, "Presses for Sheet Metal Forming." Parts formed in four-slide machines are comparable to those formed in progressive dies; however, each process has its advantages.

### Comparison Between Four-Slide and Progressive Dies

Virtually unlimited force can be applied to the work when progressive dies are used, but the amount of force applied by four-slide machines is relatively limited. Larger stampings can be produced, speeds are faster, and setup generally requires much less time with progressive dies. Progressive dies cannot provide a dwell phase in the vertical plane, but can provide a limited dwell in the horizontal plane through the use of cams.

Any type of operation that can be done in a progressive die can also be done in a four-slide machine. In fact, the dies mounted in a four-slide machine are progressive dies. The difference is that four-slide dies can dwell at closure and other operations can be performed by auxiliary slides during the dwell phase.

Difficult operations, far more complex than those possible with conventional progressive dies, can be performed with four-slide machines. Forms can be completed within the die and can also be made over a form block at the end of the die. A part emerging from a four-slide die can be severed from the strip stock and formed around a vertical mandrel, and then advanced along the mandrel for a sequence of forming operations. Limitations of four-slide machines include extensive setup time, skilled labor requirements for both tool development and machine operation, and limited workpiece sizes.

### Dies for Press Sections of Four-Slides

Two and sometimes three press sections can be mounted on the working surface of a four-slide machine. As shown in Fig. 6-87, the role of the press sections is to actuate the progressive dies used in four-slide operations. Working in conjunction with

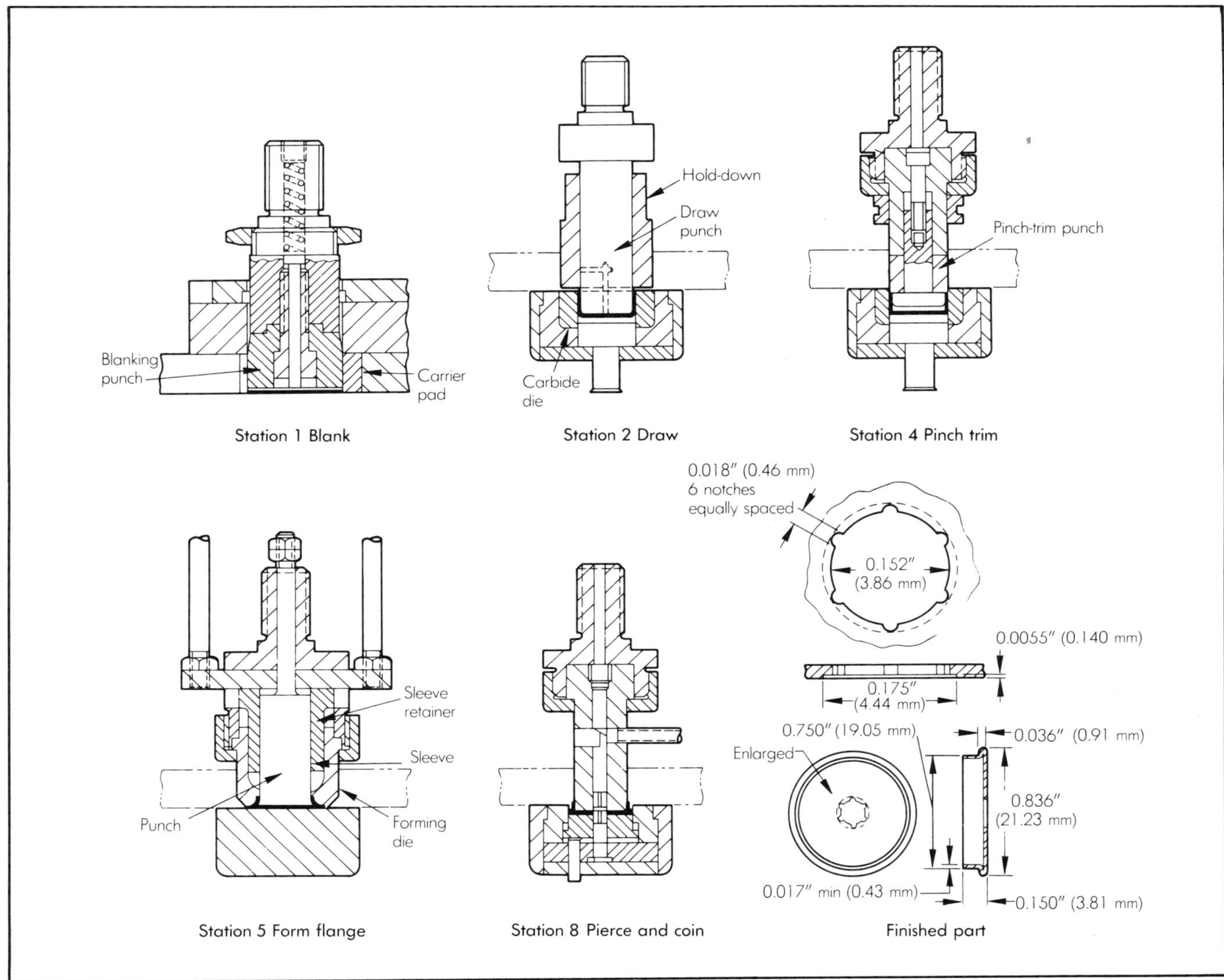


**Fig. 6-86 Dies to produce a 0.020" (0.51 mm) thick brass barrel in an eyelet machine.**

each press section is a rear auxiliary slide, a cam-actuated unit that greatly expands the capabilities of the machine.

The die sets used for most press sections are more or less conventional. In most four-slide tooling, the movable die member is equipped with fixed die posts. The mating bushings are contained in the stationary die member.

Not all press sections are the same. Some are designed for light-duty pressworking; others are designed to deliver as much as 50 tons (445 kN) of force. In even the largest and most powerful press sections, the die can be made to dwell while maintaining full force on the workpiece. However, this generates a great deal of heat between the drive cam and the contacting roller. Experience among users indicates that because of this heat buildup, the maximum dwell time should be limited to 40°.

With the exception of tooling used on the rear auxiliary slide, the dies used in four-slide machines are conventional progressive dies. A significant difference between the progressive dies used in a four-slide machine and the progressive dies used in conventional pressworking lies in the strip movement. A four-slide strip can move only in the forward direction through the die or dies and cannot move sideways. There are no stock lifters in a four-slide progressive die, and the strip always stays on the wire line, which is usually the longitudinal axis of the machine. This stock movement poses several limitations, including the following:

1. If tabs or flanges are formed downward (that is, in the direction of the stationary die), clearance for their passage must be provided in all subsequent stations. If the strip advances through a second die, it too must have clearance for passage of the tabs or flanges.
2. It is impossible to develop a sequence of downward draws. Again, the strip cannot deviate from the wire line, which means that the strip cannot be formed down into a form station and then lifted out of that station.

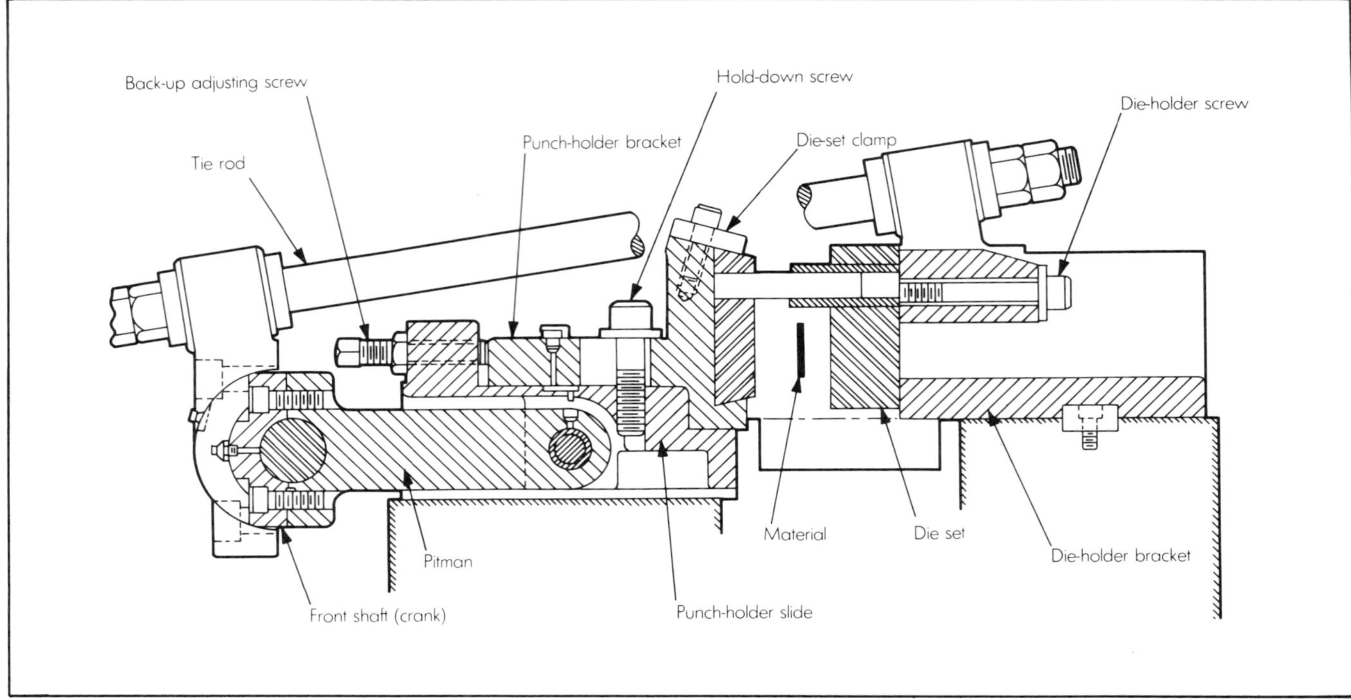


**Fig. 6-87 Typical press section of a four-slide machine carries a conventional die, usually a progressive die.**

3. It is impossible to develop a sequence of upward draws (that is, draws in the direction of the movable die), because drawing or forming in an upward direction requires that the strip be forced downward over a punch, after which it is lifted upward off the punch.

These are only apparent restrictions, however. The manufacturers of most four-slide machines have entirely eliminated the consequences of these restrictions through the use of the rear auxiliary slide.

## Tooling for the Rear Auxiliary Slide

The purpose of the rear auxiliary slide is to carry a punch through the stationary die shoe. Accordingly, the slide, which mounts on the machine bed, and the cam that drives it are behind the fixed die. It is this slide that gives the four-slide its outstanding capabilities. The potential can be grasped by hypothesizing an upright press that has two separate drive units beneath the bolster, one for the conventional slide and another for a secondary slide—and that both of these slides can dwell. This is precisely the condition that is available in a four-slide press head equipped with a rear auxiliary slide.

Several of the possibilities inherent in tooling the rear auxiliary slide are shown in Fig. 6-88. In view *a*, a lanced tab is created by the rear auxiliary slide. In this sequence, the movable die advances to the strip and enters a dwell phase. The rear auxiliary slide, carrying a lancing punch, advances, lances the strip, and forms the tab upward. The movable die retracts, but the spring-loaded shedder and the lancing punch both maintain contact with the lanced tab. When the movable die section has cleared the tab, the rear auxiliary slide begins its retraction. In view *b*, a lanced tab with a formed profile is produced. Precisely the same processing sequence as in view *a* is followed, the only difference being that the shedder in the movable die acts as a form block.

In the example shown in Fig. 6-88, *c*, piercing from both sides of the strip is required. A conventional punch in the movable die perforates a hole in the strip and then enters a dwell phase. A punch powered by the rear auxiliary slide then moves forward and perforates a hole from the reverse side. This punch immediately retracts, with stripping action provided by the die block. The punch in the movable die, now at the end of its dwell phase, also retracts. Stripping of the punch is accomplished conventionally.

Normally, holes are pierced from either or both sides of the wire line. The side selected depends on the side that should receive the breakage. This example has been given merely to show how holes can be pierced from either side in a four-slide progressive die if the machine is equipped with a rear auxiliary slide.

The two holes previously pierced are extruded with the setup shown in Fig. 6-88, *d*. Again, the rear auxiliary slide is employed. It can be noted that the upper extrusion has the breakage to the inside and the lower extrusion has the breakage to the outside. The positioning of the breakage determines whether a hole is made by conventional or rear auxiliary slide perforating. In view *e*, an embossment is produced. The movable die contacts the strip and dwells. The rear auxiliary slide advances and forms the boss. The slide retracts immediately, and the strip is free to advance. While this is an example of metal stretching, the same principle would be employed to effect a draw operation.

**Four-slide bumper.** The rear auxiliary slide and its cam comprise a massive and expensive assembly. In many instances, however, the rear auxiliary slide action required can be accomplished with relatively light equipment. When this is the case, a four-slide bumper is often employed. This is simply a

# FOUR-SLIDE OPERATIONS

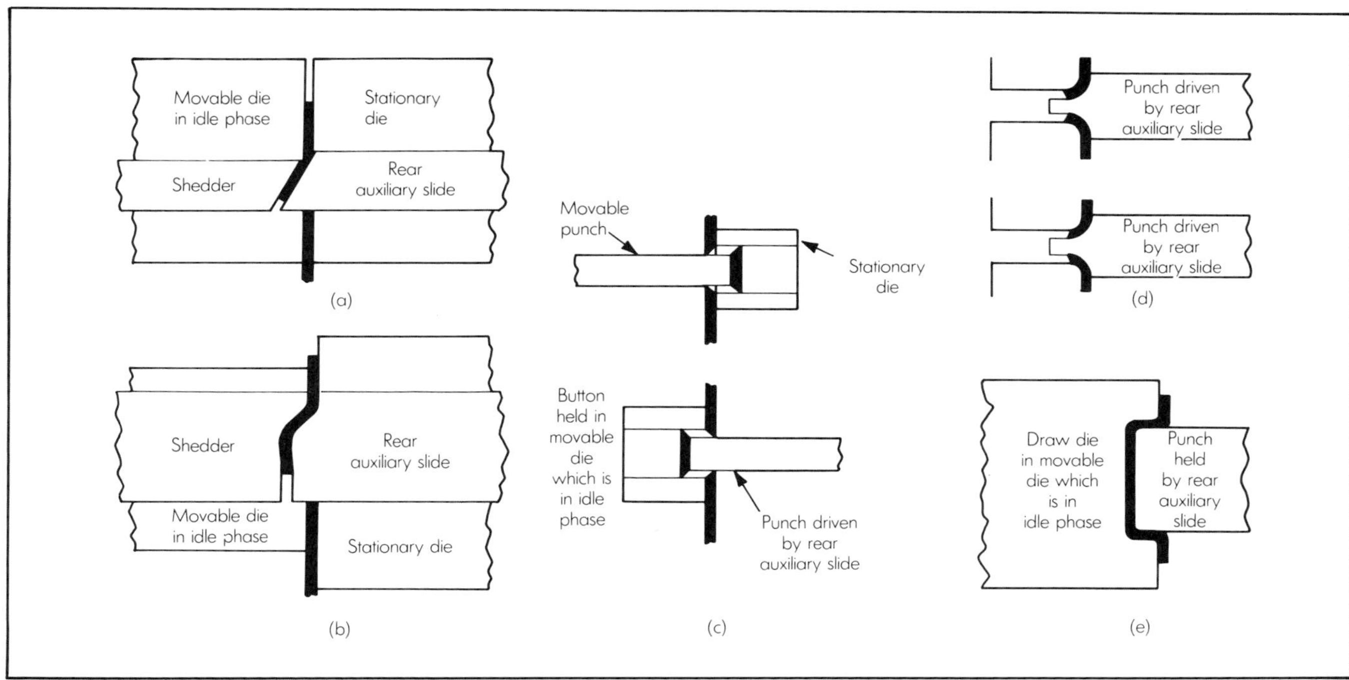


**Fig. 6-88 Possible tooling applications for the rear auxiliary slide of a four-slide machine: (a) lanced tab, (b) lanced tab with formed profile, (c) piercing from both sides, (d) extruding the pierced holes, and (e) forming an embossment.**

cam, working in opposition to the movable die. This cam is relatively small, and its action is fast and of short duration.

**Coining operations.** Coining operations are often required in four-slide machines, just as they are in conventional press-working. Virtually all four-slide machines can be equipped with heavy-duty coining heads that deliver far more force than is available from an ordinary press section. At the same time, the forces involved are so great that they preclude the possibility of dwell. This unit drives the coining tool into the stock and immediately retracts, thus keeping heat buildup due to friction at a minimum.

## Cutoff Tooling

Severing of the advancing wire or strip, like all other aspects of four-slide operation, is accomplished by cam action. Normally, cutoff is effected from the front of the machine in a horizontal four-slide operation. There are no hard and fast rules on the positioning of the cutoff tool, however, nor is its design inflexible. In some instances, the cutoff tool is knife shaped for no-scrap parting; in others, it is a punch.

The fact that the cutoff tool can take various forms and that it can be driven from either the front or rear camshaft gives the designer latitude in the development of tooling. Four cutoff methods used are illustrated in Fig. 6-89.

## Forming Tools at the Kingpost

The most complex forming accomplished in a four-slide machine is done not in the press section, but at the kingpost (see Fig. 6-90). Cutoff of the stock occurs as it leaves the press area and enters the kingpost area. Once cut off, the work undergoes various forming operations at a mandrel mounted in the kingpost. Forming is done by tooling which is mounted on the four slides that give the machine its name.

**Basic U-forms.** Only three slides are required to produce U-shaped forms (see Fig. 6-91). The three views presented in Fig. 6-91 are plan views (that is, the viewer is looking down on the mandrel, the slides, and the cutoff). In view *a*, the stock advances a predetermined distance. At the completion of this movement, the front slide and the cutoff tool begin their advance toward the strip. The timing of the cams is such that the pressure pin in the front slide contacts the strip and holds it against the mandrel before the cutoff tool makes contact.

With the workpiece firmly pinned against the mandrel, the cutoff blade advances and severs the strip. The front slide continues its forward movement, contacts the strip, and forms it against the mandrel (see Fig. 6-91, *b*). The right and left-hand slides then advance and complete the forming of the part into a U-shaped channel, as seen in view *c*. With the part fully formed, the three slides begin their retraction. The stripper (not shown) descends and pushes the part down and off the mandrel.

The slide movements described in this sequence are integrated for maximum utilization of available time. For instance, the front slide and the cutoff blade advance together with the cutoff slightly behind the pressure pin. Just as soon as the pin has firmly grasped the workpiece, the cutoff blade severs the strip and immediately retracts.

Similarly, the right and left-hand slides begin their inward movement before the front slide has completed its preliminary forming operation. The reason for this integration of slide movements is that time is limited. More specifically, all forming must be done within 180° of the machine cycle. With multiple slide movements to be completed within this time interval, it is necessary that slides at 90° to each other be moving simultaneously, with one slightly ahead of the other.

Virtually all manufacturers of four-slide machines now have special feed mechanisms in which retraction takes place within

## FOUR-SLIDE OPERATIONS

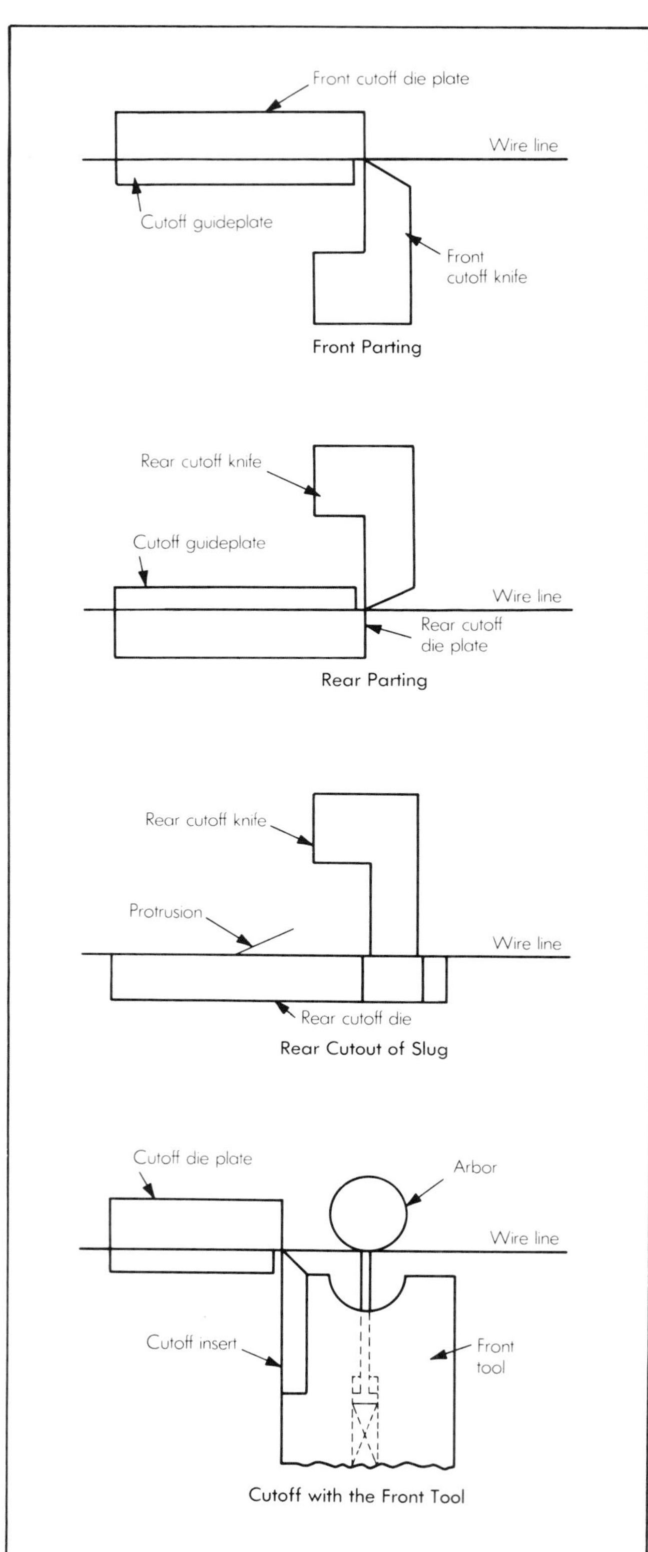


**Fig. 6-89 Four cutoff methods used on four-slide machines. Cutoff takes place between the press operations and slide operations at the kingpost.**

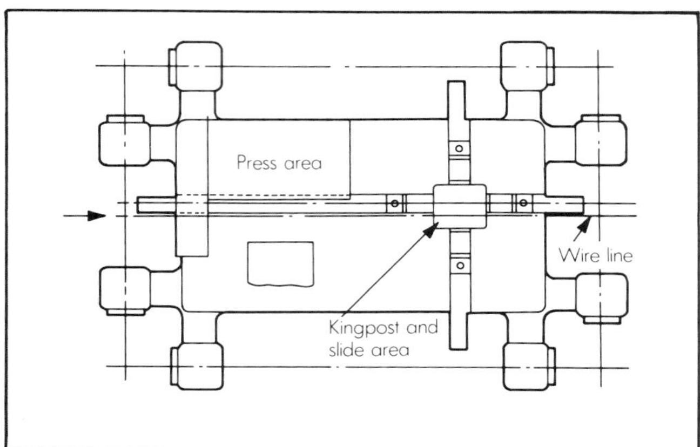


**Fig. 6-90 Schematic of a four-slide machine shows relative locations of press and kingpost/slide areas.**

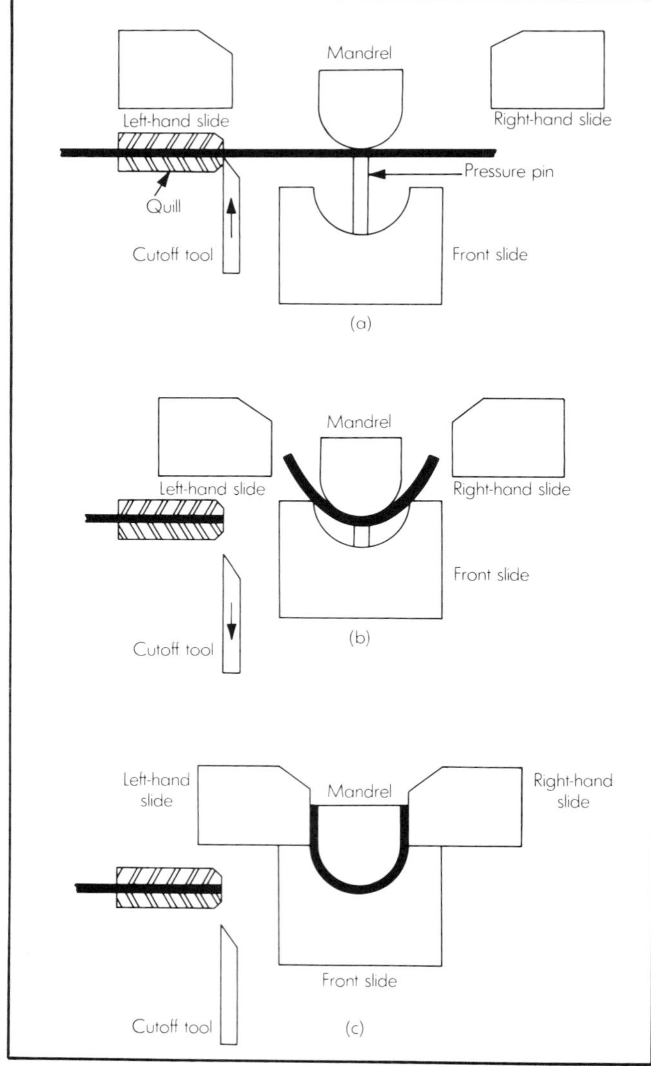


**Fig. 6-91 Plan views showing sequential movements of three slides when producing a V-form on a four-slide machine.**

90° of the machine cycle. This greatly expands the machine capabilities, since 170° are now available for forming action.

**Circular form tooling.** The tooling layout for basic circular or cylindrical forming is shown in Fig. 6-92. The sequence followed is simply an extension of the sequence described for U-forms. First, a pressure pin grasps the work and the strip or wire is severed (not shown). Next, the front slide advances to form one half of the cylindrical shape, as seen in the top view. It then enters a dwell phase. Meanwhile, the right and left-hand slides are advancing to close the form more, as shown in the center view. When these two slides have completed their advance, they too enter a dwell phase. The rear slide now advances and completes the circular form, as seen in the bottom view.

With a variation of this tooling (see Fig. 6-93), a clip with a depressed tab is formed. This necessitates minor changes in the mandrel and rear tool; otherwise, the sequence is the same. The same action takes place with the tooling shown in Fig. 6-94. The front tool forms and then dwells, a movement that is characteristic of virtually all four-slide forming operations. The side tools then accomplish their forming operations, then dwell. The rear tool advances to finish the part, then retracts. The side and front tools also retract. The finished part is stripped from the mandrel, and the cycle is complete.

**Kicker tools.** It is possible to perform more operations through the addition of a tool called a kicker (see Fig. 6-95). A kicker is simply an auxiliary tool that is carried in—or adjacent to—any of the basic slide tools previously discussed. In some instances, a kicker is a spring-loaded addition to one of the slide tools. In other instances, a kicker is independently driven by its own cam. The one shown is independently driven.

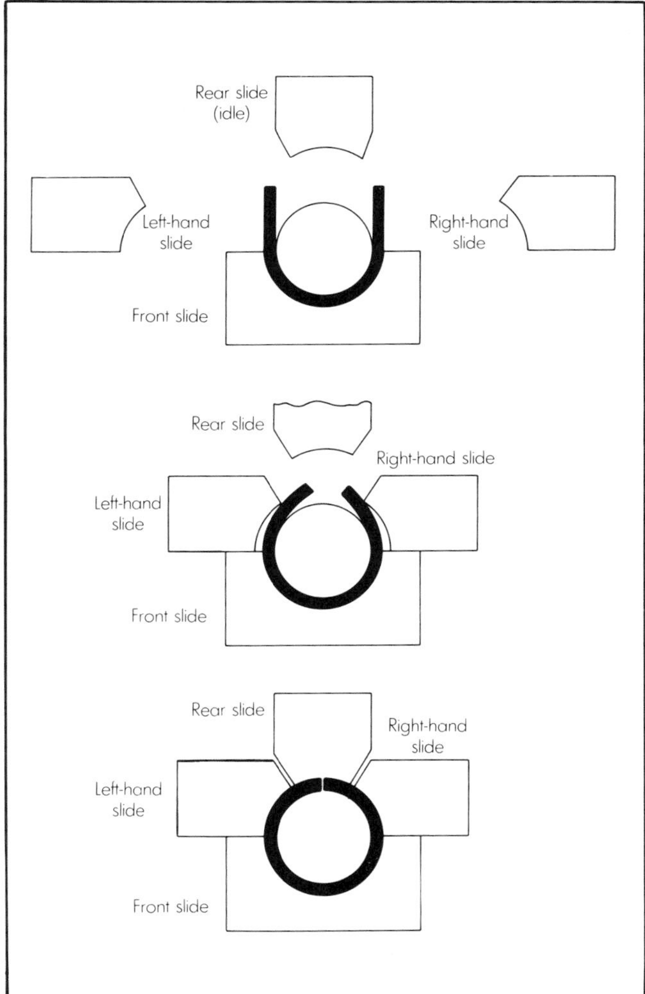


**Fig. 6-92 Tooling layout for producing circular or cylindrical forms with front, right and left-hand, and rear slides.**

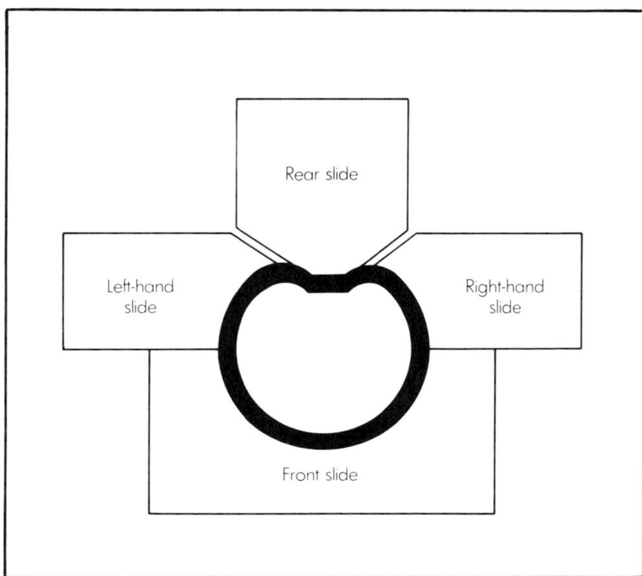


**Fig. 6-93 Clip with depressed tab is formed by variation of sequence shown in Fig. 6-92, requiring minor changes in the mandrel and rear slide tool.**

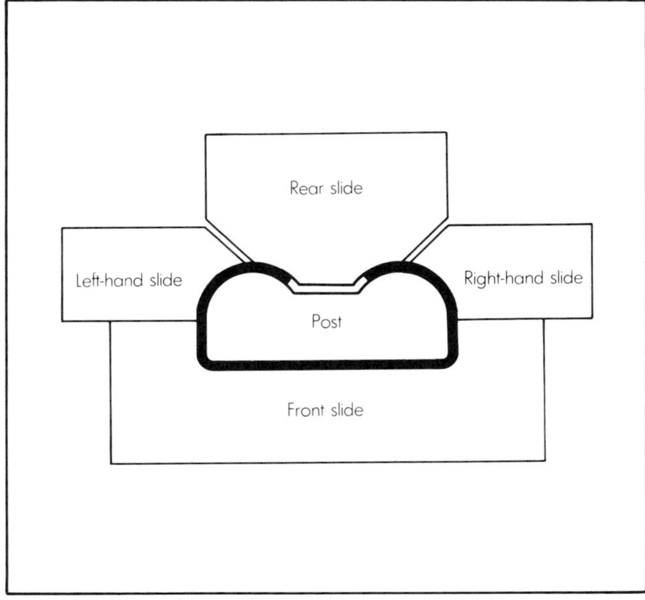


**Fig. 6-94 Another part formed by the same action shown in Fig. 6-92 and Fig. 6-93. Front and side tools dwell while rear tool finishes the forming.**

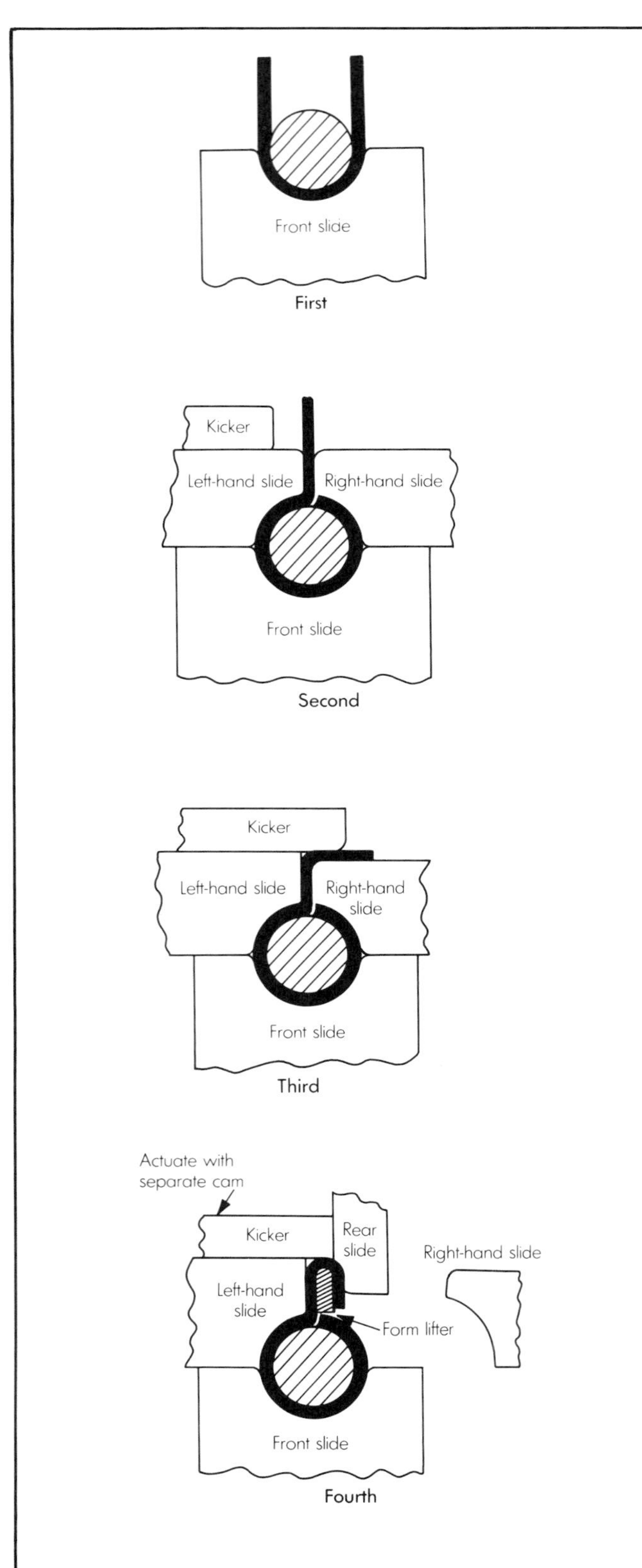


**Fig. 6-95 Kicker tool, adjacent to the left-hand slide, is driven by its own cam to form the extended leg of the part over the right-hand tool.**

In forming the circular segment of the desired part, the front and side cams follow the established sequence (that is, the front tool advances and dwells; the side tools then advance and form). First, the front tool contacts the work to form half of the cylindrical configuration. Next, the side tools enter and finish the cylinder—leaving one leg extended, however. At this point the kicker, driven by its own cam, forms the extended leg over the right-hand tool. The right-hand slide then retracts, withdrawing the tool, and a mandrel fixed to the form lifter descends. The kicker then retracts, and a form tool mounted on the rear slide completes the forming operation.

**Tool against tool.** Four-slide tooling is not limited to the forming of work around a mandrel. In many instances, a tool which pushes metal into a form can also act as a form block. A good example is seen in Fig. 6-96. First, the front tool advances to form half the cylinder and then dwells. Next, the right-hand tool advances and closes the cylinder on one side. It too dwells at this point. Subsequently, the left-hand tool advances and forms the work into a semicircular configuration in the right-hand tool, which is still in its dwell phase. At this point, the rear tool advances and completes the form against the left-hand tool. Thus, the left-hand tool is not only a forming tool—it is also a die block.

**Forming an angular part.** Production of the angular part shown in Fig. 6-97 follows the conventional sequence. First, the front slide forms the part into a radial configuration, then dwells. The right and left-hand tools then contact the work and dwell. The last movement is that of the rear tool coming in to make the final two bends. Had it been necessary, the tab formed by the rear tool could also have been formed downward. This could have been accomplished at a lower forming level, or it could have been done at the level shown through a kicker tool design. This, of course, would have required provision for clearance—for the flange to form downward—in the right-hand tool.

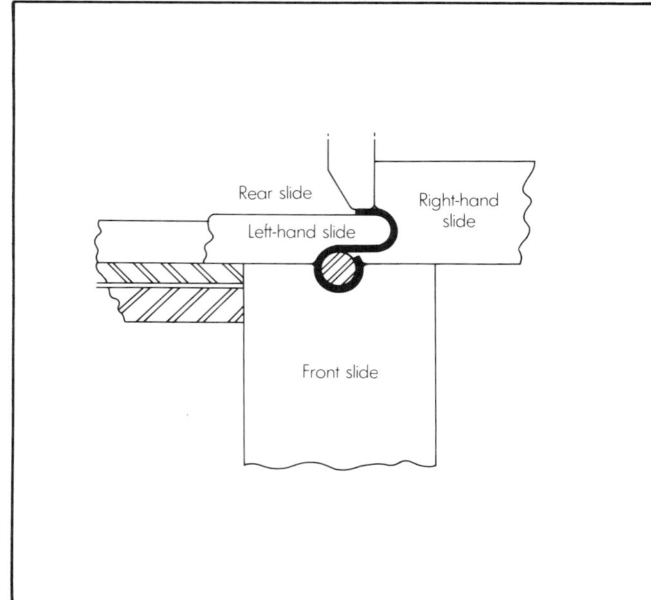


**Fig. 6-96 Left-hand tool forms work into semicircular configuration in the right-hand tool and also serves as a die block for completion of forming by the rear tool.**

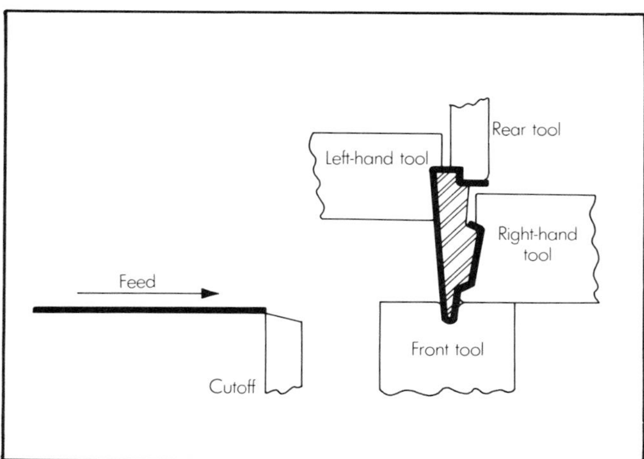


**Fig. 6-97 After forming by the front and side tools, the rear tool makes the final two bends in producing this angular part.**

**One part, two approaches.** Two or more different tooling approaches can sometimes be taken to form a single part, as illustrated in Fig. 6-98. In view *a*, the front slide makes the initial form, then dwells. Simultaneously, the left slide and the rear slide advance to finish the part.

Precisely the same part is produced in view *b*, but with totally different tooling. In this case, the front tool forms the large radius, then dwells. Next, the left-hand tool, equipped with a kicker, advances to form the side and part of the rectangular formation. The rear tool enters and finishes the part.

Use of the kicker eliminates the possibility of material locking, a condition that could arise if the forming done on the left-hand side were done with a single tool. It should be noted that when the left-hand tool seats on the workpiece, the kicker is bottomed in the upper portion of the tool. At this point, the two tools are acting as one, thus assuring a solid bottoming effect on the workpiece.

**Forming under the mandrel.** All kingpost forming operations discussed have related to forming against a mandrel held in the kingpost. The example illustrated in Fig. 6-99 shows how a slide and its tooling can form a part under a post as well as against it. The progressive die operation is relatively straightforward—a V-notch on one edge, several hole piercing operations, and a tab on the other edge. When the part is severed from the strip, it must also be formed into a locked configuration. Simultaneously, the tab, shown at the lower edge in the progressive sequence, must be formed toward the center of the closed configuration.

The operation begins with a cutoff of the part from the progressive die strip, shown in view *a* of Fig. 6-99. The front tool advances and makes a 180° radial form in the workpiece, view *b*. The left-hand tool then advances and forms the extended leg over the mandrel, view *c*. The part is ready for closure, an operation that is effected by the rear tool as the right-hand tool retracts, view *d*.

The rear tool has two working levels. The upper level of the tool closes the part; the lower level (indicated by crosshatching in Fig. 6-99) moves under the mandrel to form the tab. Lower level tabs of this type could also be produced with the front or left and right-hand tools. However, kicker tools would have to be employed. The kickers would be spring-loaded rather than independently driven.

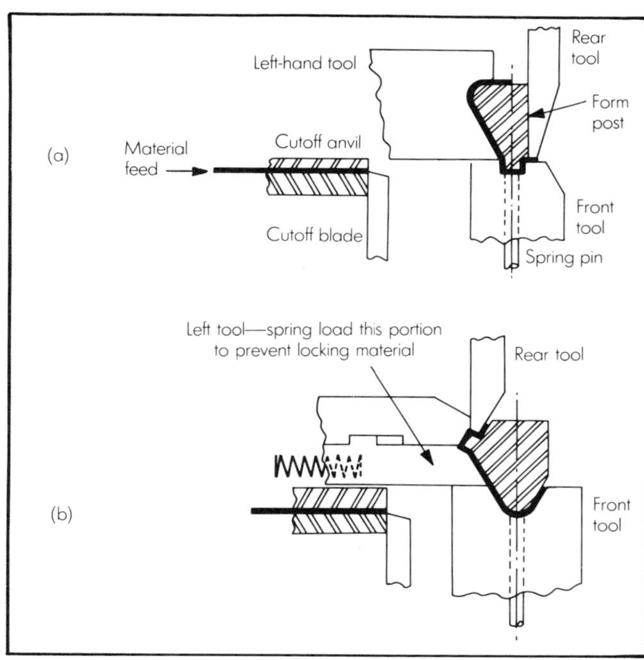


**Fig. 6-98 Two approaches for forming the same part. In view a, the left-hand tool forms the large radius. This radius is formed by the front tool in view b.**

**Dovetail seaming.** Another capability of the four-slide machine lies in its ability to perform seaming operations. The six-drawing sequence (see Fig. 6-100) illustrates the standard four-slide technique for performing a dovetail seaming operation. The progressive strip, view *a*, is the area of operation in which the seamed edges are sheared. This shearing operation does not completely separate the two adjacent parts; the punch penetrates no more than two thirds of the way through the stock. The stock is then brought into alignment at the next station with a flattening punch.

In Fig. 6-100, *b*, the part is separated from the strip by the cutoff punch and is formed into a U-shape by the front tool movement. The right-hand tool forms the male portion of the part over the kingpost mandrel, view *c*. In view *d*, the left-hand slide brings the female portion of the part into position over the male. Finally, the rear tool advances and finishes the operation by locking the dovetail, view *e*.

A technique frequently used to tighten the locking action in a dovetail seaming operation is illustrated in view *f* of Fig. 6-100. The part shown at the top in view *f* is a small punch that extends 0.002-0.003" (0.05-0.08 mm) beyond the surface of the rear tool. Because the diameter of the working portion of the punch is slightly larger than the dovetail, the punch acts to tighten the seam.

**Lockseaming.** The lockseaming sequence shown in Fig. 6-101 brings three four-slide concepts into play. The first concept is the use of a stationary tool, the second is the camming of one tool off another, and the third is the double-acting slide. In view *a*, the stock advances slightly past the stationary tool. The broken outline of the work shows the first flange, formed when the front tool advances toward the mandrel. Formation of this flange is a simple wiping action. It does require considerable blankholder force to prevent slippage, however.

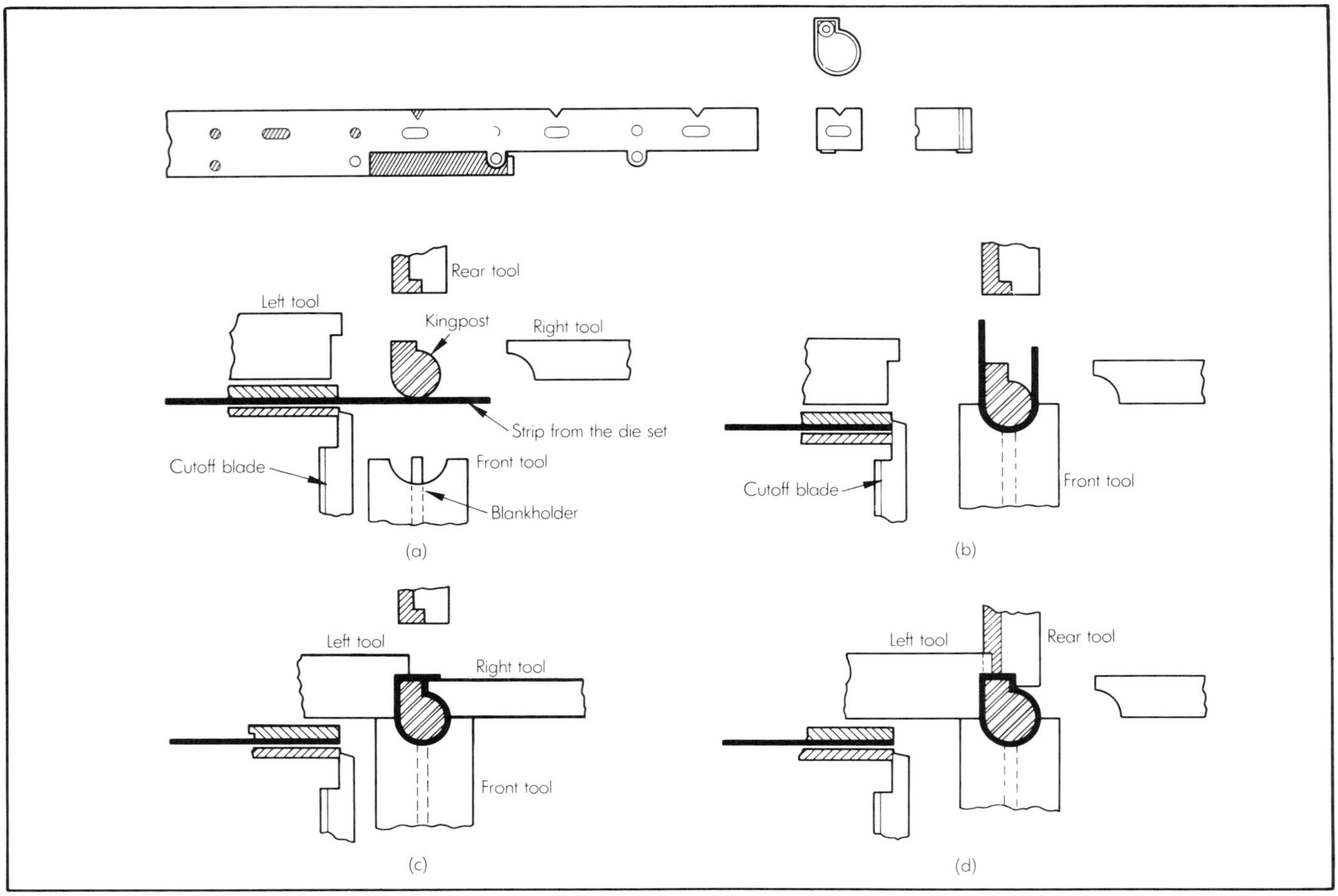

Fig. 6-99 Rear tool has two working levels: the upper level closes the part, and the lower level (indicated by crosshatching) moves under the mandrel to form the tab.

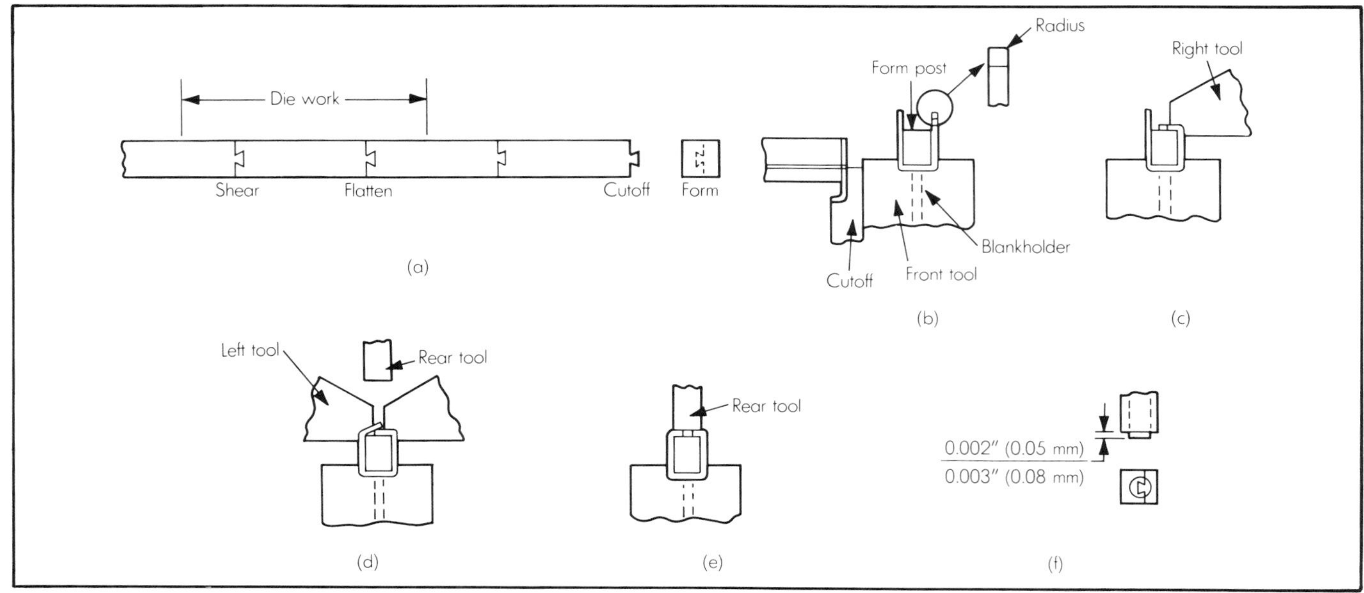


Fig. 6-100 Dovetail seaming on a four-slide machine. Seamed edges are sheared in the progressive strip (view a), with the punch penetrating only partially through the stock.

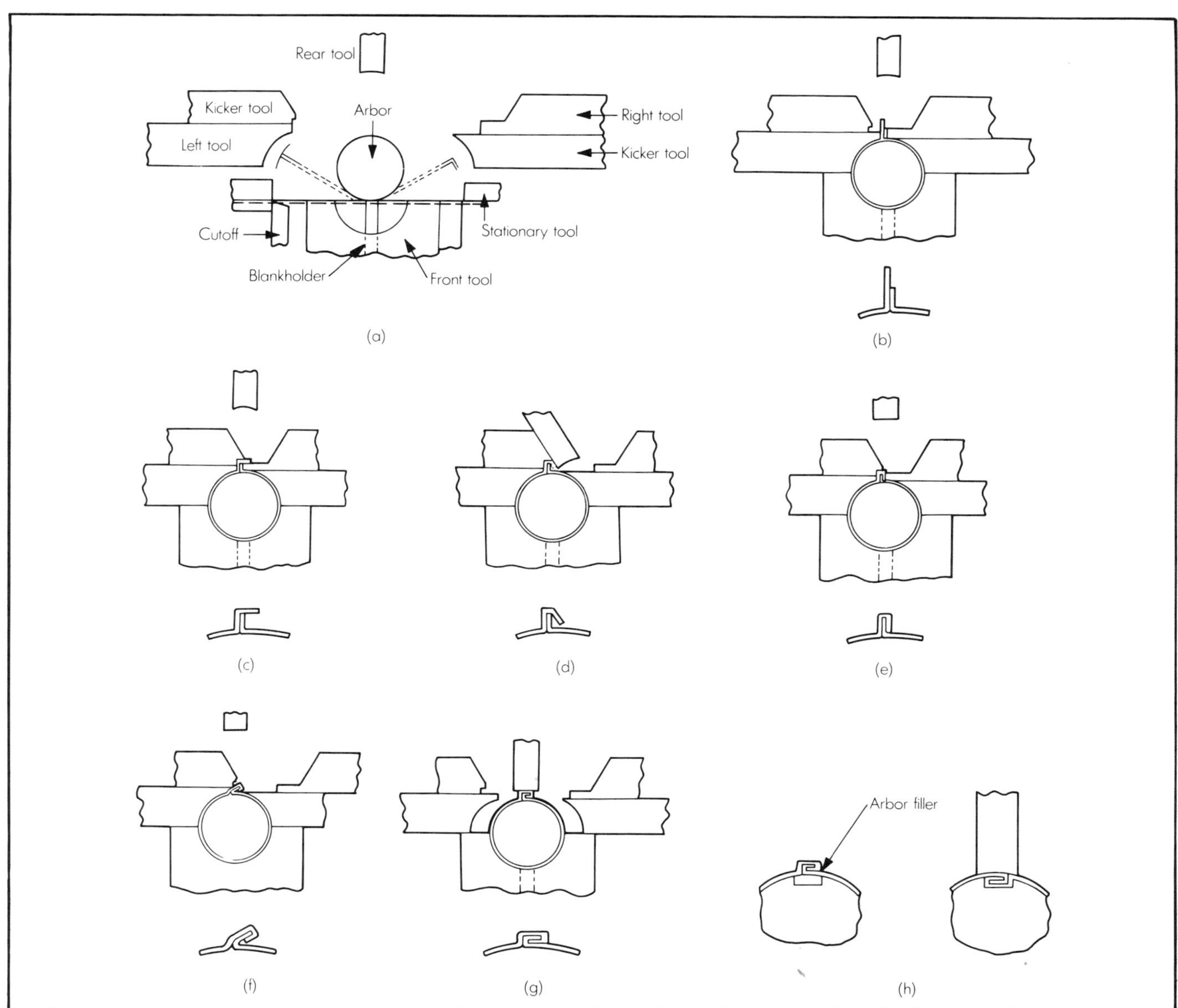


**Fig. 6-101 Lockseaming sequence makes use of a stationary tool, camming of one tool off another, and a double-acting slide. Lower member of right-hand tool and upper member of left-hand tool are kickers.**

In view *b* of Fig. 6-101, the front slide tool and side tools have advanced to close the cylinder. It should be noted that the lower member of the right-hand tool is a kicker, as is the upper member of the left-hand tool. In view *c*, the left-hand kicker advances and forms the work into a 90° bend over the right-hand tool. When this operation is complete, the right-hand tool retracts, leaving the kicker in place and the rear tool begins its advance. Unlike any of the four-slide tooling previously discussed, the rear tool is designed to pivot. It maintains its normal position (as shown in view *c*) through spring pressure; but when it contacts the left-hand kicker, it cams into an angular position and forces the seam flange downward at an angle of approximately 45°, view *d*.

The rear tool then quickly retracts and the right-hand tool quickly advances to complete the flanging operation (see view *e* of Fig. 6-101). This is an example of double action in a slide; it is the second time the right-hand tool has advanced in a single cycle of the machine. Double action is effected by a double-lobe cam. In view *f*, both the right and left-hand tools are retracting and the rear tool, also driven by a double-lobe cam, is again advancing. In view *g*, all side tooling has retracted and the rear tool is contacting and closing the rear seam, thus completing the job of forming an external lockseam.

Precisely the same tooling can be used to complete an internal lockseam, although changes in the mandrel are required. If both forms of lockseaming are to be done, the arbor must be equipped with a filler, as shown in view *h* of Fig. 6-101. This filler is removed and a slightly longer, somewhat wider rear tool is used. This tool drives the externally formed seam into the recess, thus producing an internal lockseam.

# SAFETY CONSIDERATIONS AND TROUBLESHOOTING

Built-in safety devices incorporating microswitches or sensors (discussed previously in this chapter) are often provided to protect the dies by detecting buckling of stock, incorrect positioning of blanks or parts, slug pileups, and misfeeds. These devices control the operation of the presses and, in some cases, actuate lights or alarms to warn the operators.

Also important with respect to safety is the provision of guards and devices to protect the press operators. Requirements by the Occupational Safety and Health Administration (OSHA) and details of various point-of-operation guards and devices are presented in Chapter 5, "Presses for Sheet Metal Forming." Safety programs are discussed in Chapter 20, "Safety in Forming."

A wide variety of problems can be encountered in the use of different dies, many caused by improper press selection and/or poor alignment. Some common die problems, their causes, and suggested remedies are presented in Table 6-9.

**TABLE 6-9**
**Troubleshooting Metal Stamping Dies**[1]

| Difficulty | Cause | Remedy |
|---|---|---|
| Cutting Dies: | | |
| Concave surface around edge of blank and/or around punched holes | Too much clearance between stripper and punch. | Make stripper fit closer to punch. |
| Premature dulling of punch or die | Faulty hardening. Wrong type of steel. Dirty stock. Lack of cutting compound or coolant. Nonuniform clearance. Misalignment. | More careful hardening. Selection of higher carbon tool steel. Grind shear on punch or die (approximately metal thickness). Use coolant or die lubricant. Relocate punch or die. |
| Faulty stripper action | Binding of stripper. Sloppy fit of stripper to punch. Insufficient stripping force. Unbalanced stripping forces (broken springs or poor design). | Refit stripper to punch allowing more clearance. Close up fit of stripper to punch to put stripping force as near punch as possible. Add more or heavier springs or air pressure. Balance the spring or air pressure on stripper plate. |
| Loading of punches and dies or cutting steels | Insufficient clearance. Rough surface on cutting steels. Lack of cutting compound. | Provide more clearance. Polish cutting steels. Use die lubricant. |
| Burring of stamping | Dull cutting steels. Improper clearance. | Sharpen cutting steel oftener. Reset correct clearance. |
| Tapered walls on pierced holes | Found on thick stock which requires large clearance. | Follow punching operation with shaving operation. Decrease clearance, with some sacrifice of punch life. |
| Poor shedding of scrap on trim dies | Scrap extends too far around die. | Add more scrap cutters. |
| Slugs jamming in die | Insufficient clearance angle on die. | Allow 1/16" (1.6 mm) minimum land on cutting edge and back off with 2° (minimum) angle. Sharpen punch or die oftener. |
| Excessive breakage of punches and cutting steels | Misalignment of ram of press. Loose fit on guide pins. Dull cutting steels. Running double headers. Cocked punch or die. | Align ram of press. Refit guide pins. Sharpen cutting steels oftener. Provide stock lifters and warn workers. Be sure that punch and die shoes are clean and free from burrs, and that press ram and bed are clean and free from burrs and slugs. |
| Blanks not flat | Wrong type of die operation. Poor stripping action. Too much shear. Excessive clearance. | Use return-type die. Keep shear equal to metal thickness or less. |
| Blanks or holes not to specified size | Worn punch or die. Incorrect punch or die. Material characteristics. | Replace punch and/or die. Sharpen punch and die. |

**TABLE 6-9—*Continued***

| Difficulty | Cause | Remedy |
|---|---|---|
| Slug pulling | Incorrect clearance. Excessive lubricant. Magnetized punch. | Replace punch or die. Keep lubricant to a minimum. Check magnetization. Consider shedder pins in punches. |
| Miscuts | Poor knockout action. Careless operator. Broken shedder pins. | Check setup of knockout for depth. Observe and assist operator. Replace weak shedder-pin springs. |
| Forming Dies: | | |
| Springback | Elasticity inherent in metal. | Overbending proper amount. Restrike formed area. Use heavy coining pressure at area of metal flow. |
| Ironing on sides of formed sections | Insufficient clearance. | Provide more clearance between mating sections of punch and die. |
| Formation of wrinkles on stamping | Too much clearance. Too severe a forming operation. | Make clearance equal to metal thickness. Redesign part to shallower depression. Use drawing operation. |
| Loading of forming steels | Insufficient clearance. Rough surface on forming steels. Dirty stock. | Allow more clearance. Polish friction surfaces. Change material. Use lubricants. |
| Spreading of flanging steels and breaking of die sections | Running double headers. Misalignment of punch and die because of sloppy guide pins. Ram and bed of press out of parallel. | Use more care when loading dies. Adjust press guides. Rebush and align guide pins. Check for cracks in press housing. |
| Abrasive wear on bending or flanging steel | Dirty stock. Soft forming steels. | Clean stock. Use more care when hardening die steels and/or change type of steel. |
| Tearing or thinning of stamping in area of metal flow | Too much friction on radii of punch or die. Scratches in part. Improper clearance. Tool marks in steels. | Have all friction parts smooth and use lubricant. Check and adjust clearance. |
| Flange not flat | Excessive clearance (thin stock). | Check stock and if necessary correct clearance. |
| Flange width variation | Clearance tight. Variation in location of blank or workpiece. | Correct clearance. Check locators and holding force. |
| Metal adjacent to flange not flat. | Weak spring pressure and/or worn pad. | Replace springs. Use hardened inserts in pad. |
| Draw Dies: | | |
| Wrinkling of part | Insufficient blankholder pressure. Too much clearance. Too large an area of unsupported metal between punch and draw ring. Excessive metal in area of wrinkling. | Increase air or spring pressure. Reduce clearance. Redesign punch and die to change condition. Change grain direction of draw or use more homogeneous blank metal. Use draw beads to hold back metal flow. |
| Tearing of part | Too much blankholder pressure. Incorrect radius on draw ring. Too severe a reduction in area. Rough spots on draw ring, punch, or blankholder. Poor drawability of stock. | Reduce air or spring pressure. Larger radius usually needed. Change amount of reduction or make a shallower draw. Anneal part before drawing if previously worked. Be sure all friction surfaces are polished. Use drawing compound. |
| Thinning of part | Insufficient metal flow. | Reduce blankholder pressure or flatten draw beads. |
| Broken die steels | Running double headers. | Keep parts separated. Provide workers with stock lifters. Readjust knockout. |
| Loading of punch or draw ring | Insufficient clearance. Rough surface on draw steels. Lack of drawing compound. Excessive machining marks. | Provide more clearance. Polish draw steels. Use drawing compound. |

# BIBLIOGRAPHY

TABLE 6-9—*Continued*

| Difficulty | Cause | Remedy |
|---|---|---|
| Ironing on sides of stamping | Insufficient clearance. | Provide more clearance. Increase blankholding pressure. |
| Splits or tears at edge of stamp | Nicks or scratches on blanks. | Be sure blank die makes a good clean cut at edges. Avoid scratching or denting part when handling. |
| Stretcher strains in bottom of drawn part | Too great a reduction. Insufficient clearance on sides of draw. Too much blankholding pressure. Extreme yield point condition. | Add another drawing operation and redistribute percent reduction of draws. Increase clearance between punch and draw ring. Grind draw beads or reduce pressure on blankholder. Roller level stock. Change material. |
| Ring around cup above bottom radius | Small radius in first draw. Incorrect flow path between draws. | Rework radii affecting flow path. Redistribute percentage of reduction. |
| Uneven wall height | Nonuniform blankholding pressure. Poor centering of blank in draw die. Variations in stock thickness and hardness. | Adjust or rework blankholder mechanism and locators for blank. Better distribution of drawing compound. |

(*Edward A. Reed, Metalworking Consultant*)

### References

1. Karl A. Keyes, *Stamping—Design Thru Maintenance*, Society of Manufacturing Engineers, Dearborn, MI, 1983.

### Bibliography

Dallas, Daniel B. "Four-slides: Part 1—The Press with a Difference; Part 2—The Rear Auxiliary Slide; Part 3—Forming at the Kingpost; Part 4—Advanced Forming." *Manufacturing Engineering* (February 1978), pp. 34-40; (March 1978), pp. 56-59; (April 1978), pp. 58-63; and (May 1978), pp. 40-45.

Eary, Donald F., and Reed, Edward A. *Techniques of Pressworking Sheet Metal*. Englewood Cliffs, NJ: Prentice-Hall, Inc., 1974.

Wilson, Frank W. *Die Design Handbook*. New York: McGraw-Hill Book Co., 1965.

CHAPTER

# 7

# Expanding, Shrinking and Stretch Forming

# EXPANDING, SHRINKING AND STRETCH FORMING

## EXPANDING

Expanding of metal can be done in several ways, including:

1. By conventional press operations such as bulging (see Chapter 4 of this volume, "Sheet Metal Blanking and Forming").
2. By spinning (see Chapter 9, "Spinning").
3. By extruding (see Chapter 13, "Wire Drawing, Extruding and Heading").
4. By some special forming methods (see Chapter 19, "Special Forming Methods").
5. By radial stretch forming or sizing of hollow geometric shapes on cone-type expanding machines, discussed in this section.

Radial stretch forming on cone-type expanding machines has proven to be an accurate, versatile, and economic means of producing parts in a wide range of sizes from many different materials. The circumferences of workpieces can be increased in localized areas or along their entire lengths. A variety of tapers, spherical sections, beads, offsets, and contours can be formed.

On cone-type expanding machines, the part to be formed or sized is placed around a cluster of retracted, internal forming shoes. These shoes are either jaw dies or are attached to master segments or jaws that are keyed to a slotted table (see Fig. 7-1). As a multisided cone (driver) is moved axially by a drawbar, a cam action (created by the wedge surfaces on the cone sliding along mating wedges on the inner surfaces of the master segments) forces the forming shoes radially outward against the workpiece at a constant and controlled rate. The shoes are supported and guided by a table having locating slots and retainer gibs.

Radial expansion is sufficient to cause circumferential stretching of the material beyond its yield point. This results in an increase in the diameter and the creation of a permanent set that permits accurate forming or sizing.

While many parts are expanded with only forming shoes, more intricate shapes and closer tolerance requirements necessitate the use of outer dies in conjunction with the inner shoes. Such dies are often employed for deep contouring, severe offsetting, 90° flanging, embossing, corrugating, and localized forming that can be located unsymmetrically around the periphery of the workpiece. The dies are radially retractable or are mounted in hinged rings to provide for loading and unloading the workpieces.

Hollow cylindrical shapes such as sheet metal sleeves comprise the majority of applications for this type of expanding. The process, however, is also well suited to forming other hollow shapes such as ovals, triangles, rectangles, squares, irregular polygons, and many other kinds of closed sections. Heavy sections, such as lengths of tubes, pipes, and forged or welded rings, are expanded in this way. Parts must be fabricated with high-quality welds, and their seams should be planished smooth prior to expanding.

### ADVANTAGES OF EXPANDING

Expanding produces high-quality parts having good strength. Improved strength results from stretching the metal over the entire blank surface, with uniform elongation and work hardening and the permanent deformation which takes place during expanding. There is no localized thinning, weakening, wrinkling, or distortion. Intricate contours and sharp details are easily formed.

Other important advantages include reduced material requirements and machining costs. By eliminating the binder material required for draw dies and the resultant scrap, material savings are considerable. A comparison between drawing and expanding of a typical part is illustrated schematically in Fig. 7-2. Draw forming requires multiple slow operations, and about 30% of the original blank is lost as scrap because of the trimming and piercing operations required. Expanding forms the part in a single operation without any loss of material.

Expanded cylindrical parts have a high degree of stability with respect to size and shape, even

**CHAPTER CONTENTS:**



***Contributors of sections of this chapter are:*** *Frohman C. Anderson, President, Anderson Industries, Inc.; Thomas P. Conmay, Design Engineer, Arrowsmith Industries, Inc.; Thomas F. Hill, Vice President, Grotnes Metalforming Systems, Inc.; Robert Charles McFarland, President, The Cyril Bath Co.; Arthur Joseph Moser, Management Consultant; George E. Murray, President, Aircraft Hydro-Forming, Inc.; Ralph E. Roper, President, Wallace Expanding Machines, Inc.; Felix T. Sasso, Chief Engineer, Arrowsmith Industries, Inc.*

***Reviewers of sections of this chapter are:*** *John Cole, Project Engineer/Forming, Aircraft Hydro-Forming, Inc.; Romeo Couture, Chief Applications Engineer, Greenerd Press & Machine Co., Inc.; Don Kendall, Engineering Manager, K-T Corp.; John K. Lawson, Manufacturing Research Specialist, Lockheed-California Co.; Robert G. Lown, Vice President and General Manager, Greenerd Press & Machine Co., Inc.; Robert Charles McFarland, President, The Cyril Bath Co.; Arthur Joseph Moser, Management Consultant, A. J. Moser, Inc.;*

# CHAPTER 7

## EXPANDING

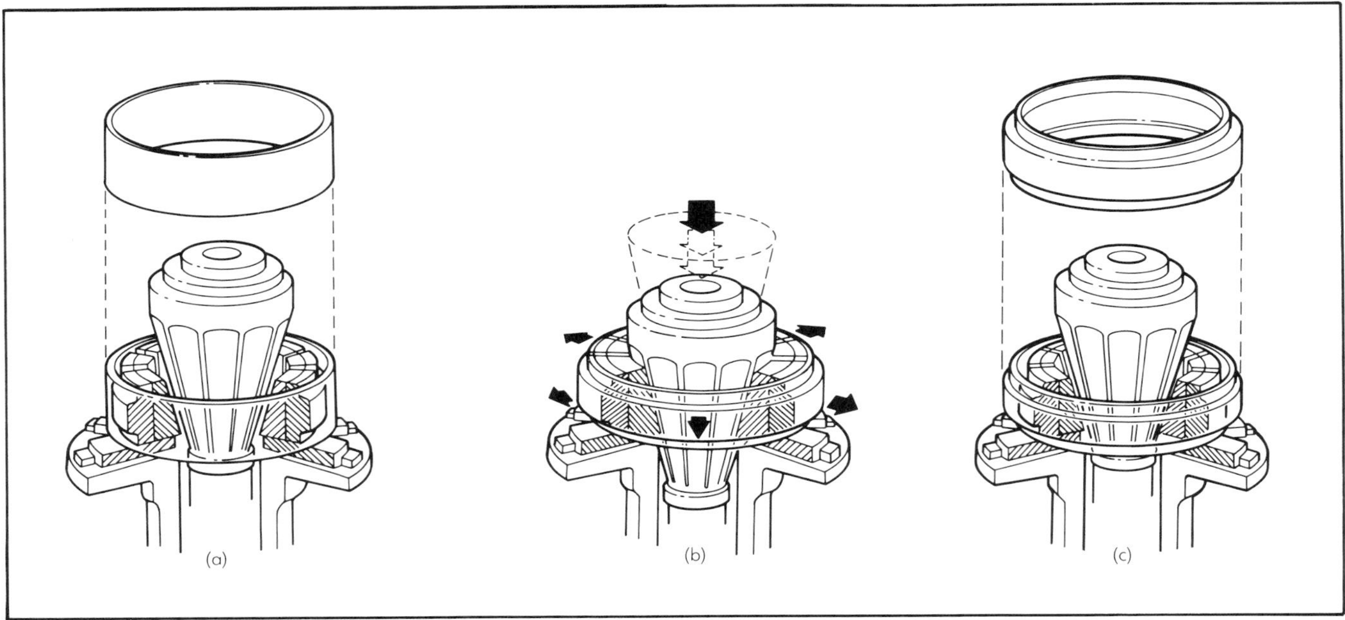


**Fig. 7-1 Successive steps in forming a workpiece on a cone-type expanding machine: (a) workpiece is positioned around collapsed tools; (b) as drawbar pulls cone down, inclined surfaces force tools outward to expand part; then (c) tools return to starting position and formed part is unloaded.** (*Grotnes Metalforming Systems, Inc.*)

when subjected to subsequent machining. Rolled ring forgings are often expanded to redistribute irregular stress concentrations, thus minimizing distortion in subsequent machining.

Expanding also serves as a quality control operation, checking the strength of any welds in the starting blanks. With respect to economy, expanding machines cost less than draw presses and tooling is less expensive (about one-half that of comparable draw dies).

### MATERIALS EXPANDED

Any material with sufficient ductility can be expanded. The materials most commonly expanded include aluminum alloys and carbon, alloy, and stainless steels. Superalloys, such as the Hastelloys and René alloys, are successfully formed by expanding. Brittle materials such as cast iron cannot be expanded.

Materials in a soft annealed condition are easiest to expand. Hard metals, including heat-treated steels, can be formed by expanding, but with less elongation. Most high-alloy materials must be normalized or stress-relieved expanding.

For parts requiring considerable forming, several expanding operations are sometimes performed. When work hardening interferes with subsequent forming, the parts are annealed between operations. Hot forming and sizing are performed on some materials, such as titanium and high-strength alloys.

#### Physical Properties

The physical properties of the workpiece material (yield point, ultimate strength, and possible work hardening effects) are important considerations for successful expanding. A typical stress-strain diagram indicating maximum ductility for two materials, a low-carbon steel and a medium-carbon, heat-treated steel, is presented in Fig. 7-3.

The maximum yield stress to be expected during expanding is indicated by the height of the stress-strain curve directly above the unit strain which represents the amount of deformation to be performed. The ultimate strength of the material must be determined for expanding within an appropriate range to prevent fracture.

#### Elongation

Expanding machines can elongate materials beyond the limits possible with drawing and stretching processes because metal is available from the entire blank without the restriction of binders or grippers. Elongation in expanding varies from a few percent in sizing operations to 40% or more in some forming applications.

Experience has shown that it is generally advisable to limit material elongations to about 75% of the limits determined by conventional tensile testing. When forming localized bosses, beads, or offsets by expanding, it is generally best to exceed by 10-50% the minimum bend radii recommended for the material being formed (refer to Chapter 10, "Bending and Straightening") because deformations occur along two axes simultaneously.

***Reviewers, cont.**: George E. Murray, President, Aircraft Hydro-Forming, Inc.; Wally Reinfelds, Senior Sales Executive, Grotnes Metalforming Systems, Inc.; Ralph E. Roper, President, Wallace Expanding Machines, Inc.; Felix T. Sasso, Chief Engineer, Arrowsmith Industries, Inc.; C. J. Sawey, Manufacturing Technology, Engineering Specialist Senior, General Dynamics, Fort Worth Div.; Wesley J. Seixas, The H. P. Townsend Manufacturing Co.; Michael W. Walton, General Sales Manager, Grotnes Metalforming Systems, Inc.; William Ward, Vice President-Engineering, Newcor Bay City; Alex Weisheit, Chief Engineer, Grotnes Metalforming Systems, Inc.*

## Springback

The amount of springback (elastic recovery) of expanded parts, which determines the accuracy that can be obtained, depends upon the dimensions of the parts, the maximum yield stress present in the material, and the modulus of elasticity. Springback is illustrated graphically in Fig. 7-3 by the steeply

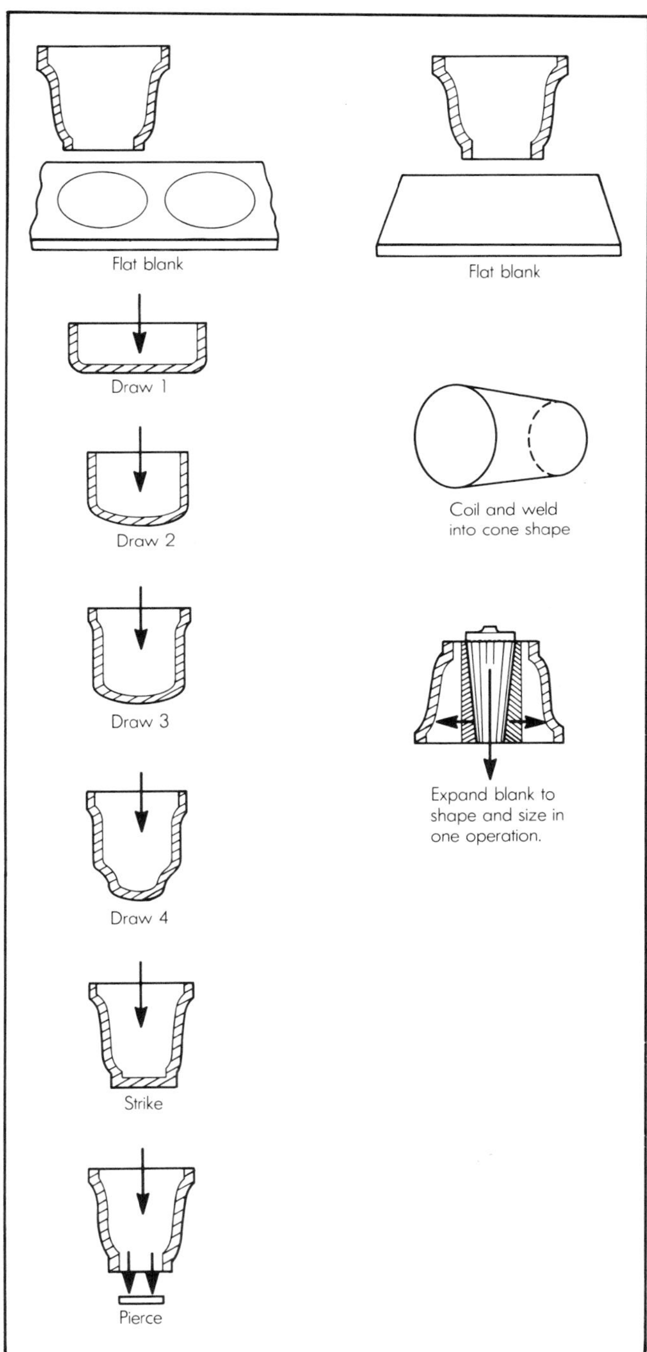


**Fig. 7-2 Part shown at upper left was originally formed by drawing, requiring six operations. Modified part (upper right) is expanded in a single operation after coiling and welding.** *(Grotnes Metalforming Systems, Inc.)*

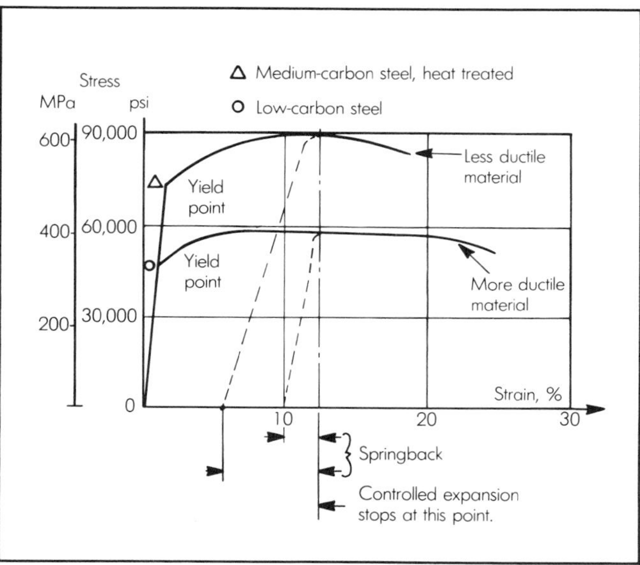


**Fig. 7-3 Stress-strain diagram for a low-carbon steel and a medium-carbon, heat-treated steel.**

sloped, broken lines connecting the stress-strain curves and the unit strain (horizontal) axis.

For relatively simple shapes, such as cylinders and conical parts, compensation can be made in the design of the tooling by using the following formula to calculate the approximate change in diameter due to springback from the following formula:[1]

$$\Delta D = D \times Y_s / E \quad (1)$$

where:

$\Delta D$ = change in diameter, in.
$D$ = workpiece diameter, in.
$Y_s$ = maximum yield stress, psi
$E$ = Young's modulus of elasticity, the ratio of psi to in./in.

For metric usage, $\Delta D$ in inches should be multiplied by 25.4 to obtain the change in diameter in millimeters.

## WORKPIECE SIZES

Parts ranging from 1-190" (25-4826 mm) diam and 1" to 80 ft (24.4 m) long have been expanded. In general, when the length of the part is about three times its diameter, the wall thickness is limited to a few percent of the part diameter. In contrast, the wall thickness of short rings can be about 30% of the part diameter. Tolerances on expanded dimensions can be 0.001-0.005" (0.03-0.13 mm), depending upon the workpiece size and material, and the machine and controls used.

Production rates attainable also vary with the workpiece and the machine. Small expanding machines typically have a production rate of several hundred parts per hour; while large machines have a rate of 50 parts per hour, depending upon material handling provisions. There are, however, exceptions. One large machine is capable of expanding 400 multiple-panel parts per hour. The parts are cut into 1600 panels.

## EXPANDING APPLICATIONS

Beads, threads, flanges, bosses, flutes, and practically any contour can be formed by expanding. Square and conical parts can be produced from cylindrical blanks. A few of the many different shapes formed or sized by expanding are illustrated in Fig. 7-4. Configurations of the expanded parts need not be geometrically symmetrical. Double-end configurations are formed by placing the workpiece between two expander heads which move together to form both ends of the workpiece simultaneously.

The appliance industry is a major user of the expanding process, with one-piece cabinets, liners, tubs, baskets, and similar components for kitchen and laundry equipment formed in this way. Expanding of refrigerator liners provides material savings of about 30%. In producing dishwasher housings, one expanding operation has replaced 20 die operations previously required.

Expanding is also used extensively in the aircraft and aerospace industry for forming fuel tanks, missile cases, rocket motor cases and thrust chambers, jet engine rings, nozzles, shrouds, and other components. There are also many applications in the automotive industry. One example is forming and sizing wheel rims for automobiles and trucks. Multiple-panel expansion applications are discussed subsequently in this section.

Other expanding applications include ring-shaped weldments or forgings for generator and motor frames, transmission gear blanks, and pulleys. Expanding is also used for many operations requiring the assembly of two or more parts. Some subassemblies are expanded to eliminate distortion from the assembly operation. In some applications, expanding is performed specifically to achieve an improvement in material strength.

## EXPANDING MACHINES

Standard expanding machines are available, but many are especially designed for specific applications. Even special machines, however, are often built to handle a range of workpiece sizes. Parts having different sizes and shapes can be expanded on the same machine by changing the forming shoes. When the height or diameter of a workpiece exceeds the limitations of the existing shoes, it is possible to use table and/or shoe extensions or to change the complete head assembly.

### Machine Operation

Expanding machines can be mechanically or hydraulically operated, of the push or pull type, and have a vertical or horizontal centerline (see Fig. 7-5). Most machines are of vertical construction and of the hydraulic pull type. Mechanical expanders are sometimes preferred for high-speed requirements and are used to expand wheel rims at rates to 20 parts per minute. For most applications, however, operating speed is limited by the time required for loading and unloading. As a result, hydraulic expanders are used more extensively because of their lower cost and greater versatility.

Push-type expanders, in which the smaller end of the driver is pushed up into the segmented master shoes from below the table, are used for workpieces having one of their ends closed or restricted, such as cones and hemispheres. For such machines, some method is generally required to hold the workpiece down on the forming shoes during expanding.

Basic elements of a small, pull-type expander actuated by a double-acting hydraulic cylinder are illustrated in Fig. 7-6. Double-acting cylinders are used to ensure adequate breakaway force during the return stroke and to control retraction of the forming shoes.

Self-contained expanding heads are made for mounting on automated lines, and expanding mandrels are available for use on existing presses. Both master segments and forming shoes on expanding mandrels are built in two sections. With the press ram in its up position (see Fig. 7-7, view *a*), the top and bottom sections are collapsed and the cone retracted. The blank to be expanded is placed around the lower section. As the press ram

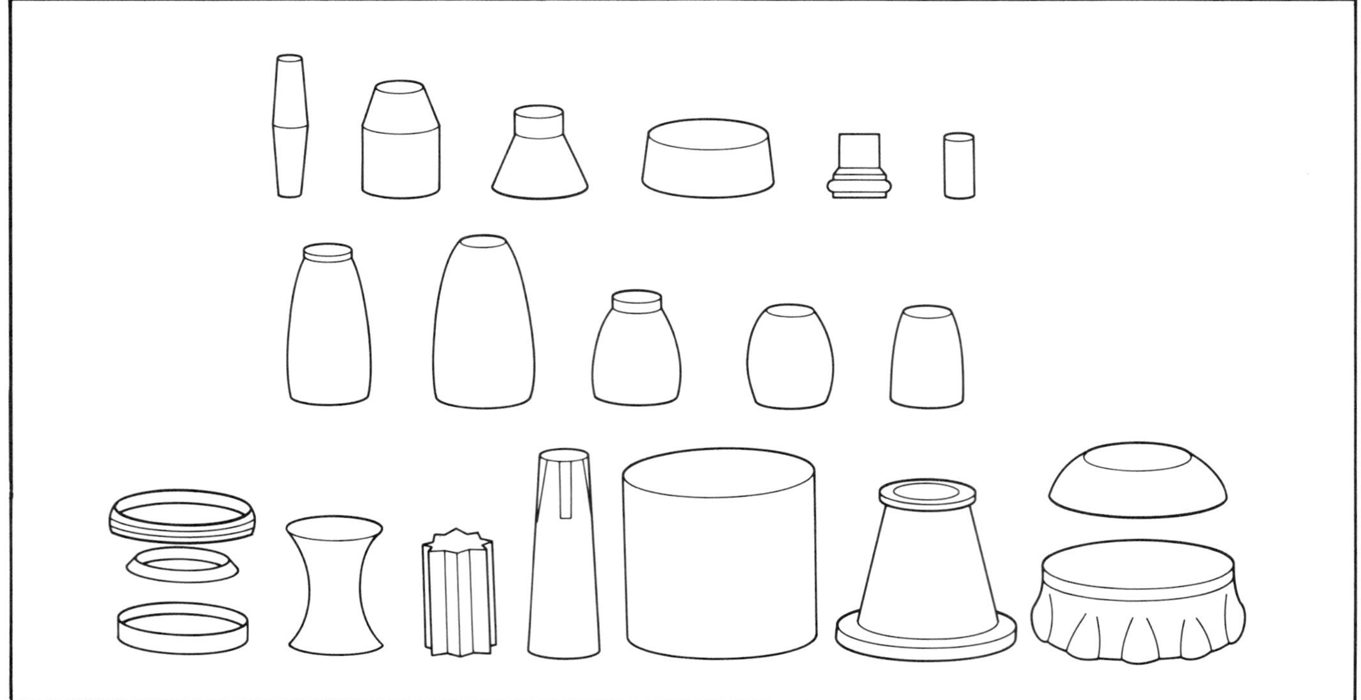

**Fig. 7-4 Typical shapes formed or sized on cone-type expanding machines.** (*Arrowsmith Industries, Inc.*)

descends (see view *b*), the tools remain collapsed until the upper and lower sections mate. Then the cone makes contact with the shoes and both sections expand as one to form the workpiece (see view *c*).

Some expanding machines are designed for mounting in an inverted position to simplify workhandling. Horn-type machines, with the expanding mandrel mounted on the end of a long tube or horn, are used for incremental expansion of long cylindrical parts such as pipes or tubes. Machines with opposed double heads are available for expanding both ends of parts. Portable machines are made for transporting to various work stations.

## Force Requirements

Expanding imposes a complex state of stress upon the workpiece material, which makes it difficult to determine the exact axial force requirements. Factors influencing the forces

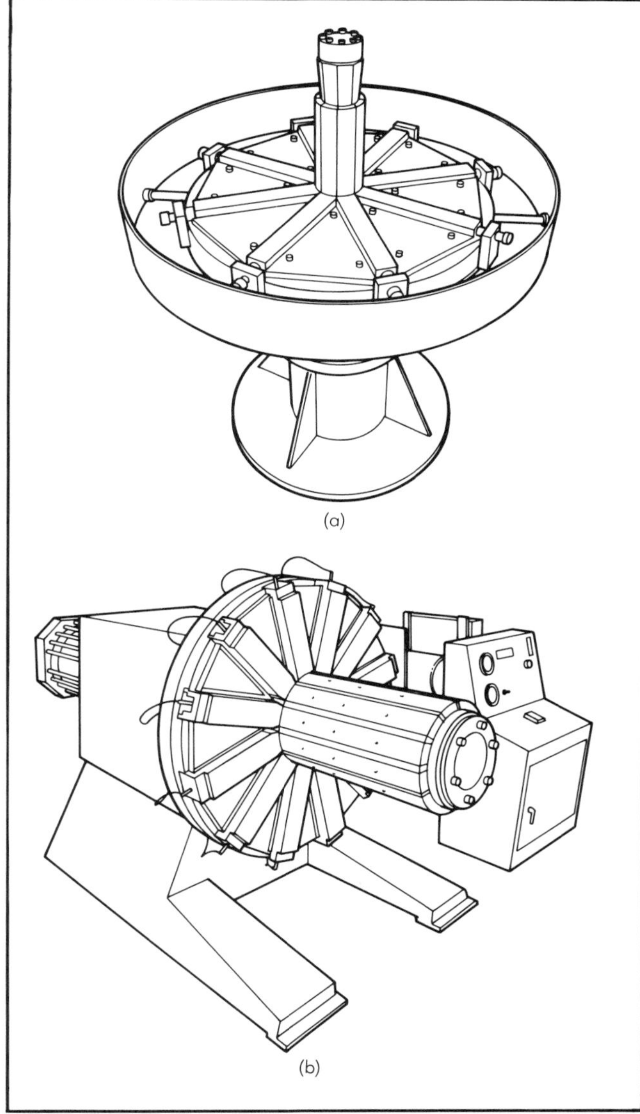


**Fig. 7-5 Hydraulic expanding machines of the (a) vertical and (b) horizontal types.** (*Grotnes Metalforming Systems, Inc.*)

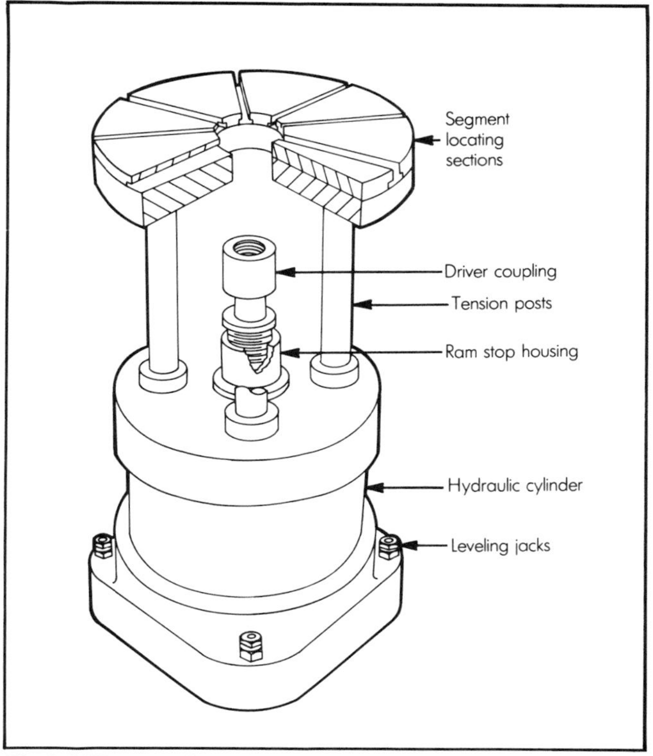


**Fig. 7-6 Elements of a small, pull-type expanding machine actuated by a double-acting hydraulic cylinder.** (*Arrowsmith Industries, Inc.*)

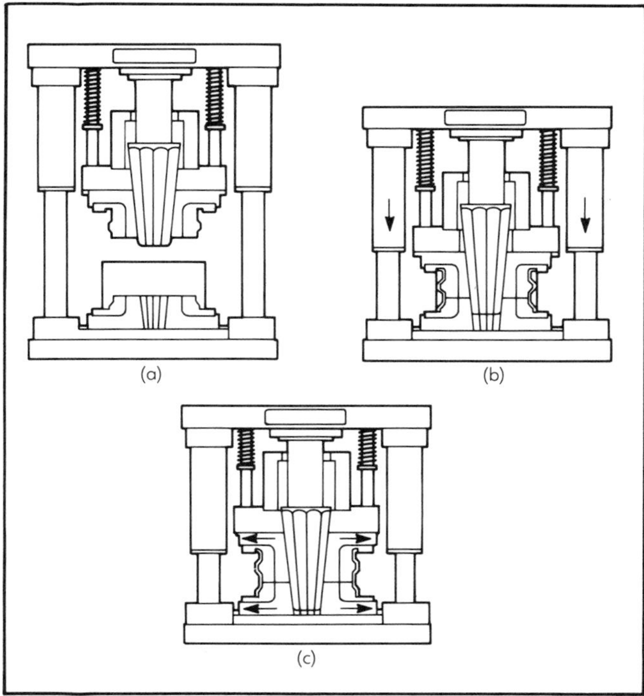


**Fig. 7-7 Expanding mandrel mounted in a press: (a) with press ram up, both tooling sections are collapsed; (b) upper and lower sections mate as ram descends; and (c) both sections expand to form the workpiece.** (*Grotnes Metalforming Systems, Inc.*)

needed include the yield strength and hoop stress of the workpiece material, the cross-sectional area of the workpiece, the angle of the wedge surfaces on the driver cone and master segments, the number of segments, and the coefficient of friction between the cone and master segments. The hoop stress, which depends upon the amount the workpiece is expanded, is mathematically related to the radial forces on the forming shoes, which in turn are related mathematically to the driver cone angle.

For simple rings and short cylinders of uniform cross section, the axial force (drawbar push or pull) required (disregarding the number of segments) may be approximated from the following formula:[2]

$$F_A = 2\pi \times Y_s \times A \times (\tan a + \mu) \quad (2)$$

where:

$F_A$ = axial force, lbf
$Y_s$ = effective yield strength, psi
$A$ = cross-sectional area of workpiece (part height times wall thickness), in.$^2$
$a$ = angle between the centerline of the machine and the wedge surfaces, degrees
$\mu$ = the coefficient of friction effective at the wedge surfaces

To determine the axial force in newtons (N), the force in pounds should be multiplied by 4.448.

The value in this formula for the effective yield strength should take into consideration the variation of this property encountered in the material as the result of expanding. The formula assumes that the hoop stress is the same on both the outside diameter and inside diameter of the workpiece, but this is not true; there can be a significant difference for workpieces having thick cross sections.

Machines have been built with drawbar push or pull forces of 15-2000 tons (133 kN-18 MN).

## Cone Angle

Geometry of the workpiece before and after expanding determines the amount of radial movement required for the forming shoes, and this determines the cone or driver angle (the angle between the centerline of the machine and the wedge surfaces). In general, an angle of 10° provides sufficient radial movement of the shoes with a reasonable stroke and mechanical advantage. The angle, however, is often varied from 2-16° to produce expansions from 0.010" (0.25 mm) or less to 10" (254 mm) or more.

For a given stroke, an increase in the cone angle decreases the force transmitted to the forming shoes, but increases the diametral travel of the shoes. Conversely, the smaller the angle, the greater the force and the shorter the travel of the shoes. As a result, the angle must be a compromise between force, shoe travel, and stroke requirements, which depend upon workpiece design and machine capacity.

The amount of springback, which varies with workpiece size and material, must also be considered because it determines the stripping force which the drive must be capable of exerting to return the cone to the starting point. In some cases, high stripping forces are required to collapse the shoes sufficiently for workpiece removal. The amount of shoe collapse affects the widths of the gaps between the shoes, which can produce marks on the workpieces. Marks can be minimized by increasing the number of shoes (discussed next in this section), by providing slave or interlocking members between the shoes, or by indexing the workpiece between expanding operations.

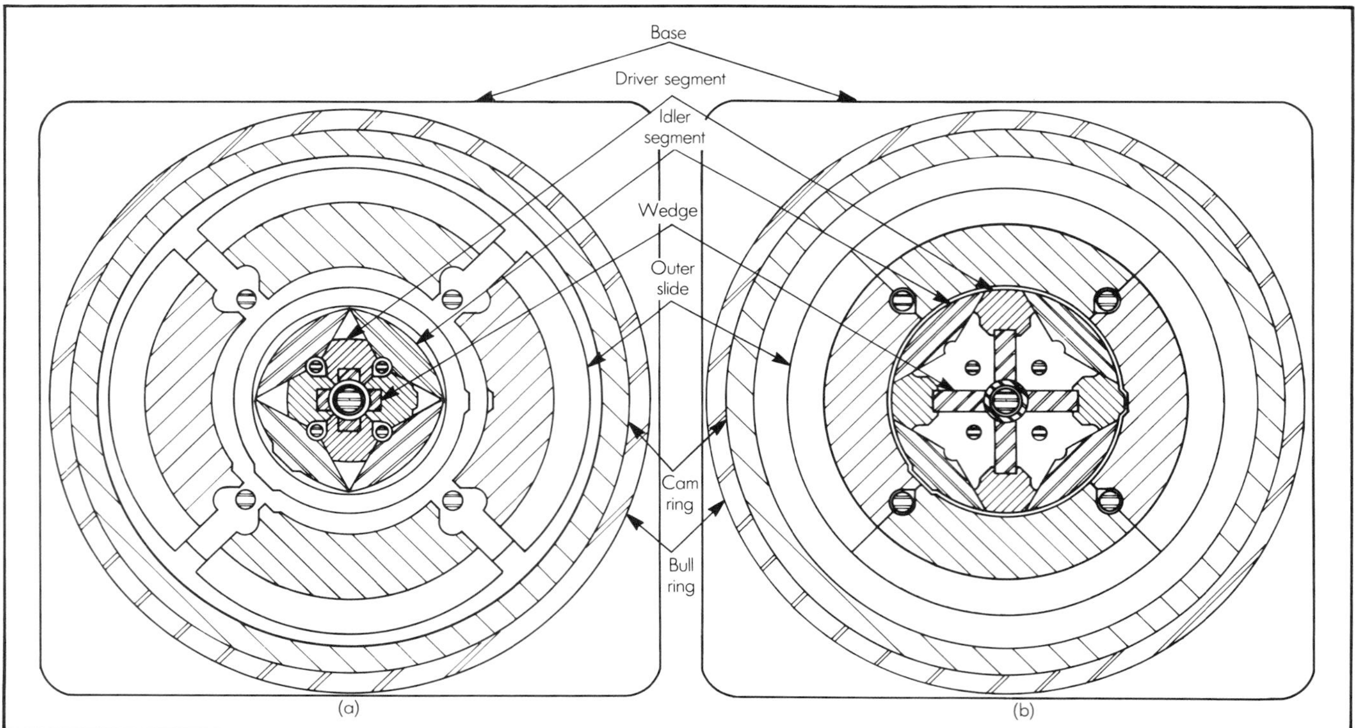


**Fig. 7-8 Gapless expanding clusters: (a) retracted and (b) expanded.** (*Wallace Expanding Machines Inc.*)

# EXPANDING

The principle of gapless expanding clusters is based upon a multiplicity of radially moving segments in which every other one is driven by a wedge that is operated vertically. All other sections that are driven by the wedge are commonly referred to as drivers, and the alternate segments in between the driven segments are commonly called idlers. They are driven by the side faces of the driver sections; and the geometry is so arranged that when the cluster is retracted (see Fig. 7-8, view *a*), the drivers withdraw at a faster rate than the idlers. This provides the capability of shrinking the periphery of the tooling and permitting a smaller diameter blank to be placed over it in the retracted position. Obviously, there is only one instance in which the gapless cluster is gapless, and that is the instance in which the cluster has reached its final position of forming (view *b*).

## Number of Forming Shoes

Expanding machines with 8 or 12 master segments and forming shoes are most common. When surface finish is critical, however, as many as 30 shoes are used. Use of fewer than six shoes is not generally recommended for sizing operations. Master segments are designed to accommodate various forming shoes, which are relatively inexpensive and easy to set up, to expand different part configurations.

Increasing the number of segments and shoes used generally increases the accuracy and improves the finish produced on the workpiece, but this increases the cost of construction. An equal number of flats must be machined on the driver, thus requiring the use of narrower wear plates and increasing the problem of fastening them to the segments.

## Machine Controls and Accessories

An essential requirement for any expanding machine is means for consistently repeating expanded diameters. Easy resetting for producing new parts and means for compensating for springback and stretch characteristics of the workpiece material are also important for many applications.

Diameter control is accomplished by limiting the distance that the driver travels during the work stroke. Common methods of controlling stroke lengths and expanded diameters on smaller machines include micrometer-adjustable, mechanically operated, positive stops; hydraulic valves; and limit switches. Pushbuttons or dials with direct readout units are used for remote control.

Through the use of automatic electronic control, operator skill requirements are minimized, a high degree of production repeatability is ensured, and versatility is increased. Control systems are available which permit the operator to program a desired finish size in increments of 0.001″ (0.03 mm). The machine automatically cycles, the expanded diameter is measured, and a readout of the diameter is displayed on a console. With such a system, the effects of springback are immediately evident and size corrections can be made while the workpiece is still in the machine. Control systems are available which permit the operator to program a desired finish size in increments of 0.001″ (0.03 mm). The machine automatically cycles, the expanded diameter is measured, and a readout of the diameter is displayed on a console. With such a system, the effects of springback are immediately evident and size corrections can be made while the workpiece is still in the machine.

Automatic return systems for the forming shoes are available for expanding machines. They consist of springs or hydraulic cylinders that keep the shoes in contact with the wedge surfaces on the cone. A stroke dwell control can be provided to hold the expanded workpiece in the expanded position for a short time to improve the set. Automatic systems for lubricating the mating wedge surfaces are a useful option. Extreme-pressure lubricants (mineral oils or synthetic fluids containing highly active chemical compounds) are generally required for expanding operations.

Another means of expanding certain metals that is sometimes desirable is a method of varying the drawbar speed. Automated parts handling equipment is available for high production requirements.

## TOOLING FOR EXPANDING

Forming shoes are clamped or bolted to the master segments; or in some cases, they are simply rested on the segment tails. One quick-change method consists of attaching the forming shoes to the master segments by means of keyhole-shaped locking lugs on the inner bearing surfaces (see Fig. 7-9). Wear plates are often provided on the master segments to extend segment life.

Thickness of the forming shoes generally varies from ½ to 1″ (12.7 to 25.4 mm) or more, depending upon the thickness of the workpiece material. For production applications, the shoes are made of Meehanite, fine-grained cast iron, carbon steel, Kirksite, or tool steel (refer to Chapter 2 of this volume, "Die and Mold Materials"). Tool steel is preferred for severe operations. When the shoes wear, they are remachined and

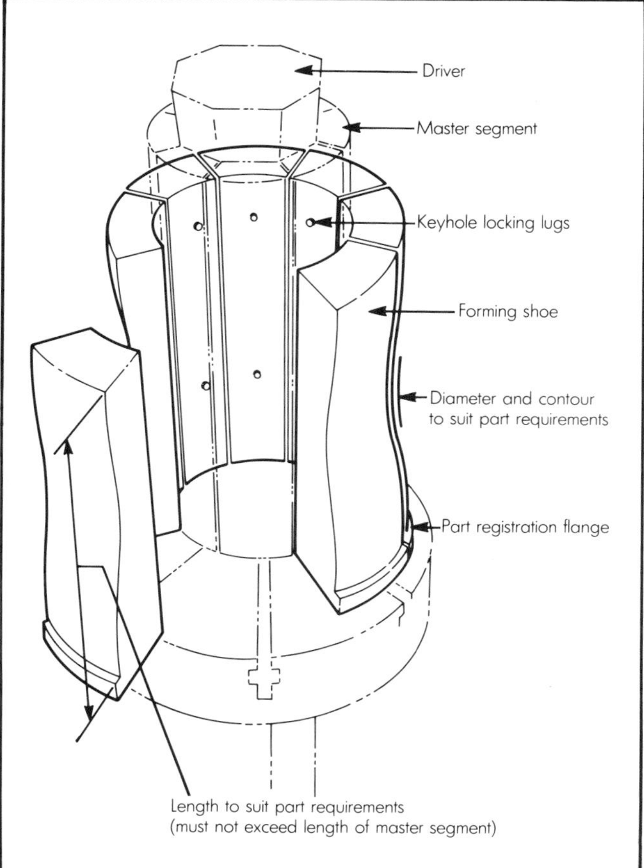


**Fig. 7-9 Keyhole-shaped locking lugs permit quick changing of forming shoes. (*Arrowsmith Industries, Inc.*)**

adjustments are made to the machine to compensate for the decrease in diameter formed.

Many expanding applications, particularly for prototype and low-volume production requirements, permit the use of hardwoods, laminated plastics, or ceramics for the forming shoes. The stresses on wood shoes, however, must be kept relatively low, usually a maximum of 1500 psi (10 MPa). This limit, however, can be exceeded by providing steel inserts in the areas of severest stress.

Forming shoes are generally machined as a cylindrical component, which is then separated radially into the required number of segments. Stepped shoes are used frequently for handling several different part diameters without the need for tooling changes.

Special machines have been built with water-cooled master segments (see Fig. 7-10, view *a*), electrical resistance heaters embedded in the forming shoes, and an insulation barrier between the segments and shoes (view *b*) for expanding alloys that require elevated temperatures to obtain reasonable yield points.

Forming shoes are heated to temperatures ranging from 500-2200° F (260-1200° C). The higher temperatures are used to form materials such as titanium alloys. Hot expanding is also used to size ring forgings made from high-strength materials, thus reducing material requirements and machining time. Hot expanding machines are equipped with controls to maintain and monitor the temperatures.

## EXPANDING MULTIPLE PANELS

The multiple-panel expansion technique was developed primarily for high production requirements. It can be used to form automotive doors, hoods, roofs, deck lids, fenders, quarter panels, floor pans, and other sheet metal components. Machines have been built which can operate at 400 cycles per hour and produce 1600 panels per hour. This method eliminates the need for gripper or binder stock, reducing material requirements 15-50%; die costs are about one-half that for press drawing.

Flat blanks are rolled into cylinders, welded, preformed into square or rectangular shapes, expanded to form the required configurations in all four sides of each blank, and then cut apart at the corners (while still in the expanding machine) to produce four panels per cycle (see Fig. 7-11).

The preforming unit on these machines is hinged and pivots downward to place the blank in the expander. Welds are positioned so that they are always in the separation area between panels. In the expander, outer die members automatically move radially inward and are locked in place. Then the cone assembly is hydraulically pulled downward to force the forming shoes (punches) radially outward to form the blank. Separated panels drop through openings in the machine base and onto chutes leading to a conveyor.

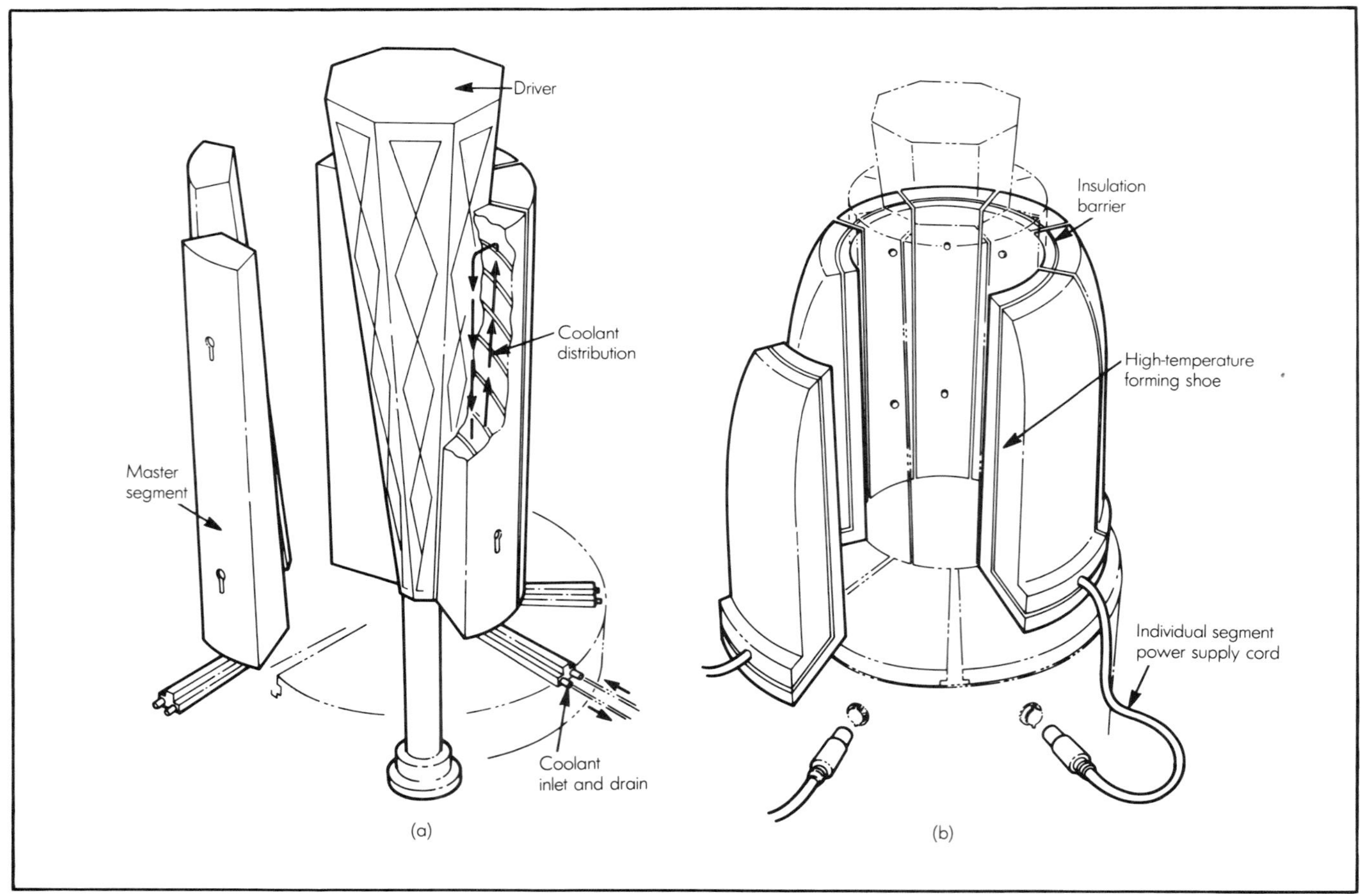


**Fig. 7-10 Tooling for hot expanding: (a) master segments are water cooled; (b) insulation is provided between segments and shoes. (*Arrowsmith Industries, Inc.*)**

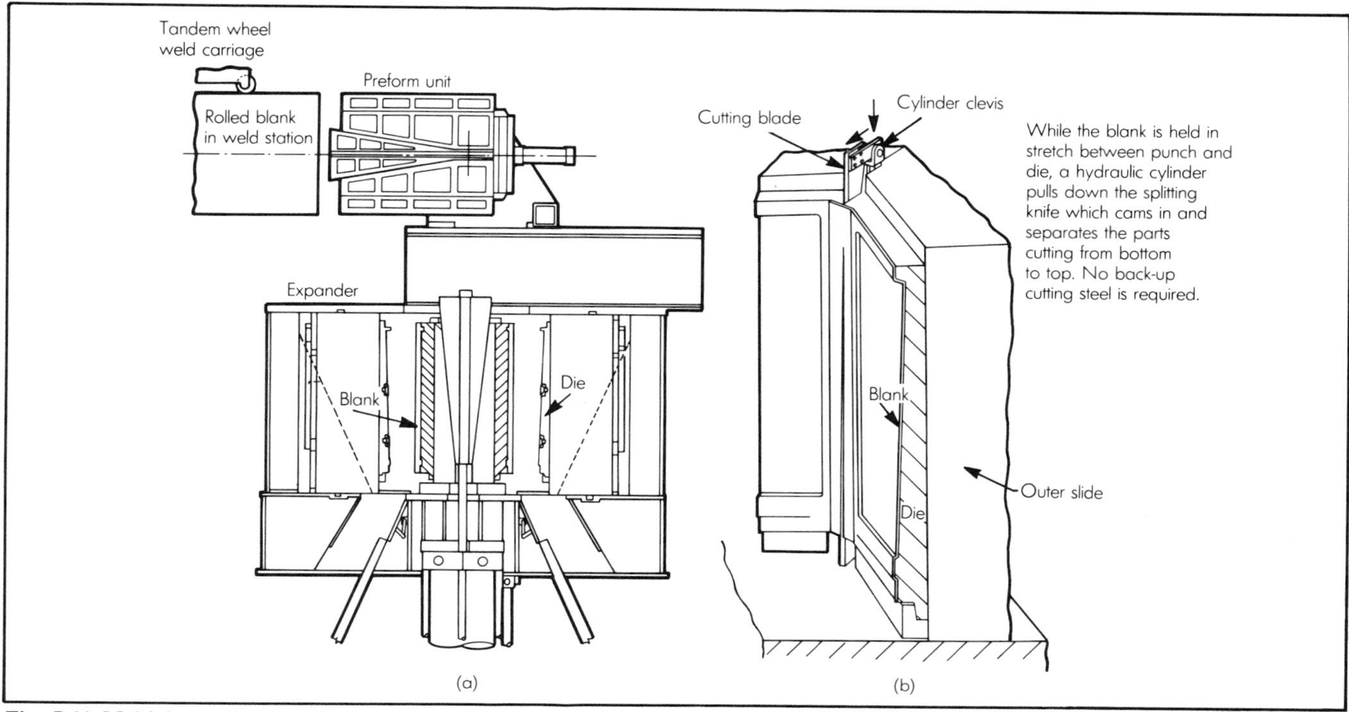


**Fig. 7-11 Multiple-panel expansion: (a) rolled blanks are welded, preformed, and expanded; (b) while still in the machine, expanded parts are split to produce four panels per cycle. (*Wallace Expanding Machines, Inc.*)**

# FLUID EXPANDING

Fluid or hydrostatic expansion is similar to the mechanical expanding process just discussed, with the exception that the inner tooling cluster is replaced with a pressurized fluid (water or oil). Since there is no inner tooling in contact with the workpiece during forming, the inside of the part is devoid of die marks.

Three types of fluid expanding now being used for commercial production applications are (1) expanding with conventional blank slippage, (2) expanding with 100% stretch, and (3) expanding with column compression and fluid expansion. All three types are similar in that an outer die surrounds the blank and injected fluid provides the forming medium. The selection of the type to be used is based upon the geometry of the workpiece.

## CONVENTIONAL BLANK SLIPPAGE

Outer die segments move radially inward to a fixed position, clamping the blank at top and bottom against a fixed, central toolpost (see Fig. 7-12). At this point, pressurized water is injected through a port in the toolpost, which expands the blank outwardly to conform with the contour of the die segments. During forming, both edges of the blank slip toward each other.

Advantages of this process are:

- Expanded parts that have no blemishes resulting from tool marks.
- Blank edges that move uniformly, eliminating wavy (scalloped) edges.
- Elimination of the need for expanding, inner-cluster tooling.
- Slightly higher expandability than is possible with conventional expanding, often permitting use of commercial quality steels instead of premium grades.

## EXPANDING WITH 100% STRETCH

With this method of fluid expanding, the ends of the blanks are locked and sealed with serrated gripper steels (see Fig. 7-13, view *a*) before expanding, thereby forcing the workpiece to be formed entirely by stretching. In addition to forming with no tooling blemishes, an important advantage of this process is economy because of material savings. Stainless steels can be formed without the need for costly electropolishing. View *b* shows stainless steel tubs for dishwashers which are expanded two at a time and then cut apart.

This method of fluid expanding, however, has a slightly reduced overall expanding capability because the blank edges cannot slide toward each other during forming. Expanding with 100% stretch creates compound elongation, thus reducing the overall blank elongation capability. This limitation may require some change in workpiece geometry near the ends of the part, such as enlarging the radii.

## COLUMN COMPRESSION AND FLUID EXPANSION

A third expanding process, combining column compression

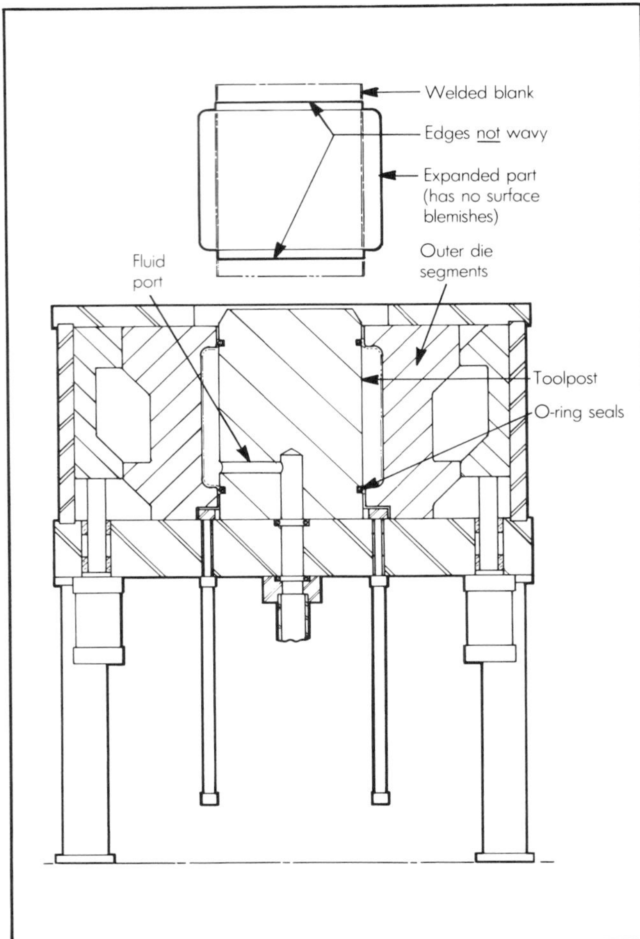


**Fig. 7-12 Fluid expanding method using conventional blank slippage.** (*Wallace Expanding Machines, Inc.*)

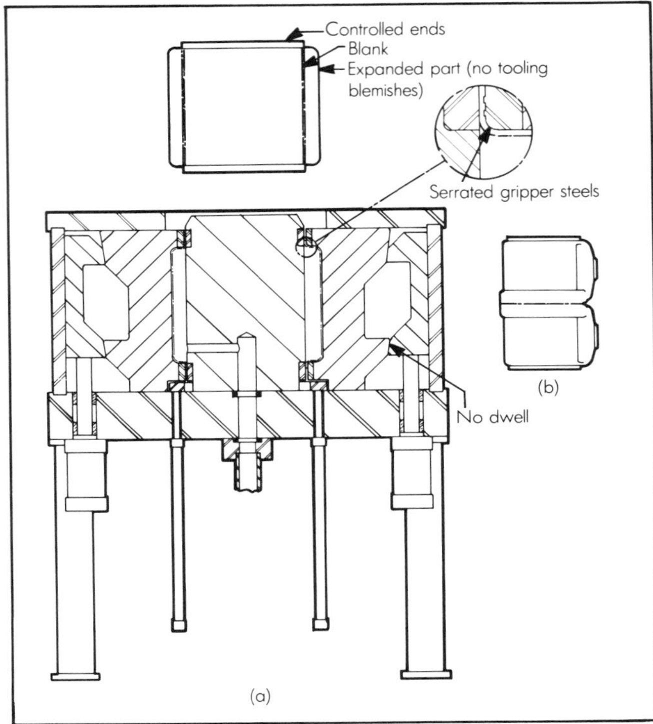


**Fig. 7-13 Fluid expanding with 100% stretch: (a) blank ends are locked and sealed with serrated gripper steels; (b) stainless steel tubs expanded two at a time and then cut apart.** (*Wallace Expanding Machines, Inc.*)

with fluid expansion, provides a higher range of expandability than any other method. It consists of mounting a die in a hydraulic press (see Fig. 7-14, view *a*); this is necessary because the forming program requires a variable ram speed. The die has no perishable fluid seals. Instead, blanks are simply trapped between special stuffing-ledge arrangements on upper and lower die halves.

When the press ram descends, a pilot in the upper die displaces water which is at a fixed level in the blank mounted in the lower die. All the air and some water is purged from the blank when the stuffing ledges contact the two ends of the blank. Water trapped inside the blank is set to a relief valve pressure of about 100-250 psi (690-1725 kPa), depending upon the application. As the ram collapses the blank, the pressurized water forces the metal outward to the configuration of the die.

Using this process to expand a welded hot-rolled steel cylinder having a wall thickness of 0.180″ (4.57 mm), the diameter is enlarged 85% and the circumference more than 200%. When forming an air conditioner orifice, the diameter is increased from 27 to 39″ (686 to 991 mm). In all cases, there is practically no thinout of the material in the formed part. One reason for this is that the low water pressure used minimizes metal stretching.

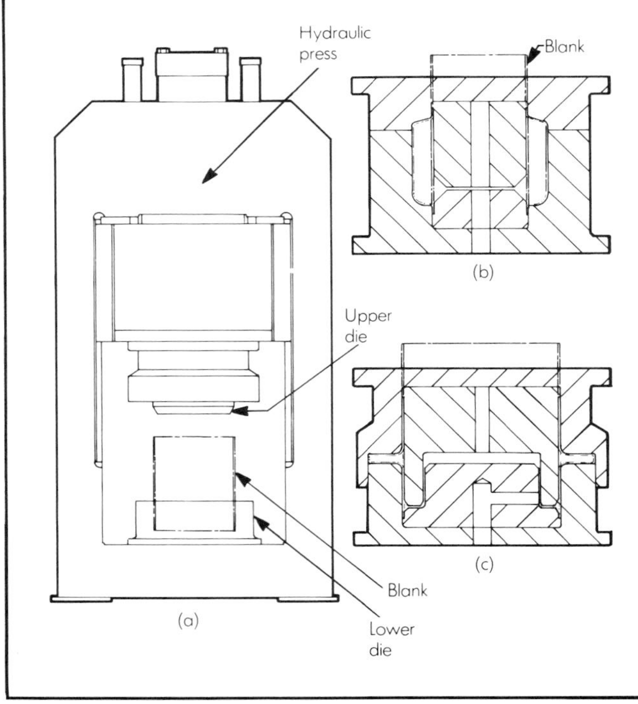


**Fig. 7-14 Fluid expanding combined with column compression: (a) die mounted in a hydraulic press, (b) common type of expanded part; (c) unusual expanded part that is separated at center to produce two identical workpieces.** (*Wallace Expanding Machines, Inc.*)

In addition to the important advantage of the higher range of expandability offered by this method, other benefits include:

- Expanded parts that have no tooling blemishes.
- A simpler, more flexible method of making round parts. The die is a mold requiring only simple circular machining.
- Lower tooling costs.
- The capability of making low-cost prototypes.
- The ability of forming sharp details.

A common type of appliance part expanded by this process is shown in Fig. 7-14, view *b*. A more unusual part that is separated at its center after expanding to produce two identical workpieces is illustrated in view *c*. In addition to its wide use in the appliance industry, the process is applicable to many multiple-panel uses such as automotive and aircraft body skins. Material savings in such applications approach 50%, and the panel quality is excellent. Welded box-shaped blanks can be made of two different types of material and even different thicknesses.

# SHRINKING

Shrinking is the opposite of expanding, with the metal workpiece being formed or sized by exceeding the material yield stress in compression rather than in tension to decrease diameters. Forces act radially inward toward the machine centerline rather than outward. The force required to form parts by shrinking can vary from the same as that required to expand an equivalent mass of material to four or five times as much. The use of fewer segments increases the shrinkability and reduces the force requirements. Parts can be accurately sized by shrinking about 0.5%, compared to the approximately 2% needed to expand to accurate size.

A typical shrinker is shown in Fig. 7-15. Principle elements include an outer reaction or pressure ring and a group of wedges. When the pressure ring and wedges are moved axially, the wedges force a set of mating jaws radially inward at a uniform rate toward a common center. The jaws have suitable die or shoe mounting provisions and are supported and guided by a table.

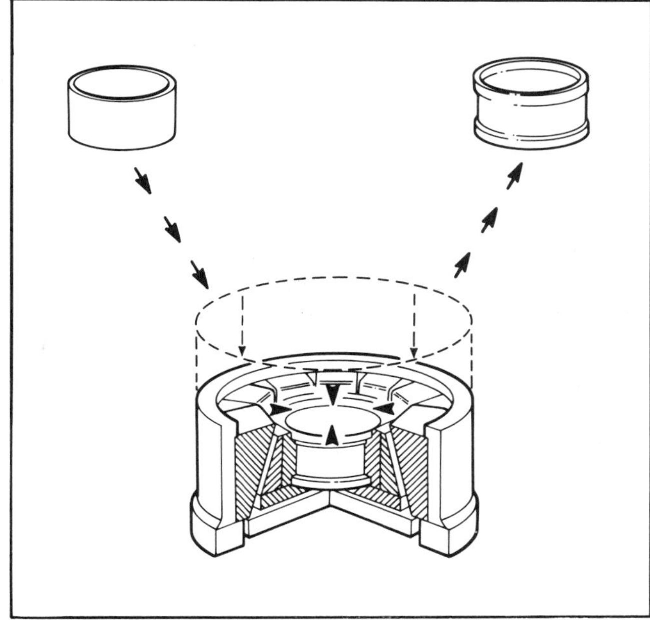

**Fig. 7-15 Shrinking consists of compressing hollow cylindrical blanks to decrease their diameters.** (*Grotnes Metalforming Systems, Inc.*)

## MATERIALS AND SHAPES

Radial compression by shrinking is applied to a wide variety of materials and workpieces having a wide range of sizes and wall thicknesses. Typical hollow cylindrical blanks include lengths of tubing, pipe, or fabricated parts made from flat stock that is cut to length, coiled, welded, and trimmed.

Circumferences of workpieces can be reduced either in localized areas or along their entire lengths. The process is well suited to forming a variety of tapers, spherical sections, inward beads, offsets, and contours. Forming of localized bosses or depressions requires inner restraint tooling. Localized details can be formed in unsymmetrical locations around the peripheries of the workpieces.

Diameter tolerances of 0.001-0.005" (0.03-0.13 mm) can generally be maintained, and shrinking is generally preferred over other methods of forming when the area of reduced diameter is relatively small and accuracy of the finished part is critical. In many cases, the need for subsequent forming or machining operations is eliminated and the amount of material, labor, and production time is reduced, thus cutting costs. Workpiece strength is increased by cold working of the material. There is no inherent limitation to the minimum diameter, the length-to-diameter ratio, or the maximum wall thickness that may be formed by shrinking.

## MACHINES USED

Shrinking machines are available in a variety of sizes and force capacities, with horizontal, vertical, angular, inverted, trunnion-mounted, and double-end configurations. Production rates generally vary from about 10-1000 parts per hour. Smaller machines usually have a single hydraulic cylinder to produce axial motion of the pressure ring or table. The hydraulic shrinker shown in Fig. 7-16 forms and sizes lock rings that are used on truck wheel rims.

Large machines are available with a group of hydraulic cylinders spaced in a circular arrangement and an open center at both ends. This permits workpieces to pass through the machine, simplifies part handling, and allows incremental shrinking of parts of any length.

Tooling for shrinking is essentially the same as for expanding, discussed previously in this chapter. An inner mandrel is sometimes used to shrink parts to produce precise inner diameters. The mandrel acts as a positive stop and can compensate for variations in wall thickness of the workpieces. Mandrels can also be used to coin surfaces or form sharp profiles on inner diameters. It is also possible to re-form the shape of a tube or ring-type part from a circle to a polygon of any number of sides, or from a square or hexagon into a circle.

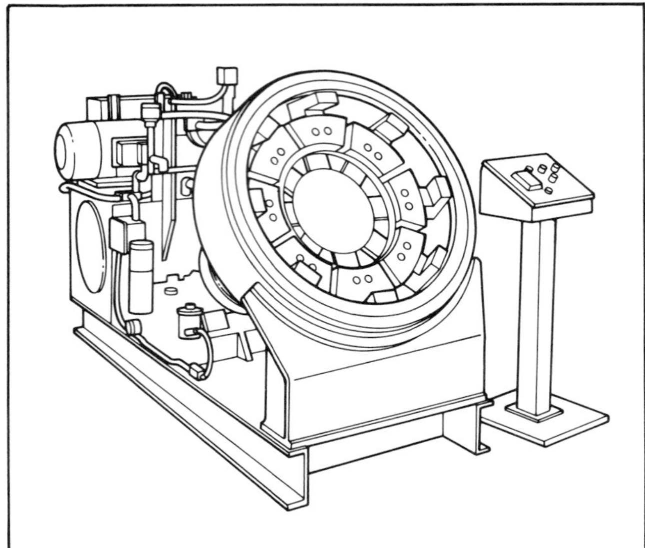

**Fig. 7-16 Hydraulic shrinking machine for forming and sizing lock rings used on truck wheel rims.** (*Grotnes Metalforming Systems, Inc.*)

## SHRINKING APPLICATIONS

Shrinking machines are widely applied in the automotive industry. One large machine, open at both ends, forms and sizes axle housings having wall thicknesses to ⅝″ (16 mm). It is part of an automated system for producing several sizes of truck and trailer axle housings. The feed system, an integral part of the machine, receives pieces from the preceding operation, positions them for two shrinking cycles on one end, repositions them for two cycles on the opposite end, and then moves them to the next operation. Shrinking provides higher production rates, closer tolerances, longer tool life, and lower costs than the hot swaging operation it replaces.

Other automotive applications include shrinking wheel rims, coining brake shoes, and forming steering linkage. Applications in the aircraft industry include forming and sizing jet engine rings. One 265 ton (2357 kN) shrinker accepts different dies to accommodate ring outside diameters ranging from 10-52″ (254-1321 mm) with wall thicknesses to 3″ (76 mm).

Shrinking is used extensively for assembly operations and is particularly effective for assembling dissimilar materials. One application consists of shrinking metal rings around rubber sleeves for use in shock absorbers. Other assembly operations include attaching connection fittings to rubber or plastic hose, shrinking the outer races of self-aligning bearings around the inner races, and locking copper rotating bands to artillery shells.

## COMBINED EXPANDING AND SHRINKING

For some applications, the principles of both expanding and shrinking are combined in a single machine. The center of such machines is an expander, while the outside elements include the pressure ring and compression tools. The machines are used for expanding applications requiring the formation of localized embossments, beads, offsets, or other contoured transitional areas along the surface of the workpiece.

The outer ring and tool assembly on combination expanding/shrinking machines is used as a locking or locating ring and has the required shapes into which the metal is expanded. Machine controls provide the capability of combining motions so that the workpiece can be initially expanded and then shrunk. The cycle sequence can be reversed to provide shrinking first and then expanding.

## LOCALIZED EXPANDING AND SHRINKING

Machines are available for localized shrinking and stretching. They are used to remove wrinkles and to fit sections normally formed in presses or drop hammers; to form rolled, extruded, and formed angles and tees; and to produce double curvatures from flat sheets.

The machines are available in foot-operated or pneumatically powered models. They consist of a C-frame head for bench or pedestal mounting. Ram actuation in a vertical plane is accomplished by foot or air power through a cam mechanism or toggle linkage in the head. No adjustments are necessary for variations in workpiece material.

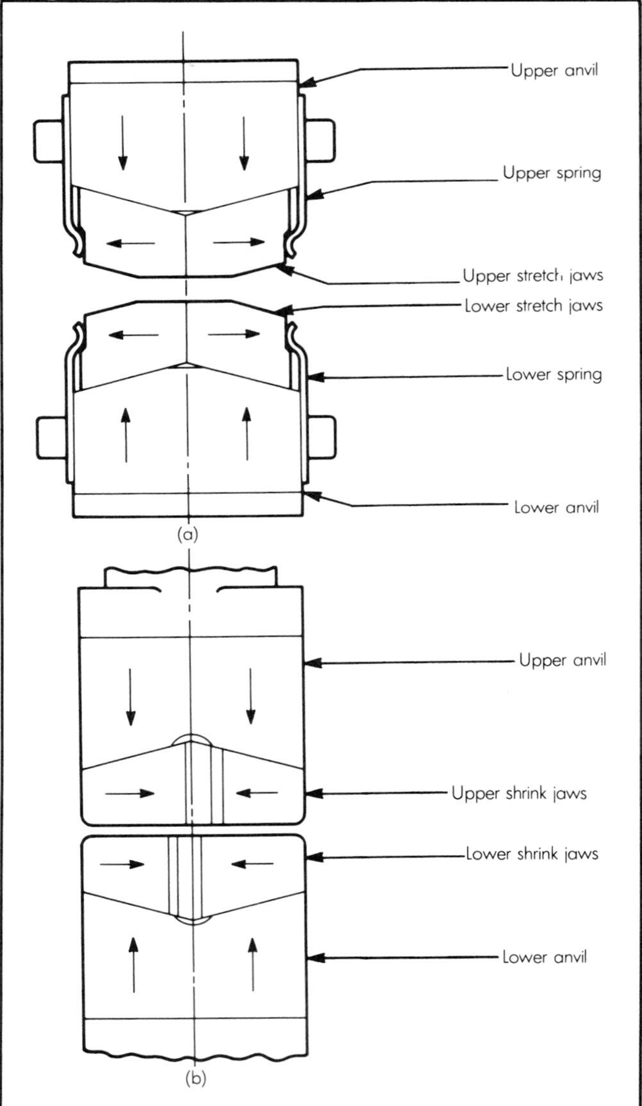


**Fig. 7-17 Interchangeable jaws and anvils permit (a) localized stretching or (b) localized shrinking. Arrows denote direction of forces.** (*The H. P. Townsend Manufacturing Co.*)

Jaws and anvils, made from wedge-shaped pieces of tool steel, are interchangeable for stretching (see Fig. 7-17, view *a*) or shrinking (view *b*). The jaws slide on the inclined surfaces of the anvils—moving toward each other for shrinking and away from each other for stretching. Parallel surfaces of the jaws grip the workpiece at two points. Action of the jaws then shrinks or stretches the material between these two points as the workpiece is fed between the jaws.

Jaw design varies with the type and thickness of material and the shape of the workpiece. Flat, stippled jaws are recommended for flat workpieces and curved sheets having large radii. Extended or offset jaws, consisting of one pair of flat-surface upper jaws and one pair of convex-surface lower jaws, are recommended for shrinking workpieces with radii. This design is required for channel sections on which the lower flange of the channel would interfere with the lower anvil or machine frame when the upper flange of the channel is inserted between the jaws.

# STRETCH FORMING

Stretching of metal occurs as a part of several types of forming operations performed on conventional presses. These operations include drawing, especially of cups having bottoms that are not flat; bulging and beading; and squeezing operations such as sizing, flattening, coining, and embossing (see Chapter 4, "Sheet Metal Blanking and Forming"). Stretching is also done in some spinning and specialized forming processes (refer to Chapters 9 and 19 in this volume).

The discussion of stretch forming and related processes (stretch-draw, stretch-wrap, compression, and radial-draw forming) in this chapter is confined to operations performed on machines specifically designed for this purpose.

Stretch forming is a method that combines controlled stretching and bending of sheet metal blanks, roll-formed sections, and extrusions around form blocks (dies) to produce accurately contoured parts without wrinkles. Usually, two opposite ends of the workpiece are gripped in jaws and pulled or wrapped around the die (form block). This is accomplished in several ways, one of which is illustrated schematically in Fig. 7-18. Various machines for different methods of stretch forming are discussed subsequently in this section.

During stretch forming, the metal is stressed in tension to slightly above its yield point to permit plastic deformation and thinning, refer to Chapter 1, "Sheet Metal Formability"). Upon release of the tension, the metal is permanently deformed; and when removed from the machine, the workpiece retains the desired contoured shape. The forces exerted during both stretching and bending must be constantly and carefully controlled and vary with the workpiece size, shape, and material.

Sufficient bending is required to produce the specified shape, but excessive bending causes unwanted wrinkling of the inner surface of the workpiece (refer to Chapter 10, "Bending and Straightening"). The application of a controlled amount of stretching, prior to or during the bending operation, prevents wrinkling and reduces the effects of springback (elastic recovery). Stretching realigns the microstructure of the metal, resulting in grain refinement and relief of residual stresses.

## ADVANTAGES OF STRETCH FORMING

Important advantages of sheet metal parts made by stretch forming, compared to those from press forming operations, include the production of higher quality, stronger workpieces, and reduced costs.

### Improved Quality and Strength

In most cases, there is practically no springback or tendency to buckle with stretch formed parts because the stresses imposed on the metal are primarily tensile and the amount of stretch is carefully controlled. As a result, accurate parts that hold their shape are produced.

Stretch formed parts have a uniform increase in tensile strength up to 10% and an increase in hardness of about 2%. Increase in strength is approximately equal to the percentage of stretch multiplied by the difference between the yield and ultimate tensile strengths of the material being formed. The workpieces are generally free of residual stresses, and stress relieving is seldom required. Warpage or distortion is seldom experienced as the result of subsequent machining or welding.

### Reduced Costs

Substantial savings result from reduced material requirements. Blanks for stretch forming are about 15% smaller than those needed for drawing on presses. The material for blank restraint is required on only two opposed edges, while for press drawing, the blank must be large enough for restraint around the entire periphery. Scrap losses for subsequent trimming operations are reduced as much as 50%.

Pressure requirements for stretch forming are from 30-70% less than that for press forming because of the increased formability of the stretched material. This reduces capital equipment costs and floor space requirements. Stretch forming machines are less expensive than presses of comparable capacity.

Tooling costs are also lower since usually only one die is required. (The exception is in stretch-draw forming between mating punch and die.) The dies for stretch forming are usually smaller and can be made of lighter, less costly materials because of lower pressure requirements, which also lengthens die life. Stretch forming dies do not generally require modification for

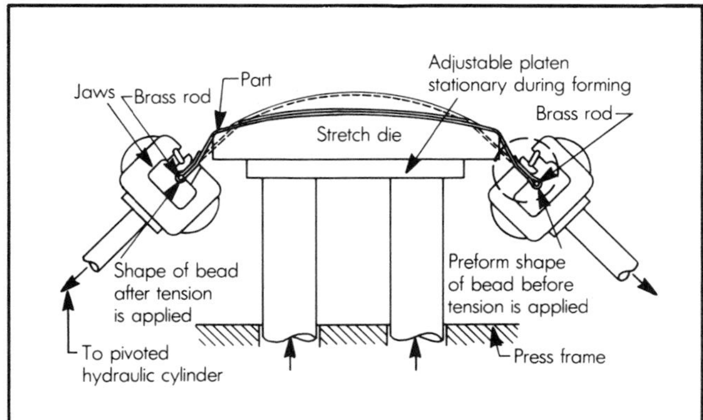


**Fig. 7-18 One method of stretch forming, with part gripped in movable jaws. (*The Cyril Bath Co.*)**

# STRETCH FORMING

springback allowance; thus, they reduce development, machining, and tryout times. The same dies can often be used to stretch form various materials by adjusting the tension exerted. Labor costs are sometimes lower because of fast, easy setup, loading, and unloading.

## PROCESS LIMITATIONS

Unless stretch forming equipment is automated, the cycle time is usually much longer than is needed for presses. Sharply defined contours cannot generally be produced readily by stretch forming. Preforming or a secondary operation may be required to form parts having such features. An exception to this limitation is stretch forming done in a press. This process, called stretch-draw forming, is discussed subsequently in this section. Parts having contours that would require deep forming, as in deep drawing operations, are not suitable for stretch forming.

A possible problem with stretch forming is that sheet metal being stretch formed does not show a uniformity of stretch because of friction and differences in contour length. Friction between the metal being formed and the die prevents it from stretching as much as the free metal—the metal between the edges of the gripping jaws and the ends of the die. As a result, it is in the area of the free metal that the workpiece most commonly fractures during stretch forming. This problem can be minimized by reducing the friction between the metal and the die by using proper die materials, sheets between the metal and the die, and/or lubricant, discussed later in this section. When required, the die can be designed to minimize or eliminate differences in contour length, but this requires a larger starting blank and a die that is larger and more expensive.

In stretch forming, the lengths of the contoured edges of the workpiece are usually only slightly greater than the initial length of the blank, while the length of the centerline contour may be much greater. When the difference in these contoured lengths is excessive, the dies must be developed (with variations in the distances from the die center to its sides) to reduce the difference.

The condition of the edges of the blanks to be stretch formed can limit the amount of elongation possible. Blanks made from some materials having rough sheared edges cannot be stretched as much as blanks with smooth edges because of the notch sensitivity of the materials.

## STRETCH FORMED MATERIALS

Practically any metal can be stretch formed providing a suitable range exists between the yield point and ultimate strength of the metal. The metals most commonly stretch formed are aluminum alloys, stainless steels, low-carbon steels, and commercially pure titanium. Metals that are less commonly formed in this way include titanium, alloys, heat-resistant alloys, and magnesium alloys. Alloys difficult to form in press operations can often be contoured easily because of the increased formability of the stretched metal.

Total allowable deformation in stretch forming, before excessive thinning and/or failure due to tearing, depends upon strain distribution, the rate of work hardening, and the amount of strain the metal can endure. Strain distribution, which is influenced by the properties of the workpiece material, die design, lubricant used, and operating parameters, should be as uniform as possible during forming. The maximum stress applied must be kept below the ultimate strength of the metal.

For severe stretch forming, the best materials are those with high ductility and elongation. Materials with ultimate strengths close to their yield strengths (such as most alloy steels, the harder aluminum alloys, and titanium alloys) require special care in maintaining a constant tension during forming.

When some metals, such as low-carbon steels and most aluminum alloys, are subjected to tensile stresses above their yield points, faint lines inclined about 45° to the direction of tension sometimes appear. If these lines (called Lüders' lines, stretch-strain marks, or slip planes) are detrimental from an appearance standpoint, they can be minimized by temper rolling the material prior to stretch forming.

With low-carbon steels, Lüders' lines generally appear at low strains. With higher strains (5-10% stretch), thinning is more even and the lines tend to blend into the material. Slower strain rates also seem to help reduce line formation. Too long a delay between temper rolling and stretching, however, may cause the lines to appear anyway because of strain aging. With aluminum alloys, the stretch-strain marks usually develop with increasingly higher strains.

### Aluminum Alloys

Both heat-treatable and nonheat-treatable aluminum alloys are shaped by stretch forming. In the case of nonheat-treatable alloys, stretch forming is best accomplished with the material in the annealed temper, because most strain-hardened tempers have limited ductility and stretchability. For heat-treatable alloys, stretch forming is usually done immediately after solution heat treatment. Elongation limits vary from about 8-15%, depending upon the aluminum alloy and its temper. Special handling during heat treatment and rolling immediately after heat treatment are sometimes done to minimize the formation of curls when aluminum alloys having a thickness of 0.032" (0.81 mm) or less are being stretch formed. Stretch forming of 7075 aluminum alloy in the full-hard (T6) condition is not recommended because of the material's low elongation values.

Thin sheets of aluminum, 0.020" (0.51 mm) thick or less, have a tendency to rupture at the gripping jaws. This rupturing can be eliminated or minimized by increasing the amount of metal extending beyond the jaws or by placing emery cloth beween the metal and the jaws. Stretch forming two parts at the same time, if the resulting difference in contour thickness is not objectionable, also reduces the tendency to rupture. Another method sometimes used to decrease rupturing is to cool the material to a temperature of -30° F (-34° C) or less before immediately stretching.

### Stainless Steels

The high ductility of stainless steels permits them to be stretch formed easily. All grades have maximum ductility when fully annealed. Differences in other properties of these materials, however, generally make it necessary to use more force in forming; consequently, the tooling usually wears faster. More springback is also often encountered and work hardening may necessitate annealing between operations, especially with severe forming, to attain final shape and prevent stress cracking.

**Austenitic stainless steels.** In the annealed condition, austenitic stainless steels are among the most readily formed materials, with elongations of 30-40% possible. They do, however, strain harden rapidly during cold working, and formability varies with the alloy type. Stretch forming can be done with the material in the ¼ or ½-hard state; ¾-hard materials are rarely formed, and full-hard materials are almost impossible to grip without slippage. When forming ¼ or ½-hard material, a springback allowance may be required in the die.

**Ferritic stainless steels.** These materials have less stretchability than the austenitic grades; only Type 430 is capable of being elongated more than 20%. Strain hardening, however, is at a slower rate.

**Martensitic stainless steels.** These materials are less ductile than ferritic types and only the lower carbon grades, such as Types 403, 410, and to a lesser extent 414, are generally recommended for stretch forming.

**Precipitation-hardening stainless steels.** These materials are available with austenitic and martensitic structures for stretch forming.

### Steels

Hot or cold-rolled, low-carbon steels (AISI 1015 to 1020) can be stretch formed readily, but they have a tendency to show Lüder's lines. Draw-quality steel sheet is generally preferred over commercial-quality steel sheet for stretch forming because of its higher ductility. Flex-rolling of commercial-quality sheets prior to forming improves stretchability of the material.

Clad or coated steels can be stretch formed, but the ductility of the cladding or coating should be as high as that of the steels. Otherwise, the clad or coated material may crack and flake, especially during severe forming. Some grades of galvanized steel are being severely formed without flaking.

### Titanium and Titanium Alloys

Titanium is stretch formed, but the absence of strain hardening can cause failure due to premature necking. Commercially pure titanium is more readily formed than titanium alloys. Stretch forming is done both cold and hot, with hot forming done at temperatures of 400-1200° F (200-650° C), depending upon the material. If forming is done cold with a die containing lead, any lead pickup should be removed from the formed part because it may affect the properties of the material. Maximum elongation usually varies from 4-10%. If the requirement is for more than 15%, annealing is generally required between successive operations. It is important that strain rates be kept low when titanium is being formed.

### Magnesium Alloys

Magnesium alloy blanks to be stretch formed are generally heated to about 300-500° F (150-260° C), depending upon the specific alloy. Because the thin, warm sheets would rapidly lose heat to cold dies, the dies are also heated. Jaws for gripping the blanks, however, are not heated, because cold magnesium has higher strength and this helps prevent workpiece breakage at the jaws.

## APPLICATIONS OF STRETCH FORMING

Stretch forming is being used extensively by the aircraft and aerospace industries. Large machines have been built for forming wing members, tail structures, fuselage segments, and engine components. The process permits tolerances to be held as close as ±0.005" (0.13 mm) for the leading edges of wings used on large jet aircraft. Other airplane parts stretch formed from 2024, 2219, and 7075 aluminum alloys include ribs, pylons, fairings, wing attachment tees, and skins.

Helicopter blades with lengths to 312" (7925 mm) have their leading edges stretch formed from Type 301 stainless steel to a tolerance of ±0.005". External fuel tanks for the space shuttles have several of their outer ogive skins and dome gores stretch formed from sheets of 2219 aluminum alloy. These compound-contoured skins range in size from 87 x 144" (2210 x 3658 mm) to 97 x 204" (2464 x 5182 mm), with thicknesses to ½" (12.7 mm). T-shaped chords, made from 311" (7899 mm) long, 2219 aluminum alloy extrusions, are stretched 3% and formed to a radius of 165.5" (4204 mm) for supporting the skins on the external fuel tanks of the space shuttles.

Stretch forming is not limited to aircraft and aerospace manufacturing. Other applications include the production of truck bumpers, structural frames for buses and recreational vehicles, monorail guide beams, window frames for mobile homes, structural building members, telecommunication antennas, and many appliance components. The outer skins covering the corner segments of school bus frames are stretch formed from 1010 steel because other methods could not produce the complex contours required. One such skin is 4 x 8 ft (1219 x 2438 mm) in size and 0.080" (2.03 mm) thick.

## STRETCH FORMING MACHINES

Many different types and sizes of machines are built to perform stretch forming and related processes. Machine selection depends upon force requirements, workpiece size, and the final shape desired. The types of machines are often categorized by the kind of forming they do: stretching (including drape forming and combined stretching and bending); stretch-drawing; stretch-wrapping; compression; and radial-drawing.

Sheet stock, because of its thin cross section, experiences little elongation through moderate bending and forming and must rely on stretching for permanent deformation. In the type of stretch forming referred to as drape forming, the bending action consists simply of draping or folding the blank over the die for subsequent stretching.

### Drape Forming

Drape forming is the most extensively used method of stretch forming because there are more machines available that are limited to forming in this manner. The single-purpose machines cost less than other forming equipment, especially for handling large sheets; and they are simple to operate.

A drape forming machine consists basically of an opposing set of stationary gripper jaws attached to a base structure and a table, usually powered hydraulically, to force the form block (die) upward into the workpiece (see Fig. 7-19). Control of the machine is limited to actuating and limiting the stroke of the die

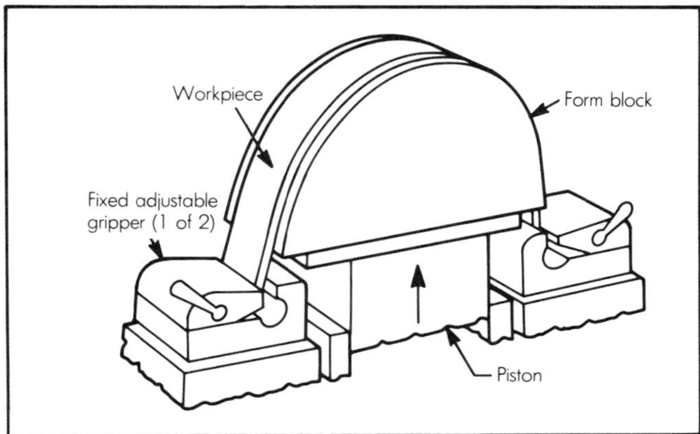


**Fig. 7-19 Drape forming machine in which blank is gripped by opposed jaws and the form block is forced into the workpiece.**[3] (*The Cyril Bath Co.*)

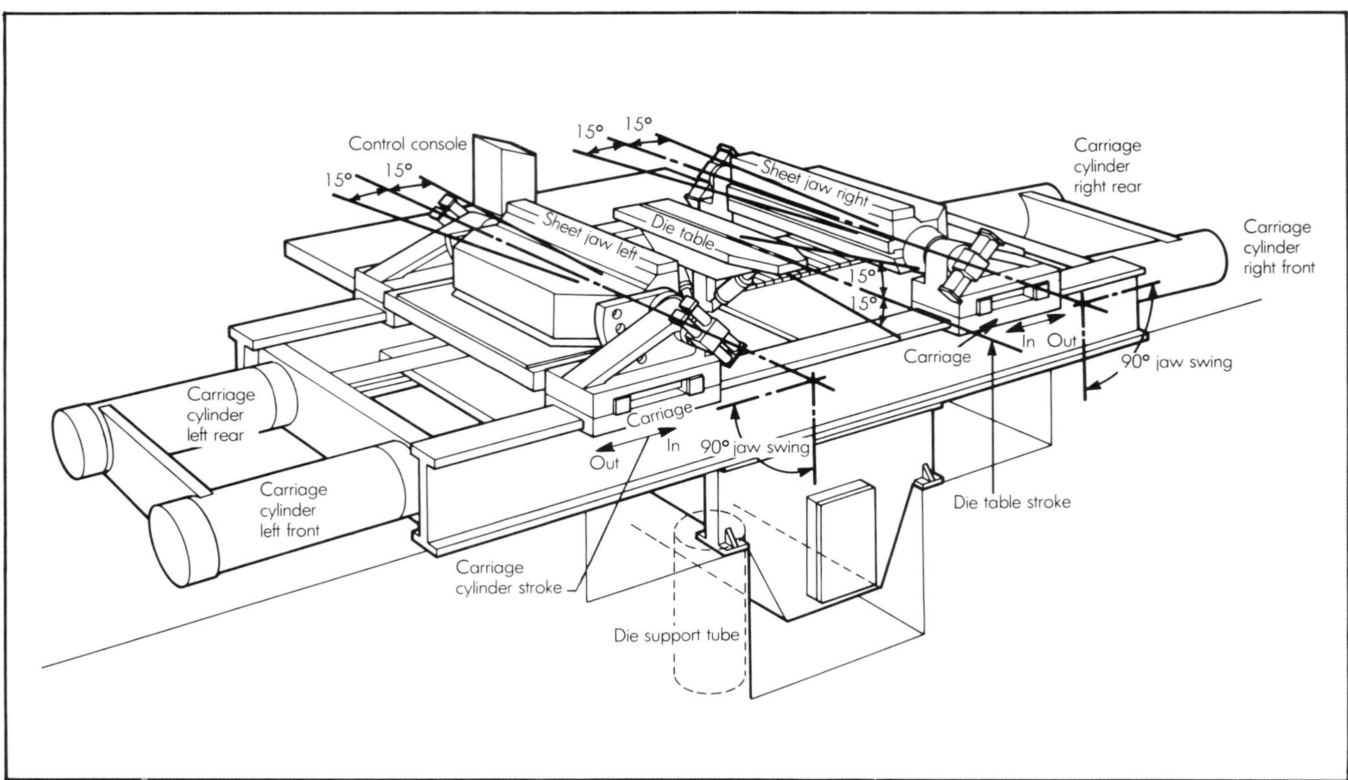


**Fig. 7-20 Transverse stretch forming machine having movable and tiltable die table and swiveling, movable jaws.** (*L & F Industries*)

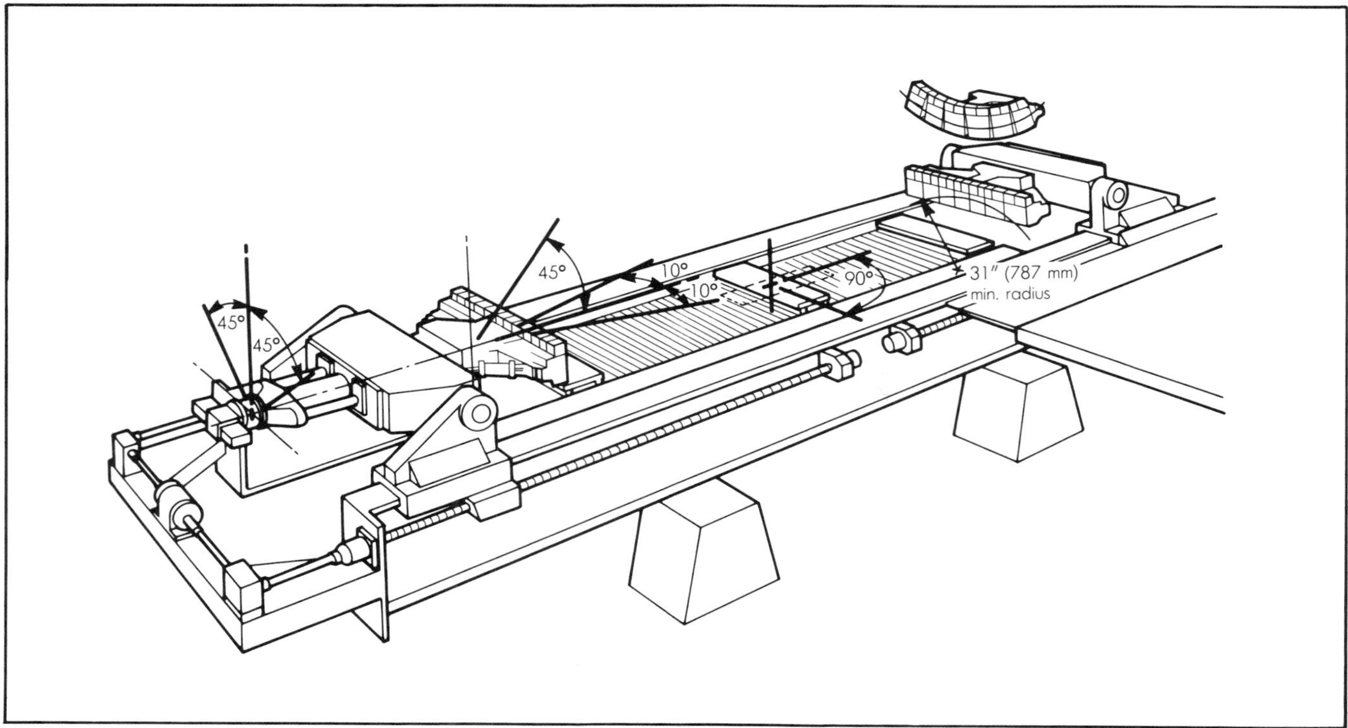


**Fig. 7-21 Longitudinal stretch forming machine having leadscrew-actuated jaws that can be curved and swiveled both horizontally and vertically.** (*L & F Industries*)

table. Since there are no tension cylinders, these machines are rated in respect to their stretching capacity based upon the amount of thrust (push) their tables can exert. Each jaw assembly need only be capable of withstanding half the thrust rating of the machine.

## Combined Stretching and Bending

Stretch forming machines that combine stretching and bending have increased capacity and versatility compared to drape forming machines. In such machins, bending the workpiece around the die elongates the material fibers, but wrinkling is prevented and springback minimized by stretching prior to or during the bending.

These machines are available in two basic types:

1. With moving jaws only, to stretch the blanks around a stationary form block.
2. With a combination of moving jaws and a moving die (form block) table.

The machines are also available as transverse or longitudinal models, as well as combination transverse and longitudinal models. All the machines can be built with any jaw width, distance between jaws, and force required. Selection of a specific type and model depends primarily upon workpiece specifications.

The jaws of transverse machines, on which workpieces are stretched and bent transversely, must be as long as the workpiece, requiring substantial material for gripping. The die table on such machines must stretch the sheet against a jaw pull determined primarily by the length of the workpiece. With longitudinal machines, thrust requirements for the die table are lower because the smaller dimension of the blank is pulled and the pull-off angle is shallower. Jaw size is also smaller, and material requirements for gripping are reduced.

A transverse stretch forming machine with powered jaws and die table is shown in Fig. 7-20. For stretch forming complex shapes, the movable die table can be tilted to 15 above or below the horizontal. The jaws, which move toward and away from each other on hydraulically operated carriages, can be swiveled 30° in a horizontal plane and 90° in a vertical plane so that the direction of stretching can be aligned with the contour of the die. This machine is rated at 750 tons (6672 kN), a die table stroke of 82″ (2083 mm), a distance between jaws of 1-144″ (25-3658 mm), and a forming speed of 1-18 ipm (25-457 mm/min). Such machines are used primarily for forming large sheets, including leading edges of airplane wings and fuselage skins. By changing or adapting jaws, large, heavy extrusions such as wing spars are formed.

A longitudinal stretch forming machine with a die table that can be swiveled 90°, but that cannot be raised is shown in Fig. 7-21. The hydraulically powered, leadscrew-actuated jaws, 100″ (2540 mm) wide, are made in sections for curvature to various radii, and they can be swiveled both horizontally and vertically. This machine develops a tensile force of 750 tons (6672 kN) at each jaw and can form sheet metal skins to 40 ft (12.2 m) long by 8 ft (2.4 m) wide. Adapter jaws are bolted to the standard jaws for forming long extruded frame members weighing as much as 1000 lb (454 kg).

## Stretch-Draw Forming

The stretch-draw forming process combines the advantages of stretch forming with shallow drawing. It is done on special presses or with prestretch blankholders mounted on the beds of

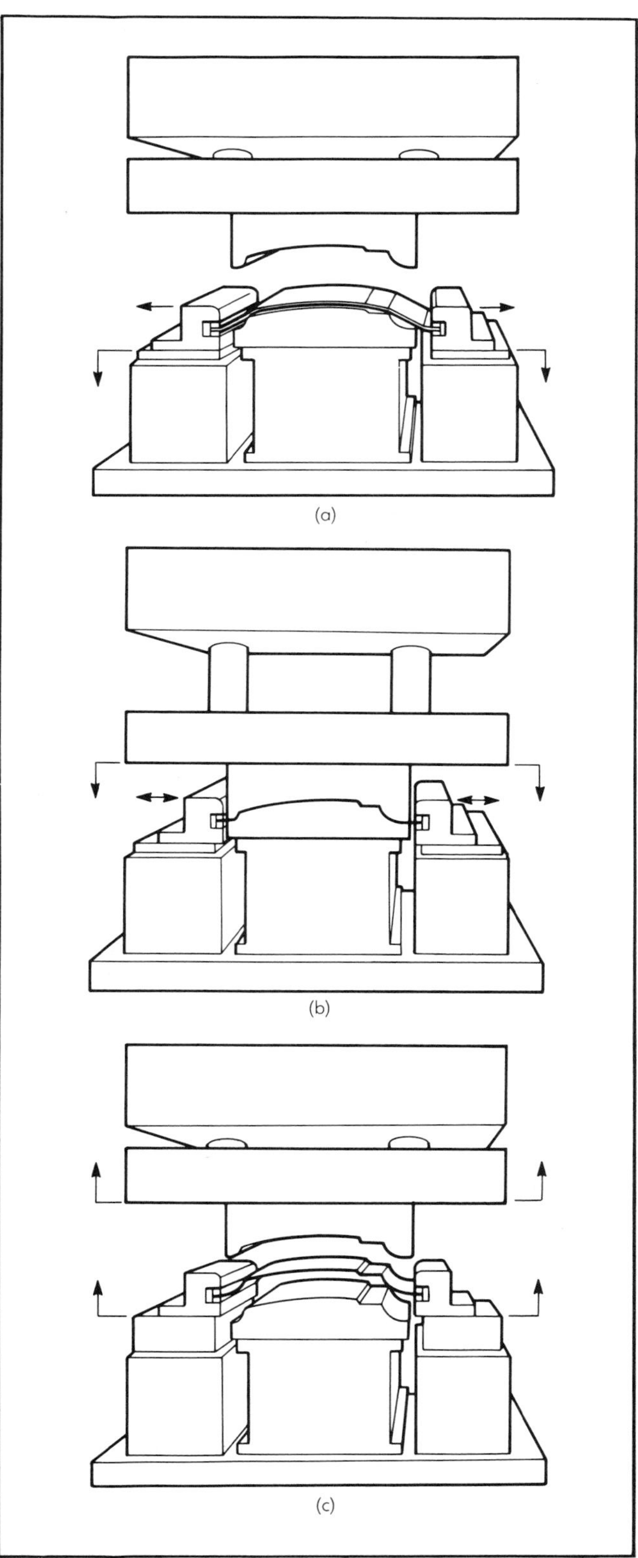


**Fig. 7-22 Stretch-draw forming on a press: (a) blank is prestretched and wrapped over lower die, (b) upper die is lowered to complete forming, and (c) formed panel is raised for unloading. (*The Cyril Bath Co.*)**

standard presses, mechanical or hydraulic. As shown in Fig. 7-22, a blank is prestretched 2-3% and wrapped over a lower die (view *a*), an upper die on the press ram is lowered to complete the required forming (view *b*), and the formed panel is raised for unloading (view *c*).

This economical process is used to contour, with reduced material requirements, automobile body panels and other parts made from sheet metal blanks. Because the metal under tension is more plastic, smaller presses can be used. For example, parts normally drawn on a 1000 ton (8896 kN), double-acting press can be stretch-draw formed on a 300 ton (2669 kN), single-acting press. Since the cycle time is slightly longer than that of conventional press drawing, however, the process is best suited for low to medium volume production requirements.

Stronger, lighter weight parts can be produced in this way. Work hardening of the material during stretch-draw forming usually results in a 10-12% increase in tensile strength, a 2-3% increase in hardness, and a 12-15% increase in yield strength compared with the blank material before forming.

One automotive manufacturer is stretch-draw forming inner hood panels for a truck cab. The material is 0.035" (0.89 mm) thick mild steel. Compared with conventional drawing, tooling costs for stretch drawing are almost 70% lower, material costs are reduced about 15%, and direct labor requirements are about 10% lower.

Another automotive manufacturer is using stretch-draw forming to produce hood outer panels from aluminum and steel, and front fenders from steel. Compared to conventional drawing, smaller blank sizes are used because large binder surfaces for material flow are not required, thus reducing costs. Material cost reductions vary to 31% per part, depending upon the model. The hood panels and fenders produced in this way have improved physical properties and surface finishes, and they are uniformly thinned over their entire surfaces, rather than only in the corners as is the case with conventional drawing.

In this application, a lower holding ring is mounted on a nitrogen-actuated pressure pad in a double-acting press. An upper holding ring closes on the lower ring and forms beads in the blank. Both upper and lower rings lower to a dwell position (see Fig. 7-23), stretching the material over the lower die. The upper die then closes to complete the forming operation. Common tooling is used for both steel and aluminum hood panels.

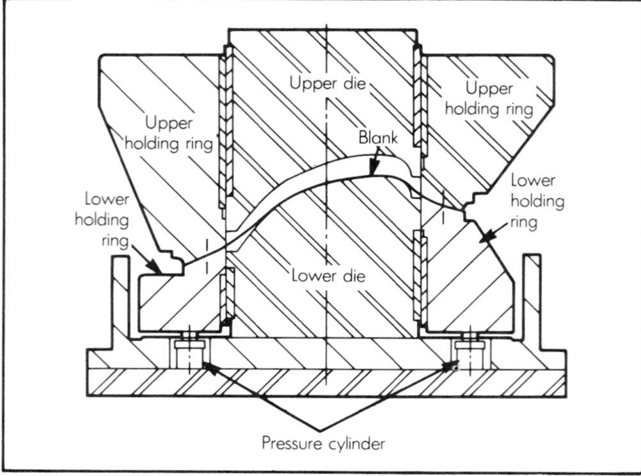


**Fig. 7-23 Tooling for stretch-draw forming fenders from steel blanks.** (*Oldsmobile Div., General Motors Corp.*)

## Stretch-Wrap Forming

The stretch-wrap forming process also combines stretching and bending to form sheet stock, rolled or brake-formed sections, and extrusions. Workpieces are held tangent to the front of a die and initially stretched to or slightly past the yield point of the material by tension devices. With tension maintained, workpieces are wrapped around the die. Upon completion of the wrapping, workpieces are given a final stretch to slightly above the elastic limit of the material, thus permanently setting the contoured shapes. Progressive forming with this method reduces the number of separate forming operations that would otherwise be required.

Bends produced with this method need not have uniform radii. Contours can vary throughout the shape, and reverse bends and offsets are easily produced. Tubular and hollow sections, and shapes with unsupported legs, such as channels, can also be contoured by the use of mandrels or fillers to maintain their shape during the forming operations.

Stretch-wrap forming is done on both swing-arm and rotary-table machines. Hydraulic cylinders are used to apply controlled tension and generally to apply leverage for bending. Machines are equipped with jaws to grip the ends of the workpieces, a support for the die, and adjustments to permit forming a range of part sizes and shapes.

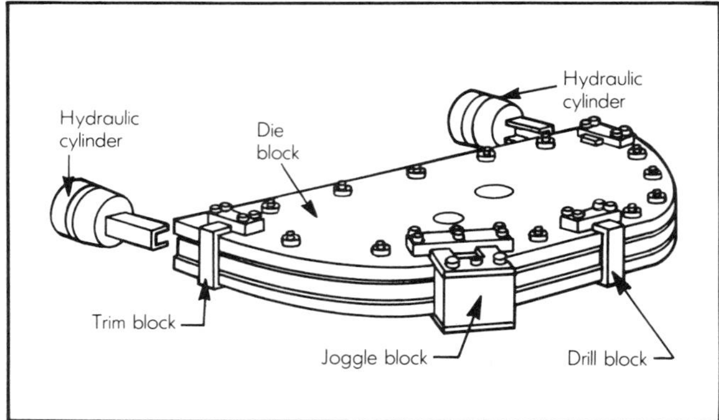


**Fig. 7-24 Swing-arm machine for stretch-wrap forming.** (*The Cyril Bath Co.*)

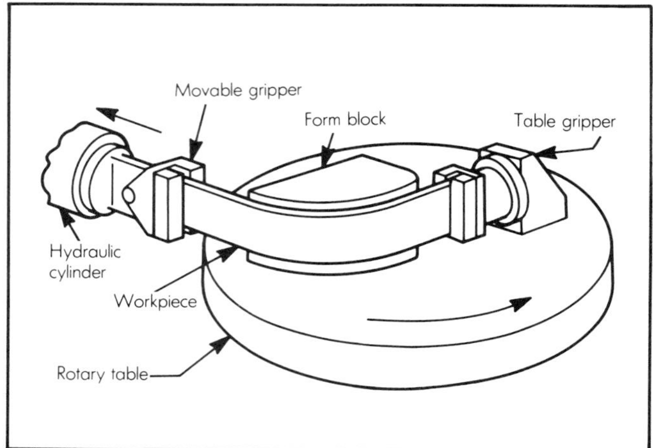


**Fig. 7-25 Rotary-table machine for stretch-wrap forming.**[3] (*The Cyril Bath Co.*)

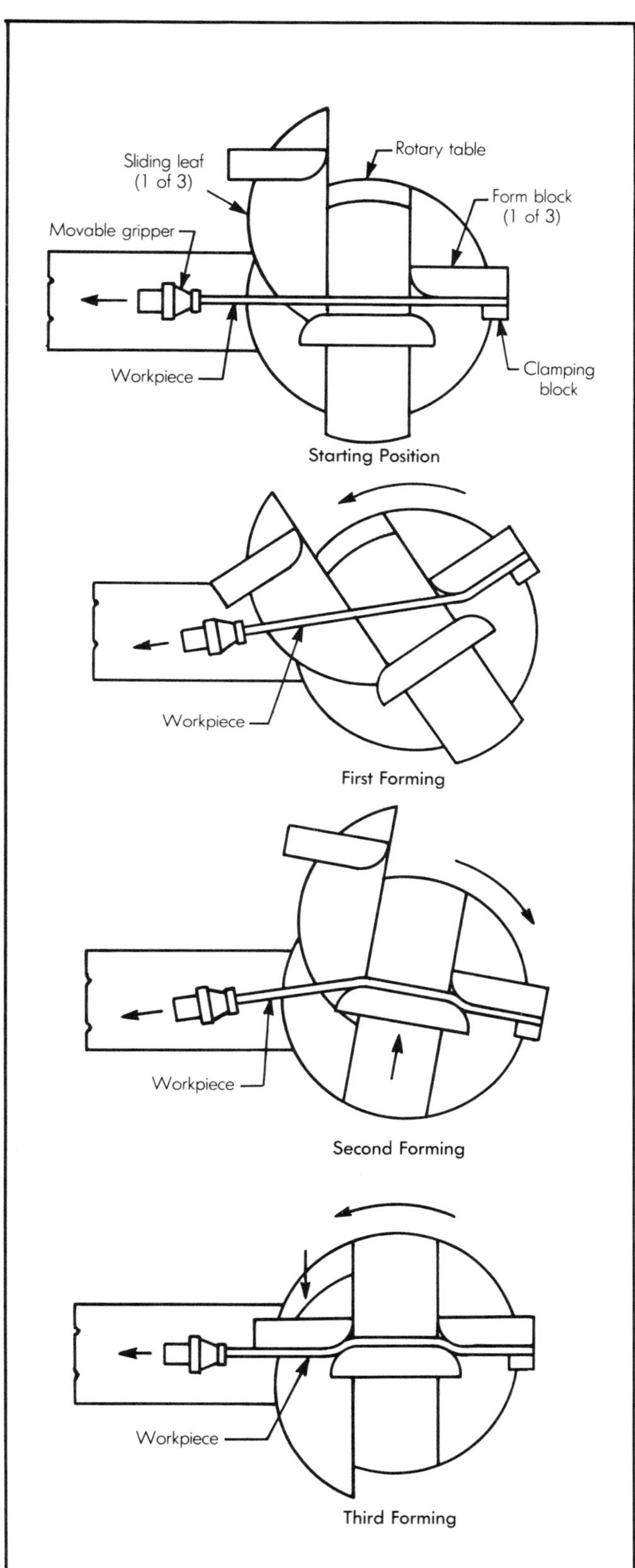


**Fig. 7-26 Stretch-wrap forming machine with three form blocks on rotary table for making reverse bends.**[3] (*The Cyril Bath Co.*)

**Swing-arm machines.** These machines have a fixed base for supporting the die. Attached by pivot pins to either side of the base are two arms upon which two opposing hydraulic tension cylinders are mounted (see Fig. 7-24). Gripping jaws are fixed to the piston rods of the cylinders. A second pair of hydraulic cylinders cause rotation of the arms, carrying them independently when actuated. Machines are also available with a single hydraulic cylinder attached to the arms by links to provide simultaneous arm motion.

**Rotary-table machines.** The most widely used machines of this type consist basically of a single hydraulic tension cylinder and a power-driven, variable-speed rotary table (see Fig. 7-25). On simpler machines, one gripper is mounted in pivots and can be bolted anywhere on the table, while a second gripper is mounted on the rod end of the tension cylinder. With a workpiece gripped in the opposing jaws, the table is rotated to wrap the workpiece around the form block (die). Wrapping (bending) starts near one end of the workpiece, rather than at the middle as on swing-arm machines.

Reverse bends can be made on these machines by using a rotary table consisting of three separately actuated leaves, each leaf carrying a form block (see Fig. 7-26). The leaves are sliding blocks contained in gibs. Table rotation is reversed for the actuation of each leaf and for changing bend direction.

For structural shapes, no springback allowance is needed in the form block. The tool, however, should allow for some shrinkage of the section in the radial and transverse directions.

## Compression Forming

In this process, material to be shaped is compression formed locally with hydraulic pressure against a table-mounted die by either shoes or rollers. Workpieces are traversed past the shoes or rollers by rotating a table (see Fig. 7-27), or the hydraulic cylinder can be traversed past a stationary die table. Pressure is concentrated at the point of tangency between the workpiece and the die. Spirals and other rise-and-fall shapes can be formed by compression forming by causing the shoe or roller to move vertically as the workpiece is being drawn past the shoe or roller by the rotating form block (see Fig. 7-28).

Rise-and-fall bends can also be produced on stretch-wrap forming machines of the rotary-table type. This is accomplished by controlled vertical movement of the gripper jaw that is mounted to the hydraulic tension cylinder.

Contouring by compression forming is advantageous for workpieces requiring sharper radius bends in deep cross sections. This process is also desirable when the size and shape

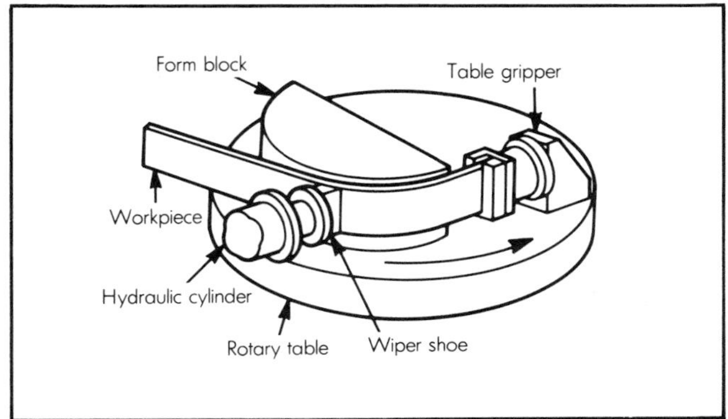


**Fig. 7-27 Compression forming with a wiper shoe mounted on the rod end of a hydraulic cylinder.**[3] (*The Cyril Bath Co.*)

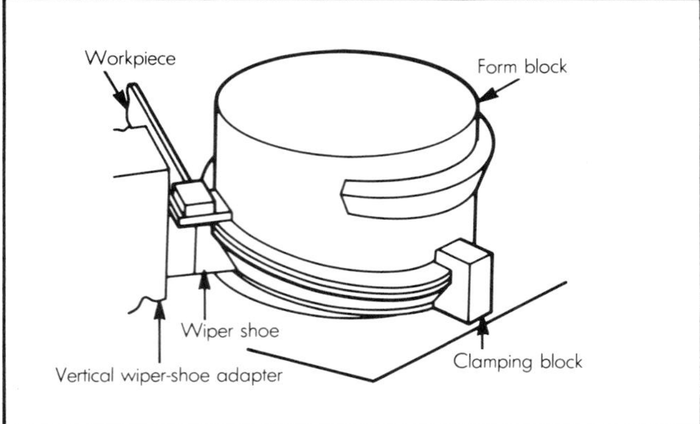


**Fig. 7-28 Compression forming of a spiral.**[3] (*The Cyril Bath Co.*)

of the cross section must be maintained within close tolerances throughout the contour. This is possible because the metal is confined between the die and the shoe or roller as the contour is being formed.

## Radial-Draw Forming

This method combines the advantages of initial stretching provided by stretch-wrap forming and features of the compression forming process to produce difficult shapes. Radial-draw forming is performed on either swing-arm or rotary-table machines (see Fig. 7-29, view *a*), with the addition of a compression forming unit. Workpieces are held in controlled tension while radial forming is done by the wrapping action of the machine arms or a die mounted on the rotary table. Simultaneously, compressive force is applied by a hydraulically operated wiper shoe shaped to mate with the cross-sectional profile of the die.

Offsets can be formed, with the workpiece held in tension after forming, by repositioning the compression unit. If the wiper shoe does not have the required offset contour, a loose block with the proper contour is placed in position by the wiper shoe (see Fig. 7-29, view *b*).

Radial-draw forming can also be used to form the legs of structural shapes to varying angles with respect to their webs at the same time that the overall longitudinal contours of the parts are being formed.

## Machine Controls

Continuous improvements have been made in controls for the operation of stretch forming machines. Control of mechanical cycling (proper sequencing of machine elements) has advanced from the use of hand-operated valves for controlling direction, pressure, and flow rate of the hydraulic fluid, to automatic operation with electronic controls and programmable controllers.

Even more important advances have been made in controlling the forming process, particularly the amount of bending and stretching. These critical factors must vary with the workpiece size, geometry, and material. Overstretching can reduce fatigue life, destroy the usefulness of the workpiece, and even break it; understretching also makes the part unusable.

With one control system, tension is applied to the workpieces by hydraulic cylinders through load cells equipped with strain gages. Rotary potentiometers on the tension cylinder carriages produce voltage differentials proportional to the carriage

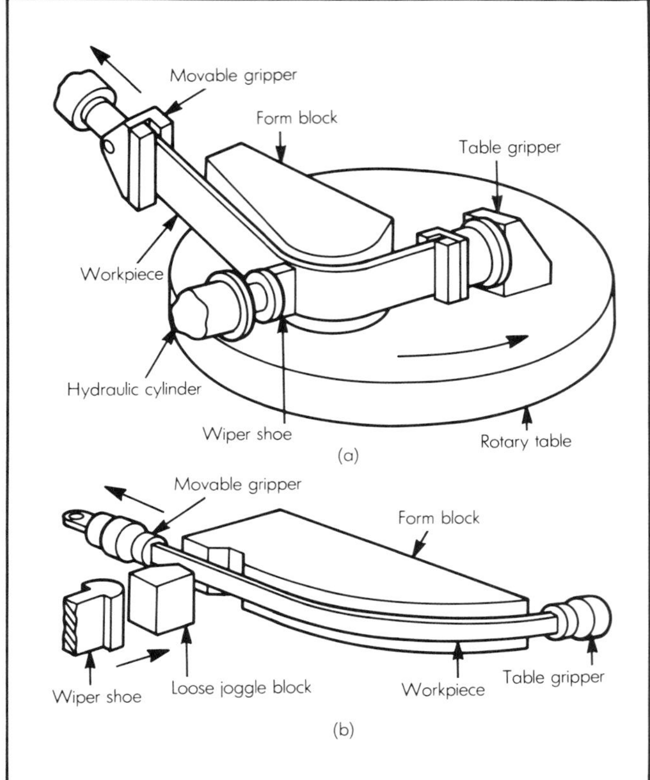


**Fig. 7-29 Radial-draw forming: (a) on a rotary-table machine and (b) for producing offsets with a loose joggle block.**[3] (*The Cyril Bath Co.*)

positions. Stress readings from the strain gages and voltage readings from the potentiometers are fed to an electronic yield-detector control.

When the yield point of the workpiece material is reached, elongation increases at a faster rate than the applied load. This creates an unbalance in the electronic circuitry and produces a signal that is fed to a servomotor. This motor drives a hydraulic relief valve and maintains the stretch tension at a fixed level relative to the yield point during the remainder of the forming cycle. A recording chart can be used to provide a permanent record of the stress imposed, thus ensuring that the workpiece was not overstressed during forming.

Modern CNC systems are also being used to provide automatic elongation control. Once a correct forming cycle has been established, it is recorded and can be transferred from the memory of the control to a magnetic tape cassette. The cassettes can be inserted into the control console of the machine to produce identical parts at any future time.

Another innovation involves yield point detection by laser measurement, used in conjunction with CNC. This permits stretch forming with a tension that exceeds the yield point of the material, but does not exceed the ultimate strength of the material.

While the likelihood of workpiece breakage during stretch forming is minimized by the use of yield point detection and tension control, defects in the material can result in a broken part. Some means should be provided, especially on larger machines, to absorb the energy released and thereby prevent machine damage in the event of such breakage. One method of accomplishing this is to mount gas/oil accumulators directly on the tension cylinders of the machine. If a workpiece breaks, the energy released drives the tension piston to displace oil from the tension cylinder, which drives the accumulator piston and compresses the gas, thus absorbing the recoil energy.

## TOOLING FOR STRETCH FORMING

Tooling requirements for stretch forming include the gripping jaws and the dies (form blocks), which vary depending upon whether sheets, plates, or sections are to be formed. Accessories often needed include blocks to form depressions (joggles) in the workpiece at desired locations, drill jigs for uniform hole positions with relation to the contour, scribe blocks to produce trim lines on the workpieces, and snakes (flexible filler pieces) to prevent the collapse or deformation of light extrusions during forming.

### Jaws

Three basic types of jaws are used to grip workpieces for stretch forming. They are straight, articulating, and extrusion jaws. Jaw selection depends upon the initial and final shapes of the workpieces, as well as the type of machine to be used for stretch forming. Articulating-type jaws (see Fig. 7-30), available in various widths, can be curved to any required radius. For stretch forming roll-formed and extruded blanks, the jaws have gripping surfaces to match the cross-sectional contour of the workpieces.

Clamping surfaces of the jaws vary with the material to be stretch formed. For aluminum alloys, the surfaces are generally serrated and partially smoothed and have a slightly tapered opening to help prevent the metal from rupturing. As previously mentioned in this section, emery cloth is sometimes placed between the metal and the jaw surfaces to minimize rupturing when thin sheets of aluminum are being stretch formed.

For stretch forming steels, including stainless steels softer than 1/4 hard, 10 to 32-pitch knurled surfaces are superior to serrated surfaces. Knurled surfaces provide a gripping force of about one-fourth the clamping pressure. Except for partially shallow sections, the clamping pressure applied with knurled-surface jaws is not always adequate for clamping stainless steel 1/4-hard or harder.

Higher clamping pressures are obtained when double-action presses—presses having outer rams which can exert high pressures to the gripping areas—are used. If the force developed by the outer ram approaches the tensile strength of the material being clamped, smooth clamping surfaces must be used. Smooth surfaces are ideal because they do not present any stress-raising conditions, which occur when serrated or knurled edges are embedded in the material. If the clamping pressure with this arrangement is not sufficient, beads may have to be formed in the gripping surfaces.

### Dies

Because stretch-formed parts experience little or no springback after forming, the dies (form blocks) are generally made to the same contour as that required on the workpiece. When springback is encountered, the dies are reworked on material-and-error basis.

Dies are made from a wide variety of materials (refer to Chapter 2, "Die and Mold Materials"). Material selection depends primarily upon the forces of the stretch-forming operation, the size and shape of the dies, the thickness and properties of the material to be formed, and the number of

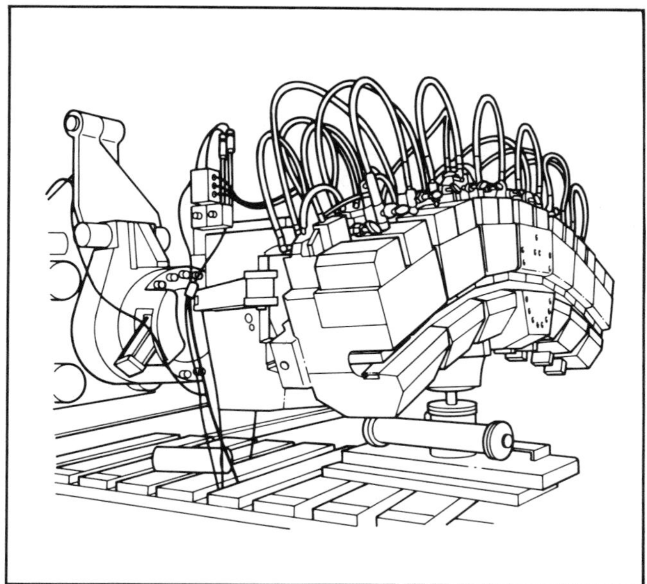

**Fig. 7-30 Articulating-type jaws can be curved to any required radius.** (*Aircraft Hydro-Forming, Inc.*)

workpieces to be produced. Die materials must retain their contour under forming pressure, resist abrasion, and have and retain smooth finishes. It is also important that large dies be lightweight.

Materials commonly used to stretch form sheet metal blanks include Kirksite (zinc alloy), plastic, and hardwoods. Kirksite is good for dies requiring compound contours because it offers minimum friction with the workpiece material. After casting, a smooth finish can be easily produced on Kirksite dies by hand grinding; and after use, the material can be reclaimed by melting. A disadvantage of this material is that it is too heavy for large dies.

Hardwoods, such as beech and maple, are sometimes used for low production requirements of parts having less severe contours and needing only light forming loads. The dies can be faced with metal or plastic, or they can have steel inserts for more severe forming requirements. These materials, however, are too heavy for large dies.

Plastic dies are employed extensively, primarily because they are lightweight. One popular design consists of epoxy/fiberglass laminations. The fiberglass die surface is supported by synthetic resins, volcanic rock, concrete, and structural tubing for ample strength, enabling even large dies to remain lightweight. Soft surfaces of the dies can be sanded or polished to final contour and dimensions, and material is easily added or removed. For lightweight, high-strength, and shock-resistant dies, epoxy/fiberglass laminations are beonded to steel fabrications.

For stretch forming extrusions, die materials most commonly used include steel, aluminum, Masonite, and wood. Steel dies are the most expensive, but their long life makes them economical for permanent tooling. When friction between the die and workpiece is a problem, the steel dies can be plated. Steels such as SAE 1020 are often used for the dies. Plastic-faced hardwood dies also have long life provided they are fastened to steel plates and have proper backing.

Aluminum plate, cast or wrought, is easy to machine, has a fairly long life (but shorter than steel), and can be anodized to improve wear and reduce friction. Masonite and wood dies tend to wear rapidly, varying with the workpiece being stretch formed, and are generally restricted to low-production applications.

Dies used for stretch forming magnesium alloys, titanium and titanium alloys, and some other materials are often heated. This is accomplished with rod or strip heaters in the dies or through the use of heat lamps around the dies. Die materials for hot forming may be cast ceramic, Meehanite, or high-nickel alloy.

## OPERATING PARAMETERS

Variables that influence stretch forming include the size and shape of the workpiece, material from which it is made, type of forming operation to be performed, machine and tooling to be used, and production requirements. Operating parameters that must be established prior to forming include force requirements and the lubricant to be used.

Sheet metal blanks used for stretch forming can also influence the success of the operation. For maximum elongation, the blanks should be cut, when possible, with the grain direction of the material longitudinal to the direction of stretch. Blank edges may also be critical. Shearing can introduce a notch effect in the edge surfaces, which can impair the stretchability of some materials. In most cases, the notch effects due to surface roughness can be eliminated by filing, sanding, or polishing the edges.

### Force Requirements

The application of excessive tension in stretch forming can cause breakage of the workpiece; too little tension can result in poor contouring, wrinkling, or springback of the formed part. An estimate of the force required for stretch forming, which determines the capacity of the machine needed, can be calculated from the following formula:

$$F = \frac{Y_s + UTS}{2} \times A \qquad (3)$$

where:

$F$ = stretch forming force, lb
$Y_s$ = yield strength of the material, psi
$UTS$ = ultimate tensile strength of the material, psi
$A$ = cross-sectional area of the workpiece, in.$^2$

For metric usage, the force in pounds is multiplied by 4.448 to obtain newtons (N).

Example:

To stretch form a workpiece having a cross section of 0.50 x 120″ (60 in.$^2$), made from a 2219 aluminum alloy having a yield strength of 36,000 psi and an ultimate tensile strength of 52,000 psi, the approximate force required is:

$$F = \frac{88{,}000}{2} \times 60 = 2{,}640{,}000 \text{ lb}$$

which equals 1320 tons or 11.7 MN.

The value obtained for force with this formula is generally an average. For some applications, force is increased an additional 25% to compensate for work hardening, friction, more complex contours, and other variables.

### Lubricants Used

To attain the required contours in stretch forming, the surface of the metal is forced into contact with the die. This creates friction (the sharper the contour, the greater the friction), which decreases the amount of stretching that takes place. To reduce friction, minimize breakage, and increase the efficiency of the operation, a lubricant is necessary (refer to Chapter 3 of this volume, "Lubricants").

A high-quality, extreme-pressure lubricant of the type used for deep drawing operations on presses usually gives good results in stretch forming. The specific lubricant to be used, however, can vary, depending upon the workpiece material, the die material, and the forming pressure.

Water-soluble oils are often used because they can easily be removed from the formed parts. If the forming pressures are low, a light-viscosity (SAE 20) oil may be used. For higher forming pressures, a heavier oil should be used. Many other lubricants, such as paraffin and wax, and many other methods are used to reduce friction and minimize die wear. Sometimes a sheet of polyvinyl chloride, wax paper, or other material is placed between the die and workpiece to reduce friction and prevent marring of polished surfaces.

Oil may be applied by brushing, wiping, or spraying, but spraying generally requires the use of more oil. Depending upon the severity of the operation, it is not always necessary to lubricate the die before forming each part. For some applications, a certain amount of friction is necessary to help prevent the metal from slipping into buckling deformation. In such cases, the lubricant should be applied sparingly. Excessive lubrication is indicated by the formation of blisters or bulges resulting from trapped lubricant.

## TROUBLESHOOTING

Problems encountered in stretch forming can be minimized by using the proper machine, tooling, setup, force, and lubricant. Elongation of the workpiece must be kept within safe limits because the primary cause of failures is tearing at the points of maximum elongation.

Sheets requiring a large curvature in a plane at 90° to the direction of stretching usually fail between the jaws and the die. Sharp curvatures cause failures at the crowns of the curves—in most cases, about halfway between the jaws.

Saddleback-shaped parts, in which the maximum stretch occurs at the edges of the sheets, generally fail at the sheet edges. It is also possible to get compression failures because of wrinkling during the forming of saddleback-shaped parts. Such parts have a tendency to slide toward the center of the die, causing wrinkles extending lengthwise between the jaws. The tendency toward folding can be reduced by decreasing the workpiece's width and/or increasing its thickness, and by using a lower strength material. Another solution is to use a matching top die which can be clamped against the part surface.

Buckling of thin sheets can be minimized by forming two or more parts at a time. Buckling of thick sheets may be reduced by allowing the metal width to overlap the ends of the dies and/or by using confinement devices. The ends of the stretch dies may require development to either hold the metal or let it flow when certain parts are being formed.

# ANDROFORMING

The patented Androform process is a method used to form sheet or plate stock into shallow, compound-curved parts. Among the major advantages of Androforming over stretch forming is that without having to make any dies, flat blanks can be elongated differentially to produce a variety of convex shapes. Forming extends to the side edges of the blanks without changing their lengths and without necking, even when the blanks are triangular or trapezium shaped.

Most production applications of Androforming consist of zero elongation at the blank edges or elongation only at the edges. A few applications, however, consist of elongation at the central area of the blanks and shrinkage along the edges. Materials can be formed at room temperature in the hard-rolled or heat-treated condition, thus eliminating the need for heat treating after forming. Flatness of the blanks is not critical because the machine that is used irons out wrinkles and warps during forming.

Androforming is being used to form compound-curved surfaces for aircraft skins and petals for parabolic antennas employed in radio telescope systems, which require precise tolerances and consistent repeatability. It can also be applied to the forming of panels for automobile bodies, appliances, and ship hulls.

The process is not suitable for producing deep drawn shapes. Limitations with respect to the depth of draw depend upon the properties, widths, and thicknesses of the materials to be formed. Maximum depths of draw are generally limited to a minimum spherical radius of about 1 ½ times the blank width.

## FORMING PRINCIPLE

The Androform process operates on the principle of selective differential elongation of metal blanks by drawing them through a series of dynamically controlled forming elements. With jaws pulling one end of the blank through the forming elements, the blank traverses a path consisting of a series of reverse bends and variable differential steps.

The path traversed is adjustably different for each increment of the blank width and is also variable along its length. With this variable pattern of individual paths, the blank is differentially stressed according to a predetermined program. The program is selected to localize the strain pattern at the low portion of the plastic range of the material.

## ANDROFORMING MACHINES

A typical machine is shown schematically in Fig. 7-31. It consists essentially of a support and guide for feeding blanks, a

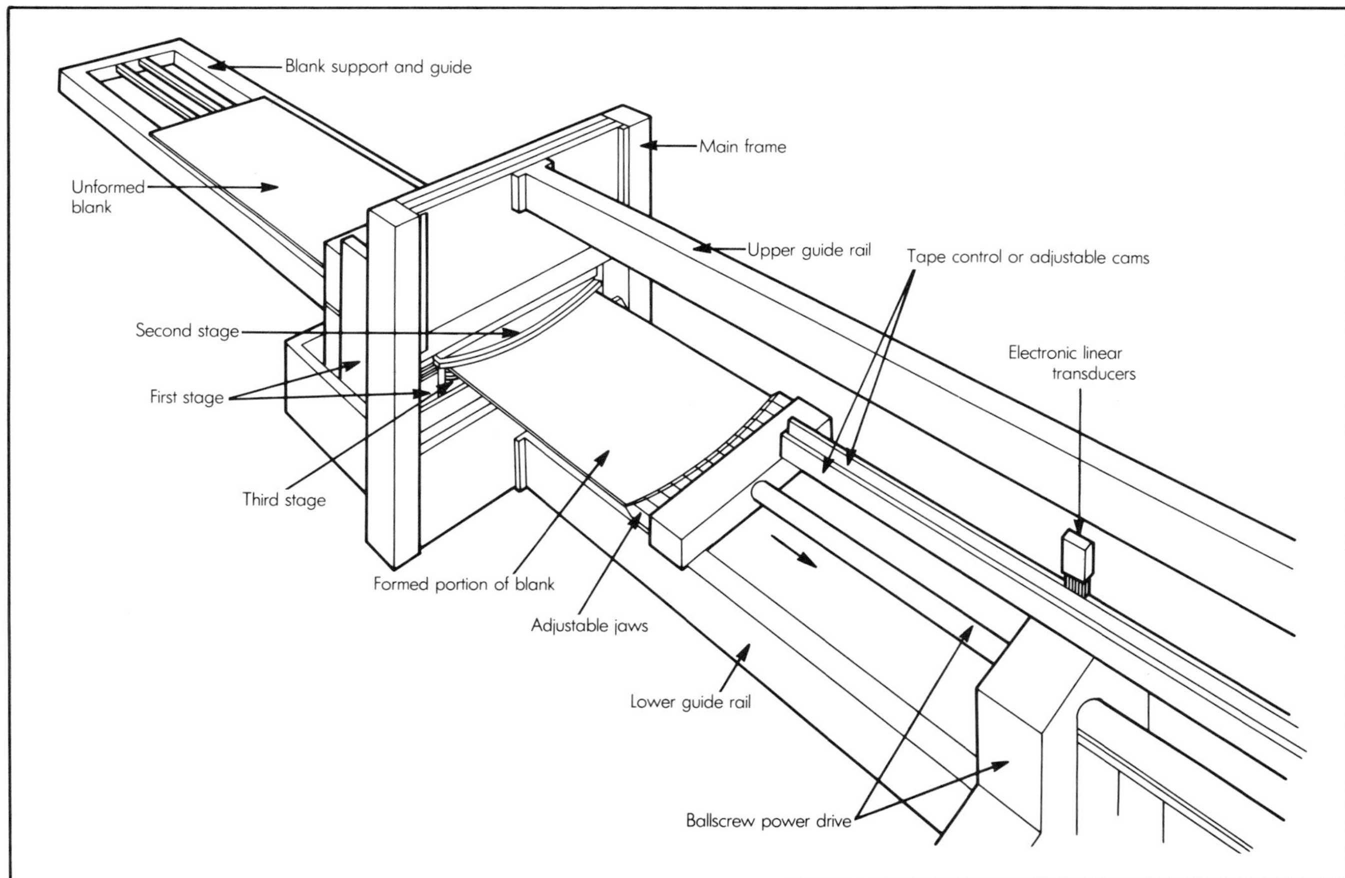


**Fig. 7-31 Androform machine for forming sheets into shallow curved parts.** (*Anderson Industries, Inc.*)

frame for holding the programmable forming elements, guide rails, a tape control or adjustable cams, and a power drive and adjustable jaws for pulling one end of the blank. The tensile load at the jaws is only about 12% of the yield point of the material.

Machines have been built to form blanks to 9/16" (14.3 mm) thick x 8 ft (2.4 m) wide x 36 ft (11 m) long. Tolerances of 0.001" /ft (0.08 mm/m) are held, and production rates of 150-180 parts per hour have been attained. Setup time for producing new parts varies from a few minutes to several hours. By proper selection of the forming elements, the largest machines have formed stainless steel as thin as 0.008" (0.20 mm).

As the blank travels over and under certain beads of the forming elements, it is subjected to simultaneous bending and tensile loads. This results in severe gradients of stress throughout the thickness and full width of the material, with the greatest tensile stress at the outer layers of the bends. The degree of the stress gradient is controlled by the dynamic actions and positioning of the forming element stages, relative to each other and their geometric differential.

Almost all the differential elongation of the blank surface takes place between the last bead of the first stage and the single bead in the second stage, where the bend is reversed. The tangent portion of the blank between the first and second-stage beads is not elongated since the tensile load is below the yield point of the material. The third-stage tooling co-acts with the second-stage bead and the horizontal lands of the second stage to control the final differential elongation throughout the material thickness; this tooling is programmed to produce the desired longitudinal curvature of the part.

## TOOLING FOR ANDROFORMING

Universally adjustable forming elements (see Fig. 7-32) eliminate the need for dies. The elements are preadjusted to shape according to formulas, calculations, and measurements taken from form-checking fixtures used for inspection.

Distances that the elements are apart and above or below each other, combined with the contours of the elements in the second and third stages, determine the shape produced. Automatic positioning of the elements to produce the desired curvature is controlled by punched tapes or a series of adjustable cams and linear transducers.

Working surfaces of the forming elements are interchangeable inserts which are selected according to the metal thickness to be formed. Profiles of these element inserts perform best when the bead radius is eight times the metal thickness. They have highly polished, hardened surfaces. Element inserts for the first stage are rigid; those for the second and third stages are adjustable to a curve proportional to the transverse curve of the part to be formed.

Before the blank enters the first-stage elements, it passes between two rigid flat plates. The plates are lined with flat hardened tool-steel sections arranged in a zig-zag pattern to provide grooves for the passage of oil. The oil lubricant is automatically forced under pressure against both faces of the blank. In addition, when titanium is being formed, a plastic coating is applied to both sides of the sheet and dried before forming. This coating, which prevents galling, is easily peeled from the sheet after forming.

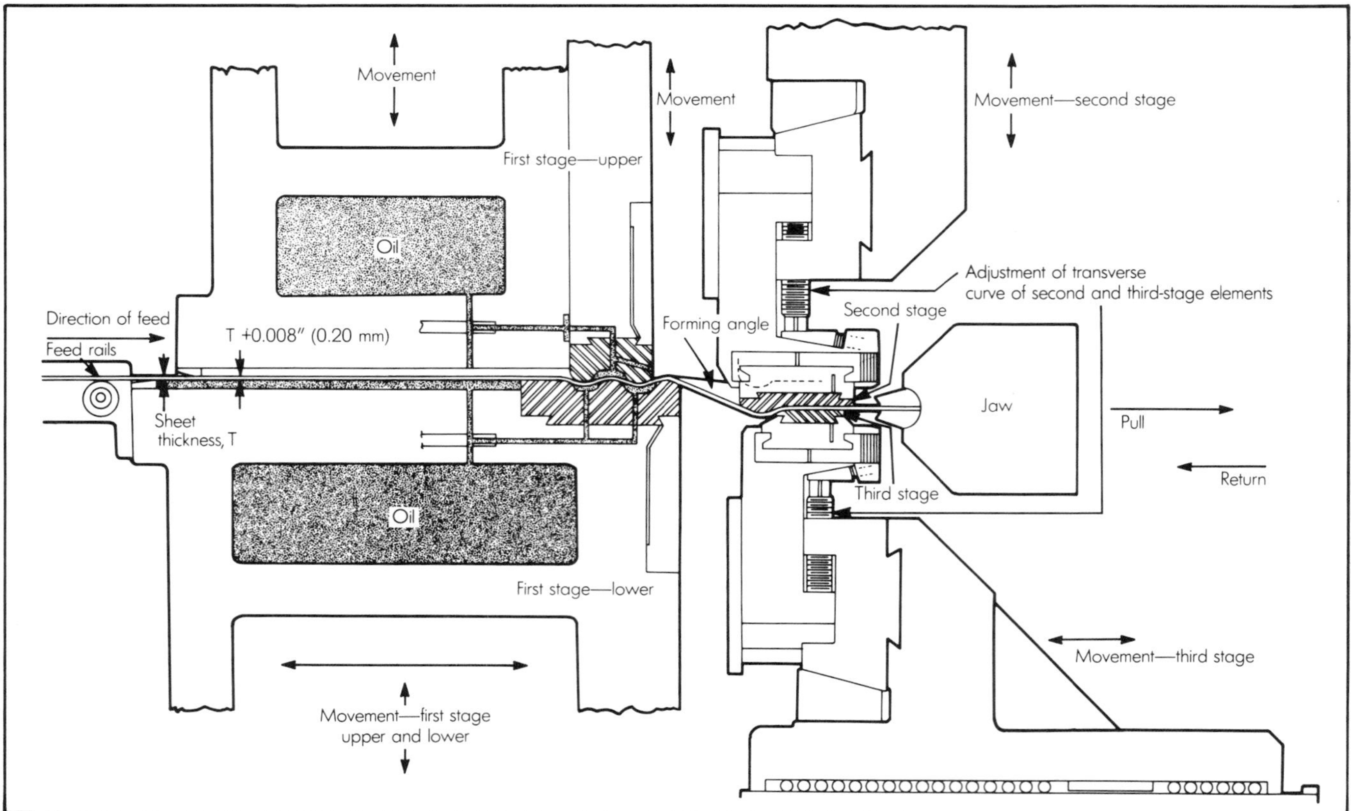


**Fig. 7-32 Forming elements for Androforming are arranged in three stages.** (*Anderson Industries, Inc.*)

# REFERENCES

## References


1. Vernon Fencl, *Metalforming by Expanding, Shrinking, and Rotary Roll Forming*, SME Technical Paper MF72-518, 1972.
2. Private communication from Thomas F. Hill, Vice President, Grotnes Metalforming Systems, Inc., Chicago, June 29, 1982.
3. American Society for Metals, *Metals Handbook*, Vol. 4, Forming, 8th ed., Metals Park, OH, 1969.


## Bibliography


Brauer, E. H. *Stretch and Compression Forming*. SME Technical Paper MF74-605, 1974.

Williams, Ralph P. "Precision Stretch Forming Large Shapes." *Manufacturing Engineering* (February 1977), pp. 44-46.

Roper, Ralph E. *The Wallace Expanding Process*. SAE Paper 660067. Presented at SAE Automotive Engineering Conference, Detroit, January 10-14, 1966.

CHAPTER

# 8

# Roll Forming

# ROLL FORMING

Roll forming is a continuous process for forming metal from sheet, strip, or coiled stock into shapes of essentially uniform cross section. The material is fed between successive pairs of rolls, which progressively shape it until the desired cross section is produced. During the process, only bending takes place; the material thickness is not changed except for a slight thinning at bend radii. Chapter 10, "Bending and Straightening," discusses sheet metal bending in greater detail.

## ROLL FORMING METHODS

The two methods used when shaped parts are roll formed are the precut or cut-to-length method and the post-cut method. Method selection is based on the complexity of the cross section and the production length specification.

### Precut Method

In precut operations, the material is cut to length prior to entering the roll forming machine. This process usually incorporates a stacking and feeding system to move the blanks into the roll forming machine, a roll forming machine running at a fixed speed of about 50-250 fpm (15-76 m/min), and an exit conveyor and stacking system. The cut-to-length process is used primarily for lower volume parts and whenever notching cannot be easily accomplished in a post-cut line; for example, miter cuts in vertical legs. Many times, the material is run from coil into a shear or blanking press and then mechanically fed into the roll former.

Tooling cost is inexpensive with this method because cutting requires only a flat shear die or end notch die. However, end flare is more pronounced and side roll tooling is required to obtain a good finished shape.

### Post-Cut Method

Even though some configurations require the cut-to-length method, the most efficient, most productive, most consistent, and least troublesome is the post-cut method. This method requires an uncoiler, a roll forming machine, a cutoff machine, and runout table. In most segments of the industry, this is the most widely used method. It can be augmented by various auxiliary operations, including prenotching, punching, embossing, marking, trimming, welding, curving, coiling, and die forming. Any or all of these procedures can be combined to eliminate the need for secondary operations, resulting in a complete or net shape product. However, the cost of tooling and the tooling changeover time for this method are greater than the tooling cost and changeover time for the precut method.

## DESIGN CONSIDERATIONS

The cross section or shape to be roll formed can be as varied as the materials used. The most effective and trouble-free operations involve shapes that are designed (or modified) with the roll forming process in mind. Many sections that traditionally have been produced by press braking, extruding, or stamping can be successfully converted to roll forming by keeping a few simple rules in mind.

### Symmetry

Many nonsymmetrical sections are roll formed without difficulty, but the section that is symmetrical about its vertical centerline when formed results in an equal amount of forming being done on each edge of the metal as it passes through the form rolls. When this condition is achieved, the stresses imparted by the forming process are equalized.

### Cross Section Depth

Extreme depth in a cross section should be avoided. The stresses produced in roll forming are much more complex than those in other types of bending. In deep sections, the metal movement around the arc of the bend is much greater—and so is the resulting edge stress.

### Bend Radii

The minimum bend radius is largely determined by the ductility of the material to be formed. Generally, sharper radii can be obtained by roll forming than by other forming methods. Given a material of sufficient ductility, bend radii should be equal to or greater than the material thickness (see Fig. 8-1). To form a radius smaller than the metal thickness, grooving or beading of the metal must be done (see Fig. 8-2). However, this practice, combined with the inherent thinning that occurs during bending, can result in fracturing of the metal at the bends (see Fig. 8-3).

### Blind Corners

A blind corner is a bend or area of a bend that cannot be controlled by direct contact of the rolls

CHAPTER CONTENTS:



***Contributors of sections of this chapter are:*** *Henry F. Classe, P.E., J.D., Chief Manufacturing Methods Engineer, Cupples Products Div., H. H. Robertson Co.; Eugene F. Gorman, P.E., Manager, Engineering, Teledyne Metal Forming; Timothy A. Gutowski, President, Contour Roll Company; George T. Halmos, Consulting Engineer, President, Delta Engineering Ltd./LTEE; Donald R. Hill, Vice President, Hill Engineering, Inc.; Richard O. Pearson, Roll Form Consultant, Roll Form Consultant Services; Donald D. Penick, Tool Design Engineer, Kirsch Company; Charles Prochaska, President, Roll Design Services.*

***Reviewers of sections of this chapter are:*** *Bruce Blacklaw, Chief Design Engineer, Samson Roll Formed Products Co.; Barlow Brooks, Jr., President, Roll Forming Corporation; William Buitenhuis, Tool Design Specialist, Teledyne Metal Forming; Henry F. Classe, P.E., J.D., Chief Manufacturing Methods Engineer, Cupples Products Div., H. H. Robertson Co.; L. C. Colleran, Vice President-Sales, Roll Formed Products Co.;*

(see Fig. 8-4). Whenever a blind corner is present, sectional dimensions cannot be controlled accurately unless the corner is accessible by slides or side idler forming rolls.

## Leg Length

The minimum practical leg length is three times the material thickness (see Fig. 8-1). A leg length shorter than this does not allow the rolls to properly form the leg. In fact, attempting to form short legs results in nipping the edge of the material. This nipping can cause edge stretch and can result in a wave along the edge of the finished part.

## Section Width

Sections with wide flat areas that are exposed when the sections are assembled into the end product should be viewed with caution. The stresses developed during roll forming can cause these areas to lose their flatness. Longitudinal ribs, based on material thickness, can be evenly spaced across the flat area to mask or hide coil imperfections such as wavy edges or lack of flatness in the center (oil canning). Roll forming cannot remove coil imperfections in wide flat areas; it can only try to hide or bury them in the cross section.

## Notches and Punched Holes

Whenever possible, prepunched holes and notches should be kept away from bend lines or edges. Generally, holes are placed three to five times material thickness beyond bend radius (see Fig. 8-1). Slight distortions in their size and shape during forming is highly possible and should be expected. To minimize distortion, the number of forming passes should be increased.

## Part Length

Cutting the roll-formed cross section to length is accomplished using the precut or the post-cut method. To minimize post cutoff distortion, it is recommended that the shape be designed or roll formed in such a way as to facilitate cutoff. The shortest length for precut parts is twice the horizontal center distance between roll forming stations.

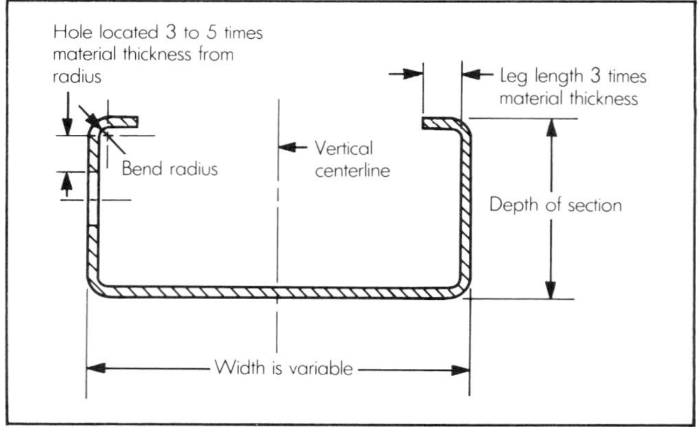


**Fig. 8-1 Several rules must be taken into consideration when designing a part to be produced on a roll forming machine.** (*Contour Roll Co.*)

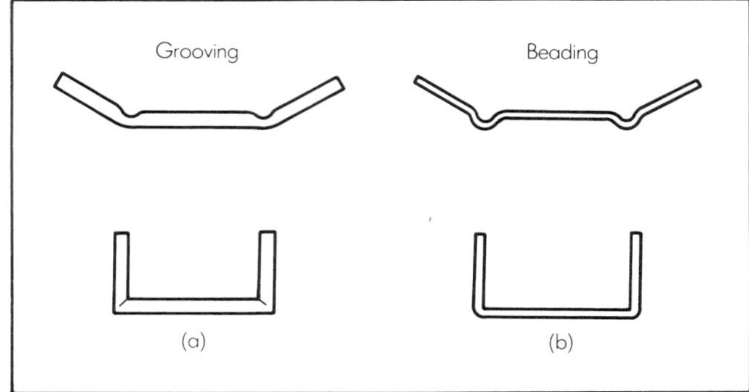


**Fig. 8-2 Grooving or beading the metal enables a smaller radius to be formed, but may result in fracturing the metal.** (*Lockformer Co.*)

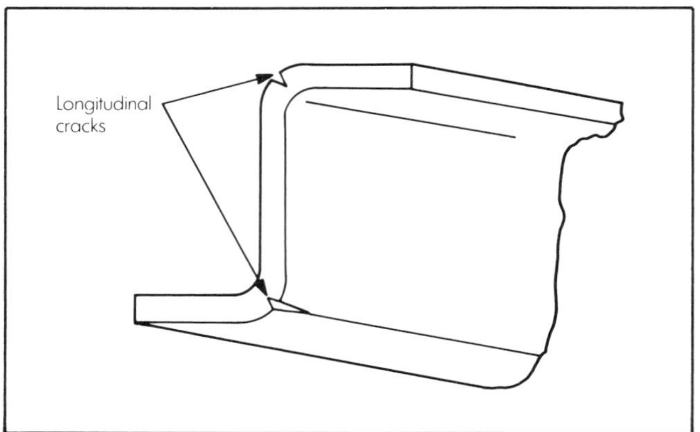


**Fig. 8-3 A bend radius that is too small results in longitudinal cracks at the bend.** (*Lockformer Co.*)

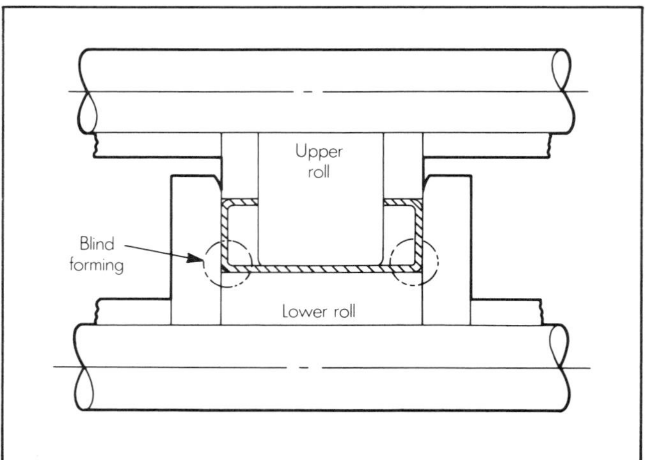


**Fig. 8-4 Blind corners cannot be controlled by direct contact of the rolls.** (*Lockformer Co.*)

***Reviewers, cont.**: Don Coulson, Vice President, Engineering, North Star Company, Inc.; Nigel C. Eiloart, President and General Manager, Brockhouse Canada Ltd.; Leo R. Gale, Executive Vice President, The Lockformer Company; Eugene F. Gorman, P.E., Manager, Engineering, Teledyne Metal Forming; Carl F. Granzow, Vice President and General Manager, Tishken Products Company; Timothy A. Gutowski, President, Contour Roll Company; Ivan Haaseth, Manufacturing Engineer, Mills Products Incorporated; George T. Halmos, Consulting Engineer, President, Delta Engineering Ltd./LTEE; Donald R. Hill, Vice President, Hill Engineering, Inc.;*

# ADVANTAGES AND LIMITATIONS

## ADVANTAGES AND LIMITATIONS

Roll forming is a high-volume process of producing uniform, accurately dimensioned parts. Production speeds of approximately 50-600 fpm (15-185 m/min) are obtained, with 100-180 fpm (30-55 m/min) an average. Parts are produced with a minimum of handling, requiring only the loading of coils at the starting end of the machine and removal of finished parts at the exit end, generally accomplished by a minimum of operators. Roll forming can also be used for low-volume production because setup or changeover time from one cross section to another rarely takes more than a few hours, and length changes generally take only a few minutes on simple shapes. However, considerable time is required for more complex shapes.

The process is readily adaptable for combination with other operations and processes to form automatically a broad variety of metal parts. The initial cost of a roll forming line can be compared quite favorably with the cost of a standard stamping line or progressive die operation.

Maintenance costs are generally low. With proper roll design, the right tooling materials, good forming material, and proper lubricant, the form rolls can produce several million feet (900 000 m) of product before shape and tolerance problems develop. If through-hardened steel rolls are used, they can be recut or retrofitted, at a fraction of replacement cost, to produce for many more years.

The designing of rolls for complicated shapes must be done by experienced roll engineers. Complicated tubular or closed shapes sometimes require mandrels to form the shape properly, and delicate breakable parts require frequent replacement when high-production runs are made.

## MATERIALS ROLL FORMED

Any material known today that can withstand bending to a desired radius can be roll formed. The material can be ferrous or nonferrous, cold rolled, hot rolled, polished, prepainted, or plated. Thicknesses of 0.005 to 3/4" (0.13 to 19 mm) and material widths of 1/8 to 72" (3 to 1830 mm) or more can be used in roll forming. Length of the finished part is limited only by the length that can be conveniently handled after it leaves the roll forming machine.

In some instances, multiple sections can be formed from a single strip or several strips can be fed simultaneously and combined to produce one composite section. The only absolute requirement for a material, whatever the type, coating, thickness, or width, is that it be capable of being formed at room temperature to the specified radii. Some materials, such as certain titanium alloys, have poor forming characteristics at room temperature. Therefore, the material must be heated and then formed on specially designed roll forming machines.

## TOLERANCES

Cross-sectional tolerances on part dimensions are a result of variations in material width and thickness, physical properties of the material, quality of the tooling, conditions of the machine, and operator skill. Dimensional cross-sectional tolerances of ±0.010 to ±0.031" (0.25 to 0.78 mm) and angular tolerances of ±1° are common. These tolerances are slighty greater when wide building panels and deep sections are being formed. If a closer tolerance, such as ±0.005" (0.13 mm), is required, material will probably need to be obtained that has a controlled tolerance of ±0.002" (0.05 mm) on the thickness and ±0.004" (0.10 mm) on the width.

Length tolerances are dependent on material thickness, part length, line speed, equipment quality and condition, and type of measuring and cutoff system used. For thin material, 0.015-0.025", tolerances of ±0.020 to ±0.093" (0.51 to 2.36 mm) are obtainable. For material greater than 0.025" (0.63 mm) thick, tolerances of ±0.015" to ±0.060" (0.38 mm to 1.52 mm) are obtainable. The minimum tolerances are based on part lengths up to 36" (915 mm), and the maximum tolerances are based on lengths up to 144" (3 660 mm). Tolerances would generally be greater on parts longer than those specified.

When considering roll forming, it is generally advisable to order the material to be formed with somewhat tighter than commercial quality tolerances. If this is done, a great many dimensional problems can be eliminated. Failure to consider material quality results in needless problems and frustrations.

### Straightness

In addition to cross-sectional, angular, and length tolerances, another tolerance to consider is the straightness of the material and the formed section. Some of the parameters that determine straightness include camber, curve or sweep, bow, and twist. The terms *camber*, *curve*, and *bow* are often used synonymously when describing straightness. The horizontal and vertical planes of the formed part are determined by the position in which the part is being formed.

**Camber.** Camber is the deviation of a side edge from a straight line (see Fig. 8-5). Measured prior to roll forming, the maximum allowable camber is 3/8" (9.5 mm) in 10 ft (3 m). Excessive camber contributes to curve, bow, and twist in the finished part.

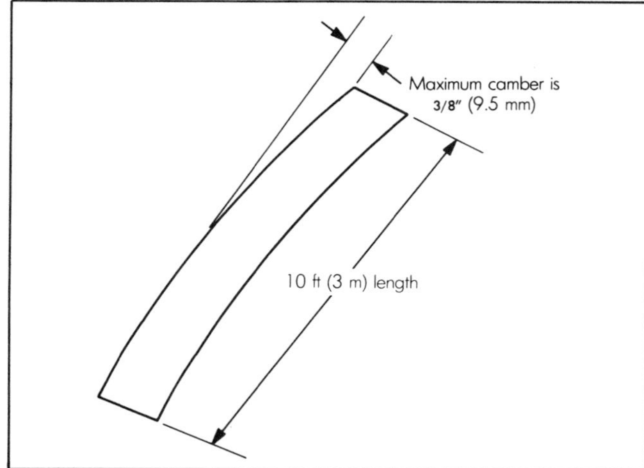


**Fig. 8-5 Camber is the deviation of a side edge from a straight line that is measured prior to roll forming.**

*__Reviewers, cont.:__ Joseph Ivaska, Jr., Director of Engineering, Tower Oil and Technology Co.; Frederick J. Krause, CMfgE, President, Design Data Systems Corporation; Richard O. Pearson, Roll Form Consultant, Roll Form Consultant Services; Donald D. Penick, Tool Design Engineer, Kirsch Company; Delbert Jack Phebus, Foreman—Roll Forming, Teledyne Metal Forming; George Powell, Vice President—Manufacturing, Brockhouse Canada Ltd.; Charles Prochaska, President, Roll Design Services; William E. Sornborger, President, North Star Company, Inc.; Ted. R. Wrubleski, Sales Engineer, Superior Roll Forming Company.*

# TOLERANCES

**Curve or sweep.** Curve or sweep is the deviation from a straight line in the horizontal plane measured after the part has formed (see Fig. 8-6). The curve in a formed part can be held to within ±1/8″ (±3 mm) in 10 ft (3 m). Curve or sweep can result from incorrect horizontal roll alignment and uneven forming pressure in a pair of rolls (see Fig. 8-7).

**Bow.** Bow is the deviation from a straight line in the vertical plane and can be in the form of cross bow or longitudinal bow (see Fig. 8-8). Bow results from uneven vertical gaps on symmetrical sections and from uneven forming areas on unsymmetrical sections. Generally, bow can be held to within ±1/8″ (±3 mm) in 10 ft (3 m).

**Twist.** Twist in a formed part resembles a corkscrew effect and often results from excessive forming pressure (see Fig. 8-9). Twist is generally held to less than 5° in 10 ft (3 m).

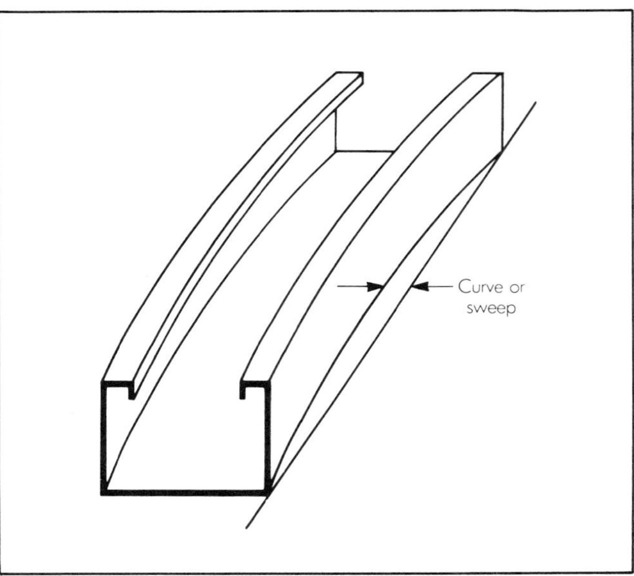


**Fig. 8-6 Curve or sweep is the deviation from a straight line in the horizontal plane measured after the part has been formed.**

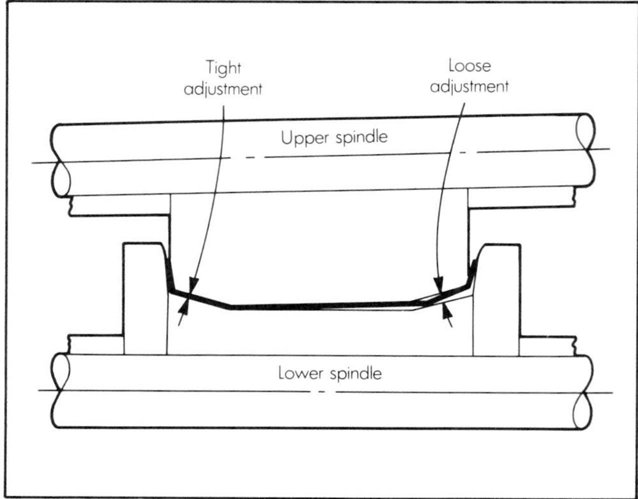


**Fig. 8-7 Improper roll adjustment contributes to curve or sweep in a rolled part.** (*Lockformer Co.*)

## Quality and Accuracy

Two areas that can affect the quality and accuracy of a roll-formed section are springback and end flare.

**Springback.** Springback is a phenomenon that occurs when the material being formed has not been stressed beyond its elastic limit. This distortion becomes evident after the straining of the part has been discontinued. The amount of springback varies with different metal properties such as yield and elastic modulus. Springback can be compensated for in the tool design by overforming. Overforming forms the material past its expected final shape.

**End flare.** End flare is the distortion that appears at the ends of a roll-formed part. The internal stresses incurred in roll

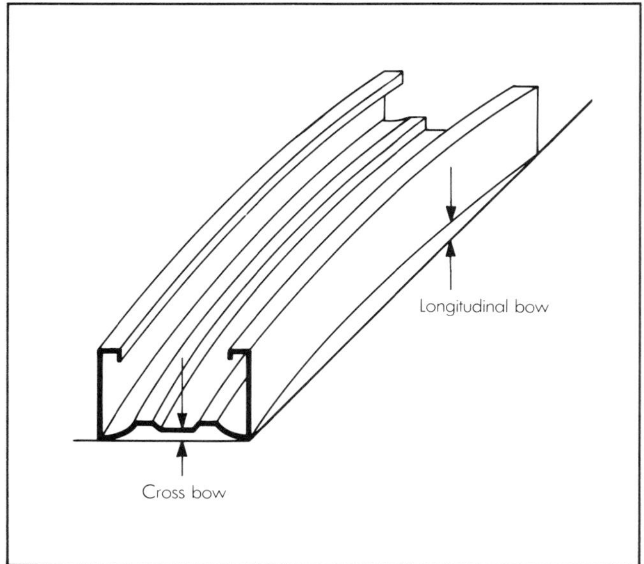


**Fig. 8-8 Bow is the deviation from a straight line in the vertical plane measured after the part has been formed.**

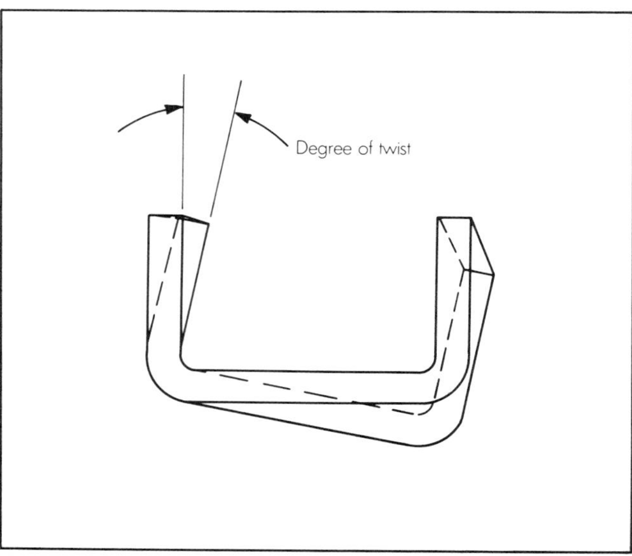


**Fig. 8-9 Twist in a roll-formed part resembles a corkscrew effect.** (*Lockformer Co.*)

forming are much more complex than in other types of bending. These stresses usually are higher in the edges of the material being formed and are released when the part is cut off. End flare can be minimized by using proper tool design. For example, extra roll passes, avoidance of prepunched edges at the cutoff zone, and more ductile materials help to reduce end flare.

### ROLL FORMING APPLICATIONS

Roll forming as a metal fabricating process is used in many diverse industries to produce a variety of shapes and products. Figure 8-10 illustrates several complicated shapes that can be produced on a roll forming machine. Roll forming is also used for parts that were manufactured by extrusion processes. This is limited, however, to parts that can be redesigned to have a constant wall thickness. Some industries that use roll-formed products are the automotive, building, office furniture, home appliances and products, medical, rail car, aircraft, and heating ventilation and air conditioning (HVAC) industries.

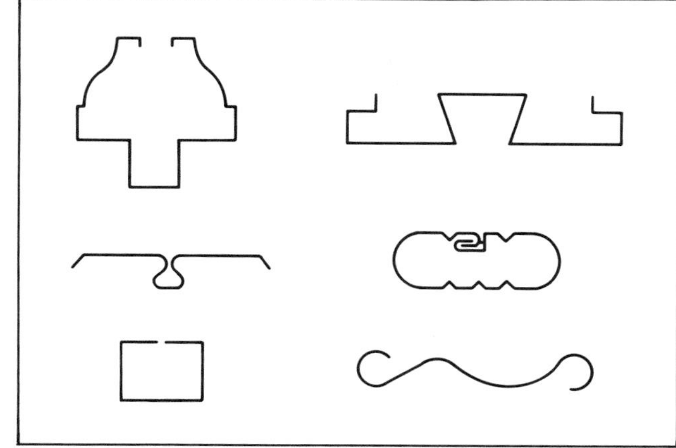

**Fig. 8-10 Complicated profiles are attainable with roll forming.**

## ROLL FORMING MACHINES

The roll forming machine (roll former) most commonly used has a number of individual units, each of which is actually a dual-spindle roll forming machine, mounted on a suitable baseplate to make a multiple-unit machine (see Fig. 8-11). The flexibility of this construction permits the user to purchase enough units for immediate needs only. By purchasing additional length of baseplate on the machine, units can be added at any time for future needs. Some of these machines are provided with machined ends on the baseplates, making it possible to couple several machines together, in tandem, to provide additional units as required.

Adjusting screws, for making vertical adjustment of the top rolls, are designed with dials and scales to provide micrometer adjustment and a means of recording the position of the top shaft for each roll pass and each shape being formed. The shaft diameter of most machines is from 1-4″ (25-90 mm).

### TYPES OF ROLL FORMING MACHINES

Several different types of roll forming machines or roll formers are used. They can be classified according to spindle support, station configuration, and drive system.

### Spindle Support

Roll forming machines can be classified according to the method by which the spindles are supported in the unit. Generally, two types exist: (1) inboard or over-hung spindle machines and (2) outboard machines.

**Inboard machine.** Inboard-type machines have spindle shafts supported on one end which are 1 to 1 1/2″ (25 to 38 mm) in diameter and up to 4″ (100 mm) in length. They are used for forming light-gage moldings, weather strips, and other simple shapes. The material thickness is limited to about 0.040″ (1.0 mm), and the top roll shaft is generally geared directly to the bottom shaft. This direct-mesh gearing permits only a small amount of roll redressing (no more than the thickness of the material being formed) on top and bottom rolls. Tooling changeover is faster on this machine than on the outboard type of machine.

**Outboard machine.** Outboard machines have housings supporting both ends of the spindle shafts (see Fig. 8-12). The outboard housing is generally adjustable along the spindles, permitting shortening of the distance between the supports to accommodate small shapes of heavy gage material. This

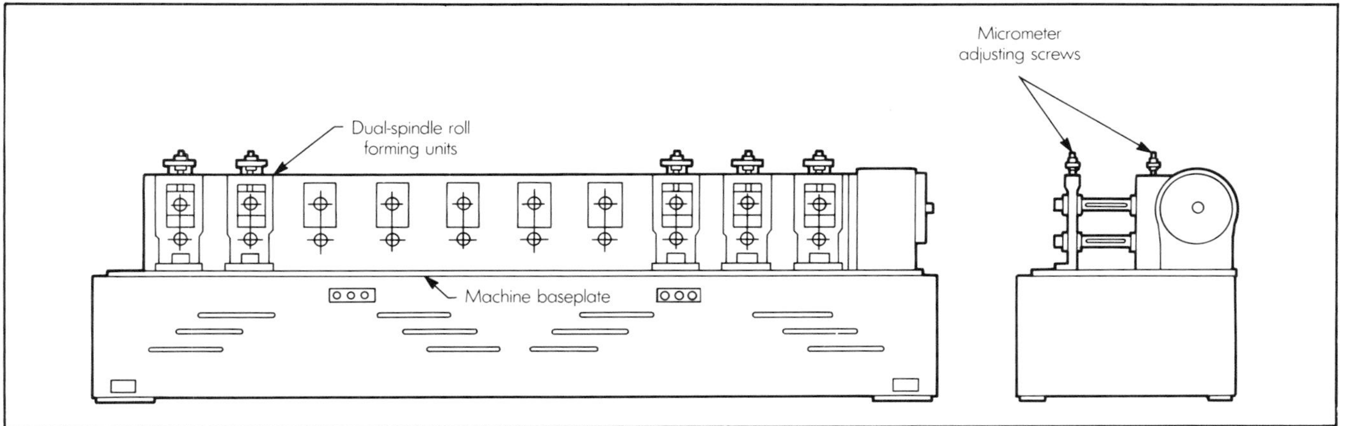


**Fig. 8-11 A roll former consists of several forming units mounted on a common baseplate.** (*Lockformer Co.*)

# ROLL FORMING MACHINES

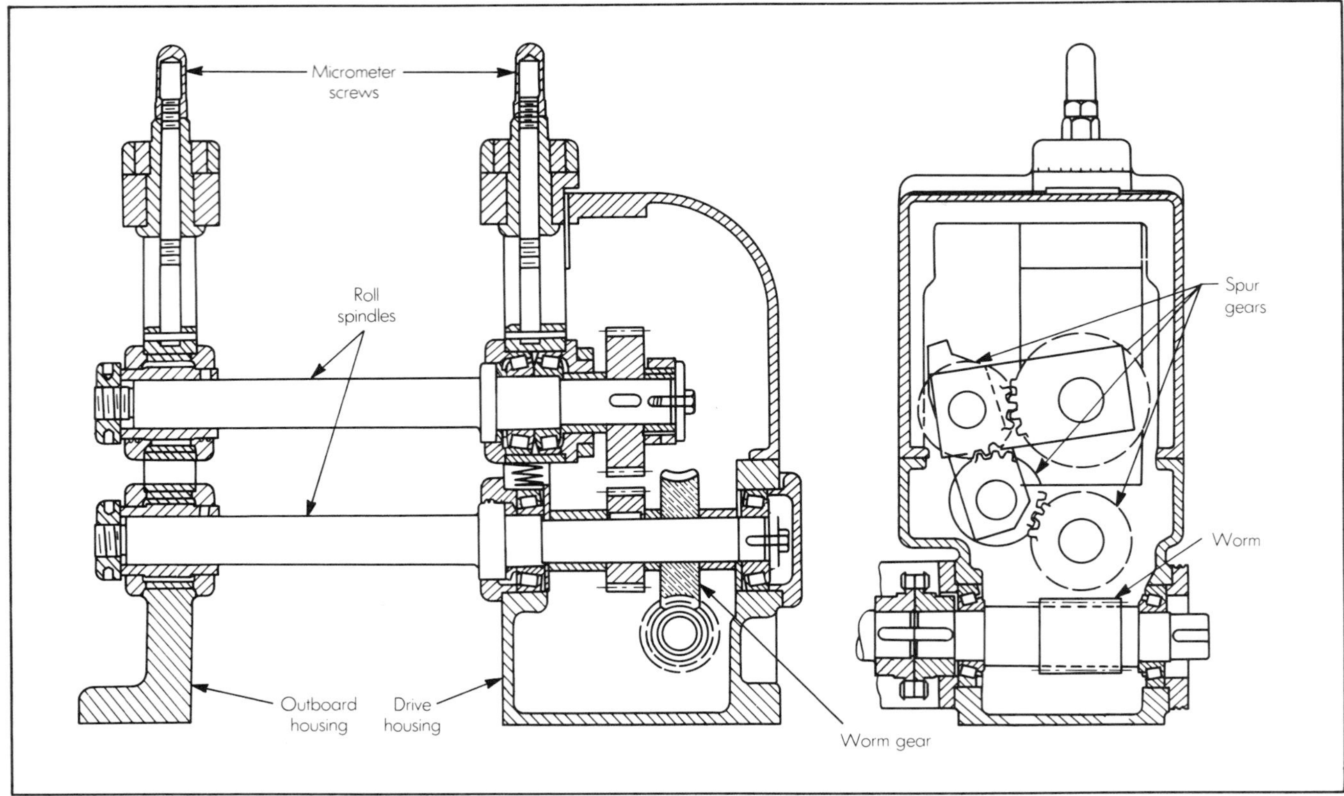


**Fig. 8-12 Cross section of an outboard roll stand with square gearing.**

adjustment also permits the machine to be used as an inboard type of machine when desired. Outboard machines can be readily designed to accommodate any width of material by making the spindle lengths to suit the material width and then mounting the individual units and spindles on a baseplate of suitable width. This type of machine is built with spindle sizes from 1 1/2 to 4" (38 to 100 mm) diam and width capacities up to 72" (1830 mm).

Generally, for roll forming material over 3/16" (5 mm) in thickness, machines are constructed so that both top and bottom shafts can be removed by lifting them vertically from the housings after the housing caps have been removed. This permits rolls to be mounted on the shafts away from the machine, an important consideration when heavy rolls are being handled. This type of machine is built in spindle sizes from 2-15" (50-380 mm) diam.

## Station Configuration

As was previously mentioned, a typical roll forming machine consists of several individual roll forming units mounted on a common baseplate. The manner in which they are mounted determines to a great extent the type of shapes that are formed on the machine.

**Single-duty machine.** This type of machine is built and designed for a one-purpose profile or for one particular set of roll tooling and is not normally designed for convenient roll changing. The cost of this machine is low in comparison to the other styles and is generally used for long production runs.

**Conventional or standard machines.** This particular type of machine is more versatile than the single-duty machine because the outboard supports are easily removed. This permits the roll tooling to be interchanged with other profiles to make it more suitable for a variety of production requirements.

To change the tooling, the top and bottom spindle lock nuts are removed and the outboard housing is pulled off the spindles. The tooling can then be removed and replaced with the desired profile.

**Side-by-side machine.** This machine is designed for multiple profiled tooling and provides the flexibility of having more than one set of roll tooling mounted on the spindle shaft at the same time (see Fig. 8-13). Generally, this type of machine is limited to two sets of rolls at a given time, but there can be up to three or four sets of rolls when small profiles are being run in production. Changeover from one production profile to another is accomplished by shifting the machine bed to the desired profile. The main advantages of the side-by-side configuration are low initial investments, fast tooling change, and reduced floor space requirement. Roll wear, however, can create problems because one set cannot be reground without regrinding the others at the same time. Adjusting for material variations can also be a problem.

**Double-high machines.** The double-high configuration consists of one set of roll tooling mounted on its own roll shafts and housings at one level on the bed frame, and a second complete set of roll tooling and housings mounted at a different level on the same common frame (see Fig. 8-14). This particular type of machine is used in the metal building industry for forming building panels up to 60" (1520 mm) wide.

**Rafted machine.** The rafted configuration resembles the single-duty and conventional configurations since each configuration has housings and spindle shafts with one particular set of roll tooling mounted on it. However, the rafted configuration has several roll forming units mounted on rafts or subplates that are removable from the roll former base (see Fig. 8-15). During tool changeover, the individual rafts are removed from the base and the replacement rafts with the roll forming units and tooling are installed. On a typical 16-stand roll forming machine, there are four sets of rafts containing four forming units each.

**Double-head machine.** This type of machine is designed and constructed with two separate sets of housings and roll shafts mounted so that they face one another. Each housing is mounted on an adjustable plate mechanism to allow the housing to be shifted for a change in overall width while at the same time maintaining the same profile for the edge formation.

This type of machine is very popular in the shelving industry, in which large, flat panels are rolled on a production basis and the panel widths change regularly. A disadvantage of this type of machine is that it does not lend itself to forming the center of the panel. Two of these machines, connected by an automatic transfer mechanism, are used to form the four edges of a shelf; the first machine would form the two long edges, and the second machine would form the two end configurations.

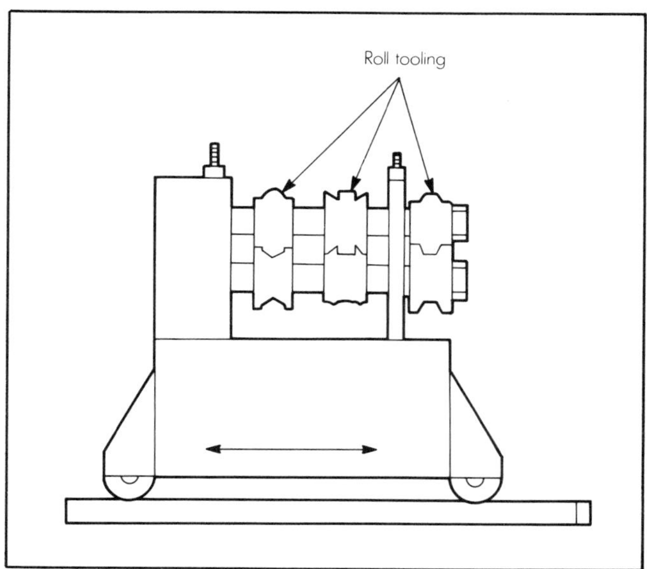

**Fig. 8-13 The side-by-side configuration permits roll forming of several different profiles on the same machine.**

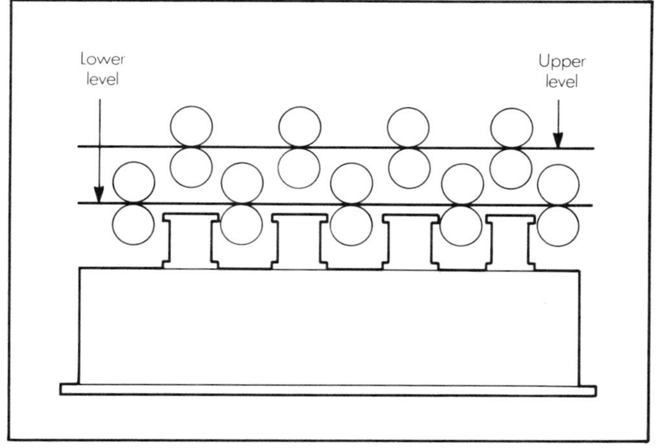

**Fig. 8-14 The double-high configuration consists of two independent sets of roll forming stations, one mounted above the other.**

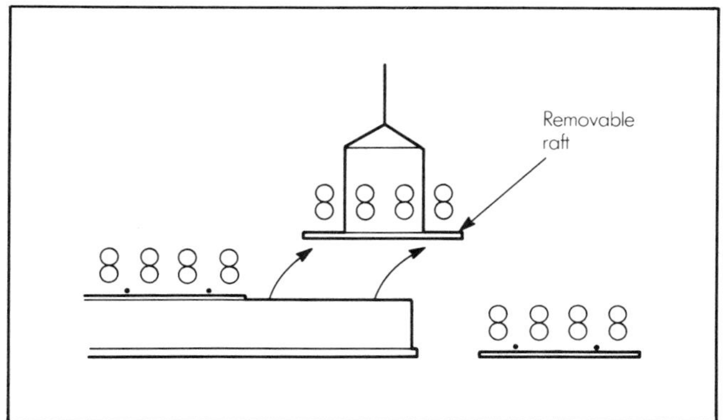

**Fig. 8-15 The rafted configuration permits quick roll tooling changeover and flexibility in tooling profile.**

## Drive System

The five basic methods used to drive the roll forming unit are chain drive, spur gear drive, worm gear drive, square gearing, and universal drive.

**Chain drive.** The chain drive consists of a sprocket attached to the individual roll forming unit and connected to the main drive by means of a roller chain. This is accomplished using a continuous roller chain, one long chain driving each unit, or a shorter chain connected to each individual unit. This drive system is inexpensive and allows flexibility in the construction of the machine.

**Spur gear drive.** The spur gear drive consists of a continuous train of spur gears mounted at the rear end of each spindle shaft. Idler gears are positioned between each unit to transfer the drive equally to all the units (see Fig. 8-16).

**Worm gear drive.** The worm gear drive is very similar to the spur gear drive. However, instead of using the idler gear to transfer the drive to each unit, an individual worm gear box is mounted on the bottom spindle of each unit. The worm gear boxes are coupled in-line which permits the machine designer to spread out the horizontal centers of each roll forming station without being concerned about properly meshing the gear train to the idler gear.

**Square gearing.** Another type of drive system that incorporates both the spur gears and the worm gear is the square gearing system (see Fig. 8-12). This type of gearing permits a vertical adjustment of the upper spindle and allows a wide range of roll diameters to be used.

**Universal drive.** This particular style or design of drive eliminates the need for any spur gearing or roller chain and sprocket drives. It consists of a series of worm driven gear boxes with top and bottom outputs that transfer the power source to the individual shafts through a double-jointed universal coupling. On certain applications, only the bottom spindle is driven.

This drive system is generally used with rafted style machines to permit quick tool changeover (see Fig. 8-17). Simplicity of design and minimal maintenance are two important advantages of this drive system.

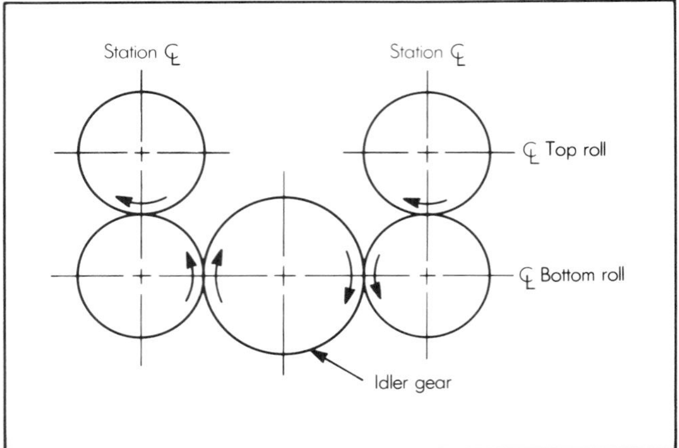


**Fig. 8-16 Idler gears are positioned between the stations to transfer the drive to each unit.**

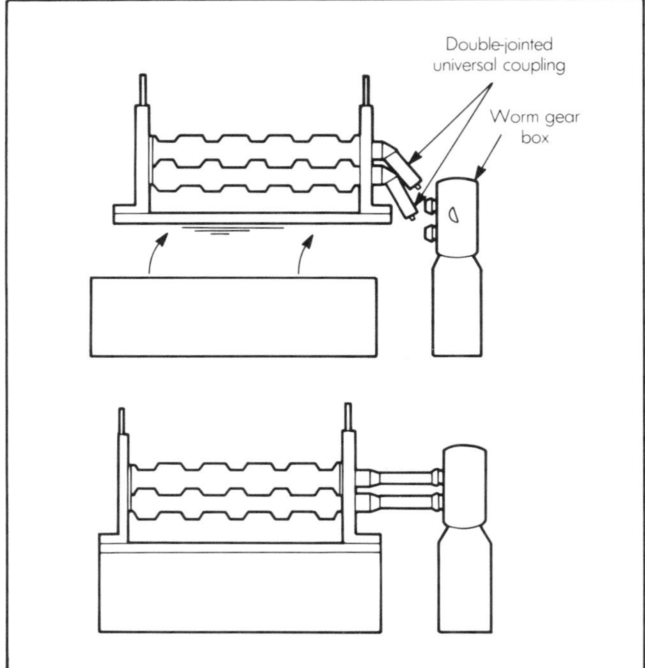


**Fig. 8-17 Universal-type drives combine a worm gear box with a double-jointed universal coupling to drive the spindle shafts.**

## MACHINE SELECTION

Several factors need to be taken into consideration when selecting a machine to be used in a roll forming operation. These include load capacity, section size, section shape, and roll changeover.

### Load Capacity

The type and thickness of the material determine to a large extent the load capacity that a given roll forming machine is required to produce. If material type and thickness change, it is best to select a machine that can provide the additional capacity.

When material up to 0.060" (1.50 mm) thick is being formed, a machine with 1 1/2" (38 mm) diam spindles should be used as long as the part is not too wide. With material over 0.060" (1.5 mm), but less than 0.080" (2 mm), a machine with 2" (50 mm) diam spindles should be used. As the material thickness increases, the diameter of the spindles must also increase to provide strength to create the pressure required to do the forming. Center distances must be increased as the size of the shape and the movement of material between forming stations increases. These distances are usually determined by the machine builder.

### Size of Section

Wide roll-formed sections require wide roll spaces. To support the pressure of the rolls, the spindle shafts must be large enough in diameter to prevent shaft deflection when forming. The distance between the centerline of the bottom spindle and the machine bed determines the maximum roll diameter and hence maximum section depth.

### Shape of Section

The more complex the shape, the greater number of passes (pairs of rolls) required to roll form the section. It is best to select a machine that provides the flexibility to add or subtract pairs of rolls in accordance to the part design.

### Roll Changeover

Roll changeover can be costly and time consuming as material variations may require different roll pressure settings. When several part configurations must be run on one machine, it is best to select a machine that permits the tooling to be changed quickly. If only two or three profiles are run, the side-by-side and the double-high machines are possible selections. The changeover can be performed quickly without losing valuable production time. Another machine to consider is the rafted machine.

## AUXILIARY EQUIPMENT

A wide variety of equipment is used in conjunction with the roll forming machine to produce quality workpieces during a continuous forming operation. This equipment can generally be divided into five categories: (1) material handling equipment, (2) measuring systems, (3) preroll forming equipment, (4) roll forming accessory equipment, (5) post roll forming equipment.

### Material Handling Equipment

This equipment transfers the material from one piece of equipment to the other and permits continuous line operation. This equipment includes an uncoiler, an accumulator, a pre-punch table, and a runout table.

**Uncoiler.** An uncoiler supports the coil while permitting the material to be fed into the roll forming machine without causing excessive drag and overrun. The two primary types of uncoilers used in the roll forming operation are the expandable mandrel or reel type and the cradle type.

*Expandable mandrel.* On the expandable mandrel type of uncoiler, the inside diameter of the coil is gripped and supported by the mandrel. The mandrel is expanded manually, hydraulically, or pneumatically. A drive mechanism and built-in drag brake can also be incorporated to facilitate the feeding of the material. The mandrel can support a wide range of coil widths and weights and can also be designed to support multiple coils. An expandable type of uncoiler is suited for high-speed roll forming lines and for situations in which material surface appearance is critical as a result of the surface's being precoated or highly polished.

*Cradle.* A cradle type of uncoiler is usually less expensive then the expandable mandrel type. The coil is supported in the cradle on rollers by the outside diameter of the coil. Power-driven cradles are available. Generally, the use of cradle-type uncoilers is limited to line speeds less than 150 fpm (45 m/min). Because the coil rotates in the cradle, it is not recommended for precoated material and for situations in which material edge and surface appearance are critical.

**Accumulator.** An accumulator stores material in an amount sufficient for a continuous flow to the roll forming machine when a new coil is installed and then welded to the old coil. It is generally incorporated in the roll forming line after the shear and end welder and before any other preroll forming equipment. Figure 8-18 shows an accumulator that utilizes two concentric rolls to store the incoming material. The material is stored in the accumulator when the coil is uncoiled at a faster rate than the speed of the roll forming line.

An accumulator can handle up to 3000 ft (900 m) of stock and permits roll forming speeds up to 500 fpm (150 m/min). The thickness of stock that can be handled ranges from 0.015-0.25" (0.4-6 mm).

**Prepunch or prenotch table.** The main purpose of the prepunch or prenotch table is to support the material as it comes out of the punch press and before it enters the roll forming machine. It also serves as a mounting surface for the trip-mechanism that actuates the punch press. Generally, the table should be longer than the longest part that is to be roll formed. The selection of the table surface is based on the finish of the material sliding on it. Some of the common surfaces vary from flat stock to "U" channel using hot-rolled steel; cold-rolled steel; chrome-plated, cold-rolled steel; hard plastic; or nylon for the sliding surface.

**Runout table.** Runout tables are used to handle the roll formed part after it has been cut off. It can have a flat, inclined,

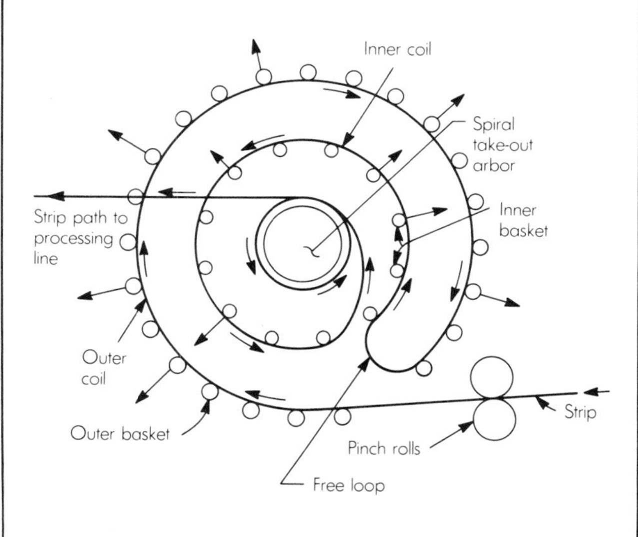


**Fig. 8-18 An accumulator stores material in the concentric rolls to permit a continuous flow of material during coil changeover.** (*Kent Corp.*)

or roller surface, or a conveyor may be used. Some tables have a material push-off system designed into them; others act as a dump table. On occasion, the runout table has the cutoff press triggering mechanism incorporated into it.

## Measuring Systems

When using coil or precut material on a roll forming line, it is necessary to measure the flat material or formed part to punch the material or cut the part to length. The measuring device used depends on the speed of the line and the length accuracy desired.

**Punch press.** To trigger the punch press, a mechanical-type mechanism mounted on the prepunch table is connected to the flying die by an adjustable rod (see Fig 8-19). As the material is fed, fingers in the mechanism drop into the prepunched holes, moving the mechanism and die forward. The movement actuates a switch which triggers the press. An adjustable cam or air cylinder disengages the fingers from the holes allowing the mechanism and die to return to their original position. This mechanism can maintain length tolerances of ±1/32" (0.8 mm) at line speeds up to 160 fpm (50 m/min).

Electronic rotary encoders consisting of a measuring wheel and an encoder can also be used to trigger the punch press. The wheel rotates as the material is fed through the roll forming line and sends signals to the encoder. At the specified part length, the encoder triggers the press. This device is usually used with a die accelerator and can maintain length tolerances of ±1/16 to ±3/32" (1.5 to 2.5 mm) at speeds up to 160 fpm (50 m/min). Length changes can be made quickly, but accuracy can be affected by vibration, measuring wheel slippage or distortion, machine reversal, and material acceleration or deceleration.

**Cutoff devices.** Several devices are used to trigger a cutoff system. Some of these include the positive stop, flag trip, spring-loaded die fingers, electronic rotary encoders, and closed-loop devices.

*Positive stop.* A positive stop is made up of a traveling plate mounted on the runout table and is attached to the cutoff die. When the rolled part hits the stop plate, the stop plate pulls the die forward and triggers the press. After the part is cut, the stop plate opens to allow the part to pass. This device can maintain length tolerances of ±1/32" (0.8 mm), but is limited to shapes that are rigid enough to move the stop plate and die. To prevent weaker parts from buckling, a die accelerator, activated by a limit switch in front of the stop plate, is used to start the entire mass moving.

*Flag trip.* A flag trip consists of a plate attached to a pivot shaft and limit switch on the runout table. When the rolled part hits the plate, the plate pivots out of the way actuating a microswitch that triggers the cutoff press. Length tolerances are generally ±1/8" (3 mm). Since this device does not have to move the die, there are no problems due to the rolled part buckling out of shape. This device is economical and can accommodate higher line speeds than the positive stop when cutting the same part.

*Spring-loaded die fingers.* Spring-loaded fingers ride on the rolled section of the material and enter holes or slots that have been punched prior to roll forming. The fingers pull the sliding die forward and trigger the press. The fingers are disengaged from the cut part using the blade, a cam, or an air cylinder.

*Electronic rotary encoder.* The electronic rotary encoder used for cutoff systems is the same as the encoders used for the punch press.

*Closed-loop device.* The closed-loop device is the most expensive measuring device used for length measurement. It

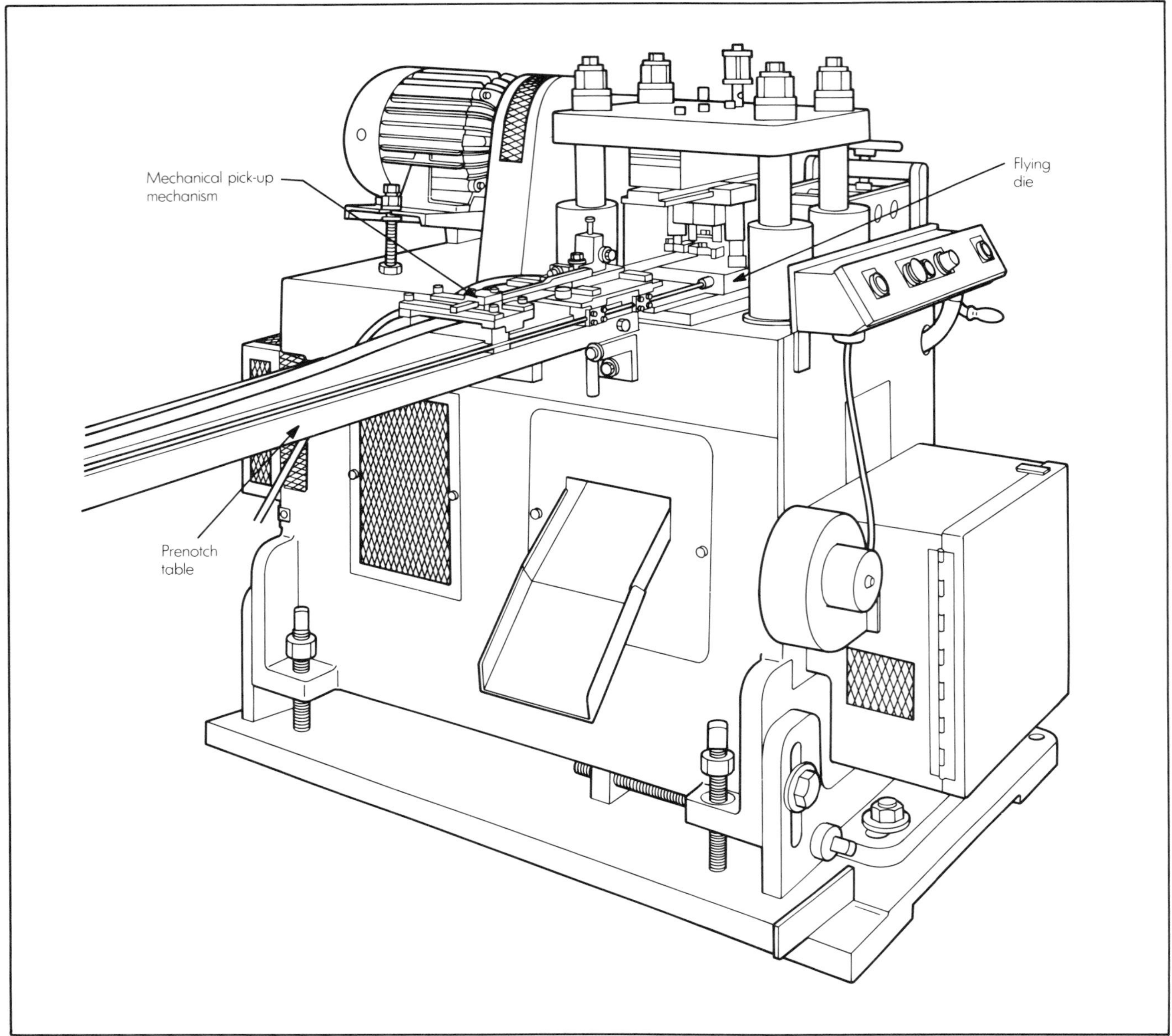


**Fig. 8-19 A four-post, mechanical punch press incorporating a flying die.** (*Tishken Products Co.*)

consists of a direct-current motor that is connected to the die accelerator and incorporates a tachometer and a pulse generator to monitor the position and speed. Before the cutoff press or saw is triggered, the motor accelerates the die to line speed. After the cut, the motor returns the die to its original position. This device can maintain length tolerances of ±1/32″ (0.8 mm).

## Preroll Forming Equipment

This group of equipment performs operations that must be done before the material can be fed into the roll forming machine. These operations include straightening, joining, notching, punching, and knurling.

**Leveler.** A leveler is used to remove the coil set from the material as it comes off the uncoiler so that the material entering the punch press or roll forming machine will be flat.

The leveler consists of a series of cylindrical rolls through which the material is driven or pulled. The upper rolls are adjustable so that the desired flatness can be obtained. Generally, the leveler is used when material greater than 3/16″ (5 mm) thick is roll formed or when coil set from lighter gages will affect the roll forming operation.

**End joiner.** An end joiner usually consists of a shear and a welder and is used to connect the ends of the coils to permit a continuous strip of metal to enter the roll forming machine. The shear is used to square the coil ends before they are joined. In some cases, the ends of the coils are overlapped and then the shear is triggered. The proper gap is adjusted manually or automatically. When the two ends are in the proper position, the torch, by means of a horizontal traverse, is passed over the ends either manually or automatically. The most common type of welder for material up to 0.06″ (1.5 mm) is the tungsten inert gas (TIG) welder; for thicker material, the metallic inert gas (MIG) welder is used.

If the end joiner is used in conjuction with an accumulator, the roll forming machine can operate continuously. Without an accumulator, the line must be stopped to permit the two ends to be joined. The end joiner also eliminates the problem of always having to thread the material through the rolls and eliminates the waste of material that is too short for part production, providing a weld can be tolerated in the finished part.

**Punching or notching press.** Punching or notching can be performed before or after the material has been formed. If close tolerances must be maintained, it is better to perform the punching after the material has been roll formed. On certain part designs, a punching die can be incorporated with the cutoff die to eliminate the need for an extra operation.

A four-post punching or notching press (see Fig. 8-19) is more versatile than a two-post press because it permits the use of larger dies as well as off-center punching. When a long punching pattern is required, it is possible to use a series of dies and connect them with a link. The press can be powered mechanically, hydraulically, or pneumatically. Two advantages of hydraulically and pneumatically powered presses are the ability to adjust the stroke and the die height.

Presses can be equipped with a stationary or flying type of die. With the stationary type, the die remains fixed during the punching or notching operation. This type of die requires a means for material accumulation before and after the press so that the roll forming machine can operate continuously. The flying type incorporates a die that slides with the material as it is being punched. A cushion or snubber should be installed on the entry end of the slide to cushion the return of the die.

**Embossing machine.** An embossing machine is used for both decorative and functional purposes. For producing products such as aluminum siding, embossing can give the aluminum a wood grained pattern. This enables the manufacturer to use a lower cost grade of material and/or material that has minor surface defects. Embossing also strengthens the material, which in turn strengthens the part. Generally, embossing is performed prior to the roll forming operation. However, it can be performed on larger panels to increase their rigidity after they are roll formed.

The embossing machine can be incorporated into the roll forming machine, or it can be a separate unit. Embossing rolls can either be mated or unmated. Mated rolls are two engraved rolls, male and female, that are driven by a pair of gears. Unmated rolls have one driven, engraved roll that is run against a rubber, paper, or polyurethane roll. Generally, the engraved rolls are steel.

## Roll Former Accessories

These accessories are used to aid the roll former in forming and conditioning the part. The accessories include guides, edge conditioners, knurling units, rotary punch units, intermediate rolls, straighteners, stock puller units, and coiling and curving units. Other accessories, such as embossers, slitters, and rotary markers, can also be incorporated to perform the necessary operations.

**Guides.** Two types of guides align the stock to the forming rolls: (1) entrance guides and (2) intermediate guides.

*Entrance guides.* An entrance guide is designed to keep the material in proper alignment with the first pass of forming rolls. To assist the entrance guide, it is beneficial for the first several passes to have edge guides designed in them. This helps to ensure good strip tracking. Most entrance guides are adjustable vertically as well as horizontally and are made with hardened steel rollers or blocks. When painted or polished material is formed, entrance guides are often bronze, aluminum, or wear-resistant synthetic material.

*Intermediate guides and shoes.* When parts are being formed, it is sometimes necessary to add guides between roll passes to lead the material from one roll pass to the next without damaging the leading edge of the material or possibly breaking the rolls. To keep the number of these guides to a minimum, they can be added at the time the rolls are being tested in the machine and need only be used when necessary. The need for these guides is also minimized by employing several more roll passes than would normally be used for forming a shape.

When a flat strip of metal has the edges bent up to form a channel section, the tendency is for the whole length of the piece to assume a curve downward. The shoe and guide arrangement shown in Fig. 8-20 can be employed to control the lateral movement.

The exit end of the guide should be positioned as close to the next set of rolls as possible to ensure proper guiding action. The entry end of the guide should be belled out to allow easy entry of the material and should gradually conform to the shape of the part being rolled.

If a fine finish on the product is not necessary, guides and shoes can be made of nickel, iron, or semisteel. Chrome plating on the wearing surfaces increases life and reduces galling. For coated and decorative finished pieces, bronze, nylon, and hard polyurethanes are good materials for guides and shoes. A big drawback, however, is their short life. Guides and shoes tend to scratch and cut the stock, so great care is necessary in their design and adjustment.

**Edge conditioners.** Grooved side rolls can be mounted at or near the entrance of the roll forming machine to remove sharp edges left from the slitting operation.

**Rotary punch unit.** A special type of punching is done using a rotary punch unit consisting of an independently mounted stand in which a top rotary punch wheel is mounted over a bottom rotary die wheel. As the material is fed into the roll forming machine, the rotary wheel punches out the desired pattern in a continuous manner. This method is generally limited to thinner materials and is used when high speed and production quantities are required. It can also be used for producing many different configurations in flat material. The units can be free-wheeling or power driven.

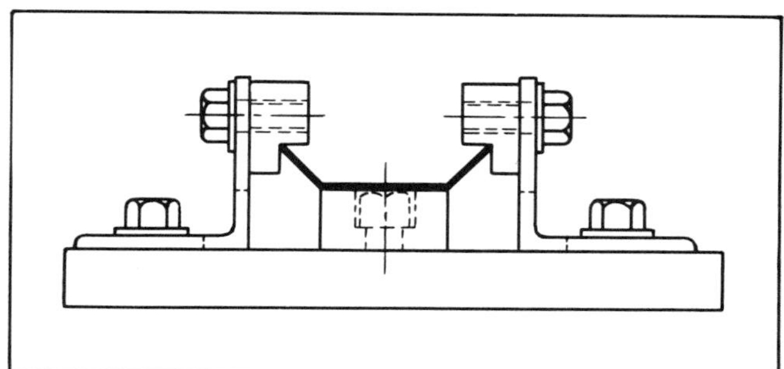

**Fig. 8-20 Typical shoe and guide arrangement.**

## ROLL FORMING MACHINES

**Knurling unit.** A knurling unit mounted at the entrance of the roll forming machine in an adjustable guide contains two pairs of upper and lower knurling wheels. The pattern is a straight, serrated type of knurl rather than the diamond or crosshatch type that is generally associated with machining. Normally the knurl is located on the outer area of the material, but it can be located anywhere on the material. Pressure on the wheels is adjusted manually to achieve the proper depth for the knurl.

The knurling unit is normally used in conjunction with the arbor or mandrel seam attachment when lock-seamed tubing is fabricated. Knurling the edges of the lock seam provides a positive gripping action which prevents the seam from shifting.

**Intermediate rolls.** In many cases work can be accomplished more effectively with auxiliary or intermediate rolls mounted between or beside main forming rolls. The two most frequently used types are idler rolls and driven rolls.

*Idler rolls.* Idler rolls are bronze-bushed or run on ball bearings and are mounted on a nonrotating pin or shaft. The roll rotates on the pin or shaft as the part passes through; the speed of the part passing through determines the speed of the idler rolls. Within reasonable limits, the diameter of these rolls can be made any convenient diameter with regard to space available, diameter of pin, etc.

For certain types of sections, idler rolls are the only means to obtain the required form unless guides are employed. Guides have been found less satisfactory than rolls because of the sliding action and resulting heat and friction.

Roll forming of tubing, both butt and lock seamed, is an example in which much of the forming is done by idler rolls. As shown in Fig. 8-21, idler rolls are also used to carry the side downward from 90°. In this case the rolls are mounted on the outside of the section and back each other up; in the case of an unsymmetrical section, the edge might be turned down on only one side with the rolls placed as shown in Fig. 8-21, *d*.

Mounting is generally the most troublesome drawback of idler rolls. In most cases, idler rolls should be designed to permit some adjustability. In a machine where the space is limited, considerable ingenuity is necessary to achieve a mounting to give the right forming action and the necessary rigidity in the working position and yet have the necessary flexibility of adjustment.

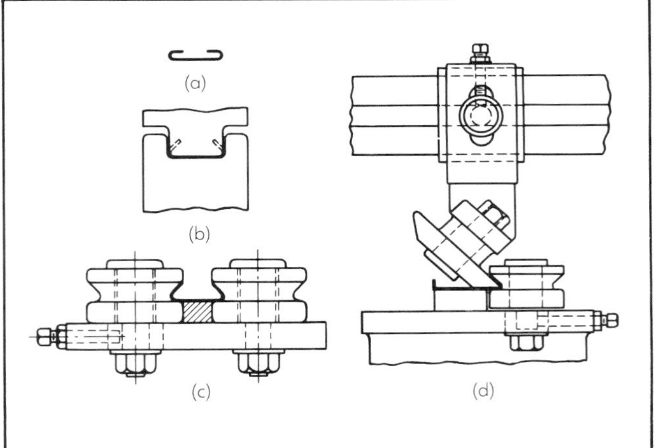


**Fig. 8-21 Channel section (a) is first formed with right-angled sides by main drive rolls at (b); vertical idler rolls (c) turn down the edges. Only one edge of section is formed by idler roll arrangement (d).**

*Driven rolls.* Driven rolls are used to finish-form a section like the one shown in Fig. 8-22. This section is rolled in the flat, and the sides formed up as far as possible; that is, as long as it is possible to get a top roll in to drive a section. After the sides are formed up, a pair of driven side rolls must be employed to close the section and drive it out of the machine.

To install driven side rolls, the top shaft would have to be removed. The machined slide ordinarily used by the top box can be used as a guiding surface for the bracket (Fig. 8-22). The driven side roll can be mounted on the hub of the bevel pinion which is bushed on a vertical pin anchored to a bracket on the housing. The bevel pinion in turn meshes with a bevel gear mounted on the bottom shaft of the roll stand. Ordinarily, the driven side rolls are smaller in diameter than the vertical rolls; consequently, their speed of rotation must be greater to give the same linear speed. To accomplish this, the bevel gears are proportioned to give the correct ratio.

**Straighteners.** Generally, all roll-formed pieces require a certain amount of straightening to achieve a straight finished part. The problem of straightening a section as it comes from the rolling machine is that it is often difficult to determine the direction of the deviation. To be of practical value, a straightener must be adjustable to compensate for bow, sweep, or spiral twist.

Straighteners must be kept as close as possible to the last set of rolls. A tendency to crookedness can be removed by light pressure in the right direction if the straightener is mounted close to the last set of rolls. If the space between the straightener and the last roll pass is allowed to become large, it will be difficult to overcome the crookedness. The last set of rolls is actually used as the fulcrum point for any type of straightener. Letting the material run out too far would mean an increased tendency to run out of line. Moreover, the last end of the piece would be unstraightened for a length equal to the distance from the centerline of the rolls to the front of the straighteners.

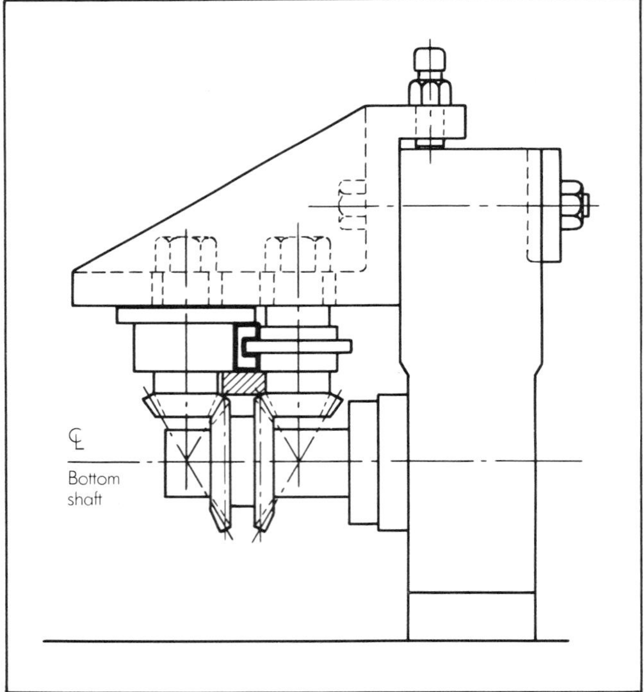


**Fig. 8-22 Driven side rolls are used for forming complicated sections.**

The three main types of straighteners used are roller, shoe/die, and guide type (see Fig. 8-23). Another type of straightner is the "Turk's head." Turk's heads are used to straighten and reshape tubing. Additional information on straightening is given in Chapter 10.

*Roller straightener.* The roller straightener consists of two to five rolls that match the outer shape of the part being straightened. It is best suited for straightening material that requires a good surface finish and for operating at higher production speeds.

*Shoe/die straighteners.* Shoe/die straighteners have the same cross-sectional shape as the material and are usually made out of bronze. They are best suited for sections having prenotched areas because they help to control end flare. The length of the shoe is generally 4-10" (100-250 mm) long. The life of the shoe straightener is not as long the roller straightener, but it is less expensive to replace the shoe for a different part configuration than it is to replace the rolls.

*Turk's head straightener.* The Turk's head contains four separate rollers, 90° apart, that are adjusted individually to achieve the desired straightness or shape. It is primarily used to straighten tubing and is not suited for products that contain deep grooves or flutes or similar cross sections. It is also used to reshape round tubes into various other shapes, such as squares, rectangles, triangles, or other variations of the original round tube. Usually more than one Turk's head must be mounted in series to form the different shapes.

**Stock puller unit.** A stock puller unit is used to pull the remaining portion or tail of the rolled material out of the rolls. A puller reduces the problem of roll slippage on the material which results in galling on the rolls. This unit is useful when lock-seamed sections are formed or when arbors or mandrels are used to form the section part.

The stock puller unit is located on the exit end of the roll forming machine and consists of two horizontally mounted shafts. The upper shaft moves downward pneumatically or mechanically to contact the material, and the lower shaft has a serrated roll on it to grip the material. Power to the driveshaft is usually through the roll former drive.

**Coiling and curving attachments.** Rings and sweeps of uniform radius can be produced in the roll forming process by substituting curving devices in place of the straightening devices. For coiling rings, a curving shoe, fitted very closely into the last roll stage, is generally used. This curving shoe is best suited for producing small-diameter rings of light-gage material. For curves of large radius and for curving heavy-gage material, a bending or curving roll is mounted after the final forming stage. It is adjustably mounted to provide for variations in material and to change the radius of the curve when necessary. Special flying-shear cutoff equipment is sometimes used to cut off individual rings, but often a long helix is formed and individual rings are cut from the helix in a separate operation.

## Post Roll Forming Equipment

Equipment in this category enables the manufacturer to produce roll-formed pieces that are cut to their proper length and to punch holes and slots in the finished part. Special curving and bending equipment can also be incorporated that would normally require secondary operations.

As most roll-formed products are produced from coil stock, a means of cutting the formed shape to length must be provided. The two types of cutoff systems that are generally used are the flying die type and the circular saw cutter. Both systems can be

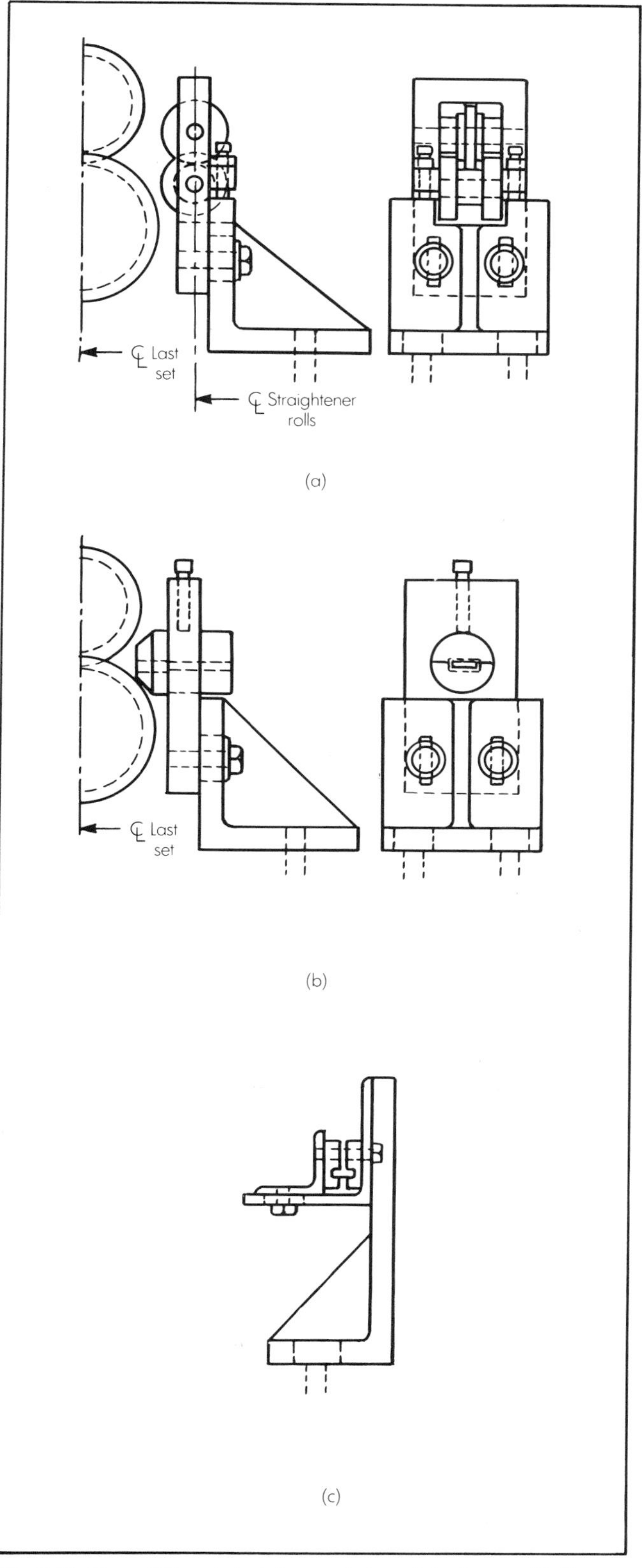


**Fig. 8-23 Three different straightener designs: (a) roll type, (b) die type, and (c) guide type.**

triggered manually or automatically. To correctly select the proper cutoff system, it is necessary to consider the volume (daily production as well as total job production), material thickness, line speed, length and cross section of piece, end product finish, and required machine versatility.

**Flying die cutoff system.** The flying die type of cutoff system is usually the fastest, most efficient, and least expensive of the various cutoff systems. Within this classification are two separate types: the slug-type and the slugless-type die. The flying dies are generally mounted on die slide rails and are actuated by a press that is mechanically, hydraulically, or pneumatically powered. The die travels with the material as it is cut; after completing the "up-stroke," the die returns to its starting position.

**Circular saw.** This type of cutoff system incorporates a circular saw mounted on a movable table. It has the capacity to cut both light and heavy stock and does not flatten or deform the ends. Generally, the circular saw is required to run at slower forming speeds than the die-type machine and it has a tendency to create burrs. Instead of using the metal blade, an abrasive wheel may be used which reduces the amount of burr by grinding the material instead of milling it. One advantage of the circular saw is that it has the capacity to cut the workpiece at various angles.

# ROLL FORMING TOOLING

Tooling used in roll forming includes the forming rolls and the dies for punching and cutting off the material. Rotary punch units, knurling units, guides, and intermediate rolls are discussed in the section "Auxiliary Equipment." Tube mills require some additional tooling to weld, size, and straighten the tubes as they are produced on the machine.

## FORMING ROLLS

The rolls are the tools that do the actual forming of the material as it moves through the roll forming machine. Several factors need to be considered when designing the rolls to form a particular part. These include the number of required passes, the material width, the flower design, the roll design parameters, and the roll material. "Flower" is the name given to the progressive section contours starting with the flat material and ending with the desired section profile.

### Number of Passes

Roll forming material into a desired final shape is a progressive operation in which small amounts of forming are performed at each pass or pair of rolls. The amount of change of shape or contour in each pass must be restricted so that the required bends can be formed without elongating the material. Too few passes can cause distortion and loss of tolerances; too many passes increase the initial tooling cost.

Generally, the number of passes depends upon the properties of the material and the complexity of the shape. Other areas to consider are part width, horizontal center distance between the individual stations, and part tolerances. The number of passes must be increased as the tolerances of the shape become tighter.

**Material.** Material thickness, hardness, and composition all affect the number of passes required to achieve a desired shape. As the thickness of the metal increases, the number of passes required to form the material increases. Steel that has a high yield strength should be overformed approximately 2° and then brought back to finish size on the final pass. Overforming compensates for springback that is encountered when steels having high yield strength are formed. Material that is coated or that has a polished surface generally requires more passes than uncoated material. Precut material may also require more passes so that the rolls can pick up the leading end of each section.

**Shape complexity.** Shape complexity is determined by the number of bends and the total number of degrees that the formed part must be bent. It is also influenced by the symmetry of the part design. The forming angle method is a rule of thumb which roll designers use to determine the approximate number of passes.

On simple shapes, a forming angle of 1-2° is recommended. This forming angle is based on the amount of bending performed for every inch of distance between station centers (horizontal center distances). The minimum forming length for a single bend is determined by multiplying the height of the desired section by the cotangent of the forming angle. This length is then divided by the distance between station centers on a given machine to determine the approximate number of passes. For multiple bends, the number of passes must be determined for each bend and then, after the formation of bends have been combined where possible, the approximate number of passes can be determined.

For shapes containing short legs, such as in lock-seamed tubing (see Fig. 8-24), it is necessary to follow a particular forming sequence. Although the metal could be formed in one pass, several passes are required to achieve the final shape, due to the inability to make a roll to form this shape.

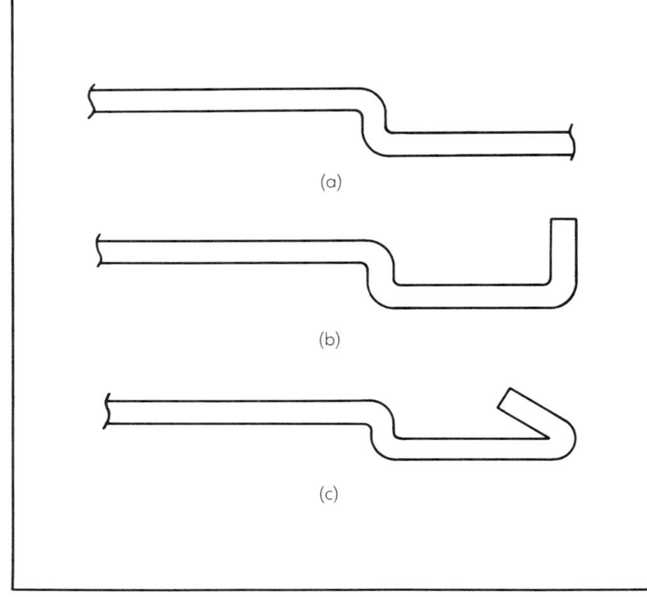


**Fig. 8-24 Certain shapes must follow an order of forming: (a) first station, (b) second station, and (c) third station.**

**Horizontal center distance.** If the machine on which the section must be run is predetermined, the machine's specifications and limitations have a bearing on the number of passes required. The machine's distance between stations (horizontal center distance) may dictate more stations if that distance is too short. The total distance from flat material to the finished section is more critical than the number of stations, since undue stresses are created by forming too fast.

## Strip Width

The width of the flat material needed to produce the shape can be determined by making an enlarged layout of the part and dividing it into its component curved and straight sections. The bend allowance for the curved sections must be calculated. The width of material required for producing the shape is obtained by totaling the individual lengths of these sections. This width is theoretical only and usually must be modified slightly when the part is run.

**Bend allowance.** Bend allowance or developed width is the amount of material required to properly form a curved section of a particular shape. Several methods are used, and each designer has a particular preference. Of the three methods described in this section, methods one and two use general equations and can be employed for all shapes. Method three is generally employed only for welded tubing. The equations given are applicable when low-carbon steel is formed; therefore, the values should be increased slightly when less-formable material is formed. For additional information on bend allowance, refer to Chapter 10, "Bending and Straightening."

**Method one.** Using this method, bend allowance is calculated as follows:

$$BA = R\frac{\alpha}{57.3} \quad (1)$$

If the inside bend radius is less than two times the material thickness, then:

$$R = R_i + 0.4T \quad (2)$$

where:

$BA$ = bend allowance, in. (mm)
$R$ = bend radius, in. (mm)
$\alpha$ = angle through which material is bent, degrees
$R_i$ = inside bend radius, in. (mm)
$T$ = metal thickness, in. (mm)

Example:

Determine the bend allowance for the bend shown in Fig. 8-25, *a*. Since $R_i$ is less than two times the material thickness, then:

$$R = R_i + 0.4T = 0.062 + 0.4(0.04) = 0.078'' \text{ (2 mm)}$$

$$BA = R\frac{\alpha}{57.3} = 0.078\frac{90}{57.3} = 0.122'' \text{ (3.1 mm)}$$

If the inside bend radius is greater than two times the material thickness, then:

$$R = R_i + 0.5T \quad (3)$$

Example:

Determine the bend allowance for the bend shown in Fig. 8-25, *b*. Since $R_i$ is greater than two times the material thickness, then:

$$R = R_i + 0.5T = 0.125 + 0.5(0.04) = 0.145'' \text{ (3.7 mm)}$$

$$BA = R\frac{\alpha}{57.3} = 0.145\frac{90}{57.3} = 0.228'' \text{ (5.8 mm)}$$

If the material is bent through a 90° zero radius or a 180° zero radius, the bend allowance, $BA$, is 1/3 T or 2/3 T respectively.

**Method two.** Another method used to determine the bend allowance for a roll-formed part is with the equation:

$$BA = (T \times P + R_i)0.01745\alpha \quad (4)$$

where:

$BA$ = bend allowance, in. (mm)
$T$ = material thickness, in. (mm)
$P$ = material thickness, %
$R_i$ = inside bend radius, in. (mm)
$\alpha$ = angle through which the material is bent, degrees

The percentage of material thickness (bend factor) is based on the ratio of the inside bend radius and the material thickness. The ratio is obtained by dividing the inside bend radius by the material thickness. After the ratio is obtained, the percentage of material thickness is determined using Fig. 8-26 or the following calculations:

For a ratio less than one:

$$P = R_A \times 0.04 + 0.3 \quad (5)$$

For a ratio greater than one or equal to one:

$$P = (R_A - 1.0)0.6 + 0.34 \quad (6)$$

where:

$P$ = material thickness, %
$R_A$ = inside bend radius/material thickness, $R_i/T$

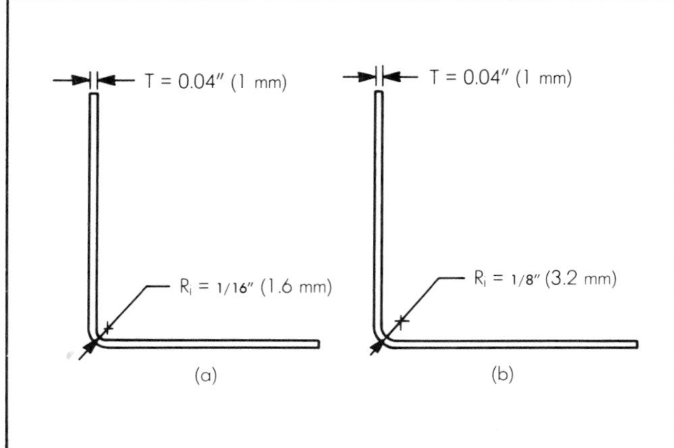


**Fig. 8-25 Determining the bend allowance for a bend: (a) inside radius is less than two times material thickness; (b) inside radius is greater than two times material thickness.**

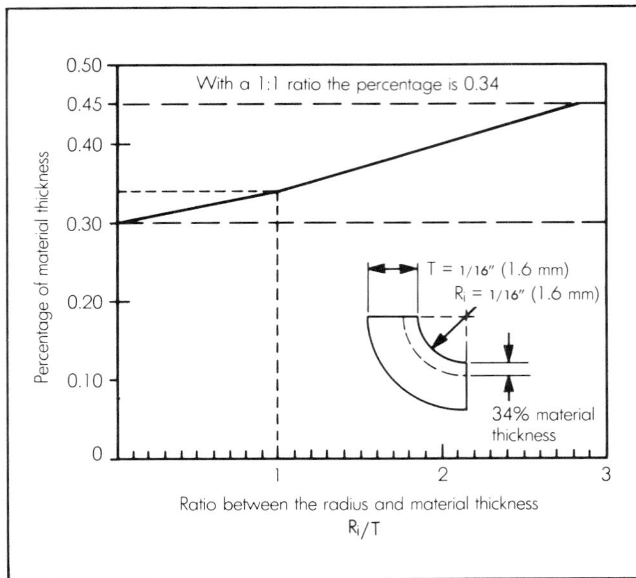


**Fig. 8-26 Chart used to determine percentage of material thickness required when calculating bend allowance.** (*Design Data Systems Corp.*)

If the percentage is calculated to be greater than 0.45, the value is 0.45.

Example:

Calculate the bend allowance of a section using Fig. 8-26. The material thickness and inside bend radius are both 1/16" (1.6 mm).

$$R_A = \frac{R_i}{T} = \frac{0.062}{0.062} = 1$$

From Fig. 8-26, the percentage of material thickness, $P$, is 0.34, therefore:

$$BA = [(0.062 \times 0.34) + 0.062]0.01745(90)$$
$$= 0.130'' \text{ (3.3 mm)}$$

**Method three.** When forming welded tubing, it is necessary to allow for welding and sizing the tube to its finished size. The material width for a given diameter and wall thickness can be determined using:

$$W = (OD - T)\pi + A_S + A_W \qquad (7)$$

where:

$W$ = material width, in. (mm)
$T$ = material or wall thickness, in. (mm)
$OD$ = outside diameter of tube, in. (mm)
$\pi$ = 3.1416
$A_S$ = sizing allowance; 2% over finished OD, in. (mm)
$A_W$ = weld allowance, in. (mm)
Note: wall thickness less than 0.040" (1 mm), $A_W = T$; wall thickness 0.040-0.120" (1-3 mm), $A_W = 2/3T$; wall thickness greater than 0.120" (3 mm), $A_W = 1/2T$

Example 1:

Determine material width required to form a 2" OD welded tube having a 1/16" wall thickness.

$$W = (2.00 - 0.062)3.1416 + 0.04 + 0.041 = 6.17''$$

Example 2:

Determine material width required to form a 50 mm OD welded tube having a 1.5 mm wall thickness.

$$W = (50 - 1.5)3.1416 + 1 + 1 = 152.4 \text{ mm}$$

## Flower Design

The development of the flower is the initial step in the design of roll tooling. This is the station-by-station overlay of progressive section contours starting with the flat strip width before forming, and ending with the final desired section profile (see Fig. 8-27). The flower can also be obtained by starting with the finished profile and unfolding it into a flat strip. The intermediate profiles between flat material and finished profile are graduated at a rate that enables the section to be completed in the fewest number of stations or passes without compromising general roll forming parameters. The flower shows graphically the number of passes required to roll form the given profile.

The two prime considerations in designing the flower are (1) a smooth flow of material from first to last pass and (2) maximum control over fixed dimensions while roll forming. Getting the smoothest flow of material might be visualized by considering a roll of paper rolled out long enough to crimp the end of the roll into the shape of the desired cross section. By holding both the roll and cross section taut, the flow of material will be smooth and natural. If cross sections were taken at equally spaced intervals between beginning and end, a flower would be generated, perfect in flow, but lacking in dimensional control. Most corners formed in this manner would be air formed rather than positively formed by direct roll contact. The distance from flat material to finished profile is critical; forming too fast would be unnatural to the flat strip and would create problems in a number of ways. Forming usually starts near the center and works toward the edges. This avoids tearing which might occur if the edges were formed and acted as a lock against material flow toward the center.

The second consideration, dimensional control, would best be achieved by forming each corner to its completed angle with total or maximum roll contact before proceeding to form the next corner. The object being to eliminate air forming or blind corners. This approach would require more passes to complete the section, and the flower would show a jerky, step-to-step motion rather than a flowing motion. This deviation from a smooth flow in the flower shows itself as stress in the forming process and results in forming problems.

The earlier and later passes in the flower should show less forming than the intermediate passes. The early passes must overcome the material inertia. Intermediate passes have a tendency to continue forming at the same angle as the early passes. Forming should be slowed down at the later passes so that the section loses its tendency to continue forming at its predetermined rate. Slowing the forming down in the later passes helps to eliminate flare. While the middle of a section may be dimensionally correct, the ends of the section length may not be within satisfactory tolerances due to flare.

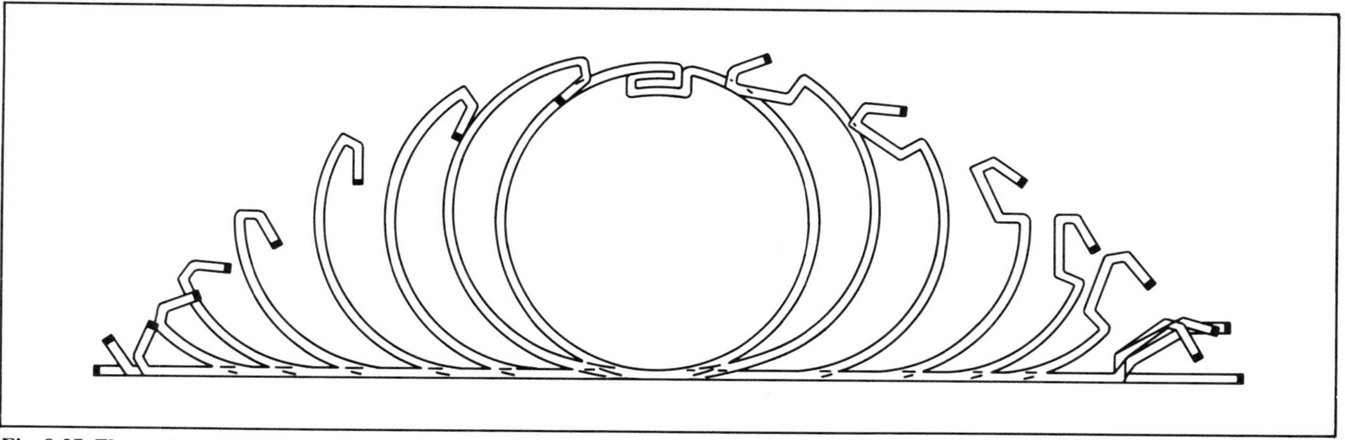

**Fig. 8-27 Flower development of a lock-seamed tube showing the progressive section contours starting with the flat strip and ending with the final section.** (*Roll Design Service*)

A compromise must be reached between optimum material flow and optimum dimensional control. When specific machines are designated to do a job, some sacrifices may be made, but design sacrifices may result in tolerance sacrifices.

**Forming position.** Several factors should be considered when deciding the position in which a section should be roll formed. A section is usually positioned so that forming is in an upward direction. For example, a channel or angle is roll formed with the legs pointing upward. Deviations from this are sometimes necessary in view of other operational or handling problems. Cutting off in a flying shear may require a certain position of the workpiece. Material with a highly polished surface on one side is sometimes better formed with the polished surface on top. This is also true of prepainted material.

**Vertical reference line.** Once the flower design has been determined, the position of the vertical reference line must be established with respect to the number and severity of bends. On symmetrical sections, it is located on the centerline of the part. For nonsymmetrical sections, the position should be determined based upon the following criteria:

1. Horizontal forming forces for bending and drawing should be balanced.
2. Vertical reference line passes through the deepest part of the section.
3. Metal movement is accomplished by forming rather than drawing.

Fulfilling these criteria is an ideal situation, and it is not always possible to do so.

**Drive line.** The drive line is a straight line from the first to the last set of rolls which is the optimum placement for equal top and bottom surface speeds. However, the rolls have variable diameters throughout their contour, and therefore various surface speeds contact the section material.

The drive line may be easily distinguishable as the longest flat area in a flat section or as the horizontal centerline through a corrugated section. The drive line is not always easily placed; and when it is, it must be placed by the roll designer in the position that previous experiences dictate. Correct choice of drive-line position allows the top and bottom rolls to pull the section material in unison. Poor choice of a drive line results in a fighting or scuffing action between top and bottom rolls, wasted horsepower, and problems in creating the desired profile.

## Roll Design Parameters

A well-designed roll set includes a well-planned flower, followed by a thoroughly thought-out roll design and carefully developed roll calculation. Roll design parameters and the type of material to be roll formed must be considered throughout the entire design process.

After the roll forming flower is completed to the satisfaction of the designer, rolls may be drawn around each overlay. For small sections, the roll material should contact the section material as much as possible. It is possible, however, to go too far and overdesign rolls, thereby creating too much roll contact, which can be detrimental. Each pass of rolls must be examined not only by itself but as part of the total job to determine where to make contact with the section material, where to exaggerate pressures or dimensions, where to clear out rolls so that material flows without restriction from one pass to another, and how to accept the section material from the previous configuration.

Early roll passes should assist the entrance guide in controlling the section laterally. Once lateral control is established with the use of roll flanges (see Fig. 8-28, *a*), further minor control may be exercised with roll stops (see Fig. 8-28, *b*). When sufficient center forming is completed to establish tracking, no further edge control is necessary (see Fig. 8-28, *c*). Symmetrical sections have a natural tendency to form evenly around the centerline and require less control than a nonsymmetrical section whose rolls may have a tendency to push or pull the section out of its correct track.

Rolls are usually made progressively larger in diameter from one pass to the next to permit the surface speed of each succeeding station to increase. The diameter increase is called "step-up." The speed differential between passes creates a tension in the section material and eliminates the possibility of an overfeed between passes. Overfeed is created by an excessive amount of work done in a single pass which stretches the section material.

Normal step-up is approximately 1/32" (0.8 mm) per pass on diameter, but varies depending upon gage of section and the particular amount of forming being done in those passes. Step-up need not be the same throughout the entire job and may diminish or disappear in later passes. Earlier passes are more susceptible to overfeed since the section material is still in a flat state and is easier to stretch. Later passes, being partially formed, become more rigid in cross section and cause the section to slip against the rolls rather than stretch the material. Thinner gages require more step-up than heavy gages since heavy gages do not stretch as readily and therefore buckle between passes. Special care should be taken in stepping up prepunched material since excessive tension between passes can stretch the length of the prepunched hole or slot.

Male corners on roll tooling do the work in the tool set, and it is usually unnecessary to back up the female radii. Angles are usually drawn to outside sharp corners, which are an ideal place to split rolls if required in that area. Outside sharp corners should not come in contact with the material to ensure that no marking occurs on the section material. Roll splits in a roll segment that touch the section material should be avoided whenever possible to avoid marking the section. Roll width should be 1 1/2 times the roll shaft diameter to prevent the rolls from cutting into the roll shafts.

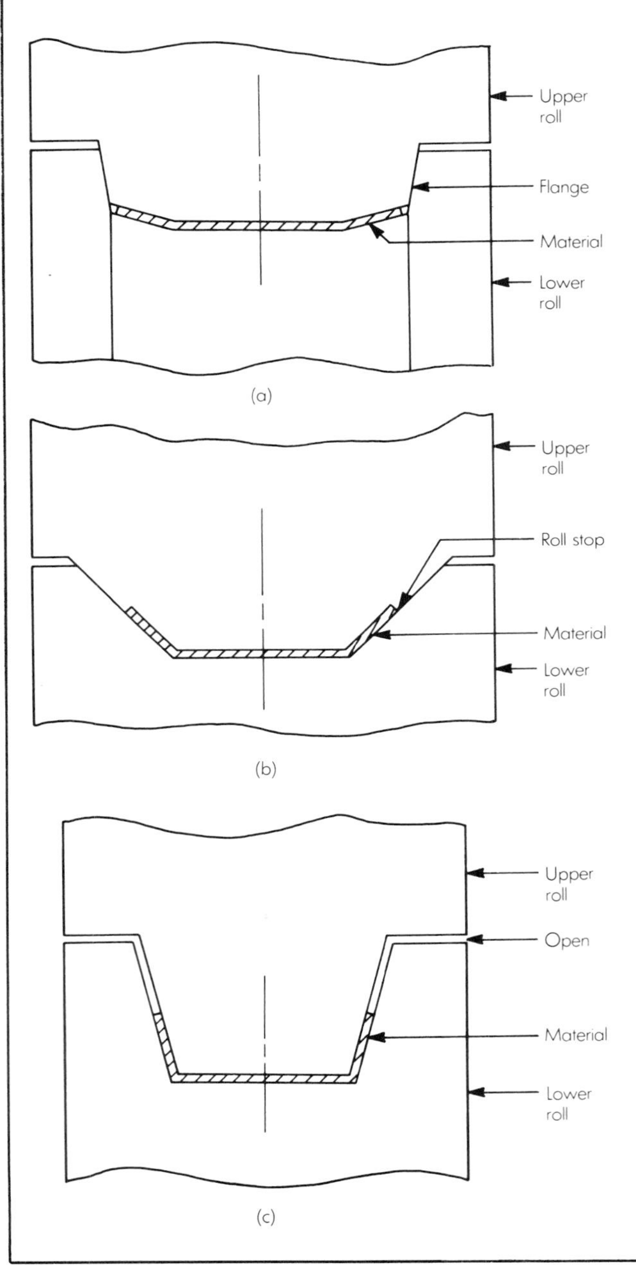


**Fig. 8-28 Roll design should incorporate (a) roll flanges to assist in lateral control, (b) roll stops to assist in minor lateral control, and (c) open roll gaps when edge control is not necessary.** (*Roll Design Service*)

Rolls may be solid or segmented (split) depending upon the complexity of the section. Solid rolls are more desirable, since fewer pieces require less handling in both manufacturing and setup and are less expensive to manufacture and handle. Rolls may be split due to weight (for ease in handling), for machinability, for insertion of shims or combination tooling, to make easily broken or wearing rolls replaceable, or to anticipate tryout changes where dimensions may be particularly critical. Very often the shape of a roll determines where it must be split.

A thin fin or projection on a roll, such as would be necessary to form the center rib as shown in Fig. 8-29, *a*, would not survive the hardening process without cracking or breaking out on the edge. This roll should be split as shown in Fig. 8-29, *b*. Its inside periphery is mounted on a hub turned on the adjoining roll, while it is driven by a pin tightly fitted in the same roll. If such a thin piece is mounted directly on the shaft with the heavy pressure to which it is subjected, it would cut into the shaft and damage it very quickly; but on the larger hub diameter of the hardened roll, it will last much longer without injury to the shaft. A roll of this shape should be made of the highest grade of tool or shock-resistant tool steel and should be very carefully hardened.

Another case in which the shape of the roll determines the location of the split is shown in Fig. 8-29, *c*. In this instance, the very sharp corners or combinations of angles and radii shown determine the placing of the split to make machining and grinding possible.

In the average shop, it is sometimes difficult to handle larger rolls and it is especially hard to mount them on the shafts of the machine if the individual sections are too unwieldy. Splitting them, in this case, makes handling easier. Designers should bear in mind that every split in a roll means the cost of at least two more ground surfaces; hence, the number of roll pieces should be as few as is consistent with good design.

In designing a set of rolls, side rolls should be used sparingly since they are more difficult to adjust properly than driven rolls; however, some sections might be impossible to make without assistance from side rolls. Sizing the width of a section directly from the side has several advantages. Driven passes have a wiping effect on all vertical legs of a section that causes friction; whereas, side rolls have a direct rolling effect. The cross section of the desired shape determines where side rolls are needed. In the forming of tubes, side rolls are an integral part of the forming process.

After rolls have worn to the point that they can no longer produce a satisfactory shape, they can be reground to produce the same shape as the original. Generally, a number of regrinds can be made before the rolls become too small to produce the desired shape.

## Material

Several types of material are used in manufacturing rolls for roll forming. The selection of the roll material is based on the type and shape of material being rolled and the quantity of parts being produced.

The most widely used type of material for roll manufacturing is an oil-hardened tool steel that has been hardened to $R_C$57-60. For extended tool life, it is best to use a high-carbon, high-chrome tool steel (D2) hardened to $R_C$59-62. On extremely tough forming applications involving high temperatures and abrasive materials, high-speed steel (M4) or carbide rolls may be required.

Forming deep sections that have sliding motion requires a material that has good frictional qualities. Cast aluminum bronze is a good choice for this type of application. To maintain a highly polished finish or prevent painted surfaces from being marred, it is advisable to chrome plate the rolls. For additional information concerning roll materials, refer to Chapter 2, "Die and Mold Materials."

## Tooling Procedure Example

The procedure for designing the rolls for a slat for roller-curtain doors (see Fig. 8-30), commonly used in warehouses and factories, would typically consist of the following steps: calculating the width of the flat material, selecting the proper size of machine, determining the flower design, and designing the rolls.

**Width calculation.** The width of the flat material necessary to produce the shape is obtained by making an enlarged layout of the part and dividing it into its component curve and straight sections. By using either Eq. (1) or Eq. (4), the bend allowance can be calculated for each of the curved sections. The width is obtained by totaling the lengths of the curved and straight sections.

**Machine selection.** When a roll forming machine for forming a shape is being selected, the type of material, hardness of material, number of bends and overall dimensions of the part must be considered, in addition to the shape, thickness, and material width. When the number of passes required to form the given shape has been determined, it is possible to determine whether an existing machine can be used.

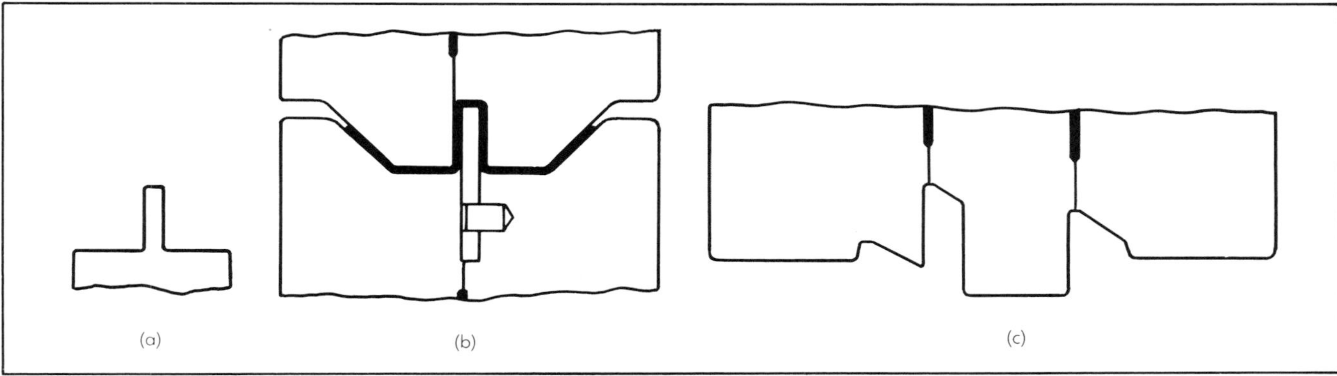


**Fig. 8-29 Split-roll design considerations: (a) thin fin projection on roll to be avoided, (b) split-roll design to overcome weakness at thin fin projection, and (c) roll splits determined by corners and grinding requirements.**

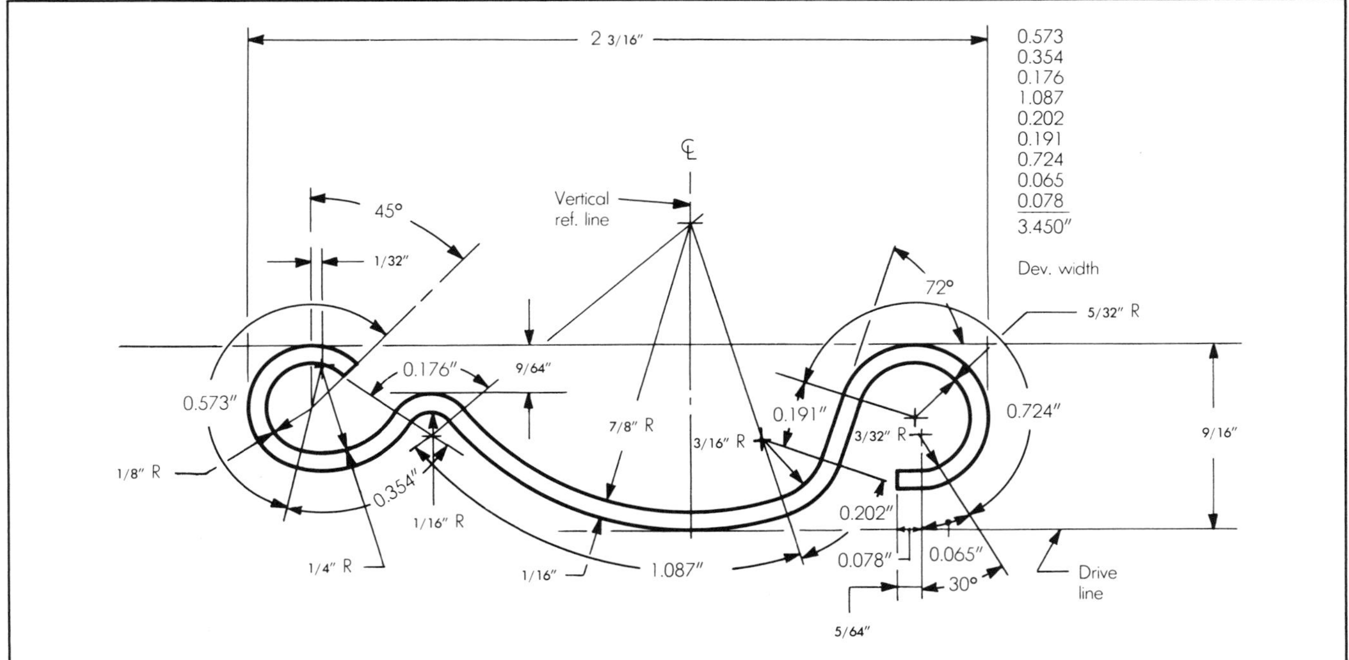


**Fig. 8-30 Cross section of part with calculated, developed strip width.**

A machine with 2 1/2″ (64 mm) diam spindles is chosen for roll forming the roller-curtain door slat in this example because the machine will be used in production over a long period of time and may possibly encounter extreme variations in thickness and hardness of material. Another reason is that the slat has a greater number of bends than the average shape, and these bends must be held to a close tolerance because the two edges of the slat form a hinge when the pieces are assembled into a door.

The gear ratio between the top and bottom rolls on this machine is 1.3:1. The slat could have been formed on a machine having a 1:1 gear ratio, but the larger machine was purchased with the probability of forming other deeper shapes.

**Flower design.** Determining the number of passes required is best done by superimposing each stage on the others in a sketch as shown in Fig. 8-31. It was decided to form this part with eight sets of horizontal rolls, one set of vertical rolls, and a guide-type straightening device. A set of horizontal rolls consists of the top and bottom roll and a vertical set of rolls consists of the inner and outer roll.

From the superimposed sketch (see Figs. 8-30 and 8-31), the vertical reference lines and drive line were established and a separate layout for each operation was made so that the rolls could be designed.

**Designing the rolls.** Since the last set of horizontal rolls is generally used to calculate the speed of the machine, the bottom roll diameter is enough greater than the minimum for the machine that it allows for redressing of the rolls to compensate for wear. The minimum diameter of the bottom roll on this machine is 5″; allowing 1 1/4″ for redress of the rolls, the pitch diameter of the last roll was established as 6.250″. To maintain tension on the strip, the pitch diameter is reduced 0.031″ on each preceding roll. Thus, the pitch diameter of the first bottom roll is 6.033″.

The pitch diameter of the upper rolls is determined by multiplying the respective pitch diameter by 1.3. The diameter of the last upper roll is 8.125″; diameter of the first roll is 7.843″.

The vertical reference line was established at 7.500″ from the flange on the inside of the roll forming stand. Since this dimension must be maintained on each set of rolls, accurately ground spacers are placed between the flange and the inside of the roll for each set of rolls. Spacers on the outside need not have an accurate width because they are backed up by a threaded nut.

The bottom roll of the first set of rolls (see Fig. 8-32) has flanges which are tapered 10° from the vertical on the sides that contact the metal and have a 3/8″ radius to guide the flat strip into the roll. The diameter of the flanges is such that the space between the flanges at the outside is more than the width of the material as it enters the rolls. The material is then guided by the flanges into correct forming position. The second and third sets of rolls have flanges of the same design for the same purpose.

Forming flanges are on the bottom roll when the metal is formed upward and on the top roll when the metal is formed downward. Both conditions occur in the fourth, fifth, sixth, and seventh sets of rolls in Fig. 8-32. All changes on contour of the rolls are dimensioned for both diameter and width; all angles are generally given from the horizontal to avoid confusion.

When the middle of the shape has been formed to the final contour and the curling of the sides is started, it is no longer necessary to confine the edges of the strip (see Fig. 8-32). Flanges are at the right of the top roll and at the left of the bottom roll because they are needed to force the material down and up, respectively.

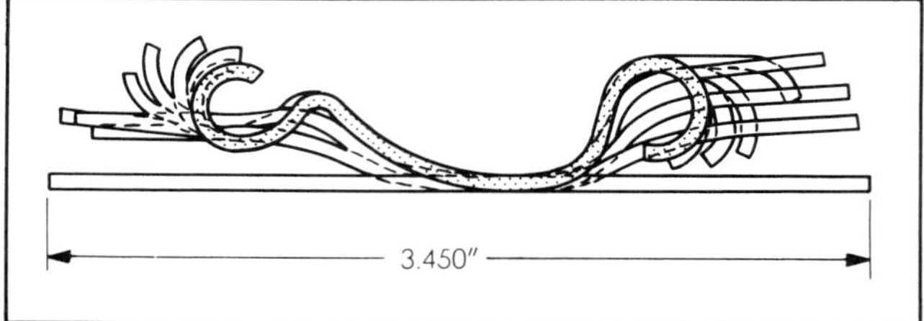


**Fig. 8-31 Superimposed forming stages show the amount of change in cross section from one stage to the next.**

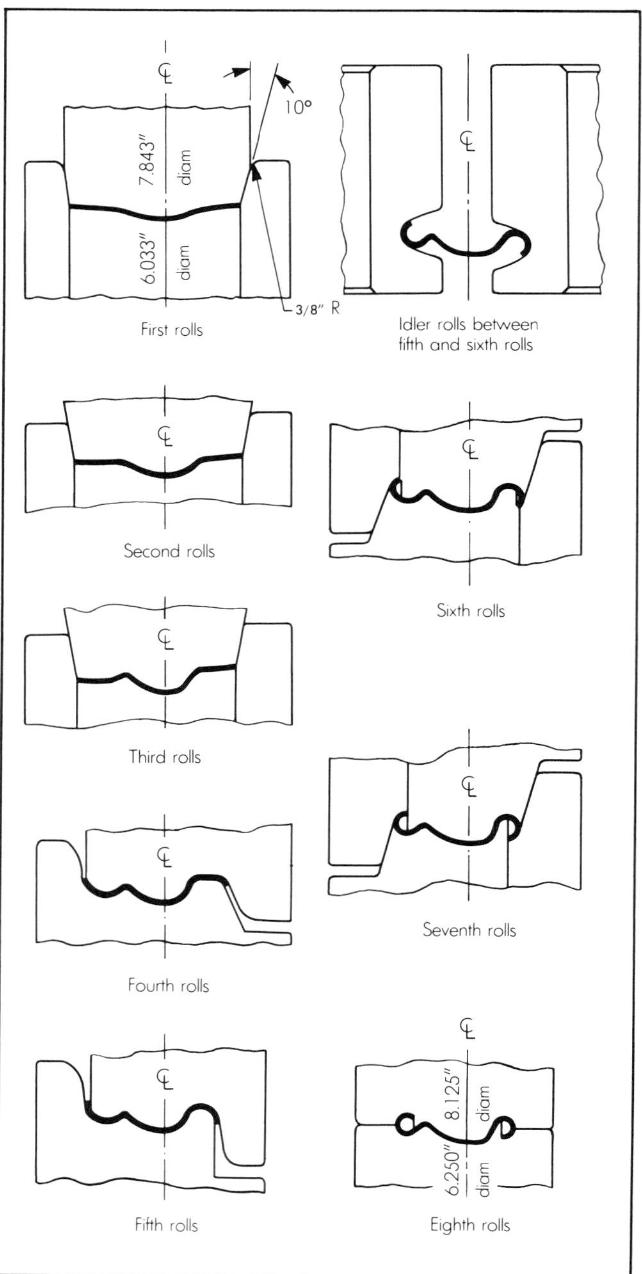


**Fig. 8-32 Rolls for forming the part illustrated in Fig. 8-30.**

In the fifth set of rolls, the middle of the slat section for the roller-curtain door remains the same but the edges are starting to be formed (see Fig. 8-32). The middle portions of all succeeding horizontal sets of rolls are the same because no further forming is required in this section of the shape.

The next pass uses a set of rolls mounted on vertical spindles that are adjustable horizontally. These rolls are not driven, but are mounted on antifriction bearings so that they rotate from the action of the shape being passed through them. Vertical rolls are necesary because the shape is being formed in a horizontal direction and without these rolls the shape would not enter the succeeding rolls without scuffing.

The first pass beyond the vertical rolls progressively shapes the sides of the strip. The seventh and eighth sets of rolls complete the shape of the strip and are designed to surround the material as much as possible. Figure 8-33 shows a simple but effective straightener guide for this shape.

## Computer Application

Computers are becoming an important aid in the design of roll forming tooling. Consistency, accuracy, and speed enable the designer to determine the optimum design for each roll pass in less time than is required when the calculations are performed by hand. The capability to display the profile of the part enables the designer to see how the material flows through each pass. This profile enables the designer to determine whether too much work is being performed at a particular pass.

The numerical information compiled by the computer can be employed to produce punched tapes used by numerically controlled machines. These tapes ensure that the rolls are accurately produced. The computer also aids in the setup of the rolls on the machine by specifying the size and locations of the required shims and spacers. All this information and data can be stored for future use and reproduced whenever necessary.

To design the rolls, information about the roll forming machine, the cross section of the final shape, and the initial forming sequence are entered in the computer program. The computer defines the coordinates of each corner numerically and displays the profile of the part at each pass and various perspectives of the flower diagram on the computer terminal. Input changes can be made to vary the material flow through the roll forming machine so that the optimum flow is achieved. Computer output includes flower diagrams, drawings of the cross-sectional shape (see Fig. 8-34), drawings of the rolls, and the tabular data defining the material and rolls. The computer can also produce the tapes used in the manufacturing of the rolls on numerically controlled machines.

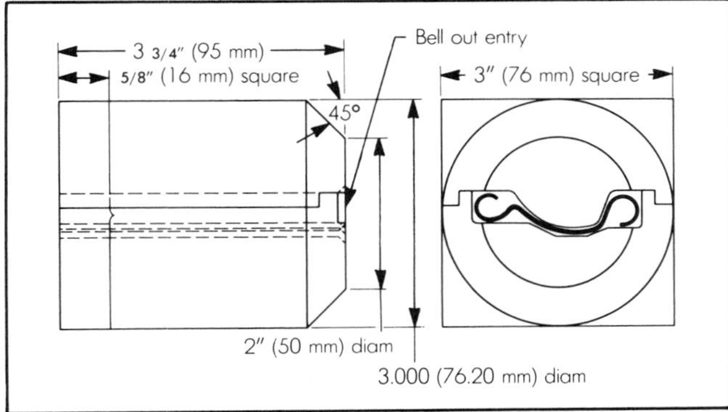


**Fig. 8-33 Straightening guide for part illustrated in Fig. 8-30.**

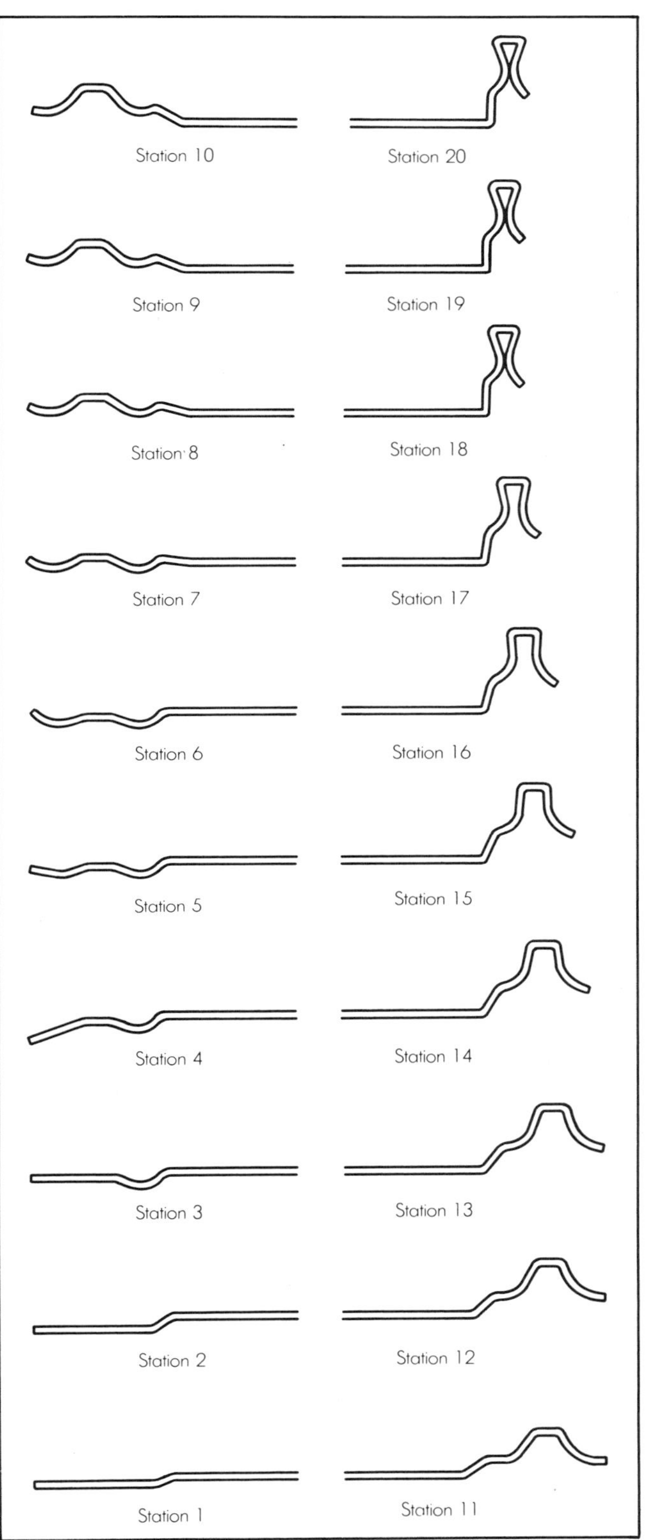


**Fig. 8-34 Using the computer for roll design provides the designer with drawings of the cross-sectional shape of the part at each station. This is the output for a part requiring 20 passes. (Only half of the cross section is shown here since the part is symmetrical.)**

## FLYING CUTOFF DIES

Although there are many variations, generally only two basic types of flying cutoff dies are used. They are most commonly referred to as the slug-type die and the slugless-type die. The decision as to which type of die to use in each case is determined by the contour of the shape to be cut, the gage of the material to be cut, the maintenance involved when cutting certain materials, the line speed to be achieved, the available press stroke, the ability to match prepunched areas, and whether other operations must be performed in the cutoff die.

### General Design Principles

Die weight can be critical in flying die operation. The goal should be to keep a happy medium between die weight and die strength.

Several means are used to reduce the die weight. Hard aluminum can be used for the die shoes and punch holders. Holes drilled in the die shoe, punch holder, punch pad, die blocks and stripper remove excess material that contributes to unnecessary weight. In the case of high shutheights, extensions can be placed on top of the punch holder to raise the rails or extensions can be placed below the die shoe to raise the pass line. Instead of using thick plates for backup of crop-off blades (in slugless dies), thinner plates with welded gusseting are often used. Die strength can be increased by using gussets wherever possible, running a reinforcement bar across the die shoe, and splitting die sections and punch pads so that they also act as reinforcing bars.

Die block surface integrity is also important for long life. Therefore, to remove the oxidized soft skin created by the heat-treating process, the die contour should be ground after the block is hardened. To keep wide dies squarely aligned with the workpiece, roller bearings with an integral stud or a bronze rail can be used to guide one of the die slide rails or an extra rail can be added for center die support. The exit side of the die blocks should always have the contour ground 0.005-0.010″ (0.13-0.25 mm) larger than the entrance side of the die blocks.

### Slug-Type Dies

Slug-type dies or blade-type dies contain two die sections through which the rolled part is fed (see Fig. 8-35). The sections are separated by a space to permit the blade to descend and cut the pieces. The cutter blade is designed for each size and shape of part, and usually follows a vertical and perpendicular path when cutting the parts. For cleaner cuts and reduced blade wear, the blade can be hinged to travel in a vertical and diagonal path or to swing in from the side (see Fig. 8-36). During this process, a slug from the cut piece is produced.

**Specific design principles.** To ensure that cutoff is accurate and high quality, several specific principles need to be considered when designing the slug-type cutoff die. The blade should be guided in the die sections to prevent it from flexing and possibly breaking. Pivoting or shuttling the blade back and forth as it travels down through the part minimizes blade galling. Increasing the cutting clearance between the blade and die block by 15% per side also helps to reduce galling.

Camming in the die jaws around the tube supports the tube walls when they are cut (see Fig. 8-36). On lock-seamed tubing, the blade should be swung in from the side to cut toward the lock seam and prevent the tube from collapsing.

Slug pulling can be reduced by relieving the die sections and by breaking up the slug into several pieces. The dies should be relieved approximately 1/16″ (1.6 mm) deep to within 1/8″ (3 mm) of the cut edge.

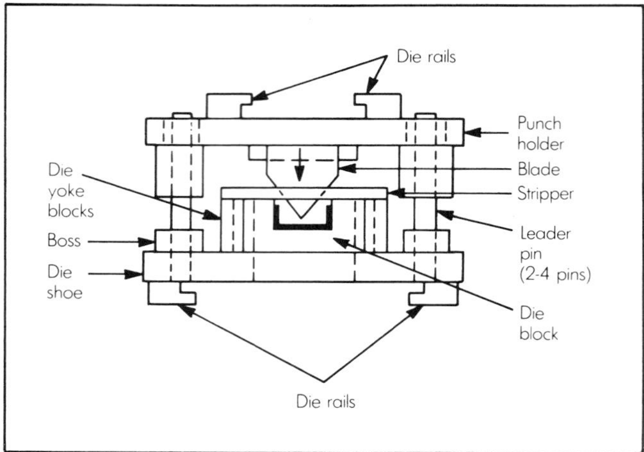


**Fig. 8-35 The slug-type die cuts the roll-formed part as the blade is moved down.** (*Hill Engineering, Inc.*)

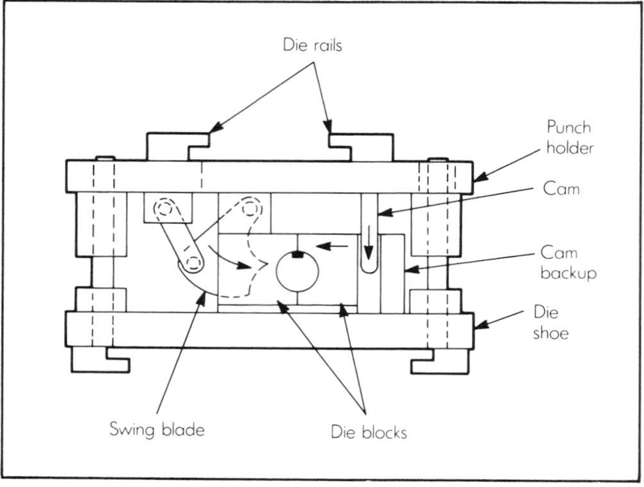


**Fig. 8-36 Swinging the blade in from the side permits cleaner cuts and reduces blade wear.** (*Hill Engineering, Inc.*)

The die blocks should be adjusted against a center gage surface rather than being shimmed in after sharpening to reduce die damage due to blade misalignment. The die set leader pins should always be supported by bosses mounted to the die shoe to provide pin stability.

**Advantages and limitations.** Slug-type dies are extremely versatile and can be used to cut off closed shapes (tubing) to heavy gage structural shapes. Since the blade can be easily contoured, the force required to cut areas that are by necessity supported with fragile die sections can be minimized to reduce die breakage. The same dieholder can be used with additional die inserts or a blade to cut off different parts. Punching and forming can be combined in the die because the part is supported by die sections on both sides of the cut.

Since the blade must travel through the entire roll-formed shape, deep cross sections require a longer linear die travel. The blade also requires more maintenance to prevent excessive galling. The slugs produced using this method tend to jam between the sections and stop the flow of material. Crank-type presses generally require increased force ratings when cutting high vertical cross sections.

**Material.** Blades are made from several types of material; the selection is based upon the material being cut, the number of parts to be cut, and the cross section of the part. These materials include a PM high-speed steel hardened to $R_C$60-62; high-speed steel (M2) hardened to $R_C$62-64; or high-chrome, high-carbon steel (D2) hardened to $R_C$60-62.

Die blocks are made from D2 steel or chromium steel (A2) and are hardened to $R_C$60-62. The die inserts are generally made from shock-resistant steel (S7) and hardened to $R_C$56-58. The yoke blocks and die rails can be made from prehardened steel or an oil-hardening steel.

## Slugless-Type Dies

A slugless-type die or crop-off die contains two die sections, similar to the blade-type die, but with a gap of 0.001-0.008″ (0.03-0.20 mm) separating the two since no blade clearance is necessary. When the press is actuated, the movable die section is forced down and cuts the piece with a scissor-type motion. The cutting motion can be vertical, on an angle, or pivoting.

**Specific design principles.** Three different methods of blade designs are used in the construction of slugless-type dies. One method is to make both die sections, stationary and movable, from tool steel and to use both sections as the blades. The two sections slide in the gibs without any wear plates (see Fig. 8-37). The second method uses blade inserts fastened to the hardened die sections. The die sections are used as holders for the inserts. To minimize deflection, blade backup plates are reinforced with gussets or tie-in bolts. The third method is to use a four-post die set and move the blade in a vertical direction. The blade is ground to have the same contour as the cross section of the rolled part (see Fig. 8-38).

The angle at which the blade should move is determined by the greatest angle of the surfaces to be cut. The contour openings should be ground so that the total contour is closed at the same time. This prevents the part from being distorted when it is cut. Hardened blade-return stop blocks maintain alignment between stationary and movable blades.

**Advantages and limitations.** Slugless-type dies can operate at a faster speed than slug-type dies because the die closing distance, and therefore time, is much less than for the slug-type dies. Scrap is also reduced because no slugs are produced. Maintenance of the blades is usually 1/2 to 1/10 the frequency of the slug-type die.

Combining other operations in the cutoff die is difficult because one blade is stationary and the other is movable. Parts that have been prepunched are difficult to cutoff; and on occasion, thinner inserts are required and are therefore more susceptible to breakage. The holders for the inserts are generally limited to one set of inserts rather than many different sets.

**Material.** Blades are generally made from a high-chrome, high-carbon steel (D2) or an air-hardening chromium steel (A2) heat treated to $R_C$60-62. The steel inserts are made from a shock-resistant steel (S7) heat treated to $R_C$56-58. The die rails can be made from prehardened steel or an oil-hardening steel.

The blade gibs are made from several different types of material. These include an air-hardening chromium steel (A2), an oil-hardening graphite steel (O6), or cold-rolled steel that has been carburized and hardened to a depth of 1/32″ (0.8 mm). The air-hardening and oil-hardening steel are heat treated to $R_C$60-62.

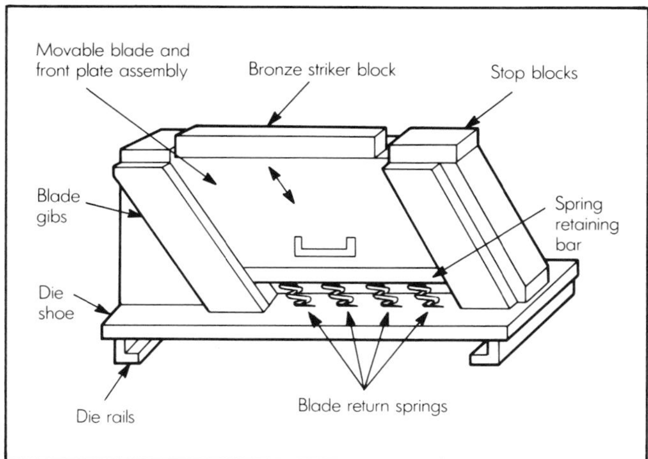


**Fig. 8-37 A slugless-type die contains a movable and a stationary blade to cut the roll-formed part.** (*Hill Engineering, Inc.*)

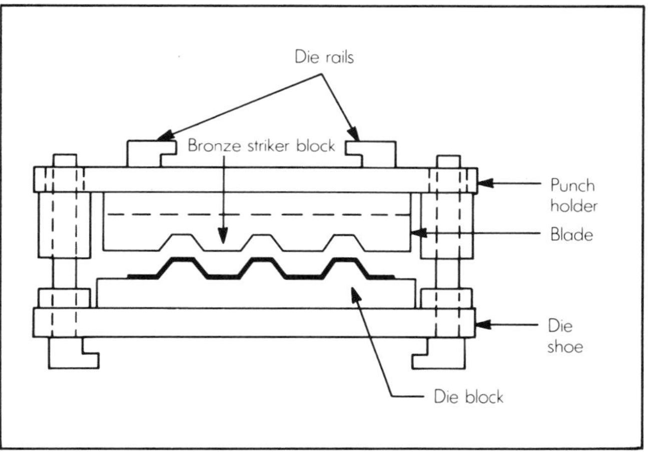


**Fig. 8-38 A four-post die set with the blade ground to the same contour as the cross section is another style of slugless-type dies.** (*Hill Engineering, Inc.*)

# TUBE AND PIPE ROLLING

Tube mills produce welded tube and pipe in a range of sizes from 1/4 to 24″ (6 to 600 mm) diam and with wall thicknesses from several thousandths of an inch to 3/4″ (19 mm) thick. The mill generally consists of a machine for forming the strip of material into a tubular shape, a welder to weld the seam, a cooling unit, a sizing and straightening machine for cutting the tube to the required lengths. The tooling for a given size of tube for these mills consist of forming tools, welder tooling, weld-flash-removing devices, sizing rolls, and cutoff tooling.

## Roll Design

A number of methods and designs are used for forming strip into a tubular shape suitable for welding, with many factors involved in choosing the proper design of rolls for producing a particular tube.

Figure 8-39 illustrates one of the most commonly used designs of rolls for forming the tube before welding. The rolls are designed with a single forming radius in each roll pass. This radius progressively decreases in each roll pass until the final pass. The radius of the final roll pass is slightly larger than the finished tube size to permit a thin fin to be inserted in the top roll to act as a guide for the two edges of the material. Generally, the last two or three roll passes are provided with fin rolls in the top rolls to guide the two edges of the strip, to prevent twisting of the tube, and to ensure accurate positioning of the seam entering the welder. Idler rolls mounted on vertical spindles between the driven-roll passes are positioned to prevent excessive rubbing and scuffing of the side of the tube as it passes through the succeeding driven-roll pass. The number of driven-roll passes can vary, increasing as the tube diameter increases, but five driven passes are considered a minimum.

With the forming radii on the rolls designed for a given thickness of material, rolls of this design produce a satisfactory tube from material as much as 40% less in thickness than that for which the rolls are designed. To accommodate other thicknesses, new top rolls can be provided to maintain the proper fit between top and bottom rolls. The same final fin roll passes are used for all thicknesses of material. Rolls of this design produce high-grade tubing when the ratio between the wall thickness or gage of the material and the outside diameter of the finished tube is between 3 and 10% and the material being formed is half hard or softer.

For forming tube with either a very thin wall or a very heavy wall (wall thickness under 3% of outside diameter of tube, or over 10% of outside diameter of tube), a modification of the design shown in Fig. 8-39 is used. This modification is obtained by forming the portion of the strip that is adjacent to the edges to the finished radius of the tube in the first forming pass, instead of depending on the fin passes to finish-form at the edges. This finished form at the edges of the strip helps to prevent buckles and waviness at the edges of the strip as it passes through the forming rolls when very thin material is being formed, and it helps to avoid the necessity of extreme pressures at the fin rolls when extra-heavy-gage material is being formed. Figure 8-40 illustrates the first four sets of rolls used in this method of tube forming. The remaining rolls are similar to those shown in Fig. 8-39.

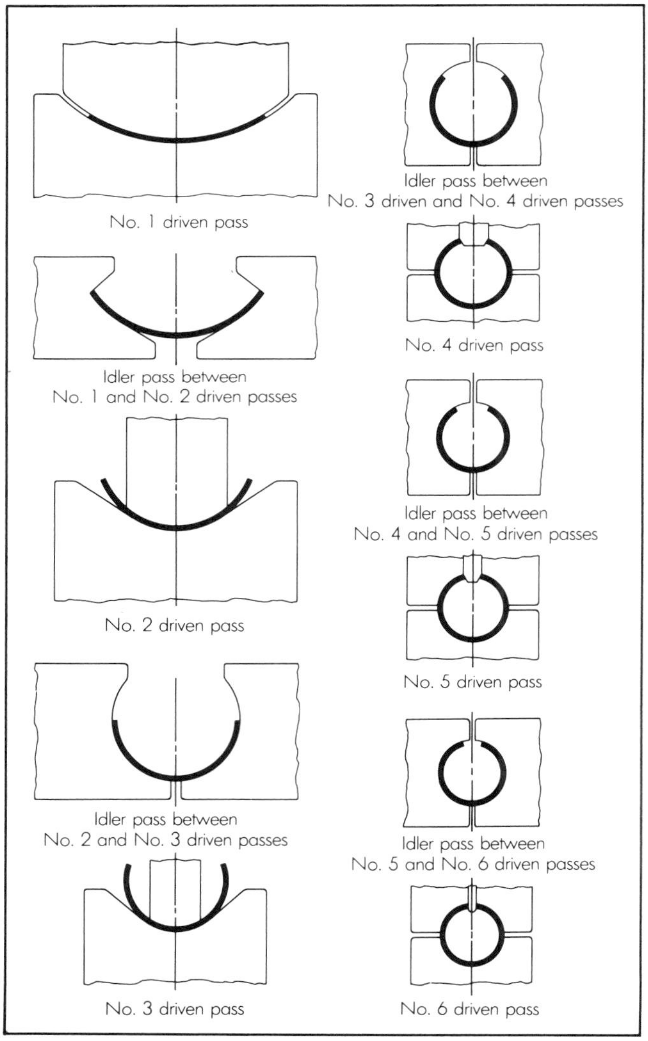

**Fig. 8-39 Rolls for forming tubing from strip material.**

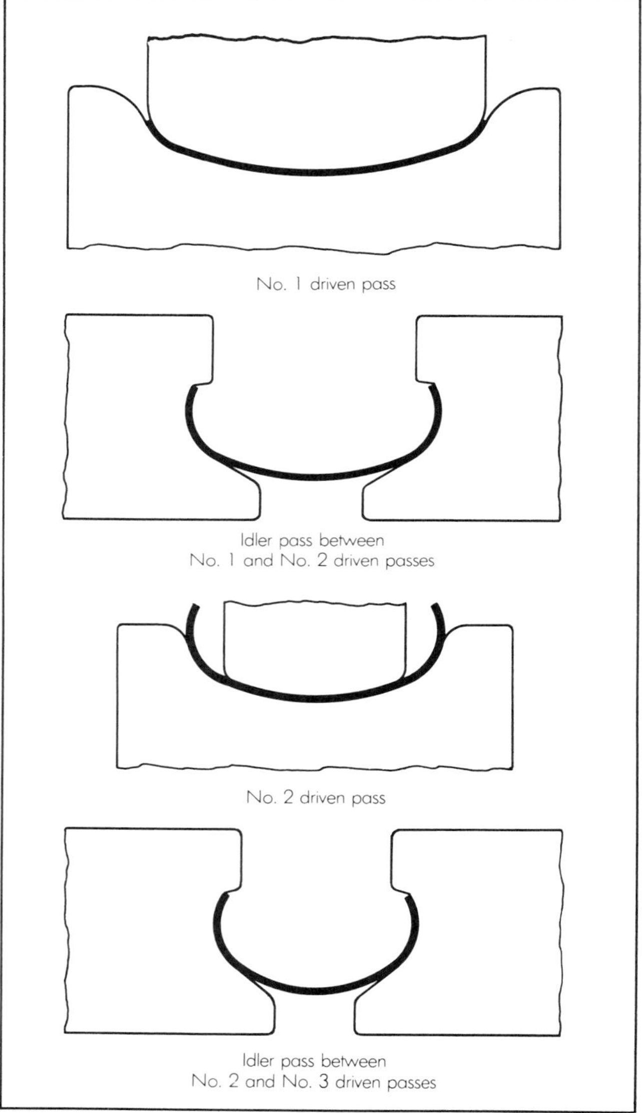


**Fig. 8-40 First group of rolls for forming tubing from thin material from the edges inward.**

In forming material of high tensile strength when springback of the metal is a factor, a third method of forming is sometimes used. In this design a part of the strip is formed to the finished tube radius in each roll pass, progressing from the two edges toward the middle until the fin passes are reached. The forming radius on the rolls is less than the finished radius of the tube to compensate for the springback of the material. The first six passes for this method of forming are illustrated in Fig. 8-41.

A number of slight variations from the designs shown can be found in practice. The number of driven forming passes can vary. Some of the vertically mounted idler rolls are sometimes omitted. The number of fin passes varies from one to three; and on some designs, the tube is closed completely in the final forming pass, eliminating a fin entirely. The shape and diameter of the roll flanges vary slightly. Rolls are sometimes split, especially in the larger sizes, for ease in mounting and also to permit regrinding the sides of the flanges when worn, compensating for the amount of regrinding by face grinding the rolls at the splits.

## Welding

Seam welding of pipe and tubing is generally performed using either low-frequency, rotary-electrode welding or high-frequency welding. High-frequency welding has become more predominant in recent years in the production of welded tubing. With rotary-electrode welding, the maximum wall thickness that is economically feasible is 0.180″ (4.5 mm). Using high-frequency welders, wall thicknesses as thick as 0.75″ (19.0 mm) and as thin as 0.005″ (0.13 mm) are obtainable. Figures 8-42 and 8-43 show the sliding contact type and induction coil type of high-frequency welder. After the welding operation, the piece is usually sized and then straightened before being cut to length.

**Sizing and straightening.** Tube and pipe are welded to an outside diameter slightly larger than the finished diameter. The sizing rolls can then produce round, accurately dimensioned,

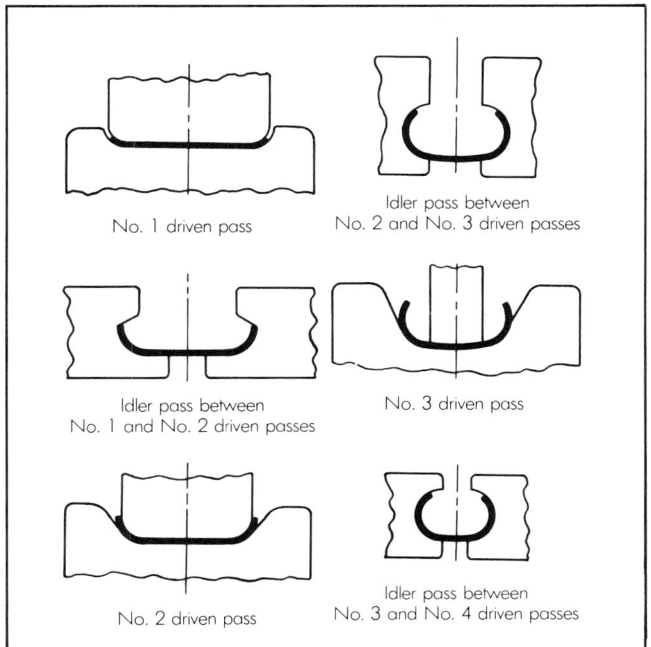


**Fig. 8-41 First group of rolls for forming high-tensile-strength material into tubing.**

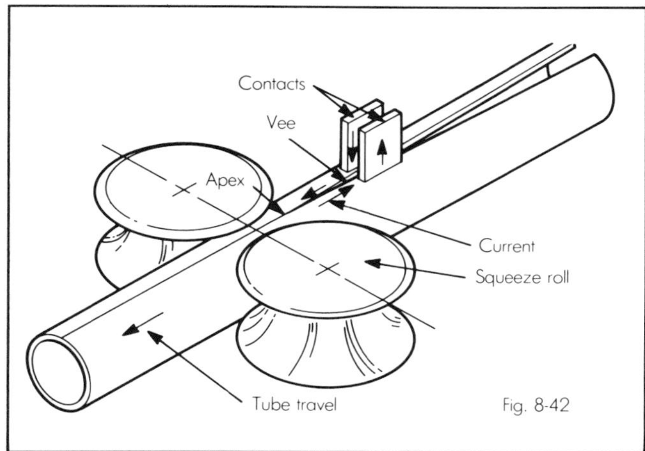


**Fig. 8-42 Two sliding contacts introduce the current to the tube edges in high frequency contact welding. (*Fabricating Manufacturers Assn. and Thermatool Corp.*)**

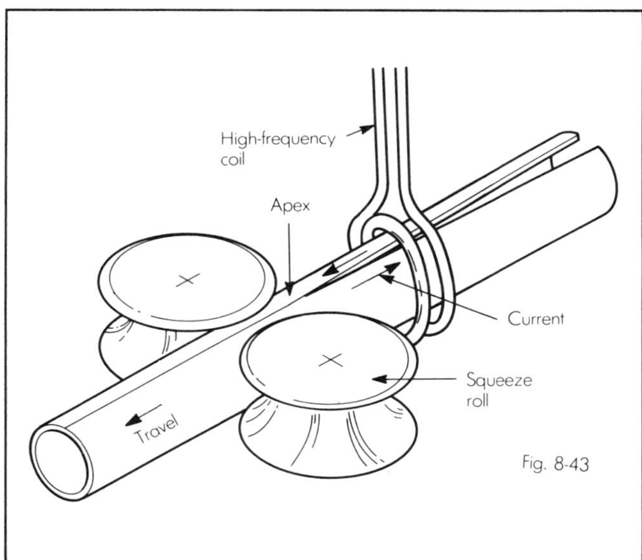


**Fig. 8-43 A multiturn induction coil induces current to the tube edges in high frequency induction welding. (*Fabricating Manufacturers Assn. and Thermatool Corp.*)**

straight finished tube. A typical set of sizing and straightening rolls consists of three driven-roll passes, vertically mounted idler rolls between each driven pass, and finally a set of idle cluster rolls which are adjustable both vertically and horizontally for final straightening of the tube. The roll radius for each driven roll successively decreases to size the tube down to its proper diameter. For example, to produce a 1.000″ (25.40 mm) diam tube, the radius in the first driven sizing pass is made 0.502″ (12.75 mm), in the second driven pass 0.500″ (12.70 mm), and in the third driven pass 0.497″ (12.62 mm). The idler rolls between the driven passes would have a 0.515″ (13.08 mm) radius, and the final cluster rolls for straightening the tube would have the nominal radius of 0.500″ (12.70 mm).

**Reshaping of round tubing.** Although reshaping of round tube into a square, rectangle, or other similar shape is often accomplished in the final cluster rolls on a tube mill, a more uniform cross section and more uniformly straight tube are produced when the entire sizing mill is used to reshape the round tube. This is especially true when heavy-walled tube is being reshaped.

Figure 8-44 shows a set of sizing-mill rolls for producing a square tube. It should be noted that the rolls are designed to form the tube slightly off from a 45° diagonal. This is done to position the weld, which is exactly on the top of the round tube before squaring and slightly off the corner of the finished square tube. If the location of the weld on the square tube is unimportant, the squaring is done on a 45° angle, making all the rolls symmetrical. Figure 8-45 illustrates the forming of an oval tube from the round.

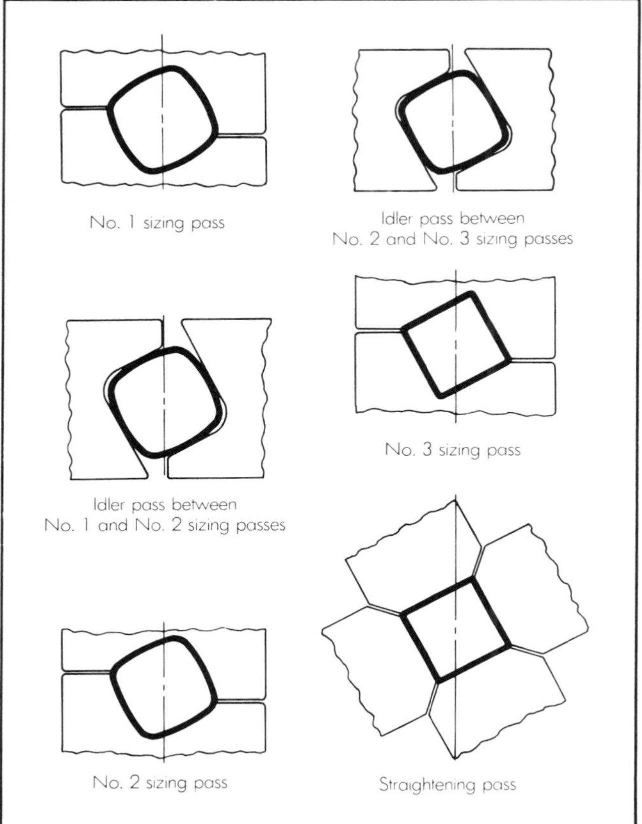


**Fig. 8-44 Rolls for reshaping round tubing into square tubing.**

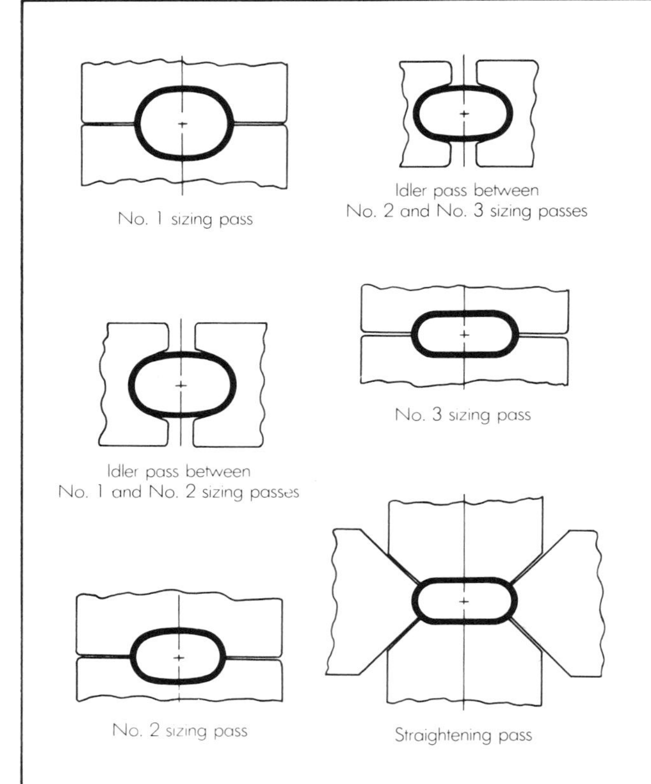


**Fig. 8-45 Roll forming an oval tube from round tubing.**

# OPERATING PARAMETERS

The roll forming operation progressively forms material as it passes from one station to another. The variable parameters in a roll forming operation include power requirement, speed, and type of lubricant used. These parameters are determined by width, thickness and type of material, complexity of cross section, coating on material, and accuracy required.

Auxiliary operations such as prepunching, embossing, curving and coiling, and cutoff incorporated in the roll forming line also influence the parameters at which a roll former must operate. Another area to consider is the area of equipment setup.

## POWER REQUIREMENT

The power required by a roll forming machine is dependent on the torque loss through the drive gearing and the friction between the material and the rolls as the material is being roll formed. The type and thickness must be taken into consideration when looking at the effect of material on power requirements. Generally, the power of roll forming machines is from 10-50 hp (7.5-37 kW) on small machines and from 50-125 hp (37-90 kW) on larger machines.

## SPEED

As was previously mentioned, the speed of roll forming machines is in the range of approximately 50-600 fpm (15-185 m/min), with 100-180 fpm (30-55 m/min) an average. The machine can be designed for operating at a constant speed, but it can also be equipped with a variable speed drive. Variable speed enables the machine to be more versatile and is achieved mechanically, electrically, or hydraulically. The most popular method is electrical, using a direct-current motor or a variable frequency drive and a standard alternating-current motor. The speed of the machine is regulated with a rheostat.

The speed at which a roll forming machine can be operated is determined by several factors. These factors include cross-section complexity; part length, width, and thickness; accuracy; and type of auxiliary operations. To a large extent, the speed of a roll forming line is limited to the fastest speed of the other in-line operations that must be performed.

## EQUIPMENT SETUP

The time that it takes to change from one tooling setup to another is often costly not only in dollars but in production time. To ensure a low amount of downtime, it is essential that as much of the machine and as many accessories as possible be permanent in setup. Some areas to consider are machine lineup, spacers, roll tooling, pass line height, roll diameters, self-threading material, cross-section templates, and setup charts. Each setup may vary slightly due to variations in material characteristics and, therefore, may require tooling adjustment.

### Machine Lineup

Using common length inboard spacers ensures a straight machine face lineup. This eliminates the need to search for shims and special spacers when setting up the tooling rolls.

### Spacers

Spacers should be hardened with the ends ground parallel to each other. The inside diameter of the spacer should be made 0.015-0.020″ (0.35-0.50 mm) oversize. A keyway is optional but desirable.

### Roll Tooling

Bolting small rolls or small segments of larger rolls together eliminates time lost during setup due to missing segments. By doing so, any shims put between roll segments for proper spacing can be permanently fixed in place, reducing time that would be required to locate proper shims during setup.

### Pass Line Height

When possible, a dimension should be established from the base of the roll forming machine to the top, bottom, or center of the cross section, and all tooling should be designed around this dimension (see Fig. 8-46). This eliminates the need for excessive movement of both the straightener and cutoff press when tooling is changed.

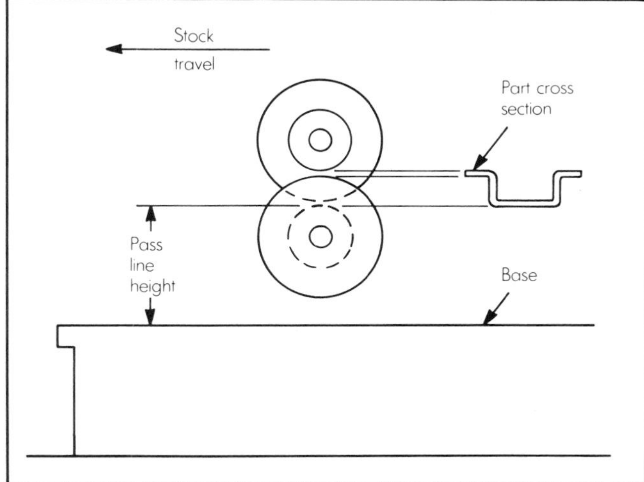


**Fig. 8-46 Establishing a pass line height eliminates excessive movement of auxiliary equipment during toolchanging.** (*Contour Roll Co.*)

### Roll Diameters

Roll diameters are determined by the depth of the shape and the capacity of the machine. The use of larger roll diameters, permits higher speeds, reduces roll wear, and permits more roll regrinds.

### Self-Threading Material

The material being fed through the rolls should enter each pair of rolls with little or no assistance from the operator after the initial setup. This is often difficult to accomplish, but very desirable if achievable.

### Cross-Section Templates

Cross-section templates enable the operator to detect improper shapes at each station. When improper shapes are produced, a quick analysis with the templates can help determine where adjustments are needed.

### Setup Charts

A setup or tooling chart (see Fig. 8-47) is a catalog of particulars involved in placing a set of rolls in the machine. It is designed for use by the operator and should be considered part of the actual tooling. This chart shows the operator the number of forming stations required, in and out spacing, placement of guides and side rollers, and type and size of material to be formed. It also enables the operator to record any shim or setup changes.

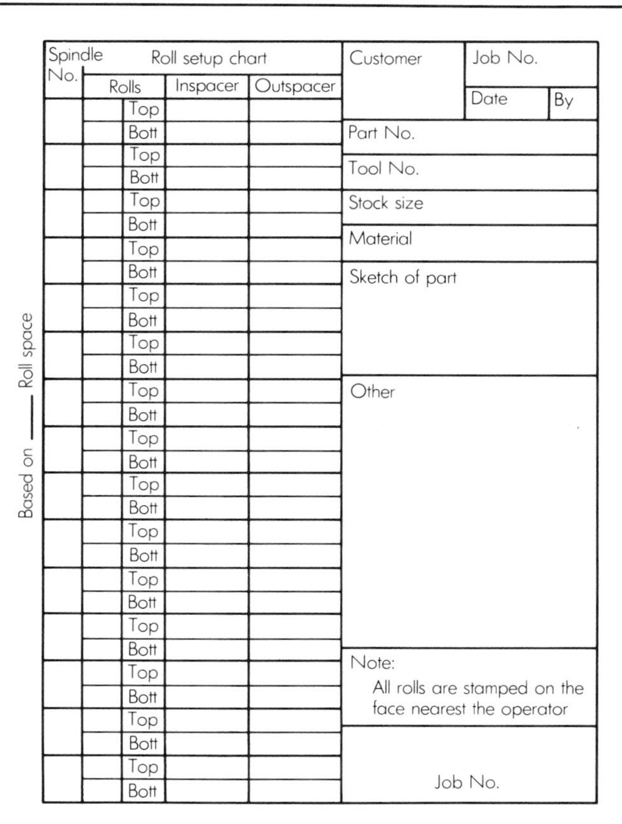


**Fig. 8-47 Setup or tooling charts aid the operator when setting up the roll forming machine for a particular part.** (*Contour Roll Co.*)

# CHAPTER 8

# OPERATING PARAMETERS

## LUBRICATION

Boundary friction, which is associated with almost all metalforming operations, is caused by the relative movement of two adjacent surfaces under pressure. In roll forming, the relative movement between the rolls and workpiece is enhanced by the surface speed differential of the rolls and workpiece.

A thin film of lubricant deposited between the two moving surfaces may reduce or eliminate the undesired effect of friction. In addition to surface problems, the heat generated by forming, compounded by heat caused by friction and, in certain lines, by welding, can be a source of additional problems. The lubricant, when used in liberal amounts, may also act as coolant for the roll forming lines. The lubricant/coolant can also serve other purposes, such as washing away contaminants and particles; improving the corrosion resistance of the formed product; prolonging the life of the cutoff die, punches, and other tools; and reducing energy consumption.

A detailed discussion covering principles of lubrication, lubricant types, lubricant quality control, waste treatment and disposal, and cleaning is found in Chapter 3, "Lubricants," of this volume. Additional information can be found in Chapter 4, Volume I, *Machining*, of this Handbook series.

### Lubricating Systems

Two basic types of lubricating systems are used in roll forming operations: the once-through system and the recirculating system. In a once-through system, the applied lubricant leaves the equipment either adhered to the material or separately as waste. In a recirculating system, most of the lubricant is captured and reused. Generally, the recirculating system is the more economical lubricating system.

Roll forming lubricants can be applied using dripping, wiping, roller coating, airless spraying, and flooding techniques. Flooding with large amounts of lubricant acts as a coolant to dissipate heat and helps flush away oxide and metal fines. Flooding is required when hot-rolled steel and heavy sections are being roll formed and when welding processes are incorporated in the line. For a detailed explanation of each lubricating technique, see Chapter 3, "Lubricants," in this volume.

### Lubricant Selection

Lubricants for a roll forming operation are selected based on the material being formed, auxiliary operations, and the place in which the roll-formed part is to be used. The selection of the lubricant should be conducted in the preplanning stage with the assistance of the machine manufacturer or a lubricant supplier.

**Material.** Most lubricants can be applied to several materials. Frequently, however, to achieve the best result economically, a specific lubricant needs to be selected. On precoated material, it is important to conduct a static check for compatibility between the lubricant and coating. This prevents the material from becoming scrap because of checking, blistering, peeling, blotching, and staining on the surface. Tables 8-1 and 8-2 provide recommendations for lubricants to be used when roll forming various materials.

**Auxiliary operations.** Operations such as prepunching, cutoff, and post notching are included in the roll forming line to produce a finished product at the end of the line. It is not uncommon to use the same lubricant for these auxiliary operations that is being used in the roll forming operation. However, this practice can shorten tool life and slow down the entire roll forming line. Generally, it is recommended that a separate lubricant be selected for these auxiliary operations.

Heavy concentrations of water-soluble lubricant work well in prepunching operations. For cutoff dies, heavy-duty, superwet soluble compounds mixed in high strengths are excellent.

**TABLE 8-1**
**Recommended Lubricants for Roll Forming Various Uncoated Materials**

| Material Formed | Recommended Lubricant | Precautions and Comments |
|---|---|---|
| Cold-rolled and pickled and oiled hot-rolled steel | Light oils, multipurpose solubles, and EP-type solubles | For heavy-gage and/or high-strength steel formed at high speeds, use liberal amounts of lubricant to dissipate heat. Use water-soluble lubricants sparingly to prevent rusting. |
| Pre-oiled steel coils | Usually none required | If lubricant is used, make sure it is compatible with treatment from steel mill. |
| Hot-rolled steel | Light, high-wetting, water-soluble and synthetic lubricants | Iron oxide must be flushed away from tooling guides, straighteners, dies, and measuring devices. Chrome rolls where large amount of fines are generated. Flooding required. |
| Stainless steel | Heavy-duty evaporating compounds with EP agents, heavy-duty solubles, apparent viscosity synthetics | Wet complete surface to prevent spotty discoloration. |
| Aluminum | Water-soluble synthetic, evaporating compounds, and water-soluble oils | Some lubricants leave marks on surface. Chrome-plated rolls require lubricant with good polarity and wetting properties along with EP additive. |
| Copper, bronze, brass | Water-soluble synthetic or water-soluble oil | High-penetrating, high-wetting properties preferred. |

**TABLE 8-2**
**Recommended Lubricants for Roll Forming Various Coated Materials**

| Material Formed | Recommended Lubricant | Precautions and Comments |
|---|---|---|
| Galvanized steel | Special water-based and evaporating-type lubricants, light oils | Dry sheets formed with water-soluble lubricants to prevent white rust. Apply lubricant with fine spray. Usually coated steel requires only small amounts of lubricant. |
| Painted stock | Some evaporating compounds and solubles | Check with lubricant supplier. Perform static check on sample piece. |
| Vinyl-coated stock | Evaporating compounds or light soluble oils | Perform static check on sample piece. |
| Lacquer-coated stock | High-wetting evaporating compounds and some synthetic solubles | Perform static check on sample piece. |
| Paper-clad stock | Light solubles | Use lubricants sparingly. Perform static check on sample piece. |
| Polymer-coated stock | Use special lubricants such as plastic film. | |

An impulse spraying technique is recommended for slug-type cutoff dies to provide a short burst of lubricant on both sides of the blade.

**Post-forming operations and end use.** Operations following roll forming and the final application in assembly or erection can influence or restrict the type of lubricant used. The following should be considered when lubricants are selected:

1. Painting or plating after forming requires either a dry surface (that is, evaporating lubricants) or compatible solvents. It is usually recommended to refrain from using silicone-type lubricants.
2. Water-soluble lubricants, adhering to the surface of the product (especially if trapped by nesting configuration and stored for prolonged periods), can cause corrosion, rusting on "black" steel, white rust on galvanized steel, and staining on aluminum.
3. Lubricants trapped in beads or grooves can cause explosion hazards if products are to be hot-dip galvanized after forming. Flashpoint and flame spreading of lubricants should be checked when products are welded or heated after forming.
4. Oiled roof sheets installed at a slope or used for similar applications can create safety hazards during erection.
5. Drying oil or tacky lubricant, acting as an adhesive, can make separation of nested products difficult.
6. Lubricants applied for products subsequently used in direct contact with foodstuff such as grain bins, food containers, etc., must be free of harmful materials and usually must have health authority approval.
7. Oily, nonevaporating lubricants on office partitions, door frames, and similar products may stain carpets and floors.

# TROUBLESHOOTING AND MAINTENANCE

When the roll forming machine starts producing parts that are improperly formed, crooked, scratched or score-marked, twisted, or of incorrect size, it is sometimes difficult to pinpoint the cause. Faulty tooling; incorrect setup; or lack of proper maintenance, both of machine and tooling, could be the areas of trouble.

## TROUBLESHOOTING

The lack of proper lubrication or coolant, faulty setups, and excessive pressures are the main causes of roll wear. The type, size, thickness, and quality of material being formed; the kind of tooling material used; the shape of cross section; and the required tolerances for an acceptable part also contribute to roll wear.

Roll wear can be best determined when the tooling is being changed. The areas to visually inspect for wear are the critical angles and the curve profiles. Actual wear is determined by placing each pair of rolls, flat side down, on a surface plate and inserting a round feeler gage of the correct diameter between the profiles of the rolls. If the gap is greater than the gap specified, excessive wear has occurred and the rolls should be reground or replaced.

When difficulty in forming arises, the first area to investigate is the material being used. The quality and dimensional accuracy of the material have a significant bearing on the quality and accuracy of the finished product. Table 8-3 lists some problems encountered in roll forming and presents some of the causes along with possible solutions.

Difficulties are also encountered during the initial installation and setup of the equipment. When possible, it is best to secure the services of the equipment manufacturer for assistance.

A thorough knowledge of the equipment and how each piece operates is important to determine the source of the problem. Prior to testing the complete line, each component should be tested to verify its operation. If a piece of equipment fails to operate, how it is driven and whether it is electrically interlocked with another piece of equipment should be determined. Safety is always of great importance. If the equipment fails to produce the desired part design, it is necessary to determine whether the problem is in the setup, material, or tooling. Improper roll design necessitates the modification of one or more pairs of rolls.

## MAINTENANCE

Improper maintenance of a roll forming machine can lead to defective parts. It is therefore important to follow the manufacturers recommendations on equipment maintenance. Some areas to consider are spindle bearings, bent spindles, machine and roll alignment, drive system, and metal build-up on the rolls. If the roll forming machine is to form various types of material, it is advisable to thoroughly clean the rolls before forming different materials.

**TABLE 8-3**
**Troubleshooting Roll Forming Operations**

| Problem | Possible Cause | Suggested Solutions |
|---|---|---|
| Metal pick-up on rolls | Metal particles in roll-forming operation | Add baffles and magnets to sump. Incorporate filtering system. Use emery cloth wipers or V-type compression rolls. |
| | Burrs from slitting operation | Polish forming rolls. Add felt wiper to forming rolls. |
| | Lubricant leaking from gear boxes | Check oil level. Reduce excessive greasing or use grease that resists water washout. Replace seals and gaskets on gear boxes. |
| | Roll stands trap metal fines in tramp oil | Design closed-loop coolant system. Use oil skimmers. |
| | Improper tool design | Redesign rolls. |
| Accelerated tool wear | Improper tooling material | Use material conducive to type of roll forming being performed and production required. |
| | Large amounts of metal fines | Wipe off and/or flush metal fines. |
| | Improper lubrication application technique | Use appropriate lubrication technique. |
| | Overworking caused by improper tool design | Redesign rolls to balance forming between stations. |
| Excessive wear on one or two pairs of rolls | Loose and/or misaligned spindles | Examine bearings, replace if necessary. Shim bearing housings for proper alignment. |
| | Worn bearing housing ways on stand | Replace as required. |
| Part does not retain desired cross-sectional shape | Material not stressed beyond elastic limit (springback) | Overform past desired shape, then bring back to desired shape on final roll pass. |
| | Too much forming per pass | Increase number of passes for freer flow. |
| | Horizontal center distance between roll-forming units too close | Increase horizontal center distance. |
| End flare in part | | Use continuous forming when applicable. |
| | Stress build up in material | Install straightener at end of roll-forming machine. |
| | Too much forming per pass | Increase number of passes for freer material flow. |
| Metal fracture at bend | Bend radius too tight | Increase radius and redesign rolls (use maximum radius permissible). |
| | Too much forming per pass | Increase number of passes for freer material flow. |
| | Improper material | Select material with proper ductility. |
| Leg of roll-formed part is wavy | Leg length too short | Increase leg length to at least three times material thickness. |

TABLE 8-3—*Continued*

| Problem | Possible Cause | Suggested Solutions |
|---|---|---|
| Distorted holes and slots | Hole or slots too close to bend or edge causing material to be stretched | Place holes 3 to 5 times material thickness away from bends or edges. Increase distance for other cutouts. Increase number of passes or horizontal center distances for freer material flow. |
| Wide flat end of roll-formed part is wavy | Material edge is stretched | Incorporate leg or groove three times material thickness from end. Form slight bend in end. Increase number of passes for freer material flow. |
| | Material is wavy | Change material. |
| Oil canning in middle of wide, flat sections | Material not perfectly flat | Stretch in rectangular or V-shaped ribs in flat area after desired cross section is formed. Maximum width of flat sections should be 5-6″ (127-152 mm). Design part with rib distance of 2-3″ (50-76 mm) between centers. |
| | Improper roll design | Redesign rolls. |
| Part bowed | Excessive material camber | Install straightener on exit end of roll-forming machine. Change material. |
| | Post roll forming equipment not aligned | Check alignment and realign if necessary. |
| | Uneven pass line height for tooling | Check pass line height and realign if necessary. |
| | Uneven forming and pressures | |
| Part twisted | Excessive material camber | See solutions for "Part Bowed." |
| | Uneven roll gap | Check gap clearance. |
| Part curved | Excessive material camber | See solutions for "Part Bowed." |
| | Roll gaps too tight | Check clearance and adjust. |
| | Incorrect roll alignment | Check shoulder alignment, spaces, and roll design. |
| | Incorrect alignment of straightener or post roll forming equipment | Check alignment and realign. |
| Poor dimensional tolerances (length and cross sectional) | Poor material quality and dimensional accuracy | Check material and change if necessary. |
| | Roll-forming machine and equipment in poor condition or misaligned | Inspect and repair where needed. |
| | Incorrect machine setup | Check setup. |
| | Spindle deflection caused by excessive pressure | Check roll gap. Check spindle bearings. |
| | Incorrect measuring system for material and required tolerances | Change measuring system. |
| | Line speed too fast for part being run | Reduce line speed. |
| Roll abrasions on coated surfaces | Improper roll finish | Use highly finished or polished rolls. |
| | Improper lubricant | Use correct lubricant (refer to Table 8-1). |

**TABLE 8-3—*Continued***

| Problem | Possible Cause | Suggested Solutions |
|---|---|---|
| Abrasions on edges of painted metal strip | Edges of material are dry causing friction | Lubricate edges. |
| | Dirty entrance guide | Clean entrance guides regularly. |
| | Improper entrance guide or intermediate guide material | Use brass or wear-resistant, synthetic material. |
| | Intermediate guides or shoes rubbing | Align guides. |
| Coating fracture at bend radii | Bend radius too tight | Increase radius and redesign rolls (use maximum radius permissible). |
| | Improper coating | Select coating for specific application. |
| | Too much forming per pass | Redesign rolls and increase number of rolls for freer material flow. |

# SAFETY CONSIDERATIONS

In any operation in which workers utilize various machines to perform specific tasks, the safety of the worker always needs to be considered when designing and operating the machine. In roll forming, the two main areas of concern are the roll forming machine and the auxiliary equipment. Chapter 20, "Safety in Forming," discusses other aspects of worker safety.

The roll forming machine consists of individual head units driven by gears, belts, or driveshafts. The drive system should be covered by housings that are permanently fastened to the machine to prevent hands or hair from being pulled into the unit. ANSI Standard B15.1, "Mechanical Power Transmission Apparatus," should be consulted for specific requirements. The rolls and rotating spindles should also be covered to eliminate pinch points and to contain pieces of the roll within the guard in case of breakage.

Since the rolls must be examined periodically, it is advisable to use guards that can hinge out of the way and that are electrically interlocked with the roll forming machine. This allows easy access to the rolls and shuts the machine off when the guard is lifted. For a more complete description of roll forming machine safety standards, refer to ANSI Standard B11.12. A roll forming machine using a hinged guard is shown in Fig. 8-48.

During the setup phase or during troubleshooting opera-

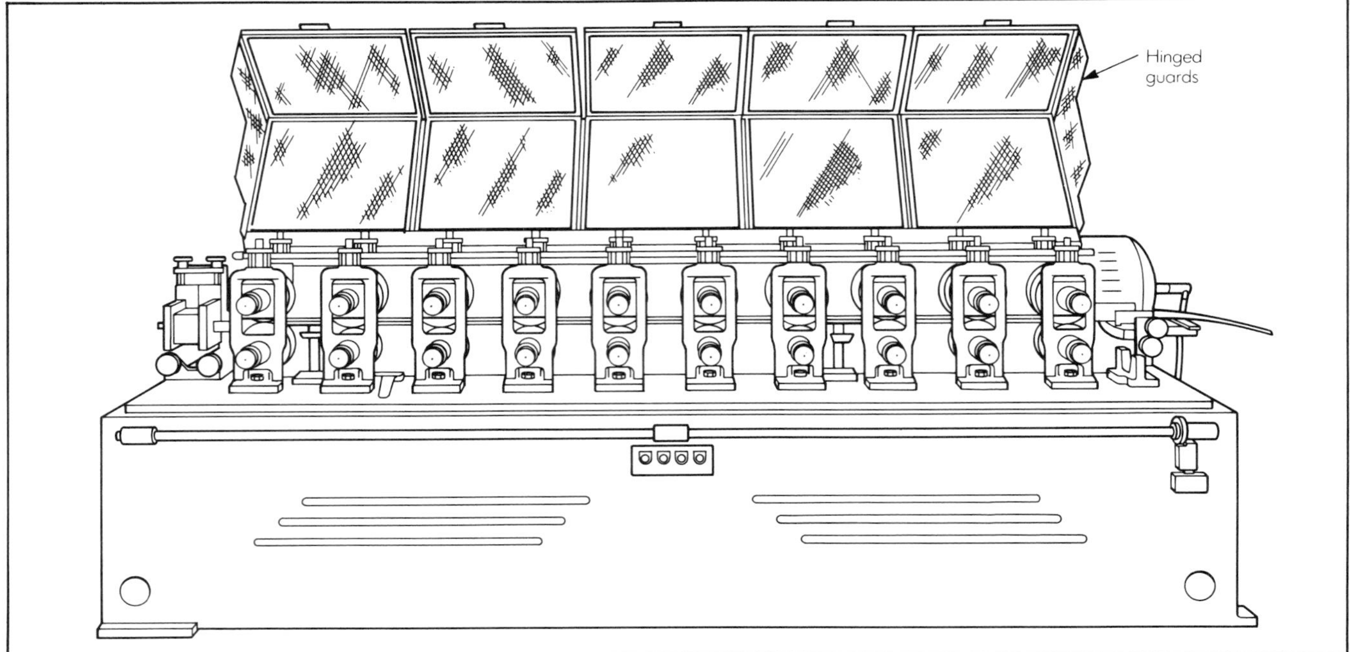


**Fig. 8-48 A hinged guard is used to cover rolls and rotating spindles while allowing the rolls to be examined periodically.** (*Tishken Products Co.*)

tions, stop/start controls should be accessible from any worker's position along with inching speeds in the forward and reverse directions. A panic (emergency) stop button is also beneficial during the production. Safety considerations when using lubricants are covered in Chapter 3, "Lubricants," of this volume.

In the case of auxiliary equipment, specific standards apply to each piece of equipment. Safety of power presses is discussed in Chapter 5, and safety of cutoff saws is discussed in Volume I, Chapter 6, of this Handbook series. Table 8-4 lists established safety standards that can be obtained from the American National Standards Institute.

**TABLE 8-4**
**Published Safety Standards**

| ANSI Number | Subject |
|---|---|
| B11.1 | Mechanical Power Presses |
| B11.2 | Hydraulic Power Presses |
| B11.10 | Metal Sawing Machines |
| B11.12 | Roll Forming and Roll Bending Machines |
| B15.1 | Mechanical Power Transmission Apparatus |
| B30.9 | Slings |
| B30.11 | Monorail Systems and Underhung Cranes |
| B30.16 | Overhead Hoists |
| Z49.1 | Welding and Cutting |
| ANSI-NFPA 51 | Oxygen-Fuel Gas Systems for Welding and Cutting |
| ANSI-NFPA 51B | Fire Prevention in Welding and Cutting Processes |

## Bibliography

Bradbury, David. *Eliminating Roll Tool Changeover*. FMA Technical Paper F-2600A, 1977.

Bridgman, Ted. *Feeding Systems for Rollformers Including Levelers, Straighteners and Decoilers*. FMA Technical Paper F-2200, 1976.

Halmos, George T., ed. *High Production Roll Forming*. Society of Manufacturing Engineers (SME), 1983.

Hill, Don. *Flying Dies (Pre-Notch and Cut-off); Measuring Systems; Their Design and Economic Impact*. FMA Technical Paper F-1930, 1975.

Hogse, Eric. *Digitally Controlled Die Accelerators*. FMA Technical Paper F-1950, 1977.

Rathbun, Melvin. *Basic Design of Tool Design for Tube Mills*. FMA Technical Paper T-2100, 1977.

CHAPTER

# 9

# Spinning

# SPINNING

Spinning is a chipless production method of forming axially symmetrical metal shapes. It is a point deformation process by which a metal disc, cylindrical workpiece, or preform is plastically deformed into contact with a rotating chuck (mandrel) by axial or axial-radial motions of a tool or rollers. Shapes produced include cones, hemispheres, tubes, cylinders, and other radially symmetrical, hollow parts in a wide variety of sizes and contours. Elliptical shapes are also spun; however, forming these shapes is not as easy as producing symmetrical cylindrical parts.

Spinning is an economical, efficient, versatile method of producing parts, especially if the cost of stamping or deep-drawing dies would be substantial. The method is used for requirements ranging from prototypes to high production parts. Parts ranging from 1/4" (6.4 mm) to 26 ft (7.9 m) diam have been spun from metals up to 3" (76 mm) or more in thickness.

**CHAPTER CONTENTS:**



# TYPES OF METAL SPINNING

The spinning process can be classified into four basic types: manual (hand) spinning, power spinning, shear forming, and tube spinning, as illustrated in Fig. 9-1. These types can be further subdivided into other categories, some of which are discussed in this section.

## MANUAL SPINNING

Manual or hand spinning is a technique for spinning conical, hemispherical, or cylindrical cup shapes requiring several axial-radial tool or roller passes to bend the metal into contact with the chuck or mandrel. The process results in only a slight reduction in the blank thickness or preform thickness.

Manual spinning is one of the oldest known methods of metalforming. It is generally done on lathe-type machines with no mechanical assistance to increase the force. A large mechanical advantage is achieved, however, when using tools of scissor design, discussed later in this section. Normally, a circular disc of metal, called the blank, is clamped between a rotating mandrel (chuck) and a follower on the tailstock of the machine. Manual pressure is applied to a levered tool to progressively bend or flare the metal over the mandrel, practically always with multiple passes of the tool.

Manual spinning is still widely used for development work, prototypes, and both short and long production runs in forming thin metal blanks. The process is limited to relatively thin blanks—up to about 1/4" (6.4 mm) thick in aluminum—and the diameter of parts that can be hand spun depends upon the machine available. Some simple shapes can be formed without a mandrel. Tolerances of the spun parts vary with the skill, strength, and fatigue of the operator.

### Underarm-Tool Manual Spinning

With this method of manual or hand spinning, the operator applies tool pressure by forcing the tip of the tool back and forth across the rotating disc by means of muscle power and body weight (see Fig. 9-2).

An adjustable toolrest provides a movable fulcrum pin which can be positioned in any one of a number of holes in the rest. With an underarm tool over the rest and against the pin, the operator can apply pressure to the revolving blank below its center of rotation. Working from the center axis outward, the blank is gradually forced to flow until it finally conforms to the shape of the chuck.

### Scissor-Tool Manual Spinning

By using a scissor or lever tool for manual or hand spinning (see Fig. 9-3), the operator can apply considerably more pressure with less exertion by means of the lever and fulcrum principle.

The operator uses the right-hand lever to guide the tool point back and forth across the revolving disc, and the left-hand lever to move the fulcrum in and out through an arc as needed. The compound levers can be easily lifted and repositioned into various holes in the toolrest when required. A bearing-mounted roller is sometimes mounted in the yoke of the compound scissor, although a blunt tool or other forming tools are used for different results.

### Dishing or Push-In Spinning

Rather than always using a male spinning chuck or mandrel for manual spinning, it is sometimes advantageous to fasten the outer periphery of the disc to a concave form which has been turned to the shape desired. The disc can be fastened by bolting it under a ring, or it can be

*Contributors of sections of this chapter are: Jeffrey M. Downing, Executive Vice President, Lake Geneva Spindustries, Inc.; Gary Gates, Kansas City Div., The Bendix Corp.; Tony Hudson, President, Electrologic, Inc.; Burton F. Lewis, BFL Associates.*

*Reviewers of sections of this chapter are: N. K. Banks, Jr., Bomco Inc.; Jeffrey M. Downing, Executive Vice President, Lake Geneva Spindustries, Inc.; Jack Frank, Vice President, L & F Industries, Inc.; Gary Gates, Kansas City Div., The Bendix Corp.; L. F. Glasier, Jr., Chief Technical Staff, Kaiser Rollmet; Robert Hudson, Vice President, Autospin, Inc.; Tony Hudson, President, Electrologic, Inc.; Burton F. Lewis, BFL Associates; John F. McGeever, Jr., President, Charles H. Schillinger Co.; William G. Meyers, Chief Engineer, Metal Spinners, Inc.; Leland W. Nichols, President, Floturn, Inc.*

# CHAPTER 9

## TYPES OF METAL SPINNING

Metal spinning

Manual spinning

Metal blank
Roller
Forming lever
Chuck
Compound lever
Backup lever (optional)
Steady rest

Power spinning

Same as manual with exception of:
1. Increased force by power assistance
2. More rigid machine structure

Shear forming

Tube spinning

Mandrel
Blank
Backward (reverse) spinning
Forward spinning
Roller
Tube
Die
Internal spinning

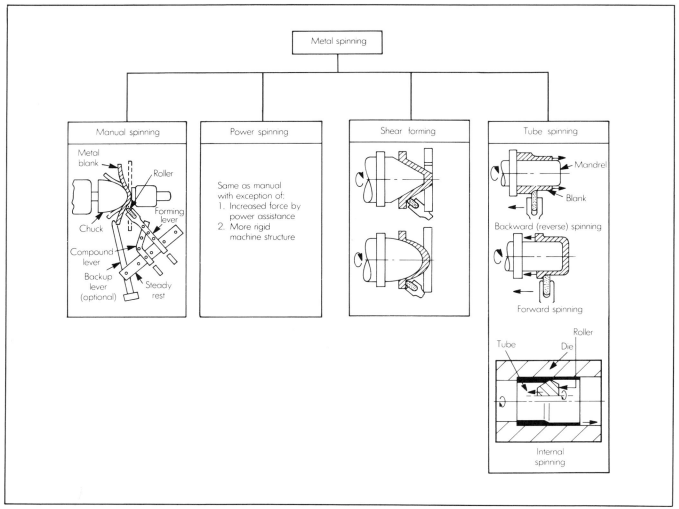

**Fig. 9-1 Types of metal spinning processes.**

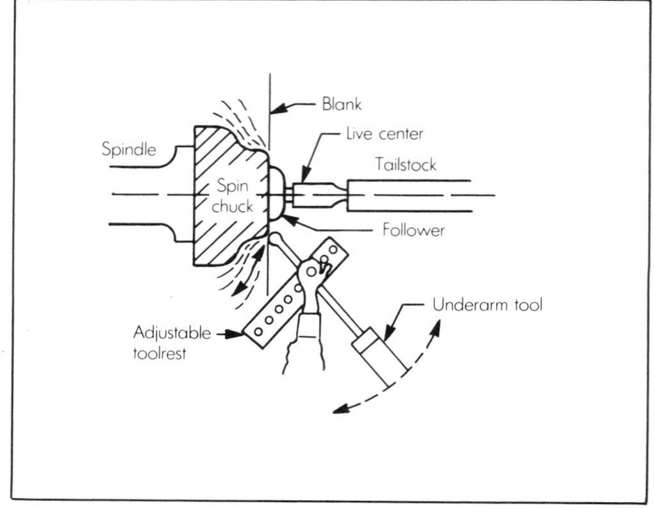


**Fig. 9-2 Underarm-tool manual spinning.**

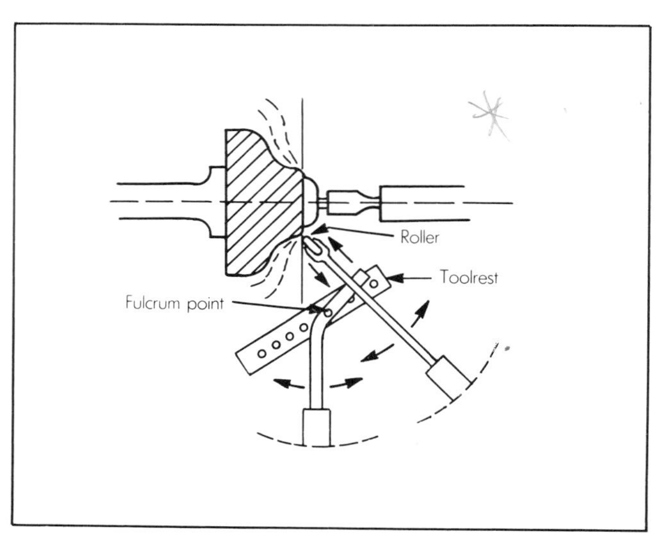


**Fig. 9-3 Scissor-tool manual spinning.**

fastened with quick-acting clamps, keyhole slots, or bayonet pins. If these methods are employed, a smooth-surfaced, spun or machined ring is placed over the bolts or clamps to prevent accidents that could result from the projections. If time and money permit, recessed fasteners should be used.

This dishing method of forming a fairly deep shape, such as a dome or dished head (see Fig. 9-4), is occasionally employed because it is possible to spin inward to a greater depth without annealing than can be accomplished by spinning downward. Spinning lines are produced on the inner surfaces of the workpieces rather than on the outer surfaces, which can provide aesthetic advantages. However, if the workpiece is made of work-hardening material, a dish formed in this manner to a greater depth also has more work stress imparted to it. Care should be taken when the workpiece is removed from the chuck, unless a stiffening flange is spun on the outer periphery prior to dishing, to prevent damaging the part. It is sometimes necessary to stress relieve or anneal spun parts prior to subsequent cutting or other fabricating, but this can cause distortion.

This same general peripheral-clamping concept is sometimes used in spinning internal flanges on a disc which has previously had a center hole cut into it and has been carefully deburred (see Fig. 9-5). Relatively deep internal flanges are made by cutting a groove or channel in the spin chuck, which provides the conical or cylindrical sidewall of the desired shape and additional clearance for the forming tool as it progresses inward. Reversing the blank thus formed exposes the spun, irregular edge for trimming to proper dimension.

### Vacuum Dishing

If equipment is available, vacuum can be employed to assist in the forming. Atmospheric pressure against the disc aids in flowing the metal uniformly. The vacuum enables the operator to have positive control of the metal thickness desired. The clamping method described for push-in spinning can be used; however, it is necessary to enclose the chuck material in metal or plastic to hold a vacuum, and to provide rubber or neoprene rings between the workpiece and the chuck to permit a seal, thus introducing tooling limitations.

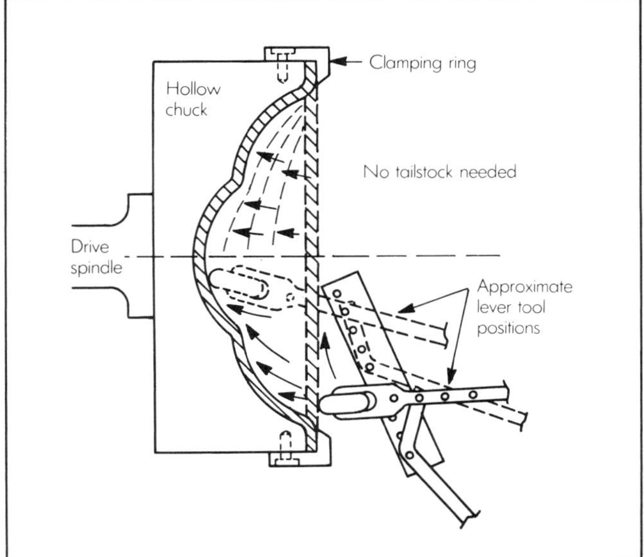


**Fig. 9-4 Dish (push-in) spinning with peripheral fastening of workpiece.**

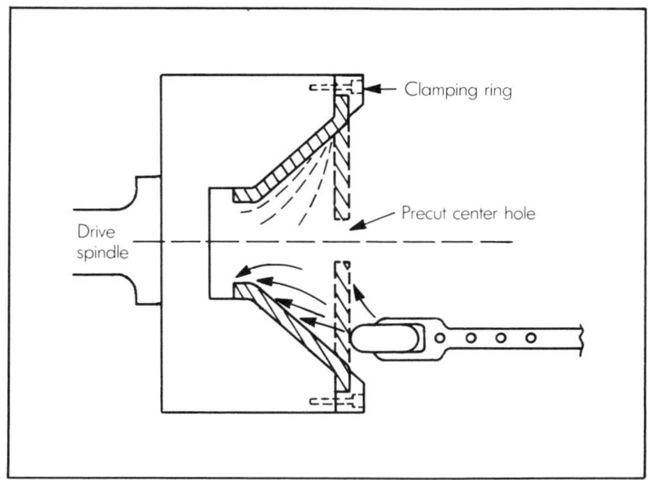


**Fig. 9-5 Forming a taper with a center flange in a precut hole by push-in spinning.**

Air in the chamber is exhausted through a hole in the spindle to which the vacuum hose line is attached with a rotary seal. If a hole in the spindle is not available, a set of matched wear plates can be incorporated into the rear face of the chuck. Such plates are made of steel and phosphor bronze to prevent galling and use flat Teflon rings to maintain a running vacuum seal. This method of forming has been used occasionally with both underarm tools and lever or scissor tools.

## POWER SPINNING

Power, power-assisted, or mechanical spinning employs the same principles as manual spinning, but uses various devices for applying force. The devices employed include (1) toolholding carriages or compounds powered by mechanical, air, hydraulic, or mechanical/hydraulic means and (2) hydraulic or electronic tracing and copying systems using single, multiple, or swivel templates. Machines controlled by CNC (discussed later in this chapter) are also used. The scope of spinning applications has been broadened, and thicker blanks can be spun with power spinning.

Power spinning is commonly used to describe shear forming (discussed next in this section), but the two processes differ greatly. With both manual and power-assisted spinning, the starting blank diameters must be considerably larger than the diameters of the finished workpieces; there is no appreciable or intentional thinning of the material and less working of the metal during spinning than during shear forming. The blank size depends upon the surface area of the spun part. With shear forming, starting blank diameters are approximately the same as the diameter of the finished parts, and there is a controlled reduction in blank thickness.

### Power-Assisted Spinning

This technique is actually a combination of manual spinning and power spinning and can be utilized for either spindown operations or dish-in operations. It is, in fact, a refinement of the lever or scissor tool and gives the operator considerably more forming power than can be exerted with the leverage system. The operator can, by manipulating two levers, cause the tool to move through any series of arcs with in-and-out and back-and-forth motions as indicated by arrows in Fig. 9-6.

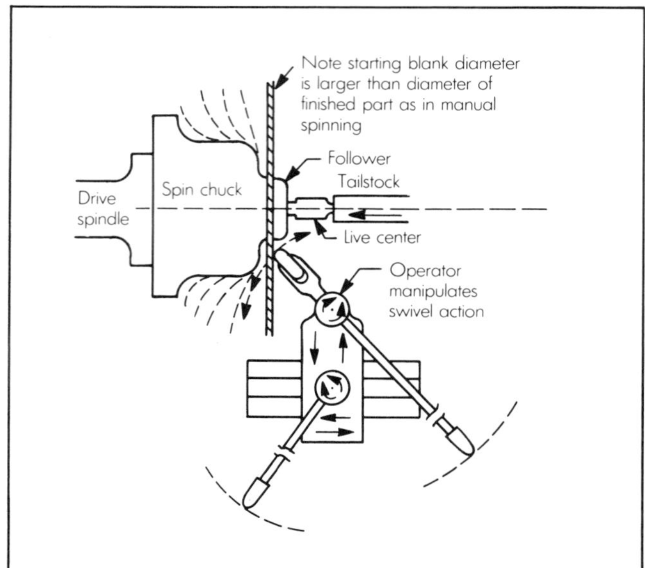


**Fig. 9-6 Power-assisted spinning.**

However, a sensitivity for the reaction of the metal can still be retained. This method requires considerable operator skill and coordination in manipulating the levers. For ironing out wrinkles and stretching deep-drawn parts, a fixed roller and feedscrew on the machine can be used.

### Dieless Dishing

Dieless dishing has been in use for many years to make spun heads for milk and chemical storage tanks, concrete mixers, etc. A special lathe with a large spider faceplate accepts a wide range of sizes of master rings bolted into predetermined dowel holes. The solid or welded blank is fastened around its periphery in the same manner as in the dishing or push-in methods previously described. The forming roller is mounted on a two-dimensional carriage and is moved back and forth across the surface of the blank under power, thus forcing the disc to stretch as it moves into the open chamber. A tracer-controlled mechanism governs the action, and the shape of the tracer template determines the final shape of the head (see Fig. 9-7).

Such spun heads have a horizontal flange which may or may not be cut off depending upon usage. In rapidly work-hardening materials, these shapes have latent stresses which can be relieved by annealing if necessary.

## SHEAR FORMING

Shear forming is a rotary-point extrusion process for spinning conical or hemispherical shapes. One axial-radial pass of the roller(s) produces a significant reduction in blank thickness. This produces high compressive shear stresses in the transverse (material thickness) direction, resulting in a thickness reduction that obeys the sine law equation (see Fig. 9-8).

The process is a variation of power spinning that is sometimes referred to as shear spinning, Hydrospinning, Flo-turning, flow turning, spin forging, compression spinning, Rotoforming, and rotary extrusion. Required shapes are spirally generated by the metal as it is progressively displaced axially between the rotating mandrels and the power-fed rolls. Metal required for forming is obtained from the blank or preform thickness, and starting diameters are approximately the same as those of the finished parts. The final shape can be conical, parabolic, hemispherical, or any other surface of revolution within reason.

### Straight-Sided, Conical Parts

Straight-sided, conical parts are shear formed from two types of blanks: flat and conical.

**Flat blanks.** Shear forming of straight-sided, conical parts from the flat blanks generally conforms to the sine law (see Fig. 9-8). The normal wall thickness, $t$, of the spun cone equals the original blank thickness, $T$, times the sine of half the included angle, $A$, of the cone. Only one thickness can be produced on straight-sided, conical parts when a flat blank with a given thickness is shear formed at a certain angle. The smallest included angle considered practical in shear forming steel into conical shapes from flat plates, without preforming operations, is 30°. This results in approximately 75% reduction in the thickness of the blank in accordance with the sine law.

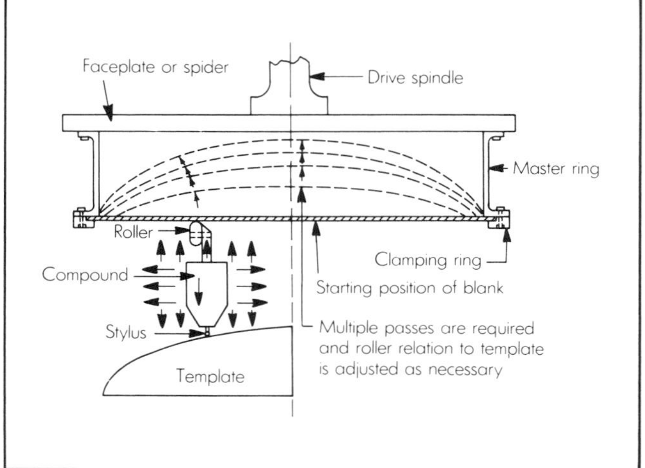


**Fig. 9-7 Dieless dishing of a tank head.**

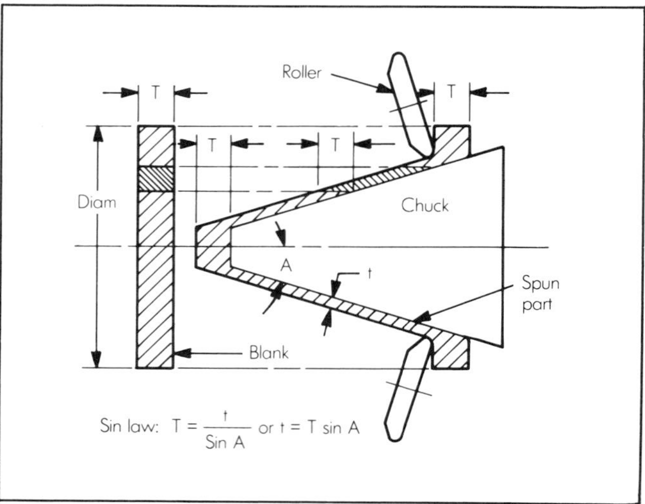


**Fig. 9-8 Sine law relationship in shear forming straight-sided conical parts from flat blanks.**

When the required finished thickness, $t$, and the side angle, $A$, are known, the blank thickness, $T$, can be calculated by the sine law.

Example:

> To spin a part with a 0.125″ (3.17 mm) thick wall at a 30° side angle, the thickness, $T$, of the starting blank equals 0.250″ (6.35 mm).

Strict adherence to the sine law, however, only occurs under ideal conditions. Under conditions of true shear forming, the flange of the workpiece is theoretically stress free, the axial thickness of the cone wall remains the same as the original blank, and the bottom and flange on the spun part also maintain the original thickness. The minimum angle to which a metal may be shear formed from a flat blank is about 15°.

When a part is shear formed to a wall thickness which deviates from the sine law, it is said to be overreduced or underreduced. Overreduction results when the workpiece wall is too thin; underreduction results when the wall is too thick. With overreduction, tensile stresses are induced in the workpiece flange, causing it to lean forward (towards the large diameter of the cone) and resulting in a part having a wall thickness larger than the clearance between the roller and the chuck or mandrel.[1] Severe overreduction causes a preform effect which, by the sine law, leads to further reduction until the part bulges behind the roller or locks to the mandrel in front of the roller, causing the part to break.[2]

When underreduction occurs, compressive stresses are induced and the flange of the workpiece tends to lean backward toward the roller(s). This usually causes the workpiece to wrinkle, break, or loosen on the mandrel, which can cause eccentricity. Underreduction induces tensile stresses in the workpiece flange and localized stretching of the blank, resulting in a wall thickness that is less than the gap set between the roller and mandrel. Forward leaning of the flange can also be caused by too large a tool radius; and backward leaning, by too small a tool radius or too fast a feed rate.[3] Flanges can be straightened by using a backup roller, which is mounted 180° from the forming roller, or by providing a shoulder on the mandrel.

**Conical blanks.** Straight-sided, conical parts are also shear formed from conical blanks, such as those drawn on presses, machined from forgings, or spun previously. This method is used when the angle required on the workpiece is such that reduction from a flat blank in one operation would be more than the material could withstand; it is also used when the flat blank required would have to be thicker than the machine could handle. Formulas giving the relationship between starting and finished thicknesses when straight-sided, conical parts are shear formed from conical blanks are presented in Fig. 9-9.

## Shear Forming Contoured Parts

Contoured parts are shear formed from either flat or shaped blanks.

**Flat blanks.** When contoured parts are shear formed from flat blanks, the thickness of the parts varies throughout the contour. As the side angle becomes smaller, the thickness is reduced.

**Shaped blanks.** To obtain a uniform thickness when shear forming contoured parts, a tracer attachment must be used on the machine or a CNC machine must be used; premachined or preformed blanks must also be used. Starting blanks are sometimes machined to the required shape; however, this can be costly and it is generally more economical to use press-drawn preforms.

Forged preforms incorporating the graduated metal thickness required are sometimes used for shear forming deeply curved or compound shapes. As shown in Fig. 9-10, each portion of the preform incorporates the necessary starting thickness for that portion. The finished part thicknesses are then divided by the sines of the various angles to the centerline as though the part were being made from a blank at 90° to the axis of rotation. The 0.177″ (4.50 mm) thickness equals 0.125″ (3.17 mm) divided by the sine of 45°, and the 0.483″ (12.27 mm) thickness equals 0.125″ (3.17 mm) divided by the sine of 15°.

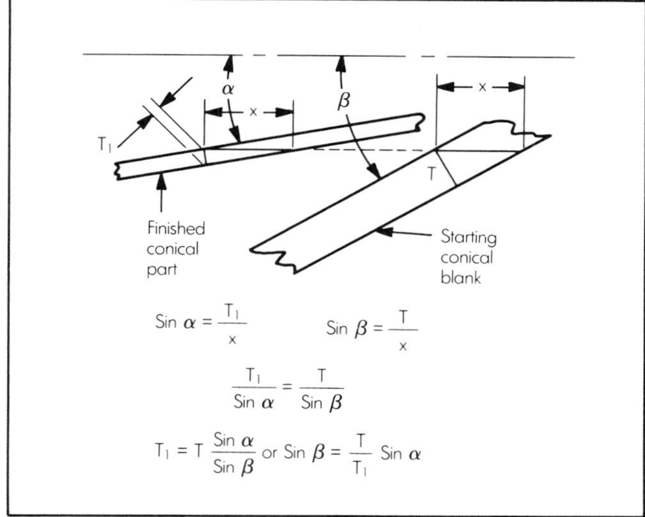


**Fig. 9-9 Relationship between starting and finished thickness when shear forming conical parts from conical blanks.** (*Floturn, Inc.*)

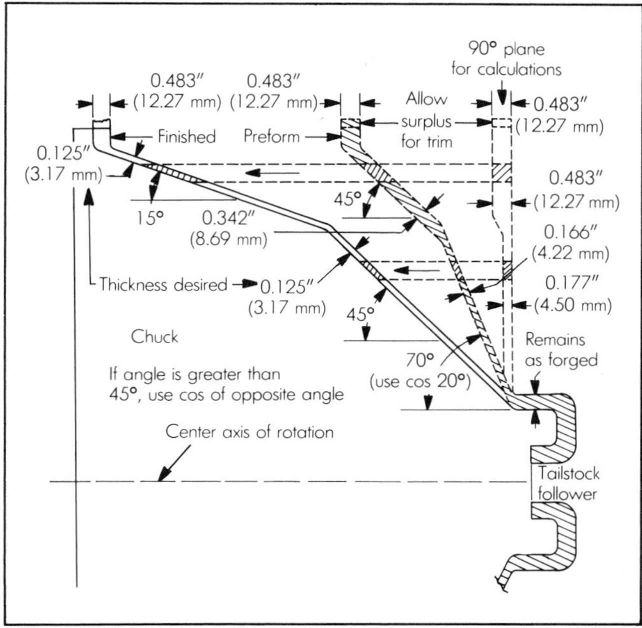


**Fig. 9-10 Forged preform with graduated metal thickness required is used to shear form deep, curved shape.**

From these determined thicknesses, the corresponding axial thickness of the preform is calculated. The 0.166″ (4.22 mm) thickness of the preform equals 0.177″ (4.50 mm) times the cosine of 20°, and the 0.342″ (8.69 mm) thickness equals 0.483″ (12.27 mm) times the sine of 45°. Slight, additional thickness should always be allowed to compensate for roller pressure variations due to changing angles.

### Curvilinear Surfaces of Revolution

Shear forming of curvilinear surfaces of revolution—including hemispheres, ellipses, and ogive shapes—from flat blanks produces tapered walls (thinner near the flanges). Constant wall thicknesses can be obtained by using blanks with varying thicknesses. Figure 9-11 shows an example of a premachined blank to obtain uniform thickness in the shear-formed part. The center area of the blank is machined thinner, and the thickness gradually increases toward the outer edge of the blank.

## TUBE SPINNING

Tube spinning is used to reduce the wall thickness and increase the length of tubes or preformed shapes (cast, roll formed and welded, forged, machined, pressed, or spun) without changing their inside diameters. Reductions in wall thicknesses of 90% and increases in length of 800% have been accomplished in this way without annealing between passes. This method follows a purely volumetric rule, and the sine law does not apply because there is no included angle. Limitations depend upon the amount of reduction the specific metal can withstand without the need for annealing; the percentage reduction necessary to make the metal flow, usually about 15-25%; and the force capacity of the machine.

In addition to reducing wall thicknesses and increasing lengths, with resultant improvements in strength due to plastic deformation, this process is often used to form shaped parts from tubing or preforms, such as parts with flanges at various locations. Varying wall thicknesses can also be produced by employing a tracing attachment on the machine or by using a CNC machine.

### Forward Tube Spinning

In the forward tube spinning method of forming tubes or cylinders, metal flows ahead of the roller(s) in the same direction as the roller feed, usually toward the headstock (spindle) of the machine. While the required thickness reduction and lengthening can often be done in a single operation, two or more passes may be required for some applications. A two-pass operation on a preform is illustrated in Fig. 9-12.

This method has been used for many years to iron out wrinkles and to stretch tubes, particularly in the manufacturing of utensils and cookware. It is also used in the aircraft and aerospace industries for making long, thin-walled, rocket-motor and missile cases and for making special fuel tanks. Advantages of forward spinning include close control of the lengths spun and elimination of distortion problems due to eccentric starting tubes or preforms. The surface finish on the bore of the spun part is almost identical to the finish on the outer surface of the mandrel.

Forward tube spinning is particularly advantageous when a closed-end preform is being worked and the rollers can form stiffener ribs or other forms by tracer or CNC programming. The process has two disadvantages, however, compared with reverse spinning (discussed next): the roller tool must traverse the entire length of the part being formed, thus reducing production speed, and it is limited by the working stroke of the machine.

### Reverse (Backward) Tube Spinning

In the reverse or backward method of tube spinning, metal is extruded beneath the roller(s) in the opposite direction of the roller feed (see Fig. 9-13), usually toward the tailstock of the machine. It is used primarily to produce straight, thin-walled cylinders, but stiffener ribs or other forms can be produced if close tolerances are not required. Preforms are not clamped (as is generally the case in forward spinning), but are slid over the mandrel to the headstock (spindle) end of the machine.

Advantages of reverse tube spinning include the ability to use simpler and more economical blanks, shorter mandrels, and smaller capacity machines than required with forward spinning

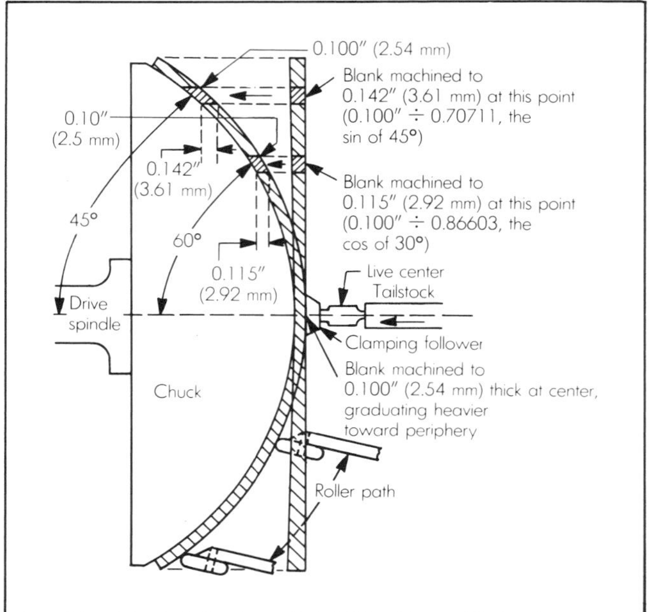


**Fig. 9-11 Shear forming of a premachined blank to obtain uniform thickness in the finished dome.**

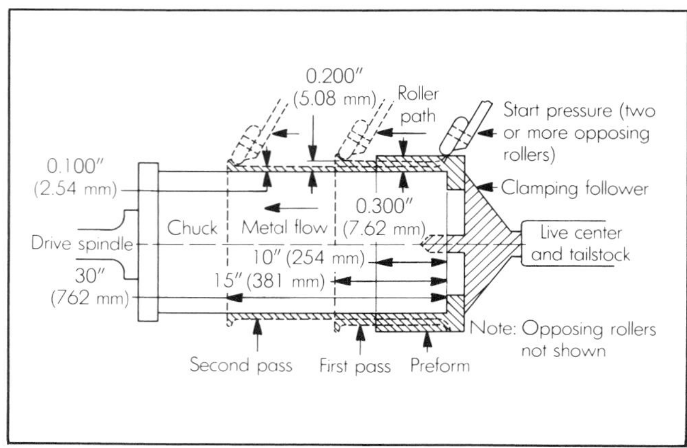


**Fig. 9-12 Forward method of spinning, employing two passes of the rollers to attain the required thickness reduction and lengthening of a preform.**

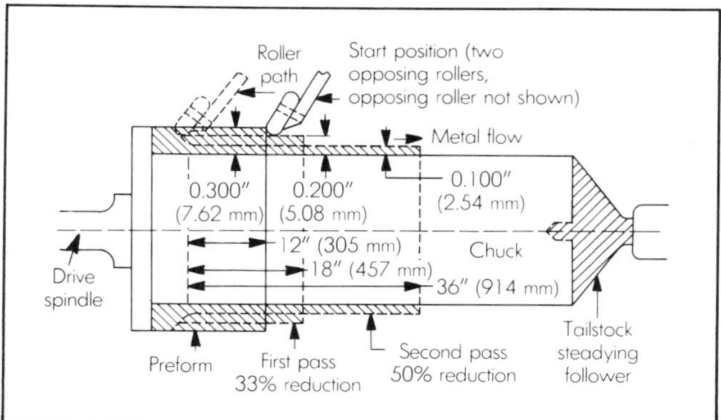


**Fig. 9-13 Reverse (backward) spinning. Position of roller after second pass is not shown.**

to produce the same parts. Good diameter control can be obtained, regardless of the tolerances on the preforms. Only compressive stresses are exerted on the preforms, which is a benefit in spinning materials of limited ductility, such as castings. Increased productivity is also possible because no workpiece clamping is required and a shorter roller travel can be used to produce the same finished length. Surface finishes as smooth as 6 $\mu$ in. (0.15 $\mu$ m) have been produced with this method.

A possible limitation of reverse spinning may be caused by variations in the wall thickness of the preform, which results in a proportional variation in length and some problems with straightness. In the case of forward spinning, inaccuracies in the preform are moved ahead of the roller and subsequently trimmed off.

### Internal Tube Spinning

Internal tube spinning, or roll extrusion, is similar to forward or reverse tube spinning, but it is done from the inside of the preform or cylindrical blank rather than from the outside. Two or more rollers are affixed to a sturdy central shaft to exert deforming pressure against the inside surface. The preform or tube is contained within an external die ring and is drawn down tightly by a separate internal clamping system. As the rollers move slowly downward (in the vertical extrusion process), the metal between the rollers and the restraining die ring is extruded upward as in reverse spinning. Internal spinning is also performed horizontally. As in forward or reverse spinning, great reductions in wall thickness may be achieved and weld seams are so well worked into the parent metal that they are almost impossible to detect.

Internal spinning increases the length of the preform through reduction of the initial wall thickness (see Fig. 9-14). Tapers, flanges, internal stiffeners, and other shapes of variable wall thicknesses can be produced by programming the rollers. Diameters and wall thicknesses can be controlled within ±2%. Diameters to 50" (1270 mm) or more and wall thicknesses down to 0.005" (0.13 mm) are produced.

## ELEVATED TEMPERATURE SPINNING

When the workpiece material, thickness, configuration, or size dictates, the starting blanks and/or mandrels are often heated to facilitate metal movement. Applications requiring multipass spinning at room temperature, with intermediate annealing between passes, can often be done in a single pass, or

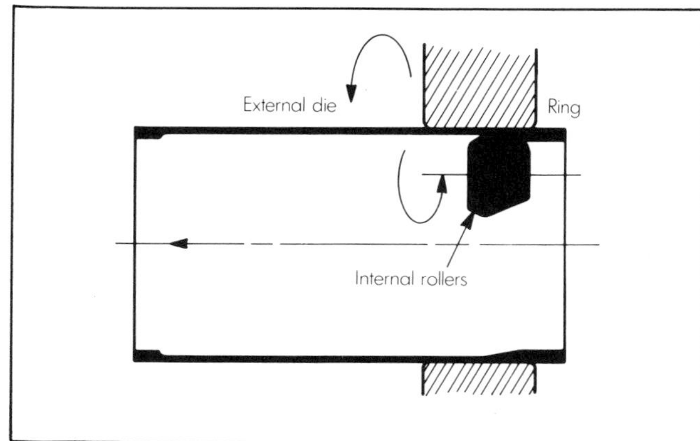


**Fig. 9-14 Internal tube spinning or roll extrusion.** (*Kaiser Rollmet*)

fewer passes, by raising the temperature of the blank or preform. Heating also decreases the force requirements of the machine used.

### Materials Spun Hot

The application of heat for spinning increases the forming limits for most materials. Materials that generally require heating are those with low ductility at room temperature. These include titanium alloys, tungsten, beryllium, high-strength and temperature-resistant alloys, refractory metals, and most of the superalloys.

Temperatures to which the blanks or preforms are raised are discussed later in this chapter. Overheating must be avoided. When shear forming is accomplished below the recrystallization temperature of the material, mechanical working occurs, with a substantial increase in the mechanical properties of the spun part.

### Methods of Heating

Several methods are employed to heat the workpieces for spinning. One effective and common method is to heat the blank or preform locally with gas-torch flames directly ahead of the roller(s). Radiant tube heaters and heat lamps are sometimes employed; and in some cases, the workpieces are preheated in a furnace before being transferred to the spinning mandrel.

For hot shear forming of tubes and cylinders, an induction coil is sometimes used to heat the band of material directly ahead of the roller(s). Correct coil design and operating parameters are critical, however, in this type of operation.

### Equipment Employed

The basic equipment and process for elevated-temperature spinning are the same as for room-temperature spinning. Some equipment modifications may be necessary, however, to protect the operator and machine from the heat. Two problems that may occur in hot shear forming are the cooling action of the tools and mandrels (if not heated) and the adverse effect of heat on the lubricant used.

## COMBINED AND SUPPLEMENTARY OPERATIONS

Other processes often used to produce preforms for spinning include casting, forging, and deep drawing. Operations sometimes performed in the same spinning setup include turning, facing, beading, crimping, flanging, trimming, and cutoff, thus eliminating the need to transfer workpieces to another machine. A multiposition, swiveling toolpost is mounted on the machine for such operations.

Necking-in (shrinking) operations are performed on the open ends of cylindrical preforms with a number of spinning passes, thus controlling shape and material thickness in the necked-in area. Hollow cylindrical parts are also expanded by having the roller apply force to the inside of the part.

# SPINNING CAPABILITIES

Properly applied, spinning has many advantages, but it also has some limitations. A wide variety of materials can be spun and shapes produced, and numerous successful applications exist.

## PROCESS ADVANTAGES

Major advantages of spinning include lower production costs for many applications, reduced tooling costs, close tolerances and smooth finishes, and improved mechanical properties.

### Lower Production Costs

Many parts can be produced at lower cost by spinning. This is especially true for prototypes and limited-production quantities, but it also applies to higher production requirements in some applications. Some firms specializing in spinning consider about 5000 identical parts a practical and economical maximum for spinning. This depends, however, upon the size and shape of the part, and the material from which it is made. For some parts, much longer production runs are more economical with spinning. The high production rates of automatic shipping machines, discussed later in this chapter, also make longer runs economical. Spinning often permits simplified manufacturing, allowing large parts to be made in one piece and generally in one setup, instead of requiring welding or assembling of components, and thus reducing costs and eliminating possible distortion from welding.

Lower production costs are also obtainable from the small investment required in capital equipment, simple and inexpensive tooling needed, high material utilization, shorter lead and setup times, and ability to make design and material changes at minimum cost. Unskilled operators can be employed to attend automatic spinning machines, thus reducing production costs.

Material savings result from the need for less starting stock than required for metal removal processes. Subsequent machining is seldom required, and scrap losses in the form of chips are practically eliminated. Low-cost sheet and strip stock can generally be used for spinning. In one case, a part is now being produced from a sheet metal blank instead of a forging previously used, resulting in a savings in material cost of more than 80%. Such savings are particularly important with the costly materials used for many aircraft and aerospace applications.

### Reduced Tooling Costs

Tooling costs are much less than the cost for stamping or deep-drawing dies, particularly for complex shaped and larger parts, and the tools often last longer. As a result, small quantities of parts can usually be produced economically by spinning. Also, if complex contours are being produced, power spinning or shear forming is usually more economical than deep drawing. For long production runs, however, deep drawing (when applicable) may be less costly unless the part contour is especially complex. Some shapes, such as venturis, however, are generally more easily formed by spinning.

In comparing spinning and deep drawing, several factors must be considered. The deep-drawing method is, of course, governed by the speed of the press operation, the labor cost of the operator, and the tool cost, which is generally higher than that of spinning tools. In large-quantity production, the labor cost per part in drawing can be substantially lower than that in spinning. Certain shapes, however, especially conical shapes, lend themselves much more economically to spinning than to any other method, particularly if automated spinning is used. Both methods are limited only by the size of equipment and the power available to make the metal flow.

Figure 9-15 shows a rough dollar ratio between spinning and deep drawing in producing a cone, a hemisphere, and a cylindrical pot. A cone is relatively easy to produce by spinning, but the cylindrical pot shape is more difficult. The relative cost, however, must be independently determined for each of the processes, as well as for other possible methods. The advantage of lower cost tooling for spinning is sometimes lost on longer production runs because of the greater production time per part required for loading and unloading; however, this is not true with machines featuring automatic loading and unloading.

The cost per part and time required to produce a number of parts by spinning or deep drawing may be compared by inserting the spinning data first, then the deep-drawing data, in the following equations:

$$X = M + L + C \quad (1)$$

$$T = S + \frac{N}{R} \quad (2)$$

where:

$X$ = cost per part
$T$ = production time
$M$ = material cost per part
$L$ = labor cost per part
$C$ = tool cost per part
$S$ = time to build tools, hr
$N$ = total number of parts
$R$ = production rate, parts per hr

Normally, less time is required to make tools with spinning than is needed with deep drawing, and the cost of modification is generally lower.

The production of a limited number of rather deep parts can sometimes be done at considerable savings if deep drawing (on standard drawing tools) and spinning to final shape can be combined. Some spinning companies rely heavily on this combination of facilities and have drawing presses and a wide variety of deep-drawing, round-par tooling available.

## Close Tolerances

Another advantage of automatic spinning and shear forming is that close tolerances can be consistently maintained. With manual spinning, the tolerances held depend upon the skill of the operator.

Tolerances that can be maintained also depend upon the contour accuracy of the mandrel and blanks or preforms, material from which the parts are spun, size of the parts, machine rigidity, control accuracy, and setup. Diametral tolerances for different-size parts, both commercial and special, are presented in Table 9-1. The tolerances given for special applications indicates that supplementary machining (after spinning) is sometimes necessary.

The greatest economy is attained by specifying the most liberal tolerances allowable. Where greater precision is necessary, sufficient stock can be left on the spun part to permit subsequent machining or grinding. Accuracy of the blank or preform is an important consideration, especially with regard to its effect on the length of the power-spun part. Since the process involves the translation of constant volume increments, more metal in the preform wall causes an increased finished part length at a given wall thickness.

## Smooth Finishes

The surface finish produced on the outer surfaces of workpieces by spinning depends upon the material being formed, spinning speed, rate of feed, tool design, and percentage reduction. The finer the feed and the larger the radius on a roller tool, the smoother the finish. Incorrectly shaped rollers (discussed later in this chapter), however, can undercut the blank or preform, causing a burr and producing a rough surface. Surface finishes produced on inner surfaces of the workpieces depend primarily upon the surface finish of the mandrel. Rollers made of bronze, nylon-covered aluminum, or other materials are sometimes used to improve surface finish.

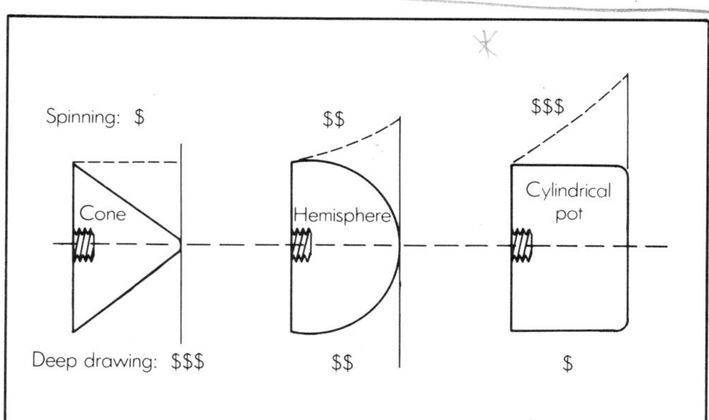


**Fig. 9-15 Approximate cost comparison of spinning vs. deep drawing for producing several different shapes.**

Surface finishes obtained generally range from 32-65 μ in. (0.81-1.65 μ m), but it is possible to produce a finish as smooth as 6 μ in. (0.15 μ m). Minor surface imperfections on the blanks or preforms are generally eliminated. In many instances, finishing or polishing costs incurred from secondary finishing operations can be reduced or eliminated because of the smooth, uniform finish obtainable on spun parts.

## Improved Mechanical Properties

The working of metal during spinning refines and elongates the grain structure, generally in the direction of metal flow (parallel to the workpiece contour), resulting in improved mechanical properties. Tensile and yield strengths, as well as hardness, are all increased (40% or more). This often makes it possible to design products that are lighter because of reduced material requirements, and sometimes permits the substitution of lower cost materials. Also, flaws or inclusions in the material usually result in metal failure during spinning, which eliminates costly subsequent processing and the possibility that an unsatisfactory part will be used in an assembly. Grain refinement of hot spun components, with proper temperature control, is often superior to that obtained in forging because of the high pressures involved with the small contact area between roller(s) and workpiece.

Despite the work hardening during cold deformation, residual stresses in the spun part are generally low. This is because the temperature at the roller/workpiece interface, generally about 1000° F (538° C), relieves the stresses developed. When spinning thick materials with lower interface temperatures, however, the residual stresses can be relatively high. Work hardening does, however, reduce the elongation of the material, but the amount of reduction is controllable. The amount of increase in hardness depends primarily upon the workpiece material and the severity of the operation.

Thermomechanical spin forming, in which a portion or all of the required heat treatment is incorporated into the processing, offers considerable opportunity for improving both efficiency

**TABLE 9-1**
**Diametral Tolerances Maintained in Spinning**

| Diameter of Spun Part, in. (mm) | Tolerance on Diameter, ±, in. (mm) | |
|---|---|---|
| | As Spun, for Most Commercial Applications | Special Applications |
| to 24 (610) | 1/64 to 1/32 (0.4 to 0.8) | 0.001 to 0.005 (0.03 to 0.13) |
| 25 to 36 (635 to 914) | 1/32 to 3/64 (0.8 to 1.2) | 0.005 to 0.010 (0.13 to 0.25) |
| 37 to 48 (940 to 1219) | 3/64 to 1/16 (1.2 to 1.6) | 0.010 to 0.015 (0.25 to 0.38) |
| 49 to 72 (1245 to 1829) | 1/16 to 3/32 (1.6 to 2.4) | 0.015 to 0.020 (0.38 to 0.51) |
| 73 to 96 (1854 to 2438) | 3/32 to 1/8 (2.4 to 3.2) | 0.020 to 0.025 (0.51 to 0.63) |
| 97 to 120 (2464 to 3048) | 1/8 to 5/32 (3.2 to 4.0) | 0.025 to 0.030 (0.63 to 0.76) |
| 121 to 210 (3073 to 5334) | 5/32 to 3/16 (4.0 to 4.8) | 0.030 to 0.040 (0.76 to 1.02) |
| 211 to 260 (5359 to 6604) | 3/16 to 5/16 (4.8 to 7.9) | 0.040 to 0.050 (1.02 to 1.27) |
| 261 to 312 (6629 to 7925) | 5/16 to 1/2 (7.9 to 12.7) | 0.050 to 0.060 (1.27 to 1.52) |

(*Spincraft*)

and product performance. This is especially true for precipitation-hardenable alloys which display a multitude of transition phases during aging. Thermomechanical working utilizes spinning deformation to promote strengthening through dislocation interactions and microstructural refinement, and to generate and manipulate modest defects for accelerated diffusion during phase transformation reactions.[4] These principles have been used successfully in spin forming of low-cost, high-quality hemispheres for missile propellant tanks from commercial 2219 and 6061 aluminum-alloy plate stock.

## LIMITATIONS OF SPINNING

Manual or hand spinning is limited with respect to the workpiece material and thickness, and the size and shape of part that can be spun. Skilled operators are required. A common problem with manual spinning is wrinkling of the flanges, the amount of wrinkling depending upon the skill of the operator.

Power spinning and shear forming are also limited with respect to the shape and size of the parts produced, as well as the workpiece material and thickness, as discussed later in this section.

### Productivity

Manual and power spinning, as well as shear forming, are usually slower than many other forming methods, especially pressworking. Productivity of the processes can be increased, however, with automatic machines and the simultaneous use of two or more forming tools. Multiple-spindle spinning machines permit production rates to 2000 parts per hour, comparable to many press operations.

### Property Changes

Reduced ductility or elongation, excessive grain deformation and orientation, unidirectional properties, and too much of an increase in hardness may be undesirable, depending upon the application of the part. Such effects, however, can generally be corrected by controlling the reduction, intermediate thermal processing, and/or subsequent heat treatment.

### Workpiece Distortion

For some applications, springback of the workpiece material after spinning or circumferential growth during spinning may be a problem. The amount of springback or growth varies with the material, the feed of the forming tool, and the roller geometry. Geometry of the contact area with respect to workpiece dimensions is the significant parameter.

In external spinning, low feeds, small roller angles, and large nose radii on the rollers tend to increase the circumferential dimension of a tube.[5] In internal spinning, however, the same conditions cause the tube to become tight against the mandrel. Annealing between successive spinning passes minimizes springback, but may result in distortion. For some applications, especially when forming thick materials, mandrels are undercut to compensate for springback due to residual stresses.

Distortions such as bellmouthing, buckling, and bowing may occur with some spinning applications, making it necessary to provide stock allowance on the spun part for subsequent machining. In forward spinning of a tube, the feed end of the tube (the unspun end) has a tendency to expand circumferentially, even though the section being reduced in thickness is still quite a distance away (see Fig. 9-16). One solution to this problem is to use a simple retaining ring on the free end of the tube. However, the parameters that play a role in this phenomena are related to the surface deformation that takes place adjacent to the roller/workpiece contact zone.

Surface deformation, also called buildup or wave formation, is governed by reduction in wall thickness, roller angle (or if round, nose radius), the angle of tilt of the roller axis with respect to the mandrel axis, and feed.[7] Buildup becomes more predominant as the deformation zone progresses along the length of a particular workpiece. It further appears that ductility of the material also plays a role to the extent that soft ductile materials have a greater tendency to form buildup ahead of the roller. The buildup increases with increasing reduction, roller angle, and feed; it decreases with increasing roller tilt angle and roller nose radius. There is no appreciable difference in buildup between forward and backward spinning of tubes under otherwise similar processing conditions.

Skewing the roller axis from the axis of the mandrel serves to minimize the relative velocity (axial) between the roller and the deforming workpiece.[8] This has been observed to be the only parametric modification that simultaneously alleviates both buildup and diametrical growth. In addition to controlling relative parameters, a practical method of reducing buildup is to use a second, flat roller that has a cylindrical surface tangent to the outer diameter of the unspun section of the tube. In this way any tendency toward buildup is continually suppressed by the cylindrical roller. It is also possible to design the working roller to have an approach or depressor angle (that is, flat land ahead of the contact angle) to serve the same purpose. Through such techniques a buildup-free deformation zone can be generated, thus minimizing surface defects on the spun surfaces (see Fig. 9-16).

## SHAPES PRODUCED

Spinning is employed to produce hollow parts in a wide variety of contours (see Fig. 9-17), including multidiameter shapes. While most parts that are spun are circular in cross section and radially symmetrical about their axes, it is possible to spin nonconcentric and elliptical parts with special tooling (discussed later in this chapter). Spun parts are sometimes cut apart and used in various assemblies.

Conical parts, which are generally difficult to draw in press operations, are the easiest and most economical parts to produce by spinning. The angle at which the metal meets the mandrel is small, allowing good control of the metal during spinning. Also, the metal is not subjected to severe strain.

Hemispherical shapes are more difficult to spin than cones, but are still ideally suited for the spinning process. Initial spinning is relatively easy because of the small angles between the metal and mandrel; however, as the angles become larger, spinning becomes more difficult.

Straight-sided cylinders with sharp corners are not as easily produced by metal spinning as cones or hemispheres. Spinning the sharp corner angles exposes the metal to high strain and requires more time and skill. In many cases, press-drawn cylindrical shapes are used as preforms for spinning. For some applications, lower production costs can be attained by using welded cylinders as the preforms for spinning operations.

Corner radii should be as generous as possible because sharp corners cause the metal to thin during spinning. Minimum recommended radii are about 1 1/2 times the metal thickness. Smaller radii or sharp corners generally require subsequent machining. Angles between the metal and the mandrel should be as small as possible, with a gradual transition from one angle

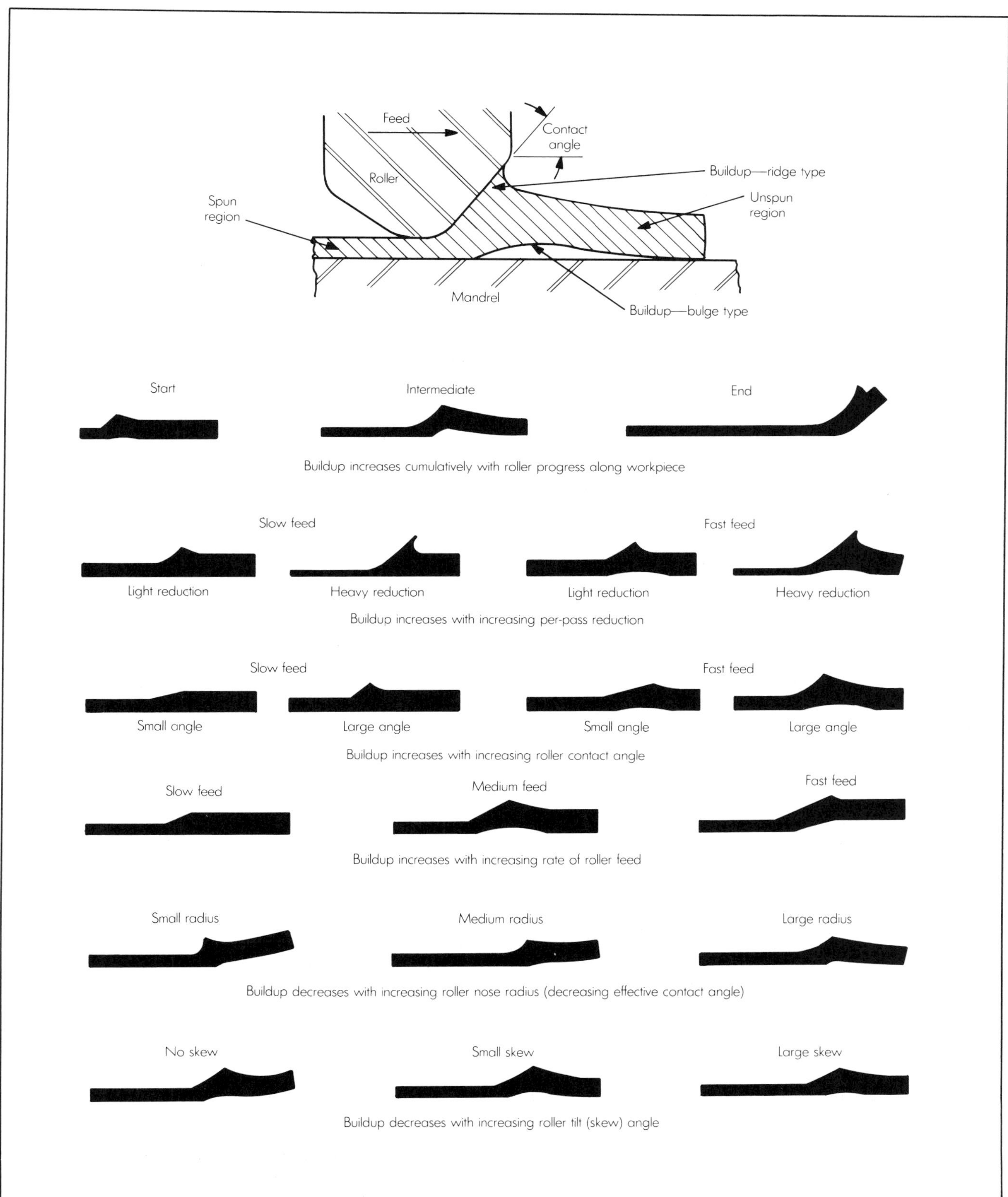


**Fig. 9-16 Influence of process parameters in tube spinning.[6]**

# SPINNING CAPABILITIES

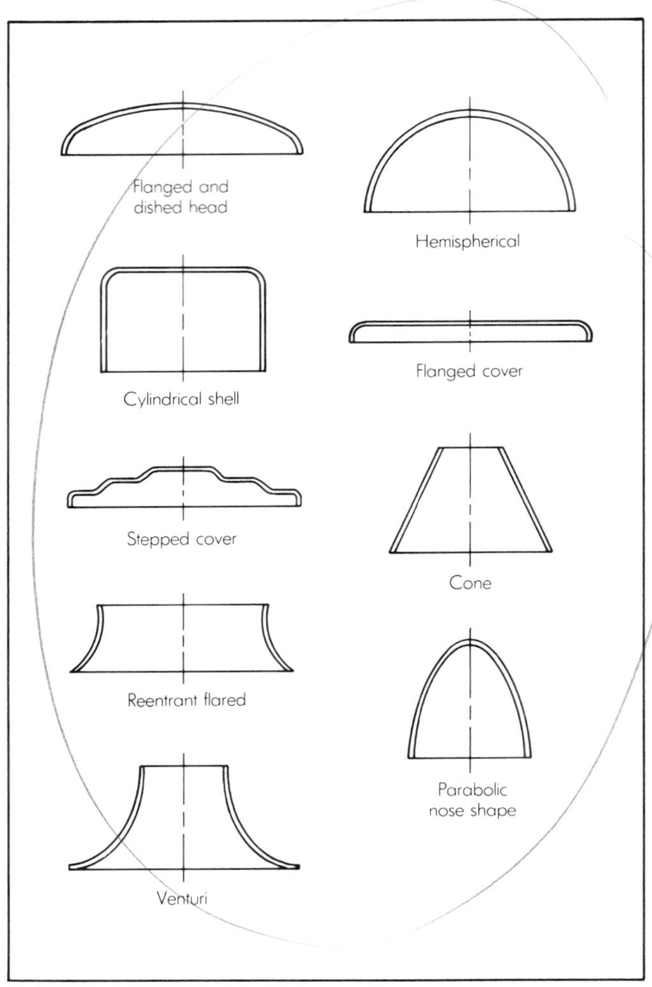


**Fig. 9-17 Variety of basic metal shapes that can be spun.** (*Metal Spinners, Inc.*)

to another. Workpieces with smooth flowing contours generally result in greater rigidity and lower spinning costs.

Reentrant shapes are more costly to spin because additional tooling is required, but they are difficult or impossible to produce by stamping. While outside beads and flanges can generally be formed on a single spinning mandrel, secondary operations and tools are needed to form inside beads or flanges.

## MATERIALS SPUN

Any metal that is ductile enough to be formed by other methods can be spun. The most suitable materials for spinning have good ductility, low hardness, high elongation (10% or more as determined in a pull test), an adequate spread between yield and ultimate strengths, a slow rate of work hardening, and a fine grain size.

Ferritic and pearlitic steel microstructures readily deform in a plastic manner, whereas coarser iron carbide lamina are fractured and redistributed in the highly oriented structure of the cold-worked section. Frequently, it is desirable to subject high-carbon alloy steel preforms to a spheroidizing anneal before power spinning them to place the free carbide in its most easily worked form. When critical, expensive parts are to be spun, it may be desirable to use vacuum-melted metals to ensure sound blanks.

Metals that are formed by spinning include carbon and alloy steels, including stainless and coated steels, and tool steels; aluminum and its alloys; copper, brass, and alloys; precious metals; lead and lead-tin alloys; high-temperature, high-strength, iron-base alloys, including the Hastelloys, Inconels, and René 41; nickel and its alloys; superstrength steels such as Vascojet 1000 and D6AC; and refractory metals such as titanium, zirconium, molybdenum, tungsten, and tantalum alloys.

Most metals are spun at room temperature, with material hardnesses to $R_C35$. Some metals, such as beryllium, magnesium, tungsten, most titanium alloys, and refractory alloys are preheated or heated during spinning to increase their ductility. Other metals are sometimes heated to compensate for insufficient spinning machine capacity or to permit thicker materials to be spun. Many metals which can be formed at room temperature are more readily spun at elevated temperature if thick sections are involved.

Blanks or preforms used for spinning are usually flat sheets or plates, tubes, rolled and welded cylinders and cones, pressed parts, forgings, extrusions, or castings. Preformed blanks drawn on presses are also employed extensively. Blank thicknesses should be held to fairly close tolerances. If the blank is too thick, excess material accumulates at the entry side of the roller and may cause the blank to deflect into a shallow cone. Also, this condition increases the roll pressure and may cause the finished part to lift from the mandrel. If the blank is too thin, the material stretches and may cause failure.

When welded cylindrical and conical preforms are used, high-quality welding and sound welds are essential and planishing and annealing of the weld area is generally recommended. Slag inclusions or voids may cause failure. With proper spinning techniques and reductions of 50% or more, the cast structure of the weld becomes a homogeneous wrought structure 95% or more as strong as the parent metal itself and nearly undetectable. A detailed discussion of welding is presented in Volume IV of this Handbook series.

Any laps, segregations, or inclusions that exist in the material may result in tearing during power spinning. Laminations tend to open up during rolling; when they do, the part usually breaks immediately. If, however, the lamination is close to the surface, it may appear as a blister or "orange peel" on the finished part. Also, in the case of extremely heavy reductions, even tool marks on the blank surfaces may cause fractures. Scale should be removed from forged or cast preforms that are not machined prior to spinning.

### Work Hardening

All metals undergo a change in grain structure during deformation. The metal becomes more resistant to flow as it is spun, and the operator in manual spinning must learn to recognize when it is necessary to stop the process in order to prevent tearing, edge cracking, and wrinkling. The irregular crystalline microstructure is changed to a generally elongated crystalline structure with each grain presenting more surface tension with its neighbor. If the workpiece is removed and annealed, the original structure is restored and the spinning operation can be continued. The extent to which the part must be further worked governs the number of heat treatments necessary. Such heat treatments, properly applied, prevent abnormal grain growth and may be controlled to refine the grain structure.

## Formability Limits

The geometric limit to which a material can be formed without failing by either splitting or buckling is one of the principle factors to be considered when any metalforming operation is analyzed. A purely theoretical approach to this problem in manual and power spinning has not been made to date. Empirical relationships have been developed for manual spinning of straight-walled cups in which limiting geometric parameters are related to material properties (the formability index).[9] These relationships have proved to be of practical value to manufacturing engineers and eliminate, or at least significantly reduce, costly cut-and-try techniques. This type of systematic approach can also be developed for other basic shapes, such as cones and hemispheres.

In manual and power spinning, the outer diameter decreases as the blank is spun against the mandrel. The resulting tangential compressive stresses induce elastic buckles at the edge of the part when a certain limiting cup depth to cup thickness ratio, $H/t$, is exceeded. The limiting cup depth to thickness ratio is related, in turn, to the ratio of the material's compressive modulus and compressive yield strength. This ratio is called the formability index, as expressed by the following formula:

$$\text{Formability index} = \frac{E_c}{S_{cy}} \tag{3}$$

where:

$E_c$ = compressive modulus of workpiece material
$S_{cy}$ = compressive yield strength of workpiece material

Beyond a limiting cup depth to diameter ratio, plastic buckling occurs. This value is a constant (not a function of $H/t$) and is related to the material's tension modulus to tensile strength ratio. Exceeding the forming limits so defined eventually causes shear splitting or circumferential splitting, since the forces necessary to remove or prevent the formation of buckles causes high tensile stresses in the axial and circumferential directions. A guide to the percentage of reduction for shear forming or tube spinning various materials without intermediate annealing is presented in Table 9-2.

Applying heat to the workpiece during spinning increases forming limits in most materials. The affect of temperature on the elastic and plastic-buckling formability indexes for manual spinning is given in graphical form in Figs. 9-18 and 9-19 for several aerospace materials. Some interesting observations can be made from these graphs. Figure 9-19 illustrates a significant rapid increase in the plastic-buckling formability index in the 1000-1500° F (538-816° C) temperature range for the following alloys: 8Al-1Mo-1V and 13V-11Cr-3Al titanium alloys; A-286 austenitic stainless steel; and PH 15-7 Mo and Am-350 semiaustenitic, precipitation-hardenable stainless steels. For René 41, a nickel-based superalloy, the temperature range for increased formability is from 1500-2000° F (816-1093° C). The plastic-buckling formability index for TZM molybdenum and pure tungsten peaks at 1500° F, decreases to a minimum in the 2000° F range, and then starts increasing slightly.

The maximum reduction in shear forming and tube spinning can be predicted from the tensile reduction in area.[10] The curve and experimental data are shown in Fig. 9-20. As the curve indicates, the maximum spinning reduction of about 80% is obtained at a tensile reduction in area of 50%. Beyond this point, there is no further increase in spinnability. The spinnability of materials with a reduction of area of less than 50% depends upon the ductility of the materials.

An increase in temperature generally results in an increase in tensile reduction in area when shear forming or tube spinning, as illustrated in Figs. 9-21, 9-22, and 9-23 for titanium alloys, ultrahigh-strength steels, and refractory alloys, respectively. The temperature required to spin a particular part can be ascertained by referring to these curves and the curve in Fig. 9-20. Other factors must be considered; for example, in Fig. 9-23, it can be noted that pure molybdenum, Mo-0.5 Ti, and TZM molybdenum have room temperature reductions in area greater than 50%, indicating that an 80% spin reduction can be attained. Room-temperature shear forming, however,

**TABLE 9-2**
**Recommended Maximum Percentages of Reduction for Shear Forming or Tube Spinning Various Metals Without Intermediate Anneals**

| | Shear Forming | | Tube |
|---|---|---|---|
| | Cone | Hemisphere | Spinning |
| Metal | Percentages of Reduction, % | | |
| Aluminum alloys: | | | |
| 2014 | 50 | 40 | 70 |
| 2024 | 50 | -- | 70 |
| 3000 | 60 | 50 | 75 |
| 5086 | 65 | 50 | 60 |
| 5256 | 50 | 35 | 75 |
| 6061 | 75 | 50 | 75 |
| 7075 | 65 | 50 | 75 |
| Pure beryllium* | 35 | -- | -- |
| Copper | 75 | -- | 75 |
| Molybdenum* | 60 | 45 | 60 |
| Nickel alloys: | | | |
| Waspaloy | 40 | 35 | 60 |
| René 41 | 40 | 35 | 60 |
| Steels: | | | |
| 4130 | 75 | 50 | 75 |
| 4340 | 70 | 50 | 75 |
| 6434 | 70 | 50 | 75 |
| D6AC | 70 | 50 | 75 |
| H11 | 50 | 35 | 60 |
| Stainless steels: | | | |
| 321 | 75 | 50 | 75 |
| 347 | 75 | 50 | 75 |
| 410 | 60 | 50 | 65 |
| 17-7PH | 65 | 45 | 65 |
| A286 | 70 | 55 | 70 |
| Titanium: | | | |
| Commercially pure* | 45 | -- | 65 |
| Ti-6Al-4V* | 55 | -- | 75 |
| Ti-3Al-13V-11Cr* | 30 | -- | 30 |
| Ti-6Al-6V-2.5Sn* | 50 | -- | 70 |
| Tungsten* | 45 | -- | -- |

* Spun at elevated temperatures; all other metals are spun at room temperature.

# SPINNING CAPABILITIES

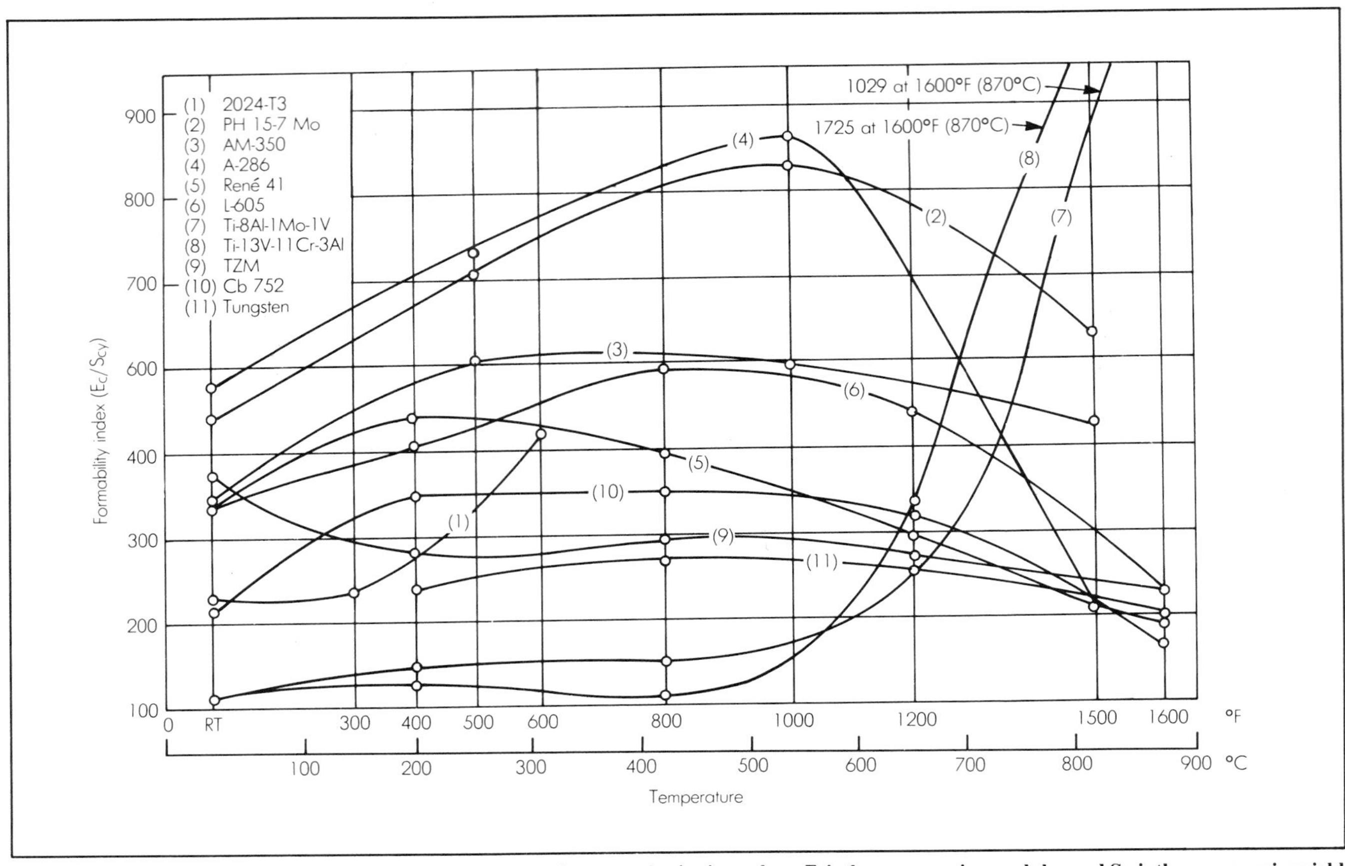


**Fig. 9-18 Elastic-buckling formability index vs. temperature for manual spinning, where $E_c$ is the compressive modulus and $S_{cy}$ is the compressive yield strength of the workpiece material.**

causes the molybdenum to laminate, and thus fail. For the prevention of lamination, a minimum temperature of 800° F (427° C) is required to shear form pure molybdenum. In this case, ductility is not the prime criteria.

The curve in Fig. 9-24 can be used in analyzing problems when cones are being shear formed. As a hypothetical example, one approach to producing a cone with a 60° included angle from a material that can be shear formed only 20% at room temperature would be to spin the material in three passes, with intermediate annealing between passes. In this case, the first breakdown mandrel would have an included angle of 108°; the second, an angle of 80°; and the final mandrel, an angle of 60°. Another approach would be to spin the part conventionally to an included angle of 80°, anneal, and then spin the preform to 60°. If an elevated temperature could be used to increase the permissible reduction of 50%, the part could be shear formed from a flat blank in one pass, thus eliminating the extra tooling required in the cold-forming operations.

While light reductions may be desirable for work hardening the surface layers of the product, they can have strong adverse affects on product quality.[12] This is because reductions result in high nonuniform deformation. The surface layers of a tube experience virtually all the deformation, with little deformation of the bulk of the underlying material. Thus, the plastic zone under the roller does not fully penetrate the thickness of the tube. This, subsequently, generates a hydrostatic tensile stress component which can cause cracks on the mandrel side of the tube wall. The mechanism is the same as that obtained in drawing and extrusion of solid and tubular parts (refer to Chapter 13, "Cold Drawing, Extruding, Heading, and Automatic Forming"), the fracture being called by a variety of names such as center burst, chevron, arrowhead, and cuppy core. The generation of these cracks is further accelerated by the presence of impurities and inclusions, particularly if they are hard.

To avoid such fractures in tube spinning, two important parameters have to be controlled.[13] One is the per pass reduction in thickness. Under otherwise identical conditions, higher reductions decrease or eliminate fracture by ensuring that the plastic zone penetrates through the thickness of the tube. The other parameter is the roller geometry. The smaller the roller angle (equivalent to the die angle in drawing), the larger and deeper the deformation zone. Furthermore, the radius between the roller angle and its relief angle is important. This is because the larger this radius, the smaller the effective roller angle, particularly with small reductions on thin-wall tubes.

## Part Sizes and Material Thicknesses

Limitations with respect to workpiece size and metal thickness in spinning depend upon the maximum swing of the spinning machine and the power available to form the metal. The maximum size and thickness limits shown in Table 9-3 are used by at least one company specializing in power spinning. Limitations for most other metals fall under the limits given in the table, depending upon the shape and depth of the workpiece,

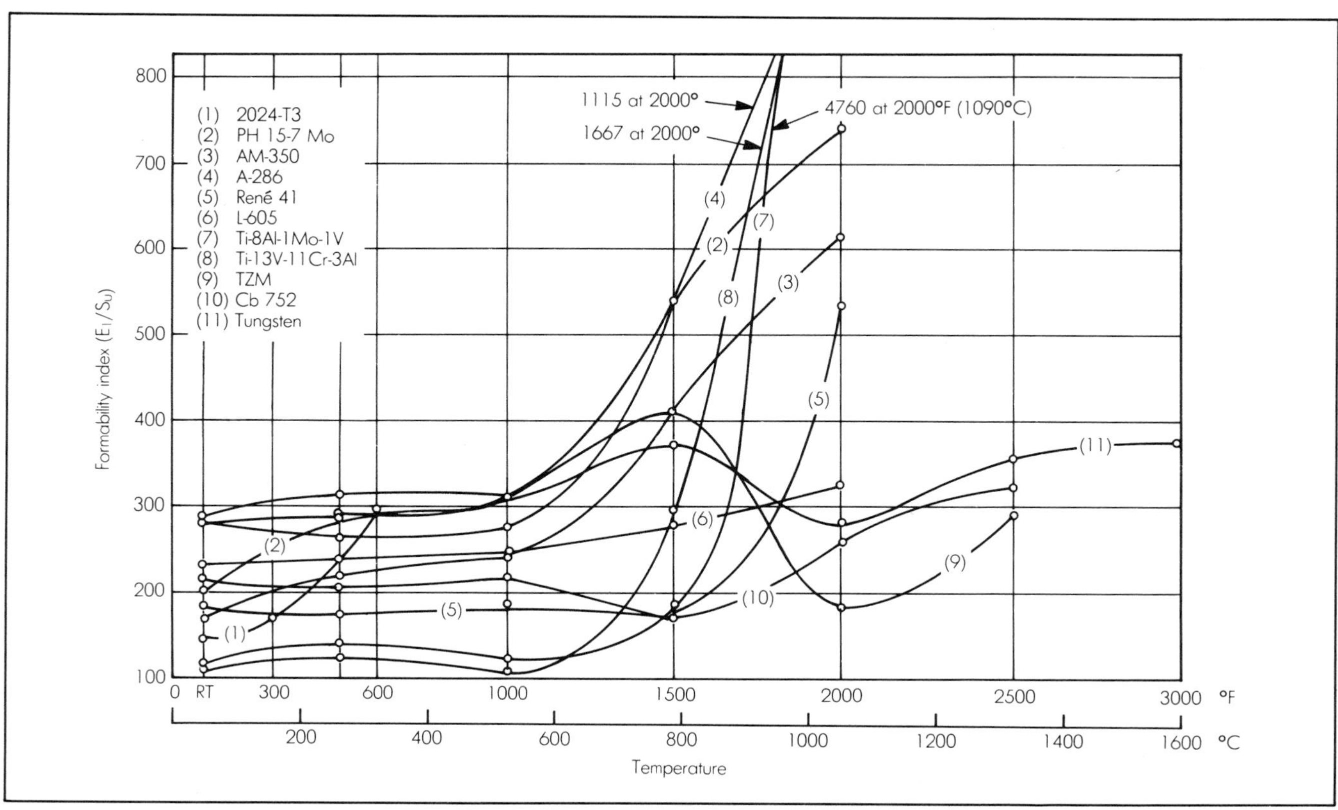


**Fig. 9-19 Plastic-buckling formability index vs. temperature for manual spinning, where $E_t$ is the tensile modulus and $S_u$ is the ultimate modulus of the workpiece material.**

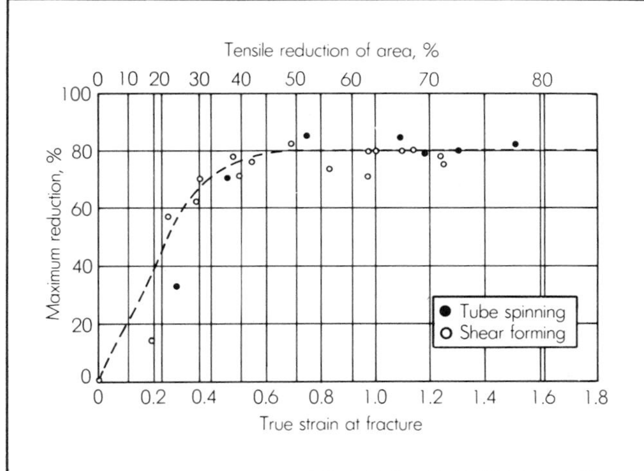


**Fig. 9-20 Maximum reduction in shear forming and tube spinning of various materials.**[11]

type of operation and tooling, and tolerance requirements. This same firm also spins parts as small as 1/4″ (6.3 mm) diam and materials as thin as 0.004″ (0.10 mm).

With manual spinning, the maximum practical thickness of low-carbon steel that can be spun is about 1/8″ (3.2 mm), with diameters to approximately 72″ (1829 mm). Larger diameter parts can be spun with thinner blanks of low-carbon steel.

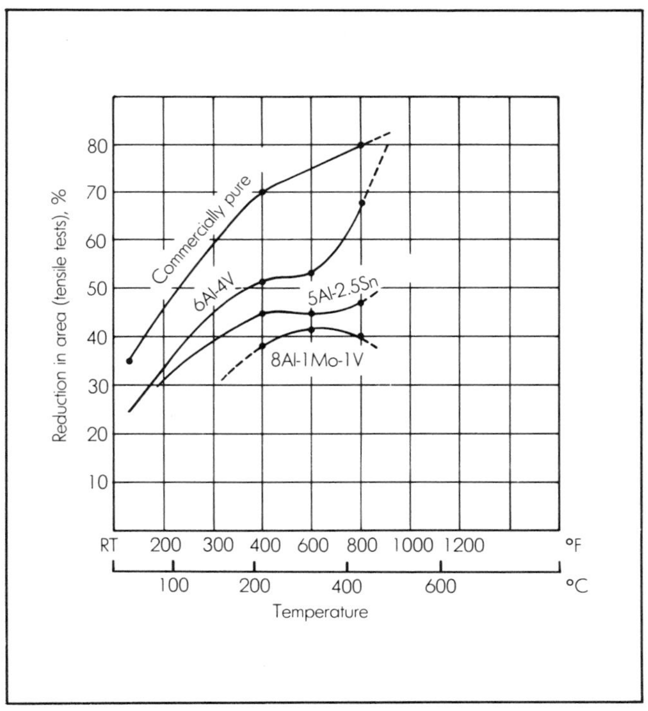


**Fig. 9-21 Tensile reduction in area for titanium alloys.**

Aluminum alloys to about 1/4" (6.3 mm) thick can be spun manually. With power spinning, parts to 300" (7620 mm) diam by 6" (152 mm) thick have been spun.

## APPLICATIONS OF SPINNING

Spun parts are used extensively by the automotive, appliance, air handling, aircraft and aerospace, machinery, ordnance, power generation, and petroleum industries. The wide variety of parts produced include tank heads, pressure vessels, air diffusers and deflectors, housings, cooking utensils, light fixtures, cylinders, holloware, milk cans, television picture tubes, cream-separator centrifuge discs, turbine engine components, nose cones, missile cases, and weapon components.

### Forming Compressor Cases

Compressor cases for aircraft turbine engines are shear formed from forgings for increased strength-to-weight ratios. The forgings, made from AISI 410 stainless steel, are about 28 1/2" (724 mm) diam x 6 1/4" (159 mm) long, with a wall thickness of 0.510" (12.95 mm). Spinning blanks are prepared by machining the forgings, producing a wall thickness of 0.194" (4.93 mm). Shear forming is done in two passes. In the first pass, wall thickness is reduced to 0.125" (3.17 mm); in the second pass, the wall thickness is reduced to only 0.042" (1.07 mm) in specified areas between internal ribs. This is accomplished with a template and hydraulic tracer control of the forming roller, and an undersized, grooved mandrel.

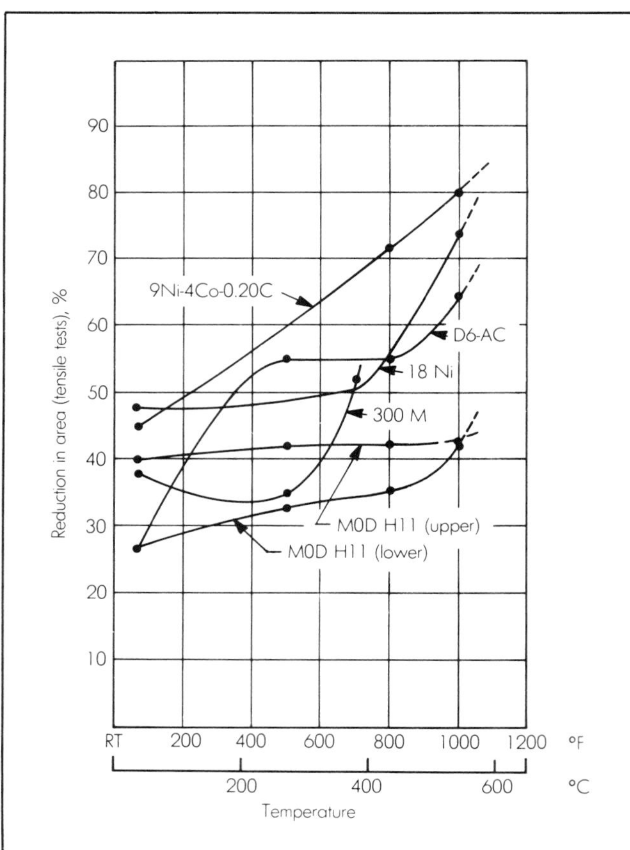


**Fig. 9-22 Tensile reduction in area for wrought ultrahigh-strength steels.**

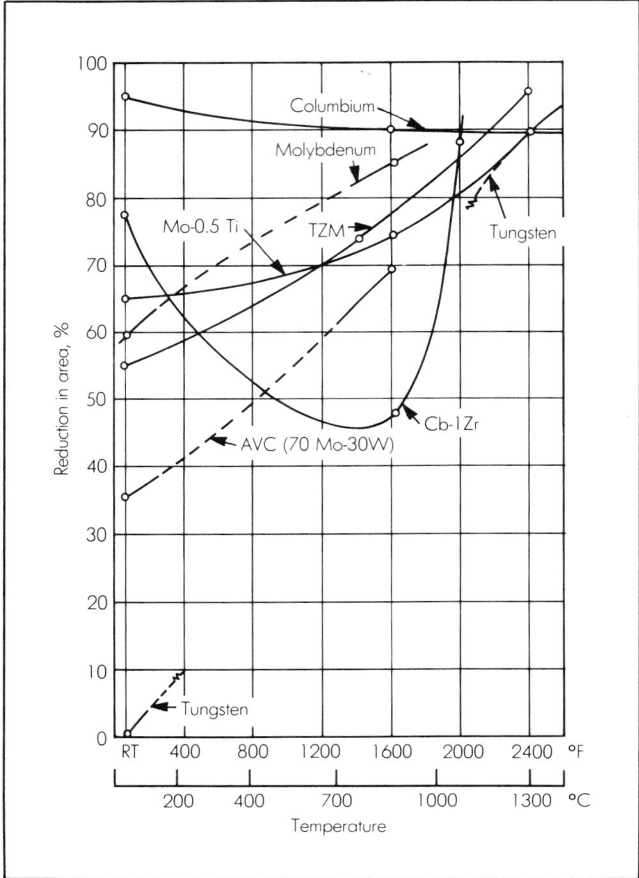


**Fig. 9-23 Tensile reduction in area for refractory alloys.**

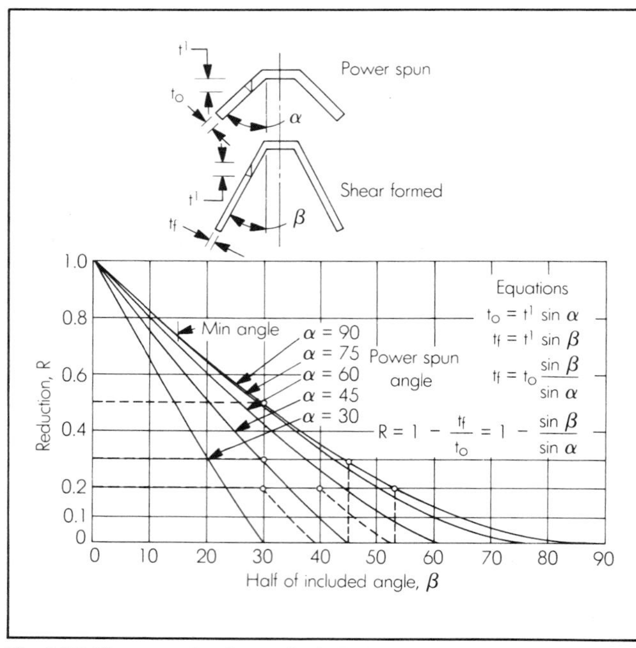


**Fig. 9-24 Percent reduction vs. included angle for shear forming cones.**

## Producing Missile Cases

Substantial reductions in material and processing costs are being obtained by shear forming missile cases. The Minuteman missile cases were originally made from four rolled rings and two end pieces, requiring five welds. By using shear forming, the cases are produced from a single rolled ring, thus eliminating three rings and welds and saving more than half the material cost.

Short-range attack missile (SRAM) cases are shear formed on a two-roll machine. A reduction in wall thickness of 70% is attained in one pass, which is about the maximum in shear forming the iron-base, D6AC material used. Ogive-shaped reinforcements on the ends of these cases are also formed on the same machine.

## Truck Wheel Disc Production

Dish-shaped truck wheel discs (see Fig. 9-25) are being shear formed from flat steel blanks, 23.214″ (589.64 mm) diam, to a depth of 4.71″ (119.6 mm) in a single pass. Metal thickness is reduced from 0.406″ (10.31 mm) near the center to 0.165″ (4.19 mm). This operation is done on a two-roll machine equipped with tracer/template control and automatic loading/unloading equipment that permits the production of more than 100 parts per hour.

Other truck wheel discs are being produced on tracer-controlled, three-roller shear forming machines with production rates in excess of 130 parts per hour from each machine. One disc is formed from a 0.330″ (8.38 mm) thick, flat steel blank in a single pass, with the tapered thickness decreased to 0.125″ (3.17 mm) at the outer edge.

**TABLE 9-3**
**Typical Size and Thickness Limits for Spinning**

| Workpiece Diameter Range, in. (mm) | Aluminum Alloys | Low-Carbon Steels | Stainless Steels and Superalloys |
|---|---|---|---|
| | Material Thickness, in. (mm) | | |
| To 48 (1219) | 3.000 (76.20) | 1.500 (38.10) | 1.500 (38.10) |
| 49-72 (1245-1829) | 2.000 (50.80) | 1.250 (31.75) | 0.625 (15.87) |
| 73-120 (1854-3048) | 1.250 (31.75) | 0.750 (19.05) | 0.375 (9.52) |
| 121-210 (3073-5334) | 0.625 (15.87) | 0.500 (12.70) | 0.250 (6.35) |

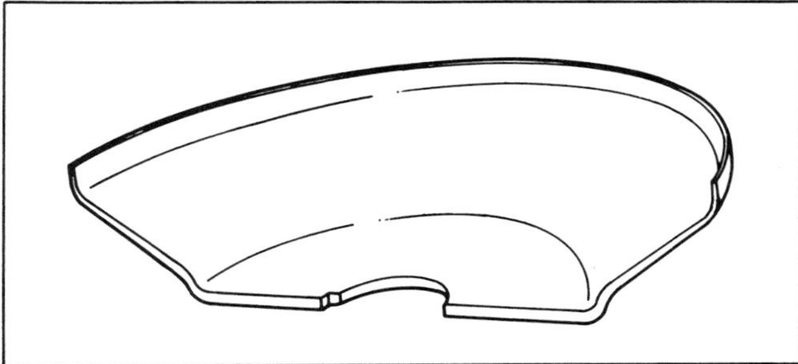

**Fig. 9-25 Sectioned truck-wheel disc is shear formed from flat steel blank at rate of more than 100 parts per hour.** (*L & F Industries*)

## Nuclear Piping

High-strength, thin-wall piping for nuclear power plants is being produced from preforms. Raw material savings are more than 75% compared to the conventional method of machining from solid steel billets, and the tensile strength of the material is increased by 30%. This operation is performed on a vertical, two-roll machine. The metal is forward extruded to reduce the wall thickness of the preform and increase its length about three times. Stainless-steel nuclear pipe has been shear spun on horizontal machines to 16″ (406 mm) diam x 20 ft (6.1 m) long, and by internal roll extrusion, to 28″ (711 mm) diam x 20 ft long.

## Thin-Wall Tubing

Internal roll extrusion has been used to produce brass and stainless steel tubes 6″ (152 mm) diam, with a wall thickness of only 0.0040″ (0.102 mm) ±0.0002″ (0.005 mm).

## Aluminum Nose Cones

Production spinning of missile nose cones is done in three passes, starting with 1/2″ (12.7 mm) thick blanks of annealed 6061 aluminum alloy. The finished cones, 34″ (864 mm) long, have a tapered wall thickness ranging from 0.078″ (1.98 mm) at the closed end to 0.125″ (3.17 mm) at the open end. Required wall thicknesses are maintained with ±0.006″ (0.15 mm) in spinning.

## Hot Spinning Applications

As stated previously, spinning at elevated temperatures is employed for many applications, especially with workpiece materials that are difficult to form at room temperature. The details of five typical applications are presented in Table 9-4.

Cup-shaped titanium supports are being hot spun in six passes, with a total forming time of about three minutes, on a two-roller CNC machine. Flat blanks of 6 Al-4V titanium alloy, 11.7″ (297 mm) diam x 1″ (25 mm) thick, are heated to 1650° F (899° C) for this operation, and the mandrel is heated to 400° F (204° C). Spin forming produces supports about 7″ (178 mm) long with a minimum wall thickness of approximately 23/32″ (18 mm). The spun-formed supports are vacuum annealed prior to rough machining and then solution treated and aged prior to finish machining.

Stainless steel rings having spherical outside and inside diameters are being hot spin formed in five passes requiring two minutes on a two-roller CNC machine. Flat discs of annealed, type 304L stainless steel, 13 1/2″ (343 mm) diam x 3/8″ (9.5 mm) thick, are heated to 2000° F (1093° C). The spun-formed rings are 3.37″ (85.7 mm) wide, with a spherical radius of 4.58″ (116.3 mm). Minimum wall thickness of the formed rings is 0.29″ (7.5 mm).

Machines are being used extensively for the hot forming of necks and the closing of ends of tubular components. Heated tubes or preforms are generally transferred by a loading unit to the shear forming machine and are clamped in a collet chuck. An ejector, built into the headstock of the machine, ejects the finished part onto a transfer conveyor. Integral domes and necks are being spun on tubing to 20″ (508 mm) diam for pressure vessels. One automated line, consisting of induction heaters, automatic material handling equipment, and a CNC shear forming machine, is producing in excess of 100 pressure cylinders per hour. Necks are formed on open-end forgings, 9 1/4″ (235 mm) diam x 54″ (1372 mm) long and weighing 130 lb (59 kg) each.

## SPINNING CAPABILITIES

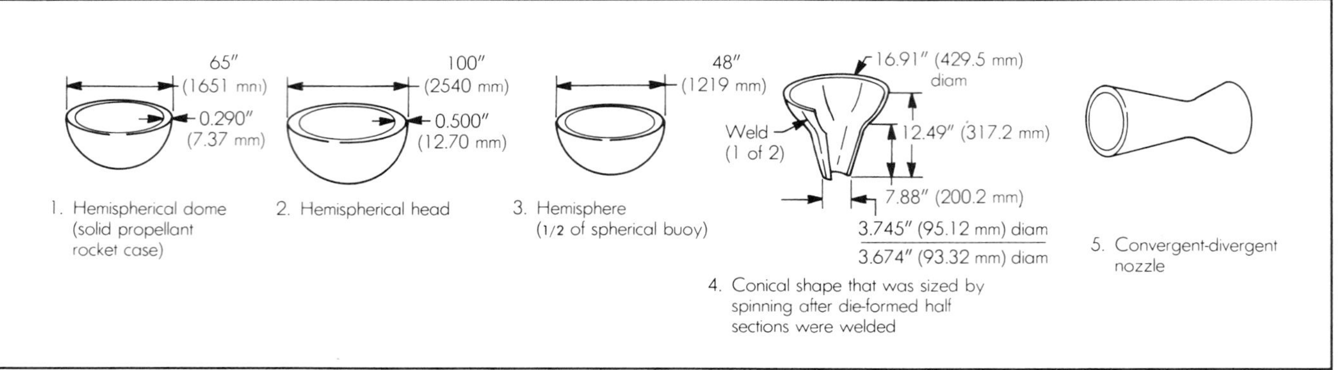


**TABLE 9-4**
**Typical Hot-Spinning Applications**

| | Part Number (see drawing above) | | | | |
|---|---|---|---|---|---|
| | 1 | 2 | 3 | 4 | 5 |
| Workpiece material | PH15-7 MO, AM-340 | D6AC | 6061-0 aluminum alloy | HK31A-H24 MAG | Tungsten |
| Material thickness, in. (mm) | 0.290 (7.37) | 0.500 (12.70) | 1 1/4 (32) | 0.180 (4.57) | 0.030-0.250 (0.76-6.35) |
| Blank configuration | 83″ (2108 mm) diam | 144″ (3658 mm) diam | 65″ (1651 mm) diam | Die-formed half sections welded together | 1. Shear form flat blank into 30° cone (two passes). 2. Conventional spin to 9°. |
| Tolerance, in. (mm) | ±0.020 (0.51) | --- | --- | --- | --- |
| Thickness reduction, % | 30 | 35 | --- | --- | --- |
| Mandrel temperature, °F (°C) | --- | --- | 450 (232) | 650 (343) | 900-1000 (482-538) |
| Blank temperature, °F (°C) | 1600 (871) | 1550 (843) | 600 (361) | 650 (343) | 1800-2100* (982-1149) |
| Heat source | Propane oxygen (four torches) | Oxyacetylene torches | Gas torch | Gas torch | Oxyacetylene torches |
| Mandrel material | Steel | Gray iron | Gray iron | Cast iron | --- |
| Forming tool material | --- | H11 tool steel | --- | --- | --- |
| Temperature sensor | Pyrometer | Optical pyrometer | Temperature-sensitive crayon | Pyrometer | --- |
| Lubricant | --- | Molybdenum disulfide in oil | --- | Graphite | Molybdenum disulfide or water-graphite suspensions |

**TABLE 9-4—*Continued***

| | Part Number (see drawing above) | | | | |
|---|---|---|---|---|---|
| | 1 | 2 | 3 | 4 | 5 |
| Rotary speed of workpiece | --- | 800-1200 sfm | 24 rpm (heating) 78 rpm (spinning) | --- | --- |
| Machine | Hydraulic power assist | Hydraulic power assist | Hydraulic power assist | --- | --- |
| Number of operations | Two breakdown mandrels, two hot-forming passes | Three mandrels, three hot passes | One mandrel, multiple forward and backward passes | Size part by spinning subsequent to welding | Conventional spin 9° cone into convergent divergent nozzle |
| Subsequent operations | Stress relieve and cold finish form | Stress relieve, sandblast, and inspect magnetically | Rough trim at 600° F (316° C) and finish trim at 250° F (121° C) | Clean part and stress relieve at 500° F (260° C) for one hour | Hydrohone part and stress relieve at 1750° F (954° C) for one hour in dry hydrogen |

* A temperature of 2100° F (1149° C) is the maximum due to recrystallization of the tungsten above this temperature.

# SPINNING MACHINES

Machines used for spinning are available in a wide variety of types and capacities. Major types include manual, powered, and automatic machines. Standard spinning machines are available, but many are specifically designed to produce a particular part or family of parts.

## MANUAL SPINNING LATHES

Machines used for manual or hand spinning are similar to lathes and are often called spinning lathes, but they do not have leadscrews or compound slides. They consist essentially of a headstock and a tailstock mounted on a bed and are equipped with an adjustable toolrest. Some machines have handwheels or levers on a compound slide for longitudinal and transverse movements of the tools, eliminating the need to use hand-held tools.

Some manual spinning machines have headstocks with reduction gears to permit turning the required spinning mandrels on the machines. Variable spindle speeds are sometimes provided to allow spinning at a constant surface speed. Some machines have slidable beds to provide gaps for spinning large-diameter parts.

## POWER-ASSISTED MACHINES

Power-assisted spinning machines also resemble lathes, but are equipped with mechanical, hydraulic, or air-actuated slides. They have headstocks with power trains, tailstocks, and main slides that move the cross slides, which support the forming rollers. One machine has been built that can spin parts to 26 ft (7.9 m) diam.

Machines are available with horizontal or vertical-spindle structures and can be equipped with tracing systems to control the paths of the rollers. Some machines have hollow spindles for handling long tubes and pipes. The forming rollers are generally free wheeling (rotated by frictional contact with the workpiece); but on some machines, they are brought to operating speed by a hydraulic motor with a slip clutch.

On a horizontal-spindle, hydraulic spinning machine of one design (see Fig. 9-26), a separate hydraulic power unit operates both the tailstock cylinder and two feed systems in the compound rest, which is clamped to the machine bed. A hydraulic motor rotates a feedscrew for longitudinal movement of the spin roller. Mounted on the bottom slide and connected to the feedscrew by a recirculating ball nut is a top slide. This top slide contains a hydraulic cylinder for transverse movement of the spin roller.

### Tracer Control

While the operator does not have to provide power for spinning on these machines, skill is still required unless tracer or automatic path control of the forming roller(s) is provided.

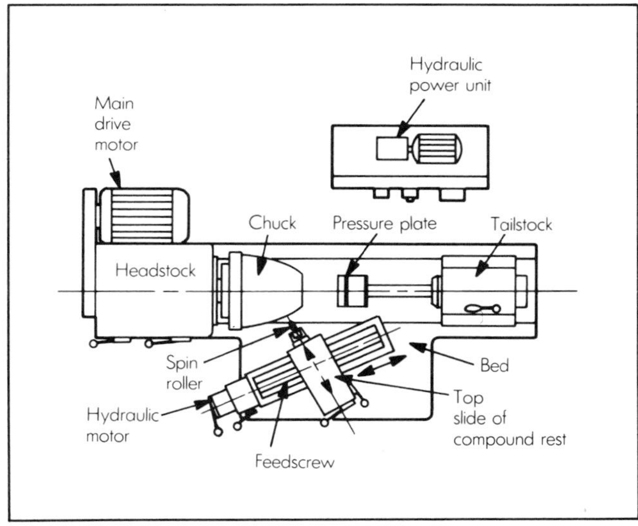


**Fig. 9-26 Hydraulic spinning machine.** (*Leifeld & Co.*)

Hydraulic or electronic tracing systems are employed, and the templates are generally made from flat steel plates. With some systems, the stylus on the tracing head is coupled to a variable-volume pump by electrohydraulic servovalves to control the output volume from the pump.

The use of a multiple template for spinning is illustrated in Fig. 9-27. The tracer unit is mounted on the top slide of the compound rest. A swivel template rotates about a pin projecting from the underside of a fixed template. By retracting the swivel template in increments, either by means of a handwheel (not shown) or programming on an automatic machine, the workpiece is progressively spun. Roller movement for the final pass is controlled by the fixed template.

### Automatic Control

Semiautomatic or fully automatic spinning, requiring even less operator skill than tracer control, is being used to attain higher production rates and to maintain closer tolerances. For semiautomatic operation, automatic positioning of the saddles, cross slides, and tailstocks during the cycle can be controlled by limit switches. Fully automatic spinning is attained by electrical sequential programming, NC, or CNC. A comprehensive discussion of sequence controllers, NC, and CNC is presented in Chapter 5, "Machine Controls," of Volume I, *Machining*, of this Handbook series.

On some machines equipped for sequential programming, plug-in diode pins are inserted in pegboard-type matrix control panels. Once the machine has been programmed, it is only necessary to load blanks or preforms and unload spun parts. Program charts indicating the proper locations for inserting the diode pins are retained for future setups.

Some machines are equipped with digital playback systems for automatic control. The machine is manually operated to produce the first part. A control unit automatically records and stores all movements (changed into electrical signals) on a cassette. The program data is stored on a floppy disc with some systems. For immediate or future production requirements, the control is switched to automatic replay.

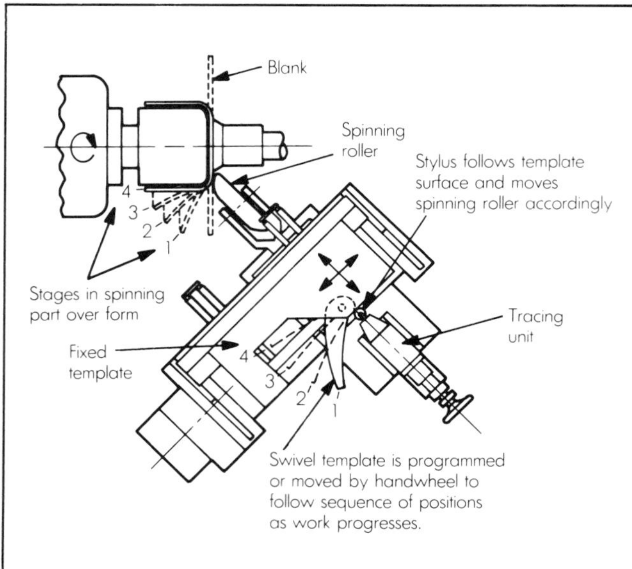


**Fig. 9-27 Multiple-template tracing setup for power-assisted spinning.** (*Spincraft*)

### Advantages of CNC

Computer numerical control (CNC) is being applied extensively to spinning for many of the same reasons that have made it such a popular control technology for metal removal (refer to Chapter 5, Volume I). Primary advantages include improved accuracy, consistent repeatability, and elimination of possible human errors. The additional cost of such controls is offset by reduced labor costs, quick setup, and increased productivity.

With CNC, there is a transition of technical expertise from the shop floor to an engineering data base. In an engineering environment, the process can be studied, programmed, and reviewed in the form of graphic plots before execution on the machine tool. Once the program is at the machine, CNC editing capabilities permit a fast change to an acceptable sequence of forming geometries. Furthermore, more complex forming geometries can be accommodated than are possible with multiple or swiveling template controls.

Once programmed, CNC spinning machines can be used economically for limited production runs because their setup time is short. Minimum labor requirements, especially when automated loading/unloading means are provided, also allow CNC spinning to be used for large-volume production, competing successfully with deep-draw operations in many instances. Spinning machines with CNC have been built for simultaneous contouring control of two, three, and four rollers, requiring as many as eight axes.

Programming a CNC for spinning is more complex than for metalcutting. Because of the plastic deformation of material and deflections of machine components in spinning, the resulting spun geometry is not identical to the programmed contour. Programming is facilitated by integral interactive-graphics hardware and software.

Software modules for spinning are available from machine and control manufacturers. Standard features available on some CNC units include contouring selection, spindle speed control, and axis speed orientation and control. Most controls can be interfaced with and react to other on-line auxiliary equipment, such as optical pyrometers, pressure transducers, and other force or electrical current measuring devices, often used in spinning superalloys. With the addition of a computerized data-acquisition system, it is possible to provide process traceability of the parts produced.

## SHEAR FORMING MACHINES

Shear forming machines are available in horizontal and vertical models, with various capacities and one to three forming rollers. In many cases, shear forming machines are also suitable or adaptable for power-assisted spinning; and for some applications, power-assisted spinning and shear forming are combined in one continuous cycle. While these machines also resemble metalcutting lathes, they generally exert higher forces in both the longitudinal and transverse directions and provide higher feed rates.

Most shear forming machines are hydraulically operated and can be fitted with tracer control or CNC. They generally have variable speed drives and variable feed mechanisms. More sophisticated models incorporate electronic and hydraulic controls to integrate the spindle speed and roller feed rate, thus producing constant feed per revolution and constant surface speed for varying workpiece diameters.

Many shear forming machines are of two-roller design. The

rollers may be set opposed to each other, or one roller can be offset to feed ahead of the other roller. With the rollers offset, roughing and finishing passes can be performed simultaneously, thus permitting higher reductions per cycle. The roller housings on most machines can be swiveled to position the rollers for various shapes of parts.

Horizontal-spindle, shear forming machines made by one builder have tailstocks that are positioned by motor-driven screws and clamped hydraulically. Standard horizontal models are available for forming parts to 45″ (1143 mm) diam x 70″ (1778 mm) long. They are powered by direct current (d-c), adjustable-speed drive motors to 200 hp (149 kW) and can exert forces to 75,000 lb (333.6 kN) for each slide unit.

Standard vertical models for heavier, larger diameter workpieces are built for parts to 75″ (1905 mm) diam, with motors to 350 hp (261 kW) and forces to 250,000 lb (1112 kN) per tool slide. On vertical machines, a carriage holding the roller slides is moved vertically on columns by hydraulic cylinders. Special vertical machines have been made to form parts 120″ (3048 mm) diam, with a vertical capacity of 150″ (3810 mm) under the tailstock. With the vertical acting tailstock retracted to the rear of the machine, tubular parts exceeding 300″ (7620 mm) in length can be spun, loading and unloading through the top of the machine.

A machine has been built for the reverse (backward) method of shear forming that can produce tubes 3 1/2 to 27″ (89 to 686 mm) diam with wall thicknesses of 0.015-1.5″ (0.38-38 mm). The machine (see Fig. 9-28) can accommodate horizontal mandrels to 30 ft (9 m) long, supported by the headstock, a sliding tailstock, and intermediate supports. Three work rolls are mounted on a carriage that is moved longitudinally by two leadscrews, with transverse motion controlled by a hydraulic tracer system. Steel tubes to 58 ft (17.7 m) long have been produced, and it has been estimated that aluminum tubes to 150 ft (45.7 m) long could be formed.

One manufacturing firm has two horizontal shear forming machines that can operate in the forward or reverse modes to produce diameters to 24″ (610 mm) and lengths to 22 ft (6.7 m). The larger of the two machines can exert a force of 800 tons (7.1 MN).

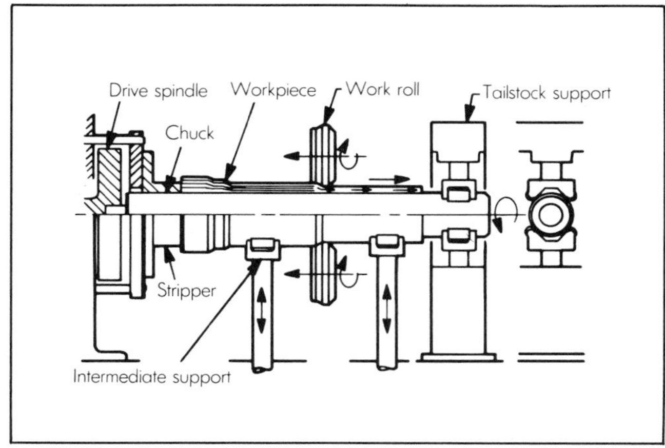


**Fig. 9-28 Machine using the reverse (backward) method of shear forming to produce long tubular components.** (*Floturn, Inc.*)

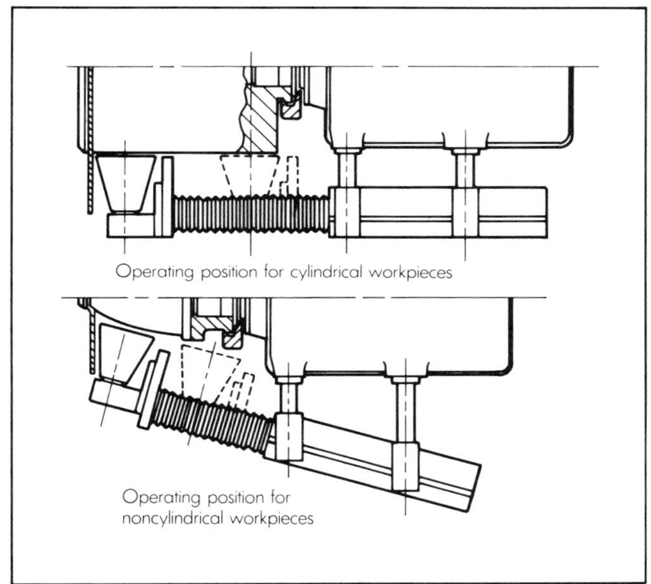


**Fig. 9-29 Counterpressure (backup) roller helps prevent wrinkling of edges of thin blanks.**

## MACHINE ACCESSORIES AND ATTACHMENTS

Many accessories and attachments are available for spinning machines to increase productivity and/or improve the quality of the parts produced. One useful device is a centering attachment that supports and automatically centers blanks. The hydraulic unit mounts on the machine bed and is adjustable for different sizes of blanks. It eliminates the need for prepunching center holes, if required, and frees the operator to perform other operations.

A counterpressure or backup roller (see Fig. 9-29) can be helpful in preventing the formation of wrinkles at the edges of thin blanks. The rotating roller supports the edge of the blank by exerting an adjustable hydraulic force, normally permitting the use of fewer passes and a higher infeed. Such attachments are mounted on the headstocks of the machines. Crimpers that bend the edges of the blanks are also used to minimize wrinkling.

Stripper mechanisms and ejector devices are employed to remove spun parts from mandrels. Some have a rod extending through the machine spindle to eject the finished parts; others have a stripping-finger mechanism housed in the tailstock spindle. Indexing-type universal toolholders, turrets, or toolchangers are desirable for performing secondary operations on the spun parts. For large vertical machines, floor-level faceplates are available to facilitate loading and unloading of large workpieces and tooling. Closed-circuit television systems are sometimes used for close-up viewing of spinning operations from remote locations.

Various types of automatic loading and unloading equipment are available. One type for vertical machines has a shuttle mechanism with an upper and a lower cradle on its end. When the tailstock has retracted, the shuttle rapidly advances into the machine. A blank on the lower loading cradle is released on the top of the mandrel. Simultaneously, the spun part is released onto the upper cradle and the shuttle returns to its outside position. This signals the tailstock to advance and the automatic spinning cycle to begin. Industrial robots are being used increasingly for automatic loading and unloading.

## MULTISPINDLE MACHINES

Vertical, four-spindle, automatic spinning machines are available (see Fig. 9-30) for producing tapered and contoured parts from 2-10" (51-254 mm) diam, with a maximum height of 6" (152 mm). The multispindle design, with built-in automatic load/unload mechanism, permits production rates of 500-2000 parts per hour.

Four parts are produced automatically with each revolution of the continuously rotating spindle-tool carrier. Mild steel blanks to 0.062" (1.57 mm) thick and aluminum alloy blanks to 0.125" (3.17 mm) thick can be spun. Beading and rolling operations can be performed simultaneously with attachments.

A roller-type spinning tool, workpiece hold-down, and form mandrel are provided for each of the four spindles. Cam-actuated, adjustable pressure arrangements progressively form a part as the carrier moves each spindle through the work sector. Loading of flat blanks or drawn cups and unloading of spun parts takes place automatically at the same time that parts are being formed on the other three spindles. The automatic loading and unloading units have positive cam-controlled motions synchronized with the other machine functions. They are capable of moving vertically, swinging in an arc, and sliding horizontally. Spindle speeds are variable from 400-3000 rpm. Optional equipment includes a flood coolant arrangement, beading attachment, and blank support units.

Tool actuation and forming pressures are programmable for each individual work spindle. This provides the ability to produce as many as four different parts with each rotation of the spindle-tool carrier—a major advantage when parts are not required in large quantities.

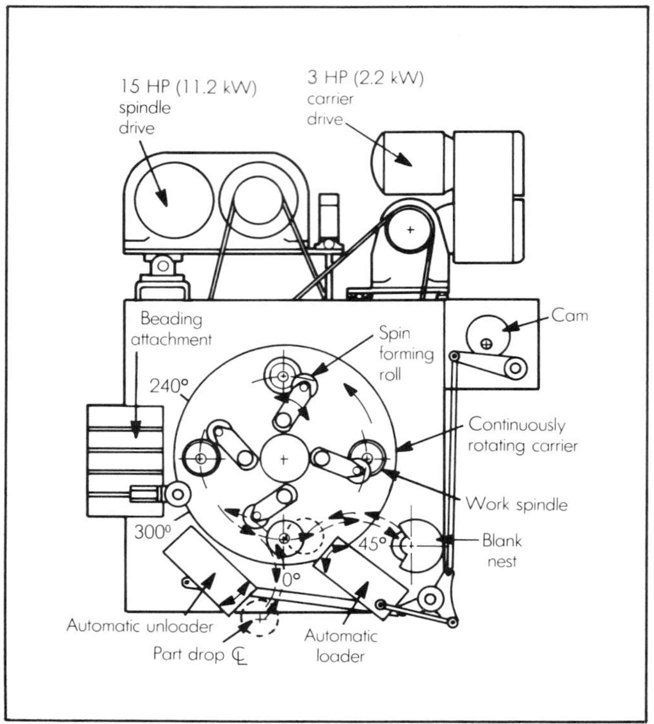


**Fig. 9-30 Top view of a vertical, four-spindle, automatic spinning machine.** (*BFL Associates*)

# TOOLING FOR SPINNING

Major tooling requirements for spinning are the chucks (mandrels) and the forming tools or rollers.

## CHUCKS

Spinning chucks, or mandrels, determine the internal shape and size of the finished workpiece, as well as the surface finish produced in the bore of the part. These tools are often referred to as spinning forms, arbors, blocks, or patterns.

Makeup of the chuck is governed by the following factors:

1. Tolerance requirements on the part to be spun.
2. Quantity of parts to be spun.
3. Type of metal to be spun, which may require hot spinning.
4. Thickness of the metal.
5. Workpiece size.
6. Desired life for the chuck or mandrel.

In general, high production requirements (500-5000 parts) for close-toleranced parts require precision steel tooling or possibly iron castings, whereas 1-100 pieces of loose-toleranced, soft-metal parts might be made on wood or wood-composition tooling. Chucks need to be balanced only if rotational speed induces vibration. Generally, static balancing is adequate, but if rotational speeds are high, dynamic balancing should also be used. It is seldom necessary to balance wood or composition spin chucks.

Springback of the metal to be spun, which occurs primarily on the flanges, is of vital concern in the geometry and makeup of the chuck. Sometimes undercutting at the finished edge is necessary. It is generally possible to produce a limited number of soft-metal parts, such as aluminum, copper, and low-carbon steel, on wood or composition chucks, but it is frequently necessary to build tooling which has an extremely dense, hardenable surface to obtain proper flow and metal finish. In addition, many of the chucks used for spinning heat-treatable alloys and space-age metals necessitate extremely complicated geometry to provide finished part dimensions within tolerance. Hot-spinning techniques are usually employed for these materials.

### Materials for Chucks

Chucks for low production requirements, especially for manual and power-assisted spinning, are sometimes made of wood, such as hard maple, that is carefully selected, cured, and kiln dried. The blocks used normally consist of strips or layers of wood that are cross laminated and glued together prior to turning to the required shape. Blanks of hard maple are available commercially. Hard maple chucks for large parts are sometimes fitted with steel reinforcing rings at areas where high forming pressures are exerted or where corners with small radii are required on the workpieces. Chucks made of less costly wood-resin or wood-fiber compositions are satisfactory for some applications where the pressure of the forming tools or rollers is closely controlled. An advantage of high-quality wood-resin tools is less distortion with changes in humidity.

For closer tolerance requirements, higher pressure forming, and the production of smoother finishes, chucks are generally made of cast iron or steel. As-cast gray iron is commonly used for the low-production spinning of soft metals. Alloy cast irons, sometimes selectively flame hardened, are employed for slightly higher production requirements. Chucks made from steels such as AISI Grades 4150 or 52100, hardened to $R_C$55-60, provide even longer life for high production.

Tool steels, such as AISI Types 01, 06, A2, D2, or D4, hardened to $R_C$60-63, are used extensively for small and medium-sized chucks, especially for shear forming operations. Such chucks have a long life.

## Number and Types of Chucks

Many spun items can be produced on a single chuck turned to the inside shape of the part, but it is frequently necessary for the sake of economy or metal-thickness control to spin through several progressions or breakdown operations similar to those of deep drawing (see Fig. 9-31). Fewer operations are generally required when spinning thinner materials. Reentrant shapes can generally be made on segmented or split chucks, such as that illustrated in Fig. 9-32, or on internal rollers, as shown in Fig. 9-33, when the part has a smaller open-end diameter than its largest diameter. There are other methods to achieve this forming that are not so commonly used, such as spinning over semihard rubber balloons; over a low-melting-temperature bismuth alloy chuck; or when making just one piece, over wood which is then chipped or burned out.

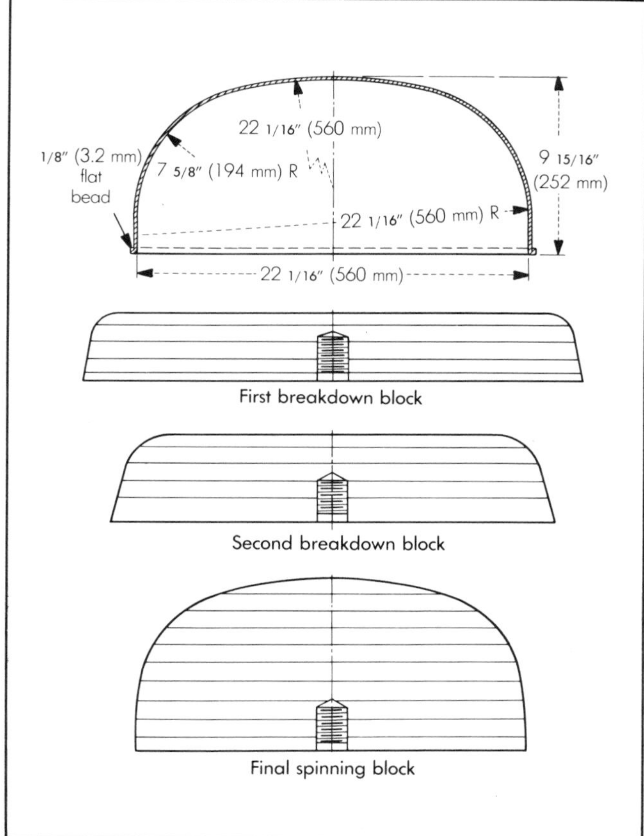


**Fig. 9-31 Progressive chucks or breakdown blocks for producing the spun part shown in the top view. Fewer operations can generally be employed for thinner materials.**

When using low-melting tooling for semiclosed shapes, the bismuth alloy is molded on a steel mandrel and the required contour is machined. After spinning, the bismuth alloy is melted and the mandrel removed. This method is best suited for ductile materials such as aluminum and copper, small-sized parts, and limited production requirements.

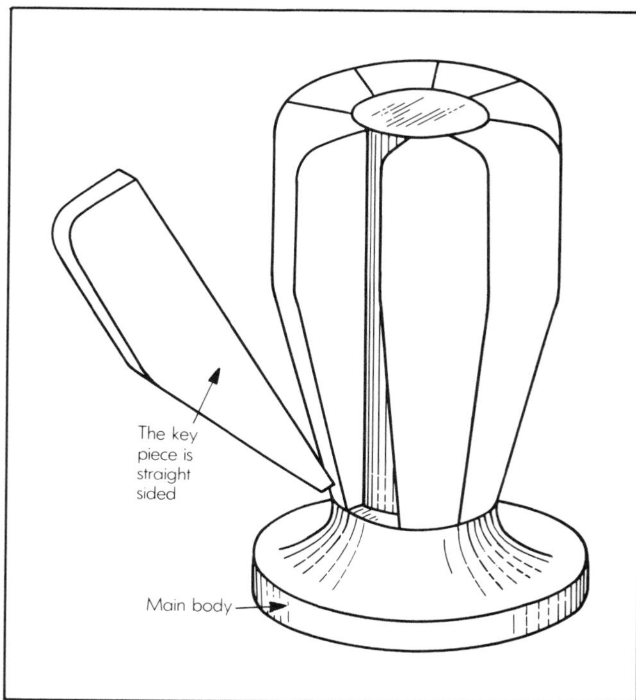


**Fig. 9-32 Collapsible sectional chuck used for spinning a vase or pitcher. After part is formed, the split tool ring is removed, starting with the key piece having parallel sides.**

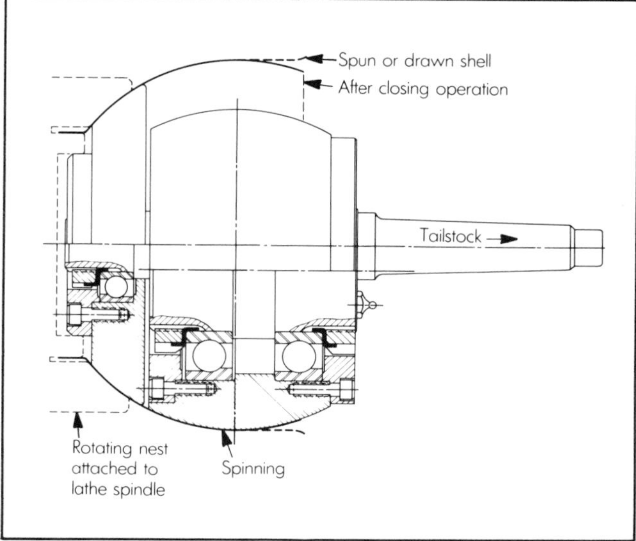


**Fig. 9-33 Off-center chuck for spinning reentrant shapes.** (*Spincraft*)

# CHAPTER 9

## TOOLING FOR SPINNING

Cross sections of different chucks used to shear form various shapes of parts are shown in Fig. 9-34. Multistage tooling employed to produce a part having a nonconcentric shape is illustrated in Fig. 9-35.

### TOOLS FOR MANUAL SPINNING

Tools used for manual (hand) spinning generally fall into three categories:

1. Laydown tools.
2. Beading or finishing tools.
3. Cutting or trimming tools.

Laydown tools usually have a round end or ball nose. Sometimes the upper part of the tool is made round for laydown operations and the bottom is slightly crowned for planishing. Beading tools for finishing the edges of spun parts have a sharp nose or are provided with a wheel. Cutting or trimming tools have diamond-shaped tips.

Underarm tools are made in a wide range of shapes, sizes, and compositions. Polished hickory sticks are sometimes used for laydown operations. More commonly, round, tool-steel bars with tips forged to the shape desired are generally hardened and polished, and sometimes chrome plated. Tools made of aluminum bronze in rod form are highly satisfactory for spinning steel. Such tools are usually fitted into wooden handles (see Fig. 9-36).

Hardened and polished steel rollers (see Fig. 9-37), which revolve in contact with the workpieces, are used extensively with lever or scissor tools, especially for spinning large parts and thick materials. The diameters, thicknesses, and contours

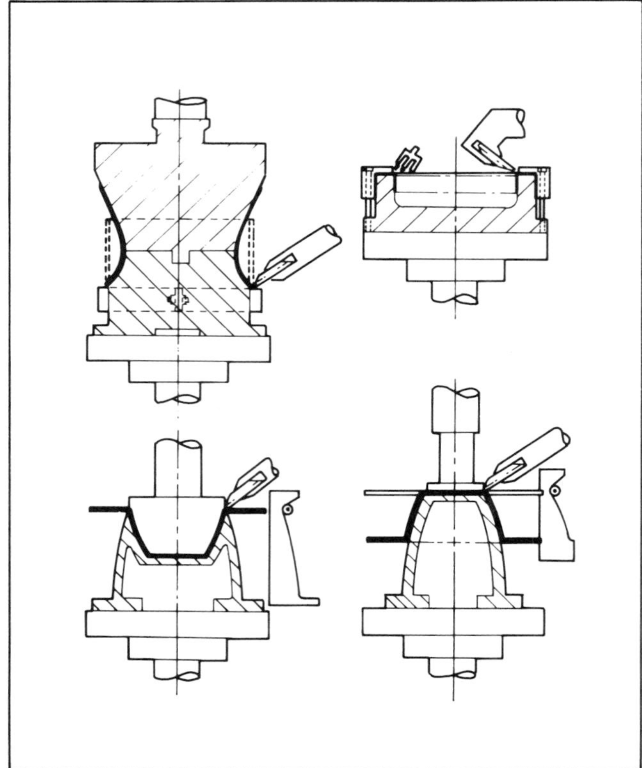

**Fig. 9-34 Sectional views of several chucks for shear forming various shapes of parts.** (*L & F Industries*)

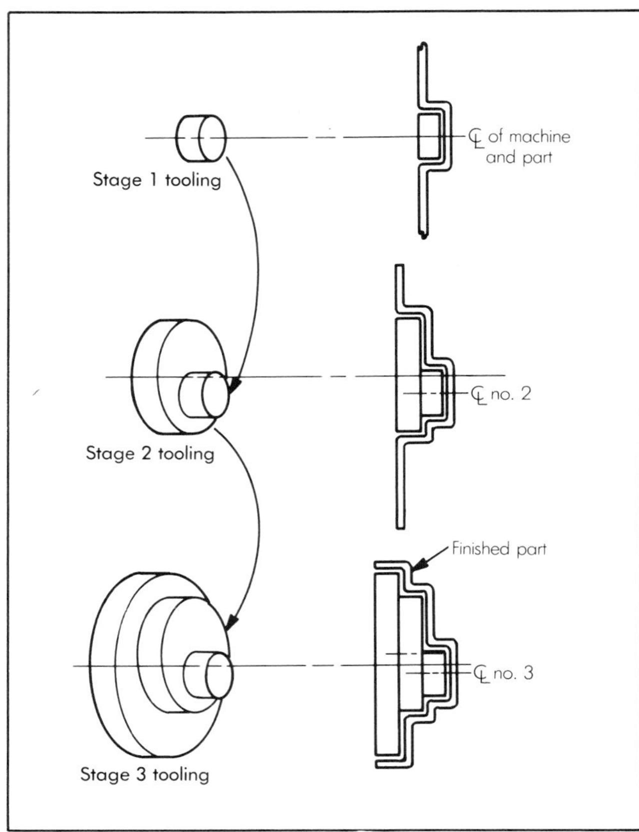


**Fig. 9-35 Three-stage tooling used to spin a nonconcentric part.** (*Spincraft*)

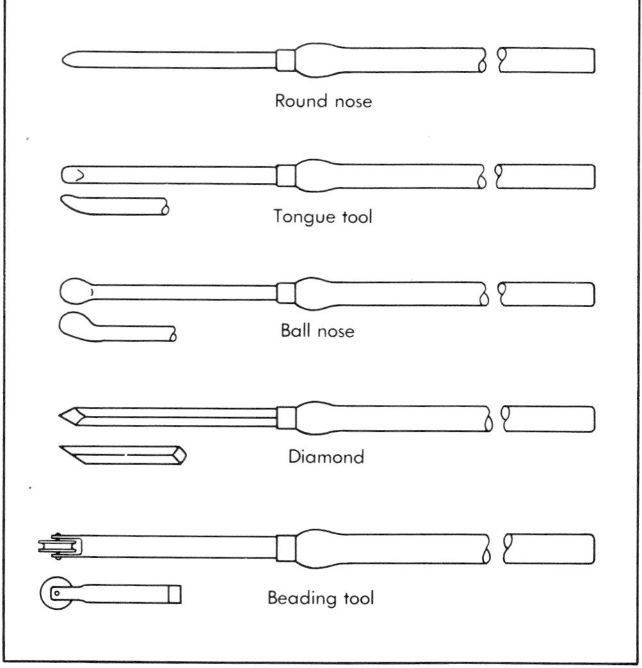


**Fig. 9-36 Common underarm tools used for manual spinning.**

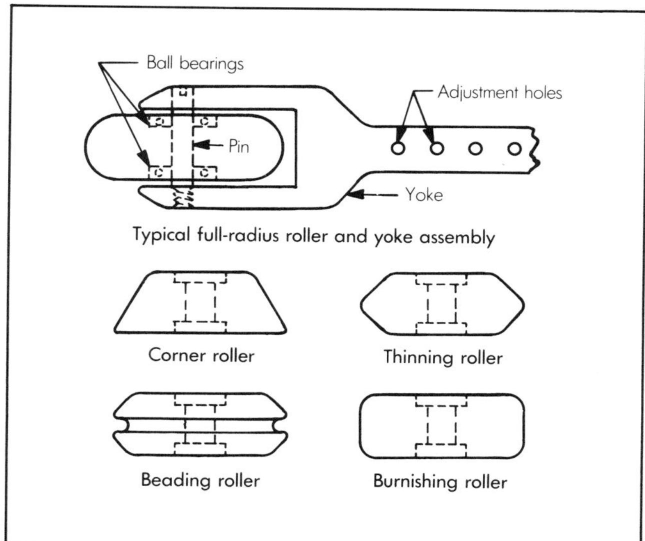


**Fig. 9-37 Variety of rollers used with lever tools for manual spinning.**

of the rollers vary widely, depending upon the results required. An oil-hardening tool steel, such as AISI Type 01, hardened to $R_C$58-62, is a satisfactory roller material for most applications.

## ROLLERS FOR SHEAR FORMING AND TUBE SPINNING

Most shear forming machines are equipped with two rollers, sometimes called tool rings, but some machines have three or more rollers. With multiple rollers, they can be set opposite each other or offset from each other. The rollers are interchangeable to handle various applications.

On machines with two rollers, stepped cones and compound conical parts having two or more progressively smaller included angles can be shear formed in several passes, using one or both rollers to form each conical wall on stepped or separate mandrels. Alternatively, one roller is set to spin the first cone and, in the same setup, the second roller is used to spin the second cone. This method, however, requires a stepped mandrel. With a third method, one or both rollers are tracer controlled to traverse the entire length of the part, using a stepped mandrel. For thicker materials, however, problems may be encountered in using the same rollers to form different included angles.

### Roller Geometry

The rollers for shear forming are often about 10-14" (254-356 mm) or more in diam x 2" (51 mm) or more thick, and are mounted on roller bearings to minimize friction. Geometry of the rollers, which depends upon the configuration of the workpieces, is critical. For shear forming conical-shaped parts from flat blanks in a single pass, a radius on the roller periphery equal to 1 1/2 times the thickness of the blank is generally satisfactory. For shear forming curvilinear parts or cones made from preforms, a roller radius of 1 1/2 to 3 times the thickness of the starting material is preferable.

For tube or cylindrical shear forming, two roller geometries (see Fig. 9-38) are commonly used. Pure radius rollers (view *a*) are used extensively for producing large cylindrical components, such as missile cases, by the forward spinning method of shear forming. Using a large radius on such tools permits high feed rates while still producing a smooth surface finish. A limitation is the high power requirements for rapid metal deformation, thus prohibiting the use of lighter machines because of lack of adequate power and rigidity.

Tube spinning rollers (see Fig. 9-38, view *b*) are used more frequently for the reverse (backward) method of shear forming, and their design is similar to extrusion dies. These rollers provide optimum results only when an effective bite (depth) is used. Larger bites can be taken on a given machine, however, because the work contact area of this type of roller is less than that of a pure radius roller; consequently, the power requirement is less. Width of the roller land influences the surface finish produced on the periphery of the part—the shorter the land, the rougher the finish.

The use of staggered rollers having a pure radius configuration (see Fig. 9-39) permits an infinite number of different bites or reductions with the same rollers. The lead roller is generally set for a bite about 30% that of the total bite. With this setup, the lead roller acts in much the same way as a tube spinning roller (see Fig. 9-38, view *b*) with a 3° lead angle. Resetting the pure radius rollers between successive passes permits faster production than does the use of tube spinning rollers, which would have to be changed between passes.

### Materials for Rollers

Rollers for shear forming are generally made from castings or forged blanks of tool steel that are hardened ($R_C$60-65), ground, and polished. A variety of tool steels are used, depending primarily upon the application. When maximum wear resistance is not required, less costly materials—for example, a medium-alloy, air-hardening, cold-work tool steel such as Type A2 or an oil-hardening, cold-work tool steel such as Type 06—are often used.

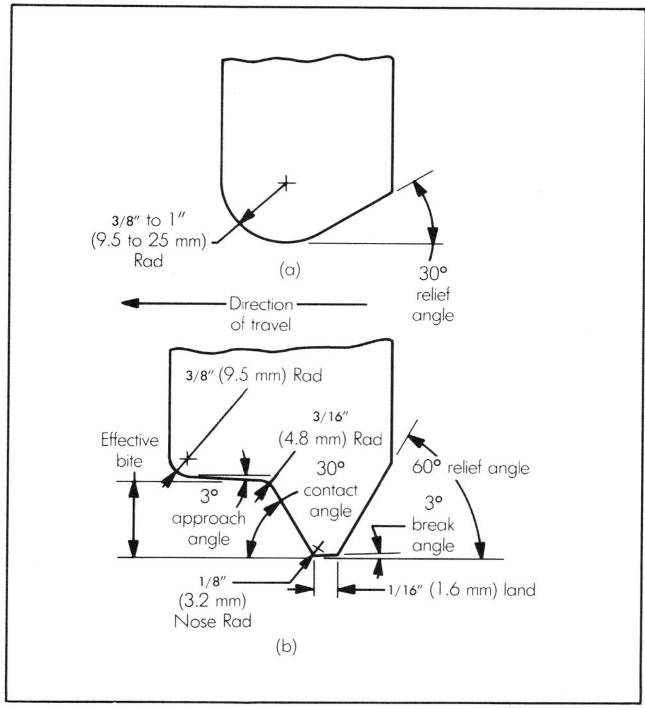


**Fig. 9-38 Roller geometries: (a) pure radius and (b) tube spinning. (*L & F Industries*)**

For increased wear resistance, high-carbon, high-chromium, cold-work tool steels such as Types D2 or D4 are commonly employed. For greater toughness and wear resistance, chromium-type, hot-work tool steels such as Type H11 or molybdenum-type, high-speed tool steels such as M4 or M42 are sometimes used. Carbide rollers are used only infrequently because of the high cost of the material, but they are advantageous for some high-production applications. More extensive information on materials is presented in Chapter 2, "Die and Mold Materials."

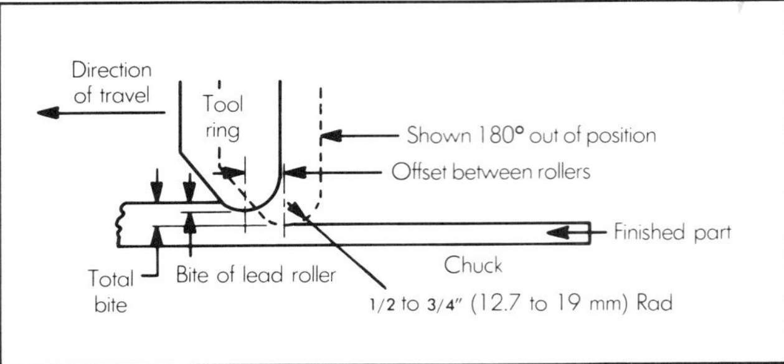


**Fig. 9-39 Use of two pure radius rollers, offset to permit different reductions.** (*L & F Industries*)

Rollers can be reworked a number of times, thus providing long life. Redrawing (heat treatment) of the rollers after every reworking is recommended.

### TEMPLATE MATERIALS

Tracing templates for spinning are made from many different materials, depending primarily upon the desired life, the type of machine used, and the tracing system. For electronic tracer systems, templates have been made from aluminum, laminated plastics, and Micarta. For hydraulic tracers, mild or heat-treated steel, sometimes flash chrome plated, is common. Some spinning firms use 6061-T6 aluminum alloy.

## OPERATING PARAMETERS FOR SPINNING

For maximum economy and optimum results in spinning, the operating parameters that must be determined include power and force requirements, the forming speed and feed rate, and the lubricant and coolant to be used. Variables influencing the selection of parameters include the size and shape of the workpiece; the material from which it is made; the kind of spinning operation to be performed; the type of machine to be used and its rigidity; and the production rate, tolerance, and surface finish requirements. Often, operations have to be performed with trial parameters before optimum conditions can be established.

### POWER AND PRESSURE REQUIREMENTS

Power requirements for power spinning and shear forming depend primarily upon the metal being spun; the included angle, diameter, and thickness of the blank and workpiece; the feed rate; the radius on the forming roller; and the percent reduction. There are no reliable formulas to determine power requirements for forming various materials, blank thicknesses, and workpiece diameter, but Table 9-5 can be used as an approximate guide for some applications.

The amount of pressure applied to the material by the forming rollers is a function of the radius on the rollers used. Pressures exceeding 400,000 psi (2758 MPa) are used for some applications, and some machines have been built that can exert a pressure of about 1,600,000 psi (11 032 MPa).

When the sine law is used, the amount of pressure on the roller and the rate of transverse travel must be carefully determined. Pressure must be sufficient to flow the material tightly against the mandrel, and the rate of travel must permit the unspun portion of the blank to remain generally at 90° to the axis of rotation. A rate of travel that is too fast or a pressure that is too light tends to tilt the unspun blank in the direction of travel; as a consequence, the metal does not thin in compliance with the sine law nor does it spin tightly to the mandrel. Improper travel rate leads to a spiral waviness (called squirrel tail) and to wrinkles in the spun part. Likewise, if the rate of travel is too slow, causing the roller to dwell, or if the inward pressure against the blank is too great, the unspun portion tends to deflect away from the direction of travel; consequently, the metal thins too much under the roller, builds up ahead of the roller, and may rupture. Needless to say, these factors (pressure and rate of travel) differ widely with metals having widely different hardness, ductility, and tensile properties.

### SPEEDS AND FEEDS

Proper speed and feed are essential for optimum results in spinning. Inside and outside diameters, as well as wall thickness, can be controlled more accurately when the correct speed and feed rate are employed.

Speed limitations include the weight and balance of the mandrel and the size, thickness, and type of material being spun. Small, thin parts can be spun at higher speeds, while large, thick parts require slower speeds. Soft, ductile metals are generally spun at higher speeds than less-formable metals.

Surface speeds used for spinning can affect the metallurgical properties of the parts produced. The properties and results obtained at low speeds are generally less desirable. Higher speeds, however, require more power.

The speeds employed for manual spinning also depend upon the contour of the workpieces and the experience and skill of the operator. Aluminum alloys can generally be manually spun with an average speed of 3000 sfm (914 m/min), with copper and brass alloys requiring slower speeds. Table 9-6 presents some approximate rotary speeds for spinning annealed, aluminum-alloy blanks of various diameters and thicknesses.

Approximate speeds and feed rates for shear forming various materials are presented in Table 9-7. As can be seen, slower speeds and feed rates are required for stainless and high-alloy steels. These recommendations apply to the spinning of cones from flat blanks in one pass. Higher feed rates, 0.060-0.090 ipr (1.52-2.29 mm/rev) for aluminum alloys, can generally be employed for spinning curvilinear-shaped parts from preforms.

Some spinning machines are designed to maintain any preselected, constant surface speed. This feature, together with the capability of automatically changing the feed rate as the workpiece diameter changes, ensures a constant volumetric

**TABLE 9-5**
**Approximate Force and Power Requirments for Shear Forming Various Materials and Part Sizes***

| Force, lb (kN) | Workpiece Diameter, in. (mm) | Power Required, hp (kW) | Type of Material, Annealed Blanks: Aluminum Alloys: 3003, 6061, 7075 | Mild Steel, 0.30% Maximum Carbon | Stainless Steels: Types 321, 347, & 410 | High-Alloy Steels: D6AC, A286, and Maraging Steels |
|---|---|---|---|---|---|---|
| | | | Maximum Blank Thickness, in. (mm) | | | |
| 4000 (17.8) | 20 (508) | 10 (7.5) | 0.187 (4.75) | 0.125 (3.17) | 0.080 (2.03) | 0.040 (1.02) |
| 8000 (35.6) | 30 (762)<br>40 (1016) | 20 (14.9)<br>30 (22.4) | 0.375 (9.52) | 0.250 (6.35) | 0.125 (3.17) | 0.062 (1.57) |
| 15,000 (66.7) | 15 (381) | 40 (29.8) | 0.500 (12.70) | 0.375 (9.52) | 0.250 (6.35) | 0.125 (3.17) |
| 50,000 (222) | 20 (508)<br>30 (762)<br>60 (1524) | 50 (37.3)<br>75 (55.9)<br>190 (141.7) | 1.000 (25.40) | 0.750 (19.05) | 0.625 (15.87) | 0.500 (12.70) |
| 75,000 (334) | 12 (305)<br>18 (457)<br>45 (1143) | 50 (37.3)<br>75 (55.9)<br>190 (141.7) | 1.125 (28.57) | 1.000 (25.40) | 0.750 (19.05) | 0.625 (15.87) |
| 100,000 (445) | 30 (762) | 190 (141.7) | 1.500 (38.10) | 1.250 (31.75) | 1.000 (25.40) | 0.750 (19.05) |

* Data based on a maximum wall reduction of 50%. *(L & F Industries)*

**Table 9-6**
**Approximate Speeds for Manual Spinning Annealed Aluminum Alloy Blanks of Various Size**

| Blank Diameter, in. (mm) | Blank Thickness, in. (mm) | Metal Temperature | Speed, rpm |
|---|---|---|---|
| to 12 (305) | 0.003-0.125 (0.08-3.17) | Room | 900-1800 |
| 12-24 (305-610) | 0.015-0.125 (0.38-3.17) | Room | 700-1200 |
| 24-36 (610-914) | 0.030-0.188 (0.76-4.78) | Room | 400-1000 |
| 36-72 (914-1829) | 0.188-0.375 (4.78-9.52) | 400° F (204° C) max | 50-250 |

displacement of the metal during spinning.

The relationship between the height of the feed marks on the workpiece, the feed per revolution, and the radius on the nose of the roller are illustrated in Fig. 9-40. Decreasing the feed rate and increasing the radius on the roller tends to produce a smoother finish.

When spinning thin blanks, reducing the infeed and increasing the number of passes helps decrease the formation of wrinkles at the edges of the workpieces. The use of counterpressure or backup rollers, described previously in this chapter, can reduce the number of passes required and can permit the use of increased feed rates in forming thin blanks without wrinkles.

## LUBRICANTS AND COOLANTS

Lubrication of the blanks is usually necessary for manual spinning to prevent marring the workpiece surfaces. Common lubricants for manual spinning include yellow naptha soap,

**TABLE 9-7**
**Approximate Speeds and Feed Rates for Shear Forming Various Materials***

| Material, Annealed Blanks | Speed, sfm (m/min): Range | Speed: Average | Feed Rate per Roller, ipr (mm/rev): Range | Feed Rate: Average |
|---|---|---|---|---|
| Aluminum alloys: 3003, 6061, & 7075 | 800-1200 (244-366) | 1000 (305) | 0.020-0.040 (0.51-1.02) | 0.030 (0.76) |
| Mild steels, 0.30% max. carbon | 600-800 (183-244) | 700 (213) | 0.015-0.030 (0.38-0.76) | 0.022 (0.56) |
| Stainless steels: Types 321, 347, & 410 | 400-600 (122-183) | 500 (152) | 0.010-0.020 (0.25-0.51) | 0.015 (0.38) |
| High-alloy steels: D6AC, A286, & maraging steels | 200-400 (61-122) | 300 (91) | 0.005-0.015 (0.13-0.38) | 0.010 (0.25) |

* Speeds and feeds vary with angle of laydown. *(L & F Industries)*

# OPERATING PARAMETERS FOR SPINNING

hard cup grease, and combinations of beeswax, paraffin, oil, and petroleum jelly.

Both a coolant and a lubricant are generally necessary in power spinning and shear forming—the coolant to rapidly remove the heat caused by plastic deformation, and the lubricant to prevent galling at the area of contact between the roller and work. For low-pressure spinning of thin, ductile metals, a soluble oil sometimes provides adequate cooling and lubrication. However, when pressures are high and the material more difficult to spin, it is often preferable to use separate cooling and lubricating media. For hot spinning, cooling is undesirable.

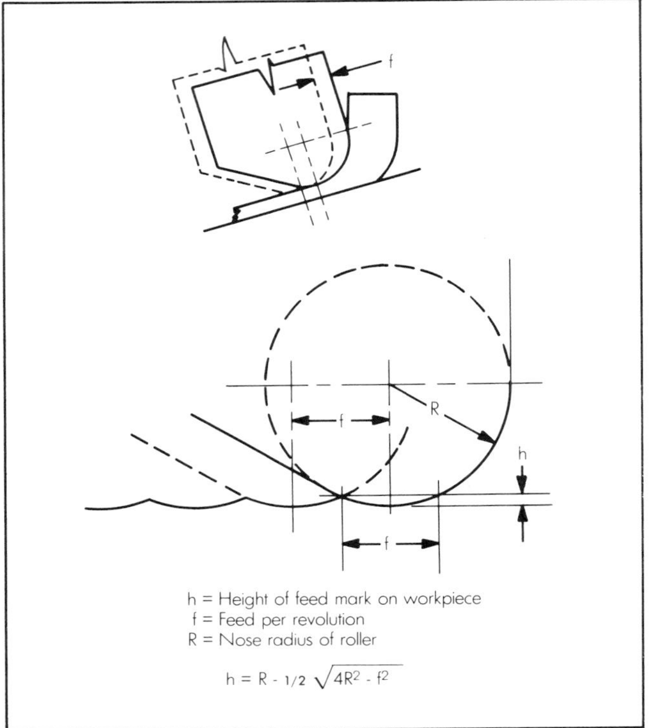


**Fig. 9-40 Relationship between the height of feed mark on workpiece, the feed per revolution, and the radius on the roller nose.**

Coolants should have a high specific heat and contain a rust inhibitor. Soluble oils and water-based coolants (1 part coolant to 20 parts water) with high heat-absorption qualities have been used satisfactorily. For lubricating, both sides of the blank (and sometimes the mandrel) should be swabbed or brushed with a colloidal zinc suspension; a moly-disulphide paste; or a non-drying, nonhardening drawing compound. Table 9-8 lists some lubricants used for spinning various metals. Good viscous properties are necessary to insure that the lubricant adheres to the mandrel, and the lubricant used must not be soluble in the coolant. For extremely severe operations, the blank can be phosphate coated prior to lubricating. A comprehensive discussion of lubricants is presented in Chapter 3 of this volume, "Lubricants."

Other factors influencing the choice of a lubricant for spinning include:

1. Temperature of the work blank. (At room temperature, lubrication and sometimes cooling are required because of the heat generated by metal deformation. At elevated temperatures, the principal requirement is for surface lubrication, usually by chemical, boundary, or solid mechanisms.)
2. Potential reactive effects on the work surface.
3. Requirement for adherence to the rotating work blank.
4. Suitable fluidity under pressure of application. (A solid precoating may be applied to the blank before setting up work.)
5. Lubricant/coolant fluidity for pump circulation systems.
6. Removal of the lubricant after forming.

**TABLE 9-8**
**Lubricants for Power Spinning and Shear Forming**

| Metal Spun | Spinning at Room Temperature | Spinning at 300-600° F (149-316° C) | Spinning Above 600° F (316° C) |
|---|---|---|---|
| Copper and brass | Soap/wax coating or fatty/mineral oil | | |
| Bronze alloys | Soap/wax or fatty compounds | | |
| Aluminum and alloys | Soap/wax coating, silicone waxes, fatty/mineral oils | | |
| Magnesium and alloys | | Soap/wax coating, tallow/graphite, fiberglass | Colloidal graphite, $MoS_2$, fiberglass |
| Carbon and low-alloy steels | Mineral/fatty oils, zinc/lithium soap disperson, $MoS_2$ paste, dry soap | | |
| Stainless steels* | Mineral/fatty oils, dry soap/borax, wax, glycerin | | Solid pigmented coatings, mica, conversion coatings |

# REFERENCES

**TABLE 9-8—*Continued***

| Metal Spun | Spinning at Room Temperature | Spinning at 300-600° F (149-316° C) | Spinning Above 600° F (316° C) |
|---|---|---|---|
| Titanium and alloys** | Colloidal graphite, $MoS_2$, phosphate-fluoride conversion coatings, fatty oil/glycerin, silicone bases | Graphite greases, pigmented graphite grease coatings, $MoS_2$, bentonite clay, powdered mica | Bentonite greases, graphite compounds, $MoS_2$, $MoS_2$ greases, powdered mica, metallic coatings |
| Other refractory metals: | | | |
| Columbium and tantalum | Graphite dispersion, $MoS_2$, greases, silicone waxes | Not done | Not done |
| Molybdenum | Not done | Castor oil Beeswax | Graphite and $MoS_2$, soap |
| Tungsten | Not done | | Copper coatings or pigmented solution |

* When formed at temperatures above 1450° F (788° C), on thick sections of 1/4 to 1/2" (6.3 to 12.7 mm), S, Cl, Zn, or $MoS_2$ lubricants are not used because of surface effects on stainless steel.

** S, Cl, or Zn coatings are not used at elevated temperatures because of surface effects and toxicity.

### References


1. R. A. C. Slater, "A Review of Analytical and Experimental Investigations of the Spin-Forging of Sheet Metal Cones," presented at the First International Conference on Rotary Metal-Working Processes, London, November 20-22, 1979.
2. Jack D. Stewart, "Shear Spinning—A Substitute for Forgings," presented at the SAE National Aeronautic and Space Engineering and Manufacturing Meeting, Los Angeles, October 6-10, 1969.
3. Slater, *op. cit.*
4. E. H. Rennhack, "Thermomechanical Spin Forming of Aluminum Alloys," *Aluminium*, Vol. 58, No. 3 (1982), pp. 166-169.
5. S. Kalpakjian and S. Rajagopal, "Spinning of Tubes: A Review," *Journal of Applied Metalworking*, Vol. 2, No. 3 (July 1982), pp. 211-223.
6. *Ibid.*
7. *Ibid.*
8. *Ibid.*
9. "Advanced Theoretical Formability Manufacturing Technology," U. S. Air Force Report AFML-TR-64-41, Project 8-143, Vols. I and II, Air Force Materials Laboratory, Wright-Patterson Air Force Base, OH, January 1965.
10. Richard L. Kegg, "A New Test Method for Determination of Spinnability of Metals," ASME Paper 60-Prod-3, 1960.
11. *Ibid.*
12. Kalpakjian and Rajagopal, *op. cit.*
13. Kalpakjian and Rajagopal, *op. cit.*


### Bibliography


American Metal Stamping Association. *Metal Spinning, Book 1, Basic Metal Spinning.* Richmond Heights, OH.

Steed, Stanley. *Manufacturing Techniques for Producing Metal Tubes with D/T Ratios Greater Than 250.* SME Technical Paper 615, 1964.

Wick, Charles. "Metal Spinning...A Review and Update." *Manufacturing Engineering* (January 1978), pp. 73-77.

CHAPTER

# 10

# Bending and Straightening

# BENDING AND STRAIGHTENING

Bending is a method of producing shapes by stressing metal beyond its yield strength, but not past its ultimate tensile strength. The forces applied during bending are in opposite directions, just as in the cutting of sheet metal. Bending forces, however, are spread farther apart, resulting in plastic distortion of metal without failure.

This chapter covers processes, equipment, and operations for sheet and plate metal, tube, pipe, and rod bending. Information on bending as related to drawing, and on flange forming, appears in Chapter 4, "Sheet Metal Blanking and Forming."

The general term *straightening* is applicable to the straightening of metal stock prior to processing and also to the straightening of workpieces and manufactured parts. Information in this chapter deals with applications, equipment, and operations for the various straightening methods.

CHAPTER CONTENTS:



## SHEET AND PLATE BENDING

The bending process appears to be simple; yet, in reality, it is a rather complex process involving a number of technical factors. Included are characteristics of the workpiece material, the material flow and reactions during various stages of deformation, the effect of tooling design on force required to form the bend, and the type of equipment used.

In the large, varied field of sheet metal and plate fabricating, several types of bending machines are used. Press brakes predominate in shops that process heavy-gage materials, because they are well suited to such applications and also because they are adaptable to other metalworking operations, such as punching, piercing, blanking, notching, perforating, embossing, shearing, and drawing.

Light-gage metal typically is formed with specialized bending machines, which are also described as leaf, pan, or box brakes; as wing folders; and as swivel benders. Equipment of this type is often manually operated.

The principal kinds of equipment used to bend sheet metal and plate can be grouped into the following categories:

- Mechanical press brakes—elongated presses with numerous tooling options. Work is performed by means of energy released from a motor-driven flywheel. These machines normally have a 3″ or 4″ stroke length.
- Hydraulic press brakes—stretched C-frame presses that are likewise compatible with a wide range and diversity of tooling. High-pressure oil in hydraulic cylinders supplies the force, which is directed downward in most models. The stroking length usually exceeds 6″.
- Hydraulic-mechanical press brakes—presses with drives that combine hydraulic and mechanical principles. In operation, oil forces a piston to move arms that push the ram toward the bed.
- Pneumatic press brakes—low-tonnage bending machines that are available with suitable tooling options.
- Bending brakes—powered or manual brakes commonly used for bending light-gage sheet metal.
- Special equipment—custom-built benders and panel formers designed for specific forming applications.

### BENDING NOMENCLATURE

Terms used to describe various aspects of sheet metal bending are illustrated in Fig. 10-1. Additional bending terms are defined in the following glossary:

**air bending** A press brake bending operation in which the punch and the workpiece do not bottom on the die.

**bend allowance** Length of the curved strip comprising a bend, measured along the neutral axis from one bend tangent line to another.

**bend angle** (a) Usually, the "included" angle of the workpiece. (b) Also, the angle through which a bend is performed; that is, the supplementary angle to that formed by the two bend tangent lines or planes.

**bend radius** The inside radius of a bent section.

**bend tangent** A tangent line where the flat, straight section of the part stops and the radius of the bend begins.

**bending** The straining of material, usually flat sheet or strip metal, by moving it around a straight axis which lies in the neutral plane. Metal flow takes place within the plastic range of the metal, so that the bent part retains a permanent set after removal of the applied

*Contributors of sections of this chapter are: Rune G. Adolfsson, Technical Dept. HK, ASEA, AB; Reed Bertolette, President, Bertolette Machines, Inc.; John A. Gillanders, Director—Technical Development, International Piping Systems, Ltd.; David A. Johnson, Program Administrator, Fabricating Manufacturers Association; Norman R. Judge, General Sales Manager, Industrial Metal Products Corp.; George M. Kimmel, Marketing Manager, Machine Tool Division, Conrac Corp.; Patrick E. Oldenburg, Training Center Manager, Di-Acro Div., Houdaille Industries, Inc.; Dale D. Oliver, Application Engineer, Di-Acro Div., Houdaille Industries, Inc.; Richard I. Phillips, Assistant Professor, Department of Industrial Education and Technology, Southwest Missouri State University; Ralph Scroggins, Consultant-Technical Field Representative, Tower Oil and Technology Corp.;*

# CHAPTER 10

# THEORY OF METAL FLOW

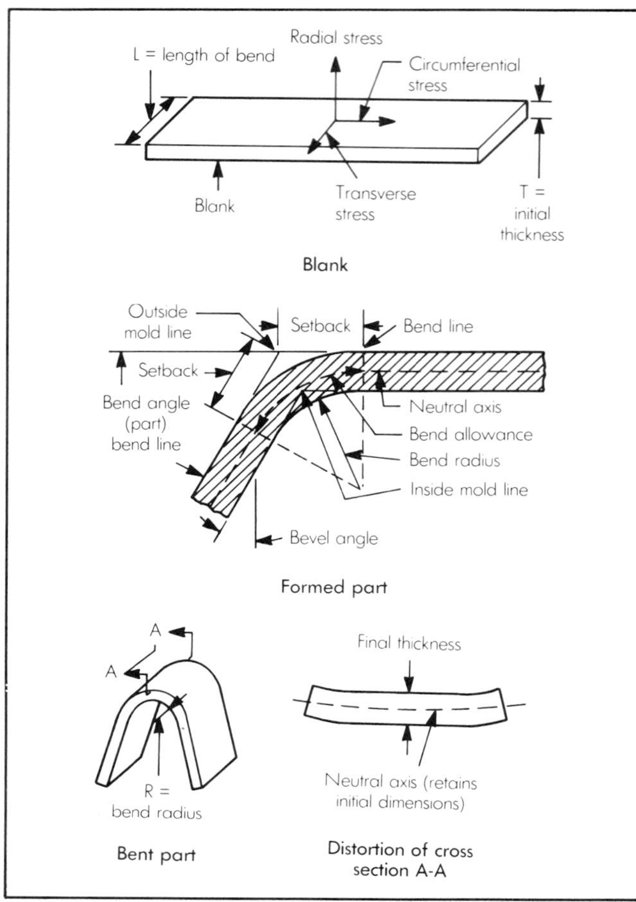


**Fig. 10-1 Illustration of bending terms.**

stress. The cross section of the bend inward from the neutral plane is in compression; the rest of the bend is in tension.

**bending brake or press brake** A form of open-frame, single-action press comparatively wide between the housings, with bed designed for holding long, narrow forming edges or dies. It is used for bending and forming strips and plates, as well as sheets (made into boxes, panels, roof decks, etc.).

**bending dies** Dies used in presses for bending sheet metal or wire parts into various shapes. The work is done by the punch pushing the stock into cavities or depressions of similar shape in the die or by auxiliary attachments operated by the descending punch.

**bending rolls** Various types of machinery equipped with two or three rolls to form curved sheet and sections.

**coining** A press brake bending operation in which the punch bottoms against the workpiece and the die.

## THEORY OF METAL FLOW

In an analysis of bending, it is helpful to think of the metal part to be formed as being made up of a number of longitudinal fibers enclosed in the part's cross section.

Such a part, undergoing a bending action perpendicular to its longitudinal axis, behaves according to the known laws of physics, in a predictable manner: As the part is bent, its fibers experience a distortion such that those nearer its outside, convex surface are forced to stretch. Thus, a portion of the part's cross section is put in tension and another portion in compression.

### Neutral Axis

Somewhere in the cross section, a plane of demarcation separates the tension and compression zones. The fibers lying in this plane are affected by the bending in a neutral manner, neither forced to stretch nor to compress. This plane, situated in the cross section parallel to the surface around which the part is bending, is called the neutral axis of the part's cross section. The neutral axis is shown schematically in Fig. 4-18 (Chapter 4) and in the "formed part" drawing in Fig. 10-1.

Although not precisely true under all conditions, for purposes of analysis, it can be assumed that the neutral axis of a cross section coincides with the center of gravity. The location of the center of gravity for a given cross section is determined by the geometry of its configuration. Therefore, for practical applications, the same can be said of the cross-section's neutral axis. The center of gravity of a symmetrical cross section falls exactly on its centerline, while being displaced from the centerline in the case of an unsymmetrical cross section.

### Fiber Deformation

Knowing the location of the neutral axis of a part helps in analyzing the results that take place when bending occurs. It is the deformation of the part's fibers during a bending action that is significant. The outer and inner surfaces are of particular interest, and the deformation of their fibers is greatly influenced by the location of the neutral axis in the part's cross section. The extent to which a fiber distorts, whether in compression or tension, can be considered to be proportional to the fibers perpendicular distance from the neutral axis. This distance acts on the fibers as a lever, using the neutral axis as a fulcrum. Thus, the outer surface and inner surface fibers experience the most distortion, while the other fibers of the cross section are subjected to only a proportionate share.

When bent around a die, a thin part, such as a sheet, experiences little distortion of its outer fibers, perhaps not enough to reach the yield state. On the other hand, the outer fibers of an extrusion of substantial depth, when bent around the same die, might undergo sufficient elongation to cause rupture. The reason is that the lever distances acting on the

***Contributors, cont.***: *Richard A. Sprick, Product Specialist, Di-Acro Div., Houdaille Industries, Inc.; Ronald R. Stange, President, Tools for Bending, Inc.; Alan Williamson, Eastern Regional Sales Manager, Machine Tool Division, Conrac Corp.*

***Reviewers of sections of this chapter are***: *Rune G. Adolfsson, Technical Dept. HK, ASEA AB; Daniel P. Baumann, Executive Vice President, Bracker Corp.; Reed Bertolette, President, Bertolette Machines, Inc.; James W. Bowman, Director of Marketing, Pacific Press & Shear Co.; Ronald Carr, Advertising & Promotion Specialist, Di-Acro Div., Houdaille Industries, Inc.; Martin Doot, Manager—Press Brake Tooling Department, Verson Allsteel Press Co.; Frank M. DuMez, General Sales Manager, Teledyne Pines; Richard J. Ferry, Manufacturing Engineer, Aerospace Div., UOP, Inc.; Ann F. Florine, Marketing Support Manager, Di-Acro Div., Houdaille Industries, Inc.; Irvan W. Gellerstedt, Asst. Sales Manager, Williams-White & Co.; John A. Gillanders, Director—Technical Development, International Piping Systems, Ltd.; Erhard Hoffman, Vice President, Eitel Presses, Transmares Corp.; Joseph Ivaska, Director of Engineering, Tower Oil and Technology Corp.;*

fibers of the sheet are small, while those acting on fibers of the deeper sectioned extrusion are great.

Since the neutral axis accompanies the center of gravity, in a geometrical sense, the inner fibers of an unsymmetrical extrusion, such as a T-section with flanges of unequal thickness, may have only slight compression if the part is formed with the heavy flange inward against the die. Consequently, wrinkling of the inner fibers does not occur. The outer fibers, on the other hand, elongate considerably. This is because the center of gravity of the section, and hence its neutral axis, is close to the inner fibers and relatively far from the outer fibers. The lever distances, causing distortion of the inner and outer fibers, therefore are different. Such parts, having their neutral axis located very near the inside concave surface, can be formed by bending alone.

If the part were bent the other way, with the heavy flange outward, the situation would be reversed. The outer fibers might not be elongated enough to reach yield, while the inner fibers, with their long lever distances, could be caused to compress to such an extent that the inner flange would buckle, as well as wrinkle.

Thus, it is apparent that the neutral axis location is a major factor in determining metal flow and forming characteristics of a part during bending operations, and that the reactions of the inner and outer surfaces depend on the part's geometry as a key determinant for the center of gravity and the neutral axis.

## BEND ALLOWANCE

Bend allowance is the dimensional amount added to a part through elongation during the bending process. It is used as a key factor in determining the initial blank size.

The length of the neutral axis, or bend allowance, is the length of the blank. Since the length of the neutral axis depends upon its position within the bend area, and this position is dictated by the material type and thickness and the radius and degree of bend, it is impossible to use one formula for all conditions. However, for simplicity, a reasonable approximation with sufficient accuracy for practical usage when air bending is given by the following equation:

$$L = \frac{A}{360} \times 2\pi(R + kt) \quad (1)$$

or:

$$L = 0.017453A(R + kt)$$

where:

$L$ = bend allowance (arc length of the neutral axis), in. or mm
$A$ = bend angle, deg
$R$ = inside radius of part, in. or mm
$t$ = metal thickness, in. or mm
$k$ = constant, neutral-axis location

Theoretically, the neutral axis follows a parabolic arc in the bend region; therefore, the $k$ factor is an average value that is sufficiently accurate for practical applications. A value of 0.5 for $k$ places the neutral axis exactly in the center of the metal. This figure is often used for some thicknesses. One manufacturer specifies $k$ according to sheet thickness and inside radius of the bend: when $R$ is less than $2t$, $k = 0.33$; when $R$ is $2t$ or more, $k = 0.50$.

Table 10-1 lists bend allowances obtained using Eq. (1) for 90° air bends on various thicknesses of mild steel. Bend allowances based on Eq. (1), using a value of 0.45 for $k$, are charted in the nomograph in Fig. 10-2 with their corresponding setback allowances. Using the nomograph, given a 90° bend of 1/8″ (3.2 mm) radius in 0.040″ (1.02 mm) stock:

1. Draw a line connecting 1/8″ on the Scale $R$ with 0.040″ on the Scale $t$.
2. Note that this line intersects Scale $BA$ (bend allowance) and Scale $SB$ (setback) and establishes 0.228″ (5.79 mm) and 0.0105″ (0.27 mm), respectively, for bend allowance and setback (defined in Fig. 10-1).

## BENDING FORCE REQUIRED

Most bending-load charts, such as the one given in Table 10-2, are based on air bending. When simple flanges are air bent, forming loads are easily determined. Many load charts similar to the one illustrated are available listing loads for mild steel in various thicknesses for a range of V-die openings. Most such charts are based on empirical equations developed from a series of tests. The force required to bend metal depends upon the type of material and its physical properties, thickness of the stock, length of the bend, width of the die, whether or not a lubricant is used, and the amount of wiping, ironing, or coining. V-dies in which the punch does not bottom (air bending), commonly used in press brakes, require the least force. Bending tonnage (force) required varies directly with tensile and yield strengths of various materials. As a precaution, it should be noted that this relationship does not always apply when the material's tensile strength exceeds 70,000 psi (484 MPa). Approximate conversion factors for a variety of materials other than mild steel are listed in Table 10-3.

### Force Calculation

Two general types of bending are used in modern pressworking. One is V-die bending, which is used extensively in brake die operations as well as in stamping die operations. The other is wiping die bending. Equations are available for both forms of bending.[1]

*__Reviewers, cont.:__ David A. Johnson, Education Program Administrator, American Fabricating Institute of Technology; Norman R. Judge, General Sales Manager, Industrial Metal Products Corp.; George M. Kimmel, Marketing Manager, Machine Tool Division, Conrac Corp.; H. Merritt Kinsey, Vice President—Marketing, Bertsch and Co., Inc.; Joseph J. Kirby, Vice President—Engineering, Eaton Leonard Corp.; Nicholas J. Marracino, Engineering Manager, Bertolette Machines, Inc.; J. C. Montgomery, President, J. M. Montgomery Manufacturing, Inc.; Jerome B. Pfeffer, Manager—Quintus Department, ASEA Pressure Systems; Richard I. Phillips, Assistant Professor, Department of Industrial Education and Technology, Southwest Missouri State University; Bernard L. Rapien, Chief Die Engineer, Cincinnati Incorporated; Fred Rifler, Vice President—Research and Development, Bracker A.G.; Ralph Scroggins, Consultant Technical Field Representative, Tower Oil and Technology Corp.; Ronald R. Stange, President, Tools for Bending, Inc.; George H. Trautman, Jr., Mgr.—Press Brake Engineering, Niagara Machine and Tool Works; Alan Williamson, Eastern Regional Sales Manager, Machine Tool Division, Conrac Corp.; Robert L. Wonsetler, Sr., Vice President—Engineering, Bertsch and Co., Inc.*

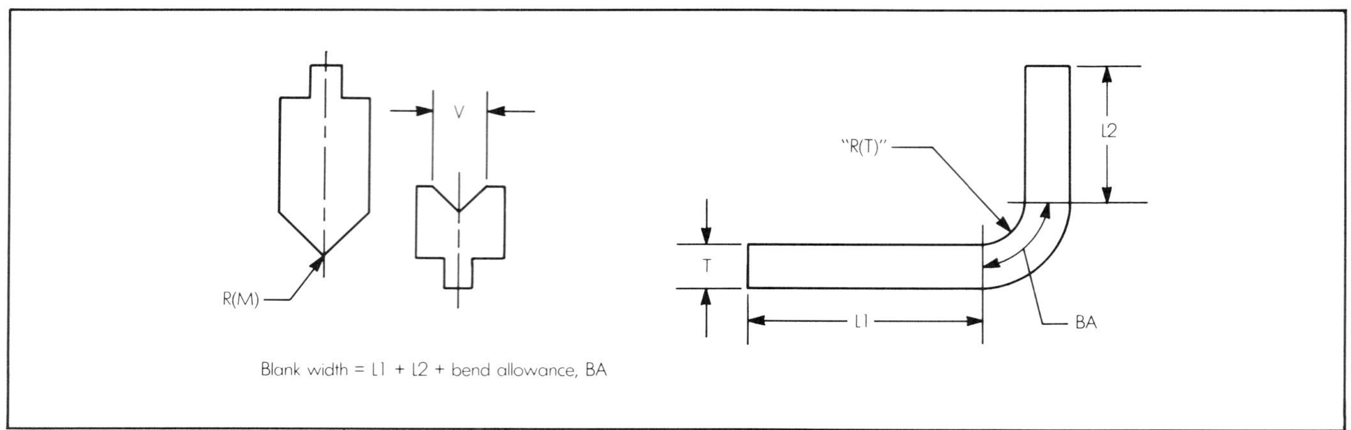


**TABLE 10-1**
**Bend Allowances for Air Bends in Mild Steel Sheet Metal**

| | Material Thickness, T | | Recommended Die Width, V | | Recommended Male Die Radius, R (M) | | Theoretical Bend Radius, R (T) = 5/32 V | | Allowance for 90° Bend, BA | |
|---|---|---|---|---|---|---|---|---|---|---|
| | in. | mm | in. | mm | in. | mm | in. | mm | in. | mm |
| 5/8 | 0.625 | 15.9 | 6 | 152 | 15/16 | 23.8 | 0.937 | 23.80 | 1.864 | 47.35 |
| 1/2 | 0.500 | 12.7 | 5 | 127 | 3/4 | 19.1 | 0.781 | 19.84 | 1.541 | 39.14 |
| 1/2 | 0.500 | 12.7 | 4 | 102 | 5/8 | 15.9 | 0.625 | 15.88 | 1.295 | 32.89 |
| 3/8 | 0.375 | 9.5 | 3 | 76 | 7/16 | 11.1 | 0.469 | 11.91 | 0.971 | 24.66 |
| 5/16 | 0.313 | 7.9 | 2 1/2 | 64 | 3/8 | 9.5 | 0.391 | 9.93 | 0.809 | 20.55 |
| 1/4 | 0.250 | 6.4 | 2 | 51 | 5/16 | 7.9 | 0.312 | 7.92 | 0.648 | 16.46 |
| 3/16 | 0.188 | 4.8 | 1 1/2 | 38 | 3/16 | 4.8 | 0.234 | 5.94 | 0.486 | 12.34 |
| 10 gage | 0.134 | 3.4 | 1 1/16 | 27 | 1/8 | 3.2 | 0.176 | 4.47 | 0.361 | 9.17 |
| 11 gage | 0.119 | 3.0 | 1 | 25.4 | 1/8 | 3.2 | 0.156 | 3.96 | 0.320 | 8.13 |
| 12 gage | 0.104 | 2.6 | 7/8 | 22.2 | 1/8 | 3.2 | 0.137 | 3.48 | 0.280 | 7.11 |
| 13 gage | 0.089 | 2.3 | 3/4 | 19.1 | 1/16 | 1.6 | 0.117 | 2.97 | 0.240 | 6.10 |
| 14 gage | 0.074 | 1.8 | 5/8 | 15.9 | 1/16 | 1.6 | 0.098 | 2.49 | 0.200 | 5.08 |
| 15 gage | 0.067 | 1.7 | 1/2 | 12.7 | 1/16 | 1.6 | 0.078 | 1.98 | 0.165 | 4.19 |
| 16 gage | 0.060 | 1.5 | 1/2 | 12.7 | 1/16 | 1.6 | 0.078 | 1.98 | 0.154 | 3.91 |
| 18 gage | 0.050 | 1.3 | 3/8 | 9.5 | 1/32 | 0.8 | 0.059 | 1.50 | 0.118 | 3.00 |
| 20 gage | 0.036 | 0.9 | 1/4 | 6.4 | 1/32 | 0.8 | 0.039 | 0.99 | 0.080 | 2.03 |
| 21 gage | 0.033 | 0.8 | 1/4 | 6.4 | 1/32 | 0.8 | 0.039 | 0.99 | 0.079 | 2.01 |
| 22 gage | 0.030 | 0.7 | 1/4 | 6.4 | 1/32 | 0.8 | 0.039 | 0.99 | 0.077 | 1.96 |
| 23 gage | 0.027 | 0.7 | 1/4 | 6.4 | 1/32 | 0.8 | 0.039 | 0.99 | 0.075 | 1.91 |

Note: Formulas are for right angles only. Bend allowances are approximate.
Neutral axis location:
For thicknesses up to 14 gage, k = 0.4.
For thicknesses from 15-23 gage, k = 0.33.

(*Cincinnati Incorporated*)

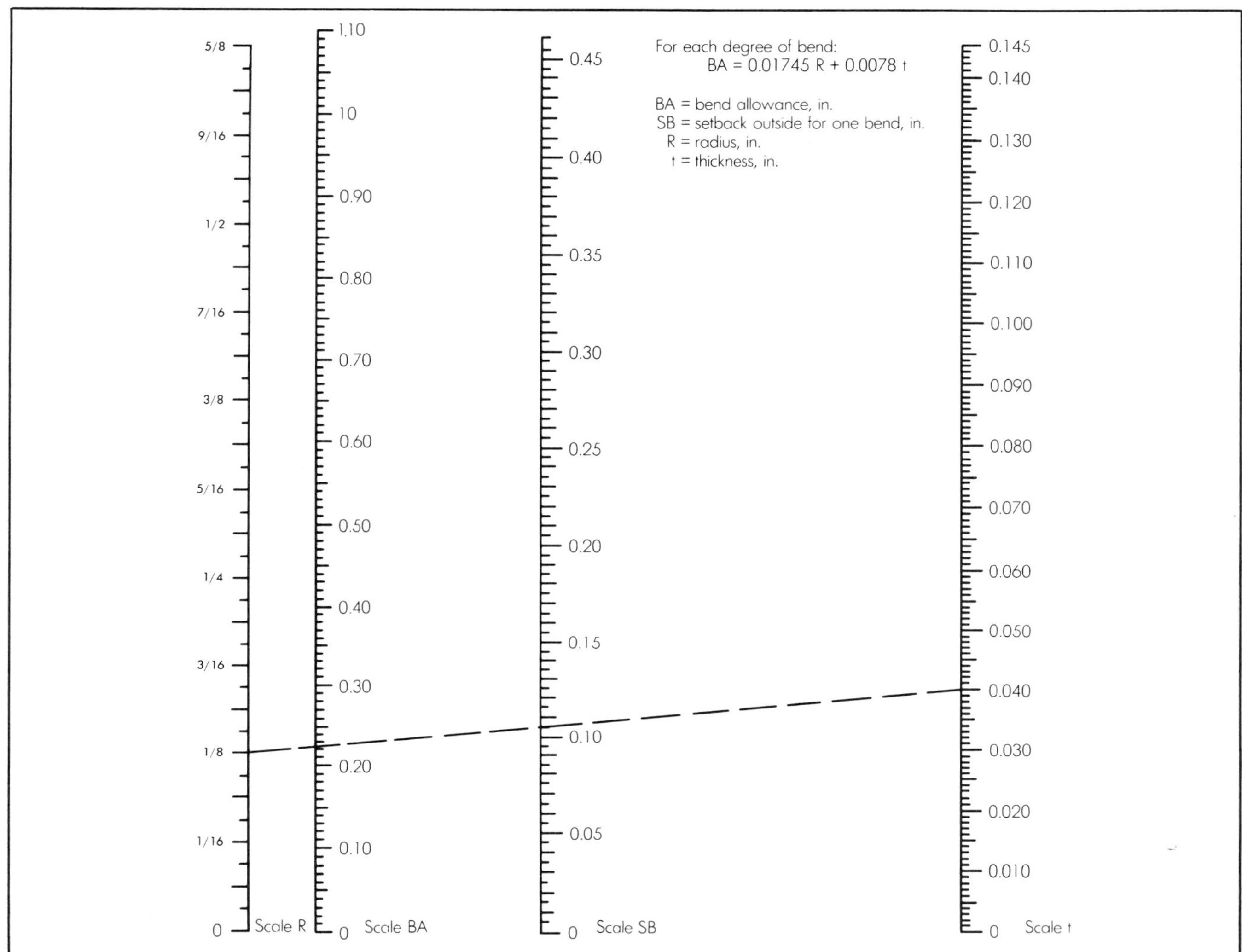


**Fig. 10-2 Nomograph for bend allowance and setback for 90° bends.**

**The V-bend equation.** A typical V-bend operation is shown in Fig. 10-3. The equation to determine bending force is:

$$F = \frac{1.33SWt^2}{D} \qquad (2)$$

where:

$F$ = force, lbf
$S$ = ultimate tensile strength, psi
$W$ = length of the bend, in.
$t$ = stock thickness, in.
$D$ = the V-die opening, in.

*Sample calculation.* Calculate the force required to V-bend a piece of high-carbon steel, 3/16″ thick. Its tensile strength is 120,000 psi. The bend, performed in a press brake, is 10′ long. The die opening is 3 1/2″. The force required is:

$$F = \frac{1.33 \times 120{,}000 \times 120 \times 0.035156}{3.5}$$

$$= 192{,}375 \text{ lbf}$$

By soft conversion (multiplying the answer by the 4.448 conversion factor), the force required to effect this bend is 855 684 newtons. This value is properly stated as 855.68 kN.

*Metric calculation.* For direct calculation of force in metric units, it is necessary to express $S$ in kilopascals; and $w$, $t$, and $D$ in meters. Also, by direct computation, with appropriate substitution of terms, it must be ascertained that the same constant (1.33) is valid for metric units. The bending force calculation, then, is:

$$F = \frac{1.33(120\,000 \cdot 6.895)(120)(0.0254)(0.1875 \cdot 0.0254)^2}{3.5 \cdot 0.0254}$$

$$= \frac{1.33(827\,400)(3.048)(0.000\,022\,7)}{0.0889}$$

$$= 856.458 \text{ kN}$$

A discrepancy of 0.774 kilonewtons between the two calculations is noted. The difference (less than 1/10 of 1%) is inconsequential.

## BENDING FORCE REQUIRED

**TABLE 10-2**
**Approximate Force, Tons per Linear Foot (kilonewton per linear meter*) Required to Make 90° Air Bends on Mild Steel**

| Width of V-Die Opening, in. (mm) | Thickness of Metal in. (mm) | | | | | | | | | | | | | | | | | | | | |
|---|---|---|---|---|---|---|---|---|---|---|---|---|---|---|---|---|---|---|---|---|---|
| | 24 gage 0.024 (0.61) | 22 gage 0.030 (0.76) | 20 gage 0.036 (0.91) | 18 gage 0.048 (1.22) | 16 gage 0.060 (1.52) | 14 gage 0.075 (1.91) | 13 gage 0.090 (2.29) | 12 gage 0.105 (2.67) | 11 gage 0.120 (3.05) | 10 gage 0.135 (3.43) | 9 gage 0.149 (3.79) | 7 gage 3/16 (4.7) | 1/4 (6.4) | 5/16 (8.0) | 3/8 (9.53) | 7/16 (11.1) | 1/2 (12.7) | 5/8 (15.9) | 3/4 (19.1) | 7/8 (22.2) | 1 (25.4) |
| 1/8 (3.2) | 2.1 (61) | 3.6 (105) | | | | | | | | | | | | | | | | With these thicknesses, usual practice is to use die openings that are at least 10 times metal thickness. | | | |
| 3/16 (4.8) | **1.4 (41)** | 2.5 (73) | 4.1 (120) | | | | | | | | | | | | | | | | | | |
| 1/4 (6.4) | 1.1 (32) | **1.8 (53)** | 2.9 (85) | 5.4 (158) | | | | | | | | | | | | | | | | | |
| 5/16 (7.9) | 0.7 (20) | 1.4 (41) | **2.2 (64)** | 4.0 (117) | 7.0 (204) | | | | | | | | | | | | | | | | |
| 3/8 (9.5) | | 1.0 (29) | 1.7 (50) | **2.9 (85)** | 5.6 (164) | 8.8 (257) | | | | | | | | | | | | | | | |
| 1/2 (12.7) | | | 1.2 (35) | 2.2 (64) | **3.6 (105)** | 6.0 (175) | 10.0 (292) | | | | | | | | | | | | | | |
| 5/8 (15.9) | | | | 1.6 (47) | 2.7 (79) | **4.5 (131)** | 6.8 (199) | 10.1 (295) | | | | | | | | | | | | | |
| 3/4 (19.0) | | | | 1.3 (38) | 2.2 (64) | 3.4 (99) | **5.4 (158)** | 7.4 (216) | 10.5 (307) | | | | | | | | | | | | |
| 7/8 (22.2) | | | | | 1.7 (50) | 3.0 (88) | 4.3 (126) | **6.3 (184)** | 8.8 (257) | 11.3 (330) | | | | | | | | | | | |
| 1 (25.4) | | | | | 1.4 (41) | 2.5 (73) | 3.7 (108) | 5.4 (158) | **7.2 (210)** | 9.6 (280) | 13.1 (383) | | | | | | | | | | |
| 1 1/8 (28.6) | | | | | | 2.1 (61) | 3.3 (96) | 4.4 (128) | 6.2 (181) | **8.4 (245)** | 11.9 (348) | 16.4 (479) | | | | | | | | | |
| 1 1/4 (31.8) | | | | | | 1.7 (50) | 2.9 (85) | 4.0 (117) | 5.4 (158) | 7.0 (204) | **9.0 (263)** | 14.0 (409) | 28.8 (841) | | | | | | | | |
| 1 1/2 (38.1) | | | | | | | | 3.2 (93) | 4.3 (126) | 5.6 (164) | 6.7 (196) | **11.2 (327)** | 22.0 (642) | 38.0 (1110) | | | | | | | |

**TABLE 10-2—*Continued***

| Width of V-Die Opening, in. (mm) | Thickness of Metal in. (mm) | | | | | | | | | | | | | | | | | | | | |
|---|---|---|---|---|---|---|---|---|---|---|---|---|---|---|---|---|---|---|---|---|---|
| | 24 gage 0.024 (0.61) | 22 gage 0.030 (0.76) | 20 gage 0.036 (0.91) | 18 gage 0.048 (1.22) | 16 gage 0.060 (1.52) | 14 gage 0.075 (1.91) | 13 gage 0.090 (2.29) | 12 gage 0.105 (2.67) | 11 gage 0.120 (3.05) | 10 gage 0.135 (3.43) | 9 gage 0.149 (3.79) | 7 gage 3/16 (4.7) | 1/4 (6.4) | 5/16 (8.0) | 3/8 (9.53) | 7/16 (11.1) | 1/2 (12.7) | 5/8 (15.9) | 3/4 (19.1) | 7/8 (22.2) | 1 (25.4) |
| 2 (50.8) | | | | | | | | | 3.2 (93) | 4.1 (120) | 5.2 (151) | 7.6 (222) | **15.3 (447)** | 26.0 (759) | 41.0 (1197) | | | | | | |
| 2 1/2 (63.5) | | | | | | | | | | 2.4 (70) | 3.5 (102) | 5.8 (169) | 11.5 (336) | **19.2 (561)** | 29.9 (873) | 45.2 (1320) | | | | | |
| 3 (76.2) | | | | | | | | | | | 2.2 (64) | 4.5 (131) | 9.1 (266) | 16.0 (467) | **24.0 (701)** | 35.0 (1022) | 47.9 (1399) | 86.2 (2517) | 138.0 (4030) | | |
| 3 1/2 (88.9) | | | | | | | | | | | | | 7.5 (219) | 12.5 (365) | 19.4 (566) | **28.0 (818)** | 39.0 (1139) | 69.5 (2029) | 108 (3154) | | |
| 4 (102) | | | | | | | | | | | | | 6.2 (181) | 10.6 (310) | 16.0 (467) | 24.0 (701) | **33.1 (967)** | 58.0 (1694) | 92.0 (2686) | | |
| 5 (127) | | | | | | | | | | | | | | 7.6 (222) | 12.3 (359) | 17.0 (496) | 24.0 (701) | 42.2 (1232) | 69.0 (2015) | 104.0 (3037) | |
| 6 (152) | | | | | | | | | | | | | | | 9.3 (272) | 14.6 (426) | 19.0 (555) | **32.4 (946)** | 52.2 (1524) | 80.0 (2336) | 112.2 (3276) |
| 7 (178) | | | | | | | | | | | | | | | | 11.1 (324) | 15.6 (456) | 26.0 (759) | 42.2 (1232) | 63.0 (1840) | 90.2 (2634) |
| 8 (203) | | | | | | | | | | | | | | | | | 12.7 (371) | 23.0 (672) | **36.0 (1051)** | 52.5 (1533) | 76.0 (2219) |
| 10 (254) | | | | | | | | | | | | | | | | | | 16.5 (482) | 27.0 (788) | **39.4 (1150)** | **56.2 (1641)** |
| 12 (305) | | | | | | | | | | | | | | | | | | | 21.0 (613) | 31.2 (911) | 44.0 (1285) |
| 16 (406) | | | | | | | | | | | | | | | | | | | 14.3 (418) | 21.5 (628) | 31.0 (905) |
| 20 (508) | | | | | | | | | | | | | | | | | | | | 15.9 (464) | 23.0 (672) |



* The newton per linear millimeter also is being considered for adoption in the United States. Numeric values are the same for kN/linear m and N/linear mm.

Note: Figures in bold type are the forces required using a punch with a radius equal to the metal thickness and die opening approximately eight times metal thickness. This combination produces an air bend with an inside radius nearly equal to metal thickness—a good practical minimum for 90° bends. When forming metal heavier than 1/2" (12.7 mm) (and all gages of high-tensile steels), V-die openings of 10 times metal thickness or greater are recommended.

# BENDING FORCE REQUIRED

**TABLE 10-3**
**Factors for Determining Bending Forces for Metals Other Than Mild Steel**

| Material | Ultimate Tensile Strength MPa | ksi | Conversion Factor |
|---|---|---|---|
| Aluminum: | | | |
| Soft sheet | 104 | 15 | 0.25 |
| Half hard sheet | 131 | 19 | 0.35 |
| Hard sheet | 193 | 28 | 0.50 |
| Brass: | | | |
| Soft sheet for drawing | 324 | 47 | 0.80 |
| Half hard sheet | 414 | 60 | 1.00 |
| Hard sheet | 587 | 85 | 1.40 |
| Bronze | | | |
| Gun metal | 276 | 40 | 0.70 |
| Phosphor soft sheet | 311 | 45 | 0.75 |
| Manganese | 483 | 70 | 1.20 |
| Copper, rolled | 255 | 37 | 0.60 |
| Duralumin | | | |
| Soft sheet | 242 | 35 | 0.60 |
| Treated | 380 | 55 | 0.90 |
| Treated and cold rolled | 518 | 75 | 1.25 |
| Iron, wrought | 345 | 50 | 0.85 |
| Lead | 21 | 3 | 0.05 |
| Monel metal, rolled sheet | 656 | 95 | 1.60 |
| Silver | 262 | 38 | 0.60 |
| Steel | | | |
| 0.25 Carbon (mild) | 414 | 60 | 1.00 |
| S.A.E. 1040 (cold drawn) | 621 | 90 | 1.50 |
| 0.50 Carbon | 656 | 95 | 1.60 |
| S.A.E. 2330 (cold drawn) | 725 | 105 | 1.75 |
| S.A.E. 3240 (hot rolled annealed) | 725 | 105 | 1.75 |
| 0.75 Carbon | 794 | 115 | 1.90 |
| 1.00 Carbon | 897 | 130 | 2.20 |
| 1.20 Carbon (annealed) | 1035 | 150 | 2.50 |
| Stainless (low carbon) | 552 | 80 | 1.30 |
| Stainless 18.8 | 656 | 95 | 1.60 |
| Tin, sheet | 35 | 5 | 0.08 |
| Zinc, rolled | 166 | 24 | 0.40 |

(*Niagara Machine & Tool Works*)

*Metric equation.* From the preceding sample calculation performed with both inch-pound units and metric units, it has been established that the V-bend equation for use with metric units is:

$$F = \frac{1.33SWt^2}{D} \qquad (3)$$

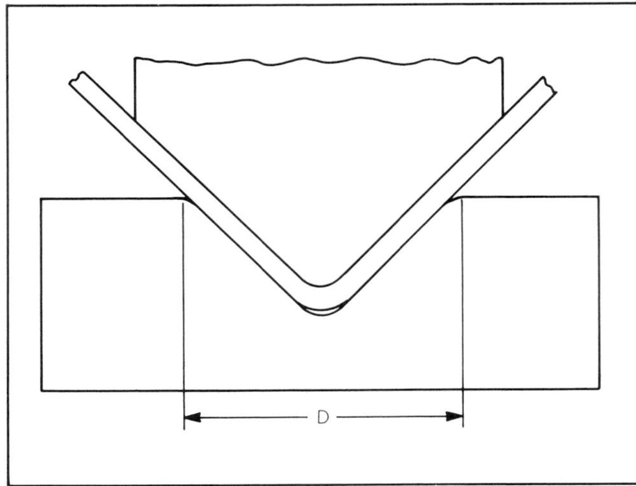


**Fig. 10-3 Typical V-bend operation.**

where:

$F$ = force, kN
$S$ = ultimate tensile strength, kPa
$W$ = length of bend, m
$t$ = stock thickness, m
(Note: For validity of equation, express thickness in meters.)
$D$ = die opening dimension, m

**The wiping equation.** A typical wiping operation is shown in Fig. 10-4. The wiping force equation in U.S. customary inch-pound units is:

$$F = \frac{0.333SWt^2}{D} \qquad (4)$$

where:

$F$ = force, lb
$S$ = tensile strength, psi
$W$ = length of bend, in.
$t$ = metal thickness, in.
$D$ = distance between radial centers, in.

*Sample calculation.* Assuming a tensile strength of 120,000 psi, a bend length of 4", a stock thickness of 3/16", and a die dimension, $D$, of 2.18", the force equation becomes:

$$F = \frac{0.333(120{,}000) \times 4 \times (0.1875)^2}{2.18}$$

$$= 2577.7 \text{ lbf}$$

$$= 11.466 \text{ kN}$$

*Metric calculation.* The same wiping force value can be obtained with Eq. (4) when tensile strength is expressed in kilopascals and the linear dimensions in meters. Thus:

$$F = \frac{0.333(120\,000 \cdot 6.895)(4 \cdot 0.0254)(0.1875 \cdot 0.0254)^2}{2.18 \cdot 0.0254}$$

$$= 11.466 \text{ kN}$$

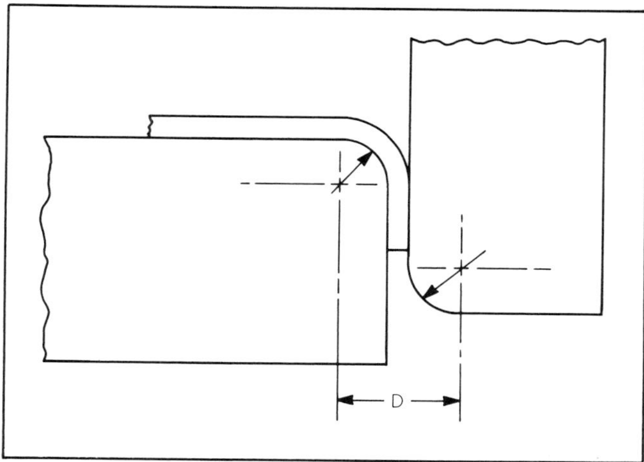


**Fig. 10-4 Typical wipe operation.**

## Bending Force Nomograph

Bending force can be estimated by use of the nomograph in Fig. 10-5, which is based on the following equation:

$$F = \frac{KLSt^2}{2W} \qquad (5)$$

where:

$F$ = bending force required, tons
$K$ = die-opening factor: varies from 1.20 for a die opening of 16 times metal thickness to 1.33 for a die opening of 8 times metal thickness
$L$ = length of bent part, in.
$S$ = ultimate tensile strength, ksi
$t$ = metal thickness, in.
$W$ = width of the V, channel, or U lower die, in.

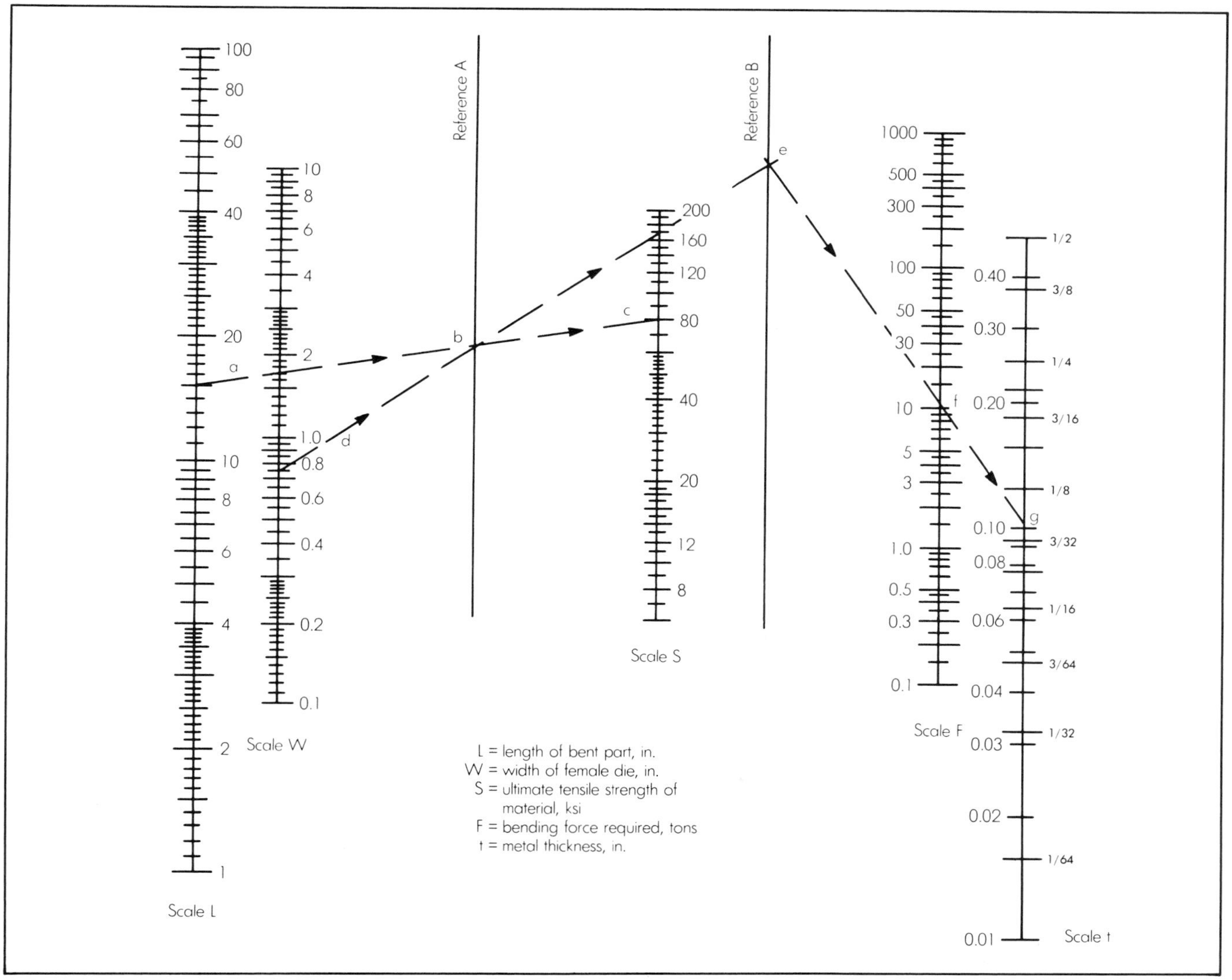

L = length of bent part, in.
W = width of female die, in.
S = ultimate tensile strength of material, ksi
F = bending force required, tons
t = metal thickness, in.

**Fig. 10-5 Nomograph for determining bending force in V-dies.**

To prevent the chart from becoming too complex, a die-opening factor of 1.33 was used in all cases. Ultimate tensile strengths (ksi and MPa) and a bending force conversion factor for various materials are given in Table 10-3.

The bending force nomograph in Fig. 10-5 is applicable only to V-shaped dies. For channel forming and U forming, the result is multiplied by four. In forming a channel with a flat bottom, a blankholder is necessary. The blankholder area is multiplied in square inches by 0.15 and added to the bending force derived from the nomograph.

To illustrate use of the nomograph in Fig. 10-5, using a 15″ long, 0.10″ thick steel strip (80 ksi ultimate tensile strength), proceed as follows to estimate the force necessary to bend this strip in a 3/4″ V-shaped die:

1. Enter the nomograph at 15″ on Scale *L* and draw Line *abc* through 80 ksi on Scale *S*.
2. Draw Line *dbe* from 0.75″ on Scale *W* to the intersection of Line *abc* with Reference Axis *A*, and extend to intersect Reference Axis *B* at Point *e*.
3. Connect Point *e* and 0.10″ (Scale *t*) by Line *efg*.
4. At Point *f*, read the bending force, 11 tons.
5. To express the result in metric units, use the conversion factor (8.9) and obtain a bending force of 98 kN.

## TYPES OF BENDING

The basic types of bending applicable to sheet metal forming are straight bending, flange bending, and contour bending. Examples of these three types of bending are shown in Fig. 10-6.

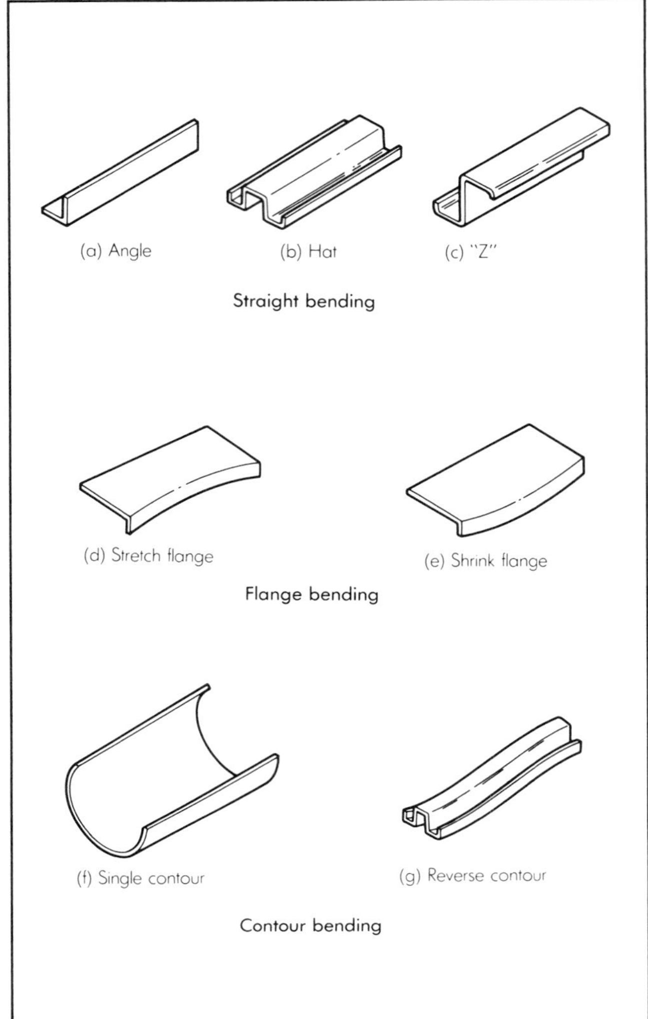


**Fig. 10-6 Types of bend forming.**

### Straight Bending

The terminology for a straight bend is shown in Fig. 10-7. During the forming of a straight bend, the inner grains are compressed and the outer grains are elongated in the bend zone. Tensile strain builds up in the outer grains and increases with the decreasing bend radius. Therefore, the minimum bend radius is an important quantity in straight bending since it determines the limit of bending beyond which splitting occurs.

Figure 10-8 illustrates a typical splitting-limit curve for straight bend forming. The limiting ratio of bend radius to material thickness, $r/t$, below which splitting occurs is a function of the bend angle up to a critical bend angle, at which point it becomes constant, $r/t_c$. The curve is defined by good parts above the line and by failed parts below the line. Material bendability can be improved by the application of heat during bending. This resultant increase in ductility tends to lower the curve in Fig. 10-8 and provide lower $r/t$ values. Lower $r/t$ values result in smaller bend radii, which permit smaller part flanges to reduce weight in structures.

A second factor to be considered in straight bending is springback. As the forming pressure is released from the part, the part tends to regain its original shape through elastic recovery. Normally, in room-temperature forming the metal is overformed to allow for springback; that is, it is formed to a smaller bend angle. The amount of overform is found through experimentation and may vary between heat applications for a given sheet metal because of slight variation in mechanical and physical properties. A second method of springback control is to maintain a low residual-stress level in the formed part. Springback is a function of the residual-stress level in the formed part, and the application of heat during bending tends to reduce residual stress.

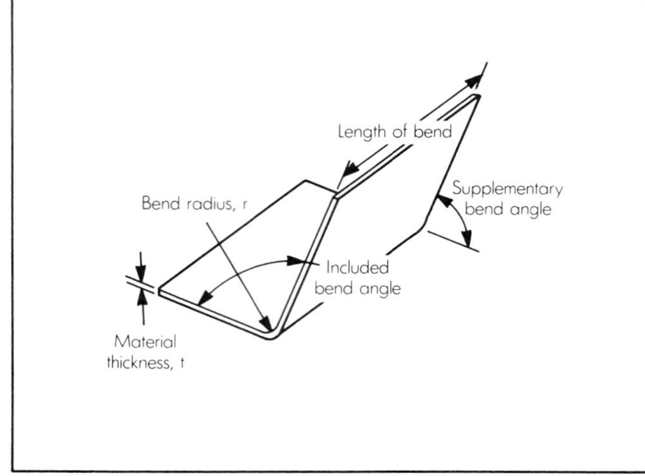


**Fig. 10-7 Terminology for a straight bend.**

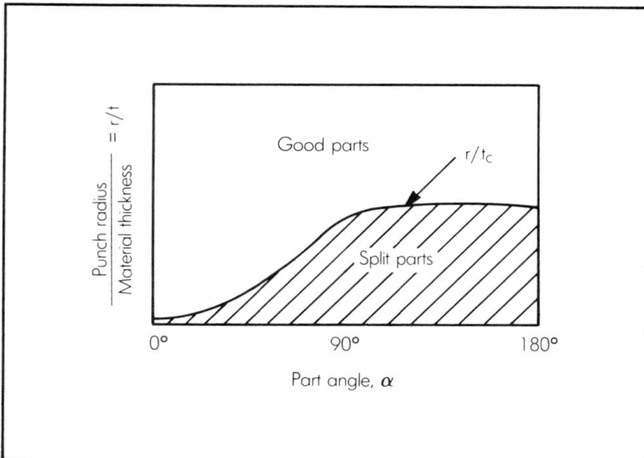


**Fig. 10-8 Limit curve for straight bending.**

## Flange Bending

Flange bend forming consists of forming shrink and stretch flanges as illustrated by views *d* and *e* in Fig. 10-6. This type of bending is normally produced on a hydrostatic or rubber-pad press at room temperature (see Chapter 5, "Presses for Sheet Metal Forming") for materials such as aluminum and light-gage steel.

Parts requiring very little handwork are produced if the flange height and free-form-radius requirements are not severe. However, forming metals with low modulus of elasticity to yield strength ratios, such as magnesium and titanium, may result in undesirable buckling and springback as shown in Fig. 10-9, *a* and *b*. Also, splitting may result during stretch-flange forming as a function of material elongation (see Fig. 10-9, *c*). Elevated temperatures utilized during the bending operation enhance part formability and definition by increasing the material ductility and lowering the yield strength, providing less springback and buckling. Detailed information on flanging is provided in Chapter 4, "Sheet Metal Blanking and Forming."

## Contour Bending

Contour bending is illustrated by the single-contoured part in Fig. 10-6, *f*, and the reverse-contoured part in Fig. 10-6, *g*. Single-contour bending is performed on a 3-roll bender, or by using special feeding devices with a conventional press brake. Higher production rates are attained using a three-roll bending machine, as described later in this chapter. Contour radii are generally quite large; forming limits are not a factor. However, springback is a factor because of the residual-stress buildup in the part; therefore, overforming is necessary to produce a part within tolerance. (Refer to Chapter 8, "Roll Forming," for additional information.)

Long-angle, Z-shaped, and hat cross-section parts are fabricated by straight bending, but they may contain generous single or reverse contouring along their longitudinal axes. Typical parts would be used for aircraft structural applications such as stringers. Normally, parts of this type are contoured at room temperature on a conventional three-roll bending machine requiring a skilled operator to produce the correct amount of overform to allow for part springback. Some contouring along the longitudinal axis can be formed on contoured press brake dies. Examples are hat channels for roof ribs on semitrailers. Their rise is 3/8" (10 mm) over a 96" (2.4 m) chord. The contour radius must be large, or buckling in the part flange or web occurs. Parts having a small contour radius must be processed through the yield point during the contouring operation to prevent buckling. This type of forming is performed on a linear stretch press. (Refer to Chapter 7, "Expanding, Shrinking, and Stretch Forming.")

In contour bending of materials such as titanium, it may become necessary to apply elevated temperatures during the forming operation to eliminate springback, and then perform a stress-relieving heat-treatment operation.

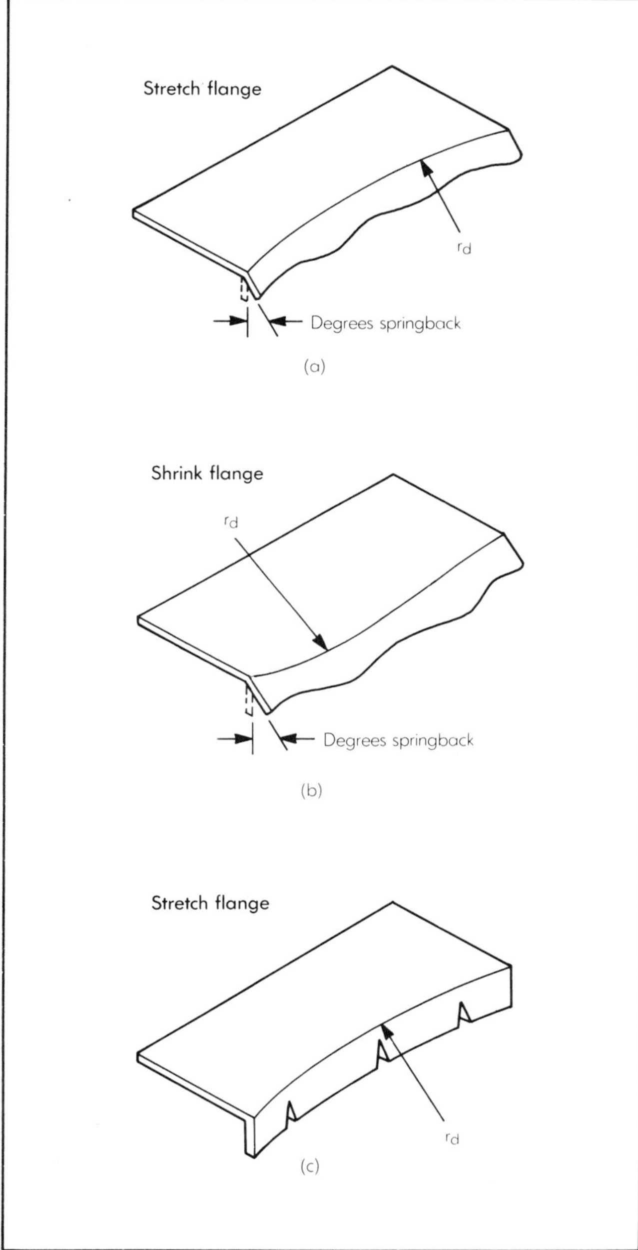


**Fig. 10-9 Flange forming failure modes: (a) and (b) buckling and springback; (c) splitting.**

# CHAPTER 10

# BENDING WITH PRESS BRAKES

## BENDING WITH PRESS BRAKES

Press brake bending is a process by which a piece of metal is placed between upper and lower dies and formed through the force and pressure exerted by lowering the ram. The press brake is a specialized type of press consisting of a long, narrow ram and bed. Almost any type of straight bend can be produced using a press brake. This versatility has led to wide use of press brake bending in the metal fabricating industry. The press brake can be used for prototype and short-run custom work, as well as for lengthy production runs.

### Equipment

In precision metal fabricating, which usually involves working with sheet metal that is less than 10 gage (0.141″; 3.57 mm) thick, the press brake is the basic bending machine. Press brakes are available in a variety of sizes and capabilities, ranging from hand-operated units to machines with a capacity of 3000 tons (27 MN). Tonnage (force) capacity is, of course, a primary consideration in press brake selection. Key operating parameters, such as speed, accuracy, stroke length, and controllability also should be taken into account. These characteristics have a significant influence on productivity, and they differ among the various types of press brakes.

### Basic Construction

As shown in Fig. 10-10, a press brake is a rather simple machine tool consisting of the following basic components or subsystems: housings, bed, ram, and a drive that activates the ram.

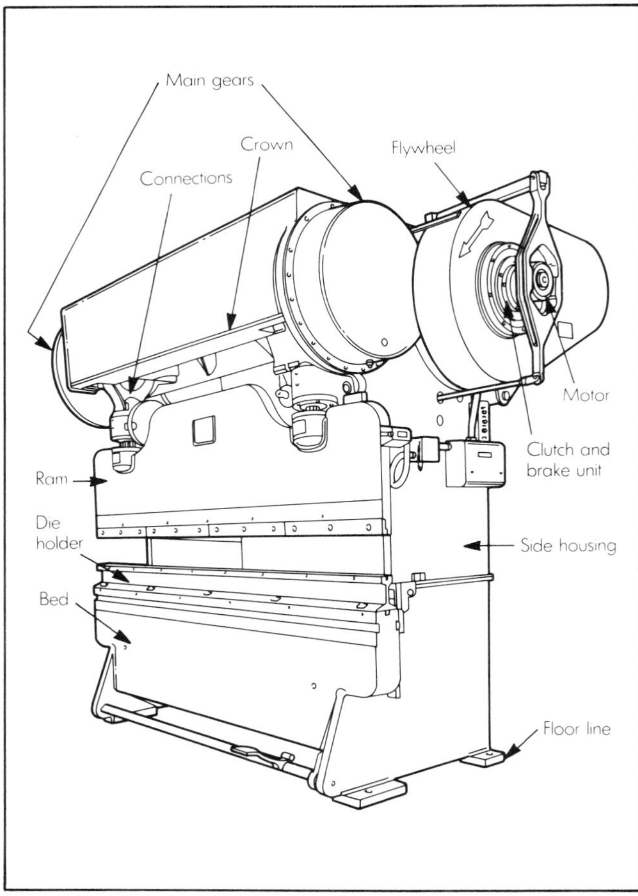


**Fig. 10-10 Typical mechanical press brake.** (*Verson Allsteel Press Co.*)

The housings are the side frames and serve as basic supports for the bed (and the lower die), as well as for ram guides and ram drive mechanisms. Housings also serve as mounting surfaces for control system elements and for gaging systems. Steel weldments are generally used for various press brake components that are assembled by bolting or welding them together.

### Press Brake Nomenclature

The following list of terms commonly used in press brake operations was compiled from various sources, including American National Standard B11.3[2] and "The Art of Forming."[3] Terms common to various power presses are defined in Chapter 5, "Power Presses for Sheet Metal Forming." (Some of these terms apply to press brakes; however, care is needed when applying generic terminology, because a press brake is not classified as a press.)

**bed** The stationary portion of a power press brake that supports the lower (female) die. The bed usually rests on uprights or housings and is subjected to the pressing load.

**bend allowance** Length of material that must be included in a flat blank to form bends of desired size.

**bottoming bending** Press brake bending process in which the upper die (punch) enters the lower die and coins or sets the material to eliminate springback.

**brake** The mechanism used to stop the motion of the power press brake ram; when engaged, it holds the power press brake ram in a stopped position.

**clutch** An assembly that connects the flywheel to the crankshaft either directly or through a gear train; when engaged, it imparts motion to the mechanical power press brake ram.

**coining** Similar to bottoming; however, greater force is applied. Coining alters the radius, and bottoming sets the bend open but does not affect shape.

**connection** The part of the power press brake that transmits motion and force from the revolving crank or eccentric to the power press brake ram. (*See* pitman.)

**die** The tool that determines the bend and the shape that will be produced. Commonly used in reference to both the upper and lower dies.

**eccentric** The offset portion of the crankshaft that governs the stroke or distance the ram moves on a mechanical power press brake.

**flange** Usually refers to the surface that is formed (by bending) from the body of the part.

**flattening dies** Dies used to flatten hems; that is, dies that can flatten a bend by closing it. Consist of a top and bottom die with a flat surface that can close one section (flange) to another (hem, seam).

**foot control** The foot-operated control mechanism (other than mechanical foot pedal) designed to control the movement of the ram on mechanical, hydraulic, or special-purpose power press brakes.

**forming** In relation to press brakes, means bending.

**gage, back-gage** A bar or fingers (located behind the press brake) which can be positioned accurately and quickly so that a sheet inserted into the press brake for bending is positioned to make a bend at the desired point.

**gibs** The parts that guide the ram. Matching gibs are located on the ram and housing.

**gooseneck punch** A punch that permits making deep, narrow channels, because its shape permits the flange to bend beyond the centerline of the ram. The upper die is relieved on one side past the centerline, to provide clearance for previously formed blanks.
**hatchet punch** A sharp upper die that permits making bends down to 30° included angle (also called acute angle punch).
**hemming** A bend of 180° made in two steps: First, a sharp-angle bend is made; next, the bend is closed by means of a flat punch and a die.
**housing** The stationary portion of the power press brake structure on which the ram is guided and to which the bed, crown, and drive are attached.
**hydraulic press brake** A press brake with the ram actuated directly by hydraulic cylinders.
**hydraulic-mechanical-press brake** A mechanical press brake that utilizes hydraulic cylinders attached to mechanical linkages to power the ram through its working stroke.
**leaf brake** A press brake on which bending action is produced manually by a "leaf" operated by two long handles, or by powered means. (Also called box and pan, or finger brake.)
**mechanical press brake** A press brake utilizing a mechanical drive consisting of a motor, flywheel, crankshaft, clutch, and eccentric to generate vertical motion.
**pitman** That portion of the connection assembly that couples to the eccentric. (*See* connection.)
**punch** Upper die.
**ram** The powered, movable portion of the power press brake structure, with die-attachment surface, which imparts the pressing load through male dies onto the piece part and against the stationary portion of the press brake bed.
**rib** A long, V-shaped or radiused indentation used to strengthen large panels.
**run mode** A single stroke or continuous stroking of a power press brake.
**shut height** The distance from the bed to the ram when the ram is at the bottom of its stroke and the adjustment is up. Normally called the maximum die space.
**single stroke** One complete stroke of the ram, usually from a full open position through a closed position back to a full open position.
**springback** Tendency of material (metal) to move toward its original form after bending force is released. Springback typically ranges from 2-4°.
**stop control** An operator control designed to immediately stop the ram motion.
**stroke (up or down)** The vertical movement of the power press brake ram during half of the cycle, from full open to full closed position or vice versa.

## Types of Press Brakes

Generally, press brakes can be divided into two categories—mechanical and hydraulic—depending on the type of ram drive that is used. An additional category (or sub-group) is the hybrid type, which incorporates both hydraulic and mechanical design elements for ram actuation. Schematic drawings of the three types of press brakes are shown in Fig. 10-11.

**Mechanical.** In a mechanical press brake (see Fig. 10-12), the up-and-down motion of the ram is produced by an eccentric shaft driven by an electric motor via a clutch and a flywheel. Since the eccentric shaft produces exactly the same displacement during every stroke and the energy stored in the flywheel is usually considerably more than required for an operation, the

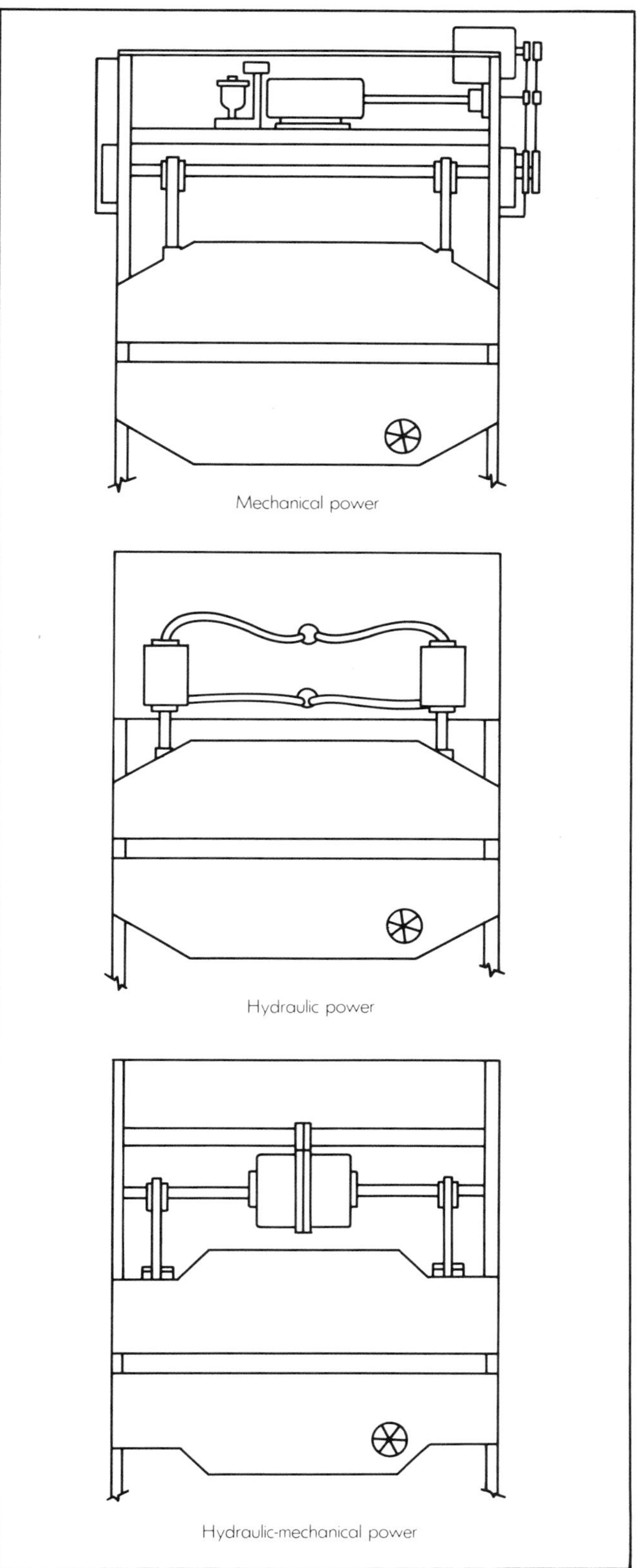


**Fig. 10-11 Press brake ram drive methods.** (*Di-Acro Div., Houdaille Industries, Inc.*)

mechanical press brake provides both accuracy and high operating speeds (up to 60 strokes per minute). A mechanical press brake is subject to damage by overloading, and the clutch may require a skilled operator to control bending speed. Current design practice uses an air-electric clutch to enable control of speed.

**Hydraulic.** A hydraulic press brake (See Fig. 10-13) is driven by two hydraulic cylinders; hence, it provides the controllability that is common to hydraulic systems. The stroke is readily adjustable, and full tonnage (force) is available throughout the stroke. One of the latest machines has a single ram-and-cylinder design that combines the desirable operating features of fast advance and return speed with slow forming speeds.

The hydraulic press brake is not susceptible to overload; hence, the machine is protected from overload damage and less operator skill is needed. Multispeed equipment, combining fast advance and return speeds with slow forming speeds, compensates partially for the characteristically slower speeds of the hydraulic press brake.

**Hybrid.** Both mechanical and hydraulic elements are embodied in the ram drive of hybrid machines. As produced by one manufacturer and illustrated in Fig. 10-14, the hydraulic-mechanical hybrid is, essentially, a mechanical press brake driven by a rotary hydraulic motor. Instead of a piston (as used in a hydraulic cylinder), the rotary hydraulic motor has a vane that rotates 270° between stops. During its motion between the two stops, the motor drives the eccentric shaft through one complete cycle. This action drives the ram to the stroke bottom and back to the top.

Accuracy of the hydraulic-mechanical drive is the same as that of the mechanical drive. The speed of this drive is also quite high because the rotary motor produces a ram stroke for each rotation cycle. The stroke length is adjustable and offers good controllability.

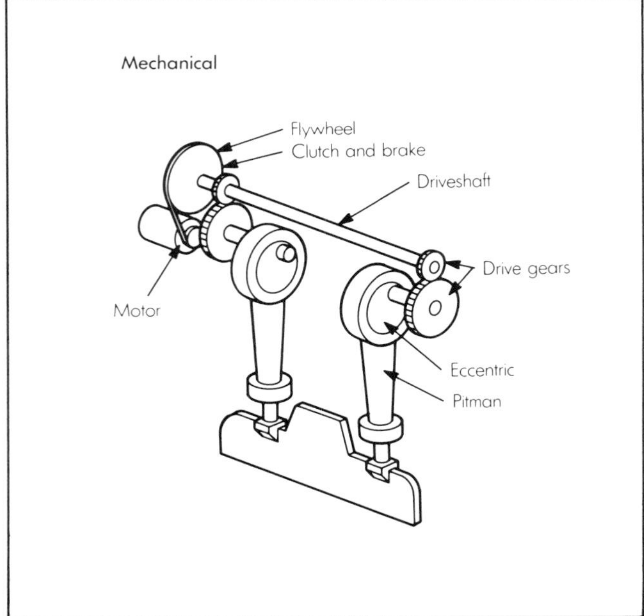


**Fig. 10-12 Mechanical press brake drive system. Ram motion is produced by an eccentric shaft driven by clutch and flywheel that are powered by an electric motor. Principal advantages are high operating speeds and accuracy.** (*Di-Acro Div., Houdaille Industries, Inc.*)

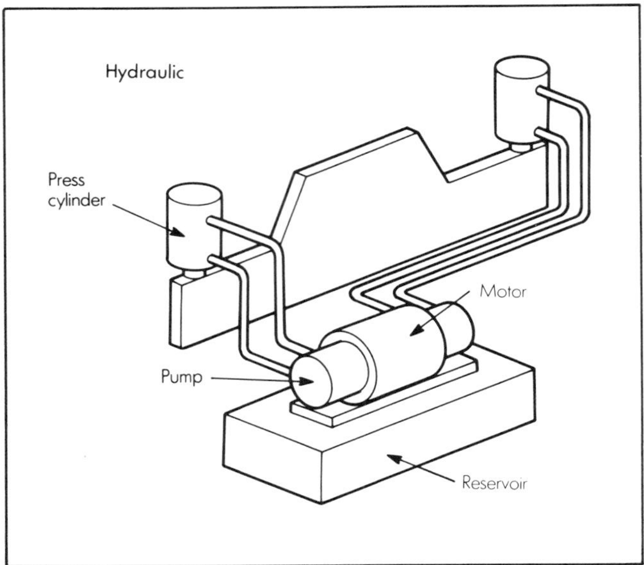


**Fig. 10-13 Hydraulic press brake drive system. The ram is operated by two hydraulic cylinders. Principal advantages are stroke control, variable applied force, and protection from overloading.** (*Di-Acro Div., Houdaille Industries, Inc.*)

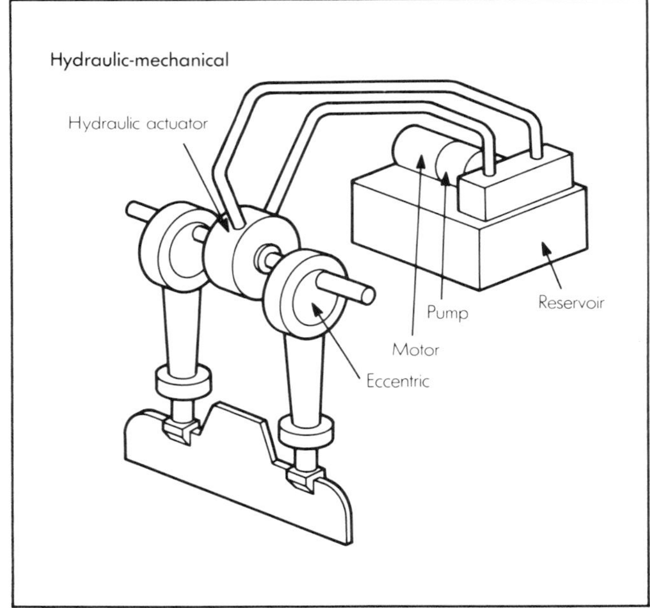


**Fig. 10-14 Hydraulic-mechanical press brake drive system. Both mechanical and hydraulic elements are incorporated in the ram drive. In essence, this is a mechanical press brake driven by a rotary hydraulic motor.** (*Di-Acro Div., Houdaille Industries, Inc.*)

## BENDING METHODS

With a few exceptions, hand-operated press brakes generally fall into the so-called leaf or finger press brake category while power units are simply called press brakes. Both types of brakes perform a similar basic operation—bending sheet metal to some desired shape. However, they accomplish this bending in a different manner.

Figure 10-15 depicts bending action as performed in a leaf press brake. In this operation, the material is literally bent around a finger die. Because the bending force is applied manually by the operator, press brakes of this type generally are limited to 16-gage (0.061″; 1.56 mm) mild steel.

Most press brake forming is done on power press brakes. In performing the operation, as illustrated in Fig. 10-16, *a*, a sheet of metal is laid over a die opening and a matching upper male die bends the material by penetrating into the lower die. The bending action involves three points, as shown in Fig. 10-16, *b*: the tip of the punch (*A*) and two points (*B*) on the female die. The material is bent to the desired angle as the punch enters the die. The larger the die opening, the smaller the force that is required to form a given angle.

Power press brake forming operations can be divided into two broad categories—air bending and bottom bending. Press brake selection depends greatly upon which method is to be used.

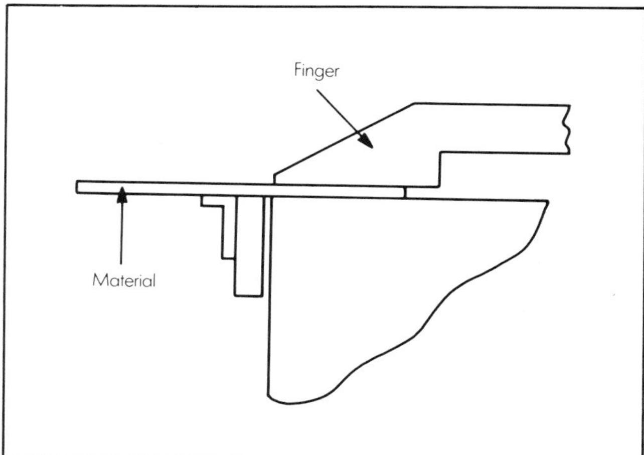


**Fig. 10-15 Bending action in a leaf press brake.**

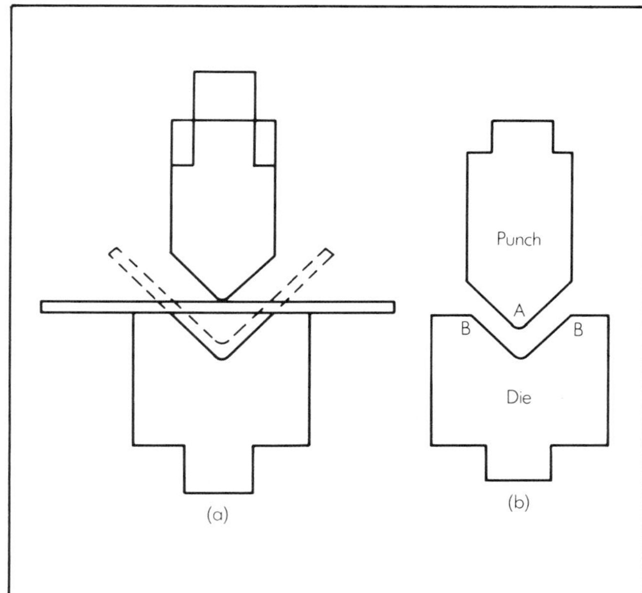


**Fig. 10-16 Typical power press brake bending action.**

## Air Bending

In air bending (see Fig. 10-17, *a*), the punch does not seat fully in the die; the sheet metal, supported by high points of the die, wraps around the tip of the punch to form the bend. Air bending is a versatile operation; a large variety of parts can be made from a single set of dies. Accuracy of the parts must be closely monitored, however, because springback is a factor.

Angular accuracy is obtained in air bending by overbending and then permitting the material to spring back to the desired angle. Depending on the material, springback may or may not be consistent. Low-carbon steels, for instance, may have widely varying tolerances that affect the springback consistency. An advantage of air bending is that it requires considerably less press-brake tonnage (force) to produce a given bend—four to six times less than in bottoming bending. Thus, some shops prefer air bending even if they have to rerun rejected parts to obtain the desired angle. With the air bending method, the formed angle can be specified anywhere from 180° to the included angle of the female die. The sharpness of a bend is a function of the distance between the two edges of the female die and the distance that the punch tip travels into the die.

Once a female die opening is selected, the repeatable accuracy of bending each successive piece part is determined by how consistently the punch tip penetrates the die. Variations in punch travel are particularly pronounced in forming lighter gages of sheet metal. A variation of 0.005″ (0.13 mm), for instance, while forming 16-gage (0.063″; 1.60 mm) mild steel may result in angular deviations of up to 7° when making 90° bends. In other words, air bending accuracy of a press brake is directly related to its ability to bring the punch tip to the same lowest point repeatedly during each stroke.

## Bottom Bending

Bottom bending and coining form bends by letting the punch penetrate the female die as far as the dies and the formed material will permit, Fig. 10-17, *b*. Generally, bottom bending results in more consistently accurate parts than air bending. Furthermore, a radius smaller than metal thickness can be obtained with bottom bending and coining.

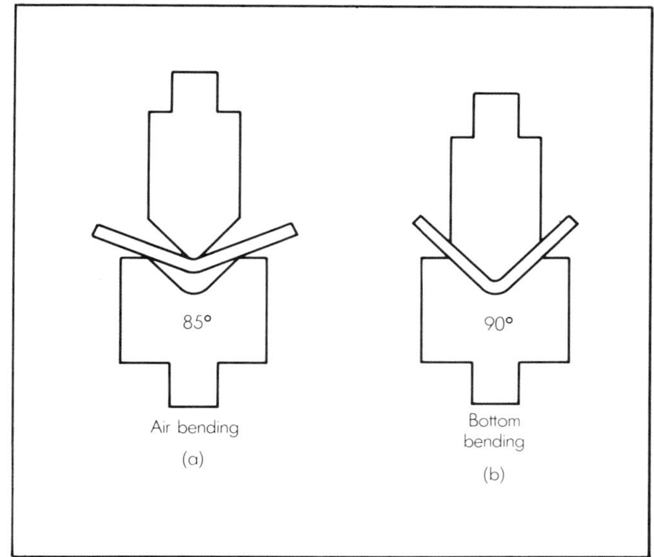


**Fig. 10-17 Two basic methods of press brake bending.**

To help overcome springback, the clearance between the punch and the die is set slightly less than the material thickness. The resulting coining action counteracts the springback, provided a sufficient dwell time at the bottom of the stroke is used to allow the material to make a compressive shift.

While bottom bending results in consistent part quality, three to five times the press brake tonnage is required to produce a given part in comparison to air bending. Furthermore, to avoid damage from overloading (particularly with press brakes using mechanical drives), clearances between punches and dies must be set very carefully: If the clearance is too loose, reject parts will be formed; if the clearance is too tight, full-length overloading may occur. In practice, a press brake usually is set up with material thickness clearance between the upper and lower dies.

For this reason, bottom bending should be used only where it is really needed—in applications requiring a high degree of accuracy and sharp corners. For example, metal furniture, cabinets, and partitions usually require bottom bending. Because of the higher tonnage (force) requirement, bottom bending is generally limited to bending steel that is no heavier than 12 gage (0.109″; 2.77 mm).

## PRESS BRAKE DIES

In addition to bending, other types of work, such as punching, countersinking, dimpling, and embossing, can be done on press brakes. Press brakes can perform virtually any forming job that can be accomplished with a relatively short stroke of the ram under power. However, although the press brake is a highly versatile machine, bending dies comprise the bulk of press brake tooling. These dies are the focus of information presented in the following section.

### V-Type Dies

The most extensive family of punches and dies for bending are the V-type dies. In every case, the lower dies are available with different die openings to accommodate various material thicknesses. Dies for air bending have included angles of 85°, while dies for bottom bending normally have 90° angles. V-type tooling can be ordered with various material capacities and with acute-angle dies that permit forming angles as small as 30°.

### Rotary Bending

Traditionally, press brake bending has been performed in one of three ways: with a V-die, with a wiping die, or with a U-die. In recent years, however, another (patented) method, rotary bending, is gaining acceptance. The main advantage of rotary bending is that it significantly reduces the force required to perform bending.

The rotary bending design eliminates the need for any type of hold-down pad or device. It provides its own inherent holding action at the same time the bending operation is proceeding.

The rotary bender is comprised of three components: the saddle (punch), the adjustable rocker, and the die anvil. The rocker is cylindrical in shape with an 88° V-notch cut out along the length. The edges of the rocker jaws are flatted and radiused to minimize marking. Three stages of a rotary bender operation are illustrated in Fig. 10-18. In view *a*, the material is clamped and the rocker rotation has begun; view *b* shows that humping is controlled and limited to space between edges of the rocker; and view *c* shows how the rocker clamps the workpiece in position and overbends it sufficiently to allow for springback.

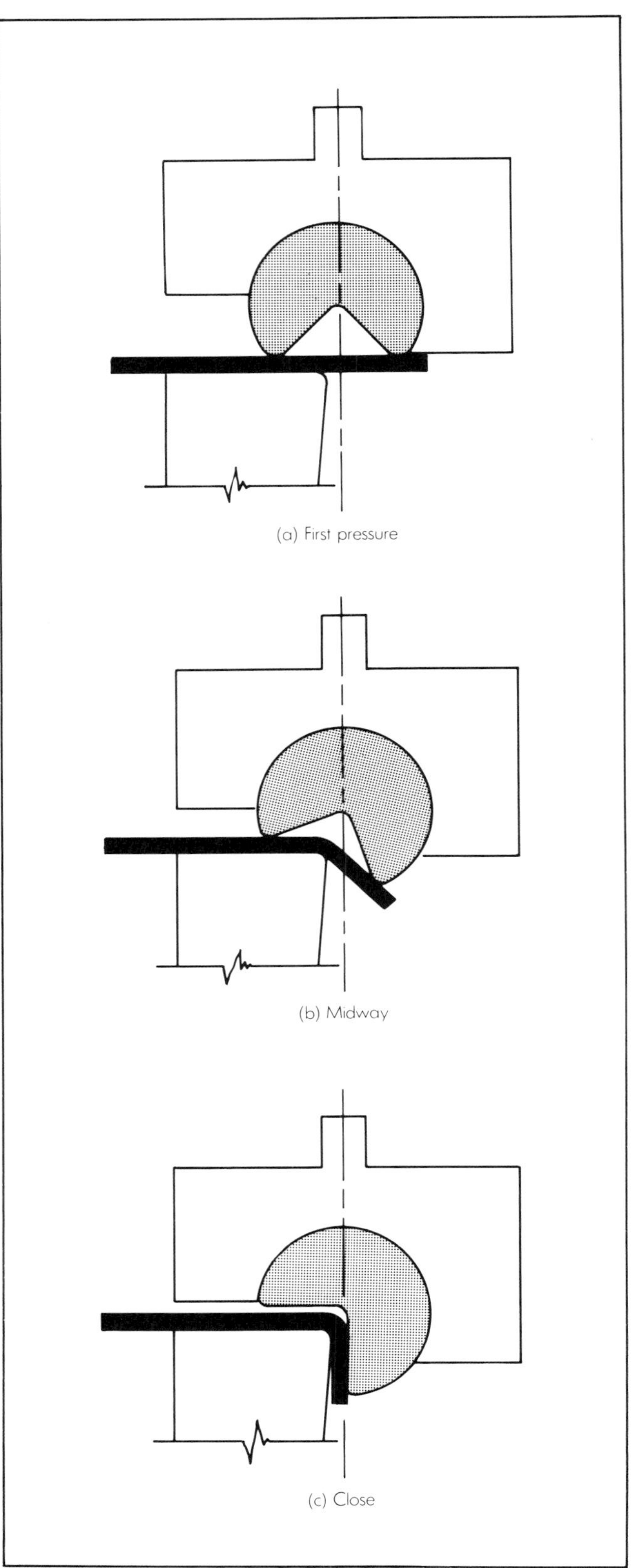


**Fig. 10-18 Sequence of operations for press brake rotary bending.**

# PRESS BRAKE DIES

The primary application for rotary benders is in progressive dies. Z-bends and short leg bends can be made in a single operation; and where needed, dart stiffeners can be rolled into the workpiece at the same time it is being bent.[4]

## Diversity of Tooling

As stated previously, the press brake is a highly versatile machine, capable of performing a variety of operations, including a considerable range and diversity of bending jobs. The demarcation between a pure bending operation and a pure forming operation is not clear cut; hence, a stamping operation sometimes classified as either bending or forming may include both. Since bending and flanging basically produce straight-line shapes, most of the tools do not require contouring and can be produced by shaping, milling, and planing. Representative sets of commonly used tooling are illustrated in Fig. 10-19.

**90° forming dies.** Figure 10-19, *a*, illustrates a typical 90° forming die, which is one of the most common dies used in press brakes. Most 90° dies are bottoming dies, and in using them, characteristics of bottoming must be considered. In general, the bend radius should not be less than the thickness of the material and the V-die opening should be eight times the metal thickness. High-tensile-strength materials require larger radii and wider vees than this, and plates over 1/2" (12.7 mm) thick also require V-die openings of more than eight times the metal thickness.

**Acute-angle or air-forming dies.** The dies shown in Fig. 10-19, *b*, are known as acute-angle dies because of the acute angles they can form. They are usually air-bending dies and may be used for 90° bends when accuracy is not critical. These dies may also be used to form a wide range of both acute and obtuse angles simply by adjusting the ram of the press, which in turn determines how far the punch enters the die.

**Gooseneck dies.** Figure 10-19, *c*, shows a typical gooseneck or return-flanging die. These dies are essentially simple V-bend dies with clearance for return flanges. Care must be taken in using these dies because the neck is usually out beyond the centerline and can easily be bent by overloading.

**Offset dies.** An offset can be formed by making two reverse bends with a 90° or acute-angle die. However, for long runs or sharp offsets, dies of the type shown in Fig. 10-19, *d*, are generally used. The force required sometimes is high, being from four to twenty times the force for a single bend, depending on the nature of the offset. Dies used to form each bend to more than 90° are usually referred to as Z-dies.

**Hemming dies.** The edges of a sheet are sometimes hemmed or turned over to provide stiffness or a smooth edge. Hemming can be done in two operations, starting with an acute-angle die and finishing with a flattening die such as that shown in Fig. 10-19, *e*. However, most hemming is done on regular hemming dies, which are two-stage dies combining an acute-angle die

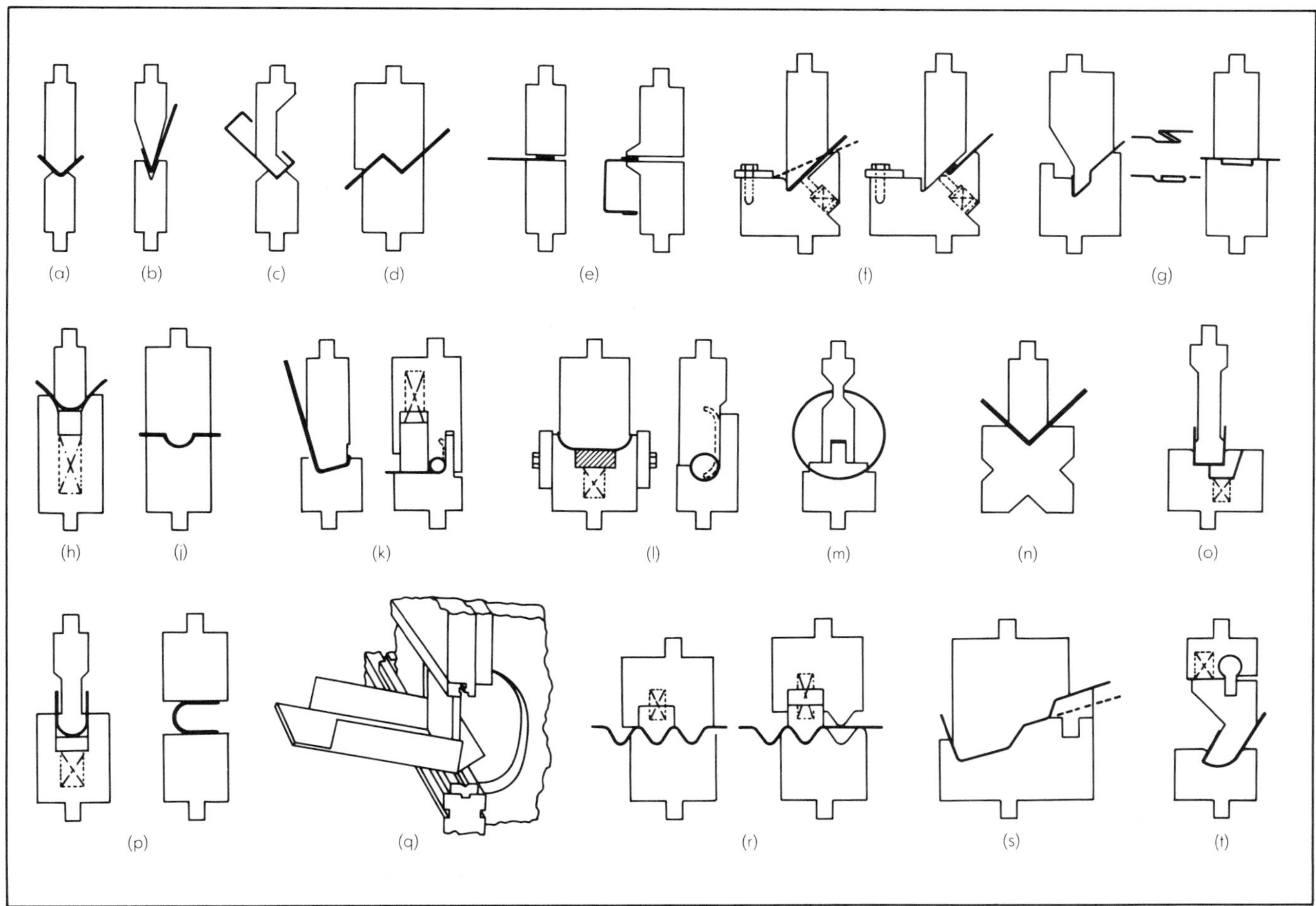


**Fig. 10-19 Typical press brake bending and forming dies.** (*Cincinnati Incorporated*)

with some sort of flattening arrangement. One type is shown in Fig. 10-19, *f*. Forces required vary greatly with thickness of the hem and degree of flatness.

**Seaming dies.** Seams in sheets or tubes can be made in a variety of ways. A set of dies for making simple seams is shown in Fig. 10-19, *g*.

**Radius dies.** These dies are usually employed when the radius exceeds four times the material thickness. Such bends can be made with a V-die machined to less than 90° and a full-radius punch. However, better results are sometimes obtained with springloaded dies such as that shown in Fig. 10-19, *h*. Instead of spring pads, rubber pads may be used. The angle of bend is adjusted by varying the distance that the punch enters the die. Punches with different radii may be used with the same die for different radii on the bend. The inside radius on air bends is commonly controlled by the die opening. This inside radius, with normal dies, is very nearly one quarter of the die opening.

**Beading dies.** In power press work, beads are used to stiffen flat sheets; in press brake operations, a bead is called a "stopped rib." In presses, the dies provide either open beads that extend from edge to edge of the sheet, or closed beads that fade out in the sheet. Open beads usually are formed by simple dies such as those shown in Fig. 10-19, *j*. Closed beads, on the other hand, require the use of spring-pressure pads at the ends, which fade out to minimize wrinkling of the metal.

**Curling dies.** These dies provide a curled or coiled-up end on the piece. Hinge dies make use of a curling operation. The curl may be centered, or it may be tangent to the sheet as shown in Fig. 10-19, *k*. In press brake work, a curl also is called a bead.

**Tube and pipe-forming dies.** These dies are similar to curling dies. The edges of the metal must be bent as a first operation. The piece then rolls up properly. Figure 10-19, *l*, shows a two-operation die for forming small tubes. For larger tubes, a bumping die such as that in Fig. 10-19, *m*, is necessary. For accurate work, such bumped tubes should be sized over a sizing mandrel. Seams can be formed on the edges of these tubes before they are rolled.

**Four-way die blocks.** For small-production runs or for a job shop, the four-way die block as shown in Fig. 10-19, *n*, is quite useful and represents savings in tool cost.

**Channel-forming dies.** Channels may be formed in gooseneck dies or in single-stroke channel dies as shown in Fig. 10-19, *o*. Such dies are commonly made with a spring-pressure pad release of some sort to eject the formed part from the die. Strippers are sometimes provided to strip the part from the punch.

**U-bend dies.** U-bend forming is similar to channel forming, but springback is usually more pronounced and a means must be provided to overcome it. One way of accomplishing this is shown in Fig. 10-19, *p*.

**Box-forming dies.** While box forming consists of simple angle bending, problems exist that are peculiar to the nature of the work. In general, a high punch and a low die are required, as seen in Fig. 10-19, *q*. Sometimes the punch is cut into sections so that the side of the box can come up between them. Certain shapes of boxes may be formed on horn presses.

**Corrugating dies.** Corrugating dies can be provided to produce a variety of corrugations. Figure 10-19, *r*, shows one type of corrugating die.

**Multiple-bend dies.** Multiple-bend dies offer an infinite variety of possibilities. Commonly used on large-production runs, one die can accomplish, in a single stroke, an operation that would require several operations with single-bend dies. Figure 10-19, *s*, shows such a die. This die requires greater forming pressure than dies for the individual operations.

**Rocker-type dies.** Rocker-type dies can be used to form parts that would be impossible with a die acting only vertically. A typical example is shown in Fig. 10-19, *t*. Rocker inserts are also often used to increase the number of bends per hit, or to produce an overbend in one hit either to improve quality or to increase production by eliminating a restrike for angle control.

**Cam-driven dies.** Cam or wedge-driven dies can be used to increase production and quality. For example, in normal acute-angle bending, the sheet moves through a large arc, and at normal press speeds, this arc may result in a bend at the outside die edge. This undesired bending may be reduced by slowing the machine, but a better solution is the wedge-driven die, in which the sheet can be laid flat and the press run at normal speeds.

## Plastic Tooling[5]

Urethanes and other plastic materials are used for tooling that embodies deformable dies. A key characteristic is the inherent property of changing shape while retaining a constant volume. When used as a female die, the urethane material forces the work material around the tip of the punch to conform to the punch contour as illustrated in Fig. 10-20.

**Advantages.** Urethane tooling systems offer a number of advantages over conventional tooling:

- Savings in tooling costs and setup time by eliminating the need for a female die and alignment adjustments.
- Elimination of the springback effects for small-radius bends, because a urethane die acts as a female bottoming die.
- Elimination of metal thickness variations effects. (If the stroke is set for the thinnest anticipated material tolerance, other bends will be at least as good as those made at the thin points.)
- Minimal metal fracturing and/or thinout in the bend area.
- Elimination of blank slippage prior to forming due to high blankholding pressure.
- High (and consistent) forming accuracy, for parts less than 4′ (1.3 m) long.
- Versatility, since one die can accommodate a wide variety of punches, and stock of various types and thicknesses can be formed with the same soft-tool combination.

**Limitations.** The force required with plastic tooling is approximately three times the force for air bending. Also, gaging can be a problem. Another drawback of plastic tooling is that it cannot form flanges narrower than half the pad width. The pad material flows upward past the workpiece and thus does not exert the required force.

The use of soft tooling requires careful consideration of press brake capacity. Polyurethane, the material commonly used, can sustain very high loads, about triple those required in conventional bending. Punch ends must be adequately rounded, or they may eventually cut the pad. Foreign material should be cleaned from pad surfaces regularly to prevent workpiece abrasion and scratching.

**Die availability.** The grade and size of the urethane die required for a forming operation are determined by the application and available press brake tonnage. Grade and pad size recommendations, together with application tips, can be found in the catalogs of suppliers who offer this type of tooling.

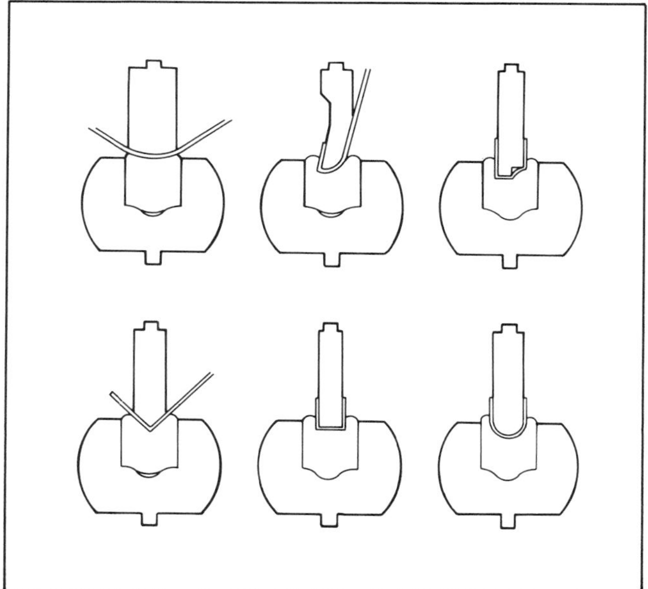

**Fig. 10-20 Urethane pads are used as dies in some power press brake operations.** (*Di-Acro Div., Houdaille Industries, Inc.*)

## PRESS BRAKE GAGING

The position of the workpiece and the stroke of the tool are two critical variables in the bending process. Traditionally, in press brake operations, operator skill has been a significant factor—particularly, for the jobs requiring loading each workpiece properly and resetting the machine frequently.

Two press brake operating considerations determine the angle and the location of a bend—how deep the punch penetrates the female die (in air bending) and how far the material is inserted into the dies. Until recently, settings for both of these considerations had to be adjusted manually; and such adjustments were time-consuming. This often dictated that production of parts would be done one bend at a time.

### Automatic Gaging

In the past decade, rapid advancements have been made in the area of automatic gaging. The advent of press brakes with a higher degree of controllability and the development of inexpensive, electronic, digital controls resulted in the introduction of gages that permit economical manufacturing of multiple-bend, multiple-stroke, air-formed piece parts in one handling.

### Various Gages Available

A wide variety of gaging devices help the press brake operator position workpieces with consistent accuracy. These gages are made by companies that specialize in gaging devices, as well as by press-brake manufacturers. Several firms offer press brakes with sophisticated control systems that regulate ram stroke as well as the workpiece gages. Capability is expressed in terms of axes, and some machines control as many as eight axes.

**Adjustable gages.** Many press brake manufacturers provide adjustable arms, or rods, that are mounted on the machine beds and function as front or back stops against which workpiece edges and flanges are positioned prior to the ram stroke.

Although their basic function is similar, back-gages and front-gages (their location with respect to the press-brake bed) differ widely in configuration, versatility, and cost. The equipment is included as original equipment on new press brakes. It is also sold for retrofitting on existing machines.

**Computer-controlled gages.** Computer numerical control (CNC) gaging systems were initially developed to control flange lengths within a specified tolerance. Back-gages that are CNC controlled are motor driven and can be programmed for multiple flange lengths that may be required for a specific part. Once a program is entered into the CNC gage's memory, the back-gage changes its position in accordance with the program after every bending operation.

Computer-controlled back-gaging systems can also be programmed to accommodate bend allowances so that the operator merely feeds the material into the press brake after the gage has been programmed.

For hydraulic and hydraulic-mechanical brakes, an additional factor to be controlled is the degree of bend; CNC gaging was developed to control the female die penetration, that is, how far the punch travels. Thus, in air forming under ideal conditions, angle variations of 30-160° theoretically can be repeated within $\pm 1/2°$.

Multiple-axes CNC gages are available to control the height of the gage bar, the position of the fingers, and other gaging variables.

Even when controlling only the flange length and/or bend angle, CNC gages can provide worthwhile productivity improvement. With all controllable axes linked together, however, they effectively convert a press brake into a computer numerically controlled machine tool. The role of the operator is reduced to feeding material into the press brake, stacking the complete parts, and monitoring the tooling and machine performance.

## PRESS BRAKE SAFETY

From a user's point of view, the question of safety actually consists of two parts: the inherent press-brake safety and the overall operational safety. The first of these—the inherent press-brake safety—largely depends on how a given press brake is designed and built and how it is controlled. The overall operational safety is a function of how well a given shop uses the machine features and how well it applies sound shop practices.

### Protective Equipment

Protective equipment for a press brake is almost identical with that for a power press (discussed in Chapter 5, "Presses for Sheet Metal Forming"). The hazards are the same: inadvertent closure of the ram and accidental separation of a component from the machine. For special equipment such as panel formers, operation is largely automatic, hazards are minimal, and safeguarding is tailored to the particular application.

**Tools and devices.** In addition to hand tools for workpiece loading/removal and mechanized devices—including robots—that do the same thing without requiring an operator to reach into the die area, there are a number of systems designed to eliminate or at least minimize the hazards. The various types and uses of these systems are described in manufacturers' literature. Procedures are also set forth in ANSI Standard B11.3, "American National Standard for Machine Tools—Power Press Brakes—Safety Requirements for Construction, Care and Use," issued by the American National Standards Institute.

**Photoelectric systems.** An electronic fence, or curtain, immediately stops a press brake if it is interrupted by the operator during a downstroke. A press brake deactivates during the loading and removal parts of the cycle. Both photoelectric (visible-light) systems and those that operate in the infrared invisible-light spectrum are in common use.

**Barriers.** Positive-deterrence devices include barriers and gates made with screens, bars, or solid material in a wide variety of designs. Some guard the end zones of a press brake, while others can be set up to span the unused portions of the bed.

**Restraints.** Operator restraints include pullback systems in a wide range of designs, and such machine-actuation devices as dual pushbuttons which require that both hands be safely away from the machine's die area during the working stroke. The pushbuttons are in cups that thwart their actuation by a hold-down of some sort. One make of pullback designed especially for press brakes tethers the operator's wrists to rings that slide freely on the transverse bar of an overhead frame; the frame is linked to the machine's ram and moves away from the die area during the working stroke.

### Machine Construction

Other protective devices built into press brakes as original equipment include:

- A sturdy enclosure for the flywheel of a mechanical press brake to contain any component that might become detached.
- Pedals that prevent inadvertent actuation. (They cannot be depressed unless mechanically unlatched by the operator's toe.)
- Systems that monitor braking performance to permit imminent failure to be foreseen and corrective action to be taken.
- Ram-reversing systems for hydraulic press brakes to prevent the ram from falling if power should fail.

A general safety feature associated with practically every control or adjustment is that various knobs, handles, pushbuttons, etc., which actuate the controls are placed in such a way as not to require any part of the operator's body to be placed in the dies. In fact, about the only time that the operator's hands need be placed near the ram and the bed area is when changing dies.

### Maintenance

In relative terms, a press brake is a simple machine tool; hence, its scheduled maintenance requirements are also simple. However, for safe, reliable operation, the user should follow the manufacturer's recommended procedures.

## ROLL BENDING

Rolling or curving metal into cylinders or cylindrical segments is carried out on machines which use two or more rolls that rotate and bend the metal as it passes between them. Flattened cylinders and elliptical cylinders can also be formed. One type of machine using three rolls, as well as a special version of a two-roll machine, can be employed to form truncated cones. These shapes find application as hoppers, bins, vertical storage tanks, appliance parts, and ordnance parts.

Any metal that can be conventionally formed can also be formed by these machines. Thicknesses of metals commonly used range from 16-gage (0.061"; 1.56 mm) to 10" (254 mm) plate, although many parts are thicker or thinner. Maximum thickness that can be curved depends upon the type, size, and power of machine. Minimum thickness usually is determined by the ability of the metal to be curved without damage.

While various machines can handle a wide range of metal thicknesses, it is not practical to roll metals varying from one extreme of the thickness range to the other extreme on three-roll machines. Two-roll machines can readily handle a wide range of sheet metal, up to the limit of their gage capacity.

The minimum diameter of a workpiece to be formed depends upon the type of machine, size of rolls, and the springback of the material. The maximum diameter is limited primarily by the work space available and by practical handling considerations. The width of the sheet or plate to be curved is limited by the working length of the rolls in the machine.

Accuracy of the workpieces is also dependent upon the type of machine used and upon variations in the temper of the material.

### Machine Types for Sheet Metal

Cylinder rolling machines for sheet metal are made in a wide variety of models and sizes; however, they can be classified according to the number of rolls. The three-roll machines can be further classified into pyramid or pinch types.

**Three-roll machines.** Conventional pinch-type, three-roll machines have rolls arranged as shown in Fig. 10-21. All three rolls are power driven on most models. The top roll on this type of machine is fixed, while the lower roll can be adjusted vertically for blank thickness. The rear roll can be adjusted angularly for the diameter of the cylinder to be formed.

Pyramid-type, three-roll machines (Fig. 10-22) have the top roll mounted between the two bottom rolls. The bottom rolls, which in larger models are supported by two smaller rolls, usually cannot be adjusted. The top roll is adjustable vertically to control the diameter of the cylinder to be formed. The two bottom rolls are gear driven, while the top roll rotates through contact with the blank.

An advantage of three-roll machines is that no tooling is required. Adjustment of relative roll position provides variation in workpiece curvature. A disadvantage is that when bending is performed with the pyramid-type machine, large flat areas occur at the leading and trailing edges of the blank. A smaller flat area, however, is left on the trailing edge by the pinch-type machine than by the pyramid-type machine, since the former type holds the workpiece more firmly. This flattening problem can be overcome by preforming the workpiece either in the rolling machine or with dies in a press brake. Another solution is to curve an oversize blank and then trim the edges. Inherent springback makes it difficult to bend sheet metal on any machine without 1-1.5" (25.4-38 mm) of end flat.

Curving or rolling with either of these two machines usually requires multiple passes, with roll adjustment between passes. Considerable operator skill is required to avoid out-of-roundness, and tight tolerances cannot be obtained. Also, the curving of blanks having holes or cutouts results in workpieces that have flutes or kinks because of metal-thickness variations. Another drawback is inability to curve small cylinders, particularly when the diameter of the cylinder is close to that of the rolls. Curving parts having an inside diameter of 2" (51 mm) less than the outside diameter of the rolls should be avoided on these machines.

The pinch-type and pyramid-type rolls can be used to curve cold or hot metal and full, flattened, or elliptical cylinders. To compensate for deflection, these machines commonly have crowned rolls. However, for any single machine, the degree of crowning is not necessarily the same for all rolls.

**Two-roll machines.** The two-roll machine, as shown in Fig. 10-23, has a steel roll located directly above a urethane roll. The top roll is fixed, while the lower roll can be adjusted vertically for metal and slip-on-tube thicknesses. The lower roll is driven, while the top roll rotates through contact with the blank.

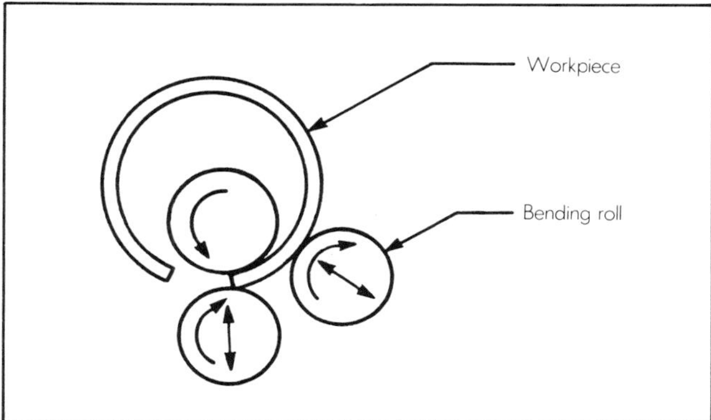


**Fig. 10-21 Roll arrangement for a three-roll, pinch-type roll bending machine.**

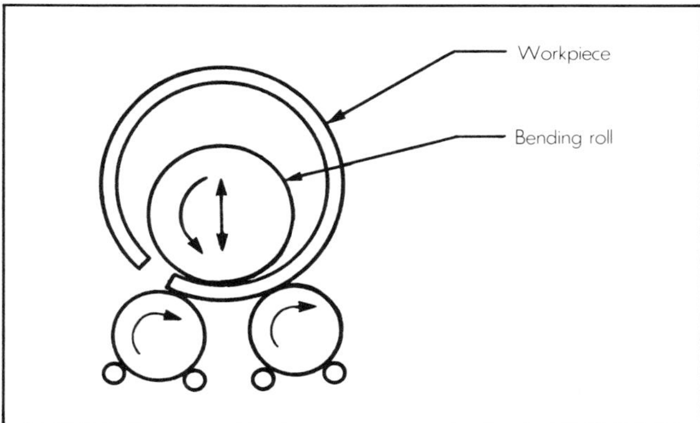


**Fig. 10-22 Roll arrangement for a three-roll, pyramid-type roll bending machine.**

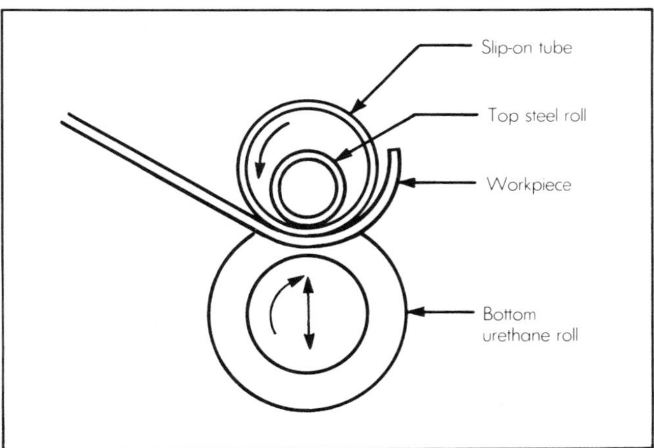


**Fig. 10-23 Roll arrangement for a two-roll bending machine.**

In operation, the rolls are set so that the top roll penetrates the lower urethane roll. Bending is accomplished under very high pressure, the urethane roll literally wrapping the blank around the top roll. The diameter of the workpiece is governed by the diameter of the top roll, the inner diameter of the part being equal to the outer diameter of the top roll plus springback of the metal.

The two-roll machine's major advantages include (1) one-pass curving—that is, the workpiece is accurately formed to its final diameter in one pass—and (2) consistently repeated accuracy from part to part. The machine curves the workpiece with minimal flats at leading and trailing edges. In lighter gage and softer metals, flats are equal to or slightly less than metal thickness; in heavier gage and tougher metals, they can range up to four times metal thickness.

The machine curves blanks having cutouts or flats, and even perforated stock, without fluting or kinking because of the high blankholding and forming pressures that it develops. The machine curves the blank without marring or scratching it because of the urethane roll. It, therefore, finds wide application in curving etched and painted nameplates. Also, due to elasticity of the urethane roll, this machine is capable of curving double metal thicknesses and can therefore be used to form an overlap.

The two-roll machine readily curves complete cylinders as well as short arc segments. It can also curve U-shaped parts, but cannot be used for curving elliptical or flattened cylinders. The machine can curve to diameters as small as 1" (25.4 mm) with proper accessories, and as large as space and handling facilities permit. Different models can curve blanks as narrow as 0.5" (12.7 mm) and as wide as 8' (2.4 m). This machine is limited to a maximum sheet thickness of 1/4" (6.4 mm) mild steel and cannot be used for hot forming. Unlike three-roll machines, two-roll units do not have crowned rolls. They compensate for roll deflection with a patented antideflection system that is incorporated into the rolls.

Two-roll machines obtain accurate curvature by using slip-on tubes. These tubes are developed for desired diameter, springback, and thickness of the metal and, in effect, constitute the tooling for a job. The tubes are slipped over the top roll of the machine, this roll being sized for the forces that are developed in the machine during curving. For curving parts to diameters smaller than the top roll, a special bridge support or small outer diameter attachment can be used. This attachment replaces the top roll and provides a support for roll mandrels down to 1" (25.4 mm) in diameter. The attachment provides the machines with the capability of curving to any diameter smaller than the top roll which it replaces.

## Special Equipment

The feed tables of two-roll machines can be provided with gages, and the drive with a timer and brake motor. These accessories permit accurate starting and stopping for curving such parts as U-shaped troughs, brake bands with loops at each end, and motor-mounted brakes with right-angle legs.

Truncated cones can be curved on the pyramid-type, three-roll machine as well as special models of the two-roll machine. With the three-roll machine, blank edges are preformed and a great deal of operator skill is required. With the two-roll machine, no preforming is required and curving is automatic once the blank has been gripped by the rolls.

The two-roll machine for curving cones has a developed steel roll and a developed urethane roll. These rolls, instead of being cylindrical, are tapered. They are made to accommodate the part they are to form, taking springback of the material into consideration. Cones are formed in one pass with repeated accuracy.

## PLATE BENDING

A variety of machines are used for bending metal plate in thicknesses from 1/4 to 10″ (6.4 to 250 mm) or more. Included among machines for plate bending and curving are press brakes; initial (single)-pinch, pinch-pyramid, and pyramid, three-roll benders; double-pinch, four-roll machines; and vertical (roll) presses that bend heavy plate up to 10″ (250 mm) thick. Most machines that roll thick plate material have a slip clutch to compensate for the separate inside diameter (ID) and outside diameter (OD) dimensions of the material being rolled.

Sheet metal machines for bending stock of up to 1/4″ (6.4 mm) thick are usually of lighter construction and are less complex than plate bending machines. Rolls can be made of bar stock, without crowning, and the ID/OD speed variation is less significant. Plate bending machines, on the other hand, normally include a higher degree of sophistication, because the compression and stretch factors, torque requirements, speed variations, and metal thicknesses vastly increase the number of variables involved in the bending operation. Sheets that are more than 10′ (3 m) wide also require a sophisticated machine, because of the potential deflection that is inherent in long bending machines.

### Press Brakes

Press brake size is based on bending a given thickness of mild-steel plate over a female die having an opening at the top equivalent to eight times stock thickness. This is an accepted standard and provides an inside radius equal to approximately 15% of the die opening. For example, when 1/4″ (6.4 mm) plate is being formed, the die opening should be 2″ (51 mm) wide. This provides an inside radius equal to approximately 0.31″ (7.9 mm). (These various approximations, inter-relating metal thickness, die opening, and bend radius, generally are invalid for steels with a tensile strength that exceeds 70,000 psi (483 MPa). Equipment manufacturers offer formability charts to indicate the appropriate tonnage (force) required for various materials.

By increasing the size of the die opening, the force required to make the same bend becomes considerably less. For instance, a force of approximately 15 tons per linear foot (438 kN/m) must be applied to form 1/4″ stock over a 2″ die opening whereas, if a 2 1/2″ (63.5 mm) die opening were employed, only 11.5 tons (336 kN/m) would be required to make the same bend. However, in this case, the inside radius would be approximately 0.39″ (9.9 mm).

Care must be exercised when increasing the die opening to reduce required force. If too large a die opening is used, an excessive amount of metal is drawn into the die opening, causing a bulge to form in the metal on the outside radius.

If this same stock were to be formed over a die opening less than eight times stock thickness, considerably more pressure would be required and, in addition, the stock would be likely to fracture.

When steel having a tensile strength greater than 60,000 psi (414 MPa) is processed, the force required rises in direct ratio to the increase in strength. For example, to brake 1/4″ (6.4 mm) plate of 60,000 psi (414 MPa) tensile strength over a 2″ (51 mm) die opening requires 15 tons (133 kN) and, if this material had a tensile strength of 120,000 psi (827 MPa), the required force would be 30 tons (267 kN) for the same length of bend.

High-tensile-strength materials are generally formed over V-die openings greater than eight times stock thickness. This is done to avoid fracturing the stock. The opening used should be 10-12 times stock thickness.

Heavy plate or plate in excess of 1″ (25.4 mm) thickness also has a tendency to fracture if formed over a die opening eight times stock thickness. The die opening recommended for high-tensile-strength material should be employed; however, if it is necessary for the inside radius to be equal or close to stock thickness, then special flanging steel or boiler plate should be used.

When an inside radius less than stock thickness is required, it should not be obtained by coining (bottoming) the stock. A die having a smaller opening should be used and the machine's rated bending capacity should be carefully checked to ensure that the use of the smaller die opening is well within the rated capacity of the machine.

### Roll Benders

When selecting a plate bending roll, it is important to undertake a thorough review of the factors related to sizing the machine. Capacity of bending rolls is determined by: (1) grade and physical properties of the material to be formed, (2) material thickness and width, and (3) minimum diameter to be formed.

For successful roll bending, the machine must have adequate capacity for the ultimate tensile strength and the yield strength of the material that is to be formed. Prebending capacity also should be checked, since the usual rolling specification is not established for fully forming a plate entirely within the machine. The three basic types of plate bending rolls in common use are initial-pinch type, the pinch-pyramid type, and the double-pinch, four-roll type. Table 10-4 summarizes key comparative characteristics of the three basic types of machines.

**Initial-pinch type.** The initial-pinch roll bender is widely used for general-purpose operations and is the type of machine used by most plate fabricators. The typical roll forging configuration of the initial-pinch roll bender is illustrated in Fig. 10-24. The top roll is fixed, and the two lower rolls are adjustable. The lower front roll is slightly offset from the top roll and is adjustable vertically to accommodate plate thickness. The rear roll or bending roll is adjustable angularly (usually 30° from vertical) and is positioned to control the diameter or curvature of the workpiece. On standard pinch-type machines, all three rolls are driven. This type of bender requires two plate entries, or passes, to complete the forming operation. The initial-pinch type of machine is capable of producing more accurate cylindrical shapes and curvatures than any other type of three or four-roll bending machine.

**Pinch-pyramid type.** Figure 10-25 represents schematically the basic layout of the pinch-pyramid, three-roll, plate-bending machine. Like the pinch-type machine, the top roll is fixed and both lower rolls are adjustable. However, usually only the lower rolls are powered; the top roll is an idler and is symmetrically positioned above the lower rolls. The primary advantage of this type of machine construction is that it allows both preforming and rolling of completed cylinders with only one entry of the work material into the machine. The pinch-pyramid type of machine is particularly applicable to the fabrication of shell segments or large-diameter tanks. Because it requires a considerable amount of positioning of the roll forgings to complete a forming cycle, the production capability of this type of machine is usually lower than the floor-to-floor output of other types of bending machines.

**Double-pinch, four-roll type.** Figure 10-26 illustrates the configuration of the roll forgings in the double-pinch, four-roll machine. The top roll position is fixed and the lower pinch roll is adjustable vertically for various plate thicknesses. The pinch roll is directly below the top roll, without offset, and the two side rolls are adjustable angularly. The top roll and lower pinch roll are powered for plate-feeding action, and both side rolls are idlers that depend upon pressure from the work material for rotation. All four rolls are crowned to provide accurate forming action. This machine is designed for one-entry forming. Usually, it is run as a three-roll machine, with the fourth roll active only during the preforming operation.

This type of bender (four roll) is especially suitable for production runs of the same size of rolled product on a regular basis. The roll position settings for production items can be recorded, and the rolls may be preset to form, not only cylindrical shapes, but conical sections and parts with varying radii on a production basis. This machine also is advantageous for bending long plates that are difficult to form on other types of equipment. In addition to the capability for one-pass forming, another advantage of the four-roll machine is that the plate being formed is always gripped between the pinch rolls, thereby eliminating accidental slippage during positioning adjustments of the side bending rolls. One disadvantage is that since the side rolls are not driven, a large-capacity machine cannot process thin plates, because of insufficient force to rotate the side rolls, and therefore the work material could be marred or scratched. Another consideration is that the cost of the four-roll machine is usually 20-30% higher than that of three-roll machines of similar capacity.

**TABLE 10-4**
**Comparison Chart for Plate Bending Roll Selection**

| Work Requirement | Initial Pinch | Pinch Pyramid | Four Roll |
|---|---|---|---|
| High accuracy, close tolerance | 1 | 3 | 2 |
| Flats or peaked seams eliminated | 1 | 3 | 1 |
| Good results on all thicknesses | 1 | 3 | 2 |
| Widest pinch opening for bar work or structurals | Modified Only | 1 | 2 |
| One entry for long plates | --- | 1 | 1 |
| Clamps plate firmly to eliminate accidental slippage | 1 | --- | 1 |
| Preset for duplicate production runs | --- | --- | 1 |
| Superior edge forming | 1 | 3 | 1 |
| Interchangeable top rolls | 1 | 1 | 1 |

(*Bertsch and Co., Inc.*)

Key:
1 = best; 2 = good; 3 = marginal; dash (---) = not recommended

## Vertical Press Plate Bending

Vertical presses, such as shown in Fig. 10-27, are especially suitable for forming cylindrical vessels from heavy metal plate. The bending method is based on a three-line principle wherein the central tool has a comparatively large radius that is smaller than the vessel radius, and the other two bending wedges can have flat surfaces dimensioned for low tool wear and contact pressures. Pivot bearings in the wedges provide increased capacity. Stepwise feeding of the plate between pressing operations is accomplished with hydraulic driving rolls mounted on the press beam. The installation setup can be changed to a driven roll for high-volume production and continuous eccentric bending.

These vertical presses with computer control are built in capacities up to 12,000 tons (83 kN) for cold-bending plates up to 10" (250 mm) thick. Vertical press design facilitates the use of a crane for handling the plate and removing the formed cylinder or conical shell when the operation is completed. During the bending process, the plate is supported by small, wheeled platforms ("roller skates") running on a flat floor. Through stepwise feeding of the plate and pressing the tools to a predetermined depth, the cylindrical surface is formed. Pressing depth is computer controlled to provide close tolerances with automatic correction for springback. Plates weighing up to 75 tons (68 Mg), with heights up to 220" (5.6 m), can be formed to close tolerances. Radial deviations are held to less than 1/8" (3.2 mm) for cylindrical vessel diameters from 24" (610 mm) to 320" (8 m).

Inherent advantages of the vertrical type press include one-pass forming, close tolerances, and minimal difficulty with flat ends, because the computer program is used to calculate parameters for the prebending operation.

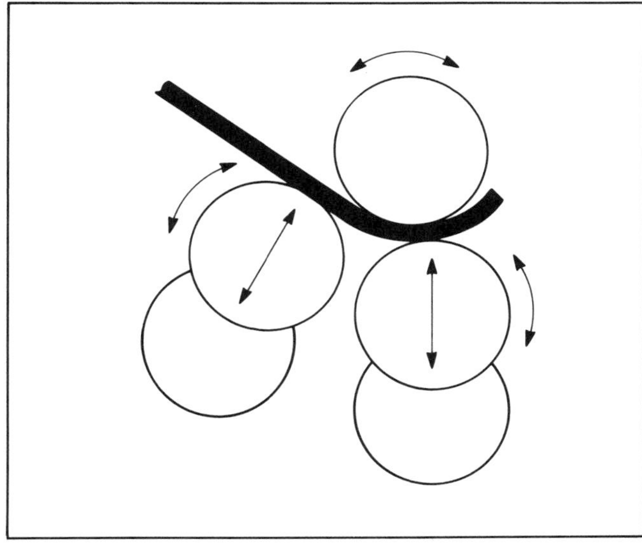

**Fig. 10-24 Roll configuration of an initial-pinch roll bending machine. This machine is a versatile, general-purpose machine that is capable of bending a range of plate thicknesses to various diameters. Accuracy is inherent in this type of design.** (*Bertsch & Co., Inc., Subsidiary of Deem International, Inc.*)

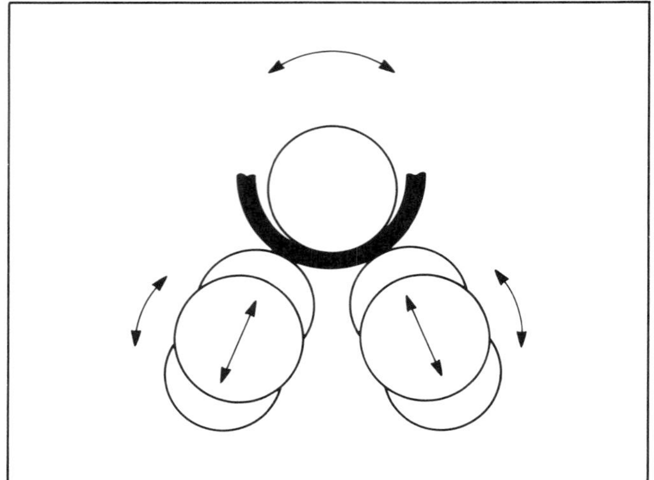

**Fig. 10-25 Roll configuration of a pinch-pyramid bending machine. The design allows both preforming and roll bending of complete cylinders with only one entry of the work material into the machine. This equipment is especially suited to production of large-diameter tanks and shell segments. (*Bertsch & Co., Inc., Subsidiary of Deem International, Inc.*)**

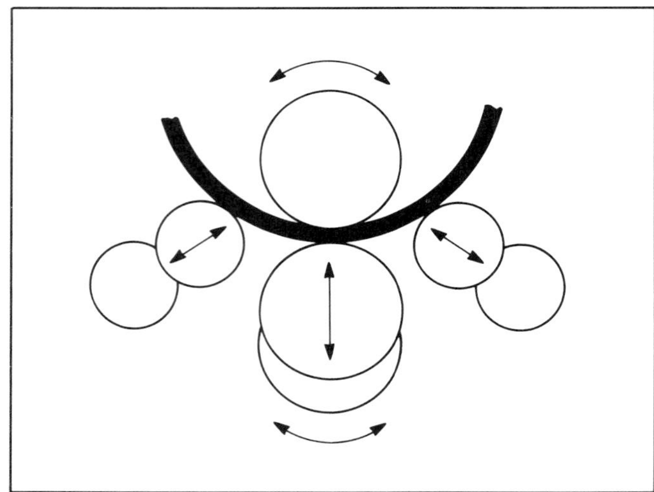

**Fig. 10-26 Roll configuration of a four-roll, double-pinch bending machine. This layout is similar to that of the initial-pinch roll, with the addition of a fourth roll. Suitable for applications involving production runs of same-size rolled products on a regular basis. An advantage is the capability of forming plate with one entry or pass. (*Bertsch & Co., Inc., Subsidiary of Deem International, Inc.*)**

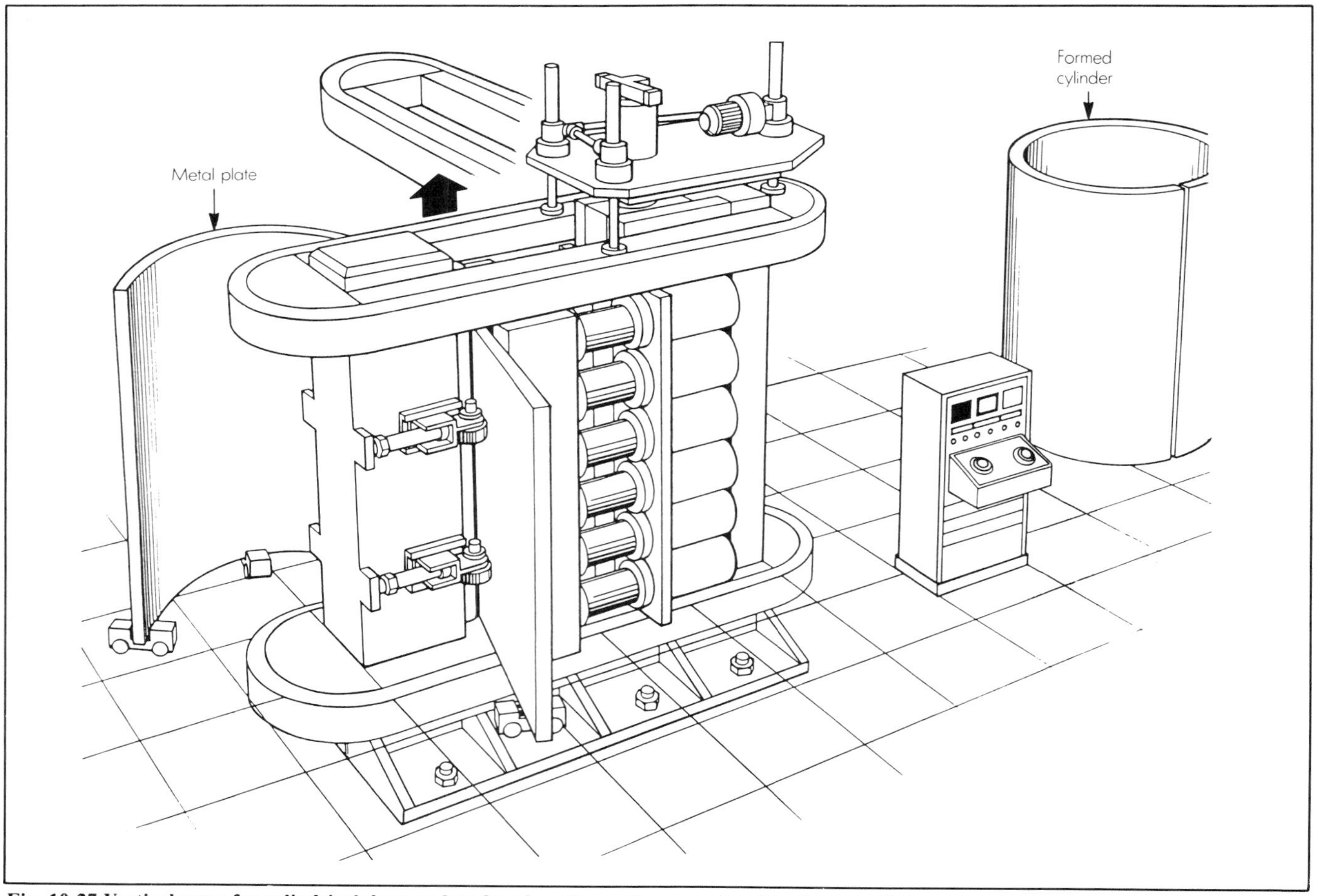

**Fig. 10-27 Vertical press for cylindrical, heavy-plate forming. Computer control enables heavy cylinders to be formed accurately in one pass with minimum flat ends. (*ASEA Pressure Systems, Inc.*)**

# TUBE, PIPE, AND BAR BENDING

The uses of bent or curved metal tube, pipe, angles, channels, rods, bars, and flat strip in industrial and consumer products are virtually limitless. Product manufacturers and metal fabricators require an endless variety and a vast quantity of bent parts and fluid conveyors.

High-volume requirements for such parts are best met by using high-speed conventional and automated machines. However, numerous applications in job-shop parts, limited-volume production parts, and a broad mix of diverse parts in relatively small quantities are produced faster and more economically on relatively small, manual or powered bending machines.

Simple machines and tooling (such as described later in this chapter) are more versatile than the sophisticated dedicated systems. They are relatively inexpensive, easy to set up and operate, and use fairly simple tooling. They are often the fastest means to produce finished parts in low-to-medium volumes—and frequently are used for prototype and one-of-a-kind work, even by firms that have more complex or sophisticated bending equipment.

The latest techniques and machines permit bending almost any ductile material ranging from small-diameter tubing to thin-wall, large-diameter tubing, and from large-diameter pipe to massive, structural iron beams. The ductile materials cover a wide range of ferrous and nonferrous metals, including carbon steel, stainless steel, aluminum, copper, and titanium.

The current state-of-the-art offers a greatly expanded range in using the strength-weight advantages of the tubular section in various engineering applications. In bending tubular sections, the radius and angular degree of bend can be precisely controlled and outer wall thickness can be reduced uniformly without collapsing. Repetitive accuracy is excellent, and close dimensional tolerances can be maintained.

With present technology, it is feasible to cold bend a long tubular element having a complex internal section through a configuration of bends and loops, holding precise dimensions and wall thicknesses throughout. The repeated accuracy of automatic equipment permits locating the plane of bend to ±0.10 and positioning the bend to ±0.005" (0.13 mm) at high-production rates.

Considerable progress has been made in all aspects of equipment involved in tube, pipe, and bar-bending processes. The machines, dies, mandrels, tooling, and automatic controls have undergone substantial development in recent years. The need for filler materials, such as sand and resin, has been eliminated in most applications by the use of flexible mandrels. Completely automatic precision bending now is performed with computers and numerically controlled equipment.

## BENDING THEORY AND PROCESS

Practically all methods of pipe and tube bending are based on the theory of applying a bending force great enough to stress the material beyond its elastic limit, but not so great as to cause stresses exceeding the materials ultimate strength, to the point at which the structure would fail and rupture.

As illustrated in Fig. 10-28, under the influence of an applied force, the material is made to flow, resulting in plastic deformation that thins the outside and thickens the inside wall of the bend throughout its length. This thinning, and hence the decrease in strength of the outer wall, together with a corresponding thickening and strength increase in the inner wall, causes a shift of the tube's neutral axis. The neutral axis, which originally was located in the center of the tube, shifts toward the compression side, resulting in a relatively larger displacement of metal in the outer portion of the bend.

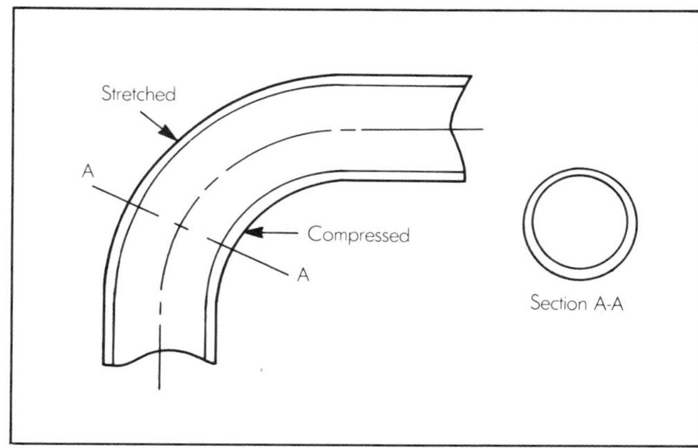


**Fig. 10-28 Stretching and compression and ovality in bent tube.** (*H & H Tool Division, Teledyne Pines*)

Whenever the likelihood exists that this metal flow would weaken the outer wall or flatten the bend excessively (especially in the case of thin-wall tubes), the metal flow must be held within well-defined limits.

This is done in various ways by supporting the tube or pipe wall during the bending operation. The support may be internal, in the form of loose, hard, granular filler material; a temporary solid rounded core; or a mandrel placed at the point of bending. The support may be external and may consist of a grooved pressure shoe and a forming shoe, or grooved rollers that enclose the tube at the location of the bend. In some bending machines, the tubing wall support is provided by a combination of rollers or shoes and a temporary solid core that is inserted in the tube.

### Material Selection

Ductility—the ability of a material to deform plastically without fracturing—is a major factor that must be considered in selecting a material for bending. Information on ductility is often available from the material supplier, or it can be measured by the percentage of elongation in a tensile test. This data should be examined, because it normally indicates whether or not a problem might develop in bending a particular material. The lower the percentage of elongation, the more difficult the bending. Elongation of the outside of a bend is one of the key factors in determining the minimum radius of bend possible in any material. In the case of nonferrous materials, 1/4 to 1/2-hard materials are best.

### Workpiece Configuration

With respect to workpiece dimensions, the smallest recommended radius for round tubing, measured to the centerline of the tube, is one and one-half times the outside diameter (OD) of the tube. However, in numerous special applications, tubing is bent to a radius that is equal to the diameter. Bending to these minimum radii requires an inside mandrel to produce a good symmetrical bend, and possibly a wiper die to eliminate wrinkling of the inner wall. A minimum centerline radius of at least two to three times the tube OD and a suitable wall factor are required to permit bending without a mandrel, and the thickest acceptable tubing wall should be used. The wall factor, as defined in Fig. 10-29, *b*, equals the tube OD divided by wall thickness. The "D" of bend (see Fig. 10-29, *b*) equals the centerline bending radius divided by the tube OD.

Bending square or rectangular tubing without distortion almost always requires a mandrel. Crush or collapse bends, such as those made on vertical compression benders, can be made by deforming the tube during the bending operation.

Bends in solid, rectangular shapes can be made with radii much smaller than in tubing if bending is done in the "easy plane"—the direction of the narrower dimension. For such parts, the bend is normally measured from the inner surface rather than from the centerline. Ductility of the material determines the smallest bend radius that can be produced without fracturing. Material springback must also be taken into consideration, since it may be impossible to form closed eyes or complete circles with certain materials.

When channels, angles, and rectangular stock are being bent in the "hard plane"—the direction of the thicker dimension—the radius is normally measured to the inside of the workpiece. In such cases, the radius should be at least three times the workpiece width.

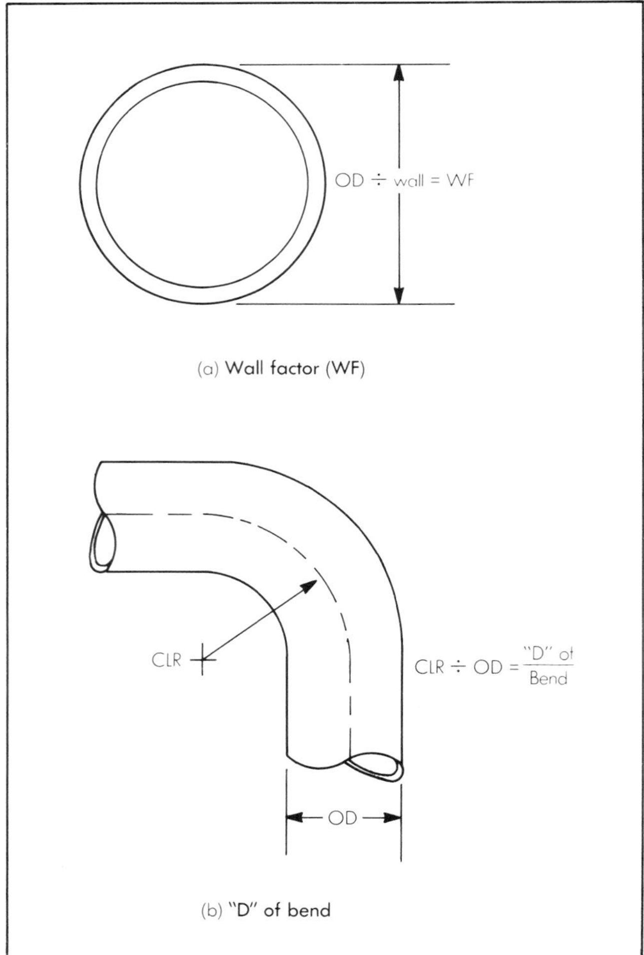


**Fig. 10-29 Wall factor and "D" of bend are critical factors in determining bend radius. (*Tools for Bending, Inc.*)**

## TUBE AND BAR BENDING

Regardless of the method used, most tube-bending processes involve the same principle and use similar fundamental tools, although hand-operated, manual benders and the powered bending machines on the market vary widely in appearance, construction, output capability, and field of application.

### Basic Principles of Tube Bending

In bending, the material is stressed beyond its yield strength, but below its ultimate strength. This is done by holding (clamping) the part with tooling while applying a force sufficient to surpass the yield strength of the material. If the applied force is below the proportional elastic limit of the material, the material returns to its original shape when the force is relaxed.

When the applied force exceeds the yield strength, however, stretching of the material under tension is suddenly increased along the outside radius of the workpiece and the material is compressed along the inside radius. Under these conditions, the material enters the plastic range and the part is permanently formed to the desired shape. The boundary line between tensile and compressive stresses is known as the neutral axis (see Fig. 10-30).

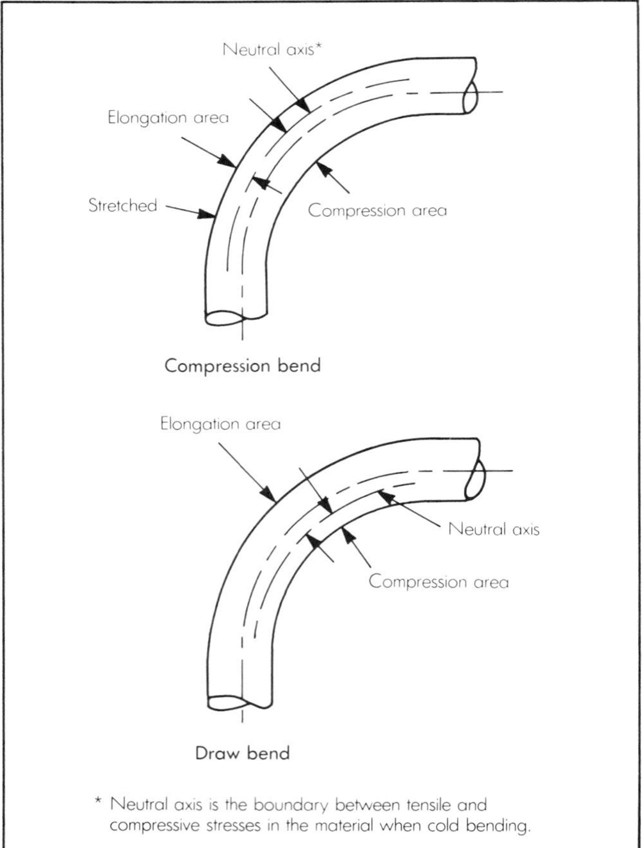


**Fig. 10-30 Characteristic neutral-axis shift for tube compression and draw bending.**

The tendency of a part to return to its original shape, even after the material is formed in its plastic range, is known as springback. This can be overcome by slight overbending, accompanied, in some instances, by bending to a smaller radius.

## Metal Flow

When a uniform workpiece such as a tube or bar is bent, the outer side of the workpiece is in tension and the inner side is in compression. The stresses are parallel and symmetrical about a neutral axis. When these stresses exceed the yield strength of the material, a permanent change in shape, or set, occurs. The basic effects of bending are:

- Lengthening of the outside of the bend and shortening of the inside of the bend.
- Thinning of the outside of the bend and thickening of the inside of the bend in tubes and hollow sections.
- Displacement of the neutral axis in both solid and hollow sections.

**Neutral axis.** Shortening of the inside and lengthening of the outside of a bend is illustrated in Fig. 10-31. The length of the neutral axis remains unchanged. Thinning and thickening effects on tubing are illustrated in Fig. 10-32; thinning results from tensile or stretching load on material outside the neutral axis, and thickening results from compressive load on material inside the neutral axis. If the material is bent without being heated, the thinning effect does not necessarily weaken the structure. Cold work hardening makes the metal on the outside of the bend stronger than the original material, with no loss of overall structural strength. There are practical limits to thinning, of course; and if thin material is bent excessively, thinning reduces it to the breaking point.

**Neutral-axis movement.** Displacement of the neutral axis occurs in all bends. Examination of a cross section of a bent tube proves this; the inner wall is thicker, and the outer wall thinner.

The neutral axis changes constantly during deformation and can be influenced by type of machine, tooling, surface condition, etc. Generally, however, the neutral axis moves toward the inside of the bend in both solid and hollow sections.

Movement of the neutral axis varies from 5% of width or diameter in heavy sections bent to large radii to about 25% for very thin sections bent to small radii.

**Elongation effect.** During bending, the pipe or tube is both elongated and compressed. Elongation occurs along the outside of the bend; compression along the inside. The actual elongation at the center of the bend may be up to 30% more than the average theoretical elongation. The theoretical line between the elongated and compressed portions, which is neither stretched nor compressed, is the neutral axis.

The principle of tension stress in the outside surface of the bend and compression of the inside surface is similar in all bending. However, the position of the neutral axis, as illustrated in Fig. 10-33, depends on the process used.

*Plastic flow.* Bending physically deforms the metal; and with the metal flow occurring in the plastic range, the shape is permanently changed. During bending, the outer wall of a tube or hollow section is thinned and the inner wall is thickened, as shown previously in Fig. 10-33.

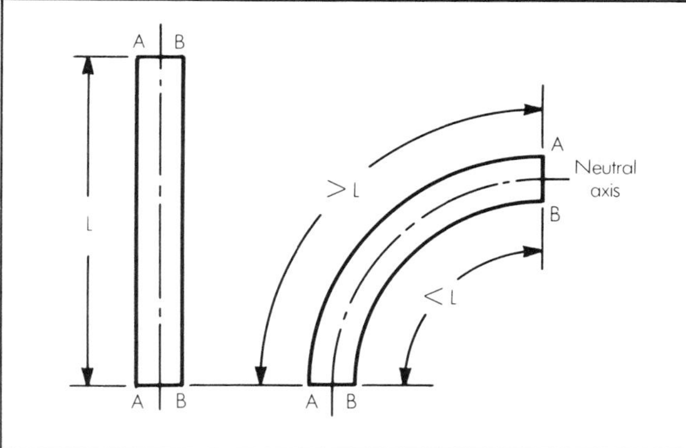


**Fig. 10-31 Comparison of key length elements of a bar or tube before and after bending.**

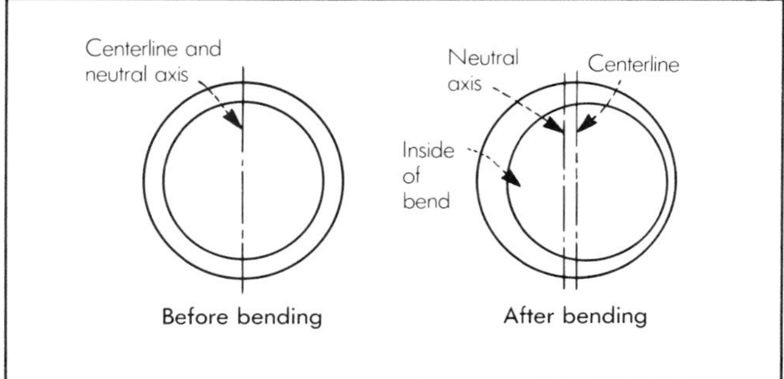


**Fig. 10-32 Thickening of material at inside of bent tube.**

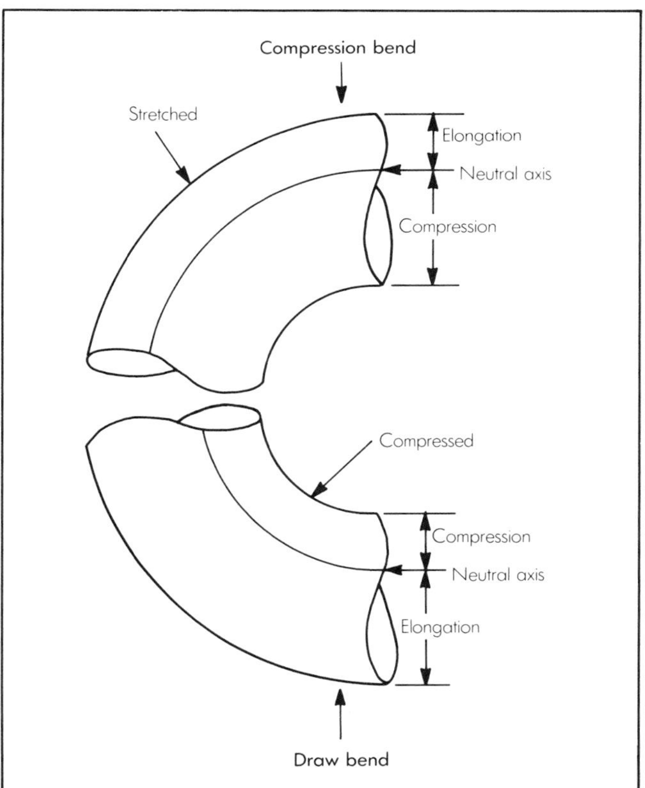


**Fig. 10-33 The neutral axis typically moves to the outer third of the cross section during compression bending, and to the inner third during draw bending.**

# TUBE AND BAR BENDING

The plastic flow of metal produces complex and interrelated changes in the metal structure. The process is further complicated because different materials have different yield points and ultimate strengths.

*Percentage elongation.* The elongation of the outside of a bend is the governing factor in determining the minimum radius of the bend possible in any material and has a direct relation to the ductility of the material as expressed by the percentage of elongation. In the bend shown in Fig. 10-31, the length before bending is the same as the length along the neutral axis, which (after bending) is longer than *BB* and shorter than *AA*. In bending, the material has been stretched on the outside to *AA* and compressed on the inside to *BB*. Assuming that a 1″ (25 mm) tube is bent to a radius of 2″ (51 mm), the initial length of the tube is 3″ (76 mm). The bent outside length, *AA*, is then almost 4″ (101 mm), so the stretch is 1″ (25 mm) and the percentage of elongation is approximately 33%.

## Design Guidelines

When bent tubing is to be utilized in a product, proper attention to manufacturing considerations is of significant importance at the inception of and throughout all stages of design and development. Insufficient attention to such considerations can lead to undue manufacturing difficulties and increased cost. The factors of primary importance in designing a bend are the ductility of the material, the radius of the bend, and the wall factor.

**General discussion.** As previously discussed, for successful bending, material selection is of crucial importance. Ductility must be sufficient to produce the smallest required radius; and at the same time, the material must have sufficient strength to provide the required rigidity. For maximum efficiency and economy, parts should have the largest acceptable radii. A large radius permits the designer to select from a much wider variety of materials, thus permitting higher strength, better appearance, and possibly, lower cost.

Part production is greatly simplified and less costly if most of the bends of multibend parts have the same radius. This permits making a series of progressive bends without taking the parts off the machine—thus eliminating additional setups, material handling, tooling, and part loading and unloading.

Whenever possible, a straight length between bends sufficient to permit reliable clamping should be provided on the workpiece. A straight length equal to three and one-half times the OD can reduce tooling costs by eliminating compounded clamp areas in the bending form and clamp blocks. It can also eliminate bending problems and tooling changeover required with compound tooling. Compound bends are more difficult to perform because material must flow from areas that have been work hardened by previous bending.

Product designers and manufacturing engineers should keep in mind that bends cannot be made close to the end of a tube without distorting the edge of the material. A straight length equal to one to two times the part OD should be provided between the end and the last bend to avoid distortion. If a bend is required closer to the end, a longer blank must be used during bending and must be trimmed afterwards.

**Bend radius.** The minimum radius of a bend (that is, the smallest radius possible without undue distortion) relates to a number of the factors discussed previously. Analysis of metal flow for a tube during bending shows that either excessive thinning of the outside of the bend or improper flow of the metal can cause the tube to collapse or rupture. In effect, this means the absence of sufficient metal at the region of greatest stretch to sustain the applied stress.

*General rules.* Whether bending round, square, or rectangular tubing, or angles, channels, or profiled sections, the following "rules of thumb" may be useful:

- Round tubing—the bending radius measured to the centerline of the bend should not be less than two and one-half times the outside diameter of the tubing. The wall factor (see Fig. 10-29) should be 15 or less to avoid the need for costly bending tools. This broad guideline should not be applied to heavy piping, boiler tube, and other large-diameter work—where bends to tight radii can be performed by using "pinched" tooling, without a mandrel or a wiper die.
- Square and rectangular tubing—the bending radius should not be less than approximately four times the inner wall thickness of the material.
- Minimum bend radius—this is determined by the shape, dimensions, thickness, strength, and ductility of the metal to be formed. In particularly favorable circumstances, and using special bending tools, a radius equal to the diameter of the material can be achieved.

*Minimum radius.* For making estimates, an approximation of the minimum centerline radius on which a tube can be bent can be determined by using the following formula. When the elongation factor is known, the formula is a practical means for making this determination even though friction between tools and tubing is not taken into consideration.

$$R = 50\frac{D}{E} \qquad (7)$$

where:

$R$ = minimum centerline radius of bend, in.
$D$ = tube OD, in.
$E$ = percentage of elongation in 2″ (Based on standard tensile test data, and not the tube's outer wall during bending.)

Example:

In calculating the minimum centerline radius of bend for a 2″ OD, Type 304 stainless steel tube with 50% elongation:

$$R = \frac{50 \times 2}{50} = 2$$

therefore, the minimum centerline radius of bend, $R$, on which 2″ OD, Type 304 stainless steel tube can be bent is 2″, or one $D$.

Note: This is an empirical formula; hence, it should not be used for metric computations.

*Tube length.* In determining the required length of a tube or pipe before bending, the lengths of the straight sections are added to the lengths of the curved sections. The following procedures may be used to approximate the lengths of the curved sections:

- To find the length of a 90° (right-angle) bend, multiply the bend radius by 1.57. (Radius is measured to center of tube.)
- To find the length of a 180° bend (U-bend), multiply the

bend radius by 3.14. (Radius is measured to center of tube.)

- To find the bent lengths of sections with curvature other than 90° or 180°, multiply the bend radius by the included angle (degrees) and then multiply the product by the constant 0.0175. (Radius is measured to center of tube.)

## BENDING METHODS

Several different methods are commonly used for bending tube, pipe, and extruded metal shapes. Key factors in making a bending operation economically productive are the method, tooling, and bending technique used. The operator is, of course, a factor, but the equipment should minimize the degree of skill or artisanship required. The various methods of bending embodied in manual benders, powered bending machines, and automatic bending machines can be divided basically into draw, compression, roll, and stretch bending.

### Draw Bending

The method generally considered to be the most versatile and accurate for bending tubing is draw bending, illustrated schematically in Fig. 10-34. With the workpiece clamped against the bending die and locked in position, the die and clamp are rotated, moving the workpiece through a pressure tool. The pressure tool can be a roller, sliding shoe, or static shoe. The mandrel remains stationary, and the tube is drawn over the mandrel during the bending operation; hence, the term *draw bending* is used.

Draw bending is the most suitable method for tight radius bending or any bending that requires a mandrel or mandrel-and-wiper-die combination. Main applications for this method are the bending of pipe, thin-wall tubing, and extrusions. The basic limitation of draw bending is that the workpiece must have a straight length to permit it to be clamped to the bending form. The straight length keeps the material from slipping as it is drawn against the force applied by the pressure tool.

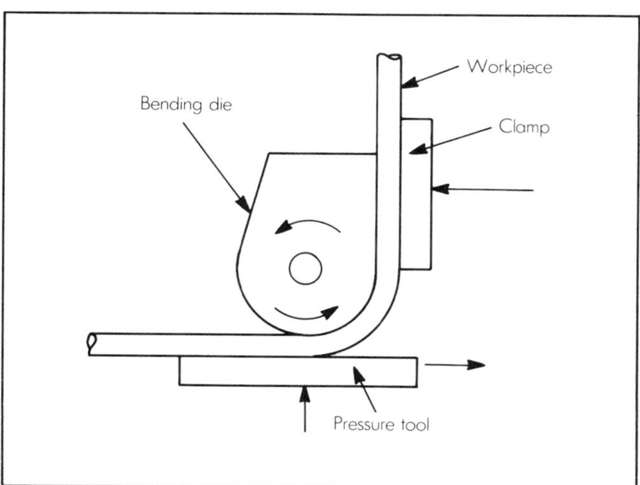


**Fig. 10-34 In draw bending, the bending form and clamp rotate to pull the workpiece and the pressure die. This method is accurate and versatile.**

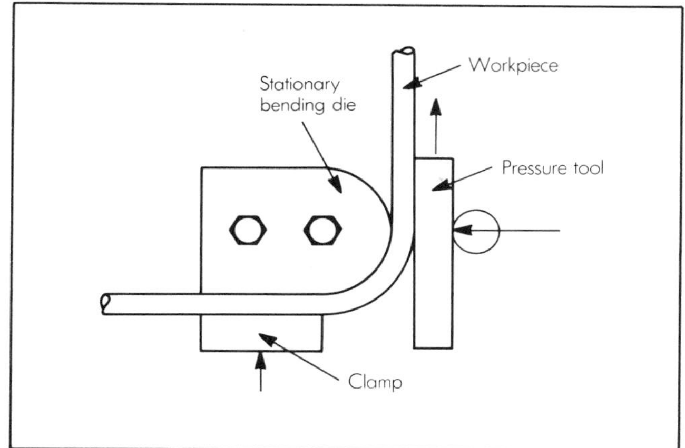


**Fig. 10-35 In compression bending, the bending form is stationary. This technique works well when little clamping distance is available between bends on the workpiece.**

### Compression Bending

The compression-bending method is used primarily to bend pipe, tube, rod, bar, and various other extruded shapes. As shown in Fig. 10-35, the workpiece is clamped to a stationary bending form and wrapped around it. A variety of pressure tools can be used—a static wiper shoe, a follower block, or a roller. This method works well for applications in which little clamping distance is available between bends.

Compression bending requires much less clamping area than draw bending, because the pressure tool forces the material to flow and become wrapped around the bending form. This method is capable of producing bends in various planes with practically no straight sections between the bends. Since the flow of metal in compression bending is not controlled as well as it is in draw bending, however, some distortion should be expected when bending tubing. Mandrels cannot be used in compression bending, because they would have to move with the workpieces as they are wrapped around the bending form.

The main theoretical difference between draw and compression bending lies in the position of the neutral axis. In draw bending, the neutral axis lies within the inner third of the cross section, which means that approximately two-thirds of the tube's cross section is in tension; whereas, in compression bending, the neutral axis lies in the outer third. This accounts for the flattening effect in draw bending being more severe than in compression bending. As a result, machines for draw bending usually require the use of an internal mandrel.

### Press Bending

An extension of compression bending, known as press, or ram, bending (see Fig. 10-36), is a means of obtaining two simultaneous compression bends. Each of the two bends is equal to one-half of the total desired included angle. In press bending, the bending form is mounted on the ram of a press and two wiping or pressure shoes pivot to wipe the material around the bending form. This method is used primarily for high-volume production bending of tube, bar, and pipe, typically when wall thickness and bending radius are relatively large.

### Roll Bending

This method, shown schematically in Fig. 10-37, is similar to the basic process employed for rolling sheet metal and plates. It is possible to adjust the rolls to give a wide range for the radius selection. For bending tubing, the roll method is limited to heavy-wall material, because it produces a high degree of wall thinning. This method can be practical in bending solid shapes into circular parts. It is also used to produce full circles, to produce helical coils, and to bend pipe, heavy tube, and solid bars.

### Stretch Bending

Stretch bending (see Fig. 10-38) is probably the most sophisticated bending method, and requires expensive tooling and machines. Furthermore, stretch bending requires lengths of material beyond the desired shape to permit gripping and pulling. The material is stretched longitudinally, past its elastic limit, by pulling both ends and then wrapping around the bending form. This method is used primarily for bending irregular shapes; it is generally not used for high production.

Draw bending, compression bending, press bending, and roll bending all stretch and compress the metal in various areas of the bend. Stretch bending, on the other hand, elongates the metal in all sections. Wall thickness, in general, is reduced; but in the stretching process greater uniformity is obtained. Thickness reduction in stretch bending amounts to approximately 40% of the total elongation.

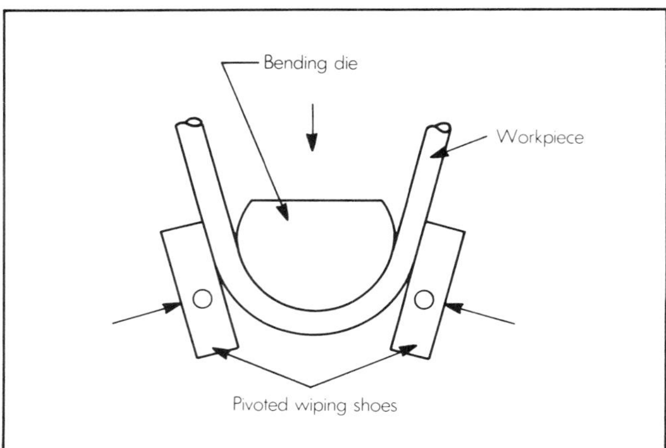


**Fig. 10-36 Press (ram) bending is performed with a bending form mounted on a press ram. This is a high-speed method for producing two simultaneous compression bends.**

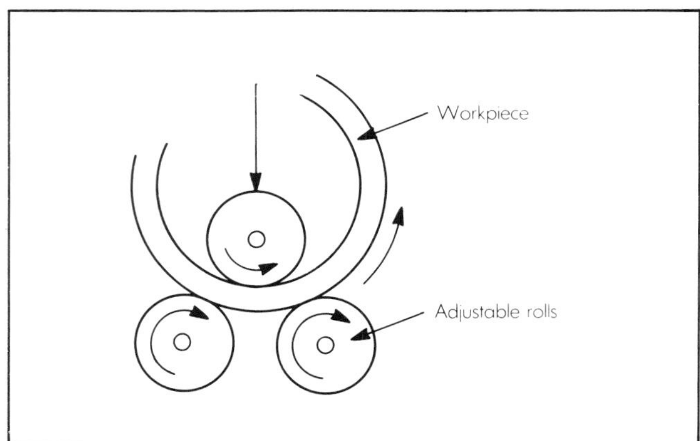


**Fig. 10-37 Roll bending is useful for forming solid bars, rods, special shapes, and heavy tubing into circular parts.**

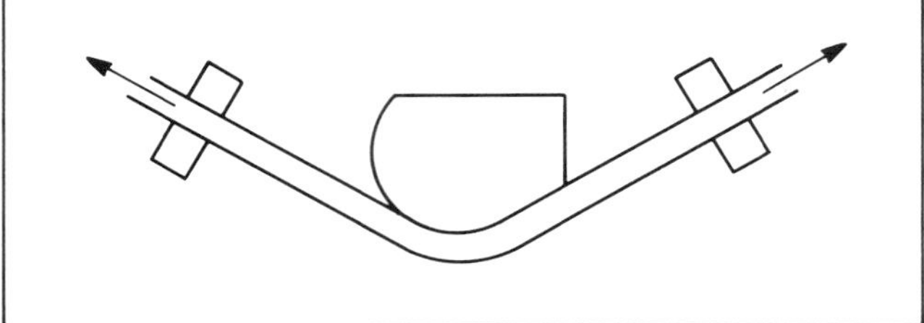

**Fig. 10-38 Stretch bending is a sophisticated method that requires costly tooling and machines, as well as extra material for gripping and pulling.**

## BENDING EQUIPMENT

The different types of bends can be made on a variety of commercially available bending machines—small and large capacity, manually operated and power driven, and general and special purpose. For specialized operations, such as bending thin-wall tubing at high production rates, an automatic draw bender would be best. If the bending operation requires high production rates, but close tolerances are not necessary and the "D" of bend and wall factor permit; some type of press bender should probably be used. However, if the requirements are for bending a wide variety of materials and shapes, then a universal, general-purpose bender—most likely a draw type—should be used.

### Bender Selection

Regardless of the requirements, bender selection should include a careful study of specifications, capacities, and operational features of machines available. In studying specifications, it should be kept in mind that most published data is generally based on capabilities for bending mild steel. To determine whether a part made from a different material can be bent on a given machine, the data for mild-steel capacity must be modified.

### Material Conversion Factor

The largest cross sections of the parts to be bent should be converted into section moduli ratings for mild steel; then, these ratings can be compared with the section modulus capacity of the bender. Since such comparisons can be made only for the same material, additional computations must be made for materials other than mild steel. This entails comparing the workpiece section modulus times the yield strength of the material with the corresponding product of the section modulus and the yield strength of mild steel (or other material for which the bender is rated).

The section modulus for tubing can be calculated from the following formula:

$$Z = 0.098\frac{D^4 - d^4}{D} \quad (8)$$

For rod, the section modulus can be calculated as follows:

$$Z = 0.098D^3 \quad (9)$$

where:

$Z$ = section modulus, in.$^3$
$D$ = outside diameter, in.
$d$ = inside diameter, in.

Note: Metric units should not be used in these empirical equations.

# BENDING EQUIPMENT

## Types of Production Machines

Three basic types of machines are used in production tube bending: (1) ram benders, including specialized, hydraulic ram benders as well as mechanical power presses; (2) roll benders; and (3) rotary benders, including rotary-compression, rotary-draw, and stretch-forming machines. The parameters that govern equipment choice are:

- Shape and size of the part.
- "D" of bend and wall factor.
- Tolerances to be held.
- Quantity of parts required.
- Production rate.

**Ram benders.** Most types of ram benders are hydraulically operated. They are commonly used for bending tubular parts, but can bend solid sections as well. They embody a moving ram that forces the workpiece between two relatively fixed dies. These dies may be completely fixed, or they may be allowed to pivot in such a way that they accommodate the part moving through the die, as in the high-volume production vertical ram bender shown in Fig. 10-39. In this way, it is possible to make a 180° bend in a single pass. With fixed-radius tooling, the angle of bend can be controlled by the final ram position. Appropriate set fixtures on the machine allow bending relative to stock ends or previous bends. Thus, by using the machine's "positive stops," a multiple-bend part can be produced with minimum tool cost.

**Power presses.** Press bending is probably the most common type of bending because of the wide variety of techniques and tooling that can be used. It is normally desirable to use two or four-post die sets to maintain better accuracy. Tolerances from ±0.02 to ±0.06" (0.5 to 1.5 mm) can be held depending upon tools, material, and equipment. Reasonable accuracy can be maintained, but care should be taken to allow for springback and pulling or stretching.

Ram-mounted cams may be employed to actuate drivers, turn rotating drivers, and even bend the part directly. Accuracy is primarily a function of the type of tooling.

There is a wide variation in tool cost, from low for hand-loaded plate dies to high for automated multiplane benders. Presses are the most flexible machines for additional operations such as coining, trimming, piercing, or upsetting. Production-quantity requirements vary also, with complex parts requiring highest volumes. Operating speeds with automation run from 30 spm for tube diameters larger than 3/4" (19 mm), to 250 spm for small-diameter tubing.

**Roll benders.** Roll benders (see Fig. 10-40) consist of three rolls set in a pyramid arrangement in either a horizontal or vertical plane. The piece to be rolled is laid across the two bottom rolls, which are power driven, and the top roll is brought into contact with the piece to be bent by means of a leadscrew or hydraulic-cylinder arrangement.

Roll benders are particularly adapted to the production of rings and coils. Spirals and multiturn coils are easily produced by the addition of deflectors to offset the emerging end of the part. One disadvantage of roll benders is that a short, straight section at each end of the stock is left unbent. If this is objectionable, it may either be cut off or be bent in a press as a separate operation. The tools are simple, consisting of rolls suitably grooved to match the stock. These are often made adjustable by spacers, especially for the bending of structural shapes and bars. Work produced on these machines is quite accurate, and very little flattening of tubes takes place.

**Rotary bending.** Rotary-bending machines wrap the workpiece around a tool called the bend die or form block. The basic rotary processes are rotary-compression bending and rotary-draw bending. Stretch forming is a form of rotary-draw bending with an additional preload on the part; it is especially useful for bending special-shaped workpieces, such as angles, through their deepest leg.

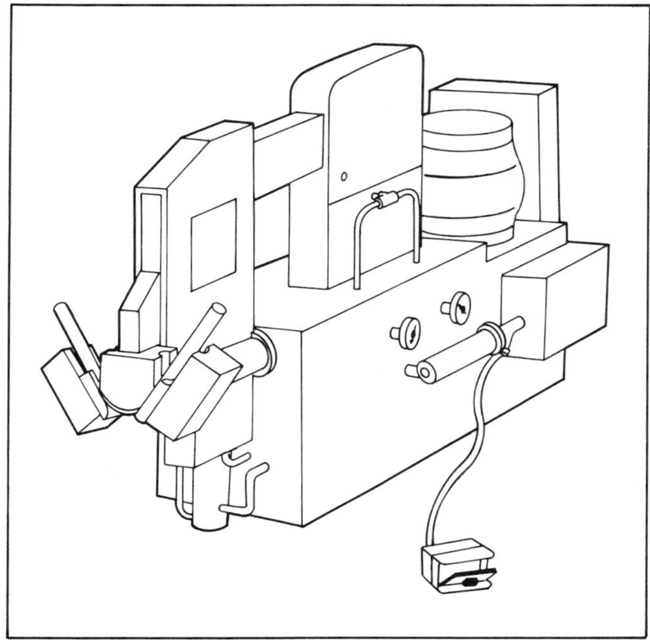

**Fig. 10-39 General view of a hydraulic-ram vertical bending machine. (*Teledyne Pines*)**

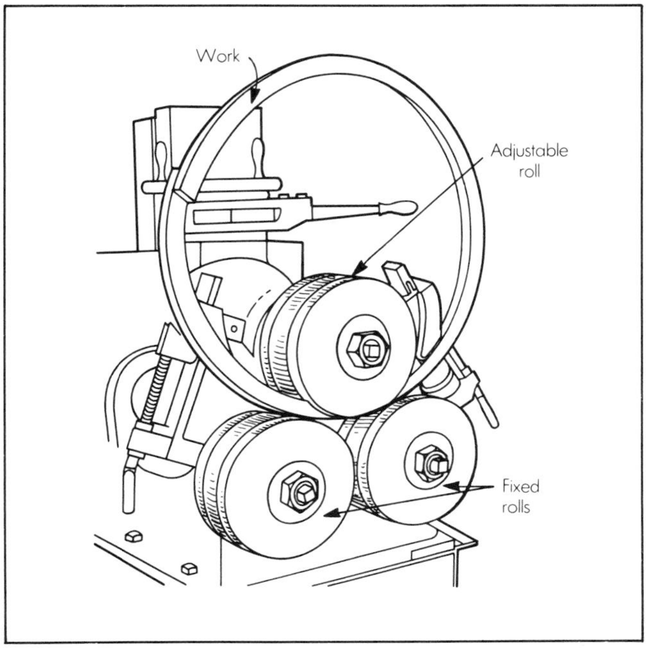


**Fig. 10-40 Typical elements and application of a three-roll bending machine. (*Buffalo Forge Co.*)**

*Rotary-compression machines.* The rotary-compression machine (see Fig. 10-41, *a*) comprises a fixed radius die; a fixed stop block, against which the piece to be bent is placed; and a movable roller (fastened to the bull gear) that wipes the piece to be bent into the radius die. No clamps are required when bending pipe or tube to normal radii, since the neutral axis is on the outer section of the piece being bent; about two-thirds of the piece are in compression; and the piece tends to expand along the center of gravity, thereby locking it into the radius die. The friction resulting from this locking action is sufficient to prevent the piece from creeping.

When bar stock is being bent against a flat radius block, clamping is often necessary. The action of the roller on the stock is sometimes through a wiper block whose contour fits the piece being bent on one side and has a flat surface to contact the roller on the other side. The wiper block converts the single fixed load of the roller into a uniformly distributed load on the stock.

This type of bender is often built for manual actuation (see Fig. 10-42) for light manufacturing operations. Tolerances are normally ±0.03" (0.8 mm), and production rates are low; however, tool costs are low, and design freedom is high. Such machines are often used for prototype work.

*Rotary-draw machines.* On this type of machine the bending die is keyed to a shaft with provision for clamping the workpiece to the form block with a clamping die. A pressure die restrains the free end of the material and allows the material to move in a straight line. As the shaft rotates, the material is drawn through the pressure die and is wrapped around the bend die (see Fig. 10-41, *b*).

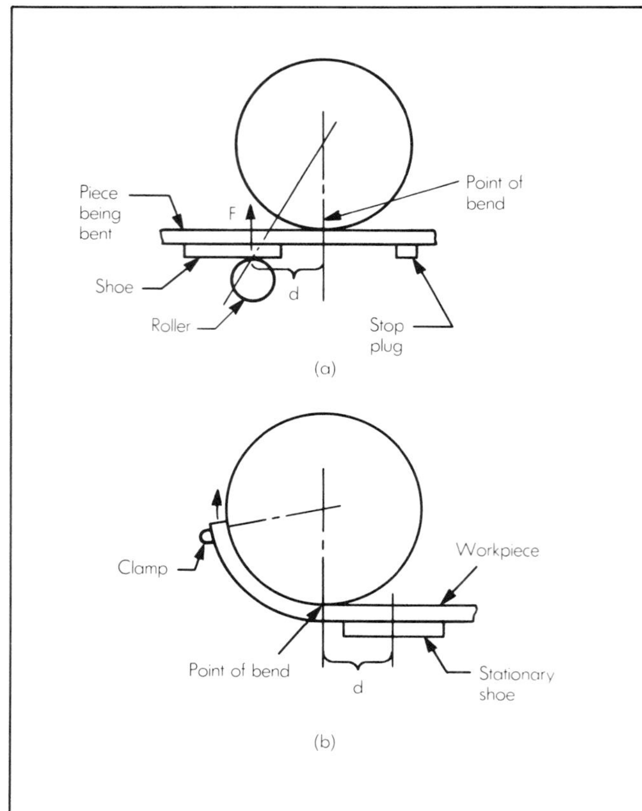


**Fig. 10-41 Rotary bending: (a) compression and (b) draw.**

When hollow sections such as pipe and tube are being bent and flattening is to be kept at a minimum, a mandrel must be included in the tooling. A wiper die (shoe) is often placed behind the pressure die to prevent wrinkling and buckling of the workpiece.

Some machines are equipped with a collet chuck mounted on a graduated plate and are used when multiple bends of the same radius are required in tubing. The device fits over the mandrel and grips the tube during the bending operation. The distance between bends, the rotations, and the degree of each bend are controlled and indexed automatically by adjustable cam stops along a calibrated rail, rotation stop bands, and self-indexing turret stops. Figure 10-43 shows a typical rotary-draw bender.

Table 10-5 provides recommended values for the minimum bend radius on materials of various ductilities, from 10-70% elongation, bent by the draw-bending method. Table 10-6 indicates the rapid increase in tensile stress on a rod as the bend radius is decreased. Extreme care must be taken when the bend radius is less than the stock width in the plane of the bend. Elongation of 50% is minimum. As in all bending, the load should be gradually applied and notches caused by sharp tools and grippers should be avoided in the bend area.

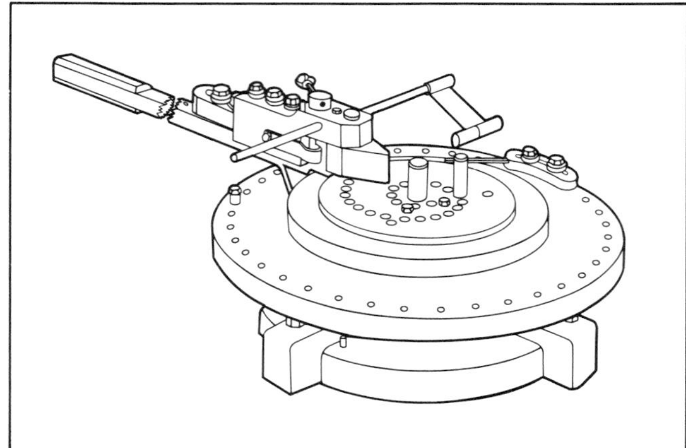

**Fig. 10-42 A manually operated, rotary-compression tube bender.** (*Di-Acro Div., Houdaille Industries, Inc.*)

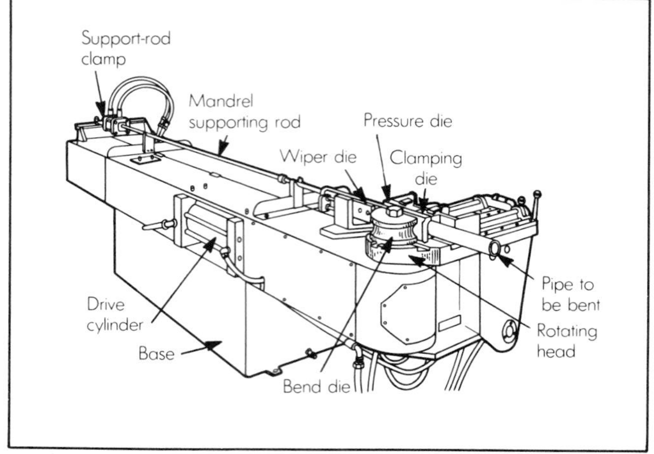


**Fig. 10-43 A rotary-draw bending machine.**

Very sharp bends are made in multiple passes. In this technique, conventional bending is performed first, then followed by another bending operation in which a compressive preload moves the neutral axis to the outside of the bend. The rebending causes considerable thickening of the stock on the inside, but eliminates tensile breaks on the outside. Too much rebending in one pass may result in cold shuts or folds and subsequent part failure.

**TABLE 10-5**
**Minimum Radius of Bend in Relation to Percentage Elongation**

| Elongation of material, % | Minimum Radius, Draw-Bending 50-100 mm: Up to 2″ (50 mm) wide (or diam) | 2-4″ (50-100 mm) wide (or diam) | Over 4″ (100mm) wide (or diam) |
|---|---|---|---|
| 10 | 5 x width | 6 x width | 6 x width |
| 20 | 2 1/2 x width | 3 x width | 4 x width |
| 25 | 2 x width | 2 1/2 x width | 3 x width |
| 30 | 1 3/4 x width | 2 1/4 x width | 3 x width |
| 40 | 1 1/3 x width | 2 x width | 3 x width |
| 50 | 1 x width | 1 1/2 x width | 2 1/2 x width |
| 60 | 1 x width | 1 1/2 x width | 2 1/2 x width |
| 70 | 1 x width | 1 1/2 x width | 2 1/2 x width |

(*Wallace Supplies Manufacturing Co.*)

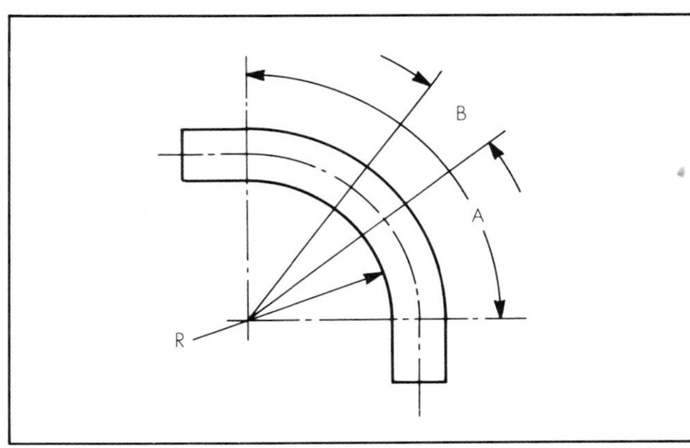


**TABLE 10-6**
**Rod Tensile Stress Increases as Bend Radius Decreases**

| | | | |
|---|---|---|---|
| R, radius of bend, in. (mm) | 0.50 (12.7) | 1.0 (25.4) | 2.0 (50.8) |
| A, elongation, avg. at outside of bend, % | 66 | 43 | 25 |
| B, elongation, max. at midpoint of bend, % | 86 | 55 | 32.5 |

## Tolerances

Complexity in a part is affected more by the number of planes of bending than by the number of bends. The tolerances for parts produced by bending vary considerably and depend on many variables, some of which are:

- Type and condition of machine.
- Type and condition of tooling.
- Material and hardness or previous cold working.
- Shape and tolerances of the part entering the machine.

Typical tolerance on tube length from most cutoff machines is ±0.015″ (0.38 mm) on diameters of stock up to 7/16″ (11 mm), and ±0.032″ (0.81 mm) on larger diameters. Closer tolerances can be held, but equipment must be in good condition or special tooling must be used.

Tolerances for bending usually increase with the stock width or diameter, and it is more difficult to obtain a uniform section throughout. Table 10-7 gives three classifications of tolerances for the production bending of tubular sections.

## Bending Tools

As shown in Fig. 10-44, five basic tools are associated with rotary-draw bending: (1) radius block or bend die, (2) clamp die, (3) pressure die, (4) mandrel, and (5) wiper die. The first three are always required; the last two are support tools employed in tube and pipe bending when the tube lacks sufficient strength for self-support.

**Bend die.** The bend die is the primary tool around which the workpiece is formed to produce a specific bend radius. It must have a groove equal in depth to at least half the workpiece diameter, and radial degrees equal to the bend degrees desired plus overbend for springback compensation. Minimum groove

**TABLE 10-7**
**Tolerances on Terminal Locations and Reference Points on Bent Parts**

| | Tolerance, (plus or minus) | | | | |
|---|---|---|---|---|---|
| | Close | | Average | | Widest |
| OD, in. (mm) | Pipe, in. (mm) | Tube, in. (mm) | Pipe, in. mm) | Tube, in. mm) | in. (mm) |
| 1/8 to 1/2 (3 to 13) | 1/64 (0.4) | 0.001 (0.03) | 1/16 (1.6) | 1/32 (0.8) | 1/16 (1.6) |
| 3/4 to 1 1/4 (19 to 32) | 1/32 (0.8) | 0.015 (0.38) | 1/16 (1.6) | 1/32 (0.8) | 3/32 (2.4) |
| 1 1/2 to 2 (38 to 51) | 1/16 (1.6) | 0.020 (0.51) | 3/32 (2.4) | 1/16 (1.6) | 1/8 (3.2) |
| 2 1/4 to 3 (57 to 76) | 1/16 (1.6) | 0.030 (0.76) | 1/8 (3.2) | 1/16 (1.6) | 3/16 (4.8) |
| 3 1/4 to 4 (83 to 102) | 3/32 (2.4) | 0.065 (1.65) | 1/8 (3.2) | 1/8 (3.2) | 1/4 (6.4) |
| 4 1/4 to 7 (108 to 178) | --- | --- | 3/16 (4.8) | 1/8 (3.2) | 3/8 (9.5) |
| 8 to 12 (203 to 305) | --- | --- | 1/4 (6.4) | 3/16 (4.8) | 1/2 (12.7) |

# CHAPTER 10

## BENDING EQUIPMENT

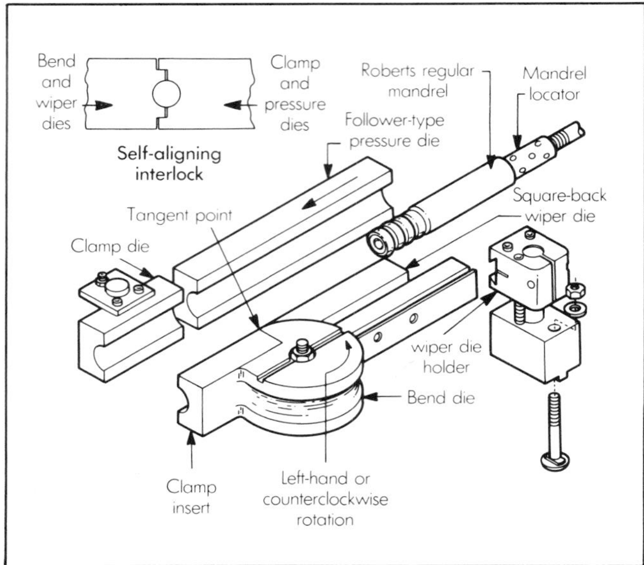


**Fig. 10-44 Basic tooling elements for rotary-draw tube bending.** (*Tools for Bending, Inc.*)

dimensions should be nominal in the outer diameter. Plus-or-minus manufacturing variations should not produce less than nominal grooves, as tube pinching results. It is good practice to establish tube groove dimensions several thousandths of an inch over nominal, allowing a plus-or-minus manufacturing tolerance that does not go below nominal when manufactured to the minus dimension. Concentricity of the groove to the locating ring or counterbore should not exceed $\pm 0.002''$ (0.05 mm). Tolerances that exceed these standards result in a cam action during die rotation that affects bend quality.

Die material must be harder than the workpiece material to avoid deformation of the groove when wrinkles occur. Bend die material must also be at least 10 points ($R_C$) harder than wiper-die material to avoid tip galling by the wiper die. Once a die is galled in the groove, tube marking results. Since tool life is a function of hardness, most steel wiper dies are approximately $R_C30$; so the form block requires hardness of $R_C40$ or greater to maintain the 10-point spread.

Standard heat treatment of alloy tool steels in a bend die configuration induces unacceptable warpage and loss of dimensional tolerance. A low-temperature, case-hardening method such as nitriding is a preferable process, but it requires a nitrogen-content alloy. This process elevates hardness into the low $R_C50$ range, with minimal loss of dimensional tolerance.

**Clamp die.** The clamp die is the matching half to the bend die grip-length section. Together they must form a true circle when closed. Maximum gripping occurs before ovality can occur. If a closed clamp does create an oval shape, gripping action is reduced and tubing is distorted; in addition, the risk of mandrel breakage is high when a ball mandrel is used.

Clamp length is a function of workpiece resistance to bending. The smaller the bend radius, the more the workpiece material is required to stretch and compress. This induces higher bend resistance and requires longer clamp lengths. Bends on radii equal to, or greater than, three times the tube diameter require a clamp length equal to three times the tube outer diameter. Bends with radii two times the tube outer diameter or less require clamp lengths of four times the tube outer diameter.

In many cases, the straight length between bends conflicts with these standards. In such cases cleats, clamp plugs, compound clamps, and pressure-die boosting can be employed to offset tool compromises for short grip lengths.

The groove of the clamp die is often conditioned by grit blasting, metallic or carbide sprays, cleats, and/or serrations to increase gripping friction. The particular finish depends on the bend quality desired, since excessively rough conditioning marks the tube. Clamp dies should be heat treated to protect the abraded finish and increase wear life. Again, a minimum-distortion heat treatment is desirable.

**Pressure die.** The pressure die functions to contain the tube in the bend die groove during the bend cycle. It has two critical dimensions. The first dimension is the tube groove size, which must match the bend die groove, since it contains the outside of the tube in the bend. If it does not match the actual dimension of the bend-die groove, ovality may occur. Under extreme compressive forces during mandrel bending, wrinkles will be induced if the tube is not properly contained.

In some applications, a different tooling technique is used to prevent ovality. The pressure die is contoured to a slightly oval shape with a deeper root diameter than would be normal for a given tube diameter. This prevents ovality by forcing the outside of the bend further outward.

The second critical dimension is groove lineal parallelism. This parallelism is related to the rise or recess of the groove as it advances during the bend cycle and causes varying pressures at tangent. If the variance exceeds $0.002''$ per linear foot (0.17 mm/m), tube pinching or excessive clearance occurs, causing tube tear or wrinkles. This condition presents the same problem as a bend die with dimensional irregularity that causes cam action. Tools must neither rise nor recess as a result of improper tolerances. This is the most common cause of wasteful bending with high scrap losses.

Pressure dies do not require hardness standards as high as those of bend dies. They track with the workpiece and have no contact wear with other tools. A standard hardness of $R_C30$ is adequate.

**Mandrel.** A mandrel is employed to prevent tube flattening or tube collapse and wrinkling during tube or pipe bending. It is fixed in position during a bend cycle; the tube is then drawn over the mandrel, thus causing wear contact. Because of wear contact, a variety of nongalling tool materials and finishes must be used. Mandrels are lathe turned, machine finished, and ground finished or plated, depending on bend quality and tool economy.

Tool steels that can be hardened to $R_C70$ with a buffed finish finer than 32 $\mu$ in. (0.8 $\mu$ m) are commonly used mandrel materials. Chromium plating is also a common practice. In those cases in which workpiece materials such as stainless steel and titanium are susceptible to galling by steel or chromium finishes, aluminum-bronze alloys and chrome-impregnated teflon materials are used successfully.

Mandrel design includes three basic types—the plug, the form, and the ball. Mandrels are shown in Fig. 10-45. When a ball mandrel is required, two design features should be considered—pitch and linkage. Pitch refers to the distance between mandrel balls at their contact points with the tube. This dimension should not exceed one-half the tube diameter. On thin-wall tubes, pitch is further reduced and is best determined by an engineering layout of the tube bend, with ball spacing designed for the closest nesting, yet allowing mandrel flexing as required by the bend radius.

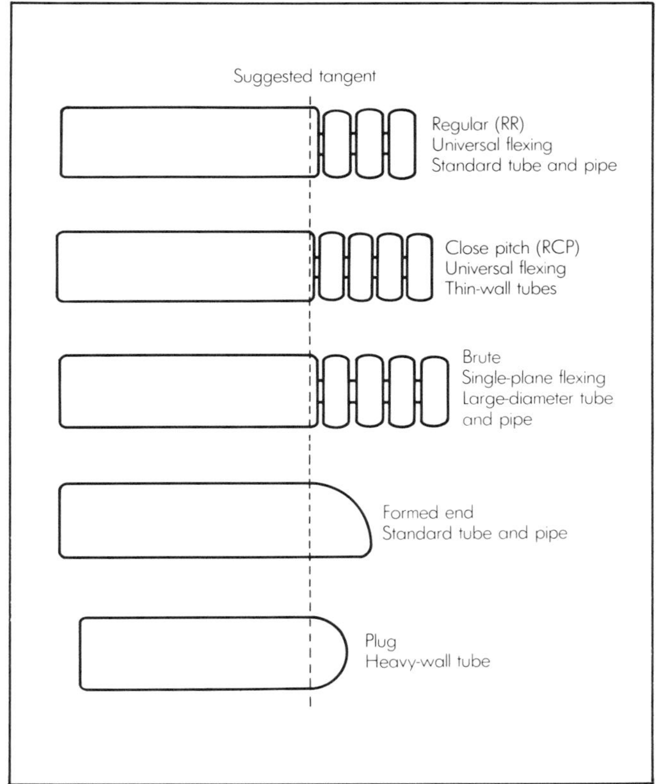


**Fig. 10-45 Types of tube-bending mandrels.** (*Tools for Bending, Inc.*)

There are three types of linkages for mandrel balls—hinge-pin, cable, and ball-and-socket. Hinge-pin mandrels provide flexing in one plane only, which usually involves the risk of breakage from improper setup while restricting wear to one contact area because of flex-axis orientation.

Ball-and-socket linkage is superior in some respects to the hinge-pin or the cable type. It is stronger, flexes universally, and can be manufactured from a variety of materials. Ball strings must be smaller in diameter than the mandrel shank, since they are positioned within the clamping area. A standard drop from the mandrel shank size is 0.005″ (0.13 mm).

Mandrel fit to the inner diameter of the tube can cause problems if the inner diameter varies more than ±0.002″ (0.05 mm). Mandrel clearance is predicated upon a maximum tube-flattening standard, generally not to exceed 3%, and a maximum clearance to avoid tube wrinkling. Normal mandrel sizing is 10% of the tube-wall thickness when tube specifications and consistency permit. A common practice is to develop clearance dimensions from a sample tube or to use a mandrel selection guide such as presented in Table 10-8.[6]

**Wiper die.** The wiper die establishes a straight line behind the tangent on the inside of a bend. This line is required when the tube material's resistance to compression is high.

The wiper die is grooved in the same dimensions as specified for the bend die and pressure die. In addition, a radius tip is required to extend the supporting groove close to the tangent where the compressive force begins. The radius tip of a wiper die must come as close to the tangent as possible. The tip cannot extend all the way, because it is not feasible to feather it to the exact tangent point, but best quality wiper dies are lathe turned for minimum tip thickness. Wiper-die grooves are preferably ground to minimize friction, since the tube sliding contact is a friction surface similar to that of the mandrel contact with the tube.

Wiper-die materials are selected to produce good service life yet avoid a brittle tip. The tip is under extreme pressure because of bending forces, so it must have sufficient ductility to avoid breaking. Wiper dies are seldom softer than $R_C30$. Aluminum bronze or chrome-impregnated teflon is commonly used when the possibility of galling exists because of tube hardness and incompatibility with tool steels. Wiper-die fit or match to the bend die is important. It may be necessary to blue and hand-dress the tip to the bending die to achieve close tangent contact.

## Lubrication[7]

Lubrication is often a significant factor in tube-fabrication operations. In most applications, it is unwise to use improvised, "home-brew" lubricants (especially for draw bending).

Several lubricant suppliers formulate specialized lubricants for tube fabrication. The application and control of such professionally formulated lubricants involve shop training of personnel in mixing drawing-process solubles properly, identifying the lubricant color codes, and ensuring continuing cleanliness of the lubricant.

Manual application techniques may be unsatisfactory, and more positive methods, such as those involving mandrel rod lubricators, spray systems, or recirculating systems, may be needed.

Lubricant cleansing is another factor that is deserving of careful attention. Some of the new, multiphase, soluble lubricants clean readily in low-temperature cleaners. Heavy residual oils clean best in high-temperature, strong, alkaline systems or in vapor degreasers.

**Lubricant selection.** When selecting a lubricant for tube, bar, and rod draw bending, the following important considerations should be taken into account:

- An assessment should be made of the lubricant's capabilities for performing the draw-bending operation and other (subsequent) operations on the tubular or rod workpiece. In most applications, a water-soluble drawing compound; an extendable homogeneous paste (either in neat form or extended); or special high-temperature lubricants can be used for tube bending. The lubricant must fulfill several requirements, including the following:

    1. It must provide a physical barrier to protect the mandrel and the inside of the tube.
    2. The lubricating qualities must be such that the lubricating film remains intact and does not dry out from the heat of deformation.
    3. The lubricant must be capable of overcoming the frictional drag of the tube over the mandrel.
    4. The lubricant should be compatible with the tooling and the workpiece material.

- The lubricant's antiwipe properties should be given careful consideration. The film strength should be sufficient to resist wipeoff when the mandrel is extracted from the bend area. Scoring and pickup can occur when the overall film strength is inadequate. Heavy-duty, water-soluble lubricants provide the necessary lubricity to reduce the heat of deformation during the drawing operation. As a side benefit, the cooler tubing is easier for the operator to handle.

**TABLE 10-8**
**Mandrel Selection Guide**

Ratio of centerline radius / tube outside diameter (columns); Ratio of tube outside diameter / wall thickness (rows)

| Bend Angle | | 1 x D 90° | 1 x D 180° | 1.50 x D 90° | 1.50 x D 180° | 2 x D 90° | 2 x D 180° | 2.50 x D 90° | 2.50 x D 180° | 3 x D 90° | 3 x D 180° | 5 x D 90° | 5 x D 180° |
|---|---|---|---|---|---|---|---|---|---|---|---|---|---|
| 10 | Ferrous | P | P | P | P | P | P | P | P | -0- | P | -0- | -0- |
| | Nonferrous | P | P | P | P | P | P | P | P | P | P | -0- | -0- |
| 20 | Ferrous | RR-1 | RR-1 | RR-1 | RR-1 | RR-1 | RR-1 | P | P | P | P | P | P |
| | Nonferrous | RR-1 | RR-2 | RR-1 | RR-2 | RR-1 | RR-2 | RR-1 | RR-2 | RR-1 | RR-2 | P | P |
| 30 | Ferrous | RR-2 | RR-3 | RR-2 | RR-3 | RR-2 | RR-3 | RR-1 | RR-2 | RR-1 | RR-2 | P | P |
| | Nonferrous | RR-3 | RR-3 | RR-3 | RR-3 | RR-3 | RR-3 | RR-3 | RR-3 | RR-2 | RR-3 | RR-1 | RR-2 |
| 40 | Ferrous | RR-3 | RR-3 | RR-3 | RR-3 | RR-3 | RR-3 | RR-3 | RR-3 | RR-2 | RR-3 | P | RR-1 |
| | Nonferrous | RCP-3 | RCP-4 | RCP-3 | RCP-4 | RR-3 | RR-4 | RR-3 | RR-3 | RR-3 | RR-3 | RR-2 | RR-2 |
| 50 | Ferrous | RCP-3 | RCP-4 | RCP-3 | RCP-4 | RR-3 | RR-4 | RR-3 | RR-4 | RR-3 | RR-3 | RR-1 | RR-2 |
| | Nonferrous | RCP-4 | RCP-5 | RCP-4 | RCP-5 | RCP-4 | RCP-5 | RCP-3 | RCP-4 | RR-3 | RR-4 | RR-2 | RR-3 |
| 60 | Ferrous | RCP-4 | RCP-5 | RCP-4 | RCP-5 | RCP-3 | RCP-4 | RR-3 | RR-4 | RR-3 | RR-4 | RR-2 | RR-3 |
| | Nonferrous | RCP-4 | RCP-5 | RCP-4 | RCP-5 | RCP-4 | RCP-5 | RCP-4 | RCP-5 | RCP-3 | RCP-4 | RR-3 | RR-3 |
| 70 | Ferrous | RCP-4 | RCP-5 | RCP-4 | RCP-5 | RCP-3 | RCP-4 | RCP-3 | RCP-4 | RR-3 | RR-4 | RR-3 | RR-3 |
| | Nonferrous | J-4 | J-5 | J-4 | J-5 | RCP-4 | RCP-5 | RCP-4 | RCP-5 | RCP-4 | RCP-5 | RR-4 | RR-5 |
| 80 | Ferrous | RCP-4 | RCP-5 | RCP-4 | RCP-5 | RCP-3 | RCP-4 | RCP-3 | RCP-4 | RCP-3 | RCP-4 | RR-3 | RR-4 |
| | Nonferrous | J-4 | J-5 | J-4 | J-5 | J-4 | J-5 | RCP-4 | RCP-5 | RCP-4 | RCP-5 | RCP-3 | RCP-4 |
| 90 | Ferrous | J-4 | J-5 | J-4 | J-5 | RCP-4 | RCP-5 | RCP-4 | RCP-5 | RCP-4 | RCP-5 | RR-4 | RR-5 |
| | Nonferrous | J-4 | J-5 | J-4 | J-5 | J-4 | J-5 | J-4 | J-5 | RCP-4 | RCP-5 | RCP-4 | RCP-5 |
| 100 | Ferrous | J-4 | J-5 | J-4 | J-5 | J-4 | J-5 | RCP-4 | RCP-5 | RCP-4 | RCP-5 | RCP-4 | RCP-5 |
| | Nonferrous | J-5 | J-6 | J-4 | J-5 | J-4 | J-5 | J-4 | J-5 | J-4 | J-5 | RCP-4 | RCP-5 |
| 125 | Ferrous | J-4 | J-5 | J-4 | J-5 | J-4 | J-5 | J-4 | J-5 | RCP-4 | RCP-5 | RCP-4 | RCP-5 |
| | Nonferrous | J-5 | | J-5 | J-6 | J-4 | J-5 | J-4 | J-5 | J-4 | J-5 | RCP-4 | RCP-5 |
| 150 | Ferrous | J-4 | J-5 | J-4 | J-5 | J-4 | J-5 | J-4 | J-5 | J-4 | J-5 | RCP-4 | RCP-5 |
| | Nonferrous | | | J-5 | | J-5 | J-6 | J-4 | J-5 | J-5 | J-6 | J-5 | J-6 |
| 175 | Ferrous | J-5 | | J-5 | J-6 | J-4 | J-5 | J-4 | J-5 | J-4 | J-5 | RCP-5 | RCP-6 |
| | Nonferrous | | | | | J-7 | | J-7 | J-8 | J-6 | J-7 | J-6 | J-7 |
| 200 | Ferrous | | | J-6 | | J-5 | J-6 | J-5 | J-6 | J-4 | J-5 | J-6 | J-7 |
| | Nonferrous | | | | | | | J-9 | | J-9 | | J-9 | J-10 |

(*Tools for Bending, Inc.*)

Note: A wiper die is suggested for applications falling beneath the dotted line. Number indicates suggested number of balls in mandrel.

Key: P—Plug; RCP—Roberts Close Pitch; RR—Roberts Regular; J—Roberts Inserted

**Lubricant application.** Effective application of lubricant to the mandrel is of significant importance. Tubes with multibends make proper lubrication of the tool difficult without a mandrel lubricator that automatically lubricates the mandrel before and during each bend. The automatic lubricator pumps lubricant through a hollow mandrel rod and a special mandrel body made for this type of accessory, thereby providing lubricant to the tangent area of the bend. This accessory also conserves lubricant by applying the proper amount to lubricate the tube and the tooling, rather than wasting lubricant by applying excessive quantities or insufficient lubricant to protect the tool.

Wiper-die lubrication should be provided; however, it is important to avoid over-application of lubricant on this tool. A light coating of lubricant reduces frictional drag and heat build-up on the thin tip of the wiper die. This reduces metal pickup and tube scratching and avoids premature failure of the wiper die.

## Troubleshooting

Tube bending is influenced by a number of variables related to materials, tooling, and operating parameters. When the tube breaks repeatedly, the material may be too hard. Hard material is unable to stretch sufficiently to accommodate the bend. Working with annealed materials can alleviate this problem. Mandrel size and location are critical factors affecting springback, wrinkling, humping, and bend radius. When the mandrel is set too far forward or when the tube slips slightly in the clamp die, tube breakage may occur. Figures 10-46 to 10-50 illustrate various common problems and their causes.

Springback control is illustrated in Fig. 10-46. Springback causes the tube to unbend 2-10° and increases the bend radius of the tube. This factor should be considered when selecting a bend die. The smaller the bend radius, the smaller the springback. Springback can be affected by the location and pressure of the pressure die.

The tube may kink or buckle, as shown in Fig. 10-47. This may be due to hard material that does not compress on the inside radius of the bend. The condition can be corrected (if the tube is not too hard) by setting up the tools as shown in Fig. 10-46, *a*. A plug mandrel may be needed if the tube buckling persists.

Figure 10-48 illustrates wrinkling that can occur when the mandrel is too far back. In this instance, the mandrel is not far enough forward to generate sufficient pressure on the inside of the bend to compress the material. The bend may begin smoothly, but as it progresses beyond approximately 20°, the material pushes back, forming a ripple or wave at Point *A*. When the bent tube is removed from the bend die, it is buckled at Point *A*.

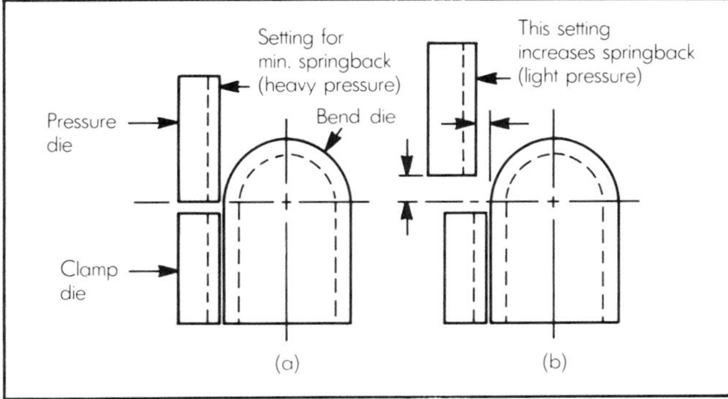


**Fig. 10-46 Illustration of pressure die setting for controlling springback in tube bending. (*H & H Tool Division, Teledyne Pines*)**

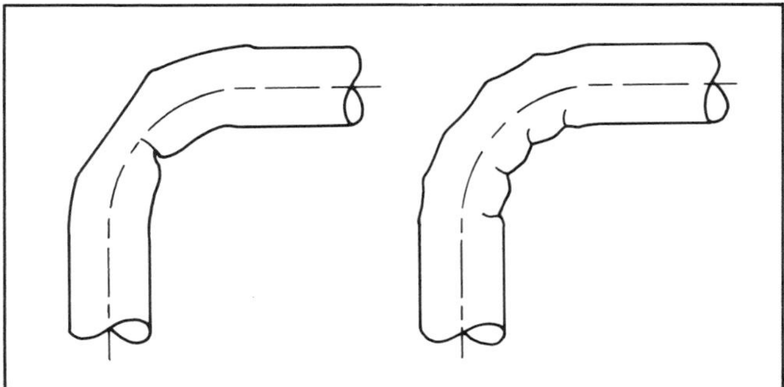

**Fig. 10-47 Typical appearance of kinked or buckled tube bends. (*H & H Tool Division, Teledyne Pines*)**

When the mandrel is too far forward, as shown in Fig. 10-49, several problems are observed. Bumps appear on the outside of the bend at the terminal tangent, and a step is formed on the inside of the bend at the starting tangent. The bump is caused by the mandrel, and the step is formed by the end of the mandrel prying the tube away from the bend die.

As shown in Fig. 10-50, deep scratches sometimes occur throughout the bend and in the wiper-die area. The corrective measures for this condition are: (1) increase rake or relief in the wiper die [the flat end of the wiper die should have 0.030-0.060" (0.76-1.52 mm) clearance from the tube]; (2) review lubricant type and amount applied; (3) recut the tube groove to remove galling.

**Tube breakage.** Tube breakage may be caused by a number of factors, including the following:

- Material lacking proper ductility and elongation.
- Tube slippage in the clamp die.
- Pressure die that is too tight, causing excess drag.
- Material wrinkling and becoming locked between mandrel balls.
- Clamp die that presses on the mandrel balls.
- Improper or insufficient lubrication.
- Mandrel too far forward.

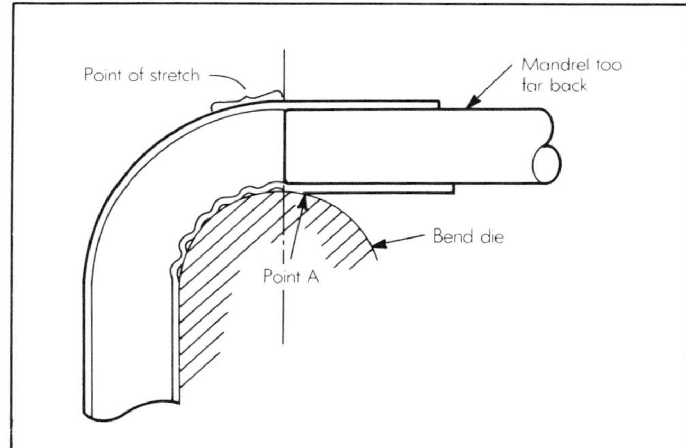


**Fig. 10-48 Tube wrinkling caused by mandrel location too far back in the bend area. (*H & H Tool Division, Teledyne Pines*)**

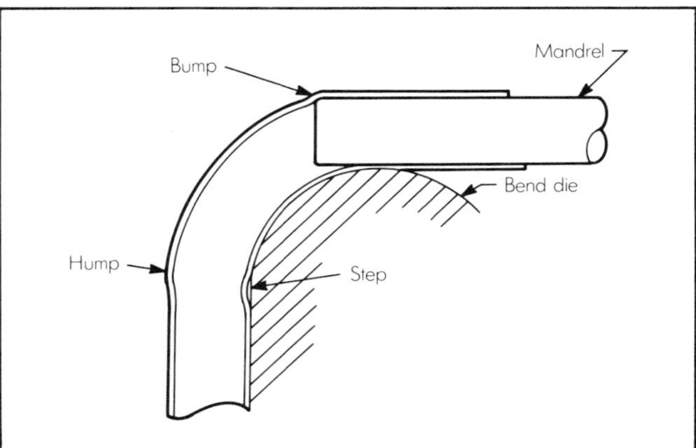


**Fig. 10-49 Tube-bending problems typically caused by a mandrel that is positioned too far forward. (*H & H Tool Division, Teledyne Pines*)**

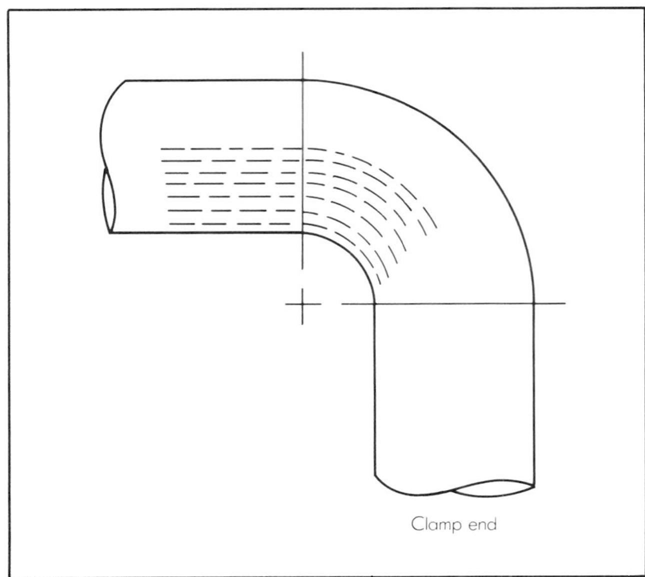


**Fig. 10-50 Deep scratches on bent tubes sometimes appear throughout the bend and in the wiper-die area.** (*Tools for Bending, Inc.*)

**Tube wrinkling.** Tube wrinkling may be caused by any of the following factors:

- Tube slippage in the clamp die.
- Mandrel that is not far enough forward.
- Wiper die that is not seated properly in the bend die.
- Wiper die that is worn or does not fit properly.
- Too much clearance between the mandrel (undersized) and tube.
- Not enough pressure on the pressure die.
- Improper or excessive lubricant.

## Automated Tube Bending[8]

The use of computers in the fabrication of tube assemblies began in the early 1960's. The subsequent development of microcomputers and large, computer-aided-design systems has dramatically accelerated the growth in automated tube fabrication technology. The following text summarizes current automated bending technology, beginning with the concept of automated tube bending and the bend accuracy and setup problems that first brought the computer into the tube shop.

**The concept.** Tube bend contours are defined in terms of intersecting vectors that define the straight portions of the tube in relation to a static reference point. This information is converted to lengths, rotations, and angles and entered into a programmable bending machine. The machine automatically uses the information to precisely control its operation.

**Bend accuracy considerations.** In the rotary-bending process, material, setup, and machine variables change from job to job. This means that the machine feed and rotation commands that worked well on one job may not work on another. Each setup usually requires modifications in the program for producing a part.

In addition, the machine precision on the feeds and rotations that form the tube does not relate directly to the "goodness of fit" tolerances. An accurate frame of reference is essential in the tube shop to objectively evaluate goodness of fit and to make the frequent bend-data corrections. In the past this absolute reference was either a master tube or a hard fixture. By positioning the tube in the fixture or comparing it to a master tube, the operator could estimate the required corrections and could eventually produce a good part.

Many companies are now using computer-controlled tube-measurement systems that inspect the tube against an absolute framework of XYZ coordinates and make corrections on the bend data based on the centerline "tunnel" tolerances. The inspection consists of digitizing the part shape and mathematically converging the best fit to the XYZ coordinates specified in the master shape. As indicated in Fig. 10-51, a report is generated and, if the tube is not within tolerance, the bend data may be automatically corrected and sent to the bending machine.

Measurement systems have also been used to calculate and store linear estimates on the corrections needed for a particular setup. This setup data can be obtained by measuring two bends and storing elongation and springback constants.

**Additional features.** The measurement computer can be used to scan the stored data for a series of part numbers and sort the parts by diameter, bend radius, and material to minimize the number of setup changes.

In addition to the setup gains, some tube shops use the measurement computer as a small manufacturing data center. With bulk data storage and high-speed peripherals, they can store and retrieve setup and bend data as well as the master shape definitions, as depicted in Fig. 10-52.

Bending machine microcomputers increase productivity by controlling simultaneous motions and part/machine interfaces. Over a period of several years, some manufacturers have made significant improvements in the production cycle time of their equipment. For one firm, Table 10-9 compares the fastest rotary bender offered three years ago with current versions. It can be noted that the improvement in cycle times is disproportionate to the gains in axis motion speeds. This is because the new controls maximize the number of overlapping motions by keeping track of potential interferences. This example is illustrative of recent design progress by a particular company. Other firms offer comparable state-of-the-art machinery, including a numerically controlled mandrel bender that can produce a "typical six-bend part" in a cycle time of 20 seconds.

Computer control also brings a number of convenience

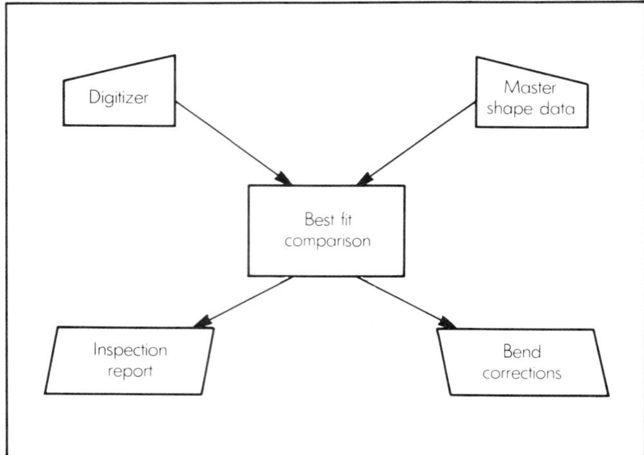


**Fig. 10-51 Block diagram related to generating an inspection report during a computer-controlled, automatic-tube-bending operation.** (*Eaton Leonard Corp.*)

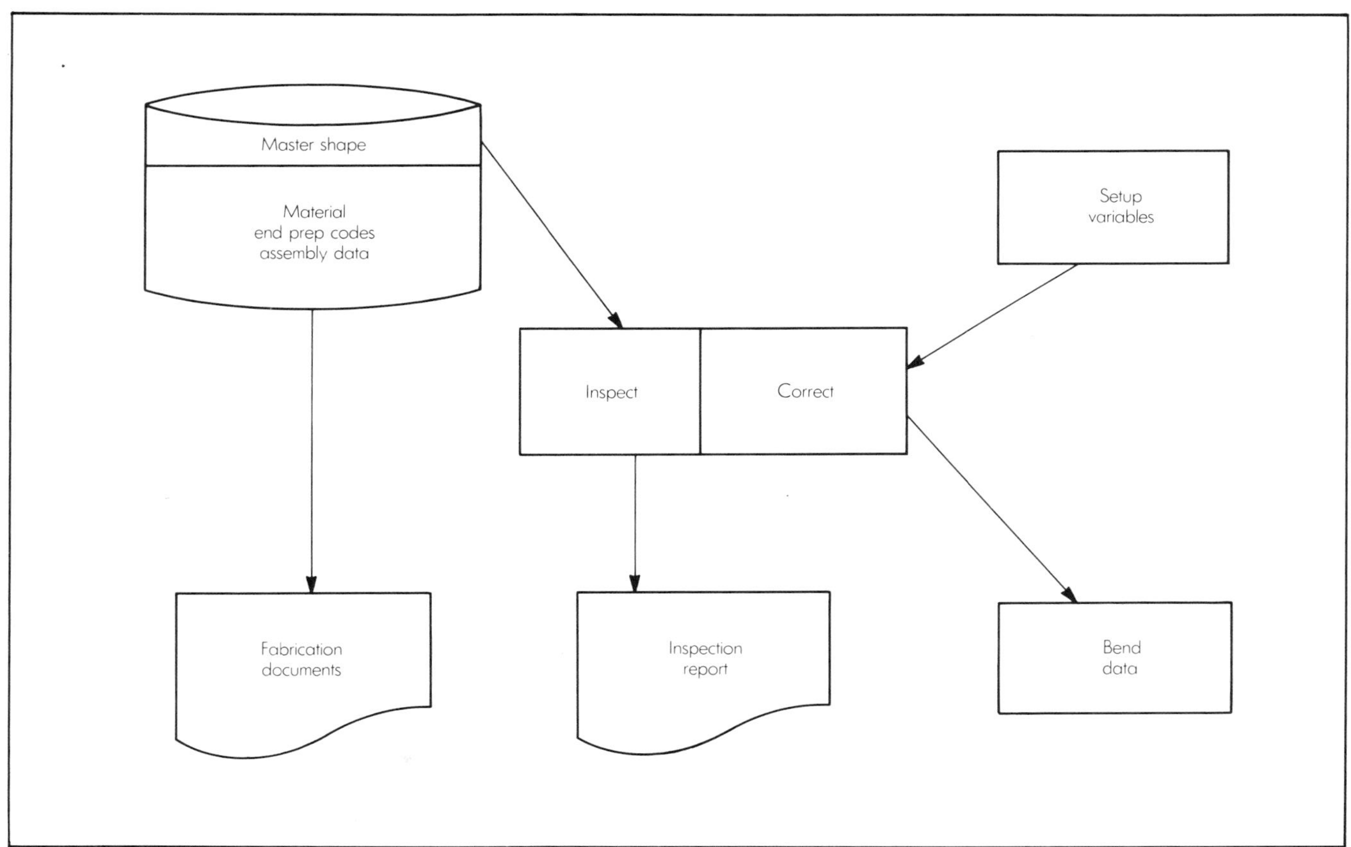


**Fig. 10-52 Block diagram depicts use of the tube-bending measurement computer for a small manufacturing data center.** (*Eaton Leonard Corp.*)

**TABLE 10-9**
**Bending Machine Productivity**

| | 1979 | 1982 | % Change |
|---|---|---|---|
| Bend-arm Rotation, rpm | 20 | 25 | 25% |
| Collet Rotation, rpm | 35 | 35 | 0% |
| Carriage Feed, ipm | 1500 | 1700 | 13.3% |
| m/min. | 38.1 | 43.2 | |
| Cycle Time, sec* | 38.6 | 26.4 | 31.6% |

*Mandrel bending, typical 6-bend part (*Eaton Leonard Corp.*)

features to tube-bending machines. Controls now keep track of tooling interference points which formerly required limit-switch settings that changed with each tooling setup.

Special sequences can be created to move the tube or tooling to prevent an interference. For example, to move the bend arm out of the way to drop a tube on a conveyor, a single program code would keep the pressure die in, open the clamp, and move the bend arm to 180° before releasing the part. Most controls also offer sophisticated part-program editing, in-process monitoring, and diagnostic routines.

**CAD/CAM application.** Computer-aided-design (CAD) systems are readily adaptable to tube bending. The advantage to the design group is the capability for making a series of contour evaluations that provide realistic tolerances and fits. Analysis programs can be used to evaluate stress induced by installation of the tubing. These systems promote design standardization, which in turn reduces tooling and fabrication costs while controlling the dimensional fits.

Figure 10-53 shows the main elements of a CAD/CAM tube system. In the early planning stages, the user outlines the data paths that are to connect the functional blocks. Types of tube data include tube geometry, tube fabrication data, tube assembly definition, manufacturing work orders, and security backup files. Obviously, the interconnection path on this diagram changes depending on the company and industry. Frequently, a manufacturer connects the engineering data base directly to the tube-shop measuring system for security and data integrity. Fabrication information can be quickly obtained even if the design center is miles (kilometers) away. In some cases when a tube is formed for the first time, a machine interference is discovered. With a data link, the tube shop may go ahead and make the part so that it clears the machine and then send this data back to the CAD system to evaluate the fit.

**Applications.** The following examples in different industries illustrate the wide variety of applications for automation in tube fabricating.

The first example of microprocessor-controlled, high-speed, automatic-bending-machine usage is in the furniture and motorcycle industries in which there are parts with more than one bend radius. A fast tool change is needed to make all the bends in one operation. In this application, a radius change is made by sliding the bend head up and shifting the centerline

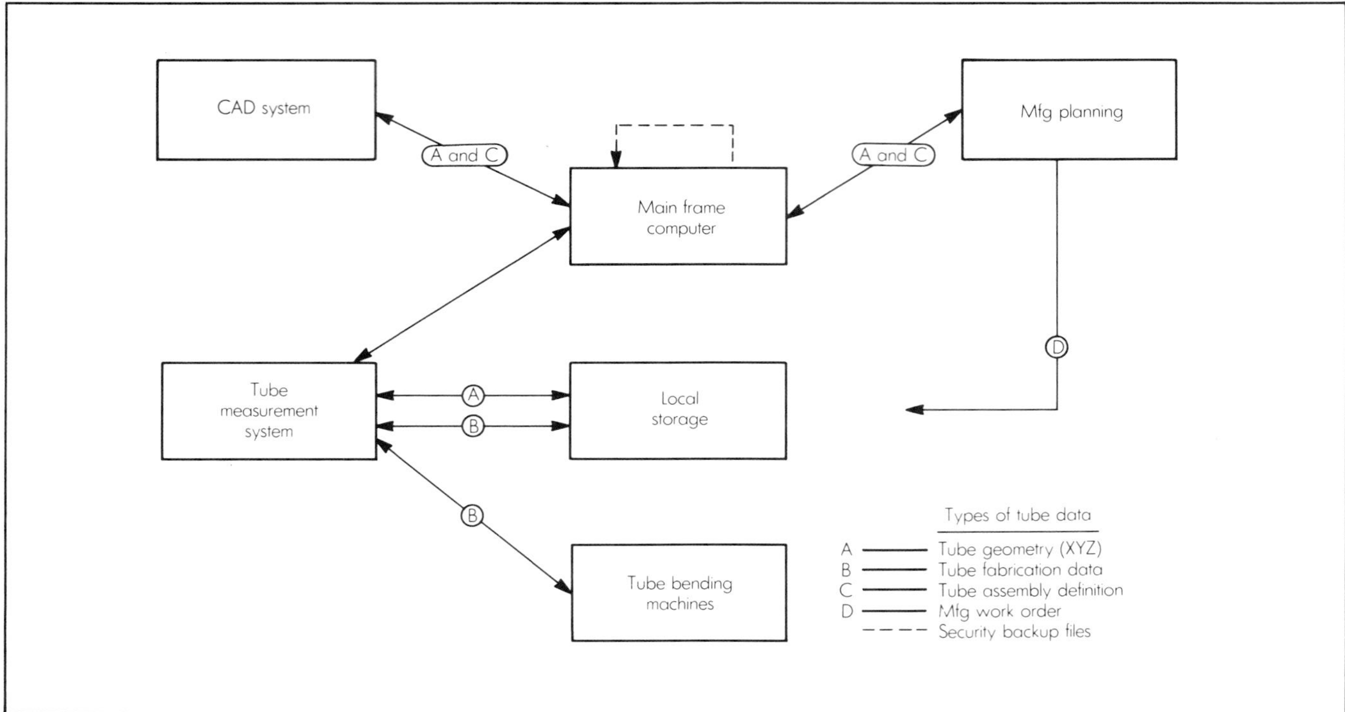


**Fig. 10-53 Main elements of CAD/CAM system for automatic tube bending.** (*Eaton Leonard Corp.*)

across. A computing-type control is needed to calculate the interferences and to sequence the tooling to clear the part. The rotation must be held back until the part clears the top die. These are sequences which depend on the bend radii as well as the part shape. Without computer control, this type of setup would be impractical to automate.

In the aerospace power-plant industry, one company uses a tube measurement system and a main-frame computer to simulate tube deflection when the ends of the tube are forced into alignment according to the assembly dimension. This new deflected-tube contour enables simulation of the bending moments on the tube ends to align them with the mating parts. In the final step, loads are simulated at the clamp points and tube clearances are checked. The computer restricts the simulated loads and stresses to the specified limits.

The appliance industry was the first to integrate fully automatic end-finishing with tube bending. In one installation, two hopper-fed, end-finishing lines unload onto conveyors that transport the tubes through a wash tank to bending machines that have fully automatic loaders and special unloading sequences to eject the finished part.

## PIPE BENDING

From post World War II until the early 1980's many improvements were made in tube and pipe-bending technology. The advancements occurred mainly in the areas of machine design and mechanical function, computer control, tooling, and lubrication. The basic principle of draw bending, however, was retained.

The relatively simple, basic, hydraulically operated draw-bending machine of the late 1940's with manual controls, static pressure die, and plug mandrel for generous radius bends has now evolved into the CNC machine with a fully boosted pressure die that has springback compensation sensors; a swing-away wiper die; an oscillating and/or multiball, autolubricating-mandrel, drop-away clamp; preset sequenced changes of plane and distances between bends; and other sophisticated options. It is, however, basically a draw-bending machine using the same principles as applied in the past—yet vastly improved in terms of performance and product quality control.

One major technological advancement in tube and pipe bending was the machine concept described earlier in the "Automatic Tube Bending" section of this chapter. This tube-bending machine combines tube making and tube bending into a single, continuous operation and utilizes a rotary bending head that changes the plane of bends without rotating the tube itself. It is a machine with a high rate of production.

### Induction Bending

In 1978, another significant advancement in bending technology occurred with the introduction in the United States of commercially designed and manufactured induction-bending machines. Until then, large-diameter, heavy-wall pipe was bent by the traditional hot-slab method in which the pipe was first sand-filled and packed, then heated in an oven to approximately 2000° F (1093° C) before being removed, placed on a bending table, clamped at one end, and pulled around forming blocks by means of a cable attached to the opposite end—hopefully completing the bend before the pipe cooled down to 1600° F (871° C).

The process, which is still used today, is slow, highly labor intensive, and costly. It is also limited, in most cases, to radii of 5 times the diameter or larger. Nevertheless, for material with wall thicknesses in excess of 4″ (102 mm), it is still the only feasible means of bending.

The new induction benders were designed specifically for

large-diameter pipe in wall thicknesses of up to 4″ (102 mm); however, they had the capability of achieving bends of less than 5 times the diameter and, in fact, could in many instances go as low as 1 1/2 times the diameter—well below the limits of hot-slab bending. Furthermore, the process was much quicker, was far less labor intensive, and achieved better wall-thinning and ovality tolerances.

**Machine description.** The principle of hot bending by the induction process is a significant departure from other methods. The pipe is contained in the body of the machine and clamped at the front end, beyond the tangent or starting point of the bend, by means of a swing arm extended from a fixed pivot point. The distance from the pivot point to the centerline of the pipe in the clamp and along its length determines the radius of the bend. This radius distance is infinitely adjustable to as small as 0.10″ (2.5 mm). Thus, within the minimum and maximum radius limits of the machine, almost any desired radius is possible, taking into consideration such factors as material type, diameter, and wall thickness. A general view of an induction bender for large-diameter (32″; 813 mm) pipe is shown in Fig. 10-54.

The body or main frame of the machine rests on transverse rails and adjusts to the radius set for the bend, not only initially when the operation is set up for the bend but continuously during bending, to compensate for irregularities in the pipe.

At the tangent point at which the bend starts and finishes, an inductor ring circumscribes the pipe. This ring may be perforated or may be adjoining another ring which provides a cooling spray. In some cases, there may be several rings for both water and air cooling. This helps to contain the heat band directly under the inductor ring and returns the ductile material to hardness as it travels through the ring.

**Operation.** When the machine is powered, electricity is transmitted to the ring which heats the pipe in a narrow band beneath it to the required temperature for bending. This preheating may take from one to several minutes depending upon a number of factors, such as material type and wall thickness, and is monitored by two pyrometers which transmit the temperature information to the machine controls. When required bending temperature has been reached, the machine initiates the bending process by means of a pusher bar or clamp at the rear end of the pipe, which pushes the pipe through the inductor. Because the pipe is clamped to a fixed pivot point, by means of the swing arm, and because the front end of the pipe itself is ductile at the tangent point, a bend is induced. A combination of forces, carefully monitored and controlled by the machine, dictates the rate of travel, amount of heat, pressures, etc., constantly during the entire bending cycle until the required degree of bend has been reached. The machine then shuts itself off, and the bent pipe is ready to be removed from the machine.

The pipe is empty—it need not be filled with sand, nor is a mandrel necessary. On completion of the bend, the pipe is cool enough to handle. The entire process, from start to finish, including loading, bending, and unloading, can be carried out by the operator and an assistant, using an overhead crane, in a relatively short time in comparison to the traditional hot-slab method—often in less time than it would take to sand-fill and pack the pipe.

**Status.** By 1982 several such machines were in steady production in the United States, ranging in capacity from 28″ (711 mm) for the smallest machine to 64″ (1.6 m) for the largest, and induction bending became a state-of-the-art process.

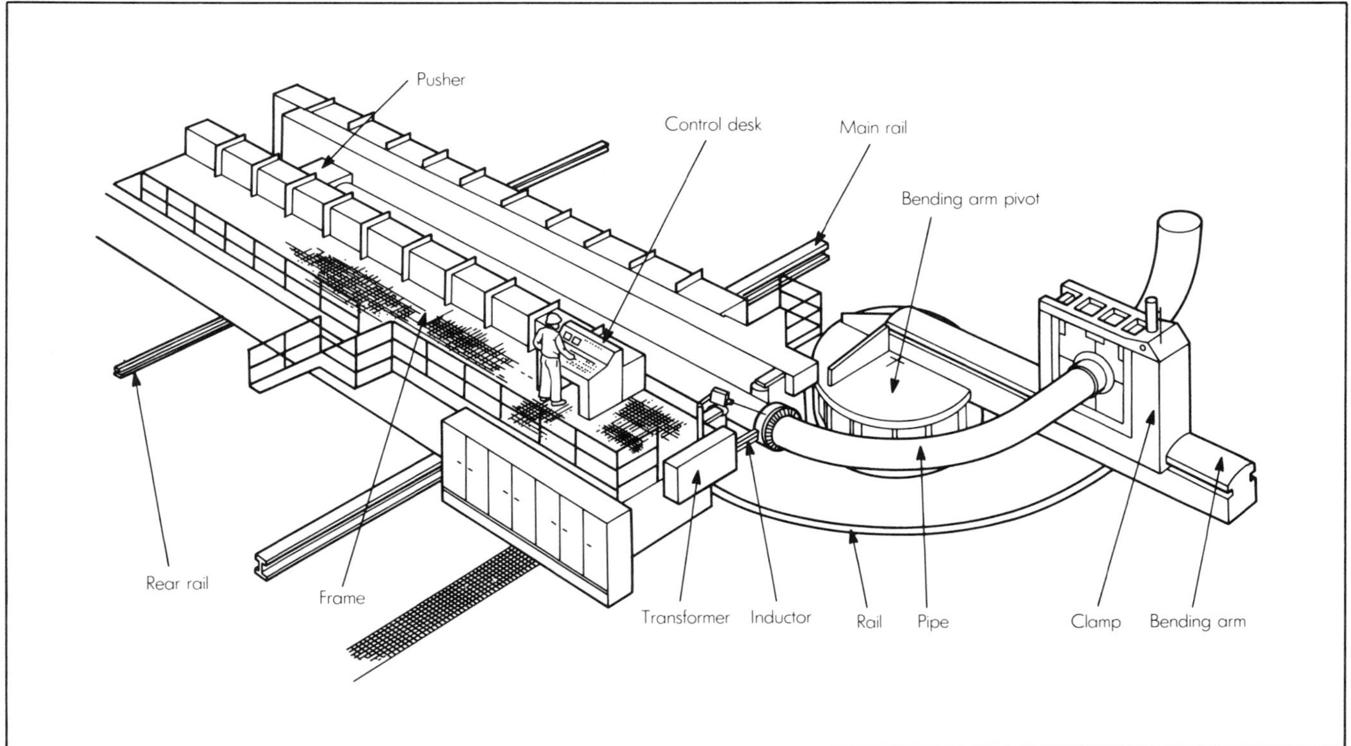


**Fig. 10-54 Induction-bending machine for large-diameter pipe (32″; 813 mm). Example of operational data: 16″ (406 mm) pipe, 3.6″ (91 mm) wall thickness, 48″ (1.2 m) bending radius, 1.4% ovality, and 11.5% wall thinning.** (*Inkamaf Corp., Cojafex B.V., Pipebending Div.*)

# PIPE BENDING

Standards applicable to hot-slab bending no longer applied to induction bending, which offered far better wall-thinning and ovality tolerances and which could achieve bends beyond the limitations of the older method.

**Small induction machines.** In 1982, further advancement in bending technology occurred with the introduction of a small induction machine designed specifically for bending pipe up to 12" (305 mm) diam in most wall thicknesses. This second generation of machinery, shown in Fig. 10-55, includes engineering advances that perform bends from 1 1/2 to 3 times the diameter, with wall thinning of less than 12 1/2%, as specified for a standard butt-weld fitting. One firm offers equipment that is said to have a capability for making bends on a radius of 1 1/2 times the pipe size, thereby enabling a bend to be used in lieu of a conventional pipe fitting.

Computer-controlled and capable of making single, multiple, and multiplane bends on infinitely variable radii without additional cost or downtime, the new generation of small machines is bringing about significant changes in piping design and production.

Computer-aided piping system design, hitherto restricted to conventional configurations of 1 1/2 times the diameter, can now achieve optimum configuration. At the same time, production facilities are becoming automated and computer controlled. Quality assurance, also, is linked into the computer system.

Theoretically, it is possible to design a piping system entirely by computer; make a half-dozen copies of the tape; send the copies out to bidders who will review the tape, indicate the location of field welds, put in cost and other factors, and return the copy with the bid price; and have the contract awarded to the successful bidder without producing drawings.

The successful bidder then has the necessary drawings produced by computer and interfaces the main frame with shop production computers. The purchasing department, in the meantime, orders materials and schedules their delivery to meet production dates. When production starts, much of it is controlled by the original computer tape. Pipe is drawn, cleaned, measured, cut, end-bevelled, flanged, and bent by computer-controlled machinery and equipment. Finished-pipe spool pieces are then checked for accuracy by equipment interfaced with the original tape on the plant's mainframe computer.

## Future Developments

Research is under way to fuse pipe ends by an electro-hydraulic process that may virtually eliminate material wastage.

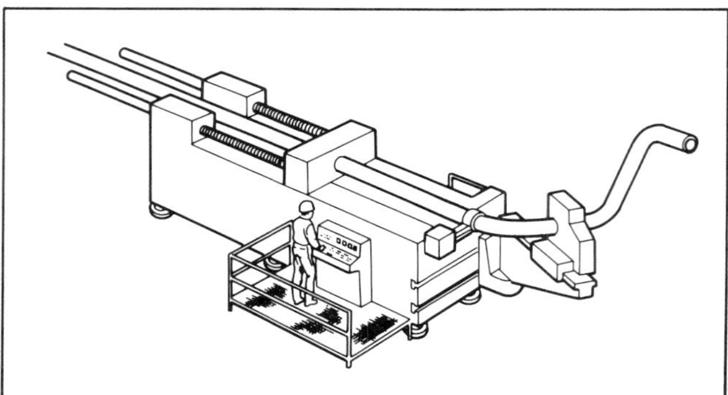

**Fig. 10-55 Induction-bending machine for pipe in diameters ranging from 2-12" (51-305 mm), with wall thicknesses up to double extra-heavy dimensions.** (*Inkamaf Corp., Cojafex B.V., Pipebending Div.*)

One significant advantage of such a process would apply to bending costly exotic materials in which, to make the bend, more pipe is used than would be required for the final developed length and the minimum tangents. Additional, nonexotic pipe can be fused on at each end before bending and trimmed off afterward, thus reducing the normally required scrap to as little as 1/2" (12.7 mm). Also, pipe can be fed on a continuous basis into machines for measuring and cutting to required lengths. There is no scrap such as normally is produced when cutting the last piece before changing jobs and sizes. Alternatively, the pipe can be fed into a small induction bender and each spool piece cut after completion of the final bend while still on the machine. When the cut spool piece is removed, the pipe feeds forward again for the next one—again, no scrap or precut lengths are required.

Research also is directed toward areas of bending that have, until now, been infeasible simply because the machinery and technology have not been available. For example, it has become possible to bend certain types of pipe that could not be bent cold because of the size and wall thickness. (There were no machines with the necessary capability.) Also, it was not possible to bend the material by the traditional hot-slab method, because that method would have a detrimental effect on the metallurgical structure. (There would be too much heat for too long a period of time.) Now, the induction process bends pipe with less heat applied to the tangent point for a minimal time without significantly altering the fiber structure.

Considerable development and updating of codes, specifications, and standards are needed to keep pace with technical advancements in this field and to avoid deterring utilization of state-of-the-art capabilities, for example, in the use of thinner walls for pressure piping that is fabricated with induction equipment.

## Hydraulic Pipe Benders[9]

Rotary-draw pipe benders have attained a state of development that enables them to meet pipe wall thickness and ovality specifications when cold bending pipe on small radii down to 1 1/2 times the diameter. The state-of-the-art in this type of equipment is represented by the microprocessor-controlled, pipe-bending machine shown in Fig. 10-56.

**Wall thinning and ovality.** According to American Society for Testing and Materials (ASTM) specifications, wall thickness for straight pipe shall not be more than 12 1/2% under the nominal wall thickness specified. Several specifications for pipe fittings are commonly cited:

- ASTM A-234 for piping fittings of wrought carbon steel and alloy steel for moderate and elevated temperatures.
- ASTM A-403 for wrought austenitic stainless steel piping fittings.
- American National Standards Institute (ANSI) B16.28 for wrought steel, butt-welded, short-radius elbows and returns.
- ANSI B16.9 for factory butt-welded fittings.

None of these specifications give any allowance for wall thinning from bending, so the applicable standard for bent pipe sections is not more than 12 1/2% under the nominal wall thickness.

No generally accepted specification exists for allowable ovality in the middle of a bend or for fittings at tangent or end points. There are, however, allowable inside and outside-

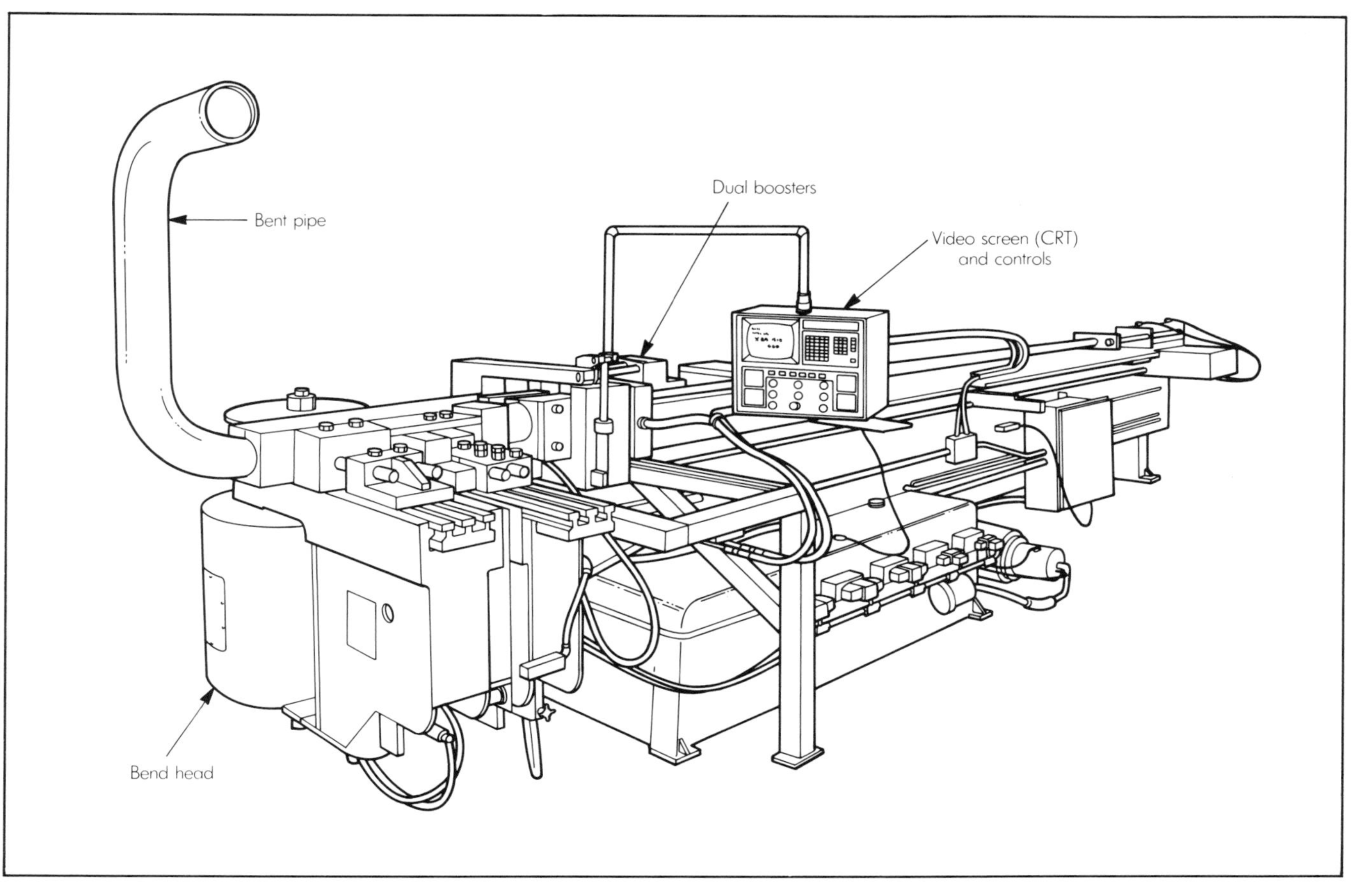


**Fig. 10-56 A modern, rotary-draw, microprocessor-controlled automatic bending machine that is capable of fulfilling pipe wall thickness and ovality specifications.** (*Conrac Machine Tool Div.*)

diameter tolerances for fitting end or tangent points, which vary according to pipe size.

**Pipe specification.** When determining pipe wall thickness specifications to meet wall-thinning specifications after bending, it is necessary to recognize that in the natural phenomenon of rotary-draw bending, the material thins on the outside of the bend. Furthermore, straight pipe can be as much as 12 1/2% under the nominal wall thickness and still be within specifications. The fabricator must know exactly how much thinning will occur during bending. This information enables calculation of the minimum acceptable wall thickness to be specified for purchased pipe.

Equipment and tooling are available to reliably limit wall thinning to 12 1/2% of nominal wall thickness for bending that is 1 1/2 times the diameter; hence, a straightforward arithmetical calculation can be made to determine the minimum original wall thickness that is necessary. As a precaution, it should be noted that the wall thicknesses of certain categories of pipe (Schedules 5 and 10) are insufficient to allow for nominal specification variations and 12 1/2% wall thinning (during bending), whereas pipes within the range of Schedules 40 and 80 are adequate and should readily accommodate the bending operations.

**Equipment factors.** A thorough understanding of machine and tooling characteristics and expert knowledge of pipe wall thinning tendencies are needed to meet rigorous requirements for specifications and productivity while fully utilizing the capabilities of highly sophisticated equipment. Equipment design is fundamental to accurate wall-thinning and ovality control. High degrees of accuracy, repeatability, and rigidity are needed in pipe-bending machines to control wall thinning and ovality and to achieve acceptable pipe tolerances.

The critical design factors for ensuring accurate, repeatable wall-thinning and ovality control include boost force and effectiveness, boost pressure, boost speed, and machine rigidity.

*Boost force.* A twin-boost system, which clamps the pipe at midsection and uses two hydraulic cylinders to push it into the bend, provides from 50-100% more boost than pressure-die-assist systems. This reduces elongation and flattening of the pipe and controls wall thinning and ovality through the bend. Tooling controls ovality at the tangent.

*Boost effectiveness.* By employing 360° clamping of the pipe, slippage is eliminated and total boost force is transmitted to the pipe.

*Variable boost pressure.* With high and low boost pressure presets, bending fabricators can eliminate the bulges associated with too much or too constant boost force through the bending process.

*Boost speed.* A tachometer feedback system precisely regulates boost travel to coordinate with bend-die rotation.

*Machine rigidity.* Spindles, bearings, bend-die posts, bend-die bolsters, clamp-die bolsters, and pressure-die bolsters should be appropriately sized and designed to provide maximum rigidity. Lack of machine rigidity creates unpredictable machine movements which in turn create nonrepeatable machine error.

**Microprocessor controls.** The advent of the microprocessor control, coupled with existing bending technology, has greatly simplified the bending operation. In the past, it was necessary for the operator to have a great deal of skill. The operator had to compensate for machine and material deficiencies. Now, trial-and-error bending has been virtually eliminated and machinery is accurate, repeatable, and automatic.

For example, on one firm's microprocessor-controlled, twin-booster benders, degrees of bend (DOB) and planes of bend (POB) are controlled to within ±0.1°. Distances between bends (DBB) are controlled to within ±0.010" (0.25 mm). Fabricators can routinely make multiple bends (as many as required) with multiple planes of rotation.

All functions can be programmed at the control or via interface with a main-frame computer. This includes automatic springback compensation, which automatically adds the correct amount of overbend where necessary, based on operator-entered data regarding type of material, outside diameter, and wall thickness. Bend data for each part can be stored in the control and recalled when needed. As much storage space as required can be added.

# STRAIGHTENING

Cold or hot metal forming processes can cause residual stresses in rod, bar, sheet, wire, or tubing—and in components made from these materials—as a result of nonuniform plastic flow of the material. Metallurgically, residual stress occurs because of many conditions inherent in the structure and properties of the metal, including molecular disorientation, and the presence of this stress can cause part deformation in shape and size. Such stresses are often induced in the cold or hot working of stock material and later cause deformations when the stock is cut or formed into components or shapes.

In rods or tubes, residual stresses usually take the form of bows or snakes (a series of bows) in the part (see Fig. 10-57). In flat rectangular or irregularly shaped parts, deviation from a straight line is generally in the form of camber (see Fig. 10-58). Another out-of-straight condition that can occur in all parts is twist, in which the face of the part is out-of-plane (see Fig. 10-59). Stock materials and piece parts can have any or a combination of all of these conditions.

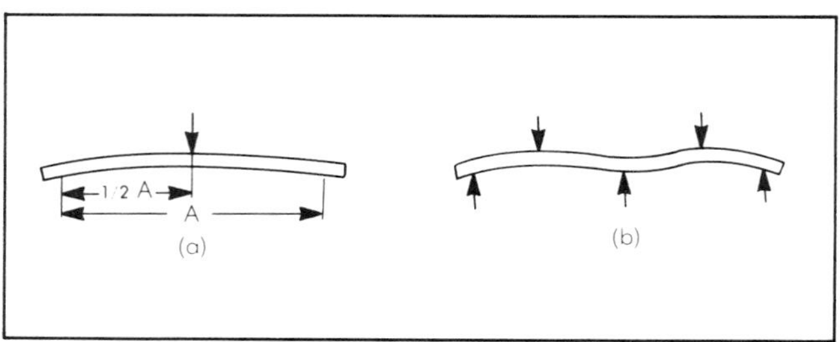


**Fig. 10-57 Types of stress deformation in rods and tubes: (a) simple bow and (b) snaking or multiple bows.**

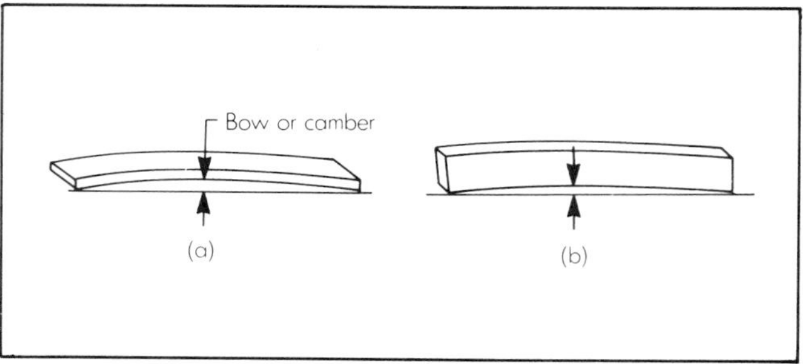


**Fig. 10-58 Types of stress deformation in rectangular bars: (a) face bow or camber and (b) edge camber.**

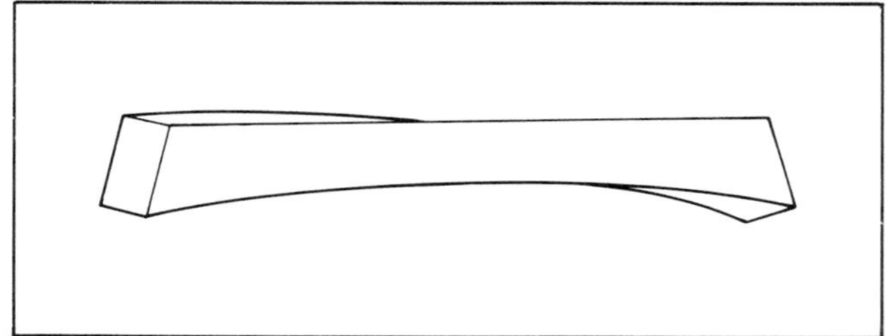

**Fig. 10-59 Stress deformation—twist.** (*Bertolette Machines, Inc.*)

## INSPECTION METHODS

Various methods are used to check straightness. Generally, round parts, rods, and tubes are placed on rolls or in V-grooves, and the deviation from straightness is read with a dial indicator as the part is rotated. Deviation can be expressed by total indicator reading (TIR), which is equal to twice the bow or camber of the part. Rods are sometimes placed on centers for checking straightness. Flat or rectangular parts are normally checked for camber by placing a straight edge on the part or by setting the part on a flat-surface plate and using a feeler gage or a dial indicator to measure the farthest distance that the part is bowed away from a straight line. Camber is measured on both the face and the edge of such parts. Laser beams of straight light are sometimes used in special instrumentation in which extremely close accuracy or high-volume measuring is required. Also, when checking straightness on a flat-surface plate, it is helpful to have a "light box," against which the profile of the part can be readily checked visually.

## PRINCIPLES OF STRAIGHTENING

The general principle of straightening deformations in stock or component parts is to move the material beyond its elastic limit. Figure 10-60 illustrates the application of the general beam-bending formula to the calculation of force required in the straightening process.

At normal room temperatures, straightening can be done by locating a deformation and moving the material in the opposite direction, so that when pressure is removed, the deformation is equalized. Stock or parts can also be heated to high temperatures and placed under continuous pressure for a period of time, allowing the molecular structure to equalize while the material cools. Stretching or drawing of stock materials through dies can

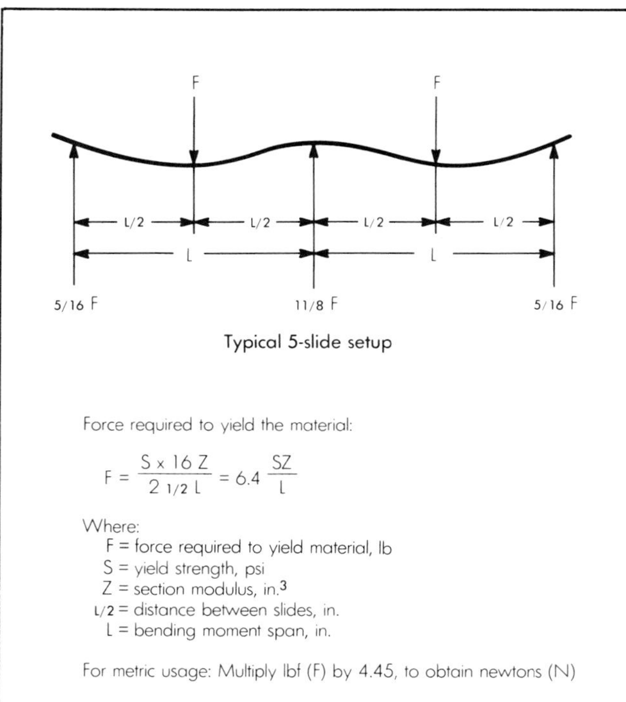

F
F
L/2
L/2
L/2
L/2
L
L
5/16 F
11/8 F
5/16 F
Typical 5-slide setup
Force required to yield the material:
$F = \frac{S \times 16\,Z}{2\,1/2\,L} = 6.4\,\frac{SZ}{L}$
Where:
F = force required to yield material, lb
S = yield strength, psi
Z = section modulus, in.$^3$
L/2 = distance between slides, in.
L = bending moment span, in.
For metric usage: Multiply lbf (F) by 4.45, to obtain newtons (N)


**Fig. 10-60 Principal elements of basic formula for force required to straighten a workpiece by deforming the material beyond its elastic limit.** (*Bertolette Machines, Inc.*)

equalize molecular surface tensions and overcome deformations. Flexing stock or component parts back and forth, returning them to a straight line, can stress relieve them and bring them to a straight condition.

## ADVANTAGES

Straightness is important in stock materials, since component parts manufactured from straight stock tend to remain straight. Straightness is obviously necessary for component parts that are used in assembly with other parts, since proper functioning of the assembly depends upon the correct relationship of one part to another. Other advantages of straightness include:

- Parts can be consistently held to close dimensions.
- Relief of residual stresses enhances part stability.
- Straight parts can be machined at greater production rates.
- Less labor and skill are required in subsequent machining operations.
- Part life is increased, since stability of a part provides better resistance to fatigue and improved yield strength.
- Less material is needed when allowances are made for cuts as a means of obtaining straightness.
- Parts which are used alone (that is, hand tools) have a better and more salable appearance.

## LIMITATIONS

Straightening does not always overcome all stresses; and after machining or heat treatment, a part may need to be restraightened. Straightening does not correct out-of-round conditions such as those caused by mismatch in forgings or ovality.

## STOCK OR CONTINUOUS MATERIALS

Stock material can be defined as wire, tubing, sheet metal, or extrusions. It generally is received in coil form. When the stock is used to produce parts, residual curves result from the coiling. On round, cross-section stock, twisting can occur about the axis of the material. This twisting (deformation) may be caused by axial movement during coiling, or it may result from production operations such as welding of tubing, drawing of wire, or feeding and processing of sheet metal.

Stock and continuous materials can be straightened in a separate operation or in line with cutoff or machining operations. Sheet metal straightening equipment that is installed with coil-handling and press-feeding lines is discussed in Chapter 5 "Presses for Sheet Metal Forming."

### Stretch Straightening

In the stretch straightening method, the ends are clamped and tension is placed on the material. This method is not widely used; it is slow and limited in effectiveness.

### Parallel-Roll Straightening

As shown in Fig. 10-61, in this method a series of rolls is arranged so that the material moves between them, overbending in diminishing amounts as it moves forward. Sheet, plate, and strip materials are generally straightened only in the flat plane, although some edge guiding can be provided. Wire or tubing, with a round or multisided cross section, can generally be straightened in two planes, one 90° to the other. When necessary, three planes, each 120° from the other can be used successfully. Rolls in such straighteners can have V-grooves for solid materials or grooves matching the cross section of tubular materials so that they do not distort under the straightening pressure.

The sets of rolls are often without their own power or drive mechanism and are located between coiled stock and a feeding mechanism which pulls or pushes the material through the rolls. Forming, stamping, or cutoff machines with integral feeds often pull material through the straightening rolls into these specific operations. Some materials (such as welded stainless steel tubing) with relatively high column strengths can be pushed through straightening rolls by feed units on a welding mill.

Parallel-roll straightening devices can also be self-powered for pulling and straightening materials from coil to cutoff or other operations. In such cases, depending on the resistance of the material to the straightening process, all of the rolls in each plane can be interconnected by chain or belt drives and powered, or only pairs of directly opposed rolls at the beginning and end of the straightener can be driven. Figure 10-62 shows a typical setup.

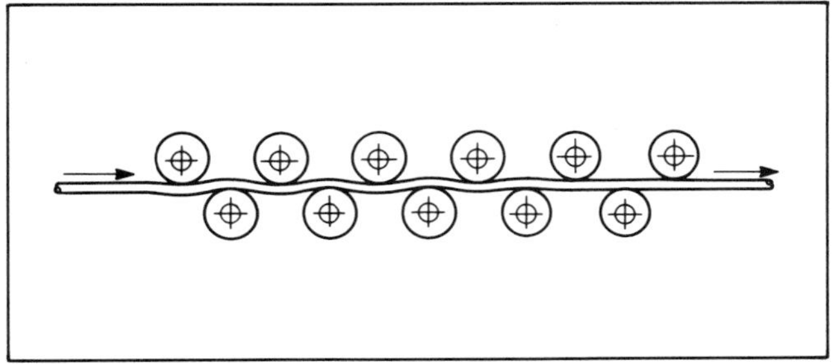

**Fig. 10-61 Parallel-roll straightening—single plane, strip stock.** (*Bertolette Machines, Inc.*)

The main advantage of parallel-roll straightening is the high speed at which material can be moved through the rolls. Linear speeds of 500-600 fpm (152-183 m/min) are feasible. A disadvantage is that straightness is attained only in the specific planes that are being worked and material often bends in other places in subsequent machining or heat treating, requiring further straightening. Another disadvantage is that the degrees of integral bends in coils can vary from the outside of the coil to the center, requiring setting changes in the straightening rolls as the material moves through them.

### Revolving-Arbor Straightening

Wire, tubing, or small-diameter, coiled rod is pulled through a rotating mechanism that usually contains cast-iron straightening dies, as illustrated in Fig. 10-63. The outer dies on each end are set to keep the wire in the center; the middle sets of dies bend the material as the arbor spins around the material moving through the mechanism. Trial and error determines the setting of the dies. A major advantage of this method is that straightening occurs around the entire circumference of the material as it moves through, covering all planes. A disadvantage is that it cannot generally be performed on material moving any faster than 150-200 fpm (46-61 m/min).

## METAL PARTS AND COMPONENTS

Metal parts and components in any shape or form can be straightened by a wide choice of methods, all of which embody the application of the principles discussed previously. Such components can be parts cut to length from stock, stampings, formed parts, forgings, castings, extrusions, or die castings.

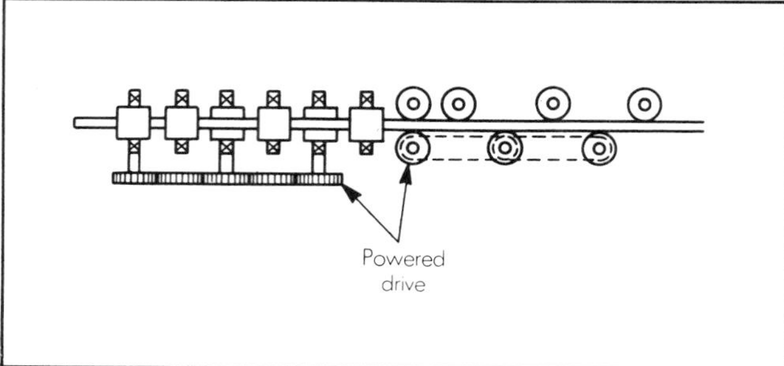


**Fig. 10-62 Horizontal and vertical-plane-shape straightener with multiple effects in each plane.**

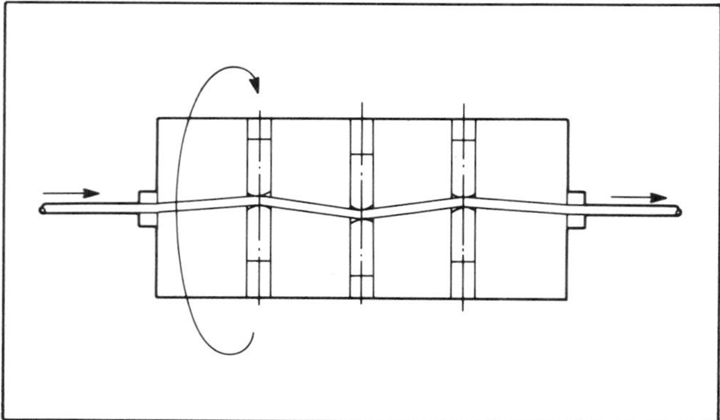

**Fig. 10-63 Diagram of revolving-arbor straightening, as used for wire, tubing, and small-diameter rod.** (*Bertolette Machines, Inc.*)

Deformations in manufactured parts can occur from the transfer of deformations or the release of stresses in the cold stock materials when the parts are produced. They can result from heat treating, wherein the materials may be heated to temperatures beyond their elastic limits and thereby conform to the position in which they are placed, resulting in a deformed set when they are quenched to cool. Also, deformations can result from rapid quenching in the hardening process, in which uneven stresses cause distortion.

Two general methods of straightening are used with most metal parts and components. One of these is to determine the location, direction, and amount of deformation in a part and then overbend the part in an opposite, correcting direction (see Fig. 10-64, *a*). The other general method is to establish an amount of overbending required to correct the maximum deformation in a quantity of parts and to apply this amount of corrective overbending to all of the parts, over the entire surface or in any series of locations. A number of different ways and types of equipment exist for applying these two methods, with a correspondingly wide range of skill requirements and results. Production rates range from several minutes per part to 1200 pieces per hour.

The main advantage of the first, selective, straightening method is that straightness can sometimes be achieved on hardened parts with a minimum of movement, thereby avoiding breakage. A disadvantage results because parts do not always retain their straightness in subsequent operations or movement. Advantages of the second, random, straightening method are minimum operator skill requirements and generally higher production rates; a disadvantage is possibly easier breakage on hardened components.

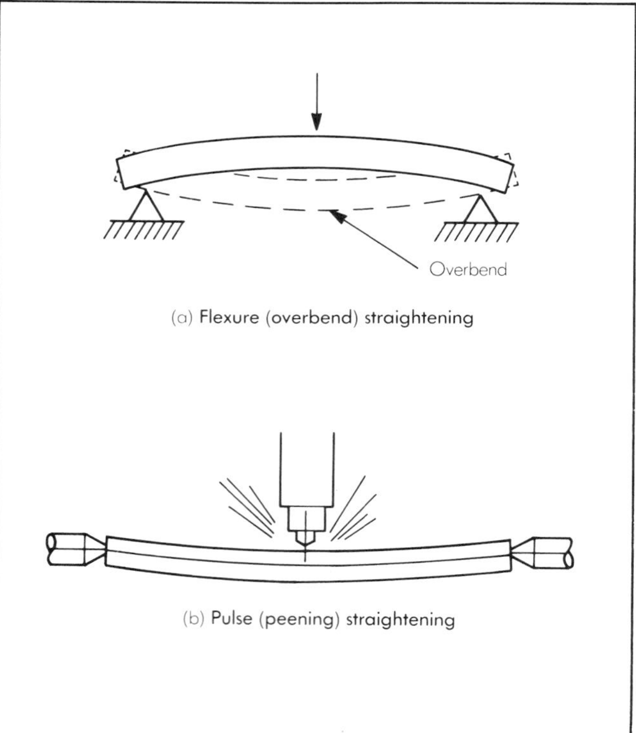


**Fig. 10-64 Schematic illustrations of principles involved in (a) flexure, or overbend, straightening and (b) straightening by automatic peening.** (*Industrial Metal Products Corp.*)

## Manual Straightening

One of the most common types of straightening is manual straightening in which the part is clamped or placed on a heavy, flat anvil or table and struck with a hammer until it is straight. Among the tools used in manual straightening are vises, anvils, grooved blocks, twisting tools, fixtures, and welding or heating torches. The twist often found in parts should be corrected before bow is straightened. The simplest means of straightening a twist is to clamp one end of the part in a vise and twist the part in the opposite direction with a wrench until the twist is removed.

Manual straightening is often done by heating an isolated spot at the outside point of the maximum deformation, followed by rapid quenching. The heat expands the part; but upon cooling, some straightening takes place. The operation generally has to be repeated several times, and one of the drawbacks of straightening by heating is that the part usually retains its straightness only temporarily. The heat can also cause soft spots in the metal.

The manual method is satisfactory for relatively low-volume work and unusually large shapes. Its advantage lies in its low investment cost. Its disadvantages are low production rates and high labor content, with a high degree of skill and judgment required.

## Clamping and Heating

Individual parts can be clamped in fixtures to a desired flatness and then heated beyond the material flow temperature, after which they are set to the desired flatness as they cool. This is a satisfactory method for relatively low volume requirements or large and intricate shapes. Disadvantages are low production rates and the need for some tempering of the material.

## Material Displacement Straightening

Material displacement, or peening, is an effective method of straightening in some applications; however, it has not been used as widely as other methods.

**Manual peening.** Some round parts with a high degree of hardness, such as drill-bit blanks, can be straightened by placing them on heavy, flat plates and peening or rapidly hammering the surface of the concave side of the distortion. This removes the distortion and allows the part to lie flat. This method is relatively slow and requires a high degree of skill.

**Flexure straightening.** In the traditional flexure ("flex") straightening process, a part usually is set between two blocks and rotated to enable sensors to detect the "bow" or amount of distortion. Then, a pressure pad comes down, pushes the bowed area back past its point of elasticity, and allows it to spring back to a calculated zero point. The problem with this process is that stress remains in the part and vibration from further processing or part handling may cause it to regain as much as 60% of its original warped shape. A further drawback of "flex" straightening is the susceptibility to breakage of certain parts, such as cast-iron camshafts and heat-treated parts.

**High-production peening.** In peen straightening, called pulse straightening by one machine manufacturer, the workpiece is pulsed on the low side, opposite the high point of the bend. The material is compressed by the pulsating tooling, and the surface is lightly burnished. This expands the surface, counteracting existing stresses in the workpiece and thereby straightening the part, as illustrated in Fig. 10-64, *b*. The metal structure is stabilized, and the part retains its straight configuration in storage or when subjected to shock and vibration during subsequent grinding, machining, etc.

A graphic plot of events during a typical peen-straightening cycle on a camshaft is shown in Fig. 10-65. Cycle time is plotted against a total indicator reading (TIR), which is displayed during operation by digital readouts for the camshaft's two inner bearings. Each straightener uses a programmable controller to handle all control functions, including part transfer and lubrication.

Plots for one bearing on each of five camshafts are shown at the top of Fig. 10-65. One of the plots, for camshaft *C*, is enlarged to show the sequence of gaging and peening operations. In five revolutions of this camshaft, three of which allow the gaging head to check part condition, a total runout of 0.011" (0.28 mm) was reduced to 0.002" (0.05 mm). This typical operation required 11 seconds; and when loading and unloading time is added to obtain the full cycle time, the result is a gross production rate of 200 parts per hour. This method is finding growing applications in high-volume production operations. Uses include straightening of cast and forged-steel camshafts, hardened-steel transmission shafts, crankshafts, disc plates, and other parts.

## Press Straightening

Machines for press straightening include arbor presses, both mechanical and hydraulic, ranging in size from very small units to heavy-duty presses for parts with larger cross sections. Round parts are placed on V-blocks or between centers on the press table and revolved under a dial indicator to find the high points. As shown in Fig. 10-66, the part is supported at Points *A* and *B*, with the high point of the bow at Point *C*. Sufficient force is then applied at Point *C* to deflect the part through its elastic limit. This operation may need to be performed several times and in various spots along the part until the part is straight. Parts that are not round can also be straightened in this manner; however, they are normally checked against a straight edge or on a flat plate to determine straightness. Press straightening is often used in conjunction with the application of heat in the deformed area. Heavy stampings or plates are sometimes straightened in confined dies in large presses, in which the entire surface is put under pressure.

The advantage of such straightening is a relatively low investment, with a minimum amount of overbend and the least possibility of breakage. Disadvantages are high labor and skill requirements, relatively low production rates, and the fact that parts do not always stay straight.

## Automatic Press Straightening

Press straightening as just described on round parts with a common central axis can be performed automatically on equipment with walking-beam or magazine loaders, automatic sensors, automatic bending movements (hydraulic or mechanical), and automatic unloaders.

The advantages of automatic straightening are high production rates and the need for little operator skill. Its disadvantages include a high investment cost and some straightness instability in subsequent movement or machining operations.

**Typical operation.** Automatic straightening machines locate a part on centers or in V-blocks and rotate it, measuring the amount of overbend at a specific location. The part is then rotated 180° opposite this bend, and pressure is applied, after which the part is again rotated to measure its straightness. This can be repeated several times until straightness is within desired tolerances, and the bending ram then can be moved to another predetermined location where the process is repeated. It is

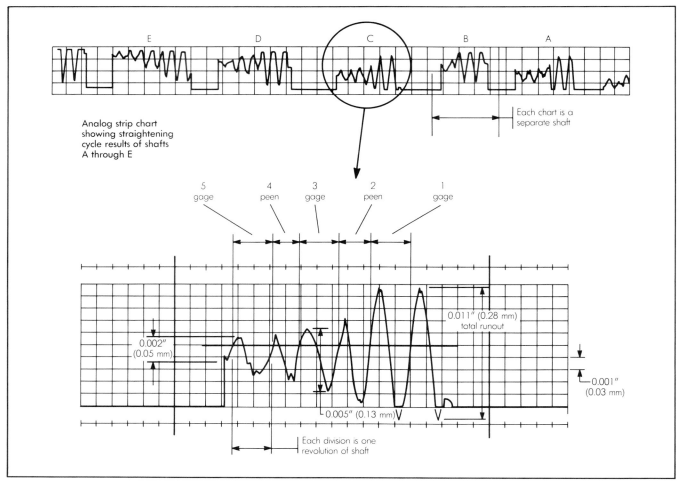

**Fig. 10-65 Graphic strip chart readout of operations and results in a typical peen-straightening cycle, applied to five camshafts.** (*Industrial Metal Products Corp.*)

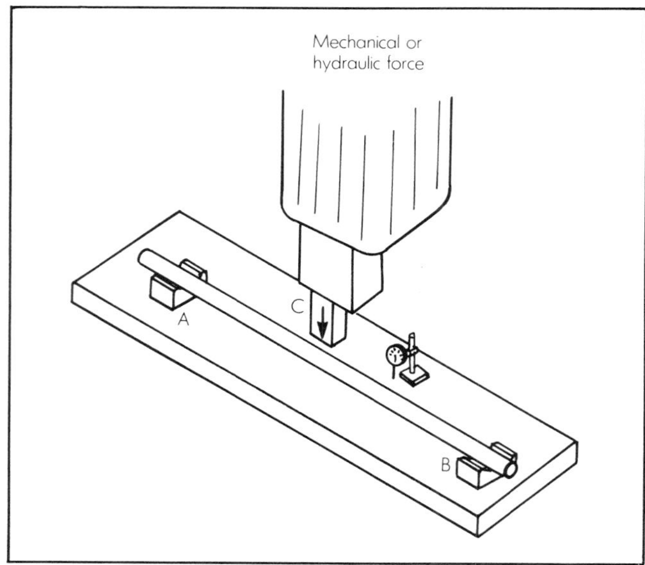


**Fig. 10-66 Press straightening.**

generally used on long-run straightening jobs of heavy shafts and intricate crankshafts.

**Universal machine.** Figure 10-67 illustrates, schematically, a fully automatic universal machine, capable of straightening a variety of parts, such as transmission shafts, camshafts, and crankshafts. Production rates range from 60-300 pieces per hour. The tolerances for each straightening position are continuously displayed on a digital readout. The carriage moves the part horizontally to the required position under the ram for straightening. Anvil supports are positioned automatically below the part to remove S-bends or to straighten long parts. Each part usually requires its own straightening program. A selector enables quick changeover for multiple part programs, which are controlled by a microprocessor and/or a programmable controller.

**Stroke-control.** One type of straightening press uses a stroke-controlled system. This system differs from the more commonly used pressure-controlled systems in which the straightening force must be carefully adjusted to remain above the metal's elastic limit, yet below the yield point.

In stroke-controlled automatic straightening presses, stroke length is calculated and adjusted individually, based on automatic measurement of results from each successive straightening

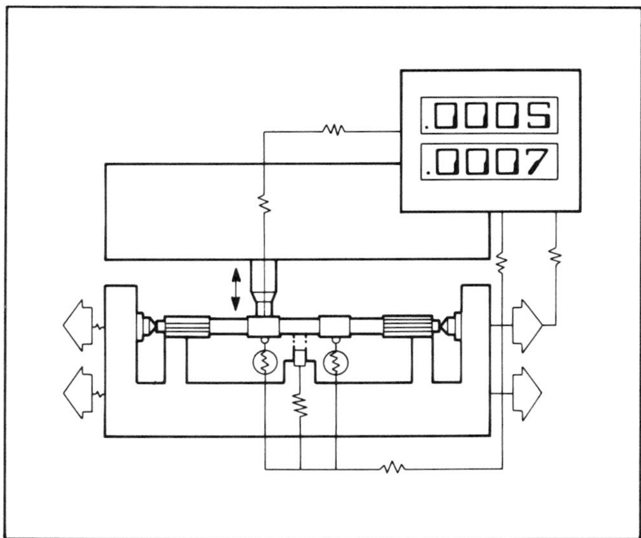


**Fig. 10-67 Fully automatic universal straightening machine with digital readout. The part is supported on centers and rotated to the correct radial position automatically, as indicated by the readout.** (*Industrial Metal Products Corp.*)

stroke. No programming is needed, and stepless adjustment of stroke length is provided. The zero runout value is determined for each workpiece; this eliminates the need for setting an absolute zero value on the measuring device.

Automatic compensation of the stroke setting is based on the difference in daylight, as well as on punch and anvil lengths. A variety of shafts and bars can be straightened at production rates up to 350 parts per hour, with minimal reliance on operator skill.[10]

## Bulldozer

Hydraulic presses are widely used for straightening because they offer excellent control of the ram stroke and speed for incremental operations on large plate and structural sections. (Refer to Chapter 5, "Presses for Sheet Metal Forming," for additional information on hydraulic presses.) These presses are available in a wide variety of designs and capacities, ranging from simple, low-tonnage, shop presses to very large, horizontal bulldozers. Tonnages range from 25-1000 tons (222-8896 kN) and larger.

The hydraulic bulldozer (see Fig. 10-68) is a commonly used straightening-type press. It is a heavy-duty machine that incorporates the basic design of a large gap press laid on its back. Main components consist of a large, horizontal frame with the cylinder mounted on one end. A movable end-lug substitutes for the conventional bed bolster. The hydraulic power unit may be mounted directly behind the cylinder, or it can be a separate floor-mounted unit behind the main frame. The throat area and stroke lengths can be sizable, but the main advantage is the ability to handle work that is brought into the press from overhead. This is a considerable benefit for large structural members or heavy steel plates that must be handled by overhead cranes and then formed in the horizontal plane. Applications include straightening, bending, and punching of plate and structural shapes (I-beams, rails, and bars). Additionally, hoops, rings, and large irregular shapes can be formed due to the relatively unrestricted die area.

## Parallel-Roll Straightening

Square or rectangular bars are often straightened by parallel rolling, which is similar to parallel-roll straightening of stock described previously. This operation also can be performed on stamped parts. Its primary advantage is a relatively high production rate, with the disadvantage of satisfactory straightening generally only on flat or symmetrical-shaped parts. The outer ends of parts also may tend to be slightly distorted.

## Rotary-Roll (Cross-Axis) Straightening

Cross-axis, or skewed, rotary-roll straighteners are composed of two or more rolls with roll axes at an angle to the axis of the part, as shown schematically in Fig. 10-69. On the two-roll straightener, one roll is concave and the other straight, and both rolls are driven. The pressure of the straight roll forces the part into the concave roll. Top and bottom guides align the axis of the part with the centerline of its path through the rolls. The angularity of the rolls and the roll pressure determine the amount of bend put into the part. The rolls being driven feed the part through the straightener. The part is straightened because the surface of the part is being alternately subjected to compressive and tensile stresses as it rotates through the straightener. This type of straightening is particularly suited to short lengths. One of its advantages is that all bending occurs within one set of rolls with no variance in size. It can rough-straighten hot-rolled, round bars; it can straighten and size cold-rolled bars; it can burnish or polish ground bars; and it can round out the ends of bars flattened when sheared.

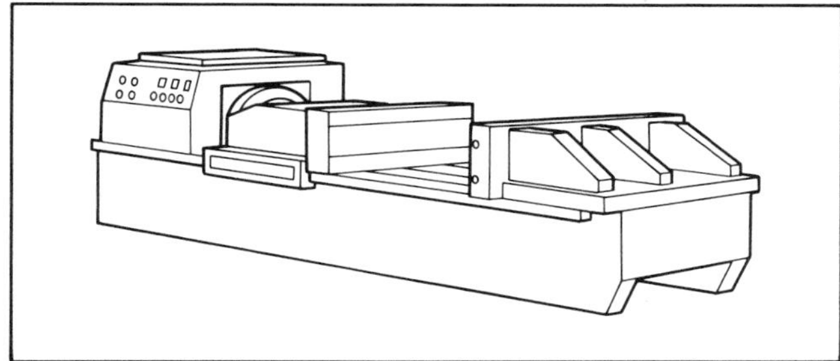

**Fig. 10-68 Hydraulic bulldozer.** (*Pacific Press and Shear Co.*)

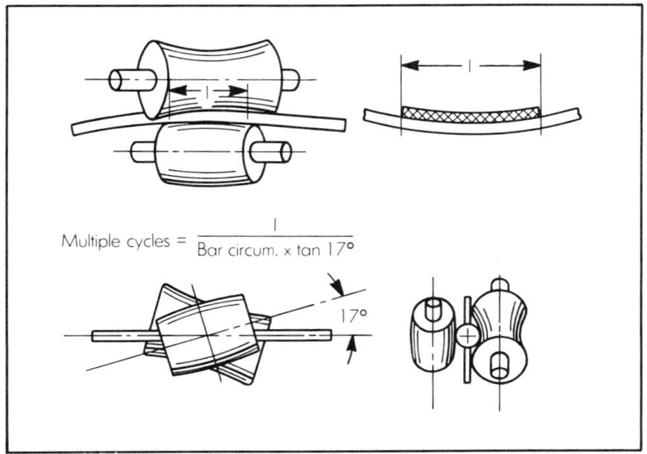


**Fig. 10-69 Operating principle of two-roll, cross-axis, skewed, rotary straightener.** (*The Medart Co.*)

Another form of this type of straightener is the multiple-roll unit. These straighteners generally have from five to nine rolls. The advantages of the multiple-roll straightener are faster operation than is possible on the two-roll type, a higher production rate, a much more symmetrical stress pattern, and less tendency to work harden the part. Disadvantages are the possibility of varying size over the length of the part and the need for the part to be of a constant cross section.

## Automatic Press Roll Straightening

The roll straightening method is used primarily for soft shafts; it is among the fastest straightening processes available. The rolling method uses support and straightening roll assemblies similar in construction to a roller V-block and a headstock unit equipped with a drive mechanism to rotate the part. Hardened shafts generally up to $R_C38$ may be straightened, provided the depth of hardness is not excessive. As illustrated in Fig. 10-70, this type of straightener utilizes a press frame with a hydraulically powered ram. Mounted on the bed of the machine are two or more lower support roll assemblies. Mounted on the ram are one or more upper support roll assemblies. One upper and two lower rolls are used when a simple bow is to be straightened. A series of bows, or snaking, requires additional roll assemblies. A driving mechanism is mounted on one end of the base and drives either a chuck or driver. This type of equipment is designed to straighten solid parts that are basically cylindrical and tubular parts that have sufficient wall thickness to prevent deformation from the pressure of the rolls.

The part is placed on the lower idler rolls. The chuck or driver moves forward, engages the part, and starts it rotating. Pressure is applied by one or more sets of overhead rolls, deflecting the part in a bow-like arc while it rotates. This action places a plastic strain within the material. When the material has been carried through the yield point, the ram action is reversed until the cycle is completed.

Advantages of this type of straightening are a stretch-relieving action, as well as a straightening action, and the ability to handle a variety of types and degrees of out-of-straightness. Concentric parts with no ovality can be held to a fine tolerance and a minimal operator skill requirement. A disadvantage is that it cannot straighten parts that are not round, thin-wall tubes, or parts that have variable diameters.

Production rates vary depending upon the mass of the part, the amount of ovality, and the tolerance of the straightness required. Small concentric parts can run as high as 1200 per hour, while larger parts, such as cold extrusions for axles and transmission shafts, may run as low as 225 per hour.

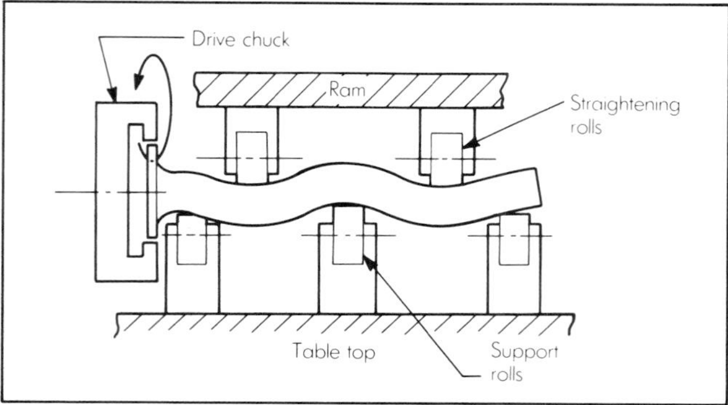


**Fig. 10-70 Automatic press roll straightening.** (*Industrial Metal Products Corp.*)

## Parallel-Rail Straightening

As used for cylindrical or tubular parts, this method employs a series of parallel rails located on a slide, with corresponding parallel rails located on a ram or head above and between the bottom rails. As shown in Fig. 10-71, a round or tubular part is placed between the rails, the ram lowers an adjustable amount by hydraulic pressure, thereby overbending the part. At the same time, the lower slide moves forward and rotates the part, and the pressure decreases to zero by the end of the stroke. At that point, the part has then been straightened.

Symmetrically round parts, or parts with multiple diameters and heads (such as bolts and spindles), can be straightened in such a manner by allowing the unlike diameters to locate between the straightening rails. The number and position of rails can be adjusted according to the size and characteristics of the part.

With hand loading and unloading, production rates of 500-600 pieces per hour can be achieved. Production rates of 1000 pieces or more per hour can be reached with automatic loading and unloading. The advantages of parallel-rail straightening are that the required operator skill is minimal; adjustment for different sizes of parts is easy; a relatively high production rate is possible; no straightness measuring, other than an occasional quality-control check, is necessary; parts with headed areas or multiple diameters can be straightened; and tooling costs are low. The disadvantage is that part length is limited to the width of the machine, generally a maximum of 24" (610 mm) long and 0.8" (20 mm) diam.

## Epicyclic Straightening

This type of straightener is particularly suited to straightening linear parts, tubing, and solid cylindrical sections in a variety of shapes. In operation, the part is securely supported in locating fixtures at either end. The straightening arm secures the part in the approximate center of its length. (Some parts require the use of additional straightening arms because of their length and/or configuration.) The arm is powered to move in a preprogrammed trajectory about the neutral axis of the part. The motion is increased in amplitude until the cross section of the part is taken through its elastic limit. At this point, the motion decreases, moving the arm to a stationary position at the part's neutral axis and producing a straight and stable part.

Among the parts for which this type of straightener is used are I-beam axles; trailer axles; asymmetrical forgings; and thin-wall, propeller-shaft or drive-shaft tubes. Production rates vary from 80 parts per hour (trailer axles) to 300 parts per hour (propeller-shaft tubes).

The motion for round parts is a circular path; but for parts with varying cross sections, such as an I-beam section, the motion is elliptical. The feed rate to bring the part to the yield point is set to work as rapidly as possible. The feed rate to bring the part back to its neutral axis is set for the degree of straightness required, while the time cycle desired is also considered. Figure 10-72 shows circular and elliptical paths of the epicyclic-motion arm.

## Moving-Insert Straightening

For linear, flat, or irregularly shaped parts, moving-insert straightening consists of reciprocal strokes transmitted to tooling inserts by a rotary cam motion. A part is positioned between a series of these inserts in a tool, with spacing set to give the desired bending moments to produce straightness. Alternate reciprocal strokes overbend the part a preset amount, with the amplitude of movement reducing during the cycle to a straight line, at which point the part is straight. The amount of bending movement and the number of bending cycles are adjustable, and different insert spacing can be used for a wide variety of soft or heat-treated components. Figure 10-73 illustrates a setup for moving-insert straightening.

The advantages of this type of straightening are its ability to straighten flat or irregularly shaped parts, with or without projections, bends, etc.; the ability to produce straightness or slight curves if desired (such as in scissors and shear blades); the availability of close tolerances throughout the length of a part, to under 0.001″ (0.03 mm) in certain types of parts; and a minimum operator skill requirement, with only quality-control checking required. Also, when the tooling inserts are at rest, they act as a straightness gage for the part.

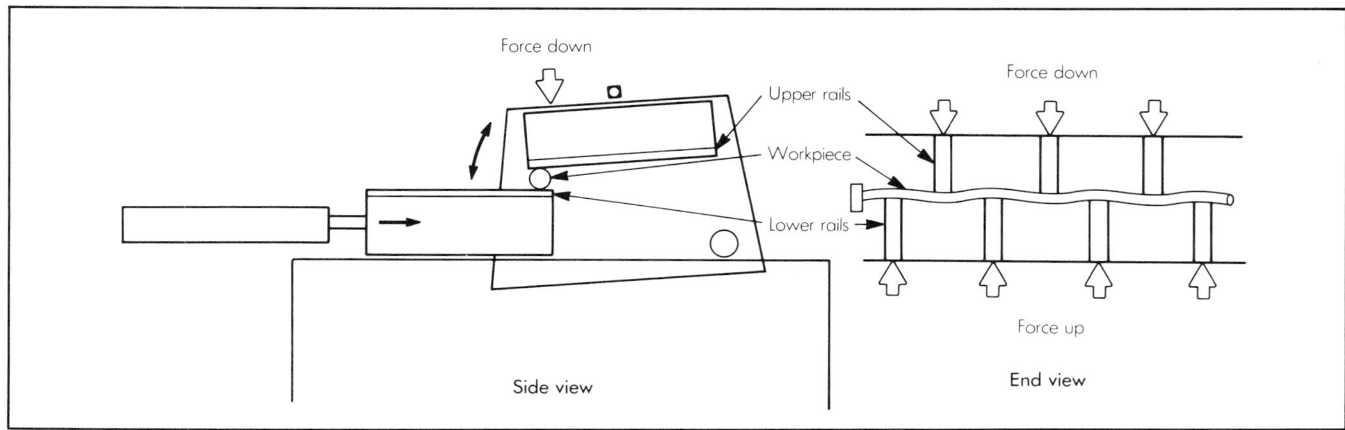


**Fig. 10-71 Parallel-rail straightening, for cylindrical or tubular parts, either symmetrical or with variations in diameter.** (*Bertolette Machines, Inc.*)

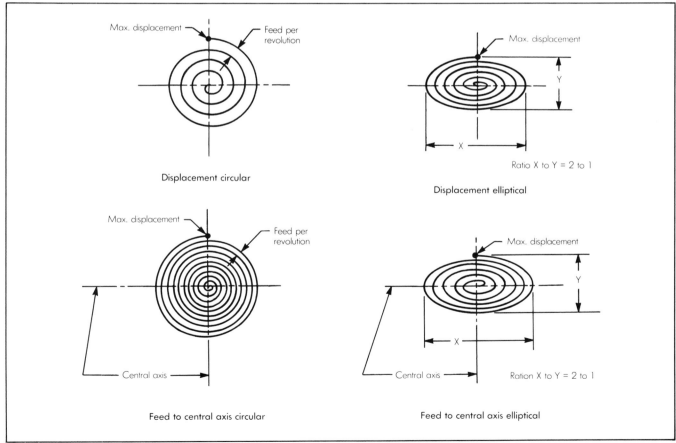

**Fig. 10-72 Circular and elliptical paths of the motion arm on an epicyclic straightener.**

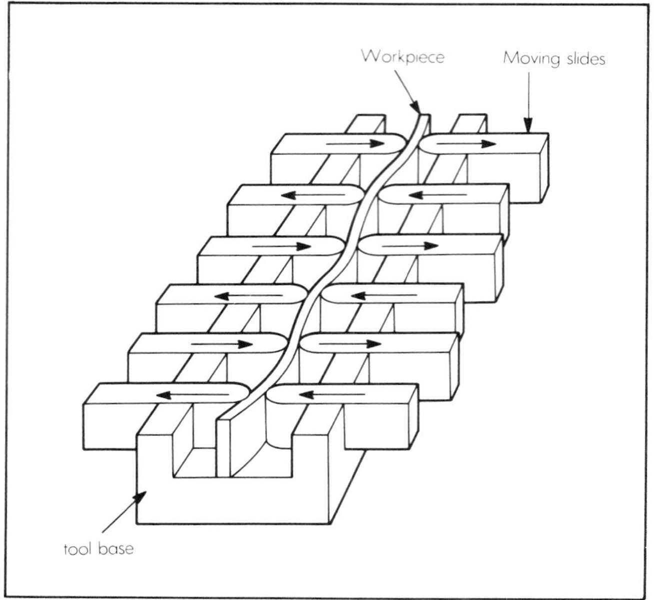


**Fig. 10-73 Moving-insert straightening—for linear, flat, or irregularly shaped parts.** (*Bertolette Machines, Inc.*)

## TOOLING

Tooling requirements for straightening vary with the type of equipment used. Tools range from hammers, mallets, grooved blocks, vises, and levers for the simplest types of manual straightening to hardened-steel rolls of various contours, including concave, grooved, and flat, required for the parallel and rotary-roll straightening equipment. For the automatic press roll straighteners, tooling consists of crowned rolls, hardened and ground, and hardened-steel chuck jaw inserts or hardened-steel lug drivers. The tooling for eipcyclic straighteners consists of interchangeable inserts for the fixed arm and movable arm clamps to accommodate various sizes and shapes of parts. For parallel-rail straightening, a series of hardened and ground rails are used. Moving-insert straightening requires individual sets of tools, or parts of them, for different sizes and shapes of components.

Handling devices for straightening range from manual handling devices to various types of walking-beam transports used with automatic straightening equipment. Many of the newer types of straighteners can be equipped with automatic controls. Integrated straightening and machining lines are available that can be equipped with pregaging and regaging equipment. Sonic test equipment, particularly adapted to check for chevrons in cold-extruded shafts such as axle shafts and main shafts, can be integrated into these systems. In fully automated systems, inspection operations can be linked with rejection stations to provide automatic rejection of parts that do not conform to the specifications.

### References

1. Daniel B. Dallas, "Metricating the Pressworking Equations," *Manufacturing Engineering* (February 1976), pp. 36-41.
2. American National Standards Institute, "American National Standard for Machine Tools—Power Press Brakes—Safety Requirements for Construction, Care, and Use," ANSI B11.3-1982.
3. Patrick E. Oldenburg, *The Art of Forming*, Di-Acro Division, Houdaille Industries, Inc.
4. Gary S. Vasilash, "A New Approach to Bending," *Manufacturing Engineering* (March 1982), pp. 87-89.
5. Oldenburg, *op. cit.*
6. Ronald Stange, Catalog No. 1071 and Rotary Draw Bending Guide (Wall Chart), Tools for Bending, Inc. Presented at AFIT/FMA Conference, 1982.
7. Joseph Ivaska and Ralph Scroggins, "Lubrication Expertise—A Productive Tool in Tube Fabrication," FMA Paper No. G-1250, American Fabricating Institute of Technology (AFIT), an educational affiliate of the Fabricating Manufacturers Association, Tube Fabricating Conference, 1982.
8. Joseph J. Kirby, "Automated Tube Bending—A Technology Update," Presentation at AFIT/FMA Conference, 1982.
9. Alan Williamson, "Meeting Wall Thinning and Ovality Specifications When Bending Pipe," Conrac Machine Tool Co., Pipe wall thinning tutorial paper.
10. Transmares Corporation, Technical information on Eitel straightening presses, and Eitel Bulletin 12.101.

### Bibliography

Altan, Taylan. "Metalforming's New Shape." *American Machinist* (December 1981), pp. 122-123.

Berkeley, Harrison C. *Production Tube Cut-Off.* SME Technical Paper MF79-447, 1979.

Dallas, Daniel B. *Pressworking Aids for Designers and Diemakers (Metric & Customary Units).* Society of Manufacturing Engineers, Dearborn, MI, 1978.

Eary, Donald F., and Reed, Edward A. *Techniques of Pressworking Sheet Metal.* Prentice-Hall, Inc., Englewood Cliffs, NJ, 1974.

Fenn Manufacturing Company. "Wire Flattening Formulas for Determining Proper Mill Size."

Foley, Robert L. "Rotary Bending Offers a New Approach to Press Brake Bending." *FMA's Journal of the Fabricator* (October 1982), pp. 1 and 18-19).

Hill, Larry. *Gauging Improvements for Increased Productivity from Power Press Brakes.* SME/FMA Technical Paper presented at FabTech International, 1981.

Houston, David L. *Multiple Axis CNC Hydraulic Press Brakes.* SME Technical Paper MF79-613, 1979.

Maropis, Nicholas. *Fabricating Miniature Tubing.* SME Technical Paper MF80-930, 1980.

McRae, Robert C. *The Economics of 1 1/2 x D Welds Ells Vs. 3 x D Bends.* SME/FMA Technical Paper presented at FabTech International, 1981.

Nussbaum, A.I. "Wire Flattening—An Appraisal of Theory and Practice." *Wire and Wire Products* (February and March 1955).

Pozzo, Richard W. *Automatic Backgauging for Press Brakes.* SME/FMA Technical Paper presented at FabTech International, 1981.

Stange, Ronald R. *Tooling Specifications and Bending Techniques.* SME Technical Paper MF79-451, 1979.

*Tooling, Manufacturing Engineering and Management*, vol. 69, no. 4 (October 1972), pp. 15-16.

Verson Allsteel Press Co. *Die Manual*, Catalog DM-73.

Weinmann, K.J. *Deformation and Springback on 90° V-Die Bending of Steel Plate.* SME Technical Paper MF79-601, 1979.

Wilson, Frank W. *Die Design Handbook*, 2nd ed. Society of Manufacturing Engineers, McGraw-Hill Book Co., NY, 1965.

CHAPTER

11

# Shearing

# SHEARING

Shearing is a process by which large sheets of material are cut into pieces of smaller length and width. These pieces are often used in subsequent operations such as punching and forming. Shearing is also used to produce blanks or slugs to be used in subsequent forming and machining processes. Because shearing is often the initial step in a series of processes, it is essential that the operating procedures result in an accurate workpiece.

Other operations related to shearing such as notching, nibbling, and piercing are included in Chapter 12, "Punching." For information on blanking, Chapter 4, "Sheet Metal Blanking and Forming," should be referenced.

**CHAPTER CONTENTS:**



## GLOSSARY OF SHEARING TERMS

**back-gage** A surface on two or more supports located behind the shear that can be positioned accurately either manually or automatically to control part size.

**bed** The stationary part of the shear frame that supports the material being sheared and the fixed blade.

**blade** A replaceable tool having one or more cutting edges.

**bow** The tendency of material being sheared to curl downward during shearing, particularly when shearing long narrow strips.

**brake** A mechanism used to stop the motion of the shear ram and hold it in a stopped position when the clutch is disengaged.

**burnishing** The result of the movable blade rubbing against the edge of the sheared material due to a blade clearance that is adjusted too tight.

**camber** The tendency of material being sheared from a sheet to bend away from the sheet in the same plane.

**clearance** The distance between the blades of a shear.

**clutch** An assembly that connects the flywheel to the driveshaft either directly or through a gear train to impart motion to the crosshead.

**continuous operation** Uninterrupted multiple strokes of the crosshead without intervening stops at the end of individual strokes.

**counterbalance** A mechanism, apart from the drive, that is used partially or wholly to balance or support the weight of the crosshead assembly.

**crosshead** A moving member on which the upper knife is mounted.

**cycle** A complete move of the crosshead from an initial start position and return to that same starting position.

**drop** The part of a sheared sheet that drops behind the shear after shearing.

**eccentric** The offset portion of the driveshaft that governs the stroke or distance the crosshead moves on a mechanically or manually powered shear.

**fixed blade** The stationary blade having one or more cutting edges.

**front-gage** Same as back-gage except that the locating fingers or surfaces are in front of the shear bed blade.

**full-revolution clutch** A type of clutch that, when tripped, cannot be disengaged until the crosshead has completed a full cycle.

**gaging mechanism** The mechanism for locating the workpiece relative to the blade cutting edge.

**gap** An opening or recess in the housings to permit shearing or slitting material longer than the width of the shear. Also referred to as a throat.

**gap frame** Frame with a cutout to allow slitting or notching.

**gibbing** Guide bars that guide the crosshead as it moves down the sideways.

**hold-down** The mechanism used to clamp the workpiece to the bed so that it does not move during shearing.

**hold-down beam** A full-length member extending between the endframes on which hold-downs are mounted.

**hydraulic shear** A shear with its crosshead actuated by hydraulic cylinders.

**knife** *See* Blade.


***Contributors of sections of this chapter are:*** *James W. Bowman, Director of Marketing, Pacific Press and Shear Company; John Buta, Vice President of Engineering, Paxson Machine Company; R. L. Butchart, Jr., Vice President-Marketing, Wysong and Miles Company; John Gehring, Sales Manager, Paxson Machine Company; Patrick E. Oldenburg, Training Center Manager, Di-Acro Division, Houdaille Industries, Inc.; Dale D. Oliver, Application Engineer, Di-Acro Division, Houdaille Industries, Inc.; Robert L. Rachor, President, Lynch Machinery Co., Inc.; Richard A. Sprick, Product Specialist, Di-Acro Division, Houdaille Industries, Inc.; Ronald E. VanWieringen, Product Manager, Wiedemann Division, Warner and Swasey Company.*

***Reviewers of sections of this chapter are:*** *James W. Bowman, Director of Marketing, Pacific Press and Shear Company; Watson Brown, Assistant Manager, Cleveland Knife Division, The Hill Acme Company; John D. Bryzgel, Product Manager of Cutoff Equipment, The Fenn Mfg. Co., A Unit of AMCA International; John R. Buta, Vice President of Engineering, Paxson Machine Company; Robert L. Butchart, Jr., Vice President-Marketing, Wysong and Miles Company; Ralph H. Caldwell, Engineer, Wysong and Miles Company; Larry Conley, Senior Project Engineer, Di-Acro Division, Houdaille Industries, Inc.; John H. Gehring, Sales Manager, Paxson Machine Company; Paul Lancaster, Vice President of Engineering, W.A. Whitney Corp.; Robert L. Rachor, President, Lynch Machinery Co., Inc.; Ronald E. VanWieringen, Product Manager, Wiedemann Division, Warner and Swasey Company; L. Frank Wagoner, Engineer, Wysong and Miles Company.*

# SHEARING PRINCIPLES

**mechanical shear** A shear with its crosshead driven by an eccentric which is engaged by a flywheel-clutch combination.

**movable blade** A blade having one or more cutting edges that is attached to the crosshead.

**part-revolution clutch** A type of clutch that may be engaged or disengaged during any part of the cycle.

**penetration** The actual percentage of total material thickness that the blade has to enter to shear the material.

**pin gaging** A variation of front-gaging in which the sheet is accurately positioned over pins by means of prepunched holes.

**programmable gaging** Back-gaging in which the gage bar is driven by an encoder signal or servomotor that can be programmed by the operator.

**rake** The inclination of one blade with respect to the other in the shearing plane.

**rotary blade** A shearing tool whose cutting edge makes a complete revolution about a fixed axis.

**secondary shear** The condition occurring on material when the blades are too tight.

**shearing** The parting of material resulting when one blade forces the material past an opposing blade.

**shear lance gaging** Gaging by means of reference points made during punching.

**slideway** A member that guides the crosshead downward during the shearing cycle.

**swing beam** A shear design in which the crosshead swings from a bearing point to the rear of the shear.

**twist** The tendency of material (strip) that is being sheared off to curve about a central longitudinal axis.

## SHEARING PRINCIPLES

The term *shearing* is derived from the method in which the blade edges meet in a progression from one side to the other, the same as an ordinary pair of scissors. The angle at which the blades are aligned to one another is termed blade rake angle, and the distance that the blades are separated is termed blade or knife clearance.

The principle of shearing is simply that as the blades come together and contact the material being sheared, the blades penetrate the material until the tensile strength is overcome and a crack or tear, called the slip plane, develops from both sides (see Fig. 11-1, *a*). Blade clearance has a considerable effect on the quality of the sheared edge. If the planes match, a clean cut is produced. If they do not match, a tear occurs if the gap is too great; if the gap is too small, a tongue develops and is recut as the blade passes (see Fig. 11-1, *b*). Insufficient blade clearance results in a poor edge condition; and recutting the tongue is commonly called secondary shear.

During the shearing process, as the knife continues down, freeing the sheared piece from the original metal, the wall of the knife rubs against the metal to cause an area of burnish that extends along the length of the metal where the knife makes contact with it. The sheared piece of metal rubs against the wall of the lower knife, causing a second burnish area on the metal.

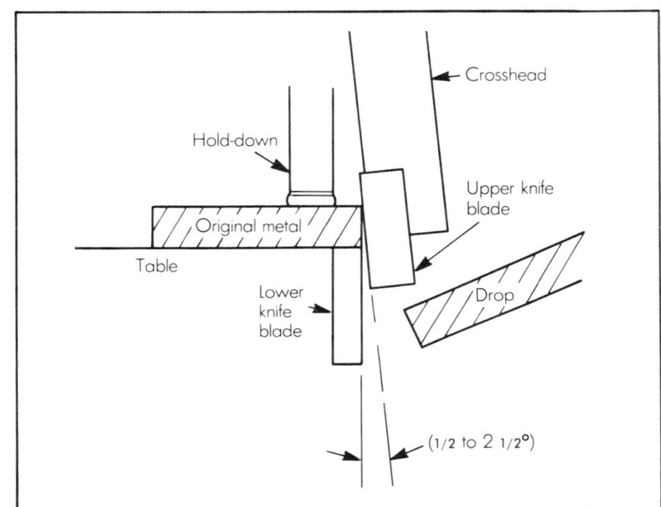


**Fig. 11-2 Alignment of upper knife with respect to the vertical plane.** (*Edward A. Lynch Machinery Co.*)

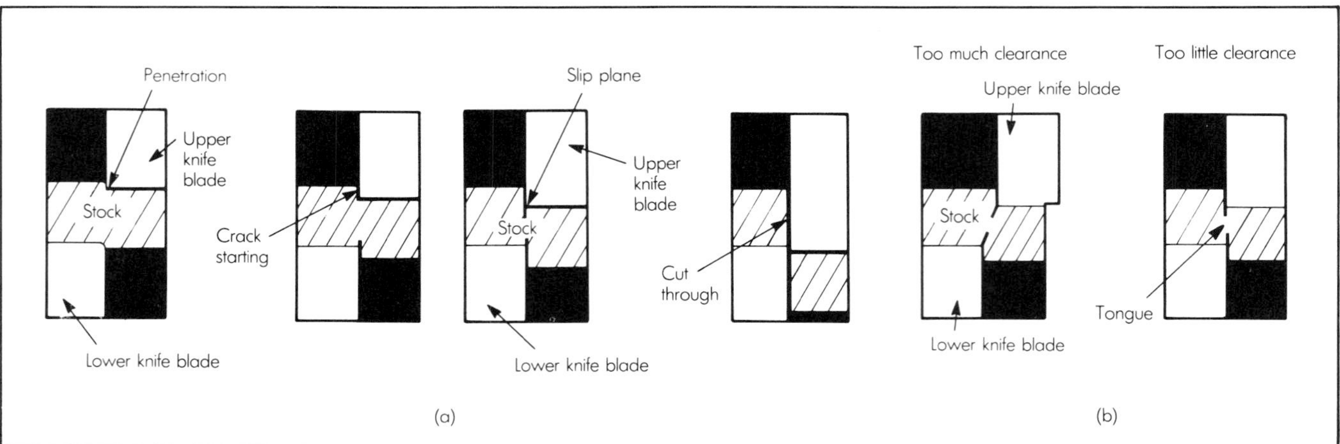


**Figure 11-1 Sequence of steps in shearing action: (a) with proper blade clearance and (b) with improper blade clearance.** (*Di-Acro Division, Houdaille Industries, Inc.*)

A burr occurs on the sheared piece because the fracture starts just above the cutting edge of the knife, not at the exact corner of the knife edge. Another burr is formed on the original metal piece by the fracture starting just off the exact corner of the knife edge.

On the top of the original metal, some plastic deformation can be seen as a slightly rounded edge. This same rounded edge can be seen on the sheared piece. (The sheared piece is also called a "drop.") The amount of plastic deformation (rounded edge) is a function of the percent of penetration and the clearance between the knife blades. For example, if the percent of penetration is high, say 50%, the knife must enter the metal halfway before the fracture occurs. This causes more plastic deformation than would result with a piece of harder metal with a percent of penetration of 25%, because the knife does not have to enter the harder material more than a quarter of its thickness to achieve shearing.

On most shears, the upper knife is slanted at an angle (see Fig. 11-2). Generally, this angle is set between 1/2 and 2 1/2°. An angle of 2 1/2° reduces the shear load by as much as 25%, but the squareness of cut and edge quality are affected. This inclination causes the knife to move down and to back away from the lower knife. This action ensures that the sheared piece will not become wedged between the two knife blades, and it helps to concentrate the shearing force in the exact area of blade engagement between the two knives. This action also causes the fractures to start on a straight line approximately parallel to the surface of the knife.

# SHEARING CAPABILITIES AND ADVANTAGES

To be considered shearing, the cutting process must take place along a straight line on the workpiece. This limits the type of work performed on a shear. However, the shear is frequently used to cut wide coils into large blanks, to cut coils into narrow strips, to square blank edges in order to produce accurate blanks, and to cut parts to specific size.

Shearing offers several advantages over most metalcutting operations. Since shearing is a chipless operation, waste scrap is reduced. The shearing process is a much faster process because the blades do not have to cut through the full thickness of the material, as is required in some of the typical metalcutting processes. Instead, the blades penetrate only slightly into the material, causing a slip plane to develop which then severs the material.

On properly sheared workpieces, secondary operations to remove burrs from edges are generally not necessary. The accuracy of a shear is high. Using machines that are not fully automated, accuracies of ±1/64" (±0.4 mm) are not uncommon; and using automated equipment, accuracies of ±0.005 to ±0.010" (±0.13 to ±0.25 mm) are readily obtained. Most shear blades have cutting edges on all four sides; therefore, the length of time before regrinding becomes necessary is extended. Shearing is more economical than some operations because expensive tooling is not required to produce accurate blanks.

**TABLE 11-1**
**Shear Capacity for Different Metals and Alloys Relative to Mild Steel**

| Material | Material Thickness, in. (mm) | | | | | | |
|---|---|---|---|---|---|---|---|
| Mild steel* | 10 gage (3.4) | 3/16 (4.8) | 1/4 (6.4) | 3/8 (9.5) | 1/2 (12.7) | 5/8 (15.9) | 3/4 (19) |
| Aluminum alloys | | | | | | | |
| 1100-0, 2024-0 | 7/32 (5.6) | 5/16 (7.9) | 3/8 (9.5) | 5/8 (15.9) | 3/4 (19) | 1 (25.4) | 1 3/16 (30.2) |
| 2024-T3, 6061-T6, 7075-T4 | 1/4 (6.4) | 3/8 (9.5) | 1/2 (12.7) | 3/4 (19) | 1 (25.4) | 1 1/4 (31.8) | 1 1/2 (38) |
| Titanium GAL-4V | 10 gage (3.4) | 3/16 (4.8) | 1/4 (6.4) | 3/8 (9.5) | 1/2 (12.7) | 5/8 (15.9) | 3/4 (19) |
| Steel | | | | | | | |
| 1020, 1040, 4340 | 10 gage (3.4) | 3/16 (4.8) | 1/4 (6.4) | 3/8 (9.5) | 1/2 (12.7) | 5/8 (15.9) | 3/4 (19) |
| A242, A374, A375 | 11 gage (3) | 3/16 (4.8) | 1/4 (6.4) | 5/16 (7.9) | 7/16 (11) | 9/16 (14.3) | 11/16 (17.5) |
| A36, A212 | 10 gage (3.4) | 3/16 (4.8) | 1/4 (6.4) | 3/8 (9.5) | 1/2 (12.7) | 5/8 (15.9) | 3/4 (19) |
| Stainless steel | | | | | | | |
| 302, 304, 410 | 12 gage (2.7) | 10 gage (3.4) | 3/16 (4.8) | 9/32 (7) | 3/8 (9.5) | 1/2 (12.7) | 5/8 (15.9) |

* Based on 50,000 psi (345 MPa) shear strength.

# SHEAR CONSTRUCTION

Shears are used to cut mild, high-strength alloy, and other steels, as well as nonferrous and nonmetallic materials of all kinds. In general, materials should be no harder than $R_C30$.

The workpiece capacity of shears generally ranges from very light gages to 1 1/2″ (1.5 to 38 mm) in thickness and from 12 to 240″ (305 to mm) in width. The capacity in alloy and high-strength steels generally is 2/3 to 3/4 the mild steel capacity of the shear. For aluminum, the capacity is generally 1 1/4 to 1 1/2 times the mild steel capacity. Table 11-1 gives the capacity of a shear for different metals and alloys relative to mild steel.

Tensile strength alone is commonly employed as the indicator of the shearing load, but it is not the only factor. Elongation is also a factor; for example, copper with low tensile strength but high elongation requires as much pressure to shear as mild steel.

## SHEAR CONSTRUCTION

Most shears are constructed from either steel plate that is welded or bolted (or a combination of the two) or from ductile iron castings.

Shear frames constructed from steel plate are less expensive than ductile iron frames and permit the fabrication of odd sizes. However, on mechanical shears, a special reinforced foundation may be required to reduce the effects of shock that are transmitted to the foundation. Ductile iron frames are generally heavier than steel frames due to the inherent design, but they provide greater strength and rigidity than the steel frames. The shock absorbing capability of ductile iron frames is also another advantage.

The elements of a typical shear are illustrated in Fig. 11-3. The upper knife is mounted at an angle or slope with respect to the horizontal lower knife. The lower knife is rigidly supported by the table and bed for accurate alignment and knife clearance. The frame can be constructed with or without a gap depending upon the work that is to be performed on the shear.

A workholding device is as important in shearing as it is in precision machining. Hold-down feet clamp the sheet or plate to the table to prevent movement during the shearing operation. Hold-downs can be either mechanically or hydraulically actuated. Mechanical hold-downs utilize springs whose pressure is automatically determined by the spring deflection. Hydraulic hold-downs use hydraulic pressure to clamp the material to the table; the pressure can be adjusted so that soft or highly polished surfaces are not damaged or marred. With either method, the hold-down feet can be furnished with mar-resistant caps to prevent surface damage or marring. Some hold-down feet can be offset, decreasing the distance between the shear knife edge and the hold-down, to facilitate the shearing of narrow sheets.

The three basic shear design configurations for crosshead action are (1) overdriven, (2) underdriven, (3) swing beam.

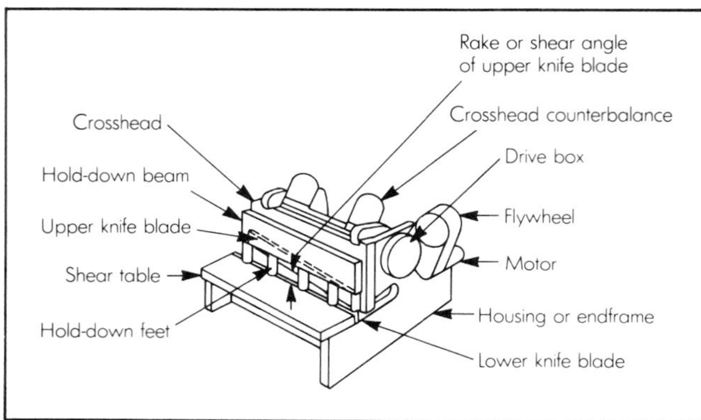


**Fig. 11-3 Components of a typical shear.**

### OVERDRIVEN SHEARS

Overdriven shears (see Fig. 11-4) were formerly quite popular and still offer several advantages. These include the capability of slitting or notching by moving the sheet through the machine. If the machine uses a swing beam design, it will offer an easy adjustment of the blade clearance. Since the machine has nothing in back of it, a clear area exists for the drop to fall and for sheared parts to be stacked.

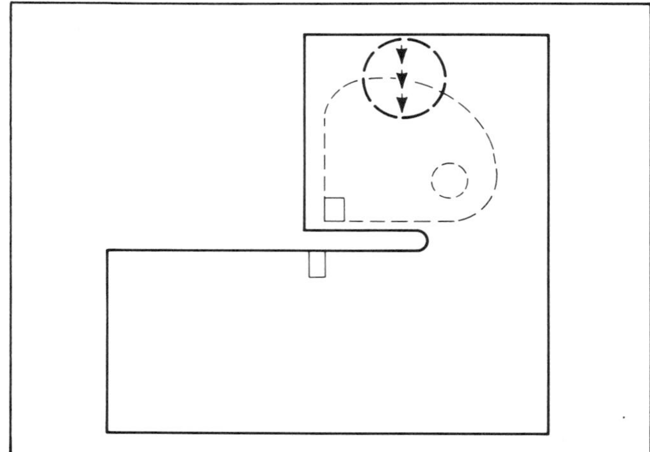

**Fig. 11-4 Overdriven ram design with gap frame.** (*Di-Acro Division, Houdaille Industries, Inc.*)

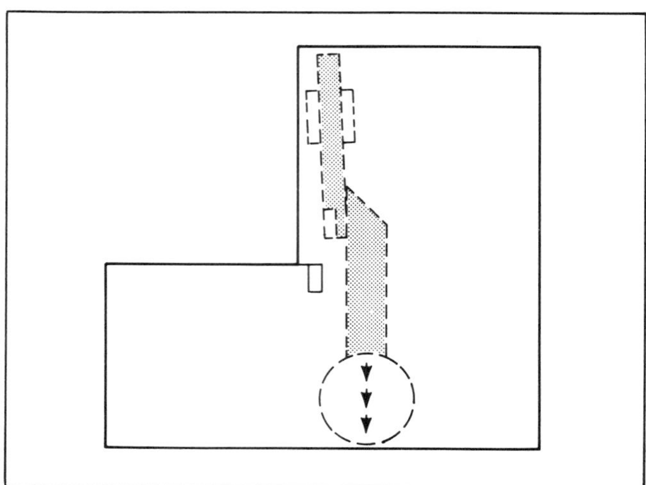

**Fig. 11-5 Underdriven ram design.** (*Di-Acro Division, Houdaille Industries, Inc.*)

### UNDERDRIVEN SHEARS

Underdriven shears (see Fig. 11-5) offer lower silhouette, lower weight, and lower cost than overdriven shears. Since generally no gap exists (the side plates completely enclose the ends), the frame is basically highly stable without being unduly heavy. Obviously, an underdriven shear cannot slit or notch.

### SWINGING BEAM SHEARS

Swing beam shears (see Fig. 11-6) offer the advantage of a blade clearance adjustment that is quick and easy. Also,there is no need to incline the crosshead, so another variable can be eliminated from the operating parameters of the shear. However, this type of shear requires a special spirally ground top blade to compensate for the combination of the radius and the rake of the top blade. The upper blade holder must also be spirally ground.

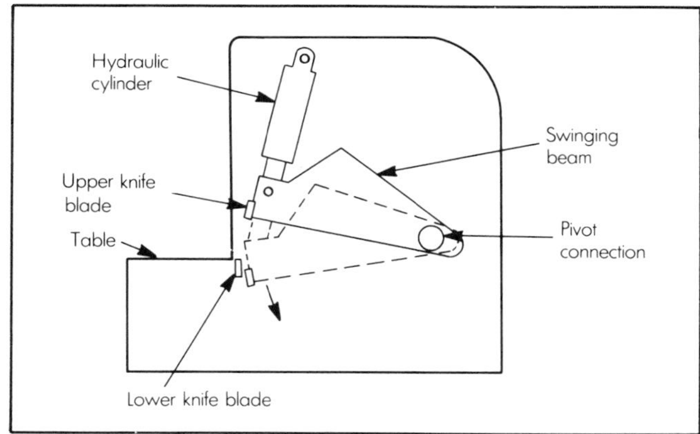


**Fig. 11-6 Swinging-beam ram design.** (*Pacific Press and Shear Company*)

# TYPES OF SHEARS

Although shears are made in a wide variety of sizes and styles to satisfy the needs of the metal fabricator, they can be classified according to either (1) the means by which the crosshead is driven or (2) the type of work that the shear was designed to perform. Some shears are capable of performing more than one type of work but can still be classified under these general categories.

## CROSSHEAD DRIVE

Crosshead drive is the means by which the crosshead is powered. It can be (1) manual, (2) mechanical, (3) hydraulic, or (4) pneumatic.

### Manual Drive

The manually driven crosshead is actuated by either a hand-operated lever or a foot treadle that extends the full length of the shear. The capacity of the manual shear is usually limited to a maximum thickness of 16 gage (1.5 mm) and a sheet width of 12-52″ (305-1320 mm).

This type of shear is often used in a prototype shop, lab, or other facility that would need to perform light shearing on an occassional basis. Advantages of these shears are that they are less expensive and take up less space than a power-driven shear.

### Mechanical Drive

On a shear with a mechanically driven crosshead, two eccentrics on the main shaft move the crosshead in an essentially vertical plane. The main shaft is driven by a reduction gear box powered by an electric motor and a V-belt. The upper blade is usually installed on the crosshead at a fixed slope or rake angle from one end to the other.

Lighter gage shears operate at speeds up to 80 spm, while shears with a capacity exceeding 1/2″ (12.7 mm) operate at speeds up to 50 spm. With these shear speeds and proper handling techniques, 20-30 parts per minute can be produced. The capacity of this type of shear can be as much as 1 1/2″ (38 mm) thick and 240″ (6096 mm) wide.

Advantages of mechanical shears are the speed at which they operate and higher production rates. Disadvantages are that since the drive is rigid and inflexible, high shock loads are common and the stroke cannot be adjusted; each stroke must be completed. Also, damage due to overloading can occur to the shear and the knives because the crosshead cannot stop in the middle of its stroke. Wear is another factor because each stroke is produced by engaging the clutch.

### Hydraulic Drive

The hydraulically driven crosshead utilizes direct-acting hydraulic cylinders or hydraulic cylinders with mechanical linkage to move the crosshead in a vertical direction. The blades of the hydraulic shear are fastened in the same manner as the blades of the mechanical shear. Figure 11-7 shows a hydraulic overdriven shear with a gap frame. Hydraulic shears cutting at full shear length are limited to a speed of 8-15 spm. The capacity, like that of the mechanical shear, can be as thick as 1 1/2″ (38 mm) and as wide as 420″ (10 668 mm).

One significant advantage of the hydraulic shear over the mechanical shear is that it stops when its capacity is exceeded. This prevents damage to the shear itself, but the knives can be damaged as a result of concentrated loading. Controllability is another important feature which allows the operator to adjust the length of the stroke for shearing material of varying thicknesses and hardnesses. A shorter stroke results in a faster cycle time. The hold-down pressure can be adjusted to prevent the marring of highly finished material. The rake angle can be adjusted on hydraulic shears, enabling the operator to increase the shear capacity; however, this reduces workpiece quality.

### Pneumatic Drive

The power of a pneumatically driven ram is derived from one or two air cylinders mounted to move the crosshead in an essentially vertical plane. The flow of air into the cylinder controls both shearing force and speed of the crosshead. Air pressure is also used to return the crosshead to top center, ready for another cut. Air flow is controlled by a pneumatic foot valve or a solenoid air valve that uses a foot-operated electric switch. The air pressure to operate this shear is from an external source.

This type of shear is normally used for sheet material thinner than 20 gage (0.9 mm), but it can be used for material as thick as 14 gage (1.9 mm) mild steel. Any overloading causes the shear to

# CHAPTER 11

## TYPES OF SHEARS

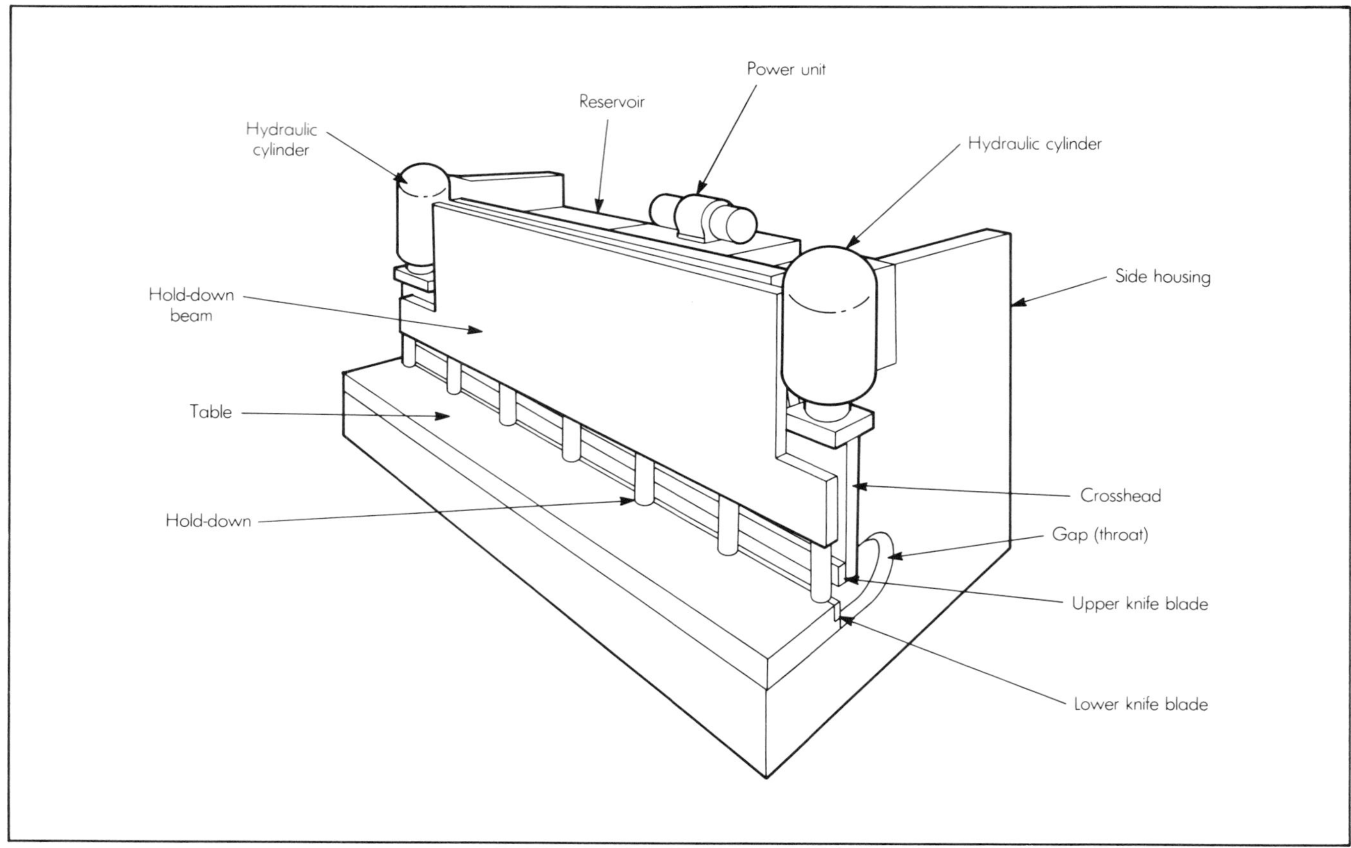


**Fig. 11-7 Hydraulic overdriven shear incorporating a gap frame to facilitate notching and slitting.** (*Pacific Press and Shear Company*)

stop before damage occurs to the shear. The knives, however, can be damaged due to concentrated loading. The pneumatic or air shear can handle sheet lengths ranging from 12-72″ (305-1829 mm). The average speed of the pneumatic shear is between 20 and 30 spm. Advantages of the pneumatic shear over a mechanical shear are the low initial cost and low maintenance.

## SHEAR DESIGN

Design of the shear determines to a large extent the type of work that can be performed. Some of the more common designs are (1) gapless shears, (2) gap shears, (3) alligator or pivot shears, (4) ironworkers, (5) cutoff machines, (6) bar-billet shears, (7) computer numerical control (CNC) shears, and (8) rotary shears.

### Gapless Shears

Gapless shears follow the same concept found in modern press brakes. Two side frames support the power unit and are joined together by the bed and crosshead. Gapless shears are powered manually, mechanically, hydraulically, or pneumatically. Capacity ranges from thin sheet metal to 1 1/2″ (38 mm) plate. The length handled on these shears ranges from 12-240″ (305-6096 mm).

Gapless shears are normally used for the production of large and small straight-sided blanks from sheet and plate. They can also be used for cutting accurate blanks which are used in subsequent metal forming operations.

### Gap Shears

The principle of the gap shear frame is the same as in a gap press. A driving mechanism is located on top of a basically C-type side frame and forces the blade down. Since the frame must support the weight of the power unit as well as the shearing forces, the frame tends to be heavier than a frame used for a gapless shear.

Powered manually, mechanically, hydraulically, or pneumatically, the gap shear has a maximum capacity of 1 1/2″ (38 mm) thick plate. Because of the gap (throat) in the side frames, the sheet length which can be handled on the gap shear is not as limited as that which can be handled on the gapless shear.

Gap shears are used for squaring sheets and producing blanks; because of the gap in the frame, they can be used to slit long sheets. Notching can also be performed on a gap shear.

### Alligator or Pivot Shears

Alligator shears have a shearing action similar to that of scissors. The pivoting blade is actuated either mechanically or hydraulically. This type of shear is generally used to shear bar stock, rods, and narrow plates and to cut metal into scrap.

The shearing capacity is dependent upon the size of the machine. One manufacturer builds pivot shears that shear bars up to 4 1/4″ (108 mm) diam and plates to 1 x 30″ (25.4 x 762 mm). Speeds for shears with mechanical drive range from 25-60 spm, whereas speeds for those with hydraulic drive are limited to 10-16 spm.

Some of the accessories that can increase accuracy and

productivity are automatic feed rolls, length gages, automatic hold-downs, bar supports for long cuts, and blades that enable shearing of more than one bar at a time.

## Ironworkers

Ironworkers (see Fig. 11-8) are machines which utilize the shearing principle and enable the operator to perform several different operations on the same machine. Some of these operations include punching, shearing, notching, coping, and forming. These operations can be performed simultaneously or singly.

The punching capacity of one machine is a 1 3/8″ (35 mm) hole in a plate 3/4″ (19 mm) thick. Shearing can be performed on bars that are 1/4″ x 24″ (6 x 610 mm) or rods to 1 1/4″ (32 mm) diam. The press and shear are hydraulically actuated and operate at speeds from 9-55 spm.

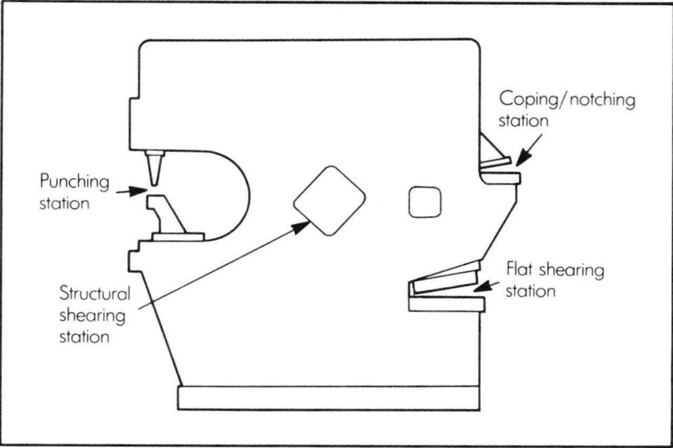


**Fig. 11-8 Ironworker showing typical work stations.** (*American National Standards Institute Inc.*)

## Cutoff Machines

Cutoff-type shearing machines are used for cutting round, square, flat, or special-shaped bars into blanks or slugs. This process can be performed on a machine specifically designed for slug cutoff, or it can be performed using a box-type shearing die in conjunction with a press.

One manufacturer of cutoff machines utilizes a double-cutting principle to shear the blanks or slugs. The dies (see Fig. 11-9) are actuated with short strokes by two flywheel-cam assemblies that rotate at a constant speed. The capacity of the machine is a 2 1/2″ (63.5 mm) diam bar having a maximum length of 36″ (914 mm).

This method is fast, efficient, and economical when large quantities are required. Some machines are capable of maintaining the length to within ±0.005″ (±0.13 mm), as well as maintaining square cuts and ends that are free of burrs, distortion, and rollover. Production can be as high as 150 pieces per minute.

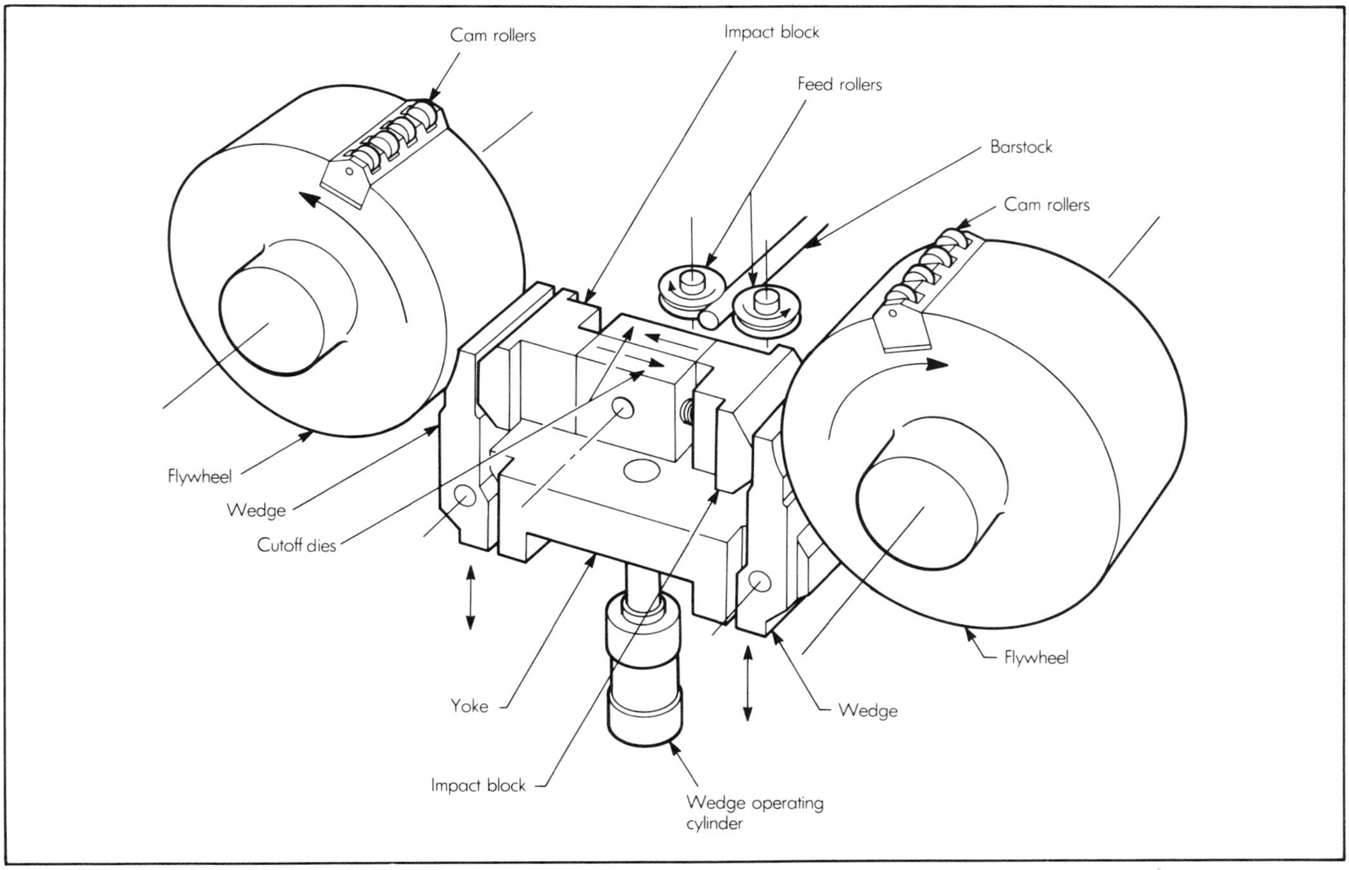

**Fig. 11-9 Cutoff machine operation utilizing twin cutoff dies to shear stock.** (*Fenn Manufacturing Co.*)

# CHAPTER 11

# TYPES OF SHEARS

## Bar-Billet Shears

Bar-billet shears usually form part of a completely automated system to produce blanks that are used in subsequent metal-forming and machining operations. The shear is designed to incorporate either a nutcracker (pivot) or a guillotine type of cutting action.

The cutting action of a pivot-type shear is the same as that of scissors closing. With the guillotine action, the upper blade descends toward the lower blade; this is the same action that is used with the conventional underdriven or overdriven shear.

The shearing force is supplied by either a hydraulic cylinder or mechanical linkage. A typical bar-billet shear has a capacity of 7" (178 mm) for round stock and 6 3/8" (162 mm) for square stock; it operates at a speed of 15-28 spm.

## CNC Shears

Computer numerical control (CNC) technology applied to shearing is generally limited to a single-axis positioning table attached to a conventional hydraulic or mechanically driven shear. A sheet to be sheared is placed in the workholders of a direct-current servo driven carriage and positioned in the shear for each cut. The CNC unit can be programmed so that a variety of lengths can be sheared from a single sheet, as well as a variety of initial trimming cuts.

All the advantages of CNC machining apply to CNC shearing, including accuracy, repeatability, increased production, hands-off safe operation, and predictable production rates. When prepunched parts are sheared, errors are not cumulative, as could be the case when back-gaging is used with manually operated shears. Accuracy and repeatability are generally good.

Occasionally, two single-axis shears are operated in tandem or at 90° angles, enabling the second shear to cut the material into smaller parts as it comes from the first shear.

One manufacturer combines two sets of blades at right angles (mounted in a C-type shear frame), a two-axis positioning table, a CNC unit, and a conveyor to transport finished parts out of the frame (see Fig. 11-10). This effectively combines two single-axis shears and thereby enables patterns to be sheared that would be impossible on conventional shears. Productivity is increased by the fact that the right-angle blade is also able to shear different-sized parts (in both length and width) with a single stroke. A computer program is used in conjunction with this system so that scrap is minimized and sheet metal utilization is maximized.

Sheets to be sheared are loaded into the workholders of the positioning table at the load station (see Fig. 11-11). The sheet is positioned against end locators to provide a reference point for the shearing operation. The shearing cycle is started, and the table positions the sheet for the initial trimming cuts, providing square starting edges. While the shear is trimming the sheet, the blanks can be unloaded and stacked as they come off the conveyor.

The right-angle CNC shear is best suited to applications for which requirements differ from day to day and to those for which accuracy and squareness of finished blanks are critical. These shears can be combined with one or more punch presses to provide an automated fabrication system.

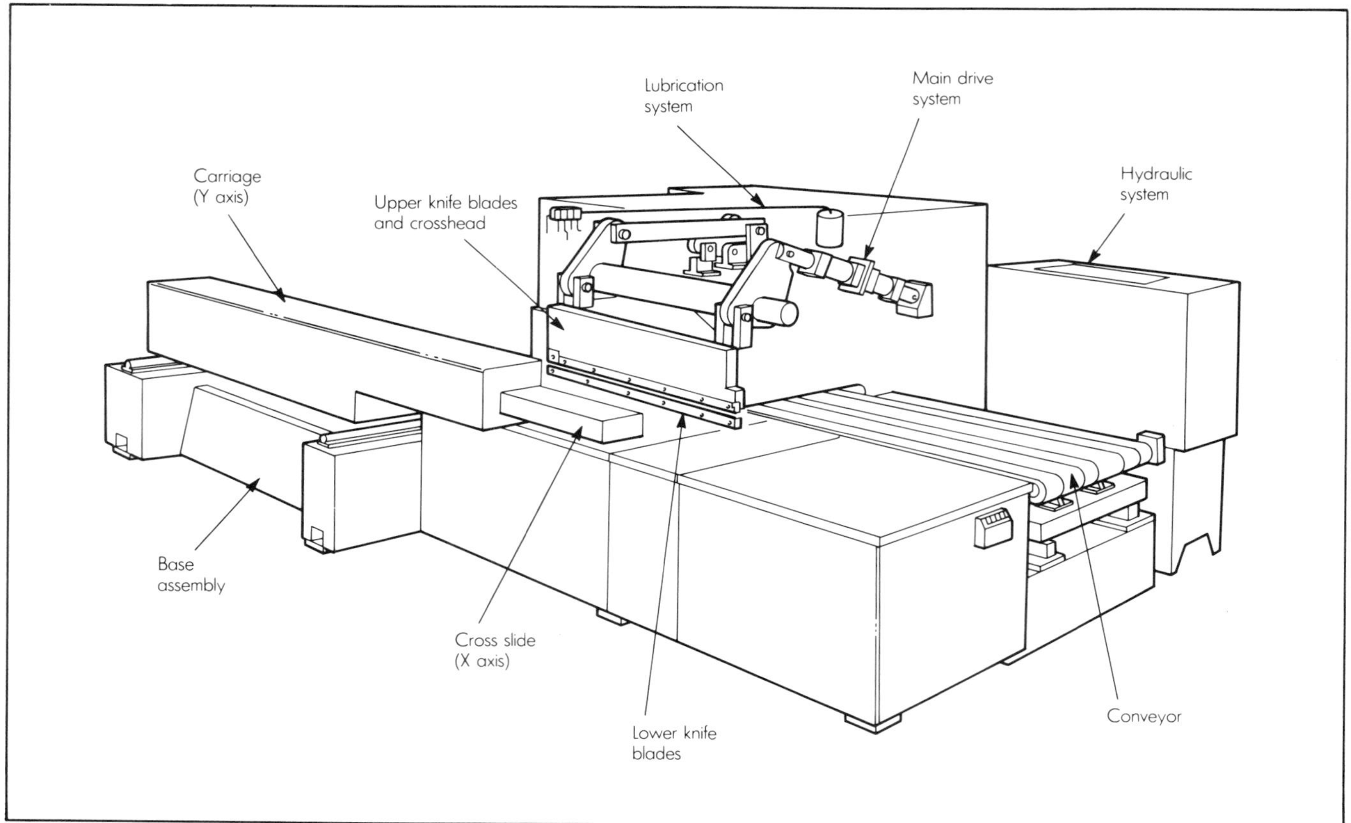


**Fig. 11-10 CNC shear incorporating a right-angle shear and a two-axis positioning table.** (*Wiedemann Div., Warner & Swasey Co.*)

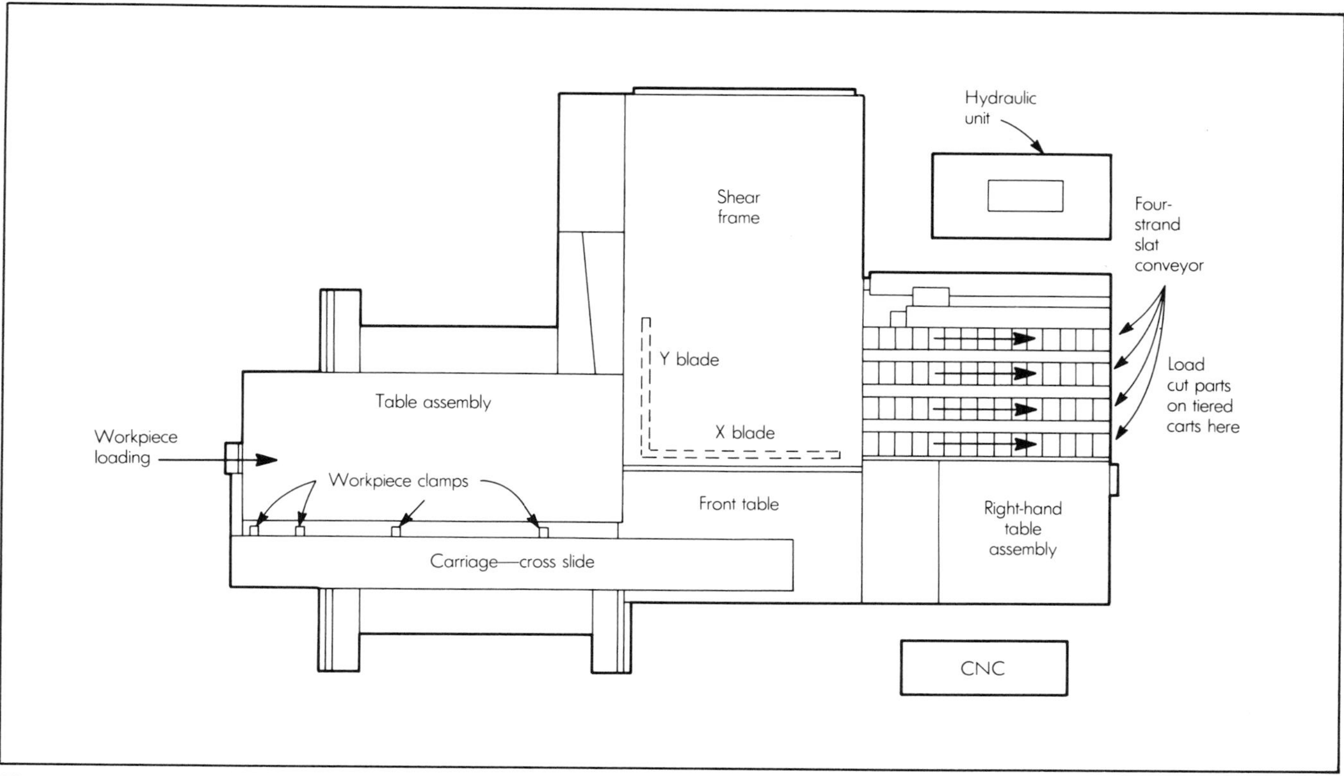


**Fig. 11-11 Workpiece being sheared in CNC shear.** (*Wiedemann Div., Warner & Swasey Co.*)

## Rotary Shear

Rotary shearing is used to produce circular and irregular shapes from steel plate. It can also be used for straight-line cutting. It is practical for shearing applications up to a maximum plate thickness of 1″ (25.4 mm). Two revolving, tapered, circular cutters or knives cut the material. Because the blades are round, no restrictions need be made to the movement of the workpiece right or left. This permits circles, irregular shapes with small radii, and straight lines to be cut. Bevel cuts can also be made. Holding fixtures are used to support and guide the workpiece during the cutting operation. Production is relatively limited on straight-line cutting. A rotary shear is illustrated in Fig. 11-12.

## Shear Lines

Shear lines, also called cut-up or cut-to-length lines, are high-production setups for producing accurately cut flat sheets from coiled stock. Two basic types of shear lines exist: the stationary-shear type and the flying-shear type.

The stationary-shear line consists of an uncoiler, flattening rolls to remove the set from the uncoiled sheet and to feed the sheet over the hump table, a stationary shear, a gage table with a retractable stop, and a stacker that stacks the cut sheets as they are discharged from the gage table. The uncoiled sheet approaches the gage stop and trips a limit switch that actuates the shear. The stop holds the sheet in accurate position on the gage table while it is being cut. In the meantime, the uncoiling continues and the excess material forms a loop over the hump table. When the cut is completed, the stop retracts and the cut sheet is discharged to the stacker. A second limit switch resets the stop. The shear meanwhile opens and permits the sheet to slide out of its loop onto the gage table for the gaging of the next piece and a repetition of the cycle.

The flying shear line includes an uncoiler, flattening rolls, measuring rolls, a sliding die shear, a runout conveyor, and a stacker. There is no hump table, and the sheet does not stop since the sliding die travels with the sheet while it is cutting. After the cut is completed, the die returns to the initial position for the next cut. A flying shear line costs more than a stationary shear line and can be justified only for very high production.

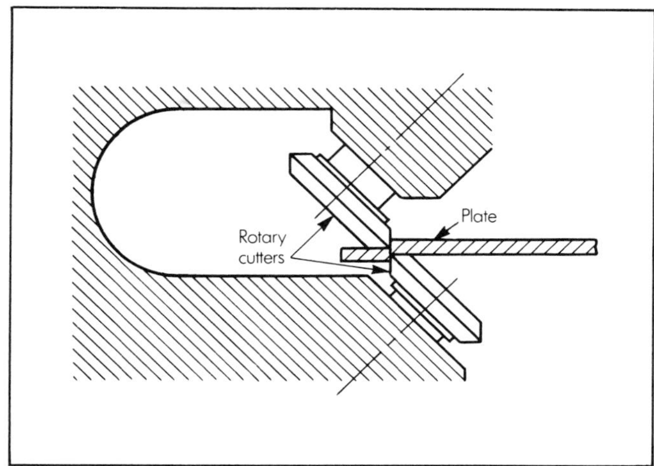


**Fig. 11-12 Rotary shear for cutting curves and contours.**

# CHAPTER 11

# TYPES OF SHEARS

## SLITTING

A slitting line is a group of machines designed to reduce a single-width coil into multiple narrower width coils (see Fig. 11-13). The slitting process shears the coiled strip in the lengthwise direction. A basic slitting line consists of an uncoiler or pay-off reel, a slitter, and a recoiler. Other equipment can be added for scrap disposal, coil handling and packaging, leveling, and edge conditioning.

### Process Description

The coil of material to be slit is held on a mandrel of the pay-off reel. The mandrel expands to tightly grip the inside diameter of the coil. The coil is unwound by rotating the mandrel and using auxiliary equipment to thread the material to the slitter arbors. The work and equipment required to unwind or unbend the material varies greatly with the width, thickness, and yield strength.

The material to be slit passes between two parallel shafts containing the rotary cutting knives (see Fig. 11-14). These knives shear the material on a continuous basis in much the same manner as a conventional shear. The force required to maintain the two shafts parallel, and therefore maintain the vertical clearance of the rotary knives, is directed through the end housings of the machine. The horizontal knife clearance is adjusted using tool steel spacers and shims during the tooling setup.

Normally the edge is trimmed on each side of the coil. The trimmed edge is a register cut and provides a reference point from which the other cuts can be made. If burr-free edges are required, the edges of the strips must be edge-rolled. The edge trim can be chopped, wound, or balled depending on the application. The multiple widths are rewound on an expandable mandrel by inserting the lead edges into a gripper slot in the rewind mandrel. The rewind mandrel is driven, and the strips are wound into slit width coils. The slit coil is kept separated at approximately the tangent point to the mandrel by separator discs to prevent interleaving of the slit width coils. The wound slit coil is removed from the mandrel by collapsing the mandrel and pushing the slit width coils off onto auxiliary handling equipment.

### Types of Slitting Lines

Three basic types of slitting lines exist: pull through, single loop, and double loop slitting. Each type of slitting has its own particular application depending on material, yield strength, thickness, and other requirements such as tightness of the coil.

The single and double-loop slitting lines are primarily used on light-gage material or where pulling tension on the strip can change the grain structure of the material. The pull-through slitting line is the more common type in general use.

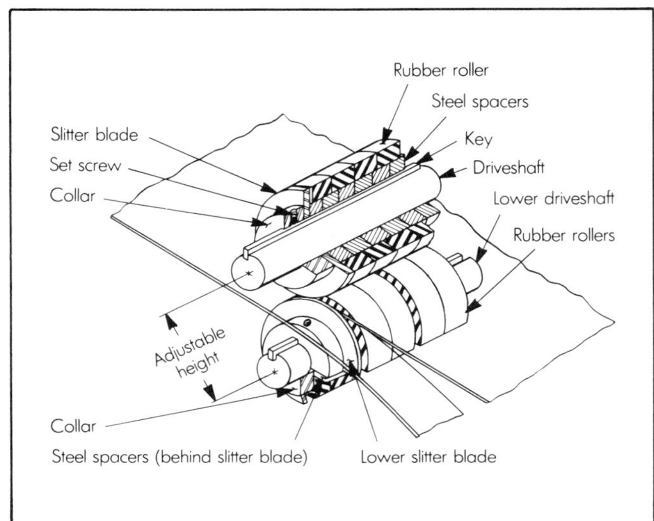


**Fig. 11-14 Rotary knives used to slit material.**

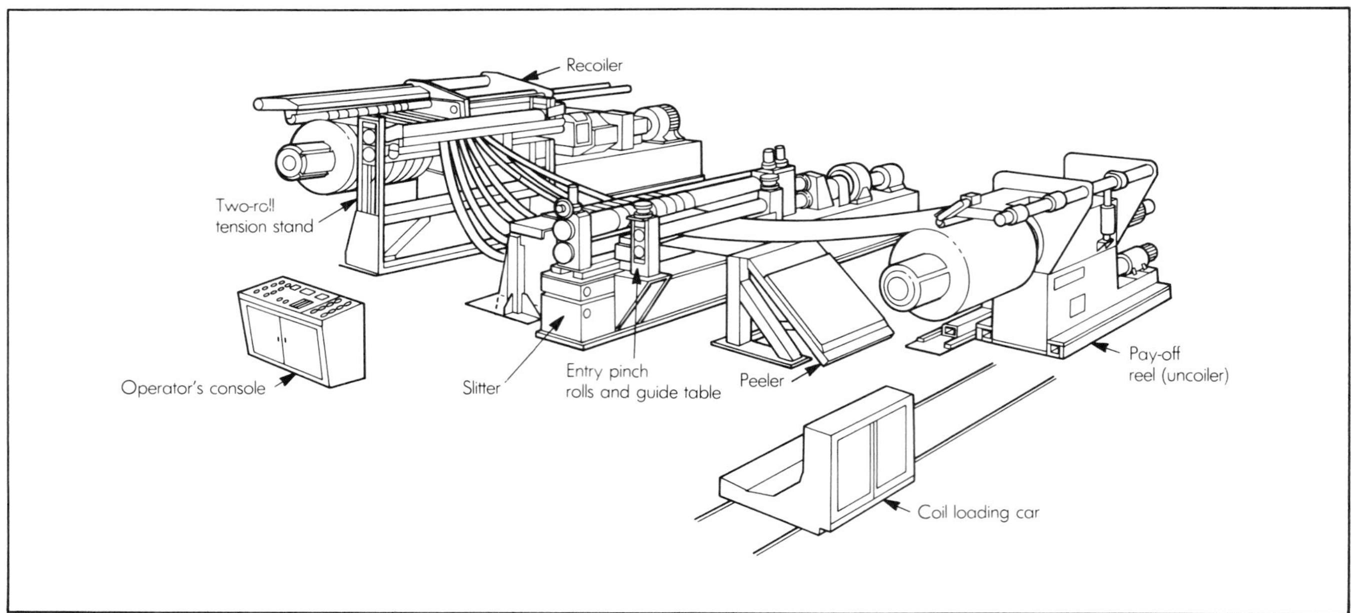


**Fig. 11-13 Slitting line incorporating pay-off reel, slitter, tensioner, and recoiler.** (*Paxson Machine Co.*)

**Pull-through slitting.** This type of slitting uses the recoiler drive to provide the power to unwind, shear, and rewind the coil (see Fig. 11-15).

**Single-loop slitting.** In single-loop slitting, the recoiler is used to provide the power to rewind the material, while the slitter provides the power to both shear and unwind the material (see Fig. 11-16). A tension device is incorporated in this line to develop the proper strip tension before entering the recoiler.

**Double-loop slitting.** In this type of slitting, the recoiler is used to provide the power to rewind, the slitter to provide power to shear, and the uncoiler to provide power to unwind. This line also incorporates a tension device to maintain proper strip tension (see Fig. 11-17).

## Specialized Slitting Lines

Various types of specialized slitters have been designed to accomplish specific tasks. Among these types are scroll slitters designed to scroll cut the multiple widths. The scroll pattern allows irregularly shaped items to be nested and blanked with a minimum of scrap loss. A consideration of scroll slitting lies in the cost and nature of the tooling.

## Slitting Applications and Materials

Most slitting lines are used to generate slit width material for press feeding or roll forming, or specific width material for cut-to-length blanking. The obvious advantage of slit width material is evident in the increased productivity obtained in feeding strip in various forming operations. Typical examples of slit width usage include tubing manufacturing, roll forming of shapes, and high-volume stamping operations.

Almost any product that can be coiled can also be slit. The material can be as thin as foil or as thick as 1″ (25.4 mm) plate. The material to be slit can be paper, cardboard, metal, etc. Each application requires a specific type of slitter. Most manufacturers of slitting equipment specialize in a specific area.

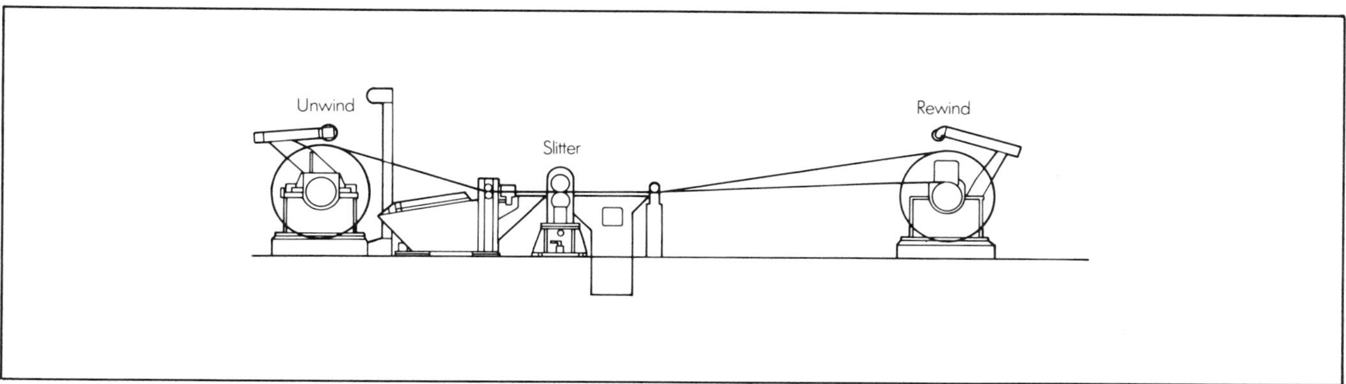


**Fig. 11-15 Pull-through slitting line.** (*Stamco, Div. of Monarch Machine Tool Co.*)

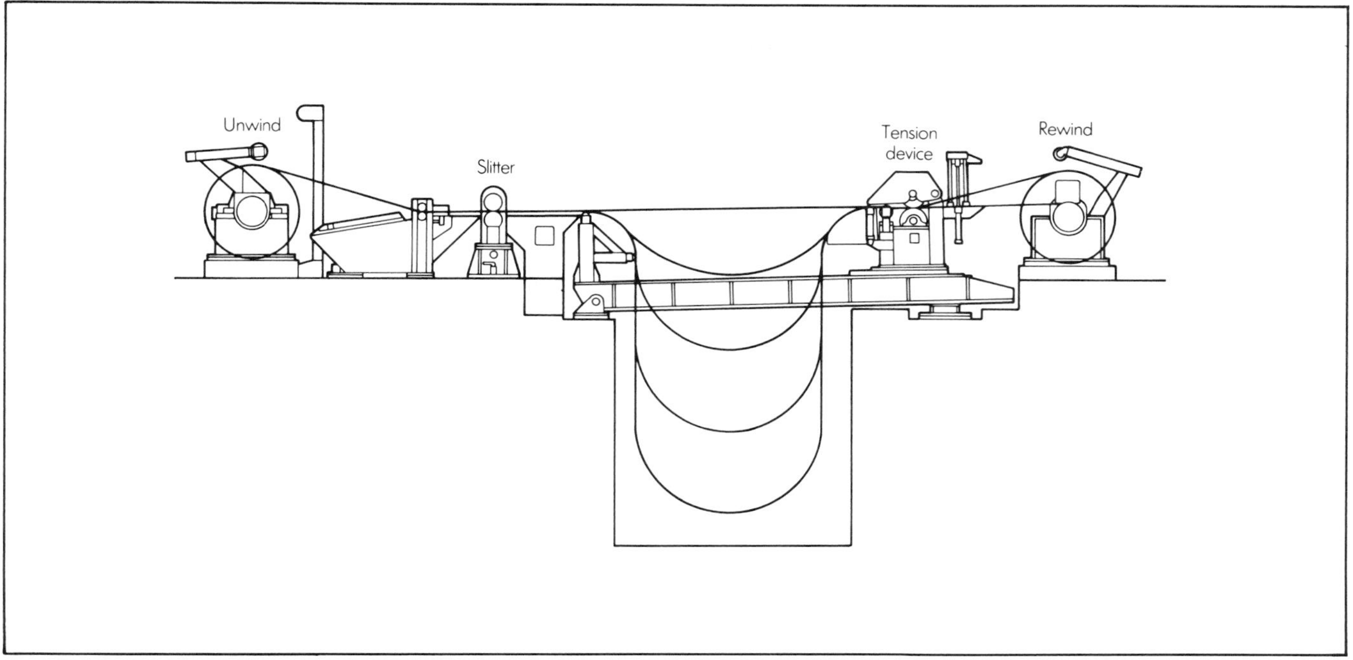


**Fig. 11-16 Single-loop slitting line.** (*Stamco, Div. of Monarch Machine Tool Co.*)

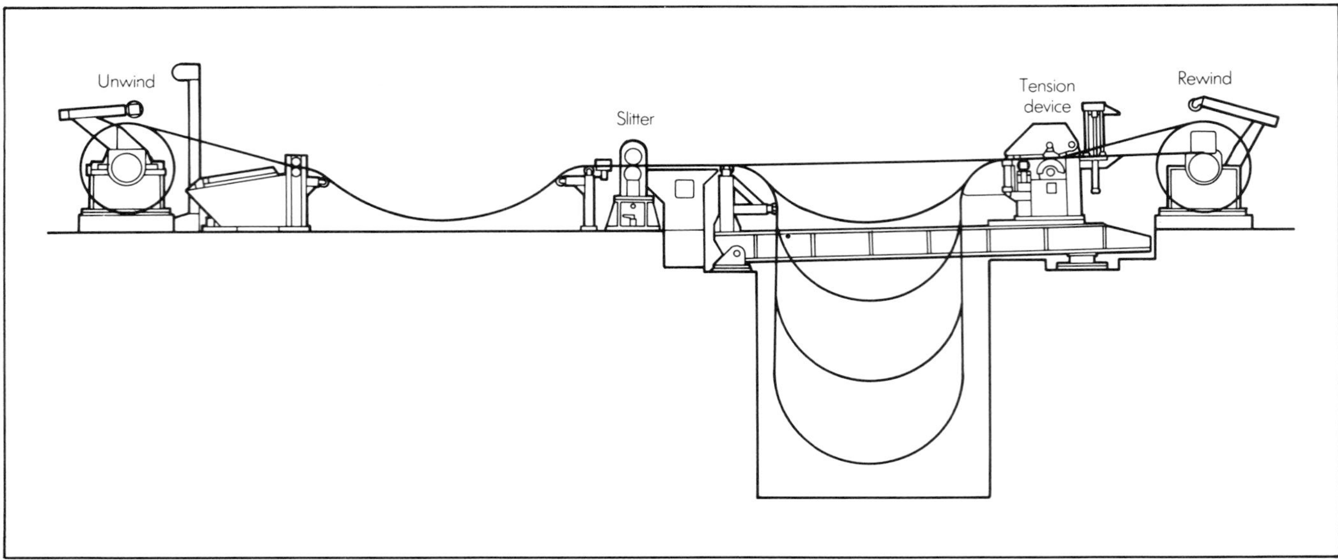


**Fig. 11-17 Double-loop slitting line.** (*Stamco, Div. of Monarch Machine Tool Co.*)

## SHEAR ACCESSORIES

Many accessories are available to enable a shear to perform the required operations while maintaining the desired accuracy. These accessories are either standard or optional equipment and can be divided into two categories: (1) shear accuracy and (2) shear production.

Some of the accessories used to maintain accuracy are back-gages and front-gages, sheet support systems, and shadow lights. Production or material handling accessories are front-feeding systems, ball transfers, conveyor systems, and automatic stackers.

### Gaging

Regardless of its type, the shear must have some kind of gage on it for measuring blanks or parts to be sheared. The particular type of gage depends on the application and the desired accuracy. There are six basic types and methods of gaging:

1. Back-gaging.
2. Front-gaging.
3. Squaring-arm gaging.
4. Pin gaging.
5. Programmable gaging.
6. Shear lance gaging.

**Back-gaging**. In back-gaging, the operator pushes the material between the knives and housings into the shear against an adjustable stop or back-gage. Modern shears have back-gages controlled from the operator's position at the front of the shear, either by power or manually. Pushbutton control on power-operated back-gages provides a selection of fast traverse speed and slow location speed for accurate final setting. Accurate gage screws, compensating nuts, precision slides and guides, and digital readouts make gage setting of 0.001″ (0.02 mm) accuracy possible. For rapid, accurate cutting, electronic sensors in the back-gage angle automatically trip the shear only when the sheet is in accurate position. Back-gages are also retractable so that the angle can be moved out of the way and mill plate of almost any depth can be fed into the shear and cut at any point desired.

**Front-gaging**. In front-gaging, the sheet or plate is located with respect to the cutting edge by means of adjustable stops or gages located in the table or in the front support arms. A disadvantage of front-gaging is the length of time needed to accurately set up the front-gages. However, this time is justifiable for long production runs and is generally necessary when material is being sheared that is deeper than the back-gage capacity.

**Squaring-arm gaging**. Mounted on the end of the shear, the squaring arm enables the operator to shear a 90° corner on the material. Adjustable stainless steel scales in both the shear table and the squaring arm assist in locating the multiple stops (see Fig. 11-18). The squaring arm can be mounted on either end of the shear to distribute wear on the knives.

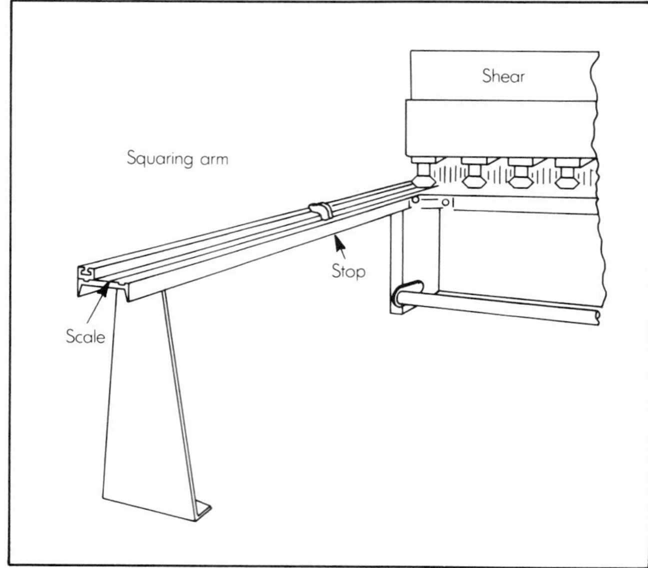


**Fig. 11-18 Typical squaring arm with adjustable stop.**

**Pin gaging**. Pin gaging (see Fig. 11-19) is a variation of front-gaging which makes use of locator pins that fit into prepunched holes. The advantage in using it is that it is highly accurate, as accurate as the press used to punch the locator holes.

**Programmable gaging**. Programmable gaging offers a high degree of accuracy, but generally is not used in general shearing. A form of programmable gaging is incorporated in CNC shearing.

**Shear lance gaging**. Shear lance gaging is an accurate way to gage sheared pieces and/or blanks. The lances (see Fig. 11-20) are produced on a separate press. This type of gaging requires a minimum amount of setup and is fast.

## Sheet Supports

When the back-gage is used to shear wide drops of thin metal, the metal often sags and causes an inaccurate measurement. To eliminate this problem, a sheet support system can be added to the back of the shear.

Two methods are used to support the sheets. One method utilizes a pneumatically operated bar to hold the workpiece in a horizontal plane until the workpiece is cut (see Fig. 11-21). After the cut, the bar is lowered and the workpiece is permitted to drop. An advantage of this support system is that both ferrous and nonferrous materials can be supported. Another method utilizes magnetic rollers that are attached to the crosshead to hold a ferrous workpiece in a horizontal position during shearing (see Fig. 11-22). After the cut, the workpiece is released. Generally, these support systems are limited to material less than 1/8″ (3.2 mm) thick.

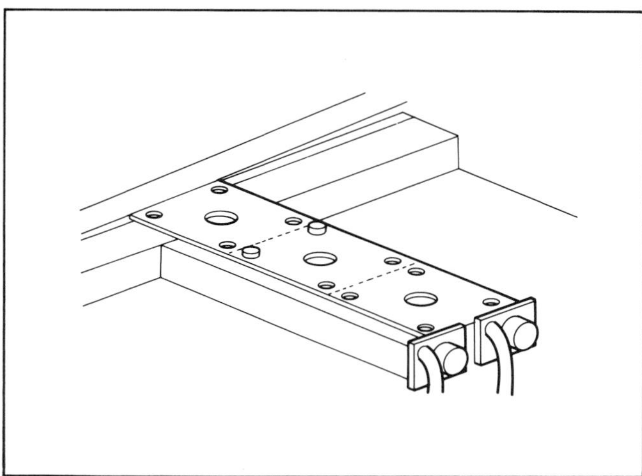

**Fig. 11-19 Pin gaging is a very accurate method of positioning material to be sheared.** (*Di-Acro Division, Houdaille Industries Inc.*)

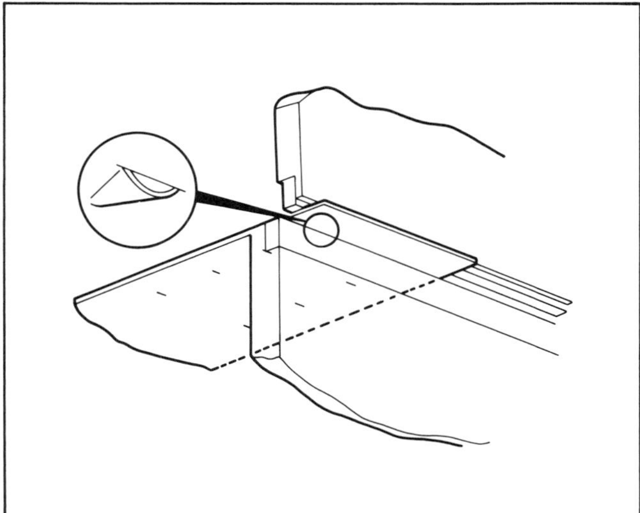

**Fig. 11-20 Shear lance gaging requires little setup and is accurate. The lancing is performed on a separate press.** (*Di-Acro Division, Houdaille Industries Inc.*)

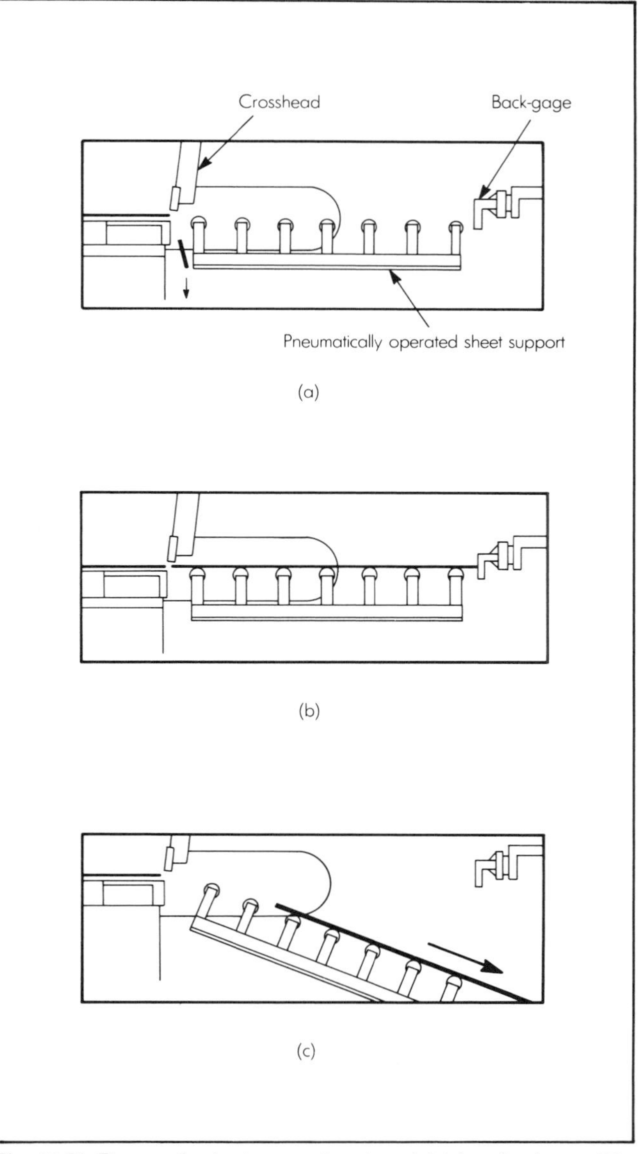


**Fig. 11-21 Pneumatic sheet support system: (a) trimming is possible with support in position; (b) support holds sheet in horizontal position during shearing; (c) support pivots down and enables sheet to drop.** (*Di-Acro Division, Houdaille Industries Inc.*)

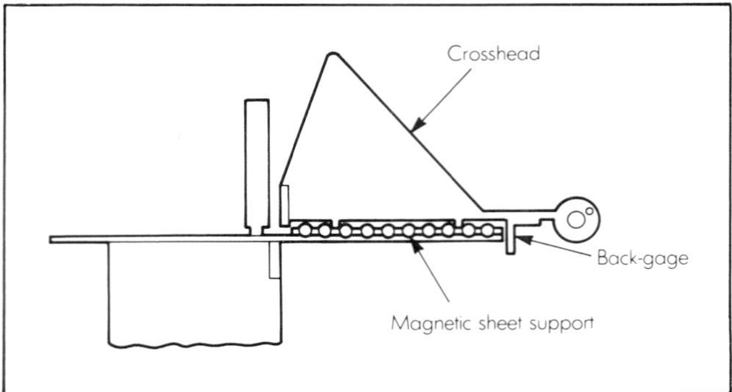


**Fig. 11-22 Magnetic sheet support enables accurate shearing of thin sheets.** (*Niagara Machine and Tool Works*)

### Shadow Lights

Shadow lights, which are located above the crosshead, permit cutting from a scribed line.

### Material Handling

A variety of accessories are available to facilitate the handling of material before and after the shearing process. Front feeding systems and front handling systems reduce the amount of work and time required to shear blanks on a production basis. Ball transfers, located in the bed and extension arms, enable the operator to maneuver thick plates with a minimum amount of difficulty. After the material is sheared, conveyors can automatically transfer the material to other work stations or to an automatic stacker.

# SHEAR KNIVES

Shear knives are precision cutting tools that are usually rectangular in cross section. In general, each knife has four cutting edges. Special applications call for either the upper or lower knife to be specially shaped to cut corrugated material, wire mesh, and other items of unusual geometry. Bow knives have no advantage in standard shears except for special applications.

## KNIFE SELECTION

Knives should be carefully selected according to the type and thickness of the material to be cut. Generally, the best grade of knife suitable for the maximum thickness to be sheared is the most economical investment. The best grade of knife is imperative when alloy steels, high-strength steels, and abrasive materials are being cut. It is also important to determine whether the material is to be sheared hot or cold. Normally, knives for cold shearing are not designed for hot shearing.

For maximum life, knives should be as hard as possible without spalling. The general hardness range is from $R_C$53-55 for heavy plate applications to approximately $R_C$59-61 for light-gage applications. It is interesting to note that a knife can cut alloys as hard as itself because a sharp knife edge concentrates the shearing force in a very small area of the metal.

Shear knives come in many grades and hardnesses, but three grades are used most often. These grades are: (1) Grade I, (2) Grade II, and (3) Grade III.

Grade I is a tool steel that is normally used in low-production, general-purpose applications. This grade is relatively inexpensive and is satisfactory for intermittent shearing of mild steel, brass, and aluminum.

Grade II is an intermediate alloy that is shock resistant and is used for shearing plate 5/16″ (8 mm) and thicker. It can also be used for light-gage shearing with reasonable life. This alloy is more durable than Grade I, and the added cost is usually well justified.

Grade III is a high-carbon, high-chrome alloy that is used for shearing mild steel up to 1/4″ (6.3 mm) thick. It is usually recommended for continuous shearing of steels up to 1/4″ (6.3 mm) in thickness. It is also used for shearing aluminum, brass, and stainless steel up to 3/16″ (4.8 mm) thick. Because this grade is hard and somewhat brittle, it is not recommended for shearing mild steel greater than 1/4″ (6.3 mm) thick since edge chipping and spalling can result. Grade III can, however, give excellent results on certain materials over 1/4″ (6.3 mm) in thickness.

Table 11-2 can be used as a guide in selecting common knives for a given material thickness in mild steel. However, it is best to consult the shear manufacturer for the proper knife selection based on type of material and quantity of material being sheared.

**TABLE 11-2**
**Selection of Shearing Knife Material Based on Mild Steel and Varying Metal Thicknesses**

| Knife Material Grade | Mild Steel Capacity, in. (mm) | AISI No. |
|---|---|---|
| Standard | All thicknesses | L6 |
| High-carbon, high-chrome | Through 1/4″ (6.4 mm) | D2 |
| High-carbon, high-chrome | 5/16 to 3/8″ (8 to 9.5 mm) | D1 |
| Shock-resisting | 5/16 to 5/8″ (8 to 16 mm) | A2 |
| Shock-resisting | Over 5/8″ (16 mm) | S5 |

## KNIFE SHARPNESS

Sharpness of the knife plays an important role in both edge quality and shearing force (tonnage) requirements. Figure 11-23 compares the cutting action of a sharp blade with that of a dull blade.

A sharp edge on the shear knife bites into the material more quickly, avoiding excessive deformation of the surface because the shear stress is concentrated in a small area. Dull edges of shear knives deform the metal surface to a greater degree than sharp edges because the shear stresses are spread out over a larger area. This means that more shearing force is necessary to start the fractures and make them meet. In addition, with dull edges the tension-compression stage lasts much longer because the fractures have not relieved the stressed areas by separating the metal at those points. Dullness can also cause heavy burrs on the sheared edge of the stock and excessive wear on the ram

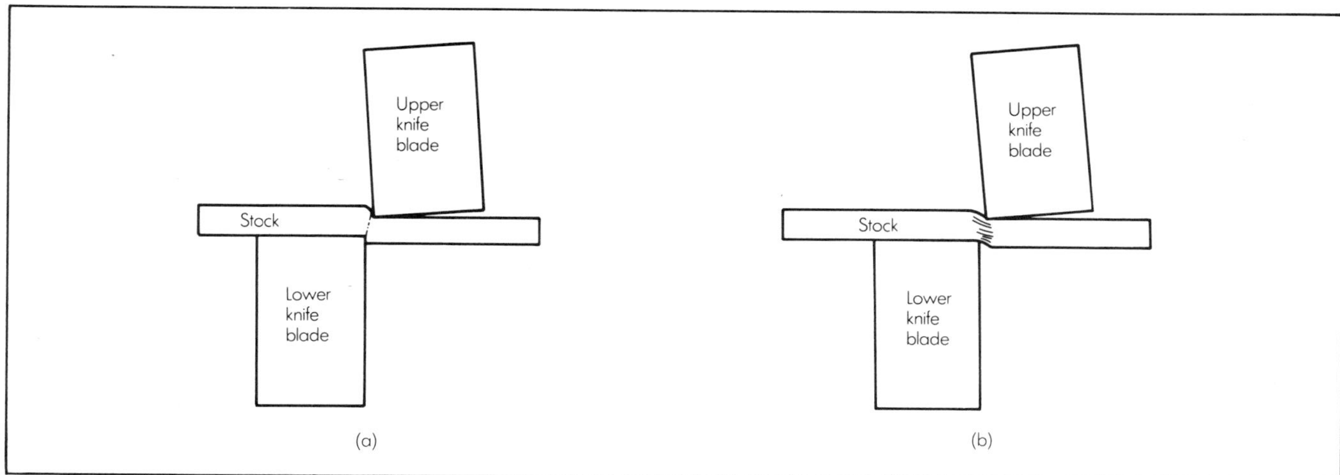


**Fig. 11-23 Shearing stock: (a) with a sharp knife blade, the sharp edges bit into the metal and start the fracture easily; (b) with a dull knife blade, the dull edges pull and tear the metal apart.** (*Di-Acro Division, Houdaille Industries Inc.*)

guides; it may also overload components of the shear if the shear is already being operated at capacity. This is especially true of mechanical shears due to the rigidity of their drive system.

Operating a shear that has dull knives can be very expensive in the long run, both in terms of quality and additional maintenance on the shear. Therefore, every shear owner should have a controlled resharpening program, with at least one extra set of knives available to prevent excessive downtime.

# OPERATING PARAMETERS

Variables that determine the type and size of the shear used include the type and thickness of the material and the job to be performed. As was previously stated, certain shears are designed for particular applications. Gap shears are used for squaring blanks as well as for slitting and notching. Bar-billet shears and alligator shears are best suited for shearing bars and billets.

The material has a direct influence on the speed, shearing force, knife clearances, and rake of the shear. Another important consideration is proper maintenance to ensure trouble-free operation.

## POWER

The power of the motor driving the shear, rated in horsepower or kilowatt, should correspond to the recommendations of the manufacturer. High-slip motors are recommended on mechanical shears. Rapid cutting—that is, cutting on each stroke of the shear with the clutch continuously engaged—requires greater power than does intermittent cutting. Hydraulic shears require larger motors than equivalent mechanical shears; their motors are of the squirrel-cage type.

## SHEARING FORCE

When a shear makes a cut on a piece of metal, it exerts considerable force to start the cut and to continue the shearing action. The shear, therefore, must be capable of supplying sufficient force to shear the material and to hold the material firmly in place until the cut is completed.

In normal shearing, only part of the material is sheared; the remaining portion is broken through due to the shearing action. The force required to shear the material depends on the thickness and type of material, the rake of the upper knife, and the percent of penetration required. The percent of penetration is equivalent to the percent elongation in 2" (51 mm). Values for the percent penetration and shear strength of various materials can be found in Table 11-3. Generally, the shear strength is 50-80% of the tensile strength; the shear strength of aluminum and its alloys is 50-70%; and the shear strength of low-carbon steels is 70-80%.

The required shear force for a given type and thickness of material and a designated rake can be calculated using the formula:[1]

$$F = \left(\frac{S \times P \times T^2 \times 12}{R}\right)\left(1 - \frac{P}{2}\right) \tag{1}$$

where:

$F$ = shear force, lb
$S$ = shear strength (stress), psi
$P$ = penetration of knife into material, %
$T$ = thickness of material, in.
$R$ = rake of the knife blade, in./ft

For metric usage, the force is multiplied by 4.448 to obtain newtons (N).

Example:

To shear a sheet of 0.10C steel, 10 gage (0.135") thick, having a shear strength of 43,000 psi and a 38% penetration on a shear having a rake of 1/4, the required force is:

$$F = \left(\frac{43{,}000 \times 0.38 \times 0.135^2 \times 12}{1/4}\right)\left(1 - \frac{0.38}{2}\right) = 11{,}578\ lb$$

which is 5.8 tons or 51.5 kN.

**TABLE 11-3**
**Values of Percent Penetration and Shear Strength for Various Materials**

| Material | Percent Penetration | Shear Strength, psi (MPa) |
|---|---|---|
| Lead | 50 | 3500 (24.1) |
| Tin | 40 | 5000 (34.5) |
| Aluminum | 60 | 8000 (55.2) |
| Zinc | 50 | 14,000 (96.5) |
| Cold worked | 25 | 19,000 (131) |
| Copper | 55 | 22,000 (151.7) |
| Cold worked | 30 | 28,000 (193) |
| Brass | 50 | 32,000 (220.6) |
| Cold worked | 30 | 52,000 (358.5) |
| Tobin bronze | 25 | 36,000 (248.2) |
| Cold worked | 17 | 42,000 (289.6) |
| Steel, 0.10C | 50 | 35,000 (241.3) |
| Cold worked | 38 | 43,000 (296.5) |
| Steel, 0.40C | 27 | 62,000 (427.5) |
| Cold worked | 17 | 78,000 (537.8) |
| Steel, 0.80C | 15 | 97,000 (668.8) |
| Cold worked | 5 | 127,000 (875.6) |
| Steel, 1.00C | 10 | 115,000 (792.9) |
| Cold worked | 2 | 150,000 (1034.2) |
| Silicon steel | 30 | 65,000 (448.2) |
| Nickel | 55 | 35,000 (241.3) |

## RAKE

The rake is the angular slope formed between the lower knife and the upper knife (see Fig. 11-24). Generally, the rake is expressed as a single number, 3/4, which means that the knife rises 3/4″ for every foot in length. In metric units, the rake would be expressed as the rise measured in millimeters for every meter in length.

The amount of blade engagement can also be used to express rake. As the rake decreases, the amount of upper knife blade engagement increases. This results in a greater shearing force being required, since there is more metal to offer resistance to the knife as it travels through the material. Increasing the rake, decreases the knife blade engagement and the shearing force.

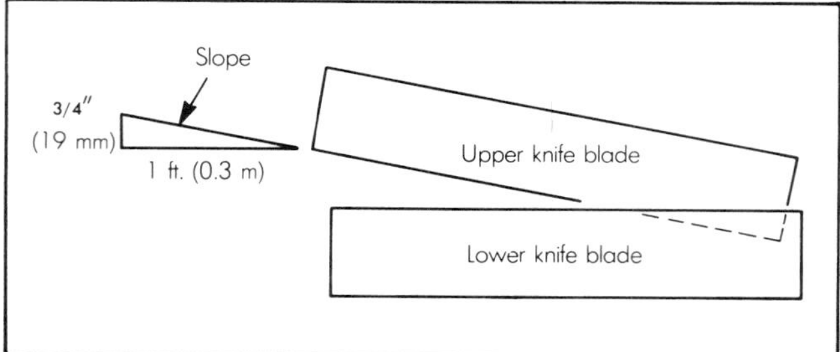


**Fig. 11-24 The rake is the angular slope formed by the cutting edges of the upper and lower knives.**

Rake should be as low as possible to reduce the amount of distortion in the sheared material. A higher rake reduces the cutting force, but increases the distortion in the sheared material. Hydraulic shears generally have an adjustable rake, whereas mechanical shears usually have a fixed rake.

## KNIFE CLEARANCE

Knife clearance is the clearance between the upper (movable) knife and the lower (fixed) knife as they pass one another. There are two extremes in setting the clearance between the knife blades with respect to the metal being sheared. One extreme is insufficient clearance wherein the two fractures do not meet in a line. The result is that a transverse, secondary fracture must occur to free the drop from the original stock. The pressure of the knife descending causes this secondary fracture to occur, and the cut edge displays a characteristic ragged shape. The knife rubbing against this secondary shear area often creates a second burnish area along the length of the cut (see Fig. 11-25).

The other extreme is excessive clearance, which results in an edge that resembles a tear more than a clean cut. The clearance between the knife blades could be so great that excessive deformation would occur on the upper edge of the original metal stock with corresponding deformation on the bottom surface of the drop. Excessive clearance wastes shearing force because it brings more bending forces into play and the shear encounters more resistance in the metal which it must overcome. A general knife blade clearance for most shears is 8% of the material thickness. Recommended knife clearances based on edge quality and drop width can be found in Tables 11-4 and 11-5.

The principal effect of knife clearance is the appearance of the cut, particularly in shearing wide drops. A second effect is the squareness of the cut. In addition to its effect on appearance and squareness of the cut, knife clearance affects to a slight degree the twist of the drop, if the drop is narrow. Knife clearance also affects the shearing force, which in certain circumstances can be lowered by opening the clearance. It is essential to maintain an appropriate knife clearance when shearing extremely thin sheets or extremely heavy plate. Very thin stainless steel, for example, can only be sheared with tight knife clearance and very sharp knives. In contrast, to get a smooth cut when shearing very heavy plate, the knife clearance must be opened.

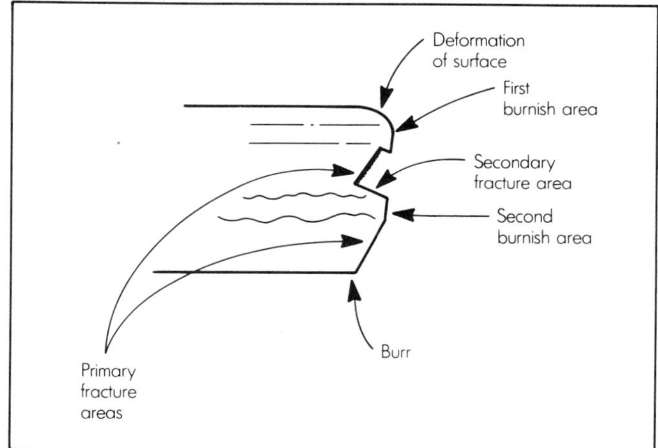


**Fig. 11-25 Secondary fracture occurs when there is insufficient knife clearance. (*Edward A. Lynch Machinery Co.*)**

**TABLE 11-4**
**Recommended Knife Clearances for Shearing Wide Drops in Mild Steel Plates when Edge Appearance is not Critical**

| Metal Thickness, in. (mm) | Knife Clearance, in. (mm) |
|---|---|
| 1/4 (6.4) | 0.025-0.030 (0.63-0.76) |
| 3/8 (9.5) | 0.038-0.050 (0.97-1.27) |
| 1/2 (12.7) | 0.050-0.070 (1.27-1.78) |
| 3/4 (19) | 0.075-0.110 (1.90-2.79) |
| 1 (25.4) | 0.100-0.150 (2.54-3.81) |
| 1 1/4 (32) | 0.125-0.180 (3.17-4.57) |
| 1 1/2 (38) | 0.150-0.220 (3.81-5.59) |

**TABLE 11-5**
**Recommended Knife Clearances for Trimming Mild Steel when Edge Appearance is Critical**

| Metal Thickness, gage/in. (mm) | Knife Clearance, in. (mm) |
|---|---|
| 10 gage (3.4) | 0.005-0.009 (0.13-0.23) |
| 3/16 (4.8) | 0.007-0.013 (0.18-0.33) |
| 1/4 (6.4) | 0.010-0.018 (0.25-0.46) |
| 3/8 (9.5) | 0.020-0.028 (0.51-0.71) |
| 1/2 (12.7) | 0.030-0.040 (0.76-1.02) |
| 5/8 (16) | 0.040-0.050 (1.02-1.27) |
| 3/4 (19) | 0.050-0.065 (1.27-1.65) |
| 1 (25.4) | 0.070-0.090 (1.78-2.29) |
| 1 1/4 (32) | 0.090-0.120 (2.29-3.05) |
| 1 1/2 (38) | 0.110-0.150 (2.79-3.81) |

On mechanical shears, the knife clearance should be set to an optimum setting, then all thicknesses (up to capacity) can be sheared without changing the knife clearance. Hydraulic shears require that the knife clearance be changed when wide drops are being sheared because the wide drops increase the required shearing force. As was stated previously, increasing the knife clearance reduces the shearing force and prevents the hydraulic shear from stalling. Mechanical shears have the extra capacity to make such cuts without additional clearance. The knife clearance must also be changed on hydraulic shears when different thicknesses of material are being sheared. This is due to the hydraulic shear operating at a slower speed.

### SHEARING SPEED

Two factors that determine how fast a shear should operate are the operator and the type of work.

The shear should operate at a comfortable work pace. If it is operating at a speed faster than the operator is able to feed work safely, there is a potential for trouble. Similarly, shear speed should be suited to the job performed. Small pieces can be cut at a faster speed than larger pieces, and thin gage material can be cut at a faster speed than heavy plate.

Material handling is another factor to consider when determining shear speed, since more time is spent handling the material than shearing the material. Handling time increases with the size and thickness of the sheet. Therefore, handling time can exceed 70% of the required total operating time. To reduce this time, automatic feeding, stacking, and transporting systems can be used.

### MAINTENANCE

Proper maintenance of shears ensures many hours of trouble-free operation. The two most important maintenance areas are lubrication and knife blade sharpening.

To facilitate the lubrication of the moving parts on a shear, many manufacturers incorporate either a centralized or an automatic lubrication system. One manufacturer incorporates an operation time counter so that maintenance can be carried out according to schedule.

Shear knives are available with multiple cutting edges, and the majority of shears have knives with four blades. These knives are desirable as their blades can be rotated three times before regrinding or replacement is necessary; therefore, maintenance costs are reduced.

As was previously stated, dull knives affect shearing force, edge quality, and slideway wear. It is, therefore, important to have a controlled sharpening program. Intervals between sharpening are determined by material being sheared and the type of knife blade material. Using dull knives not only affects edge quality but also causes the knife edge to suffer from fatigue. This in turn causes spalling, breaking, and chipping of the knife and requires more material to be removed by grinding when the knife is resharpened.

When stock coated with a rust preventive material is sheared, the lower knife blade should be swabbed with oil several times a day. The upper blade picks up lubrication from the stock. Knives should be kept clean and free of metal particles. If knives become magnetized, they should be removed and demagnetized to prevent further damage.

## TROUBLESHOOTING

Other than the condition of the sheared edge, there are three characteristic indicators of the quality of the sheared part or drop. These are the camber, bow, and twist that remain in the part after shearing (see Fig. 11-26).

If the edges are being trimmed from a part, the drop becomes scrap and the amount of distortion is of no consequence. However, if the drops are the parts to be used, then attention must be given to the width of the drop and the resultant distortion. The problem of distortion is particularly important when narrow strips are being sheared. The part of the workpiece

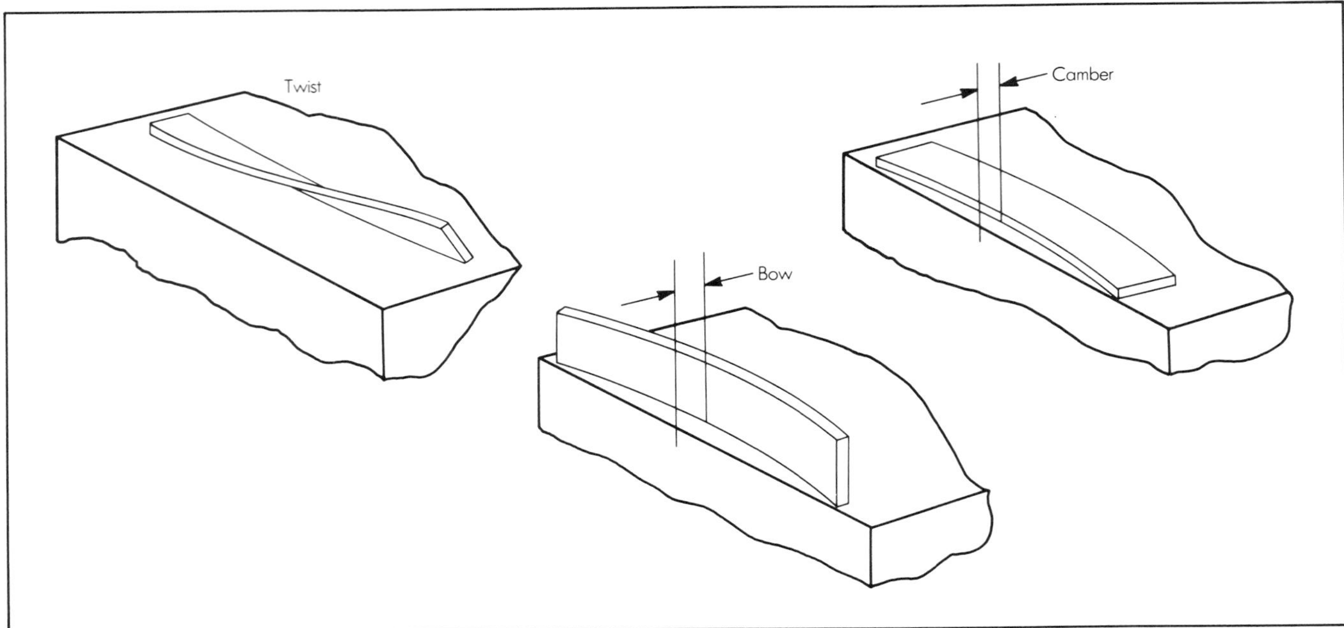


**Fig. 11-26 Common distortions in sheared metal.**

Bow
mm/m in./ft
80 1.0
65 0.8
50 0.6
35 0.4
20 0.2
1 1/2" (38 mm) drop
2" (51 mm) drop
3" (76 mm) drop
4" (102 mm) drop
1/8 1/4 3/8 1/2 5/8 in./ft
10 20 30 40 50 mm/m
Blade rake

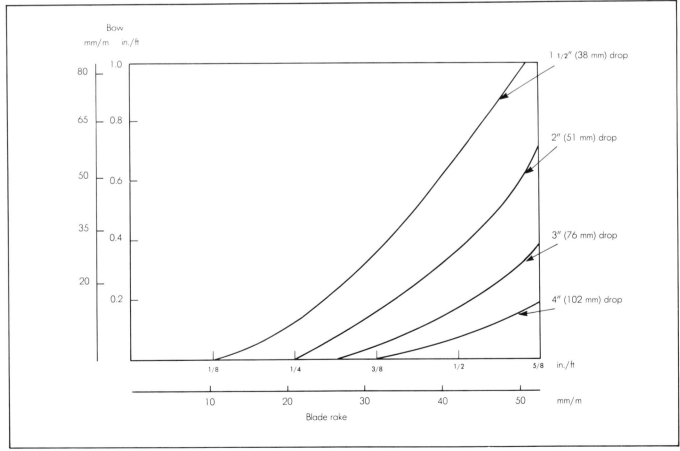

**Fig. 11-27 The effects of blade rake and drop width on bowing.** (*Pacific Press and Shear Co.*)

which remains on the table remains flat while the smaller part that extends beyond the knives is subject to distortion. Although a bow, twist, or camber can mean rejection of the sheared part, each of these problem conditions can usually be reduced or minimized.

## CAMBER

Camber cannot be eliminated, but can sometimes be reduced by lowering the rake angle of the upper knife. It can also occur if there is insufficient hold-down pressure. On the other hand, reasonable accuracy can often be obtained by taking deep trim cuts from the edges of the work material, providing the remaining dimensions of the trimmed material are sufficient for the subsequent shearing job.

## BOW

When narrow strips are being cut, bowing is almost directly proportional to the rake angle of the upper knife because a high rake angle causes the material to bend during the cut. The bow, however, decreases as the width of the drop increases and becomes negligible if the drop exceeds 4″ (102 mm) in width (see Fig. 11-27). Therefore, by reducing the rake angle, bowing can be minimized when narrow strips are being cut.

A shear that has a high rake and limited power is sufficient for cutting wide pieces, but does not perform well on narrow strips. A shear that has a lower rake angle, or an adjustable rake angle, and ample shearing capacity produces better quality drops on both wide and narrow pieces.

It should be noted that a shear must exert a certain force to cut a specific material thickness and it may not be possible to reduce the rake angle sufficiently to completely eliminate bowing.

## TWIST

Twist in the material is generally proportional to the rake of the upper knife and to the width of the cut piece that drops off under the knife. Soft materials twist more than hard materials; thick materials, more than thin materials; and narrow strips, more than wide cuts. Table 11-6 shows the various factors that affect twist in sheared material. Figure 11-28 is a graph relating twist to drop width, material thickness, and shear rake.

When 1/4″ (6.4 mm) plate is being cut, there is some twist even with a 1″ (25.4 mm) drop. If the drop is increased to 4″ (102 mm), virtually no twisting occurs. When 1″ (25.4 mm) plate is being sheared, the drop must be greater than 5″ (127 mm) to eliminate or substantially reduce twist.

**TABLE 11-6**
**Factors Affecting Twist in Sheared Material**

| Factor | More Twist | Less Twist |
|---|---|---|
| Material thickness | Thicker | Thinner |
| Material hardness | Softer | Harder |
| Width of drop | Narrower | Wider |
| Length of material | Longer | Shorter |
| Material stresses | More stresses | Stress-free |
| Rake angle | Higher | Lower |
| Speed of knife | Slower | Faster |

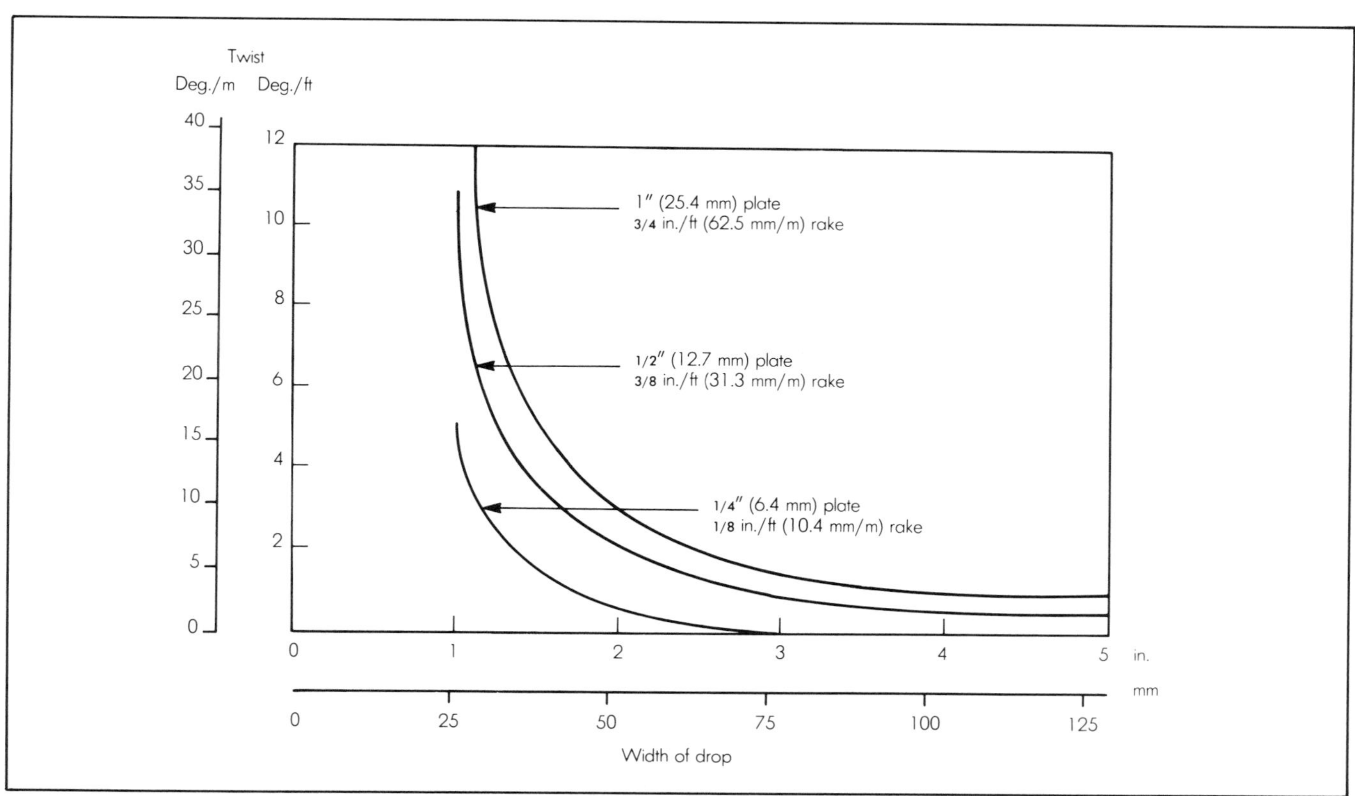


**Fig. 11-28 The effects of blade rake and drop width on twisting.** (*Pacific Press and Shear Co.*)

**TABLE 11-7**
**Minimum Drop Width to Prevent Distortion in Mild Steel at Various Blade Rakes**

| Plate Thickness, in. (mm) | Blade Rake, in./ft (mm/m) | | | | | |
|---|---|---|---|---|---|---|
| | 1/4 (20.8) | 3/8 (31.3) | 1/2 (41.7) | 5/8 (52.1) | 3/4 (62.5) | 7/8 (72.9) |
| | Drop Width, in. (mm) | | | | | |
| 1/8 (3.2) | 1 (25.4) | 1 (25.4) | 2 (51) | 3 (76) | 5 (127) | 7 (178) |
| 1/4 (6.4) | 2 (51) | 3 (76) | 4 (102) | 5 (127) | 7 (178) | 9 (229) |
| 3/8 (9.5) | 3 (76) | 5 (127) | 6 (152) | 8 (203) | 10 (254) | 12 (305) |
| 1/2 (12.7) | 4 (102) | 6 (152) | 8 (203) | 11 (279) | 14 (356) | 16 (406) |
| 5/8 (15.9) | 5 (127) | 8 (203) | 11 (279) | 14 (356) | 18 (457) | 21 (533) |
| 3/4 (19) | 6 (152) | 9 (229) | 12 (305) | 16 (406) | 21 (533) | 24 (610) |
| 7/8 (22.2) | 7 (178) | 11 (279) | 14 (356) | 18 (457) | 24 (610) | 28 (711) |
| 1 (25.4) | 8 (203) | 12 (305) | 16 (406) | 21 (533) | 27 (686) | 32 (813) |
| 1 1/4 (31.8) | 10 (254) | 15 (381) | 20 (508) | 27 (686) | 34 (864) | 40 (1016) |
| 1 1/2 (38.1) | 12 (305) | 18 (457) | 25 (635) | 32 (813) | 41 (1041) | 48 (1219) |

(*Pacific Press and Shear Co.*)

There is a practical limit to how much the rake angle can be reduced to minimize twist. Shear manufacturer's recommendations are, generally, a compromise which produces commercially acceptable cuts with optimum practical force. Table 11-7 shows the minimum drop width for mild steel that may be cut at various rake angles without distortion. For example, if the material is 1/2" (12.7 mm) mild steel and the required drop is 8" (203 mm), the rake angle should be 1/2 in./ft (41.7 mm/m); otherwise, distortion in the form of bowing and twisting becomes evident.

## SAFETY IN SHEARING OPERATIONS

Safety of the shear operator, as well as other personnel working around a shear, should be of paramount importance at all times because a shear, like any machine tool, can be a potential hazard if precautionary measures and common sense are ignored.

Most shear manufacturers design and construct their equipment to conform to ANSI Standard B11.4, "Safety Requirements for the Construction, Care, and Use of Shears." Another standard (ANSI Standard B11.5, "Safety Requirements for the Construction, Care, and Use of Iron Workers") is followed when an ironworker is designed or operated. Every effort is made to minimize the operator's exposure to possible hazardous conditions and situations that may occur during the operation of the shear. Design hazards such as pinch points, exposure to moving parts, and access to hazardous areas are either eliminated or provided with protective guards and/or warning signs in accordance with the standards.

Because of the diversified applications and conditions in which a shear is required to perform, it is not always possible for the manufacturer to equip each machine with guards and safety devices that would accommodate every adaptation. Therefore, owners, managers, supervisors, and operators themselves must assume responsibility for the safe operation of shear equipment under their control.

Each application should be evaluated in regards to the maintenance setup of the shear, the type and size of the material to be sheared, the method of handling the material, and the best method of protecting personnel from injury during the operation. Adequate guarding and safe operating procedures should be implemented at all times.

Two major areas of a shear offer the greatest potential hazards for the operator: (1) the point-of-operation and (2) the rear of the shear. Safeguarding the point-of-operation entails the use of guards (see Fig. 11-29), awareness barriers, or devices that prevent the operator from inadvertently placing his fingers or hands in the knife area or under the hold-downs. In this respect, fixed guards offer the most positive means of protection. They can be securely attached to the shear and must conform to the dimensions given in ANSI Standard B11.4. They provide clearance for moving the material into the knives, yet do not allow sufficient clearance for insertion of the operator's fingers.

Adjustable guards represent another alternative for guarding the point-of-operation on shears. They must adhere to the same dimensions as the fixed guards. These, however, can be inadequate if they are not adjusted properly. Suitable guards and presence-sensing devices that are interlocked with the shear controls can be used successfully to prevent actuation of the shear if the guard is not in place or if the operator's hand is detected in the sense field of the device.

One of the most effective means of guarding the point-of-operation when it is not practical to conform to the specific dimensions given in ANSI Standard B11.4 is the awareness barrier. This barrier is similar to a fixed guard, but it has movable lower sections that provide additional clearances

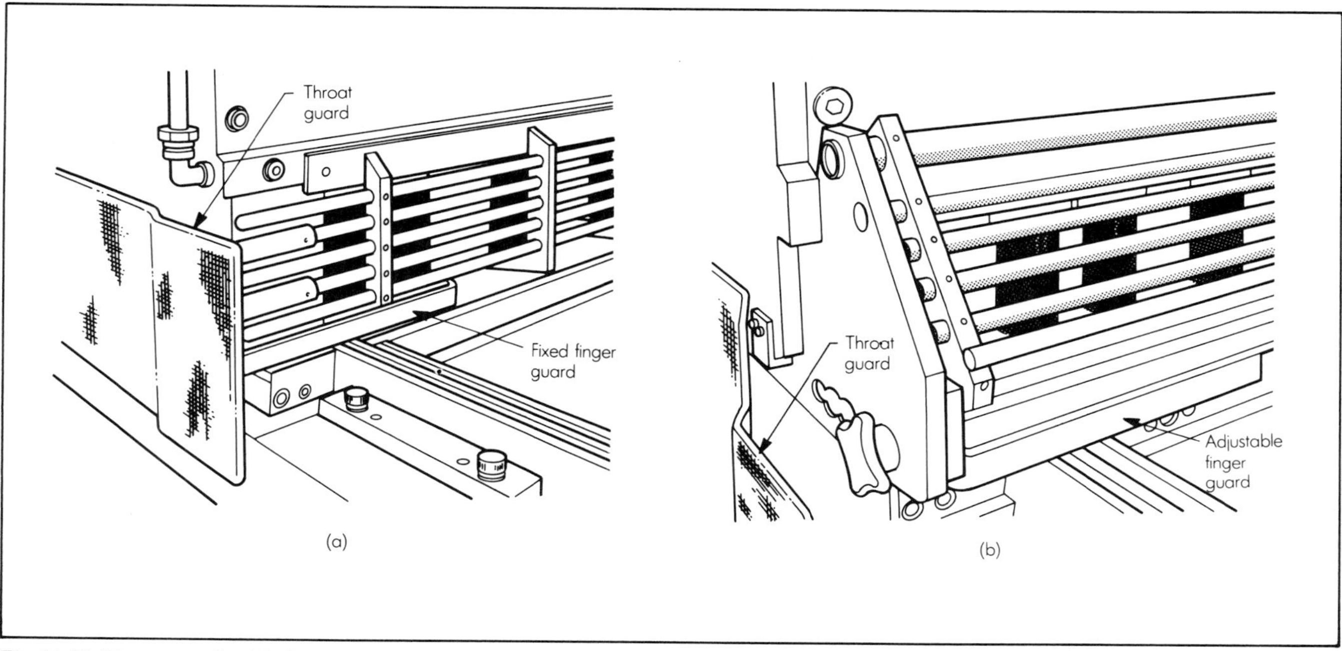


**Fig. 11-29 Finger guards with throat guard in place: (a) fixed-type guard for shears up to 5/16" (8 mm) capacity; (b) adjustable guard for shears with 3/8" (9.5 mm) capacity and greater.** (*Di-Acro Division, Houdaille Industries Inc.*)

greater than the 1/4" (6.4 mm) minimum required for material entry. When the material is inserted, the sectioned pieces lift but remain in contact with the inserted material by virtue of their own weight. Any remaining clearance is guarded by the movable sections. These provide a physical resistance to entry, thus creating an awareness barrier for the hazardous area.

Various mechanical and passive methods are available to protect the operator from injury by preventing or stopping the stroking of the shear, or restraining or withdrawing the operator's hands if they are placed in the danger zone. These, however, do not provide the consistent protection of fixed guards or awareness barriers since their effectiveness is dependent upon adjustment and the willingness of the operator to use the methods consistently.

If the shear has a throat (gap), throat guards are required to safeguard the knife area. Full or partial enclosures should be used to provide protection from entry from both sides of the point-of-operation at the throat. The guards should be movable to facilitate changing the knife and to permit shearing and slitting of material that is longer than the shear.

The area between the housings at the rear of the shear is an ever present hazard because it cannot, within the scope of practicality, be eliminated by design. Not only do the exposed shear knives present a danger, but the moving back-gage and the falling or sliding drops from the sheared material require safeguarding measures.

Since it is frequently necessary for the operator or helpers to enter the hazard area to remove scrap or sheared pieces, a warning sign and a removable barrier that extends the full length between the housings is essential. Rear-actuated presence-sensing devices, interlocked barriers, or disconnect switches that prohibit operation of both the shear and the back-gage are other safeguarding methods that protect personnel working within this area. Chapter 20, "Safety in Forming," presents other safety related topics in metalforming.

### References

1. Private communication from Larry Conley, Senior Project Engineer, Di-Acro Division, Houdaille Industries, Inc., Lake City, MN, October 30, 1982.

### Bibliography

Fischer, Fedrick R.; Huyvaert, Robert N.; Skinner, Robert L.; Wesstrom, Alfred. *The Serpentine-Slitting Process*, SME Technical Paper EM76-981, 1976.

Oldenburg, Patrick E. *The Art of Shearing*. Di-Acro Division, Houdaille Industries, Inc. 1979.

CHAPTER

# 12

# Punching

# PUNCHING

CHAPTER CONTENTS:



Punching involves the cutting of holes and results in scrap slugs. It can be performed with punching presses specifically designed to hold the tooling or with stamping presses and unitized tooling. Operations related to punching include nibbling, notching, piercing, perforating, slotting, pointing, and marking.

Both ferrous and nonferrous metals are punched, as well as nonmetallic materials. For a discussion on the theory of punching and the various materials punched, refer to Chapter 4, "Sheet Metal Blanking and Forming."

## ADVANTAGES

Punching on a punch press is fast and economical. A variety of shapes and sizes can be punched with standard tooling. Many presses are capable of nibbling large cutouts and contours in workpieces that would generally be produced with other, more costly metalcutting techniques. Plasma and laser cutting attachments permit small internal angles, scrolls, spirals, etc., to be cut on the punch press.

## WORKPIECE SIZES

Most punch presses are rated based on both the punching force they are able to deliver and the maximum hole size they can punch in a given thickness of material at a specified shear strength. The largest hole size is limited only by the punching force, punch and die size limit, and material thickness limit of the machine. One press is capable of punching a 6" (152 mm) diam hole in 3/8" (9.5 mm) thick mild steel plate. Generally, the maximum thickness punched is 1 1/8" (29 mm) on machines specifically designed for heavy plate and structural steel.

The size of the workpiece is generally determined by the throat opening in the punch press (distance from punch center to rear of press), weight of workpiece, and area in which the carriage moves. Several NC punch presses are capable of repositioning the workpiece, which in effect enables any length of material to be punched as long as the workpiece does not exceed the weight limit capacity of the machine and auxiliary tables are used to support the overhanging material. Manually rotating workpieces on presses with rear address clamping enables the width of the workpiece to be doubled. The largest workpiece capable of being punched prior to repositioning or rotation is 82" (2083 mm) wide by 100" (2540 mm) long.

Incorporating numerical control (NC) on the punch press increases the accuracy of the hole locations. Accuracy with a 1" (25.4 mm) center distance between holes varies from ±0.003 to ±0.010" (0.076 to 0.25 mm). On presses that use gaging or duplicating techniques, hole accuracy is maintained at ±0.015 to ±0.03" (0.38 to 0.76 mm).

## APPLICATIONS

Punch presses are used to punch holes of different shapes and sizes in various types of materials. Some of the applications for punch presses are in the production of electronic metal work, electrical boxes, appliances, construction equipment, farm machinery, trucks, office furniture, and vending machines. Figure 12-1 shows a few of the many products that are produced with modern punch presses.

Other operations that can be performed on the punch press include notching, forming, tapping, nibbling, and louvering.

# PRESSES

Punch presses are made with different force capabilities, frame configurations, tool-mounting capabilities, and controls. However, the mode of operation for all punch presses is the same.

The workpiece is generally positioned and firmly held down on the worktable prior to punching. When the controls are actuated, the ram descends and the punch knocks out the material as determined by the size of the punch and die (see Fig. 12-2). The stripper holds the material firmly in place until the punch has fully withdrawn. If the press is numerically controlled, the workpiece is then automatically moved to the next punching location. On certain presses, lifting devices in the die block prevent burrs created during punching from holding the workpiece on the die.

Power to the ram is derived manually, mechanically, or hydraulically. Manual punch presses are equipped with a long lever that converts the pull of a human hand to the forces necessary to punch the workpiece. Punching force for these presses is usually limited to about 4 tons (36 kN). Mechanical punch presses utilize flywheel energy which is transferred to the ram by gears, cranks, or

***Contributors of sections of this chapter are:*** *Howard Abbott, C. Behrens Machinery Co., Inc.; Victor Carbone, Engineering Manager, Strippit Division, Houdaille Industries, Inc.; Jim Mishek, National Sales Manager, Wilson Tool; Gary Pappas, Raskin, Datason Corporation; Jerry Rush, U.S. Amada, Ltd.; Jack Schneider, Production Manager, Mate Punch and Die Co.; Richard M. Stein, P.E., Chief Product Engineer, Strippit Division, Houdaille Industries, Inc.; Ronald E. VanWieringen, Product Manager, Wiedemann Division, The Warner & Swasey Co.; Frederic J. Vezina, Jr., Product Specialist, Strippit Division, Houdaille Industries, Inc.; Laurie Videle, Product Manager CNC Machines, W. A. Whitney Corp.*

# CHAPTER 12

# PRESSES

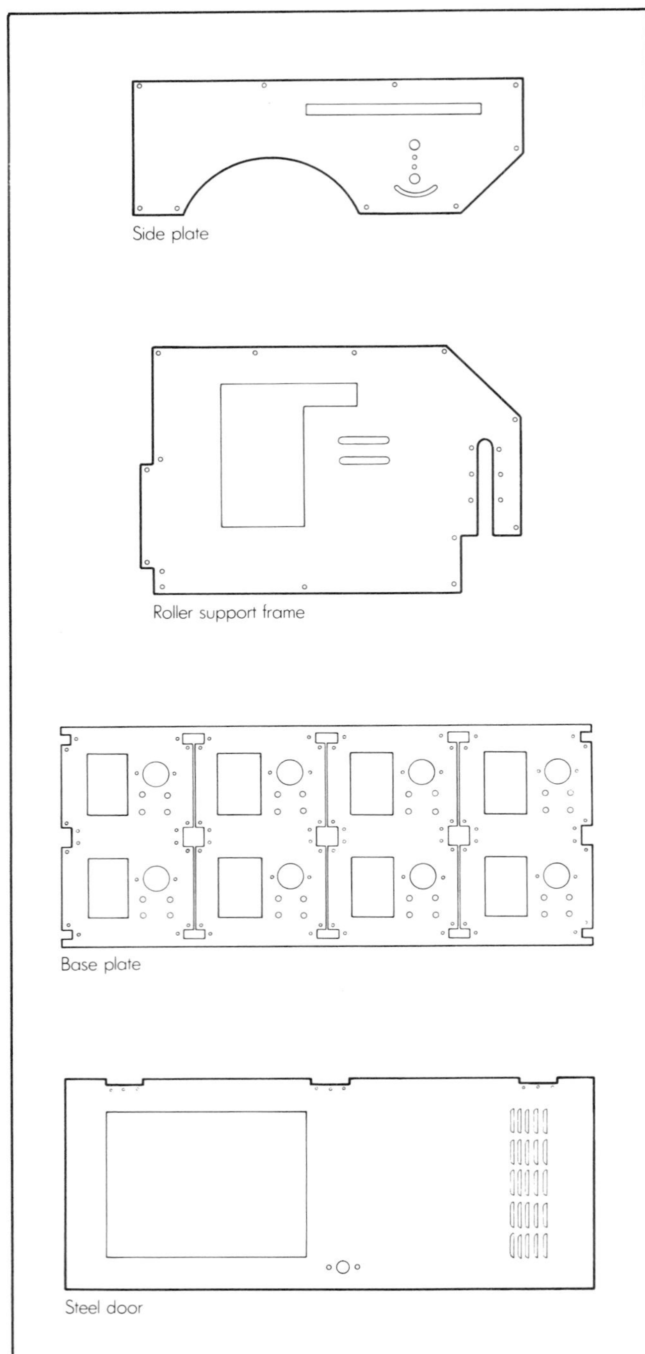


**Fig. 12-1 A few of the many different products fabricated on a punch press.** (*Wiedemann Div., Warner & Swasey Co.*)

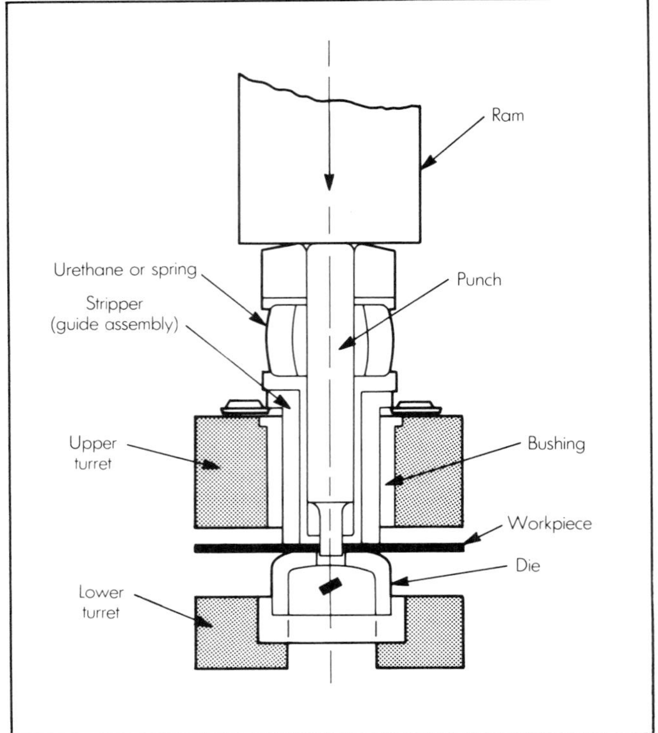


**Fig. 12-2 The punch knocks out the material as the ram descends.** (*Raskin, Datason Corp.*)

eccentrics to punch the workpiece as shown in Fig. 12-3. Hydraulic punch presses develop the punching force through the application of fluid pressure on a piston using pumps, valves, intensifiers, and accumulators. Hydraulic presses are capable of maintaining full punching force throughout their entire stroke lengths. Punching forces for mechanical and hydraulic punch presses range from 8-60 tons (71-534 kN). Presses specifically designed for heavy plate and structural steel are capable of producing up to 154 tons (1370 kN) of punching force. For additional information on mechanical and hydraulic press design and construction, refer to Chapter 5, "Presses for Sheet Metal Forming."

## CONSTRUCTION

Generally, most punch presses consist of a frame to which all the other components are attached, a mechanism to produce the punching force, a ram to transmit the force to the punch, and a table upon which the workpiece is mounted. The punch and die are the tooling used to produce the desired shapes in the workpiece.

Frames are usually made from steel weldments or solid steel plate and follow either a C-frame design or a bridge-frame design (see Fig. 12-4). A variation of the C-frame design is the

***Reviewers of sections of this chapter are:*** *Howard Abbott, C. Behrens Machinery Co., Inc.; Christian Bergerson, Product Manager-Machinery, Strippit Division, Houdaille Industries, Inc.; Tom Boyer, Vice President Marketing, Peddinghaus Corp.; Victor Carbone, Engineering Manager, Strippit Division, Houdaille Industries, Inc.; Dick Eckert, Manager Tooling, Strippit Division, Houdaille Industries, Inc.; John Holland, Central Region Manager, Peddinghaus Corp.; Jim Mishek, National Sales Manager, Wilson Tool; David J. Moellering, Moeller Manufacturing Co.; Thomas M. Ose, Service Engineer, Unitec Service Division, Marshall & Huschart Machinery Co.; Gary Pappas, Raskin, Datason Corporation; Bernard L. Rapien, Chief Die Engineer, Cincinnati Incorporated; Mike Rose, Sales Manager, Unitec National;*

# PRESSES

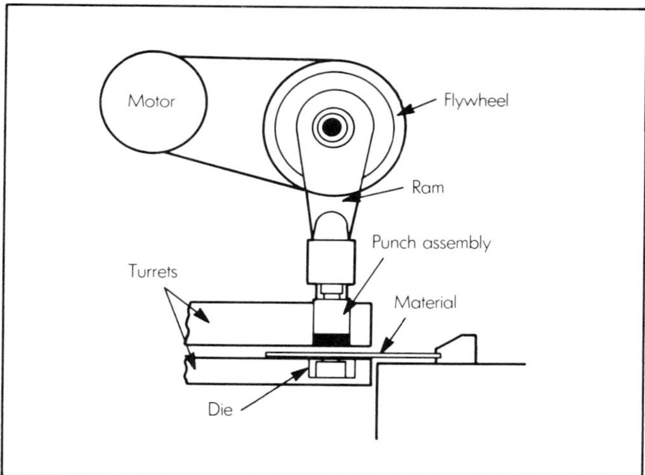


**Fig. 12-3 Mechanical punch presses utilize flywheel energy transferred to the ram to punch the workpiece.** (*Di-Acro Division, Houdaille Industries, Inc.*)

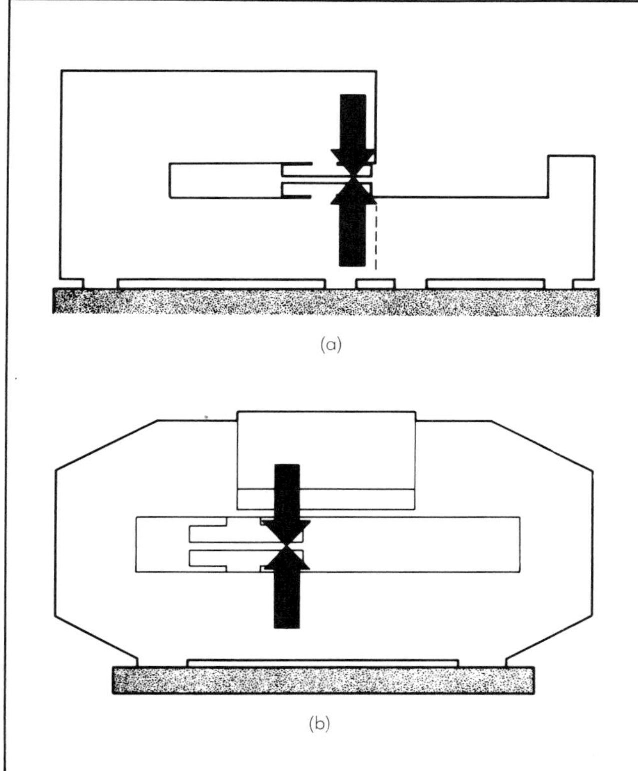


**Fig. 12-4 The frames of most punch presses follow either a (a) C-frame design or (b) bridge-frame design.** (*U.S. Amada Ltd.*)

J-frame design which eliminates the need for a special machine foundation normally associated with C-frame presses. The most popular design among manufacturers is the C-frame which is designed with either front address or rear address clamping. However, the bridge-frame design minimizes the deflection that occurs as a result of the uneven opposing forces acting upon the upper and lower frame members.

## TYPES OF PUNCH PRESSES

The two types of punch presses built are the single-station press and the multiple-station press. Multiple-station punch presses are generally referred to as turret presses. However, some multiple-station presses are built that contain two or three punching stations. The tooling is mounted individually in the toolholder. These presses fall into a classification between single-station presses and turret presses and are generally used when heavy plate, angles, or beams are being punched for structural steel fabrication.

Another type of multiple-station press contains two punching stations, but incorporates removable cartridges to mount the tooling. The cartridges are capable of holding up to 12 different styles of punches and are positioned under the punching head with servo-drive motors. The advantage of this type over the turret press is that the tooling can be mounted in the cartridges for another workpiece while the press is in operation. This type of press is particularly useful when two identical workpieces are being punched simultaneously.

### Single-Station Punch Presses

Single-station punch presses are equipped with a single, rigid tool adapter in which a punch of the required size and configuration is mounted. The corresponding die is mounted in the machine pedestal. Toolchanging can be performed manually, semiautomatically, or automatically and is discussed in greater detail in a section on "Tooling For Punch Presses" later in this chapter.

The single tool adapter allows the tooling to be changed quickly during programmed pauses on NC presses. It also provides good punch guidance and allows standard punches to be used in heavy, off-center-loaded situations without excessive tool wear. On presses with manual toolchanging, it is important to store the tools in a convenient place to provide ready access to them during the punching process.

### Turret Punch Presses

The turret punch press derives its name from the manner in which the tools are mounted in the press. An upper turret holds the punches, and a lower turret holds the respective dies.

Turret movement is achieved manually on small, hand-operated punch presses and semiautomatically or automatically on NC or CNC punch presses. Automatic turret movement is obtained by connecting a closed-loop, direct or alternating-current drive to the upper and lower turret assemblies (see Fig. 12-5). This movement can be unidirectional or bidirectional, and the direction of the turret rotation is generally determined

***Reviewers, cont.**: Jerry Rush, U.S. Amada, Ltd.; Jack Schneider, Production Manager, Mate Punch and Die Co.; Richard M. Stein, P.E., Chief Product Engineer, Strippit Division, Houdaille Industries, Inc.; Joe Troiani, Manager of Applications, Trumpf America Inc.; Ronald E. VanWieringen, Product Manager, Wiedemann Division, The Warner & Swasey Co.; Laurie Videle, Product Manager CNC Machines, W. A. Whitney Corp.; George Werbos, Project Engineer, Wiedemann Division, The Warner & Swasey Co.; D. J. Williams, Jr., Vice President Marketing, Producto Machine Co.*

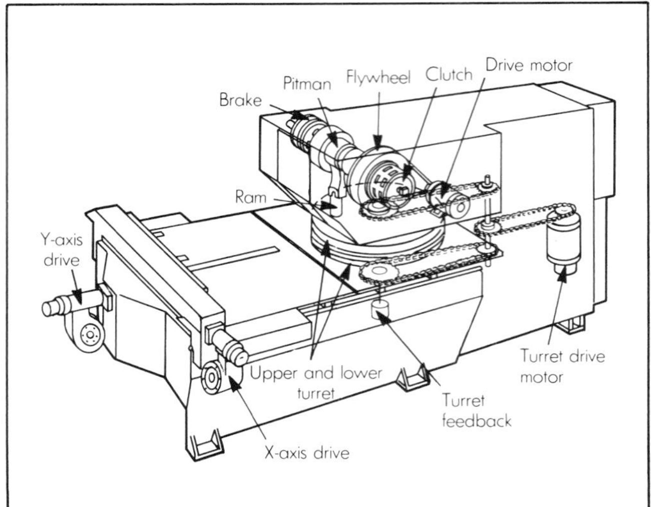


**Fig. 12-5 CNC punch presses have the upper and lower turret driven by a closed-loop, direct-current servo drive.** (*Wiedemann Div., Warner & Swasey Co.*)

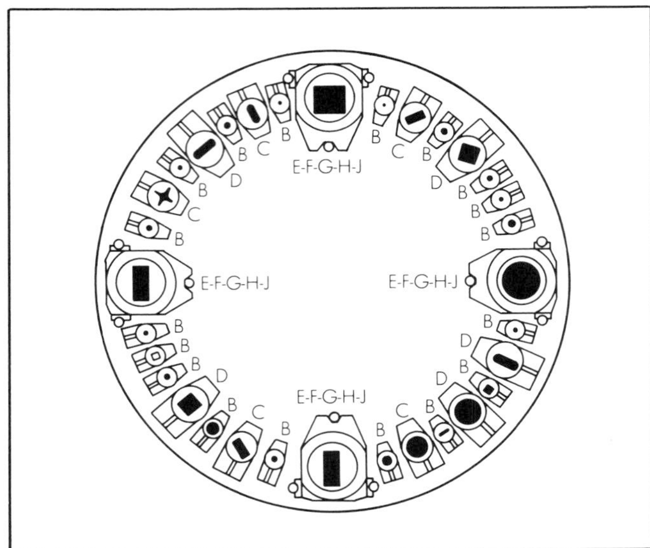


**Fig. 12-6 A 32-station turret designed to hold various punch and die sizes in certain locations.** (*Wiedemann Div., Warner & Swasey Co.*)

by the programmed punching sequence. Certain CNC presses offer an "optimization" feature which automatically determines the most efficient punching sequence for a particular workpiece. When a hole is to be punched, the turret is rotated until the proper tool is positioned under the ram.

Turret presses have the capability of holding tools of a variety of shapes and sizes. The variety of tools enables the operator to punch many different hole shapes and sizes without having to change the tools in the turret. However, tools of the proper size and shape must be mounted in the proper location in the turret as shown in Fig. 12-6. The number of tools contained in the turret ranges from 12 to a maximum of 72 depending on the manufacturer. Since the tools can be stored in the turret when they are not used, they are less likely to be damaged due to improper storage.

## PRESS CONTROL

Three methods are used to control the operation of the press: manual, semiautomatic (manual data input), and automatic control.

### Manual Control

On a manually controlled press, the operator is in complete control and is involved with each aspect of part production. From the drawing, the operator determines the tooling and the punching sequence for the required operation. The accuracy of the part produced is dependent on the skill of the operator and the accuracy of the press.

### Semiautomatic Control

The semiautomatic, sometimes referred to as manual data input (MDI), punch press offers productive capabilities between a manual punch press and an automatic punch press.

**Operation.** The operator initially selects the reference position for the workpiece and then loads the part on the worktable. The press is then set to operate automatically, and the operator inputs the data from the drawing into the press using programmable codes. When the data input is completed, the cycle is started and the part is positioned and/or punched automatically. If more than one part is to be punched, the press can be programmed to repeat the cycle over again.

**Advantages and limitations.** Two of the main advantages of the semiautomatic punch press are the cost of the machine and simplicity of operation. The cost of a semiautomatic punch press is approximately one-half that of a CNC punch press. Programming and editing is performed right at the machine using the programming codes instead of at a computer terminal. This enables an operator to learn how to program and operate the press in about two hours. The codes used indicate the work positioning speed, subroutines used, type of data input (inch, metric, or absolute), stops, returns to initial positions, positional coordinates, and the tool that is used. Although most CNC presses have MDI capabilities, their inputting procedure is more difficult and they require more time than the semiautomatic punch press. The MDI press is more accurate than the manually controlled press and can achieve the same degree of accuracy as the CNC press.

Generally, the maximum work positioning speed of an MDI press is limited to about 1000 ipm (25 400 mm/min) whereas the CNC press attains speeds as high as 4400 ipm (111 760 mm/min). Since the press uses fewer programmable codes than the CNC press, the operations that can be performed with the semiautomatic punch press are less than those that can be programmed on a CNC press.

**Applications.** Semiautomatic punch presses are especially suited for small job shops in which cost and training prohibit the use of CNC punch presses. They can also be used by large firms that perform prototype work and produce parts in limited quantities.

### Automatic Control

Automatic punch press control is achieved using either NC or CNC. For a comprehensive discussion of NC and CNC operation, refer to Chapter 5 in Volume I of this Handbook series. The punch press generally consists of a punching mechanism, a workpiece positioner, and a structure upon which these mechanisms are mounted. Automatic control is used for both single-station and turret punch presses.

Presses with C-type frames have the workpiece positioned in both the X-axis and the Y-axis directions while the turret or tool adapter remains in a fixed position. The X axis is generally used in conjunction with the workpiece length; and the Y axis, with the workpiece width (see Fig. 12-7). The clamps that grip the workpiece can be located on the front or back of the press table; this feature is referred to as front address or rear address clamping. Presses with rear address clamping are capable of punching parts that are twice the specified press Y axis or throat depth by manually rotating the workpiece. Presses with bridge-type frames have the workpiece positioned in the X-axis and Y-axis directions also, with the exception of some presses that position the workpiece in the X axis and the turret in the Y axis.

The turrets are rotated automatically to properly position the selected punch and die. Tool changes on single-station presses are also achieved automatically with specially designed removal/insertion mechanisms.

**Operation.** The first step in processing a part is to generate a program containing the dimensional and geometric data of the part from the print. This is usually performed by a programmer rather than a press operator. The program is stored in binary code on a narrow strip of paper or mylar tape. Cassette floppy disks are also used for storing programs. The tape and a list of the required tools are given to the press operator who inserts the tape into the tape reader on the press. After the tools and workpiece are loaded, the press is activated and the part is punched out according to the tape. The program can be stored in the press control to facilitate the production of multiple parts.

**Advantages and limitations.** Numerically controlled punch presses ensure greater productivity capabilities in most short to medium runs and greater workpiece accuracy. Prototype parts can be made quickly, and the need for models and templates is eliminated. Cost estimating is also simplified because of the precise time keeping.

With the addition of computer numerical control (CNC), programming is easier and requires 1/5 to 1/4 the time. Canned cycles and subroutines enable the programmer to program the punching operation in fewer steps. An "optimization" feature enables the programmer to program the punching operations in any order. The computer then determines the most efficient punching sequence. The control unit is also used in conjunction with the various press accessories that can be incorporated with the press to permit the press to be more versatile. The control unit has built-in diagnostic features to inform the operator of press malfunctions.

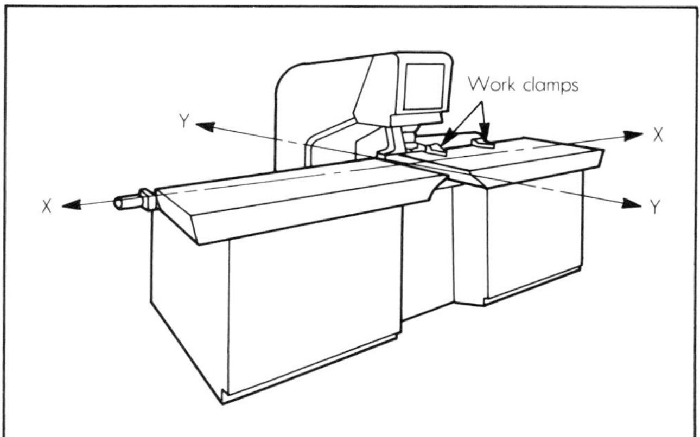


**Fig. 12-7 The workpiece on numerically controlled presses is positioned in both the X axis and the Y axis.** (*W. A. Whitney Corp.*)

The cost of the press is generally four times the cost of a manual press. The time required to learn how to program and operate the press is greater than that necessary for manual and semiautomatic presses.

**Applications.** Automatic presses are used in a wide range of fabricating shops where many different contours and cutouts are required. The ability of the CNC press to store the punching program for different workpieces enables this type of press to be used in limited production runs as well as long production runs. Plasma and laser cutting sometimes permit the press to produce intricate cutouts and contours that are not normally permissible with standard tooling.

## PUNCH PRESS SELECTION

Many different punch presses are available, ranging from a manually controlled, single-station press to a computer-controlled turret press. To properly select a punch press, it is therefore beneficial to consider press construction, capacity and capabilities, and controls as they relate to the type of work currently being performed and the production requirements. It is also important to select a press based on production growth that is anticipated in the future.

### Press Construction

As was mentioned in a previous section, the two styles of press construction used are the C-frame design and the bridge-frame design. Although the C-frame is a more popular design among manufacturers, some of the larger presses require a special foundation to maintain accuracy between press frame and worktable. However, presses with this style of frame and rear address clamping enable the press to punch workpieces that are twice the rated throat depth by manually rotating the workpiece. Bridge-frame presses and C-frame presses with front address clamping do not permit punching workpieces that are wider than the rated throat depth.

### Press Capacity and Capabilities

The force rating of a press directly affects the thickness of material that can be punched and also the maximum size of hole that can be punched in a workpiece. Whether the press is a single-station or multistation determines the amount of time required for tool changes. Hydraulic presses have a more even punching force than mechanical presses which is useful when punching thick material. However, mechanical presses permit a faster speed, strokes per minute (spm), than hydraulic presses. A higher stroke speed is advantageous when large cutouts and contours are being nibbled. Other capabilities to consider are workpiece weight limits, workpiece positioning speed, workpiece repositioning, and the ability to do minor forming. Plasma arc and laser cutting attachments permit the punch press to be more versatile.

### Press Control

How the press is controlled determines the accuracy and the speed at which parts can be produced. Automatic and semiautomatic controls provide the greatest accuracy in hole positioning and part repeatability. Automatic controls on presses provide the greatest flexibility in the contours that can be produced. However, they require more time to program than semiautomatic presses. Since semiautomatic presses are simple to program, they can be used when producing noncomplex and simple prototype parts and production parts on a limited basis.

# PRESSES

## PUNCH PRESS ACCESSORIES

Several accessories, when incorporated with the punch press, enable the press to perform a greater variety of work with a minimum of special tooling. These accessories also provide the means by which the press can operate automatically and thus reduce the number of operators needed for production. Some of these accessories include a plasma cutting torch, a laser cutting attachment, and material loading and unloading equipment. A useful feature is the capability of repositioning the workpiece during punch press operation.

### Plasma Arc Cutting

The plasma arc cutting process is accomplished by ionizing a gas with an electric arc and then forcing the gas and the arc through a small orifice. This process provides a clean, high-speed cut with little or no slag formation, requiring no preheat, and produces a minimum heat-affected zone (HAZ), resulting in little or no distortion.

A typical plasma arc cutting system incorporates a cutting torch mounted integrally in a CNC punch press, a floor-mounted power supply to provide the high amperage requirements, a slag removal system, a filtering system, and a torch-head height control system. The CNC unit is generally the same one that is used with the punch press.

**Plasma cutting applications.** Plasma cutting in sheet metal applications can be performed on any electrically conductive material ranging in thickness from 20 gage to over 1" (0.91 to 25.4 mm). It is employed to make contours, slots, and large cutouts which are not practical when using a punching machine. Nibbling, however, can be performed on thin materials on certain occasions, faster and less expensively than plasma cutting. Generally, plasma cutting can be performed at speeds to 500 ipm (12 700 mm/min). Speed, however, is dependent on material thickness and composition. Table 12-1 and Table 12-2 give the recommended torch speeds for cutting mild steel, stainless steel, and aluminum with a water injection plasma arc torch. For additional information concerning plasma cutting applications, refer to Chapter 14 in Volume I of this Handbook series.

**Quality and accuracy.** The quality and accuracy of a plasma arc cut are dependent on thickness, flatness, and quality of material, cutting speed, and the amount of current used during the cutting process. Beveled cuts are a result of an unequal distribution of thermal energy across the faces of the cut (see Fig. 12-8). Generally, the good side of the cut is within ±3° of being square. With a clockwise gas swirl, the good side is on the right side of the cut while looking in the direction of the cutting. The opposite side has approximately a 7-10° bevel when material thicker than 1/4" (6.4 mm) is being cut. On material less than 1/4" thick, both sides of the cut are beveled approximately 5-10°.

To obtain a sharp outside corner, it is necessary to program the torch to perform a triangular or semicircular loop (see Fig. 12-9). The triangular loop is easier to program on the computer. Generally, the inside corner is a radius equal to one-half the kerf width. Kerf width is dependent on nozzle diameter and generally varies from 1/16 to 3/8" (1.6 to 9.5 mm) wide.

Cutting accuracy for typical production runs is limited to ±0.020 to ±0.030" (0.51 to 0.76 mm) due to component wear and arc fluctuations. This can be improved by employing automatic cutter compensation techniques.

**Torch operation.** In the plasma torch (see Fig. 12-8), cool gas swirls around an electrode. When the torch is operating, an arc is established between the electrode and the workpiece. A column of plasma (heated and partially ionized gas) leaves the torch in a constricted arc at approximately 750 ft/s (230 m/s) through the small nozzle opening. As the plasma stream is forced through the nozzle, a large amount of heat [from 40,000-90,000° F (22 204-49 982° C)] is concentrated into a confined area. When this high-speed, high-temperature stream contacts the workpiece, the heat rapidly melts the metal and the ionized gas blows away the molten metal.

The electrode and nozzle require occasional replacement as a result of wear during the cutting process. Nozzles are generally in two sizes, and the selection of the correct nozzle is determined by the thickness of the material being cut.

**Torch adjustment.** Several methods are used to adjust the torch head to its proper height in relation to the workpiece. The least expensive method is a manual adjustment performed by the operator. This is not a very satisfactory means to control the height because damage can be incurred to the head if the nozzle is unprotected and the material is bowed.

Two methods are used to automatically maintain a fixed but variable torch height adjustment. One method is to utilize a voltage feedback system that senses the voltage potential between the electrode and the workpiece. The initial height is set by a proximity switch; and when the arc is struck, the voltage potential is maintained by raising or lowering the torch head with a stepping motor. Another method is to fix the torch head at a specified distance in a housing that floats on the workpiece. Both methods permit the cutting of bowed material while the torch head is maintained at the required distance.

**Torch systems.** Several torch systems are employed in plasma cutting. Each system has its own particular operation and advantages. Modifying the torch head enables the torch to be used with more than one type of torch system.

*Air plasma.* Air plasma is the most economical system employed and operates best on low-carbon steel. The air used in this system is generally taken from the atmosphere and then compressed and dried for use in the cutting operation. This system eliminates the need to purchase other gases and is capable of producing high cutting speeds.

*Oxygen injection.* Oxygen injection is similar to the air plasma system. Instead of using air for the plasma stream, this system uses bottled oxygen for the cutting process. A disadvantage of both the oxygen injection and air plasma systems is that surface hardening takes place on the cut edges.

*Dual gas.* Dual-gas plasma cutting utilizes two different gases for the cutting operation. One of the gases is ionized to a plasma state while the other serves as a shield gas to prevent oxide formation on the cut edges. The gases used are generally argon and hydrogen, or nitrogen and carbon dioxide.

*Water shielding.* Water shielding utilizes low-pressure water to shield the cut edges and to cool the material. Nitrogen is generally used as the gas. This system is recommended for cutting aluminum, titanium, and stainless steel.

*Water injection.* Water injection employs nitrogen as the plasma gas and water under a greater pressure than the water shielding system. The pressurized water shields the cut edges and constricts the plasma flow into a smaller, cross-sectional area. As with the water shielding system, the water cools the material to enable thinner material to be cut without distortion. To remove and dispose of the injection water and any smoke or grit generated from the cutting process, the water injection torch incorporates an annular vacuum suction ring (see Fig. 12-10). This system is slightly more expensive to operate than other systems, but can be used for nearly all types of material.

**TABLE 12-1**
**Recommended Operating Parameters for Plasma Arc Torch with Water Injection and Using 100% Nitrogen Gas**

| Thickness, in. (mm) | Table Speed, ipm (mm/min) | Arc Voltage, volts | Arc Current, amps | Nozzle Diameter, in. (mm) |
|---|---|---|---|---|
| Mild Steel: | | | | |
| 0.035 (1) | 450 (11 430) | 125 | 250 | 0.120 (3.05) |
| 0.075 (2) | 300 (7620) | 130 | 250 | 0.120 (3.05) |
| 1/8 (3) | 200 (5080) | 135 | 260 | 0.120 (3.05) |
| 1/8 (3) | 200 (5080) | 140 | 300 | 0.166 (4.20) |
| 1/4 (6) | 150 (3810) | 145 | 260 | 0.120 (3.05) |
| 1/4 (6) | 150 (3810) | 145 | 350 | 0.166 (4.20) |
| 3/8 (10) | 125 (3175) | 150 | 380 | 0.166 (4.20) |
| 1/2 (13) | 100 (2540) | 155 | 400 | 0.166 (4.20) |
| 1/2 (13) | 115 (2920) | 160 | 500 | 0.187 (4.75) |
| 3/4 (19) | 75 (1905) | 165 | 500 | 0.187 (4.75) |
| 1 (25) | 60 (1525) | 165 | 600 | 0.187 (4.75) |
| 1 1/4 (32) | 45 (1145) | 175 | 600 | 0.187 (4.75) |
| 1 1/4 (32) | 50 (1270) | 185 | 700 | 0.220 (5.60) |
| 1 1/2 (38) | 40 (1015) | 195 | 700 | 0.220 (5.60) |
| 1 3/4 (44) | 35 (890) | 200 | 725 | 0.220 (5.60) |
| 2 (50) | 30 (760) | 205 | 725 | 0.220 (5.60) |
| Stainless Steel: | | | | |
| 0.035 (1) | 450 (11 430) | 125 | 250 | 0.120 (3.05) |
| 0.075 (2) | 300 (7620) | 130 | 250 | 0.120 (3.05) |
| 1/8 (3) | 200 (5080) | 135 | 260 | 0.120 (3.05) |
| 1/8 (3) | 200 (5080) | 140 | 300 | 0.166 (4.20) |
| 1/4 (6) | 150 (3810) | 145 | 260 | 0.120 (3.05) |
| 1/4 (6) | 150 (3810) | 145 | 350 | 0.166 (4.20) |
| 3/8 (10) | 125 (3175) | 150 | 380 | 0.166 (4.20) |
| 1/2 (13) | 100 (2540) | 155 | 400 | 0.166 (4.20) |
| 3/4 (19) | 50 (1270) | 160 | 400 | 0.166 (4.20) |
| 3/4 (19) | 75 (1905) | 165 | 500 | 0.187 (4.75) |
| 1 (25) | 30 (760) | 165 | 400 | 0.166 (4.20) |
| 1 (25) | 60 (1525) | 165 | 550 | 0.187 (4.75) |
| 1 1/2 (38) | 30 (760) | 170 | 580 | 0.187 (4.75) |
| 2 (50) | 20 (510) | 170 | 600 | 0.187 (4.75) |
| 2 (50) | 25 (635) | 190 | 700 | 0.220 (5.60) |
| 3 (75) | 12 (305) | 200 | 750 | 0.220 (5.60) |
| Aluminum: | | | | |
| 0.035 (1) | 540 (13 715) | 125 | 250 | 0.120 (3.05) |
| 0.075 (2) | 360 (9145) | 130 | 250 | 0.120 (3.05) |
| 1/8 (3) | 240 (6095) | 135 | 260 | 0.120 (3.05) |
| 1/8 (3) | 240 (6095) | 140 | 300 | 0.166 (4.20) |
| 1/4 (6) | 180 (4570) | 145 | 260 | 0.120 (3.05) |
| 1/4 (6) | 180 (4570) | 145 | 325 | 0.166 (4.20) |
| 3/8 (10) | 150 (3810) | 150 | 350 | 0.166 (4.20) |
| 1/2 (13) | 120 (3050) | 155 | 375 | 0.166 (4.20) |
| 3/4 (19) | 60 (1525) | 160 | 400 | 0.166 (4.20) |
| 1 (25) | 35 (915) | 165 | 400 | 0.166 (4.20) |
| 1 (25) | 70 (1830) | 165 | 500 | 0.187 (4.75) |
| 1 1/2 (38) | 35 (915) | 170 | 550 | 0.187 (4.75) |
| 2 (50) | 25 (610) | 170 | 600 | 0.187 (4.75) |
| 2 (50) | 30 (760) | 190 | 700 | 0.220 (5.60) |
| 3 (75) | 15 (355) | 200 | 750 | 0.220 (5.60) |

(*Hypertherm, Inc.*)

**TABLE 12-2**
**Recommended Operating Parameters for Plasma Arc Torch with Water Injection and Using 65% Argon and 35% Hydrogen**

| Thickness, in. (mm) | Table Speed, ipm (mm/min) | Arc Voltage, volts | Arc Current, amps | Nozzle Diameter, in. (mm) |
|---|---|---|---|---|
| Stainless Steel: | | | | |
| 3 (75) | 15 (380) | 215 | 900 | 0.250 (6.35) |
| 4 (100) | 10 (255) | 225 | 1000 | 0.250 (6.35) |
| 5 (130) | 6 (150) | 235 | 1000 | 0.250 (6.35 |
| Aluminum: | | | | |
| 3 (75) | 18 (460) | 210 | 900 | 0.250 (6.35) |
| 4 (100) | 12 (305) | 210 | 900 | 0.250 (6.35) |
| 5 (130) | 8 (200) | 210 | 1000 | 0.250 (6.35) |
| 6 (150) | 7 (180) | 210 | 1000 | 0.250 (6.35) |

(*Hypertherm, Inc.*)

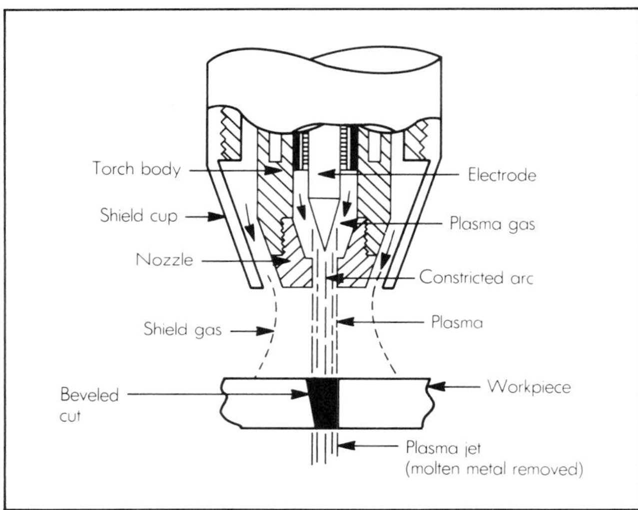


**Fig. 12-8 Typical plasma arc cutting torch with shield gas.** (*W. A. Whitney Corp.*)

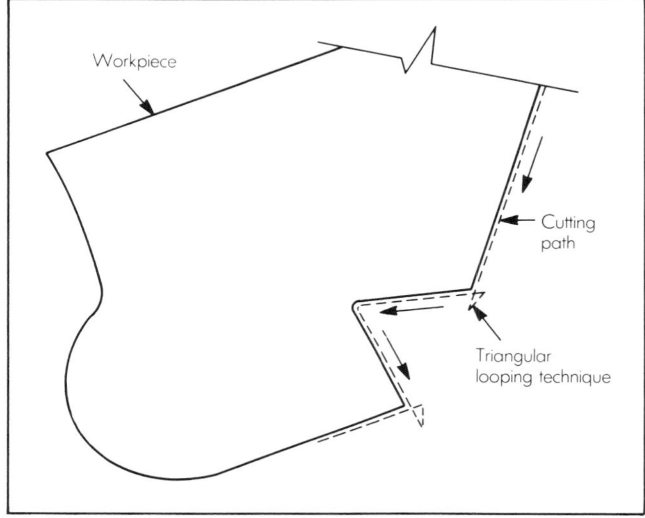


**Fig. 12-9 Looping is required to achieve a sharp outside corner when cutting with plasma arc.**

## Laser Cutting Attachment

The versatility of a punch press to produce holes in sheet metal is dependent on the number and shape of the punches available. A laser cutting attachment further enhances the punch press such that virtually any part shape is achievable through programmed motion of the workpiece with respect to the cutting beam.

The most popular type of laser for cutting sheet metal is the $CO_2$ laser. Its popularity derives from the fact that relatively high-powered beams can be generated at a laser frequency which is suitable for cutting a wide range of materials. Generally, $CO_2$ industrial lasers used in combination with a punch press range in output power from 400-1500 watts. A punch press laser system consisting of a punch press, laser cabinet, cutting head, laser control pedestal, and CNC machine control is shown in Fig. 12-11. Elevating the punch press on air pads during punching and nibbling operations reduces vibrations and prevents mirror misalignment.

**Application.** Materials which absorb the laser energy to create heat can be cut using the laser attachment. The cut materials are not confined to metals only. Plastics, wood,

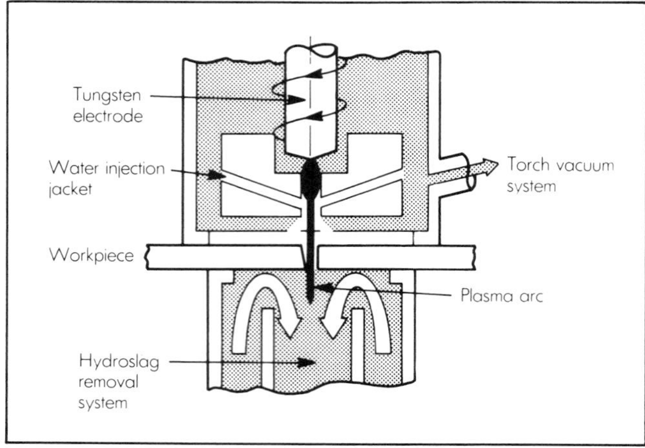


**Fig. 12-10 A water-injected plasma arc cutting torch incorporates a vacuum system in the torch head to remove water, smoke, or grit during cutting operation.** (*Trumpf America Inc.*)

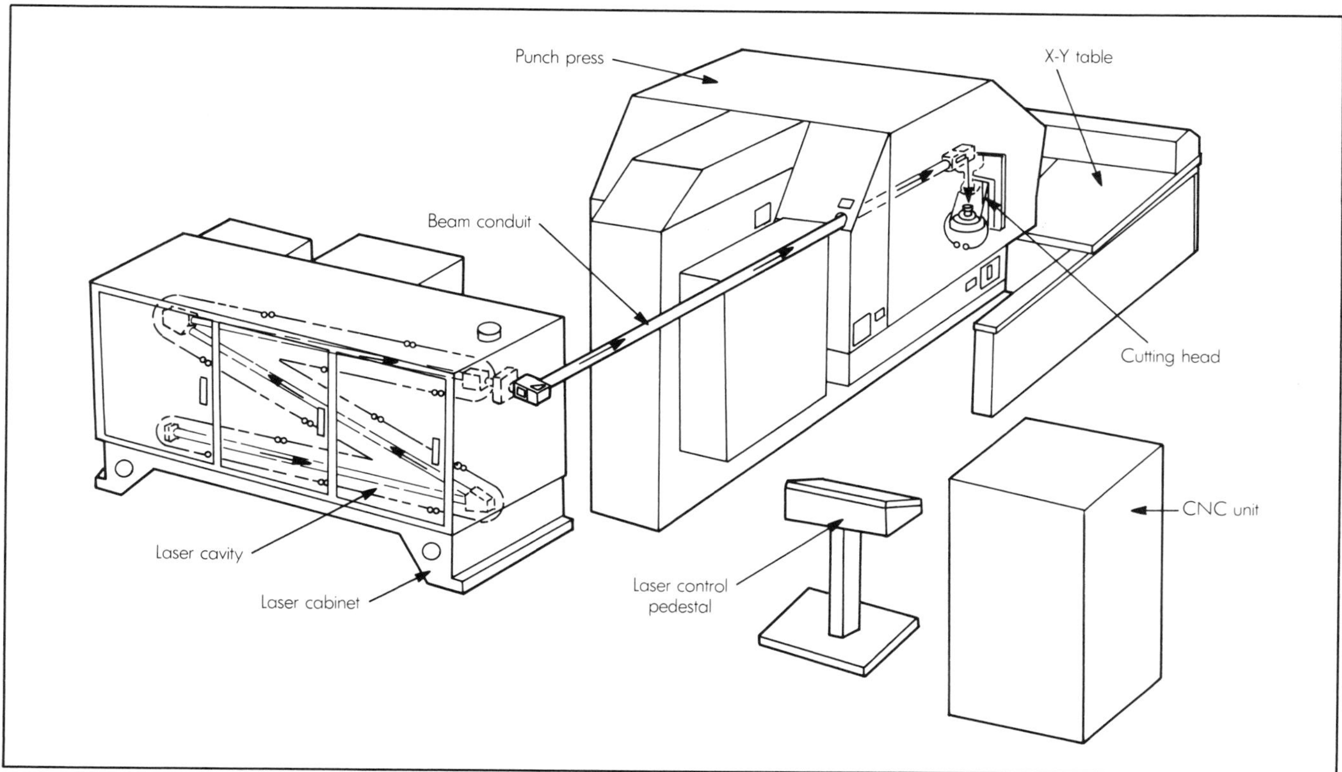


**Fig. 12-11 Punch press with laser cutting attachment and related equipment.** (*Strippit Div. of Houdaille Industries, Inc.*)

leather, rubber, and mica can be successfully cut with the laser. Titanium, spring steel, high-carbon steel, and high-nickel alloys are also easily cut by laser.

The cutting speed of the laser depends on available power, material characteristics, material thickness, and desired quality of cut. Speeds range from about 20-400 ipm (500-10 000 mm/min). Table 12-3 and Table 12-4 provide a list of materials that can be cut with a laser and the recommended cutting speeds.

The laser cutting attachment is employed to make large contours and cut-outs in material that normally require nibbling. Small contours and special shapes are possible without the use of special punches. The laser can also be used for etching material by employing a faster cutting speed or by regulating the pulse rate and width of the laser if so equipped. However, it is difficult to regulate the depth of the cut. For additional information on laser applications, refer to Chapter 14 in Volume I of this Handbook series.

**Laser operation.** In laser operation, a vacuum is applied to a series of tubes located in the laser cabinet and small amounts of carbon dioxide, helium, and nitrogen are then introduced into these tubes. A high voltage potential is applied to the gas mixture causing a light to be given off in random directions. This light is reflected by mirrors and strikes gas atoms within the tube. The striking of the gas atoms provides more energy to the light beam. When the energy of the light beam is great enough, the light beam is transmitted through the mirror and conducted toward the cutting head of the laser attachment.

The unfocused beam, generally about 0.4″ (10 mm) diam, is concentrated to a beam of about 0.005-0.020″ (0.13-0.51 mm) diam by a focusing lens (see Fig. 12-12). When the focused beam contacts the material surface, the surface temperatures increase to over 18,000° F (10 000° C), causing the material to melt and vaporize. An assist gas is injected into the nozzle to aid in the vaporizing of the material being cut. For ferrous materials, oxygen is used as the assist gas and helps to keep the nozzle clean, create an exothermic reaction, and blow away molten material. Compressed air is generally used as an assist gas when cutting nonferrous materials. Bearings, mounted in the cutting head, ride on the material surface to maintain the focusing lens at the proper height with respect to the material.

**Advantages of laser cutting.** A laser cutting attachment provides the fabricator with a greater flexibility in producing holes and contours in the workpiece. This is because the laser attachment eliminates the need for the special tools that are required when large holes, cut-outs, or contours are being produced. Changing the assist gas, gas pressure, or cutting speed enables the laser attachment to cut a wide range of material types and thicknesses. Since the laser is not in contact with the workpiece, tool wear is eliminated and sharp corners can be produced. The quality of the cut edge is good and generally eliminates the need for secondary operations. The narrow kerf of the focused beam minimizes the heat-affected zone of the workpiece which in turn reduces workpiece distortion.

**Limitations of laser cutting.** Materials that reflect light rather than absorb it, such as aluminum, copper, and brass, are difficult to cut. Since the maximum power attainable with a laser attachment is around 1500 watts, the thickest mild steel that can be cut is 3/8″ (9.5 mm). Cutting speeds are generally lower than those using the plasma cutting attachment. Initial alignment through the cutting head is difficult due to the invisible laser beam.

**TABLE 12-3**
**Recommended Laser Attachment Table Speeds (475 Watt Laser)**

| Material | Thickness, in. (mm) | 5″ Lens, ipm (mm/min) | 2.5″ Lens, ipm (mm/min) |
|---|---|---|---|
| Mild steel | 0.048 (1.22) | 130 (3302) | 250 (6350) |
| | 0.060 (1.52) | 120 (3048) | 220 (5588) |
| | 0.120 (3.05) | 60 (1524) | 120 (3048) |
| | 0.134 (3.40) | 50 (1270) | 90 (2286) |
| | 0.250 (6.35) | 20 (508) | --- |
| Stainless steel | 0.090 (2.29) | 80 (2032) | 100 (2540) |
| | 0.125 (3.18) | 30 (762) | 40 (1016) |
| Plywood | 3/4 (19) | 20 (508) | --- |
| Polystyrene | 1/8 (3.2) | 390 (9906) | --- |
| Polyvinyl chloride | 1/2 (12.7) | 120 (3048) | --- |
| Rubber | 1/8 (3.2) | 80 (2032) | --- |
| Quartz glass | 1/16 (1.6) | 45 (1143) | --- |

(*Strippit Div. of Houdaille Industries*)

**TABLE 12-4**
**Recommended Laser Attachment Table Speeds (1000 Watt Laser)**

| Material | Thickness, in. (mm) | 5″ Lens, ipm (mm/min) | 2.5″ Lens ipm (mm/min) |
|---|---|---|---|
| Mild steel | 0.048 (1.22) | 250 (6350) | 300 (7620) |
| | 0.060 (1.52) | 190 (4826) | 290 (7366) |
| | 0.120 (3.05) | 120 (3048) | 150 (3810) |
| | 0.134 (3.40) | 110 (2794) | 140 (3556) |
| | 0.250 (6.35) | 50 (1270) | 45 (1143) |
| | 0.375 (9.52) | 18 (457) | --- |
| Stainless steel | 0.090 (2.29) | 140 (3556) | 160 (4064) |
| | 0.125 (3.18) | 90 (2286) | 110 (2794) |
| Aluminum | 0.090 (2.29) | 20 (508) | 30 (762) |

(*Strippit Div. of Houdaille Industries*)

## Material Handling

Improving the methods by which the material is handled increases the production rate of the NC punch press. Incorporating a workpiece load/unload system and a workpiece repositioning system in a punch press enables the press to operate automatically. Some presses can also be equipped with an automatic part sorter to separate and sort different parts produced from the same workpiece.

**Load/unload system.** A load/unload system enables the workpiece to be automatically loaded, positioned, and unloaded from the punch press (see Fig. 12-13). Depending on the design, the various components can be positioned on the same side of the press or on opposite sides. The load/unload components are interfaced with the CNC unit for the press to provide a completely interactive system.

The loading component consists of a carrier mounted on an overhead rail. Suction cups, located in the retractable head of the carrier, transfer the workpiece from the storage rack to the worktable of the punching machine. When the CNC unit calls for a new workpiece, the retractable head lowers the workpiece to its initial position on the worktable. Generally, the workpiece is loaded and held in a ready position during the punching cycle. Pneumatically operated slides position the workpiece for punching, and sensors in the work clamps and end-stop ensure that the workpiece is positioned correctly and ready for punching.

When the punching is completed, the table moves to the load/unload position and the unload arm grips the finished workpiece. The work clamps are then released, and the workpiece is pulled off onto the scissor table. Cycle time for the loading and unloading sequence varies from 15-30 seconds. Part-discharging systems utilize a trap door and a conveyor belt controlled by the CNC unit to remove cut-out parts or scrap created by nibbling, laser cutting, or plasma arc cutting.

**Automatic sheet repositioning.** Automatic repositioning makes it possible for the work clamps to move along the edge of the sheet, regrip the sheet, and bring into the working area a portion of the workpiece which was not within punching range previously. There is no theoretical limit to the number of repositioning moves that can be made within a part nor to the length of the piece that can be handled. In practice, however, repositioning approximately doubles the length of the sheet that can be punched. When punching long sheets, it is necessary to use auxiliary tables to fully support the sheets.

The first operation in a repositioning cycle is for the sheet to be moved into position underneath repositioning cylinders located on either side of the turret/toolholder toward the front. The distance *L1* is the working area before repositioning, and *N1* is the area that cannot be punched before repositioning (see Fig. 12-14, *a*). The repositioning pads come down and hold the sheet stationary, and the work clamps open and move back approximately 0.05" (1.3 mm). The clamps then move along the edge of the sheet a preprogrammed distance, the clamps move back into the workpiece, the piece is reclamped and the repositioning pads are released. The distance *L2* is the working area after repositioning, and the distance *N2* is the area that cannot be punched after repositioning (see Fig. 12-14, *b*). The new punching cycle is ready to begin.

Repositioning is completely automatic and actuated by programmed command. Elapsed time is up to 10 seconds, depending on the distance of the repositioning move. The hole-to-hole accuracy of the move from a hole punched before a

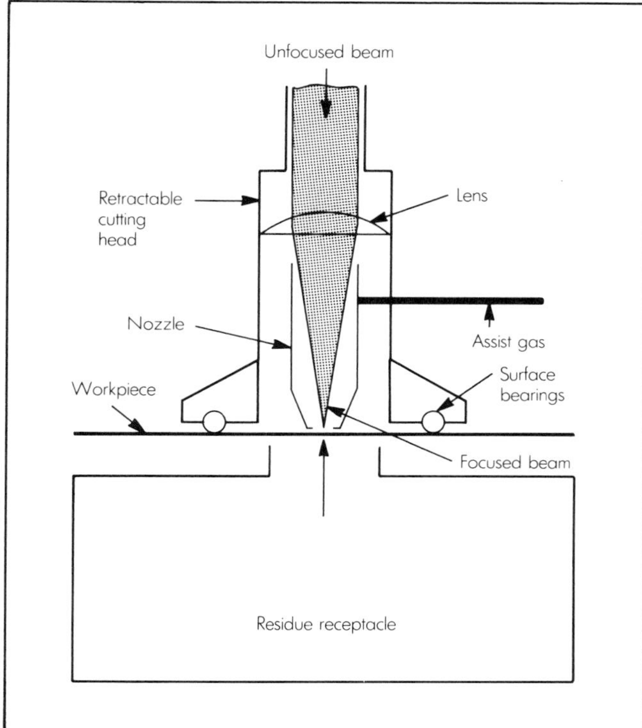


**Fig. 12-12 A focusing lens concentrates the unfocused beam to a diameter of 0.005-0.020" (0.13-0.51 mm). (*Strippit Div. of Houdaille Industries, Inc.*)**

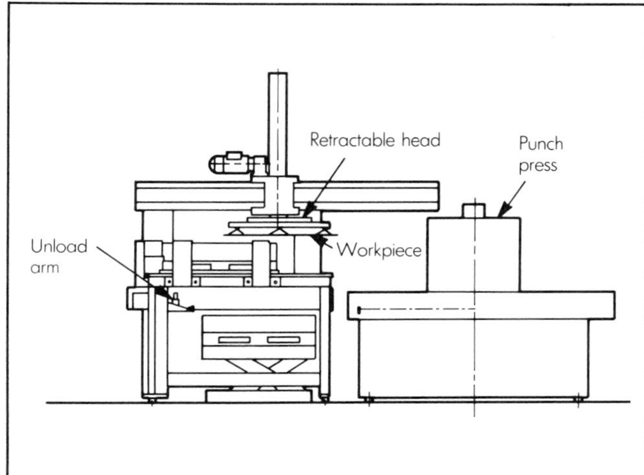


**Fig. 12-13 A loading/unloading system automatically loads, positions, and unloads the workpiece from the punch press. (*C. Behrens Machinery Co., Inc.*)**

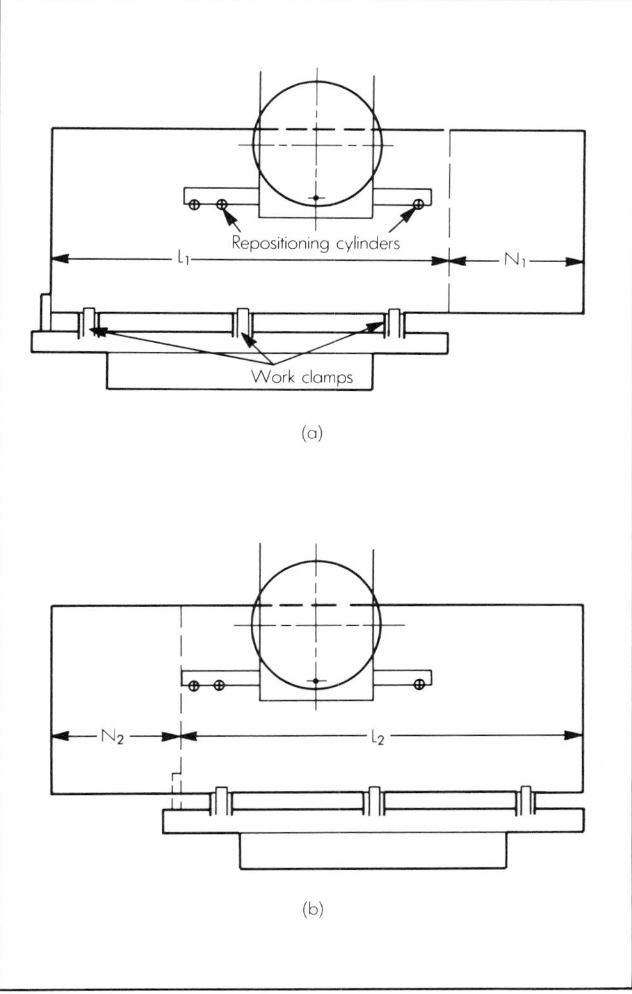


**Fig. 12-14 Repositioning cylinders hold the workpiece stationary while the work clamps move down the edge of the sheet a preprogrammed distance. (a) Workpiece before repositioning; (b) workpiece after repositioning. (*C. Behrens Machinery Co., Inc.*)**

repositioning cycle to a hole punched after the cycle is diminished by one-half as compared to the accuracy of holes punched within the same cycle.

Wide sheets can be repositioned manually on C-type frame machines that have sheet locating pins and rear address clamping (see Fig. 12-15). This allows sheets that are twice the width capacity of the machine to be punched. However, there is generally a limit to the amount of weight that can be supported. Auxiliary tables are also necessary to fully support the additional sheet width.

### Other Accessories

To provide even greater flexibility and versatility to the punching press, several other accessories can be incorporated in the press. A carbide-tipped stylus can be programmed to create numbers, letters, and marks for parts identification or center marks for bend lines, fit-up, welded parts, etc. A tapping attachment mounted on the side of the ram or under the worktable is capable of tapping holes up to 3/4″ (19 mm). A milling attachment mounted under the table can be used to remove the scalloped edges produced when contours or cutouts are nibbled.

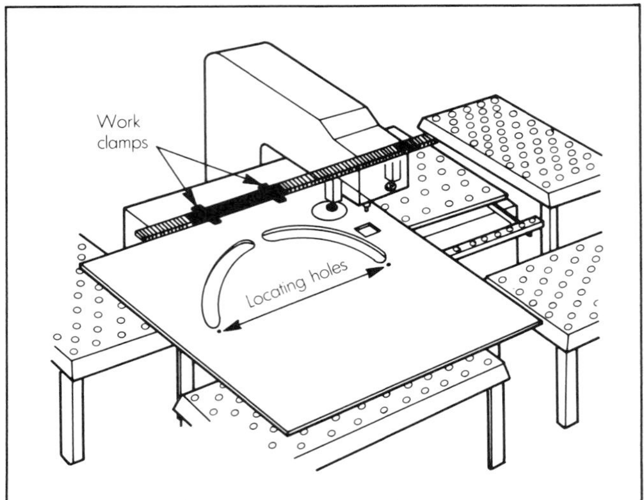


**Fig. 12-15 Work clamps located at the rear of the table permit the workpiece to be manually rotated, doubling the width capacity of the press. (*W. A. Whitney Corp.*)**

# NOTCHING MACHINES

When sheet metal is being processed, notching the corners or sides of a workpiece is often necessary to ensure that when the part is formed, the sides meet at sharp, well-matched corners. On parts on which the forms are shallow, the corner notching can be performed by a single-station or turret punch press. As the forms become deeper, it becomes more desirable to process parts on a notching machine capable of cutting notches greater than 8″ (203 mm) on a side in a single stroke.

A notching machine is a stand-alone unit with dedicated tooling capable of cutting 90° corners and V-notches in sheet metal. The basic unit generally includes a base, ram, hydraulic power pack and cylinder for actuation of the ram, tooling, a worktable, and positioning guides for supporting and locating the workpiece (see Fig. 12-16). The cutting action is initiated by either a foot switch or microswitches in the positioning guides.

The capacity of typical machines can range from an 8.75 x 8.75″ (222.2 x 222.2 mm) corner notch in 20 gage (0.9 mm) material to a 8.62 x 8.62″ (219.0 x 219.0 mm) notch in 0.250″ (6.40 mm) thick mild steel. Standard adjustments are applicable when stainless steel is being notched.

Accuracy of the 90° cut angle is ensured because the fixed relation of the blades is controlled by the machining of their seats. The accuracy of the cut lengths is controlled by setting the positioning to the scales that are fixed to the tabletop. Micrometer adjusters are normally available for closer tolerance work.

## OPERATION

The setup of a notching machine involves the relocation of the positioning guides for the desired notch depth and the adjustment of the blade clearance to the setting required for the material thickness being cut. Insufficient blade clearance causes secondary shearing and too much blade clearance generates excessive burrs on the underside of the workpiece. Each of these conditions causes premature blade wear due to excessive forces on the cutting edges.

## TOOLING

The tooling for these machines is made up of two pairs of shear blades set at a right angle to one another. The upper blades are mounted to the ram and set on an angle to provide a rake to the lower blades which reduces the input force necessary to cut. The lower blades are mounted in a recess of the tabletop which presets the 90° angle. To adjust blade clearance, the lower blades are moved simultaneously by sliding the tabletop in or out as required.

The sharpening of the blades is done on a surface grinder to hold parallelism, taking into account rake and relief angles where necessary.

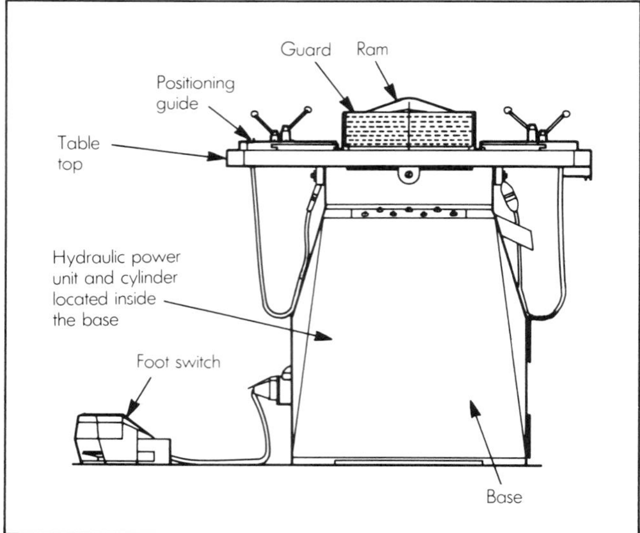


**Fig. 12-16 Typical components on a sheet metal notching machine. (*Strippit Div. of Houdaille Industries Inc.*)**

# TOOLING FOR PUNCH PRESSES

Tooling for a punch press consists of a punch, a die, and a stripper. The size of the punched hole is determined by the punch size, while the die size (opening) affects the condition of the hole and tool life. The clearance between the die and punch is based on the type and thickness of material. Some manufacturers use a punch holder with the punch and a dieholder with the die. Generally, tooling is interchangeable between presses of the same manufacturer, but not presses of other manufacturers. For a detailed description of punch and die design, see Chapter 6, "Die Design for Sheet Metal Forming." Figure 12-17 shows the installation of the tooling components in a turret punch press.

The punch is stripped from the metal using either a positive stripping method or a self-stripping method. The force necessary for positive stripping is derived from the press. Positive stripper plates and urethane strippers are used with the positive stripping plate to reduce workpiece distortion as the punch is being stripped. The positive stripper plates are mounted on the bottom of the turret or toolholder and can be set at a fixed distance from the workpiece or adjusted to contact the workpiece. The force for the self-stripping method is achieved from stripper springs incorporated in the tooling. The stripper or guide assembly is in contact with the workpiece during punching and until the punch is stripped from the workpiece.

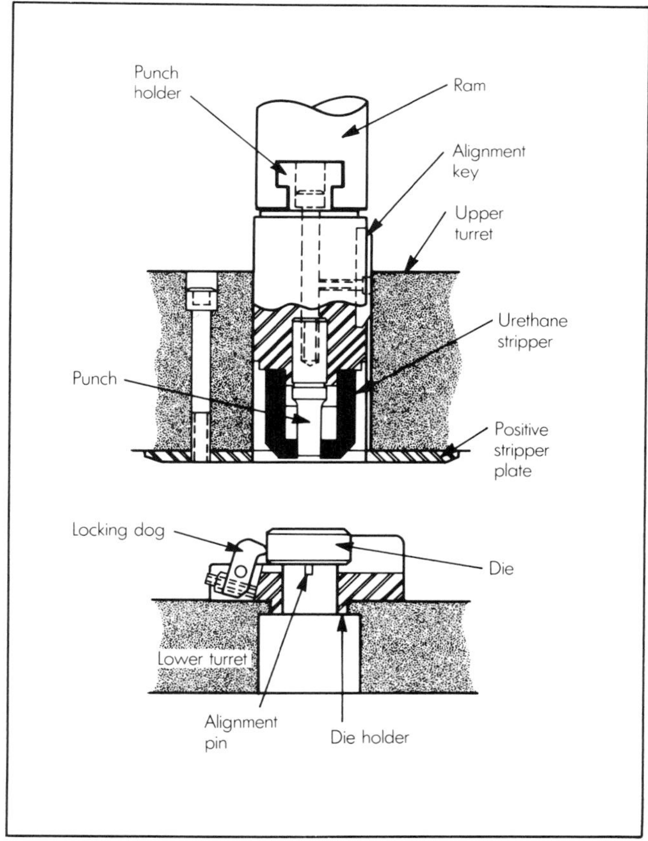


**Fig. 12-17 Typical tooling components on a turret press.** (*Wiedemann Div., Warner & Swasey Co.*)

## PUNCH SELECTION

Punches for a punch press generally are selected based on the size and contour of the hole to be punched in a given material and the material thickness. Tip configuration also affects punch selection. The two most common configurations are the flat tip and the shear ground tip. Shear ground punches reduce the required punching force and the punching noise. Figure 12-18 illustrates the different types of shear ground on a punch tip, and Table 12-5 lists the advantages and limitations of each type of shear.

### Size

When the size of the punch is being selected, it is important that the punch's compressive strength be greater than the force required to punch the hole. Punch failure normally occurs before the compressive strength of the punch has been reached. Punches smaller than 0.12" (3.0 mm) diam generally buckle at about 70% of their compressive strength. The compressive strength in the punch can be calculated from the equation:

$$S_c = \frac{T \times S_s \times L}{A} \tag{1}$$

where:

$S_c$ = compressive stress in the punch, psi (MPa)
$T$ = thickness of material being punched, in. (mm)
$S_s$ = shear strength of material being punched, psi (MPa)
$L$ = circumference of the punch shape, in. (mm)
$A$ = cross-sectional area of the punch, in.$^2$ (mm$^2$)

The maximum allowable compressive stress, $S_c$, depends upon the composition and hardness of the steel from which the punch is made. Generally, a good grade of oil-hardened, shock-resistant tool steel can withstand 300,000 psi (2068.5 MPa)

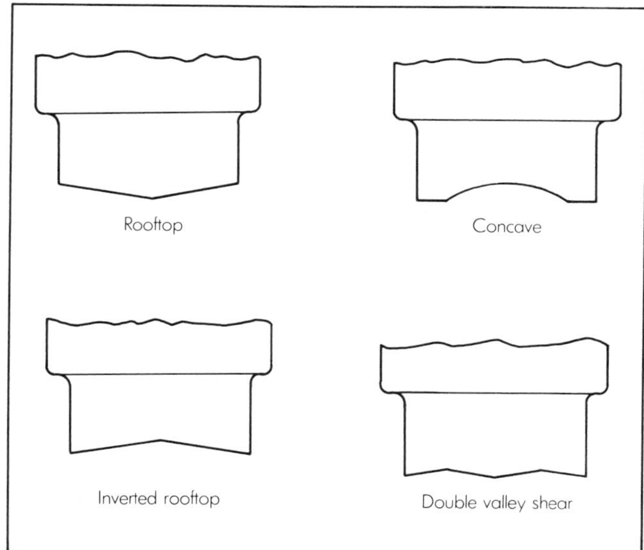


**Fig. 12-18 Punches with different types of shear ground on them.** (*Wilson Tool*)

compressive stress before breaking. Therefore, a punch with a compressive stress of 250,000 psi (1728 MPa) can be used safely and will provide good tool life.

Example:

Determine the compressive stress in a punch when a 1/2″ diam hole is punched in a 1/2″ steel plate with a 50,000 psi shear strength.

$$S_c = \frac{\frac{1}{2} \times 50000 \times 3.14159 \times \frac{1}{2}}{\frac{3.14159 \times \frac{1}{2}^2}{4}} = 200{,}000 \text{ psi} = 1379 \text{ MPa}$$

Figure 12-19 shows the minimum punch diameter that can be punched through a given thickness of material. Three different materials are illustrated. The upper edge of the shaded areas represent the breaking point for the punch. Punching hole diameters within the shaded area results in a shortened punch life.

To use the graph, locate the thickness of material along the vertical scale and follow across horizontally to the lower edge of the shaded area for the material being punched. From this point, drop down to the horizontal scale and read the minimum recommended punch diameter. For example, when punching 3/4″ (19 mm) thick mild steel, 19/32″ (15 mm) is the recommended minimum punch diameter; the punch would fail prematurely if a 1/2″ (12.7 mm) diam punch were chosen.

Another method for determining the size of punch is to consult Fig. 12-20 which gives the thickness-to-diameter ratio for materials with a given shear strength. The curve shown as a broken line represents the maximum compressive stress that a punch can withstand; the solid curve represents the recommended compressive stress for a punch. For example, the recommended thickness-to-diameter ratio for mild steel with a shear strength of 50,000 psi (345 MPa) is 1 1/4. This means that the material thickness can be 1 1/4 times greater than the punch diameter.

**TABLE 12-5**
**Advantages and Disadvantages of Different Types of Shear for Punches**

| Type of Shear | Advantages | Limitations |
|---|---|---|
| Rooftop | Best shear for punching at maximum forces. | Nibbling must be done at 75% of bite or excessive side loading results. |
| Concave or Double Concave | Best shear for nibbling because it inverts the stresses and reduces side loading. | Because of inverted stresses, the punch can break when punching at high forces. Difficult to grind. |
| Inverted Rooftop | Good shear for nibbling because of inverted stresses and reduced side loading. | More susceptible to breakage if it has a sharp focal point for stresses. Radiusing the focal point reduces susceptibility to breakage. |
| Double Valley Shear | Best shear for nibbling when shape is long and narrow. | Because of inverted stresses, the punch can break when punching is done at high forces. |

*(Wilson Tool)*

## Shape

Punches are available in many styles to accommodate the various contours that must be punched with the punch press. Figure 12-21 shows the shapes of the standard types of punches. Special shapes are also available to enable the fabricator to punch holes for specific applications. Some of these punches are employed in the formation of louvers, electrical knockouts, multiple holes, and tap extrusions. Figure 12-22 illustrates the shapes of some of these special punches.

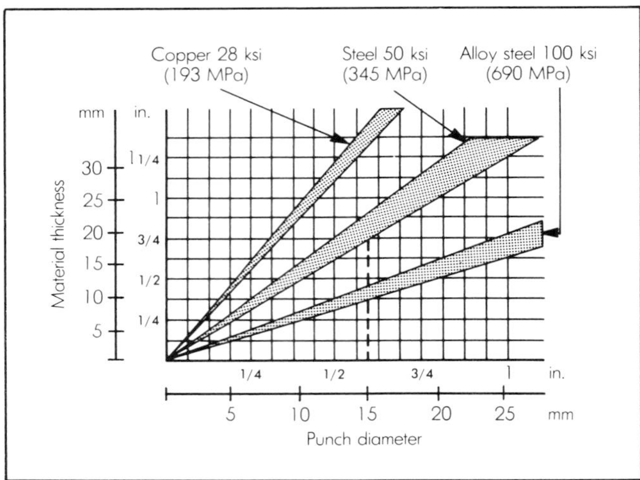


**Fig. 12-19 Graph used to obtain the minimum punch diameter based on the type and thickness of the workpiece material.** (*W. A. Whitney Corp.*)

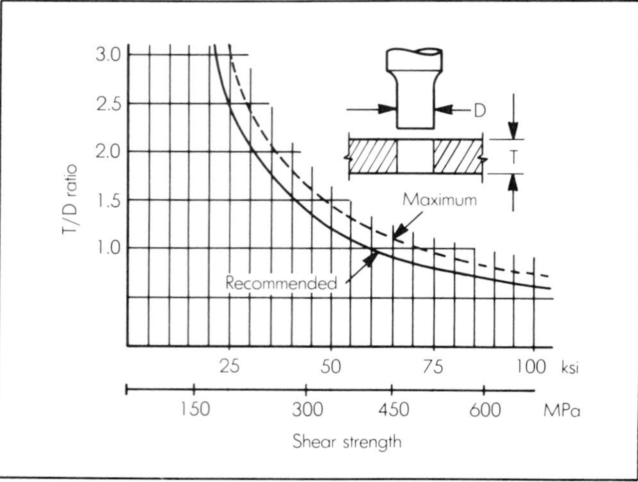


**Fig. 12-20 Graph used to determine the correct material thickness to punch diameter ratio when punching material with a given shear strength.** (*W. A. Whitney Corp.*)

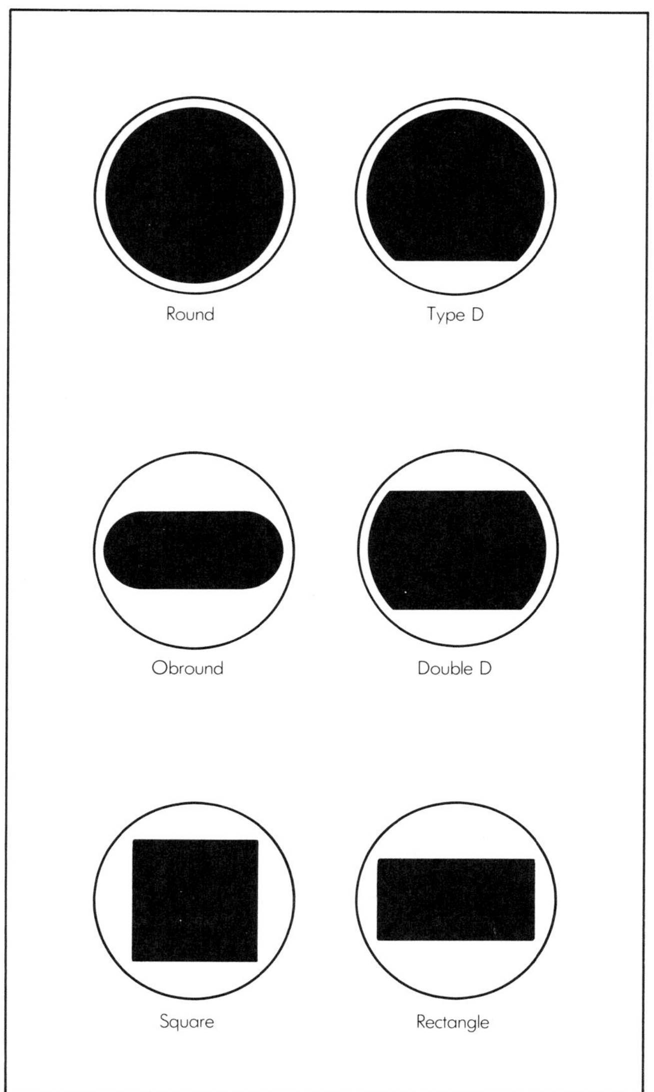


Fig. 12-21 Shapes of punches commonly used on punch presses.

## TOOL MOUNTING

Punches and dies for single-station punch presses are mounted in the tool adapter and a machine pedestal. Turret-type presses have the tools mounted in the upper and lower turret. Radial tool alignment of shaped punches is achieved with pins or keys in the punches and dies. A special rotary adapter permits the punch and die to be rotated to any desired angle. This reduces the number of special form tools required and the total tooling costs. After the tools are inserted in their holder, they are locked into position manually, hydraulically, or pneumatically.

Toolchanging is accomplished manually, semiautomatically, or automatically. Manual toolchanging is generally found on turret-type presses and certain single-station presses. This is not an inconvenience with turret presses because the turret usually contains all the tools required for the specific production run. On presses with a semiautomatic toolchanging system, the punch, stripper, and die are mounted in a cartridge mechanism

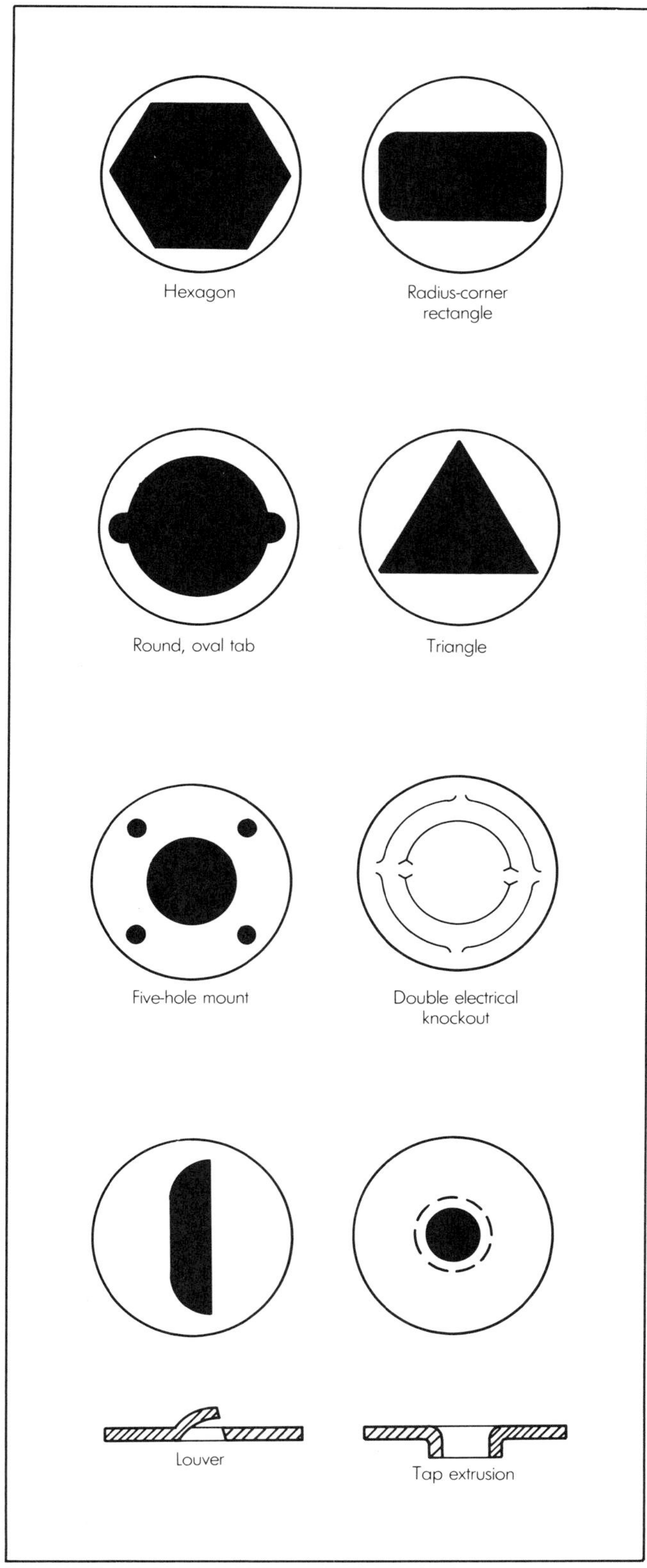


Fig. 12-22 Special-shaped punches permit the fabricator to punch holes for special applications with only one punch.

before being inserted into the tool adapter (see Fig. 12-23). During a programmed stop, one set of tools is removed and the other set is installed. During the punching operation, another set of tools can be loaded in the cartridge. Toolchanging takes place in less than 15 seconds. Automatic toolchangers generally have a bidirectional tool magazine in which the tool sets are mounted. During programmed tool changes, the tool adapter unloads the tools into the magazine and the magazine positions the programmed tool to the active location and then inserts the next set of tools into the adapter (see Fig. 12-24). The tool sets are inserted into the magazine either manually or with a set-up cartridge.

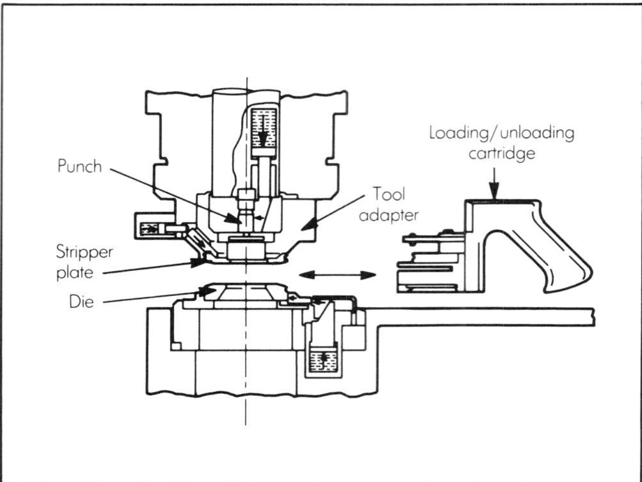


**Fig. 12-23 The punch, stripper, and die are inserted into the tooling adapter with a loading/unloading cartridge on presses with semi-automatic toolchanging systems.** (*Trumpf America, Inc.*)

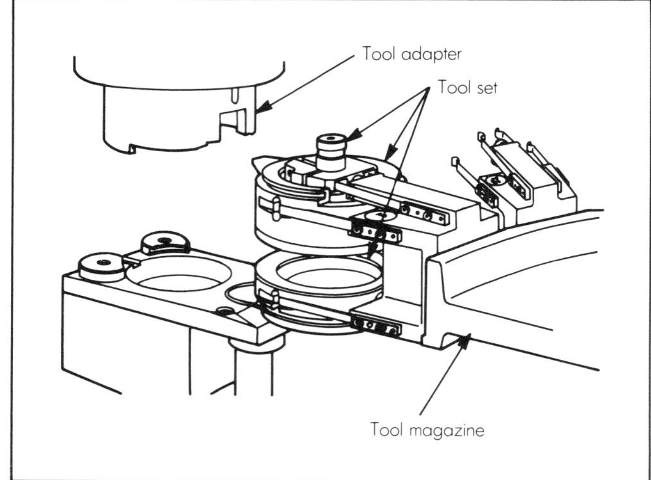


**Fig. 12-24 During a programmed tool change, the tool adapter unloads the tool set into the tool magazine and the magazine then rotates and inserts the next set of tools into the adapter.** (*W. A. Whitney Corp.*)

# OPERATING PARAMETERS

The type and thickness of material and the hole size determine to a large extent the force required to punch a hole in the workpiece. Punch clearance and type of material determine the amount of force required for stripping the punch from the workpiece. Punching and stripping force calculations are discussed in detail in Chapter 4, "Sheet Metal Blanking and Forming." Clearances between punches and dies are discussed in Chapter 6, "Die Design for Sheet Metal Forming."

## SPEED

The number of strokes per minute (spm) for a press is dependent upon how the ram is driven, the speed at which the workpiece can be positioned under the punch, and the thickness of material being punched. Generally, the maximum spm made by a punch press is fixed, rated at the maximum material thickness that the press is capable of punching, and cannot be varied by the operator. Based on 1" (25.4 mm) centers, the speed of the various presses ranges from 55-265 spm. In a continuous punching mode used for nibbling, the press can attain 500 spm. One manufacturer provides the capability to have two different speed settings for nibbling.

The workpiece positioning speed is dependent on the weight of the moving parts and the type of carriage drive motors that are used. The distance that the workpiece must travel during a punching operation is also a factor. Axis positioning speeds up to 3150 ipm (80 010 mm/min) are attained if the workpiece is moved in only one direction and up to 2400 ipm (111 760 mm/min) if the workpiece is moved in both directions at the same time.

## NIBBLED PATH EVALUATION

When it is necessary to nibble openings in sheet or plate material with a round punch, a scalloped condition often results on the finished edge. The scallop can create problems for clearance of mating parts and for safety if the opening is used as an access.

### Scallop Height

The scallop height (see Fig. 12-25) for an opening when utilizing a specified punch size and punching center distance can be determined using the formula:

$$S = r - \sqrt{r^2 - (R/2)^2} \qquad (2)$$

where:

$S$ = scallop height, in. (mm)
$r$ = punch radius, in. (mm)
$R$ = distance between punch centers, in. (mm)

Example:

Determine the scallop height of a nibbled opening using a 1" (25.4 mm) diam punch and a 0.350" (8.89 mm) center distance.

$$S = r - \sqrt{r^2 - (R/2)^2} = 0.50 - \sqrt{0.50^2 - (0.350/2)^2}$$
$$= 0.031'' \text{ (0.78 mm)}$$

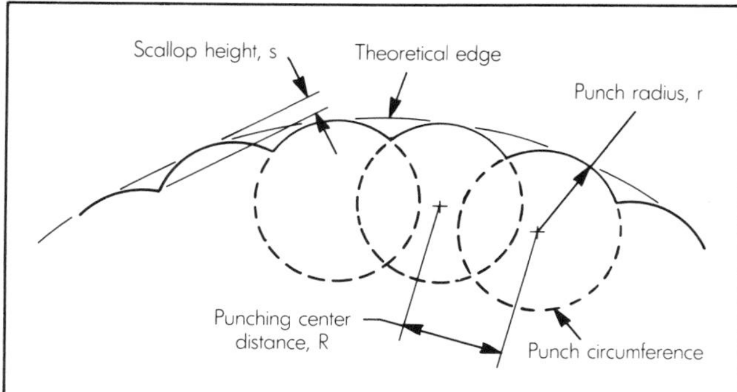


**Fig. 12-25 Nibbling openings and contours with a round punch often results in a scalloped condition.** (*W. A. Whitney Corp.*)

### Punch Center Distance

The required punching center distance (see Fig. 12-25) for a given punch diameter and scallop height can be determined using the formula:

$$R = 2\sqrt{2rs - s^2} \tag{3}$$

where:

$R$ = distance between punch centers, in. (mm)
$r$ = punch radius, in. (mm)
$S$ = scallop height, in. (mm)

Example:

Determine the required punching center distance when nibbling an opening with a 1″ (25.4 mm) diam punch and a 0.015″ (0.38 mm) scallop height.

$$R = 2\sqrt{2rs - s^2} = 2\sqrt{2(0.50)(0.015) - 0.015^2}$$
$$= 0.243'' \text{ (6.17 mm)}$$

These formulas are applicable to straight line and circular operations when utilizing point-to-point or linear interpolation NC programming on contouring machines. The formula acccuracy for circular interpolation is only approximate and becomes increasingly accurate when the nibbled arc radius increases. Table 12-6 indicates the center distance required to obtain a specified scallop height when punches with various diameters are to be used. It is important to consider material thickness and punch diameter during nibbling operations to prevent punch breakage or punch/die contact due to unsymmetrical loading of the punch. The punching center distance should be 33% of the material thickness or 20% of the punch diameter.

## FORMING ON A PUNCH PRESS

The NC punch press is one of the most productive machine tools in the modern sheet metal fabricating industry. The machines are universally accepted for their ability to rapidly and precisely punch parts in runs of 1-100,000 and more. In addition to simple hole punching, they can be used to perform forming operations, including forming the interior of a workpiece with the proper tooling. Figure 12-26 illustrates the basic forms produced on an NC punch press. Table 12-7 provides a description of the various forming operations, suggested applications, material types and thicknesses, and force requirements for these operations.

Interior forms are defined as those forms that commonly appear within the workpiece as opposed to bends which are normally accomplished on a press brake. A few of the general rules governing the design and fabrication of interior forms when forming is performed on an NC punch press include:

1. Always form upward so that the form projects from the top side of the sheet.
2. Observe the maximum height limitation of the form.
3. Stay within the force capacity of the press.
4. Consider the mechanical properties of the workpiece.

### Forming Position

Forming done on an NC punch press must always be performed upward so that the forms generated are on the top face of the workpiece. The rapid movement of the workpiece in the machine does not allow for any projections to exist on the underside of the sheet. The underside of the sheet slides across the dies in the lower turret, and any form projecting downward can be caught in the openings of these dies. Any design

**TABLE 12-6**
**Recommended Punching Center Distances, in. (mm)**

| Scallop Height | Distance Between Punch Centers | | | | | | | | | | | |
|---|---|---|---|---|---|---|---|---|---|---|---|---|
| 0.015 (0.38) | 0.081 (2.05) | 0.119 (3.02) | 0.147 (3.73) | 0.170 (4.32) | 0.191 (4.85) | 0.210 (5.33) | 0.227 (5.76) | 0.243 (6.17) | 0.272 (6.91) | 0.298 (7.57) | 0.323 (8.20) | 0.346 (8.79) |
| 0.032 (0.81) | 0.108 (2.74) | 0.167 (4.24) | 0.209 (5.31) | 0.245 (6.22) | 0.275 (6.98) | 0.303 (7.70) | 0.328 (8.33) | 0.352 (8.94) | 0.395 (10.03) | 0.433 (11.00) | 0.469 (11.91) | 0.502 (12.75) |
| 0.047 (1.20) | 0.120 (3.05) | 0.195 (4.95) | 0.248 (6.30) | 0.292 (7.42) | 0.329 (8.35) | 0.363 (9.22) | 0.394 (10.00) | 0.422 (10.72) | 0.475 (12.06) | 0.523 (13.28) | 0.566 (14.38) | 0.606 (15.39) |
| 0.062 (1.57) | 0.124 (3.15) | 0.216 (5.48) | 0.278 (7.06) | 0.329 (8.35) | 0.373 (9.47) | 0.413 (10.49) | 0.449 (11.40) | 0.482 (12.24) | 0.543 (13.79) | 0.597 (15.16) | 0.647 (16.43) | 0.693 (17.60) |
| Punch radius | 0.062 (1.57) | 0.125 (3.17) | 0.187 (4.75) | 0.250 (6.35) | 0.312 (7.92) | 0.375 (9.52) | 0.437 (11.10) | 0.500 (12.70) | 0.625 (15.87) | 0.750 (19.05) | 0.875 (22.22) | 1.000 (25.40) |

(*W. A. Whitney Corp.*)

# OPERATING PARAMETERS

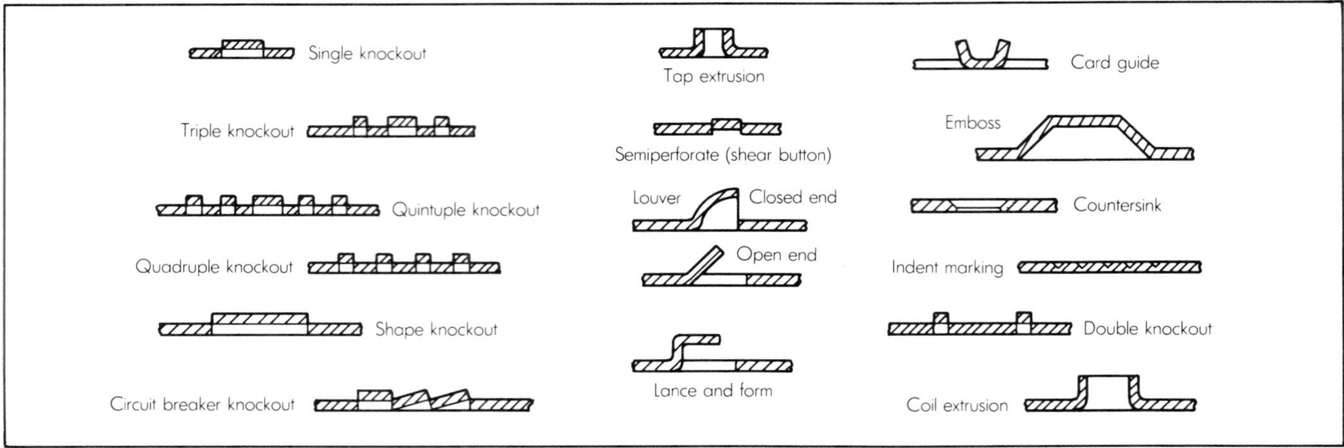


**Fig. 12-26 Numerically controlled punch presses are capable of producing these typical forms with upward forming tools.** (*Mate Punch and Die Co. and* NC ShopOwner)

requiring downward forming should be carefully evaluated; if downward forming is still required, careful programming and, perhaps, special workpiece handling are necessary. However, on a manually controlled press, downward forming is permissible because the workpiece is moved manually.

## Form Height

Another important consideration when forming is done on an NC punch press is the maximum height of the form. Each model of a punch press has a different vertical gap which determines the maximum form height the press can produce. The gap is the dimension from the lowermost surface on the upper turret or toolholder (most often the bottom side of the stationary, machine-mounted stripper) to the top surface of the standard die (see Fig. 12-27). The gap dimension is translated to maximum form height according to the following formula:

$$H = G\frac{(C + T)}{2} \tag{4}$$

where:

$H$ = maximum form height, in. (mm)
$G$ = vertical gap, in. (mm)
$C$ = clearance, 0.12″ (3.0 mm)
$T$ = workpiece thickness, in. (mm)

All forming must be completed at the standard die height. This requirement dictates that the forming start above standard die height so that when the operation is completed the workpiece is in the normal working plane. This also means the lower forming tool must be higher (by the height of the form/length of the form tool stroke) than the standard tool. The formed sheet lies on top of the form die after the actual forming stroke has been completed. The additional 0.12″ (3.0 mm) in the formula is to accommodate any workpiece distortion which could occur and still allow the workpiece to safely pass under the upper turret or toolholder.

The normal work sequence of an upward-forming operation on an NC punch press is as follows:

1. The material is positioned under the forming tool. Figure 12-28, view *a*, shows the various components of a typical form-up tool.
2. The upper tool comes down and contacts the workpiece and lower part of the forming tool (view *b*).
3. The upper tool continues to move down compressing the springs so that the forming insert is exposed and the form is completed (view *c*).
4. The upper tool moves upward to top dead center allowing the lower stripper to lift the workpiece off the forming insert (view *d*). The workpiece is then moved to the next forming position.

## Force Capacity

Force capacity in any press working operation is always a consideration. There are, unfortunately, some misconceptions in this area. Forming operations are more difficult to quantify than are punching operations, because the mechanics involved are more than just a momentary loading and release as is the case with simple punching. Additionally, forming operations are completed at bottom dead center (BDC), whereas punching is completed before BDC. Most presses are rated at the position at which the punching is normally completed. Therefore, in a forming operation in which heavy coining of the workpiece is required, sufficient attention must be given to force calculations and/or estimates. High-strength and/or highly alloyed materials such as stainless steel require higher pressing loads than do lower strength materials such as mild steel. For detailed information regarding force calculations for forming, refer to Chapter 4, "Sheet Metal Blanking and Forming."

## Mechanical Properties

The mechanical properties of the workpiece may dictate a particular approach to forming or may limit form size or height. As a rule, very brittle materials and those with low tensile strength do not lend themselves readily to single-hit forming. Formability is mainly dependent on the elongation characteristics of the material. Mild steels, most common stainless steels, and many aluminum grades are quite suitable for forming. The suitability is, of course, dependent on the shear form itself. While a given material may not be suitable for a deep emboss or extrusion, for example, it may pose no special problem for a lance and form (such as a louver). Grain direction is also an important consideration particularly when working with stainless steel. All forming should, if at all possible, be done at right angles to the grain of the material. This practice reduces the probability of cracking and produces a part that is less susceptible to fatigue failure in service. For a more comprehensive discussion on material formability, refer to Chapter 1, "Sheet Metal Formability."

## LUBRICANTS

The most serious problem encountered in punching occurs when the punch is stripped from the workpiece. Metal slivers adhere to the punch, causing galling and rapid tool wear.

Applying conventional mill oils to both sides of the workpiece minimizes galling and rapid wear when punching either carbon or low-alloy steels. However, lubrication of the workpiece increases slug pulling. For metals thicker than 1/4" (6 mm), extreme pressure (EP) oils are used to extend tool life. Sulfurized and sulfochlorinated oils with the proper viscosity are generally used when stainless steel is punched. When stainless steels are nibbled, emulsions are employed to reduce

**TABLE 12-7**
**Forming Tools Used on an NC Punch Press**

| Punch Form | Description | Application | Material Type and Thickness, in. (mm) | Force Requirements | Comments |
|---|---|---|---|---|---|
| Single knockout | Round hole punched through, with slug retained in place by thin uncut tabs ("ties"). | | | | Knockouts must be punched fully through—so that light shows—then flattened about half way back on a subsequent hit. |
| Double knockout | Ring of metal punched up, held in place by ties. | Mainly electrical, electronic enclosures. Provides an optional opening. | | | |
| Triple knockout | Ring and central slug. | Knockout tools may be used together. A single and a double yield a triple; two doubles make a quad. Two singles do not make a double. | Mild steel, 0.024-0.120 (0.61-3.05) Aluminum, 0.036-0.120 (0.91-3.05) (Results very good on both.) | Calculate as a punching operation. No shear on punch face. | A knockout tool is made for only a narrow range of stock thickness. For a wider range, more hits may be needed. |
| Quadruple knockout | Two rings. | | | | Setup is fairly easy. Some hand work on the tie reliefs may be necessary. |
| Quintuple knockout | Two rings and a slug. | | | | |
| Shape knockout | Single shape; rectangle, double D, ellipse, etc. | | | | |
| Circuit breaker knockout | Stock is fractured on three sides, and fourth side is cut on a subsequent hit. | Electrical enclosures—twist out for circuit breaker. | | | Form slopes slightly. Light should be seen through the front edge only. |
| Tap extrusion | Material is extruded up and ID is burnished to a size. Initial through hole is previously pierced. | Mainly for where sheet is too thin for threading or for a bearing diameter. | Steel—good Aluminum—poor Stainless—poor 0.02-0.12 (0.51-3.0) | Under 4 tons (35.6 kN) | Select pre-pierce punch size carefully. It controls height and appearance. Maximum thickness—two times material thickness. |
| Coil extrusion | Hole is punched down and material is extruded up to yield a hole about as long as 2X thickness. | Mainly for header plates for tube-construction heat exchangers. | Aluminum—fair Copper—good Brass—good 0.02-0.06 (0.5-1.5) | Under 4 tons (35.6 kN) | |

# OPERATING PARAMETERS

TABLE 12-7—*Continued*

| Punch Form | Description | Application | Material Type and Thickness, in. (mm) | Force Requirements | Comments |
|---|---|---|---|---|---|
| Semiperforate | Stock is cut with minimum clearance, producing straight-wall sides. Slug is held by small uncut ties. | Locating lug for post-shearing, weld locator, or a dowel to limit motion. | Aluminum—good Stainless—poor Steel—best 0.05-0.12 (1.3-3.0) | Low | Set up to desired height. One and one half times thickness is maximum form height. |
| Louver | Stock is cut on three sides and lifted up on one side and formed. | Variety of applications where it permits air flow but not penetration. | All kinds 10 gage (3.4 mm) | Low to medium high | Louver direction and program sequence are important as multiple hits are required. |
| Lance and form | Stock is cut on one side and formed. | Also air flow, spring attachment, end stop, etc. | | | |
| Card guide | Stock is pierced and formed to a channel shape with lead-ins at ends. | Guides for printed circuit boards and similar. | Steel—good Aluminum—fair 0.04-0.06 (1.0-1.5) | Low | |
| Emboss | Stock is formed, flowing plastically. No pierce. | Endless variety. | Steel—best Aluminum—poor Stainless—good 0.01-0.18 (0.25-4.5) | Low to very high | High forces can develop if tool is set up improperly, causing tool to coin at stroke bottom. |
| Countersink | Stock is cold forged down into a prepunched hole. Underside is featureless. | For screw heads and rivets and for deburring. | Steel—good Aluminum—fair Stainless—good 0.03-0.25 (0.8-6.4) | Low to quite high | Maximum depth is 60% of stock thickness. If fastener head is too high, make a larger hole. |
| Indent marking | Material is cold forged. | For numbering, serial codes, etc. | Steel—good Aluminum—good Stainless—poor 0.03-0.25 (0.8-6.5) | High | Maximum chisel marking should be 0.005″ (0.13 mm) deep. |

(*Mate Punch and Die Co. and* NC ShopOwner)

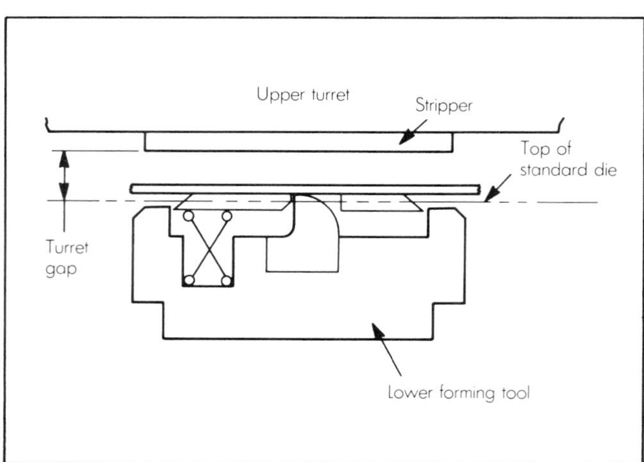


**Fig. 12-27 The turret gap is the distance from the lower surface on the upper turret to the top surface of the standard die.** (*Mate Punch and Die Co.*)

the punching temperature and increase tool wear. Soap solutions, emulsions, low-viscosity oils, mineral spirits, and chlorinated solvents are used when copper and its alloys are punched. For additional information on lubricant types and application methods, refer to Chapter 3, "Lubricants."

## MAINTENANCE

Two types of maintenance are necessary: punch press maintenance and tooling maintenance.

### Punch Press Maintenance

Proper maintenance of the punch press helps to ensure that the press is functional and in good working condition. This can be accomplished by following the manufacturer's recommendations and setting up a preventive maintenance program for each press. Chapter 5, "Presses for Sheet Metal Forming," discusses the different components to maintain on both hydraulic and mechanical presses.

## Tooling Maintenance

Tooling maintenance is more involved than press maintenance because it must be performed more frequently. Some of the routine maintenance procedures performed on punches and dies include cleaning punches, dies, and their holders; sharpening the punch and die; and checking center alignment of the punch and die.

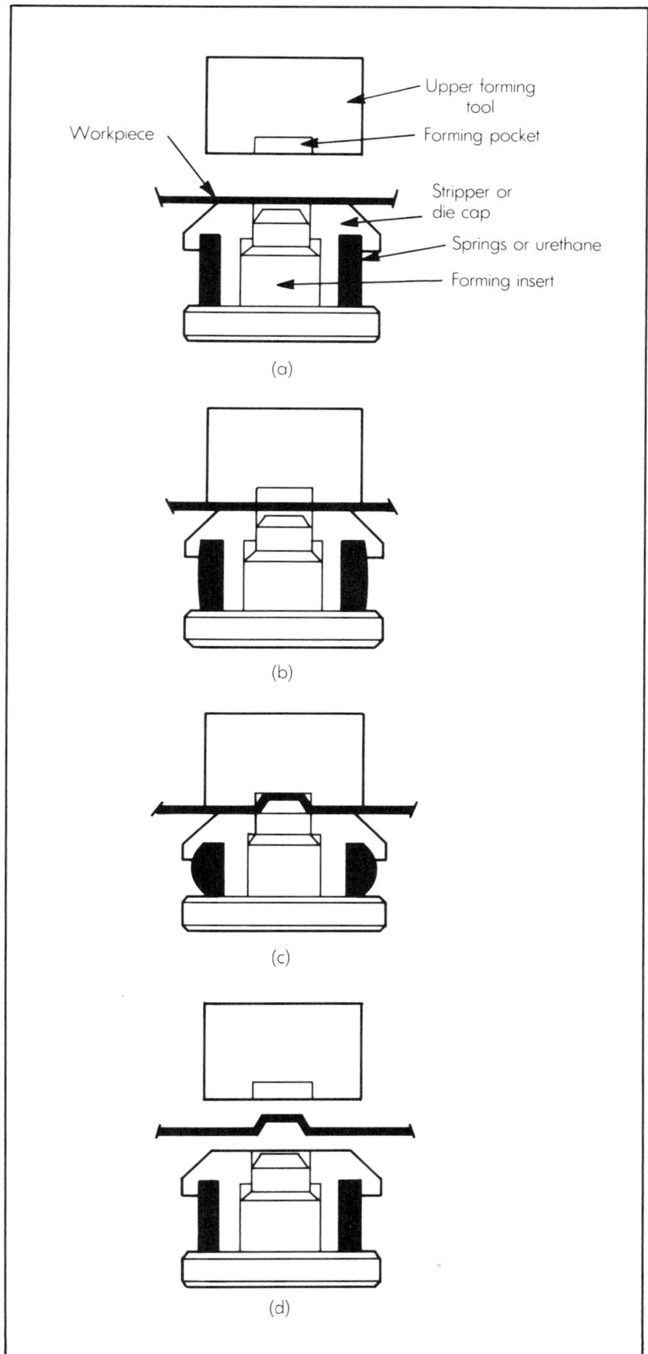


**Fig. 12-28 When forming is performed on an NC punch press, the forming is always done in an upward direction. (a) Workpiece positioned under forming tool; (b) upper tool moves down and contacts workpiece; (c) upper tool continues to move downward, depressing springs and forming workpiece in forming pocket; (d) upper tool moves upward, and lower stripper lifts workpiece off of forming insert. (*Wilson Tool*)**

**Cleaning.** Guide bores of the punches and mating parts should be cleaned as often as required. Any dirt or burrs at the bottom of the dieholder may result in a die-to-punch misalignment. Tar and gum accumulates on punches and dies when oil is used to lubricate the workpiece during punching. An abrasive tar is formed when the scale from hot-rolled steel mixes with the lubrication oil and causes premature wear on the punch and guide. Certain plastic laminates, such as fiberglass, also produce abrasive powder which causes excessive wear of tooling and related components.

**Sharpening.** Punches and dies wear with use, and sharpening at the proper time is very important for maximum tool life. Normally, punch and die wear are determined by the amount of burr produced on the workpiece (see Fig. 12-29). When the burr exceeds the allowable height, the tooling is sharpened. However, in some cases, waiting until the allowable burr height is exceeded necessitates removing too much stock from the tool to sharpen it.

Another means of determining when a punch and die need to be sharpened is by the amount of wear on the punch cutting edge. Sharpening is generally recommended when the cutting edge has worn to a 0.010-0.015″ (0.25-0.38 mm) radius or if the tool is damaged, such as being chipped or galled. Therefore, the tools must be inspected periodically for wear or damage. If a dull punch or die is maintained in use beyond the sharpening point, the wear multiplies rapidly and not only shortens tool life but could cause a complete punch or die failure which would expose operators to hazardous working conditions.

Punches wear about three times as fast as dies because the punch must penetrate the material and then be stripped out of it. Consequently, they should be sharpened more frequently than dies. Dies should not always be sharpened at the same time as the punch, since to do so results in shorter die life.

The number of hits that a punch can make before being sharpened is referred to as the production life. The production life is determined by several factors, including hole size and configuration, punch and die clearance, type of stripping, tool alignment, punch material and hardness, type and thickness of

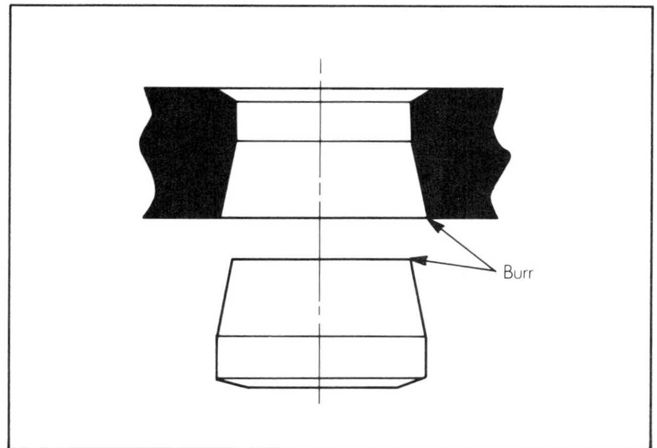


**Fig. 12-29 Punches and dies should be sharpened when the burr reaches the allowable height for the particular workpiece. (*W. A. Whitney Corp.*)**

material being punched, punching speed, and type of lubrication used. Generally, the production life of a punch in mild steel up to 0.075″ (1.90 mm) thick is 25,000-30,000 hits. One manufacturer incorporates a tool hit counter on the press to record the number of hits for each tool in the turret. This provides the information necessary for sharpening the tools at the proper time.

When sharpening punches and dies, it is necessary to follow the tooling manufacturer's recomendations to ensure that the correct grinding angles are maintained. After sharpening, the dead-sharp corner of the cutting edge should be removed with a fine oilstone to produce a working radius of 0.0005-0.005″ (0.013-0.13 mm). This spreads the stress at the cutting edge over the radius rather than the sharp corner and prevents premature chipping or flaking of the cutting edge.

**Tooling alignment.** To ensure long punch and die life and good hole quality, punches and dies must be accurately centered. Accurate tooling alignment is accomplished with an aligning punch and die.

The die and dieholder are placed in the die shoe/bolster assembly or lower turret. The bolster plate is not tightened down until the alignment procedure is completed. The aligning punch has a tapered lower section which, when slowly inched into the die, automatically centers the die to the punch. The bolster plate is then tightened, and the proper tooling may be installed in the press. On turret presses, the alignment procedure must be performed under the ram rather than at the loading station.

A regular schedule for checking tooling alignment is good practice. However, the frequency for checking the alignment varies with the severity of the punching applications. When changing from heavy punching applications (where high breakthrough shock is experienced) to lighter applications that require closer punch-to-die clearance, it is recommended that the tooling be realigned prior to using the tighter clearance tooling. In situations in which the press is used frequently by different operators, it is recommended that each operator realign the tooling prior to using it. This is extremely important in cases in which the operator is not advised of the previous press application. The time required to align the tooling can save many dollars that would ordinarily be spent to repair damaged tooling or would be wasted on downtime caused by the wait for replacement parts for the press.

## SAFETY

Safety to both the operator and the press is always an important consideration during punching operations. Operator accidents usually occur when the general safety rules have been violated, press installation instruction and operating instructions have been ignored, and the press's safety devices have been modified. Press accidents occur as a result of failing to follow the correct operating procedures, modifying the safety devices installed on the press, and failing to properly maintain the press. Figure 12-30 shows various devices used to prevent accidents to the operator and the press.

### Operator Safety

It is important that the press's point of operation be designed in such a way to prevent the operator's hands or fingers from entering during the punching operation. Since most openings are less than 1/4″ (6 mm), guards or other devices may not be required. Table movement and ram operation can be deactivated through the use of pressure-sensitive safety mats and safety interlocks. The operating zone of the press should also be clearly designated with a guard rail and warning strips. When a plasma torch or a laser cutting attachment are incorporated into the press, it is important that the proper operating instructions are followed and that the appropriate safety devices are installed.

### Press Safety

A punch press can be damaged by attempting to punch a hole in a workpiece that exceeds its rated capacity. Some manufacturers of hydraulic-powered presses incorporate an overload protection device in the press which reverses the ram action in case of press overload. Sensors in the stripper prevent table movement before the punch is fully extracted from the workpiece. Many CNC presses have diagnostic messages on the control panel to assist the operator with press-related malfunctions.

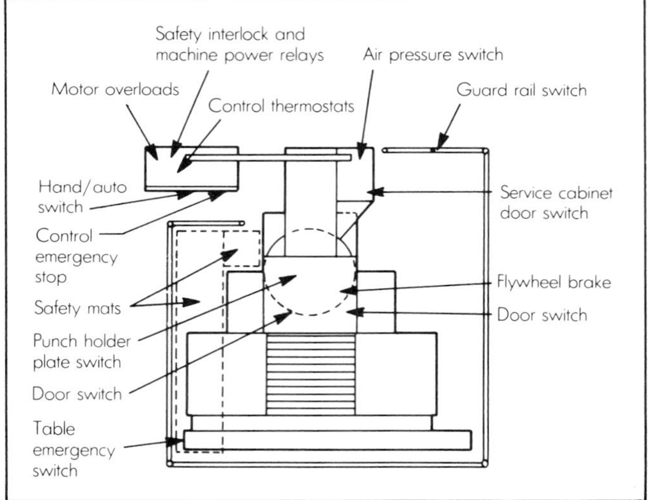


**Fig. 12-30 Typical safety devices used on a punch press to ensure protection to the operator and the punch press.** (*Wiedemann Div., Warner & Swasey Co.*)

# TROUBLESHOOTING

When problems arise during punching operations, it is necessary to determine which operating parameters or punching techniques are incorrect, as well as which press components have worn due to extended use. Some of the common problems that exist during punching are rapid tool wear, punch galling, slug pulling, and workpiece distortion, accuracy, and noise. Table 12-8 provides a list of the common problems along with the possible causes, suggested solutions, and any additional comments to explain the results occurring from a particular solution. Figure 12-31 illustrates the suggested solution to tool-wear problems caused by nibbling.

**TABLE 12-8**
**Troubleshooting Punching Operations**

| Problem | Possible Cause | Suggested Solution | Comments |
|---|---|---|---|
| Rapid tool wear | Inadequate die clearance | Increase die clearance to 20-25%. | Increased "breakway." Decreased burnished area. |
| | Poor tool alignment | Realign station(s). | |
| | | Level turrets. | |
| | Misalignment as a result of wear | Replace toolholder. | Expensive. |
| | | Rework turret or receiver. | Expensive |
| | Punch overheating | Use lubricant. | Slug pulling can result. |
| | | Use more than one punch of the same size in the punching sequence. | More toolchanging time required. |
| | Poor sharpening practices | Use coarser softer wheel. | |
| | | Dress wheel more rapidly. | |
| | | Reduce metal removal rates. | |
| | | Use generous amounts of coolant. | |
| | | Use conventional surface grinder. | Expensive. |
| | Nibbling | Increase distance between punch cutters. | Results in larger scallops. |
| | | Punch slot or opening following specific sequence (see Fig. 12-31). | More difficult to program. |
| | | Use specially coated HSS punch. | Expensive. |
| Punch galling | Die clearance too small | Increased die clearance. | |
| | Dull punch | Sharpen punch following manufacturer's recommendations. | Stone punch tip longitudinally after grinding to break down grinding marks. |
| | | Grind back taper on punch tip. | Back taper reduces punch tip size upon sharpening. |
| | Inadequate lubrication | Apply correct lubricant to workpiece. | Lubrication may cause slug pulling to occur. |
| Slug pulling | Die | Decrease die clearance 10% (small holes). | Faster tool wear. |
| | | | More tool breakage. |
| | | | Increased burr height on workpiece. |
| | | Increase die clearance on holes greater than 2″ (51 mm). | |
| | | Use die with a negative taper die land. | Faster tool wear. |
| | | Use thinner lubricant or eliminate lubrication. | Faster tool wear. |
| | | Decrease die land. | Less sharpening life. |
| | Punch | Increase punch penetration into the die. | Faster tool wear. |
| | | | More difficult to strip punch. |
| | | Use slug ejectors. | Not possible on very small punches. |
| | | | More frequent punch breakage. |
| | | Use shear ground punches and increase punch penetration. | Faster tool wear. |
| | | | More difficult to maintain. |
| Workpiece distortion | Lateral movement in workpiece | Increase die clearance. | |
| | Bending of workpiece | Increase stripper pressure. | |
| | | Turn sheet over after hitting. | Some loss of accuracy. |
| | | Alternate holes on first operation. | Time consuming. |
| | | Reprogram punching sequence. | Time consuming. |

**TABLE 12-8—*Continued***

| Problem | Possible Cause | Suggested Solution | Comments |
|---|---|---|---|
| Workpiece accuracy (hole-to-hole reference) | Lateral movement of workpiece material | Increase die clearance. | |
| | Movement of workholders | Adjust or replace. | |
| | Movement of workpiece in workholders | Replace gripping surfaces of workholders. | |
| | Table not aligned to press | Realign table. | |
| | Tools misaligned | Realign stations, check tooling. | |
| | Turrets out of level | Level turrets. | |
| | Station locating housing worn | Inspect and replace. | |
| | Pin housing worn | Inspect and replace. | |
| | Ball screws or nut worn or misaligned | Move to a single point from two directions and check accuracy. | |
| | Turret bores worn | Inspect for punch holder play and repair bores or replace cartridges. | |
| Workpiece noise | Poor stripping | Increase die clearance. | |
| | | Use correct lubricant. | |
| | | Increase stripping pressure. | Sheet marking may occur. |
| | | Use soft-face stripper. | Stripper face more susceptible to cutting. |
| | Poor workpiece support | Fill all die holders with "dummy" dies. (Recommended standard procedure) | |
| | | Reduce workpiece size. | Usually not possible to achieve. |
| | | Increase workpiece thickness. | |
| | Warped workpiece | Straighten before running. | Expensive. |

(*Mate Punch and Die Co.*)

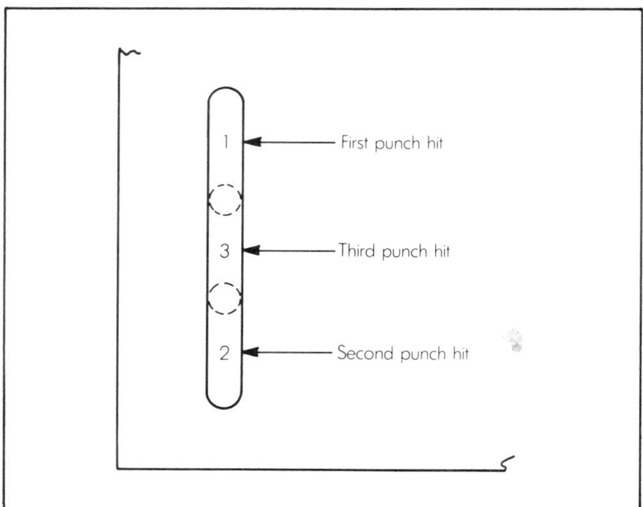


**Fig. 12-31 The sequence for punching this slot in the workpiece is programmed to prevent off-center loading on the punch.** (*W. A. Whitney Corp.*)

## Bibliography

Broland, Ted F. *Punching and Shearing Science*. W. A. Whitney Technical Paper 100C.

Mishek, Tim. *Which Turret Punch Press is Best for You*. Wilson Tool, 1982.

Palko, Michael P. *Laser and the CNC Turret Punch Press*. SME Technical Paper MF79-611, 1979.

Rakowski, Leo R. "Fabricating Capacities Soar with NC Punching Machines." *Machine and Tool Blue Book* (November 1978).

Rolland, Burton A. *The Fabrication Center Plasma-Arc and Punching Combination*. SME Technical Paper MR78-599, 1978.

Troiani, Joseph. "How to Apply Water Injection Plasma Cutting to a CNC Punching and Nibbling Machine." *The Fabricator* (April 1982).

Winshop, John T. "A New Area in NC Punching." *American Machinist* (November 1979).

CHAPTER

# 13

# Drawing, Extruding and Upsetting

# DRAWING, EXTRUDING AND UPSETTING

## COLD DRAWING OF BAR, WIRE AND TUBE

The cold drawing of a metal bar, rod, or wire consists essentially of pulling the part through a die of similar shape but smaller size (see Fig. 13-1). For a tubular part, an internal bar or mandrel can be introduced for simultaneous working of the interior surface (see Fig. 13-2). As the name implies, cold drawing is usually performed with the bar, rod, or wire at room temperature.

Drawing can also be done with the material preheated to temperatures up to the metal's recrystallization temperature. Called warm drawing, this technique can make drawing easier or impart special mechanical properties to the workpiece. For example, brittle materials generally require drawing at an elevated temperature at which the material remains ductile; prior processing of the material by rolling, extruding, or other compression deformation processes to improve the ductility of the material; or a combination of these techniques.

In addition to the production of bar, wire, and tube, many special sections are also cold drawn, thus reducing subsequent processing requirements. Parts produced are generally steel bars having the same cross-sectional shape throughout their length. Individual components are obtained by cutting pieces from the bars. Shapes possible are virtually unlimited and include intricate, nonsymmetrical shapes. Starting stock can be flat, square, round, or hexagonal bars, bars of other shape, or coils. Flat stock, however, is the most common starting material for drawing.

### PURPOSES OF COLD DRAWING

Cold drawing is performed for one or several of the following purposes:

1. To obtain a smaller size. (There is usually a limitation as to how small a wire can be to be hot rolled or extruded; and with tubes, a parallel situation exists with wall thicknesses.)
2. To produce longer lengths than are available in the hot-worked state.
3. To obtain shapes other than rounds, squares, etc., which often cannot be produced in any other way.
4. To secure better surface finishes than are available from hot-working processes.
5. To obtain closer dimensional tolerances than those generally possible with hot-working processes.
6. To obtain better straightness or alignment along the length of the workpiece than is possible in hot working.
7. To increase certain mechanical properties. Properties increased by cold drawing include tensile strength and hardness.
8. To improve other properties such as machinability. (For example, in certain steels an improvement of as much as 15-25% in machinability can be realized when workpieces are cold drawn.)
9. To make small lots of products of odd sizes or other variables that do not justify a hot mill run.

### DRAFT, REDUCTION AND ELONGATION

Cold-drawing applications range from the production of fine wire that is substantially less than 0.001" (0.03 mm) diam to tubes 12" (305 mm) or more in diameter. Regardless of size, however, several unifying relationships are maintained. These relationships are the draft, reduction in area, and elongation.

#### Draft and Area Reduction

In the cold drawing of bar, rod, and large-diameter wire, especially for upsetting, draft is

CHAPTER CONTENTS:



***Contributors of sections of this chapter are:*** *Robert G. Backus, Assistant Chief Engineer, The Ajax Manufacturing Co.; R. F. Boshold, Assistant Vice President, Mannesmann Demag Wean Co., Hydraulic Machinery Div.; Thomas G. Johannisson, ASEA AB; Paul D. Noble, Product Manager, Tubular and Bar Div.; Mannesmann Demag Wean Co., Engineering Center; Jerome B. Pfeffer, Manager—Quintus Dept., ASEA Pressure Systems; Ted A. Schiebold, Engineer, Imerman Industries, Inc.; J. E. Spearman, Manager of Administration, Vaughn Div., Wean United, Inc.*

***Reviewers of sections of this chapter are:*** *Professor Betzalel Avitzur, Department of Metallurgy and Materials Engineering, Lehigh University, Whitaker Laboratory #5; Robert G. Backus, Assistant Chief Engineer, The Ajax Manufacturing Co.; A. M. Bayer, Technical Director, Teledyne Vasco; R. F. Boshold, Assistant Vice President, Mannesmann Demag Wean Co., Hydraulic Machinery Div.; John Budrean, General Manager—Tooling, Verson Allsteel Press Co.; Russell W. Burman, Manager/Technical Development, Refractory Metals Div., AMAX Specialty Metals Corp.; Terry D. Capuano, P.E., Vice President—New Product Development, Russell, Burdsall & Ward Corp.; R. William Carlson, Orbital Forging Sales Manager, VSI Automation; L. C. Carrison, Program Engineer, Industrial Programs, Specialty Materials Dept., General Electric Co.;*

# COLD DRAWING OF BAR, WIRE AND TUBE

generally referred to as the difference between the original and final diameters:

$$\text{Draft} = D_o - D_f \quad (1)$$

where:

$D_o$ = original diam, in. or mm
$D_f$ = final diam, in. or mm

In cold drawing small-diameter wire, draft is referred to as the percentage of area reduction and is calculated as follows:

$$\text{Percent area reduction} = \frac{A_o - A_f}{A_o} \times 100 \quad (2)$$

where:

$A_o$ = original cross-sectional area ($0.7854\ D_o^2$), in.$^2$ or mm$^2$
$A_f$ = final cross-sectional area ($0.7854\ D_f^2$), in.$^2$ or mm$^2$

Example:

When reducing a 17/32" (13.49 mm) diam rod to a 1/2" (12.70 mm) diam rod by cold drawing:

$$\text{Draft} = 17/32 - 1/2 = 1/32 \text{ in. } (0.79 \text{ mm})$$

$$\text{Percent area reduction} = \frac{0.2217 - 0.1963}{0.2217} \times 100 = 11.46\%$$

For a single cold-drawing pass, the percent area reduction that can be taken depends upon many factors including the type of material, its size, and the starting metallurgical condition; the final size and mechanical properties required; die design; and lubrication efficiency. The percentage of area reduction per pass can range from near zero to 45% for solid parts and 50% for tubes drawn on a bar that is free to move with the tube.

More than one cold-drawing pass is usually required if higher total reductions are necessary. Multipass drawing, however, may also require intermediate annealing, particularly for metals with high work-hardening characteristics. Other intermediate operations, such as recleaning, recoating, and repointing, may also be required. The additional costs of these intermediate operations must be considered when cold-drawing operations requiring high reductions are planned.

In continuous drawing, as accomplished on multiblock or continuous-type drawing machines (discussed later in this section), two types of drafting are used: straight-line and taper drafting; the type of drafting used depending upon the drawing equipment employed. In straight-line drafting, each pass or reduction is of equal percentage. For example, drawing 1/4" (6.4 mm) diam rod to a diameter of 0.100" (2.54 mm)—a total area reduction of 84%—can be accomplished by drawing the material through five holes, with an approximate area reduction of 31% between successive holes, the diameters progressively decreasing from 0.250" (6.35 mm) to 0.210" (5.33 mm), to 0.174" (4.42 mm), to 0.145" (3.68 mm), to 0.120" (3.05 mm), and finally, to 0.100".

In taper drafting, the area reduction between passes varies. Using the same example, reducing a 0.250" (6.35 mm) diam rod to a finish size of 0.100" (2.54 mm), taper drafting could be accomplished with the diameters progressively decreasing from 0.250 to 0.195" (4.95 mm), an area reduction of 39%; to 0.160" (4.06 mm), a reduction of 33%; to 0.135" (3.43 mm), a reduction of 29%; to 0.115" (2.92 mm), a reduction of 27%; and finally to 0.100", a reduction of 24%.

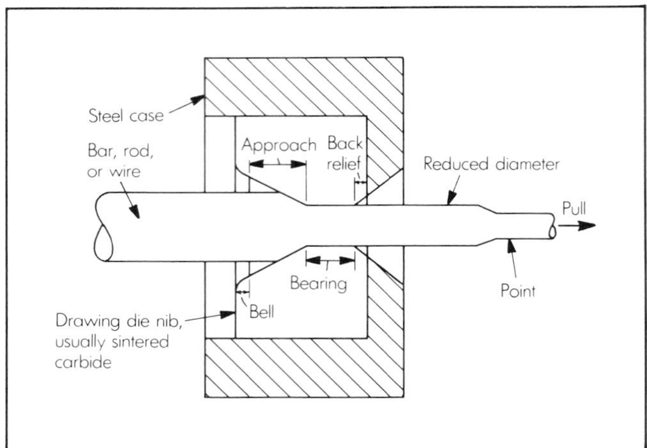


**Fig. 13-1 Die for drawing bar, rod, or wire.**

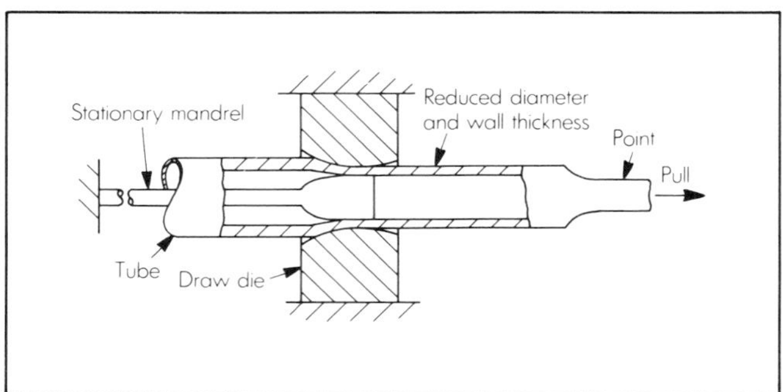


**Fig. 13-2 Die and internal mandrel for drawing tube.**

*__Reviewers, cont.__: D. R. Casagranda, Manager—Technical Services, Metal Treating Chemicals Div., Witco Chemical Corp.; Budd R. Catlin, Manager—Wire Drawing Machinery Dept., Morgan Construction Co.; Corporate Engineering, Camcar Div., Textron Inc.; Charles Dekker, Technical Sales Manager, Metal Flow Forming, Schuler Inc.; Jack Dennehy, Mossberg Industries, Inc.; R. S. Dusseau, CMfgE, Vice President—Sales, Abbey Etna Machine Co.; Thomas A. Fairman, Laboratory Manager, The H.A. Montgomery Co.; Barry M. Glasgal, General Manager, Quality Control and Metallurgical Services, Republic Steel Corp.; Nicholas L. Grace, Senior Research Project Engineer, Gleason Machine Div., The Gleason Works; Irv Hertzberg, President, Cold Header Machine Corp.; Peter B. Hopper, Product Metallurgist, Specialty Metals Div., Crucible Inc., Colt Industries; Dale W. Hutchinson, Product Manager—Metalworking Products, Acheson Colloids Co.; Tom Johannisson, ASEA AB; George Kaase, Chief Engineer, Cold Draw Dept., Abbey Etna Machine Co.; Herbert S. Kalish, Vice President, Technical and International Director, Adamas Carbide Corp.; Ron Keller, General Manager, Indiana Wire Die Co.; Bob Knight, Coldforge; William A. Kurnot, Chief Engineer, Forming Technology Co., Div. of Masco Corp.; Elmer D. Latvala, Metal Forming Manager, Parker Surface Treatment Products, Occidental Chemical Corp.; Earl Leach, Manager—Metal Forming Industry, Surface Treatments, Inc.; H. W. Long, Vice President, Texas, Extrusion Presses; James L. Maloney, Jr., Manager—SMS Engineering;*

# COLD DRAWING OF BAR, WIRE AND TUBE

## Die Pull

Approximate die pull—the force which is required to pull stock through the die and which determines the machine capacity needed—can be calculated as follows:

$$F = T \times C \times (A_o - A_f) \qquad (3)$$

where:

$F$ = die pull—force required to pull stock through die, lb
$T$ = tensile strength of material before drawing, psi
$C$ = constant varying with percent area reduction (see Table 13-1)
$A_o - A_f$ = difference between original and final cross-sectional areas, in.$^2$

Values obtained for die pull with this formula are approximate; lubrication and die design influence the pull required. For metric usage, the die pull, $F$ (lb), should be multiplied by 4.448 to obtain newtons (N).

**TABLE 13-1**
**Constants to be Used in Equation (3) for Determining Die Pull—the Force Required to Pull Stock Through the Draw Die**

| Percent Area Reduction, from Eq. (3) | Constant, C |
|---|---|
| 0-10 | 3.0 |
| 12 | 2.8 |
| 14 | 2.7 |
| 16 | 2.6 |
| 18 | 2.5 |
| 20 | 2.4 |
| 22 | 2.3 |
| 24 | 2.2 |
| 26 | 2.1 |
| 28 | 2.0 |
| 30 | 2.0 |
| 32 | 1.9 |
| 34 | 1.8 |
| 36 | 1.7 |

(*Ajax Manufacturing Co.*)

## Percentage of Elongation

Another unifying relationship which holds for any cold-drawing pass, regardless of size, is the percentage of elongation. To compute the percentage of elongation, the equation is:

$$\text{Percent elongation} = \frac{L_f - L_o}{L_o} \times 100 \qquad (4)$$

where:

$L_o$ = original length, in. or mm
$L_f$ = final length, in. or mm

This formula can be simplified for solid round shapes, using the same terms already used to find the percentage of area reduction, as follows:

$$\text{Percent elongation} = (\text{Percent area reduction}) \div \left(\frac{D_f}{D_o}\right) \qquad (5)$$

From this form of the percentage-of-elongation formula, it can be seen that a given percentage of area reduction always produces a larger percentage of elongation, a fact also true for cold drawing of nonround workpieces.

## PREPARING FOR COLD DRAWING

One or more of three basic preparation steps are usually required prior to successful cold drawing. These three steps, naturally dependent on the state of the part before drawing and on the desired drawing results, are heat treatment, surface preparation, and pointing.

### Heat Treatment

Heat treatment usually involves annealing or softening of one type or another so that the material is ductile enough for the intended percentage reduction. This is particularly necessary in the case of certain metals that are quite hard or brittle in the hot-worked state, or in the case of previously cold-drawn parts that have already been work-hardened too much to allow further reduction. Heat treatment before cold drawing can also involve other treatments, such as patenting, which together with the cold drawing produce certain desirable and often unique mechanical properties. Details of heat treating are presented in Volume III, *Materials, Finishing and Coating*, of this Handbook series.

### Surface Preparation

To prevent damage to the workpiece surface or the draw die during cold drawing, the starting stock must first be cleaned of surface contaminants, such as scale, glass, and heavy rust. This cleaning usually involves the use of various pickling or shot blasting methods. In many cases, especially when tubes are being drawn, the surface can also be coated or prelubricated by phosphatizing, plating, soaping, or liming methods. Provided no intermediate annealing is required, some of the prelubricating

*__Reviewers, cont.__: Robert F. Mitchell, Executive Vice President, Waterbury Headers, Inc., A Subsidiary of SFM Corp.; Robert F. Morton, President, Apex Alkali Products Co.; Elliott S. Nachtman, Tower Oil & Technology Co.; Richard A. Neal, Director of Research and Development, R. H. Miller Div., Pennwalt Corp.; Paul D. Noble, Product Manager, Sales, Tubular and Bar Div., Mannesmann Demag Wean Co., Engineering Center; Gerald A. O'Brien, Chief Manufacturing Engineer, Metal Forming, Saginaw Steering Gear Div., General Motors Corp.; Richard H. Parsons, Press Forming Services; John A. Passeri, Jr., Reynolds Aluminum, Reynolds Metals Co.; Product Quality and Assurance Section, Steel Production Group, Bethlehem Steel Corp.; B. Mitchel Robin, Vice President—Technical, E. F. Houghton & Co.; Ted A. Schiebold, Engineer, Imerman Industries, Inc.; Everett E. Schields, Product Metallurgist, Republic Steel Corp.; William R. Sonnenberg, Manufacturing Development Manager, Caterpillar Tractor Co.; Jim Souder, Sales Communications Manager, National Machinery Co.; J. E. Spearman, Manager of Administration, Vaughn Div., Wean United, Inc.; Jerry R. Spindler, Manufacturing Engineer, General Electric Co.; Clark O. Stockdale, Alcoa Laboratories, Alcoa Technical Center (retired); Otto W. Swierad, CMfgE, Manufacturing Manager, Branford Wire and Manufacturing Co.; Ike Tripp, Jr., Product Manager, Etna Products, Inc.; David C. Vale, Product Manager, Specialty Products Group, Kennametal Inc.; Richard Weinandy, Form Flow Inc.*

methods permit several cold-drawing passes without repeated treatment. Solid bars or rods are generally lubricated by oil during the drawing process.

## Pointing

Pointing, sometimes called chamfering, involves the preparation of a short length of one end of the starting part to a size slightly smaller than the draw die. The prepared end, called the *point*, is thereby ready for insertion through the draw die for gripping. The actual pointing operation is usually performed at room temperature by swaging, rolling, or turning. However, it can be performed after preheating and can also be done by hammering, acid etching, or grinding.

In some cases, these pointing operations can be avoided through the use of push pointing, a technique which involves pushing the end a short distance through the die. Pushing forces, however, are much higher than pulling forces. As a result, starting parts having small diameters and slender sections may buckle during the push-pointing process. This buckling action can be minimized by proper support, but parts having a diameter of about 3/8" (9.5 mm) or less must generally be prepointed by one of the methods previously described.

## DRAWING ROD AND WIRE

Methods and equipment used for cold drawing of rod and wire, as well as small-diameter tubing, are generally designed so that the products can be uncoiled and then recoiled after drawing. On multiple-die continuous machines, uncoiling, drawing, and recoiling are repeated at successive stations. Rod coils, when ready for processing, are usually butt welded together for continuous drawing.

Currently, hot-rolled rods available in coil form range from about 7/32" (5.6 mm) to 1 3/4" (44.4 mm) diam. For subsequent continuous drawing, rod is normally rolled to 3/8" (9.5 mm) diam for aluminum, 5/16" (7.9 mm) diam for copper alloys, 1/4" (6.3 mm) diam for stainless steels, and 7/32" diam for low and high-carbon steels. Lengths can vary from a few feet (meters) to many miles (kilometers). In the cold-drawing industry, wire is defined as being rod which has been drawn at least once. Wire less than 3/16" (4.8 mm) diam generally requires more than one drawing pass.

In the drawing process, cleaned and coated coils of rod or wire are first placed on a payoff tray, stand, or reel (see Fig. 13-3), which permits free unwinding of the stock. The leading end of the rod or wire, after being pointed, is then inserted through the drawing die and seized by a gripper attached to a powered cylindrical block or capstan. On so-called dry machines, the die is mounted in an adapter within a box. This die box contains, if necessary, grease, dry soap, oil, or other lubricants through which the stock must pass before reaching the die.

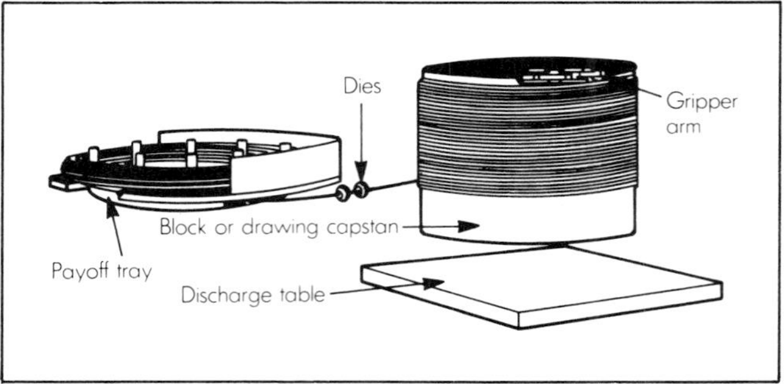


**Fig. 13-3 Payoff tray and capstan for drawing coil stock.** (*Vaughn Div., Wean United*)

## Bull Blocks

Bull blocks are single-die drawing machines with individual drive systems. They are used extensively for breakdown, finishing, or sizing operations on large diameter rod and wire, made from both ferrous and nonferrous metals, by firms with production requirements that do not warrant more sophisticated, continuous machines (discussed next in this section).

The spindles of these machines are generally vertical, with spindle blocks revolving in a horizontal plane. Occasionally, especially for applications involving large-diameter stock, the arrangement is reversed, with the spindles horizontal and the blocks revolving in a vertical plane.

Many design variations are available with bull blocks. For example, a double-deck arrangement permits two drafts to be performed, with the second draft maintaining a fixed percentage of area reduction. Other refinements include external air cooling and internal water cooling of the block, and riding-type, block-stripping spiders for direct coiling and wire removal. These spiders, with collapsible feet, can be equipped with automatic discharging mechanisms to transfer drawn coils to wire carriers or stems.

Usually, especially when large bundles are not required, the wire being drawn on the block is coiled around block pins which provide an extension to the height of the block. Then, a stripper, with the feet temporarily collapsed, is inserted through the eye of the coil, the feet fitting into stripper slots or recesses in the block flange. The feet are then locked in their extended positions, and the bundle is lifted free of the block.

With the development of floating plugs (see Fig. 13-4), long lengths of thin-walled, small-diameter, nonferrous tubing are being drawn on special types of single-spindle machines. Instead of a conventional mandrel being used that is attached to a rod, as is done in drawbench operations, a specially designed plug is inserted in the leading end of the tube prior to pointing and passing the tube through the draw die. The plug is free to ride in the throat of the die during drawing, thus controlling the inside diameter of the tube (while the die controls the outside diameter) and maintaining the desired wall thickness.

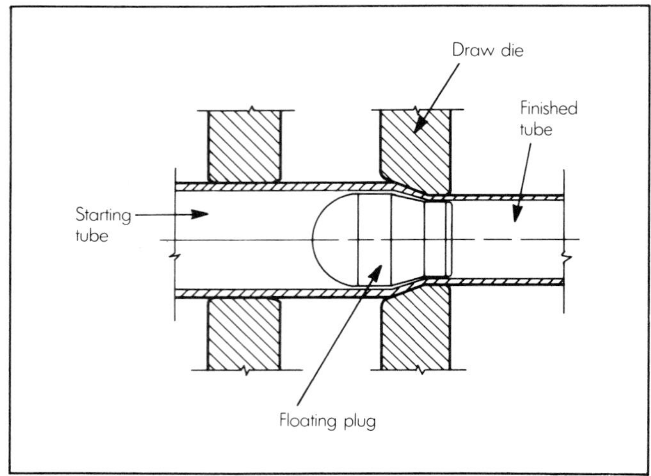


**Fig. 13-4 Floating plug used to draw long, thin-walled, small-diameter, nonferrous tubes.** (*Vaughn Div., Wean United*)

Drawing methods and machines, particularly material handling arrangements, are generally more sophisticated for single-spindle tube drawing than for the more conventional bull blocks used in drawing rod and wire. Machine configurations available for single-spindle tube drawing include horizontal, vertical upright, and inverted vertical designs.

## Dry-Drawing, Nonslip Continuous Machines

For the dry drawing of ferrous metals, four types of nonslip continuous machines are in general use: accumulating-type machines; double-block, accumulating-type machines; controlled-speed machines; and straight-through machines.

**Accumulating type.** The simplest continuous machine for dry drawing is the accumulating-type, or storage, machine. Originally, machines of this type were powered by a single drive with lineshafts extending the lengths of the machines. Gearing was selected so that wire would accumulate on the initial blocks. When a station became full, it was necessary to stop it, and those preceding it, and to deplete the accumulated storage of wire by permitting the blocks at succeeding stations to continue to run. This resulted in inefficient operation and demanded considerable operator attention.

Modern versions of accumulating machines, with individual direct-current drives for each block, permit more precise regulation and efficient operation. The geometry of these machines, however, imparts a twist to the wire with each revolution of the flyer (a sheave that revolves around the block), which for certain products is undesirable.

A multiblock, accumulating-type continuous machine for automatic drawing of wire is shown in Fig. 13-5. This dry-drawing, nonslip machine is equipped with electromagnetic block clutches. Photocells sense high and low wire accumulation on each block and disengage or engage appropriate block clutches. A single direct-current motor drives a coupled lineshaft which carries the clutches. Only the inlet block has to be stopped in case of a payoff snarl, allowing the machine to continue production while the snarl is removed. A programmable controller enables rapid checkout and simple alteration to input and output circuits, and serves as a continuous fault-monitoring system to simplify maintenance.

**Double-block accumulating machines.** Another of the nonslip continuous machines is the double-block accumulating machine with individually driven blocks. With this arrangement, wire is transferred from the first drawing block by means of an

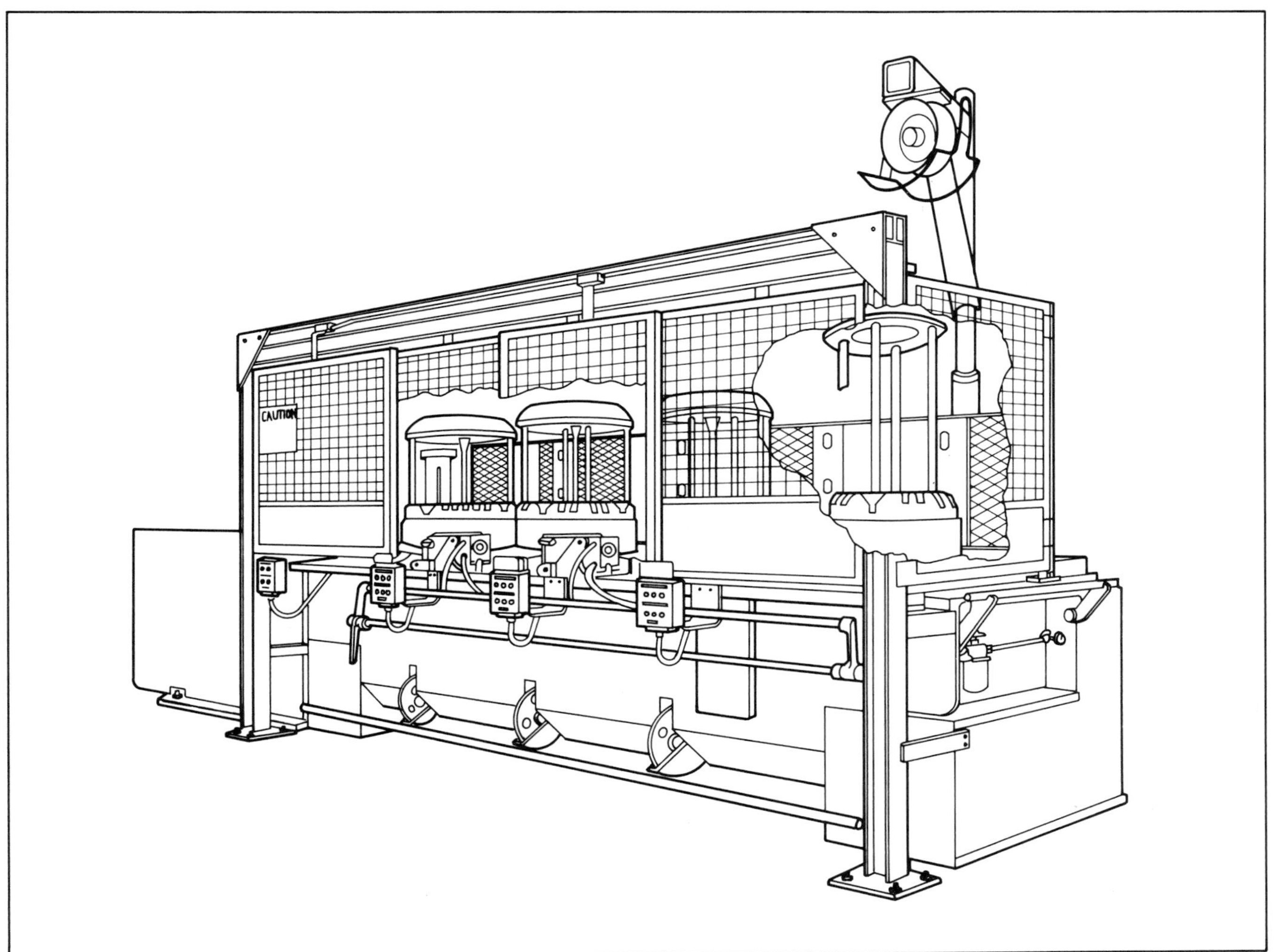


**Fig. 13-5 Accumulating-type, continuous wire drawing machine.** (*Morgan Construction Co.*)

# COLD DRAWING OF BAR, WIRE AND TUBE

intermediate flyer sheave which reverses the direction of the wire (without twisting it) onto a coiling block mounted immediately above the first drawing block. Here, the wire is held temporarily in storage until demanded by the second drawing block.

Fully automatic, electrical drive systems can be used to start and stop, or slowdown and speedup, the individual blocks to accumulate or deplete wire as conditions require. With excellent cooling characteristics, these machines are capable of operating at high speeds.

**Controlled-speed machines.** A third type of nonslip continuous machine for drawing ferrous wires is the controlled-speed machine. On such machines, the wire follows an essentially flat path from block to block with a constant, unvarying amount of wire storage, without twisting and slipping. A tension arm between blocks, activated by a loop of the wire being drawn, regulates the speed of the adjustable-speed, direct-current motor on the preceding block.

For breaking down larger rod sizes, controlled-speed machines offer the advantage of easier string-up (threading of the stock). Also, for drawing tubing continuously in a sinking operation (drawing without an internal bar or mandrel), in which excessive flexing of the roll-formed or lapped material might rupture the strand being drawn, the machines provide a superior drawing method because of minimum flexing. Both vertical and horizontal-spindle machines are used, with the vertical-spindle arrangement being more common.

**Straight-through machines.** Straight-through, dry-drawing, nonslip continuous machines, without tension arms, are also available. In many instances, particularly those in which large-size workpieces are required, the spindles are canted from the vertical axis to accommodate wire buildup on the blocks and to provide unimpeded, straight entry into the succeeding die. In general, these machines require skillful operators because to make the electrical systems function properly, the operators may need to alter torque adjustments at each block when stringing up the machines.

### Wet-Drawing, Slip-Type Continuous Machines

The continuous drawing of nonferrous rod and wire, as well as some intermediate and fine sizes of ferrous wire, is generally done on wet-drawing, slip-type machines. On these machines, the surface speed of the capstans, except for the final (pull-out) capstans, exceeds the speed of the wire being drawn, thus creating slip of the wire on the capstans. Brighter surface finishes are generally produced with these machines, but the machines are limited to smaller reductions per pass than with dry-drawing nonslip continuous machines.

With these machines, the drawing operation is generally confined to an enclosed chamber, with the lubricant bathing the dies and wire as it is being drawn. These machines are less complicated electrically than nonslip machines, and only one drive system is employed. They are designed with either tandem or cone-type configurations, usually with horizontal spindles, but sometimes with a vertical spindle for the finishing capstan. Cone capstans have drawing surfaces (usually hard faced) that are stepped outwards to provide increasing peripheral speeds. This compensates for the elongation and increasing speed of the wire as it is reduced in diameter during drawing.

**Dead-block units.** Recent interest in obtaining large, heavy-weight bundles (coils) of wire at maximum efficiency has promoted the use of dead (stationary) block drawing and/or coiling units at the finishing ends of drawing machines. With dead-block units, the problems normally attendant to coiling large, eccentrically loaded coils at high speeds on a revolving, slotted, stripper block, plus stopping for the removal of accumulated wire, are effectively eliminated.

Centrifugal force cannot affect the wire as it is being coiled on a stationary block. A rotating flyer lays the wire, a strand at a time, on the surface of the fixed block. Full and empty wire receivers can be interchanged under the dead block without stopping the coiling process.

With horizontal dead-block units, large, snarl-free coils can be laid in a geometric pattern with a slowly orbiting or revolving, tilted or level turntable carrying a properly positioned receiving stem or carrier. Inverted, vertical-spindle dead-block units can, in some instances, be used successfully for drawing. These units, however, have gained widest use for take-up applications in plating and other wire-processing operations.

**Spoolers.** Various types of spoolers are also used in conjunction with machines for taking up drawn wire. An important consideration with spooling systems is to provide controlled tension when laying the wire on the spool. This is necessary to ensure that subsequent operations are not adversely affected during paying off from the spool.

## DRAWING BARS

Bars about 1 1/4" (32 mm) and smaller in diameter are cold drawn from coil stock by various methods. With one method, cold-drawn coils of rod and wire produced on the various machines described are straightened and cut into bars in a separate operation on machines designed for that purpose. Some in-line methods and equipment begin by unwinding the starting coil, then pull the stock through a draw die without recoiling, and finally straighten and cut the material into bars in a continuous operation.

The continuous machine illustrated in Fig. 13-6 has a fixed die box with a recirculating wet-die lubricating system. Drawing is accomplished with three moving grip slides: one slide for push pointing before the die box and two opposed-motion drawing slides after the die box. The push-pointing grip runs twice as fast as the drawing grips to minimize production loss when push pointing. This machine also has one set each of vertical and horizontal straightening rollers, and a set of feed-out rolls. Most cold-drawn bars are produced from hot-rolled or extruded bars up to 55 ft (16.8 m) long x 6" (150 mm) diam, with seldom more than one cold-drawing pass performed.

### Drawbenches for Bars

The cold drawing of cleaned and pointed hot-rolled bars is generally performed on a high-powered, rigidly built, long, horizontal machine called a drawbench (see Fig. 13-7). The drawbench consists essentially of a table of entry rollers (an elevating entry conveyor is shown), a die stand, a carriage, and an exit rack (not shown). Entry rollers support the hot-rolled bars and are usually powered to help bring the pointed ends of the bars into the draw dies. An upright head can hold as many as four dies to permit drawing four bars at a time. If lubrication is required, a lubricating oil system is provided on the entry side of the head.

On most drawbenches, the entry side of the head is provided with a hydraulic pushing device, which for a normal draft, can be used to push-point the ends of the bars. Pneumatically operated grips on the carriage grasp the pointed ends of the bars protruding through the dies. The carriage is powered by a motor-driven

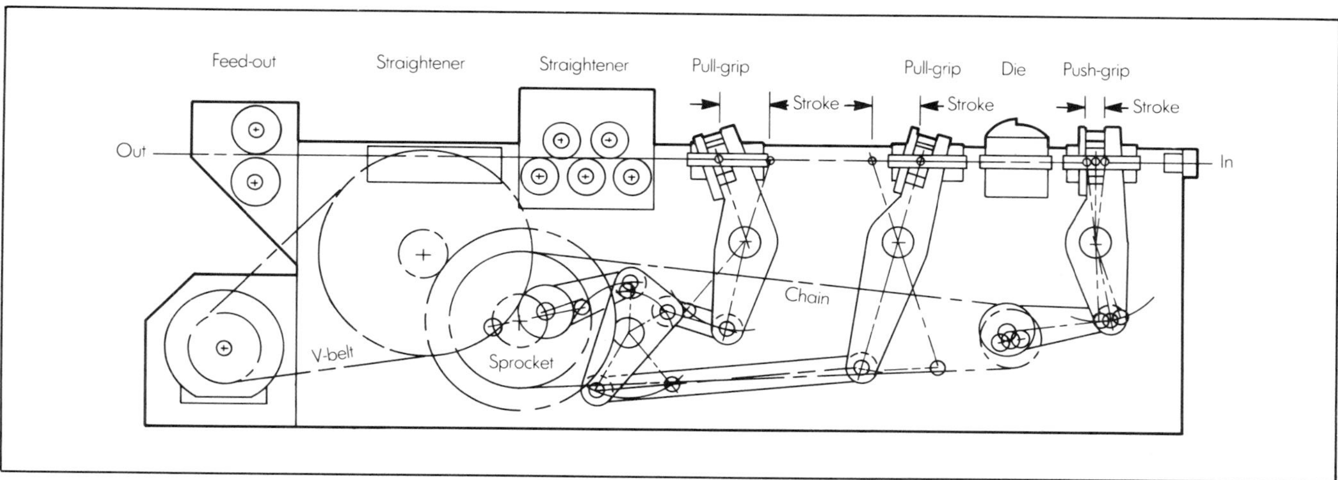


**Fig. 13-6 In-line drawing and straightening machine for producing cold-drawn bars from hot-rolled steel coils or bars.** (*Ajax Manufacturing Co.*)

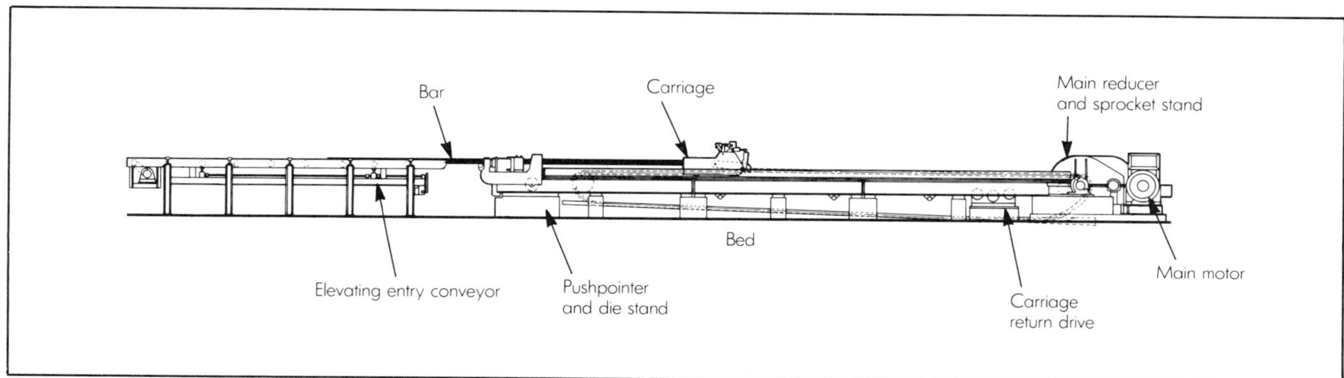


**Fig. 13-7 Typical arrangement of a drawbench for producing cold-drawn bars from hot-rolled bars.** (*Wean United*)

chain(s) or hydraulic piston(s) to slide or roll along ways to pull the bar(s) through the die(s), as shown in Fig. 13-8.

As soon as the bar being pulled exits from the draw die, the carriage automatically releases the bar and stops. The drawn bar is then free to fall, usually onto discharge arms for removal from the drawbench. The carriage is then rapidly returned to the die stand, by a separately powered return system on chain benches or by means of a piston on hydraulic benches, for drawing the next bar.

### Capacities of Bar Drawbenches

Drawbenches for hot-rolled bars are available with pulling forces to 1,000,000 lb (4448 kN) and capacities for drawn lengths to about 65 ft (19.8 m). They can have pulling speeds, usually adjustable, to 360 sfm (109.7 m/min). Return speeds of the carriages are generally faster, to about 500 sfm (152.4 m/min). Chain-operated drawbenches are usually controlled automatically to permit low speeds at the start of the pulling action, followed by rapid acceleration to the preset pulling speed.

## DRAWING TUBES

Tubes, particularly those having small diameters and requiring working only of their outer surfaces, are produced from cold-drawn coils on machines that straighten the stock and cut it to required lengths. As with bars, however, most tubes are produced from straight lengths rather than coiled stock. With four exceptions, the methods and equipment used for cold drawing tubes in straight lengths are basically identical to those used for bar drawing. The four exceptions are:

1. There are tubes that require more than one drawing pass.
2. Tubes are usually longer than bars. Drawbenches for tubes are usually correspondingly longer, some permitting drawn lengths of over 100 ft (30.5 m).
3. Tube diameters are generally larger than bar diameters, ranging to about 12" (305 mm). The bigger tube drawbenches have larger components than do bar drawbenches.
4. Tubes require internal mandrels or bars for simultaneous working or support of the interior surface during drawing. Tube drawbenches are usually equipped with one of several available devices, usually powered, for ready assembly of the cleaned, coated, and pointed workpiece onto internal bars or rod-supported mandrels. If rod-supported mandrels are used, they are usually air-operated so that the mandrel can be placed and maintained in the plane of the draw die after pulling starts. Butt or electric-welded tubes are sometimes drawn to smooth the weld seams and tube walls.

# COLD DRAWING OF BAR, WIRE AND TUBE

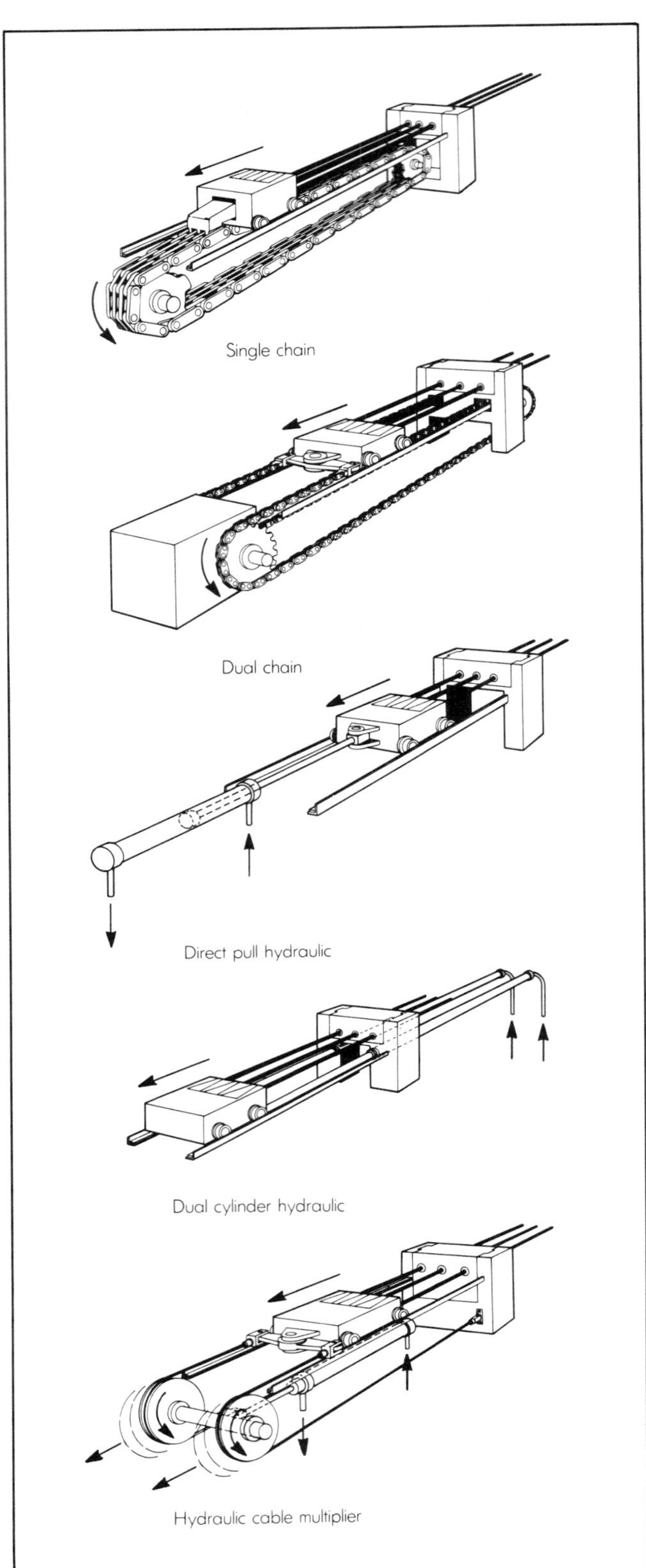


**Fig. 13-8 Various methods of powering carriage to pull hot-rolled bars through cold-drawing dies. (*Wean United*)**

## OTHER DRAWING METHODS

Many other methods of cold drawing are employed, but these methods are not used as extensively as those methods just described.

### Combined Rolling and Drawing

Rolling and drawing are combined in integrated systems for the close-tolerance production of nonferrous, flat wire and wire of other shape. Coils of round wire are pulled through a rolling mill, line, or Turk's head; a cooling box to remove heat from the wire; a measuring device; a draw die; and a cleaning box.[1]

### Pultrusion

The pultrusion process, discussed in Chapter 18, "Plastics Forming," is related to drawing in that material is pulled through a die; however, it is not a cold-drawing method because heating is required for curing (polymerizing) the resin-coated fiber reinforcements in the parts produced.

### Vibration-Assisted (Ultrasonic) Drawing

Ultrasonic vibrations imposed on the drawing die, plug, or mandrel are advantageous for some applications. While this process is not being used extensively, it is considered beneficial for drawing hard-to-deform materials and profiled wires, and for some tube drawing operations. Advantages include reduced friction and force requirements, increased reductions per pass, production of improved surface finishes, and reduced die wear. Limitations include the need for high-cost vibrating equipment and low-speed production.

In ultrasonic drawing, the die is expanded and contracted radially or the plug or mandrel is vibrated axially. This is accomplished by magnetostrictive transducers that convert electrical energy to mechanical vibrations. Electrical power is supplied to the transducers by a generator and frequency converter. Force-insensitive tool mountings are provided to isolate the vibrations from the machine structure.

### Dieless Drawing

This process, which involves heating the workpiece material during drawing, has limited application. It has been reported that one aircraft engine manufacturer is using the process to make titanium tubes, and that large area reductions are possible with low draw loads. A limitation is the difficulty of achieving uniform input of heat to the workpiece.

In dieless drawing, one end of a rod or tube is gripped in a fixed head and the other end is held in a movable drawhead. The workpiece is heated locally, near the drawhead, by a movable induction-heating coil encircling the workpiece. When the desired reduction in cross-sectional area occurs at the heated zone, the drawhead continues to move away from the fixed head and the heating coil moves toward the fixed head. Speed of the drawhead and heat from the coil are adjusted to provide uniform reduction.

## DIES FOR DRAWING

Proper design of the dies is critical for optimum cold drawing. The dies are basically conical, with a bell-shaped mouth and a cylindrical land. Drawing starts in the conical section and is completed at the intersection of the conical approach section and the bearing. The die land helps to maintain size as the conical approach section wears. Design recommendations presented in Table 13-2 can be used as a

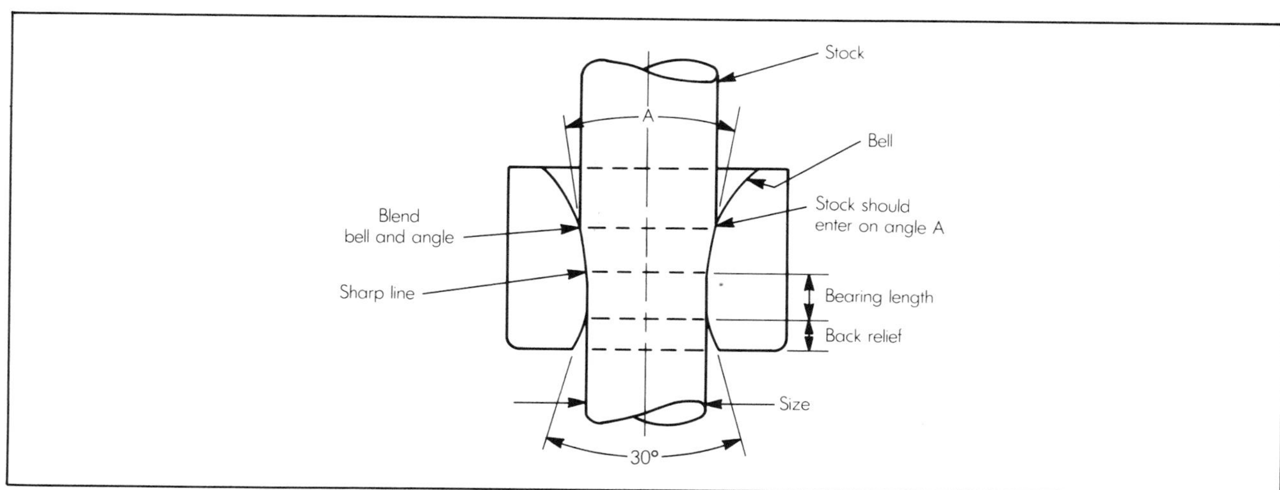


**TABLE 13-2**
**Design Guides for Cold-Drawing Dies**

| Workpiece Material | Finished Size, in. (mm) | Angle A, degrees | | Bearing Length, percent size or in. (mm) | | Back Relief, percent nib height or in. (mm) |
|---|---|---|---|---|---|---|
| Low-carbon steel | 0.006-0.015 (0.15-0.38) | 16 | | 50% | | 0.005-0.010 (0.13-0.25) |
| | 0.016-0.128 (0.41-3.25) | 16 | | 50% | | 15% |
| | 0.129-0.230 (3.28-5.84) | 16 | | 50% | | 15% |
| | 0.231-0.516 (5.87-13.11) | 16 | | 1/4 (6.4) | | 15% |
| | 0.517-0.750 (13.13-19.05) | 16 | | 5/16 (7.9) | | 15% |
| High-carbon steel | 0.006-0.015 (0.15-0.38) | 12 | | 66% | | 0.005-0.010 (0.13-0.25) |
| | 0.016-0.128 (0.41-3.25) | 12 | | 66% | | 15% |
| | 0.129-0.230 (3.28-5.84) | 12 | | 66% | | 15% |
| | 0.231-0.516 (5.87-13.11) | 12 | | 1/4 (6.4) | | 15% |
| | 0.517-0.750 (13.13-19.05) | 12 | | 5/16 (7.9) | | 15% |
| | | Tungsten Carbide or Natural Diamond | Synthetic Diamond | Tungsten Carbide or Natural Diamond | Synthetic Diamond | |
| Copper | 0.040-0.250 (1.02-6.35) | 16 | 18 | 50% | 10-25% | 15% |
| | 0.250-0.516 (6.35-13.11) | 16 | 18 | 1/4 (6.4) | 10-25% | 15% |
| | 0.517-0.750 (13.13-19.05) | 16 | 18 | 5/16 (7.9) | 10-25% | 15% |

*(Indiana Wire Die Co.)*

# COLD DRAWING OF BAR, WIRE AND TUBE

guide for dies to cold draw round wire, bar, and tube when standard drawing practice and reductions are employed: 20-30% reduction per pass on steel wire and 3/64 to 1/16" (1.2 to 1.6 mm) per pass on steel bar stock. For higher reductions and for certain applications, special dies have to be designed.

## Materials for Draw Dies

Draw dies are subjected to severe wear, compressive forces, thermal stresses, and chemical reaction. Selection of the die material is therefore important; it depends primarily upon the workpiece material, the size and shape of the part to be drawn, the quantity of parts required, and the cost of the die material. Most draw dies are made with diamond or tungsten carbide inserts, but tool steels and ceramics are used for some applications. A comprehensive discussion of tool steels and carbides is presented in Chapter 2, "Die and Mold Materials."

**Tool steels.** Hardened tool steels are generally limited to large draw dies, primarily because they are more economical for such dies. They also provide cost savings for short-run production requirements.

Tool steels commonly used for draw dies include AISI Type M2, a molybdenum-type, high-speed steel; D2, a high-carbon, high-chromium, cold-work tool steel; O1, an oil-hardening, cold-work tool steel; and W1, a water-hardening tool steel. AISI Type A11, an air-hardening, cold-work tool steel produced by the powder metallurgy (PM) process is being used successfully as an alternative to more costly carbide. This material has a toughness equivalent to Types M2 and D2 and has superior wear resistance.

The tool steels are generally hardened to about $R_C$64 for dies to be used for small reductions in cold drawing. A lower hardness, about $R_C$60, is usually recommended for large reductions. Tool steels with lower hardness are less prone to breakage, but they generally wear faster.

Chromium plating of draw dies made from tool steels is a common practice. Good results are being obtained with respect to reduced wear and longer life by coating tool steel dies with titanium nitride. Coated dies, however, produce inferior surface finishes and require careful polishing.

**Carbides.** For cold drawing, most medium-sized dies and many large ones are made from tungsten carbides cemented with a cobalt binder. Advantages of carbides, compared to tool steels, include higher abrasion (wear) resistance and compressive strength than seen with tool steels, generally providing longer life. Carbides, however, are more expensive, requiring long production runs for economic justification. Carbides are also more brittle than tool steels, requiring careful designing and mounting (refer to Chapter 2), and are more difficult to grind. Adjustable carbide sections are used extensively for drawing square and rectangular bars when sharp corners are required.

Selection of carbide grades depends upon the size of the dies and the severity of their application. Grades having high cobalt contents (9-13%) are often preferable for cold-drawing dies. These grades can withstand greater stock reductions per pass without breaking than can grades having low cobalt contents. For optimum performance and maximum wear resistance, however, it is generally preferable to use grades with low cobalt contents (6-9%) for small-sized dies. If carbide dies are not damaged or broken in drawing operations, they can sometimes be reworked and used as large-sized dies.

As with tool steel dies, good results, in respect to reduced wear and longer life, are being obtained for some applications by coating carbide dies with titanium nitride. Such dies must be carefully polished prior to and after coating to produce smooth surface finishes.

**Diamonds.** Diamond dies are extensively used in the wire industry, especially for cold drawing small-diameter round wire, regardless of workpiece material and production requirements. Advantages of diamond dies include the exceptionally smooth surface finishes produced and long life—five or more times that of carbide dies is common. Both synthetic, polycrystalline diamonds and natural, single-crystal, industrial-grade, mined diamonds are employed for cold-drawing dies. The use of diamond dies is restricted only by their non-availability in large sizes and their high cost.

Natural diamond dies generally produce a smoother surface finish than synthetic diamonds because of their single-crystal structure. The performance of such dies, however, may be erratic because of possible flaws (hard and soft directions) or unfavorable cleavage planes in the crystals. Larger natural diamonds are more costly than synthetic diamonds, and the supply is limited; but smaller natural diamonds may cost less than synthetic diamonds.

A major advantage of synthetic diamond dies is slow, uniform wear, which generally results in a consistently longer life than that of natural diamond dies. A possible limitation is that synthetic diamond dies may produce a duller, more striated finish than natural diamond dies produce because of their polycrystalline crystal structure. Finishes can be improved by careful polishing. Some wire-drawing firms are using synthetic diamond dies for breakdown operations and natural diamond dies for finishing.

Synthetic diamond die blanks are available from several producers. General Electric Co.'s Compax blanks are a combination of two materials: a polycrystalline diamond core surrounded by a cemented tungsten carbide support ring. The two materials are produced as an integral blank by a high-pressure/high-temperature process, with the diamond crystals randomly oriented and bonded to each other and to the carbide ring.

Because of the random orientation of the synthetic diamond crystals, the blank core has uniformly high hardness and wear resistance in all directions. There are no hard or soft directions or cleavage planes and therefore no need to preferentially orient the blank in the die casing, as is normally required with single-crystal mined diamonds. The carbide ring provides compressive support to the diamond core, making the blank more resistant to fracture in drawing applications. Blanks are generally mounted in metal casings, using either a brazed metal powder matrix or shrink-fit procedures. Temperatures, however, must be kept below about 650° C (1200° F) to prevent damage to the polycrystalline diamond core.

**Refractories.** These materials, especially ceramics such as zirconia oxide or silicon nitride, are being used as draw dies or as linings for steel dies. Advantages claimed for these materials include minimized metal-to-metal pickup and improved surface finish.

## Materials for Mandrels

Mandrels for drawing tubes are generally made from hardened tool steels or cemented tungsten carbide. Sometimes, carbide or diamond nibs are brazed or mechanically attached to steel mandrels.

## LUBRICANTS FOR COLD DRAWING

Die wear in cold drawing occurs because of mechanical

abrasion, compressive forces, thermal stresses, and chemical reactions. To minimize wear, lubricants are used. Since no single lubricant is best for all applications, a wide variety is employed. Details on lubrication principles, lubricant types, application methods, waste treatment, quality control, and troubleshooting are presented in Chapter 3, "Lubricants." To ensure selection of a proper lubricant for optimum performance in a specific application, consultation with specialized lubricant manufacturers is recommended. Chapter 10 of the *Steel Wire Handbook*, Volume 4, published by the Wire Association International, Gilford, CT, is also helpful.

For some applications, surface coatings of lime or borax, or phosphate coatings, are applied to the bars, rods, or wire to form a base for lubricant retention. Proprietary alkaline coatings have, to a great extent, replaced lime or borax. This is due to advanced chemical technology and the ability to improve adhesion, toughness, and low-moisture characteristics. Dry-film, soap, and wax lubricants are used in many applications; and water-emulsifiable, tallow-based soaps are commonly employed in drawing copper rods. Oil-based greases, generally thickened with a wax, polymer, or stearate and filled with pigments, are also used extensively.

Fluid lubricants are often preferred to dry lubricants for reduced friction, longer die life, and improved dimensional accuracy of the drawn workpieces. Straight mineral, synthetic, and water-soluble oils are used as lubricants for cold drawing finer sizes of wire. Water-soluble oils generally result in shorter die life than straight mineral oils, but are used extensively for drawing nonferrous metals. High-viscosity oils are sometimes preferred for better adhesion to the workpiece material. With the many antiwear additives now available, however, lower viscosity oils with such additives provide the best combination of good lubrication and superior cooling for high-speed drawing equipment.

Many different application methods are used in an attempt to apply the lubricant as close as possible to the die/workpiece interface. Metered application systems are available to dispense a preset amount of oil at frequent intervals.

# HOT EXTRUSION

Extrusion is a plastic deformation process in which material is forced under pressure to flow through one or more die orifices to produce products of the desired configuration. In hot extrusion, heated billets are reduced in size and forced to flow through dies to form products of uniform cross section along their continuous lengths. With special tooling, stepped and tapered extrusions are produced. Cold and warm extrusion are discussed subsequently in this chapter; the extrusion of metal powders is covered in Chapter 17, "Powder Metallurgy"; and extruding of plastics is covered in Chapter 18, "Plastics Forming."

## HISTORY OF HOT METAL EXTRUSION

In 1797, Joseph Bramah was granted a patent describing a press for making pipes of lead or other soft metals; the pipes could have various diameters and any given length without joints. The process consisted of forcing preheated metal through a die by means of a hand-operated plunger.

There was no development of Bramah's idea until 1820, when Thomas Burr constructed a hydraulic powered press for producing lead pipes by extrusion, or as it was then called, squirting. In 1894, Alexander Dick adapted the process to the hot extrusion of copper and brass, using billets in a horizontal extrusion press.

Rapid development of the electrical industry during the second half of the nineteenth century created the need for protective envelopes for cables to shield them against mechanical damage and make them impervious to water. In 1879, Borel in France and Wesslau in Germany devised methods for directly extruding lead sheathing onto cables. The presses used worked successfully; however, continuous lengths of cable could not be sheathed because the cable needed to be cut for inserting fresh billets. Two years later, Huber in Germany developed a press for sheathing long lengths of cable without the need for soldered joints. The press permitted charging consecutive billets of lead into the container at the end of each extrusion stroke.

Since successful extrusion of metals such as lead, copper, and brass was made possible, the process has been adapted to aluminum and steel. Today, many other metals and alloys are being extruded. These include magnesium, nickel, molybdenum, titanium, zirconium, uranium, and many superalloys and metal powders, as discussed later in this chapter.

## ADVANTAGES OF EXTRUSION

The extrusion process provides a practical forming method for producing a limitless variety of parallel-surfaced shapes to meet almost any design requirement. Other advantages include improving the microstructure and physical properties of the material, maintaining close tolerances, material conservation, economical production, and increased design flexibility.

### Shapes and Sizes Produced

Extruded sections can be hollow or solid, thick or thin, of simple or intricate shape, and of any size within the capacity of the press. A few examples of aluminum extrusions are illustrated in Fig. 13-9. Gears, airfoils, and many other shapes are produced.

Some shapes which cannot be rolled because of their geometry (such as those with reentrant angles) can be readily extruded. Also, some alloys which cannot be hot rolled because of a severe decrease in temperature during rolling can sometimes be extruded. Other alloys which break up when deformed unless they are contained on all sides can be extruded more readily than they can be rolled.

The size of an extrusion is measured by the diameter of the smallest circle that will enclose its cross section. This dimension is called the circle size. Aluminum extrusions with circle sizes ranging from 1/4 to 31" (6.4 to 787 mm) are produced, often in lengths more than 100 ft (30.5 m).

### Improved Properties

The rapid and severe reduction of the material under high pressure in hot extrusion refines the grain structure, minimizes decarburization or coating, and usually imparts improved and uniform properties to the extruded product. For many applications, the products are used as extruded, after stretch straightening. For other applications, the properties of the

# HOT EXTRUSION

**Fig. 13-9 Examples of aluminum extrusions.** (*Aluminum Extruders Council, Aluminum Assn.*)

extrusions are further improved by subsequent heat-treating or cold-working processes, such as drawing.

## Tolerances Maintained

The tolerances that are maintained in hot extruding depend primarily upon the workpiece material (difficulty in extruding), the size and geometry of the workpiece, and the press and tooling used. Associations such as the Aluminum Association, Aluminum Extruders Council, and the International Magnesium Association publish dimensional standards. The tolerances for hot extrusions of steel or titanium generally range from ±0.015 to ±0.062″ (0.38 to 1.57 mm).

Cross-sectional dimensional tolerances of extrusions made from aluminum and some other metals are specified in two ways: (1) metal dimensions (where 75% or more of the dimension is metal) and (2) space dimensions, measured by their distances from the places at which the metal segments are connected together. Tolerances for space dimensions are generally several times greater than those for metal dimensions.

## Surface Quality

The surface finish of aluminum extrusions is generally 63 μin. (1.60 μm) or less. For magnesium extrusions, the surface quality is generally described in terms of the depth of imperfections, which varies from a maximum of 0.0015″ (0.038 mm) deep for section thicknesses of 0.063″ (1.60 mm) or less, to 0.008″ (0.20 mm) deep for section thicknesses of 0.501″ (12.73 mm) or more. The surface finish of steel extrusions is typically 125 μin. (3.175 μm), but finishes of 63 μin. have been produced on close-tolerance extrusions of steel and titanium.

## Economy of Extrusion

The extruding process competes with many other metal-forming processes, including machining, welding, roll forming, casting, forging, and drawing. Often, extruding is the only feasible method that can be used.

**Machining.** Producing many lengths of metal to the required cross section by machining is almost always more costly than extruding a similar number of workpieces. With machining, costs are additive since each additional piece requires practically the same amount of time and labor, and material losses resulting from the production of chips are considerable.

**Welding.** Fabricating shapes by welding is also costly. The cost of producing the individual components to be welded can be high, and the welding costs do not decrease much with increased volume requirements. In some instances, the cost of necessary welding fixtures is higher than the cost of an extrusion die.

**Rolling.** For small-production requirements, the cost of a set of forming rolls and the setup for production can be a major part of the product cost. In such cases, the cost of extrusion tooling can be nominal and the setup costs for extruding a product are generally lower than those for rolling a similar product. Extrusion is therefore ideal for small orders of nonstandard items. With extruding, changes can be made to the design of the product with no significant increase in cost; however, such changes with rolling and other metalforming methods can be expensive.

Order sizes for extrusions range from as small as several pounds to as large as many tons [one short ton (2000 lb) equals 907 kg], with the economical order size varying with the material to be extruded, the capacity of the press, and the weight of the shape produced. There is a crossover point for extrusion cost versus rolling cost wherein the economies swing from one process to another. This critical point occurs somewhere around 50,000 lb (22 680 kg) for some extruded shapes made from certain steels.

**Casting.** Sand casting and permanent-mold casting result in workpieces that may require extensive finishing before they can be used. Extrusions, however, have fairly smooth surface finishes and relatively close dimensional control. The cost of casting molds also rises far more rapidly than that of extrusion dies as the complexity of the workpieces increase.

## POSSIBLE LIMITATIONS

Because of limitations with respect to the diameter and

length relationship of the starting billets, production rates from extrusion presses may be lower than for some other metal-forming processes. For example, about 95% of all carbon-steel tubing produced is made on tube mills rather than extrusion presses because tube mills permit faster production rates. The concentricity of tubing can generally be held to closer tolerances with tube mills than with extrusion presses. The initial investment required for an extrusion plant, however, is far less than for a tube mill. Also, when the cross sections of required shapes embody elements of various thicknesses, miscellaneous appendages, heavy sections, or voids, extruding is more economical and may be the only method of forming possible.

### Crew Size

The number of operators (the crew size) required for extrusion operations varies widely, depending upon the age and condition of the plant and equipment, degree of automation of the process, and work quality of the operators and management. Even with some automation and efficient operation, a crew size of four or more may be required. More operators are generally needed for extruding steel and refractory metals because of increased lubricating requirements and shorter die life, thus boosting labor costs.

### Design Requirements

Many standard shapes are available from commercial extruders, and considerable savings are possible by selecting such shapes if they are suitable. Sometimes, minor and acceptable changes can be made in the product design to permit the use of standard shapes. If special shapes are required, close cooperation should be maintained with the extruder during the design stages to permit obtaining the most economical extrusions. Extrusion designs with a high ratio of thick-to-thin walls, sharp corners, and abrupt metal transitions should be avoided.

### Extrusion Defects

Defects sometimes occur in extrusions as the result of a nonuniform flow of metal in the billet container. Such defects include funnel-shaped, hollow forms in the center of the billet (usually restricted to the unextruded portions of the billet); pipes, which are internal separations of the metal; and surface defects, such as scale, blisters, and die lines.

## METHODS OF EXTRUDING

The extrusion process can be classified into two main groups: direct and indirect extrusion, with direct extrusion being more common. Another method of extrusion is the hydrostatic process, which is used with both heated and unheated billets.

### Direct Extrusion

In direct, or forward, extrusion (see Fig. 13-10), a billet of metal (No. 4) is placed in a heavy-walled container (Nos. 7 and 8) and the extruded product (No. 1) exits through a die (No. 3) secured in a holder. The force for extruding is applied by a pressing stem or ram (No. 6), with an intermediate, reusable dummy block (No. 5). Metal flow from the die is in the same direction as the forward movement of the stem.

The direct method is by far the most common method of extrusion, but it does have some disadvantages. The surface of the entire length of the billet must slide along the container wall. The ease with which this is done depends upon the material being extruded and whether a lubricating film is present. In all cases, part of the extrusion load (the amount depending upon the length of the billet) is expended in overcoming the friction between the billet and the container, or in shearing inner billet material from the slower moving, peripheral layer of billet material adjacent to the container wall.

Force requirements in direct extrusion increase rapidly as the billets are upset to fill the containers (see Fig. 13-11). There is then a further increase, commonly known as breakthrough force, before extrusion begins. When the maximum force has been reached, the force requirements fall as the billet length decreases until a minimum is reached, and then they rapidly increase again. This increase occurs because only a thin disc of the billet remains and the metal has to flow radially towards the die aperture. Resistance to deformation increases considerably as the thicknesses of the butt ends (the unused portions of the billets) decrease.

### Indirect Extrusion

In indirect, or backward, extrusion, the billet remains stationary relative to the container wall while the die is pushed into the billet by a hollow stem (ram); or the container and billet are pushed over the stationary stem and stem-mounted die (see Fig. 13-12). The die is loosely attached to the end of the stem, and the extrusion exits through the hollow stem. Lengths of the billets used in indirect extrusion are limited only by the column strengths of the stems. Since there is no relative motion between the outer surface of the billet and the bore of the container, friction between these two surfaces is eliminated and the force necessary is decreased.

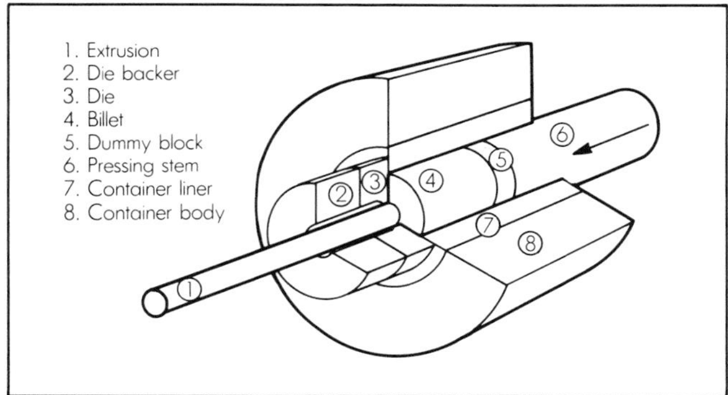


**Fig. 13-10 Direct method of hot extrusion.** (*Wean United*)

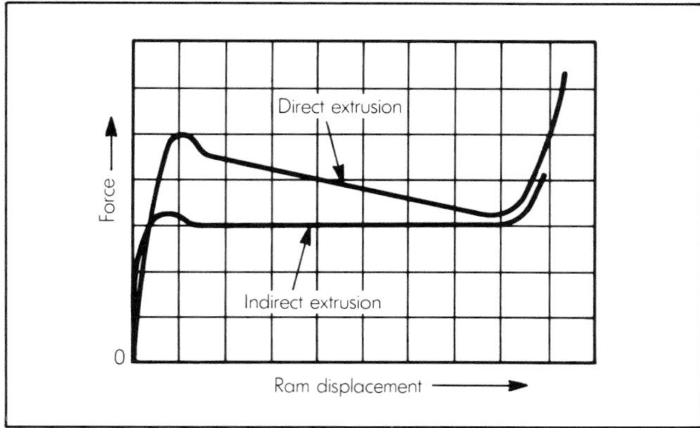


**Fig. 13-11 Force vs. ram displacement for direct and indirect extrusion.** (*Wean United*)

# CHAPTER 13

# HOT EXTRUSION

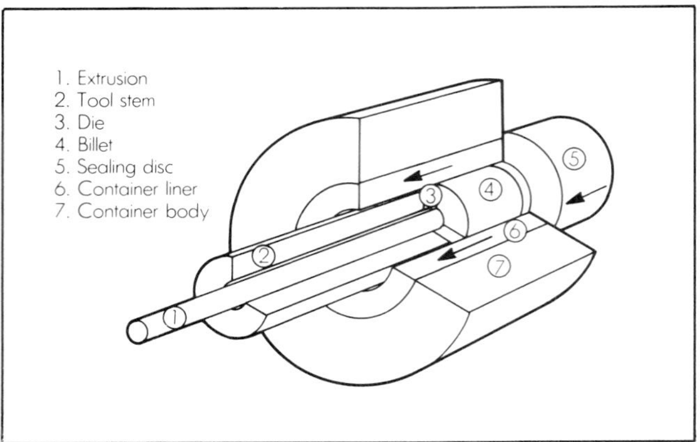


**Fig. 13-12 Indirect method of hot extrusion.** (*Wean United*)

Breakthrough force needed with indirect extrusion is significantly lower than that needed with direct extrusion (see Fig. 13-11). After breakthrough, the force requirements remain essentially constant throughout the extrusion stroke. Near the end of the stroke, as the unextruded butt thickness becomes thinner, the force necessary rises significantly, as is also the case with direct extrusion.

**Advantages.** The advantages of indirect extrusion are the results obtained through both decreased force requirements and a more uniform flow pattern of the material being extruded. The major advantages of indirect extrusion are:

1. A 25-30% reduction in force requirements compared to those needed in direct extrusion provides the capability for extruding larger billets and smaller extruded sections, decreasing the temperatures of the billets, and permitting higher speed extrusion.
2. Billet lengths are limited only by the length and stability of the hollow stem needed for a given container length, rather than by force requirements.
3. There is less tendency for surfaces and edges of aluminum alloy extrusions to crack, even at higher extrusion speeds, because no heat is produced by friction between the billet and the container. (A temperature increase at the billet surface toward the end of the extrusion cycle is typical in the direct extrusion of aluminum alloys.)
4. Tooling life may be increased, especially that of inner container liners, because of the almost total absence of friction.
5. More uniform deformation of the complete cross section of the billet is attained, with a reduced tendency to form extrusion defects or coarse-grained peripheral zones.

**Disadvantages.** A major disadvantage of indirect extrusion is that impurities or defects on the surfaces of the billets affect the surfaces of the extrusions. Impurities or defects on the extrusion surfaces preclude the use of the extrusions for architectural purposes and make them unacceptable for anodizing. For applications of indirect extrusion, wire-brushed, machined, or chemically cleaned billets have to be used in many cases, adding to production costs. With direct extrusion, impurities or defects on the billets are automatically retained as shells or discard butts in the containers.

Another limitation of the indirect process is that the cross-sectional area of the extrusion is limited by the size of the opening possible in the hollow stem. As a result, indirect extrusion is less versatile than direct extrusion and cannot be used for all products.

## Hydrostatic Extrusion

In hydrostatic extrusion, the billet is surrounded by a pressurized liquid acting on all surfaces of the billet except that at which the billet contacts the die opening. As with indirect extrusion, virtually no friction exists between the billet and the container wall. Hydrostatic extrusion is not exclusively a hot process; it is frequently performed with the billets at room temperature or with the billets only warmed. In fact, the billet temperature is limited by the stability of the fluid medium used.

Pressure for hydrostatic extrusion is provided in either of the following two methods:

1. The ram or plunger of the extrusion press is forced into the container to increase the pressure of the fluid acting on the billet (see Fig. 13-13). This method is often called constant-rate extrusion.
2. A pump, with or without a pressure intensifier, applies the pressurized medium directly to the billet, and no ram or plunger is used in the container. This is referred to as constant-pressure extrusion. Constant-rate extrusion is easier to control than constant-pressure extrusion and permits a reduction in pressure requirements for the supply fluid.

When the fluid pressure on the billet is sufficient, material is extruded through the die to form the product. To produce hollow products, such as tubes, a mandrel (normally stationary) is used to form the inner surface of the product, as illustrated in Fig. 13-13.

**Advantages.** Many materials subjected to high hydrostatic pressures generally have increased ductility. As a result, hydrostatic extrusion is suitable for both brittle and ductile metals. The lack of friction between billet and container reduces force requirements (see Fig. 13-14), permitting high reduction ratios, fast speeds, and/or low billet temperatures. In the warm hydrostatic extrusion of high-strength aluminum alloys, speeds are being attained that are from 50 to 100 times faster than those employed for hot direct extrusion.

Other advantages of hydrostatic extrusion include an even flow of material, the absence of a residue of extruded material on the container wall, the ability to extrude large-diameter and long billets, and the freedom for the billets to rotate during extrusion. An even flow of material facilitates the manufacturing of clad products. The pressurized medium used also helps lubricate the surfaces between the billet and the die.

**Disadvantages.** One disadvantage of hydrostatic extrusion is the prior preparation required for the billets. Every billet has to be tapered at one end to match the die entry angle. This is necessary to form a seal at the start of the extrusion cycle. Also, the entire surface of the billet generally has to be machined, particularly if cast billets are being used, to remove surface defects. Containing the fluid medium under the high pressures employed can present problems and necessitates special design considerations.

In hydrostatic extrusion, the radial and axial pressures exerted by the fluid medium are equal; whereas, in conventional extrusion, the radial pressure on the container is 20-80% lower than the axial pressure applied by the ram. As a result, the tooling for hydrostatic extrusion has to withstand significantly higher pressures, necessitating stringent requirements with respect to tooling design and materials. However, the equal

# HOT EXTRUSION

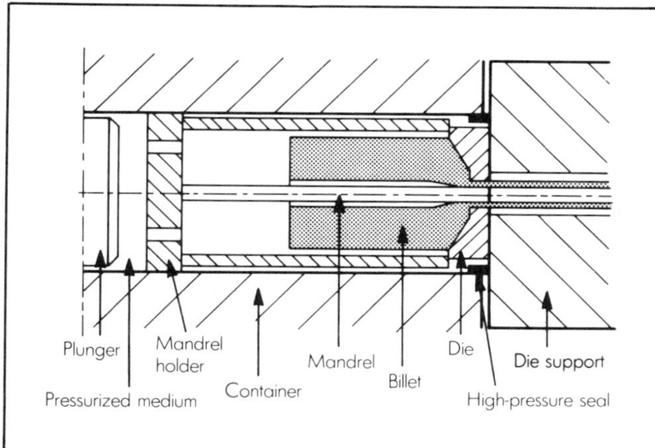


**Fig. 13-13 Principle of hydrostatic extrusion of tubes. (*ASEA*)**

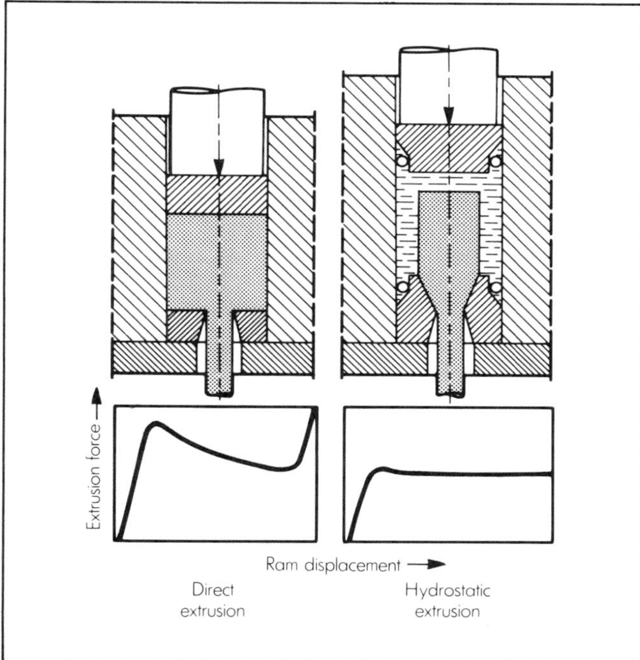


**Fig. 13-14 Extrusion force vs. ram displacement for direct and hydrostatic extrusion. (*Wean United*)**

pressurization in hydrostatic extrusion permits higher reduction ratios at lower preheating temperatures in comparison to conventional extrusion methods.

## MATERIALS EXTRUDED AND APPLICATIONS

The uses to which extrusions are applied appear endless and are expanding constantly. A large proportion of metal consumption is in the form of extrusions. Depending upon the material used, extrusions serve the transportation, construction, mechanical, and electrical sectors of the economy. They are used for durable goods, for industrial equipment, and for heating and air conditioning applications, as well as in deep-well drilling and in the production of nuclear power.

Practically all metals can be extruded, but their extrudability varies with their deformation properties. Soft metals are easier to extrude, while hard metals require higher billet temperatures and extruding pressures and sturdier presses and dies.

### Lead and Tin

Lead and tin have high ductility and are easily extruded. The addition of alloying elements increases the force required, but extruding presents no problem and is done with billets heated to a maximum temperature of about 575° F (300° C). Major applications include pipes, wire, tubes, and sheathing for cable. For many applications, molten lead is used instead of billets. Protective sheathings of lead on electrical conductors are sometimes produced on vertical extrusion presses, filling the container with molten lead.

### Aluminum and Aluminum Alloys

Aluminum is probably the most ideal metal for extrusion and is the most commonly extruded. Most commercially available aluminum alloys can be extruded. Depending upon the alloy, billet temperatures generally range from about 575 to 1100° F (300 to 600° C). Major applications include pipes, wire, rods, bars, tubes, hollow shapes, cable sheathing, architectural and structural sections, and automotive trim. A wide, thin section, an aluminum truck-trailer wear band, extruded from rectangular billets, is illustrated in Fig. 13-15. The V-groove, radii, thickness, and center-to-center dimensions are maintained to close tolerances. Most sections are extruded from heat-treatable, high-strength aluminum alloys.

### Magnesium and Magnesium Alloys

Extruded products of magnesium and magnesium alloy are used in the aircraft, aerospace, and nuclear power industries. The extrudability of these materials is about the same as that of aluminum, with similar billet temperatures; however, longer heating periods are generally required to ensure uniform temperatures throughout the billets.

### Zinc and Zinc Alloys

Extruding of zinc and zinc alloys requires higher pressures than needed for lead, aluminum, and magnesium. Billet temperatures generally range from about 400 to 650° F (200 to 350° C). Applications include rods, bars, tubes, hardware components, fittings, and handrails.

### Copper and Copper Alloys

Extrusions of copper and copper alloys are used extensively for wire, rods, bars, pipes, tubes, electrical conductors and connectors, and welding electrodes. Architectural shapes are extruded from brass, but usually in limited quantities. Billet temperatures vary from about 1100 to 1825° F (600 to 1000° C), and extrudability ranges from easy to difficult, depending upon

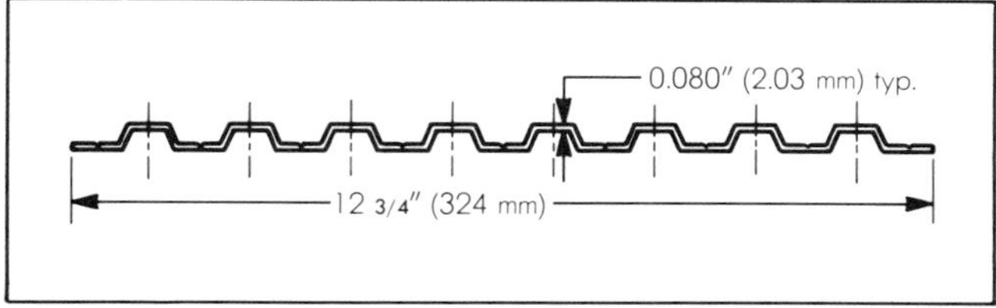


**Fig. 13-15 Aluminum section extruded from rectangular billets to close tolerances. (*Wean United*)**

the alloy. High pressures—100 ksi (690 MPa) or more—are needed to extrude many copper alloys.

### Extruding Steels

The hot extrusion of steel requires the use of glass as a lubricant or other high-temperature lubricant to prevent excessive tooling wear that can result from the high billet temperatures required, 1825-2375° F (1000-1300° C). High ram speeds are also essential to minimize contact time between the billets and the tooling. Products produced include structural sections, generally required in small quantities, and tubes with small bores. For economic reasons, steel structural shapes, especially those needed in large quantities, are better suited to the rolling process. The materials extruded are generally plain carbon steels, but some alloy and stainless steels are also extruded.

### Extruding Other Metals

Many other metals are being hot extruded, including titanium and titanium alloys, nickel and its alloys, superalloys, zirconium, beryllium, uranium, and molybdenum. Titanium alloys are more difficult to extrude than steels, but lower billet temperatures, 1100-1825° F (600-1000° C), and higher speeds are generally employed. Nickel and nickel alloys are also very difficult to extrude, and billet temperatures above 1825° F (1000° C) are used. Some of the exotic metals are extruded into tubes, rods, and bars, and the bars are often used as forging stock in subsequent operations.

### Metal Powders and Plastics

Metal powders (discussed in Chapter 17, "Powder Metallurgy") are extruded into long shapes by both cold and hot processes, depending upon the characteristics of the powders. Powders extruded include aluminum, copper, nickel, stainless steels, beryllium, and uranium. The powders are often compressed into billets that are heated before being placed in the extrusion press. For many applications, the powders are encapsulated in protective metallic cans, heated, and extruded with the cans.

The extrusion of plastic moldings is discussed in Chapter 18, "Plastics Forming." Major applications for extruded plastics include the production of film, sheets, and various profiles, and the coating of cable, wire, and metal strips. Plastics in pellet, granular, or powder form are heated in the container of an extruding machine. The stem of the machine is replaced by a rotating screw which forces the material through the die orifice. Plastic extrusion is thus more of a continuous operation since no interruption is needed to load billets into the container.

## PRESSES FOR HOT EXTRUSION

Both horizontal and vertical presses are available for hot extrusion, with the horizontal type being predominant. Hot extrusion is also done on hydrostatic presses, discussed later in this section, and on high-energy-rate forming (HERF) machines described in Chapter 19, "Special Forming Methods."

### Press Drives

The majority of all modern extrusion presses are driven hydraulically although mechanical drives are used in some applications, such as the production of small tubes. There are basically two types of hydraulic drives: direct-drive oil type and accumulator water type. In the past, accumulator water-driven presses were predominant; however, today, direct-drive oil presses are being used more extensively.

**Accumulator water drives.** The hydraulic circuit of accumulator water-driven presses consists essentially of one or more air-over-water accumulators charged by high-pressure water pumps. The accumulator bottle, or bank of bottles, is designed to give the amount of water needed to provide necessary pressure requirements throughout the extrusion stroke, with a pressure drop not exceeding about 10%. For applications involving marginal, difficult-to-extrude shapes, this drop in pressure is often critical. This limitation, plus the high cost of high-pressure water pumps, accumulators, and valves, as well as the substantial floor-space requirements, resulted in the increasing popularity of direct-drive, oil-hydraulic extrusion presses. An important advantage of accumulator water drives, however, is higher stem speeds—to 15 ips (381 mm/s)—making them desirable for the extrusion of steel. Water is also a nonflammable hydraulic medium, a consideration when extruding very hot billets.

**Direct-drive oil presses.** A typical direct-drive, oil-hydraulic press for hot extrusion is illustrated in Fig. 13-16. The development of reliable, high-pressure, variable-delivery oil pumps—some operating at pressures exceeding 5000 psi (34.5 MPa)—has been primarily responsible for the increasing use of these presses. They are self-contained, require less floor space, and are less expensive than accumulator water-driven presses. More importantly, they provide a constant force during the entire extrusion stroke, with no pressure drop. A limitation of direct-drive oil presses is slower stem speeds than are available with accumulator drives. Stem speeds to 2 ips (51 mm/s) are common, but speeds to 8 ips (203 mm/s) are possible by using oil accumulators with oil-hydraulic drives.

### Improvements in Extrusion Presses

Major improvements available on modern extrusion presses include simplified hydraulic circuits for easier troubleshooting, manifolded piping for reduced leakage and maintenance, and improved valves that minimize wear. Closed-loop, constant-rate speed controls simplify the production of smooth finishes and uniform extrusion properties. The presses are also faster operating for increased productivity.

On many presses, magnetic relays have been replaced with solid-state programmable controllers for increased versatility, simplified troubleshooting, and ease of interfacing with computers. The use of computers, for the presses and auxiliary equipment in an integrated extruding system, permits monitoring all operations and instantaneously providing data regarding production, downtime, inventory, and other information necessary for an efficient and profitable extrusion plant.

### Force and Pressure Capacities

Presses for hot extrusion are usually rated in force capacity—the total force the press is capable of exerting upon the billet. Press operation, however, is dependent upon the actual unit pressure exerted on the metal. For a press with a given force capacity, which equals the cross-sectional area of the container multiplied by the unit pressure, higher unit pressures can be obtained if the billet container is smaller in diameter. As the container diameter increases, the unit pressure capability decreases, with a resultant decrease in the ability to extrude. This is illustrated in Table 13-3, which shows maximum unit pressures in relation to billet (container) diameters on

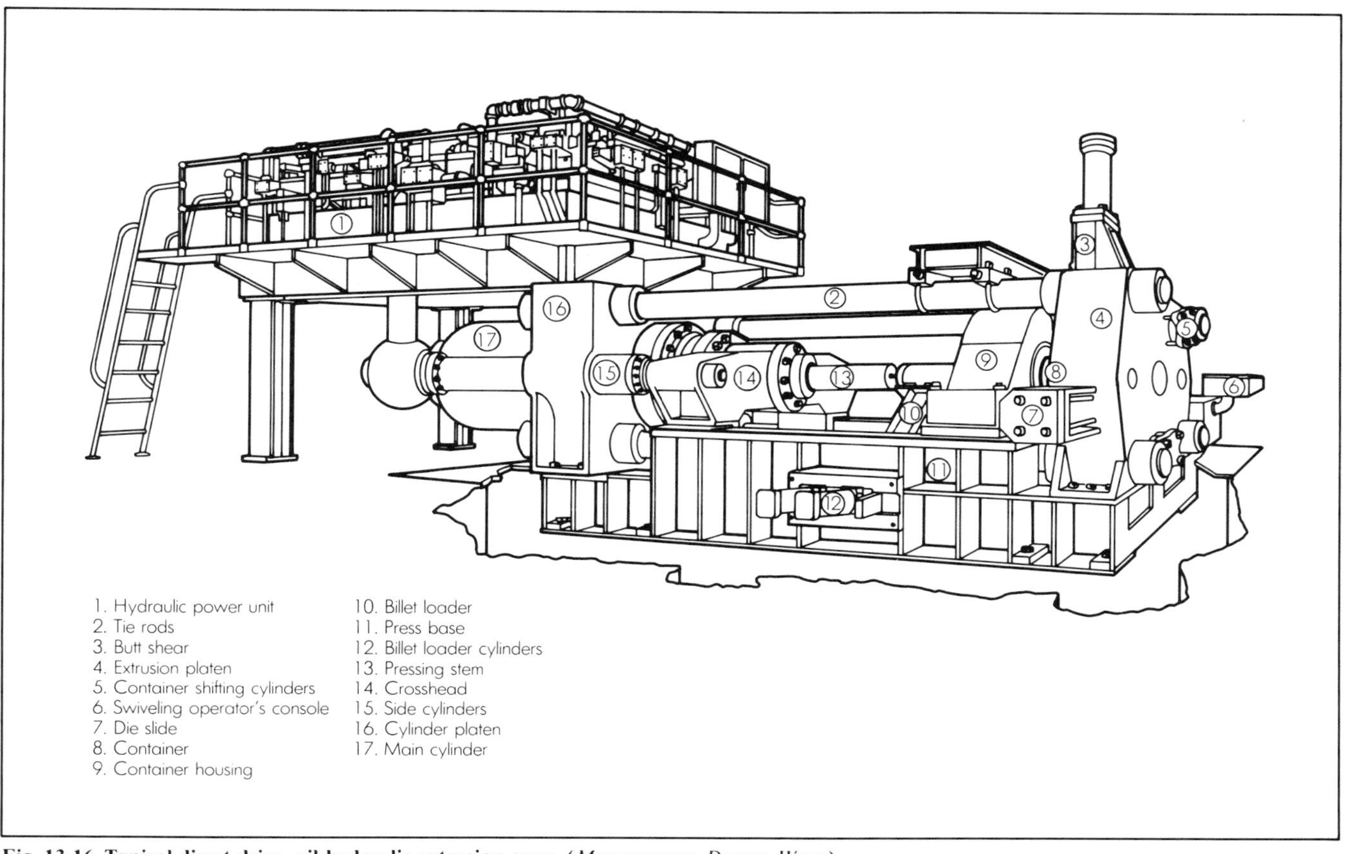


**Fig. 13-16 Typical direct-drive, oil-hydraulic extrusion press.** (*Mannesmann Demag Wean*)

**TABLE 13-3**
**Typical Capacities of Presses for Hot Extrusion of Aluminum and Aluminum Alloys**

| Max Press Force | | Max Billet Length | | Max Billet Diam | | Max Billet Weight | | Max Unit Pressure on Metal | |
|---|---|---|---|---|---|---|---|---|---|
| tons | MN | in. | mm | in. | mm | lb | kg | ksi | MPa |
| 500 | 4.45 | 12 | 305 | 3 1/2 | 89 | 11.5 | 5.2 | 91 | 627.4 |
| | | | | 4 | 102 | 15 | 6.8 | 70.5 | 486.1 |
| 900 | 8.0 | 18 | 457 | 4 1/2 | 113 | 28.5 | 12.9 | 101.5 | 699.8 |
| | | | | 5 | 127 | 35 | 15.9 | 79.5 | 548.1 |
| 1400 | 12.5 | 24 | 610 | 5 | 127 | 47 | 21.3 | 123 | 848.1 |
| | | | | 6 | 152 | 67.5 | 30.6 | 88 | 606.7 |
| 1650 | 14.7 | 32 | 813 | 6 | 152 | 90 | 40.8 | 103 | 710.2 |
| | | | | 7 | 178 | 123 | 55.8 | 77 | 530.9 |
| | | | | 8 | 203 | 160 | 72.6 | 60 | 413.7 |
| 1675 | 14.9 | 26 | 660 | 6 | 152 | 73 | 33.1 | 104.5 | 720.5 |
| | | | | 7 | 178 | 100 | 45.4 | 78 | 537.8 |
| | | | | 8 | 203 | 130 | 59.0 | 61 | 420.6 |
| 1800 | 16.0 | 34 | 864 | 7 | 178 | 130 | 59.0 | 84 | 579.2 |
| | | | | 8 | 203 | 170 | 77.1 | 65.5 | 451.6 |
| 2000 | 17.8 | 34 | 864 | 7 | 178 | 130 | 59.0 | 93.5 | 644.7 |
| | | | | 8 | 203 | 170 | 77.1 | 73 | 503.3 |

*(continued)*

TABLE 13-3—*Continued*

| Max Press Force | | Max Billet Length | | Max Billet Diam | | Max Billet Weight | | Max Unit Pressure on Metal | |
|---|---|---|---|---|---|---|---|---|---|
| tons | MN | in. | mm | in. | mm | lb | kg | ksi | MPa |
| 2200 | 19.6 | 36 | 914 | 7 | 178 | 138 | 62.6 | 103 | 710.2 |
| | | | | 8 | 203 | 180 | 81.6 | 80 | 551.6 |
| | | | | 9 | 229 | 228 | 103.4 | 65.5 | 451.6 |
| 2500 | 22.2 | 36 | 914 | 7 | 178 | 138 | 62.6 | 117 | 806.7 |
| | | | | 8 | 203 | 180 | 81.6 | 91 | 627.4 |
| | | | | 9 | 229 | 228 | 103.4 | 74.5 | 513.7 |
| 2750 | 24.5 | 36 | 914 | 8 | 203 | 180 | 81.6 | 100 | 689.5 |
| | | | | 9 | 229 | 228 | 103.4 | 82 | 565.4 |
| | | | | 10 | 254 | 282 | 127.9 | 66.5 | 458.5 |
| 3000 | 26.7 | 38 | 965 | 8 | 203 | 190 | 86.2 | 109 | 751.5 |
| | | | | 9 | 229 | 241 | 109.3 | 89 | 613.6 |
| | | | | 10 | 254 | 298 | 135.2 | 72.5 | 499.9 |
| 3500 | 31.1 | 38 | 965 | 9 | 229 | 241 | 109.3 | 104 | 717.1 |
| | | | | 10 | 254 | 298 | 135.2 | 85 | 586.1 |
| | | | | 12 | 305 | 429 | 194.6 | 59 | 406.8 |
| 3750 | 33.4 | 38 | 965 | 9 | 229 | 241 | 109.3 | 111.5 | 768.8 |
| | | | | 10 | 254 | 298 | 135.2 | 91 | 627.4 |
| | | | | 12 | 305 | 429 | 194.6 | 63.5 | 437.8 |
| 4000 | 35.6 | 40 | 1016 | 10 | 254 | 314 | 142.4 | 97 | 668.8 |
| | | | | 12 | 305 | 452 | 205.0 | 68 | 468.8 |
| | | | | 13 | 330 | 530 | 240.4 | 57.5 | 396.4 |
| 4500 | 40.0 | 42 | 1067 | 10 | 254 | 330 | 149.7 | 109 | 751.5 |
| | | | | 12 | 305 | 475 | 215.5 | 76 | 524.0 |
| | | | | 14 | 356 | 647 | 293.5 | 56 | 386.1 |
| 5000 | 44.5 | 45 | 1143 | 12 | 305 | 508 | 230.4 | 85 | 586.1 |
| | | | | 14 | 356 | 698 | 316.6 | 62 | 427.5 |
| | | | | 16 | 406 | 904 | 410.1 | 47.5 | 327.5 |
| 5500 | 48.9 | 45 | 1143 | 12 | 305 | 508 | 230.4 | 93.5 | 644.7 |
| | | | | 14 | 356 | 698 | 316.6 | 68 | 468.8 |
| | | | | 16 | 406 | 904 | 410.1 | 52.5 | 362.0 |
| 6000 | 53.4 | 54 | 1372 | 12 | 305 | 610 | 276.7 | 102 | 703.3 |
| | | | | 14 | 356 | 831 | 376.9 | 74.5 | 513.7 |
| | | | | 16 | 406 | 1085 | 492.2 | 57 | 393.0 |
| | | | | 18 | 457 | 1374 | 623.2 | 45 | 310.3 |
| 8000 | 71.2 | 64 | 1626 | 13 | 330 | 851 | 386.0 | 115 | 792.9 |
| | | | | 16 | 406 | 1286 | 583.3 | 76 | 524.0 |
| | | | | 18 | 457 | 1628 | 738.5 | 60 | 413.7 |
| | | | | 20 | 508 | 2010 | 911.7 | 49 | 337.8 |

(*Mannesmann Demag Wean Co.*)

direct-drive hydraulic presses of various force capacities made by one press builder.

For extruding most metals, a press is generally not being used to its full capacity if the unit pressure is lower than 65 ksi (448.2 MPa).

The maximum unit pressure that can be used safely or economically on most extrusion presses is about 150 ksi (1034.2 MPa). This pressure is near the upper limit of the mechanical strengths of most tool steels used for extrusion, and higher pressures are likely to cause premature tooling failure.

The largest direct-drive oil press in the United States has a rated force capacity of about 8000 tons (71.2 MN). Hot extrusion presses with accumulator water drives are available with higher force capacities. One vertical press for extruding seamless, carbon and alloy steel pipe to 48" (1219 mm) diam x 80 ft (24.4 m) long is rated at 35,000 tons (311.5 MN). This press is powered by a 5000 psi (34.5 MPa), air-ballasted, water accumulator system, with 12 accumulator bottles.

## Press Selection

The unit pressures needed for extrusion, which are a major consideration in press selection, vary with the metal to be extruded and its condition, the length and temperature of the billet, the complexity of the cross section of the product, the speed of extrusion, and the reduction ratio. The reduction (extrusion) ratio equals the cross-sectional area of the container liner divided by the cross-sectional area of the combined die openings.

Higher pressures are generally necessary at the beginning of the extrusion cycle, as previously discussed (see Fig. 13-11). Pressure requirements diminish as extrusion progresses and then rise again as the butt of the billet is reduced to a thickness of about 1/2 to 1" (12.7 to 25.4 mm). Methods of determining press force and pressure requirements to extrude various products are discussed subsequently in this chapter under the subject of operating parameters.

Advantages of using a press with ample capacity include (1) the ability to use lower billet temperatures and faster speeds and (2) the ability to obtain improved metallurgical properties in the extruded products. Using a press with inadequate capacity can result in the inability to extrude (billets sticking in the containers) or in extrusions of poor quality.

Accurate and adjustable alignment of the stem, container, and die, as well as a rigid structure, are essential for any extrusion press. Most press structures use prestressed tie-rod construction. Modern presses permit longer die-stack lengths than possible with earlier models, thus providing better tool stability and improved tolerances on extruded products.

## Press Accessories

A wide variety of accessories are available as either standard or optional items for hot-extrusion presses.

**Die changing.** Die slides and revolving die arms are available on most presses to facilitate changing dies. Multistation die slides (see Fig. 13-17) permit die setups to be made while the press is operating, thus minimizing downtime. On the unit illustrated in Fig. 13-17, a shifting cylinder is located integrally, within the slide. A long cylinder stroke permits die changing at the front or back of the press. Adjustable end stops allow accurate alignment of die stations in their operating positions.

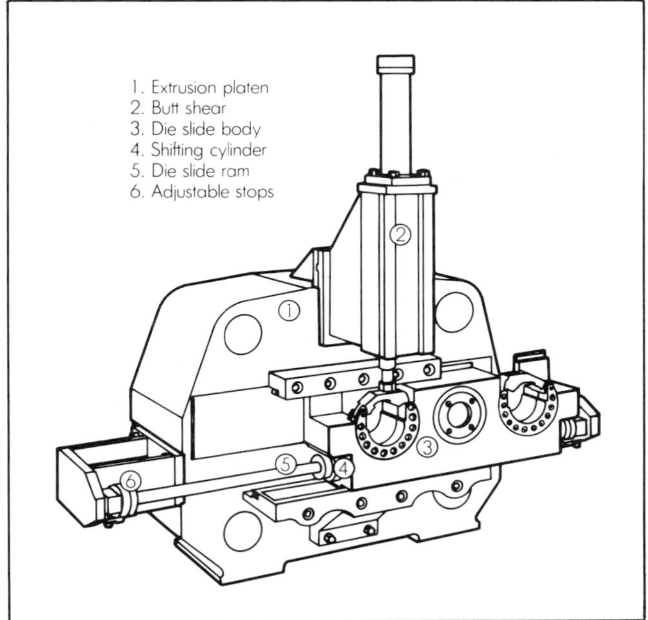


**Fig. 13-17 Multistation die slide with internal shifting cylinder.** (*Wean United*)

Copper and steel extrusion requires frequent die changes because of the high billet temperatures. Often, the dies have to be changed after extruding each billet to allow the dies to cool. Automatic die changers are available to remove the hot die and insert a replacement. A number of dies are used in rotation, being fed from a magazine.

**Container changing and heating.** With each change in billet diameter, the container on the press must be changed. Different press builders offer various devices to permit changing the container in a minimum of time. Some presses have been built with three indexing containers to permit simultaneous billet loading, extruding, and cleaning/lubricating, or to facilitate changing containers, thus increasing production. Presses used to extrude wide, thin sections or sheets can be equipped with containers that accept rectangular billets and reduce the force and pressure requirements.

Controlled operating temperature of the container is essential for proper press operation. This is generally accomplished with electrical heating elements, located either externally in the container housing or internally in drilled holes in the container body. For some applications, a combination of external and internal heating is provided. Container cooling is also used for certain applications, such as the extruding of copper, brass, and steel, to extend tool life.

**Billet piercing.** When prepierced or predrilled billets are used for tube extrusion, the presses are equipped with integral mandrel manipulators for moving the mandrels into the bores of the billets prior to extrusion. For solid billets, the tube extruding presses are equipped with piercing units to drive the mandrels through the centers of the heated billets. Both internal and external piercers are available, with the internal units generally being preferred because of more precise centering capabilities and reduced space requirements compared to external units.

**Billet loading.** Loaders of internal and external types (see Fig. 13-18) are available for automatically feeding billets and dummy blocks into the press. Some loaders are of two-section design, with both sections receiving a billet and dummy block and swinging into charging position as a unit. As the press ram advances, the two sections retract in sequence so that the billet and dummy block remain fully supported and aligned until they have entered the container. For high-production requirements, three-section loaders are available.

**Butt separating.** Separating the butt from the extruded product on presses is done with either cutoff saws or shears. For most materials, other than aluminum, cutoff is generally done with a saw rather than a shear. This is normally a vertical, down-cutting saw fitted with a toothed blade or, in some cases, an abrasive wheel. Shears must be rigidly supported and fully guided throughout their stroke to prevent deflection and smearing of the metal being sheared. For some applications, the presses are equipped with both a saw and shear.

**Butt unloading.** Mechanized butt and dummy block handling systems are available for extrusion presses to eliminate manual lifting of these heavy pieces. Features offered on various systems include the following:

1. A cushioned receiver to catch the butt and dummy block after sawing or shearing.

2. A means to transfer the butt and dummy block outside the press.
3. An intermediate air or water quench.
4. An elevator to raise the butt and dummy block to a convenient handling and inspection level.
5. A shear to separate the butt from the dummy block.
6. A chute to orient and return the dummy block to a convenient position for loading.

On presses on which a die slide is shifted during the operating cycle, the slide can be designed to remove the dummy block and butt from the press.

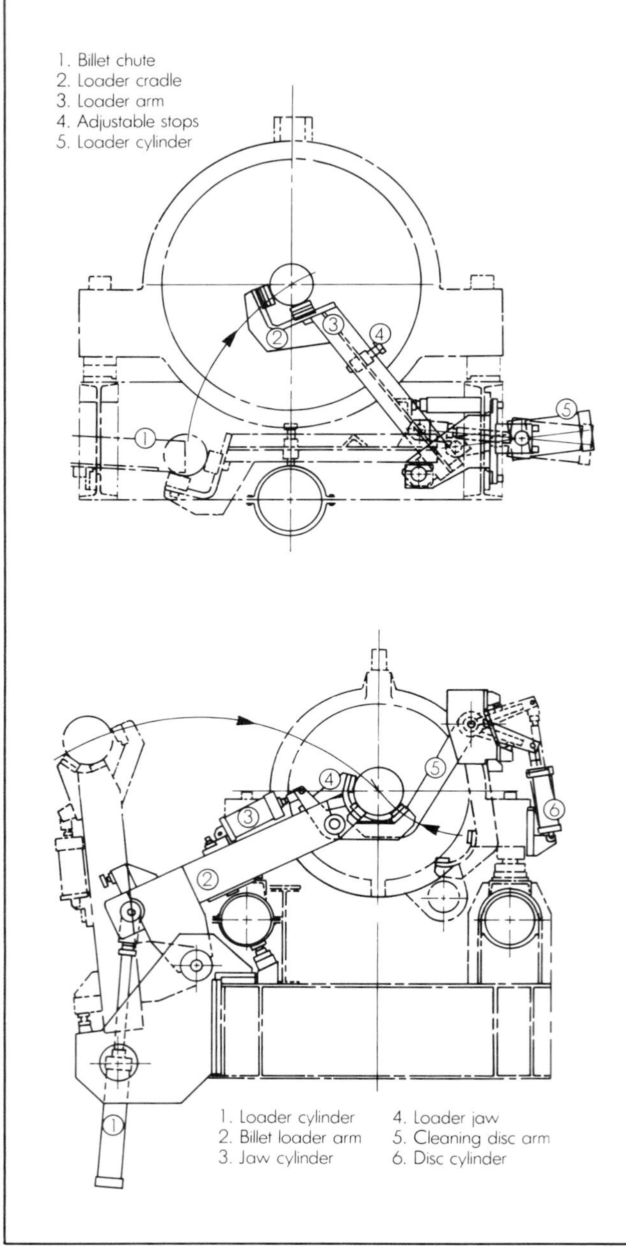


**Fig. 13-18 Two types of billet loaders: internal (top) and external (bottom).** (*Wean United*)

## Auxiliary Equipment

In addition to the press, other equipment is required for complete extrusion facilities, some of which are completely automated. Such equipment includes billet heaters, stretchers, pullers, sawing equipment, and system controls. For many installations, especially for aluminum extrusion, gas-fired and induction billet heaters have been replaced by gas-fired log heaters. Heating aluminum logs that are 12-20 ft (3.7-6.1 m) long and cutting them to the required length as they emerge from the heater has eliminated the need to store billets of varying lengths. Log shears allow the press operator to tailor billet lengths to provide maximum yield from each billet with a minimum of scrap. Computer control ensures shearing the logs to the optimum billet length for the particular die being used and for the extrusion length desired.

Reliable extrusion pullers have been developed that reduce operator responsibilities, eliminate twisting of the extruded products, and ensure that equal-length extrusions are obtained from multiple-hole dies. Such pullers also improve the efficiency of extrusion stretching operations. Fewer manipulations of the stretcher tailstock are required to accommodate unequal extrusion lengths, and the need for detwisting extruded shapes prior to stretching is virtually eliminated. In many instances, stretching requires only one operator, located at the headstock, with tailstock manipulation controlled by the same operator by means of a TV camera. Several installations have completely programmed puller/stretcher combinations.

Beyond the stretcher, automatic saw tables are frequently provided and, in many cases, cut-to-length extrusions are automatically stacked for subsequent heat treatment.

Enclosed, water-filled chambers have been provided at the ends of several presses that are used to extrude copper tubing. The tubing is extruded directly into the chamber and remains submerged for the full length of the runout. A special gate prevents backflow through the dies, and an end crimper prevents water from filling the tube. The result of this arrangement is the production of copper tubing having a refined grain structure, with consistent grain orientation.

## Hydrostatic Extrusion Presses

Hydrostatic extrusion presses have been built for production applications with pressure capacities to 200 ksi (1379 MPa), using an intensifier in a 6500 psi (44.8 MPa) hydraulic system. Speeds in excess of 2.8 ips (70.6 mm/s) have been attained. Castor oil is generally used as the pressure medium because of its good lubricity and high-pressure properties.

Hydrostatic presses made by one builder have a frame consisting of two semicylindrical yokes and four columns held together by numerous layers of prestressed high-strength steel wire wound around the frame (see Fig. 13-19). This construction keeps the columns in a compressed state, even under maximum frame load conditions. Wire winding is also used for the high-pressure billet container, made from a forged steel cylinder with replaceable liners.

# TOOLING FOR HOT EXTRUSION

Successful and economical hot extrusion requires careful consideration with respect to the design of the tooling components, selection of the materials from which they are made, and method by which they are manufactured and heat treated. High-quality materials are essential because the tooling must operate under high pressures and high temperatures, and is subjected to severe strain and abrasive wear.

## Tooling Components

Tooling for hot extrusion consists of many components, including containers, container liners, stems (rams), dummy blocks, mandrels, spider or bridge dies for producing hollow extrusions, and flat or feeder plate dies. Complete die assemblies are often called tooling stacks.

Two common types of dies are flat faced and shaped. Flat-faced dies, sometimes called square dies, have one or more openings (apertures) similar in cross section to that of the desired extruded product. Shaped dies, also referred to as converging or streamlined dies, have a smooth entry opening with circular cross section that changes progressively to the final extruded shape required. Flat-faced dies are easier to design and manufacture than shaped dies, and are commonly used for the hot extrusion of aluminum, copper, brass, and magnesium alloys. Shaped dies, which are more difficult and costly to design and manufacture, are used for the hot extrusion of steels, titanium alloys, and other metals.

**Dies for solid shapes.** A typical die-slide tooling arrangement for the direct extrusion of solid shapes is shown in Fig. 13-20. Stepped extrusions having two or more cross-sectional dimensions are produced by using two or more separate dies. The die with the smallest opening is used first. This die is then removed and progressively larger dies are employed.

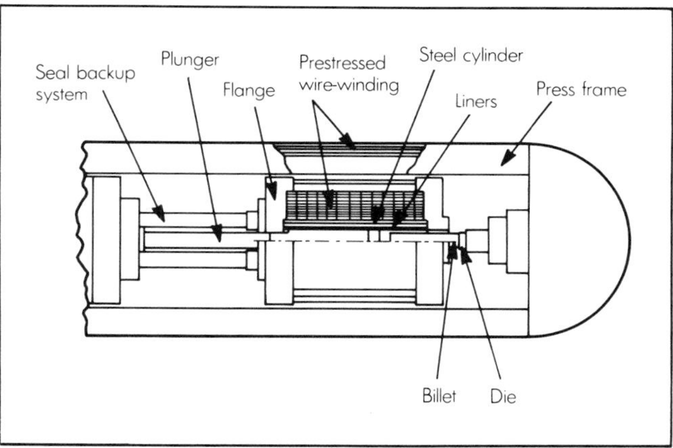


**Fig. 13-19 Hydrostatic extrusion press with prestressed wire-wound frame and billet container.** (*ASEA*)

Aluminum extruders sometimes use rectangular containers to produce wide shapes or smaller shapes side by side. Rectangular containers having the same areas as round containers can extrude much wider shapes. Liners for rectangular containers generally consist of two or more pieces.

**Dies for hollow shapes.** Hollow or semihollow shapes are extruded from hollow or solid billets. Fixed or floating mandrels, separate from the dies, are used to extrude hollow billets. Mandrels fixed to the ends of the stems are referred to as German types. Floating mandrels, called French types, are generally set in slots in the dummy blocks and center themselves in the dies as the metal is extruded.

For solid billets, hollow dies classified as spider, porthole, or bridge types are used. These dies have stub mandrels as integral parts of the dies. The extrusions produced have one or more seams (longitudinal weld lines) resulting from the metal's dividing to flow around the mandrel supports and welding together before passing through the die.

Spider dies have steel spiders supporting the stub mandrels that extend through the dies. Porthole dies (see Fig. 13-21) are similar except that the spiders are replaced with mandrels having annular holes and die caps supported in die rings. Bridge dies (see Fig. 13-22) have the stub mandrels supported by bridges over the cavities.

**Tooling for indirect extrusion.** Two recent developments in tooling for indirect extrusion, both patented by Texas Extrusion Corp., are noteworthy. These developments involve the use of multihole, segmented stems for increased productivity and hollow gag blocks for "buttless" extrusion.

Instead of a one-piece tubular stem that is used on conventional indirect extrusion presses, a stack of short, identical stem segments is assembled in a tube (see Fig. 13-23). The use of segments facilitates machining of multiple cavities of any configuration and permits the use of long stems. Segments extend the full length of the stems, minimizing deflection of the dies. This design permits using practically the entire die face, rather than just the center portion, thus allowing more holes per die.

The use of a hollow gag block allows practically the complete extrusion of billets, with up to 94% metal utilization.

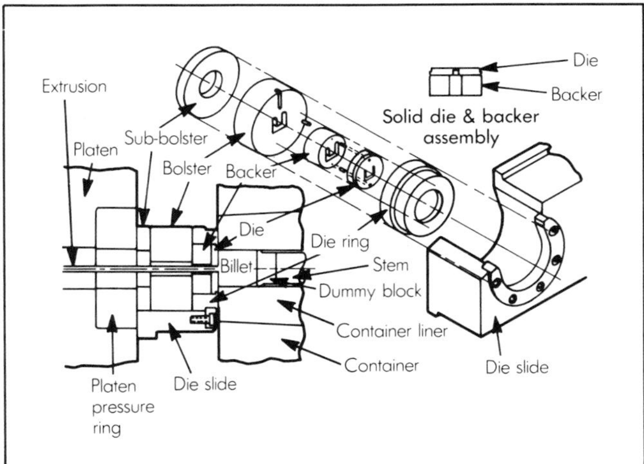


**Fig. 13-20 Typical die-slide tooling arrangement for hot, direct extrusion of solid shapes.** (*Wean United*)

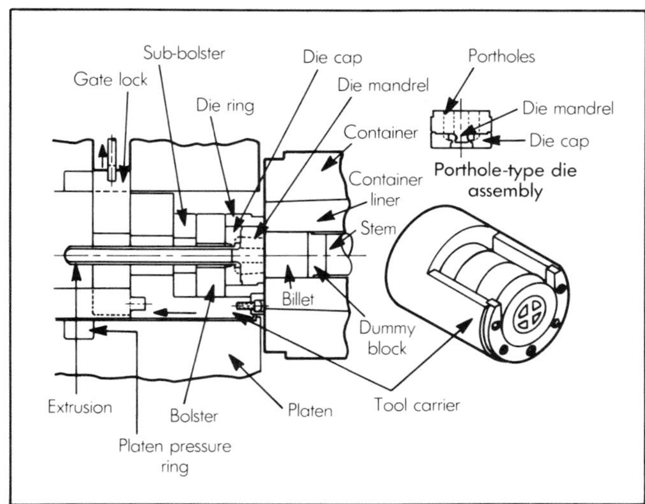


**Fig. 13-21 Typical carrier tooling arrangement for porthole-type die.** (*Wean United*)

The gag block is a plate with a cavity and is located at the fixed platen end of the press. It seals the billet-loading end of the container. With conventional indirect extrusion, the press stroke stops when the die approaches the solid face of a gag block, separated from the extruded product by the butt of the billet. With a hollow gag block, the blind cavity in the block is filled with metal. Extrusion continues until the die reaches the end of the container, thus eliminating the butt. In effect, the metal in the gag-block cavity becomes a reusable butt, with the same metal serving as a butt for all subsequent billets. Any impurities in or on the billet surface, however, end up in or on the surface of the extrusion.

## Die Design

Die design is a critical aspect of the extrusion process and embodies both science and art. Optimum design is influenced by many factors, including the circle size of the shape to be produced, the maximum and minimum wall thicknesses, the press capacity, the length of the runout table, the stretcher capacity, the tool-stacking limitations, an understanding of the properties and characteristics of the metal to be extruded, and the press operating procedures and maintenance.

**Use of CAD/CAM.** Computers are being used by some extruders to design and manufacture (with CNC machines) dies and to select process variables such as extruding speed and billet temperatures. Software employed is based primarily upon an analysis of metal flow. Various design stages are displayed on a CRT screen, and the designer interacts with a computer to change or modify the design, based upon experience.

**Design considerations.** Since all metals shrink upon cooling after hot extrusion, a shrinkage allowance must be provided in designing the dies. Deformation of the die under high pressures and expansion resulting from the high temperatures must also be considered in die design.

Another important consideration is the tendency for metal to flow faster through a larger opening than a smaller one. This must be compensated for in designing dies for use in extruding certain sections. For example, when a section to be extruded has both a thick wall and a thin wall, various means are employed to retard metal flow through the thick section and increase the flow rate through the thin section of the die.

Fine adjustments to the die for correcting or changing the rates of metal flow are made by varying the length of the land, also called the bearing (see Fig. 13-24), directly behind the die opening. By decreasing the length of the bearing, the rate of flow is increased; increasing the bearing length reduces the flow rate.

The geometry of the die aperture at the front and back of the bearing surface is known as the choke and relief respectively (see Fig. 13-24). If the die designer expects to encounter difficulty in filling sharp corners or completing thin sections of the extruded product, a choke may be provided on certain portions of the bearing surface. This slows the rate of metal flow and consequently fills the die aperture. Increasing the amount of back relief at the exit side of the bearing surface increases the rate of metal flow.

For the hot extrusion of some materials, such as brass, bronze, and other soft metals, the dummy block is made smaller in diameter than the billet. In extruding, no lubrication is provided between the bore of the container liner and the outer surface of the billet. As a result, friction prevents the outer surface of the billet from sliding and the undesirable skin of the billet is left in the container as the dummy block shears the metal during its forward stroke. An additional press stroke is required to remove this retained metal before the next billet can be charged into the container.

## Tooling Materials

Materials used for hot-extrusion tooling vary with the actual

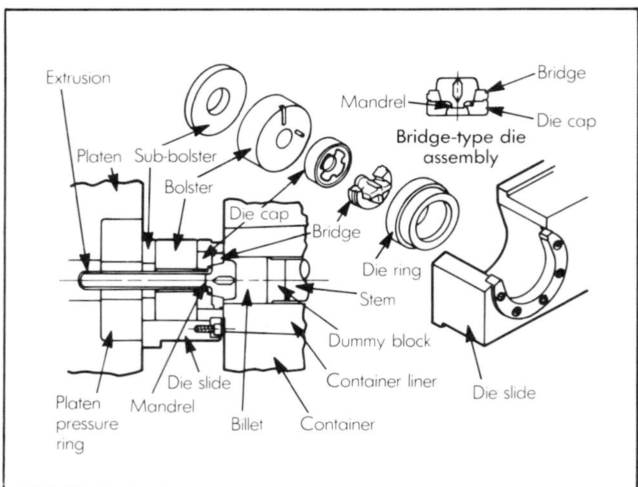


**Fig. 13-22 Typical slide tooling arrangement for bridge-type die.** (*Wean United*)

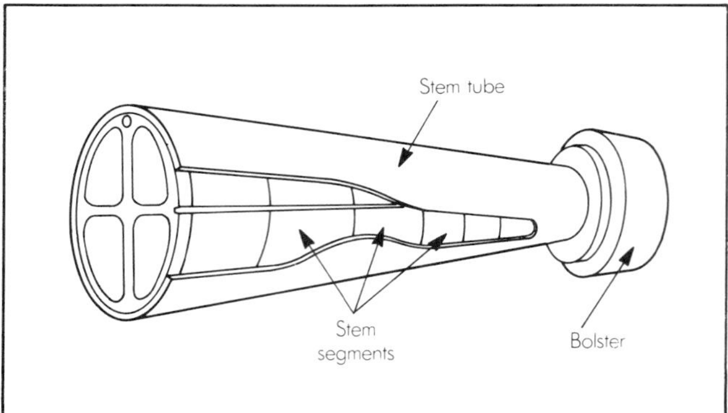


**Fig. 13-23 Multihole segmented stem for indirect extrusion.** (*Texas Extrusion Corp.*)

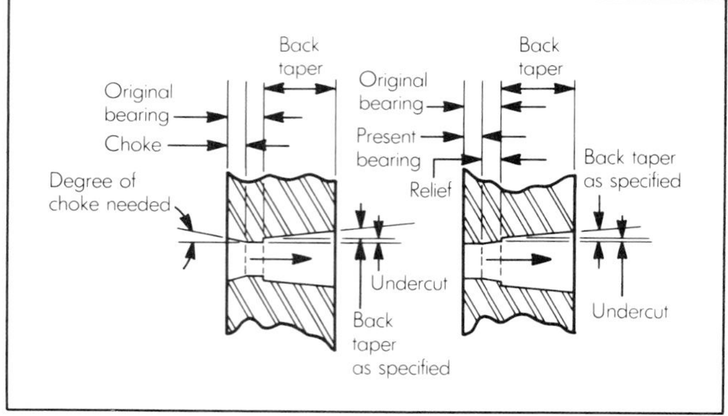


**Fig. 13-24 Shaped die (left) and flat-faced die (right) for hot extrusion.** (*Wean United*)

application. High-quality materials, however, are essential for all applications. Desirable properties for tooling materials to withstand the high mechanical and thermal stresses encountered include:

1. High toughness and resistance to softening.
2. High resistance to abrasive wear.
3. Adequate strength at high temperatures.
4. Resistance to distortion and cracking from tensile stresses developed during heat treatment, as well as from temperature changes during extruding, which can initiate hot cracking.
5. High thermal conductivity to continuously remove heat from the area of contact with the hot billets.

**Tool and alloy steels.** Resistance to softening is an important requirement for tooling materials operating at high temperatures. When tool and alloy steels are used, this resistance is controlled primarily by the additions of tungsten, molybdenum, and vanadium alloying elements. The most common tool steels used for hot extrusion are the hot-work steels, both chromium and tungsten types, classified by AISI with the symbol H, such as H11, H12, H13, H19 and H21.

The selection of tool and alloy steels for the hot extrusion of aluminum and aluminum alloys presents few problems because of the relatively low temperatures employed. Static stresses rather than thermal considerations are the primary limitation in the choice of a steel.

Hot extrusion of copper, copper alloys, steels, and superalloys, however, involves high temperatures, 1400-2200° F (760-1200° C), and results in repeated, gradual softening of the tooling. This can only be compensated for by cooling the tools, using high extrusion speeds to limit the contact time of the tools with the hot metals, and/or by properly selecting and using suitable lubricants.

The choice of tooling materials for a specific extrusion application is influenced by many factors; in most choices, however, the question of economics is involved. Tooling cost per part extruded is the subject of continuing research to develop materials and methods of treatment to make the process more economical. Tool and alloy steels recommended for use in the hot extrusion of aluminum and aluminum alloys, copper and copper-based alloys, and steels are presented in Table 13-4. These recommendations are based on years of research and practical applications.

Increased toughness, ductility, and fatigue strength, as well as a fine, uniform grain structure and longer life, have been obtained with tool steels produced by the electroslag remelting (ESR) and vacuum arc remelting (VAR) processes.

**Hard surfacing.** The bearing surfaces of hot-extrusion dies are often hardened by the use of surface treatments, coatings, or

**TABLE 13-4**
**Suggested Steels for Tools Used in Hot Extrusion**

| | Metals to be Hot Extruded | | | | | |
|---|---|---|---|---|---|---|
| | Aluminum and Aluminum Alloys | | Copper and Copper-Based Alloys | | Steels | |
| | Steels for Tools | | | | | |
| Tooling Application | AISI/SAE | Bhn | AISI/SAE | Bhn | AISI/SAE | Bhn |
| Dies | H12<br>H13 | 430-460<br>460-510 | H21 | 400-440 | H21 | 400-440 |
| Backers | H12<br>H13 | 400-460<br>460-510 | H19 | 400-440 | H19 | 430-470 |
| Dieholders | H12 | 400-440 | H19 | 400-440 | H19 | 400-440 |
| Dummy blocks | H12<br>H13 | 400-460<br>430-460 | H12 | 360-400 | H19 | 420-460 |
| Bolsters | H12<br>4340 | 460-510<br>460-510 | 4340<br>H12 | 340-380<br>400-440 | H12<br>4340 | 430-470<br>340-380 |
| Mandrels | H12<br>H13 | 460-510<br>460-510 | H11 | 380-420 | H11 | 380-420 |
| Mandrel holders | 4340<br>4150 | 360-400<br>360-400 | 4340<br>4150 | 360-400<br>360-400 | 4150 | 360-400 |
| Stems | H12 | 440-510 | H12 | 440-480 | H13 | 440-480 |
| Liners | H12<br>4340 | 430-460<br>370-410 | H12<br>A286 | 360-400<br>310-330 | H13 | 360-400 |
| Liner holders | 4150 | 360-400 | 4150 | 320-360 | 4150 | 320-360 |
| Containers | 4340<br>4150 | 300-350<br>300-350 | 4150<br>4340 | 280-320<br>280-320 | 4150<br>4340 | 280-320<br>280-320 |

(*Mannesmann Demag Wean Co.*)

inserts, especially for producing complex shapes and sections, thus increasing die life. The surface treatment used most frequently is nitriding. Coatings employed include tungsten carbide deposits, usually by electrodeposition, and titanium nitride, applied by vapor deposition.

Insert materials used for hot-extrusion dies include cemented tungsten carbide and aluminum oxide ceramics. The use of carbide is generally limited to the extrusion of small and medium-sized, round or simple shapes. Grades of tungsten carbide used generally have coarse grain structure and high cobalt contents, sometimes with tantalum carbide added. Additional information on tooling materials is presented in Chapter 2, "Die and Mold Materials."

## OPERATING PARAMETERS

The method of billet preparation and heating, the amount of pressure and rate of speed used for extruding, and the type of lubricant employed are critical parameters for successful and economical hot extrusion.

### Billet Preparation

The more common metals that are to be extruded are generally cast in the form of cylindrical logs 12-20 ft (3.7-6.1 m) or more in length. These logs are sawed or sheared into billets of varying length, depending upon the cross-sectional area and length of the product to be extruded.

Further billet preparation is sometimes required, depending upon the material to be extruded. For example, the outer surfaces of some steel billets must be machined prior to being heated, and then must be descaled after being heated to the extrusion temperature. When extruding is performed indirectly, best results are obtained by scalping the billets prior to extrusion to remove oxides and other impurities from the billet skin; otherwise, these impurities would find their way onto the surfaces of the extrusion due to the inherent nature of the metal flow in indirect extrusion.

Aluminum billets are usually homogenized by heat treatment before they are extruded. This treatment improves extrudability of the material and the surface finish produced, and reduces the appearance of a streaked texture that often results after anodizing.

Billet temperatures, which vary with the metals extruded, and methods of heating the billets are discussed in a previous part of this section. Too high a billet temperature can result in blisters or other surface defects, including cracking. Too low a temperature increases the extruding pressure requirements and shortens tool life.

### Pressure Requirements

Unit pressures needed for hot extrusion, which are major considerations in press selection (discussed previously), vary with the following factors:

1. The metal to be extruded and its condition.
2. The length and temperature of the billet.
3. The complexity of the cross section of the product to be extruded (die shape).
4. The speed of extrusion.
5. The reduction (extrusion) ratio.
6. The lubricant used and resultant friction.

Determining pressure requirements is difficult for extruding complicated shapes and sections, especially those having thin walls; and careful judgments based on past experience have to be made for estimates. Formulas for estimating pressure requirements have been developed using shape and friction parameters, as well as other parameters. However, for less complicated shapes, such as round bars and tubes, a fair approximation of pressure requirements can be calculated by using the following formula:

$$P = k \log_e \frac{A}{a} \tag{6}$$

where:

$P$ = extrusion pressure required, psi or MPa
$k$ = numerical value representing the resistance to deformation, usually based on past experience in extruding a specific metal at a specific temperature (see Table 13-5)
$A$ = cross-sectional area of the container liner; or in the case of tubes or other hollow shapes, the cross-sectional area of the liner minus the cross-sectional area of the mandrel, in.$^2$ or mm$^2$
$a$ = total cross-sectional area of the extruded product (the shape area times the number of openings in the die), in.$^2$ or mm$^2$

While extrusion pressure requirements that are determined by using this formula are useful, the values obtained are only approximations. The resistance to the deformation factor, $k$, varies with the billet temperature, type of metal extruded, amount of reduction (extrusion ratio), stem speed, configuration of the extruded product, and other factors. Additional factors influencing pressure requirements include billet length, nonhomogeneous metal flow, and friction.

For optimum, efficient use of extrusion press capacity, unit pressures generally range from 65-110 ksi (448.2-758.4 MPa), with a maximum of about 150 ksi (1034.2 MPa). When practical, the use of a press having a capacity higher than

**TABLE 13-5**
**Factor $k$ for Various Materials to be Used in Equation (6) for Determining Extrusion Pressures***

| Metal to be Extruded | $k$, ksi (MPa) |
|---|---|
| Carbon steel | 21 (145) |
| Stainless steel | 30 (207) |
| Tool steel | 50 (345) |
| Zirconium | 34 (234) |
| Titanium | 25 (172) |
| Hastelloy | 64 (441) |
| Inconel 600 | 50 (345) |
| A-286 | 61 (421) |
| Copper | 15 (103) |

(*Mannesmann Demag Wean Co.*)

* The $k$ factors are average values and vary with the billet temperature, extrusion ratio, stem speed, shape of the extrusion, and other factors.

actually required is generally desirable. This permits using lower billet temperatures and faster stem speeds, and provides improved properties in the extruded products.

## Stem Speeds

Optimum stem speeds are essential for hot extrusion. Excessive speed can result in overheating of the billet and in tears and other surface defects. Too slow a speed reduces productivity and increases the required extruding pressure because of billet cooling. Slow speeds can also decrease tool life because of prolonged contact time between the tools and the hot billet. Commonly used stem speeds and billet temperatures for various metals are presented in Table 13-6.

The use of variable-delivery pumps and adjustable valves facilitates setting the stem speed. Automatic control means are available to maintain constant speed throughout the extruding cycle.

## Lubrication

The use of lubricants in hot extrusion is desirable to improve metal flow by reducing friction and to protect tooling, but it is impractical for some applications. Lubricants are necessary in the billet containers and on conical dies for extruding many metals, such as some copper alloys and steels. Lubricants are seldom used, however, with flat dies, which are commonly employed in extruding aluminum, because the metal flow is inhomogeneous and surface defects can be produced on the extruded product as the result of trapped lubricant. Extrusion with flat dies involves shearing away the billet surface; if any lubricant is used, it is to facilitate subsequent removal of this residual material and to prevent adhesion to the die.

For extrusion temperatures below about 1850° F (1000° C), grease and graphite mixtures are frequently employed as lubricants. Colloidal additives, such as molybdenum disulfide, are often added to the mixtures. For extrusion temperatures above 1850° F, glass is generally used as the lubricant. Glass is applied as a powder or as fiberglass and forms a viscous film upon contact with the hot billet. After extrusion, the glassy layer can be removed by pickling in a hydrofluoric acid solution, immersing in a molten salt bath, or blasting.

# SAFETY CONSIDERATIONS

Safety requirements for the construction, care, and use of horizontal, hydraulic extrusion presses are presented in ANSI Standard B11.17. The noise generated by pumps on large extrusion presses can be minimized by remote location of the pumps.

**TABLE 13-6**
**Commonly Used Billet Temperatures and Stem Speeds for Extruding Various Metals**

| Metal Extruded | Common Range of Billet Temperatures, °F (°C) | Common Range of Stem Speeds, ips (mm/s) |
|---|---|---|
| Steel | 1900-2100 (1038-1149) | 6-8 (152-203) |
| Copper | 1500-1600 (816-871) | 2-3 (51-76) |
| Aluminum | 700-900 (371-482) | 0.5-1 (13-25) |
| Brass | 1300-1400 (704-760) | 1-2 (25-51) |

(*Mannesmann Demag Wean Co.*)

In addition to normal industrial safety precautions (discussed in Chapter 20, "Safety in Forming"), one manufacturer of extrusion presses recommends that the following guidelines be observed:

1. Never use the equipment beyond specified limits.
2. Never operate, service, or adjust the equipment without proper instruction.
3. Never energize the control circuits or initiate operation without first checking to see that all personnel are clear of the equipment. Always set the control to "Manual" before energizing the circuit.
4. While working on the press or auxiliaries, immobilize the equipment by following these precautions:
   *a.* Cut off power to the control panels and all motors.
   *b.* Cut off air pressure by closing the air supply line.
   *c.* Wherever possible, mechanically block the equipment to prevent movement.
5. Observe the utmost precautions when working between platen and open container, between stem and container, and inside platen.
6. When performing maintenance to electrical circuits, shut off all power to the equipment. Never jumper-out any interlocking or safety circuits.
7. Never use the equipment without the guards or safety devices that have been provided to prevent accidents.
8. Never have any part of the body in the path of any moving machine parts while the press or auxiliary equipment are in operation, while oil or air lines are under pressure, while motors are running, or while control panels are receiving power.
9. Keep away from the die shifting mechanism and auxiliaries when the press is in operation.
10. Do not look into the platen exit hole when a billet is about to be extruded or the press is under load.
11. Do not reach into the platen hole when the press is in operation.
12. Keep away from leaks in high-pressure pipe lines, valves, and cylinder connections when pressure is on. Turn off the pressure supply and bleed pressure from the system before making repairs. Stay clear of high-pressure oil or air jets when bleeding off excess pressure or air. Especially protect the eyes.
13. Do not move equipment at full speed until limit switches and interlocking safety switches are properly adjusted.
14. Eject billets that cannot be extruded because they are too cold (or cannot be extruded for any other reason) from the container only if this can be accomplished with moderate force. When doing so, the ram should be set for movement at minimum speed. The shock caused by a sudden release of energy when the billet is freed could damage the press. Therefore, if the billet cannot be ejected with moderate force, it should be removed from the container outside the press.
15. Do not eject liners from the container in the press.
16. Use protective gloves when doing any work on or near the container and housing.

# COLD AND WARM EXTRUSION

Cold and warm extrusion differ from hot extrusion, discussed previously in this chapter, in that the starting workpieces (often called slugs) are cold (at room temperature) or warm (heated to below the critical temperature of the metal). Metal is forced to flow by plastic deformation under compression around punches and into or through shape-forming dies to produce parts of the desired configuration. Since the temperatures of the slugs are always below the recrystallization temperatures of the metals to be formed, the process is essentially one of cold working. Most steels, nonferrous metals, and superalloys can be extruded cold or at low deformation temperatures, with stresses in the tooling being the primary limiting factor.

## ADVANTAGES OF THE PROCESS

Important advantages of cold and warm extrusion include substantial cost savings in many applications, fast production rates, improved physical properties, close tolerances, energy conservation, and elimination of pollution problems.

### Cost Savings

Reduced costs are the result of material savings, the reduction or elimination of subsequent machining, less material handling, and high production rates. In some cases, assemblies of several components can be replaced with a single extruded part.

Since extrusion reshapes metal without removing any material, less raw material is required. Subsequent machining requirements are often minimal or eliminated, and no flash has to be removed. Firms utilizing the cold-extrusion process claim an average material savings of 25% compared to the amount of material used in screw machining, and savings to 70% or more have been reported. For some applications, less costly materials can be employed.

In one application, idler pulley shafts for crawler-tractor track mechanisms were originally machined from AISI 1141 resulfurized steel bars, each weighing 38.9 lb (17.6 kg). Finished weight of each shaft was 22.2 lb (10.1 kg)—a scrap loss of 16.7 lb (7.6 kg) per part in machining. Now, the shafts are being cold extruded from less costly 1035 steel. Each extrusion weighs 24.9 lb (11.3 kg), resulting in a scrap loss of only 2.7 lb (1.2 kg) in machining; and no heat treating of the finished shafts is required.

### Improved Physical Properties

Work hardening during cold extrusion results in the improvement of some physical properties of most metals, often eliminating the need for subsequent hardening; and grain flow lines generally follow the contour of the extruded part. The mechanical properties obtained by cold working are higher than those obtainable with hot extrusion if the heat generated by deformation does not initiate recrystallization. In the case of low and medium-carbon steels, increases in tensile strengths range from 25-100% or more and increases in yield strengths, from 100-300%, depending upon the amount of deformation (see Table 13-7). Hardnesses are also increased, but elongation and reduction in area are decreased.

### Tolerances and Surface Finishes

**Diameter tolerances.** The tolerances maintained on diameters in cold extrusion depend upon finished part requirements, toolmaking practice, tool wear, and life expectancy of the tooling. As a general rule, diameter tolerances of ±0.005" (0.13 mm) can be consistently held with acceptable tool life. Closer diameter tolerances, to ±0.002" (0.05 mm) are feasible, but tool costs increase accordingly. The use of carbide tooling components can contribute to maintaining close diameter tolerances because of reduced tool wear.

**Length tolerances.** Overall length tolerances are more

**TABLE 13-7**
**Properties of Some Steels Before and After Cold Extrusion**

| Steel AISI | Condition | Reduction, % | Hardness | Ultimate Tensile Strength, ksi (MPa) | Ultimate Yield Strength, ksi (MPa) |
|---|---|---|---|---|---|
| 1016 | Before extrusion | | $R_B$ 67 | 61.8 (426) | 45.3 (312) |
| | After extrusion | 50 | $R_B$ 93 | 109 (752) | 105 (724) |
| | | 70 | $R_B$ 96 | 114 (786) | 111 (765) |
| 1045 | Before extrusion | | $R_B$ 81 | 85.8 (592) | 43.2 (298) |
| | After extrusion | 50 | $R_B$ 96 | 146 (1007) | 140 (965) |
| | | 65 | $R_B$ 100 | 154 (1062) | 146 (1007) |
| 1340 | Before extrusion | | $R_B$ 80 | 79.6 (549) | 46.9 (323) |
| | After extrusion | 50 | $R_B$ 98 | 140 (965) | 135 (931) |
| | | 65 | $R_C$ 28 | 148 (1020) | 142 (979) |
| 8620 | Before extrusion | | $R_B$ 70 | 67 (462) | 48.1 (332) |
| | After extrusion | 50 | $R_B$ 98 | 122 (841) | 118 (814) |
| | | 65 | $R_B$ 99 | 130 (896) | 124 (856) |

difficult to control in cold extrusion for various reasons, but primarily because of volume control of the starting slug. Diameter tolerance of the starting stock affects the slug volume. To control the volume, the weight of the slugs is checked. Weight tolerances generally range from as close as ±0.02 oz (0.5 g) on small parts to ±0.2 oz (5.7 g) on large parts.

**Surface finishes.** Surface finishes produced by cold extrusion depend primarily upon the application, the condition of the starting slug, the lubricant used, and the die design. When preturned bars are used, cold extrusion can produce finishes as smooth as 20-30 μin. (0.51-0.76 μm). There is no oxidation, as is common in hot extrusion.

## LIMITATIONS OF COLD EXTRUSION

One disadvantage of cold extrusion is its limitations with respect to the shapes, length-to-diameter ratios, and maximum size to which parts can be produced, as discussed next in this section. Warm extrusion, in which the slugs or preforms are heated to a maximum temperature of about 1800° F (980° C), generally less than 1400° F (760° C), but more than 1000° F (538° C) for steels, permits the production of more intricate shapes and larger parts on smaller capacity presses, and the extrusion of metals that cannot be cold formed.

### Production Requirements

A complete cold-extrusion facility is expensive, requiring capital investment in slug production (including cleaning, coating, lubricating, and annealing), extruding presses, and tooling. As a result, substantial production requirements are necessary to make the investment economically viable. Some firms specializing in cold extrusion feel that about 10,000-50,000 large parts or approximately 100,000 small parts per month are necessary to make the process economically justifiable. However, when extrusion is combined with other operations on multistation, automatic forming machines equipped for fast tool changeover (discussed later in this chapter), lot sizes tend to be smaller—as few as 1000 for large parts [to 100 lb (45.4 kg)] and 20,000 for small parts [1/4 to 1 lb (0.11 to 0.45 kg)].

### Center Burst (Chevron) Defects

Center bursts, often called chevrons, are internal defects sometimes formed during cold extrusion. These defects are not common, occurring primarily when a large reduction in area is followed by a smaller reduction in the extruding of multi-diameter parts. The problem can generally be eliminated by changing the die angle or the reduction in area. The relationship between included die angle and reduction in area with respect to central bursting is illustrated in Fig. 13-25.

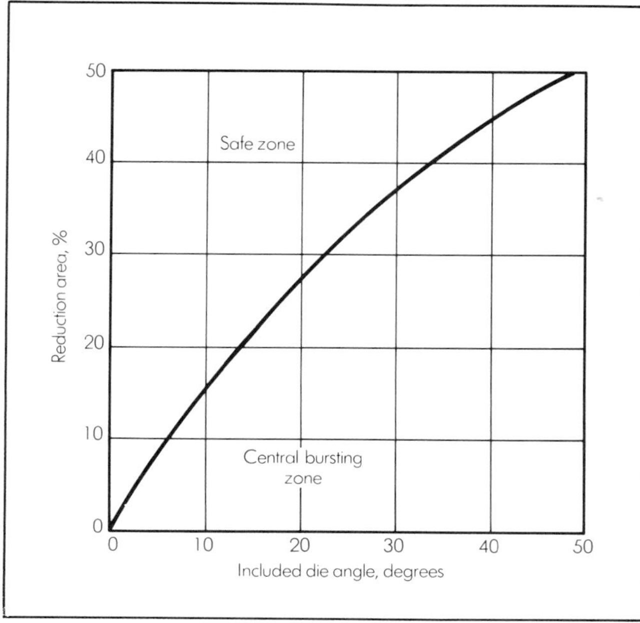


**Fig. 13-25 Relationship between included die angle and reduction in area with respect to central bursting.** (*Bethlehem Steel Corp.*)

## SHAPES AND SIZES PRODUCED

The most economical applications of cold extrusion are generally limited to the forming of symmetrical parts with solid or hollow cross sections. Parts with other geometries, including noncircular and complex-shaped components, are formed, but at a higher cost. When cross-sectional shapes are highly unsymmetrical, unequalized pressures are exerted on the tools and can cause breakage.

The length of cold-extruded parts is generally several times the diameter. In fact, shaft-type shapes account for about 80% of the total cold-extruded output. Upsetting (heading), discussed later in this chapter, is often combined with extrusion, as in the production of flanged parts. While cylindrical parts are most common, other shapes extruded include internal or external splines, squares, flats, hexagons, ovals, and tapers. Hollow parts having bottoms thicker than the sidewalls are also common.

The bases of closed-end parts can be flat, conical, hemispherical, or other shapes, and projections or depressions can be formed in one or both faces. Inner and/or outer surfaces of the side walls can be provided with beads, flutes, grooves, ribs, splines, teeth, or any other longitudinal projections or depressions. Axial holes can be produced if they are not too small in diameter or too long. Figure 13-26 illustrates a part cold extruded from AISI 4140 steel in a single hit.

Although straight, parallel, or bevel splines and gear teeth can be formed, helical gears having helix angles greater than 15° are not feasible for production. However, close dimensional accuracies, smooth surface finishes, and contoured grain flow make extruded parts ideal for subsequent rolling or cutting of gear teeth.

While most cold-extruded parts produced are small and medium sized, large parts are also produced. The majority of extrusions have a diameter range of 3/4 to 2 1/2" (19 to 63.5 mm), with lengths varying from 3-24" (76-610 mm). When cold extruding is combined with upsetting, however, part diameters to 8" (203 mm) and lengths to 80" (2032 mm) have been produced. The weight of most cold-extruded parts ranges from 1-50 lb (0.45-22.7 kg), depending upon the size and capacity of the press used. Larger presses, improved die design, and improved lubricants have made possible the cold extrusion of parts weighing as much as 100 lb (45.4 kg).

## MATERIALS EXTRUDED

Most metals can be cold extruded, providing enough pressure can be applied to exceed the yield strengths of the materials and tooling of sufficient strength is available. Material selection depends primarily upon the desired properties in the extruded product, a sufficient spread between yield and ultimate strengths of the material, a fair degree of ductility, and the availability of a press and of tooling capable of withstanding the required pressure and produce the cold extrusions economically.

With respect to steels, cold extruders predominantly use the softer, lower carbon grades. However, the use of alloy steels is increasing because of the need for higher strength in smaller, more lightweight components. Carbon steels employed include the AISI 1005 to 1070 types, some of the resulfurized 1100 series, and the higher manganese 1500 series. Popular alloy steels for cold extruding include AISI 4023, 4037, 4130, 4140, 4820, and the 5100 and 8600 series.

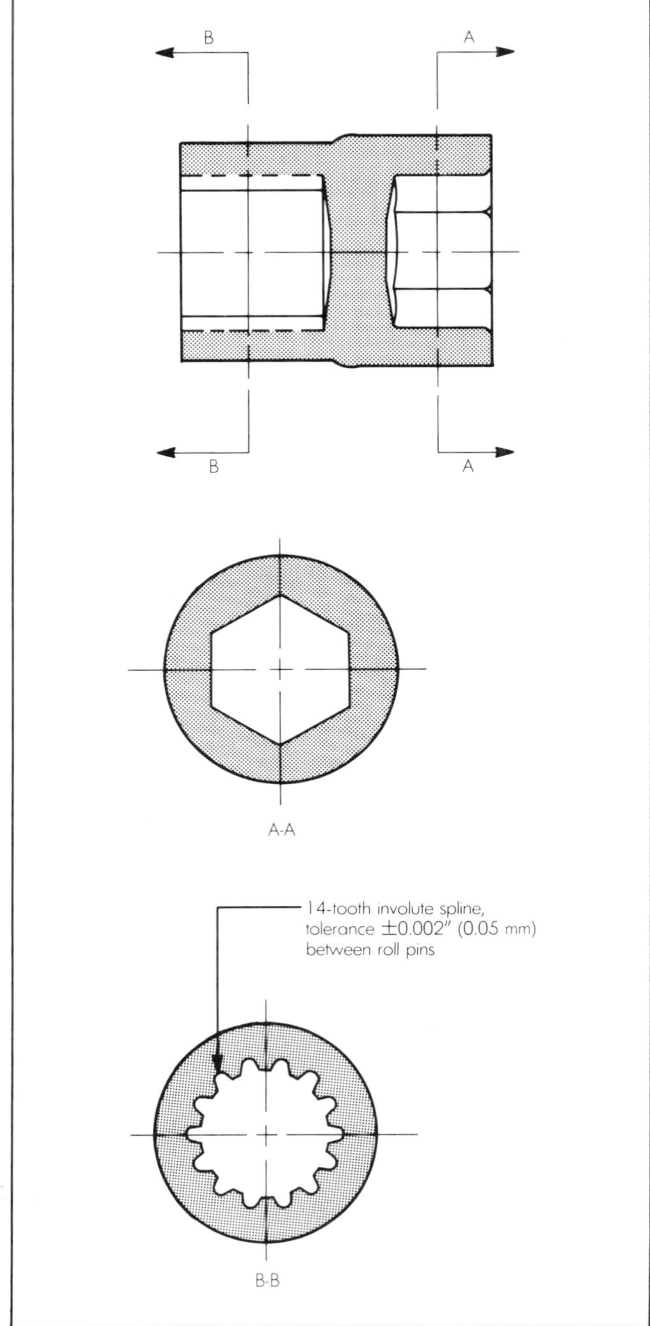


**Fig. 13-26 Part cold extruded from AISI 4140 steel in a single hit.** (*Imerman Industries, Inc.*)

Many stainless steels are cold extruded. Nonferrous metals that are cold extruded include aluminum, lead, magnesium, and copper alloys.

## Chemical Composition of Steels

With plain-carbon steels, more pressure is required as the carbon content of the steel is increased. Backward extrusion of unheated slugs is generally limited to steels containing a maximum of about 0.35% carbon, while forward extrusion can be performed on steels containing 0.60% or more carbon.

The silicon content of plain-carbon steels should be limited to a maximum of about 0.35% because higher silicon contents increase the resistance to plastic flow and the rate of work hardening. The effect of manganese is not as strong as that of silicon, and steels containing up to 1.5% manganese have been cold extruded. Sulfur content should generally be limited to a maximum of about 0.05%, and resulfurized steels are not recommended for cold extrusion, although they are used successfully in limited applications. Phosphorus contents greater than 0.04% cause significantly higher pressure requirements.

As the alloying content of steels increases, extruding becomes more difficult. The nickel content of alloy steels must generally be limited to a maximum of about 1.00% for successful and economical extrusion, and chromium to about 0.90% maximum. For best results, the molybdenum content should be limited to a maximum of approximately 0.50%. With alloy steels containing 0.20-0.30% carbon, the manganese content should not exceed about 0.90%. However, alloy steels with low carbon contents (to about 0.12%) can contain as much as 1.35% manganese.

Boron-treated steels are becoming increasingly popular for cold extrusion. The addition of boron, which improves hardenability, permits the use of easier-to-extrude grades, while providing the heat-treatment results of more costly steels. In one application, a 1018 boron steel has replaced 1024 steel, reducing pressure requirements and increasing tool life.

## Desirable Properties

Steels having the lowest yield strength and the greatest range between their yield and ultimate strengths are the most ideal for maximum deformation by cold extrusion. Another important property is the hardness of the metal. The optimum hardness before extrusion for plain-carbon steels containing a maximum of about 0.15% C is $R_B$ 65 or lower. Since such a low hardness is often impractical, starting hardnesses to $R_B$ 85 are commonly used. Higher starting hardnesses require more careful tool design and smaller reductions in area for economical extrusion. The properties of steels to be used for cold extrusion can be improved by thermal treatments, such as spheroidize annealing.

## Annealing Practice

A fully annealed microstructure is optimum for plastic flow of steels by cold extrusion. For higher carbon (above about 0.25%) and alloy steels, as well as for most applications of backward extrusion, thermal treatment to anneal or spheroidize anneal is generally necessary. A detailed discussion of annealing and other heat-treating processes is presented in Volume III, *Materials, Finishing and Coating*, of this Handbook series.

### Steel Melting Practice

In most cases, rimmed steels are not satisfactory for cold extrusion because they characteristically do not have the high degree of chemical and microstructural uniformity required. Killed steels, which have good homogeneity, are generally needed. Grain size uniformity is critical, especially for backward extrusion. Coarse-grain steels deform more easily and require less pressure than those having a fine-grain structure, but they have lower mechanical properties and are more prone toward in-process failures. Fine-grain steels from ASTM No. 5 to No. 8 are generally preferable for cold extrusion.

### Undesirable Imperfections and Deficiencies

Several imperfections and deficiencies resulting from ingot pouring and rolling practice in the steel mills are undesirable for cold extrusion. These imperfections and deficiencies, vary with the quality of the steel and may include pipe, gross inclusions, segregation, seams, and laps.

**Pipe.** Depending upon steel mill practice and ingot design, primary or secondary pipe may form in the top sections of ingots during solidification. When rolled into bars, rods, or wire, ingot pipe results in center discontinuities, which may cause poor flow or ruptures during extruding.

**Inclusions.** Solid, nonmetallic inclusions, such as manganese sulfide, silicate, and aluminum oxides, present to some extent in all steels, may cause trouble in extruding, especially if they are gross in size or locally concentrated.

**Segregation.** Excessive chemical segregation is a variation in chemical composition across the cross section of a bar, rod, or wire, resulting from the solidification pattern of steel after pouring. It can affect the uniformity of mechanical properties, the pressures required for extrusion, and the concentricity required in backward extrusion. Investigations have found segregation present when center bursts (chevrons) occurred.

**Seams and laps.** These imperfections, when present in the starting steels, remain as imperfections in extruded parts. They may be tightly closed at the surfaces, but tend to elongate and become shallower in depth with radial progression into the workpieces. Seam-free steel, which has surface stock removed to eliminate surface imperfections, is available from mills.

### Specifying Surface Quality and Structure

Surface quality in terms of seams can be defined in several ways. The normal maximum seam depth expectancy in regular-quality alloy steels or special-quality carbon steels is 1.6% of the ordered diameter. Seam depths less than normal may be acquired by agreement between the steel supplier and the purchaser, or cold-working quality steel may be specified. Specifications pertaining to cold-forging or cold-working quality define better surface quality and uniform internal structure. Unfortunately, these specifications are not absolute standards and can vary from mill to mill.

Steels used for cold extrusion vary from lower cost, commercial hot-rolled grades to special, more expensive types having definitive requirements as to surface and internal quality. Economic considerations are necessary to justify the cost of increased quality. The degree of surface quality needed generally depends upon the severity of expansion of the surface taking place during forming. External surface quality is therefore more important for upsetting operations. Longitudinal seams have little effect on backward or forward-extrusion operations, but the depth of the seams determines the stock allowance that must be provided for removal of the seams. The cost of improved quality should be weighed against the cost of steel with increased stock allowance and the cost of removing the stock.

## APPLICATIONS

Cold extrusion is now being used for producing more economically a wide variety of parts that were previously cast, forged, or machined by metal-removal processes. Some large, hollow extrusions, such as wheel spindles and axles, are replacing parts formerly shaped from tubing by hot swaging. Industries using cold-extruded products include automotive, aircraft and aerospace, appliance, ordnance, hardware, farm and construction equipment, electrical equipment, and air conditioning. Typical parts produced by cold extrusion include bearing races, a variety of fasteners, piston pins, spark plug shells, socket wrenches, track link bushings, transmission and axle shafts, pinions and gear blanks, ball joint sockets, switch housings, and steering and suspension components.

The use of cold extrusion should be considered when the parts to be produced require one or more of the following:

- Strength, toughness, and grain structure superior to those machined from hot-rolled carbon steel.
- Close tolerances and smooth surface finishes.
- A hollow cross section with one end closed or partially closed and having bosses, projections, or recesses.
- Walls of zero draft and/or variable thickness.
- Longitudinal projections or depressions on either the inside or outside walls.
- A base thickness greater than the side walls.
- Multiple diameter surfaces.
- Liquid or gas pressure tightness.
- Flanges on either the open or closed ends.

Warm extruding is being increasingly applied, especially on high-alloy and some stainless steels. Heating the slugs reduces the flow stress (resistance to deformation), increases the ductility, and reduces the strain hardening of the workpiece material. Warm extruding, however, increases the production costs because of the need for heating and often requires the use of tooling materials and lubricants that are more heat resistant and higher in cost.

## METHODS OF EXTRUDING

Cold and warm extrusion are performed in several ways. Methods employed include backward, forward, radial, combination, impact, and continuous extrusion.

### Backward Extrusion

In backward (indirect or reverse) extrusion, metal is forced to flow in the opposite direction to the travel of the punch (see Fig. 13-27). Backward extrusion is most commonly employed for the production of hollow parts, but metal can also be forced to flow into recesses in the punch to form splines and other shapes. The outside diameters of the parts formed take on the shapes of the dies and/or recesses in the punches, and the inside diameters of hollow parts are controlled by the punches.

Backward extrusion should be considered when one or more of the following conditions pertain:

1. The ratio of shell length to diameter is high. Shell length is limited by the column strength of the punch, the metal being extruded, the lubricant spread during extrusion, and other factors. For aluminum alloys, the maximum

length is usually about six times the inside diameter of cylindrical shells (see Fig. 13-28, *a*), and for steels, about three times.

2. A heavy bottom is combined with a sidewall of thin gage (view *b*).
3. The bottom design includes hollow or solid studs, necks, plug caps, or cavities on the inside or outside (view *c*).
4. Square, rectangular, oval, or unusual shell shapes are required (view *d*).
5. Walls of varying cross-sectional thickness, or with longitudinal ribs, are required (view *e*).

Combinations of the above conditions may be required in a single shell. In such cases, the bottom is the limiting design factor. When sidewall thickness varies at different points in the cross section, there must be sufficient metal in the shell bottom to avoid resultant tensile stresses as material flows into the heaviest wall section. Generally, depending on production conditions and the type of metal being formed, the bottom thickness should not exceed about 90% of the greatest wall thickness.

Any lack of symmetry in the sidewalls of a shell creates lateral pressures which force the punch out of alignment. For this reason ribs or similar designs on the inside or outside walls of a shell should be symmetrical. Bosses, indentations, or cavities on the inside or outside of the bottom of cup shapes should likewise be symmetrical where possible. The limits of backward extrusion of steel are governed by the percentage of reduction in area and the relationship of the punch diameter to the length of the punch.

## Forward Extrusion

In forward (direct) extrusion, metal is forced to flow ahead of the punch through an orifice in the die (see Fig. 13-29). Forward extrusion is most commonly employed to produce shaft-type components, but is also used to form other shapes (see Fig. 13-30). The punch closely fits the die cavity to prevent backward flow of the metal.

With forward extrusion, very high reductions in cross-sectional area can be produced in one operation. The length of

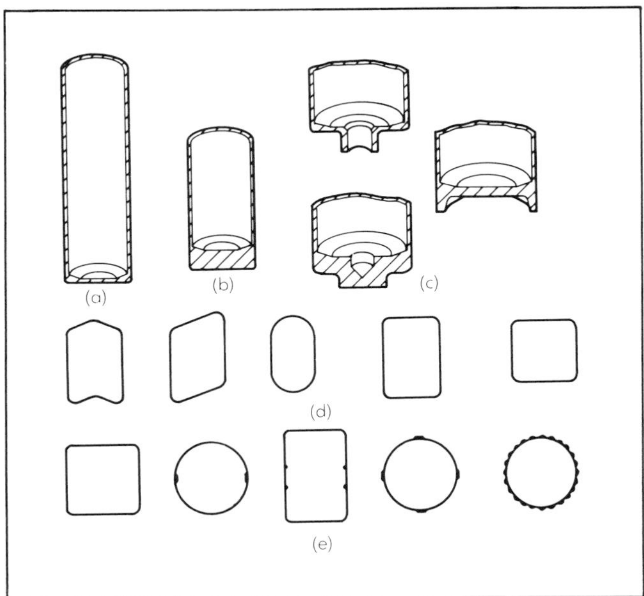


**Fig. 13-28 Product shapes and proportions efficiently produced from aluminum alloys by cold and impact extrusion.**

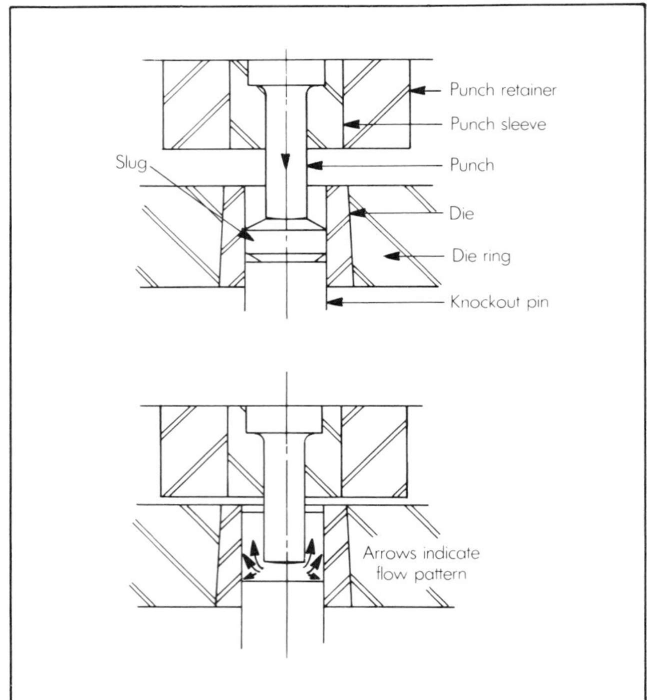


**Fig. 13-27 Backward extrusion.**

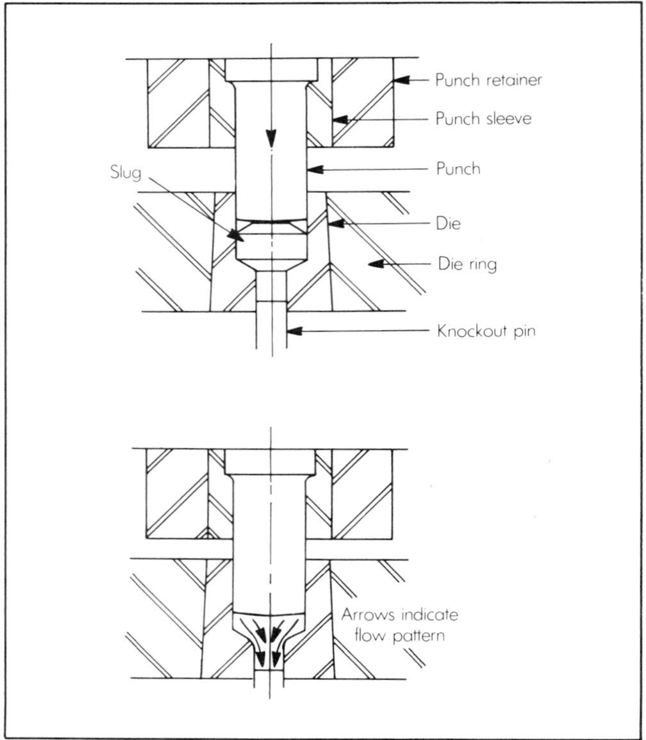


**Fig. 13-29 Forward extrusion.**

the extrusion depends upon the material, the lubricant spread, and the space in the press beyond the die orifice. Aluminum-alloy tubes over 40 ft (12.2 m) in length and 5" (127 mm) diam are in production.

Designers of stressed parts should consider cold-forward extrusions when:

1. Walls must contain no draft.
2. A strong pressure-tight container is required.
3. Strength and toughness are required.
4. Assemblies can be replaced by a one-piece design.
5. Workpiece and precision forming can eliminate or minimize subsequent machining operations.
6. Production quantities are high.

## Radial Extrusion

Radial extrusion, sometimes called cross, lateral, or transverse extrusion, is an adaptation of forward extrusion in which the die orifices allow the metal to flow radially, usually at an angle of 90° to the direction of punch travel.

## Combination Extrusion

Backward, forward, and radial extrusion are sometimes performed simultaneously with a single press stroke, permitting the forming of more-complex-shaped parts. Examples of simultaneous backward and forward extrusion are illustrated in Fig. 13-31. Upsetting (heading), discussed later in this chapter, is also often combined with extrusion to enlarge the diameters of parts at desired sections.

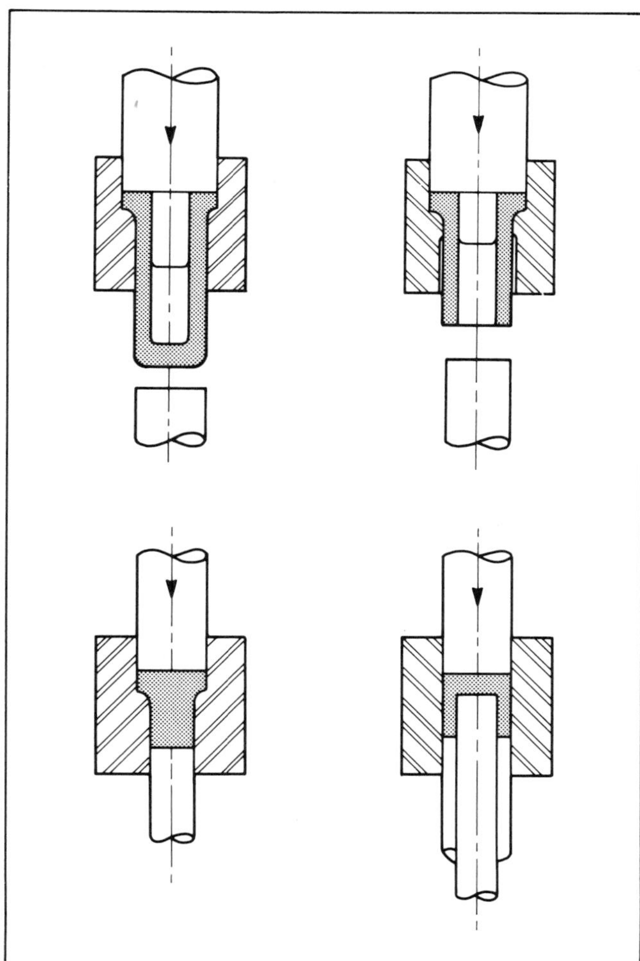

**Fig. 13-30 Various shapes produced by forward extrusion.** (*Verson Allsteel Press Co.*)

## Impact Extrusion

Impact extrusion, often called simply impacting, is similar to backward, forward, and combination extrusion except that faster speeds, shorter strokes, and shallower dies are employed. Impact of the punch causes the metal to move upward, downward, or both upward and downward (see Fig. 13-32), without being confined by the punch or die walls. Large reductions are possible because of the impulsive force applied. Production rates to 18,000 parts per hour have been achieved with automatic feeding equipment.

Cold impacting is used extensively for the easy extrusion of nonferrous metals having low melting points and good ductility, such as lead, tin, zinc, aluminum, copper, and alloys of these metals. Applications include the production of collapsible tubular containers (such as used for toothpaste), battery cases, cartridge cases, and beverage cans. Impacting is sometimes done hot, especially for extruding steels, as in the production of valves and tubes.

The Hooker process of impact extrusion is similar to forward impacting except that preformed cups are used instead of slugs. The punch is provided with a shoulder or chamfer (see Fig. 13-33) that first upsets the cup and then causes the metal to flow through an annulus formed between a projection on the punch and the die, thus elongating and thinning the walls of the cup. Harder metals can be formed in this way, and the process is

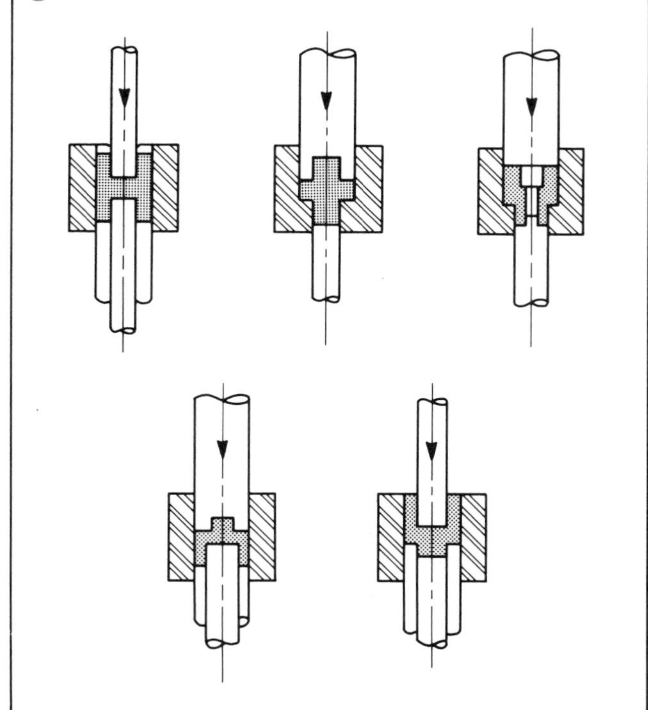

**Fig. 13-31 Simultaneous backward and forward extrusion can produce complex-shaped parts.** (*Verson Allsteel Press Co.*)

# CHAPTER 13

## COLD AND WARM EXTRUSION

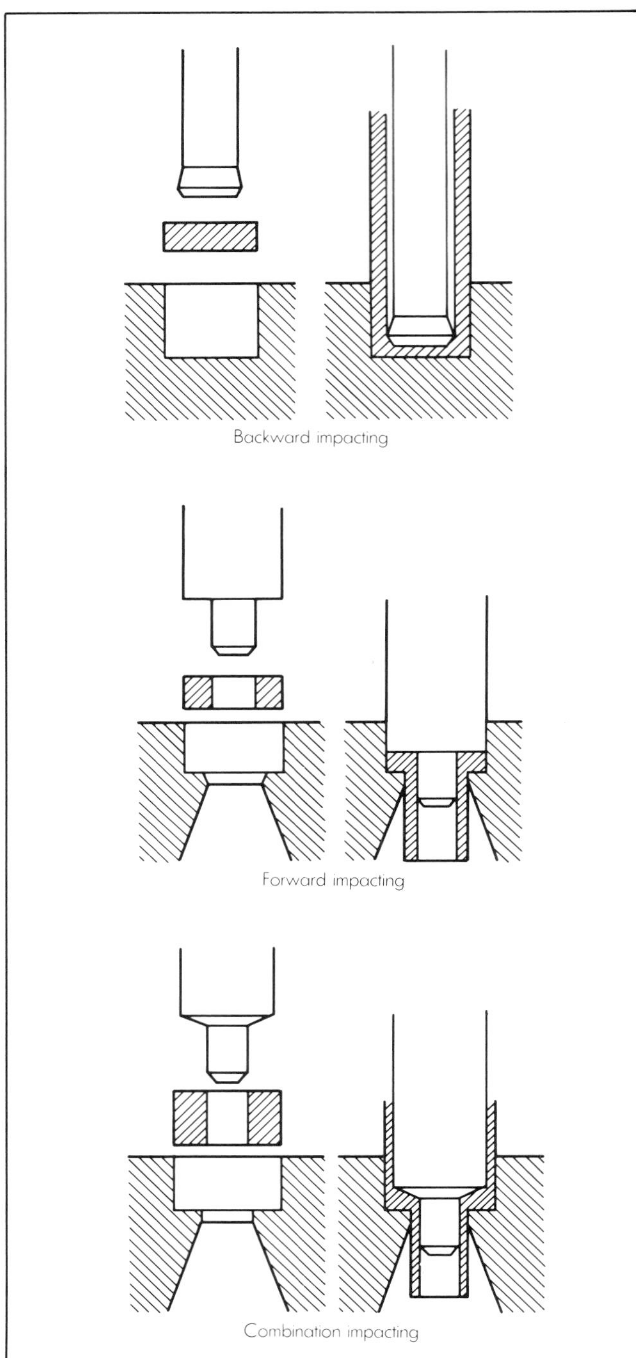


**Fig. 13-32 Various methods of impact extrusion.** (*The Aluminum Assn.*)

used extensively to form closed-end tubular containers of special cross section.

### Continuous Extrusion

Several methods have been developed for semicontinuous and continuous extrusion. One hydrostatic continuous extrusion machine developed by the Western Electric Engineering Research Center reduces 5/16" (7.9 mm) diam aluminum rod to 0.015" (0.38 mm) diam conductor wire at speeds over 12,000 fpm (3658 m/min).[2] Rod is fed from a coil into a roller-straightener and then passes through a coating head where it is coated with a thin film of viscous medium. The viscous medium serves as both the hydrostatic fluid and a lubricant for the die.

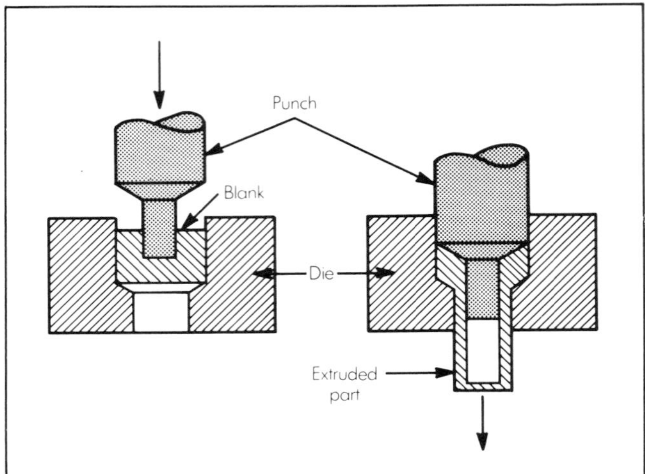


**Fig. 13-33 The Hooker process of forward impacting.**

Coated rod is pulled into the pressure chamber of the extrusion machine. The chamber is an endless, traveling-block design consisting of circumferentially quartered, driven segments divided into short, axial lengths. As the segments pass over the die, the rod is forced to extrude through it by the pressure generated at the die. Segment quadrants are automatically returned to the rod-entrance end of the machine. Pressures in the chamber during extrusion have exceeded 286 ksi (1972 MPa). Simultaneous extrusion of multiple wires has been done on this machine.

Two types of machines developed by Derek Green of the United Kingdom Atomic Energy Authority[3] are available from Mossberg Industries, Providence, RI, for the continuous extrusion of aluminum and other soft metal rods or powder at atmospheric pressure and room temperature. On both the Conform rotary machine and the Linex linear machine, continuous extrusion is performed by direct frictional contact between the feedstock and one or more moving members of the machines.

**Conform system.** In Conform machines, the extrusion chamber is comprised of a three-sided groove in the periphery of a rotating wheel with a stationary shoe making up the fourth side of the chamber. One type of machine has the wheel in the vertical plane (horizontal shaft) to accept powder metal as the feedstock, although it can also use solid feedstock. The other type, with the wheel in the horizontal plane, is designed for use with either solid or bunched scrap feedstocks and incorporates a Turk's head to preform the feedstock before it reaches the groove.

As shown in Fig. 13-34, three sides of the groove in the rotating wheel grip and advance the feedstock, while sliding friction against the stationary shoe acts to retard this advancement. Advancement occurs, however, because the groove walls have more surface area than the shoe. A die, supported in the groove, blocks passage of the stock, causing the stock to upset. As the wheel rotates, pressure at the die face increases, causing

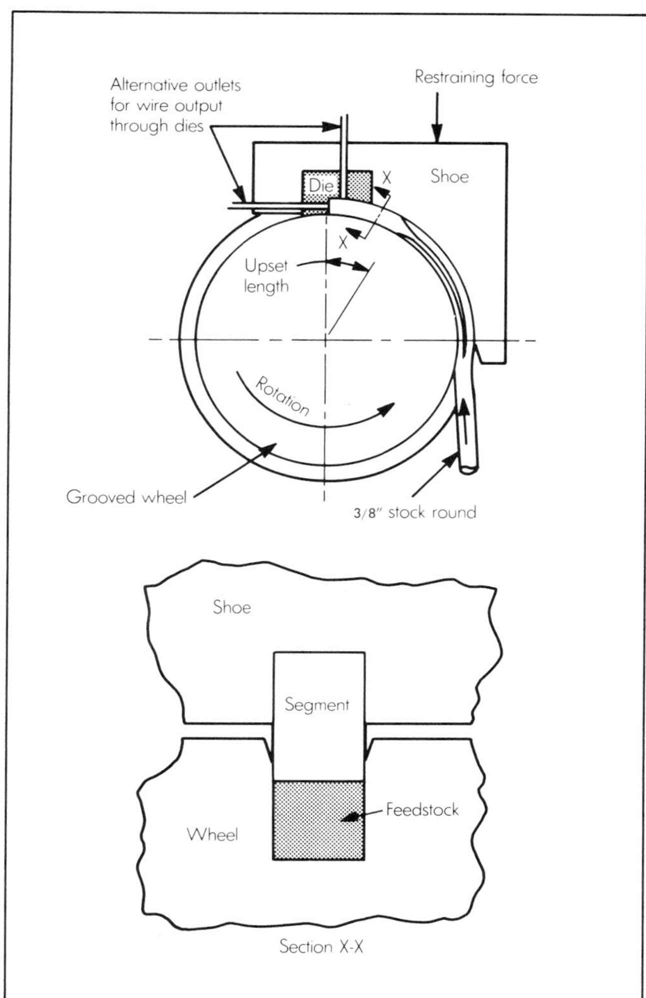


**Fig. 13-34 Feedstock is advanced by a grooved wheel, while friction against a stationary shoe acts to retard the advance.**

the upset length to increase. The process continues until pressure is sufficient for extrusion to take place, at which point the upset length stabilizes and the process runs continuously. When powder is used, the combination of pressure and heat developed during extrusion causes welding between the individual grains, making the resulting extrusion as strong and dense as any extrusion made from solid feedstock.

**Linex system.** For the Linex linear-type continuous extrusion machine, feedstock is preformed to a roughly rectangular cross section. Preforming round feedstock to a rectangular cross section is accomplished by pulling the stock through a Turk's head. Lubrication is provided to the opposing ungripped surfaces of the feedstock before it upsets against the constraining walls of the extrusion chamber (see Fig. 13-35). Two sides of the extrusion chamber, composed of the legs of a fork-shaped die, are fixed. Top and bottom gripping surfaces, making up the other two sides of the chamber, are hardened steel blocks assembled on two chains which are pulled by drive sprockets past the die.

The gripper blocks compress the feedstock, deform it plastically to a point beyond its yield strength, and carry it into

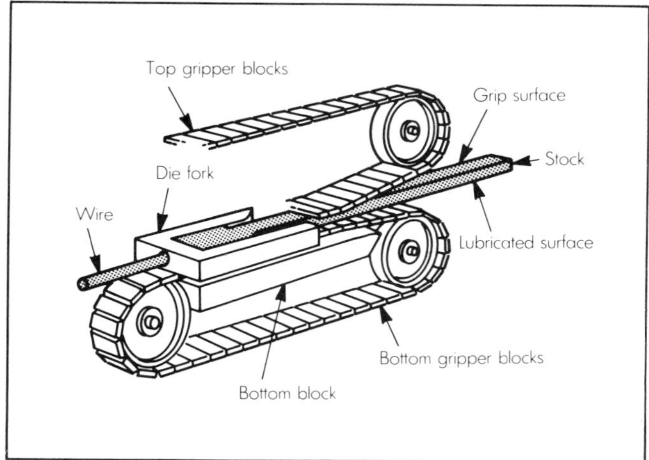


**Fig. 13-35 Friction-actuated, linear-type continuous extruder uses feedstock preformed to a rectangular cross section.**

the die fork. Lubricant on the ungripped sides of the feedstock reduces the coefficient of sliding friction between the upset feedstock and the legs of the die fork. The stock is made narrower than the opening between the die fork legs and fills the extrusion chamber as it is upset. As in the Conform process, the upset length stabilizes when sufficient pressure for extrusion has been developed. Feedstock diameters for the Linex machines may vary from 0.280-0.475" (7.11-12.06 mm).

There are several applications in which the Linex process is preferable to the Conform process. For example, if work hardening is desirable during extrusion, the Linex process is preferable because the temperature is considerably lower. During Conform extrusion of aluminum, the temperature is sufficiently high for annealing to take place. Another area in which the Linex process offers an advantage is in coextrusion, in which a cladding and a concentric core are extruded simultaneously.

**Extrolling.** This process, developed and patented by Professor Betzatel Avitzur of Lehigh University, combines the extrusion process with rolling.[4] Feedstock is fed to the extrusion die, which can be multiholed, by friction between grooved rolls (see Fig. 13-36). The stock is reduced in cross-sectional area between the rolls, pressure builds up in front of the obstructing die, and the material is extruded.

**Helical extrusion.** This process, also invented by Derek Green of the United Kingdom Atomic Energy Commission, combines hydrostatic and conventional extrusion with "machining." A billet is hydrostatically extruded over a piercing cone (see Fig. 13-37). The upper end of the tube formed is cut by the edge of a helical ramp on a rotating, conventional extrusion die, and the metal is extruded through the aperture in this die.

## PRESSES FOR COLD AND WARM EXTRUSION

Cold and warm extrusion are performed on both mechanical and hydraulic presses, as well as on upsetting (heading) machines and multistation, automatic forming machines, discussed later in this chapter. Major factors influencing press selection include the size and shape of the part to be extruded, material from which it is made, reduction in area required, production rate and total number of parts needed, tolerances to be held, initial cost, and maintenance costs.

In general, mechanical presses are preferable for short stroke and high speed requirements, which are applicable to the large-quantity production of small to medium-sized parts. Mechanical presses are always used for impact extrusion because of the short stroke and high speed requirements. Hydraulic presses offer advantages for long stroke, high and uniform force, and slower speed requirements and for the small-quantity production of large and long parts. Presses of vertical and horizontal construction are available in both mechanical and hydraulic designs.

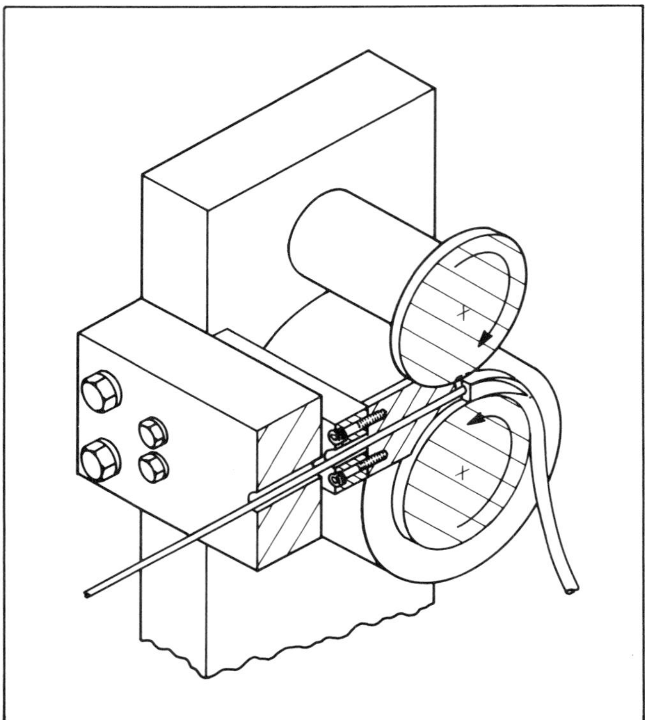

**Fig. 13-36 Extrolling combines the extrusion process with rolling.**

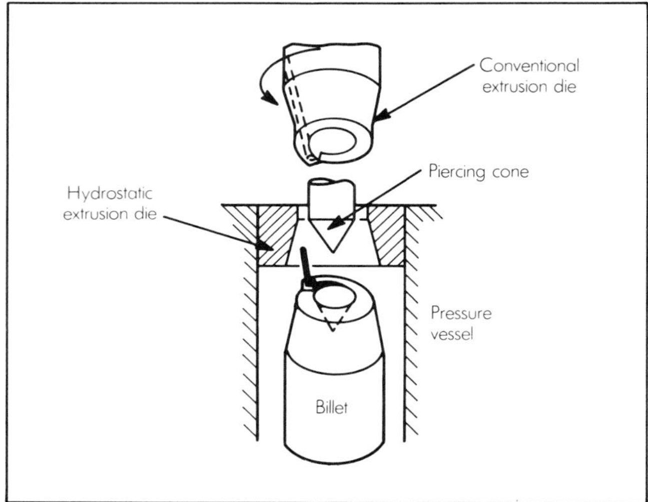


**Fig. 13-37 Helical extrusion combines hydrostatic and conventional extrusion with cutting.**

## Requirements for All Presses

Whether a mechanical or a hydraulic press is selected, good rigidity, with a minimum of deflection, is essential. Press slides must be well guided with long, close-fitting, adjustable gibs, and the frames must minimize bending of the extruding punches. Ample press size, force, energy, and speed are necessary for the specific application(s). The press force rating selected should be at least 30% greater than the requirements calculated (discussed later in this section), or the requirements established by strain-gage equipment on mechanical presses, or those obtained by gage readings on hydraulic presses during experimental and development tryouts. A detailed discussion of both mechanical and hydraulic presses is presented in Chapter 5, "Presses for Sheet Metal Forming."

## Mechanical Presses

A major advantage of mechanical presses is their high-speed capability. The slide speed is highest at midstroke and can be variable. Possible limitations include a variable force (depending upon slide position) and a maximum practical force capacity of about 6000 tons (53 MN). To establish the drive capacity for mechanical presses, the force required must be determined for a specific distance up on the stroke.

Most mechanical presses used for cold or warm extrusion are the straight-side type, with slide actuation by crankshaft, eccentric gear, knuckle joint, or drag links. Presses with crankshaft actuation of the slides are frequently used for long extrusions because of their positive action. Crankshafts are most common for presses to about 600 tons (5338 kN), but are available on presses with capacities to 3000 tons (26.7 MN) and stroke lengths to 48" (1219 mm).

Presses with eccentrics for actuating their slides have the advantage of no torsional stresses in their shafts, and high forces can be transmitted efficiently. On presses having their slides actuated by knuckle joints, even higher pressures can be exerted near the bottoms of the strokes. Knuckle-joint presses, however, have limited stroke lengths that are shorter than those of standard crank presses of comparable force ratings.

Design versatility is an important advantage of presses having slides actuated by drag links. Drag-link mechanisms generally consist of a power-driven crank, two intermediate links, and a fourth link connecting the drive to the press slide. By changing the relative lengths and geometric arrangement of the links, a variety of motions can be provided. With one design, the full force capacity of the press is exerted high above the bottom of the stroke and maintained nearly constant throughout the working stroke. Another possibility is designing the link drive to reduce impact velocity, with fast approach and return of the slide.

## Hydraulic Presses

Important advantages of hydraulic presses include relatively constant force throughout the stroke; long stroke capabilities, 100" (2540 mm) or more; and high force capacities, 50,000 tons (445 MN) or more. A possible limitation is lower speeds, as determined by the hydraulic pump capabilities.

Horizontal hydraulic presses with multiple die stations and work transfer devices are used extensively for the cold extrusion of shaft-type parts. For the extrusion of automotive control arms, three-action hydraulic presses have been built with two opposed horizontal platens, one vertical platen, multiple die stations, and automatic work transfer.

### Automation of Presses

For single-operation applications (in which extrusion is completed in one stroke) and low production requirements, the slugs are generally fed by hand. Methods of hand feeding are discussed in Chapter 5, "Presses for Sheet Metal Forming." For single-operation, high production requirements, automation should be considered. When production requirements are sufficient to warrant the added investment, lower cost production can generally be obtained by using automatic loading, feeding, and ejection equipment.

When several operations have to be performed on parts in a single press, the workpieces can be moved from station to station by transfer or shuttle-type feeding units. Rotary-indexing, dial-type feeds are also often used.

## TOOLING FOR COLD AND WARM EXTRUSION

Tool design and tool material selection are critical to successful cold extrusion. The punch profile must be such that the tool properly meters the lubricant, allowing the tools to last for a sufficient number of blows and making the process economically feasible. Typically, punches and dies are encased in retainers and shrink rings so that they are under compressive stresses at all times. Surface finish of the tools in contact with the workpiece should be 5 $\mu$in. (0.13 $\mu$m) or less.

### Tooling Materials

Recommended materials for extrusion punches are M2 and M4 molybdenum-type, high-speed tool steel and tungsten carbide. Tool-steel punches should be heat treated to a hardness of $R_C$ 62-66 and should have a high compressive yield strength. Die nibs and inserts are usually made of high-grade alloy tool steels, such as D2, M2, and M4, and are heat treated to a hardness of $R_C$ 58-64, depending on the steel. Tooling materials used by one major forming company are presented in Table 13-8.

For high production rates, long life, and good dimensional control, tungsten carbide material is often used, especially for backward-extrusion punches. Retainers or housings should have sufficient strength and toughness to prevent splitting and failure of the working tools. Shrink rings should be made from hot-work die steels, such as H11 or H13, heat treated to a hardness of $R_C$ 46-48. Outer housings are frequently made from H13 steel or SAE 4340 steel.

Detailed information on die materials, including tool steels and tungsten carbides, is presented in Chapter 2, "Die and Mold Materials." This information includes formulas for calculating shrink allowances and guidelines for designing extrusion punches and dies made from tungsten carbide.

### Design of the Tooling

A typical backward-extrusion die is shown in Fig. 13-38. A carbide die insert and its ring are tapered in the holder, which consists of two members shrunk or pressed together. The carbide insert and die ring are supported by toughened steel plates that enable the high local loads to be distributed. The extruding punch is guided by a spring-loaded guideplate which must clear the punch nose and is positioned by being piloted in a ring on the lower die. Ejection of the part from the die is by means of a delayed-action stripper which lifts the bottom portion of the die cavity. Figure 13-39 illustrates one design of a forward-extrusion die.

Because of the many variables involved, such as part design, metal properties, production and tolerance requirements, and pressures exerted, no inflexible rules of tool design exist that are suitable for all applications. Experience is the best guide in analyzing requirements and developing efficient, economical tooling for a specific operation.

General recommendations for any tooling used for cold or warm extrusion include the following:[5]

1. Provide good tool support and direct extrusion forces into press components.
2. Balance the metal flow for uniform extrusion and design the shape-forming orifice to allow the metal to flow naturally.
3. Design the die with open construction whenever practical to allow excess metal in the slugs or preforms to escape. It is generally more economical to use open-cavity dies and then trim the extruded parts to length if trimming is required.
4. Provide proper venting between dies for "breathing."
5. Use a good die set or ensure accurate alignment of the tooling components through the use of adequate guiding and proper design. This minimizes the possibility of deflection and bending that could shorten tool life.
6. Avoid high stress concentration areas. Sectional construction can minimize stresses where sharp corners are required.
7. Design for easy replacement of tooling components most subject to wear or breakage.
8. Minimize the heat generated during extrusion. While heat increases the plasticity of the metal and reduces pressure requirements, it can cause the lubricant to break down and shorten tool life.
9. Design extrusion punches to meter the surface flow of the lubricant.
10. Minimize the surface area of contact between the tooling and material being extruded by undercutting or relieving the punch or die, or both, beyond the shape-forming orifice. Care is required, however, to prevent the trapping of metal in such undercuts or reliefs.

**Backward-extrusion punches.** To reduce the possibility of bending, punches used for backward extrusion should be supported by guide bearings or bushings whenever possible. The clearance between punch and guide is generally 0.005-0.0005" (0.13-0.013 mm), depending upon the punch diameter.

The contour of the punch nose is critical and varies with the material to be extruded, the depth of penetration, the lubricant spread on the inner surface of the extrusion, and other variables. A typical punch nose contour used to extrude parts such as automotive piston pins is shown in Fig. 13-40. The major diameter, *A*, of the punch nose, often called the bearing land diameter, is made approximately equal to the bore size required in the extrusion, but varies with the increase in diameter produced by axial strain of the metal as it passes over the radius, *B*, which is commonly 0.030" (0.76 mm).

The bearing land, dimension *D* in Fig. 13-40, on a backward-extrusion punch is made as narrow as possible to minimize contact friction and yet maintain dimensional control of the extrusion. For the same reasons, as well as to facilitate stripping of the extrusion, the punch shank is often relieved immediately above the land. Diameter *E* is usually 0.004-0.024" (0.10-0.61 mm) less than the land diameter, depending upon the punch diameter. The relief angle, *F*, is generally 1-3°; but when depth

**TABLE 13-8**
**Tooling Materials for Cold Forming**

| Tool | Material | Hardness | Application |
|---|---|---|---|
| Punches, forming | S5 | $R_C$ 56-58 | Normal |
| | M2 | $R_C$ 59-61 | Medium |
| | M4 | $R_C$ 62-64 | High load |
| Punches, extrusion | T4 | $R_C$ 64-66 | Special purpose |
| | M2 | $R_C$ 61-63 | Special purpose |
| | M4 | $R_C$ 64-66 | Special purpose |
| | Tungsten carbide (Kennametal 3109 or equivalent) | $R_A$ 88 | Normal |
| Punches, piercing | T4 | $R_C$ 60-62 | Normal |
| Die inserts | O1 | $R_C$ 58-60 | Special purpose |
| | S5 | $R_C$ 56-58 | Special purpose |
| | M2 (or T1 modified) | $R_C$ 59-61 | Normal |
| | M4 | $R_C$ 62-64 | Severe forming |
| | Tungsten carbide (20-25% Co) | $R_A$ 84-86 | Highest wear |
| Trim dies | M2 (or T1 modified) | $R_C$ 59-61 | Normal speed |
| Die cases | H13 | $R_C$ 47-51 | Normal |
| Upset dies | W1 | $R_C$ 53-56 | Medium |
| | A2 | $R_C$ 59-61 | Heavy |
| | H13 | $R_C$ 47-51 | Interference-fit inserts |
| Cutter and quills, for shearing | O1 | $R_C$ 58-60 | Medium |
| | M2 (or T1 modified) | $R_C$ 59-61 | Heavy |
| | Tungsten carbide (20-25% Co) | $R_A$ 84-86 | Highest wear |
| Fillers, hardplates, and backing blocks | O1 | $R_C$ 58-60 | Medium |
| | L6 | $R_C$ 57-59 | Heavy |
| | M2 (or T1 modified) | $R_C$ 59-61 | Special purpose |
| Knockout pins | O1 | $R_C$ 58-60 | Light |
| | M2 (or T1 modified) | $R_C$ 59-61 | Medium |
| | M4 | $R_C$ 62-64 | Heavy |
| Sleeves and knockout stripper | O1 | $R_C$ 58-60 | Light |
| | M2 (or T1 modified) | $R_C$ 59-61 | Medium |
| | M4 | $R_C$ 62-64 | Heavy |
| | S5 | $R_C$ 56-58 | Heavy |
| Sleeves, for die insert support | H13 | $R_C$ 47-51 | Material selection based on degree of forming, geometry of pieces involved, and insert material. |
| | S5 | $R_C$ 56-58 | |
| | M2 (or T1 modified) | $R_C$ 59-61 | |

(*Imerman Industries, Inc.*)

of penetration exceeds four times the punch diameter, a double radius is often used instead of an angle.

To conserve lubricant by decreasing the surface flow, an angle (*H* in Fig. 13-40) is generally provided on the punch nose. This angle varies depending upon the metal being extruded, the severity of the operation, and the design of the part extruded. An angle of 5° is common for cold extrusion of most steels; however, the angle can range to 10° for some steels and can be as small as 1° for extruding aluminum alloys. High nose angles reduce pressure requirements, but cause rapid depletion of the lubricant and increased tool wear. A flat having a diameter about 35% that of the bearing land is sometimes provided on the bottom of a tapered punch nose to meter the lubricant spread. When high angles or spherical-shaped punch noses are required, the amount of reduction per operation must be reduced.

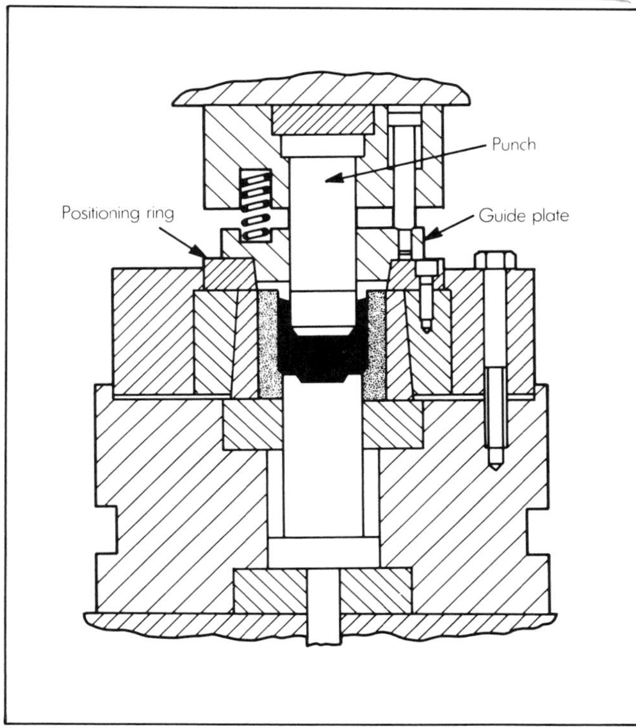


**Fig. 13-38 Typical backward-extrusion die with a carbide insert.**

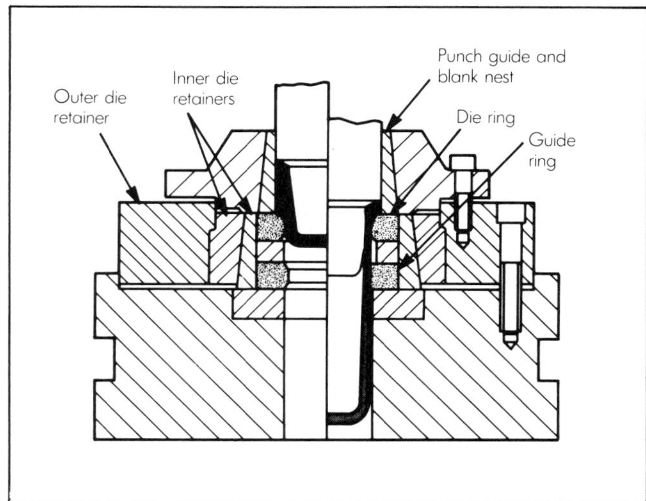


**Fig. 13-39 One design of a forward-extrusion die with carbide inserts in a compression ring.**

Overall lengths of the punches should be as short as possible to minimize bending. The extruding ends of the punches should be gradually blended into larger diameter, upper ends to distribute the loads.

**Dies for backward extrusion.** The design of dies for backward extruding varies widely, depending primarily upon the design of the extrusion, the material to be extruded, and the severity of the operation. A die nib typical of those used to backward extrude parts such as automotive piston pins is illustrated in Fig. 13-41. The upper portion of the die bore is tapered, angle *C*, generally from 5-10 min, to facilitate entry of slugs or preforms, allow free flow of metal upward, and provide clearance so that metal does not close in on the punch.

The straight portion of the die bore, diameter *A* in Fig. 13-41, controls the outside diameter of the extrusion. Angle *B* tapers the extrusion, and the outside diameter, *D*, is from 1.8 to 2 times the bore diameter, dimension *A*. Die nibs are generally assembled in one or more restraining rings by using tapered or shrink fits and pressing the rings together.

**Forward extrusion tooling.** Dies for forward extrusion have an upper bore that is 0.004-0.010" (0.10-0.25 mm) larger in diameter than the slugs and is 25-75% longer. A tapered shoulder immediately below the upper bore forces the metal to flow through the orifice formed between the die land and the punch. The dies are generally a tapered or shrink fit in restraining rings.

A sectional view of a die for forward extruding the ends of armature shafts for automotive starting motors is shown in Fig. 13-40. Bars of AISI 1040 hot-rolled steel are cold drawn to a diameter between 0.739 and 0.742" (18.77 and 18.55 mm) for extrusion. The forward-extruding operation reduces the diameter at one end of the shaft to 0.4685" (11.900 mm), a 60% reduction in area.

Carbide guide bearings and the extrusion die (see Fig. 13-42) are a shrink fit 0.006" (0.15 mm) on diameter in restraining rings, made from AISI H13 tool steel that has been hardened to $R_C$43 and ground. Bores of the carbide guide bearings, which resist wear, provide a clearance of 0.003-0.006" (0.08-0.15 mm) for the slugs as they are pushed into the extrusion die by the

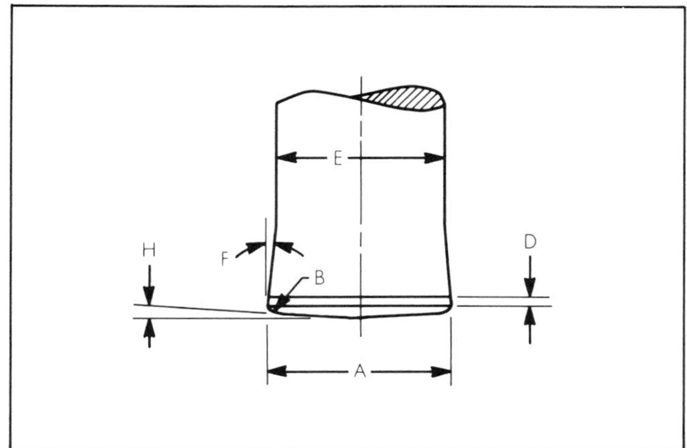


**Fig. 13-40 Typical punch-nose contour used for cold extruding parts such as automotive piston pins.** (*Verson Allsteel Press Co.*)

punch. Sectional construction (short lengths) of these bearings and the extrusion die reduce the cost and facilitate assembly and replacement. The bearings and die and their restraining rings are encased in a dieholder, made from H13 tool steel hardened to $R_C47$ and ground, with a locknut that is tightened while holding the die assembly under a force of 150 tons (1334 kN).

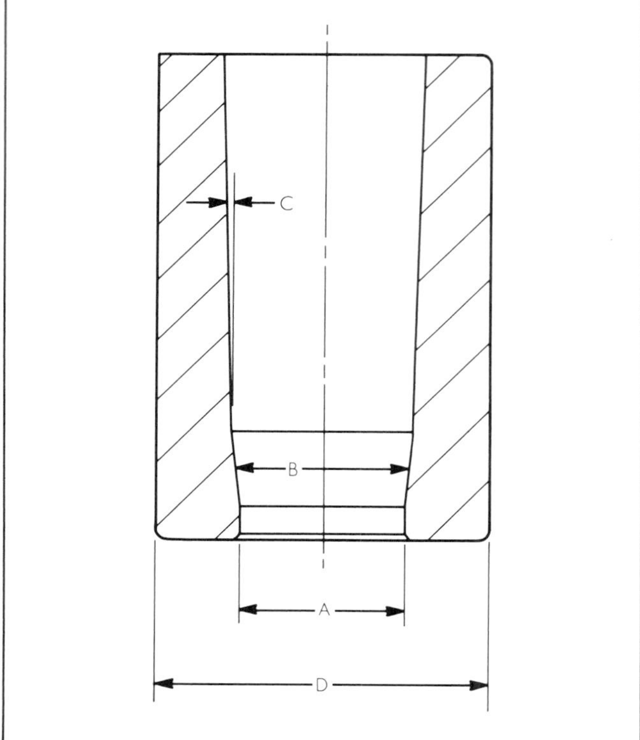


**Fig. 13-41 Typical die nib used for the backward extrusion of parts such as automotive piston pins. (*Verson Allsteel Press Co.*)**

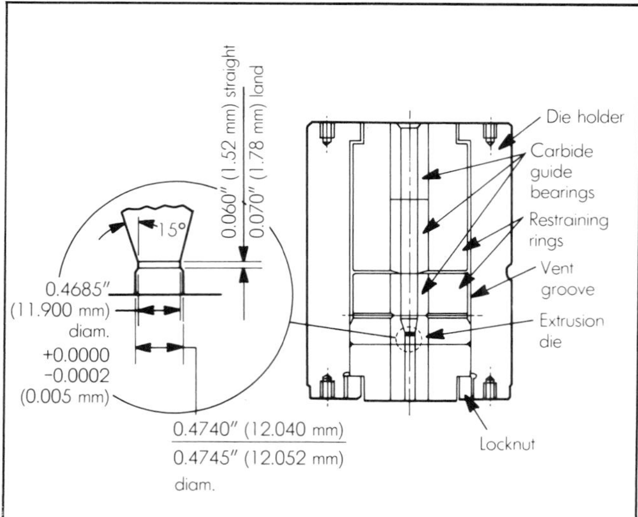


**Fig. 13-42 Sectional view of forward-extruding die. Enlargement (left) shows tapered bore and bearing land that controls the OD of the extrusion.**

The carbide extrusion die member, shown enlarged at the left in Fig. 13-42, has a tapered 15° bore to force the metal to flow through the orifice formed by the bearing land; the bore diameter of the land controls the outside diameter (OD) of the extruded surface. This straight bearing land is kept short—0.065" (1.65 mm)—to minimize friction and facilitate ejection. Friction is also reduced by undercutting the die bore below this land. Careful blending is required between the tapered bore and orifice-forming land of the extrusion die to facilitate metal flow, and all inside diameters (guide bearings and extrusion die) are sized and lapped to prevent steps at the parting lines. Surface finish on all internal surfaces is held to 5 $\mu$in. (0.13 $\mu$m) or less. Vent grooves on the faces and OD's of the restraining rings, and top surface of the extrusion die, are provided to allow trapped oil and air to escape. Life of this extrusion die has been averaging about 250,000 shafts.

### Computer Design and Manufacture

Computer-aided design and manufacture (CAD/CAM) are being employed extensively for extrusion dies. The CAD/CAM systems use interactive software based on the geometries of the desired extrusions, properties of the metals to be extruded, and analyses of the metal flow. Machines for producing the dies are equipped with computer numerical control (CNC) units.

## PRODUCING SLUGS FOR EXTRUDING

The production of slugs for cold or warm extrusion is a costly part of the complete processing. Slugs must have accurate dimensions, smooth surfaces, and uniform volumes, especially if closed dies are used. Tolerances that must be maintained on the size and shape of slugs depend primarily upon the accuracy required in the extruded parts. Slugs that fit closely into the die are particularly important for backward-extruding operations, but preformed slugs need not conform closely to the contour of the die, except at locating surfaces.

Shapes and dimensions of slugs should generally conform as closely as possible to those of the extrusions. When a part can be extruded in a single operation, the slug diameter is usually made equal to the maximum diameter of the extruded part. When several extrusions are required, however, slug diameters are often smaller than the maximum diameter of the required part.

Controlling only the lengths of slugs is not generally sufficient because of volume variations that can result from differences in diameters of the slugs. It is usually best to control the weights of the slugs, which are a direct indication of their volumes. Slug weights are often controlled within 1% or less. Flat, parallel ends; perpendicularity of the ends to the sides; and clean, smooth surfaces are also important.

### Slug Production Methods

A number of methods are employed to produce slugs, including blanking, sawing, cutoff, shearing, coining, and upsetting (heading). Variables that should be considered before selecting the most cost effective method include the size and shape of the slugs, dimensional and weight tolerances necessary, number of operations needed, production requirements, material losses in producing the slugs, tooling costs, existing equipment for slug production, and cost of new equipment.

Most slugs that are sawed, cutoff, or sheared from rods, bars, or coil stock are produced from hot-rolled steel. There is a trend, however, toward cold drawing or turning the hot-rolled material prior to producing the slugs. The use of turned bars is increasing, the objective being to remove decarburization and imperfections from the hot-rolled surfaces. This ensures fewer production rejects due to seam ruptures, and results in improved finishes on the extrusions. About 0.001" (0.03 mm) per 1/16" (1.6 mm) of diameter is generally removed from the surfaces by turning.

**Blanking.** The blanking of slugs from sheet, plate, or coil stock is employed only infrequently because of the considerable material loss. This process, however, offers advantages for certain applications, especially when the ratios of required slug diameters to thicknesses are large. A limitation is that variations in thickness of the sheet, plate, or coil stock can result in nonuniform slug volumes. Such variations may necessitate surface grinding of the material before blanking, or grinding the slugs after blanking. Blanked slugs may also have to be shot blasted or tumbled to smooth their edges. Another possible limitation is that work hardening of the slug edges as a result of blanking may cause tearing during extrusion. Details of the blanking process are presented in Chapter 4, "Sheet Metal Blanking and Forming."

**Sawing.** Many long, small-diameter slugs are produced from bar stock on bandsaws, hacksaws, circular saws, or abrasive-wheel cutoff machines. When the required slugs have a large diameter-to-length ratio, however, loss of material from the sawing kerf often makes this method uneconomical. Also, the edges of sawed blanks generally require chamfering or deburring prior to extrusion, thus adding to production costs. Details of the various sawing processes are presented in Chapter 6, "Sawing," in Volume I, *Machining*, of this Handbook series.

**Cutoff.** Cutoff tools are used to chamfer and separate some slugs from bar stock, especially if lathes, multiple-spindle automatics, or similar equipment are available for this purpose. As with the sawing process, however, the slugs should have a small diameter-to-length ratio to prevent excessive metal losses from chips. Care must be exercised to remove any projections left at the centers of the cutoff slugs prior to extrusion.

**Shearing.** The fastest, most efficient, lowest cost, and most commonly used method of producing slugs is the shearing of wire, rod, bar, or coil stock. However, high-quality shearing is necessary to produce clean breaks, with both ends of each slug square with the longitudinal axis and having a minimum of distortion. Also, shearing is generally limited to bars having a maximum diameter of about 2" (51 mm). Bars to 4" (102 mm) diam are being sheared, but the greater the length of the slug in relation to its diameter, the less the relative economy of shearing. Not all materials are suitable for shearing. For example, it is difficult, if not impossible, to produce quality sheared surfaces on steels having carbon contents greater than 0.50%, or an unfavorable crystal structure. Details of the shearing process are presented in Chapter 11, "Shearing."

**Coining.** The coining process (refer to Chapter 4, "Sheet Metal Blanking and Forming") is sometimes employed to form flat, square faces on the ends of slugs; to produce desired indentations in the bases and tops of the slugs; to alter the size or shape of the slugs; and/or to cold work the material before preextrusion annealing. Cold working by coining or upsetting (discussed next in this section) facilitates the subsequent annealing of slugs made from high-alloy steels by reducing the temperature and heating time requirements.

**Upsetting (heading).** Upsetting, commonly called heading, is discussed in detail later in this chapter. This process is used for the same purposes as coining and is employed instead of coining when it is necessary to gather metal at a specified area of the slug for subsequent extrusion or to develop a predetermined profile. With profiled slugs, less initial pressure is required to deform the metal before extrusion pressure is applied, thus reducing impact on the punch. Upsetting, often combined with shearing and/or forming, also tests the quality of the metal; surface seams open during upsetting, and the slugs are rejected before further processing.

**Other slug production methods.** Preformed slugs made by casting molten metal or compacting powdered metals have been used. Cast slugs are generally limited to nonferrous metals and have not been used with much success. Slugs made from powdered metals are economical for certain applications. Hot-forged preforms have also been used for cold and warm extrusion.

## Slug Treatment Before Extruding

Slugs to be used for cold or warm extrusion generally require annealing and must be cleaned, coated, and lubricated.

**Annealing.** Most slugs require annealing to provide the necessary ductility for extrusion. When more than one extruding operation is to be performed, reannealing is often needed. The higher the reduction required, the harder the extruded part becomes. When the hardness of the extrusion reaches about $R_B$ 100, annealing, recoating, and relubrication are generally required before further reduction is possible. A detailed discussion of annealing is presented in Volume III, *Materials, Finishing and Coating*, of this Handbook series.

**Cleaning.** Grease, oil, soil, scale, and surface oxides must be removed prior to coating and lubricating slugs to be extruded. A common process for preparing slugs for extrusion consists of alkali cleaning, hot water rinsing, acid pickling, cold water rinsing, and hot water rinsing prior to coating. Then the slugs are rinsed in cold water and a neutralizing medium prior to lubricating. Additional information on chemical cleaning and acid pickling of metals is presented in Volume III, *Materials, Finishing and Coating*, of this Handbook series.

**Coating.** The purpose of conversion coatings applied to slugs to be extruded is for the coatings to serve as a separating layer between the workpiece and tools, and as a lubricant carrier. Zinc phosphate coatings are the most common for cold and warm extrusion, but oxalate coatings are used for corrosion-resistant steels. For less severe applications, the need for coatings can sometimes be eliminated by using proprietary lubricating compounds containing sulfur, phosphorus, and/or chlorine.

Small crystals of the phosphate coating absorb or react with the lubricant applied, thus bonding the lubricant to the surface and minimizing spread of the lubricant during extrusion. Weights of the coatings applied vary with the severity of the extruding operation, but are always heavier than prepaint treatments. Phosphate coatings can be removed from the extrusions, if necessary, by immersing the parts in a hot, alkali cleaning solution and then rinsing with hot water. Details of the metal coating processes are presented in Volume III, *Materials, Finishing and Coating*, of this Handbook series.

**Lubricating.** Many different lubricants are used for cold and warm extrusion, but the following solid-phase lubricants are most commonly applied:

1. Soaps, fortified with soluble salts and made up in a heated water solution in which the phosphate-coated slugs are immersed.
2. Specially formulated soaps, also in a heated water solution, which react with the zinc phosphate coating to

convert a portion of it to a water-insoluble metal soap, zinc stearate.

3. Lime over phosphate-coated rods or slugs, which is commonly used in less severe operations.

For some warm extruding operations, graphite is occasionally added to the lubricant, but graphite is difficult to remove from the extrusions if removal is necessary. For other severe operations, molybdenum disulfide is sometimes used in place of or with fatty soaps on phosphate coated slugs. For extruding aluminum alloys, cleaned and pickled slugs are often tumbled in zinc stearate powder, but heat-treatable alloys require zinc phosphate and reactive soap coatings.

Other lubricants are available, and new ones are continually being developed. One dry lubricant, designated as a fluorotelomer, consists of a finely divided solid dispersed in a nonflammable fluorocarbon. When applied to a metal slug, the diluent evaporates, leaving the dry film as the lubricant. Additional information on lubrication principles and various lubricants is presented in Chapter 3, "Lubricants."

## PRESSURE REQUIREMENTS FOR COLD EXTRUSION

Many variables affect the pressure requirements for cold extrusion. These variables include the metal to be extruded and its condition, the reduction in area required, the shape of the extruded part, the press employed, the type and amount of coating and lubricant employed, the design of the die, and the speed of extruding. Because so many variables exist, it is impossible to precisely estimate the pressure and energy requirements for extruding a specific workpiece.

Reductions up to 85% of cross-sectional area by extrusion on cold steel slugs in one operation have been successfully made. Under normal conditions, it is good practice to limit the first reduction to approximately 60% and subsequent operations to about 40%. Reductions exceeding 65% should be restricted to steels of $R_B$ 60 or less. In-process annealing is recommended in most cases when hardness rises above $R_B$ 100. In aluminum and magnesium alloys, reductions above 90% require extremely high pressures and are not recommended.

Pressure requirements for backward extrusion of some parts can vary from as little as 20 tons/in.$^2$ (276 MPa) if the parts are made from certain magnesium alloys, to more than 180 ton/in.$^2$ (2482 MPa) if the parts are made from some high-alloy steels. In addition, pressure requirements at the start of the extruding cycles can be as much as 30% higher than those necessary to maintain plastic flow after extrusion begins. Some typical pressure ranges for cold extruding various materials are presented in Table 13-9.

Helpful information and recommendations with respect to pressure requirements for extruding specific parts can be obtained from press builders, material suppliers, and toolmakers. Two of many curves plotted by one press builder on the basis of numerous tests using strain gages and similar equipment during actual operation are presented in Fig. 13-43 and Fig. 13-44. Both of these curves were plotted for slugs 1.244" (31.60 mm) diam x 0.99" (25.1 mm) long.

The nomographs shown in Fig. 13-45 and Fig. 13-46, based on an empirical equation developed by General Motors Corp., can be used to estimate extrusion parameters.[6] Given any three of four important extrusion factors (area reduction, extrusion or punch angle, material extruded, and ram pressure), the fourth factor can be determined from the graphs. For the forward-extrusion example shown in Fig. 13-45, with an area reduction of 65%, an extrusion die angle of 120°, and an extruded material of AISI 1032 steel, the ram pressure is about 232 ksi (1600 MPa). For the backward-extrusion example (see Fig. 13-46), with an area reduction of 55%, a punch angle of

**TABLE 13-9**
**Typical Pressure Ranges for Cold Extruding Various Materials**

| Materials Cold Extruded | Pressure Range* tons/in.$^2$ | Pressure Range* MPa |
|---|---|---|
| Aluminum alloys (7075, 6061, 2014, 1100) | 40-80 | 552-1103 |
| Brass, soft | 30-50 | 414-690 |
| Copper, soft | 25-80 | 345-1103 |
| Steels, plain carbon, annealed (1008, 1016, 1018, 1020, 1038, 1060) | 60-200 | 827-2758 |
| Steels, alloy, annealed (4024, 4137, 4188, 5130, 8620) | 70-200 | 965-2758 |
| Steels, stainless | 70-200 | 965-2758 |

* Backward extrusion requires higher pressures in the ranges given than forward extrusion.

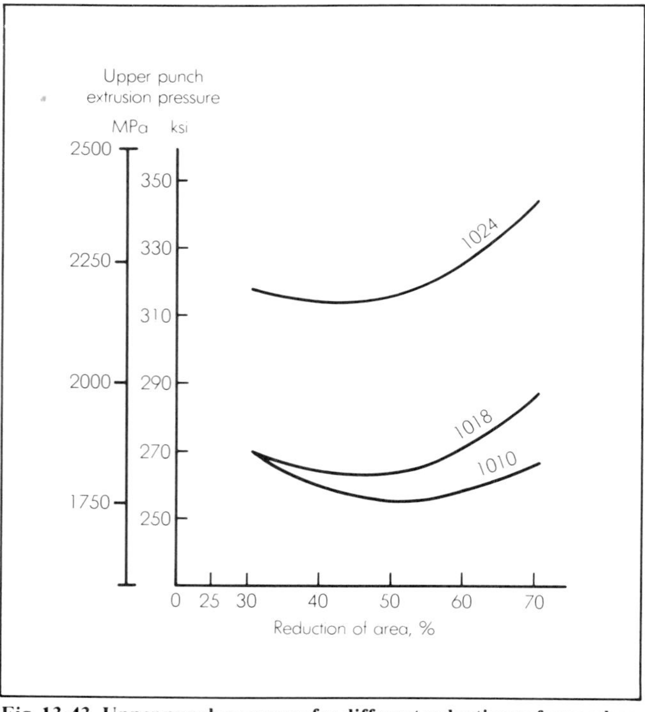


**Fig. 13-43 Upper punch pressures for different reductions of area when backward extruding various steels.** (*Verson Allsteel Press Co.*)

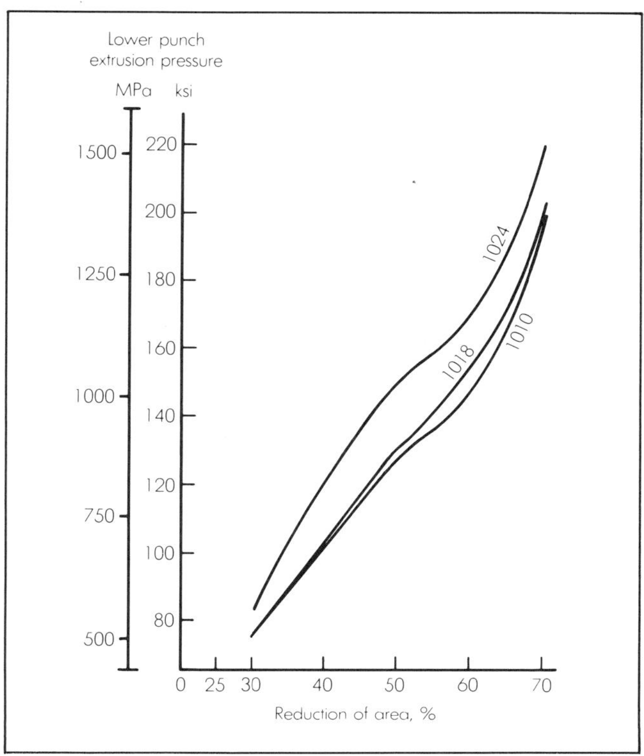


**Fig. 13-44 Lower punch pressures for different reductions of area when backward extruding various steels.** (*Verson Allsteel Press Co.*)

150°, and an extruded material of AISI 1032 steel, the ram pressure approximates 260 ksi (1793 MPa).

Computers are being used increasingly to determine process variables such as extrusion pressures, as well as to design and manufacture the tooling with CAD/CAM techniques and press selection. An analysis of metal-flow characteristics, stress concentrations, and stored data on material properties and press characteristics are employed in developing interactive software for the computer program.

When material deformation in cold extrusion is limited by low ductility of the material and/or the capacity of the press or tooling, warm extrusion is often employed. Less pressure is required with warm extrusion because of the reduction in flow stress (resistance to deformation), increase in ductility, and reduction in strain hardening of the workpiece material.

## EXTRUDING SPEEDS

Slide speeds (velocity at contact between tools and slugs) for cold extrusion generally vary from 7-15 ips [35-75 fpm (10.7-22.9 m/min)], depending upon the metal being extruded, the reduction in area required, and the shape of the slugs. Operating speeds of the presses, in strokes per minute, vary with the required stroke lengths and depths of punch penetration.

## SAFETY CONSIDERATIONS

Considerations and requirements with respect to press safety for cold and warm extrusion are similar to those discussed in detail in Chapter 5, "Presses for Sheet Metal Forming." Press construction and controls, guards, and devices described in that chapter are all applicable to extruding operations.

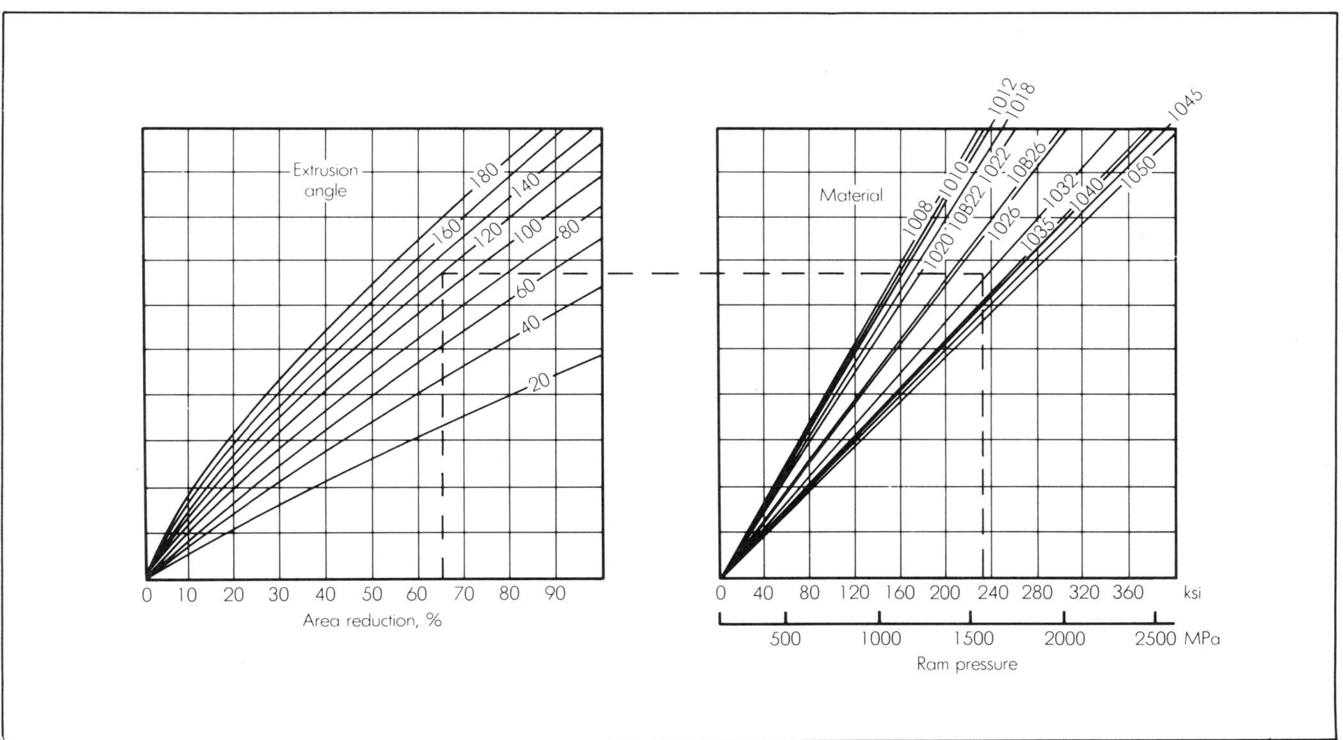


**Fig. 13-45 Relation of parameters for the forward extrusion of various steels.**

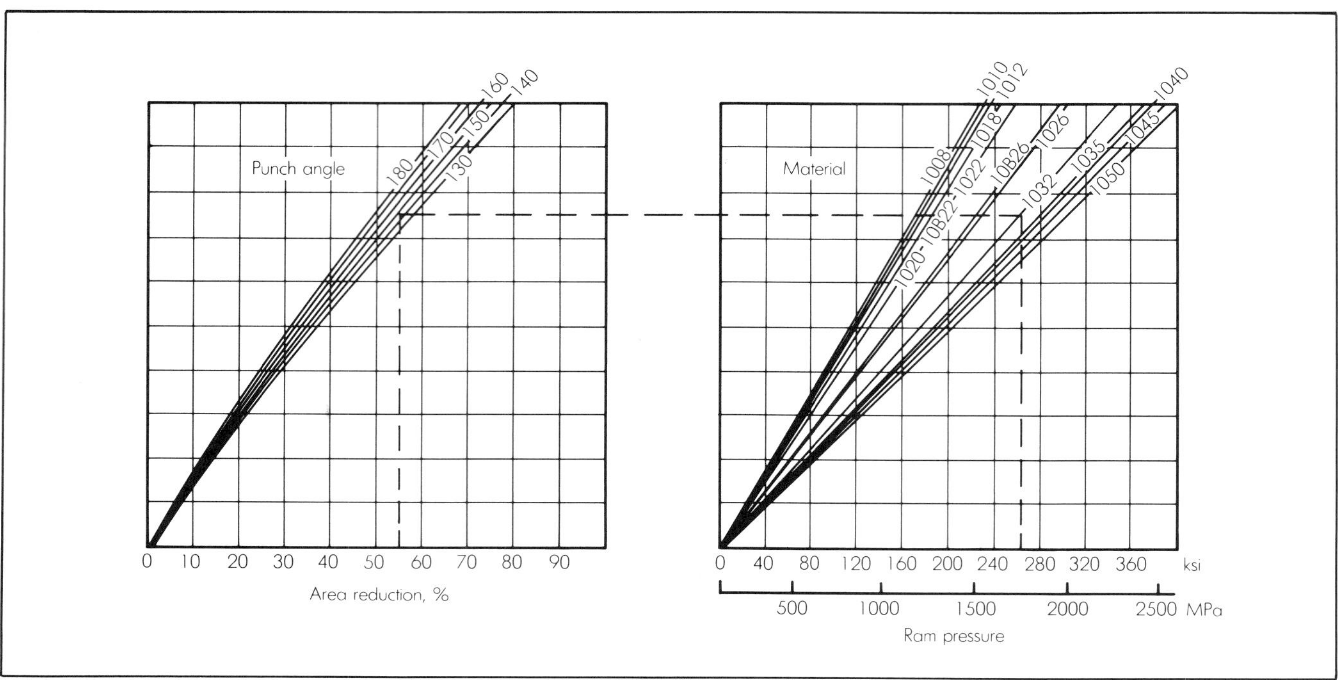


**Fig. 13-46 Relation of parameters for the backward extrusion of various steels.**

# COLD AND WARM UPSETTING (HEADING)

Upsetting is a forming operation for reshaping metal by plastic flow. Force applied to the end of a blank, contained between a punch and a die, causes metal flow, increasing the diameter and decreasing the length of the blank. Upsetting is commonly called heading because the process was first used to form heads on nails. The method is now employed extensively to form the heads on bolts, screws, rivets, and other fasteners. The name *heading*, however, is misleading in that metal can be gathered anywhere along the length of the blank or all of the stock can be increased in diameter.

Cold upsetting is performed with the metal blanks at room temperature. In warm upsetting, the starting material is heated to a temperature below its recrystallization temperature, typically 800-1200° F (427-649° C), with a maximum temperature of about 1800° F (982° C). Hot upsetting, discussed in Chapter 15, "Hot Forging," is done with the metal heated above its recrystallization temperature, typically 1900-2300° F (1038-1260° C), depending upon the specific metal.

Upsetting is accomplished by inserting a blank of a specific length into a stationary die. A punch, moving parallel to the axis of the blank, contacts the end of the blank protruding from the die and compresses the metal. Impressions in the punch or die, or both, determine the upset shape produced. Some parts are upset in the punch, some in the die, some in both, and some in an open space between the punch and the die (see Fig. 13-47).

## ADVANTAGES OF UPSETTING

Major advantages of upsetting are economical production, the forming of high-quality parts, increased part strength, and versatility in product design.

### Economical Production

Economy in upsetting is the result of high production rates, low labor costs, and material savings. Production rates range from 35 per minute for large parts to 900 per minute for small balls. Fewer machines are needed to meet production requirements, resulting in reduced costs for capital equipment, maintenance, and floor space. Labor costs are minimal because most operations are completely automatic, requiring labor only for machine setups, supervision, and parts handling.

Material savings result from the elimination or reduction in the amount of chips produced. When upsetting is combined with other operations, such as extruding, trimming, and thread rolling, savings are considerable. In some cases, no subsequent machining or finishing of the upset parts is required.

### Quality of Upset Parts

**Improved properties.** Cold working during upsetting increases tensile, yield, and shear strengths of the metal, as well as its fatigue life. The uninterrupted grain flow pattern produced follows the part contour. For some applications, the upset parts can be made smaller without sacrificing strength, or lower cost metals can be substituted for more expensive raw materials.

**Smooth finishes.** Upsetting produces smooth surface finishes. The exact finish obtained depends upon the condition of the raw material, the surface coating and/or lubricant employed, the finish on the tools, and other factors. Surface finishes from 10-100 μin. (0.25-2.54 μm) are common. Cold-drawn raw material is used extensively for upsetting, and the smooth surfaces produced in drawing are retained in upsetting.

**Close tolerances.** The tolerances that can be maintained in upsetting depend upon many variables, including the style of the upset, the length-to-diameter ratio of the blank, the severity of the operation, the type of workpiece material and size of workpiece, and the quality of the tooling and machine. Dimensional tolerances as close as 0.0005" (0.013 mm) on shank diameter and 0.005" (0.13 mm) on overall length are held in some applications, but such close tolerances increase production costs. The tolerances specified should be as liberal as possible, depending upon functional requirements. Practical tolerances commonly used are 0.002-0.022" (0.05-0.56 mm) on diameters and 1/32 to 3/16" (0.8 to 4.8 mm) on lengths, the tighter tolerances being applicable to smaller parts.

### Design Versatility

A wide variety of different-shaped parts, including some that are difficult to produce by any other method, can be formed by upsetting. The upset sections can be concentric or eccentric and formed anywhere along the part. Gears and cams can be formed integral with shafts; holes or recesses can be formed in the ends of parts; and designs previously requiring the assembly of several components can sometimes be upset as a single part. For some applications, the cross-sectional area of the part can be reduced because of the added strength imparted by cold working of the metal. Redesigning of a machined part can significantly improve its functionality and reduce its cost if full advantage is taken of cold heading design capabilities.

## LIMITATIONS OF UPSETTING

Possible limitations of upsetting include the need for substantial production requirements and the limit to the maximum size of parts that can be formed, which depends upon the capacity of the machine with respect to force, energy, and cutoff capability. The maximum size of parts that can be formed by cold upsetting seldom exceeds 1 1/4" (32 mm) diam, but machines are in use that produce parts to 2 1/8" (54 mm) diam or more. Bar stock is used for large parts because coil stock more than 1 5/8" (41 mm) diam is not readily available. Another possible limitation is that some upsetting operations may require the use of annealed wire or rods, which must be cold drawn to a specified diameter, thus adding to production costs.

When low-carbon steel is upset, some general limitations relate to the ability of that metal to deform without cracking or splitting. Figure 13-48 shows the generally accepted limits to the maximum diameter obtainable. Free upsets between the die and the punch do not contain the metal at the sides of the upset. Under these conditions, maximum upset diameter is about 2 1/2 times the blank diameter. If the metal is contained in or controlled by punch surfaces (which tend to hold the metal together), maximum upset diameter is about three times the blank diameter. The exact maximum diameter, of course, depends on the quality of the material, and there are examples of upsetting carried out at four times the blank diameter.

Because of the substantial cost of machines and tooling, as well as the long setup time, upsetting is generally restricted to high-production requirements. Exact production requirements vary with the size and design of the part, the metal from which it is made, the cost of alternative production methods, and other factors. In general, however, the minimum quantity for economical upsetting of large parts varies from about 10,000-25,000. For small parts, requirements can range from 25,000-50,000 or more. Accumulating parts required in smaller quantities into similar families, thereby minimizing setup changes or adjustments, permits more economical production.

## UPSET LENGTHS

At the point of contact between the punch and the blank, the portion of the blank to be upset extends out of the die, unsupported by either die or punch. If this length is too great, the blank bends instead of upsetting uniformly. The maximum length that can be upset without bending is expressed in multiples of the blank diameter. For example, if the blank is 1/2" (12.7 mm) diam and 1" (25.4 mm) extends outside the die, there are two diameters of unsupported length outside the die. One general rule is that 2 1/4 to 2 1/2 diameters in length can be upset in one blow.

If the volume of metal in 2 1/4 diameters of stock length is not enough to form the required upset, two blows must be used. According to a second general rule, up to about 4 1/2 diameters in length can be upset in two blows. The first blow upsets the stock to a larger size and reduces its height, thereby reducing the number of few diameters unsupported for the second blow. For

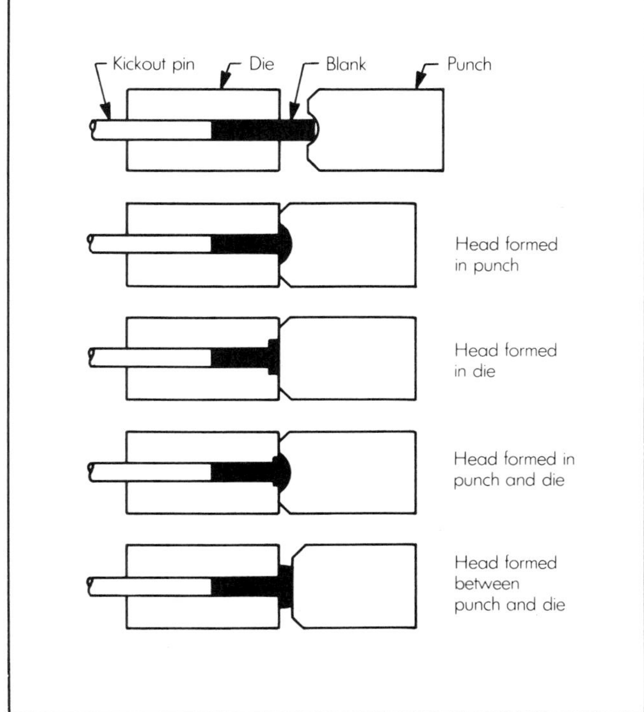


**Fig. 13-47 Various types of upsetting.**

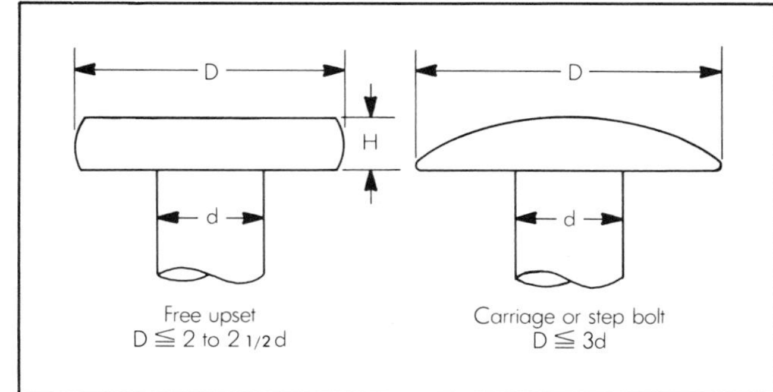


**Fig. 13-48 Generally accepted limits for maximum upset diameters.**

# COLD AND WARM UPSETTING (HEADING)

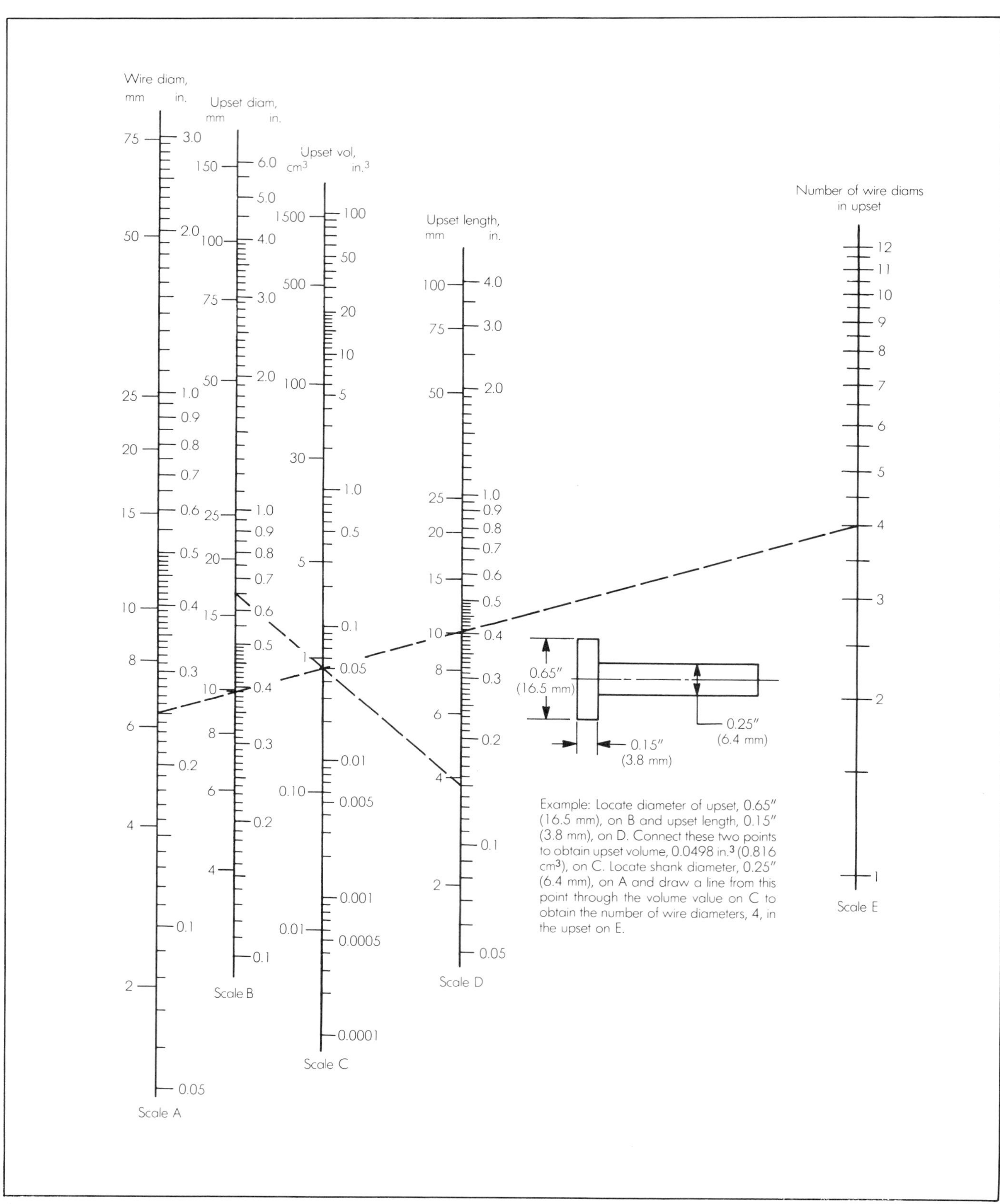


**Fig. 13-49 Upset dimensioning nomograph. (*Industrial Fasteners Institute*)**

many parts, the first blow produces a long frustum of a cone and the second or finish blow finishes the upset. Industry also uses other terms. For example, the first blow or punch is sometimes called cone operation, bulb upset, bulbing, gathering blow, cone hammer, first hammer, upsetting punch, or simply cone. The second blow or punch is sometimes called finish operation, finish upset, heading blow, heading operation, finish hammer, heading hammer, second hammer, or finish. When a sliding punch supports part of the blank during upsetting, up to approximately 6 1/2 diameters in length can be upset in two blows.

In multidie machines, the total number of diameters in the length of an upset is limited by the number of blows available and the work hardening of the material. Normally an average of about two diameters of material can be coned in one blow, about four diameters in two blows, six diameters in three blows, eight diameters in four blows, etc. By using a sliding cone tool in the first blow, larger volumes can be gathered with fewer blows, allowing other operations in remaining dies.

Upsetting is often combined with extrusion in multidie machines to form large-headed, small-shanked parts. In contrast to upsetting, extrusion reduces the diameter of the initial stock while increasing its length, with the amount of diameter reduction expressed as reduction in area. For reductions in area of 30-40% or more, the blank is trapped (or totally enclosed) before extrusion. Smaller reductions can usually be performed without trapping, depending on the material. Some materials have been trap-extruded to over 90% reduction in the area of the initial stock. Through extrusion and upsetting, parts can be made that have more than 6, 8, or 10 shank diameter equivalents in the upset length.

Since extruding and heading are separate operations, each having its own limits, the maximum capability of each must be calculated separately. By starting with stock larger than the shank, then extruding the shank and upsetting the head, maximums can be reached for both upsetting and extrusion based on the initial stock size. For example, 1/2" (12.7 mm) diam stock extruded to an 80% reduction in area and upset using 6 diameters of initial stock length results in an upset representing 70 diameters of the after-extruded shank size; however, the rules for upsetting (6 1/2 diameters in two upsetting blows) and extrusion are not surpassed.

## UPSET VOLUMES

Upset volume is the amount of material required to form an upset. The volume of cylindrical upset, stated as length in multiples of blank diameter, is the basis of calculation with the following equation:

$$n = \frac{HD^2}{d^3} \tag{7}$$

where:

$n$ = number of stock diameters in upset
$H$ = upset length, in. or mm
$D$ = upset diameter, in. or mm
$d$ = stock diameter, in. or mm

The upset dimensioning nomograph (see Fig. 13-49) can also be used to calculate the number of diameters in cylindrical upsets. The dimensions of the equation and the nomograph are illustrated in Fig. 13-50.

A third method of calculating number of diameters is by unit weight. Tables 13-10 and 13-11 give the weights of unit lengths of steel wire and are used in conjunction with the following equation:

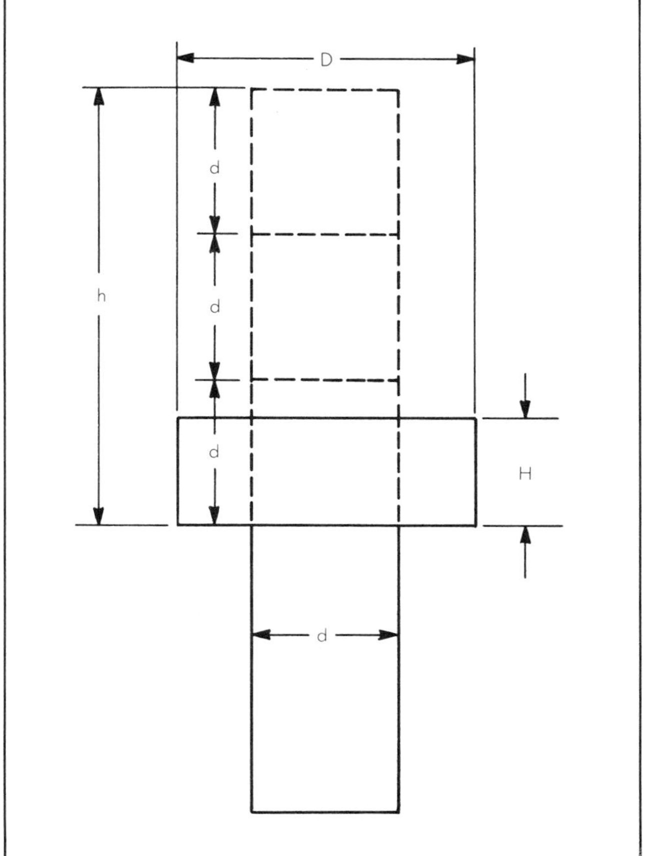

Fig. 13-50 Upset dimensions.

$$n = \frac{W_D H}{W_d d} \tag{8}$$

where:

$W_d$ = unit weight based on stock diameter
$W_D$ = unit weight based on upset diameter

Figure 13-51 gives an example from Table 13-10. In Table 13-10, the unit weight of 0.625" diam $D$ is found by moving to the right across the top row to the column 0.600, then down to the unit weight across from 0.025, which is 0.08694. Next, the unit weight of 0.312" is found by moving across to 0.300, then down to the weight (0.02167) opposite 0.012. By substituting these unit weights in the unit-weight equation, the answer of 3.0 diameters in the upset is found.

If the upset part has a complicated head shape, the following weight method can be used to determine the number of diameters in the head:

1. Accurately weigh the sample.
2. From Table 13-10 or 13-11, find the weight of the stem or shank by looking up the diameter and multiplying it by the shank length.

# COLD AND WARM UPSETTING (HEADING)

3. Subtract this weight from the total weight. The remainder is the weight of the head, or $W_D H$ in the equation. Divide this weight by $W_d d$ to get the number of diameters in the head.

## HEIGHT REDUCTION

The amount of upsetting is sometimes referred to as the reduction in height expressed as a percentage. For example, upsetting bolt and cap-screw heads usually results in a 50-60% reduction in height. Reduction in height is calculated by the equation:

$$\frac{L - H}{L} \times 100 = \text{percent reduction in height} \qquad (9)$$

where:

$L$ = length of stock to be upset, in. or mm
$H$ = height of finished upset, in. or mm

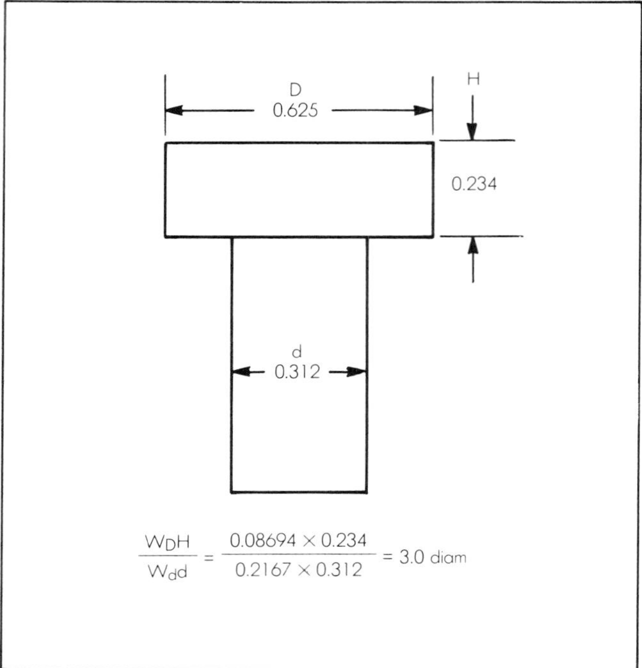


**Fig. 13-51 Example of upsetting illustrating the use of Table 13-10.**

## MATERIALS UPSET

A wide variety of ferrous and nonferrous metals are formed by cold and warm upsetting. The degree of upsetting possible varies for different metals. Desirable chemical compositions, melting practices, and properties, as well as undesirable defects, of metals to be upset are essentially the same as those discussed previously in this chapter for cold and warm extrusion.

Low-carbon steels, containing up to about 0.20% carbon, are the most common for upsetting. This carbon content is too low to permit a marked response to heat treatment, but the steel's strength is substantially improved by cold working. Medium-carbon steels, up to about 0.40-0.45% carbon, respond to quench-and-temper heat treatment. They are fairly easy to cold work, but as their carbon content increases, their capability of being upset decreases. Alloy steels with more than 0.45% carbon fall in the difficult-to-head range. These, plus some grades of stainless steel, present a challenge to upsetting techniques and result in shortened tool life as compared with low-carbon steels. As an aid to forming parts like Phillips screws from this type of material, the wire is sometimes heated as it enters the machine. Heat reduces the yield and tensile strengths of the material, making it easier to head. Copper, aluminum, and their alloys, in most grades, fall into the group of metals that are upset with substantial improvements due to cold working.

**TABLE 13-10**
**English Weights of Unit Lengths of Steel Wire**

| | Weight, 0.001 lb | | | | | | | | |
|---|---|---|---|---|---|---|---|---|---|
| Diam, in. | 0.000 | 0.100 | 0.200 | 0.300 | 0.400 | 0.500 | 0.600 | 0.700 | 0.800 |
| 0.000 | --- | 2.23 | 8.90 | 20.03 | 35.61 | 55.64 | 80.13 | 109.06 | 142.45 |
| 0.001 | --- | 2.27 | 8.99 | 20.17 | 35.79 | 55.87 | 80.39 | 109.38 | 142.81 |
| 0.002 | --- | 2.32 | 9.08 | 20.30 | 35.97 | 56.09 | 80.66 | 109.69 | 143.17 |
| 0.003 | --- | 2.36 | 9.17 | 20.43 | 36.15 | 56.31 | 80.93 | 110.00 | 143.52 |
| 0.004 | --- | 2.41 | 9.26 | 20.57 | 36.33 | 56.53 | 81.20 | 110.31 | 143.88 |
| 0.005 | --- | 2.45 | 9.35 | 20.71 | 36.51 | 56.76 | 81.47 | 110.63 | 144.24 |
| 0.006 | --- | 2.50 | 9.45 | 20.84 | 36.68 | 56.99 | 81.74 | 110.94 | 144.60 |
| 0.007 | --- | 2.55 | 9.54 | 20.98 | 36.87 | 57.21 | 82.01 | 111.26 | 144.95 |
| 0.008 | --- | 2.60 | 9.63 | 21.12 | 37.05 | 57.44 | 82.28 | 111.57 | 145.31 |
| 0.009 | --- | 2.64 | 9.72 | 21.25 | 37.23 | 57.67 | 82.55 | 111.89 | 145.67 |
| 0.010 | --- | 2.69 | 9.82 | 21.39 | 37.41 | 57.89 | 82.82 | 112.20 | 146.03 |
| 0.011 | --- | 2.74 | 9.91 | 21.53 | 37.60 | 58.12 | 83.09 | 112.52 | 146.40 |
| 0.012 | --- | 2.79 | 10.00 | 21.67 | 37.78 | 58.35 | 83.36 | 112.84 | 146.76 |
| 0.013 | --- | 2.84 | 10.10 | 21.81 | 37.96 | 58.58 | 83.64 | 113.15 | 147.12 |
| 0.014 | --- | 2.89 | 10.19 | 21.95 | 38.15 | 58.80 | 83.91 | 113.47 | 147.48 |
| 0.015 | --- | 2.94 | 10.29 | 22.09 | 38.33 | 59.03 | 84.18 | 113.79 | 147.84 |

**TABLE 13-10—*Continued***

| | Weight, 0.001 lb. | | | | | | | | |
|---|---|---|---|---|---|---|---|---|---|
| Diam, in. | 0.000 | 0.100 | 0.200 | 0.300 | 0.400 | 0.500 | 0.600 | 0.700 | 0.800 |
| 0.016 | --- | 2.99 | 10.38 | 22.23 | 38.52 | 59.26 | 84.46 | 114.11 | 148.21 |
| 0.017 | --- | 3.05 | 10.48 | 22.37 | 38.70 | 59.49 | 84.73 | 114.43 | 148.57 |
| 0.018 | --- | 3.10 | 10.58 | 22.51 | 38.89 | 59.72 | 85.01 | 114.75 | 148.93 |
| 0.019 | --- | 3.15 | 10.68 | 22.65 | 39.08 | 59.95 | 85.29 | 115.07 | 149.30 |
| 0.020 | --- | 3.20 | 10.77 | 22.79 | 39.26 | 60.19 | 85.56 | 115.39 | 149.66 |
| 0.021 | --- | 3.26 | 10.87 | 22.93 | 39.45 | 60.41 | 85.84 | 115.71 | 150.03 |
| 0.022 | --- | 3.31 | 10.97 | 23.08 | 39.64 | 60.65 | 86.11 | 116.03 | 150.39 |
| 0.023 | --- | 3.37 | 11.07 | 23.22 | 39.83 | 60.88 | 86.39 | 116.35 | 150.76 |
| 0.024 | --- | 3.42 | 11.17 | 23.37 | 40.01 | 61.12 | 86.67 | 116.67 | 151.13 |
| 0.025 | --- | 3.48 | 11.27 | 23.51 | 40.20 | 61.35 | 86.94 | 116.99 | 151.49 |
| 0.026 | --- | 3.53 | 11.37 | 23.65 | 40.39 | 61.58 | 87.22 | 117.32 | 151.86 |
| 0.027 | --- | 3.59 | 11.47 | 23.80 | 40.58 | 61.82 | 87.50 | 117.64 | 152.23 |
| 0.028 | --- | 3.65 | 11.57 | 23.95 | 40.77 | 62.05 | 87.78 | 117.96 | 152.60 |
| 0.029 | --- | 3.70 | 11.67 | 24.09 | 40.96 | 62.29 | 88.06 | 118.29 | 152.97 |
| 0.030 | --- | 3.76 | 11.77 | 24.24 | 41.16 | 62.52 | 88.34 | 118.61 | 153.34 |
| 0.031 | --- | 3.82 | 11.88 | 24.39 | 41.35 | 62.76 | 88.62 | 118.94 | 153.70 |
| 0.032 | --- | 3.88 | 11.98 | 24.53 | 41.54 | 62.99 | 88.90 | 119.26 | 154.08 |
| 0.033 | --- | 3.94 | 12.08 | 24.68 | 41.73 | 63.23 | 89.19 | 119.59 | 154.44 |
| 0.034 | --- | 4.00 | 12.19 | 24.84 | 41.92 | 63.47 | 89.47 | 119.92 | 154.82 |
| 0.035 | --- | 4.06 | 12.29 | 24.98 | 42.12 | 63.71 | 89.75 | 120.24 | 155.19 |
| 0.036 | 0.288 | 4.12 | 12.40 | 25.13 | 42.31 | 63.95 | 90.03 | 120.56 | 155.56 |
| 0.037 | 0.305 | 4.18 | 12.50 | 25.28 | 42.50 | 64.18 | 90.32 | 120.90 | 155.93 |
| 0.038 | 0.321 | 4.24 | 12.61 | 25.43 | 42.70 | 64.42 | 90.60 | 121.23 | 156.31 |
| 0.039 | 0.338 | 4.30 | 12.71 | 25.58 | 42.90 | 64.66 | 90.88 | 121.56 | 156.68 |
| 0.040 | 0.356 | 4.36 | 12.82 | 25.73 | 43.09 | 64.90 | 91.17 | 121.88 | 157.05 |
| 0.041 | 0.374 | 4.43 | 12.93 | 25.88 | 43.29 | 65.15 | 91.45 | 122.21 | 157.42 |
| 0.042 | 0.393 | 4.49 | 13.04 | 26.03 | 43.48 | 65.39 | 91.74 | 122.54 | 157.79 |
| 0.043 | 0.411 | 4.55 | 13.14 | 26.19 | 43.68 | 65.63 | 92.03 | 122.87 | 158.18 |
| 0.044 | 0.431 | 4.62 | 13.25 | 26.34 | 43.88 | 65.87 | 92.31 | 123.21 | 158.55 |
| 0.045 | 0.451 | 4.68 | 13.36 | 26.49 | 44.07 | 66.11 | 92.60 | 123.54 | 158.93 |
| 0.046 | 0.471 | 4.74 | 13.47 | 26.65 | 44.27 | 66.35 | 92.88 | 123.87 | 159.30 |
| 0.047 | 0.491 | 4.81 | 13.58 | 26.80 | 44.47 | 66.60 | 93.17 | 124.20 | 159.68 |
| 0.048 | 0.513 | 4.88 | 13.69 | 26.96 | 44.67 | 66.84 | 93.46 | 124.53 | 160.06 |
| 0.049 | 0.534 | 4.94 | 13.80 | 27.11 | 44.87 | 67.08 | 93.75 | 124.87 | 160.44 |
| 0.050 | 0.556 | 5.01 | 13.91 | 27.27 | 45.07 | 67.33 | 94.04 | 125.20 | 160.82 |
| 0.051 | 0.579 | 5.07 | 14.02 | 27.42 | 45.27 | 67.57 | 94.33 | 125.53 | 161.19 |
| 0.052 | 0.602 | 5.14 | 14.13 | 27.58 | 45.47 | 67.82 | 94.62 | 125.87 | 161.57 |
| 0.053 | 0.625 | 5.21 | 14.25 | 27.74 | 45.68 | 68.07 | 94.91 | 126.20 | 161.95 |
| 0.054 | 0.649 | 5.28 | 14.36 | 27.89 | 45.88 | 68.31 | 95.20 | 126.54 | 162.33 |
| 0.055 | 0.673 | 5.35 | 14.47 | 28.05 | 46.08 | 68.56 | 95.49 | 126.88 | 162.71 |
| 0.056 | 0.698 | 5.42 | 14.59 | 28.21 | 46.28 | 68.81 | 95.78 | 127.21 | 163.09 |
| 0.057 | 0.723 | 5.49 | 14.70 | 28.37 | 46.48 | 69.05 | 96.08 | 127.55 | 163.47 |
| 0.058 | 0.749 | 5.56 | 14.82 | 28.53 | 46.69 | 69.30 | 96.37 | 127.89 | 163.86 |
| 0.059 | 0.774 | 5.63 | 14.93 | 28.69 | 46.89 | 69.55 | 96.66 | 128.22 | 164.24 |
| 0.060 | 0.801 | 5.70 | 15.05 | 28.85 | 47.10 | 69.80 | 96.95 | 128.56 | 164.62 |
| 0.061 | 0.828 | 5.77 | 15.16 | 29.01 | 47.30 | 70.05 | 97.25 | 128.90 | 165.00 |
| 0.062 | 0.856 | 5.84 | 15.28 | 29.17 | 47.50 | 70.30 | 97.54 | 129.24 | 165.39 |
| 0.063 | 0.883 | 5.91 | 15.40 | 29.33 | 47.71 | 70.55 | 97.84 | 129.54 | 165.77 |
| 0.064 | 0.911 | 5.99 | 15.51 | 29.49 | 47.92 | 70.80 | 98.13 | 129.92 | 166.15 |
| 0.065 | 0.940 | 6.06 | 15.63 | 29.65 | 48.13 | 71.05 | 98.43 | 130.26 | 166.54 |

*(continued)*

**TABLE 13-10—*Continued***

| Diam, in. | Weight, 0.001 lb. | | | | | | | | |
|---|---|---|---|---|---|---|---|---|---|
| | 0.000 | 0.100 | 0.200 | 0.300 | 0.400 | 0.500 | 0.600 | 0.700 | 0.800 |
| 0.066 | 0.970 | 6.13 | 15.75 | 29.82 | 48.33 | 71.30 | 98.73 | 130.59 | 166.93 |
| 0.067 | 0.999 | 6.21 | 15.87 | 29.98 | 48.54 | 71.56 | 99.02 | 130.94 | 167.31 |
| 0.068 | 1.03 | 6.28 | 15.99 | 30.14 | 48.75 | 71.81 | 99.32 | 131.28 | 167.70 |
| 0.069 | 1.06 | 6.36 | 16.11 | 30.31 | 48.96 | 72.07 | 99.62 | 131.63 | 168.08 |
| 0.070 | 1.09 | 6.43 | 16.23 | 30.47 | 49.17 | 72.32 | 99.92 | 131.97 | 168.47 |
| 0.071 | 1.12 | 6.51 | 16.35 | 30.64 | 49.38 | 72.57 | 100.21 | 132.31 | 168.86 |
| 0.072 | 1.15 | 6.58 | 16.47 | 30.80 | 49.59 | 72.82 | 100.51 | 132.65 | 169.25 |
| 0.073 | 1.19 | 6.66 | 16.59 | 30.97 | 49.80 | 73.08 | 100.81 | 133.00 | 169.63 |
| 0.074 | 1.22 | 6.74 | 16.71 | 31.13 | 50.01 | 73.33 | 101.11 | 133.34 | 170.02 |
| 0.075 | 1.25 | 6.82 | 16.83 | 31.30 | 50.22 | 73.59 | 101.41 | 133.69 | 170.41 |
| 0.076 | 1.29 | 6.89 | 16.96 | 31.47 | 50.43 | 73.85 | 101.71 | 134.03 | 170.80 |
| 0.077 | 1.32 | 6.97 | 17.08 | 31.63 | 50.64 | 74.10 | 102.01 | 134.38 | 171.19 |
| 0.078 | 1.35 | 7.05 | 17.20 | 31.80 | 50.86 | 74.36 | 102.32 | 134.72 | 171.58 |
| 0.079 | 1.39 | 7.13 | 17.33 | 31.97 | 51.07 | 74.62 | 102.62 | 135.07 | 171.98 |
| 0.080 | 1.42 | 7.21 | 17.45 | 32.14 | 51.28 | 74.87 | 102.92 | 135.42 | 172.37 |
| 0.081 | 1.46 | 7.29 | 17.58 | 32.31 | 51.50 | 75.13 | 103.22 | 135.77 | 172.76 |
| 0.082 | 1.50 | 7.37 | 17.70 | 32.48 | 51.71 | 75.39 | 103.53 | 136.11 | 173.15 |
| 0.083 | 1.53 | 7.45 | 17.83 | 32.65 | 51.92 | 75.65 | 103.83 | 136.46 | 173.54 |
| 0.084 | 1.57 | 7.54 | 17.95 | 32.82 | 52.14 | 75.91 | 104.14 | 136.81 | 173.94 |
| 0.085 | 1.61 | 7.62 | 18.08 | 32.99 | 52.36 | 76.17 | 104.44 | 137.16 | 174.33 |
| 0.086 | 1.65 | 7.70 | 18.21 | 33.19 | 52.57 | 76.43 | 104.74 | 137.51 | 174.72 |
| 0.087 | 1.68 | 7.78 | 18.33 | 33.33 | 52.79 | 76.69 | 105.05 | 137.86 | 175.12 |
| 0.088 | 1.72 | 7.87 | 18.46 | 33.51 | 53.00 | 76.95 | 105.36 | 138.21 | 175.52 |
| 0.089 | 1.76 | 7.95 | 18.59 | 33.68 | 53.22 | 77.22 | 105.66 | 138.56 | 175.91 |
| 0.090 | 1.80 | 8.03 | 18.72 | 33.85 | 53.44 | 77.48 | 105.97 | 138.91 | 176.31 |
| 0.091 | 1.84 | 8.12 | 18.85 | 34.03 | 53.66 | 77.74 | 106.28 | 139.26 | 176.70 |
| 0.092 | 1.88 | 8.20 | 18.98 | 34.20 | 53.88 | 78.01 | 106.58 | 139.62 | 177.10 |
| 0.093 | 1.92 | 8.29 | 19.11 | 34.38 | 54.10 | 78.27 | 106.89 | 139.97 | 177.50 |
| 0.094 | 1.97 | 8.38 | 19.24 | 34.55 | 54.32 | 78.53 | 107.20 | 140.32 | 177.89 |
| 0.095 | 2.01 | 8.46 | 19.37 | 34.73 | 54.54 | 78.80 | 107.51 | 140.68 | 178.29 |
| 0.096 | 2.05 | 8.55 | 19.50 | 34.90 | 54.76 | 79.06 | 107.81 | 141.03 | 178.69 |
| 0.097 | 2.09 | 8.64 | 19.63 | 35.08 | 54.98 | 79.33 | 108.13 | 141.39 | 179.09 |
| 0.098 | 2.14 | 8.73 | 19.77 | 35.26 | 55.20 | 79.60 | 108.44 | 141.74 | 179.49 |
| 0.099 | 2.18 | 8.81 | 19.90 | 35.43 | 55.42 | 79.86 | 108.75 | 142.09 | 179.89 |

**TABLE 13-11**
**Metric Weights of Unit Lengths of Steel Wire**

| Diam, mm | Weight, g | Diam, mm | Weight, g | Diam, mm | Weight, g |
|---|---|---|---|---|---|
| 1.6 | 0.0556 | 5.5 | 0.6576 | 14 | 4.2610 |
| 1.8 | 0.0704 | 6 | 0.7826 | 15 | 4.8915 |
| 2 | 0.0870 | 6.5 | 0.9185 | 16 | 5.5654 |
| 2.2 | 0.1052 | 7 | 1.0652 | 17 | 6.2828 |
| 2.5 | 0.1359 | 7.5 | 1.2229 | 18 | 7.0437 |
| 2.8 | 0.1704 | 8 | 1.3914 | 19 | 7.8481 |
| 3 | 0.1957 | 9 | 1.7609 | 20 | 8.6960 |
| 3.5 | 0.2663 | 10 | 2.1740 | 21 | 9.5873 |
| 4 | 0.3478 | 11 | 2.6305 | 22 | 10.5221 |
| 4.5 | 0.4402 | 12 | 3.1305 | 23 | 11.5004 |
| 5 | 0.5435 | 13 | 3.6740 | 24 | 12.5222 |
| | | | | 25 | 13.5874 |

The microstructure of steel also affects its upsettability. Cold working can sometimes take place prior to heading during the wire-drawing process. The metal work-hardens, and tensile strength increases over its hot-rolled condition. For difficult-to-form materials or severe deformation, annealing after drawing can be specified. For optimum formability, steel should be spheroidize annealed.

While some ductile metals are upset without a lubricant, most metals are lubricated. Zinc phosphate coating and soap lubricants, or oils, discussed previously in this chapter for cold and warm extrusion, are commonly employed.

## APPLICATIONS OF UPSETTING

Upsetting, often combined with extruding, trimming, thread rolling, and other operations, has long been employed for the production of nails, bolts, screws, nuts, rivets, and other fasteners. More recently, the process has been applied to the low-cost, mass production of many other components. Parts being manufactured in this way include pipe fittings and plugs, spark-plug shells, ball studs, shafts, bearing pins and spacers, and wrist pins.

Other components being produced by upsetting include cams, gears, worms, ratchets, hose clamps, electrical terminals, ordnance parts, balls and rollers, and shifter forks. The process is also being used extensively to form slugs to required size and shape for subsequent extruding, forming, or machining. Upsetting tests the quality of the starting material, opening any surface seams and eliminating the need for further processing.

Upsetting can also be used to bend or flatten metal on specific parts of the blanks. However, this is usually done on only one end of each blank unless double-end machines are employed. To form shanks having cross sections other than round, wire or rod of the required cross section is sometimes used. In other cases, shanks are shaped by pressing round stock into dies of the desired shape.

## METHODS OF UPSETTING

Most upsetting is done on horizontal mechanically powered machines, often called headers or formers, described later in this section. The process is also performed on conventional vertical presses and special machines, powered either mechanically or hydraulically, with the starting metal unheated (cold upsetting) or heated (warm upsetting). Mechanical presses are generally preferred for forming because of their higher production capability, but they cost more than hydraulic presses of comparable force capacity. Hydraulic presses generally provide longer tool life when cold forming; for warm forming, the longer contact time between the tools and the workpieces tends to shorten punch life. Hot upsetting is discussed in Chapter 15, "Hot Forging."

### Warm Upsetting

Heating the metal to a temperature below its recrystallization temperature adds to the capabilities of upsetting. Most metals undergo a drastic reduction in tensile strength and increase in formability when heated to a temperature range of about 1100-1300° F (600-700° C). This is especially important in forming alloy steels, some stainless steels, and other metals having high tensile strengths, or in making parts that require considerable deformation.

Warm upsetting reduces force requirements, permitting a smaller press (about 20-30% less force capacity) to produce the same formed part by cold upsetting. For parts requiring more than one operation, warm upsetting generally eliminates the need for reannealing, recoating, and relubricating. Another important advantage is minimized die breakage because of reduced loading on the tooling, but faster tool wear generally occurs because of the higher contact temperatures. Good lubricant coating of the workpiece and tooling is also more difficult.

A limitation with respect to warm upsetting is the need for heating the metal, which adds to production costs. Induction heating is the most popular method for heating material for warm upsetting, especially when higher temperatures are required, but resistance heating is used for some applications. Another possible limitation of warm upsetting is that higher cost tooling materials with heat-resistant properties are generally required. The tendency of the slugs to buckle also increases with higher temperatures, due to reduction in column strength.

### Controlled-Flow Heading

Many applications of cold or warm extrusion require so-called "pancake-type" slugs having a thickness considerably less than their diameter. An economical method of producing such slugs is to shear them from small-diameter stock and upset them to the required diameter and thickness. To accomplish upsetting in a single stroke on standard vertical presses, Verson Allsteel Press Co. has developed a technique called controlled-flow heading. This process permits upsetting of sheared slugs having length-to-diameter ratios in excess of the standard limits of 2 1/2 or 3:1 for conventional heading. The process can also be used for the production of finished parts.

In controlled-flow heading, slugs are upset after they are guided in a die. A typical die stack is shown in Fig. 13-52. In this application, slugs 3/4" (19 mm) diam x 3" (76 mm) long, sheared from AISI 5120 steel bar stock, are upset into pancake shaped slugs 2 1/8" (54 mm) diam x 3/8" (9.5 mm) thick in a single press stroke. Sheared slugs are inserted through the top of a restraining guide bushing and fall through the bushing bore against an anvil. The guide bushing is supported within its retainer at a predetermined height by a cushion mounted under the press bolster.

As the press ram descends, the punch upsets the slug within the controlled space which the cushion maintains between the bushing and anvil. When the lower face of the punch holder contacts the top face of the guide bushing (at which point, the leading edge of the punch coincides with the lower face of the guide bushing), the punch and bushing move downward as a single unit against the action of the cushion. This movement

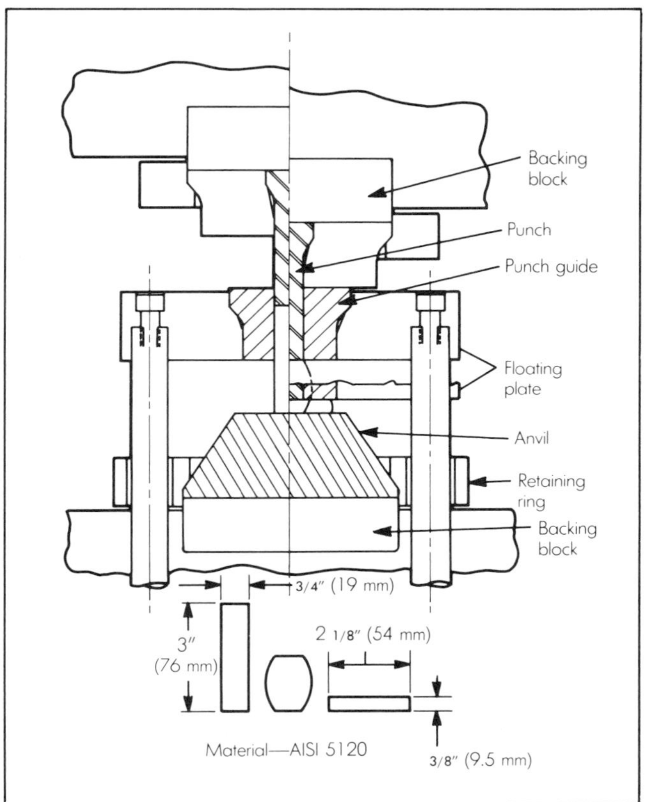


**Fig. 13-52 Typical die stack for controlled-flow heading.** (*Verson Allsteel Press Co.*)

continues until the press reaches the bottom of its stroke, thus completely forming the pancake slug.

On the upward stroke of the press ram, the cushion forces the bushing to follow the punch holder to a predetermined height, thus leaving the pancake slug free to be swept off the anvil, clearing the die for the next part. After the bushing comes to rest at this height, the punch and press ram continue moving upward, thus providing an opening for insertion of the next sheared slug.

When designing tool stacks for controlled-flow heading, it is important that sufficient adjustment be provided to allow precise setting of the distance between guide bushing and anvil. Since this distance represents the length of unsupported column in the controlled-flow process, it is usually necessary to determine the initial distance by tryout. However, the final distance established should be that which produces the most satisfactory results on headed parts.

To maintain close control of diameters of pancake slugs, a floating restraining member can be mounted on top of the anvil to limit radial flow of material. However, it is not advisable to restrain the slug over its entire length or thickness, since this would trap material, would increase force requirements, and could lead to die damage in the event of an over-volume slug.

### Cold-Flow Forming

Gleason Machine Div. has developed a patented G-Flow machine for cold-flow forming. The machine has three working elements: a ram punch, an anvil, and a power pad, each hydraulically driven and activated independently by an electronic solid-state control system. All three elements are programmable for velocity, displacement, and force. In cold-flow forming, the slug is subjected to pressure by the ram and anvil punches until it reaches a plastic state. The material then flows until the part is fully formed. The metal may flow backward, forward, or radially under this steady, uniformly controlled pressure.

In typical closed-die systems (see Fig. 13-53, *a* and *b*), the stationary die nib and the power pad clamp together to form a two-piece die. The ram punch and the anvil travel from opposite sides to form the part in the closed die. In an open-die system (view *c*), the dies are initially closed, the ram punch and the anvil travel from opposite sides, and the power pad retracts under the working pressure to control flow of the metal. The controlled pressures exerted on the slug from both directions allows the formation of complex shapes with close tolerances and allows the formation of thin-walled parts without rupture.

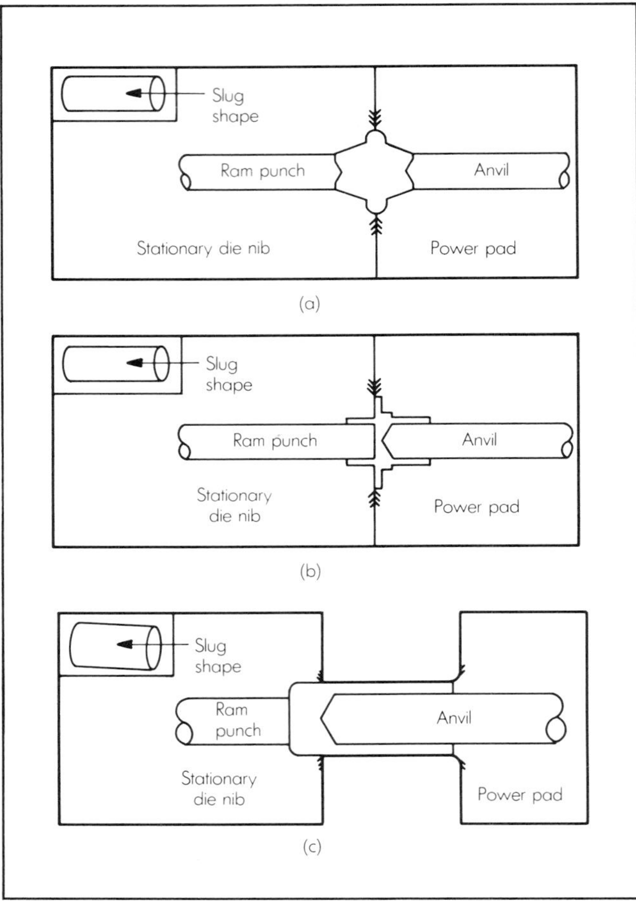


**Fig. 13-53 Cold-flow forming: closed-die systems (views a and b), and open-die system (view c).** (*Gleason Machine Div.*)

### Orbital Forming

Orbital forming, a relatively new process of cold forging, is a method for producing shapes by lateral upsetting or vertical displacement, or by a combination of these operations. An upset ratio of 4:1 can be obtained. Metal is plastically deformed progressively between a lower die moved vertically by a hydraulic ram and an orbiting upper die having a conical working face (see Fig. 13-54). Since there is no impact between the tooling and workpiece, the process is quiet; and because only a small area is formed at a time, pressure requirements are low (about one-fourth of normal forging pressures). The axis of the upper die is inclined, usually at an angle of 1-2°. Hot orbital forming is discussed in Chapter 15, "Hot Forging."

Applications include forming flanges on shafts and tubing, in addition to intricate parts, such as gears, hubs, and pins. Further densification of PM parts is also achieved. The process is particularly suitable for parts that have thin cross sections in relation to their diameters. Four types of upper die movement are available. Orbital motion is best for round parts, especially if considerable reduction of thickness is needed on the periphery. A spiral motion is used for round parts having complex shapes in their center portions. Planetary motion is best suited for round parts with lugs, ribs, gear teeth, or fins. A straight-line movement is used for asymmetrical parts when metal flow has to be directed in a specific direction.

## MACHINES FOR UPSETTING

Horizontal machines (presses) for upsetting are generally called headers or formers. They are available in small to large sizes, with varying degrees of capability. With a blank held in a stationary die on a horizontal press, the end protruding from the face of the die is struck axially by an upsetting tool. Since only so much metal can be formed in one blow, the number of dies, blows, and wire-size capacities usually describe specific machines. Most machines have automatic wire feeding, cutoff, transferring, and kickout capabilities. Horizontal upsetters or heading machines are similar to the forging machines used for hot forging, described in Chapter 15, "Hot Forging."

### Single-Stroke Headers

These machines have one die and one punch. They make

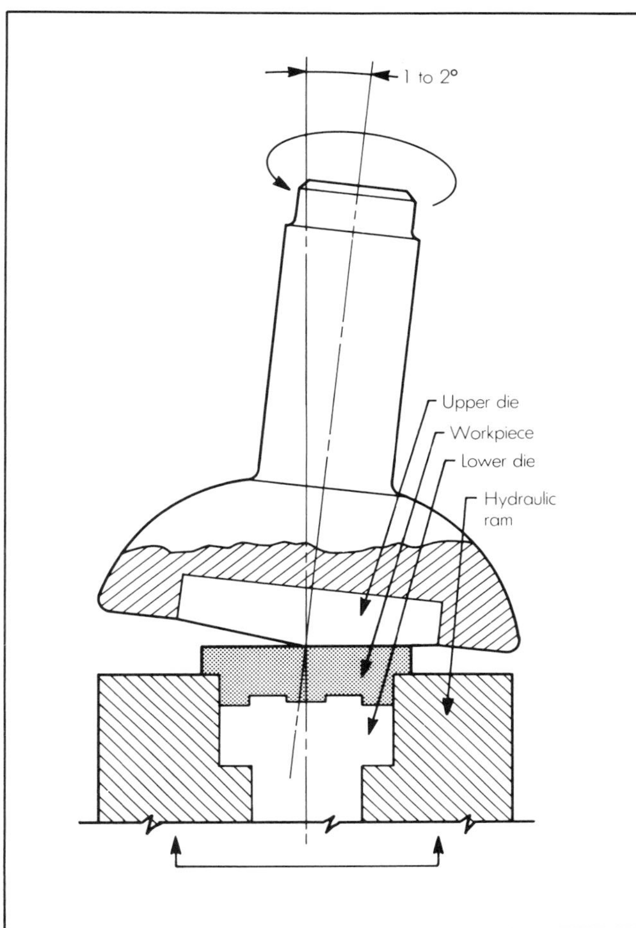


**Fig. 13-54 In orbital forming, the upper die has a conical working face.** (*VSI Automation*)

simple parts that can be formed on one blow. Ball headers are a variation of this type of machine. Speeds range up to 900 parts per minute. Double-stroke headers have one die and two punches. Cone and finish punches change position between blows. This is the most popular machine for producing screw blanks and other fasteners. Wire-capacity sizes range up to 3/4" (19 mm), and machines are also built as slug headers. High-speed, double-stroke headers produce up to 550 parts per minute. Some tubular rivet headers are double-stroke machines with mechanisms specially designed for heading and extruding semitubular rivets.

Three-blow, two-die headers have two dies and three punches. Of basic double-stroke header design, these headers offer the added advantage of allowing extruding or upsetting to be performed in the first die before double-blow heading or heading and trimming are performed in the second die. They produce large-headed, small-shanked, special parts by combining trapped extrusion and upsetting in one simple machine. They are also suitable for stepped parts when transfer between dies would be difficult.

### Progressive or Transfer Headers

These upsetters are multistation machines with two, three, four, five, or more dies and a like number of tools. A transfer unit moves workpieces from the cutter through a succession of dies, either straight through, with end-for-end turnaround between stations, or a combination of the two. Multiple upsetting blows combined with extrusion, piercing, and trimming make these versatile machines ideal for producing long-shank or complex-shaped parts. Sizes range up to 1 3/16" (30 mm) diam and 25 3/4" (654 mm) in length under the head.

Three or four-die headers combining heading, trimming, pointing, and threading in one machine are referred to as boltmakers. They are the accepted machine for making completely finished hex-head cap screws. Their versatility has led them to be the leading producers of threaded special parts. Sizes range up to 1 1/4" (32 mm).

New high-speed boltmakers offer two to three times greater output of standard hex-head cap screws. Cold nut formers are four and five-die machines specially designed for producing standard and special nuts. The simple, production-proved transfer unit can turn nut blanks end for end between dies or can transfer them straight through. This allows working the metal on both sides for well-filled, high-quality nut blanks with insignificant waste of metal. Sizes include to 2" (51 mm) and larger. Some machines designed to produce long-shank parts have provisions for setup changeover to produce nut-type parts.

## TOOLING FOR UPSETTING

Design and material selection for tooling are critical for successful and economical upsetting. Various tooling components required include those for cutoff, coning, and kickout.

### Cutoff Tooling

Good cutoff quality is important to accurate upsetting. Ends with a minimum of distortion are easier on tooling, provide better control of metal flow, and give good ends on the finished parts. Quality of the cutoff blank is determined by the type of wire used (its material and hardness), the type of cutoff tooling, and the type of cutoff quill (or stationary cutter) in the die block and by the movement of a cutter insert in a plate mounted on a slide or lever. The wire feeds through both quill and cutter to a stationary stock gage or stop (see Fig. 13-55). The inside diameter of the quill should be about 1% larger than wire size, and the inside diameter of the cutter should be about 1/2% larger than the quill hole (or 1 1/2% more than the wire). Clearance between the cutter and the quill varies with the type of material being sheared. As a starting point in determining clearance, the wire diameter should be multiplied by a factor of

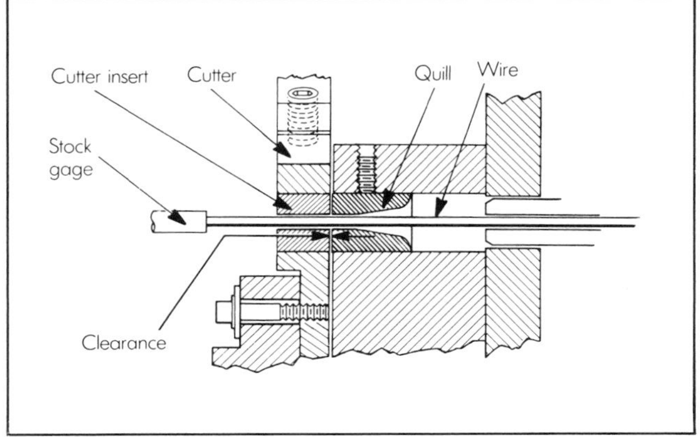


**Fig. 13-55 Wire cutoff method used on typical heading machines.**

0.020. Soft-steel wires may require more clearance, and harder wires usually shear best with less. Cutoff quality determines final clearance.

## Cone Tool Design

The importance of the cone operation cannot be overstressed. Just as the preparation of the wire is of prime importance, the cone operation is the foundation upon which the final upset is to be built. The function of a coning operation in two-blow heading is to reduce the amount of unsupported length to less than 2 1/4 times the average cone diameter for the finish blow. As shown in Fig. 13-56, $(E + F) - J = 2\ 1/4$ or less. This amount of unsupported length upsets satisfactorily in the second blow.

Figure 13-56 also shows the detail of the cone tool design and cone upset. Cone tool design is very specific; in attempting a two-blow upset, some bending takes place in the first blow and the cone tool holds this bending to acceptable limits.

Diameter $B$ in the cone tool (see Fig. 13-56) is only 0.001-0.002" (0.03-0.05 mm) larger than the wire diameter. Distance $G + H$ is the unsupported length at the start of upsetting. If the die is counterbored, distance $G + H$ must include the depth of the counterbore because this depth adds to the unsupported length. In this case, $H$ may become greater than $G$, requiring a sliding cone tool (discussed later in this section).

As stated previously, 4 1/2 stock diameters can be upset in two blows, whereas strict adherence to the rules shown in Fig. 13-56 would appear to allow only 3 1/4 diameters. The rules are safe, but very often exceeded. For example, diameter $C$ might be increased to diameter $B$ times 1.33, and the 2 1/4 times mean diameter equal to cone length might be stretched to 2.4 or 2.5 times the mean diameter. Just the combination of these two increases would allow approximately four diameters in stock length to be upset in two blows. It should be kept in mind that concentricity, appearance, grain-flow characteristics, or general quality of the part must be sacrificed with each stretch of a rule. In some cases, such a sacrifice may not matter, but in others it may be a disadvantage.

The means of obtaining the rest of the 4 1/2 diameters of stock in two blows is by bellmouthing the cone tool as shown in Fig. 13-57. First the buckle point of the stock, which is halfway between the points of support $A/2$, is determined. Next the cone tool is located at the start-of-cone-upset position. The one tool can be bellmouthed in front of the buckle point, thus allowing more stock in the cone. This bellmouthing must be done with care; otherwise, an abrupt transition from the shallow angle of the cone to the bellmouth slope causes the finished upset to have a cold shut (a fold or lap where the material has folded back upon itself). Controlling the buckle point is the prime consideration in making a cone tool that adequately controls the stock. According to the equations in Fig. 13-56, the angle of the sides of the cone varies depending on the amount of stock to be upset. The diameter of the cone at the buckle point should be no larger than necessary to make either the next cone or the finished upset, as the case may be.

If the die is counterbored, it can cause the buckle point of the unsupported stock to fall close to or outside the front end of the cone tool, resulting in a defective cone upset (see the left-hand view in Fig. 13-58). To correct this condition, a sliding cone tool must be used, even though there are fewer than 4 1/2 diameters of unsupported stock initially. This permits the cone tool to move forward of the buckle point (see Fig. 13-58, right-hand view).

As stated previously, 2 1/4 diameters of material can be upset in one blow. This procedure works well for rivets and other simple parts. However, coning before finish heading, even for upsets with less than two diameters' volume, adds extra control and helps produce more concentric and uniform heads. Many first blows are not cone-shaped but are actually preforms. Figure 13-59 shows a few typical examples of coned and finished head shapes for two-blow heading. The shape of the cone punch, in these examples, is usually determined by the shape of the finished head. Figure 13-60 shows an example of a part progressively coned in multiple dies.

**Fixed cone tools.** Figure 13-61, *a*, shows a typical assembly of a fixed cone tool; a hard plate is used to distribute load and protect machine parts, and the pin in the tool is separate to facilitate toolmaking and easy replacement. View *b* illustrates a

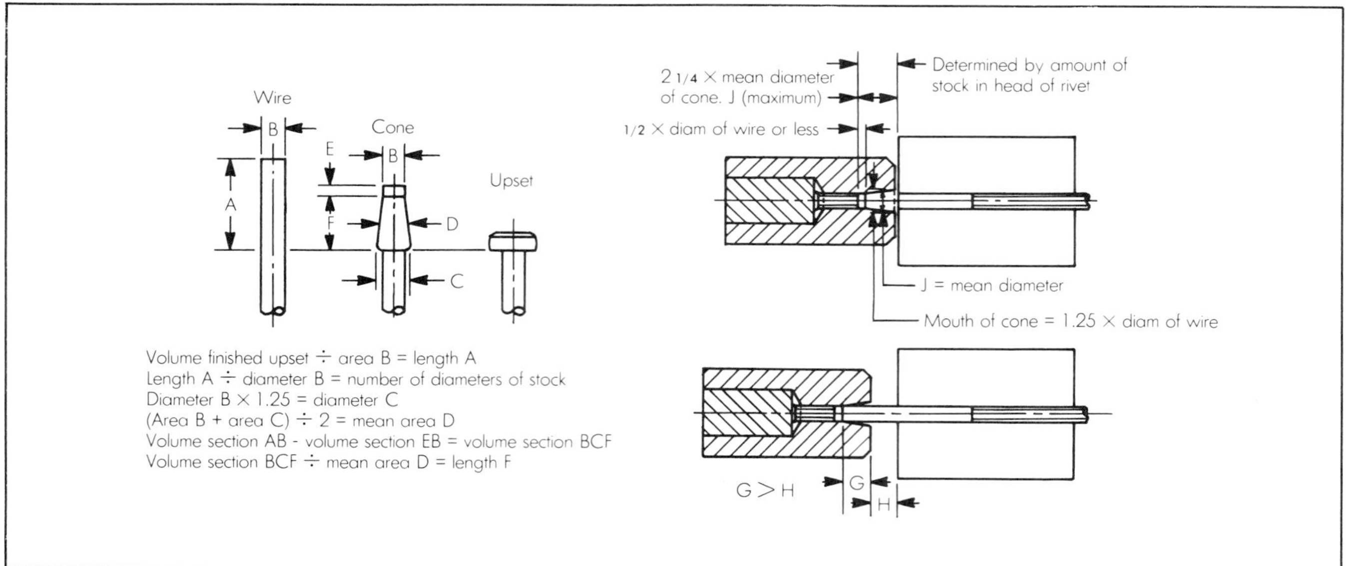


**Fig. 13-56 Two-blow upsetting sequence showing the relationship of the cone dimensions.**

fixed tool with a spring pin, necessary when the blank length is short. Transfer fingers, used to move the blank to the die, must retain control until the blank is pushed into the die far enough to keep it from falling. The spring pin, being advanced from the forming position, moves the blank into the die sooner, thus allowing more time for the transfer fingers to move out of the way of the advancing cone tool. Once the blank seats in the die, the cone pin moves to the same position as shown in view *a*. View *c* shows a sliding cone tool for upsetting long lengths or for controlling concentricity. View *d* shows the spring pin and sliding tool combined for upsetting large heads on short shanks.

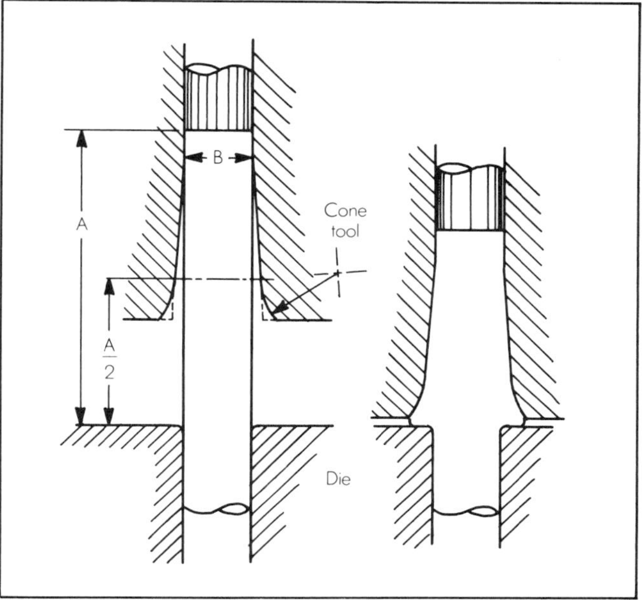


**Fig. 13-57 Cone-tool bellmouthing.**

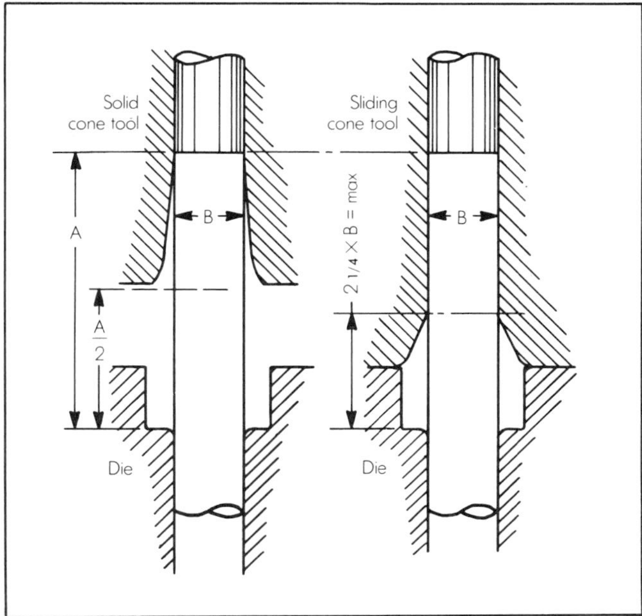


**Fig. 13-58 Counterbored cone tools: solid (left) and sliding (right).**

**Sliding cone tools.** Figure 13-62 shows three steps in the operation of a sliding cone tool with a spring pin. Although this assembly is the most complicated, it is also the most versatile. As stated previously, about six diameters of material can be upset in two blows with such a tool. As shown in view *a*, a spring behind the cone tool holds it forward in the holder to the limit of the notch against a tangent pin. A second spring holds the cone pin forward and works in the same manner. In view *a*, the blank is about to be pushed into the die. In view *b*, the blank is fully in the die and the cone tool; metal flow is about to begin. At this point, length *R* is the only length unsupported outside the die, and it is 2 1/4 diameters or less. The cone tool supports the rest of the length. As the heading slide continues forward, the cone-tool pin pushes the metal out of the straight bore into the cone-tool cavity, as shown in view *c*. In this manner up to six diameters of material can be upset in two blows by leaving only 2 1/4 mean diameters unsupported after the first blow.

The sliding cone tool offers two advantages; it permits large upsets and provides better control of metal flow and therefore more concentric upsets. The sliding cone tool is frequently ideal for upsets of less than four or even two diameters because of added control. For example, in the first blow on recessed-drive screw heads, most of the head shape is established in the cone blow, and concentric upsets are essential.

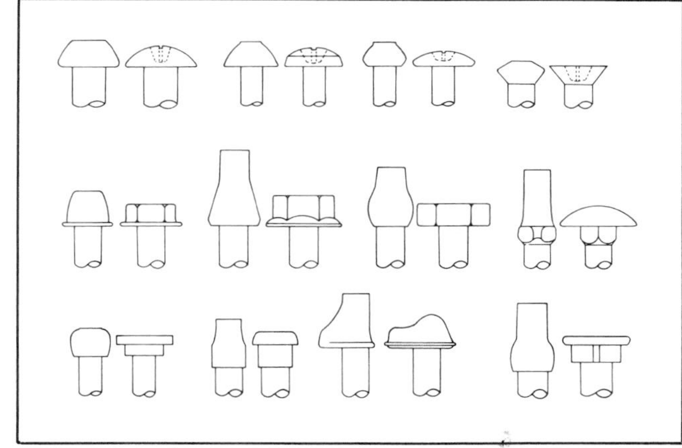

**Fig. 13-59 Coned and finished head shapes for two-blow upsetting.**

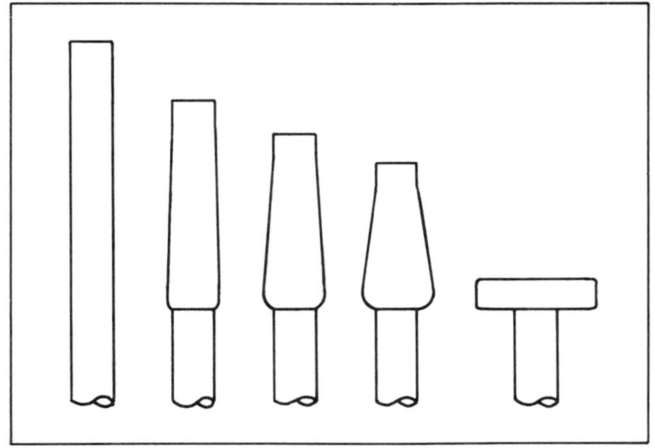

**Fig. 13-60 Steps in progressive multiple-die coning.**

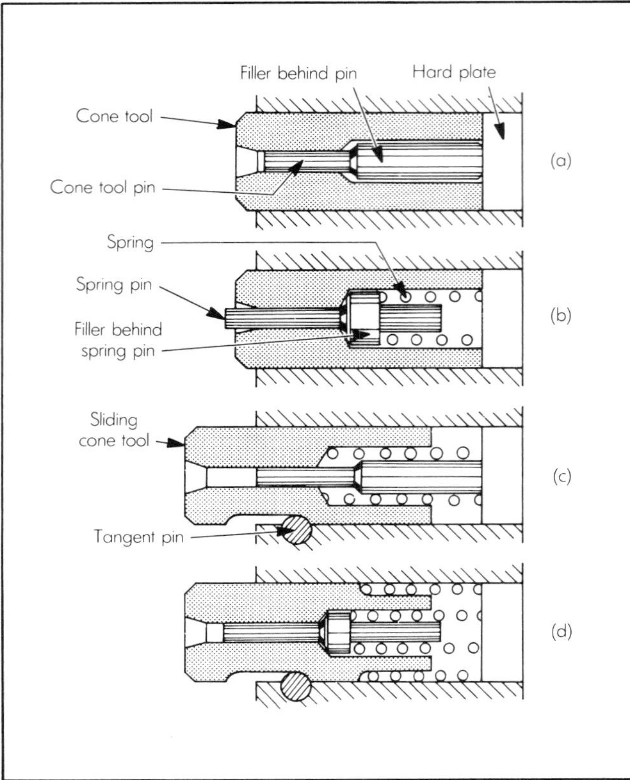


Fig. 13-61 Typical cone tools: (a) fixed, (b) fixed with spring pins, (c) sliding, and (d) combination sliding and spring pin.

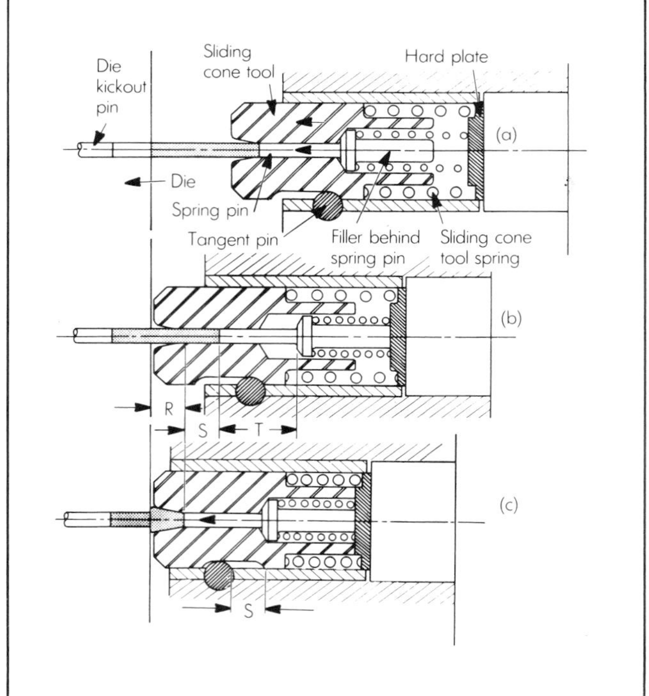


Fig. 13-62 Sequence of operations of sliding cone tool with spring pin.

The maximum amount of slide, *S* in view *b* of Fig. 13-62, is normally three to four diameters or less. However, the amount of slide should be no more than required to make the upset. The end positions of the pin before and after sliding indicate the amount of slide required. The amount of slide actually used is the length of the tangent pin slot, *S* in view *c*, and should be equal to *S* in view *b*. The pin length, *T*, should be no longer than necessary for the amount of tool slide used plus about three pin diameters in length retained in the tool bore for guidance.

Cold headers are built precisely to allow the maximum length of cutoff to transfer between the cone tool and the die before the cone tool contacts the blank. Since the sliding cone tool extends forward of its normal position, the amount of slide must be subtracted from the maximum blank length that the machine can normally transfer. Otherwise, the cone tool hits the end of the blank as it approaches the die. This also applies to a spring pin in the cone tool if it projects beyond the face of the tool.

## Kickout Pins

When the workpiece has been headed, it must be ejected by a kickout pin to clear the die for the next blank. At the start of the operation, the blank enters the die until the kickout pin stops it and upsetting begins. Therefore, the kickout pin must support some of the upsetting pressure as shown in Fig. 13-63, *a*. If the unsupported length of the kickout pin is more than 10-12 diameters, it tends to bend or break under upsetting pressure or kickout load. However, the second function of the kickout pin is to eject the part from the die, and pin length is even more critical (and apparent) when the blank is die-pointed, as shown in view *b*. Even though the part diameter and length are unchanged, the kickout pin is smaller in diameter and therefore weaker. In such a case, the die supports some of the upsetting load, but the pin would probably fail quickly from kickout loads.

When more than 10 or 12 unsupported diameters of pin length are necessary, a supported kickout-pin assembly is recommended. Figure 13-64 shows the kickout pin for 17 diameters of die kickout length. The center support, *A*, reduces the unsupported length to less than 10 or 12 diameters on each side of the center support. During the kickout stroke, the kickout-pin head, *C*, moves against support *A*. The support, being pinned to the telescoping sleeve, *B*, moves with the pin head to complete the kickout stroke. As the kickout pin moves out of the die for the next blow, the kickout pin pushes the filler, *D*, against the shoulder in sleeve *B*, returning support *A* to its center position.

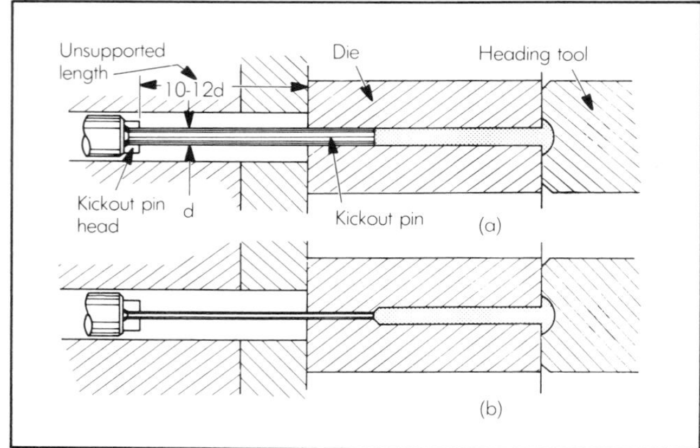


Fig. 13-63 Unsupported kickout pins.

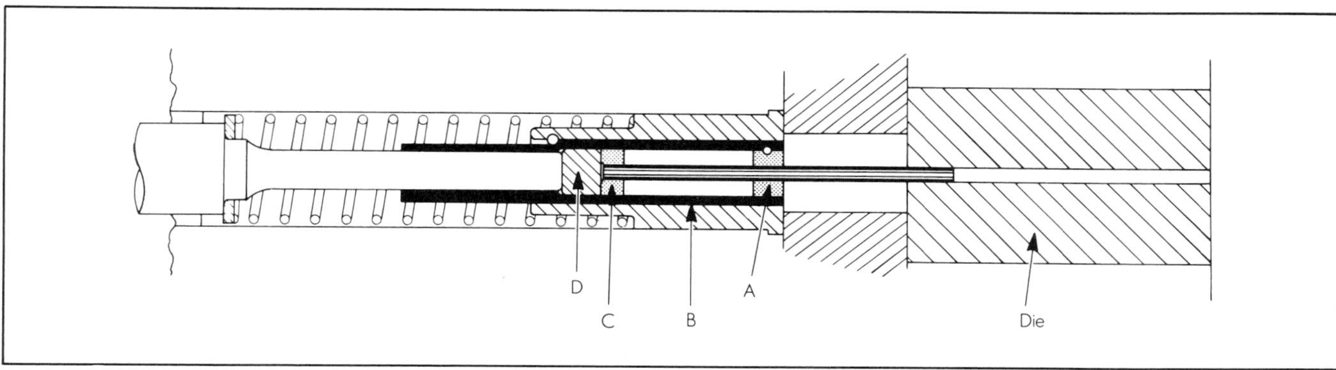


**Fig. 13-64 Supported knockout-pin assembly.**

Kickout-pin breakage is also often due to poor stock lubrication. A coating may be used to lubricate the workpiece, but a rough or rusted surface makes the workpiece difficult to kick from the die; so the wire coating should be smooth and clean.

As the end of the kickout pin wears, it is possible for metal to extrude around it. This can cause a tight spot in the die where the pin and workpiece overlap, resulting in enough pressure to break the pin. The same effect occurs when the diameter of the kickout pin is too large. Because the pin stops the workpiece when it enters the die, it often absorbs the heading pressures. If the pin is too large (fits the die too closely), the end of the pin can swell and bind in the die. A back taper in the die (a smaller inner diameter at the die face than toward the kickout) may allow the metal to upset to a larger diameter at the end of the shank rather than under the head. The kickout pin must then try to force this larger diameter through a smaller hole during kickout; and if the pressure to kick the part becomes too great, the pin may break. Excessive kickout pressure can also be created by machining rings left in the die. The inside of the die should be smooth and free of rust or machining marks.

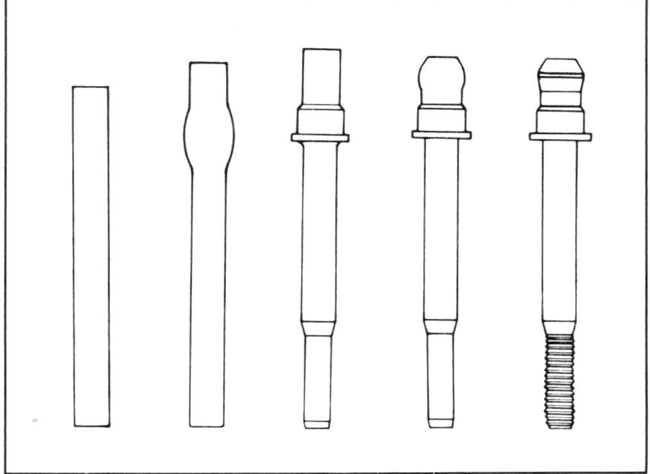

**Fig. 13-65 Spark-plug center post produced by progressive upsetting.**

## Special Tooling

Great strides are taking place in upsetting capabilities as experience increases with the growth in the variety of tool materials and designs used. The part in Fig. 13-65 exemplifies unique tool design and points out the versatility and range of upsetting. This drawing shows the progression of upsets and extrusions to make a spark-plug center post. The small diameter between two large diameters on the head is usually expected to require a secondary cutting operation.

Figure 13-66 shows how a third punch makes this secondary upset. As the punch case approaches the die, an air-loaded pin pushes the blank into the die (view *a*). Inserts mounted to a taper in the punch case are held forward (open) by air pressure. The punch case continues to advance until the inserts touch the die, after which the die forces the inserts back along the taper to the closed position (view *b*). At this point, the punch case remains stationary and the inserts have formed a cavity for the

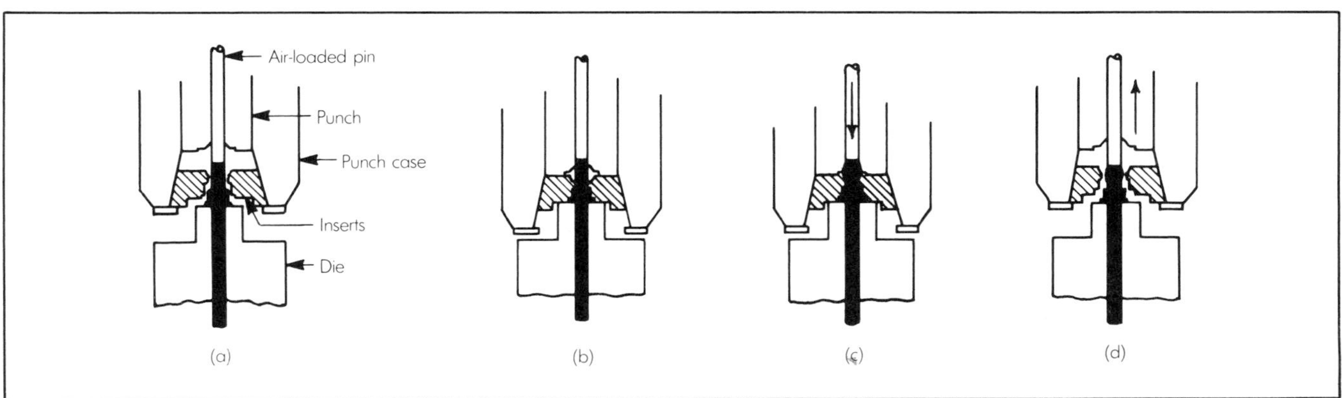


**Fig. 13-66 Steps in the formation of a secondary upset on the part shown in Fig. 13-65.**

# COLD AND WARM UPSETTING (HEADING)

metal to flow into. The pin continues to advance and upset metal into this cavity, forming the head and the second upset (view *c*).

As the punch case withdraws from the die (see Fig. 13-66), the inserts move to their forward (open) position, allowing the inserts to clear the largest diameter of upset (view *d*). After the blank is formed in the third die, it is transferred to the last die position, from which it is blown up a tube to tracks leading to the machine's integrated threader. In the threader, concentric rings are rolled on the end of the post and a final roll-coining operation is performed on the head by the same set of dies. A finished center post falls from the rolling station at each stroke of the machine.

## Tooling Materials

Selection of materials for upsetting tools is usually governed by personal preference and experience. Since tooling is perishable, some users consider more costly, longer lasting tools more economical, especially for long production runs. Others feel lower cost and shorter tool life are more practical. The decision is usually based on the shape of the upset part, the type of material used in the part, and the quantity of parts needed. Table 13-12 lists a few typical materials for header tooling and their heat treatment.

Carbides are frequently used for long-run jobs or tough-to-form materials. Sometimes carbides are the only tool materials that last satisfactorily. Carbides are hard and strong; however, as their hardness increases for wear resistance, their rupture strength decreases. The best grade of carbide for the job is one that is as hard as possible without breaking apart under the heading impact. Carbides used for cutters and cutoff quills need good wearing quality, while their impact resistance is of less importance; consequently, in obtaining higher impact resistance with a carbide die upsetting insert, hardness may be sacrificed.

Because one-piece dies for upsetting are large and carbides are expensive, smaller carbide inserts are mounted in steel casings. The casing has two functions: it positions the small, less-costly insert, and it provides support. It is usually made of a very tough material. The insert presses into a smaller hole in the case. The amount of interference fit depends on the inner and outer diameters of the insert and the outer diameter of the casing. Carbide-tooling suppliers can provide details, and additional information is provided in Chapter 2, "Die and Mold Materials."

## SAFETY CONSIDERATIONS

Safety requirements for the construction, care, and use of cold headers and cold formers are presented in ANSI Standard B11.7.

**TABLE 13-12**
**Typical Steels and Heat Treatments for Upsetting Dies and Tools**

| Tooling Components | Type of Steel | Heat Treatment |
|---|---|---|
| Quills, cone punches, finish punches, dies | Water-hardening tool steel, AISI Type W1 | Heat to 1475° F (802° C), water quench, draw at 450° F (232° C). . .$R_C$58-60 |
| Cone punches, finish punches, dies for wire 1/4" (6.4 mm) diam and smaller | Air-hardening tool steel, AISI Type A2 | Heat to 1775° F (968° C), cool in air, draw at 450° F (232° C). . .$R_C$59-61 |
| Cutters (open), fillers | Special-purpose tool steel, AISI Type L6 | Heat to 1475° F (802° C), oil quench, draw at 350° F (177° C). . .$R_C$58-60 |
| Kickout pins, cutters (solid) | Oil-hardening tool steel, AISI Type O1 | Heat to 1475° F (802° C), oil quench to 400° F (204° C), cool in air to room temperature, draw at 400° F. . .$R_C$59-61 |
| Extrusion inserts | Tungsten-type high-speed tool steel, AISI Type T1 | Preheat to 1450° F (788° C), transfer to high heat. . .2300° F (1260° C), air quench, draw at 1050° F (566° C), air cool, redraw at 1120° F (604° C), air cool. . .$R_C$60-61 |
| Kickout-pin heads | SAE 4140 | Heat to 1500° F (816° C), oil quench, draw at 850° F (454° C). . .$R_C$43-45 |
| Piercer pins | Tungsten-type high-speed tool steel, AISI Type T4 | Same treatment at T1. . .$R_C$61-62 |
| Cases for die inserts | Chromium-type, hot-work tool steel, AISI Type H13 | Heat to 1850° F (1010° C), air cool, draw at 1025° F (552° C), air cool, two redraws at 1025° F, air cool. . .$R_C$47-51 (Note: Steel tends to decarburize; atmosphere-controlled furnace recommended) |

# AUTOMATIC COLD AND WARM FORMING

Automatic cold and warm forming is done on completely automated, multistation machines equipped with a high-speed device for automatically transferring parts through a series of punch and die setups. Operations commonly performed on these machines include extruding and upsetting (discussed previously in this chapter), shearing (cutoff), coining, piercing, trimming, threading, and knurling. Hot forming is discussed in Chapter 15, "Hot Forging."

## ADVANTAGES AND LIMITATIONS

Advantages and limitations of automatic forming are similar to those given earlier in this chapter for extruding and upsetting. A major advantage is cost savings resulting from reduced material requirements and handling, the elimination or reduction of subsequent machining, and high production rates. Other benefits include improved physical properties, smooth surface finishes, and close tolerances of the parts formed.

An additional advantage of automatic forming, compared to extruding and heading, is the capability of performing more operations in the same setup. Production rates on automatic forming machines vary from about 35 to as many as 120 parts per minute, depending upon the size and shape of the parts, and the material being formed.

Possible limitations of automatic forming are the size and shape of the parts that can be produced (discussed next in this section) and the need for substantial production requirements to make the process economical. The substantial cost of automatic forming machines and necessary tooling makes high production requirements essential. However, advances in machine design and controls have reduced the time required for changeover, thus making shorter production runs feasible.

## PART SHAPES AND SIZES FORMED

Symmetrical parts having solid, hollow, or cup-shaped cross sections are the most economical to form and the most widely produced. However, parts with other geometries, including noncircular and complex-shaped components are also formed, but at higher cost.

Cylindrical parts are the most common shapes produced by automatic forming, but components having square, rectangular, hexagonal, oval, tapered, splined, or toothed surfaces, as well as multiple diameters, are also formed. Projections or depressions can be formed on or in one or both faces and can be flat, conical, hemispherical, or other shape. Figure 13-67 illustrates a part produced by shearing, combination forward and backward extruding, upsetting, and piercing. Thin wall sections are produced on this part, and the cam form is held to ±0.003" (0.08 mm).

While many small components are formed automatically, there is an increasing number of large parts now being produced in this way. Limitations with respect to maximum reductions in area and unsupported lengths of stock that can be upset without bending in a single blow are discussed earlier in this chapter.

Close tolerances can be maintained in automatic forming, but the tighter the tolerances, the more costly the production. Part diameters can be held to ±0.0005" (0.013 mm) by using sizing dies, but ±0.002" (0.05 mm) is a more common tolerance. Lengths are sometimes held to 0.005" (0.13 mm), but ±0.015" (0.38 mm) is a more usual tolerance.

## MATERIALS FORMED

A wide variety of ferrous and nonferrous metals are cold and warm formed on automatic machines. The severity of forming possibilities varies for different metals. Desirable chemical compositions, melting practices, and properties of metals to be formed, as well as undesirable defects of the metals, are discussed earlier in this chapter.

Soft, low-carbon grades of steel are the most common materials used for cold automatic forming. As the carbon and alloy contents of steels increase, forming becomes more difficult. For some materials, heating and warm forming are required. Warm forming is used extensively for the production of parts made from high-alloy steels and some stainless steels.

A fully annealed microstructure is desirable for the maximum formability of steels, and spheroidize annealing is often preferable for severe forming operations. For certain applications, the use of boron-treated steels may eliminate the need for annealing prior to forming. For some applications interprocess annealing between forming stations may be required.

Most formed products are made from wire that is cold drawn from hot-rolled rod, bar, or coil stock for close control of diameter and smooth finishes. Forming immediately, with the use of in-line drawing machines, facilitates forming by avoiding age hardening that normally follows drawing. Many automatic forming machines are equipped with in-line drawing units. Some machines have sonic or magnetic-particle inspection devices to monitor incoming stock for imperfections.

## APPLICATIONS OF AUTOMATIC FORMING

Parts produced on automatic forming machines are used by many different industries for a wide variety of applications. They have replaced many components which were previously cast, forged, machined, or produced by other processes. The versatility of automatic forming machines has led to their being referred to as parts makers. Considerable savings can be realized by forming different parts of similar size and shape. This minimizes tooling costs and changeover time, and makes the production of smaller lot sizes more economical.

### Producing Multidiameter Shafts

Many different types of multidiameter shafts are produced on automatic forming machines. A typical shaft produced on a four-die cold former at the rate of 35 parts per minute is shown in Fig. 13-68. For this application, starting blanks, 250 mm

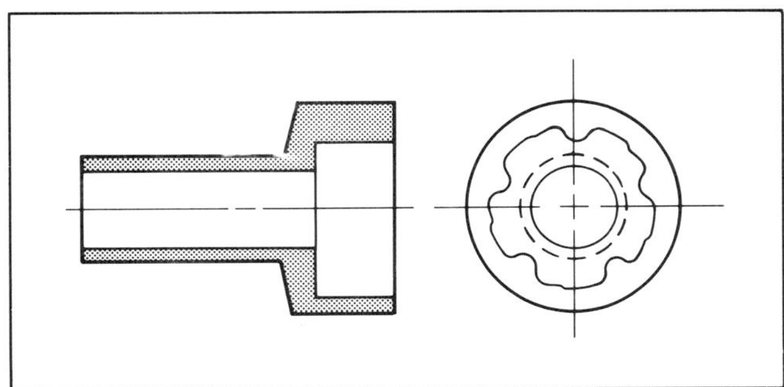

**Fig. 13-67 Part produced by shearing, combined forward and backward extruding, upsetting, and piercing.** (*Imerman Industries, Inc.*)

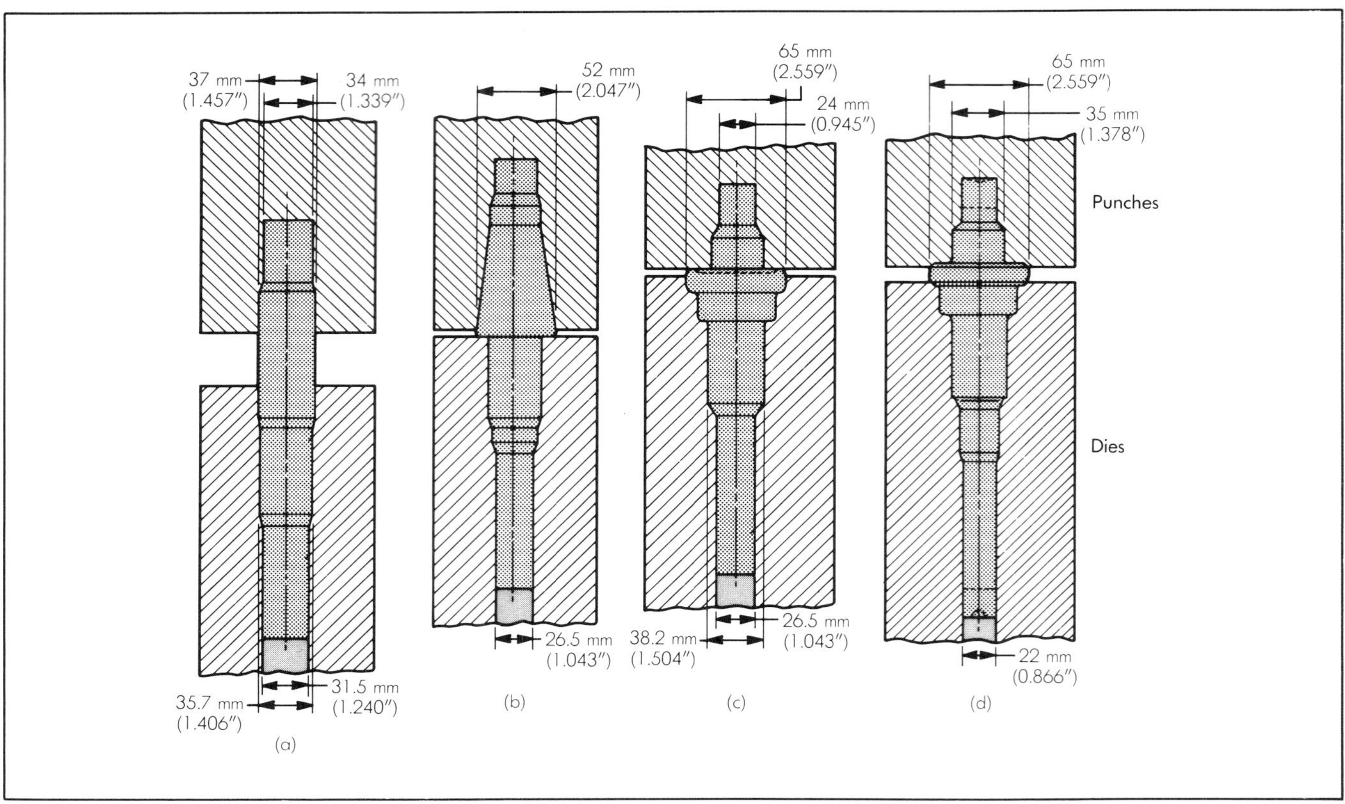


**Fig. 13-68 Multidiameter shaft produced on a four-die cold former at the rate of 35 parts per minute.**

(9.84 ") long, are sheared off-line from steel bars (similar to SAE 4130), 37 mm (1.457"). Weight of the blanks is held to 2118 ±5 g (4.67 ±0.01 lb). After shearing, the blanks are annealed, phosphate coated, and lubricated before they enter the cold-forming machine.

In the first cold-forming operation (see Fig. 13-68, *a*), three small diameters (two on one end and one on the opposite end of the blank) are extruded to effect an area reduction of about 27%. Open extrusion, with space between the punch and die, is employed for this operation. The phosphate coating and lubricant on the blank, combined with the reduction in diameter, prevents upsetting and ensures extruding.

In the second cold-forming operation (see Fig. 13-68, *b*), another small diameter is extruded and a cone is upset in the punch section of the tooling. The close control of blank weight in shearing ensures that no flash is produced in the small gap between the punch and die. In this same operation, several small diameters are extruded in the die section of the tooling to achieve an area reduction of about 30%.

In the third cold-forming operation (see Fig. 13-68, *c*), one small diameter is further extruded and another surface is sized in the punch. No flash is produced in the gap between the punch and die. In the die, a flange and supporting diameter are upset, the diameter of another surface is sized, and radii are formed. No operation is performed on the smallest diameter surface of the shaft.

The fourth and final cold-forming operation is illustrated in Fig. 13-68, *d*). Here, the punch section of the tooling coins (flattens) the top of the flange on the shaft. The die section coins the bottom of this flange and extrudes small-diameter surfaces. Unfilled areas on both ends of the shaft (denoted by broken lines in view *d*) are sheared off-line after forming and before subsequent machining. These unfilled areas result from differences in the speed of metal flow between the inner and outer material during the different extrusions.

Another shaft, this one produced on a five-die cold former at the rate of 45 parts per minute, is illustrated in Fig. 13-69. Blanks, 200 mm (7.87") long, are sheared from 35.15 mm (1.384") diam steel bars, similar to SAE 4130 but with less carbon (0.16-0.22%). Blank weight is held to 1511 ±5 g (3.33 ±0.01 lb).

In the first cold-forming operation (see Fig. 13-69, *a*), two smaller diameter surfaces are extruded to effect an area reduction of about 27%. A cone is upset by the punch in the second forming operation (view *b*). A gap between the punch and die sections allows the metal to flow unrestricted to form the conical shape. Extruding of the opposite end of the shaft in the die during this operation effects a total area reduction of about 25%.

In the third operation (see Fig. 13-69, *c*), flash is formed in the gap between the punch and die sections as the conical portion of the shaft is sized. Further extrusion of the small-diameter surfaces is performed in the die during the fourth operation (view *d*). The punch consists merely of a flat plate used to drive the part into the die section of the tooling, reducing the area about 22%.

The final cold-forming operation is shown in Fig. 13-69, *e*). The die section of the tooling in this station operates in a sequential manner, performing two distinct operations on the shaft. As the punch (a flat plate) pushes the part into the die section, the flash around the conical portion of the part is sheared to provide consistent stock for subsequent machining operations. Then, the upper portion of the die bottoms out, and the lower portion of the die extrudes another minor diameter on the opposite end of the workpiece. The unfilled excess on the end of the part (represented by broken lines) is sheared from the part in a subsequent operation.

## Cold Forming Ball Joints

The ball joint illustrated in Fig. 13-70 is produced at the rate of 40 per minute on a six-die cold former. Made of steel similar to SAE 5147, the ball joint is produced at a rate of about 50,000 per month. The wire is first drawn through a straightening die before it enters the cutoff station. At the cutoff station, the 22 mm (0.866") diam wire is cut to a length of 97.5 mm (3.839"), holding total weight of the blank to 295 ± 1 g (0.760 ± 0.002 lb).

The first forming operation in the automatic sequence is shown in Fig. 13-70, *a*. The major diameter of the blank is not changed; the operation is performed to square the blank and produce a small chamfer on one end. The second forming operation (view *b*) is an extruding process. The minor diameter produced in the operation represents an area reduction of about

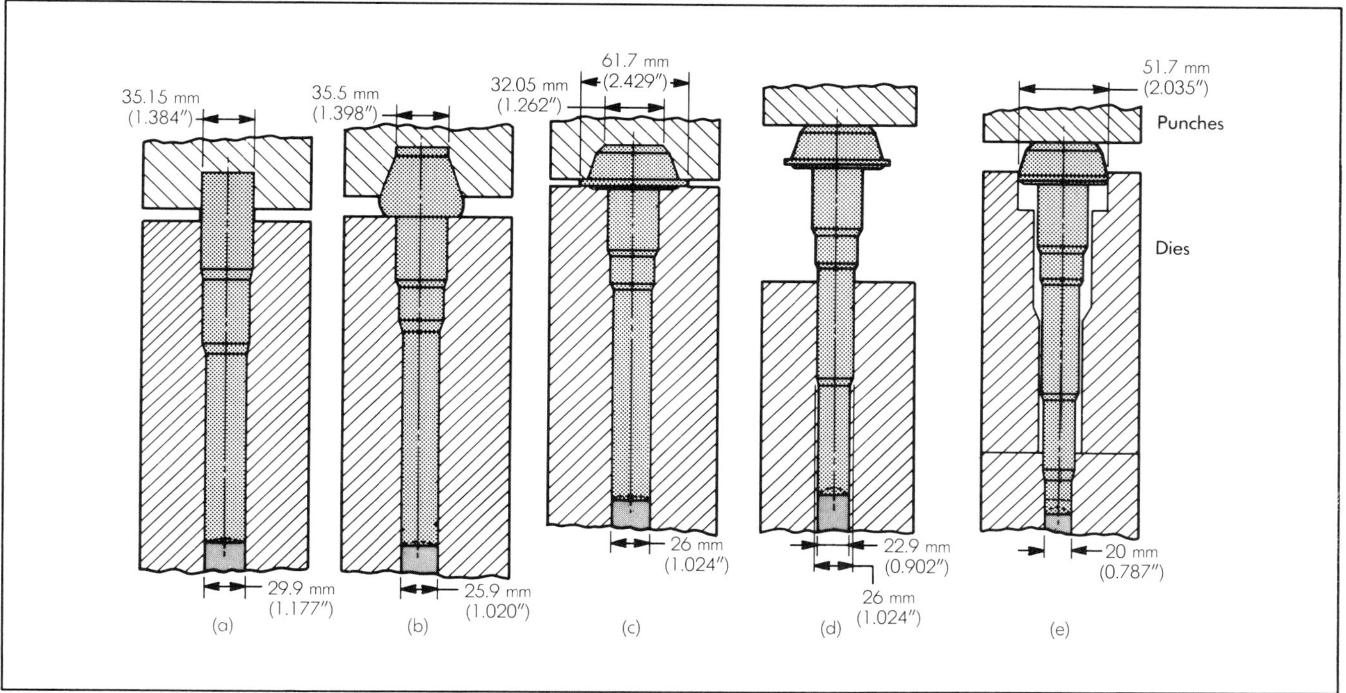


**Fig. 13-69 Multidiameter shaft produced on a five-die cold former at the rate of 45 parts per minute.**

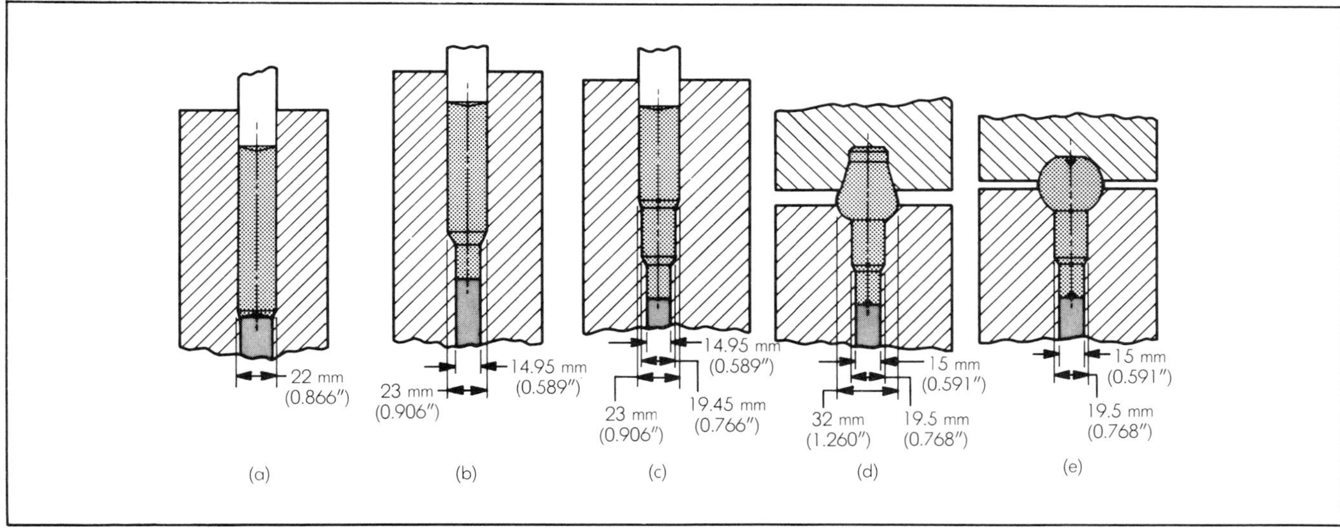


**Fig. 13-70 Ball joint produced on a five-die cold former at the rate of 40 parts per minute.**

58%. View *c* depicts the third operation. Here, another minor diameter is produced—an area reduction of about 28%.

The fourth forming operation (see Fig. 13-70, *d*) shows the preparation of the spherical portion of the part. The tooling is designed with a gap between the punch and die. In a controlled manner, metal is allowed to flow into the gap, forming a portion of the spherical section. As part of this operation, a center is formed in one end of the part.

The final operation (see Fig. 13-70, *e*) finishes the spherical portion of the part and simultaneously forms a center in the sphere for subsequent turning and threading operations. By using the cold forming process to produce centers, subsequent centering operations are eliminated, saving time and money.

### Gear Blank Forming

Gear blanks with integral stems are cold formed in the sequence shown in Fig. 13-71 on a five-die forming machine at the rate of 40 parts per minute. Blanks are sheared off-line to a weight tolerance of 875 ± 2 g (1.929 ± 0.004 lb) from 40.5 mm (1.594") diam bar stock. Blank length is about 89 mm (3.504"). View *a* shows the first cold-forming operation performed on the blank. The entire operation is accomplished inside the die section of the tooling under force provided by the punch. The operation consists of extruding a taper and minor diameter.

The second cold-forming operation (see Fig. 13-71, *b*) consists of a cone preparation (upsetting) and a slight expansion of the minor diameter. View *c* shows the third station of the machine in which a large upsetting operation is performed. Again, the minor diameter is allowed to expand slightly.

Recesses in the gear are formed in the fourth station as shown in Fig. 13-71, *d*. Also, the configuration of the major diameter is refined, but the minor diameter is held constant. In the final operation (depicted in view *e*), the minor diameter is extruded to final size and the major diameter is held constant. In this final station, the punch is a flat plate used only to force the stem of the part through finish extrusion.

It is interesting to note that this part was previously formed on a vertical press. The recesses could not be formed, so they were machined in subsequent operations. By switching to progressive cold forming, the expensive machining operation was entirely eliminated. Today, only the gear teeth are machined.

### Forming Fasteners

A wide variety of fasteners are produced on automatic forming machines. The forming sequence used to produce a special nut on a six-station, five-die machine is shown in Fig. 13-72. These nuts were previously made from malleable iron castings. Now, stronger and more uniform nuts are being obtained by cold forming them from 1030 steel coil stock at the rate of 50 per minute. Savings are obtained and energy is conserved by eliminating the need to cast the nuts.

## MACHINES FOR AUTOMATIC FORMING

Machines used for automatic cold and warm forming are available in various sizes and capacities to handle stock to 2" (51 mm) diam or larger. The machines are usually special, built to specific customer requirements, and are often sold fully tooled. They are all equipped with high-speed transfer units that automatically move the workpieces from station to station.

Most automatic forming machines are designed with the stations arranged and work transfer accomplished in a horizontal plane. Figure 13-73 shows a cross section of the tooling area on a four-die horizontal machine. Some machines, however, have the stations arranged vertically, with the workpieces being transferred from the top of the machine to the bottom as they progress through the forming sequence.

Automatic forming machines, supported with an uncoiler, are generally equipped with a wire straightener, a roll-feed unit, and a cutoff station to shear blanks of the required length. When equipped with a cutoff station, the machines are identified by the number of stations and number of dies; for example, a six-station, five-die forming machine. The starting coil stock is usually phosphatized and lubricated, and sometimes annealed. In-line cold-drawing machines are occasionally employed to size and smooth the stock.

### Machine Operation

Practically all automatic forming machines are mechanically operated. A motor-driven flywheel drives an eccentric shaft that is connected to the machine slide by a pitman. The reciprocating slide carries a punch at each station to force metal into the stationary dies mounted on the machine opposite the punches. Normally, a forming operation is completed with each stroke of

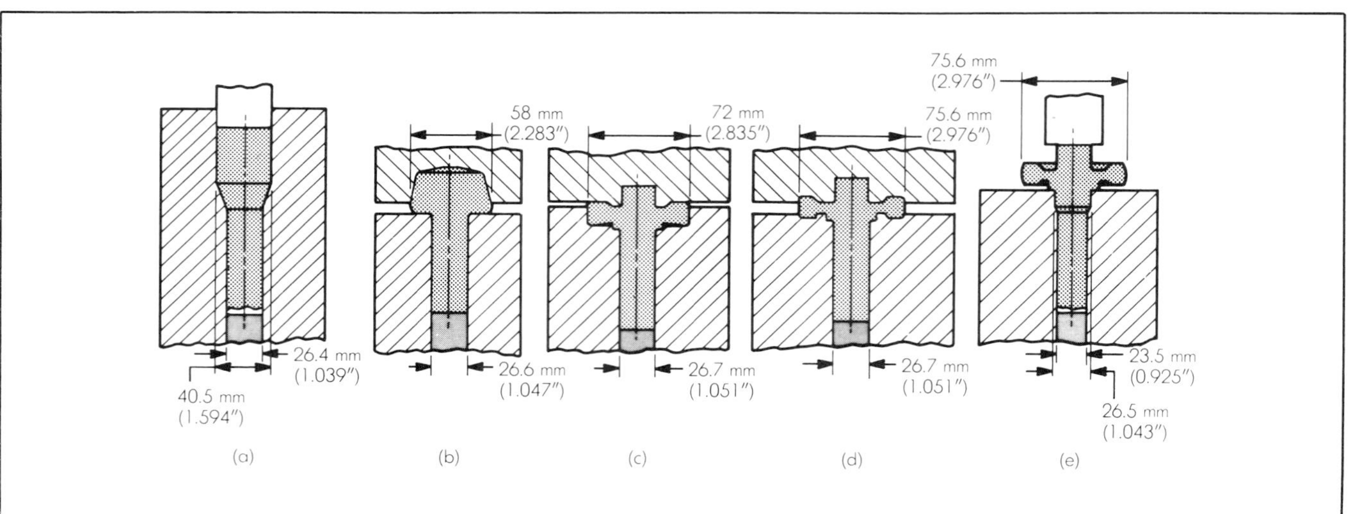


**Fig. 13-71 Forming sequence for producing gear and stem blanks on a five-die cold former at the rate of 40 parts per minute.**

the slide, with the partially formed part being removed from the die by a kickout mechanism. At the final station, a completely formed part is removed from the die.

## Workpiece Transfer

Cutoff blanks are mechanically transferred to and from the successive forming stations by cam-controlled grippers. Automatic transfer units are available with the capability for end-for-end turnaround of the workpieces between stations. Some units also permit 90° rotation of the workpieces for piercing or forming operations at a right angle to their longitudinal axes. For increased versatility, some machines are provided with two interchangeable transfer units, one for short workpieces and the other for longer parts. Other machines utilize the same transfer unit for both short or long parts, requiring only adjustments to change from one to the other.

## Tooling Changeover

Recent advances in machine design have resulted in faster tooling changeover, thus making shorter production runs more feasible. One machine manufacturer offers setup fixtures for both punch and die components, including punch-to-die alignment features. Such fixtures facilitate handling of the tooling and shorten the changeover time by allowing operators to complete many setup adjustments off the machine. Once set up, the tooling units are lifted from the fixtures, placed into the machine, and installed with few, if any, secondary adjustments. This approach to quick changeover involves replacing all dies and punches in their respective holders with in-machine clamping systems that quickly secure them in place. The complete changeover of punches and dies for the production of another part can be accomplished in 30 minutes or less.

Another approach to quick toolchanging is to hydraulically

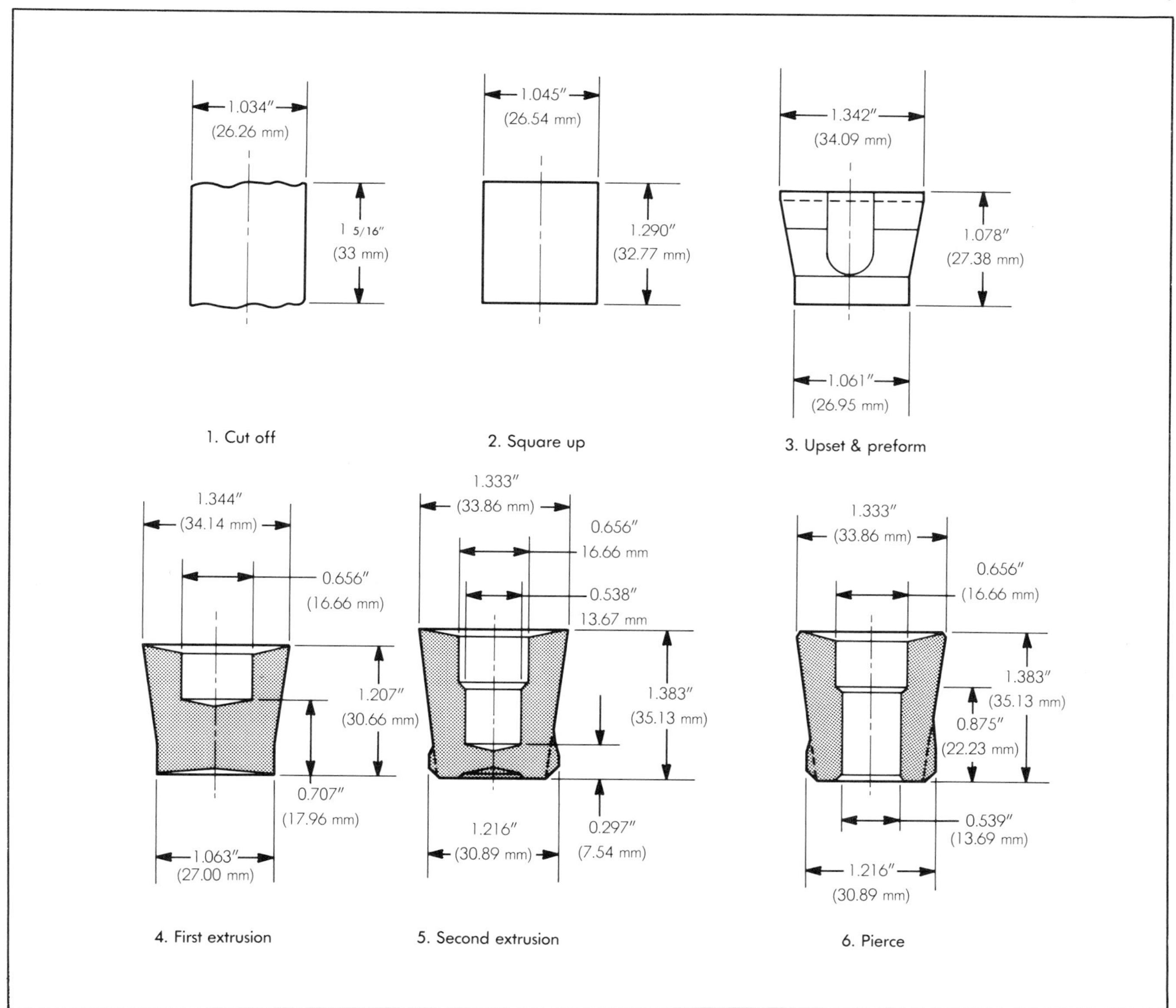


**Fig. 13-72 Special nuts are cold formed from 1030 steel coil stock at the rate of 50 per minute.**

# AUTOMATIC COLD AND WARM FORMING

clamp each punch and die for individual removal. This design may be more practical for long production runs in which individual tools wear at different rates and require changing at various times. Individual toolchanging can be partially or fully automated with robot-type devices that move into the tooling area, remove a specific die or punch assembly, and replace it from a storage rack of tooling.

Some toolchanging systems are computer controlled, with a single command actuating the changing of all tools or a specific punch or die. With such systems, five punches and five dies can be changed in less than 15 minutes. Other systems rely on less computerization, and some have actuation of the robot device by operator push-button control.

## Machine Controls

Improved in-process control systems have been developed for automatic forming machines. Microprocessor control units are available with sensing devices, such as strain gages or piezoelectric voltage transducers, to monitor and analyze forming forces. Deviations from normal, such as short feeds, misfeeds, tool wear or breakage, and excessively hard workpiece material, are detected and displayed. If such deviations exceed preset values, the machine is automatically stopped. Such controls prevent machine overloading and damage to the machine and tooling, resulting in longer tool life, reduced scrap, and improved quality of the parts formed.

## Noise Reduction

As with many other manufacturing machines, excessive noise is often a problem with forming machines. Soundproof enclosures and integral acoustic covers are available to reduce noise levels without hampering access to vital machine areas. They are equipped with mist-precipitating ventilators.

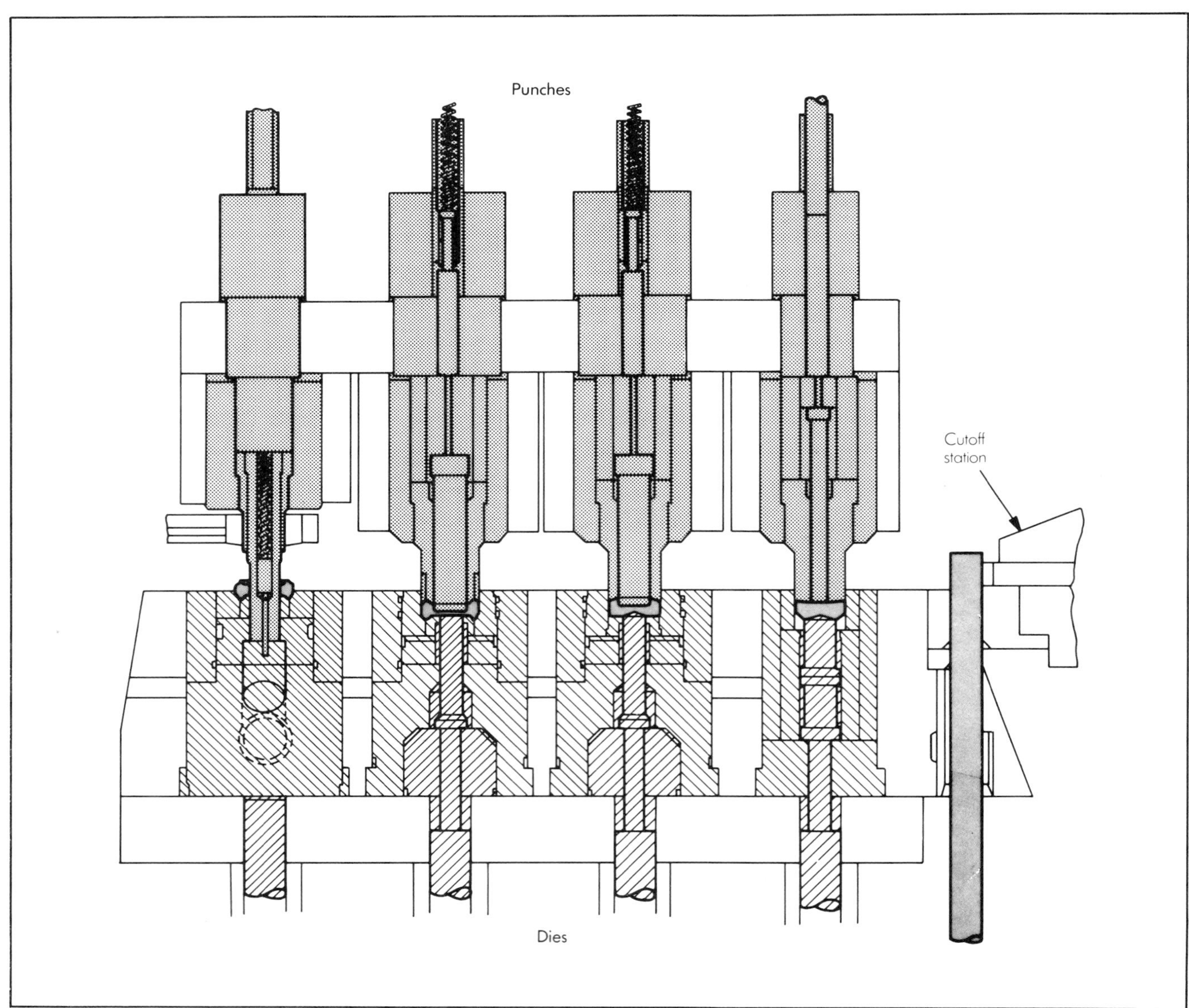


**Fig. 13-73 A four-die automatic forming machine tooled to produce gear blanks.**

## TOOLING AND OPERATING PARAMETERS

Design and materials for extruding and upsetting tools, as well as pressure requirements and slide speeds for these operations, are discussed earlier in this chapter. Information on piercing, coining, and sizing is presented in Chapter 4, "Sheet Metal Blanking and Forming," and Chapter 6, "Die Design for Sheet Metal Forming." Information on shearing (cutoff) is presented in Chapter 11, "Shearing"; and information on threading and knurling is presented in Volume I, *Machining*, of this Handbook series.

## SAFETY CONSIDERATIONS

Safety requirements for the construction, care, and use of cold headers and cold formers are presented in ANSI Standard B11.7.

### References

1. Ike Tripp, Jr., *Lubrication and Manufacturing Techniques for the Roll Drawing of Nonferrous Shaped Wire*, SME Technical Paper MF82-336, 1982.
2. Paul Andrus, *Continuous Hydrostatic Wire Extrusion*, SME Technical Paper MF76-409, 1976.
3. J. T. Black, W. G. Voorhes, and D. Breneiser, *Linex—Linear Continuous Extrusion of Metals*, SME Technical Paper MF76-141, 1976.
4. Betzatel Avitzur, "Extrolling: Update 1977" *Wire Journal*, March 1978, pp. 78-84.
5. Verson Allsteel Press Co., *Impact Machining*, Chicago, 1969.
6. Ronald Drake and James Throop, *Force Predictions in Cold Extrusion Operations*, SME Technical Paper MR70-139, 1970.

### Bibliography

"Continuous Metal Extrusion." *Manufacturing Engineering* (February 1977), pp. 42 and 43.

Drozda, Thomas J. "Money-saving Innovations in Automatic Forming." *Manufacturing Engineering*, February 1983, pp. 32-39.

Laue, Kurt, and Stenger, Helmut. *Extrusion*. Metals Park, OH: American Society for Metals, 1981.

Roberts, Peter R. *The Extended Application of the Extrusion Process Using Encapsulated Billets*. SME Technical Paper MF76-391, 1976.

"The Case for Extruded Parts." *Manufacturing Engineering* (May 1979), pp. 64 and 65.

Wick, Charles. "Cold Extruding Motor Shafts." *Manufacturing Engineering* (February 1977), pp. 37-39.

CHAPTER

# 14

# Swaging

# SWAGING

Swaging is a metalforming process in which a rapid series of impact blows is delivered radially to either solid or tubular work. This causes a reduction in cross-sectional area and/or a change in geometric shape. The method is basically a forging process, especially similar to radial forging, discussed in Chapter 15 of this volume, "Hot Forging." Applications of swaging include tapering, pointing, reducing, external and internal forming, compacting, sizing, and assembling.

CHAPTER CONTENTS:



## THE SWAGING PROCESS

In swaging, impact blows are transferred to the work in rapid succession by dies in the machine. The contour built into the dies controls the cross section formed.

### METAL FLOW

Under normal operating conditions, each swaging blow to a solid bar produces a flow of metal, as shown in Fig. 14-1. It is often supposed that the metal moves entirely in the direction of the feed, but this is not the case. Flow takes place in all directions in amounts dependent upon conditions surrounding the metal in question. Pressure in an ordinary swaging die is exerted across a single axis. Free flow of the metal is resisted by high surface friction within the die. If this friction is overly large, no longitudinal flow takes place and excessive localized stresses in the groove of the die spall or break out the hardened surface. This stressing takes place when the length of the work under compression exceeds ten times the diameter.

In accordance with the physical laws governing the flow of metals under pressure, more metal normally moves out of the taper in opposition to the feed than flows through the straight blade. Some flow also takes place in the plane of the cross section, but it is restricted by the oval in the dies and cannot properly be called free flow.

The action of the material opposing the feed can be felt by the operator; and although it is sometimes incorrectly called kickback, its proper name is feedback. Feedback is entirely the result of slippage of the work in the taper of the die, usually because of oily surfaces or a taper that is too steep. It is observed as a heavy longitudinal vibration offering considerable resistance to feeding. Mechanical feeds are sometimes used to overcome feedback if it is not too heavy.

The ideal taper angles are 8° or less for average work. On larger sizes, an included angle of 6° is more desirable. In those cases in which steeper angles need to be used or the work is unavoidably greasy, and the finish is not too important, die tapers can be crosshatched to provide a certain amount of seizure to the work being fed.

### WORK ROTATION

Another action which takes place in swaging is slow rotation of the work. Apparently, this rotation is a steady motion; and for practical purposes it may be considered so, although actually it is intermittent, with intervals so close together that they cannot be seen or felt. The dies intermittently compress the work and rotate around it, and it is during the compression that the dies grip the piece, causing it to rotate at approximately spindle speed. After the swaging blow, the dies release the work, which continues to rotate at a slower rate from its own inertia. This performance is repeated at very rapid intervals, thus giving the impression that the work rotates steadily.

Because of the rotational action, frictional resistance must be supplied to the work so it does not actually rotate at spindle speed. If resistance is not provided, the die action takes place in one position on the work and produces excessive oval or flash, causing the work to stick in the dies. The operator's hands are one means of controlling the rotation of the work, but mechanical means are often employed. Under actual production conditions, a comparison of machine for machine reveals that a hand-fed swager sometimes produces more work than one fed mechanically, because the flexibility of the operator's hands and arms provides better frictional control and shock-absorbing qualities. Mechanical holders and feeds should provide this flexibility as much as practicable without sacrificing strength; at the same time, rotational inertia of the holders must be light to avoid twisting the piece.

### EFFECTS ON MATERIAL PROPERTIES

Whether or not the physical effects of swaging actually penetrate the bar depends upon whether the machine is heavy enough for the job. A light machine on a heavy piece has only a surface effect,

***Contributors of sections of this chapter are:*** *R. S. Dusseau, CMfgE, Vice President, Abbey Etna Machine Co.; Clarence Miller, Director of Field Sales, Abbey Etna Machine Co.*

***Reviewers of sections of this chapter are:*** *John D. Bryzgel, Product Manager, Swaging Equipment, Fenn Manufacturing Co.; R. S. Dusseau, CMfgE, Vice President, Sales, Abbey Etna Machine Co.; Richard Kelley, Senior Sales Engineer, Machinery Div., The Torrington Co.; Clarence J. Miller, Director U.S. Field Sales, Abbey Etna Machine Co.; Dr.-Eng. Bernhard Mueller, Owner, Heinrich Mueller Maschinefabrik; Kenneth A. Turnquist, Plant Manager, Machinery Div., The Torrington Co.; Jack Ussin, President, Steinel-America.*

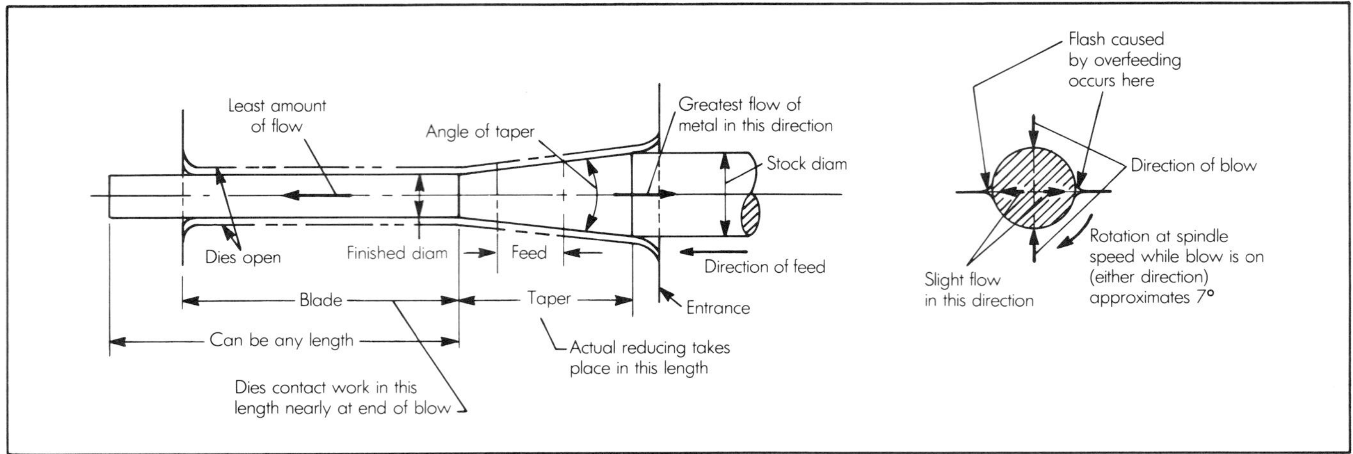


**Fig. 14-1 Metal flow during swaging of a solid bar.** (*Machinery Div., The Torrington Co.*)

and the tensile strength is not increased in proportion to the apparent surface hardness. On the other hand, if the machine is heavier than the job actually requires, both the hardness and strength are increased. The effects of these two conditions are visible on a swaged piece. A rod that is cold worked only on the surface is concave on the end, while a bar that is thoroughly cold worked has a definite convex bulge at the same point.

### DIMENSIONAL CHANGES

In solid reduction, all the metal goes into elongation; basically, the workpiece diameter is converted into length. The change in dimension can be easily calculated by equating the initial volume and swaged volume, then solving as follows:

$$A = 100\left(1 - \frac{D_2^2}{D_1^2}\right) \qquad (1)$$

where:

$A$ = cross-sectional area reduction, %
$D_1$ = original diam, in. or mm
$D_2$ = swaged diam, in. or mm

Example:

The reduction of a 1.000" (25.40 mm) diam bar to 0.750" (19.05 mm) diam is:

$$A = 100\left(1 - \frac{0.750^2}{1.000^2}\right) = 43.75\%$$

or

$$A = 100\left(1 - \frac{19.05^2}{25.40^2}\right) = 43.75\%$$

# ADVANTAGES AND LIMITATIONS OF SWAGING

Economy, versatility, and improved workpiece quality are important advantages of the swaging process.

### ECONOMY OF SWAGING

Swaging is one of the most economical processes available for forming cylindrical parts required in medium to large production quantities. Machines used are relatively inexpensive, and they are simple to set up, operate, and maintain. Skilled operators are not required; for machines having automatic feeds, one operator can attend several machines, thus reducing labor costs. Since no metal is removed in swaging, material savings add to the economy of the process. A variety of shaped sections (square, hexagonal, etc.) can be formed from low-cost round stock. Assemblies made by swaging eliminate the cost of fastening devices or joining operations.

High productivity also makes swaging economical. Production rates generally vary from about 100-3000 or more parts per hour, depending upon the amount of reduction, the type of part (solid or tubular), angle of reduction, ductility and cleanliness of the workpiece material, method of feeding, and other factors. Swaging machines are easily automated to increase production rates.

### VERSATILITY OF SWAGING

For some applications, swaging can produce parts that cannot be economically made in any other way. One example is the forming of copper welding tips having angular holes that are drilled before the tips are reduced, tapered, and elongated by swaging. Wire mandrels are inserted to prevent deformation of the holes during swaging.

Most metals can be swaged, as discussed later in this section. The amount of deformation possible varies with the specific material to be formed.

### IMPROVEMENTS IN QUALITY

Swaging refines, rearranges, and improves the grain structure of the metal, resulting in increases in surface hardness, elastic limit, and tensile strength of both ferrous and nonferrous materials. Stainless and alloy steels exhibit such increases to a greater extent than other metals. Carbon steels show an increase in tensile strength of about 1000 psi (6.9 MPa) for each 10% of area reduction.

Flow of the metal during swaging causes a burnishing action at the surface. This generally results in an improved surface finish comparable with that of a ground part and often eliminates the need for subsequent finishing operations. Surface irregularities such as scratches, burrs, and tool marks are often eliminated, depending upon the size of the irregularities and the amount of reduction during swaging.

Flats, flash, and other surface markings can occur during swaging because of poor die construction. Spiral patterns show if excessive speeds are used, and prior removal of surface contaminants such as paint, scale, and abrasives is important. Occasionally, lubricants are used in swaging to give better surface finishes and to improve die life, but lubricants increase workpiece feedback, which is a serious problem in manual feeding. Many factors affect the finish of the finished swaged part, but finishes in the range of 10-40 $\mu$ in. (0.25-1.02 $\mu$ m) can be achieved in closely controlled processes.

Close dimensional tolerances can be consistently maintained in swaging, depending upon the condition and size of the machine and dies. New dies, properly designed and made, can sometimes swage initial parts to tolerances of 0.0001" (0.003 mm) or less. Die wear, however, generally makes such tolerances impractical for production applications. The dies are usually manufactured to produce parts at the low limit of required tolerance, and they gradually wear to the high tolerance limit in a straight line variation over a period of time.

Table 14-1 can be used as a general guide to normal tolerances for solid reductions in ductile materials or for swaging tubes over hard mandrels. Closer tolerances can be maintained with a reduction in the amount of deformation and a reduction in production rates for a given operation; they can also be maintained if care is applied in die maintenance. When die wear results in forming parts that exceed the required tolerance, the dies should be restored to their original dimensions.

**TABLE 14-1**
**Normal Tolerances for Solid Reductions in Ductile Materials or for Swaging Tubes Over hard Mandrels**

| Diameter | | Tolerance, ±, | |
|---|---|---|---|
| in. | mm | in. | mm |
| 0 to 1/2 | 12.7 | 0.001 | 0.03 |
| 1/2 to 1 | 12.7 to 25.4 | 0.002 | 0.05 |
| 1 to 1 1/2 | 25.4 to 38.1 | 0.003 | 0.08 |
| 1 1/2 to 3 | 38.1 to 76.2 | 0.005 | 0.13 |
| 3 to 4 1/2 | 76.2 to 114.3 | 0.007 | 0.18 |
| 4 1/2 | 114.3 and over | 0.010 | 0.25 |

As feed rates are reduced, tolerances can also be reduced, but generally by no more than 50%. Variations in wall thicknesses of the starting tube blank are compounded as the wall of the tube thickens during swaging. The accuracy of tubes swaged without an internal mandrel depends upon the variation of the wall thickness of the starting blank.

### LIMITATIONS OF SWAGING

Limitations of swaging include the need for workpieces of symmetrical cross section and restrictions on the angles and lengths of taper that can be formed in one operation. If more than one pass is used, lines of demarcation may be visible where one die overlaps the other. Forming of sharp tapers or swaging close to shoulders is difficult.

Swaging is a noisy operation, which can be objectionable. The noise level, however, can be reduced by proper mounting of the machine and the use of baffles and/or enclosures. For many applications, the use of ear protectors is required.

## MATERIALS SWAGED

Any metal having a reasonable amount of ductility and elongation can be swaged. Hot-rolled steel is usually more ductile and can be swaged more easily than cold-rolled or drawn stock because cold working can reduce the deformation properties.

Among the ferrous metals, the low-carbon steels, such as 1010, 1015, or 1020 steel, are the easiest to swage and normally can be reduced 40% or more in cross-sectional area in one operation. Multiple operations are necessary to secure greater area reductions. As the metal's carbon content or alloy content is increased, its capability of being cold formed by swaging is decreased. Alloys such as manganese, nickel, and chromium increase metal strength and thereby decrease the cold-forming capabilities of the metal.

The plain carbon steels can generally be reduced 40% or more in cross-sectional area before annealing is required. As the alloy content is increased to the point at which the steel becomes tool steel, however, area reduction is lowered to 15-20%. Certain varieties of stainless steel, such as 302, 304, 305, 321, 403, 410, 430, and 443, are well adapted to area reductions of 35-40%. However, the adaptability of other grades varies from 20-35% depending upon the ductility of each grade. With steels that cold work readily, stress-relieving the material between successive operations is necessary to restore ductility.

Experience has shown that steels with hardnesses of up to $R_B85$ swage well since they are usually ductile enough for cold forming. When the material exceeds $R_B105$, cold swaging is impractical because of the excessive wear on the swager's internal parts and dies. Materials in excess of $R_B105$ should be swaged hot so that they are plastic enough to take deformation.

The addition of free-machining elements such as lead, phosphorus, and sulfur increases the possibility of material splitting during swaging. These additives cause weaknesses in the structure of the steel; and with the application of forming loads, the weak points tend to fracture. They should be avoided in all swaging procedures.

All too often, material for swaging is purchased without any regard to its physical properties, with the result being that it is unsuitable for the job. In cold swaging steel, maximum results are obtained when the microstructure is spheroidize-annealed. This heat treatment is important for the medium and high-carbon steels. A pearlitic microstructure is not conducive to good swaging. Consequently, spheroidizing should be emphasized when material for cold forming is specified.

Depending upon the alloy, nonferrous metals such as copper, brass, and aluminum usually adapt readily to swaging. It is possible to obtain taper reductions of as much as 70% in cross-sectional area, because of the high ductility of these metals. Leaded brass is generally not recommended for swaging, since it usually fractures under the stress of cold working. With proper die design, however, leaded brass can sometimes be swaged to area reductions of about 10%.

The maximum included angle of reduction for aluminum should be kept under 25°. Under the high feeding pressures of steep angles, aluminum has a tendency to be picked up by the dies. Consequently, a reduction in the die angle helps overcome this condition.

Materials such as tungsten and molybdenum, which have low ductility, are formed better with hot-swaging techniques. Many materials that are brittle at room temperature must be preheated before insertion into a swaging machine. Those having tensile strengths in excess of 100,000-120,000 psi (690-827 MPa) are normally heated to the high end of the forging temperature range and then swaged.

# METHODS OF SWAGING

The various methods of swaging include solid, tube, mandrel, cold (room temperature), hot, and internal methods. Swagers can be through-fed to reduce an entire bar or tube, or the workpiece can simply be fed in and out to reduce only the end. Multiple passes may be necessary to make long tapers. In central reductions, the part is advanced into the swager for a given distance, the diameter is reduced for a specified length, and the entire part is removed from the machine. It is possible to produce regular or irregular internal shapes. Stationary-spindle machines can swage external shapes.

## TUBE SWAGING

The swaging of tubing involves somewhat different factors from those involved in swaging solid material. Each time a blow is struck, part of the action is used to increase the thickness of the tube wall. The movement of metal longitudinally also occurs; the amount of this movement, or lengthening, as well as the amount of wall thickening, depends on the original proportion of wall thickness to outer diameter, amount of reduction, angle of taper, and other factors.

The reason the wall thickness increases is that each time a blow is struck, the short columns of material adjacent to the grooved edges where the die faces meet are compressed. As in any column, if too much metal is compressed in one blow, the column buckles and either wrinkles the tubing or breaks the wall. For this reason, thin-wall tubing must be fed more slowly than tubing with a heavier wall. The crushing effect on the wall is easily seen on the inside of a tube that has had considerable reduction without the use of a mandrel, appearing as a comparatively rough or slightly crinkled surface. Because of the endwise flow of the metal, some loss of area occurs between the original and swaged sections. As the material is progressively reduced and approaches a solid section, it performs more as a solid, with a solid's inherent flow characteristics.

Figure 14-2 shows the inner cone surface being compressed not as a straight line but as the curved surface, *A*. As this surface approaches a point, compression lines, *B*, build up to roughen the surface increasingly. Ordinarily this roughening is of no consequence. When tube diameters become theoretically solid, the material is not completely or actually solid, but contains laps and seams resulting from the collapse of the original inner surface, *C*. In aluminum or other soft materials, a cold weld sometimes takes place and the seams disappear.

It is possible to estimate either the inner diameter or the outer diameter of any swaged tubular cross section if one or the other is known. Ordinarily these dimensions cannot be determined accurately, but they can be established closely enough that a single minor alteration in the die produces the required dimension. In tubular reductions, approximately 10% of the metal goes into elongation, with the remaining 90% going into thickening the wall of the tube.

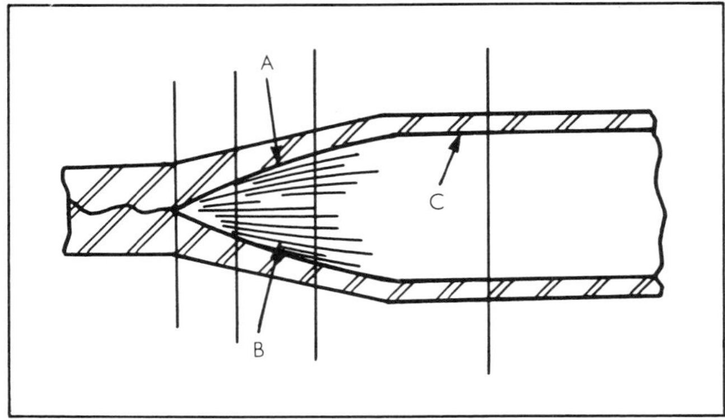


**Fig. 14-2 Reduction flow pattern during tube swaging.** (*Machinery Div. The Torrington Co.*)

A limit exists as to the thinness of a tube wall that can be swaged. Usually the diameter should not be greater than about 25-30 times the wall thickness for good swaging. If the ratio is greater than this, the wall will collapse and wrinkle. Sometimes thin-wall tubes can be swaged by using an internal mandrel for support during the reduction. However, in all cases the tube should have sufficient column strength to withstand the feeding forces necessary.

Either seamless or welded tubing can be swaged. However, seamless tubing is generally more eccentric in its relationship between inner and outer diameters. This irregularity cannot be corrected by swaging and should be borne in mind when material is specified.

Welded tubing tends to camber when reduced, since the metal in the weld area flows differently from the parent metal. If the quality of the weld is inferior or if the weld area is hard, the tube will split during swaging. Annealed tubing is often required to eliminate these problems.

## MANDREL SWAGING

For certain applications it is desirable to maintain or reduce the wall thickness of a tube or to meet a specific inner diameter. In such cases, a mandrel is used. Mandrels are also used to support thin-wall tubes during reduction and to form internal shapes. When extended through the front of the dies, the mandrel can be used as a pilot to support the first part of an assembly to be swaged.

When swaging is performed with a mandrel, the solid capacity of a particular machine must be used to select the proper swager to prevent overloading. Even though the work just touches the mandrel, a machine with suitable solid capacity to handle the diameter in question should be selected. It is possible to thin the wall of the tube approximately 10% per pass. However, if the tube is 0.025″ (0.63 mm) thick or less, further thinning is extremely difficult. In general practice the mandrel is tapered slightly to aid in removal of the work after swaging. If tolerances permit, a taper of 0.001 in./in. (mm/mm) is acceptable. The dies used in mandrel swaging should be manufactured with a considerable amount of ovality, for it is the ovality that springs the work from the mandrel. The amount of ovality is a function of the tube diameter, the wall thickness, and the material.

The mandrel can be held by hand with the work loaded onto it and the entire unit fed into the swager, as illustrated in Fig. 14-3, view *a*. The mandrel may also be mounted in the spindle so that it floats in the die cavity as shown in view *b*. When this approach is taken, the mandrel must also be free to rotate; otherwise, torsional stress will cause the mandrel to fail. Another method consists of mounting the mandrel in the die. By altering the shape of the mandrel, the internal contour can be changed to almost any desired shape. A round mandrel, however, is best for ease of removal. The mandrel is lubricated with a thin film of lubricant, which must not get into the die cavity or serious feeding problems will result. It is sometimes more practical to apply the lubricant to the interior of the part than to the mandrel.

Piano wire can be used for smaller diameter mandrels (up to 0.060″; 1.52 mm diam). For larger diameters, a shock-resistant tool steel, hardened to about $R_C$55-57 and ground to a high finish, is used. In some cases a flash chromium plate on the mandrel increases its abrasive wear resistance.

## HOT SWAGING

While most metals are swaged at room temperature, some materials require heating prior to swaging, as discussed previously in this chapter under the subject of "Materials Swaged." Hot swaging is also used to form long or steep tapers, and for large reductions. Caution must be used when hot swaging, however, since elevated temperatures can cause the column strength of the material to be lowered so that it cannot sustain the feeding forces of swaging without bending. The maximum reduction that an alloy can be given without the generation of flaws varies significantly with the chemical composition and metallurgical structure of the workpiece, the swaging sequence to be used, and the shape into which the workpiece is to be formed.

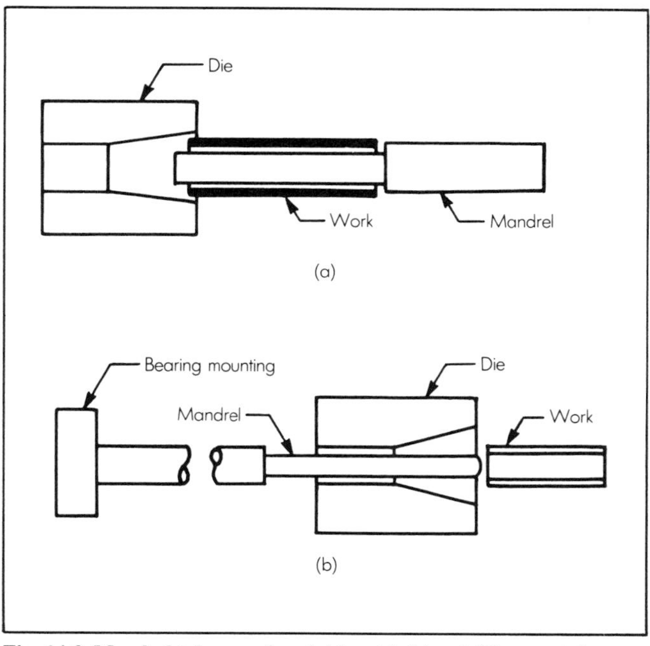


**Fig. 14-3 Mandrel tube swaging: (a) hand-held and (b) mounted.**

## INTERNAL SWAGING

Several types of machines (discussed later in this chapter) have been built specifically to form complex profiles in the bores of cylindrical workpieces. Such special-purpose machines, however, are costly and applications are limited.

# SWAGING APPLICATIONS

Swaging is used for a wide variety of applications, including tapering, pointing, reducing, external and internal forming, compacting, sizing, and assembling. A few typical examples are illustrated in Fig. 14-4. Typical cross sections of internal shapes produced by swaging tubular stock over shaped mandrels are shown in Fig. 14-5.

Reductions are made to diameters as small as 0.005″ (0.13 mm) and on workpieces of unlimited length. The amount of reduction possible per pass varies with the material swaged. An application of reducing in the production of piston rods is shown in Fig. 14-6, in which a groove must be produced in the outside diameter of a tube, near the center (view *a*). If the groove were machined, the tubing wall below the groove would be too thin for the intended application. Instead, the groove is formed by swaging (view *b*) and then machining (view *c*), allowing sufficient wall thickness below the groove.

In reducing or pointing tubing, a mandrel is only required when the tubing has very thin walls. Thickening of the walls, however, usually occurs when tubing is swaged without a mandrel. To control the diameters, a mandrel is used.

The length of tapers that can be swaged depends upon the capacity of the machine. Long tapers can be formed in a single operation on large machines. On smaller machines, tapers longer than about 18″ (457 mm) are generally formed in two or more operations. Two or more sets of dies are required for such operations, with the successive sets overlapping the preceding sets; but this requires care in blending the tapers produced.

The 14½″ (368 mm) long taper on the tubular part shown in Fig. 14-7 is completed in 15 seconds or less on a swager equipped with an automatic hydraulic feed. Production rates

## SWAGING APPLICATIONS

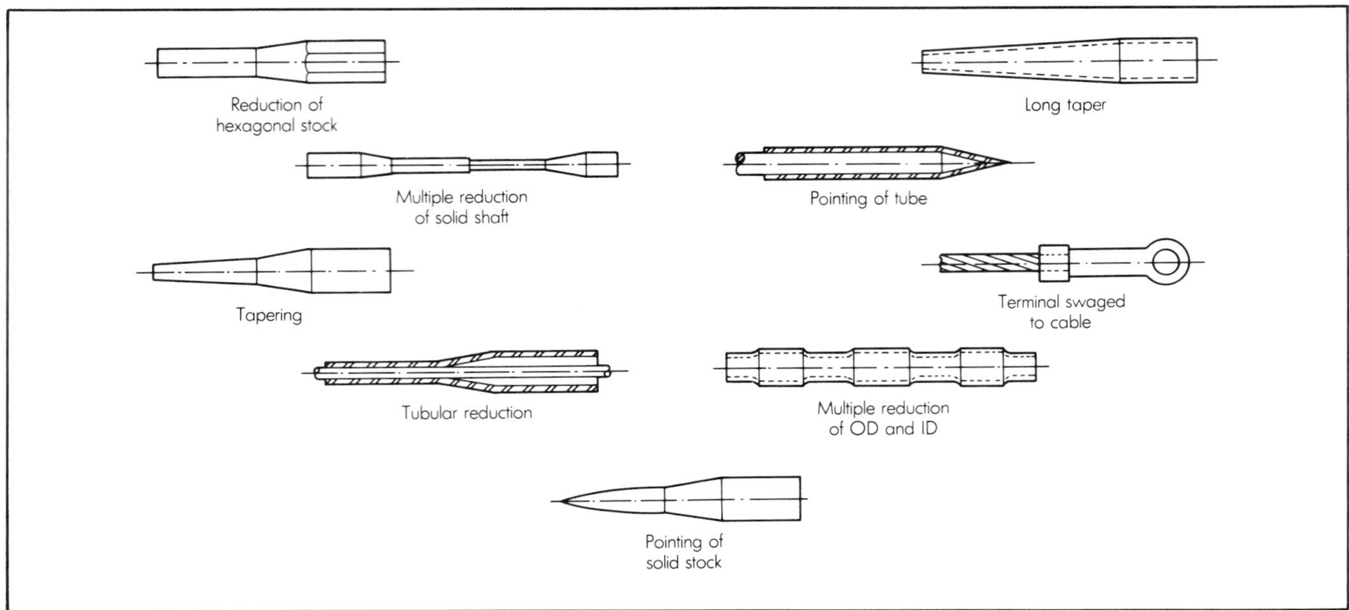


**Fig. 14-4 Examples of typical swaging applications.** (*Machinery Div., The Torrington Co.*)

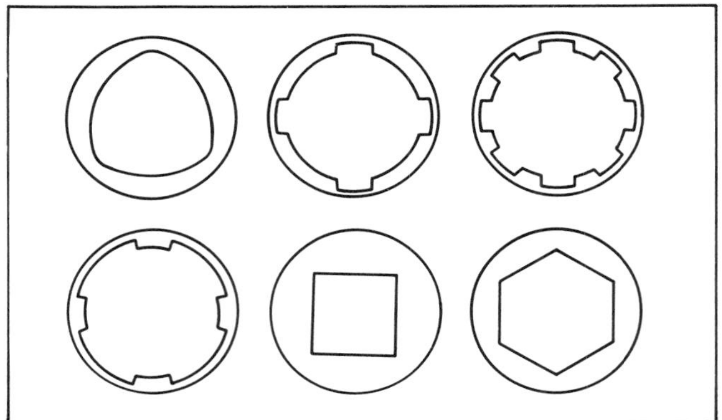

**Fig. 14-5 Various cross sections produced by swaging tubes over shaped mandrels.** (*Abbey Etna Machine Co.*)

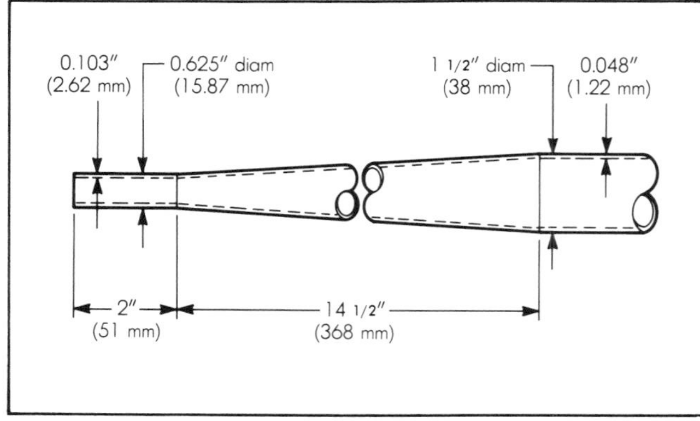


**Fig. 14-7 Swaging the 14½" (368 mm) long taper on this tubular part requires only 15 seconds.** (*Abbey Etna Machine Co.*)

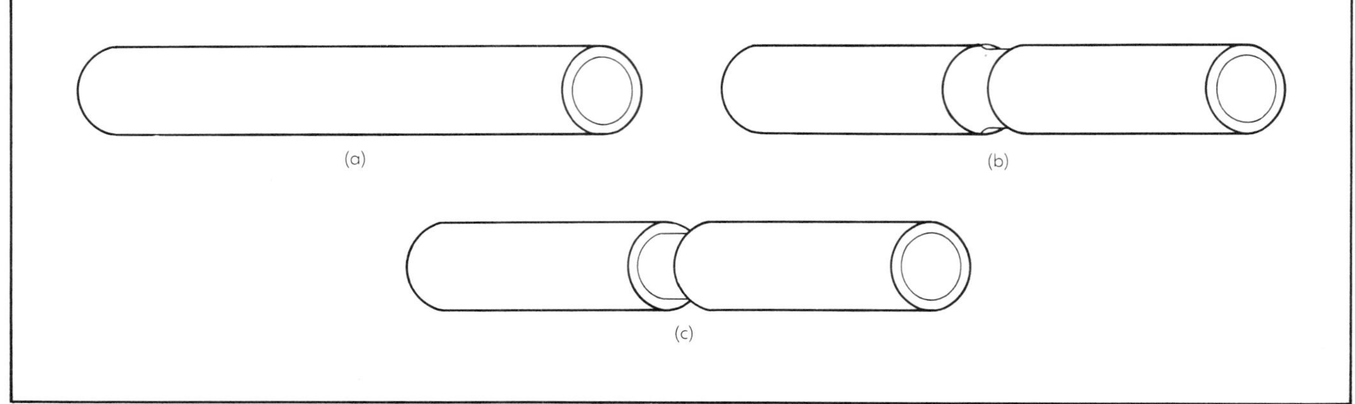


**Fig. 14-6 Tube to be used for a piston rod (a) is grooved by swaging (b) and then machined (c) to allow sufficient wall thickness below the groove.** (*Abbey Etna Machine Co.*)

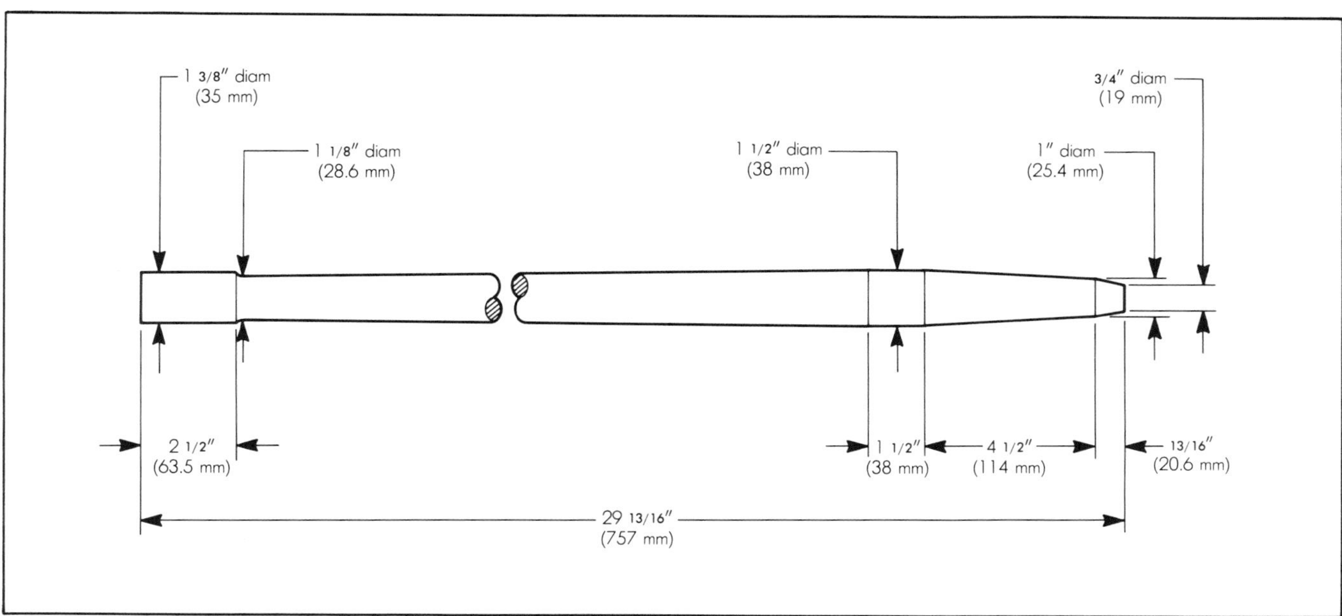


**Fig. 14-8 Swaging of this part provided a material savings of 40% over the machining method previously employed.** (*Abbey Etna Machine Co.*)

average 250-300 parts per hour for this application.

The part illustrated in Fig. 14-8 was originally machined from solid bar stock. By converting to swaging, it was possible to reduce the length of the stock and its diameter. This resulted in a savings in material of 40% and a reduction in labor costs of 30%. The swaged part is 15% stronger than the one previously machined. Swaging is done in three operations: two hot, with the workpieces heated to 1750° F (954° C), and a final forming at room temperature. The first hot swaging operation requires 25 seconds; the second, 20 seconds. The cold-swaging operation requires 20 seconds.

Swaging is employed for many different assembly applications. Figure 14-9 illustrates the assembly of a nonferrous bushing inside steel tubing. Slightly oversized steel tube lengths are drilled radially at the desired location of the bushings, and the bushings are inserted into the tubes. The assemblies are then swaged over a mandrel to hold the required diameter of the bushing bore. Swaging causes the bushing material to flow into the drilled holes, thus locking the assembly.

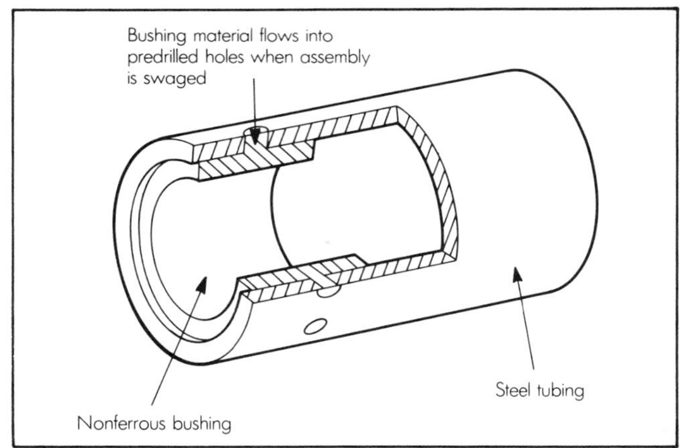


**Fig. 14-9 Nonferrous bushing is assembled and locked inside steel tube by swaging.** (*Fenn Manufacturing Co.*)

# SWAGING MACHINES

Swaging machines are available in many different types, sizes, and capacities to suit specific requirements. Machine selection requires consideration of many variables including the application; workpiece size, geometry, and material; production requirements (quality, accuracy, and finish); and cost (initial, operating, and maintenance).

## MACHINE CAPACITY

The proper machine size for a particular swaging application depends primarily upon the strength of the head designed into the machine. The load on the head is a direct result of the projected area of material under compression and the tensile strength of the material being swaged.

The rated diameter of solid stock that can be swaged on a machine can be calculated from the following formula:

$$D = \frac{C}{L \times S} \tag{2}$$

where:

$D$ = rated diameter of solid stock, in.
$C$ = capacity (safe working load), lb
$L$ = die length, in.
$S$ = tensile strength of workpiece material, psi

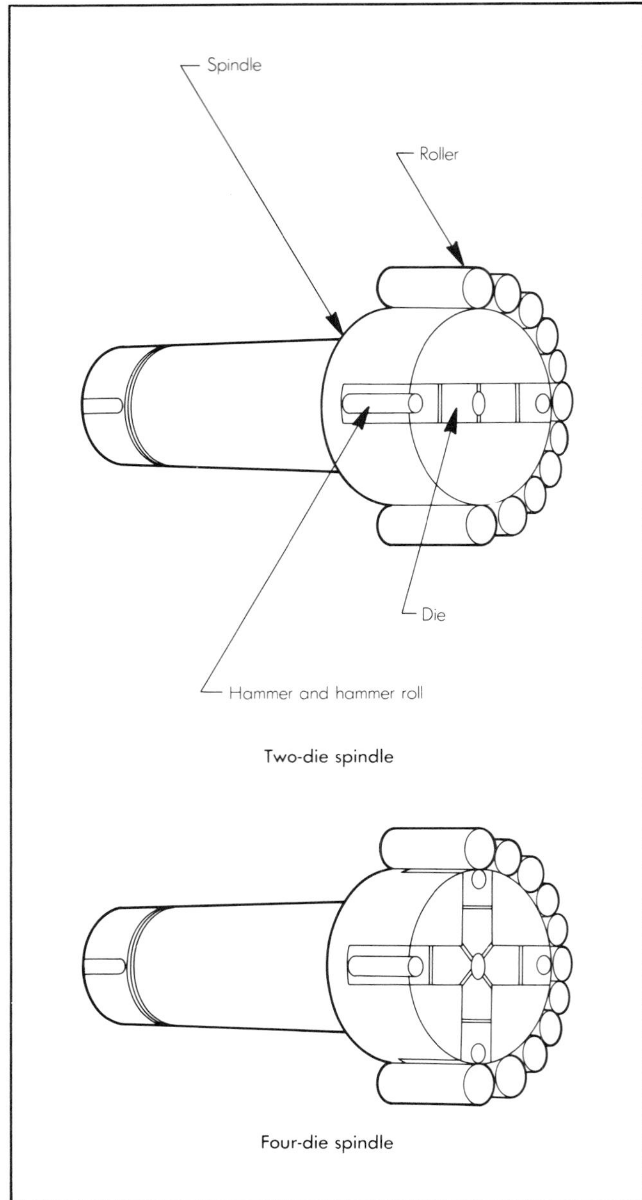


**Fig. 14-10 Typical construction of two and four-die swaging machines.** (*Abbey Etna Machine Co.*)

Example:

If the strength of the head limits the safe working load of the swaging machine to 112,500 lb (500 kN), the die is 3″ (76 mm) long, and the tensile strength of the workpiece material is 60,000 psi (414 MPa), the rated diameter for solid stock is:

$$D = \frac{112{,}500}{3 \times 60{,}000} = \tfrac{5}{8}\,'' \text{ (16 mm)}$$

For materials with lower tensile strengths, solid stock of larger diameter can be swaged; for materials with higher tensile strengths, the stock diameter must be smaller. It is possible to change the diameter capacity by varying the length of die in contact with the workpiece. If the tensile strength of the material exceeds 120,000 psi (827 MPa), cold swaging may not be satisfactory and hot swaging should be considered.

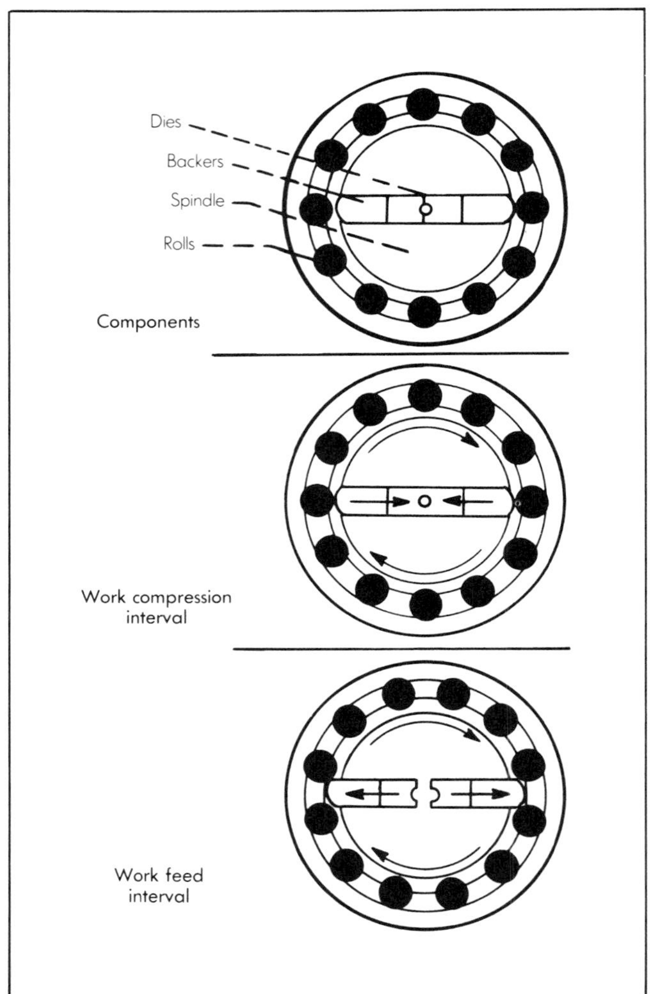


**Fig. 14-11 Components and swaging action in a rotary machine.** (*Machinery Div., The Torrington Co.*)

Safe working loads for swaging machine heads generally range from 15,000-4,000,000 lb (67-17 792 kN) or more, based on the average diameter of the tapered section of the die (not the stock diameter) and on workpiece material having a yield strength of 60,000 psi (414 MPa).

The smallest standard machines available can swage solid stock to 1/16″ (1.6 mm) diam and tubing to ¼″ (6.3 mm) diam; the largest machines can swage solid stock to 4″ (102 mm) diam and tubing to 14″ (356 mm) diam. Special machines have been built to swage larger solid stock and tubing.

## NUMBER OF DIES

Most swaging machines are of the two or four-die type (see Fig. 14-10), but three-die machines are sometimes used for swaging certain parts, such as three-flute taps. With two-die construction, the two dies are placed in a rectangular slot across the larger end of the spindle. Four-die swagers have two slots

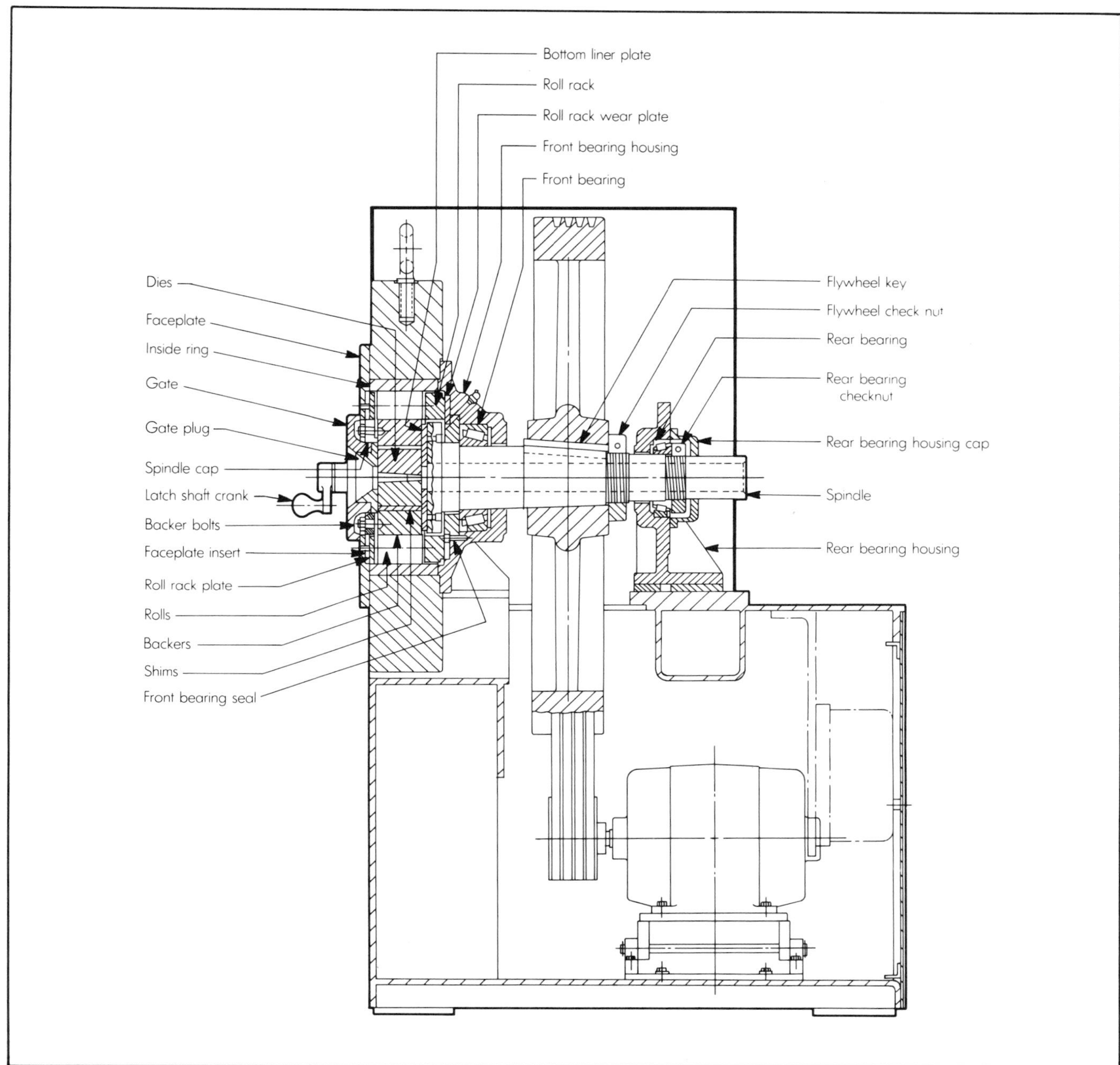


**Fig. 14-12 Cross section of a typical rotary swaging machine.** (*Machinery Div., The Torrington Co.*)

that are at right angles to each other, each slot containing a pair of dies.

Two-die construction is used on both small and large swaging machines, but four-die construction is more common on larger machines. For certain applications, such as those involving heavy reductions and those in which finish and accuracy are secondary considerations, four-die machines are more efficient than two-die types.

Four-die swaging has several advantages over two-die swaging. On the four-die swager, work reduction is quicker and is of a greater magnitude. The rolls of a four-die machine offer more direct hammering pressure and less of a bearing surface, and the maximum angle of taper can be increased over that of the two-die operation. There is less chance of the dies splitting on the four-die machine when heavy reductions are performed and less twist when a coil of stock is worked. Surface finish produced by the four-die machine, however, is not as good as that produced by the two-die machine.

To properly decide whether a two-die or four-die swager should be used, several factors must be considered. The initial and maintenance costs of the four-die swagers are higher than those of the two-die machine. For both types of swagers, the feed rate and the rate of wear of parts are generally the same. There is less flexibility in the dies of the four-die swager, and the four-die swager usually takes more time to set up. A four-die machine should, therefore, be used only for applications in which the machine has a definite advantage over the two-die machine or for operations that can be performed only on the four-die machine. For example, swaging of hexagonal and square sections on round stock requires a four-die machine with a special spindle device that rotates the stock at the same speed as the spindle.

## ROTARY SWAGING MACHINES

The action of a rotary swager is illustrated in Fig. 14-11, which shows the interior of the machine after the faceplate is removed. As the spindle is rotated, the backers strike opposing rolls and are driven inward, giving a blow to the work. As the spindle continues to revolve, centrifugal force causes the dies to separate. The number of blows delivered to the work is a function of the number of rolls and the revolution speed of the spindle, which varies from about 100 rpm in large machines to 1000 rpm or more in small machines. The amount of die movement varies from 0.005-0.375″ (0.13-9.52 mm), depending on the type of machine and the work being performed.

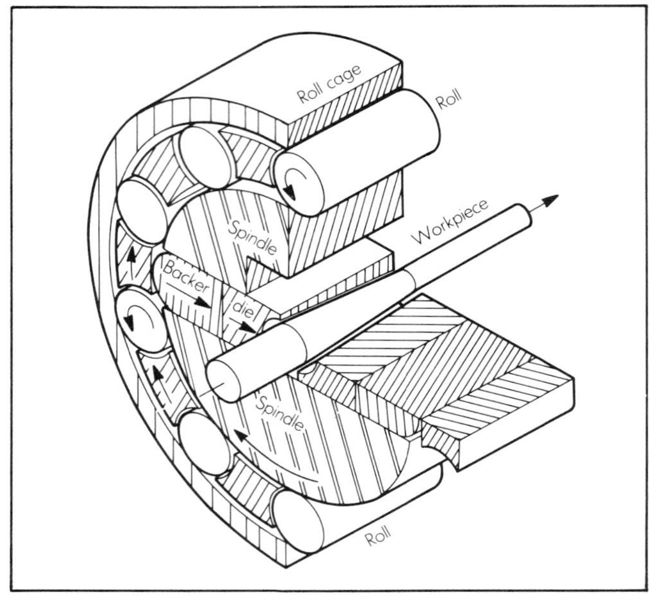


**Fig. 14-13 Components in a standard two-die rotary swaging machine.**

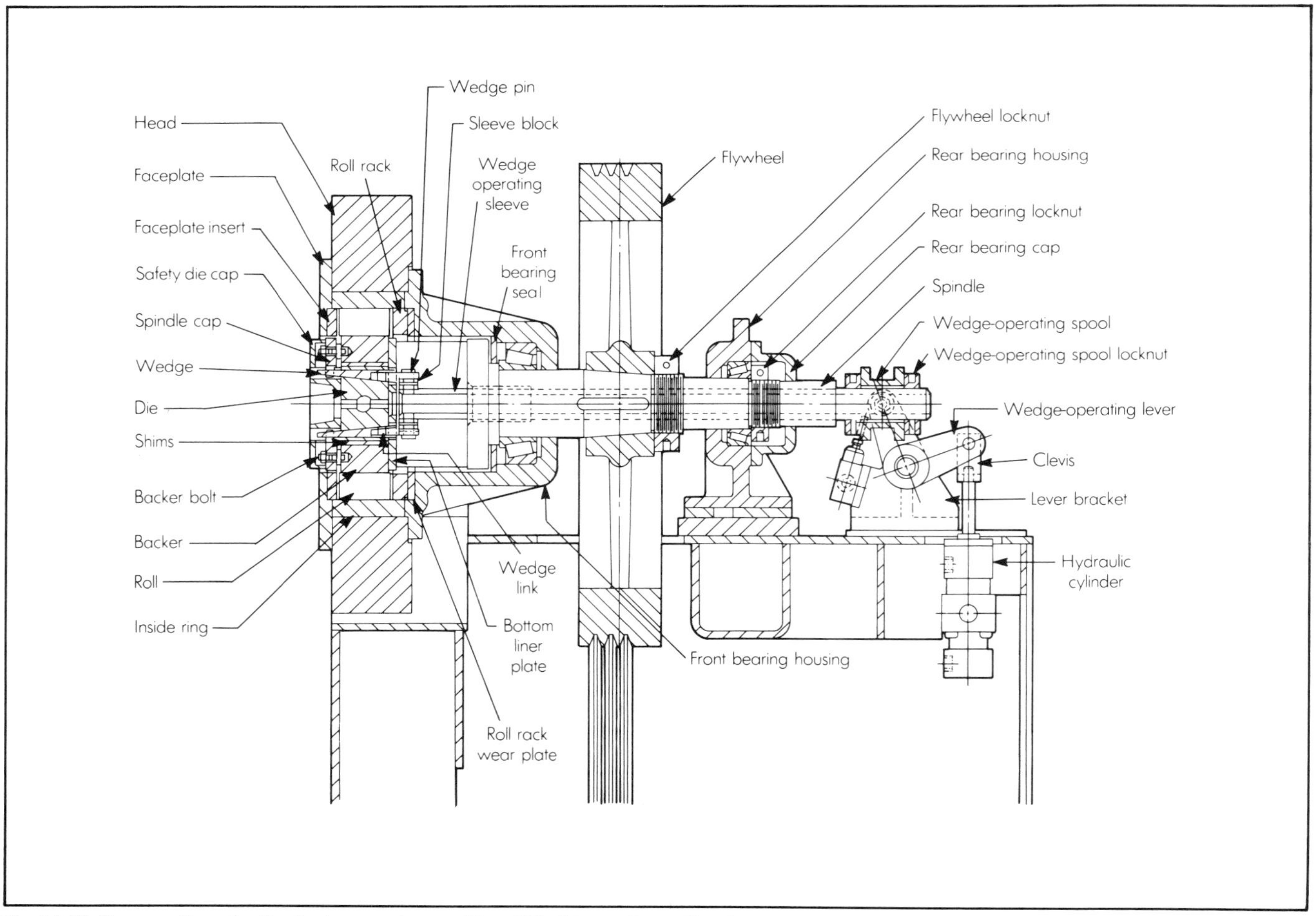

**Fig. 14-14 Cross section of a die-closing swaging machine.** (*Machinery Div., The Torrington Co.*)

Figure 14-12 shows a cross section of a typical rotary swager. The machine is constructed with a base that supports the head and bearing mountings. The spindle is rotated by a motor-driven flywheel to provide the required inertia. The head of the spindle is slotted to hold the backers and dies (see Fig. 14-13). These parts fit freely in the slot so they slide easily. The inside ring is press-fitted into the head of the machine and is under compression. This compression places the inside ring in a better condition to accept the loads imposed upon it during swaging. The rolls are mounted in a cage to keep them separated and to prevent them from skewing under heavy loads. A shim is placed between the backer and the die to allow for manufacturing tolerances and to permit the dies to be economically redressed. The amount of stock removed in reworking the dies is compensated for by the use of a thicker shim.

When the swager is being set up for operation, sufficient shimming should be used to bring the die faces together as the flywheel is rotated. During the rotation of the flywheel, the high point of the backer passes over the roll and a blow is delivered. This blow should be such that it requires moderate effort to rotate the flywheel by hand. Too heavy a blow imposes overloading and premature failure of the internal parts of the machine; but if the die faces do not meet, it is impossible to control diameter accurately.

## DIE-CLOSING SWAGERS

Die-closing swagers are used whenever it is necessary to open the die faces a greater amount for loading than is possible with rotary machines. A cross-sectional view of such a machine is shown in Fig. 14-14. The general construction is the same as that of the rotary swager in that both machines have common parts such as backers, rolls, an inside ring, and shims, but the die-closing swager differs in the addition of a wedge mechanism. The back of the die is ground at an angle, and a wedge is inserted between the angular die and the backer (see Fig. 14-15). The wedge is connected by a mechanical linkage to a hydraulic cylinder which serves as its motive power and permits precise positive control of the opening and closing rate of the dies.

The use of the wedge permits a large opening between the die faces with the wedge retracted. Therefore, work of a larger diameter can be inserted in the machine for swaging. As the wedges are advanced to the forward position, the machine functions exactly like a rotary swager. The die-closing swager can be used for center reductions and fastening operations. It is versatile to the extent that it may be used as a rotary machine by simply removing the wedges and installing the proper tooling. Reductions are limited to 25% of the diameter of the work. The angle of the wedges generally varies between 4 and 7 1/2°.

Automatic cycling for the die-closing machine has been developed so that the machine stops when the work is loaded or unloaded from the swager. This is particularly advantageous in fastening terminals to aircraft-cable assemblies. This feature eliminates the possibility of damage to highly finished or critical parts due to improper handling.

## STATIONARY-SPINDLE SWAGING MACHINES

Stationary-spindle swagers are rotary machines in reverse. As the name implies, the spindle is fixed so that the dies reciprocate in a vertical or horizontal plane; the head of the machine rotates about the spindle, thus giving the blow to the

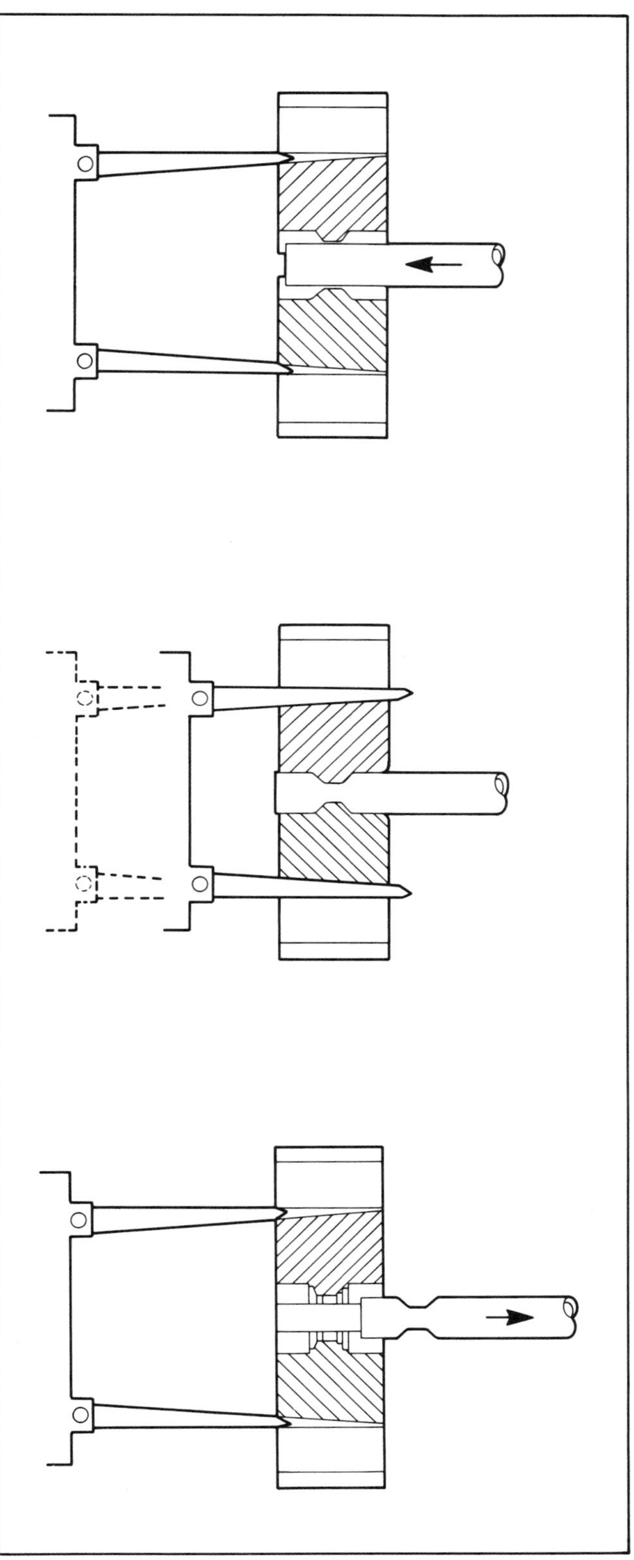

**Fig. 14-15 Die-closing unit consists of a pair of hydraulically operated wedges between the backers and the dies to permit larger die openings.** (*Fenn Manufacturing Co.*)

backers and dies. A cross section of the machine is illustrated in Fig. 14-16. The usual components of swaging machines are included, but the basic difference between this machine and others lies in its rotating head and fixed spindle. The operation still comprises an impact blow delivered to the work. Between roller contacts, the backers and dies are retracted radially outward by springs. Since the die remains in the same plane, it is possible to swage external shapes of regular or irregular geometric shape, including complex cross sections such as gundrill shanks from tubing and tap blanks with square driving ends. Parts with circular cross sections can be swaged by rotating the workpieces, thus preventing a slight parting line where the dies meet.

These machines are used to manufacture shapes that are not round. They are available in two, three, and four-die configurations to handle various applications. One limitation is the need for a transition region between changes in cross-sectional shapes when workpieces are fed into and out of the dies; 90° shoulders cannot be formed.

## CREEPING-SPINDLE SWAGERS

Creeping-spindle swaging machines employ the principles of both stationary-spindle and rotary swagers. On these machines, the spindle head is mounted on a slowly rotating shaft which is driven by a reduction gear and variable-speed motor. The spindle head, containing the hammers and dies, revolves slowly within a rapidly rotating roller cage.

One advantage of creeping-spindle swaging is more accurate control of die reciprocation. These machines are used for swaging applications that are not suitable for stationary-spindle machines, such as forming rods or tubes into coils or forming workpieces that cannot be easily oscillated. Advantages include minimum flash on the workpieces and reduced possibility of the workpieces whipping.

## HOT SWAGING MACHINES

Machines used for hot swaging are commonly water cooled. A channel is machined into the head of the swager to permit the circulation of water for extracting heat from the machine. A water-jacket swager is shown in Fig. 14-17. A flushing system (see Fig. 14-18) can be used to cascade coolant through the working parts of the machine to remove scale that tends to accumulate inside.

The method of heating workpieces for hot swaging should be one that keeps oxidation and resulting scale to a minimum. Because of its abrasiveness, scale is detrimental to the life of the internal components of the machine.

## SIMULTANEOUS-BLOW SWAGING MACHINES

In simultaneous-blow swaging, performed with four-die stationary-spindle machines, all four dies contact the work simultaneously. This method is used to form fluted shapes and other circular cross sections.

## ALTERNATE-BLOW SWAGING MACHINES

Alternate-blow swaging (see Fig. 14-19) is effective for swaging shapes in a four-die stationary-spindle machine. It is accomplished by having alternate rolls recessed. With this arrangement, when two opposing rolls hammer the dies, the rolls 90° away do not (see Fig. 14-20), thus eliminating forming fins on the workpieces. Applications include swaging chisels, screwdrivers, file tangs, tapered leaf springs, and similar products.

## INTERNAL SWAGING MACHINES

Two types of machines have been built specifically for internal swaging; but as previously discussed, they have had only limited application. These machines can rapidly produce complex profiles in the bores of cylindrical workpieces. Applications include rifle barrels, heat-exchanger tubes, sockets, internal splines and gear teeth, and ratchets. Starting workpieces can be tubing, castings, forgings, extrusions, powder metal parts, or premachined blanks.

On one type of machine, called the Intraform, four dies pulsate rapidly while revolving around the periphery of the workpiece. The dies, mounted on cams, pulsate through contact with a series of free-wheeling, hardened steel rollers located in a raceway in the machine's headstock. The cams cause the dies to produce a smooth, continuous squeezing action, with no hammering effect, at the rate of more than 1000 times per minute. Contact with the rotating dies causes the free-wheeling workpiece to revolve at about 80% of the die speed.

Operations can be performed with or without a mandrel. When a mandrel is used, the workpiece is fed over the mandrel toward the rear of the headstock (see Fig. 14-21) and the mandrel is not fed. Long workpieces can be formed with a short, relatively inexpensive mandrel. Operations on hollow or solid workpieces for which a mandrel is not required include pointing, reduction of diameters, and forming tapers.

With another type of internal swaging machine, called the Fellows-Appel for a process called Multiflow, solid or tubular workpieces are rotated and fed intermittently between four forming dies that are forced radially against the workpieces to squeeze the material. Each die is spring loaded to a crank-actuated mover. The crank arms, mounted eccentrically on four pinion shafts driven by a single bull gear, work in pairs, first moving toward then away from each other. This motion is transmitted to the four die blocks by rollers that fit the grooved ends of the cranks.

A mandrel is used in conjunction with the dies to form internal shapes. Workpieces are loaded into a feeding unit, with their ends held in a chuck for rotation. As the feeding unit moves the workpiece into the forming head in short, rapid increments, the four dies move radially toward the workpiece at rates to 1500 strokes per minute. Intermittent rotation and feeding of the workpiece is in timed relation with the die movements. After forming, the shaped workpieces are fed into a straightness control device.

## SWAGING SMALL PARTS ON PRESSES

Automatic and continuous die swaging of miniature parts required in large quantities is being done rapidly and economically on power presses. One half of the swaging die is fastened to the press bed or bolster, and the other half is attached to the press ram. Workpieces can be solid or tubular, and secondary operations can be performed simultaneously. Secondary operations that have been incorporated into this process include sawing, heading, skiving, lancing, piercing, modified knurling, and flattening. Coiled wire is used for solid parts; and strip stock, formed into tubing on the press, for hollow parts.

A progressive series of mating cavities are machined into both die halves. With each stroke of the press, the material is

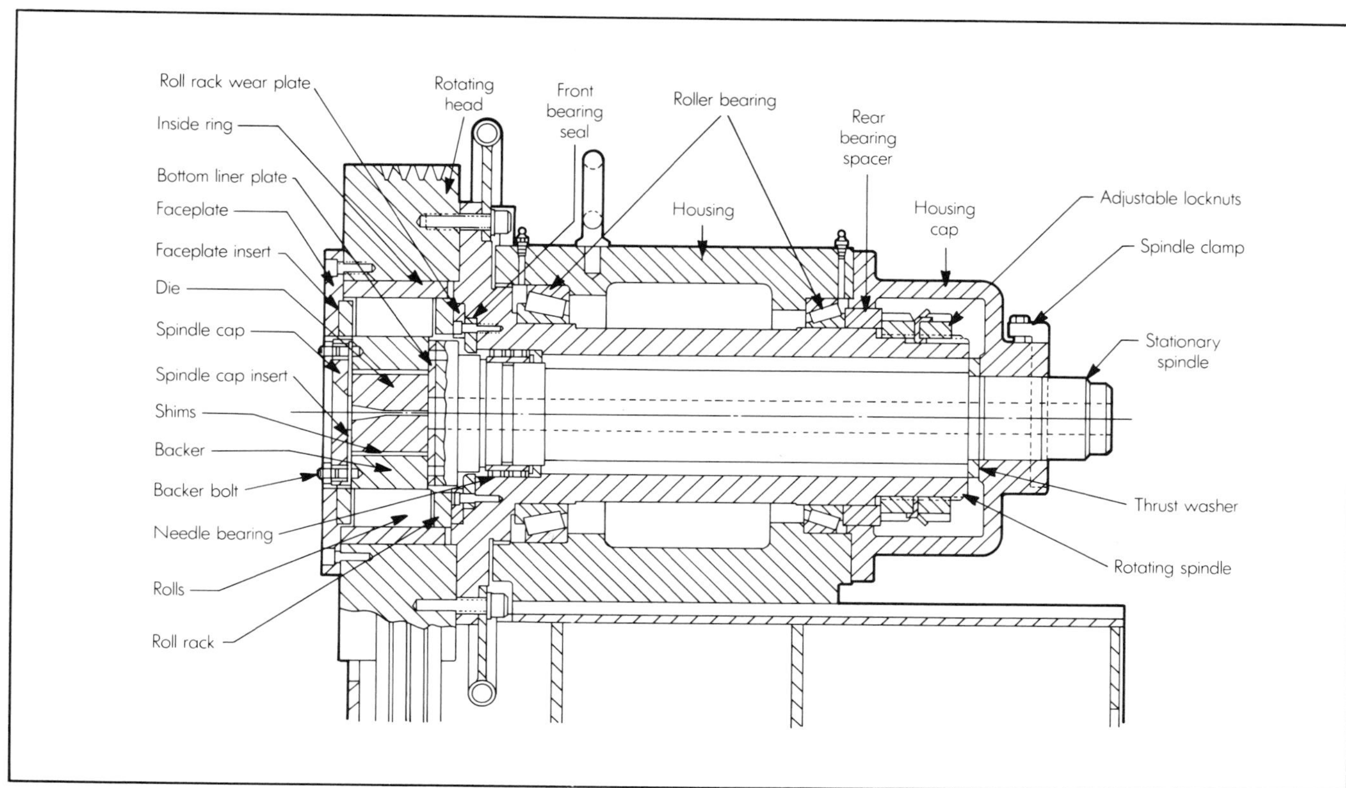


**Fig. 14-16 Cross section of a stationary-spindle swaging machine.** (*Machinery Div., The Torrington Co.*)

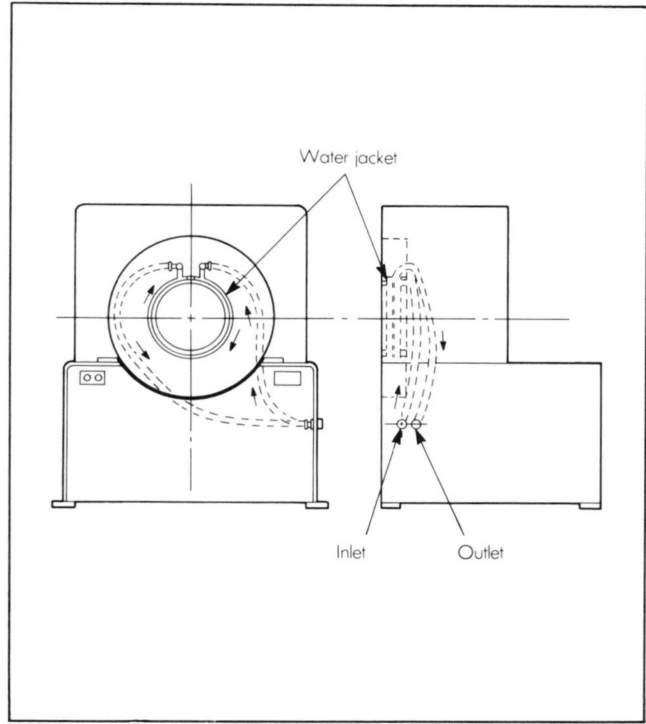


**Fig. 14-17 Water-jacketing arrangement for hot-swaging machine.** (*Machinery Div., The Torrington Co.*)

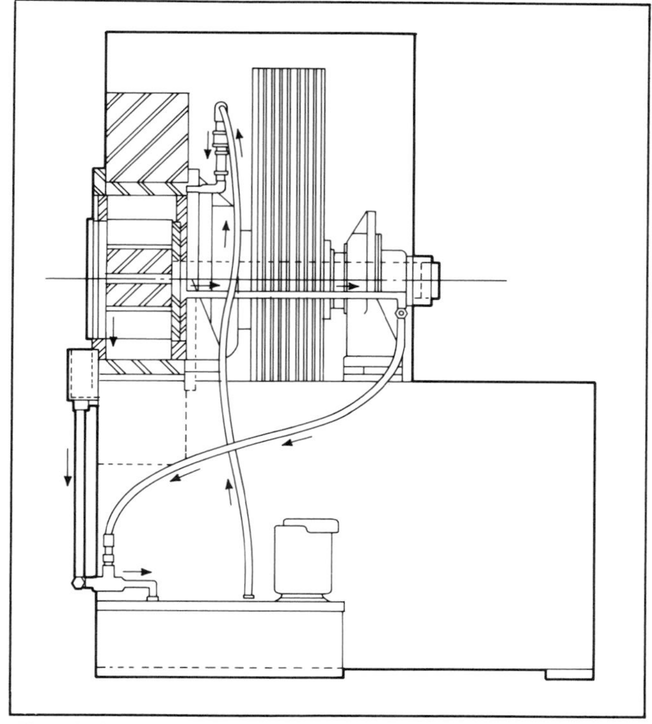

**Fig. 14-18 Flushing system for a hot-swaging machine.** (*Machinery Div., The Torrington Co.*)

# CHAPTER 14

## SWAGING MACHINES

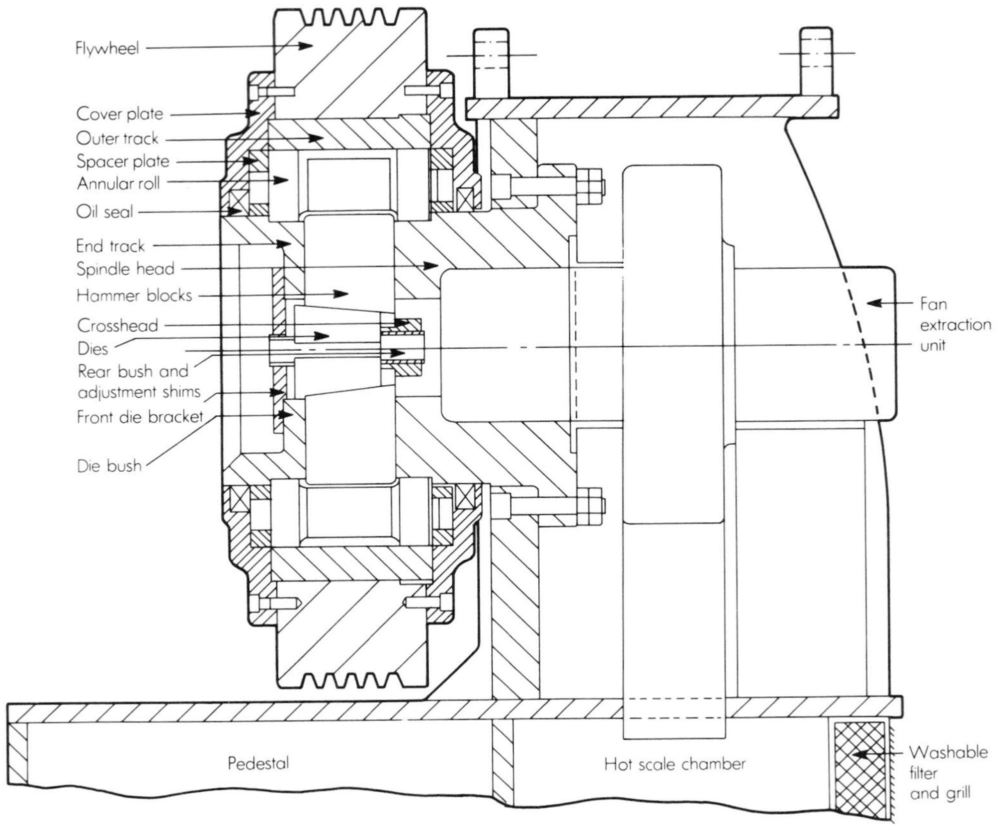

**Fig. 14-19 A four-die stationary-spindle machine equipped with rolls for alternate-blow swaging. (*Abbey Etna Machine Co.*)**

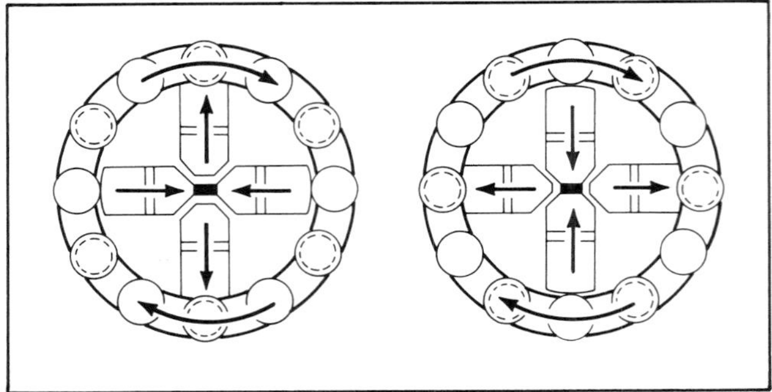

**Fig. 14-20 With alternate recessed rolls, two opposing rolls hammer two dies while the rolls 90° away do not. (*Abbey Etna Machine Co.*)**

advanced one die cavity and rotated 90° clockwise. On the next press stroke, the material is advanced to the next die cavity and is rotated 90° counterclockwise. A ratchet, mechanically operated from the press crankshaft, provides the oscillating rotary motion which ensures symmetrical shaping with uniform wall thicknesses.

Periodic advancement and partial rotation of the material and opening and closing of the dies results in progressive swaging. A completed part is cut off with each stroke of the press. Any change in diameter of the parts being formed requires a small radius between adjacent diameters to permit metal flow; sharp corners or undercuts cannot be formed. When solid wire is being swaged, only small diameter changes are feasible.

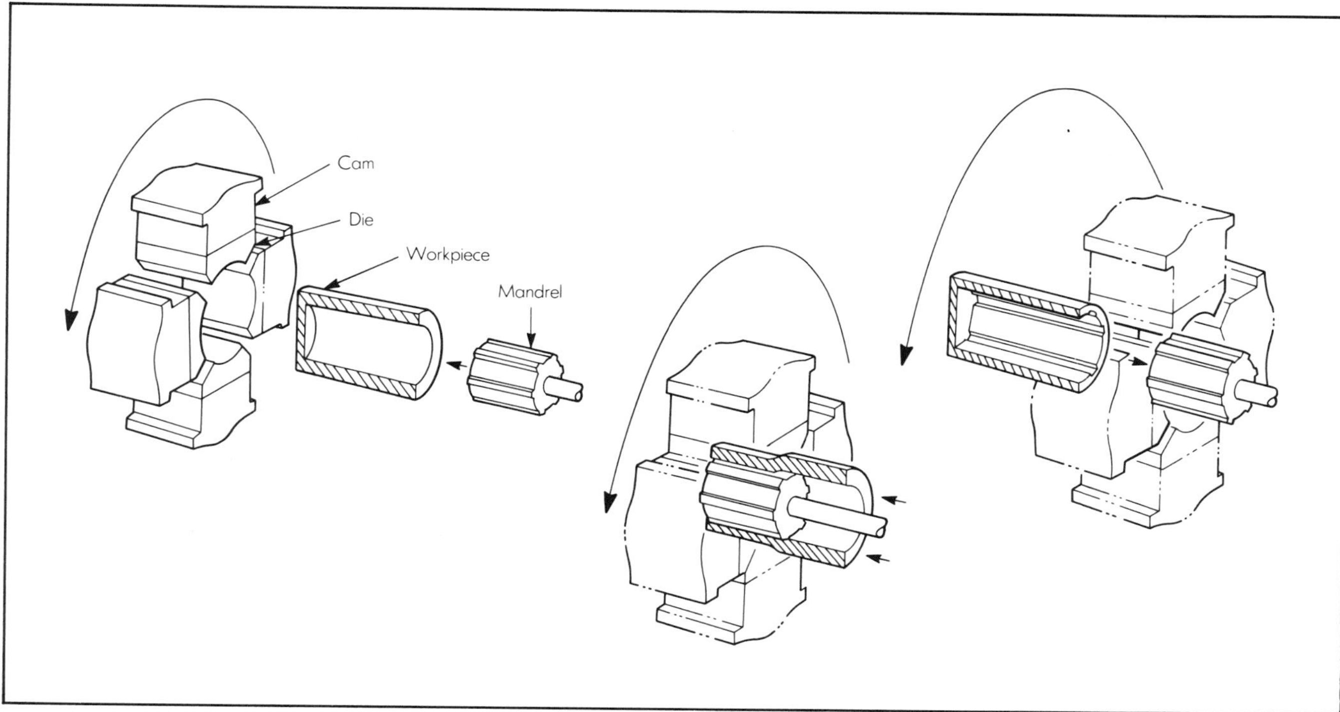


**Fig. 14-21 Internal swaging with a mandrel on an Intraform machine.** (*Cincinnati Milacron Inc.*)

# FEEDING SWAGERS

Methods of feeding swaging machines vary from hand feeding to feeding via completely automatic units. Selection of a particular type of feed depends upon the specific application.

## HAND FEEDING

Hand feeding is the most satisfactory and often fastest method for many swaging applications, especially for small work, simple shapes, and low production requirements. This method offers good control, and intermittent thrust is easily absorbed by the hands. Also, the operator can increase or decrease the feed pressure more effectively than a power unit can.

The included angle of taper in swaging, however, is generally restricted to about 8°, and swaging lengths are limited with hand feeding. Guide or feed blocks may also be necessary to ensure straight feeding.

## POWER FEEDING

For larger and/or longer workpieces, greater reductions, more complex shapes, heavy and/or unwieldly parts, and higher production requirements, power feeding is generally required. The pulsating end thrust set up by the opening and closing of the dies (feedback) can be too high for hand feeding. Power feeding permits swaging with higher included angles—to 14° and even more on small parts and copper or aluminum tubing.

Several types of standard mechanical and hydraulic swager feeding units are available. These feeders positively advance the work into the die and permit no bounce. Air feeds are not recommended because they offer a cushion to the work as it is advanced into the die, thereby permitting bounce and causing pickup by the die. However, combined hydraulic/pneumatic units are sometimes used. The choice of mechanical or hydraulic feed is dependent upon the type of application and production requirements. If high feed force is necessary, a hydraulic feed is the best selection; for modest production rates at low expense, a mechanical unit will suffice. A simple rack-and-pinion device is sometimes sufficient to increase the mechanical advantage in hand feeding.

One common method of power feeding is the use of a hydraulically actuated, traveling vise, with workpiece rotation controlled by varying the pressure on the vise jaws (see Fig. 14-22). Another method frequently used is to grip the workpiece by a rotating collet, with rotation controlled by an adjustable brake and feeding accomplished with a hydraulic cylinder.

For applications in which it is desirable to continuously feed long solid or tubular work through the dies of a swager, roll feeds of pull and/or push-through type are often used. Roll feeds can be mounted at either or both ends of the swager; they are used for sizing operations over mandrels.

Holding devices for workpieces to be swaged are available with either outside or inside diameter gripping jaws. The holding devices are usually closed by a drawbar pulled by a slide that is actuated either hydraulically or pneumatically. Holding assemblies must be designed for controlled rotation, as required for swaging. For short workpieces that cannot be held tightly, holders that apply a light friction grip are sometimes used. Spring ejectors in the holders push the workpiece out of the swager.

When production volume warrants the capital expense, it is

feasible to use a completely automatic feeder by which production rates of 2000 or more pieces per hour are practical. Because a given metal flows only at a specific rate in swaging, there can be little improvement in actual swaging time. However, there can be a decided improvement in the time spent in handling the part. This portion of the complete swaging cycle can be significantly reduced with the introduction of automatic feeding units employing hoppers or magazines for loading.

An automatic loading device for a swaging machine is illustrated in Fig. 14-23. With this device, workpieces roll down an incline and are stopped by Detent No. 1. On the back stroke of the feed ram, Detent No. 2 is in its receded position, allowing a swaged part to be discharged. At the end of the back stroke, Detent No. 2 rises and No. 1 recedes, permitting one workpiece to roll into position for feeding into the swaging machine. A secondary detent on No. 1 prevents movement of the following workpieces. As the workpiece is gripped and the feed ram advances, Detent No. 2 recedes to allow the workpiece and holder to move forward in the clearance provided by radius *R*. The cycle is then repeated for continuous operation.

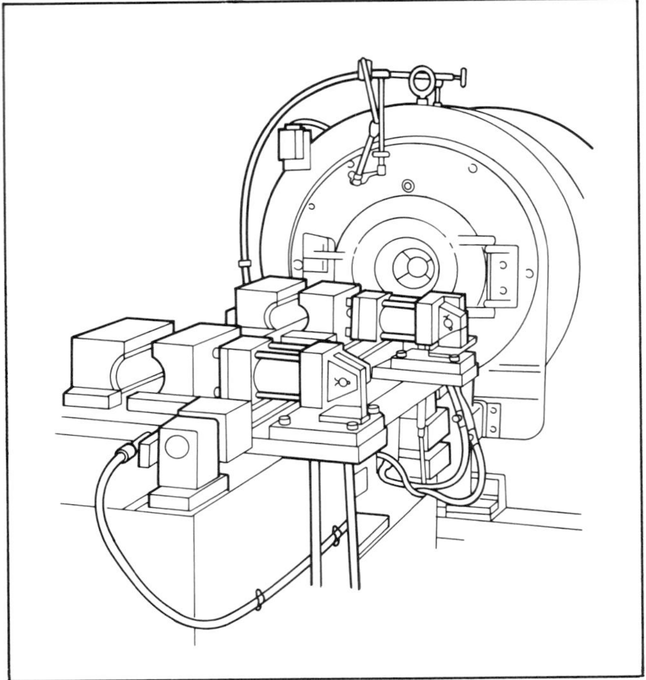

**Fig. 14-22 Hydraulically actuated, traveling-vise method of feeding a swaging machine.** (*Fenn Manufacturing Co.*)

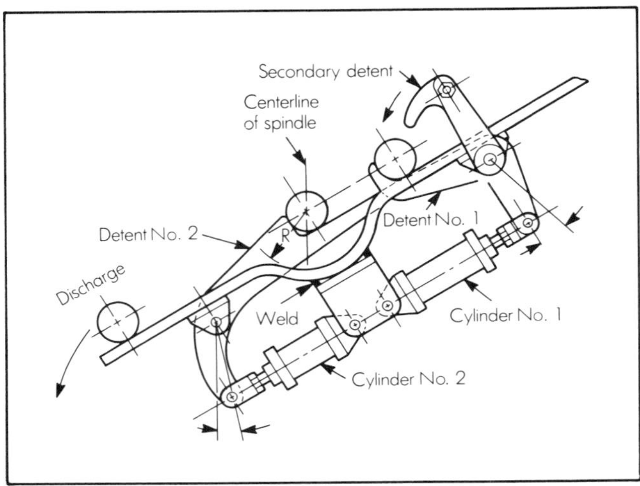


**Fig. 14-23 Automatic loading mechanism for a swaging machine employing detents for positioning the workpieces.**

# SWAGING DIES

Good swaging performance depends primarily upon the dies. Therefore, it is imperative that the dies be properly designed and carefully manufactured. Improper design can lead to feeding problems and poor surface quality such as finning, wrinkling, and rippling.

## TYPES OF OPERATIONS

Basically, swaging dies are constructed for three types of operations: (1) solid reduction, (2) tubular reduction, and (3) fastening and mandrel swaging. The difference in the dies used for these operations lies in the geometry of the die cavity. Because of the volume of metal being formed, dies for solid workpieces must have more clearance than those used for tubing. The function of the clearance is to prevent metal from being trapped and consequently overloading the dies and breaking them. Two types of construction, for solid reduction and tubular reduction, are illustrated in Figs. 14-24 and 14-25.

To ensure that a die performs well, several factors should be considered. The point at which the taper meets the blade should be well blended. A smooth transition from taper to blade has a streamlining effect which results in smooth metal flow through the die. It is desirable to have as smooth a surface finish as possible for swaging the softer metals such as lead and aluminum; rough areas on these metals induce pickup and its attendant problems. In the swaging of steel and other common metals, the surface of the die has little bearing on the type of swaged surface that results; in fact, experience has shown that in some operations a rough surface in the die is desirable.

Dies generally show wear in three ways: (1) by the production of out-of-tolerance pieces, (2) by a change in die geometry, and (3) by the development of a wear ring on the die. As a die is used over a period of time, the blade gradually wears to a larger diameter. When this wear reaches the point at which the parts are no longer within specification, it is necessary to make an adjustment. A die that is swaged out of tolerance can be corrected by grinding a few thousandths of an inch (0.03-0.05 mm) off the die face. If more than this amount of stock has to be removed to achieve the specified tolerance, the die should be reworked. Removing too much stock from the face of the die changes its geometry. The development of a wear ring can be corrected by completely reworking the die. This wear ring occurs at the point at which the workpiece first makes contact

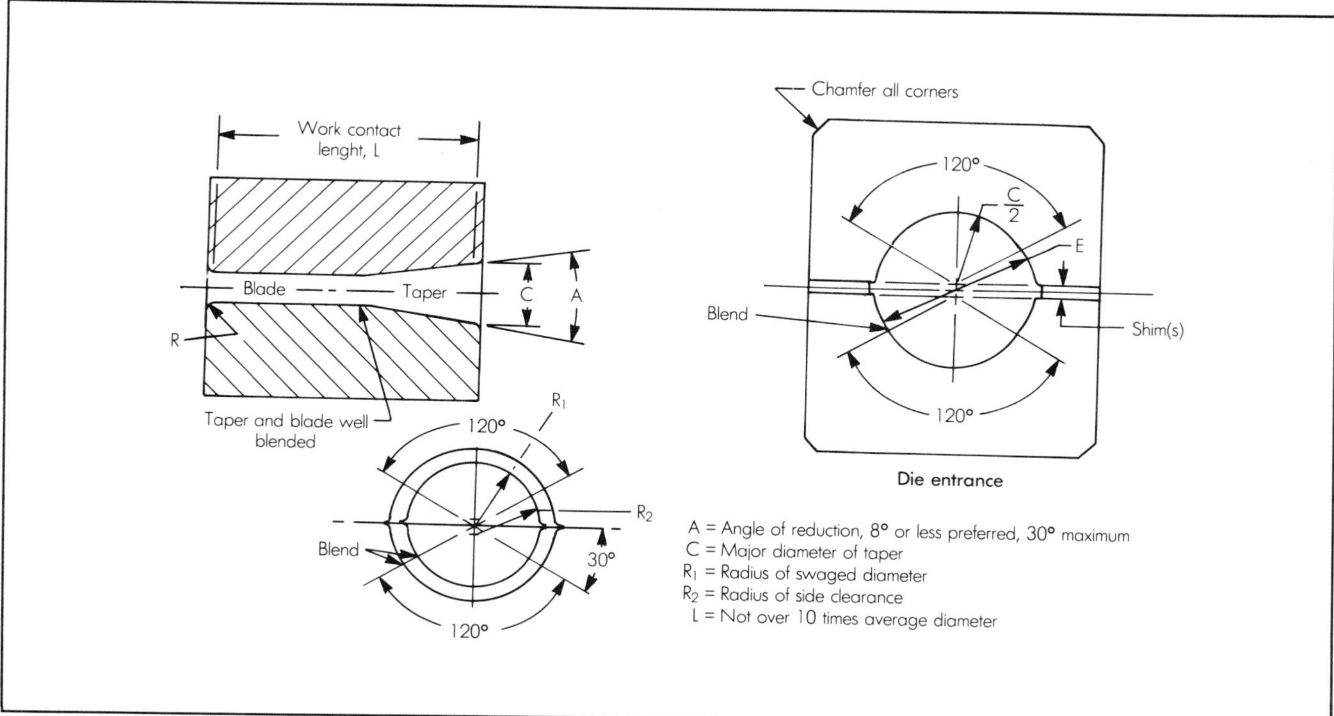


**Fig. 14-24 Swaging die for solid reduction.** (*Machinery Div., The Torrington Co.*)

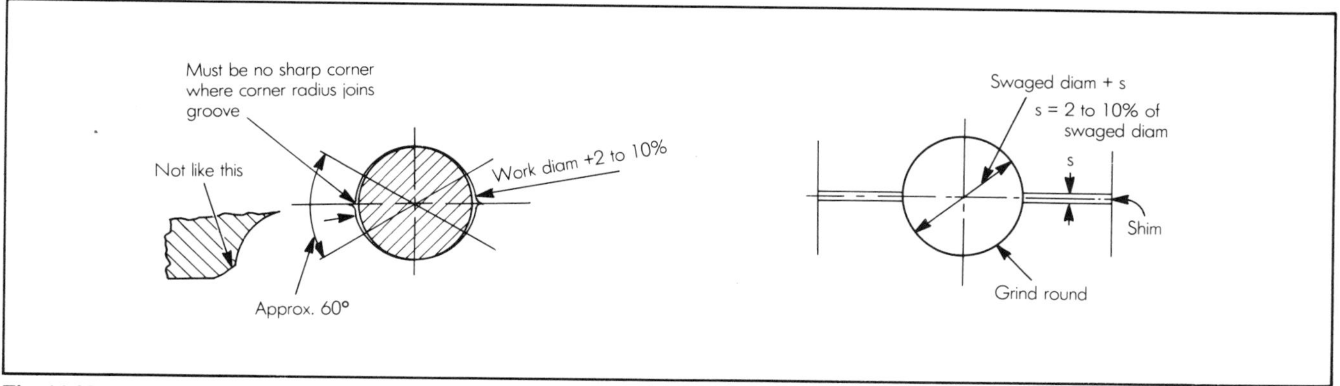


**Fig. 14-25 Swaging die for tubular reduction.** (*Machinery Div., The Torrington Co.*)

with the die. Dirty workpieces or sharp cutoff edges greatly accelerate the development of the wear ring.

Generally, the standard swaging die cavity is considered in terms of two areas. The first area is called the taper and is the tapered portion of the die; it is the area of the die at which the greatest amount of swaging is done. The second area is called the blade. The blade is the straight portion of the die cavity and the area of the die at which final sizing and surface finishing take place.

For easy hand feeding of work into the swager, the taper should have an included angle of 6-8°. As the taper angle increases, it becomes progressively more difficult to feed the work. In fact, beginning with included angles of 12-15°, a hydraulic or mechanical feed unit is required to feed the work into the machine. At included angles of 28-30°, swaging generally becomes impractical except with some tubing materials, such as copper.

## Solid Reduction

The general type of construction that has proved most satisfactory for solid reduction is illustrated in Fig. 14-24. This die has 120° of contact with the work. The 30° on either side of the 120° area is devoted to side clearance. Because of the volume of metal being formed, this side clearance is necessary to avoid trapping the material.

The junction of the blade radius with the clearance radius occurs at approximately one-half the depth of the groove. This junction should be adequately blended to form a smooth transition from one radius to the other. The side clearance is built into both the blade and the taper of the die cavity.

# SWAGING DIES

## Tubular Reduction

For tubular work, the swaging die is constructed in an oval. A round die would simply clamp onto the work, since there is no room for the metal to flow. The amount of ovality varies with the wall thickness and diameter of the tube (see Fig. 14-25). The thinner the wall of the tube, the less the ovality required. Harder materials require more ovality than softer materials, and larger diameters require more than smaller diameters. Dies used for mandrel swaging require more ovality than dies for tubular work swaged without a mandrel. The proper amount of ovality reduces the possibility of splitting under high pressure.

In general, the ratio between the wall thickness and the diameter should not exceed 25 to 30:1 when tubing is being reduced. For example, 1″ (25 mm) diam tube should have a minimum wall thickness of 0.035″ (0.89 mm). Too thin a wall results in wrinkling and collapse of the tube during the swaging operation. Tubes with heavy walls (wall thickness-to-diameter ratios greater than 10:1) should be treated as solid work.

## Fastening and Mandrel Swaging

Swaging dies for fastening operations are used in fastening cable terminals and in other operations in which two parts are swaged into an integrated assembly. Such dies are produced with completely round die cavities, the edges of which are ground just enough to prevent marking of the work. The round cavity forces a maximum amount of material radially inward to ensure a well-swaged joint. Conversely, when mandrel swaging is being performed, it is desirable to have a fair amount of ovality in the die to release the work from the mandrel.

## TYPES OF DIES

The standard single-taper die is the most common tool used in swaging. Other swaging dies include the piloted die, double-taper die, pointing die, double-extension die, cable-swaging die, and stationary-spindle die. These dies are illustrated in Fig. 14-26.

**Piloted die**. When concentricity is important in the part being produced, a piloted die is recommended. With careful attention to fits, it is possible to make production runs with a total indicator reading of 0.005-0.015″ (0.13-0.38 mm).

**Double-taper die**. When only the tapered portion of the die is being used, this die is an economical approach to tooling. Its cost is approximately one-third more than a standard die, but its life is at least twice as long.

**Pointing die**. The pointing die with cross stop has a key built into the die at the apex of the point. This key prevents overfeeding of the material into the die cavity. If overfeeding occurs, the metal flashes in between the die faces, particularly at the point, causing overloading and concentrated stress, which in turn cause fracture and failure along the die cavity. The keyway minimizes the chances of this fracture and failure occurring.

**Double-extension die.** This die is used in applications for which the longest possible taper must be secured with a minimum amount of die. It is popular in the swaging of tapered furniture legs and ski poles. The extensions are generally 1″ (25 mm) square x 1/2″ (12.7 mm) long, thereby giving 2-3″ (51-76 mm) of additional taper with any given die.

**Cable-swaging die**. The cable-swaging die is used to fasten terminals to cables. When used in a die-closing machine, these dies are normally manufactured with spring pockets to assist in keeping the dies open to prevent them from nicking the surfaces of the terminal.

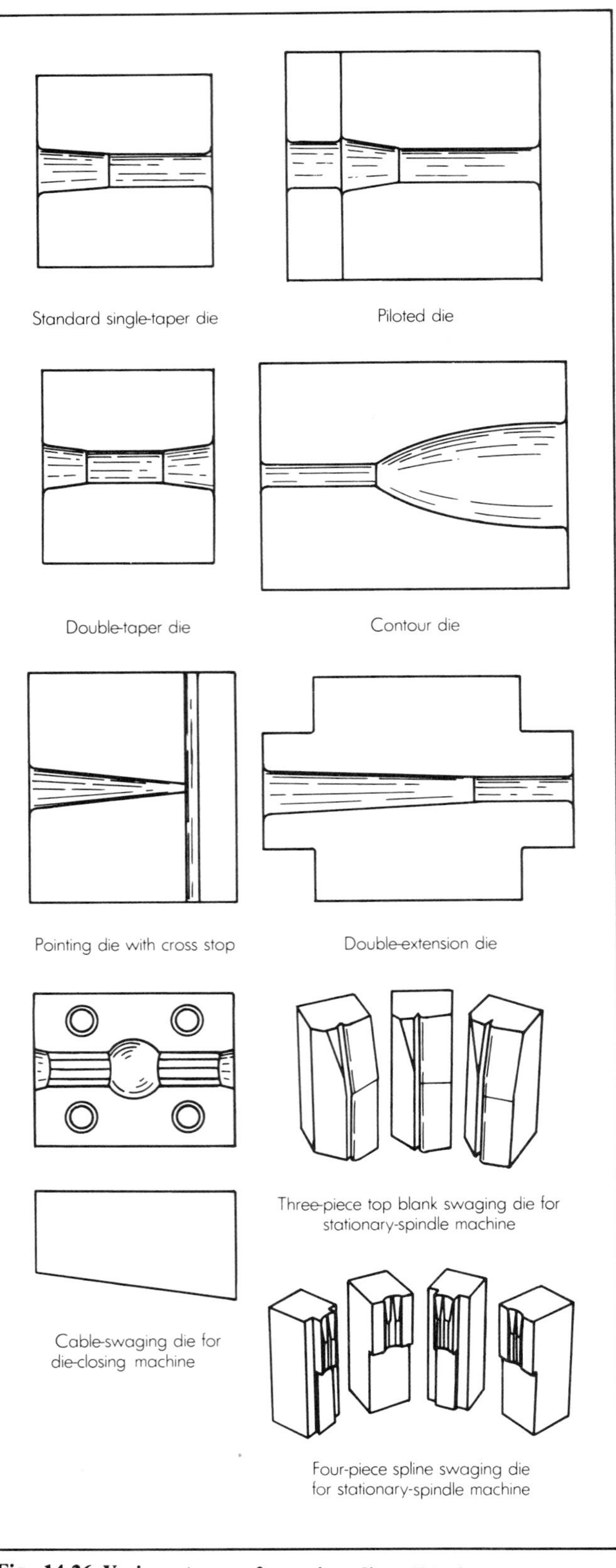


**Fig. 14-26 Various types of swaging dies.** (*Machinery Div., The Torrington Co.*)

**Stationary-spindle swager die.** This die is manufactured in two, three, or four pieces depending upon the particular application. A triangular shape requires three dies as opposed to four dies for a square shape.

## DIE MATERIALS

Dies are generally made from tool steels that have alloying elements added to provide resistance to wear. Some manufacturers heat treat the dies to obtain a hard, wear-resistant case and a tough, impact-resistant core. The hardness of the surface of the die is $R_C$60-65, whereas the core is in the $R_C$40-50 range to withstand the shock loads of swaging. Other manufacturers through-harden the dies. Impact-resistant grades of carbide are sometimes used. Normal die wear is caused by abrasion of the flowing metal in the die cavity, and contamination on the surface of the work only accelerates the deterioration of the dies.

Dies and backers used for hot swaging are commonly made from high-speed steels or from hot-work tool steels such as H11 or H21. For some special applications of hot swaging, dies are made from maraging steels, cast ceramic, 310 stainless steel, Incoloy 802, Hastelloy X, or high-silicon cast iron (Meehanite) to better withstand the high temperatures involved.

A comprehensive discussion of tool and die steels is presented in Chapter 2 of this volume, "Die and Mold Materials."

# SWAGING MANDRELS

Several types of mandrels are used for swaging, depending upon the job to be performed (see Fig. 14-27). Most mandrels, however, can be classified into the following three basic types: (1) hand mandrels, (2) floating or plug-type mandrels, and (3) built-in mandrels. A slight taper on the mandrels, if not objectionable, facilitates removal of the swaged parts.

Hand mandrels are used on workpieces that are fairly simple and that can be easily handled along with the mandrel. Hand mandrels are generally used when thin-wall tubing is swaged to avoid any wrinkling of the unswaged part and to give support to the swaged area. They are usually not employed when close control of wall thickness is required.

Floating or plug-type mandrels are used when the bead in welded tubing is ironed or the inside diameter of seamless tubing is sized. The mandrel is positioned in the die, and the work is fed by means of roll feeds on the front and exit ends of the swager.

Built-in mandrels are probably the most commonly used type of mandrel. They are used basically to size the inside diameter of a tube within the confines of the die length itself. Built-in mandrels are also used to gage lengths when mandrels and stops are manufactured as integral units.

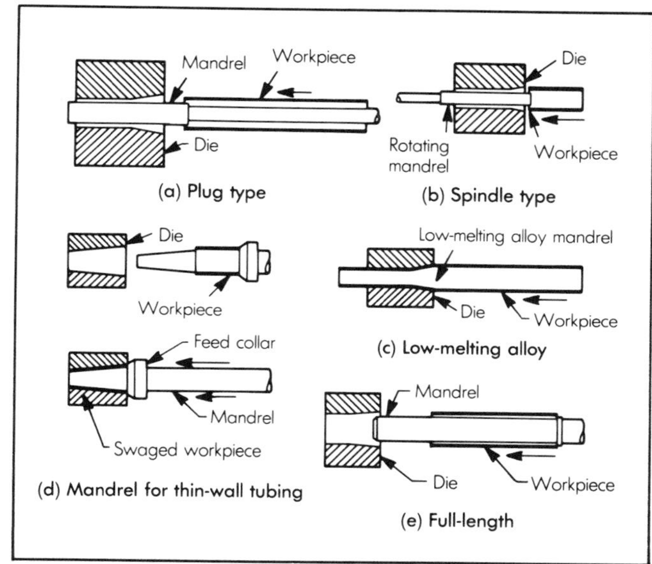


**Fig. 14-27 Various types of swaging mandrels.** (*Abbey Etna Machine Co.*)

# OPERATING PARAMETERS

Optimum results in swaging depend upon many factors including using the proper machine and tooling and employing the correct operating parameters.

## FEED RATES

The feed rate used in swaging depends primarily upon the included angle in the die; however, it is also influenced by whether the workpiece is solid or tubular; by the type, condition, and cleanliness of the workpiece materials; and by the amount of reduction. Tubing can be formed at higher feed rates than solid bars, and sizing operations can be performed faster than operations involving substantial reductions of solid bars. The highest feed rates are used for materials that are easily swaged and for applications in which surface finish is not critical. Thin-wall tubes generally must be swaged at slow feed rates to prevent collapsing.

Feed rates normally range to about 5 fpm (1.5 m/min) on two-die swagers and from 6 to 8 fpm (1.8 to 2.4 m/min) on four-die swagers. For small reductions, however, feed rates to 100 fpm (30.5 m/min.) are used. Each application requires careful study to determine the optimum feed rate. A steady feed is desirable, and variations in the feed rate or overfeeding can cause split dies.

## CLEANLINESS AND LUBRICATION

Cleanliness of workpieces to be swaged can be critical. Parts coated with grease, phosphate, or other lubricants minimize the capability of the die to restrain the work. This results in feedback of the workpiece, which causes poor feeding and reduced production rates, and can be hazardous to the operator.

# OPERATING PARAMETERS

**TABLE 14-2**
**Common Problems in Swaging, Their Causes, and Suggested Solutions**

| Problem | Probable Causes | Suggested Solutions |
|---|---|---|
| Difficult feeding | Workpieces oily or greasy. | Clean workpieces. |
| | Workpiece material tool hard. | Anneal if possible or substitute a grade more suitable for the operation. |
| | Die entrance too small. | Enlarge die entrance. |
| | Die opening too small. | Reset standard machines with thinner shims. For dies designed to be adjusted on a taper, use a thicker shim. |
| | Slight recess worn in die taper where stock first contacts the die. | Regrind the die taper. |
| | Taper in dies worn from oval to round. | Lap or regrind taper. |
| Roughened work | | |
| Long, longitudinal dents | Edges of die groove not round or groove has improper side clearance. | Lap or regrind die groove. |
| | Too much die opening. | Reset machine with proper shims. |
| | Feed too fast. | Decrease feed rate. |
| Short dents | Edge of groove where taper and blade intersect is not rounded. | Stone and/or polish the corner round to obtain a streamlined blend. |
| Small dents, unevenly distributed | Dirty head and/or work | Clean head. Remove scale or other material from work that is likely to become loose and be pounded into surface. |
| | Edges of die groove not round. | Lap or regrind die groove. |
| | Feed too fast. | Decrease feed rate. |
| Flashing | Too much die opening. | Reset machine with proper shims. |
| | Work rotating at spindle speed and getting stuck in dies. | Increase ovality in dies. |
| Peeling | Excessive pressure within die groove. | Decrease length of work in the dies with respect to diameter (swaging length should not exceed 10 x diameter). |
| Scouring and pickup | High pressure. | Use lubricant. Polish dies. Eliminate abrupt changes in groove surfaces and contours. Remove any localized high-pressure spots. Increase ovality of dies. |
| Longitudinal cracks or breaks in solid material | Seams or pipes in original stock. | Obtain better material. |
| Short cracks in solid material (running in all directions) | Material too hard. | Anneal material prior to swaging. |
| Wrinkling or corrugating in tubing | Tube OD more than 35 x wall thickness | Use a mandrel that is within the solid-material capacity of the machine. |
| | Die groove too oval. | Lap or regrind die groove. |
| | Feed too fast. | Decrease feed rate and ensure that it is steady. |

Most swaging is done dry, but coolant systems are available as optional equipment on most machines. Such systems for cooling and lubricating the workpieces and dies are generally used only for hot swaging or to produce small or large tapers. When such systems are not used, a lubricating grease should be applied to the rolls and sides of the dies, but not in the die cavities.

## TOOL MAINTENANCE

Rolls used in swaging machines decrease in diameter with continued impact, and this can produce poor results. In some cases, when the diameter at one end of each roll wears more than the other end, the rolls can be reversed end for end. Replacement of the rolls, however, is necessary eventually. The relationship of the diameters of the rolls to each other is generally more important than the individual roll diameters.

Dies having only slight wear can be reworked by lapping; those with more wear require regrinding. The dies are sometimes polished to produce smoother surface finishes in swaging. Compensation for stock removed in grinding is made by adding shims between the dies and the hammers or backers.

## TROUBLESHOOTING

Problems commonly encountered in swaging include difficult feeding and roughened workpieces. Causes of these problems and suggested solutions are presented in Table 14-2. The dies, backers, rolls, cage, and other parts of the machines should be removed periodically and inspected, cleaned, and lubricated.

Also, both the hammers and rolls should be periodically removed from the machine and stress relieved to reduce the work-hardening effects of continuous hammering. Stress relieving can be accomplished by heating the components to 500° F (260° C) for six hours, air cooling, reheating to 500° F for six more hours, and again air cooling.

**Bibliography**

Purcell, William P. *Automatic Die Swaging of Close Tolerance, Miniature and Subminiature Metal Parts.* SME Technical Paper MR80-950, 1980.

CHAPTER

# 15

# Hot Forging

# HOT FORGING

Forging is one of the oldest metalworking processes known to man. As early as 2000 BC, forging was used to produce weapons, implements, and jewelry. The process was performed by hand using simple hammers.

Hot forging is defined as the controlled, plastic deformation or working of metals into predetermined shapes by means of pressure or impact blows, or a combination of both. In hot forging, this plastic deformation is performed above the recrystallization temperature to prevent strain hardening of the metal.

During the deformation process, the crystalline structure of the base metal is refined and any nonmetallic or alloy segregation is properly oriented. In bar stock, the grain flow is only in one direction. When the contour of the part is changed, the grain flow lines are cut, rendering the metal more susceptible to fatigue and stress corrosion. Hot forging develops the grain flow so that it follows the outline of the part being formed as seen in Fig. 15-1. The directional alignment of the grains or fibers helps increase strength, ductility, and resistance to impact and fatigue in the metal.

Deformation is affected by the stress inherent in the metal, the microstructural characteristics of the starting material, the temperature at which the deformation occurs, the rate at which the deformation occurs, and the frictional restraint between the material being forged and the die surface.

**CHAPTER CONTENTS:**



## GLOSSARY OF FORGING TERMS

The following terms frequently used in the forging industry are adapted from the *Open Die Forging Manual*,[1] the *Forging Industry Handbook*,[2] and *Forging Equipment, Materials and Practices*.[3]

**air lift hammer** A gravity-drop forging hammer which uses air pressure to lift the hammer between strokes.

**anisotropy** The characteristic of exhibiting different values of a property in different directions with respect to a fixed reference system in the material.

**anvil** Large, heavy block of metal that supports structure of conventional forging hammers. Also, the block of metal on which hand forgings are made.

**bark** The decarburized layer just beneath the scale produced by heating steel in an oxidizing atmosphere.

**bed** The stationary, and usually horizontal, part of a press that serves as a table to which a bolster plate or lower die assembly is fastened.

**blank** A piece of stock (also called a slug or multiple) from which a forging is to be made.

**blister** A defect caused by gas bubbles either on the surface or beneath the surface of the metal.

**blocker dies** Blocker dies are characterized by generous contours, large radii, draft angles of 7° or more, and liberal finish allowances.

**blocker-type design** A design characterized by generous contours, large radii, draft angles of 7° or more, and liberal finish allowances.

**blocking** A forging operation often used to impart an intermediate shape to a forging, preparatory to forging of the final shape in the finishing impression of the dies. Blocking can ensure proper "working" of the material and contribute to greater die life.

**bloom** Also called slab or billet, semifinished products of rectangular cross section with rounded corners, hot-rolled or forged. Blooms can also be circular forged sections. The cross-sectional area is usually larger for blooms than for billets.

**blow** The force delivered by one stroke of forging equipment.

**blow hole** A cavity produced by gas evolved during solidification of metal.

**board hammer** A type of gravity drop hammer which uses hardwood boards attached to the ram or hammer to raise the ram after the forging stroke.

**bolster** The plate secured to the bed of a press for locating and supporting the die assembly.

**boss** A relatively short protrusion or projection on the surface of a forging, often cylindrical in shape.

**burnt** Permanently damaged metal caused by heating conditions producing incipient melting or intergranular oxidation.

***Contributors of sections of this chapter are:*** *Dr. Taylan Altan, Senior Research Leader, Battelle Columbus Laboratories; Gene G. Bates, Manager—Acme Division, The Hill Acme Company; Kay H. Beseler, Vice President, Girard Associates, Inc.; David A. Dickinson, President, Girard Associates, Inc.; Richard Edmonson, Vice President—Engineering, National Machinery Co.; Mario Farina, Product Specialist, Erie Press Systems; Charles W. Frame, Chief Engineer, Chambersburg Engineering Co.; Dale W. Hutchinson, Product Manager—Metalworking Products, Acheson Colloids Company; Otto Knapp, Product Manager, COSA Corp.; Joseph Leitersdorf, P.E., Consulting Engineer; Nick L. Matthews, Lubricant Division, Russell Products; Dr. Charles C. Reynolds, President, GESCO, Inc.; Robert W. Stansbury, Industry Manager—Metalprep Dept., Pennwalt Corp.*

***Reviewers of sections of this chapter are:*** *Dr. Taylan Altan, Senior Research Leader, Battelle Columbus Laboratories; Gene G. Bates, Manager—Acme Division, The Hill Acme Company; Kay H. Beseler, Vice President, Girard Associates, Inc.; John D. Bryzgel, Sales Manager—Machinery, The Fenn Manufacturing Co.;*

# CHAPTER 15

## GLOSSARY OF FORGING TERMS

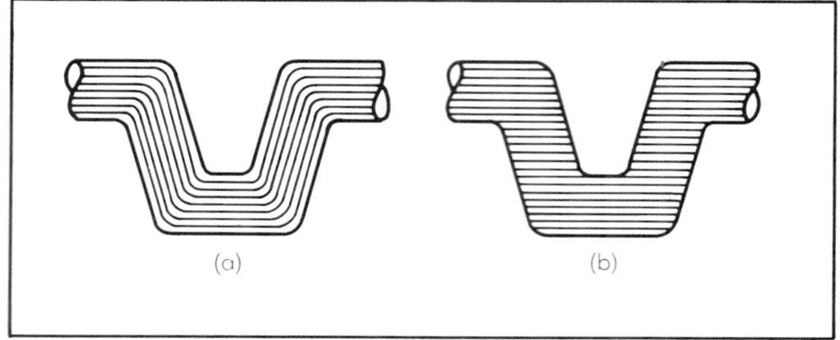


**Fig. 15-1 (a) Grain flow in hot forging follows the outline of the component. (b) During machining, the grain flow is broken.** (*Forging Industry Association*)

**burst** An internal discontinuity caused by improper forging.

**buster** A die impression used to combine preliminary forging operations such as edging and blocking to minimize number of blows.

**camber** Deviation from edge straightness, usually referring to the greatest deviation of a side edge from a straight line. Sometimes used to indicate crown on flat rolls.

**check** Crack in a die impression generally caused by excessive changes in die temperature and/or high forging pressure.

**close-finish design** A forging design combining the characteristics of close-tolerance design and close-to-finish design.

**close-to-finish design** A forging design with the minimum draft, finish allowances, and radii obtainable in conventional forging equipment. Dimensional tolerances on length, width, match, surface, and straightness are about 1/2 of the commercial tolerances, but die wear, flash extension, and die closure tolerances are about the same.

**close-tolerance design** A forging designed with commercially recommended draft radii and finish allowances, but with dimensional tolerances of less than one-half the commercial tolerances recommended for otherwise similar parts. Often little or no machining is required after forging.

**closed-die forging** *See* impression-die forging.

**cogging** The process of forging ingots to produce blooms or billets.

**coining** The process of applying necessary pressure to all or some portion of a forging's surface to obtain closer tolerances and smoother surfaces or to eliminate draft. Coining may be done while forgings are hot or cold and is usually performed on surfaces parallel with the parting line of the forging.

**cold lap** A flaw caused when a workpiece fails to fill the die cavity during first forging. A seam is formed as subsequent dies force metal over this gap to leave a seam on the workpiece surface.

**cold shut** A defect characterized by a fissure or lap on a forging's surface which has been closed without fusion during the forging operation.

**commercial designs** A forging design characterized by standard draft angles of 5-7° and radii, finish allowances, and specific dimensional tolerances that can be achieved by most commercial forging equipment and practices.

**compressive strength** The maximum stress that a material subjected to compression can withstand when loaded without deformation or fracture.

**core forging** The process of displacing metal with a punch to fill a die cavity.

**counterblow equipment** Equipment with two opposed rams that are activated simultaneously to strike repeated blows on the workpiece placed midway between them.

**counterlock** A jog in mating surfaces of dies to prevent lateral die shifting from side thrusts developed in forging irregular-shaped pieces.

**creep** Time-dependent strain occurring under stress. The resistance to creep, or creep strength, decreases with increasing temperature.

**critical (temperatures)** Temperatures at which phase changes take place in metals.

**cross forging** Preliminary working of forging stock in flat dies so that the principal increase in dimension is in the transverse direction with respect to the original axis of the ingot.

**die block** A block (usually) of heat-treated steel into which desired impressions are machined or sunk and from which closed-die forgings are produced on hammers or presses. Die blocks are usually used in pairs, with part of the impression in one of the blocks and the balance of the impression in the other.

**die forging** (1) Compression in a closed impression die. (2) A product of such an operation.

**die match** The condition in which dies, after having been set up in the forging equipment, are in proper alignment relative to each other.

**die shift** A condition requiring correction in which, after dies have been set up in the forging equipment, displacement of a point in one die from the corresponding point in the opposite die occurs in a direction parallel with the fundamental parting line of the dies.

**directional properties** Anisotropic values. Physical or mechanical properties varying with the relation to a specific direction; resulting from structural fibering and preferred orientation.

**draft** The amount of taper on the sides of the forging and on projections to facilitate removal from the dies; also, the corresponding taper on the side walls of the die impressions. Draft angles are commonly between 5-7°. In open-die forging, draft is the amount of relative movement of the dies toward each other through the metal in one application of power.

**drawing out** Stretching by a series of upsets along the length of the workpiece.

**drop forging** A forging produced in impression dies with a drop hammer.

---

***Reviewers, cont.**: Jim Comstock, Marketing Manager—Metalprep Dept., Pennwalt Corp.; Greg P. Cordones, Vice President, Graphite Products Corp.; David A. Dickinson, President, Girard Associates, Inc.; L. George Drabing, Consultant; Richard Edmonson, Vice President—Engineering, National Machinery Co.; George Elliott, Sales Manager—Induction Heating Systems, Radyne/AKO Corp.; Mario Farina, Product Specialist, Erie Press Systems; Charles W. Frame, Chief Engineer, Chambersburg Engineering Co.; J. R. Gilger, Sales Manager, Industrial Colloids; Dr. John Terence Golden, Technical and Manufacturing Manager, Renite Company; Arthur F. Hayes, Research and Development, Ladish Company; Tony Hiller, Department Manager, Metalprep Dept., Pennwalt Corp.; George A. Houston, President, Federal Forging Tools, Inc.; Dale W. Hutchinson, Product Manager—Metalworking Products, Acheson Colloids Company; Dr. Sulekh C. Jain, Technical Director, CE—Beaumont; John B. Janney, Jr., Vice President—Sales, Janney Cylinder Co., an Ampco-Pittsburg Co.;*

# GLOSSARY OF FORGING TERMS

**edger** The portion of the die impression used for preforming which distributes metal into regions that facilitate filling cavities in later operations of the forging sequence.

**extrusion forging** (1) Forcing metal into or through a die opening by restricting flow in other directions. (2) A part made by the operation.

**finish allowance** The amount of excess metal surrounding the intended final shape. Sometimes called clean-up allowance, forging envelope, or machining allowance.

**flakes** Short, discontinuous, internal fissures in ferrous metals attributed to stresses caused by localized transformation and decreased solubility of hydrogen during cooling after hot working.

**flash** Excess metal that is pushed out of the die cavity.

**flash extension** The portion of flash remaining after trimming. Flash extension is measured from the intersection of the draft and flash at the body of the forging to the trimmed edge of the stock.

**flash gutter** An additional cavity machined along the parting line of the die cavity to receive the excess metal as it flows out of the die cavity through the flash gap.

**flash land** Configuration in the finishing impression of the dies designed either to restrict or to encourage growth of flash at the parting line, whichever may be required in a particular instance to ensure complete filling of the finishing impression.

**flat-die forging** *See* open-die forging.

**flow lines** Patterns resulting from elongation of the nonhomogeneities present in the ingot in the direction that the metal flows during working. Flow lines are usually revealed in cross sections of forgings by macroetching or sulfur printing.

**flow stress** (1) The shear stress required to cause plastic deformation of solid metals. (2) The uniaxial true stress required to cause flow at a particular value of strain.

**forgeability** The relative ability of material to deform without rupture.

**forging** (1) The process of deforming to the desired shape by forming in presses, hammers, rolls, upsetters, and related machinery. (2) The product resulting from this deformation process.

**forging machine (upsetter or header)** A type of forging equipment, related to the mechanical press, in which the main forming energy is applied horizontally to the workpiece, which is gripped and held by prior action of the dies.

**forging stresses** Elastic stresses induced by forging or cooling from the forging temperature; sometimes erroneously referred to as forging strains.

**gathering** An operation which increases the cross section of part of the stock above its original size.

**grain flow** Fiberlike lines caused by orientation of the constituents of the metal in the direction of working; can be visible on etched sections.

**gravity hammer** A type of forging hammer that obtains energy for forging by the mass and velocity of a free-falling ram or hammer.

**gutter** *See* flash gutter.

**high-energy-rate forming** The process of producing forgings on equipment capable of extremely high ram velocities resulting from the sudden release of a compressed gas against a free piston. Also referred to as high-velocity or high-speed forging.

**hot working** The mechanical working of metal at a temperature above its recrystallization point, a temperature high enough to prevent strain hardening.

**hydraulic hammer** A gravity drop forging hammer which uses hydraulic pressure to lift the hammer between strokes.

**impression** A cavity machined into a forging die to produce a desired configuration in the workpiece during forging.

**impression-die forging** A forging that is formed to the required shape and size by machined impressions in specially prepared dies which exert three-dimensional control on the workpiece.

**insert** A component which is removable from a die. An insert can be used to fill a cavity or to replace a portion of the die with a material which gives better service.

**isothermal forging** A forging operation performed on a workpiece during which the temperature remains constant and uniform. Generally used when aluminum, nickel, or titanium is being forged.

**lap** Surface defect appearing as a seam which is caused by metal that is folded and subsequently rolled or forged into the surface.

**locks** Changes in the plane of mating surfaces of the dies to improve alignment during forging by counteracting lateral thrust.

**mandrel forging** *See* ring rolling.

**manipulator** A mechanical device for handling an ingot or billet during forging.

**match** A condition in which a point in one die half is aligned properly with the corresponding point in the opposite die half within specified tolerance.

**matching draft** When unsymmetrical ribs and side walls meet at the parting line, it is standard practice to provide greater draft on the shallower die to make the forging's surface meet at the parting line. This is called matching draft.

**natural draft** After the parting line has been established and a machining allowance is provided, a shape may have what is called natural draft.

**open-die forging** Hot mechanical forming of metals between flat or shaped dies where metal flow is not completely restricted. Also known as hand or smith forging.

**parting line** The line or plane along which the dies separate, sometimes called flash line or split line.

**parting plane** The plane which includes the principal die face and which is perpendicular to the direction of the ram travel. When parting surfaces of the dies are flat, the parting plane coincides with the parting line. Also referred to as the forging plane.

***Reviewers, cont.:*** *Merle E. Johnson, Vice President—Marketing, Johnston Manufacturing Co.; Walter C. Johnson, Vice President/Systems Marketing, Verson Allsteel Press Co.; Otto Knapp, Product Manager, COSA Corp.; William A. Kurnot, Chief Engineer, Forming Technology Co.; Joseph Leitersdorf, P.E., Consulting Engineer; Les Lugosi, Manager—Research and Development, Wynn Oil Company; Nick L. Matthews, Lubricant Division, Russell Products; Robert W. Pearson, Maintenance Manager, Dominion Forge Co., Ltd.; Dr. Charles C. Reynolds, President, GESCO, Inc.; Kamal Salib, Tool and Manufacturing Engineer, Letts Drop Forge; Dr. John Schey, Professor—Dept. of Mechanical Engineering, University of Waterloo; Dr. Sanjay Shah, Manager—Product and Process Engineering, Wyman-Gordon Co.; Robert B. Sparks, Manager—Research and Development, Wyman-Gordon Co.; Robert W. Stansbury, Industry Manager—Metalprep Dept., Pennwalt Corp.; Technical Committee, Forging Industry Association; Horst D. Wilms, Sales Manager, Siempelkamp Corporation.*

**press forging** Mechanical forming of metals by means of a press. The action is that of kneading the metal by relatively slow application of force as compared with the action of hammering.

**ram** The moving part of a forging hammer, forging machine, or press, to which one of the tools is fastened.

**restriking** Striking a trimmed forging an additional blow in the dies to align or size its several components or sections. The operation can be performed hot or cold.

**ring rolling** The process of shaping weldless rings from pierced discs or thick-walled, ring-shaped blanks between rolls which control wall thickness, ring diameter, height, and contour.

**roll forging** The process of shaping stock between power-driven rolls bearing contoured dies, usually used for preforming. Roll forging is often employed to reduce thickness and increase length of stock.

**seam** A crack or inclusion on the surface of forging stock which may carry through forging and appear on the finished product.

**semifinisher (semifinishing impression)** An impression in the forging die which only approximates the finish dimensions of the forging. Semifinishers are often used to extend die life or the finishing impression; to ensure proper control of grain flow during forging; and to assist in obtaining desired tolerances.

**sow block** Metal dieholder employed in a forging hammer to protect the hammer anvil from shock and wear. Also called anvil cap or shoe. Sow blocks are occasionally used to hold insert dies.

**steam hammer** A type of drop hammer in which the ram is actuated for each stroke by a double-action steam cylinder.

**swage (swedge)** Reducing or changing the cross-sectional area of the stock, usually by revolving the work between rapid impact blows.

**trimming** The process of removing flash or excess metal from a forging.

**upsetting** Working metal in such a manner that the cross-sectional area of a portion or all of the stock is increased.

**vent** A small hole in a punch or die which permits the passage of air or gas. Venting prevents trapping air that interferes with forming of a vacuum, which interferes with stripping.

# FORGING PROCESSES

Metal flow during the forging process normally falls into two categories: upsetting and extrusion. Upsetting occurs when the metal is compressed parallel to the longitudinal axis of the workpiece. This action enables the metal to flow freely in one direction as in open-die forging, or it can be restrained as in impression-die forging. Extrusion occurs when the metal is compressed parallel to the longitudinal axis of the workpiece and allowed to flow through an orifice in the die cavity. For a detailed discussion on extrusion, refer to Chapter 13, "Drawing, Extruding, Upsetting, and Automatic Forming."

## OPEN-DIE FORGING

Open-die forging, also referred to as smith forging, blacksmith forging, hand forging, and flat-die forging, is generally performed without special tooling. The forms obtained and the dimensions maintained are usually dependent upon the skill of the operator and the type of equipment used. However, with the addition of computer control to the equipment, more complex forgings can be produced and better dimensional control is maintained. This equipment may range from the simple anvil and hammer of the blacksmith to giant, computer-controlled, hydraulic presses capable of delivering up to 75,000 tons (667 MN) of force and producing single forgings weighing several thousand pounds. Most open-die forgings are simple geometric shapes such as discs, rings, or shafts. Open-die forging is also used in the steelmaking industry to cog ingots or to draw down billets from one size to a smaller one.

The open-die forging process is employed when only a few parts are needed and when the part is too large to be produced in closed dies. Quantities of less than 100 parts are generally good candidates to be produced in open dies because designing and manufacturing closed dies for such a small quantity is often too costly. However, large quantities are produced with open dies. The open-die process is also used to obtain the mechanical properties in a workpiece that are not obtainable by machining. Generally, most forgings begin with the open-die process before the final forging operation.

## IMPRESSION-DIE FORGING

In impression-die forging, the workpiece is placed between two dies containing the impression of the forging shape to be produced. The dies are brought together and the workpiece is plastically deformed until the sides come in contact with the walls of the die (see Fig. 15-2). As the deformation continues, a small amount of material begins to flow outside the die impression, forming flash. The thin flash cools rapidly, creating a pressure increase inside the workpiece. The increased pressure assists the flow of material into the unfilled portion of the impression. The majority of the forgings produced are done using impression-die forging.

Closed-die forging or flashless forging, which is a special form of impression-die forging, does not depend on the flash to achieve complete die filling. Generally, the material is deformed in a cavity that does not allow excess material to flow outside the impression. Therefore, die design and workpiece volume are more critical than in impression-die forging so that complete die filling is achieved without generating excess pressures due to overfilling.

Currently, closed-die forging is moving more and more toward near-net-shaped and net-shaped forging. Near-net-shaped parts are those parts that require minor metal removal before assembly. Net-shaped parts have finished functional surfaces that do not require additional metal removal. Gears, airfoils, and high-temperature jet engine disc forgings are being produced using this process.

## RELATED PROCESSES

Several other processes are employed when workpieces are forged for a particular application. These processes incorporate principles from both open and closed-die forging. Two of the

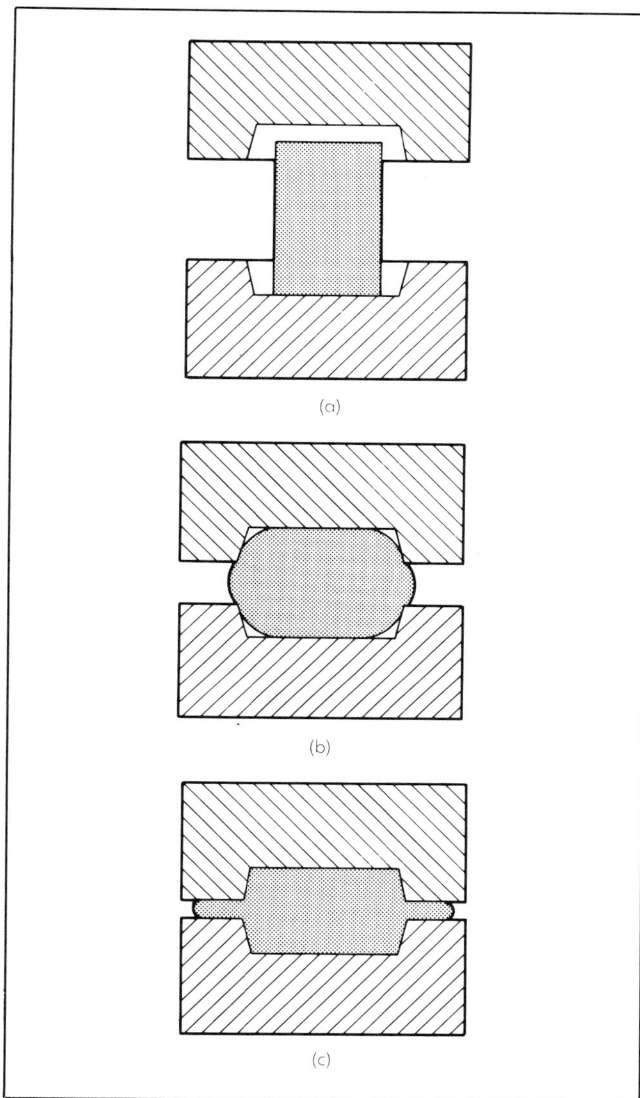


**Fig. 15-2 In impression-die forging: (a) the workpiece is inserted between the dies; (b) the dies are brought together deforming the workpiece until the sides come in contact with the walls; and (c) the thin flash assists the flow of material and completes die filling.** (*Forging Industry Association*)

more common processes are radial forging and ring rolling. Orbital forging, isothermal forging, Gatorizing (a process developed by Pratt and Whitney Aircraft), and incremental forging are special processes frequently employed in the aircraft and aerospace industries.

## Radial Forging

Radial forging is a process used to reduce the cross-sectional area of billets, bars, and tubes. Normally four different types of operations are performed by radial forging: (1) axial feed into tapered dies (see Fig. 15-3), (2) infeed of dies (see Fig. 15-4), (3) axial feed into tapered dies while simultaneously upsetting (see Fig. 15-5), (4) combination of axial feed and infeed of dies (see Fig. 15-6). A mandrel can be attached to the backstop to control internal material flow when hollow workpieces are being upset.

Radial forging permits a wide variety of shapes to be produced with a minimum amount of tooling. The process lends itself to automation. Accuracy and repeatability are dependent on the design of the dies rather than operator skill.

Radial forging is being used in several diverse industries including the railroad, power utility, construction equipment, automotive, steel, aircraft, and defense industries.

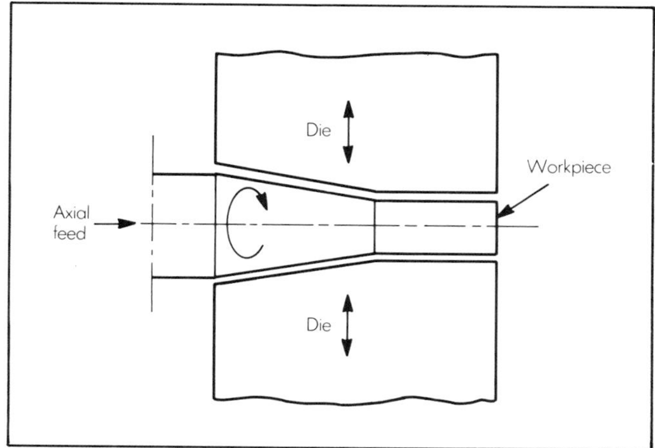


**Fig. 15-3 Reductions in cross section are achieved by axially feeding the workpiece through tapered dies.** (*Fenn Manufacturing Co.*)

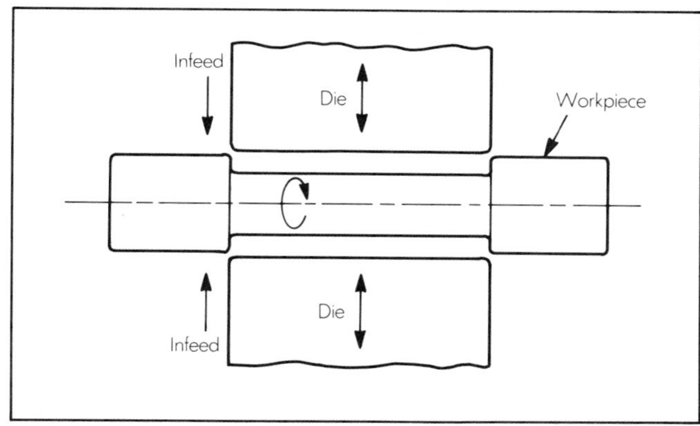


**Fig. 15-4 Reductions in cross section are also obtainable in the middle of the workpiece by controlling the die feed.** (*Fenn Manufacturing Co.*)

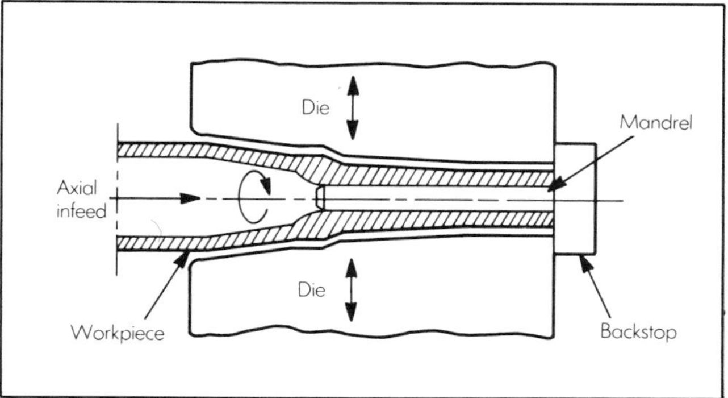


**Fig. 15-5 Radial forging machines can simultaneously upset the workpiece and reduce its cross section.** (*Fenn Manufacturing Co.*)

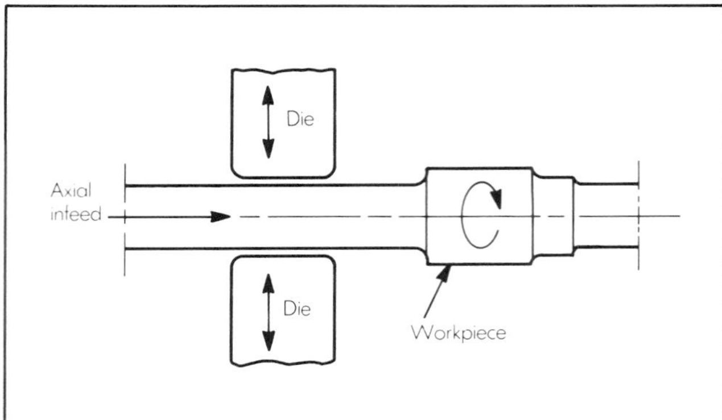


Fig. 15-6 Cross sections can be varied on the workpiece by regulating the infeed of the dies and axial feed of the workpiece. (*Fenn Manufacturing Co.*)

## Ring Rolling

Ring rolling is a process used to produce seamless rings having rectangular or contoured cross sections and specified diameters. Figure 15-7 illustrates a few of the contoured cross sections that can be produced on a ring-rolling machine. Radial ring rolling decreases the wall thickness while increasing the ring diameter. Radial-axial ring rolling decreases both the wall thickness and height of the ring while increasing the ring diameter.

Seamless rings are produced in diameters ranging from several inches (75 mm) to over 20 ft (6 m). Cross-sectional contours are limited only by the ability to design and manufacture the required main rolls and/or mandrels.

Ring rolling is less expensive than closed-die forging because less waste material results and the ring is much closer to a finished shape. The metallurgical structure and physical properties are also improved. Ring rolling is used in a variety of industries to produce products of diverse applications. Some of these industries include the automotive, agricultural, machine tool, mining, aircraft, aerospace, and defense industries.

## Orbital Forging

In orbital forging, the workpiece is subjected to a combined rolling and pressing action between a flat bottom platen and a swiveling upper die with a conical working face instead of a direct pressing action between two flat platens (see Fig. 15-8). The cone axis is inclined so that the narrow sector in contact with the workpiece is parallel to the lower platen. As the cone rotates about the cone apex, the contact zone also rotates. At the same time, the platens are pressed toward each other so that the workpiece is progressively compressed by the rolling action. Press loading is appreciably less than that of conventional upsetting because of the relatively small area of instantaneous contact.

## Isothermal Forging

Isothermal forging is a process in which the preform or billet is forged at one temperature and does not experience the die chill, surface cooling, or thermal gradients that are associated with conventional forging. This is accomplished by surrounding the billet with surfaces that are at the same temperature as the billet. Preheated tooling maintains the temperature of the billet ends or preform faces, and a die-billet heater maintains the billet temperature at the billet periphery. The deformation occurs at a speed relatively slow enough to produce a part with greater complexity using a minimum of force. In effect, time substitutes for a portion of the forging load that would normally be required. Isothermal forging has been beneficial for forging the more expensive or difficult-to-forge materials, such as titanium and superalloys.

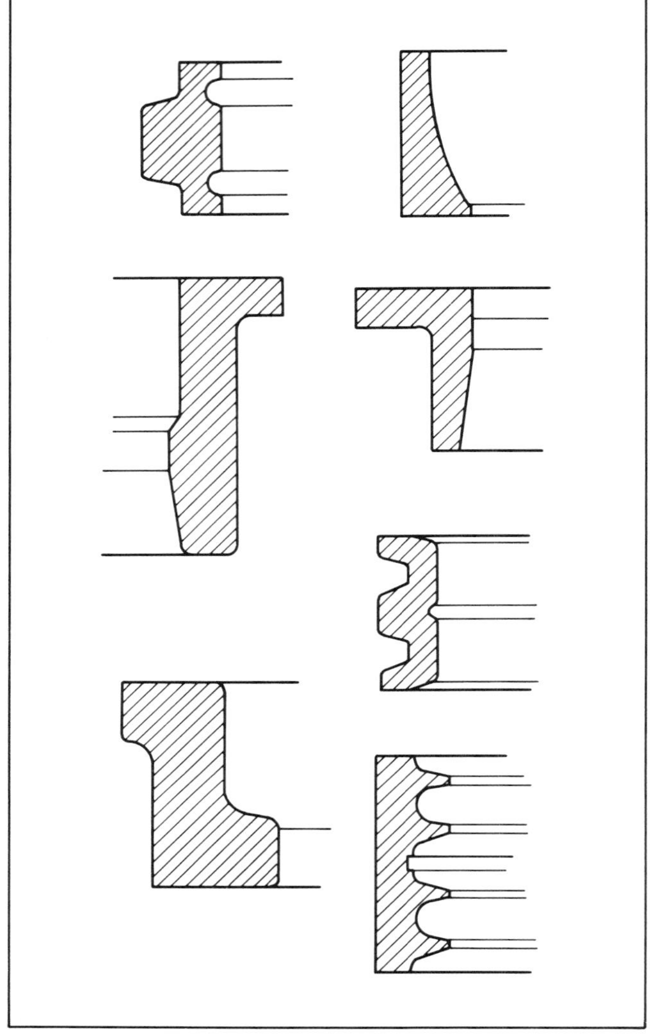

Fig. 15-7 A few of the many different ring cross sections obtainable on a ring rolling machine.

The main advantages of isothermal forging are the ability to produce complex profiles having a near-net shape; lower forging pressures, thereby permitting the use of existing equipment to forge larger components; reduced initial material weight and secondary machining; and lower part costs. Figure 15-9 compares the conventional forging process with isothermal forging. However, the advantages of increased material utilization and decreased machining cost must offset the increased cost of the dies and equipment used and the decrease in production output.

## Gatorizing

Gatorizing (developed by Pratt and Whitney Aircraft) is a forging process that includes isothermal forging as a step in the

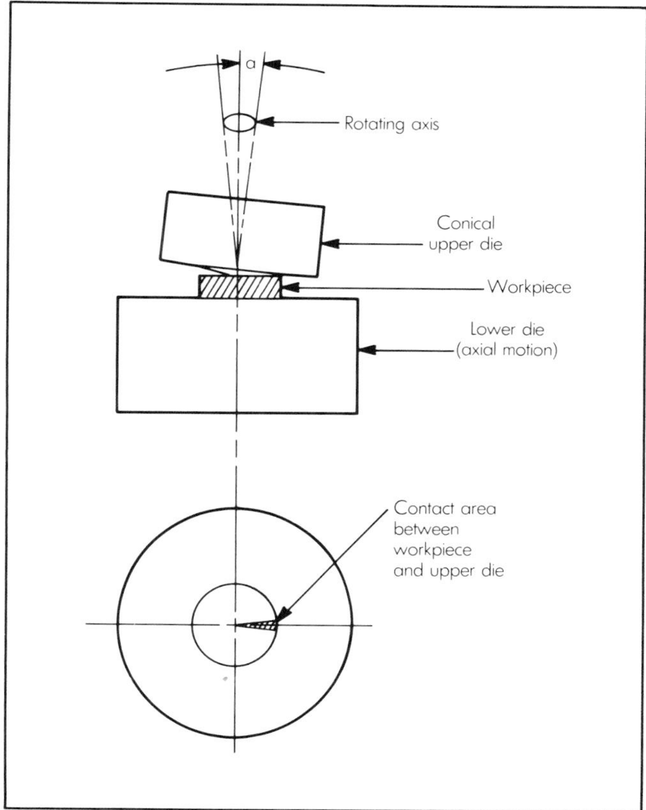


**Fig. 15-8 Orbital forging combines a rolling action and a pressing action to forge the workpiece.**

normal application of the process. The material is first preconditioned to develop a fine grain size and superplastic structure, and then forged isothermally in an atmosphere containing nitrogen or argon gas, or a vacuum. This process is frequently employed when powder metals and superalloys are being forged. For additional information on superplastic forming, refer to Chapter 1, "Sheet Metal Formability," and Chapter 4, "Sheet Metal Blanking and Forming." The forming of powder metals is discussed more thoroughly in Chapter 17, "Powder Metallurgy."

## Incremental Forging

Incremental forging is a recently developed process in which only part of the workpiece is deformed at one time. This process is similar to cogging, fullering, or drawing out and can be employed to produce rib and web-type blocker preforms that are finish formed in a closed die or machined to final dimensions. Steel, titanium, and superalloys can be forged using incremental forging.

# PREFORMING

Preforming is a forging operation used to preform, descale, and properly orient the grain flow prior to the main forging operation. In preforming, the number of operations is increased, which results in improved productivity and reduced tooling costs. Some of the machines used in preforming include hammers, presses, forging machines, forging rolls, and wedge rolling machines.

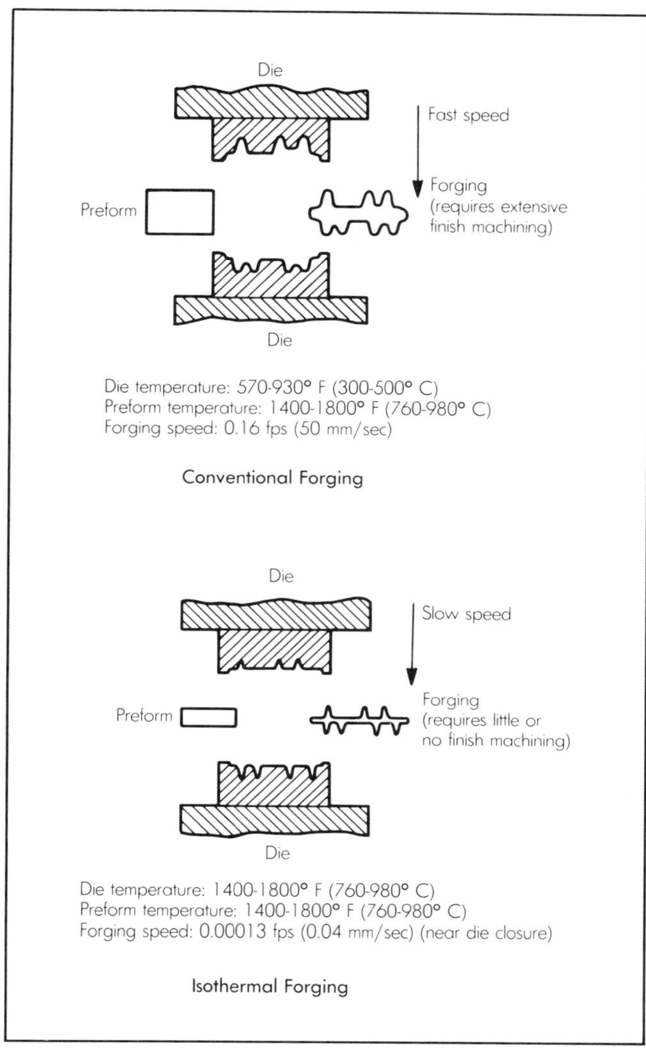


**Fig. 15-9 The isothermal process is compared to the conventional impression-die process.**

## Roll Forging

Roll forging is employed to produce a preformed blank to be finish formed in a hammer or press, or to produce parts requiring a long, tapered, symmetrical section. Crankshafts, connecting rods, and other automotive-related components are frequently roll forged prior to being finish formed. Roll forging is performed on forging rolls.

## Wedge Rolling

Wedge rolling, also referred to as transverse roll forming or cross rolling, is a process for accurately forming various shapes on the peripheries of shafts or preformed parts. Figure 15-10 illustrates some of the various shapes suitable for this process. The process is performed on machines that are self-contained or are designed for use in conjunction with other equipment in a forging shop.

A major advantage of the wedge-rolling process is the complete use of material; almost 98% of the metal is used. The process is fast, noiseless, and automatic and can form almost

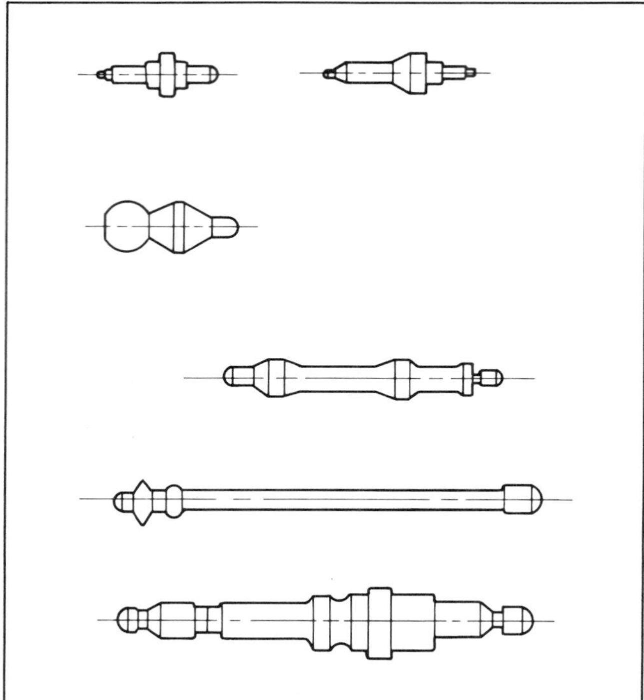

Fig. 15-10 Wedge rolling is capable of forming various cross sections on the peripheries of shafts.

any type of ferrous and nonferrous metal. Tolerances are comparable to those of machining operations, and the mechanical properties of the metal are improved. However, self-contained machines are expensive and the forming dies are difficult to design. This process is also limited to external surfaces and axisymmetric part geometries.

## Electric Upsetting

Electric upsetting is used mostly in preforming operations to gather a large amount of material at one end of a round bar. The principle of operation is illustrated in Fig. 15-11. A bar of circular cross section is gripped between the tools of the electrode and is pushed by the hydraulically or pneumatically operated upsetting head against the anvil plate on which the other electrode is secured (see view *a*). When the current is switched on, the rod section contained between the electrodes heats rapidly and the formation of the head begins (see view *b*). The cold bar is continuously fed between the gripping electrodes; thus, the metal accumulates continuously in the head (see view *c*). The anvil electrode is gradually retracted to give enough space for the formation of the head. As soon as a sufficient quantity of metal is gathered, the machine switches off and the product can be removed by its cold end. Normally, the head is formed to final shape in a mechanical or screw-type press in the same heat. The process is suitable for preforming components like valves, or steam turbine blades.

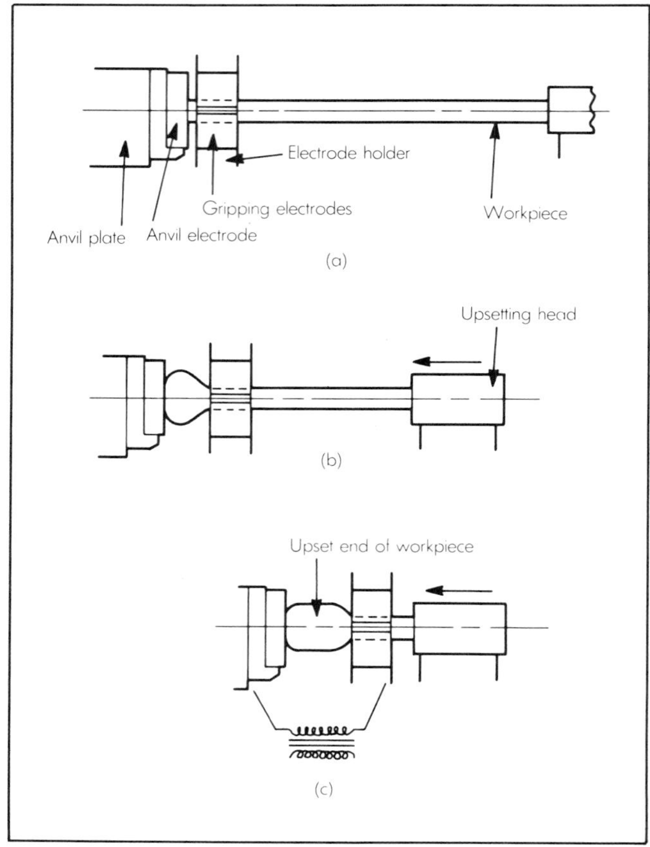


Fig. 15-11 Electric upsetting is commonly used in preforming operations to gather a large amount of material at one end of a bar.

## ADVANTAGES

Forging orients the grain flow to follow the contour of the part. This orientation provides the highest strength in the direction of the greatest stress. The higher strength-to-weight ratio permits the use of smaller, more lightweight components without the reduction of strength or toughness. Forgings can be made from a wide range of materials. Materials that are difficult to machine have been successfully forged into the desired shape. Gas pockets or voids usually found in other metal fabricating methods are eliminated, and the material's structural integrity and mechanical properties are improved. Parts can be economically produced in sizes ranging from less than 1 to 300″ (25-7600 mm) in length. Forgings are also readily adaptable to secondary operations such as heat treating, machining, welding, and surface conditioning.

## TOLERANCES

Forging tolerances represent a compromise between the accuracy desired and the accuracy that can be economically obtained. The accuracy obtained is determined by several factors. These factors include the initial accuracy of the forging dies and tooling, the complexity of the part, the type of material being forged, and the type of forging equipment that is used.

Another factor determining the forging's accuracy is the type of forging being produced. The four common types of forgings are the open-die type, the blocker type, the conventional type, and the precision type. The open-die type is least refined in shape and therefore has the widest tolerance of the four types. The precision type has the narrowest tolerance. The tolerances normally obtained in conventional-type forgings can be found in "Guideline Tolerances For Hot Forged Impression Die Forgings," published by the Forging Industry Association.

# FORGING PROCESSES

## APPLICATIONS

Forging of almost all forged components begins with open-die forging to achieve the initial material characteristics. Impression-die or closed-die forging is used to obtain a variety of shapes, sizes, and properties.

Forgings are used in a variety of industries to obtain the required component properties. In the automotive industry, forgings are used in the production of engine components, transmission components, and suspension components. High strength-to-weight ratios and reliability of forgings satisfy the stringent requirements in the aircraft and aerospace industry when airframe components, landing gear components, and other structural components are being produced. Forgings made from materials that are able to withstand elevated temperatures while maintaining strength are used in turbine engines. Other industries that use forgings include off-highway equipment, ordnance, oil field, metalworking, plumbing, railroad, and refrigeration. Table 15-1 is a list of some of the common components and characteristics produced by forging.

**TABLE 15-1**
**Components Commonly Forged[4]**

| Component | Component Characteristics |
|---|---|
| Aircraft | |
| Engine disc, blades, rings | High-temperature strength, creep and fatigue resistant. |
| Airframe structural parts | High strength, fracture toughness. |
| Chemical plant parts | Transverse ductility and toughness. |
| Crankshafts | Sound bearing surfaces; bending and torsional fatigue strength. |
| Die blocks | Toughness, internal soundness, and wear properties. |
| Electrical machinery<br>Generator rotors<br>Turbine rotors<br>Turbine discs | Internal soundness, transverse ductility and toughness, bending and torsional fatigue strength, high-temperature properties. |
| Machinery components<br>Mill spindles<br>Press columns | Internal soundness, high strength, and toughness. |
| Marine propulsion shafting | Long cylindrical configuration, torsional strength and toughness. |
| Nuclear components<br>Fittings<br>Flanges<br>Nozzles<br>Penetrations<br>Shells<br>Tube sheets | Transverse ductility and toughness, and freedom from internal discontinuities. On solid products, internal soundness is essential. |
| Oil field components<br>Valve bodies<br>Blow-out preventers<br>Head spools<br>Reamers<br>Stabilizers | High strength and wear resistance. |
| Ordnance components<br>Breech blocks<br>Gun tubes | Transverse toughness and ductility at high strength levels. |
| Pipe molds | Resistance to thermal fatigue, dimensional stability. |
| Pressure vessel components | Transverse ductility and toughness, and low-cycle fatigue strength. |
| Pump and compressor components<br>Blocks<br>Cylinders<br>Eccentrics | Transverse ductility and toughness. |
| Rolls<br>Corrugating paper rolls<br>Foil mill rolls<br>Steel mill rolls | Superior surface quality, high load-carrying capability, and good wear resistance. |

# MATERIALS FOR FORGING

The forging process is not restricted to ferrous metals. Nonferrous metals, superalloys, and refractory metals are also capable of being forged when correct forging practices are followed. This section discusses the various materials that are currently being used in forging, the material's forgeability, and the recommended practices for forging the particular material. The materials used in forging operations are obtained in bar and billet form produced to "Forging Quality." The term *forging quality* indicates that the material is free from cracks and inclusions which would reduce the materials forgeability or the performance of the finished part. For a more comprehensive discussion of materials, refer to Volume III, *Materials, Finishing, and Coating*, in this Handbook series.

An important consideration when selecting a material to be forged is its forgeability. Other considerations would be based on the mechanical properties that are inherent in the material or that can be obtained as a result of forging and heat treatment. These properties include elastic modulus, density, and strength; resistance to wear, fatigue, shock, or bending; response to heat treatment; machining characteristics; and durability or economy.

# CHAPTER 15

# MATERIALS FOR FORGING

## FORGEABILITY

Forgeability denotes a combination of resistance to deformation and the ability to deform without fracture and can be defined as the capability of the material to deform without failure regardless of the pressure and load applied. Table 15-2 is a list of the different metals and alloys in increasing order of forging difficulty. The forgeability of a particular material is based on metallurgical and mechanical factors. The temperature range over which a material can be forged also contributes to a material's forgeability. Materials with a narrow range of forging temperatures are more difficult to forge because they can only be forged for a short time. The need to obtain a fine grain structure and certain mechanical properties may further restrict the temperature and deformation range in forging.

### Metallurgical Factors

Metallurgical factors which affect a material's forgeability are crystal structure, composition, purity, number of phases present, and grain size. Materials exhibiting a face-centered cubic structure generally have the best forgeability. The forgeability progressively decreases with body-centered cubic structures and hexagonal close-packed structures respectively. The influence of the crystal structure on forgeability changes, however, when pure metals are alloyed. Alloys containing insoluble compounds exhibit brittle behavior regardless of forging temperature. If the various compounds dissolve within the metal matrix, increasing the forging temperature improves the materials forgeability. Generally, alloys containing more than one phase are more difficult to forge than single-phase alloys. Fine-grained metals are more easily forged than coarse-grained metals.

### Mechanical Factors

The two most significant factors other than forging temperature affecting forgeability are strain rate and stress distribution.

Strain rate is the amount of deformation produced within a given time interval. Hammers, which provide sharp, impacting blows, produce higher strain rates per blow than do presses with their squeezing action.[6] The rapid deformation of metal can increase the material's temperature significantly during the forging operation and can actually decrease the material's forgeability if heated sufficiently for some melting to develop. Multiphase alloys and coarse-grained metals are adversely affected by strain rates. Slow strain rate deformation, on presses, is employed to develop sophisticated, near-net-shaped designs in titanium and superalloys.

During forging, the workpiece is exposed to compressive, shear, and tensile stresses. Ruptures are usually associated with tensile and shear stresses. Therefore, compressive support must be provided when these conditions occur. Table 15-3 provides a list of forging equipment to be used when certain materials are being forged.

**TABLE 15-2**
**Forgeability of Materials in Order of Increasing Forging Difficulty[5]**

Highest forgeability
- Aluminum alloys
- Magnesium alloys
- Copper alloys
- Carbon and low-alloy steels
- Martensitic stainless steels
- Maraging steels
- Austenitic stainless steels
- Nickel alloys
- Semiaustenitic precipitation hardening (PH) stainless steels
- Titanium alloys
- Iron-based superalloys
- Cobalt-based superalloys
- Columbium alloys
- Tantalum alloys
- Molybdenum alloys
- Nickel-based superalloys
- Tungsten alloys
- Beryllium

Lowest forgeability

### Forgeability Tests

The hot-twist, Gleeble, tensile, and upset test are the common tests performed on a material to determine the forging practice and to measure lot-to-lot variability. One or more tests may be employed for a given material. The choice of test performed is based on the type of material being tested.

**Hot-twist test.** During the hot-twist test, a round bar of a given material is heated to a specified temperature. When the temperature has been attained, the bar is twisted until the bar fails. The number of twists before failing is indicative of the material's forgeability. Repeating the test over a range of forging temperatures permits the optimum temperature and deformation rate to be determined. The amount of torque required in twisting the material is related to the amount of force required to deform the material.

The hot-twist test is useful in determining the forgeability of carbon, low-alloy, and stainless steels. However, the hot-twist test is not capable of determining forgeability of materials forged at low temperatures, due to work-hardening effects induced by twisting.

**Gleeble test.** In the Gleeble test, the workpiece is heated using a resistance heating element. Both strain rates and temperature control can be varied over a broad range to determine optimum forgeability.

**Tensile test.** The tensile test is used to determine a material's forgeability by relating percent elongation and reduction as a function of temperature and strain rate. This test is particularly suited for evaluating strain-rate-sensitive and precipitation-hardenable alloys.

**Upset test.** The upset test consists of upset forging cylindrical billets to various thicknesses or to the same thickness but various height-to-diameter ratios. The reduction obtainable without failure by cracking is considered to be the forgeability. This is the most widely used test and is helpful in determining the surface quality of the forged material.

## FERROUS MATERIALS

Ferrous materials contain iron as the base element. These materials include carbon and alloy steels, tool steels, maraging steels, and stainless steels.

### Carbon and Alloy Steels

Carbon and alloy steels for forging are usually bars or billet stock hot-worked by forging and/or rolling from ingots melted by open-hearth, electric-arc, argon-oxygen degassed (AOD), or basic-oxygen furnace (BOF) methods. For certain grades and

**TABLE 15-3**
**Recommended Forging Equipment for Forging Various Materials[7]**

| Material | Choice of Equipment | Material | Choice of Equipment |
|---|---|---|---|
| Aluminum | Hydraulic presses preferred if part requires severe deformation; otherwise, optional. | Steels (carbon and low alloy) | Hammers, screw presses, and mechanical presses preferred for forgings containing thin sections or when scale removal is a problem; otherwise, optional. |
| Beryllium | Hydraulic presses preferred because of better forgeability under slower deformation rates. | | |
| Copper | Hammers, screw presses, and mechanical presses preferred because workpiece temperature is more easily maintained; hydraulic presses preferred for forging bronze alloys and high-zinc brasses that are sensitive to deformation rate. | Steels (stainless grade) | Hammers, screw presses, and mechanical presses preferred for forgings containing thin sections; otherwise, optional. |
| Columbium | Hammers, screw presses, mechanical presses; presses preferred for wrought alloys when high forging temperatures are required. | Tantalum | Hammers, screw presses, and mechanical presses preferred for wrought alloys when high forging temperatures are required. |
| Magnesium | Hydraulic presses preferred because of poor forgeability under rapid deformation rates. | Titanium | Hammers, screw presses, and mechanical presses preferred for forgings containing thin sections; otherwise, optional. |
| Molybdenum | Hammers, screw presses, and mechanical presses preferred for wrought alloys when high forging temperatures are required. | Tungsten | Hammers, screw presses, and mechanical presses preferred for wrought alloys when high forging temperatures are required. |
| Nickel | Choice depends on section thickness requirements; hammers, screw presses, and mechanical presses are preferred for forgings with thin sections (less than 1/2″ (12.7 mm); otherwise, optional. | Zirconium | Hydraulic presses preferred if billets are jacketed (for temperatures above 1400° F (760° C); optional if forging temperature is below 1400° F (760° C). |

quality requirements, vacuum-arc or electroslag remelting methods are used.

The forgeability of these materials increases as the deformation rate increases. They are forged using hammers, presses, forging machines, high-energy-rate machines, and other types of forging equipment. Heating is generally performed in batch or continuous-type furnaces that are fuel-fired, or it is performed by induction heating. Furnaces with reducing flames help to reduce the scaling that is associated with carbon steels.

Forging temperatures are based on carbon content, alloy composition, temperature range of maximum plasticity, and amount of reduction. Generally, the maximum temperature is selected since it minimizes the forging pressure. Table 15-4 provides the recommended maximum temperature when forging carbon and alloy steels. When workpieces requiring only small reductions are forged, the temperature is decreased 50-100° F (28-56° C).

Lubrication is generally not required with open-die forging. Graphite dispersed in water is commonly used as a lubricant in closed-die forgings.

## Tool Steels

Tool steels are special grades of carbon, alloy, or high-speed steels developed for specific applications. In forging, the workpiece is heated carefully to avoid cracking, then brought to forging temperature. Soaking the workpiece ensures uniformity of temperature throughout the workpiece before forging begins. Initial forging temperatures range from 2000-2200° F (1090-1200° C) depending on composition. Forging should be completed before the temperature reaches 1500-1800° F (815-980° C) to minimize cracking resulting from forging at too low a temperature. Table 15-5 provides recommended forging temperature ranges for commonly forged tool steels.

Cooling of tool steels must be performed carefully to prevent cracking. The rate of cooling is based on the composition of the various tool steels. Generally, most tool steels are air cooled to the transformation temperature to eliminate grain-boundary precipitation and then buried in an insulating compound or slowly cooled to complete transformation.

## Maraging Steels

Forging of maraging steels is performed on the same equipment that is used for forging carbon and alloy steels. Forging temperatures are selected based on the type of forging operation being performed. When large reductions are performed, forging temperatures are similar to those used for alloy

**TABLE 15-4**
**Recommended Forging Temperatures for Carbon and Alloy Steels**[8]

| Type of Steel | Grade AISI | Grade UNS | Temperature, °F (°C) |
|---|---|---|---|
| Carbon | 1010 | G10100 | 2450 (1343) |
| | 1015 | G10150 | |
| | 1020 | G10200 | |
| | 1022 | G10220 | |
| | 1025 | G10250 | 2400 (1316) |
| | 1030 | G10300 | |
| | 1035 | G10350 | |
| | 1040 | G10400 | 2300 (1260) |
| | 1045 | G10450 | |
| | 1050 | G10500 | |
| | 1060 | G10600 | 2200 (1204) |
| | 1070 | G10700 | |
| | 1075 | G10750 | |
| | 1080 | G10800 | |
| | 1095 | G10950 | |
| Manganese | 1330 | G13300 | 2300 (1260) |
| | 1340 | G13400 | |
| Nickel-Chromium | 3140 | G31400 | 2300 (1260) |
| | E3310 | G33106 | |
| Molybdenum | 4023 | G40230 | 2250 (1232) |
| | 4037 | G40370 | |
| | 4042 | G40420 | |
| | 4063 | G40630 | |
| | 4422 | G44220 | |
| | 4427 | G44270 | |
| | 4520 | G45200 | |
| Chromium-Molybdenum | 4130 | G41300 | 2300 (1260) |
| | 4140 | G41400 | |
| | 4150 | G41500 | |
| Nickel-Chromium-Molybdenum | 4320 | G43200 | 2250 (1232) |
| | 4340 | G43400 | 2350 (1288) |
| | 4718 | G47180 | 2250 (1232) |
| | 8115 | G81150 | 2150 (1177) |
| | 81B45 | G81451 | 2200 (1204) |
| | 8620 | G86200 | 2250 (1232) |
| | 8630 | G86300 | 2250 (1232) |
| | 8640 | G86400 | 2200 (1204) |
| | 86B45 | G86451 | 2200 (1204) |
| | 8660 | G86600 | 2150 (1177) |
| | 8740 | G87400 | 2250 (1232) |
| | 8222 | G82220 | 2250 (1232) |
| | E9310 | G93106 | 2250 (1232) |
| | 94B17 | G94171 | 2250 (1232) |
| | 94B30 | G94301 | 2250 (1232) |
| | 94B40 | G94401 | 2250 (1232) |
| | 9840 | G98400 | 2250 (1232) |
| | 9850 | G98500 | 2200 (1204) |
| Nickel-Molybdenum | 4615 | G46150 | 2200 (1204) |
| | 4620 | G46200 | 2300 (1260) |
| | 4815 | G48150 | 2250 (1232) |
| | 4820 | G48200 | 2250 (1232) |

**TABLE 15-4—*Continued***

| Type of Steel | Grade AISI | Grade UNS | Temperature, °F (°C) |
|---|---|---|---|
| Chromium | 5046 | G50460 | 2200 (1204) |
| | 50B46 | G50461 | 2200 (1204) |
| | 50B60 | G50601 | 2200 (1204) |
| | 5120 | G51200 | 2250 (1232) |
| | 5130 | G51300 | 2250 (1232) |
| | 5140 | G51400 | 2200 (1204) |
| | 5150 | G51500 | 2200 (1204) |
| | 5160 | G51600 | 2200 (1204) |
| | 51B60 | G51601 | 2200 (1204) |
| | E52100 | G52986 | 2200 (1204) |
| Chromium Vanadium | 6120 | G61200 | 2250 (1232) |
| | 6150 | G61500 | 2200 (1204) |
| | 6407 | | 2250 (1232) |
| | 6427 | | 2250 (1232) |
| | 7140 | | 1950-2250 (1066-1232) |
| | 8560 | | 2150 (1177) |
| Silicon-Manganese | 9260 | G92600 | 2200 (1204) |

**TABLE 15-5**
**Recommended Forging Temperature Ranges for Tool Steels**[9]

| Type | Grade | Temperature, °F (°C) |
|---|---|---|
| Water-hardening | W1 to W5 | 1800-2000 (982-1093) |
| Shock-resisting | S1,S2,S4,S5 | 1850-2100 (1010-1149) |
| Oil-hardening, cold-work | 01 | 1800-1950 (982-1066) |
| | 02 | 1800-1900 (982-1038) |
| | 07 | 1800-2000 (982-1093) |
| Medium-alloy, air-hardening, cold-work | A2,A4,A5,A6 | 1850-2000 (1010-1093) |
| High-carbon, high-chromium, cold-work | D1 to D6 | 1800-2000 (1010-1093) |
| Chromium, hot work | H11,H12,H13,H14,H16 | 1950-2150 (1066-1177) |
| | H15 | 1900-2100 (1038-1149) |
| Tungsten, hot work | H20,H21,H22,H24,H25,H26 | 2000-2200 (1093-1204) |
| Molybdenum high-speed | M1,M10 | 1900-2100 (1038-1149) |
| | M2 | 1900-2150 (1038-1177) |
| | M4 | 1950-2150 (1066-1177) |
| | M30,M34,M35,M36 | 1950-2150 (1066-1177) |
| Tungsten high-speed | T1 | 1950-2200 (1066-1204) |
| | T2,T4,T8 | 1900-2200 (1038-1204) |
| | T3 | 2000-2250 (1093-1232) |
| | T5,T6 | 1950-2200 (1066-1204) |
| Low-alloy, special purpose | L1,L2,L6 | 1800-2100 (982-1149) |
| | L3 | 1800-2000 (982-1093) |
| Carbon-tungsten, special purpose | F2,F3 | 1800-2000 (982-1093) |

(*continued*)

**TABLE 15-5—*Continued***
**Recommended Forging Temperature Ranges for Tool Steels**[9]

| Type | Grade | Temperature, °F (°C) |
|---|---|---|
| Low-carbon mold steels | P1 | 2200-2350 (1204-1288) |
| | P3 | 1900-2200 (1038-1204) |
| | P4 | 2000-2250 (1093-1232) |
| | P20 | 1950-2250 (1066-1232) |

steels. Maraging steel grades 200, 250, 280, and 350 are usually forged between 1500-2300° F (816-1260° C). If small reductions are performed on certain portions of the workpiece, the forging temperature is reduced to prevent excessive grain growth.

## Stainless Steels

Stainless steels are considerably more difficult to forge than carbon or low-alloy steels because of their strength at higher temperatures and the limitations on the temperature at which stainless steels can be forged. Table 15-6 is a list of commonly used stainless steels in order of their forgeability. Generally, the equipment used in forging stainless steel is the same as that used in forging carbon and alloy steels. The major difference is that, in forging stainless steel, the equipment must deliver more power per stroke and more blows, or a combination of both. Stainless steels are heated in fuel-fired or electric furnaces or by induction heating. Stainless steels do not form as much scale as carbon or alloy steels. However, the scale that does form is extremely hard and abrasive. The surface can be cleaned by pickling, rough turning, or grit blasting.

Hot-rolled or cold-finished, stainless steel bars are often used for forging. Semifinished round-corner squares are also used, depending on the size of the forging. The bars are generally over 1/2" (12.7 mm) round or square, and the semifinished squares are generally 4" (102 mm) square or larger.

Stainless steels are generally divided into four basic categories: martensitic stainless steels, ferritic stainless steels, austenitic stainless steels, and precipitation-hardened stainless steels.

**Martensitic stainless steels.** Martensitic stainless steels are iron-chromium alloys which are air-hardening and have forging characteristics similar to alloy steels. However, the required forging forces for high-chromium grades are increased by 50% over those required for alloy steels.

Table 15-7 provides the recommended forging temperature ranges of the more commonly forged martensitic alloys. Heating the material to a higher temperature may cause cracking during forging due to transformation of some austenite to delta ferrite.

During cooling, martensitic stainless steels are subject to thermal cracking. Therefore, martensitic alloys should be cooled slowly and shielded from the water spray used to cool the dies. Generally, martensitic forgings are cooled to 1100° F (590° C) in a furnace or in an insulating medium. The forgings are then tempered to facilitate any necessary machining.

**Ferritic stainless steels.** Ferritic stainless steels have a broad range of forgeability. Table 15-7 provides the recommended forging temperature ranges for commonly forged ferritic alloys. These alloys are not as susceptible to cracking as the martensitic alloys are, and the cooling rate is not critical. Generally, these alloys are annealed after forging.

**Austenitic stainless steels.** Austenitic stainless steels are more difficult to forge than ferritic and martensitic alloys. Table 15-7 provides the recommended forging temperature ranges of the commonly forged austenitic alloys. Austenitic alloys with a high nickel content are susceptible to attack by sulfur during

**TABLE 15-6**
**Forgeability of Commonly Used Stainless Steels**[10]

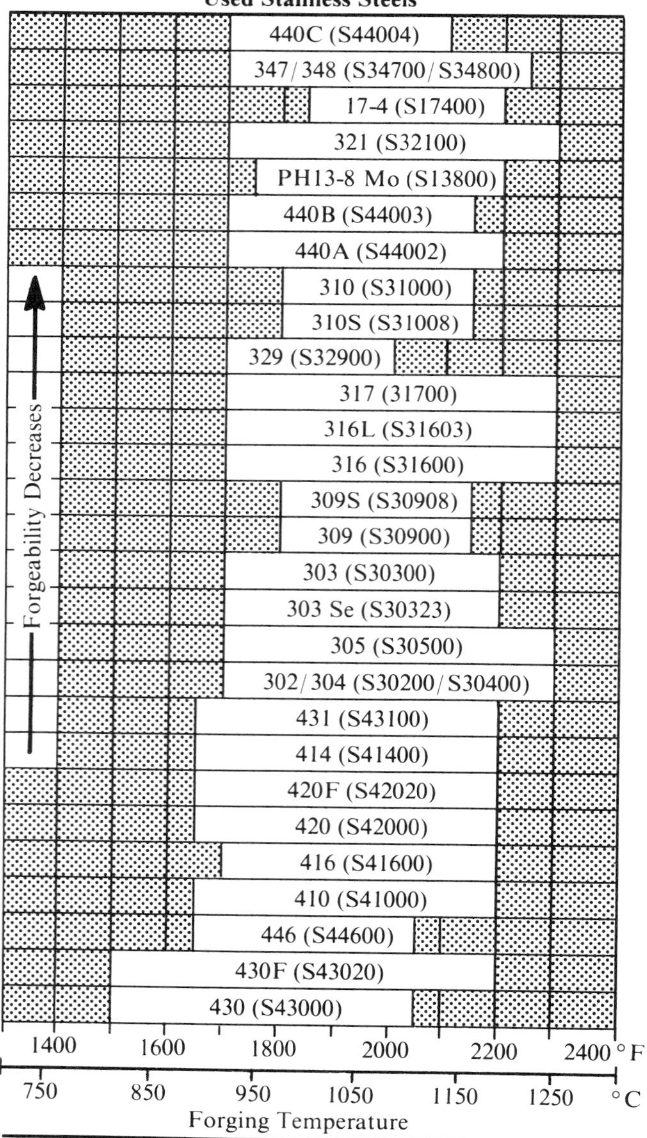

heating and should be heated in a slightly oxidizing atmosphere if sulfur-rich fuels are used.

The forgeability of austenitic alloys is not affected by forging rates. Therefore, hammers and fast-acting forging machines are recommended since they minimize the problems caused by heat transfer. However, special care must be taken in regard to the intensity of hammer blows, the amount of reduction between reheatings, and the amount of final reduction to control grain size.

Most austenitic alloys can be cooled rapidly down to ambient temperature in air or water. Annealing the forging and then cooling it rapidly from about 1950° F (1065° C) to ambient temperature is generally advisable for parts requiring corrosion resistance.

**TABLE 15-7**
**Recommended Forging Temperature Ranges for Stainless Steels**

| Types of Stainless Steel | Alloy | | Temperature, ° F (° C) |
|---|---|---|---|
| | AISI | UNS | |
| Martensitic | 403 | S40300 | 1600-2100 (871-1149) |
| | 410 | S41000 | 1650-2200 (899-1204) |
| | 414 | S41400 | 1650-2200 (899-1204) |
| | 416 | S41600 | 1700-2150 (929-1177) |
| | 420 | S42000 | 1650-2200 (899-1204) |
| | 420F | S42020 | 1650-2200 (899-1204) |
| | 431 | S43100 | 1650-2200 (899-1204) |
| | 440A | S44002 | 1750-2050 (954-1121) |
| | 440B | S44003 | 1750-2050 (954-1121) |
| | 440C | S44004 | 1700-2100 (927-1177) |
| | 501 | S50100 | 1800-2200 (982-1204) |
| | 502 | S50200 | 1800-2200 (982-1204) |
| | 619 | S42300 | 1900-2100 (1038-1177) |
| | Greek Ascoloy | S41800 | 1750-2150 (954-1177) |
| Ferritic | 405 | S40500 | 1750-2050 (954-1121) |
| | 430 | S43000 | 1500-2050 (816-1121) |
| | 430F | S43020 | 1500-2000 (816-1093) |
| | 446 | S44600 | 1650-2050 (899-1121) |
| Austenitic | 201 | S20100 | 1750-2200 (954-1204) |
| | 202 | S20200 | 1750-2200 (954-1204) |
| | 301 | S30100 | 1750-2200 (954-1204) |
| | 302 | S30200 | 1700-2300 (927-1260) |
| | 302B | S30215 | 1750-2200 (954-1204) |
| | 303 | S30300 | 1700-2300 (927-1260) |
| | 303SE | S30323 | 1700-2300 (927-1260) |
| | 304 | S30400 | 1700-2300 (927-1260) |
| | 305 | S30500 | 1700-2300 (927-1260) |
| | 308 | S30800 | 1750-2200 (954-1204) |
| | 309 | S30900 | 1800-2150 (982-1177) |
| | 309S | S30908 | 1800-2150 (982-1177) |
| | 310 | S31000 | 1800-2150 (982-1177) |
| | 310S | S31008 | 1800-2175 (982-1191) |
| | 314 | S31400 | 1750-2000 (954-1093) |
| | 316 | S31600 | 1700-2300 (927-1260) |
| | 316L | S31603 | 1700-2300 (927-1260) |
| | 317 | S31700 | 1700-2300 (927-1260) |
| | 321 | S32100 | 1700-2300 (927-1260) |
| | 329 | S32900 | 1700-2200 (927-1093) |
| | 347 | S34700 | 1700-2250 (927-1232) |
| | 348 | S34800 | 1700-2250 (927-1232) |
| Precipitation-hardened | S13800 | S13800 | 1750-2200 (954-1204) |
| | 632 | S15700 | 2000-2250 (1093-1232) |
| | 630 | S17400 | 1850-2200 (1010-1204) |
| | 635 | S17600 | 2050-2250 (1121-1232) |
| | 631 | S17700 | 1950-2200 (1066-1204) |
| | 633 | S35000 | 2100-2150 (1038-1177) |
| | 634 | S35500 | 2000-2200 (1093-1204) |

**Precipitation-hardened stainless steels.** Precipitation-hardened stainless steels are not used as extensively as the low-alloy martensitic steels and are among the most difficult to forge. Table 15-7 provides the recommended forging temperature ranges of those precipitation-hardened steels that are commonly used. Forging temperatures are based on the amount and rate of reduction, grain growth, delta ferrite transformation, and type of subsequent heat treatments.

Thick sections should not be placed directly into a furnace heated to forging temperature. Preheating the material to 1200-1400° F (650-760° C) and allowing it to equalize in temperature minimizes internal cracks. Sections thicker than 3" (75 mm) and sections containing intricate designs are generally cooled slowly. Oxidizing atmospheres are recommended for all heating operations. Scale should be removed by acid pickling if the workpiece was not finish formed. Vapor blasting is recommended for workpieces that have been finish formed to prevent intergranular attack around the carbides of the delta ferrite-austenite interfaces.

## NONFERROUS MATERIALS

Nonferrous materials do not contain iron as the base element. The common nonferrous metals currently being forged include aluminum, copper, magnesium, and titanium. Superalloys and refractory metals are also being forged and are discussed in a separate section. Zinc alloys have been forged successfully, but have only been used in limited applications.

### Aluminum and Aluminum Alloys

Aluminum and aluminum alloys have the greatest forgeability of all forged materials and can be readily forged into precise, intricate shapes. Their ease of forgeability is due to their ductility, the capability of heating the dies to the same temperature as the workpiece, their freedom from scale during forging, and the low forging forces required. However, forging forces vary with alloy composition. Aluminum forging materials are produced by press forging and rolling from continuously cast ingots.

Most alloys are forged at 100° F (56° C) below their solidus temperature. Temperature control must be carefully maintained because the recommended forging temperature range is narrow. Table 15-8 provides the recommended forging temperature ranges for commonly forged aluminum alloys in closed dies. The temperature is generally decreased approximately 50° F (28° C) when large reductions are made and/or when fast deformation rates are employed, such as on hammers or high energy rate forming (HERF) machines. The forging dies are generally heated to the temperature of the material.

Aluminum and aluminum alloys are forged with the equipment used for forging other materials. Mechanical presses are widely used in closed-die forging, but hydraulic presses are recommended when large, intricate parts are being forged. Muffle-type furnaces are recommended for heating aluminum alloys. When using gas or oil, it is important to minimize the sulfur content.

Die lubrication is necessary to prevent the aluminum-rich material from adhering to the dies. Graphite suspended in water is the most common lubricant used. To remove any oxide and lubricant residue, the workpiece is immersed in an aqueous solution containing 4-8%, by weight, sodium hydroxide (NaOH) at 160° F (71° C) for 1/2 minute to 5 minutes; rinsed in hot water, 170° F (77° C), for the same length of time; immersed in an aqueous solution containing 10% by volume of nitric acid at 190° F (88° C); and then rinsed in hot water. Aluminum forgings are usually heat treated to obtain the required mechanical properties.

### Copper Alloys

Copper alloys are forged using slugs produced by shearing or sawing. Forging brass, UNS-C37700, is the least difficult of all copper alloys to forge.

Most copper forgings are produced in mechanical presses. The dies are always heated to improve forgeability, and the optimum temperature varies from 300-600° F (149-316° C) depending on the alloy being forged. Copper alloy workpieces are generally heated in gas-fired furnaces. Table 15-9 provides the recommended temperature ranges for forging copper alloys. To minimize grain growth and scale, the workpiece should be brought to uniform temperature and then forged.

Graphite particles dispersed in water usually provide adequate lubrication. A forging oil provides additional lubrication for deep-cavity forgings.

**TABLE 15-8**
**Recommended Forging Temperature Ranges for Aluminum Alloys**[11]

| Alloy | | |
|---|---|---|
| AA | UNS | Temperature, ° F (° C) |
| 1100 | A91100 | 600-760 (315-405) |
| 2014 | A92014 | 785-860 (420-460) |
| 2025 | A92025 | 785-840 (420-450) |
| 2218 | A92218 | 760-840 (405-450) |
| 2219 | A92219 | 800-880 (427-470) |
| 2618 | A92618 | 770-850 (410-455) |
| 3003 | A93003 | 600-760 (315-405) |
| 4032 | A94032 | 780-860 (415-460) |
| 5083 | A95083 | 760-860 (405-460) |
| 6061 | A96061 | 810-900 (432-482) |
| 6151 | A96151 | 810-900 (432-482) |
| 7039 | A97039 | 720-820 (382-438) |
| 7075 | A97075 | 720-820 (382-438) |
| 7079 | A97079 | 760-850 (405-455) |

**TABLE 15-9**
**Recommended Forging Temperature Ranges for Copper Alloys**[12]

| Alloy | | |
|---|---|---|
| CDA | UNS | Temperature, ° F (° C) |
| 122 | C12200 | 1350-1550 (732-843) |
| 182 | C18200 | 1200-1400 (649-760) |
| 377 | C37700 | 1200-1400 (649-760) |
| 464 | C46400 | 1100-1300 (593-704) |
| 616 | | 1400-1600 (760-871) |
| 624 | C62400 | 1300-1500 (704-816) |
| 628 | | 1500-1650 (816-899) |
| 642 | C64200 | 1350-1650 (732-899) |
| 670 | C67000 | 1100-1300 (593-704) |
| 673 | C67300 | 1100-1350 (593-732) |
| 674 | C67400 | 1100-1350 (593-732) |
| 675 | C67500 | 1100-1300 (593-704) |

## Magnesium Alloys

Forgeability of magnesium alloys is determined by the solidus temperature, the deformation rate, and the grain size. Generally, magnesium alloys are forged at temperatures within 100° F (56° C) of the solidus temperature. Table 15-10 provides the recommended temperature ranges of commonly forged magnesium alloys and the temperature ranges for the dies. Since cold workpieces are susceptible to cracking, the dies should be heated to approximately the same temperature as the workpiece. Decreasing the forging temperature 50° F (28° C) for each successive operation in a multistep process prevents recrystallization and grain growth. For workpieces requiring only a small amount of reduction, forging at the lowest temperature is recommended to permit strain-hardening.

Hydraulic presses and slow-action mechanical presses are used when magnesium alloys are being forged. Hammers and fast-acting presses produce cracks in the workpiece. Die lubrication is usually achieved using colloidal graphite in a water-based fluid. Soot or lampblack can also be applied. It is important that the coating be thin and uniform. Fuel-fired or electric furnaces are generally used to heat the forgings, and inert or reducing atmospheres are not required below temperatures of 900° F (480° C).

Magnesium forgings are rapidly cooled in water to prevent further recrystallization and grain growth. Trimming of the workpiece is performed cold on a bandsaw when only small quantities are required. Hot trimming is performed at 400-500° F (205-260° C) on a trimming press. Cleaning is usually performed in two steps. First, the workpieces are blast cleaned to remove the lubricant residue, and then they are dipped in a solution of 8% nitric acid and 2% sulfuric acid followed by a warm water rinse. Protection against corrosion is accomplished by dipping the workpieces in a dichromate solution.

## Titanium Alloys

Titanium can be forged into intricate and unusual shapes, but it is more difficult to forge than aluminum or ferrous alloys. Titanium is produced by vacuum-arc melting in consumable-electrode furnaces.

**TABLE 15-10**
**Recommended Forging Temperature Ranges for Magnesium Alloys**[13]

| Alloy | | Temperature, ° F (° C) | |
|---|---|---|---|
| ASTM | UNS | Magnesium Alloy | Forging Die |
| ZK21A | | 575-700 (300-370) | 500-600 (260-315) |
| AZ61A | M11610 | 600-700 (315-370) | 550-650 (290-345) |
| AZ31B | M11311 | 550-650 (290-345) | 500-600 (260-315) |
| High-Strength Alloys | | | |
| ZK60A | | 550-725 (290-385) | 400-550 (205-290) |
| AZ80A | M11800 | 550-750 (290-400) | 400-550 (205-290) |
| Elevated-Temperature Alloys | | | |
| HM21A | M13210 | 750-975 (400-525) | 700-800 (370-425) |
| EK31A | | 700-900 (370-480) | 650-750 (345-400) |
| Special Alloys | | | |
| ZE42A | | 550-700 (290-370) | 575-650 (300-345) |
| ZE62 | | 575-675 (300-345) | 575-650 (300-345) |
| QE22A | M18220 | 650-725 (345-385) | 600-700 (315-370) |

Forgeability is determined by the forging temperature and the rate of deformation. Most of the alloys are forged 25-50° F (14-28° C) below the alpha-beta to beta transus temperature to obtain better tensile ductility in the finished workpiece. Table 15-11 provides the recommended temperature ranges of the commonly forged titanium alloys. Dies heated to 800° F (425° C) are used on hydraulic presses, and those heated to 500° F (260° C) are used for hammers and mechanical presses.

The forging equipment used for titanium is the same as for steel. However, forging pressures are greater. Mechanical presses are employed when parts up to 100 lb (45 kg) are being forged, and hydraulic presses are employed when parts from 20-900 lb (9-408 kg) are forged. Hammers are employed for forgings of all sizes. To minimize contamination by oxygen, nitrogen, and hydrogen, vacuum-type furnaces or furnaces providing an inert atmosphere are recommended when titanium is heated. Glass and ceramic coatings are also used to minimize material contamination during heating and forging.

Lubrication is provided by oil-graphite or water-graphite suspensions. Borosilicate-type glasses are also being employed as lubricants in forging titanium. Finished forgings are cleaned using both mechanical and chemical methods. Hot baths containing caustic soda or sodium hydroxide are frequently used to remove the heavy gray or black scale formed by forging. Acid pickling can be used to remove the oxygen-enriched surface from the forging.

## Beryllium

Beryllium forgings are produced from all commercial grades of hot-pressed blocks, from canned powder, and from solid billets made from vacuum-melted, high-purity ingots. (Refer to Chapter 17, "Powder Metallurgy," for additional information.)

Forging of beryllium is generally performed between 1300-1400° F (705-760° C) to develop high strength and minimize grain growth. Reduction of greater than 25% should be avoided unless lateral support is provided.

Special forging techniques are employed to produce crack-free parts in a hydraulic press. If cracks occur during forging, the cracks should be removed between forging steps. Surrounding the beryllium workpiece with a steel cladding is the most common technique employed. This technique helps to restrain metal flow and keep tensile stresses low enough to

**TABLE 15-11**
**Recommended Forging Temperatures for Titanium Alloys**[14]

| Alloy | Temperature, ° F (° C) |
|---|---|
| Commercially pure | 1600-1700 (870-927) |
| Ti-5Al-2.5Sn | 1800-1850 (982-1010) |
| Ti-8Al-1Mo-1V | 1800-1850 (982-1010) |
| Beta III | 1550-1650 (843-900) |
| Ti-13V-11Cr-3Al | 1600-1800 (870-982) |
| Ti-3Al-8V-6Cr-4Mo-4Zr | 1500-1600 (815-870) |
| Ti-5Al-6Sn-2Zr-1Mo-0.25Si | 1875-1950 (1025-1065) |
| Ti-6Al-4V | 1700-1750 (927-955) |
| Ti-6Al-6V-2Sn | 1600-1650 (870-900) |
| Ti-6Al-6V-4Mo-4Zr | 1525-1600 (830-870) |
| Ti-6Al-2Sn-4Zr-2Mo | 1700-1800 (927-982) |
| Ti-6Al-6Mo-4Zr-2Sn | 1625-1700 (885-927) |
| Ti-7Al-4Mo | 1500-1700 (815-927) |
| IMI Alloy 679 | 1650-1725 (900-940) |

prevent cracking. Another technique is a backward extrusion process with disposable tool elements.

Dies should be heated to approximately 800° F (425° C). Graphite dispersed in oil and glasses are generally employed as lubricants. After forging, the workpiece should be stress relieved.

## SUPERALLOYS

The forgeability of superalloys is the lowest of any materials currently being forged. Iron, cobalt, and nickel are the three basic metal systems used for superalloys. Hot-rolled or press-forged billets are generally used as the starting material. Ingot or billet quality is important. Therefore, vacuum-arc or electroslag remelting is used to produce the initial billets.

The forging of superalloys is performed successfully on both hammers and presses used to forge carbon and carbon-alloy steels. However, typical forging pressures are greater and range from 80-100 ksi (552-690 MPa). Hammers are used for producing preforms and closed-die forgings for large parts weighing 100-2000 lb (45-910 kg). Mechanical presses usually are preferred for small forgings less than 20 lb (9 kg) requiring close tolerance control. Hydraulic presses are generally used when large forgings, up to several tons (27 kN), are being produced.

The forging temperature range is narrow for superalloys and must be controlled to obtain the desired properties. Table 15-12 provides the recommended forging temperature ranges of the superalloys currently being forged. Heating the dies and decreasing the strain rate improves the forgeability of superalloys.

An insulating layer of material such as ceramic, glass, or steel protects the surface against heat losses due to radiation and conduction. It also protects the material's surface from sulfur in the furnace atmosphere and lubricants. Lubrication is provided by graphite dispersed in water or oil.

## REFRACTORY MATERIALS

Refractory metals currently being forged include tantalum, columbium, molybdenum, and tungsten. Their forgeability depends on the method used to convert the cast ingots into billets suitable for forging.

Tantalum and columbium billets are brought to forging temperature in gas-fired furnaces that have an oxidizing atmosphere. Oxidizing atmospheres are not required for tungsten and molybdenum heated in full-fired furnaces. Induction furnaces are also used when heating molybdenum to temperatures greater than 2500° F (1371° C).

Glass coatings are applied to tantalum and columbium to prevent oxidation and provide the necessary lubrication during forging. Molybdenum and tungsten form an oxide on the surface during heating that prevents surface contamination and provides lubrication during forging. Tungsten forgings must be cooled slowly to prevent thermal cracking.

**TABLE 15-12**
**Forging Temperatures for Superalloys**[15]

| Metal System | Alloy | Temperature, ° F (° C) |
|---|---|---|
| Iron | A-286 | 1800-2050 (980-1120) |
| | V-57 | 1650-2150 (900-1177) |
| | M-308 | 2150 (1177) |
| | 19-9DL | 1200-2150 (649-1177) |
| | W-545 | 1700-2000 (927-1093) |
| | Discaloy | 2200 (1205) |
| | 16-25-6 | 2100 (1150) |
| | AFC-260 | 1750-2075 (955-1135) |
| | Pyromet 860 | 1900-2050 (1038-1120) |
| Cobalt | J1570 | 1800-2150 (980-1177) |
| | J-1650 | 1850-2100 (1010-1150) |
| | HS-25 (L-605) | 1850-2250 (1010-1230) |
| | S-816 | 1900-2200 (1038-1205) |
| | HA-188 | 1800-2150 (980-1177) |
| | MP35N | 1900-2100 (1038-1150) |
| Nickel | Nickel 200 | 1600-2200 (870-1205) |
| | Hastelloy W | 1900-2200 (1038-1205) |
| | Incoloy 901 | 1800-2150 (980-1175) |
| | Inconel Alloy X-750 | 1900-2100 (1038-1150) |
| | Inconel Alloy 600 | 1900-2100 (1038-1150) |
| | Inconel Alloy 751 | 1900-2200 (1038-1205) |
| | Hastelloy R-235 | 1850-2200 (1010-1205) |
| | Hastelloy C | 1850-2250 (1010-1230) |
| | Inconel Alloy 718 | 1700-2050 (927-1120) |
| | Nimonic 90 | 1850-2100 (1010-1150) |
| | Hastelloy X | 1600-2200 (870-1205) |
| | Nimonic 115 | 2000-2150 (1093-1175) |
| | Unitemp 1753 | 1850-2150 (1010-1175) |
| | M-252 | 1800-2150 (980-1175) |
| | René 41 | 1850-2150 (1010-1175) |
| | Astroloy | 2000-2150 (1093-1175) |
| | Waspaloy | 2000-2100 (1093-1150) |
| | Udimet 700 | 1875-2050 (1025-1120) |
| | Udimet 500 | 1900-2175 (1038-1190) |
| | MAR-M Alloy 421 | 1900-2100 (1038-1150) |
| | Unitemp AF 2-1 DA | 1950-2150 (1065-1175) |
| | AF 1-1 DA | 1950-2050 (1065-1120) |
| | Udimet 710 | 1950-2150 (1065-1175) |
| | René 95 | 1950-2050 (1065-1120) |

# FORGING EQUIPMENT

Many different types of machines and equipment are used for the forging process. These include various machines for the actual forging and auxiliary equipment for heating, loading, and unloading the stock, as well as other machines to produce a completed part.

Forging machines are generally classified with respect to their principle of operation. Hammers and high energy rate forming (HERF) machines are classified as *energy-restricted* machines because the deformation results from the kinetic energy of the hammer ram. Mechanical presses are referred to as *stroke-restricted* machines because their ability to deform the material is determined by the length of the press stroke and the available force at the various stroke positions. Hydraulic presses are called *force-restricted* machines because their ability to deform the material depends on the maximum force rating of the press. Screw-type presses are other examples of *energy-restricted* machines even though they are similar in construction to mechanical and hydraulic presses.

# FORGING EQUIPMENT

## SELECTION CRITERIA

Several variables must be evaluated before a machine can be selected for a particular forging. The two most important variables to be evaluated are the force and energy capabilities of the machine relative to the requirements of the forging. The force and energy capabilities of a particular forging machine can be obtained from force versus energy diagrams supplied by the manufacturer. Force versus energy diagrams are also referred to as power diagrams. The subsequent section on operating parameters in this chapter discusses the methods used to determine the amount of force or energy required to deform the forging.

Another variable is the rate at which the deformation occurs (strain rate). Low-impact speeds are best suited for displacing material sideways, while higher speeds are beneficial for filling deep die cavities or for producing forgings having sharply defined, complex shapes or particularly thin sections. The impact speed also has an effect on the type of material that can be forged in a particular machine. However, many materials can be successfully forged with either a hammer or press, so the machine selection should be determined by the shape and definition of the forging. If the machine is going to be purchased for a particular forging, it is also necessary to consider the investment costs, existing experience in die technology and equipment, availability of skilled labor, required precision, production rate, noise pollution, maintenance requirements, and expected die set-up times.

Table 15-13 and Table 15-14 present the force and energy capabilities of hammers and presses, as well as their ranges of impact speeds. Refer to Table 15-3 for a list of the machines recommended for forging different materials.

## FORGING HAMMERS

Forging hammers are energy-restricted machines and are the most inexpensive and versatile types of machines used in forging. This is due to the hammer's capability of developing large forces and the short die contact time. The main components are a ram, frame assembly, anvil, and anvil cap. The anvil is connected directly to the frame assembly, the upper die is attached to the ram, and the lower die is attached to the anvil cap.

In operation, the workpiece is placed on the lower die. The ram moves downward, exerting a force on the anvil and causing the workpiece to deform.

Forging hammers are classified by the method used to drive the ram downward. The two common methods are by gravity or by an external power source. Another type of forging hammer is the counterblow type. Hammers used in open-die forging are slightly different from those used in closed-die forging.

### Gravity Drop Hammers

A gravity drop hammer consists of an anvil or base, supporting columns which contain the ram guides, and a device to return the ram to its starting position. The energy for deforming the workpiece is derived from the downward drop of the ram. The height of the fall and the falling weight are factors that determine the force of the blow. A foot treadle releases the ram.

Small and medium-size gravity drop hammers, with ram weights of 100-7500 lb (45-3400 kg), use hardwood boards passing between friction rolls to raise the ram. This type of hammer is often referred to as a board drop hammer and is shown in Fig. 15-12. Since the height is not readily adjustable, this type of hammer is only used when constant blows are required.

Power-lift gravity hammers incorporate a cylinder and piston to raise the ram between strokes (see Fig. 15-13). Power to lift the ram can be from hydraulic, pneumatic, or steam

**TABLE 15-14**
**Capacities of Forging Presses**

| Press Type | Force, tons (MN) | Pressing Speed, fps (m/s) |
|---|---|---|
| Mechanical | 250-16,000 (2.2-142.3) | 0.2-5 (0.06-1.5) |
| Screw | 150-31,500 (1.3-280) | 1.5-4 (0.5-1.2) |
| Hydraulic | 250-70,000 (2.2-623) | 0.1-2.5 (0.03-0.8) |

**TABLE 15-13**
**Capacities of Forging Hammers**

| Hammer Type | Ram Weight, lb (kg) | Maximum Blow Energy, ft-lb (kJ) | Impact Speed, fps (m/s) | Blows per Minute |
|---|---|---|---|---|
| Board | 100-7500 (45-3400) | 35,000 (47.5) | 10-15 (3-4.6) | 45-60 |
| Air or steam lift | 500-16,000 (225-7255) | 90,000 (122) | 12-16 (3.7-4.9) | 60 |
| Electrohydraulic drop | 1000-22,000 (450-9980) | 80,000 (108.5) | 10-15 (3-4.6) | 50-75 |
| Power drop | 1500-70,000 (680-31 750) | 850,000 (1153) | 15-30 (4.6-9) | 60-100 |
| Counterblow (vertical) | 1000-60,000 (450-27 215) | 900,000 (1220) | 15-30 (4.6-9) | 50-65 |
| Impacter | 350-21,000 (160-7710) | 3000-25,000 (4-34) | 10-17 (3-5.2) | 100-170 |

pressure. This type of hammer is capable of being adjusted for intermediate-length or full-length strokes. Power-lift gravity drop hammers are built in sizes from 500-16,000 lb (225-7255 kg) and are capable of being programmed for automatic blow control.

## Power Drop Hammers

Power drop hammers not only raise the ram but also drive the ram during the downward stroke. Pressurized air, steam, or hydraulic oil provide power to the cylinder at the top of the hammer. A piston in the cylinder transmits power to the ram

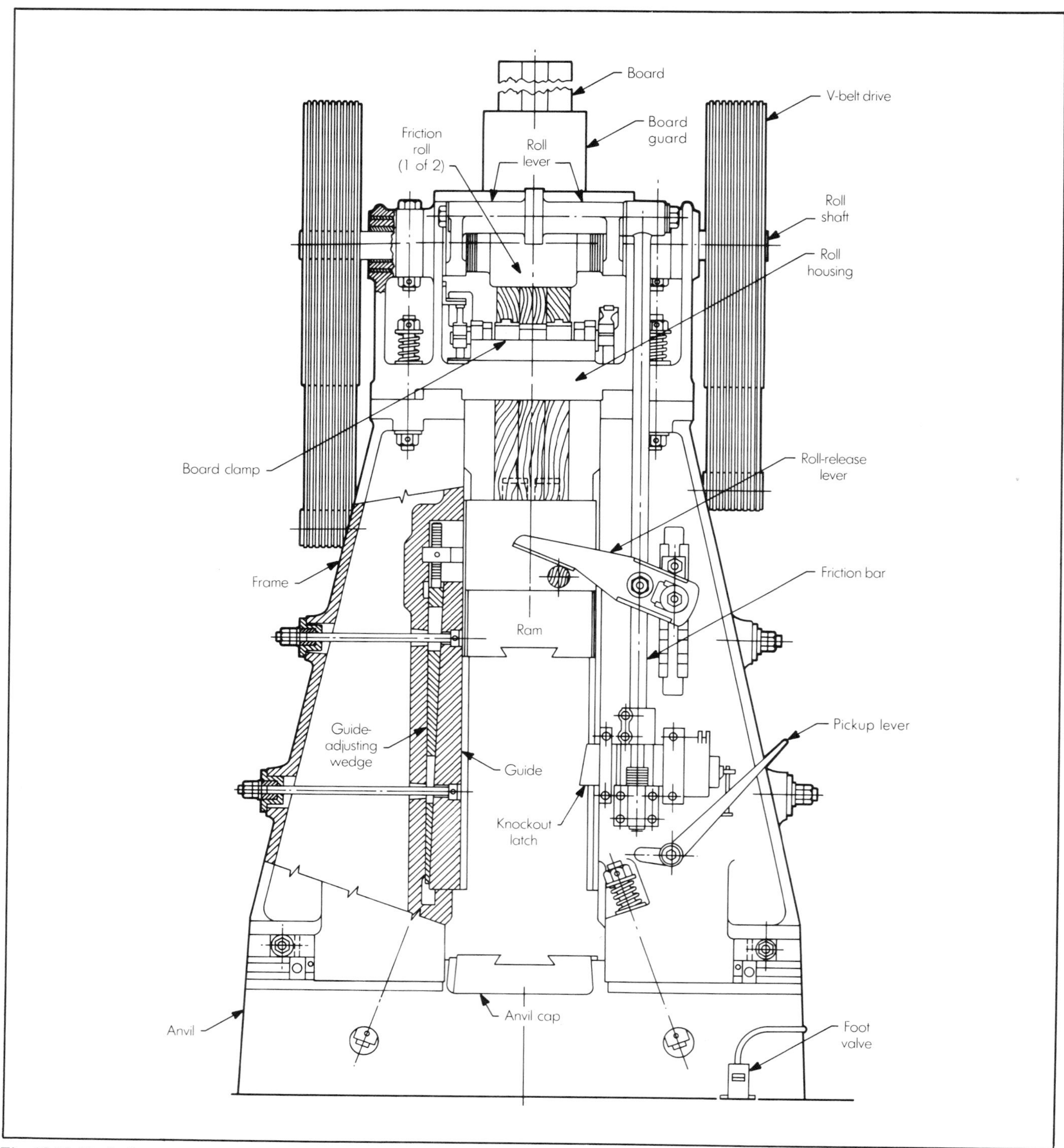


**Fig. 15-12 Typical components of a board drop hammer.** (*Erie Press Systems*)

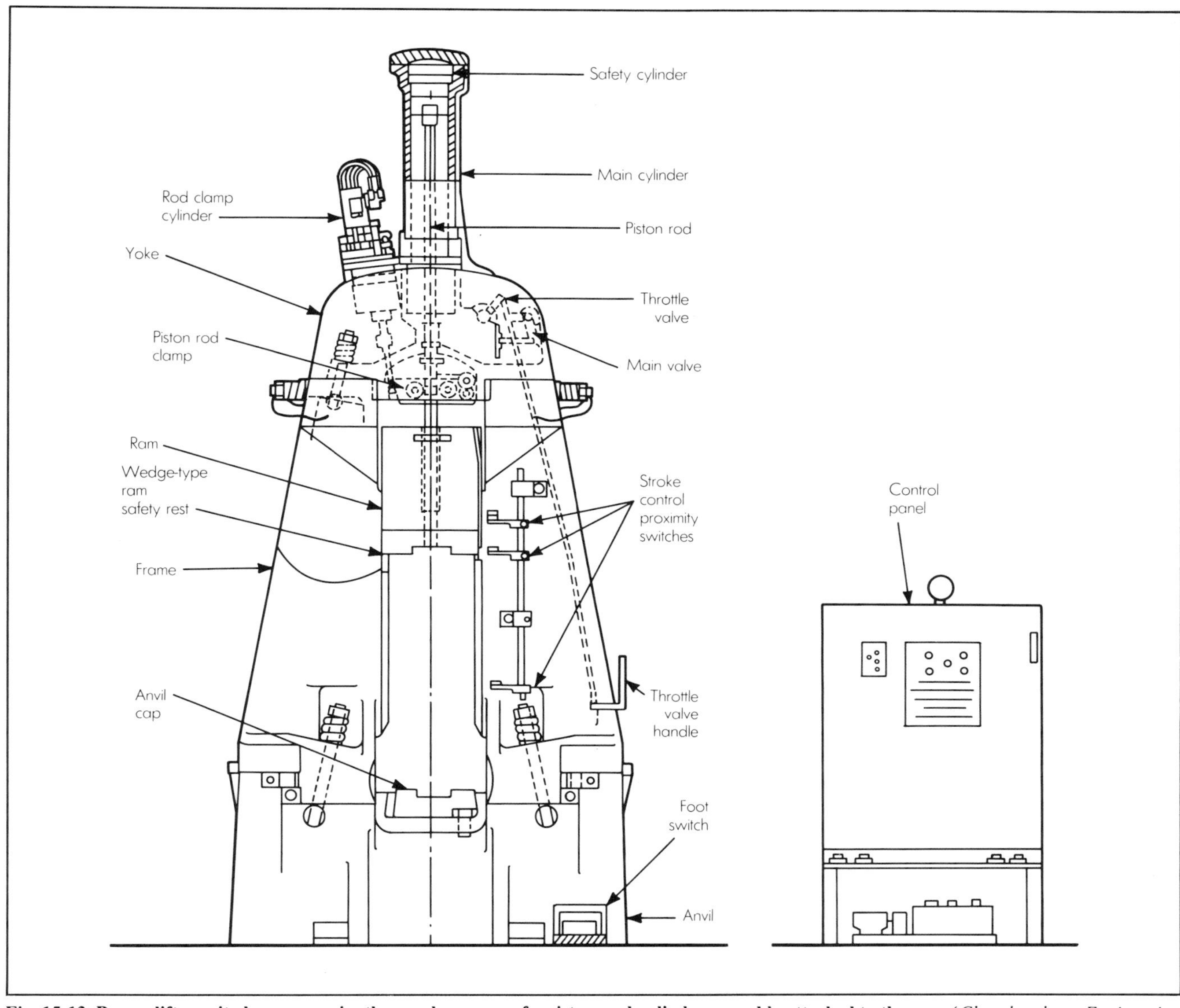


**Fig. 15-13 Power-lift gravity hammers raise the ram by means of a piston-and-cylinder assembly attached to the ram.** (*Chambersburg Engineering Co.*)

(see Fig. 15-14). Varying the opening of the valve in the cylinder regulates the ram speed. On steam and air hammers the opening is achieved manually by depressing a foot treadle. On hydraulically operated hammers, the opening can be programmed with electronic controls. Power drop hammers are rated by the weight of the free falling ram and are built in sizes from 1000-70,000 lb (450-31 750 kg).

## Die Forger Hammers

Die forger hammers are short-stroke, high-speed hammers that are similar in operation to power drop hammers (see Fig. 15-15). The ram is held at the top of the stroke by a constant source of pressurized air. During operation, the pressurized air is admitted to and exhausted from the cylinder to energize the blow. One manufacturer builds die forger hammers that are capable of delivering 4000-66,000 ft-lb (5.4-89.5 kJ) of energy per blow. The energy of the blow and the forging program is controlled from an automatic processor.

## Counterblow Hammers

Counterblow hammers incorporate two opposed rams that are activated simultaneously toward each other pneumatically or hydraulically. Depending on machine design, the rams move either in a vertical direction or a horizontal direction. The horizontal counterblow hammers are referred to as impacters.

In the conventional vertical design, the opposing rams are approximately equal in weight. The workpiece is placed in the lower die as in other forging hammers. However, when the hammer is activated, the lower die moves upward toward the descending upper die and the two dies meet approximately halfway through the stroke. Since the lower die is moving, it is difficult to do any preforming on the side of the die. If several cavities are required, more than one hammer is necessary. The workpiece also has a tendency to jump from the die during operation. Another disadvantage is that the guiding clearances are twice as large as on gravity drop hammers, causing die mismatch. However, due to the counterblow effect, a minimal amount of energy is lost to vibration and a smaller foundation can be used.

A recent vertical hammer design has the upper ram guided within the lower ram, and the lower ram has a weight four times that of the upper ram. The lower ram's speed is reduced, and the

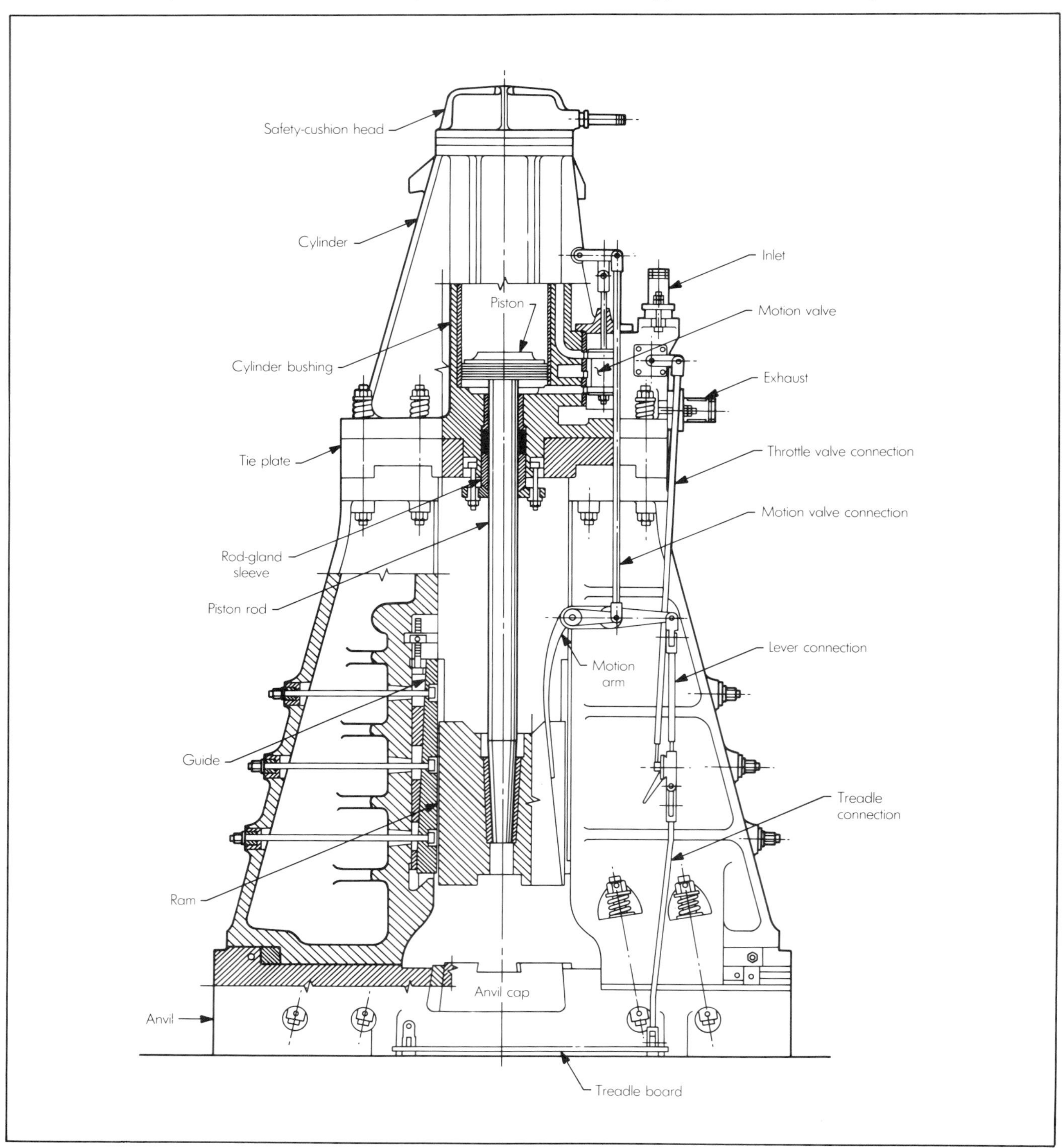


**Fig. 15-14 Power drop hammers utilize pressurized air, steam, or hydraulic oil to raise the ram and drive it downward. (*Erie Press Systems*)**

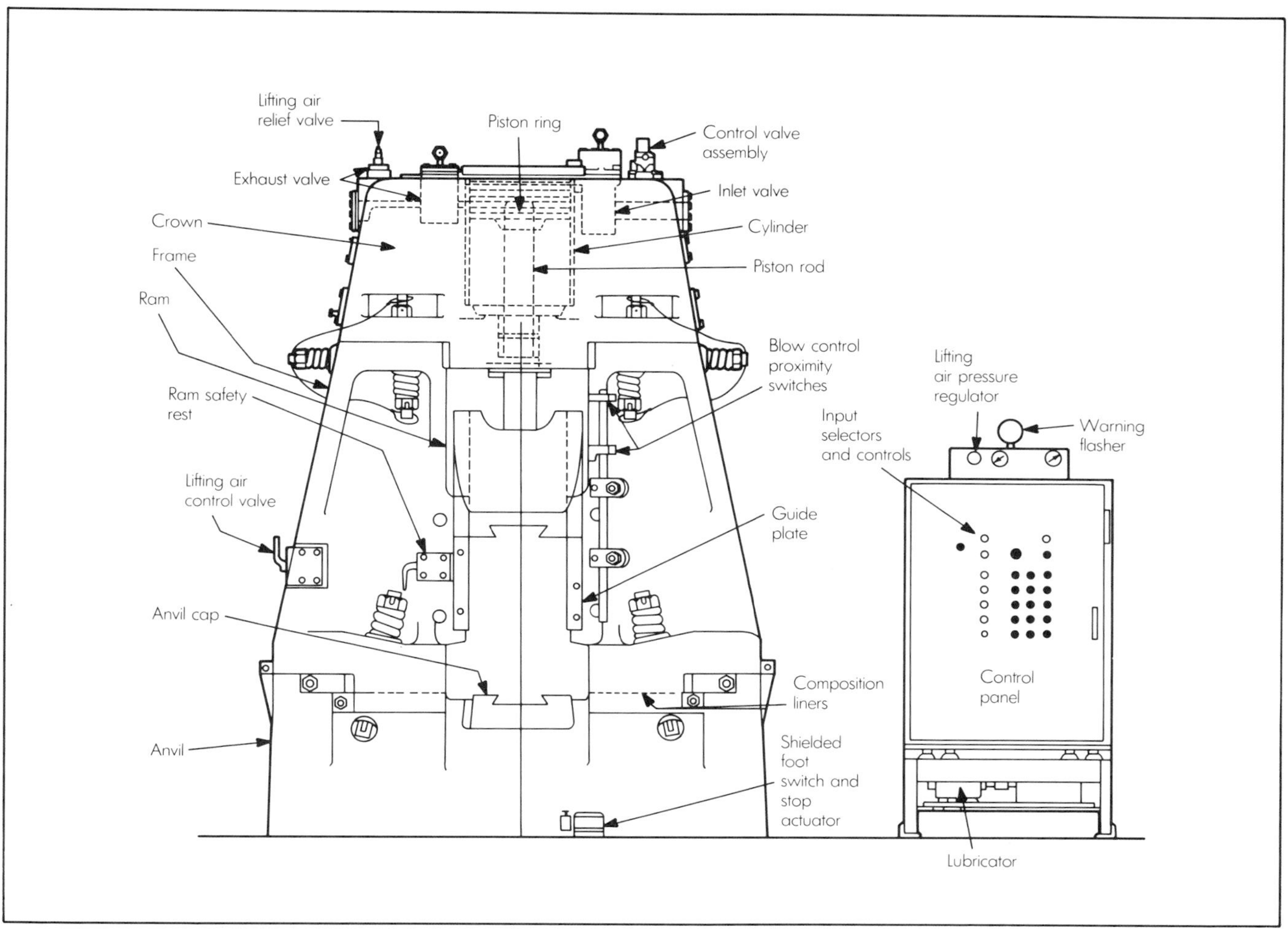


**Fig. 15-15 Front view of die forger hammer.** (*Chambersburg Engineering Co.*)

stroke distance is shortened. This design facilitates operation and reduces the excessive ram clearances encountered on conventionally designed hammers.

The horizontal counterblow hammer employs multi-impression dies and has the workpieces suspended from the top. The rams are equal in weight, and the striking velocities are equal in magnitude but opposite in direction. These hammers operate at high speed and lend themselves to automatic forging processes with the use of automatic work transfers.

### Open Die Forging Hammers

Open die forging hammers have a single or double frame (see Figs. 15-16 and 15-17). Double frames provide a more rigid and accurate ram guidance. The anvil block is independent of the frame to permit the anvil to give way under a heavy blow or series of blows without disturbing the ram. Generally, the frame and anvil are mounted on the same foundation.

Power to drive the ram down and to lift it back to its starting position is generally provided by pressurized steam or air. The steam pressure is normally set at 100-120 psi (690-825 kPa), and air pressure is set at 90-100 psi (620-690 kPa). Two manually operated control levers regulate the flow of steam or air in or out of the cylinder, and the displacement of the ram stroke.

Open die forging hammers are rated by the nominal weight of the moving parts. Single-frame hammers are built as large as 8000 lb (3630 kg), and double-frame hammers are built as large as 220,000 lb (99 790 kg). However, double-frame hammers are usually built in sizes to 24,000 lb (10 880 kg).

## HIGH ENERGY RATE FORMING MACHINES

High energy rate forming (HERF) machines are classified as load-restricted machines since the amount of deformation obtainable is determined by the kinetic energy of the ram. These machines use the sudden release of high-pressure inert gases to accelerate opposing rams at a high velocity. Since the ram velocity is from two to ten times faster than the ram of a forging hammer, the mass of the HERF machine ram is considerably less than that of the forging hammer ram. The high velocity of the ram induces metal flow at a rate greater than in other types of forging equipment. However, these high speeds often result in increased die wear and limited die life. For a comprehensive description of HERF machines and their operating characteristics, refer to Chapter 19, "Special Forming Methods."

## MECHANICAL PRESSES

Basically, mechanical forging presses are characterized by a

# CHAPTER 15

## FORGING EQUIPMENT

ram that is moved in a vertical direction. Energy to move the ram vertically is generated by a large rotating flywheel powered by an electric motor. A mechanical drive translates the rotary motion into reciprocating linear motion. All the components are contained in a heavy, rigid frame that is generally made from cast steel. Smaller presses use one-piece construction whereas larger presses use multiple-piece construction and tie rods.

During its stroke, the ram is guided at all four corners by full-length guides that are adjustable and contain replaceable liners to compensate for wear. The guides can be of the box-type or diagonal-type design.

A clutch to disengage the flywheel and a brake to stop the eccentric shaft at the end of the stroke are important components on a mechanical forging press. Small and medium-sized presses use positive-type or friction-type clutches. Large presses use air-operated clutches.

The controls are usually set to operate through a single stroke but can be adjusted to operate on a continuing, repetitive cycle. Lubrication to the various bearing points is accomplished by a pressurized central lubrication system. Part ejectors, designed into the press table or press ram, are used for removing parts from the die cavity. These ejectors are actuated by cams or levers that are operated from the main eccentric shaft.

### Press Drives

Press drives of most mechanical presses are of the eccentric-shaft design. The rotary motion of the eccentric shaft is

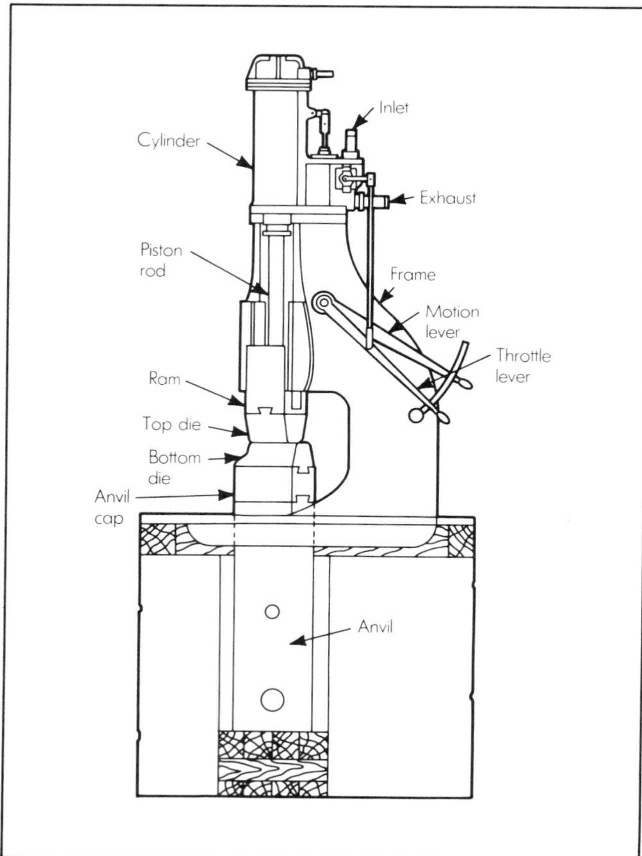


**Fig. 15-16 Typical components of a single-frame, open-die forging hammer.** (*Forging Industry Association*)

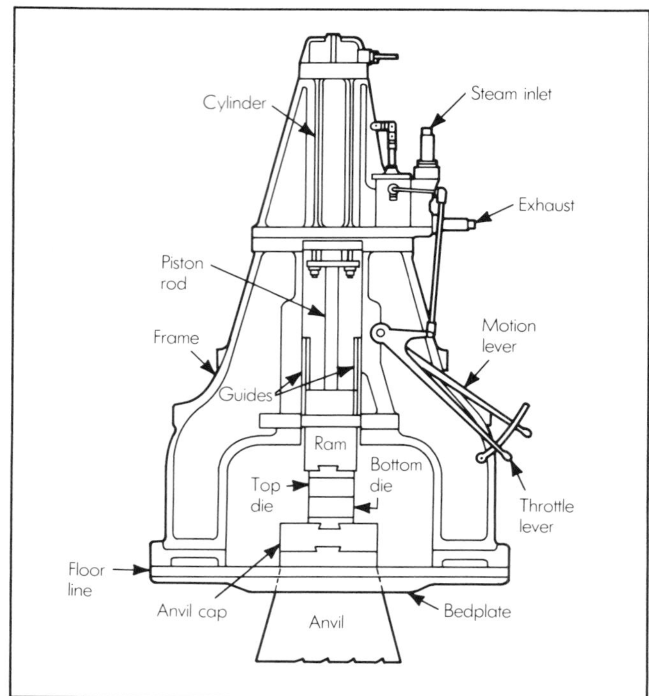


**Fig. 15-17 Typical components of a double-frame, open-die forging hammer.** (*Forging Industry Association*)

translated into linear motion through pitman arms, a pitman arm and wedge, or a scotch yoke mechanism.

**Pitman arm drive.** In a pitman arm press drive, the torque derived from the rotating flywheel is transmitted from the eccentric shaft to the ram through the pitman arm or a connecting rod (see Fig. 15-18). The pitman arm can be of a single or twin design (see Fig. 15-19). Twin-pitman design limits the tilting or eccentric action resulting from off-center loading on wide presses. The shut height of the press can be adjusted mechanically or hydraulically through wedges. Mechanical presses with this type of drive are capable of forging parts that are located in an off-center position.

**Wedge drive.** A wedge drive (see Fig. 15-20) consists of a massive wedge sloped upward at 30° toward the pitman, an adjustable pitman arm, and an eccentric driveshaft. The torque from the rotating flywheel is transmitted into horizontal motion through the pitman arm and the wedge. The wedge slides in rectangular slots on the ram and diagonal slots in the press frame. As the wedge is forced between the frame and the ram, the ram is pushed downward providing the force required to forge the part. The amount of wedge penetration between the ram and frame determines the shut height of the ram. Shut height can be adjusted by rotating the eccentric bushing on the eccentric shaft by means of a worm gear. A ratchet mechanism prevents the adjustment from changing during press operation.

Wedge drives transmit the forging force more uniformly over the entire die surface than pitman arm drives and reduce ram tilting due to off-center loading. Increases in forging accuracies during on-center and off-center loading conditions and the ability to adjust the shut height are the main advantages of wedge-driven mechanical presses. However, one of the disadvantages is a particularly long contact time between die and forged part.

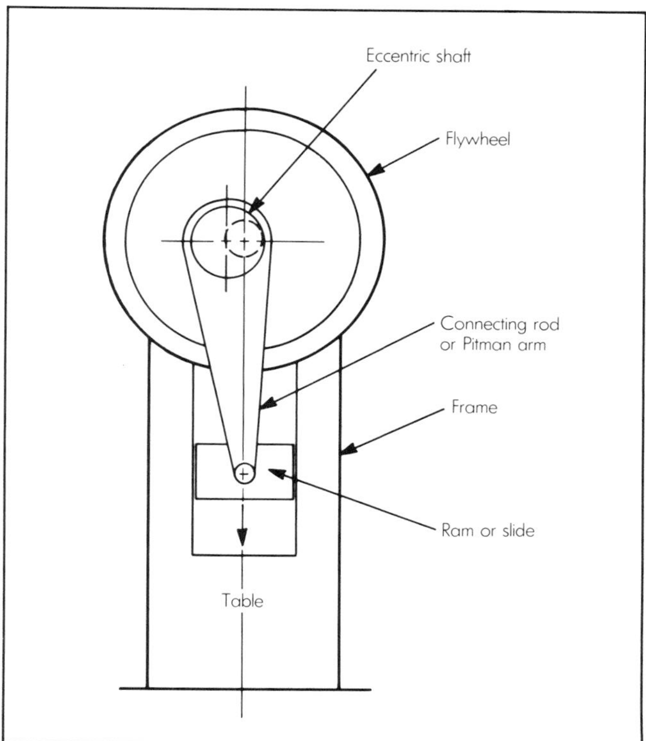


**Fig. 15-18 The eccentric shaft on a slider-crank mechanism converts rotary motion into reciprocating motion.**

**Scotch-yoke drive.** The Scotch-yoke drive contains an eccentric block that wraps around the eccentric shaft and is contained within the ram. The eccentric block consists of a top and bottom half. As the shaft rotates, the eccentric block moves in both horizontal and vertical directions while the ram is actuated by the eccentric block only in a vertical direction (see Fig. 15-21). The shut height of the ram can be adjusted mechanically or hydropneumatically through wedges.

This drive design provides a more rigid guidance for the ram which results in more accurate forgings. Forging parts off-center is also possible with this type of drive. Since the drive system is more compact than the pitman arm drive, the press has a shorter overall height. The shorter height increases frame rigidity and reduces energy loss due to press stretching.

## Capacity and Speed

Mechanical presses are considered stroke-restricted machines because the forging capability of the press is determined by the length of the stroke and the available force at the various stroke positions. The maximum force attainable by a mechanical press is at the bottom of the work stroke. Generally, the forging force of the press is determined by measuring the force at a distance of 1/8 or 1/4" (3 or 6 mm) before bottom dead center. Presses are normally built in a range of sizes varying from 300-16,000 tons (2670-106 750 kN). However, there are some presses being built that have a capacity to 18,000 tons (160 128 kN).

The stroke of the mechanical press is of a variable speed, fixed length, and a specified duration. Maximum speed on the mechanical press is achieved at the center of the ram stroke. Stroking rates vary from 30 spm on large presses to about 100 spm on smaller presses.

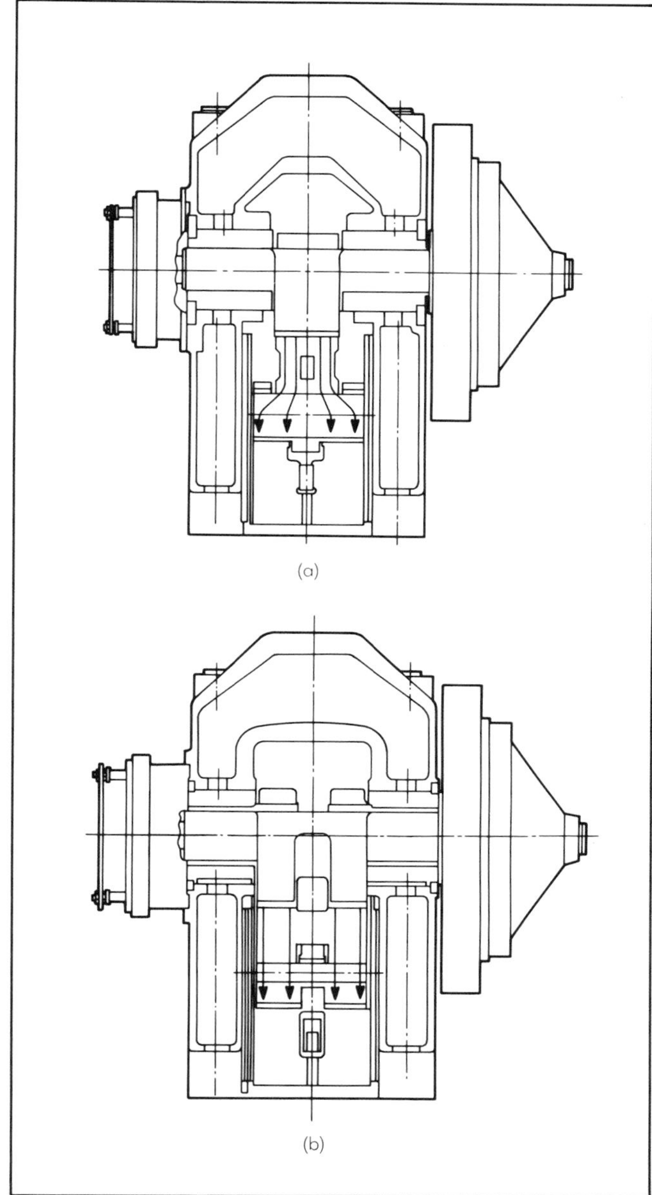


**Fig. 15-19 Pitman arms can be of (a) single or (b) twin design.** (*Verson Allsteel Press Co.*)

## Advantages and Limitations

In comparison to drop or hammer forging, mechanical press forging results in accurate, close tolerance parts. Mechanical presses permit automatic feed and transfer mechanisms to feed, pick up, and move the part from one die to the next. The dies used with these presses are lighter and less expensive than dies for forging hammers. Since the dies are subject to squeezing forces instead of impact forces, harder die materials can be used to extend die life.

One limitation of mechanical presses is that they cost approximately three times as much as forging hammers which can do the same amount of work. They are also not capable of performing as many preliminary operations as hammers.

# CHAPTER 15

## FORGING EQUIPMENT

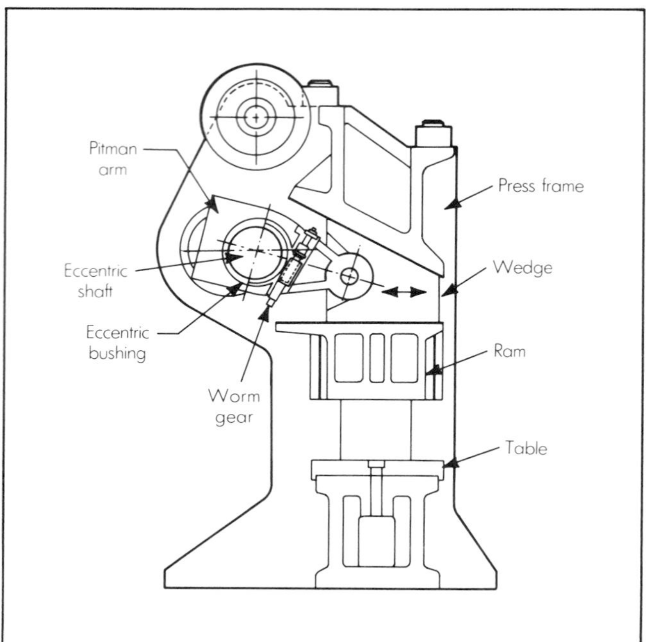


**Fig. 15-20 Wedge-driven presses use an inclined wedge to push the ram downward.** (*Verson Allsteel Press Co.*)

Generally, mechanical presses forge the preform and final shape in one, two, or three blows while hammers are capable of delivering up to ten or more blows.

### HYDRAULIC PRESSES

Hydraulic presses are essentially force-restricted machines, and metal forming results from a squeezing action rather than from impact. The capability of hydraulic presses to carry out the forging operation is determined mainly by the maximum force available. The maximum force can be limited to protect the tooling and the machine through pressure relief valves that limit the fluid pressure acting upon the ram.

A basic hydraulic press consists of a frame, piston and cylinder, power ram, and electric motor driven hydraulic pumps. The electric motor driven hydraulic pumps are usually an integral part of the press. The hydraulic pumps may also be in a central location and provide hydraulic pressure for several presses within the shop. Hydraulic presses have been built with several pistons. These pistons may act independently and in different directions to hold split dies and the workpiece during forging. The pistons may also actuate side rams which permit multiram forging of hollow components.

#### Press Frame

The frame of the press must be capable of resisting the force imposed on the press bed by the hydraulic cylinder. This is accomplished by employing cast or welded frames that have been prestressed with tie rods, or it is accomplished by assembling laminated plates together with large transverse pins. Hydraulic presses are also built using two or four-column construction (see Fig. 15-22). Four-column presses are employed for both open and closed-die forging, and two-column presses are usually employed only for open-die forging. Figure 15-23 illustrates a C-frame-design hydraulic press built using a welded-frame construction capable of performing open and closed-die forging. A counterbalance minimizes the deflection that is inherent with C-frame designs.

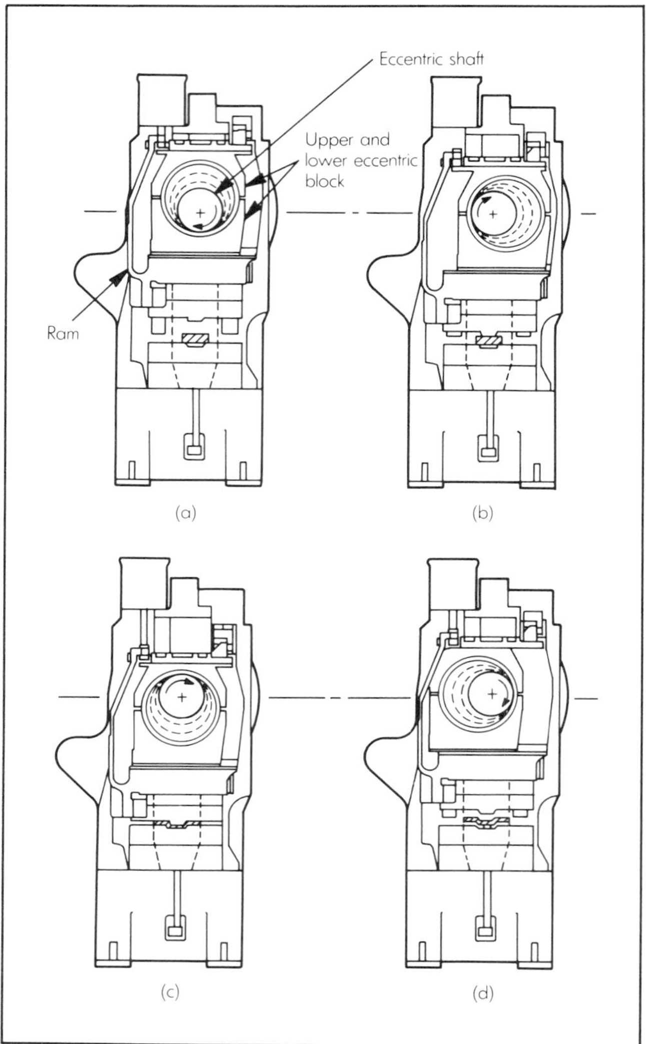


**Fig. 15-21 Side view of mechanical press with scotch-yoke drive. (a) Ram is at top of stroke; scotch yoke is centered. (b) Midway through downward stroke, scotch yoke is in extreme forward position. (c) Scotch yoke is in center of ram at bottom dead center. (d) Midway through upward stroke, scotch yoke is in extreme rear position.** (*Erie Press Systems*)

#### Press Operation

The operation of a hydraulic press is determined by the design of the drive configuration and the type of drive system that is utilized.

**Drive configuration.** The two main drive configurations for hydraulic presses are the push-down design and the pull-down design.

*Push-down design.* In the push-down drive configuration (see Fig. 15-24, *a*), the stationary cylinder and crosshead are located above the work. The cylinder crosshead and the stationary press bed are connected by four columns. These columns are designed to take up the press load and simultaneously guide the moving piston-ram assembly. During

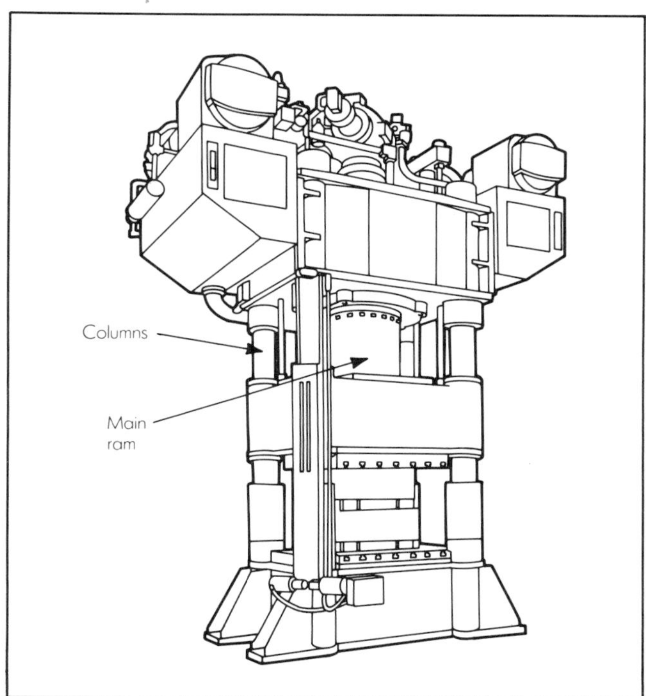


**Fig. 15-22 Typical four-column hydraulic press. (*Erie Press Systems*)**

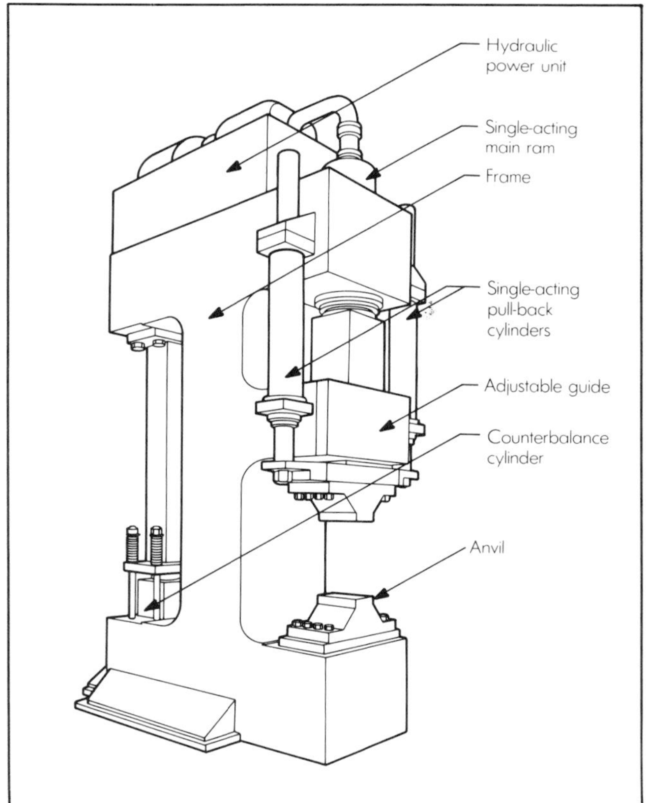


**Fig. 15-23 A C-frame-design hydraulic press incorporates a counterbalance to minimize deflection. (*Erie Press Systems*)**

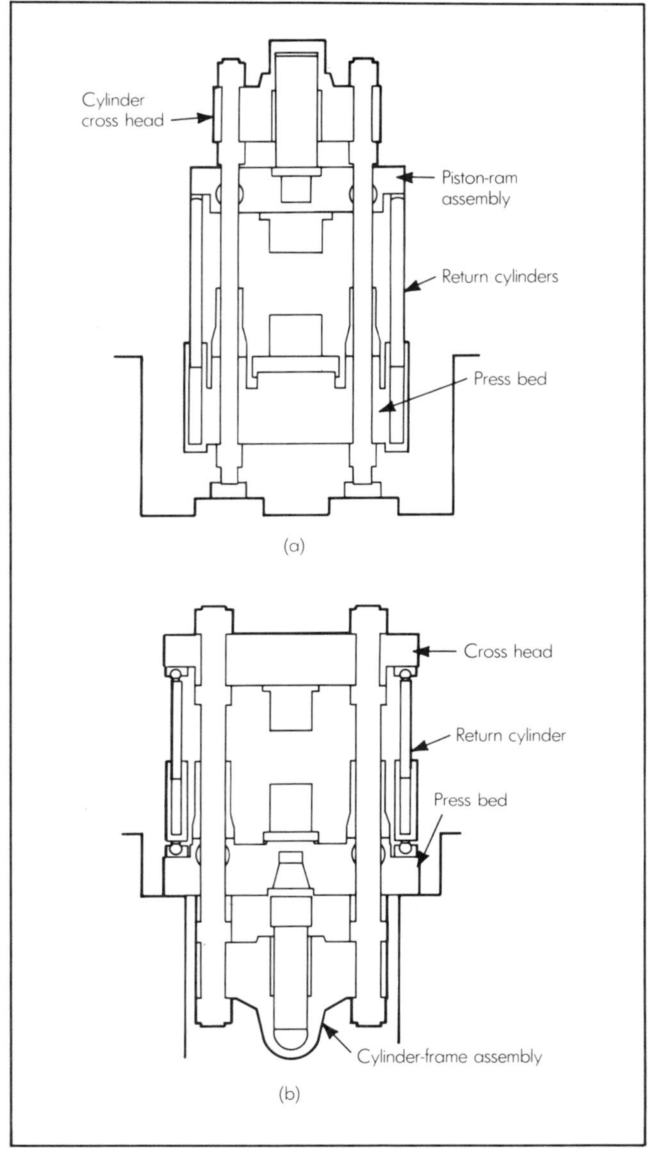


**Fig. 15-24 Hydraulic presses can incorporate either (a) a push-down drive design or (b) a pull-down drive design.**

operation, the piston-ram assembly is pushed down by the cylinder in the crosshead. Bushings in the piston-ram assembly guide the assembly as it moves. Return cylinders push the piston-ram assembly back to the proper starting position.

The push-down drive design is the least expensive drive configuration to build and does not require expensive press foundations. Since the press components are exposed, maintenance is simplified and existing problems are easily detected. However, presses utilizing the push-down drive design require greater ceiling heights than do pull-down drive presses. Since all the hydraulic system is located above the workpiece, there is a possibility of fluid leakage resulting in a fire and safety hazard. The push-down drive press exhibits elastic deflections during off-center loading and does not lend itself to two-column construction because of insufficient stability.

# FORGING EQUIPMENT

*Pull-down design.* In the pull-down drive design (see Fig. 15-24, *b*), the movable cylinder frame assembly is located below the press bed in the foundation pit. The movable crosshead and cylinder frame assembly are connected together with either two or four columns that slide in bushings located in the press bed. During operation, the crosshead is pulled down by the columns. Return cylinders push the crosshead back to the proper starting position.

Pull-down drive presses require the minimum amount of height above the floor, which results in a lower center of gravity and increased static and dynamic stiffness. Most of the hydraulic and auxiliary equipment can be located beneath the floor level. Fire hazards due to leaking hydraulic fluid are eliminated, and the length of hydraulic piping is shortened. However, the foundation for pull-down drive presses is more expensive than for push-down drive presses. Since more than half of the press weight is moving, heavy column guides are required. Maintenance generally requires working in the pit, and problems are not as easily detected as on push-down drive presses.

**Press drives.** Operation of a hydraulic press is simple and based on the motion of a hydraulic piston guided in a cylinder. Two types of drive systems are used on hydraulic presses: direct drive and accumulator drive.

*Direct drive.* Direct-drive presses usually have hydraulic oil or water-oil emulsions as the working medium. In vertical presses of early design, at the start of the downstroke the upper ram falls by gravity and oil is drawn from the reservoir into the ram cylinder through the suction of the fall. When the ram contacts the workpiece, the valve between the ram cylinder and the reservoir is closed and the pump builds up pressure in the ram cylinder. This mode of operation results in relatively long dwell times prior to the start of deformation.

In modern direct-drive presses (see Fig. 15-25, *a*), during downstroke a residual pressure is maintained in the return cylinders or in the return line by means of a pressure relief valve. The upper ram is forced down against pressure, and the dwell inherent with the free fall is eliminated. When the press stroke is completed, that is, when the upper ram reaches a predetermined position or when the pressure reaches a certain value, the oil pressure is released and diverted to lift the ram.[16] With this drive system, the maximum press load is available at any point during the working stroke.

The equipment required for direct-drive presses is generally lower in cost than the equipment on accumulator-drive presses, and the equipment is usually readily available. The electric power consumption is closely related to the power required for forging the workpiece. Forging speed is held constant throughout the stroke, and the hydraulic pressure can be adjusted without too much difficulty. The hydraulic pressure can also be instantaneously disconnected by stopping the pump motors or by adjusting the vanes on vane-type pumps. The hydraulic oil used as the working medium poses possible fire and safety hazards. However, nonflammable fluids are being employed to minimize the hazards. The number of pumps required for a given press may be greater due to a limited selection of readily available pumps.

*Accumulator drive.* Accumulator-drive presses usually have a water-oil emulsion as a working medium and use nitrogen or air-loaded accumulators to keep the medium under pressure. This type of drive is used primarily on presses larger than 10,000 tons (88 960 kN). The sequence of operations is essentially similar to that for the direct-drive press except that the pressure is built up by means of the pressurized water-oil emulsion in the accumulators (see Fig. 15-25, *b*). Consequently, the rate of penetration, the ram speed under load, is not directly dependent upon the pump characteristics and can vary depending upon the pressure in the accumulator, the compressibility of the pressure medium, and the resistance of the workpiece to deformation. Toward the end of the forging stroke, as deformation progresses, the working medium expands, the force required to forge the material increases, and the speed of penetration and the load available at the ram decrease.[17]

Accumulator-drive presses are capable of operating at faster speeds than direct-drive presses. The faster press speed permits the rapid working of materials, reduces the contact time between the tool and workpiece, and maximizes the amount of work performed between reheats. The pressure can be built up rapidly since the energy is stored in the accumulator. However, the pumps always deliver the working fluid at maximum system pressure. This results in consuming more electrical energy than the power expended in the forging operation. The working medium of all hydraulic presses must be maintained within a narrow temperature range for optimum performance. Therefore, thermostatically controlled heat exchangers or immersion heaters and cooling coils are needed. The available press force cannot be easily limited to less than the rated capacity. Speeds are not constant throughout the press stroke. Since the drive system is not contained within the press, the pipe lines are longer than on direct-drive presses.

## Capacity and Speed

Hydraulic presses are rated by the maximum amount of forging force available. Open-die presses are built from 200-14,000 tons (1.8-125 MN). Closed-die presses range in size from 500-50,000 tons (4.5-445 MN). Research is being conducted to build hydraulic presses as large as 200,000 tons (1779 MN).

The ram speeds during normal forging conditions vary from

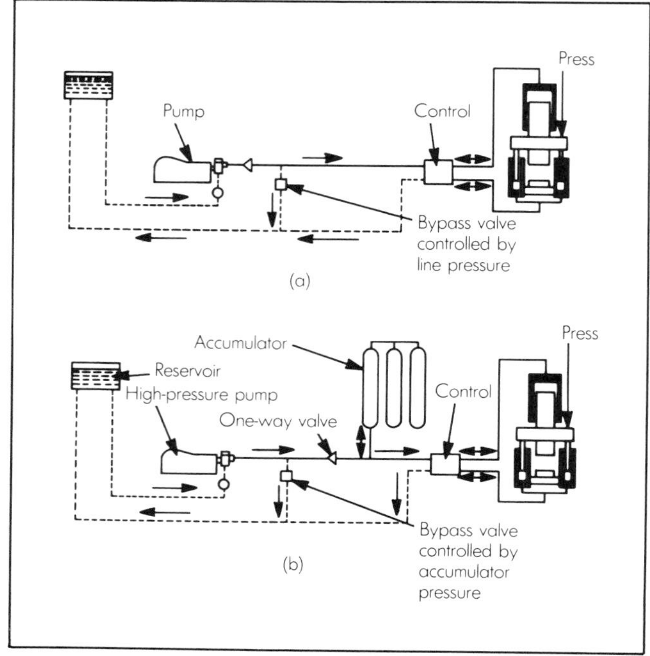


**Fig. 15-25 Operation of a hydraulic press is based on the motion of a hydraulic piston guided in a cylinder. Hydraulic press is (a) direct driven or (b) accumulator driven.**

25-300 ipm (635-7620 mm/min). To forge materials that are extremely strain-rate sensitive, press speeds have been slowed to a fraction of an inch per minute.

### Advantages and Limitations

Hydraulic presses are employed for open and closed-die forging operations. The force applied by the hydraulic press can be varied throughout the stroke by adjusting the control valve. The ram speed can also be continuously adjusted during the cycle when materials that are susceptible to rupturing under high deformation rates are being forged. Hydraulic presses are ideally suited for extrusion-type forging operations that require a fairly constant load over a long stroke and relatively large amounts of energy for the deformation.

Because hydraulic presses are relatively slow, the workpiece is in contact with the dies for a longer period of time than it is on mechanical presses, resulting in a transfer of heat from the workpiece to the dies. The heat transfer reduces the number of times that the workpiece can be forged between reheats and causes abnormal die wear. For these reasons, hydraulic presses for closed-die forging are best suited for materials that have low forging temperatures, such as aluminum and magnesium. The heat-transfer problem can be minimized by heating the dies to approximately the same temperature as the workpiece.

## SCREW PRESSES

Screw presses are energy-restricted machines and use energy stored in a flywheel to provide the force for forging. The rotating energy or inertia of the flywheel is converted to linear motion by a threaded screw attached on one end to the flywheel and on the other end to the ram.

### Drive Systems

The three main types of drive systems used on screw presses are friction drive, direct electric drive, and hydraulic drive. A fourth drive system has a flywheel that rotates constantly and a controllable clutch.

**Friction drive.** On friction-drive screw presses (see Fig. 15-26), two large, energy-storing driving discs are mounted on a horizontal shaft on top of the machine and are rotated continuously by an electric motor. To initiate the down stroke, one of the driving discs is pressed against the friction belt of the flywheel by a pneumatic cylinder. When the flywheel reaches the desired speed, the disc is disengaged. The rotating flywheel turns the screw, which moves the ram downward. Generally, on friction drives, a nut is fixed in the crown of the press and the flywheel, screw, and ram move downward and upward within the guide system. The ram stops once the energy has been dissipated. The second disc is then pressed against the flywheel to reverse the rotation of the screw and lift the ram to the starting position.

**Direct electric drive.** On direct electric drive screw presses (see Fig. 15-27), a reversible, slow-speed electric motor is built directly on the screw and press frame. The screw is fixed axially, and the nut and ram move downward and upward within the guide system. The motor is energized to initiate the downstroke and then reversed to lift the ram to its starting position. To limit the maximum force of the press, a slipping clutch is provided. Coining presses, equipped with smaller flywheels, operate without a slipping clutch.

A modification of the direct-drive screw press is the wedge screw press. The screw on this design is inclined rather than vertical, and it actuates a V-shaped wedge (see Fig. 15-28). The wedge moves the ram downward and upward. The design permits off-center forging and is suitable for eccentric precision forging.

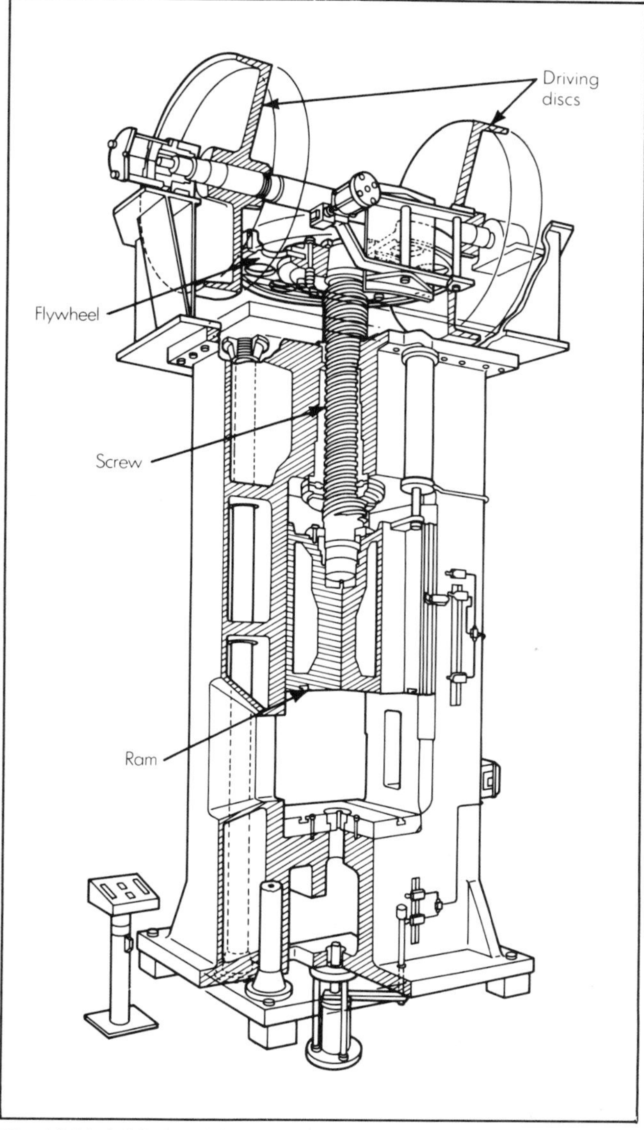


**Fig. 15-26 A friction-driven screw press applies continuously rotating discs against a flywheel to rotate the screw. (*Radyne/Ako Corp.*)**

**Gear drive.** Large forging screw presses are often driven by two to four electric or hydraulic motors. Hydraulic gear-drive screw presses have a solid flywheel connected directly to the screw shaft. During the forging operation, the flywheel is rotated moving the screw up or down in the press. On electric gear-drive screw presses, the flywheel is in two parts; the outer wheel is driven by the electric motors, and the inner wheel is attached to the screw shaft. A slipping clutch transmits the torque from the outer wheel to the inner wheel when the part is being deformed.

**Constantly rotating flywheel.** This drive system is different from conventional drive systems in that a large flywheel is rotated continuously in the same direction by an electric motor.

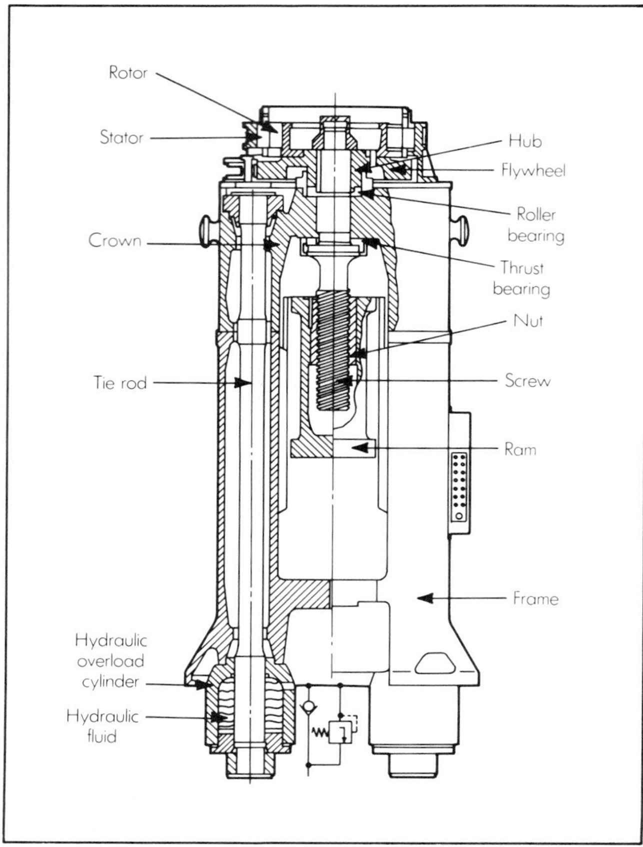


**Fig. 15-27 Cross section of a direct electric drive screw press with hydraulic overload system.** (*Maschinefabrik Weingarten AG*)

A pneumatically operated friction clutch transmits the torque to the axially fixed screw which moves the ram downward (see Fig. 15-29). At the bottom of the press stroke, the clutch is disengaged and two hydraulic cylinders return the ram to its starting position. This type of screw press is capable of off-center forging and forging nonsymmetrical parts.

### Capacities and Speed

Screw presses are generally rated by the diameter of the screw. This diameter, however, is comparable to a listing of nominal forces that can be produced by the press. The nominal force is the force that the press is capable of delivering to deform the workpiece while maintaining maximum energy. The coining or working force is approximately double the nominal force when forging occurs near the bottom of the stroke.

Friction screw presses have screw diameters ranging from 4-25" (100-635 mm) or nominal forces from 160-4000 tons (1.4-35.6 MN). Direct electric drive screw presses have been built with 24" (600 mm) diam screws or 4190 tons (37.3 MN) nominal force capacity. Hydraulic gear-drive screw presses have been built up to 31,500 tons (280 MN). Electric gear-drive presses have been built with screws up to 35" (900 mm) diam and 9900 tons (88 MN) nominal force capacity. Constantly rotating flywheel type screw presses are available with screw diameters over 22" (560 mm) and a nominal force capacity up to 6930 tons (61.6 MN). Small screw presses operate as fast as 40-50 spm while large screw presses operate at about 12-16 spm.

### Advantages and Limitations

Screw presses are used for open and closed-die forging operations. They usually have more energy available per stroke than mechanical presses, permitting them to accomplish more work per stroke. When the energy has been dissipated, the ram comes to a halt, even though the dies have not closed. Stopping the ram permits multiple blows to be made to the workpiece in the same die impression. The die height adjustment is not critical, and the press is not capable of jamming. Die stresses are minimized and are not affected by the temperature or height of the workpiece, resulting in good die life. The impact speed is much greater than with mechanical presses, ensuring the filling of deep die cavities. However, most screw presses permit full force operation only near the center of the bed and ram bolsters.

## FORGING MACHINES

Forging machines (see Fig. 15-30) are basically double-acting mechanical presses operating in a horizontal plane and are often called horizontal upsetters or heading machines. The forging is accomplished between closed dies and is referred to as upset forging.

Energy stored in a flywheel driven by an electric motor powers a main shaft which drives the header slide in a horizontal direction through a pitman arm or an eccentric. This is similar to the action of a ram in a mechanical press. The total length that the header slide travels forward is the stroke length. The advance is the distance that the header slide travels forward before contacting the stock, and the stock gather is the working portion of the stroke. The header slide is long and supported by wide bearing surfaces to ensure accurate alignment and guidance during forging. Attached to the header slide is a set of punches or forming tools that force the stock into the die cavities.

The die area consists of a die block split vertically or horizontally into two parts. The two die halves contain matching cavities or passes in which the stock is gripped and formed during forging. The fixed half is referred to as the stationary die, and the other half is referred to as the movable die. The movable die is attached to the gripper slide, which is driven in a direction perpendicular to the header slide by means of a toggle mechanism and a toggle slide. The length of travel of the movable die is the die opening. A flywheel clutch and brake mechanism controls single-stroke and nonrepeat operations as well as machine stop motion. A bed frame and crown surround the die area to provide support and rigidity during forging.

Most forging machines are designed so that the die surfaces are vertical or horizontal; the operator moves the workpiece through the sequence of passes by moving the workpiece from one die cavity to the next. Both vertical and horizontal forging machines are designed to use automatic transfer equipment.

### Operation

In operation, the workpiece is placed in the first cavity of the stationary die of the machine. The movable die mounted on the gripper slide moves against the stationary die to grip the workpiece. The header tool or punch, secured in the toolholder in the header slide, advances forward against the end of the workpiece and forces it to flow into the die cavity. The header slide then returns to its back position, and the movable die slide opens to release the stock (see Fig. 15-31). The workpiece is fed progressively through the die cavities. Once the part has been finish-formed, it is removed from the die and is ready for packaging or secondary operations.

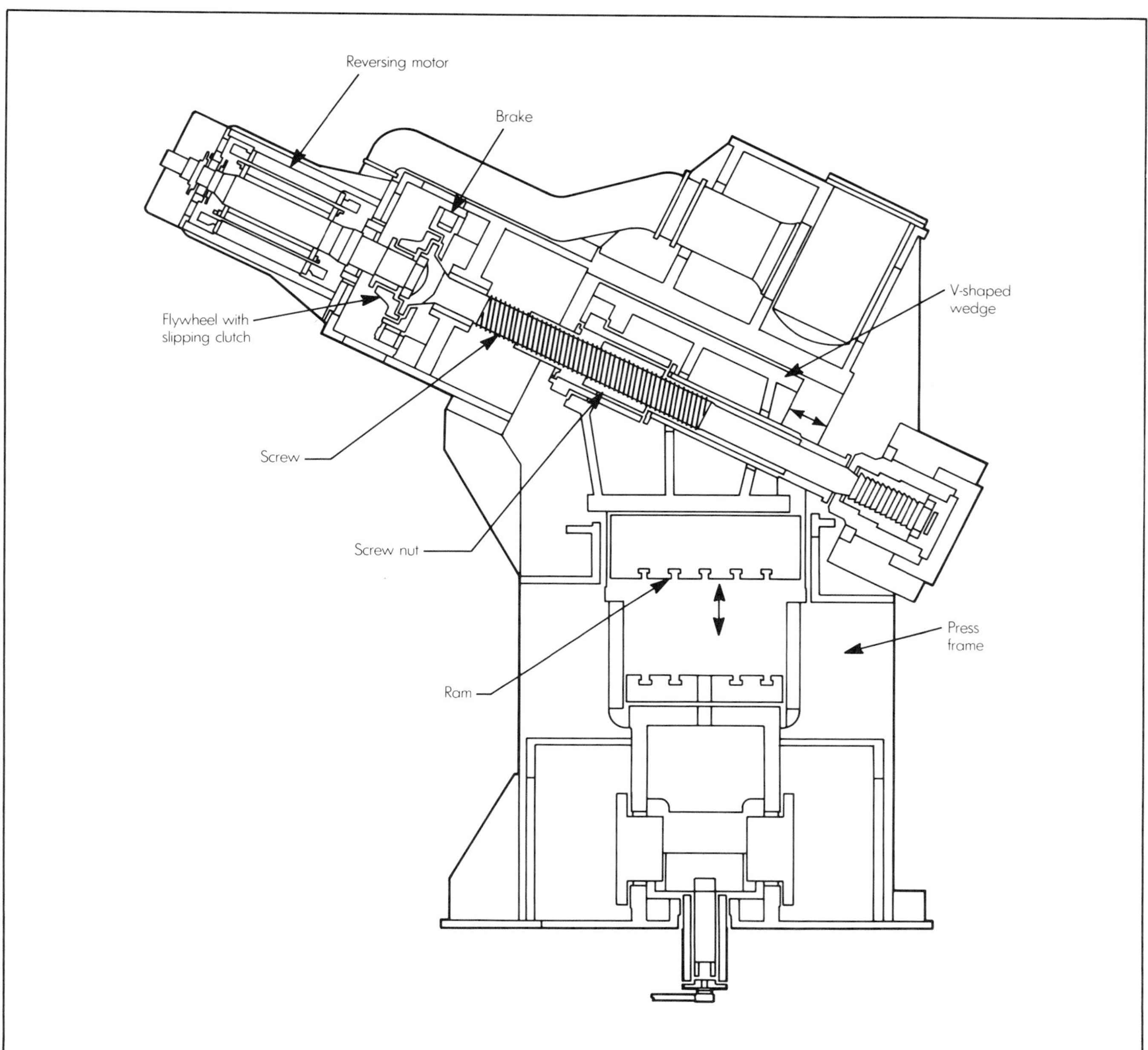


**Fig. 15-28 A wedge screw press actuates a V-shaped wedge to move the ram downward.** (*Lasco, Letts Equipment Division*)

## Capacities

Forging machines are historically sized by the maximum size bar on which a square or hexagonal head can be forged. This is the maximum diameter of upset that can be forged in a given machine and still permit the workpiece to be moved from one die cavity to the next and then be withdrawn through the throat or feed gap. These machines range in size from less than 1″ (25 mm) to over 10″ (254 mm) diam and have a corresponding force rating of 100-3000 tons (900-26 688 kN).

Generally, a forging machine incorporates from one to five die cavities in the die halves. The number of cavities is dependent upon the application and the space available in the die area. Stroke lengths on standard machines vary from 7-30″ (178-762 mm) and can be modified to accommodate specific applications. The operating speed on most machines ranges from about 90 spm on smaller machines to about 20 spm on the larger machines.

## Application

Forging machines can upset, deep-pierce, split, bend, and extrude simple or intricate shapes to close tolerances, usually with a savings in material. The tolerances obtained are based on the configuration of the forging and the accuracy of the die design. Machining the part after forging permits looser tolerances, but tighter tolerances often eliminate secondary operations. Tolerances of 0 to +1/16″ (1.6 mm) on the diameter are

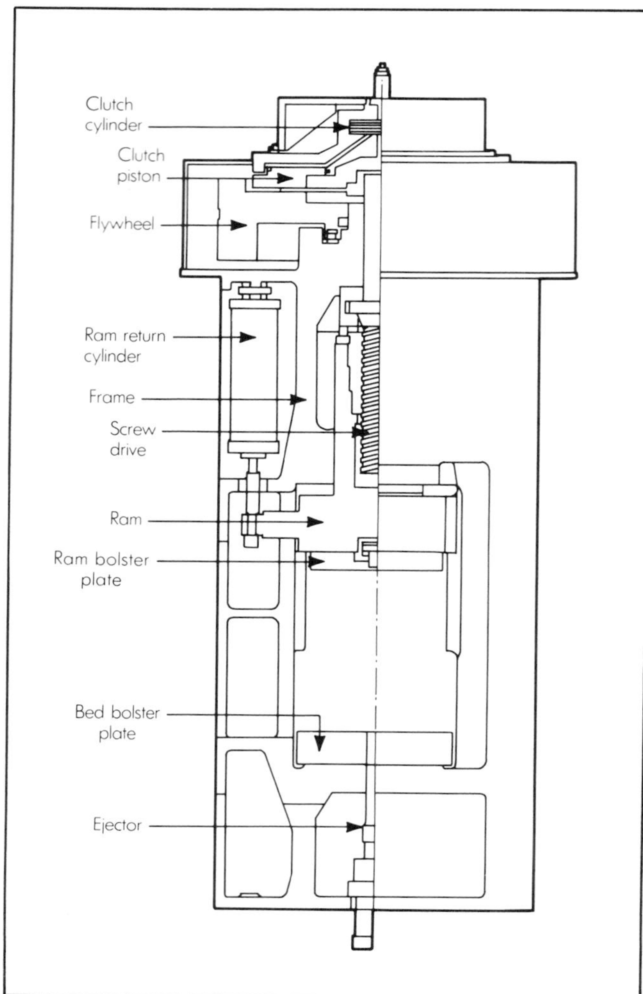


**Fig. 15-29 Screw press incorporating a constantly rotating flywheel drive for rotating the screw and moving the screw downward. Hydraulic cylinders return the ram to its initial position.** (*Siempelkamp Corp.*)

obtainable on minor upsets. For thin flanges and for upsets relatively large in ratio to stock diameter, tolerances of 0 to +3/32" (2.4 mm) are obtainable. Generally, the forging or upsetting is done symmetrically on the ends of the bar or tube. However, forging machines can gather material for upset at any point along the length of the bar, using sliding dies (see Fig. 15-32), and can be nonsymmetrical in shape with offset dies. The tools can be mounted either in the toolholder or in the movable die slide. Some typical parts that are produced on a forging machine are wheel wrenches, tubing upsets, stub pinion shafts, truck axles, mine roof bolts, and splined slip yokes. Forging machines are also used to produce preforms that are finish-forged in subsequent operations on hammers or presses.

## HOT FORMERS

Hot formers are self-contained feeding, shearing, and forging machines. They are similar to forging machines in design since they are mechanically operated, horizontal forging machines. However, the forging takes place in closed dies on hot formers, whereas on forging machines, the forging takes place in split dies.

A typical hot former installation consists of a bar rack, an in-line induction heater, and a hot former machine that usually incorporates a shear and three or four forming stations (see Fig. 15-33). An internal cooling system is also incorporated in the hot former to maintain the tooling at the proper temperature.

The hot former obtains its energy from the momentum of a motor-driven flywheel which drives an eccentric shaft. The eccentric shaft is connected to a heading slide through a pitman connection. The heading slide moves back and forth with the throw of the eccentric. Attached to the front of the heading slide is a set of three or four tools (punches) that force the metal into the die cavities during part forming. An operation is performed in each die on each stroke. At the final die, the formed part is removed from the die by a kickout mechanism, thus making a finished forging with each stroke.

### Operation

The hot forming process typically begins with the automatic feeding of a steel bar from a storage area through an induction heating system (see Fig. 15-33). In the induction heater, the bar is heated to approximately 2250° F (1232° C). The bar is partially descaled by feed rolls before it is sheared to length at the hot former cutoff area. The cutoff blank is mechanically transferred by cam-controlled grippers through three or four forming dies where upsetting, preforming, finish-forming, and piercing (as needed) take place (see Fig. 15-34). The formed part then discharges at around 1900° F (1038° C) and slowly cools. Depending on the type of material being formed, this slow cooling eliminates the need for heat treating some parts prior to any secondary operations.

### Capacity

Hot formers vary in physical size and workpiece capacity. Most hot formers usually contain three or four dies and are capable of hot shearing bars from 1 to 3 1/2" (25 to 90 mm) diam with lengths to 5 7/8" (150 mm). The speed of a hot former varies from 180 spm on small machines to 45 spm on the largest machines.

### Application

Parts forged on a hot former are typically round or square, are symmetrical in shape, and have a hole pierced through them. The part lengths are usually less than the diameter. Some typical parts include transmission gear blanks, side gears, drive flanges, and bearing races. More complex parts with irregular shapes such as trunnions, tripods, hubs and spindles, connecting rod caps, and drive yokes are also feasible with the appropriate tooling. Part diameters vary from 1 to 7 1/2" (25 to 190 mm) with a maximum weight of 16 lb (7 1/4 kg). Figure 15-35 shows some of the typical parts produced on a hot former.

Hot-formed parts have a good surface finish and close tolerances. Depending on the application, some surfaces may need no machining; others, only grinding. Diameter tolerances, as shown in Fig. 15-36, illustrate that parts forged on a hot former have much closer tolerances than press or hammer forgings, but not quite as close as cold-formed parts of comparable size.

Long production runs containing 50,000-100,000 parts are most efficient and economical. However, quantities as low as 25,000 may be considered, particularly when the part size is large or when several similar parts or part families can be grouped together for production, a situation that reduces setup time and, consequently, costs.

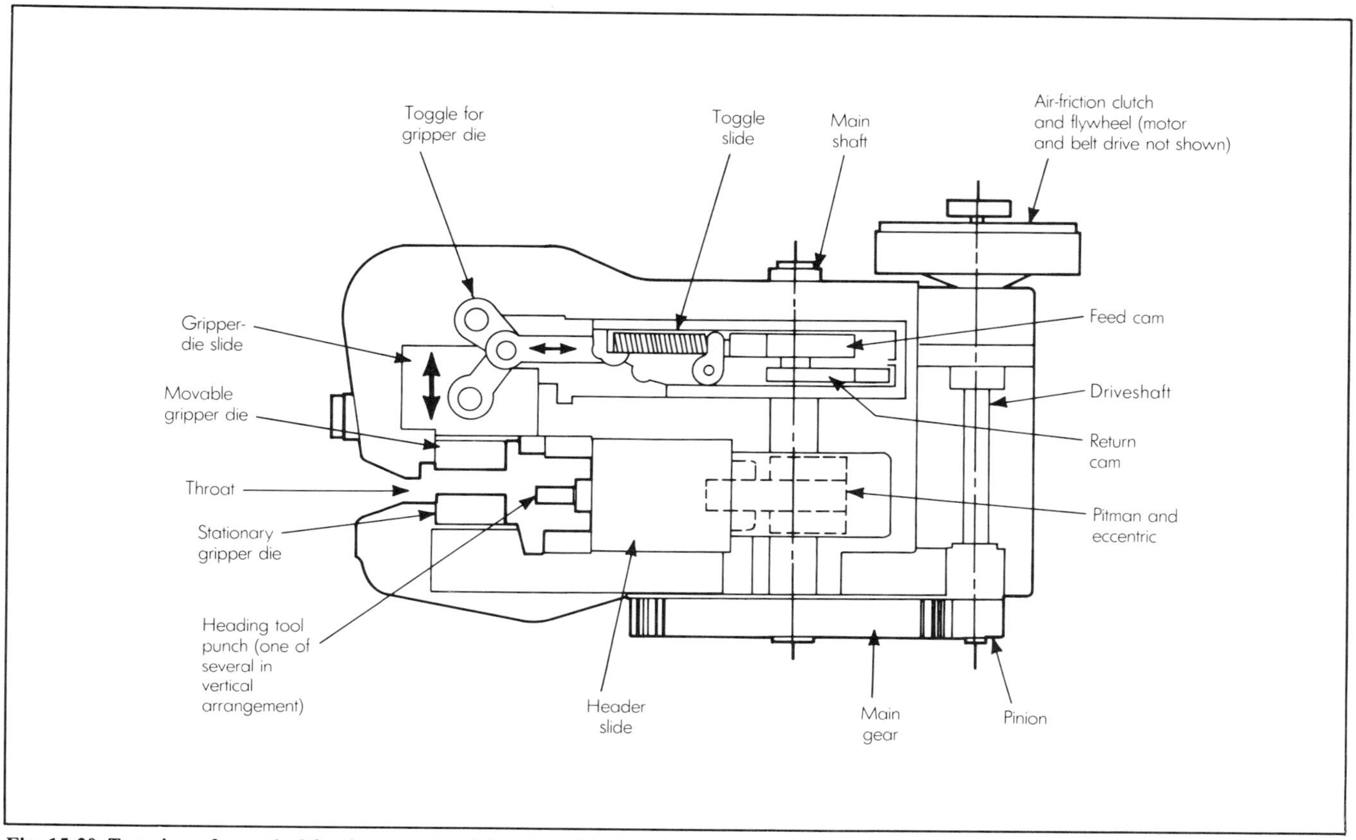

Fig. 15-30 Top view of a vertical forging machine. (*American Machinist*)

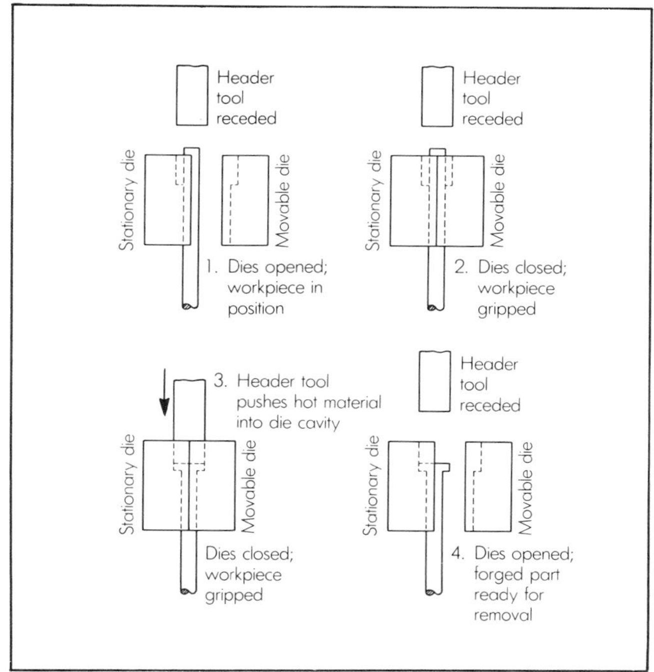


**Fig. 15-31 Plan view of successive positions of dies and header tool during forging cycle.**

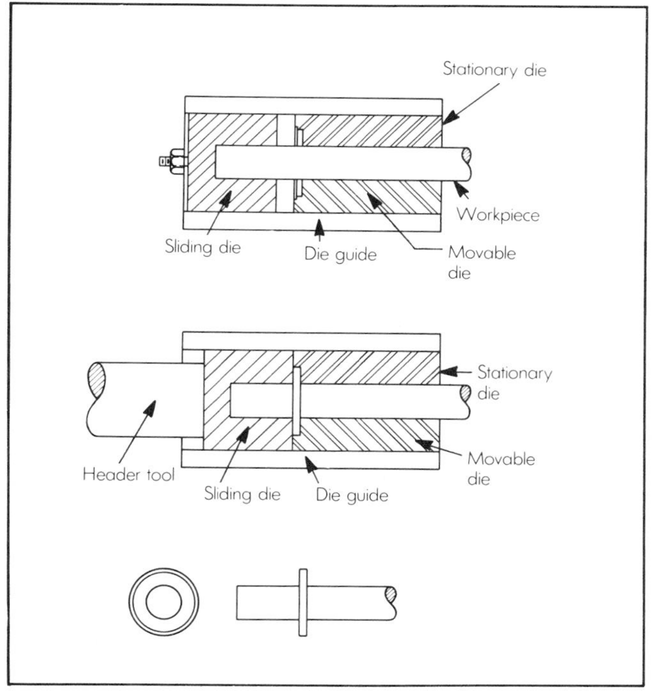


**Fig. 15-32 Sliding-type forging machine die.**

# CHAPTER 15

# FORGING EQUIPMENT

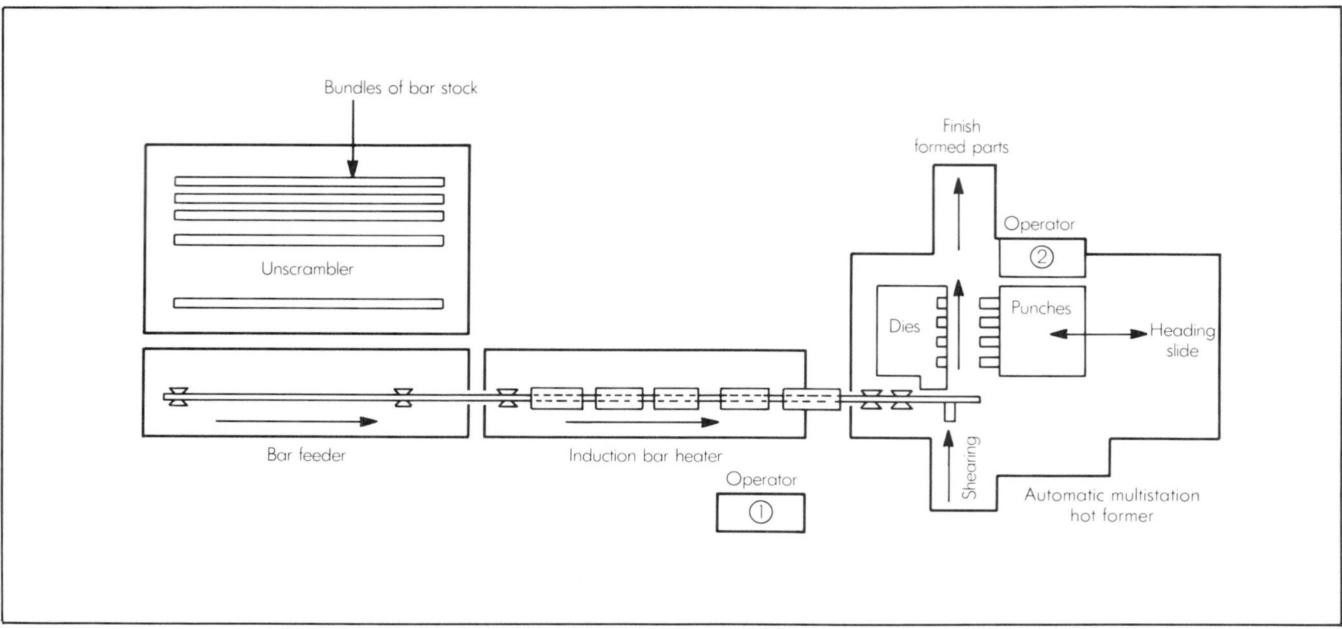


**Fig. 15-33 Typical hot former installation consists of a bar rack, an in-line induction heater, and a hot former machine.** (*Girard Associates, Inc.*)

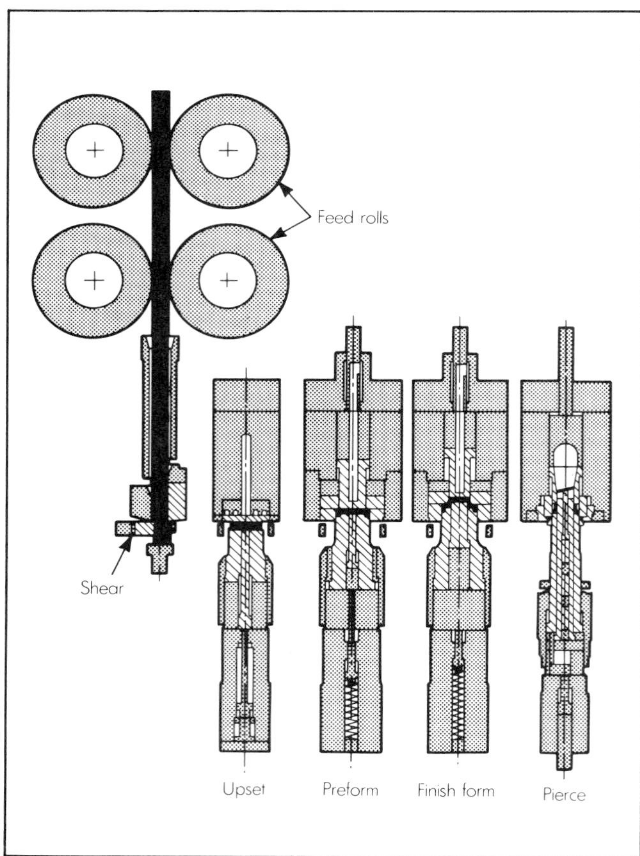


**Fig. 15-34 In the hot forming process, the cutoff blank is mechanically transferred by cam-controlled grippers to the various forming dies.** (*Girard Associates, Inc.*)

## FORGING ROLLS

Forging rolls are highly productive machines designed to preform blanks in a variety of shapes, lengths, and sizes for finish forging on presses or hammers. Forging rolls are also referred to as reducer rolls, back rolls, or gap rolls. In addition to shaping parts or preforms, forging rolls also descale the stock, an operation normally performed in the press or forging machines.

A motor-driven driveshaft supplies power for turning the lower roll shaft through reduction gears. An air-operated diaphragm clutch transmits the torque from the reduction gears to the lower roll shaft, and a disc brake ensures accurate stopping. The roll shafts are geared together to maintain timing between the rolls. The forging roll machine can be designed to permit the rolls to be overhung or supported by an outboard housing (see Fig. 15-37). Overhung rolls are chosen when the shapes are to be finish formed in other equipment, and the supported-type rolls are chosen when close tolerances are required on the workpiece. The shafts which support the rolls are capable of handling single-pass or multiple-pass roll dies.

### Operation

In single-pass operation, the workpiece is inserted between the roll dies and the machine is activated. As the rolls rotate, the two die surfaces come together and squeeze the stock between them. Continued roll motion feeds the part through and out the other side of the machine.

In multiple-pass operation (see Fig. 15-38), the workpiece is inserted between the roll dies until it comes in contact with an end-stop. The machine is activated and the die surfaces come together on the workpiece to squeeze it into the desired shape. While the workpiece is being formed, the rolls feed the workpiece back out toward the operator. The operator repeats this sequence for the next pass or passes until the final shape is obtained.

In most operations, the workpiece is fed in a horizontal direction. To prevent long workpieces from being bent or

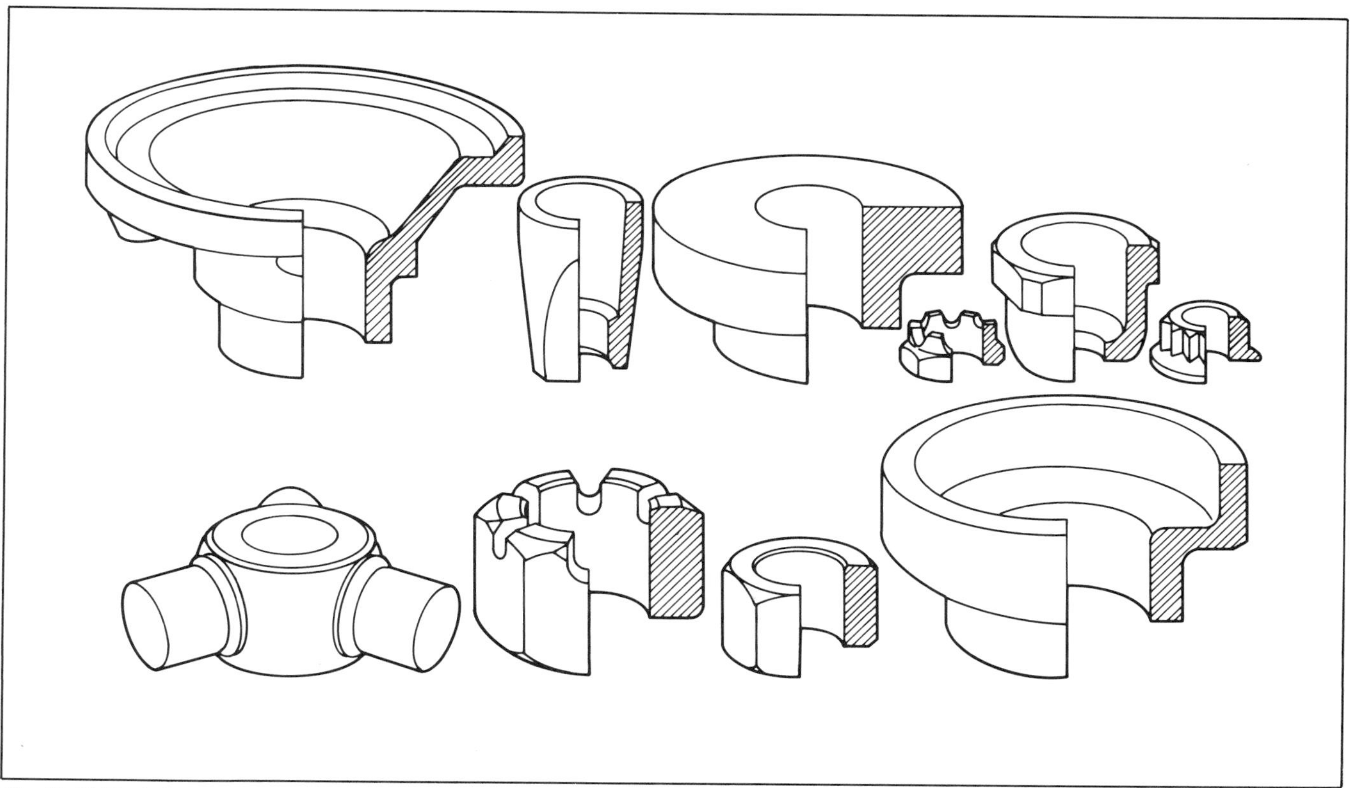

Fig. 15-35 Typical parts produced on a hot forming machine. (*Girard Associates, Inc.*)

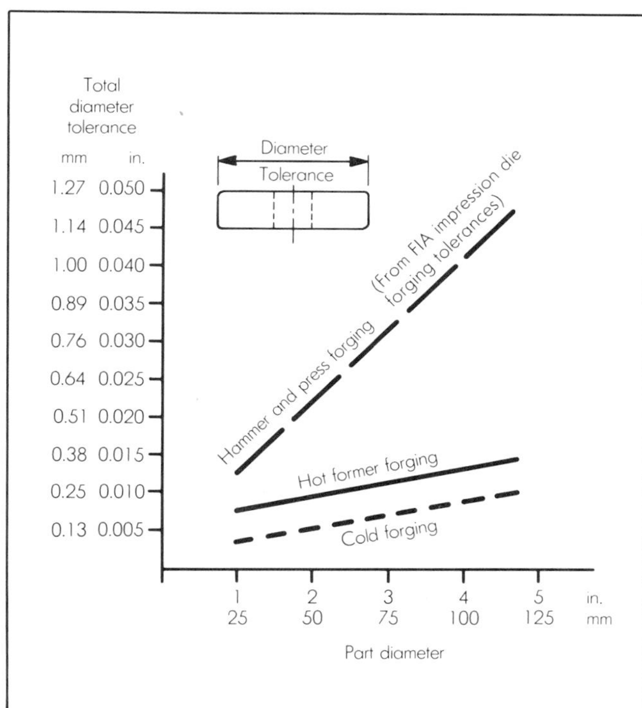


**Fig. 15-36 Comparison of diameter tolerances of parts produced by cold forging, hot former forging, and hammer and press forging.** (*National Machinery*)

deformed, the workpiece is supported from the top and automatically fed in a vertical direction. The operation of forging rolls can also be automated to permit mass production of preformed forgings.

### Capacity and Applications

Forging rolls are available in several sizes for rolling blanks up to 5″ (127 mm) thick and 40″ (1016 mm) long. Typical parts preformed are automobile crankshafts, axle shafts, connecting rods, wheel spindles, and wrenches.

## WEDGE ROLLING MACHINES

Wedge rolling machines are designed to preform balls, tapers, undercuts, 90° shoulders, or a combination of these on one shaft. The self-contained machines consist of a welded frame in which two rolls are rotated in the same direction by an electric motor (see Fig. 15-39); however, some manufacturers build the machine with three rolls. Wedge-shaped dies are bolted to T-slots in the periphery of the rolls. A feeder loads the bar into rolls, and an induction heater heats the material to the desired forging temperature. Portable machines consist of a frame and electrically driven rolls.

### Operation

Preheated bars are fed axially between the rolls until they contact the end-stop (see Fig. 15-40). As the rolls rotate, the dies progressively roll and displace the metal and elongate the bar along its centerline to the desired cross section. On certain applications, multiple parts can be produced during one roll pass. When long bars are used, the dies can be designed to cut

# FORGING EQUIPMENT

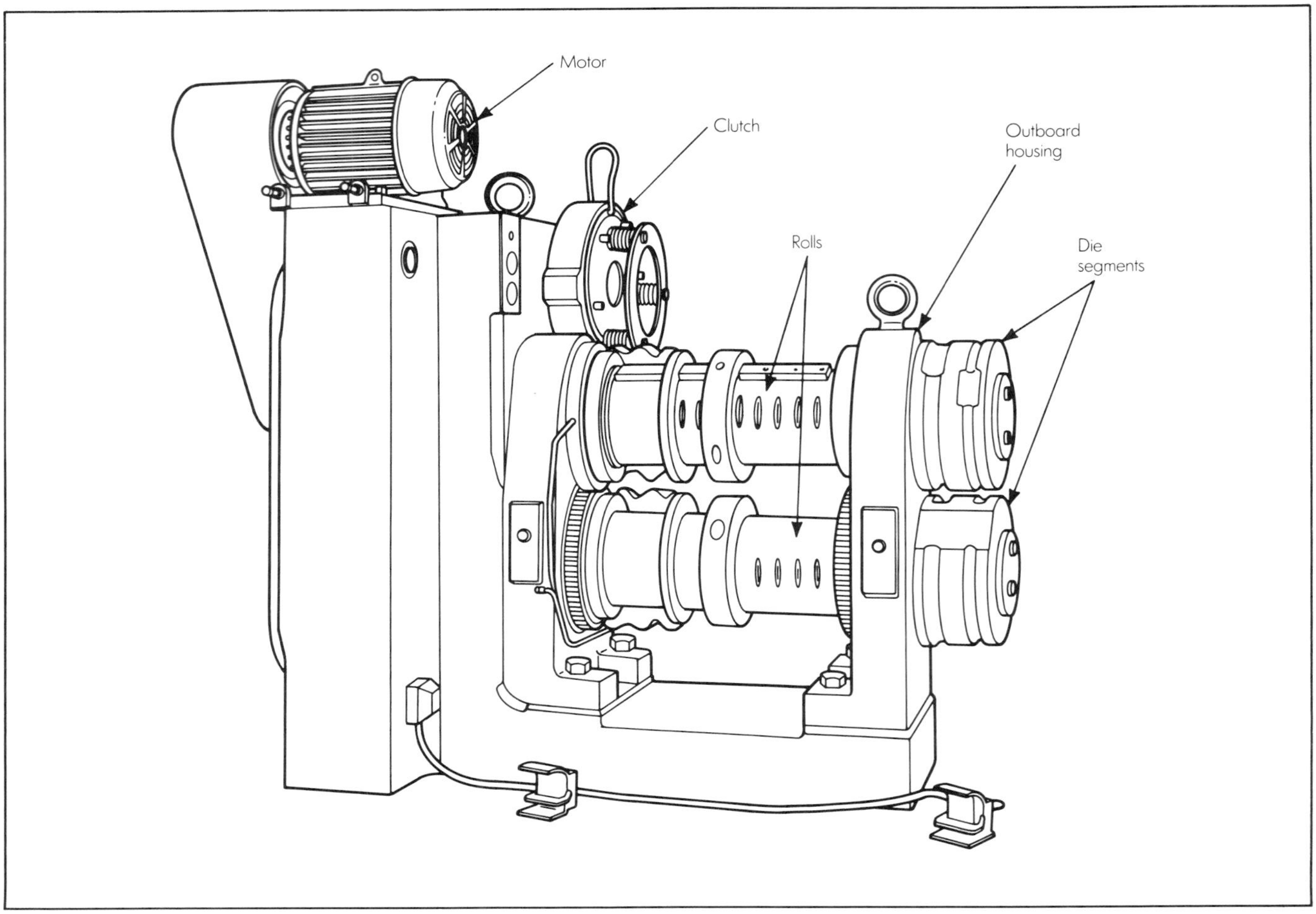

**Fig. 15-37 Roll forging machine with rolls supported by an outboard housing.** (*Verson Allsteel Press Co.*)

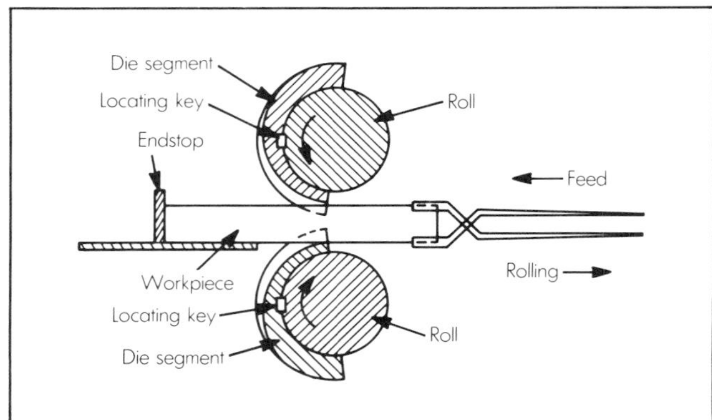


**Fig. 15-38 Schematic of roll forging operation using multiple passes.** (*Battelle Columbus Laboratories*)

off the preformed part from the bar. It is important to prevent overstressing the tooling so that good die life may be obtained.

## Capacity and Applications

The rolls on two-roll machines are as large as 48″ (1220 mm) diam x 42″ (1065 mm) wide. These machines can accept bar stock from 1/4 to 5″ (6 to 127 mm) diam and up to 36″ (915 mm) long. The rolls on three-roll machines are smaller and can preform parts from 1/2 to 1″ (12 to 25 mm) diam and from 6 to 8″ (152 to 200 mm) long.

Wedge rolling machines are capable of producing 600-1200 preforms per hour if only single parts are being run. The quantity would increase proportionately in multiple-pass runs. Tolerances can be maintained at +0.004″ (0.10 mm) diam and approximately ±0.004 to ±0.006″ (0.10-0.15 mm) in length.

Wedge rolling machines are currently being used to preform transmission output shafts, cluster gears, chassis idler arms, pitman arms, ball joints, front wheel spindles, connecting rods, stem pinions, and mining tools.

## RADIAL FORGING MACHINES

The radial forging machine deforms the workpiece between two or four opposed dies that deliver a series of short, rapid strokes. The dies are mounted in levers driven by a main driveshaft through eccentrics (see Fig. 15-41). The die holders are water cooled to maintain temperature control. The distance between the dies is controlled manually by adjusting the eccentrics or automatically by an infeed control. The workpiece is held at the proper location and is fed into the dies using either one or two chuck heads mounted on the machine bed. Two

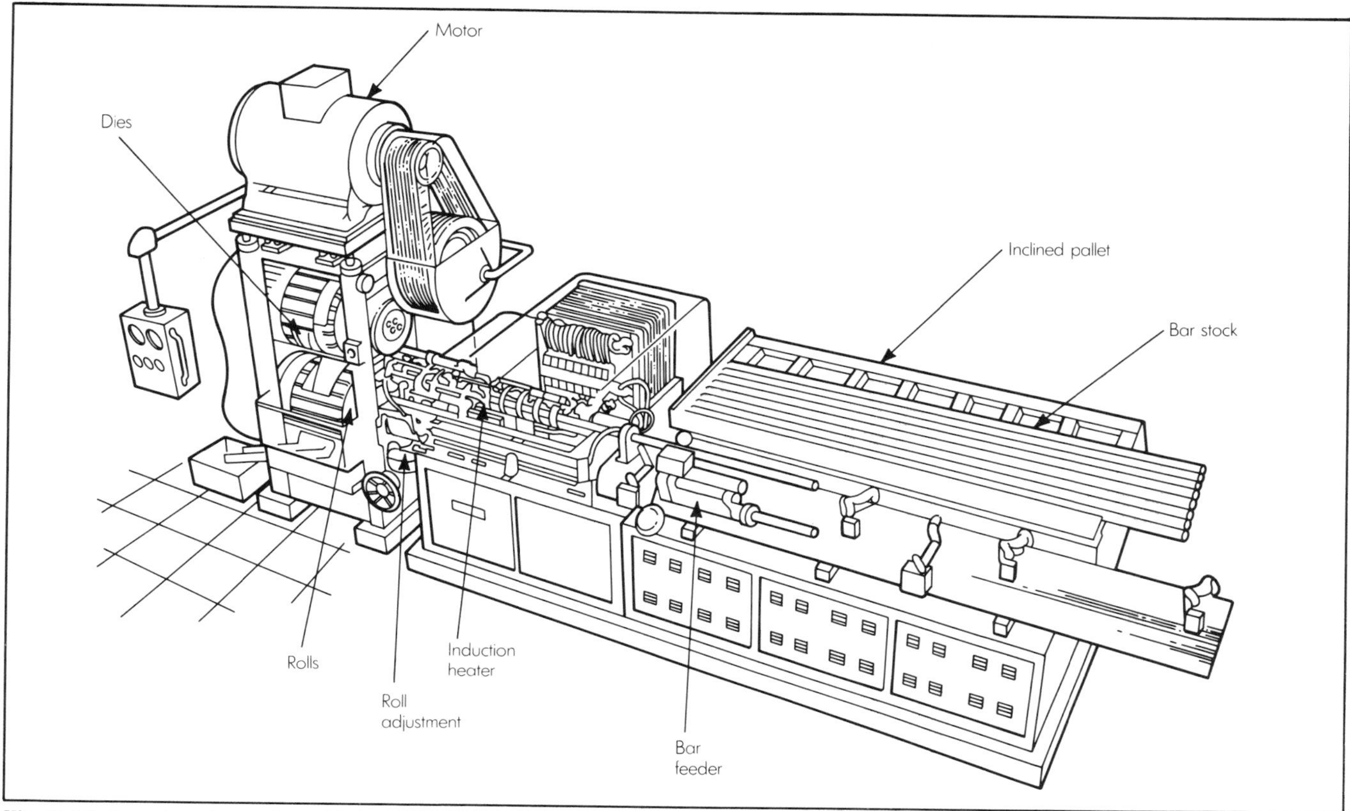

**Fig. 15-39 An automated wedge rolling machine incorporates a bar feeder, an induction heater, and the rolling machine.**

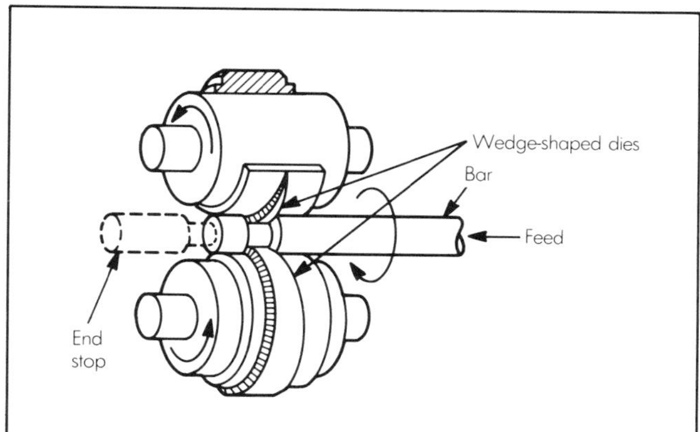

**Fig. 15-40 Wedge-shaped dies roll and displace the metal along its centerline.**

chuck heads, mounted on each side of the forging dies, are used when long parts are being forged.

## Operation

After each blow, the clamped workpiece is fed axially toward the entrance of the oscillating dies. Workpieces that are circular in cross section are also rotated between blows to obtain a good surface finish, while noncircular shapes are held in a fixed position.

In upsetting operations, the workpiece is fed against a

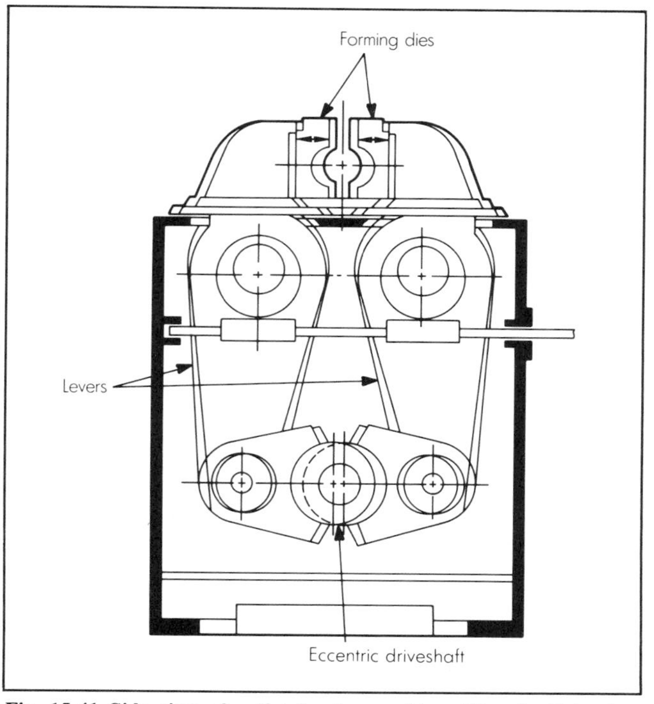

**Fig. 15-41 Side view of radial forging machine.** (*Battelle Columbus Laboratories*)

backstop located behind the dies (see Fig. 15-5). A mandrel can be attached to the backstop to control internal material flow when hollow workpieces are being upset.

### Capacity and Applications

Radial forging machines that are currently being constructed are capable of forging steel bars to 6" (150 mm) diam and tubes having a 1" (25 mm) wall thickness to 13" (330 mm) diam. These machines range in capacity from 60-250 tons (534-2244 kN) per die. Dies can be made to 20" (510 mm) in length.

Radial forging machines are widely used for precision forging of bars with round, square, and rectangular cross sections. These machines are also used for producing profiled parts, such as solid or hollow-stepped shafts, and for finishing tubes with cylindrical and conical profiles. Figure 15-42 illustrates a sample of the parts being forged on these machines.

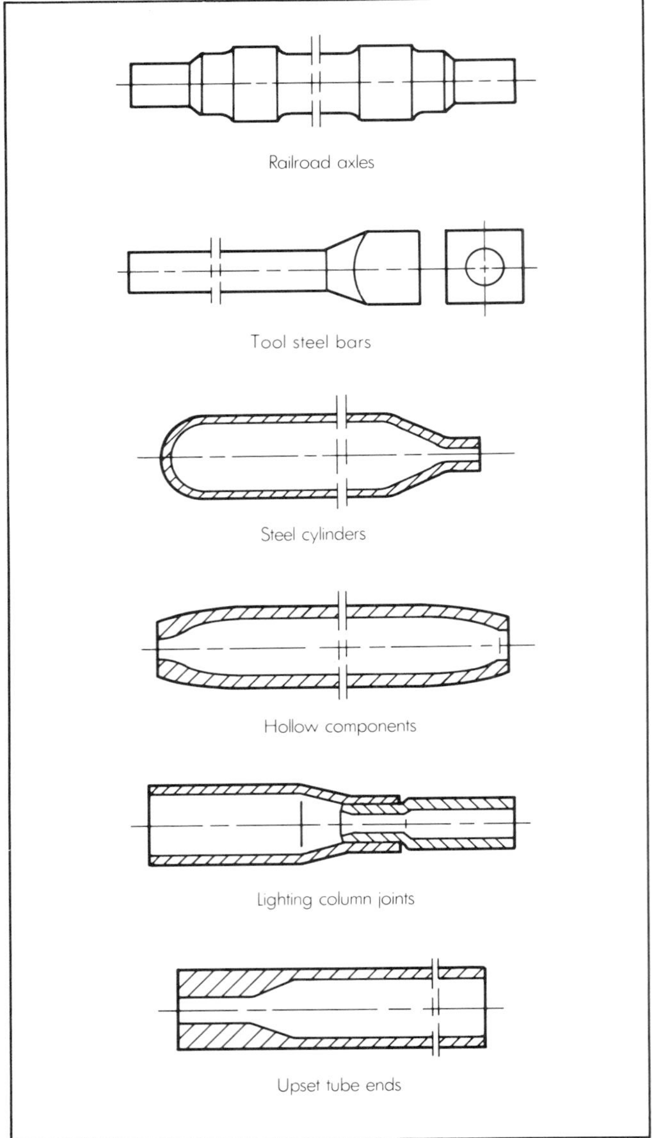


**Fig 15-42 Sample of the variety of parts that can be forged on a radial forging machine.** (*Fenn Manufacturing Co.*)

## RING ROLLING MACHINES

Seamless rings are predominantly produced on ring rolling machines. The preform required for ring rolling is produced by upsetting and piercing a heated block or billet having correct volume into a donut-shaped forging.

In operation, the blank forging is placed over the inner mandrel of the ring rolling machine. The wall thickness of the blank is reduced between the mandrel and an outer roll by moving the two rolls against each other while driving the blank with the outer roll. As the wall thickness is reduced, the diameter increases. Shaping the cross section can be performed at the same time.

The three basic types of ring rolling machines generally used are table ring mills, radial machines, and radial-axial machines.

### Table Ring Rolling Machines

Table-type ring rolling machines are horizontal machines containing a main roll and four mandrels (see Fig. 15-43). The mandrels are mounted in a turntable which rotates mandrel and blank into rolling position. When the blank is in position and the main roll makes contact with it, the drive power and rolling force are applied to the blank and the rolling begins. Guide rolls center the ring between the main roll and mandrel. A tracer roll controls the rolling process to produce the required ring diameter. Axial rolls can also be incorporated to control axial height.

These machines are generally automated and are designed for high-volume production of lightweight, small-diameter rings. They are also capable of maintaining good dimensional repeatability.

### Radial Ring Rolling Machines

Radial ring rolling machines can be designed to operate horizontally or vertically. A powered, rotating main roll is mounted on the outside along with two guide rolls (see Fig. 15-44). During operation, an unpowered mandrel is brought into contact with the ring and applies the rolling force. During rolling, the wall thickness is decreased and the ring diameter and axial height are increased. Ring diameter is controlled by a tracer wheel. A mandrel support is generally not used when forming rings with short axial heights.

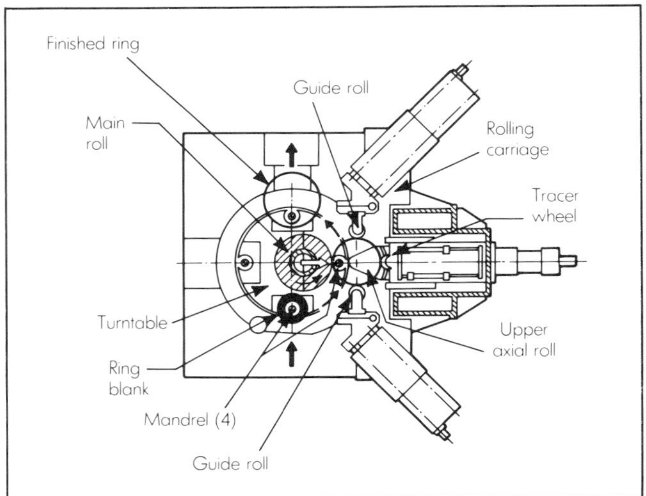


**Fig. 15-43 Plan view of table-type ring rolling machine.** (*Girard Associates, Inc.*)

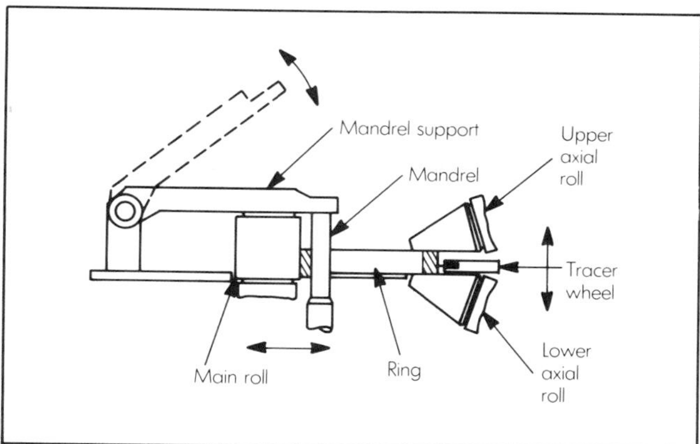


**Fig. 15-44 Side view of main components on a radial ring rolling machine with provision to control axial height.** (*Girard Associates, Inc.*)

## Radial-Axial Ring Rolling Machines

Radial-axial machines are similar in design to radial machines except they include axial rolls. Axial height of the ring is decreased by an upper and lower axial roll (see Fig. 15-44). During operation, the upper axial roll closes to achieve the predetermined axial height.

## Capacity and Application

One manufacturer produces table machines capable of rolling rings up to 24″ (600 mm) diam x 4″ (100 mm) in axial height when mandrel supports are not used. Rings up to 20″ (500 mm) diam x 6″ (160 mm) axial height are obtainable with mandrel supports. Radial and radial-axial machines are capable of rolling rings to 23 ft (7 m) diam and from 4-46″ (100-1160 mm) axial height.

Rolled rings are used for a variety of different applications. Some of these include antifriction bearing races, gear blanks, wheel bearings, commutator rings, rotating and nonrotating rings for jet engines, nuclear reactor components, and flanges. Rolled rings are also cut into segments to produce small curved parts.

# AUXILIARY EQUIPMENT

In addition to the machines used to forge the part, several other types of machines and equipment are required. These include machines to transport and hold the workpiece during forging operations, the equipment to heat the workpiece to forging temperature, and the machines and equipment used to automate the forging operation. Cleaning and finishing equipment are discussed in Volume III of this Handbook series.

## Material Handling

The type and capacity of handling equipment in a forging shop is determined by the type of work performed. Since open-die forging is generally associated with large workpieces, equipment must be provided to manipulate and hold the workpiece during the forging operation. This can be accomplished using chargers and manipulators. Bar or billet feeders are especially useful in closed-die processes when the operation is automated. Robots and positioning arms are also frequently used in automated operations.

**Chargers.** Chargers are track or wheel-mounted vehicles designed to load and hold the workpiece during the forging operation. The workpiece is clamped near the center of gravity and supported during transporting. Charging attachments are also designed to be installed on lift trucks and are used for workpieces weighing less than 12,000 lb (5400 kg). An operator controls the charger.

**Manipulators.** Manipulators are also track or wheel-mounted vehicles designed to load and hold the workpiece during the forging operation. However, manipulators grip the workpiece on one end and have the capability to rotate the workpiece. Mobile manipulators are generally used with workpieces under 40,000 lb (18 100 kg). The manipulator is controlled by an operator or by remote control. Track-mounted manipulators require an overhead crane to remove the workpieces from the furnace.

## Material Heating

In hot forging, the workpiece must be heated to its recrystallization temperature to obtain maximum material flow. The workpiece is heated in either a fuel-fired furnace or an induction heater. Furnaces used for heat treating forgings are discussed in Volume III of this Handbook series.

**Fuel-fired furnaces.** Fuel-fired furnaces use fuel oil, natural gas, or liquid petroleum (LP) gas to supply the energy for heating the workpieces. The temperatures required for various materials are discussed in a previous section. Burners in direct-fired furnaces are located in the heating chamber. In indirect-fired or muffle furnaces, they are located in a separate combustion chamber, preventing the workpieces from coming in contact with the combustion products. The workpieces in these furnaces are heated by radiation and circulation of the products of combustion. Fuel-fired forging furnaces are usually slot, box (door), or continuous types.

*Slot and box furnaces.* Slot and box furnaces consist of a rectangular shell made out of steel plate with a ceramic or refractory lining. One or more openings are designed in the furnace to load and unload the workpieces. The openings in slot furnaces are kept to a minimum height to prevent unnecessary heat loss to the outside during loading and unloading. The workpieces are loaded into the furnace in a time-rotation method—one piece out, one piece in—and then allowed to soak until the temperature is uniform throughout the workpiece.

Slot furnaces (see Fig. 15-45) are capable of heating the whole part or just the end of the workpiece, whereas box furnaces are normally capable of heating only the entire workpiece. To produce uniformly heated slugs with the least amount of scale formation, impinging of the flame on the workpiece must be avoided and a neutral atmosphere must be maintained. Modern gas-fired slot furnaces often use ceiling-mounted incandescent burners and an adjustable slot to maintain positive pressure inside the furnace.

*Continuous furnaces.* Continuous furnaces are similar in construction to box furnaces except that they incorporate a device to move the workpieces through the furnace. The movement is either linear or rotary. Usually the furnace is heated by zones. The initial zone is normally a preheat zone and can be heated by the exhaust gases of the soaking zone or by burners directed to give maximum Btu's to the work space in the shortest time cycle. In the other zones, the Btu input is gradually decreased to maintain the workpiece at the desired temperature. The speed of the moving hearth and/or piece is determined by the production, the time to preheat the workpiece, and the soaking period required.

**Induction heaters.** An induction heater consists of a water-cooled coil carrying alternating current. The coil is designed and sized to surround the workpiece as it is heated (see Fig. 15-46). As the electric current flows through the coil, a current is induced in the workpiece that raises its temperature. The depth of heating is determined by the frequency. The lower the frequency and the higher the resistance in the stock, the greater the effective depth of penetration. Frequencies range from 60-10,000 Hz; for heating billets, the maximum is approximately 960 Hz.

Induction heaters are built to perform a variety of applications. Some induction heaters are capable of heating only the ends of bars or billets, while others are capable of heating the entire billet individually or continuously.

Some of the advantages of induction heaters are fast heating, automatic temperature control, reduction in scale losses, and freedom of exhaust gases caused by combustion products.

## Automation in Forging

Automation of hot forging operations involves more difficult problems than those encountered in automating cold forging processes. The handling of the hot workpiece within a press, the lubricating of the dies, and the transporting of heated billets from furnace to forging machine require rapid handling of the billet and synchronization of the furnace and press operations. In hot forging, the method and type of automation are determined primarily by production requirements. Four main types of automation, based on the level of sophistication and on the size of the production series, can be considered.

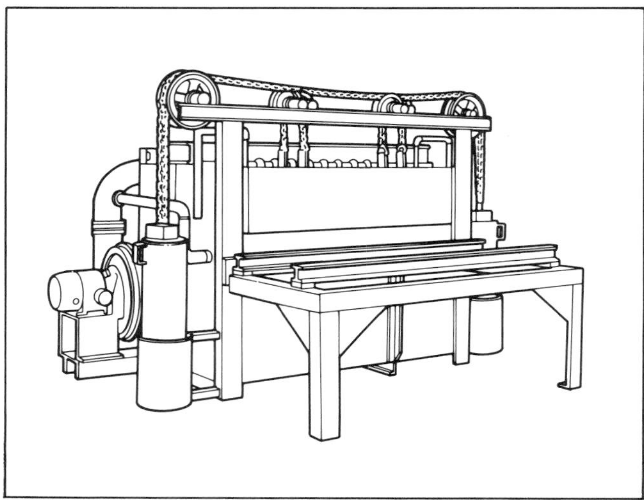

**Fig. 15-45 Slot furnaces are capable of heating either the end of the workpiece or the entire workpiece for various forging operations.** (*Johnston Manufacturing Co.*)

**Automation of forging systems.** This automating method involves the mechanization of operations such as heating, transporting the billets to be forged from furnace to forging unit, and feeding the billets to the first forging station. The workpiece is transported manually or automatically from one station to the next within the forging unit, whether press or hammer. The finished forging is transported automatically to the trimming press, where it is handled again by the trimming press operator.

**Automation within a forging machine.** This method of automating consists of equipping a standard forging machine, in general a mechanical press, with mechanical or pneumatic transfer devices. Thus, the billet or the forging is transported automatically from one forging station to the next within the same machine. The transporting mechanism usually consists of a walking beam system which is synchronized with the press operation. Thus, the high speed of the press, in terms of deformation rate and contact times, is maintained.

**Automation by linking standard machines.** In this automating method, the means of transporting workpieces outside as well as inside forging machines such as presses or hammers is mechanized using robots, hydraulically or pneumatically operated arms, and mechanically activated transfer systems. The operator is required only to supervise the sequence of operations and to stand by to stop the machines in the event of a malfunction.

In Fig. 15-47, the heated workpiece is transferred toward the press by a conveyor. When the workpiece arrives at a predetermined position, the robot rotates to pick up the workpiece and carry it to the press die area. If the die area is clear, the robot positions the workpiece in the first die station and then activates the press. The upset workpiece is then transferred to the second die station, and the press is activated. Mechanical ejectors in the die remove the forged workpiece, and the cycle is repeated.

**Automation using single-purpose automatic machines.** The single-purpose automatic forging machines are built for one

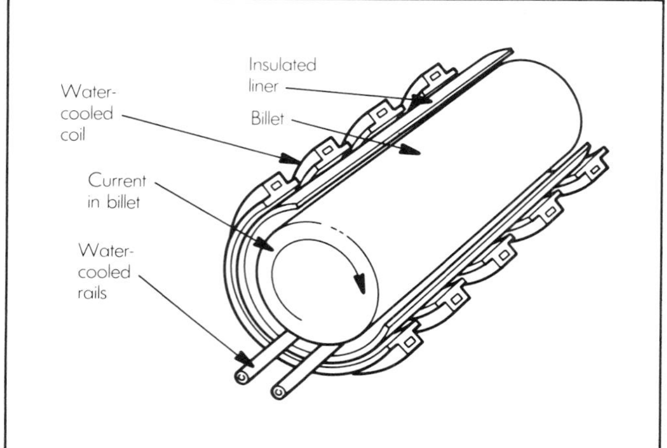


**Fig. 15-46 Cross section of an induction heater used for heating bars or billets.** (*Radyne, Inc.*)

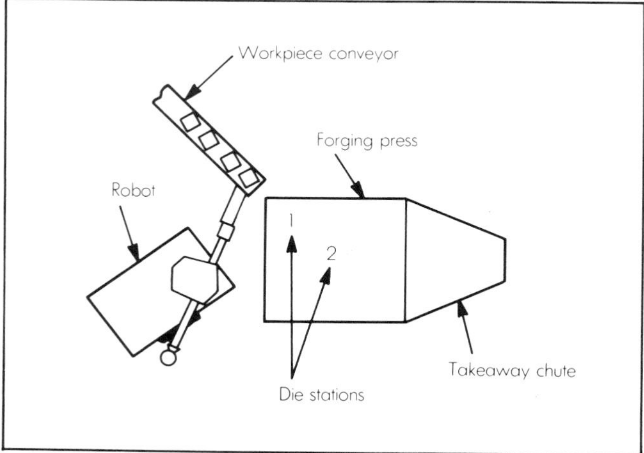


**Fig. 15-47 Typical components used when automating the forging process.** (*Battelle Columbus Laboratories*)

type of workpiece of the same or different size. These machines are economical only if the number of parts to be produced is large enough to justify the relatively high capital investment. An example of such a machine is the hot former previously described. Thus, automatic forging machines are mostly used for producing high-volume automotive parts such as bearing races, gear blanks, nuts, bolts, connecting rods, journal cross forgings, valve lifters, and axles.

# OPERATING PARAMETERS

The variable parameters in the hot forging process are influenced by the material's forgeability and flow stress characteristics, the part geometry, the volume of material to be forged, the type of forging equipment, the initial workpiece or billet size and shape, the preforming operations performed, the flash width and thickness, the temperature of material and dies, and the type of lubricant used.

The temperature ranges of commonly forged materials are provided in the previous section "Materials for Forging" in this chapter. Lubricant requirements, types, selection, and application are discussed in a subsequent section.

## FORCE

The machines used in forging operations apply either a squeezing-type force or an impact-type force. Mechanical and hydraulic presses are examples of machines that apply a squeezing force to the workpiece, and hammers and screw presses are examples of machines that apply an impact-type force.

### Presses

The impression die forging process is a nonsteady-state type of process because the metal flow, stresses, and temperatures continually change throughout it. The continual changing of these variables makes it difficult to accurately determine the force required to forge the workpiece.

In addition to these variables, a variety of geometric shapes and materials can be forged and each one requires a different analysis. Therefore, the force is generally estimated based on the past experience of a similarly forged part or it is estimated with empirical methods. The empirical methods employ simple formulas or nomograms to estimate the force requirement. Another method employs a computerized analytical technique that divides the forging into individual parts, analyzes each part, and then puts the individual parts together to analyze the complete forging.

**Simple formula.** One simple formula employed to estimate the forging force takes into consideration the surface area of the forging including the flash and then multiplies the area by an average forging pressure determined by experience. The forging pressure varies from 28.4-150 ksi (196-1034 MPa) depending on the material being forged and the part geometry.

**Nomograph.** The nomograph in Fig. 15-48 can also be used to estimate the required forging force of a particular part. Figure 15-49 provides the coefficient of difficulty, $K$, for various shaped parts. Table 15-15 provides the flow stress of steel at different forging temperatures.

To estimate the forging force, the following procedure should be followed:

1. Calculate the surface area of the forging including the flash.
2. Determine the flow stress of the material from Table 15-15.
3. Locate the area and flow stress on the appropriate scales.
4. Connect the two points with a line that extends to the press force scale.
5. Multiply the press force reading by the coefficient of difficulty, $K$, given in Fig. 15-49 to obtain the required press force.

Example:

Estimate the force required to forge a steel forging having a coefficient of difficulty, $K$, of 1.40. The surface area is 150 in.$^2$ (970 cm$^2$), and the tensile strength of the steel is 114,000 psi (786 MPa). The forging temperature is 2400° F (1316° C).

The area is located at Point 1 on the Area Scale illustrated in Fig. 15-48; and from Table 15-15, the flow stress is found to be 3400 psi (23.4 MPa), Point 2 on the Flow Stress Scale. Extending the line from Points 1 and 2 to the Press Force Scale indicates that the force is 2400 tons (21.4 MN), Point 3. Multiplying the force by the coefficient 1.4 yields a required press force of 3360 tons (29.9 MN).

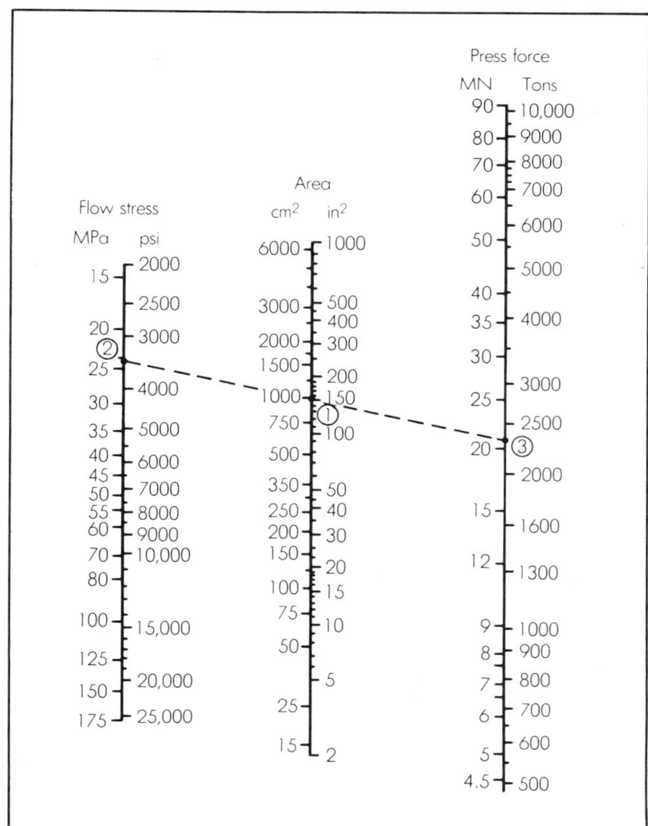


**Fig. 15-48 Nomograph for estimating the force a press needs to produce when forging a part.** (*Erie Press Systems*)

# CHAPTER 15

## OPERATING PARAMETERS

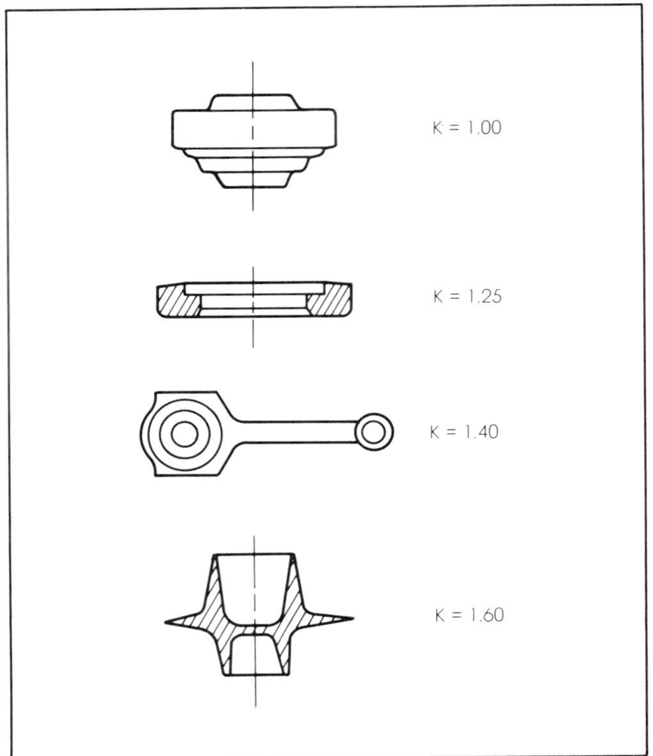


**Fig. 15-49 Coefficient of difficulty for commonly forged parts.** (*Erie Press Systems*)

### Hammers

Hammers and other types of impact equipment are normally rated according to the weight of their ram. However, it is necessary to determine whether the hammer is capable of delivering the energy required to deform the workpiece.

In a gravity drop hammer, the total energy is derived from the free fall of the ram and can be calculated from the following formula:

$$E_T = W \times H \tag{1}$$

where:

$E_T$ = nominal energy of the hammer, ft-lb (J)
$W$ = weight of ram, lb (kg × 9.81)
$H$ = length of stroke, ft (m)

For a power drop hammer, the total energy is derived from the free fall of the ram and the mean effective pressure acting on the ram cylinder. The energy can be calculated from the following formula:

$$E_T = (W + P \times A) \times H \tag{2}$$

where:

$E_T$ = nominal energy of the hammer, ft-lb (J)
$W$ = weight of ram, lb (kg × 9.81)
$P$ = air, steam, or hydraulic pressure acting on cylinder, psi (MPa)
$A$ = surface area of ram cylinder, in.$^2$ (mm$^2$)
$H$ = length of stroke, ft (m)

For a counterblow hammer having rams of equal weight, the total energy can be calculated from the following formula:

$$E_T = \frac{G \times V^2}{4} \tag{3}$$

where:

$E_T$ = nominal energy of the hammer, ft-lb (J)
$G$ = weight of one ram, lb (kg)
$V$ = actual blow velocity of rams (twice velocity of one ram), ft/s (m/s)

It is important to note that in order to obtain the energy available in a hammer from the previously mentioned formulas, the nominal energy must be multiplied by an efficiency factor. This factor is determined from the energy lost due to friction in the guides, noise, and vibration.

Even before determining how much energy a hammer or other type of impact machine can deliver, it is necessary to determine the total energy required for the forging, the minimum energy required by the hammer, and the number of blows necessary to forge the workpiece.

**Total deformation energy.** An approximate estimate of the deformation energy required for conventional-type forgings (excluding the more special forgings used in the aircraft industry) can be determined from the following formula:

$$E_D = V \times F_I \times S_F \times C \tag{4}$$

where:

$E_D$ = total deformation energy required for finished forging, ft-lb
$V$ = volume of billet to be forged, in.$^3$
$F_I$ = forgeability index of material being forged (refer to Table 15-16)
$S_F$ = shape factor obtained from square root of ratio of average width and average thickness
$C$ = constant equal to 2000

To obtain energy in joules, $J$, foot pounds force is multiplied by 1.356.

*Average width.* To estimate the average width, first the total plan area of the forging that is being compressed is calculated, including the flash in the die lands or saddles but not in the gutter. Then the average length of the forging is estimated by dividing the sum of the major lengths by two. The area is divided by the average length to obtain the average width.

*Average thickness.* To obtain the average thickness, the volume of the forging being compressed is estimated and then this value is divided by the plan area of the forging previously calculated.

**Minimum energy.** An estimate of the minimum blow energy required by the hammer can be calculated using the following formula:

$$E_M = A \times F_I \times C \tag{5}$$

where:

$E_M$ = minimum blow energy required by the hammer, ft-lb
$A$ = area of forging being compressed by dies, in.$^2$
$F_I$ = forgeability index of material being forged (refer to Table 15-16)
$C$ = constant equal to 250

**TABLE 15-15**
**Flow Stress of Steel at Forging Temperatures**

| Forging Temperature, °F, (°C) | Tensile Stress of Steel, psi (MPa) | | | |
|---|---|---|---|---|
| | 57,000 (393) | 85,000 (586) | 114,000 (786) | 142,000 (979) |
| | Flow Stress, psi (MPa) | | | |
| 1800 (982) | 4300 (29.6) | 7700 (53) | 10,700 (73.8) | 15,500 (106.9) |
| 2000 (1093) | 3130 (21.6) | 5100 (35.2) | 7300 (50.3) | 9700 (66.9) |
| 2200 (1204) | 2700 (18.6) | 3100 (21.4) | 5100 (35.2) | 7100 (48.9) |
| 2400 (1316) | 2000 (13.8) | 2850 (19.6) | 3400 (23.4) | 4300 (29.6) |

**TABLE 15-16**
**Relative Forgeability of Materials**

| Material | Forgeability Index | Material | Forgeability Index |
|---|---|---|---|
| 1010-1030 | 1.00 | Stainless Steel | |
| Brass | | 14S (Aluminum) | |
| 1035-1050 | | 300 Series | |
| Bronze | 1.10 | Stainless Steel | |
| 1112-1137 | | Tricent | |
| 9310-9315 | | Vasco Jet 1000 | 1.75 |
| 1055-1075 | | Thermold J | |
| 2300-2330 | | 756 Aluminum | |
| 3100-3135 | | 17-4 PH | |
| 4100-4140 | 1.20 | 17-7 PH | |
| 4600-4620 | | AM-350 | 2.00 |
| 5100-5140 | | AM-355 | |
| 6100-6135 | | A-286 | |
| 8600-8630 | | Discaloy | |
| 2335-2350 | | Stainless W | 2.50 |
| 3140-3150 | | Inconel X | |
| 3300-3335 | | 16-25-6 | |
| 4300-4340 | 1.30 | 19-9DL | |
| 4625-4640 | | Titanium Alloys | |
| 4815-4820 | | H-155 | 3.00 |
| 6140-6150 | | Hastelloy C | |
| 8635-8650 | | Udimet 500 | |
| HY-TUFF | | Inco 700 | |
| AMS 6407 | | René 41 | 3.50 |
| AMS 6427 | | M-252 | |
| 400 Series | 1.50 | Waspaloy | |

(*Forging Industry Association*)

To obtain energy in joules, $J$, foot pounds force is multiplied by 1.356.

**Number of blows.** The total number of blows required to forge a part can be estimated by dividing the total deformation energy, $E_D$, by the minimum energy, $E_M$. It is important to note that this value does not include any blows required for bending, rolling, and fullering.

It is best to distribute the work load between as many impressions as possible, that is, finisher, blocker, and buster impressions. Generally, it is preferable to limit the number of blows for each impression to no more than four or five. The finisher impression should normally use less energy than the other impressions.

## SPEED

The most important characteristic of a forging machine is the number of strokes per minute (spm) or blows per minute that it is capable of attaining. The spm determines the production rate of the machine. It also influences whether or not a part can be finish forged without reheating.

The contact time under pressure is the length of time that the part is being deformed between the dies. The heat transfer coefficient is larger during part deformation than when the part is not being deformed. Die wear increases as the contact time is lengthened.

The velocity of the ram under pressure is also important

because it determines the contact time and the rate of deformation, or strain rate. Certain materials cannot be forged at a high rate of deformation because they have a tendency to crack.

Table 15-17 shows the speeds and blows per minute of different forging equipment.

**TABLE 15-17**
**Speed and SPM Capabilities of Forging Equipment**

| Type of Equipment | Speed, fps (m/s) | Blows per Minute |
|---|---|---|
| Board drop hammer | 10-15 (3-4.6) | 45-60 |
| Air or steam lift hammer | 12-16 (3.7-4.9) | 60 |
| Electrohydraulic drop hammer | 10-15 (3-4.6) | 50-75 |
| Power drop hammer | 15-30 (4.6-9) | 60-100 |
| Counterblow hammer (vertical) | 15-30 (4.6-9) | 50-65 |
| Impacter | 10-17 (3-5.2) | 100-170 |
| Mechanical press | 0.2-5 (0.06-1.5) | |
| Hydraulic press | 0.1-2.5 (0.03-0.8) | |
| Screw press | 1.5-4 (0.5-1.2) | |

## COST CONSIDERATIONS

During the forging process, the objective is to produce the forging at the lowest cost, yet in uniformly good quality—not to produce the part in the machine that is lowest in cost. It is necessary to complete the forging while the material is in full forging heat. The following costs are interrelated and should be evaluated:

1. Cost of raw material.
2. Cost of tooling per forging produced.
3. Cost of labor.
4. Cost of equipment per forging produced.
5. Cost of tooling development.
6. Cost of heating each forging.

# TOOLING

Tooling used in the forging process consists mainly of the dies in which the workpieces are forged. Forging may be accomplished with open or impression-type dies, or a combination of both.

## OPEN DIES

Dies employed in open-die forging are relatively simple compared with those used for closed-die forging. The types of dies normally employed are flat dies, swage dies, and V-dies. Each die set is composed of a top and bottom half. The top half is attached to the ram, and the bottom half is attached to the hammer or press bed. Auxiliary tools are also employed to cut forged bars, control final forging size, and initiate setdowns or changes in sections on the forged parts. Piercing, punching, or trepanning tools may be used to remove the center slug when manufacturing rings from upset discs.

### Flat Dies

Flat dies, as illustrated in Fig. 15-50, are used for the majority of open-die forgings. The flat surfaces are parallel to avoid tapering the workpiece. Flat dies range from 12-20" (300-500 mm) in width, but normally are 16-18" (400-450 mm) wide. The edges are rounded to prevent the workpiece from being pinched or torn during the forging operation and to prevent the formation of laps.

Flat dies are used to forge bars, flat forgings, and other parts, either round or shaped. Wide dies are employed when transverse flow (side movement) is desired (see Fig. 15-50, view *b*) or when the workpiece is drawn out by using repeated blows. Narrow dies are employed for cutting off or for necking down various cross sections (see view *c*). Flat dies are also used in combination with other types of dies. The flat die is usually on top, and the shaped die is on the bottom.

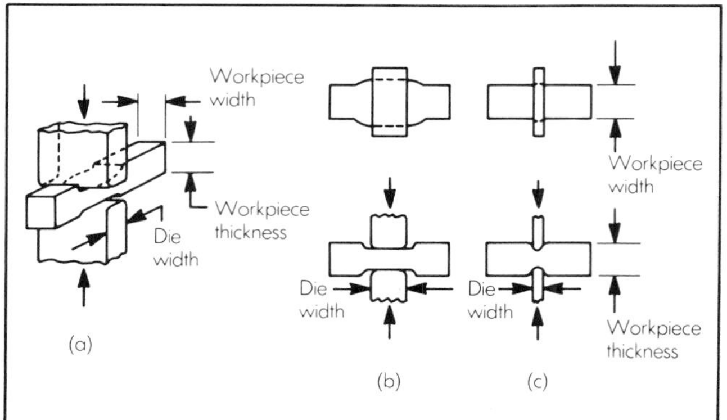


**Fig. 15-50 Typical flat dies as used in open-die forging.** (*Forging Industry Association*)

### Swage Dies

Swage dies are basically flat dies with a V shape cut in their centers (see Fig. 15-51). The V shape usually has a 120° included

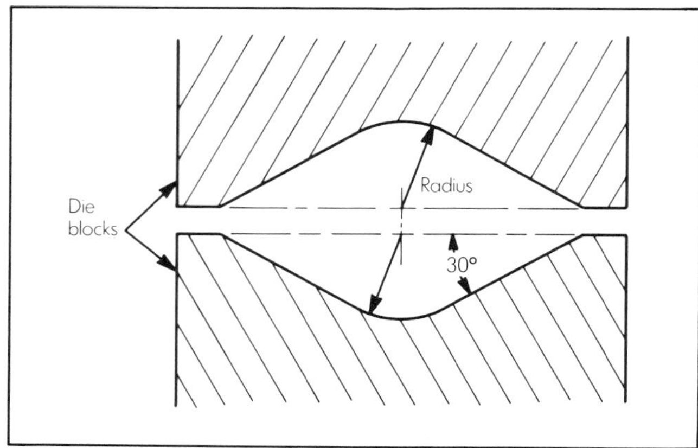


**Fig. 15-51 Cross section of swaging dies used in open-die forging.** (*Battelle Columbus Laboratories*)

angle, and the center of the V contains a radius corresponding to the minimum diameter shaft that can be produced.

When round shafts are being manufactured, swage dies can be used to round off the polygonal surfaces produced by a flat die; or if properly designed, they can be used to produce the complete shaft.

The advantages of swage dies over flat dies for forging round bars include minimal side bulging, longitudinal movement of all metal, faster operation, and greater deformation in the center of the bar. The disadvantage is that swage dies are normally designed to forge a single-size bar. Another disadvantage is that parts cannot be marked or cut off when swaging dies are used; the swaging dies must be removed and replaced with flat dies first.

## V-Dies

In V-dies, the bottom die contains a V form and the top die is always flat (see Fig. 15-52). The optimum angle for the V is usually between 90 and 120°. V-dies can be used to produce round parts, but are usually employed to forge hollow cylinders from a hollow billet. A hollow or solid mandrel is used in conjunction with the V-dies to form the inside of the cylinder.

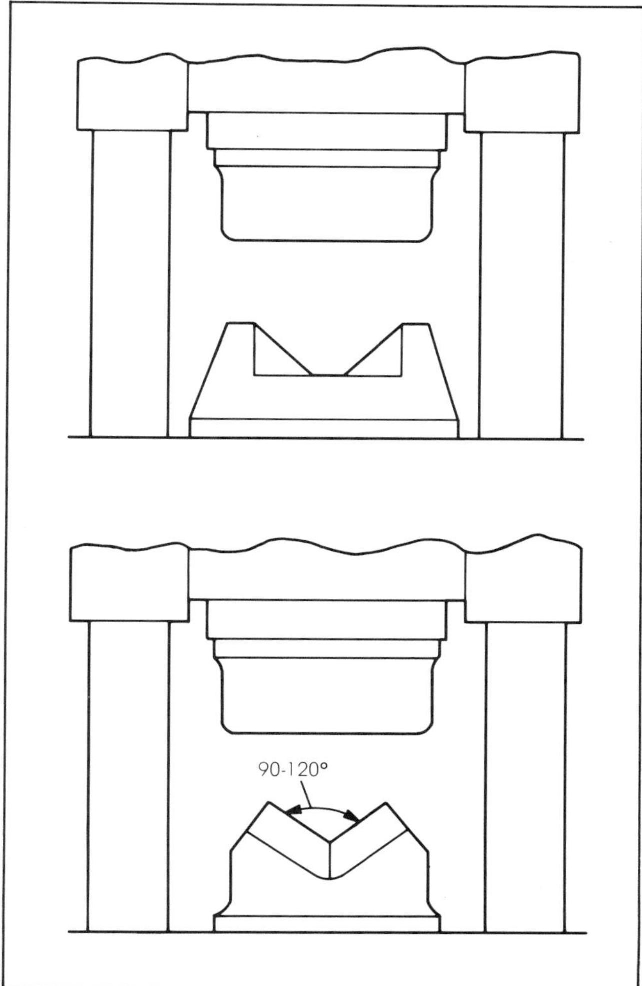


**Fig. 15-52 V-dies contain an included angle of 90-120° for the bottom die; the top die is always flat. (*Battelle Columbus Laboratories*)**

## Die Material

The die material must be capable of withstanding heat, abrasion, and rough use as well as being economical in cost. Alloy steels of the AISI 4100 or 4300 series and some proprietary tool steels containing 0.40-0.55% carbon are normally used for these dies. The hardness of these dies is lower (approximately 270-320 Bhn) than closed dies.

Die life depends on the material being forged, the type of machine used for the forging process, and most importantly the part design. Worn dies can be remachined and built up by hard face welding.

## IMPRESSION DIES

Impression-die forging (sometimes called closed-die forging) is performed on hammers and presses with dies attached to the ram and to the sow block or the bolster plate. The dies for use on presses are often designed to forge the part in one blow, and knock-out pins are often incorporated to mechanically eject the forging from the impression. Dies may contain impressions for several parts.

Hammer forgings are normally made with several blows in successive die impressions. A typical die for hammer forgings is shown in Fig. 15-53. The edger or roller impression is used to preform the workpiece so that the metal is distributed along its length for subsequent steps. If a portion of the bar stock is being reduced, the impression is referred to as a fullering impression. The bending impression bends the workpiece so that it fits the shape of the blocking impression. The blocking impression is used as an intermediate step to impart the general shape to the part. The final shape is formed in the finishing impression. Excess material flows into the gutter surrounding the finishing impression as the die halves are brought together. The excess material or flash is removed in a subsequent operation. When several forgings are produced sequentially from bar stock, a cutoff impression is machined into one corner of the die to sever the finished forging from the bar.

Since mechanical presses operate with a fixed stroke, the

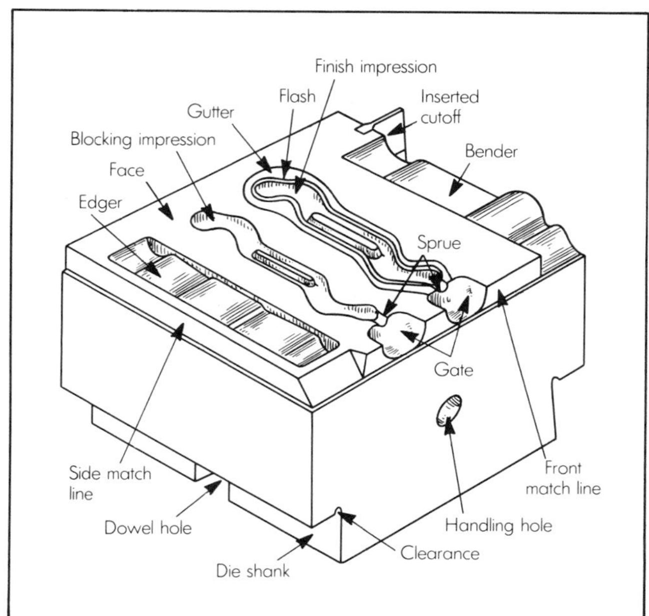


**Fig. 15-53 Elements of a die block for drop forging.**

dies used on these presses are designed so that die filling occurs without the two die halves making contact. Contact of the die halves can cause the press to lock or could possibly cause serious damage to the dies or press. Dies used on hammers and hydraulic presses are designed to have sufficient bearing area so that the dies can make contact lightly without incurring damage.

## Die Design Guidelines

The significant features of impression-die forgings imparted by tooling are illustrated in Fig. 15-54. The guidelines discussed in the preceding section apply to dies used on hammers and presses. They were adapted from material in the *Forging Industry Handbook*[18] and other material furnished by the Forging Industry Association.

**Parting line and parting plane.** The parting line is the line along which the dies meet and separate; it does not need to be located along a straight plane. When the parting surfaces of the two die blocks are in more than one plane, the dies are said to be locked dies (see Fig. 15-54). While this is not a recommended design characteristic, it is sometimes used to impart desired grain flow properties to the forged part.

The location of the parting line affects part removal, die cost and die life, grain flow, production rates, ease of flash removal, and the amount of material to be removed by finish machining. If possible, the parting line should be located in one plane, in a position that minimizes side thrusts, and in the central element of the part. Figure 15-55 illustrates a variety of simple shapes with the parting line locations indicated.

The parting plane, also referred to as the forging plane, is a plane perpendicular to the direction of the forging force. It is not always in the same plane as the parting line.

**Draft.** Draft angle is normally added to all surfaces perpendicular to the parting plane to allow the forged part to be easily removed from the die. Tilting the part in the die produces a natural draft and eliminates the need to add draft angle (see Fig. 15-56). The amount of draft does not vary widely from alloy to alloy, but it is usually greater on hard-to-forge alloys and on forgings produced with hammers. Deeper die cavities normally require greater drafts to ensure release of the forged part.

The standard draft angles are 7°, 5°, 3°, 1°, and 0°. Knockout pins must be employed to remove parts from the die halves that have been designed with small or no draft angles. Outside draft angles can normally be smaller than inside draft angles since the cooled part shrinks away from the die cavity. Since the draft angle imparted to the forged part must be machined away to final specifications, emphasis has been put on the design of near-net-shape and precision forging to improve cost savings of material and reduce overhead.

**Webs and ribs.** Webs are thin sections on the part that are parallel to the parting plane; ribs are thin sections perpendicular to the parting plane. Both sections are more difficult to forge

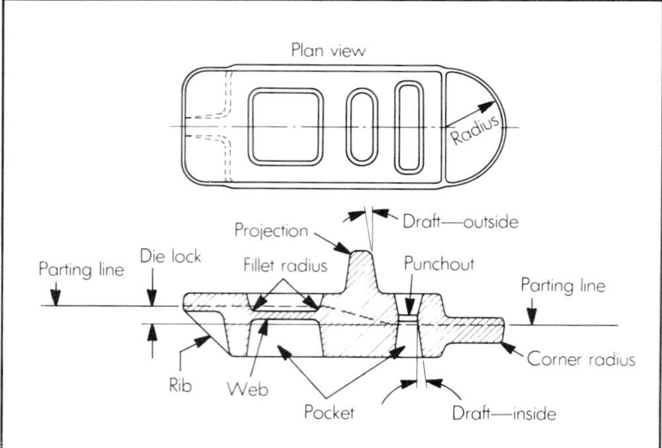


**Fig. 15-54 Significant features of impression die forgings that are imparted by tooling.**

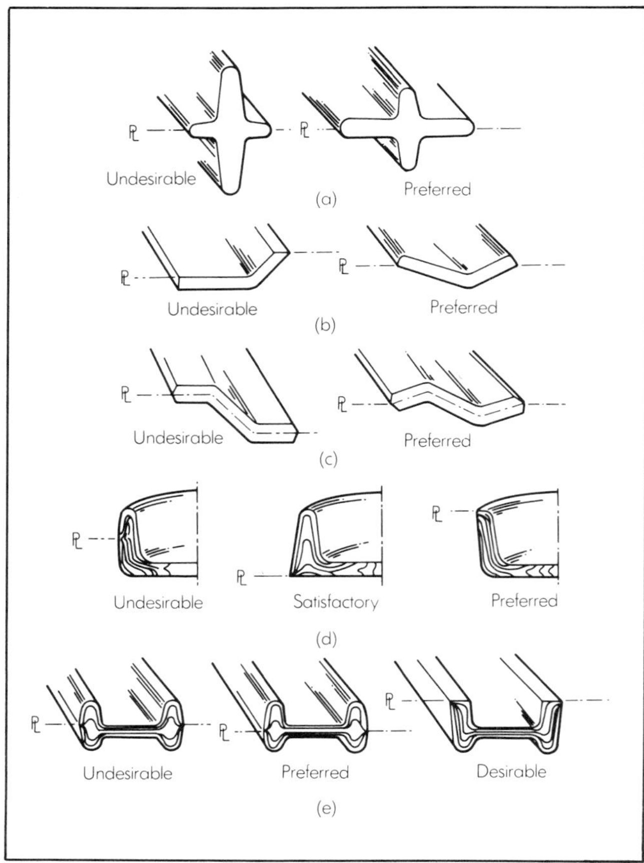


**Fig. 15-55 Cross section of several forging shapes illustrating the undesirable and preferred parting line locations. (a) Deep impressions that may promote die breakage should be avoided. (b) and (c) Side thrust that could cause dies to shift sideways should be avoided. (d) and (e) Location should be selected that permits obtaining the most desirable grain flow pattern. (*Forging Industry Association*)**

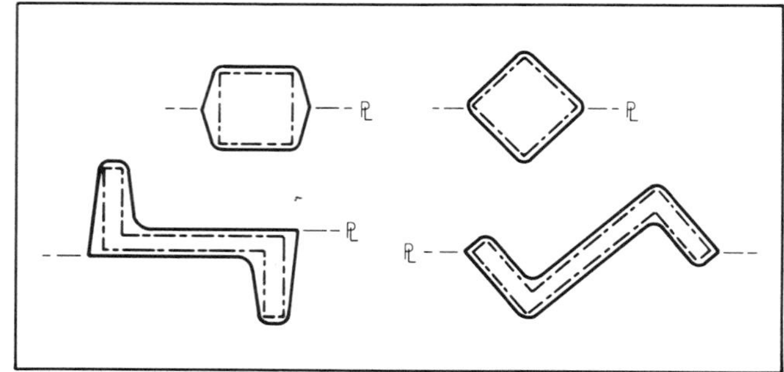

**Fig. 15-56 Natural draft on a workpiece can be obtained by changing the parting line. (*Forging Industry Association*)**

than thicker sections because the metal cools rapidly and because the force and energy requirements of these sections differ from those required by the thicker sections.

The minimum thickness of a web is determined by the minimum longitudinal dimension (for circular parts, the diameter) of the part, the type of material, and whether the metal is free to flow (unconfined) in one direction. Web thickness is greater for hard-to-forge material and confined webs. Figure 15-57 shows minimum web thicknesses for unconfined webs in steels with good forgeability.

The minimum thickness of a rib is determined by its height and the metallurgical properties of the material being forged. As a general rule, a rib confining a web should not be higher than the width of the web. Intermediate ribs should be no higher than the enclosing rib. Figure 15-58 gives rib height/thickness ratios for steels with good forgeability. Ribs in harder-to-forge materials should be thicker.

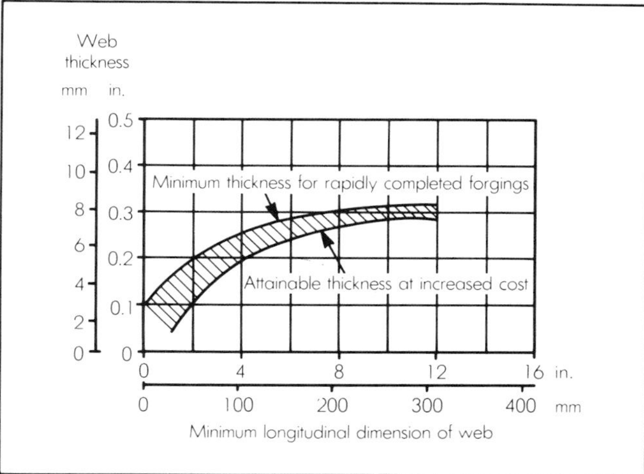


**Fig. 15-57 Graph for determining minimum web thickness for unconfined webs for steels with good forgeability. (*Forging Industry Association*)**

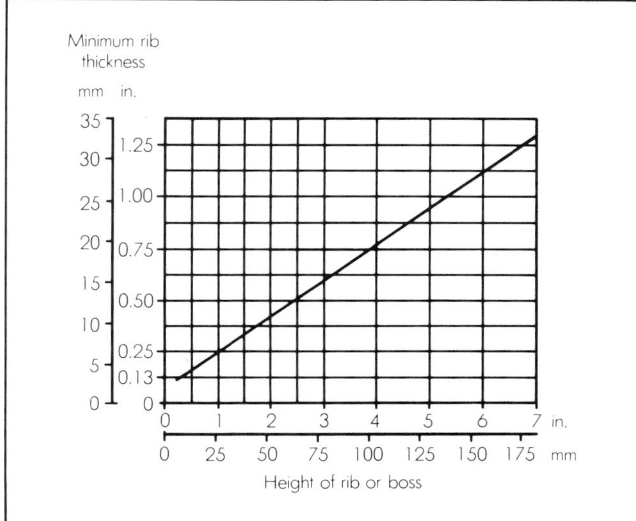


**Fig. 15-58 Graph for determining rib thickness based on rib height for steels with good forgeability. (*Forging Industry Association*)**

**Fillet and corner radii.** Fillet radii should be as large as possible to permit good metal flow and to avoid laps and cold shuts (see Fig. 15-59). To reduce fillet radii and smoothly distribute metal around the fillet, several preforming operations may be required. Smaller radii are more costly to machine in the die, can cause checking of the die surface, and can reduce die life. Corner radii should be as large as possible to permit good metal flow during forging and to reduce die wear.

**Flash.** The excess material in a closed impression die surrounds the forged part at the parting plane and is referred to as flash. Flash consists of two parts, the flash land and the gutter. The flash land is the portion of the flash adjacent to the part, and the gutter is outside the land. Flash is normally cut off in the trimming die.

*Flash land.* The flash land impression in the die is designed so that as the dies close and metal is forced between the dies, the pressure in the part cavity is sufficient to fill the cavity without breaking the die. The pressure is controlled through land geometry, thickness, and width. The flash land is generally constructed as two parallel surfaces that have the proper thickness-to-width ratio when the dies are closed.

The land thickness is determined by the forging equipment used, material being forged, weight of forging, and complexity of the forged part. The ratio of flash land width to flash land thickness varies from 2:1 to 5:1. Lower ratios are used in presses, and higher ratios are used in hammers. Figure 15-60 can be used to determine flash thickness and the thickness-to-width ratio based on the weight of the forged part when carbon and alloy steels are being forged.

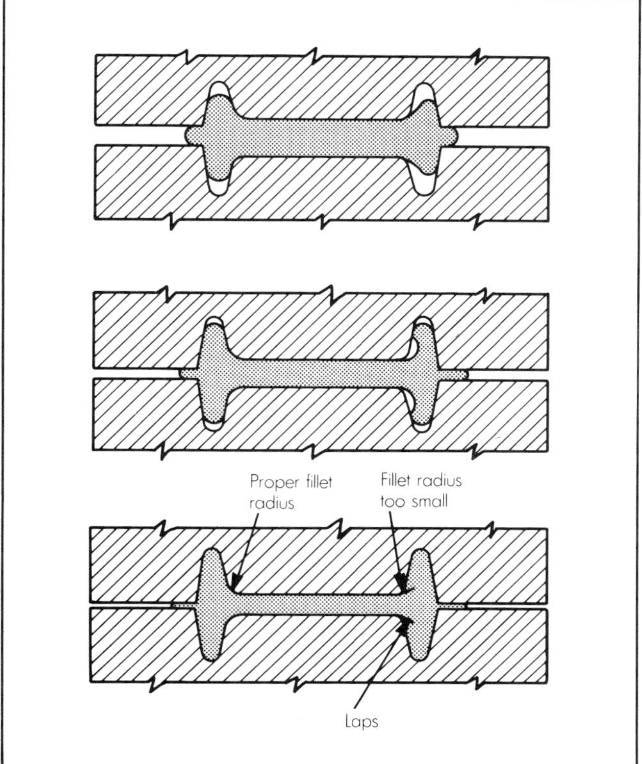


**Fig. 15-59 Illustration showing the influence of fillet radius on metal flow during progressive stages of die closure. (*Forging Industry Association*)**

# TOOLING

*Flash gutter.* The gutter is thicker than the flash land and provides a cavity in the die halves for the excess material. The gutter should be large enough so that it does not fill up with excess material or become pressurized. The four gutter designs commonly used are parallel, conventional, tapered open, and tapered closed (see Fig. 15-61). Choice of gutter design is generally determined by the type of forging equipment used, the properties of the material being forged, the forging temperature, and the overall pressures exerted in the die cavity.

## Die Material

Impression dies are usually made from low-alloy, prehardened steels containing 0.35-0.50% carbon, 1.50-5.00% chromium, and additions of nickel, molybdenum, tungsten, and vanadium. It is difficult to heat treat die blocks safely after machining because thermal distortion could destroy or reduce the dimensional accuracy of the impressions. Therefore, die blocks are machined after the desired hardness has been achieved through heat treating. Die blocks containing shallow or simple impressions can be hardened to $R_C50$. However, die blocks with deep impressions, ribs, or complex designs require softer, tougher materials to minimize cracking and die breakage.

When the volume of parts is high and the size of the forging is limited, die inserts can be incorporated in the die block to minimize wear. Inserts are generally installed in locations that are prone to excessive wear due to complexity of design and material flow. Table 15-18 lists recommended die block materials to use for forging various materials. Several proprietary tool steels are also used in manufacturing die blocks for less severe applications. Hot die and isothermal forging require nickel-based superalloys and other specialized die materials.

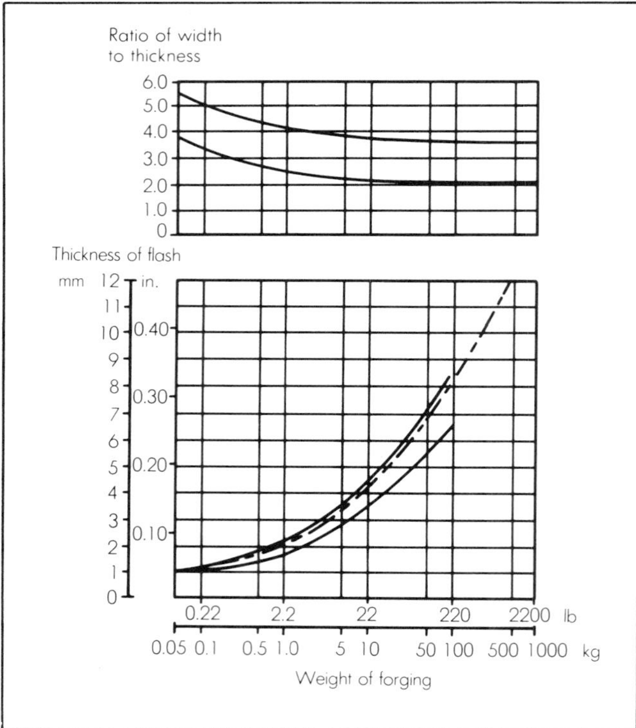


**Fig. 15-60 Graph for determining flash thickness and flash width-to-thickness ratio based on the weight of the forging. (*Battelle Columbus Laboratories*)**

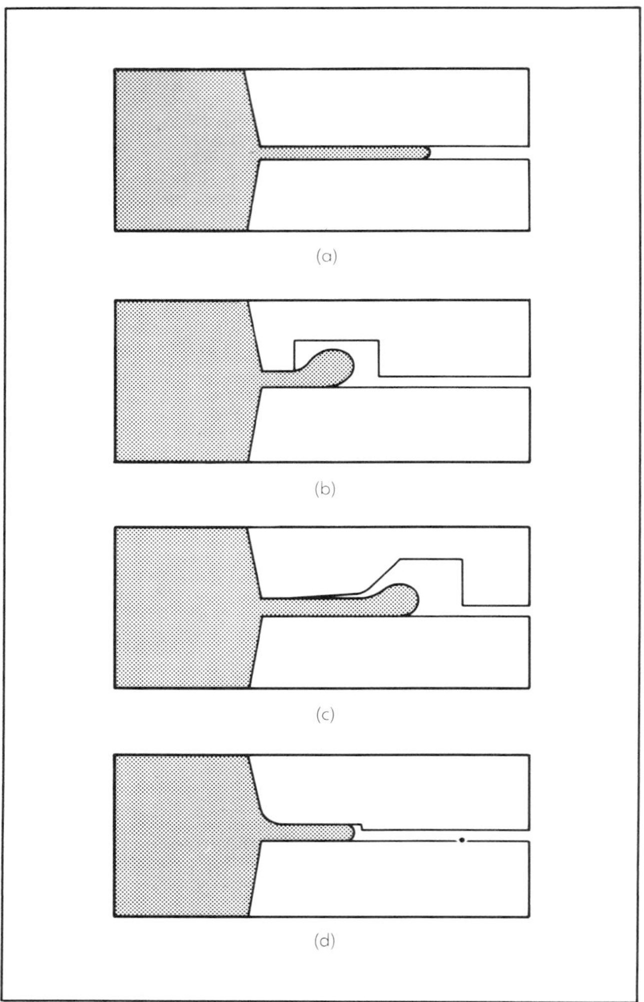


**Fig. 15-61 Four commonly used gutter designs: (a) parallel, (b) conventional, (c) tapered open, (d) tapered closed. (*American Machinist*)**

## FORGING MACHINE DIES

Forging machines are capable of upsetting, deep-piercing, splitting, bending, and extruding simple or intricate shapes. The workpiece is gripped in the cavities or passes contained in the die halves, and the header tool forces the heated material into the die cavity. Figure 15-62 illustrates a typical three-pass operation to produce gear blanks.

### Design Guidelines

The cavities can be located either in the die halves or the header tool. For some upsetting applications, the cavities may be located in both the die halves and the header tool and the upsetting may be performed in more than one pass.

Generally, each pass is forged with only one blow by the header tool. To prevent buckling during forging, the length of unsupported workpiece, $B$, should be less than three times the diameter or square of the bar, $A$ (see Fig. 15-63). When the material is upset in the die cavity (see Fig. 15-64), the unsupported workpiece length, $B$, can be greater than three times the bar diameter, $A$, if the die cavity diameter, $D$, is less

**TABLE 15-18**
**Recommended Die Materials for Closed Die Forging Dies**

| Material Forged | Application | Die Material* | Hardness, $R_C$ |
|---|---|---|---|
| Aluminum | Punches and dies | H11, H12 or H13 | 44-48 |
| | Die inserts | H11, H12 or H13 | 46-50 |
| Brass | Punches, dies, and inserts | H21, H11 or H13 | 48-52 |
| Steel | Punches, dies, and inserts | H13, H12 or H19 | 38-48 |
| | Trimmer dies | D2, A2 or hardweld on cutting edge of cold-rolled steel | 58-60 |

(*Crucible Specialty Metals Div., Colt Industries*)

* The recommended grade is listed first, and alternate grades follow.

than one and one-half times the bar diameter, *A*. An unsupported workpiece length greater than three times bar diameter can also be forged in the header tool (see Fig. 15-65). In this type of application, the header tool should have a tapered recess that contains the same volume as the unsupported workpiece. The small diameter of the taper, *d*, should be the same as the bar diameter, *A*, and the depth of the recess, *E*, should be less than two and one-half times the bar diameter, *A*.

## Die Materials

Material selection of the dies is based on the type of material forged, the design of the tools, and the number of parts produced. Inserts are often used in the header tools and the die halves to produce small quantities of a particular part and to minimize die wear inherent in certain part designs. Inserts can be held in place with adapter blocks, set screws, or press fit.

Simple cross sections made from carbon or low-alloy steels and in small quantities (approximately 100 parts) are normally forged in die halves made from 4150 alloy steel blocks hardened to $R_C$ 38-42. For larger production runs and for more complex cross sections, tool steels such as H11 hardened to $R_C$ 46-50 are selected for the die halves. For stainless steels and heat-resistant alloys, the die halves are made entirely from proprietary tool steels or tool steel inserts.

Header tools are made from tool steels such as W1 or H11 hardened to $R_C$ 42-46 and $R_C$ 46-50 respectively for parts made

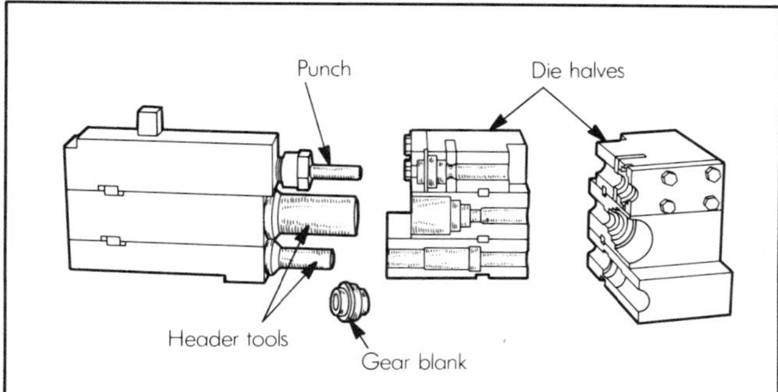


**Fig. 15-62 Set of dies used in a vertical-type forging machine. Gathering takes place in the top die; upsetting to final dimensions takes place in the center die; and separating from the bar takes place in the top die.**

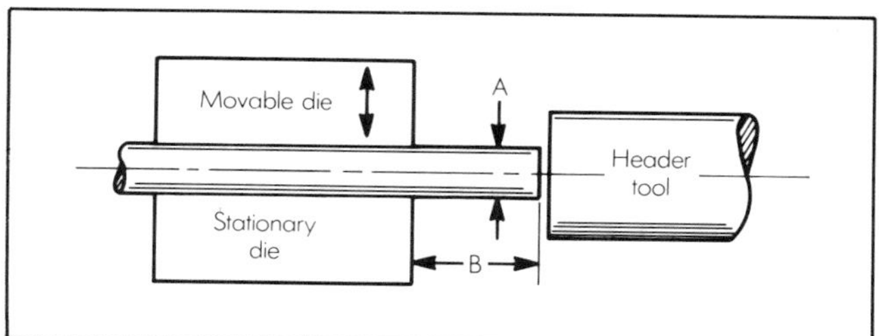


**Fig. 15-63 Dies used to forge unsupported stock in forging machine. Maximum unsupported length, *B*, is three times bar diameter, *A*.** (*Hill Acme Co.*)

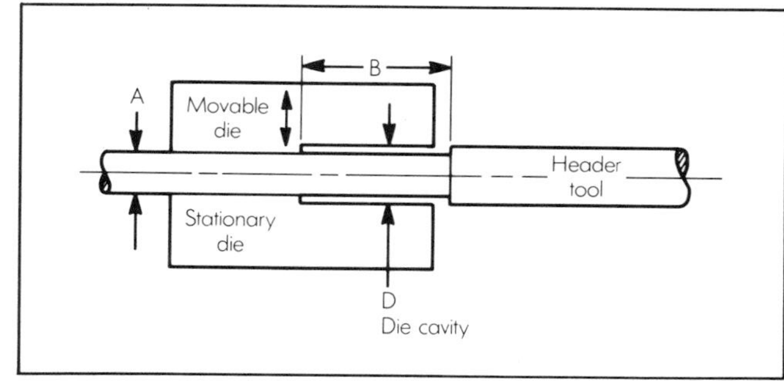


**Fig. 15-64 Dies used to forge stock in die cavity of forging machine. Diameter of die cavity, *D*, must be less than one and one half times the size of bar diameter, *A*, to prevent buckling.** (*Hill Acme Co.*)

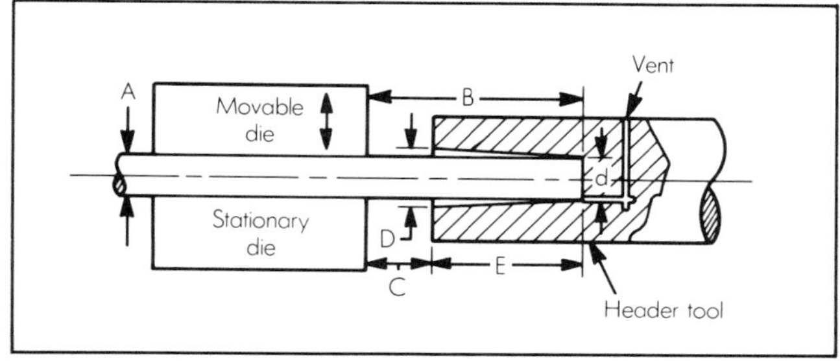


**Fig. 15-65 Design of dies when material is displaced in header tool cavity.** (*Hill Acme Co.*)

from carbon, alloy, stainless, and heat-resistant steels. Inserts made of H11 hardened to $R_C$ 48-52 are also employed for large production runs of stainless steel parts.

## TRIMMING AND PUNCHING DIES

Trimming is the removal of flash that is produced on the part during the forging operation. Trimming may also be used to remove some of the draft material thereby producing straight side walls on the part. It is usually performed by a top die and bottom die that are shaped to the contour of the part. The top die acts as a punch to push the part through the lower die containing the cutting edge. If the top die does not follow the contour of the part, the part may be deformed during the trimming operation. Figure 15-66 illustrates typical tools for trimming impression-die forgings.

An operation similar to trimming is punching in which excess material on an internal surface is removed (see Fig. 15-67). To ensure accurate cuts, punching and trimming operations are often performed simultaneously (see Fig. 15-68).

Materials for trimming and punching dies are selected based on the type of material to be trimmed and whether the part is to be trimmed hot or cold. Punches are normally made from proprietary tool steels when carbon and stainless steels are to be trimmed, and from 1020 steel that has been hard faced when nonferrous alloys are to be trimmed. The trimming die, or bottom die, can be made from D2 or A2 alloys. It can also be made from cold-rolled steel that has a high strength alloy hard facing applied to the cutting edge.

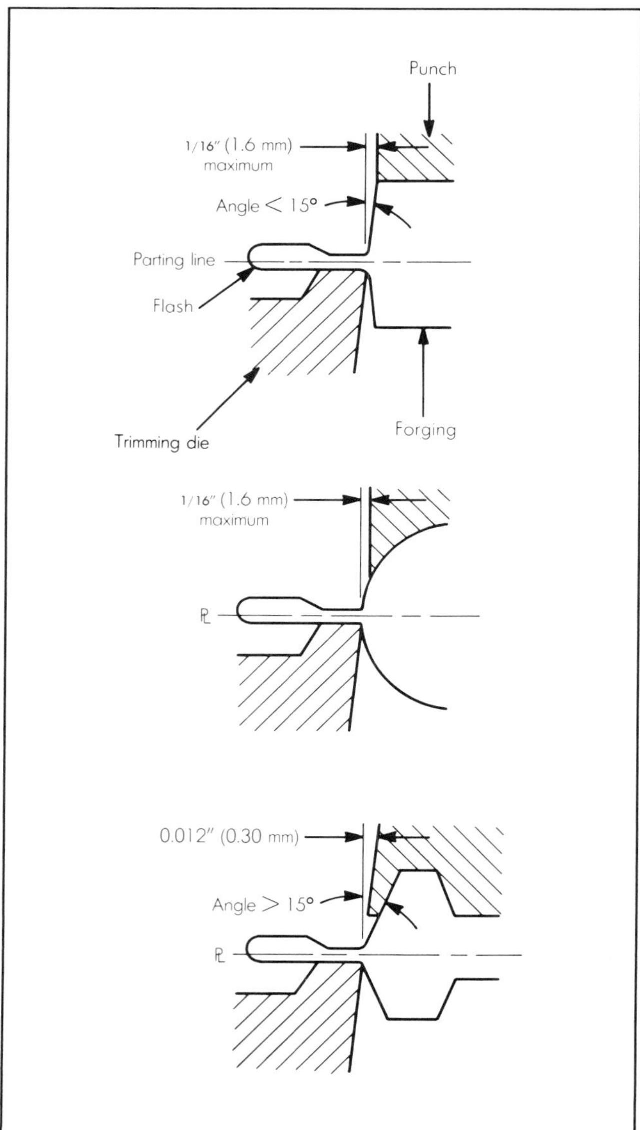


**Fig. 15-66 Typical trimming tools for removing flash from impression-die forgings. (*Forging Industry Association*)**

## OTHER TOOLING

Other types of tooling employed in forging include dies used in roll forging, wedge rolling, radial forging, and ring rolling.

### Roll Forging Tooling

The tools used in roll forging consist of a pair of ring segments, or dies, for each forming pass. The segments can be mounted on the rolls individually for single-pass operation or with other pairs of ring segments for use in multiple-pass

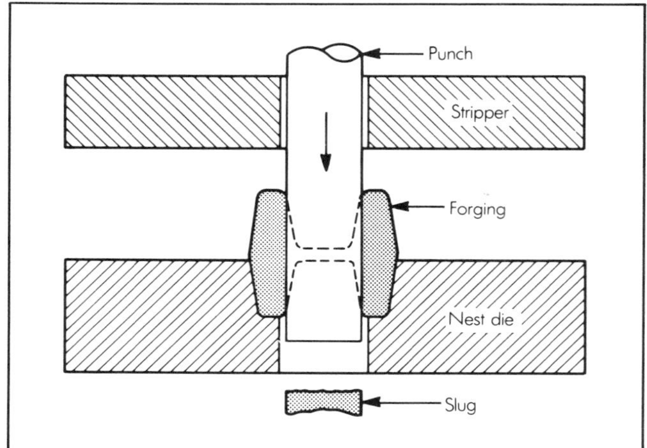


**Fig. 15-67 Schematic diagram of typical punching operation on an impression-die forging. (*Forging Industry Association*)**

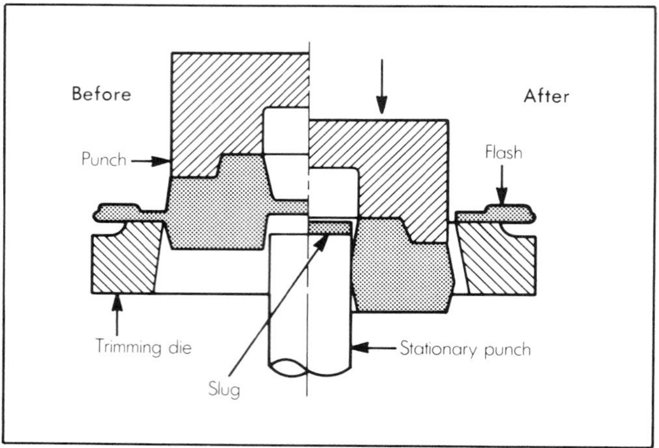


**Fig. 15-68 Schematic diagram of combined trimming and punching operation. (*Forging Industry Association*)**

operation. An undercut step maintains the rings in the proper location, and thrust bolts fasten the segments to the rolls. Keys are designed in the rolls to absorb the tangential thrust.

The lengths of the segments are determined by the length of the workpieces. Generally, the segments are designed to forge the workpiece up to half the roll circumference (see Fig. 15-69, *a*). Short workpieces can be forged in quarterly segments used in series and offset by 142° (see Fig. 15-69, *b*). Long workpieces, such as truck axles, can be forged using up to three-fourths of the ring circumference.

### Wedge Rolling Tooling

The wedge-shaped dies used in wedge rolling are bolted to T-slots in the peripheries of the rolls. The dies can be designed to permit single-pass or multiple-pass operation. Dies are usually made from H11 or H13 tool steel.

### Radial Forging Tooling

The dies used on radial forging machines contain two or four segments mounted in dieholders located on top of the drive housing. The die cross section can be designed to permit circular, square, or tapered parts to be forged. Dies can be made from nickel-chromium steel with a high strength alloy hard facing applied or from a high-strength, nickel-based alloy.

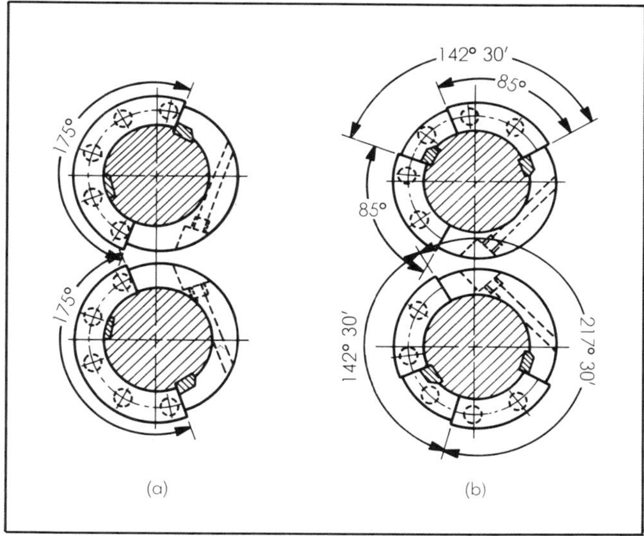


**Fig. 15-69 Roll forging dies: (a) die segments up to one half roll circumference and (b) dies used for forging short workpieces.** (*Verson Allsteel Press Co.*)

### Ring Rolling Tooling

Deformation of rings on a ring rolling machine is performed between an inner mandrel and a main roll. The inner mandrel and main roll can be cylindrical or designed to form a particular finished shape in the ring.

## COMPUTER APPLICATIONS

Computer aided design and manufacturing (CAD/CAM) techniques are being increasingly applied in forging technology. Using the three-dimensional description of a machined part, which may have been computer designed, it is possible to generate the geometry of the associated forging. For this purpose, it is best to use a CAD/CAM system with software for handling geometry, drafting, dimensioning, and numerical control (NC) machining. Thus, the forging sections can be obtained from a common database.

Using well-proven analyses based on the slab method or other techniques, the forging load and stresses can be obtained and flash dimensions can be selected for each section, permitting metal flow to be regarded as approximately two-dimensional (plane strain or axisymmetric). In some relatively simple section geometries, a computer simulation can be conducted to evaluate initial estimates on blocker or preform sections. Once the blocker and finisher sections are obtained to the designer's satisfaction, this geometric database can be utilized to write NC part programs and thereby obtain NC tapes or discs for cutting the forging die (or the die used for electrodischarge machining of the forging die).

This CAD/CAM procedure is still in a stage of development. In the near future, this technology can be expected to evolve in two main directions: (1) handling the geometry of complex forgings, for example, three-dimensional description, automatic drafting and sectioning, and NC machining, and (2) utilizing design analysis, for example, calculation of stresses in the forging and stress concentrations in the dies, prediction of elastic deflections in the dies, metal flow analysis, and blocker/preform design.

# FORGING LUBRICANTS

Since the early years of forging, lubricants of one type or another have been utilized to aid the forging process. At first, the lubricants used were essentially parting agents such as salt, soda ash, and sawdust. Recently, however, forging lubricants have come under serious scientific scrutiny, resulting in a wide range of lubricants for a variety of applications. The proper forging lubricant, correctly applied, not only pays for itself but yields a considerable profit in areas such as increased production, improved tool and die life, and a better working environment.

## LUBRICANT REQUIREMENTS

A forging lubricant, in order to be effective, must function in several different ways. The lubricant must provide a physical barrier between the die surface and the workpiece. The film deposited by the lubricant and cured by the die must adhere to the metal surface and not be removed under the pressures achieved by the workpiece's acting against the die surface during the forging operation. A poor barrier coat allows metal-to-metal contact between the workpiece and the die, causing scratching, galling of the workpiece, and excessive die wear. Under more extreme conditions, the workpiece welds to the die causing rejection of the workpiece and extensive damage to the die. Many times after severe welding, the die is irreparable. The lubricant must also provide a thermal barrier to reduce heat transfer between the workpiece and die. Excessive temperature fluctuations on the surface of the die can lead to premature die failure as a result of thermal fatigue.

# CHAPTER 15

## FORGING LUBRICANTS

The forging lubricant must permit a smooth, plastic flow of metal into the die cavity by providing the proper coefficient of friction. A forging lubricant with a coefficient of friction that is too high causes an incomplete fill and thus a rejected forging. A coefficient of friction that is too low, however, can result in a rejected forging due to a rough surface finish.

A safe working environment for personnel and equipment is another important function of the forging lubricant. The lubricant should be nontoxic, nonfuming, and nonflammable to ensure operator safety. To prevent damage to the equipment, the lubricant should be noncorrosive to the various equipment components and tooling and should form no compressed gases that result in a potentially explosive atmosphere. It should also be cost-effective in long term usage.

### TYPES OF LUBRICANTS

The three types of lubricants that are generally used in forging are oil and graphite, water and graphite, and synthetic lubricants. Table 15-19 shows the three types of lubricants with their advantages and disadvantages. (Refer to Chapter 3, "Lubricants," for a complete description of the various lubricants.)

#### Oil and Graphite

While this type of lubricant often provides satisfactory performance in the lubrication of dies, its use creates undesirable fire and smoke, as well as an atmosphere contaminated with graphite dust. The use of graphite and oil lubricants is declining throughout the forging industry and is generally restricted to hydraulic press forging of aluminum, selected military shell casings, and specialized hammer work. Oil-and-graphite forging lubricants are commonly swabbed onto the dies, in the concentrated form.

#### Water and Graphite

Water-dispersed graphite compounds have served widely as forging lubricants since about 1970. Such products use fine graphite particles as their main lubricant, along with various specific additives to enhance their performance. This type of lubricant is diluted with water and can be applied by spraying or swabbing. The spraying method is generally preferred and is readily adaptable to installations incorporating automatic spraying techniques.

Graphite lubricants have proven safe, easy to use, and cost effective. Their main drawback is in the area of housekeeping, as accumulations of graphite in the press area can be undesirable to worker safety and health. Graphite residues may also cause shorting in unshielded or exposed electrical circuits. However, proper venting procedures in the forging area help to reduce graphite accumulations.

#### Synthetic Lubricants

The desire to prevent fire, smoke, and graphite accumulation has led the forging industry to develop synthetic water-soluble lubricants. These lubricants do not contain any graphite pigments; and as with other water-based lubricants, the most effective method of application is spraying. Spraying provides sufficient atomization to ensure uniform die coverage. Extensive field evaluation of synthetic forging lubricants has demonstrated that, when properly applied, synthetic forging lubricants result in improved cost effectiveness and better working conditions. However, they have limited performance capabilities. These lubricants are generally used when metal movement is limited or when part configurations are simple.

### LUBRICANT SELECTION

Using the proper lubricant can benefit any type of forging, from simple parts in shallow cavities to intricate forms with exotic metals. It is important to recognize that there is no perfect lubricant for every operation. No single chemical formulation provides the ultimate in metal movement, the longest die life, the cleanest working environment, the lowest cost, and yet is applicable to all types of metals.

The primary factors involved in lubricant selection are the forging temperature, die temperature, type of material, forging equipment used, method of application, complexity of shape, rate of production, and environmental regulations. Selection should be done with the assistance of the lubricant supplier to achieve optimum lubricating performance and minimum lubricant cost.

#### Die Temperature

Die temperature is a critical part of lubricant selection.

**TABLE 15-19**
**Types of Forging Lubricants**

| Type | Advantages | Disadvantages |
|---|---|---|
| Oil and graphite | Can be swabbed or sprayed effectively.<br>Good die life.<br>Good performance over a wide range of die temperatures. | Produces fire and smoke.<br>Costly because of inability to dilute with water.<br>Explosive nature may shorten die life. |
| Water and graphite | Good cost effectiveness because of ability to dilute with water.<br>Improved die life when applied properly.<br>Eliminates fire and smoke.<br>Provides die cooling. | Method of application is important for success.<br>Graphite creates poor environmental conditions. |
| Synthetic (nongraphited or nonpigmented) | Improved housekeeping.<br>Operator acceptance.<br>Water dilution creates cost effectiveness.<br>Good die life when properly applied. | Spray application is important.<br>Possible metal flow problems.<br>Odd-shaped forgings can be difficult. |

(*Pennwalt Corporation*)

# FORGING LUBRICANTS

Forging lubricants are formulated to function as a dry uniform coating. Too little heat leaves a wet, ineffective coating, and too much heat does not allow the proper wetting of the entire die surface.

Normal die temperatures operate in the 250-550° F (121-288° C) range. In this temperature range, a water-based lubricant is often used to form a thin, continuous dry-graphite film. As the lubricant comes in contact with the hot die surface, the water rapidly flashes off as steam. The result is that there are no viscosity variations and no compressed gases to prevent proper cavity fill and to cause explosions which would damage the equipment.

Die temperatures in excess of 550° F (288° C) may require special lubricant formulations. A richer lubricant mixture and a higher spray pressure are helpful in coating the die at higher temperatures. Water-dispersed graphite lubricants with additives can be used if extreme care is utilized in application so that a uniform lubricant film is formed over the entire die surface. Under these conditions the water carrier flashes off as the solid film forms over the entire surface.

## Type of Material

On certain ferrous materials, the oxide film that is produced on the workpiece during heating is sufficient to provide adequate lubrication. However, this film and the scale produced may cause premature loss of die life; therefore, lubricants are generally applied during most operations. Table 15-20 provides the recommended type of lubricant to use when forging different materials.

**Aluminum.** Since aluminum does not form an oxide film when heated, direct metal-to-metal contact causes seizing and galling. Hence, it is important to have good, continuous lubrication. Lubricants used for aluminum-alloy forgings vary from kerosene to oil-graphite suspensions. In general, dies are sprayed with flake graphite mixed with water or petroleum-based carriers. Water-soluble soaps are sometimes added to the graphite mixture for forging narrow rib sections.

Another technique, referred to as black etching, consists of dipping aluminum forging blanks in 10% sodium hydroxide to produce a slightly roughened surface for better lubricant adhesion. The forging blanks are then dipped in colloidal graphite and dried prior to heating. If necessary, dies are sprayed additionally with flake-graphite mixtures. This technique reduces the heating time in the furnace, eliminates seizing and galling, and gives better lubricity and surface finish. However, this technique may cause some surface pitting if the forgings are not cleaned soon after forging. During forging, excess lubricant is blown off with compressed air.

**Magnesium.** The lubricant used in magnesium forging is usually a dispersion of fine graphite in water, light oil, or kerosene swabbed or sprayed on the hot dies. The carrier evaporates or burns off and leaves a fine film of graphite. Lampblack applied directly from the sooty flame of an oil or kerosene torch is also frequently used. Sometimes the dies are lightly lubricated after billets have been partially forged, or the forging billet is dipped in the lubricant before heating. Fluid lubricants such as grease and oils are seldom used, because they promote rupturing. With magnesium, care should be taken to ensure that the coating of lubricant is thin and has complete coverage.

**Copper.** Spraying with dispersions of graphite in water or swabbing with mixtures of graphite and oil generally serves to provide the lubrication needed for forging copper alloys.

**Steels.** A wide variety of lubricants are used for forging steel. The most popular lubricants are graphite suspensions; the new synthetics; and to a lesser extent, salts, oils, and sawdust. For forgings in dies with deep recesses, oils with graphite and water-dispersed graphite lubricants are favored; for shallow impressions, various graphited suspensions and synthetics are preferred. Austenitic stainless steels have a tendency to weld in dies during forging because they do not form much scale. Because of this, water-based and oil-based suspensions of graphite are frequently used.

In specialized cases, a glass coating is used as a lubricant in

**TABLE 15-20**
**Suggested Lubricants for Various Materials**

| Material | Pigment | Dispersing Carrier | Percent of Pigment* | Remarks |
|---|---|---|---|---|
| Aluminum | Graphite | Oil, Solvent | 5-15% | For hydraulic press forging. Used when dies are in excess of 600° F (315° C). |
| Aluminum, brass | Graphite | Solvent, Light oil, Water | 2-8% | Lower die temperatures in the range of 200° F (93° C). |
| Aluminum, brass, carbon steels | Graphite or other pigment | Water, Sol-vent, Oil | 2-8% | Normal die temperatures, 250-550° F (121-288° C). Lubricant versatile for forging a wide variety of sizes and shapes. |
| Carbon steels, high-strength alloys | Graphite | Water, Oil | 2-8% also 2-12% | Higher die temperatures, 550° F (288° C) and above, application critical particularly with water-based products. Oil can be used effectively for large hammer. |
| Superalloys, titanium | Ceramic and graphite | Alcohol, Water, Xylene, 1·1·1 Trichlore-thane | Grapite 2-8% Ceramic used as received | Ceramic coating applied to workpiece and allowed to dry. Graphite in water mixture sprayed on die surface. |

*Solids calculated at the spray orifice

(*Russell Products Co.*)

# FORGING LUBRICANTS

press forging. It is applied by either dipping the heated forging in molten glass or sprinkling it with glass powder. The disadvantage in using glass is the tendency of glass to accumulate in deep cavities, thus inhibiting metal flow and complete die filling. Also, if enough heat is not retained in the part, the glass tends to solidify and acts as an abrasive rather than as a lubricant.

In addition to the lubricants applied to the steel forging, the oxide film on the dies after tempering serves as a parting agent and provides a bond for the graphite lubricants. To reduce thermal chilling during forging, graphite-coated asbestos paper or fiberglass provides a thermal barrier between the dies and the forging and at the same time acts as a lubricant.

**Titanium.** At forging temperatures, titanium alloys are extremely reactive. Special precautions must be taken to protect the workpiece from atmospheric attack and to isolate the workpiece and die to prevent galling or welding. The titanium workpiece is sandblasted, wiped with a clean rag, coated at room temperature with a slurry of ceramic or glass, and air-dried before heating for forging. In addition, the dies are sprayed with water-based graphite mixtures. Graphite-coated asbestos paper or fiberglass is also used to provide a thermal barrier between the die and the workpiece when forging large parts on large mechanical or hydraulic presses.

**Heat-resistant superalloys.** The most common lubricants for superalloys are mixtures of oil and graphite or of water and graphite sprayed onto the dies. Certain glasses are particularly useful for coating the alloys that have narrow forging temperature ranges. Asbestos sheet, asbestos cloth, fiberglass, mica, or sawdust are sometimes used in conjunction with oil-graphite lubricants. These materials are employed mainly to minimize die chilling when parts with a minimum of detail and generous contours are to be forged in hydraulic presses. For forging nickel-based superalloys, sulfur-free lubricants should be used; lubricants containing molybdenum disulfide or other sulfur compounds are believed to have harmful effects. For these alloys, a special graphite grease is frequently sprayed onto the dies.

**Refractory metals.** The liquid oxide formed on molybdenum during heating serves as an excellent lubricant. However, to reduce metal loss, glass coatings are often used on large forgings. These coatings also reduce heat losses during forging. Colloidal graphite and molybdenum disulfide are suitable lubricants for small forgings.

For beryllium forging, the dies are heated to 800° F (427° C) and sprayed with standard oil-based graphite lubricant. The workpiece is etched in a solution of 3% sulfuric acid and 3% phosphoric acid and coated with a low-temperature, glass-frit enamel. If two or more forging stages are required for producing a part, the blanks are vapor-blasted, etched, and recoated between each operation. For forging conical shapes, the workpiece is enclosed in a can or a jacket. Lubrication techniques in this case have significant influence on the flow of both the canning material and the beryllium, which should be as uniform as possible from surface to surface. Therefore, different lubricants are preferred for the opposed dies to achieve balanced flow and to minimize the chance of jacket failure.

A coating of Al-10Cr-2Si alloy, 0.002-0.004" (0.05-0.10 mm) thick, protects columbium against atmospheric contamination at temperatures between 2000 and 2600° F (1093 and 1427° C). A glass-frit coating can also be applied to the workpiece before it is heated in a gas-fired furnace.

Two types of coatings, aluminides and glasses, have been used successfully for protection against oxidation when forging tantalum. Mixtures of graphite and molybdenum dispersed in water are also used. Aluminum-alloy coatings are applied by dipping the tantalum workpiece in the molten alloy at 1650-1700° F (900-926° C) for about 10 minutes.

A coating 0.003" (0.08 mm) thick of 50Sn-50Al on Ta-10W alloy has proved effective against oxidation for workpieces heated in air up to 3000° F (1649° C). In forging at 2150-2400° F (1177-1315° C), a hot-dipped Al-12Si alloy has provided effective protection of the Ta-30Cb-7.5V and Ta-10Hf-5W alloy. Aluminum-alloy coatings, while providing the best oxidation resistance, are generally poor lubricants. Thus, for forging, glass coatings are preferred since they offer both protection and lubrication. In the temperature range of 2000-2400° F (1093-1315° C), a variety of borosilicate glasses are generally used.

Tungsten oxide, which becomes molten and volatilizes at forging temperatures, serves as an effective lubricant for forging tungsten. Mixtures of graphite and molybdenum disulfide are also sprayed on the dies. These films provide lubricity and act as parting agents which aid in the removal of the parts from the dies. A variety of glass coatings are also used for protection and lubrication, but their progressive buildup in the dies interferes with complete die filling. To minimize die chilling, asbestos cloth, paper, or fiberglass is used between the forging blank and the die.

## LUBRICANT APPLICATION

In hot forging, the workpiece is heated to 2000-2500° F (1090-1370° C), the appropriate lubricant is applied to the die surfaces, and then the workpiece is forged.

One of the most overlooked areas in forging operations is the method of lubricant application. The method of application has a significant influence on the quality of the part being forged and is often more important than lubricant selection. If the lubricant is not in the right place, it is impossible for it to perform its function. Therefore, a great deal of care must be taken to achieve a uniform coat over the entire die surface. A bare spot or a coating of lubricant that is too light can allow metal-to-metal contact and the subsequent scratching, galling, and possibly welding which causes rejects and die damage. In a swabbing application, if the lower die cavity is coated while the upper die face is neglected, the erosion of the upper die face can increase by as much as 50%.

Lubricant application can take place by several different methods. The simplest of these is swabbing, in which the swab is immersed in a solution of the forging compound and brushed over the die surface. In many shops, this has given way to spraying, which is highly recommended for water-based lubricants. Spraying may be accomplished by the use of a hand-held gun or spray nozzles mounted to the frame. The nozzles can be fixed or reciprocating and are actuated by the operator or by a programmed spray system. When spraying methods are employed, it is important that good mixing and agitation techniques are followed. Another method of lubricant application is by dipping the heated workpiece in the lubricant solution. The dipped workpiece is usually air-dried before it is forged.

The thickness of the lubricant film depends on the type of metal being forged. An excessive amount of lubricant does not increase lubrication since the unnecessary lubricant is squeezed out during the forging process. An excessive amount of lubricant is wasteful, dirties the area and workpiece, causes die build-up, and adds to pollution in the atmosphere.

Generally, the lubricant is only applied to the die surfaces. However, when titanium, stainless steel, or superalloys are being forged, a ceramic coating is applied to the workpiece in conjunction with the die lubricant. The ceramic coating provides protection, insulation, and additional lubrication of the workpiece during the forging operation. For additional information concerning types of lubricants, application methods, waste treatment and disposal, cleaning, quality control, and lubricant troubleshooting, Chapter 3, "Lubricants," in this volume should be referenced.

# TROUBLESHOOTING AND SAFETY

Although hot forging provides the opportunity to produce parts exhibiting characteristics not normally attainable by other metal forming operations, there are several defects that may occur in the workpiece as a result of improper forging design and forging techniques. These defects are not always detectable to the eye; therefore, either nondestructive or destructive inspection techniques must be employed to detect them. Another problem that occurs in hot forging is die failure.

## FORGING DEFECTS

To ensure that forgings are free of defects, the starting material should be free of any internal or external flaws which lower the finished quality of the forging. Throughout the forging operation the temperature of the workpiece must be monitored to maintain correct forging temperatures. Correct preforming operations help to ensure proper grain orientation and material flow during the finish forging procedures. Some of the more common defects that occur are given in Table 15-21. The possible causes and suggested solutions are also provided.

## DIE FAILURE

Die failure in hot forging can generally be attributed to erosion of the die surface, plastic deformation, thermal fatigue, and mechanical fatigue. The indications that a die is beginning to fail or has failed include component dimensions falling outside the tolerance limit, ejection difficulties, and gross die breakage. Table 15-22 and Table 15-23 show the various problems related to die failure and list the possible causes of those problems along with solutions to correct the problem. Figure 15-70 shows the locations on a die at which the various problems are most likely to occur.

### Erosion

Erosion is caused by the action of the forging sliding over a point in a die. The points that first show the effects of erosion are corners in the die cavities. The frictional conditions during forging have a great deal to do with the rate at which erosion takes place. If the area of the die is unlubricated, erosion takes place very fast because of temporary local welding and removal of small particles from the die.[20]

### Plastic Deformation

Plastic deformation, like erosion, occurs at corners in the die and is caused by the softening of the top layer of die material. Areas that are greatly affected are corner radii on punches, corners of bosses in the die, and the radii between the flash land and die cavity. If plastic deformation occurs at the flash land, the flash gap is actually reduced in thickness and the radius between the cavity and flash land becomes larger than the intended radius.[21]

### Thermal Fatigue

Thermal fatigue is caused by cyclic variations in temperature. Repeated and localized heating and cooling to which die top surfaces are exposed during forging cause dimensional changes that develop fatigue stresses in this layer. The top surface of the die is rapidly heated while in contact with the hot billet, but its thermal expansion is to some extent prevented by the comparatively cooler layers surrounding it. This promotes buildup of compressive stresses in the list layer; and when it happens often enough, the surface actually cracks. Thermal fatigue is a complicated process influenced by die and stock temperatures, contact times, temperature fluctuations, and production rates.[22]

### Mechanical Fatigue

The stress changes occurring during the forging cycle can cause mechanical fatigue. Mechanical fatigue usually occurs in fillets in the die, such as the bottom of cavities, because they act as stress risers. Mechanical fatigue life of materials is much shorter when the peak stress is beyond the elastic limit of the die material. Experiments testing the fatigue strength of various alloyed steels have indicated that fatigue strength decreases with an increase in temperature.[23]

## INSPECTION TECHNIQUES

Two techniques are commonly employed when inspecting forgings: nondestructive and destructive.

### Nondestructive Techniques

A nondestructive test is an examination of an object or material in any manner that does not affect its future usefulness. The purpose of the test may be to detect internal or surface flaws, measure thickness, determine material structure or composition, or measure or detect properties of the material.

Before the forged workpiece is tested, the scale and lubricant should be removed. It is also good practice to prepare the surface by acid or caustic etching. Some of the common nondestructive tests are magnetic particle inspection, visual penetrant inspection, and ultrasonic inspection. For a more comprehensive discussion on these and other techniques, refer to Volume IV, *Quality Control and Assembly*, in this Handbook series.

**Magnetic particle inspection.** This inspection technique is used only on metallic materials that can be intensely magnetized. It may be used to detect surface discontinuities, but interpretation of the results is difficult.

**Visual penetrant inspection.** In this technique a penetrating liquid containing a die or a fluorescent filler is applied to the forging surface. A capillary action draws the penetrant into the discontinuities. The excess penetrant is wiped off, and a developing material is applied to draw out the penetrant from

# TROUBLESHOOTING AND SAFETY

**TABLE 15-21**
**Common Defects in Forged Workpieces**[19]

| Forging Operation | Problem | Possible Causes | Suggested Solutions |
|---|---|---|---|
| Upsetting | Cracking on barrel | Light seams on material. | Allow workpiece to remain in furnace for an extended time to scale off defect. |
| | | Heavy seams on material. | Reject material or remove seams by grinding. |
| | | Temperature rise during forging. | Reduce amount of reduction per pass. |
| | | Incorrect forging temperature. | Correct forging temperature. |
| | Rough surface | Coarse grain size (stainless steels, heat-resistant alloys) | Reduce forging temperature. Use billet with finer grain size. |
| Open and closed-die forging (flattening, drawing-out, fullering, rolling) | Cracking on edges | Forging temperature too high. | Reduce forging temperature. |
| | | Temperature rise during forging. | Reduce amount of reduction per pass. |
| | Center cracks (ends) | Temperature rise during forging. | Reduce amount of reduction per pass. |
| | | Coarse grain size. | Use light reductions followed by reheating to refine center grain size. |
| | | Defective center condition. | Review metallurgical quality. Replace material if necessary. |
| Closed-die forging | Laps | Incorrect preform design. | Redesign preform die. |
| | | Improper lubrication. | Use correct lubrication practice. |
| | | Die preform worn out. | Grind laps and restrike. |
| | Flow-through defect (rib-web part) | Excessive lubrication. | Reduce amount of lubricant. |
| | | Incorrect preform (blocker). | Correct preform or blocker die. |
| | Incomplete die filling | Dies too cold.<br>Improper lubricant.<br>Incorrect flash design.<br>Insufficient amount of material.<br>Incorrect preform design.<br>Equipment capacity too low.<br>Forging temperature too low.<br>Lubricant or scale build-up in die cavity. | Check all possible causes before assuming any single cause. Incorrect diagnosis can lead to die breakage. |
| | Depressions in forging surface | Improper oxide or scale cleaning techniques prior to forging. | Use correct cleaning techniques to remove oxide and scale build-up. |
| | Mismatch of forging halves | Incorrect die alignment or die shift. | Realign dies. |
| | Thermal cracks | Nonuniform material temperature. | Cool forged workpiece slowly in insulating material or in a furnace. |
| | | Forging heated too quickly. | If forging has been cooled at room temperature, reheat slowly through 1000-1500° F (540-815° C) range before heat treating. |
| | Cold shuts | Incorrect preform design. | Correct preform impressions. |
| | | Forging temperature too low. | Increase forging temperature. |
| | | Poor workmanship. | Retrain worker. |

**TABLE 15-22**
**Forging Die Failure**

| Problem | Possible Causes | Suggested Solutions |
|---|---|---|
| Erosion (Die wear) | Compressive pressure too great. | Use harder die material. |
| | Shear stresses. | Use weld overlay on die wear surfaces. |
| | Improper lubrication. | Use correct lubricant and application technique. |
| Thermal fatigue | Temperature variations. | Lower maximum forging temperature. |
| | | Use different die material containing chromium and tungsten. |
| Mechanical fatigue | Stress changes during forging cycle. | Lower forging temperatures. |
| | Exceeded stress of die material. | Harden die surfaces. |
| Plastic deformation | Die material too soft. | Use die material with higher hot hardness. |
| | | Use weld overlay on die wear surfaces. |

any discontinuities. The discontinuities can be detected by a stain that appears on the developing material or that is observed under an ultraviolet light.

**Ultrasonic inspection.** Ultrasonic inspection is the most common method used when inspecting forgings. Low-frequency mechanical vibrations are induced in the workpiece, and any defects cause a reflection of some of the energy. The reflection of the energy reduces the energy transmitted through the workpiece. A detector determines the location of the defect.

## Destructive Techniques

A destructive test is an examination of an object or material to determine its chemical composition, internal structure and grain pattern, and mechanical properties. Since these testing techniques render the product useless, they are only performed on a spot check basis or on test specimens.

## SAFETY

A primary consideration in forging is the safety of the operator. It is therefore necessary that each operator be properly trained prior to operating any forging equipment. It is also necessary that protective equipment be distributed and used by the operator to protect against injuries to the head, eyes, ears, feet, and body. This equipment is described in ANSI Standard B24.1.

The various forging machines should be equipped with the necessary controls to prevent accidental operation. This can be achieved through dual pushbutton controls and/or point-of-operation devices. Guards should be installed on all exterior moving parts to prevent accidental insertion of the hands or hair. Guards should also be installed to protect against flying scale or falling objects during the forging operation.

It is important that all forging equipment be properly maintained according to manufacturer's recommendations. During machine repair or die changing, the power to the machine should be locked out to prevent accidental operation and the ram should be blocked with blocks, wedges, or tubing capable of supporting the load. The strength and dimensions of the blocking material are given in the ANSI Standard previously mentioned. For additional information on safety, refer to Chapter 20, "Safety In Forming."

**TABLE 15-23**
**Failure of Forging Die Assemblies with Inserts and Slip Rings**

| Problem | Possible Causes | Suggested Solutions |
|---|---|---|
| Pickup and wear | Improper lubrication | Use correct lubricant and application techniques. |
| | Rough slug surfaces | |
| | Rough die surface | Regrind and finish die surface. |
| | Die insert too soft | Use harder material for die insert. |
| | Improper tool design | Redesign die insert/die. |
| Axial cracks | Insufficient prestress | Increase prestress by using additional retainer rings, increasing assembly diameter, increasing retainer rings length, or using stronger retainer rings. |
| | Working pressure exceeded | Reduce workpiece volume. Select material with proper flow stress. |
| Transverse cracks (extrusion die inserts) | Stress concentrations or triaxial stresses due to fatigue failure. | Use tougher die material. |
| | | Decrease hardness of tool steel inserts. |
| | | Redesign retainer ring. |

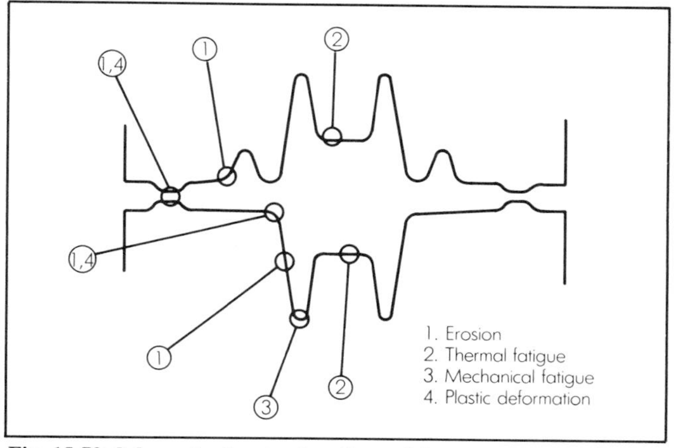


**Fig. 15-70 Schematic showing locations of the more common forging defects.** (*Battelle Columbus Laboratories*)

# CHAPTER 15

## REFERENCES

### References


1. *Open Die Forging Manual*, 3rd ed. (Ohio: Forging Industry Association, 1982), pp. 159-178.
2. Jon E. Jenson, ed. *Forging Industry Handbook* (Ohio: Forging Industry Association, 1966), pp. 417-438.
3. T. Altan et al., *Forging Equipment, Materials, and Practices* (Ohio: Battelle Columbus Laboratories Metalworking Division, 1973), pp. 461-466.
4. *Open Die Forging Manual, op. cit.*, p. 31.
5. *Ibid.* p. 91.
6. *Ibid.* p. 90.
7. T. Altan et al., *op. cit.*, p. 341.
8. John T. Winshop, "Fundamentals of Forging" *American Machinist*, (July 1978), pp. 116-117.
9. *Ibid.*
10. "Ferrous Metals," *Machine Design* (April 15, 1982), p. 34.
11. T. Altan et al., *op. cit.*, p. 197.
12. Winshop, *op. cit.*, pp. 116-117.
13. T. Altan et al., *op. cit.*, p. 204.
14. *Ibid.*, p. 206.
15. *Ibid.*, pp. 184-187.
16. *Ibid.*, p. 8.
17. *Ibid.*
18. Jon E. Jenson, ed., *op. cit.*, pp. 119-134.
19. T. Altan et al., *op. cit.*, p. 254.
20. *Ibid.*, pp. 450-451.
21. *Ibid.*
22. *Ibid.*
23. *Ibid.*


### Bibliography


Altan, T., and Nagpal, V. "Impression and Closed Die Forging," *International Metals Review* (December 1973).

Altan, Taylan. *Characteristic and Applications of Various Types of Forging Equipment*. SME Technical Paper MFR72-02, 1972.

American Society for Metals. *Metals Handbook*, Vol. 5, 8th ed. 1970.

Belmont, Kenneth J. *Wedgerolling for Preforms and as a Substitute for Machining*. SME Technical Paper MF74-606, 1974.

Beseler, Kay H. *Shape Rolling of Seamless Rings*. SME Technical Paper MF82-334, 1982.

Brass, Otto, and Altan, Taylan. *Selection of Equipment for Precision Forging of Turbine and Compressor Blades*. SME Technical Paper MF74-603, 1974.

Coyne, James E. *Recent Developments in Closed Die Forgings*. SME Technical Paper MF74-162, 1974.

Drabing, L. George. *Design Techniques for Multi-Impression Drop Forging*. SME Technical Paper MF76-919, 1976.

Forging Industry Association. "Forging Topics," Vol. 38, No. 1 (1980).

————. "Forging Topics," Vol. 38, No. 2 (1980).

————. *The Facts About Seamless Rolled Rings*, Cleveland, 1977.

Hayes, Arthur F. *History of the Production of Isothermal Forgings in Industry*. SME Technical Paper MF77-301, 1977.

Kulkarni, Kishor M. *Isothermal Forging—From Research to a Promising New Manufacturing Technology*. SME Technical Paper MF77-299, 1977.

Lahoti, G. D., and Altan, Taylan. *Design of Dies for Radial Forging of Rods and Tubes*. SME Technical Paper No. MF76-390, 1976.

Sabroff, A. M.; Boulger, F. W.; and Henning, H. J. *Forging Materials and Practices*. New York: Reinhold Book Corporation, 1968.

CHAPTER

16

# Casting

# CASTING

Casting is a manufacturing process in which molten metal is poured or injected and allowed to solidify in a suitably shaped mold cavity. During or after cooling, the cast part is removed from the mold and then processed for delivery.

Casting processes and cast-material technologies vary from simple to highly complex. Material and process selection depends on the part's complexity and function, the product's quality specifications, and the projected cost level. Table 16-1 indicates the range of materials that are feasible for use in parts made by various commonly used casting processes.[1]

Castings are parts that are made close to their final dimensions by a casting process. With a history dating back 6000 years, the various casting processes are in a state of continuous refinement and evolution as technological advances are being made.

## CASTING MOLD ELEMENTS

In Fig. 16-1, a typical green-sand mold section is depicted to illustrate the various basic elements that are common to most casting processes. In most casting processes, the terms used to describe the molds are the same. Molds are usually, but not always, made in two halves. Exceptions are the investment casting and coreless casting processes, in which one-piece molds are used, and die casting and permanent or semipermanent-mold casting, which may use molds or dies made up of more than two parts for casting complex shapes.

In most processes, the upper half of the mold is called the cope and the lower half is referred to as the drag. Cores made of sand or metal are placed in the mold cavity to form inner surfaces of the casting. The mold requires a gating system to distribute metal in the mold and risers (liquid reservoirs) to feed the casting as it solidifies. The sprue is the channel, usually vertical, through which the metal enters. A runner, usually horizontal, leads the metal into the mold. The metal leaves the runner through a gate to enter the mold cavity or a riser above or adjacent to the cavity. A riser is a reservoir connected to the cavity to provide liquid metal to the casting to offset shrinkage as the casting solidifies. (Additional definitions are provided in the Nomenclature section of this chapter.)

## GENERAL CHARACTERISTICS

In many applications, castings offer cost and performance advantages because their shape, composition, structure, and properties can be tailored for a specific end product. The precision casting processes also offer near-net-shape economic benefits in materials, labor, and energy usage.

Except for certain high-volume production items, such as automotive parts, cast materials usually are produced in batches or melt-lot quantities that are smaller than those obtained from typical wrought-material production runs; hence, castings may more easily be made to accommodate specific application requirements.

### Casting Properties

Castings generally exhibit nondirectional properties. Wrought metals, on the other hand, usually are anisotropic—stronger and tougher in one direction than in another. Some casting processes do, however, provide directional strength properties that can be utilized by part designers and manufacturing engineers to increase performance of the finished part.

In some instances, the properties and performance attainable in cast components cannot be obtained readily by other manufacturing methods. For example:

- Cast iron has desirable wear and damping properties for air-conditioner crankshaft and diesel engine cylinder liner applications.
- Compacted graphite (a recent cast iron alloy development) offers the heat and wear-resisting characteristics of gray iron and the strength approaching nodular iron.
- Cast bearing alloys have a controlled dispersion of lubricating materials.
- High rupture strength superalloy airfoils are made possible by the use of nonmachinable cast alloys with creep resistance superior to that of wrought materials.
- Castings allow the manufacture of parts from alloys that are difficult or impossible to machine or forge, and are especially advantageous for cored internal passages.
- Fine equiaxed, directionally solidified, single-crystal, eutectic structures provide a variety of useful properties made possible by modern casting processes and material technology.

For simple shapes, near-net-shape castings often cannot compete economically with forgings. However, the casting processes offer a design flexibility and a capability for size and configuration

**CHAPTER CONTENTS:**




***Contributors of sections of this chapter are:*** *Roger L. Baas, Sales Manager—Machinery Div., Prince Corp.; William M. Barron, Sales Manager—Castings, Waukesha Foundry Div., Abex Corp.; Timothy L. Coghill, Plant Manager, Precision Metalsmiths, Inc.; Ronald E. Greenwood, President, Unicast Development Corp.; Jeffrey T. Heinen, Metals Processing Engineer, Corporate Research and Development, General Electric Co.; Leo J. LeBlanc, President, Enterprise Brass Works, Inc.; Raymond W. Monroe, Research Manager, Steel Founders' Society of America; Rodney L. Naro, Business Development Manager, Ashland Chemical Div., Ashland Oil, Inc.; John M. Svoboda, Technical and Research Director, Steel Founders' Society of America; Fred E. Weil, SRI International.*

***Reviewers of sections of this chapter are:*** *Roger L. Baas, Sales Manager—Machinery Div., Prince Corp.; William M. Barron, Sales Manager—Castings, Waukesha Foundry Div., Abex Corp.; John Burczky, Manager of Special Projects, Thompson Castings Inc.; Timothy L. Coghill, Plant Manager, Precision Metalsmiths, Inc.;*

# CHAPTER 16

## GENERAL CHARACTERISTICS

**TABLE 16-1**
**Commercial Capability of Casting Processes**

| Process | Ductile Iron | Steel | Stainless Steel | Aluminum, Magnesium | Bronze, Brass | Gray Iron | Malleable Iron | Zinc, Lead |
|---|---|---|---|---|---|---|---|---|
| Die casting | | | | • | • | | | • |
| Continuous | • | | | | • | • | | • |
| Investment | • | • | • | • | • | | | |
| Ceramic cope & drag | • | • | • | • | • | • | | • |
| Permanent mold | | | | • | • | • | | • |
| Plaster mold | | | | • | • | | | • |
| Centrifugal | • | • | • | | • | • | | • |
| Resin shell | • | • | • | • | • | • | • | |
| Sand | • | • | • | • | • | • | • | • |

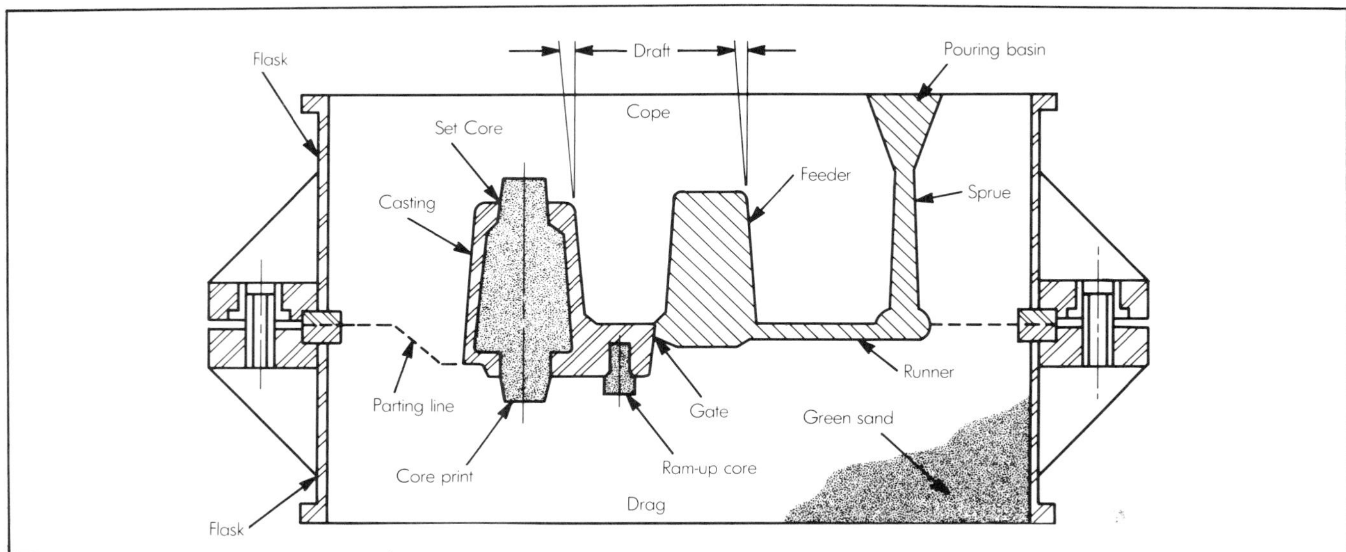


**Fig. 16-1 Cross-section view of typical cored casting and the sand mold in which it is produced.** (*Iron Castings Society, Inc.*)

complexity that are beyond the usual limits for feasible or economic use of the forging techniques. Castings are best used for complex part geometries—components that would require considerable machining and multipiece assembly if made by other processes.

### Mold Considerations

Molds are generally made by surrounding a pattern with a mixture of granular refractory and binder. This mixture may be dry or wet, and the composition varies with the mold and casting materials that are used. The choice of mold material depends on casting quality and quantity requirements, as well as on metal temperature and chemical reactivity.

The mold cavity is designed to be oversize to compensate for volume changes due to liquid-to-solid-phase transformations and thermal contraction. The pattern provides the shape and

***Reviewers, cont.**: Jack W. Douthitt, Chairman of the Board, TAM Supply Co.; Ronald E. Greenwood, President, Unicast Development Corp.; R. W. Heine, Professor of Metallurgical Engineering, Dept. of Metallurgical and Mineral Engineering, College of Engineering, University of Wisconsin—Madison; Jeffrey T. Heinen, Metals Processing Engineer, Corporate Research and Development, General Electric Co.; C. Steele Irons, Manager—Lynn Casting Technology, Aircraft Engine Business Group, General Electric Co.; Leo J. LeBlanc, President, Enterprise Brass Works, Inc.; Don K. Lewis, Metallurgist, Certified Alloys Co.; Edward J. Metzger, Jr., Vice President—Manufacturing, Multi-Cast Corp.; Leon D. Michelove, Staff—Plant Support, Product Assurance Materials and Components Engineering and Test, Raytheon Missile Systems Div., Raytheon Co.; John Mickowski, President, Tymac Controls Corp.; William Mihaichuk, Market Development Manager, Eastern Alloys Inc.;*

size of the cavity into which the molten metal is poured. Gates and risers may be attached to the pattern or molded in separately. The casting manufacturer generally uses tapered sections, chills, risers, insulation, and hot tops to provide adequate soundness through directional solidification.

Internal surfaces are formed by casting against cores. Cores are generally made from a similar mold material, but sometimes are made from a material that offers a greater resistance to the physically harsh and chemically reactive environment in the mold cavity before and during solidification. Hollow parts may also be made by one of the coreless casting techniques, such as centrifugal casting and slush casting.

After the binder hardens sufficiently, the pattern is removed. Sometimes special mold coatings are applied to improve the casting surface finish or reduce cleaning costs. A variation of this practice is found in evaporative-pattern (full-mold) casting, in which a shape made from low-density, expanded polystyrene is left in the sand to evaporate when hot metal is poured into the mold. Another variation is the use of permanent molds that may be reused several thousand times.

The mold is such an important aspect of most casting processes that the name of the molding process and the type of mold media are commonly used to identify the processes used to make castings. Examples include no-bake sand-molded steel castings, green sand molded brass castings, and investment-molded nickel-based superalloy castings.

## PROCESS SELECTION

The casting processes most often used are identified broadly as sand-mold casting, metal-mold casting, and plaster and ceramic-mold casting. As illustrated by the format used for Table 16-2, the major metal casting processes also can be characterized and grouped based on whether a reusable pattern with expendable mold, a reusable mold, or an expendable mold and pattern are employed in the process.

Each casting process has certain inherent advantages and limitations. Size and shape of the casting, dimensional accuracy and tolerance, surface finish, metallurgical properties, choice of alloys, production quantities, and cost all enter into the choice of a molding and casting process. Many sand castings, for example, have low labor and finishing costs; others are cleaned but are not ground or machined. A comparison of the molding processes with respect to these and other factors is given in Table 16-3, and a comparative rating of the processes is given in Table 16-4. For the highest quality, most cost-effective application of a casting method, advantages of the method must be fully used and its limitations must be recognized.

Effective operation of a foundry requires careful attention to the basics—part geometry, molding, gating, heat transfer, melt and mold materials, metal chemistry, cleanliness, and safety.

Process control is vitally important, because the foundry has more process variables than most other manufacturing operations. A good process control system forces the identification and understanding of key process parameters and their interrelationships. Productivity and consistent casting quality result from knowing and controlling key parameters within critical ranges. Experience indicates that a well-controlled foundry process affords an opportunity to reduce basic material costs by 25-30% while maintaining casting quality at the desired level.

## COMPUTERIZED OPERATIONS

Computer-based systems are gaining acceptance in virtually all aspects of foundry operations. Computer use extends into all functional areas, from sand control to final quality inspection; and the computer now has an integral role in the entire process, from design to the manufacture of castings.

### Computer-Aided Design

The capability for producing intricate shapes, both internal and external, is an important advantage of casting processes. A number of different casting processes may be used to make castings with complex geometric configurations. Investment casting, die casting, gravity metal-mold casting, and sand casting processes present an array of possibilities for near-net-shape component manufacturing. While each of the casting processes has advantages and limitations, the extent to which the complexity of the geometry affects the capability for near-net-shape processing is a common factor. Generally, the more complex the shape the more likely the raw shape will be different from the final shape. For complex parts, the near-net-shape casting processes offer a significant potential for saving material and lessening the need for secondary operations.

Another common problem with near-net-shape processing of complex geometries stems from representing three-dimensional (3D) shapes on a two-dimensional (2D) medium, the drawing or blueprint. The blending of external and internal joining sections is commonly done on the drawing by notation alone and must later be more fully defined by the craftsman, who is the patternmaker in the case of castings. Subsequent layouts of the component frequently do not deal with questions of near-net-shape processing, but rather whether the casting reasonably represents the drawing and whether the important dimensions to be machined are as required. Process capabilities may be ignored or accepted at this stage rather than used to their limits. It is here that the possibilities that come from computer-aided engineering can bring about substantial improvements in near-net-shape casting of components.

**Net shape.** Accurate and precise dimensional representation of casting geometry, both as cast and finished, is a necessity for near-net-shape processing. The near-net shape must be defined. The casting process can then render its best reproduction of that shape, and further processing by machining can be most economically performed. Accurate and precise 3D representation of complex casting geometries is a requirement that is not generally available to small and medium-sized foundries at an affordable cost. The 2D blueprint limitation is omnipresent.

To resolve this problem, a computer-aided design/computer-aided manufacturing (CAD/CAM) technique called solid

*__Reviewers, cont.__: Raymond W. Monroe, Research Manager, Steel Founders' Society of America; John D. Rutherford, Manager, Market Development, Certified Alloys Co.; Gerald Shroff, Manager, Metalworking and Manufacturing Equipment Program, Mining and Mechanical Industries Center, SRI International; John M. Svoboda, Technical and Research Director, Steel Founders' Society of America; J. B. Thomas, Vice President, Thompson Castings Inc.; R. A. Thomas, President, Thompson Castings Inc.; Robert Togni, Plant Engineer, Plant Engineering, Tennessee Die Casting Corp.; Lee Tuttle, Assistant Professor, Mechanical Engineering, GMI Engineering and Management Institute; Professor John J. Uicker, Professor of Mechanical Engineering, Director, Computer Aided Engineering Center, University of Wisconsin—Madison; Wayne F. Wales, General Electric Co.*

**TABLE 16-2**
**Metal Casting Processes**

| | Process | Description | Characteristics: Metals Used | Characteristics: Equipment Cost |
|---|---|---|---|---|
| Reusable pattern expendable mold | Sand Mold | Mold made by ramming sand around wood or metal pattern. Sand bonded with clay or chemicals. V-process uses vacuum to attain mechanical bond. | All common metals | Low |
| | Shell mold | Sand coated with thermosetting resin is poured over heated metal pattern to form a shell. Halves are stripped and assembled. | Primarily ferrous, copper, aluminum | Moderate |
| | Plaster mold | Molds made by casting plaster around pattern. Molds are baked after pattern removal. | Mainly aluminum, copper | Moderate |
| | Ceramic mold | Slurry of ceramic aggregate and binder, poured over pattern and chemically set. Resultant mold is stabilized and high-temperature cured. Molds can be poured hot or at room temperature. | All common metals | Moderate |
| Reusable mold | Die casting (pressure die casting) | Molten metal is forced into metallic die under high pressure. In hot-chamber machines (for zinc), metal is pumped into die. In cold-chamber units (for aluminum), metal is ladled into shot chamber. | Primarily zinc, aluminum, magnesium. Some copper and steel | Very high |
| | Low-pressure casting | Gas pressure (under 20 psi) is used to inject molten metal into a permanent mold. | Primarily aluminum | High |
| | Permanent-mold casting | Metal is poured into permanent molds made from metal or graphite. | Primarily nonferrous. Some iron and steel | High |
| | Centrifugal casting | Permanent or sand-lined mold for a symmetrical part, such as pipe, is rotated rapidly around its longitudinal axis. Centrifugal force distributes molten metal evenly along mold. | Most metals | High |
| | Squeeze casting | Combines casting and forging in one mold. | Primarily nonferrous | |
| Expendable pattern and mold | Investment casting (lost-wax process) | A wax pattern is coated with a refractory shell by casting or dipping. Assembly is then heated to melt out the wax pattern. Metal is cast into ceramic mold. | Steels, high-temperature alloys, nonferrous metals | High |
| | Evaporative pattern (full-mold process) | Pattern is made from foamed polystyrene. Sand is rammed around pattern. When metal is poured into mold, pattern vaporizes. | All metals, mainly iron. | Low |

**TABLE 16-2—*Continued***

| Characteristics | | | | |
|---|---|---|---|---|
| Tooling Cost | Labor Cost | Tolerances and Surface Finish | Usual Size Range | Status |
| Low | Low to moderate | Fair | Small to extremely large | Most widely used process for ferrous metals for both small and large-production runs. Various binder systems available. |
| Moderate | Low to moderate | Fair to good | Small to 100 lb (45 kg) | Used for production of fairly small parts for which closer tolerances are required than are obtainable from sand castings. Widely used for cores. |
| Moderate | High | Very good | Small to 100 lb (45 kg) | Used for some precision nonferrous castings in moderate quantity. Thin walls can be cast. This casting process is not widely used. |
| Moderate | Moderate | Excellent | Less than 100 lb (45 kg); sometimes several tons | Unicast and Shaw processes are most common versions. Used for precision casting, particularly for tools and dies. A special-purpose, relatively expensive process. |
| Very high | Low to moderate | Excellent | Small to over 50 lb (23 kg) | Very widely used for high production of aluminum and zinc castings. An inexpensive way of obtaining precision parts. |
| High | Low to moderate | Excellent | Under 50 lb (23 kg) | Widely used in Britain; only a few installations in the United States are used for quantities between those produced by die and permanent-mold processes. |
| High | Moderate | Good | 1 to 50 lb (0.5-23 kg) | Used for moderate quantities of semi-precision castings. Is normally less expensive than sand casting for hundreds of parts or a few thousand parts. Limited applicability for ferrous metals. |
| Moderate | Low to moderate | Fair to good | Large—over 100 lb (45 kg) | Used mainly for producing pipe and large cylinders in large quantities. |
| High | Low to moderate | Good | Small to 8 lb (4 kg) | Hybrid process, used to obtain design freedom of casting combined with properties and structural integrity of forging. Compatible with wide range of metals. |
| High | High | Excellent | Very small to 5 lb (2 kg) and over | Used for precision castings, particularly for gas turbine engines. A specialized process usually performed in foundries not used for other processes. |
| Low to moderate | Low to moderate | Fair | 5 lb (2 kg) and larger | Beginning to be used for low-production, complex casting such as machine tool frames. No draft needed in castings since pattern is not removed. Patterns are easy to machine. |

(*SRI International*)

**TABLE 16-3**
**Summary of Molding and Casting Processes**

| | Sand | Shell Mold | Permanent Mold | Die Casting |
|---|---|---|---|---|
| Choice of materials* | 1,2,3,4,5,6,7,8,9,10,11 | 1,2,3,4,5,6,9 | 1,3,4,5,6,7,8,10,11 | 4,5,7,8,10,11 |
| Complexity of part | Considerable, limited by pattern drawing. No limit with cores. | Considerable, limited by removal of mold from pattern. Less limited with cores. | Limited, restricted by the rigid molds. Ability to eject casting limits shape. | Moderate, limited by design of movable cores. |
| Number of castings relative to tool life | Wide range, type of pattern depends upon total castings. | High, metal patterns have a long life. | Moderate to high, casting metal affects life of mold. | High, mold life affected by casting metal. |
| Casting size or weight | 1 oz (28 g) to many tons. | 1 oz (28 g) to 100 lb (45 kg) and 60 in.$^2$ (0.04 m$^2$). | Several oz (100 g) to 50 lb (23 kg). | Several oz (100 g) to 75 lb (34 kg) in aluminum, 200 lb (91 kg) in zinc. Usually under 15 lb (7 kg). |
| Minimum section, in. (mm) | 1/8 to 1/4 (3-6) depending upon metal. | 1/16 (1.6) for most materials. | 3/32 (2.4) for most materials. | 0.025 (0.64) |
| Minimum diameter cored hole, in. (mm) | 3/16 to 1/4 (5-6) | 1/8 to 1/4 (3-6) | 3/16 to 1/4 (5-6) | 1/32 to 3/16 (1-5) depending upon metal. |
| Surface finishes, μin. (μm) | 250-1000 (6.4-25.4) | Somewhat better than sand. | 100-250 (2.5-6.4) | 40-100 (1-2.5) |
| Precision tolerances, in. (mm) | 1/16 to 11/64 (1.6-4.4) depending upon metal and casting size. Tolerance of ±0.010" (0.25 mm) possible on some parts. | ±0.003 in./in. (mm/mm); 0.003 (0.08) total possible on some dimensions. | ±0.015 in./in. (mm/mm) for first in. (25 mm); 0.001-0.002" (0.03-0.05 mm) for each additional in. (25 mm) | ±0.001-0.005 (0.03-0.13) depending upon material. |
| Tool costs | Low | Low to moderate | Medium | High |
| Direct labor costs | Wide range, much hand labor required. | Moderate | Moderate | Low to medium |
| Finishing costs | Wide range, high to low, depends upon cleaning, snagging, and machining required. | Low, often only a minimum required. | Low to moderate | Low, little more than trimming necessary. |

* 1. Gray iron
2. Malleable iron
3. Steel
4. Aluminum alloys
5. Copper alloys
6. Nickel alloys
7. Zinc alloys
8. Magnesium alloys
9. Heat and corrosion-resistant alloys
10. Tin alloys
11. Lead alloys

geometric modeling is being developed to facilitate computer-aided casting design and process engineering. Representing casting dimensions in 3D through solid geometric modeling is expected to quantify near-net-shape casting design definitions for further processing or machining.[2]

The key role of solid geometric modeling in computer-aided casting design and in the University of Wisconsin—Madison's "cast metals program" (CMP) project is shown on the information flow diagram illustrated in Fig. 16-2. The top area represents the component design utilized by a foundry customer and presented either on a conventional 2D drawing or blueprint or on magnetic tape. The drawing or tape represents the finished component design (net shape) without processing allowances.

**Computer input.** When the blueprint or tape is received by the foundry, process engineering may begin after the solid geometric database is developed, as illustrated in the middle area of Fig. 16-2. Wire frame data from computerized drafting systems may be converted to a solid geometric database via a translator program. Or, the blueprint may be converted to the solid geometric database either by digitizing or by using a computer-aided design terminal. After digitizing the blueprint geometry, the translator program produces the solid geometry database. Or at the CAD workstation, the solid geometric modeling software program permits the operator to directly model the casting from the blueprint.

This is done by inputting rudimentary solid geometric subshapes, such as plates, cylinders, cubes, cones, etc., and joining them as specified on the blueprint. Figure 16-3 illustrates how an air-cooled cylinder casting can be modeled. An assembly of disks (1) is joined with a cylinder (3) to produce the finned shape (2). Next, the bore is removed, bosses are added (4 and 5), and boss holes are removed (6), and a sector of fins is removed to produce the air-cooled cylinder model (7). The model can be rotated and blend lines removed (7). Cross sectioning can also be done.

This geometric assembly process is familiar to most foundry engineers because it resembles the current technique for deter-

TABLE 16-3—*Continued*

| Plaster Molding | Investment Casting | Centrifugal Casting | Solid Ceramic Casting |
|---|---|---|---|
| 4,5 | 3,4,5,6,9 | 1,3,4,5,6,9 | 1,2,3,4,5,6,7,8,9,10,11 |
| Considerable, possible to make mold of several pieces. Expendable mold. | Considerable, very complex patterns can be assembled from pieces. | Casting of circular periphery most favorable. Almost any shape can be cast. | Unlimited; almost any shape can be cast. |
| Moderate, depends on pattern material. | Moderate, type of pattern mold depends upon number of castings. | Low to moderate | High |
| 1 oz (28 g) to several hundred lb in most materials. | Under 1 oz (28 g) to 100 lb (45 kg). Best for parts under 2 lb (1 kg). | 1 oz (28 g) to many tons. | 1 oz (28 g) to many tons. |
| 0.030 (0.76) | 0.030 (0.76) | 0.030 (0.76) | 0.030 (0.76) |
| 1/2 (12.7) | 0.020-0.030 (0.51-0.76) | 3/16 to 1/4 (5-6) | 0.020-0.030 (0.51-0.76) |
| 30-50 (0.8-1.3) | 10-85 (0.3-2.2) | 100-250 (2.5-6.4) or as in sand. | 30-80 (0.8-2.0) |
| ±0.005-0.010 in./in. (mm/mm) or less | ±0.005 in./in. (mm/mm) | Same as permanent mold. | ±0.003 in./in. (mm/mm) for first in. (25 mm); ±0.001″ (0.03 mm) for each additional in. (25 mm). |
| Medium | High | Medium | Low |
| High-skilled operators necessary. | High, many hand operations required. | Moderate | Moderate to high |
| Low, little machining necessary. | Low, machining usually not necessary. | Low to moderate | Low, machining usually not necessary. |

mining total casting volume (and weight), that is, to estimate the sum of all the primitive subshape volumes making up the total casting based on component blueprint dimensions. This tedious process is now built into computer software. Having built the solid geometric model of the component, the geometric database is established and further engineering and manufacturing planning may proceed.

## Computers in Manufacturing

Computer applications in the foundry include numerous manufacturing functions. Examples include hot metal allocation to mold lines, product mix (for production scheduling), preventive maintenance monitoring, overall plant energy management, and materials management. Table 16-5 identifies a number of the computer-generated informational reports that are used for materials management.[3]

## NOMENCLATURE

The following definitions of terms commonly used in foundry manufacturing engineering and production operations are adapted from various sources, including the *Iron Castings Handbook*[4] and the *Steel Castings Handbook*.[5]

**binder** A material, other than water, added to sand to bind particles together, sometimes with the aid of heat

**blow holes** Voids or pores which may occur due to entrapped air or shrinkage during solidification of heavy sections.

**burnout** Firing a mold at a high temperature to remove pattern material residue.

**captive foundry** An organization that produces castings from its own patterns for its own use.

**castability** A complex combination of liquid-metal properties and solidification characteristics which promotes accurate and sound final castings.

**casting** 1. A metal object cast to the required shape by pouring or injecting liquid metal into a mold, as distinct from one shaped by a mechanical process. 2. The act of pouring molten metal into a mold.

**casting yield** The weight of casting or castings divided by the total weight of metal poured into the mold, expressed as a percent.

**cavity** The recess or impressions in a die in which the casting is formed.

**centrifugal casting** A process of filling molds by (1) pouring metal into a sand or permanent mold that is revolving about either its horizontal or its vertical axis or (2) pouring metal

**TABLE 16-4**
**Comparative Ratings of Casting Methods***

| Production Method | Sand Casting | Plaster-Mold Casting | Centrifugal Casting | | Permanent-Mold Casting | Die Casting | Solid Ceramic Casting |
|---|---|---|---|---|---|---|---|
| Mold material | Sand | Plaster[a] | Sand[a] | Metal[a] | Metal | Metal | Ceramic |
| Porosity | 6 | 4 | 2 | 1 | 3 | 4-5 (3-4)[b] | 1 |
| Surface | 6 | 1 | 5 | 3 | 4 | 2 (1-2)[c] | 1 |
| Tolerances | 6 | 2 | 5 | 3 | 4 | 1 | 1 |
| Strength of solid metal[d] | 6 | 5[e] | 3 | 2 | 4 | 1 | 1 |
| Thick section | 6 | 1 | 5 | 3 | 4 | 2 | 1 |
| Speed of production for small runs[f] | 1 | 4 | 2 | 3 | 3 | 5[g] | 3 |
| Speed of production for large runs[f] | 6 | 5 | 4 | 2 | 3 | 1 | 4 |
| Possibility to save machining | 5 | 1 | 4 | 2 | 3 | 1 | 1 |
| Cost per piece[h] | 5 | 6 | 4 | 2 | 3 | 1 | 5 |
| Tool cost | 1 | 3 | 2 | 4 | 4 | 5 | 3 |

* Rating given in order of preference for the particular characteristic: 1 indicates first preference, 2 second preference, etc.
[a] Copper and aluminum-based alloys.
[b] Cold-chamber machines.
[c] On specially finished dies.
[d] To be considered in conjunction with tendency to porosity.
[e] For some aluminum-based alloys lower than in sand.
[f] On basis of most economical setup, as to number of impressions on gate or in mold, for comparative production quantities.
[g] The die-casting process is a high-speed production method for large quantities. If this method is selected to produce a small amount of castings for the initial order, then the choice has been made on expected closer tolerances, less machining, better surface finish, etc.
[h] The cost per piece before machining exclusive of patterns or dies.

into a mold that is subsequently revolved before solidification of the metal is complete.

**centrifuge casting** A casting technique in which mold cavities are spaced symmetrically about a vertical axial common downgate. The whole assembly is rotated about that axis during pouring and solidification.

**ceramic molding** A molding process that uses a ceramic shell or mold made by alternately dipping a pattern in dipcoat slurry and stuccoing with coarse ceramic particles until the shell of desired thickness is obtained.

**chaplets** Metal supports or spacers used in molds to maintain cores, or parts of the mold which are not self-supporting in their proper positions during the casting process. They become a permanent part of the casting.

**charge** 1. The materials placed in a melting furnace. 2. Castings placed in a heat-treating furnace.

**check** A minute crack in the surface of a casting caused by unequal expansion or contraction during cooling.

**cold-chamber machine** A type of die-casting machine in which the metal-injection mechanism is not submerged in molten metal.

**cold shut** Lines on casting surface resulting from incomplete fusion of metal streams appearing as flow lines on the casting.

**combination die** A die having two or more cavities, each producing a different part. *See* multiple-cavity die.

**commercial foundry** An organization that produces castings for its customers from the customers' patterns.

**continuous casting** A process for forming a bar of constant cross section directly from molten metal by gradually withdrawing the bar from a die as the metal flowing into the die solidifies.

**cope** Upper or topmost section of a flask, mold, or pattern.

**core** 1. A metal insert in a die to produce a hole in pattern. 2. *See* preformed ceramic core.

**core plate** Plate for supporting cores while they are hardened.

**critical temperature** Temperature at which metal changes phase. In usual iron alloys, the temperature at which alpha iron transforms to gamma iron or vice versa. Actually, a temperature range for cast irons.

**dewaxing** The process of removing the expendable wax pattern from an investment mold or shell mold, usually accomplished by melting out the application of heat or dissolving the wax with an appropriate solvent.

**draft** The taper given to walls, cores, and other parts of the die cavity to permit easy ejection of the casting.

**draft, permanent mold** The taper in the mold cavity which allows the casting to be removed easily.

**dry-sand mold** A sand mold that is dried before being filled with liquid metal.

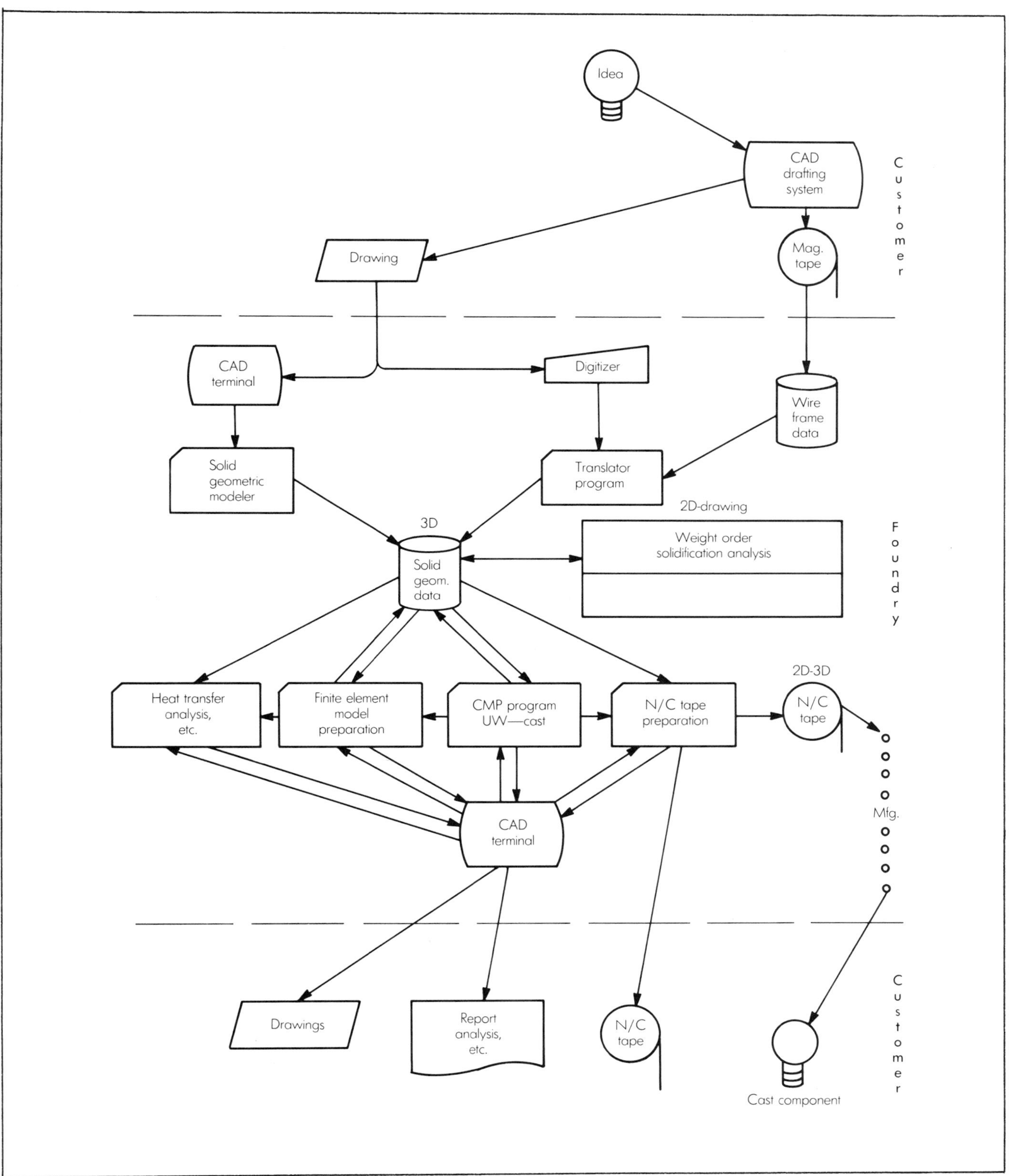


**Fig. 16-2 Information flow diagram for CAD/CAM casting design and process engineering program using solid geometric modeling.** (*University of Wisconsin—Madison*)

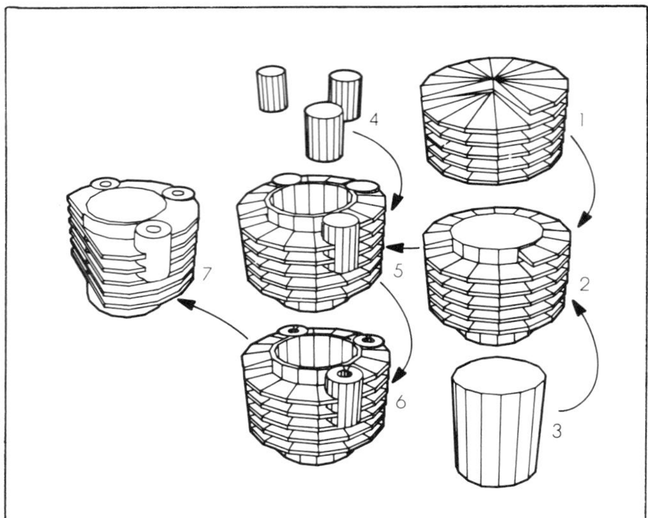


Fig. 16-3 Schematic representation of geometric modeling by assembling elemental subshapes. (*University of Wisconsin—Madison*)

**dry strength** The maximum strength of a molded sand specimen that has been thoroughly dried at 220-230° F (104-110° C) and cooled to room temperature. Also known as dry bond strength.

**ductility** The property permitting permanent deformation without rupture in a material by stress in tension.

**ejector marks** Marks left on castings by ejector pins.

**ejector pin** A rod which forces the casting out of the die cavity and off cores.

**expendable pattern** A pattern that is destroyed in making a casting. It is usually made of wax or foamed plastic.

**feeder, feed head** A reservoir of molten metal attached to a casting to compensate for the contraction of metal as it solidifies, thus preventing voids in the casting. Also known as a riser.

**flash** A thin web or fin of metal on a casting which occurs at die partings, around air vents, and around movable cores. This excess metal is due to necessary working and operating clearances in a die.

**flask** Tubular or rectangular metal form without top and without fixed bottom used to hold the refractory forming a mold. Also the complete mold with or without pattern material and with or without cast metal.

**founding** The art of melting and casting metals into useful objects.

**freezing range** That range of temperature between liquidus and solidus temperatures in which molten and solid constituents coexist.

**gate** End of the runner in a mold or die where molten metal enters the casting or mold cavity; sometimes applied to entire assembly of connected channels and to the pattern parts which form them.

**gooseneck** Spout connecting a metal pot or chamber with a nozzle or sprue hole in the die and containing a passage through which molten metal is forced on its way to the die. It is the metal-injection mechanism in a hot-chamber type of die-casting machine.

**green sand** A molding sand that has been tempered with water and is employed for casting when still in the damp condition.

**green-sand mold** A mold composed of moist molding sand that is not dried before being filled with molten metal.

**green strength** Strength of a tempered sand mixture at room temperature.

**heat checking** Formation of fine cracks in a die surface due to alternate heating and cooling. These cracks are reflected in the surface of the casting.

**hot-chamber machines** Die-casting machines which have a plunger or injection system in continuous contact with molten metal.

**impregnation** The treatment of defective castings with a sealing medium to stop pressure leaks in porous areas. Mediums used include silicate of soda, drying oils with or without styrenes, plastics, and proprietary compounds.

**injection** The process of forcing molten metal into a die.

**investing** The process of pouring the investment slurry into a flask surrounding the pattern to form the mold.

**investment process** The coating of an expendable pattern with a ceramic material so that it forms the surface of the mold that

**TABLE 16-5**
**Computer-Generated Reports**
**Used in Foundry Materials Management**

A. Production control
  1. Order status (master)
  2. Orders requiring samples
  3. Total backlog, by standard time, by week
     a. core
     b. mold
     c. finish
  4. Thirteen week master molding schedule
  5. Daily production schedule
     a. core
     b. melt
     c. mold
     d. finish
  6. Open orders
     a. by customer
     b. due date and tons
B. Inventory Control
  1. Receipts summary
  2. Inventory transaction recap
  3. Maintenance stock parts catalog
     a. by vendor
     b. by in-plant numbering identification
     c. cost center where part is normally used
  4. Cycle inventory (daily assignment of items to be cycle counted that day)
  5. Stock inventory master
  6. Daily usage activity
C. Purchasing
  1. Daily open purchase order update
     a. by vendor
     b. by purchase order number
     c. by due date
  2. Vendor dollar volume
     a. descending amount
     b. alphabetical

(*Pryor Foundry, Inc. Subsidiary of J. I. Case Co.*)
Note: Several reports are utilized by more than one department; however, they are only listed under the area of primary usage.

contacts the molten metal when the pattern is removed and the mold is poured.

**lost-wax process** A casting process in which an expendable pattern made of wax or a similar material is melted or burned out of the mold rather than being drawn out.

**multiple-cavity die** A die having more than one duplicate impression.

**nozzle** Outlet end of a gooseneck or the tubular fitting which joins the gooseneck to the sprue hole.

**parting line** A line on a pattern or casting corresponding to the separation between adjacent sections of a die.

**pattern** A form of wood, metal, plastics, or other material, around which refractory material is placed to make a mold for casting metals.

**permanent mold** A mold of two or more parts that is used repeatedly for the production of many castings of the same form. Liquid metal is poured in by gravity.

**plunger** Ram or piston which forces molten metal into a die. Plunger machines are those having a plunger in continuous contact with molten metal.

**porosity** A characteristic of being porous, with voids or pores resulting from trapped air or shrinkage in a casting.

**port** Opening through which molten metal enters the injection cylinder of a plunger machine or is ladled into the injection cylinder of a cold-chamber machine.

**preformed ceramic core** A preformed refractory aggregate inserted in a wax or plastic pattern or shape the interior of that part of a casting which cannot be shaped by the pattern. Sometimes the wax is injected around the preformed core.

**ribs** Sections joining parts of a casting to impart greater rigidity.

**riser** A reservoir of molten metal provided to compensate for internal contraction of the casting as it solidifies. Also known as feeder or feeder head.

**runner** The portion of the gate assembly that connects the downgate (sprue) with the casting ingate or riser. The term also applies to that part of the pattern which forms the runner.

**seam** 1. A surface defect on a casting related to but of lesser degree than a cold shut. 2. A ridge on the surface of a casting caused by a crack in the mold face.

**shell core process** Resin-coated sand is blown into a heated core box. The sand against the box hardens. The balance of the sand is drained out to make a hollow core.

**shell molding process** A resin-coated sand is laid on a heated pattern so that the sand against the pattern bonds together to form a hardened shell. Two mating shells make a mold.

**shot** That segment of the casting cycle in which molten metal is forced into the die.

**shrink mark** A surface depression which sometimes occurs next to a heavy section that cools more slowly than adjacent areas.

**shrinkage, solidification** Dimensional reduction that accompanies the freezing (solidification) of metal passing from the molten to the solid state.

**sprue** The vertical channel from the top of the mold to the parting line. Also a generic term to cover all gates, risers, etc., returned to the melting unit for remelting. Also applied to similar portions of patterns.

**V Process** A molding process in which the sand is held in place in the mold by vacuum. The mold halves are covered with a thin sheet of plastic to retain the vacuum.

**vent** Narrow passage at the die parting which permits air to escape from the die cavity as it is filled with molten metal.

**void** A large pore or hole within the wall of a casting, usually caused by entrapped gas. A blow hole.

# SAND-MOLD CASTING

Of all the forming processes, sand-mold casting is the most versatile and provides the greatest freedom of design in terms of size, shape, and product quantity. Sand-mold castings can be produced singly or by the millions and in sizes weighing from a fraction of an ounce to hundreds of tons (several grams to hundreds of megagrams).

One of the main advantages of sand-mold casting is the flexibility it permits in shaping the part so that the imposed load is distributed evenly throughout the part for minimum stress concentration. When well-designed castings are used, stress concentrations can be reduced as much as 50%, and in many cases significant increases in service life and strength can be achieved.

## DESIGN CONSIDERATIONS

To ensure maximum dispersal of stress, minimum stress concentration, and the most effective configuration for the function of a given design, the following guidelines are applicable to sand-mold castings:

1. External corners should be rounded with radii that are 10-20% of the section thickness (see Fig. 16-4). Rounded corners increase resistance of ductile metals to fatigue rupture, increase static strength of gray iron in bending by 4-7%, and increase gray iron's deflection by 10-20%. Rounding of corners is also the most efficient method of decreasing, or eliminating, chilled edges in gray-iron castings. If a notation to round all external corners is included in the part drawing, the patternmaker must

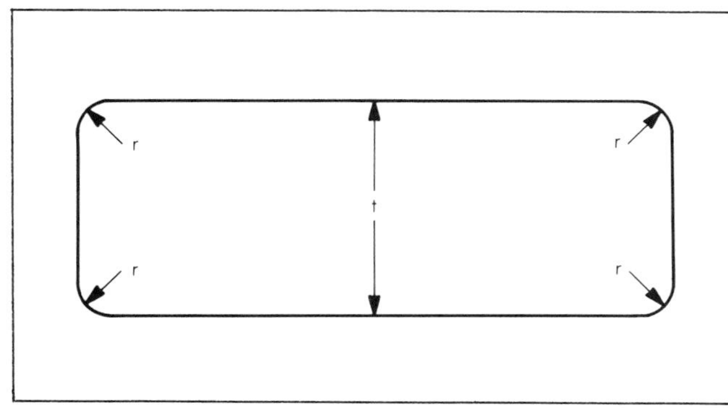


**Fig. 16-4 Sand-casting external corner radii guideline: r = 0.10 to 0.20 t.**

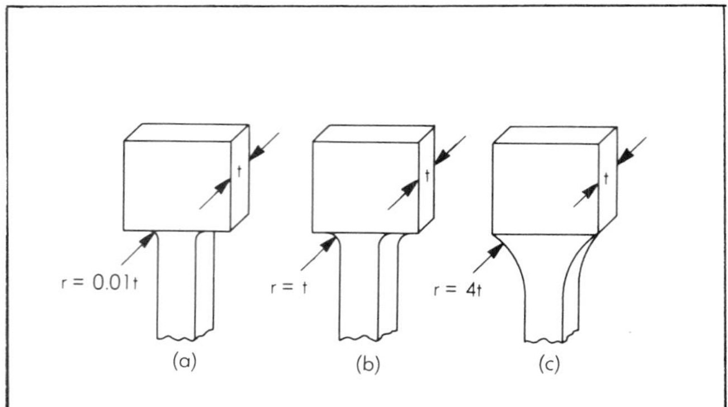


**Fig. 16-5 Sand-casting fillet radii comparison for stress endurance and fatigue strength.**

provide for rounded corners at partings and at core prints.

2. Radii equal to the thickness of the smaller section are used when sections of dissimilar size are joined or when L or T junctions are used. This proportioning provides significant increases in resistance to fatigue stresses in all metals and in resistance to static stresses in gray iron (see Figs. 16-5 and 16-6). A radius equal to the section thickness, as shown in Fig. 16-5, *b*, has a 40-50% higher endurance limit than a sharp corner, as shown in view *a*. A further increase in fillet radius to 4t, as shown in view *c*, increases the endurance limit to 120% more than that of view *a*. Figure 16-6 shows the average fatigue life of 5/8" (16 mm) thick sections with fillets stressed in tension to a maximum fiber stress of approximately 50,000 psi (345 MPa).
3. Tapered sections and irregular sections should conform to stress patterns, particularly in bending, as illustrated in Fig. 16-7. The section modulus at the plane of maximum stress *AA* is five times greater with the tapered connecting member (view *b*) than with the straight connecting member (view *a*). This increase in section modulus decreases maximum fiber stress in bending by 60%. The lower stress concentration at *AA* in design *b* decreases maximum stress even more and is particularly important in fatigue loading.
4. For complex loads, tubular and reinforced C sections should be used rather than standard I, H, and channel sections to obtain improved load-bearing capabilities (see Fig. 16-8). For a given weight and overall size, the tubular section has moments of inertia and section moduli about the X axis that are 9-17% greater than those of the standard I section. The tubular section also has design properties about the Y axis that are 140-170% greater than those of the I section. This significant increase in properties makes the tubular section ideal for complex loading. The reinforced C or U section does not have properties about the X axis (70-90% of the I section) that are as good as those of the tubular section, yet shows even better properties about the Y axis than does the tubular section.
5. The largest possible radii should be used with L junctions or when joining sections with slightly varying sectional moduli. Radii of ten or more times the thickness of the section can be used.
6. Complex sections such as X, V, Y, K, and X-T junctions should be simplified to staggered T junctions and, if possible, to corrugated sections, as illustrated in Fig. 16-9. As shown in view *a*, X junctions should be simplified to staggered T junctions; and as shown in view *b*, V, Y, and K junctions should be streamlined. The X-T junctions should be staggered to T-T junctions as shown in view *c*; and if possible, stiffness should be obtained with corrugated sections such as shown in view *d* rather than with rib-stiffened plates as in *c*.
7. Ribs should be eliminated entirely, if at all possible, particularly those stressed in tension. Corrugated or U sections should be used instead (see Fig. 16-10).

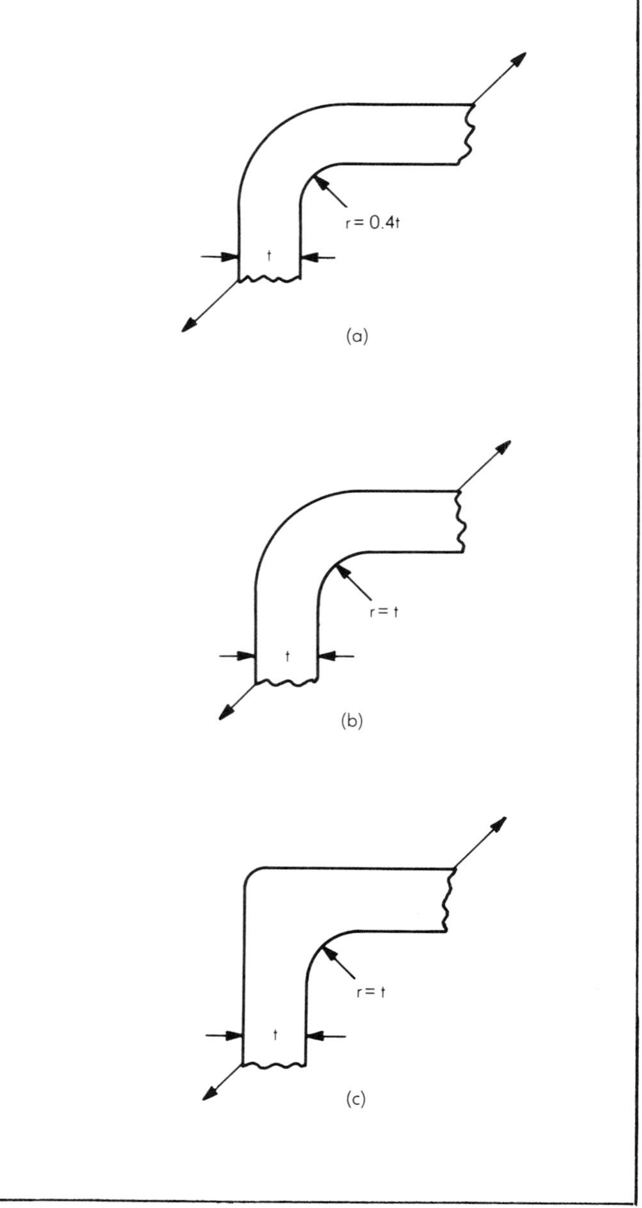


**Fig. 16-6 Average fatigue life of cast fillets tension-stressed to 50 ksi (345 MPa): (a) 270,000 cycles; (b) 1,850,000 cycles; (c) 5,900,000 cycles.**

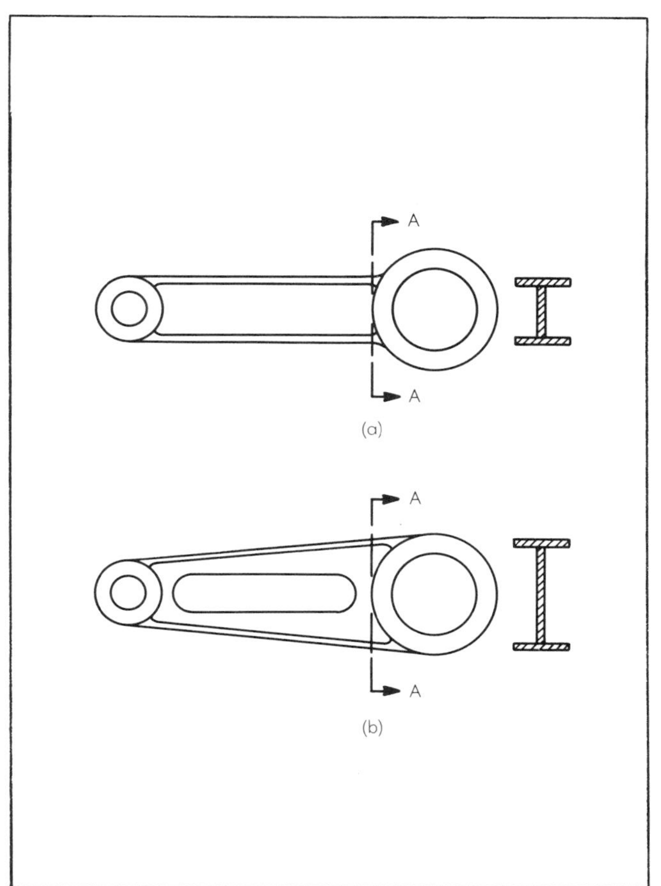

Fig. 16-7 Tapered sections increase the section modulus and fatigue strength of castings.

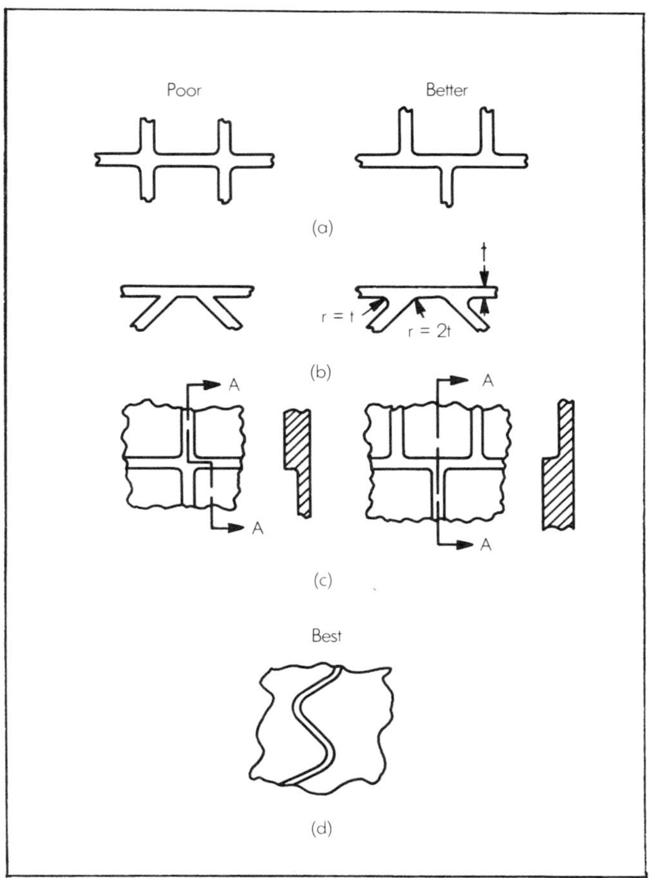

Fig. 16-9 Casting stiffness can be improved by simplifying and streamlining the cross sections.

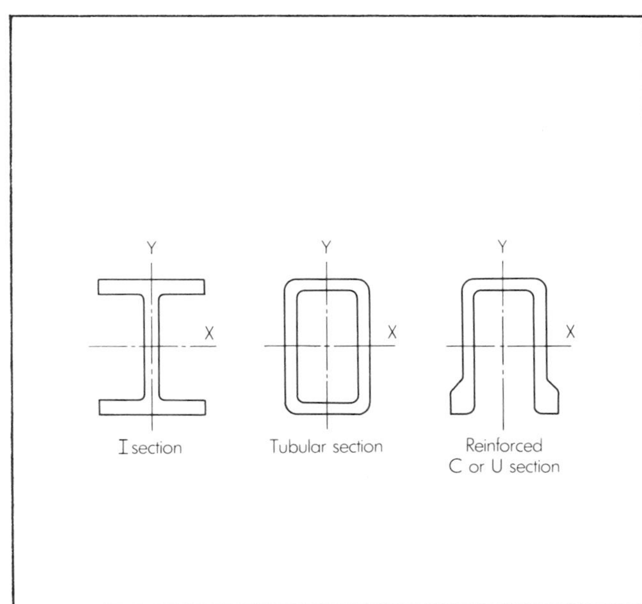

Fig. 16-8 Tubular and reinforced sections are used in castings designed to sustain complex loads.

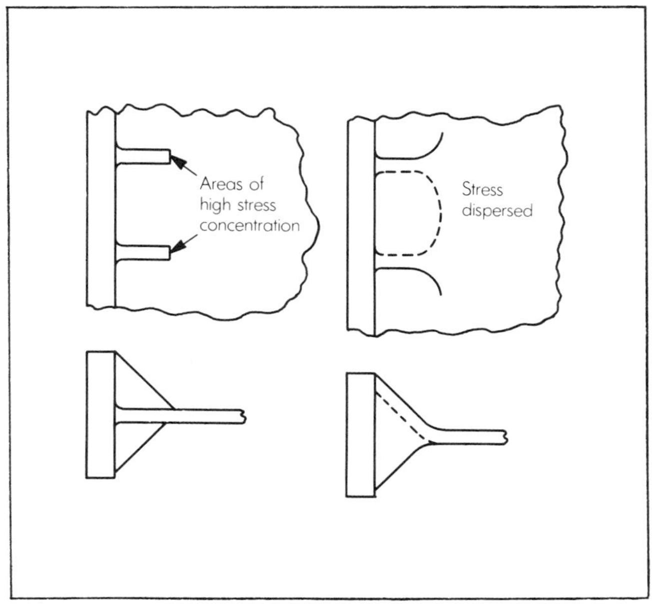

Fig. 16-10 Stress concentrations in tension-loaded castings are avoided by using U-shaped or corrugated sections instead of ribs.

# DIMENSIONAL VARIATIONS AND STOCK REQUIREMENTS

Strength of castings can be ensured by specifying minimum hardness, generally Brinell hardness. Many reports of low casting strength properties can be attributed to improper sampling, in which only the very centers of the cast sections were tested, with as much as 50-80% of the cast sections removed by machining.

If machine finishing requirements specify that less than 50% of the original cast section can be removed by machining from both sides of the section, then the physical properties of ferrous castings will approach the properties of classical test specimens. Maximum physical and mechanical properties in nonferrous castings are usually obtained with special chilling techniques.

Practically all metals are available as castings, and some metals, such as gray iron and some of the superalloys that are not forgeable, can be formed only by casting. There are, on the other hand, some immiscible alloys that cannot be cast, and these can be formed only by powder metallurgy techniques.

## DIMENSIONAL VARIATIONS AND STOCK REQUIREMENTS

In planning the dimensional accuracy and finish-stock requirements of sand-mold castings, the following important factors must be evaluated:

1. If maximum dimensional accuracy is to be obtained with any casting process, allowances must be made for slight pattern alterations after sample castings have been made. This allowance is necessary to compensate for shrinkage variations and distortion. These factors are direct functions of shape.
2. In any process involving the use of heat, the problem of thermal distortion must be considered. When a configuration has one dimension several times larger than the other two (a crankshaft, for example), distortion occurs on cooling. This distortion can easily nullify forming precision. Precision then depends on a straightening operation rather than on the molding method or molding precision. If production quantities warrant the cost of a die, some castings can be die-straightened to accuracies within thousandths of an inch (hundredths of a millimeter).
3. The theoretical rule that stock requiring a minimum amount of finishing is the most economical does not always apply in casting operations. The range from 0.020-0.060″ (0.51-1.52 mm) finish stock is difficult to finish. Finish allowances of 0.020″ (0.51 mm) are recommended for grinding, and 0.060″ (1.52 mm) should be the minimum for cutting with edged tools.

The variables governing dimensional tolerances in a given molding process are the size and shape of the casting. Dimensional tolerances are not influenced to any great extent by the type of metal used. Tables 16-6 and 16-7 show the dimensional variations of both ferrous and nonferrous castings formed by the various processes.

Finish-stock requirements are dependent on dimensional variations. It is essential that edged tools do not scrape the surface of the casting. The opportunity to alter the pattern after checking sample castings ensures that machining costs and related problems are kept to a minimum. It is possible to obtain less finish stock than that shown in Table 16-8, for example, but this depends on the particular size and shape of the casting.

In general terms, the roughness of shot-cleaned surfaces of ferrous castings lies in the range of 250-700 $\mu$ in. (6.4-17.8 $\mu$ m). By giving special attention to mold preparation and by using finer than average shot for cleaning, surface smoothness as low as 150 $\mu$ in. (3.8 $\mu$ m) can be obtained. Some precision-casting surfaces, such as those produced by investment casting, provide smoothness in the 50-100 $\mu$ in. (1.3-2.5 $\mu$ m) range. Aluminum, magnesium, and copper-alloy casting surfaces can be expected to fall in the range of 200-300 $\mu$ in. (5.1-7.6 $\mu$ m).

Stylus-type instruments generally are unsuitable for measuring cast surfaces. Visual surface comparators available for cast

**TABLE 16-6**
**Tolerance Comparison for Various Casting Methods**

| | Casting Metal* | | | |
|---|---|---|---|---|
| Casting Method | Steel, in. (mm) | Gray Iron, in. (mm) | Copper-Based Alloys, in. (mm) | Light Alloys,** in. (mm) |
| Green-sand mold | ±0.040-0.080 (1.02-2.03) | ±0.03-0.05 (0.8-1.3) | ±0.015 (0.38) | ±0.015 (0.38) |
| Shell mold | ±0.020-0.050 (0.51-1.27) | ±0.019-0.04 (0.48-1.0) | ±0.016-0.019 (0.41-0.48) | ±0.010-0.014 (0.25-0.36) |
| Permanent mold | ±0.015-0.020 (0.38-0.51) | ±0.030-0.035 (0.76-0.89) | ±0.018-0.025 (0.46-0.64) | ±0.009-0.012 (0.02-0.30) |
| Die casting | --- --- | --- --- | ±0.005-0.080† (0.13-2.03) | ±0.005-0.080† (0.13-2.03) |
| Investment | ±0.010-0.020 (0.25-0.51) | ±0.010-0.020 (0.25-0.51) | ±0.005-0.010 (0.13-0.25) | ±0.005-0.010 (0.13-0.25) |

* Casting dimension 1-6″ (25-152 mm)

** Aluminum, magnesium, zinc alloys

† These tolerances have no parting lines. If the casting passes a parting line, 0.015-0.020″ (0.38-0.51 mm) should be added for a 1″ (25 mm) casting section. If the dimension is between a core and mold surface, the difference is approximately the same.

**TABLE 16-7**
**Tolerances for Sand-Mold Castings**

| Casting Metal | Tolerance in./ft | Tolerance mm/m |
|---|---|---|
| Cast iron | ±3/64 | 99 |
| Steels | ±1/16 | 132 |
| Malleable iron | ±1/32 | 66 |
| Copper-based alloys | ±3/32 | 198 |
| Aluminum alloys | ±1/32 | 66 |
| Magnesium alloys | ±1/32 | 66 |

surfaces are usually more practical than stylus instruments. However, the size and shape of the casting are the major variables in the selection of measuring instruments. The most practical way of specifying and controlling cast surface is to provide a series of castings showing acceptable and unacceptable surfaces.

## GREEN-SAND MOLDING

More than 20 million product tons of castings are produced annually in the United States, and more than 90% of this foundry product is cast in sand molds, primarily green-sand molds (80%). In green-sand molding, a mold is formed around a pattern with sand-clay-water mixtures which may contain other additives. The molding medium is readily compacted; and when the pattern is removed, the compacted mass retains a reverse of the pattern's shape. Figure 16-11 shows typical steps involved in making a casting from a green-sand mold.

The molding mixture is formulated to withstand the heat and pressures generated as the mold is filled with molten metal. Almost all commercial castings weighing up to 500 lb (227 kg) are cast in green sand because of the preferred quality, production capability, and relatively low cost of this process. Comparatively few castings of this size and weight are produced by other casting methods.

Among the products made by green-sand molding are automotive castings such as cast-iron cylinder blocks, connecting rods, crankshafts, and differential housings. Fluid-transmission castings and plumbing castings and fittings are almost entirely produced by green-sand molding.

The railroad industry is a large consumer of steel castings produced by this method, and much of the machinery and transportation industries' equipment and components are made from cast steel, gray iron, ductile iron, and malleable iron; and from aluminum, brass, bronze, or other nonferrous castings produced in green sand.

There are a variety of ways in which castings, even the simplest types, can be made in green sand. The selection of pattern equipment, which to a large extent determines the moldmaking technique to be used, is predicated principally on production quantities. The cost of a pattern for very limited bench-scale production is relatively low, but the production costs are high. The man-hours required to produce a ton of castings ready for shipment can vary from as many as 250 man-hours to as few as 10 man-hours with green-sand castings. Production can be accomplished almost entirely by hand labor or by practically full automation. Moldmaking equipment now in use is capable of producing more than 300 molds per hour. The type of automated equipment to be used depends largely on the type and size of the casting to be produced. Although most of the automated systems use flasks, flaskless molding has found wide acceptance in industry.

## DRY-SAND MOLDING

The term *dry-sand molding* refers to the method of molding in a sand mold that has been dried after the pattern has been removed. This method is used mainly for large castings weighing up to 100 tons (91 metric tons). The drying process increases the strength of the molding sand many times. This additional strength is needed to withstand the higher static pressures of the liquid metal when casting heights are measured in feet (meters). Occasionally, the more rigid walls of dry-sand molds are used in conjunction with precision patterns to obtain more accurate casting dimensions. Generally, the dimensional tolerances and finish stock of clay-bonded, dried-mold castings are smaller than the average tolerances and finish stock for green-sand mold castings.

Molds can be dried in an oven at approximately 450° F (232° C), or they can be dried by portable heaters. A widely used variation of this method is skin drying, in which the mold surface is dried only to a depth of from 1/8 to 1" (3 to 25 mm) or slightly more. This variation is used largely to dry a mold surface that has been washed or blackened with a powder refractory suspended in liquid to improve the mold's surface finish. Some dry-sand molds are an assembly of cores that are bonded with clay, cement, sodium silicate, or any of the resin and oil bonds used for cores. The cores are baked or hardened before assembly.

## SHELL MOLDING

The shell molding process is used when extreme dimensional accuracy and precise duplication of intricate shapes are the

**TABLE 16-8**
**Nominal Finish-Stock Requirements for Green-Sand Castings**

| Casting Material | Casting Dimension, in. (mm) Less than 5 (127) | 5-10 (127-254) | 10-20 (254-508) | 20-50 (508-1270) | 50-100 (1270-2540) | Over 100 (2540) |
|---|---|---|---|---|---|---|
| Ferrous | 3/64 to 1/8 (1.2 to 3.2) | 1/8 to 3/16 (3.2 to 4.8) | 1/8 to 1/4 (3.2 to 6.4) | 5/16 to 3/8 (7.9 to 9.5) | 3/8 to 1/2 (9.5 to 12.7) | 1/2 to 3/4 (12.7 to 19.1) |
| Nonferrous | 0.045 to 0.090 (1.14 to 2.29) | 0.050 to 0.12 (1.27 to 3.1) | About the same as for ferrous castings | | | |

# SHELL MOLDING

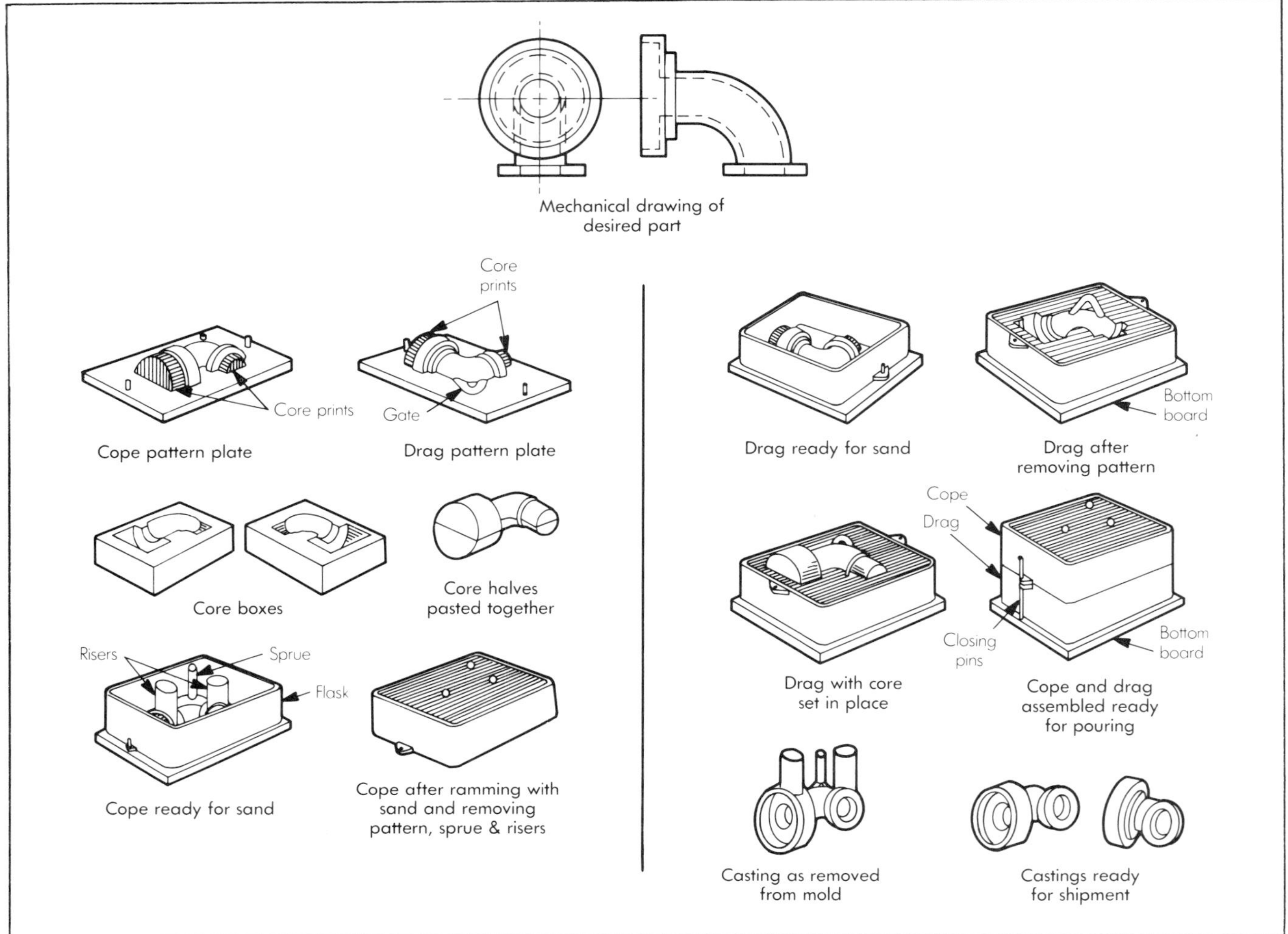


**Fig. 16-11 Typical steps involved in making a casting from a green-sand mold.** (*Steel Founders' Society of America*)

principal requirements. Basically the method consists of the following steps:

1. A metal pattern (or several patterns) is placed on a metal plate.
2. The pattern is coated with a mixture of fine sand and phenolic resin, 4-6 lb (1.8-2.7 kg) of resin to each 100 lb (45 kg) of sand.
3. The pattern is heated and the resin is allowed to melt to the specified thickness.
4. The resin is cured.
5. The excess sand is dumped.
6. The hardened mold is stripped from the pattern.

The resultant "shell" duplicates the pattern in reverse, with the shape of the pattern forming either a cavity or a projection in the shell. If the shape to be cast is such that one half duplicates the other, then one pattern may be used for both shells. The two shells can then be joined with a phenolic-resin paste or mechanical joiners to form a mold cavity that holds the molten metal and reproduces the shape of the casting desired. When the shape of the casting is unsymmetrical, two patterns must be prepared and, subsequently, two shells must be produced and joined to form the proper mold cavity. If the casting requires internal cavities, sand cores can be placed within the shell mold.

Patterns for shell molds are generally made of iron or steel, although aluminum can be used for limited-quantity production. The metal that is used is largely determined by the degree of casting accuracy specified and the number of castings to be produced. Iron and steel patterns provide greater dimensional accuracy than aluminum patterns, but aluminum patterns are generally more economical.

In casting larger and heavier parts, it is necessary to back up a shell mold, usually by placing it upright in a metal box and filling the space behind it with steel shot. This reinforces the shell and prevents it from breaking up under lateral pressure of the cast metal. After the casting has been poured and has hardened, the shell is broken away and the casting is ready for cleaning and machining, if needed.

Shell molding can be used to form almost any shape—small pipes, camshafts, bushings, spacers, valve bodies, brackets, manifolds, bearing caps, gears, and shafts. The size and weight of the casting and of the shell mold are usually the limiting factors of shell molding applications. Casting sizes of more than 20-24″ (500-600 mm) are considered large for shell molding. However, this process lends itself to the incorporation of more than one pattern on a single plate, and plates with as many as 12 patterns are commonplace.

Shell molding offers dimensional accuracy up to 0.003-0.004″ (0.08-0.10 mm). This degree of accuracy is often superior to that attainable with either green or dry-sand molding, although it cannot match the accuracy of the permanent-mold process or the precision of investment casting methods.

## THE FULL-MOLD PROCESS

The full-mold or cavityless process (also known as the evaporative-pattern process) is a method of making metal castings by the use of expanded polystyrene foam patterns that eliminate the need for traditional mold cavities. Basically, the process consists of embedding the foam patterns in sand and then pouring the casting metal directly into the foam. This vaporizes the polystyrene and leaves a casting that duplicates the original pattern (see Fig. 16-12). Since the patterns are the exact size and shape of the casting, there is no need for the patternmaker or molder to think in mirror images as with the conventional moldmaking methods.

More significantly, the process eliminates the need for draft allowances, cores, coreboxes, parting lines, and many conventional foundry operations. The reduced costs that result can make full-mold castings competitive with weldments. It is often more economical to pour metal into foam patterns made from cut-out and glued sheets of expanded polystyrene than to cut out and weld steel plates. In addition, many part shapes that would normally be made of steel (to meet welding requirements) can be made satisfactorily of iron at reduced costs.

Since its introduction (about 1960), the full-mold process has produced millions of tons of castings; and some foundries produce over a thousand tons of these castings each month. Although a pattern is required for each casting, expanded polystyrene patterns are more economical than wood patterns and consequently are widely used for large, single-unit castings. In these cases, the foam patterns are fabricated by hand. If multiple castings are needed, they can be assembled by production-line techniques.

If very large quantities are needed, the expanded polystyrene patterns can be molded on automated molding machines. To illustrate the economies attainable with the full-mold evaporative pattern process, a molded pattern of a 1740 lb (789 kg) counterweight for a forklift truck weighs only 7.5 lb (3.4 kg). This massive part was cast in unbonded sand that was simply poured around the pattern and vibrated.

### Mold Materials

Expanded polystyrene patterns are generally molded in furan-bonded silica sands that are hand-rammed around the patterns and allowed to harden. Other bonding materials, such as silicates and bentonites, are used to some extent, and even completely unbonded sand can be used. This is a major advantage shared by no other casting process. The permeability of the sand is a critical property, since the gases formed during vaporization must escape through the sand. To obtain the desired permeability, sand that is fairly large grained is used. The patterns are coated with a refractory coating to improve high-temperature properties and to impart a smooth surface to the castings.

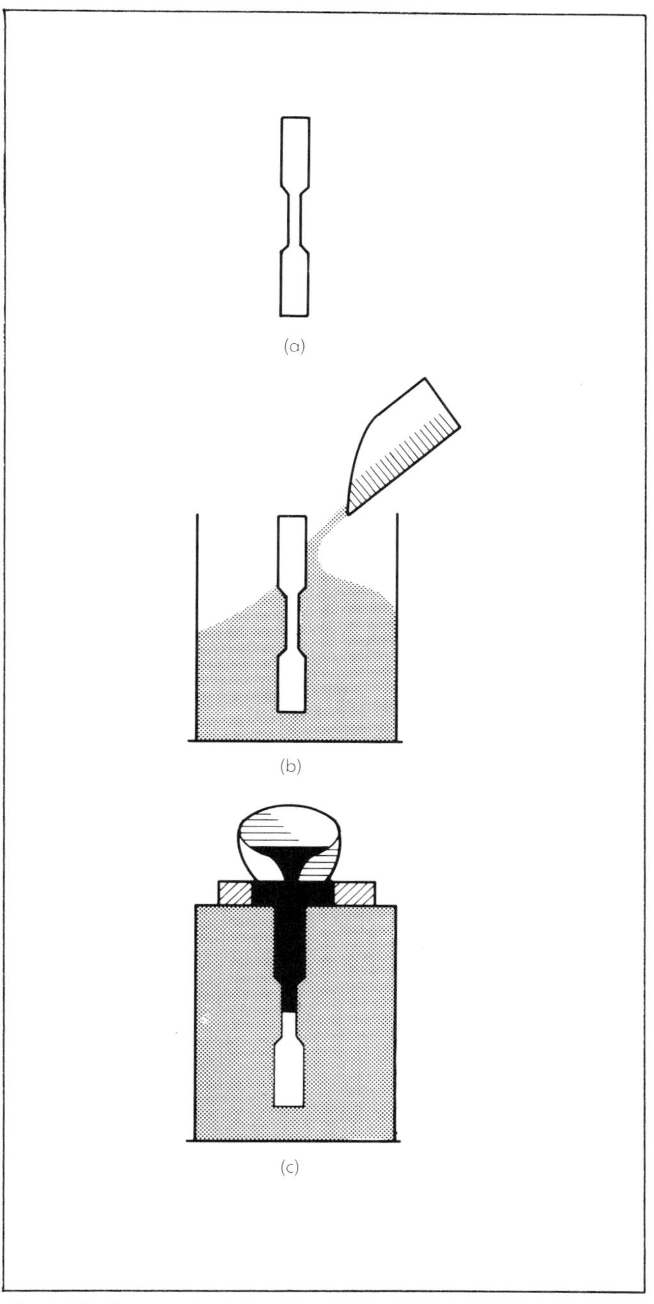


**Fig. 16-12 Steps in the full-mold (evaporative-pattern or "lost foam") casting process: the polystyrene pattern (a) is buried in sand (b) and vaporized by molten metal (c).**

### Casting Materials

The full-mold evaporative pattern process can be used with all commercial foundry metals. Because polystyrene vaporizes at 170° F, (77° C), even metals with relatively low melting points, such as lead and zinc, can be used. The interaction of the molten metal and the expanded polystyrene causes no adverse effects, with the possible exception of carbon pickup when certain low-carbon steels are used. The process is gaining wider acceptance because of the improved machinability it imparts to gray-iron castings made in furan-bonded full molds and, under the proper pouring conditions, the absence of slag inclusions.

Expanded polystyrene can also be used to make the foundry gating and riser systems which are included in the mold when the sand is rammed around the pattern. Venting of the mold can also be accomplished with polystyrene strips which vaporize in advance of the hot gases. This venting method uses rods and wires that are removed from the sand before casting or are removed by artificial evacuation. The metal can be poured as fast as the vaporization rate of the foam permits. For example, castings in the 30 ton (27 metric ton) range are poured at the rate of at least 300 lb/s (136 kg/s).

### Full-Mold Production Casting

Since each casting consumes its own pattern during pouring of the metal, large numbers of identical polystyrene patterns are needed for large-volume full-mold (evaporative-pattern) production. The large quantities of patterns can be produced rapidly in a number of ways. To make disks, for example, a bandsaw can be used to cut through 10 or 20 sheets of expanded polystyrene at a time. For more complex shapes, automatic milling machines can be used on solid foam billets. For extremely high-volume production runs, the expanded polystyrene foam can be molded to the desired shape in automatic molding machines that operate on steam and compressed air.

Polystyrene beads are preexpanded and then injected into molds on the machine; steam is then injected into the molds, causing the foam to expand further and to fuse into a solid mass. This mass is then chilled with cold water, and the pattern is ejected from the mold. Since patternmaking can be a fully automated process, many foundries have converted to a completely automated full-mold production system. This makes possible the most complete and effective use of unbonded sands, particularly in mass-production operations.

The economics of patternmaking have been a deciding factor in the growth rate of the full-mold evaporative pattern process. For many prospective applications, the tooling costs have been unacceptably high. And this, combined with the need for a separate pattern for each casting, has tended to limit the method's growth. However, the process is firmly established as a means of making automotive stamping dies and prototype machine castings. Developments currently under way indicate that the full-mold process will enable users to make multiple castings from automatically carved patterns, and high-production castings from molded patterns.

## CEMENT MOLDING

Sand molds using a cement binder are probably the most durable of all the sand-process molds. Cement molding, also called the Randupson process, is used to form large molds for ship stools and other ship parts, and for ingots.

Cement molds are made of washed and graded silica sand to which is added 10% Portland cement mixed with 4-5% (and sometimes more) water. This mixture can be mulled like a green-sand mixture and soon sets to produce an air-dried mold of great strength which may be stored for long periods without deterioration.

Two disadvantages of cement molding are that (1) once the sand-cement mixture is mulled, it must be quickly formed around the pattern before the cement sets and (2) cement is much more expensive than green sand or dry sand for molding. The chief advantage of cement molding, maximum mold-wall rigidity, can also be a disadvantage with some shapes and metals that are subject to hot tearing.

## VACUUM MOLDING

The vacuum molding method (V-Process) is a molding process in which the sand is held in place in the mold by vacuum. The mold halves are covered with a thin sheet of plastics to retain the vacuum. This is a licensed process with the North American rights being owned by the Herman-Sinto V-Process Corporation. Tilghman Wheelabrator possesses the rights in the United Kingdom. The license is purchased outright, and a royalty fee is paid for each ton of product shipped for sale.

The licensor designs, engineers, and manufactures equipment for making vacuum molds, but it is not imperative that the foundry buy the equipment. Some plants design and build their own equipment or buy from a third source. The licensor maintains a technical and service staff to aid and assist the foundries in producing castings by this method. Following are some of the salient points of the method.

### Process Description

Patterns are made in the usual manner; however, because they are not subject to the jolting and abrasive actions of sand, they do not have to be constructed as strongly as for conventional sand molding. The patterns can be distorted by the negative pressures, so they must be accurately supported in a pattern carrier to withstand the stresses. The pattern carrier is airtight and is evacuated by a connecting line at certain stages in the process.

There is also a connection to a positive air supply. Patterns and mounting boards are vented by various methods—usually by core box screens. The placement of gates and risers is similar to conventional methods. Experience indicates that it is not always necessary to use bottom entry tile gates. Simple parting-line gates also produce a clean, sound casting. However, there is one additional feature that must be included in the pattern rigging—communicators.

The communicators are vents or "flow-offs" that have a greater diameter than the sprue and should be located at the uppermost places in the mold cavity. The communicators maintain the pressure differential necessary for mold integrity. Gases are created and exhausted through the communicator. As the hot metal rises in the mold cavity, a portion of film above the metal line is vaporized, causing a vacuum leak. At this point, air enters the mold cavity through the communicators to maintain atmospheric pressure. The difference in pressure between the mold sand and the cavity and exterior surfaces keeps the mold and pattern together.

A copolymer-type plastics film, having an ethyl-vinyl-acetate blended with the polyethylene, is required. The film is heated to a plastic state, then pulled around the pattern by means of the vacuum in the pattern carrier, whereupon the plastics material takes a permanent set. The film application, or drawdown by the vacuum, should be done quickly, in five seconds or less. The V-Process molding method is illustrated schematically in Fig. 16-13 for the production of horizontally parted molds. A similar sequence applies to vertically parted molds, and it is possible to make a casting impression on both mold surfaces simultaneously.

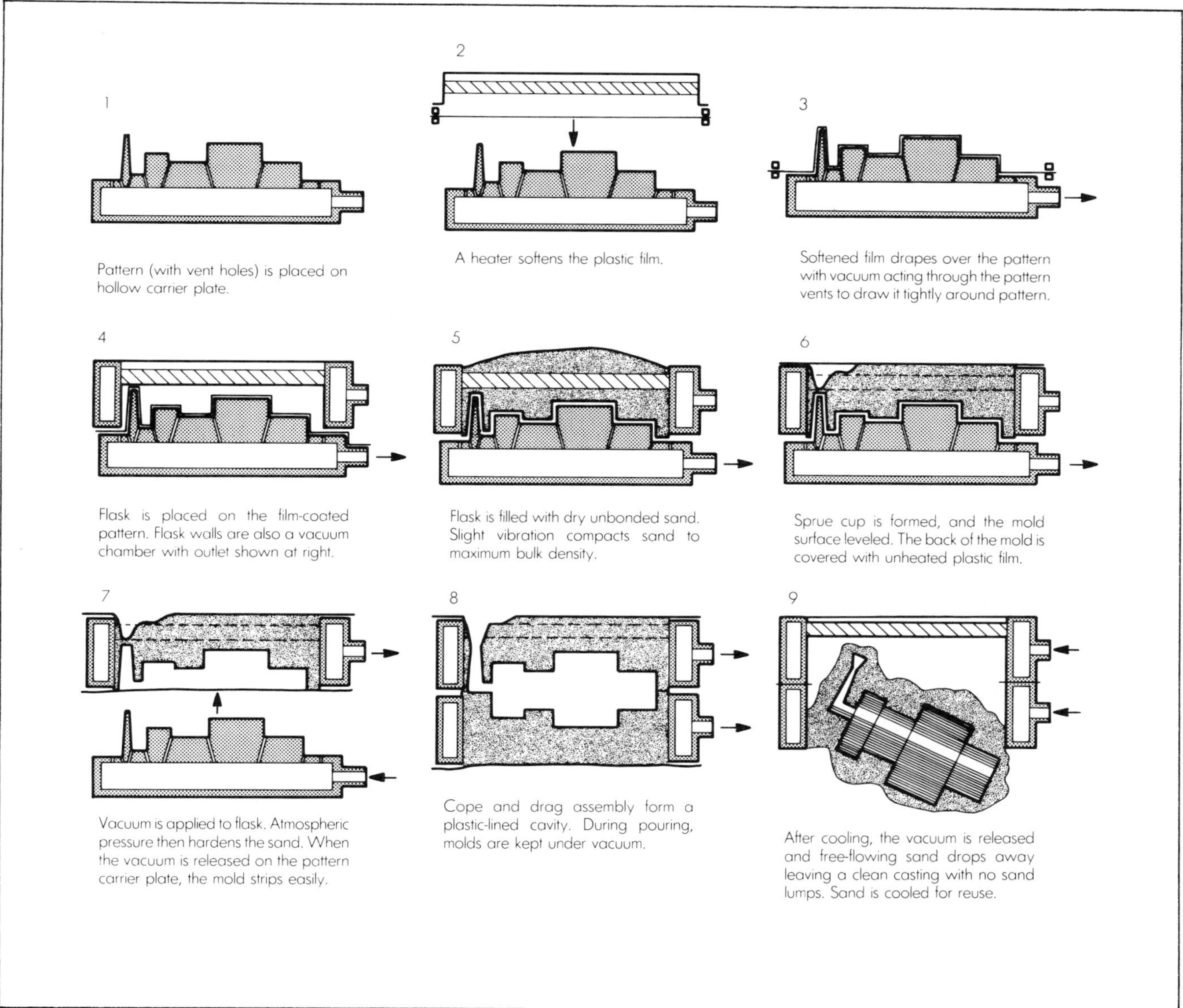


**Fig. 16-13 Schematic illustration of sequential steps in the V-Process molding method.** (*Herman-Sinto V-Process Corp.*)

## Mold Wash

A mold wash is applied to a "V" mold and serves a dual purpose. The higher refractory properties of the wash prevent sand burn-in, and the mold-wash coating on the plastics film stabilizes the sand surface layer and prevents erosion. The mold coating has a lower permeability than the sand; it acts as a heat barrier and aids the plastics in maintaining pressure differentials.

The preferred wash has a high percentage of solid material; typically, zircon flour is suspended in a volatile carrier such as isopropyl alcohol. A heavy coating, about 100 mils (2.5 mm) thick is applied and allowed to dry. Phenol resin is frequently used as a binder. It is critical to obtain a wash that adheres to the plastics film on vertical or cylindrical surfaces of the mold, because the sand tends to displace the coating during the vibration cycle.

## Flasks

Vacuum-mold flasks are about twice as expensive as conventional molding boxes. The walls are air chambers with the interior surface having a large part of its area covered with a screen that is fine enough to hold the sand yet porous enough to permit air passage. The external flask walls have at least two check-valved hose connections for vacuum attachment.

## Sands Used in Vacuum Molding

The vacuum molding process is fairly tolerant of the type of sand used. A clean, dry silica sand, having a grain fineness size of 55-60, is commonly used. Many foundries normally use this grain size; however a finer sand, 80-90 grain, has definite advantages. The finer sand forms a more densely packed mold having less voids and requiring less vacuum capacity.

# COREMAKING PROCESSES

The molding aggregate must be fluid and free-flowing to achieve maximum density. Olivine sands are used in manganese steel foundries with success, and chromite is used in one operation. Zircon, with its normal 105 grain fineness size, may prove to be economical because of its resistance to penetration and burn-in, especially on heavy section castings.

## Moldmaking

The pattern carrier is positioned on a table, to which multiple pairs of vibrators are attached. Tables have been built using vertical or horizontal vibrators. Vertical types are the most prevalent. Moldmaking is a critical part of the process because a high level of compaction is necessary.

The vibrators are of high frequency, very low amplitude type and generally require several 30-second periods of vibration to give the mold a good bulk density. Hydraulic mold draw mechanisms can be incorporated into the vibrating table. Air-lift bellows raise the table clear of the foundation during vibrating cycles.

## Vacuum Use and Equipment

After the flask has been filled with sand and the desired high bulk density achieved, vacuum lines are attached to the flask and pressure is reduced in the mold. A sheet of plastics is applied to the top surface of the mold. The vacuum is removed from the pattern carrier, and a positive pressure is applied to the pattern carrier. The mold is then stripped. The cope mold half is somewhat more complicated, since all mold cavity openings, such as sprues, open risers, and communicators, must be made airtight with the top sheet of plastics. The mold is then sent to a mold assembly area.

The vacuum system required for molding is simple. It consists of a water-sealed vacuum pump, with a drive motor, 40-150 hp (30-112 kW), a sand separator, filters, hose gages, and a silencer. A negative pressure of from 10-22 in. of Hg (33.8-74.3 kPa) is carried in the molds. The highest vacuum requirements occur during the pouring of the molds. Mold cavity size, section thickness, and sand fineness affect the vacuum volume that is necessary.

## Sand Handling

A closed sand system is very desirable for economic production. As previously discussed, no binders or moisture is required. Experience indicates a maximum loss of about 5% in carryout; fines are frequently added back into the sand. Core sand breakdown varies with the type of binder employed and the nature of the casting. Molds retain heat and are slow to cool; therefore, equipment should be provided in the return system to reduce sand temperature to below 120° F (49° C). At casting removal and mold release, the temperature of the sand is about 500° F (260° C).

## COREMAKING PROCESSES

Cores are needed to create the recesses, undercuts, and interior cavities that are often a part of castings. The sands, binders, methods, and equipment used to make these cores are described in this section, with the exception of those for shell cores, which are discussed in the previous section on shell molding. The processes described here may also be used in the production of molds as well as cores. The properties of various core binders are shown in Table 16-9. The binder manufacturers should be consulted concerning precautions necessary for the various materials.

## Oil-Oxygen Process

The oil-oxygen process is based on the oxidation and polymerization of a combination of oils containing chemical additives which, when activated by an oxygen-bearing material, gel or set in a predetermined time. More precisely, the drying oils absorb oxygen by auto-oxidation, isomerize to the conjugated form, and then polymerize to the solid state. When mixed with sand and an activator, the oil provides cores that have excellent dimensional stability, uniformity in hardness, and nondeforming properties. The oxygen-oil either eliminates or reduces the need for ramming, rodding for support, and long oven curing. The oxidation process is accelerated by metallic driers, by light and heat, and by the oxidation decomposition products that are formed concurrently.

The resulting core has better physical properties than it would have if it were made by conventional methods, and is ready for casting many hours sooner. When the finished casting is cooled and removed from the flask, the core simply collapses and pours out, eliminating the need to remove sand forcibly from recessed areas.

There are two main limitations to the oil-oxygen process. First, the sand mixture has a short bench life. Once the mix sets, it is no longer usable. Secondly, the process is limited to core production that normally does not exceed six to eight cores per box in an eight-hour period, thus lending itself to job work rather than production runs.

**Core and moldmaking procedure.** When using the oil-oxygen process to make cores or molds, the sand is prepared and mixed with binders and activators, then the core is poured, washed, finished, and oven baked.

*Sand handling.* Dry-sand storage and mulling equipment is located close to the core production area. Overhead hoppers provide the fastest discharge facilities. Coremaking stations are arranged in a straight line, usually in two rows separated by a center aisle. Overhead cranes generally deliver the sand and fill the boxes. A jib crane is sometimes used to fill boxes at one or two coremaking stations. When the boxes are filled, they are removed by a conveyor to stand until ready to be drawn.

Another widely used method of sand handling is to set up a straight-line roller conveyor that passes directly beneath a stationary hopper. The hopper is first filled with oil-oxygen sand, then the boxes are filled and rolled away until the sand has set and can be drawn.

*Sand preparation.* A typical oil-oxygen sand mix is 2% binder and 5-15% activator, depending on the amount of oil used. Almost any type of sand can be used as long as it is dry and at not more than 100° F (38° C). The amount of binder required depends on the surface area to be coated. An approximate 2% binder coats sand with a fineness of 45-55 grain. Finer sands or more angular sands require more binder.

Oxygen-bearing materials such as perborates, percarborates, permanganates, and peroxides are the principal activators in the oil-oxygen process. The amount of activator added to the sand determines the working time or setting time of that particular mix. As the activators react with the base oils, the oils begin to gel and harden. The rate of hardening is controlled by increasing or decreasing the amount of catalyst or oxidizing agent. When the sand mass has partially hardened, it is stripped from the corebox or pattern, whichever is used. The working life of the mix, generally about 30 minutes, must be controlled so that production schedules can be maintained.

*Sand mixing.* The oil-oxygen process can be carried out on all types of mixers and mullers, but a continuous-screw mixer is usually the most effective. The activator is blended into the trough by a vibrating chute or a screw-type feeder. A pump dispenses the liquid into the system. Since mixing is required only for coating purposes and the mixed sand is used immediately, setup times are faster than can be attained with batch-type mixing.

*Core pouring.* After mulling, the sand is ready to be poured into coreboxes. The prepared sand has excellent flowability and pours easily; it should not be rammed. Cores can be made as fast as the boxes or molds can be filled. The sand should be distributed evenly by hand throughout the box and tucked into corners and pockets. Rods are then positioned to carry hooks and help support overhanging areas. When the box is filled, it is struck off and the core is completed. The core is permitted to stand until the activator has reacted with the oil-oxygen binder to gel the oil films partially. When the mix has set, it is removed from the core box or mold. If necessary, oil-oxygen sand can be patched with a regular oil-sand mix.

*Core washing and finishing.* Core washing is just as important in the oil-oxygen process as in any other sand process. It reduces "burn-on," enhances core appearance, and provides better surface finishes. All types of washes can be used, including solvent-based types.

*Oven baking.* When core finishing is completed, the cores or molds are baked or oven cured long enough to complete the polymerization of the oils. Curing temperatures are from 400-450° F (204-232° C); curing time depends on core-section size and the type and efficiency of the oven. Moisture removal is no problem, since there is no water in the system. A 12" (305 mm) cube of oil-oxygen sand baked three hours at 450° F in a circulating oven bakes through and produces a scratch hardness in excess of $R_C$90. Conventional core sand mixes baked for the same length of time at the same temperature dry to a depth of only 3" (76 mm) from all sides. Depending on the type of oven, baking cycles are usually reduced 30-50% with use of the oil-oxygen process.

**Casting materials and applications.** The oil-oxygen process can be employed to cast all types of metals, including steel, gray iron, ductile iron, Meehanite iron, brass, bronze, aluminum, and aluminum alloys. The process has found its widest use in the larger ferrous-metal jobbing foundries. Large cores and molds can be produced rapidly at economically competitive rates. Typical of the castings produced by the oil-oxygen process are impeller wheels for steam turbines, 20-40 ton (19-36 metric ton) dies, bridge-saddle supports, and large gears.

## Carbon Dioxide Process

In the carbon dioxide ($CO_2$) process, clean, dry sand is mixed with a solution of sodium silicate and is rammed or blown into the corebox. When this mixture is gassed for several seconds with $CO_2$ gas, it forms a silica gel which binds the sand grains into a strong, solid form. Additional hardening of the resulting core may be carried out by baking at about 400° F (204° C), but baking is usually not necessary. The core is normally ready for use as soon as a suitable refractory coating has been applied.

Cores that are $CO_2$ gassed may be used to form all the usual alloys in a wide range of applications and sizes. A major application is the production of cores for steel, iron, aluminum, and copper-based alloy castings. Tolerances of $CO_2$ cores are equivalent to tolerances of cores developed by other processes.

Carbon dioxide consumption is an important economic factor in the $CO_2$ process. Not only is overuse of the gas costly in high-volume production, but extensive overgassing of cores may cause them to be broken easily and may reduce their shelf life. Any method of passing the $CO_2$ through the corebox may be used as long as a thorough combination of the gas with the binder in all corners and crevices of the core is ensured.

The $CO_2$ process corebox may be filled either by hand ramming or by blowing. Because the core does not need to be removed from the box before it has set, core driers and ovens are not needed and tolerances may be improved. Currently, there is no method of recovering the used sodium silicate sand mixture. Thus, the $CO_2$ process is impractical for the production of large molds.

Coreboxes for $CO_2$ process cores are usually made of metal or plastics. Most wood varnishes used on wooden coreboxes are attacked by the sodium silicate. If wood boxes must be used, they should be protected by an application of a varnish or silicone lacquer that is resistant to the effects of the binder.

## Furan No-Bake System

The development of the furan no-bake system is an outgrowth of research on the oil-oxygen process aimed at reducing or eliminating the need for oven baking. Among its advantages are a simplified sand mix (resin, activator, and sand), excellent flowability, and reduced rodding (high tensile strength restricts needed rodding to lifting hooks only). In addition, only semiskilled coremakers are needed, less core and mold finishing is required, hardness throughout the core is uniform, exact dimensions are attainable, cores are better fitting, and better shakeout is possible. The need for rough cleaning is reduced, machining and layout costs are lower, the need for oven baking is reduced or eliminated, and thermal cracks in the cores are absent.

No-bake binders are materials that convert from liquid to solid at room temperatures. It would be misleading to say that these materials never require oven drying or curing, since many cores cannot be cast successfully without some drying, usually because of the configuration of the casting and the type and temperature of the metal poured.

Furan is a generic term denoting the basic structure of a class of chemical compounds. The resins used in the no-bake system are composed of furfural alcohol, urea, and formaldehyde. When catalyzed with acids, these synthetic liquid resins form a tough, resinous film. The reaction is exothermic and forms a thermosetting resin. The temperature and type of sand, the speed and type of muller or mixer, the binder formulation, and the type and amount of activator used influence the speed of reaction.

A typical sand mix for the furan no-bake process consists of:

1. Washed and dried sand (less than 0.5% clay).
2. 2% furan no-bake resin.
3. 40% activator (phosphoric acid used in this system).

The basic reaction between the phosphoric acid and furan resin results in an acid dehydration of the resin.

Continuous mixers are best suited to this process, since they not only measure the materials and mix the ingredients but also deliver the prepared sand to the designated area. However, all types of mixers and mullers can be used successfully.

The quality of the cores is directly related to the corebox. Old coreboxes containing nicks and indentations, or boxes that have back draft, often prove difficult to draw. Takedown boxes are ideal.

Refractory coatings are generally used to wash the cores and improve the finish of the resultant castings. Alcohol, water, or chlorinated-solvent-type washes can be used. Regardless of the solvent used, it must be removed from the sand surfaces. An

**TABLE 16-9**
**Comparison of Properties for Various Mold and Core Binder Systems**

| | Protective Tensile Strength (1) | Rate of Gas Evolution (1) | Degree of Thermal Plasticity (1) | Collapsability Speed (1) | Ease of Breakout (2) | Moisture Resistance (2) | Curing Speed (1) | Strip Time, (min) (5) | Resistance to Overcure (2) | Optimum Temperature, °F (°C) | Clay and Fines Resistance (2) | Flowability (2) | Air Drying Rate (1) | Pouring Smoke (1) | Metals not Recommended |
|---|---|---|---|---|---|---|---|---|---|---|---|---|---|---|---|
| **ORGANIC** | | | | | | | | | | | | | | | |
| THERMOSETTING | | | | | | | | | | | | | | | |
| Shell Processes: | | | | | | | | | | | | | | | |
| Dry blend | H | M | L | M | F | G | H | | G | 500 (260) | F | E | N | M | |
| Warm coat (solvent) | H | M | L | M | F | G | H | | G | 500 (260) | F | E | N | M | |
| Hot coat | H | M | L | M | F | G | H | | G | 500 (260) | F | E | N | M | |
| Hot Box Processes: | | | | | | | | | | | | | | | |
| Furan | H | H | L | H | G | F | H | | F | 450 (230) | P | G | M | M | (3) |
| Phenolic | H | H | L | M | G | G | H | | F | 450 (230) | P | G | M | M | Steel |
| Oils: | | | | | | | | | | | | | | | |
| Core oil | M | M | M | H | G | G | L | | P | 400 (205) | F | F | H | M | |
| SELF-SETTING | | | | | | | | | | | | | | | |
| Furan No-Bakes: | | | | | | | | | | | | | | | |
| High nitrogen furan—acid | H | M | L | M | G | G | | 1-45 | | 80 (27) | P | G | H | M | Steel |
| Medium nitrogen furan—acid | H | M | L | M | G | G | | 1-45 | | 80 (27) | P | G | H | M | |
| Low nitrogen furan—acid | H | M | L | M | G | G | | 1-45 | | 80 (27) | P | G | H | M | |
| Phenolic No-Bakes: | | | | | | | | | | | | | | | |
| Phenolics—acid | M | M | L | M | G | G | | 2-45 | | 80 (27) | P | G | H | M | |
| Urethanes: | | | | | | | | | | | | | | | |
| Alkyd—organometallic | H | M | L | M | F | G | | 2-45 | | 90 (32) | F | F | H | H | |
| Phenolic—pyridine | M | H | L | H | G | F | | 2-20 | | 80 (27) | P | G | H | M | (4) |
| VAPOR-CURED (COLD BOX) | | | | | | | | | | | | | | | |
| Phenolic urethane—amine | M | H | L | H | G | F | H | | G | 75 (24) | P | G | H | M | (4) |
| Furan/peroxides—$SO_2$ | M | L | L | H | E | E | H | | E | 75 (24) | P | G | M | L | --- |
| Solvent evaporation—air | M | H | --- | --- | --- | G | H | | G | --- | --- | G | H | --- | --- |

**TABLE 16-9—*Continued***

| | Protective Tensile Strength (1) | Rate of Gas Evolution (1) | Degree of Thermal Plasticity (1) | Collapsability Speed (1) | Ease of Breakout (2) | Moisture Resistance (2) | Curing Speed (1) | Strip Time, (min) (5) | Resistance to Overcure (2) | Optimum Temperature, °F (°C) | Clay and Fines Resistance (2) | Flowability (2) | Air Drying Rate (1) | Pouring Smoke (1) | Metals not Recommended |
|---|---|---|---|---|---|---|---|---|---|---|---|---|---|---|---|
| **INORGANIC** | | | | | | | | | | | | | | | |
| THERMOSETTING | | | | | | | | | | | | | | | |
| Silicate (warm box) | H | L | L | M | P | F | H | | F | 250 (120) | P | G | M | M | (3) |
| SELF-SETTING | | | | | | | | | | | | | | | |
| Silicates: | | | | | | | | | | | | | | | |
| Sodium silicate—ester cured | M | L | H | L | P | P | | 5-60 | | 75 (24) | F | G | M | N | |
| Sodium silicate—FeSi cured | H | L | L | L | P | P | | 30 | | 75 (24) | F | G | H | N | |
| Sodium silicate—2 CaO $SiO_1$ cured | L | L | L | L | P | P | | 30 | | 75 (24) | F | G | H | N | |
| Cements: | | | | | | | | | | | | | | | |
| Cement—hydraulic cured | M | L | L | L | P | F | | 45 | | 75 (24) | F | F | L | N | |
| Cement (fluid sand)—hydraulic cured | L | L | L | L | P | F | | 30-60 | | 75 (24) | P | G | L | L | |
| Phosphates: | | | | | | | | | | | | | | | |
| Phosphate—oxide cured | M | L | L | M | G | P | | 30-60 | | 90 (32) | F | F | H | N | |
| VAPOR-CURED | | | | | | | | | | | | | | | |
| Sodium silicate—$CO_2$ | L | L | L | L | P | P | H | | P | 75 (24) | F | F | H | N | |

(*American Foundrymen's Society*)

Notes:
(1) H = High, M = Medium, L = Low, N = None
(2) E = Excellent, G = Good, F = Fair, P = Poor
(3) Use minimum $N_2$ levels for Steel
(4) Iron oxide required for Steel
(5) Rapid strip times require special mixing equipment

effective film of wash reduces the tendency of the sand to burn on and also reduces erosion caused by the molten metal flowing over a given area.

## Oil No-Bake Process

A significant advancement in binder development for medium to large castings, the oil no-bake process implements a synthetic-oil binder which, when mixed with basic sands and activated chemically, produces cores that can be cured at room temperature. This binder can be used either as a fast-baking oil-oxygen binder or as a substitute for the furan no-bake resin.

When compared with the oil-oxygen or the furan no-bake processes, the oil no-bake process offers optimum flowability, better depth of set, faster baking at reduced temperatures, easier draw, and lower production costs. The oil no-bake process can be used with all types of mullers and mixers; good castings are assured as long as the sand is clean and dry and well mixed with the oil no-bake ingredients.

Oil no-bake ingredients can be furnished as either three or two-component systems. A typical sand mix for a three-component system is:

| | |
|---|---|
| Sand, washed and dried | 1000 lb (454 kg) |
| Oil no-bake binder | 14 lb (6.4 kg) |
| Oil no-bake catalyst | 0.7 lb (0.3 kg) |
| Oil no-bake crosslinking agents | 2.8 lb (1.3 kg) |

For the two-component system, the mix would be:

| | |
|---|---|
| Sand, washed and dried | 1000 lb (454 kg) |
| Oil no-bake binder and catalyst | 14.7 lb (6.7 kg) |
| Oil no-bake crosslinking agents | 2.8 lb (1.3 kg) |

In the two-component system, the sand, binder, and catalyst are supplied in a premixed state.

Cores made with the oil no-bake process generally can be drawn with greater assurance of a complete set than those made with the oil-oxygen or furan no-bake processes, because the polymerization reaction results in a complete and uniform setting of the sand mass.

## Phenolic Core Binders

The trend in the foundry industry is toward increased use of room temperature curing binders to make cores and molds by cold pressing techniques. Table 16-10 provides general information on advantages and limitations of various chemical core binder systems. Recent developments in phenolic no-bake technology make this binder system an economical choice for a variety of casting applications.

**Acid-catalyzed binders.** When mixed with sand, the phenolic-based (phenol formaldehyde) acid-catalyzed binders undergo an exothermic condensation reaction to form a cured polymer. Produced by reacting phenol with formaldehyde, phenolic-based resins are subject to autopolymerization reaction at ambient or slightly higher temperatures. It is recommended that this type of binder be stored at temperatures of 80°F (27°C) or lower. Phenolic resins cannot be used with phosphoric acid, but they work well with the stronger sulfonated products such as exlene sulfonic (XSA), tulene sulfonic (TSA), and benzene sulfonic (BSA).

The curing characteristics of acid-catalyzed resins, as well as other no-bake systems, are typically monitored through the use of compressive strength cure curves, with the work and strip time defined as the time required for the sand mix to develop 1 psi (7 kPa) and 20 psi (140 kPa) compressive strength, respectively.

**TABLE 16-10**
**Chemical Core Binder Comparison***

| ACID CATALYZED NO-BAKES |
|---|
| Furan |
| + Good strength development; excellent hot strength; color change during cure; various $N_2$, $H_2O$, and FA levels |
| - Very sand sensitive; 10-60 min strip; 4 hr minimum pour-off; resin shelf life (silane degradation); acid handling; slow through-cure |
| Phenolic |
| + Zero-low $N_2$ content; good strength properties; color change during cure |
| - 15-60 min strip; sand sensitivity; 4 hr minimum pour-off; strong acid catalyst required; slow through-cure |
| URETHANE NO-BAKES |
| Alkyd oil |
| + Excellent stripping; least sensitive to control; water free; low $N_2$; no unpleasant fumes; wide strip time range; good through-cure |
| - Moderate unbaked hot strength; 18-24 hr cure before pour-off (without baking); 15-140 min strip |
| Phenolic |
| + 30 sec to 2 hr strip; low sand sensitivity; excellent flow-ability; 10 min pour-off; excellent through-cure |
| - Zero retention mixer; process layout; iron oxide for steel; release (rigid cure) |
| INORGANIC NO-BAKES |
| Sodium silicate |
| + Environmental; decreased cost; low sand sensitivity; low gas evolution; low water |
| - slow cure characteristics; poor shake-out; wet reclamation low strength; humidity sensitive |
| Cement |
| + Environmental; very low cost; non-sand sensitive |
| - Slow cure characteristics; poor shake-out and reclamation; high cement and $H_2O$ additions; release (rigid cure) |
| Aluminum phosphate |
| + Environmental; low sand sensitivity; low gas evolution; low water; good shake-out and reclamation |
| - Slow cure characteristics; low strength; humidity sensitive |
| VAPOR-CURED SYSTEMS |
| Furan/$SO_2$ |
| + Fast cure; long bench life; good hot strength; color change during cure; good shake-out |
| - Material handling; closed system gassing; corrosive; sand sensitive, resin build-up on pattern |
| Phenolic urethane/amine |
| + Very fast cure; low sand sensitivity; high productivity; medium bench life |
| - Iron oxide for steel; closed system gassing |
| Sodium silicate/$CO_2$ |
| + Environmental; low sand sensitivity; decreased cost; low gas evolution; non-hazardous gas |
| - Poor shake-out and reclamation; low strengths; humidity sensitive |

(*Ashland Chemical Company*)

* Plus (+) = advantages; minus (-) = limitations

# CORE AND COREBOX-MAKING METHODS

Sand mixes having compressive strengths approaching 1 psi lack the flowability needed to produce dense cores or molds. Likewise, 20 psi represents the point at which the sand mix has reached sufficient strength to be drawn from the pattern or corebox without sag or distortion. Ideally, a no-bake resin would have a work/strip time approaching one.

**Urethane binders.** The urethane binders fall into two categories: alkyd and phenolic. The alkyd types are actually three-part systems consisting of alkyd resin, metal driers, and/or amine catalysts and isocyanate. These binders are characterized by deep-setting curing properties because the urethane reaction does not produce detrimental by-products that may retard the curing process.

Two characteristics distinguish phenolic urethane binders from other no-bake binders: (1) the work/strip time ratio is typically on the order of 0.80 to 1, and (2) the reaction produces no by-products that affect cure rate. The phenolic binders consist of three components: phenolic resin, isocyanate, and amine-based catalysts. A typical silica sand mix is made with equal parts of phenolic and isocyanate ingredients and 2% catalyst.

The sand surface, chemistry, temperature, and moisture content have an effect on the cure of phenolic urethane resins. However, unlike acid-catalyzed binder systems, small fluctuations in sand temperature do not cause significant changes in curing properties. Moisture content should be maintained below 0.2% of sand weight.

Phenolic urethane no-bake binders are generally recognized as state of the art in chemically bonded sands. As stated previously, curing is achieved by the reaction of a phenolic polyol with a polymeric isocyanate in the presence of a base catalyst. This resin system exhibits excellent working properties and uniform deep setting. Most cores or molds develop strength rapidly and can be poured within an hour after stripping.

### Microwave Curing

The growing use of fast-reacting sand binders and the improvements in output of core and moldmaking equipment have led to a need for new technology in other foundry operations. Most cores and molds must be coated and post baked and often must be assembled by being glued together. The capability for rapid production of cores and molds must be matched with increased production rates in subsequent operations so that final casting can be accomplished in the least time.

**Microwave principle.** Microwave technology is being applied to foundry core heating and curing. When an electromagnetic wave is propagated in a heatable dielectric material, its energy is converted to heat. In the foundry field, water is a major dielectric material that can be heated by microwave energy.

The water molecules consist of hydrogen and oxygen atoms arranged so that the molecule is electrically neutral. The electrical charges within the molecule have a dipole moment and are said to be polar. An electrical field exerts a twisting force that attempts to align the molecules with the field.

When the direction of the electrical field is reversed, the molecules attempt to reverse their orientation. However, in doing so, frictional forces created by the molecules' rubbing together must be overcome and energy is dissipated as heat. Friction generates heat, and the dielectric material becomes hot.

**Dielectric materials.** In addition to water, other good, heatable dielectric materials used in foundries include phenolic resins of all types, furan hotbox resins, urethane no-bakes, and all the inorganic binder systems. Green sand is very heatable due to its water content and carbon impurities. Reactivity of the binders increases as the temperature rises. Microwave heating can raise the temperature of the binder to the point at which its exothermic property carries the curing reaction through completion.

**Advantages.** While initial microwave equipment costs are high, the following advantages merit consideration in some applications for processing cores and molds.[6]

- Speed of processing yields increased throughput.
- Cores and molds are processed at reduced temperatures, facilitating handling.
- Low core temperature eliminates sand binder thermoplasticity problems.
- Complete removal of water from cores and molds reduces casting defects.
- It is compatible with low-cost, hot-melt adhesives.
- Elimination of separate core glue curing cycle is possible.
- New microwave sand binders can be used that can be water-based and nonpolluting and that require lower cost coreblowers and coreboxes.
- Processing is effectively controlled due to uniform heating and accurate instrumentation.
- Energy savings can be made.

## CORE AND COREBOX-MAKING METHODS

The most widely accepted methods and equipment used to make cores are described in this section. For details concerning the sands, binders, and other materials that can be used to make a core, see the preceding descriptions for each process.

### Bench and Floor Coremaking

Many large cores are still made in wooden coreboxes placed on the foundry floor for packing and filling. After the core cavity is filled with sand, a heavy metal cover, or core plate, is clamped to the face of the box and the entire mass is lifted by an overhead crane. The assembly is then inverted 180° on trunnions located on opposite sides of the corebox and is lowered, plate down, to the floor. The clamps are removed, and the corebox is drawn (carefully raised from the core) by a crane. With oil-bonded or urea-bonded sand mixes that require baking before the core is hardened, the box can be removed immediately. For $CO_2$ cores, the core must be hardened by gassing while it is in the corebox. For the no-bake mixes, the cores must be left in the corebox long enough to permit catalytic reaction to harden the oil or resin, usually about 30 minutes. During this time, other coreboxes can be cycled.

### Core Blowing

The need for mass production of cores led to the development of core blowing in the late 1920s. Basically the core-blowing machine propels the premixed core sand from the machine chamber into the corebox cavity by compressed air. The chamber is alternately opened to receive the sand mix and closed to retain the air pressure when the blow-air valve is opened. The water-passage core in an automobile cylinder head is a typical example of this type of blown core. Before core blowing was developed, it took a skilled coremaker 20 minutes to produce such a core. Using the core-blowing method, a less-skilled coremaker can turn out 120 cores per hour.

Initially all blown cores were oil or urea-bonded and had to be baked for hardening. They were usually made in vertically split coreboxes with two half boxes matched with free-fitting line-up dowels. This type of box could be handled manually. It was closed, slid against stops under the blow magazine, and air clamped. The core was then blown, the clamp was released, and the box with its cores was withdrawn from under the magazine. One half of the box was then usually lifted or drawn away, leaving the soft, wet cores in the other half of the box. The simpler cores were then placed on a flat core plate adjacent to the previously blown cores, and the remaining half of the box was carefully withdrawn. The filled core plate was then put into the oven for baking. Many cores of this type required the use of core driers to support the irregular contours prior to and during baking.

The blow-tube type of horizontally split corebox, currently used to produce more complex core shapes, can be handled either manually or by machine, depending on its size and weight.

The introduction of phenolic resin-coated sands in the early 1950s revolutionized foundry core practice. It enabled cores to be provided that significantly improved the finish of the casting surface and permitted accuracies that were previously unattainable.

In the core-blowing operation, this resin-coated sand is blown into a heated corebox. For best results, the temperature range should be from 400° F (204° C) minimum to 550° F (288° C) maximum. After the box is blown full of coated sand, pauses of 15 seconds to 3 minutes in the cycle are required, depending on the thickness of the core. The corebox is then inverted to permit the excess material to drain from the corebox cavity for subsequent use. Although resin-coated sand is usually more expensive than other core-sand mixes, the additional costs are often offset by this draining technique. In addition, the lightweight cores are easy to handle, often eliminating the need for hoists, and they can be stored indefinitely before use without deterioration.

A modification of the shell coremaking method uses vertically split coreboxes mounted in core machines with the blow opening in the bottom. The coated sand is blown upward from the sand chamber below, and the blow pressure is maintained for about 5-10 seconds. When the pressure is released, the excess material drains back into the sand chamber by gravity. This method is particularly suited to small cores with shell thicknesses in the 1/8" (3 mm) range.

**Large cores.** For some of the larger cores, it is economically feasible to make the cores in two halves and join them after coremaking. This type of core does not drain. The mix is blown into a confined cavity in which the interior configuration, that portion of the core which does not face the molten metal, is built into the corebox. This arrangement permits core cross sections to be made exactly to the requirements of the job. It is also common practice to make the lightening mandrels in sections. These sections are spaced to create reinforcing ribs in the shell core to provide rigidity at points of stress. This technique makes more effective use of the core material because it increases the strength attained by curing the core from both sides. Coremaking time is also reduced as a result of faster curing.

**Venting.** In all types of core blowing, some means of exhausting the core cavity is desirable, since most core configurations cannot be blown without some type of venting. Shell coreboxes operating at elevated temperatures should have a minimum number of vents. Maintenance problems with these installations can seriously curtail production. Parting-line reliefs or vents should be machined in the joint face of the corebox to exhaust the box cavity, providing a densely blown core. If other venting is required, a self-cleaning vent should be used and daily inspection and replacement of these vents should be made a routine.

The venting of shell cores differs greatly from that of other types of cores. The original oil-sand or urea postbaked cores are blown with what is called a wet mix. This material is more resistant to blowing and requires greatly increased corebox exhausting or venting. In the case of horizontally split coreboxes blown through blow tubes, the top surface of the core cavity around the blow tubes must be covered with core vents. By contrast, the bottom of the lower half of the box has very few vents. The explosive blowing action propels the sand mass downward, creating the need for instantaneous exhausting of the air from the top of the corebox to permit dense packing. The fewer vents in the bottom of the corebox help lead or channel the sand to those core areas that are away from the direct line of the blow tubes.

For $CO_2$ cores, the coreboxes are vented in nearly the same manner as boxes for the oil-sand cores. In this case, however, the core vents serve an additional purpose. After the silicate sand mix has been blown into the corebox, it is hardened by gassing. For thorough hardening, the $CO_2$ gas must permeate the entire core. The amount of gas used can vary dramatically, depending on the number of top vents. If there are too many vents, the $CO_2$ escapes too quickly, leaving the bottom section of the core only partially cured. For this reason, the number and placement of vents in a $CO_2$ corebox must be a compromise.

**Hot box.** Making hot-box furan-sand cores differs slightly from oil-sand core blowing and shell coremaking. The hot-box mix is wet, rather than dry and free-flowing as is the shell sand. The cores are solid and can be made in a shorter cycle. Their surfaces are hard upon removal from the corebox, but the cores are relatively weak since the catalyst reaction continues after removal until the core cures through to the center. Because of their fragility, these cores are ejected from the bottom half of the corebox with ejection pins to avoid the breakage that sometimes occurs in manual removal.

**Cold box.** The relatively new cold-box technique is similar to the hot-box method except that the coreboxes operate at ambient temperatures. The main difference is that cold-box core blowing is a gassing function rather than a catalyst reaction. Cold-box gas differs from $CO_2$ in that it is slightly toxic. The coreboxes must be tightly sealed during gassing, and the gas must be vented outdoors through a filter.

## Corebox Economics

Very few coreboxes for castings of less than about 10 tons (9 metric tons) are made of wood. Production rates usually dictate the use of sturdier, longer lasting coreboxes; and in some instances, casting accuracy requirements may influence the selection of corebox material and the method of construction. For shell and hot-box coremaking, elevated temperatures usually require metal coreboxes—usually aluminum or cast iron. However, aluminum is unsatisfactory for most applications in which long corebox life is required or in which the cores are fragile. Various alloys of either gray iron or ductile iron are generally used for most hot-box or shell cores. In addition, cavity finishing is not as critical as it is with the other methods.

Plastics coreboxes can be used to make oil-sand, $CO_2$, and cold-box cores. A well-engineered, plastics-lined, metal-framed corebox works well in some medium-sized production operations. These plastics liners are generally made of epoxy or polyurethane. The complexity of the core contours encountered in farm machinery and tractor production justifies the use of plastics coreboxes in those operations. Cores of simpler configurations can be made in all-metal coreboxes that would cost less for these applications than the best-quality plastics-lined boxes.

The main consideration in corebox construction is assurance that the equipment is compatible with the foundry's coremaking facilities. If the production requirements for a new casting warrant, and if the capital costs for a new type of core machine can be amortized in a short time with reduced core costs, such expenditures should be made. It must be kept in mind that core costs represent a major portion of the cost of producing most castings.

## MELTING AND POURING

Changes in melting and pouring practices have resulted from state and federal pollution-abatement regulations, but have no effect on the finished casting. The most significant change has resulted from the air-emission regulation, which has made it necessary to replace cupola melting with electric melting of gray iron. The quality of the iron is the same for both, but the costs of controlling air emissions from a cupola are often many times higher than the costs of controlling those from an electric furnace.

### Melting Methods

As far as the user is concerned, the differences are negligible between the various electric melting methods—direct arc, indirect arc, and high and low-frequency induction. Each method is suited to a particular application, depending upon the type of metal to be melted, refractory life, and fume-control requirements. When properly operated, all these methods can provide satisfactory results.

The direct-arc electric process is almost universally used to melt carbon and low-alloy steel for castings. The open-hearth, converter, and crucible processes are practically extinct. However, the argon-oxygen decarburization (AOD) process is gaining acceptance for melting of both low and high-alloy steels due to the ability to control sulfur and gas levels and to minimize oxidation losses of chromium. The basic oxygen melting process has not been adapted to cast steels. High-frequency induction melting is used for high-alloy steels and especially for very low-carbon steels with less than 0.10% carbon; however, it is at an economic disadvantage with the direct-arc method for carbon and low-alloy steels. Low-frequency induction melting of steel is impractical because of refractory problems.

The electric melting method is advantageous for melting ductile iron because of its ability to produce low-sulfur iron (iron with less than 0.05% sulfur). However, the basic cupola produces even less sulfur than the acid electric process. Acid cupola iron can be desulfurized to give comparable low-sulfur iron. Again, airborne pollution is usually the controlling factor determining the melting process; equally acceptable metal can be produced by any of the processes.

The same pollution and economic factors are the chief determinants in the melting processes for malleable iron. Many nonferrous metals are melted by some form of the crucible process as well as by electricity. In most cases metal quality depends on skilled operators, not equipment variations.

### Pouring Methods

Only one significant exception (centrifugal force) exists to the stationary, nonpressurized pouring of sand-mold castings because any appreciable increase in pressure over that imposed by the atmosphere and gravity only forces the metal into the interstices between the grains of sand. No increase in density can be obtained in a static sand mold above that obtained by directional solidification.

Centrifugal force, however, assists in producing a large volume of iron pipe by spinning a sand or metal mold about its horizontal axis. It is not generally recognized that in using this process, tubular shapes with wall thicknesses from a fraction of an inch to several inches and diameters measured in feet are economically produced in practically any metal. The designer has more freedom with centrifugal tubular castings than would be possible if these shapes were to be formed by a wrought process. (Further details concerning centrifugal casting are included in this chapter under "Centrifugal Casting.")

## CLEANING AND FINISHING

The cleaning of castings is a critical cost factor to both the producer and the user. With costs necessarily calculated to four-decimal accuracy, it is important that the producer and user specifically define what a cleaned or finished casting should entail before signing any purchase agreement. Some of the items to be specified are: (1) finish; (2) size; (3) locators; (4) allowable ranges in hardness, chemistry, and gate and riser tolerances; (5) weight; (6) amount of machining; (7) surface condition, including oil, paint, and degree of oxidation; (8) impregnation; (9) type of cleaning medium; (10) types of repairs; (11) procedure for repairing; and (12) acceptable repaired locations.

These and many other items that apply to special alloys must be considered. Various trade associations have established standards for each alloy system. What may be a workable system for one producer may be beyond the capabilities and equipment of a competitor, and unit costs between producers could differ appreciably.

The producer should be able to provide a schematic process line layout that indicates whether the casting is accurately located for finishing. In some instances, it may be advantageous to do some preliminary machining, locating, etc., at considerable savings to the purchaser.

The line process selected for cleaning depends on whether the alloy is tough, ductile, or brittle. Proper gating design and mechanical flagging allow easy removal of gates to within 1/8" (3 mm) or less on small, brittle, mechanical-mixture alloys such as gray iron. The same problem in ductile brass, aluminum, steel, and other alloys means that gates must be sawed, flame cut, or press trimmed before the casting goes to the next step in the process. In either jobbing or production foundries, cleaning can usually be divided into two categories—rough cleaning in the foundry and finishing in a special foundry area (the cleaning or finishing room). It is recommended that as much metal as possible be removed in the foundry to prevent double and triple handling.

Castings are hauled from the foundry to the cleaning area by a variety of means. In production foundries, they are usually conveyed; in job shops, batch handling is normally used to prevent mixing. The hard, brittle alloys, with their gates and risers occasionally removed, go directly to some type of surface-cleaning device. The cleaning methods control the final finish to

# CLEANING AND FINISHING

a great degree. The general methods used are (1) wire brushing, (2) shotblasting, (3) tumbling, and (4) chemical treating.

The following are a few considerations for each process. Additional information on brushing, shotblasting, tumbling, and chemical treatment is presented in Volume III, *Materials, Finishing, and Coating*, of this Handbook series.

1. Wire brushing:
   - Type of brush—manual or power-driven.
   - Brush material.
   - Size of wire in the brush.
   - Size and shape of the casting.
   - Casting production rate.
2. Shotblasting:
   - Whether wet or dry.
   - Whether air-blown or centrifugal.
   - Size, hardness, and shape of casting.
   - Size and type of blasting material—metallic, non-metallic, organic (see also Table 16-11).
   - Finish desired.
   - Effect on physical and mechanical properties.
   - Whether continuous, by batch, or programmed.
3. Tumbling:
   - Whether wet or dry.
   - Barrel-loading design.
   - Abrasive composition and geometry.
   - Finish desired.
   - Size and shape of the casting.
4. Chemical treating:
   - Type of chemical—acid, basic, or salt.
   - Size of the casting.
   - Contamination of the casting surface.

With the emphasis on pollution abatement, many foundries clean castings prior to grinding and trimming. This reduces excessive gassing or pinholing in some melting processes and results in less slag and effluent. The next step involves cleaning the gate and riser areas to meet specified tolerances. This varies with the type of alloy and the degree of cleaning the casting has already received up to this point. The three main categories for cleaning, and the methods used in each category, are shown in Table 16-12. Detailed information on grinding, sawing, and hand-cutting gates and risers is given in Tables 16-13, 16-14, and 16-15. Additional information on grinding and sawing is presented in Volume I, *Machining*, of this Handbook series.

The final step before inspection is usually referred to as chipping. This encompasses the removal of thin sections of metal from the casting parting line and core prints, and the cleaning of the cored areas that are hard to reach by other finishing methods. Some high-production foundries have automated many of these tasks, including inspection or sizing. Techniques and equipment commonly used are hammer and chisel, pneumatic hammers, pneumatic grinders, contour grinders, definning machines, barrel tumblers, and rotary tools.

**TABLE 16-11**
**Recommended Sizes of Abrasive for Casting Shot Blasting**

| Castings | SAE Size No. |
|---|---|
| Average gray or annealed malleable, with pockets, burned in sand, etc. | S390 shot |
| Light gray iron or annealed malleable | S330 shot |
| Hard malleable | S330 shot |
| Brass (all types) | G50 or G120 grit |
| Die castings | G50 grit |
| Aluminum | G50 grit |
| Steel | S330 shot |

(*American Wheelabrator Equipment Corp.*)

## HEAT TREATMENT

Depending on specifications, the heat treatment of castings may or may not precede final inspection. The following is a breakdown of the two generally applied heat-treatment methods for castings. For details on heat treating, see *Materials, Finishing, and Coating*, Volume III of this Handbook series.

1. Softening treatments:
   - Full annealing.
   - Process annealing.
   - Spheroidizing.
   - Solution annealing.
   - Isothermal annealing.
   - Malleabilizing annealing.
   - Tempering.
   - Normalizing.
2. Hardening Treatments:
   - Quenching—brine, water, or oil.
   - Precipitation hardening.
   - Flame hardening.
   - Induction hardening.
   - Austempering.
   - Marquenching.
   - Martempering.

## INSPECTION

Final inspection depends upon the agreement between the producer and the user. Inspection can be very simple or extremely complicated, depending upon the end use of the casting. Aerospace requirements usually call for high-integrity castings; therefore, they involve extensive destructive, environmental, and nondestructive testing methods.

## FINISHING

Castings can be finished in a number of ways by a variety of painting, plating, and coating processes. However, the specific alloy used and the particular applications are the main determinants in selecting the finish for the final finished part.

**TABLE 16-12**
**Casting-Cleaning Methods**

| Cleaning Method | Alloy Type: Soft and Brittle | Hard and Brittle | Ductile Tough |
|---|---|---|---|
| Grinding | • | • | • |
| Broaching | • | | |
| Shearing | • | | • |
| Torching | | • | • |
| Snagging | | • | |
| Sawing | | | • |
| Trimming | | | • |
| Machining | | | • |
| Coining | | | • |
| Punching | | | • |

**TABLE 16-13**
**Abrasive Wheels for Grinding Castings**

| Casting | Grain Size | Wheel Type | Bond | Speed and Equipment |
|---|---|---|---|---|
| Gray iron | 16-21 | Silicon carbide | Vitreous | 5000-6000 sfm (25-31 m/s), floor stand and swing frame |
| | | Silicon carbide | Resinous | 7000-9500 sfm (36-48 m/s), floor stand and swing frame |
| Brass | 24-30 | Silicon carbide | Vitreous | 5000-6000 sfm (25-31 m/s), floor stand |
| | | Silicon carbide | Resinous | 7000-9500 sfm (36-48 m/s), floor stand |
| Steel | 14-20 | Aluminum oxide | Vitreous | 5000-12,000 sfm (25-61 m/s), swing frame, floor stand, and portable |
| | | Aluminum oxide | Resinous | 9000-16,000 sfm (46-81 m/s), swing frame, floor stand, and portable |
| Aluminum | 21-30 | Silicon carbide | Vitreous | 5000-6000 sfm (25-31 m/s), floor stand |
| | | Aluminum oxide | Resinous or shellac | 7100-9500 sfm (36-48 m/s) floor stand |
| Malleable Iron | 20 | Aluminum oxide or silicon carbide | | |

**TABLE 16-14**
**Bandsawing Conditions for Casting Gate Removal**

| | Speed, fpm (m/s) | | | | |
|---|---|---|---|---|---|
| Casting Material | Low Speed | High Speed | Feeding Force, lb (N) | Lubricant | General Information |
| Copper-based alloy | 400 (2) or less | 2000 (10) or less buttress type | 25 (111) to 1″ (25 mm) thickness | Used if chips weld to saw blade. | Sawing speed decreases as hardness increases. |
| Aluminum and magnesium | Up to 500 (2.5) buttress blade | Up to 3500 (18) on 1/2″ (12.7 mm) section | Low | Ordinarily dry | 4-pitch, 0.50″ (12.7 mm) speed increases with section thickness. |
| Ferrous (bandsawing) | 50-500 (0.2-2.5) | 1500 (7.6) or less | Moderate | May be used if chips weld to saw blade. | |
| Ferrous (friction sawing) | | 3000-15,000 (15-76) | 20-40 (89-178) | None | 1/4 to 1″ (6.4 to to 25 mm) width blade with 10-18 teeth per in. (0.4-0.7/mm) |

**TABLE 16-15**
**Operating Data for Hand-Cutting Carbon-Steel Castings**

| Section Thickness, in. (mm) | Cutting Orifice Diameter, in. (mm) | Oxygen Pressure, psi (kPa) | Cutting Speed, in./min (mm/s) | Oxygen Usage, $ft^3/hr$ ($m^3/hr$) | Acetylene Usage, $ft^3/hr$ ($m^3/hr$) |
|---|---|---|---|---|---|
| 1.0 (25) | 0.047-0.060 (1.19-1.52) | 28-40 (193-276) | 9-18 (4-8) | 130-160 (3.7-4.5) | 13-16 (0.4-0.5) |
| 2.0 (51) | 0.067-0.081 (1.70-2.06) | 22-50 (152-345) | 6-13 (3-6) | 185-231 (5.2-6.5) | 16-20 (0.5-0.6) |
| 3.0 (76) | 0.067-0.081 (1.70-2.06) | 33-55 (227-379) | 4-10 (2-4) | 207-290 (5.9-8.2) | 16-23 (0.5-0.7) |
| 4.0 (102) | 0.080-0.091 (2.03-2.31) | 42-60 (289-413) | 4-8 (2-4) | 235-388 (6.7-11.0) | 20-26 (0.6-0.7) |
| 6.0 (152) | 0.098-0.100 (2.49-2.54) | 36-80 (248-551) | 3-5.4 (1-2) | 400-567 (11.3-16.1) | 25-32 (0.7-0.9) |
| 10.0 (254) | 0.100-0.110 (2.54-2.79) | 66-96 (454-661) | 1.9-3.2 (1-2) | 610-750 (17.2-21.2) | 36-46 (1.0-1.3) |
| 12.0 (305) | 0.110-0.120 (2.79-3.05) | 58-86 (400-593) | 1.4-2.6 (1-1) | 720-905 (20.3-25.6) | 42-55 (1.2-1.6) |
| 24.0 (610) | 0.221-0.332 (5.61-8.43) | 22-48 (152-331) | --- | 1600-3000 (45-85) | --- |
| 36.0 (914) | 0.290-0.500 (7.37-12.7) | 12-38 (83-262) | --- | 3000-4600 (85-130) | --- |

(*American Welding Society*)

# METAL-MOLD CASTING

In metal-mold casting, molten metal is poured or forced into a mold made entirely of metal or into a mold in which the outer form is made of metal. The principal methods of producing castings in metal molds are high-pressure die casting, permanent and semipermanent-mold casting, low-pressure casting, and centrifugal-mold casting.

A metal-mold casting generally exhibits superior surface finish, close dimensional tolerances, and improved mechanical properties as compared to those of a sand casting. The process can be justified economically when the quantity of castings and the savings in per-piece machining justify the cost of the metal mold and associated equipment. Refinements in mechanical metal-mold cycling that increase output, reduce machine downtime, and decrease the direct labor content have greatly increased the economic return from these casting methods.

Successful metal-mold casting requires a knowledge of (1) melting, cooling, and handling of alloys; (2) metal flow in metal molds and dies; (3) solidification and shrinkage of alloys; (4) correct gating and venting for sound casting structure; (5) tolerances as they affect mold costs and casting dimensions; and (6) required production rates. In addition, knowledge of sound mechanical concepts of mold design and automation is critical.

## HIGH-PRESSURE DIE CASTING

Die casting has long been recognized as one of the most economical and effective methods of producing moderate to high-volume quantities of near-net-shape components. The primary requirements for producing commercially acceptable high-pressure die castings (referred to hereafter as die castings) are an efficiently operating casting machine; a well-designed and well-constructed die; and a suitable casting alloy. In addition, the product must be designed for production by die casting.

In die casting, molten metal is forced under pressure into metal molds or dies. Necessary equipment consists essentially of the molds and a die-casting machine that holds, opens, and closes the molds or dies. The process is economical for producing castings with complex contours; holes and contours can be cast which would be costly to produce by machining operations. Holes are cast to tolerances that often compare with those of drilled, reamed, or counterbored holes, and surfaces and dimensions of die castings usually require little or no machining or finishing.

### Casting Machines

A die-casting machine has four main elements: (1) the die mounting and clamping system, (2) the die, (3) the injection mechanism, and (4) a source of molten metal. The machine frame incorporates a stationary platen (cover) and a movable platen (ejector) to which the die halves are attached. The basic function of the casting machine is to open and close the die and to lock it against the pressure of the molten metal developed by the injection mechanism.

The opening and closing mechanism, which actuates the movable platen, can be pneumatic, mechanical, hydraulic, or a combination of these. The most common method uses compound toggles, with the force supplied by a hydraulic cylinder. Other closing methods are (1) direct hydraulic, (2) wedge-lock hydraulic, (3) cam-lock hydraulic, and (4) mechanical with hydraulic lock.

Die casting machine clamping systems generally are four-bar presses. Solid, one-piece frame machines are used to a lesser degree. Machines are normally rated by the magnitude of the clamping force, generally expressed in tons or kilonewtons. Another method specifies the shot-weight capacity of the injection system.

Recently, the "P-$Q^2$" diagram, a graphic method of rating metal pumping capacity (pressure and metal flow rate), has become an accepted way of determining whether a machine of a given clamping force can not only hold the die halves together, but can also inject a sufficient quantity of metal with adequate speed to produce acceptable parts with the particular dies intended for the machine.

An alternative technique for expressing pumping capacity is to specify the "dry shot speed" (maximum plunger speed attainable with no metal present in the shot chamber), the maximum static pressure applied to the metal at zero plunger speed, and the maximum volume of metal each shot can contain for a given plunger diameter. It is also important to determine the maximum number of shots per hour that the machine can maintain without a drop in system hydraulic pressure.

Two general types of metal injection mechanisms for high-pressure die-casting machines are the hot-chamber type and the cold-chamber type.

**Hot-chamber machines.** The oldest type of die-casting machine, and the simplest to operate, is the hot-chamber machine. Depending on size, such machines can operate at about 100 shots per hour for castings up to 50 lb (23 kg), or several thousand shots per hour for single-impression castings weighing fractions of an ounce. In the United States, hot-chamber die casting is usually limited to the zinc alloys and, in a minor way, to the lead and tin alloys. In recent years, hot-chamber magnesium has been introduced and is gaining acceptance for certain product applications.

Hot-chamber die-casting machines are limited to use with alloys that do not chemically attack or erode the submerged metal injection system. Aluminum and copper alloys are not suitable for use in the hot-chamber machines.

The submerged-plunger hot-chamber machine illustrated in Fig. 16-14 is commonly used to produce zinc, tin, lead, and some magnesium castings. While the die is open and the plunger retracted, the molten casting metal flows into the pressure chamber through the filling inlet. After the die closes, the hydraulic cylinder is actuated and the plunger forces the casting metal into the die. This type of injection is generally limited to pressures of 2000-4000 psi (14-28 MPa) and cannot be used either with an alloy having a solvent action on the melting pot or pressure chamber, or with an alloy at a temperature high enough to affect the fit of the plunger and cylinder. The submerged-plunger machine is not suitable for use with aluminum, copper, and ferrous alloys.

Recent developments in hot-chamber machine design provide quicker injection speeds to minimize cavity fill times. At the same time, new injection systems minimize final plunger impact. These features and better process control and gating technique allow for production of castings having reduced cross-sectional thickness.

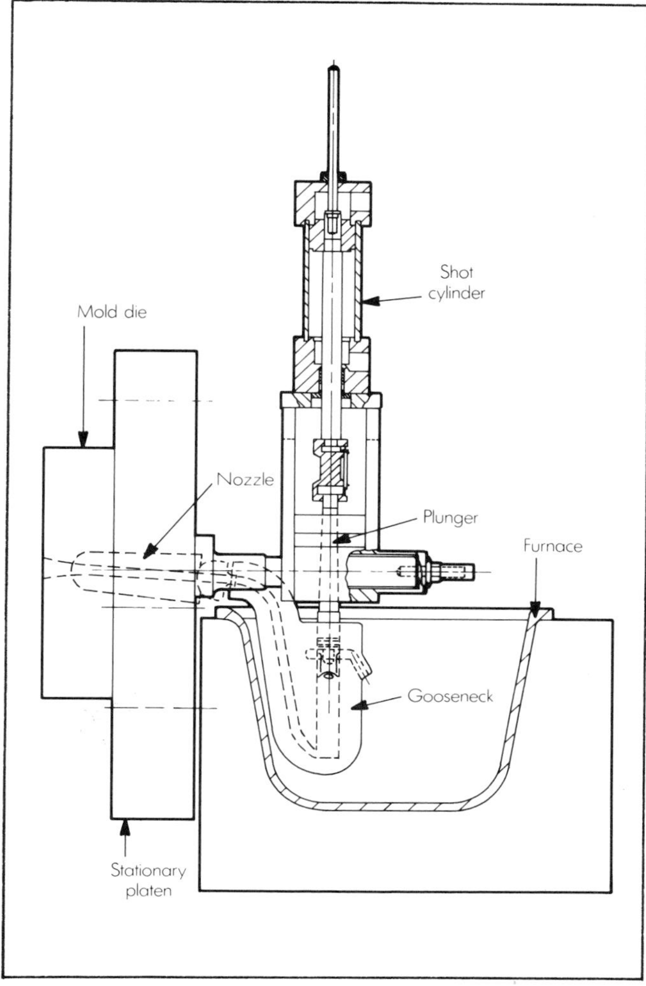


**Fig. 16-14 Hot-chamber injection system for die-casting machine.** (*Prince Corporation*)

Thin-wall zinc casting and new, highly integrated automatic machines have given the zinc casting industry the capability to be competitive with alternative metals and plastics.

**Cold-chamber machines.** In the horizontal configuration commonly used for cold-chamber machines, the pressure chamber is separate from the melting pot and is not heated. Hence, the pressure chamber is not exposed directly to the erosive and thermal characteristics of molten metal. The material, in a liquid form, is injected by a plunger to fill the die cavity. The cold-chamber machine is constructed and operated as shown in Fig. 16-15 and in the general layout drawing shown in Fig. 16-16. Molten metal from a separate holding furnace is ladled into the cold-chamber sleeve after the die is closed and all cores are locked into position as illustrated in Fig. 16-17, *a*. The hydraulic cylinder ram forces the metal into the die as shown in view *b*; and after solidification, the die is opened and the cores are withdrawn as shown in view *c*. The ejector mechanism then removes the casting from the movable, or ejector, half of the die as shown in view *d*.

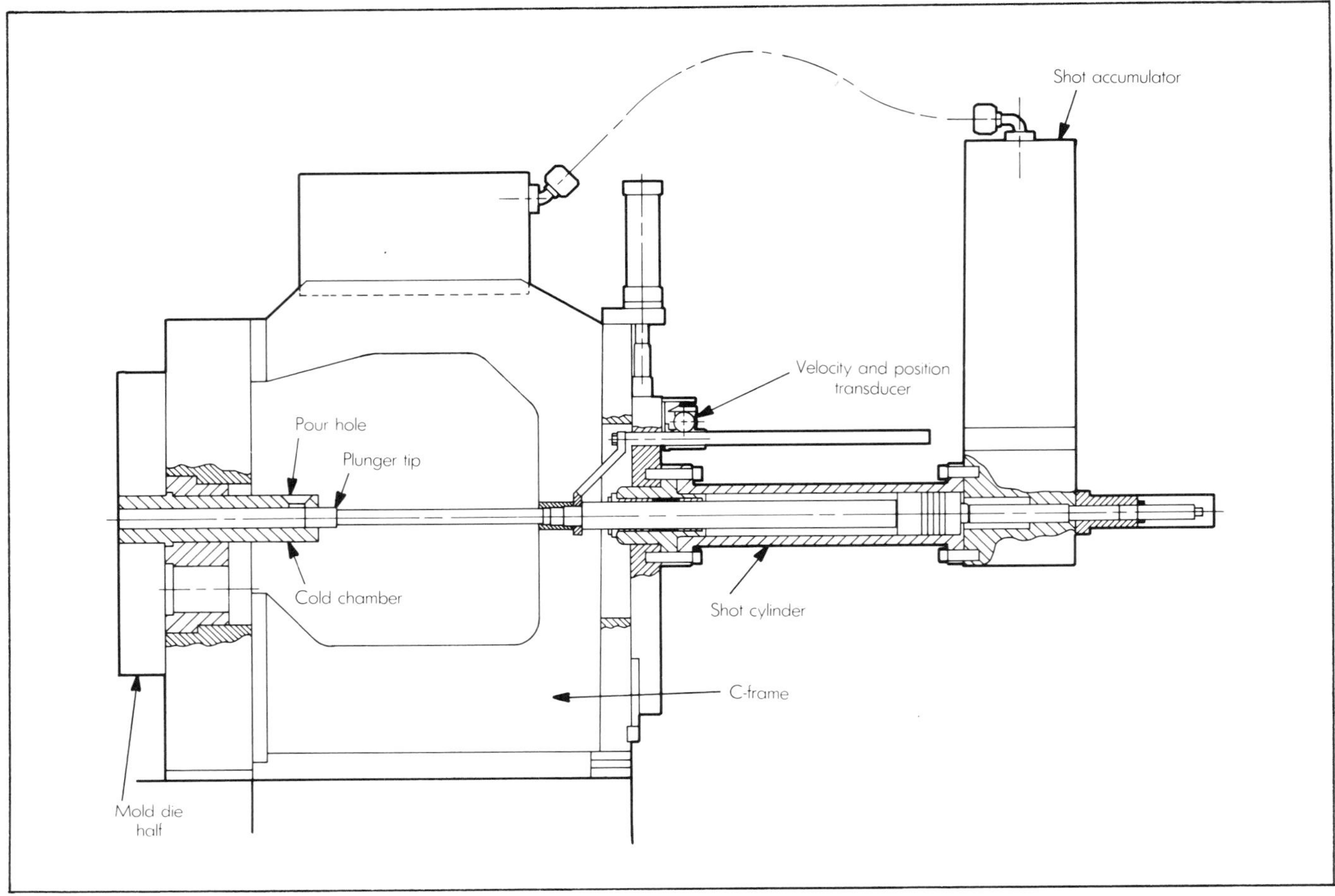


**Fig. 16-15 Cold-chamber shot system for die-casting machine. (*Prince Corporation*)**

Injection pressures in this type of machine range from 2500-20,000 psi (17-138 MPa), but most castings are made at pressures of 4000-6000 psi (28-41 MPa). Machines of the cold-chamber type are chiefly used for making castings in aluminum, brass, and magnesium alloys. Lower melting point alloys can be cast in these machines, but these alloys are generally more economically cast in the faster operating hot-chamber type of machines.

Another type of cold-chamber machine is the verticast machine wherein molten metal is drawn into a vertical shot chamber by vacuum and is then rammed into the die by a plunger operating from below. This type of machine is used to cast certain aluminum specialty alloys, in addition to the traditional aluminum alloys, and to manufacture radially symmetrical castings and castings requiring minimum porosity and maximum pressure tightness.

## New Technology

In recent years, a considerable amount of research and experimentation has been applied to cold-chamber die casting. Cavity fill times and injection profiles have been analyzed and programs written to define the proper requirements. A better understanding of flow conditions and parameters for proper gating has brought a number of significant changes in the cold-chamber type of process.

Process control equipment is being introduced and implemented in many die-casting companies. The speed, pressure, and position of the plunger during injection are monitored and recorded. New machine injection systems (see Fig. 16-18) allow digital programming of plunger speed or velocity, and some encompass a closed-loop type of injection system in which the machine automatically responds or corrects itself to maintain the selected speed.

Microcomputer-based "injection performance analyzers" are used to provide complete graphic and statistical analysis of the salient process control parameters to achieve optimum tie bar strains, injection speed, die temperatures, etc.

This data is used for setup and diagnosis of machine operating conditions and is indispensable for maintenance of low scrap rates and high-quality standards. The pertinent parameters analysis data is used on a periodic basis, typically once or twice a shift, to monitor and correct machine performance. If desired, the process controls can be installed on the machines to check each shot produced. Advanced process control equipment is available for retrofit on some machines.

As illustrated in Fig. 16-19, other elements of process control are the monitoring of metal temperature and the monitoring and control of die temperature, die cooling, and clamping tonnage (force). Some die-casting machines are available with computerized, automatic, individual tie bar adjustment. The

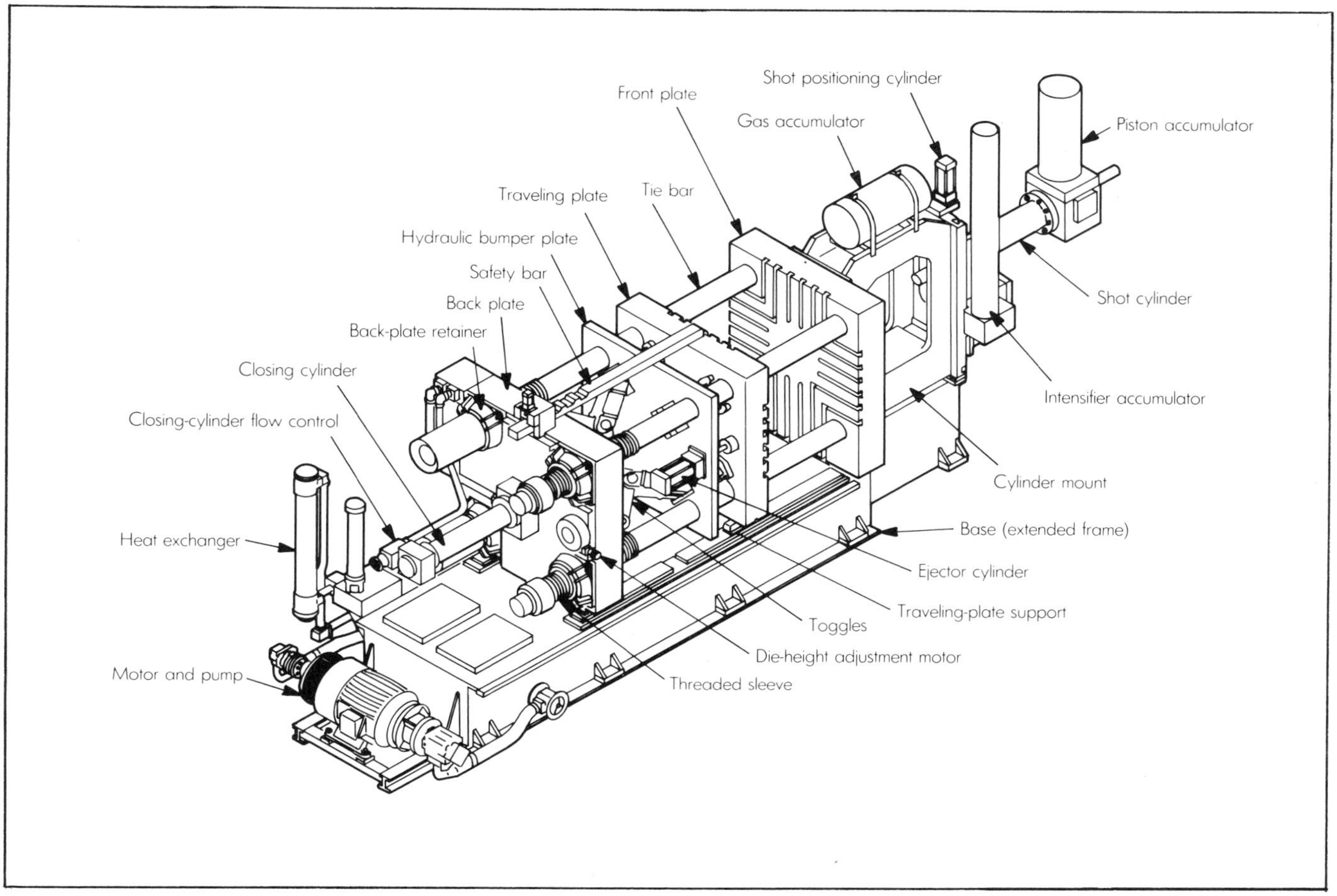

**Fig. 16-16 General layout of representative cold-chamber die-casting machine.** (*Prince Corporation*)

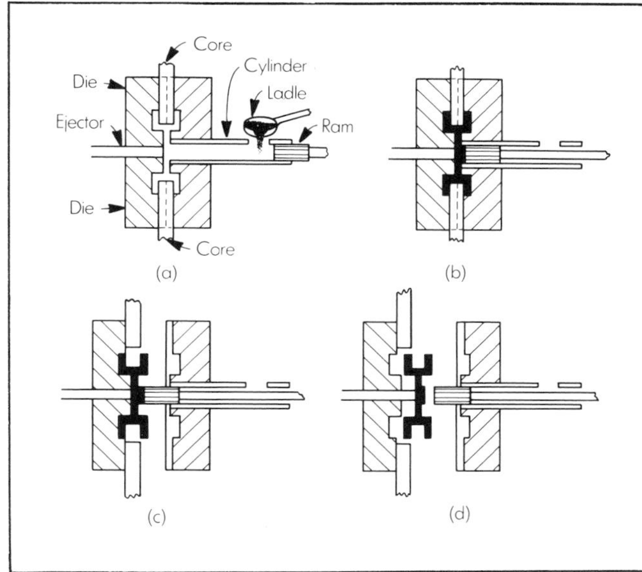


**Fig. 16-17 Cold-chamber die-casting machine sequence of operations: (a) cylinder is filled with molten metal; (b) ram forces metal into die; (c) die is opened; and (d) casting is ejected.**

force for each corner or tie bar of the machine can be preselected with high and low limits, and the machine will automatically adjust the force within the preselected limits. The application of electronics to the die-casting industry has eased or eliminated the necessity for many operator decisions.

**Critical speed.** A significant advancement in the horizontal cold chamber process is the implementation of the critical cold-chamber plunger speed or velocity. Table 16-16 shows a segment of the chart for critical, slow-shot velocity in a cold-chamber machine. In the cold-chamber process, if the plunger is accelerated too rapidly, the liquid alloy in the shot cylinder forms surf-type waves, thus trapping air in the cold chamber and subsequently injecting it into the die. If the metal is injected too slowly, the wave leaves the plunger tip and air is eventually trapped in front of the ram and towards the end of the cycle and is again injected into the die. New research has shown a direct correlation between the ram or plunger tip diameter and the percentage of fill in the cold-chamber sleeve.

When these two factors are known, a data chart is available that states the proper speed for the conditions that minimize air entrapment in the liquid metal during the slow-shot part of the injection. After the cold chamber is filled, the die cavity is filled under a fast-shot mode of operation.

At fill percentages less than 40%, the critical speed technique is not valid and it is difficult to prevent air entrapment during the slow-shot phase. Low fill percentages are therefore to be avoided whenever possible.

**Shot speed.** Other recent changes in the injection portion of the die-casting process include faster shot speeds, thus minimizing cavity fill times and implementation by most machinery builders of a low impact type shot arrangement. For years die-casting machines have had tremendous water hammer type pressure spikes associated with the injection speeds. These spikes have been eliminated with modern machine design and in many cases allow die casters to run larger castings in smaller machines (see Fig. 16-20).

**Automation.** The past several years have also shown a trend toward automation in die casting. In cold-chamber machines, automatic ladles supply metal from the remote holding furnace to the cold-chamber sleeve. Die lubricants are supplied automatically either from stationary heads or reciprocating-type devices. The plunger tip is automatically lubricated and extractors or robots are used to take the casting out of the die-casting machine, thus producing a completely automated cycle. The die-casting industry is now beginning to concentrate on robots that unload the die-casting machine and place the casting in a quench and then into either a horizontal or vertical trim press. This allows an operator to tend more than one die-casting machine.

Other features now utilized by industry include automatic tie bar pulling and automatic die clamping. These are elements of automatic die changing which the industry is adopting rapidly.

**Vacuum die casting.** Former vacuum die casting machines enclosed the die in a sealed metal box that was evacuated during the part of the cycle in which the die closed. Newer technology utilizes vacuum pulled directly through the die, with a special shutoff valve that is incorporated in the mold itself. It is reported that the vacuum process reduces porosity and improves surface finish of the castings produced.

**Pore-free die casting.** A relatively new concept in die casting is the pore-free process (patented by International Lead Zinc Research Organization, Inc.) that recognizes the porosity inherent to the cold-chamber die-casting process and uses this porosity to advantage. This process utilizes an oxygen purge before metal is injected. The metal is injected into a die after the

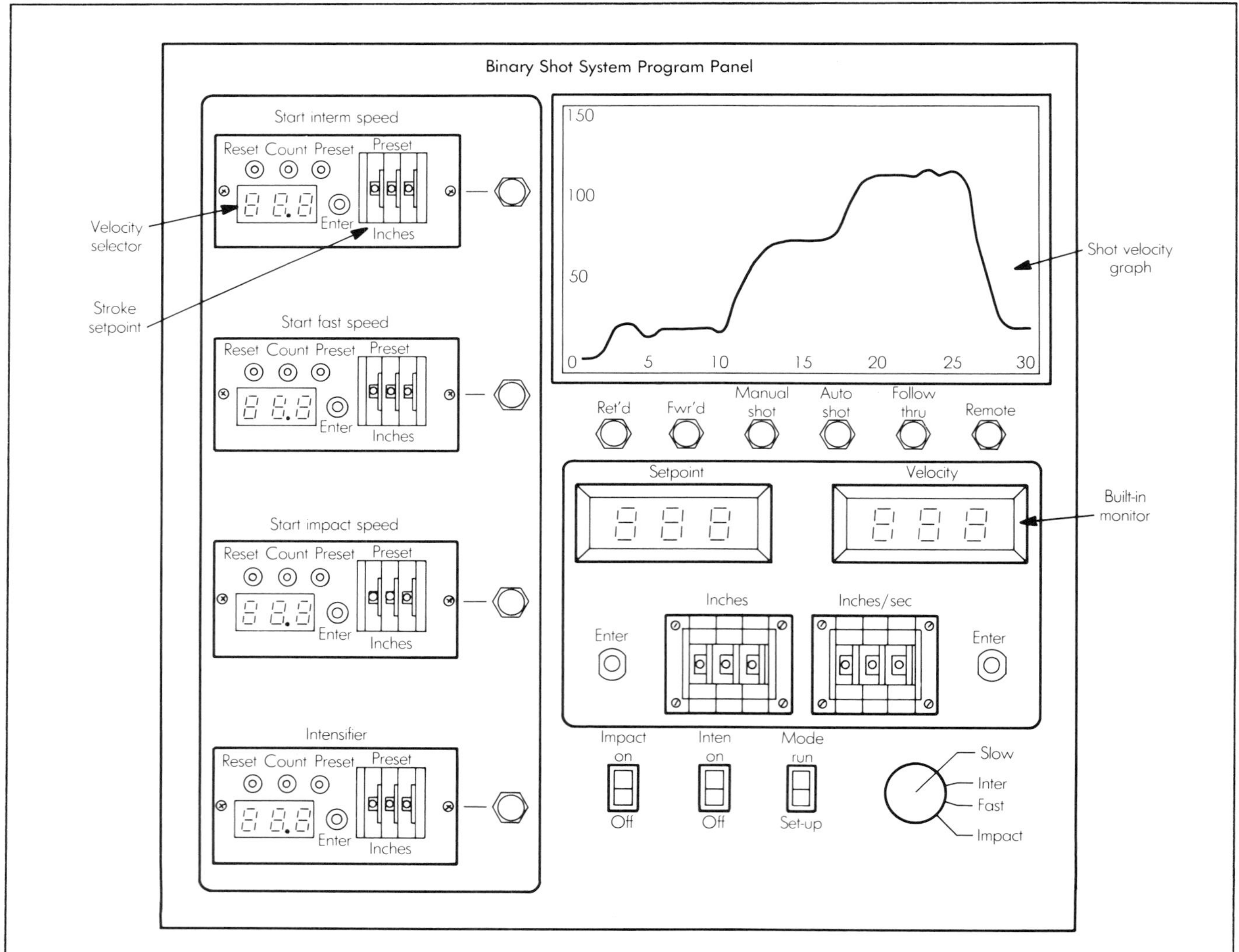


**Fig. 16-18 Illustration of control panel for die-casting process control equipment.** (*Prince Corporation*)

**TABLE 16-16**
**Critical Velocity for Cold-Chamber Die Casting**

| Initial Fill, % | Cold-Chamber Diameter, in. (mm) | | | | | | | | | | |
|---|---|---|---|---|---|---|---|---|---|---|---|
| | 1.00 (25.4) | 1.50 (38.1) | 2.00 (50.8) | 2.50 (63.5) | 3.00 (76.2) | 3.50 (88.9) | 4.00 (101.6) | 4.50 (114.3) | 5.00 (127.0) | 5.50 (139.7) | 6.00 (152.4) |
| | Critical Slow Shot Velocity, in./s (mm/s) | | | | | | | | | | |
| 40 | 13.8 (351) | 16.9 (429) | 19.5 (495) | 21.8 (554) | 23.9 (607) | 25.8 (655) | 27.6 (701) | 29.3 (744) | 30.9 (785) | 32.4 (823) | 33.8 (859) |
| 45 | 12.5 (318) | 15.3 (389) | 17.7 (450) | 19.8 (503) | 21.7 (551) | 23.5 (597) | 25.1 (638) | 26.6 (676) | 28.0 (711) | 29.4 (747) | 30.7 (780) |
| 50 | 11.3 (287) | 13.8 (350) | 16.0 (406) | 17.9 (455) | 19.6 (498) | 21.2 (538) | 22.6 (574) | 24.0 (610) | 25.3 (643) | 26.5 (673) | 27.7 (704) |
| 55 | 10.1 (257) | 12.4 (315) | 14.3 (363) | 16.0 (406) | 17.5 (445) | 19.0 (483) | 20.3 (516) | 21.5 (546) | 22.7 (577) | 23.8 (605) | 24.8 (630) |
| 60 | 9.0 (229) | 11.0 (279) | 12.7 (323) | 14.2 (361) | 15.6 (396) | 16.8 (427) | 18.0 (457) | 19.1 (485) | 20.1 (511) | 21.1 (536) | 22.0 (559) |
| 65 | 7.8 (198) | 9.6 (244) | 11.1 (282) | 12.4 (315) | 13.6 (345) | 14.7 (373) | 15.7 (399) | 16.7 (424) | 17.6 (447) | 18.5 (470) | 19.3 (490) |
| 70 | 6.8 (173) | 8.3 (211) | 9.6 (244) | 10.7 (272) | 11.7 (297) | 12.7 (323) | 13.6 (345) | 14.4 (366) | 15.2 (386) | 15.9 (404) | 16.6 (422) |
| 75 | 5.7 (145) | 7.0 (178) | 8.1 (206) | 9.0 (229) | 9.9 (251) | 10.7 (272) | 11.4 (290) | 12.1 (307) | 12.8 (325) | 13.4 (340) | 14.0 (356) |
| 80 | 4.6 (117) | 5.7 (145) | 6.6 (168) | 7.3 (185) | 8.0 (203) | 8.7 (221) | 9.3 (236) | 9.9 (251) | 10.4 (264) | 10.9 (277) | 11.4 (290) |
| 85 | 3.6 (91) | 4.4 (112) | 5.0 (127) | 5.6 (142) | 6.2 (157) | 6.7 (170) | 7.2 (183) | 7.6 (193) | 8.0 (203) | 8.4 (213) | 8.8 (224) |
| 90 | 2.5 (64) | 3.0 (76) | 3.5 (89) | 3.9 (99) | 4.3 (109) | 4.7 (119) | 5.0 (127) | 5.3 (135) | 5.6 (142) | 5.9 (150) | 6.1 (155) |
| 95 | 1.3 (33) | 1.6 (41) | 1.9 (48) | 2.1 (53) | 2.4 (61) | 2.5 (64) | 2.7 (69) | 2.9 (74) | 3.1 (79) | 3.2 (81) | 3.3 (84) |

(*Prince Corporation*)

air has been evacuated and the oxygen has been forced into the cold chamber and cavity. Any gases or entrapped air produced during the injection cycle form with the oxygen, resulting in finely dispersed microscopic oxides in the solidified metal rather than air bubbles. Thus, very strong, porosity-free castings can be produced. Recently this process was adapted to a specially designed machine and commercial castings are now being produced in a highly automated manner. Pore-free die casting is compatible with zinc and aluminum alloys.

## Furnaces

Each casting machine is generally equipped with a holding furnace that keeps the metal at a predetermined temperature. Metal is often melted in a separate foundry and carried to holding furnaces in molten form. Casting-machine holding furnaces may be of the pot type, using steel or cast-iron pots; refractory crucibles; or refractory-lined reverberatory, electric-induction, or resistance furnaces. All types are in common use, and the choice depends upon the alloy selected, economic conditions, and accuracy of control desired. Common practice is to use automatic temperature controls at each holding furnace. Breakdown furnaces are often used for initial melting and are sometimes equipped with an automatic ladling or pumping system. New, energy-efficient electric furnaces that use only 9 kW · h (32.4 MJ) to maintain metal in the molten state are being widely implemented in the cold-chamber industry. Also, various high-efficiency gas-fired furnaces are available.

## Die-Casting Dies

The key to successful die casting is the die. Although close attention must be given to die-casting production variables, such as cycling time, lubrication, and the composition and temperature of the casting metal, closer attention must be given to the variables that determine the surface quality and consistency of the part, which are determined by the die itself. These variables include die design, die material, and the die production method.

**Die design.** A die-casting die must be designed to facilitate ease of ejection of the part from the die. It must also possess the quality of thermal balance (heat input vs. heat extraction) that controls surface quality and soundness of the part and dictates cycling speed. The die must also be designed for optimum

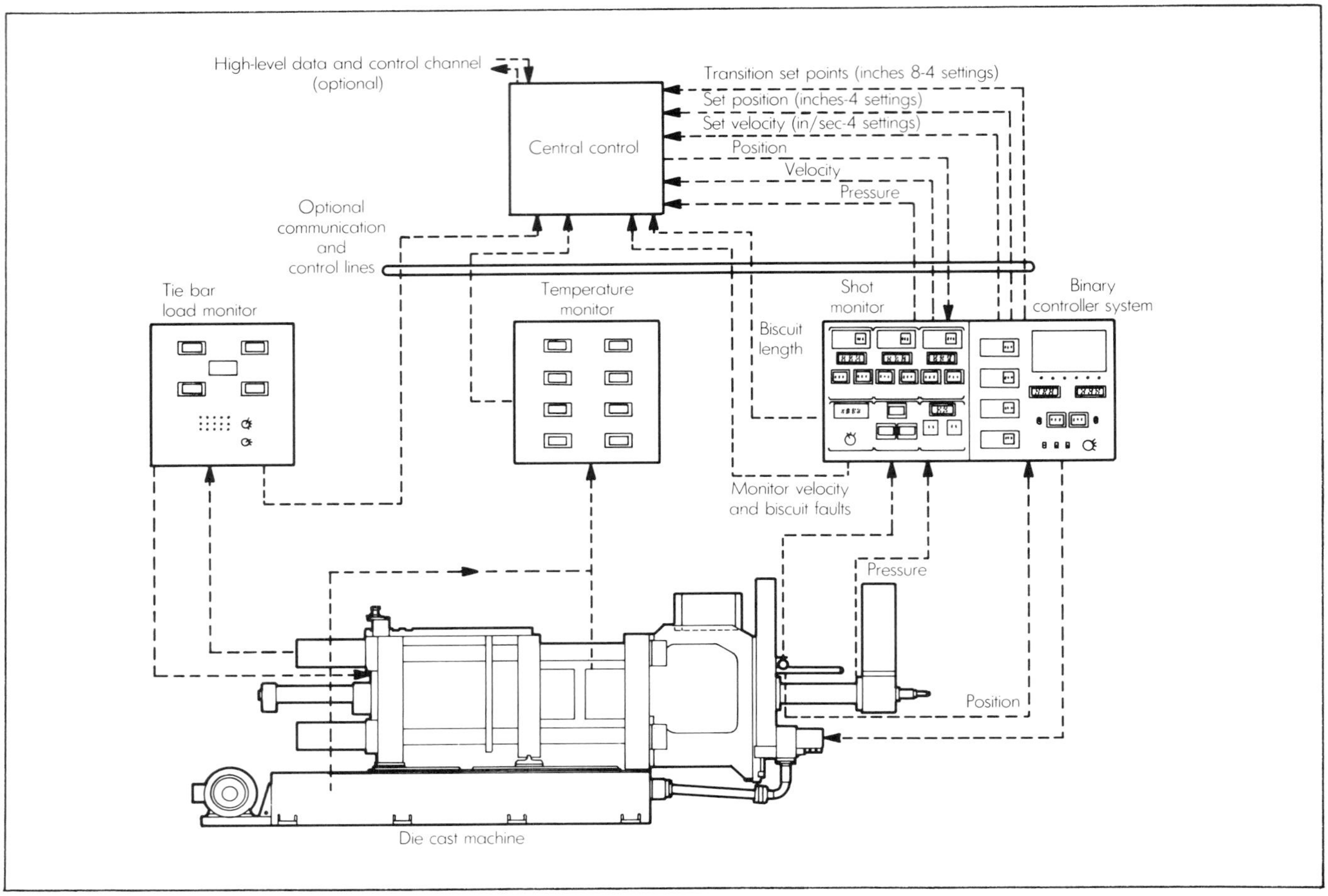

**Fig. 16-19 General view of die-casting machine linked to a process control system.** (*Prince Corporation*)

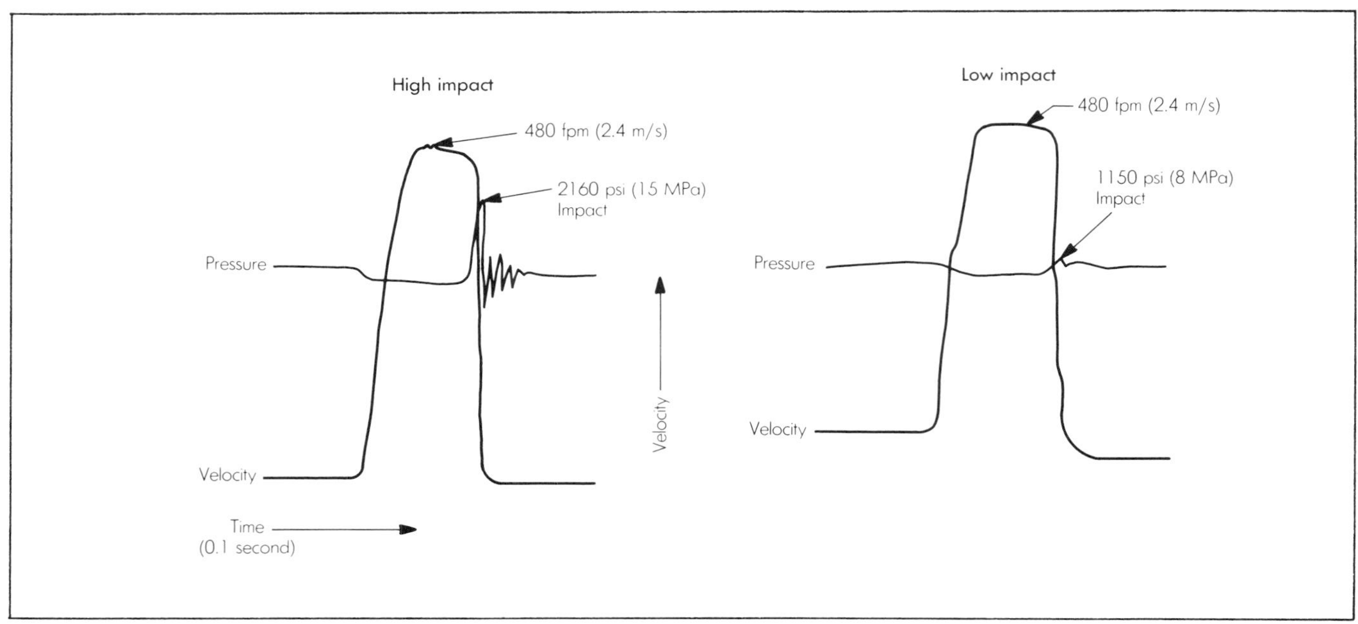


**Fig. 16-20 Shot impact diagram shows that impact pressure is reduced significantly (at same shot speed) with new design of injection systems in die-casting machines.** (*Prince Corporation*)

mechanical efficiency to attain consistent close tolerances and a fine finish on thousands of parts.

*Single-cavity dies.* A die for producing a single part consists of four components: (1) the impression blocks containing a cavity or impression identical to the casting's form, (2) the holding blocks, (3) the ejection mechanism, and (4) the die base. A single-cavity die is shown in Fig. 16-21. All cast holes in this illustration are formed by stationary cores.

*Multiple-cavity dies.* Dies can be designed to produce more than one casting at the same time, providing economy if the number of dies and casting machines needed is reduced. A typical multiple-cavity die is shown in Fig. 16-22.

*Coring.* Cores in die-casting dies may be either stationary or movable. Again, economy and the particular application are the guides to the type of core to be used. The casting shown in Fig. 16-23 has eight cored holes, three of which are formed by stationary cores in the ejector die half. Of the five other holes formed by movable cores, three are at an angle to the axis of the casting. The center hole is formed by two opposing cores which meet in the center of the hole.

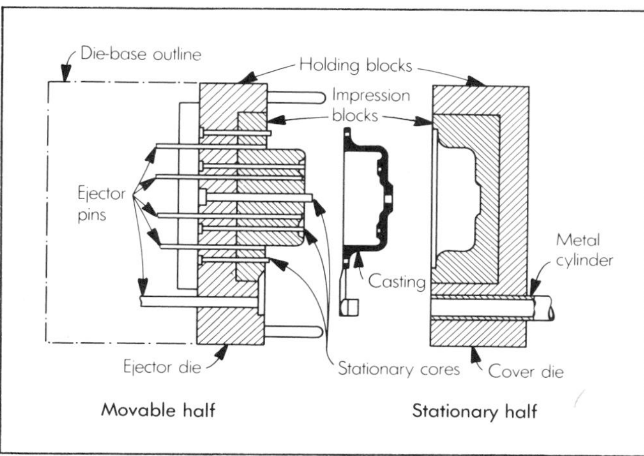


**Fig. 16-21 Typical die-casting die.**

Collapsible cores may also be used to cast internal threads or other complex internal contours. These normally incorporate a key section that is removed to allow the other sections to fall out. Collapsible cores increase die cost and generally add to cycle time.

*Ejection.* Ejector pins, mounted in a plate, are commonly used to push the finished casting out of the ejector die half. Actuation of the ejector plate may be manual or mechanical. The ejector plate is normally actuated either hydraulically by a cylinder in the die-casting machine or mechanically by the opening action of the machine. Pins or sleeves are located in such a way that no distortion or marking exists on the casting surface, which requires a good surface finish.

*Venting.* Since the die cavities are filled with air before metal enters, means must be provided for air to escape; otherwise, the casting may not fill out or will contain entrapped air. Overflow wells can be incorporated to allow air to escape and to ensure complete filling of the die cavity. To prevent clogging of vents with flash or oxide buildup, it is recommended that they be polished and be accessible to the operator for cleaning.

*Runners and feeders.* The design of gate runners and gates through which molten metal flows via passage ways and orifices into the die cavity and the part has been the subject of much research in recent years. The research and development has led to application of computerized gating programs and formulas that die designers can use to calculate proper injection velocities, runner size and shape, and gate area required. Some common sense must still be applied to keep gate thicknesses to a proper size commensurate for good trimming and finishing applications, and judgment must also be applied to attain good directional flow of the metal to the gates. The molten metal passes through the runners or feeders that direct it for uniform

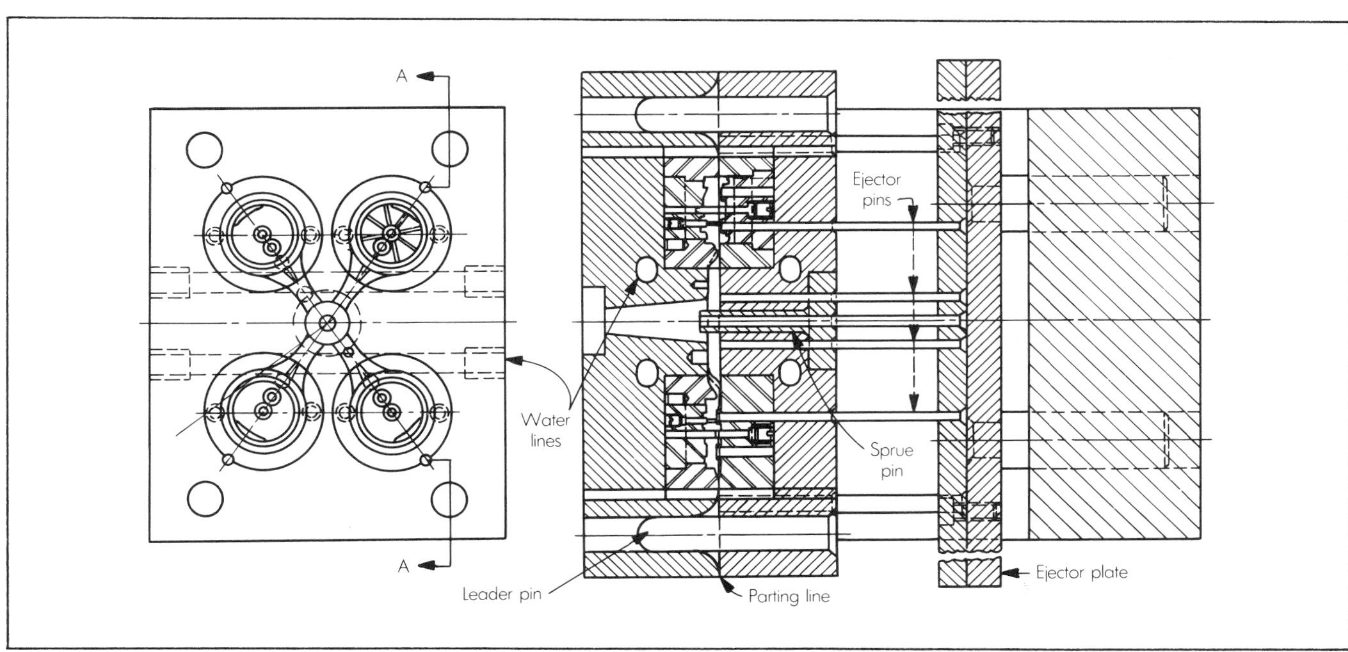


**Fig. 16-22 A typical multiple-cavity die.**

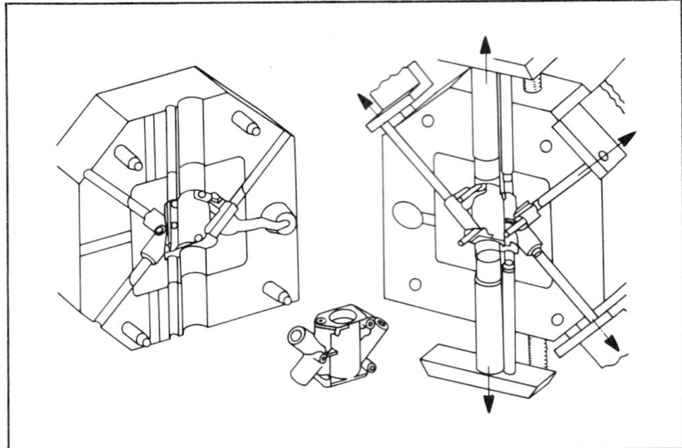

**Fig. 16-23 Intricately cored casting and dies with cores operating at various angles to the casting parting line.**

distribution into the die cavity through the gates. Figure 16-24 shows some of the more frequently used types of feeders.

*Flash control.* Flash is extraneous metal that occurs during metal injection and when a pressure spike exerts a greater force of separation than the die clamping force can constrain. Thus, metal enters the parting lines or the core sides, resulting in thin flash deposits. Flash also can occur when the key sealing areas experience excessive wear. Since flash is prevalent on all die castings, its control must be considered in the design of the die in light of its removal by power-press trim dies, sanding, filing, grinding, and other methods. Slight product-design changes can often simplify die design and flash removal. Good design minimizes the number and location of partings and intersections of die parts and therefore restricts the amount of flash.

**Die materials.** The primary die-casting die materials are the hot-work tool steels, mold steels, maraging steels, and refractory tungsten and molybdenum. Table 16-17 presents the chemical composition of the most widely used steels for die-casting dies.

The three principal modes of die failure related to die materials are heat checking, which is caused by thermal fatigue; mechanical erosion; and decarburization.

*Heat checking.* Heat checking caused directly by thermal fatigue is the most common form of die failure. Heat checking results from the difference in heating and cooling rates between the die surface and the steel below the surface, which causes tensile stress and results in minute cracks at the point of stress. Part of the solution to heat checking is to ensure proper die design—elimination of points of stress that could check. Overall, however, improved die life lies primarily in the use of materials that retain high strength at elevated temperatures.

*Mechanical erosion.* Because dies of low hardness resist heat checking but gall, erode, and deform rapidly under load, a compromise is necessary. Hot-work die steels must be soft enough to resist heat checking yet hard enough to avoid deformation under service loads. Dies should be as soft as possible while still being able to withstand washing, wearing, and peening.

*Decarburization.* Poor service life can be expected from a die whose surface has been decarburized in heat treatment. Decarburization can also occur during solidification of a cast die. A loss of carbon means a loss in surface hardness, which in turn alters the properties of the die alloy, leading to early heat checking, pitting, and washing.

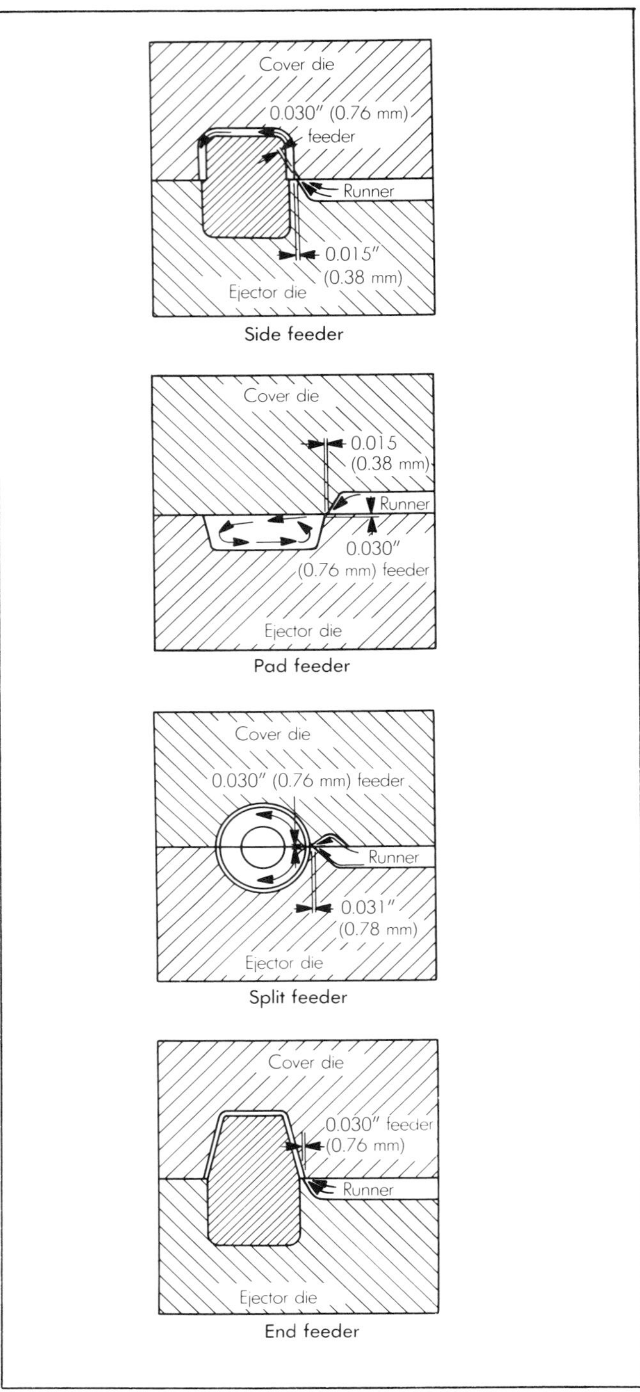


**Fig. 16-24 Various types of die feeders. The feeders must be individually tailored to each die.**

Dies for casting zinc parts can be made from AISI 4130 steels in the prehardened form P20, which has slightly higher chromium and molybdenum contents than conventional 4130. Another steel widely used for zinc casting is H11 heat treated to a minimum hardness of $R_C35$. Materials that can be used for aluminum casting dies are H12 and H13 hot-work steels.

**TABLE 16-17**
**Composition of Die-Casting Die Steels**

| Steel Type | Composition, % | | | | | | |
|---|---|---|---|---|---|---|---|
| | C | Cr | Mo | W | V | Co | Ni |
| Hot-work tool steels: | | | | | | | |
| H11 | 0.35 | 5.00 | 1.50 | --- | 0.50 | | |
| H12 | 0.35 | 5.00 | 1.50 | 1.50 | 0.40 | | |
| H13 | 0.35 | 5.00 | 1.50 | --- | 1.00 | | |
| H19 | 0.40 | 4.25 | --- | 4.25 | 2.00 | 4.25 | |
| H20 | 0.35 | 2.00 | --- | 9.00 | | | |
| H21 | 0.35 | 3.50 | --- | 9.00 | | | |
| Mold steel P2 | 0.30 | 1.70 | 0.40 | | | | |
| Maraging steel: | | | | | | | |
| 250 grade | --- | --- | 5.00 | --- | --- | 8.00 | 18.00 |
| 300 grade | --- | --- | 5.00 | --- | --- | 9.00 | 18.00 |

Because of higher casting temperatures, dies for casting copper alloys have a shorter life than dies for zinc and aluminum die casting. The conventional die materials for brass and bronze die-casting dies are hot-work steels H19 and H21. Maraging steels with yield strengths of 250,000 psi (1724 MPa) and 300,000 psi (2069 MPa) are being used increasingly for copper-alloy die casting. Recent work with refractory metals—particularly molybdenum, tungsten, and their alloys—has substantially improved die life for copper-alloy dies.

Molybdenum and tungsten have many of the properties of the ideal die material, and some of the most successful die casting of brass has been done with tungsten. Tungsten, however, is brittle at lower temperatures, and both metals wear somewhat from casting impingement into the porous structures of the sintered dies. Both tungsten and molybdenum are subject to some peening, and both cost about ten times as much as steel alloys for dies.

**Die-production methods.** Regardless of the die material, dies may be either wrought or cast. Wrought dies offer these advantages:

1. They are generally more economical when a single impression or core is required with relatively shallow machining.
2. They are more economical when cavities can be hobbed (hubbed) with simple tools and when production requirements are low enough to make the hobbing of steels economical.
3. They are generally more economical when electrical-discharge machining (EDM) can be used in shallow impressions and when EDM electrode configurations are simple and few in number (and "white-layer" problems are eliminated). When extremely close tolerances are required, this method is superior, especially on pre-hardened blocks.
4. Wrought die-casting dies are usually more economical with conventional machining and engraving when the engraving is to be raised on the casting.
5. The wrought method of die production is advantageous in applications in which cores are long and fragile.
6. Wrought dies are more economical to machine for low-production requirements and for dies with simple configurations that can be sunk in low-cost steels.
7. The die building process is being revolutionized by CAD/CAM and CNC, producing dies with very close tolerances in an economical manner.
8. The wrought methods are necessary for the production of refractory-material dies, which cannot be precision-cast at present.

Cast dies, on the other hand, offer the following advantages:

1. They are better and more economical when textures must be die cast or when engravings must be sunk into the die casting.
2. Cast dies eliminate difficult metal-removal problems when cores are deep or complex, and they allow formation of complicated water passages, etc.
3. Through the use of reversed patterns, casting allows simplified production of many dies that would normally be difficult to machine.
4. Cast-die production requires no additional costs to form complex die parting lines.
5. This method produces cavities and cores cheaply, rapidly, and accurately after patterns are made.

## Ferrous-Metal Die Casting

Because steel dies cannot withstand the temperatures of molten iron and steel, the die-casting process has not been fully applied to the casting of ferrous metals. However, advancements in the use of tungsten and molybdenum as die materials have increased interest in the die casting of iron and steel. The high melting points, low coefficients of thermal expansion, high thermal conductivity, and unusual resistance to thermal fatigue of the refractory metals make them ideal for ferrous-metal die casting. Also, the high degree of conductivity of refractory metals causes rapid solidification of the castings, in as little as tenths of a second in some cases, resulting in fine grain structure and rapid cycle time. Fine-grained steels and iron exhibit strength values that approach the properties of forged steels as indicated in Table 16-18.

# HIGH-PRESSURE DIE CASTING

**TABLE 16-18**
**Strength and Elongation of Five Types of Die-Cast Ferrous Metal**

| Type | Tensile Strength, ksi | (MPa) | Yield Strength, ksi | (MPa) | Elongation, % |
|---|---|---|---|---|---|
| 1018 as cast | 90-105 | 621-724 | 45-60 | 310-414 | 13 |
| Annealed | 70-80 | 483-552 | 45-60 | 310-414 | 25 |
| 4618 as cast | 144-192 | 993-1324 | 85-120 | 586-827 | 3 |
| Annealed | 83-150 | 573-1034 | 65-100 | 448-690 | 10 |
| 4340 as cast | 185-220 | 1276-1517 | 115-200 | 793-1379 | 1-7 |
| Annealed | 85-117 | 586-807 | 50-75 | 345-517 | 10-18 |
| 304 stainless as cast | 75-82 | 517-565 | 42-44 | 290-303 | 20-35 |
| Annealed | 82-86 | 565-593 | 40-42 | 276-290 | 35-55 |
| Nodular iron, Annealed | 103 | 710 | 76 | 524 | 5 |

**Accuracy.** Dimensional accuracy of ferrous castings produced with refractory-metal dies is equal to that of typical aluminum castings. Tolerances of ±0.002″ (0.05 mm) have been achieved across parting lines of 3/4″ (19 mm) thick castings, and closer tolerances are possible within die cavities. Draft can be held to a minimum if the casting is removed from the die while it is hot. No draft is necessary in internal die cavities, and 3-5° draft angles can be used for short, large-diameter cores. Castings with wall thicknesses of 1/8″ (3 mm) and surfaces of 32-64″ (813-1626 mm) have been obtained.

Die-life data for refractory-metal dies is, as yet, incomplete, although laboratory tests have found that certain refractory dies are capable of withstanding more than 15,000 cycles.

**Disposable dies.** Another approach to ferrous-metal die casting may lie in the use of aluminum dies that maintain their form just long enough for the steel or iron casting to solidify. The die is used only once, and the heat of the casting melts out the cores.

Low-carbon steel dies, which have high melting points, are easy to machine, and can be readily cast, have also been considered for ferrous-metal die casting. It is possible that inexpensive cast-steel dies, quickly replaced when worn, may prove to be most economical for ferrous-metal casting dies.

## Die-Casting Design

Die-cast parts are becoming increasingly complex. While considerable flexibility is permitted in the design of die castings, some major casting design factors must be observed to achieve the best die design.

**Wall thickness.** The thickness of casting walls should be as uniform as the design of the part permits, with transitions from thin to heavy sections as gradual as possible. The walls should be thick enough to permit easy flow of the metal, yet thin enough to provide the required maximum density. Ribs may be employed to increase strength and stiffness. Wall thickness is governed by the type of casting, the casting material, the amount of restriction to metal flow, and the position of the gate. Minimum recommended wall thicknesses, based on experience, are listed in Table 16-19 and may be used as a guide.

**Ribs.** The incorporation of ribs in the casting design increases rigidity, reduces weight, and facilitates good distribution of metal within the die. The height of ribs or rims around a part should rarely exceed five times the wall thickness. Drafts and fillets should be ample to obtain a smooth transition into the thinner sections. Holes and openings should be surrounded by a small rim to provide greater rigidity and to reduce edge stresses.

**Undercuts.** Internal undercuts should be avoided whenever possible since they require loose pieces that reduce production rates and increase die costs. Undercuts in the external shape of a casting require core pulls or slides in the mold and should also be avoided when possible. However, undercuts cannot always be avoided and may even be desirable for better venting. Small changes in design can lead to simplification and reduce the number of slides to a minimum. Reduction or elimination of undercuts has a direct bearing on tool life, tool maintenance, and machine uptime.

**Inserts.** Bearings, bushings, wear plates, shafts, screws, and other inserts can be cast into the parts. The inserts must be accurately located by the die and must be easily positioned in the die to obtain the fastest production rate. The surrounding material must shrink onto the insert so that it does not come loose.

**Cored holes.** Holes perpendicular to the die parting plane can be readily cast with stationary core pins. Holes in planes not perpendicular to the die parting plane require special core pulls. It is generally practical to core holes in lead and tin die castings as small as 0.032″ (0.81 mm) diam; in zinc, 0.039″ (0.99 mm) diam; in aluminum, 0.098″ (2.49 mm); in magnesium, 0.078″ (1.98 mm); and in copper, 0.118″ (3.00 mm) diam. With special care it is possible to cast smaller holes. Blind holes are necessarily not as deep as through holes, since the cores are unsupported on one end. The recommended maximum length-to-diameter relationships for unsupported cores and the draft on cores are given in Table 16-20 and Fig. 16-25.

Casting holes for subsequent tapping is generally more economical than drilling such holes. When required, cored holes in zinc, aluminum, and magnesium die castings may be tapped without first removing the draft in the holes. Recommended sizes for tapping are based on an allowance of 75% of full-depth threads at the bottom or small end of the cored hole, and 60% at the top or large end.

Slots may be cast in die castings as narrow as 0.024″ (0.61 mm) for tin alloys, 0.032″ (0.81 mm) for lead and zinc alloys, 0.047″ (1.19 mm) for aluminum, 0.039″ (0.99 mm) for magnesium, and 0.059″ (1.50 mm) for copper alloys. The maximum depth of slot for these widths is 0.394″ (10.00 mm) for all the alloys except zinc and magnesium, which may have depths up to

**TABLE 16-19**
**Minimum Wall Thickness for Die Castings**

| Surface Area,* in.$^2$ (mm$^2$) | Tin, Lead, Zinc | Aluminum, Magnesium | Copper |
|---|---|---|---|
| | Minimum Wall Thickness, in. (mm) | | |
| up to 3.9 (2516) | 0.0236-0.0394 (0.599-1.001) | 0.0315-0.0471 (0.800-1.196) | 0.0589-0.0787 (1.496-1.999) |
| 3.9-15.5 (2516-10,000) | 0.0394-0.0589 (1.001-1.496) | 0.0471-0.0707 (1.196-1.796) | 0.0787-0.0982 (1.999-2.494) |
| 15.5-77.5 (10,000-50,000) | 0.0589-0.0787 (1.496-1.999) | 0.0707-0.0982 (1.796-2.494) | 0.0982-0.118 (2.494-3.00) |
| Over 77.5 (50,000) | 0.0787-0.0982 (1.999-2.494) | 0.0982-0.118 (2.492-3.00) | 0.118-0.157 (3.00-3.99) |

* Area of a single main plane to be produced at minimum wall thickness.

0.474″ (12.04 mm). Draft is generally required only on slots in aluminum and copper alloys.

**Corner radii and fillets.** Sharp corners and corners without proper radii should be avoided in all castings. Sharp corners can induce premature die cracking. Compared with other casting processes, die casting permits use of the smallest radii because the flow of metal into the cavity is aided by the high casting pressure. The low-melting-point alloys can be cast with a fillet radius of about one-half the wall thickness. To avoid an undesirable accumulation of metal at a corner, the fillet radius should not be greater than the wall thickness. Sharp edges are preferred in the die parting plane. A more expensive die is required to cast even a small radius at the parting line. However, a bead or radius below the parting line can greatly enhance the appearance of a trimmed casting.

**Cast threads.** Internal and external threads are satisfactorily cast in die castings. External threads can be cast if the axis is along the parting plane of the die or if slides are used. Inaccuracies in the threads can result from imperfect closing of the slides or the guiding of the die halves and slides. Flash at the parting line and other imperfections often must be corrected by subsequent machining.

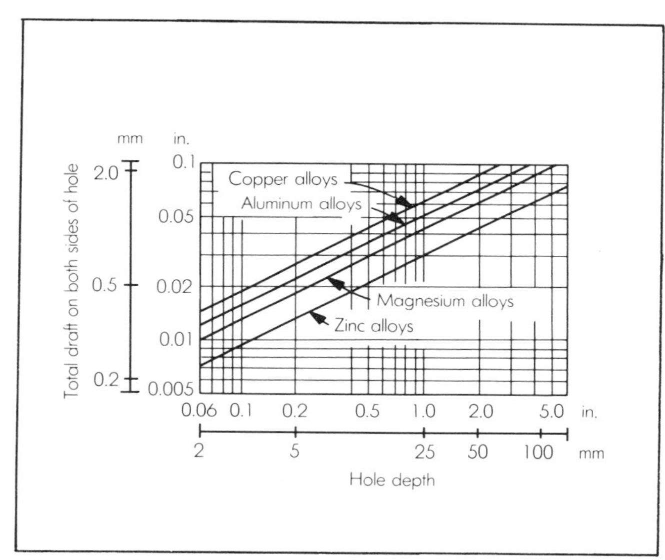


**Fig. 16-25 Draft for cored holes.**

**TABLE 16-20**
**Depths of Blind Cored Holes**

| Alloy | 1/8 (3.2) | 5/32 (4.0) | 3/16 (4.8) | 1/4 (6.4) | 3/8 (9.5) | 1/2 (12.7) | 5/8 (15.9) | 3/4 (19.1) | 1 (25.4) |
|---|---|---|---|---|---|---|---|---|---|
| | Max Depth, in. (mm) | | | | | | | | |
| Zinc | 3/8 (9.5) | 9/16 (14.3) | 3/4 (19.1) | 1 (25.4) | 1 1/2 (38.1) | 2 (50.8) | 3 1/8 (79.4) | 4 1/2 (114.3) | 6 (152.4) |
| Aluminum | 5/16 (7.9) | 1/2 (12.7) | 5/8 (15.9) | 1 (25.4) | 1 1/2 (38.1) | 2 (50.8) | 3 1/8 (79.4) | 4 1/2 (114.3) | 6 (152.4) |
| Magnesium | 5/16 (7.9) | 1/2 (12.7) | 5/8 (15.9) | 1 (25.4) | 1 1/2 (38.1) | 2 (50.8) | 3 1/8 (79.4) | 4 1/2 (114.3) | 6 (152.4) |
| Copper | --- | --- | --- | 1/2 (12.7) | 1 (25.4) | 1 1/4 (31.8) | 2 (50.8) | 3 1/2 (88.9) | 5 (127.0) |

(Column headers: Hole Diameter, in. (mm))

Difficulties are sometimes encountered when internal threads are being cast because the casting must be unscrewed from the core after it has solidified. An unscrewing device may be incorporated in the die, or the core may be removed with the part and unscrewed at the workbench. Fine threads, more than six threads in depth, incompletely filled threads, and metal shrinkage can also cause trouble in thread casting. Coring the internal threads adds cost to die construction and increases cycle time.

**Draft.** The amount and location of draft on a die-cast part depend on the arrangement of the part in the die. Outer surfaces can generally be cast in two parallel planes, while inner or cored surfaces require draft. Draft that is present on the inner or outer surfaces of a casting and is reproduced in the die impression allows ejection of the casting without galling. The values shown in Fig. 16-26 represent normal production drafts at the most economical level. Greater accuracy involving unusually close work or special care in production should be specified only when and where necessary; otherwise, additional cost may be incurred.

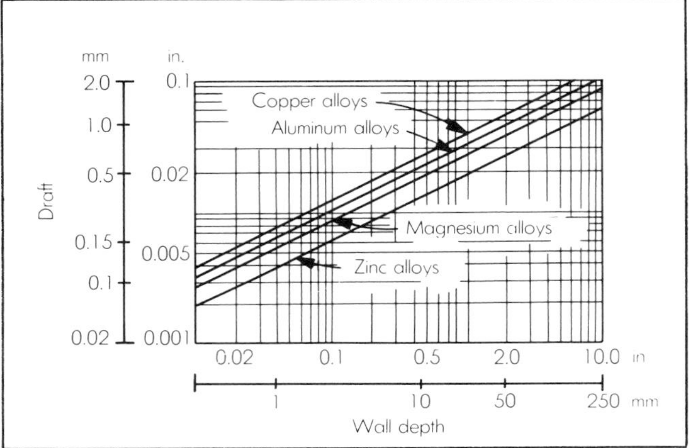


**Fig. 16-26 Draft requirements for castings.**

**Dimensional tolerances.** The dimensional accuracy that can be achieved in die casting depends upon the following factors:

1. The accuracy to which the die cavity and cores are machined or cast.
2. The possible thermal expansion of the die during operation.
3. The melting point and shrinkage of the alloy being cast.
4. The wear and erosion on the surfaces of the die cavity and cores.
5. The position of the movable die parts with respect to each other in the casting position.

The tolerances on basic linear dimensions for a die casting within one die half are summarized in Table 16-21.

When linear dimensions extend across a movable die section, the tolerances on the part in that area must be increased. Table 16-22 lists the amount by which the basic tolerance given in Table 16-21 must be changed. The additional tolerance is necessary because of the toolmaker's tolerances on the movable die, the fit between the moving parts, and the material shrinkage.

Additional allowances must be made on dimensions that extend across the parting line of a die casting. Table 16-23 lists the amount by which the tolerances of Table 16-21 should be revised for parting-line dimensions.

Flatness tolerances on die-casting surfaces are ±0.008″ (0.20 mm) on dimensions up to 3″ (76 mm). For each additional inch, 0.003″ (0.08 mm) is added to the basic tolerance. Flatness is measured with a feeler gage from three widely separated points on a continuous plane surface of the die casting.

## PERMANENT-MOLD CASTING

Permanent-mold castings are produced by forcing molten metal, under pressure of a gravity head or a low-pressure feed system, into a static mold consisting of a clamped metal assembly. In permanent-mold casting, the mold cores are also made of metal. Various metals can be cast in permanent molds, but the process is most common for the lighter nonferrous

**TABLE 16-21**
**Tolerances on Basic Linear Dimensions**

| Dimension | Die-Casting Alloy | | | |
|---|---|---|---|---|
| | Zinc | Aluminum | Magnesium | Copper |
| | Tolerances, in. (mm) | | | |
| Basic tolerance, up to 1″ (25 mm) linear dimension | ±0.003 (0.08) | ±0.004 (0.10) | ±0.004 (0.10) | ±0.007 (0.18) |
| Aditional tolerance for each additional inch (25 mm) | | | | |
| Over 1″ up to 12″ (300 mm) | ±0.001 (0.03) | ±0.0015 (0.038) | ±0.0015 (0.038) | ±0.002 (0.05) |
| Over 12″ (300 mm) | ±0.001 (0.03) | ±0.001 (0.03) | ±0.001 (0.03) | |

Example:
An aluminum die casting would have, on a 4.000″ (101.6 mm) dimension, a tolerance of ±0.0085″ (0.215 mm) if that dimension is not affected by a parting line or moving die part.

**TABLE 16-22**
**Tolerances for Movable Die Sections**

| Projected Area of Die-Casting Portion* | Die-Casting Alloy | | | |
|---|---|---|---|---|
| | Zinc | Aluminum | Magnesium | Copper |
| | Tolerances, in. (mm) | | | |
| Up to 10 in.$^2$ (6450 mm$^2$) | ±0.004 (0.10) | ±0.005 (0.13) | ±0.005 (0.13) | ±0.010 (0.25) |
| 10-20 in.$^2$ (6450-12,900 mm$^2$) | ±0.006 (0.15) | ±0.008 (0.20) | ±0.008 (0.20) | |
| 20-50 in.$^2$ (12,900-32,000 mm$^2$) | ±0.008 (0.20) | ±0.012 (0.30) | ±0.012 (0.30) | |
| 50-100 in.$^2$ (32,000-64,000 mm$^2$) | ±0.012 (0.30) | ±0.015 (0.38) | ±0.015 (0.38) | |

Note: Above tolerances are to be applied to those given in Table 16-21.
* Projected area is that portion of the die casting affected by the moving die part.

metals. When ferrous metals are cast in permanent molds, the molds are given refractory coatings to protect the surfaces from the heat and erosive action of the molten metal. It is also necessary to protect the mold when copper-based alloys are cast.

The sequence of operations in permanent-mold casting, as shown in Fig. 16-27, is as follows:

1. Apply refractory mold coating to internal areas of preheated mold sections.
2. Set mechanical, shell, or sand cores as required and close the mold.
3. Pour heated aluminum into sprue openings.
4. After the casting has solidified, remove it from the mold for the next operation, which usually involves trimming the gates and risers.

Many pressure-type castings, aircraft and missile castings, automotive pistons, pump bodies, and high-quality castings of any kind (even if the quantities required are small) are produced by the permanent-mold method. Also, the permanent-mold method is used to produce many other commercial castings because of the price advantage, superior as-cast dimensional tolerance and surface finish, and improved mechanical properties obtainable in comparison to the sand casting method. The initial cost of permanent molds is higher than that for sand casting pattern equipment; however, the lower cost of casting results in net savings over other casting methods. Weights of permanent-mold castings may range from a few ounces to 100 lb (45 kg) or more. The more complex the shape of the casting, however, the higher the cost of producing the mold and casting. In such cases, sand castings can sometimes be produced at lower cost.

## Casting Design

Permanent-mold castings usually have mechanical properties superior to those of sand or plaster-mold castings. Castings made by the permanent-mold method have better as-cast surfaces, closer dimensional tolerances, and consistent repeatability—factors critical to expeditious machining setup. Because

**TABLE 16-23**
**Additional Tolerances for Parting-Line Dimensions**

| Projected Area of Die Casting* | Die-Casting Alloy | | | |
|---|---|---|---|---|
| | Zinc | Aluminum | Magnesium | Copper |
| | Tolerances, in. (mm) | | | |
| Up to 50 in.$^2$ (32,000 mm$^2$) | ±0.004 (0.10) | ±0.005 (0.13) | ±0.005 (0.13) | ±0.005 (0.13) |
| 50-100 in.$^2$ (32,000-64,000 mm$^2$) | ±0.006 (0.15) | ±0.008 (0.20) | ±0.008 (0.20) | |
| 100-200 in.$^2$ (64,000-130,000 mm$^2$) | ±0.008 (0.20) | ±0.012 (0.30) | ±0.012 (0.30) | |
| 200-300 in.$^2$ (130,000-194,000 mm$^2$) | ±0.012 (0.30) | ±0.015 (0.38) | ±0.015 (0.38) | |

Note: Above tolerances are to be applied to those given in Table 16-21.
* Projected area is that of the die casting at the die parting plane.

# CHAPTER 16

## PERMANENT-MOLD CASTING

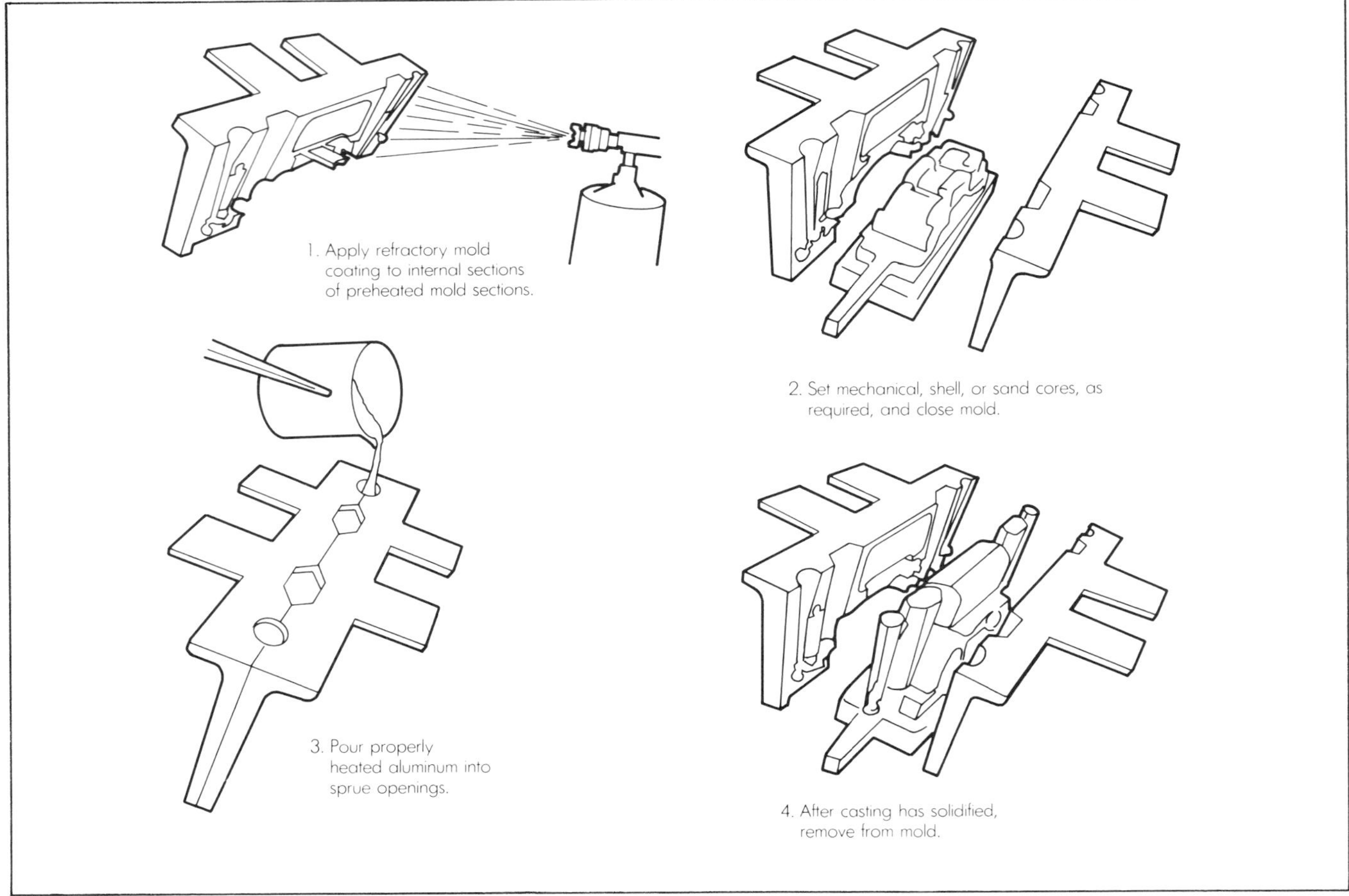

1. Apply refractory mold coating to internal sections of preheated mold sections.
2. Set mechanical, shell, or sand cores, as required, and close mold.
3. Pour properly heated aluminum into sprue openings.
4. After casting has solidified, remove from mold.

**Fig. 16-27 Basic steps in the permanent-mold aluminum casting process.** (*LA Aluminum Casting Co., Div. of REO Industries, Inc.*)

of rapid solidification in the metal molds, permanent-mold castings exhibit a finer grain structure than castings produced in slower cooling (solidification) processes such as sand casting.

**Tolerances.** Dimensional tolerances of permanent-mold castings vary with the design requirements for the part; however, for most requirements, tolerances are generally ±0.010″ (0.25 mm) for parts up to 1.000″ (25.4 mm). For each additional inch in part sizes over 1″, the tolerance would be ±0.002 in./in. (mm/mm). Across parting lines, the tolerance would be ±0.030″ (0.76 mm). For flatness as cast, 4″ (102 mm) long, it would be ±0.015″ (0.38 mm); and for each additional 1″ in length, it would be ±0.001 in./in. (mm/mm).

**Thicknesses.** To avoid premature solidification along the line of metal flow, the casting should be designed to avoid abrupt changes from thick to thin sections. Thin sections should gradually increase in thickness as they approach heavier sections, and heavy sections should not be surrounded by thin sections.

**Finish.** A finish of 125 $\mu$ in. (3.2 $\mu$ m) can be obtained in certain areas by permanent-mold casting, but this finish is limited by parting line location and by draft requirements. When the draft angle is less than 3° on outside surfaces (a little more for copper-based alloys), ejection of the casting tends to mar the surface finish. Minimum inside surface draft is 2°. Also, gating techniques that require thick spray coatings adversely affect fine finish. In most cases, however, a permanent-mold casting is readily distinguished by its superior finish.

**Cored holes.** Cored hole diameter depends on the depth of the hole. (The deeper the hole, the more a small-diameter core is apt to warp.) Minimum diameter of cored holes is 1/8″ (3 mm), and 3/16″ (5 mm) is preferred. Undercuts on a casting that require multipart cores should be eliminated if possible. Multipart cores materially increase labor costs and reduce production rates.

**Inserts.** Inserts, which are separate parts made of metals generally different from that of the casting, can easily be cast into permanent-mold castings. These inserts may be studs, bushings, pipes, etc., which provide hardness, wear resistance, strength, and other characteristics not obtainable from the casting metal. Inserts must be held in place until the molten metal solidifies around them, and they must be mechanically locked—that is, grooved, knurled, or otherwise shaped—so that the cast metal securely holds them. Sharp corners in inserts should be avoided because of their tendency to set up stress concentrations in the casting.

Electrolytic or galvanic corrosion, which occurs because of differences in the galvanic potential of the insert metal and the cast metal, can be a problem. Joints of dissimilar metals should be protected from exposure to moisture, which can lead to corrosion.

# PERMANENT-MOLD CASTING

## Mold Design and Construction

Permanent molds are made in two or more pieces that, when fitted and clamped together, define the outlines of the casting as well as the gates and risers (Fig. 16-28). Stationary or movable cores are used to form holes of any desired shape in the casting. Provision of proper draft and avoidance of undercuts facilitates part ejection and reduces sticking as the molten metal solidifies or "freezes."

In permanent-mold operations, the mold must be designed to open easily and quickly to prevent distortion that occurs if the casting sticks in the mold. If sticking does occur, the casting must be reheated by external heaters so that it can be ejected. Mold parts must be held tightly together so that uneven heating by the molten metal does not warp open the closure. The mold must be designed with parting lines, gates, vents, etc., so that the molten metal can enter the cavity preferably at the bottom, without causing turbulence or hot spots. Vents should be arranged so that air pushed ahead of the molten metal is not trapped in branches that are not directly in line with risers or overflows.

When bottom gating is impractical, the mold should be tilted at a steep angle at the start of the pour and gradually turned upright as it fills. In such gravity pouring operations, care must also be taken to prevent entrapment of air in the molten metal by a vortex in the sprue. This problem can be solved by incorporating a choked area in the sprue to control the amount of metal that enters the mold and thereby prevent a downpull of air.

**Materials.** Molds may be constructed of either iron or steel. Mold cavities are usually made of iron, while steel is most commonly used for cores. A properly inoculated pearlitic gray cast iron alloy is usually used for molds because of its high thermal conductivity and good thermal shock resistance. Molds are also built from aluminum alloys, the surfaces of which are anodized for added hardness and improved metal flow.

**Production methods.** Because of the relatively high cost of machining permanent-mold cavities, some mold builders cast the mold to size and then polish the cavities and machine mating surfaces. If casting tolerances are critical, however, this practice cannot be followed and the entire mold must be machined to size.

**Thickness.** In general, outside mold thickness should be from 1-2" (25-50 mm) depending on the thickness of the casting; extremely heavy castings should have slightly thicker molds. Molds thinner than 1" (25 mm) have a comparatively short life because of their susceptibility to cracking and warpage. Molds that are too heavy require too much time to bring to temperature and are awkward to handle. A well-proportioned mold should last for many thousands of shots. Interior mold section thicknesses may range from 1/8" (3 mm) for aluminum and copper alloys to 5/32" (4 mm) for magnesium alloys.

**Fig. 16-28 Permanent-mold casting machine showing two-part mold with center core designed to pull down and free the casting for removal.**

**Gates and risers.** Gates and risers of the mold should be designed to make possible the progressive solidification of metal in an unbroken flow from the farthest end of the casting to the risers. If the casting should freeze somewhere along the line ahead of its turn, sections of metal that are still liquid between the freezing point and the farthest end would be cut off from the flow and they would shrink, resulting in cracks or at least in dangerous internal stresses.

**Chills.** Another method of ensuring solidification in a directional flow is to vary the thickness of the mold sections or to incorporate chills in the mold to exert different chilling action on different parts of the mold. Chills can be copper, brass, or aluminum pieces inserted into the mold's inner surface, water passages in the mold, or cooling fins against which air or water mist can be blown.

**Coatings.** Mold coating is also important to directional solidification. Many different coatings may be used, but in the past a refractory paint made of calcium carbonate or French chalk in a sodium silicate binder, used as a spray, has been commonly used. The insulating spray coating, depending on its thickness, disperses the heat dissipated from the casting over a wide range. Lubricating sprays can also be used in the same way, and these coatings also help in the removal of castings and cores from the mold. For example, a coating of graphite water paint permits easy removal of a 60-40 brass casting.

A new mold should be sandblasted lightly to ensure adhesion of the spray to the mold. If properly applied, the coating should last for a 24-hour production run. To apply a coating correctly, the mold should be heated to 300° F (149° C) and a very light coating should be sprayed on the mold and wiped smooth with steel wool. Additional light coatings should then be applied until the desired thickness is reached. A mask should be used to prevent the coating from being sprayed on the parting surfaces; and gate and riser areas should be sprayed with the greatest amount of coating, since these are the areas that require the longest solidification time. Vents should be cleaned of spray before the metal is cast. After a period of use, the coating may become worn or rough and a light touchup coating should be applied. However, after the mold cools, the entire coating should be removed and the mold resprayed before it is used again.

**Mold temperature.** For each casting job, the optimum mold temperature should be ascertained and maintained. Mold temperature must be controlled within a definite range, typically between 600 and 700° F (316 and 371° C) maximum for aluminum and magnesium. Depending on alloy selection, surface and internal requirements, and production rate, a mold temperature as low as 300-400° F (149-204° C) may be used. It should be kept in mind that the temperature is not necessarily the same throughout the mold surface. Temperature can be checked at critical points by contact pyrometers or thermocouples inserted into holes in the mold. Temperature is sometimes maintained by the use of heating units embedded in the mold.

**Cores.** Cores are commonly made from steels such as 1020, H11, H13, and H14. These materials are also used for very thin sections in which warpage and cracking can create problems.

# PERMANENT-MOLD CASTING

The particular type of steel used is normally determined by the intended use of the mold. Complex internal cavities can be cast in permanent molds by use of collapsible steel cores. The production of automotive pistons is a common example.

**Ejection.** Considerable force is required to eject castings from molds properly, and hydraulic or air-pressure mechanisms may be helpful. Manual devices using a rack and pinion are also commonly used. In ejecting the casting from the mold cavity, the push-out mechanism must push the casting in a straight line to prevent it from being cocked. A cocked casting may bind and be distorted.

## Permanent Mold Casting Production

The basic steps in the production of a permanent-mold casting are as follows:

1. A general analysis of the casting drawing is made to establish parting lines, draft requirements, gating methods, core requirements, and ejection-pin placement.
2. The mold drawing is prepared to show the cavity and gating dimensions, insert locations, and ejection-pin mechanisms.
3. A master pattern is crafted if the mold is to be cast to size. From this pattern a plaster cast is made. The plaster cast is then cast in the mold material by either a sand-mold or ceramic-mold process.

   If the mold is to be machined to size, a wood pattern of the mold halves is made and finish allowance is given in the areas in which machining is required. A casting is then produced from the wood pattern and is processed to drawing requirements. Iron or steel blanks can be used as stock items and processed to mold dimensions if the mold is not too complex.
4. After the mold is formed, it is stress-relieved at its approximate operating temperature and any distortion or warpage that appears is corrected.
5. The mold is then heated and coated as described earlier.
6. Metal is poured into the cavity; and after solidification, the casting is ejected. Pouring temperature of the molten metal is critical; and after it is determined for a specific job, it should be maintained. The casting cycle, which is determined experimentally, should be held constant since castings tend to sag, warp, or break if they are removed from the mold prematurely. The casting cycle and the casting-metal temperature vary the mold temperature, which determines the quality of the casting.

   Melting the casting metal should follow the best practice. No matter how well a mold is constructed and how well a casting operation is carried out, a strong casting cannot be made unless its metal meets the prescribed composition and has been protected from oxidation, contamination, gassing, and overheating.
7. The casting is stacked to cool. Ejected castings are very hot, relatively soft, and easily bent, so racks are normally provided to prevent warpage in the cooling process.

## Permanent Mold Casting Equipment

Various permanent-mold machines are available from different manufacturers, although some companies prefer to build their own machines to suit their individual requirements. Automatically timed machines are available, and these are relatively simple to operate. Typically, they operate as follows:

1. The operator pushes a button that closes the mold by hydraulic or air pressure. The mold halves are held tightly together by the pressure, eliminating the need for clamps required on manual molds.
2. The button also starts a timer that is preset for the particular cycle time desired.
3. The operator pours the metal into the sprue or, when a tilting-mold machine is used, into a cup that pours the metal into the sprue as the machine is tilted upright.
4. After the predetermined cycle time has elapsed, the mold parts are opened and the cores are ejected.
5. The casting is then ejected by a push-out-pin mechanism.

Counters may be incorporated on automatic permanent-mold machines to show the number of castings that have been poured.

## Slush Casting

Slush-casting procedures are generally the same as those described for gravity permanent-mold casting. The difference between the two casting methods lies in the pouring technique. In slush casting, the mold is constructed so that it can be inverted, either automatically or manually depending on production requirements and ease of operation. The molten metal is poured into the mold and is allowed to solidify for a short time. After a thin shell of metal has solidified on the outside of the casting, the mold is inverted and the liquid metal in the center of the casting is poured out. This molding method leaves a hollow shell casting with a thickness from 1/32" to 1/2" (0.8 to 12.7 mm), depending on the time the metal is allowed to set. Slush casting has an advantage over conventional permanent-mold casting in that hollow castings with roughly defined interior passages can be produced.

Zinc or lead alloys are the most commonly used metals for slush casting. Thus, the mold may be constructed from cast iron, steel, brass, or aluminum. Since the metal to be cast usually has a relatively low pouring temperature, cast iron and steel molds are not as necessary as they are for permanent-mold casting of alloys that melt at high temperatures.

Generally, slush castings are used in ornamental applications, such as statues, candelabra, or lamp pedestals. This casting method may be used whenever the external appearance is the most important consideration. Because the inside of the casting is rough, it is impossible to hold to accurate interior dimensions.

## Low-Pressure Permanent-Mold Casting

Although gravity is the most common method of pouring permanent-mold castings, forced low-pressure permanent-mold machines are in use. Low-pressure permanent-mold casting resembles die casting in its use of pressure to force molten metal into the mold cavity, but the pressure required is much lower than that of die casting. Usually the quality of castings, the surface finish achieved, and the tolerances attained with low-pressure casting are at least equal to those of conventional gravity permanent-mold casting.

Low-pressure permanent-mold casting of automobile cylinder heads, manifolds, crankcases, pistons, and wheels has proved to be successful.

Recent improvements in low-pressure systems have led to the following advantages:

1. Castings of high density and decreased porosity and shrinkage are produced.

2. Casting strength can be controlled consistently.
3. High yield is attained, since risers are seldom used and runners and gates are much smaller than those in conventional gravity permanent-mold casting.
4. Casting unloader or extractor and sand core loaders, when necessary, have highly automated the low-pressure process.

Figure 16-29 shows a typical low-pressure permanent-mold machine. With this type of machine, one operator may attend to several machines at once by simply pressing a button to close the molds and start their cycles. After the mold is closed, pressurized gas, usually either air or nitrogen at 6-7 psi (41-48 kPa), enters the furnace atmosphere and forces molten metal up a hollow tube, or stalk, through a sprue, and into the mold cavity from the bottom. Pressure is maintained long enough for the casting to solidify. After the cycle is completed, the mold automatically opens and the part is ejected.

Because aluminum is the metal most commonly used for low-pressure permanent-mold castings, the stalks (usually made of cast iron) are subject to erosion and must be replaced regularly. Stalks made of silicon carbide have been tried; but although they have an indefinite wear life, they are fragile and are subject to thermal shock. Low-pressure dies can be constructed entirely of steel, or sand cores can be used for complex internal shapes.

## Graphite Permanent-Mold Process

The foundry industry has long recognized the benefits of casting metal into graphite permanent molds. Graphite's superior thermal conductivity promotes rapid solidification, which results in castings that have improved surface finish and good mechanical properties. Graphite is also known for its excellent thermal stability, and it does not warp or distort when used as a die. However, graphite tends to oxidize rapidly at elevated temperatures, and relatively short mold life results when conventional ferrous and nonferrous materials are cast in graphite molds.

During the past ten years, a process has evolved using graphite dies with new zinc-aluminum gravity casting alloys (containing 7%, 11%, or 27% aluminum). The most popular zinc alloy for graphite-mold casting contains 11% aluminum. The low casting temperatures of the zinc alloys make them suitable for graphite dies in a permanent-mold process that offers excellent finish and precision tolerances (in the range between die casting and permanent-mold casting) at low cost. In zinc-casting operations, graphite dies can provide a high-volume production tool capable of casting 20,000-50,000 parts from a single mold.

**Graphite molds.** High-quality, high-density molded graphite grades are recommended for casting dies. Graphite slabs are purchased and machined by toolmakers in much the same way as iron or steel mold materials. Graphite, however, cuts much faster and easier, and a vacuum system is incorporated to remove cuttings. Because graphite is soft, die polishing does not require power tools; instead, graphite dies are polished by hand. For profile work such as medallions, sculptures, or noncritical dies, a simple woodworking pantograph with a grinding tip is sufficient to sink die cavities. New molds are sprayed with a graphite aerosol that acts as a mold release and helps break metal surface tension during casting. After the mold is broken in, the spray is usually discontinued.

Refractory coatings are used only in the runner system to promote feeding, thus avoiding dimensional surface finish inconsistencies associated with the heavy refractory coatings used on iron dies.

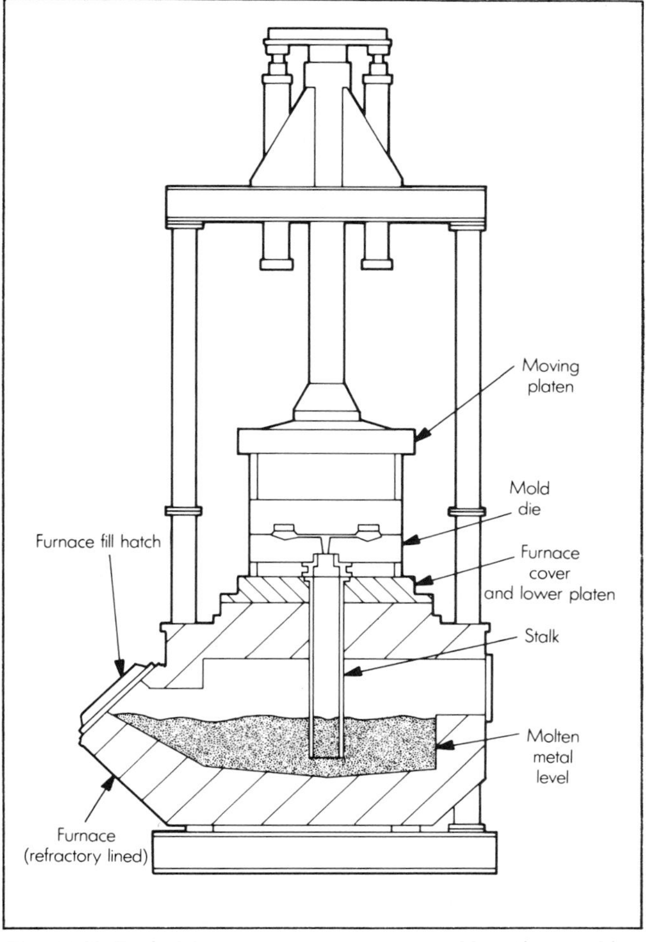


**Fig. 16-29 Typical low-pressure, permanent-mold casting machine.** (*Prince Corporation*)

**Operations.** Because graphite conducts heat rapidly, the zinc alloy casting cycle times are reduced compared to those for iron molds. In addition, machining of graphite dies is easier and faster than that of iron, and tooling cost for graphite dies is usually less than for iron. On the other hand, graphite permanent-mold castings are limited to parts under 10 lb (4.5 kg) and presently are restricted to casting sizes of approximately 12 x 14 x 7" (300 x 360 x 175 mm). Although bench hand molding is being done, the new process uses dies mounted on a simple, pneumatically actuated, semiautomatic machine that incorporates an ejector system in the opening cycle. Accurate part removal is necessary to prevent chipping or fracturing the graphite, and the timed casting cycles improve productivity.

The fact that zinc limits the attack on graphite is one reason for mold longevity. Aluminum alloys have been tried in the process, but higher casting temperatures and increased hot strength at ejection limit the useful life of a graphite die. However, aluminum alloys may be suitable for short runs or preproduction requirements for high-volume production methods such as die casting. The graphite permanent-mold process is often selected as an alternative for short-run die casting (using zinc-aluminum alloys) due to lower tooling cost and acceptable tolerance control.

### Semipermanent-Mold Casting

Semipermanent-mold casting is identical to permanent-mold casting except in the formation of the internal areas of the castings. In semipermanent-mold casting, these internal areas are formed by expendable cores.

**Core materials.** Many different types of material may be used for semipermanent-mold cores, and each has its advantage in performing a particular task. The commonly used varieties include bonded sand cores, shell cores, carbon-dioxide cores, plaster cores, graphite cores, and glass cores. New materials are constantly being developed, and a thorough search should be made of new coremaking processes before a process for a complex casting is established.

*Bonded sand cores.* For bonded sand cores, sand is washed and graded to size and then mixed with various cereal binders, oil conditioners, and other additives to improve its flowability or green strength, depending on application requirements. After the sand is mixed to the proper consistency, it is rammed into a core box which contains a pattern of the core.

In its green state, the rammed sand core is soft and fragile, and it must be supported by a drier while it is baked. Cores are placed in an oven at approximately 450° F (232° C) for about 2-4 hours, depending on the sand mix and core size.

*Shell cores.* Another type of sand core is the phenolic-bonded shell core. This type of core can be made accurately and produces good detail and surface finish. For this reason, semipermanent-mold castings are being produced in increasing numbers with shell cores.

The shell-core process begins with washed and dried fine sand that is mixed with a phenolic-resin compound. If the sand and phenolic-resin compound are not mixed thoroughly, the sand does not bond properly and will produce a bad core.

Core boxes for shell cores are constructed of steel, cast iron, bronze, brass, or aluminum. The material is determined by production requirements—cast iron and steel are best for long life and are generally used for long production jobs. Aluminum, brass, and bronze perform well in short runs, but will not give adequate service for heavy production.

The sand-resin mixture is deposited in the heated corebox, which is the pattern for the shell core. After the resin has melted to the desired thickness, the corebox is inverted and the excess sand in the center of the core (which has not reached curing temperature) is poured out. The curing of the phenolic resin is completed by the further addition of heat, the core box opens, and the core is ejected. Figure 16-30 illustrates the sequence of steps in the shell molding process.

*Carbon-dioxide sand cores.* For carbon-dioxide cores, sand is mixed with sodium silicate and is rammed into the corebox and subjected to a gentle flow of $CO_2$ gas. The subsequent reaction is referred to as "freezing" the core. The core hardens into a solid mass that can be used in the mold without baking or additional processing.

The advantages of $CO_2$ sand cores are that they are low in cost, do not need driers, and are immediately available for use. However, there are a number of limitations to this process, and product requirements should be surveyed before this core-making method is chosen.

*Plaster cores.* Plaster-of-paris cores for semipermanent-mold casting provide close dimensions as well as smooth surface finishes and fine detail. This process is expensive in comparison with the sand-core methods, but sometimes its advantages may be worth the extra cost.

*Graphite cores.* Cores made of graphite for semipermanent-mold casting may be fabricated by either molding or machining.

*Glass cores.* Glass cores may be formed by molding them into the required shape. Such cores can be leached out of the castings by a chemical process.

**Equipment.** The equipment used to produce semipermanent-mold casting cores is relatively simple. In the case of bonded sand cores, all that is needed is a sandbox, a ramming tool, and a metal plate to hold the core for baking. Machines can be used to blow a shot of sand into the corebox under air pressure, eliminating hand ramming.

Automatic or semiautomatic machines are also used for shell cores. This type of machine has a hopper to store the resin-bonded sand and a corebox clamped to the hopper. The machine is inverted to fill the corebox with sand, and the filling process may be assisted by a small amount of air pressure. A dwell time is provided to allow the heated corebox to bond the resin to the desired wall thickness. Then the machine is rolled upright to expel the excess sand and allow the core to be removed from the box.

Semiautomatic $CO_2$ sand core machines are similar to oil-bonded core machines except that they have a cycle in which the core is gassed after the sand is blown. Plaster cores are usually made by hand in brass coreboxes. The mixed plaster slurry is poured into the box, and after it sets the core is removed by hand and is fired in an oven for approximately 16 hours before it is ready for use.

Any semipermanent mold must be equipped to receive and hold its core in position while it is closed and the molten metal is poured. Further details on the preparation of cores by the various sand processes are given in the sand-mold casting section of this chapter. Preparation of plaster and other ceramic materials for coremaking is described in greater detail in the ceramic-mold casting section of this chapter.

## CENTRIFUGAL CASTING

Centrifugal castings are made by pouring molten metal into a mold that is being rotated or that starts to rotate at a certain point during pouring. The centrifugal force generated by rotation forces the metal under constant pressure against the interior mold wall until it solidifies. Cylindrical parts are usually the most preferred shapes for the centrifugal-casting processes. Tubular castings produced in permanent molds by the true centrifugal-casting method have higher structural strengths and more distinct cast impressions than castings produced by the static permanent-mold or sand-mold processes.

Metals that can be cast by ordinary static casting methods, including carbon and alloy steels, high-alloy corrosion and abrasion-resistant steels, gray iron, brass, and bronze containing up to 30% lead, aluminum, and magnesium, can be cast centrifugally. In addition many other materials, including glass, plastics, and ceramics, may be centrifugally cast.

Either permanent molds or sand molds may be used for centrifugal casting. The selection of the type of mold is determined by the shape of the casting, the quality desired, and the number of castings to be produced.

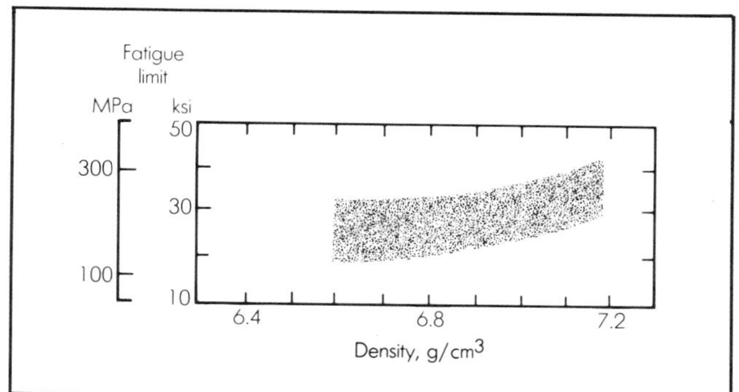


**Fig. 17-11 Fatigue strength of PM parts increases with density.**

reach 15-20% elongation. Ductility can be increased by hot or cold repressing followed by additional sintering.

**Hardness**. Because of the difference in metallurgical structure, gross indentation hardness values of PM parts and wrought parts should not be compared directly. The hardness value of a PM part is referred to as "apparent hardness." The apparent hardness is a result of powder particle hardness and porosity, as described in MPIF Standard 43.

**Corrosion resistance**. Corrosion resistance of PM parts is affected by voids. Entrapment of corrosives can lead to internal corrosion. Corrosion resistance is improved by compacting to higher density. Stainless steel and titanium PM parts have relatively good corrosion resistance in the atmosphere and in weak acids. Nonferrous PM formulations have good atmospheric corrosion resistance. Steam treating of ferrous PM parts creates a corrosion resistant, blue-black, iron oxide surface. Finishes, plating, and coatings also are applied to improve corrosion resistance. Impregnation with a resin or infiltration with metal to seal the pores against entry of plating solutions usually is recommended.

## Cost

In evaluating producibility of PM part designs and in specifying the processes to be used, the manufacturing engineer takes into account the cost-effectiveness of the processing options that are available. Figure 17-12 shows the different processes normally used for the production of structural PM parts of iron powder. When making technical judgments that balance cost against physical properties of proposed iron powder parts, the objective is to stay as far as possible toward the left-hand portion of the chart.

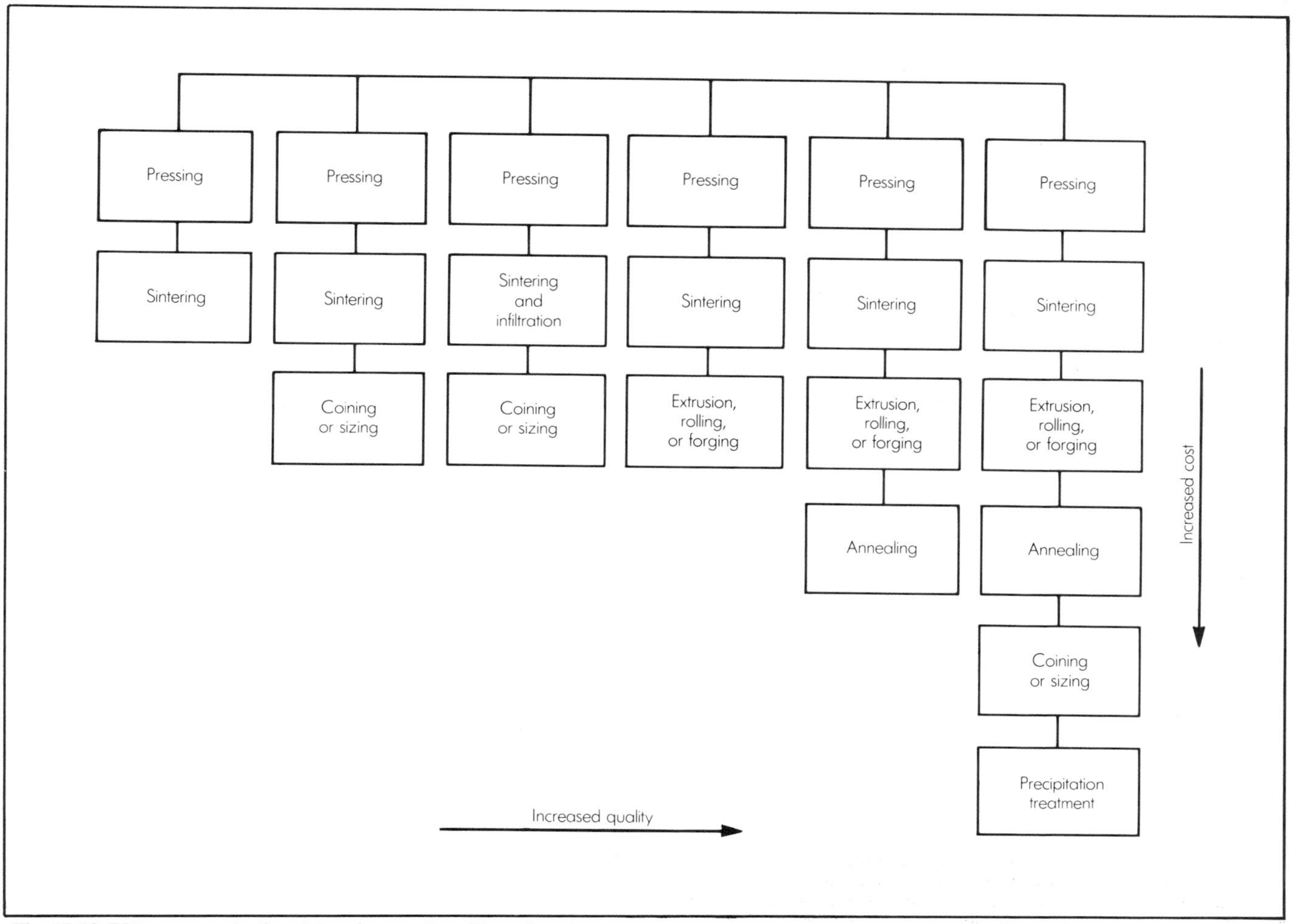

Pressing → Sintering

Pressing → Sintering → Coining or sizing

Pressing → Sintering and infiltration → Coining or sizing

Pressing → Sintering → Extrusion, rolling, or forging

Pressing → Sintering → Extrusion, rolling, or forging → Annealing

Pressing → Sintering → Extrusion, rolling, or forging → Annealing → Coining or sizing → Precipitation treatment

Increased quality →

Increased cost ↓

**Fig. 17-12 PM process selection determines part quality and cost.**

# CHAPTER 17

## PM PRODUCT DESIGN

### Guidelines

Parts should be designed specifically for fabrication by powder metallurgy, rather than adapting designs originally intended for production by other methods. For attainment of appropriate design configurations, simplified tooling, satisfactory parts, and low production costs, the key PM design recommendations may be summarized in the following six guidelines:

1. The shape of the part must permit ejection from the die.
2. The part shape must be such that the powder is not required to flow into thin walls, narrow splines, or sharp corners.
3. The part shape should permit construction of strong, durable tooling.
4. The shape of the part should make allowance for the length to which thin-walled parts can be compacted.
5. The part should be designed with the fewest possible changes in section.
6. The special capabilities afforded by powder metallurgy should be utilized, including the ability to produce certain part forms by PM that are not practicable to manufacture by other methods.

These design recommendations are the key to PM part producibility. They are illustrated and amplified in Fig. 17-13 through Fig. 17-22.

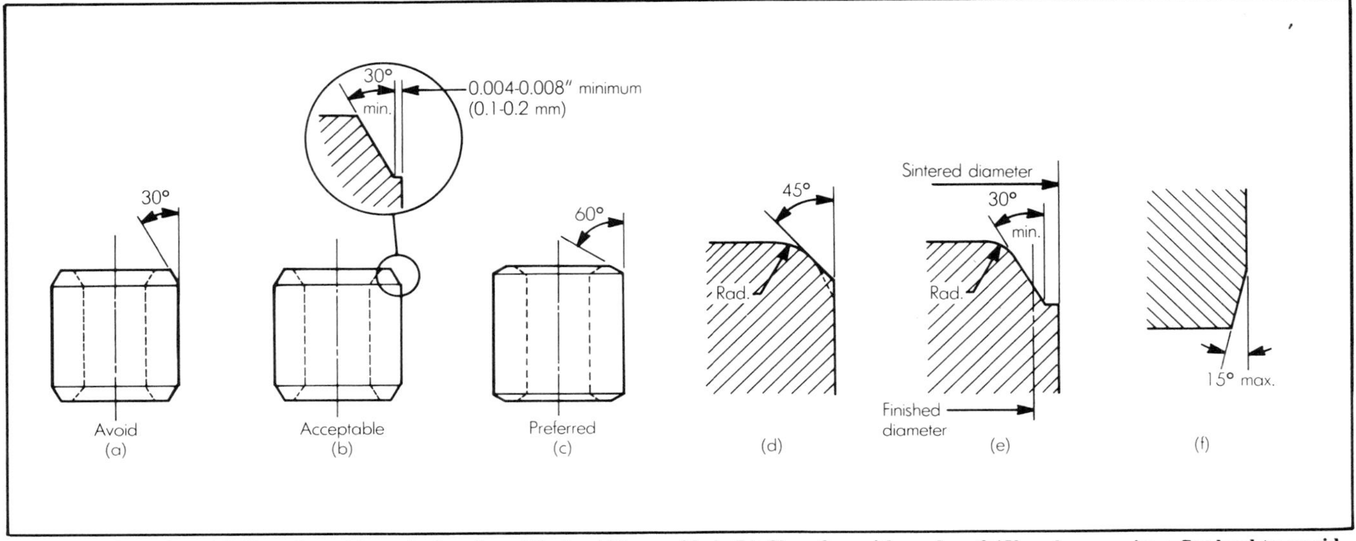


**Fig. 17-13 Chamfers: (a) Chamfers with angles less than 45° should be avoided. (b) Chamfers with angles of 45° or less require a flat land to avoid punch breakage. (c) Chamfers greater than 45° are preferred. (d) Where a radius is essential, a useful compromise is a combination of radius and chamfer. (e) When the part is to be machined or ground on the outside diameter, the form shown is practical. (f) An acute angle for a lead-in can be formed in the compacting die, or produced by a coining operation if the chamfer is short.**

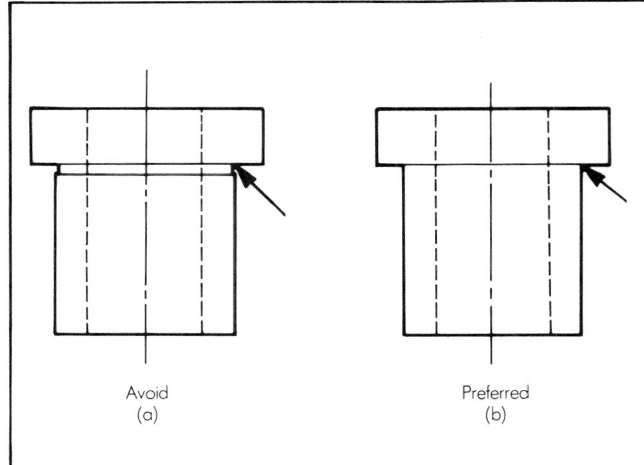


**Fig. 17-14 Undercuts: Undercuts cannot be molded. A radius should be provided between flange and body, and the housing should have a corresponding radius or chamfer. Otherwise, the undercut must be machined. If necessary, a radiused groove can be formed in the flange where it meets the hub.**

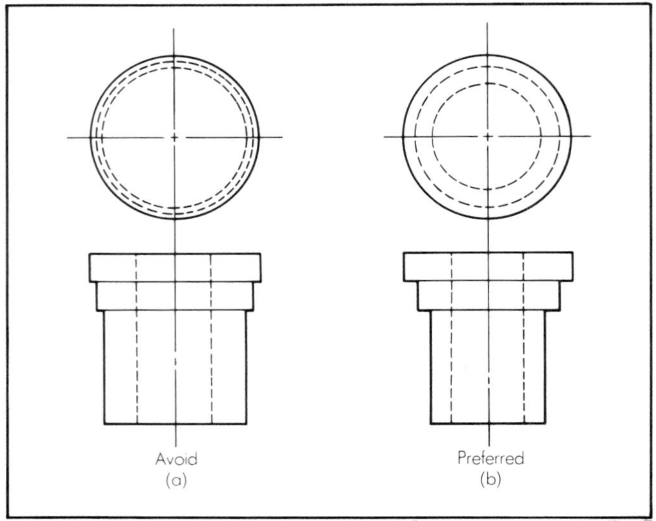


**Fig. 17-15 Steps: Parts with multiple steps should be designed with 0.035″ (0.9 mm) minimum width for each step. Thin punches increase breakdown time.**

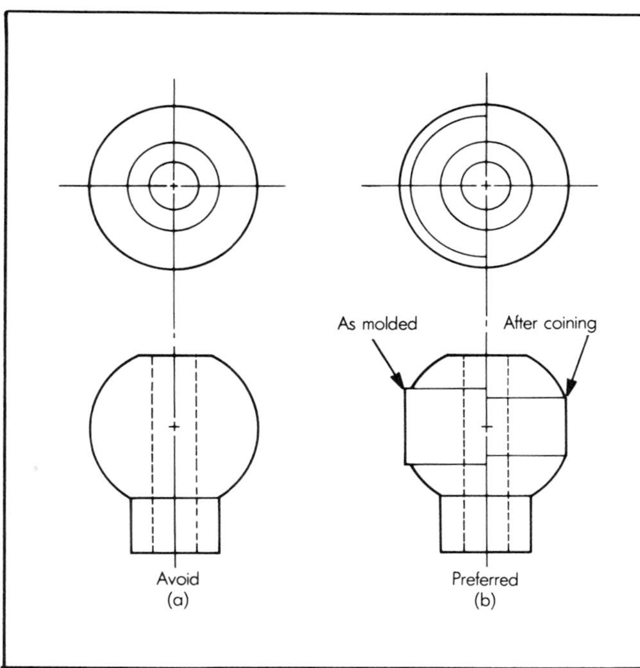


**Fig. 17-16 Spheres: (a) Complete spheres cannot be molded, because sharp edges on punches would touch and break. (b) A cylindrical section between two spherical sections can be molded. The cylindrical section will lie within the sphere after coining. If the cylindrical portion is less in height than 25% of the spherical diameter, the punches become weak.**

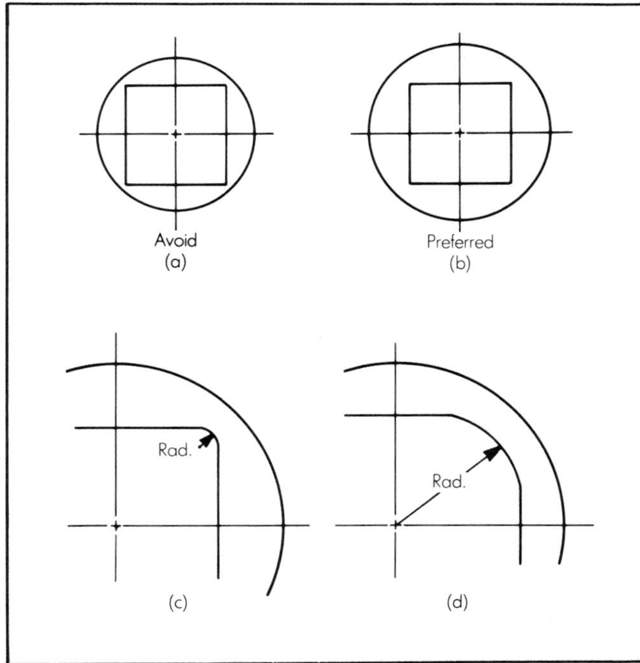


**Fig. 17-17 Wall thickness: (a) Avoid parts with a minimum wall thickness less than 0.030" (0.75 mm). For heavy, rigid, and long parts this limit must be increased. (b) The outside diameter has been increased to give reasonable strength. (c and d) Designs to increase wall thickness where a square bore is required. (d) Practical where flats are machined on a round spindle.**

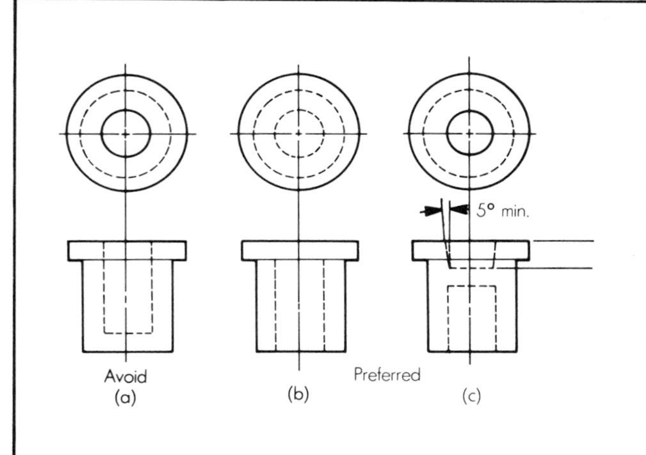


**Fig. 17-18 Flanges and holes: (a) If a flange or any projection is opposite the blind end, the design must be modified. (b) Blind hole as shown can be molded. (c) Short counterbores can be molded on the flanged face without complicating the tooling, if the area of the counterbore is not more than 20% of the total pressed area, the depth (x) is not more than 25% of the total thickness, and a minimum taper of 5° is permissible.**

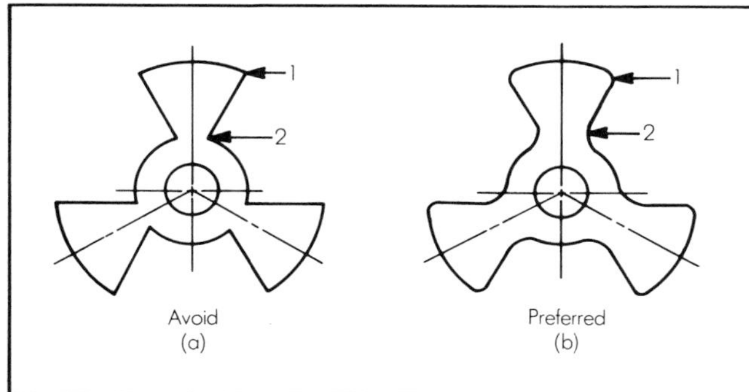


**Fig. 17-19 Edges and corners: (a) Avoid sharp edges which weaken the die (1) and corners which weaken parts (2). (b) Radiused edges (1) and radiused corners (2) add strength to tools and parts.**

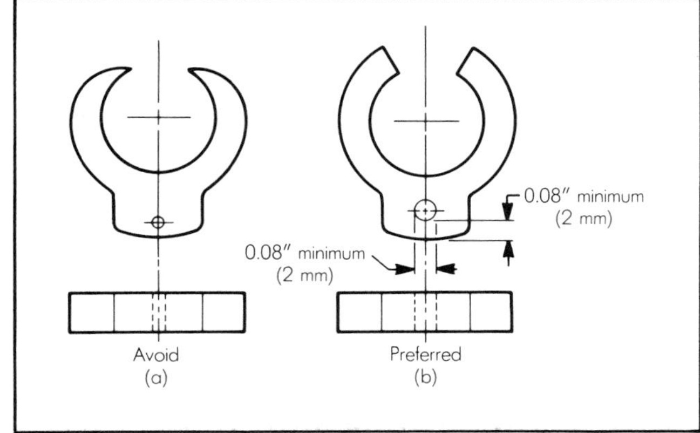


**Fig. 17-20 Featheredges: (a) Profiles requiring featheredges on punches should be avoided. Holes should not be less in diameter than 20-25% of their length. The practical minimum diameter for holes is considered to be 0.08" (2 mm). (b) Redesigned for stronger punches and hole large enough for molding.**

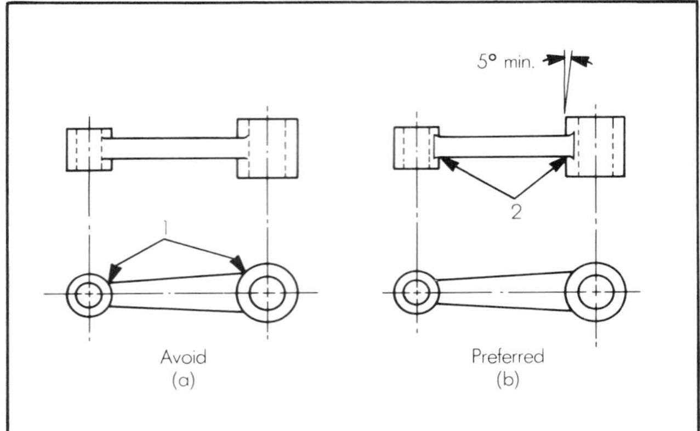


**Fig.17-21 Radii: (a) Radii (1) at change in profile require weak, featheredged punches, likely to break down. (b) Radii (2) at change in height strengthen both punches and parts. Taper on portion of boss formed by top punch assists extraction. Remainder of boss, formed by die, must be parallel.**

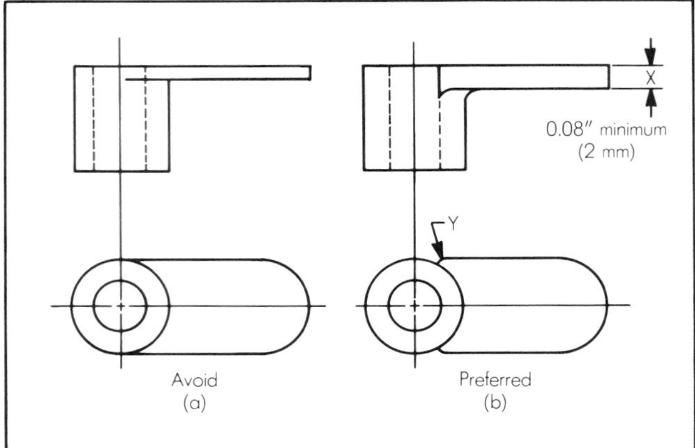


**Fig. 17-22 Thin forms: (a) Large, thin forms cannot be molded, particularly when attached to long forms. Parts crack on extraction. (b) Make projection (x) as thick as possible, add radius at root, and delete sharp edges on punch profile by radiusing as shown at (y).**

# POWDER MIXING AND BLENDING

Mixing of powders precedes compacting and includes producing mixtures of different metal powders. In addition to mixing of various metal powders, this section covers mixing of metal powders with lubricants, a procedure that almost universally precedes compacting of parts in rigid dies. Also discussed are some of the numerous variables involved in this complex process and their effects on the degree of mixing that is obtainable.

The term *mixing* of powders refers to "...the thorough intermingling of powders of two or more materials."[8] The term *blending* refers to "...the thorough intermingling of powders of the same composition."[9] In the literature concerning the science and technology of powders, these terms are frequently used interchangeably. In the following short discussion, the term *mixing* will be used exclusively.

## MIXER VARIABLES

Many different types of blenders and mixers are available. Batch mixers are commonly used in PM operations. The most widely used types include drum, cubical-shaped, double-cone (conical), twin-shell ("V"), and conical-screw (rotating auger). These types are shown in Fig. 17-23. Ribbon and paddle mixers, sigma blade mixers, and planetary blade mixers also are widely used. The selection of the best type of mixer for a given powder requires careful consideration, and tests must be made in each case.

**TABLE 17-7**
**Variables in the Mixing Process**

| | |
|---|---|
| • Type of mixer | • Interior surface of mixer |
| • Volume of the mixer | • Characteristics of powders |
| • Dimensions of mixer | • Rotational speed of mixer |
| • Volume of powder in the mixer | • Mixing temperature |
| | • Mixing time |
| • Volume ratio of component powders | • Mixing medium (gaseous or liquid) |

The most common mixing equipment for base metal powder mixes is the double-cone type, as shown in Fig. 17-24. An important consideration in mixing is that the powder must not fall freely during any stage of mixing, because this causes segregation. For this reason, the cylindrical part of double-cone mixers is kept short. This point must also be considered when other types of mixers, e.g. drum-type mixers with baffles, are used. The twin-shell "V" blender offers advantages that should be evaluated when powder uniformity is essential and precisely repeatable, predictable performance is necessary.

Many variables are involved in mixing. Table 17-7 shows some of the most important variables in the mixing process. Mixers can be characterized by their volume. However, two cylindrical mixers of identical volume perform differently when their length to diameter ratios differ. Although they may be of identical volume, the interior surface area of the two mixers is different, thereby changing the frictional effect, and the movement of the particles is quite different. It is the interior surface of the mixer that gives movement to the powder mass.

### Size of Load

For every type and size of mixer, the optimum powder charge varies. The ratio of the mixer volume to the volume of the powder is of great importance. There is always an optimum amount of powder for a given mixer, below and above this optimum amount, the mixing is inferior. This optimum amount depends on the type of powders to be mixed and on many other factors that affect the frictional behavior of the powder.

### Powder Characteristics

The powders to be mixed may differ in many respects. Tables 17-8 and 17-9 list the most important characteristics of a powder. If the powders differ significantly in density, segregation of the heavier powder may occur because gravitational forces may be stronger than the frictional forces. A change in the type of mixer and in the mixing procedure may be helpful to avoid segregation.

Powders of identical materials and identical particle size and particle size distribution may mix differently when the particle shape differs. Metal powders with oxidized surfaces flow faster and mix differently than identical metal powders with pure metallic surfaces. All these differences in the mixing behavior are due to the various friction conditions in the powders.

## Friction

Friction occurs between the particles in a powder mass. This friction and the manner of mixing determine the movement of powder particles. Studies of friction in a powder mass provide a better understanding of mixing problems.

During mixing, friction occurs between the powder particles and between the powder and the mixer wall. Friction causes an increase in temperature. If this increase in temperature occurs in an oxygen-containing atmosphere, and if some of the powders to be mixed oxidize, the mixed powders will contain particles with an oxide film. This is highly undesirable in some cases, especially when the oxide film affects further processing of the mixed powder.

The temperature during mixing has a significant effect on friction between powder particles, because the friction coefficient between most materials increases with increasing temperature. The flow of a powder is not as good at an elevated temperature as it is at a lower temperature. If it should be desirable to improve the flow or movement of powder particles during mixing, a lowering of the mixing temperature will lower friction and may improve the mixing.

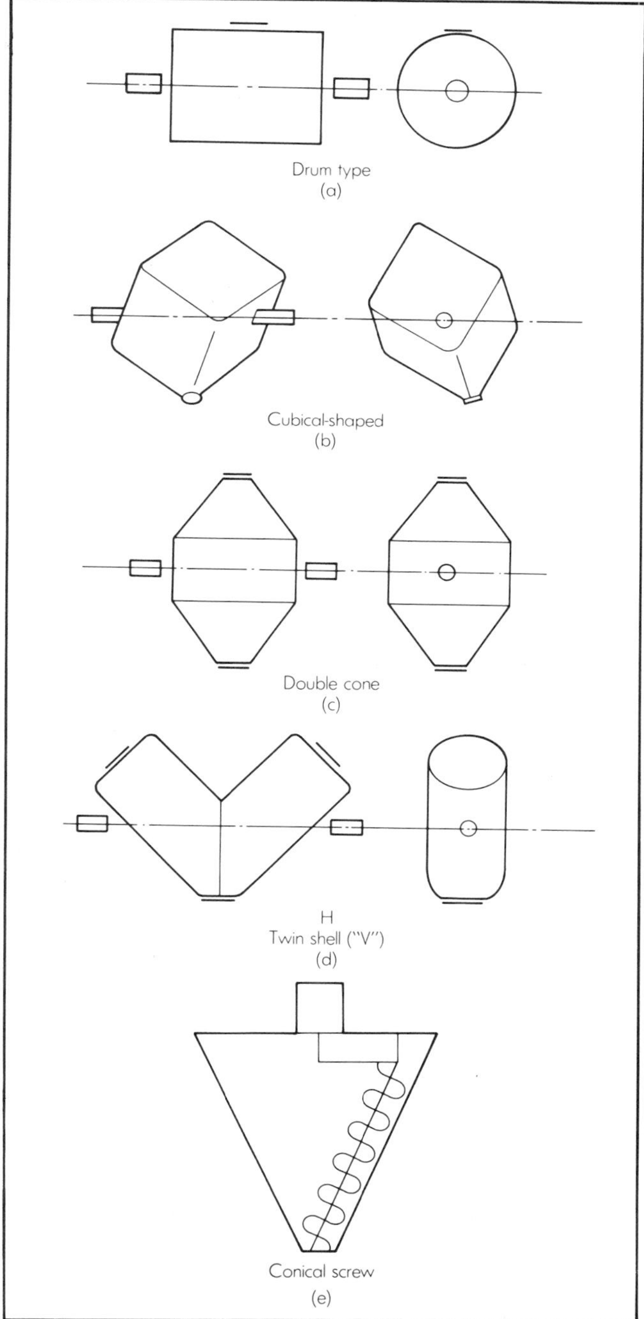

**Fig. 17-23 Diagrammatic outlines of powder mixers.**

## Rotational Speed

The rotational speed of a mixer greatly affects the mixing. Increasing the speed up to a certain point is useful in shortening the mixing time. However, for practically all types of mixers and powders, there is an optimal speed. Above this speed, the effectiveness decreases because the centrifugal forces are too strong and the powders do not move away from the wall of the mixer.

## Mixing Time

The optimum mixing time cannot be determined in advance without some testing. It is difficult to draw useful conclusions from the optimum time for one powder and to apply them to another powder in the same mixer. Mixing time strongly affects quality of the mix. Some powders are well mixed in some equipment after a relatively short time, whereas, other powders and/or other equipment require a prolonged mixing time to achieve the same degree of mixing; in other cases, a prolonged mixing time results in an even lower effectiveness.

## LUBRICANT

When parts are pressed in rigid dies, lubrication must be provided to reduce friction between powder particles and between the compact being pressed and the die wall and core

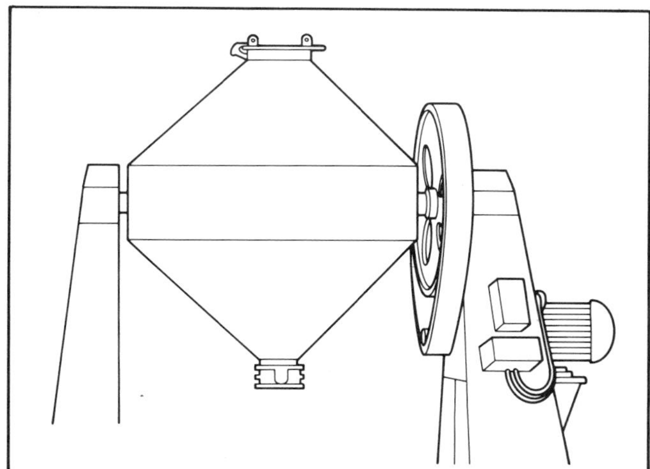
**Fig. 17-24 Double cone mixer.**

## POWDER MIXING AND BLENDING

**TABLE 17-8**
**Characteristics of a Powder Particle**

Material characteristics
- Structure
- Theoretical density
- Melting point
- Plasticity
- Elasticity
- Purity (impurities)

Characteristics due to fabrication process
- Density (porosity)
- Particle size (diameter)
- Particle shape
- Particle surface area
- Surface conditions
- Microstructure
- Type of lattice defects
- Gas content within a particle
- Adsorbed gas layer
- Amount of surface oxide
- Reactivity
- Conductivity

**TABLE 17-9**
**Characteristics of a Mass of Powder**

- Particle characteristics
- Average particle size
- Particle size distribution
- Average particle shape
- Particle shape distribution
- Specific surface (surface area per 1 gram)
- Apparent density
- Tap density
- Flow of the powder
- Friction conditions between the particles

rod. The lubricant has a low shear strength and keeps the metal surfaces apart. Complete separation is not possible even with well-lubricated surfaces, and there is friction due to contacts between metal asperities which puncture the lubricant film. Lubricants are chosen which attach themselves strongly to the metal surfaces and are not easily penetrated. The base metal powders are stearic acid; graphite; metal stearates, such as zinc and lithium stearate; and synthetic waxes, such as accrawax. Without lubrication, the pressure necessary to eject compacts from the die would increase rapidly; after a few compacts had been pressed, they would seize in the die during automatic compacting.

The lubricant is commonly introduced as a fine powder mixed with the metal powder or metal powders. The amount of lubricant added (generally 1/2 to 1% by weight) depends upon the shape of the compact. Complex shapes require larger amounts of lubricant to achieve a reasonably low ejection pressure. The mixing time and the intensity of mixing powder and lubricant affect such properties of the powder mixture as flow and apparent density. For most base metal powder mixes, mixing times of 20-40 minutes are common.

# COMPACTING

To facilitate an orderly presentation of subject matter, this section on "Compacting" is limited to conventional die pressing. Other pressure compacting techniques, including isostatic, forging, high energy rate forming, extrusion, and continuous powder rolling; are discussed subsequently in this chapter under "Special PM Processes." Slip casting and gravity compacting pressureless methods also are presented in that section.

The words *pressing, compacting,* and *briquetting* are synonymous and imply cold pressing powders into a green compact. The objectives in pressing are:

1. To achieve the required part shape.
2. To obtain the required green density (pressed, but not sintered).
3. To secure sufficient green strength to permit safe handling of the part.
4. To provide particle-to-particle contact which is necessary for sintering.

### BEHAVIOR OF POWDERS[10]

When metal powders are pressed in a die, the resulting compacts generally have enough adhesion and strength to permit handling without breaking. The green strength depends upon the type of metal powders—those from soft metals having higher strength—and upon the pressure that is applied. For soft metal powders, low pressures less than 35 MPa (5000 psi) produce compacts that can be handled. For harder powders, higher pressures are necessary. The question as to which "mechanisms" or physical forces produce adhesion between metal particles is basic to an understanding of the green strength of PM compacts. Two basic processes—bulk movement and deformation—occur during compaction under pressure.

### Bulk Movement

Bulk movement and rearrangement of particles results in a more efficient packing of the powder; that is, densification. Such movement is limited by frictional forces developed between neighboring particles and between particles and die, punch, and core rod surfaces. The relative ease of such motion increases with decreasing apparent density of the powder. With low apparent densities there is less particle-to-particle contact and more free space into which particles may move. Small particles move relatively greater distances because of their ability to pass through the small channels among the particles. Although most of the motion is in the direction of pressure application, there is some lateral motion due to the restraining action of blocking particles and the availability of free spaces. Powder characteristics that increase frictional forces reduce the extent of bulk particle movement. Movement of particles within the powder mass tends to take place at relatively low pressures and accounts for the early densification of the material. Additionally, the rate of pressure application influences bulk movement. High rates of pressure application tend to cause premature immobilization of particles due to high compressive stresses being developed on the particles, and this tends to block open passages.

## Deformation of Particles

Deformation of individual particles can also reduce the amount of porosity in the compact. Certainly with regard to the production of high-density parts, it is the major mechanism of densification. Both elastic and plastic deformation may occur. Most elastic deformation will be recovered when the stress is removed from the compact. This may take place before, during, and after ejection from the die cavity. It is for this reason that compacts usually have dimensions slightly greater than the die dimensions. The extent of elastic deformation increases with decreasing values of elastic modulus and increasing values of particle stress relative to the yield stress or elastic limit of the material.

When clean metal surfaces are made to touch each other, the adhesion between them is small because the area of contact is small. The area of contact between the surfaces increases when pressure is applied. The pressure produces some elastic deformation. For most practical cases of adhesion of surfaces under pressure, the amount of elastic deformation is negligibly small, since the weight of the powder alone causes plastic flow. Under these circumstances, the area of contact, regardless of the particle type or shape of surface asperities, is roughly proportional to the force applied; however, to produce complete contact, extremely high loads are required. The analysis of adhesion on a fundamental basis is complicated by the fact that metal surfaces, and in particular, the surfaces of metal powder particles, generally are covered with an oxide film. In addition, layers of gas molecules are absorbed on these surfaces. The oxides themselves can be cold welded, but the strength of the bond is generally low compared with that of metals. On the other hand, when metals are rubbed together, which is what happens during compacting of metal powders, the oxide films are penetrated or rubbed off and metal-to-metal contact is established.

Except for porous types of parts, plastic deformation of individual particles usually represents the most important mechanism of densification during compaction. It is evident that the greater the actual pressures on the particles, the greater the degree of plastic deformation. Rapid rates of pressure application may affect this process, but exactly how is not certain. Most materials work harden significantly so that it becomes increasingly more difficult to improve densification by increasing the pressure on the compact. On this basis, the effectiveness of the external pressure is greatest at low pressures where plastic deformation occurs relatively easily, and becomes progressively less effective with increasing pressure.

## PRESSES

There are three basic types of compacting presses. The first and most widely used is the mechanical press, which includes (a) opposed-ram pressing, (b) single-action pressing, (c) multiple-action pressing, (d) anvil-type pressing, and (e) rotary-type pressing. The second type, the hydraulic press, also can be obtained with (a) opposed-ram pressing, (b) single-action (with floating die) or withdrawal-type pressing, (c) multiple-action pressing using (a) or (b). The third major type of press, which is finding increasing usage, is the hybrid press. This press uses a combination of mechanical, hydraulic, and pneumatic forces to compact a part.

### Tonnage and Stroke Capacity

The capacity in tons, or in kilonewtons (kN) or meganewtons (MN) that a press must have to produce compacts in rigid dies at a given pressure in tons/in.$^2$ or MPa depends upon the size of the part to be pressed and is equal to the pressure multiplied by the projected area of the part in in.$^2$ or m$^2$. The compacting pressure depends upon the desired green density of the part which, in turn, is determined by the requirements for the physical and mechanical properties of the sintered part. In addition to tonnage capacity of a press, the stroke capacity of a press, i.e., the maximum ram travel, is important, because it determines the length of a part that can be pressed and ejected. In presses used for automatic compacting, the stroke capacity is related to the length available for diefill and for the ejection stroke.

Green density is the density of the part after it has been pressed, but before it has been put through the next process—sintering in the case of metal powders, or firing in the case of ceramics or ferrites. The most common way of expressing density is grams per cubic centimeter (g/cm$^3$). The amount of force required to obtain a given green density depends upon the material being pressed. It can range from 3-60 tons/in.$^2$ (41.4-827 MPa). The upper limit is usually held to 60 tons/in.$^2$ to provide a safety factor against premature tool failure under load. Table 17-10 gives some examples.

### Die Pressing

The powder metal compacting press using die compaction is the most widely accepted high-production method of producing components by the powder metallurgy process. This is regarded as the conventional technique. The press is a machine that consolidates loose powdered material into a useful form or shape by compacting the powder under high pressures. The component being produced is formed within the confines of hard tooling, comprising dies, punches, and core rods. The process is called PM die pressing. The part produced is known as a briquette and is said to be in the "green" or unsintered state after ejection from the tooling. While the presses are known as powdered metal compacting presses, they are not limited to the pressing of metal powders. Almost any material, alloys or mixture, that can be provided in powder form can be compacted.

High-production PM compacting presses are available as standard production machines and are built in a wide range of

**TABLE 17-10**
**Press Tonnage for Various Materials**

| Material | Tons per In.$^2$ | MPa |
|---|---|---|
| Aluminum | 5-20 | 69-276 |
| Brass | 30-50 | 414-689 |
| Bronze | 15-20 | 207-276 |
| Carbon | 10-12 | 138-165 |
| Carbides | 10-30 | 138-414 |
| Alumina | 8-10 | 110-138 |
| Steatites | 3-5 | 41-69 |
| Ferrites | 8-12 | 110-165 |
| Iron Parts: | | |
| low denisty | 25-30 | 345-414 |
| medium density | 30-40 | 414-552 |
| high density | 35-60 | 483-827 |
| Tungsten | 5-10 | 69-138 |
| Tantalum | 5-10 | 69-138 |

Note: Tonnage requirements are approximations and vary with changes in chemical, metallurgical, and sieve characteristics; with the amount of die lubricants used; and with mixing procedures.

# COMPACTING

capacity and production rate capabilities. Presses are designed to have the capability of producing parts of a specific classification. The Metal Powder Industries Federation (MPIF) has classified PM parts in terms of their complexity, the Class I being the least complex through Class IV, the most complex.

## Press Selection

Selection must be based primarily on the type of work to be done, whether parts are large or small, whether they are simple or complex in shape, whether high or low-volume production is required, and numerous other factors related specifically to the job.

In some situations, simple tools and versatile, multiple-action presses are more suitable than complex tools and simple presses. The availability of toolmaking facilities must be considered, as well as the economics involved as far as tool cost and maintenance are concerned. As in selecting equipment for any other process, a thorough analysis of all the conditions involved is essential to ensure the best results.

The requirements for a powder metal compacting press should include the following:

- Adequate pressure capability in the direction of pressing, and sufficient part ejection capacity.
- Controlled length and speed of compression and ejection strokes.
- Synchronized timing of press strokes.
- Capability of producing a part of the desired classification.
- Adjustable powder filling arrangements.
- Material feeding and part removal system.
- Machine safety interlocks to prevent machine and/or tooling damage in the event of a malfunction.
- Necessary safety devices for operating personnel.

In order to better understand the types of commercially available PM compacting presses and their advantages and limitations, an explanation of PM part classification and tooling systems used to produce these parts is necessary.

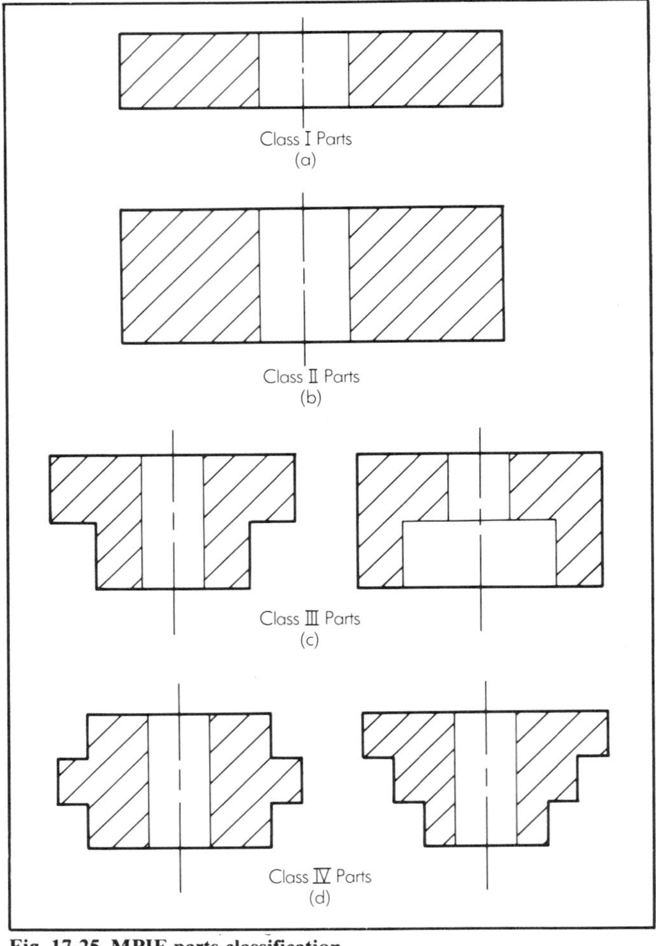


**Fig. 17-25 MPIF parts classification.**

## MPIF Part Classification

**Class I parts**. As shown in Fig. 17-25, *a*, these parts are thin, are a single level, and are pressed with a force from one direction. A slight density variation within the part results from the single direction pressing. The highest density is on the surface in contact with the moving punch, the lowest density on the opposite side. Parts with a finished thickness of approximately 0.3" (7.6 mm) can be produced by this method without significant density variation.

**Class II parts**. Figure 17-25, *b*, illustrates parts that are single level of any thickness and are pressed from both top and bottom. The lowest density region of these parts is near the center, with higher density on the top and bottom.

**Class III parts**. Figure 17-25, *c*, illustrates parts with two levels of any thickness that are pressed from both top and bottom. Individual punches are required for each of the levels to control powder fill and density in each of the two levels.

**Class IV parts**. As illustrated in Figure 17-25, *d*, these parts have multiple levels of any thickness and are pressed from both top and bottom. Individual punches are required for each level to control powder fill and density in each of the levels.

The contour of the part does not enter into the determination of part complexity classification. The part may be a gear, cam, lever, or some other configuration and may have the same classification. Only part thickness and the number of distinct levels determine classification.

# SINTERING

The briquetting or compacting of PM structural parts is followed by one or more sintering operations in which the green compacts are heated in a controlled-atmosphere furnace. The most commonly used furnaces are of the continuous type, equipped with a pusher, a conveyer belt, or other mechanical means of transporting the workpieces. A cooling section, containing the same protective atmosphere, is provided, enabling removal of the compacts from the furnace at approximately room temperature. Figure 17-26 shows a typical temperature profile in a continuous sintering furnace.

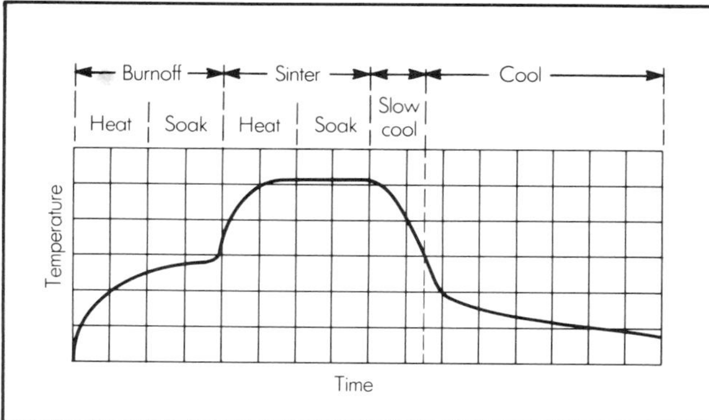


Fig. 17-26 Temperature profile in a continuous sintering furnace.

In its simplest application, sintering is intended to impart strength to the part. This is accomplished using thermal treatments to promote spontaneous bonding and agglomeration reactions between particles. Sintering can also be employed to introduce alloying elements since the diffusional processes which tend to homogenize the distribution of alloying elements are the same ones that control sintering reactions.

Two basic types of sintering processes are commercially important: solid-phase sintering and liquid-phase sintering. Solid-phase sintering involves only atomic diffusion mechanisms and is, by nature, relatively slow at temperatures less than about 80% of the melting point. Time cycles for sintering and the furnace temperature are determined by the composition of the powders and by the properties desired in the finished product. Representative sintering temperatures and times for various materials are listed in Table 17-11. For a specific metal, the temperature is below the melting point; with mixtures of metals to produce alloys, the temperature is below the melting point of the major constituent.

Furnace atmospheres are produced in cryogenic distillation or gas-reforming equipment and include partially combusted natural gas, propane, dissociated ammonia, byproduct hydrogen, and vacuum. In many installations, sufficient heat is furnished by resistance-wound or silicon carbide element electric furnaces. When gas or oil-fired equipment is used, the furnace is provided with a muffle.

## SINTERING METHODS

Sintering methods differ in such respects as the manner in which heat is applied; the medium surrounding the compact (liquid, gas, vacuum, air, powder, or a mold); conditions created by the composition of the compact; and the state of the constituents during sintering. Among the numerous methods employed are treating in a liquid salt bath, for very dense parts; treating in a liquid metal bath, for metal powder blanks that are machined after sintering; imbedding the compact in a heated powder pack of an inert or partially reducing material; and heating in a ceramic or graphite mold. All of these methods have disadvantages that limit their application to special parts.

The most common method of sintering structural parts is by externally heating the compact inside a box, or muffle, that is filled with a protective atmosphere to prevent oxidation.

In high-volume production sintering, continuous furnaces of the type used in heat treating are used. A steady stream of protective atmosphere is retained in the muffle, while the charge of work is passed through the furnace by a stoker arrangement.

**TABLE 17-11**
**Sintering Temperature and Time**

| Material | Time, Minutes | Temperature °F | Temperature °C |
|---|---|---|---|
| Bronze | 10-20 | 1400-1600 | 760-871 |
| Copper | 12-45 | 1550-1650 | 843-899 |
| Brass | 10-45 | 1550-1650 | 843-899 |
| Iron, iron graphite | 20-45 | 1850-2100 | 1010-1149 |
| Nickel | 30-45 | 1850-2100 | 1010-1149 |
| Stainless steel | 30-60 | 2000-2350 | 1093-1288 |
| Alnico magnets | 120-150 | 2200-2375 | 1204-1302 |
| Ferrites | 10-600 | 2200-2700 | 1204-1482 |
| 90-W, 6-Ni, 4-Cu | 10-120 | 2450-2900 | 1343-1593 |
| Tungsten carbide | 20-30 | 2600-2700 | 1427-1482 |
| Molybdenum | 120 | 3730 | 2054 |
| Tungsten | 480 | 4250 | 2343 |
| Tantalum | 480 | 4350 | 2399 |

The parts may be loaded in trays that are carried on a conveyor belt; frequently, the work itself is placed directly on the conveyor belt.

In addition to the conventional form of sintering, involving heating the original powder mass to a high temperature, but below its melting point, in a protective atmosphere; there are two major variations.

### Hot Pressing

This technique identifies the application of both elevated temperature (below the melting point) and an external pressure to the compact. This technique is widely used for ceramic materials and refractory metals, but not for conventional ferrous and nonferrous materials.

### Liquid Phase

Sintering usually is considered a solid-state process; that is, no molten or liquid phase is present. However, liquid-phase sintering is a process variation in which sintering temperature is high enough that one or more components of the material is liquefied. Liquid-phase sintering utilizes a second powder, mechanically mixed with the first, which has a melting point lower than the sintering temperature. The presence of a liquid phase during sintering not only enhances the bonding and agglomeration reactions between the solid particles, but also freezes upon cooling and acts in much the same manner as a solder to provide additional strength.

## FURNACES

The mesh belt conveyor furnace (Fig. 17-27)[11] is the most commonly used furnace for sintering. It usually consists of the following components:

- Charge table and belt drive.
- Burn-off furnace.
- Sintering furnace.
- Slow cooler.
- Final cooling section.
- Discharge table.

This type of furnace is commonly used for sintering nonferrous and ferrous parts up to a maximum temperature of 2100° F (1150° C).

# SINTERING

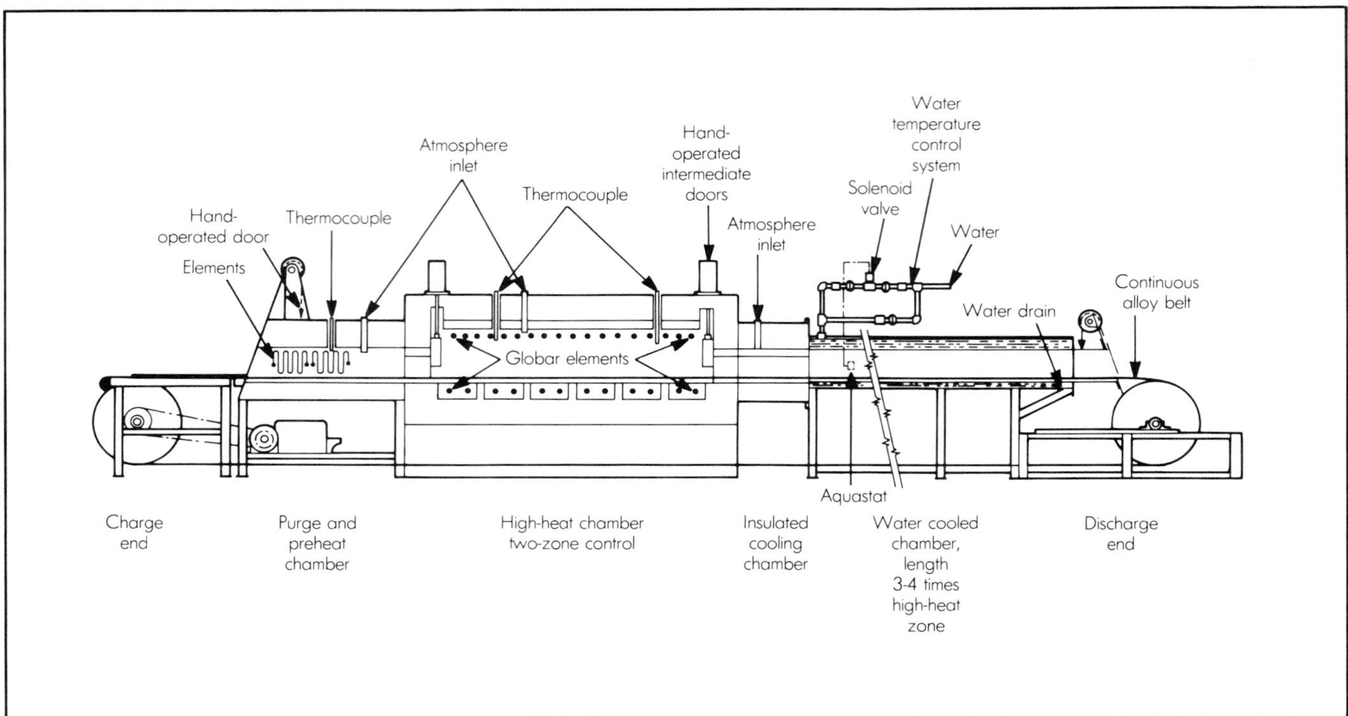


**Fig. 17-27 Mesh-belt continuous-type sintering furnace.**

When higher sintering temperatures are required, different types of furnaces are used. In the 3150° F (1732° C) temperature range, molybdenum-heated pusher furnaces may be used. In the 2100-2500° F (1150-1371° C) temperature range, walking beam furnaces may be used; and in the maximum temperature range of about 5000° F (2760° C), vacuum furnaces may be used.

When molybdenum heating elements are employed for temperatures of 2200-3150° F (1204-1730° C), it is important that hydrocarbon residues from the lubricant burn-off do not come in contact with the heating elements as they will carburize. For the hydrogen sintering of cemented carbides which is usually performed in a molybdenum-heated pusher furnace, a separate presinter and burn-off furnace is used. This keeps lubricant residues out of the molybdenum heated furnace.

Since the atmosphere in a furnace may react with brickwork or insulation, many furnaces are constructed with a metallic muffle to isolate the atmosphere from the lining. Muffle-type construction gives the best control of atmosphere and atmosphere velocity, but it is limited to a top temperature of 2200° F (1200° C) by the alloy materials that are available.

When the atmosphere is in contact with the refractories, certain precautions must be taken. When endothermic gas is used in contact with the lining materials, the lining must be of special low iron and reducible oxide composition, or carbon nodules will form at certain temperature gradients in the insulation and spall the brickwork. When low dew point reducing atmospheres such as dissociated ammonia or hydrogen are used at high temperatures, they can reduce the silica, which is the major constituent of most refractories. Under these conditions, high-alumina insulating materials are required.

Vacuum sintering is commonly used for such materials as stainless steel, tungsten carbides, tool steels, and titanium.

## LUBRICANT PURGING

Since most PM parts are compacted with a lubricant to reduce compacting pressure and to assist in ejection of the part from the die, this lubricant must be burned out of the part before it can be sintered. The removal of the lubricant is normally accomplished in a burn-off furnace, under a protective atmosphere, at temperatures ranging from 800-1500° F (427-816° C) and for a typical time of 20-30 minutes. After lubricant burn-off, the part is conveyed into the sintering furnace for the appropriate period of time at the desired temperature.

## ATMOSPHERES

During the burn-off, sintering, and subsequent cooling operations, the parts are maintained in a protective atmosphere. The purpose of this atmosphere is to prevent oxidation; to reduce oxides in the metals; to carburize, decarburize, or maintain a neutrality to carbon; and to assist in flushing lubricant residues from the furnace.

The most commonly used protective atmospheres are:

- Endothermic gas.
- Nitrogen blended with other reducing gases.
- Dissociated ammonia.
- Exothermic gas.
- Hydrogen.

A decision as to the atmosphere to select must take into consideration the atmosphere's compatibility with the materials being processed, the type of furnace needed, and the cost of the furnace. Typical sintering atmospheres are listed in Table 17-12.

**TABLE 17-12**
**Relative Cost and Uses of Sintering Atmospheres**

| Atmosphere | Relative Cost Index per 1000 ft$^3$ (28.3 m$^3$) | Uses |
|---|---|---|
| Cylinder hydrogen | 50 | All-purpose sintering atmosphere. Most powerful reducing atmosphere. Must be used for tungsten and tantalum carbides, Alnico, and stainless steels or alloys in excess of 2% chromium. Decarburizing to iron powders |
| Cracked anhydrous ammonia, 75% $H_2$ -25% $N_2$. Dew point -60° F | 10 | Used for brass sintering. Used in place of cylinder hydrogen to reduce cost. Not suitable for metals that absorb molecular nitrogen at sintering temperatures. Decarburizing to iron powders |
| Exothermically cracked gas, 17% max $H_2$. 10% max CO, 4% min $CO_2$. 1.0% $CH_4$, bal. $N_2$. Dew point, 10° F higher than cooling water. Refrigerated or dried to 40° F (4.4° C) point | 2.5 | Lowest-cost atmosphere. Used for copper, bronze, silver, and iron powders where decarburization is not a factor<br>Refrigerated or dried to 40° F (4.4° C) dew point for iron to prevent discoloration. Sulfur must be removed for copper, bronze, and silver if in excess of 8 grains/100 ft$^3$ (0.18 g/m$^3$) |
| Endothermically cracked gas, 40% $H_2$, 20% CO, 0-3% $CO_2$, 0-1.0% $CH_4$. Dew point 0-70° F. CO and dew point can be adjusted for desired carbon potential | 3 | Used for medium and high-carbon iron powders to prevent decarburization. Carbon potential adjustable for low or high carbon. Used to obtain more reducing atmosphere than exothermic type. Used for brass sintering. Used for heat-treating and carburizing powdered-iron parts |

# TOOLING FOR PM PARTS

The design of tooling for sintered metal parts begins with a study of the workpiece drawing. The most important point to consider is whether the part is feasible for the PM process. Can the part be molded? Can it be made within the capability of existing equipment in the fabricating shop? Can it satisfy the basic parameters governing a sound sintered metal part?

An understanding of what happens when powder is compacted between punches in a die is essential to design a good part and the appropriate tools for it (see "Compacting" in this chapter).

The tool engineer should participate in the design of the product as early as possible in its inception and development cycle. This helps to assure that prospective parts are designed in accordance with the capabilities and limits inherent in the PM process.

## TOOLING DESIGN FACTORS

The limitations posed by rigid dies are illustrated by the die action shown in Fig. 17-28.[12] A single punch cannot assure uniform density if the part is of varying thickness (actually, varying axial height); therefore, steps are limited to one quarter of height (Fig. 17-28, view *a*). Much larger steps are allowable with a multiple-sleeve die; however, a very thin sleeve is impractical (view *b*) and the sleeve should be radiused to prevent excessive wear. Knife-edge punches wear excessively and should be changed to present a flat face (view *c*). On withdrawal, a deeply penetrating punch would damage the compact, so it should be tapered (view *d*). Holes can be made with parallel walls, but should be a minimum of 0.2" (5 mm) diam to prevent premature core rod failure. The maximum depth-to-diameter ratio range is practically limited to 2-4 (view *e*). Even under pressure, the powder cannot fill very thin sections (view *f*).

Diecastings, forgings, extrusions, and plastic parts are made by a process with one common feature. All of these processes rely on plasticity of the component material to flow throughout the cross section of the mold tool to produce the part. Movement of material in the direction transverse to the pressing motion is a natural and necessary phenomenon of these forming techniques. Thin wall sections, or uneven cross sections, can be molded with comparative ease. Multiple levels pose no particular problem. Side coring and curved sections can be made with these molding methods.

Metal powders, on the other hand, do not share the basic characteristic of the other molding and forming methods. Powdered metal does not flow under pressure. This is a basic factor; it imposes restrictions on the tooling design and the manufacturing processing of parts by the PM technique. Since metal powder does not flow under pressure, several other related factors must be considered in tooling design. Some of the significant tooling design parameters are interrelated and can be grouped based on the following:

1. Metal powder does not flow under pressure. (This factor is fundamental and is repeated for emphasis.) Under vertical axial load, powder can, however, exert a side force. For example, when a simple shape is compacted at 30 tons/in.$^2$ (414 MPa), 10 tons/in.$^2$ (138 MPa) pressure can be exerted laterally against the die.
2. A compact (unsintered part) has very low tensile strength and ductility. For a given material, these properties are a function of density.
3. A PM part should have uniform density. Structural strength of PM parts is directly related to density. Density is the property that relates to internal transfer of applied loads within the part. To achieve uniform density, tooling design must accommodate the no-flow characteristic of metal powder. Parts with multiple-level cross sections usually require a separate tool member for each level.
4. The finished part should be free of shear planes. Shear planes develop in a sintered metal part when a level of the compact densifies without simultaneous densification of adjacent material. Densification of the adjacent material is necessary to provide support, which prevents angular slippage of the compacted material. Where a shear plane exists (even when the part is ejected as a whole piece), the rupture does not heal during sintering and causes an unsound sintered part to be produced. When the shear plane is at a point of stress concentration, the part may fail in service.
5. The part must be free of cracks. Because compacted material has little green strength, adequate ejection support must be provided for each overhanging level in the mold tooling. Cracking may result if this support is not provided.
6. A compact tends to grow or "pop" as it is ejected from the die. This "pop out" is proportional to the compacting pressure.
7. Tooling must perform reliably. Tool design practices should emphasize the importance of performing effectively, with little maintenance or setup adjustment, for high-volume production runs over a long period of time.

## TOOL MATERIAL

Tools used in the production of PM parts perform a variety of operations, such as compacting, coining, sizing, and hot forming. In the early days of the industry, when only bronze powders were compacted, little was required of tooling, other than high wear resistance. With the introduction of iron and steel powders—and, more recently, refractory metal and superalloy powders—tool materials now require the additional feature of high impact resistance. Additionally, there is an increasing demand for high-density compacts, a requirement that imposes even heavier loads on the compacting tools. And, with recent activity in the hot forming of powdered metal parts, wear resistance at elevated temperatures has been added to the growing list of tooling requirements.

### Wear Resistance or Impact Strength

The characteristics of wear resistance and high impact strength are difficult to combine in one material. Tool material selection is determined by the PM part and the powder

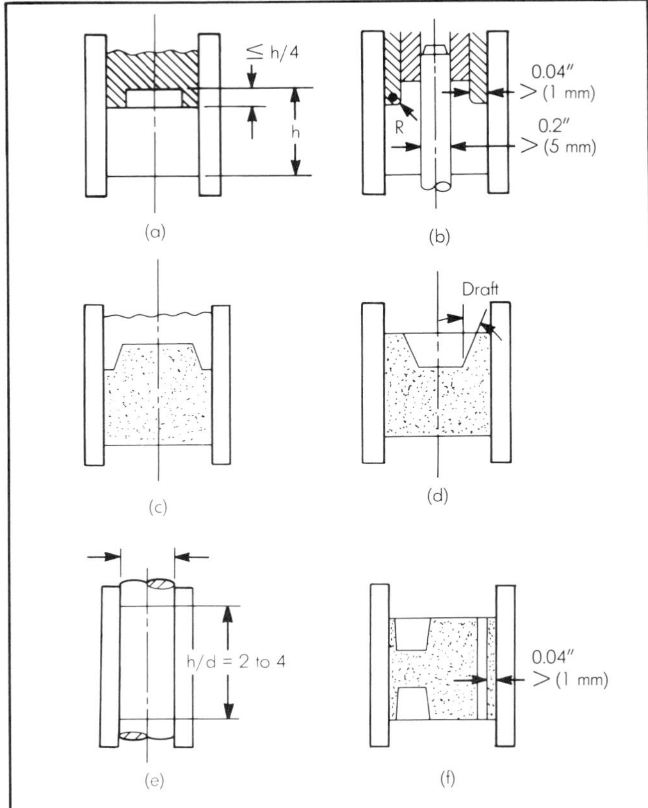


**Fig. 17-28 Design and production limitations of PM parts.**

material; the method of tool construction; and the PM processes by which the part is to be made or finished. Wear resistance is a key factor in die and core materials. For punch materials, on the other hand, impact resistance or toughness is more important than wear resistance. Refer to Chapter 2 "Die and Mold Materials" for additional information.

### Die Materials

The most commonly used die materials are the wear-resistant steels and cemented carbides. The most common steel grades are A2, D2, M2, and SAE No. 6150. Tungsten carbide is used for core rod sleeves. Cemented carbides are used in the form of shrink-fitted linings. Tough steels such as A2 and D2 are recommended for the punches. Cemented-carbide punches are not in common use.

## DIE DESIGN

Die cavities and punch faces should be lapped and polished to a very high surface finish, preferably below 10 $\mu$ in. (0.25 $\mu$ m). Clearances between die walls and punches should not exceed 0.005″ (0.13 mm); these clearances should be held between 0.0002-0.0003″ (0.005-0.008 mm) for precision parts.

To facilitate ejection and avoid excessive die wear, a slight taper, typically 0.001 in./in. or mm/mm, is machined in the die. Tapers may, however, entrap powder particles and cause fins and burrs; more wear-resistant die materials, such as cemented carbides, may be used to avoid the need for tapers in compacting dies. In coining dies, tapers may be necessary to press oversize sintered pieces into the cavity.

## Die Strength

In determining die wall thickness, it is frequently assumed that for reasons of safety, full hydraulic transmission of pressure is obtained, even though this is contrary to the no-side-flow theory.

An exact calculation of the stress on die walls is almost impossible from a practical point of view because of the nature of the work performed. In the first place, stress distribution throughout a compact under pressure, which must be taken into account as part of the structure under consideration, is extremely complicated and includes variables such as part shape, particle-size distribution, and other factors that affect transmission of compressive stress in the lateral direction. The experimental work and stress analysis required for precise calculation of these stresses require far more time than is usually available to the die designer.

## Die Dimensions

Simpler empirical methods of calculating die dimensions are usually employed. In one of these, Poisson's ratio of 0.3 for structural steel is employed with a modification of Lame's formula for cylinders of heavy wall thickness subjected to high internal hydrostatic pressures. This is:

$$D = d\sqrt{\frac{s+pu}{s-pu}} \qquad (1)$$

where:

$D$ = outer diameter of die
$d$ = diameter of the compact
$S$ = maximum allowable fiber stress of die material
$p$ = briquetting pressure
$u$ = Poisson's ratio for steel

While the pressure within a cylinder is uniform in the hydrostatic case, it is multipled by Poisson's ratio for this application.

This formula can be used only as a guide or approximation, since the ratio of die length to compact length, pressure distribution, distribution within the compact, variations in shape, and other important factors are not considered. In many applications, this formula produces safer results than are necessary.

Internal-stress distribution in irregular shapes becomes even more involved; and in sectional dies, the lateral stresses exerted by the compact are transferred from individual inserts to the die ring. As a result, corresponding allowances must be made in calculating stresses. Tool designers invariably allow a high safety factor in such calculations, because the cost of die materials is the least expensive aspect of design and fabrication.

## PM TOOLING SYSTEMS

Tooling systems applicable to the various categories of PM parts, as defined in the "Compacting" section of this chapter, include the single-action system, double-action system, floating-die system, and withdrawal system.

## Single-Action

Single-action systems, as illustrated in Fig. 17-29, are generally limited to Class I parts. During the pressing portion of the compacting cycle, the die, the core rod, and one of the punches (usually the lower punch) remain stationary. Compacting is performed by the moving punch which is driven by the action of the press. One or more core rods may be used to form any through holes in the part.

During ejection, the upper punch moves away from the formed part and the part is ejected from the die. When the core rod is stationary, the part is ejected from the die and core rod

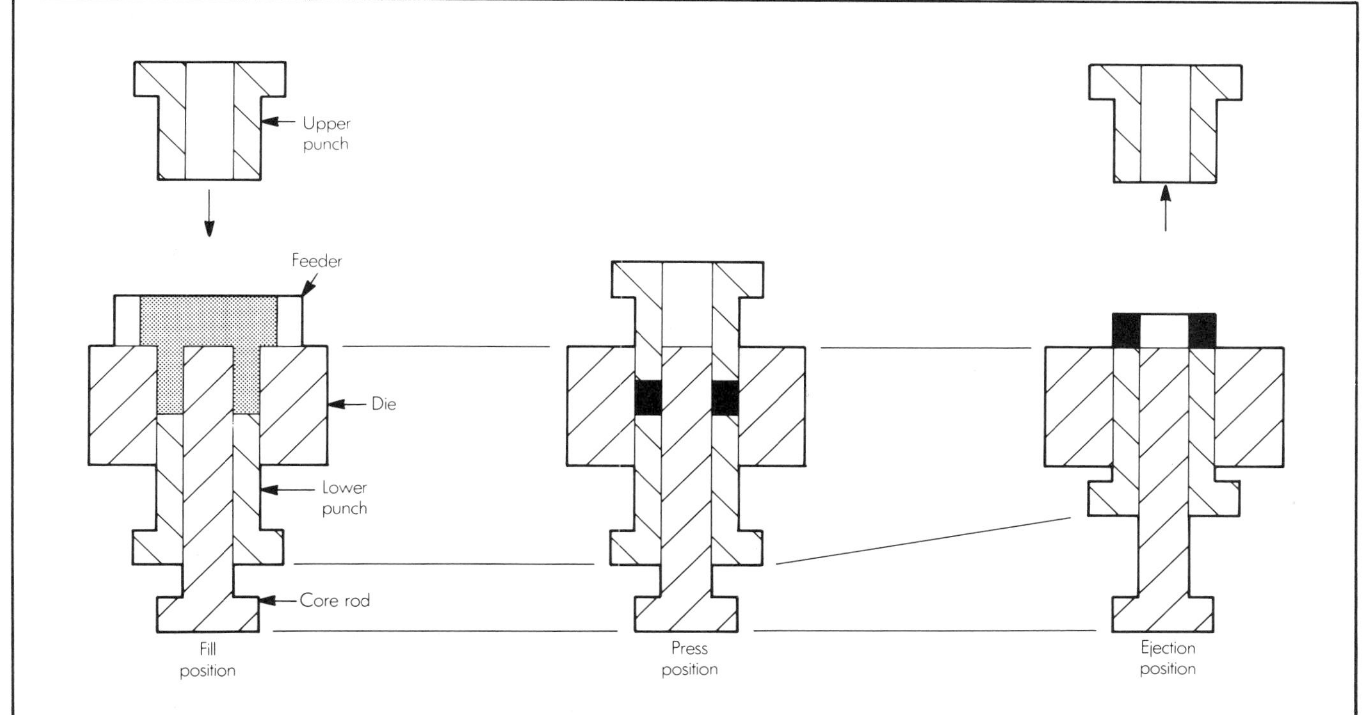


**Fig. 17-29 Single-action press system.**

simultaneously. On some presses, the core rod is free to move (float) upward with the part as it is being ejected. Upon final ejection, the compacted part elastically expands slightly. This expansion causes the part to free itself from the core rod. The core is then free to move downward to the fill position. This "floating" core arrangement offers the advantage of reduced ejection forces and reduced core rod wear.

## Double-Action

The double-action tooling system shown in Fig. 17-30 is used primarily to produce Class I and Class II parts. Pressure is applied to the top and bottom of the part simultaneously and at the same rate. The die and core rod are stationary. Densification takes place from the top and bottom toward the center with the lowest density region existing near the neutral axis of the part. Although the core rod is shown as being fixed, it can be arranged to function in the same manner as the core rod for single-action pressing, "floating" out with the part during ejection (see earlier section, "Single-Action").

## Floating Die

The floating-die tooling system is shown in Fig. 17-31. In principle, it is the same as the double-action system, except that a different means is used to accomplish the same end result. The die is mounted on a yielding mechanism. Springs are used; however, pneumatic or hydraulic cylinders are more often used because they offer an easily adjustable force. As the upper punch enters the die, starting to compact the powder, the friction between the powder and die wall causes the die to float downward. This has the same effect as an upward-moving lower punch. After pressing, the die moves upward to its fill position and the upward-moving lower punch ejects the part. The core rod can be fixed or floating as described earlier.

## Withdrawal Tooling System

The withdrawal system uses the floating die principle. The main difference is that the punch forming the bottom level of the part is always stationary. The die and other lower tooling members, including auxiliary lower punches and core rods, move downward from the time pressing begins until ejection is complete. Figure 17-32 shows the sequence of events in a multimotion withdrawal tooling system. During compaction, all elements of the tooling system move downward, except the stationary punch. The die is floating, but is counterbalanced by pneumatic or hydraulic cylinders. The auxiliary punches are mounted on press members which are counterbalanced; in addition, these press members (usually called platens) have positive pressing stops. The positive stop controls the finished length of each of the levels within the compacted part. Before ejection, these stops are released or disengaged so that the lower platens can be moved further downward. During ejection, the upper punch moves upward away from the parts, while the lower punches move downward sequentially until all tool members are level with the top of the stationary punch. The compacted parts are fully supported by the tooling members during ejection. During ejection, the compacted part does not move.

The dieplate and lower coupier then move back into the filling position, and the cycle repeats. The movement of the upper punch and die are shown schematically in the cycle diagram illustrated in Fig. 17-33.[13] Two alternate motions of the die are shown to indicate that the die travel should be adjusted with reference to travel of the upper punch in order to control density distribution along the length of the part.

If the flange thickness does not exceed 20-25% of the total compact thickness, it is possible to compact a part by using only one bottom punch. Punches can be combined with the proper "step." This is accomplished by adding a shoulder in the die

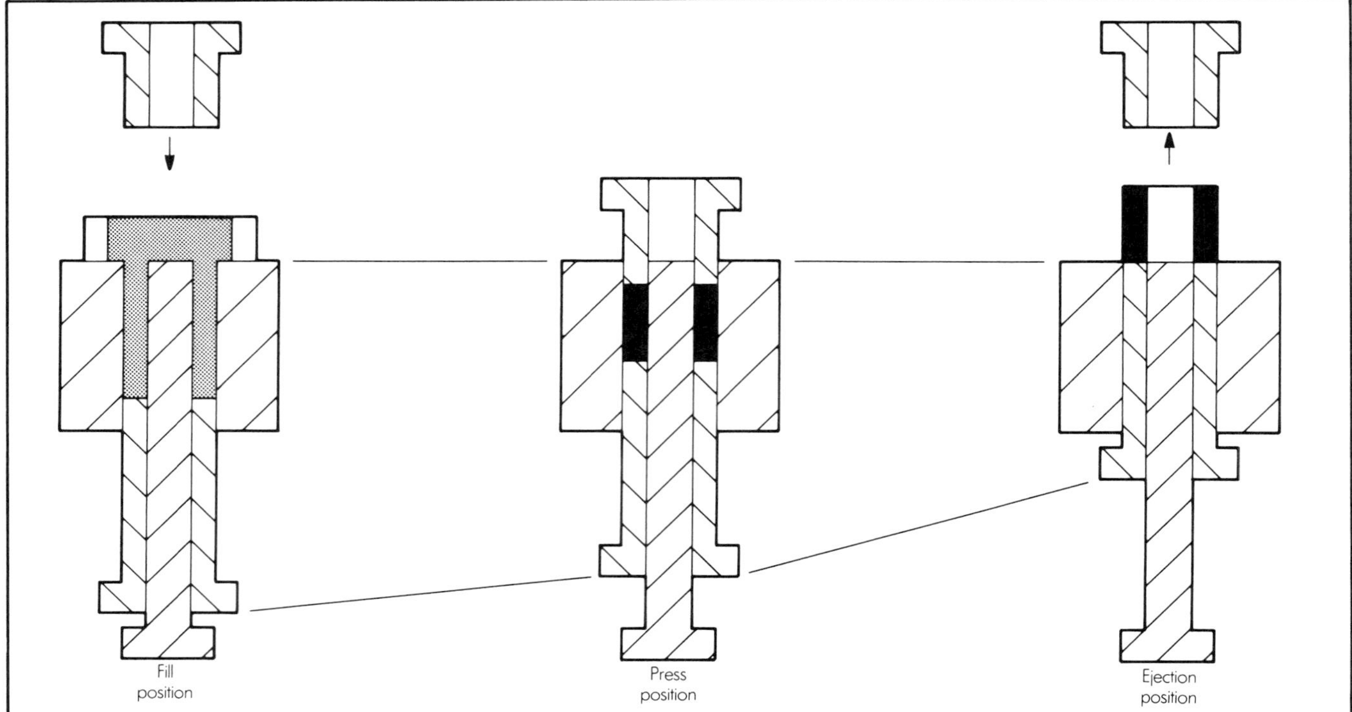


**Fig. 17-30 Double-action press system.**

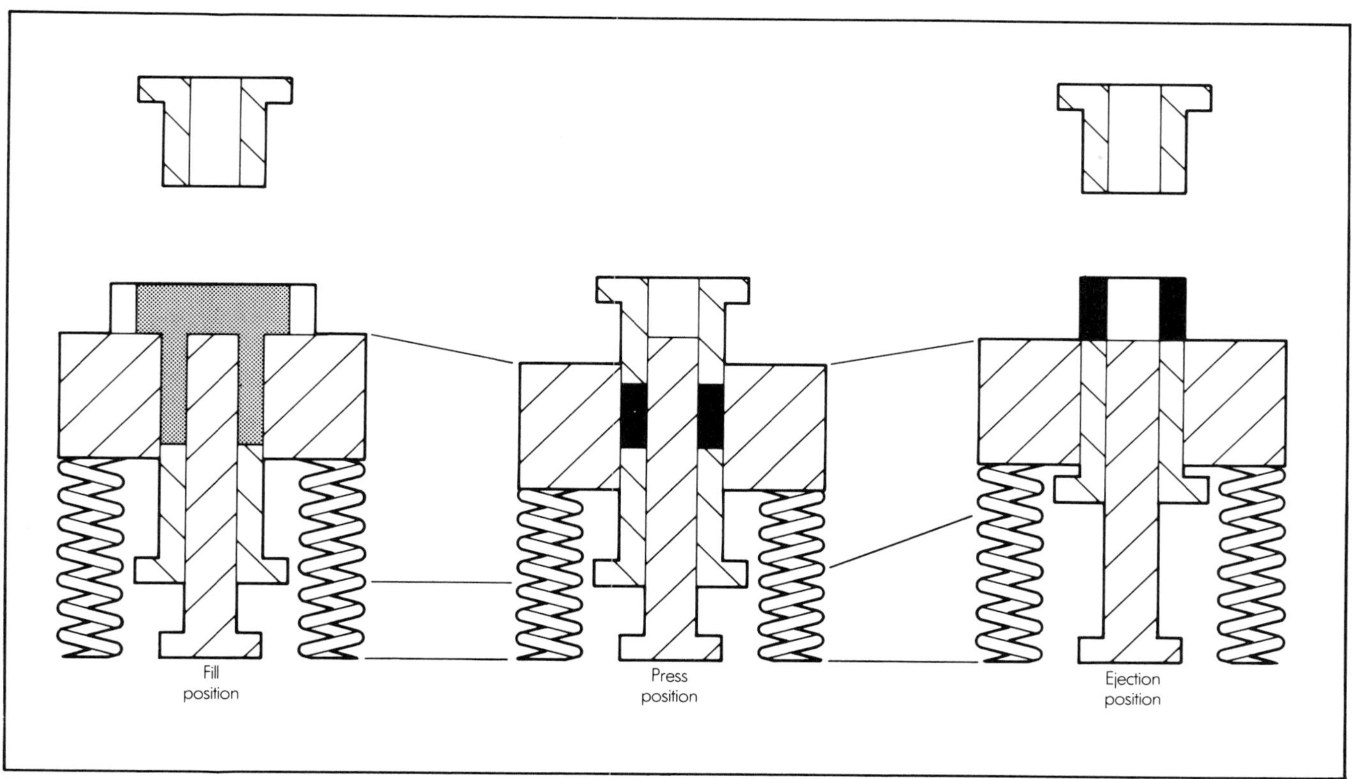


Fig. 17-31 Floating-die press tooling.

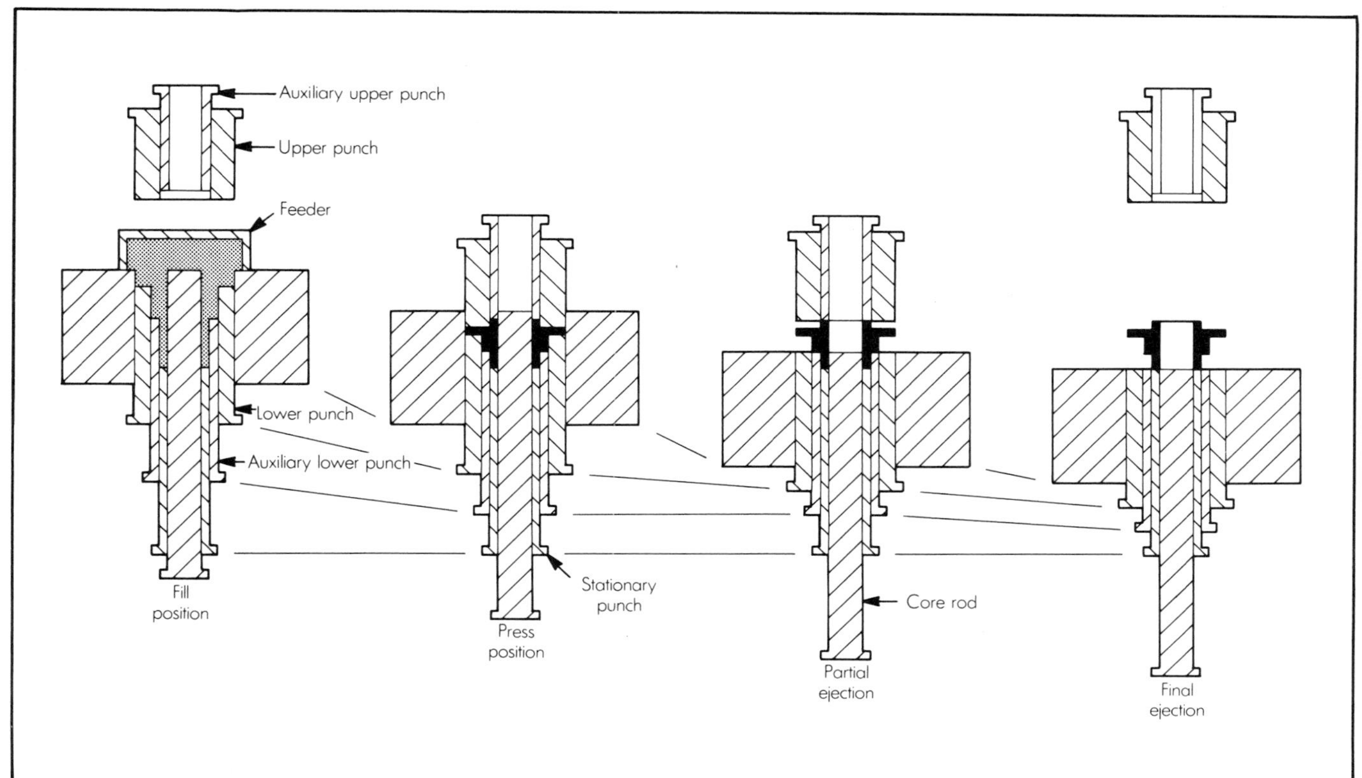


Fig. 17-32 Withdrawal floating-die multiple punches.

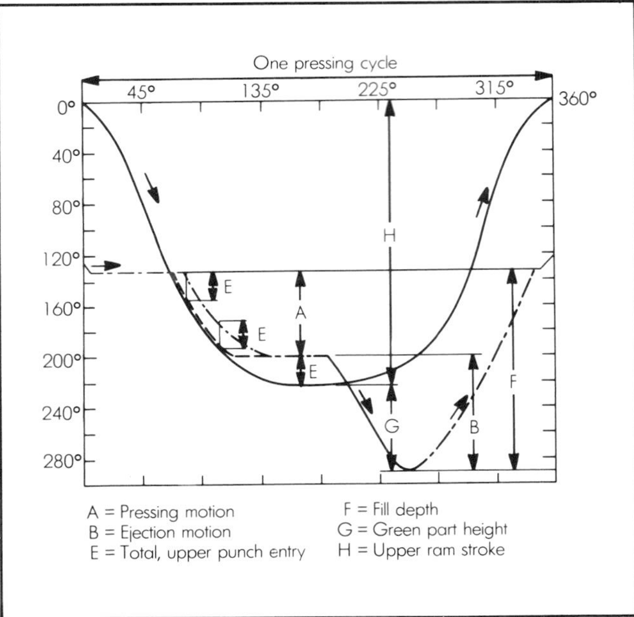


**Fig. 17-33 Cycle diagram shows movement of upper punch and die during compacting with withdrawal system.**

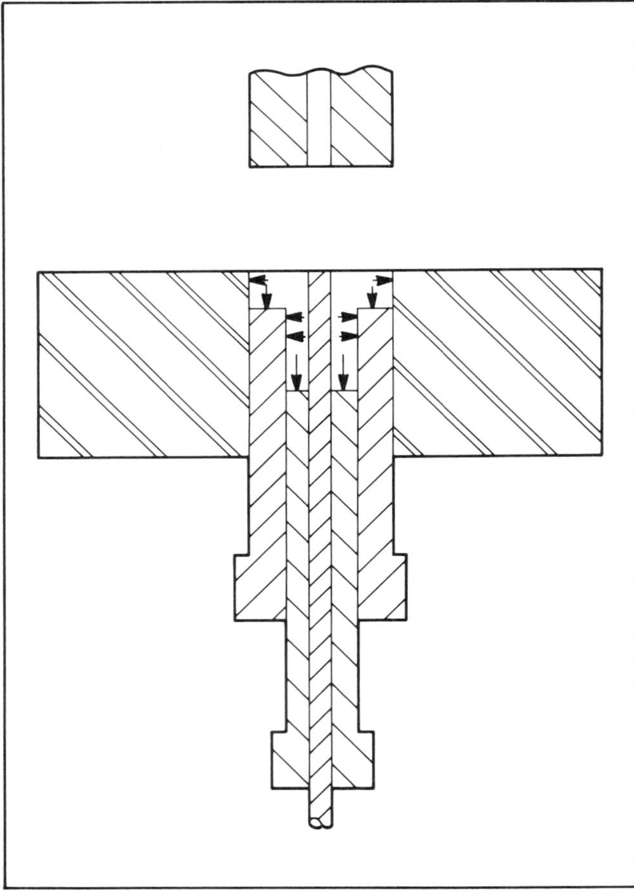

**Fig. 17-34 Multilevel part causes side forces on the punches.**

bore, as if the outer lower punch were locked in position. Some complex part designs require multiple upper, as well as multiple lower, punches. Core rods may be stationary, retractable, or floating (spring loaded). Split-segment dies are occasionally used, but are not suitable for high production rates.

## PRACTICAL OPERATING TIPS

Powder metallurgy compacting forces are high; 50 tons/in.$^2$ (690 MPa) is not uncommon for iron-based parts. Long, slender punches may be necessary in some designs; however, they should to be avoided if possible. If the punch walls are thinned to provide relief for powder escape, or for any other reason, column stresses can exceed workable limits. A punch with 1 in.$^2$ (645 mm$^2$) of effective area and anywhere from several inches to over a foot (75-300 mm) in length can be expected to repeatedly lift the equivalent of 50 small automobiles. It can be expected to do this hundreds of thousands of times, with the load cycling from full compression to rather high tensile stress if any binding or "hang-up" occurs on the fill stroke. A core rod of 1/8" (3 mm) diam making an iron part 2" (50 mm) long could be subjected to tensile stress close to its limit during either the compression or the ejection cycle.

### Punches

Poorly designed (or improperly operated) punches can be subjected to forces much higher than normal compacting pressures due to thinning of punch areas to provide relief, construction holes, sharp corners, and other stress raisers. Although punches or other tool members may tolerate these high stresses under static conditions, repeated cycling of the load would lead to premature fatigue failure. Any errors in press setup or operation that could cause an overdensity condition could shorten a tool's life expectancy or even destroy it quickly.

### Side Forces

Although design concern often focuses on the vertical forces on a punch, a punch used to make a multilevel part may be subjected to heavy side forces as well. For example, in Fig. 17-34 two lower punches are used to make a part that is a combination gear and pinion. The inner lower punch used to compact the pinion would experience only vertical forces; however, the outer lower punch would be subjected not only to vertical forces, but to radial "bursting" forces since it is also acting as the die for the pinion. This means that sufficient wall must be left between the root of the gear and the top of the pinion tooth because this wall, in fact, establishes the working thickness of the die wall for the pinion. If there is not enough wall thickness in relation to the size of the part and the tonnage to be used, the life of the punch is shortened. This type of stress must be taken into consideration whenever the part/tool design causes a punch to act as a die.

A part that uses two lower punches to put even a simple step in the parts causes side forces to act on the punch as shown in Fig. 17-34. In the example of the gear and pinion, these side forces are contained totally within the outer punch; however, in the case of the simple step, the side pressures are transmitted through the punch to the die wall. If these forces are high enough, they can cause galling between the punch and the die. This problem is magnified if the punch is shaped like a wedge where it meets the die. A problem like this can most easily be resolved by close cooperation between the part user and the PM designer.

### Pop Out

The expansion or "pop out" of the part as it leaves the die makes it essential that the top edge of the die wall be properly rounded or flared to allow the part to make a smooth transition during ejection. Breaking the top edge of the die with some kind of a shallow chamfer (as is frequently done, especially on gears and parts with sharp corners) may help, but will not do the job properly.

"Pop out" can also cause problems with parts of certain designs; for example, a plate with two hubs which would be formed by the lower punch could create problems during the ejection portion of the cycle. If the hubs were relatively small and far apart and the flange or plate were compacted to a high density, the hubs would tend to shear off as the flange cleared the die. This is illustrated in Fig. 17-35. As the flange tries to expand, the hubs, which are still held captive in the punch system, are not free to follow this expansion, and cracking can result. These problems can be minimized by making the hubs as heavy and short as possible, by decreasing the flange density, and by using one of the various methods of allowing the top punch to maintain some pressure on the part (top-punch hold down). Parts that would require a deep, thin-walled die may be difficult to produce, as the die may not fill with consistent uniformity—if it would fill at all. Also, deep, thin dies would require long delicate punches, which could cause problems. Parts that are very thin and flat could have difficulty in uniformly filling the die area, as well as difficulty in filling the die over the very thin sections. Designing in thin sections should be avoided, as the problems inherent in the use of thin sections may more than offset any gain in the material saved.

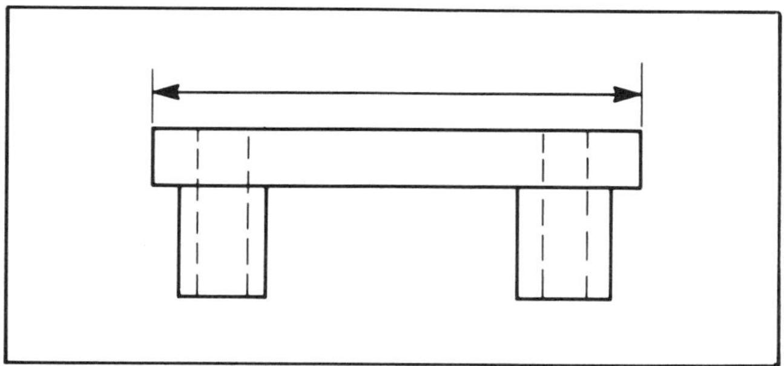

**Fig. 17-35 Hub design facilitates part molding and ejection.**

# COMPACTING PRESSES

Both mechanical and hydraulic power presses are used in PM compacting. Each drive has its advantages and limitations. Generally, presses of either type are available for producing a given PM part.

## MECHANICAL PRESSES

Mechanical presses most often use an arrangement of gears, a crankshaft, and a connecting rod to provide the necessary pressing and ejection motions and forces to compact and eject the part. This type of drive converts the rotary motion into a linear motion through an eccentric or crankshaft operating the machine slide by means of a connecting rod. Some mechanical presses are cam driven, but these types are generally limited to smaller capacity machines.

Mechanical presses are available in both top and bottom drive configuration. There is no distinct advantage of one over the other. However, maintenance and housekeeping require careful consideration whether a press is above floor level or installed in a pit, so accessibility should be considered.

Mechanical presses are available in a wide pressing tonnage range from 0.75-825 tons (6.7-7339 kN). Production rates range from 900 pieces per hour on the large machines to over 100,000 pieces per hour on the small presses. The depth of fill (depth of loose powder in the die) ranges from 0.040-7" (1.02-178 mm).

Advantages of mechanical presses include high production rates, low connected machine horsepower, and a wide range of pressing tonnages available.

## HYDRAULIC PRESSES

Hydraulic presses use one or more cylinders to provide the necessary motion and force to compact and eject the part. Standard hydraulic presses are available in capacities from 60-1250 tons (534-11 120 kN), although presses up to 3000 tons (26 668 kN) are being used in production of PM parts.

Production rates achievable with hydraulic presses are lower than rates for mechanical presses. Usually the hydraulic press has a maximum production of 600 pieces per hour. Greater depth of fill is available in hydraulic presses, with fill depths up to 15" (381 mm).

The advantages of hydraulic presses are overload protection, greater depth of fill available, versatility for complex parts, and lower initial capital investment.

## ANVIL PRESSES

Anvil-type single-action presses can compact powder parts that have at least one flat side, are very thin, have holes, and require a high degree of precision and uniformity. These parts can be Class I, II, or III, and can be compacted single or multiple cavity, single or multiple punch. As shown in Fig. 17-36, the tooling consists of a tool set that holds the lower punches, which are moved up and down by the press ram. There are no upper punches. Compacting rates are as high as 350 spm for tiny parts or 40-90 spm for larger parts. In conventional presses, parts are compacted between opposing upper and lower punches. In the anvil-type press, tooling usually is simpler; parts are compacted against an anvil by the upward action of a lower punch.

Anvil presses are available from 0.75-35 tons (6.7-311 kN) pressing capacity, with maximum depth of fill ranging from 0.040-3" (1.02-76 mm). Multiple-cavity pressing is commonly used in anvil presses with possible production rates of over 100,000 pieces per hour.

Some models of anvil presses are arranged to allow double direction pressing, using an upper punch entry system. This type of pressing can produce Class I, II, and III parts, and some Class IV parts. Typical parts that can be made with anvil or upper-punch types of presses are carbide and ceramic inserts with positive rake and chipbreaker, electronic substrates with depressions on both sides, and certain double-flanged parts.

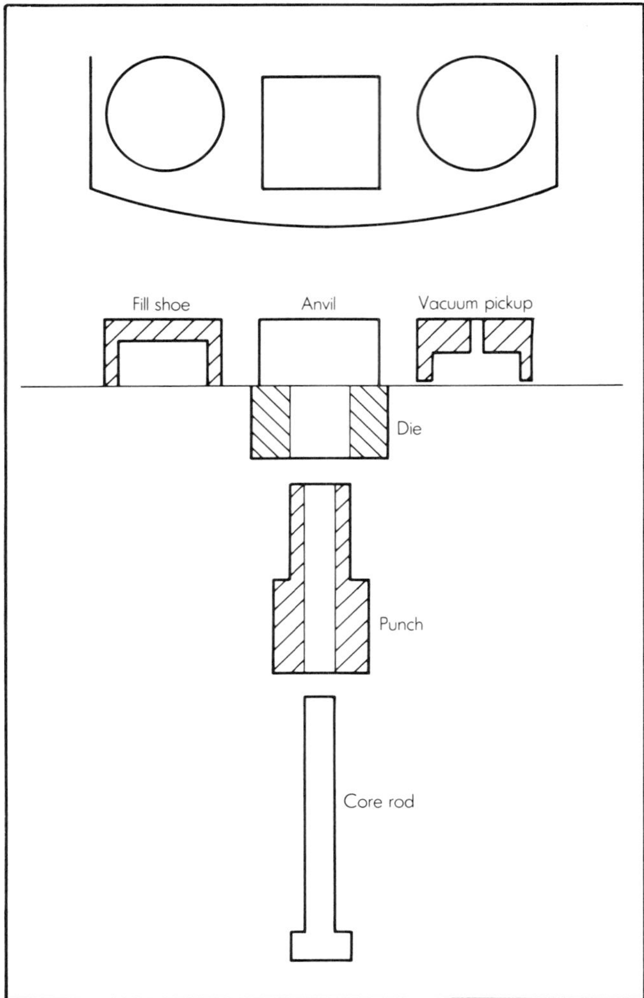


Fig. 17-36 Anvil type operation.

Anvil presses are usually mechanically driven. A schematic of the anvil press operation is shown in Fig. 17-37.

## ROTARY PRESSES

These machines generally are limited to single-level Class II types of parts, although some Class III parts such as flanged bushings are produced on rotary machines. Rotary presses are available in capacity ranges from 4-35 tons (36-311 kN) with depth of fill up to 3″ (76 mm). Production rates over 1000 pieces per minute are achievable depending on machine size and number of tooling stations. Rotary presses are mechanically driven.

## SINGLE LOWER PUNCH, OPPOSED-RAM PRESSES

Like rotary presses, these machines are limited to Class II and some Class III PM parts. These machines are available in both top-drive and bottom-drive models with capacities ranging from 4-110 tons (36-979 kN) with maximum depth of fill up to 4″ (102 mm). Production rates up to 50 ppm are possible with single cavity tooling, although production rates of 15-30 ppm are more common. Ejection of the part is by the lower punch moving upward. Both mechanical and hydraulic presses of this type are available.

## SINGLE LOWER PUNCH WITHDRAWAL PRESS

This machine has essentially the same part-making capabilities as described for the single-punch, opposed-ram press, in terms of pressing capacity, depth of fill, and production rate. The major difference is that the floating-die principle is used to achieve top and bottom pressing. The die is moved downward to effect ejection of the part.

## MULTIPLE MOTION DIE SET PRESSES

Presses of this type can be arranged to produce the most complex PM parts. Machines of this type all use the floating-die, withdrawal tooling concepts. Machines with both bottom drive and top drive are available. Pressing capacities range from 3-550 tons (27-5000 kN), with maximum depth of fill of 7″ (178 mm). Production rates vary from over 100 ppm on the smaller machines to 10 ppm on the 550 ton models. In addition to being able to produce complex parts, the removable die set (toolholder) minimizes press downtime needed to changeover from part to part. This is accomplished by having two or more die sets per press. One of the extra die sets is set up outside the press and is ready for installation into the machine. Pressing position for each level being produced by a separate tooling member is controlled by fixed-height tooling blocks (stop blocks), which are usually ground to the proper height to produce a given dimension on the part. A change in this dimension on the part requires the tooling block to be changed accordingly.

## MULTIPLE MOTION ADJUSTABLE STOP PRESSES

Presses of this type have the same part-making capability as die set presses and use the same tooling concepts. Presses available range from 110-825 tons (979-7339 kN), with a maximum depth of fill of 6″ (152 mm). The major difference between this type of press and the removable die set press is that the die set is not removable; however, the press stop positions are adjustable and a change of any dimension on the part in the direction of pressing is easily accomplished.

## PM PRESS CONTROLS AND GUARDING

Powder metallurgy presses and tooling, especially multimotion machines, are complex and capital intensive. As a result, the machine must have controls and electrical interlocks that monitor the functions of the machine and tooling as a manufacturing system. Machines of the latest technology are controlled by microprocessors. The microprocessor system has the capability, speed, and reliability to monitor the many machine functions that occur during each cycle of the press, stopping the machine if any malfunction occurs. The microprocessor system can also provide diagnostic information when a malfunction occurs. This facilitates repair of the malfunction and keeps machine downtime to a minimum.

The press guarding must meet all federal, state, and local regulations regarding mechanical and hydraulic-power PM compacting presses. The guarding used to enclose the point of operation should be made of clear, shock-resistant material such as acrylic plastic, rather than expanded metal. The clear

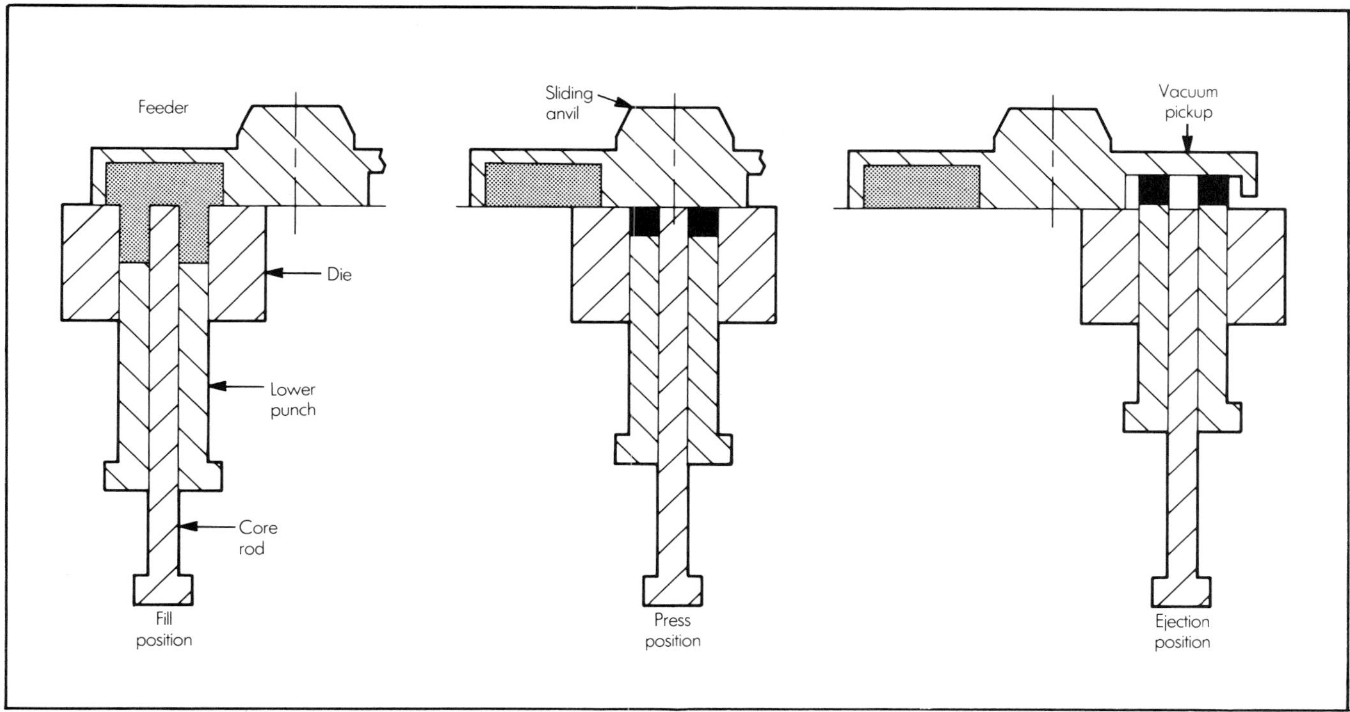


**Fig. 17-37 Sliding anvil press tooling system.**

plastic materials offer improved visibility and reduce the breathable airborne powder at the operator station.

## POWDER FEEDING SYSTEM

Powder metallurgy presses are provided with an automatic powder feeding system. Another function in addition to feeding the powder to the tooling is that the feeder also provides an automatic part removal system. As the feeder or feed shoe approaches the die, the part that has just been compacted and ejected from the tooling is pushed away from the tooling or the point of operation by the feed shoe.

The most common type of feeder has an in-line reciprocating motion. The feed shoe rides on the die table and is spring loaded to provide a clean wiping action. It is connected directly to a press-mounted hopper by means of a flexible hose, and powder is fed to it by gravity. The press-mounted hopper should have a powder level control to maintain a constant head of powder to assure uniform die filling. The feed shoe moves over the die cavity when the tooling is flush and in the ejection mode. The press then moves to its fill position, filling the die cavity volumetrically. With a properly designed powder feeding system, part weight control of +0.75% is easily achievable in a production environment.

On hydraulic presses, the feed shoe is actuated by a hydraulic cylinder that is timed sequentially with the press stroke.

On mechanical presses, the feeder has traditionally been cam driven and timed mechanically with the press stroke. The latest technology in feeder drives is the use of a d-c servomotor driving a ballscrew to actuate the feed shoe. When used in conjunction with a microprocessor, the feeder stroke can be optimized to provide maximum time over the die cavity. The feeder stroke can be varied when using the d-c drive, while a cam-driven feeder has a fixed stroke.

## PRESS MAINTENANCE

The most important rule in PM press maintenance is to keep the press clean. Powder particles can be extremely small, as small as 5 microns; and if allowed to accumulate, they will work into critical bearing and guiding surfaces, even though the bearings are protected with wiper, seals or boots. Loose powder on and around the press can be caused by any of the following:

1. Poor bulk powder handling—spillage while loading the press hopper. Automatic bulk loading systems are available and are considered a sound investment. They reduce spillage and improve loading efficiency.
2. Poorly maintained press feed shoes. Feed shoes normally have a replaceable wiper. If they are not properly maintained, a small amount of powder will be lost with each stroke of the press. This can amount to a considerable amount of expensive powder loss during a single shift of operation.
3. Powder loss through tooling clearances. The running clearance in PM tooling is small, generally 0.001 in./in. (0.025 mm/mm) diam. Small amounts of powder sift through this clearance and accumulate. Little can be done to prevent this loss. This is an area that requires frequent cleaning.

A modern PM press should be equipped with an automatic lubrication system with fault monitors. The press manufacturer should include in the operator and maintenance manual a routine maintenance checklist that specifically identifies areas and frequency of critical maintenance items. Some press builders offer, through their service department, a preventative maintenance program in which a service representative visits the customer's plant at intervals to maintain the equipment.

# SECONDARY OPERATIONS

Powder metallurgy parts processing and fabrication can be divided into two major categories: primary and secondary. Primary operations, which are covered earlier in this chapter, include powder mixing, compacting, and sintering. Secondary operations, which, if required, are applied selectively to PM structural parts after sintering, include sizing, coining, and repressing (sometimes followed by sintering or annealing); forging; impregnation; infiltration; heat treatment and steam treatment; machining; joining; and plating and other surface finishing.

## REPRESSING

Repressing, sometimes called coining or sizing, is used to increase density, provide greater dimensional accuracy, and improve surface smoothness and hardness. In these operations, the sintered structural part is inserted in a confined die and struck by a punch. A principal purpose of "sizing" is to correct distortions that occur during sintering. This operation sometimes is called "coining," although coining actually describes an operation that gives a profile to the part, as in coining a blank to produce a coin. Repressing can be used to produce complex shapes that are not attainable from a single-press operation, or to reshape or emboss a surface. Repressing may be followed by resintering—a second sintering operation to improve mechanical properties and relieve the cold work introduced during repressing.

## FORGING

To obtain the same properties in PM parts as in wrought materials, the porosity must be eliminated. This may be done by producing preforms from metal powders and hot forging the preforms to obtain parts of closely controlled dimensions and complete or near complete density. (A general discussion of forging is presented in "Hot Forging," Chapter 15 of this volume.)

### General Description

The forging of PM preforms permits the production of accurate and complex-shaped parts requiring little or no machining and having properties equal to or exceeding those made from comparable wrought materials. Lower cost compared to the cost of conventional forging, coupled with higher strength compared to the strength of conventional powder metallurgy, are the basic advantages of this technique. Material utilization is often close to 100%. Since the forging is done in a closed die, precisely the proper amount of metal is used; no flash is generated. The powders used are generally more costly than comparable wrought materials. Purity is critical. Powder metallurgy forged parts often cost slightly more than unmachined forgings, but the savings in machining often offset this differential.

Unlike conventional PM which is normally limited to axial deformation, PM forging can create lateral flow to produce shapes not possible with conventional compacting. Surface finish is also better than that possible with conventional forging or casting. The parts are formed accurately in a single blow. This minimizes subsequent machining or the need for multiple dies, as are needed in the case of step forging. The fine grain and homogenous structure produced provide uniform strength in all directions. Intermediate forging steps also are eliminated. These include shearing or cutting the billets, multihit forming (requiring several dies), and the trimming of flash. Other advantages include precise repeatibility and minimal labor requirements when the process is automated. Also, alloys or composite materials can be created by combining immiscible metals, since no melting takes place.

### Powder Forging Process

As illustrated schematically in Fig. 17-38, the production of a PM forging consists essentially of making a preform; heating it, usually by induction; placing the preform in a heated die; and forming (forging) it to final shape in a single blow. The die design for hot compaction is such that the flash is eliminated. The design of the preform and the temperature and pressure of the final forging stage ensure complete densification throughout the part. The metal can flow in all directions, thus differentiating it from conventional hot restriking, coining, or densifying, in which the part is already close to final shape and metal flow is primarily in the direction of pressing. The process differs from conventional forging in that lower temperatures are used, only a single hit is required, there is no scaling or flash, close tolerances are maintained, and a longer die life is obtained. Before a preform is forged it must be heated to the forging temperature. For preforms of low alloy steel composition, the forging temperature is in the same range as for conventional forgings, i.e., from 1470-2200° F (800-1200° C).

In conventional forging (see Chapter 15) a fully dense blank is forged. The type of conventional forging closest to powder forging is precision forging in which the blank is forged in a closed die. The weight and geometry of the forging blank as well as the preheating and forging cycle are closely controlled. Nevertheless, even in precision forging, a flash is formed which must be trimmed and the forging must generally be machined. In powder forging, the blank is a more precise preform produced from metal powders by compacting and sintering. As diagrammed in Fig. 17-39, three different approaches are used in forging the preforms.

**Hot repressing**. The first of these approaches is hot repressing, sometimes called hot densification, in which the shape of the preform is close to that of the final piece except for its length in the forging direction. In this process, the friction

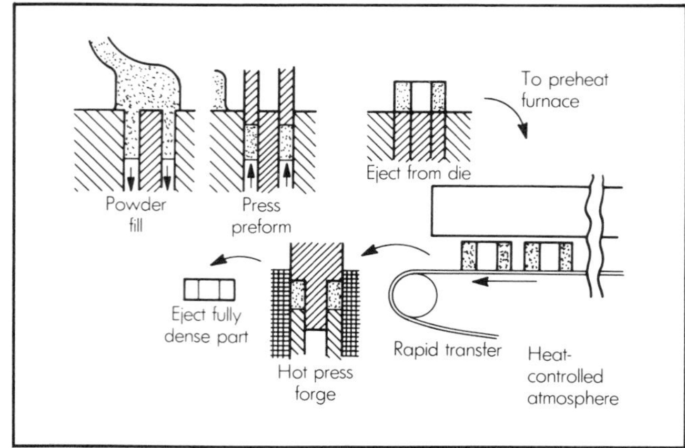


**Fig. 17-38 Schematic diagram of powder forging process.**

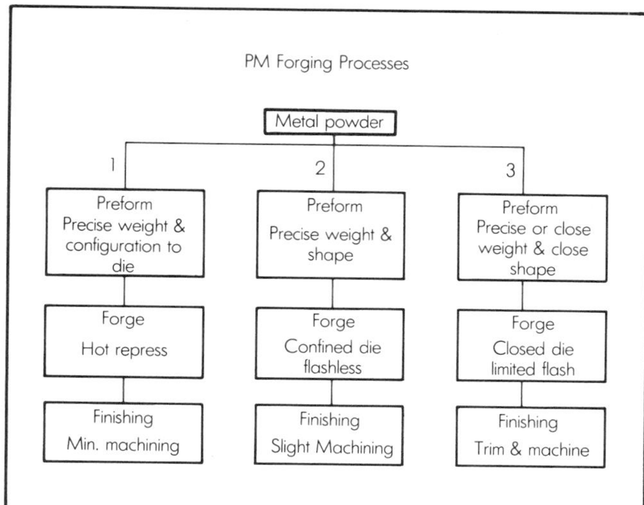


**Fig. 17-39 Processes used for PM forging.**

between die and preform during hot forging is high and, therefore, the pressure necessary for complete densification also is high. This causes rapid wear of the forging tools. Hot repressing is generally used in applications in which densities on the order of 98% of theoretical are satisfactory.

**Flashless.** The second approach is the one most widely used industrially. It is a precision forging process without flash. The shape of the preform is simpler than that of the final part, so the desired final shape is produced to closely controlled dimensions in the hot forging step. This is not a hot repressing operation; the preform is upset (and extruded) in hot forging. The advantages of hot forging by upsetting (and extrusion) over hot forging by repressing are attributed to much more lateral flow, especially in the beginning of deformation. This leads to more rapid initial densification and also involves more shear stress at pore surfaces, producing relative motion between opposite sides of the collapsed pore. Mechanical rupturing of any oxide film present at the pore surface exposes the metal and ensures a sound metallurgical bond across collapsed pore surfaces. Upset forging also produces fibering of inclusions in the lateral direction. Toward the end of the forging stroke, by upsetting when the preform has reached the die wall, the mode of deformation becomes the same as in repressing.

**Limited flash.** A third approach to hot forging of PM preforms involves the process as it pertains to the conventional forge shop. In this situation, the results of the forging step must not necessarily be a product with dimensions as closely or nearly as closely controlled as those of conventional PM structural parts. The forging may even have a flash which must be trimmed after forging.

## Materials

Carbon and low alloy steel powders are widely used and some aluminum powders are formed in this way. Oxidation and decarburization can be critical. Nickel and molybdenum are common additions; and copper, cobalt, manganese and chromium are also used. The dies are generally maintained at a temperature between 500-600° F (260-316° C). Forging pressure is normally between 40-75 tons/in.$^2$ (552-1034 MPa). Graphite is sprayed on the components as a lubricant prior to forging. Some producers can hold 0.001″ (0.03 mm) on outside diameters and lateral dimensions; however, the parts are costly, because of short die life and close control requirements. A tolerance of ±0.003 or ±0.004″ (±0.08 or ±0.10 mm) is realistic and economical for these dimensions. Dimensions in the direction of pressing are more difficult to hold to close tolerance. While ±0.005″ can be maintained in some cases, as much as ±0.015″ (±0.38 mm) may be necessary, depending on part size, configuration, and density required, as well as the press and tooling used.

## PM Forging Machines

Forging machines for powder forging must meet certain requirements:

- The force-displacement characteristics must match deformation characteristics of the preforms.
- Workpiece-tool contact times should be as short as possible.
- The machines should be stiff, and the ram should have effective guidance to obtain desired tolerances in the powder forgings.
- Mechanisms for ejection of the parts are necessary.

Because of these requirements, forging hammers that do not have sufficiently accurate guidance and hydraulic presses that are too slow are inappropriate for powder forging. Mechanical presses, in particular crank presses with short, fast strokes and short contact times, are used. This applies mainly to precision hot forging by upsetting to closely controlled dimensions without a flash.

When the conventional forging approach is applied in forging PM preforms, the same equipment as in conventional forging may be used. Flow stress and the force for forging preforms are initially lower than for conventional forging, but they rise toward the end of the forging stroke as density increases. Tooling for powder forging is quite different from that for conventional forging and closely resembles tooling for powder compacting. On the other hand, the provisions necessary in tooling for powder compacting to obtain uniform density in multilevel parts are not required. An example of a relatively simple tool design for powder forging is shown in Fig. 17-40. The powder preform is upset during forging and ejected after forging.

Only limited data is available on tool life of forging tools for preform forgings. Since the preforms are heated in a protective atmosphere, tool wear due to scale formation is less of a problem than in conventional forging. Also, the flow stress in preform forging is lower and no flash need be formed, which adds to tool life. On the other hand, the dimensional tolerances in preform forging are closer than in conventional forging, which means that tools, or at least those parts of the tooling subjected to wear, must be replaced more often. A tool life of 5000-10,000 forgings for readily replaceable high-wear components of the tooling and of 10,000-20,000 forgings for other components has been attained.

# HEAT TREATMENT AND STEAM TREATMENT

Powder metallurgy structural parts can be heat treated by conventional methods that are used for wrought or cast parts. Best results are obtained with dense PM structures. Porosity influences the rate of heat flow through the part, and internal contamination occurs if salt-bath heat-treating chambers are used in the process. For this reason, in heat-treating PM steel

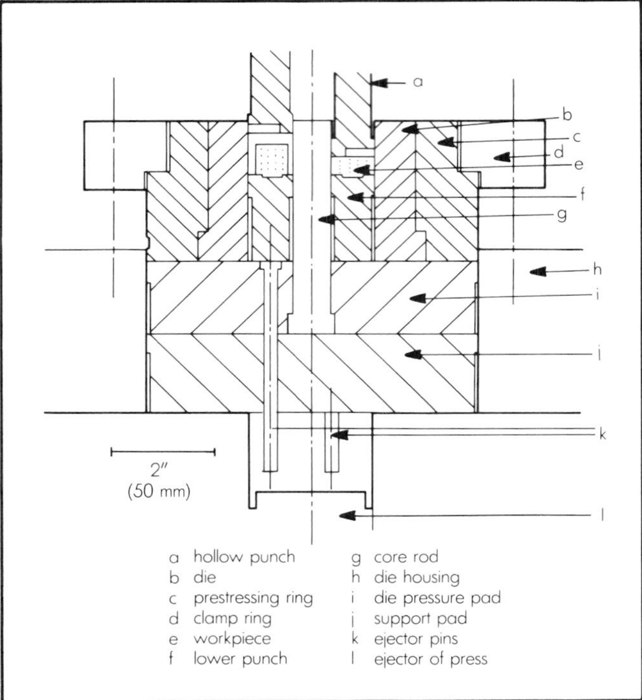


**Fig. 17-40 Powder forging tooling construction.**

parts, austenitizing in salt baths and particularly in cyanide baths is avoided.

## Heat Treatment

The surface hardness of PM steel parts may be increased by carburizing and carbonitriding. Ferrous PM parts, containing 0.3% or higher combined carbon, can be quench-hardened for increased strength and wear resistance. The percentages of carbon and other alloying elements combined in the material and density of the part determine the degree of hardening for any given quench condition. Surface hardness of 500-600 Knoop (file hard) is possible with quench hardening.

Ferrous parts without carbon can be carburized by standard methods. Low-density parts carburize throughout, while high-density parts develop a distinct carburized case. Case depth is a function of the part density. Very-high-density parts respond well to fused salt carbonitriding, but density must be high enough to prevent absorption of salt into the pores. Low and medium-density parts absorb brines and salts during salt-bath carbonitriding which can lead to subsequent corrosion. Thus, oil quench hardening is recommended for low and medium-density parts.

The properties of as-sintered aluminum PM parts are improved by a series of thermal treatments. Aluminum PM parts achieve higher strength by solution and precipitation of soluble alloying elements. As-sintered strength is affected by the rate of cooling from sintering temperature. Parts cooled very slowly, about 50° F (10° C) per hr develop the lower strengths of annealed tempers.

## Steam Treatment

Steam treating is widely used for PM structural parts. In steam treating, the porosity of PM structural parts is directly used. The parts are treated in dry steam at approximately 1020° F (550° C). The steam reacts with the surfaces of the part, not only the outer surface, but also the inner surface along the pores connected to the outside. A layer of magnetic black oxide forms on the outside surface, and a skeleton of magnetic black oxide forms throughout the part's interior. This not only provides some corrosion resistance, but also improves mechanical properties, since it increases the density, hardness, wear resistance, and compressive strength of the part.

# IMPREGNATION AND INFILTRATION

The controlled porosity of PM parts makes it possible to infiltrate them with another metal or impregnate them with oil or a resin, either to improve mechanical properties or to provide other performance characteristics.

## Impregnation

When structural PM parts serve as bearings, they may be impregnated with a lubricant, as is done with self-lubricating bearings. Such bearings are among the most widely used products of powder metallurgy. Porosities ranging from 25-35% generally are used, since higher values result in lower bearing strength. Oil-impregnated bearings hold from 10-30% oil by volume. Impregnation is accomplished either by immersing sintered bearings in heated oil or by means of a vacuum treatment. Most self-lubricating bearings are of porous bronze or iron composition.

When a porous part is to be made impervious to liquids or gases, it is impregnated with a viscous liquid thermosetting polymer or anaerobic resin. The polymer or other impregnating resin is changed to a solid by low temperature or vacuum processes. This treatment is used on PM parts which must be made pressure tight and on parts to which a surface finishing operation, such as plating, is to be applied. During plating operations, the impregnation treatment prevents absorption or entrapment of the plating solution in the pores of the part.

The following are general guidelines for impregnating PM parts:

1. A density range should be planned that is between 80-90% theoretical, or 6.2-7.1 g/cc for iron parts. This is the best range for maximum penetration without bleeding.
2. Parts should be heat treated prior to vacuum sealing. Anaerobic sealants are limited to upper temperatures of 400° F (204.4° C). Also, quenching oils should be removed prior to impregnation by baking, annealing or vapor degreasing.
3. The optimum time for sealing is immediately after sintering. Clean, open pores aid penetration. Tumbling, burnishing, and machining tend to smear surfaces and block the sealant entry. Also, fluids used in these operations can penetrate the pores and inhibit impregnation.
4. PM parts can be coined, sized, and repressed after vacuum sealing. Volume changes of up to 2% can be tolerated without difficulty.
5. Impregnation improves machinability and tool life. Machinability is increased by eliminating the chattering that develops as the tool jumps across pore openings. Although the impregnating resin does not replace machining oil, it does help to lubricate the machining process (see *Machining,* Volume I of this Handbook series).

# SECONDARY OPERATIONS

## Infiltration

Infiltration is the process of filling the pores of a sintered solid with molten metal or alloy. In this operation, the melting point of the liquid metal must be considerably lower than that of the solid metal. The purpose of infiltration is to obtain a relatively pore-free structure. Liquid metal is infiltrated into the PM part either by allowing it to enter from above or by absorbing it from below. For example, copper placed upon a piece of presintered iron and heated to 2100° F (1150° C) is drawn into the iron by capillarity.

Properties resulting from infiltration with another metal depend upon the metals that constitute the structure of the infiltrated part, together with the manner and the proportions in which they are combined. Infiltration is used to improve mechanical properties, seal pores prior to electroplating, improve machinability, and make parts gas or liquid tight. Advantages of infiltration include:

1. Increased mechanical properties. Higher tensile strength and hardness, greater impact energy and fatigue strength, and other improvements.
2. Uniform density. Parts that contain nonuniform and/or heavy sections can be infiltrated to even out density variations.
3. Higher density. Infiltration increases sintered part weight without changing the size.
4. Removal of porosity for secondary operations. Infiltration may be used in place of impregnation as a method to seal surface porosity. This enables such operations as pickling and plating to be performed without damaging the interior of the part. Infiltration is also a method of sealing a part used for application in which no porosity is desired.
5. Selective property variation. By infiltrating only selected areas of a part, it is possible to obtain a controlled variation of properties such as density, strength, and hardness. This is known as localized infiltration.
6. Assembly of multiple parts. Different sections of the final part, pressed separately, can be assembled by sintering the individual pieces together and bonding them into one part through common infiltration.

## MACHINING

Whenever possible, PM structural parts are compacted and sintered to final dimensions, thereby eliminating the need for subsequent machining needed. However, products requiring such features as threads, grooves, undercuts, or side holes cannot be produced directly by powder metallurgy methods and must be finish-machined. Tungsten carbide tools are recommended, although high-speed-steel tools may be used in some low-volume applications (see *Machining,* Volume I of this Handbook series).

Machining characteristics of PM parts are similar to those of cast materials. Small amounts of lead, sulfur, copper, or graphite are common additives that improve the machinability of ferrous PM parts. Lead is also used to increase machinability of nonferrous parts. Machining speeds and feeds for high-density parts (above 92% of theoretical density) are similar to those for wrought metals. Lower density parts require adjustment of feed and speed to obtain optimum results. In general, high speeds, light feeds, and very sharp carbide tools are recommended. Lubricants and coolants should be used with caution, especially when porous parts are machined, to avoid entrapping solutions that could cause corrosion. Grinding of PM parts is similar to grinding of wrought materials; however, when surface porosity is required, it should be remembered that grinding tends to reduce porosity (see Chapter 11 "Grinding," in *Machining,* Volume I of this Handbook series).

## FINISHING

Virtually all of the commonly used finishing methods are applicable to PM parts. Some of the more frequently used methods include plating, coating, tumbling, burnishing, and coloring. (For additional information on finishing, see *Materials and Finishing,* Volume III of this Handbook series.)

### Plating

Powder metallurgy parts may be plated by electroplating or other plating processes. To avoid penetration and entrapment of plating solutions in the pores of the part, an impregnation or infiltration treatment is usually applied before plating.

Copper, nickel, chromium, cadmium, and zinc plating may be applied. High-density (7 g/cc) and infiltrated parts can be plated by using methods similar to those used for wrought parts. Lower density parts should be sealed, as noted earlier. Electroless nickel plating can be used as well as electroplating, which is applicable to nonimpregnated ferrous parts in the 6.6-7.2 g/cc density range.

### Coating

Parts manufactured by pressing and sintering metal powders are more susceptible to environmental degradation than cast and machined parts. Powder metallurgy parts have interconnected porosity. Internal as well as external surfaces are exposed to the atmosphere. Conventional coatings cannot effectively seal all of the reactive surface. Special protective coatings have been developed for PM parts.

In one coating system an aluminum/ceramic material is used for PM part corrosion protection. The coating eliminates the need for impregnation or plating. The process provides a passivated aluminum coating that serves as a base for application of topcoats that seal the coating and the PM part surface from the atmosphere. Coatings of this type are available as either sacrificial or protective (barrier) coatings.

### Tumbling

During tumbling, rust inhibitors should be added to the water. After tumbling, parts should be spun dry and heated to evaporate water from the pores. Tumbling is done after machining to avoid abrasive pickup in the pores, which can cause rapid tool wear.

### Burnishing

Burnishing can be used to improve part finish and dimensional accuracy or to work-harden the surfaces. Closer tolerances can be held on PM parts than on wrought parts, because the surface porosity allows metal to be displaced more easily.

### Coloring

Ferrous PM parts can be colored by several methods. For indoor corrosion resistance, parts are blackened by heating to the blueing temperature and then cooled. Oil dipping gives a deeper color and slightly more corrosion resistance. Ferrous PM parts also can be blackened chemically, using a salt bath. On parts with density below 7.3 g/cc, care must be taken to avoid entrapment of salt. Nickel and copper-bearing parts are adversely affected by blackening baths.

## JOINING

Many of the conventional joining operations for wrought materials can be performed on PM structural parts. Of the various welding techniques, electrical resistance welding is better suited than oxyacetylene welding and arc welding, in which oxidation of the interior porous material is possible. However, argon arc welding is used for stainless steel parts. Copper brazing is applicable to copper infiltrated parts, and in some instances, copper infiltration and copper brazing may be combined into one operation. Powder metallurgy parts also may be joined by using somewhat different compositions for the components—one that expands slightly during sintering and another that shrinks slightly. The composition that grows is used for the inner portion of the assembly, and the one that shrinks is used for the outer portion. The parts are assembled as compacted; an excellent joint forms during sintering. (A general coverage of welding processes is presented in *Assembly, Testing, and Quality Control,* Volume IV of this Handbook series.)

# SPECIAL PM PROCESSES

In the field of powder metallurgy, die compaction is the most widely used method and is considered the "conventional" technique. It is discontinuous; employs either low pressures (under 10 tons/in.$^2$ or 138 MPa) or high pressures (40 tons/in.$^2$ or 550 MPa). It applies force only in the axial (vertical) direction to one or both ends of the powder mass, and involves relatively little time (about 1-2 seconds) and a punch movement of about 20 fps (6 m/s). No liquid is used to suspend the powder. The die is a rigid, solid mass with a relatively long lifetime. Both low-density and high-density structural parts with a very broad range of complexities and sizes are made by the conventional die pressing PM techniques. These conventional methods as well as the equipment used in them are covered earlier in this chapter, in the section on "Compacting."

This section presents information on various special PM pressure and pressureless compacting methods. Also included is information on the wrought processes for hot consolidation of metal powders to fully dense compacts, an operation that combines sintering with the application of pressure to the powder at elevated temperature.

## PRESSURE COMPACTION METHODS

One of the more frequently used pressure compacting methods is isostatic compaction, either cold or hot; other PM pressure methods include hot pressing, spark sintering, high energy forming, extruding, injection molding, and isothermal PM forging.

## ISOSTATIC COMPACTION

In isostatic compaction, pressure is applied simultaneously from all directions on a metal powder compact. Powder is placed in a flexible mold or container that is immersed in a fluid bath within a pressure vessel. The fluid is put under high pressure and exerts hydrostatic pressure on the powder. Isostatically compacted products are characterized by their uniform, high density. With selection of the correct encapsulation technique and knowledge of the influence of the pressure, powder products can be pressed close to their final shape and dimension.

Pressing is done at room temperature in the cold isostatic process. Hot isostatic pressing, on the other hand, involves pressing compacts under high temperature conditions. Powder is contained in a metal or glass mold or can and is placed in an autoclave.

**Cold isostatic compacting.** Cold isostatic compacting is a "room temperature" process by which pressure is applied uniformly to a deformable container holding the metal powder to be compacted. This technique is especially useful in the manufacturing of parts having a large length-to-diameter ratio.

The system generally includes a pressure vessel designed to contain a fluid under high pressure, a deformable container, and arbors (or cores) if tubes or special shapes are being made. A representative schematic drawing is shown in Fig. 17-41.

*Advantages.* Variations exist in cold isostatic pressing, and the pressure may not always be completely uniform; however, the friction between powder and die, which is a characteristic of other methods of PM pressing, is absent in cold isostatic pressing. The commercial advantages of cold isostatic over other methods of pressing are:

1. Greater uniformity in density is achieved.
2. Shapes with high ratios of length to diameter which cannot be readily pressed in rigid dies can be cold isostatically pressed.
3. Parts with reentrant angles and undercuts can be pressed.
4. Parts with thinner wall sections can be pressed.
5. The equipment for cold isostatic pressing, dies in particular, is less costly than that for rigid die pressing.
6. Lubricants do not have to be mixed with metal powders.

*Disadvantages.* On the other hand, cold isostatic pressing has certain disadvantages, including the following:

1. Dimensional control of the green compacts is less precise than in rigid die pressing.
2. The surfaces of cold isostatically pressed compacts are less smooth.
3. The production rate in cold isostatic pressing is considerably lower.
4. The flexible molds used in cold isostatic pressing have shorter lives than rigid steel or carbide dies.

*Applications.* Cold isostatic pressing is less widely used for metal than for ceramic powders, for which the automatic fabrication of such components as spark plugs is highly mechanized. However, the production of isostatically pressed metal compacts has grown rapidly. Applications include:

- Complex shapes that cannot be pressed in rigid dies. Such shapes are found in powder metallurgy products made from relatively expensive metals such as titanium, for which material savings are important. Examples include an aircraft hydraulic fitting made from a mixture of titanium powder and an aluminum-vanadium alloy,

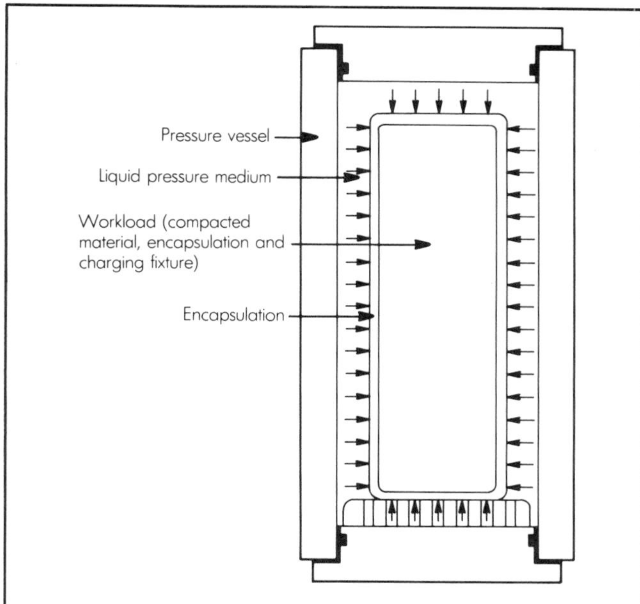


**Fig. 17-41 Cold isostatic pressing is performed at room temperature with liquid as the pressure medium.** (*ASEA*)

which is isostatically pressed before being sintered and hot forged; and isostatically pressed titanium ball valves for controlling flow of sea water.

- Shapes such as long, slender, hollow cylinders, which are often used for porous filters because of their large ratio of surface area to volume. Such cylinders generally are isostatically pressed from powder. Stainless steel and titanium powders are commonly used.
- Large shapes, such as rocket nozzles, made from tungsten powder, which are isostatically pressed because production quantities do not justify the cost of building rigid dies. The nozzle shape also is readily producible by the isostatic process.
- The shapes of compacts that are to be fabricated by hot consolidation which are often well suited to cold isostatic pressing as a first step. Examples are compacts from tungsten and molybdenum and their alloys which are to be hot rolled into sheet or hot forged into the shape of dies.

**Hot isostatic compacting**. Hot isostatic pressing (HIP) is a manufacturing process in which PM parts are compressed by gas at high temperatures and pressure. Commercial HIP systems are typically capable of temperatures to 3632° F (2000° C ) and pressure to 30,000 psi (207 MPa).

In forming a part from powder, the powder is placed in a flexible, gas-tight capsule having the shape of the finished part. The capsule is placed in a pressure vessel in which it is heated and subjected to isostatic pressure applied by high-purity argon or helium gas. The part is compressed equally on all sides by the application of heat and pressure. The principle of hot isostatic pressing is illustrated in Fig. 17-42.

*Advantages.* Hot isostatic pressing provides some important commercial advantages:

- Unique microstructures which substantially improve performance and reliability.

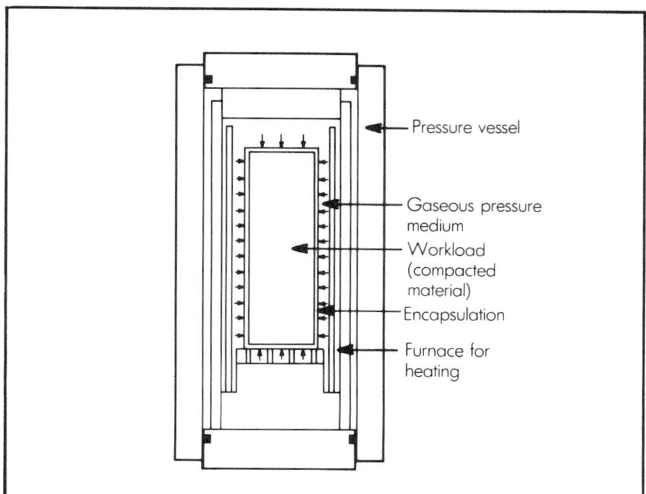


**Fig. 17-42 Hot isostatic pressing is performed at elevated temperature with gas as the pressure medium.** (*ASEA*)

- Alloys and shapes which are impossible to achieve by other means.
- Complex "near net" shapes which require little or no machining.
- Reduced consumption of energy and scarce or expensive materials.
- Reduced overall production costs.

*Disadvantages.* A significant limitation of HIP processing, even without the mold, is the lengthy cycle time to load, heat, pressurize, hold, cool, and unload. Until recently, cycle times of 12-24 hours were not uncommon. New systems, which incorporate furnaces with forced convection heating and cooling, reduce cycle time to 8 hours or less. The time improvements are at both ends (heating and cooling) of the cycle only. With present technology, parts must be held at a specific temperature and pressure for a predetermined time.

Size of the work chamber is another limiting factor. Autoclaves built for PM parts and billets range from 15-36" diam (381-914 mm) by 60-108" (1524-2743 mm) long. Larger HIP units have been built for special aircraft uses and for experimentation.

*Applications.* Hot isostatic pressing was first commercially used in the aerospace industry. Current applications have grown to encompass the consolidation of high-speed steels and superalloy powders, densification of cemented tungsten carbides and oxides, upgrading of investment castings, and fabrication of high-performance ceramics. With system capabilities expanding and becoming increasingly cost efficient, even the more common metallic and ceramic alloys are being processed commercially using HIP.

While most HIP-processed PM parts have been made directly from powders, another trend is toward eliminating the disposable can. Conventionally pressed and sintered parts (at about 90-95% density) are loaded into the chamber directly for full densification.

## Other PM Pressure Compaction Methods

**Hot pressing**. Hot pressing can produce compacted products with a high level of strength, hardness, accuracy, and density. During hot pressing, the total amount of deformation of the compact is relatively limited in comparison to hot extrusion and hot forging, but complete densification generally is achieved. Factors that limit the use of hot pressing include die cost, difficulties in heating and atmospheric control, and length of time required for the cycle. Temperatures are too high for steel dies; and a principal problem is the choice of suitable mold material. It must be strong enough at the hot-pressing temperature to withstand the applied pressure without plastic deformation, and it should not react with the powder. A widely used material for hot pressing beryllium and cemented carbides is graphite.

**Spark sintering**. A method of hot consolidating metal powders closely related to hot pressing is electrical resistance sintering under pressure. Powder or a green powder preform is placed between two punches that also serve as electrodes for conducting a low-voltage, high-amperage current. The powder is heated to the hot-pressing temperature by the electric current and simultaneously pressed. This process is mainly used in pressing beryllium powder and titanium alloy powder compacts in graphite molds, under conditions in which a dense compact is produced in 12-15 seconds.

**High-energy-rate forming.** In commercial PM practice, limited use is made of high-energy-rate forming techniques for closed die powder compaction. Various methods of energy production have been developed, including pneumatic, mechanical, explosive, and spark discharge. Two unique features are the very short duration of pressure application, ranging from 50 ms to 5 $\mu$ s, and the high amounts of energy imparted to the material. Benefits sought are high green densities, high green and sintered strength, and uniform density of the compacts.

One type of high-energy-rate forming uses dies similar to those in conventional compacting, but the upper punch is an impactor that moves at high velocity through a barrel to compact the powder. The impactor may be actuated by an explosive charge or by compressed gas. Another method is explosive compacting, in which the powders are loaded into a steel tube; the tube ends are welded shut; and explosives are taped to the tube and tapered at one end to attach an explosive cap. Available information indicates that explosive compacting activity is limited to experimental investigations and developmental work.

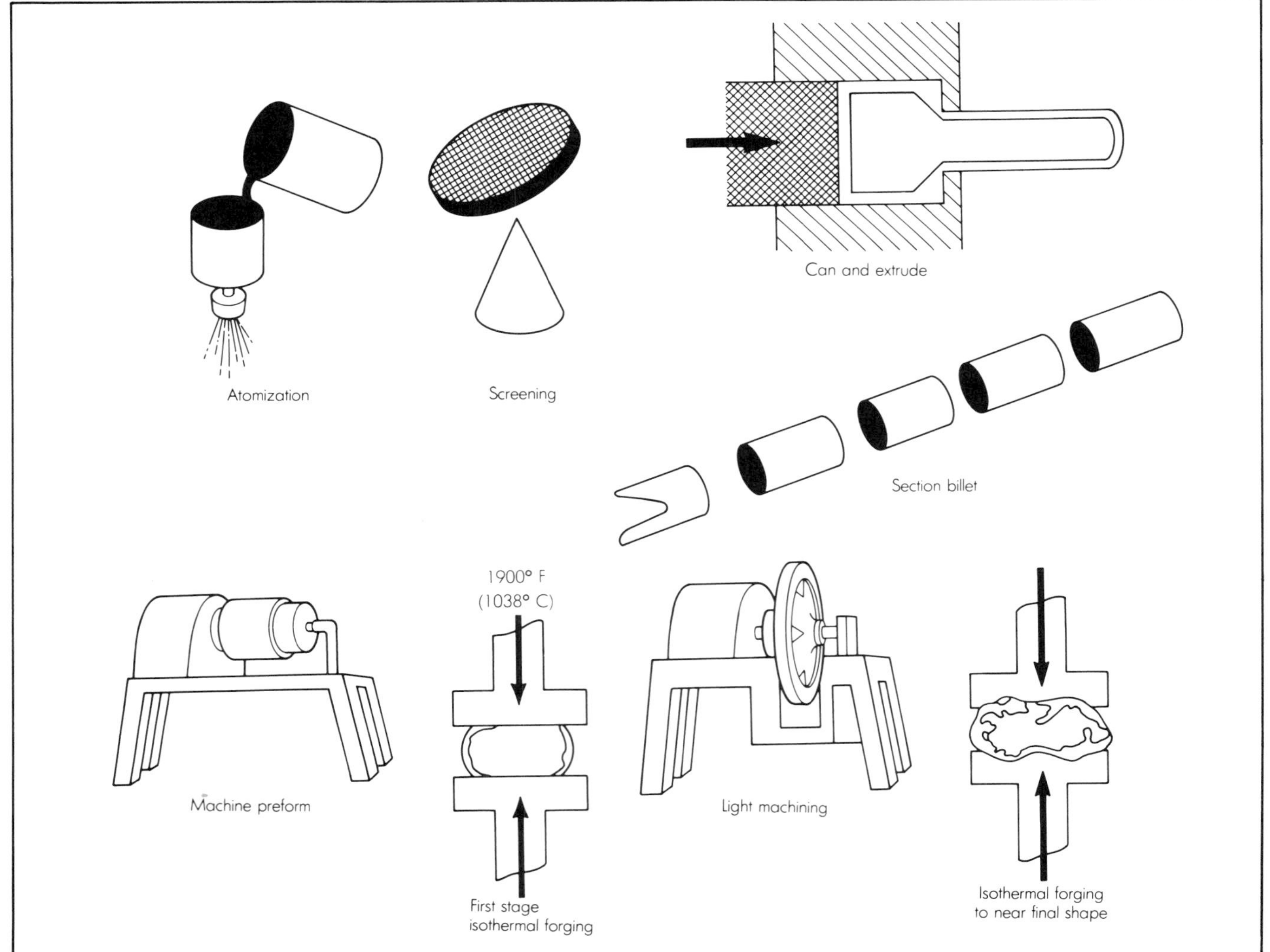


**Fig. 17-43 Schematic flow chart shows hot isostatic pressing followed by forging for producing turbine discs.**

# SPECIAL PM PROCESSES

**Extruding**. Long shapes produced from metal powders are extruded. Developments in this field make it possible to produce extruded shapes with very high densities and excellent mechanical properties. Methods used for extruding depend upon the characteristics of the powder; some powders are extruded cold with a binder, while others can be heated to a suitable extruding temperature. Hot extrusion combines hot compacting and hot mechanical working, yielding a fully dense product. (General information on extruding is provided in Chapter 13, "Wire Drawing, Extruding and Heading," in this volume.) Generally, the powder is first compressed into a billet and is then heated or sintered in a nonoxidizing atmosphere before being placed in the press. Although various methods are used for PM hot extrusion, in most applications, the metal powders are placed in a metallic capsule or "can," heated, and extruded with the can. Although the greatest use of this process has been to produce nuclear solid fuel elements and other materials for high-temperature applications; aluminum, copper, nickel, beryllium, and other powder metals can be extruded. The process also is used for producing seamless tubing from stainless steel powder.

**Injection molding**. Complex shapes, with wall thicknesses from 0.2" (5 mm) to 0.023" (0.6 mm), and shapes with cross-cored holes, which are impossible to compact by conventional powder metallurgy processes, can be produced by applying to metal powders (and ceramic powders) the technology of injection molding of plastics. Additional information on injection molding is provided in Chapter 18, "Plastics Forming," in this volume.

Injection molding of powder metals is a three-step process, starting with metal powder in a plastic binder. In the first step, part preforms—which are about 20% larger than finished size—are injection molded in a manner similar to that of plastic injection molding. In the second step, the preforms are heated to drive off the plastic binder. In the third step, they are sintered much like traditional powder metal parts. The final parts have a density of 95-98% that of wrought material, are fully annealed, and often require no additional machining.

The principal advantage of powder metal injection molding is its ability to produce complex parts to near net shape, minimizing machining and leading to cost savings in both materials and processing. The batch nature of the process, and the long cycle times, preclude using it in some applications, however. The maximum part size can also be a limitation.

An example of a part produced by injection molding from nickel powder is a 2" (50.8 mm) diam screw seal with a discontinuous internal thread. The seal is used in an aircraft wing flap ballscrew assembly.

**Isothermal PM forging**. Gatorizing is a Pratt & Whitney patented hot die forging process that uses a powder metal billet as the input material. The process work is performed as a hot isothermal operation in which both the dies and forging stock are heated to the established forging temperature and maintained at that temperature during forging. The billet is made by consolidating the metal powder by either extrusion or hot isostatic pressing into a log that is in a superplastic (low-strength; high-ductility) condition. The reduced forging pressure requirement eliminates the need for a large tonnage press that would be used for conventional forging of the superalloys in high-performance aircraft jet engines. For example, a press with a 3000 ton (27 MN) capacity is used to Gatorize compressor rotor discs, made from IN100 (nickel-base superalloy); whereas, a press with 20,000 ton (178 MN) or larger capacity would be required to produce an equivalent part conventionally. Another advantage of this process is the fabrication of parts to near net shape. The Gatorizing process is illustrated, schematically, in Fig. 17-43.

## PRESSURELESS PM COMPACTION METHODS

The various pressureless PM compaction methods include gravity compaction, continuous compaction, and slip casting.

### Gravity Compaction

Gravity compaction refers to filling a die with loose powder and sintering the powder in the die. This method also is called "pressureless molding," "gravity sintering," and "loose sintering." Principal commercial application is for the production of PM filters.

### Continuous Compaction

Continuous pressureless compaction is used to produce porous sheet. The process (sometimes referred to as "slurry coating"), consists of preparing a slurry of the metal powder, a liquid, and chemical additives. The slurry then can be coated on a metal screen or solid sheet. It is passed through a set of rolls that apply little pressure, but control slurry thickness. Drying and sintering complete the process. Applications include production of high-porosity sheet for electrodes in rechargeable batteries and the application of porous coatings of various metals to ferrous sheet stock to produce unusual properties.

### Slip Casting

Although green compacts for tungsten, molybdenum, and other powders are sometimes made by slip casting, the process is used only to a limited extent for metals; it is more widely used for ceramics. The powder, converted to a slurry mixture, is poured into a plaster-of-paris mold. Since the mold is porous, the liquid drains into the plaster, leaving a solid layer of material deposited on the surface. Upon drying, the green compacts are sintered in the usual manner. The procedure is simple and permits considerable variation in size and complexity; however, it is not suited to high production rates.

## WROUGHT PM PROCESSES

Powder metallurgy often is associated with structural parts, or self-lubricating parts of specific shapes produced by rigid die pressing and sintering. However, from its inception, PM also has been applied to wrought materials. These are metal structures that begin as powders; but through processing, they become fully dense, high-performance products that possess unusual metallurgical characteristics. By beginning with metal powders instead of melting and casting the metal, a homogeneous, segregation-free microstructure is achieved, with resulting benefits in uniformity of mechanical properties. This section covers significant commercial processes that use metal powders as a starting point for production of wrought products.

### An Early Example

One of the first applications of PM was for a wrought product—the production of tungsten wire for lamp filaments. To produce tungsten wire, specially treated tungsten powder is pressed into bar form using a breakaway die which avoids stress-induced cracking of the very low green strength compact. The green bar is presintered in hydrogen at a relatively low temperature to impart a degree of interparticle bonding and strength and to remove reducible impurities (primarily oxygen), then it is sintered at a high temperature to full density by a process of electric resistance sintering in hydrogen. Finally, the sintered bar is worked into wire by hot swaging followed by warm and cold wire drawing.

The main rationale for powder processing in this instance is that tungsten, because of its high melting point, cannot be processed readily by other methods. Secondarily, lamp filaments are treated with specialized minor additions to control grain growth, an important process step that is possible only through a PM approach.

Other important driving forces which can lead to the choice of a specialized powder metallurgy process include:

1. Cost reduction through minimizing process steps and through lower requirements for equipment investment. For example, powder rolling of strip, and tube extrusion.
2. Material savings achieved through more efficient use of materials by processing directly to near net shape. For example, HIP for aircraft components of superalloys or titanium.
3. Improved properties for highly alloyed materials through fine dispersion of phases which are a normal part of the alloy microstructure. For example, tool steels and superalloys.
4. Achieving unique combinations of materials not possible by a melting process. For example, tungsten-silver and tungsten-copper materials and oxide dispersion hardened materials.

## Powder Processing

The success of the specialized powder processing methods depends upon the powder quality. In an extreme instance, superalloy powders used for aircraft parts such as turbine discs are produced under rigid conditions of exclusion from oxygen and other contaminants. Vacuum-melted metal is argon atomized and then further processed through the point of final consolidation without being exposed to air or any impurity. The cost of such rigorous treatment is offset by savings in the amount of material removed and the cost of removing it using conventional melting, forging, and machining processes.

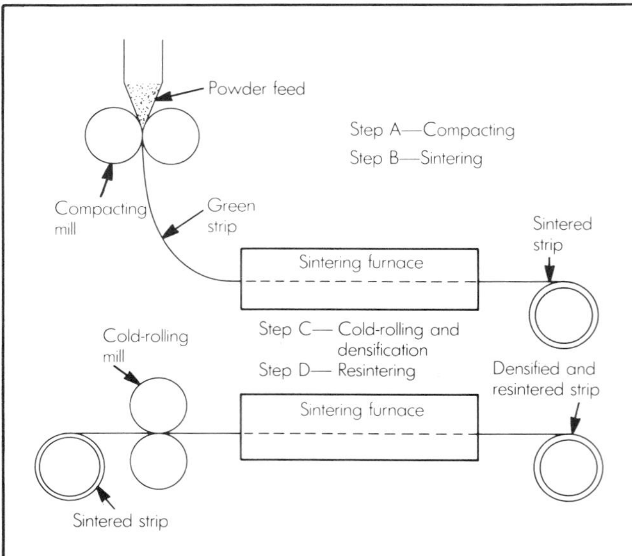


**Fig. 17-44 Powder cold-rolling process with in-line sintering.**

One method of producing extremely clean powders for a relatively low cost involves vacuum melting metals in the largest available furnaces (five tons) and atomizing them with nitrogen.

Although not requiring such extreme freedom from contamination as powders for aircraft parts, powders for successful powder rolling of specialty metal strip or HIP plus extrusion of tube materials must be quite free of nonmetallic inclusions and consistent in all other properties. Such processes can be adjusted to work well with different powders, but adjustment is difficult if not impractical once the production process conditions have been set.

## Powder Rolling

Metal powder can be converted directly into strip by a powder rolling process whereby the powders are consolidated in a rolling mill to form a green strip which is sintered and further rolled to full density. An important purpose in using powder rolling is the elimination of processing steps including melting, ingot casting, homogenizing, conditioning, hot forging, hot rolling, and pickling. Avoiding the capital equipment expense necessary to perform such processing steps also is an important economic consideration.

**Cold rolling**. One powder rolling approach, illustrated in Fig. 17-44, is characterized by the fact that all working steps are carried out cold (room temperature). The powder is normally fed by a controlled metering system into the roll gap at the top of two horizontally opposed rolls. Such a mill is ordinarily a conventional two-level rolling mill turned on its side. Powder may also be fed to rolls which are vertically aligned as in normal metal rolling using appropriate feed controls. A greater danger of segregation and nonuniform engagement of the two roll surfaces with the powder must be dealt with in the latter case.

Strip monitoring of thickness and density is provided by feedback and by control of the powder feed and roll adjustment to achieve uniformity and desired green strip properties. Green density can vary over a wide range for specific process requirements; but for each specific process and material, it must be controlled within narrow limits. A lower limit would undoubtedly be that which allows strip integrity in the system, and an upper limit should be 90% or less of theoretical density, since a density that is any higher negates the potential benefits of chemical refinement during sintering, and blistering by entrapped gases or reaction products can occur.

The next step in the process is strip sintering to develop metallurgical bonding between the particles. This process is carried out in line with the compacting mill and under a protective atmosphere such as a hydrogen or dissociated ammonia atmosphere. Usually a belt or roller hearth furnace is selected. The belt furnace gives good support to the strip during the sintering operation, but requires heating of the belt, (usually weighing as much or more than the strip). The open mesh belts also drag oxygen into the furnace and result in lower purity for the atmosphere. Roller hearth furnaces are more energy efficient, but provide less support for the strip and must use a specially bricked furnace to achieve good atmosphere purity.

Cold rolling of the sintered strip at densities under 90% theoretical is limited in amount of reduction to no greater than 10-15% because of the low ductility of the sintered porous strip. Greater amounts of cold reduction at this point result in excessive strip cracking. The cold-rolling step at this stage does, in fact, accomplish densification more than strip elongation. If

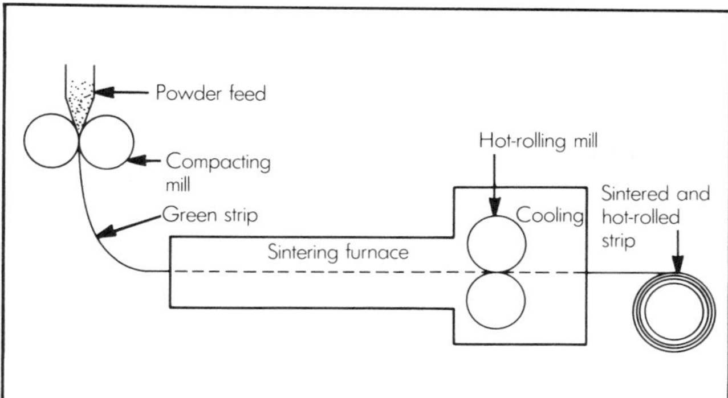


**Fig. 17-45 Powder hot-rolling process.**

the strip is cold worked after the initial in-line sintering, it must again be sintered in-line since it is at that point too fragile (brittle) to be recoiled. Following a second in-line sintering, however, the strip is close to full density and may be subjected to substantial cold working followed by conventional annealing.

**Hot rolling**. In-line sintering is limited as to time at temperature by the amount of heating time, line speed, and furnace length. A sufficient degree of sintering allows the strip to be coiled for further processing steps or to be consolidated further by a cold or hot-rolling step in line with the sintering furnace. Such a hot-rolling step is carried out while the strip is still heated from the sintering furnace and under a protective atmosphere as illustrated in Fig. 17-45.

**Applications**. Metals in strip form made on a commercial scale by powder rolling include nickel and nickel iron alloys for electronic and coinage uses; nickel iron and nickel iron cobalt controlled expansion alloys; cobalt and ductile cobalt alloys for welding applications; and an aluminum-backed, aluminum lead alloy which, after roll bonding to a steel backing, is used widely for automotive bearings.

## Tool Steels Production

The manufacture of tool steels by consolidation to full density billets of gas-atomized powders has been a commercial reality since the early 1970's. The fully dense PM billets are worked to finished shapes by conventional hot-forging and hot-rolling methods. Additional information on tool steels made by PM processes is contained in Chapter 3, "Cutting Tool Materials," in *Machining*, Volume I of this Handbook series.

A major advantage of the PM production of tool steels is the ability of this approach to achieve a relatively fine and uniform dispersion of carbide phases compared to the coarse carbide network and heavy segregation usually encountered with normal melting, casting technology. Not only does the PM structure give good product yields, but the end properties are significantly improved, especially for certain applications. It has also been reported that higher alloying levels and, therefore, higher properties can be achieved with PM. Three different approaches are known to be in commercial practice at this time.

**Consolidation at Atmospheric Pressure**. This process (CAP), developed by Cyclops Corporation, has been used to produce tool steels T-15, M-2, and M-3. Clean, relatively fine, gas-atomized powders are enclosed in glass bottles which are evacuated and sealed and then sintered loose to +99% density preforms or billets which are subsequently forged and rolled. It is reported that a boron-containing addition is used in the powder mix as a sintering activator. For high-speed steels, the metal powder is produced by air melting and nitrogen atomizing with a resultant nitrogen level of 150 ppm.

This same method is also used to produce high-density preforms or billets of high-temperature nickel-base alloys.

**Crucible Particle Metallurgy (CPM)**. A second method for producing billets and preforms is the Crucible Particle Metallurgy (CPM) process developed by Crucible Specialty Metals Div., Colt Industries. This process consists of pouring gas-atomized alloy powders into a steel can which is evacuated and sealed. The filled and sealed container is hot isostatically pressed to full density and can then be worked to desired shapes by conventional hot forging and rolling while still in the container. Crucible Particle Metallurgy high-alloy steels can be characterized by complete homogeneity in the compact and in the products produced from the compact. The carbide particle size is finer and more uniformly distributed than it is in conventionally produced high-alloy steels.

The Crucible Particle Metallurgy (CPM) process is used to produce conventional tool steel compositions and has also enabled development of higher alloyed grades than are possible with conventional melt-cast technology.

**Anti-Segregation Process (ASP)**. A third and similar method is the Anti-Segregation Process (ASP) developed by NYBY Uddeholm Steel Corp. of Sweden. It includes a cold isostatic pressing (CIP) treatment of the sealed can of powder followed by heating and hot isostatic pressing (HIP). Again, the billet or preform, after hot isostatic pressing to full density is capable of being processed by hot forging and rolling.

## Specialty Alloy Tubing

The advances in PM consolidation consisting of gas atomization of powders and powder consolidation to produce high quality tool steel compositions have spurred the development of additional alloys and products along similar lines. One of the noteworthy developments is the production of high-quality specialty alloys in tube form. A process developed and used by NYBY Uddeholm Steel Corp. of Sweden produces seamless tubing from powders in such alloy systems as 304L stainless steel; 316L stainless steel; and various other austenitic, ferritic, and martensitic grades of specialty stainless steels; as well as nonferrous alloys including nickel copper alloy 400.

In the process, a gas-atomized powder is poured into a steel capsule which is vibrated so that the packed density is above 70% of theoretical. After being filled, the capsule is sealed and leak tested. It is then cold isostatically pressed (CIP) under very high pressures (500 MPa, 72,500 psi) to consolidate the powder to a theoretical density of 85-90% and allow it to undergo the extrusion step in a controlled manner. The capsule is heated in two stages to 2200° F (1200° C) and extruded in a conventional extrusion press at an extrusion ratio of 20-30 to 1 based on theoretical density.

Advantages of this process over normal melting, casting, and extruding production methods for seamless tubing are (1) a lower inclusion rate because of the powder cleanliness; (2) closer composition control in the finished tube because of the better control in composition of powders achievable by blending and because of the absence of segregation from the solidification step; (3) and a more homogeneous structure.

## Oxide Dispersion Strengthening

Powder metallurgy allows the consolidation of materials which contain fine dispersions of oxide or other insoluble phases that are stable up to the melting point of the base metal.

Perhaps the most sophisticated approach is the INCO Mechanical Alloying process whereby through intensive ball milling (attriting), the individual powder ingredients of an alloy including oxide phases such as $Y_2O_3$ are formed into homogeneous powders, each particle having the desired final composition and degree of dispersion. This alloying occurs by a complex dynamic equilibrium of particle fracture and recombination by welding. The alloyed particles are then consolidated by canning and hot extrusion into shapes which can be further worked as desired for aircraft parts.

### Tungsten, Tantalum and Molybdenum

In addition to the lamp filaments described earlier, the high melting refractory metals, such as tungsten, tantalum, and molybdenum and their alloys, are fabricated to wrought intermediate shapes by powder metal technology. Frequently, the powders are formed into large green billets by cold isostatic pressing (CIP); vacuum sintered at high temperature to achieve at least a closed porosity state; and then further worked by hot forging, rolling, swaging, etc.

# NONFERROUS PM METALS

As in most other metal-oriented fields, powder metallurgy (PM)is linked strongly to the development and use of ferrous materials. It is, however, being increasingly applied in the fabrication of structural (and nonstructural) parts from the light, high strength to weight ratio, nonferrous metals, such as aluminum, magnesium, beryllium, and titanium. When processed by PM, these metals (usually in alloy form), exhibit high levels of mechanical properties that are suited to a wide range of applications—especially in aircraft, aerospace, and nuclear fields. In addition to these metals, structural PM parts make considerable use of copper and copper alloys.

## ALUMINUM

The commercial production of precision parts by powder metallurgy techniques is an important development in the fabrication of aluminum alloys. Their high strength, light weight, corrosion resistance, high thermal and electrical conductivity, and response to a variety of finishing processes are utilized in automobiles, appliances, business machines, power tools, and many other applications.

Aluminum PM parts are competitive with many aluminum castings, extrusions, and screw machine products that involve machining operations. They also compete with PM parts manufactured from other metal powders in which some features of aluminum are needed.

### Material Characteristics

The commercially available aluminum powder alloys are blends of carefully sized, atomized, aluminum powder mixed with powders of various alloying metals such as copper and magnesium.

### Properties and Performance

**Properties**. Aluminum PM parts can be produced with a wide range of property values. Tensile strength can vary from 16,000-50,000 psi (110-345 MPa) depending on composition, density, sintering practices, thermal treatment, and repressing operations. Figure 17-46 illustrates the general point that aluminum PM parts can be produced with strength levels comparable to the commonly used ferrous PM parts.

**Corrosion resistance**. Aluminum alloys are widely used in both structural and nonstructural applications because of their resistance to corrosion. The corrosion resistance of aluminum PM alloys can be improved appreciably through the application of chemical conversion coatings or through anodizing treatments. Amorphous chromate coatings are especially useful in providing economical protection to parts exposed to saline environments. When exceptional corrosion resistance is required, anodizing treatments are best.

**Light weight**. A distinguishing characteristic of aluminum PM parts is their lighter weight in comparison to other common PM materials. Aluminum has a 3 to 1 weight advantage over iron and a 3.3 to 1 advantage over copper.

**Conductivity**. Another advantage of aluminum is its excellent conductivity, both electrical and thermal, in comparison with most other metals. Aluminum PM parts, therefore, may be utilized as heat sinks or as electrical conductors.

### Manufacturing Process

The fabrication of aluminum PM parts involves the same basic manufacturing operations, equipment, and tooling that are employed for other metal powders. There are some differences, however.

**Compacting**. Aluminum PM premixes exhibit excellent compressibility and yield high-density parts at lower compaction and ejection pressures than are needed for iron powders. Lower compacting pressures permit the use of smaller, faster presses to produce larger parts; or in some cases, multiple-cavity tooling is used for high-production rates. Aluminum powder transfers more readily under pressure in the die than do iron powders. This allows the molding of complex shapes such as slopes and multilevels.

**Sintering**. Aluminum PM parts can be sintered in various types of furnaces and atmospheres. Sintering time and temperature typically are less than for other materials. Reproducible dimensions can be achieved with proper attention to compact density, sintering, temperature, dew point, and atmosphere. Most parts are sintered in a $N_2$ atmosphere at 1100° F (593° C) with the dew point controlled to -40° F (-40° C) or better.

The high strength and good ductility of sintered aluminum PM parts are attributable to the sintering process and the liquid-phase sintering that aluminum PM powders undergo. When aluminum premixes are sintered, liquid-phases form as aluminum combines with the added soluble elements—copper, silicon, and magnesium. These liquid constituents migrate along particle boundaries; penetrate the aluminum oxide envelope; and diffuse into the powder particles. This reduces porosity and increases homogeneity.

**Secondary operations**. Secondary operations performed on aluminum PM parts are similar to those for most other PM materials. These include sizing or coining, heat treatment, machining, finishing, and joining. Cold or hot forming can be added when optimum properties are desired.

# NONFERROUS PM METALS

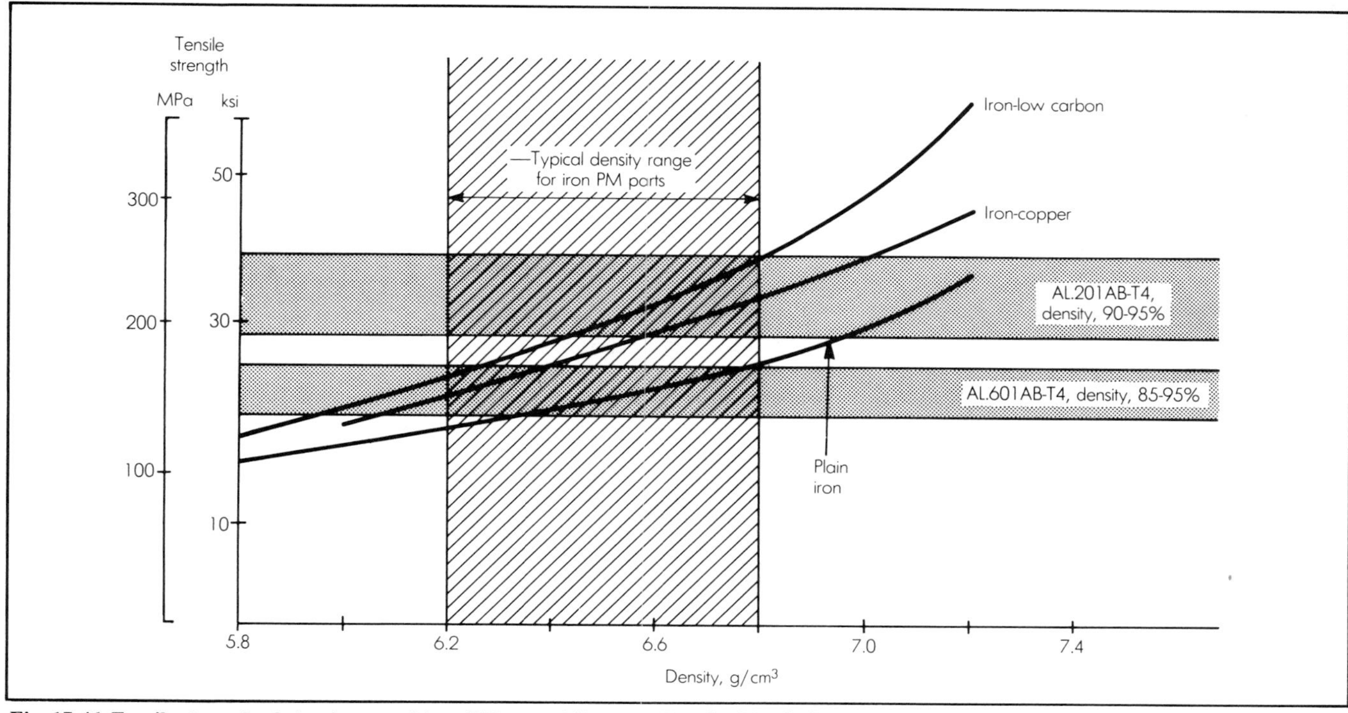


**Fig. 17-46 Tensile strength of aluminum and iron PM parts (*American Powder Metals Co.*).**

## MAGNESIUM

Magnesium alloy powders are processed by a hot-extrusion method in which loose powder is loaded into the heated extrusion chamber and extruded directly through the die. No atmospheric protection is provided, and the heat of the container is used to raise the powder temperature sufficiently to allow for extrusion. The metallurgical structure of magnesium and its alloys is such that coarse-grained alloys have a lower compressive yield strength than tensile yield strength. When magnesium alloys are sufficiently fine grained, they have about the same yield strength in tension and compression.

Fine-grained alloys can be produced from coarse magnesium alloy powders by hot extrusion. Any shape that can be extruded conventionally can be extruded from the magnesium alloy powders or "pellets." These pellet extrusions have a finer grain size than extrusions from chill-cast magnesium alloy ingots—and, therefore, have a ratio of compressive to tensile yield strength near one.

## BERYLLIUM

Most beryllium parts are produced by powder metallurgy, because it enables a fine-grained product to be produced. Beryllium powder is consolidated by loose powder sintering. Commercial purity beryllium is produced by vacuum hot pressing in graphite molds. Vacuum hot pressed beryllium, depending on the grade, has yield strengths of 30,000-36,000 psi (200-250 MPa) with 2-4% elongation, or yield strengths of 60,000 psi (410 MPa) with 1-2% elongation.

Better mechanical properties have been obtained from high purity impact attrited powder which is cold isostatically pressed in evacuated bags at 60,000 psi (410 MPa) and then hot isostatically pressed in evacuated and sealed steel cans at 15,000 psi (105 MPa) pressure and peak temperatures of 1679-2120° F (915-1160° C). Typical mechanical properties of this hot isostatically pressed beryllium are:

- Yield strength: 41,000 to 66,000 psi (280 to 460 MPa)
- Tensile strength: 67,000 to 87,000 psi (470 to 600 MPa)
- Elongation: 4 to 6 1/2%

Hot-pressed beryllium can be extruded and rolled. The extrusions have good ductility in the extrusion direction; 10% elongation with 130,000 psi (900 MPa) tensile strength and 80,000 psi (550 MPa) yield strength. Because of this preferred orientation during plastic working, it is also possible by cross rolling to produce beryllium sheet that is relatively ductile in the plane of the sheet, but very brittle in the direction perpendicular to the plane of the sheet.

Beryllium is finding increasing use in aircraft applications, particularly jet engine parts. It is used in gyroscopes and other guidance instruments. Among the aerospace applications of beryllium were heat sinks that were used for the Apollo space capsules. In nuclear applications, the principal advantage of beryllium is its outstanding ability to slow down neutrons to thermal velocities and at the same time not react with the neutrons.

## TITANIUM

The high cost of titanium has restricted its use to products that require exceptional corrosion resistance or a high strength to weight ratio. Its chemical reactivity mandates specialized equipment and technology to produce conventional castings or wrought shapes. Furthermore, numerous costly processing steps are involved, as shown in Fig. 17-47.

The powder metallurgy (PM) process has been instrumental in expanding applications for titanium. It is attractive from a raw material cost point of view, since the ore refining process produces a sponge product from the magnesium or sodium reduction of $TiCl_4$. Processing temperatures for PM are a fraction of the melting point of the titanium metal, thus reducing the reactivity problem; and substantially fewer processing steps may be required, as shown in Fig. 17-47. The process offers the generic attributes of powder metallurgy products—fine grain size and homogeneous composition. Perhaps the strongest advantage of PM titanium is its ability to produce near net shape components. This advantage is manifested in a substantially lower initial material cost than that for ingot metallurgy material, and in reduced machining cost.

## General Methods

A few applications, primarily those demanding exceptional corrosion resistance, use commercially pure titanium powder consolidated to a near net shape product. The product application may be structural, in which case, a high-density product is required; or it may be nonstructural, in which case, the high specific surface area and/or the permeability of a porous product is required. Strength can be controlled by varying the oxygen content of the starting material.

More often the applications for titanium relate to the high strength to weight ratio characteristic of its alloys. Two PM methods are routinely used to prepare alloys. In one method, prealloyed ingot metallurgy bar stock is converted to powder form by an atomization process. The resulting product, spherical in form, is of uniform chemical composition and has the strength of the parent alloy. This latter attribute requires the use of special consolidation techniques. In the other PM method, the most economical, elemental alloying constituents are blended with the commercially pure powder to form a mixture having a bulk composition that meets the specifications of the desired alloy. Because the blended elemental powder is composed primarily of soft, commercially pure titanium, it is readily fabricated into shapes by common methods. Homogenization and the full alloy strength are developed in subsequent processing steps.

**Fabrication**. The chemical reactivity of titanium, especially

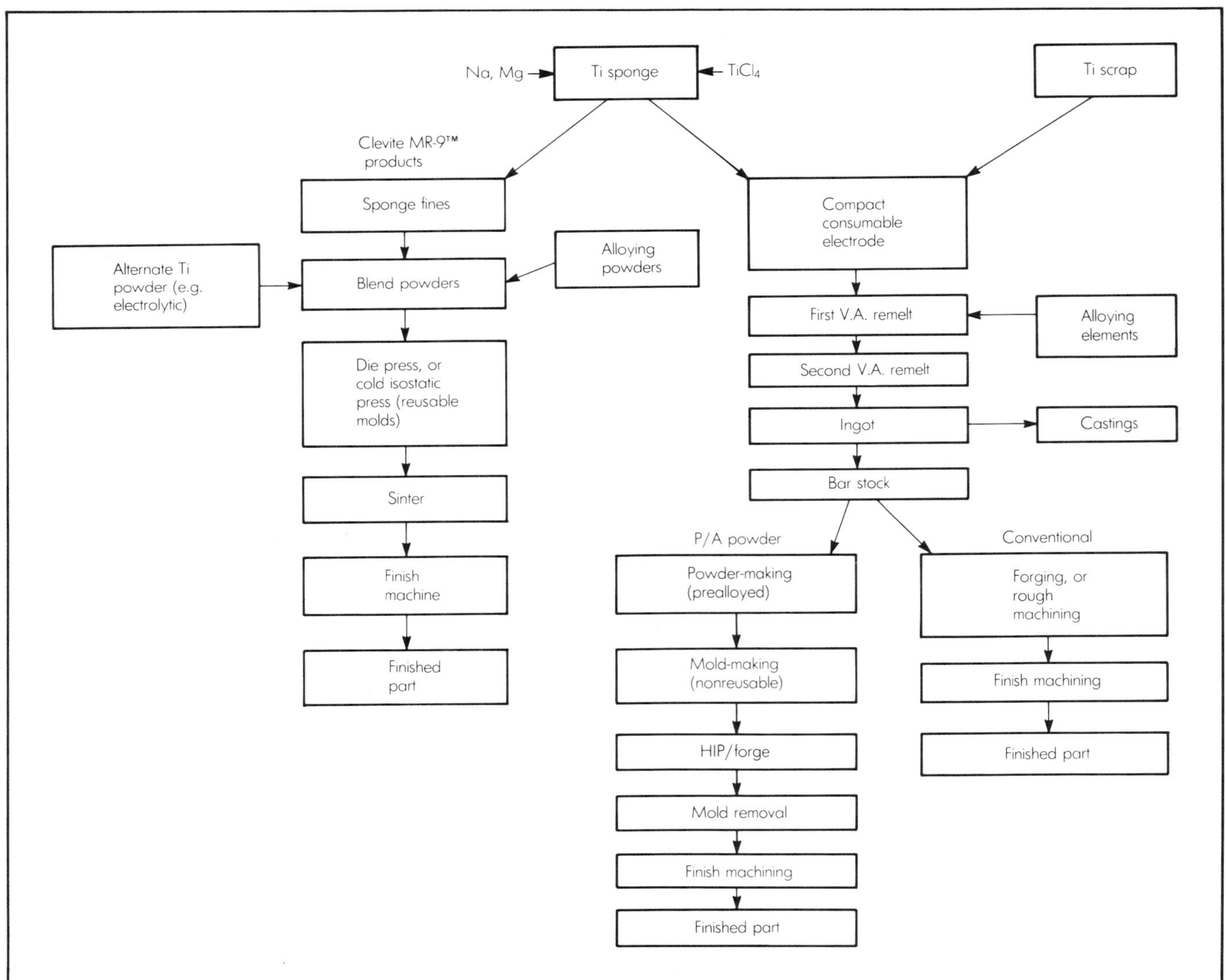


**Fig. 17-47 Manufacturing processes for PM and conventional cast and wrought shapes.**

The characteristics of wear resistance and high impact strength are difficult to combine in one material. Tool material selection is determined by the PM part and the powder material; the method of tool construction; and the PM processes by which the part is to be made or finished. Wear resistance is a key factor in die and core materials. For punch materials, on the other hand, impact resistance or toughness is more important than wear resistance. Refer to Chapter 2 "Die and Mold Materials" for additional information.

in fine powder form dictates that particular care be used in fabrication. Electrical equipment must be explosion proof, and reasonable care must be exercised to preclude fire or explosion. Good housekeeping is mandatory.

In general, the methods used to fabricate titanium PM parts are similar to those for PM fabrication of other metals. Commercially pure powder and blended elemental mixtures can be consolidated inexpensively in rigid dies or cold isostatic pressing (CIP) molds. In the first case, carbide dies are recommended and clearances should be generous. Polyurethane makes a durable CIP mold which, on the average, has a life of 50 parts. Compacting pressures range from 30-50 tons/in.[2] (415-690 MPa). Blended elemental parts exhibit green densities of 80-85% of theoretical and can be easily handled without breakage. If the product application calls for sheet or foil shapes, the commercially pure or blended elemental powder can be powder rolled directly to these configurations.

**Compacting**. Prealloyed powder, because of its inherent strength, requires more costly consolidation procedures. The most common process is hot isostatic pressing (HIP). This process requires that the powder be encapsulated in a container and subjected to high temperature. The container is evacuated and sealed for pressing. The pressing cycle is relatively long, and the container must be removed following the HIP cycle. The fluid die process developed for consolidation of high-strength powders eliminates the need for specialized equipment and shortens the production cycle, but still employs an expendable mold for each part. Both processes have the capability of producing fully dense components of intricate shape.

Vacuum hot pressing may be used for either blended elemental or prealloyed powders, with the resulting parts being fully dense. Tooling resembles rigid dies of the reusable type, and special capital equipment is required.

**Sintering**. Because of its affinity for oxygen, sintering of titanium and its alloys is done in vacuum. It is critically important to control oxygen absorption during processing. Sinter densities range from 95-99.5% for standard parts. In controlled surface area or permeability parts, porosity may vary from 40-80% depending upon design.

**Equipment**. Fabrication equipment is typically employed throughout the PM industry. Rigid die presses may be either mechanical or hydraulic type. Isostatic compaction chambers, both cold (CIP) and hot (HIP), are commercially available. Vacuum sintering furnaces capable of maintaining pressures below 5 x $10^{-4}$ Torr are employed and may use inert gas recirculating systems to rapidly cool alloys to obtain the required structure. Finishing equipment parallels equipment that is used universally by the PM industry.

**TABLE 17-13**
**Composition and Density of Titanium P M Alloys**

| Alloy | Nominal Composition, % | | | | | | | Density, g/cm$^3$ |
|---|---|---|---|---|---|---|---|---|
| | Al | V | Sn | Zr | Mo | $O_2$ | Ti | |
| C.P. | --- | --- | --- | --- | --- | 0.15 | 99. | 4.19 |
| Ti-64 | 6 | 4 | --- | --- | --- | 0.2 | Bal. | 4.38 |
| Ti-662 | 6 | 6 | 2 | --- | --- | 0.2 | Bal. | 4.47 |
| Ti-6242 | 6 | --- | 2 | 4 | 2 | 0.2 | Bal. | 4.47 |

(*Imperial Clevite, Inc.*)

**TABLE 17-14**
**Typical Mechanical Properties of Titanium P M Alloys**

| Alloy | Yield Strength, (MPa) | Ultimate Tensile Strength, (MPa) | Elongation, % | Hardness, $R_A$ |
|---|---|---|---|---|
| C.P. | 35 | 48 | 13 | 12 |
| Ti-64 B/E | 120 | 133 | 12 | 24 |
| PRE | 127 | 136 | 17 | 33 |
| Ti-64 STA | 140 | 155 | 3 | 5 |
| Ti-662 B/E | 140 | 150 | 7 | 10 |
| Ti-6242 B/E | 130 | 145 | 12 | 15 |

(*Imperial Clevite, Inc.*)

## Properties

Performance of PM alloys is strongly influenced by product integrity. Controlled-porosity parts have lower performance characteristics than fully dense parts. Since the majority of applications for PM titanium are structural, properties given in this section are representative of state-of-the-art materials processed for optimum performance unless otherwise noted.

Nominal composition and typical densities of some commonly used PM alloys are presented in Table 17-13. The density for commercially pure material is based on its use as a structural component. The density of porous parts may be as low as 1.8 g/cm$^3$. Other physical properties may be estimated from ingot metallurgy data, allowing for a proportional decrease in value depending on the degree of porosity in the final part. Typical mechanical properties are listed in Table 17-14.

## Applications

Titanium PM has produced parts for a wide range of applications, and the list is steadily expanding. Commercially pure titanium fasteners have been used by the chemical industry for many years. More recently, this industry has moved toward porous titanium electrodes for conversion cells when high specific surface area is advantageous.

Prealloyed and blended alloys have been used in static applications by the aerospace industry. The near net shape capability accounts for much of the demand for PM titanium. A good example is a missile warhead, for which titanium PM offered material savings of one third of that of the previously used forging. At the other extreme, PM titanium alloys are receiving consideration as prosthetic implants, for which excellent corrosion resistance to body fluids, coupled with high strength and near net shape potential, creates a powerful driving force.

## COPPER

Copper has a combination of properties not found in any other metal. It has exceptionally high electrical and thermal conductivity. It has excellent resistance to corrosion, is highly ductile, exhibits good strength, and is nonmagnetic. In addition, it can be welded, brazed, and soldered. It can also be plated. Its pleasing color finds many applications in the decorative field. These factors make copper a useful PM material.

An increasing number of PM manufacturers are producing pure copper parts. Copper parts for electrical and thermal applications, such as wires, contacts, and tubing, are produced by PM. Thin sheet and refrigeration tubing made by PM methods allow parts to be produced with properties comparable to those made by conventional methods.

## Copper Powder

One of the best known powder metallurgy applications of copper powder is self-lubricating bronze bearings, which are produced from mixtures of elemental copper and tin powders. The grades of copper powder used are free-flowing granular powders with density in the range of 2.5-3.2 g/cm$^3$. Copper powders similar to those for self-lubricating bearings are used:

- As an ingredient in mixes for iron-based structural parts.
- For metallic brushes pressed from mixtures of copper and graphite powder.
- For structural parts with a bronze composition.
- For straight copper powder structural parts for electrical and electronic applications.

A variety of copper powders is available. Their properties are strongly related to the methods by which they are produced. The principal methods for producing copper powder for PM applications are:

- Electrolytic deposition of copper powder.
- Gaseous reduction of copper oxide.
- Atomization.

## Copper-Alloy Powders

For producing bronze structural parts, either elemental powders or a prealloyed atomized bronze powder is used. Structural parts from brasses (copper-zinc alloys) and nickel

**TABLE 17-15**
**Typical Tensile Properties and Electrical Conductivity of Copper P M Parts**

| Property | Electrical Conductivity Type I | Type II |
|---|---|---|
| Density, g/cm$^3$ | 8.0 | 8.3 |
| Ultimate tensile strength, psi (MPa) | 23,000 (159) | 28,000 (193) |
| Elongation, % | 20 | 30 |
| Electrical conductivity, % of IACS (Ohm$^{-1}$m$^{-1}$) | 85 (0.493 x 10$^8$) | 90 (0.522 x 10$^8$) |

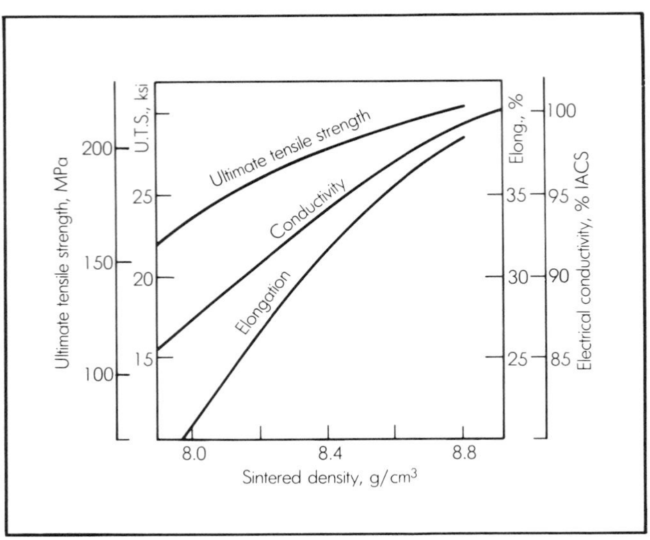


**Fig. 17-48 Effect of density on properties of parts made from electrolytic copper powder.**

silvers (copper-nickel-zinc alloys) are produced from prealloyed powders. Copper-aluminum alloy powder produced by atomizing the molten alloy with a stream of nitrogen forms the basis for the fabrication of copper that is dispersion strengthened with alumina.

Copper-lead powders are used in the production of bearings that consist of a bearing alloy lining on a steel shell primarily for main and connecting rod bearings. Since copper and lead are not completely miscible even in the liquid state, the alloys from which the powder is produced are melted in electric induction furnaces that have a stirring action to keep the metals finely dispersed. The alloys are then water atomized into powder.

Copper-based metallic filter materials have a copper-tin-bronze composition and are produced from spherical powder. Loose powder sintering of powders with a narrow particle size distribution results in filters having an optimum combination of properties required in filters: retention of fine impurity particles and reasonable fluid permeability.

## Properties and Specifications

The data presented in this section relates primarily to compositions that are widely used commercially for structural parts.

**TABLE 17-16**
**Composition and Properties of P M Bronze**

Composition of PM Bronze, MPIF CT-0010: 86.3-90.5% Cu, 9.5-10.5% Sn, 0-1.7% graphite, 0-1.0% Fe. Other elements total 0.5% max.
Properties of PM Bronze CT-0010

| Density Range | Ultimate Tensile Strength psi | Ultimate Tensile Strength MPa | Compressive Yield Strength, 0.2% Offset psi | Compressive Yield Strength, 0.2% Offset MPa | Elongation, % | Comparable Specifications |
|---|---|---|---|---|---|---|
| N:5.6-6.0g/cm$^3$ AS | 8000 | 55 | 7000 | 48 | 1.0 | SAE 840 |
| R:6.4-6.8g/cm$^3$ | 14,000 | 97 | 11,000 | 76 | 1.0 | SAE 841 |
| S:6.8-7.2g/cm$^3$ | 18,000 | 124 | 17,500 | 121 | 2.5 | SAE 842<br>ASTM B255 Type II |

**TABLE 17-17**
**Composition and Properties of Sintered Brass and Sintered Leaded Brass**

| Density Range | Ultimate Tensile Strength psi | Ultimate Tensile Strength MPa | Tensile Yield Strength 0.2% Offset psi | Tensile Yield Strength 0.2% Offset MPa | Elongation, % | Hardness |
|---|---|---|---|---|---|---|
| Composition of PM 90/10 Brass Designation CZ-0010: 88.0-91.0% Cu, 8.3-12.0% Zn, 0-0.3% Fe. Total other elements 0.4% max. Properties of PM 90/10 Brass CZ-0010 | | | | | | |
| T:7.2-7.6g/cm$^3$ | 20,000 | 138 | 9000 | 62 | 13 | Rockwell H57 |
| U:7.6-8.0g/cm$^3$ | 27,000 | 186 | 10,000 | 69 | 18 | Rockwell H70 |
| Composition of PM 90/10 Leaded Brass, MPIF Designation CZP-0210: 86.0-90.0% Cu, 7.3-13.0% Zn, 1.0-2.0% Lead, 0-0.3% Fe. Total other elements 0.4% max. Properties of PM 90/10 Leaded Brass, CZP-0210 | | | | | | |
| T:7.2-7.6g/cm$^3$ | 18,000 | 124 | 7000 | 48 | 14 | Rockwell H46 |
| U:7.6-8.0g/cm$^3$ | 25,500 | 176 | 8000 | 55 | 20 | Rockwell H60 |

**Structural parts from pure copper.** The raw material for PM structural parts from pure copper must be a high-purity copper powder. Green compacts from copper powder pressed to high densities tend to expand during sintering because of gas entrapment in the pores. The usual practice in producing copper parts with high final densities is to compact the powder at moderate pressures of 15-18 tons/in.[2] (207-248 MPa); sinter the compact at 122-302° F (50-150° C) below the melting point of copper; repress the sintered compact to the desired high density; and then resinter the compact to obtain an annealed structure, if desired. The effect of density on physical properties and on electrical conductivity of copper powder is shown in Fig. 17-48. Typical tensile properties and electrical conductivity of copper PM parts are listed in Table 17-15.

**PM bronze structural parts.** Powder metallurgy bronze parts usually are produced from mixtures of copper and tin powders by methods similar to those used for self-lubricating bronze bearings. The compositions and properties contained in MPIF Standard 35 are shown in Table 17-16.[14]

**PM brass structural parts.** In contrast to bronze structural parts, PM parts from brass and leaded brass are produced from prealloyed atomized powder. The purpose of lead in the lead bearing compositions is to make it easier to compact the powder and to facilitate machining of the sintered parts. Adding lithium stearate as a lubricant (instead of zinc stearate as used for iron powder) to the powder improves the mechanical properties of brass. The composition and properties listed in MPIF Standard 35 for a 90/10 brass and 90/10 leaded brass are shown in Table 17-17.

## POWDER METALLURGY SUPERALLOYS

The term *superalloy* is applied to alloys of iron, nickel, and cobalt which have high strength at temperatures of 1100° F (600° C) and higher. They are of primary interest for components in jet aircraft engines and for aerospace applications. A large amount of work has gone into the development of superalloys by powder metallurgy. The development work is concerned with nickel-based superalloys having compositions near those of alloys produced by casting or by casting and working, and with dispersion-strengthened alloys.

### Nickel Base

The high temperature strength of nickel-based superalloys is attributed to the presence of coherent precipitates, which are nickel-aluminum and nickel-titanium intermetallic compounds produced by solution treatment and aging. In addition to high temperature strength, the alloys must have corrosion resistance, which requires sufficient chromium in the composition. The advanced alloys developed to obtain balanced stress rupture and corrosion resistance exhibit in the cast condition gross segregation and structural inhomogeneity, which is a principal reason why these alloys are produced by powder metallurgy methods.

A principal application of powder metallurgy superalloys is turbine discs in jet engines. In this application, stresses up to 70,000 psi (480 MPa) and temperatures as high as 1400° F (760° C) are encountered. Until this temperature is reached, a relatively fine grained material has better strength than a coarse-grained material. The principal methods of producing superalloy powders are argon atomization, vacuum atomization, and the rotating electrode process. One method for hot consolidating superalloy powders is "Gatorizing" (see Fig. 17-43, which is described earlier under "Special PM Processes").

### Dispersion-Strengthened Superalloys

A great amount of research has been done on oxide dispersion strengthened superalloys. The aim in this work is to produce alloys that retain their strength at higher temperatures than the nickel-based superalloys strengthened by precipitation strengthening with the gamma prime phase. The oxides in the fine dispersion in nickel, iron, and cobalt are generally thorium or yttrium oxide. These oxides have been found to be stable, while aluminum oxide is not stable. In addition to work on oxide dispersion strengthened nickel alloys primarily of a fundamental character, three commercial approaches to producing the alloys based on wet methods were developed. Among the well-known methods is "TD-Nickel" (Thoria Dispersed Nickel) developed by the DuPont Company; the so-called "DS-Nickel" of Sherritt Gordon Mines Ltd.; and oxide dispersion strengthened nickel and cobalt-based alloys developed by Sylvania Electric Products, Inc.

# QUALITY CONTROL

When parts are produced in large numbers by a high-volume process such as powder metallurgy, 100% inspection is not only slow and costly, but impractical. In addition, reliance on inspection does not assure elimination of all defective parts. Mass inspection tends to be careless; operators become fatigued; and inspection gages become worn or out of adjustment. In relying on inspection, the risk of overlooking defective parts is variable and of unknown magnitude; whereas, in a planned sampling program, the risk can be calculated.

Powder metallurgy technology is well suited to the application of quality control practices based on statistical sampling principles. Using this approach, mathematical concepts underlie the inspection of parts being produced, to determine whether or not the entire stream of production is acceptable. To apply these quality control techniques in inspection, the following steps are implemented:

- Sample the stream of manufactured parts.
- Measure the critical "monitoring" dimensions.
- Calculate deviations of dimensions from the "mean."
- Construct a control chart.
- Plot succeeding data on the control chart.

For detailed information on an effective, systematic approach to tolerance control, refer to Chapter 2, "Tolerance Control," in Volume I, *Machining*, of this Handbook series. (A general discussion of quality control is presented in Volume IV, *Assembly, Testing and Quality Control,* of this Handbook series.)

## POWDER TESTS

Standard methods for sampling finished lots of metal powder have been developed by ASTM Committee B-9 and the standards committee of MPIF. A description of these methods can be found in ASTM Standard B215 and in MPIF Standard 1. The two tests which have been standardized by ASTM and MPIF for chemical analysis of metal powders are:

- ASTM Standard E 159, MPIF Standard 2 for the so-called hydrogen loss of copper, tungsten, and iron powder.
- ASTM Standard E 194, MPIF Standard 6 for acid-insoluble content of copper and iron powder.

The following methods are used for determining particle size, particle size distribution, particle shape and structure, and specific surface:

- Sieving.
- Microscopic sizing.
- Methods based on Stokes' Law:
  - ($c_1$) The roller air analyzer.
  - ($c_2$) The micromerograph.
  - ($c_3$) Light and X-ray (sedigraph) turbidimetry.
- Coulter counter and particle analysis by light obscuration.
- Laser light scattering; the microtrac particle analyzer.

For powders with a particle size distribution that includes primarily particle sizes larger than 1732 μ in. (44 μ m), sieving is the most important method. The roller air analyzer, the micromerograph, the Coulter counter, the light obscuration particle analyzer and the microtrac analyzer are used for powders with finer particle sizes, under 1732 μ in. and most commonly in the range from 39-1575 μ in. (1-40 μ m). The turbidimetric methods have been developed for the very fine refractory metal and refractory compound powders with particle sizes from less than 39-390 μ in. (1-10 μ m).

Two methods used for determining the specific surface of metal powders are:

- The Fisher subsieve sizer which is based on permeametry.
- The gas adsorption (BET) method.

## QUALITY CONTROL PROGRAM[15]

Following is a representative in-house PM quality control program, as practiced by a manufacturer of approximately 200 different high-density structural PM parts. Most of the parts weigh 6.8 g/cm$^3$, which is 88% of theoretical density, or higher. Part production runs range from 10,000-100,000 pieces. The metal powder is primarily iron with copper or nickel and some graphite. The quality control system locates unacceptable parts in process, at the operations where they occur—rather than waiting to find them when they have progressed to finished parts.

### Powder Quality Control

The initial quality control checks are divided between various departments. When the powder is received, receiving inspection personnel make a visual check of each 2500 lb (1134 kg) bulk pack. They determine if there are any rust balls in the powder, if there is any graphite or lubricant segregation, or if the powder is contaminated with foreign material. Inspection personnel also take a powder sample from each container and forward it to the metallurgical laboratory for testing.

Laboratory personnel check each sample of powder for apparent density and flow rate. If the results do not fall within specifications, the containers are rejectable. These results, if acceptable, are returned to the inspection personnel, who list this information on each container. Depending upon the sampling plan prescribed for each supplier and each specification, physical properties of the incoming blend are determined in the metallurgical laboratory.

In some instances, suppliers may be required to submit a preshipment sample for testing. In all cases, the supplier's in-house test data is sent to the metallurgical engineering quality control section. All suppliers are audited by complete test work on one blend per month. Physical tests performed in the laboratory determine the following:

1. Compressibility—Transverse rupture bars are compacted on a tensile testing machine. Each specification requires that a minimum green density be attained when compacted at a specified tonnage.
2. Green transverse rupture strength—Transverse rupture bars are pressed to a specified density and then broken as per ASTM Standard B312-76.
3. Sintered transverse rupture strength—Transverse rupture bars are pressed to a specified density and sintered in a production furnace. They are then broken as per ASTM Standard B528-76. Transverse rupture bars from a standard lot of powder are pressed and sintered at the

same time as the incoming blend bars. This standard lot is one which has been tested extensively in the metallurgical laboratory and which has known physical properties. This standard is used as a control to ensure sintering conditions are acceptable and to validate the results of incoming lots.

4. Sintered ultimate tensile strength—Tensile bars are pressed to a specified density and sintered in a production furnace. Bars from the standard powder are pressed and sintered at the same time. These are then broken as per MPIF Standard 10-63.
5. Sintered dimensional change—Transverse rupture bars of a specified density are sintered with standard bars of the same density. The difference between the die length and sintered transverse rupture bar length is determined for both the test bars and the standard bars. The incoming powder test bars must be within 0.05% of the standard bars.
6. Sintered hardness—Apparent hardness of sintered tensile and transverse bars is determined.
7. Sintered density—Sintered density is determined by spraying the bars with "krylon" or another appropriate sealer and checking density by weighing wet and dry. For transverse rupture bars, the density may be determined using dry weight, and volume by direct measurement.
8. Composition—C, Mn, Ni, Cr, Mo and Cu content are determined for sintered bars.

After the necessary test work is performed and the results are found to be acceptable, the powder is released for use by production.

### Pressing Quality Control

Quality responsibilities during the compaction of the piece parts are divided as follows:

- Manufacturing Responsibilities:
  1. After release from the laboratory, and prior to compaction, all of the powder is screened to remove any rust balls, graphite lumps, or foreign material. Manufacturing personnel are also responsible for cleaning the hoppers before screening, to remove any powder or graphite buildup which may be accumulating.
  2. During the setup, the press operator is responsible for checking all thickness dimensions, overall density, and section densities, as well as for detecting any cracks or shear which may be in the part.
  3. During the production run, the press operator makes visual checks, dimensional checks, overall density and section density checks a minimum of once per hour. These results are entered into an operator's log book. An operator who is having difficulties is required to make as many checks as necessary to ensure that quality is being maintained.
- Inspection Responsibilities:
  1. After a new setup, a line inspector checks all sizes, overall density, and section densities, and makes a visual check for imperfections on the part prior to giving setup approval.
  2. Inspection personnel are required to make visual, size, and density checks two times per shift for each press.

  The results are then entered into an inspection log, and notations are made of any problems found.

### Sintering Quality Control

As the parts are being sintered or sintered and hardened, quality responsibilities are divided as follows:

- Manufacturing Responsibilities:
  1. During setup, the furnace operator is responsible for setting the belt speed, dew point, and temperatures, and for belt loading. As the first pieces exit the furnace, the operator checks for sizes and hardness and performs any physical testing that may be required.
  2. During the production run, the furnace operator is responsible every hour for measuring critical dimensions and hardness and for any physical testing. He also checks dew point, belt speed, and temperatures every hour. All of this information is entered into the operator's log book.
- Inspection Responsibilities:
  1. After a setup, the line inspector takes some of the first parts out of the furnace, checks dimensions and hardness, performs any necessary physical testing, and visually inspects the parts.
  2. During production sintering, the inspector makes the same checks as the line inspector, two times per shift. This information is entered into the inspection log book.
- Metallurgical Engineering Responsibilities:

  Every week, inspection personnel submit sintered samples to metallurgical engineering personnel as an audit of sintering practices. One sample per furnace per material specification is submitted for microexamination and cross-sectional hardness. If problems with dew point, hardness, or functional tests occur during daily sintering runs, samples are submitted to engineering personnel for disposition.

**Steam oxidation quality control**. If parts are being steam oxidized for pressure tightness, three pieces from each furnace load are checked for hardness and leak resistance.

**Final inspection quality control**. As the parts are finished, the line inspector makes a final quality check. Parts from each load are randomly selected, checked for accuracy of all dimensions and hardness, and inspected visually. Any necessary physical tests or pressure tightness checks also are performed. The audit frequency is strictly dependent upon the past quality history of the particular parts, materials, or processing.

## NONDESTRUCTIVE EVALUATION

The problems inherent in obtaining accurate and meaningful data useful in quality control have prompted the development and application of nondestructive tests particularly suited for powder metallurgy materials. In one method the specimen is excited by a piezoelectric or electromagnetic transducer. At the fundamental resonant frequency, the amplitude of vibration reaches a maximum. Another technique consists of measuring the ultrasonic velocity by placing transducers on opposite faces of a specimen and measuring the time necessary to transmit a pulse.

# CHAPTER 17

## QUALITY CONTROL

Nondestructive techniques, such as ultrasonic velocity and resonant frequency measurements, hold considerable promise for evaluating the quality of PM parts. A principal benefit of these techniques is that they can provide nondestructive assessment of pore size, pore shape, and the extent of interparticle bonding, in addition to detecting gross flaws, such as cracks. This is an especially valuable capability with PM materials, which often exhibit wide ranges of strength arising from variations in processing variables and powder characteristics, even when cracks are not present.

Variations in sintering time, temperature, atmosphere, powder type, contaminants, and other variables can produce parts that appear sound but have undesirably low mechanical properties. The ability to rapidly assess the extent of sintering in individual parts is a useful technique for monitoring product quality.

### Data Correlation

The ultrasonic velocity through a material is the speed of transmission of a high-frequency (MHz range) sound wave. The velocity is dependent on the interatomic forces in the metal, but microstructural features have an important effect. In recent years it has been found that the microstructural characteristics which control the mechanical strength of some materials, such as PM and cast irons, also control their ultrasonic velocity.

Figure 17-49 compares mechanically measured tensile strengths with nondestructively predicted strengths for specimens sintered for 20 min. Very little deviation existed between the predicted and the actual strength values. Most predicted values differed no more than 1 or 2 ksi from the measured values, and the greatest deviation was 4 ksi. The correlation of velocity and resonant frequency with both yield and tensile strength indicates that these methods provide a useful nondestructive means for assessing quality of PM parts.

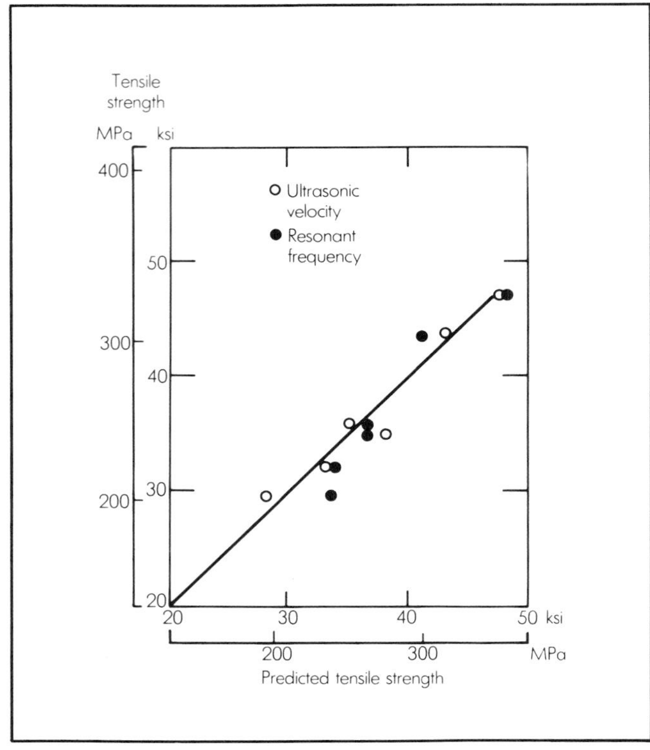


**Fig. 17-49 Comparison between measured strength and strength predicted from ultrasonic velocity and resonant frequency.**

### Testing of Production Parts

Ultrasonic velocity and resonant frequency measurements have been used to get information on the extent of sintering in PM materials. In practice, differences in the techniques used to take the measurements and differences in part size and shape may affect the choice of equipment and technique to be used. Ultrasonic velocity measurements can be taken by placing a small [approximately 1/2″ (13 mm) diam] transducer on one flat surface and measuring the time required to receive a reflected signal. Alternatively, two transducers can be used on plane parallel surfaces of a part. The shape of the part is not as important as the ability to transmit the sound wave from one surface to the other. Curved transducers are available for testing curved parts. The ultrasonic velocity measurement is quick and relatively simple to perform, and a variety of equipment for industrial use is available.

Ultrasonic velocity is influenced to some extent by the length and thickness of the part, and subtle differences in measurement technique can result in different measured values. Measurements of similarly shaped parts by a consistent technique should provide a good comparison of material properties.

Resonant frequency is measured by vibrating an exciter plate adjacent to the part being examined. At the resonant frequency, the part vibrates at an increased amplitude which is detected by a pick-up plate. The frequency of vibration depends on the part shape as well as sintering conditions, but comparison of similar parts eliminates the shape variable and allows evaluation of the extent of sintering.

## SAFETY

Until recent years, powder metallurgy has worked with comparatively safe materials such as tungsten carbide, copper, tin, brass, nickel, and iron. Now, aluminum, magnesium, titanium, zirconium, and even uranium are being processed by powder metallurgy and, therefore, special precautions must be taken to avoid the hazards of fire and explosions.

Metal powders of even such active materials as aluminum, magnesium, titanium, and zirconium can be used with complete safety if dust clouds are avoided and proper precautions are taken in handling them to avoid sources of ignition or chemical reaction. Manufacturers of PM parts should thoroughly review their plant operations and establish the appropriate safety procedures.

For employee/operator protection, various safety procedures and devices are applicable. Among the latest developments are retrofit units that utilize infrared light to provide a safety "curtain" as an invisible protective barrier on PM compacting machines. These devices are connected into the emergency-stop circuit of mechanical clutches and hydraulic compactors. Also included among safety devices are capacitance-type (radio frequency), optical, and ultrasonic presence-sensing devices. Additional information is provided in Chapter 5, "Presses for Sheet Metal Forming," and Chapter 20, "Safety in Forming."

## EXPLOSION HAZARDS

The Bureau of Mines' laboratories have investigated dust explosions for over 30 years and have published a number of reports detailing their extensive findings. The summary in Table 17-18 is based on the ignition and explosion characteristics of each metal compared with coal, which is the dividing point between moderate and strong explosions. While this is a useful guide to the relative explosibility hazard, fires and/or explosions have occurred with iron, lead, nickel, and zinc when in extremely fine form (with resulting high surface area). The Bureau of Mines has tested a variety of screen sizes on various metals and found that explosibility increases with the fineness of powders. There are many indications that practically all metal dusts can become explosive if they are fine enough—and powders are continually being made finer.

### Fire Hazard Avoidance

A fire or an explosion is a chemical reaction which has three requirements: fuel, a source of ignition, and oxidant. A fire or an explosion can be prevented by removing any one of these factors.

**Dust**. If no dust cloud is present, there will be no fuel; so metal powder users should avoid the formation of dust clouds. Equipment should be designed to avoid the open dumping of powder. Proper ventilation and dust collection equipment should be used wherever dust clouds may occur. Good housekeeping is also essential, since dust accumulating on high horizontal places, such as rafters and windowsills, can be easily dislodged by drafts, bumps, and other means to create a dust cloud.

**Ignition**. Open-ignition sources can be prevented in the powder-handling area, and this is sufficient for the less dangerous metal powders. But the active metals such as aluminum, magnesium, titanium, and zirconium require additional care, since static electricity or small sparks can set them off. The following precautions are necessary to eliminate potential sources of ignition throughout the area in which such powders are to be handled:

1. Electrical grounding of all equipment, including all containers should be thorough. Because static cannot be grounded through an oil or grease film in bearings, it is necessary to provide wire "jumpers" around lubricating films.
2. All electric wiring equipment and lighting in the area involved must be explosion proof, conforming to National Electrical Manufacturers Association (NEMA) rating Class II, Group E.
3. All sources of mechanical friction should be eliminated wherever a dust cloud can exist.
4. When tools are required, nonsparking types should be used. It is important to remember that friction, as by hammering, sliding, or rubbing, etc., must be avoided, even with nonsparking-type tools.
5. Sparks caused by metal striking metal must be avoided.
6. Open flames in the area where the powders are being handled must be avoided. No smoking should be permitted.
7. All equipment and the surrounding area should be completely cleaned before repairs are made, particularly if a torch or welding equipment is to be used in the area.

**Oxidant**. The oxidant can be made ineffective or removed from the mixture, and this should always be done when a dust cloud is being created, as in the blending of metal powders. When possible, it is preferable to use premix powders and let the powder producer assume the responsibility of performing the hazardous blending operation.

### Explosive Mix Precautions

To eliminate an explosive mix, it is not generally necessary to remove all the oxygen. The Bureau of Mines has studied the effect of various mixtures of inert gases with air—a process referred to as "inerting." The Bureau has published data for

**TABLE 17-18**
**Explosibility of Metal Powders**

| Severe | Strong | Moderate | Weak | None |
|---|---|---|---|---|
| Atomized aluminum | Titanium hydride | Silicon | Aluminum-iron alloy | Aluminum-bronze alloy |
| Aluminum premixes | Zirconium hydride | Boron | Zinc | Beryllium-bronze alloy |
| Aluminum-magnesium alloy | Aluminum-silicon alloy | Aluminum-nickel alloy | Gold bronze | Manganese-bronze alloy |
| Magnesium | Calcium silicide | Aluminum-lithium alloy | Ferrosilicon | Nickel |
| Thorium hydride | Iron-carbonyl | Aluminum-cobalt alloy | Vanadium | Selenium |
| Zirconium | Ferrotitanium | Ferromanganese | Antimony | Stainless steel |
| Uranium hydride | Coal | Aluminum-copper alloy | Cadmium | |
| Titanium | | Chromium | Ferrovanadium | |
| Uranium | | Manganese | Ferrochromium | |
| Thorium | | Tantalum | Lead | |
| | | Tin | Tellurium | |
| | | Iron-hydrogen reduced | Molybdenum | |
| | | | Cobalt | |
| | | | Tungsten | |
| | | | Beryllium | |
| | | | Copper | |

most reactive metal powders, indicating the maximum amount of oxygen which may be present when inerting with carbon dioxide or nitrogen.

**Atmosphere**. Great care must be taken in selecting a suitable atmosphere, since many metals react with supposedly inert gases. The limiting percent of oxygen for 100-mesh atomized aluminum ranges from 3% with an air-$CO_2$ mixture to 9% with air-$N_2$. Most magnesium, titanium, uranium, and zirconium powders cannot be inerted with $CO_2$, while the oxygen content must be less than 2-3% with air-$N_2$ mixtures. Helium is generally recommended for inerting magnesium, and is probably advisable with titanium, uranium, zirconium, etc.

Before inerting, reference should be made to the Bureau of Mines report and the National Fire Protection Association standard, and operations should be conducted well below the minimum oxygen levels indicated. When a mixture of powder is to be inerted, it may be necessary to run special explosibility tests to determine a safe atmosphere, particularly if $CO_2$ might be the inerting ingredient.

**Blending**. The blending of metal powders is probably the most hazardous operation undertaken by a powder metallurgy plant. The blending equipment must be filled with the protective atomosphere before powder is charged into it, and any other equipment or container must be similarly purged prior to receiving the product. Care must be exercised to minimize dust clouds when filling or discharging the powder, even with the above precautions; and all sources of ignition must be avoided, as previously discussed. The blender should be operated at the lowest practical speed to avoid abrading the powder particles.

**Dust collection**. In operating a dust collection system, special precautions are necessary because of the suspension of the finest metal dust in air. The powder should be conveyed in a concentration well below that designated as the "minimum explosive limit." A dry collector, operated where dust is concentrated, will contain an explosive dust cloud and must be located in an isolated area well away from any source of ignition. No personnel should be allowed in the immediate vicinity of the collector while it is operating.

Wet collectors, which collect dust under water, are safer, but the metal powder usually ends up as scrap. Since chemical reactions between water and metal are possible with the evolution of hydrogen and the development of heat, sources of ignition must be avoided in the gas-stream discharge. The sludge containing the metal powder should be brought to a safe area as soon as possible so that the reaction can proceed to its conclusion. When working with metal powders, one should also be careful that combinations of metal powders, together or with other chemicals, are safe. The well-known thermite mixture of aluminum powder and iron oxide is safe under controlled conditions, but could cause trouble under certain circumstances.

**Halogenated hydrocarbons**. The National Aeronautics and Space Administration (NASA) has investigated the reactions of metal powders with halogenated hydrocarbons and has concluded that great care should be exercised when combining any metal powder with any halogenated hydrocarbon. Aluminum, magnesium, titanium, barium, lithium, and beryllium have been found to explode on impact with various halogenated hydrocarbons including Freon MF, Freon TF, carbon tetrachloride, trichloroethylene, and perchloroethylene. This problem could arise with the use of an aerosol lubricant spray on the compacting press (which would supply the necessary impact).

## FIRE FIGHTING

Special fire fighting procedures must be planned for areas containing metal dusts, particularly those of active metals. The local fire department should be advised of the plans, and the plant personnel should be carefully trained.

Drums in a storage area would probably not be subject to a fire, but they should be kept cool. Extreme heat may increase the pressure of the air in the drums to the point at which the drums would burst.

### Loose Powder Fire

Loose metal powder is not generally processed or stored in the vicinity of combustible material, so it is unlikely that a metal powder fire will occur. If a fire should develop in the area of loose metal powder, it should be left alone to burn out by itself. Dry sand can be carefully spread on the fire, working from the outside edges to avoid creating a dust cloud. Many of the more dangerous materials from an explosive standpoint, such as atomized aluminum, magnesium, and titanium, require a high temperature before igniting and probably would not ignite. However, uranium ignites spontaneously, and zirconium, gold, bronze, and many hydrides ignite at less than 400° F (204° C).

Streams of water or gas (for instance, from a carbon dioxide extinguisher) should be avoided, since they could stir up a dust cloud that could result in an explosion. It is most important that the fire department be aware of this and of the plant areas requiring special precautions. Plant fire-protection systems should be designed so that automatic sprinklers and $CO_2$ jets used for building protection do not contact the metal powders in such fashion that they stir up dust.

### Fire Fighting Residue

The residues of fires and fire fighting may also be hazardous. For example, the following reactions can occur, resulting in heat and/or dangerous gases:

1. Metal + $H_2O$ ⟶ metal oxide + $H_2$ = heat
2. Metal + $CO_2$ ⟶ metal oxide + C
   Metal + $CO_2$ ⟶ metal oxide + CO
3. Metal + $CCl_4$ ⟶ metal chloride + C + heat

Temperatures above 9000° F (5000° C) are possible from these reactions. Therefore, it is important to be very careful when cleaning up after a fire. If powder is in a container, it can be moved to an isolated location and left until the reaction ceases and the drum cools. If the drum is sealed, the cover should be gently loosened to relieve the pressure and the powder should be left to burn itself out.

**References**

1. Joel S. Hirschhorn, *Introduction to Powder Metallurgy*, (New York: American Powder Metallurgy Institute, 1969).
2. Fritz V. Lenel, *Powder Metallurgy Principles and Applications*, (Princeton, NJ: Metal Powder Industries Federation, 1980).
3. American Society for Testing and Materials, *Definitions of Terms Used in Powder Metallurgy*, ASTM Standard B243, Philadelphia.

# BIBLIOGRAPHY

4. B. H. Amstead, Phillip F. Ostwald, Myron L. Begeman, *Manufacturing Processes*, 7th ed., (New York: John Wiley & Sons, 1979).
5. H. W. Blakeslee, *Powder Metallurgy in Aerospace Research*, NASA SP-5098, (Philadelphia: Franklin Institute; and Washington: NASA, 1971).
6. Samuel Bradbury, ed., *Source Book on Powder Metallurgy*, (Metals Park, OH: American Society for Metals, 1979).
7. Hoeganaes Corp., *Creating with Metal Powders*, 5th ed., (Riverton, NJ: Hoeganaes Corp., 1979).
8. American Society for Testing and Materials, *op. cit.*
9. *Ibid.*
10. Lenel, *op. cit.*
11. Powder Metallurgy Equipment Association, *Powder Metallurgy Equipment Directory*, 13th ed., (Princeton, NJ: Metal Powder Industries Federation, 1982).
12. John A. Schey, *Introduction to Manufacturing Processes*, (New York: McGraw-Hill, 1977).
13. Powder Metallurgy Equipment Association, *op. cit.*
14. Schey, *op. cit.*
15. Loren C. Bone, "Quality Control System of P/M at Caterpillar Tractor Co." (technical paper), Metal Powder Industries Federation, Princeton, NJ. 1982.

### Bibliography

Alves, A. L. *The Application of Robots to Production of Hot P/M Forgings.* SME Technical Paper MS79-779, 1979.

Billiett, Romain. "Plastic Metals: From Fiction to Reality with Injection Molded P/M Materials." Paper presented at the National Powder Metallurgy Conference, May 1982. Sponsor: Metal Powder Industries Federation (MPIF).

Clapp, David D. *A Departure from Traditional Production of P/M Parts.* SME Technical Paper MF76-397, 1976.

Dallas, Daniel B. "A New Approach to Injection Molding." *Manufacturing Engineering* (May 1975), pp. 26-27.

DeGroat, George H. *Tooling for Metal Powder Parts.* New York: McGraw-Hill Book Co., Inc., 1958.

Dreger, Donald R. "Progress in Powder Metallurgy." *Machine Design* (November 9, 1978), pp. 116-121.

*Engineering Properties of Zinc Alloys.* New York: International Lead Zinc Research Organization, Inc., 1980.

Feneberger, K., and Feichtinger, A. R. "Characterization of Graphite/Carbon Powders for use in Iron Powder Metallurgy." Paper presented at the National Powder Metallurgy Conference, May 1982. Sponsor: Metal Powder Industries Federation (MPIF).

Froes, F. H., Eylon, D., Wirth, G., Grundhoff, K. J., and Smarsly, W. "Fatigue Properties of Hot Isostatically Pressed Ti-6A1-4V Powders." Paper presented at the National Powder Metallurgy Conference, May 1982. Sponsor: Metal Powder Industries Federation (MPIF).

Globus, Alfred R. *Titanium Metal Powder.* New York: Vantage Press, Inc., 1963.

Hegland, Donald E. "Gaining Ground with the Nonmachining Processes." *Production Engineering* (May 1982), pp. 44-48.

"Integrated Powder Compacting Process." *Manufacturing Engineering* (December 1975), pp. 44-45.

*International Powder Metallurgy Directory.* Shrewsbury, Shropshire, England: MPR Publishing Services Ltd., 1982.

Irving, Robert R. "All Systems are Go for Powder Metallurgy." *Iron Age* (July 28, 1980), pp. 41-45.

Jandeska, William F. *Strength and Ductility Enhancement of Low Temperature Sintered Iron Powder Structures.* SAE Paper No. 820231, 1982.

Jones, P. K., and Wisker, J. W. Production of Precision Automotive Components by the Powder Forging Process. SAE Technical Paper 780361, 1978.

Jones, W. D. *Fundamental Principles of Powder Metallurgy.* London: Edward Arnold (Publishers) Ltd., 1960.

Kibrick, E. H.; Rennhack, E. H.; and Runkle, J. C. "Hot Isostatic Pressing of Niobium C-103 Alloy Shapes." Paper presented at National Powder Metallurgy Conference, May 1982. Sponsor: Metal Powder Industries Federation (MPIF).

Kosinski, Edward J. "The Mechanical Properties of Titanium P/M Parts Produced from Superclean Powders." Paper presented at the National Powder Metallurgy Conference, May 1982. Sponsor: Metal Powder Industries Federation (MPIF).

Kuhn, Howard A. *Designing Powder Preforms.* SME Technical Paper MF76-395, 1976.

Kunkel, Robert N. *Tooling Design for Powder Metallurgy Parts.* Dearborn, MI: American Society of Tool and Manufacturing Engineers, 1968.

Leone, Frank D. "A New High Strength P/M Alloy Steel and Case Histories." Paper presented at the National Powder Metallurgy Conference, May 1982. Sponsor: Metal Powder Industries Federation (MPIF).

McManus, George J. "Cyclops' 'CAP' Process Moves P/M to a New Level." *Iron Age* (February 1, 1982), pp. MP14-16.

Metal Powder Industries Federation. *Material Standards and Specifications.* MPIF Standard 35, Princeton, NJ, 1981.

Peck, L. D. "Metal Injection Molding Comes Out of the Laboratory." *Machine and Tool Blue Book* (October 1981), pp. 80-91.

"P/M Forging Leaps Ahead." *Production* (October 1981), pp. 106-108.

"P/M Parts Pack New Punch." *Product Engineering* (August 1979).

*Powder Metallurgy Equipment Manual.* Princeton, NJ: Powder Metallurgy Equipment Assoc., 1977.

Price, Peter E. "Hot Isostatic Pressing in the Aerospace Industry." *Metal Progress* (February 1982), pp. 46-47.

"Robot Ends Worker Fatigue in Hot P/M Forging." *Iron Age* (January 23, 1978).

Roll, Kempton H. *The Role of Powder Metallurgy in Modern Manufacturing.* SME Technical Paper EM78-279, 1979.

Stephenson, Henry R. *Design Capabilities for Powder Metal Miniature Parts.* SME Technical Paper MR79-510.

Veidis, Mikelis V. *The Forging of Sintered Preforms.* SME Technical Paper MF79-129, 1979.

Weggel, Ralph W. "The basics of Force Feed Roll Briquetting." *Manufacturing Engineering* (March 1982), pp. 107-109.

Wick, Charles. "Hot Forming P/M Preforms." *Manufacturing Engineering* (May 1978), pp. 34-39.

Wigotsky, Victor. "Full Density P/M Hits Its Stride." *Design Engineering* (April 1982).

Zovas, Peter; Hwang, K.S.; Li, Chaojin; and German, R. M. "Activated and Liquid Phase Sintering: Progress and Problems." Paper presented at the National Powder Metallurgy Conference, May 1982. Sponsor: Metal Powder Industries Federation (MPIF).

CHAPTER

# 18

# Plastics Forming

# PLASTICS FORMING

The commercially important plastics resins are all derived from natural resources that are in plentiful supply. Many of the plastics are byproducts from gasoline refining operations. Principal raw material sources for plastics are coal, air, water, petroleum, natural gas, limestone, salt, sulfur, and agricultural byproducts. Products called intermediates are made from these basic materials and are subsequently combined to make plastics resins. In the plastics industry, the sectors involved with the production of plastics products include resin producers, compounders, processors, mold and die makers, manufacturing companies, consultants, and chemical additive suppliers.

Thermoplastics is the family of plastics that can be recycled. Thermosets, the other key family of plastics, is so named because once it is set it cannot be reset in any other shape or cannot be recycled, although byproduct uses are found for thermoset scrap material. Processors usually receive the thermoset plastics resins in a partially polymerized state to facilitate molding by the traditional techniques.

*Plastics* as a word is not the precise name of all the available materials, hence the need to adopt the term *polymer*. This term denotes a material that has gone through a polymerization cycle, which is essentially a chemical process for which the original base material can be oil, gas, or coal. The primary polymer groups and typical applications are listed in Tables 18-1 and 18-2.[1]

CHAPTER CONTENTS:



## NOMENCLATURE

This section provides definitions of selected terms of interest to manufacturing engineers who are involved with the production of plastics parts.[2]

**A-stage** An early stage in the reaction of a thermosetting resin in which the material is fusible and still soluble in certain liquids.

**ABS** *See* acrylonitrile butadiene styrene.

**acetal resin** The molecular structure of this polymer is that of a linear acetal, consisting of unbranched poly-oxymethylene chains.

**acrylic resin** A synthetic resin prepared from acrylic acid or from a derivative of acrylic acid.

**acrylonitrile butadiene styrene (ABS)** Acrylonitrile and styrene liquids and butadiene gas are polymerized in a variety of ratios to produce the family of ABS resins.

**additives** Products that are combined with resins and polymers as extenders or modifiers to alter the properties of the base polymer.

**air-assist forming** A method of thermoforming in which air flow or air pressure is used to partially preform the plastics sheet immediately prior to the final pulldown onto the mold using vacuum.

**air-slip forming** A variation of snap-back forming in which the male mold is enclosed in a box in such a manner that when the mold moves forward toward the hot plastics, air is trapped between the mold and the plastics sheet. As the mold advances, the plastics is kept away from it by the air cushion until the full travel is attained, at which point a vacuum is applied, removing the air cushion and forming the part against the plug.

**allyl diglycol carbonate (ADC)** A crystal clear thermosetting plastics with outstanding scratch resistance; used for goggles, etc.

**alloy** Composite material produced by blending polymers or copolymers with other polymers or elastomers under controlled conditions.

**allyl resin** A synthetic resin formed by the polymerization of chemical compounds containing the group $CH_2 = CH—CH_2—$.

**amino plastics** Urea and melamine formaldehyde. Also applicable to the polyamide (nylon) resins.

**amorphous polymers** Polymers that have a andomly oriented molecular structure with no definite order or regularity.

**aniline formaldehyde resins** Members of the aminoplastics family made by the condensation of formaldehyde and aniline in an acid solution. These resins are thermoplastic and have high dielectric strength.

**Antioxidant** A substance that prevents or slows down oxidation of plastics material that is exposed to air.

**antistatic agents** Materials and treatments used during or after the molding process to minimize static electricity in plastics materials.

**B-stage** An intermediate stage in the reaction of thermosetting resin in which the material softens when heated and swells in contact with certain liquids, but does not entirely fuse or dissolve. A B-stage resin is ready for curing.

*Contributors of sections of this chapter are: Robert W. Bainbridge, Bainbridge Consultants, Inc.; Glenn L. Beall, President, Glenn Beall/Engineering Inc.; D. M. Bigg, Projects Manager, Polymer Science and Technology, Battelle Columbus Laboratories; Christopher M. Hall, Product Manager RIM Machinery, Plastics Machinery Division, Cincinnati Milacron Marketing Co.; Joseph Hansmann, General Manager—Research and Development, Magna International, Inc.—Concord; John Kovalchuck, Director of Manufacturing Technology, Firelands College, Bowling Green State University; Roy L. Manns, President, Boston Plastics Group, Medical Electronic Independent Plastics Engineering Centre, Inc. (MEIPEC); William K. McConnell, Jr., President, McConnell Company, Inc.; Travis H. Meister, Consultant—Plastics; Dario Ramazzotti, President, Ramazzotti Design and Engineering.*

# CHAPTER 18

## NOMENCLATURE

**bag molding** A method of applying pressure during bonding or molding, in which a flexible cover exerts pressure on the material being molded, through the application of air pressure or the drawing of a vacuum.

**Bakelite** The proprietary name for phenolic and other plastics materials produced by the Union Carbide Corp.

**blow molding** A method of extrusion in which a parison (hollow tube) is forced into the shape of a mold cavity by internal air pressure.

**butadiene** A gas, insoluble in water but soluble in alcohol and ether, obtained from the cracking of petroleum and other methods. Butadiene is widely used in forming copolymers with styrene and other monomeric substances.

**butadiene styrene** A thermoplastic polymer used for film and sheet.

**C-stage** The final stage in the reactions of a thermosetting resin in which the material is relatively insoluble and infusible. Thermosetting resins in fully cured plastics are in this stage.

**cast** (1) The act of forming a plastics object by pouring a fluid monomer-polymer into an open mold, where it finishes polymerizing; (2) the act of forming plastics film and sheet by pouring liquid resin onto a moving belt or by precipitation in a chemical bath.

**centrifugal casting** A method of forming thermoplastics resins in which the granular resin is placed in a rotatable container, heated to a molten temperature and rotated to force the liquid resin to conform to the shape of the container.

**coextrusion** A process for extruding two or more materials in a single film or sheet. Two identical polymers can be laminated by coextrusion. Two or more extruders are used, and the extrudate is usually moved through a common die.

**commodity plastics** The term *commodity* identifies a group of plastics that are characterized by high-volume usage and general availability from sources other than the prime resin suppliers. Polyethylene, polystyrene, and polyvinylchloride are examples of commodity plastics.

**compression molding** A technique for thermoset molding in which the molding compound is placed in the open mold cavity, the mold is closed, and heat and pressure are applied until the material is cured.

**compression ratio** In an extruder screw, compression ratio is the ratio of volume available in the first flight at the hopper to the last flight at the end of the screw.

**continuous tube process** A blow-molding process that uses a continuous extrusion of tubing to feed into the blow molds.

**copolymer** *See* polymer and homopolymer.

**cross-linking** Applied to polymer molecules, the setting-up of chemical links between the molecular chains. The thermoset plastics are cross-linked at the molecular level.

**crystallinity** A state of molecular structure in some resins which denotes uniformity and compactness of the molecular chains that form the polymer.

**cure** The act of changing the physical properties of a material by chemical reaction, which may be condensation or addition-type polymerization, or vulcanization; accompanied by heat and catalysts, with or without pressure. For room-temperature curing systems, heat is generated by an exothermic reaction.

**drape-assist frame** In sheet thermoforming, a frame (made of wires or bars) shaped to the peripheries of the depressed areas of the mold and suspended above the sheet that is to be formed.

**drape forming** A method of forming thermoplastic sheet in which the sheet is clamped into a movable frame, heated, and draped over the high points of a male mold. Vacuum or air pressure is then applied to complete the forming operation.

**dry coloring** The method commonly used for coloring plastics by tumble blending uncolored particles of the plastics material with selected dyes and pigments.

**elastomer** A material which, at room temperature, stretches under low stress to at least twice its length and snaps back to the original length upon release of the stress. The term *elastomer* is commonly applied to synthetic rubber polymers.

**engineering plastics** Thermoset and thermoplastic materials whose characteristics and properties enable them to withstand mechanical loads (tension, impact, flexure, vibration, friction, etc.) combined with temperature changes. The reliability and predictability of engineering plastics makes them suitable for application in structural and load-bearing product design elements. Polycarbonate, ABS, acetal, and nylon are among the widely used engineering plastics.

**ethylene tetrafluoroethylene copolymer (ETFE)** A moldable variety of fluorocarbon (fluoroplastic) polytetrafluoroethylene (PTFE), for example, teflon (TFE)

**expanded plastics** *See* foamed plastics.

**filler** An inert substance added to a plastics resin to reduce cost and improve physical properties. The filler particles usually are small, in comparison to those used in reinforcements, but there is some overlap between the two additives.

**flake** The dry, unplasticized base of cellulose plastics.

**flock** Short fibers of cotton and other materials, used as fillers for molding materials.

**fluorocarbons** The family of plastics including polytetrafluoroethylene (PTFE), polychlorotrifluoroethylene (PCTFE), polyvinylidene and fluorinated ethylene propylene (FEP).

**foam molding** A molding process whereby heat-softened plastics containing a foaming (blowing) agent are injection molded into a cavity where they harden to produce a product that has a solid skin contiguous with a foam core. See also structural foam and sandwich molding.

**foamed plastics** Resins in sponge form.

**gate** In injection and transfer molding, the gate is the orifice through which the melt enters the cavity.

**glass transition temperature** A reversible change that occurs in an amorphous polymer when it reaches a certain temperature range in which the material undergoes a transition from a hard, brittle, glassy state to a flexible condition. At the glass

***Reviewers of sections of this chapter are:*** *Robert W. Bainbridge, Bainbridge Consultants, Inc.; D. M. Bigg, Projects Manager, Polymer Science and Technology, Battelle Columbus Laboratories; James E. Cserr, Supervisor, Materials Engineering, Rubber/Plastics Dept., Engineering Office, Chrysler Corp.; Paul E. Fina, Coordinator—Plastics Technology, College of DuPage; Christopher M. Hall, Product Manager RIM Machinery, Plastics Machinery Division, Cincinnati Milacron Marketing Co.; Joseph Hansmann, General Manager—Research and Development, Magna International, Inc.—Concord; Christopher Irwin, Technical Manager, Mold Operations, Plastics Machinery Division, Hoover Universal, Inc.; John Kovalchuck, Director of Manufacturing Technology, Firelands College, Bowling Green State University;*

transition temperature, the polymer chains become free to rotate and to slide past each other. Above the so-called "glass temperature," the material acts like a viscous liquid; below the glass temperature, it behaves like a solid.

**homopolymer/copolymer** These terms are used frequently to differentiate between single and multiple monomers. For example, among acetal resins, Delrin is a homopolymer, whereas Celcon is a copolymer. Polypropylene is available in both molecular forms.

**hot-runner mold** A mold in which the runners are insulated from the chilled cavities and are kept hot so the material can be used again.

**injection blow molding** A blow molding process in which the parison to be blown is formed by injection molding and then blow molded as a secondary operation.

**injection mold** A mold into which a plasticated material is introduced from an exterior heating cylinder.

**injection molding** A molding procedure whereby heat-softened thermoplastic or thermoset material is forced from a plasticating barrel into a relatively cool mold cavity for hardening.

**injection pressure** The pressure on the face of the injection ram and the pressure at which molding material is injected into the mold.

**isocyanate resins** Most applications for this resin are based on its combination with polyols (polyesters, polyethers, etc.). During the reaction, the ingredients join through formation of the urethane linkage; hence, this technology is generally known as urethane chemistry.

**laminated plastics** A plastics material consisting of superimposed layers of a synthetic resin-impregnated or coated filler which have been bonded (by heat and pressure) to form a single piece.

**L/D ratio** A term used to define an extrusion screw. Denotes the ratio of screw length to diameter.

**mat** A randomly distributed felt of glass fibers used in reinforced plastics lay-up molding.

**matched metal molding** Method of molding reinforced plastics between two close-fitting metal molds mounted in a hydraulic press (similar to compression molding).

**melamine formaldehyde** A synthetic resin derived from the reaction of melamine with formaldehyde or its polymers.

**methacrylonitrile** A vinyl nitrile compound that is similar to ABS.

**monomer** A relatively simple compound that can react to form a polymer.

**movable platen** The large back platen of an injection molding machine to which the back half of the mold is secured.

**nylon** The generic name for all synthetic fiber-forming polyamides. These polyamides can be formed into monofilaments and yarns characterized by a high degree of toughness, strength, and elasticity, as well as high melting point and good resistance to chemicals, but poor resistance to water absorption and penetration.

**parison** The hollow plastics tube from which a container, toy, etc., is blow molded.

**phenolic resin** A synthetic resin produced by the condensation of an aromatic alcohol with an aldehyde. Phenolic resins are used for thermosetting molding materials and laminated sheets.

**phthalate esters** A main group of plasticizers, produced by the direct action of alcohol on phthalic anhydride.

**plastic** (a) Pliable and capable of being shaped by pressure. The word *plastic* is incorrectly used as the generic term for the industry and its products.

**plastics** (n) A generic term for the industry and its products. This term is properly used only as a plural word. The plastics products include polymeric substances, natural or synthetic, and exclude rubber materials.

**plasticate** To soften a material by mixing and heating to prepare it for molding.

**plasticize** To soften a material and make it moldable by the use of a plasticizer.

**plasticizer** Chemical agent (elastomer or plastics) added to plastics compositions to make them softer, more flexible, and more workable.

**platform blowing** A special technique for blowing large parts by use of a movable table to support the material.

**plug-and-ring** Method of sheet forming in which a plug, functioning as a male mold, is forced into a heated plastic sheet that is held in place by a clamping ring.

**plug forming** A thermoforming process in which a plug or male mold is used to partially preform the part before forming is completed by the use of vacuum or pressure. Also called plug assist.

**polyester** A resin formed by the reaction between a dibasic acid and a dihydroxy alcohol, both organic. Polyesters modified with fatty acids are called alkyds.

**polyethylene** A thermoplastic material comprised of polymers of ethylene. Normally it is a crystalline, translucent, tough, waxy solid that is unaffected by water and a large variety of chemicals.

**polymer** A high-molecular-weight organic compound, natural or synthetic, whose structure can be represented by repeated small units (mers). Examples include polyethylene, cellulose, and rubber. Synthetic polymers are formed by addition or condensation polymerization of monomers. If two or more monomers are involved, a copolymer is obtained. Some polymers are elastomers, others are plastics.

**polymerization** A chemical reaction in which the molecules of a monomer are linked together to form large molecules whose molecular weight is a multiple of that of the original monomer.

**polypropylene** A tough, lightweight, rigid, crystalline plastics made by the polymerization of high-purity propylene gas in the presence of an organo-metallic catalyst at relatively low pressures and temperatures.

**polystyrene** A water-white thermoplastic produced by the polymerization of styrene (vinyl benzene). The electrical insulating properties of polystyrene are very good and the material is relatively unaffected by moisture, but it generally is brittle.

**polyurethane resins** A family of resins produced by reacting

***Reviewers, cont.***: *Seymour E. Lavitt, Engineering Associate, Plastics Design/Development Associates; Roy L. Manns, President, Boston Plastics Group, Medical Electronic Independent Plastics Engineering Centre, Inc. (MEIPEC); William K. McConnell, Jr., President, McConnell Company, Inc.; Travis H. Meister, Consultant—Plastics; Dewey Rainville, General Manager, Rainville Operation, Hoover Universal, Inc.; Dario Ramazzotti, President, Ramazzotti Design and Engineering; Chris Rauwendaal, Manager, Process Research, Corporate Research and Development, Raychem Corporation.*

## NOMENCLATURE

diisocyanate with organic compounds containing two or more active hydroxyl units to form polymers having free isocyanate groups. These groups, under the influence of heat or catalysts react with each other, or with water, glycols, etc., to form thermosetting or thermoplastic materials.

**polyvinyl chloride (PVC)** A thermoplastic material composed of polymers of vinyl chloride. Polyvinyl chloride is a colorless plastics with outstanding resistance to water, alcohols, and concentrated acids and alkalies.

**reciprocating screw** An extruder system in which the screw when rotating is pushed backward by the molten polymer which collects in front of the screw. When sufficient material has been collected, the screw moves forward and forces the material at high velocity through the head and the nozzle into a mold.

**reinforcement** A strong inert material that is bound into plastics to improve the strength, stiffness, and impact resistance. Reinforcements are usually long fibers of sisal, cotton, glass, etc., in woven or nonwoven form.

**resin** Any of a class of solid or semisolid organic products of natural or synthetic origin. Resins generally are of high molecular weight and have no definite melting point. Most resins are polymers.

**rotational molding (or casting)** A method used to make hollow products from powdered plastics, plastisols, and lattices. Powdered plastics or plastisol is charged into a hollow mold that can be rotated in one plane or in two planes. Heat is applied to melt, fuse, or cure the polymer. Cooling is usually required before removing the casting.

**roving** A form of fibrous glass in which spun strands (filaments) are woven into a tubular rope. Chopped roving is commonly used in preforming.

**rubber** An elastomer capable of rapid recovery after being stretched to at least twice its length at temperatures from 0 to 150°F (-18 to 66°C); specifically, Hevea or natural rubber, which is the standard of comparison for elastomers.

**runner** In an injection or transfer mold, the channel, usually circular, that connects the sprue with the gate to the cavity.

**sandwich molding** A molding process in which two different materials are injected consecutively into a mold cavity to produce products having surfaces of one plastics with desirable characteristics and a core of another material with its desired characteristics.

**set** To convert a liquid resin or adhesive into a solid state by curing, by evaporation of solvent or suspending medium, or by gelling.

**sheet molding compound (SMC)** A combination of polyester resin, filler, and reinforcement rolled into a sheet form. Thermoplastic resin often is added to obtain a surface with desired characteristics.

**silicone** One of a family of polymeric materials in which the recurring chemical group contains silicon and oxygen atoms as links in the main chain. Silicons are derived from silica (sand) and methyl chloride.

**spray-up** The term for a number of techniques in which a spray gun is used as the processing tool.

**stretch forming** A plastics sheet forming technique in which the heated thermoplastic sheet is stretched over a mold and then cooled.

**structural foam** This product has a rigid cellular core and a solid integral skin.

**styrene acrylonitrile (SAN)** A thermoplastic copolymer with good stiffness, along with good resistance to chemicals, scratching, and stress cracking.

**thermoforming** The processes for forming thermoplastic sheet by heating the sheet and using air, vacuum, or mechanical methods to form it onto the surface contour of a mold.

**thermoplastics** Polymers that are capable of being repeatedly softened by heating and hardened by cooling.

**thermoset** A material that will undergo or has undergone a chemical reaction by the action of heat, catalysts, or ultraviolet light and will achieve or has achieved a relatively infusible state.

**transfer molding** A method of molding thermosetting materials, in which the plastics is softened by heat and pressure in a transfer chamber, then forced by high pressure through sprues, runners, and gates into a closed mold for final curing.

**urea or urea formaldehyde resin** A synthetic resin derived from the reaction of urea (carbamide) with formaldehyde or its polymers.

**urethane** *See* isocyanate resins.

**vacuum forming** A thermoforming method of sheet forming in which the plastics sheet is clamped in a stationary frame, heated, and drawn down by vacuum into a mold.

**vacuum metalizing** A process in which surfaces are thinly coated with metal by exposing them to the vapor of metal that has been evaporated under vacuum.

**viscoelasticity** The characteristic that causes plastics materials to respond to stress as though they are a combination of elastic solids and viscous fluids. This property is exhibited in varying degrees by all plastics. This term is not applicable to elastomers.

**window** A defect in a thermoplastic film, sheet, or molding, caused by the incomplete plasticizing of a piece of the material during processing. It appears as a globule in an otherwise blended mass.

# PLASTICS MATERIALS

Plastics are nonmetallic basic engineering materials that can be shaped and formed by many different processes. There are many kinds of chemically different plastics, and each kind may be made into hundreds of compositions or alloys. Each formulation provides some special desirable combinations of properties.

Plastics are a large, varied group of synthetic materials that contain a mixture of molecules. Chemically, the plastics materials are combinations of carbon with oxygen, hydrogen, nitrogen, and other organic and inorganic materials. Although a plastics is solid in the finished state, it is semiliquid at some stage of the manufacturing process and is capable of being formed into shapes of any desired contour or degree of complexity. Forming is usually done through the application of heat and/or pressure, in processes such as molding, extruding, and casting. There are nearly 50 different families of plastics in commercial use, and each family has numerous variations and subtypes.

# PLASTICS MATERIALS

## MOLECULAR STRUCTURE

Plastics generally are not found in nature, although many additives and pigments are based upon naturally formed substances. Plastics are made synthetically from basic chemical raw materials called monomers. The generic titles of most plastics begin with the prefix "poly." This may be confusing initially, but the prefix is simply a term coined to indicate that the material is a long molecular chain made up of a very large number of relatively simpler molecules of the immediate source material, which is indicated by the second part of the name. The immediate source material is known as a monomer; the long chain plastics molecule produced from it is called a polymer. The process by which the monomers are induced to link up to form a polymer is called polymerization (a process that emulates the natural formation and growth of molecules).

To cite a few examples: polystyrene is the polymer produced from the monomer styrene; polyethylene is produced from ethylene; polypropylene from propylene; and polyvinyl chloride is produced from vinyl chloride.

In general, the polymerization process is carried out by the large suppliers of plastics, since the chemical reaction is complex and costly and often has to be done on a large scale to produce the final material at an economic selling price. In some instances, however, the actual polymerization is carried out by the processor, since it occurs during the molding or shaping process. This is the case with thermosetting materials, for example, in which the chemical change taking place under heat in the molding process is the final stage of polymerization in which the molecular chains interlink to form a three-dimensional network. This process, known as "cross-linking" is what makes the resulting plastics hard, rigid, and unaffected by further heating. Cross-linking does not, however, take place with thermoplastics, and thus there are no links between the molecular chains; so on application of heat they are able to slide against each other, making the solid material soften and melt.

Polymers are always comprised of carbon atoms in combination with other elements. In current practice, polymer chemists use only eight of the 100 known elements to create many hundreds of different plastic formulations. These eight elements are: carbon, hydrogen, nitrogen, oxygen, fluorine, silicon, sulfur, and chlorine. Figure 18-1 illustrates the monomers that compose several common thermoplastics.

## PRINCIPAL TYPES OF POLYMERS

The three primary types of polymers are thermoplastics, thermosets, and elastomers. Elastomers, which are materials that at room temperature can stretch to twice their length and snap back to the original length, are outside the scope of this chapter. While the main polymer groups have many significant differences, they also have a common link in that they need a range of temperature and pressure within which to perform at their optimal levels. Some individual plastics can withstand temperatures up to 500° F (260° C) and pressures up to 100 psi (690 kPa) for periods of 5 minutes to 4 hours. Some plastics would soften in boiling water, but are capable of withstanding subzero frigid environments.

### Thermoplastic Materials

A thermoplastic material will repeatedly soften when heated and harden when cooled. The material's characteristics and properties are unaffected by repeated cycles of heating and cooling. Typical materials in the thermoplastic group are the styrene polymers and copolymers, acrylics, cellulosics, polyethylenes, vinyls, nylons, and various fluorocarbon materials. Commonly used thermoplastics and typical applications are listed in Table 18-1.

### Thermoset Plastics

Thermoset plastics are made quite differently from thermoplastics. Polymerization (curing) of thermoset plastics is done in two stages: partly by the materials supplier and partly by the molder.

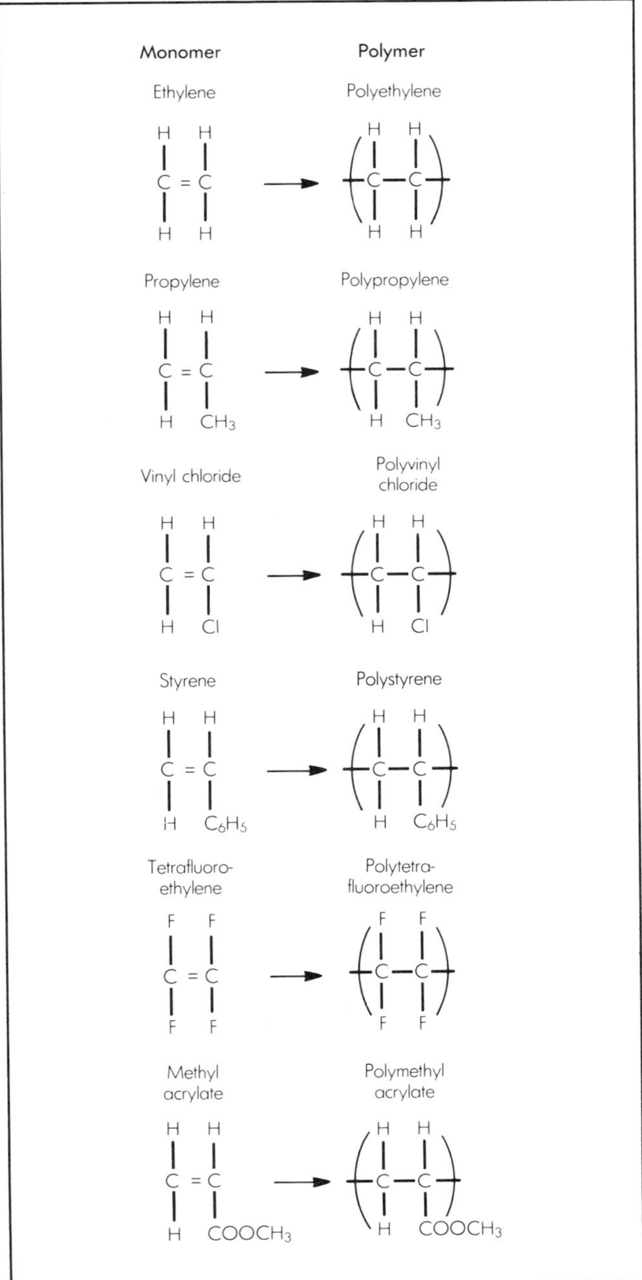


**Fig. 18-1 Plastics molecular structure showing typical monomers and their repeating units.**

## CHAPTER 18

# PLASTICS MATERIALS

**TABLE 18-1**
**Commonly Used Thermoplastics and Typical Applications**

| Plastics (Chemical Name) | Typical Properties | Typical Applications |
|---|---|---|
| Acetal (polymerized formaldehyde) | Tough, strong, resilient, rigid, resistant to common solvents, resists creep | Gears, bushings, cams, fan blades, fasteners, valves, shower heads, tool handles, instrument housings |
| Acrylic (polymethyl methacrylate) | Clarity, optical properties, weather resistance, easily colored, rigid, strong | Replaces glass in many applications, windows, lenses, instrument panels, domes, displays, voltage line spacers |
| Acrylonitrile-butadiene-styrene (ABS) | Hard, tough, rigid (but can be made flexible), good electrical properties | Business machine and camera housings, telephones, wheels, gears, grilles, impellers, pipe, bearings, handles |
| Cellulosics: | | |
| cellulose acetate | Tough, resilient, good insulator, transparent to translucent, easily colored | Household appliances, toys, beads, knobs, sunglass frames, packaging materials, lampshades, pipe and tubing |
| cellulose acetate-butyrate | Tough, moisture resistant, dimensionally stable, easily colored, extrudable | Steering wheels, football helmets, goggle frames, sound tapes, trays, belts, extruded tubing, furniture trim |
| cellulose nitrate, pyroxylin | Tough, water resistant, workable, easily colored, flammable, poor weathering | Shoe heels, fabric coating, brushes, combs, photographic film, buttons, spectacle frames, mirror coverings |
| cellulose propionate | Short molding cycle, tough, impact resistant, good color retention and weathering | Toys, pens, automotive parts, handles, toothbrushes, appliance housings, telephones, steering wheels, novelties |
| ethyl cellulose | Low density, stability, alkali resistant, heat/cold resistant, impact strength | Coating materials, decorative trim, tool handles, cosmetic packages, refrigerator components, toys |
| Chlorinated polyether | Dimensional stability, heat and corrosion resistant, good electrical properties | Bearing retainers, water meters, tanks and tank linings, laboratory and chemical handling equipment |
| Fluorocarbons: | | |
| polychlorotrifluoroethylene (PCTFE) | Tough, dimensionally stable, chemical resistant, excellent electrical insulating qualities | Chemical handling equipment, wire insulation, packaging for lubricants and pharmaceuticals, coil forms |
| tetrafluoroethylene (TFE) | Heat and chemical resistant, nonstick surface, ultraviolet and moisture resistant | Missile components, high-temperature wire and cable insulation, frying pans, gaskets, chemical apparatus |
| fluorinated ethylene propylene (FEP) | Good electrical properties and thermal range, hard, stiff, dimensional stability | Laboratory ware and bottles, liners, insulators, seals, rings, gaskets, rollers, spacers, bushings |
| polyvinylidene fluoride, (PCTFE-$VF_2$) | Strong, tough, good heat stability, solvent and chemical resistant, weather resistant | Paints, high-temperature valve seats, capacitor film, wire insulation, chemical-handling equipment |
| Nylon (polyamides) | Tough, strong, low friction, heat and abrasion resistant, resists most organic solvents | Brush bristles, hosiery, bushings, gears, washers, protective coatings, cooking bags, tubing, pipe fittings |
| Phenoxy (epichlorohydrin and bisphenol-A) | Good creep resistance, clarity, low shrinkage, impermeability properties, self-extinguishing | Special bottles, coatings, adhesives, laminate bonding, blow and injection moldings, and extrusions |
| Polyimides | Heat resistant, acid and organic-solvent resistant, radiation resistant, dielectric | High-temperature bearings, valves, piston rings, compressor parts, abrasive-wheel binders |
| Polycarbonate | Impact strength, chemically stable, good temperature stability, good weathering | Hammer handles, street-light globes, centrifuge bottles, appliance parts, coffee pots, high-temperature lenses |

TABLE 18-1—*Continued*

| Plastics (Chemical Name) | Typical Properties | Typical Applications |
|---|---|---|
| Polyethylene | Moisture resistant, good electrical and chemical properties, weather resistant | Packaging, toys, bottles, pipes, tubing, ice trays, electrical insulation, surgical implants |
| Polyphenylene oxide (PPO) | Broad thermal range, good acid and base resistance, nontoxic, low moisture absorption | Autoclave parts, micromembrane filters, surgical tools, pump housings, valves, pipe fittings |
| Polypropylene (PP) | Low density, resists boiling water, translucent, readily colored, good thermal range | Clothes washer and dishwasher parts, automotive ducts and trim, dishes, radio and TV cabinets, hinges, pipe |
| Polystyrene (PS) | Transparent, easily colored, weather resistant, excellent dielectric, acid resistant | Jewelry, light fixtures, packages, clock cases, radio cabinets, bottles, houseware, capacitors, syringes |
| Polysulfone | Good arc resistance, self-extinguishing, good thermal and oxidation resistance | Hot-water pipes, automotive underhood parts, switches, circuit breakers, appliance housings, lenses |
| Polyurethane (PUR) | Thermal insulation properties, tough, hard, mar-resistant, flexible, chemical resistant | Cushions, toys, rocket fuel tank insulator, gears, industrial wheels, truck tires, pump impellers, belts |
| Styrene acrylonitrile (SAN) | Heat resistant; good stiffness; scratch, paint-solvent, chemical, and stress-crack resistant | Chemical apparatus, piano and organ keys, telephone parts, bristles, films, lenses, food packages |
| Vinyl: | | |
| polyvinyl chloride (PVC) | Strong, self-extinguishing, easily colored, good abrasion and chemical resistance, weatherability | Pipe, conduit, wire and cable insulation, bottles, rain gutters, garden hose, gaskets, raincoats, toys |
| polyvinyl acetate | Impervious to petroleum, naptha, turpentine, mineral oil, and vegetable oil; good dielectric | Paints, sealers, coatings, electrical tape, insulation for wires and pipes, films |
| polyvinylidene chloride | Transparent, low gas and moisture permeability, nonflammable, tough, abrasion resistant, strong | Food packaging, auto seat covers, film, bristles, pipe lining, filters, valves, carpeting, fittings |

Note: Thermoplastic materials undergo no chemical change in processing and do not become permanently hard with the application of heat and pressure. They remain soft at elevated temperatures; are hardened by cooling; and may be remelted repeatedly by successive applications of heat. Thermoplastic materials are processed principally by injection or blow molding, extrusion, thermoforming, and calendering.

As illustrated in Fig. 18-2, phenolic (a typical thermoset plastic) is first partically polymerized by reacting phenol with formaldehyde under heat and pressure. The reaction is stopped at the point at which mostly linear chains have been formed. The linear chains still contain unreacted portions which are capable of flowing under heat and pressure.

The final stage of polymerization is completed in the molding press, in which the partially reacted phenolic is liquefied under pressure, producing a cross-linking reaction between molecular chains. Unlike a thermoplastic monomer, which has only two reactive ends for linear chain growth, a thermoset monomer must have three or more reactive ends so that its molecular chains cross-link in three dimensions.

After it has been molded, a thermoset plastics has virtually all of its polymer molecules interconnected with strong, permanent physical bonds that are not heat reversible. If a thermoset is heated at a high enough temperature, or too long, chain breakage and physical degradation can occur.

Phenolic, urea, and melamine thermoset plastics are polymerized by a "condensation" reaction, wherein a byproduct (water, for example) is created during the reaction in the mold. Such volatile byproducts cause some dimensional instability

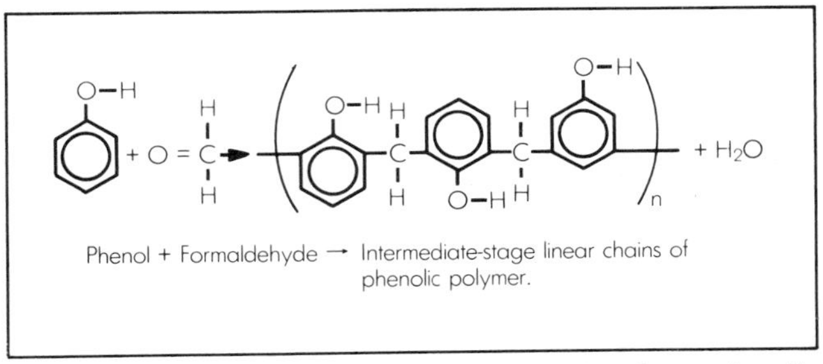

**Fig. 18-2 Condensation polymerization reaction for a phenolic polymer. The reaction is completed during molding, to create a single, giant molecule.**

and low part strength unless they are carefully removed during molding. Degassing is easily accomplished during the molding operations.

Other thermoset plastics, such as epoxy, polyester, and elastomeric silicones, cure by an "addition" reaction, resulting in no volatile byproducts and hence fewer molding problems. Most addition-cured thermoset plastics can be liquid at room temperature; the two ingredients (along with a catalyst and a promoter) can be simply mixed and poured into molds in which they cross-link (cure) at room temperature into permanent form—in much the same way as in casting concrete. Molds are often heated, however, to speed the curing process. In this case, a promoter is not needed.

In general, thermoset plastics, because of their tightly cross-linked structure, resist higher temperatures and provide greater dimensional stability than most thermoplastics. Examples of thermoset plastics products include glass-reinforced-polyester boat hulls and circuit-breaker components, epoxy printed-circuit boards, and melamine dinnerware. Commonly used thermoset plastics and typical applications are listed in Table 18-2. Additional information on plastics, including representative data for characteristics and properties, is provided in *Materials, Finishing, and Coating,* Volume III of this Handbook series.

## ADDITIVES[3]

Plastics are materials that are composed not only of large, polymeric-molecule materials, but also additional small-molecule materials that are added to provide some particular characteristic. The plastics industry uses the word *additives* to describe ingredients that are combined with the basic resins and polymers to extend them, to modify their properties, to facilitate processing, or to achieve special color and finish. For example, the characteristics of color, flexibility, rigidity, flame resistance, weathering behavior, and processibility can be altered significantly by the use of additives. The additives are particularly applicable to polyvinyl chloride and the various thermoset plastics.

**TABLE 18-2**
**Commonly Used Thermoset Plastics and Typical Applications**

| Plastics (Chemical Name) | Typical Properties | Typical Applications |
|---|---|---|
| Epoxy (EP) | Toughness, adhesion, chemical resistance, bonding strength, good electrical properties | Coatings, molds, tooling, dies, electrical insulation, pipe fittings, automotive and aircraft parts |
| Melamine formaldehyde (cyanamide) | Hard, strong, elastic, easily colored, good electrical qualities | Tableware, buttons, hearing aids, organ keys, electrical devices, knobs, table tops, engine ignition parts |
| Phenolic (phenol formaldehyde) | Hard, strong, heat and water resistant, weather resistant, easily colored | Radio and TV cabinets, telephones, washing machine agitators, jewelry, knife handles, toys, knobs, bottle caps |
| Polyester (unsaturated polyester) | High impact strength, good dielectric strength, low electrical loss | Switchgear, numerous reinforced plastics items, laundry tubs, fan blades, pump housings, boats, automobile bodies |
| Silicone (organo-silicon oxide) | Heat and water resistance, good low-temperature properties, long-term stability | Water repellants, protective coatings, lubricants, laminates, molds, adhesives, electrical encapsulation |
| Urea formaldehyde (cyanamide) | Easily colored, hard, strong, good dielectric strength, resists heat and chemicals | Lampshades, scale and appliance housings, buttons, electrical devices, adhesives, laminates, drip-dry clothing |
| Urethane (polyester di-isocyanate) | Tough, strong, good insulating properties for electricity and heat, weather resistant | Padding for automobiles and furniture, insulation for coolers, gaskets, toys, tires, sponges, conveyor belts, brushes |
| Alkyd (alkyd polyester) | Flow freely with low molding pressure, easily colored, good shock resistance | Electrical switchgear, computer components, TV insulation, engine ignition parts, fuses, coatings |
| Allyl (DAP) (diallyl phthalate) | Exceptional resistance to heat and chemicals, low electrical loss, dimensional stability | Rocket and missile components, electrical connectors, power-circuit breakers, plywood, surface laminates |

Note: Thermosetting plastics are formed to shape with heat, with or without pressure, resulting in a product that is permanently hard. The plastics hardens by a chemical change known as polymerization and cannot be resoftened. Polymerization is a chemical process that forms a new compound whose molecular weight is a multiple of that of the original substance. Processes used for the thermosetting plastics include compression or transfer molding, casting, laminating, and impregnating. Some thermosets also are used for making rigid and flexible foams.

In general, plastics additives may be grouped into two main categories. One group comprises additives that modify the base polymer's characteristics by physical means. Additives of this type perform as plasticizers, lubricants, impact modifiers, fillers, and pigments. The other group of additives achieves its effect by chemical reactions. Additives of this type include flame retardants, stabilizers, ultraviolet absorbers, and antioxidants.

### Physical Agents

Physical agents of plastics include antistatic agents, colorants, fillers, lubricants, and plasticizers.

**Antistatic agents.** Some plastics tend to develop an undesirable electrostatic charge on their surface during use. Antistatic agents are added to minimize the buildup of the electrostatic charge. An antistatic agent is a surface-active additive that is slightly incompatible with the polymer so that it migrates slowly to the surface and helps reduce the electrostatic charge. Effectiveness of antistatic agents usually diminishes over a period of time.

**Colorants.** Plastics in their natural state are often colorless, or a bland, milky white color. The ingredients used for coloring plastics materials are dyes, organic or inorganic pigments, and various special coloring compounds. In general, dyes are used to obtain brilliant transparent colors. Organic pigments are discrete solid particles of dyes. Inorganic pigments are non-brilliant salts and oxides of metals that are dispersed throughout the polymer. The specialty pigments include metallic flakes, pearlescent pigments, or fluorescent pigments blended with other pigments. Colors combined within the resin are pelletized. These color concentrates then are mixed with the basic polymer and molded to final form.

**Fillers.** Important functions in the manufacturing of plastics compounds are performed by fillers. Fillers reduce cost; provide body; speed the cure or hardening process; minimize shrinkage; reduce crazing; improve thermal endurance; add strength; and provide special chemical, mechanical, and electrical properties. Some commonly used fillers are listed in Table 18-3.[4]

**Lubricants.** Lubricants are used to improve the processibility and appearance of the plastics product. Internal lubricants act within the plastics material itself to reduce the forces acting between molecules. Other additives act as external lubricants to reduce adhesion of the plastic to the metal surfaces of the molds and the process machinery.

**Plasticizers.** Chemically and thermally stable materials, called plasticizers, are added to plastics to improve the softness, flexibility, and processibility of the polymeric materials. Plasticizers reduce the intermolecular secondary bond forces between polymer chains, with the result that the plastics become more flexible. Polyvinyl chloride is the polymer that is most commonly used with plasticizers.

### Chemical Reaction Additives

Chemical reaction additives include antioxidants, flame retardants, and stabilizers.

**Antioxidants.** The antioxidants are additives that inhibit or retard oxidative degradation of the plastic material within the anticipated processing and usage limits of the end-product and its applications.

**Flame retardants.** Organic materials char when subjected to high temperatures, and most such materials can be ignited with a flame. Since polymers are organic materials, they will burn. Some polymers burn more easily than paper, and others are harder to ignite than wood. The flammability of plastics may be reduced by addition of certain other materials, known as flame retardants. These materials usually are mixed into the plastic formulation after the polymerization stage. Most effective flame retardants are insoluble in polymers; hence, they must be used in plastics in which transparency is not a principal requirement.

**Stabilizers.** The degradation of materials during high-temperature processing can be prevented, and extension of life-cycle stability under degrading environmental conditions can be achieved by using stabilizers. Changes in size and shape of the polymer molecules have significant effects on properties of the plastics. Both ultraviolet radiation and oxidation can cause the primary covalent bonds in polymer chains to break. This in turn can create free radicals which can recombine in a variety of ways—sometimes in the form of cross-links that tend to make the material more rigid and brittle.

As described previously in this section, antioxidants are added to resist the onset of degradation due to oxidation. Also, since most polymers are adversely affected by exposure to ultraviolet radiation (sunlight), protection is afforded by the inclusion of suitable ultraviolet absorbers in the plastic formulation.

## PROPERTIES AND LIMITATIONS

As the spectrum of end-uses for plastics grows, so also does the demand for greater sophistication in terms of physical and mechanical properties. Selection of materials is the critical factor insofar as polymers are concerned and must take into account, not only the materials' advantages but also their inherent limitations.

These limitations are necessarily influenced to some extent by the end-use and the working environment, but mainly include the following limiting factors common to the major thermoplastics sector:

- Working temperature.
- Flexural modulus.
- Impact resistance.
- Creep resistance.
- Tensile modulus.
- Elongation.
- Compressive strength.
- Environmental stability.
- Wear resistance.

### Scope for Selection

The list of thermoplastics, thermosets, and elastomers coming within the terminology of polymers can be confusing; each material class or type is distinctive in one property or another. Any plastics resin is capable of almost endless variation either in terms of chemical structure or physical modification through mixing, blending, filling, reinforcing, or alloying. The importance of additives and polymer alloys in achieving a considerable upgrading of properties in many polymers can be significant. Thus, a wide scope is offered by polymers and it is often possible that several polymer types could be regarded as generally satisfactory for any one potential application or end-use.

**TABLE 18-3**
**Plastics Fillers and Reinforcements**

| Filler or Reinforcement | Properties Improved | | | | | | | | | | | | | |
|---|---|---|---|---|---|---|---|---|---|---|---|---|---|---|
| | Chemical resistance | Heat resistance | Electrical insulation | Impact strength | Tensile strength | Dimensional stability | Stiffness | Hardness | Lubricity | Electrical conductivity | Thermal conductivity | Moisture resistance | Processability | Recommended for use in* |
| Alumina tabular | • | • | | | | • | | | | | | | | S/P |
| Alumina trihydrate, fine particle | | | • | | | | • | | | | | • | • | P |
| Aluminum powder | | | | | | | | | | • | • | | | S |
| Asbestos | • | • | • | • | | • | • | • | | | | | | S/P |
| Bronze | | | | | | | • | • | | • | • | | | S |
| Calcium carbonate** | | • | | | | • | • | • | | | | | • | S/P |
| Calcium metasilicate | • | • | | | | • | • | • | | | | • | | S |
| Calcium silicate | | • | | | | • | • | • | | | | | | S |
| Carbon black† | | • | | | | • | • | | | • | • | | • | S/P |
| Carbon fiber | | | | | | | | | | • | • | | | S |
| Cellulose | | | | • | • | • | • | • | | | | | | S/P |
| Alpha cellulose | | | • | | • | • | | | | | | | | S |
| Coal, powdered | • | | | | | | | | | | | • | | S |
| Cotton (macerated/chopped fibers) | | | • | • | • | • | • | • | | | | | | S |
| Fibrous glass | • | • | • | • | • | • | • | • | | | | • | | S/P |
| Fir bark | | | | | | | | | | | | | • | S |
| Graphite | • | | | | • | • | • | • | • | • | • | | | S/P |
| Jute | | | | • | | | • | | | | | | | S |
| Kaolin | • | • | | | | • | • | • | • | | | • | • | S/P |
| Kaolin (calcined) | • | • | • | | | • | • | • | | | | • | • | S/P |
| Mica | • | • | • | | | • | • | • | • | | | • | | S/P |
| Molybdenum disulphide | | | | | | | • | • | • | | | • | • | P |
| Nylon (macerated/chopped fibers) | • | • | • | • | • | • | • | • | • | | | | • | S/P |
| Orlon | • | • | • | • | • | • | • | • | | | | • | • | S/P |
| Rayon | | | • | • | • | • | • | • | | | | | | S |
| Silica, amorphous | | | • | | | | | | | | | • | • | S/P |
| Sisal fibers | • | | | • | • | • | • | • | | | | • | | S/P |
| TFE-fluorocarbon | | | | | | • | • | • | • | | | | | S/P |
| Talc | • | • | • | | | • | • | • | • | | | • | • | S/P |
| Wood flour | | | • | | • | • | | | | | | | | S |

* Symbols: P—in thermoplastics only; S—in thermosets only; S/P—in both thermoplastics and thermosets.
** In thermosets, calcium carbonate's prime function is to improve molded appearance.
† Prime functions are imparting of U-V resistance and coloring; also is used in cross-linked thermoplastics.

## Requirements for Selection

Three fundamental requirements guide the plastics materials selection for a particular application:

1. Optimum properties.
2. Optimum processing or fabrication.
3. The lowest economic factor.

The critical choice factor is therefore a synthesis of these key requirements and calls for extensive and practical experience with material class, type, and likely modification or variation. Manufacturers and processors of polymers have extensive knowledge of the materials within their production capability, but the optimal choice could well lie beyond the range offered by a single source. Even when a reasonably positive material choice has been made, it is advisable in truly structural or demanding applications to carry out functional testing on realistic prototypes to avoid expensive failures or modifications at a later stage in production.

## Properties of Polymers (Unfilled)

Thermoplastics are viscoelastic solids (or melts) whose properties are very dependent on temperature within their own melting range.

Two distinct types of thermoplastic polymers exist: those that are amorphous and those that are primarily crystalline. In the amorphous polymers such as polymethyl methacrylate, polyethersulphone and, essentially, polyvinyl chloride, the molecular chains cannot pack themselves together in any regular sort of order. Random entanglement is the mode of molecular joining. Such polymers soften (but do not melt) and become highly viscoelastic over an extended temperature range.

Other polymers, such as polyethylene, polypropylene, nylon and polyethylene terephthalate are, or may be, partially crystalline in their solid states. The similarity of the molecular structures along the polymer chains encourages crystallization. Complete crystallization, however, is prohibited largely by the lengths of the chains (which entangle one another) and by irregularities of detailed chain structures. Any one molecule may thus pass through more than one crystalline region or crystallite. The crystallites are therefore joined to their neighbors by unordered, amorphous lengths of polymer chain.

Partially crystalline polymers have a more sharply defined melting point—at least it can be measured optically as the temperature at which the last traces of crystallinity vanish. Melt viscosities are usually lower than those of the amorphous polymers; in the case of nylon and polyethylene terephthalate, they are very much lower.

## Properties of Polymers (Filled)

To tailor a polymer, a wide range of fillers (described earlier in this chapter) in the form of liquid, particulate, fiber and pigment additives are used in levels from 1-35%. Glass beads (microspheres) also are used to increase the modules, since glass fiber orientation in injection molding cannot be easily controlled and can cause warpage.

In general terms, the properties and characteristics of polymers can be improved by particulate or fiber fillers. Impact strength can be improved by adding a rubbery filler such as butadiene to styrene. Rigidity and/or compression strength can be increased by a chemical agent to foam the material. At the same time, weight also is reduced (by foaming), but a particulate filler such as talc or slate powder can be added to increase the specific gravity.

# PART DESIGN AND PROCESSING

The technology of plastics, including prediction of performance and endurance, is significantly different from that of metals and other traditional materials. Of critical importance to the design of plastics parts is the realization that the meaningful tests for engineering characteristics and properties of plastics are different, and so is the interpretation of tensile strength, stress-strain modulus, Izod impact resistance, and other data obtained from the tests commonly used for metals. The most important reason that such test data cannot be used directly is that plastics are viscoelastic; creep can occur when the plastics material's elastic limit is exceeded.

The standard physical properties data normally available in the technical literature is not sufficient for plastics material selection or for the design of parts—because this data, alone, does not adequately account for the effect of time under load or for the response to sustained temperature exposure, nor does the data relate directly to functional part performance in which a complex pattern of stresses and various environmental factors are encountered. A set of stress-strain curves at different ambient temperatures more realistically indicates the physical properties of plastics materials.

The fundamental engineering material properties required to overcome these limitations include strength and rigidity as a function of time, temperature, and stress (creep and creep rupture), as well as realistic information on strength at high rates of loading (impact) and repeated loading (fatigue).[5]

## DESIGN CONSIDERATIONS

The design of a plastics product must reflect functional design aspects, such as production and assembly-related design factors, and material design factors, including consideration of the plastics material's design limits, performance strengths, and inherent weaknesses.[6]

### Functional Design Factors

A number of production and assembly-related design principles require thorough consideration at the inception of the design and during the engineering development program. Some of the basic functional performance design practices are summarized in this section.

**Radii.** In the design of plastics parts, loads should be distributed over as large an area as possible. This means that sharp corners should be avoided so that no stress-concentration points exist. Radii (as large as possible) should be located at the intersections of angular surfaces, such as the bases of ribs or bosses.

**Ribs.** Ribs increase rigidity and strength of a molded part without greatly increasing the weight or cost.

**Width.** The width of the rib base should be no larger than 1/2 to 3/4 the thickness of the wall to which it is attached.

**Height.** Ribs should not be higher than three times the thickness of the wall to which they are attached.

**Spacing.** When two or more ribs are required, the spacing of centers should not be less than two times the rib base thickness.

**Taper.** Rib taper may vary from 1/2° to 2° per side.

**Corrugations.** Ribs cannot be formed in plastics sheet for rigidizing thermoformed parts as is done in injection molding. When it is impracticable to fasten the plastics to more rigid materials (metal or wood), corrugation can be specified. Corrugation angles should be generously radiused (not less than one-half the material thickness). When aesthetic considerations preclude corrugations, doming may be used.

**Gussets.** Gussets are supporting structures for the edge of a part or for bosses. Gusset design guidelines for thickness, spacing, taper, and draft are similar to those for ribs.

**Bosses.** Studs or pads, called bosses, provide sites for locating fasteners such as self-tapping screws or threaded inserts. Included among design guidelines for bosses are the use of corner locations, the provision of proper draft, and the specification of an adequate radius at the junction of the boss and the wall section. The boss wall thickness should not be more than 3/4 (preferably 1/2) the thickness of the wall to which it is attached.

**Holes.** Holes should be designed and located to minimize part weakening and to avoid production problems. When holes parallel to the draw are too small to be molded, they should be drilled after the part has been molded. For holes molded in ABS plastics parts for which structural requirements are specified, the following design practices are applicable:

- Distance from a hole to the edge of a part should be no less than three times the hole diameter.
- Minimum distance between holes should equal five times the hole diameter.
- Hole size should be between 120-140% of the fastener (or shaft) outside diameter, to avoid thermal stress problems.

**Threads.** Threads in molded ABS plastics parts are generally designed for either of the following two thread classes:

Class 1: A loose fit for quick, easy assembly.
Class 2: A moderate or free fit for interchangeable parts.

Parts with molded external threads can be removed from the mold either by unscrewing the molded articles from the mold member or by splitting the mold. Internal threads can be molded by using a threaded pin from which the article is unscrewed.

## Material Design Factors

The designer must know the end-use performance and functional requirements for a proposed application. A proposed design should reflect the careful consideration of processing advantages and limitations, as well as projected part cost parameters. The plastics material supplier can provide information on design stress limits to determine the wall thickness and the amount of support ribbing or number of corrugations necessary to carry the anticipated loads at the projected temperatures. Data is also needed on the plastics material's resistance to various factors related to the part's environment, including possible outdoor exposure.

A substantial amount of information is needed to develop a product design from the initial concept through development and selection of the appropriate manufacturing process. Five key factors involved in the conceptual development are shown in the grid depicted in Fig. 18-3.

**End-use.** The product's end-use requirements should be established. Generally, the lower strength properties of plastics (compared to metals) requires that parts be designed to utilize a larger percentage of the ultimate strength of the plastics grade that is selected. Material selection must be keyed to the provision of specific properties that are critical to part performance. To correctly select materials that are compatible with end-use requirements, information is needed on: structural requirements, environmental factors, cost limits, and relevant standards and regulations.

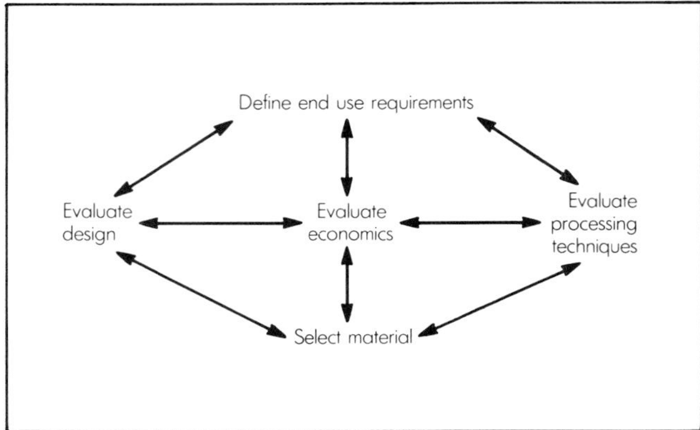


**Fig. 18-3 Five interrelated factors comprise a "thinking grid" for orderly plastics material selection and product design.** (*Borg-Warner Chemicals, Borg-Warner Corp.*)

**Preliminary design.** Preparation of a preliminary design sketch can reveal which aspects of the design are inflexible and which may be varied to obtain the desired level of structural performance.

**Material selection.** The typical property data sheet provided by the material supplier is the initial document used to select the plastics grade for a particular application. The initial material selection should be refined by reviewing the time-dependent, temperature-dependent, and environment-dependent property behavior. Supplementary data on abrasion resistance, tensile elongation at rupture, etc., may be needed to confirm the final choice. Material properties such as proportional limit, coefficient of expansion, and specific gravity are useful for mathematical design calculations. Other properties, such as hardness, impact strength, weathering resistance, and flammability, require experience and judgment to correlate the property data validly to a particular part application.

**Design modification.** The preliminary design should be modified to reflect:

- Specific property balance of the material selected.
- Processing limitations.
- Assembly methods.

Using data on material design limits, calculations should be made for wall thicknesses, interference fit tolerances, and other factors. At this stage of the part design and development, a prototype usually is built and tested.

**Performance tests.** In normal good practice, simulated end-use tests and (if necessary) simulated product storage tests are conducted. It is important to determine which part performance tests accurately represent realistic end-use requirements and can be performed in the laboratory. In many instances, the test equipment and methods developed during the engineering development stage can be adapted for future production quality control testing.

## STANDARD TESTS

Since the phenomena that can cause failure of plastics parts are more varied than those for metals, it is necessary to examine carefully the characteristics of a proposed plastics material relative to its intended use. All possible failure modes should be identified and evaluated in relation to characteristics and properties of the proposed material. Depending on the part's functional specifications and its operating environment, information and data may be needed on the proposed plastics material's thermal, optical, electrical, and environmental properties, in addition to the more familiar data on mechanical properties.

### Principal Standards

Three primary groups of test standards for plastics materials are used in the United States and Europe: ASTM (American Society for Testing and Materials), BSI (British Standards Institute), and DIN (Deutscher Normenausschuss; German standards organization). The ASTM standards are the most commonly used in North America and many parts of Europe. Table 18-4 lists some of the principal ASTM tests and standards for plastics.

### Technical Discussion

When plastics are being tested, the temperature and moisture content of the specimen are critical. Processing conditions also are important. While the ASTM methods provide useful preliminary data, the final properties in the actual application can vary substantially and are primarily affected by the design of the part. Materials manufacturers and independent testing laboratories usually develop empirical testing methods to supplement the standard ASTM test methods listed in Table 18-4.

In general, when using test load-deformation data for the evaluation of polymers, the following guidelines apply:

- Tough materials have a high elongation factor.
- Hard materials have a high modulus of elasticity.
- Strong materials have a high tensile strength factor.
- The tensile strength of a polymer molding is greater along flow lines than across. The importance of gating is critical for a structural part.
- Extra strength or toughness usually cannot be achieved with increased wall section. Considerable strength in polymers is attained by design configuration, and up to 25% can be lost by environment (humidity) with some polymers, for example, nylon.
- Toughness and impact strength are a function of temperature. The impact strength is quite low at low temperatures, at which the material is brittle, rising in strength value at intermediate temperature level and falling at higher temperatures as the material softens.

**Thermal expansion.** The thermal expansion of polymer materials is relatively large. Plastics expand or contract more with temperature changes than do other materials, such as metals. A critical plastics part dimension may, however, be held to close tolerance with the aid of a shrink fixture or a cooling aid designed for that purpose.

The high thermal expansion of plastics generally affects the use of molded metal inserts which are sometimes required for electrical contacts, screw thread mountings, or parts needing increased strength. Such inserts are commonly used in phenolics because the coefficient of expansion for phenolics is among the lowest of the common plastics. Thermal expansion characteristics may play an important part when synthetic resins are used as cements and bonding agents.

**Creep and cold flow.** Any material subjected to continuous stress will show a permanent deformation, even though the stress is below the proportional limit of the material. The magnitude of this deformation is quite variable. For metals at ordinary temperatures, this slow deformation may not be measurable during the life of the equipment; while for plastics, it might well be a limiting factor in their use.

**TABLE 18-4**
**Standard Tests for Plastics**

| ASTM Test Method* | Property or Characteristic |
|---|---|
| | Mechanical Tests |
| D638 | Tensile properties |
| D790 | Flexural properties |
| D747 | Stiffness in flexure |
| D256 | Izod impact |
| D1822 | Tensile impact |
| D2990 | Tensile creep |
| D695 | Compressive properties |
| D732 | Shear strength |
| D621 | Deformation under load |
| D785 | Rockwell hardness |
| D2240 | Indentation hardness (durometer) |
| D2236 | Dynamic mechanical properties |
| | Thermal Tests |
| D1525 | Vicat softening point |
| D648 | Deflection temperature |
| D1238 | Flow rate (melt index) |
| C177 | Thermal conductivity |
| D696 | Coefficient of thermal expansion |
| D746 | Brittleness temperature |
| D635 | Flammability |
| | Electrical Tests |
| D257 | Electrical resistance |
| D150 | Dielectric constant and dissipation factor |
| D149 | Dielectric strength |
| D495 | Arc resistance |
| D618 | Conditioning procedures |
| | Analytical Tests |
| D1505 | Density by density gradient method |
| D1895 | Apparent density |
| D792 | Specific gravity |
| | Permanence Tests |
| D1435 | Outdoor weathering |
| G23 | Accelerated weathering |
| D2565 | Water-cooled xenon arc type |
| 18FR | Atlas type fade-ometer |
| D1598 | Pipe tests |
| D794 | Permanent effect of heat |
| D570 | Water absorption |
| D543 | Resistance to chemicals |

* ASTM standards describing these tests are available from American Society for Testing and Materials.

# PART DESIGN AND PROCESSING

The creep characteristics of plastics are very much influenced by the applied stress and temperature, and a range exists, although not sharply defined, above which creep is very pronounced. This characteristic forms an effective limit to the conditions that plastics may withstand in service.

The creep characteristics of a plastics material can be correlated with its percentage of elongation found in the tensile test. Materials with the greater elongation show greater creep deformations, corresponding to greater molecular slippage. Thus in general, thermoplastics are more subject to creep than are thermosetting materials. Similarly, the effect of reinforcing with a fabric filler is to reduce both elongation at break and creep characteristics in approximately the same ratio.

The creep characteristics of plastics seriously limit their use as structural materials. Creep must always be taken into account in design of plastics members that carry a continuous load. No matter how small the stress, and whether it is due to compression, tension, or shear, creep will occur.

**Shrinkage and warping.** Plastics may be dimensionally unstable, not only because of creep under load, but also because of a tendency to shrink. The shrinkage may be quite appreciable, particularly with thermosetting materials in which it is attributed to the slow continuation of the curing process. In some applications, shrinkage effects tend to counteract the creep tensile stress and may give an apparent negative creep. For compression, however, the creep and shrinkage are additive and frequently of the same order of magnitude in normal service life.

In thermoplastic materials, shrinkage may result from loss of moisture or plasticizers or may simply be a process of relieving internal stresses introduced previously by molding or forming. A large amount of warping may be associated with shrinkage of this type.

Warping is particularly noticeable in injection-molded parts, in which large, locked-up stresses can be introduced by the sudden chilling that occurs during the molding process. Such stresses are sometimes of high magnitude and produce cracks and tears. Even small, locked-up stresses reduce the apparent strength of a material by a proportionate amount. Shear strength is particularly affected by these stresses. In clear materials, internal stresses may be detected with polarized light.

**Fatigue characteristics.** Fatigue failures are among the most common service failures. Repeated stresses weaken a material; and if a stress is repeated often enough, failure may occur—even though the stress is well below the ultimate strength. A failure of this type, called a fatigue failure, is characterized initially by the appearance of miniature cracks.

## PROCESSING METHODS

Plastics materials differ greatly from each other and lend themselves to a wide variety of processing methods. Each material usually is best adapted to one particular method, although as indicated in Tables 18-5 and 18-6, many plastics can be fabricated readily by several different methods. The material used in most processes is in a powder or granular form; and in some operations, there is a preliminary stage of preforming the plastics resin before further processing to produce the part.

### Compounding and Preforming

Although a few plastics are molded without additives, most industrial products embody a combination of properties that necessitates mixing certain ingredients before molding. Most thermoplastic material is purchased in granular form and hence is compounded dry. Thermosetting material, on the other hand, is purchased as a liquid or as a partially polymerized compound.

The compounding process is normally carried out in a muller into which any of several ingredients are mixed, including resins, stabilizers, color pigments, plasticizers, and fillers. Materials that have been mixed, and sometimes melted, are placed into the feed hoppers of injection, extrusion, or calendering machines. Some thermoplastic materials are preformed into small pellets of the proper size and shape for a given mold cavity. Preforms are of uniform density and weight, and the operation avoids waste of material in loading molds and, in general, speeds up production by enabling faster loading of molds , with no possibility of overloading. In the preforming operation, the thermosetting powder is cold-molded and no curing takes place. Preforms are used only in compression and transfer-molding processes.

A rotary preforming press is used in making disk pellets of various molding compounds. The powder is fed by gravity from the hopper into the mold cells, and excess powder is scraped off. As the unit revolves, pressure is applied uniformly on both sides, compressing the powder charge. Reciprocating machines, having only a single set of dies, are also used for a wide variety of preforming operations.

### Summary of Processes

The plastics materials are fabricated into end-products by many different processes. The molding, extrusion, and fabricating techniques are similar to those developed for metals and for rubber compounds. A large proportion of plastics parts are made by some form of molding. Compression molding is performed in hand-tended presses or in fully automatic molding machines.

The plastics injection molding process is similar to the die casting of metals (see Chapter 16, "Casting"). In the latest application of advanced technology, fast mold changing systems (automatic and semiautomatic) are being applied increasingly to injection-molding operations. The major components of fast mold changing are the mold clamping devices, mold transport systems, standardized tooling, and electronic controls. The end result is a "flexible manufacturing" capability in producing a variety of plastics molded parts.

Reaction injection molding (RIM) is a relatively new processing technique that involves simultaneous high-pressure injection of two or more reactive liquid streams into a small impingement mixing chamber, followed by low-pressure injection into a mold cavity. The new liquid injection molding (LIM) process which now is entering production applications pumps (at low pressure) the two or more liquid materials directly from shipping containers through a mixer and injects the stream into a heated mold.

Plastics extrusion molding is similar to the extrusion of metals, except that a long screw is used to melt and plasticize the plastics material by heat and mechanical working. Film or plastics sheets are often made by the extrusion process.

In one blow-molding process, a tube of hot, molten plastics is extruded into the blow mold, which clamps and seals off each end but permits air to be blown into the sealed tube of molten plastics. The laminated, high-pressure plastics are produced from a pile of sheets of cloth or paper that has been impregnated with the desired thermosetting resin. The laminates then are subjected to high pressure and heat, which plasticize the resin and bond the sheets together while the chemical hardening takes place. Laminated and many extruded thermoplastics are fabricated into end products by conventional machining, stamping, and forming processes. Welding and adhesive-bonding techniques are used to bond the thermoplastics during assembly operations.

Cast plastics use a hardening process without the application of pressure. Casting of film is done by pouring the heat-plasticized plastics on a wheel or belt from which it is stripped after it hardens by cooling. Some film is precipitated in a chemical bath that hardens the plastics as it leaves the bath. Casting of molded plastics products is accomplished by methods similar to those for the casting of metals. A number of components for motor vehicles, boats, missiles, and other products are produced from reinforced plastics made by a low-pressure molding process. Many different methods are used for making the reinforced plastics. In general, the resins utilize a hardening catalyst and are often mixed with the filler materials in the mold.

In the rotational process, a liquid or powdered plastics is introduced into a mold which spins under conditions that cause the plastics to harden on the surface of the mold, in a process that is similar to the slush casting of metals. The fluidized bed

**TABLE 18-5**
**Thermoplastics Parts Manufacturing Processes**

| Thermoplastics | Compression molding | Transfer molding | Injection molding | Extrusion | Rotational molding | Blow molding | Thermoforming | Reaction injection molding | Casting | Forging | Foam molding | Reinforced plastic molding | Vacuum molding | Pultrusion | Calendering |
|---|---|---|---|---|---|---|---|---|---|---|---|---|---|---|---|
| Acetal | | | • | • | • | • | • | | | | • | • | | | • |
| ABS | | | • | • | • | • | • | | | • | | | | | • |
| Acrylic | • | | • | • | | • | • | | • | | | | | | • |
| Cellulose acetate | • | | • | • | | | • | | | | | | | | • |
| Cellulose acetate-butyrate | • | | • | • | • | | • | | | | | | | | • |
| Cellulose nitrate | • | | • | • | | | • | | | | | | | | • |
| Cellulose propionate | • | | • | • | | | • | | | | | | | | • |
| Ethyl cellulose | | | • | • | | | • | | | | | • | | | • |
| Chlorinated polyether | | | • | • | • | • | • | | | | | | | | |
| CTFE | • | • | • | • | | | • | | | | | | | | • |
| Tetrafluoroethylene (TFE) | • | • | • | • | | | | | | | | | | | • |
| FEP | • | • | • | • | | • | | | | | | | | | • |
| CTFE-$VF_2$ | • | • | • | • | | • | | | | | | | | | • |
| Nylon | | | • | • | • | • | | • | • | • | | • | | | • |
| Phenoxy | | | • | • | | • | | | | | | | | | |
| Polyimide | | | • | | | | | | | | | | | | |
| Polycarbonate | | | • | • | | • | • | | | | | | | | • |
| Polyethylene | | | • | • | • | • | • | | | • | • | • | | | • |
| Polyphenylene oxide (PPO) | | | • | • | | • | | | | | | • | | | |
| Polypropylene (PP) | • | | • | • | • | • | • | | • | • | | • | | | • |
| Polystyrene | | | • | • | • | • | • | | | | • | • | | | • |
| Polysulfone | | | • | • | | • | • | | | | | • | | • | |
| Polyurethane | | | • | • | • | | | | | | • | • | • | | • |
| SAN | | | • | • | | • | | | | | | | | | |
| PVC | • | • | • | • | • | • | • | | | | • | • | • | | • |
| Polyvinyl acetate | • | • | • | • | • | • | • | | | | • | | | | • |
| Polyvinylidene chloride | | | • | | | | | | | | | | | | |

**TABLE 18-6**
**Thermoset Plastics Parts Manufacturing Processes**

| Thermosetting Plastics | Compression molding | Transfer molding | Injection molding | Rotational molding | Thermoforming | Reaction injection molding | Casting | Foam molding | Reinforced plastics molding | Laminating |
|---|---|---|---|---|---|---|---|---|---|---|
| Alkyd | • | • | • | | | | • | | • | |
| Allyl | | | | | • | | • | | • | • |
| Epoxy | | | | • | | • | • | • | • | • |
| Melamine | • | • | • | | | | | • | • | • |
| Phenolic | • | • | • | | | | • | • | • | • |
| Polyester (unsaturated) | • | | | | | • | • | • | • | |
| Polyurethane | | | | | | • | | | | |
| Silicone | | | | | | | • | • | • | |
| Urea | • | • | • | | | | | • | | |

process employs a preheated metal insert that is dipped into a bed of finely divided plastics powder that melts and fuses to the metal.

An electrostatic spray process operates on the principle that oppositely charged particles attract each other. The piece that is to be coated is grounded and thereby attracts the charged plastics particles.

Foamed, expanded, or bubbled plastics are produced by many molding and extrusion procedures that use a blowing agent in the plastics to cause foaming during the process.

Thermoforming consists of heating a thermoplastic sheet until it softens and then forcing it to conform to a mold either by differential air (or vacuum) pressure or by mechanical means.

### DESIGN/MANUFACTURING INTERACTION

Early in the product design schedule, the combined engineering and manufacturing judgments are brought to bear on selection of the production process. Injection molding, thermoforming, compression and transfer molding, blow molding, and the other manufacturing processes each have their advantages and disadvantages; each process is best suited for certain parts-production applications.

The product design must reflect the influence of the processing method that is to be used; and to a significant extent, the process itself dictates some of the design features. Some key parameters are:

- Part size.
- Number of parts to be produced.
- Tooling cost.
- Use of "family" molds.
- Ease or difficulty of design changes.

For a sound, producible part design, careful consideration must be given to:

- Tolerances.
- Mold shrinkage.
- Draft or cavity wall taper.
- Wall thickness.
- Finished part appearance.
- Quality control.
- Cost.

## THERMOSET PLASTICS MOLDING

Types of thermoset materials that are capable of being molded include phenolic, urea, melamine, melamine-phenolic, diallyl phthalate, alkyd, polyester, epoxy, and the silicones. Thermosetting molding compounds processed from the individual heat-reactive resin systems are available in a wide range of formulations to satisfy specific end-use requirements. Depending upon the type of material, products may be supplied in granular, nodular, flaked, diced, or pelletized form. Polyester materials are supplied in granular, bulk, log, rope, or sheet form, and polyurethanes are made in many forms, ranging from flexible and rigid foams to rigid solids and abrasion-resistant coatings.

### PRINCIPLES OF PLASTICS MOLDING

As the term implies, thermoset molding compounds when placed within the confines of a mold (generally hardened steel) are subjected to heat to plasticize and cure the material, and to pressure to form the desired shape. The mold is held closed, under pressure, sufficiently long to polymerize or cure the material into a hard, infusible mass.

#### Molding Conditions

Successful plastics molding is dependent upon the mold temperature, material temperature, and molding pressure.

**Mold temperature.** Thermoset molding compounds may be molded in a temperature range of 285-400°F (141-204°C). Material suppliers should be consulted for recommended temperatures for a specific material and molding method. The heating media are steam, hot oil, and electric cartridge or strip heaters.

**Material temperature.** Minimum cure time is a function of increased mold temperature and maximum material temperature when loaded in the mold. It is desirable to preheat most compounds. Extrudates are formed from screw feed material in a heated barrel. The temperature range is 180-260°F (82.2-127°C) depending on type of preheat equipment.

**Molding pressure.** The pressure is required to flow the compound within the confines of the mold cavities and force it to completely fill out the part with minimum flash thickness. The required pressure is dependent on method of molding.

### Molding Methods

All of the thermoset compounds, except epoxies and silicones, may be molded by the following methods: compression, transfer, thermoset injection, and the new runnerless injection compression process. Table 18-7 lists factors to be considered in the selection of a molding method.

## COMPRESSION MOLDING

In compression molding, the plastics compound is placed in a heated mold. The compound softens and becomes plastic as the upper part of the die moves (down or up, depending on the movable platen location), compressing the material to the required shape and density. Continued heat and pressure produce the chemical reaction that hardens the thermosetting material.

### Molding Equipment

A vertical molding press is required, with one stationary platen and one movable platen providing the molding and clamp pressure. The press may close in either direction. Pressure is made available using air or hydraulic cylinders (or a combination of the two) or a mechanical toggle. Presses are generally self-contained and have provisions for top and bottom knock-out systems. The press operation may be either automatic or semiautomatic. Presses available have clamp ratings of 50-2000 tons (445-17 800 kN).

Preform presses, high-frequency preheaters, and preheat extruders are commonly used as auxiliary equipment in the compression-molding process.

### Molding Process

The mold consists of two halves, one containing the cavity or cavities (the female member) and one containing the force or forces (the male member). Each is mounted on press supports or grids which are in turn fastened to the stationary or moving platens. Generally, the cavities are in the lower half to permit easy loading of the molding compound. This operation may be manual or automatic. In the case of automatic operation, movable loading trays are incorporated in conjunction with trays or forks to receive molded parts from the mold.

A typical cycle with the mold at recommended temperature and with adequate pressure available would proceed as follows:

1. Air-clean the mold of all flash or foreign matter.
2. Load the material into the cavities.
3. Close the mold completely; or before closing it, interject a brief "breathe cycle" by opening the mold slightly to release any air and gases trapped in the molding compound.
4. Complete the cure time.
5. Open the mold and activate the knock-out assembly.
6. Remove the molded parts.
7. Clean the mold with an air blast.

The cure duration is dependent upon the type of molding compound, mold temperature, and material temperature. Cross-sections 0.125-0.500" (3.18-12.7 mm) thick may cure in 30 seconds to 2 minutes when preheated material is used (which is always desirable).

### Molding Conditions

Factors to be considered during compression molding

**TABLE 18-7**
**Selection of Molding Method—Compression or Transfer**

| Factors to Consider: Advantages—Limitations | Compression | Transfer |
|---|---|---|
| Close tolerances, projected area | • | |
| Close tolerances, over flash line, minimum flash | | • |
| Lowest mold shrinkage | • | |
| Uniform shrinkage, all directions | • | |
| Maximum uniform density | • | |
| Reduced cure, thick sections | | • |
| No weld lines, less molded-in strains | • | |
| Small holes, longer length, through holes | | • |
| Extremely thin mold sections, telescoping | | • |
| No venting problems | • | |
| Impact strength | • | |
| Molds with movable sections or cores | | • |
| Molded-in inserts | | • |
| Large projected area parts | • | |
| Lowest mold-flash scrap | • | |
| Generally less mold maintenance | | • |
| Gate or sprue removal necessary | | • |
| Maximum number cavities per clamp force | • | |
| Mold erosion, sprues, runners, gates | | • |
| Generally higher mold cost | | • |

include the type of molding compound, the mold temperature, and the molding pressure.

**Compound.** Using a molding compound with the desired functional performance characteristics, the specifications should provide a bulk factor not greater than three to one, good funnel flow rating, and proper plasticity.

**Temperature.** The mold temperature should be specified after consulting with the material supplier. As stated previously, temperatures range from 285-400° F (141-204° C).

**Pressure.** Generally, all thermoset compounds recommended for compression molding require the same molding pressure; polyesters are the exception and are considered low-pressure materials. Epoxy and silicone materials are not generally molded by compression.

A material of recommended plasticity, at room temperature, requires pressures of 2000-3000 psi (13.8-20.7 MPa) on the projected molding and land area of each cavity. Parts greater than 1″ (25 mm) in depth require an additional 600 psi (4.1 MPa) per inch of depth. Preheated material may reduce pressures 50% or more. The material supplier should be consulted when molding pressure is specified for polyesters.

## Mold Construction

Factors influencing mold construction include the mold cavity and forces and the materials and method of construction.

**Cavity and forces.** The molds may contain a single cavity or multicavities. The number of cavities is determined by the production requirements, part size, type of material, and clamp capacity of the molding press.

Determining factors that dictate mold design of cavity and force include the type of material, part design, flash line restrictions, part dimensions and tolerances, and end-use requirements. Shrinkage of material during curing and cooling is built into mold dimensions.

**Mold types.** Five basic types of compression mold cavity and force are available for selection.

*Flash type.* The flash-type mold, illustrated in Fig. 18-4, is simple in construction and low in cost. Disadvantages are that it creates minimal back pressure within the cavity needed to control density and molded part dimensions and it has high flash scrap loss. The flash mold is not recommended for parts requiring maximum density and strength.

*Semipositive, vertical-flash type.* The semipositive, vertical-flash-type mold, shown in Fig. 18-5, requires double fitting of force to cavity and is costly. It controls maximum density and critical dimensions as related to cavity and force, offers ease of flash removal on large parts, and leaves no flash line scar on the side of the part.

*Semipositive, horizontal-flash type.* The semipositive, horizontal-flash-type mold, shown in Fig. 18-6, controls conditions in a manner similar to that of the horizontal-flash type, but it is less costly and more popular. It is recommended for close-tolerance parts and assures minimum flash fin.

*Direct-positive type.* The direct-positive-type mold, illustrated in Fig. 18-7, is used for high-bulk materials and deep-draw parts when maximum density is required. It is a single-cavity mold that uses an accurately weighed charge of material.

*Landed-positive type.* The landed-positive-type mold, shown in Fig. 18-8, is used as a single-cavity mold on a rotary press, on which molding pressure is controlled at each station. Maximum density may be maintained by clearance between the side wall of the force and the cavity. Overall height of the part is controlled by land areas on mating surfaces of the force and cavity.

**Mounting and retainer plates.** Cavities and forces are assembled on mounting plates and may be held in the confines of a retainer plate. Heat sources are contained in one or both units.

**Part-removal systems.** A top and bottom knockout system is necessary in automatic operations. One set of pins may act as hold-down or hold-up pins while the second set facilitates part removal.

**Mold design.** Mold design is a special area and requires expertise in steel types and hardness specifications, machining methods, and other factors that may vary in the molds for producing different parts.

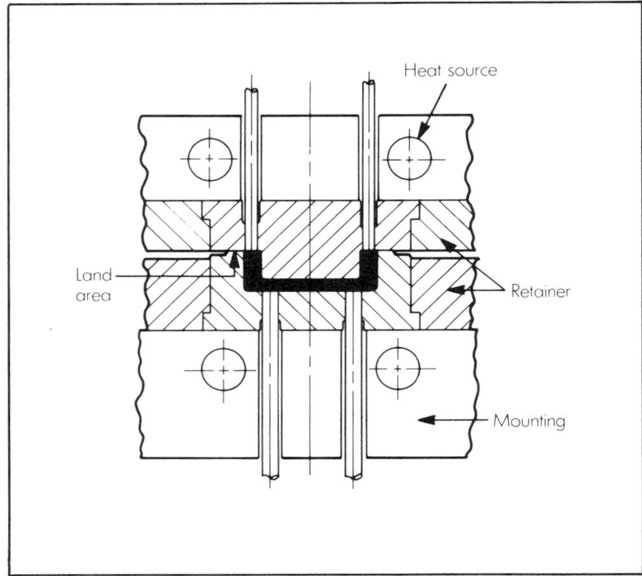


**Fig. 18-4 Flash-type compression mold.** (*R. W. Bainbridge*)

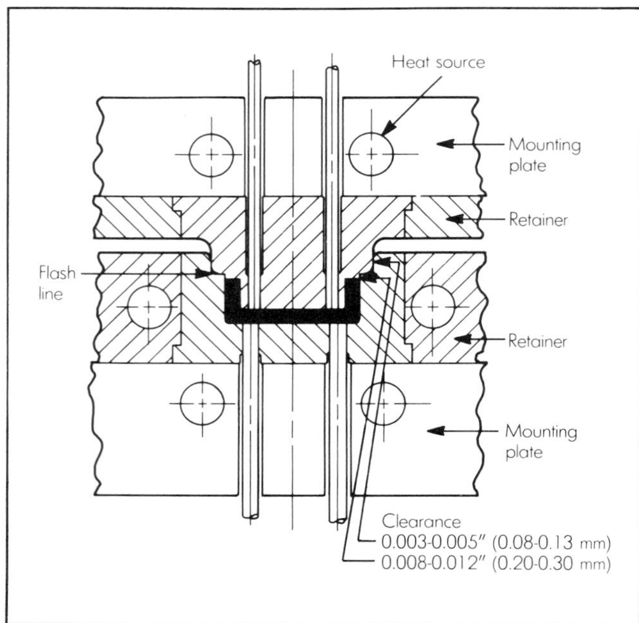


**Fig. 18-5 Semipositive, vertical-flash compression mold.** (*R. W. Bainbridge*)

**Mold making.** The principal kinds of steel used for making plastics molds are prehardened, carburizing, oil hardening, air hardening, stainless, and maraging. These materials are supplied in rolled, forged, and cast sections. The primary methods used to form cavities in steel molds are conventional machining, hobbing, and electrical discharge machining (EDM). Heat treatment is part of the mold-making process, unless a prehardened steel is selected. Finishing of the mold cavity surface is usually done by grinding and polishing. For additional information, refer to Chapter 2, "Die and Mold Materials."

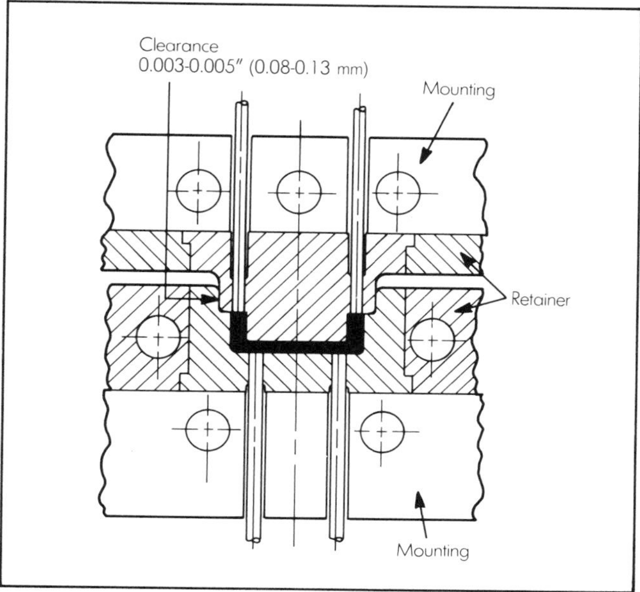


**Fig. 18-6 Semipositive, horizontal-flash-type compression mold.** (*R. W. Bainbridge*)

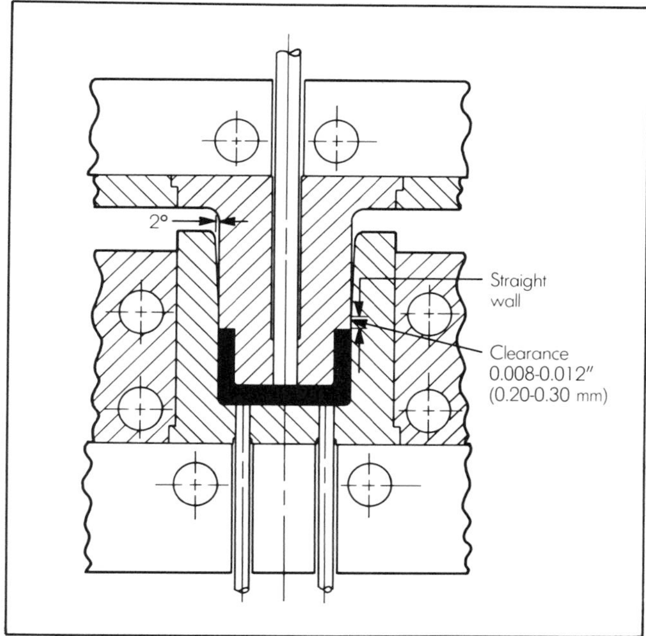


**Fig. 18-7 Direct-positive-type compression mold.** (*R. W. Bainbridge*)

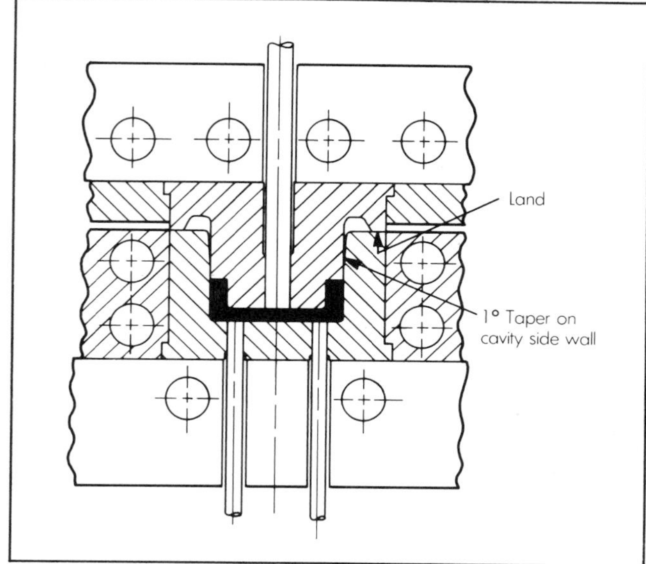


**Fig. 18-8 Landed-positive-type compression mold.** (*R. W. Bainbridge*)

## TRANSFER MOLDING

Transfer molding, as the name implies, is a method of molding specific parts when it is desirable that the two halves of the mold, containing the shape of the part, are closed before any material is introduced. The material is loaded into a pot or transfer sleeve, and transfer pressure is applied to cause material to flow into the closed section of the mold. In a single-cavity mold, the material flows generally through a sprue bushing and is gated directly into the part. In the case of a multicavity mold, it flows from a sprue bushing or transfer sleeve into a runner system and is gated into each cavity and part.

There are two distinct transfer methods of molding. One is known as pot-type transfer, and the other (more widely used) is the plunger transfer method.

### Molding Equipment

Pot-type transfer molding is generally done in a conventional bottom-clamp compression press. Plunger transfer molding is done in a conventional vertical press. A transfer press has a hydraulic clamp cylinder with a separate transfer cylinder applying force (pressure) in the opposite direction of the clamp force (pressure). For automatic operation, a top clamp force and a bottom transfer force are desirable for ease of loading preheated preforms. Plunger transfer presses are generally self-contained and have provisions for top and bottom knockout systems which are available for semiautomatic or automatic operations. Users should contact press manufacturers or molders for available press sizes.

Auxiliary equipment is similar to the units identified under "Compression Molding."

### Molding Processes

Depending upon whether the molding method is pot-type or plunger, one of two types of molds are employed in transfer molding.

**Pot-type mold.** A pot-type transfer mold, illustrated in Fig. 18-9, generally has one cavity. The mold consists of two halves, with the cavity section assembled to the lower mounting plate, which is fastened to the supports or grids and is bolted to the movable lower platen. The lower platen is activated up and down by the clamp ram. The force section is assembled to the lower surface of the movable floating platen. The pot or chamber is contained in the upper area. These components are fastened together as a complete assembly. The plunger that enters the pot area is mounted to the head of the press or to the grids.

In a typical cycle using recommended mold temperature, the operator loads preheated preforms or extrudates into the pot

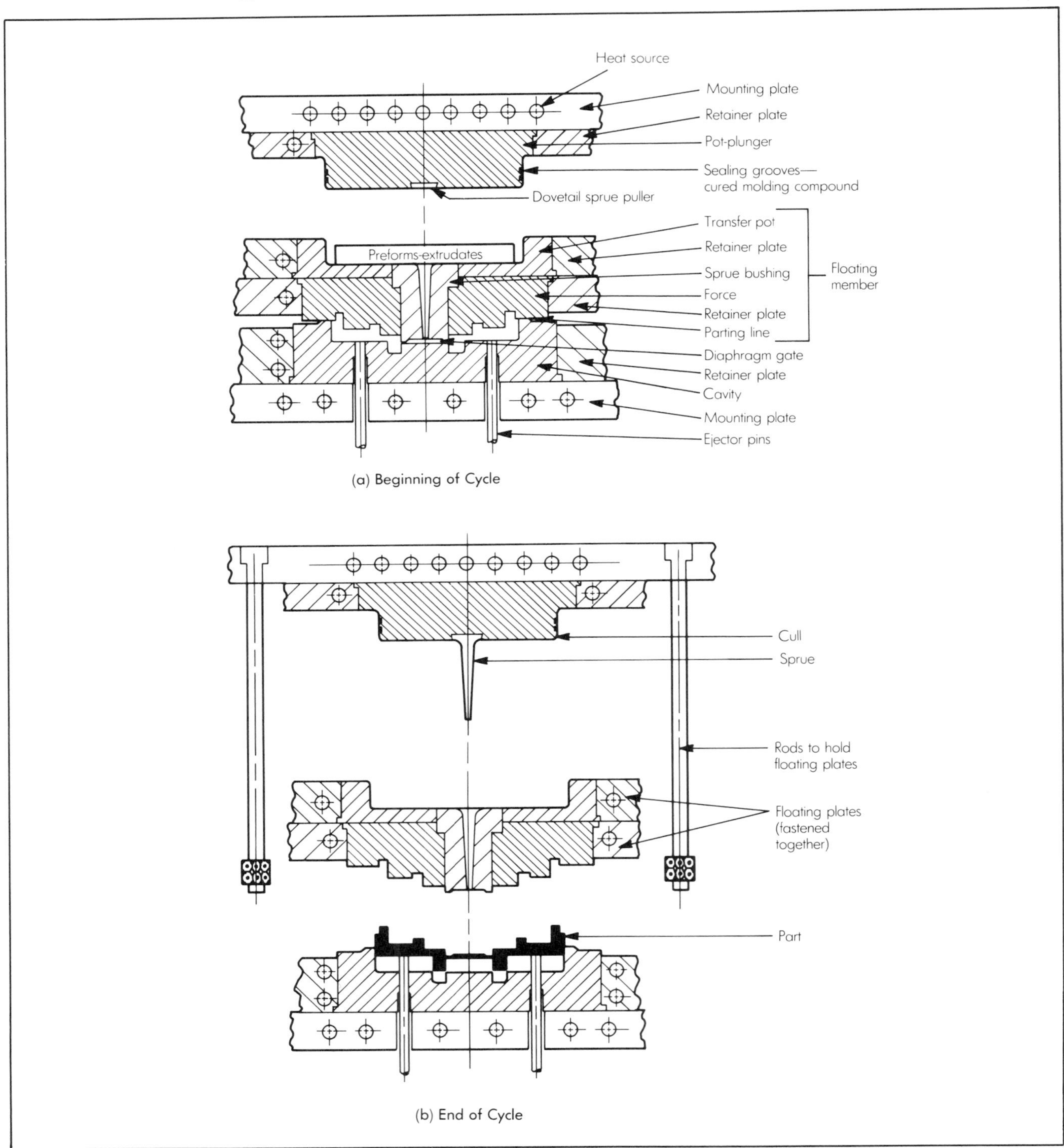


**Fig. 18-9 Pot-type transfer mold.** (*R. W. Bainbridge*)

area, the press is activated upward using low pressure, and the press picks up the floating member (see Fig. 18-9, *a*), which engages the plunger. High pressure is applied, forcing the material through the sprue bushing directly into the cavity and force area or through a diaphragm gate in the case of a circular part. The cure cycle is completed under pressure; the clamp ram is moved downward; and the mold opens. The pot and plunger separate and the movable floating platen is pulled away from the lower half of the mold by means of rods fastened to the head of the press. The part-removal assembly raises the part from the cavity, and the operator removes the part. The operator removes cull and sprue from the plunger, uses an airblast to clean the remainder of the mold, and places the preforms in a preheater or activates the extruder for the following cycle, as shown in Fig. 18-9, *b*.

**Plunger mold.** A plunger transfer mold (shown in Fig. 18-10) consists of two halves, one containing the cavity or cavities and one containing the force or forces. The transfer sleeve and plunger are located in the center of the mold; the plunger is fastened to the transfer cylinder. The press design dictates location of the clamp ram and transfer cylinder. The halves of the mold are mounted on grids or support pillars in the proper

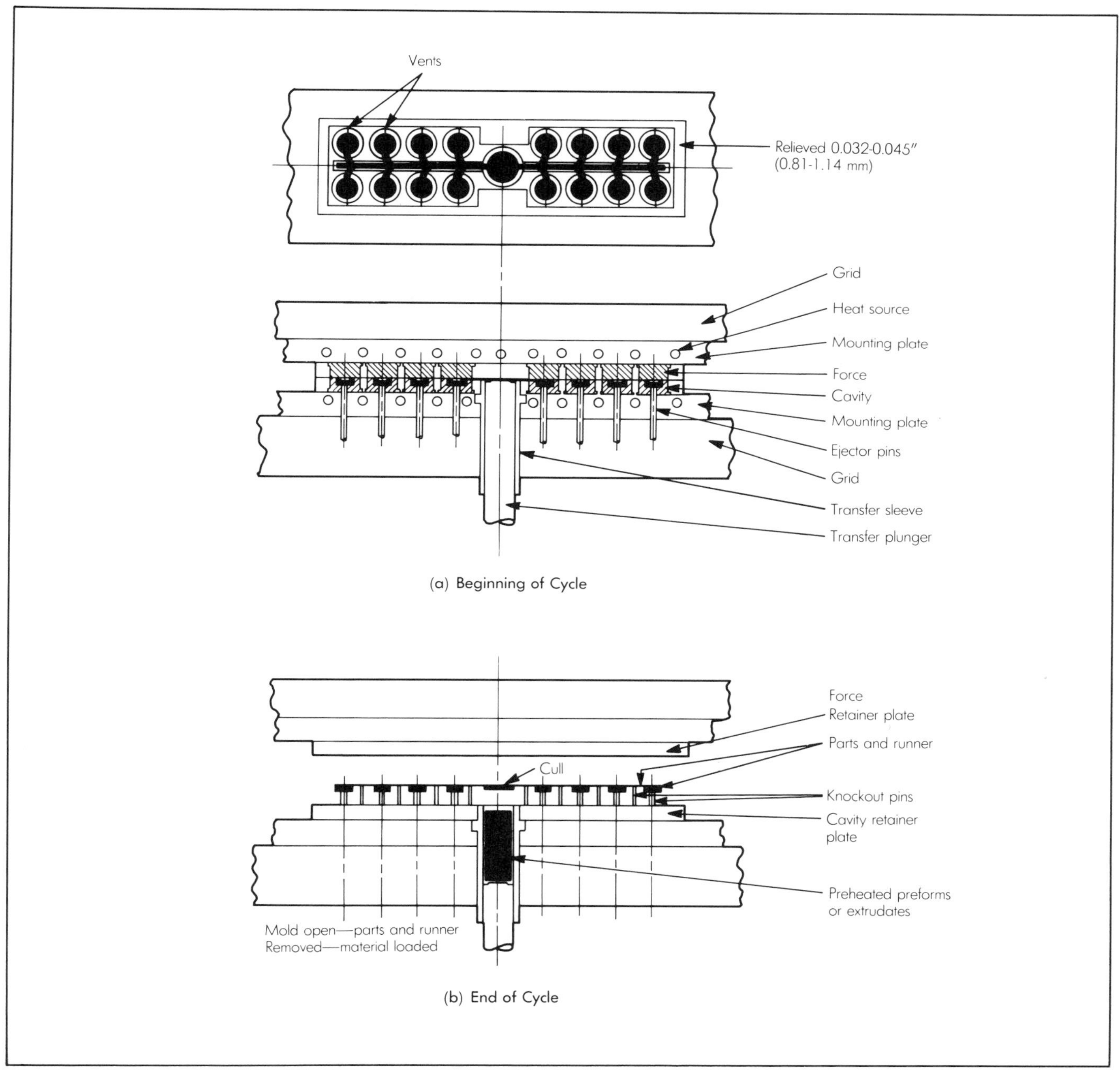


**Fig. 18-10 Plunger-type transfer mold.** (*R. W. Bainbridge*)

location. In a typical operation with a bottom plunger transfer press, with molding performed at recommended mold temperature, preheated preforms or extrudates are loaded into the transfer sleeve, and the press is closed. Activation of the transfer plunger forces material into the runner system, through a gate, into the mold cavity. After completing the cure cycle, the press is opened, and parts and runners are removed from the mold. The cull is removed from the top of the transfer plunger, and the transfer plunger is activated downward. An airblast is used to clean the mold, making sure vents are clean. The final step is to activate the preheater or extrudate equipment. Figure 18-10 shows a plunger transfer mold at the beginning and the end of a cycle.

### Molding Conditions

Factors to be considered during transfer molding include the type of molding compound, the mold temperature, and the molding pressure.

**Compound.** The molding compound should have soft plasticity properties suitable for preforming and/or making extruded shapes in extrusion equipment using a screw to feed and preheat material in a temperature-controlled barrel.

**Temperature.** Mold temperature can range from 285-400° F (141-204° C), depending upon the specific plastic materials used.

**Pressure.** Technical considerations related to pressure specification differ for pot and plunger-type transfer molds. Polyester, epoxy, and silicone molding compounds require less tranfer pressure than other materials. The plastics supplier should be consulted for recommended pressure.

*Pot-type transfer.* The transfer pressure in this type of mold is the pressure developed within the pot area. The projected pot area must be equal to or 10% greater than the projected area of the part. Failure to provide sufficient area in the pot can cause the mold to "blow open" at the parting line of the cavity and the force. Recommended transfer pressure developed in the pot area is 6000-10,000 psi (41.1-69 MPa).

*Plunger transfer.* The transfer pressure recommended is 6000-8000 psi (41.4-55.1 MPa). The significant area is made up of combined projected areas of the parts and the transfer plunger, plus total runner and gate area of all cavities. Clamp force must be sufficient to keep the mold from flashing at the parting line of the cavities, runners, and cull area.

### Mold Design

The mold design engineer must consider part design, dimensional tolerances, gate location, type of material, type and size of molding presses, and mold design options before making the decision to mold a part either by pot-type or by plunger transfer. The majority of parts requiring transfer molding are suitable for the plunger transfer method. As in the case of compression molding, the final mold design is the result of considerable study. Types of steel, method of machining, and hardness vary for each part. Transfer molds must be supported well, especially in the center area, to keep the mold from flashing.

## MOLDING PROCESS COMPARISON

A thorough evaluation should be made of the advantages and disadvantages of molding by the compression method as compared to the transfer method. It is desirable for the design engineer, process engineer, and material representative to meet and discuss all options before deciding upon the best method of molding a particular part.

### Compression Molding

Although it is the oldest method of molding, compression molding probably will continue to be a major technique for processing most thermoset molding compounds. The following applications are representative of the market areas for which many parts are molded by compression:

- Wiring devices—wall plates, outlet boxes and receptacles, switches.
- Closures—bottle and tube caps for drugs and cosmetics.
- Electrical switch gear—home and low-voltage circuit breakers.
- Automotive parts—brake and transmission parts, grilles and body parts, ignition parts.
- Dishware—melamine dishware.
- Small appliances—knobs, handles, bases for motor mounts and cookers.
- Housings—sanitary tubs, stall shower units or bases, electrical outlet boxes.

### Transfer Molding

Because of the part design, dimensional tolerances, mold design options, etc., many parts are well suited for molding by the transfer method. The following applications are representative of the market areas for which many parts are molded by transfer:

- Electronic devices—capacitors, transistors, integrated circuits, wire-wound power resistors, diodes, semiconductors, rectifiers, connectors, data processing devices.
- Electrical switch gear and motor starters—heavy switch gear circuit breaker and related parts.
- Automotive parts—transmission parts, solenoid covers, ignition parts.
- Cookware—handles, stick handles, housing.
- Appliances—housing for motors, pumps, and timers.

### Other Methods of Molding

With the trend toward more automatic operations requiring no operators or one operator for several presses, there have been some conversions to the injection process and some new parts are being molded using it. Currently, the runnerless injection/compression process is being adopted for some applications. Faster cycles are generally possible when the part and material are adaptable to this new process. Process engineers must consider and evaluate the significant factors and parameters and make the decision as to the most suitable operation.

# INJECTION MOLDING

Injection molding is a versatile process for forming thermoplastic and thermoset materials into molded products of intricate shapes, at high production rates and with good dimensional accuracy. Injection molding makes use of the heat-softening characteristics of thermoplastic materials. These materials soften when heated and reharden when cooled. No chemical changes take place when the material is heated or cooled, the change being entirely physical. For this reason the softening and rehardening cycle can be repeated several times. While this is true for thermoplastics, with certain thermosets and rubbers that can be injection molded, a chemical reaction does occur.

## MOLDING PROCESS

The basic injection molding process involves the injection, under high pressure, of a metered quantity of heated and plasticized material into a relatively cool mold—in which the plastics material solidifies. The granular molding material is loaded into a hopper which gravity feeds to a rotating screw, as shown in Fig. 18-11. The screw melts the plastic and conveys it to a reservoir at the end of the screw. Melting is accomplished by both frictional heat generation and conduction from a heated barrel. When sufficient material has accumulated in the reservoir, the screw is moved forward, injecting the plastics into the mold. A special ring at the end of the screw prevents the plastics from flowing back into the screw. In the mold, the material is solidified, then the mold is opened, and the part is ejected.

The temperature to which the material is raised in the heating cycle can vary from 350-700° F (177-371° C) depending on the type of plastics and its viscosity. The higher the temperature, the lower the viscosity of the material and the easier it is to inject material into the mold. The more complex the workpiece, the greater the number of parts per mold. Long runners and the presence of fillers in the plastics tend to increase the temperature requirement of the material. The material temperature also affects the physical properties of the molded part, as does the rate at which it is cooled in the mold.

When the plastics material is pushed from the nozzle end of the cylinder, it enters through channels into the closed mold. In the majority of cases, the mold is kept cold to cool the molded pieces rapidly to the point at which it can be opened and the pieces ejected without distortion. This is done by circulating water through the mold frame. For certain jobs, it is necessary to use a mold that has been heated to temperatures as high as 240° F (116° C). However, the material sets faster in a cold die, and the cycles are shorter. Automatic control devices are used to maintain mold temperatures at desired levels.

## ADVANTAGES AND LIMITATIONS

Since speed is one of the main advantages in injection molding, complex molds with inserts should be avoided whenever possible. Injection molds need not be single-cavity, but the high rate of production reduces the need for a large number of cavities. The savings resulting from higher production rates are partially offset by higher capital expenditure for machines and molds, and higher operating costs.

Injection molding is generally limited to forming thermoplastic materials, but equipment is available for converting the machines to enable molding thermosetting plastics and compounds of rubber.

The size of the article that can be molded is determined by the pressure and heating-cylinder capacities of the machine.

## EQUIPMENT

Injection molding machines are comprised of two basic sections: the clamp unit and the injection unit. The clamping

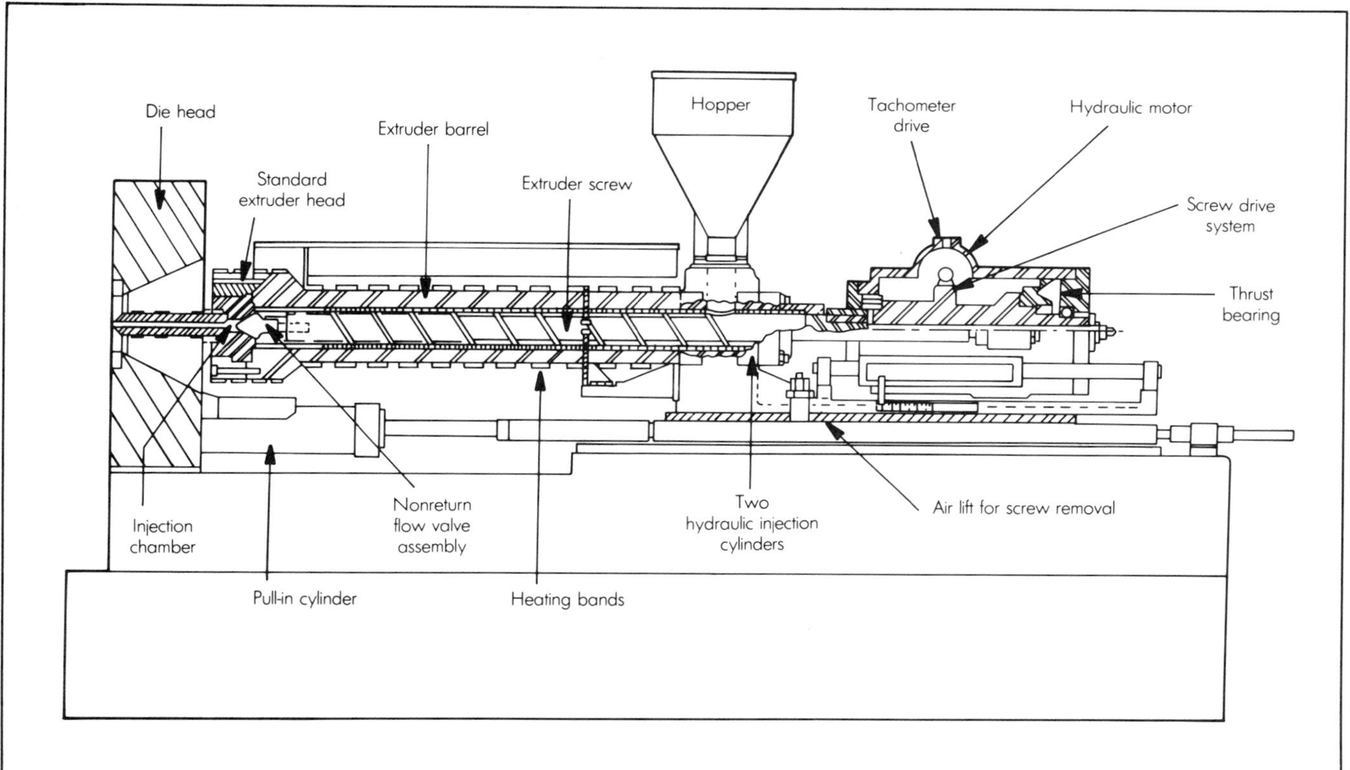


**Fig. 18-11 Schematic illustration showing injection end of reciprocating screw machine.** (*HPM Div., Koehring Co.*)

unit supports, opens, and closes the mold and maintains it in the closed position under suitable clamping pressure. The injection unit converts the plastics from solid particles into a continuous, semifluid mass and injects it into the closed mold.

Injection machines are commonly self-contained, hydraulically actuated machines that are operated from a central hydraulic system. Suitable valves control the sequence of operations.

Injection machines are usually classified by the capacity or quantity of molding material that the heating cylinder can deliver in one stroke of the injection ram. The capacity is expressed in ounces (grams). The rated capacity is the amount of plastics deliverable in one shot, including the weight of the part, runners, and sprue. Flat parts impose another additional limiting factor; the pressure requirements for their projected area cannot surpass the capacity of the clamping pressure on the mold.

## Injection Molds

Various materials are employed in the construction of cavities and punches for injection molds. Molds for high-production parts are generally made of an oil-hardening, nondeforming-quality tool steel or stainless steel. Pretempered steels are used for large or intricate cavities and punches which might distort during heat treatment. These steels are suitable for large production runs if proper care is taken of the molds.

Mold cavities of steel are most frequently used, although beryllium copper molds centrifugally cast around a hardened mandrel or formed by electroplating are frequently used. Beryllium copper is preferred for molding decorative parts requiring complex design detail and for parts requiring several cavities. Electroplating of nickel around a mandrel is used for cavities requiring fine detail and close tolerances. Stainless steel is used to prevent corrosion, and chrome plating is also used to provide hard, corrosion-resistant surfaces. Mold cavities and punches are also produced by a precision investment casting process. Additional information is provided in Chapter 2, "Die and Mold Materials."

Designs for the molding of threads, undercuts, inserts, and side holes have been developed which may reduce production speeds and introduce uncertainties in the uniformity of the product. Many of the design details are the result of practical shop experience rather than research. For this reason the sizes and shapes of nozzles, sprues, runners, and gates have been developed as the result of actual experience on various jobs. It is sound practice to specify that minimum sizes of openings and channels have adequate cross section to ensure a fast, easy flow of material into the cavity sections without resorting to a complicated cycle. Passages that are too small result in improperly filled parts which show uneven flow, shrink marks, and weld lines.

## Gates for Injection Molding

The six types of gates commonly used for injection molding are shown in Fig. 18-12. It is generally good practice to locate gates as close to the appearance surface as practicable. The final mass of material entering the mold is generally the hottest and gives the best weld and finish. When a core is used, a gate near the appearance surface causes the weld to occur at a point farther from that surface than it would be otherwise.

The standard gate (see Fig. 18-12, view *a*,) is adaptable to most articles injection-molded from acetates. It is usually used when there are many small cavities in the mold, and it minimizes the extent of the finishing operation. The fan-type gate (view *b*) is used for molding thin, flat pieces of large area. It helps to spread the material out and to reduce the tendency toward surface-flow lines. The ring-type gate (view *c*) is employed in molding hollow, cylindrical pieces. Runner and gate both encircle the core pin and cause material to flow more evenly into the cavity, thus eliminating the weld that would otherwise occur if the material entered at one side, flowed around the core pin, and joined on the opposite side. The finishing operation for a disk gate (view *d*) consists of punching out the thin disk that forms the gate.

For injection molding of acrylics and vinyl materials, a tab gate (see Fig. 18-12, *e*) is cut between the regular gate and the cavity wall. The small gate between the tab and ball end of the full-round runner builds up temperature by restriction and causes the hot plastic material to strike against the blank wall of the tab. The plastic front is smoothed out and fills the cavity area with an even, flat flow of plasticized material. Tab-gating permits a lower plunger pressure; therefore, it is not necessary to pack the cavity to obtain completely filled parts. This type of gate usually produces well-formed parts of good appearance. It also reduces welds and sinks, and improves craze resistance and dimensional stability.

The pinpoint gate (view *f*) is particularly suited to the molding of polystyrene. It has a round runner with a spherical end from which the gate continues to the cavity. The gate should be about 3/32" (2.4 mm) long and 0.040" (1 mm) wide, either round or square in shape. To ensure best results with this gate, water at 140-150° F (60-66° C) should be circulated through the mold.

A variation of the pinpoint or restricted-gate design, for vinyl elastomers, is the use of a pin or plate deflector in an enlarged area between the runner and the gate.

## Sprues

Heated material from the cylinder nozzle enters the mold through a sprue which is a 3-5° tapered, polished hole through a stationary part of the mold. The small end of the taper is directed toward the nozzle, to facilitate removal. It is slightly greater in diameter than the nozzle orifice. The large end of the sprue feeds the runners or feeds material directly into the cavity. Hardened-steel sprue bushings with a spherical seat to fit the nozzle of the injection cylinder are commercially available.

When sprues are designed to feed into runners, a sprue lockpin with a hook machined into its end is used to pull the sprue. The lockpin is short enough to clear the bottom of the runner and to provide a depression that fills first and catches the small amount of material that cools at the tip of the nozzle between cycles.

## Runners

The runners are channels leading from the sprue to the gates of the individual cavities. The best shaped runners have a round cross section because they have the least friction surface. One-half of this type of runner must be machined in each mold block and be accurately located and machined so as to match accurately when the mold is closed. As a compromise, trapezoidal or semicircular cross-sectioned runners are frequently machined into one half of the mold only.

## Ejection and Venting

Ejection is accomplished by knockout or ejector pins, sleeves, or stripper plates supported on the ejector bar. In general, ejector pins have been found to be more satisfactory for injection molding practice than other means.

Trapped air is vented from close-fitting molds during injection by means of vents placed at the cavity edge on one parting plane of the mold. The vent location is extremely important. If not properly located, a vent can become plugged with material before the trapped air is relieved. The vents should have a maximum depth of 0.002″ (0.05 mm) and should be about 1/8″ (3 mm) wide. Baffles or obstructions at the gate are sometimes used to divert the flow of material within the cavity, to move the entrapped air to an escape vent, or to change the location of the flow lines to a position where they

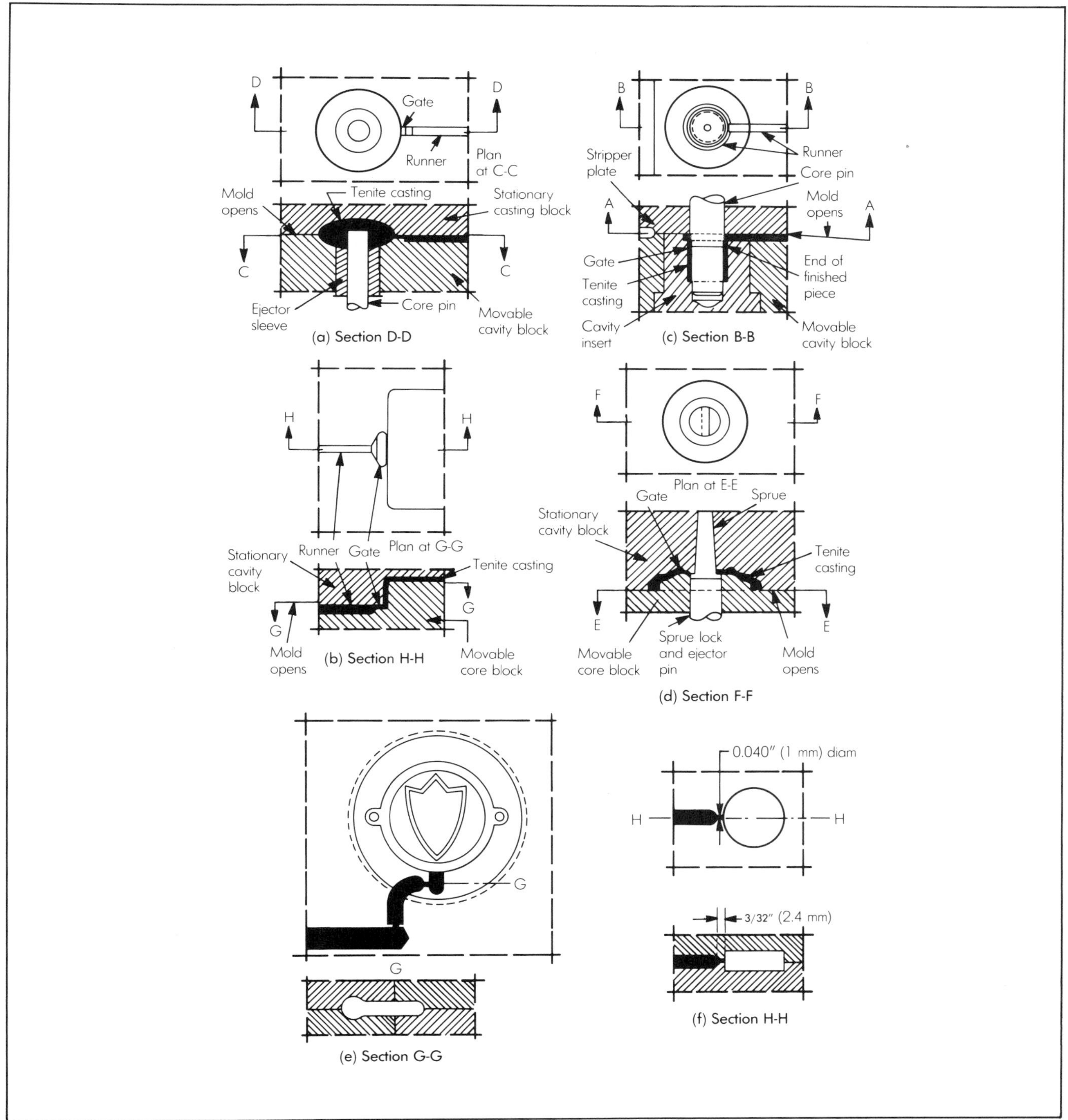


**Fig. 18-12 Types of gates used in injection molding.**

will not affect the strength or appearance of the part. Ejector pins should be located in a position that allows air to escape around them.

## Hot-Runner Molds

In the hot-runner method of molding, the die design allows a nozzle or an arrangement of nozzles to gate directly into the cavities. The sprue bushing and runner plate become an extension of the heating cylinder and are usually electrically heated. A thermocouple at each sprue bushing controls the material heat. Figure 18-13 shows a schematic drawing of a hot-runner mold system.

Lower maintenance requirements and faster cycling are among the advantages of hot-runner molds. This method also brings the material closer to the plasticized condition and provides uniform filling of multiple-cavity molds while eliminating sprue and runner waste.

## Automatic Injection Molding

The fully automatic injection-molding machines are designed to operate continuously without constant operator attention. Because of a uniform operating cycle, molds with fewer cavities can turn out greater production than the manually operated machines. Microprocessor control is a standard feature on most new units.

Many machines have a two-stage pressure arrangement on the mold-closing mechanism to prevent damage to the mold in case of incomplete ejection of parts or runners. Low pressure is used to close the mold; after the mold is completely closed, a limit switch actuates the high-pressure stage to lock the mold closed. If a piece of material is left in the mold, the limit switch cannot function and a warning light flashes.

The part design should lend itself to automatic or mechanical ejection upon opening of the mold. Self-shearing gates and a sorting arrangement to separate the parts from the runners can make this a more economical setup.

As noted earlier in this chapter under "Summary of Processes," in current applications of advanced technology, fast mold changing systems are utilized for injection-molding operations. Advantages include reduced time for tooling changes, which contributes to productivity gains. Varying levels of fast mold changing are available—from automatic, push-button setups to less sophisticated semiautomatic systems that require more operator assistance. The end result is a capability for integrating injection-molding operations into a flexible manufacturing system for producing a variety of plastics parts.

## Examples of Injection Molds

Figure 18-14 shows a partial section through a mold for a cylindrical part having four equally spaced ribs, a threaded base, and slots in the side walls between the ribs. The part was positioned horizontally in the mold to eliminate the need for complicated side cores to form the slots in the side walls and the threads in the base of the part. A 3″ (76 mm) diam hydraulic cylinder is used to pull the simple side core. The upper and lower cavities and the core are made of SAE 6150 steel, hardened and tempered to $R_C$ 52-54, polished to a high-luster mirror finish, then flash chrome plated. The runner is 5/16″ (8 mm) diam with a pinpoint gate.

A single-cavity injection mold for a rectangular cup with tapered walls is shown in Fig. 18-15. The cavity is made of cast beryllium copper finished to a high-luster mirror polish. The punch is made of SAE 6150 steel hardened to $R_C$ 52-54 and given the same finish as the cavity. The ejector pin passes through an insert designed for the passage of water. The sprue extends to the molded part without using a runner.

An interchangeable, multiple-cavity mold is illustrated in Fig. 18-16. Sixteen cavities in groups of four are incorporated in this mold. The core pins are fastened to a slide operated by pins in the upper plate. A heel block ensures that the core slide is in proper position during the injection of the molding material.

## Mold-Design Check List

Many of the following steps should be taken when designing a compression, transfer, or injection mold for plastics parts.

1. Check the location of cavities in a multiple-cavity mold for balance of side pressure and pressure balance, as it may become necessary to use only part of the cavities.

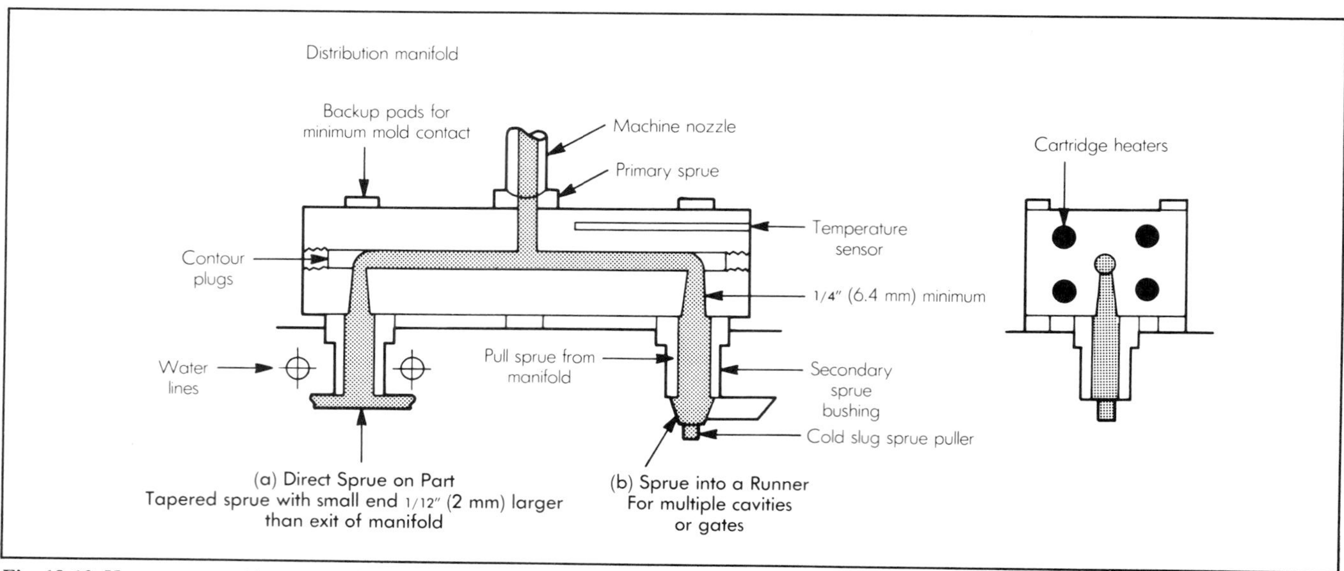


**Fig. 18-13 Hot-runner mold system.** (*General Electric Co.*)

2. Design dowel cores, cavities, and punches in place when possible.
3. Specify the maximum draft allowable.
4. Specify solid-brass, tapered pipe plugs for steam lines to prevent leaks. Steam lines should be baffled to ensure uniform circulation.
5. Specify return pins in the ejector bar to ensure its return and to prevent the ejector pins from hitting the opposite half of the mold.
6. Specify guide pins in the punch half of the mold. These pins should be longer than the punches so they enter the guide bushings before the punch enters the cavity. This design also provides a resting place for the punch half while on a work bench.
7. If the guide pins and bushings are of the press type, specify a method of locking them in place.
8. Check the location of holes with respect to steam lines to prevent breaking through the lines and causing leaks.
9. If the part has threads, check the termination of the thread on the core or cavity to permit removal. Be sure the hand of thread is specified.
10. For a multiple-cavity mold, locate parts to facilitate segregation when broken from runners.
11. Ensure that holes in guide-pin bushings are all the way through, permitting flash or stray material to fall out.
12. Check to ascertain if support pillars are needed under ejector bars and steam plates.
13. Where possible, support core pins in the opposite half of

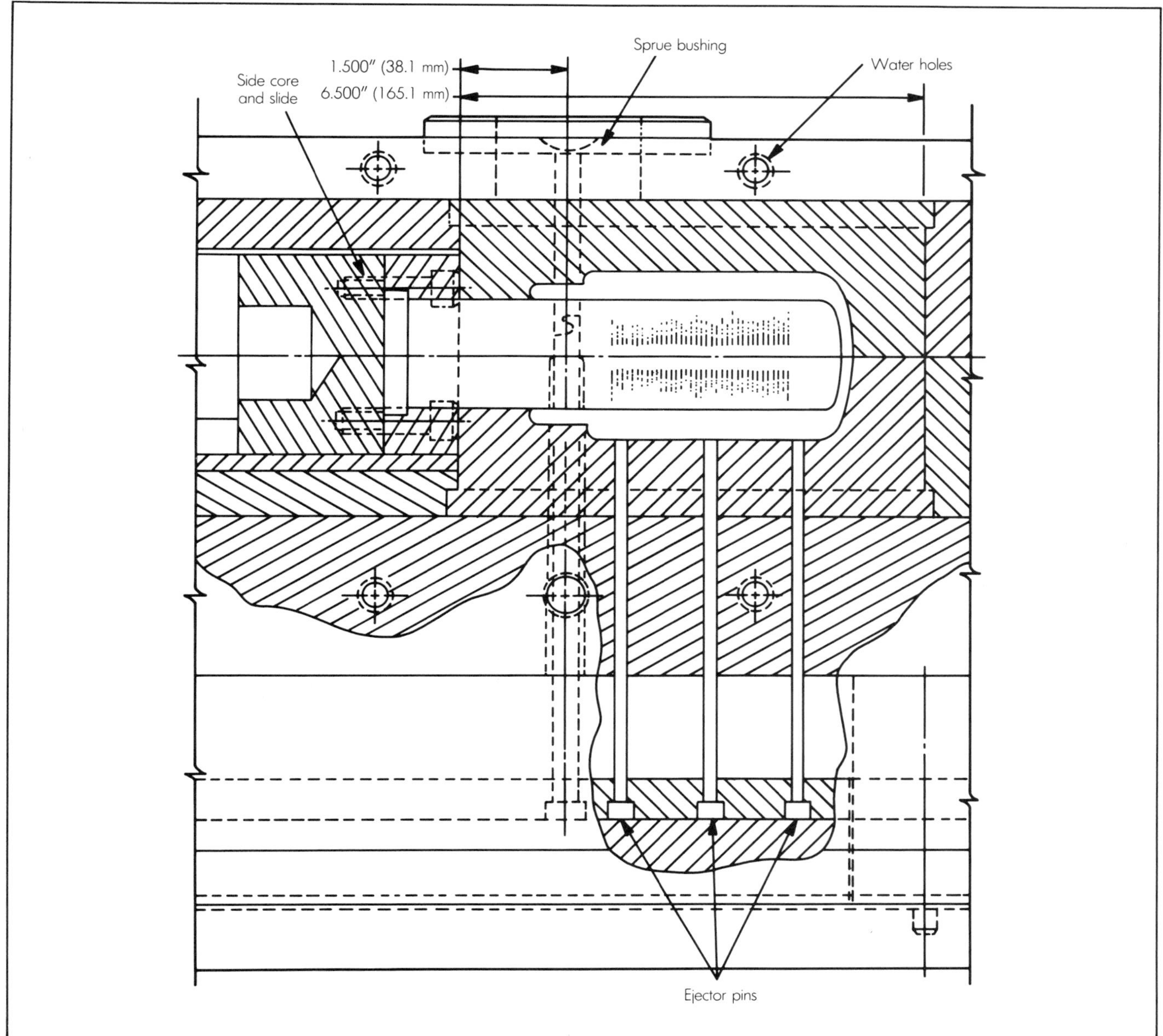


**Fig. 18-14 Injection mold for cylindrical part with screw threads.**

the mold to reduce deflection under molding pressure.
14. Check for sufficient ejector pin movement.
15. Specify headed ejector pins. Hold thickness of head and depth of counterbore to close tolerances to prevent high or low pins. Use standard, commercially available pins where possible, since they are easily replaced.

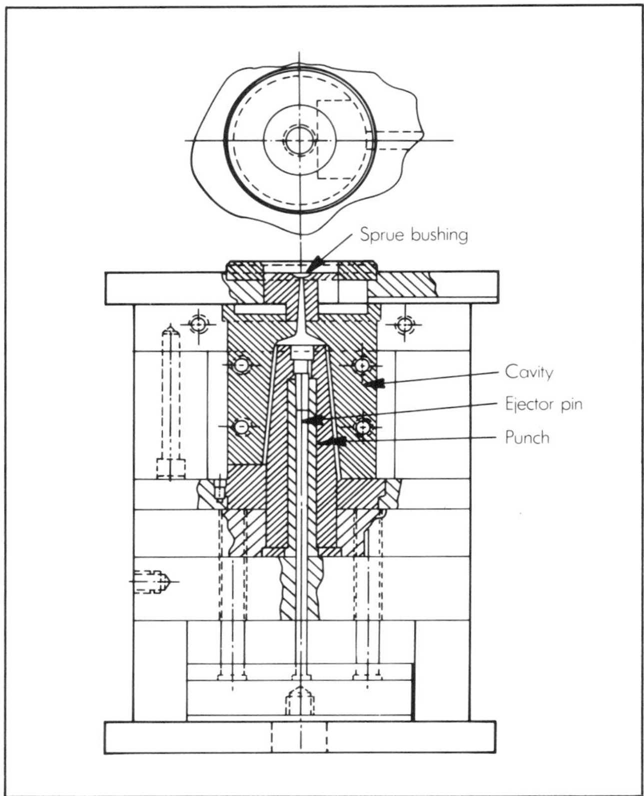


Fig. 18-15 Injection mold with sprue leading to the cavity.

16. To overcome side pressure and possible shifting, use heel blocks on large irregular-cavity molds. Pocket the punch and cavity halves in steam plates to prevent shifting.
17. Use stop blocks to absorb some of the locking pressure.
18. Check the size of the loading well according to the preform or bulk-powder requirements.
19. Specify steam lines where required to ensure uniform heating.
20. Make sure the mold fits into the press used.
21. If inserts are required in the part, obtain them in advance to ensure proper fit when the mold is constructed.
22. Divide the cavities into sections to simplify machining.
23. If the mold is to be electrically heated, ensure that the holes for the thermocouples are located for proper and uniform control of temperatures in the mold areas.
24. Give special attention to mold rigidity to ensure dimensional accuracy of the molded part. It is essential that adequate support be provided to prevent undue deformation of the mold under pressure.
25. Check the rigidity of the ejector bar.
26. Check the mold, for the press in which it is to be used, for the (a) mold-clamping arrangement, (b) steam and water connections, (c) ejector arrangement and travel, (d) clamping and transfer pressure, (e) capacity of transfer cylinder, (f) ease of loading material into the mold.
27. Provide clearance holes for telescoping pins and cores.
28. Ensure that guide-pin centers are unsymmetrical about one or more mold center lines. Position guide pins to permit use of a loading board if required.
29. Place most of the cores in the ejector half of the mold where possible.
30. Use ejector pins to remove the part from deep pockets.
31. Locate pullers or pickups near ejector pins to prevent cracking or deforming the part on ejection.
32. Harden all plates, core slides, heel blocks, and other components that are subject to wear.
33. Mark cavity, punch, and core material on each part.
34. To ensure maximum heat utilization, insulate heated

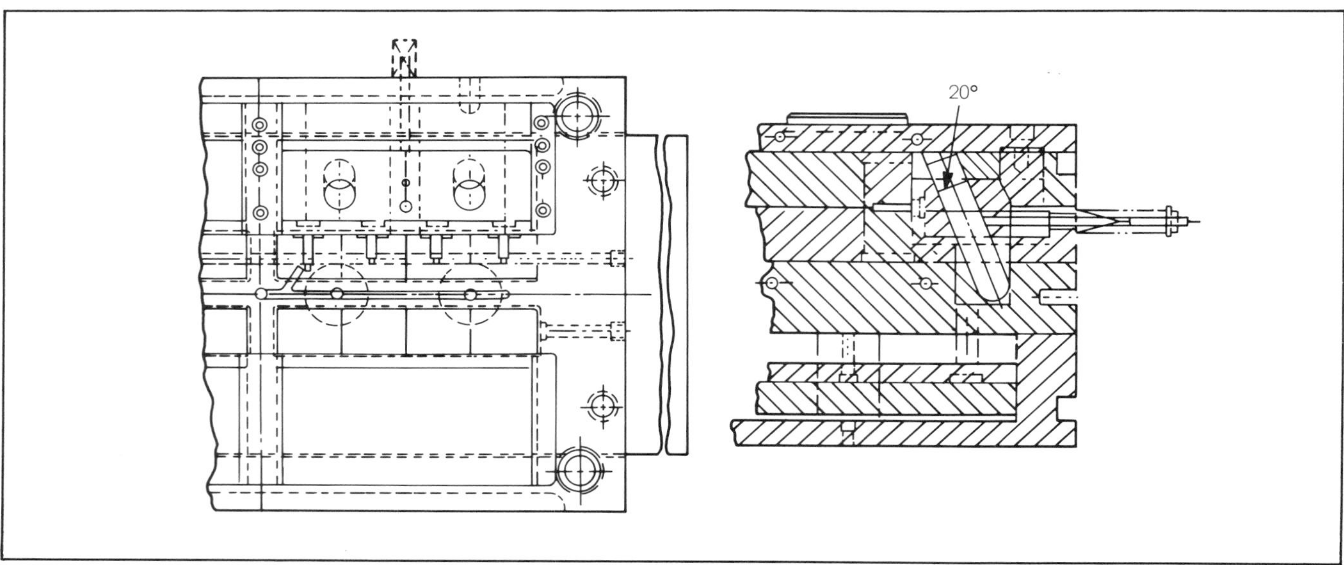


Fig. 18-16 An interchangeable, multiple-cavity injection mold.

parts of the mold from the unheated parts.
35. Provide eyebolt holes for lifting and disassembling the mold.
36. Ensure that molded parts bear the molder's trademark and cavity number where permissible.
37. Ensure that loose cores have proper identification and fit the mold in one position only.
38. Check the shrinkage factor of the molding material.
39. Design the position of the gate to prevent washing away the core pins and inserts. Also, position the gate to minimize finishing.
40. Specify the finish of the mold; flash hard-chrome plate if

**TABLE 18-8**
**Injection Molding Troubleshooting Chart**

| Color Streaking | Short Shots | Sink Marks | Flash | Weak Weld | Brittleness | Poor Surface Finish | Blush at Gate | Jetting | Weld Burns | Lamination | Warpage | Wave Marks | Poor Dimensional Stability | Sticking in Cavity | Sprue Sticking | SUGGESTED REMEDIES |
|---|---|---|---|---|---|---|---|---|---|---|---|---|---|---|---|---|
| | 2 | 2 | | 4 | | 3 | 6 | | | | | 4 | 4 | | | Increase injection pressure |
| | | | 1 | | | | | | 8 | 8 | 5 | | | 1 | | Decrease injection pressure |
| | 8 | | | | | | | | | | 3 | | | 3 | 5 | Increase cycle time |
| | | 3 | | | | | | | | | | 3 | 3 | | | Increase injection hold-time |
| | | | | | | | | | | | | | | 2 | 4 | Decrease injection hold-time |
| 9 | 7 | 7 | | 6 | | 7 | 7 | 7 | 7 | | | | | | | Increase sprue, runner or gate size |
| 10 | 9 | 8 | | | | | | 6 | | 7 | | | | | | Decrease gate land length |
| | | | | | | | | 5 | 6 | 6 | | | | | | Use larger opening in nozzle |
| | 1 | 1 | | | | | | | | | | 1 | | | | Adjust feed |
| | | | 2 | | | | | | | | | | | | | Increase clamp pressure |
| 3 | 4 | | | 3 | | | 5 | 3 | 3 | 4 | | | 2 | | | Increase stock temperature |
| 2 | | 4 | 4 | | 2 | 4 | 4 | 2 | 2 | | 2 | 5 | 1 | | | Decrease stock temperature |
| 4 | 5 | | | 1 | 4 | 5 | 2 | 4 | | 2 | | | 6 | | | Increase mold temperature |
| | | 5 | 5 | | | | | | | | 1 | 2 | 7 | | 3 | Decrease mold temperature |
| | | | | | | | | | | | 7 | | 8 | | | Change of water channels |
| | | | 6 | | | | | | | | | | | | | Rematch mold parting line |
| | 6 | 6 | | 5 | 7 | | | | 7 | | | 6 | | | | Add more gas vents |
| | | | | | 1 | 1 | 1 | | | 3 | | | | | | Predry material |
| | | 9 | | | 8 | | | | 9 | 9 | | | | | | Change location of gate |
| | | | | | | 6 | | | | | | | | | 7 | Polish surface of mold |
| | 3 | | | 2 | | | | | | | | | | | | Increase injection speed |
| 1 | | | 3 | | 9 | | 3 | 1 | 1 | 5 | 4 | | | | | Decrease injection speed |
| | | | | | | | | | | | | | | | 2 | Reseat nozzle (machine) |
| 8 | | | | | | | | 8 | | | | | | | 6 | Check nozzle heating band |
| 5 | | | | | 3 | 2 | | | | 1 | | | | | 8 | Check material for contamination |
| | | | | | | | | | | | | | | | 1 | Polish sprue bushing |
| 6 | | | | | 5 | | | | 4 | | | | | | | Decrease screw RPM |
| | | 10 | | | | | | | | | | | 5 | | | Back pressure (Increase) |
| 7 | | | 7 | | 6 | | | | 5 | | 6 | | | | | Back pressure (Decrease) |

(*Borg-Warner Chemicals, Inc.*)

Note: Numbers 1-10 signify suggested sequence of adjustments to make when attempting to remedy a particular problem.

required. Ensure that the mold material finishes to the required specifications.

41. Provide shrink or cooling fixtures if required to maintain dimensions and to prevent warping of the part.
42. If an ejector shedder is used, locate ejectors in the line to give maximum strength to the shedder.
43. Ensure that molds for automatic presses have ejector pins in both halves if possible, to obtain proper ejection.
44. Dimension all cavities, punches, and cores to the correcting side of tolerance.
45. Provide channels for water or air cooling of injection punches, cavities, and cores.
46. Maintain uniform wall sections by using material-saving cores where possible.
47. Ensure that the sprue bushing fits properly.

### TROUBLESHOOTING

Table 18-8 lists suggested remedies for problems encountered in injection molding operations. As an example of how to use this troubleshooting chart, if the problem is poor surface finish on the molded part, the user would read downward under the "Poor Surface Finish" column to remedy No. 1. This remedy indicates the easiest solution to the problem. If predrying does not correct the situation, remedy No. 2 in the same column would be used. If the problem persists, subsequent remedies are prescribed until the condition is corrected. The same procedure is followed to troubleshoot the various abnormal conditions listed. Any one of the suggested remedies may solve a particular problem; however, some problems may require a combination of suggested remedies.

## EXTRUSION FORMING

The extrusion process is a continuous operation in which hot plasticized material is forced through a die opening that produces an extrudate of the desired shape. The most commonly extruded materials are rigid and flexible vinyl, ABS, polystyrene, polypropylene, and polyethylene. Nylon, polycarbonate, polysulfone, acetal, and polyphenylene are included among other plastics that can be extruded.

The extrusion process is used to produce film (thinner than 0.030"; 0.76 mm), sheets (thicker than 0.030", 0.76 mm), filaments, tubes, and a variety of profiles. The process of plastics extrusion also is used to coat cables, wires, and metal strips.

### EXTRUSION PROCESS

In the profile extrusion process, the material in pellet, granular, or powder form is placed into a feed hopper which feeds the cylinder of the extruding machine as required (see Fig. 18-17). The cylinder is heated by electricity, oil, or steam, and closely controlled temperature zones are set up along its length. A rotating screw carries the material through the cylinder, mixing and working the material where necessary, and forcing it through a die orifice of the proper shape.

The extruded shape coming from the die is carried through a cooling medium; and when it has been cooled sufficiently to retain shape, it is cut to length or coiled. In some instances the material must be held to shape during cooling. Cooling is done by exposure to air at room temperature, by passing through a liquid bath held at a controlled temperature, or by jets of compressed air. Too-rapid cooling must be prevented because it causes warpage and sets up internal stains in the finished pieces.

The raw material must have a uniform particle size and a controlled moisture content to maintain close dimensional tolerances and a smooth surface on the finished extrusion. The temperature of each heat zone of the cylinder must be held constant to ensure a good extrusion.

The speed of extrusion (pounds or kilograms per hour handled by the machine) varies considerably depending upon the size of the die opening, the delivery of the screw, and the nature of the material being processed. Variable-speed machines are generally considered best for all-round flexibility, particularly in job shops. A wide variation of temperatures, speeds, methods of handling, and design of equipment is necessitated by the wide variation in characteristics of different thermoplastics.

Plastic extrusions are produced as tubes, rods, sheets, flat strips, profiles, filaments, and coatings for wire, cable, pipe, and rope.

### EXTRUSION EQUIPMENT

Common extruders consist of three basic units: the drive (power source); the process unit (screw and barrel); the forming unit (head and die).

The screw is the heart of the extruder and consists basically of feed, transition, and metering sections. The feed section is deep flighted and intended to convey solid or sometimes half-molten or molten plastics (for example, the second extruder in a multistage extrusion line) out of the feed throat area to the transition zone—which begins compressing the preheated material. This section forces the plastics against the heated barrel and continues or begins the melting process, which should be completed at the end of the transition or the beginning of the metering zone.

In the transition zone the depth of the flights becomes continuously shallower until the final depth of the transition zone phases into the metering zone. As homogenously as possible, the metering zone conveys the molten plastics to the head and die at uniform rates and high pressure. The compression ratio (c.r.) is dependent on the material, the different melt densities, and the bulk densities.

The extrusion machine has a pilot for the attachment of adapter rings or plates on the outboard end of the cylinder. A die base is placed within the adapter ring to direct the flow of the material toward the die orifice.

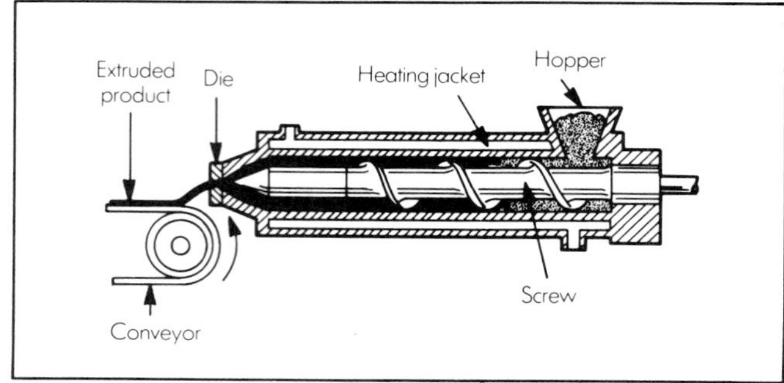


**Fig. 18-17 Schematic arrangement of a plastic extrusion machine.**

## Extrusion Dies

The die is usually made of flat, ground tool steel and is mounted as shown in Fig. 18-18. The design of the extrusion die, unlike that of injection or compression molds, cannot be predetermined precisely. A great deal of secondary work is often required to obtain extruded shapes of the desired dimensions. It is usually necessary to alter an extrusion die by filling or blocking to direct the flow of material to obtain a completely filled shape. Some designers make the orifice 10-30% oversize to allow for shrinkage upon cooling of the finished shape or to allow for controlled tension which pulls the shape to the required size or cross section.

A crosshead is widely used for coating wire with plastics. It is an adapter bolted on the face of the machine which directs the material at right angles to the centerline of the screw. The crosshead is usually T-shaped, having two faces upon which the dies are fastened. The wire emerges from the die and is cooled and carried away. The crosshead can be swung through 360° and thus is adaptable to many coating jobs.

## Multiscrew Extruders

Multiscrew extruders have been developed for compounding and pelletizing and (among many applications) for the extrusion of polyvinylchloride (PVC) materials. Advantages of the multi-screw machine are outstanding homogenization and higher output. The four-screw machine is used extensively in the production of PVC pipe. The twin-screw type of machine, illustrated in Fig. 18-19, also is gaining in usage.

Multiscrew extruders differ significantly in both construction and operation from the single-screw extruding machine. A twin-screw extruder with closely intermeshing counterrotating screws can be represented by two series of C-shaped chambers—one series for each screw. These chambers convey the

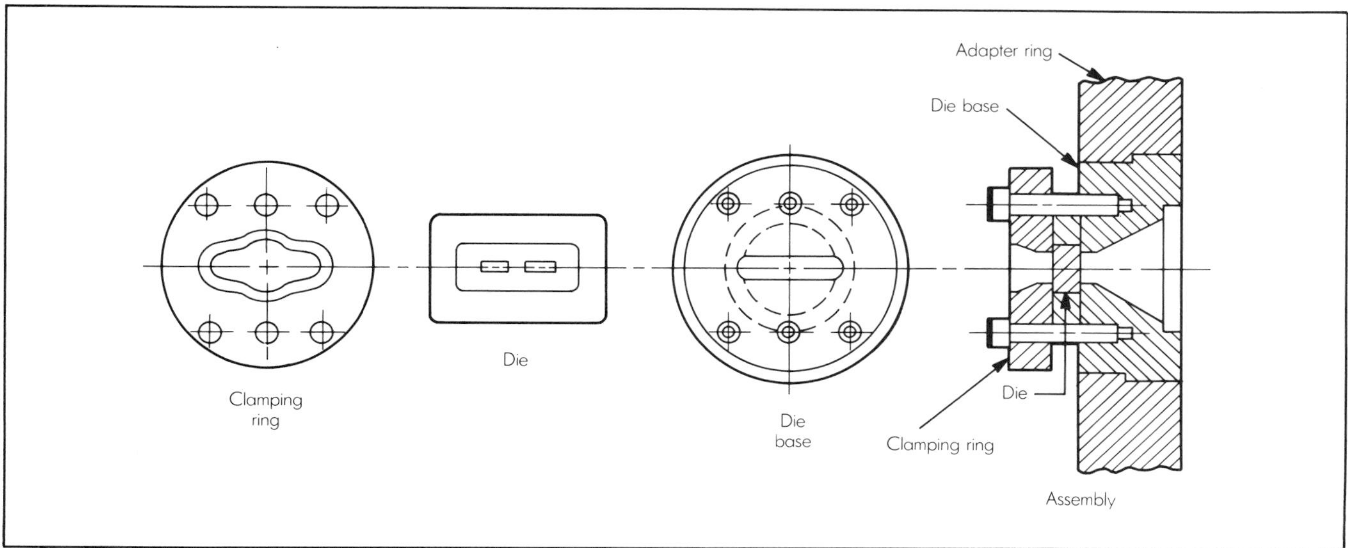


**Fig. 18-18 Die assembly for extruding plastics materials.**

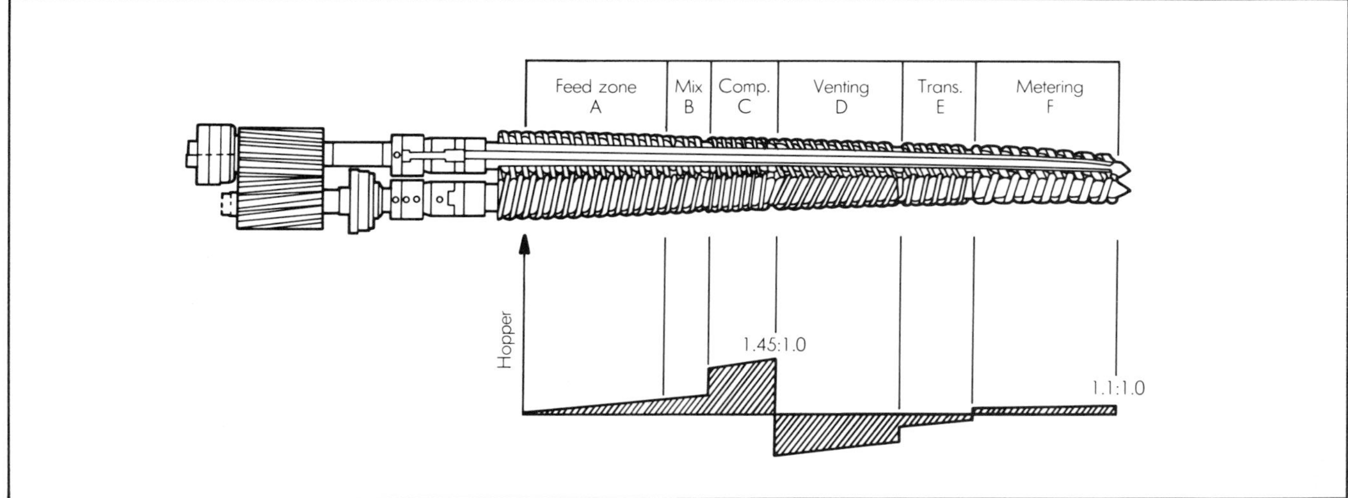


**Fig. 18-19 Schematic diagram of conical twin screw layout with compression ratios at each zone.** (*Cincinnati Milacron Inc.*)

processing material positively from the hopper to the die by rotation of the screws. In the pump zone, leakage gaps provide an interaction between the chambers. The output can be controlled either by varying the speed of revolution or by controlling the feed. Because of the design of twin-screw machines, a much larger screw and barrel area (surface) is in contact with the material being extruded. Rate of wear is significantly higher than for single-screw and barrel, even though the twin-screw extruders are usually shorter (in the range of $L/D$ = 7 to 17) and the screw speed is lower. The circumference surface speed is also quite different, as indicated in Table 18-9.

**TABLE 18-9**
**Circumference Surface Speed**
**(Single-Screw vs. Twin-Screw Extruder)**

| Diameter, in. (mm) | Surface Speed: Single-Screw, ft/min (m/s) | Surface Speed: Twin-Screw, ft/min (m/s) |
|---|---|---|
| 2.5 (64) | 12-118 (0.06-0.6) | 6-30 (0.03-0.15) |
| 3.5 (89) | 59-256 (0.3-1.3) | 2-20 (0.01-0.1) |

# REACTION INJECTION MOLDING

Reaction injection molding (RIM) is a form of injection molding that brings temperature and ratio-controlled, liquid-reactant streams together under high-pressure impingement mixing to form a polymer directly in the mold. Two liquid reactants (monomers) are mixed together as they enter the mold. A chemical reaction produces the plastics as it forms the part.

When compared to other molding systems, RIM offers more design flexibility, lower energy requirements, lower pressures, lower tooling costs, and lower capital investment. Significant advantages in design and production are gained from the RIM fabricating capability for incorporating a load-bearing, structural skin and a lightweight, rigid, cellular core into a part in one processing operation.

While initial RIM applications were primarily automotive, nonautomotive uses are increasing in industrial, business, and consumer-product applications. Recent production applications include business machine cabinets and vacuum cleaner housings. Thermosetting polyurethanes are the most commonly used RIM materials. Recently, however, the successful completion of development and testing programs on other plastics, such as nylons and epoxies, has led to RIM production usage of these materials. Table 18-10 compares the properties of various RIM materials systems.

## RIM ADVANTAGES

Where RIM polymer physical properties are suited for an application, a comparison of RIM to conventional injection molding and sheet molding compound (SMC), discussed later in this chapter, reveals advantages to using RIM.

### Design Freedom

With RIM, the designer has exceptional freedom. Parts can be complex and large, and produced without molded-in stresses. Inserts are easily incorporated. Properly designed RIM parts can include ribs, bosses, cutouts, attaching ears, etc., as well as a variety of cross-section thicknesses without sink marks. For flexible RIM with 25-50 ksi (172-345 MPa) flexural modulus, undercuts are attainable on visible surfaces.

### Low Pressures

Pressures within the RIM mold are 50-100 psi (345-690 kPa) and require correspondingly low clamp capacities—about 100 lbf (445N) for each square inch of projected part area (0.7N for each square mm) or about 3-5% of the clamp force required for injection molding or SMC.

### Low Energy Requirements

For RIM, the connected horsepower is about 25% of the power required for injection molding, and the percentage of time the maximum horsepower is required during an average cycle is about 25% of that for injection molding.

### Lower Capital Investment

Reaction injection molding equipment requires lower capital investment for mixers, clamps, presses, molds, etc., compared to other systems. The cost of RIM machinery is about one-third to one-half that of injection molding machinery to mold the same size of part, and considerably lower than that of sheet molding compound (SMC) machinery.

### Lower Tooling Costs

Low molding pressures allow the use of less expensive tooling, because lightweight, easily machined materials can be used. However, the mold must be capable of producing the required finish, since the RIM process precisely duplicates the mold surface. Reaction injection molding allows prototyping and low-volume applications with low-cost molds.

## RIM LIMITATIONS

Reaction injection molding applications have been limited by the availability of and properties of materials suitable for the process. Originally, RIM materials were primarily polyurethanes. However, recent commercial availability of suitable epoxy and nylon formulations is broadening the potential for RIM applications. Relatively long cycle time, low production rates, and limited applicability have been among the other principal drawbacks of the RIM method. Progress is occurring at a rapid rate, however, and developments in methods, materials, and equipment may eliminate the need for postcuring and mold-spraying in the RIM process—and thereby make it faster and more versatile.

## RIM MATERIALS AND APPLICATIONS

Urethanes currently dominate commercial RIM production and can be formulated to produce a wide range of densities, flexible or rigid, from low-density foam to rigid structural foam and from low to high-modulus elastomers.

Reaction injection molding urethane elastomers provide design freedom combining damage resistance, corrosion resistance, and parts consolidation with large and complex shapes. Current automotive applications include front and rear fascia,

**TABLE 18-10**
**Typical Properties of RIM Systems**

| Property | Urethane Rigid Structural Foam 1/2" (13 mm) Thick | Urethane* Low-Modulus Elastomer | Urethane* High-Modulus Elastomer | Nylon 6* High-Modulus | Epoxy* High-Modulus |
|---|---|---|---|---|---|
| Density, lb/ft$^3$ | 37 | 62 | 62 | 71 | 69 |
| (kg/m$^3$) | (593) | (993) | (993) | (1137) | (1105) |
| Tensile strength, psi | 3400 | 3200 | 4650 | 6000 | 10,000 |
| (MPa) | (23.4) | (22.1) | (32.1) | (41.4) | (69.0) |
| Elongation, % | < 5 | 235 | 105 | 250 | 6 |
| Flexural modulus, ksi | 160 | 34 | 120 | 115 | 398 |
| (MPa) | (1103) | (234) | (827) | (793) | (2744) |
| Coefficient of thermal expansion, $10^{-6}$ in./in./° F | --- | --- | 60 | 70 | 31 |
| ($10^{-6}$ mm/mm/° C) | --- | --- | (108) | (126) | (56) |

* 1/8" (3 mm) thick

bumpers, fenders, and spoilers. Other transportation uses of urethane RIM products include bus bumpers, truck fender extensions, and interior trim panels.

Nonautomotive urethane RIM applications are increasing and include electronic equipment enclosures; recreation items; shoes; and products for the construction, furniture, agriculture, and appliance fields. Specific product applications include hay rollers, tractor grilles and cab roofs, water-bed frames, tennis backboards, window frames, office furniture, work surfaces, marine boarding ladders, shoe soles, boots, beer kegs, oar blades, file cabinets, bookshelves, computer housings, snowmobiles, golf carts, television screens, and lawn and garden equipment housings.

## Urethane Development

Commercially available RIM machinery to process materials at a higher temperature increases the versatility of urethanes. Material suppliers are seeking superior urethane properties, such as formulations that can pass through automotive paint ovens at 325° F (163°C), while retaining damage resistance. Such formulations could involve solid components such as pure diphenylmethane diisocyanate (MDI), which is solid at room temperature and melts at 100° F (38°C), and solid chain extenders such as hydroquinone di (beta-hydroxyethyl) ether (HQEE). Higher processing temperatures can also reduce urethane viscosities to shoot onto and to wet fibrous mat inserts.

## Nylon RIM

Nylon (caprolactam polymerization) for RIM is now commercially available and has potential for automotive applications and agricultural, appliance, electronic enclosure, and other nonautomotive applications. (Reaction injection molding machinery to process nylon is commercially available.)

## Epoxies

Epoxies have been developed for RIM production applications. Potential applications are high-performance, large-size structural parts, including sheet metal replacement in the automotive and appliance industries. Epoxies for RIM can achieve high structural strength and impact strength by shooting over continuous fiber mat in a closed mold. (Reaction injection molding machinery to process epoxies is commercially available.)

## Polyesters

Polyester plastics for RIM are undergoing development programs in which material properties are being improved to compete with alternative RIM materials.

## Reinforced RIM

Reinforcement and filler additions make stiffer, more heat-resistant parts that are less sensitive to temperature changes and have significantly reduced coefficients of thermal expansion. Table 18-11 compares properties of reinforced reaction injection molding (RRIM) systems. The greatest interest has been in applications using 1/16" (1.6 mm) milled glass fibers, a fiber length that provides the best reinforcing properties consistent with reliable production. Since fiber orientation can be a problem, attention has turned to flake glass because of its isotropic properties. When added to the reactant monomers, the flake glass increases viscosity and imposes a high abrasive load on machine parts through which the filled components flow. Flake glass is significantly more abrasive than milled glass fibers.

# RIM PROCESS

To produce quality plastics parts, the reaction injection molding machine and the RIM system must accurately control material conditioning, temperature, metering rates, mix ratio, and injection pressures. The basic components of a RIM processing system are shown in Fig. 18-20. Typical RIM processing parameters for various materials are listed in Table 18-12.

## Elements of the Process

Elements of the RIM process include the material supply injection and mixing.

**Material supply.** The material supply system includes monomer onditioning (feed) tanks, with agitators and heat exchangers for temperature control, and low-pressure recirculation pumps for constant flow from the tanks to the mixhead supply lines.

**Injection.** The injection system delivers the preconditioned reactant monomers to the mixheads at controlled pressures and ratios using lance displacement of the liquid in a high-pressure cylinder. An alternate approach utilizes high-pressure, variable-displacement pumps.

**Mixing.** The mixhead is mounted directly to the mold and contains the small, cylindrical mixing chamber in which the reactive streams undergo thorough blending through high-pressure impingement mixing. The streams enter the mixing chamber from precise orifices while the shot is being made. A piston cleans the mixing chamber after the shot is completed. This method eliminates the solvent flush required with mechanical mixing devices.

**TABLE 18-11**
**Typical Properties of Reinforced RIM Systems**

| Property | Urethane High-Modulus Elastomer | Nylon 6 | Epoxy |
|---|---|---|---|
| Glass content, % | 23* | 25* | 45-52** |
| Tensile strength, psi | 6490 | 7580 | 28,000-44,000 |
| (MPa) | (44.7) | (52.3) | (193-303) |
| Elongation, % | 37 | 13 | 2-4 |
| Flexural modulus, ksi | 380 | 275 | 2600-3700 |
| (MPa) | (2620) | (1896) | (17 927-25 511) |
| Coefficient of thermal† expansion, $10^{-6}$ in./in./° F | 25 | 29 | 15 |
| ($10^{-6}$ mm/mm/° C) | (45) | (52) | (27) |

* 1/16" (1.6 mm) milled glass
** Continuous glass
† Parallel to fibers

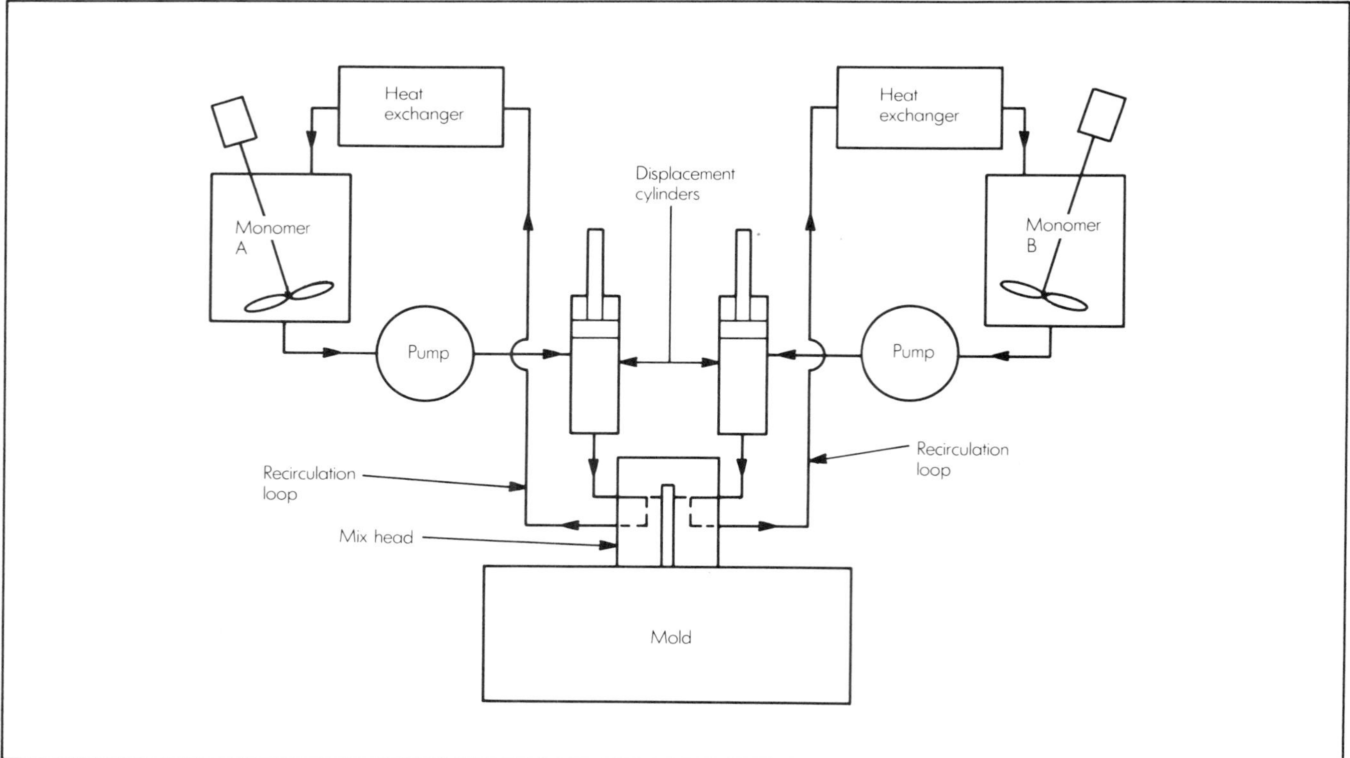


**Fig. 18-20 Basic elements of reaction injection molding (RIM) process.** (*Modern Plastics Encyclopedia, 1980-81*)

**TABLE 18-12**
**Typical RIM Processing Parameters**

| | Urethane | Nylon 6 | Epoxy |
|---|---|---|---|
| Processing temperature (monomers), | | | |
| °F | 90-120 | 160-265 | 100-160 |
| (°C) | (32-49) | (71-129) | (38-71) |
| Mold temperature, | | | |
| °F | 150-200 | 265-280 | 200-300 |
| (°C) | (66-93) | (129-138) | (93-149) |
| Injection pressure, | | | |
| psi | 1500-3000 | 200-800 | 500-1500 |
| (MPa) | (10.4-20.7) | (1.4-5.5) | (3.5-10.4) |

### Mold Considerations

The type of mold material, mold filling, and mold carriers should be considered prior to RIM molding.

**Mold material.** The mold can be made from steel, aluminum, epoxy-reinforced nickel, Kirksite, and epoxy (in descending order of durability). Reinforced epoxy and sprayed metal molds offer a low-cost option for prototyping and low-volume RIM applications. The importance of mold surface temperature control varies with the RIM material and the mold material. These parameters directly affect shrinkage of the part out of the mold.

**Mold filling.** Mold filling occurs as the mixture flows from the mixing chamber at greatly reduced pressure. The mold is equipped with a simple static aftermixer (to ensure thorough mixing of reactants), a runner, and a gate. The cross-section area of the runner and gate should be designed to ensure laminar flow into the mold at a rate of approximately 3-9 fps (0.9-2.7 m/s). Turbulent flow causes undesirable entrainment of air bubbles in the molded part. Controlled venting of the mold is essential to avoid trapped air. A range of mold release sprays is available for the urethane RIM process for easier part removal. Development programs now are being culminated on internal mold release technology that can eliminate or significantly reduce mold spraying and reduce cycle time by as much as 50%.

**Mold carrier.** The mold carrier units (clamp, press, etc.) provide mold clamping and opening functions, including positioning movements in some cases to present the mold to the operator. Mold carriers can also be the vertical-pillar press type, or they can be self-contained molds.

### Areas of Progress

In addition to the increase in varieties of plastics materials that are suitable for reaction injection molding, other major developments are fostering rapid growth for the RIM process.

Advancements in internal mold release agents are leading to significant reductions in cycle time (as previously stated). Fast-cycling RIM is no longer limited to amine-extended systems. Conventional glycol-extended systems have been greatly improved and now are competitive with the amines.

Light-stable RIM materials have been developed to simplify the coloring of RIM parts and eliminate the need for painting and finishing. And the new nylon RIM resins with improved dimensional stability will tend to broaden the applications for RIM.

# REINFORCED THERMOSET PLASTICS

The reinforced plastics described in this chapter primarily encompass polyester and fiberglass systems. The most commonly used processes can be divided into two categories: high and low volume. Several less-common intermediate volume processes also are described in this chapter.

The low-volume processes fall in the 2000-25,000 parts per year range. They are characterized by essentially low-pressure to pressureless hand or spray lay-up in low-cost molds with a high labor cost. High-volume processes are those in which more than 30,000 parts per year are produced (100,000 parts per tool for automotive components). They involve an initial high cost for tooling and equipment, but the labor intensity is low. These processes are not competitive with the metal stamping process unless they eliminate the need for multipiece assembly operations. Table 18-13 identifies typical thermosetting materials that are used for the various reinforced plastics processes.

## HIGH-VOLUME PROCESSES

The high-volume processes for reinforced thermoset plastics are sheet molding compound (SMC), thick molding compound (TMC), bulk molding compound (BMC), pultrusion, and pulforming.

### Sheet Molding Compound

Sheet molding compound is a mixture of chopped fiberglass and thermosetting polyester resins that is formed into a sheet up to 1/4" (6.4 mm) thick. This sheet can be easily handled and can be cut into strips or squares and used as a compression molding compound.

The resin system initially has a low viscosity to ensure complete mixing of the additives and wettability of the glass reinforcement. The viscosity is increased after the sheet compound has been formed. This creates a tack-free sheet for handling purposes.

A typical manufacturing process is shown schematically in Fig. 18-21. The numbers on this illustration correlate with the following steps:

1. The thermoset polyester is mixed with a thermoplastic resin (low-shrink additive), fillers, catalysts, thickeners, and internal release agents. This mixing operation can consist simply of batch weighing the ingredients by hand and funneling them into a tank with a mixer, or it may be a sophisticated operation for weighing and mixing ingredients by means of a highly automated system controlled by computer.
2. The blended resin compound is pumped to the upper and lower carrier film and spread in a uniform layer at the required thickness with a doctor blade (a movable bar that regulates the amount of viscous material on the rollers of the spreader).
3. The fiberglass rovings are in creels and are set in racks to facilitate the feeding of the required number of rovings

to the cutter. This depends upon the width and percentage of glass needed for a specific SMC.

4. Rovings are chopped to the required length and fed by gravity to the lower carrier film or sheet, which has the resin compound spread upon it.
5. The two carrier sheets are brought together with the chopped fiberglass between them.
6. The combined systems are pressed together with heated rollers to wet the surface of the glass fibers and eliminate the entrapped air. The heat from the rollers initiates the required increase of the resin viscosity.
7. The SMC sheet is cut off when a predetermined weight per roll is obtained. The SMC sheet is approximately 1/4″ (6.4 mm) thick. The carrier sheets then are used as a barrier to prevent the evaporation of volatile ingredients in the resin system. The carrier sheets are polyethylene or nylon. Nylon is used when greater control over the loss of volatile compounds is required.

**TABLE 18-13**
**Production Processes for Reinforced Thermoset Plastics**

| | Processes | | | | | | | | | |
|---|---|---|---|---|---|---|---|---|---|---|
| Resin | SMC | TMC | BMC | Pultrusion | Open Mold | Vacuum Bag | Pressure Bag | Preform | Resin Injection | Filament |
| Alkyd | | | • | | | | | | | |
| Epoxy | | | | • | • | • | • | | | • |
| Phenolic | • | | | | | | | | | |
| Polyester | • | • | • | • | • | • | • | • | • | • |

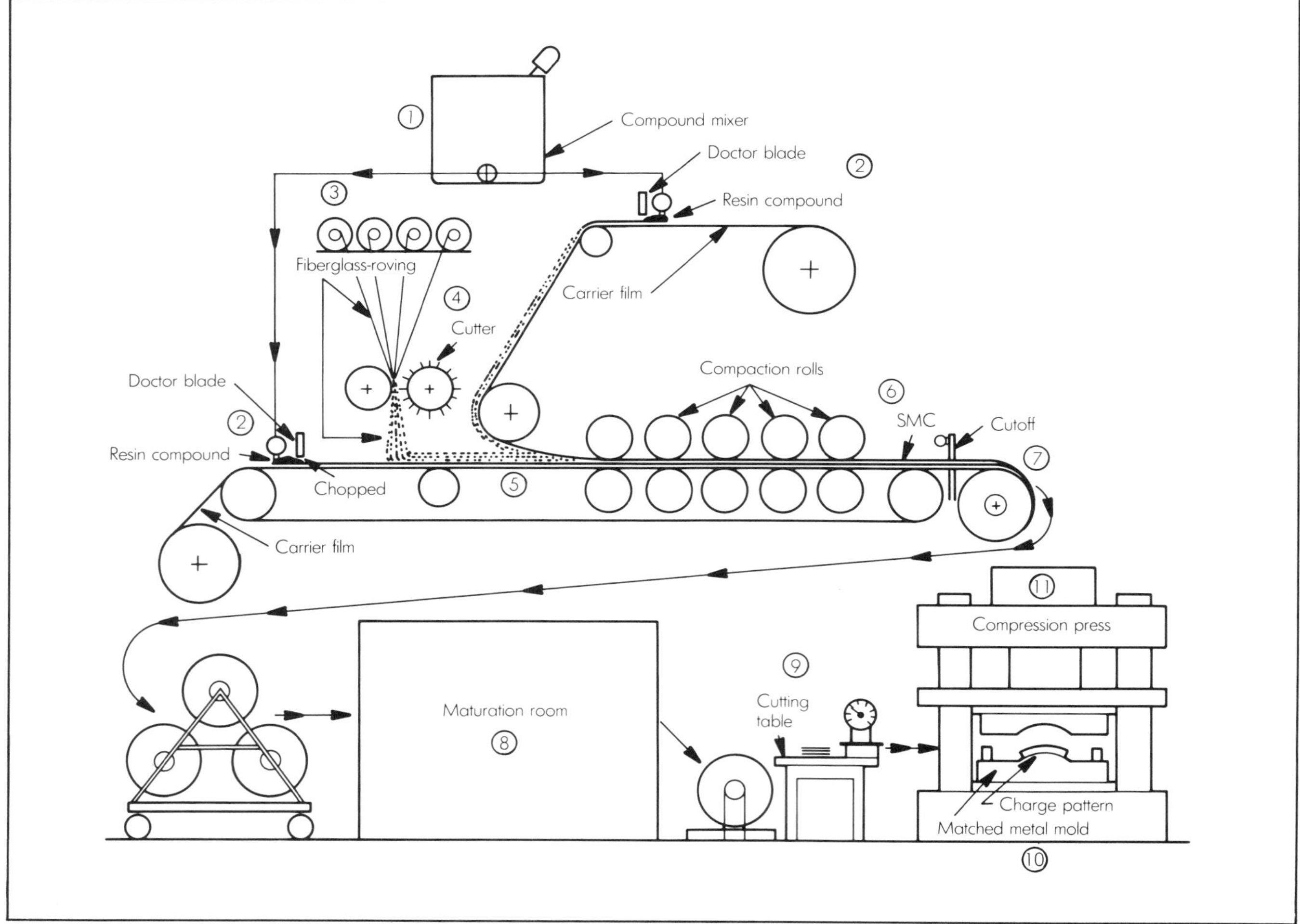


**Fig. 18-21 Sheet molding compound (SMC) manufacturing process.** (*T. H. Meister*)

8. The resin system is sent to the maturation room where it is brought to the required viscosity. This is a time/temperature-related pre-curing reaction. It requires several hours and is determined for a specific formulation.
9. After maturation, the rolls are sent to the press area where the sheet is slit and cut or diecut to a predetermined size, shape, and weight. The carrier sheets are stripped off at this location.
10. A specific charge pattern for the sheet is determined by experimentation. A charge pattern's weight and placement is dictated by the part design and by the flow characteristics of the SMC. These factors must be consistent to maintain the desired quality of parts. For additional reinforcement, glass cloth may be added at stress locations.
11. The SMC process is performed on a hydraulic press capable of producing a pressure of 500-1200 psi (3.5-8.3 MPa) on the mold. Pressures are dependent upon the formulation and the complexity of the part. Generally, for maximum density, strength, and good surface quality, a pressure of 1000-1200 psi (6.9-8.3 MPa) is needed.

The matched metal dies may be heated to 320-330° F (160-166° C) to cure the resin system. Curing time is controlled by the thickest section on the part (bosses and/or ribs).

## Thick Molding Compound (TMC)

This manufacturing process uses a mixture of chopped fiberglass and thermosetting polyester resins that is formed into a sheet up to 2″ (51 mm) thick or into a billet shape for compression and injection molding.

The thick molding compound system has a 50% advantage in production rates over SMC systems. Greater filler contents can also be tolerated. The production of thick sheets reduces handling costs and consumption of carrier sheets.

The use of the TMC process for some large automotive parts (grille opening panels) has been successful in providing good strength and improved surfaces (in comparison to the use of the SMC process). The injection-molding method is used.

A typical process is shown schematically in Fig. 18-22. The following list corresponds with the numbers in the illustration.

1. Resin compounding and reinforcing is basically the same as that for the SMC process, except it does not require a thickening agent and uses higher filler loadings. Fiberglass rovings are chopped in the cutter and introduced along with the metered resin compound into the impregnating rolls. The secondary wiping rolls deposit the resin-coated fiberglass onto the carrier sheets or films to provide improved wettability of the fibers.
2. The carrier sheets (polyethylene or nylon) sandwich the TMC.
3. The compaction rolls reduce the compound to the desired thickness and also lower the entrapped air content.
4. The finished TMC is slit and cut to predetermined width and length. The slabs or billets are shipped to the molding area (injection and/or compression).
5. The injection-molding method uses billets that are introduced into the barrel with a hydraulic stuffer. Depending upon the temperature required for specific formulations, the barrel is heated in excess of 100° F (38° C) to obtain a consistent flow characteristic. The reciprocating screw is of a special design for handling TMC, since standard screws could break the glass fibers. The compound is injected at 5000-12,000 psi (34.5-82.7 MPa) into the heated mold at 325° F (163° C) where its curing is accomplished. The curing time depends upon the geometry of the part. The heaviest sections (bosses, etc.) are the governing factor, as they are with SMC.

   Experience has shown that the higher pressure applied in this process minimizes surface porosity, which is a serious problem with SMC parts. This problem is of a major concern for automotive applications requiring high-temperature finishes. Also, the TMC process has the ability to produce thinner sections with greater dimensional accuracy. Injection gives directional orientation of the reinforcing fiber, and this can create weak areas parallel to the fiber flow. Also, it sometimes happens that material flowing around core pins adjacent to mounting lugs can produce areas that are rich in resin and weak in reinforcement. These problems can be minimized through careful part design. Parts produced by this system have minimal deflashing requirements when compared with compression molding.
6. Compression molding of TMC is performed by the same method as used with SMC. Fewer sheets are required (only one may be used) in the load pattern, as compared to the multiple plies needed with SMC. Also, improved physical properties and minimal porosity are attained. All of these factors tend to make TMC superior to SMC.

## Fabrication

Most TMC and SMC parts require some secondary fabricating operations, depending on the design of part (injection-molded TMC requires much less). For automotive components, typical SMC and TMC secondary operations consist of:

- Deflashing or trimming edges.
- Punching large openings.
- Drilling or piercing small holes.
- Driving attachment studs.
- Light surface sanding and pit filling.

Most deflashing is done at the press by the press operator during the closed-mold phase of the molding cycle. This is a manual operation utilizing a rasp file if the flash is light, or a hand power sander if the flash is heavy. The outer periphery of the part is cleared of flash; and large openings are cleared, depending on the amount of time the operator has available. This is best done at the press while the part is still hot from the mold.

Large openings are molded in the tool either with a small amount of flash or with a thin web of material covering the entire opening. This is removed with a trim die in a mechanical or hydraulic punch press.

Smaller openings may be molded in the tool in the same way if they are in the direction of the mold opening; if not, they may be molded in the tool by retractable cores. Often, if the holes are in areas in which problems of material flow in the mold may exist, or if an effort is being made to reduce costs, it is preferrable to drill holes in automatic drill fixtures or pierce them in a punch press.

For purposes of parts attachment in assembly operations, parts are designed with bosses molded on the back side. Attachment studs are driven into the bosses either manually or in gang stud-driving operations performed in a single unit that operates sequentially under pneumatic logic control.

Exterior automotive parts produced by the SMC and TMC

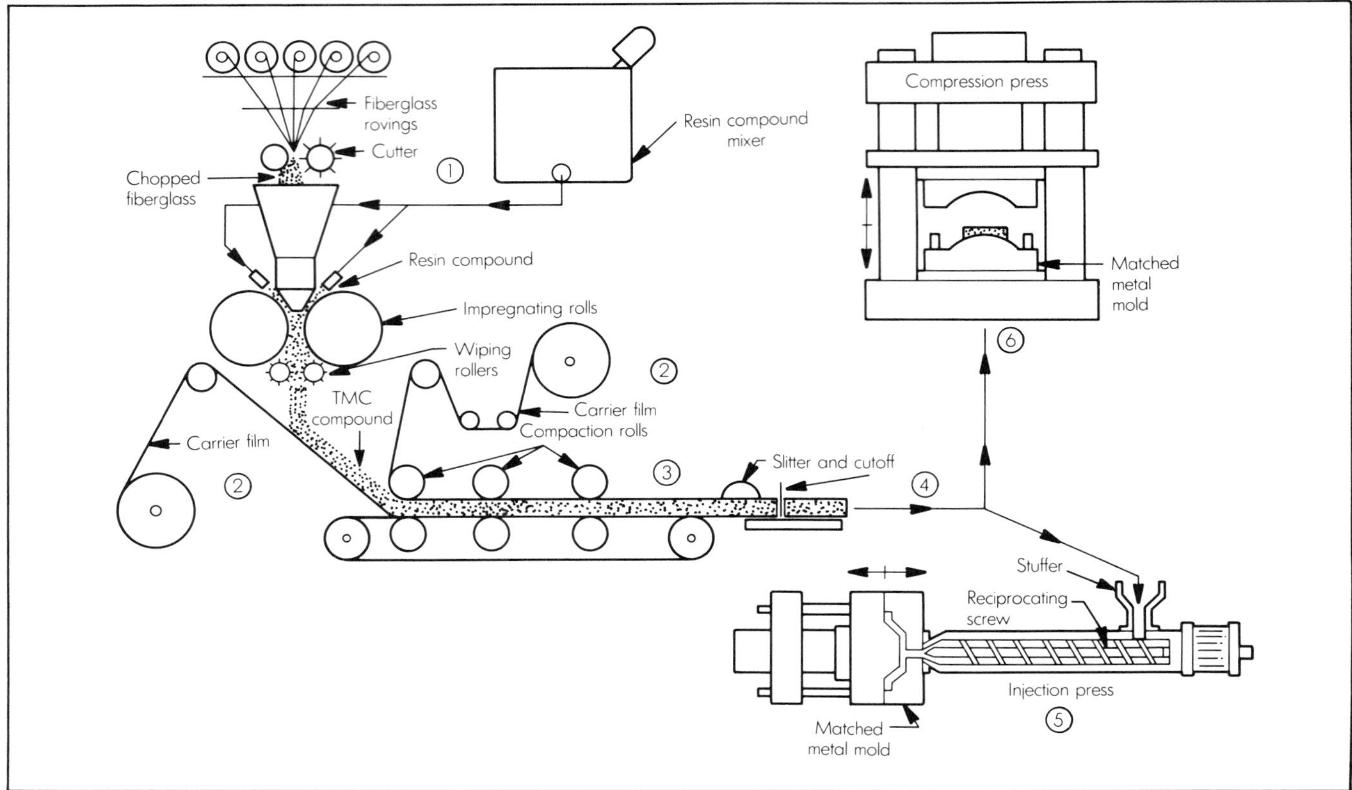


**Fig. 18-22 Thick molding compound (TMC) manufacturing process.** (*T. H. Meister*)

processes are painted and must achieve a Class A surface. This means that the plastics painted surfaces must be free of blemishes and must match the adjacent sheet metal painted surf'aces.

Wiping with a penetrating sealer, to detect any voids or porosity on the surface which might have to be repaired, and light scuff sanding are combined with inspection of parts before priming. Additional information on fabrication and assembly is provided in Volume IV, *Assembly, Testing, and Quality Control,* of this Handbook series.

## Bulk Molding Compound

The bulk molding compound (BMC) manufacturing process predates the SMC and TMC systems and has been used to produce a large number of automotive and electrical parts. The automotive companies use large amounts of BMC for heater and air conditioning housings. Some compounders have used sisal as the primary reinforcing fiber.

A typical BMC process is shown in Fig. 18-23. The following list corresponds with the numbers in the illustration.

1. This process is a batch system using a sigma blade mixer that gives versatility in the compound selections. Bulk molding compound is low in strength because of glass length degradation during mixing. When a large quantity of the same compound is being produced day after day (heater housings, etc.), a continuous compounding unit can be used. The fiberglass may also be purchased as a chopped roving and introduced by hand. The resin compound consists of a polyester resin, filler, catalyst, internal lubricants, and in some instances a low-shrink additive. Sheet molding compounds and thick molding compounds were derived from similar basic formulations.
2. The bulk compound is dumped from the mixer into a ram extruder to form billets that are cut to length for a given weight. The billets then are taken to the molding area. Polyethylene sheeting covers the billets to prevent evaporation of volatile constituents if storage for more than a few hours is required.
3. Compression molding is accomplished on a heated (280-325° F; 138-163° C), matched metal mold using a standard hydraulic press capable of producing 300-700 psi (2.1-4.8 MPa). Molding pressures vary with part design (thickness, intricate ribbing, bosses, and dimensional tolerances).

   A modification of the compression method is transfer molding. This involves working to a closed mold; the BMC is introduced through a pot with a ram that forces it into the closed mold. This method is used when close thickness tolerance is needed or when inserts are contained in the molded part.
4. Injection molding of BMC is accomplished in much the same manner as injection molding of TMC—using a reciprocating screw (or a plunger); heated barrel (100° F; 39° C, or higher); heated, matched metal mold; and a stuffer. Injection pressure is in the 5000-12,000 psi (34.5-82.7 MPa) range.

Some companies produce BMC for sale to custom molders who do not have sufficient requirements to warrant in-house compounding facilities. These companies have also developed highly specialized compounds that are beneficial to a small custom molder who does not have development capabilities.

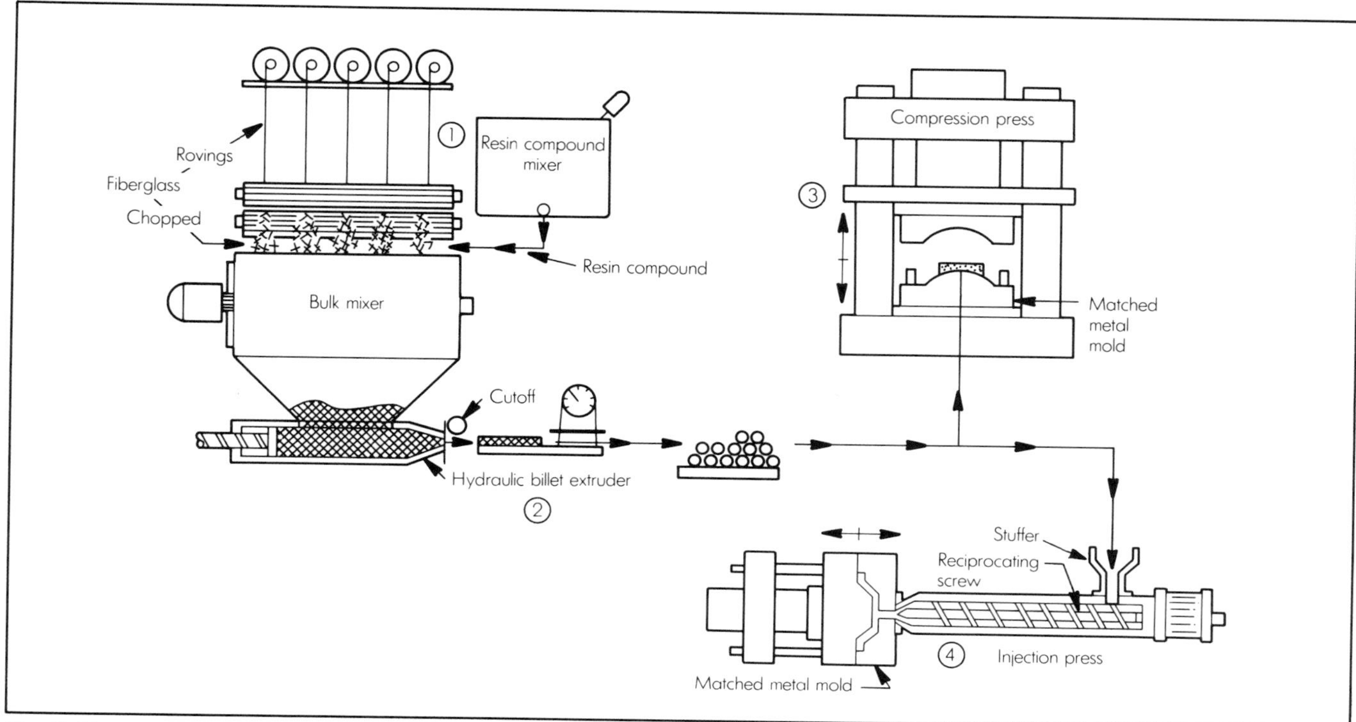


**Fig. 18-23 Bulk molding compound (BMC) manufacturing process.** (*T. H. Meister*)

## Pultrusion Manufacturing Process

Pultrusion is a continuous method of manufacturing various reinforced plastic shapes of uniform cross sections (rods, tubes, and I beams). This method consists of pulling various reinforcing materials through a resin bath and subsequently forming and curing them. The cured section of material is then cut to any predetermined length.

Figure 18-24 is a schematic drawing of this process. The numbers in this illustration correlate with the following list:

1. The reinforcing materials are primarily fiberglass rovings, mat, and woven cloth. Other fibers in sheet or woven form, such as carbon fiber, can be incorporated for high-strength aerospace products.
2. The reinforcing materials are pulled through a catalyzed resin bath that has low viscosity to ensure proper wet out of the fibers. The reinforcements then pass through a resin-control orifice to eliminate excess resins prior to forming. Resins used are either polyester (approximately 90%) or epoxies (approximately 10%).
3. The impregnated materials pass through a preforming tool. An example of this is a progression from a flat to a partial "U" shape just prior to final die configuration. The dies are made of chrome-plated tool steel and are heated. Radio-frequency curing is a commonly used system. Fluorocarbon-TFE linings are applied to the mold surfaces when this curing technique is used.
4. The pulling is a function of the section size and may require only a simple belt or wheel device attached to a caterpillar unit that is capable of thousands of pounds (kilonewtons) of pulling force. The process exerts a lateral pulling force, thus densifying the material.
5. A flying cutoff saw is used to obtain the required lengths.

The forms produced vary from small-diameter rods (1/8"; 3 mm) to large formed sections (6-10"; 152-250 mm). Many forms are available as off-the-shelf items.

## Pulforming Manufacturing Process

Pulforming (see Fig. 18-25) is a continuous process similar to pultrusion, except the finished product is not a uniform, straight section cut to length. This process is used to produce a curved part that has a constant volume, yet also has a changing geometry. An example is an automotive monoleaf spring which has a square cross section in the center and a flat, rectangular shape at each end. This is a recent development to meet high strength requirements.

Figure 18-25 illustrates the pulforming process. Numbers on the illustration correspond with the following list:

1. Initially this process is basically the same as pultrusion. Reinforcement is impregnated in a catalyzed resin (polyester or epoxy).
2. The low-viscosity resin impregnates the rovings, and the excess is wiped off at the control orifice and passes through a radio-frequency preheater.
3. The die table rotates and acts as a capstan while containing the female cavities. The impregnated rovings are forced into these cavities by the stationary die shoe, which forms a closed cavity. The cured parts are cut off on the farside table after curing, and the empty cavity is rotated into position to receive a new "charge". This technique is repeated continuously and can be used to produce a uniform cross-sectional part that requires a curvature. The curvature of the part is determined by the table diameter. Different curvature requirements dictate the need for different tables to satisfy those dimensions.

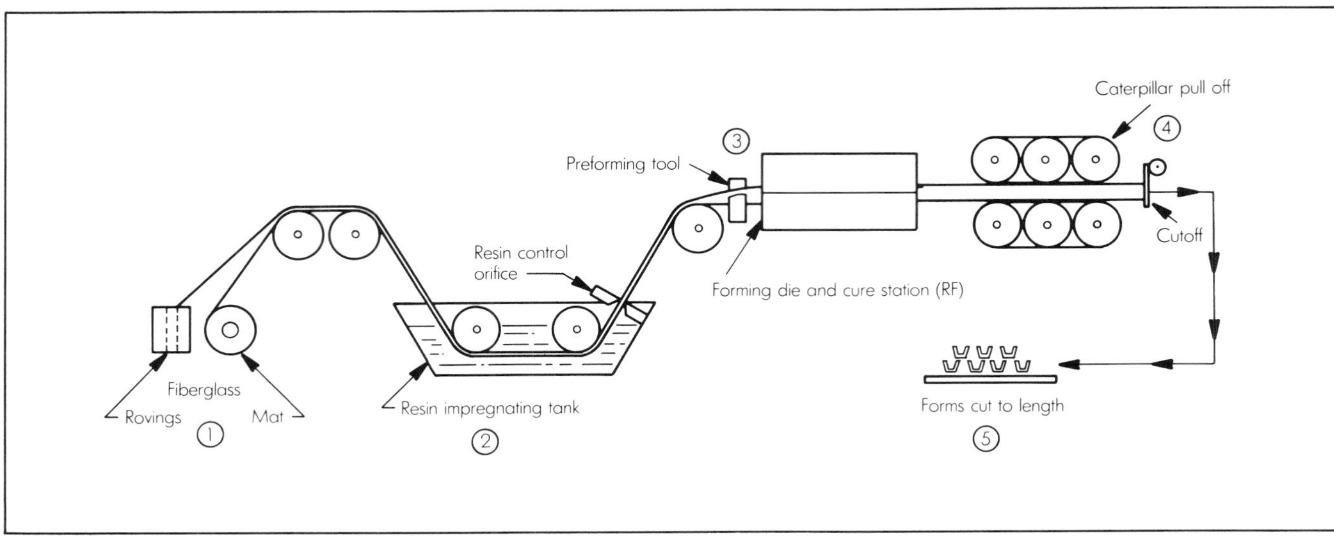


**Fig. 18-24 Pultrusion manufacturing process.** (*T. H. Meister*)

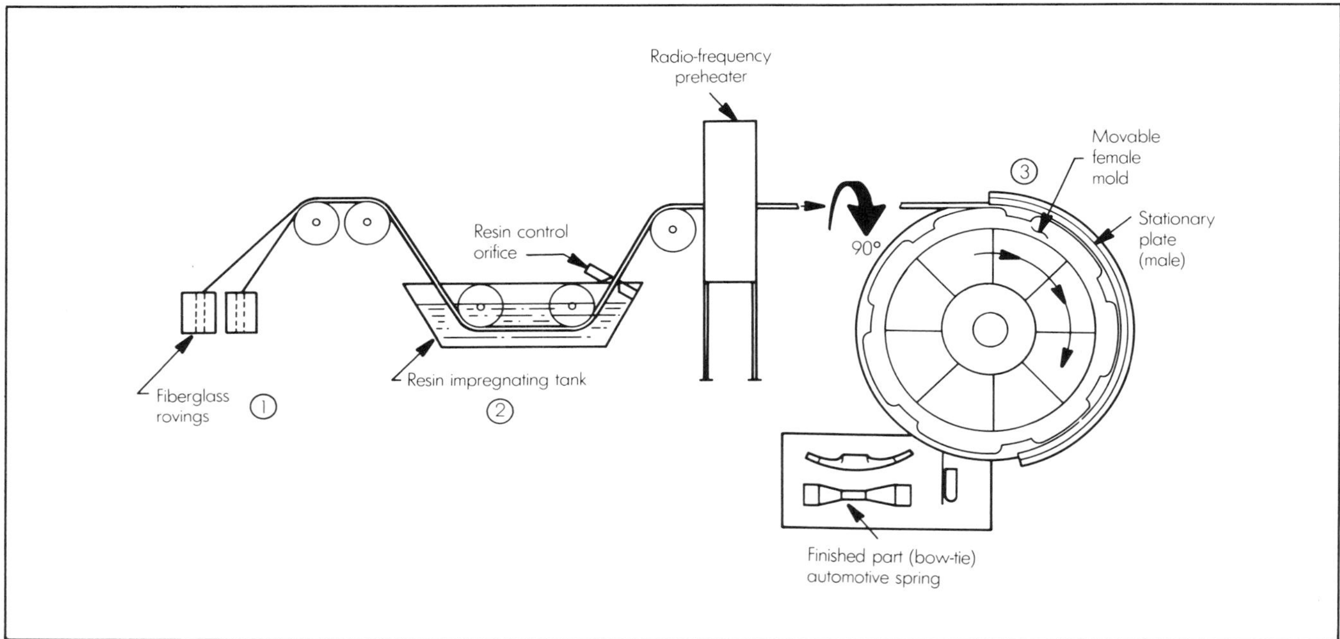


**Fig. 18-25 Pulforming manufacturing process.** (*T. H. Meister*)

Pulforming can be adapted (without a circular table) to produce a straight-line pull product that has a changing geometry within a constant volume.

## LOW-VOLUME PROCESSES

Commonly used low-volume processes include (1) hand or spray lay-up, (2) vacuum bag, (3) pressure bag, (4) autoclave, (5) wet preform, (6) resin injection, and (7) filament winding. The second and third processes make use of the hand or spray lay-up, but embody a low-pressure system to improve glass content. The wet preform, resin injection, and filament winding processes also are suitable for intermediate-volume operations.

### Hand or Spray Lay-up

The hand or spray lay-up (see Fig. 18-26) is an open-mold system. The mold may be a simple wood or plaster unit (male or female) or a cast or sheet metal construction for which permanence is required. The size can vary from a 12″ (305 mm) box to a large yacht.

The mold surface must be heavily waxed and then sprayed with a polyvinyl alcohol solution to prevent the laminate from sticking to the surface. To make a smooth surface, a gel coat is applied. Thickness of the gel coat, which is either brushed or sprayed on, is approximately 0.020″ (0.51 mm). The gel is a catalyzed polyester resin that is highly filled (may be pigmented

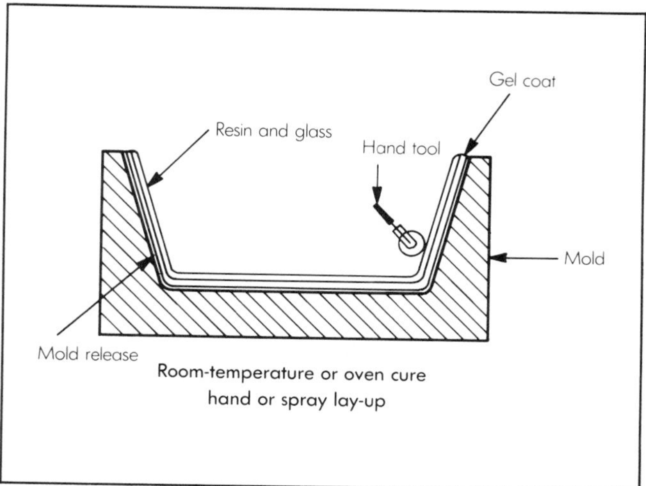


**Fig. 18-26 Open mold hand or spray lay-up process.** (*T. H. Meister*)

for color) and stabilized for weather resistance. It must be allowed to partially cure before the subsequent resin and glass system is applied. A smooth surface is produced if the mold has a smooth surface. The laminate is built up by spraying catalyzed polyester resin onto the gel coat, then laying a glass mat on it and working the resin up through the mat with a hand (squeegee) tool. Subsequent resin and glass layers are applied to attain the required thickness.

An alternative is to use a chopper spray gun (see illustration under "Wet Preform" section) to build up the thickness. Again, the hand tool is used to compact the laminate and force entrapped air out. The laminate is cured by either allowing the mold to stand at room temperature, or it is force cured in an oven. Room-temperature curing takes much more time (overnight), but it gives the mold a longer life. Oven curing shortens the curing time and the mold life.

## Vacuum Bag, Pressure Bag, and Autoclave

The vacuum bag (see Fig. 18-27), pressure bag (see Fig. 18-28), and autoclave molding processes are modifications of

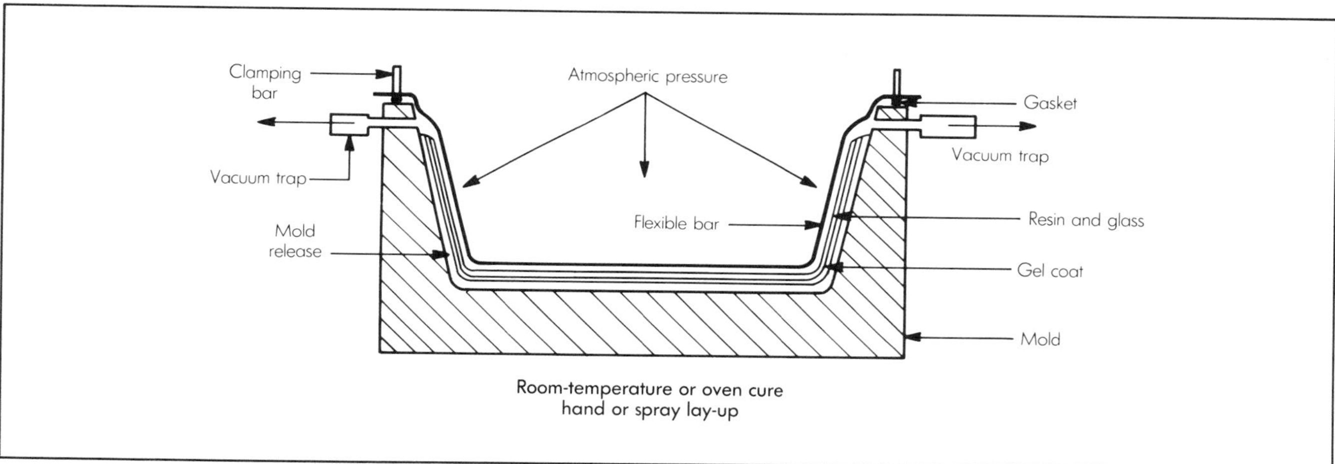


**Fig. 18-27 Vacuum bag process.** (*T. H. Meister*)

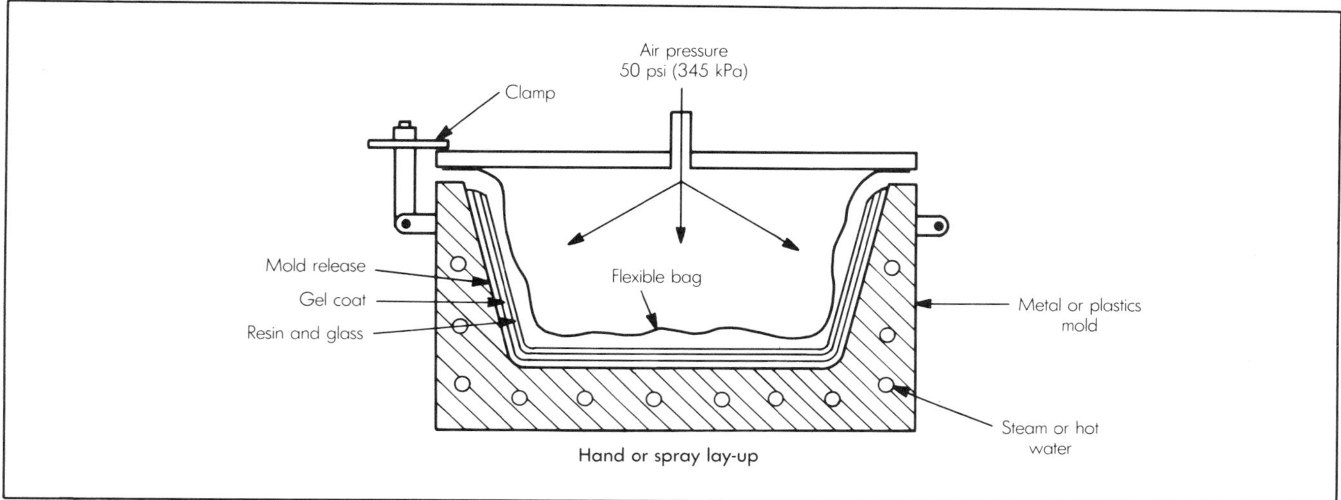


**Fig. 18-28 Pressure bag process.** (*T. H. Meister*)

the open-mold process. Pressure is applied to the laminate to control thickness and glass content. The pressure bag is generally used in conjunction with a heated metal mold. This is an expensive mold that is justified by a long-life part that should undergo only minor changes. The vacuum bag and pressure bag systems are used extensively in the aerospace industry and in the manufacturing of boats and fishing rods.

**Vacuum bag.** The vacuum bag method uses a film of styrene-resistant plastics (mylar or cellophane). The film is sealed around the mold, and a vacuum is created under the bag. This flattens the fibers, draws air from the resin, and produces a glazed surface on the back of the part.

**Pressure bag.** The pressure bag process differs from the vacuum bag process in that positive pressure is applied to the top surface of the film. Steam heat sometimes is introduced into the mold cavity.

**Autoclave.** The autoclave method is widely used in the aerospace industry to produce parts from impregnated epoxy. A woven fabric is impregnated with epoxy resin. It then is dried and heated to a stage at which it is partially polymerized and is susceptible to heat.

The impregnated fabric is cut and placed in a mold, which may have a phenolic or aramid honeycomb core. The mold then is covered with a vacuum bag and placed in an autoclave. Vacuum is held at 28 in. Hg (95 kPa), while the autoclave is pressurized to 50 psi (345 kPa). The mold is heated to 250-350°F (121-177°C) for about 2 1/2 hours.

## Wet Preform

The wet-preform process (see Fig. 18-29) has been used for heavy truck front ends in the past, but is giving way to the SMC process. It is still a viable process for intermediate-volume applications that do not specify Class A surface requirements. The process consists of making a fiberglass form that roughly represents the part shape (preform). The form is made by two methods. One is through the use of a plenum chamber that deposits chopped rovings on a revolving screen with air and a polyester resin binder sprayed on the preform. The form is baked on the screen to retain its shape. The form is placed in a matched metal mold, catalyzed resin (predetermined amount) is poured on, and pressure and heat are applied. The plenum chamber is used for small parts that are not complicated in design so that a uniform layer of glass fibers can be deposited on the screen.

The other form-making method is used for large parts (truck front ends). The fiber and binder are applied with a chopper spray gun by an operator. A significant amount of operator skill is required to obtain a uniform fiber buildup over the entire geometry of these large, multicontoured parts. The binder is oven-cured. The more sophisticated units have an attached oven, and the preform is rotated into the oven while another form is being sprayed up.

It should be noted that these processes generally do not use a low-shrink additive in the resin system. Therefore, the part has a

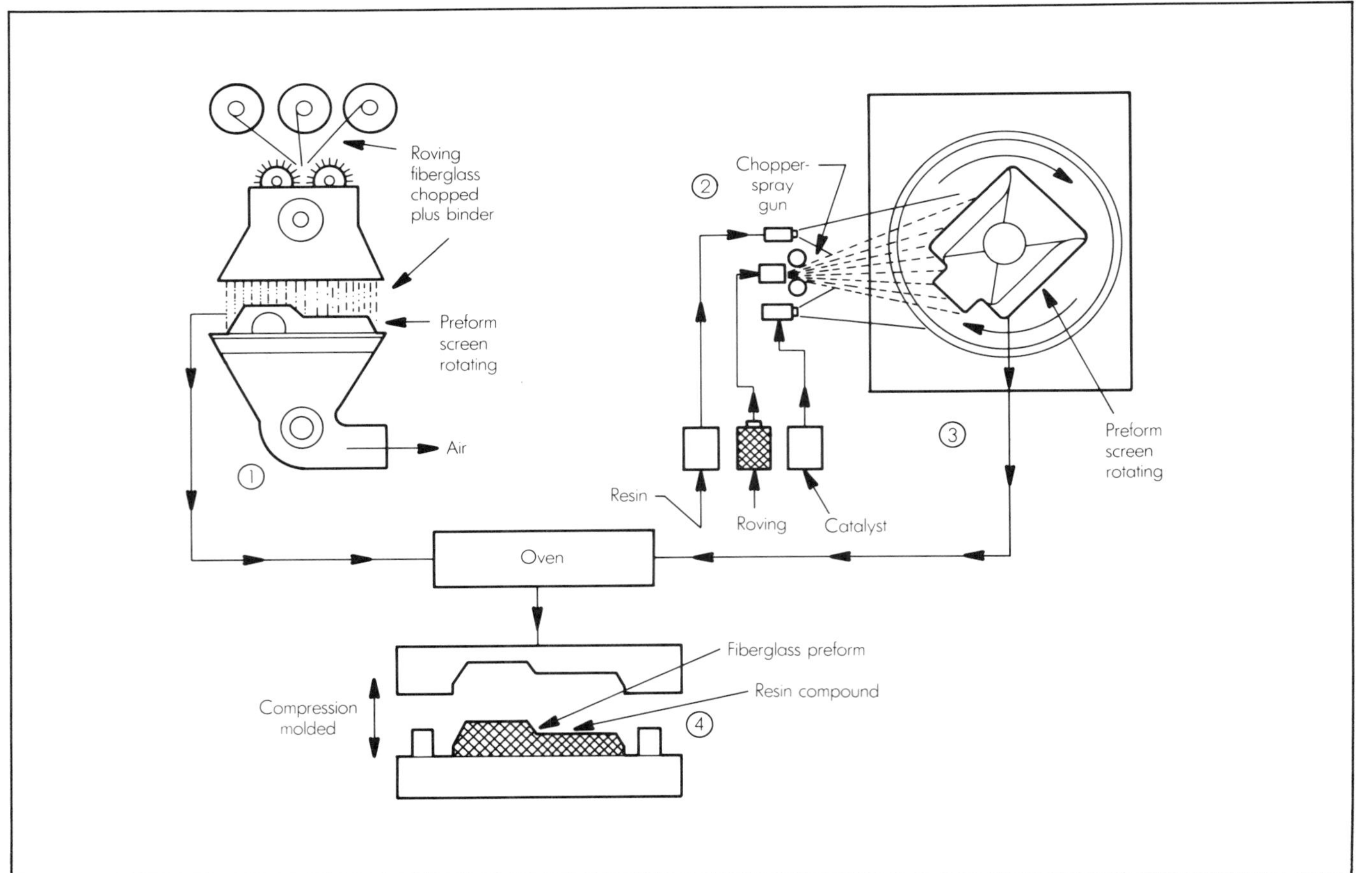


**Fig. 18-29 Wet preform process.** (*T. H. Meister*)

high shrink factor, which leaves a fiberglass pattern on the surface. A gel coat can help to minimize the pattern. For parts requiring sheet-metal-like surfaces (automotive-appearance items), it is not a suitable process.

## Resin Injection

Resin injection molding (see Fig. 18-30) as an intermediate-volume process uses tooling and equipment that is lower in cost than that used in conventional compression or injection-molding techniques. Molding cycles are much slower than those for compression and injection methods, but production rates far exceed those for the open-mold techniques.

The closed mold made from plastics or spray metal or cast aluminum produces parts with smooth surfaces on both sides. A gel coat may be used to obtain a desired color, improve weatherability, increase corrosion resistance, and permit post-finishing operations. The mold has cooling coils for exotherm control, a perimeter gasket to prevent resin and pressure leakage, and air vents to bleed off air and to determine part fill. The resin compound, including catalyst and filler, is pumped into the mold through an injection port. The curing cycle is about 10-20 minutes because the resin is injected rapidly and

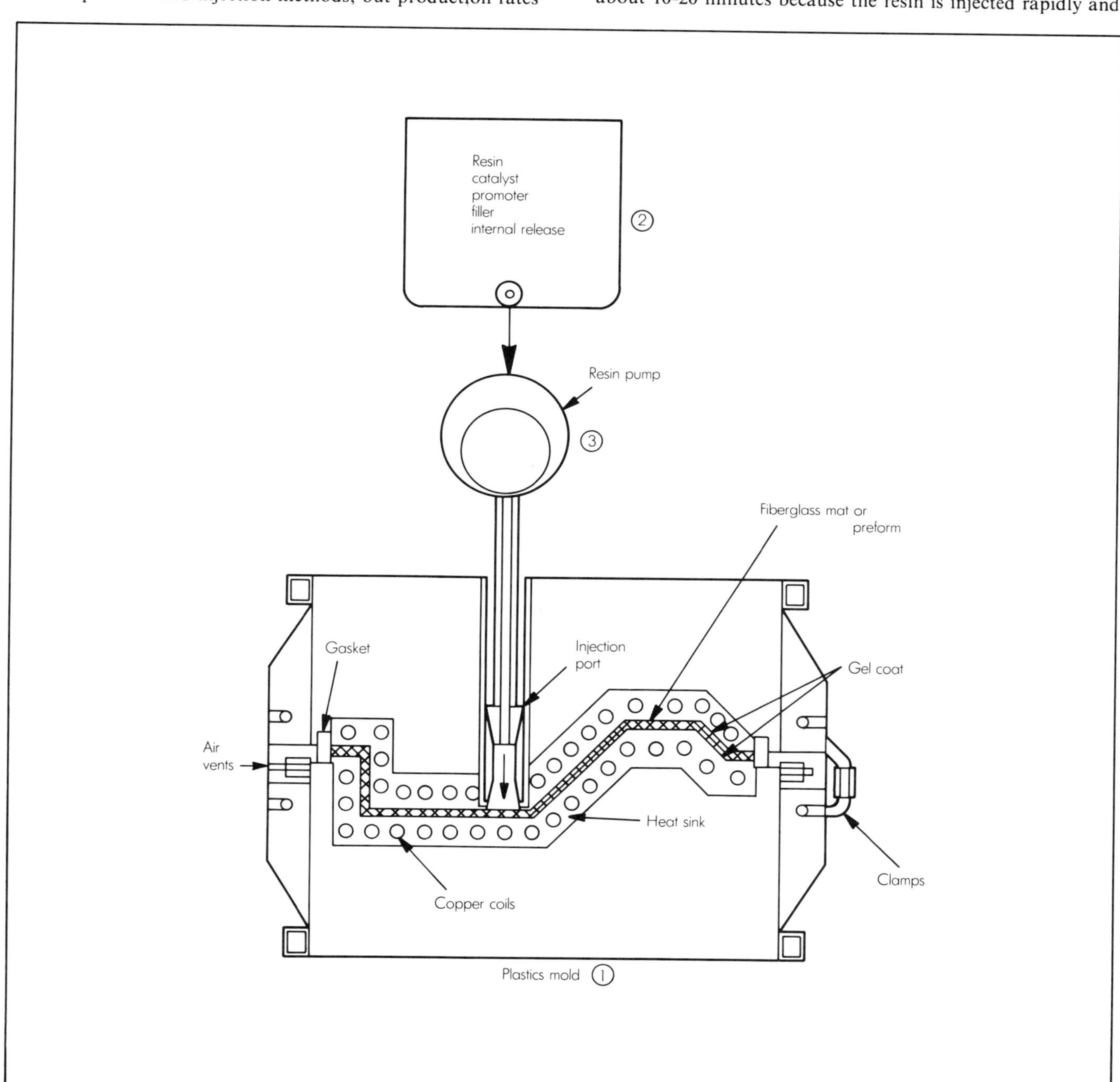


**Fig. 18-30 Resin injection molding.** (*T. H. Meister*)

thus allows for the faster gelling and curing permitted in lay-up systems. This closed-mold technique also allows for foam encapsulation and the use of ribs and inserts.

### Filament Winding

Filament winding (see Fig. 18-31) uses continuous fiberglass rovings fed through a catalyzed resin bath (polyester or epoxy) onto a revolving mandrel by a traveling head on the winder. The fiber is wound to a predetermined pattern under an applied tension that provides an even share of load bearing by the fiberglass reinforcement. In some instances, inflatable or soluble mandrels are used to facilitate their removal from the completed part. The filament winding process produces storage tanks and various aerospace items, as well as high-strength, lightweight pipes and tubes.

This process is also used to make high-strength molding sheet. A simple round mandrel is used to produce a laminate that is formed by a wide-angle winding operation. When the desired thickness is reached, the laminate is slit lengthwise to make a flat sheet. This sheet is cut into suitable strips and compression molded with SMC into parts that have high-strength areas provided by the filament-wound material.

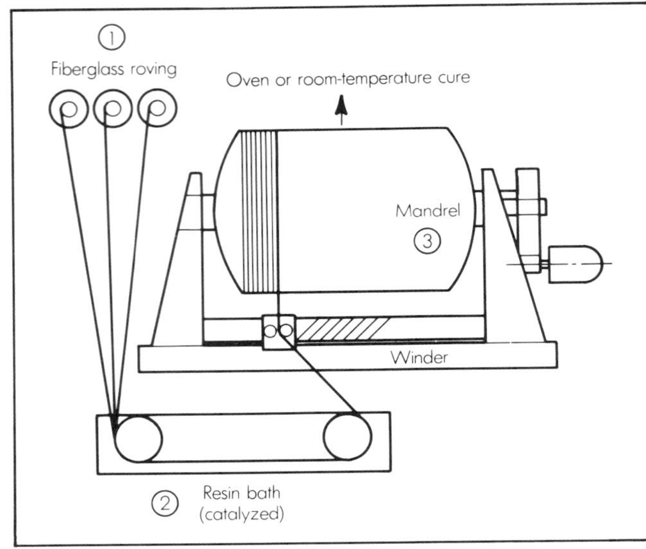


**Fig. 18-31 Filament winding process.** (*T. H. Meister*)

# THERMOFORMING PLASTIC SHEET AND FILM

Thermoforming consists of heating a thermoplastic sheet to its processing temperature and forcing the hot, flexible material against the contours of a mold. This pliable material is rapidly moved either mechanically with tools, plugs, matched molds, etc., or pneumatically with differentials in pressure created by a vacuum or by compressed air.

When held to the contours of the mold and allowed to cool, the plastics material retains the detail and shape of the mold. Figure 18-32 shows a typical thermoforming system employing a cast-aluminum mold. To obtain better optics, some parts, such as skylights and aircraft windshields, can be thermoformed without molds, using only vacuum or compressed air and holding fixtures.

Thermoforming has several advantages including (1) low costs for machinery and tooling because of low processing pressures; (2) low internal stresses and good physical properties in finished parts; (3) capability of being predecorated, laminated, or coextruded to obtain different finishes, properties, etc.; (4) capability of forming light, thin, and strong parts for packaging and other uses; and (5) capability of making large, one-piece parts with relatively inexpensive machinery and tooling. The main disadvantages are: (1) higher cost of using sheet or film instead of plastics pellets and (2) necessity of trimming the finished part.

## MACHINERY REQUIREMENTS

Equipment for thermoforming ranges from the widely used, hand-fed type of machine utilizing a straight vacuum forming cycle to sophisticated equipment that is capable of converting thermoplastic pellets to the finished thermoformed product. Typical facilities consist of a sheet extruder, sheet cooling equipment, a reheat oven to bring the sheet to the proper thermoforming state, an automatic thermoforming press, and a die-cutting machine to cut the finished product from the sheet web. Waste material from the web is reground automatically and then pneumatically conveyed to the raw material bin, where it is mixed with virgin pellets for the start of another cycle. Products such as refrigerator door liners are made by this method.

### Heating

Thermoforming requires thorough, fast, uniform, radiant heat with a minimum of 4.0 kW/ft$^2$ (43 kW/m$^2$). Top and bottom sandwich-type heater banks should always be used on any gage sheet material over 0.040" (1.02 mm) thick. This

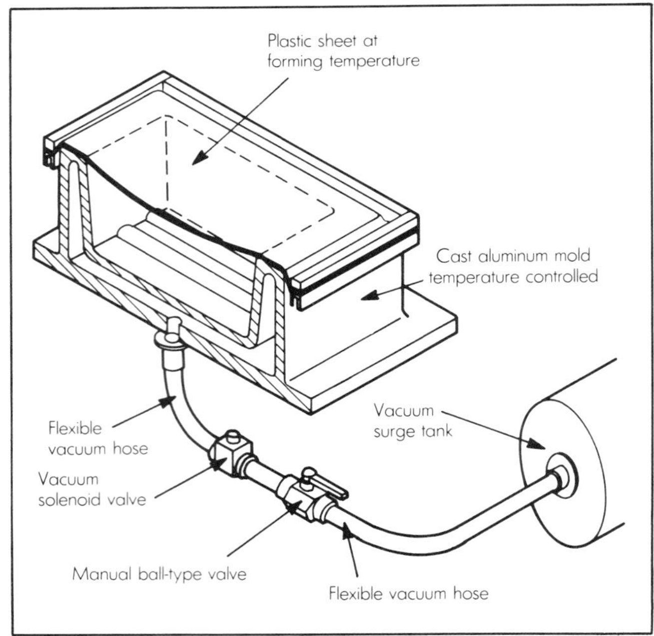


**Fig. 18-32 Thermoforming vacuum system.** (*McConnell Co., Inc.*)

ensures uniform heat throughout the sheet and improves the physical properties of the thermoformed part. The most important factor in thermoforming is heating the sheet to its proper forming temperature. The temperature of the emitting surface of the radiant heater should be adjustable from 400° F (204° C) to 1200° F (649° C), where the radiated infrared waves vary from 236-126 $\mu$ in. (6.0-3.2 $\mu$ m). This is the best range for the plastics sheet to absorb energy. Various wave-lengths are required by different plastics. Several types of heating elements are used, as listed in Table 18-14.

## Vacuum

The second most important factor in thermoforming is adequate vacuum. A thermoforming machine must have a vacuum surge tank of ample capacity for the particular machine size, with properly sized valves and tubing. High, continuous vacuum after the part has been formed ensures faster cooling, better dimensional tolerances, and sharp detail. The vacuum gage should not drop below 20 in. Hg (68 kPa) during forming. At sea level, 20 in. Hg provides only 9.82 psi (67.7 kPa) of atmospheric pressure on the part; and, as the part cools, this is barely sufficient to form most material and hold it against the mold. The best parts and cycles are achieved with 25 in. Hg (12.3 psi; 85 kPa) or more on the formed part. Representative data is given in Table 18-15.

**Surge tank.** The following formula can be used to determine vacuum reservoir (surge tank) size:

$$V_o P_o + V_m P_m = V_1 P_1 \quad (1)$$

where:

$V_o$ = surge tank volume (capacity), including piping to vacuum control valve, ft$^3$
$P_o$ = pressure in surge tank, psia. Use 0.5 psia (equivalent to 29 in. Hg Vac). (See Table 18-14.)
$V_m$ = mold area volume (consumption per cycle), ft$^3$
$P_m$ = initial pressure of the mold, at sea level either 14.7 (atmospheric pressure) or 17.7 psi when using pre-stretch forming
$V_1 = V_o + V_m$ (ft$^3$)
$P_1$ = desired working pressure, psia (psia × 6.9 = kPa)

**Sample calculation.** To determine surge tank volume, $V_o$, for the system shown in Fig. 18-32, assume:

$V_m$ = volume of mold and piping, 4 ft$^3$
$P_o$ = vacuum pump can pull approximately 29 in. Hg. Use 0.5 psia surge tank pressure
$P_1$ = desired working pressure, 2.42 psia (25 in. Hg)
$P_m$ = initial mold pressure, 14.7 psi (at sea level)
$V_1 = V_o + 4$ ft$^3$

From Eq. (1):

$$(V_o \times 0.5) + (4 \times 14.7) = (V_o + 4) \times 2.42$$

$$0.5V_o + 58.8 = 2.42V_o + 9.68$$

$$V_o = 25.58 \text{ ft}^3 \times 7.48 \text{ gal/ft}^3 = 191 \text{ gal} = 723 \text{ L}$$

**Prestretched bubble.** Frequently, in thermoforming, it is necessary to prestretch (preblow) the plastics sheet and then vacuum form the part. A general view of this process is shown in Fig. 18-33. The prestretched bubble is usually accomplished with 3-5 psig (20.7-34.5 kPa) of compressed air. This results in an even greater amount of air at atmospheric pressure. To compute the increased air volume of the prestretched bubble, 2.4 ft$^3$ is added to the mold volume for a total of 6.4 ft$^3$ and the pressure differential needed for blowing the bubble (3-5 psig) is added to the initial atmospheric pressure in the mold; for example: 14.7 + 3 = 17.7 psig.

Using the sample calculation for determining the surge tank volume, but with prestretching and plug-assist:

**TABLE 18-14**
**Various Types of Radiant Heating Elements**

| Type of Heating Element | Efficiency When New, % | Efficiency After 6 Months, % | Average Life, hrs. | Comments |
|---|---|---|---|---|
| Coiled nichrome wire | 16-18 | 8-10 | 1500 | Cheapest initially, very inefficient, heat nonuniformly with use |
| Tubular rods | 42 | 21 | 3000 | Inexpensive, heat non-uniformly with use, difficult to screen or mask for profile heat |
| Ceramic panels<br>Quartz panels | 62<br>55 | 55<br>48 | 12-15,000<br>8-10,000 | Best buy, uniform heat, efficient, ideal for heat profiling |
| Gas-fired infrared | 40-45 | 25 | 5-6,000 | Cheapest to operate but many disadvantages |

Note: After 6 months use, 4-8% efficiency can be gained by replacing side wall and back-side reflectors. Sanding/polishing oxidized tubular heaters can improve their efficiency 10-15%. Steel clamping frames should be nickel-copper-chrome-plated to reflect heat to sheet edges. The angle of incidence equals the angle of reflection.

$$(V_o \times 0.5) + (6.4 \times 17.7) = (V_o + 6.4) \times 2.42$$
$$0.5V_o + 113.3 = 2.42V_o + 15.5$$
$$V_o = 50.9 \text{ ft}^3 \times 7.48 \text{ gal/ft}^3 = 381 \text{ gal} = 1442 \text{ L}$$

Vacuum surge tanks should be located close to the thermoformer and the vacuum control valve. A flexible vacuum hose should be used from the tank to the valve and then to the mold, as indicated in Fig. 18-33. Straight-in connections should be made. Elbows, tee, and reducers should not be used in plumbing the vacuum line. Vacuum and air-control valves must be full-opening types. Table 18-16 provides data for vacuum line and part sizing.

### Mechanical Operation

In addition to heat and vacuum, another requirement for a thermoforming machine is good mechanical operation. With movable top and bottom platens and compressed air and vacuum available separately to both platens, all thermoforming techniques can be accomplished. Thermoformers also must have a method of clamping the plastics sheet securely during the heating and forming operations. Controls and safety devices complete the machine. For low-volume production, sheet or roll-fed, single-station machines are used. For higher production, multiple stations are employed. Figures 18-34 and 18-35 show examples of these machines.

**TABLE 18-15**
**Basic Vacuum Pressure Measurements**

| Units | | | |
|---|---|---|---|
| Gage Pressure, PSIG | Absolute Pressure, PSIA | In. Hg | kPa |
| 0 | 14.7 | 0 | 0 |
| -1 | 13.7 | 2.0 | 6.9 |
| -2 | 12.7 | 4.1 | 13.8 |
| -4 | 10.7 | 8.1 | 27.6 |
| -6 | 8.7 | 12.2 | 41.4 |
| -8 | 6.7 | 16.3 | 55.2 |
| -9 | 5.7 | 18.3 | 61.1 |
| -10 | 4.7 | 20.4 | 69.0 |
| -11 | 3.7 | 22.4 | 75.8 |
| -12 | 2.7 | 24.4 | 82.7 |
| -12.3 | 2.4 | 25.0 | 84.7 |
| -13 | 1.7 | 26.5 | 89.6 |
| -13.7 | 1.0 | 27.9 | 94.5 |
| -14 | 0.7 | 28.5 | 96.5 |
| -14.2 | 0.5 | 29.0 | 97.9 |
| -14.6 | 0.1 | 29.7 | 100.7 |
| -14.7 | 0 | 29.9 | 101.4 |

Note: PSIA— Absolute pressure (pounds per square inch) is measured with respect to zero-absolute vacuum. In a vacuum system, it is equal to the negative gage pressure subtracted from atmospheric pressure.

PSIG— Gage pressure (pounds per square inch) is the amount by which pressure exceeds the atmospheric pressure.

Hence: Gage pressure + atmospheric pressure = absolute pressure

## TOOLING

One of the most advantageous features of the thermoforming process is its relatively low tooling cost requirements.

### Construction

A wide variety of materials can be used to manufacture molds, because of the relatively low pressures required. Atmospheric pressure of 14.7 psi (101 kPa) up through 50-100 psi (345-690 kPa) is all that is used. This means wood, plaster, epoxy, urethane, aluminum, etc., are practical mold materials. The best all-around material is aluminum with a nominal wall thickness of 3/8″ (10 mm), because of its good thermal conductivity, ease of fabrication by casting or machining, light weight, and low cost.

Production molds are usually temperature controlled, with tubing or channels provided for temperature-controlled coolant to pass through the mold continuously. Table 18-17 shows a comparison of heat-transfer rates with various materials. Wood and epoxy work well for prototypes or short runs. The more generous the radii and the draft on molds, the more easily the part forms. Material distribution is also better. Sharp angles and corners cause stress concentrations and lead to part failure. Figure 18-36 illustrates typical mold construction, in which a moat is designed into the mold to prevent warpage of polyolefin formed parts.

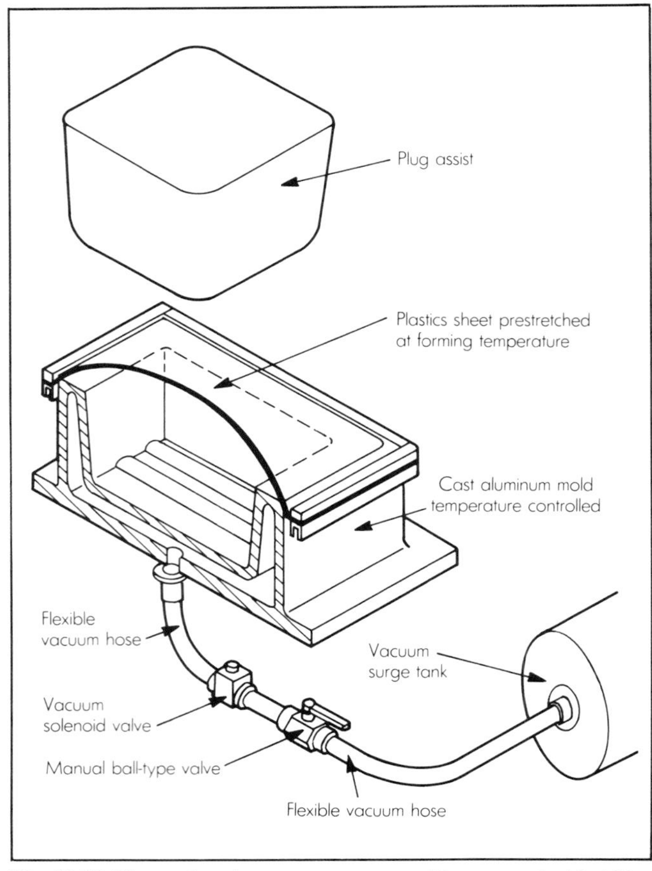


**Fig. 18-33 Thermoforming vacuum system with prestretched bubble.** (*McConnell Co., Inc.*)

## Male vs. Female Molds

Male molds are suitable for use more often than female molds because they are cheaper to make. However, many other factors besides cost must be taken into account when selecting a mold. Close tolerances can only be held on a thermoformed part on the side that is formed against the mold, unless matched tooling is used. When parts are to be mated or joined, and fine detail is desired, these surfaces must be formed next to the mold.

During straight, drape-type forming, the portion of the hot sheet that first touches the mold freezes (solidifies) with very little stretch. This creates thick sections at the point at which the sheet first touches the mold and thin areas where it contacts the mold last. For more uniform wall thickness and deep draw ratios, the plastics sheet can be prestretched evenly while at thermoforming temperatures and then rapidly formed to the mold, as discussed previously.

**TABLE 18-16**
**Vacuum Line and Port Sizing**

| Thermoforming Machine Forming Area | Vacuum Line and Control Valve Sizes, diam |
|---|---|
| Up to 30 x 36″ (0.8 x 0.9 m) | 1″ (25 mm) |
| 3 x 4′ to 7 x 9′ (0.9 x 1.2 m) to (2.1 x 2.7 m) | 1.5″ (38 mm) |
| 8 x 10′ and up (2.4 x 3.0 m) | 2″ (51 mm) |

## Vacuum

All thermoforming molds used with vacuum and/or air pressure require holes, channels, or ducts for evacuation of air between the hot, pliable sheet and the mold. Normally, the faster the vacuum application, the better the part. Slots, slits, or channels are used wherever possible. The slot-type vacuum mold is built in segments to permit evacuation of the air between the respective mold surfaces and the sheet. The segments and male molds are mounted on baseplates, using shims as needed for vacuum slots. Plastics sheet materials that are quite fluid at forming temperature, such as the polyolefins, require small vacuum openings of 0.010-0.020″ (0.25-0.51 mm) to avoid vacuum holes in the finished part.

Larger holes or slots can be tolerated with other materials and big holes can be formed in areas of the part that is to be trimmed. The polyolefins also require a sandblasted surface finish or use of porous molds for smooth areas. Porous-type tooling has thousands of microscopic holes on the surface and enables extremely fast vacuum attainment with resultant fine detailing in the part.

## Temperature Control

As stated previously, mold temperature must be controlled for high-quality parts (see Fig. 18-36). Production tooling normally has cast-in cooling tubes or machined channels for passage of a temperature-controlled cooling liquid. All thermoplastic materials have a mold shrinkage factor. Table 18-18 lists shrinkage factors for various mold materials. The various types of sheet shrink from 1/4% to as much as 4% smaller than the mold by the time they have reached room temperature.

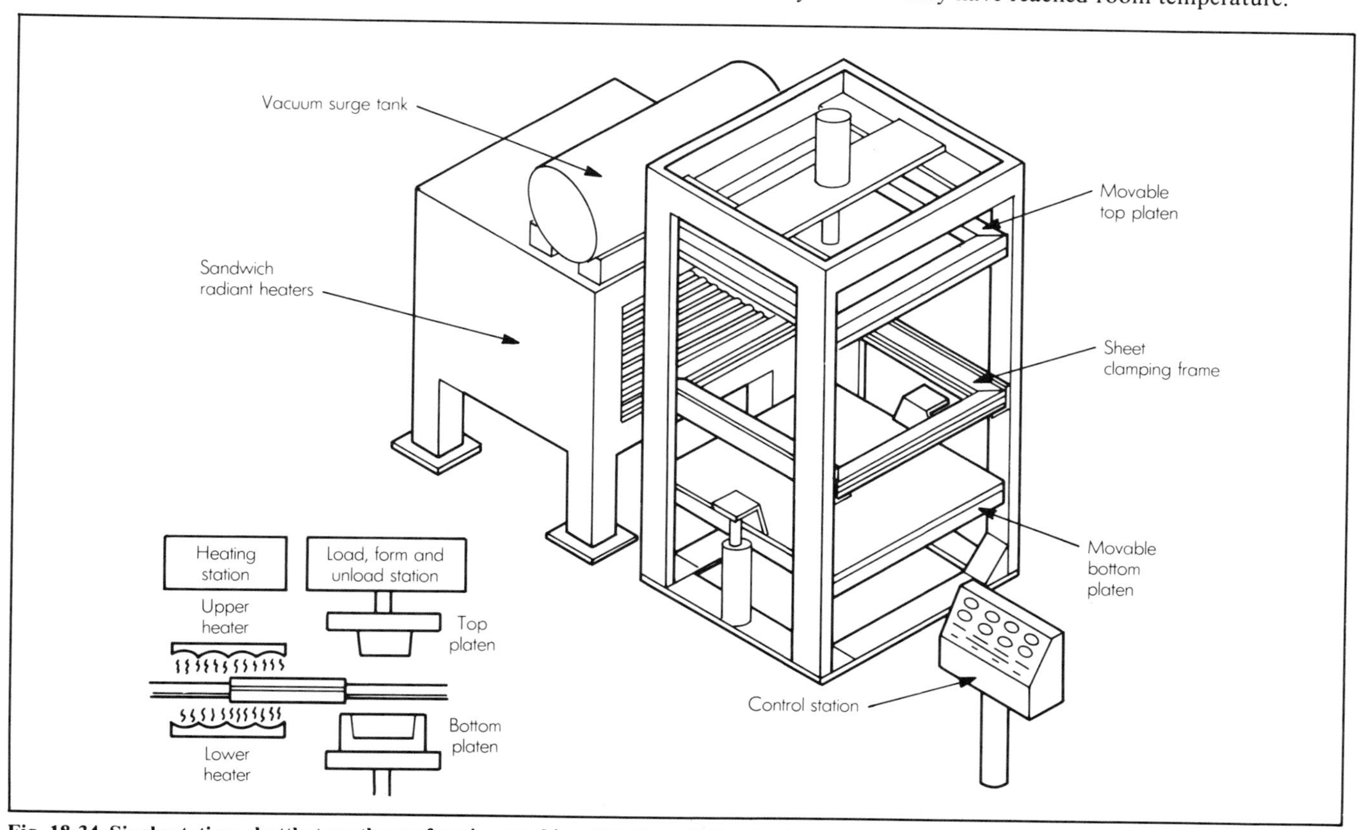


**Fig. 18-34 Single-station, shuttle-type thermoforming machine.** (*McConnell Co., Inc.*)

# THERMOFORMING PLASTIC SHEET AND FILM

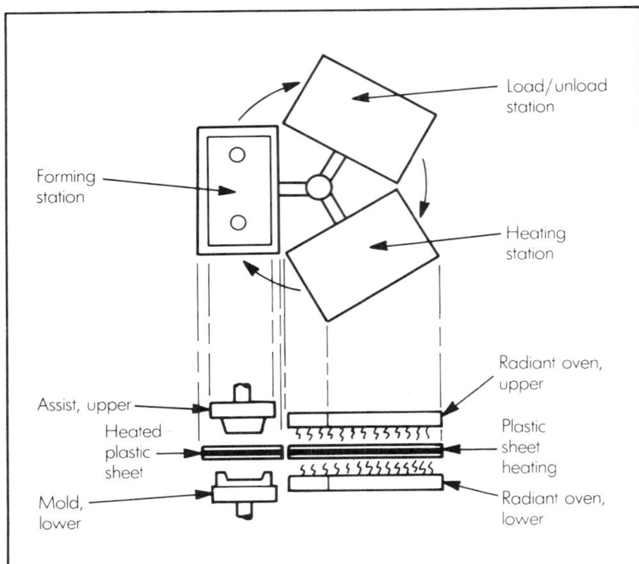


**Fig. 18-35 Rotary thermoforming machine.** (*McConnell Co., Inc.*)

**TABLE 18-17**
**Material Heat Transfer Rate Comparison**

| Material | Heat Transfer Rate Factor | k Value* |
|---|---|---|
| Aluminum | 1500 | 130 |
| Aluminum-filled epoxy | 6-10 | 0.52-0.87 |
| Epoxy | 1.5 | 0.13 |
| Plaster | 2 | 0.17 |
| Steel | 300 | 26 |
| Wood | 1 | 0.09 |

* k = Btu/hr/ft$^2$/° F/ft

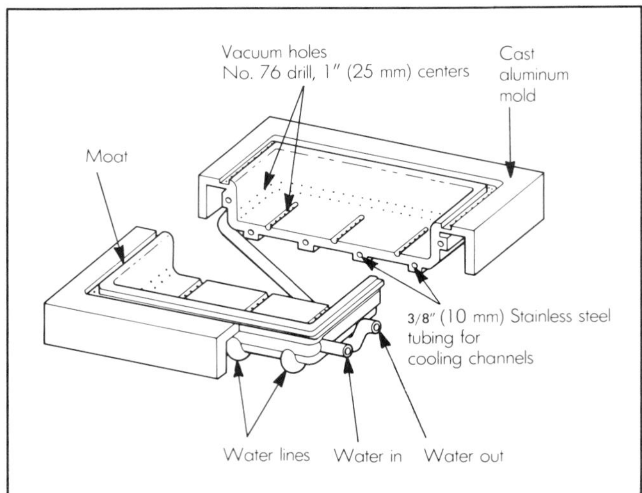


**Fig. 18-36 Typical temperature-controlled mold construction.** (*McConnell Co., Inc.*)

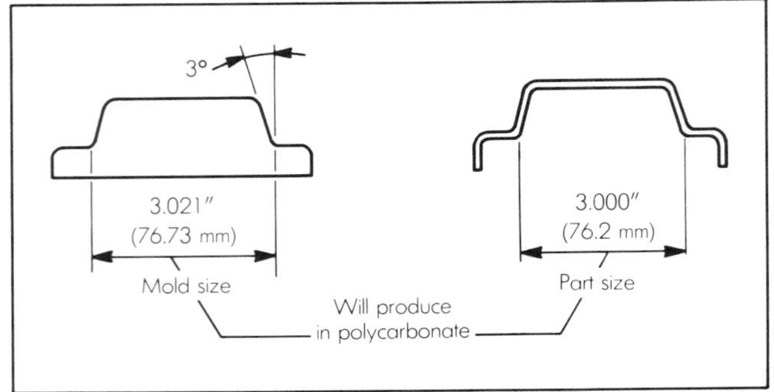


**TABLE 18-18**
**Typical Draft and Shrinkage**

| Material | Shrinkage Range, in./in. or mm/mm | Shrinkage Normally Used, in./in. or mm/mm |
|---|---|---|
| ABS | 0.003-0.008 | 0.005 |
| Acrylic | 0.003-0.008 | 0.0055 |
| Butyrate | 0.002-0.005 | 0.0035 |
| Polycarbonate | 0.006-0.008 | 0.007 |
| Polyethylene, high density | 0.020-0.035 | 0.025 |

Approximately 75% of the part shrinkage occurs as the material cools from the processing temperature to the set temperature (material heat distortion temperature at 66 psi; 455 kPa). Consistent mold temperatures and cooling rates are important for good parts. Changing these temperatures changes the size and physical properties of the finished part. For example, the hotter the mold, the greater the final shrinkage of the part. Ideally, molds should be designed to provide a temperature differential between the entering and exiting water of no more than 5° F (2.4° C). Coolant should have a fast, turbulent flow for efficient cooling.

## Breakaway Molds

Undercuts in molds can be handled with dovetailed slots, removable split rings, segmented cavities, movable side cores, unscrewing-type cavities, etc. These can be hinged to move as the mold is retracted from the part; segments can come out with the part or can be mechanically retracted before the part is removed. Figure 18-37 shows a mold with breakaway segment (removable insert).

## Mechanical Helpers

Mechanical helpers are used as a means of preventing webbing (bridging, gathering, or sticking together of a sheet material) and as a plug-assist to carry material into an area and/or to compression-mold a portion of the part. Generally, the plug-assist is used to move the material. Therefore, it should be made of a very low heat conducting material, such as wood, felt-covered wood, epoxy, or synthetic foam, or it should be heated. Usually, if it is heated, its temperature should be approximately the same as that of the sheet, to avoid chilling. In this case, Teflon-coated aluminum with rheostat-controlled strip heaters works well for the plug-assist device. To determine the correct plug dimensions, a first approximation should be about 85% of the size and shape of the cavity to be plugged.

# THERMOFORMING PLASTIC SHEET AND FILM

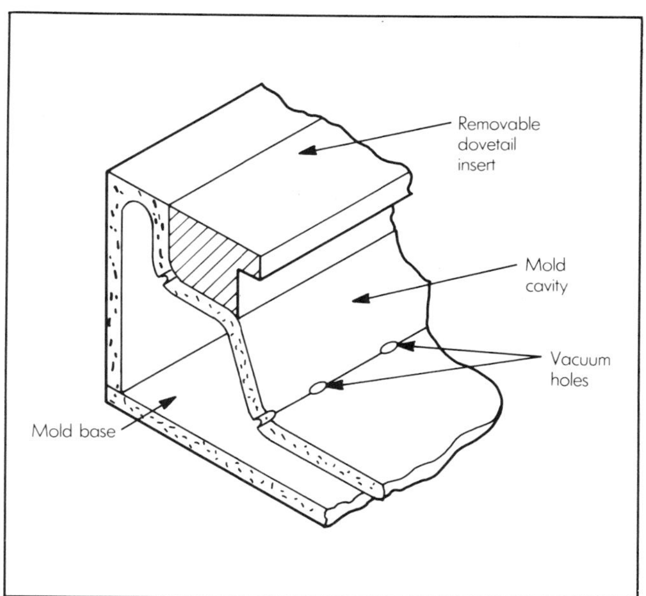


**Fig. 18-37 Breakaway segment for undercut in mold.** (*McConnell Co., Inc.*)

## THERMOFORMING TECHNIQUES

A variety of techniques is used for the thermoforming of plastics sheets. They include vacuum forming, free forming, drape forming, plug and ring forming, vacuum snap-back forming, airslip forming, plug-assist forming, matched-die forming, and twin-sheet forming. Most of the processes are based on the principle of forcing a heated, pliable thermoplastic sheet to conform to the contours of a mold, then allowing the formed material to cool. The most commonly used thermoforming techniques can be classified as vacuum, pressure, mechanical, prestretching, twin-sheet, and rigidizing methods.

### Thermoforming Temperatures

As mentioned earlier under "Heating" (refer to the 'Machinery Requirements" section), proper heating of the thermoplastic sheet from the core out is the most important factor in thermoforming. Table 18-19 presents the various processing temperature ranges for some of the commonly used materials.

### Vacuum Forming Technique

The most popular forming method is by use of vacuum. The mold is closed into the hot plastics sheet, creating a mechanical seal between the mold and the sheet. A vacuum is then used to rapidly remove the air between them. Thus, atmospheric pressure (14.7 psi; 101 kPa, at sea level) is used to force the hot,

**TABLE 18-19**
**Thermoforming Processing Temperature Ranges**

| Material | Ideal Mold Temperature, °F (°C) | Set Temperature, °F (°C) | Lower Processing Limit, °F (°C) | Normal Forming Temperature, °F (°C) | Upper Limit, °F (°C) |
|---|---|---|---|---|---|
| ABS | 180 (82) | 208 (98) | 260 (127) | 300 (149) | 360 (182) |
| Acrylic | 190 (88) | 208 (98) | 300 (149) | 350 (177) | 380 (193) |
| Butyrate | 150 (66) | 176 (80) | 260 (127) | 295 (146) | 360 (182) |
| Polycarbonate | 260 (127) | 288 (142) | 355 (168) | 375 (191) | 400 (204) |
| Polyethylene, high density | 160 (71) | 176 (80) | 260 (127) | 300 (149) | 360 (182) |
| Polysulfone | 325 (163) | 358 (181) | 390 (199) | 475 (246) | 575 (302) |
| Styrene | 180 (82) | 200 (93) | 260 (127) | 300 (149) | 360 (182) |
| Vinyl, rigid | 140 (60) | 163 (73) | 220 (104) | 280 (138) | 310 (154) |

Notes:

1. *Mold Temperature.* High mold temperatures provide high-quality parts, better impact strength and other physical properties, minimum internal stresses, better detail, material distribution and optics. On the other hand, thin-gage disposables and like items can frequently be thermoformed on molds of 35-90° F (17-32° C), lowering cycles greatly. The additional stresses produced are not as pronounced in the thin gages and can usually be tolerated.
2. *Set Temperature.* This is the temperature at which the part may be removed from the mold without warpage. Sometimes parts can be removed at higher temperatures if cooling fixtures are used. The set temperature is usually the heat-distortion temperature at 66 psi (455 kPa).
3. *Lower Processing Limit.* This represents the lowest temperature at which material can be formed without creating undue stresses. This means that the sheet material should touch every corner of the mold before it reaches this lower limit. Material processed below the lower limit will have greatly increased stresses and strains that later could cause warpage, lower impact, and/or other physical changes in the finished item.
4. *Normal Forming Temperature.* This is the temperature at which the sheet should be formed under normal operation. This temperature should be reached throughout the sheet and should be measured just before the mold and sheet come together. Shallow-draw projects with fast vacuum and/or pressure forming will allow somewhat lower sheet temperature and thus a faster cycle. Higher temperatures are required for deep draws, prestretching operations, detailed molds, etc.
5. *Upper Limit.* This is the temperature point at which the thermoplastic sheet begins to degrade or at which the sheet becomes too fluid and pliable to thermoform. These temperatures normally can be exceeded only with an impairment of the material's physical properties. Injection molding and extruding do use much higher temperatures, although only for short durations; however, they create additional degradation of material.

pliable sheet onto the mold, holding it there until it cools and hardens, as shown in Fig. 18-38. The sheet can be draped over a male or female mold or can be "free" drawn into a vacuum box and cooled while only touching the clamping flange area.

### Pressure Forming Technique

Forming by compressed air up to 100 psi (690 kPa) is common in production of thin-gage containers and other parts. Faster cycles, finer details, and better material distribution are some features of the pressure forming technique. The hot plastics sheet is locked between a pressure box or plate and the mold. Then, compressed air is quickly applied to the one side of the mold and vacuum is applied to the other side, as illustrated in Fig. 18-39. Air blowing is also used to produce optically clear parts by "free blowing" acrylic, etc., for aircraft canopies, skylights, food covers, etc.

### Mechanical Forming Technique

This method involves stretching and forming a thermoplastic sheet by mechanical means or devices. Mechanical forming techniques include (1) pulling a plastics sheet at forming temperature mechanically to the mold, using a ring and plug arrangement; (2) forming with matched tools, using a single mold with a pressure blanket; and (3) forming with strip heaters. Figure 18-40 shows the principle of mechanical forming with matched molds.

### Prestretching

Parts with depths equal to or greater than the narrowest width dimension usually need to be prestretched just prior to final forming. The prestretching is done (when the sheet is at the proper thermoforming temperature) either by vacuum, compressed air, plug-assist, or a combination of techniques. Prestretching provides very uniform walls.

**Prestretching by vacuum snap-back.** In this universal method of obtaining uniform thickness of the part, a prestretch box is pushed into the hot plastics sheet, causing a seal to form around its entire periphery. The hot material is then moved by a vacuum or by compressed air into a bowl shape with uniform thickness throughout. As the bowl-shaped area of the plastics has not touched anything, it is still at forming temperature. At this moment, the mold is forced into the bubble and "snapped" against it by vacuum. Figure 18-41 illustrates this technique.

**Prestretching with plug-assist forming.** Using a female mold either on a top or bottom-movable platen, the hot plastics sheet is sealed against its periphery. A plug-assist can now be moved into the hot sheet at a fast enough speed (8-22 in./s; 203-559 mm/s) to keep the material next to the plug and away from the relatively cool mold. When the plug has carried the hot sheet close to the mold surfaces, vacuum and/or air pressure is applied instantly. The hot sheet can also be blown by compressed air into a bubble and then plugged. This manner of forming results in very even wall thicknesses on the finished product. Figure 18-42 illustrates this method.

To obtain the best consistency in overall part thickness, the plug-assist should only carry or move a prestretched bubble without cooling the sheet material. Any cooling at this point leaves "chill marks" on the finished part where the plug touched it. Heating the plug to the same temperature as the sheet or using a very low heat-conducting surface on the plug can eliminate or minimize this condition.

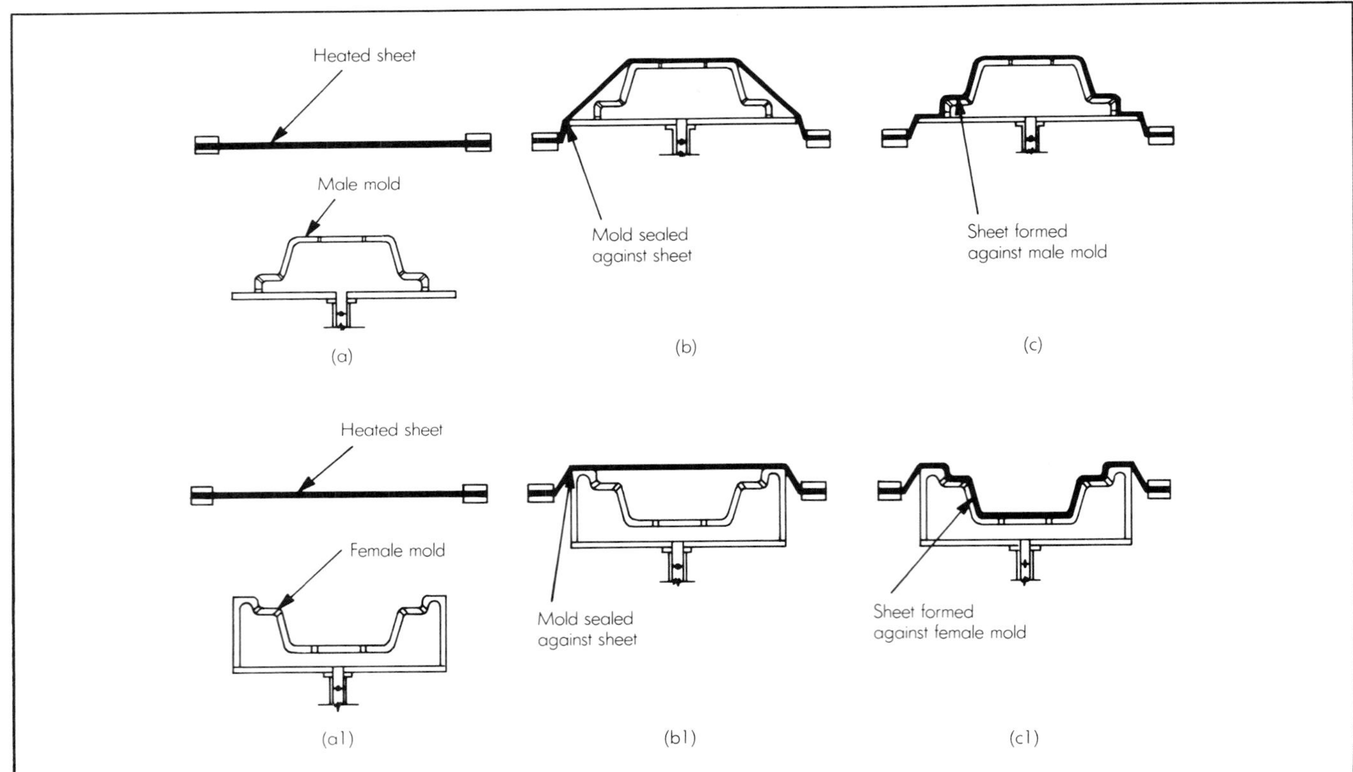


**Fig. 18-38 Vacuum forming—drape process.** (*McConnell Co., Inc.*)

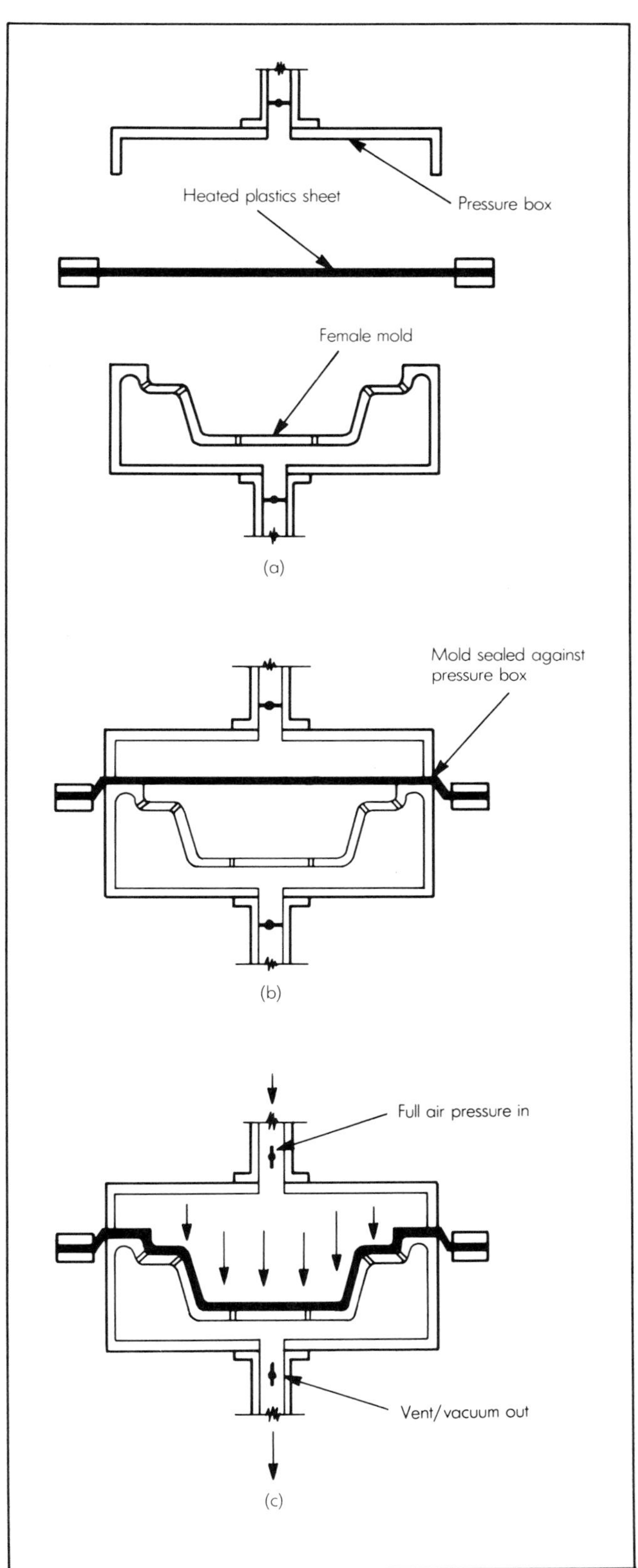


**Fig. 18-39 Pressure forming.** (*McConnell Co., Inc.*)

## Twin Sheet Forming

Hollow products are produced at high rates of speed using two sheets of plastics. The sheets are usually heated to forming temperature in separate clamping frames, and sandwich heating can be used. The sheets are then mechanically placed one over the other. At this stage, opposing molds are moved into the hot sheets with a vacuum drawn in the molds and air pressure applied between the two sheets.

The molds pinch off around the entire perimeter, and the item is formed. Figure 18-43 depicts twin-sheet thermoforming.

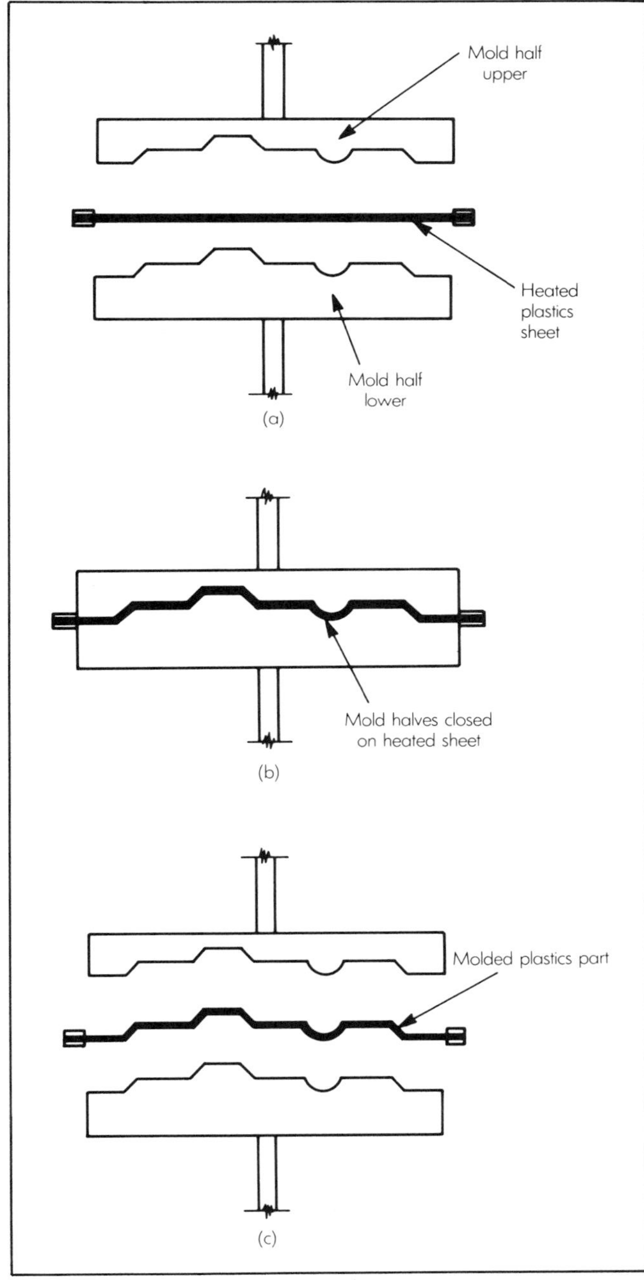


**Fig. 18-40 Mechanical forming with matched molds.** (*McConnell Co., Inc.*)

# THERMOFORMING PLASTIC SHEET AND FILM

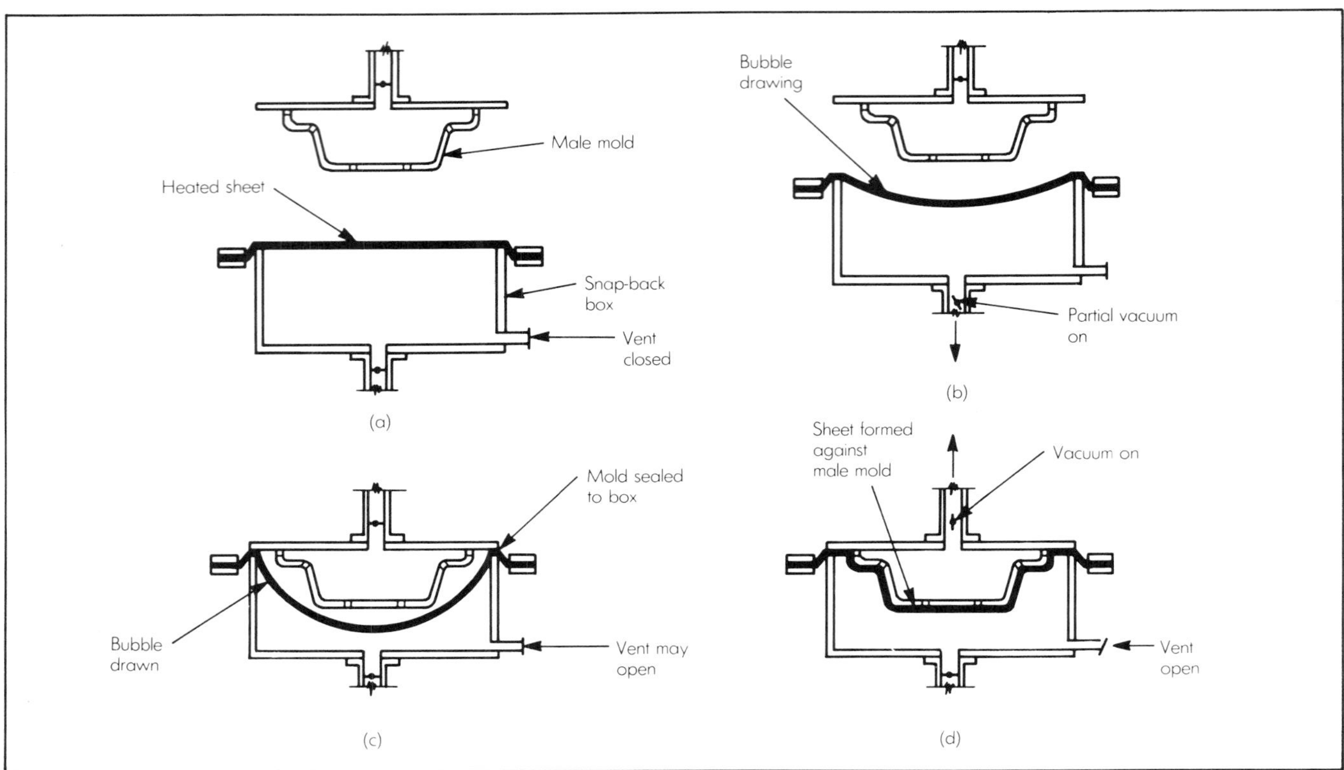


**Fig. 18-41 Vacuum snap-back forming.** (*McConnell Co., Inc.*)

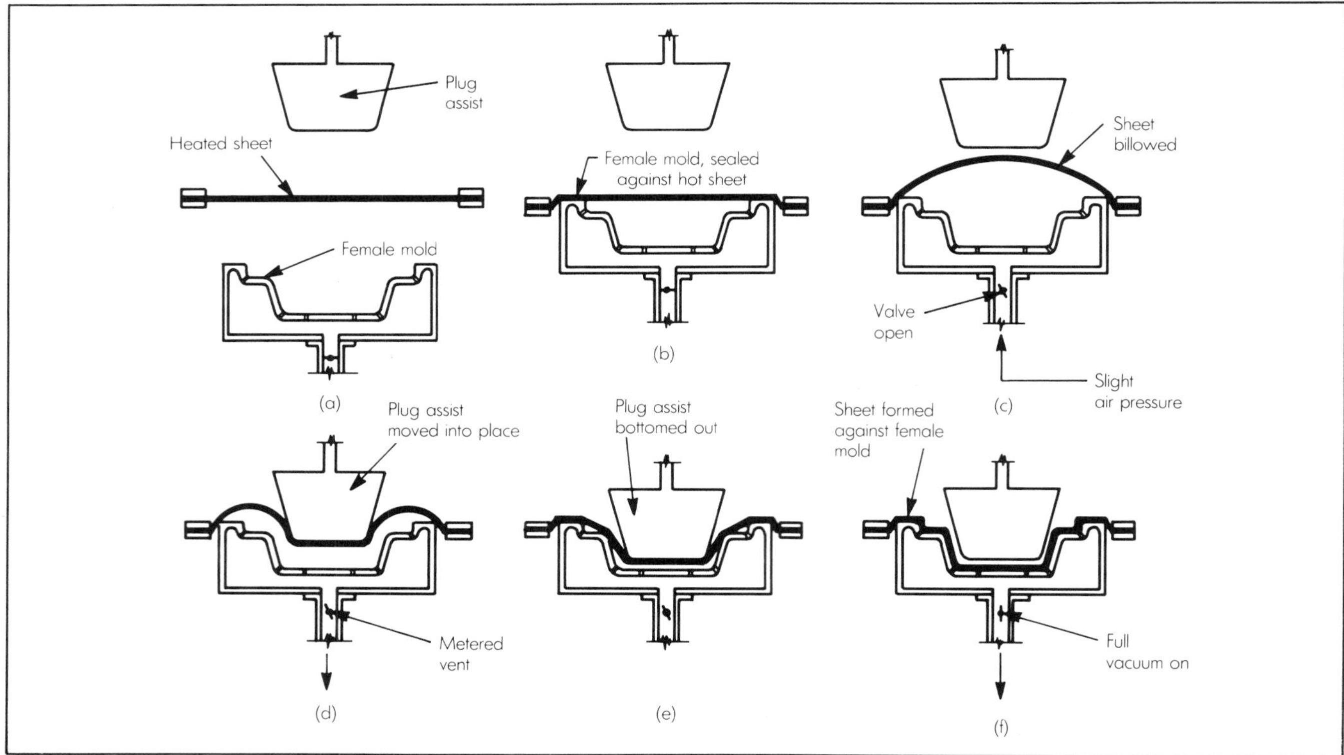


**Fig. 18-42 Billow molding with plug assist.** (*McConnell Co., Inc.*)

Several variations of this process are used in industry. Boats, bifold doors, garage door segments, material handling skids, dock floats, etc., are among articles thus formed.

## Rigidizing

Thermoplastics are not normally considered for structural uses because of their creep and cold flow characteristics. However, one way of designing around these deficiencies is to thermoform the outside "skin" for the product out of thermoplastic sheet. The finished thickness should be approximately 0.04″ (1 mm). The skin is then rigidized by spraying about 1/8″ (3 mm) of chopped fiberglass and polyester on the reverse side, or a minimum of 3/8″ (10 mm) polyurethane foam. When it has cured, a strong, substantial product is obtained. Acrylic is very compatible with polyester-reinforced fiberglass, and many items are made by combining the two materials. Applications include sanitary wear, panels, and outdoor furniture. Polyurethane and ABS also bond well together and are used successfully in ice chests, boats, surfboards, serving trays, and other products.

## HIGH-PRESSURE LAMINATES

High pressure laminates consist of superimposed layers of a thermoset, resin-impregnated or resin-coated filler polymerized (fused) together by heat and pressure. A minimum of 1100 psi (7.6 MPa) and maximum of 2000 psi (13.8 MPa) pressure is used for high-pressure laminating. Fillers and reinforcements are composed of various materials, such as cotton mats, paper, glass fibers or fabric, glass mats, graphite, boron fibers, felted asbestos, and nylon fabric.

These sheets or mats are macerated with such thermosetting resins as phenolic, melamine, polyester, epoxy, and silicone. The heat and pressure during lamination creates a chemical reaction that causes the entire laminate to cure into a hard, nearly homogeneous, insoluble mass. Sheets, tubes, rod, and molded forms are produced. After thermoset resins have polymerized, they cannot be resoftened or reshaped by heat or solvents. Large volumes of decorative, high-pressure laminates are used in the furniture and building industries. Industrial laminates are used throughout industry in aircraft, auto, electronic, and appliance fields, as well as in other fields.

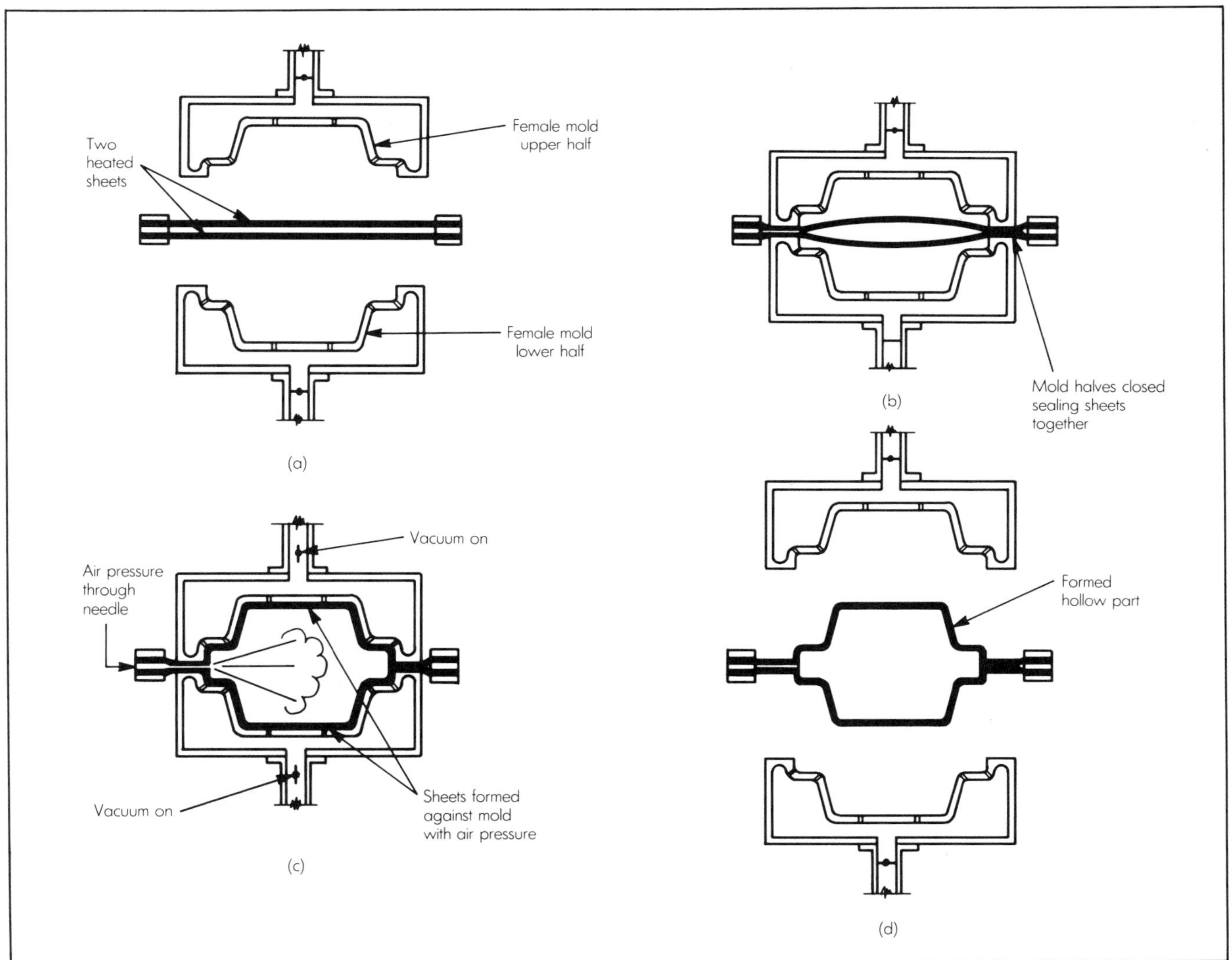


**Fig. 18-43 Twin sheet thermoforming.** (*McConnell Co., Inc.*)

# OTHER PROCESSING METHODS

A variety of special techniques is used in processing plastics, in addition to the basic procedures described previously in this chapter. Combinations of several processes often may be used advantageously for producing specialty plastics products.

## BLOW MOLDING

Blow molding is a process for shaping thermoplastic materials into one-piece, hollow articles by means of heat and air pressure. The method consists basically of stretching a hot thermoplastic tube with air pressure, then hardening it against a relatively cool mold. A wide variety of blow molding techniques and equipment is used to suit specific applications.

The principal difference between blow molding glass and blow molding plastics is attributed to the different material properties. Molten glass is much less sensitive than plastics—not only in the melt viscosity, but also in its chemical stability. For this reason, modified glass blowing machines cannot be used for plastics. Another difference is that glass blowers start with a drop of molten glass, while the plastics blowers use a preformed plastics part, which usually is a tube of molten plastics called a parison.

### Extrusion Blow Molding

The extrusion blow molding process is the most commonly used method, and its basic steps are applicable to other blow molding processes. The principle involved in extrusion blow molding involves inflating a softened plastics tube (the parison) while it is confined between the cavity halves of a mold. When the expanding parison contacts the cold mold wall, it becomes rigid and assumes the shape of the mold cavity.

In the extrusion blow molding process an extruder plasticizes the plastics and pumps it through a crosshead fitted with a die and core or a mandrel to produce a parison (hollow tube of molten plastics) of suitable diameter for the product. In extrusion blow molding, the mold is then positioned with the parison between the two female mold halves. The mold closes over the parison, pinching one end of the parison tube and enclosing a blowing pin, or compressed air entry pipe, at the other end. The closed parison is inflated by air pressurized at approximately 100 psi (700 kPa).

The parison expands onto the relatively cold walls of the mold and solidifies into the mold surface shape. After the product is cool enough to retain its shape, the mold is opened and the part is ejected. Two commonly used processes are continuous extrusion and intermittent extrusion.

**Continuous extrusion.** For heat-sensitive plastics such as polyvinylchloride, the continuous extrusion process is very suitable. In this process, the parison is being formed continuously at a rate that is controlled by the rate of molding, cooling, and part removal. To avoid interference with parison formation, the mold clamp must be moved (out of the way) to the blowing station. This is done with either a rotary wheel or a side shuttle.

Continuous extrusion is often used for producing containers in sizes up to 1 gal (3.8 L). For containers up to 5 gal (19.9 L) capacity, a reciprocating screw is used; and for large, heavy, industrial containers, the ram or accumulator head systems are used.

**Intermittent extrusion.** Intermittent extrusion is best suited for processing polyolefins. With this method, the parison is extruded immediately after the part is removed from the mold. All operations of molding, cooling, and part removal take place under the diehead; a shuttle is not required. Variations of the intermittent extrusion process include the reciprocating screw, side ram/plunger accumulator, and accumulator head with tubular plunger processes.

### Injection Blow Molding

Applications of the injection blow molding process have been increasing rapidly in recent years. In the past, the process was used to produce small containers; currently, it is commonly used to produce 32 oz (1 L) bottles and jars.

In this process, the parison is created by injecting the resin around a core rod in a parison mold. Immediately after injection (and before the material is completely cooled), the mold opens and the parison on the core rod is transferred to the blowing mold. Air to expand the parison to the shape of the blow mold is blown through the core rod, and the finished bottle is formed on the rod. When the mold halves separate, the finished bottle is blown or stripped from the core rod, which returns to the injection station to repeat the cycle.

Containers molded by this process have accurately molded neck finishes and require no trimming or finishing. Bottle weight also is held to close tolerances, and weight distribution in the bottle can be effectively controlled. The injection blow molding process can be used with all of the thermoplastics, including heat-sensitive materials such as polyvinylchloride (PVC).

### Stretch-Blow Molding

The stretch-blow molding process was developed to provide improved properties and more uniform wall thickness to bottles for carbonated and alcoholic beverages, syrups, edible oils, etc. During the conventional blow molding processes, forming is done with plastics materials in the viscous and elastoviscous states in the parison. The stretch-blow process uses preforms that are in the viscoelastic stage.

Products made by the stretch-blow process have higher strength, better clarity, and stronger barrier properties to prevent the passage of oxygen, carbon dioxide, and water vapor. These properties are attributable to biaxial orientation of the resin molecules, shown in Fig. 18-44, which is attained by stretch-blowing preforms into bottles along two planes at the same time. The biaxial stretching occurs on both axes, resulting in a strong, even-walled container.

The two basic types of processes for stretch-blow molding are (1) a single-stage process in which preforms are made and bottles blown on the same machine and (2) the two-stage process in which preforms are made in one machine and then blown later on another machine. Single-stage equipment is capable of processing polyethylene terephthalate (PET) and polyvinylchloride (PVC). Two-stage machines generally are used to make PET and polypropylene (PP) bottles.

The single-stage and the two-stage processes have the following in common:

- A preform that is shorter and smaller than the desired container. The preform is made either by extruding a tube, by the extrusion blow-molding of a "test-tube"

shape, or by the injection molding of a "test-tube" shape.
- A predetermined preform "orientation temperature" that is dependent upon the material.
- Processing at the orientation temperature, to stretch the preform to the desired size and shape.
- A cooling cycle that brings the material to a solid stage.

A variation, called injection stretch-blow molding, is gaining increasing usage. Bottles made with a hemispherical bottom configuration for pressurized contents such as carbonated beverages require a separate, injection-molded base cup to provide a flat bottom for free standing. A special mold with a separate retracting bottom section permits forming pedestal bottles, or the concave "wine bottle" bottom. The special mold eliminates the need for a separate base cup.

A typical sequence of two-stage, injection stretch-blow operations is illustrated in Fig. 18-45. In view *a*, the heat-conditioned preform is positioned in the blow mold. The center rod follows the preform as it is blown downward and holds the center of the preform against the center of the mold. In view *b*, air expands the preform to final shape against the mold walls. View *c* shows a variation in which a separate section forms a typical wine bottle bottom.

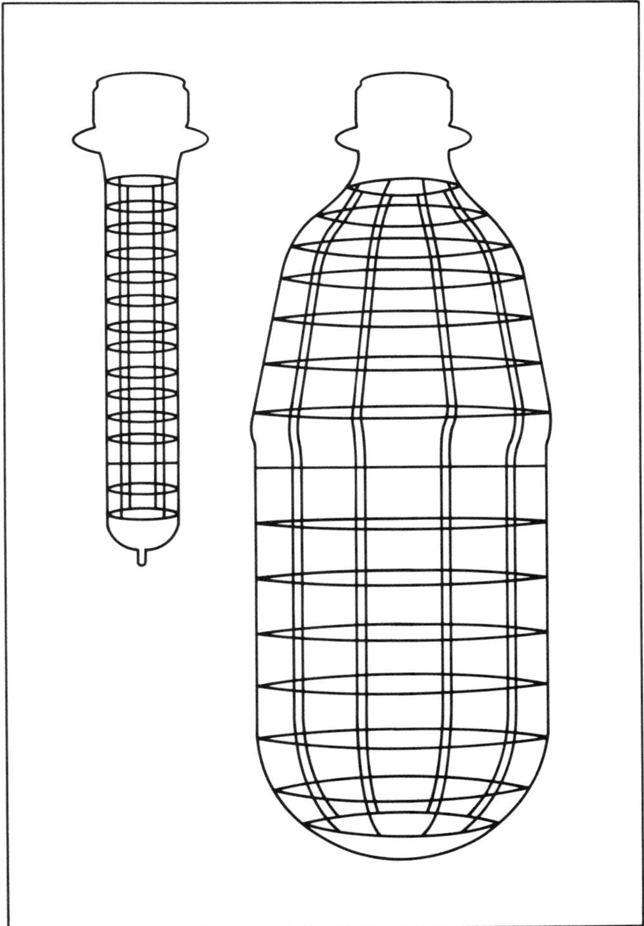

**Fig. 18-44 Polyethylene terephthalate (PET) bottle blow molding begins with a preform. Crosshatching shows biaxial stretching for uniform wall thickness.** (*Plastics Machinery Division, Cincinnati Milacron, Inc.*)

## LIQUID INJECTION MOLDING

In comparison to other processes, the new liquid injection molding (LIM) method has the potential necessary to replace compression and transfer molding of thermoset plastics in some applications.

### The LIM Process

Instead of being charged into the cavity of a compression mold or a transfer pot as powder, pellets, or other molding compound, two LIM material components are pumped directly from the shipping containers through a mixing device and injected into a heated mold, where they cure.

Liquid injection molding differs considerably from reaction injection molding (RIM), with which it sometimes is confused. The pumping systems used in LIM are generally lower pressure systems than those used for RIM, and mixing in LIM is accomplished more often mechanically than by impingement. Also, while RIM parts usually are large, LIM parts typically are quite small.

### LIM Applications

Most of the early LIM development activity and production applications involve the use of silicone elastomers. Although LIM experimental work is underway with epoxies, polyesters, and urethanes, most applications relate to the use of liquid silicones as replacements for gum-silicone rubbers and organic rubbers.

Liquid injection molding applications are found in the automotive, aerospace, furniture, and pharmaceutical industries. Products include such diverse items as ignition system parts, weather seals, diaphragms, connectors, valves, grommets, O-rings, and other types of seals.

## ROTATIONAL MOLDING

Rotational molding is a process for forming hollow plastics parts. The process utilizes the principle that finely divided plastics material becomes molten in contact with a hot metal

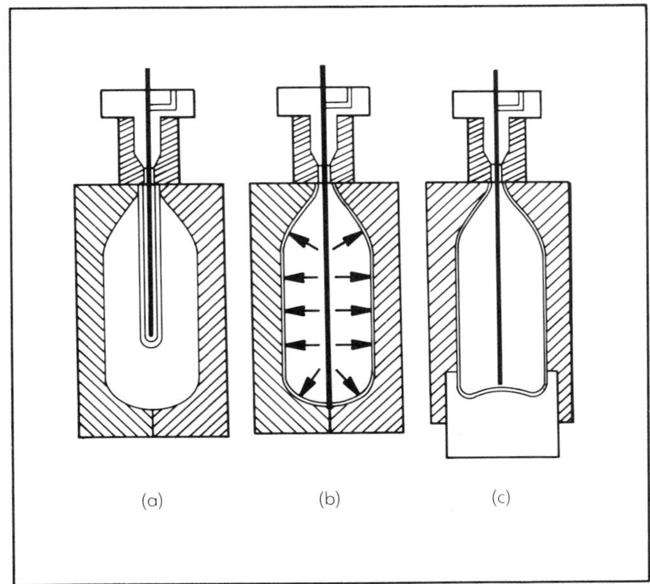


**Fig. 18-45 Schematic drawing of process for two-stage injection, stretch-blow operations.**

surface, and then takes the shape of that surface. When the polymer is cooled while in contact with the metal, a reproduction of the mold's interior surface is produced.

### The Process

Rotational molding employs the simultaneous rotation of thin-walled molds about two axes, primary and secondary, which are perpendicular to each other. After being charged with plastics material, the molds are heated externally while rotating. This causes the particles to melt on the inner surface of the mold as they tumble. Successive layers are deposited until all of the material is uniformly distributed and fused. The molds are cooled by air or external water spray while still rotating. They are then opened for removal of the finished article and recharged.

The process is employed for the production of hollow objects from thermoplastic materials. The main benefit of the rotational molding process is its versatility and applicability to the production of parts ranging from small, intricate products, to larger items such as automobile fuel tanks, to very large (5000 gal; 19 000 L) liquid storage tanks. Figure 18-46 illustrates a setup for the rotational molding of very large tanks.

Rotational molding differs from other molding processes in that, while the others require both heat and pressure to plasticize the resin, rotational molding requires only that the mold is heated. Because of its long time/temperature cycle, this process cannot be used with all polymers. A material with good oxidative stability and high melt flow characteristics is required.

### Operations

Rotational speeds of the two mold axes usually are controlled by separate motors; typically, a ratio of 3:1 is specified for speeds of the primary and secondary axes. Rotational speed of the primary axis generally is under 18 rpm and mold temperatures range from 500-800° F (260-426° C), depending on the materials used and the end products that are to be made.

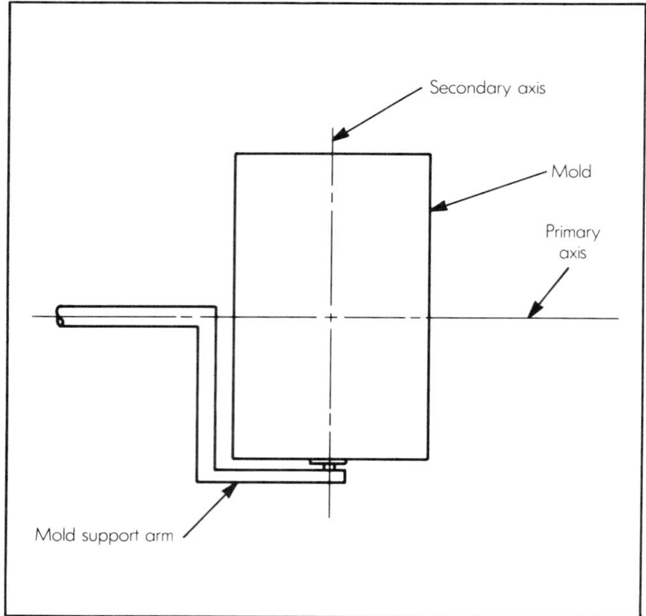


**Fig. 18-46 Typical offset support arm for rotationally molding a large (5000 gal; 19 000 L) tank.** (*D. Ramazzotti*)

## STRUCTURAL FOAM MOLDING

A structural foam is a plastics product with a rigid cellular core and an integral skin. The solid skin is typically 0.030-0.080" (0.76-2.03 mm) thick. Density reductions compared with solid plastics are in the range of 20-40%, depending upon part configuration, thickness, and molding conditions. Structural foams can be molded and extruded. Since the bending stiffness of parts increases proportionately to the cube of the part's thickness, structural foam parts can be made quite rigid, with good strength-to-weight ratios.

All thermoplastics can be foam-molded. Typical materials are polystyrene, polyethylene, polypropylene, polycarbonate, acrylonitrile butadiene styrene (ABS), and vinyl. The plastics used in this process range from preblended resins and foaming agents, to materials that are dry blended with the foaming agent in a machine-mounted hopper blender. The foaming agents usually are combined with inorganic solids which when decomposed by the heat in the plasticizing cylinder, generate carbon monoxide or nitrogen gases.

In the foam-molding process, the solid skin is formed when the injected foaming mass is chilled by cool mold surfaces. This skin creates an insulating barrier that still permits the central mass to complete its expansion to form the foamed core. Because of the heat insulating properties of the foam-molded products, the molding cycle times are slower than the cycle times normally attained in injection molding operations.

The basic processes fall into two categories: high pressure and low pressure. Both processes are performed with reciprocating screw, injection molding machines. In a typical operation, an inert gas (nitrogen) is introduced into the resin melt under pressure. The resin-gas mixture is subsequently expanded into a mold at low pressure. The gas then expands, causing the mixture to foam and fill the mold. When contact is made with the cool mold surface, the gas bubbles collapse and form the solid skin.

The inherently low molding pressures associated with polymer melt expansion make the structural foam process advantageous for large, complex parts. Table 18-20 provides a summation of the various processing methods with respect to their capabilities for producing large, complex parts. For structural foam, mold pressures are approximately 1000 psi (6.9 MPa), compared to typical pressures 10 times higher for injection molding. Currently, structural foam parts are molded into consoles, overhead innerliners and doors in agricultural and construction machinery, business machine housings, and motor vehicle body components.

## CASTING

Casting processes are applicable to some thermoplastics and thermosets. These materials can be cast at atmospheric pressure in inexpensive molds to form large parts with section thicknesses that would be impracticable for other manufacturing processes. Casting resins are molded on a production basis in lead, plaster, rubber, and glass molds.

In a typical operation, the liquid resin is poured into the mold and the product is cured in an oven by applying heat, or it is cured exothermically with a catalyst. Shrinkage during curing facilitates removal of the product from the mold. Finishing operations include the removal of flash and, in cold molds, removal of the gate. In some instances, the parts are buffed or tumble polished to improve the appearance.

Plastics products made by the casting process include sheets,

**TABLE 18-20**
**Structural Foam vs. Other Processes for Large, Complex Parts**

| Process | Design Flexibility | Structural Integrity | Secondary Operations | Relative Tooling Cost | Assembly Flexibility |
|---|---|---|---|---|---|
| Structural foam molding | Due to low pressures, significant design flexibility possible (parts consolidation, etc.).<br>High rigidity allows for high load-bearing structural members.<br>No sink marks with integral function. | Good structural integrity.<br>Low, molded-in stress provides low warp, dimensionally stable parts. | Sprue removal.<br>Painting required for appearance surfaces. | Lower tooling cost; aluminum tools possible. | Vibration welding, ultrasonic bonding, self-tapping screws, ultrasonic inserts, adhesive bonding possible.<br>Many parts can be integrally molded. |
| Injection molding | Some flexibility possible, but due to high pressures, large complex parts not cost effective.<br>Ribs required for high load-bearing parts.<br>Sink marks in thick sections. | Good structural integrity. | Sprue removal.<br>Class A finish. | Higher pressures require expensive steel tools: high-strength, pre-hardened. | In thermoplastics, vibration welding, ultrasonic bonding, self-tapping screws, ultrasonic inserts, and adhesive bonding possible.<br>Parts can be consolidated. |
| Sheet molding | Fiber orientation and resin-rich areas may occur in complex, load-bearing areas.<br>Lower fatigue strength limits complex, dynamic parts.<br>Limited deep draws on complex/large surfaces. | Possible nonuniform physical properties.<br>Lower impact strength. | Deflashing<br>Large or small openings must be trimmed or cut out. | Steel tools required. | Thermoset materials require molded-in inserts. |
| Sheet metal | Only simple shapes and contours possible.<br>Requires multiple dies for part complexity.<br>Inferior dimensional control. | Minimal integral component strength due to multiple component assembly. | Multiple assembly operations: drilling, tapping, welding. | Low-cost tooling.<br>Complex, deep-draw dies, etc.<br>High piece-part cost. | Screws, nuts, bolts, rivets, welding.<br>Parts consolidation nearly impossible. |
| Die casting | Limited complex-part capability.<br>Large parts are heavier. | Good structural integrity.<br>Lower impact strength. | Trim dies required.<br>Machining of critical surfaces. | High tooling cost.<br>Tool maintenance required due to potential wear damage. | Hardware assembly. |
| Reaction injection molding | Good design flexibility due to low pressures, but large complex structural parts not feasible due to lower material properties.<br>Thicker sections required.<br>Batch process. | Lower properties can prohibit complex, high-stressed features.<br>Lower impact and creep resistance. | Flashing must be trimmed. | Low tooling cost. | Thermoset process such that thermal fastening techniques not possible. |

(*General Electric Co.*)

rods, tubes, and profile shapes. Embedments and encapsulations are also accomplished by casting. Other important uses of casting resins are for tooling such as draw, bending, and drop-hammer dies (refer to Chapter 2, "Die and Mold Materials"), as well as for many types of fixtures.

### Casting of Thermoplastics

Acrylics and nylons are available in cast form. Acrylic sheets, rods, and tubing are produced by casting. Very large nylon parts, unsuitable for molding by other methods, can be cast. Plastics parts often are cast when the number of parts needed is not sufficient to justify the cost of dies.

The thermoplastics are polymerized and cast simultaneously. A mixture of monomer, catalyst, and other necessary additives is heated and poured into a mold at atmospheric pressure. A polymerization reaction occurs, and the material, either acrylic or nylon, is formed.

This process is capable of producing large parts of contoured form, free from voids, and several inches (100 mm) thick. Nylon parts weighing from 1 to 1500 lb (1/2 to 700 kg) have been cast. Minimum recommended section thickness is 1/4" (6.4 mm), although thinner sections can be achieved. Normal casting tolerances are ±1%. Critical tolerance dimensions are controlled by subsequent machining. Typical applications include bearings, wheels, large gears, and elevator buckets for foundry sand.

### Casting of Thermosets

Thermosetting materials used for casting include the phenolics, epoxies, polyesters, and the polyurethanes. These resins have a wider use in casting than the thermoplastics, because they have a greater fluidity for pouring. Epoxies and polyesters are commonly cast. A mixture of a monomer, a catalyst, and additives is poured into a mold. Open molds are used for parts that can be withdrawn from the mold cavity. Flexible molds permit the casting of undercut parts. Both filled and clear casting resins are used in a variety of items ranging from bowling balls to flower pots. Extensive use is made of cast epoxy tooling in the manufacturing of metal parts by stamping, bending, etc. (See Chapter 2, "Die and Mold Materials.")

Polyurethane castings are made from either one-shot or prepolymer systems. The prepolymer or isocyanate is mixed with a diamine, polyol, or polyester curing agent. The mixture is degassed and poured into a prepared, heated mold. Curing takes place at atmospheric pressure.

### Centrifugal Casting

The centrifugal casting process is generally used for making large round forms. The process involves rotating a heated tube that is uniformly charged with powdered plastics along its length, thereby creating a molded tube of the desired wall thickness.

Various methods are used to melt the resin and to coat the inner wall of the tube. When the melting is completed, the heat source is deactivated while the tube mold continues to rotate, thus maintaining uniform wall thickness of the tube during cooling. Upon completion of the cooling cycle, the tube, which has shrunk away from the mold, is removed.

An advantage of the centrifugal casting technique for resin powder molding is the capability to quickly produce prototypes at minimum mold and product cost. Molds are relatively inexpensive cavity forms. Commonly used mold materials are sheet steel; spun, machined, or cast aluminum; and electroformed copper and nickel. In many cases, the production economics are attractive, even when relatively high-volume production is required and especially when the items produced are large and heavy. Product length and diameter are limited mainly by machine size. Current production items range from 6-30" (152-762 mm) diam and up to 96" (2438 mm) in length.

## FORGING

The forging process sometimes is used in manufacturing thermoplastic parts that would be difficult to produce by other processes. The forging technique is capable of producing thick parts with abrupt changes in sections. An example of the application of forging is its use to produce thick, large-diameter gears from polypropylene.

Although identified by the term *forging*, this process is misnamed since it is not truly a forging process, but rather a reforming operation. In this process, a preheated blank or billet of the required shape and volume is placed between a pair of forging dies, which are then closed to deform the work blank and fill the die cavity. The dies remain closed for 16-60 seconds to minimize elastic recovery of the part when it is released from the dies.

Typical forging equipment is a hydraulic press or a mechanical toggle press. Forming pressures range from 1-10 ksi (6.9-69 MPa). Dies are generally made of a machinable prehardened steel, similar to the steel used for injection molds. The most commonly used plastics in the forging process are those that are difficult to process by the usual injection methods. The blank used for forging is made by cutting it from an extruded bar, or by compression molding.

## FILM AND SHEET FORMING

The basic methods for producing film or thin sheets are calendering, extrusion, blowing, and casting. The method chosen for a particular application is determined mainly by the type of thermoplastic that is to be processed.

### Calendering

Calendering, illustrated in Fig. 18-47, is the formation of a thin sheet by squeezing a thermoplastic material between rolls. In principle, it is a continuous "extrusion" process in which a pair of mating rolls establishes the thickness and surface characteristics of the sheet that is formed.[7]

The material, composed of resin, plasticizer, filler, and color pigments, is compounded and heated before being fed into the

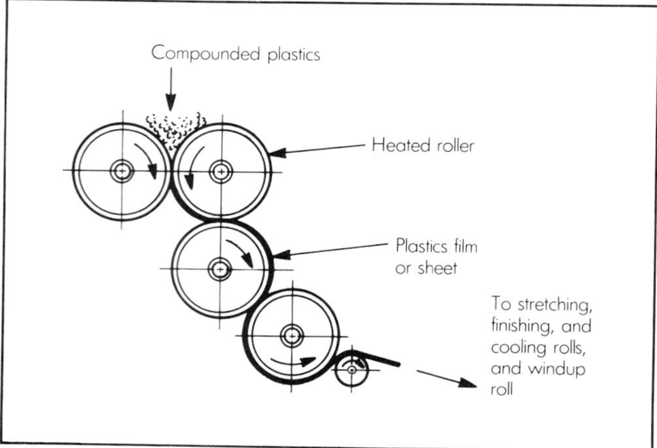


**Fig. 18-47 Diagram of film forming by the calendering process.**

calender. The thickness of the sheet produced depends upon the roll spacing and the speed of the finishing rollers that stretch the plastics material. Before the sheet (film) is wound, it passes through water-cooled rolls. Vinyl, polyethylene, cellulose acetate films and sheeting, and vinyl floor tile are products of calendering.

### Extrusion

In making sheets of polypropylene, polyethylene, polystyrene, or ABS, an extrusion process is used. This process is illustrated schematically in Fig. 18-48. After the material has been compounded, it is placed in the feed hopper. The material is heated to 320-425° F (160-240° C) and forced into the die area at pressures of 2-4 ksi (14-28 MPa) by the screw conveyor. The thickness of the sheet is controlled by a combination of the choker bar and the die opening. After extrusion, the sheet passes through oil or water-cooled, chromium-plated rolls before being cut to size. Plastics sheet and film materials produced by extrusion can range in thickness from 0.001-0.126″ (0.03-3.2 mm). [Material with a thickness less than 0.01″ (0.3 mm) is called film.]

### Blown Tubular Extrusion

The blown tubular extrusion process produces film by first extruding a tube vertically through a ring die and then blowing it with air into a large-diameter cylinder. The blown cylinder is air cooled as it rises, and then it is flattened by driven rolls before reaching the winder. This technique is used to produce thin film such as that used in trash bags and packaging materials.

### Film and Cell Casting

In film casting, the plastics resins are dissolved in a solvent and spread on a polished continuous belt or large drum and conveyed through an oven in which they are cured and the solvent is removed. In cell casting, a cell is made up of two sheets of polished glass, separated according to the film thickness that is desired. Gaskets retain the liquid catalyzed monomer. The cell is heated to the desired temperature in an oven in which it is held until curing is completed. Cell casting is used for the production of acrylic transparent sheets.

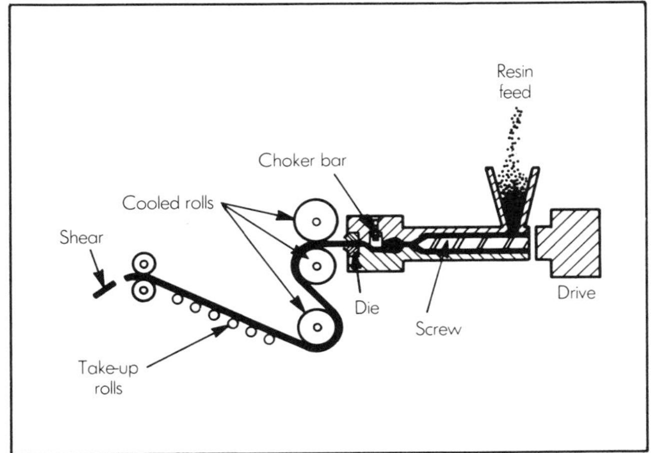


**Fig. 18-48 Process for extruding thin plastic sheets and film.**

# MACHINING AND FINISHING

For low-volume production or prototypes, most plastics can be machined with standard woodworking and metalworking equipment and cutting tools; however, different tool angles are necessary when high-volume production of parts is required. When more than a few pieces are to be machined, the need for cooling should be given careful consideration.

Although most plastics can be machined dry, some require a coolant, particularly when machined at high speeds and feeds. The machining process results in the generation of frictional heat. Virtually all the heat generated by the cutting friction of the plastics and the metal cutting tool is absorbed by the cutting tool. Therefore, very little heat is transferred to the core of the material. This heat must be kept to a minimum or must be removed by a coolant for optimum results. Cooling by air jets, vapor mists, or a solution of between 10-20% soluble oil and water may be necessary.

If the heat produced during machining is allowed to build up, the surface of the plastics expands. Friction increases, causing poor tolerance control, and the finish may be marred by oxidation and discoloring. For these reasons, adequate cutting tool clearances are essential. A summary of machining variables for various thermoplastics is given in Table 18-21.

## GUIDELINES FOR MACHINING

Adhering to the following guidelines will facilitate the plastics machining process:

1. Machining and finishing of plastics parts should be avoided or minimized wherever possible through careful design of the part and the mold. Proper positioning of gates and flash lines helps to simplify finishing.
2. In many applications, the part can be redesigned to eliminate or minimize the need for machining. In all (or most) cases of design, this is a desirable objective.
3. Tools must be sharp, with proper chipbreakers or relief, to allow the efficient removal of chips.
4. Water-soluble oil and water, vapor mists or an air jet can be used to aid the machining process. Vacuums can be utilized to collect the chips at or near the point of machining.
5. Cutting tools should be ground with no rake or 2-3° negative rake to allow a scraping action, rather than a cutting action.
6. Plastics are relatively resilient when compared to metals. Stock material should be properly supported to minimize distortion.
7. Elastic recovery occurs in thermoplastics both during and after machining, so provisions must be made in tool geometry for sufficient clearance to provide relief.

## TURNING

As stated previously, machining of plastics is generally done dry. However, some thermosetting plastics, such as phenolics and ureas, contain abrasive fillers that require frequent tool sharpening. This can be lessened when an air-jet or water-based

**TABLE 18-21**
**Machining Variables for Thermoplastics**

| Plastics | | Sawing (Circular) | Sawing (Band) | Lathe (Turn) | Lathe (Cutoff) | Drilling | Milling | Reaming |
|---|---|---|---|---|---|---|---|---|
| Acetal | Speed (sfm) (m/min) | 4000-6000 (1219-1829) | 600-2000 (183-610) | 450-600 (137-183) | 600 (183) | 300-600 (91-183) | 1000-3000 (305-914) | 350-450 (107-137) |
| | Feed, ipr (mm/rev) | Fast, smooth | Fast, smooth | 0.0045-0.010 (0.11-0.25) | 0.003-0.004 (0.08-0.10) | 0.004-0.010 (0.10-0.25) | 0.004-0.016 (0.10-0.41) | 0.0055-0.015 (0.14-0.38) |
| | Tool | HSS, carbide | HSS | HSS, carbide | HSS, carbide | HSS, carbide | HSS, carbide | HSS, carbide |
| | Clearance (deg) | 20-30 | --- | 10-25 | 10-25 | 10-25 | 10-20 | --- |
| | Rake (deg) | 15 (positive) | 0-15 (positive) | 0-15 (positive) | 0-15 (positive) | 0-10 (positive) | 0-10 (positive) | 0-10 (positive) |
| | Set | Slight | Slight | --- | --- | --- | --- | --- |
| | Point Angle (deg) | --- | --- | --- | --- | 118 | --- | --- |
| | Cooling | Dry, air jet, vapor | Dry, air jet | Dry, air jet, vapor | Dry, air jet, vapor | Dry, air jet, vapor | Dry, air jet, vapor | Dry, air jet, vapor |
| Acrylic | Speed (sfm) (m/min) | 8000-12,000 (2438-3658) | 8000-12,000 (2438-3658) | 300-600 (91-183) | 450-500 (137-152) | 200-400 (61-122) | 300-600 (91-183) | 250-400 (76-122) |
| | Feed, ipr (mm/rev) | Fast, smooth | Fast, smooth | 0.003-0.008 (0.08-0.20) | 0.003-0.004 (0.08-0.10) | Slow, steady | 0.003-0.010 (0.08-0.25) | 0.006-0.012 (0.15-0.30) |
| | Tool | HSS, carbide | HSS | HSS, carbide | HSS, carbide | HSS, carbide | HSS, carbide | HSS, carbide |
| | Clearance (deg) | 10-20 | --- | 10-20 | 10-20 | 12-15 | 15 | --- |
| | Rake (deg) | 0-10 (positive) | 0-10 (positive) | 0-10 (negative) | 0-15 (negative) | 0-10 (positive) | 0-10 (negative) | 0-10 (negative) |
| | Set | Slight | Slight | --- | --- | --- | --- | --- |
| | Point Angle (deg) | --- | --- | --- | --- | 90-118 | --- | --- |
| | Cooling | Dry, air jet, vapor | Dry, air jet, vapor | Dry, air jet, vapor | Dry, air jet, water solution | Dry, air jet, vapor | Dry, air jet, vapor | Dry, air jet, vapor |
| Fluorocarbon | Speed (sfm) (m/min) | 8000-12,000 (2438-3658) | 5000-7000 (1524-2134) | 375-500 (114-152) | 425-475 (130-145) | 200-500 (61-152) | 1000-3000 (305-914) | 300-600 (91-183) |
| | Feed, ipr (mm/rev) | Fast, smooth | Fast, smooth | 0.004-0.008 (0.10-0.20) | 0.003-0.004 (0.08-0.10) | 0.002-0.010 (0.05-0.25) | 0.004-0.016 (0.10-0.41) | 0.006-0.015 (0.15-0.38) |
| | Tool | HSS, carbide | HSS | HSS, carbide | HSS, carbide | HSS, carbide | HSS, carbide | HSS, carbide |
| | Clearance (deg) | 20-30 | --- | 15-30 | 10-25 | 20 | 7-15 | 10-20 |
| | Rake (deg) | 0-5 (positive) | 0-10 (positive) | 3-20 (positive) | 3-15 (positive) | 0-10 (negative) | 3-15 (positive) | 0-10 (negative) |
| | Set | Heavy | Heavy | --- | --- | --- | --- | --- |
| | Point Angle (deg) | --- | --- | --- | --- | 90-118 | --- | --- |
| | Cooling | Dry, air jet, vapor | Dry, air jet | Dry, air jet, vapor | Dry, air jet, vapor | Dry, air jet, vapor | Dry, air jet, vapor | Dry, air jet, vapor |

**TABLE 18-21—*Continued***

| Plastics | | Sawing (Circular) | Sawing (Band) | Lathe (Turn) | Lathe (Cutoff) | Drilling | Milling | Reaming |
|---|---|---|---|---|---|---|---|---|
| Nylon | Speed (sfm) (m/min) | 4000-6000 (1219-1829) | 4000-6000 (1219-1829) | 500-700 (152-213) | 700 (213) | 180-450 (55-137) | 1000-3000 (305-914) | 300-450 (91-137) |
| | Feed, ipr (mm/rev) | Fast, smooth | Fast, smooth | 0.002-0.016 (0.05-0.41) | 0.002-0.016 (0.05-0.41) | 0.003-0.012 (0.08-0.30) | 0.004-0.016 (0.10-0.41) | 0.005-0.015 (0.13-0.38) |
| | Tool | HSS, carbide | HSS | HSS, carbide | HSS, carbide | HSS, carbide | HSS, carbide | HSS, carbide |
| | Clearance (deg) | 20-30 | --- | 5-10 | 7-15 | 10-15 | 7-15 | --- |
| | Rake (deg) | 15 (positive) | 0-15 (positive) | 0-5 (positive) | 0-5 (positive) | 0-10 (positive) | 0-5 (positive) | 0-10 (positive) |
| | Set | Slight | Slight | --- | --- | --- | --- | --- |
| | Point Angle (deg) | --- | --- | --- | --- | 118 | --- | --- |
| | Cooling | Dry, air jet, vapor | Dry, air jet | Dry, air jet, vapor | Dry, air jet, vapor | Dry, air jet, vapor | Dry, air jet, vapor | Dry, air jet, vapor |
| Polycarbonate | Speed (sfm) (m/min) | 6000-8000 (1829-2438) | 800-3000 (244-914) | 500-1000 (152-305) | 500-1000 (152-305) | 300-800 (91-244) | 1000-3000 (305-914) | 400-500 (122-152) |
| | Feed, ipr (mm/rev) | Fast, smooth | Fast, smooth | 0.005-0.025 (0.13-0.64) | 0.004-0.010 (0.10-0.25) | 0.001-0.0015 (0.03-0.04) | 0.006-0.020 (0.15-0.51) | 0.004-0.012 (0.10-0.30) |
| | Tool | HSS, carbide | HSS | HSS, carbide | HSS, carbide | HSS, carbide | HSS, carbide | HSS, carbide |
| | Clearance (deg) | 20-30 | --- | 3 | 5-10 | 15 | 5-15 | --- |
| | Rake (deg) | 15 (positive) | 5-15 (positive) | 0-10 (negative) | 0-15 (positive) | 0-5 (negative) | 0-5 (negative) | 0-15 (positive) |
| | Set | Slight | Slight | --- | --- | --- | --- | --- |
| | Point Angle (deg) | --- | --- | --- | --- | 118 | --- | --- |
| | Cooling | Dry, air jet | Dry, air jet | Dry, air jet, vapor | Dry, air jet vapor | Dry, air jet | Dry, air jet, vapor | Dry, air jet, vapor |
| Polyolefin (UHMW) | Speed, (sfm) (m/min) | 1650-5000 (503-1524) | 3900-5000 (1189-1524) | 300-450 (91-137) | 425-475 (130-145) | 200-600 (61-183) | 1000-3000 (305-914) | 280-600 (85-183) |
| | Feed, ipr (mm/rev) | Fast, smooth | Fast, smooth | 0.0015-0.004 (0.04-0.10) | 0.003-0.004 (0.08-0.10) | 0.004-0.020 (0.10-0.51) | 0.006-0.020 (0.15-0.51) | 0.006-0.012 (0.15-0.30) |
| | Tool | HSS, carbide | HSS, carbide | HSS, carbide | HSS, carbide | HSS, carbide | HSS, carbide | HSS, carbide |
| | Clearance, (deg) | 15 | --- | 15-25 | 15-25 | 10-20 | 10-20 | 10-20 |
| | Rake (deg) | 0-8 (positive) | 0-10 (positive) | 0-15 (positive) | 3-15 (positive) | 0-5 (negative) | 0-10 (positive) | 0-10 (negative) |
| | Set | Heavy | Heavy | --- | --- | --- | --- | --- |
| | Point Angle (deg) | --- | --- | --- | --- | 90-118 | --- | --- |
| | Cooling | Dry, air jet, vapor | Dry, air jet, vapor | Dry, air jet, vapor | Dry, air jet, vapor | Dry, air jet, vapor | Dry, air jet, vapor | Dry, air jet, vapor |

(*Cadillac Plastic and Chemical Co.*)

Note: This information is intended as a guideline and is not to be construed as absolute. Because of the variety of work and diversity of finishes required, it may be necessary to depart from the suggestions in the table. A good practice to follow is to run a test workpiece before starting a production run.

# MACHINING AND FINISHING

coolant is used. In machining some plastics, friction heats the surface of the plastic and causes it to become "gummy." As a result, the tools build up a film of burned resin. In the case of high-speed drills, this causes sticking and possible cracking, and consequently causes inaccurate work.

### Tool Materials

Tool cutting angles should be lessened to avoid "gummy" buildup of resin, and a coolant should be used to reduce friction at the cutting edge. Cast cobalt-based, carbide-tipped, and carbide-insert metalcutting tools are excellent for machining all types of plastics and are economical for long production runs. Standard, high-speed-steel toolbits are acceptable for use in low-volume production and for making laboratory samples.

### Turning Speeds

Most thermoplastics may be turned with surface speeds to 600 sfm (183 m/min) with feeds of 0.002-0.005" (0.05-0.13 mm). The speed and feed must be determined largely by the type of plastics, the finish desired, and the kind of tool used.

Turning of acrylic plastics is done with tools having 0° rake and about 12° clearance, set at an angle of 60° to the spindle. Cuts should be made at a surface speed of about 65 sfm (20 m/min) and a feed of 0.010 ipr (0.25 mm/rev). A smooth surface is obtained with a 0.020" (0.51 mm) depth of cut. The top surface of the tool should be lapped to a bright finish.

Cutoff tools should also be ground with increased front and side clearances. The surface speed should be reduced to approximately one-half that used while turning. Slower speeds tend to roughen the cut surfaces, whereas faster speeds may cause overheating of the material.

**Screw machines.** For screw-machine operations on laminated tubes such as phenolic, it is better to specify a smaller inside diameter than is required for finished size, or to use a laminated rod and drill it to size. Cutting feeds recommended are 0.007-0.015 ipr (0.18-0.38 mm/rev) for cutoff and 0.002-0.003 ipr (0.05-0.08 mm/rev) for forming.

The following spindle speeds are recommended for hand screw machines: 1" (25 mm) diam and larger, 800-1000 rpm; 1 to 1/2" (13 mm) diam, 1500-2000 rpm; 7/16 to 5/8" (11 to 16 mm) diam, 3600 rpm; 1/8" (3 mm) and under, 5000 rpm. In many cases, due to the intended application of the fabricated plastics part, it is not permissible to use cutting lubricants. Tungsten-carbide-tipped or carbide insert tools increase production and tool life.

**Phenolics and ureas.** The machining of molded phenolics and ureas destroys their lustrous surface; hence, they should not be machined unless the desired shape cannot be molded. Molded and cast phenolics are machined with feeds, speeds, and tools similar to those needed for machining brass (refer to Volume I, *Machining,* of this Handbook series). The tools should have 10-20° clearance with slightly negative or zero rake and should be set 1-2° above center.

## FILING

While one of the primary considerations in the production of plastics is limited postprocessing, it is often necessary to remove flash and gates from the body of some parts. Some manufacturers have production employees who use scrapers on parts after removing them from machines. The scrapers are often a piece of brass shaped to allow efficient material removal.

Many parts removed from molds and other processing methods are warm, and this property allows easier removal of flash. For soft thermoplastics, a coarse, single-cut, shear-tooth file having teeth set at a 45° angle should be used. The combination of coarse teeth and long angle promotes self-cleaning. Milled tooth files are recommended for filing edges of sheet stock.

The shape and type of file used on thermosetting materials depends on the filler and resin in the plastics and the shape of the part surface to be filed.

When fillers are added to the plastics, they cause difficulties in machining and filing in the following order: (1) wood flour (least), (2) fabric, (3) cotton, (4) mineral, and (5) glass (most). Mill files are used to remove the flash from the surfaces of molded articles, to bevel corners, and to remove burrs after sawing. Swiss-pattern files of various shapes and tooth coarseness are used on small, intricate moldings in which the surfaces to be filed are difficult to reach. Rat-tail and half-round files are used for cleaning out holes and rounded slots.

Mill, swiss-pattern, rat-tail, and half-round files can be used depending on the material to be filed and shaped and the amount of material that is to be removed.

## ROUTING AND SHAPING

Shapers are used for a variety of operations, such as machining of rabbetted edges to permit flush mounting, machining to predetermined cross sections, and cutting of both flat and formed parts to size.

Routers should have a no-load spindle speed of 10,000-20,000 rpm. Two or three-flute cutters under 1 1/2" (38 mm) diam running at these speeds produces the smoothest cut. At slower spindle speeds, the cutter should have more flutes or blades and should be larger in diameter to produce the necessary peripheral speed. Cutters should be kept sharp and should have a back clearance angle of 10° and a 0° rake angle.

It is advisable to grind a slight radius on the corner of the cutter so that it produces a fillet in the shoulder of a rabbet. Unless this precaution is taken, the piece may fail at this sharp corner. Work should be fed to the cutter slowly and continuously to reduce cracking and to avoid overheating. It is advisable to use either an airblast or suction system to remove chips and to help cool the cutter.

Because of thickness variations in cast acrylic sheet, it is not possible to maintain close tolerances in both toe and depth of rout. Relatively small tolerances can be maintained in either the toe or the depth; but when the tolerances of both are critical, a second routing operation is required, with a corresponding increase in fabricating costs.

Tolerances of ±0.015" (0.38 mm) can be maintained in the depth or toe of the rout in a single operation. Tolerances of ±0.030" (0.76 mm) or better can be held in the length of shoulder of the rout. Standard, high-speed end mills may also be used for rabbetting acrylic sheet.

Portable routers can be used whenever the acrylic part is too large or awkward to bring to the machine. They are useful for obtaining a normal or right-angle cut when trimming the edge of a formed piece. When a number of flat panels are to be trimmed, with other than straight edges, it is sometimes advisable to use routers or shapers.

## GEAR CUTTING

When cutting laminated gear blanks, the feed should be the maximum that is possible without showing marks on the teeth. A coarse feed tends to reduce wear on the cutter edges. In hobbing, it is not necessary to make roughing and finishing cuts; a single cut to the required depth is sufficient. Hobs of 3-4" (76-102 mm) pitch diam may be run at 140-210 rpm with feeds of 0.040-0.080 ipr (1.02-2.03 mm/rev).

On shapers, gears are cut at 100-130 spm with fairly fine feed, unless both roughing and finishing cuts are taken. In the latter case, 0.010" (0.25 mm) of stock for finishing may be removed at any desired feed or speed. In all gear cutting operations, the laminated stock should be backed with wood or cast iron where the cutter breaks through the surface, to avoid fraying or rough edges.

## SAWING

For short runs or prototype preparation, all types of saws have been adapted to cutting plastics. Hand saws, hacksaws, saber saws, backsaws, and even jewelers' saws have been used. The shape of the individual tooth is important in the cutting operation.

Circular saws and bandsaws are the most common tools used for sawing operations. While table saws used in woodworking successfully cut plastics up to 1" (25 mm) thick with speeds at 10,000-12,000 fpm (3050-3660 m/min), carbide-tipped blades are recommended for production jobs. The carbide-tipped blades should be hollow ground, with zero rake (or slightly negative) and 12-15 teeth/in. (0.5-0.6 teeth/mm) depending on the thickness of the material.

### Bandsawing

Bandsaws provide an important advantage over circular saws. The blade is longer, which allows each tooth to cool as well as chips to be cleared during the sawing operation. Although bandsaws run cooler than tablesaws they are not as accurate for straight cutting and the cuts produced are not as smooth. Bandsaw manufacturers recommend saw teeth with 60° angle and set about one-half the thickness of the blade on each side, so that the bandsaws give a width of cut double their thickness.

Narrower saw blades and more set are needed for cutting curves than are required for straight cuts. Bandsaws just soft enough to be filed are recommended; they must be kept sharp. Dull blades cause chipping and may result in saw breakage. Sawing is usually done dry, but water or mist cooling may be used in production runs. Saw teeth should be set from 8-18 teeth/in. (0.3-0.7 teeth/mm), and the saw should run at 1800-2500 rpm.

### Circular Sawing

Sawing of polystyrene or cellulose acetate can be done with circular saws having 9-12 teeth/in. (0.4-0.5 teeth/mm) for thin sheets and 6 teeth/in. (0.2 teeth/mm) for thicknesses over 1/4" (6 mm). Saws of 6-9" (152-229 mm) diam are run at speeds of 3000-3600 rpm. Saw blades should be hollow ground and are usually 1/32 to 1/16" (0.8 to 1.6 mm) thick. A water spray or mist facilitates a cleaner cut. A stream of water running in the kerf while cutting produces very satisfactory results. This is applicable to both circular saws and bandsaws; otherwise, the thermoplastic materials will fuse. Recommended circular saws are 14" (356 mm) diam, 12 gage (0.11"; 2.8 mm) and 9 gage (0.16"; 3.9 mm) thick, with 130 teeth and 10° rake, and operated at 3000 rpm. These blades are made of a special alloy steel stock.

Table 18-22 lists the number of teeth and other saw specifications for cutting different thicknesses of plastics materials. Chipping is caused by dull saws or by setting the saw too high or too low in reference to the table. When cutting is done without a coolant, an exhaust system should be used to remove the dust. Smoother cuts are sometimes obtained by heating the material.

**TABLE 18-22**
**Circular-Saw Blades for Cutting Plastics**

| Thickness to be Cut, in. (mm) | Saw-Blade Thickness, in. (mm) | Teeth per in. | Blade Type |
|---|---|---|---|
| 0.04-0.08 (1.0-2.0) | 0.06-0.09 (1.5-2.3) | 8 to 14 | Hollow ground |
| 0.10-0.15 (2.5-3.8) | 0.09-0.25 (2.3-6.4) | 6 to 8 | Hollow ground |
| 0.19-0.38 (4.8-9.7) | 0.09-0.13 (2.3-3.3) | 5 to 6 | Spring set |
| 0.44-0.75 (11.2-19.1) | 0.13 (3.3) | 3 to 4 | Spring set or swaged |
| 1.00-4.00 (25.4-102) | 0.13-0.16 (3.3-3.9) | 3 to 3 1/2 | Spring set, swaged, and cemented carbide |

**Underwater saw.** The most satisfactory method of sawing parts molded of vinyl plastics is with an underwater saw. When unfilled resin is sawed, equipment should be fitted with hardened-steel saw blades. The rotary speed recommended is 3500-4000 rpm, and the saw blade should have 10-14 teeth/in. (0.4-0.6 teeth/mm). The teeth should have no set. An average speed of travel through the stock is approximately 3-4 ipm (102 mm/min). The finish of the sawed surface and the possibility of the stock's chipping at the leading edge are affected by the rate of travel of the saw through the stock, the sharpness of the saw, and whether the stock being sawed is a solid piece or made of several small ones clamped together.

Although filled resin compounds can also be satisfactorily sawed with an underwater saw, the effective life of the saw is materially reduced by the filler. Fine-abrasive cutoff wheels are preferable to metal saws. The abrasive wheels produce an equally good finish on the cut surface at a considerable increase in tool life. Rubber-bonded cutoff wheels are not recommended, but resin-bonded saws are satisfactory. Notching the wheel helps to promote self-cleaning.

**Hollow-ground saw.** For laminated stock, circular saw blades that are hollow-ground and have no set are generally recommended when cuts must be smooth. When rougher edges are permissible, saws with teeth set as for wood are satisfactory; the set makes it unnecessary to hollow-grind. Decreased set as diameter increases is advocated by some; others recommend radial teeth with 0° rake.

## THREADING AND TAPPING

High-speed, nitrided, chromium-plated taps are best for threading small holes. Speeds used range from 40-54 rpm. Tools have three flutes rather than the four commonly used in metalworking. A negative rake of about 5° on the front face of the land helps prevent binding of the tap in the holes when the tap is backed out. Small holes can be tapped dry. Water is a better tapping medium than lard oil or kerosene. Machine taps 0.002-0.006" (0.05-0.15 mm) oversize are recommended; these give 75% of full thread. A slight chamfer or countersink minimizes uplifting of material around the edge of the hole.

# MACHINING AND FINISHING

Holes larger than 1/4" (6 mm) diam should be molded rather than threaded or tapped, except when very thin sections are involved.

Standard machines and pipe-tapping and threading dies can be used satisfactorily on parts molded of vinyl plastics. The traverse should be single and uniformly continuous. Speed, which should be moderate to slow, is limited only by the rate of heat development. On lathe operations, the threading or chasing tool should be relieved considerably in order to reduce side friction. Any form of thread can be used, but the Unified inch (or equivalent metric) thread for machine screws is most satisfactory. In applications in which the threads are subject to wear or abuse, metal inserts are molded to the part. These inserts may be tapped or threaded before or after molding.

## DRILLING

For maximum efficiency in drilling holes up to 1/4" (6 mm) diam, it is recommended that drills especially designed for plastics be used. These drills are available in 60-90° included-angle points with polished flutes; they are wider than the standard machine drill and have a slow helix. A 60° included angle is desirable for sections up to 3/16" (5 mm) thick, and a 90° point is desirable for thicker sections. A slow helix works best for through holes; a fast helix is best on blind holes. A 15° lip clearance is provided on the tool.

Drills must be backed out and cleared frequently. This frees chips, especially during the drilling of deep blind holes. Speeds of 100-300 sfm (30-91 m/min) are ordinarily used for drilling; but for materials containing inert or abrasive fillers, a slow speed of approximately 75 sfm (23 m/min) should be used.

When cast phenolics are drilled, the drills sometimes cut 0.003" (0.08 mm) undersize. Speed should be as high as possible without burning, and the tool should be backed out often. Negative rake helps the drill to clear.

### Drill Speeds and Feeds

For cellulose acetate, polystyrene, and acrylics, slow drill speed minimizes the tendency to overheat. The use of water as a coolant can prevent the material from softening. Liquid soap can be used as a lubricant for holes over 1/8" (3 mm) diam. Drills should be backed out frequently to clear chips. Light feed rates avoid strain and limit the tendency of the material to chip or develop strain cracks after being worked. Highly polished or chromium-plated drills prevent subsequent cracking or crazing of the piece.

Parts molded from vinyl plastics can be drilled in much the same manner as other synthetic materials. Standard drills and the usual feeds are used. For holes with depths exceeding twice the drill diameter, drills with extralarge flutes should be used.

For drilling small holes in styrene or vinyl plastics, speeds of 4000-6000 rpm are recommended. When the feed is kept as high as practical, the drilling time is minimized. The shorter the drilling time, the less tendency for the bit to raise burrs around the edge of the hole.

### General Considerations

When the hole is being drilled properly and the operation is most efficient, chips emerge in a tight spiral similar to those produced in drilling mild steel. However, this type of chip is not always produced; chips are smaller if greater amounts of filler are present in the resin.

In the design of jigs for drilling, close-fitting bushings should be avoided, since they may increase the friction on the drill and may also increase the tendency of the chips to plug the drill flutes. If the operation is such that a drill bushing is essential, a floating leaf or template should be employed. When a template is used, the hole should be spotted with the template in place, using the drill size corresponding to the final hole size; then the template should be removed and the hole completed. Pilot holes should be avoided, except in special instances when the hole is to be reamed or counterbored. High-speed steel drills having polished flutes are generally recommended. The use of soapy water or plain water as a coolant also facilitates the drilling operation. Table 18-23 provides data on drill design.

## PUNCHING

Punching, blanking, shearing, and shaving are done extensively on laminated plastics. Punching grades of phenolic laminates have a letter *P* in the designation standardized by the National Electrical Manufacturers Association (NEMA). Thickness of sheet, character of filler, and temperature of the sheet are factors that determine the operations employed.

Some sheets can be punched cold, up to a certain thickness; others require heating. Usually the thickness that can be punched is greater when the sheet is hot. Heating can be done on hot plates or in ovens. The recommendations of the supplier of laminated stock, as to both temperature and length of heating, should be followed. Some materials can be heated to 380° F (193° C) without damage, and others only to 250° F (121° C). Too high a temperature may affect the finish of the sheet; heating for too long may make it brittle. Punching would be done within two minutes or less after heating.

Laminated materials yield somewhat when punched; as a result, the hole produced is slightly smaller than the punch. Allowance of about 3% of the thickness punched must be made for this in punching as well as in blanking. A very close fit between punch and die, approaching a sliding fit for cold work, is required. Stripper plates should fit the punch closely to prevent lifting at the edge of the hole as the punch is withdrawn. Progressive dies are satisfactory, but best results are secured with compound dies that place a spring load on the stripper. Blanking punches should be from 0.001-0.998" (0.03-25.3 mm) smaller than the size of blank required. Press speeds are about 200 spm.

Punched blanks often have rough edges. This can be remedied by shaving in a hollow die with a 45° cutting edge (which must be sharp) using a brass or soft-steel plunger. (Some companies prefer hardened-steel plungers for longer life.) Shaving is generally performed hot, but can be done cold on some materials up to about 1/8" (3 mm) thick.

Cellulose acetate sheets can be punched and blanked with sharp-edged tools. To obtain smooth edges, the sheet is warmed to about 125° F (52° C), not hot enough to affect its polish. As the material is compressed by the cutting action, one edge becomes concave and the other becomes convex. This is hardly noticeable on thin sheets. Acrylics are blanked similarly with sharp-edged punches, but heating to 180° F (82° C) is recommended for this type of material.

## EMBOSSING

Embossing, as a stamping or letter pressing operation, often is done in branding parts of plastics materials. Heated brass dies are used; and in some cases, the stock is also heated. Letters are often filled in with paint or enamel by wiping after embossing. However, they can be made to stand out readily by covering the area to be marked with metal leaf before embossing; the pressure causes the leaf to cling in the recesses.

**TABLE 18-23**
**Drills for Thermoplastics**

| | Ratio of hole depth to drill diameter | | |
|---|---|---|---|
| | Shallow, up to 1.5:1 | Medium (1.5:1 to 3:1) | Deep (over 3:1) |
| Chip removal | No problem | Continuous ribbon cleared by flutes without clogging. | Material removed in form of powder or minute chips. |
| Point angle | 55-60° | Depends on size of flute | 140° |
| Type of flute | Wide polished spiral | Wide polished spiral | Wide polished spiral |
| Rake angle | 0° | 0° | 0° |
| Lip or clearance angle | 15-20° | 12-15° | 12-15° |
| Coolant | None | None | Wet |
| Rate of feed | High as practical | As necessary to cut continuous chip | Slow, approx. 2 1/2 min. (Do not form powder.) |

In embossing, cast-phenolic blanks, previously heated until soft, are pressed in steel dies to form a design on one surface. This sometimes involves a fairly deep impression requiring considerable flow of material and may include punching of holes, as in buttons. Embossing of grained surfaces is often done on thermoplastic sheets.

## BUFFING

The equipment used for buffing usually consists of an electric motor with a double-end spindle. When the spindle is of sufficient length; two wheels may be mounted, one on each end. A spacer of adequate length between the two wheels is then essential. One wheel is used for the cutting operation, and the other for buffing. With this operation, two operators can work on one unit. This method is particularly suitable for smaller work. The operator is able to perform both operations within a minimum of space and with considerable savings of motion and time.

Buffing wheels for phenolic materials are usually made of soft muslin cloth, with loose stitches widely separated. This allows the wheel to adjust itself readily to the contour of the molded surface and also provides better and more uniform cutting properties.

Abrasives such as tripoli, crocus, and rouge are mixed with wax as a bond. These preparations are usually cast into convenient bars to simplify the application of the compound to the wheel surface.

The terms *cutting* and *buffing* are commonly used in the plastics industry. The cutting operation is mainly used when the mold parting line is actually on an important surface and must be removed by sanding or filing. Cutting is also used to remove scratches or when an inferior surface must be eliminated.

Light buffing is used to restore the lustrous surface to molded parts that have been handled during the various finishing operations. Finger marks and stacking marks are removed by buffing, and this generally is done without using a buffing or finishing compound.

## POLISHING

Ashing, polishing, and buffing are done on nearly all types of plastics either to improve the finish or to remove sanding marks or toolmarks left by preceding operations. Ashing is done with wet pumice; polishing is done with special compounds containing wax and sometimes a fine abrasive.

For larger pieces and some small parts requiring an extrafine surface finish, hand polishing or wheel buffing is necessary. The correct speed of lathes for phenolics and ureas, using a 10-12″ (254-305 mm) diam wheel that is 4-5″ (102-127 mm) wide, is approximately 2500 rpm. A speed of approximately 1500 rpm is used for styrenes and acetate materials. It is desirable to work with manufacturers of polishing supplies and to perform trial-and-error experimentation (depending upon the material used and the design of the part) to determine optimum speeds for different compositions and wheel constructions.

Articles molded from vinyl plastics can be buffed and polished with fabric wheels of the standard types. Only light pressure should be used on the work. If the pressure is too great, sufficient heat may be generated to soften the stock and cause sticking to the fabric wheel. For general-purpose work, a muslin wheel with a 1 1/2″ (38 mm) swing and operating at 3700 sfm (1128 m/min) may be used.

Where appreciable amounts of stock are to be removed during a polishing operation, (particularly for the removal of wheel or machining marks from unfilled compounds) it is best to use a cutting compound on a loose, cotton wheel operating at approximately 6100 sfm (1859 m/min).

If the polishing operation can be performed wet, good results can be obtained with a suspension of finely divided pumice in water and a loose muslin wheel operating at a peripheral speed of approximately 6100 sfm (1859 m/min). A constant stream of water and pumice fed to the wheel produces the best results. This operation is similar to the ashing commonly used in the polishing of all plastics and is the most effective way of obtaining a good surface luster on a production basis.

For laminated phenolics, grinding or sanding with No. 220 grit cotton buffing wheels, with tripoli or other polishing compounds, restores luster. Buffing without prior sanding can be done with tripoli to restore surfaces that have not been scratched too deeply in handling. In general, buffing wheels for plastics should have loose stitching.

# CHAPTER 18

# BIBLIOGRAPHY

Small plastics parts are often tumbled in pumice and then in polishing compounds as a substitute for, or as a supplement to, wheel ashing and polishing. Tumbling is also done extensively to remove thin fins. Generally, tumbling is performed dry; but for cutting down operations and for subsequent polishing on acrylics, tumbling in wet pumice is advocated.

### References


1. B. H. Amstead, Phillip F. Ostwald, and Myron L. Begeman, *Manufacturing Processes, SI Version*, 7th ed., (New York: John Wiley & Sons, 1979).
2. J. Harry DuBois and Frederick W. John, *Plastics*, 5th ed., (New York: Van Nostrand Reinhold Co., 1974).
3. R. L. E. Brown, *Design and Manufacture of Plastic Parts*, (New York: John Wiley & Sons, 1980), p. 10.
4. DuBois, *op. cit.*, p. 12.
5. DuBois, *op. cit.*, p. 229.
6. *ABS Product Design Manual*, (Parkersburg, WV: Borg-Warner Chemicals, Borg-Warner Corp., 1980), p. 7.
7. Amstead, *op. cit.*, p. 277.


### Bibliography


Celanese Plastics Co., Division of Celanese Corp. *Standard Tests on Plastics*. Bulletin G1C, 8th ed., 1977.

"Chemicals and Additives." *Modern Plastics*, Special Report (September 1982), pp. 55-74.

Dane, Mark. "CIM Makes the Shoe Mold." *American Machinist* (February 1983), pp. 73-76.

Design Guide—Valox Resins. General Electric Co., Plastics Operations, VAL-50A.

Deslorieux, A. M. "Structural Foam." *Mechanical Engineering* (February 1983), pp. 41-45.

Dreger, Donald R. "New Thrust for Polymer Technology." *Machine Design* (June 24, 1982), pp. 51-55.

E. I. du Pont de Nemours & Co., Inc. *Engineering Guide to DuPont Elastomers*, E-41875.

"Engineering Thermoplastic Resins." Composite Data Sheet (Vydyne), Monsanto Polymer Products Co., MPR-2-215.

Fried, Joel R. "Polymer Technology—Part 5." *Plastics Engineering* (December 1982), pp. 21-26.

General Electric Co., Plastics Div. *Designing with Lexan Resin*, CDC-536B.

General Electric Co., Plastics Operations. *Injection Molding*, VAL-15C (Valox) and CDX-81 (Noryl).

__________. *Guide to Material Properties, Design, Processing, and Secondary Operations, Ultem*, ULT-201.

__________. *Secondary Operations*, CDC-538B.

Helmons, J. M., and Philips, N. V. *Process Control in Plastic Injection Molding*. SME Technical Paper EM78-660, 1978.

Hunkar, Denes B. *Technology of Process Controls for Plastics Molding*. SME Technical Paper EM77-182, 1977.

Mauro, Brian E. *The Role of Urethane Coatings in Decorating Plastics*. SME Technical Paper FC77-649, 1977.

"Modular Mold System Provides Flexible Crate-Making Capability." *Plastics Technology* (February 1983), pp. 15-17.

Nelson, Kenneth W. "Engineering Plastics Can Cut Fuel System Cost." *Automotive Engineering* (March 1983), pp. 25-29.

O'Connor, G. G., and Fath, M. A. "Thermoplastic Elastomers: Can TPE's Compete Against Thermoset Rubbers?" *Rubber World* (December 1981 and January 1982).

Pitzer, Robert R. "Plated Plastics? For Best Results Think Early." *Production Engineering* (October 1982), pp. 60-62.

"Plastics." *Machine Design*, Materials Reference Issue, (April 15, 1982), pp. 95-176.

"Primary Processing." *Modern Plastics Encyclopedia*, 1981-1982.

Simon, Robert M. "EMI Shielding Can Be Made of Conductive Plastics." *Industrial Research & Development* (June 1982).

Smith, Richard F. *Silicone Fluids as Processing Aids for Thermoplastics*. SAE Technical Paper 780357, 1978.

Spier, Martin I. *Simultaneous Injection Molding of Dissimilar But Compatible Materials*. SME Technical Paper EM79-138, 1979.

Storms, Charles D. *Functional Primers for Plastics*. SME Technical Paper FC77-651, 1977.

__________. *Painting Plastics*. SME/AFP Technical Paper FC81-440, 1981.

Swanson, Frank O. "ASTM D-4000: A Classification System for Plastics." *ASTM Standardization News* (October 1982), pp. 31-34.

"Thermoplastics for the Engineer." *Chartered Mechanical Engineer* (May 1982), pp. 27-31.

"Thermoplastics Technology." UFE Incorporated.

Todd, William H. *Compression Molding Equipment Development*. Technical Paper, The Society of the Plastics/Composites Institute, Washington, DC, 1976.

Uniroyal Engineered Polymer Products. *Royalite Applications Bulletin R59-AB-1/81*.

Wynes, Thomas, and Castro, Anthony. "Antistatic Agents." *Modern Plastics Encyclopedia*, 1975-1976.

CHAPTER

# 19

# Special Forming Methods

# SPECIAL FORMING METHODS

A group of techniques, commonly referred to as the high-energy-rate forming (HERF) processes, predominates the general category of special forming methods. Some argument exists (and not without justification) that HERF might more accurately be termed high-velocity forming (HVF). No matter which nomenclature is preferred, however, of importance is the fact that these processes share a common feature: each technique imparts, through the application of high rates of energy transfer, a high rate of strain to the material being formed. While the exact means used to achieve this high rate of energy transfer varies from process to process, the effect for most processes is the same: the velocity component of the forming operation becomes very large and, in sheet metal forming, improved formability and closer tolerances can result.

It has been suggested that a HERF process can be defined as any process in which forming speeds of more than 50 fps (15 m/s) are utilized. Historically, the usual list of HERF processes has included the explosive, electrohydraulic, electromagnetic, and compressed-gas forming methods. In subsequent sections of this chapter, each of these techniques is described in detail and a comprehensive discussion of the theory, equipment, application, and limitations of each method is provided as well.

Because of their increased utilization and importance as forming methods, ultrasonic forming and stress peen forming, though not conceded to be HERF processes, have been added to the list of special forming methods discussed in this chapter. Finally, it is acknowledged that the acronym HERF has, on occasion, been used elsewhere as an abbreviation for high-energy-rate forging. This topic is included in the section on high velocity forging.

**CHAPTER CONTENTS:**



## DESCRIPTION OF SPECIAL FORMING METHODS

The conventional forming processes typically accomplish plastic deformation by applying forming stresses at relatively low velocities. In some of these processes (for example, drop hammer forming), the kinetic energy of massive tools moving fairly swiftly provides the means for applying the needed forming stresses. A key difference between conventional methods and the HERF processes is the very high kinetic energies obtained in the latter.

For example, deformation velocity for the drop hammer may reach 10 fps (3 m/s) or slightly higher, while velocities in some of the HERF processes may range to above 700 fps (200 m/s). Although the mass, $m$, being moved may be much less for the HERF process than for the drop hammer, the velocity, $V$, in the expression for kinetic energy ($KE = 1/2\, mV^2$) is several orders of magnitude greater for the HERF process. A compressed-gas, HERF forging press can deliver in excess of 200,000 ft-lb (271 kJ) of energy, versus 35,000 ft-lb (47 kJ) for a forging hammer. The energy transfer in one of the fastest and largest steam hammers can produce pressures up to 100,000 psi (689 MPa) on the workpiece, while high explosives can provide transient pressures 10-20 times as high.

Each of the special forming methods that, together, compose the family of HERF processes utilizes one of three basic energy sources: chemical, electrical, or mechanical.

Chemical energy, provided in the form of explosives, propellants, or gas mixtures, is used in the group of processes known as explosive forming. This group includes high-explosive forming, low-explosive forming, cartridge-actuated forming, propellant forming, and combustible gas forming.

Large stores of electrical energy, released through high-voltage capacitor discharge, are used in electrohydraulic and electromagnetic forming. In the electrohydraulic (or electrospark) process, forming pressures are obtained from a shock wave within a pressure-distributing medium, usually water. The shock wave is produced by providing sufficient energy either to explode a bridgewire, or to create a high-energy arc (or spark discharge). In electromagnetic forming (sometimes called magnetic or magnetic-pulse forming), deformation occurs as the result of the force applied by a high-density magnetic field upon a current-carrying workpiece.

Mechanical energy is applied (via compressed gas) in high-velocity hammers to perform operations such as forging and extrusion.

***Contributors of sections of this chapter are:*** *Charles Barrett, Manager—Special Projects, Metal Improvement Company; John K. Lawson, Manufacturing Research Specialist, Lockheed California Co.; Michael M. Plum, Manager of Magneform Business Development, Maxwell Laboratories; Professor S. A. Tobias, Head of Department, Dept. of Mechanical Engineering, University of Birmingham.*

***Reviewers of sections of this chapter are:*** *Thomas E. Alves, Supervisory Mechanical Engineer, Manufacturing Engineering Section, Naval Ordnance Section; John Banker, Sales Manager, Explosive Fabricators, Inc.; Charles Barrett, Manager—Special Projects, Metal Improvement Company; T. Z. Blazynski, Reader in Applied Plasticity, Dept. of Mechanical Engineering, University of Leeds; Francis W. Boulger, Battelle Institute;*

# CHAPTER 19

## DESCRIPTION OF SPECIAL FORMING METHODS

The high-energy-rate forming of sheet metal or hollow, tubular-shaped parts frequently takes place by stretching the material, but (depending upon the process) many applications can involve drawing or compression. Operations such as flanging, expanding or bulging, swaging, punching, sizing, heading, coining, cutting, forging, extruding, powder compaction, surface hardening, and welding or bonding can be performed by using one or more of the HERF techniques.

In peen forming, small shot or beads are mechanically hurled or pneumatically blasted at high velocity against the workpiece material. Residual compressive stresses are generated in the peened surfaces. When of sufficient magnitude, these stresses can cause the material to deform slightly. Hence, in thin sections, stress peen forming can be used for sizing purposes, or for forming shallow bends and contours.

Ultrasonic forming takes advantage of the useful effects of macrosound, or large amounts of acoustic energy, upon the flow properties of some materials. In this respect, the process can be compared to hot forming, wherein the addition of thermal energy is used to reduce the force required and to improve upon the amount of elongation that can be obtained with conventional forming equipment.

### ADVANTAGES AND LIMITATIONS

The variety of energy sources available for HERF processes helps provide a high degree of versatility in metalworking capabilities. However, this same variety can complicate the selection of the best technique for a given application.

Although the explosive, propellant, combustible gas, electrohydraulic, and electromagnetic forming processes and the high-velocity forging process are usually best suited for a particular application, they do share certain advantages. Typical advantages of HERF processes include:

1. Uniform application of pressure.
2. High degree of repeatability.
3. Reduced springback.
4. Improved surface finish.
5. Improved tolerances with sheet metal.
6. Ductility marginally improved in some metals when sheet metal is being formed.
7. Reduced tooling costs.
8. Relatively low energy costs.
9. Reduced production costs for small-to-large production runs (except in explosive forming, which is labor intensive).

Peen forming induces surface stresses that are compressive in nature; and since no dies are used, lead time is minimal. Sharp bends are not suitable to this process. (For additional advantages of a particular process, refer to the subsequent sections discussing each process in detail.)

### MATERIAL FORMED

If a material is formable by conventional methods, then one or more of the special methods should also be capable of forming the material. Accordingly, the materials that can be fabricated using the HERF processes include aluminum, magnesium, copper, carbon and alloy steels, stainless steels, superalloys, titanium, beryllium, zirconium, the refractory metals, and many composites. However, some individual HERF processes (notably electromagnetic forming) are limited in the materials that can be formed. Peen forming has been employed to form aluminum and high-strength steel alloys. Ultrasonic forming has been employed to form nickel, titanium, and stainless steel alloys.

### WORKPIECE SIZES AND TOLERANCES

Table 19-1 can be used to find general information on part size limitations. Of course, the actual size of the workpiece that can be formed depends upon the capacity (physical, electrical, etc.) of the available equipment; though in some cases, a relatively simple or inexpensive modification can be made that will significantly expand the capacity of the equipment.

#### Explosive Forming

With respect to workpiece size and material thickness, high-explosive forming is by far the most versatile of HERF methods. For this process, part blanks do not necessarily have to be limited to mill stock sizes for sheet or plate since even welded material has been formed successfully. Material thicknesses ranging to a few inches (100 mm) have been formed, though sheet gages are much more common in applications. Tolerances in explosive forming are at least as good as in conventional methods; while for large parts, the accuracy obtainable by explosive techniques is generally superior. In fact, in order to obtain required tolerances on large parts, explosive forming is sometimes used to final-size blanks that have been preformed using conventional techniques. In explosive forming, a tolerance of ±0.015" (0.38 mm) is more or less typical. Closer tolerances of ±0.008" (0.20 mm) and less can be obtained depending on workpiece material, the size and shape of the part, the dimensional accuracy of the tooling, and

***Reviewers, cont.***: *Otto Brass, Vice President—Engineering, Precision Metal Products; James Daly, Vice President Operations, Metal Improvement Company, Inc.; A. E. Doherty, Jr., President, A & T Engineering; Dr. Joseph El Gomayel, Industrial Engineering, Michael Golden Laboratories, Purdue University; Blaine Fluth, President, Diversico Industries, Inc.; Chet Hoggatt, Head of Laboratories for Applied Science, Denver Research Institute, University of Denver; W. R. King, Supervisor Manufacturing Technology, Fort Worth Division, General Dynamics; Philip C. Krause, Vice President, Sonobond Corp.; John K. Lawson, Manufacturing Research Specialist, Lockheed California Co.; Alan Male, Manager of Metal Processing Research, Westinghouse Research; Ted R. Marshall, Engineering Technician, Manufacturing Engineering Section, Naval Ordnance Station; Alan McMechan, Chief Materials and Process Engineer, McDonnell Douglas Canada, Ltd.; Jim Mote, Head of Chemical and Materials Sciences, Denver Research Institute, University of Denver; Joseph S. Newman, Section Head Process Engineering, Grumman Aerospace Corp.; Thad A. Peake, Head of Manufacturing Technology Branch, Product Support Div., Production Dept., Naval Ordnance Station; Michael M. Plum, Manager of Magneform Business Development, Maxwell Laboratories; D. H. Sansome, Professor of Applied Plasticity, Dept. of Production Technology and Production Management, University of Aston in Birmingham; Professor S. A. Tobias, Head of Department, Dept. of Mechanical Engineering, University of Birmingham; E. S. Vitolo, Manager of Sales Promotion, Foster Wheeler Energy Corp.; Jack Yoblin, President, Precision Forge Company, Inc.*

the care exercised in establishing and following process parameters and procedures.

### Electrohydraulic Forming

Although theoretically capable of forming very large parts, electrohydraulic forming is limited, in a practical sense, by the cost of the required electrical components. Component costs increase with larger workpieces because of the additional amount of energy required. Parts ranging from a few tenths of an inch (10 mm) to 5 ft (1.5 m) diam can be formed from materials that are a few thousandths of an inch (0.30 mm) to about 1″ (25 mm) in thickness. In many applications, very close tolerances are possible. External dimensions on tubular parts are readily held to within ±0.010″ (0.25 mm). With moderate effort and adequate tooling, critical dimensions can be held to within ±0.005″ (0.13 mm). Selected dimensions can be held to within ±0.002″ (0.05 mm) by special effort.

### Electromagnetic Forming

In appropriate materials, workpieces up to 72″ (1830 mm) diam and 1/4″ (6 mm) thick can be electromagnetically formed. A typical tolerance is ±0.015″ (0.38 mm), though accuracy to within ±0.005″ (0.13 mm) has been obtained in certain electromagnetic swaging (compression) applications. In expansion forming operations, a practical minimum outside diameter (OD) of tubing appears to be about 1.5″ (40 mm); while in compression operations, tubing down to 0.125″ OD can be formed. Tubes up to 72″ (1830 mm) OD have been sized electromagnetically.

### High-Velocity Forging

Typical tolerances for high-velocity forging are ±0.030″ (0.76 mm) for forging operations and as low as ±0.015″ (0.38 mm) for coining operations. Billet size can be 12″ (305 mm) diam, and flat stock can be 18″ (460 mm) diam.

### Peen Forming

In peen forming, the maximum workpiece size currently being formed is 10 ft wide x 100 ft long (3 x 30 m). Longer workpieces can also be formed. The contour tolerances obtained are approximately ±0.025″ (0.63 mm).

# SELECTION CRITERIA

An approach to the problem of choosing the most appropriate manufacturing method for a particular application involves, typically, a preliminary study of the economic and performance characteristics of the processes being considered. Sometimes, even the performance characteristics may appear attractive mainly for economic reasons.

In evaluating these methods from an economic standpoint, the costs of capital equipment, ancillary facilities, and required tooling, taken with the estimated unit labor and materials costs, must be compared with the same factors as applied to the relevant conventional processes. From a performance standpoint, comparisons may show that one of these methods is capable of producing a much simpler, more lightweight, or higher quality part.

In general, the reasons for using one of these methods to form a particular material or to produce a specific shape are:

1. To obtain parts that are not producible by other methods because of size, complexity, material characteristics, or some combination of these factors.
2. To facilitate the making of parts from materials that are not readily formed by conventional methods.
3. To obtain required dimensional tolerances.
4. To reduce the size or cost of needed equipment.
5. To achieve faster production rates.
6. To realize lower tooling or production costs.
7. To reduce the costs of small runs or "one-of-a-kind" parts.

Table 19-1 provides significant information relating to economic and performance characteristics of the various forming processes. This information can be utilized by the engineer to determine the potential of each process for a specific application.

## ECONOMIC CHARACTERISTICS

While the information presented in Table 19-1 can help in preparing an estimate of the costs associated with the various methods (that is, required capital investment, tooling, labor, and energy costs), such condensed data must of necessity be generalized and, therefore, cannot reflect fully the many possible factors that should be considered. Furthermore, this data is subject to change as new developments become available or as different economic conditions prevail. When making a cost comparison to aid in selecting between one of these special processes and a conventional one, or when choosing between two different special processes, each of which appears capable of accomplishing the necessary forming, the engineer is advised, therefore, to contact manufacturers of the respective equipment to obtain the most current information available.

Experience indicates that the HERF processes are generally more useful in the production of smaller quantities of parts. Figure 19-1 illustrates idealized cost-comparison curves for forming by HERF and by conventional methods. For the production of a small number of parts, the unit cost makes a HERF operation more favorable because of the generally lower initial cost of tooling, capital equipment, etc. However, as the number of parts is increased, the crossover point, $P$, is reached and the unit cost for the conventional method becomes the lower figure. Hence, in industries that produce extremely large numbers of parts, such as the stamping industry, the operations fall to the right of $P$ and, for the most part, are not economically feasible for most HERF techniques.

Exceptions do exist. For example, studies by Tobias at the University of Birmingham, England have shown that, when properly designed and controlled, automated pneumatic-mechanical, high-velocity hammers can be competitive with conventional stamping and high-production forging equipment.[1] Also, electromagnetic forming can be used to assemble detail parts by compression swaging at rates of 300-12,000 units per hour.

There is yet another facet to the cost-comparison problem. A plot of the type shown in Fig. 19-1 assumes that conventional equipment is available and that a direct comparison can be

# SELECTION CRITERIA

**TABLE 19-1**
**Characteristics of High-Energy-Rate Forming Processes**

| | Electrohydraulic | | High-Explosive Standoff | High-Explosive Direct Contact | Explosive Propellant Closed Die |
|---|---|---|---|---|---|
| | Exploding Bridge Wire | Spark Discharge | | | |
| Metalworking operations | Tube bulging, sizing, drawing, flanging, coining, blanking, stretching | Tube bulging, drawing, sizing, expanding, flanging, coining, embossing, blanking, stretching | Draw forming, stretch forming, flanging, coining, blanking, embossing, sizing, beading, cutting, expanding, powder compacting, stretching, joining | Hardening, welding, cutting, perforating, cladding, powder compacting | Tube bulging, powder compacting, sizing, perforating, stud driving, machining, flanging |
| Size limitations | 0.25-60″ (6-1524 mm) diam or larger | 0.25-60″ (6-1524 mm) diam or larger | Limited only by available blank size; presently, 144-180″ (3658-4572 mm) | Part size not limiting | Limited by equipment |
| Shape complexity | Complex surfaces and shapes, especially tubular | Complex surfaces and shapes, especially tubular | Small and intricate, large and simple | Simple shapes | Compound surfaces, non-symmetrical shapes |
| Principal advantage | Controllability and repeatability | Controllability and repeatability | Neither pressure nor energy limited, i.e., large parts | Extremely high pressures | Reduces number of operations to produce complex parts |
| Capital investment | Moderate | Moderate | Low | Low | Low |
| Tooling costs | Low | Low | Low | None to low | Moderate |
| Labor costs | Moderate | Moderate | Moderate | Moderate | Low to moderate |
| Production rate | 360 parts per hr depending on part complexity and equipment | Up to 360 parts per hr depending on part complexity and equipment | 0.5-4 parts per hr or less depending on part and facility | 0.5-4 parts per hr depending on part and facility | 2-12 parts per hr depending on part and facility |
| Cycle time | Long | Medium | Medium | Medium | Medium |
| Energy costs | Low | Low | High | High | High |
| Lead time required to place facility in operation | Moderate to long | Moderate | Short | Short | Short |
| Safety considerations | Equipment interlocks, high-voltage safety practices, trained personnel | Equipment interlocks, high-voltage safety practices, trained personnel | Trained personnel | Trained personnel | Trained personnel |
| Facility location | In-plant | In-plant | Field or plant | Field or plant | In-plant or separate facility |
| Method of energy release | Vaporization of wire | Vaporization of medium | Chemical detonation | Chemical detonation | Chemical burning |
| Pressure-wave velocity, fps (m/s) | 20,000 (6096) | 20,000 (6096) | 4000-25,000 (1219-7620) | 4000-25,000 (1219-7620) | 1000-8000 (305-2438) |
| Pressure-wave duration | Microseconds | Microseconds | Microseconds | Microseconds | Milliseconds |
| Energy range, ft - lb (kJ) | 20,000-175,000 (27-237) | 10,000-110,000 (13.5-150) | 100,000-2,000,000 (136-2712) per lb of explosive; up to 100 lb (45 kg) detonator | 0.5-8 psf high explosive | Low to moderate (detonation wave in gas) |
| Workpiece-deformation velocity, fps (m/s) | 50-700 (15-213) | 50-700 (15-213) | 60-400 (18-122) | Not applicable | 50-200 (15-61) |
| Energy transfer medium | Water or other suitable liquid | Water or other suitable liquid | Water, elastomers, sand, molten salts | Direct contact or buffer material | Air or water; high-velocity projectile or ram |

**TABLE 19-1—*continued***

| Gas Mixtures | | | HERF Hammers | |
|---|---|---|---|---|
| Combustion | Detonation | Electromagnetic | Pneumatic-hydraulic | Combustion-pneumatic |
| Tube bulging, flanging, draw forming, stretch forming, sizing, stretching | Draw forming, stretch forming | Swaging, shrinking, tube bulging, sizing, flanging, shallow drawing, blanking, coining, joining, welding | Hot/warm/cold forming, powder compacting, coining, piercing, upsetting, extruding | Hot/warm/cold forming, powder compacting, powder forging, cropping, blanking, piercing, coining |
| Up to 60" (1524 mm) diam | 12" (305 mm) diam | 0.1-72" (2.5-1830 mm) diam and larger in some operations | Up to 24" (610 mm) diam; larger on future machines | Up to 10" (254 mm) diam; larger on future machines |
| Compound surfaces, nonsymmetrical shapes | Simple dishes, domes, surfaces of revolution | Compound surfaces, corrective forming on large complex shapes | Complex shapes, thin forged sections | Complex shapes, thin forged sections |
| Uniform pressures permitting accurate forming of thin parts | Adaptability to production forming | Controllability and repeatability, swaging operations | Controllability and repeatability | Controllability and repeatability |
| Moderate | Moderate to high | Moderate to high | Moderate | Low |
| Moderate to high | Low | High if work coil is regarded as part of tooling | Moderate | Moderate |
| Moderate to high | Moderate | Moderate to low | Moderate | Low |
| 2 parts per hr or less | 6-12 parts per hr | Up to 12,000 parts per hr for simple parts and automated transfer equipment | 60-100 parts per hr with automatic equipment, depending on part complexity | With automatic handling, 2000-3000 parts per hr; with manual feeding, 300-400 parts per hr |
| Long | Long | Medium to short | Long | Short |
| Low | Very low | Low | Moderate | Low |
| Moderate | Moderate to long | Moderate to long | Moderate | Very short |
| Trained or experienced personnel | Trained or experienced personnel | Equipment interlocks, high-voltage safety practices, trained personnel | Guards and shields, trained personnel | Guards and shields, trained personnel |
| Separate facility | In-plant | In-plant | In-plant | In-plant |
| Chemical burning | Chemical detonation | Expanding magnetic field | Quick-release valve | Quick-release valve |
| 1000-8000 (305-2438) | 2000-20,000 (610-6096) | Not applicable | Not applicable | Not applicable |
| Milliseconds | Milliseconds-microseconds | Microseconds | Milliseconds | Milliseconds |
| Low (burning gas mixtures) | 4500-175,000 (6-237) | 0-175,000 (0-237) | Up to 400,000 (542) | Up to 25,000 (34) |
| 60-100 (18-30) | 60-200 (18-61) | 50-1000 (15-305) | 50-700 (15-213) | 50-700 (15-213) |
| Gas pressure | Gas pressure | Magnetic field (could be operated in vacuum) | High-velocity ram | High-velocity ram |

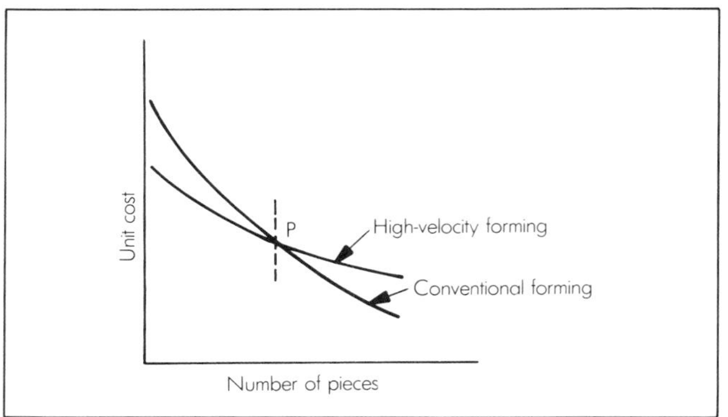


**Fig. 19-1 Cost comparison between conventional forming and high-energy-rate forming.**

made, as would be the case in a heavily industrialized community. One of the attractive features of some HERF processes, and especially of explosive forming, is that the processes can be established in those areas in which heavy industrial equipment is not available. Also, by means of the HERF processes, small manufacturers can, with only a modest capital outlay, enter areas of production formerly closed to them because of the excessive cost of heavy equipment.

## PERFORMANCE CHARACTERISTICS

Before attempting to determine whether the physical requirements of a part can best be met through using one of the special methods or a conventional method, the engineer should become acquainted with the basic features of the processes being considered, including any singular capabilities that these processes may have to offer.

The manufacturing engineer would do well to avoid relying too heavily upon claims that are strictly hearsay, especially unsubstantiated claims that high-velocity forming methods improve the properties of the deformed material. Well-documented, verifiable claims are, of course, another matter. For example, in specific applications, it has been well demonstrated that HERF can produce metallurgical advantages not readily produced by conventional methods, such as shock hardening (especially surface and through hardening), rapid cold working (hardening and strengthening when subsequent heat treatment is not used), explosive and magnetic welding of different (normally incompatible) metals, and compaction of metal powders to high green densities.

Although it is true that, in the as-formed condition, a high-energy-rate formed material can exhibit metallurgical properties that are superior to those possessed by the material prior to forming, many metals and alloys are subjected to post-forming heat treatment, which generally eliminates the effects of the forming operation.

It is perhaps more practical for the manufacturing engineer to understand that high strain rates, per se, have no apparent adverse effects upon material properties. It is important to recognize that some materials possess greater strain-rate sensitivity than others and that for such materials, a greater amount of energy may be required to overcome hardening and to obtain the desired degree of forming. However, it is generally safe to assume that for a given amount of strain, the rate at which the strain is produced will have a negligible effect on the material's final properties from the standpoint of either increasing or decreasing the utility of the part.

Conversely, the HERF processes have displayed uncommon capabilities to produce certain kinds of workpiece configurations. Therefore, the processes can normally be used to best advantage when new parts are designed with the particular forming method (and its inherent advantages and limitations) firmly in mind. A working knowledge of these capabilities facilitates the design of specifically HERF-producible parts or assemblies, which may feature a lighter weight, higher quality, and/or reduced complexity and cost.

# FORMING METHODS

In the following sections, each of the special forming methods is described with an aim toward providing the tooling or manufacturing engineer with a practical understanding of how the processes work and how to go about evaluating the processes as possible alternatives to the more traditional forming methods. A great deal of technical information relating to HERF has been published, and this information can aid the engineer in taking a scientific approach toward implementing the processes. A certain amount of "art" is always involved, however; and (as regulated by the amount of experience possessed by the engineer) some trial and error is usually required for any given combination of process and workpiece. To the novice who is seriously considering the use of any of the HERF processes, it is suggested that the references listed at the end of this chapter can provide much valuable assistance.

## EXPLOSIVE FORMING

Explosive forming is a high-velocity process in which the punch or diaphragm is replaced by an explosive charge. The explosives used are generally highly explosive chemicals, gaseous mixtures, or propellants. Explosive joining and cladding techniques are discussed in Volume 4, *Quality Control and Assembly*, of this Handbook series.

### High-Explosive Forming

The two methods of high-explosive forming used are the standoff method and the contact method. Explosives such as dynamite should be avoided when possible, and only stable explosives should be used. Some of the more commonly used high explosives are cyclotrimethylene trinitramine (RDX), pentaerythritol tetranitrate (PETN), trinitrotoluene (TNT), or Detasheet (trademark of E. I. du Pont de Nemours & Company, Inc.). Properties of the various high explosives used are given in Table 19-2. The type of explosive used depends upon the material being formed.

**Standoff method.** In the standoff method of high-explosive forming, the explosive charge is located at some predetermined distance from the workpiece (see Fig. 19-2). Water is generally used as the energy transfer medium to ensure a uniform transmission of energy and to muffle the sound of the explosive blast. After detonation of the explosive, a pressure pulse of high intensity is produced. A gas bubble is also produced which expands spherically and then collapses until it vents at the surface of the water. When the pressure pulse impinges against the workpiece, the metal is displaced into the die cavity with a velocity of 60-400 fps (18-122 m/s). To ensure proper die filling, the die cavity must be evacuated.

Measurements indicate that the pressure pulse accounts for 60% of the energy available, the first oscillation of the gas bubble for 25%, and the remaining oscillations for the other 15%. These values, however, vary with charge weight and type of explosive used. For many forming operations, the charge weight and standoff distance combinations are chosen so that the bubble breaks over the workpiece during the first expansion.

**Contact method.** In contact forming, the explosive charge is held in direct contact with the workpiece while the detonation is

**TABLE 19-2**
**Properties of Selected High Explosives**[2]

| Explosive | Relative Power, % TNT | Form of Charge | Detonation Velocity, fps (m/s) | Energy, ft · lb/lb (kJ/kg) | Detonator Required | Storage Life | Maximum Pressure, ksi (MPa) |
|---|---|---|---|---|---|---|---|
| Trinitrotoluene (TNT) | 100 | Cast | 23,000 (7010) | 262,000 (780) | J-2* | Moderate | 2400 (16 548) |
| Cyclotrimethylene trinitramine (RDX) | 170 | Pressed granules | 27,500 (8380) | 425,000 (1270) | No. 6 | Very good | 3400 (23 443) |
| Pentaerythritol tetranitrate (PETN) | 170 | Pressed granules | 27,200 (8290) | 435,000 (1300) | No. 6 | Excellent | 3200 (22 064) |
| Pentolite (50/50) | 140 | Cast | 25,000 (7620) | 317,000 (950) | No. 8 | Good | 2800 (19 306) |
| Tetryl | 129 | Pressed granules | 25,700 (7835) | | Special** | Excellent | |
| Composition C-3 | 115 | Hand-shaped putty | 26,400 (8045) | | No. 6 | Good | |
| 40% straight dynamite | 94 | Cartridge granules | 15,500 (4725) | 202,000 (605) | No. 8 | Fair | 970 (6688) |
| 50% straight ditching dynamite | 103 | Cartridge granules | 17,400 (5305) | 220,000 (660) | No. 6 | Fair | |
| 60% extra dynamite | 109 | Cartridge granules | 12,500 (3810) | 240,000 (715) | No. 6 | Fair | 620 (4275) |
| Blasting gelatin | 99 | Cartridge plastic | 26,200 (7985) | 408,000 (1220) | J-2 | Fair | 2600 (17 927) |
| Bituminous coal D permissible explosive | | Cartridge granules | 4600 (1400) | | No. 8 | Fair | |
| Primacord, 40 g/ft | | Plastic or cotton cord | 20,800 (6340) | | No. 6 | Excellent | |
| Mild detonating cord, 10 g PETN/ft | | Metal-coated cord | 24,000 (7315) | | Special† | Excellent | |
| Detasheet† | | Cut to shape | 23,700 (7225) | | No. 8 | Very good | |
| Cyadyn 3‡ | 90 | Cartridge granules | 7000 (2135) | | No. 6 | Fair-good | |
| IRECO DBA-10HV§ | 20 | Slurry (two parts) | 11,500 (3505) | | Special | Excellent (unmixed components) | |

* With booster.
** Special engineer's blasting cap.
† Registered trademark, E. I. du Pont de Nemours & Company, Inc.
‡ Registered trademark, American Cyanamid Company.
§ Intermountain Research and Engineering Corp.

# CHAPTER 19

## EXPLOSIVE FORMING

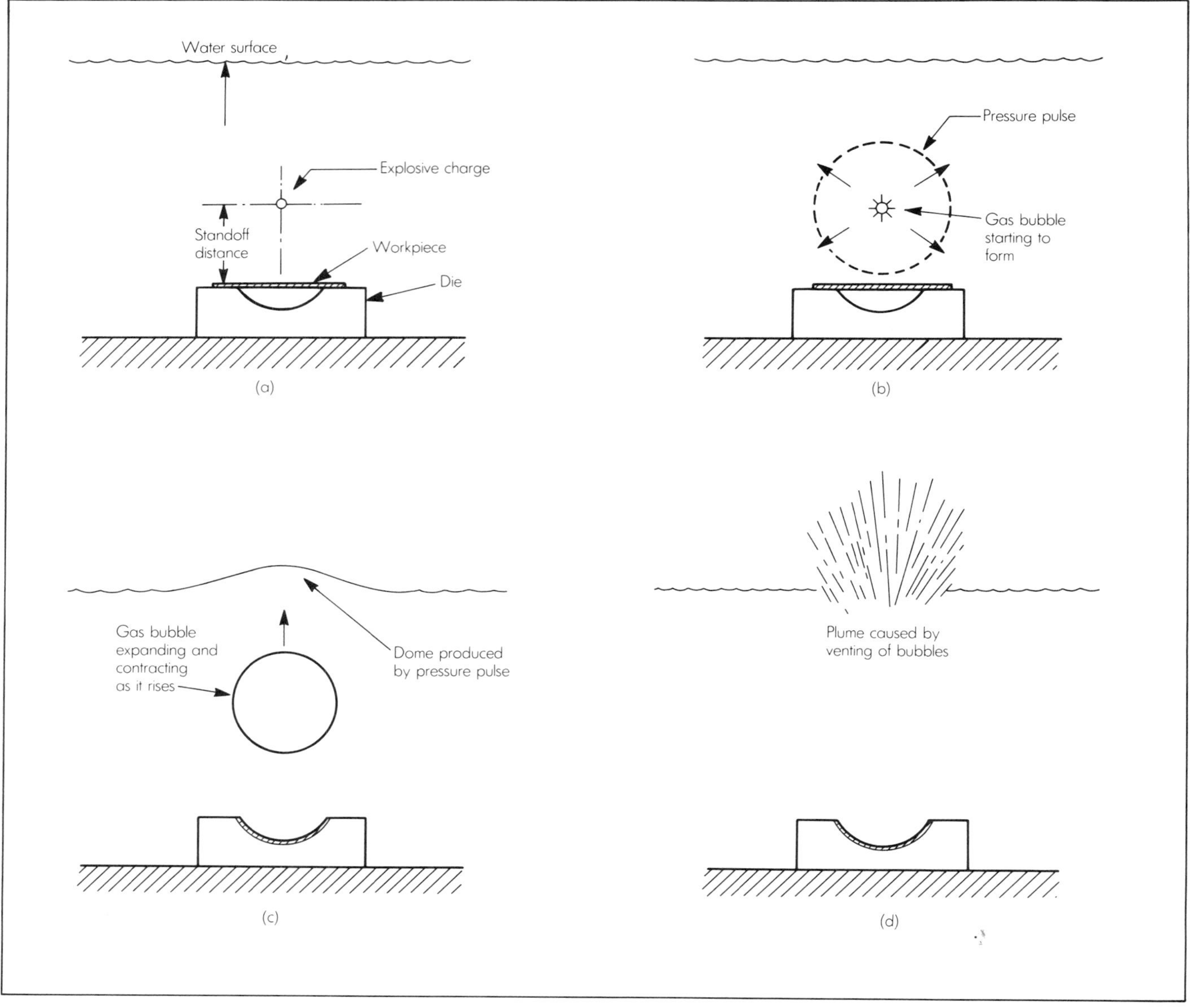


**Fig. 19-2 Sequence of underwater explosive-forming operations: (a) explosive charge is set in position, (b) detonation occurs producing pressure pulse and gas bubble, (c) workpiece deformed, and (d) gas bubble vents at surface of the water.**

initiated. The detonation produces interface pressures on the surface of the metal up to several million psi (35 000 MPa). Pressures, working times, and impulse values are directly related to the properties of the workpiece and the explosive, and to the geometry of the operational system. In most contact operations, high-intensity, transient stress waves are induced in the workpiece which then propagate through the metal, resulting in displacement, deformation, and possible fracture. The working of the metal during contact forming is due to the action of the applied loads and subsequent stress-wave effects.

**Scaling.** Generally, scaling permits the development of the necessary forming parameters on a scale model and the subsequent accurate application of the developed data to a full-scale component. For scaling to be applied effectively, the following requirements must be met:

1. Complete geometrical similitude is required between the scale model and the full-scale components.
2. The ratio between the explosive standoff distance and the die-opening diameter must remain constant.
3. The same explosive must be used on the full-scale component as on the model.
4. The blank yield strength, modulus of elasticity, and ductility must be the same for all sizes.
5. The ratio of the blank thickness to the die-opening diameter must remain constant.
6. The clamping-system stiffness must remain the same.
7. The coefficient of friction must remain constant.
8. The hold-down force increases by the square of the scale factor. [5000 lb (22.2 kN) on a 6″ (152.4 mm) die would require 500,000 lb (2220 kN) on 60″ (1524 mm) die.]

The application of scaling to high-explosive forming has permitted the economical development of many parts that would otherwise have required considerable experimental data on full-scale parts. Further steps to refine high-explosive forming by computerizing the major factors affecting metal deformation have resulted in usable computer programs for predicting metal-deforming parameters. Once perfected, the computer techniques should greatly reduce the amount of empirical work necessary to describe and set up a specific production process.

## Combustible Gas Forming

In combustible gas forming, the workpiece is placed between the mixing head and the lower die (see Fig. 19-3). The mixing head is then bolted or hydraulically clamped to the lower die. A synthetic rubber seal is incorporated in the mixing head and the lower die to ensure sealing of the combustible gases and to permit a vacuum in the die cavity. On-off valves and pressure regulators control the flow of the gases into the combustion chamber. Check valves in the inlet lines protect against backfiring in the inlets. The gas is usually ignited by an electrically heated glow wire which extends into the chamber. Normally, one ignition point is sufficient. However, several ignitors, fired simultaneously, are used to produce the correct flame front when large workpieces are being formed. Working pressures from 1000-110,000 psi (7-760 MPa) can be obtained by varying the gas mixture and initial gas pressure. After the reaction is completed, the residual gas pressure and exhaust gases are released through the exhaust outlet.

High-energy-rate forming using combustible gases differs considerably from high-explosive forming. The major differences are the rate at which the metal is strained and the length of time that the energy is applied to the workpiece. High-explosive forming produces strain rates ranging from 400-600 in./in./s (mm/mm/s), whereas combustible gas forming produces strain rates of only 2-5 in./in./s (mm/mm/s). Deformation times for high-explosive forming are usually measured in microseconds, and times for combustible gas forming are measured in milliseconds. The longer deformation times in combustible gas forming can result in the workpiece being heated up and thereby producing undesirable properties in the metal.

The selection of fuels, oxydizers, and diluents for combustible gas forming is also more restrictive than is the selection of high explosives. Table 19-3 lists the common mixtures used for combustible gas forming. Generally, acceptable gas fuels must satisfy the following conditions:

1. Detonation must be stable with a controlled pressure release.
2. Combustion products must not be toxic.
3. Gases should be permanent gases at charging pressure and temperature to ensure thorough mixing and uniform combustion.
4. Fuel gas, oxidizing gas, and diluent gas should be practical in cost.

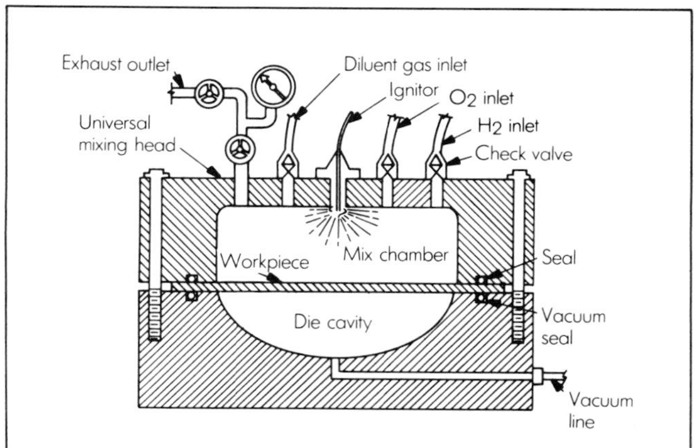


**Fig. 19-3 Schematic view of typical combustible gas forming operation employing a spark igniter to initiate uniform shock front.**

## Advantages and Limitations

High explosives are probably the most versatile of the various energy sources used in high-energy-rate forming. They lend themselves to forming by open and closed-die techniques; and since the pressure wave produced by the explosive takes the place of the punch used in conventional forming, tooling costs are reduced. High explosives are capable of producing extremely high but controllable pressures, and they permit workpieces of unlimited sizes to be formed. Close workpiece tolerances can be maintained, and a variety of metals can be formed. However, skilled personnel are required and the forming is usually performed in remote areas rather than in the plant.

Combustible gas explosive forming is safe and quiet and can be performed in a normal factory environment. An intermediate medium is not needed, as it is with high-explosive forming. The workpiece can be deformed at room temperature or heated above its recrystallization temperature. Combustible gas explosive forming can also be used in large-volume production runs. Compared with the form dies required in high-explosive forming, tooling for combustible gas explosive forming is relatively expensive.

## Applications

Explosive forming is largely used in the aerospace and aircraft industries and has been successfully employed in the production of automotive-related components. In general, explosive forming has found its greatest potential in limited-production prototype forming and in forming large parts for which conventional tooling costs are high. Explosive forming can be used to form a wide variety of metals, from aluminum to exotic high-strength alloys. Combustible gas explosive forming is best suited to complex shapes, large sections of thin-gage materials, and operations in which rapid automatic cycles are required.

Some of the operations performed in explosive forming include draw forming, stretch forming, flanging, coining, blanking, embossing, sizing, beading, cutting, expanding, powder compacting, stretching, joining, hardening, welding, cladding, and tube bulging.

**TABLE 19-3**
**Types of Gases Used in Combustible Gas Forming**

| Fuels | Oxidizers | Diluents |
|---|---|---|
| Hydrogen | Oxygen | Helium |
| Ethane | Air | Nitrogen |
| Methane | Ozone 13 | Carbon dioxide |
| Natural gas | | Argon |

# CHAPTER 19

## EXPLOSIVE FORMING

### Equipment and Tooling

The equipment required in explosive forming consists of either a male or female die and the energy source in the form of an explosive charge or a combustible gas. High-explosive forming dies can be designed to permit deep drawing, compression forming, or sizing of preformed parts (see Fig. 19-4) and generally incorporate a vacuum port to ensure proper die filling. Combustible gas forming requires a mixing head to regulate the gas mixture and pressure (see Fig. 19-3).

Tooling materials are determined by several factors including part quantity, strength of material being formed, and tolerances needed in the final part. For quantities of 10-20 parts that do not require close tolerances, dies have been made from plastics, concrete, and sheet metal. Dies made from concrete sacrifice tolerance as well as surface finish. Prototype parts have been successfully formed using dies made from fiberglass or cast epoxies.

For quantities of 50 or more parts, dies are made from zinc-based alloys when light-gage aluminum, steel, or copper is to be formed and from hardened tool steel when titanium, high-strength steels, or superalloys are to be formed. Combustible gas forming dies are usually made from wrought alloy steel, carbon steel, or cast iron.

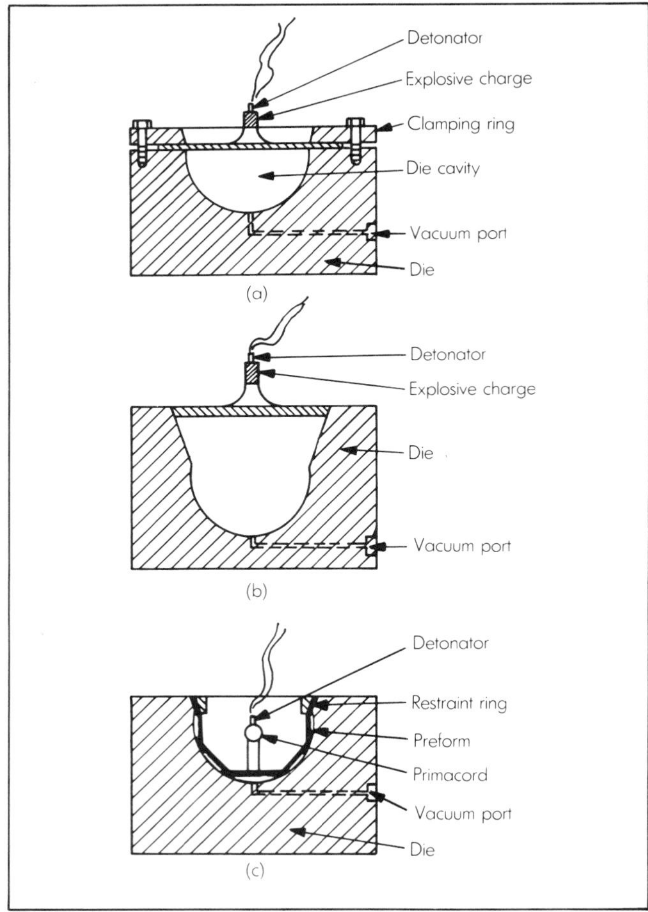


Fig. 19-4 Schematic views of typical explosive-forming arrangements: (a) deep-drawing die, (b) compression-forming die, (c) preform sizing die.

High-explosive forming dies must be carefully designed, since high-impulsive loads occur during forming. To prevent spalling and die deterioration due to tensile forces, high-explosive forming dies are designed to maintain a compressive-stress state. Sharp corners must also be avoided to promote good die life. To reduce die weight, sheet metal dies have been backed with water.

## ELECTROHYDRAULIC FORMING

Electrohydraulic forming (EHF) is a process that converts electrical energy into mechanical energy for the forming of metallic parts. The amount of electrical energy discharged is controlled by varying the charging voltage from zero to its maximum. The discharged electrical energy causes explosions inside the hollow workpiece, which is filled with water or another suitable medium. These explosions produce shock waves that emanate in all directions until some obstruction is encountered. If the energy is of sufficient magnitude, the workpiece is deformed. The deformation is controlled by applying external restraints in one or more of three ways: in the form of dies, by varying the magnitude of the energy released, and by using shapers within the transfer medium (see Fig. 19-5).

### Forming Methods

Two common methods employed to convert the electrical energy into mechanical energy are the spark discharge method and the exploding bridge wires method.

**Spark discharge.** The spark transducer is a device that discharges electrical energy without the use of bridge wires. It operates in a manner similar to a common automotive spark plug. The energy is discharged from the transducer when it jumps across an air gap between two electrodes.

Research has shown that the transducer is only 60% as efficient as bridge wires. However, for some operations this is offset by the ease of operation and the ability to make successive shots without removing the energy converter from inside the part being formed. Electrohydraulic forming with spark trans-

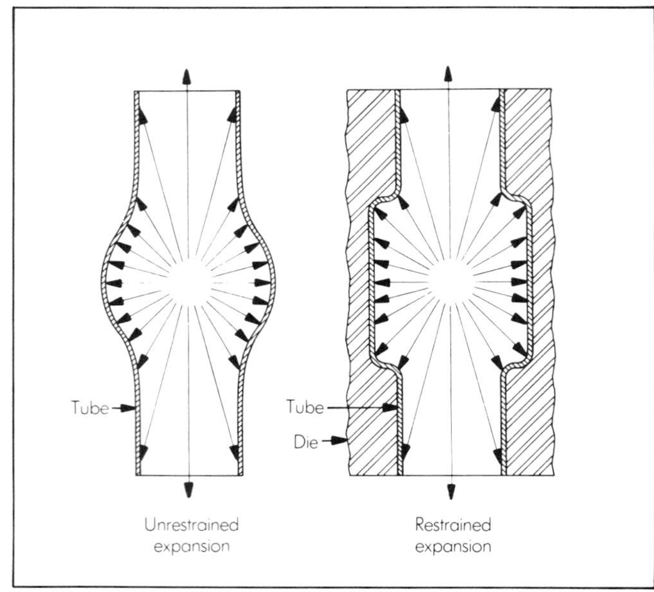


Fig. 19-5 Energy patterns in unrestrained and restrained electrohydraulic forming.

ducers can be improved through the use of shock reflectors or shapers that help to concentrate the energy into selected areas of the part.

**Exploding bridge wires.** The use of exploding bridge wires in EHF provides greater versatility and more accurate control than the use of spark transducers. However, a disadvantage of this method is that a new wire must be installed on the electrode for each successive shot, thus increasing production time.

In this method, a wire filament is attached between the two electrodes. As the electrical energy flows through the wire, the wire vaporizes or explodes exerting a high pressure on the medium. The pressure developed by this action is important to the operation of EHF. Table 19-4 shows pressures observed by several investigators under varying conditions. The pressure acting at a given point depends upon the distance of the point from the discharged energy's origin. Higher pressures are attained if the wire is exploded in a liquid rather than air. Wire length and wire diameter also have an important effect on the operation. Figure 19-6 shows peak pressures recorded by Bagnoli and Molella for energy discharges into wires of several different materials and diameters.

## Advantages and Limitations

The main advantage of EHF is its ability to form hollow shapes that would normally require more expensive fabricating techniques. Generally, the process is not recommended for forming ordinary parts that are readily adaptable to conventional forming processes. When EHF is used, the cost of tooling is usually less than that of conventional tooling. The nature of the process is such that large amounts of energy can be directed into isolated areas, as is required in some piercing operations. Electrohydraulic forming is also more adaptable to automatic production processes than are most explosive methods. The greatest advantage of EHF is that it facilitates the production of small-to-intermediate sized parts that do not require excessive energy levels.

One of the most significant limitations of the process is the required energy rating of the capacitor bank. Another limitation is the ability of the triggering device to discharge the energy into the hollow blank.

**Accuracy.** Accuracy of the EHF process depends on the dimensional accuracy of the dies used and on the control of both the magnitude and location of energy discharges. Modern equipment provides infinite control of the energy within specified limits, so the primary factor is the die. External dimensions on tubular parts are readily held within ±0.010" (0.25 mm) and can be held within ±0.002" (0.05 mm) with special effort. Internal dimensions vary according to the external tolerances plus any variations which occur in material thickness.

**Economy.** Equipment, tooling, and manufacturing all play a part in the economics of EHF. The condenser banks increase the equipment cost, but the workholding devices or tool clamping facilities are less expensive than those used with press forming equipment to form an equivalent part.

The economics of the EHF process can be analyzed best by comparing the fabrication of a given part with another process. For example, from the part illustrated in Fig. 19-7, 31" (787 mm) of welding were eliminated by EHF in place of fabrication as a subassembly consisting of three pieces welded together. In such cases, not only is the cost of the part reduced by

**TABLE 19-4**
**Pressure Observations of Exploding Bridge Wires**

| Energy Released, J | Capacitance, μF | Wire Size, in. (mm) | Wire Material | Standoff Distance, in. (mm) | Pressure, psi (MPa) | Investigator |
|---|---|---|---|---|---|---|
| 588 | 24 | 0.025 (0.63) | Copper | 1.00 (25.4) | 1600 (11) | Picatinny Arsenal |
| 3888 | 24 | 0.025 (0.63) | Copper | 1.00 (25.4) | 4800 (33) | Picatinny Arsenal |
| 4500 | 600 | 0.045 (1.14) | Aluminum | 1.00 (25.4) | 15,000 (103) | General Dynamics—Fort Worth |
| 8000 | 1200 | 0.045 (1.14) | Aluminum | 1.00 (25.4) | 20,000 (137.9) | General Dynamics—Fort Worth |
| 12,000 | 1200 | 0.045 (1.14) | Aluminum | 1.00 (25.4) | 25,000 (172) | General Dynamics—Fort Worth |
| 18,000 | 1800 | 0.045 (1.14) | Aluminum | 1.00 (25.4) | 35,000 (241) | General Dynamics—Fort Worth |
| 4320 | 240 | 0.062 (1.57) | Magnesium | 4.00 (101.6) | 400 (2.8) | Republic Aviation |
| 12,000 | 240 | 0.062 (1.57) | Magnesium | 4.00 (101.6) | 4325 (29.8) | Republic Aviation |
| 17,280 | 240 | 0.062 (1.57) | Magnesium | 4.00 (101.6) | 6500 (44.8) | Republic Aviation |
| 130,000 | | 0.062 (1.57) | Titanium | 2.36 (60.0) | 42,000 (289.6) | George C. Marshall Space Flight Center |

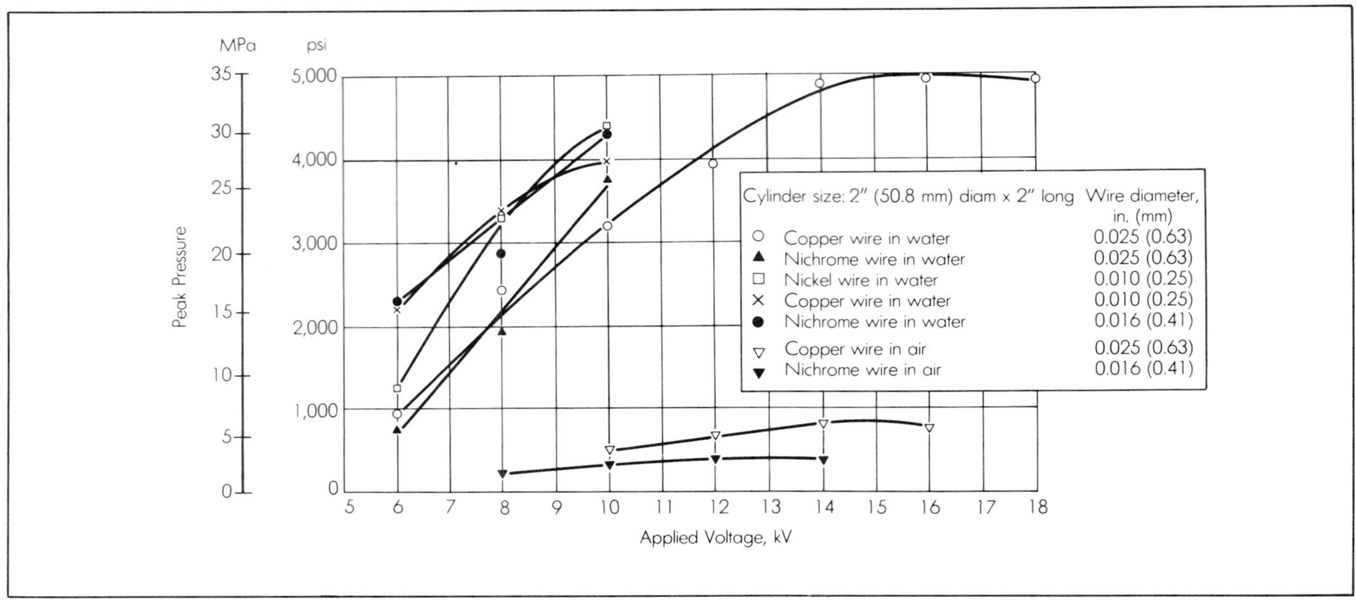


**Fig. 19-6 Peak pressures vs. discharge voltages of a 24 $\mu$ F capacitor bank.**[3]

eliminating the welding, but considerable savings are realized from the reduction of as much as 90% of the normally required manufacturing time.

**Materials formed.** Most materials formed by conventional processes are also formable by EHF. Some of the materials include aluminum alloys, stainless steels, heat-treatable stainless steel (17-7), nickel alloys, titanium, Inconel 718, and Hastelloy. Materials having critical impact velocities less than 100 fps (30 m/s) or low ductility are not practical for electrohydraulic forming.

## Applications

Electrohydraulic forming can be employed to form a variety of materials in a wide range of part sizes. It is well suited for the formation of hollow shapes. These shapes may be round and symmetrical, round and nonsymmetrical, or irregular in cross section. The EHF process provides the capability to pierce some parts while they are being formed. Forming pan shapes and deep recesses is also possible, but these shapes and recesses are usually best formed by conventional equipment. In the aerospace industries, EHF is employed to perform bulging, forming, beading, drawing, blanking, and piercing operations (see Fig. 19-8).

In general, this process should not be expected to produce any more part deformation than can be produced by other processes. However, strains can be produced more uniformly in certain parts. Electrohydraulic forming is selected when the part design requires an operation that is peculiar or not within the capabilities of conventional equipment, at least without some special tooling.

## Equipment

The equipment normally used in EHF consists of a high-voltage power supply (such as a rectifier), a charging resistor, a bank of capacitors to store the charge, switching circuits, a discharge mechanism or energy converter, and die clamping devices (see Fig. 19-9). The energy capacity of the equipment is normally rated in kilojoules (1 kJ = 738 ft-lb) and ranges from 6-150 kJ or more. Maximum energy can usually be attained within 10-25 seconds.

Tubular part sizes of 8-12" (200-300 mm) diam x 24-36" (600-915 mm) long and pan or recessed shapes up to 24" (600 mm) diam x 8" (200 mm) deep can be formed. Die clamping is performed hydraulically in most cases with clamping forces of 100-125 tons (890-1112 kN).

The electrode assembly shown in Fig. 19-10 is designed to accept replaceable electrode rods of variable length. The receptacles of the electrode rods are also replaceable since they are subject to deterioration from spark erosion. The face of the electrode assembly is also subject to deterioration, so a replaceable fiberglass disc is bonded to the electrode base. Polyurethanes are employed for the potting compounds because they are tough and have a high tear strength.

## Tooling Design Requirements

Die design technology for electrohydraulic forming is slightly different from that for conventional forming processes. Because EHF normally utilizes a liquid as a medium for transferring pressures to the workpiece, and because of the speed at which the operation occurs, there should be a provision to allow air to escape from behind the workpiece and a provision to prevent the liquid from entering the die cavity. The die requires no punch; otherwise, it would be similar to a die for forming a drawn shape by mechanical means. Dies for hollow-body or tubular parts are usually split to permit removal of the part after forming (see Fig. 19-11). The split configuration requires an accurate means of indexing, such as dowel pins, to prevent mismatching of the die halves. During forming operations, the halves must be firmly clamped together to prevent unwanted marking of the part at the split line. Internal finish of the die must be of a quality equal to or better than the required finish on the workpiece.

The EHF process seems to function best when the forming action is initiated at the bottom of the part and is successively worked up as additional shots are required. This procedure

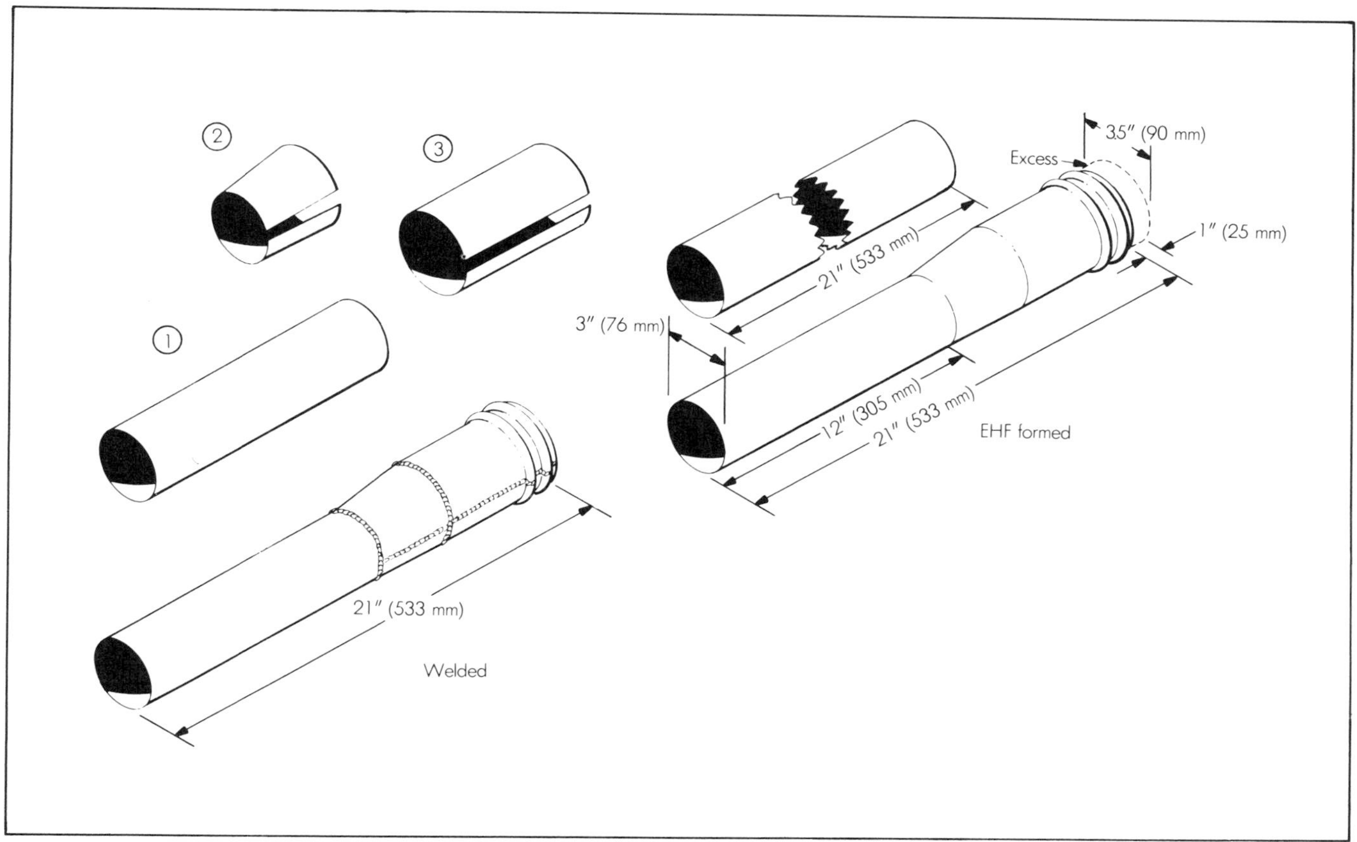


**Fig. 19-7 Comparison of conventionally formed and welded part with the electrohydraulically formed replacement.**

places the smallest inside diameter of the die, which is a slip fit for the tubular blank, at the bottom. This diameter must remain constant for a distance sufficient to accommodate a seal plug for the liquid. The seal plug can be made of rubber (approximately 60 durometer hardness) for small parts, but should be a metal plug with an "O" ring for parts 2" (50 mm) diam or more.

If the part shape is simple in design, air vent holes at the top of the die are adequate for air removal; if it is complex, a vacuum must be applied to the die cavity to prevent air entrapment. It is good practice to provide an excess length of at least one-half the tube diameter at the top of the part to ensure full forming and a good part definition. The excess area is also an ideal place to locate the air vent holes or the vacuum hole. The die shape and finish in the area of excess metal should be such that friction between the part and the die is held to a minimum. By reducing friction, the length of the part blank is allowed to draw inward, minimizing thinning that results from the expansion. The less resistance there is to a change of length, the less thinning there will be in the walls of the part.

## Die Materials

Die materials are selected based on the operations to be performed and the quantity of parts to be produced. Low-carbon steel is the most common material for dies used for forming only. Except when the forming is very extreme or when cutting action is required, dies from this material will suffice for forming several hundred parts. If cutting action is required, or if very long die life is desired, a heat-treated tool steel should be used, as is the case in the design of dies for conventional processes. Aluminum can be used as a die material if special care is taken not to overshoot when the part is being formed. Spark discharges of sufficient energy intensity can carry the part material against the face of the die with an impact capable of compressing the die surface.

Dies for electrohydraulic forming can also be fabricated from epoxy casting resins. Such dies are inexpensive to make and require little or no machining because they are molded to a pattern of the required shape. Physical requirements for dies made from plastics are basically the same as those stipulated for metal dies. Dies of this type can last for a dozen or more parts if the required forming is gentle and the dies are handled with care. Care must also be exercised during casting and curing to avoid porosity. Voids leave weak spots in the die that break down under the impulsive loading of the forming operation. If severe transitions are required in the part, the epoxy die may produce no more than two or three parts before the breakdown. Plastics can be used to provide an economical means to make feasibility studies of the process for a particular part configuration. This type of die can also be recommended whenever only two or three parts may be required for experimental or test purposes.

Dies cast from SAE 925 die metal have performed satisfactorily for short runs of aluminum parts. This material, used extensively for drop-hammer dies, has a melting point of 727° F (386° C) and a compressive strength of 153,000 psi (1055 MPa).

**Fig. 19-8 Typical applications of electrohydraulic forming.** (*General Dynamics/Fort Worth Division*)

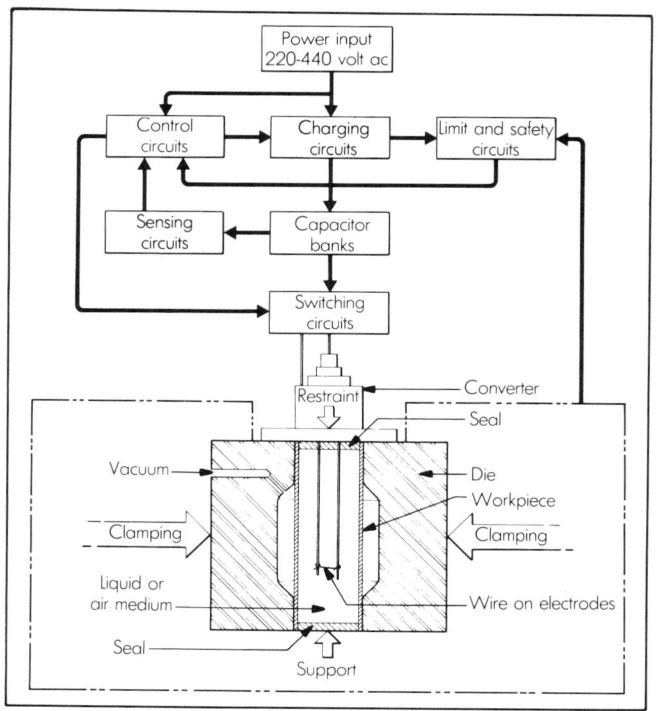


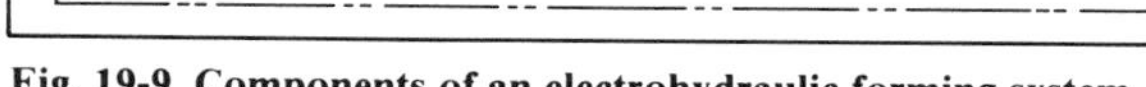
**Fig. 19-9 Components of an electrohydraulic forming system.**

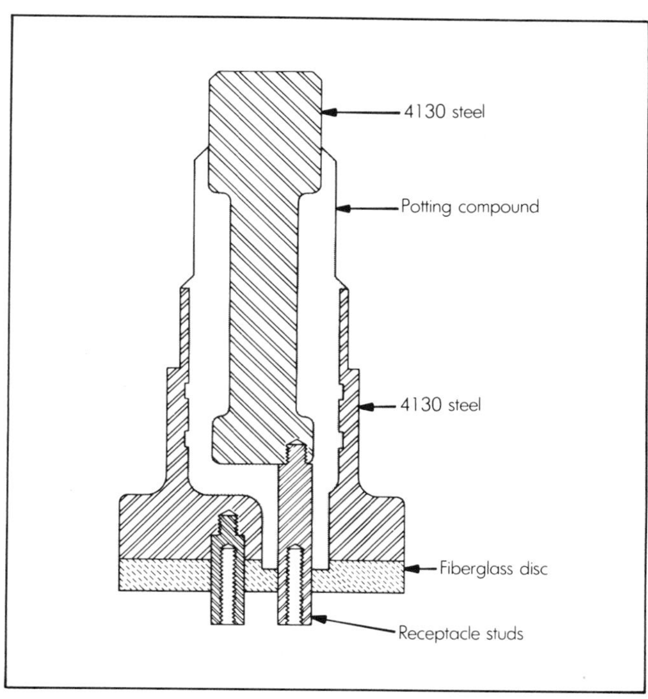


**Fig. 19-10 Cross section of a serviceable electrohydraulic electrode assembly.**

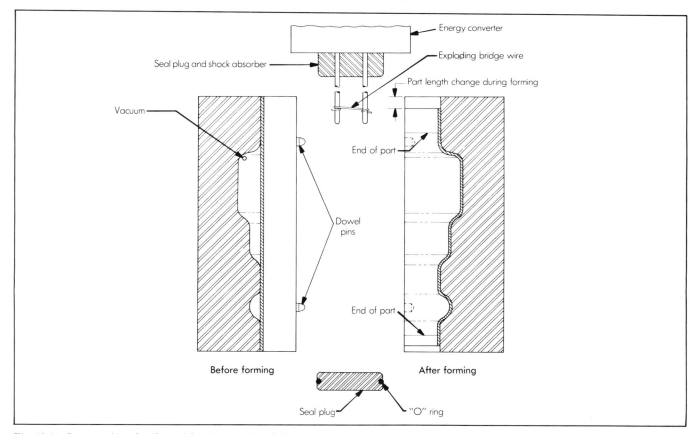

**Fig. 19-11 Cross section of a die used for electrohydraulic forming showing workpiece orientation before and after forming.**

# CHAPTER 19

# ELECTROMAGNETIC FORMING

For severe forming operations, cutting operations, or part quantities in excess of a few hundred, dies for electrohydraulic forming should be manufactured from heat-treated alloy steels. The SAE 4130 and 4340 steels are excellent for most applications. These materials have optimum heat-treating characteristics that permit them to be machined in their heat-treated condition. The SAE 4130 steel is usually heat treated to a strength level of 160,000-180,000 psi (1100-1240 MPa); SAE 4340 steel has an optimum strength level after heat treatment of around 220,000 psi (1500 MPa). Heat treated to 220,000 psi (1500 MPa), D6AC steel is also an excellent material for EHF dies. If a die is required to cut tough materials, special-purpose tool steels such as AISI Type S2 or AISI Type L6 should be used.

## ELECTROMAGNETIC FORMING

Electromagnetic forming, also referred to as magnetic pulse forming, was developed in the 1960s as a means for shaping, forming, and assembling metallic parts. It is currently the most widely used HERF process in industry. In this process, electrical energy is converted into mechanical energy by means of a magnetic field that exerts a force on a current-carrying conductor, the workpiece.

### Theory

When an electric current flows through a conductor, such as a length of wire, a magnetic field is created that fills the space closely surrounding the conductor. The magnetic field envelops the wire as long as the current flows. As inferred from the ability of a simple bar magnet to either attract or repel a second magnet, magnetic fields possess definite orientations, or directions of influence. When a magnetic field is produced by flow of an electric current within a conductor, the direction of the field is derived from the direction of the current flow.

If a loop of wire is moved through an existing magnetic field, an electric current is generated in the wire loop because of a phenomenon known as induction. The same effect (that is, the generation of an electric current in a loop of wire) occurs if, instead, the wire loop is held stationary while the source of the field is moved closely past the loop, causing proximate relative motion to occur again between the loop and the field. When the source of the magnetic field is an electromagnet, the field-producing current is usually called the primary current. The induced current, however, has variously been termed the secondary current, the eddy current, or the image current.

Finally, if in the preceding example, the magnetic field were produced electromagnetically (for example, by flow of an electric current through a helical coil of wire), the direction of the generated (or induced) electric current in the wire loop would be in the opposite direction of the field-producing current in the coil winding. Each of the two electric currents (primary and induced) establishes its own magnetic field. However, since the primary and induced currents flow in opposite directions, the magnetic fields established will be oriented in the opposite direction. The magnetic field associated with the helical coil interacts with the magnetic field associated with the wire loop to cause a repelling force (or pressure) against one side of the wire loop, as illustrated in Fig. 19-12.

A basic type of electromagnetic forming circuit is depicted in Fig. 19-13. The circuit employs a voltage source, a capacitor for energy storage, an appropriate switch, and a helically wound work coil that can apply compressive forces on a cylindrical workpiece. In actual practice, forming machines employ one or more banks of several parallel-connected capacitors, which can be charged by a high voltage (usually around 8 kV maximum). In operation, the capacitors are charged to a preselected voltage and then rapidly discharged into the work coil. The current flowing through the coil produces a magnetic field of high intensity between the coil and workpiece as shown in Fig. 19-13. The flux lines indicate the boundaries of areas containing the magnetic field; close spacing indicates a high magnetic field intensity; and wider spacing indicates a lower magnetic field intensity.

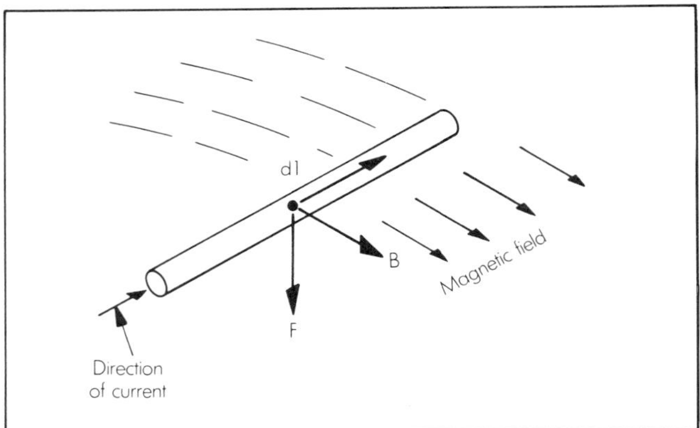

**Fig. 19-12 Force on a current-carrying conductor in a magnetic field.**

The type of circuit shown generally delivers a current that can be represented by a rapidly decaying oscillation, as illustrated in Fig. 19-14. The damping of the current reflects the loss of energy due to the mechanical work performed, as well as the resistive losses in both the coil discharge circuit and the workpiece itself. As the capacitors are discharged, the magnetic field builds and collapses with the same oscillation as the primary current; and secondary current, resulting from the motion of the field relative to the stationary workpiece, is induced in the workpiece material. The interaction between the magnetic field produced by the induced current and the magnetic field produced by the coil current create a high magnetic pressure between the coil and the tubular workpiece that tends to collapse the workpiece.

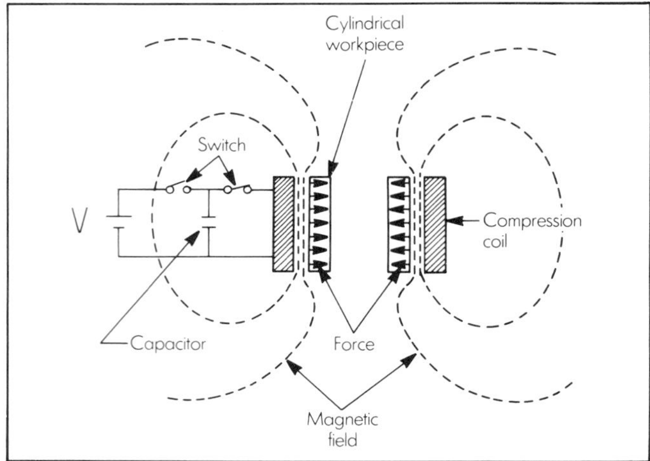

**Fig. 19-13 A magnetic field of high intensity between the coil and workpiece produces a magnetic pressure which deforms the workpiece.**

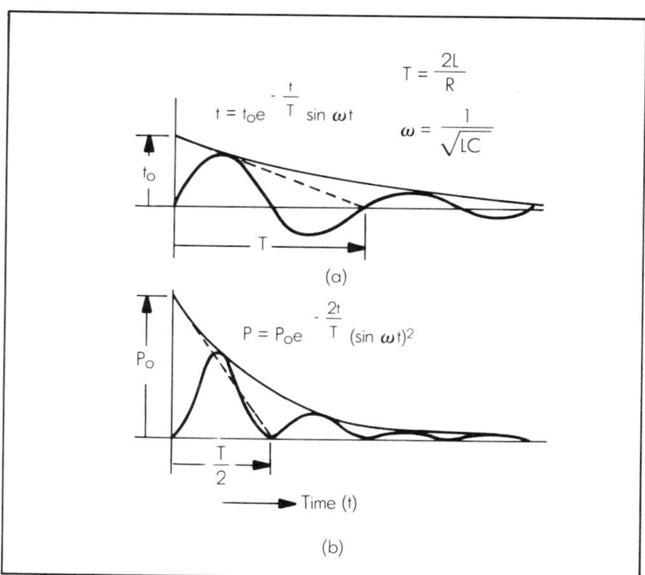


**Fig. 19-14 Typical damped current and pressure wave forms of a magnetic-pulse forming discharge.**

Corresponding to the oscillations of the primary (coil) current, the magnetic pressure is generated in a brief series of pulses, with succeeding pulses decreasing rapidly in strength. The rate of pulsation is known as the ringing frequency. The first pulse, which is much larger than the following ones, does most of the work. The duration of the magnetic pulse is very short (between 10 and 100 $\mu$ sec), so the magnitude of the pressure must be sufficient to exceed the yield stress of the workpiece and to accelerate the material to a very high velocity. In fact, it is because of the high kinetic energy imparted to the workpiece, after the brief pressure pulse has ended, that most of the forming takes place.

Throughout the entire pulse, some electromagnetic energy is lost due to resistance heating in both workpiece and coil-winding material. The amount of deformation that is produced depends mainly upon the velocity acquired by the workpiece material. Likewise, the velocity imparted is a function of the magnitude and duration of the magnetic pulse. These characteristics of the pulse are, in turn, dependent on several factors, which include basic circuit parameters as well as properties of the workpiece and coil-winding materials.

Under conventional circumstances, a long pressure pulse would probably be considered desirable, since it would lengthen the period of acceleration and increase the velocity of the material. In electromagnetic forming, however, the magnetic field of the coil in time permeates the workpiece material, despite the opposing field of the induced current; also, as more of the coil field penetrates beyond the workpiece, the net force dwindles to zero. The length of the pulse, therefore, should be limited so that, ideally, it coincides with the time required for the field to penetrate no further than a shallow layer at the surface of the workpiece. The depth of this layer is the same as the skin depth (described subsequently).

The duration of the pulse is established by the ringing frequency of the current discharge; and since the ringing frequency is inversely proportional to the square root of the product of the circuit capacitance and the circuit inductance, the numerical value of this product should preferably be limited to some maximum value. Hence, the practice of electromagnetic forming requires that some consideration be given to the effects that coil and workpiece properties may have upon one another (mutual induction, for example) and upon other circuit factors that are basically machine constants.

The amount of magnetic pressure that is required for a specific application is a function of the geometry of the workpiece, the configuration of the die, and the strength of the workpiece material. Because forming depends on accelerating the material to a high velocity, it is also a function of the specific gravity of the workpiece material.

The magnitude of the magnetic pressure is proportional to the square of the field intensity (see Fig. 19-15). The field intensity, however, depends on such factors as the number of capacitors being used and the sum of their capacitance, the voltage to which the capacitors are charged, the basic machine circuit impedances, the resistivity of the coil-winding material, the resistivity of the workpiece material, the ringing frequency of the discharge circuit, and the volume of the effective gap between the forming coil and the workpiece. These factors, in

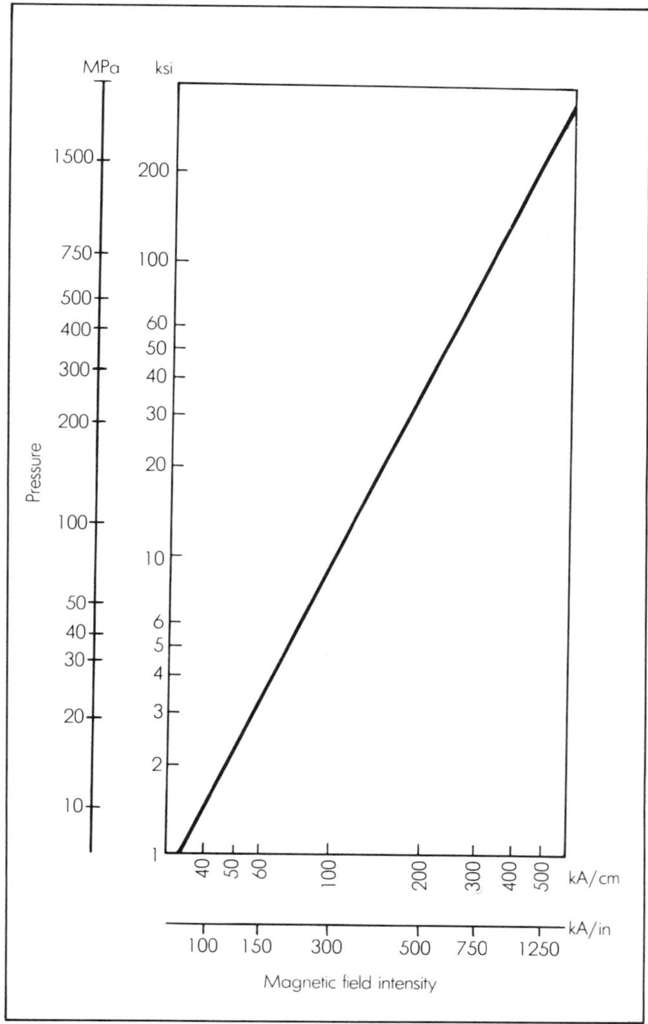


**Fig. 19-15 Relationship of magnetic field intensity to pressure produced.**

turn, establish the amount of energy needed to meet a certain forming pressure requirement, and they effectively limit the amount of energy that is available.

Essential to an understanding of the electromagnetic forming process is an awareness of how these factors may interrelate and thus affect the amount of pressure that can be developed from a set measure of stored energy. For example, pressures that are adequate for metalforming applications require magnetic fields of high intensity, while very high currents (in coil and workpiece) are needed to produce the high intensity fields. A fundamental requirement, therefore, is that coil-winding and workpiece materials be selected that have relatively low resistivity.

At frequencies that typify the discharge of current in electromagnetic forming applications, the current tends to flow through a narrow surface layer, rather than be evenly distributed throughout the cross section of a thick conductor. This characteristic is known as the skin effect, and the thickness of the layer of current flow is called the skin depth. In general, it is desirable for the skin depth to be minimized. This is true especially in workpieces of thin cross section, wherein a theoretical skin depth that is less than the material gage should be maintained. Because skin depth is proportional to the square root of the material's resistivity and inversely proportional to the square root of the ringing frequency, low resistivity and high frequency are desirable characteristics. The relationship between resistivity and skin depth is shown in Fig. 19-16.

To facilitate the loading and unloading of parts, some clearance must be provided between workpiece and coil. From Fig. 19-13, however, it should be apparent that for a given energy input, the wider the gap between coil and workpiece, the lesser will be the field intensity. It follows that in order to maximize the pressure which can be developed from the same energy input, the effective gap should be kept as small as possible. The total effective gap, however, includes more than just the air space between coil and part. For the process to work at all, the coil winding must be kept well insulated from the workpiece; and it is usually most practical to apply the required dielectric material as a permanent covering to the coil winding.

In addition to the thicknesses of the air space and the dielectric material, the total effective gap includes the sum of the skin depths for the coil winding and the workpiece. Besides insulation materials that provide the maximum dielectric strength per unit thickness and work coils that are fabricated to fit the workpieces with minimum practical clearance, low resistivity and high ringing frequency are preferred characteristics.

For a given application, the pressure required to obtain static yield can be estimated using standard analytical methods. For example, in swaging or compression-forming applications, the pressure requirement based on hoop strength can be compared with the beam or cantilever strength, depending on the shape being formed. However, due to such factors as inertia effects, the increase in yield strength that can occur at high strain rates, and the complexity of the shape being formed, the magnetic pressure actually needed will, in general, be three to eight times the pressure required to exceed the static yield strength of the material. Various approaches to estimating the necessary amount of energy have been devised. These generally involve using instruments to measure the field intensity and the ringing frequency for a particular setup. Once experience with the process has been obtained, however, simple trial-and-error techniques are usually found to suffice.

### Advantages and Limitations

Electromagnetic forming works well with materials that are good conductors, such as copper, aluminum, brass, or low-carbon steel. A maximum resistivity of 15 microhm-cm is generally recommended for workpiece materials. Table 19-5 lists the values of electrical resistivity for a number of materials.

Electromagnetic forming provides increased ductility from aluminum alloys. Many parts that would normally require several forming steps with interstage annealing can be formed electromagnetically in a single operation. When high percentages of stretching are required, however, the edges of part blanks must be carefully smoothed to avoid tearing.

For materials having higher resistivity, such as stainless steel, a special technique can be employed to produce limited amounts of deformation. The technique uses an intermediate piece of conductive material, called a driver, that is placed between the work coil and the part blank. As the driver deforms, it transfers the pressure to the high-resistivity workpiece material. Because of the added costs of fabricating the driver pieces (which can only be used once) and of separating the driver from the workpiece after the forming operation, the practicality of using this technique for a given application should be carefully considered.

The configuration of the workpiece must be such that the area to be formed constitutes a closed loop, as in the case of rings, tubes, circular areas on flat workpieces, etc., thus permitting the induced currents to flow closely parallel to the coil currents. Small holes in the area to be formed are of little consequence, but slits interrupting the paths of the induced currents have a detrimental effect. Because the magnetic field can pass through nonconductive materials, however, it is possible to form through nonmetallic coatings or liners.

The electromagnetic pulses can be precisely controlled in both magnitude and timing. Controlling the magnitude of the pulses affords excellent shape repeatability and the maintenance of close tolerances. Because the timing of the magnetic pulse can be controlled with microsecond accuracy, machines can be designed for repetition rates of hundreds of operations per minute. Though limited in theory only by the charge time of the capacitors, the repetition rate is in fact limited either by the speed with which parts can be loaded and unloaded or by the cooling time required for electrical components and coils between cycles. With manual loading, operations at rates of 200-600 parts per hour are maximum; with automated handling, some operations at rates of thousands of parts per hour are feasible. In general, assembly operations (via magnetic swaging) are more easily performed at high cycle rates than are forming operations. Even when forming operations are not automated, cycle times are normally faster than for other HERF methods.

The work coils used in electromagnetic forming can require a substantial investment when parts are formed in a wide variety of shapes and sizes. This cost can be reduced by adapting larger compression coils to smaller parts with field shapers. Also, the strength of the work coil is generally the limiting factor in the amount of forming pressure produced by the electromagnetic forming machine. Currently, compression coils and expansion coils designed for moderately high repetition rates are capable of withstanding pressures up to 60,000 psi (400 MPa) and 15,000 psi (100 MPa) respectively.

Form dies for electromagnetic forming are relatively inexpensive. Almost without exception, most applications require just a single die or mandrel. Because magnetic pressure

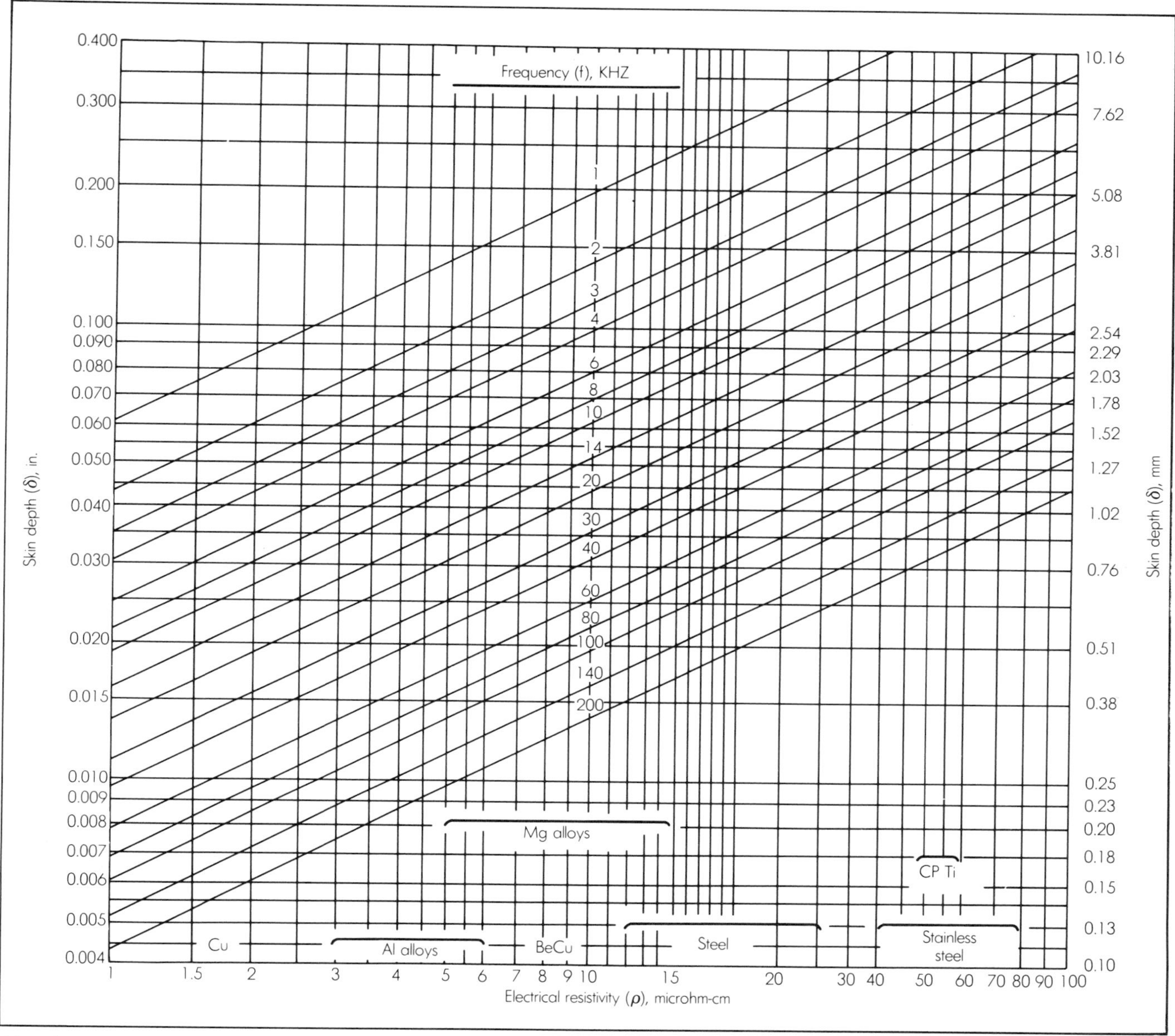


**Fig. 19-16 Relationship of skin depth to electrical resistivity at various ringing frequencies.**

takes the place of a punch, matched punch and die sets are hardly ever used. (Contrary examples exist in assembly swaging, in which neither die nor mandrel is needed, and in certain applications in which a flat coil, for example, has been used to propel a punch-shaped tool to "coin" tight contour radii in preforms.) Opportunities for unwanted tool marks are usually limited to one surface of the workpiece only. However, since the workpiece normally strikes the die surface with substantial impact, tooling flaws can easily be transferred.

A similar problem can occur when split form dies must be used to facilitate removal of the formed parts. Unless the die halves match closely at the parting line, impact pressures can reproduce the mismatch along the sides of the part. Also, if the die is metal, induced currents in the die can create electrical arcing between die halves. The probability of burn marks developing on the parts and of erosion of the die parting line increases with the presence of mismatch. For certain applications, the electrical arcing can be eliminated using dies made from nonconductive and impact-resistant plastics.

One claim made for electromagnetic forming is potentially misleading. It has been implied that since no friction exists between the magnetic pressure and the workpiece, lubricants are not required. This is true in so far as it applies to the actual forming mechanism. However, broad experience has established that a dry-film lubricant, judiciously applied to the forming surfaces of solid mandrels or to the inside of hollow, cylindrically shaped form dies (which do not split in two for part removal), may be required to separate the workpiece from the tool.

# ELECTROMAGNETIC FORMING

**TABLE 19-5**
**Electrical Resistivity of Common Materials ($\rho$), microhm-cm**

| Materials | $\rho$ | Materials | $\rho$ |
|---|---|---|---|
| Aluminum | | Magnesium | |
| 1100-0 | 2.9 | AZ80A | 14.5 |
| 2024-0 | 3.5 | Molybdenum | 5.2 |
| 2024-T3 | 5.8 | Platinum | 10.7 |
| 2024-T6 | 4.5 | Silver | 1.6 |
| 2219-T37 | 6.2 | Steels | |
| 2219-T62 | 5.7 | 10XX | 12 |
| 3003-0 | 3.4 | 11XX | 14.3 |
| 3003-H18 | 4.3 | 13XX | 17 |
| 5052-ALL | 4.9 | 23XX | 28.4 |
| 6061-0 | 3.8 | 40XX | 19 |
| 6061-T4 | 4.3 | 41XX | 22.3 |
| 6061-T6 | 4.3 | 43XX | 30 |
| 7075-T6 | 5.7 | 48XX | 30 |
| 7178-T6 | 5.6 | 51XX | 21 |
| Beryllium | 5.0 | 61XX | 21 |
| Beryllium-Cu, Berylco 25 | 7.9 | Stainless steels | |
| Brass | | Austenitic | 69-79 |
| 70%, annealed | 6.2 | Ferritic | 60-67 |
| 80%, annealed | 5.4 | Martensitic | 40-72 |
| leaded | 6.6 | Tantalum | 12.4 |
| red, 85%, annealed | 4.7 | Thorium | 18 |
| yellow, annealed | 6.4 | Tin | 11.6 |
| Bronze, 90%, annealed | 3.9 | Tin-lead-antimony alloys | 25.6-28.7 |
| Columbium | 14.2 | Titanium | |
| Copper | | Commercially pure | 48-57 |
| annealed | 1.72 | 5Al-2.5Sn | 157 |
| hard | 1.77 | 6Al-4V | 172 |
| Gold | 2.35 | 8Al-1Mo-1V | 199 |
| Hafnium | 35 | Tungsten | 5.5 |
| Lead | 22 | Vanadium | 25 |
| Magnesium | | Wrought iron | 12 |
| M1A | 5 | Zinc | 6.1 |
| AZ31B | 9.2 | Zirconium and alloys | 40-74 |
| AZ61A | 12.5 | | |

## Applications

Within the size, gage, and resistivity limitations of the material, the electromagnetic forming process is capable of an unusually wide variety of forming and assembly operations. As a forming method, it has proven exceptionally useful in the fabrication of hollow, noncircular, or asymmetrical shapes from tubing stock, for which conventional processes such as spin forming could not be employed. Using this method, diverse configurations that would otherwise require forming separate details and then welding for assembly can be formed in one piece. The method can also be used on heated workpieces, but thermal insulation must be provided to protect the coil.

The principal compression applications involve swaging to produce tensile, compression, and torque joints or sealed pressure joints; swaging to apply compression bands or shrink rings for fastening components together; and sizing of tubing on mandrels to improve roundness or to alter diameter. Expansion coils are used in applications that require tubing to be formed. Examples of shapes that can be formed in tubing using expansion coils include circumferential bulges (spherical and other shapes), side-wall bulges, straight-tapered transitions, noncircular cross sections, end expansions with angular offsets, and end flanges at angles ranging from 45-90° to the tube centerline. Flat coils are primarily used on flat sheet to produce stretch (internal) and shrink (external) flanges on ring and disc-shaped workpieces; shallow hat, cup, or dome shapes having generous radii; and many dimple-type shapes. Semi-portable flat coils have been used to restore flatness or contour to locally distorted areas of panels and other large-scale parts.

Electromagnetic forming has also been used to perform piercing; shearing; riveting; and via the same operating principles, pulsed magnetic welding. Additional information on this last process may be found in Volume IV, *Quality Control and Assembly,* in this Handbook series.

To determine whether a particular application can be performed using electromagnetic forming techniques, the ratio of the outside diameter of the material to be formed to its wall thickness can serve as a practical guideline. For copper and aluminum, this ratio should be approximately 20:1; for brass, 30:1; and for low-carbon steel, 40:1. However, the primary consideration is the yield strength of the material.

## Application Examples

Typical examples of how the electromagnetic process is employed in producing individual parts and an assembly of parts include forming a duct in a die, joining tubular members, assembling motors, and attaching rubber parts to metal subassemblies.

**Forming.** Most forming operations shape a piece by propelling it against a die. Several complex operations can sometimes be performed simultaneously with simple tooling. Figure 19-17 shows a duct being formed with two lateral holes and the ends rolled over, all in a single operation.

**Joining tubular members.** Tubular members can be joined to end fittings by magnetic swaging. In the case of parts designed to undergo tension or compression loading, such as aircraft control rods, the end pieces are grooved and the surrounding tube is swaged into these grooves. By properly designing the groove spacing and size, joints can be produced that equal or exceed the strength of the riveted design. Joints that are subject to torque loading are produced by magnetically swaging the tubular member over toothlike protrusions. Metal-to-metal seals have also been obtained by carefully selecting the proper combination of materials to be used for the parts so that the outer part remains in tension and the inner part in compression after forming and elastic recovery. However, metal-to-metal seals have not been produced in commercial applications.

**Assembly of motors.** The assembly of small appliance motors by electromagnetic forming makes it possible to retain precisely the relative positions of several parts in an assembly when they are positioned in a fixture and subsequently joined by magnetic assembly.

Figure 19-18 shows a schematic cross section of a motor assembled by swaging a clamping ring around the assembled parts. The swaging pressure forces the ring into intimate contact with the arms of the end bells, leaving the ring in a stressed condition similar to a shrink fit and retaining the concentricity of the assembly.

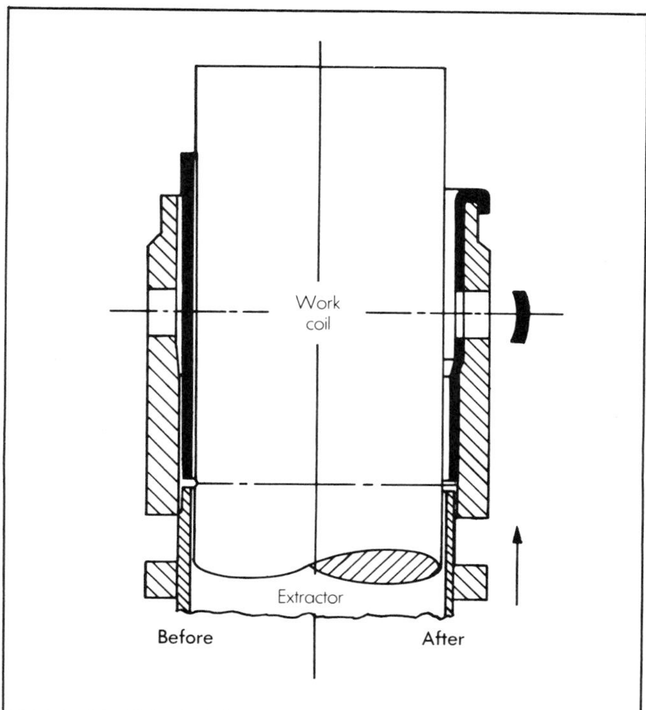


**Fig. 19-17 Setup used to form tubular aluminum part with two punched holes and a rolled end.**

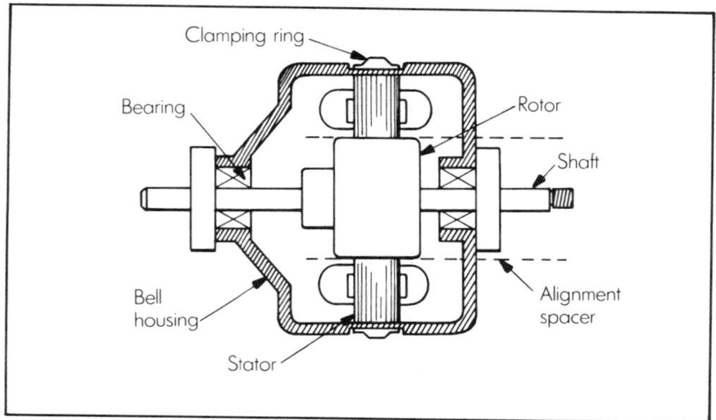


**Fig. 19-18 Cross section of motor showing how clamping ring may be magnetically installed without loss of stator-rotor concentricity.**

**Attachment of rubber parts.** The assembly of metal and rubber parts makes use of the high velocity attained by the workpiece. Figure 19-19 shows schematically how a ring can be swaged onto a steel tube to ensure a solid axial attachment of the rubber boot. The high velocity of the movement of the outer ring does not permit the rubber sufficient time to escape laterally and thereby prevents the ring from cutting through the rubber. Instead, the force is transmitted to the underlying steel tube, which is indented.

The attachment of rubber boots, as used in automotive ball joints, is a common magnetic-forming application. It has the advantage of a reliable connection that is tamperproof and economical.

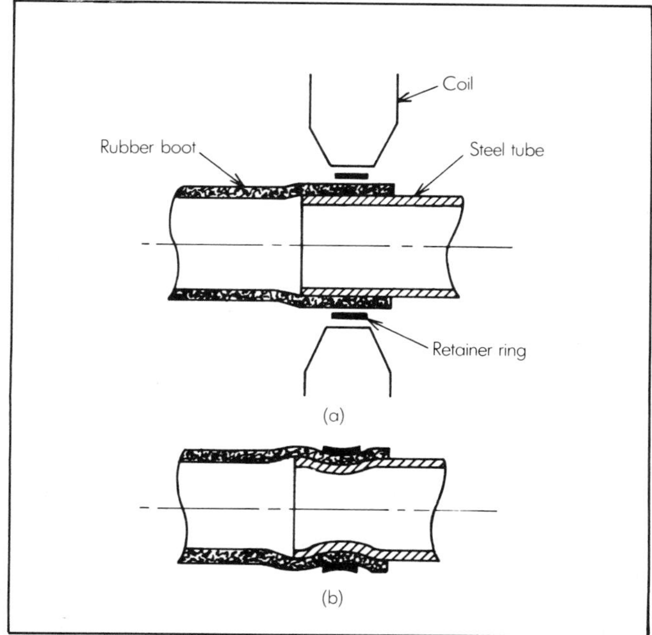


**Fig. 19-19 Cross-sectional view showing rubber boot (a) before and (b) after ring is swaged onto steel tube.**

# ELECTROMAGNETIC FORMING

## Equipment

The main components in an electromagnetic forming machine are the power supply, energy storage capacitors, control circuitry, switching devices for rapidly discharging the capacitors, transmission lines and busses, and work coils. The machines are typically rated according to their energy storage capacity; the common unit of energy capacity is the kilojoule (1 kJ = 738 ft-lb). Machines have been made commercially available in sizes ranging from 2 to over 100 kJ. One manufacturer supplies modules of 12 kJ capacity that can be stacked to provide machines of increased capacity.

The maximum voltage that can be used is generally limited by the dielectric strength of the insulators. Although insulators are generally constructed to withstand 10 kV, operating voltages are normally held to a maximum of around 8 kV to provide extended service life.

The maximum safe current is usually established by the limitations of the switching devices, which are typically ignitron tubes. Because the discharge current is a function of the frequency, as well as the voltage, machines may have a critical ringing frequency above which the operating voltage level must be prudently selected to avoid exceeding the current rating of the ignitrons. The discharge current in electromagnetic forming is usually between 100 and 400 kA.

Typically, control circuits are provided that permit a continuously variable selection of the operating voltage level. If the machine employs more than one bank of capacitors, controls are generally provided to facilitate switching-in of the banks, either singly or in multiples, thereby allowing the working capacitance of the system to be varied in steps.

To help constrain field penetration to the workpiece material, by minimizing the length of the magnetic pulse, the power transmission lines should have low inductance. This also helps to maximize delivery of discharge energy to the work coil.

The purpose of the work coil is to generate a high-intensity magnetic field at the surface of the workpiece. Hence, for production work, the coil should also be capable of withstanding the pressure developed by the opposed magnetic fields. Coils meant for use at high cycle rates must not only be durable, but should be designed with passages for water cooling. Production coils should have integral coverings of high dielectric strength, and the coil windings should possess high tensile strength and low electrical resistivity. When one-of-a-kind parts, or parts in very limited numbers, are required, savings in tooling costs can often be realized by simply hand-winding heavy electrical wire or light cable around a suitable core of nonconductive material (for example, phenolic-impregnated fiberglass) to make an expendable coil.

Work coils can be designed to be mounted directly on the machine or positioned in a separate location. Depending on the application, coils can be constructed either with a single winding of heavy cross section or with multiple-turn windings. In any case, it is important that work coils be designed to provide clearance with the workpiece. Generally, a radial clearance of 0.025-0.030″ (0.64-0.76 mm) is adequate to accommodate standard out-of-round conditions in tubing used as part blanks, without causing an excessive loss in field intensity. Work coils can usually be purchased through the manufacturers of electromagnetic forming machines. Three types of coils most commonly used in electromagnetic forming are compression, expansion, and flat forming coils.

**Compression coils.** Compression coils enclose a portion of the workpiece as shown in Fig. 19-20, *a*, and are used to collapse the workpiece inwards in a radial direction. They may have either a helical or wafer-type construction and can be designed as specific shapes or as general-purpose coils for use with field shapers.

Compression coils, with or without field shapers, are used to produce structural joints, hermetic joints and seals, metal-to-ceramic seals, and swaged connections and to uniformly reduce the cross sections of tubular shapes. The most common applications range in size from less than 1/8″ (3 mm) to 24″ (610 mm) diam.

**Expansion coils.** Expansion coils are inserted within tubular workpieces as shown in Fig. 19-20, *b*, and are used to expand the workpiece outwards in a radial direction. Like compression coils, they may be built either with single or multiturn, helical windings, as required by the application. Field shapers have, on occasion, been used to slightly extend the effective diameter of expansion coils, usually while shortening the formed length.

Expansion coils are used primarily to bulge, shape, and flange tubular parts. Durable coils have been built in sizes suitable for forming tubing ranging in diameter from 1.5-72″ (38-1820 mm) OD and having lengths up to 24″ (610 m).

**Flat coils.** Flat coils (or pancake coils, as they are sometimes called) have a spiral-shaped winding and can be placed either above or below a flat workpiece (see Fig. 19-20, *c*). In larger sizes, they have been made with two parallel spiral windings to provide greater strength. As with compression and expansion coils, the winding is usually made of beryllium copper. Typically, flat coils have a "dead" area in their center in which no magnetic pressure is developed. The size of this area depends on the individual coil's design.

Flat coils are generally used in conjunction with a die to form, coin, blank, or dimple the workpiece. Flat coils have also been used to correct unwanted local deformations in very large parts. Although larger coils have been constructed, flat coils are usually built in sizes to about 8″ (200 mm) diam.

## Tooling

Field shapers and forming dies are also used in conjunction with the work coils to achieve a variety of forming applications.

**Field shapers.** Field shapers are single-turn coils, usually made from beryllium copper or hardened aluminum, that are inserted between the work coil and the workpiece (see Fig. 19-21). They receive energy from the work coil and transfer it to the workpiece by induction. However, field shapers must be electrically insulated from both the work coil and the workpiece.

Field shapers are used to adapt large-diameter compression coils to smaller diameter workpieces and, within limitation, can be built to concentrate the pressure to a specific location on the workpiece. In some instances, field shapers can be designed to adapt expansion coils to larger workpieces.

**Forming dies.** Although parts of adequate shape can sometimes be free-formed by simply varying the amount of voltage to the capacitors until the proper level has been determined, parts for which a specific contour is desired are usually formed using external form dies or internal mandrels. When production requires total quantities of more than one or two dozen parts, the high impact forces that normally occur between part blank and die will usually necessitate that the die be made of steel, preferably heat-treat hardenable. The die or mandrel should be polished if surface finish is important. When low impact pressures are expected to occur or production

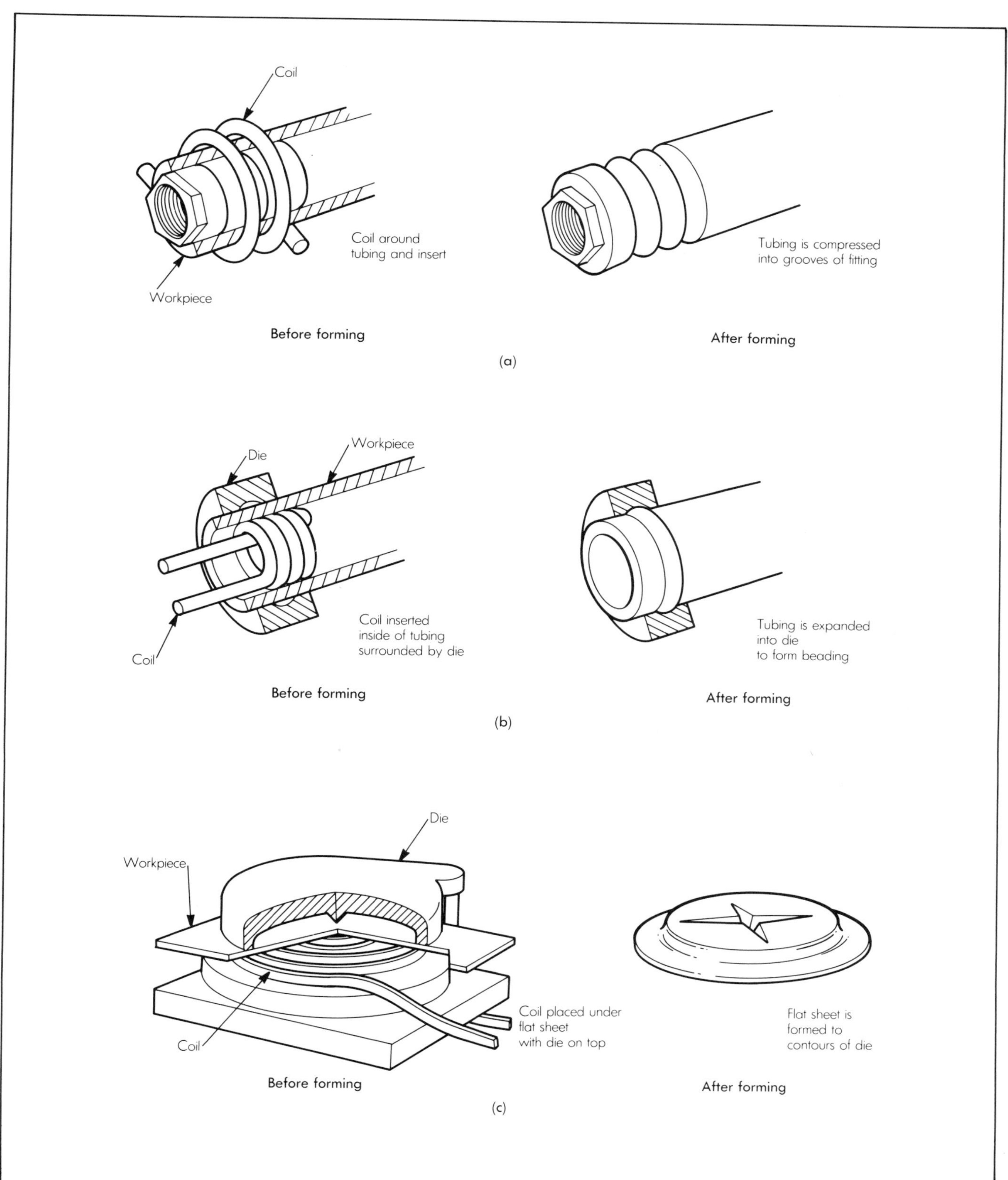


**Fig. 19-20 Three basic electromagnetic forming coils: (a) compression coil, (b) expansion coil, and (c) flat coil.**

# ELECTROMAGNETIC FORMING

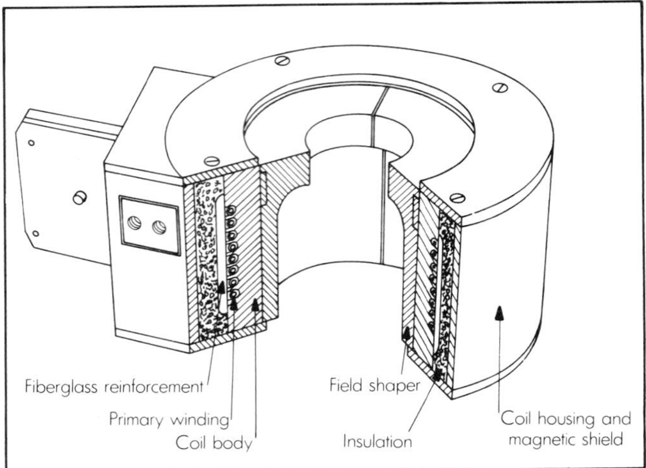


**Fig. 19-21 Cutaway section of a compression coil with a removable field shaper in place.**

quantities are limited, aluminum or brass can sometimes be used. To avoid the high costs of machining complex contours, impact-resistant, castable plastics have been successfully used as liners in dies made for bulging operations.

In general, dies for expansion forming do not require allowances for elastic recovery (springback) of the workpiece material. When parts are formed to a net length, the dies for forming bulges and end flanges must allow room for using an over-length part blank, which subsequently either foreshortens (in expanding operations) or draws out slightly from the die (in flanging operations). Once the correct length for the part blank has been determined experimentally, a ring-shaped shim can be made that, when used in conjunction with a machined shoulder in the die, precisely locates the workpieces for net-length forming. In other respects, dies for expansion forming should be designed to facilitate easy insertion and removal of the workpiece. Springback is generally a more important consideration in compression-forming and swaging operations.

## Forming Techniques

In forming operations, the initial gap between the workpiece and the die surface is called the fly distance. The fly distance must be sufficient to permit the material to deform plastically. From an energy standpoint, the ideal pressure pulse would have just enough magnitude to accelerate the part material to some maximum velocity and then let the part coast to a zero velocity by the time it covered the full fly distance. In many applications, however, the required deformation is not constant for the entire part, so the fly distance varies along its surface. A forming procedure must then be developed, which avoids using either too much or too little pressure in local areas.

For example, if the pressure pulse is too small, the material stops forming before it reaches the die surface. Conversely, if the pressure pulse gives the material too great a velocity, it may actually rebound from the die surface. The difficulty is in deciding whether to use either just enough energy to balance the pressure between too much and too little, if this produces a part within tolerance, or to purposely use too little energy, then systematically produce the required deformation in a series of steps, using multiple forming "hits."

In applications requiring moderately abrupt changes in part contour, a pressure pulse that imparts high kinetic energy may be desirable, since very high forming pressures can be developed when the material is rapidly decelerated on impact with the die. Sharp, reversing contours are not generally feasible using electromagnetic methods.

In certain enclosed dies or in dies having large cavities, air can become entrapped between the part blank and the die as a result of the high forming speed. When this happens, compression of the air can slow the workpiece, causing it to form incompletely. In some cases, small vent holes in the die may be adequate to allow the air to escape. Such holes, however, must be the proper size and in the proper location so that they do not produce objectionable marks on the workpiece. The process can be used to expand tubes in gradual tapers (for example, "reducers" from one diameter to another); however, when the total amount of expanded area is substantial, forming must take place in a series of steps, moving axially along the length of the workpiece for each successive forming "hit." This procedure prevents air from being trapped between the part blank and die, but labor costs should be compared with those for conventional methods. A possible alternative would be to design the tooling with vacuum fittings and seals, as required in explosive and electrohydraulic forming tools.

## Safety

Because extremely high voltages and currents are employed in electromagnetic forming, it is important that production and maintenance personnel become familiarized with proper operational and safety procedures. The sudden release of high levels of electrical energy can create hazards that range from thoroughly unnerving to potentially lethal in their effects.

Adequate insulation must be provided and maintained between points of substantially different potential, such as between coil and workpiece. Field shaper and coil insulations should be visually examined at least daily. A short between coil and workpiece takes the form of an intense arc, and energy is released in an explosive burst that can impel small pieces of coil or workpiece material to high velocities and create very loud sound levels. Coils, coil clamps, field shapers, and form dies must also be inspected and kept clean and free of metallic dust and chips.

All forming coils fail, sooner for expendable coils or later for durable coils. The first symptom of trouble in water-cooled coils is usually a reduced flow of the coolant. Decreasing flow, though seemingly innocuous, should be investigated immediately; it may signal an impending failure of the coil. The second stage of coil breakdown can be a sudden parting of the coil winding, again with explosive force. Of course, coils can be made to fail prematurely (and catastrophically) if an excessive amount of energy is applied. Because there is a lack of predictability in coil breakdowns, a safety shield should be used between personnel and the work coil. The shield also provides extra protection against the effects of electrical shorts, which can result from insulation failure in the coil or field shaper, or from arcs caused by metal chips.

Another reason for using a safety shield around the work setup occurs when the workpiece does not receive a symmetrically applied pressure. This can happen, for example, when a tubular workpiece does not cover the entire working length of an expansion coil winding. A strong axial thrust against the workpiece occurs, which may expel the workpiece from the die at high velocity.

In expansion forming operations in which greater amounts of deformation take place, the high velocity of the part causes compression of the air between the part and the die surface and forms acoustic shock waves as the air tries to escape. When parts are manually loaded, so that the cycle rate is not very fast and discharges occur at irregular intervals, it is recommended that an audible warning signal be provided just prior to each forming "hit." This helps to prevent nearby personnel from being severely startled by the shock noise. Hearing protection may also be required for the operator and others close by, or acoustical shielding can be provided around the workstation.

Although the potential dangers may seem obvious, all personnel should be strongly warned against touching or holding a coil, field shaper, driver piece, die, or workpiece during the forming operation.

## HIGH-VELOCITY FORGING

In high-velocity forging, the energy stored in a high-pressure gas or the energy from a burning fuel-oxydizer mixture is used to accelerate a ram to high velocity for accomplishing the forging. The ram velocities attained in this process are about three to four times those of conventional drop hammers. The concept of using compressed gases as an energy source to drive machines was applied in the late 1940s in the testing of materials, and a shock loading device was developed in 1955. The concept of using a burning fuel-oxydizer to develop the high-pressure gas is basically derived from the principles of an internal combustion engine.

### Advantages and Limitations

High-velocity forging results in both process advantages and equipment advantages.

**Process advantages.** High-velocity forging is capable of forming groups of components that are difficult, if not impossible, to form with conventional methods. Because parts can be made closer to finished dimension, savings in raw material and subsequent machining can be substantial. The rapid deformation and resulting reduced component cooling improves the forgeability and grain structure of some materials. However, for some magnesium and nickel alloys, serious rupturing can occur when large billet reductions are made.

High-velocity forging has not measured up to its original expectations. Originally, it was thought that this process would be a universal solution to the problems facing the forging industry. However, it is only one among several processes that can be profitable providing they can be properly matched to the components and materials to be formed.

**Equipment advantages.** High-velocity forging machines are much smaller in size and lighter in weight than conventional forging equipment capable of performing the same operation, and usually they do not require any special foundations. These advantages result in reduced initial capital requirements and lower installation costs. Although ram velocities are three to four times faster than conventional machines, the overall cycle time is usually much slower. The slow cycle time reduces die life due to longer contact (dwell time) with the workpiece. Die design is usually more complex and costly than the die design needed for conventional methods.

### Applications

High-velocity forging is being employed for hot forging; cold and warm forming; powder compaction/forging; and, to a limited extent, blanking and piercing. Cropping billets to size has also been performed. In hot forging, high-velocity forging can be applied to a wide variety of metals to obtain more complex shapes with thinner cross sections, closer tolerances, and better surface finish than are possible with some of the more conventional forming methods. For additional information on hot forging, refer to Chapter 15, "Hot Forging"; for additional warm and cold forming information, refer to Chapter 13, "Drawing, Extruding and Upsetting," in this volume.

The shapes usually selected to be formed by high-velocity forging are symmetrical and are characterized by webs and outside ribs measuring as thin as 1/8" (3 mm). Thin, radial fins can also be forged, providing the fins are spaced far enough apart to prevent excessive temperature rises in the dies. Grossly asymmetrical shapes are usually not formed by high-velocity forging due to complexity in die design. Table 19-6 contains a list of some parts that are suitable for high-velocity forging and some that are unsuitable.

### Machines

The machines used in high-velocity forging are essentially high-speed hammers which fall into the category of work-restricted machines. For additional information on hammers and work-restricted machines, refer to Chapter 15, "Hot Forging," in this volume.

High-velocity forging hammers can be divided into two different groups based on their method of actuation; that is, the energy source from which the blow is derived, and the method employed to separate the dies after the forming stroke and to prepare the machine for the next blow. As was stated previously, the energy is developed either from a compressed gas or from the combustion of a mixture of hydrocarbon fuel and air.

**Pneumatic-hydraulic hammers.** Two different designs of pneumatic-hydraulic hammers are currently being employed. Both hammers use a pressurized gas (either nitrogen or air) to produce the energy to deform the workpiece and also use hydraulic cylinders to return the ram to its initial position.

The first design (see Fig. 19-22) contains a drive unit at the top of the inner frame, which is supported by air springs. The driving chamber, located in the drive unit, contains the pressurized gas that acts upon the ram. Hydraulic jacks in the frame prevent the ram from descending until the hammer is ready to be activated. When the hammer is activated, the hydraulic rams descend and the blow is initiated by a high-pressure gas pulse which breaks a seal (pneumatic latch). The broken seal permits the pressurized gas contained in the drive

**TABLE 19-6**
**Typical Parts That Are Suitable or Unsuitable for High-Velocity Forging**

| Suitable | Generally Unsuitable |
|---|---|
| Gear blanks | Crankshafts |
| Spherical segments | Wheel spindles |
| Cones | |
| Cup shapes | |
| Discs | |
| Flanges | |
| Twisted blades | |
| Symmetrical structures | |
| Asymmetrical structures | |

# CHAPTER 19

# HIGH-VELOCITY FORGING

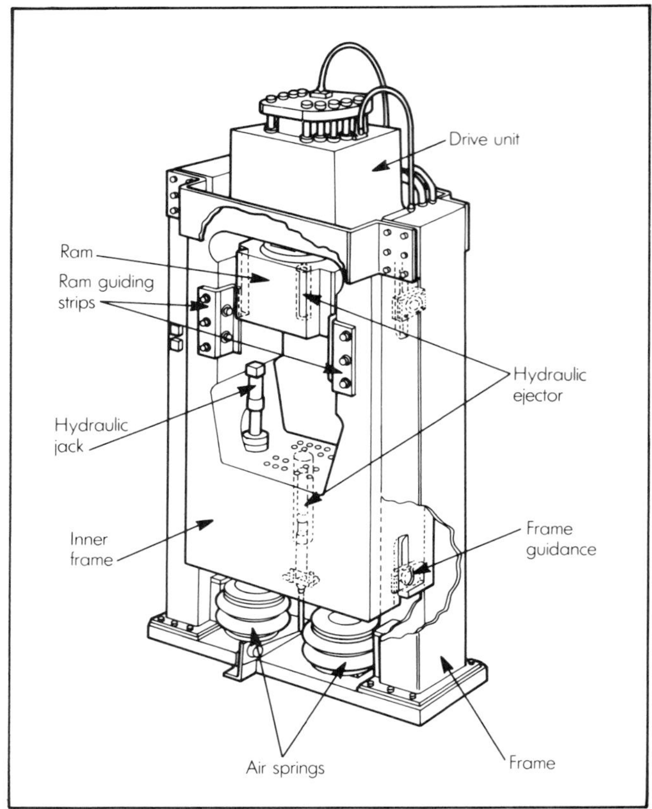


**Fig. 19-22 Pneumatic-hydraulic hammer incorporating single drive unit design.**

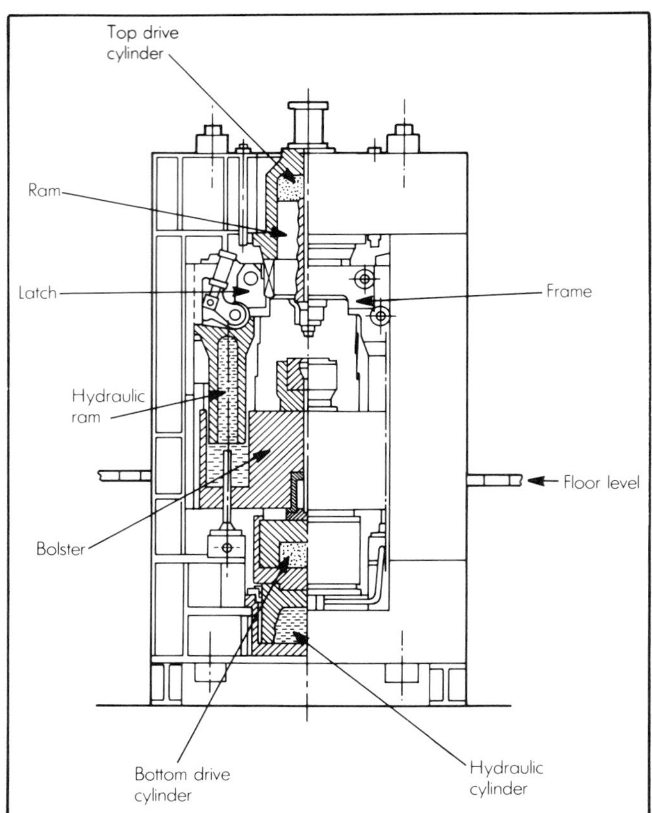


**Fig. 19-23 Pneumatic-hydraulic hammer incorporating twin drive cylinder design.**

unit to force the ram downward while the inner frame moves upward simultaneously. After the workpiece has been deformed, the hydraulic jacks return the ram to its initial position. This design of hammer is capable of delivering up to 225,000 ft-lb (305 kJ) of energy, and the nominal cycle time is 3-8 seconds, depending on hammer size.

The second design (see Fig. 19-23) contains an upper and lower cylinder located within the frame. The upper cylinder drives the ram downward, and the lower cylinder drives the bolster upward. The gas pressure is adjusted between the cylinders to balance the momentum which, in turn, prevents shocks from being transmitted to the foundation. Hydraulically controlled latches hold the ram up. To deform the workpiece, the latches are disengaged and the ram and bolster are accelerated toward each other. A hydraulic ram returns the ram and bolster to their starting positions and restores the gas to its initial pressure. These hammers are capable of delivering up to 397,650 ft-lb (539 kJ) of energy with a nominal cycle time of 5-8 seconds, depending on hammer size.

**Combustion-pneumatic hammers.** At the start of the cycle, the piston/ram assembly is held at top dead center by low-pressure air in the back pressure chamber (see Fig. 19-24, *a*). A cylindrical projection on the top of the piston provides a seal between the combustion chamber and the expansion chamber. Since the exhaust valve is open, the pressure in the combustion chamber is atmospheric. When the firing button is pushed, the exhaust valve closes and the gas valve opens allowing the gaseous fuel to flow into the combustion chamber.

The combustion chamber is then charged with compressed air entering the inlet valve to form a combustible mixture that, depending on the blow energy required, can reach a final pressure of up to 150 psi (1034 kPa), view *b*. A spark plug ignites the fuel-air mixture, producing a pressure increase of 7-8 times. The increased pressure forces the piston downward, overcoming the upward force of the back pressure. As soon as the seal is broken, the pressure acts over the entire surface area of the piston, accelerating the piston/ram assembly downward to impinge on the workpiece, view *c*. As the piston/ram assembly moves downward, the back pressure intensifies and returns the assembly to its initial position. The upward movement of the piston/ram assembly expels the exhaust gases through the exhaust duct, view *d*.

Combustion-pneumatic hammers are essentially a hybrid of the internal combustion engine and a forging hammer. The hammers currently being built are capable of delivering 5000-10,000 ft-lb (6.8-13.6 kJ) of energy when operating continuously. They are capable of delivering up to 20,000 ft-lb (27 kJ) when making occasional hard blows. The energy delivered is controlled by the amount of air and fuel introduced into the combustion chamber. Cycle time is usually one second, and ram velocities are as high as 50-70 fps (15-21 m/s), depending on energy output.

## Tooling

High-velocity forging dies are mostly of the closed type, though the more conventional flash and gutter impression type

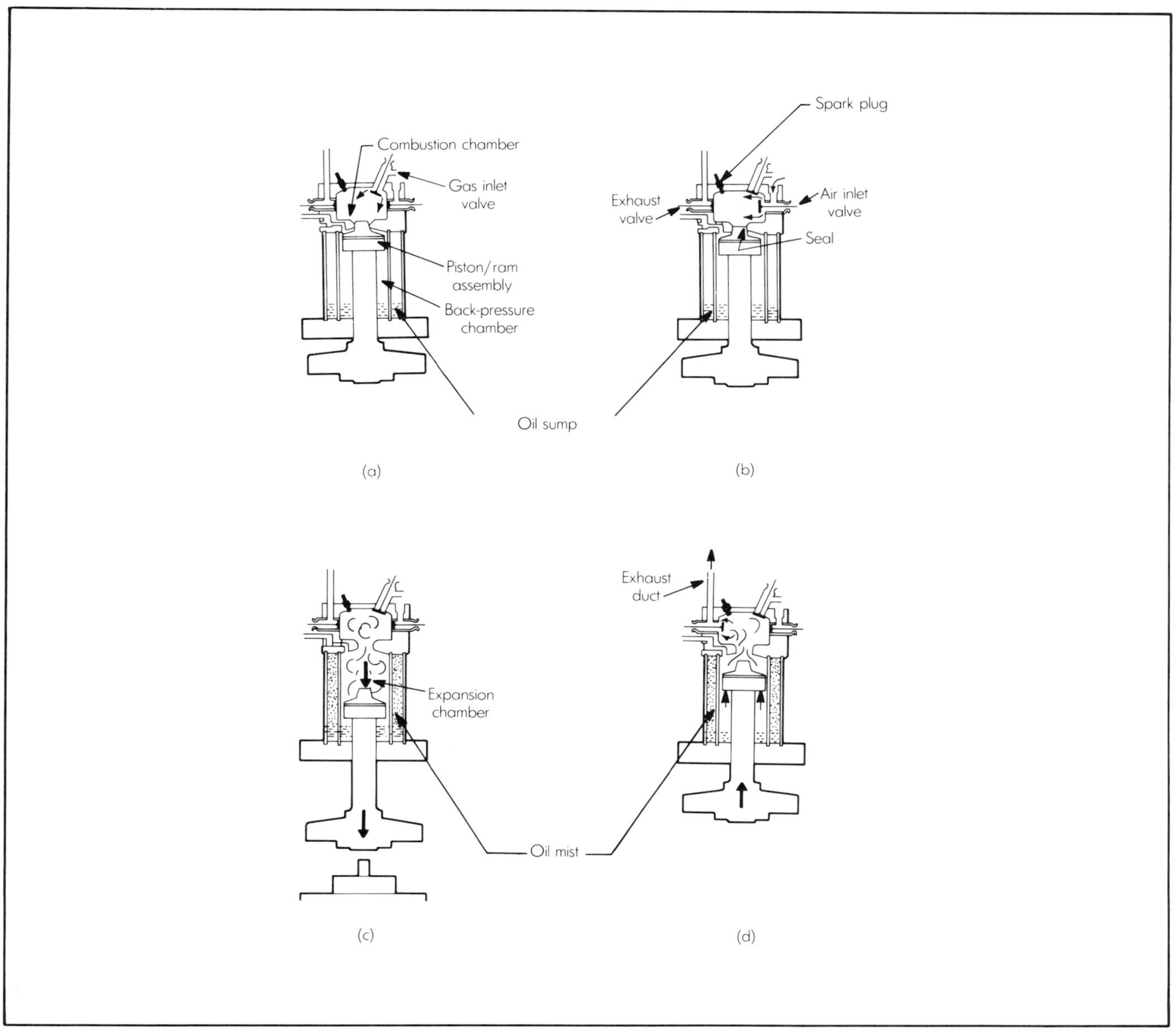


**Fig. 19-24 Operating cycle of combustion-pneumatic hammer: (a) injection, (b) charging and ignition, (c) working stroke, and (d) return stroke.**

are also employed. The dies resemble dies used in conventional impact extrusion or cold forming. The most successful tooling assemblies incorporate shrink-fitted or press-fitted inserts into the dieholders. A fairly common tool set consisting of a lower shoe, a shrink-type insert holder, an interference-fitted die insert, and an ejector is shown in Fig. 19-25. The upper die consists of a simple punch having a clearance at the edge to permit the flash to flow around it.

Selecting the correct material and heat treatment of the tooling minimizes plastic deformation of the punches or fracturing of the dies during forming operations. Material selection is primarily based on tooling material and manufacturing costs, but also depends on the size and shape of the part to be formed, type of material used, tolerance requirements, and number of parts to be produced. Figure 19-26 shows the materials and hardnesses of a tooling assembly used for forging gear shafts.

Nonstandard, low-alloy tool steels (such as 6F2 and 6F3) are usually selected when parts requiring low forging stresses and short production runs are hot forged. When parts requiring higher stresses and longer production runs are forged, H11, H12, and H13 chromium tool steels have been employed. Molybdenum high-speed tool steel, M2, is used in warm forming operations; cold-forming operations use D2 and D3 tool steels hardened to $R_C$ 58-60 for the dies and A2 or D2 tool steel hardened to $R_C$ 56-58 for the punches. Punches have also been made from M2 and S1 tool steels hardened to $R_C$ 58-60. Cropping blades are generally made from D2 and A2 tool steels hardened to $R_C$ 54-56.

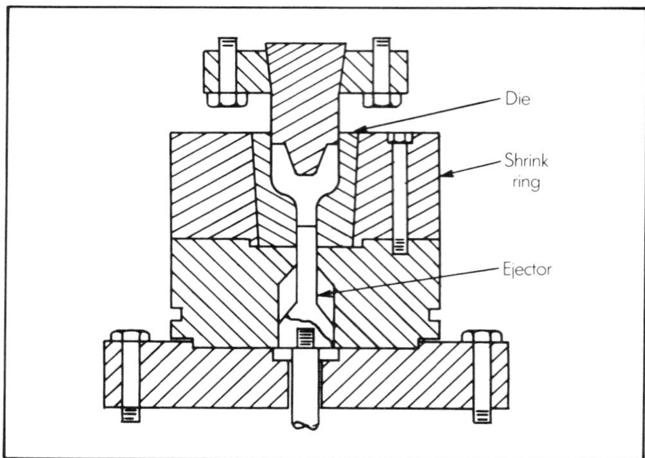


Fig. 19-25 Cross section of simple tooling assembly.

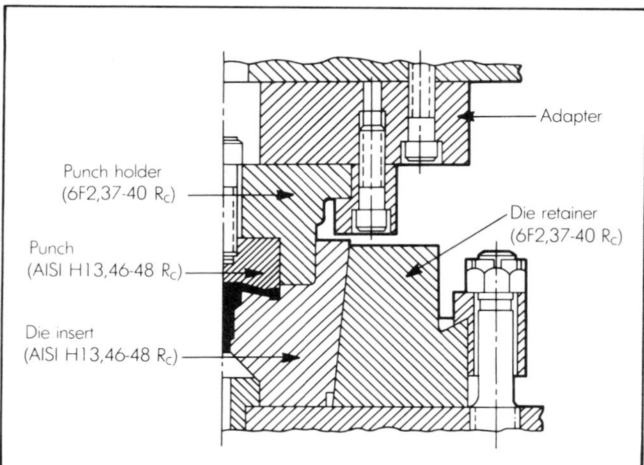


Fig. 19-26 Cross section of tooling used to form gear shafts showing tooling assembly material and hardnesses.

## PEEN FORMING

Peen forming is a dieless forming process performed at room temperature. During the process, the surface of the workpiece is impacted by pressure from small, round steel shot. Every piece of shot impacting the surface acts as a tiny hammer, producing elastic stretching of the upper surface as shown in Fig. 19-27. The impact pressure of the peening shot causes local plastic deformation that manifests itself as a residual compressive stress. The surface force of the residual compressive stress combined with the stretching causes the material to develop a compound, convex curvature on the peened side (see Fig. 19-28). When curvatures are being formed within the elastic range of the metal, the core of the metal remains elastic with a small, balancing, residual tensile stress. Other mechanical forming processes that require overforming with subsequent springback induce high tensile stress. Although high tensile stress can be minimized by stretch forming techniques, stretch forming is usually not performed on tapered or sculptured sections.

The size, velocity, and angle of impingement of the shot as well as the distance of the wheels or nozzles (the wheels or nozzles propel the shot) from the workpiece are automatically controlled in specially designed machines. Peen forming can be performed with or without an external load applied on the workpiece.

### Stress Peen Forming

Stress peen forming is an auxiliary technique of applying an external mechanical load on the workpiece to assist the peen forming operation. The workpiece to be formed is stressed in an arc within 90% of its material yield point and then peen formed to the required specifications. The prestressed radii is critical and is developed mathematically and experimentally so that the material's yield point is not exceeded prior to peen forming. Mechanical or hydraulic devices are designed to deflect the workpiece for specific applications.

Prestressing increases the effect of peen forming in one direction and sharply decreases the effect in the opposite direction. The radius of curvature induced by stress peen forming on a specific thickness of metal can be as large as four times the radius obtainable by peen forming without an external load applied.

### Advantages and Limitations

Parts formed by peen forming exhibit increased resistance to flexural bending fatigue. Another distinct advantage with peen forming, unlike most other forming methods, is that all surface stresses generated are of a compressive nature. Although peen-formed workpieces usually require shot peening on one side only, both sides have compressive stresses in the surface. These

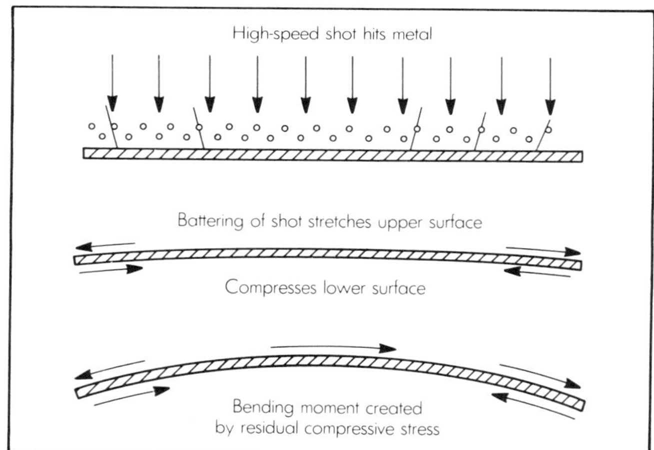


Fig. 19-27 Peen forming uses high-speed metal shot to form the workpiece. (*Metal Improvement Co.*)

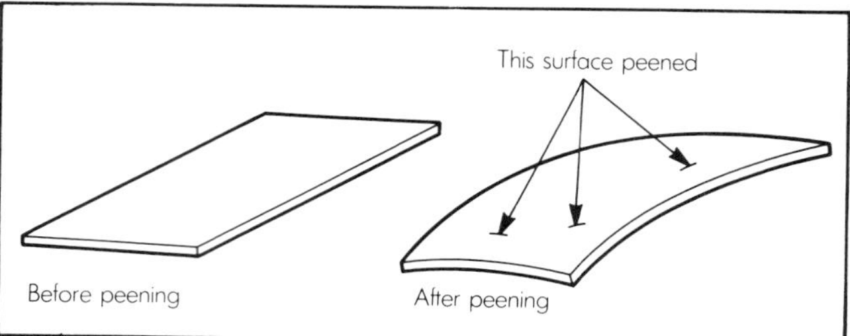


Fig. 19-28 Compound curvatures can be produced with peen forming. (*Metal Improvement Co.*)

compressive stresses serve to prevent stress corrosion cracking. Some workpieces should be shot peened all over prior to or after peen forming to further improve fatigue and stress corrosion characteristics. Workpieces which have been cold formed by other processes are often shot peened to overcome the harmful tensile stresses set up by the bending process. Sharp bends, such as right-angle flanges and deep-drawn or spun shapes, are not suitable to this process.

Being a dieless process, peen forming requires minimal lead time. The costly development and manufacturing time required to make hard dies is eliminated, reducing start-up cost. The process permits design changes and reworking of the part to improve fit when necessary.

## Applications

Peen forming is used to form large or small panel-shaped objects that do not contain abrupt changes in curvature. The process is capable of rolling, stretching, or twisting the material to develop the shape. Obtaining compound or saddle-backed shapes is also possible. The aircraft industry uses peen forming to form the wing panels on civilian and military aircraft.

Peen forming is applicable to all metals and can be performed on tapered or integrally stiffened machined panels, honeycomb skins, and isogrid (diamond patterned) panels. This process is usually best suited for forming curvatures having radii within the metal's elastic range. Metal thicknesses in aluminum range from 0.05-2.00″ (1.2-50 mm); in high-strength steel alloys, the thickness range is from 0.016-1.00″ (0.40-25.0 mm). Workpiece sizes currently being formed are 10 ft (3 m) wide x 100 ft (30 m) long, and contour tolerances are approximately ±0.025″ (0.63 mm). Table 19-7 shows the curvatures obtained in different metal thicknesses of aluminum when the shot size is varied.

Shot peening is also used for surface preparation. For additional information on this application, refer to Volume 3, *Materials, Finishing, and Coating,* in this Handbook series.

## Machines

Peen forming is usually performed by automatic machines within a cabinet enclosure. When close tolerances are required, forming is performed manually by skilled technicians. Two basic types of machines are used, differing only in how the peen forming media is delivered to the part being formed.

**TABLE 19-7**
**Curvatures Obtained in Aluminum Alloys of Varying Metal Thickness Using Different Diameter Shot**

| Material Thickness, in. (mm) | Shot Diameter, in. (mm) | |
|---|---|---|
| | 0.093 (2.36 mm) | 0.132 (3.35 mm) |
| | Radius of Curvature, in. (mm) | |
| 0.125 (3.2) | 11.5 (292) | 10 (254) |
| 0.19 (4.8) | 26.5 (673) | 21 (533) |
| 0.25 (6.3) | 47 (1194) | 40 (1016) |
| 0.31 (7.9) | 85 (2159) | 80 (2032) |
| 0.375 (9.5) | 150 (3810) | 121 (3073) |
| 0.50 (12.7) | 285 (7239) | 256 (6502) |
| 0.75 (19.0) | 980 (24 892) | 790 (20 066) |
| 1.00 (25.4) | 1570 (39 878) | 1260 (32 000) |

(*Metal Improvement Co.*)

**Nozzle-type machines.** In nozzle-type machines, compressed air or gravity is used to propel the steel shot to the workpiece. These machines may have as many as 20 nozzles, and each nozzle (see Fig. 19-29) is capable of delivering 50 lb (23 kg) of shot per minute to a specific location or area of the workpiece. Each nozzle is independently controlled by a pressure gauge and shutoff valves. The nozzle direction is adjustable so that the optimum angle of impingement can be achieved when workpieces are formed containing surface areas with unusual geometry.

Nozzle-type machines can automatically compensate for varying curvature requirements along the workpiece length or width. Thickness variations, cutouts, and reinforcements, as well as distortion caused by machining stresses or heat treatment, can also be compensated for with these machines.

Figure 19-30 shows a nozzle-type, gantry peen forming machine. In this machine design, the gantry, which houses the nozzles, traverses over the workpiece while the workpiece is stationary. Another machine design has the workpiece moving through the stationary machine that houses the nozzles.

**Centrifugal wheel machines.** Centrifugal wheel peen forming is another method by which the shot media is delivered to the workpiece (see Fig. 19-31). These machines use solid-state electronic controls to regulate rotating speeds of a paddle wheel that flings the shot at the workpiece, as shown in Fig. 19-32. A typical wheel can deliver 300 lb (136 kg) of shot per minute. Production-type centrifugal wheel machines have 6-8 wheels, providing the machine with a capacity to peen form using more than 2000 lb (900 kg) of shot per minute. The ability to deliver shot media at a controlled velocity in such large volumes permits higher production rates on these machines than obtainable on nozzle-type machines.

Workpieces formed by centrifugal wheel machines are usually of broad, uniform cross section, with all areas accessible

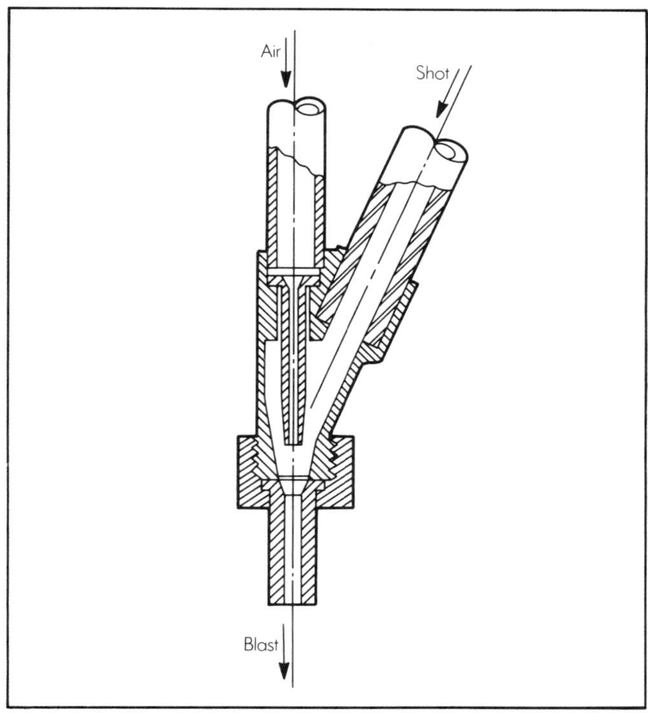


**Fig. 19-29 Cross section of a nozzle used on a nozzle-type peen-forming machine (*Metal Improvement Co.*)**

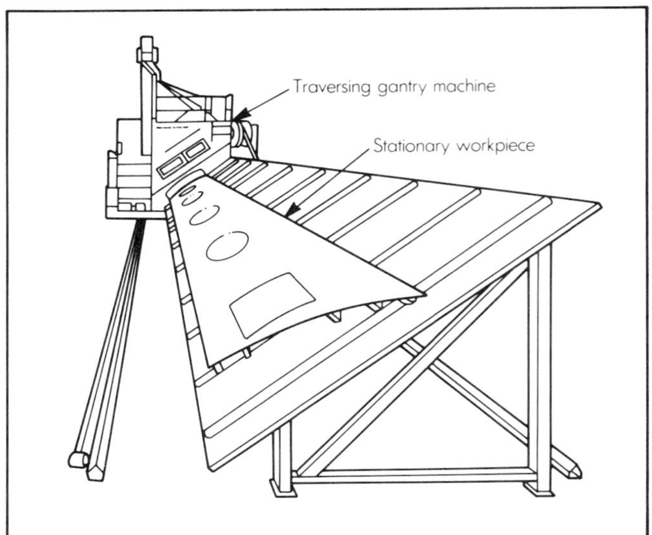


**Fig. 19-30 Gantry-type peen-forming machine transverses the workpiece while the workpiece is stationary. (*Metal Improvement Co.*)**

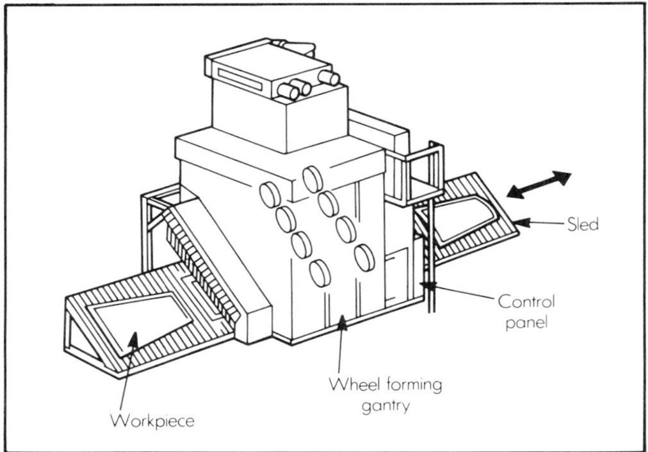


**Fig. 19-31 Centrifugal wheel peen-forming machine with a movable bed. (*Metal Improvement Co.*)**

to the shot stream. Minor changes to the shot stream direction can be made by indexing the position of the shot delivered to the wheel paddle.

## ULTRASONIC-ACTIVATED FORMING

Ultrasonic-activated forming is a metalforming process that applies high-frequency vibrations to the workpiece through the tooling. The vibrations are usually greater than 15,000 cycles per second (cps) and are generally no more than a few thousandths of an inch (0.08 mm) in amplitude.

Metalforming with the aid of ultrasonic energy dates back to the mid-1950s. Tests showed that when a wire was stressed in tension with ultrasonic activation, the yield strength of the material appeared to be reduced and the elongation seemed to increase. It was also determined that this effect increased linearly with an increase in vibratory power and was independent of the frequency. This phenomenon was attributed to

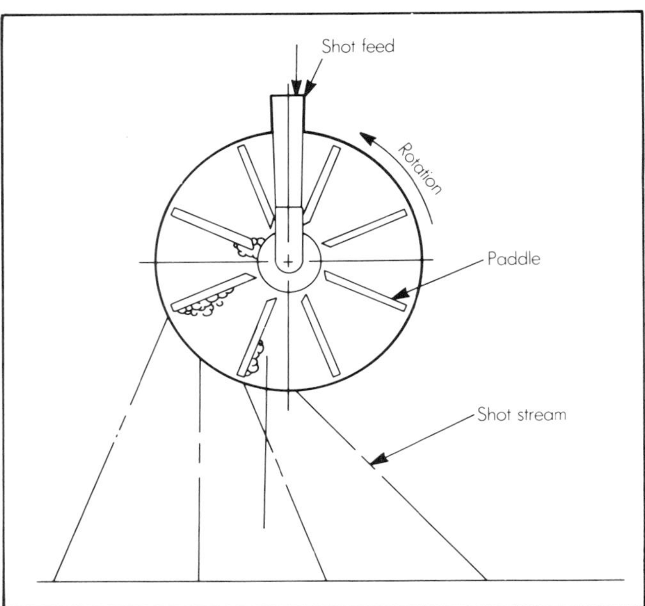


**Fig. 19-32 The wheels on a centrifugal wheel peen-forming machine fling the metal shot at the workpiece. (*Metal Improvement Co.*)**

ultrasonically facilitated formation and movement of dislocations within the crystal lattice structure that assisted intercrystalline slip.

### Advantages and Limitations

Applying ultrasonic energy in the form of high-frequency vibrations during cold-forming operations reduces the forming force required, increases the deformation rate, decreases the total number of processing steps, and improves the quality of the finished product, particularly the surface finish and the dimensional tolerances. Experience has also shown that friction between a vibrating tool and the workpiece is reduced and, most importantly, that the workpiece may be swaged, which reduces or even eliminates the critical tensile stresses in the workpiece. A major limitation of the process is the amount of power required.

### Application

Ultrasonic activation can be applied to both slow-speed and high-speed forming processes. Slow-speed forming processes are those processes in which the strain rate is low, and high-speed processes are those in which the strain rate is high. Some of the slow-speed forming processes include deep drawing, tube drawing, draw ironing, tube flaring, dimpling, bending, and straightening. High-speed forming processes include wire drawing, extrusion, and rolling. For additional information on ultrasonic or vibration-assisted tube drawing, refer to Chapter 13, "Drawing, Extruding and Upsetting," in this volume.

Ultrasonic-activated forming has been successfully employed when forming aluminum, copper, steel, titanium, and nickel alloys. It has also been used to form both thermoplastic and thermosetting polymers.

### Equipment

The main components required for ultrasonic-assisted forming are the press or draw bench, the ultrasonic frequency converter, and the transducer-coupling system. The frequency converter changes the current supply frequency of approximately 50/60 cps into a high-frequency alternating current. The high-frequency alternating current is fed to the transducer-coupling system, which changes the electrical impulses to mechanical vibrations.

In tube-drawing operations, either the draw die or the plug can be ultrasonically activated. Activating the die is generally preferred since the effect of the vibration is greatest, the number of passes can be greatly reduced, and the tools can be more easily interchanged than with plug-activated systems. Figure 19-33 illustrates the setup used in ultrasonic plug-activated tube-drawing systems.

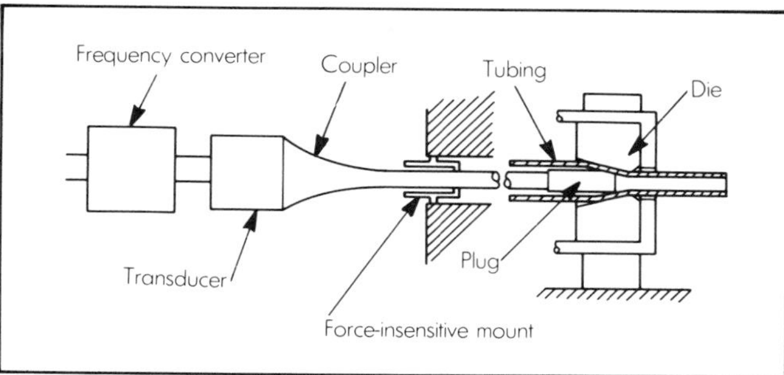


**Fig. 19-33 Schematic of ultrasonic plug-activated system.**

## References

1. S. A. Tobias, "Automation of High Energy Rate Forming Processes," *Proceedings of First International Conference of the Center for High Energy Forming*, (June 1967).
2. M. C. Noland, *et al*, "High-Velocity Metalworking," NASA SP-5062 (National Aeronautics and Space Administration, Washington, DC, 1967), p. 183.
3. D. L. Bagnoli and D. J. Mollela, "Applications of High Velocity Hydro-electrical Discharge as a Nondestructive Testing and Metal Forming Tool," Technical Report 3238 (Picatinny Arsenal, NJ, 1965), pp. 13 and 29.

## Bibliography

Bruno, E. J., ed. *High-Velocity Forming of Metals*. Dearborn, MI: American Society of Tool and Manufacturing Engineers, 1968.

Cunningham, J. W. *Effects of Superimposed High-frequency Vibrations on Deformation Processes*. SME Technical Paper MF67-968, 1967.

Devine, Janet, and Krause, Philip C. "Ultrasonic Cold Forming of Aircraft Sheet Materials." Report No. TR81-F-3. U.S. Army Aviation Research and Development Command, January 1981.

Jones, J. Byron. *Ultrasonic Metal Deformation Processing*. SME Technical Paper MF67-969, 1967.

Metal Improvement Company, Inc. *Shot Peening Applications*, 6th ed. New Jersey, 1980.

Miller, Paul C. "High-Energy-Rate Forming Joins the Productivity Race." *Tooling and Production* (October 1981).

Nielson, John H. "Tube Drawing with Ultrasonics." *ASTME Student Quarterly* (Spring 1969).

Sprow, Eugene E. "Peen Forming Becomes a CNC Art." *Tooling and Production* (December 1982).

Stauffer, Robert N. "Electromagnetic Metalforming." *Manufacturing Engineering* (February 1978).

Zittel, Guenter. *Evolution in the Forming and Assembly of Metal Parts with Magneform*. SME Technical Paper AD75-796, 1975.

CHAPTER

# 20

# Safety in Forming

# SAFETY IN FORMING

This chapter contains general information on safety program development, administration, principles and practices. Specific safety information related to the various forming processes and equipment is provided in previous chapters, such as Chapter 5, "Presses for Sheet Metal Forming"; Chapter 10, "Bending and Straightening"; Chapter 12, "Punching"; and Chapter 17, "Powder Metallurgy."

Safety is the principal subject matter of this chapter and is presented as an integral part of manufacturing engineering and management responsibility. Industrial hygiene and in-depth treatment of employee health practices and noise control are outside the scope of coverage. Additional information on noise control can be obtained from Chapter 18, "Safety and Noise Control," in *Machining*, Volume I of this Handbook series.

CHAPTER CONTENTS:



## SAFETY PROGRAM FUNDAMENTALS

What conditions should exist for an effective safety program? First, a management commitment must be evident. Secondly, responsibility for the safety function must be assigned to a qualified person who serves as a focal point and coordinator for the program. Thirdly, a safety program cannot succeed without acceptance and support by employees. Sustained effort and constant attention are needed. Solutions to safety problems require application of sound management principles and practices similar to those used to solve production quality and cost problems. It is important that management "close the loop" by providing a systematic means of verifying that the intended safety program is being carried out.

Small business operations may have special problems in dealing with workplace safety and health hazards. While large companies usually can justify the full-time services of safety engineers and industrial hygienists, small firms often cannot. Yet the workplace hazards that cause injury and illness are as prevalent in small businesses as in large firms. A principal purpose of this chapter is to provide basic information that can help manufacturing companies of all sizes to establish their own safety programs.

### GENERAL CONSIDERATIONS

At the outset, it is fundamentally important to distinguish between the meaning of "accident" and the term "act of God," as used in the insurance business. The distinction can be made clearly: floods and tornadoes cannot be prevented by the manager of a manufacturing plant, but workplace accidents can be prevented or reduced in number and severity. The key requirements are recognition of the problem and application of recognized accident prevention principles and techniques.

An accident may be defined simply as an unplanned event. In a carefully planned manufacturing operation, when an unplanned event or incident occurs, corrective action should be taken to avoid repetition. The unplanned event (accident) may have caused interruption of the planned production sequence, damage to parts or equipment, damage to property, or injury to employees.

It is also important to distinguish between physical provisions for safety and the training of people to act safely. No matter how well working conditions are designed and constructed, few situations can be safeguarded to the extent that the human element is completely absent. For example, an adjustable barrier guard is a standard safeguard on a power press, but unless employees are trained to have it in place, it does not prevent injuries. Thus, maximum safety is attained by the combination of safe facilities and people who are properly trained in safe procedures.

Operators and maintenance and setup personnel should be trained to make sure safeguards and safeguarding devices are in place and functioning properly before a machine is put into operation. Thus maximum safety is attained by the combination of safe facilities and people trained in safe procedures.

***Contributors of sections of this chapter are:*** *Benjamin J. Cieslik, Safety Director, General Motors Corporation; Hillman E. Deaton, Director of Human Resources, Riley-Beaird Co., Division of U.S. Riley Corp.; Eugene J. Dreger, Compliance Officer, Occupational Safety and Health Administration, U.S. Department of Labor; William E. Gaskin, Vice President, American Metal Stamping Association; Herbert W. Goetz, Vice President, Manager—Product Safety, Cincinnati Incorporated; Susan Hanke, Publications and Library, Wausau Insurance Companies; Roger P. Harrison, Training Director, Rockford Safety Equipment Co.; Joseph W. Hart, Director—Industrial Service, Loss Prevention Department, Liberty Mutual Insurance Co.; Cathy Shutway, Special Assistant, Safety & Health, Forging Industry Association.*

***Reviewers of sections of this chapter are:*** *John J. Ahern, Consultant; Julien Christensen, Chief Scientist—Human Factors, General Physics Corporation; Benjamin J. Cieslik, Safety Director, General Motors Corporation; J. R. Crawford, Manager—Employee Safety, Chrysler Corporation; R. W. Dean, Assistant to President, Niagara Machine & Tool Works; Hillman E. Deaton, Director of Human Resources, Riley-Beaird Co.; Dennis R. Ebens, Executive Vice President, Rockford Safety Equipment Co.; Roger Harrison, Training Director, Rockford Safety Equipment Co.; Joseph W. Hart, Director—Industrial Service, Liberty Mutual Insurance Co.; Frederick W. Lang, Assistant Director, Occupational Safety and Ergonomics, General Motors Corporation; Courtlandt Layng, Vice President—Sales and Marketing, W. I. Martin Safety Equipment Co.*

# CHAPTER 20

## SAFETY PROGRAM FUNDAMENTALS

An accident prevention program should be concerned with only the types of accidents that can occur in a particular area or workplace. Because each workplace is different, the safety programs vary and each program should be adapted to the circumstances in a particular plant. However, while the details of safety programs may vary considerably, effective programs share the common elements listed in Table 20-1.[1]

**TABLE 20-1**
**Key Factors in Workplace Safety**

- Management leadership
- Assignment of responsibility
- Identification and control of hazards
- Employee and supervisor training
- Safety and health recordkeeping
- First-aid and medical assistance
- Employee awareness, acceptance and participation
- Management follow-up

### Management Leadership

The top local executive should assume a leadership role. The attitude of management personnel toward job safety and health is reflected by other employees. If management is not interested in preventing accidents, workers are unlikely to be safety conscious.

At all times, the manager should demonstrate interest in safety and health and give these matters the attention they require. There should be no doubts about genuine personal concern for employee safety and health and the priority placed on them in the workplace. The safety policy must be clearly set. Procedures and actions, taken with management support, demonstrate its importance. Some action items for consideration include:

- Posting the OSHA workplace poster, "Job Safety and Health Protection," where employees can see it. (This is an OSHA requirement.)
- Meeting with employees to discuss job safety and health matters. Discussion should cover mutual responsibilities under the Act. (The text of the OSHA workplace poster can aid in this task.)
- Showing all employees a copy of the Act and a copy of OSHA standards that apply to their business. They should be told where these documents are kept and where they may have access to them.
- Writing a "policy statement" and posting it near the OSHA workplace poster so that everyone is reminded of the concern for safety.
- Establishing a "Code of Safe Practices and Operating Procedures" to provide specific instruction for employees.
- Including job safety and health topics in meetings or in conversations with employees.
- Personally reviewing inspection and accident reports to ensure follow-up when needed.
- Commenting on good or bad safety records and providing accident prevention guidance on a routine basis.
- Setting a good example. If, for instance, eye protection is required to be worn in specific areas, then the manager must wear eye protection when visiting that area, too.

### Assignment of Responsibility

Responsibility for safety and health activities must be clearly assigned. In terms of management responsibility, the direct supervisors of employees are usually the key personnel.

After top management has set the basic safety policy, detailed responsibility for carrying out the program can be delegated to the same persons who oversee the operating and production details. Supervisors, group leaders, "straw bosses" or other key persons, can be assigned specific responsibilities for safety and health and should be held accountable for getting the job done.

A good rule of thumb is to assign safety and health responsibilities along with production responsibilities. It then becomes "part of the job" to operate safely.

When considering responsibility, all employees should be included. Each employee has the responsibility to follow safety and health procedures and instructions, and each has the responsibility for recognizing hazards in his or her immediate work area and for taking action to control them. A general understanding of this key point should be fostered. Supervisors should be evaluated and rated on the degree to which they assume responsibility for safety, as well as on the usual criteria such as production quantity and quality, etc. Safety must be treated as an integral part of the ongoing operations.

### Identification and Control of Hazards

Possible accident causes should be properly identified and either eliminated or controlled. To maintain a safe and healthful workplace, it is necessary to do two things:

1. Identify workplace hazards that exist now or could develop.
2. Install procedures to control these hazards or to eliminate them if possible.

When beginning the planning process, it is helpful to keep in mind that the safety program should be tailored for the particular operations to which it is applied. It should deal with the specific materials, processes, equipment, employees, and production operations in a particular plant or manufacturing area. Safety program planning and implementation may be viewed as a two-stage process:

1. Getting started and working up to a satisfactory level.
2. Maintaining the safety activity at a satisfactory level over a period of time.

### Employee and Supervisor Training

Appropriate safety-related training should be instituted. An effective accident prevention program requires proper job performance from everyone in the workplace.

The manager must ensure that all employees know about the materials and equipment they work with, what known hazards are in the operation, and how the hazards are controlled or eliminated.

All employees need to know the following (especially if these items have been included in a policy and in a code of safe practices):

- No employee is expected to undertake a job until he or she has received job instructions on how to do it properly and has been authorized to perform that job.

- No employee should undertake a job that appears to be unsafe.
- Mechanical and electronic safeguards must be kept in place.
- Each employee should report unsafe conditions encountered during work.
- Any injury or illness, even a slight one, suffered by an employee must be reported at once. Accidents should be investigated and corrective action taken when necessary.

In addition, any safety rules that are a condition of employment, such as the use of protective footwear or eye protection, should be explained clearly and enforced.

The direct supervisors must know how to train employees in the proper approach to doing their jobs. Appropriate training for the supervisors should be provided. (Many community colleges offer management training courses for little or no cost.)

There are some specific training requirements in the OSHA standards which must be met. Included are those pertaining to first aid, powered industrial trucks (including forklifts), power presses, and welding. In general, they deal with situations in which the use of untrained or improperly trained operators on machinery requiring skill could cause hazardous situations to develop not only for the operator but also for nearby workers.

## Safety and Health Record-Keeping

Records of financial, engineering, and manufacturing data are essential to all successful businesses. They enable the owner or manager to learn from experience and to make corrections for future operations. Records of accidents, related injuries, illnesses, and property losses can serve the same purpose if they are used effectively.

The record-keeping provisions in OSHA regulations require employers to collect and store factual information about accidents that occur. When the facts have been determined, causes of accidents can often be identified and control procedures can be instituted to prevent a similar occurrence from happening.

**Injury/illness records.** The injury/illness record-keeping requirements under OSHA necessitate some paperwork. These records provide information for evaluating the success of safety and health activities. Success would generally mean a lack of, or a reduced number of, employee injuries or illnesses during a calendar year. Five important steps are required by the OSHA record-keeping system:

1. Obtain a report on every injury requiring medical treatment (other than first aid).
2. Record each injury on OSHA Form No. 200 according to the instructions provided.
3. Prepare a supplementary record of occupational injuries and illnesses for recordable cases either on OSHA Form No. 101 or on workers' compensation reports giving the same information.
4. Every year, prepare the annual summary (OSHA Form No. 200); post it no later than February 1 and keep it posted until March 1.
5. Retain these records for at least five years.

During the year, the records should be reviewed to see where injuries are occurring. Recurring patterns or repeat situations should be noted. These records can help to identify high risk areas that require immediate attention.

The basic OSHA records include only injuries and illnesses. However, in some plants the system is extended to include all incidents, including those in which no injury or illness results. This is done to aid in pinpointing unsafe conditions and/or procedures. Safety councils, insurance companies, and other service organizations can assist in instituting such a system.

Injury/illness record-keeping can be useful and is advisable if done on a reasonable basis. However, companies that employ 10 or fewer employees are not required to keep records under the OSHA injury/illness record-keeping system.

Regardless of the number of employees, a plant or shop may be chosen by the Federal Bureau of Labor Statistics (BLS) or a related State agency for inclusion in an annual sample survey. Instructions are provided in letters sent by the agency directly to plants and shops selected for the BLS survey.

**Exposure records.** The injury/illness records may not be the only records to be maintained. Certain OSHA standards which deal with toxic substances and hazardous exposures require records on the exposure of employees, physical examination reports, employment records, etc.

As the work is done to identify possible exposure hazards, determination can be made, on a case-by-case basis, concerning possible applicability of the additional record-keeping provisions. It is necessary to be aware of this category of record-keeping so that, if required, such records can be embodied into the safety program control procedures and the self-inspection activities.

**Documentation of activities.** Essential records, including those legally required for workers' compensation, insurance audits, and government inspections must be maintained as long as the actual need exists. The employer must ensure the ready availability of medical personnel for advice and consultation on matters of employee health. This does not mean that on-site health care must be provided; but if health problems develop in the workplace, the employer is expected to get medical help to treat them and their causes.

To fulfill the above requirements, the following actions should be considered:

- Develop an emergency medical procedure for handling injuries, transporting ill or injured workers, and notifying medical facilities with a minimum of confusion. Posting emergency telephone numbers is a good idea.
- Survey the nearby medical facilities and make arrangements for them to handle routine and emergency cases. Cooperative agreements possibly could be made with larger plants having medical personnel.
- Install a procedure for reporting injuries and illnesses that is understood by all employees.
- If the business location is remote from medical facilities, ensure that at least one trained first-aid person is available at all times. Arrangements for training this person can be made through the local Red Cross Chapter, an insurance company, the local safety council, and other service organizations.
- Check battery-charging stations, maintenance operations, laboratories, heating and ventilating operations, and any corrosive-material areas to make sure they have the required eye wash facilities and showers.
- Consider retaining a local doctor or an industrial nurse on a part-time or as-needed basis to advise in medical and first-aid planning.

It is worthwhile to maintain records of safety activities, such as policy statements, training sessions for management and

# SAFETY PROGRAM FUNDAMENTALS

employees, safety and health meetings, information distributed to employees, and medical arrangements. Maintaining essential records: (1) demonstrates sound business management as supporting proof for credit applications, for showing "good faith" in reducing any proposed penalties from OSHA inspections, for insurance audits, etc., and (2) affords an efficient means to review safety and health activities for better control of operations and to plan improvements.

### First-Aid and Medical Assistance

A medical and first-aid system should be ready for use when needed. Large manufacturing companies usually have the necessary systems and services. However, most small businesses do not have an organized medical and first-aid system, nor are they expected to have one. But all businesses are required to have the following:

- In the absence of a nearby infirmary, clinic, or hospital that can be used for the emergency treatment of injured employees, the employer must ensure that a person or persons be trained and available to render first aid. Adequate first-aid supplies must be readily available for emergency use.
- When the eyes or body of any employee may be exposed to injurious corrosive materials, suitable equipment for quick drenching or flushing of the eyes and body must be provided in the work area for immediate emergency use. Employees should be trained in using the equipment.

### Employee Involvement

A properly conducted safety program is an on-going activity designed to foster an on-the-job awareness and acceptance of safety and health responsibility by every employee. Employee awareness, acceptance, and participation are vitally important in determining the effectiveness of a safety program.

Large companies have the advantages of size, including in-house expertise and a number of resources. They can, however, tend to become impersonal unless special attention is paid to retaining "the human touch." Small companies have inherent advantages in the area of safety and health, such as close contact with the employees, a specific acquaintance with the problems of the whole business, and usually a low labor turnover. Small business owners and managers often have developed a personal relationship of loyalty and cooperation which can be built upon when establishing a safety program.

Some tips for persuading employees to accept their responsibilities for safety and health are as follows:

- The manager must be convinced of the need to have a safe and healthful workplace. If management acts without conviction, the employees sense it quickly.
- Each employee needs to know that management is sincerely interested in preventing accidents. Realistically, it is known that accidents may occur, but it is also recognized that almost all accidents can be prevented.
- Genuine effort should be made to "sell" the idea to employees, and to impress upon them that job safety and health is a condition of their employment. It is, of course, essential to be reasonable and rational in communicating the safety requirements and benefits.
- A job safety analysis (JSA) should be prepared for all jobs and work stations, and a commitment should be undertaken to implement the JSA program's principal findings.
- A start should be evident; some specific safety activities should be initiated. While it may not be possible to anticipate all of the job-related hazards, the necessity for developing sound safety practices should begin to be recognized. Employees should become aware that management shares their concerns and is interested in doing something about safety problems.
- Safety pamphlets should be displayed on a workplace safety bulletin board; safety and health-related posters and information devices maintain awareness of the concern for on-the-job safety.
- All employees should become involved in inspecting, detecting and correcting. Employees should participate in planning, and they should be asked for suggestions and assistance.
- It is important to let employees know when they are doing a good job, and also when their lack of response to a safety program is unacceptable and is a cause for mutual concern.

Consideration should be given to forming a joint labor-management safety committee. This committee can assist in starting a program and can help maintain interest in the program once it is operating. Committees can be an excellent way of communicating safety and health information. If there are few employees, consideration should be given to rotating them so that all can have an active part in the safety and health programming.

## HOW TO BEGIN

A basic approach to the startup stage of a safety program involves developing an action plan to lay the groundwork prior to beginning the program. Whether the motivation is voluntary or is derived from a realization that "safe and healthful working conditions" are required by law, periodic self-initiated review is worthwhile. If problems and deficiencies are identified, a plan can be formulated and appropriate actions can be taken to improve the safety practices.

### Obtain Up-To-Date Information

The original Occupational Safety and Health Act was enacted in 1970. A number of changes have been made since the Act became law in December 1970. For example, the federal law contains provisions for allowing a state to develop and operate its own occupational safety and health program in place of the federal OSHA program. It is possible that the regulatory aspect of the law (setting of mandatory minimum standards and conducting inspections of workplaces) is now being operated by the state government in a particular locale.

Knowing which level of government has current jurisdiction over a plant is important. Persons who are not sure of this may telephone the nearest OSHA area office to find out. Various federal OSHA publications are available for use in safety and health activities in areas that are not subject to state-operated programs. They include:

- Workplace posters from OSHA (Job Safety and Health Protection). A federal or state OSHA poster must be displayed in the workplace.
- Standards that apply to the plant's operations. These are needed for reference material. They are the regulations OSHA uses when inspecting for compliance with the Act. These standards are the baseline for voluntary, self-conducted inspections and are useful in determining the

specific changes that need to be made when hazards are identified. Most businesses come under OSHA's general industry standards. In states with OSHA programs, it is necessary to use and to conform to the appropriate state standards (see Table 20-2).

- Recordkeeping requirements and the necessary forms. These are needed by companies that have 11 or more employees. The forms are similar to information forms for workers' compensation and to other records.
- Occupational Safety and Health Act. This basic reference document provides authoritative information.

Federal materials are available free of charge through the OSHA area offices. Area offices supply publications, films and training materials on health and safety programs and specific hazards, and material on an employer's rights and responsibilities. Information on the locations of OSHA area offices can be obtained from: Office of Public and Consumer Affairs, U.S. Department of Labor, Occupational Safety and Health Administration, Room N-3641, Third and Constitution Ave. NW, Washington, DC 20210.

## Clean Up The Plant

Poor housekeeping is a major contributor to low morale and sloppy work in general, even if it is not usually the cause of major accidents. Most safety action programs start with an intensive clean-up campaign in all areas of business. Actions include:

- Collect rubbish and dispose of it.
- Provide proper trash containers.
- Ensure that flammables are properly stored.
- Ensure that exits are unobstructed.
- Mark aisles and passageways where necessary.
- Provide adequate lighting.
- Establish neat, well-planned work stations.

It is important to involve all employees and to impress upon them what must be done to make their workplace safer, more healthful, and more productive.

## Take Inventory

A start should be made to gather specific facts and information about the manufacturing operations. This can be done by taking an inventory. The purpose is to assemble useful information about the equipment, materials, employees, facilities, etc. At the start, it is sufficient to accept and use the information that is obtained from a reasonable amount of effort. The review or inventory should cover:

- Equipment—Make a list of major equipment, principal operations, and the locations of each. Special attention should be given to inspection schedules, maintenance activities, and plant and office layouts.
- Employees' capabilities—Make an alphabetical list of all employees, showing the date they were hired, their job functions, and the experience and training they have had. Special attention should be given to new employees and to employees with handicaps.
- Accident and injury/illness history—Examine the files for first-aid cases and workers' compensation insurance payments, and compensation awards, if any. Review any losses. Determine how the insurance rate compares with others that are available. Special attention should be given to recurring accidents, types of injuries, etc.

**TABLE 20-2**
**State-Operated Compliance Programs**

The following are operating under OSHA-approved state plans as of May 4, 1983:

| | |
|---|---|
| Alaska | New Mexico |
| Arizona | North Carolina |
| California | Oregon |
| Connecticut | Puerto Rico |
| Hawaii | South Carolina |
| Indiana | Tennessee |
| Iowa | Utah |
| Kentucky | Vermont |
| Maryland | Virginia |
| Michigan | Virgin Islands |
| Minnesota | Washington |
| Nevada | Wyoming |

With whatever facts have been assembled, make a preliminary check to determine if any major problem areas can be identified. Useful clues are such things as interruptions in the normal operations, too many employees taking too much time off, too many damaged products, etc. General assistance in this kind of problem identification can often be obtained from compensation carriers, local safety councils, state agencies, major suppliers, and even, perhaps, a competitor.

If a major problem exists, determine what can be done to solve it. When a problem is identified, work can begin on the corrective action or a plan for controlling the problem. It is advisable to take immediate action at this point and make a record of all that is done. The reviewer should avoid becoming overly involved in looking for major problem areas during this fact-finding stage. It should be remembered that no one hazardous situation causes all of the safety and health problems. Therefore, no single action greatly improves the safety and health program.

If no major problem is found at this point, the investigation should not be terminated. The self-inspection technique should be used to be sure that sound safety practices are being followed.

## Make a Self-Inspection of the Operations

The most widely accepted method of identifying hazards is to conduct safety and health inspections. The only way to be certain of the actual situation is to look at it from time to time. Preparations for planning and installing a safety program must include a self-inspection of the workplace. Self-inspection can reveal where probable hazards exist and whether they are under adequate control. The generalized "self-inspection scope" list contained in Table 20-3 can serve as a starting point for development of an appropriate list identifying areas to be included within the scope of an inspection at a specific location. The OSHA offices provide general checklists to assist the self-inspection fact-finding process. A review of the checklisted items can provide an indication of where action should begin to improve the provisions for employee safety.

The checklists obtained from OSHA are not all-inclusive. Users of the lists should add to them or delete portions that are not applicable. When the self-inspection (with aid of checklists) has been completed, the information obtained should be added to the file that contains injury information and other employee records. This material, along with information on processes and equipment, is a body of resource information containing factual data that helps in determining the locations and seriousness of problems that may exist. Using this internal information and the OSHA standards in the problem-solving process then enables sound judgments and decisions to be made concerning actions needed to solve safety problems.

After the hazards have been identified, control procedures can be instituted using the OSHA standards as guidelines. These control procedures will be the basic means for preventing accidents. The OSHA standards can be of great assistance since they address controls in order of effectiveness and preference:

1. Eliminating the hazard from the machine, the method, the material, or the plant structure.
2. Abating the hazard by limiting exposure or controlling it at its source.
3. Training personnel to be aware of the hazard and to follow safe work procedures to avoid it.
4. Prescribing personal protective equipment for protecting employees from the hazard.

Technical assistance in self-inspection may be available to the small business owner or manager through the insurance carrier; local safety council; and many local, state, and federal agencies, including the state consultation programs and OSHA area offices. Useful checklists are available from the National Safety Council, trade associations, insurance companies, and other service organizations. Appropriate information on regulations and compliance requirements is available from states that have OSHA-approved plans; and some states provide free safety and health training programs.

**TABLE 20-3**
**Safety Self-Inspection Scope**

**Processing, Receiving, Shipping and Storage**—equipment, job planning, layout, heights, floor loads, projection of materials, materials-handling and storage methods.

**Building and Grounds Conditions**—floors, walls, ceilings, exits, stairs, walkways, ramps, platforms, driveways, aisles.

**Housekeeping Program**—waste disposal, tools, objects, materials, leakage and spillage, cleaning methods, schedules, work areas, remote areas, storage areas.

**Electricity**—equipment, switches, breakers, fuses, switch-boxes, junctions, special fixtures, circuits, insulation, extensions, tools, motors, grounding, NEC compliance.

**Lighting**—type, intensity, controls, conditions, diffusion, location, glare and shadow control.

**Heating and Ventilating**—type, effectiveness, temperature, humidity, controls, natural and artificial ventilation and exhausting.

**Machinery**—points of operation, flywheels, gears, shafts, pulleys, key ways, belts, couplings, sprockets, chains, frames, controls, lighting for tools and equipment, brakes, exhausting, feeding, oiling, adjusting, maintenance, lock out, grounding, work space, location, purchasing standards.

**Hand and Power Tools**—purchasing standards, inspection, storage, repair, types, maintenance, grounding, use and handling.

**Chemicals**—storage, handling, transportation, spills, disposals, amounts used, toxicity or other harmful effects, warning signs, supervision, training, protective clothing and equipment.

**Fire Prevention**—extinguishers, alarms, sprinklers, smoking rules, exits, personnel assigned, separation of flammable materials and dangerous operations, explosive-proof fixtures in hazardous locations, waste disposal.

**Maintenance**—regularity, effectiveness, training of personnel, materials and equipment used, records maintained, method of locking out machinery, general methods.

**Personnel**—training, experience, methods of checking machines before use, type of clothing, personal protective equipment, use of guards, tool storage, work practices, method of cleaning, oiling, or adjusting machinery.

**Personal Protective Equipment**—type, size, maintenance, repair, storage, assignment of responsibility, purchasing methods, standards observed, training in care and use, rules of use, method of assignment.

# SAFETY PROGRAM DEVELOPMENT

Responsibility for the safety program usually is assigned to individuals holding staff positions in large plants, and line positions in small plants. In a large plant, the safety director should have management staff rank and authority. When the overall safety function is delegated as a collateral duty for a line executive who then has dual responsibilities that extend beyond the person's line authority, the safety assignment is regarded as a staff function. In each instance, determination of the appropriate organizational placement of the safety function should be made in terms of policies, hazards, problems, and other factors.[2]

The first duty of a newly appointed safety director is to review the existing safety policy and, if none exists, to prepare a suitable safety statement for approval and signature by a member of top management. The safety policy statement may be brief, but it must be composed and formatted as an official document.

The content of this statement should be concise; it should be directly to the point, relevant, and clearly understandable by the employees. To achieve maximum awareness and benefit, this policy statement should be given wide internal distribution. The *OSHA Handbook for Small Businesses* contains the following model safety policy statement:[3]

> "The Occupational Safety and Health Act of 1970 clearly states our common goal of safe and healthful

working conditions. The safety and health of our employees continues to be the first consideration in the operation of this business.

It is the intent of this company to comply with all laws. To do this we must constantly be aware of conditions in all work areas that can produce injuries. No employee is required to work at a job he or she knows is not safe or healthful. Your cooperation in detecting hazards and, in turn, controlling them is a condition of your employment. Inform your supervisor immediately of any situation beyond your ability or authority to correct."

## EXAMPLES OF SAFETY DIRECTIVES

A large manufacturer of motor vehicles extensively distributes internally the "Seven Basic Principles of Safety" shown in Fig. 20-1. Bearing the signature of the company's Chairman of the Board, the directive states that the safety program is based on a concept that safety is the responsibility of everyone, management and employee alike. The directive includes the following statement:

> "Each year a substantial investment of time and money is made to insure that the equipment and tools in our plants are properly designed from the standpoint of safety and that our plant layouts are as safe as it is possible to make them. But physical things have to be operated and used by people. In the final analysis, their safety depends on the factor of people, the human factor. It is the individual who is ultimately responsible for his or her own safety and for the safety of those around them..."

Additional examples of safety policy statements and related internal communication elements are provided in the *OSHA Handbook for Small Businesses*[4] and *Safety Training Methods*.[5]

### Seven Basic Principles of Safety

**1 Provide Active Top Management Support**

A good safety record is clear evidence of good management. Accordingly, general managers and other top divisional and plant executives will make safety their responsibility by . . .

- Maintaining a comprehensive safety program at all times
- Meeting with key supervisory personnel at least once a month to review safety performance
- Taking any action necessary to improve safety conditions. This way management lends meaningful and feasible support to a continuing safety effort.

**2 Maintain Adequate Safety Personnel**

Each plant should have sufficient, well-trained personnel to assure continuous, careful attention to safety. A qualified person should be assigned to direct the safety program, handle safety education and assist the supervisory force in maintaining safe working conditions. The safety staff should be sufficient in numbers to monitor all operations.

**3 Develop Safety Instructions For Every Job**

Written rules and instructions setting out safe practices for each job assignment are necessary. This material should be used as the basis for safety instruction of new employees and of employees transferred to new jobs, and then reviewed on a timely basis with all employees.

**4 Instruct All New Employees**

All new employees should be thoroughly instructed in general safety policies, rules and procedures before being referred to their supervisor for job training. In turn, the supervisor should review with them thoroughly the safety measures of the particular job, before they start to work. Subsequently, the safety performance of new employees should be reviewed regularly. This will assure that they both understand and carry out the written safety rules and instructions applicable to their jobs.

**5 Operate Through Supervision**

Supervisors are the key people in the safety program because they are in constant contact with employees. Superintendents should hold meetings with their supervisors at least once a month to review safety conditions, general safety policies and specific situations.

Also, supervisors should take the initiative in making a success of the safety program in their own departments. As a part of this effort, they should personally contact each employee at least monthly, to discuss safety and health matters.

**6 Make Every Employee Safety Minded**

The cooperation of the individual employee is vital to the success of a safety program. Continued education is required to make certain that all concerned—management and employees alike—do their part in protecting the safety of the individual at all times. Every available medium—safety booklets, posters, signs, and plant papers—may be used to good advantage in furthering the objectives of such a program.

**7 Extend Efforts Beyond The Plant**

Special attention should be given to off-the-job safety as employees have more accidents away from work than they do on the job. Our objectives should include efforts to promote the safety of employees and their families by. . .

- Maintaining a comprehensive safety program for employees driving company-owned vehicles
- Providing material on highway safety to aid employees driving their own cars
- Encouraging employees to develop safe practices in the home, on the farm, and in recreational activities.
- Participating in community safety activities.

**Fig. 20-1 Example of internal company directive stating key elements in a manufacturing company management commitment to employee safety.** (*General Motors Corporation*)

# CHAPTER 20

# SAFETY PROGRAM DEVELOPMENT

## SAFETY PROGRAM METHODOLOGY

Based upon more than 25 years experience in steel fabricating, one company uses an orderly method of safety program planning and administration structured around four key elements: examination, diagnosis, prescription, and treatment. Known by the abbreviation, EDPT, this system has been instrumental in achieving a reduction in total work injuries (per million man-hours) from 1349 in 1957, to 60 in 1982, as illustrated in Fig. 20-2.[6]

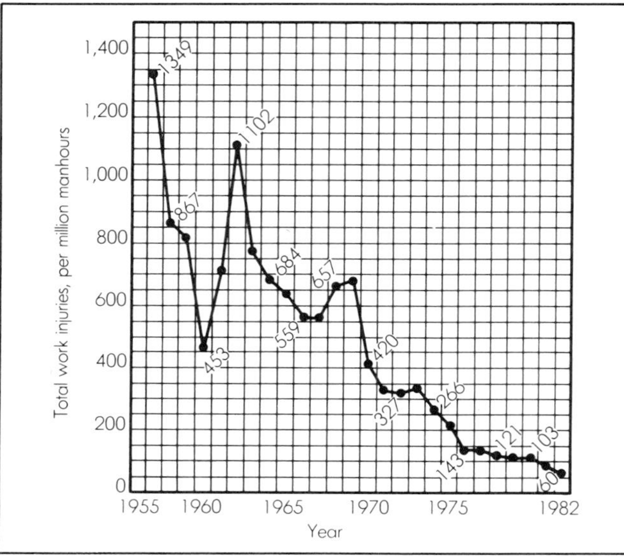


**Fig. 20-2 Graph showing decline in total work injuries per million man-hours of operation.** (*Riley-Beaird Division, United States Riley Corporation*)

## Program Rationale

The systematic EDPT approach designed to abate hazards associated with the work environment at any level of exposure is depicted in Table 20-4. The four-phase process includes examining a safety perspective; diagnosing the exposure, if any; and prescribing control techniques. This approach is reinforced by treating or monitoring the prescribed effect to achieve an optimum response. The method has been applied to a wide range of situations in manufacturing plants of varying size, diversity of products and operations, and geographic locale.

The EDPT concept is versatile and susceptible to adaptation because it is simple and the four-phase structure provides an organized approach that is too often omitted in risk abatement attempts. Additionally, however, each phase of the concept interrelates to the other phase to provide continuity of reinforcement in safety control applications.

## Examination

The essence of examination, safety program Phase 1, is summarized in Table 20-5. This phase is designed to pinpoint a problem area in terms of statistical results. The techniques composing this phase are explained in the following discussion.

**Total incident accountability.** The rationale in applying this technique is that there often is little understanding concerning the point that accident causation, number of injuries, and injury severity are intricately associated with the total number of accidents and noninjury incidents. These interrelationships may be inadvertently overlooked when only the more serious incidents, such as disabling injuries and recordable cases, are considered. However, this oversimplification, in effect, tends to deter reliable safety performance measurements. If severity does identify with gross number accumulations in accident causation, as has been observed over the years, it is reasonable

**TABLE 20-4**
**A Systematic Four-Phase Safety Program Matrix (EDPT)**

| Phase 1 EXAMINATION | Phase 3 PRESCRIPTION | Phase 4 TREATMENT |
|---|---|---|
| • Current audio process | • Policy development | • System testing |
| • Total incident accountability | • Executive mandate | • Design approval |
| • Unit related averages | • Organizational adjustment | • Standards development |
| • Structured assessment | • Selective applicability | • Train/retrain provision |
| Phase 2 DIAGNOSIS | • Assigned managerial accountability | • Support reinforcement |
| • Critical awareness reinforcement | • Central monitoring system | • Emergency handling direction |
| • Analytical survey | • Structured assessment | • Predictability provision |
| • Operational audit | • Sustained monitoring provisions | • Professional consultation |
| • Indentifiable deviations | • Performance efficiency audits | |
| | • Employee response ratings | |
| | • Data base input | |
| | • Structured compliance | |

(*Riley-Beaird*)

**TABLE 20-5**
**Examination, Safety Program, Phase 1**

What is the problem? Who is involved? Where is it occurring? When is it occurring?

1. EXAMINATION *(Risk Evaluation)*
   Investigation or analysis of the cause or nature of a condition, situation, or problem—statistically:
   a. To inspect closely
   b. To test conditions
   c. To inquire into carefully

*(Riley-Beaird)*

to consider total incident accountability critical to safety goal achievement.

**Unit related averages.** Averages are compiled for a number of subunits that compose a plant on the basis of an incident rate computed on all work injuries (total incident accountability). A tabular format is used to compile two kinds of useful information: an experience rate and the degree of deviation.

*Experience rate.* An individual experience rate is calculated for all subunits versus an overall plantwide average. This data identifies the achievers and nonachievers.

*Deviation.* The degree of deviation is apparent on both a short and long-term basis in the columnar tabulation that is prepared. The left-hand column represents a current month. The center column reflects the year-to-date accumulated rate versus the same period the prior year in the right-hand column. Additionally, the production bays are separated from the service departments to more closely align the type of work performed by each group. This data arrangement facilitates study of all of the subunits unfavorable to or below the overall plant average to ascertain the degree of deviation of a particular subunit.

## Diagnosis

Using information gathered during the examination process, the diagnostic phase can begin. Diagnosis starts with a technique termed critical awareness reinforcement and proceeds to an operational audit and the use of data on deviations.

**Awareness.** When the safety performance measurement is relevant and reliable and considered on the basis of total incident accountability and performance-related averages, at least to the point at which its margin of error is reflected, as shown in Table 20-6, it is useful in feeding back information for clearly identifying systematic needs associated with risk abatement. This technique is called critical awareness reinforcement.

**Audit.** Inasmuch as injury incident rates alone have not always been satisfactory indicators of safety performance, an additional technique (the operational audit), employed in the diagnostic phase, supports the statistical indicators and contributes to a realistic conclusion concerning the nature and cause of safety incidents.

A physical audit in the form of a walk-through observation is an invaluable aid in establishing the true identity of an indicated statistical risk trend. This can be done by a safety professional and/or a delegated representative so long as the person to whom the responsibility is delegated is appropriately trained. The immediacy, extent of the risk, and visibility of a potential solution related to a possible consequence can normally be confirmed through this technique.

For example, if the statistics indicate that eye injuries are recurring in a given work unit, the observer may be able to establish certain identifiable needs, such as enclosure separations, revised work procedures, or even protective apparel, in the process of the operational audit. An accurate prognosis in terms of a prescribed safeguard then can be established.

**Deviations.** The accumulated data on identifiable deviations, described previously in this section, is of critical importance in optimizing safety control. It helps to isolate the problem areas to which remedial action should be applied and leads to the next phase of the safety program (see Table 20-7).

## Prescription

The prescriptive phase of the EDPT concept is concerned with the advantages and disadvantages of the various safety options available. Most professional safety practitioners are aware that manufacturing productivity achievements may increase exposure to risk. But how much risk and what type of tolerance is acceptable in an identifiable risk, or if a risk can be controlled at a certain level, are questions that can only be answered by a trained professional who applies a prescriptive approach.

Yet, in reality, it seems that the determination of what constitutes an effective safeguard is based on a fluid set of values among most safety professionals and, therefore, is often viewed on the basis of what appears to be practical in a given situation.

Perhaps this limitation is due partly to the absence of clearly defined prescriptive methods designed to influence the risk abatement process. Over the past 25 years, substantial progress has been made in developing and testing prescriptive applications designed to optimize risk abatement.

Implemented and tested on a trial-and-error basis, the various prescriptive techniques have undergone extensive research and testing and have proved to be an effective body of prescriptive applications for use in neutralizing risk exposures and enhancing safety program developments.

**TABLE 20-6**
**Diagnosis, Safety Program, Phase 2**

What are the results of the examination? How can the risk be eliminated or minimized?

2. DIAGNOSIS (recognition of a risk by symptoms—*Risk Identification*)
   A conclusion concerning the nature or cause of a phenomenon. (The "what" aspect of the problem.)

*(Riley-Beaird)*

**TABLE 20-7**
**Prescription, Safety Program, Phase 3**

How can the control process best be effected? What is the best method of approach? Who is responsible to initiate control measures? When?

3. PRESCRIPTION *(Risk Elimination)*
   An expressed direction for a therapeutic or corrective agent. To prescribe a guide, a direction, or a rule of action.

*(Riley-Beaird)*

# SAFETY PROGRAM DEVELOPMENT

## Treatment

The final phase of the EDPT concept is the treatment aspect. The treatment phase is designed to reinforce all of the other steps in the system concept as summarized in Table 20-8.

The variable in the treatment phase (see Fig. 20-3), includes functions that only a safety professional can perform. Functions such as record design, incident predictability, projection system testing, communication network adjustments, support reinforcement, purchasing and design consultation, and structured reinforcement are among those to be performed.

## History and Experience

A company whose safety program is based on the EDPT methodology has been cited by the National Safety Council 16 times in the past 22 years for outstanding performance. The company's latest safety achievement occurred between July 3, 1981, and June 8, 1982, when, for the first time since its inception in 1918, the company operated in excess of 2 million man-hours without any disabling injuries.[7]

## Application to Forming Operations

The EDPT concept can be the basis for an organized approach to planning, devising, and implementing a safety program. It provides the framework for a process that systematically assembles, analyzes, and details data that is useful in the ongoing safety control activity.

The EDPT concept applied to safety in forming is, in principle, similar to its use in other fields. However, it should be recognized that many characteristics are unique to the forming and shaping of in-process materials.

**Safety programming.** The first step of the examination phase routinely enables the practitioner, whether a lay or professional safety person, to identify factors for establishing general parameters common to the manufacturing field being considered and the objective—which is the safety improvement to be attained.

In this perspective, the user of this method should examine where the work is being done, what is being utilized to accomplish the work, how the application is developed, and to which operator or employee responsibility is delegated to perform the work. The overall plant facility, the material being used, and the method of application are also prime considerations.

It is in this context that the examination process of the EDPT concept is applied to the forming processes in the manufacturing field. The fact that forming involves various types of machine processes requires an awareness of the capabilities of the operator involved and of the environmental effects of the location in which work is performed.

The diagnostic phase, or second phase, of the EDPT concept goes a step further. It involves the attachment of measurement

**TABLE 20-8**
**Treatment, Safety Program, Phase 4**

4. TREATMENT *(Risk Control)*
   To act or apply an agent (something that produces or is capable of producing an effect) to improve or alter a condition, situation, or problem. (What are the overall results?)

*(Riley-Beaird)*

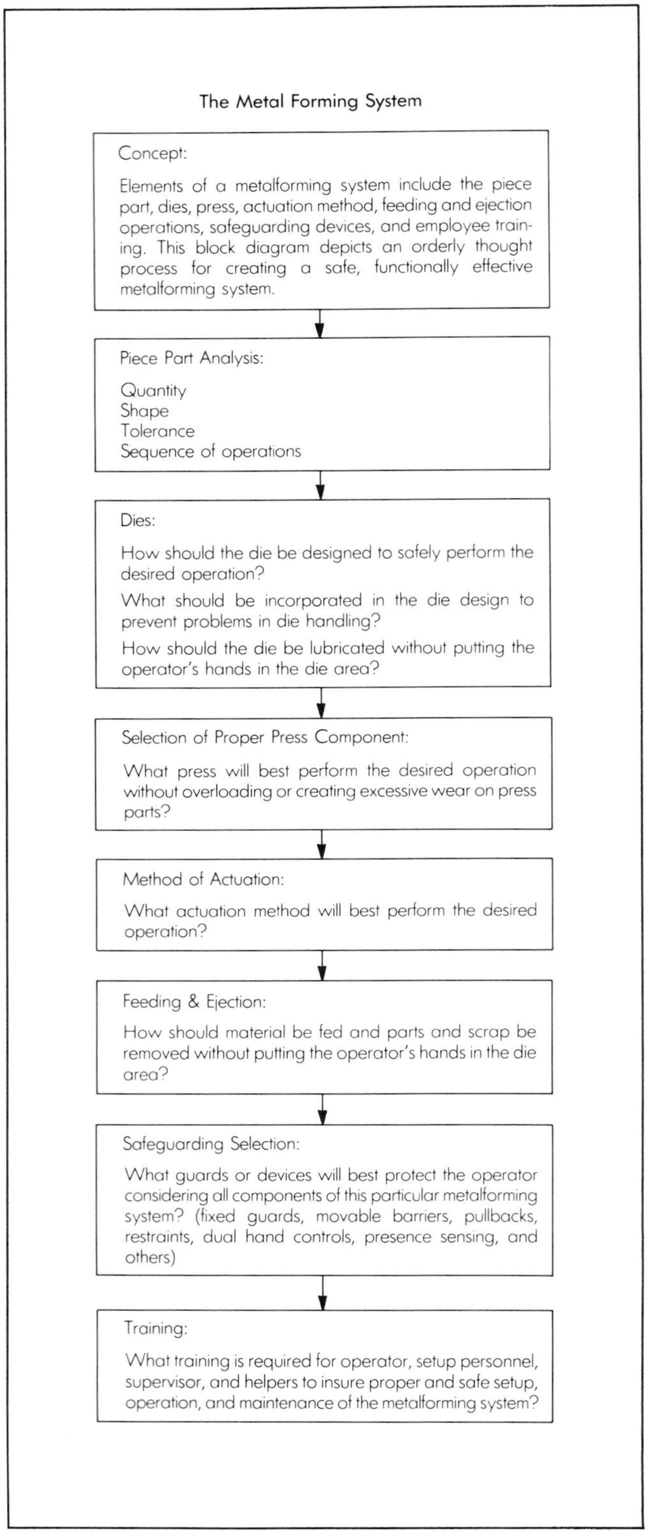

The Metal Forming System

Concept:

Elements of a metalforming system include the piece part, dies, press, actuation method, feeding and ejection operations, safeguarding devices, and employee training. This block diagram depicts an orderly thought process for creating a safe, functionally effective metalforming system.

↓

Piece Part Analysis:

Quantity
Shape
Tolerance
Sequence of operations

↓

Dies:

How should the die be designed to safely perform the desired operation?

What should be incorporated in the die design to prevent problems in die handling?

How should the die be lubricated without putting the operator's hands in the die area?

↓

Selection of Proper Press Component:

What press will best perform the desired operation without overloading or creating excessive wear on press parts?

↓

Method of Actuation:

What actuation method will best perform the desired operation?

↓

Feeding & Ejection:

How should material be fed and parts and scrap be removed without putting the operator's hands in the die area?

↓

Safeguarding Selection:

What guards or devices will best protect the operator considering all components of this particular metalforming system? (fixed guards, movable barriers, pullbacks, restraints, dual hand controls, presence sensing, and others)

↓

Training:

What training is required for operator, setup personnel, supervisor, and helpers to insure proper and safe setup, operation, and maintenance of the metalforming system?

**Fig. 20-3 Schematic block diagram illustrates a broad systems view of safety and shows how selection of safeguarding method is linked into the overall safety system.** (*E.W. Bliss Division, Gulf & Western Manufacturing Company*)

standards which are known by the practitioner to foster safety achievements from which effects can be appraised.

An evaluation guide for appraising these effects is provided in Table 20-9. The table's chart format includes suggested numerical rating values that are apportioned appropriately within each of the five areas designated for evaluation, including facilities, materials handling, machinery, operator, and housekeeping. Although not included in the chart, equipment maintenance is vitally important to safety since poorly maintained machines can cause accidents.

The user can evaluate and appraise a specific variable in terms of whether it is in full compliance, reasonably adequate (good) compliance, or fair-to-poor compliance.

The benefits of a valued measurement of safety are many. The data provides a means to convey to management in understandable, quantified terms, information on the existing level of safety and the status of the safety program. Whenever necessary, prescriptive controls can be established to minimize a risk or alleviate a problem.

**Safety maintenance.** The fourth phase of the EDPT concept, the treatment phase, consists of maintaining the prescriptive effects selected by the practitioner at an optimum level. The task

**TABLE 20-9**
**Performance Guide for Evaluating Safety in Forming**

| | Degrees | | | | |
|---|---|---|---|---|---|
| | EXCELLENT 3 | GOOD 2 | FAIR 1 | POOR 0 | |
| Factors | Full Compliance | Minor Deviation | Partial Compliance | General Non-Compliance | |
| 1. Facility: | | | | | |
| Adequate aisles and direct access | 20 | 16 | 12 | 0 | |
| Work area free of congestion | 20 | 16 | 12 | 0 | |
| Adequate process accommodations, racks, etc. | 20 | 16 | 12 | 0 | |
| Adequate lighting and ventilation effects | 20 | 16 | 12 | 0 | |
| Work platforms 4 ft (1.2 m) or more above floor level, adequately guarded | 20 | 16 | 12 | 0 | |
| | 100 | 80 | 60 | 0 | x 0.20 = ______ |
| 2. Materials Handling: | | | | | |
| Equipment adequate for job | 25 | 20 | 15 | 0 | |
| Equipment free of overloading | 25 | 20 | 15 | 0 | |
| Planned and organized movements of material | 25 | 20 | 15 | 0 | |
| Adequate safeguards against unexpected movement | 25 | 20 | 15 | 0 | |
| | 100 | 80 | 60 | 0 | x 0.20 = ______ |
| 3. Machinery: | | | | | |
| Operated by authorized and trained operators | 15 | 12 | 9 | 0 | |
| Cut off when not in operation | 10 | 8 | 6 | 0 | |
| All moving parts such as flywheels, shafts, gears, pulley sets 7 ft (2.1 m) or less from floor, adequately guarded | 15 | 12 | 9 | 0 | |
| Point of operation guarded or catch point avoided by use of special tools* | 15 | 12 | 9 | 0 | |
| Electrical circuits grounded | 15 | 12 | 9 | 0 | |
| Machine secured free of vibration and maintenance defects | 15 | 12 | 9 | 0 | |
| Repairs, oiling, and/or adjusting of equipment never made while machine is in operation | 15 | 12 | 9 | 0 | |
| | 100 | 80 | 60 | 0 | x 0.20 = ______ |

(*continued*)

TABLE 20-9—*Continued*

| | Degrees | | | | |
|---|---|---|---|---|---|
| | EXCELLENT 3 | GOOD 2 | FAIR 1 | POOR 0 | |
| Factors | Full Compliance | Minor Deviation | Partial Compliance | General Non-Compliance | |
| 4. Operator: | | | | | |
| Authorized to operate and properly maintain | 15 | 12 | 9 | 0 | |
| Job procedures defined and followed | 15 | 12 | 9 | 0 | |
| Refrains from taking positions exposing self or others | 15 | 12 | 9 | 0 | |
| Refrains from attempting to repair, oil, and/or adjust machinery in operation | 15 | 12 | 9 | 0 | |
| Refrains from horseplay, joking, etc., that is dangerous | 15 | 12 | 9 | 0 | |
| Wears required safety apparel. Refrains from wearing rings | 15 | 12 | 9 | 0 | |
| Maintains equipment to the best of his/her ability—reports defects immediately | 10 | 8 | 6 | 0 | |
| | 100 | 80 | 60 | 0 | x 0.20 = ______ |
| 5. Housekeeping: | | | | | |
| Work surface clear of tripping hazards such as loose tools, in-process materials, spilled oil, water, etc. | 25 | 20 | 15 | 0 | |
| Workbenches, tables, etc., at work station orderly | 25 | 20 | 15 | 0 | |
| In-process tools and materials properly arranged and secured | 25 | 20 | 15 | 0 | |
| Adequate disposal accommodations | 25 | 20 | 15 | 0 | |
| | 100 | 80 | 60 | 0 | x 0.20 = ______ |

* Although hand tools are used as an adjunct to safety devices and guards, the tools are not sanctioned as the sole means of operator protection. Such tools do, however, qualify as a "no hands in die" method of safe operation.

of maintaining safety control at a satisfactory level is facilitated by actions performed during development of the safety program. These actions enable possible hazards to be identified and some change to be instituted to correct or eliminate them. Once the problems are known and the appropriate people know what is being done about them, it is necessary to ensure continuance of sound safety practices. If special controls or a workplace code of safe practices and operating procedures has been instituted, the controls or code must be monitored and maintained. To ensure that this is done, it is helpful to use a periodic self-inspection program, such as described earlier in this chapter and amplified in the guidelines given in the following section.

## A SYSTEMATIC APPROACH TO METALFORMING SAFETY

Amputations and bone fractures are among the most common types of injuries. Typically, an accident occurs when the worker reaches into the machine's point of operation while loading, unloading, or holding a part in process. In many instances, the machine is not stopped for loading or unloading and there is insufficient space or distance for the worker to safely handle the part while loading it into or removing it from the machine.

Failure to use a brush or an appropriate hand tool is a major cause of finger amputations. Frequently, gloves, loose sleeves, and bulky jackets are caught in the tooling, resulting in injury. Whenever the operator is handling stampings, gloves should be worn to protect the hands from cuts caused by burrs and sharp edges.

When determining the most appropriate safeguarding means to be applied to metalforming equipment, consideration must be given to the job requirements and, in particular, to the level of skill needed to perform the task. In one accident study, analysis showed that only a minority of the injured workers were considered journeymen. The majority were in the general category of "operator."[8]

In the safety field, for an effective, professional approach to the overall goal of accident and injury prevention or to the important area of machine safeguarding, a broad systems view is essential. Figure 20-3 illustrates, schematically, in that context how the systems concept is applied to metalforming operations and the selection of proper safeguarding methods and devices.

For effective safety planning, it is critically important to recognize and consider the multipurpose functions of many types of machinery. To develop a forming system that provides adequate safety, an account must be taken of the following:

- Size and type of machine.
- Method of control.
- Tooling design and operation.

- Blank or piecepart size.
- Shape and contours of the formed part.
- Method of feeding the blank into the machine.
- Method of removing the formed part from the machine.

Experience has shown that a thorough, systematic approach must be taken in controlling employee injuries on machines, since no single accident control measure (alone) can be effective. In a given plant situation—taking account of variations in type of forming machine, operation, and workers—specific guidelines for machine safeguarding can be developed by considering key factors such as machine design, provision for "hands out of danger area," machine controls, and guards.

## Machine Design and Use

The machine and the associated equipment must be well designed for the job for which they are to be used. Selecting the proper size and capacity of machine for the job is essential. The machine must have adequate capacity and strength and should be operated within the design capacity. When there is a choice of machines available for performing a specific job, full consideration should be given to whether optimum worker protection can be provided on the machine selected. The job should be so well planned that neither overloading nor overspeeding of the machine is likely to occur. In regard to the safety requirements for machine tools, the B11 series of the American National Standards provides good guidance for both the manufacturer and the user.

## Hands Out of Danger Area

Whenever possible, metalforming operations should be planned to eliminate the need for the worker to reach into the point of operation. This is accomplished through the use of well-designed tooling and alternative methods of feeding, part removal, and scrap removal, including the use of special hand tools.

Particularly with power presses, press brakes, shears, hammers and other machines that can be cycled, the first objective for safe operation is to plan the operation so that it is unnecessary for the operator to place a hand into the point of operation. The second objective is to prevent the operator, through the application of effective safeguarding methods, from placing a hand in the point of operation when the slide or ram is closing.

To avoid an operational requirement that could endanger the operator's hands, the job designer or process engineer should plan the material feeding, part removal, scrap removal, and tooling lubrication to eliminate, whenever possible, the need for workers to reach into the danger area. Various feeding methods commonly used include automatic feeding (requiring no manual operation other than replacing of stock); semi-automatic feeding by means of manually operated feeding devices; hand-tool feeding (permitting hands to be kept away from the point of operation); and manual feeding of large pieces of such size or shape that when holding them, the hands are positioned well away from the point of operation or danger area. The die and the forming system should be designed to facilitate a "hands out of the die" operation.

## Machine Controls

The design and location of machine controls can have a major bearing on safe operation of the machine. Operating controls should be convenient; should be identifiable as to their function; and except for stopping controls, should be protected against accidental actuation. Stopping or deactivation controls must be convenient and obvious. Location of machine controls is critical for two reasons. First, the machine control should be conveniently located so that the operator need not reach into or be unnecessarily close to a danger area to operate the controls. Secondly, the machine controls should be placed so that the operator can control the machine, yet be in a safe location outside the danger area.

Pendant controls allow good visibility and control and help the operator to remain in a safe location. There should be supervisory control over certain modes of operation or control stations through the use of key-operated selector switches to obtain the optimum level of employee safety. Not only should the stop buttons be convenient, but also there should be a sufficient number of them to allow quick stopping in case of emergency. Electrical foot switches that are used as operator controls should be covered or guarded.

## Guards and Devices

A wide variety of safeguarding methods can be applied to metalforming machines to reduce the inherent exposures to employee injuries (see Chapter 5, "Presses for Sheet Metal Forming"). The hazards are primarily at the point of operation, but can also include drive mechanisms and the loading and unloading equipment. Figure 20-4 shows a diagrammatic

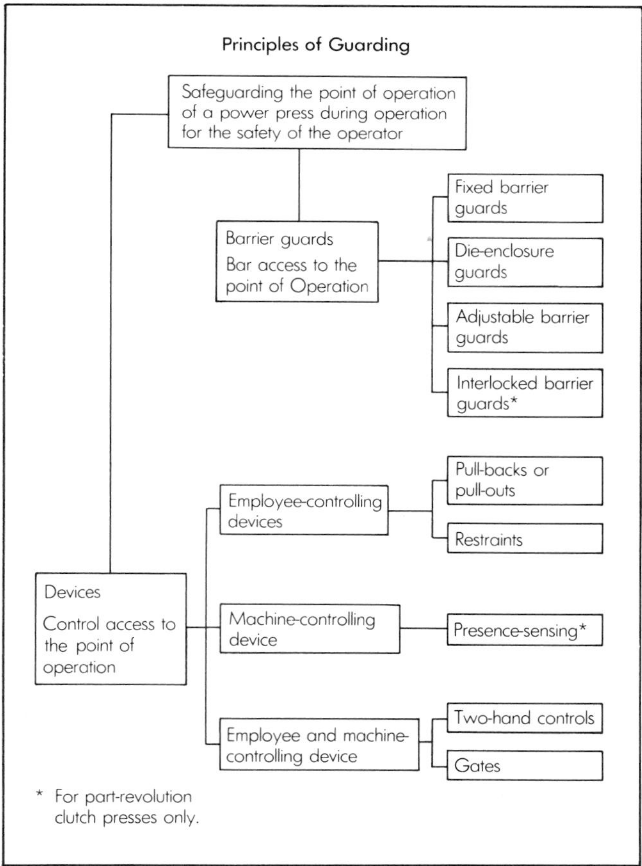


**Fig. 20-4 This diagrammatic overview identifies basic principles of machine safeguarding and shows their interrelationships. (*E. W. Bliss Division, Gulf & Western Manufacturing Company*)**

representation of the principles applicable to safeguarding power press point of operation for operator safety. Details of guards and devices for presses are presented in Chapter 5.

The type and extent of application of safeguarding is dependent upon several factors, including the exposure to injury and the experience-based probability of injury. All press operations should be safeguarded. As stated previously, the type of safeguarding depends upon the machine type, the tooling, the part size and configuration, the feeding method, the part removal method, and the provisions for scrap disposal. Users of multifunctional equipment should consider all elements of the forming system when selecting point of operation safeguarding or when determining safe methods of operation.

Other factors to consider include the level of skill needed to perform the job, the ability of the worker, and the responsibility for decision-making on the part of the operator. The most effective and practical method of safeguarding should be selected for each machine operation. The factors to be considered when selecting a safeguarding device for a press brake are diagrammed in Fig. 20-5. Many general-purpose metal-forming machine tools must be provided with more than one available method of safeguarding because of the different types of operations that can be performed on them. Table 20-10 identifies safeguarding methods that are recommended for various types of work.

## Preventive Maintenance

Along with the machines on which they are installed, guards and safety devices should be the object of a regular preventive maintenance program. This includes proper adjustment, regular inspection, replacement of critical parts before failure when that may be anticipated, and maintenance of reasonable records. Trained personnel should be designated to carry out the program to ensure that the standards as established by management are maintained. As an example of good practice, Table 20-11 shows a maintenance checklist for a hydraulic shear machine.

## Lockout/Tagout

Means must be provided for locking out all power and releasing all stored energy when maintenance and repair

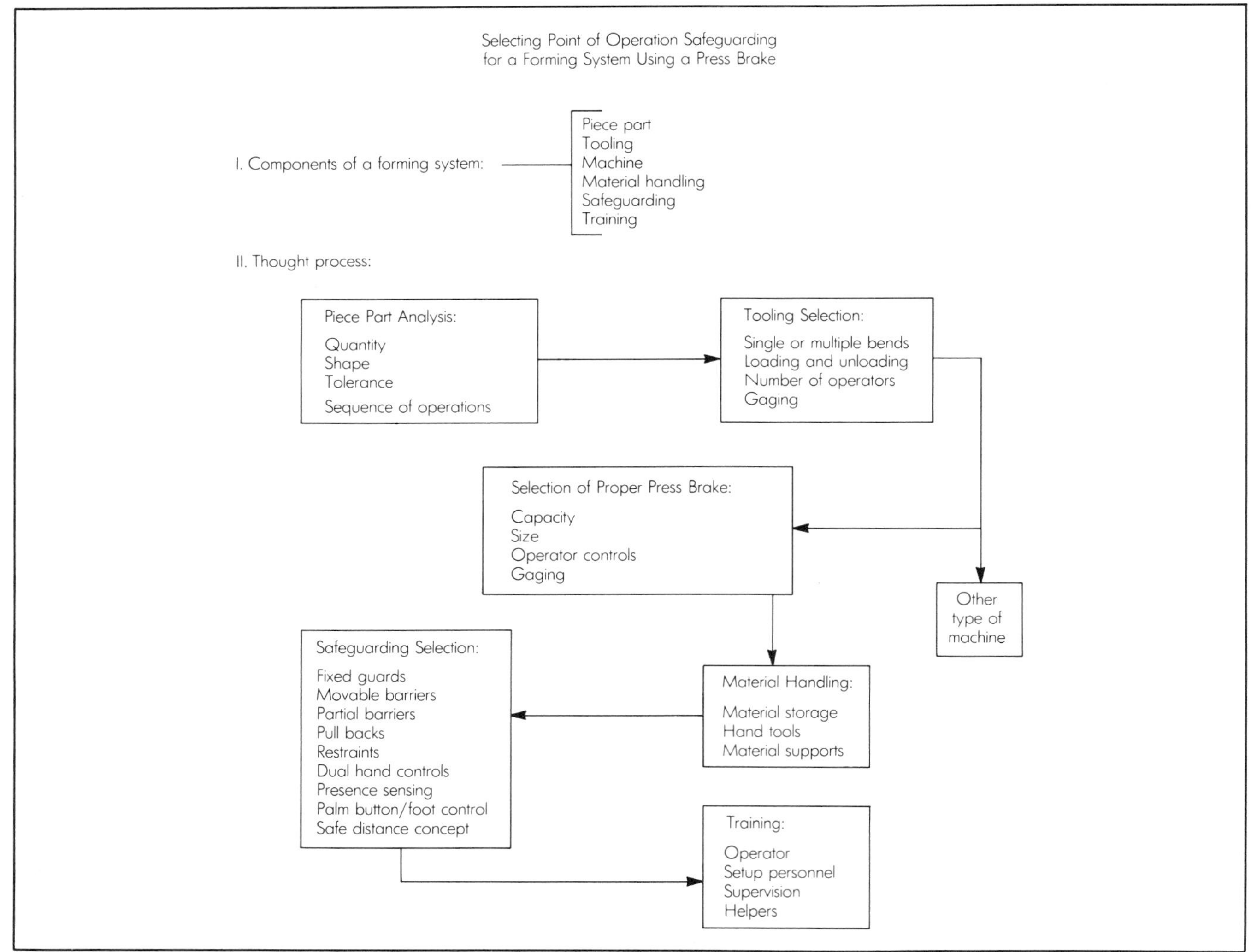


**Fig. 20-5 Factors related to selection of safeguarding method for a press brake.** (*Cincinnati Incorporated*)

**TABLE 20-10**
**Press Brake Safeguarding: Point of Operation Selection Chart**

| Type of Work Performed in Press Brake | Mechanical Press Brake with Foot Treadle | | Mechanical or Hydraulic Press Brake with Foot Switch | |
|---|---|---|---|---|
| | Without Helper | With Helper | Without Helper | With Helper |
| V-Bend with work supported by operator(s) over 20″ (508 mm) from die | E & C or G & C | E & C or GG & C | E & C or GG & C | E & C or GG & C |
| V-Bend with work supported by operator(s) 20″ (508 mm) or less from die | C, D & F or C, D & G | C, D & FF or C, D & GG | C, D & F or C, D & G | C, D & FF or C, D & GG |
| Work placed completely in the die area by operator(s) | B, C, D & E or B, C, D & G | B, C, D & E or B, C, D & GG | B, C, D & A | B, C, D & AA |
| Progressive forming such as a tube, cone, or bumping operation | C & F or C & G | C & FF or C & GG | C & F or C & G | C & FF or C & GG |
| Bends on third and fourth side such as a box | C, D & E or C, D & F | C, D & E or C, D & FF | C, D & E or C, D & F | C, D & E or C, D & FF |
| Single-station or Multiple-station, press-type work | DO NOT USE | DO NOT USE | C, D & A | C, D & AA |
| Horn-type work | D & G | DO NOT USE | D & G | DO NOT USE |
| Wiping die | C, D & G | C, D & GG | C, D & A | C, D & AA |

(*Cincinnati Incorporated*)

Note: The types of work in this chart do not necessarily reflect all possible types. The user is instructed to utilize a safety device or guard appropriate to the particular press brake operations. Each guard or device should be used, maintained, and adjusted in accordance with the safety device manufacturer's instructions. Hand tools or another mechanism must be used to feed or remove any part that would otherwise require hands to be placed in the die. Placing hands in the die is not recommended under any condition.

The letters refer to types of safety devices or guards as follows:

- A— Dual palm buttons.
- AA— Multiple two-hand palm buttons.
- B— Hand tools (for small parts not to be used in place of safety device).
- C— Plastics end guards on each end.
- D— Plastics guard sections on unused area.
- E— Photoelectric presence sensing device.
- F— Restraints.
- FF— Two restraints.
- G— Pullbacks.
- GG— Two pullbacks.

activities are in progress. The power disconnects should be convenient for shutting off and locking out all power, including air, electric, hydraulic, and steam. Unexpected startup of machines must be prevented through the use of an effective lockout/tagout program. Additional information on lockout practices may be obtained from ANSI Z244.1 "Safety Standard for Lockout/Tagout of Energy Sources."

## Environmental Hazards

Areas surrounding machines should be kept clear of slip, trip, and fall hazards. Good working surfaces of the nonslip type should be provided on all platforms surrounding machines. Lighting and good layout of machines with room for material movement are important items to consider.

## Worker/Job Demands

It is important to evaluate the physical as well as the mental requirements for performing metalforming machine tasks. The job should be designed to fit the worker. Adequate provision must be made for handling of heavy, sharp, or bulky materials to reduce the exposure to muscle strain and other employee injuries.

## Safe Clothing and Equipment

Unrestrained long hair should not be allowed around moving machinery. Hair should be restrained, such as under a cap; and jewelry, such as rings and watches, should not be allowed. Short sleeves are generally preferable to long sleeves when operating machine tools. Eye protection should be provided and worn.

**TABLE 20-11**
**Maintenance Checklist for Hydraulic Shears**

| Check or Adjustment | Daily | Weekly | Monthly | Three Months | Six Months | Annually | Two Years |
|---|---|---|---|---|---|---|---|
| 1. Check hold-downs for proper operation—correct if necessary | • | | | | | | |
| 2. Inspect blades for nicks or wear—turn, replace or resharpen if necessary | • | | | | | | |
| 3. Check to see that all guards and barriers are in place and in good condition | • | | | | | | |
| 4. Wipe machine with clean rags, especially the clevis pin | | • | | | | | |
| 5. Check stroke control—adjust if necessary | | | • | | | | |
| 6. Check rake control—adjust if necessary | | | • | | | | |
| 7. Check blade bolts and ram adjusting nuts—tighten if necessary | | | • | | | | |
| 8. Check blade and ram guide clearance—adjust if necessary | | | • | | | | |
| 9. Clean strainer in water line to heat exchanger | | | | | • | | |
| 10. Check machine level—relevel if necessary | | | | | • | | |
| 11. Check entire machine for loose fasteners, especially back-gage and hold-down beam bolts—tighten if necessary | | | | | • | | |
| 12. Remove magnetic trap and clean | | | | | • | | |
| 13. Replace bypass filter cartridge | | | | | • | | |
| 14. Clean intake strainer | | | | | | • | |
| 15. Replace air cleaner | | | | | | | • |
| **Lubrication Schedule** | | | | | | | |
| 1. Check automatic lubrication oil level and turn crank 24 turns—and oil if necessary | • | | | | | | |
| 2. Fill back-gage nut reservoirs with oil | | • | | | | | |
| 3. Check hydraulic reservoir oil level—add oil if necessary | | | • | | | | |
| 4. Check oil temperature in reservoir—clean and adjust temperature control valve if necessary | | | | | • | | |
| 5. Drain, clean, and refill hydraulic reservoir—see operator's manual | | | | | | • | |
| 6. Check and reset hydraulic pressures | | | | | | • | |

Note: Intervals are based on one shift operation

(*Cincinnati Incorporated*)

## Training

Operators, helpers, and maintenance and setup personnel should be well trained in safe work practices through the application of a well-planned training program. Machine manufacturers are good sources for training materials.

Particular attention must be given to new employees. Immediately upon starting work, new employees begin to learn things and form attitudes about their company, their job, their boss, and other employees. They do so whether or not the employer makes an effort to train them. If people are trained during the first few hours and days to do things the right way, considerable losses over a period of time can be avoided.

Attention must, however, be paid to all employees. Old habits can be wrong habits. An employee who continues to repeat an unsafe procedure is not working safely, even if an accident has not resulted from this condition.

Some general indicators that might show a need for training or retraining are:

- Excessive waste or scrap.
- High labor turnover.
- An increase in the number of "near misses" which could have resulted in accidents.
- A recent upswing in actual accident experience.
- High injury and illness incidence.
- Expansion of business and/or new employment.
- A change in manufacturing process, or introducing a new process.

## Supervision

After workers have been trained, the level and quality of supervision should be such that the applicable guards and devices are utilized along with the previously taught safe work practices and procedures.

While every employee's attitude should be one of determination that accidents can be prevented, one thing more may be needed. Management should stress the responsibility assigned to the person in charge of the job—as well as to all other supervisors—to be sure that there is a concerted effort to follow every safe work procedure and health practice applicable to that job. It should be explained to the supervisors that they must not silently condone unsafe or unhealthy activity in or around the workplace.

# FIRE PROTECTION

The general objective of fire prevention and protection can be subdivided into three basic areas: (1) preventing the outbreak of fire; (2) extinguishing the fire and averting its spread; and (3) preventing casualties and limiting damage from the fire. For information on the chemical principles of combustion, the classification of fires, and recommended types of fire extinguishers, refer to "Safety and Noise Control," Chapter 18, Volume I, *Machining*, of this Handbook series.

Although many industries have special fire prevention and control problems that are related specifically to the materials used and the processes that are performed, the most frequent causes of industrial fires are similar among various industries. Most of the causes can be eliminated or controlled. The following list indicates the approximate percent to which the five most common causes contributed to industrial fires.[9]

- Electrical causes—22%.
- Matches and smoking—18%.
- Friction (hot bearings, machine parts, jammed material)—11%.
- Hot surfaces—9%.
- Overheated materials—7%.

## Fire Protection Information

To develop and maintain an effective fire control program, use should be made of information and assistance that are available from insurance companies, fire protection societies and associations, government agencies, and fire-engineering consultants. It is advisable to refrain from limiting the inquiry to seeking advice on the solution of specific fire problems. The greater benefit is gained from a more general line of inquiry that is aimed at knowing what the problems are. Then, when the problems have been identified, professional fire control expertise can render valuable assistance. Table 20-12 provides a rudimentary checklist for fire safety.

**TABLE 20-12**
**Fire Safety Checklist**

| General | OK | Action Needed |
|---|---|---|
| 1. Are all exits visible and unobstructed? | ☐ | ☐ |
| 2. Are all exits marked with a readily visible sign that is properly illuminated? | ☐ | ☐ |
| 3. Are there sufficient exits to ensure prompt escape in case of emergency? | ☐ | ☐ |
| 4. Are areas with limited occupancy posted and is access/egress controlled to persons specifically authorized to be in those areas? | ☐ | ☐ |
| 5. Are approved safety cans or other acceptable containers used for handling and dispensing flammable liquids? | ☐ | ☐ |
| 6. Are all flammable liquids that are kept inside buildings stored in proper storage containers or cabinets? | ☐ | ☐ |
| 7. Are oxidizing chemicals stored in areas separate from all organic material? | ☐ | ☐ |

| Housekeeping and Work Environment | OK | Action Needed |
|---|---|---|
| 1. Is smoking permitted in designated "safe areas" only? | ☐ | ☐ |
| 2. Are NO SMOKING signs prominently posted in areas containing combustibles and flammables? | ☐ | ☐ |
| 3. Are covered metal waste cans used for oily and paint-soaked waste? | ☐ | ☐ |
| Are they emptied at least daily? | ☐ | ☐ |
| 4. Are paint spray booths, dip tanks, etc., and their exhaust ducts cleaned regularly? | ☐ | ☐ |
| 5. Is fire-safety-related housekeeping sustained at a satisfactory level? | ☐ | ☐ |

| Equipment and Facilities | OK | Action Needed |
|---|---|---|
| 1. Is there sufficient clearance from stoves, furnaces, etc., for stock, woodwork, or other combustible materials? | ☐ | ☐ |
| 2. Is there clearance of at least 4 ft (1.3 m) in front of heating equipment involving open flames, such as gas radiant heaters, and fronts of firing doors of stoves, furnaces, etc.? | ☐ | ☐ |
| 3. Are all oil and gas-fired devices equipped with flame failure controls that will prevent flow of fuel if pilots or main burners are not working? | ☐ | ☐ |
| 4. Is there at least a 2" (50 mm) clearance between chimney brickwork and all woodwork or other combustible materials? | ☐ | ☐ |
| 5. Does equipment meet OSHA standards for all spray painting or dip tank operations using combustible liquids? | ☐ | ☐ |

| Fire Protection | OK | Action Needed |
|---|---|---|
| 1. Are portable fire extinguishers provided in adequate number and type? | ☐ | ☐ |
| 2. Are fire extinguishers inspected monthly for general condition and operability and noted on the inspection tag? | ☐ | ☐ |
| 3. Are fire extinguishers recharged regularly and properly noted on the inspection tag? | ☐ | ☐ |
| 4. Are fire extinguishers mounted in readily accessible locations? | ☐ | ☐ |
| 5. Have plant personnel been instructed in the use of extinguishers and fire hose? | ☐ | ☐ |
| 6. Does the automatic sprinkler system cover the entire plant area? | ☐ | ☐ |

### Fire Protection Fundamentals

The details involved in fire prevention and the limitation of fire loss are complex and numerous; however, the underlying principles may be summarized straightforwardly:[10]

- Know the hazardous characteristics, including the fire and explosion potentials, of all materials handled.
- Prevent the start of a fire by adequate inspection, effective maintenance, good housekeeping, and the segregation and reduction in usage of combustible materials.
- Limit the spread of fire by using protected passageways and door openings, enclosing critical work areas with fire-resistant construction, and installing fire walls at appropriate locations.
- Devise a fire protection plan, obtain the necessary fire-fighting devices and equipment, and maintain the system in a state of readiness for a fire emergency.

### Fire Protection Program

The following are some key items that should be considered when a fire protection program is being implemented.[11]

**Electrical equipment.** All electrical equipment should be included in a schedule of periodic inspections. Maintenance and inspection of motors and other electrical items should be performed by qualified personnel.

**Smoking.** Smokers can be a special problem. Despite all cautions and warnings, some people persist in smoking in hazardous places. Yet, in view of the danger, a strong effort should be made to confine smoking and the use of matches to designated areas.

**Housekeeping.** Rubbish, waste, and other debris should be cleaned up and removed daily, with disposal provided in suitable containers (preferably located outside the plant). Oily or paint-soaked rags or clothing left in lockers can be a hazard. Lint, dust, and oil collecting in flues and vents can ignite spontaneously. Thorough housekeeping measures, regularly performed, contribute to prevention of fires.

**Open flames.** Open flames sometimes are used for heating materials and as an aid to forming operations. In these instances, it is advisable to use protective clothing for employees and to provide fireproof materials around the work area. Fire extinguishers of the proper type also should be readily available.

**Heated surfaces.** Hot surfaces on in-process materials; and heated surfaces on furnaces, flues, heating devices, and electric lamps can cause fires when flammable materials are too close to them. Care should be taken to guard against exposure of combustibles to heated surfaces.

**Molten metal.** Molten metal can ignite flammable material when contact occurs. Precautions should be taken to provide protective clothing and a flameproof environment in foundry areas.

**Volatile liquids.** Solvents, petroleum derivatives, paints, varnishes, and lacquers are common sources of fires and explosions. While, in some instances, the liquids do not burn, heat causes vaporization and the resulting mist or vapor may be ignited by sparks from electrical devices, static electricity, or contact between metal objects, as well as by open flames. Flameproof cabinets, tight metal containers, color coding, and rigorous storage and handling procedures are necessary for volatile liquids.

**System elements.** Portable fire extinguishers; fixed extinguisher systems using automatic sprinklers or standpipes and hoses; fire alarms; fire walls; and fire doors are the elements of an effective fire protection system. Of the various system elements, automatic sprinklers are the most extensively used installations of fixed fire extinguisher units and are considered to be the most dependable form of fire protection. Sprinkler systems provide around-the-clock protection and have been effective in many thousands of fires.

*Precautions.* Sprinkler system failures sometimes are caused by water supply valves that are *not* turned on. Other failures are attributed to inadequate water supply, improper installation, and high-piled materials and congested conditions that impede the water distribution. Regular inspection and maintenance should be performed to ensure reliable operation of the sprinkler system when needed to extinguish a fire.

*Complete coverage.* A key point in fire protection is the importance of equipping the manufacturing plant with a *complete* sprinkler system that covers the entire plant area rather than a partial system located only in selected places in the plant. Installation of a complete automatic sprinkler system is especially important in the new one-story plants having a configuration and large size that may limit internal access by fire department personnel attempting to fight a fire from outside the building.

# EFFECTIVE SAFETY PROGRAMS

Studies were sponsored by the U.S. Department of Health, Education, and Welfare (DHEW); Public Health Service; and National Institute for Occupational Safety and Health (NIOSH), and then reported in NIOSH Research Report No. 79-136, "Safety Program Practices in Record-Holding Plants." The series of investigations was conducted in three phases and consisted primarily of surveys in plants that were recognized as industry leaders in man-hours worked without a disabling injury.

During the course of the investigations, site visits to the companies were undertaken to verify in detail the key elements of successful safety programming. The findings indicated that, although similar safety program organizational structures and techniques were used by the record-holding companies, no safety program was exactly like any other. However, all of the programs had one major characteristics in common: safety in each instance was a real priority item in corporate policy and action.

## COMMON CHARACTERISTICS

The plants involved in the NIOSH survey shared some general features that appear to represent basic elements in effective safety programs. First, the programs set safety goals, assigned safety responsibilities, provided adequate resources, and evaluated safety performance. Second, they identified problems, applied preplanned solutions, and evaluated management and employee effectiveness. And, finally, the programs motivated and included employees.

From the NIOSH study, the following are among principal conclusions concerning characteristics associated with superior safety performance.[12]

1. A strong management commitment to safety expressed not only through stated policy and adequate financial support, but also through active involvement in program implementation and demonstrated concern for worker well-being.
2. Efficient hazard identification, engineering control, job safety training, and safety evaluation programs designed to anticipate and manage hazards, not just to count and investigate accidents (after the fact).
3. Good housekeeping practices and general plant cleanliness; along with favorable environmental qualities such as comfortable levels of heat and noise, and effective ventilation and lighting.
4. An effective employee communication, feedback, and involvement program designed to motivate management and employees to deal with one another and with safety problems in a positive "humanistic" manner.
5. A safety program that is integrated into the larger management system and is designed to deal with safety as an intrinsic part of plant operations.

## MODEL SAFETY PROGRAM

As discussed earlier in this chapter, after completing the preliminary processes of general information gathering and planning, a safety program typically is launched with issuance of a policy statement and appointment of a safety director. The next stages entail development, promulgation, and implementation of the safety program. As a starting point for formulation of a suitable program for a particular plant or group of manufacturing forming operations, Table 20-13 provides a generalized example of a model safety program.

**TABLE 20-13**
**Safety Program Model**

### People Make It Work

The human element is the most important aspect of a safety program. Management, the safety director, safety committee, foremen, supervisors and employees all play critical roles.

**Management Responsibility:**
Safety starts at the top. The chief executive, and all other "top management" must provide the example and moving force for the safety program. The person responsible for administering the program should report directly to the top executive.

Primary responsibilities of management personnel should include:
- Development of realistic program objectives.
- Development of safety policies.
- A commitment to provide the financial and personnel resources necessary to implement and sustain a safety program.
- Definition of duties and safety-related responsibilities of personnel at each administrative level.
- Ensuring that a safety analysis is conducted for each job description or operation.
- Requiring that instructions, rules of procedure and safeguarding techniques are established for each operation.
- Insisting that specified safeguarding and safety equipment be utilized at all times.
- Requiring a hazards analysis of all equipment before purchase.

**The Safety Director:**
In most small and medium-size plants, the safety director's responsibilities are combined with other duties. In the performance of safety functions, the safety director should:
- Direct and supervise the overall safety program.
- Coordinate safety committee meetings and activities.
- Work with process engineering or others on job safety analysis and creation of operational instructions.
- Investigate or coordinate the investigation of any serious injury and take corrective action if necessary.
- Make periodic safety inspections.
- Deal with inspections by OSHA or other governmental agencies.

**Foremen and Supervisors:**
Accident prevention must be of concern to all employees. However, it is the direct responsibility of foremen and supervisors who deal directly with the workforce to administer and enforce safe work practices. Their responsibility involves:
- Instruction and supervision of subordinates in safe work practices.
- Enforcement of safety rules, including safety requirements for each operation and use of proper safety equipment.
- Departmental housekeeping.
- Condition of equipment.
- Training.
- Complaint and accident investigation.

**Hourly Workers:**
Since production workers have the greatest injury potential, their commitment should be to:
- Adhere to instructions and observe all safety rules in performance of the job.
- Report any hazardous operation or condition.
- Use protective safety equipment provided or needed on the job.
- Operate machinery in the safest manner possible, paying strict attention to instructions and safeguarding systems.

(*American Metal Stamping Association*)

# STANDARDS AND INFORMATION SOURCES

Employee safety must be a primary consideration in company planning, decision-making, and operations. Provision of a safe workplace is a humane and moral requirement for employers. It also is a legal requirement, backed by the regulatory force of government agency authority and power.

The Williams-Steiger Occupational Safety and Health Act of 1970, commonly referred to as OSHA, is one of the most comprehensive laws ever passed by the U.S. Congress to regulate the working conditions of workers in the United States. The law became effective on April 28, 1971.

## REQUIREMENTS OF THE OSHA LAW

Under OSHA, all employers who are in any way engaged in interstate commerce, or in a business that affects interstate commerce, must maintain employee workplaces that are free from recognized hazards, and must comply with a voluminous body of specific standards pertaining to plants, equipment, and operating practices. Also, all companies with seven or more employees must comply with the OSHA record-keeping requirements. The United States Department of Labor is empowered to determine what constitutes "recognized hazards." Further, the Department of Labor is responsible for the development, adoption, and enforcement of safety standards—and industry is measured and evaluated continually against these government-mandated standards.

### Responsibility of the Employer

In what often is called the current "era of OSHA," the employer must apply prudence, humane concern, and sound business practice to the maintenance of a safe working environment; and this must be done in specific and standard ways. Also, the employer must be able to prove it is being done. The U.S. Federal OSHA Act provides strong enforcement powers. Industry must comply or face severe penalties. A compilation that lists some of the principal safety standards applicable to metalforming machines is given in Table 20-14. Under the federal Act, the employer must:

- Observe all OSHA standards that are applicable to a particular business.
- Keep company employees informed of their protection and their obligations under the Act.
- Permit government inspection of the workplace and premises.

**Inform.** Among the basic OSHA provisions is a requirement that the employer inform employees of the protection provided by the Act. One of the key stipulations is that the U.S. Labor Department's informational poster, "Safety and Health Protection on the Job," be prominently displayed in the workplace.

**Conform.** The employer must comply with all safety and health standards that are applicable to a particular business or manufacturing operation. To ensure availability of complete, authoritative information on which to base plans for meeting all standards that apply, an employer may order a copy of the "Federal Occupational Safety and Health Standards," from the Superintendent of Documents, Government Printing Office, Washington, DC, 20402.

**Keep records.** It is necessary to establish OSHA injury records. For injury record-keeping requirements under the Act, an employer should obtain the necessary forms and the booklet "Record-Keeping Requirements Under OSHA," from the nearest Department of Labor office.

The law requires that an employer notify the nearest Area Director, Occupational Safety and Health Administration, Department of Labor, within 48 hours, if any accident or health hazard results in one or more fatalities or the hospitalization of five or more people.

**Meet the general requirement.** The general duty clause of the Act requires that "...Each employer shall furnish, to each of the employees, employment and a place of employment which are free from recognized hazards that are causing or likely to cause death or serious physical harm..."

The chairman of the Occupational Safety and Health Review Commission has suggested that the following kind of evidence be considered as a basis for citing "recognized hazards" under the OSHA general duty clause.[13]

*Detectable by senses.* The situation or condition must be something that can readily be detected with the use of only the basic human senses.

*Readily recognized.* The situation or condition must be such that it would be recognized by all reasonably prudent people as a hazard likely to cause death or serious physical harm.

### Responsibility of the Employee

The employee is obliged to comply with OSHA standards. This includes obedience to all rules, regulations, and orders issued in connection with the Act, which are applicable to

**TABLE 20-14**
**Safety Standards for Metalforming Machines**

American National Standards Institute
- B11.1—Mechanical Power Presses
- B11.2—Hydraulic Power Presses
- B11.3—Power Press Brakes
- B11.4—Shears
- B11.5—Iron Workers
- B11.6—Lathes
- B11.7—Cold Headers and Cold Formers
- B11.12—Roll Forming and Bending
- B11.14—Coil Slitting Machines
- B11.15—Pipe, Tube and Shape Bending Machines
- B11.17—Horizontal Hydraulic Extrusion Presses
- B11.18—Coil Processing Systems
- B11.19—Guards and Devices
- B15.1—Mechanical Power Transmission Apparatus
- B24.1—Forging Industry
- B244.1—Lock out/Tag out of Energy Sources

Metal Powder Industries Federation
- MPIF Standard No. 47, P/M Presses

U.S. Department of Labor
Occupational Safety and Health Administration
OSHA Safety & Health Standards
- 29 CFR 1910.211—Definitions
- 1910.212—General Requirements for All Machines
- 1910.217—Mechanical Power Presses

the employee's own actions and conduct on the job. The Act, however, does not provide penalties for employee infractions of rules.

## NOISE CONTROL

For general information on relevant OSHA standards, hearing protection, and a noise control program, refer to "Safety and Noise Control," Chapter 18, in *Machining*, Volume I of this Handbook series.

Employers are responsible for providing and ensuring permissible noise levels. Permissible noise exposure for employees varies from a maximum level of 90 dB(A) for a duration of 8 hours per day to 115 dB(A) for 1/4 hour or less. In OSHA's Occupational Noise Exposure Hearing Conservation Amendment that became effective April 17, 1983 (for implementation by March 1, 1984), a key rule requires baseline audiograms for employees who are exposed to more than 85 dB(A) for an 8-hour, time-weighted average. Employers are required to ". . .administer a continuing, effective hearing conservation program. . ." A summary of permissible sound levels and allowable exposure times is presented in Table 20-15.

### Typical Operating Conditions

Figure 20-6 shows typical sound levels encountered in common, everyday situations and in industrial operations. Metal stamping and forming operations commonly have ambient noise levels ranging from 85-95 dB(A); hence, noise controls are mandatory. The required degree of control is greater where the 8-hour, time-weighted exposures exceed 90 dB(A). Also, as interpreted in the formal OSHA rule, hearing protection is accepted as an "interim" measure only and officially permitted while engineering and/or administrative controls are being devised and implemented.

### A Sample Program

The 1983 OSHA Hearing Conservation Amendment defines and specifies the components of an effective hearing conservation program to include noise monitoring, audiometric testing, hearing protection, employee training, and recordkeeping. For employer compliance with the OSHA requirements, a suitable program must be instituted and maintained. To assist employers, a representative program is administered jointly by the American Metal Stamping Association (AMSA) and the Industrial Services Division of the Colorado Hearing and Speech Center (CHSC).[14]

**Program elements.** Baseline and annual hearing tests are conducted by employees of CHSC who are certified as Occupational Hearing Conservationists by the Council for Accreditation in Occupational Hearing Conservation (CAOHC). Mobile hearing-test vans are not used.

Participating companies provide a quiet room in which the overall sound level does not exceed 50 dB(A) as measured with either a Type I or Type II sound level meter. Prior to the actual hearing testing, the CHSC technician measures the sound level in the room and performs an octave band analysis to ensure that the testing environment is in compliance with OSHA requirements for background noise levels.

*Testing.* Hearing testing is conducted in a one-on-one situation using a calibrated portable air conduction audiometer whose earphones are equipped with ear-muff-type enclosures to reduce the effects of ambient background noise.

Tests take about five minutes per employee. The individual nature of the testing encourages the employee to report any past history of hearing or ear problems.

The intent is to foster a feeling of trust and confidence on the part of the employees so that audiometric testing can be viewed as a service instead of harassment from management.

*Analysis.* Results of the hearing tests are sent to CHSC where they are processed for computer input and analyzed. Each hearing test form (audiogram) is reviewed by a certified audiologist who makes comments and recommendations on the audiogram. A computer summary sheet and the original audiogram for each employee are returned to the company. Result slips are provided to inform employees about the outcome of their hearing tests.

*Additional services.* Area sound level surveys and a one-hour training program about noise are other services that can be performed in conjunction with the hearing testing, if desired.

The one-hour employee training program covers topics such as the effects of noise on hearing and the purpose of hearing protection. The program also includes an explanation of the purpose of hearing tests and the test procedure, and a showing of a CHSC film. This presentation meets, and in most cases exceeds, the OSHA requirements for an annual training program.

**TABLE 20-15**
**OSHA Limits for Noise Exposure**

| Hours of Exposure | Sound Level, dB(A) |
|---|---|
| 8 | 90 |
| 6 | 92 |
| 4 | 95 |
| 3 | 97 |
| 2 | 100 |
| 1 1/2 | 102 |
| 1 | 105 |
| 1/2 | 110 |
| 1/4 or less | 115 |

OSHA standards establish limits on workplace noise exposure for given time periods. The limit for average exposure during an 8-hour shift is 90 decibels, or dB(A). Exposure to impulse noise should never exceed 140 decibels.

### Noise Control Methods[15]

Methods of controlling noise include the use of sound barriers, absorption, damping, and isolation and shock.

**Sound barriers.** A simple way to reduce noise is to place a barrier between the source of noise and the receiver. Erecting a wall, barrier, or enclosure around the noise source will reduce the sound transmission by making the noise travel a longer distance and by reducing the noise intensity as it passes through the barrier.

The effectiveness of the barrier material in reducing sound transmission is measured in terms of the number of decibels by which airborne sound is reduced as a result of passing through the barrier.

This reduction is called the transmission loss (TL) of the barrier. The TL of a barrier or structure is a fixed property of the material, but varies with the frequency of sound.

Loaded vinyl, vinyl-foam combinations and other high mass materials are effective barrier materials.

**Absorption.** When a sound wave enters a porous material, part of the energy is converted into heat by friction between the air and the material. This process is called sound absorption.

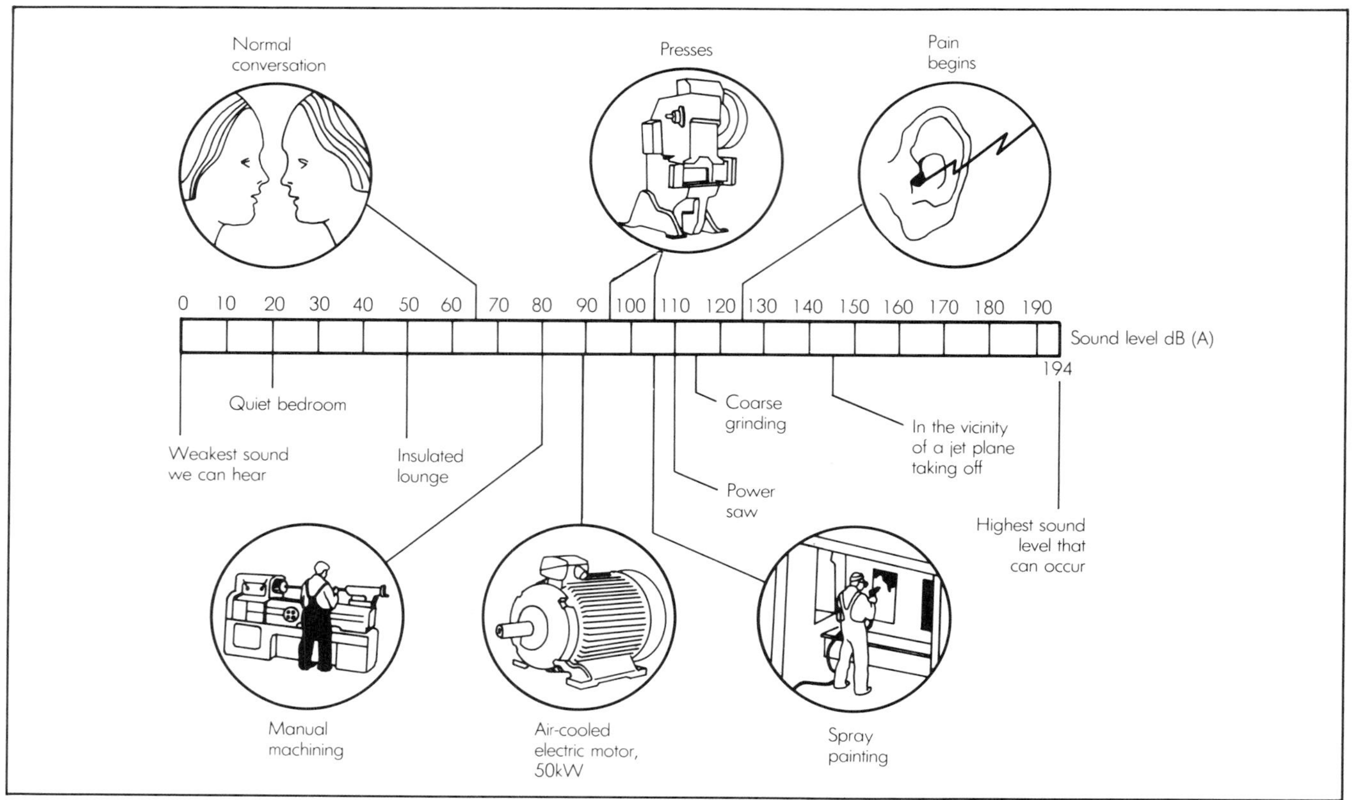


**Fig. 20-6 Typical sound levels for stamping and punching operations, shown in relation to various other sound and noise levels.** (*"Noise Control—A Guide for Workers and Employers," OSHA*)

Sound absorption materials can be designed directly into a finished product to reduce the noise level at its point of origin. Treating the noise at the source can often be the most efficient and cost effective solution. Fiberglass and polyurethane foams are among the most efficient sound absorbers.

Sound absorptive materials are also used as finished surfaces on walls and ceilings or in the form of absorbing baffles to reduce reflection and lower noise levels within a room or an area.

*Tuning.* Absorbers can be tuned to provide optimum absorption at a given frequency by spacing the absorbers at fixed distances from the wall being treated. The separation distance in a given application is determined by the average frequency of the sounds being generated.

Because of their porous nature, sound absorbers are not air tight and, therefore, make very inefficient noise barriers. Their role in industrial noise control is to reduce reverberation within a room. Only when placed near a sound reflecting surface can they produce maximum absorption.

The efficiency of an absorbing material is measured by its "coefficient of absorption." For many materials, this coefficient increases with both the frequency of the noise and the thickness of the material.

*Maintenance.* Sound absorbers can pick up dust, dirt, grease, and oil, which can reduce their efficiency by as much as 80%. In addition to rendering the absorber inefficient for noise control, this situation can create a serious fire hazard. Absorption materials can be supplied with an impervious film facing which alleviates this problem while maintaining a useful absorption rating of above 70%.

*Calculation.* The effect of installing baffles for sound absorption can be calculated with reasonable accuracy as follows:[16]

$$NR = 10 \log\left(\frac{A_o + A_a}{A_o}\right) \qquad (1)$$

where:

$NR$ = sound pressure level, dB(A)
$A_o$ = original absorption, sabins
$A_a$ = added absorption, sabins
sabins (of absorption) = Surface area in square feet multiplied by the absorption coefficient. (When using SI metric units, the "metric sabin" is defined by expressing surface area in square meters.)

Example:

A factory space measures 100 x 100 x 20 ft. (In metric this would be 30.5 x 30.5 x 6.1 m.) The total area (walls, floor, and ceiling) equals 28,000 $ft^2$ (Metric: 2601 $m^2$). The average absorption coefficient is 0.15. Therefore, the total sabins, before treatment, is 4200.

If absorbers are installed overhead, one for each 8 $ft^2$ (0.7 $m^2$) of ceiling area, the added absorption equals approximately 12,000 sabins.

$$NR = 10 \log \frac{4200 + 12{,}000}{4200} = 5.86 \text{ db(A)}$$

The example holds true for a wide range of dimensions. However, greater reduction is realized where ceilings are lower and vice versa.

**Damping.** Instead of waiting until noise is generated, it is sometimes possible to stop, or at least attenuate, vibrations before they produce sound. This is damping.

In true damping, energy is removed from a system and mechanical or vibrating energy is converted through internal friction to heat. Of the several types of damping, control of noise most often requires hysteretic damping. This is the energy dissipation due to the viscous properties engineered into various plastics and rubbers.

Damping materials such as viscoelastic sheet material, mastics, and impregnated felt can be effective in reducing vibration, particularly in highly resonant members. The choice of damping materials depends upon the type of structure, its environment, and the temperature range and frequency range of vibrations.

Viscoelastic sheet materials are generally the most efficient. On a pound-for-pound basis, viscoelastic sheet materials are generally more expensive than asphalt-impregnated felts. When compared on the basis of vibration reduction, however, they are less expensive. They also offer ease and safety of application, and often greater durability.

Damping material efficiency is usually measured in terms of the fraction of vibration reduction per cycle (that is, the loss factor). Commercial viscoelastic damping sheet material is designed to provide maximum loss at room temperature on structural sheet up to 1/4" (6.4 mm). The damping sheet is adhered to either side of the substrate to be damped. This is referred to as extensional damping and is quite effective. The rule of thumb is to use damping sheet at a thickness approximately equal to one and one half times the substrate thickness to be damped. The use of damping materials often provides a simple, practical method for reducing noise caused by impacts and resonating surfaces.

**Isolation and shock.** Vibration isolation prevents vibration in one structure from reaching an attached or adjacent structure. Isolation can be accomplished with steel springs; cork, felt, rubber, plastics, high-density fiberglass pads; or air mount systems.

Isolating, either by designing the vibration isolation material into new equipment or by retrofitting existing equipment, is an important means for overall noise control. It is a first consideration in the designing of new equipment and machinery. It is also important in retrofit noise control.

For example, vibration isolation of a punch press will not reduce the noise level of the operating press by more than one dB(A). It will, however, prevent induced structure-borne noise that can show up as secondary airborne noise.

It is possible for structure-borne noise to be transmitted several hundred feet from the noise source to a light fixture or similar object. The noise then "generated" by this fixture may reach objectionable levels. Elimination of the vibration eliminates this secondary noise source. Figure 20-7 shows an

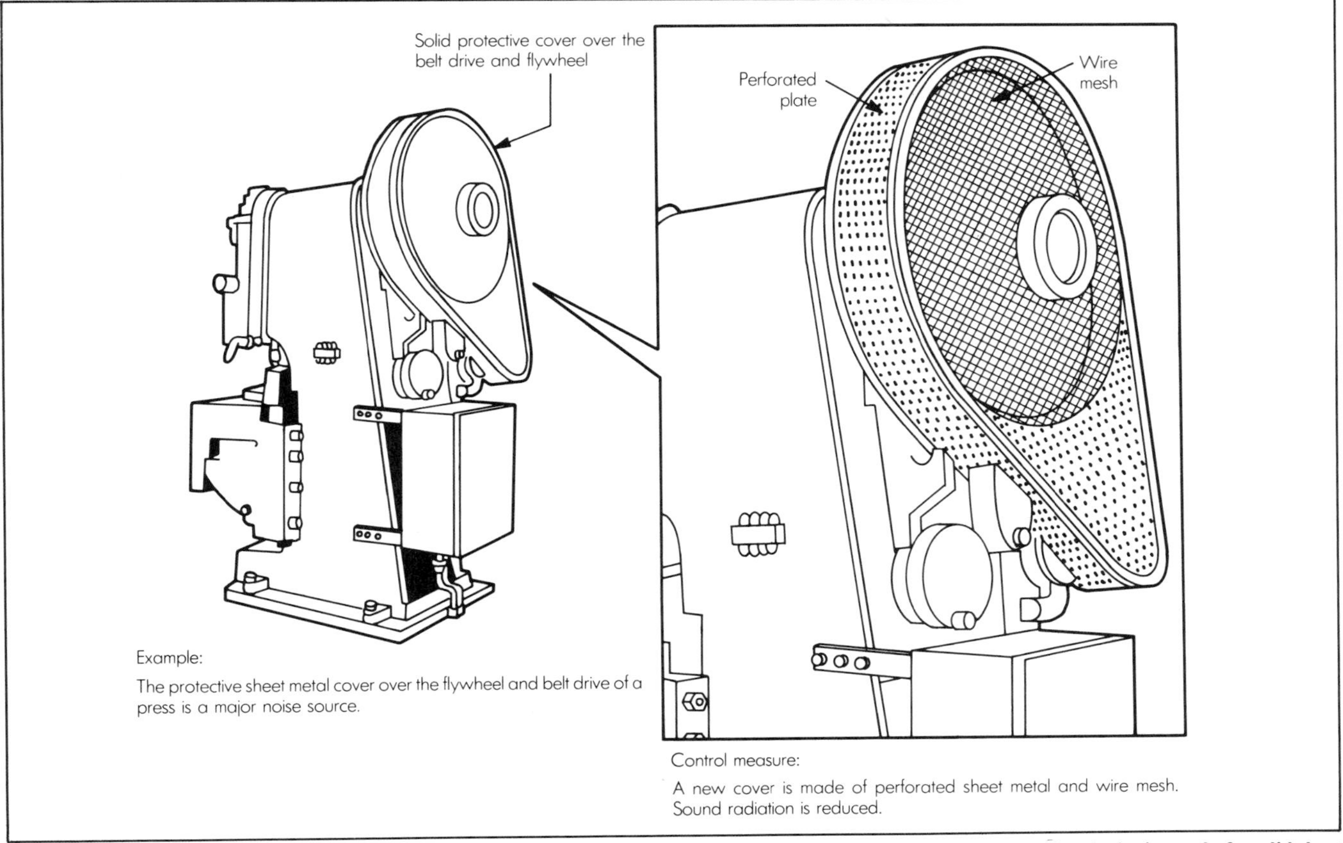

Solid protective cover over the belt drive and flywheel
Perforated plate
Wire mesh
Example:
The protective sheet metal cover over the flywheel and belt drive of a press is a major noise source.
Control measure:
A new cover is made of perforated sheet metal and wire mesh. Sound radiation is reduced.


**Fig. 20-7 Sound radiation from a press drive can be reduced by using a protective cover made of perforated sheet metal and wire instead of a solid sheet metal covering.** (*"Noise Control—A Guide for Workers and Employers," OSHA*)

# STANDARDS AND INFORMATION SOURCES

example of noise reduction modification in the flywheel cover for a press.

## INFORMATION SOURCES

The *Federal Register* is authoritative and is among the best sources of information on standards since all OSHA standards are published in it when adopted, as are all amendments, corrections, insertions, or deletions. The *Federal Register* is available in many public libraries. Annual subscriptions are available from the Superintendent of Documents, U.S. Government Printing Office, Washington, DC 20402.

Each year the Office of the Federal Register publishes all current regulations and standards in the *Code of Federal Regulations (CFR)*, available at many libraries and from the U.S. Government Printing Office. OSHA's regulations are collected in Title 29 of the CFR, Part 1900-1999.

### Current Information

To assist in keeping current with OSHA standards, the OSHA Subscription Service was developed. This service provides all standards, interpretations, regulations, and procedures in loose-leaf form. All changes and additions are issued for an indefinite period of time. The service is available from the Superintendent of Documents only, and is not available from OSHA or from the Department of Labor. Individual volumes of the OSHA Subscription Service are available. (For current prices, contact the nearest OSHA office.)

The OSHA standards fall into four major categories: general industry, agriculture, maritime, and construction. For manufacturing companies having work that includes a variety of forming operations, the general industry standards are most relevant. The appropriate standards are available (from government sources) in two ways:

1. A complimentary copy of the appropriate set of OSHA standards may be obtained from the nearest OSHA office. A self-addressed mailing label should be sent to assist in responding to the request.
2. "General Industry Standards and Interpretations" (including Agriculture) is available as Volume 1 of the Occupational Safety and Health Subscription service described earlier.

### General Information Sources

In the startup of a safety program and the resolution of specific problems, consideration should be given to obtaining useful information and assistance from various nongovernmental sources. These include trade associations, technical societies, professional safety organizations, electrical and fire inspection agencies, insurance company consultants, machinery manufacturers, and specialists in the safety field. Some safety information sources are listed in Table 20-16.

**TABLE 20-16**
**Safety Information Sources**

Acoustical Society of America
335 East 45th Street
New York, NY 10017

American Chemical Society
1155 16th Street N.W.
Washington, DC 20036

American Industrial Hygiene Association
210 Haddon Avenue
Westmont, NJ 08108

American Medical Association
Department of Occupational Health
535 North Dearborn Street
Chicago, IL 60610

American Metal Stamping Association
27027 Chardon Road
Richmond Heights, OH 44143

American National Red Cross
Safety Services
17th and D Streets N.W.
Washington, DC 20006

American National Standards Institute
1430 Broadway
New York, NY 10018

American Public Health Association
1740 Broadway
New York, NY 10019

American Society for Testing and Materials
1916 Race Street
Philadelphia, PA 19103

American Society of Safety Engineers
850 Busse Highway
Park Ridge, IL 60068

Forging Industries Association
55 Public Square, Suite 1121
Cleveland, OH 44113

Industrial Hygiene Foundation of America, Inc.
5231 Centre Avenue
Pittsburgh, PA 15232

Industrial Medical Association
55 East Washington Street
Chicago, IL 60602

Metal Powder Industries Federation
Princeton Forrestal Center
105 College Road East
Princeton, NJ 08540

National Bureau of Standards
U.S. Department of Commerce
Washington, DC 20234

National Machine Tool Builders Association
7901 Westpark Drive
McLean, VA 22102

**TABLE 20-16—*Continued***
**Safety Information Sources**

National Fire Protection Association
60 Batterymarch Street
Boston, MA 02110

National Safety Council
425 North Michigan Avenue
Chicago, IL 60611

Society of Automotive Engineers
400 Commonwealth Drive
Warrendale, PA 15096

Society of Fire Protection Engineers
60 Batterymarch Street
Boston, MA 02110

Society of Manufacturing Engineers
One SME Drive, P.O. Box 930
Dearborn, MI 48121

Superintendent of Documents
U.S. Government Printing Office
Washington, DC 20402

Underwriters Laboratories, Inc.
333 Pfingsten Road
Northbrook, IL 60062

U.S. Department of Labor
Occupational Safety and Health Administration
OSHA Technical Data Center, Room N-2439-Rear
200 Constitution Avenue N.W.
Washington, DC 20210

U.S. Department of Health, Education and Welfare
National Institute for Occupational Safety and Health
4676 Columbia Parkway
Cincinnati, OH 45226

### References


1. Occupational Safety and Health Administration, U.S. Department of Labor, *OSHA Handbook for Small Businesses*, OSHA 2209.
2. Jack B. ReVelle, *Safety Training Methods* (New York: John Wiley & Sons, Inc., 1980), p. 10.
3. Occupational Safety and Health Administration, *op. cit.*, p. 46.
4. Occupational Safety and Health Administration, *op. cit.*
5. ReVelle, *loc. cit.*
6. Hillman Deaton, Riley-Beaird Div., United States Riley Corp., treatise provided with private correspondence.
7. *Ibid.*
8. Joseph W. Hart, "Safeguarding Metalcutting Machines," *Professional Safety* (January 1983), pp. 13-16.
9. ReVelle, *op. cit.*, p. 122.
10. Russell DeReamer, *Modern Safety and Health Technology* (New York: John Wiley & Sons, Inc., 1980), p. 515.
11. ReVelle, *op. cit.*, p. 123.
12. Robert J. Cleveland, Alexander Cohen, H. Harvey Cohen, and Michael J. Smith, *Safety Program Practices in Record-Holding Plants*, DHEW (NIOSH) Publication No. 79-136, U.S. Department of Health, Education, and Welfare, Public Health Service, National Institute for Occupational Safety and Health.
13. Employers Insurance of Wausau, *The Era of OSHA*, p. 3.
14. Wayne G. Bodenhemier, "AMSA/CHSC—A Partnership That Works," *Metal Stamping* (April 1983), pp. 20-23.
15. E-A-R Division, Cabot Corporation, *Leadership in Noise Control*, 1982.
16. Industrial Noise Control, Inc., *1983-1984 Catalog of Products for In-Plant Noise Control*.


### Bibliography


Acoustical Society of America. "Catalog of Acoustical Standards," ASA Catalog 4-1983. NY.

American Metal Stamping Association. *Guidelines to Safety and Health in the Metal Forming Plant*. Richmond Heights, OH, 1982.

American National Standards Institute. "American National Standard for Machine Tools—Hydraulic Presses—Safety Requirements for Construction, Care, and Use." ANSI B11.2. NY.

__________. "American National Standard—Safety Requirements for the Construction, Care, Use, and Safeguarding of Roll Forming and Roll Bending Machines." ANSI B11.12. NY.

__________. "American National Standard for Machine Tools—Power Press Brakes—Safety Requirements for Construction, Care, and Use." ANSI B11.3. NY.

__________. "American National Standard—Safety Requirements for the Construction, Care, and Use of Shears." ANSI B11.4. NY.

Anderson, C. Richard. *OSHA and Accident Control Through Training*. New York: Industrial Press Inc., 1975.

Asfahl, C. Ray. "A Ten-Point Scale for Workplace Hazards." *Professional Safety* (January 1983).

Bell, Lewis H., and Mull, Harold R. *Guidelines to Power Press Noise Reduction*. SME Technical Paper TE80-338, 1980.

Booth, Walter. *Press Room Guards and Barriers*. SME Technical Paper MM77-426, 1975.

Deaton, Hillman E. "A New Dimension in Safety Application." *Professional Safety* (February 1983).

Ebens, Dennis R. "Point of Operation Safeguarding Mechanical Power Presses." POS/SP1M/2-82. Rockford Safety Equipment Co. Rockford, IL.

Henderson, Truman M. "An Auditing System for Health and Safety." *Professional Safety* (May 1981), pp. 23-27.

Huber, Lee J. "Audiometric Testing." *Professional Safety* (February 1983), pp. 17-19.

Lawrence, Kenneth; Lewis, David P.; and Bryant, Roscoe C. *Noise Control in the Workplace*. Germantown, MD: The Center for Compliance Information, Aspen Systems Corp., 1978.

Metal Powder Industries Federation. "Safety Requirements for the Construction, Safeguarding, Care, and Use of P/M Presses." MPIF Standard No. 47. Princeton, NJ, 1979.

Occupational Safety and Health Administration. *All About OSHA*. OSHA 2056. U.S. Department of Labor, Washington, DC, 1982.

__________. *Concepts and Techniques of Machine Safeguarding*. OSHA 3067. U.S. Department of Labor, Washington, DC, 1981.

__________. *Field Operations Manual (FOM)*. OSHA Subscription Service, Superintendent of Documents, U.S. Government Printing Office, Washington, DC.

__________. *General Industry*. OSHA 2206. OSHA Safety and

# CHAPTER 20

## BIBLIOGRAPHY


Health Standards (29 CFR 1910). U.S. Department of Labor, Washington, DC, 1983.

———. *Noise Control*. Superintendent of Documents, U.S. Government Printing Office, Washington, DC.

"Operator's Safety Test." *Industrial Machinery News* (January 1983), pp. 80-83.

Pinkstaff, Carlos D. *Retrofit of Power Presses for Safety—A Systems Approach*. SME Technical Paper MF74-620, 1974.

*Power Press Safety Manual*. EP-233 (0382). Cincinnati Incorporated, Cincinnati, 1982.

*Power Press Safety Manual*, 3rd ed. Stock No. 129.68. National Safety Council, Chicago, 1979.

*Press Brake Safety*. Manual No. B-22. Niagara Machine & Tool Works, Buffalo, 1975.

*Safety Precautions and Suggestions*. 30M 2-83. E.W. Bliss Division, Gulf & Western Manufacturing Co., Southfield, MI, 1983.

*Think Safety*. 2M880 WP. Danly Machine Corp., Chicago.

Weck, M. *Machine Tool Noise—Assessment and Reduction*. SME Technical Paper 1979-382, 1979.

Weimer, George A. "What It Takes to Make Your Plant Safe and Sound." *Iron Age* (November 1, 1982), pp 46-50.

Weisner, Ralph H. *Power Shears Safety*. SME Technical Paper MF74-815, 1974.

Worn, H. *Safety Equipment for Industrial Robots*. SME Technical Paper MS80-714, 1980.

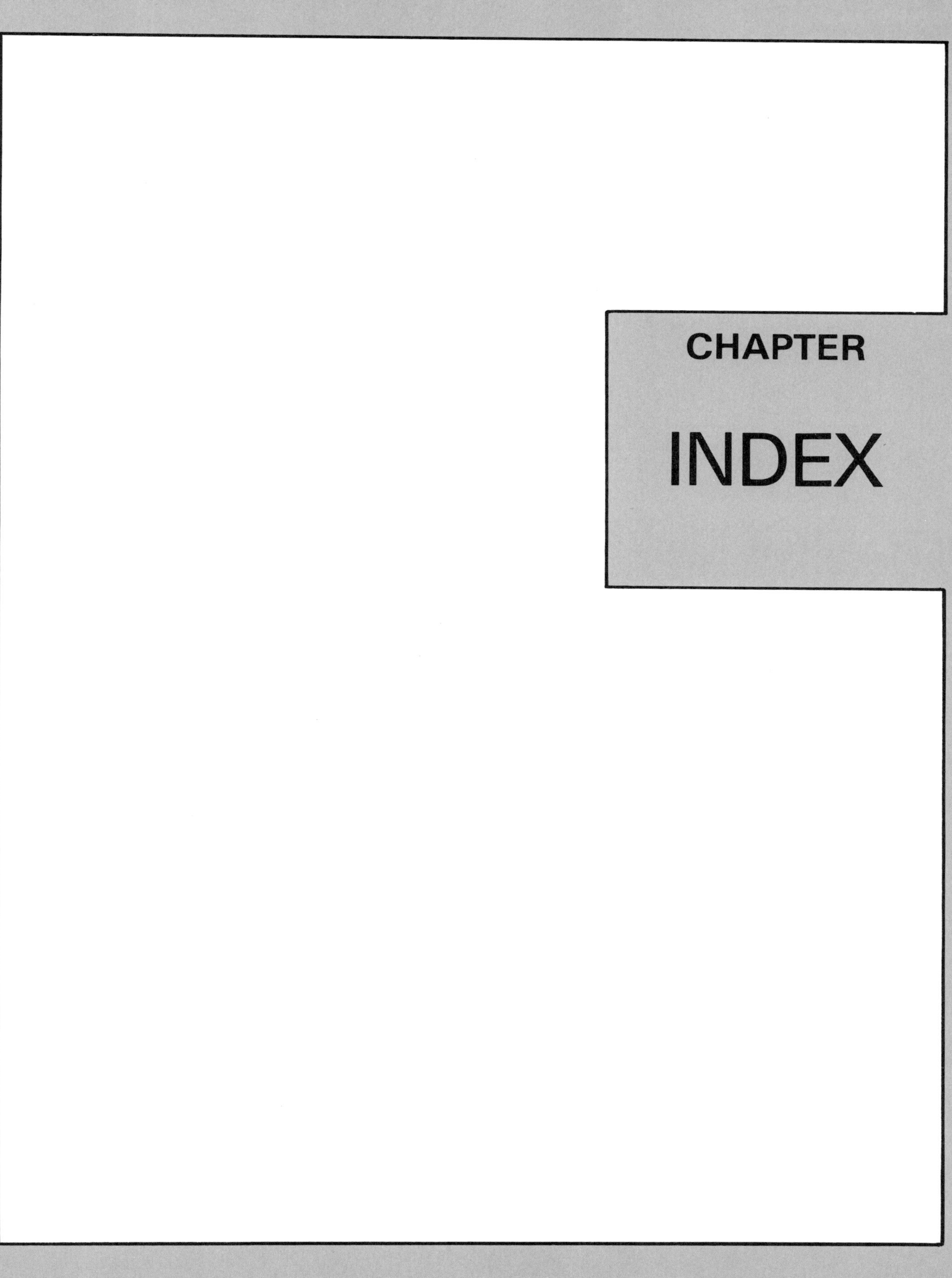

CHAPTER

# INDEX

## D

## E

## F

## K



## L



## M

## N



## O



## P

# INDEX

## Q



## R

# INDEX

## T

## U



## V



## W



## Y



## Z